The Merriam-Webster Dictionary

The Merriam-Webster Dictionary

Merriam-Webster, Incorporated
Springfield, Massachusetts

A GENUINE MERRIAM-WEBSTER

The name *Webster* alone is no guarantee of excellence. It is used by a number of publishers and may serve mainly to mislead an unwary buyer.

Merriam-Webster™ is the name you should look for when you consider the purchase of dictionaries or other fine reference books. It carries the reputation of a company that has been publishing since 1831 and is your assurance of quality and authority.

ISBN 978-0-87779-095-2

MADE IN THE UNITED STATES OF AMERICA

3rd Printing OPM Dallas, PA 3/2023

Contents

PREFACE

This new edition of *The Merriam-Webster Dictionary* continues the line of Merriam-Webster paperback dictionaries which began in 1947. It is based on and preserves the best aspects of preceding editions, but it now includes the most important recent vocabulary that was added to the *Merriam-Webster.com Dictionary* over the past decade. Throughout the dictionary, over 8,000 usage examples illustrate meanings and help to clarify definitions. All the new material has been based on examples of actual use found in the Merriam-Webster citation files and in edited texts online.

The nearly 65,000 entries and more than 75,000 definitions in this dictionary give coverage to the most frequently used words in the language. The heart of the dictionary is the A-Z vocabulary section, where readers will find information about meaning, spelling, pronunciation, etymology, and synonyms. This section is followed by others that users have long found useful: the section Foreign Words and Phrases covers words and phrases from other languages that often occur in English texts but have not become part of the English vocabulary; the section Geographical Names identifies places of importance in the United States and the world.

The Merriam-Webster Dictionary was created by a company that has been publishing dictionaries for more than 175 years and continues to maintain an in-house staff of experienced lexicographers. For this edition, the primary editing was done by Linda Picard Wood, Serenity H. Carr, and Susan L. Brady. Specialist editors included Emily A. Vezina for cross-reference, Joshua S. Guenter for pronunciation, James L. Rader for etymology, Daniel B. Brandon for physical science, and Joan I. Narmontas for life science. Data entry and data-file processing were handled by Anne McDonald. Paul S. Wood acted as production editor, guiding the book through its typesetting stages. Proofreaders included Faith Bell, Tasha R. Bigelow, Faith de Castro, Allison M. DeJordy, Joanne M. Despres, Michael Metivier, and Diana Oshorun, as well as some of the other editors mentioned above. All the editors join in the hope that users will find *The Merriam-Webster Dictionary* to be a concise, handy, and reliable guide to the English language of today.

EXPLANATORY NOTES

The dictionary contains so much information, that is necessary to condense much of it to accommodate the limitations of the printed page. This section provides information on the conventions used throughout the dictionary, from the styling of entries and pronunciations to how information on usage and meaning is presented. An understanding of the information contained in these notes will make the dictionary both easier and more rewarding to use.

ENTRIES

A boldface letter or a combination of such letters, including punctuation marks and diacritics where needed, that is set flush with the left-hand margin of each column of type is a main entry. The main entry may consist of letters set solid, of letters joined by a hyphen or a diagonal, or of letters separated by one or more spaces:

alone . . . *adj*
avant–garde . . . *n*
and/or . . . *conj*
assembly language *n*
av·a·lanche . . . *n*

The material in lightface type that follows each main entry on the same line and on succeeding indented lines presents information about the main entry.

The main entries follow one another in alphabetical order letter by letter: *bill of attainder* follows *billion; Day of Atonement* follows *daylight saving time*. Those containing an Arabic numeral are alphabetized as if the numeral were spelled out: *4-H* comes between *fourfold* and *Four Hundred; 3-D* comes between *three* and *three-dimensional*. Those that often begin with the abbreviation *St.* in common usage have the abbreviation spelled out: *Saint Valentine's Day*. Main entries that begin with *Mc* are alphabetized just as they are spelled.

A pair of guide words is printed at the top of each page. These indicate that the entries falling alphabetically between the words at the top of the outer column of each page are found on that page.

The guide words are the first and last main entries printed on the page:

antithesis • aphelion

When one main entry has exactly the same written form as another, the two are distinguished by superscript numerals preceding each word:

^{1}**melt** . . . *vb*
^{2}**melt** *n*
^{1}**pine** . . . *n*
^{2}**pine** *vb*

Full words come before parts of words made up of the same letters; solid compounds come before hyphenated compounds; hyphenated compounds come before open compounds; and lowercase entries come before those with an initial capital:

²super *n*
super- . . . *prefix*
run·down . . . *n*
run–down . . . *adj*
run down *vb*
dutch . . . *adv*
Dutch . . . *n*

The centered dots within entry words indicate division points at which a hyphen may be put at the end of a line of print or writing. Thus the noun *cap·puc·ci·no* may be ended on one line and continued on the next in this manner:

cap-
puccino
cappuc-
cino
cappucci-
no

Centered dots are not shown after a single initial letter or before a single terminal letter because typesetters seldom cut off a single letter:

abyss . . . *n*
flighty . . . *adj*
idea . . . *n*

Nor are they usually shown at the second and succeeding homographs unless they differ among themselves:

¹sig·nal . . . *n*
²signal *vb*
³signal *adj*
but
¹min·ute . . . *n*
²mi·nute . . . *adj*

There are acceptable alternative end-of-line divisions just as there are acceptable variant spellings and pronunciations, but no more than one division is shown for any entry in this dictionary.

A double hyphen at the end of a line in this dictionary (as in the definition at **citronella**) stands for a hyphen that is retained when the word is written as a unit on one line. This kind of fixed hyphen is always represented in boldface words in this dictionary with an en dash, longer than an ordinary hyphen.

When a main entry is followed by the word *or* and another spelling, the two spellings are equal variants. Both are standard, and either one may be used according to personal inclination:

ocher *or* **ochre**

If two variants joined by *or* are out of alphabetical order, they remain equal variants. The one printed first is, however, slightly more common than the second:

¹plow *or* **plough**

When another spelling is joined to the main entry by the word *also*, the spelling after *also* is a secondary variant and occurs less frequently than the first:

ab·sinthe *also* **ab·sinth**

Secondary variants belong to standard usage and may be used according to personal inclination. Once the word *also* is used to signal a secondary variant, all following variants are joined by *or*:

²wool·ly *also* **wool·ie** *or* **wooly**

Variants whose spelling puts them alphabetically more than a column away from the main entry are entered at their own alphabetical places as well as at the main entry:

²gage *var of* GAUGE
¹gauge *also* **gage**
²gauge *also* **gage**

Variants having a usage label appear only at their own alphabetical places:

me·tre . . . *chiefly Brit var of* METER

To show all the stylings that are found for English compounds would require space that can be better used for other information. So this dictionary limits itself to a single styling for a compound:

peace·mak·er
pell–mell
high five

When a compound is widely used and one styling predominates, that styling is shown. When a compound is uncommon or when the evidence indicates that two or three stylings are approximately equal in frequency, the styling shown is based on the comparison of other similar compounds.

A main entry may be followed by one or more derivatives or by a homograph with a different functional label. These are run-on entries. Each is introduced by a long dash and each has a functional label. They are not defined, however, since their meanings are readily understood from the meaning of the root word:

> **fear·less** . . . *adj* . . . — **fear·less·ly** *adv* — **fear·less·ness** *n*
> **hic·cup** . . . *n* . . . — **hiccup** *vb*

A main entry may be followed by one or more phrases containing the entry word or an inflected form of it. These are also run-on entries. Each is introduced by a long dash but there is no functional label. They are, however, defined since their meanings are more than the sum of the meanings of their elements:

> [1]**set** . . . *vb* . . . — **set sail** : . . .
> [1]**hand** . . . *n* . . . — **at hand** : . . .

Defined phrases of this sort are run on at the entry defining the first major word in the phrase. When there are variants, however, the run-on appears at the entry defining the first major word which is invariable in the phrase:

> [1]**seed** . . . *n* . . . — **go to seed** *or* **run to seed 1** : . . .

Boldface words that appear within parentheses (as **co·ca** at **co·caine** and **jet engine** and **jet propulsion** at **jet–propelled**) are run-in entries.

Attention is called to the definition of *vocabulary entry* on page 823. The term *dictionary entry* includes all vocabulary entries as well as all boldface entries in the sections headed "Foreign Words and Phrases" and "Geographical Names."

PRONUNCIATION

The matter between a pair of reversed slashes \ \ following the entry word indicates the pronunciation. The symbols used are explained in the chart at the end of this section.

A hyphen is used in the pronunciation to show syllabic division. These hyphens sometimes coincide with the centered dots in the entry word that indicate end-of-line division:

> **ab·sen·tee** \ˌab-sən-ˈtē\

Sometimes they do not:

> **met·ric** \ˈme-trik\

A high-set mark ˈ indicates major (primary) stress or accent; a low-set mark ˌ indicates minor (secondary) stress or accent:

> **heart·beat** \ˈhärt-ˌbēt\

The stress mark stands at the beginning of the syllable that receives the stress.

A syllable with neither a high-set mark nor a low-set mark is unstressed:

> [1]**struc·ture** \ˈstrək-chər\

The presence of variant pronunciations indicates that not all educated speakers pronounce words the same way. A second-place variant is not to be regarded as less acceptable than the pronunciation that is given first. It may, in fact, be used by as many educated speakers as the first variant, but the requirements of the printed page are such that one must precede the other:

> **apri·cot** \ˈa-prə-ˌkät, ˈā-\
> **for·head** \ˈfȯr-əd, ˈfȯr-ˌhed\

Symbols enclosed by parentheses represent elements that are present in the pronunciation of some speakers but are absent from the pronunciation of other speakers, or elements that are present in some but absent from other utterances of the same speaker:

> [1]**om·ni·bus** \ˈäm-ni-(ˌ)bəs\
> **ad·di·tion·al** \ə-ˈdi-sh(ə-)nəl\

Thus, the above parentheses indicate that some people say \ˈäm-ni-ˌbəs\ and others say \ˈäm-ni-bəs\; some \ə-ˈdi-shə-nəl\, others \ə-ˈdi-shnəl\.

When a main entry has less than a full pronunciation, the missing part is to be supplied from a pronunciation in a preceding entry or within the same pair of reversed slashes:

cham·pi·on·ship \-ˌship\
pa·la·ver \pə-ˈla-vər, -ˈlä-\

The pronunciation of the first three syllables of *championship* is found at the main entry *champion*. The hyphens before and after \ˈlä\ in the pronunciation of *palaver* indicate that both the first and the last parts of the pronunciation are to be taken from the immediately preceding pronunciation.

In general, no pronunciation is indicated for open compounds consisting of two or more English words that have own-place entry:

dental floss *n*

Only the first entry in a sequence of numbered homographs is given a pronunciation if their pronunciations are the same:

[1]**re·ward** \ri-ˈwȯrd\ *vb*
[2]**reward** *n*

The absent but implied pronunciation of derivatives and compounds run on after a main entry is a combination of the pronunciation at the main entry and the pronunciation of the other element as given at its alphabetical place in the vocabulary:

— **quick·ness** *n*
— **hold with**

Thus, the pronunciation of *quickness* is the sum of the pronunciations given at *quick* and *-ness;* that of *hold with*, the sum of the pronunciations of the two elements that make up the phrase.

FUNCTIONAL LABELS

An italic label indicating a part of speech or another functional classification follows the pronunciation or, if no pronunciation is given, the main entry. The eight traditional parts of speech are indicated as follows:

bold . . . *adj*
forth·with . . . *adv*
[1]**but** . . . *conj*
ge·sund·heit . . . *interj*
bo·le·ro . . . *n*
[2]**un·der** . . . *prep*
[1]**it** . . . *pron*
slap . . . *vb*

Other italicized labels used to indicate functional classifications that are not traditional parts of speech include:

AT *abbr*
self- *comb form*
un- . . . *prefix*
-ial *adj suffix*
[2]**-ly** *adv suffix*
[2]**-er** . . . *n suffix*
-ize *vb suffix*
Fe *symbol*
may . . . *verbal auxiliary*

Functional labels are sometimes combined:

afloat . . . *adj or adv*

INFLECTED FORMS

NOUNS

The plurals of nouns are shown in this dictionary when suffixation brings about a change of final *-y* to *-i-*, when the noun ends in a consonant plus *-o* or in *-ey*, when the noun ends in *-oo*, when the noun has an irregular plural or an uninflected plural or a foreign plural, when the noun is a compound that pluralizes any element but the last, when a final consonant is doubled, when the noun has variant plurals, and when it is believed that the dictionary user might have reasonable doubts about the spelling of the plural or when the plural is spelled in a way contrary to what is expected:

[2]**spy** *n, pl* **spies**
si·lo . . . *n, pl* **silos**
val·ley . . . *n, pl* **valleys**
[2]**shampoo** *n, pl* **shampoos**
mouse . . . *n, pl* **mice**
moose . . . *n, pl* **moose**
cri·te·ri·on . . . *n, pl* **-ria**
son–in–law . . . *n, pl* **sons–in–law**
[1]**quiz** . . . *n, pl* **quiz·zes**
[1]**fish** . . . *n, pl* **fish** *or* **fishes**
pi . . . *n, pl* **pis**
[3]**dry** *n, pl* **drys**

Cutback inflected forms are used when the noun has three or more syllables:

ame·ni·ty . . . *n, pl* **-ties**

The plurals of nouns are usually not shown when the base word is unchanged by suffixation, when the noun is a compound whose second element is readily recognizable as a regular free form entered at its own place, or when the noun is unlikely to occur in the plural:

night . . . *n*
fore·foot . . . *n*
mo·nog·a·my . . . *n*

Nouns that are plural in form and that regularly occur in plural construction are labeled *n pl*:

munch·ies . . . *n pl*

Nouns that are plural in form but that are not always construed as plurals are appropriately labeled:

lo·gis·tics . . . *n sing or pl*

VERBS

The principal parts of verbs are shown in this dictionary when suffixation brings about a doubling of a final consonant or an elision of a final *-e* or a change of final *-y* to *-i-*, when final *-c* changes to *-ck* in suffixation, when the verb ends in *-ey*, when the inflection is irregular, when there are variant inflected forms, and when it is believed that the dictionary user might have reasonable doubts about the spelling of an inflected form or when the inflected form is spelled in a way contrary to what is expected:

[2]**snag** *vb* **snagged; snag·ging**
[1]**move** . . . *vb* **moved; mov·ing**
[1]**cry** . . . *vb* **cried; cry·ing**
[1]**frol·ic** . . . *vb* **frol·icked; frol·ick·ing**
[1]**sur·vey** . . . *vb* **sur·veyed; sur·vey·ing**
[1]**drive** . . . *vb* **drove** . . . **driv·en** . . . **driv·ing**
[2]**bus** *vb* **bused** *or* **bussed; bus·ing** *or* **bus·sing**
[2]**visa** *vb* **vi·saed** . . . **vi·sa·ing**
[2]**chagrin** *vb* **cha·grined** . . . **cha·grin·ing**

The principal parts of a regularly inflected verb are shown when it is desirable to indicate the pronunciation of one of the inflected forms:

learn . . . *vb* **learned** \\ˈlərnd, ˈlərnt\\; **learn·ing**
[1]**al·ter** \\ˈȯl-tər\\ *vb* **al·tered; al·ter·ing** \\-t(ə-)riŋ\\

Cutback inflected forms are usually used when the verb has three or more syllables, when it is a two-syllable word that ends in *-l* and has variant spellings, and when it is a compound whose second element is readily recognized as an irregular verb:

elim·i·nate . . . *vb* **-nat·ed; -nat·ing**
[2]**quarrel** *vb* **-reled** *or* **-relled; -rel·ing** *or* **-rel·ling**
[1]**re·take** . . . *vb* **-took** . . . **-tak·en** . . . **-tak·ing**

The principal parts of verbs are usually not shown when the base word is unchanged by suffixation or when the verb is a compound whose second element is readily recognizable as a regular free form entered at its own place:

[1]**jump** . . . *vb*
pre·judge . . . *vb*

Another inflected form of English verbs is the third person singular of the present tense, which is regularly formed by the addition of *-s* or *-es* to the base form of the verb. This inflected form is not shown except at a handful of entries (as *have* and *do*) for which it is in some way unusual.

ADJECTIVES & ADVERBS

The comparative and superlative forms of adjectives and adverbs are shown in this dictionary when suffixation brings about a doubling of a final consonant or an elision of a final *-e* or a change of final *-y* to *-i-*, when the word ends in *-ey*, when the inflection is irregular, and when there are variant inflected forms:

> [1]**red** . . . *adj* **red·der; red·dest**
> [1]**tame** . . . *adj* **tam·er; tam·est**
> [1]**kind·ly** . . . *adj* **kind·li·er; -est**
> **hors·ey** *also* **horsy** . . . *adj* **hors·i·er; -est**
> [1]**good** . . . *adj* **bet·ter** . . . **best**
> [1]**far** . . . *adv* **far·ther** . . . *or* **fur·ther** . . . **far·thest** *or* **fur·thest**

The superlative forms of adjectives and adverbs of two or more syllables are usually cut back:

> [3]**fancy** *adj* **fan·ci·er; -est**
> [1]**ear·ly** . . . *adv* **ear·li·er; -est**

The comparative and superlative forms of regularly inflected adjectives and adverbs are shown when it is desirable to indicate the pronunciation of the inflected forms:

> [1]**young** \ˈyəŋ\ *adj* **youn·ger** \ˈyəŋ-gər\ **youn·gest** \ˈyəŋ-gəst\

The inclusion of inflected forms in *-er* and *-est* at adjective and adverb entries means nothing more about the use of *more* and *most* with these adjectives and adverbs than that their comparative and superlative degrees may be expressed in either way: *lazier* or *more lazy; laziest* or *most lazy*.

At a few adjective entries only the superlative form is shown:

> [2]**mere** *adj, superlative* **mer·est**

The absence of the comparative form indicates that there is no evidence of its use.

The comparative and superlative forms of adjectives and adverbs are usually not shown when the base word is unchanged by suffixation, when the inflected forms of the word are identical with those of a preceding homograph, or when the word is a compound whose second element is readily recognizable as a regular free form entered at its own place:

> [1]**near** . . . *adv*
> [3]**good** *adv*
> **un·wor·thy** . . . *adj*

Inflected forms are not shown at undefined run-ons.

CAPITALIZATION

Most entries in this dictionary begin with a lowercase letter. A few of these have an italicized label *often cap*, which indicates that the word is as likely to be capitalized as not and that it is as acceptable with an uppercase initial as it is with one in lowercase. Some entries begin with an uppercase letter, which indicates that the word is usually capitalized. The absence of an initial capital or of an *often cap* label indicates that the word is not ordinarily capitalized:

> **salm·on** . . . *n*
> **gar·gan·tuan** . . . *adj, often cap*
> **Mo·hawk** . . . *n*

The capitalization of entries that are open or hyphenated compounds is similarly indicated by the form of the entry or by an italicized label:

dry goods . . . *n pl*
french fry *n, often cap 1st F*
un–Amer·i·can . . . *adj*
Par·kin·son's disease . . . *n*
lazy Su·san . . . *n*
Jack Frost *n*

A word that is capitalized in some senses and lowercase in others shows variations from the form of the main entry by the use of italicized labels at the appropriate senses:

Trin·i·ty . . . *n* . . . **2** *not cap*
To·ry . . . *n* . . . **3** *often not cap*
ti·tan . . . *n* **1** *cap*
re·nais·sance . . . *n* . . . **1** *cap* . . . **2** *often cap*

ETYMOLOGY

This dictionary gives the etymologies for a number of the vocabulary entries. These etymologies are inside square brackets preceding the definition. Meanings given in roman type within these brackets are not definitions of the entry, but are meanings of the Middle English, Old English, or non-English words within the brackets.

The etymology gives the language from which words borrowed into English have come. It also gives the form of the word in that language or a representation of the word in our alphabet if the form in that language differs from that in English:

philo·den·dron . . . [NL, fr. Gk, neut. of *philodendros* loving trees . . .]
[1]**sav·age** . . . [ME, fr. AF *salvage, savage*, fr. LL *salvaticus,* alter. of L *silvaticus* of the woods, wild . . .]

An etymology beginning with the name of a language (including ME or OE) and not giving the foreign (or Middle English or Old English) form indicates that this form is the same as the form of the entry word:

le·gume . . . [F]
[1]**jour·ney** . . . [ME, fr. OF . . .]

An etymology beginning with the name of a language (including ME or OE) and not giving the foreign (or Middle English or Old English) meaning indicates that this meaning is the same as the meaning expressed in the first definition in the entry:

ug·ly . . . *adj* . . . [ME, fr. ON *uggligr* . . .] **1** : FRIGHTFUL, DIRE

USAGE

Three types of status labels are used in this dictionary—temporal, regional, and stylistic—to signal that a word or a sense of a word is not part of the standard vocabulary of English.

The temporal label *obs* for "obsolete" means that there is no evidence of use since 1755:

[3]**post** *n* **1** *obs*

The label *obs* is a comment on the word being defined. When a thing, as distinguished from the word used to designate it, is obsolete, appropriate orientation is usually given in the definition:

cat·a·pult . . . *n* **1** : an ancient military machine for hurling missiles

The temporal label *archaic* means that a word or sense once in common use is found today only sporadically or in special contexts:

[1]**mete** . . . *vb* . . . **1** *archaic*
[1]**thou** . . . *pron, archaic*

A word or sense limited in use to a specific region of the U.S. has an appropriate label. The adverb *chiefly* precedes a label when the word has some currency outside the specified region, and a double label is used to indicate considerable currency in each of two specific regions:

[2]**wash** *n* . . . **8** *West*
do·gie . . . *n, chiefly West*
crul·ler . . . *n* . . . **2** *Northern & Midland*

Words current in all regions of the U.S. have no label.

A word or sense limited in use to one of the other countries of the English-speaking world has an appropriate regional label:

chem·ist . . . *n* . . . **2** *Brit*
loch . . . *n, Scot*
[2]**wireless** *n* . . . **2** *chiefly Brit*

The label *dial* for "dialect" indicates that the pattern of use of a word or sense is too complex for summary labeling: it usually includes several regional varieties of American English or of American and British English:

[2]**mind** *vb* **1** *chiefly dial*

The stylistic label *slang* is used with words or senses that are especially appropriate in contexts of extreme informality:

[3]**can** . . . *vb* . . . **2** *slang*
[2]**grand** *n* . . . *slang*

There is no satisfactory objective test for slang, especially with reference to a word out of context. No word, in fact, is invariably slang, and many standard words can be given slang applications.

The stylistic labels *offensive* and *disparaging* are used for those words or senses that in common use are intended to hurt or that are likely to give offense even when they are used without such an intent:

dumb . . . *adj* **1** *often offensive*
half–breed . . . *n, often disparaging*

Additional labels that are self-explanatory, such as *informal*, are used at some entries and senses.

Definitions are sometimes followed by verbal illustrations that show a typical use of the word in context. These illustrations are enclosed in angle brackets, and the word being illustrated is usually replaced by a lightface swung dash. The swung dash stands for the boldface entry word, and it may be followed by an italicized suffix:

[1]**jump** . . . *vb* . . . **5** . . . ⟨~ town⟩
all–around . . . *adj* **1** . . . ⟨best ~ performance⟩
[1]**can·on** . . . *n* . . . **3** . . . ⟨the ~*s* of good taste⟩
en·joy . . . *vb* . . . **2** . . . ⟨~*ed* the concert⟩

The swung dash is not used when the form of the boldface entry word is changed in suffixation, and it is not used for open compounds:

[2]**deal** *vb* . . . **2** . . . ⟨*dealt* him a blow⟩
drum up *vb* **1** . . . ⟨*drum up* business⟩

Definitions are sometimes followed by usage notes that give supplementary information about such matters as idiom, syntax, and semantic relationship. A usage note is introduced by a lightface dash:

[2]**cry** *n* . . . **5** . . . — usu. used in the phrase *a far cry*
[2]**drum** *vb* . . . **4** . . . — usu. used with *out*
[1]**jaw** . . . *n* . . . **2** . . . — usu. used in pl.
[1]**ada·gio** . . . *adv or adj* . . . — used as a direction in music
hajji . . . *n* . . . — often used as a title

Sometimes a usage note is used in place of a definition. Some function words (as conjunctions and prepositions) have chiefly grammatical meaning and little or no lexical meaning; most interjections express feelings but are otherwise untranslatable into lexical meaning; and some other words (as honorific titles) are more amenable to comment than to definition:

or . . . *conj* — used as a function word to indicate an alternative
[1]**at** . . . *prep* **1** — used to indicate a point in time or space
auf Wie·der·seh·en . . . *interj* . . . — used to express farewell
sir . . . *n* . . . **2** — used as a usu. respectful form of address

SENSE DIVISION

A boldface colon is used in this dictionary to introduce a definition:

equine . . . *adj* . . . : of or relating to the horse

It is also used to separate two or more definitions of a single sense:

no·ti·fy . . . *vb* . . . **1** : to give notice of : report the occurrence of

Boldface Arabic numerals separate the senses of a word that has more than one sense:

add . . . *vb* **1** : to join to something else so as to increase in number or amount **2** : to say further . . . **3** : to combine (numbers) into one sum

A particular semantic relationship between senses is sometimes suggested by the use of one of the two italic sense dividers *esp* or *also*.

The sense divider *esp* (for *especially*) is used to introduce the most common meaning included in the more general preceding definition:

crys·tal . . . *n* . . . **2** : something resembling crystal (as in transparency); *esp* : a clear colorless glass of superior quality

The sense divider *also* is used to introduce a meaning related to the preceding sense by an easily understood extension of that sense:

chi·na . . . *n* : porcelain ware; *also* : domestic pottery in general

The order of senses is historical: the sense known to have been first used in English is entered first. This is not to be taken to mean, however, that each sense of a multisense word developed from the immediately preceding sense. It is altogether possible that sense 1 of a word has given rise to sense 2 and sense 2 to sense 3, but frequently sense 2 and sense 3 may have developed independently of one another from sense 1.

When an italicized label follows a boldface numeral, the label applies only to that specific numbered sense. It does not apply to any other boldface numbered senses:

craft . . . *n* . . . **3** *pl usu* **craft**
[1]**fa·ther** . . . *n* . . . **2** *cap* . . . **5** *often cap*
dul·ci·mer . . . *n* . . . **2** *or* **dul·ci·more** \-ˌmōr\
[2]**lift** *n* . . . **5** *chiefly Brit*

At *craft* the *pl* label applies to sense 3 but to none of the other numbered senses. At *father* the *cap* label applies only to sense 2 and the *often cap* label only to sense 5. At *dulcimer* the variant spelling and pronunciation apply only to sense 2, and the *chiefly Brit* label at *lift* applies only to sense 5.

CROSS-REFERENCE

Four different kinds of cross-references are used in this dictionary: directional, synonymous, cognate, and inflectional. In each instance the cross-reference is readily recognized by the lightface small capitals in which it is printed.

A cross-reference following a lightface dash and beginning with *see* is a directional cross-reference. It directs the dictionary user to look elsewhere for further information:

eu·ro . . . *n* . . . — see MONEY table

A cross-reference following a boldface colon is a synonymous cross-reference. It may stand alone as the only definition for an entry or for a sense of an entry; it may follow an analytical definition; it may be one of two or more synonymous cross-references separated by commas:

pa·pa . . . *n* FATHER
[1]**par·tic·u·lar** . . . *adj* . . . **4** : attentive to details : PRECISE
[2]**main** *adj* **1** : CHIEF, PRINCIPAL
[1]**fig·ure** . . . *n* . . . **6** : SHAPE, FORM, OUTLINE

A synonymous cross-reference indicates that an entry, a definition at the entry, or a specific sense at the entry cross-referred to can be substituted as a definition for the entry or the sense in which the cross-reference appears.

A cross-reference following an italic *var of* ("variant of") is a cognate cross-reference:

pick·a·back . . . *var of* PIGGYBACK

Occasionally a cognate cross-reference has a limiting label preceding *var of* as an indication that the variant is not standard American English:

aero·plane . . . *chiefly Brit var of* AIRPLANE

A cross-reference following an italic label that identifies an entry as an inflected form (as of a noun or verb) is an inflectional cross-reference:

calves *pl of* CALF
woven *past part of* WEAVE

Inflectional cross-references appear only when the inflected form falls at least a column away from the entry cross-referred to.

SYNONYMS

A bold italic ***Synonyms*** preceded by a small black diamond figure near the end of an entry introduces words that are synonymous with the word being defined:

alone . . . *adj* . . . ♦ ***Synonyms*** LONELY, LONESOME, LONE, SOLITARY

Synonyms are not definitions although they may often be substituted for each other in context.

COMBINING FORMS, PREFIXES, & SUFFIXES

An entry that begins or ends with a hyphen is a word element that forms part of an English compound:

-wise . . . *adv comb form* . . . ⟨slant*wise*⟩
ex- . . . *prefix* . . . **2** . . . ⟨*ex*-president⟩
-let *n suffix* **1** . . . ⟨book*let*⟩

Combining forms, prefixes, and suffixes are entered in this dictionary for two reasons: to make understandable the meaning of many undefined run-ons and to make recognizable the meaningful elements of words that are not entered in the dictionary.

LISTS OF UNDEFINED WORDS

Many words that begin with the prefixes or combining forms *anti-*, *in-*, *non-*, *over-*, *re-*, *self-*, *semi-*, *sub-*, *super-*, and *un-* are self-explanatory combinations of the prefix or combining form and a word entered elsewhere in the dictionary, and they are listed undefined at the bottom of the page or spread on which they would normally appear if defined.

ABBREVIATIONS & SYMBOLS

Abbreviations and symbols for chemical elements are included as main entries in the vocabulary:

RSVP *abbr* . . . please reply
Ca *symbol* calcium

Abbreviations have been normalized to one form. In practice, however, there is considerable variation in the use of periods and in capitalization (as *vhf*, *v.h.f.*, *VHF*, and *V.H.F.* for the entry **VHF**), and stylings other than those given in this dictionary are often acceptable.

ABBREVIATIONS IN THIS WORK

abbr	abbreviation
abl	ablative
A.D.	anno Domini
adj	adjective
adv	adverb
AF	Anglo-French
alter	alteration
Am	American
AmerF	American French
AmerSp	American Spanish
Ar	Arabic
B.C.	before Christ
Brit	British
C	Celsius
CanF	Canadian French
cap	capital, capitalized
cen	central
cent	century
Chin	Chinese
comb	combining
compar	comparative
conj	conjunction
constr	construction
D	Dutch
dial	dialect
dim	diminutive
E	English
Eng	English
esp	especially
est	estimated
F	Fahrenheit, French
fem	feminine
fr	from
ft	feet
G	German
Gk	Greek
Gmc	Germanic
Heb	Hebrew
imper	imperative
interj	interjection
Ir	Irish
irreg	irregular
It	Italian
Jp	Japanese
K	Kelvin
km	kilometers
L	Latin
LGk	Late Greek
lit	literally
LL	Late Latin
m	meters
masc	masculine
MD	Middle Dutch
ME	Middle English
MexSp	Mexican Spanish
MF	Middle French
MGk	Middle Greek
mi	miles
ML	Medieval Latin
modif	modification
Mt	Mount
n	noun
neut	neuter
NL	New Latin
No	North
n pl	noun plural
obs	obsolete
OE	Old English
OF	Old French
OIt	Old Italian
ON	Old Norse
orig	originally
part	participle
Per	Persian
perh	perhaps
Pg	Portuguese
pl	plural
pp	past participle
prep	preposition
pres	present, president
prob	probably
pron	pronoun, pronunciation
prp	present participle
Russ	Russian
Sc	Scotch, Scots
ScGael	Scottish Gaelic
Scot	Scottish
sing	singular
Skt	Sanskrit
So	South
Sp	Spanish
St	Saint
superl	superlative
trans	translation
Turk	Turkish
US	United States
USSR	Union of Soviet Socialist Republics
usu	usually
var	variant
vb	verb
VL	Vulgar Latin
W	Welsh

PRONUNCIATION SYMBOLS

ə	abut, collect, suppose
ˈə, ˌə	humdrum
^{ə}	(in ^{ə}l, ^{ə}n) battle, cotton; (in l^{ə}, m^{ə}, r^{ə}) French table, prisme, titre
ər	operation, further
a	map, patch
ā	day, fate
ä	bother, cot, father
är	car, heart
au̇	now, out
b	baby, rib
ch	chin, catch
d	did, adder
e	set, red
er	bare, fair
ē	beat, easy
f	fifty, cuff
g	go, big
h	hat, ahead
hw	whale
i	tip, banish
ir	near, deer
ī	site, buy
j	job, edge
k	kin, cook
k̲	German Bach, Scots loch
l	lily, cool
m	murmur, dim
n	nine, own
^{n}	indicates that a preceding vowel is pronounced through both nose and mouth, as in French bon \bō^{n}\
ŋ	sing, singer, finger, ink
ō	bone, hollow
ȯ	saw
ȯr	boar, port
œ	French bœuf, feu, German Hölle, Höhle
ȯi	toy
p	pepper, lip
r	rarity
s	source, less
sh	shy, mission
t	tie, attack
th	thin, ether
t̲h̲	then, either
ü	boot, few \ˈfyü\
u̇	put, pure \ˈpyu̇r\
u̇r	boor, tour
æ	French rue, German füllen, fühlen
v	vivid, give
w	we, away
y	yard, cue \ˈkyü\
^{y}	indicates that a preceding \l\, \n\, or \w\ is modified by having the tongue approximate the position for \y\, as in French digne \dēn^{y}\
z	zone, raise
zh	vision, pleasure
\	slant line used in pairs to mark the beginning and end of a transcription: \ˈpen\
ˈ	mark at the beginning of a syllable that has primary (strongest) stress: \ˈshə-fəl-ˌbȯrd\
ˌ	mark at the beginning of a syllable that has secondary (next-strongest) stress: \ˈshə-fəl-ˌbȯrd\
-	mark of a syllable division in pronunciations (the mark of end-of-line division in boldface entries is a centered dot •)
( )	indicate that what is symbolized between sometimes occurs and sometimes does not occur in the pronunciation of the word: **bakery** \ˈbā-k(ə-)rē\ = \ˈbā-kə-rē, ˈbā-krē\

A

[1]**a** \ˈā\ *n, pl* **a's** *or* **as** \ˈāz\ *often cap* **1** : the 1st letter of the English alphabet **2** : a grade rating a student's work as superior

[2]**a** \ə, (ˈ)ā\ *indefinite article* : ONE, SOME — used to indicate an unspecified or unidentified individual ⟨there's ~ man outside⟩

[3]**a** *abbr, often cap* **1** absent **2** acre **3** alto **4** answer **5** are **6** area

AA *abbr* **1** Alcoholics Anonymous **2** antiaircraft **3** associate in arts

AAA *abbr* American Automobile Association

A and M *abbr* agricultural and mechanical

A and R *abbr* artists and repertory

AAPI *abbr* Asian American and Pacific Islander

aard•vark \ˈärd-ˌvärk\ *n* [obs. Afrikaans, fr. Afrikaans *aard* earth + *vark* pig] : a large burrowing African mammal that feeds on ants and termites with its long sticky tongue

[1]**ab** \ˈab\ *n* : an abdominal muscle

[2]**ab** *abbr* about

AB *abbr* **1** able-bodied seaman **2** airman basic **3** [NL *artium baccalaureus*] bachelor of arts

ABA *abbr* American Bar Association

aback \ə-ˈbak\ *adv* : by surprise ⟨taken ~⟩

aba•cus \ˈa-bə-kəs\ *n, pl* **aba•ci** \-ˌsī, -ˌkē\ *or* **aba•cus•es** : an instrument for making calculations by sliding counters along rods or grooves

[1]**abaft** \ə-ˈbaft\ *prep* : to the rear of

[2]**abaft** *adv* : toward or at the stern : AFT

ab•a•lo•ne \ˌa-bə-ˈlō-nē, ˈa-bə-ˌ\ *n* : any of a genus of large edible sea mollusks with a flattened slightly spiral shell with holes along the edge

[1]**aban•don** \ə-ˈban-dən\ *vb* [ME *abandounen,* fr. AF *abanduner,* fr. (*mettre*) *a bandun* to hand over, put in someone's control] : to give up completely : FORSAKE, DESERT — **aban•don•ment** *n*

[2]**abandon** *n* : a thorough yielding to natural impulses; *esp* : EXUBERANCE

aban•doned \ə-ˈban-dənd\ *adj* : morally unrestrained ♦ ***Synonyms*** PROFLIGATE, DISSOLUTE, REPROBATE

abase \ə-ˈbās\ *vb* **abased; abas•ing** : HUMBLE, DEGRADE — **abase•ment** *n*

abash \ə-ˈbash\ *vb* : to destroy the composure of : EMBARRASS — **abash•ment** *n*

abate \ə-ˈbāt\ *vb* **abat•ed; abat•ing** **1** : to put an end to ⟨~ a nuisance⟩ **2** : to decrease in amount, number, or degree

abate•ment \ə-ˈbāt-mənt\ *n* **1** : DECREASE **2** : an amount abated; *esp* : a deduction from a tax

ab•at•toir \ˈa-bə-ˌtwär\ *n* [F] : SLAUGHTERHOUSE

ab•ba•cy \ˈa-bə-sē\ *n, pl* **-cies** : the office or term of office of an abbot or abbess

ab•bé \a-ˈbā, ˈa-ˌ\ *n* : a member of the French secular clergy — used as a title

ab•bess \ˈa-bəs\ *n* : the superior of a convent for nuns

ab•bey \ˈa-bē\ *n, pl* **abbeys** **1** : MONASTERY **2** : CONVENT **3** : an abbey church

ab•bot \ˈa-bət\ *n* [ME *abbod,* fr. OE, fr. LL *abbat-, abbas,* fr. LGk *abbas,* fr. Aramaic *abbā* father] : the superior of a monastery for men

abbr *abbr* abbreviation

ab•bre•vi•ate \ə-ˈbrē-vē-ˌāt\ *vb* **-at•ed; -at•ing** : SHORTEN, CURTAIL; *esp* : to reduce to an abbreviation

ab•bre•vi•a•tion \ə-ˌbrē-vē-ˈā-shən\ *n* **1** : the act or result of abbreviating **2** : a shortened form of a word or phrase used for brevity esp. in writing

[1]**ABC** \ˌā-(ˌ)bē-ˈsē\ *n, pl* **ABC's** *or* **ABCs** \-ˈsēz\ **1** : ALPHABET — usu. used in pl. **2** : RUDIMENTS — usu. used in pl.

[2]**ABC** *abbr* American Broadcasting Company

Ab•di•as \ab-ˈdī-əs\ *n* : OBADIAH

ab•di•cate \ˈab-di-ˌkāt\ *vb* **-cat•ed; -cat•ing** : to give up (as a throne) formally — **ab•di•ca•tion** \ˌab-di-ˈkā-shən\ *n*

ab•do•men \ˈab-də-mən, ab-ˈdō-\ *n* **1** : the cavity in or area of the body between the chest and the pelvis **2** : the part of the body posterior to the thorax in an arthropod — **ab•dom•i•nal** \ab-ˈdä-mə-nᵊl\ *adj* — **ab•dom•i•nal•ly** *adv*

ab•duct \ab-ˈdəkt\ *vb* : to take away (a person) by force : KIDNAP — **ab•duc•tion** \-ˈdək-shən\ *n* — **ab•duc•tor** \-tər\ *n*

abeam \ə-ˈbēm\ *adv or adj* : on a line at right angles to a ship's keel

abed \ə-ˈbed\ *adv or adj* : in bed

Abe•na•ki \ˌa-bə-ˈnä-kē\ *also* **Ab•na•ki** \ab-ˈnä-kē\ *n, pl* **Abenaki** *or* **Abenakis** *also* **Abnaki** *or* **Abnakis** : a member of a group of Algonquian-speaking Indigenous peoples of northern New England and southern Quebec

ab•er•ra•tion \ˌa-bə-ˈrā-shən\ *n* **1** : deviation esp. from a moral standard or normal state **2** : failure of a mirror or lens to produce exact point-to-point correspondence between an object and its image **3** : unsoundness of mind : DERANGEMENT — **ab•er•rant** \a-ˈber-ənt\ *adj*

abet \ə-ˈbet\ *vb* **abet•ted; abet•ting** [ME *abetten,* fr. AF *abeter,* fr. *beter* to bait] **1** : INCITE, ENCOURAGE **2** : to assist or support in the achievement of a purpose ⟨~ a fugitive⟩ — **abet•tor** *or* **abet•ter** \-ˈbe-tər\ *n*

abey•ance \ə-ˈbā-əns\ *n* : a condition of suspended activity — **abey•ant** \-ənt\ *adj*

ab•hor \əb-ˈhȯr, ab-\ *vb* **ab•horred; ab•hor•ring** [ME *abhorren,* fr. L *abhorrēre,* fr. *ab-* + *horrēre* to shudder] : LOATHE, DETEST — **ab•hor•rence** \-əns\ *n*

ab•hor•rent \-ənt\ *adj* : LOATHSOME, DETESTABLE ⟨~ crimes⟩

abide \ə-ˈbīd\ *vb* **abode** \-ˈbōd\ *or* **abid•ed; abid•ing** **1** : BEAR, ENDURE **2** : DWELL, REMAIN, LAST — **abide by** : to conform or acquiesce to ‹*abide by* the law›

abil·i·ty \ə-ˈbi-lə-tē\ *n, pl* **-ties** : the quality of being able : POWER, SKILL

-ability *also* **-ibility** *n suffix* : capacity, fitness, or tendency to act or be acted on in a (specified) way ‹flamm*ability*›

ab·ject \ˈab-ˌjekt, ab-ˈjekt\ *adj* : low in spirit, hope, or state ‹~ poverty› — **ab·jec·tion** \ab-ˈjek-shən\ *n* — **ab·ject·ly** *adv* — **ab·ject·ness** *n*

ab·jure \ab-ˈju̇r\ *vb* **ab·jured**; **ab·jur·ing** **1** : to renounce solemnly : RECANT **2** : to abstain from — **ab·ju·ra·tion** \ˌab-jə-ˈrā-shən\ *n*

abl *abbr* ablative

ab·late \a-ˈblāt\ *vb* **ab·lat·ed**; **ab·lat·ing** : to remove or become removed esp. by cutting, abrading, or vaporizing

ab·la·tion \a-ˈblā-shən\ *n* **1** : surgical cutting and removal **2** : loss of a part (as the outside of a nose cone) by melting or vaporization

ab·la·tive \ˈab-lə-tiv\ *adj* : of, relating to, or constituting a grammatical case (as in Latin) expressing typically the relation of separation and source — **ablative** *n*

ablaze \ə-ˈblāz\ *adj or adv* : being on fire : BLAZING

able \ˈā-bəl\ *adj* **abler** \-b(ə-)lər\; **ablest** \-b(ə-)ləst\ [ME, fr. AF, fr. L *habilis* apt, fr. *habēre* to hold, possess] **1** : having sufficient power, skill, or resources to accomplish an object **2** : marked by skill or efficiency — **ably** \-blē\ *adv*

-able *also* **-ible** *adj suffix* **1** : capable of, fit for, or worthy of (being so acted upon or toward) ‹break*able*› ‹collect*ible*› **2** : tending, given, or liable to ‹knowledge*able*› ‹perish*able*›

able–bod·ied \ˌā-bəl-ˈbä-dēd\ *adj* : having a sound strong body

abloom \ə-ˈblüm\ *adj* : BLOOMING

ab·lu·tion \ə-ˈblü-shən, a-\ *n* : the washing of one's body or part of it

ABM \ˌā-(ˌ)bē-ˈem\ *n, pl* **ABM's** *or* **ABMs** : ANTIBALLISTIC MISSILE

Abnaki *var of* ABENAKI

ab·ne·gate \ˈab-ni-ˌgāt\ *vb* **-gat·ed**; **-gat·ing** **1** : DENY, RENOUNCE **2** : SURRENDER, RELINQUISH ‹~ her powers› — **ab·ne·ga·tion** \ˌab-ni-ˈgā-shən\ *n*

ab·nor·mal \ab-ˈnȯr-məl\ *adj* : deviating from the normal or average — **ab·nor·mal·i·ty** \ˌab-nȯr-ˈma-lə-tē\ *n* — **ab·nor·mal·ly** *adv*

[1]**aboard** \ə-ˈbȯrd\ *adv* **1** : ALONGSIDE **2** : on, onto, or within a car, ship, or aircraft **3** : in or into a group or association ‹welcome new workers ~›

[2]**aboard** *prep* : ON, ONTO, WITHIN

abode \ə-ˈbōd\ *n* **1** : STAY, SOJOURN **2** : HOME, RESIDENCE

abol·ish \ə-ˈbä-lish\ *vb* : to do away with : ANNUL ‹~ slavery› — **ab·o·li·tion** \ˌa-bə-ˈli-shən\ *n*

ab·o·li·tion·ism \ˌa-bə-ˈli-shə-ˌni-zəm\ *n* : advocacy of the abolition of slavery — **ab·o·li·tion·ist** \-ˈli-sh(ə-)nist\ *n or adj*

A–bomb \ˈā-ˌbäm\ *n* : ATOMIC BOMB — **A–bomb** *vb*

abom·i·na·ble \ə-ˈbä-mə-nə-bəl\ *adj* : causing disgust or hatred : DETESTABLE

abominable snow·man \-ˈsnō-mən, -ˌman\ *n, often cap A&S* : a mysterious creature with human or apelike characteristics reported to exist in the high Himalayas

abom·i·nate \ə-ˈbä-mə-ˌnāt\ *vb* **-nat·ed**; **-nat·ing** [L *abominari,* lit., to deprecate as an ill omen, fr. *ab-* away + *omen* omen] : to hate or loathe intensely

abom·i·na·tion \ə-ˌbä-mə-ˈnā-shən\ *n* **1** : something abominable **2** : extreme disgust or hatred : LOATHING

ab·orig·i·nal \ˌa-bə-ˈri-jə-nəl\ *adj* : ORIGINAL, INDIGENOUS

ab·orig·i·ne \ˌa-bə-ˈri-jə-nē\ *n* : a member of the original people to inhabit a region : NATIVE

aborn·ing \ə-ˈbȯr-niŋ\ *adv* : while being born or produced

[1]**abort** \ə-ˈbȯrt\ *vb* **1** : to cause or undergo abortion **2** : to terminate prematurely ‹~ a spaceflight› — **abor·tive** \-ˈbȯr-tiv\ *adj*

[2]**abort** *n* : the premature termination of a mission of or a procedure relating to an aircraft or spacecraft

abor·tion \ə-ˈbȯr-shən\ *n* : the spontaneous or induced termination of a pregnancy after, accompanied by, resulting in, or closely followed by the death of the embryo or fetus

abor·tion·ist \-sh(ə-)nist\ *n* : one who induces abortions

abound \ə-ˈbau̇nd\ *vb* **1** : to be plentiful : TEEM **2** : to be fully supplied

[1]**about** \ə-ˈbau̇t\ *adv* **1** : reasonably close to; *also* : on the verge of ‹~ to join the army› **2** : on all sides **3** : NEARBY

[2]**about** *prep* **1** : on every side of **2** : near to **3** : CONCERNING

about–face \-ˈfās\ *n* : a reversal of direction or attitude — **about–face** *vb*

[1]**above** \ə-ˈbəv\ *adv* **1** : in the sky; *also* : in or to heaven **2** : in or to a higher place; *also* : higher on the same page or on a preceding page

[2]**above** *prep* **1** : in or to a higher place than : OVER ‹storm clouds ~ the bay› **2** : superior to ‹he thought her far ~ him› **3** : more than : EXCEEDING **4** : as distinct from ‹~ the noise›

above·board \-ˌbȯrd\ *adv or adj* : without concealment or deception : OPENLY

abp *abbr* archbishop

abr *abbr* abridged; abridgment

ab·ra·ca·dab·ra \ˌa-brə-kə-ˈda-brə\ *n* **1** : a magical charm or incantation against calamity **2** : GIBBERISH

abrade \ə-ˈbrād\ *vb* **abrad·ed**; **abrad·ing** **1** : to wear away by friction **2** : to wear down in spirit : IRRITATE — **abra·sion** \-ˈbrā-zhən\ *n*

[1]**abra·sive** \ə-ˈbrā-siv\ *n* : a substance (as pumice) for abrading, smoothing, or polishing

[2]**abrasive** *adj* : tending to abrade : causing irritation ‹~ relationships› — **abra·sive·ly** *adv* — **abra·sive·ness** *n*

abreast \ə-ˈbrest\ *adv or adj* **1** : side by

side **2** : up to a standard or level esp. of knowledge ⟨kept ~ of the news⟩

abridge \ə-ˈbrij\ *vb* **abridged; abridg·ing** [ME *abregen,* fr. AF *abreger,* fr. LL *abbreviare,* fr. L *ad* to + *brevis* short] : to lessen in length or extent : SHORTEN — **abridg·ment** *or* **abridge·ment** *n*

abroad \ə-ˈbrȯd\ *adv or adj* **1** : over a wide area **2** : away from one's home **3** : outside one's country

ab·ro·gate \ˈa-brə-ˌgāt\ *vb* **-gat·ed; -gat·ing** : ANNUL, REVOKE — **ab·ro·ga·tion** \ˌa-brə-ˈgā-shən\ *n*

abrupt \ə-ˈbrəpt\ *adj* **1** : broken or as if broken off **2** : SUDDEN, HASTY ⟨an ~ turn⟩ **3** : so quick as to seem rude ⟨an ~ reply⟩ **4** : DISCONNECTED **5** : STEEP — **abrupt·ly** *adv*

abs *abbr* absolute

ab·scess \ˈab-ˌses\ *n, pl* **ab·scess·es** [L *abscessus,* lit., act of going away, fr. *abscedere* to go away, fr. *abs-, ab-* away + *cedere* to go] : a localized collection of pus surrounded by inflamed tissue — **abscessed** \-ˌsest\ *adj*

ab·scis·sa \ab-ˈsi-sə\ *n, pl* **abscissas** *also* **ab·scis·sae** \-ˈsi-(ˌ)sē\ : the horizontal coordinate of a point in a plane coordinate system obtained by measuring parallel to the x-axis

ab·scis·sion \ab-ˈsi-zhən\ *n* **1** : the act or process of cutting off **2** : the natural separation of flowers, fruits, or leaves from plants — **ab·scise** \ab-ˈsīz\ *vb*

ab·scond \ab-ˈskänd\ *vb* : to depart secretly and hide oneself

ab·sence \ˈab-səns\ *n* **1** : the state or time of being absent **2** : WANT, LACK **3** : INATTENTION ⟨~ of mind⟩

[1]**ab·sent** \ˈab-sənt\ *adj* **1** : not present **2** : LACKING **3** : INATTENTIVE

[2]**ab·sent** \ab-ˈsent\ *vb* : to keep (oneself) away

[3]**ab·sent** \ˈab-sənt\ *prep* : in the absence of : WITHOUT

ab·sen·tee \ˌab-sən-ˈtē\ *n* : one that is absent or keeps away

absentee ballot *n* : a ballot submitted (as by mail) in advance of an election by a voter who is unable to be present at the polls

ab·sen·tee·ism \ˌab-sən-ˈtē-ˌi-zəm\ *n* : chronic absence (as from work or school)

ab·sent·mind·ed \ˌab-sənt-ˈmīn-dəd\ *adj* : unaware of one's surroundings or actions : INATTENTIVE — **ab·sent·mind·ed·ly** *adv* — **ab·sent·mind·ed·ness** *n*

ab·sinthe *also* **ab·sinth** \ˈab-ˌsinth\ *n* [F] : a liqueur flavored esp. with wormwood and anise

ab·so·lute \ˈab-sə-ˌlüt, ˌab-sə-ˈlüt\ *adj* **1** : free from imperfection or mixture **2** : free from control, restriction, or qualification ⟨~ power⟩ **3** : lacking grammatical connection with any other word in a sentence ⟨~ construction⟩ **4** : POSITIVE ⟨~ proof⟩ **5** : relating to the fundamental units of length, mass, and time **6** : FUNDAMENTAL, ULTIMATE ⟨~ knowledge⟩ — **ab·so·lute·ly** *adv*

absolute pitch *n* **1** : the position of a tone in a standard scale independently determined by its rate of vibration **2** : the ability to sing a note asked for or to name a note heard

absolute value *n* : a nonnegative number equal to a given real number with any negative sign removed

absolute zero *n* : a theoretical temperature marked by a complete absence of heat and motion and equivalent to exactly -273.15°C or -459.67°F

ab·so·lu·tion \ˌab-sə-ˈlü-shən\ *n* : the act of absolving; *esp* : a remission of sins pronounced by a priest in the sacrament of reconciliation

ab·so·lut·ism \ˈab-sə-ˌlü-ˌti-zəm\ *n* **1** : the theory that a ruler or government should have unlimited power **2** : government by an absolute ruler or authority

ab·solve \əb-ˈzälv, -ˈsälv\ *vb* **ab·solved; ab·solv·ing** : to set free from an obligation or the consequences of guilt

ab·sorb \əb-ˈsȯrb, -ˈzȯrb\ *vb* **1** : to take in and make part of an existent whole **2** : to suck up or take in in the manner of a sponge **3** : to engage (one's attention) : ENGROSS **4** : to receive without recoil or echo ⟨a ceiling that ~*s* sound⟩ **5** : ASSUME, BEAR ⟨~ all costs⟩ **6** : to transform (radiant energy) into a different form esp. with a resulting rise in temperature — **ab·sorb·er** *n* — **ab·sorb·ing** *adj* — **ab·sorb·ing·ly** *adv*

ab·sor·bent *also* **ab·sor·bant** \əb-ˈsȯr-bənt, -ˈzȯr-\ *adj* : able to absorb ⟨~ cotton⟩ — **ab·sor·ben·cy** \-bən-sē\ *n* — **absorbent** *also* **absorbant** *n*

ab·sorp·tion \əb-ˈsȯrp-shən, -ˈzȯrp-\ *n* **1** : a process of absorbing or being absorbed **2** : concentration of attention ⟨~ in his work⟩ — **ab·sorp·tive** \-tiv\ *adj*

ab·stain \əb-ˈstān\ *vb* : to refrain from an action or practice — **ab·stain·er** *n* — **ab·sten·tion** \-ˈsten-chən\ *n*

ab·ste·mi·ous \ab-ˈstē-mē-əs\ *adj* : sparing in use of food or drink : TEMPERATE — **ab·ste·mi·ous·ly** *adv* — **ab·ste·mi·ous·ness** *n*

ab·sti·nence \ˈab-stə-nəns\ *n* : voluntary refraining esp. from eating certain foods, drinking liquor, or engaging in sexual intercourse — **ab·sti·nent** \-nənt\ *adj*

abstr *abbr* abstract

[1]**ab·stract** \ab-ˈstrakt, ˈab-ˌstrakt\ *adj* **1** : considered apart from a particular instance **2** : expressing a quality apart from an object ⟨*honesty* is an ~ word⟩ **3** : having only intrinsic form with little or no pictorial representation ⟨~ painting⟩ — **ab·stract·ly** *adv* — **ab·stract·ness** *n*

[2]**ab·stract** \ˈab-ˌstrakt; *2 also* ab-ˈstrakt\ *n* **1** : a written summary **2** : an abstract thing or state

[3]**ab·stract** \ab-ˈstrakt, ˈab-ˌstrakt; *2 usu* ˈab-ˌstrakt\ *vb* **1** : REMOVE, SEPARATE **2** : to make an abstract of : SUMMARIZE **3** : to draw away the attention of **4** : STEAL — **ab·stract·ed·ly** \ab-ˈstrak-təd-lē, ˈab-ˌstrak-\ *adv*

abstract expressionism *n* : art that expresses the artist's attitudes and emotions through abstract forms — **abstract expressionist** *n*

ab•strac•tion \ab-ˈstrak-shən\ *n* **1** : the act of abstracting : the state of being abstracted **2** : an abstract idea **3** : an abstract work of art

ab•struse \ab-ˈstrüs\ *adj* : hard to understand : RECONDITE — **ab•struse•ly** *adv* — **ab•struse•ness** *n*

ab•surd \əb-ˈsərd, -ˈzərd\ *adj* [MF *absurde,* fr. L *absurdus,* fr. *ab-* from + *surdus* deaf, stupid] : RIDICULOUS, UNREASONABLE — **ab•sur•di•ty** \-ˈsər-də-tē, -ˈzər-\ *n* — **ab•surd•ly** *adv*

abun•dant \ə-ˈbən-dənt\ *adj* [ME, fr. AF, fr. L *abundant-, abundans,* prp. of *abundare* to abound, fr. *ab-* from + *unda* wave] : more than enough : amply sufficient ♦ ***Synonyms*** COPIOUS, PLENTIFUL, AMPLE, BOUNTIFUL — **abun•dance** \-dəns\ *n* — **abun•dant•ly** *adv*

[1]**abuse** \ə-ˈbyüs\ *n* **1** : a corrupt practice **2** : MISUSE ⟨drug ~⟩ **3** : coarse and insulting speech ⟨verbal ~⟩ **4** : MISTREATMENT ⟨child ~⟩

[2]**abuse** \ə-ˈbyüz\ *vb* **abused; abus•ing 1** : to put to a wrong use : MISUSE **2** : to use excessively ⟨~ alcohol⟩ **3** : MISTREAT **4** : to attack in words : REVILE — **abus•er** *n* — **abu•sive** \-ˈbyü-siv\ *adj* — **abu•sive•ly** *adv* — **abu•sive•ness** *n*

abut \ə-ˈbət\ *vb* **abut•ted; abut•ting** : to touch along a border : border on

abut•ment \ə-ˈbət-mənt\ *n* **1** : the place at which one thing borders another **2** : the part of a structure (as a bridge) that supports weight or withstands lateral pressure

abut•ter \ə-ˈbə-tər\ *n* : one that abuts; *esp* : the owner of a contiguous property

abuzz \ə-ˈbəz\ *adj* : filled or resounding with activity or excitement ⟨an office ~ with rumors⟩

abys•mal \ə-ˈbiz-məl\ *adj* **1** : immeasurably deep : BOTTOMLESS **2** : absolutely wretched ⟨~ living conditions⟩ — **abys•mal•ly** *adv*

abyss \ə-ˈbis\ *n* **1** : the bottomless pit in old accounts of the universe **2** : an immeasurable depth

abys•sal \ə-ˈbi-səl\ *adj* : of or relating to the bottom waters of the ocean depths

ac *abbr* account

-ac *n suffix* : one affected with ⟨hypochondri*ac*⟩

Ac *symbol* actinium

AC *abbr* **1** air-conditioning **2** alternating current **3** [L *ante Christum*] before Christ **4** [L *ante cibum*] before meals **5** area code

aca•cia \ə-ˈkā-shə\ *n* : any of a genus of leguminous trees or shrubs with round white or yellow flower clusters and often feathery leaves

acad *abbr* academic; academy

ac•a•deme \ˈa-kə-ˌdēm, ˌa-kə-ˈ\ *n* : SCHOOL; *also* : academic environment

[1]**ac•a•dem•ic** \ˌa-kə-ˈde-mik\ *n* : a person who is academic in background, outlook, or methods

[2]**academic** *adj* **1** : of, relating to, or associated with schools or colleges **2** : literary or general rather than technical **3** : theoretical rather than practical — **ac•a•dem•i•cal•ly** \-mi-k(ə-)lē\ *adv*

ac•a•de•mi•cian \ˌa-kə-də-ˈmi-shən, ə-ˌka-də-\ *n* **1** : a member of a society of scholars or artists **2** : ACADEMIC

ac•a•dem•i•cism \ˌa-kə-ˈde-mə-ˌsi-zəm\ *also* **acad•e•mism** \ə-ˈka-də-ˌmi-zəm\ *n* **1** : a formal academic quality **2** : purely speculative thinking

acad•e•my \ə-ˈka-də-mē\ *n, pl* **-mies** [Gk *Akadēmeia,* school of philosophy founded by Plato, fr. *Akadēmeia,* gymnasium where Plato taught, fr. *Akadēmos* Greek mythological hero] **1** : a school above the elementary level; *esp* : a private high school **2** : a society of scholars or artists

acan•thus \ə-ˈkan-thəs\ *n, pl* **acanthus 1** : any of a genus of prickly herbs of the Mediterranean region **2** : an ornamentation (as on a column) representing the leaves of the acanthus

a cap•pel•la *also* **a ca•pel•la** \ˌä-kə-ˈpe-lə\ *adv or adj* [It *a cappella* in chapel style] : without instrumental accompaniment

acc *abbr* accusative

ac•cede \ak-ˈsēd\ *vb* **ac•ced•ed; ac•ced•ing 1** : to become a party to an agreement **2** : to express approval **3** : to enter upon an office ♦ ***Synonyms*** AGREE, ACQUIESCE, ASSENT, CONSENT, SUBSCRIBE

ac•cel•er•ate \ik-ˈse-lə-ˌrāt, ak-\ *vb* **-at•ed; -at•ing 1** : to bring about earlier **2** : to speed up : QUICKEN — **ac•cel•er•a•tion** \-ˌse-lə-ˈrā-shən\ *n*

ac•cel•er•a•tor \ik-ˈse-lə-ˌrā-tər, ak-\ *n* **1** : one that accelerates **2** : a pedal for controlling the speed of a motor-vehicle engine **3** : an apparatus for imparting high velocities to charged particles

ac•cel•er•om•e•ter \ik-ˌse-lə-ˈrä-mə-tər, ak-\ *n* : an instrument for measuring acceleration or vibrations

[1]**ac•cent** \ˈak-ˌsent, ak-ˈsent\ *vb* : to give stress to : EMPHASIZE

[2]**ac•cent** \ˈak-ˌsent\ *n* **1** : prominence given to one syllable of a word esp. by stress **2** : a distinctive manner of pronunciation ⟨a foreign ~⟩ **3** : a mark (as ´, `, ˆ) over a vowel used usu. to indicate a difference in pronunciation from a vowel not so marked — **ac•cen•tu•al** \ak-ˈsen-chə-wəl\ *adj*

ac•cen•tu•ate \ak-ˈsen-chə-ˌwāt\ *vb* **-at•ed; -at•ing** : STRESS, EMPHASIZE — **ac•cen•tu•a•tion** \-ˌsen-chə-ˈwā-shən\ *n*

ac•cept \ik-ˈsept, ak-\ *vb* **1** : to receive willingly **2** : to agree to **3** : to assume an obligation to pay

ac•cept•able \ik-ˈsep-tə-bəl, ak-\ *adj* : capable or worthy of being accepted — **ac•cept•abil•i•ty** \ik-ˌsep-tə-ˈbi-lə-tē, ak-\ *n*

ac•cep•tance \ik-ˈsep-təns, ak-\ *n* **1** : the act of accepting **2** : the state of being accepted or acceptable **3** : an accepted bill of exchange

ac•cep•ta•tion \ˌak-ˌsep-ˈtā-shən\ *n* : the generally understood meaning of a word

[1]**ac•cess** \ˈak-ˌses\ *n* **1** : capacity to enter

or approach **2** : a way of approach : ENTRANCE

[2]**access** *vb* : to get at : gain access to

ac·ces·si·ble \ik-ˈse-sə-bəl, ak-, ek-\ *adj* **1** : capable of being reached ⟨~ by train⟩ **2** : capable of being used or seen ⟨~ archives⟩ **3** : capable of being understood ⟨an ~ film⟩ — **ac·ces·si·bil·i·ty** \-ˌse-sə-ˈbi-lə-tē\ *n*

ac·ces·sion \ik-ˈse-shən, ak-\ *n* **1** : increase by something added **2** : something added **3** : the act of coming to a high office or position

ac·ces·so·ry *also* **ac·ces·sa·ry** \ik-ˈse-sə-rē, ak-\ *n, pl* **-ries** **1** : a person who though not present abets or assists in the commission of an offense **2** : something helpful but not essential ♦ ***Synonyms*** APPURTENANCE, ADJUNCT, APPENDAGE, APPENDIX — **accessory** *adj*

ac·ci·dent \ˈak-sə-dənt\ *n* **1** : an event occurring by chance or unintentionally **2** : CHANCE ⟨met by ~⟩ **3** : a nonessential property

[1]**ac·ci·den·tal** \ˌak-sə-ˈden-tᵊl\ *adj* **1** : happening unexpectedly or by chance **2** : happening without intent or through carelessness ♦ ***Synonyms*** CASUAL, FORTUITOUS, INCIDENTAL, CHANCE — **ac·ci·den·tal·ly** \-ˈden-tᵊl-ē\ *also* **ac·ci·dent·ly** \-ˈdent-lē\ *adv*

[2]**accidental** *n* : a musical note foreign to a key indicated by a signature

ac·claim \ə-ˈklām\ *vb* **1** : to give strong approval or praise to **2** : to declare by acclamation ♦ ***Synonyms*** EXTOL, LAUD, COMMEND, HAIL — **acclaim** *n*

ac·cla·ma·tion \ˌa-klə-ˈmā-shən\ *n* **1** : loud eager applause **2** : an overwhelming affirmative vote by shouting or applause rather than by ballot

ac·cli·mate \ˈa-klə-ˌmāt, ə-ˈklī-mət\ *vb* **-mat·ed; -mat·ing** : to accustom or become accustomed to a new climate or situation — **ac·cli·ma·tion** \ˌa-klə-ˈmā-shən, -ˌklī-\ *n*

ac·cli·ma·tise *Brit var of* ACCLIMATIZE

ac·cli·ma·tize \ə-ˈklī-mə-ˌtīz\ *vb* **-tized; -tiz·ing** : ACCLIMATE — **ac·cli·ma·ti·za·tion** \-ˌklī-mə-tə-ˈzā-shən\ *n*

ac·cliv·i·ty \ə-ˈkli-və-tē\ *n, pl* **-ties** : an ascending slope

ac·co·lade \ˈa-kə-ˌlād\ *n* [F, fr. *accoler* to embrace, ultim. fr. L *ad-* to + *collum* neck] : an expression of praise : AWARD

ac·com·mo·date \ə-ˈkä-mə-ˌdāt\ *vb* **-dat·ed; -dat·ing** **1** : to make fit or suitable : ADAPT, ADJUST **2** : HARMONIZE, RECONCILE **3** : to provide with something needed **4** : to hold without crowding **5** *of the eyes* : to undergo involuntary adjustment for seeing at different distances

ac·com·mo·dat·ing *adj* : OBLIGING

ac·com·mo·da·tion \ə-ˌkä-mə-ˈdā-shən\ *n* **1** : something supplied to satisfy a need; *esp* : LODGINGS — usu. used in pl. **2** : the act of accommodating : ADJUSTMENT **3** : the involuntary adjustment of the eye for seeing at different distances

ac·com·pa·ni·ment \ə-ˈkəm-pə-nē-mənt, -ˈkəmp-nē-\ *n* : something that accompanies another; *esp* : subordinate music to support a principal voice or instrument

ac·com·pa·ny \-nē\ *vb* **-nied; -ny·ing** **1** : to go or occur with : ATTEND **2** : to play an accompaniment for — **ac·com·pa·nist** \-nist\ *n*

ac·com·plice \ə-ˈkäm-pləs, -ˈkəm-\ *n* : an associate in wrongdoing

ac·com·plish \ə-ˈkäm-plish, -ˈkəm-\ *vb* : to bring to completion ♦ ***Synonyms*** ACHIEVE, EFFECT, EXECUTE, PERFORM — **ac·com·plish·er** *n*

ac·com·plished \-plisht\ *adj* **1** : EXPERT, SKILLED ⟨an ~ pianist⟩ **2** : established beyond doubt ⟨an ~ fact⟩

ac·com·plish·ment \ə-ˈkäm-plish-mənt, -ˈkəm-\ *n* **1** : COMPLETION **2** : something completed or effected **3** : an acquired excellence or skill

[1]**ac·cord** \ə-ˈkȯrd\ *vb* [ME, fr. AF *acorder,* fr. VL **accordare,* fr. L *ad-* to + *cord-, cor* heart] **1** : GRANT, CONCEDE **2** : AGREE, HARMONIZE ⟨his interpretation does not ~ with the facts⟩ — **ac·cor·dant** \-ˈkȯr-dᵊnt\ *adj*

[2]**accord** *n* **1** : AGREEMENT, HARMONY **2** : willingness to act ⟨gave of their own ~⟩

ac·cor·dance \ə-ˈkȯr-dᵊns\ *n* **1** : ACCORD **2** : the act of granting

ac·cord·ing·ly \ə-ˈkȯr-diŋ-lē\ *adv* **1** : in accordance **2** : CONSEQUENTLY, SO

according to *prep* **1** : in conformity with ⟨paid *according to* ability⟩ **2** : as stated or attested by ⟨*according to* you⟩

[1]**ac·cor·di·on** \ə-ˈkȯr-dē-ən\ *n* [G *Akkordion,* fr. *Akkord* chord] : a portable keyboard instrument with a bellows and reeds — **ac·cor·di·on·ist** \-ə-nist\ *n*

[2]**accordion** *adj* : folding like the bellows of an accordion ⟨~ pleats⟩

ac·cost \ə-ˈkȯst\ *vb* [MF *accoster,* ultim. fr. L *ad-* to + *costa* rib, side] : to approach and speak to esp. aggressively

[1]**ac·count** \ə-ˈkau̇nt\ *n* **1** : a statement of business transactions **2** : a formal business arrangement for regular dealings or services ⟨an advertising ~⟩ ⟨an email ~⟩ **3** : a statement of reasons, causes, or motives **4** : VALUE, IMPORTANCE ⟨his opinion is of little ~⟩ **5** : a sum of money deposited in a bank and subject to withdrawal by the depositor — **on account of** : BECAUSE OF — **on no account** : under no circumstances — **on one's own account** : on one's own behalf

[2]**account** *vb* **1** : CONSIDER ⟨I ~ him lucky⟩ **2** : to give an explanation ⟨~ for the money you spent⟩ — used with *for*

ac·count·able \ə-ˈkau̇n-tə-bəl\ *adj* **1** : ANSWERABLE, RESPONSIBLE **2** : EXPLICABLE — **ac·count·abil·i·ty** \-ˌkau̇n-tə-ˈbi-lə-tē\ *n*

ac·coun·tant \ə-ˈkau̇n-tᵊnt\ *n* : a person skilled in accounting — **ac·coun·tan·cy** \-tᵊn-sē\ *n*

account executive *n* : a business executive in charge of a client's account

ac·count·ing \ə-ˈkau̇n-tiŋ\ *n* : the art or system of keeping and analyzing financial records

ac·cou·tre *or* **ac·cou·ter** \ə-ˈkü-tər\ *vb*

-cou·tred *or* **-cou·tered**; **-cou·tring** *or* **-cou·ter·ing** \-ˈkü-t(ə-)riŋ\ : EQUIP, OUTFIT ⟨the knights were *accoutred* for battle⟩

ac·cou·tre·ment *or* **ac·cou·ter·ment** \ə-ˈkü-trə-mənt, -ˈkü-tər-\ *n* [F] **1** : an accessory item — usu. used in pl. **2** : an identifying characteristic

ac·cred·it \ə-ˈkre-dət\ *vb* **1** : to endorse or approve officially **2** : CREDIT — **ac·cred·i·ta·tion** \-ˌkre-də-ˈtā-shən\ *n*

ac·cre·tion \ə-ˈkrē-shən\ *n* **1** : growth or enlargement esp. by addition from without **2** : a product of accretion

accretion disk *n* : a disk of usu. gaseous matter surrounding and gradually accumulating onto a massive celestial object

ac·crue \ə-ˈkrü\ *vb* **ac·crued**; **ac·cru·ing** **1** : to come by way of increase **2** : to be added by periodic growth — **ac·cru·al** \-əl\ *n*

acct *abbr* account; accountant

ac·cul·tur·a·tion \ə-ˌkəl-chə-ˈrā-shən\ *n* : cultural modification of an individual or group by borrowing and adapting traits from another culture

ac·cu·mu·late \ə-ˈkyü-myə-ˌlāt\ *vb* **-lat·ed**; **-lat·ing** [L *accumulare*, fr. *ad-* to + *cumulare* to heap up] : to heap or pile up ♦ ***Synonyms*** AMASS, GATHER, COLLECT, STOCKPILE — **ac·cu·mu·la·tion** \-ˌkyü-myə-ˈlā-shən\ *n* — **ac·cu·mu·la·tive** \-ˈkyü-myə-lə-tiv\ *adj* — **ac·cu·mu·la·tor** \-ˈkyü-myə-ˌlā-tər\ *n*

ac·cu·rate \ˈa-kyə-rət\ *adj* : free from error : EXACT, PRECISE — **ac·cu·ra·cy** \-rə-sē\ *n* — **ac·cu·rate·ly** *adv* — **ac·cu·rate·ness** *n*

ac·cursed \ə-ˈkərst, -ˈkər-səd\ *or* **ac·curst** \ə-ˈkərst\ *adj* **1** : being under a curse **2** : DAMNABLE, EXECRABLE

ac·cus·al \ə-ˈkyü-zəl\ *n* : ACCUSATION

ac·cu·sa·tive \ə-ˈkyü-zə-tiv\ *adj* : of, relating to, or being a grammatical case marking the direct object of a verb or the object of a preposition — **accusative** *n*

ac·cu·sa·to·ry \ə-ˈkyü-zə-ˌtȯr-ē\ *adj* : expressing accusation ⟨an ~ tone⟩

ac·cuse \ə-ˈkyüz\ *vb* **ac·cused**; **ac·cus·ing** : to charge with an offense : BLAME — **ac·cu·sa·tion** \ˌa-kyə-ˈzā-shən\ *n* — **ac·cus·er** *n*

ac·cused \ə-ˈkyüzd\ *n, pl* **accused** : the defendant in a criminal case

ac·cus·tom \ə-ˈkəs-təm\ *vb* : to make familiar through use or experience

ac·cus·tomed \ə-ˈkəs-təmd\ *adj* : USUAL, CUSTOMARY; *also* : being in the habit ⟨~*ed* to winning⟩

[1]**ace** \ˈās\ *n* [ME *as* a die face marked with one spot, fr. AF, fr. L, unit, a copper coin] **1** : a playing card bearing a single large pip in its center **2** : a point (as in tennis) won on a serve that goes untouched **3** : a golf score of one stroke on a hole **4** : a combat pilot who has downed five or more enemy planes **5** : one that excels **6** : the best pitcher on a baseball team

[2]**ace** *vb* **aced**; **ac·ing** **1** : to score an ace against (an opponent) or on (a golf hole) **2** : to defeat decisively **3** : to perform extremely well in or on ⟨*aced* the quiz⟩

[3]**ace** *adj* : of first rank or quality

ACE in·hib·i·tor \ˌā-ˌsē-ˈē-in-ˈhi-bə-tər, ˈās-\ *n* : any of a group of drugs that lower blood pressure by relaxing the arteries

acer·bic \ə-ˈsər-bik, a-\ *adj* : acid in temper, mood, or tone ⟨~ wit⟩

acer·bi·ty \ə-ˈsər-bə-tē\ *n, pl* **-ties** : SOURNESS, BITTERNESS

acet·amin·o·phen \ə-ˌsē-tə-ˈmi-nə-fən\ *n* : a crystalline compound used in chemical synthesis and in medicine to relieve pain and fever

ac·e·tate \ˈa-sə-ˌtāt\ *n* **1** : a salt or ester of acetic acid **2** : a textile fiber made from cellulose and acetic acid; *also* : a fabric or plastic made of this fiber

ace·tic acid \ə-ˈsē-tik-\ *n* : a colorless pungent liquid acid that is the chief acid of vinegar and is used esp. in making chemical compounds

ac·e·tone \ˈa-sə-ˌtōn\ *n* : a volatile flammable fragrant liquid compound used in making other chemical compounds and as a solvent

ace·tyl·cho·line \ə-ˌsē-tᵊl-ˈkō-ˌlēn\ *n* : a compound that is released at nerve endings of the autonomic nervous system and is active in the transmission of nerve impulses

acet·y·lene \ə-ˈse-tᵊl-ən, -tᵊl-ˌēn\ *n* : a colorless flammable gas used as a fuel (as in welding and soldering)

ace·tyl·sal·i·cyl·ic acid \ə-ˈsē-tᵊl-ˌsa-lə-ˌsi-lik-\ *n* : ASPIRIN 1

ache \ˈāk\ *vb* **ached**; **ach·ing** **1** : to suffer a usu. dull persistent pain ⟨an *aching* back⟩ **2** : LONG, YEARN ⟨*aching* to go home⟩ — **ache** *n* — **ach·ing·ly** \ˈā-kiŋ-lē\ *adv*

achieve \ə-ˈchēv\ *vb* **achieved**; **achiev·ing** [ME *acheven*, fr. AF *achever* to finish, fr. *a-* to (fr. L *ad-*) + *chef* end, head, fr. L *caput*] : to gain by work or effort ♦ ***Synonyms*** ACCOMPLISH, ATTAIN, REALIZE — **achiev·able** \-ˈchē-və-bəl\ *adj* — **achieve·ment** *n* — **achiev·er** *n*

Achil·les' heel \ə-ˌki-lēz-\ *n* [fr. the story that the Greek warrior Achilles was vulnerable only in the heel] : a vulnerable point

Achil·les tendon \ə-ˌki-lēz-\ *n* : the tendon joining the muscles in the calf of the leg to the bone of the heel

ach·ro·mat·ic \ˌa-krə-ˈma-tik\ *adj* : giving an image almost free from extraneous colors ⟨~ lens⟩

achy \ˈā-kē\ *adj* **ach·i·er**; **ach·i·est** : afflicted with aches — **ach·i·ness** *n*

[1]**ac·id** \ˈa-səd\ *adj* **1** : sour or biting to the taste; *also* : sharp or sour in manner **2** : of or relating to an acid — **acid·i·ty** \ə-ˈsi-də-tē\ *n* — **acid·ly** *adv*

[2]**acid** *n* **1** : a sour substance **2** : a usu. water-soluble chemical compound that has a sour taste, reacts with a base to form a salt, and reddens litmus **3** : LSD — **acid·ic** \ə-ˈsi-dik\ *adj*

acid·i·fy \ə-ˈsi-də-ˌfī\ *vb* **-fied**; **-fy·ing** **1** : to make or become acid **2** : to change into an acid — **acid·i·fi·ca·tion** \-ˌsi-də-fə-ˈkā-shən\ *n*

ac·i·do·sis \ˌa-sə-ˈdō-səs\ *n, pl* **-do·ses** \-ˌsēz\ : an abnormal state of reduced alkalinity of the blood and body tissues

acid precipitation *n* : precipitation with above normal acidity that is caused esp. by atmospheric pollutants

acid rain *n* : acid precipitation in the form of rain

acid test *n* : a severe or crucial test

acid·u·lous \ə-ˈsi-jə-ləs\ *adj* : somewhat acid or harsh in taste or manner

ack *abbr* acknowledge; acknowledgment

ac·knowl·edge \ik-ˈnä-lij, ak-\ *vb* **-edged; -edg·ing 1** : to recognize the rights or authority of **2** : to admit as true **3** : to express thanks for; *also* : to report receipt of ⟨~ a letter⟩ **4** : to recognize as valid — **ac·knowl·edg·ment** *or* **ac·knowl·edge·ment** *n*

ACL \ˌā-ˌsē-ˈel\ *n* : ANTERIOR CRUCIATE LIGAMENT

ACLU *abbr* American Civil Liberties Union

ac·me \ˈak-mē\ *n* [Gk *akmē*] : the highest point

ac·ne \ˈak-nē\ *n* [Gk *aknē,* manuscript var. of *akmē,* lit., point] : a skin disorder marked by inflammation of skin glands and hair follicles and by pimple formation esp. on the face

ac·o·lyte \ˈa-kə-ˌlīt\ *n* **1** : one who assists a member of the clergy in a liturgical service **2** : FOLLOWER

ac·o·nite \ˈa-kə-ˌnīt\ *n* **1** : MONKSHOOD **2** : the dried root of a common Eurasian monkshood used formerly as a drug

acorn \ˈā-ˌkȯrn, -kərn\ *n* : the nut of the oak

acorn squash *n* : an acorn-shaped dark green winter squash with a ridged surface and yellow to orange flesh

acous·tic \ə-ˈkü-stik\ *or* **acous·ti·cal** \-sti-kəl\ *adj* **1** : of or relating to the sense or organs of hearing, to sound, or to the science of sounds **2** : deadening sound ⟨~ tile⟩ **3** : operated by or utilizing sound waves **4** : having a sound that is not electronically modified ⟨~ guitar⟩ — **acous·ti·cal·ly** \-k(ə-)lē\ *adv*

acous·tics \ə-ˈkü-stiks\ *n sing or pl* **1** : the science of sound **2** : the qualities in a room that make it easy or hard for a person in it to hear distinctly

ac·quaint \ə-ˈkwānt\ *vb* [ME, ultim. fr. L *ad-* + *cognoscere* to know] **1** : to cause to know personally **2** : INFORM

ac·quain·tance \ə-ˈkwān-tᵊns\ *n* **1** : personal knowledge **2** : a person with whom one is acquainted — **ac·quain·tance·ship** *n*

acquaintance rape *n* : rape committed by someone known to the victim

ac·qui·esce \ˌa-kwē-ˈes\ *vb* **-esced; -esc·ing** : to accept, comply, or submit without open opposition ♦ ***Synonyms*** CONSENT, AGREE, ASSENT, ACCEDE — **ac·qui·es·cence** \-ˈe-sᵊns\ *n* — **ac·qui·es·cent** \-sᵊnt\ *adj* — **ac·qui·es·cent·ly** *adv*

ac·quire \ə-ˈkwī(-ə)r\ *vb* **ac·quired; ac·quir·ing** : to gain possession of : GET — **ac·quir·able** \-ˈkwī-rə-bəl\ *adj*

acquired *adj* **1** : gained by or as a result of effort or experience **2** : caused by environmental forces and not passed from parent to offspring in the genes ⟨~ characteristics⟩

acquired immune deficiency syndrome *n* : AIDS

acquired immunodeficiency syndrome *n* : AIDS

ac·quire·ment \ə-ˈkwī(-ə)r-mənt\ *n* **1** : ATTAINMENT, ACCOMPLISHMENT **2** : the act of acquiring

ac·qui·si·tion \ˌa-kwə-ˈzi-shən\ *n* **1** : ACQUIREMENT **2** : something acquired

ac·quis·i·tive \ə-ˈkwi-zə-tiv\ *adj* : eager to acquire : GREEDY — **ac·quis·i·tive·ly** *adv* — **ac·quis·i·tive·ness** *n*

ac·quit \ə-ˈkwit\ *vb* **ac·quit·ted; ac·quit·ting 1** : to pronounce not guilty **2** : to conduct (oneself) usu. satisfactorily — **ac·quit·tal** \ə-ˈkwi-tᵊl\ *n*

acre \ˈā-kər\ *n* **1** *pl* : LANDS, ESTATE **2** — see WEIGHT table

acre·age \ˈā-k(ə-)rij\ *n* : area in acres

ac·rid \ˈa-krəd\ *adj* **1** : sharp and biting in taste or odor **2** : deeply bitter : CAUSTIC — **ac·rid·i·ty** \a-ˈkri-də-tē\ *n* — **ac·rid·ly** *adv* — **ac·rid·ness** *n*

ac·ri·mo·ny \ˈa-krə-ˌmō-nē\ *n, pl* **-nies** : harsh or biting sharpness of language or feeling — **ac·ri·mo·ni·ous** \ˌa-krə-ˈmō-nē-əs\ *adj* — **ac·ri·mo·ni·ous·ly** *adv* — **ac·ri·mo·ni·ous·ness** *n*

ac·ro·bat \ˈa-krə-ˌbat\ *n* [F *acrobate,* fr. Gk *akrobatēs,* fr. *akros* topmost + *bainein* to go] : a performer of gymnastic feats — **ac·ro·bat·ic** \ˌa-krə-ˈba-tik\ *adj* — **ac·ro·bat·i·cal·ly** \-ti-k(ə-)lē\ *adv*

ac·ro·bat·ics \ˌa-krə-ˈba-tiks\ *n sing or pl* : the performance of an acrobat

ac·ro·nym \ˈa-krə-ˌnim\ *n* : a word (as *radar*) or abbreviation (as *FBI*) formed from the initial letter or letters of each of the successive parts or major parts of a compound term

ac·ro·pho·bia \ˌa-krə-ˈfō-bē-ə\ *n* : abnormal dread of being in a high place : fear of heights

acrop·o·lis \ə-ˈkrä-pə-ləs\ *n* [Gk *akropolis,* fr. *akros* topmost + *polis* city] : the upper fortified part of an ancient Greek city

¹**across** \ə-ˈkrȯs\ *adv* **1** : to or on the opposite side **2** : so as to be understandable ⟨get the point ~⟩

²**across** *prep* **1** : to or on the opposite side of ⟨ran ~ the street⟩ **2** : on so as to cross or pass at an angle ⟨a log ~ the road⟩

across–the–board *adj* **1** : placed to win if a competitor wins, places, or shows ⟨an ~ bet⟩ **2** : including all classes or categories ⟨an ~ wage increase⟩

acros·tic \ə-ˈkrȯs-tik\ *n* : a composition usu. in verse in which the initial or final letters of the lines taken in order form a word or phrase — **acrostic** *adj*

acryl·ic \ə-ˈkri-lik\ *n* **1** : ACRYLIC RESIN **2** : a paint in which the vehicle is acrylic resin **3** : a quick-drying synthetic textile fiber

acrylic resin *n* : a glassy thermoplastic used for cast and molded parts or as coatings and adhesives

[1]**act** \ˈakt\ *n* **1** : a thing done : DEED **2** : STATUTE, DECREE **3** : a main division of a play; *also* : an item on a variety program **4** : an instance of insincere behavior : PRETENSE

[2]**act** *vb* **1** : to perform by action esp. on the stage; *also* : FEIGN, SIMULATE, PRETEND **2** : to take action **3** : to conduct oneself : BEHAVE **4** : to perform a specified function **5** : to produce an effect

[3]**act** *abbr* **1** active **2** actual

ACT *abbr* Australian Capital Territory

actg *abbr* acting

ACTH \ˌā-(ˌ)sē-(ˌ)tē-ˈāch\ *n* : a protein hormone of the pituitary gland that stimulates the adrenal cortex

act·ing \ˈak-tiŋ\ *adj* : doing duty temporarily or for another ⟨~ president⟩

ac·tin·i·um \ak-ˈti-nē-əm\ *n* : a radioactive metallic chemical element

ac·tion \ˈak-shən\ *n* **1** : a legal proceeding **2** : the manner or method of performing **3** : ACTIVITY **4** : ACT, DEED **5** : the accomplishment of a thing usu. over a period of time, in stages, or with the possibility of repetition **6** *pl* : CONDUCT **7** : COMBAT, BATTLE ⟨units that saw ~⟩ ⟨soldiers missing in ~⟩ **8** : the events of a literary plot **9** : an operating mechanism ⟨the ~ of a gun⟩; *also* : the way it operates ⟨stiff ~⟩

ac·tion·able \ˈak-sh(ə-)nə-bəl\ *adj* : affording ground for an action or suit at law — **ac·tion·ably** \-blē\ *adv*

ac·ti·vate \ˈak-tə-ˌvāt\ *vb* **-vat·ed**; **-vat·ing 1** : to spur into action; *also* : to make active, reactive, or radioactive **2** : to treat (as carbon) so as to improve adsorptive properties **3** : to set up (a military unit) formally; *also* : to call to active duty — **ac·ti·va·tion** \ˌak-tə-ˈvā-shən\ *n* — **ac·ti·va·tor** \ˈak-tə-ˌvā-tər\ *n*

ac·tive \ˈak-tiv\ *adj* **1** : causing or involving action or change **2** : asserting that the grammatical subject performs the action represented by the verb ⟨~ voice⟩ **3** : BRISK, LIVELY **4** : erupting or likely to erupt ⟨~ volcano⟩ **5** : presently in operation or use **6** : tending to progress or to cause degeneration ⟨~ tuberculosis⟩ — **active** *n* — **ac·tive·ly** *adv* — **ac·tive·ness** *n*

ac·tive–ma·trix \ˈak-tiv-ˌmā-triks\ *adj* : of, relating to, or being an LCD in which each pixel is individually controlled

ac·tive·wear \ˈak-tiv-ˌwer\ *n* : clothing designed for recreation or informal wear

ac·tiv·ism \ˈak-ti-ˌvi-zəm\ *n* : a doctrine or practice that emphasizes vigorous action for political ends — **ac·tiv·ist** \-vist\ *n or adj*

ac·tiv·i·ty \ak-ˈti-və-tē\ *n, pl* **-ties 1** : the quality or state of being active **2** : forceful or energetic action **3** : an occupation in which one is engaged

ac·tor \ˈak-tər\ *n* : a person who acts in a play, motion picture, television show, etc.

ac·tress \ˈak-trəs\ *n* : a woman or girl who is an actor

Acts \ˈakts\ *or* **Acts of the Apostles** *n* — see BIBLE table

ac·tu·al \ˈak-chə-wəl, -shə-\ *adj* : really existing : REAL — **ac·tu·al·i·ty** \ˌak-chə-ˈwa-lə-tē, -shə-\ *n* — **ac·tu·al·i·za·tion** \ˌak-chə-wə-lə-ˈzā-shən, -shə-\ *n* — **ac·tu·al·ize** \ˈak-chə-wə-ˌlīz, -shə-\ *vb*

ac·tu·al·ly \ˈak-chə-wə-lē, -shə-\ *adv* : in fact or in truth : REALLY

ac·tu·ary \ˈak-chə-ˌwer-ē, -shə-\ *n, pl* **-ar·ies** : a person who calculates insurance risks and premiums — **ac·tu·ar·i·al** \ˌak-chə-ˈwer-ē-əl, -shə-\ *adj*

ac·tu·ate \ˈak-chə-ˌwāt\ *vb* **-at·ed**; **-at·ing 1** : to put into action **2** : to move to action — **ac·tu·a·tion** \ˌak-chə-ˈwā-shən, -shə-\ *n* — **ac·tu·a·tor** \ˈak-chə-ˌwā-tər, -shə-\ *n*

act up *vb* **1** : MISBEHAVE **2** : to function improperly ⟨the car is *acting up* again⟩

acu·ity \ə-ˈkyü-ə-tē\ *n, pl* **-ities** : keenness of perception

acu·men \ə-ˈkyü-mən\ *n* : mental keenness and penetration ♦ ***Synonyms*** DISCERNMENT, INSIGHT, PERCIPIENCE, PERSPICACITY

acu·pres·sure \ˈa-kyu̇-ˌpre-shər\ *n* : a finger massage of those points on the body stimulated in acupuncture

acu·punc·ture \-ˌpəŋk-chər\ *n* : an orig. Chinese practice of inserting thin needles through the skin at specific points esp. to cure disease or relieve pain — **acu·punc·tur·ist** \ˌa-kyu̇-ˈpəŋk-chə-rist\ *n*

acute \ə-ˈkyüt\ *adj* **acut·er**; **acut·est** [ME, fr. L *acutus*, pp. of *acuere* to sharpen, fr. *acus* needle] **1** : SHARP, POINTED **2** : containing less than 90 degrees ⟨an ~ angle⟩ **3** : sharply perceptive; *esp* : mentally keen **4** : SEVERE ⟨~ distress⟩; *also* : having a sudden onset, sharp rise, and short duration ⟨~ inflammation⟩ **5** : of, marked by, or being an accent mark having the form ´ — **acute·ly** *adv* — **acute·ness** *n*

acy·clo·vir \(ˌ)ā-ˈsī-klō-ˌvir\ *n* : a drug used esp. to treat the genital form of herpes simplex

ad \ˈad\ *n* : ADVERTISEMENT

AD *abbr* **1** after date **2** [L *anno Domini*] in the year of our Lord — often printed in small capitals and often punctuated **3** assistant director **4** athletic director

ad·age \ˈa-dij\ *n* : an old familiar saying

[1]**ada·gio** \ə-ˈdä-j(ē-ˌ)ō, -zh(ē-ˌ)ō\ *adv or adj* [It] : at a slow tempo — used as a direction in music

[2]**adagio** *n, pl* **-gios 1** : an adagio movement **2** : a ballet duet or trio displaying feats of lifting and balancing

[1]**ad·a·mant** \ˈa-də-mənt, -ˌmant\ *n* [ME, fr. AF, fr. L *adamant-*, *adamas* hardest metal, diamond, fr. Gk] : a stone believed to be impenetrably hard — **ad·a·man·tine** \ˌa-də-ˈman-ˌtēn, -ˌtīn\ *adj*

[2]**adamant** *adj* : very determined : INFLEXIBLE, UNYIELDING — **ad·a·man·cy** \ˈa-də-mən-sē\ *n* — **ad·a·mant·ly** *adv*

Ad·am's apple \ˈa-dəmz-\ *n* : the projection in front of the neck formed by the largest cartilage of the larynx

adapt \ə-ˈdapt\ *vb* **1** : to make suitable or fit (as for a new use or for a different situation) **2** : to adjust to environmental conditions ♦ ***Synonyms*** ADJUST, ACCOMMODATE, CONFORM — **adapt·abil·i·ty** \ə-ˌdap-tə-ˈbi-lə-tē\ *n* — **adapt·able** *adj* — **ad·ap·ta·tion** \ˌa-ˌdap-ˈtā-shən\ *n* — **ad·ap·ta·tion·al** \-sh(ə-)nəl\ *adj* — **adap·tive** \ə-ˈdap-tiv\ *adj* — **ad·ap·tiv·i·ty** \ˌa-ˌdap-ˈti-və-tē\ *n*

adapt·er *also* **adap·tor** \ə-ˈdap-tər\ *n* **1** : one that adapts **2** : a device for connecting two dissimilar parts of an apparatus **3** : an attachment for adapting apparatus for uses not orig. intended

adaptive optics *n sing or pl* : a telescopic system that improves image resolution by compensating for distortions from atmospheric turbulence

ADC *abbr* **1** aide-de-camp **2** Aid to Dependent Children

add \ˈad\ *vb* **1** : to join to something else so as to increase in number or amount **2** : to say further ⟨let me ∼ this⟩ **3** : to combine (numbers) into one sum

ADD *abbr* attention deficit disorder

ad·dend \ˈa-ˌdend\ *n* : a number to be added to another

ad·den·dum \ə-ˈden-dəm\ *n, pl* **-da** \-də\ [L] : something added; *esp* : a supplement to a book

[1]**ad·der** \ˈa-dər\ *n* [ME, alter. (by false division of *a naddre*) of *naddre,* fr. OE *nædre*] **1** : a poisonous European viper or a related snake **2** : any of various harmless No. American snakes (as the hognose snake)

[2]**add·er** \ˈa-dər\ *n* : one that adds; *esp* : a device that performs addition

[1]**ad·dict** \ə-ˈdikt\ *vb* **1** : to devote or surrender (oneself) to something habitually or excessively **2** : to cause addiction to a substance, activity, or behavior in (someone) — **ad·dic·tive** \-ˈdik-tiv\ *adj*

[2]**ad·dict** \ˈa-(ˌ)dikt\ *n* : one who is addicted to a habit-forming substance, behavior, or activity

ad·dic·tion \ə-ˈdik-shən\ *n* **1** : the quality or state of being addicted **2** : a compulsive need for a habit-forming substance, activity, or behavior characterized by well-defined physiological symptoms upon withdrawal **3** : a strong inclination to do, use, or indulge in something repeatedly

ad·di·tion \ə-ˈdi-shən\ *n* **1** : the act or process of adding; *also* : something added **2** : the operation of combining numbers to obtain their sum ♦ ***Synonyms*** ACCRETION, INCREMENT, ACCESSION, AUGMENTATION

ad·di·tion·al \ə-ˈdi-sh(ə-)nəl\ *adj* : coming by way of addition : ADDED, EXTRA

ad·di·tion·al·ly \ə-ˈdi-sh(ə-)nə-lē\ *adv* : in or by way of addition : FURTHERMORE

[1]**ad·di·tive** \ˈa-də-tiv\ *adj* **1** : of, relating to, or characterized by addition **2** : produced by addition — **ad·di·tiv·i·ty** \ˌa-də-ˈti-və-tē\ *n*

[2]**additive** *n* : a substance added to another in small quantities to effect a desired change in properties ⟨food ∼*s*⟩

ad·dle \ˈa-dᵊl\ *vb* **ad·dled**; **ad·dling** **1** : to throw into confusion : MUDDLE **2** : to become rotten ⟨*addled* eggs⟩

addn *abbr* addition

addnl *abbr* additional

add–on \ˈad-ˌȯn, -ˌän\ *n* : something (as a feature or accessory) added esp. as an enhancement

[1]**ad·dress** \ə-ˈdres\ *vb* **1** : to direct the attention of (oneself) **2** : to direct one's remarks to : deliver an address to **3** : to mark directions for delivery on **4** : to identify (as a memory location) by an address

[2]**ad·dress** \ə-ˈdres, ˈa-ˌdres\ *n* **1** : skillful management **2** : a formal speech : LECTURE **3** : the place where a person or organization may be communicated with **4** : the directions for delivery placed on mail; *also* : the designation of a computer account from which one can send or receive email **5** : a location (as in a computer's memory) where particular data is stored; *also* : URL

ad·dress·ee \ˌa-ˌdre-ˈsē, ə-ˌdre-ˈsē\ *n* : one to whom something is addressed

ad·duce \ə-ˈdüs, -ˈdyüs\ *vb* **ad·duced**; **ad·duc·ing** : to offer as argument, reason, or proof ♦ ***Synonyms*** ADVANCE, ALLEGE, CITE, SUBMIT — **ad·duc·er** *n*

-ade *n suffix* **1** : act : action ⟨block*ade*⟩ **2** : product; *esp* : sweet drink ⟨lime*ade*⟩

ad·e·nine \ˈa-də-ˌnēn\ *n* : a purine base that codes genetic information in the molecular chain of DNA and RNA

ad·e·noid \ˈa-də-ˌnȯid, ˈad-ˌnȯid\ *n* : an enlarged mass of tissue near the opening of the nose into the throat — usu. used in pl. — **adenoid** *or* **ad·e·noi·dal** \ˌa-də-ˈnȯi-dᵊl\ *adj*

aden·o·sine tri·phos·phate \ə-ˈde-nə-ˌsēn-trī-ˈfäs-ˌfāt\ *n* : ATP

ad·e·no·vi·rus \ˌa-dᵊn-ō-ˈvī-rəs\ *n* : any of a family of viruses causing infections of the respiratory tract, conjunctiva, and gastrointestinal tract

[1]**ad·ept** \ˈa-ˌdept\ *n* : EXPERT

[2]**adept** \ə-ˈdept\ *adj* : highly skilled : EXPERT — **adept·ly** *adv* — **adept·ness** *n*

ad·e·quate \ˈa-di-kwət\ *adj* : equal to or sufficient for a specific requirement — **ad·e·qua·cy** \-kwə-sē\ *n* — **ad·e·quate·ly** *adv* — **ad·e·quate·ness** *n*

ad·here \ad-ˈhir\ *vb* **ad·hered**; **ad·her·ing** **1** : to give support : maintain loyalty **2** : to stick fast : CLING — **ad·her·ence** \-ˈhir-əns\ *n* — **ad·her·ent** \-ənt\ *adj or n*

ad·he·sion \ad-ˈhē-zhən\ *n* **1** : the act or state of adhering **2** : the union of bodily tissues abnormally grown together after inflammation; *also* : the newly formed uniting tissue **3** : the molecular attraction between the surfaces of bodies in contact

[1]**ad·he·sive** \-ˈhē-siv, -ziv\ *adj* **1** : tending to adhere : STICKY **2** : prepared for adhering

[2]**adhesive** *n* : an adhesive substance

adhesive tape *n* : tape coated on one side

with an adhesive mixture; *esp* : one used for covering wounds

[1]**ad hoc** \ˈad-ˈhäk, -ˈhōk\ *adv* [L, for this] : for the case at hand apart from other applications

[2]**ad hoc** *adj* : concerned with or formed for a particular purpose ⟨an *ad hoc* committee⟩ ⟨*ad hoc* solutions⟩

adi·a·bat·ic \ˌa-dē-ə-ˈba-tik\ *adj* : occurring without loss or gain of heat — **adi·a·bat·i·cal·ly** \-ti-k(ə-)lē\ *adv*

adieu \ə-ˈdü, -ˈdyü\ *n, pl* **adieus** *or* **adieux** \ə-ˈdüz, -ˈdyüz\ : FAREWELL — often used interjectionally

ad in·fi·ni·tum \ˌad-ˌin-fə-ˈnī-təm\ *adv or adj* : without end or limit

ad in·ter·im \ad-ˈin-tə-rəm, -ˌrim\ *adv* : for the intervening time — **ad interim** *adj*

adi·os \ˌa-dē-ˈōs, ˌä-\ *interj* [Sp *adiós*, lit., to God] — used to express farewell

ad·i·pose \ˈa-də-ˌpōs\ *adj* : of or relating to animal fat : FATTY

adj *abbr* **1** adjective **2** adjutant

ad·ja·cent \ə-ˈjā-sᵊnt\ *adj* : situated near or next ♦ ***Synonyms*** ADJOINING, CONTIGUOUS, ABUTTING, JUXTAPOSED, CONTERMINOUS — **ad·ja·cent·ly** *adv*

ad·jec·tive \ˈa-jik-tiv\ *n* : a word that typically serves as a modifier of a noun — **ad·jec·ti·val** \ˌa-jik-ˈtī-vəl\ *adj* — **ad·jec·ti·val·ly** *adv*

ad·join \ə-ˈjȯin\ *vb* : to be situated next to

ad·join·ing *adj* : touching or bounding at a point or line ⟨~ rooms⟩

ad·journ \ə-ˈjərn\ *vb* **1** : to suspend indefinitely or until a stated time **2** : to transfer to another place — **ad·journ·ment** *n*

ad·judge \ə-ˈjəj\ *vb* **ad·judged; ad·judg·ing 1** : JUDGE, ADJUDICATE **2** : to hold or pronounce to be : DEEM **3** : to award by judicial decision

ad·ju·di·cate \ə-ˈjü-di-ˌkāt\ *vb* **-cat·ed; -cat·ing** : to settle judicially — **ad·ju·di·ca·tion** \ə-ˌjü-di-ˈkā-shən\ *n*

ad·junct \ˈa-ˌjəŋkt\ *n* : something joined or added to another but not essentially a part of it ♦ ***Synonyms*** APPENDAGE, APPURTENANCE, ACCESSORY, APPENDIX — **adjunct** *adj*

ad·jure \ə-ˈju̇r\ *vb* **ad·jured; ad·jur·ing** : to command solemnly : urge earnestly ♦ ***Synonyms*** BEG, BESEECH, IMPLORE — **ad·ju·ra·tion** \ˌa-jə-ˈrā-shən\ *n*

ad·just \ə-ˈjəst\ *vb* **1** : to bring to agreement : SETTLE **2** : to cause to conform : ADAPT, FIT **3** : REGULATE ⟨~ a watch⟩ — **ad·just·able** *adj* — **ad·just·er** *also* **ad·jus·tor** \ə-ˈjəs-tər\ *n* — **ad·just·ment** \ə-ˈjəst-mənt\ *n*

ad·ju·tant \ˈa-jə-tənt\ *n* : one who assists; *esp* : an officer who assists a commanding officer by handling correspondence and keeping records

ad·ju·vant \ˈa-jə-vənt\ *n* : one that helps or facilitates; *esp* : something that enhances the effectiveness of medical treatment — **adjuvant** *adj*

[1]**ad–lib** \ˈad-ˈlib\ *vb* **ad–libbed; ad–lib·bing** : IMPROVISE — **ad–lib** *n*

[2]**ad–lib** *adj* : spoken, composed, or performed without preparation

ad lib \ˈad-ˈlib\ *adv* [NL *ad libitum*] **1** : at one's pleasure **2** : without limit

adm *abbr* administration; administrative

ADM *abbr* admiral

ad·man \ˈad-ˌman\ *n* : one who writes, solicits, or places advertisements

admin *abbr* administration; administrative

ad·min·is·ter \əd-ˈmi-nə-stər\ *vb* **1** : MANAGE, SUPERINTEND **2** : to mete out : DISPENSE ⟨~ punishment⟩ **3** : to give ritually or remedially ⟨~ quinine for malaria⟩ **4** : to perform the office of administrator — **ad·min·is·tra·ble** \-strə-bəl\ *adj* — **ad·min·is·trant** \-strənt\ *n*

ad·min·is·tra·tion \əd-ˌmi-nə-ˈstrā-shən\ *n* **1** : the act or process of administering **2** : MANAGEMENT **3** : the officials directing the government of a country **4** : the term of office of an administrative officer or body — **ad·min·is·tra·tive** \əd-ˈmi-nə-ˌstrā-tiv\ *adj* — **ad·min·is·tra·tive·ly** *adv*

ad·min·is·tra·tor \əd-ˈmi-nə-ˌstrā-tər\ *n* : one that administers; *esp* : one who settles an intestate estate

ad·mi·ra·ble \ˈad-m(ə-)rə-bəl\ *adj* : worthy of admiration : EXCELLENT — **ad·mi·ra·bil·i·ty** \ˌad-m(ə-)rə-ˈbi-lə-tē\ *n* — **ad·mi·ra·ble·ness** *n* — **ad·mi·ra·bly** \-blē\ *adv*

ad·mi·ral \ˈad-m(ə-)rəl\ *n* [ME, ultim. fr. Ar *amīr-al-* commander of the (as in *amīr-al-baḥr* commander of the sea)] : a commissioned officer in the navy ranking next below a fleet admiral

ad·mi·ral·ty \ˈad-m(ə-)rəl-tē\ *n* **1** *cap* : a British government department formerly having authority over naval affairs **2** : the court having jurisdiction over questions of maritime law

ad·mire \əd-ˈmī(-ə)r\ *vb* **ad·mired; ad·mir·ing** [MF *admirer*, fr. L *admirari*, fr. *ad-* to + *mirari* to wonder] : to regard with high esteem — **ad·mi·ra·tion** \ˌad-mə-ˈrā-shən\ *n* — **ad·mir·er** *n* — **ad·mir·ing·ly** \-ˈmī-riŋ-lē\ *adv*

ad·mis·si·ble \əd-ˈmi-sə-bəl\ *adj* : that can be or is worthy to be admitted or allowed : ALLOWABLE ⟨~ evidence⟩ — **ad·mis·si·bil·i·ty** \-ˌmi-sə-ˈbi-lə-tē\ *n*

ad·mis·sion \əd-ˈmi-shən\ *n* **1** : the act of admitting **2** : the privilege of being admitted **3** : a fee paid for admission **4** : the granting of an argument **5** : the acknowledgment of a fact

ad·mit \əd-ˈmit\ *vb* **ad·mit·ted; ad·mit·ting 1** : PERMIT, ALLOW **2** : to recognize as genuine or valid **3** : to allow to enter ⟨*admitted* to the club⟩ **4** : to accept into a hospital as an inpatient

ad·mit·tance \əd-ˈmi-tᵊns\ *n* : the act or process of admitting : permission to enter

ad·mit·ted·ly \əd-ˈmi-təd-lē\ *adv* **1** : as has been or must be admitted **2** : it must be admitted

ad·mix \ad-ˈmiks\ *vb* : to mix in

ad·mix·ture \ad-ˈmiks-chər\ *n* **1** : something added in mixing **2** : MIXTURE

ad•mon•ish \ad-ˈmä-nish\ *vb* : to warn gently : reprove with a warning ♦ ***Synonyms*** CHIDE, REPROACH, REBUKE, REPRIMAND, REPROVE — **ad•mon•ish•er** *n* — **ad•mon•ish•ing•ly** *adv* — **ad•mon•ish•ment** *n* — **ad•mo•ni•tion** \ˌad-mə-ˈni-shən\ *n* — **ad•mon•i•to•ry** \ad-ˈmä-nə-ˌtȯr-ē\ *adj*

ad nau•se•am \ad-ˈnȯ-zē-əm\ *adv* [L] : to a sickening or excessive degree

ado \ə-ˈdü\ *n* **1** : heightened fuss or concern **2** : TROUBLE

ado•be \ə-ˈdō-bē\ *n* **1** : sun-dried brick; *also* : clay for making such bricks **2** : a structure made of adobe bricks

ad•o•les•cence \ˌa-də-ˈle-sᵊns\ *n* : the process or period of growth between childhood and maturity — **ad•o•les•cent** \-sᵊnt\ *adj or n*

adopt \ə-ˈdäpt\ *vb* **1** : to take (a child of other parents) as one's own child **2** : to take up and practice as one's own **3** : to accept formally and put into effect — **adopt•able** \-ˈdäp-tə-bəl\ *adj* — **adopt•er** *n* — **adop•tion** \-ˈdäp-shən\ *n*

adop•tive \ə-ˈdäp-tiv\ *adj* : made or acquired by adoption ⟨the ~ father⟩ — **adop•tive•ly** *adv*

ador•able \ə-ˈdȯr-ə-bəl\ *adj* **1** : worthy of adoration **2** : extremely charming ⟨an ~ child⟩ — **ador•able•ness** *n* — **ador•ably** \-blē\ *adv*

adore \ə-ˈdȯr\ *vb* **adored**; **ador•ing** [ME *adouren,* fr. AF *aurer, adourer,* fr. L *adorare,* fr. *ad-* to + *orare* to speak, pray] **1** : WORSHIP **2** : to regard with loving admiration ⟨~*s* his wife⟩ **3** : to be extremely fond of ⟨~*s* pecan pie⟩ — **ad•o•ra•tion** \ˌa-də-ˈrā-shən\ *n*

adorn \ə-ˈdȯrn\ *vb* : to enhance the appearance of esp. with ornaments ⟨blouses ~*ed* with sequins⟩ — **adorn•ment** *n*

ad•re•nal \ə-ˈdrē-nᵊl\ *adj* : of, relating to, or being a pair of endocrine organs (**adrenal glands**) that are located near the kidneys and produce several hormones and esp. epinephrine

adren•a•line \ə-ˈdre-nə-lən\ *n* : EPINEPHRINE

adrift \ə-ˈdrift\ *adv or adj* **1** : afloat without motive power or moorings **2** : without guidance or purpose

adroit \ə-ˈdrȯit\ *adj* [F, fr. OF, fr. *a-* to + *droit* right] **1** : dexterous with one's hands **2** : SHREWD, RESOURCEFUL ♦ ***Synonyms*** CANNY, CLEVER, CUNNING, INGENIOUS — **adroit•ly** *adv* — **adroit•ness** *n*

ad•sorb \ad-ˈsȯrb, -ˈzȯrb\ *vb* : to take up (as molecules of gases) and hold on the surface of a solid or liquid — **ad•sorp•tion** \-ˈsȯrp-shən, -ˈzȯrp-\ *n*

ad•u•la•tion \ˌa-jə-ˈlā-shən\ *n* : excessive admiration or flattery — **ad•u•late** \ˈa-jə-ˌlāt\ *vb* — **ad•u•la•tor** \-ˌlā-tər\ *n* — **ad•u•la•to•ry** \-lə-ˌtȯr-ē\ *adj*

¹**adult** \ə-ˈdəlt, ˈa-ˌ\ *adj* [L *adultus,* pp. of *adolescere* to grow up, fr. *ad-* to + *alescere* to grow] : fully developed and mature — **adult•hood** *n*

²**adult** *n* : one that is adult; *esp* : a human being after an age (as 18) specified by law

adul•ter•ant \ə-ˈdəl-tə-rənt\ *n* : something used to adulterate another

adul•ter•ate \ə-ˈdəl-tə-ˌrāt\ *vb* **-at•ed**; **-at•ing** [L *adulterare,* fr. *ad-* to + *alter* other] : to make impure by mixing in a foreign or inferior substance — **adul•ter•a•tion** \-ˌdəl-tə-ˈrā-shən\ *n*

adul•tery \ə-ˈdəl-t(ə-)rē\ *n, pl* **-ter•ies** : sexual unfaithfulness of a married person — **adul•ter•er** \-tər-ər\ *n* — **adul•ter•ess** \-t(ə-)rəs\ *also* **adul•tress** \-trəs\ *n* — **adul•ter•ous** \-t(ə-)rəs\ *adj*

ad•um•brate \ˈa-dəm-ˌbrāt\ *vb* **-brat•ed**; **-brat•ing** **1** : to foreshadow vaguely : INTIMATE **2** : to suggest or disclose partially **3** : SHADE, OBSCURE — **ad•um•bra•tion** \ˌa-dəm-ˈbrā-shən\ *n*

adv *abbr* **1** adverb **2** advertisement

ad va•lor•em \ˌad-və-ˈlȯr-əm\ *adj* [L, according to the value] : imposed at a percentage of the value ⟨an *ad valorem* tax⟩

¹**ad•vance** \əd-ˈvans\ *vb* **ad•vanced**; **ad•vanc•ing** **1** : to assist the progress of ⟨~ a cause⟩ **2** : to bring or move forward ⟨~ a pawn⟩ **3** : to promote in rank **4** : to make earlier in time **5** : PROPOSE **6** : LEND **7** : to raise in rate : INCREASE — **ad•vance•ment** *n*

²**advance** *n* **1** : a forward movement **2** : IMPROVEMENT **3** : a rise esp. in price or value **4** : a first step made esp. to start a relationship **5** : something supplied ahead — **in advance** : BEFOREHAND

³**advance** *adj* : made, sent, or furnished ahead of time ⟨~ payment⟩

ad•van•tage \əd-ˈvan-tij\ *n* **1** : superiority of position **2** : BENEFIT, GAIN **3** : the 1st point won in tennis after deuce — **ad•van•ta•geous** \ˌad-van-ˈtā-jəs\ *adj* — **ad•van•ta•geous•ly** *adv*

ad•vent \ˈad-ˌvent\ *n* **1** *cap* : a penitential period beginning four Sundays before Christmas **2** *cap* : the coming of Christ **3** : a coming into being or use

ad•ven•ti•tious \ˌad-vən-ˈti-shəs\ *adj* **1** : ACCIDENTAL, INCIDENTAL **2** : arising or occurring sporadically or in other than the usual location ⟨~ buds⟩ — **ad•ven•ti•tious•ly** *adv*

¹**ad•ven•ture** \əd-ˈven-chər\ *n* **1** : a risky undertaking **2** : a remarkable and exciting experience — **ad•ven•tur•ous** \-ch(ə-)rəs\ *adj*

²**adventure** *vb* **-ven•tured**; **-ven•tur•ing** \-ˈven-ch(ə-)riŋ\ **1** : RISK, HAZARD ⟨~ their capital in foreign trade⟩ **2** : to engage in adventure

ad•ven•tur•er \əd-ˈven-ch(ə-)rər\ *n* **1** : a person who engages in new and risky undertakings **2** : a person who follows a military career for adventure or profit **3** : a person who tries to gain wealth by questionable means

ad•ven•ture•some \əd-ˈven-chər-səm\ *adj* : inclined to take risks

ad•ven•tur•ess \əd-ˈven-ch(ə-)rəs\ *n* : a female adventurer

ad•verb \ˈad-ˌvərb\ *n* : a word that typically serves as a modifier of a verb, an adjective, or another adverb — **ad•ver•bi•al** \ad-ˈvər-bē-əl\ *adj* — **ad•ver•bi•al•ly** *adv*

[1]**ad·ver·sary** \ˈad-vər-ˌser-ē\ *n, pl* **-sar·ies** : FOE
[2]**adversary** *adj* : involving antagonistic parties or interests
ad·verse \ad-ˈvərs, ˈad-ˌvərs\ *adj* **1** : acting against or in a contrary direction ⟨~ winds⟩ **2** : UNFAVORABLE ⟨~ criticism⟩ — **ad·verse·ly** *adv*
ad·ver·si·ty \ad-ˈvər-sə-tē\ *n, pl* **-ties** : serious difficulty : MISFORTUNE
ad·vert \ad-ˈvərt\ *vb* : REFER ⟨~ to a previous remark⟩
ad·ver·tise \ˈad-vər-ˌtīz\ *vb* **-tised; -tis·ing** **1** : INFORM, NOTIFY **2** : to call public attention to esp. in order to sell — **ad·ver·tis·er** *n*
ad·ver·tise·ment \ˌad-vər-ˈtīz-mənt; əd-ˈvər-təs-mənt\ *n* **1** : the act of advertising **2** : a public notice intended to advertise something
ad·ver·tis·ing \ˈad-vər-ˌtī-ziŋ\ *n* : the business of preparing advertisements
ad·vice \əd-ˈvīs\ *n* **1** : recommendation with regard to a course of action : COUNSEL **2** : INFORMATION, REPORT
ad·vis·able \əd-ˈvī-zə-bəl\ *adj* : proper to be done : EXPEDIENT ⟨~ to stay fit⟩ — **ad·vis·abil·i·ty** \-ˌvī-zə-ˈbi-lə-tē\ *n*
ad·vise \əd-ˈvīz\ *vb* **ad·vised; ad·vis·ing** **1** : to give advice to : COUNSEL **2** : INFORM, NOTIFY **3** : CONSULT, CONFER ⟨~ with your friends⟩ — **ad·vis·er** *also* **ad·vi·sor** \-ˈvī-zər\ *n*
ad·vised \əd-ˈvīzd\ *adj* : thought out : CONSIDERED ⟨well-*advised*⟩ — **ad·vis·ed·ly** \-ˈvī-zəd-lē\ *adv*
ad·vise·ment \əd-ˈvīz-mənt\ *n* **1** : careful consideration ⟨take the matter under ~⟩ **2** : the act of advising
ad·vi·so·ry \əd-ˈvi-zə-rē\ *adj* **1** : having or exercising power to advise **2** : containing or giving advice
[1]**ad·vo·cate** \ˈad-və-kət, -ˌkāt\ *n* [ultim. fr. L *advocare* to summon, fr. *ad-* to + *vocare* to call] **1** : one who pleads another's cause **2** : one who argues or pleads for a cause or proposal — **ad·vo·ca·cy** \-və-kə-sē\ *n*
[2]**ad·vo·cate** \-ˌkāt\ *vb* **-cat·ed; -cat·ing** : to plead in favor of — **ad·vo·ca·tion** \ˌad-və-ˈkā-shən\ *n*
advt *abbr* advertisement
adze *also* **adz** \ˈadz\ *n* : a tool with a curved blade set at right angles to the handle that is used in shaping wood
AEC *abbr* Atomic Energy Commission
ae·gis \ˈē-jəs\ *n* **1** : SHIELD, PROTECTION ⟨under the ~ of the constitution⟩ **2** : PATRONAGE, SPONSORSHIP ⟨under the ~ of the museum⟩
ae·o·li·an harp \ē-ˈō-lē-ən-\ *n* : a box with strings that produce musical sounds when the wind blows on them
ae·on *chiefly Brit var of* EON
aer·ate \ˈer-ˌāt\ *vb* **aer·at·ed; aer·at·ing** **1** : to supply, impregnate, or combine with a gas and esp. air **2** : to supply (blood) with oxygen by respiration — **aer·a·tion** \ˌer-ˈā-shən\ *n* — **aer·a·tor** \ˈer-ˌā-tər\ *n*
[1]**ae·ri·al** \ˈer-ē-əl\ *adj* **1** : inhabiting, occurring in, or done in the air **2** : AIRY **3** : of or relating to aircraft
[2]**aer·i·al** \ˈer-ē-əl\ *n* : ANTENNA 2
ae·ri·al·ist \ˈer-ē-ə-list\ *n* : a performer of feats above the ground esp. on a trapeze
ae·rie \ˈer-ē, ˈir-ē\ *n* : a highly placed nest (as of an eagle)
aer·o·bat·ics \ˌer-ə-ˈba-tiks\ *n sing or pl* : spectacular flying feats and maneuvers
aer·o·bic \ˌer-ˈrō-bik\ *adj* **1** : living or active only in the presence of oxygen ⟨~ bacteria⟩ **2** : involving or increasing oxygen consumption; *also* : of or relating to aerobics — **aer·o·bi·cal·ly** \-bi-k(ə-)lē\ *adv*
aer·o·bics \-biks\ *n sing or pl* : strenuous exercises that produce a marked temporary increase in respiration and heart rate; *also* : a system of physical conditioning involving these
aero·drome \ˈer-ə-ˌdrōm\ *n, chiefly Brit* : AIRPORT
aero·dy·nam·ics \ˌer-ō-dī-ˈna-miks\ *n* : the science dealing with the forces acting on bodies in motion in a gas (as air) — **aero·dy·nam·ic** \-mik\ *also* **aero·dy·nam·i·cal** \-mi-kəl\ *adj* — **aero·dy·nam·i·cal·ly** \-mi-k(ə-)lē\ *adv*
aero·naut \ˈer-ə-ˌnȯt\ *n* [F *aéronaute,* ultim. fr. Gk *aēr* air + *nautēs* sailor] : one who operates or travels in an airship or balloon
aero·nau·tics \ˌer-ə-ˈnȯ-tiks\ *n* : the science of aircraft operation — **aero·nau·ti·cal** \-ti-kəl\ *also* **aero·nau·tic** \-tik\ *adj*
aero·pho·bia \ˌer-ō-ˈfō-bē-ə\ *n* : fear or strong dislike of flying
aero·plane \ˈer-ə-ˌplān\ *Brit var of* AIRPLANE
aero·sol \ˈer-ə-ˌsäl, -ˌsȯl\ *n* **1** : a suspension of fine solid or liquid particles in a gas; *also, pl* : the particles themselves **2** : a substance (as an insecticide) dispensed from a pressurized container as an aerosol
aero·space \ˈer-ō-ˌspās\ *n* : the earth's atmosphere and the space beyond — **aerospace** *adj*
aery \ˈer-ē\ *adj* **aer·i·er; -est** : having an aerial quality : ETHEREAL ⟨~ visions⟩
aes·thete *also* **es·thete** \ˈes-ˌthēt\ *n* : a person having or affecting sensitivity to beauty esp. in art
aes·thet·ic *also* **es·thet·ic** \es-ˈthe-tik\ *adj* **1** : of or relating to aesthetics : ARTISTIC **2** : appreciative of the beautiful — **aes·thet·i·cal·ly** *also* **es·thet·i·cal·ly** \-ti-k(ə-)lē\ *adv*
aes·thet·ics *also* **es·thet·ics** \-tiks\ *n* : a branch of philosophy dealing with the nature, creation, and appreciation of beauty
ae·ti·ol·o·gy *chiefly Brit var of* ETIOLOGY
AF *abbr* **1** air force **2** audio frequency
[1]**afar** \ə-ˈfär\ *adv* : from, at, or to a great distance
[2]**afar** *n* : a great distance
AFB *abbr* air force base
AFC *abbr* **1** American Football Conference **2** automatic frequency control

AFDC *abbr* Aid to Families with Dependent Children

af·fa·ble \ˈa-fə-bəl\ *adj* : courteous and agreeable in conversation — **af·fa·bil·i·ty** \ˌa-fə-ˈbi-lə-tē\ *n* — **af·fa·bly** \ˈa-fə-blē\ *adv*

af·fair \ə-ˈfer\ *n* [ME *afere,* fr. AF fr. *afaire,* fr. *a faire* to do] **1** : something that relates to or involves one : CONCERN **2** : a romantic or sexual attachment of limited duration

¹af·fect \ə-ˈfekt, a-\ *vb* **1** : to be fond of using or wearing **2** : to pretend that an attitude or behavior is genuine

²affect *vb* : to produce an effect on : INFLUENCE

³af·fect \ˈa-ˌfekt\ *n* : EMOTION; *also* : an observable display of emotion ⟨an expressionless ~⟩

af·fec·ta·tion \ˌa-ˌfek-ˈtā-shən\ *n* : an attitude or behavior that is assumed by a person but not genuinely felt

af·fect·ed \a-ˈfek-təd\ *adj* **1** : given to or marked by affectation **2** : artificially assumed to impress others — **af·fect·ed·ly** *adv*

af·fect·ing \a-ˈfek-tiŋ\ *adj* : arousing pity, sympathy, or sorrow ⟨an ~ story⟩ — **af·fect·ing·ly** *adv*

af·fec·tion \ə-ˈfek-shən\ *n* : tender attachment — **af·fec·tion·ate** \-sh(ə-)nət\ *adj* — **af·fec·tion·ate·ly** *adv*

af·fec·tive \a-ˈfek-tiv\ *adj* : relating to, influencing, or expressing an emotion or feeling : EMOTIONAL ⟨an ~ disorder⟩

af·fer·ent \ˈa-fə-rənt, -ˌfer-ənt\ *adj* : bearing or conducting inward toward a more central part and esp. a nerve center (as the central nervous system)

af·fi·ance \ə-ˈfī-əns\ *vb* **-anced; -anc·ing** : to promise oneself or another in marriage

af·fi·da·vit \ˌa-fə-ˈdā-vət\ *n* [ML, he has made an oath] : a sworn statement in writing

¹af·fil·i·ate \ə-ˈfi-lē-ˌāt\ *vb* **-at·ed; -at·ing** : to associate as a member or branch — **af·fil·i·a·tion** \-ˌfi-lē-ˈā-shən\ *n*

²af·fil·i·ate \ə-ˈfi-lē-ət\ *n* : an affiliated person or organization

af·fin·i·ty \ə-ˈfi-nə-tē\ *n, pl* **-ties** **1** : KINSHIP, RELATIONSHIP **2** : attractive force : ATTRACTION, SYMPATHY

affinity card *n* : a credit card issued in affiliation with an organization (as a charity or an airline) the use of which benefits the organization or possessor of the card

af·firm \ə-ˈfərm\ *vb* **1** : CONFIRM **2** : to assert positively **3** : to make a solemn and formal declaration or assertion in place of an oath ♦ ***Synonyms*** AVER, AVOW, AVOUCH, DECLARE, ASSERT — **af·fir·ma·tion** \ˌa-fər-ˈmā-shən\ *n*

¹af·fir·ma·tive \ə-ˈfər-mə-tiv\ *adj* : asserting that the fact is so : POSITIVE

²affirmative *n* **1** : an expression of affirmation or assent **2** : the side that upholds the proposition stated in a debate

affirmative action *n* : an active effort to improve the employment or educational opportunities of members of minority groups and women

¹af·fix \ə-ˈfiks\ *vb* : ATTACH, ADD

²af·fix \ˈa-ˌfiks\ *n* : one or more sounds or letters attached to the beginning or end of a word that produce a derivative word or an inflectional form

af·fla·tus \ə-ˈflā-təs\ *n* : divine inspiration

af·flict \ə-ˈflikt\ *vb* : to cause pain and distress to ♦ ***Synonyms*** RACK, TRY, TORMENT, TORTURE — **af·flic·tion** \-ˈflik-shən\ *n*

af·flic·tive \ə-ˈflik-tiv\ *adj* : causing affliction : DISTRESSING ⟨~ emotions⟩ — **af·flic·tive·ly** *adv*

af·flu·ence \ˈa-ˌflü-ən(t)s, a-ˈflü-\ *n* : abundant supply; *also* : WEALTH, RICHES — **af·flu·ent** \-ənt\ *adj*

af·ford \ə-ˈfȯrd\ *vb* **1** : to manage to bear or bear the cost of without serious harm or loss **2** : PROVIDE, FURNISH ⟨the roof ~*ed* a fine view⟩

af·for·es·ta·tion \a-ˌfȯr-ə-ˈstā-shən\ *n* : the act or process of establishing a forest — **af·for·est** \a-ˈfȯr-əst, -ˈfär-\ *vb*

af·fray \ə-ˈfrā\ *n* : FIGHT, FRAY

af·fright \ə-ˈfrīt\ *vb, archaic* : FRIGHTEN, ALARM — **affright** *n*

af·front \ə-ˈfrənt\ *vb* **1** : INSULT **2** : CONFRONT ⟨~ death⟩ — **affront** *n*

af·ghan \ˈaf-ˌgan\ *n* **1** *cap* : a native or inhabitant of Afghanistan **2** : a blanket or shawl of colored wool knitted or crocheted in sections — **Afghan** *or* **Afghani** \af-ˈga-nē, -ˈgä-\ *adj*

Afghan hound *n* : any of a breed of tall slim swift hunting dogs with a coat of silky thick hair and a long silky top-knot

af·ghani \af-ˈga-nē\ *n* — see MONEY table

afi·cio·na·do \ə-ˌfi-sh(ē-)ə-ˈnä-dō, -sē-ə-\ *n, pl* **-dos** [Sp, fr. pp. of *aficionar* to inspire affection] : DEVOTEE, FAN

afield \ə-ˈfēld\ *adv or adj* **1** : to, in, or on the field **2** : away from home **3** : out of the way : ASTRAY

afire \ə-ˈfī(-ə)r\ *adj or adv* : being on fire : BURNING

AFL *abbr* American Football League

aflame \ə-ˈflām\ *adj or adv* : FLAMING

AFL–CIO *abbr* American Federation of Labor and Congress of Industrial Organizations

afloat \ə-ˈflōt\ *adj or adv* **1** : borne on or as if on the water **2** : CIRCULATING ⟨rumors were ~⟩ **3** : ADRIFT

aflut·ter \ə-ˈflə-tər\ *adj* **1** : FLUTTERING **2** : nervously excited ⟨~ at the news⟩

afoot \ə-ˈfu̇t\ *adv or adj* **1** : on foot **2** : in action : in progress

afore·men·tioned \ə-ˈfȯr-ˈmen-chənd\ *adj* : mentioned previously

afore·said \-ˌsed\ *adj* : said or named before

afore·thought \-ˌthȯt\ *adj* : planned beforehand : PREMEDITATED ⟨with malice ~⟩

a for·ti·o·ri \ˌä-ˌfȯr-tē-ˈȯr-ē\ *adv* [NL, lit., from the stronger (argument)] : with even greater reason

afoul of \ə-ˈfau̇l-əv\ *prep* **1** : in or into

conflict with **2** : in or into collision or entanglement with
Afr *abbr* Africa; African
afraid \ə-ˈfrād\ *adj* **1** : FRIGHTENED, FEARFUL **2** : filled with concern or regret ⟨~ I won't be able to go⟩
A–frame \ˈā-ˌfrām\ *n* : a building having triangular front and rear walls with the roof reaching to the ground
afresh \ə-ˈfresh\ *adv* : ANEW, AGAIN
Af•ri•can \ˈa-fri-kən\ *n* **1** : a native or inhabitant of Africa **2** : a person and esp. a Black person of African ancestry — **African** *adj*
African American *also* **Af•ri•can–Amer•i•can** \-ə-ˈmer-ə-kən\ *n* : an American of African and esp. of Black African descent — **African American** *also* **African–American** *adj*
Af•ri•can•ized bee \ˈa-frə-kə-ˌnīzd-\ *n* : a highly aggressive hybrid honeybee accidentally produced from Brazilian and African stocks that has spread from So. America into Mexico and the southern U.S.
Africanized honeybee *n* : AFRICANIZED BEE
African violet *n* : a tropical African plant widely grown indoors for its velvety fleshy leaves and showy purple, pink, or white flowers
Af•ri•kaans \ˌa-fri-ˈkäns\ *n* : a language developed from 17th century Dutch that is one of the official languages of the Republic of So. Africa
Af•ro \ˈa-(ˌ)frō\ *n, pl* **Afros** : a hairstyle of tight curls in a full evenly rounded shape
Af•ro–Amer•i•can \ˌa-frō-ə-ˈmer-ə-kən\ *n* : AFRICAN AMERICAN — **Afro–American** *adj*
aft \ˈaft\ *adv* : near, toward, or in the stern of a ship or the tail of an aircraft
AFT *abbr* American Federation of Teachers
[1]**af•ter** \ˈaf-tər\ *adv* : AFTERWARD, SUBSEQUENTLY
[2]**after** *prep* **1** : behind in place **2** : later than ⟨~ dinner⟩ **3** : in pursuit or search of ⟨he's ~ your job⟩
[3]**after** *conj* : following the time when ⟨we will come ~ we make plans⟩
[4]**after** *adj* **1** : LATER ⟨in ~ years⟩ **2** : located toward the rear
af•ter•birth \ˈaf-tər-ˌbərth\ *n* : the placenta and membranes of the fetus that are expelled after childbirth
af•ter•burn•er \-ˌbər-nər\ *n* : a device incorporated in the tail pipe of a turbojet engine for injecting fuel into the hot exhaust gases and burning it to provide extra thrust
af•ter•care \-ˌker\ *n* : the care, nursing, or treatment of a convalescent patient
af•ter•deck \-ˌdek\ *n* : the rear half of the deck of a ship
af•ter•ef•fect \-ə-ˌfekt\ *n* : an effect that follows its cause after an interval
af•ter•glow \-ˌglō\ *n* : a glow remaining where a light has disappeared
af•ter•im•age \-ˌim-ij\ *n* : a usu. visual sensation continuing after the stimulus causing it has ended
af•ter•life \-ˌlīf\ *n* : an existence after death
af•ter•math \-ˌmath\ *n* **1** : a second-growth crop esp. of hay **2** : CONSEQUENCES, EFFECTS ♦ *Synonyms* AFTEREFFECT, UPSHOT, RESULT, OUTCOME
af•ter•noon \ˌaf-tər-ˈnün\ *n* : the time between noon and evening
af•ter•shave \ˈaf-tər-ˌshāv\ *n* : a usu. scented lotion for the face after shaving
af•ter•taste \-ˌtāst\ *n* : a sensation (as of flavor) continuing after the stimulus causing it has ended
af•ter–tax \ˈaf-tər-ˈtaks\ *adj* : remaining after payment of taxes and esp. of income tax ⟨an ~ profit⟩
af•ter•thought \-ˌthȯt\ *n* : an idea occurring later
af•ter•ward \-wərd\ *or* **af•ter•wards** \-wərdz\ *adv* : at a later time
Ag *symbol* [L *argentum*] silver
AG *abbr* **1** adjutant general **2** attorney general
again \ə-ˈgen, -ˈgin\ *adv* **1** : once more : ANEW ⟨come see us ~⟩ **2** : on the other hand ⟨we may, and ~ we may not⟩ **3** : in addition : BESIDES
against \ə-ˈgenst\ *prep* **1** : in opposition to **2** : directly opposite to : FACING **3** : as defense from **4** : so as to touch or strike ⟨threw him ~ the wall⟩; *also* : TOUCHING
[1]**aga•pe** \ä-ˈgä-pā, ˈä-gə-ˌpā\ *n* [LL, fr. Gk *agapē*, lit., love] : unselfish unconditional love for another
[2]**agape** \ə-ˈgāp\ *adj or adv* : having the mouth open in wonder or surprise : GAPING
agar \ˈä-ˌgär\ *n* **1** : a jellylike substance extracted from a red alga and used esp. as a gelling and stabilizing agent in foods **2** : a culture medium containing agar
agar–agar \ˌä-ˌgär-ˈä-ˌgär\ *n* : AGAR
ag•ate \ˈa-gət\ *n* **1** : a striped or clouded quartz **2** : a playing marble of agate or of glass
aga•ve \ə-ˈgä-vē\ *n* : any of a genus of spiny-leaved plants (as a century plant) related to the amaryllis
agcy *abbr* agency
[1]**age** \ˈāj\ *n* **1** : the length of time during which a being or thing has lived or existed **2** : the time of life at which some particular qualification is achieved; *esp* : MAJORITY **3** : the latter part of life **4** : a long time **5** : a period in history
[2]**age** *vb* **aged**; **ag•ing** *or* **age•ing** **1** : to grow old or cause to grow old **2** : to become or cause to become mature or mellow
-age *n suffix* **1** : aggregate : collection ⟨track*age*⟩ **2** : action : process ⟨haul*age*⟩ **3** : cumulative result of ⟨break*age*⟩ **4** : rate of ⟨dos*age*⟩ **5** : house or place of ⟨orphan*age*⟩ **6** : state : rank ⟨vassal*age*⟩ **7** : fee : charge ⟨post*age*⟩
aged \ˈā-jəd *for 1;* ˈājd *for 2*\ *adj* **1** : of advanced age **2** : having attained a specified age ⟨a man ~ 40 years⟩
age•ism \ˈā-ˌji-zəm\ *n* : discrimination

against persons of a particular age and esp. the elderly — **age·ist** \-jist\ *n*
age·less \ˈāj-ləs\ *adj* **1** : not growing old or showing the effects of age **2** : TIMELESS, ETERNAL ⟨~ truths⟩
agen·cy \ˈā-jən-sē\ *n, pl* **-cies** **1** : one through which something is accomplished : INSTRUMENTALITY **2** : the office or function of an agent **3** : an establishment doing business for another **4** : an administrative division (as of a government) ♦ ***Synonyms*** MEANS, MEDIUM, VEHICLE
agen·da \ə-ˈjen-də\ *n* : a list of things to be done
agen·der \(ˌ)ā-ˈjen-dər\ *adj* : of, relating to, or being a person whose gender identity is genderless or neutral
agent \ˈā-jənt\ *n* **1** : one that acts **2** : MEANS, INSTRUMENT **3** : a person acting or doing business for another **4** : a computer program designed to automate certain tasks (as gathering information online) ♦ ***Synonyms*** ATTORNEY, DEPUTY, PROXY, DELEGATE
Agent Orange *n* : an herbicide widely used in the Vietnam War that is composed of 2,4-D and 2,4,5-T and contains a toxic contaminant
agent pro·vo·ca·teur \ˈä-ˌzhäⁿ-prō-ˌvä-kə-ˈtər, ˈā-jənt-\ *n, pl* **agents provocateurs** \ˈä-ˌzhäⁿ-prō-ˌväk-ə-ˈtər, ˈā-jənts-prō-\ [F] : a person hired to infiltrate a group and incite its members to illegal action
age of consent : the age at which one is legally competent to give consent esp. to marriage or to sexual intercourse
age–old \ˈāj-ˈōld\ *adj* : having existed for ages : ANCIENT
ag·er·a·tum \ˌa-jə-ˈrā-təm\ *n, pl* **-tum** *also* **-tums** : any of a genus of tropical American plants that are related to the daisies and have small showy heads of usu. blue or white flowers
age spots *n pl* : benign flat spots of dark pigmentation on the skin occurring esp. among older people
Ag·ge·us \a-ˈgē-əs\ *n* : HAGGAI
[1]**ag·glom·er·ate** \ə-ˈglä-mə-ˌrāt\ *vb* **-at·ed**; **-at·ing** [L *agglomerare* to heap up, join, fr. *ad-* to + *glomer-, glomus* ball] : to gather into a mass : CLUSTER — **ag·glom·er·a·tion** \-ˌglä-mə-ˈrā-shən\ *n*
[2]**ag·glom·er·ate** \-rət\ *n* : rock composed of volcanic fragments
ag·glu·ti·nate \ə-ˈglü-tᵊn-ˌāt\ *vb* **-nat·ed**; **-nat·ing** **1** : to cause to adhere : gather into a group or mass **2** : to cause (as red blood cells or bacteria) to collect into clumps — **ag·glu·ti·na·tion** \-ˌglü-tᵊn-ˈā-shən\ *n*
ag·gran·dise *Brit var of* AGGRANDIZE
ag·gran·dize \ə-ˈgran-ˌdīz, ˈa-grən-\ *vb* **-dized**; **-diz·ing** : to make great or greater ⟨~ an estate⟩ — **ag·gran·dize·ment** \ə-ˈgran-dəz-mənt, -ˌdīz-; ˌa-grən-ˈdīz-\ *n*
ag·gra·vate \ˈa-grə-ˌvāt\ *vb* **-vat·ed**; **-vat·ing** **1** : to make more severe : INTENSIFY **2** : IRRITATE — **ag·gra·va·tion** \ˌa-grə-ˈvā-shən\ *n*
[1]**ag·gre·gate** \ˈa-gri-gət\ *adj* : formed by the gathering of units into one mass
[2]**ag·gre·gate** \-ˌgāt\ *vb* **-gat·ed**; **-gat·ing** : to collect into one mass
[3]**ag·gre·gate** \-gət\ *n* : a mass or body of units or parts somewhat loosely associated with one another; *also* : the whole amount
ag·gre·ga·tion \ˌa-gri-ˈgā-shən\ *n* **1** : a group, body, or mass composed of many distinct parts **2** : the collecting of units or parts into a mass or whole
ag·gres·sion \ə-ˈgre-shən\ *n* **1** : an unprovoked attack **2** : the practice of making attacks **3** : hostile, injurious, or destructive behavior or outlook esp. when caused by frustration — **ag·gres·sor** \-ˈgre-sər\ *n*
ag·gres·sive \ə-ˈgre-siv\ *adj* **1** : tending toward or exhibiting aggression; *esp* : marked by combative readiness **2** : marked by driving energy or initiative : ENTERPRISING **3** : more intensive or comprehensive esp. in dosage or extent — **ag·gres·sive·ly** *adv* — **ag·gres·sive·ness** *n*
ag·grieve \ə-ˈgrēv\ *vb* **ag·grieved**; **ag·griev·ing** **1** : to cause grief to **2** : to inflict injury on : WRONG
ag·gro \ˈa-ˌgrō\ *adj* : aggressive or aggressively daring in style or manner ⟨~ music⟩ ⟨~ surfing⟩
aghast \ə-ˈgast\ *adj* : struck with amazement or horror
ag·ile \ˈa-jəl\ *adj* : able to move quickly and easily — **ag·ile·ly** *adv* — **agil·i·ty** \ə-ˈji-lə-tē\ *n*
ag·i·ta \ˈa-jə-tə\ *n* [southern It dial. pron. of It *acido,* lit., heartburn, acid] : a feeling of agitation or anxiety
ag·i·tate \ˈa-jə-ˌtāt\ *vb* **-tat·ed**; **-tat·ing** **1** : to move with an irregular rapid motion **2** : to stir up : EXCITE **3** : to discuss earnestly **4** : to attempt to arouse public feeling — **ag·i·ta·tion** \ˌa-jə-ˈtā-shən\ *n* — **ag·i·ta·tor** \ˈa-jə-ˌtā-tər\ *n*
ag·it·prop \ˈa-jət-ˌpräp\ *n* [Russ] : political propaganda promulgated esp. through the arts
agleam \ə-ˈglēm\ *adj* : GLEAMING ⟨eyes ~ with tears⟩
aglit·ter \ə-ˈgli-tər\ *adj* : GLITTERING
aglow \ə-ˈglō\ *adj* : GLOWING
ag·nos·tic \ag-ˈnäs-tik\ *adj* [Gk *agnōstos* unknown, unknowable, fr. *a-* un- + *gnōstos* known] : of or relating to the belief that the existence of any ultimate reality (as God) is unknown and prob. unknowable — **agnostic** *n* — **ag·nos·ti·cism** \-ˈnäs-tə-ˌsi-zəm\ *n*
ago \ə-ˈgō\ *adj or adv* : earlier than the present time ⟨10 years ~⟩
agog \ə-ˈgäg\ *adj* [MF *en gogues* in mirth] : full of excitement : EAGER
a–go–go \ä-ˈgō-ˌgō\ *adj* [*Whisky à Gogo,* café and disco in Paris, France, fr. F *à gogo* galore] : GO-GO
ag·o·nise *Brit var of* AGONIZE
ag·o·nize \ˈa-gə-ˌnīz\ *vb* **-nized**; **-niz·ing** : to suffer or cause to suffer agony — **ag·o·niz·ing·ly** *adv*

ag·o·ny \'a-gə-nē\ *n, pl* **-nies** [ME *agonie,* fr. L *agonia,* fr. Gk *agōnia* struggle, anguish, fr. *agōn* gathering, contest for a prize] : extreme pain of mind or body ♦ ***Synonyms*** SUFFERING, DISTRESS, MISERY

ago·ra \ˌä-gə-'rä\ *n, pl* **ago·rot** \-'rōt\ — see *shekel* at MONEY table

ag·o·ra·pho·bia \ˌa-gə-rə-'fō-bē-ə\ *n* : abnormal fear of being in a helpless, embarrassing, or inescapable situation characterized esp. by avoidance of open or public places — **ag·o·ra·pho·bic** \-'fō-bik, -'fä-\ *adj or n*

agr *abbr* agricultural; agriculture

agrar·i·an \ə-'grer-ē-ən\ *adj* **1** : of or relating to land or its ownership ⟨~ reforms⟩ **2** : of or relating to farmers or farming interests — **agrarian** *n* — **agrar·i·an·ism** *n*

agree \ə-'grē\ *vb* **agreed**; **agree·ing** **1** : ADMIT, CONCEDE ⟨~*s* that he was wrong⟩ **2** : to be similar : CORRESPOND ⟨both copies ~⟩ **3** : to express agreement or approval **4** : to be in harmony **5** : to settle by common consent **6** : to be fitting or healthful : SUIT ⟨this climate ~*s* with her⟩

agree·able \ə-'grē-ə-bəl\ *adj* **1** : PLEASING, PLEASANT ⟨an ~ fragrance⟩ **2** : ready to consent ⟨I'm ~ to their proposal⟩ **3** : being in harmony : CONSONANT — **agree·able·ness** *n* — **agree·ably** \-blē\ *adv*

agree·ment \ə-'grē-mənt\ *n* **1** : harmony of opinion or action **2** : mutual understanding or arrangement; *also* : a document containing such an arrangement

ag·ri·busi·ness \'a-grə-ˌbiz-nəs, -nəz\ *n* : an industry engaged in the manufacture and sale of farm equipment and supplies and in the production, processing, storage, and sale of farm commodities

agric *abbr* agricultural; agriculture

ag·ri·cul·ture \'a-gri-ˌkəl-chər\ *n* : FARMING, HUSBANDRY — **ag·ri·cul·tur·al** \ˌa-gri-'kəl-ch(ə-)rəl\ *adj* — **ag·ri·cul·tur·ist** \-ch(ə-)rist\ *or* **ag·ri·cul·tur·al·ist** \-ch(ə-)rə-list\ *n*

agron·o·my \ə-'grä-nə-mē\ *n* : a branch of agriculture that deals with the raising of crops and the care of the soil — **ag·ro·nom·ic** \ˌa-grə-'nä-mik\ *adj* — **agron·o·mist** \ə-'grä-nə-mist\ *n*

aground \ə-'graůnd\ *adv or adj* : on or onto the bottom or shore ⟨ran ~⟩

agt *abbr* agent

ague \'ā-gyü\ *n* : a fever (as malaria) with recurrent chills and sweating

ahead \ə-'hed\ *adv or adj* **1** : in or toward the front **2** : into or for the future ⟨plan ~⟩ **3** : in or toward a more advantageous position

ahead of *prep* **1** : in front or advance of **2** : in excess of : ABOVE

ahoy \ə-'hȯi\ *interj* — used in hailing ⟨ship ~⟩

AI *abbr* artificial intelligence

[1]**aid** \'ād\ *vb* : to provide with what is useful in achieving an end : ASSIST

[2]**aid** *n* **1** : ASSISTANCE **2** : ASSISTANT

AID *abbr* Agency for International Development

aide \'ād\ *n* : a person who acts as an assistant; *esp* : a military officer assisting a superior

aide–de–camp \ˌād-di-'kamp, -'kän\ *n, pl* **aides–de–camp** \ˌādz-di-\ [F] : AIDE

AIDS \'ādz\ *n* [*a*cquired *i*mmuno*d*eficiency *s*yndrome] : a serious disease of the human immune system that is characterized by severe reduction in the numbers of helper T cells and increased vulnerability to life-threatening illnesses and that is caused by infection with HIV commonly transmitted in infected blood esp. during illicit intravenous drug use and in bodily secretions (as semen) during sexual intercourse

AIDS–related complex *n* : a group of symptoms (as fever, weight loss, and lymphadenopathy) that is associated with the presence of antibodies to HIV and is followed by the development of AIDS in a certain proportion of cases

AIDS virus *n* : HIV

ai·grette \ā-'gret, 'ā-ˌ\ *n* [F, plume, egret] : a plume or decorative tuft for the head

ail \'āl\ *vb* **1** : to be the matter with : TROUBLE **2** : to be unwell

ai·lan·thus \ā-'lan-thəs\ *n* : any of a genus of Asian trees or shrubs with pinnate leaves and ill-scented greenish flowers; *esp* : TREE OF HEAVEN

ai·le·ron \'ā-lə-ˌrän\ *n* : a movable part of an airplane wing used in banking

ail·ment \'āl-mənt\ *n* : a bodily disorder

[1]**aim** \'ām\ *vb* [ME, fr. AF *aesmer & esmer;* AF *aesmer,* fr. *a-* to (fr. L *ad-*) + *esmer* to estimate, fr. L *aestimare*] **1** : to point a weapon at an object **2** : to direct one's efforts : ASPIRE **3** : to direct to or toward a specified object or goal

[2]**aim** *n* **1** : the pointing of a weapon at an object **2** : the ability to hit a target **3** : OBJECT, PURPOSE ⟨my ~ is to win⟩ — **aim·less** \-ləs\ *adj* — **aim·less·ly** *adv* — **aim·less·ness** *n*

AIM *abbr* American Indian Movement

ain't \'ānt\ **1** : are not **2** : is not **3** : am not — though disapproved by many and more common in less educated speech, used in both speech and writing to catch attention and to gain emphasis

Ai·nu \'ī-nü\ *n, pl* **Ainu** *or* **Ainus** **1** : a member of an Indigenous people of northern Japan **2** : the language of the Ainu people

[1]**air** \'er\ *n* **1** : the gaseous mixture surrounding the earth **2** : a light breeze **3** : MELODY, TUNE **4** : the outward appearance of a person or thing : MANNER **5** : an artificial manner **6** : COMPRESSED AIR ⟨~ sprayer⟩ **7** : AIRCRAFT ⟨traveled by ~⟩ **8** : AVIATION ⟨~ safety⟩ **9** : the medium of transmission of radio waves; *also* : RADIO, TELEVISION

[2]**air** *vb* **1** : to expose to the air ⟨~ clothes⟩ **2** : to expose to public view **3** : to broadcast on radio or television

air·bag \'er-ˌbag\ *n* : a bag designed to in-

flate automatically to protect automobile occupants in case of collision
air·boat \ˈer-ˌbōt\ *n* : a shallow-draft boat driven by an airplane propeller
air·borne \-ˌbȯrn\ *adj* : done or being in the air
air brake *n* **1** : a brake operated by a piston driven by compressed air **2** : a surface projected into the airflow to lower an airplane's speed
air·brush \ˈer-ˌbrəsh\ *n* : a device for applying a fine spray (as of paint) by compressed air — **airbrush** *vb*
air con·di·tion·er \ˌer-kən-ˈdi-sh(ə-)nər\ *n* : an apparatus for filtering air and controlling its humidity and temperature — **air–con·di·tion** \-ˈdi-shən\ *vb*
air·craft \ˈer-ˌkraft\ *n, pl* **aircraft** : a vehicle for traveling through the air
aircraft carrier *n* : a warship with a deck on which airplanes can be launched and landed
air·drop \ˈer-ˌdräp\ *n* : delivery of cargo or personnel by parachute from an airplane in flight — **air–drop** *vb*
Aire·dale terrier \ˈer-ˌdāl-\ *n* : any of a breed of large terriers with a hard wiry coat
air·fare \ˈer-ˌfer\ *n* : fare for travel by airplane
air·field \-ˌfēld\ *n* : AIRPORT
air·flow \-ˌflō\ *n* : the motion of air relative to a body in it
air·foil \-ˌfȯi(-ə)l\ *n* : an airplane surface designed to produce reaction forces from the air through which it moves
air force *n* : the military organization of a nation for air warfare
air·frame \ˈer-ˌfrām\ *n* : the structure of an aircraft, rocket, or missile without the power plant; *also* : AIRCRAFT
air·freight \-ˈfrāt\ *n* : freight transport by aircraft in volume; *also* : the charge for this service
air gun *n* **1** : a gun operated by compressed air **2** : a hand tool that works by compressed air; *esp* : AIRBRUSH
air·head \ˈer-ˌhed\ *n* : a mindless or stupid person
air lane *n* : AIRWAY 1
air·lift \ˈer-ˌlift\ *n* : transportation (as of supplies or passengers) by aircraft — **airlift** *vb*
air·line \-ˌlīn\ *n* : a transportation system using airplanes
air·lin·er \-ˌlī-nər\ *n* : a large passenger airplane operated by an airline
air lock *n* : an airtight chamber separating areas of different pressure
air·mail \ˈer-ˌmāl\ *n* : the system of transporting mail by aircraft; *also* : mail so transported — **airmail** *vb*
air·man \-mən\ *n* **1** : AVIATOR, PILOT **2** : an enlisted person in the air force ranking next below an airman first class
airman basic *n* : an enlisted person of the lowest rank in the air force
airman first class *n* : an enlisted person in the air force ranking next below a senior airman
air mass *n* : a large horizontally homogeneous body of air
air·mo·bile \ˈer-ˌmō-bəl, -ˌbēl\ *adj* : of, relating to, or being a military unit whose members are transported to combat areas usu. by helicopter
air·plane \-ˌplān\ *n* : a powered heavier-than-air aircraft that has fixed wings from which it derives lift
air·play \-ˌplā\ *n* : the playing of a musical recording on the air by a radio station
air pocket *n* : a condition of the atmosphere (as a local downdraft) that causes an airplane to drop suddenly
air police *n* : the military police of an air force
air·port \ˈer-ˌpȯrt\ *n* : a place from which aircraft operate that usu. has paved runways and a terminal
air rage *n* : an airline passenger's uncontrolled anger that is usu. expressed in aggressive or violent behavior
air raid *n* : an attack by armed airplanes on a surface target
air·ship \ˈer-ˌship\ *n* : a lighter-than-air aircraft having propulsion and steering systems
air·sick \-ˌsik\ *adj* : affected with motion sickness associated with flying — **air·sick·ness** *n*
air·space \-ˌspās\ *n* : the space above a nation and under its jurisdiction
air·speed \-ˌspēd\ *n* : the speed of an object (as an airplane) with relation to the surrounding air
air·strip \-ˌstrip\ *n* : a runway without normal airport facilities
air·tight \ˈer-ˈtīt\ *adj* **1** : so tightly sealed that no air can enter or escape **2** : leaving no opening for attack
air–to–air *adj* : launched from one airplane in flight at another; *also* : involving aircraft in flight
air·waves \ˈer-ˌwāvz\ *n pl* : AIR 9
air·way \-ˌwā\ *n* **1** : a regular route for airplanes **2** : AIRLINE
air·wor·thy \-ˌwər-t͟hē\ *adj* : fit for operation in the air ⟨an ~ plane⟩ — **air·wor·thi·ness** *n*
airy \ˈer-ē\ *adj* **air·i·er**; **-est** **1** : LOFTY ⟨~ perches⟩ **2** : lacking in reality : EMPTY **3** : DELICATE **4** : BREEZY
aisle \ˈī(-ə)l\ *n* [ME *ile*, fr. AF *ele*, lit., wing, fr. L *ala*] **1** : the side of a church nave separated by piers from the nave proper **2** : a passage between sections of seats
ajar \ə-ˈjär\ *adj or adv* : partly open
AK *abbr* Alaska
aka *abbr* also known as
AKC *abbr* American Kennel Club
akim·bo \ə-ˈkim-bō\ *adj or adv* : having the hand on the hip and the elbow turned outward
akin \ə-ˈkin\ *adj* **1** : related by blood **2** : similar in kind
Al *symbol* aluminum
AL *abbr* **1** Alabama **2** American League **3** American Legion
¹-al *adj suffix* : of, relating to, or characterized by ⟨direction*al*⟩
²-al *n suffix* : action : process ⟨rehears*al*⟩
Ala *abbr* Alabama

al•a•bas•ter \ˈa-lə-ˌbas-tər\ *n* **1 :** a compact fine-textured usu. white and translucent gypsum often carved into objects (as vases) **2 :** a hard translucent calcite

à la carte \ˌa-lə-ˈkärt, ˌä-\ *adv or adj* [F] **:** with a separate price for each item on the menu

alac•ri•ty \ə-ˈla-krə-tē\ *n* **:** cheerful readiness **:** BRISKNESS

à la mode \ˌa-lə-ˈmōd, ˌä-\ *adj* [F, according to the fashion] **1 :** FASHIONABLE, STYLISH **2 :** topped with ice cream

[1]**alarm** \ə-ˈlärm\ *also* **ala•rum** \ə-ˈlär-əm, -ˈler-\ *n* [ME *alarme,* fr. MF, fr. OIt *all'arme,* lit., to arms] **1 :** a warning signal or device **2 :** the terror caused by sudden danger

[2]**alarm** *also* **alarum** *vb* **1 :** to warn of danger **2 :** FRIGHTEN

alarm•ist \ə-ˈlär-mist\ *n* **:** a person who alarms others esp. needlessly

alas \ə-ˈlas\ *interj* — used to express unhappiness, pity, or concern

al•ba•core \ˈal-bə-ˌkȯr\ *n, pl* **-core** *or* **-cores :** a large tuna that is a source of canned tuna

Al•ba•nian \al-ˈbā-nē-ən\ *n* **:** a native or inhabitant of Albania

al•ba•tross \ˈal-bə-ˌtrȯs, -ˌträs\ *n, pl* **-tross** *or* **-tross•es :** any of a family of large web-footed seabirds

al•be•do \al-ˈbē-(ˌ)dō\ *n, pl* **-dos :** the fraction of incident radiation that is reflected by a body or surface

al•be•it \ȯl-ˈbē-ət, al-\ *conj* **:** even though **:** ALTHOUGH

al•bi•no \al-ˈbī-nō\ *n, pl* **-nos :** a person or animal lacking coloring matter in the skin, hair, and eyes — **al•bi•nism** \ˈal-bə-ˌni-zəm\ *n*

al•bum \ˈal-bəm\ *n* **1 :** a book with blank pages used for making a collection (as of stamps or photographs) **2 :** one or more recordings (as on tape or disk) produced as a single unit

al•bu•men \al-ˈbyü-mən\ *n* **1 :** the white of an egg **2 :** ALBUMIN

al•bu•min \al-ˈbyü-mən\ *n* **:** any of numerous water-soluble proteins of blood, milk, egg white, and plant and animal tissues

al•bu•min•ous \al-ˈbyü-mə-nəs\ *adj* **:** containing or resembling albumen or albumin

al•bu•ter•ol \al-ˈbyü-tə-ˌrȯl, -ˌrōl\ *n* **:** a drug used as an aerosol or in tablet form to treat asthma

alc *abbr* alcohol

al•cal•de \al-ˈkäl-dē\ *n* **:** the chief administrative and judicial officer of a Spanish or Spanish-American town

al•ca•zar \al-ˈkä-zər, -ˈka-\ *n* [Sp *alcázar,* fr. Ar *al-qaṣr* the castle] **:** a Spanish fortress or palace

al•che•my \ˈal-kə-mē\ *n* **:** medieval chemistry chiefly concerned with efforts to turn base metals into gold — **al•che•mist** \ˈal-kə-mist\ *n*

al•co•hol \ˈal-kə-ˌhȯl\ *n* [NL, fr. ML, powdered antimony, fr. Sp, fr. Ar *al-kuḥul* the powdered antimony] **1 :** a colorless flammable liquid that is the intoxicating agent in fermented and distilled liquors **2 :** any of various carbon compounds similar to alcohol **3 :** beverages containing alcohol

[1]**al•co•hol•ic** \ˌal-kə-ˈhȯ-lik, -ˈhä-\ *adj* **1 :** of, relating to, caused by, or containing alcohol **2 :** affected with alcoholism — **al•co•hol•i•cal•ly** \-li-k(ə-)lē\ *adv*

[2]**alcoholic** *n* **:** a person affected with alcoholism

al•co•hol•ism \ˈal-kə-ˌhȯ-ˌli-zəm\ *n* **:** continued excessive and usu. uncontrollable use of alcoholic drinks; *also* **:** a complex chronic psychological and nutritional disorder associated with such use

al•cove \ˈal-ˌkōv\ *n* **1 :** a nook or small recess opening off a larger room **2 :** a niche or arched opening (as in a wall)

ald *abbr* alderman

al•der \ˈȯl-dər\ *n* **:** any of a genus of trees or shrubs related to the birches and growing in wet areas

al•der•man \ˈȯl-dər-mən\ *n* **:** a member of a city legislative body

ale \ˈāl\ *n* **:** a beer that is usu. darker and more bitter than a lager

ale•a•tor•ic \ˌā-lē-ə-ˈtȯr-ik\ *adj* **:** characterized by chance or random elements ⟨~ music⟩

ale•a•to•ry \ˈā-lē-ə-ˌtȯr-ē\ *adj* **:** ALEATORIC

alee \ə-ˈlē\ *adv* **:** on or toward the lee

ale•house \ˈāl-ˌhau̇s\ *n* **:** a place where ale is sold to be drunk on the premises

[1]**alert** \ə-ˈlərt\ *adj* [It *all'erta,* lit., on the ascent] **1 :** watchful against danger **2 :** quick to perceive and act — **alert•ly** *adv* — **alert•ness** *n*

[2]**alert** *n* **1 :** ALARM 1 **2 :** the period during which an alert is in effect

[3]**alert** *vb* **1 :** WARN **2 :** to make aware of

Aleut \ˌa-lē-ˈüt, ə-ˈlüt\ *n* **1 :** a member of a people of the Aleutian and Shumagin islands and the western part of Alaska Peninsula **2 :** the language of the Aleuts

ale•wife \ˈāl-ˌwīf\ *n, pl* **ale•wives** \-ˌwīvz\ **:** a food fish related to the herring that is abundant esp. along the Atlantic coast

Al•ex•an•dri•an \ˌa-lig-ˈzan-drē-ən\ *adj* **1 :** HELLENISTIC **2 :** of or relating to Alexander the Great

al•ex•an•drine \-ˈzan-drən\ *n, often cap* **:** a line of six iambic feet

al•fal•fa \al-ˈfal-fə\ *n* **:** a leguminous plant widely grown for hay and forage

al•fres•co \al-ˈfres-kō\ *adj or adv* [It] **:** taking place in the open air

alg *abbr* algebra

al•ga \ˈal-gə\ *n, pl* **al•gae** \ˈal-(ˌ)jē\ **:** any of a group of lower plants having chlorophyll but no vascular system and including seaweeds and related freshwater plants — **al•gal** \-gəl\ *adj*

al•ge•bra \ˈal-jə-brə\ *n* [ML, fr. Ar *al-jabr*] **:** a generalization of arithmetic in which letters representing numbers are combined according to the rules of arithmetic — **al•ge•bra•ic** \ˌal-jə-ˈbrā-ik\ *adj* — **al•ge•bra•i•cal•ly** \-ˈbrā-ə-k(ə-)lē\ *adv*

Al•gon•qui•an \al-ˈgän-kwē-ən, -ˈgäŋ-\ *or* **Al•gon•quin** \-kwən\ *n* **1** *usu Algonquin* **:** a First Nations people of the Ottawa

River valley **2** *usu Algonquian* : a family of languages spoken by Indigenous peoples of eastern and central No. America

al·go·rithm \ˈal-gə-ˌri-t͟həm\ *n* : a procedure for solving a problem esp. in mathematics or computing — **al·go·rith·mic** \ˌal-gə-ˈrit͟h-mik\ *adj* — **al·go·rith·mi·cal·ly** \-mi-k(ə-)lē\ *adv*

[1]**ali·as** \ˈā-lē-əs, ˈāl-yəs\ *adv* [L, otherwise, fr. *alius* other] : otherwise called

[2]**alias** *n* : an assumed name

[1]**al·i·bi** \ˈa-lə-ˌbī\ *n* [L, elsewhere, fr. *alius* other] **1** : a plea offered by an accused person of not having been at the scene of an offense **2** : an excuse (as for failure)

[2]**alibi** *vb* **-bied**; **-bi·ing** **1** : to furnish an excuse for **2** : to offer an excuse

[1]**alien** \ˈā-lē-ən, ˈāl-yən\ *adj* **1** : relating or belonging to another person, place, or thing : STRANGE ⟨an ~ environment⟩ **2** : relating, belonging, or owing allegiance to another country or government : FOREIGN **3** : EXOTIC 1 **4** : EXTRATERRESTRIAL

[2]**alien** *n* **1** : a person who is not of a particular group or place **2** : a foreign-born resident who has not been naturalized **3** : an extraterrestrial being

alien·able \ˈāl-yə-nə-bəl, ˈā-lē-ə-nə-\ *adj* : transferable to the ownership of another ⟨~ property⟩

alien·ate \ˈā-lē-ə-ˌnāt, ˈāl-yə-\ *vb* **-at·ed**; **-at·ing** **1** : to make hostile : ESTRANGE **2** : to transfer (property) to another — **alien·ation** \ˌā-lē-ə-ˈnā-shən, ˌāl-yə-\ *n*

alien·ist \ˈā-lē-ə-nist, ˈāl-yə-\ *n, dated* : PSYCHIATRIST

[1]**alight** \ə-ˈlīt\ *vb* **alight·ed** *also* **alit** \ə-ˈlit\; **alight·ing** **1** : to get down (as from a vehicle) **2** : to come to rest from the air
♦ ***Synonyms*** SETTLE, LAND, PERCH

[2]**alight** *adj* : lighted up

align *also* **aline** \ə-ˈlīn\ *vb* **1** : to bring into line **2** : to array on the side of or against a cause — **align·er** *n* — **align·ment** *also* **aline·ment** *n*

[1]**alike** \ə-ˈlīk\ *adv* : EQUALLY ⟨denounced by teachers and students ~⟩

[2]**alike** *adj* : LIKE ⟨~ in their beliefs⟩
♦ ***Synonyms*** AKIN, ANALOGOUS, SIMILAR, COMPARABLE

al·i·ment \ˈa-lə-mənt\ *n* : NOURISHMENT 1 — **aliment** *vb*

al·i·men·ta·ry \ˌa-lə-ˈmen-t(ə-)rē\ *adj* : of, relating to, or functioning in nourishment or nutrition

alimentary canal *n* : the tube that extends from the mouth to the anus and functions in the digestion and absorption of food and the elimination of residues

al·i·mo·ny \ˈa-lə-ˌmō-nē\ *n, pl* **-nies** [L *alimonia* sustenance, fr. *alere* to nourish] : an allowance made to one spouse by the other for support pending or after legal separation or divorce

A–line \ˈā-ˌlīn\ *adj* : having a flared bottom and a close-fitting top ⟨an ~ skirt⟩

alive \ə-ˈlīv\ *adj* **1** : having life **2** : being in force or operation **3** : SENSITIVE ⟨~ to the danger⟩ **4** : ALERT, BRISK **5** : ANIMATED ⟨streets ~ with traffic⟩ — **alive·ness** *n*

alk *abbr* alkaline

al·ka·li \ˈal-kə-ˌlī\ *n, pl* **-lies** *or* **-lis** **1** : a substance (as a hydroxide) that has a bitter taste and neutralizes acids **2** : a mixture of salts in the soil of some dry regions in such amount as to make ordinary farming impossible — **al·ka·line** \-kə-lən, -ˌlīn\ *adj* — **al·ka·lin·i·ty** \ˌal-kə-ˈli-nə-tē\ *n*

al·ka·loid \ˈal-kə-ˌlȯid\ *n* : any of various usu. basic and bitter organic compounds found esp. in seed plants

al·kane \ˈal-ˌkān\ *n* : a hydrocarbon in which each carbon atom is bonded to 4 other atoms

al·kyd \ˈal-kəd\ *n* : any of numerous synthetic resins used esp. for protective coatings and in paint

[1]**all** \ˈȯl\ *adj* **1** : the whole of ⟨sat up ~ night⟩ **2** : every member of **3** : EVERY ⟨~ manner of problems⟩ **4** : any whatever ⟨beyond ~ doubt⟩ **5** : nothing but ⟨~ ears⟩ **6** : being more than one person or thing ⟨who ~ is coming⟩

[2]**all** *adv* **1** : WHOLLY ⟨sat ~ alone⟩ **2** : selected as the best — used in combination ⟨*all*-state champs⟩ **3** : so much ⟨~ the better for it⟩ **4** : for each side ⟨the score is two ~⟩

[3]**all** *pron sing or pl* **1** : the whole number, quantity, or amount ⟨~ of it is gone⟩ **2** : EVERYBODY, EVERYTHING ⟨~ are members⟩ ⟨that is ~⟩

[4]**all** *n* : the whole of one's resources ⟨gave his ~⟩

Al·lah \ˈä-lə, ˈa-; ˈä-ˌlä, ä-ˈlä\ *n* [Ar *allāh*] : GOD 1 — used in Islam

all along *adv* : all the time ⟨knew it *all along*⟩

all–Amer·i·can \ˌȯl-ə-ˈmer-ə-kən\ *adj* **1** : selected as the best in the U.S. **2** : composed wholly of American elements **3** : typical of the U.S. — **all–American** *n*

all–around \ˌȯl-ə-ˈrau̇nd\ *adj* **1** : considered in all aspects ⟨best ~ performance⟩ **2** : competent in many fields : VERSATILE ⟨an ~ athlete⟩

al·lay \ə-ˈlā\ *vb* **1** : ALLEVIATE **2** : CALM
♦ ***Synonyms*** LIGHTEN, RELIEVE, EASE, ASSUAGE

all clear *n* : a signal that a danger has passed

al·lege \ə-ˈlej\ *vb* **al·leged**; **al·leg·ing** **1** : to assert without proof **2** : to offer as a reason — **al·le·ga·tion** \ˌa-li-ˈgā-shən\ *n* — **al·leged** \ə-ˈlejd, -ˈle-jəd\ *adj* — **al·leg·ed·ly** \ə-ˈle-jəd-lē\ *adv*

al·le·giance \ə-ˈlē-jəns\ *n* **1** : loyalty owed by a citizen to a government **2** : loyalty to a person or cause

al·le·go·ry \ˈa-lə-ˌgȯr-ē\ *n, pl* **-ries** : the expression through symbolism of truths or generalizations about human experience — **al·le·gor·i·cal** \ˌa-lə-ˈgȯr-i-kəl\ *adj* — **al·le·gor·i·cal·ly** \-k(ə-)lē\ *adv*

[1]**al·le·gro** \ə-ˈle-grō, -ˈlā-\ *n, pl* **-gros** : an allegro movement

[2]**allegro** *adv or adj* [It, merry] : at a brisk lively tempo — used as a direction in music

al·lele \ə-ˈlēl\ *n* : any of the alternative

forms of a gene that may occur at a given site on a chromosome — **al·le·lic** \-ˈlē-lik, -ˈle-\ *adj*

al·le·lu·ia \ˌa-lə-ˈlü-yə\ *interj* : HALLELUJAH

Al·len wrench \ˈa-lən-\ *n* [*Allen* Manufacturing Company, Hartford, Conn.] : an L-shaped hexagonal metal bar of which either end fits the socket of a screw or bolt

al·ler·gen \ˈa-lər-jən\ *n* : something that causes allergy — **al·ler·gen·ic** \ˌa-lər-ˈje-nik\ *adj*

al·ler·gist \ˈa-lər-jist\ *n* : a specialist in allergies

al·ler·gy \ˈa-lər-jē\ *n, pl* **-gies** [G *Allergie,* fr. Gk *allos* other + *ergon* work] : exaggerated or abnormal reaction (as by sneezing) to substances or situations harmless to most people — **al·ler·gic** \ə-ˈlər-jik\ *adj*

al·le·vi·ate \ə-ˈlē-vē-ˌāt\ *vb* **-at·ed; -at·ing** : RELIEVE, LESSEN ⟨~ pain⟩ ♦ ***Synonyms*** LIGHTEN, MITIGATE, ALLAY — **al·le·vi·a·tion** \ə-ˌlē-vē-ˈā-shən\ *n*

al·ley \ˈa-lē\ *n, pl* **alleys 1** : a garden or park walk **2** : a place for bowling **3** : a narrow passageway esp. between buildings

al·ley–oop \ˌa-lē-ˈyüp\ *n* : a basketball play in which a player catches a pass above the basket and immediately dunks the ball

al·ley·way \ˈa-lē-ˌwā\ *n* : ALLEY 3

all–fired \ˈȯl-ˌfī(-ə)rd\ *adv* : EXTREMELY, EXCESSIVELY ⟨~ stubborn⟩

All·hal·lows \ȯl-ˈha-lōz\ *n, pl* **Allhallows** : ALL SAINTS' DAY

all hours *n pl* : a very late time ⟨stayed up until *all hours*⟩

al·li·ance \ə-ˈlī-əns\ *n* : a union to promote common interests ♦ ***Synonyms*** LEAGUE, COALITION, CONFEDERACY, FEDERATION

al·li·ga·tor \ˈa-lə-ˌgā-tər\ *n* [Sp *el lagarto* the lizard] : either of two large short-legged reptiles resembling crocodiles but having a shorter and broader snout

alligator pear *n* : AVOCADO

¹**all–in·clu·sive** \ˌȯl-in-ˈklü-siv\ *adj* : including everything; *esp* : sold for one price that includes charges that are often added separately ⟨an ~ vacation package⟩

²**all–inclusive** *n* : an ~ resort

al·lit·er·ate \ə-ˈli-tə-ˌrāt\ *vb* **-at·ed; -at·ing 1** : to form an alliteration **2** : to arrange so as to make alliteration

al·lit·er·a·tion \ə-ˌli-tə-ˈrā-shən\ *n* : the repetition of initial sounds in adjacent words or syllables — **al·lit·er·a·tive** \-ˈli-tə-ˌrā-tiv\ *adj*

al·lo·cate \ˈa-lə-ˌkāt\ *vb* **-cat·ed; -cat·ing** : ALLOT, ASSIGN — **al·lo·ca·tion** \ˌa-lə-ˈkā-shən\ *n*

al·lot \ə-ˈlät\ *vb* **al·lot·ted; al·lot·ting** : to distribute as a share ♦ ***Synonyms*** ASSIGN, APPORTION, ALLOCATE — **al·lot·ment** *n*

all–out \ˈȯl-ˈau̇t\ *adj* : made with maximum effort

¹**all over** *adv* : EVERYWHERE

²**all over** *prep* **1** : in eagerly affectionate, attentive, or aggressive pursuit **2** : in or into a state marked by excessive criticism

al·low \ə-ˈlau̇\ *vb* **1** : to assign as a share ⟨~ time for rest⟩ **2** : to count as a deduction **3** : to make allowance ⟨~ for expansion⟩ **4** : ADMIT, CONCEDE ⟨~*ed* that the situation was serious⟩ **5** : PERMIT ⟨~*s* the dog to roam⟩ ⟨work on it as time ~*s*⟩ — **al·low·able** *adj*

al·low·ance \-əns\ *n* **1** : an allotted share **2** : money given regularly for expenses **3** : a taking into account of extenuating circumstances

al·loy \ˈa-ˌlȯi, ə-ˈlȯi\ *n* **1** : a substance composed of metals melted together **2** : an admixture that lessens value — **al·loy** \ə-ˈlȯi, ˈa-ˌlȯi\ *vb*

all right *adv* **1** — used interjectionally esp. to express agreement or resignation or to indicate the resumption of a discussion ⟨*all right,* let's go⟩ **2** : beyond doubt **3** : SATISFACTORILY ⟨does *all right* in school⟩ — **all right** *adj*

All Saints' Day *n* : a Christian feast on November 1 in honor of all the saints

All Souls' Day *n* : a day of prayer observed by some Christian churches on November 2 for the souls of the faithful departed

all·spice \ˈȯl-ˌspīs\ *n* : the berry of a West Indian tree related to the European myrtle; *also* : the mildly pungent and aromatic spice made from it

all–star \ˈȯl-ˌstär\ *n* : a member of a team of star performers — **all–star** *adj*

all–ter·rain vehicle *n* : a small motor vehicle with three or four wheels for use on a wide range of terrain

all told *adv* : with everything or everyone counted ⟨expecting eight guests *all told*⟩

al·lude \ə-ˈlüd\ *vb* **al·lud·ed; al·lud·ing** [L *alludere,* lit., to play with] : to refer indirectly — **al·lu·sion** \-ˈlü-zhən\ *n* — **al·lu·sive** \-ˈlü-siv\ *adj* — **al·lu·sive·ly** *adv* — **al·lu·sive·ness** *n*

al·lure \ə-ˈlu̇r\ *vb* **al·lured; al·lur·ing** : to attract by something desirable — **allure** *n* — **al·lur·ing·ly** *adv*

al·lu·vi·um \ə-ˈlü-vē-əm\ *n, pl* **-vi·ums** *or* **-via** \-vē-ə\ : soil material (as clay) deposited by running water — **al·lu·vi·al** \-vē-əl\ *adj or n*

all–wheel \ˈȯl-ˈwēl\ *adj* : acting independently on or by means of all four wheels of a vehicle

al·ly \ə-ˈlī, ˈa-ˌlī\ *vb* **al·lied; al·ly·ing** : to enter into an alliance — **al·ly** \ˈa-ˌlī, ə-ˈlī\ *n*

-ally *adv suffix* : ²-LY ⟨specific*ally*⟩

al·ma ma·ter \ˌal-mə-ˈmä-tər\ *n* [L, fostering mother] **1** : an educational institute that one has attended **2** : the song or hymn of an alma mater

al·ma·nac \ˈȯl-mə-ˌnak, ˈal-\ *n* **1** : a publication esp. of astronomical and meteorological data **2** : a usu. annual publication of miscellaneous information

al·man·dite \ˈal-mən-ˌdīt\ *n* : a deep red garnet

al·mighty \ȯl-ˈmī-tē\ *adj* **1** *often cap* : having absolute power over all ⟨*Almighty* God⟩ **2** : relatively unlimited in power — **al·might·i·ness** *n*
Almighty *n* : GOD 1
al·mond \ˈä-mənd, ˈa-; ˈal-\ *n* : a small tree related to the peach; *also* : the edible nutlike kernel of its fruit
al·mo·ner \ˈal-mə-nər, ˈä-mə-\ *n* : a person who distributes alms
al·most \ˈȯl-ˌmōst, ȯl-ˈmōst\ *adv* : very nearly but not exactly
alms \ˈämz, ˈälmz\ *n, pl* **alms** [ME *almesse, almes,* fr. OE *ælmesse, ælms,* fr. L *eleemosyna* alms, fr. Gk *eleēmosynē* pity, alms, fr. *eleēmōn* merciful, fr. *eleos* pity] : something given freely to relieve the poor
alms·house \-ˌhau̇s\ *n* : POORHOUSE
al·oe \ˈa-lō\ *n* **1** : any of a large genus of succulent chiefly southern African plants related to the lilies **2** *pl* : the dried juice of the leaves of an aloe used esp. formerly as a laxative
aloe vera \-ˈver-ə, -ˈvir-\ *n* : an aloe with leaves that yield a jellylike emollient extract used esp. in cosmetics; *also* : this extract
aloft \ə-ˈlȯft\ *adv* **1** : high in the air **2** : in flight
alo·ha \ə-ˈlō-ə, ä-ˈlō-hä\ *interj* [Hawaiian] — used to greet or bid farewell
alone \ə-ˈlōn\ *adj* **1** : separated from others **2** : not including anyone or anything else : ONLY ⟨she ~ knows why⟩ ♦ ***Synonyms*** LONELY, LONESOME, LONE, SOLITARY — **alone** *adv*
¹**along** \ə-ˈlȯŋ\ *prep* **1** : in a line matching the direction of ⟨sail ~ the coast⟩ **2** : at a point on or during ⟨stopped ~ the way⟩
²**along** *adv* **1** : FORWARD, ON ⟨move ~⟩ **2** : as a companion ⟨bring her ~⟩ **3** : at an advanced point ⟨plans are far ~⟩
along·shore \ə-ˈlȯŋ-ˈshȯr\ *adv or adj* : along the shore or coast ⟨walked ~⟩
¹**along·side** \-ˌsīd\ *adv* : along or by the side
²**alongside** *prep* **1** : along or by the side of **2** : in association with
alongside of *prep* : ALONGSIDE
aloof \ə-ˈlüf\ *adj* : removed or distant physically or emotionally — **aloof·ly** *adv* — **aloof·ness** *n*
al·o·pe·cia \ˌa-lə-ˈpē-sh(ē-)ə\ *n* : BALDNESS
aloud \ə-ˈlau̇d\ *adv* : with the speaking voice ⟨read ~⟩
alp \ˈalp\ *n* : a high rugged mountain
al·paca \al-ˈpa-kə\ *n* : a domesticated mammal esp. of Peru that is prob. descended from the vicuña; *also* : its woolly hair or a thin cloth made from this hair
al·pha \ˈal-fə\ *n* **1** : the 1st letter of the Greek alphabet — Α or α **2** : something first : BEGINNING
al·pha·bet \ˈal-fə-ˌbet\ *n* : the set of letters or characters used in writing a language
al·pha·bet·i·cal \ˌal-fə-ˈbe-ti-kəl\ *or* **al·pha·bet·ic** \-ˈbe-tik\ *adj* **1** : arranged in the order of the letters of the alphabet **2** : of or employing an alphabet — **al·pha·bet·i·cal·ly** \-ti-k(ə-)lē\ *adv*
al·pha·bet·ize \ˈal-fə-bə-ˌtīz\ *vb* **-ized**; **-iz·ing** : to arrange in alphabetical order — **al·pha·bet·iz·er** *n*
al·pha·nu·mer·ic \ˌal-fə-nu̇-ˈmer-ik, -nyu̇-\ *adj* : consisting of letters and numbers and often other symbols ⟨an ~ code⟩; *also* : being a character in an alphanumeric system
alpha particle *n* : a positively charged particle identical with the nucleus of a helium atom that is ejected at high speed in certain radioactive transformations
alpha rhythm *n* : ALPHA WAVE
alpha wave *n* : an electrical rhythm of the brain often associated with a state of wakeful relaxation
Al·pine \ˈal-ˌpīn\ *adj* **1** : relating to, located in, or resembling the Alps **2** *often not cap* : of, relating to, or growing on upland slopes above timberline **3** : of or relating to competitive ski events consisting of slalom and downhill racing
al·ready \ȯl-ˈre-dē\ *adv* : by this time : PREVIOUSLY
al·right \ȯl-ˈrīt\ *adv* : ALL RIGHT
al·so \ˈȯl-sō\ *adv* : in addition : TOO
al·so–ran \-ˌran\ *n* **1** : a horse or dog that finishes out of the money in a race **2** : a contestant that does not win
alt *abbr* **1** alternate **2** altitude
Alta *abbr* Alberta
al·tar \ˈȯl-tər\ *n* **1** : a structure on which sacrifices are offered or incense is burned **2** : a table used as a center of ritual or worship
altar server *n* : a usu. young person who assists the celebrant at a church service
¹**al·ter** \ˈȯl-tər\ *vb* **al·tered**; **al·ter·ing** \-t(ə-)riŋ\ **1** : to make or become different **2** : CASTRATE, SPAY — **al·ter·able** \ˈȯl-tə-rə-bəl\ *adj* — **al·ter·a·tion** \ˌȯl-tə-ˈrā-shən\ *n*
²**alter** *abbr* alteration
al·ter·ca·tion \ˌȯl-tər-ˈkā-shən\ *n* : a noisy or angry dispute
al·ter ego \ˌȯl-tər-ˈē-gō\ *n* [L, lit., second I] : a second self; *esp* : a trusted friend
al·ter·i·ty \ȯl-ˈter-ə-tē\ *n* : the quality or state of being radically alien to the conscious self or a particular cultural orientation
¹**al·ter·nate** \ˈȯl-tər-nət, ˈal-\ *adj* **1** : arranged or succeeding by turns **2** : every other **3** : being an alternative ⟨an ~ route⟩ — **al·ter·nate·ly** *adv*
²**al·ter·nate** \-ˌnāt\ *vb* **-nat·ed**; **-nat·ing** : to occur or cause to occur by turns — **al·ter·na·tion** \ˌȯl-tər-ˈnā-shən, ˌal-\ *n*
³**alternate** *n* : SUBSTITUTE
alternating current *n* : an electric current that reverses its direction at regular intervals
al·ter·na·tive \ȯl-ˈtər-nə-tiv, al-\ *adj* **1** : offering a choice ⟨several ~ plans⟩ **2** : different from the usual or conventional — **alternative** *n*
alternative medicine *n* : any of various systems of healing (as homeopathy) not

typically practiced in conventional Western medicine
al·ter·na·tor \ˈȯl-tər-ˌnā-tər, ˈal-\ *n* : an electric generator for producing alternating current
al·though *also* **al·tho** \ȯl-ˈt͟hō\ *conj* : in spite of the fact that : even though
al·tim·e·ter \al-ˈti-mə-tər, ˈal-tə-ˌmē-tər\ *n* : an instrument for measuring altitude
al·ti·tude \ˈal-tə-ˌtüd, -ˌtyüd\ *n* **1** : angular distance above the horizon **2** : vertical distance : HEIGHT **3** : the perpendicular distance in a geometric figure from the vertex to the base, from the vertex of an angle to the side opposite, or from the base to a parallel side or face
al·to \ˈal-tō\ *n, pl* **altos** [It, lit., high, fr. L *altus*] : the lower female voice part in a 4-part chorus; *also* : a singer having this voice or part
[1]**al·to·geth·er** \ˌȯl-tə-ˈge-t͟hər\ *adv* **1** : WHOLLY ⟨stopped raining ~⟩ **2** : in all ⟨spent $100 ~⟩ **3** : on the whole ⟨~ their efforts were successful⟩
[2]**altogether** *n* : NUDE ⟨posed in the ~⟩
al·tru·ism \ˈal-trü-ˌi-zəm\ *n* [F *altruisme*, fr. *autrui* other people, fr. OF, oblique case form of *autre* other, fr. L *alter*] : unselfish interest in the welfare of others — **al·tru·ist** \-ist\ *n* — **al·tru·is·tic** \ˌal-trü-ˈis-tik\ *adj* — **al·tru·is·ti·cal·ly** \-ti-k(ə-)lē\ *adv*
al·um \ˈa-ləm\ *n* : either of two colorless crystalline aluminum-containing compounds used esp. as an emetic or as an astringent and styptic
alu·mi·na \ə-ˈlü-mə-nə\ *n* : the oxide of aluminum occurring in nature as corundum and in bauxite
al·u·min·i·um \ˌal-yə-ˈmi-nē-əm\ *n, chiefly Brit* : ALUMINUM
alu·mi·nize \ə-ˈlü-mə-ˌnīz\ *vb* **-nized**; **-niz·ing** : to treat with aluminum
alu·mi·num \ə-ˈlü-mə-nəm\ *n* : a silver-white malleable ductile light metallic element that is the most abundant metal in the earth's crust
aluminum oxide *n* : ALUMINA
alum·na \ə-ˈləm-nə\ *n, pl* **-nae** \-(ˌ)nē\ : a woman or girl who is a graduate or former student of a college or school
alum·nus \ə-ˈləm-nəs\ *n, pl* **-ni** \-ˌnī\ [L, foster son, pupil, fr. *alere* to nourish] : a graduate or former student of a college or school
al·ways \ˈȯl-wēz, -wəz, -(ˌ)wāz\ *adv* **1** : at all times : INVARIABLY **2** : FOREVER
Alz·hei·mer's disease \ˈälts-ˌhī-mərz-, ˈalts-\ *n* : a degenerative brain disease of unknown cause that is characterized esp. by progressive mental deterioration and memory loss
am *pres 1st sing of* BE
[1]**Am** *abbr* America; American
[2]**Am** *symbol* americium
[1]**AM** \ˈā-ˌem\ *n* : a broadcasting system using amplitude modulation; *also* : a radio receiver for broadcasts made by such a system
[2]**AM** *abbr* **1** ante meridiem — often not cap. and often punctuated **2** [NL *artium magister*] master of arts
AMA *abbr* American Medical Association
amah \ˈä-(ˌ)mä\ *n* : a female servant in eastern Asia; *esp* : a Chinese nurse
amain \ə-ˈmān\ *adv, archaic* : with full force or speed
amal·gam \ə-ˈmal-gəm\ *n* **1** : an alloy of mercury with another metal used in making dental cements **2** : a mixture of different elements
amal·gam·ate \ə-ˈmal-gə-ˌmāt\ *vb* **-at·ed**; **-at·ing** : to unite or merge into one body — **amal·ga·ma·tion** \-ˌmal-gə-ˈmā-shən\ *n*
aman·u·en·sis \ə-ˌman-yə-ˈwen-səs\ *n, pl* **-en·ses** \-ˌsēz\ : one employed to write from dictation or to copy what another has written : SECRETARY
am·a·ranth \ˈa-mə-ˌranth\ *n* **1** : any of a large genus of coarse herbs sometimes grown for their showy flowers **2** : a flower that never fades
am·a·ran·thine \ˌa-mə-ˈran-thən, -ˌthīn\ *adj* **1** : relating to or resembling an amaranth **2** : UNDYING
am·a·ryl·lis \ˌa-mə-ˈri-ləs\ *n* : any of various plants related to the lilies; *esp* : an autumn-flowering South African bulbous herb widely grown for its large showy red to whitish flowers
amass \ə-ˈmas\ *vb* : ACCUMULATE
am·a·teur \ˈa-mə-(ˌ)tər, -ˌtu̇r, -ˌtyu̇r, -ˌchu̇r, -chər\ *n* [F, fr. L *amator* lover, fr. *amare* to love] **1** : a person who engages in a pursuit for pleasure and not as a profession **2** : a person who is not expert — **am·a·teur·ish** \ˌa-mə-ˈtər-ish, -ˈtu̇r-, -ˈtyu̇r-, -ˈchu̇r-, -ˈchər-\ *adj* — **am·a·teur·ism** \ˈa-mə-(ˌ)tər-i-zəm, -ˌtu̇r-, -ˌtyu̇r-, -ˌchu̇r-, -ˌchər-\ *n*
am·a·tive \ˈa-mə-tiv\ *adj* : indicative of love : AMOROUS — **am·a·tive·ly** *adv* — **am·a·tive·ness** *n*
am·a·to·ry \ˈa-mə-ˌtȯr-ē\ *adj* : of or expressing sexual love
amaze \ə-ˈmāz\ *vb* **amazed**; **amaz·ing** : to fill with wonder : ASTOUND ♦ ***Synonyms*** ASTONISH, SURPRISE, DUMBFOUND — **amaze·ment** *n* — **amaz·ing·ly** *adv*
am·a·zon \ˈa-mə-ˌzän, -zən\ *n* **1** *cap* : a member of a race of female warriors of Greek mythology **2** : a tall strong often masculine woman — **am·a·zo·ni·an** \ˌa-mə-ˈzō-nē-ən\ *adj, often cap*
amb *abbr* ambassador
am·bas·sa·dor \am-ˈba-sə-dər\ *n* : a representative esp. of a government — **am·bas·sa·do·ri·al** \-ˌba-sə-ˈdȯr-ē-əl\ *adj* — **am·bas·sa·dor·ship** *n*
am·ber \ˈam-bər\ *n* : a yellowish or brownish fossil resin used esp. for ornamental objects; *also* : the color of this resin
Amber Alert *n* : a widely publicized bulletin that alerts the public to a recently abducted or missing child
am·ber·gris \ˈam-bər-ˌgris, -ˌgrēs\ *n* : a waxy substance from the sperm whale used in making perfumes
am·bi·dex·trous \ˌam-bi-ˈdek-strəs\ *adj* : using both hands with equal ease — **am·bi·dex·trous·ly** *adv*

am·bi·ence *or* **am·bi·ance** \ˈam-bē-əns, ä^{n}-ˈbyä^{n}s\ *n* : a pervading atmosphere

[1]**am·bi·ent** \ˈam-bē-ənt\ *adj* : existing on all sides

[2]**ambient** *n* : music intended to serve as an unobtrusive accompaniment to other activities

am·big·u·ous \am-ˈbi-gyə-wəs\ *adj* : capable of being understood in more than one way — **am·bi·gu·i·ty** \ˌam-bə-ˈgyü-ə-tē\ *n* — **am·big·u·ous·ly** *adv*

am·bi·tion \am-ˈbi-shən\ *n* [ME, fr. MF or L; MF, fr. L *ambition-, ambitio,* lit., act of soliciting for votes, fr. *ambire* to go around] : eager desire for success or power

am·bi·tious \-shəs\ *adj* : characterized by ambition — **am·bi·tious·ly** *adv* — **am·bi·tious·ness** *n*

am·biv·a·lence \am-ˈbi-və-ləns\ *n* : simultaneous attraction toward and repulsion from a person, object, or action — **am·biv·a·lent** \-lənt\ *adj*

[1]**am·ble** \ˈam-bəl\ *vb* **am·bled**; **am·bling** \-b(ə-)liŋ\ : to go at an amble

[2]**amble** *n* : an easy gait esp. of a horse

am·bro·sia \am-ˈbrō-zh(ē-)ə\ *n* : the food of the Greek and Roman gods — **am·bro·sial** \-zh(ē-)əl\ *adj*

am·bu·lance \ˈam-byə-ləns\ *n* : a vehicle equipped for carrying the injured or sick

am·bu·lant \ˈam-byə-lənt\ *adj* : AMBULATORY

[1]**am·bu·la·to·ry** \ˈam-byə-lə-ˌtȯr-ē\ *adj* **1** : of, relating to, or adapted to walking **2** : able to walk or move about

[2]**ambulatory** *n, pl* **-ries** : a sheltered place (as in a cloister) for walking

am·bus·cade \ˈam-bə-ˌskād\ *n* : AMBUSH

am·bush \ˈam-ˌbu̇sh\ *n* **1** : a trap in which concealed attackers wait to attack by surprise **2** : the concealed position from which a surprise attack is made — **ambush** *vb*

amdt *abbr* amendment

ameba, ameboid *var of* AMOEBA, AMOEBOID

ame·lio·rate \ə-ˈmēl-yə-ˌrāt\ *vb* **-rat·ed**; **-rat·ing** : to make or grow better : IMPROVE — **ame·lio·ra·tion** \-ˌmēl-yə-ˈrā-shən\ *n*

amen \(ˌ)ā-ˈmen, (ˌ)ä-\ *interj* — used esp. at the end of prayers to affirm or express approval

ame·na·ble \ə-ˈmē-nə-bəl, -ˈme-\ *adj* **1** : ANSWERABLE ⟨~ to the law⟩ **2** : agreeable to something asked for

amend \ə-ˈmend\ *vb* **1** : to change for the better : IMPROVE **2** : to alter formally in phraseology — **amend·able** \-ˈmen-də-bəl\ *adj*

amend·ment \ə-ˈmend-mənt\ *n* **1** : correction of faults **2** : the process of amending a parliamentary motion or a constitution; *also* : the alteration so proposed or made

amends \ə-ˈmendz\ *n sing or pl* : compensation for injury or loss

ame·ni·ty \ə-ˈme-nə-tē, -ˈmē-\ *n, pl* **-ties** **1** : AGREEABLENESS **2** : a gesture observed in social relationships **3** : something that serves as a comfort or convenience

Amer *abbr* America; American

amerce \ə-ˈmərs\ *vb* **amerced**; **amerc·ing** **1** : to penalize by a fine determined by the court **2** : PUNISH — **amerce·ment** *n*

Amer·i·ca·na \ə-ˌmer-ə-ˈka-nə, -ˈkä-\ *n pl* : materials concerning or characteristic of America, its civilization, or its culture

American Indian *n* : a member of any of the Indigenous peoples of the western hemisphere except often certain peoples (such as the Inuit) who live in arctic regions; *esp* : an American Indian of No. America and esp. the U.S.

Amer·i·can·ism \ə-ˈmer-ə-kə-ˌni-zəm\ *n* **1** : a characteristic feature of English as used in the U.S. **2** : attachment or loyalty to the traditions, interests, or ideals of the U.S. **3** : a custom or trait peculiar to the U.S. or to Americans

Amer·i·can·ize \ə-ˈmer-ə-kə-ˌnīz\ *vb* : to make or become American — **Amer·i·can·i·za·tion** \ə-ˌmer-ə-kə-nə-ˈzā-shən\ *n*

Amer·i·can·ness \ə-ˈmer-ə-kən-nəs\ *n* : the quality or state of being American

American plan *n* : a hotel plan whereby the daily rates cover the cost of room and three meals

American Sign Language *n* : a sign language for the deaf in which meaning is conveyed by a system of hand gestures and placement

am·er·i·ci·um \ˌam-ə-ˈrish-ē-əm, -ˈris-\ *n* : a radioactive metallic chemical element produced artificially from plutonium

AmerInd *abbr* American Indian

Am·er·in·di·an \ˌa-mə-ˈrin-dē-ən\ *n* : AMERICAN INDIAN — **Amerindian** *adj*

am·e·thyst \ˈa-mə-thəst\ *n* [ME *amatiste,* fr. AF & L; AF, fr. L *amethystus,* fr. Gk *amethystos,* lit., remedy against drunkenness, fr. *a-* not + *methyein* to be drunk, fr. *methy* wine] : a gemstone consisting of clear purple or bluish-violet quartz

ami·a·ble \ˈā-mē-ə-bəl\ *adj* **1** : AGREEABLE ⟨an ~ comedy⟩ **2** : having a friendly and sociable disposition — **ami·a·bil·i·ty** \ˌā-mē-ə-ˈbi-lə-tē\ *n* — **ami·a·ble·ness** *n* — **ami·a·bly** \ˈā-mē-ə-blē\ *adv*

am·i·ca·ble \ˈa-mi-kə-bəl\ *adj* : FRIENDLY, PEACEABLE ⟨an ~ settlement of differences⟩ — **am·i·ca·bil·i·ty** \ˌa-mi-kə-ˈbi-lə-tē\ *n* — **am·i·ca·bly** \ˈa-mi-kə-blē\ *adv*

amid \ə-ˈmid\ *or* **amidst** \-ˈmidst\ *prep* : in or into the middle of : AMONG

amid·ships \ə-ˈmid-ˌships\ *adv* : in or near the middle of a ship

ami·no acid \ə-ˈmē-nō-\ *n* : any of numerous nitrogen-containing acids that include some which are used by cells to build proteins

amir *var of* EMIR

[1]**amiss** \ə-ˈmis\ *adv* **1** : WRONGLY **2** : ASTRAY ⟨something had gone ~⟩ **3** : IMPERFECTLY

[2]**amiss** *adj* **1** : WRONG **2** : out of place

am·i·ty \ˈa-mə-tē\ *n, pl* **-ties** : FRIEND-

SHIP; *esp* : friendly relations between nations

am·me·ter \ˈa-ˌmē-tər\ *n* : an instrument for measuring electric current esp. in amperes

am·mo \ˈa-mō\ *n* : AMMUNITION

am·mo·nia \ə-ˈmō-nyə\ *n* [NL, fr. L *sal ammoniacus* sal ammoniac (ammonium chloride), lit., salt of Ammon, fr. Gk *ammōniakos* of Ammon, fr. *Ammōn* Ammon, an Egyptian god near one of whose temples it was extracted] **1** : a colorless gaseous compound of nitrogen and hydrogen used in refrigeration and in the making of fertilizers and explosives **2** : a solution (**ammonia water**) of ammonia in water

am·mo·ni·um \ə-ˈmō-nē-əm\ *n* : an ion or chemical group derived from ammonia by combination with hydrogen

ammonium chloride *n* : a white crystalline volatile salt used in batteries and as an expectorant

am·mu·ni·tion \ˌam-yə-ˈni-shən\ *n* **1** : projectiles fired from guns **2** : explosive items used in war **3** : material for use in attack or defense

Amn *abbr* airman

am·ne·sia \am-ˈnē-zhə\ *n* **1** : abnormal loss of memory **2** : the selective overlooking of events or acts not favorable to one's purpose — **am·ne·si·ac** \-zhē-ˌak, -zē-\ *or* **am·ne·sic** \-zik, -sik\ *adj or n*

am·nes·ty \ˈam-nə-stē\ *n, pl* **-ties** : an act granting a pardon to a group of individuals — **amnesty** *vb*

am·nio·cen·te·sis \ˌam-nē-ō-ˌsen-ˈtē-səs\ *n, pl* **-te·ses** \-ˌsēz\ : the surgical insertion of a hollow needle through the abdominal wall and uterus of a pregnant female esp. to obtain fluid used to check the fetus for chromosomal abnormality and to determine sex

am·ni·ot·ic fluid \ˌam-nē-ˈä-tik-\ *n* : the watery fluid in which the embryo or fetus is immersed

amoe·ba *also* **ame·ba** \ə-ˈmē-bə\ *n, pl* **-bas** *or* **-bae** \-(ˌ)bē\ : any of various tiny one-celled protozoans that lack permanent cell organs and occur esp. in water and soil — **amoe·bic** \-bik\ *adj*

amoe·boid *also* **ame·boid** \-ˌbȯid\ *adj* : resembling an amoeba esp. in moving or readily changing shape

amok \ə-ˈmək, -ˈmäk\ *or* **amuck** \-ˈmək\ *adv* : in a violent, frenzied, or uncontrolled manner ⟨run ∼⟩

among \ə-ˈməŋ\ *also* **amongst** \-ˈməŋst\ *prep* **1** : in or through the midst of **2** : in the number, class, or company of **3** : in shares to each of **4** : by common action of

amon·til·la·do \ə-ˌmän-tə-ˈlä-dō\ *n, pl* **-dos** [Sp] : a medium dry sherry

amor·al \ā-ˈmȯr-əl\ *adj* **1** : neither moral nor immoral; *esp* : being outside the sphere to which moral judgments apply **2** : lacking moral sensibility — **amor·al·ly** *adv*

am·o·rous \ˈa-mə-rəs\ *adj* **1** : inclined to love **2** : being in love **3** : of or indicative of love — **am·o·rous·ly** *adv* — **am·o·rous·ness** *n*

amor·phous \ə-ˈmȯr-fəs\ *adj* **1** : SHAPELESS, FORMLESS **2** : not crystallized

am·or·tize \ˈa-mər-ˌtīz, ə-ˈmȯr-\ *vb* **-tized; -tiz·ing** : to extinguish (as a mortgage) usu. by payment on the principal at the time of each periodic interest payment — **amor·ti·za·tion** \ˌa-mər-tə-ˈzā-shən, ə-ˌmȯr-\ *n*

Amos \ˈā-məs\ — see BIBLE table

¹amount \ə-ˈmau̇nt\ *vb* **1** : to be equivalent **2** : to reach a total : add up

²amount *n* **1** : the total number or quantity **2** : a principal sum plus the interest on it

amour \ə-ˈmu̇r, ä-, a-\ *n* **1** : a love affair esp. when illicit **2** : LOVER

amour pro·pre \ˌa-ˌmu̇r-ˈprōprᵊ, ˌä-, -ˈprȯprᵊ\ *n* [F] : SELF-ESTEEM

¹amp \ˈamp\ *n* **1** : AMPERE **2** : AMPLIFIER; *also* : a unit consisting of an electronic amplifier and a loudspeaker

²amp *vb* : EXCITE, ENERGIZE ⟨tried to ∼ up the crowd⟩

am·per·age \ˈam-p(ə-)rij\ *n* : the strength of a current of electricity expressed in amperes

am·pere \ˈam-ˌpir\ *n* : a unit of electric current equivalent to a steady current produced by one volt applied across a resistance of one ohm

am·per·sand \ˈam-pər-ˌsand\ *n* [alter. of *and per se and,* spoken form of the phrase *& per se and,* lit., (the character) & by itself (stands for the word) *and*] : a character & used for the word *and*

am·phet·amine \am-ˈfe-tə-ˌmēn, -mən\ *n* : a compound or one of its derivatives that stimulates the central nervous system and is used esp. to treat hyperactive children and to suppress appetite

am·phib·i·an \am-ˈfi-bē-ən\ *n* **1** : an amphibious organism; *esp* : any of a class of vertebrate animals (as frogs and salamanders) intermediate between fishes and reptiles **2** : an airplane that can land on and take off from either land or water

am·phib·i·ous \am-ˈfi-bē-əs\ *adj* [Gk *amphibios,* lit., living a double life, fr. *amphi-* + *bios* mode of life] **1** : able to live both on land and in water **2** : adapted for both land and water **3** : made by joint action of land, sea, and air forces invading from the sea; *also* : trained for such action

am·phi·bole \ˈam-fə-ˌbōl\ *n* : any of a group of rock-forming minerals of similar crystal structure

am·phi·the·ater \ˈam-fə-ˌthē-ə-tər\ *n* **1** : an oval or circular structure with rising tiers of seats around an arena **2** : a very large auditorium

am·pho·ra \ˈam-fə-rə\ *n, pl* **-rae** \-ˌrē\ *or* **-ras** : an ancient Greek jar or vase with two handles that rise almost to the level of the mouth

am·ple \ˈam-pəl\ *adj* **am·pler** \-plər\; **am·plest** \-pləst\ **1** : LARGE, CAPACIOUS **2** : enough to satisfy : ABUNDANT — **am·ply** \-plē\ *adv*

am·pli·fy \ˈam-plə-ˌfī\ *vb* **-fied; -fy·ing 1** : to expand by extended treatment **2** : to increase in magnitude or strength; *esp* : to make louder — **am·pli·fi·ca·tion** \ˌam-plə-fə-ˈkā-shən\ *n* — **am·pli·fi·er** \ˈam-plə-ˌfī(-ə)r\ *n*
am·pli·tude \-ˌtüd, -ˌtyüd\ *n* **1** : ample extent : FULLNESS **2** : the extent of a vibratory movement (as of a pendulum) **3** : the height or depth of an oscillation (as of an alternating current or a radio wave) compared to its average value
amplitude modulation *n* : modulation of the amplitude of a radio carrier wave in accordance with the strength of the signal; *also* : a broadcasting system using such modulation
am·poule *or* **am·pule** *also* **am·pul** \ˈam-ˌpyül, -pül\ *n* : a small sealed bulbous glass vessel used to hold a solution for hypodermic injection
am·pu·tate \ˈam-pyə-ˌtāt\ *vb* **-tat·ed; -tat·ing** : to cut off ⟨∼ a leg⟩ — **am·pu·ta·tion** \ˌam-pyə-ˈtā-shən\ *n*
am·pu·tee \ˌam-pyə-ˈtē\ *n* : one who has had a limb amputated
AMSLAN *abbr* American Sign Language
amt *abbr* amount
amuck *var of* AMOK
am·u·let \ˈam-yə-lət\ *n* : an ornament worn as a charm against evil
amuse \ə-ˈmyüz\ *vb* **amused; amus·ing** : to entertain in a light or playful manner : DIVERT — **amuse·ment** *n* — **amusing** *adj* — **amus·ing·ly** *adv*
amusement park *n* : a commercially operated park having various devices (as a roller coaster) for entertainment and booths for selling refreshments
AM·VETS \ˈam-ˌvets\ *abbr* American Veterans (of World War II)
am·y·lase \ˈa-mə-ˌlās, -ˌlāz\ *n* : any of several enzymes that accelerate the breakdown of starch and glycogen
an \ən, (ˈ)an\ *indefinite article* : A — used before words beginning with a vowel sound
[1]**-an** *or* **-ian** *also* **-ean** *n suffix* **1** : one that belongs to ⟨Americ*an*⟩ ⟨crustace*an*⟩ **2** : one skilled in or specializing in ⟨phoneti*cian*⟩
[2]**-an** *or* **-ian** *also* **-ean** *adj suffix* **1** : of or belonging to ⟨Americ*an*⟩ **2** : characteristic of : resembling ⟨Shakespeare*an*⟩
AN *abbr* airman (Navy)
an·a·bol·ic steroid \ˌa-nə-ˈbä-lik-\ *n* : any of a group of synthetic steroid hormones sometimes abused by athletes in training to increase the size and strength of their muscles
anach·ro·nism \ə-ˈna-krə-ˌni-zəm\ *n* **1** : the error of placing a person or thing in the wrong period **2** : one that is chronologically out of place — **anach·ro·nis·tic** \ə-ˌna-krə-ˈnis-tik\ *adj* — **anach·ro·nous** \-ˈna-krə-nəs\ *adj*
an·a·con·da \ˌa-nə-ˈkän-də\ *n* : a large So. American snake that suffocates and kills its prey by constriction
anad·ro·mous \ə-ˈna-drə-məs\ *adj* : ascending rivers from the sea for breeding ⟨shad are ∼⟩
anae·mia, anae·mic *chiefly Brit var of* ANEMIA, ANEMIC
an·aer·obe \ˈa-nə-ˌrōb\ *n* : an anaerobic organism
an·aer·o·bic \ˌa-nə-ˈrō-bik\ *adj* : living, active, occurring, or existing in the absence of free oxygen
an·aes·the·sia, an·aes·thet·ic *chiefly Brit var of* ANESTHESIA, ANESTHETIC
ana·gram \ˈa-nə-ˌgram\ *n* : a word or phrase made by transposing the letters of another word or phrase
[1]**anal** \ˈā-nᵊl\ *adj* **1** : of, relating to, situated near, or involving the anus **2** : of, relating to, or characterized by the stage of psychosexual development in psychoanalytic theory during which one is concerned esp. with feces **3** : of, relating to, or characterized by personality traits (as frugality and neatness) considered typical of fixation at the anal stage of development — **anal·ly** *adv*
[2]**anal** *abbr* **1** analogy **2** analysis; analytic
an·al·ge·sia \ˌa-nᵊl-ˈjē-zhə\ *n* : insensibility to pain — **an·al·ge·sic** \-ˈjē-zik, -sik\ *adj*
an·al·ge·sic \-ˈjē-zik, -sik\ *n* : an agent for producing analgesia
analog computer *n* : a computer that operates with numbers represented by directly measurable quantities (as voltages)
anal·o·gous \ə-ˈna-lə-gəs\ *adj* : similar in one or more respects — **anal·o·gous·ly** *adv*
an·a·logue *or* **an·a·log** \ˈa-nə-ˌlȯg, -ˌläg\ *n* **1** : something that is analogous to something else **2** : an organ similar in function to one of another animal or plant but different in structure or origin
anal·o·gy \ə-ˈna-lə-jē\ *n, pl* **-gies 1** : inference that if two or more things agree in some respects they will probably agree in others **2** : a likeness in one or more ways between things otherwise unlike — **an·a·log·i·cal** \ˌa-nə-ˈlä-ji-kəl\ *adj* — **an·a·log·i·cal·ly** \-k(ə-)lē\ *adv*
anal–re·ten·tive \ˈā-nᵊl-ri-ˈten-tiv\ *adj* : ANAL 3
an·a·lyse *chiefly Brit var of* ANALYZE
anal·y·sis \ə-ˈna-lə-səs\ *n, pl* **-y·ses** \-ˌsēz\ [NL, fr. Gk, fr. *analyein* to break up, fr. *ana-* up + *lyein* to loosen] **1** : separation of a thing into the parts or elements of which it is composed **2** : an examination of a thing to determine its parts or elements; *also* : a statement showing the results of such an examination **3** : PSYCHOANALYSIS — **an·a·lyst** \ˈa-nə-list\ *n* — **an·a·lyt·ic** \ˌa-nə-ˈli-tik\ *or* **an·a·lyt·i·cal** \-ti-kəl\ *adj* — **an·a·lyt·i·cal·ly** *adv*
an·a·lyte \ˈa-nə-ˌlīt\ *n* : a chemical substance that is the subject of chemical analysis
an·a·lyze \ˈa-nə-ˌlīz\ *vb* **-lyzed; -lyz·ing** : to make an analysis of
an·a·pest \ˈa-nə-ˌpest\ *n* : a metrical foot of two unaccented syllables followed by one accented syllable — **an·a·pes·tic** \ˌa-nə-ˈpes-tik\ *adj or n*
an·ar·chism \ˈa-nər-ˌki-zəm\ *n* : the theo-

ry that all government is undesirable — **an·ar·chist** \-kist\ *n or adj* — **an·ar·chis·tic** \ˌa-nər-ˈkis-tik\ *adj*

an·ar·chy \ˈa-nər-kē\ *n* **1** : a social structure without government or law and order **2** : utter confusion — **an·ar·chic** \a-ˈnär-kik\ *adj* — **an·ar·chi·cal·ly** \-ki-k(ə-)lē\ *adv*

anas·to·mo·sis \ə-ˌnas-tə-ˈmō-səs\ *n, pl* **-mo·ses** \-ˌsēz\ **1** : the union of parts or branches (as of blood vessels) **2** : NETWORK

anat *abbr* anatomical; anatomy

anath·e·ma \ə-ˈna-thə-mə\ *n* **1** : a solemn curse **2** : a person or thing accursed; *also* : one intensely disliked

anath·e·ma·tize \-ˌtīz\ *vb* **-tized**; **-tiz·ing** : to pronounce an anathema against : CURSE

anat·o·mise *Brit var of* ANATOMIZE

anat·o·mize \ə-ˈna-tə-ˌmīz\ *vb* **-mized**; **-miz·ing** : to dissect so as to examine the structure and parts; *also* : ANALYZE

anat·o·my \ə-ˈna-tə-mē\ *n, pl* **-mies** [LL *anatomia* dissection, fr. Gk *anatomē*, fr. *anatemnein* to dissect, fr. *ana-* up + *temnein* to cut] **1** : a branch of science dealing with the structure of organisms **2** : structural makeup esp. of an organism or any of its parts **3** : a separating into parts for detailed study : ANALYSIS — **an·a·tom·i·cal** \ˌa-nə-ˈtä-mi-kəl\ *or* **an·a·tom·ic** \-mik\ *adj* — **an·a·tom·i·cal·ly** \-mi-k(ə-)lē\ *adv* — **anat·o·mist** \ə-ˈna-tə-mist\ *n*

anc *abbr* ancient

-ance *n suffix* **1** : action or process ⟨further*ance*⟩ : instance of an action or process ⟨perform*ance*⟩ **2** : quality or state : instance of a quality or state ⟨protuber*ance*⟩ **3** : amount or degree ⟨conduc*tance*⟩

an·ces·tor \ˈan-ˌses-tər\ *n* [ME *ancestre*, fr. AF, fr. L *antecessor* predecessor, fr. *antecedere* to go before, fr. *ante-* before + *cedere* to go] : one from whom an individual is descended

an·ces·tress \ˈan-ˌses-trəs\ *n* : a female ancestor

an·ces·try \ˈan-ˌses-trē\ *n* **1** : line of descent : LINEAGE **2** : ANCESTORS — **an·ces·tral** \an-ˈses-trəl\ *adj*

an·cho \ˈän-chō\ *n, pl* **anchos** : a poblano chili pepper esp. when mature and dried to a reddish black

[1]**an·chor** \ˈaŋ-kər\ *n* **1** : a heavy metal device attached to a ship that catches hold of the bottom and holds the ship in place **2** : something that serves to hold an object firmly **3** : ANCHORPERSON **4** : a large store that attracts customers and other businesses to a shopping mall

[2]**anchor** *vb* : to hold or become held in place by or as if by an anchor

an·chor·age \ˈaŋ-k(ə-)rij\ *n* : a place suitable for ships to anchor

an·cho·rite \ˈaŋ-kə-ˌrīt\ *n* : HERMIT

an·chor·man \ˈaŋ-kər-ˌman\ *n* **1** : the member of a team who competes last **2** : an anchorperson who is a man

an·chor·per·son \-ˌpər-sən\ *n* : a broadcaster who reads the news and introduces the reports of other broadcasters

an·chor·wom·an \-ˌwu̇-mən\ *n* : an anchorperson who is a woman

an·cho·vy \ˈan-ˌchō-vē, an-ˈchō-\ *n, pl* **-vies** *or* **-vy** : any of a family of small herringlike fishes often used as food

an·cien ré·gime \äⁿs-yaⁿ-rā-ˈzhēm\ *n* **1** : the political and social system of France before the Revolution of 1789 **2** : a system no longer prevailing

[1]**an·cient** \ˈān-shənt\ *adj* **1** : having existed for many years ⟨~ customs⟩ **2** : belonging to times long past; *esp* : belonging to the period before the Middle Ages

[2]**ancient** *n* **1** : an aged person **2** *pl* : the peoples of ancient Greece and Rome; *esp* : the classical authors of Greece and Rome

an·cil·lary \ˈan-sə-ˌler-ē\ *adj* **1** : SUBORDINATE, SUBSIDIARY ⟨a factory's ~ plants⟩ **2** : AUXILIARY, SUPPLEMENTARY ⟨~ evidence⟩ — **ancillary** *n*

-ancy *n suffix* : quality or state ⟨flamboy*ancy*⟩

and \ənd, (ˈ)and\ *conj* **1** — used to indicate connection or addition esp. of items within the same class or type or to join words or phrases of the same grammatical rank or function **2** — used to join one finite verb to another so that together they are equivalent to an infinitive of purpose ⟨come ~ see me⟩

[1]**an·dan·te** \än-ˈdän-ˌtā, -tē\ *adv or adj* [It, lit., going, prp. of *andare* to go] : moderately slow — used as a direction in music

[2]**andante** *n* : an andante movement

and·iron \ˈan-ˌdī(-ə)rn\ *n* : one of a pair of metal supports for firewood in a fireplace

and/or \ˈand-ˈȯr\ *conj* — used to indicate that either *and* or *or* may apply ⟨apples ~ oranges means that the possibilities include apples, oranges, or both⟩

an·dro·gen \ˈan-drə-jən\ *n* : a male sex hormone (as testosterone)

an·drog·y·nous \an-ˈdrä-jə-nəs\ *adj* **1** : having the characteristics of both male and female **2** : suitable for either sex ⟨~ clothing⟩ — **an·drog·y·ny** \-nē\ *n*

an·droid \ˈan-ˌdrȯid\ *n* : a mobile robot usu. with a human form

an·ec·dot·al \ˌa-nik-ˈdō-tᵊl\ *adj* **1** : relating to or consisting of anecdotes **2** : based on reports of an unscientific nature — **an·ec·dot·al·ly** *adv*

an·ec·dote \ˈan-ik-ˌdōt\ *n, pl* **-dotes** *also* **-dota** \ˌa-nik-ˈdō-tə\ [F, fr. Gk *anekdota* unpublished items, fr. *a-* not + *ekdidonai* to publish] : a brief story of an interesting, amusing, or biographical incident

ane·mia \ə-ˈnē-mē-ə\ *n* **1** : a condition in which blood is deficient in quantity, in red blood cells, or in hemoglobin and which is marked by pallor, weakness, and irregular heart action **2** : lack of vitality — **ane·mic** \ə-ˈnē-mik\ *adj*

an·e·mom·e·ter \ˌa-nə-ˈmä-mə-tər\ *n* : an instrument for measuring the force or speed of the wind

anem·o·ne \ə-ˈne-mə-nē\ *n* : any of a large genus of herbs related to the buttercups that have showy flowers without petals but with conspicuous often colored sepals

anent \ə-ˈnent\ *prep* : CONCERNING

an·es·the·sia \ˌa-nəs-ˈthē-zhə\ *n* : loss of bodily sensation

an·es·the·si·ol·o·gy \-ˌthē-zē-ˈä-lə-jē\ *n* : a branch of medical science dealing with anesthesia and anesthetics — **an·es·the·si·ol·o·gist** \-jist\ *n*

¹**an·es·thet·ic** \ˌa-nəs-ˈthe-tik\ *adj* : of, relating to, or capable of producing anesthesia

²**anesthetic** *n* : an agent that produces anesthesia

anes·the·tist \ə-ˈnes-thə-tist\ *n* : one who administers anesthetics

anes·the·tize \ə-ˈnes-thə-ˌtīz\ *vb* **-tized**; **-tiz·ing** : to subject to anesthesia

an·eu·rysm *also* **an·eu·rism** \ˈan-yə-ˌri-zəm\ *n* : an abnormal blood-filled bulge of a blood vessel

anew \ə-ˈnü, -ˈnyü\ *adv* **1** : over again ⟨begin ~⟩ **2** : in a new form ⟨this film tells the story ~⟩

an·gel \ˈān-jəl\ *n* [ME, fr. OE *engel* & AF *angele,* both fr. L *angelus,* fr. Gk *angelos,* lit., messenger] **1** : a spiritual being superior to humans **2** : an attendant spirit **3** : a winged figure of human form in art **4** : MESSENGER, HARBINGER ⟨~ of death⟩ **5** : a person held to resemble an angel **6** : a financial backer — **an·gel·ic** \an-ˈje-lik\ *or* **an·gel·i·cal** \-li-kəl\ *adj* — **an·gel·i·cal·ly** \-k(ə-)lē\ *adv*

an·gel·fish \ˈān-jəl-ˌfish\ *n* : any of several brightly colored tropical fishes that are flattened from side to side

an·gel·i·ca \an-ˈje-li-kə\ *n* : a biennial herb related to the carrot whose roots and fruit furnish a flavoring oil

¹**an·ger** \ˈaŋ-gər\ *vb* : to make angry

²**anger** *n* [ME, affliction, anger, fr. ON *angr* grief] : a strong feeling of displeasure ♦ ***Synonyms*** WRATH, IRE, RAGE, FURY, INDIGNATION

an·gi·na \an-ˈjī-nə\ *n* : a disorder (as of the heart) marked by attacks of intense pain; *esp* : ANGINA PECTORIS — **an·gi·nal** \an-ˈjī-nᵊl\ *adj*

angina pec·to·ris \-ˈpek-t(ə-)rəs\ *n* : a heart disease marked by brief attacks of sharp chest pain caused by deficient oxygenation of heart muscles

an·gio·gen·e·sis \ˌan-jē-ō-ˈje-nə-səs\ *n* : the formation of blood vessels — **an·gio·gen·ic** \-ˈje-nik\ *adj*

an·gio·gram \ˈan-jē-ə-ˌgram\ *n* : a radiograph made by angiography

an·gi·og·ra·phy \ˌan-jē-ˈä-grə-fē\ *n* : the use of radiography to make blood vessels visible after injection of a substance opaque to radiation

an·gio·plas·ty \ˈan-jē-ə-ˌplas-tē\ *n* : surgical repair of a blood vessel esp. by using an inflatable catheter to unblock arteries clogged by atherosclerotic deposits

an·gio·sperm \-ˌspərm\ *n* : FLOWERING PLANT

¹**an·gle** \ˈaŋ-gəl\ *n* **1** : a sharp projecting corner **2** : the figure formed by the meeting of two lines in a point **3** : a point of view **4** : a special technique or plan : GIMMICK — **an·gled** *adj*

²**angle** *vb* **an·gled**; **an·gling** \-g(ə-)liŋ\ : to turn, move, or direct at an angle

³**angle** *vb* **an·gled**; **an·gling** \-g(ə-)liŋ\ : to fish with a hook and line — **an·gler** \-glər\ *n* — **an·gling** \-gliŋ\ *n*

an·gle·worm \ˈaŋ-gəl-ˌwərm\ *n* : EARTHWORM

An·gli·can \ˈaŋ-gli-kən\ *adj* **1** : of or relating to the established episcopal Church of England **2** : of or relating to England or the English nation — **Anglican** *n* — **An·gli·can·ism** \-kə-ˌni-zəm\ *n*

an·gli·cize \ˈaŋ-glə-ˌsīz\ *vb* **-cized**; **-ciz·ing** *often cap* **1** : to make English (as in habits, speech, character, or outlook) **2** : to borrow (a foreign word or phrase) into English without changing form or spelling and sometimes without changing pronunciation — **an·gli·ci·za·tion** \ˌaŋ-glə-sə-ˈzā-shən\ *n, often cap*

An·glo \ˈaŋ-glō\ *n, pl* **Anglos** : a non-Hispanic white inhabitant of the U.S.; *esp* : one of English origin and descent

An·glo·cen·tric \ˌaŋ-glō-ˈsen-trik\ *adj* : centered on or favoring England or things English

An·glo–French \ˌaŋ-glō-ˈfrench\ *n* : the French language used in medieval England

An·glo·phile \ˈaŋ-glə-ˌfī(-ə)l\ *also* **An·glo·phil** \-ˌfil\ *n* : one who greatly admires England and things English

An·glo·phobe \ˈaŋ-glə-ˌfōb\ *n* : one who is averse to England and things English

An·glo–Sax·on \ˌaŋ-glō-ˈsak-sən\ *n* **1** : a member of any of the Germanic peoples who invaded England in the 5th century a.d. **2** : a member of the English people **3** : Old English — **Anglo–Saxon** *adj*

an·go·ra \aŋ-ˈgȯr-ə, an-\ *n* **1** : yarn or cloth made from the hair of an Angora goat or rabbit **2** *cap* : any of a breed of cats, goats, or rabbits with a long silky coat

an·gry \ˈaŋ-grē\ *adj* **an·gri·er**; **-est** : feeling or showing anger ♦ ***Synonyms*** ENRAGED, WRATHFUL, IRATE, INDIGNANT, MAD — **an·gri·ly** \-grə-lē\ *adv*

angst \ˈäŋst\ *n* [G] : a feeling of anxiety

ang·strom \ˈaŋ-strəm\ *n* : a unit of length equal to one ten-billionth of a meter

an·guish \ˈaŋ-gwish\ *n* : extreme pain or distress esp. of mind — **an·guished** \-gwisht\ *adj*

an·gu·lar \ˈaŋ-gyə-lər\ *adj* **1** : sharp-cornered **2** : having one or more angles **3** : being thin and bony — **an·gu·lar·i·ty** \ˌaŋ-gyə-ˈler-ə-tē\ *n*

An·gus \ˈaŋ-gəs\ *n* : any of a breed of usu. black hornless beef cattle originating in Scotland

an·hy·drous \an-ˈhī-drəs\ *adj* : free from water

an·i·line \ˈa-nᵊl-ən\ *n* : an oily poisonous liquid used in making dyes, medicines, and explosives

an·i·mad·vert \ˌa-nə-ˌmad-ˈvərt\ *vb* : to remark critically : express censure — **an·i·mad·ver·sion** \-ˈvər-zhən\ *n*

[1]**an·i·mal** \ˈa-nə-məl\ *n* **1** : any of a kingdom of living things typically differing from plants in capacity for active movement, in rapid response to stimulation, and in lack of cellulose cell walls **2** : a lower animal as distinguished from human beings; *also* : MAMMAL

[2]**animal** *adj* **1** : of, relating to, or derived from animals **2** : of or relating to the physical as distinguished from the mental or spiritual ♦ ***Synonyms*** CARNAL, FLESHLY, SENSUAL

an·i·mal·cule \ˌa-nə-ˈmal-kyül\ *n* : a tiny animal usu. invisible to the naked eye

[1]**an·i·mate** \ˈa-nə-mət\ *adj* : having life

[2]**an·i·mate** \-ˌmāt\ *vb* **-mat·ed**; **-mat·ing** **1** : to impart life to **2** : to give spirit and vigor to **3** : to make appear to move ⟨~ a cartoon for motion pictures⟩ — **an·i·mat·ed** *adj* — **an·i·mat·ed·ly** *adv*

an·i·ma·tion \ˌa-nə-ˈmā-shən\ *n* **1** : VIVACITY, LIVELINESS **2** : a motion picture made from a series of drawings, computer graphics, or stop-motion images simulating motions by means of slight progressive changes

an·i·ma·tron·ic \ˌa-nə-mə-ˈträ-nik\ *adj* : of, relating to, or being an electrically animated mechanical figure (as a puppet)

an·i·mism \ˈa-nə-ˌmi-zəm\ *n* : attribution of conscious life to objects in and phenomena of nature or to inanimate objects — **an·i·mist** \-mist\ *n* — **an·i·mis·tic** \ˌa-nə-ˈmis-tik\ *adj*

an·i·mos·i·ty \ˌa-nə-ˈmä-sə-tē\ *n, pl* **-ties** : ILL WILL, RESENTMENT

an·i·mus \ˈa-nə-məs\ *n* : deep-seated resentment and hostility

an·ion \ˈa-ˌnī-ən, -ˌnī-ˌän\ *n* : a negatively charged ion

an·ise \ˈa-nəs\ *n* : an herb related to the carrot with aromatic seeds (**aniseed** \-sēd\) used in flavoring

an·is·ette \ˌa-nə-ˈset, -ˈzet\ *n* [F] : a usu. colorless sweet liqueur flavored with aniseed

ankh \ˈäŋk\ *n* : a cross having a loop for its upper vertical arm and serving esp. in ancient Egypt as an emblem of life

an·kle \ˈaŋ-kəl\ *n* : the joint or region between the foot and the leg

an·kle·bone \ˈaŋ-kəl-ˌbōn\ *n* : the bone that in human beings bears the weight of the body and with the tibia and fibula forms the ankle joint

an·klet \ˈaŋ-klət\ *n* **1** : something (as an ornament) worn around the ankle **2** : a short sock reaching slightly above the ankle

ann *abbr* **1** annals **2** annual

an·nals \ˈa-nᵊlz\ *n pl* **1** : a record of events in chronological order **2** : historical records — **an·nal·ist** \-nᵊl-ist\ *n*

an·neal \ə-ˈnēl\ *vb* **1** : to make (as glass or steel) less brittle by heating and then cooling **2** : STRENGTHEN, TOUGHEN

[1]**an·nex** \ə-ˈneks, ˈa-ˌneks\ *vb* **1** : to attach as an addition **2** : to incorporate (as a territory) within a political domain — **an·nex·a·tion** \ˌa-ˌnek-ˈsā-shən\ *n*

[2]**an·nex** \ˈa-ˌneks, -niks\ *n* : a subsidiary or supplementary structure

an·nexe *chiefly Brit var of* ANNEX

an·ni·hi·late \ə-ˈnī-ə-ˌlāt\ *vb* **-lat·ed**; **-lat·ing** : to destroy completely — **an·ni·hi·la·tion** \-ˌnī-ə-ˈlā-shən\ *n*

an·ni·ver·sa·ry \ˌa-nə-ˈvər-sə-rē\ *n, pl* **-ries** : the annual return of the date of a notable event and esp. a wedding

an·no Do·mi·ni \ˌa-nō-ˈdä-mə-nē, -ˈdō-, -ˌnī\ *adv, often cap A* [ML, in the year of the Lord] — used to indicate that a time division falls within the Christian era

an·no·tate \ˈa-nə-ˌtāt\ *vb* **-tat·ed**; **-tat·ing** : to furnish with notes — **an·no·ta·tion** \ˌa-nə-ˈtā-shən\ *n* — **an·no·ta·tor** \ˈa-nə-ˌtā-tər\ *n*

an·nounce \ə-ˈnau̇ns\ *vb* **an·nounced**; **an·nounc·ing** **1** : to make known publicly **2** : to give notice of the arrival or presence of — **an·nounce·ment** *n*

an·nounc·er \ə-ˈnau̇n-sər\ *n* : a person who introduces radio or television programs, makes commercial announcements, or gives station identification

an·noy \ə-ˈnȯi\ *vb* : to disturb or irritate esp. by repeated acts : VEX ♦ ***Synonyms*** IRK, BOTHER, PESTER, TEASE, HARASS — **an·noy·ing·ly** *adv*

an·noy·ance \ə-ˈnȯi-əns\ *n* **1** : the act of annoying **2** : the state of being annoyed **3** : NUISANCE ⟨the delay was a minor ~⟩

[1]**an·nu·al** \ˈan-yə-wəl\ *adj* **1** : covering the period of a year ⟨~ rainfall⟩ **2** : occurring once a year : YEARLY **3** : completing the life cycle in one growing season ⟨~ plants⟩ — **an·nu·al·ly** *adv*

[2]**annual** *n* **1** : a publication appearing once a year **2** : an annual plant

annual ring *n* : the layer of wood produced by a single year's growth of a woody plant

an·nu·i·tant \ə-ˈnü-ə-tənt, -ˈnyü-\ *n* : a beneficiary of an annuity

an·nu·i·ty \ə-ˈnü-ə-tē, -ˈnyü-\ *n, pl* **-i·ties** : an amount payable annually; *also* : the right to receive such a payment

an·nul \ə-ˈnəl\ *vb* **an·nulled**; **an·nul·ling** : to make legally void — **an·nul·ment** *n*

an·nu·lar \ˈan-yə-lər\ *adj* : ring-shaped

an·nun·ci·ate \ə-ˈnən-sē-ˌāt\ *vb* **-at·ed**; **-at·ing** : ANNOUNCE

an·nun·ci·a·tion \ə-ˌnən-sē-ˈā-shən\ *n* **1** *cap* : March 25 observed as a church festival commemorating the announcement of the Incarnation **2** : ANNOUNCEMENT

an·nun·ci·a·tor \ə-ˈnən-sē-ˌā-tər\ *n* : one that annunciates; *specif* : a usu. electrically controlled signal board or indicator

an·ode \ˈa-ˌnōd\ *n* **1** : the positive electrode of an electrolytic cell **2** : the negative terminal of a battery **3** : the electron-collecting electrode of an electron tube — **an·od·ic** \a-ˈnä-dik\ *also* **an·od·al** \-ˈnō-dᵊl\ *adj*

an·od·ize \ˈa-nə-ˌdīz\ *vb* **-ized**; **-iz·ing** : to subject (a metal) to electrolytic action as the anode of a cell in order to coat with a protective or decorative film

an·o·dyne \'a-nə-ˌdīn\ *n* : something that relieves pain : a soothing agent

anoint \ə-'nȯint\ *vb* **1** : to apply oil to esp. as a sacred rite **2** : CONSECRATE — **anoint·ment** *n*

anom·a·lous \ə-'nä-mə-ləs\ *adj* : deviating from a general rule : ABNORMAL

anom·a·ly \ə-'nä-mə-lē\ *n, pl* **-lies** : something anomalous : IRREGULARITY

[1]**anon** \ə-'nän\ *adv* : SOON

[2]**anon** *abbr* anonymous; anonymously

anon·y·mous \ə-'nä-nə-məs\ *adj* : of unknown or undeclared origin or authorship — **an·o·nym·i·ty** \ˌa-nə-'ni-mə-tē\ *n* — **anon·y·mous·ly** *adv*

anoph·e·les \ə-'nä-fə-ˌlēz\ *n* [NL, genus name, fr. Gk *anōphelēs* useless, fr. *a-* not + *ophelos* advantage, help] : any of a genus of mosquitoes that includes all mosquitoes which transmit malaria to human beings

an·o·rec·tic \ˌa-nə-'rek-tik\ *adj* : ANOREXIC — **anorectic** *n*

an·orex·ia \ˌa-nə-'rek-sē-ə\ *n* **1** : loss of appetite esp. when prolonged **2** : ANOREXIA NERVOSA

anorexia ner·vo·sa \-nər-'vō-sə\ *n* : a serious disorder in eating behavior marked esp. by a pathological fear of weight gain leading to faulty eating patterns, malnutrition, and usu. excessive weight loss

an·orex·ic \ˌa-nə-'rek-sik\ *adj* **1** : lacking or causing loss of appetite **2** : affected with or as if with anorexia nervosa — **anorexic** *n*

[1]**an·oth·er** \ə-'nə-thər\ *adj* **1** : some other ⟨do it ~ time⟩ **2** : being one in addition : one more ⟨~ piece of pie⟩

[2]**another** *pron* **1** : an additional one : one more **2** : one that is different from the first or present one

ans *abbr* answer

[1]**an·swer** \'an-sər\ *n* **1** : something spoken or written in reply to a question **2** : a solution of a problem

[2]**answer** *vb* **1** : to speak or write in reply to **2** : to be responsible **3** : to be adequate — **an·swer·er** *n*

an·swer·able \'an-sə-rə-bəl\ *adj* **1** : subject to taking blame or responsibility **2** : capable of being refuted

answering machine *n* : a machine that receives telephone calls by playing a recorded message and usu. by recording messages from callers

answering service *n* : a commercial service that answers telephone calls for its clients

[1]**ant** \'ant\ *n* : any of a family of small social insects related to the bees and living in communities usu. in earth or wood

[2]**ant** *abbr* antonym

Ant *abbr* Antarctica

ant- — see ANTI-

[1]**-ant** *n suffix* **1** : one that performs or promotes (a specified action) ⟨cool*ant*⟩ **2** : thing that is acted upon (in a specified manner) ⟨inhal*ant*⟩

[2]**-ant** *adj suffix* **1** : performing (a specified action) or being (in a specified condition) ⟨propell*ant*⟩ **2** : promoting (a specified action or process) ⟨expector*ant*⟩

ant·ac·id \ant-'a-səd\ *n* : an agent that counteracts acidity — **antacid** *adj*

an·tag·o·nism \an-'ta-gə-ˌni-zəm\ *n* **1** : active opposition or hostility **2** : opposition in physiological action — **an·tag·o·nis·tic** \-ˌta-gə-'nis-tik\ *adj*

an·tag·o·nist \-nist\ *n* : ADVERSARY, OPPONENT

an·tag·o·nize \an-'ta-gə-ˌnīz\ *vb* **-nized**; **-niz·ing** : to provoke the hostility of

ant·arc·tic \ant-'ärk-tik, -'är-tik\ *adj, often cap* : of or relating to the south pole or the region near it

antarctic circle *n, often cap A&C* : the parallel of latitude that is approximately $66\frac{1}{2}$ degrees south of the equator

[1]**an·te** \'an-tē\ *n* : a poker stake put up before the deal to build the pot; *also* : an amount paid : PRICE

[2]**ante** *vb* **an·ted**; **an·te·ing** **1** : to put up (an ante) **2** : PAY

ant·eat·er \'ant-ˌē-tər\ *n* : any of several mammals (as an aardvark) that feed mostly on ants or termites

an·te·bel·lum \ˌan-ti-'be-ləm\ *adj* : existing before a war; *esp* : existing before the U.S. Civil War of 1861-65

an·te·ced·ent \ˌan-tə-'sē-dᵊnt\ *n* **1** : a noun, pronoun, phrase, or clause referred to by a personal or relative pronoun **2** : a preceding event or cause **3** *pl* : the significant conditions of one's earlier life **4** *pl* : ANCESTORS — **antecedent** *adj*

an·te·cham·ber \'an-ti-ˌchām-bər\ *n* : ANTEROOM

an·te·date \'an-ti-ˌdāt\ *vb* **1** : to date (a paper) as of an earlier day than that on which the actual writing or signing is done **2** : to precede in time

an·te·di·lu·vi·an \ˌan-ti-də-'lü-vē-ən, -dī-\ *adj* **1** : of the period before the biblical flood **2** : ANTIQUATED, OUT-OF-DATE

an·te·lope \'an-tə-ˌlōp\ *n, pl* **-lope** *or* **-lopes** [ME, fabulous heraldic beast, prob. fr. MF *antelop* savage animal with sawlike horns, fr. ML *anthalopus,* fr. LGk *antholops*] **1** : any of various deerlike ruminant mammals that chiefly inhabit Africa and have a slender build and horns extending upward and backward **2** : PRONGHORN

an·te me·ri·di·em \'an-ti-mə-'ri-dē-əm\ *adj* [L] : being before noon

an·ten·na \an-'te-nə\ *n, pl* **-nae** \-(ˌ)nē\ *or* **-nas** [ML, fr. L, sail yard] **1** : one of the long slender paired segmented sensory organs on the head of an arthropod (as an insect or crab) **2** *pl usu -nas* : a metallic device (as a rod or wire) for sending out or receiving radio waves

an·te·pe·nult \ˌan-ti-'pē-ˌnəlt\ *also* **an·te·pen·ul·ti·ma** \-pi-'nəl-tə-mə\ *n* : the 3d syllable of a word counting from the end — **an·te·pen·ul·ti·mate** \-pi-'nəl-tə-mət\ *adj or n*

an·te·ri·or \an-'tir-ē-ər\ *adj* **1** : situated before or toward the front **2** : situated near or nearer to the head **3** : coming before in time ♦ ***Synonyms*** PRECEDING, PREVIOUS, PRIOR, ANTECEDENT

anterior cruciate ligament *n* : a cross-shaped ligament of the knee that connects the tibia and femur

an·te·room \ˈan-ti-ˌrüm, -ˌru̇m\ *n* : a room forming the entrance to another and often used as a waiting room

an·them \ˈan-thəm\ *n* **1** : a sacred vocal composition **2** : a song or hymn of praise or gladness

an·ther \ˈan-thər\ *n* : the part of a stamen of a seed plant that produces and contains pollen

ant·hill \ˈant-ˌhil\ *n* : a mound thrown up by ants or termites in digging their nest

an·thol·o·gy \an-ˈthä-lə-jē\ *n, pl* **-gies** [NL *anthologia* collection of epigrams, fr. MGk, fr. Gk, flower gathering, fr. *anthos* flower + *logia* collecting, fr. *legein* to gather] : a collection of literary selections — **an·thol·o·gist** \-jist\ *n* — **an·thol·o·gize** \-ˌjīz\ *vb*

an·thra·cite \ˈan-thrə-ˌsīt\ *n* : a hard glossy coal that burns without much smoke

an·thrax \ˈan-ˌthraks\ *n* : an infectious and usu. fatal bacterial disease of warm-blooded animals (as cattle and sheep) that is transmissible to humans; *also* : a bacterium causing anthrax

an·thro·po·cen·tric \ˌan-thrə-pə-ˈsen-trik\ *adj* : interpreting or regarding the world in terms of human values and experiences

an·thro·poid \ˈan-thrə-ˌpȯid\ *n* **1** : any of several large tailless apes (as a gorilla) **2** : a person resembling an ape — **anthropoid** *adj*

an·thro·pol·o·gy \ˌan-thrə-ˈpä-lə-jē\ *n* : the science of human beings and esp. of their physical characteristics, their origin and ancestry, their environment and social relations, and their culture — **an·thro·po·log·i·cal** \-pə-ˈlä-ji-kəl\ *adj* — **an·thro·pol·o·gist** \-ˈpä-lə-jist\ *n*

an·thro·po·mor·phism \ˌan-thrə-pə-ˈmȯr-ˌfi-zəm\ *n* : an interpretation of what is not human or personal in terms of human or personal characteristics : HUMANIZATION — **an·thro·po·mor·phic** \-fik\ *adj*

an·ti \ˈan-ˌtī, -tē\ *n, pl* **antis** : one who is opposed

anti- \ˌan-ti, -tē, -ˌtī\ *or* **ant-** *or* **anth-** *prefix* **1** : opposite in kind, position, or action **2** : opposing : hostile toward **3** : counteractive **4** : preventive of : curative of

an·ti·abor·tion \ˌan-tē-ə-ˈbȯr-shən, ˌan-ˌtī-\ *adj* : opposed to abortion — **an·ti·abor·tion·ist** \-shə-nist\ *n*

an·ti·bal·lis·tic missile \ˌan-ti-bə-ˈlis-tik-, ˌan-ˌtī-\ *n* : a missile for intercepting and destroying ballistic missiles

an·ti·bi·ot·ic \-bī-ˈä-tik, -bē-\ *n* : a substance isolated from cultures of certain microorganisms (as fungi) or of synthetic origin that is administered topically, orally, or by injection to treat or prevent infections by killing or inhibiting the growth of bacteria in or on the body — **antibiotic** *adj*

an·ti·body \ˈan-ti-ˌbä-dē\ *n* : any of a large number of proteins of high molecular weight produced normally by specialized B cells after stimulation by an antigen and acting specifically against the antigen in an immune response

[1]**an·tic** \ˈan-tik\ *n* [It *antico* ancient thing or person, fr. *antico* ancient, fr. L *antiquus*] : an often wildly playful or funny act or action

[2]**antic** *adj* **1** *archaic* : GROTESQUE **2** : PLAYFUL

an·ti·can·cer \ˌan-ti-ˈkan-sər, ˌan-ˌtī-\ *adj* : used against or tending to arrest or prevent cancer ⟨~ drugs⟩

An·ti·christ \ˈan-ti-ˌkrīst\ *n* **1** : one who denies or opposes Christ **2** : a false Christ

an·tic·i·pate \an-ˈti-sə-ˌpāt\ *vb* **-pat·ed; -pat·ing** **1** : to foresee and provide for beforehand ⟨~*s* problems⟩ **2** : to look forward to — **an·tic·i·pa·tion** \-ˌti-sə-ˈpā-shən\ *n* — **an·tic·i·pa·to·ry** \-ˈti-sə-pə-ˌtȯr-ē\ *adj*

an·ti·cli·max \ˌan-ti-ˈklī-ˌmaks\ *n* : something (as the ending of a story) that is strikingly less important or dramatic than expected — **an·ti·cli·mac·tic** \-klī-ˈmak-tik\ *adj*

an·ti·cline \ˈan-ti-ˌklīn\ *n* : an arch of layers of rock in the earth's crust

an·ti·co·ag·u·lant \ˌan-ti-kō-ˈa-gyə-lənt\ *n* : a substance that hinders the clotting of blood — **anticoagulant** *adj*

an·ti·cy·clone \ˌan-ti-ˈsī-ˌklōn\ *n* : a system of winds that rotates about a center of high atmospheric pressure — **an·ti·cy·clon·ic** \-sī-ˈklä-nik\ *adj*

an·ti·de·pres·sant \ˌan-ti-di-ˈpres-ᵊnt, ˌan-ˌtī-\ *n* : a drug used to relieve psychic depression — **antidepressant** *adj*

an·ti·dote \ˈan-ti-ˌdōt\ *n* : a remedy to counteract the effects of poison

an·ti·drug \ˈan-ˌtī-ˌdrəg\ *adj* : acting against or opposing illicit drugs

an·ti·fer·til·i·ty \ˌan-ti-fər-ˈti-lə-tē\ *adj* : tending to reduce or destroy fertility : CONTRACEPTIVE ⟨~ agents⟩

an·ti·freeze \ˈan-ti-ˌfrēz\ *n* : a substance added to a liquid to lower its freezing temperature

an·ti·fun·gal \ˌan-tē-ˈfəŋ-gəl, ˌan-ˌtī-\ *n* : FUNGICIDE — **antifungal** *adj*

an·ti·gen \ˈan-ti-jən\ *n* : any substance (as a toxin) foreign to the body that induces an immune response — **an·ti·gen·ic** \ˌan-ti-ˈje-nik\ *adj* — **an·ti·ge·nic·i·ty** \-jə-ˈni-sə-tē\ *n*

an·ti·grav·i·ty \ˌan-ti-ˈgra-və-tē, ˌan-ˌtī-\

---

antiaging	**antiapartheid**	**anticolonial**	**antifascist**
anti-AIDS	**antibacterial**	**anticommunism**	**antigovernment**
antiaircraft	**anticapitalist**	**anticommunist**	**anti-HIV**
antialcohol	**anti-Catholic**	**antidemocratic**	**anti-imperialism**
anti-American	**anticholesterol**	**antidiscrimination**	**anti-imperialist**
antianxiety	**anticlerical**	**antiestablishment**	**antiknock**

adj : reducing or canceling the effect of gravity

an·ti·he·ro \ˈan-ti-ˌhē-rō, ˈan-ˌtī-\ *n* : a protagonist who is notably lacking in heroic qualities (as courage)

an·ti·his·ta·mine \ˌan-ti-ˈhis-tə-ˌmēn, ˌan-ˌtī-, -mən\ *n* : any of various drugs used in treating allergies and colds — **antihistamine** *adj*

an·ti·hy·per·ten·sive \-ˌhī-pər-ˈten-siv\ *n* : a substance that is effective against high blood pressure — **antihypertensive** *adj*

an·ti–in·flam·ma·to·ry \-in-ˈfla-mə-ˌtȯr-ē\ *adj* : counteracting inflammation — **anti–inflammatory** *n*

an·ti–in·tel·lec·tu·al \-ˌin-tə-ˈlek-chə-wəl\ *adj* : opposing or hostile to intellectuals or to an intellectual view or approach

an·ti·lock \ˈan-ti-ˌläk, ˈan-ˌtī-\ *adj* : being a braking system designed to prevent the wheels from locking

an·ti·log·a·rithm \ˌan-ti-ˈlȯ-gə-ˌri-thəm, ˌan-ˌtī-, -ˈlä-\ *n* : the number corresponding to a given logarithm ⟨if the logarithm in base *x* of *a* equals *b* then the antilogarithm in base *x* of *b* equals *a*⟩

an·ti·ma·cas·sar \ˌan-ti-mə-ˈka-sər\ *n* : a cover to protect the back or arms of furniture

an·ti·mat·ter \ˈan-ti-ˌma-tər, ˈan-ˌtī-\ *n* : matter composed of antiparticles

an·ti·mo·ny \ˈan-tə-ˌmō-nē\ *n* : a brittle silvery white metallic chemical element used esp. in alloys

an·ti·neu·tron \ˌan-ti-ˈnü-ˌträn, ˌan-ˌtī-, -ˈnyü-\ *n* : the antiparticle of the neutron

an·ti·no·mi·an \ˌan-ti-ˈnō-mē-ən\ *n* : one who denies the validity of moral laws

an·tin·o·my \an-ˈti-nə-mē\ *n, pl* **-mies** : a contradiction between two seemingly true statements

an·ti·nov·el \ˈan-ti-ˌnä-vəl, ˈan-ˌtī-\ *n* : a work of fiction that lacks all or most of the traditional features of the novel

an·ti·nu·cle·ar \ˌan-ti-ˈnü-klē-ər, -ˈnyü-\ *adj* : opposing the use or production of nuclear power

an·ti·ox·i·dant \ˌan-tē-ˈäk-sə-dənt, ˌan-ˌtī-\ *n* : a substance that inhibits oxidation — **antioxidant** *adj*

an·ti·par·ti·cle \ˈan-ti-ˌpär-ti-kəl, ˈan-ˌtī-\ *n* : a subatomic particle identical to another subatomic particle in mass but opposite to it in electric and magnetic properties

an·ti·pas·to \ˌan-ti-ˈpas-tō, ˌän-ti-ˈpäs-\ *n, pl* **-ti** \-(ˌ)tē\ : any of various typically Italian hors d'oeuvres

an·tip·a·thy \an-ˈti-pə-thē\ *n, pl* **-thies** **1** : settled aversion or dislike **2** : an object of aversion — **an·ti·pa·thet·ic** \ˌan-ti-pə-ˈthe-tik\ *adj*

an·ti·per·son·nel \ˌan-ti-ˌpər-sə-ˈnel, ˌan-ˌtī-\ *adj* : designed for use against military personnel ⟨~ mine⟩

an·ti·per·spi·rant \-ˈpər-spə-rənt\ *n* : a preparation used to reduce perspiration

an·tiph·o·nal \an-ˈti-fə-nᵊl\ *adj* : performed by two alternating groups — **an·tiph·o·nal·ly** *adv*

an·ti·pode \ˈan-tə-ˌpōd\ *n, pl* **an·tip·o·des** \an-ˈti-pə-ˌdēz\ [ME *antipodes,* pl., persons dwelling at opposite points on the globe, fr. L, fr. Gk, fr. pl. of *antipod-, antipous* with feet opposite, fr. *anti-* against + *pod-, pous* foot] : the parts of the earth diametrically opposite — usu. used in pl. — **an·tip·o·dal** \an-ˈti-pə-dᵊl\ *adj* — **an·tip·o·de·an** \(ˌ)an-ˌti-pə-ˈdē-ən\ *adj*

an·ti·pol·lu·tion \ˌan-ti-pə-ˈlü-shən\ *adj* : designed to prevent, reduce, or eliminate pollution ⟨~ laws⟩

an·ti·pope \ˈan-ti-ˌpōp\ *n* : one elected or claiming to be pope in opposition to the pope canonically chosen

an·ti·pro·ton \ˌan-ti-ˈprō-ˌtän\ *n* : the antiparticle of the proton

an·ti·psy·chot·ic \ˌan-tē-sī-ˈkä-tik\ *n* : any of the powerful tranquilizers used to treat psychosis — **antipsychotic** *adj*

an·ti·quar·i·an \ˌan-tə-ˈkwer-ē-ən\ *adj* **1** : of or relating to antiquities **2** : dealing in old books — **antiquarian** *n* — **an·ti·quar·i·an·ism** *n*

an·ti·quary \ˈan-tə-ˌkwer-ē\ *n, pl* **-quar·ies** : a person who collects or studies antiquities

an·ti·quat·ed \ˈan-tə-ˌkwā-təd\ *adj* : OUT-OF-DATE, OLD-FASHIONED

[1]**an·tique** \an-ˈtēk\ *n* : an object made in a bygone period

[2]**antique** *adj* **1** : belonging to antiquity **2** : OLD-FASHIONED **3** : of a bygone style or period

[3]**antique** *vb* **-tiqued**; **-tiqu·ing** **1** : to finish or refinish in antique style : give an appearance of age to **2** : to shop around for antiques — **an·tiqu·er** *n*

an·tiq·ui·ty \an-ˈti-kwə-tē\ *n, pl* **-ties** **1** : ancient times **2** : great age **3** *pl* : relics of ancient times **4** *pl* : matters relating to ancient culture

an·ti·re·tro·vi·ral \ˌan-tē-ˈre-trō-ˌvī-rəl, ˌan-ˌtī-\ *adj* : effective against retroviruses ⟨~ drugs⟩ — **antiretroviral** *n*

antis *pl of* ANTI

an·ti–Sem·i·tism \ˌan-ti-ˈse-mə-ˌti-zəm, ˌan-ˌtī-\ *n* : hostility toward Jews as a religious or social minority — **an·ti–Sem·ite** \-ˈse-ˌmīt\ *n* — **an·ti–Se·mit·ic** \-sə-ˈmi-tik\ *adj*

an·ti·sep·tic \ˌan-tə-ˈsep-tik\ *adj* **1** : killing or checking the growth of germs that cause decay or infection **2** : scrupulously clean : ASEPTIC **3** : coldly impersonal ⟨an ~ greeting⟩ — **antiseptic** *n* — **an·ti·sep·ti·cal·ly** *adv*

an·ti·se·rum \ˈan-ti-ˌsir-əm, ˈan-ˌtī-\ *n* : a serum containing antibodies

an·ti·so·cial \ˌan-ti-ˈsō-shəl\ *adj* **1** : disliking the society of others **2** : contrary or hostile to the well-being of society ⟨crime is ~⟩; *esp* : deviating sharply

antilabor	**antimicrobial**	**antipoverty**	**antispasmodic**
antimalarial	**antinausea**	**antislavery**	**antistatic**

from the social norm — **an·ti·so·cial·ly** *adv*
an·tith·e·sis \an-ˈti-thə-səs\ *n, pl* **-e·ses** \-ˌsēz\ **1** : the opposition or contrast of ideas **2** : the direct opposite
an·ti·thet·i·cal \ˌan-tə-ˈthe-ti-kəl\ *also* **an·ti·thet·ic** \-tik\ *adj* : constituting or marked by antithesis — **an·ti·thet·i·cal·ly** \-ti-k(ə-)lē\ *adv*
an·ti·tox·in \ˌan-ti-ˈtäk-sən\ *n* : an antibody that is able to neutralize a particular toxin or disease-causing agent; *also* : an antiserum containing an antitoxin
an·ti·trust \ˌan-ti-ˈtrəst\ *adj* : of or relating to legislation against trusts; *also* : consisting of laws to protect trade and commerce from unlawful restraints and monopolies or unfair business practices
an·ti·ven·in \-ˈve-nən\ *n* : an antitoxin to a venom; *also* : a serum containing such antitoxin
ant·ler \ˈant-lər\ *n* [ME *aunteler,* fr. AF *antiler,* fr. VL **anteocularis* located before the eye, fr. L *ante-* before + *oculus* eye] : one of the paired deciduous solid bone processes on the head of a deer; *also* : a branch of this — **ant·lered** \-lərd\ *adj*
ant lion *n* : any of various insects having a long-jawed larva that digs a conical pit in which it lies in wait for insects (as ants) on which it feeds
an·to·nym \ˈan-tə-ˌnim\ *n* : a word of opposite meaning
ant·sy \ˈant-sē\ *adj* **1** : RESTLESS, IMPATIENT ⟨~ children⟩ **2** : APPREHENSIVE ⟨~ investors⟩
anus \ˈā-nəs\ *n* [L] : the lower or posterior opening of the alimentary canal
an·vil \ˈan-vəl\ *n* **1** : a heavy iron block on which metal is shaped **2** : INCUS
anx·i·ety \aŋ-ˈzī-ə-tē\ *n, pl* **-et·ies** **1** : painful uneasiness of mind usu. over an anticipated ill **2** : abnormal apprehension and fear often accompanied by physiological signs (as sweating and increased pulse), by doubt about the nature and reality of the threat itself, and by self-doubt
anx·ious \ˈaŋk-shəs\ *adj* **1** : uneasy in mind : WORRIED ⟨~ parents⟩ **2** : earnestly wishing : EAGER ⟨~ to leave⟩ — **anx·ious·ly** *adv*
[1]**any** \ˈe-nē\ *adj* **1** : one chosen at random **2** : of whatever number or quantity
[2]**any** *pron* **1** : any one or ones ⟨take ~ of the books you like⟩ **2** : any amount ⟨~ of the money not used is to be returned⟩
[3]**any** *adv* : to any extent or degree : AT ALL ⟨could not walk ~ farther⟩
any·body \-ˌbä-dē, -bə-\ *pron* : ANYONE
any·how \-ˌhaů\ *adv* **1** : in any way **2** : NEVERTHELESS; *also* : in any case
any·more \ˌe-nē-ˈmȯr\ *adv* **1** : any longer ⟨won't bother you ~⟩ **2** : at the present time
any·one \ˈe-nē-(ˌ)wən\ *pron* : any person
any·place \-ˌplās\ *adv* : ANYWHERE 1
any·thing \-ˌthiŋ\ *pron* : any thing whatever
any·time \ˈe-nē-ˌtīm\ *adv* : at any time whatever
any·way \-ˌwā\ *adv* : ANYHOW
any·where \-ˌhwer\ *adv* **1** : in or to any place **2** : to any extent ⟨not ~ near done⟩
any·wise \-ˌwīz\ *adv* : in any way whatever
A–OK \ˌā-ō-ˈkā\ *adv or adj* : very definitely OK
A1 \ˈā-ˈwən\ *adj* : of the finest quality
aor·ta \ā-ˈȯr-tə\ *n, pl* **-tas** *or* **-tae** \-tē\ : the main artery that carries blood from the heart — **aor·tic** \-tik\ *adj*
ap *abbr* **1** apostle **2** apothecaries'
AP *abbr* **1** American plan **2** Associated Press
apace \ə-ˈpās\ *adv* : SWIFTLY
Apache \ə-ˈpa-chē\ *n, pl* **Apache** *or* **Apach·es** \-ˈpa-chēz, -ˈpa-shəz\ : a member of a group of Indigenous peoples of the southwestern U.S.; *also* : any of the languages of the Apache people — **Apach·e·an** \ə-ˈpa-chē-ən\ *adj or n*
apanage *var of* APPANAGE
apart \ə-ˈpärt\ *adv* **1** : separately in place or time **2** : ASIDE **3** : in two or more parts : to pieces
apart·heid \ə-ˈpär-ˌtāt, -ˌtīt\ *n* [Afrikaans] : racial segregation; *esp* : a policy of racial segregation formerly practiced in the Republic of So. Africa
apart·ment \ə-ˈpärt-mənt\ *n* : a room or set of rooms occupied as a dwelling; *also* : a building divided into individual dwelling units
ap·a·thy \ˈa-pə-thē\ *n* **1** : lack of emotion **2** : lack of interest : INDIFFERENCE — **ap·a·thet·ic** \ˌa-pə-ˈthe-tik\ *adj* — **ap·a·thet·i·cal·ly** \-ti-k(ə-)lē\ *adv*
ap·a·tite \ˈa-pə-ˌtīt\ *n* : any of a group of minerals that are phosphates of calcium and occur esp. in phosphate rock and in bones and teeth
apato·sau·rus \ə-ˌpa-tə-ˈsȯr-əs\ *n* : any of a genus of large 4-footed dinosaurs of the Jurassic : BRONTOSAURUS
APB *abbr* all points bulletin
[1]**ape** \ˈāp\ *n* **1** : any of the larger tailless primates (as a baboon or gorilla); *also* : MONKEY **2** : MIMIC, IMITATOR; *also* : a large uncouth person
[2]**ape** *vb* **aped; ap·ing** : IMITATE, MIMIC
ape–man \ˈāp-ˌman\ *n* : a primate intermediate in character between Homo sapiens and the higher apes
aper·i·tif \ˌä-ˌper-ə-ˈtēf\ *n* : an alcoholic drink taken as an appetizer
ap·er·ture \ˈa-pər-ˌchůr, -chər\ *n* : OPENING, HOLE
apex \ˈā-ˌpeks\ *n, pl* **apex·es** *or* **api·ces** \ˈā-pə-ˌsēz, ˈa-\ : the highest point : PEAK
apha·sia \ə-ˈfā-zh(ē-)ə\ *n* : loss or impairment of the power to use or comprehend words — **apha·sic** \-zik\ *adj or n*
aph·elion \a-ˈfēl-yən\ *n, pl* **-elia** \-yə\ [NL, fr. *apo-* away from + Gk *hēlios* sun] : the point in an object's orbit most distant from the sun

antisubmarine **antitumor** **antiviral** **antiwar**
antitank

aphid \ˈā-fəd\ *n* : any of numerous small insects that suck the juices of plants
aphis \ˈā-fəs, ˈa-\ *n, pl* **aphi•des** \-fə-ˌdēz\ : APHID
aph•o•rism \ˈa-fə-ˌri-zəm\ *n* : a short saying stating a general truth : MAXIM — **aph•o•ris•tic** \ˌa-fə-ˈris-tik\ *adj*
aph•ro•di•si•ac \ˌa-frə-ˈdi-zē-ˌak, -ˈdē-zē-\ *n* : an agent that excites sexual desire — **aphrodisiac** *adj*
api•ary \ˈā-pē-ˌer-ē\ *n, pl* **-ar•ies** : a place where bees are kept — **api•a•rist** \-pē-ə-rist\ *n*
api•cal \ˈā-pi-kəl, ˈa-\ *adj* : of, relating to, or situated at an apex — **api•cal•ly** \-k(ə-)lē\ *adv*
apiece \ə-ˈpēs\ *adv* : for each one
aplen•ty \ə-ˈplen-tē\ *adj* : being in plenty or abundance
aplomb \ə-ˈpläm, -ˈpləm\ *n* [F, lit., perpendicularity, fr. MF, fr. *a plomb,* lit., according to the plummet] : complete composure or self-assurance
APO *abbr* army post office
Apoc *abbr* **1** Apocalypse **2** Apocrypha
apoc•a•lypse \ə-ˈpä-kə-ˌlips\ *n* **1** : a writing prophesying a cataclysm in which evil forces are destroyed **2** *cap* — see BIBLE table — **apoc•a•lyp•tic** \-ˌpä-kə-ˈlip-tik\ *also* **apoc•a•lyp•ti•cal** \-ti-kəl\ *adj*
Apoc•ry•pha \ə-ˈpä-krə-fə\ *n* **1** *not cap* : writings of dubious authenticity **2** : books included in the Septuagint and Vulgate but excluded from the Jewish and Protestant canons of the Old Testament — see BIBLE table **3** : early Christian writings not included in the New Testament
apoc•ry•phal \-fəl\ *adj* **1** : not canonical : SPURIOUS **2** *often cap* : of or resembling the Apocrypha — **apoc•ry•phal•ly** *adv* — **apoc•ry•phal•ness** *n*
apo•gee \ˈa-pə-(ˌ)jē\ *n* [F *apogée,* fr. NL *apogaeum,* fr. Gk *apogaion,* fr. *apo* away from + *gē, gaia* earth] : the point at which an orbiting object is farthest from the body being orbited
apo•lit•i•cal \ˌā-pə-ˈli-ti-kəl\ *adj* **1** : having an aversion for or no interest in political affairs **2** : having no political significance — **apo•lit•i•cal•ly** \-k(ə-)lē\ *adv*
apol•o•get•ic \ə-ˌpä-lə-ˈje-tik\ *adj* : expressing apology — **apol•o•get•i•cal•ly** \-ti-k(ə-)lē\ *adv*
ap•o•lo•gia \ˌa-pə-ˈlō-j(ē-)ə\ *n* : APOLOGY; *esp* : an argument in support or justification
apol•o•gise *Brit var of* APOLOGIZE
apol•o•gize \ə-ˈpä-lə-ˌjīz\ *vb* **-gized**; **-giz•ing** : to make an apology : express regret — **apol•o•gist** \-jist\ *n*
apol•o•gy \ə-ˈpä-lə-jē\ *n, pl* **-gies** **1** : a formal justification : DEFENSE **2** : an expression of regret for a wrong
ap•o•plexy \ˈa-pə-ˌplek-sē\ *n* : STROKE 3 — **ap•o•plec•tic** \ˌa-pə-ˈplek-tik\ *adj*
ap•o•pto•sis \ˌa-pəp-ˈtō-səs, -pə-ˈtō-\ *n, pl* **-pto•ses** \-ˌsēz\ : a genetically directed process of cell self-destruction
aport \ə-ˈpȯrt\ *adv* : on or toward the left side of a ship
apos•ta•sy \ə-ˈpäs-tə-sē\ *n, pl* **-sies** : a renunciation or abandonment of a former loyalty (as to a religion) — **apos•tate** \ə-ˈpäs-ˌtāt, -tət\ *adj or n*
a pos•te•ri•o•ri \ˌä-pō-ˌstir-ē-ˈȯr-ē\ *adj* [L, lit., from the latter] : relating to or derived by reasoning from observed facts — **a posteriori** *adv*
apos•tle \ə-ˈpä-səl\ *n* **1** : one of the group composed of Jesus' 12 original disciples and Paul **2** : the first prominent missionary to a region or group **3** : a person who initiates or first advocates a great reform — **apos•tle–ship** *n*
ap•os•tol•ic \ˌa-pə-ˈstä-lik\ *adj* **1** : of or relating to an apostle or to the New Testament apostles **2** : of or relating to a succession of spiritual authority from the apostles **3** : PAPAL ⟨~ authority⟩
[1]**apos•tro•phe** \ə-ˈpäs-trə-(ˌ)fē\ *n* : the rhetorical addressing of a usu. absent person or a usu. personified thing (as in "O grave, where is thy victory?")
[2]**apostrophe** *n* : a punctuation mark ' used esp. to indicate the possessive case or the omission of a letter or figure
apos•tro•phise *Brit var of* APOSTROPHIZE
apos•tro•phize \ə-ˈpäs-trə-ˌfīz\ *vb* **-phized**; **-phiz•ing** : to address as if present or capable of understanding
apothecaries' weight *n* : a system of weights based on the troy pound and ounce and used chiefly by pharmacists — see WEIGHT table
apoth•e•cary \ə-ˈpä-thə-ˌker-ē\ *n, pl* **-car•ies** [ME *apothecarie,* fr. ML *apothecarius,* fr. LL, shopkeeper, fr. L *apotheca* storehouse, fr. Gk *apothēkē,* fr. *apotithenai* to put away] : DRUGGIST
ap•o•thegm \ˈa-pə-ˌthem\ *n* : APHORISM
apo•the•o•sis \ə-ˌpä-thē-ˈō-səs, ˌa-pə-ˈthē-ə-səs\ *n, pl* **-o•ses** \-ˌsēz\ **1** : DEIFICATION **2** : the perfect example
[1]**app** \ˈap\ *n* : APPLICATION 6
[2]**app** *abbr* **1** apparatus **2** appendix
ap•pall *also* **ap•pal** \ə-ˈpȯl\ *vb* **ap•palled**; **ap•pall•ing** : to overcome with horror : DISMAY
Ap•pa•loo•sa \ˌa-pə-ˈlü-sə\ *n* : any of a breed of saddle horses developed in western No. America and usu. having a white or solid-colored coat with small spots
ap•pa•nage *also* **a•pa•nage** \ˈa-pə-nij\ *n* **1** : provision (as a grant of land) made by a sovereign or legislative body for dependent members of the royal family **2** : a rightful adjunct
ap•pa•ra•tus \ˌa-pə-ˈra-təs, -ˈrā-\ *n, pl* **-tus•es** *or* **-tus** [L] **1** : a set of materials or equipment for a particular use **2** : a complex machine or device : MECHANISM **3** : the organization of a political party or underground movement
[1]**ap•par•el** \ə-ˈper-əl\ *vb* **-eled** *or* **-elled**; **-el•ing** *or* **-el•ling** **1** : CLOTHE **2** : ADORN
[2]**apparel** *n* : CLOTHING, DRESS
ap•par•ent \ə-ˈper-ənt\ *adj* **1** : open to view : VISIBLE **2** : EVIDENT, OBVIOUS **3** : appearing as real or true : SEEMING
ap•par•ent•ly \-lē\ *adv* : it seems apparent

ap·pa·ri·tion \ˌa-pə-ˈri-shən\ *n* : a supernatural appearance : GHOST

ap·peal \ə-ˈpēl\ *vb* **1** : to take steps to have (a case) reheard in a higher court **2** : to plead for help, corroboration, or decision **3** : to arouse a sympathetic response — **appeal** *n*

ap·pear \ə-ˈpir\ *vb* **1** : to become visible **2** : to come formally before an authority **3** : SEEM **4** : to become evident **5** : to come before the public

ap·pear·ance \ə-ˈpir-əns\ *n* **1** : outward aspect : LOOK **2** : the act of appearing **3** : PHENOMENON

ap·pease \ə-ˈpēz\ *vb* **ap·peased**; **ap·peas·ing** **1** : to cause to subside : ALLAY **2** : PACIFY, CONCILIATE; *esp* : to buy off by concessions — **ap·pease·ment** *n* — **ap·peas·able** \-ˈpē-zə-bəl\ *adj*

ap·pel·lant \ə-ˈpe-lənt\ *n* : one who appeals esp. from a judicial decision

ap·pel·late \ə-ˈpe-lət\ *adj* : having power to review decisions of a lower court

ap·pel·la·tion \ˌa-pə-ˈlā-shən\ *n* : NAME, DESIGNATION

ap·pel·lee \ˌa-pə-ˈlē\ *n* : one against whom an appeal is taken

ap·pend \ə-ˈpend\ *vb* : to attach esp. as something additional : AFFIX

ap·pend·age \ə-ˈpen-dij\ *n* **1** : something appended to a principal or greater thing **2** : a projecting part (as an antenna) of an animal or plant body; *esp* : an arm, leg, or similar part ♦ ***Synonyms*** ACCESSORY, ADJUNCT, APPENDIX, APPURTENANCE

ap·pen·dec·to·my \ˌa-pən-ˈdek-tə-mē\ *n, pl* **-mies** : surgical removal of the intestinal appendix

ap·pen·di·ci·tis \ə-ˌpen-də-ˈsī-təs\ *n* : inflammation of the intestinal appendix

ap·pen·dix \ə-ˈpen-diks\ *n, pl* **-dix·es** *or* **-di·ces** \-də-ˌsēz\ [L] **1** : supplementary matter added at the end of a book **2** : a narrow blind tube usu. about three or four inches long that extends from the cecum in the lower right-hand part of the abdomen

ap·per·tain \ˌa-pər-ˈtān\ *vb* : to belong as a rightful part or privilege

ap·pe·tis·er, ap·pe·tis·ing *Brit var of* APPETIZER, APPETIZING

ap·pe·tite \ˈa-pə-ˌtīt\ *n* [ME *apetit,* fr. AF, fr. L *appetitus,* fr. *appetere* to strive after, fr. *ad-* to + *petere* to go to] **1** : natural desire for satisfying some want or need esp. for food **2** : TASTE, PREFERENCE ⟨an ~ for adventure⟩

ap·pe·tiz·er \ˈa-pə-ˌtī-zər\ *n* : a food or drink taken just before a meal to stimulate the appetite

ap·pe·tiz·ing \-ziŋ\ *adj* : tempting to the appetite — **ap·pe·tiz·ing·ly** *adv*

appl *abbr* applied

ap·plaud \ə-ˈplȯd\ *vb* : to show approval esp. by clapping

ap·plause \ə-ˈplȯz\ *n* : approval publicly expressed (as by clapping)

ap·ple \ˈa-pəl\ *n* : a rounded fruit with firm white flesh and a seedy core; *also* : a tree that bears this fruit

ap·ple·jack \-ˌjak\ *n* : a liquor distilled from fermented cider

ap·plet \ˈa-plət\ *n* : a short computer program esp. for performing a simple specific task

ap·pli·ance \ə-ˈplī-əns\ *n* **1** : INSTRUMENT, DEVICE **2** : a piece of household equipment (as a stove or toaster) operated by gas or electricity

ap·pli·ca·ble \ˈa-pli-kə-bəl, ə-ˈpli-kə-\ *adj* : capable of being applied : RELEVANT — **ap·pli·ca·bil·i·ty** \ˌa-pli-kə-ˈbi-lə-tē, ə-ˌpli-kə-\ *n*

ap·pli·cant \ˈa-pli-kənt\ *n* : one who applies ⟨a job ~⟩

ap·pli·ca·tion \ˌa-plə-ˈkā-shən\ *n* **1** : the act of applying **2** : assiduous attention **3** : REQUEST; *also* : a form used in making a request **4** : something placed or spread on a surface **5** : capacity for use **6** : a program (as a word processor) that performs one of a computer's major tasks

ap·pli·ca·tor \ˈa-plə-ˌkā-tər\ *n* : a device for applying a substance (as medicine or polish)

ap·plied \ə-ˈplīd\ *adj* : put to practical use ⟨~ art⟩

ap·pli·qué \ˌa-plə-ˈkā\ *n* [F] : a fabric decoration cut out and fastened to a larger piece of material — **appliqué** *vb*

ap·ply \ə-ˈplī\ *vb* **ap·plied**; **ap·ply·ing** **1** : to put to practical use **2** : to place in contact : put or spread on a surface **3** : to employ with close attention **4** : to have reference or connection **5** : to submit a request

ap·point \ə-ˈpȯint\ *vb* **1** : to fix or set officially ⟨~ a day for trial⟩ **2** : to name officially **3** : to fit out : EQUIP

ap·poin·tee \ə-ˌpȯin-ˈtē, ˌa-\ *n* : a person appointed

ap·point·ive \ə-ˈpȯin-tiv\ *adj* : subject to appointment

ap·point·ment \ə-ˈpȯint-mənt\ *n* **1** : the act of appointing **2** : an arrangement for a meeting **3** *pl* : FURNISHINGS, EQUIPMENT **4** : a nonelective office or position

ap·por·tion \ə-ˈpȯr-shən\ *vb* : to distribute proportionately : ALLOT — **ap·portion·ment** *n*

ap·po·site \ˈa-pə-zət\ *adj* : APPROPRIATE, RELEVANT ⟨an ~ quotation⟩ — **ap·po·site·ly** *adv* — **ap·po·site·ness** *n*

ap·po·si·tion \ˌa-pə-ˈzi-shən\ *n* : a grammatical construction in which a noun or pronoun is followed by another that has the same referent (as *the poet* and *Burns* in "a biography of the poet Burns")

ap·pos·i·tive \ə-ˈpä-zə-tiv, a-\ *adj* : of, relating to, or standing in grammatical apposition — **appositive** *n*

ap·praise \ə-ˈprāz\ *vb* **ap·praised**; **ap·prais·ing** : to set a value on — **ap·prais·al** \-ˈprā-zəl\ *n* — **ap·prais·er** *n*

ap·pre·cia·ble \ə-ˈprē-shə-bəl\ *adj* : large enough to be recognized and measured — **ap·pre·cia·bly** *adv*

ap·pre·ci·ate \ə-ˈprē-shē-ˌāt\ *vb* **-at·ed**; **-at·ing** **1** : to value justly **2** : to be aware of **3** : to be grateful for **4** : to increase in value — **ap·pre·ci·a·tion** \-ˌprē-shē-ˈā-shən\ *n*

ap·pre·cia·tive \ə-ˈprē-shə-tiv, -shē-ˌāt-\ *adj* : having or showing appreciation — **ap·pre·cia·tive·ly** *adv*

ap·pre·hend \ˌa-pri-ˈhend\ *vb* **1** : ARREST **2** : to become aware of **3** : to look forward to with dread **4** : UNDERSTAND — **ap·pre·hen·sion** \-ˈhen-chən\ *n*

ap·pre·hen·sive \-ˈhen-siv\ *adj* : viewing the future with anxiety — **ap·pre·hen·sive·ly** *adv* — **ap·pre·hen·sive·ness** *n*

[1]**ap·pren·tice** \ə-ˈpren-təs\ *n* **1** : a person learning a craft under a skilled worker **2** : BEGINNER — **ap·pren·tice·ship** *n*

[2]**apprentice** *vb* **-ticed**; **-tic·ing** : to bind or set at work as an apprentice

ap·prise \ə-ˈprīz\ *vb* **ap·prised**; **ap·pris·ing** : INFORM ⟨*apprised* him of his rights⟩

ap·proach \ə-ˈprōch\ *vb* **1** : to move nearer to ⟨~ the bench⟩ **2** : to be almost the same as **3** : to make advances to esp. for the purpose of creating a desired result **4** : to take preliminary steps toward ⟨~ the subject carefully⟩ — **approach** *n* — **ap·proach·able** *adj*

ap·pro·ba·tion \ˌa-prə-ˈbā-shən\ *n* : APPROVAL

[1]**ap·pro·pri·ate** \ə-ˈprō-prē-ˌāt\ *vb* **-at·ed**; **-at·ing** **1** : to take possession of **2** : to set apart for a particular use

[2]**ap·pro·pri·ate** \ə-ˈprō-prē-ət\ *adj* : fitted to a purpose or use : SUITABLE ♦ ***Synonyms*** PROPER, FIT, APT, BEFITTING — **ap·pro·pri·ate·ly** *adv* — **ap·pro·pri·ate·ness** *n*

ap·pro·pri·a·tion \ə-ˌprō-prē-ˈā-shən\ *n* : something (as money) set aside by formal action for a specific use

ap·prov·al \ə-ˈprü-vəl\ *n* : an act of approving — **on approval** : subject to a prospective buyer's acceptance or refusal

ap·prove \ə-ˈprüv\ *vb* **ap·proved**; **ap·prov·ing** **1** : to have or express a favorable opinion of **2** : to accept as satisfactory : RATIFY ⟨~ the treaty⟩

approx *abbr* approximate; approximately

[1]**ap·prox·i·mate** \ə-ˈpräk-sə-mət\ *adj* : nearly correct or exact ⟨an ~ count⟩ — **ap·prox·i·mate·ly** *adv*

[2]**ap·prox·i·mate** \-ˌmāt\ *vb* **-mat·ed**; **-mat·ing** : to come or bring near or close — **ap·prox·i·ma·tion** \ə-ˌpräk-sə-ˈmā-shən\ *n*

appt *abbr* appoint; appointed; appointment

ap·pur·te·nance \ə-ˈpərt-nəns, -ˈpər-tə-nəns\ *n* : something that belongs to or goes with another thing ♦ ***Synonyms*** ACCESSORY, ADJUNCT, APPENDAGE, APPENDIX — **ap·pur·te·nant** \ə-ˈpərt-nənt, -ˈpər-tə-nənt\ *adj*

Apr *abbr* April

APR *abbr* annual percentage rate

apri·cot \ˈa-prə-ˌkät, ˈā-\ *n* [alter. of earlier *abrecock,* ultim. fr. Ar *al-birqūq,* ultim. fr. L (*persicum*) *praecox,* lit., early-ripening (peach)] : an oval orange-colored fruit resembling the related peach and plum in flavor; *also* : a tree bearing apricots

April \ˈā-prəl\ *n* [ME, fr. AF & L; AF *avrill,* fr. L *Aprilis*] : the 4th month of the year

a pri·o·ri \ˌä-prē-ˈȯr-ē\ *adj* [L, from the former] **1** : characterized by or derived by reasoning from self-evident propositions **2** : independent of experience — **a priori** *adv*

apron \ˈā-prən\ *n* [ME, alter. (fr. misdivision of *a napron*) of *napron,* fr. MF *naperon,* dim. of *nape* cloth, modif. of L *mappa* napkin] **1** : a garment tied over the front of the body to protect the clothes **2** : a paved area for parking or handling airplanes — **aproned** *adj*

[1]**ap·ro·pos** \ˌa-prə-ˈpō, ˈa-prə-ˌpō\ *adv* [F *à propos,* lit., to the purpose] **1** : OPPORTUNELY **2** : in passing : INCIDENTALLY

[2]**apropos** *adj* : being to the point

apropos of *prep* : with regard to

apse \ˈaps\ *n* : a projecting usu. semicircular and vaulted part of a building (as a church)

[1]**apt** \ˈapt\ *adj* **1** : well adapted : SUITABLE **2** : having an habitual tendency : LIKELY **3** : quick to learn — **apt·ly** *adv* — **apt·ness** \ˈapt-nəs\ *n*

[2]**apt** *abbr* **1** apartment **2** aptitude

ap·ti·tude \ˈap-tə-ˌtüd, -ˌtyüd\ *n* **1** : natural ability : TALENT **2** : capacity for learning **3** : APPROPRIATENESS

aqua \ˈa-kwə, ˈä-\ *n* : a light greenish blue color

aqua·cul·ture \ˈa-kwə-ˌkəl-chər, ˈä-\ *n* : the cultivation of aquatic organisms (as fish or shellfish) for human use esp. as food — **aqua·cul·tur·ist** \-chə-rist\ *n*

aqua·ma·rine \ˌa-kwə-mə-ˈrēn, ˌä-\ *n* **1** : a bluish green gem **2** : a pale blue to light greenish blue

aqua·naut \ˈa-kwə-ˌnȯt, ˈä-\ *n* : a person who lives in an underwater shelter for an extended period

aqua·plane \-ˌplān\ *n* : a board towed behind a motorboat and ridden by a person standing on it — **aquaplane** *vb*

aqua re·gia \ˌa-kwə-ˈrē-j(ē-)ə\ *n* [NL, lit., royal water] : a mixture of nitric and hydrochloric acids that dissolves gold or platinum

aquar·i·um \ə-ˈkwer-ē-əm\ *n, pl* **-i·ums** *or* **-ia** \-ē-ə\ **1** : a container (as a glass tank) in which living aquatic animals or plants are kept **2** : a place where aquatic animals and plants are kept and shown

Aquar·i·us \ə-ˈkwer-ē-əs\ *n* [L, lit., water carrier] **1** : a zodiacal constellation between Capricorn and Pisces usu. pictured as a man pouring water **2** : the 11th sign of the zodiac in astrology; *also* : one born under this sign

[1]**aquat·ic** \ə-ˈkwä-tik, -ˈkwa-\ *adj* **1** : growing or living in or frequenting water **2** : performed in or on water

[2]**aquatic** *n* : an aquatic animal or plant

aqua·vit \ˈä-kwə-ˌvēt\ *n* : a clear liquor flavored with caraway seeds

aqua vi·tae \ˌa-kwə-ˈvī-tē, ˌä-\ *n* [ME, fr. ML, lit., water of life] : a strong alcoholic liquor (as brandy)

aq·ue·duct \ˈa-kwə-ˌdəkt\ *n* **1** : a conduit for carrying running water **2** : a structure carrying a canal over a river or hollow **3** : a passage in a bodily part

aque·ous \ˈā-kwē-əs, ˈa-\ *adj* **1 :** WATERY **2 :** made of, by, or with water

aqueous humor *n* **:** a clear fluid occupying the space between the lens and the cornea of the eye

aqui·fer \ˈa-kwə-fər, ˈä-\ *n* **:** a water-bearing stratum of permeable rock, sand, or gravel

aq·ui·line \ˈa-kwə-ˌlīn, -lən\ *adj* **1 :** of or resembling an eagle **2 :** hooked like an eagle's beak ⟨an ~ nose⟩

ar *abbr* arrival; arrive

Ar *symbol* argon

AR *abbr* Arkansas

-ar *adj suffix* **:** of or relating to ⟨molecul*ar*⟩ **:** being ⟨spectacul*ar*⟩ **:** resembling ⟨oracul*ar*⟩

Ar·ab \ˈa-rəb\ *n* **1 :** a member of a Semitic people of the Arabian peninsula in southwestern Asia **2 :** a member of an Arabic-speaking people — **Arab** *adj* — **Ara·bi·an** \ə-ˈrā-bē-ən\ *adj or n*

ar·a·besque \ˌa-rə-ˈbesk\ *n* **:** a design of interlacing lines forming figures of flowers, foliage, and sometimes animals — **arabesque** *adj*

[1]**Ar·a·bic** \ˈa-rə-bik\ *n* **:** a Semitic language of southwestern Asia and northern Africa

[2]**Arabic** *adj* **1 :** of or relating to the Arabs, Arabic, or the Arabian peninsula in southwestern Asia **2 :** expressed in or making use of Arabic numerals

Arabic numeral *n* **:** any of the number symbols 0, 1, 2, 3, 4, 5, 6, 7, 8, 9

ar·a·ble \ˈa-rə-bəl\ *adj* **:** fit for or used for the growing of crops ⟨~ land⟩

arach·nid \ə-ˈrak-nəd\ *n* **:** any of a class of usu. 8-legged arthropods comprising the spiders, scorpions, mites, and ticks — **arachnid** *adj*

Ar·a·ma·ic \ˌa-rə-ˈmā-ik\ *n* **:** an ancient Semitic language

ar·a·mid \ˈa-rə-məd, -ˌmid\ *n* **:** any of several light but very strong heat-resistant synthetic materials used esp. in textiles and plastics

Arap·a·ho *or* **Arap·a·hoe** \ə-ˈra-pə-ˌhō\ *n, pl* **-ho** *or* **-hos** *or* **-hoe** *or* **-hoes :** a member of an Algonquian-speaking Indigenous people of the Great Plains

ar·bi·ter \ˈär-bə-tər\ *n* **:** one having power to decide **:** JUDGE

ar·bi·trage \ˈär-bə-ˌträzh\ *n* [F, fr. MF, arbitration] **:** the purchase and sale of the same or equivalent securities in different markets in order to profit from price discrepancies

ar·bi·tra·geur \ˌär-bə-(ˌ)trä-ˈzhər\ *or* **ar·bi·trag·er** \ˈär-bə-ˌträ-zhər\ *n* **:** one who practices arbitrage

ar·bit·ra·ment \är-ˈbi-trə-mənt\ *n* **1 :** the act of deciding a dispute **2 :** the judgment given by an arbitrator

ar·bi·trary \ˈär-bə-ˌtrer-ē\ *adj* **1 :** AUTOCRATIC, DESPOTIC **2 :** determined by will or caprice **:** selected at random — **ar·bi·trari·ly** \ˌär-bə-ˈtrer-ə-lē\ *adv* — **ar·bi·trari·ness** \ˈär-bə-ˌtrer-ē-nəs\ *n*

ar·bi·trate \ˈär-bə-ˌtrāt\ *vb* **-trat·ed; -trat·ing 1 :** to act as arbitrator **2 :** to act on as arbitrator **3 :** to submit for decision to an arbitrator — **ar·bi·tra·tion** \ˌär-bə-ˈtrā-shən\ *n*

ar·bi·tra·tor \ˈär-bə-ˌtrā-tər\ *n* **:** one chosen to settle differences between two parties in a controversy

ar·bor \ˈär-bər\ *n* [ME *erber, herber* garden, fr. AF, fr. *herbe* herb, grass] **:** a shelter formed of or covered with vines or branches

ar·bo·re·al \är-ˈbȯr-ē-əl\ *adj* **1 :** of, relating to, or resembling a tree **2 :** living in trees ⟨~ monkeys⟩

ar·bo·re·tum \ˌär-bə-ˈrē-təm\ *n, pl* **-retums** *or* **-re·ta** \-tə\ [L, plantation of trees, fr. *arbor* tree] **:** a place where trees and plants are grown for scientific and educational purposes

ar·bor·vi·tae \ˌär-bər-ˈvī-tē\ *n* **:** any of various evergreen trees and shrubs with scalelike leaves that are related to the cypresses

ar·bour *chiefly Brit var of* ARBOR

ar·bu·tus \är-ˈbyü-təs\ *n* **:** TRAILING ARBUTUS

[1]**arc** \ˈärk\ *n* **1 :** a sustained luminous discharge of electricity (as between two electrodes) **2 :** a continuous portion of a curved line (as part of the circumference of a circle)

[2]**arc** *vb* **arced** \ˈärkt\; **arc·ing** \ˈär-kiŋ\ **:** to form an electric arc

ARC *abbr* **1** AIDS-related complex **2** American Red Cross

ar·cade \är-ˈkād\ *n* **1 :** an arched or covered passageway; *esp* **:** one lined with shops **2 :** a row of arches with their supporting columns **3 :** an amusement center having coin-operated games

ar·cane \är-ˈkān\ *adj* **:** SECRET, MYSTERIOUS

[1]**arch** \ˈärch\ *n* **1 :** a curved structure spanning an opening (as a door) **2 :** something resembling an arch **3 :** ARCHWAY

[2]**arch** *vb* **1 :** to cover with an arch **2 :** to form or bend into an arch

[3]**arch** *adj* **1 :** CHIEF, EMINENT ⟨my ~ enemy⟩ **2 :** ROGUISH, MISCHIEVOUS; *also* **:** deliberately playful or impudent ⟨~ comments⟩ — **arch·ly** *adv* — **arch·ness** *n*

[4]**arch** *abbr* architect; architectural; architecture

ar·chae·ol·o·gy *or* **ar·che·ol·o·gy** \ˌär-kē-ˈä-lə-jē\ *n* **:** the study of past human life as revealed by relics left by ancient peoples — **ar·chae·o·log·i·cal** \-ə-ˈlä-ji-kəl\ *adj* — **ar·chae·ol·o·gist** \-ˈä-lə-jist\ *n*

ar·cha·ic \är-ˈkā-ik\ *adj* **1 :** having the characteristics of the language of the past and surviving chiefly in specialized uses ⟨~ words⟩ **2 :** belonging to an earlier time **:** ANTIQUATED — **ar·cha·i·cal·ly** \-i-k(ə-)lē\ *adv*

arch·an·gel \ˈär-ˌkān-jəl\ *n* **:** a chief angel

arch·bish·op \ärch-ˈbi-shəp\ *n* **:** a bishop of high rank

arch·bish·op·ric \-shə-(ˌ)prik\ *n* **:** the jurisdiction or office of an archbishop

arch·con·ser·va·tive \(ˌ)ärch-kən-ˈsər-və-tiv\ *n* : an extreme conservative — **archconservative** *adj*

arch•dea•con \-ˈdē-kən\ *n* : a church official who assists a diocesan bishop in ceremonial or administrative functions

arch•di•o•cese \-ˈdī-ə-səs, -ˌsēz\ *n* : the diocese of an archbishop

arch•duke \-ˈdük, -ˈdyük\ *n* **1** : a sovereign prince **2** : a prince of the imperial family of Austria

Ar•che•an \är-ˈkē-ən\ *adj* : of, relating to, or being the earliest eon of geologic history — **Archean** *n*

arch•en•e•my \ˌärch-ˈe-nə-mē\ *n, pl* **-mies** : a principal enemy

Ar•cheo•zo•ic \ˌär-kē-ə-ˈzō-ik\ *adj* : ARCHEAN — **Archeozoic** *n*

ar•chery \ˈär-chə-rē\ *n* : the art or practice of shooting with bow and arrows — **ar•cher** \ˈär-chər\ *n*

ar•che•type \ˈär-ki-ˌtīp\ *n* : the original pattern or model of all things of the same type — **ar•che•typ•al** \ˌär-kə-ˈtī-pəl\ *adj*

arch•fiend \ˌärch-ˈfēnd\ *n* : a chief fiend; *esp* : SATAN

ar•chi•epis•co•pal \ˌär-kē-ə-ˈpis-kə-pəl\ *adj* : of or relating to an archbishop

ar•chi•man•drite \ˌär-kə-ˈman-ˌdrīt\ *n* : a dignitary in an Eastern church ranking below a bishop

ar•chi•pel•a•go \ˌär-kə-ˈpe-lə-ˌgō, ˌär-chə-\ *n, pl* **-goes** *or* **-gos** : a group of islands

ar•chi•tect \ˈär-kə-ˌtekt\ *n* **1** : a person who plans buildings and oversees their construction **2** : a person who designs and guides a plan or undertaking

ar•chi•tec•ture \ˈär-kə-ˌtek-chər\ *n* **1** : the art or science of planning and building structures **2** : a method or style of building **3** : the manner in which the elements (as of a design) or components (of a computer) are arranged or organized — **ar•chi•tec•tur•al** \ˌar-kə-ˈtek-chə-rəl, -ˈtek-shrəl\ *adj* — **ar•chi•tec•tur•al•ly** *adv*

ar•chi•trave \ˈär-kə-ˌtrāv\ *n* : the supporting horizontal member just above the columns in a building in the classical style of architecture

ar•chive \ˈär-ˌkīv\ *n* **1** : a place for keeping public records; *also* : public records — often used in pl. **2** : a repository esp. of information

ar•chi•vist \ˈär-kə-vist, -ˌkī-\ *n* : a person in charge of archives

ar•chon \ˈär-ˌkän, -kən\ *n* : a chief magistrate of ancient Athens

arch•ri•val \ˈärch-ˈrī-vəl\ *n* : a principal rival

arch•way \ˈärch-ˌwā\ *n* : a passageway under an arch; *also* : an arch over a passage

arc lamp *n* : a gas-filled electric lamp that produces light when a current arcs between incandescent electrodes

¹**arc•tic** \ˈärk-tik, ˈär-tik\ *adj* [ME *artik,* fr. L *arcticus,* fr. Gk *arktikos,* fr. *arktos* bear, Ursa Major, north] **1** *often cap* : of or relating to the north pole or the region near it **2** : FRIGID

²**arc•tic** \ˈär-tik, ˈärk-tik\ *n* : a rubber overshoe that reaches to the ankle or above

arctic circle *n, often cap A&C* : the parallel of latitude that is approximately 66½ degrees north of the equator

-ard *also* **-art** *n suffix* : one that is characterized by performing some action, possessing some quality, or being associated with some thing esp. conspicuously or excessively ⟨bragg*art*⟩ ⟨dull*ard*⟩

ar•dent \ˈär-dᵊnt\ *adj* **1** : characterized by warmth of feeling : PASSIONATE **2** : FIERY, HOT ⟨an ~ sun⟩ **3** : GLOWING ⟨~ eyes⟩ — **ar•dent•ly** *adv*

ar•dor \ˈär-dər\ *n* **1** : warmth of feeling : ZEAL **2** : sexual excitement

ar•dour *chiefly Brit var of* ARDOR

ar•du•ous \ˈär-jə-wəs, -dyü-wəs\ *adj* : DIFFICULT, LABORIOUS — **ar•du•ous•ly** *adv* — **ar•du•ous•ness** *n*

¹**are** *pres 2d sing or pres pl of* BE

²**are** \ˈer\ *n* — see METRIC SYSTEM table

ar•ea \ˈer-ē-ə\ *n* **1** : a flat surface or space **2** : the amount of surface included (as within the lines of a geometric figure) **3** : range or extent of some thing or concept : FIELD **4** : REGION

area code *n* : a usu. 3-digit number that identifies each telephone service area in a country (as the U.S. or Canada)

are•na \ə-ˈrē-nə\ *n* [L *harena, arena* sand, sandy place] **1** : an enclosed area used for public entertainment **2** : a sphere of activity or competition

ar•gen•tite \ˈär-jən-ˌtīt\ *n* : a dark gray or black mineral of metallic luster that is an important ore of silver

ar•gon \ˈär-ˌgän\ *n* [Gk, neut. of *argos* idle, lazy, fr. *a-* not + *ergon* work; fr. its relative inertness] : a colorless odorless gaseous chemical element found in the air and used for filling electric lamps

ar•go•sy \ˈär-gə-sē\ *n, pl* **-sies** **1** : a large merchant ship **2** : FLEET

ar•got \ˈär-gət, -ˌgō\ *n* : the language of a particular group or class

argu•able \ˈär-gyü-ə-bəl\ *adj* : open to argument, dispute, or question

ar•gu•ably \ˈär-gyü-(ə-)blē\ *adv* : as may be argued or shown by argument

ar•gue \ˈär-gyü\ *vb* **ar•gued; ar•gu•ing** **1** : to give reasons for or against something **2** : to contend in words : DISPUTE ⟨*argued* about money⟩ **3** : DEBATE **4** : to persuade by giving reasons

ar•gu•ment \ˈär-gyə-mənt\ *n* **1** : a reason offered in proof **2** : discourse intended to persuade **3** : QUARREL

ar•gu•men•ta•tion \ˌär-gyə-mən-ˈtā-shən\ *n* : the art of formal discussion

ar•gu•men•ta•tive \ˌär-gyə-ˈmen-tə-tiv\ *adj* : inclined to argue

ar•gyle *also* **ar•gyll** \ˈär-ˌgī(-ə)l\ *n, often cap* : a geometric knitting pattern of varicolored diamonds on a single background color; *also* : a sock knit in this pattern

aria \ˈär-ē-ə\ *n* : an accompanied elaborate vocal solo forming part of a larger work

ari•a•ry \ˌä-rē-ˈä-rē\ *n, pl* **ariary** — see MONEY table

ar·id \ˈa-rəd\ *adj* : very dry; *esp* : having insufficient rainfall to support agriculture — **arid·i·ty** \ə-ˈri-də-tē\ *n*
Ar·i·es \ˈer-ˌēz, -ē-ˌēz\ *n* [L, lit., ram] **1** : a zodiacal constellation between Pisces and Taurus pictured as a ram **2** : the 1st sign of the zodiac in astrology; *also* : one born under this sign
aright \ə-ˈrīt\ *adv* : RIGHT, CORRECTLY
arise \ə-ˈrīz\ *vb* **arose** \-ˈrōz\; **aris·en** \-ˈri-zᵊn\; **aris·ing** \-ˈrī-ziŋ\ **1** : to get up **2** : ORIGINATE **3** : ASCEND ♦ ***Synonyms*** RISE, DERIVE, SPRING, ISSUE
ar·is·toc·ra·cy \ˌa-rə-ˈstä-krə-sē\ *n, pl* **-cies 1** : government by a noble or privileged class; *also* : a state so governed **2** : the governing class of an aristocracy **3** : UPPER CLASS — **aris·to·crat** \ə-ˈris-tə-ˌkrat\ *n* — **aris·to·crat·ic** \ə-ˌris-tə-ˈkra-tik\ *adj*
arith *abbr* arithmetic; arithmetical
arith·me·tic \ə-ˈrith-mə-ˌtik\ *n* **1** : a branch of mathematics that deals with computations usu. with nonnegative real numbers **2** : COMPUTATION, CALCULATION — **ar·ith·met·ic** \ˌer-ith-ˈme-tik\ *or* **ar·ith·met·i·cal** \-ti-kəl\ *adj* — **ar·ith·met·i·cal·ly** \-ti-k(ə-)lē\ *adv* — **arith·me·ti·cian** \ə-ˌrith-mə-ˈti-shən\ *n*
arithmetic mean *n* : the sum of a set of numbers divided by the number of numbers in the set
Ariz *abbr* Arizona
ark \ˈärk\ *n* **1** : a boat held to resemble that of Noah's at the time of the Flood **2** : the sacred chest in a synagogue representing to Hebrews the presence of God; *also* : the repository for the scrolls of the Torah
Ark *abbr* Arkansas
¹**arm** \ˈärm\ *n* [ME, fr. OE *earm*] **1** : a human upper limb and esp. the part between the shoulder and wrist; *also* : a corresponding limb of a 2-footed vertebrate **2** : something resembling an arm in shape or position ⟨an ~ of a chair⟩ ⟨the eight ~*s* of an octopus⟩ **3** : POWER, MIGHT ⟨the ~ of the law⟩ — **armed** \ˈärmd\ *adj* — **arm·less** *adj*
²**arm** *vb* [ME, fr. AF *armer,* fr. L *armare,* fr. *arma* weapons, tools] : to furnish with weapons
³**arm** *n* **1** : WEAPON **2** : a branch of the military forces **3** *pl* : the hereditary heraldic devices of a family
ar·ma·da \är-ˈmä-də, -ˈmā-\ *n* : a fleet of warships
ar·ma·dil·lo \ˌär-mə-ˈdi-lō\ *n, pl* **-los** [Sp, fr. dim. of *armado* armed one] : any of several small burrowing mammals with the head and body protected by an armor of bony plates
Ar·ma·ged·don \ˌär-mə-ˈge-dᵊn\ *n* : a final conclusive battle between the forces of good and evil; *also* : the site or time of this
ar·ma·ment \ˈär-mə-mənt\ *n* **1** : military strength **2** : arms and equipment (as of a tank or combat unit) **3** : the process of preparing for war
ar·ma·ture \ˈär-mə-ˌchu̇r, -chər\ *n* **1** : a protective covering or structure (as the spines of a cactus) **2** : the rotating part of an electric generator or motor; *also* : the movable part in an electromagnetic device (as a loudspeaker)
arm·chair \ˈärm-ˌcher\ *n* : a chair with armrests
armed forces *n pl* : the combined military, naval, and air forces of a nation
Ar·me·nian \är-ˈmē-nē-ən\ *n* **1** : a native or inhabitant of Armenia **2** : the Indo-European language of the Armenians
arm·ful \ˈärm-ˌfu̇l\ *n, pl* **armfuls** *or* **arms·ful** \ˈärmz-ˌfu̇l\ : as much as the arm or arms can hold
arm·hole \ˈärm-ˌhōl\ *n* : an opening for the arm in a garment
ar·mi·stice \ˈär-mə-stəs\ *n* : temporary suspension of hostilities by mutual agreement : TRUCE
arm·let \ˈärm-lət\ *n* : a band worn around the upper arm
ar·mor \ˈär-mər\ *n* **1** : protective covering **2** : armored forces and vehicles — **ar·mored** \-mərd\ *adj*
ar·mor·er \ˈär-mər-ər\ *n* **1** : a person who makes arms and armor **2** : a person who services firearms
ar·mo·ri·al \är-ˈmȯr-ē-əl\ *adj* : of or bearing heraldic arms
ar·mory \ˈär-mə-rē\ *n, pl* **ar·mor·ies 1** : a place where arms are stored **2** : a factory where arms are made
ar·mour, ar·moury *chiefly Brit var of* ARMOR, ARMORY
arm·pit \ˈärm-ˌpit\ *n* : the hollow under the junction of the arm and shoulder
arm·rest \-ˌrest\ *n* : a support for the arm
ar·my \ˈär-mē\ *n, pl* **armies 1** : a body of persons trained and organized for war **2** *often cap* : the complete military organization of a country for land warfare **3** : a great number **4** : a body of persons organized to advance a cause
army ant *n* : any of various nomadic social ants
ar·my·worm \ˈär-mē-ˌwərm\ *n* : any of numerous moths whose larvae move about destroying crops
aro·ma \ə-ˈrō-mə\ *n* : a usu. pleasing odor : FRAGRANCE — **ar·o·mat·ic** \ˌar-ə-ˈma-tik\ *adj*
aro·ma·ther·a·py \ə-ˌrō-mə-ˈther-ə-pē\ *n* : massage with a preparation of fragrant oils extracted from herbs, flowers, and fruits
arose *past of* ARISE
¹**around** \ə-ˈrau̇nd\ *adv* **1** : in a circle or in circumference ⟨a tree five feet ~⟩ **2** : in or along a circuit ⟨the road goes ~ by the lake⟩ **3** : on all sides ⟨nothing for miles ~⟩ **4** : NEARBY ⟨wait ~ awhile⟩ **5** : from one place to another ⟨travels ~ on business⟩ **6** : in an opposite direction ⟨turn ~⟩ **7** — used with some verbs to indicate continued action ⟨joking ~⟩ **8** : APPROXIMATELY ⟨cost ~ $5⟩
²**around** *prep* **1** : SURROUNDING ⟨trees ~ the house⟩ **2** : to or on another side of ⟨~ the corner⟩ **3** : NEAR ⟨stayed right ~ home⟩ **4** : along the circuit of ⟨go ~ the world⟩

arouse \ə-ˈrau̇z\ *vb* **aroused; arous·ing** **1** : to awaken from sleep **2** : to stir up : EXCITE — **arous·al** \-ˈrau̇-zəl\ *n*

ar·peg·gio \är-ˈpe-jē-ˌō, -ˈpe-jō\ *n, pl* **-gios** [It fr. *arpeggiare* to play on the harp, fr. *arpa* harp] : a chord whose notes are performed in succession and not simultaneously

arr *abbr* **1** arranged **2** arrival; arrive

ar·raign \ə-ˈrān\ *vb* **1** : to call before a court to answer to an indictment **2** : to accuse of wrong or imperfection — **ar·raign·ment** *n*

ar·range \ə-ˈrānj\ *vb* **ar·ranged; ar·rang·ing** **1** : to put in order **2** : PLAN ⟨~ an interview⟩ **3** : to adapt (a musical composition) to voices or instruments other than those for which it was orig. written **4** : to come to an agreement about : SETTLE ⟨~ a business deal⟩ — **ar·range·ment** *n* — **ar·rang·er** *n*

ar·rant \ˈa-rənt\ *adj* : being notoriously without moderation : EXTREME

ar·ras \ˈa-rəs\ *n, pl* **arras** **1** : TAPESTRY **2** : a wall hanging or screen of tapestry

[1]**ar·ray** \ə-ˈrā\ *vb* **1** : to dress esp. splendidly **2** : to arrange in order (as in an array)

[2]**array** *n* **1** : a regular arrangement **2** : rich apparel **3** : a large or varied group

ar·rears \ə-ˈrirz\ *n pl* **1** : a state of being behind in the discharge of obligations ⟨in ~ with the rent⟩ **2** : overdue debts

[1]**ar·rest** \ə-ˈrest\ *vb* **1** : STOP, CHECK **2** : to take into legal custody

[2]**arrest** *n* **1** : the act of stopping; *also* : the state of being stopped **2** : the taking into custody by legal authority

ar·rhyth·mia \ā-ˈrith-mē-ə\ *n* : an alteration of the heartbeat's rhythm

ar·riv·al \ə-ˈrī-vəl\ *n* **1** : the act of arriving **2** : one that arrives

ar·rive \ə-ˈrīv\ *vb* **ar·rived; ar·riv·ing** **1** : to reach a destination **2** : to make an appearance ⟨the guests have *arrived*⟩ **3** : to attain success

ar·ro·gant \ˈer-ə-gənt\ *adj* : offensively exaggerating one's own importance — **ar·ro·gance** \-gəns\ *n* — **ar·ro·gant·ly** *adv*

ar·ro·gate \-ˌgāt\ *vb* **-gat·ed; -gat·ing** : to claim or seize without justification as one's right — **ar·ro·ga·tion** \ˌar-ə-ˈgā-shən\ *n*

ar·row \ˈer-ō\ *n* **1** : a missile shot from a bow and usu. having a slender shaft, a pointed head, and feathers at the butt **2** : a pointed mark used to indicate direction

ar·row·head \ˈer-ō-ˌhed\ *n* : the pointed end of an arrow

ar·row·root \-ˌrüt, -ˌru̇t\ *n* : an edible starch from the roots of any of several tropical American plants; *also* : a plant yielding arrowroot

ar·royo \ə-ˈrȯi-ə, -ō\ *n, pl* **-royos** [Sp] **1** : a watercourse in a dry region **2** : a water-carved gully or channel

ar·se·nal \ˈärs-nəl, ˈär-sə-nəl\ *n* [ultim. fr. Ar *dār ṣināʿa* house of manufacture] **1** : a place for making and storing arms and military equipment **2** : STORE, REPERTOIRE ⟨an ~ of tools⟩

ar·se·nic \ˈärs-nik, ˈär-sə-nik\ *n* **1** : a solid brittle poisonous chemical element of grayish metallic luster **2** : a very poisonous oxygen compound of arsenic used in making insecticides

ar·son \ˈär-sᵊn\ *n* : the willful or malicious burning of property — **ar·son·ist** \-ist\ *n*

[1]**art** \ˈärt\ *n* **1** : skill acquired by experience or study **2** : a branch of learning; *esp* : one of the humanities **3** : an occupation requiring knowledge or skill **4** : the use of skill and imagination in the production of things of beauty; *also* : works so produced **5** : ARTFULNESS

[2]**art** *adj* : produced as an artistic effort ⟨an ~ film⟩

[3]**art** *abbr* **1** article **2** artificial **3** artillery

-art — see -ARD

ar·te·fact *chiefly Brit var of* ARTIFACT

ar·te·ri·al \är-ˈtir-ē-əl\ *adj* **1** : of or relating to an artery; *also* : relating to or being the oxygenated blood found in most arteries **2** : of, relating to, or being a route for through traffic

ar·te·ri·ole \är-ˈtir-ē-ˌōl\ *n* : any of the small terminal branches of an artery that ends in capillaries — **ar·te·ri·o·lar** \-ˌtir-ē-ˈō-lər\ *adj*

ar·te·rio·scle·ro·sis \är-ˌtir-ē-ō-sklə-ˈrō-səs\ *n* : a chronic disease in which arterial walls are abnormally thickened and hardened — **ar·te·rio·scle·rot·ic** \-ˈrä-tik\ *adj or n*

ar·tery \ˈär-tə-rē\ *n, pl* **-ter·ies** **1** : one of the tubular vessels that carry blood from the heart **2** : a main channel of transportation or communication

ar·te·sian well \är-ˈtē-zhən-\ *n* : a well from which the water flows to the surface by natural pressure; *also* : a deep well

art·ful \ˈärt-fəl\ *adj* **1** : performed with, showing, or using art or skill **2** : CRAFTY — **art·ful·ly** *adv* — **art·ful·ness** *n*

ar·thri·tis \är-ˈthrī-təs\ *n, pl* **-thri·ti·des** \-ˈthri-tə-ˌdēz\ : inflammation of the joints — **ar·thrit·ic** \-ˈthri-tik\ *adj or n*

ar·thro·pod \ˈär-thrə-ˌpäd\ *n* : any of a phylum of invertebrate animals comprising those (as insects, spiders, or crabs) with segmented bodies and jointed limbs — **arthropod** *adj*

ar·thros·co·py \är-ˈthräs-kə-pē\ *n, pl* **-pies** : visual examination of the interior of a joint (as the knee) with a special surgical instrument; *also* : surgery on a joint using arthroscopy — **ar·thro·scope** \ˈär-thrə-ˌskōp\ *n* — **ar·thro·scop·ic** \ˌär-thrə-ˈskä-pik\ *adj*

Ar·thu·ri·an \är-ˈthu̇r-ē-ən\ *adj* : of or relating to King Arthur and his court

ar·ti·choke \ˈär-tə-ˌchōk\ *n* [It dial. *articiocco,* ultim. fr. Ar *al-khurshūf*] : a tall thistlelike herb related to the daisies; *also* : its edible flower head

ar·ti·cle \ˈär-ti-kəl\ *n* [ME, fr. AF, fr. L *articulus* joint, division, dim. of *artus* joint, limb] **1 :** a distinct part of a written document **2 :** a nonfictional prose composition forming an independent part of a publication **3 :** a word (as *an, the*) used with a noun to limit or give definiteness to its application **4 :** a member of a class of things; *esp* **:** COMMODITY

ar·tic·u·lar \är-ˈti-kyə-lər\ *adj* **:** of or relating to a joint ⟨~ cartilage⟩

[1]**ar·tic·u·late** \är-ˈti-kyə-lət\ *adj* **1 :** divided into meaningful parts **:** INTELLIGIBLE **2 :** able to speak; *also* **:** expressing oneself readily and effectively ⟨an ~ orator⟩ **3 :** JOINTED — **ar·tic·u·late·ly** *adv* — **ar·tic·u·late·ness** *n*

[2]**ar·tic·u·late** \-ˌlāt\ *vb* **-lat·ed; -lat·ing 1 :** to utter distinctly **2 :** to unite by or as if by joints — **ar·tic·u·la·tion** \-ˌti-kyə-ˈlā-shən\ *n*

ar·ti·fact \ˈär-tə-ˌfakt\ *n* **:** something made or modified by humans usu. for a purpose; *esp* **:** an object remaining from another time or culture ⟨prehistoric ~*s*⟩

ar·ti·fice \ˈär-tə-fəs\ *n* **1 :** TRICK; *also* **:** TRICKERY **2 :** an ingenious device; *also* **:** INGENUITY

ar·ti·fi·cer \är-ˈti-fə-sər, ˈär-tə-fə-sər\ *n* **:** a skilled worker

ar·ti·fi·cial \ˌär-tə-ˈfi-shəl\ *adj* **1 :** produced by art rather than nature; *also* **:** made by humans to imitate nature **2 :** not genuine **:** FEIGNED — **ar·ti·fi·ci·al·i·ty** \-ˌfi-shē-ˈa-lə-tē\ *n* — **ar·ti·fi·cial·ly** *adv* — **ar·ti·fi·cial·ness** *n*

artificial insemination *n* **:** introduction of semen into the uterus or oviduct by other than natural means

artificial intelligence *n* **:** the capability of a machine and esp. a computer to imitate intelligent human behavior

artificial respiration *n* **:** the rhythmic forcing of air into and out of the lungs of a person whose breathing has stopped

ar·til·lery \är-ˈti-lə-rē\ *n, pl* **-ler·ies 1 :** crew-served mounted firearms (as guns) **2 :** a branch of the army armed with artillery — **ar·til·ler·ist** \-rist\ *n*

ar·ti·san \ˈär-tə-zən, -sən\ *n* **:** a worker who practices a trade or handicraft

art·ist \ˈär-tist\ *n* **1 :** one who practices an art; *esp* **:** one who creates objects of beauty **2 :** ARTISTE **3 :** a person who is very good at something ⟨a scam ~⟩

ar·tiste \är-ˈtēst\ *n* **:** a skilled public performer

ar·tis·tic \är-ˈtis-tik\ *adj* **:** showing taste and skill — **ar·tis·ti·cal·ly** \-ti-k(ə-)lē\ *adv*

art·ist·ry \ˈär-tə-strē\ *n* **:** artistic quality or ability

art·less \ˈärt-ləs\ *adj* **1 :** lacking art or skill **2 :** free from artificiality **:** NATURAL **3 :** free from guile **:** SINCERE — **art·less·ly** *adv* — **art·less·ness** *n*

art nou·veau \ˌär-nü-ˈvō, ˌärt-\ *n, often cap A&N* [F, lit., new art] **:** a late 19th century design style characterized by sinuous lines and leaf-shaped forms

art·work \ˈärt-ˌwərk\ *n* **:** an artistic production or work

arty \ˈär-tē\ *adj* **art·i·er; -est :** showily or pretentiously artistic — **art·i·ly** \ˈär-tə-lē\ *adv* — **art·i·ness** *n*

aru·gu·la \ə-ˈrü-gə-lə\ *n* **:** a yellowish-flowered herb related to the mustards with edible leaves used esp. in salads

ar·um \ˈa-rəm\ *n* **:** any of a family of plants (as the jack-in-the-pulpit or a skunk cabbage) with flowers in a fleshy enclosed spike

ARV *abbr* American Revised Version

[1]**-ary** *n suffix* **:** thing or person belonging to or connected with ⟨function*ary*⟩

[2]**-ary** *adj suffix* **:** of, relating to, or connected with ⟨budget*ary*⟩

Ary·an \ˈa-rē-ən, ˈer-e-; ˈär-yən\ *adj* **1 :** INDO-EUROPEAN **2 :** NORDIC — **Aryan** *n*

[1]**as** \əz, (ˌ)az\ *adv* **1 :** to the same degree or amount **:** EQUALLY ⟨~ green as grass⟩ **2 :** for instance ⟨various trees, ~ oak or pine⟩ **3 :** when considered in a specified relation ⟨my opinion ~ distinguished from his⟩

[2]**as** *conj* **1 :** in the same amount or degree in which ⟨green ~ grass⟩ **2 :** in the same way that ⟨farmed ~ his father before him had farmed⟩ **3 :** WHILE, WHEN ⟨spoke to me ~ I was leaving⟩ **4 :** THOUGH ⟨improbable ~ it seems⟩ **5 :** SINCE, BECAUSE ⟨~ I'm not wanted, I'll go⟩ **6 :** that the result is ⟨so guilty ~ to leave no doubt⟩

[3]**as** *pron* **1 :** THAT — used after *same* or *such* ⟨it's the same price ~ before⟩ **2 :** a fact that ⟨he's rich, ~ you know⟩

[4]**as** *prep* **:** in the capacity or character of ⟨this will serve ~ a substitute⟩

As *symbol* arsenic

AS *abbr* **1** American Samoa **2** Anglo-Saxon **3** associate in science

asa·fet·i·da *or* **asa·foe·ti·da** \ˌa-sə-ˈfe-tə-dē, -ˈfē-\ *n* **:** an ill-smelling plant gum formerly used in medicine

ASAP *abbr* as soon as possible

as·bes·tos \as-ˈbes-təs, az-\ *n* **:** a noncombustible grayish mineral that occurs in fibrous form and has been used as a fireproof material

as·cend \ə-ˈsend\ *vb* **1 :** to move upward **:** MOUNT, CLIMB **2 :** to succeed to **:** OCCUPY ⟨he ~*ed* the throne⟩

as·cen·dan·cy *also* **as·cen·den·cy** \ə-ˈsen-dən-sē\ *n* **:** controlling influence **:** DOMINATION

[1]**as·cen·dant** *also* **as·cen·dent** \ə-ˈsen-dənt\ *n* **:** a dominant position

[2]**ascendant** *also* **ascendent** *adj* **1 :** moving upward **2 :** DOMINANT

as·cen·sion \ə-ˈsen-chən\ *n* **:** the act or process of ascending

Ascension Day *n* **:** the Thursday 40 days after Easter observed in commemoration of Christ's ascension into heaven

as·cent \ə-ˈsent\ *n* **1 :** the act of mounting upward **:** CLIMB **2 :** degree of upward slope

as·cer·tain \ˌa-sər-ˈtān\ *vb* **:** to learn with certainty — **as·cer·tain·able** *adj*

as·cet·ic \ə-ˈse-tik\ *adj* **:** practicing self-denial esp. for spiritual reasons **:** AUSTERE — **ascetic** *n* — **as·cet·i·cism** \-ˈse-tə-ˌsi-zəm\ *n*

ASCII \ˈas-kē\ *n* [*A*merican *S*tandard *C*ode for *I*nformation *I*nterchange] : a computer code for representing alphanumeric information

ascor·bic acid \ə-ˈskȯr-bik-\ *n* : VITAMIN C

as·cot \ˈas-kət, -ˌkät\ *n* [*Ascot* Heath, racetrack near Ascot, England] : a broad neck scarf that is looped under the chin

as·cribe \ə-ˈskrīb\ *vb* **as·cribed**; **as·crib·ing** : to refer to a supposed cause, source, or author : ATTRIBUTE — **as·crib·able** *adj* — **as·crip·tion** \-ˈskrip-shən\ *n*

asep·tic \ā-ˈsep-tik\ *adj* : free or freed from disease-causing germs

asex·u·al \ā-ˈsek-shə-wəl\ *adj* **1** : lacking sex or functional sex organs **2** : occurring or formed without the production and union of two kinds of gametes ⟨~ reproduction⟩ **3** : devoid of sexuality **4** : neither male nor female — **asex·u·al·ly** *adv*

as for *prep* : with regard to : CONCERNING ⟨*as for* the others, they were late⟩

[1]**ash** \ˈash\ *n* **1** : any of a genus of trees related to the olive and having winged seeds and bark with grooves and ridges **2** : the tough elastic wood of an ash

[2]**ash** *n* **1** : the solid matter left when material is burned **2** : fine mineral particles from a volcano **3** *pl* : the remains of the dead human body after cremation or disintegration

ashamed \ə-ˈshāmd\ *adj* **1** : feeling shame **2** : restrained by anticipation of shame ⟨~ to say anything⟩ — **asham·ed·ly** \-ˈshā-məd-lē\ *adv*

ash·en \ˈa-shən\ *adj* : resembling ashes (as in color); *esp* : deadly pale

ash·lar \ˈash-lər\ *n* : hewn or squared stone; *also* : masonry of such stone

ashore \ə-ˈshȯr\ *adv* : on or to the shore

as how *conj* : THAT ⟨allowed *as how* she was glad to be here⟩

ash·ram \ˈäsh-rəm\ *n* : a religious retreat esp. of a Hindu sage

ash·tray \ˈash-ˌtrā\ *n* : a receptacle for tobacco ashes

Ash Wednesday *n* : the 1st day of Lent

ashy \ˈa-shē\ *adj* **ash·i·er**; **-est** : ASHEN

Asian \ˈā-zhən\ *adj* : of, relating to, or characteristic of the continent of Asia or its people — **Asian** *n*

Asian American *also* **Asian-Amer·i·can** \-ə-ˈmer-ə-kən\ *n* : an American of Asian descent — **Asian American** *also* **Asian-American** *adj*

[1]**aside** \ə-ˈsīd\ *adv* **1** : to or toward the side **2** : out of the way : AWAY ⟨putting ~ savings⟩

[2]**aside** *n* : an actor's words heard by the audience but supposedly not by other characters on stage

aside from *prep* **1** : BESIDES ⟨*aside from* being pretty, she's intelligent⟩ **2** : with the exception of ⟨*aside from* one D his grades are excellent⟩

as if *conj* **1** : as it would be if ⟨it's *as if* nothing had changed⟩ **2** : as one would if ⟨he acts *as if* he'd never been away⟩ **3** : THAT ⟨it seems *as if* nothing ever happens around here⟩

as·i·nine \ˈa-sə-ˌnīn\ *adj* [L *asininus,* fr. *asinus* ass] : STUPID, FOOLISH — **as·i·nin·i·ty** \ˌa-sə-ˈni-nə-tē\ *n*

ask \ˈask\ *vb* **asked** \ˈaskt\; **ask·ing** **1** : to call on for an answer ⟨she ~*ed* him about his trip⟩ **2** : UTTER ⟨~ a question⟩ **3** : to make a request of ⟨~ him for help⟩ **4** : to make a request for ⟨~ help of her⟩ **5** : to set as a price ⟨~*ed* $800 for the car⟩ **6** : INVITE

askance \ə-ˈskans\ *adv* **1** : with a side glance **2** : with distrust

askew \ə-ˈskyü\ *adv or adj* : out of line : AWRY

ASL *abbr* American Sign Language

[1]**aslant** \ə-ˈslant\ *adv or adj* : in a slanting direction

[2]**aslant** *prep* : over or across in a slanting direction

asleep \ə-ˈslēp\ *adv or adj* **1** : in or into a state of sleep **2** : DEAD **3** : NUMB **4** : INACTIVE

as long as *conj* **1** : provided that ⟨do as you like *as long as* you get home on time⟩ **2** : INASMUCH AS, SINCE ⟨*as long as* you're up, turn on the light⟩

aso·cial \(ˌ)ā-ˈsō-shəl\ *adj* : ANTISOCIAL

as of *prep* : AT, DURING, FROM, ON ⟨takes effect *as of* July 1⟩

asp \ˈasp\ *n* : a small poisonous African snake

as·par·a·gus \ə-ˈsper-ə-gəs\ *n* : a tall branching perennial herb related to the lilies; *also* : its edible young stalks

as·par·tame \ˈas-pər-ˌtām, ə-ˈspär-\ *n* : a crystalline low-calorie sweetener

ASPCA *abbr* American Society for the Prevention of Cruelty to Animals

as·pect \ˈas-ˌpekt\ *n* **1** : a position facing a particular direction **2** : APPEARANCE, LOOK **3** : PHASE

as·pen \ˈas-pən\ *n* : any of several poplars with leaves that flutter in the slightest breeze

as per \ˈaz-ˌpər\ *prep* : in accordance with ⟨*as per* instructions⟩

as·per·i·ty \a-ˈsper-ə-tē\ *n, pl* **-ties** **1** : ROUGHNESS **2** : harshness of temper

as·per·sion \ə-ˈspər-zhən\ *n* : a slanderous or defamatory remark

as·phalt \ˈas-ˌfȯlt\ *also* **as·phal·tum** \as-ˈfȯl-təm\ *n* : a dark substance found in natural beds or obtained as a residue in petroleum refining and used esp. in paving streets

asphalt jungle *n* : a big city or a specified part of a big city

as·pho·del \ˈas-fə-ˌdel\ *n* : any of several Old World herbs related to the lilies and bearing flowers in long erect spikes

as·phyx·ia \as-ˈfik-sē-ə\ *n* : a lack of oxygen or excess of carbon dioxide in the body that results in unconsciousness and often death and is usu. caused by interruption of breathing

as·phyx·i·ate \-sē-ˌāt\ *vb* **-at·ed**; **-at·ing** : SUFFOCATE — **as·phyx·i·a·tion** \-ˌfik-sē-ˈā-shən\ *n*

as·pic \ˈas-pik\ *n* [F, lit., asp] : a savory meat jelly

as·pi·rant \ˈas-pə-rənt, ə-ˈspī-rənt\ *n* : one who aspires ⟨a presidential ~⟩ ♦ ***Synonyms*** CANDIDATE, SEEKER

¹**as·pi·rate** \ˈas-pə-rət\ *n* **1** : an independent sound \h\ or a character (as the letter *h*) representing it **2** : a consonant having aspiration as its final component

²**as·pi·rate** \ˈas-pə-ˌrāt\ *vb* **-rat·ed**; **-rat·ing** : to draw, remove, or take up or into by suction

as·pi·ra·tion \ˌas-pə-ˈrā-shən\ *n* **1** : the pronunciation or addition of an aspirate; *also* : the aspirate or its symbol **2** : a drawing of something in, out, up, or through by or as if by suction **3** : a strong desire to achieve something noble; *also* : an object of this desire

as·pire \ə-ˈspī(-ə)r\ *vb* **as·pired**; **as·pir·ing** **1** : to seek to attain or accomplish a particular goal **2** : to rise aloft

as·pi·rin \ˈas-pə-rən\ *n, pl* **aspirin** *or* **aspirins** **1** : a white crystalline drug used to relieve pain and fever **2** : a tablet of aspirin

as regards *also* **as respects** *prep* : in regard to : with respect to

ass \ˈas\ *n* **1** : any of several long-eared mammals smaller than the related horses; *esp* : one of Africa ancestral to the donkey **2** *informal + impolite* : a stupid person

as·sail \ə-ˈsāl\ *vb* : to attack violently — **as·sail·able** *adj* — **as·sail·ant** *n*

as·sas·sin \ə-ˈsa-sᵊn\ *n* [ML *assassinus*, fr. Ar *ḥashshāshīn*, pl. of *ḥashshāsh* worthless person, lit., hashish-user, fr. *hashīsh* hashish] : a murderer esp. for hire or fanatical reasons

as·sas·si·nate \ə-ˈsa-sə-ˌnāt\ *vb* **-nat·ed**; **-nat·ing** : to murder by sudden or secret attack — **as·sas·si·na·tion** \-ˌsa-sə-ˈnā-shən\ *n*

as·sault \ə-ˈsȯlt\ *n* **1** : a violent attack **2** : an unlawful attempt or threat to do harm to another — **assault** *vb* — **as·sault·ive** \ə-ˈsȯl-tiv\ *adj*

assault rifle *n* : a military automatic rifle with a large-capacity magazine

¹**as·say** \ˈa-ˌsā, a-ˈsā\ *n* : analysis to determine the quantity of one or more components present in a sample (as of an ore or drug)

²**as·say** \a-ˈsā, ˈa-ˌsā\ *vb* **1** : TRY, ATTEMPT **2** : to subject (as an ore or drug) to an assay **3** : JUDGE 3

as·sem·blage \ə-ˈsem-blij, *3 & 4 also* ˌas-ˌäm-ˈbläzh\ *n* **1** : a collection of persons or things : GATHERING **2** : the act of assembling **3** : an artistic composition made from scraps, junk, and odds and ends **4** : the art of making assemblages

as·sem·ble \ə-ˈsem-bəl\ *vb* **-bled**; **-bling** **1** : to collect into one place : CONGREGATE **2** : to fit together the parts of **3** : to meet together : CONVENE

as·sem·bly \ə-ˈsem-blē\ *n, pl* **-blies** **1** : a gathering of persons : MEETING **2** *cap* : a legislative body; *esp* : the lower house of a legislature **3** : a signal for troops to assemble **4** : the fitting together of parts (as of a machine)

assembly language *n* : a computer language consisting of mnemonic codes corresponding to machine-language instructions

as·sem·bly–line \ə-ˈsem-blē-ˌlīn\ *adj* : made by or as if by an assembly line; *esp* : lacking originality or creativity

assembly line *n* : an arrangement of machines, equipment, and workers in which work passes from operation to operation in a direct line

as·sem·bly·man \ə-ˈsem-blē-mən\ *n* : a member of an assembly

as·sem·bly·wom·an \-ˌwu̇-mən\ *n* : a woman who is a member of an assembly

as·sent \ə-ˈsent\ *vb* : AGREE, CONCUR — **assent** *n*

as·sert \ə-ˈsərt\ *vb* **1** : to state positively **2** : to demonstrate the existence of ♦ ***Synonyms*** DECLARE, AFFIRM, PROTEST, AVOW, CLAIM — **as·ser·tive** \-ˈsər-tiv\ *adj* — **as·ser·tive·ly** *adv* — **as·ser·tive·ness** *n*

as·ser·tion \ə-ˈsər-shən\ *n* : a positive statement

as·sess \ə-ˈses\ *vb* **1** : to fix the rate or amount of **2** : to impose (as a tax) at a specified rate **3** : to evaluate for taxation — **as·sess·ment** *n* — **as·ses·sor** \-ˈse-sər\ *n*

as·set \ˈa-ˌset\ *n* **1** *pl* : the entire property of a person or company that may be used to pay debts **2** : ADVANTAGE, RESOURCE ⟨my wit is my chief ~⟩ **3** : an item of value owned

as·sev·er·ate \ə-ˈse-və-ˌrāt\ *vb* **-at·ed**; **-at·ing** : to assert earnestly — **as·sev·er·a·tion** \-ˌse-və-ˈrā-shən\ *n*

as·sid·u·ous \ə-ˈsi-jə-wəs\ *adj* : steadily attentive : DILIGENT — **as·si·du·i·ty** \ˌa-sə-ˈdü-ə-tē, -ˈdyü-\ *n* — **as·sid·u·ous·ly** *adv* — **as·sid·u·ous·ness** *n*

as·sign \ə-ˈsīn\ *vb* **1** : to transfer (property) to another **2** : to appoint to or as a duty ⟨~ a lesson⟩ **3** : FIX, SPECIFY ⟨~ a limit⟩ **4** : ASCRIBE ⟨~ a reason⟩ — **as·sign·able** *adj*

as·sig·na·tion \ˌa-sig-ˈnā-shən\ *n* : an appointment for a meeting; *esp* : TRYST

assigned risk *n* : a poor risk (as an accident-prone motorist) that an insurance company is forced to insure by state law

as·sign·ment \ə-ˈsīn-mənt\ *n* **1** : the act of assigning **2** : something assigned

as·sim·i·late \ə-ˈsi-mə-ˌlāt\ *vb* **-lat·ed**; **-lat·ing** **1** : to take up and absorb as nourishment; *also* : to absorb into a cultural tradition **2** : COMPREHEND **3** : to make or become similar — **as·sim·i·la·tion** \-ˌsi-mə-ˈlā-shən\ *n*

¹**as·sist** \ə-ˈsist\ *vb* : HELP, AID ⟨~*ed* the injured⟩ — **as·sis·tance** \-ˈsis-təns\ *n*

²**assist** *n* **1** : an act of assistance **2** : the action of a player who enables a teammate to make a putout (as in baseball) or score a goal (as in hockey or basketball)

as·sis·tant \ə-ˈsis-tənt\ *n* : a person who assists : HELPER

as·sis·ted living \ə-ˈsīs-təd-\ *n* : a system of housing and limited care for senior citizens who need assistance with daily activities but do not require care in a nursing home

as·sis·tive \ə-ˈsis-tiv\ *adj* **:** providing aid or assistance ⟨~ technology⟩

as·size \ə-ˈsīz\ *n* [ME *assise,* fr. AF, session, legal action, fr. *asseer, asseoir* to seat, fr. VL **assedēre,* fr. L *assidēre* to sit beside] **1 :** a judicial inquest **2** *pl* **:** the former regular sessions of superior courts in English counties

assn *abbr* association

assoc *abbr* associate; associated; association

[1]**as·so·ci·ate** \ə-ˈsō-shē-ˌāt, -sē-\ *vb* **-at·ed; -at·ing 1 :** to join in companionship or partnership **2 :** to connect in thought

[2]**as·so·ciate** \-shē-ət, -sē-; -shət\ *n* **1 :** a fellow worker **:** PARTNER **2 :** COMPANION **3** *often cap* **:** a degree conferred esp. by a junior college ⟨~ in arts⟩ — **associate** *adj*

as·so·ci·a·tion \ə-ˌsō-shē-ˈā-shən, -sē-\ *n* **1 :** the act of associating **2 :** an organization of persons **:** SOCIETY

as·so·cia·tive \ə-ˈsō-shē-ˌā-tiv, -sē-; -shə-tiv\ *adj* **1 :** of, relating to, or involved in association esp. of ideas or images **2 :** of, having, or being the property of producing the same mathematical value regardless of how an expression's elements are grouped as long as their order is the same

as·so·nance \ˈa-sə-nəns\ *n* **:** repetition of vowels esp. as an alternative to rhyme in verse — **as·so·nant** \-nənt\ *adj or n*

as soon as *conj* **:** immediately at or shortly after the time that ⟨we'll start *as soon as* they arrive⟩

as·sort \ə-ˈsȯrt\ *vb* **1 :** to distribute into like groups **:** CLASSIFY **2 :** HARMONIZE

as·sort·ed \-ˈsȯr-təd\ *adj* **:** consisting of various kinds

as·sort·ment \-ˈsȯrt-mənt\ *n* **:** a collection of assorted things or persons

asst *abbr* assistant

as·suage \ə-ˈswāj\ *vb* **as·suaged; as·suag·ing 1 :** to make (as pain or grief) less **:** EASE **2 :** SATISFY ♦ ***Synonyms*** ALLEVIATE, RELIEVE, LIGHTEN, MITIGATE

as·sume \ə-ˈsüm\ *vb* **as·sumed; as·sum·ing 1 :** to take upon oneself **2 :** to pretend to have or be **3 :** to take as granted or true though not proved

as·sump·tion \ə-ˈsəmp-shən\ *n* **1 :** the taking up of a person into heaven **2** *cap* **:** August 15 observed in commemoration of the Assumption of the Virgin Mary **3 :** a taking upon oneself **4 :** PRETENSION **5 :** SUPPOSITION

as·sur·ance \ə-ˈshu̇r-əns\ *n* **1 :** PLEDGE **2** *chiefly Brit* **:** INSURANCE **3 :** SECURITY **4 :** SELF-CONFIDENCE; *also* **:** AUDACITY

as·sure \ə-ˈshu̇r\ *vb* **as·sured; as·sur·ing 1 :** INSURE **2 :** to give confidence to **3 :** to state confidently to **4 :** to make certain the coming or attainment of

as·sured \ə-ˈshu̇rd\ *n, pl* **assured** *or* **as·sureds :** INSURED

as·ta·tine \ˈas-tə-ˌtēn\ *n* **:** an unstable radioactive chemical element

as·ter \ˈas-tər\ *n* **:** any of various mostly fall-blooming leafy-stemmed composite herbs with daisylike purple, white, pink, or yellow flower heads

as·ter·isk \ˈas-tə-ˌrisk\ *n* [L *asteriscus,* fr. Gk *asteriskos,* lit., little star, dim. of *astēr* star] **:** a character * used as a reference mark or as an indication of the omission of letters or words

astern \ə-ˈstərn\ *adv or adj* **1 :** in, at, or toward the stern **2 :** BACKWARD

as·ter·oid \ˈas-tə-ˌrȯid\ *n* **:** any of the numerous small celestial bodies found esp. between Mars and Jupiter

asth·ma \ˈaz-mə\ *n* **:** a chronic lung disorder marked by recurrent episodes of labored breathing, a feeling of tightness in the chest, and coughing — **asth·mat·ic** \az-ˈma-tik\ *adj or n*

as though *conj* **:** AS IF

astig·ma·tism \ə-ˈstig-mə-ˌti-zəm\ *n* **:** a defect in a lens or an eye causing improper focusing and blurred vision — **as·tig·mat·ic** \ˌas-tig-ˈma-tik\ *adj*

astir \ə-ˈstər\ *adj* **1 :** being in action **:** MOVING **2 :** being out of bed

as to *prep* **1 :** ABOUT, CONCERNING ⟨uncertain *as to* what went on⟩ **2 :** ACCORDING TO ⟨graded *as to* size⟩

as·ton·ish \ə-ˈstä-nish\ *vb* **:** to strike with sudden and usu. great wonder **:** AMAZE — **as·ton·ish·ing·ly** *adv* — **as·ton·ish·ment** *n*

as·tound \ə-ˈstau̇nd\ *vb* **:** to fill with bewilderment or wonder — **as·tound·ing·ly** *adv*

[1]**astrad·dle** \ə-ˈstra-dᵊl\ *adv* **:** on or above and extending onto both sides

[2]**astraddle** *prep* **:** ASTRIDE

as·tra·khan \ˈas-trə-kən, -ˌkan\ *n, often cap* **1 :** karakul of Russian origin **2 :** a cloth with a usu. wool, curled, and looped pile resembling karakul

as·tral \ˈas-trəl\ *adj* **:** of, relating to, or coming from the stars

astray \ə-ˈstrā\ *adv or adj* **1 :** off the right path or route **2 :** into error

[1]**astride** \ə-ˈstrīd\ *adv* **1 :** with one leg on each side **2 :** with legs apart

[2]**astride** *prep* **:** with one leg on each side of

[1]**as·trin·gent** \ə-ˈstrin-jənt\ *adj* **:** able or tending to shrink body tissues — **as·trin·gen·cy** \-jən-sē\ *n*

[2]**astringent** *n* **:** an astringent agent or substance

astrol *abbr* astrologer; astrology

as·tro·labe \ˈas-trə-ˌlāb\ *n* **:** an instrument formerly used for observing the positions of celestial bodies

as·trol·o·gy \ə-ˈsträ-lə-jē\ *n* **:** divination based on the supposed influence of the stars upon human events — **as·trol·o·ger** \-jər\ *n* — **as·tro·log·i·cal** \ˌas-trə-ˈlä-ji-kəl\ *adj* — **as·tro·log·i·cal·ly** \-kə-lē\ *adv*

astron *abbr* astronomer; astronomy

as·tro·naut \ˈas-trə-ˌnȯt\ *n* **:** a traveler in a spacecraft

as·tro·nau·tics \as-trə-ˈnȯ-tiks\ *n* **:** the science of the construction and operation of spacecraft — **as·tro·nau·tic** \-tik\ *or* **as·tro·nau·ti·cal** \-ti-kəl\ *adj*

as·tro·nom·i·cal \ˌas-trə-ˈnä-mi-kəl\ *also* **as·tro·nom·ic** \-mik\ *adj* **1** : of or relating to astronomy **2** : extremely large ⟨an ~ amount of money⟩

astronomical unit *n* : a unit of length used in astronomy equal to the mean distance of the earth from the sun or about 93 million miles (150 million kilometers)

as·tron·o·my \ə-ˈsträ-nə-mē\ *n, pl* **-mies** : the science of objects and matter beyond the earth's atmosphere — **as·tron·o·mer** \-mər\ *n*

as·tro·phys·ics \ˌas-trə-ˈfi-ziks\ *n* : astronomy dealing esp. with the physical properties and dynamic processes of celestial objects — **as·tro·phys·i·cal** \-zi-kəl\ *adj* — **as·tro·phys·i·cist** \-ˈfi-zə-sist\ *n*

as·tute \ə-ˈstüt, -ˈstyüt, a-\ *adj* [L *astutus,* fr. *astus* craft] : shrewdly discerning; *also* : WILY ⟨an ~ lawyer⟩ — **as·tute·ly** *adv* — **as·tute·ness** *n*

asun·der \ə-ˈsən-dər\ *adv or adj* **1** : into separate pieces ⟨torn ~⟩ **2** : separated in position from each other

ASV *abbr* American Standard Version

[1]**as well as** *conj* : and in addition : and moreover ⟨brave *as well as* loyal⟩

[2]**as well as** *prep* : in addition to : BESIDES ⟨the coach, *as well as* the team, is ready⟩

asy·lum \ə-ˈsī-ləm\ *n* [ME, fr. L, fr. Gk *asylon,* neut. of *asylos* inviolable, fr. *a-* not + *sylon* right of seizure] **1** : a place of refuge **2** : protection given to esp. political fugitives **3** : an institution for the care of the needy or sick and esp. of the mentally ill

asym·met·ri·cal \ˌā-sə-ˈme-tri-kəl\ *or* **asym·met·ric** \-trik\ *adj* : not symmetrical — **asym·met·ri·cal·ly** \-tri-kə-lē\ *adv* — **asym·me·try** \(ˌ)ā-ˈsi-mə-trē\ *n*

asymp·tom·at·ic \ˌā-ˌsimp-tə-ˈma-tik\ *adj* : presenting no symptoms of disease ⟨an ~ infection⟩

as·ymp·tote \ˈa-səmp-ˌtōt\ *n* : a straight line that is approached ever more closely by a curve that never coincides with it — **as·ymp·tot·ic** \ˌa-səmp-ˈtä-tik\ *adj* — **as·ymp·tot·i·cal·ly** \-ti-k(ə-)lē\ *adv*

[1]**at** \ət, (ˈ)at\ *prep* **1** — used to indicate a point in time or space ⟨be here ~ 3 o'clock⟩ **2** — used to indicate a goal ⟨swung ~ the ball⟩ **3** — used to indicate position or condition ⟨~ rest⟩ **4** — used to indicate means, cause, or manner ⟨sold ~ auction⟩

[2]**at** *also* **att** \ˈät\ *n, pl* **at** *also* **att** — see *kip* at MONEY table

At *symbol* astatine

AT *abbr* automatic transmission

at all *adv* : in any way : in any circumstances ⟨not *at all* likely⟩

at·a·vism \ˈa-tə-ˌvi-zəm\ *n* : appearance in an individual of a character typical of an ancestral form; *also* : such an individual or character — **at·a·vis·tic** \ˌa-tə-ˈvis-tik\ *adj*

atax·ia \ə-ˈtak-sē-ə\ *n* : an inability to coordinate muscular movements

ate *past of* EAT

[1]**-ate** *n suffix* **1** : one acted upon (in a specified way) ⟨distill*ate*⟩ **2** : chemical compound or complex derived from a (specified) compound or element ⟨ace*tate*⟩

[2]**-ate** *n suffix* **1** : office : function : rank : group of persons holding a (specified) office or rank ⟨episcop*ate*⟩ **2** : state : dominion : jurisdiction ⟨emir*ate*⟩

[3]**-ate** *adj suffix* **1** : acted on (in a specified way) : being in a (specified) state ⟨temper*ate*⟩ ⟨degener*ate*⟩ **2** : marked by having ⟨vertebr*ate*⟩

[4]**-ate** *vb suffix* : cause to be modified or affected by ⟨pollin*ate*⟩ : cause to become ⟨activ*ate*⟩ : furnish with ⟨aer*ate*⟩

ate·lier \ˌa-tᵊl-ˈyā\ *n* **1** : an artist's or designer's studio **2** : WORKSHOP

athe·ist \ˈā-thē-ist\ *n* : one who denies the existence of God — **athe·ism** \-ˌi-zəm\ *n* — **athe·is·tic** \ˌā-thē-ˈis-tik\ *adj*

ath·e·nae·um *or* **ath·e·ne·um** \ˌa-thə-ˈnē-əm\ *n* : LIBRARY 1

ath·ero·scle·ro·sis \ˌa-thə-rō-sklə-ˈrō-səs\ *n* : arteriosclerosis characterized by the deposition of fatty substances in and the hardening of the inner layer of the arteries — **ath·ero·scle·rot·ic** \-ˈrä-tik\ *adj*

athirst \ə-ˈthərst\ *adj* **1** *archaic* : THIRSTY **2** : EAGER, LONGING

ath·lei·sure \ath-ˈlē-zhər, -ˈle-, -ˈlā-\ *n* : casual clothing designed to be worn both for exercising and for general use

ath·lete \ˈath-ˌlēt\ *n* [ME, fr. L *athleta,* fr. Gk *athlētēs,* fr. *athlein* to contend for a prize, fr. *athlon* prize, contest] : a person who is trained to compete in athletics

athlete's foot *n* : ringworm of the feet

ath·let·ic \ath-ˈle-tik\ *adj* **1** : of or relating to athletes or athletics **2** : VIGOROUS, ACTIVE **3** : STURDY, MUSCULAR — **ath·let·i·cal·ly** \-ti-kə-lē\ *adv* — **ath·let·i·cism** \-tə-ˌsi-zəm\ *n*

ath·let·ics \ath-ˈle-tiks\ *n sing or pl* : exercises and games requiring physical skill, strength, and endurance

athletic supporter *n* : an elastic pouch used to support the male genitals and worn esp. during athletic activity

[1]**athwart** \ə-ˈthwȯrt\ *prep* **1** : ACROSS **2** : in opposition to

[2]**athwart** *adv* : obliquely across

atilt \ə-ˈtilt\ *adv or adj* **1** : in a tilted position **2** : with lance in hand

-ation *n suffix* : action or process ⟨flirt*ation*⟩ : something connected with an action or process ⟨discolor*ation*⟩

Atl *abbr* Atlantic

at–large \ˈat-ˈlärj\ *adj* : of or being a political representative who is elected to serve an entire area rather than one of its subdivisions

at·las \ˈat-ləs\ *n* : a book of maps

atm *abbr* atmosphere; atmospheric

ATM *n* : a computerized electronic machine that performs basic banking functions

at·mo·sphere \ˈat-mə-ˌsfir\ *n* **1** : the gaseous envelope of a celestial body; *esp* : the mass of air surrounding the earth **2** : a surrounding influence **3** : a unit of pressure equal to the pressure of air at sea level or about 14.7 pounds per square inch (10 newtons per square centimeter) **4** : an intriguing or singular tone, effect, or appeal — **at·mo·spher·ic** \ˌat-mə-ˈsfir-ik, -ˈsfer-\ *adj* — **at·mo·spher·i·cal·ly** \-i-k(ə-)lē\ *adv*

at·mo·sphe·rics \ˌat-mə-ˈsfir-iks, -ˈsfer-\ *n pl* : radio noise from atmospheric electrical phenomena

atoll \ˈa-ˌtȯl, -ˌtäl, ˈā-\ *n* : a coral island consisting of a reef surrounding a lagoon

at·om \ˈa-təm\ *n* [ME, fr. L *atomus,* fr. Gk *atomos,* fr. *atomos* indivisible, fr. *a-* not + *temnein* to cut] **1** : a tiny particle : BIT **2** : the smallest particle of a chemical element that can exist alone or in combination

atom·ic \ə-ˈtä-mik\ *adj* **1** : of or relating to atoms; *also* : NUCLEAR 2 ⟨~ energy⟩ **2** : extremely small

atomic bomb *n* : a very destructive bomb utilizing the energy released by splitting the atom

atomic clock *n* : a very precise clock regulated by the natural vibration of atoms or molecules (as of cesium)

atomic number *n* : the number of protons in the nucleus of an element

atomic weight *n* : the mass of one atom of an element

at·om·ise, at·om·is·er *Brit var of* ATOMIZE, ATOMIZER

at·om·ize \ˈa-tə-ˌmīz\ *vb* **-ized**; **-iz·ing** : to reduce to minute particles

at·om·iz·er \ˈa-tə-ˌmī-zər\ *n* : a device for dispensing a liquid (as perfume) as a mist

atom smasher *n* : ACCELERATOR 3

aton·al \ā-ˈtō-nᵊl\ *adj* : marked by avoidance of traditional musical tonality — **ato·nal·i·ty** \ˌā-tō-ˈna-lə-tē\ *n* — **aton·al·ly** \ā-ˈtō-nə-lē\ *adv*

atone \ə-ˈtōn\ *vb* **atoned**; **aton·ing** **1** : to make amends **2** : EXPIATE ⟨~ for sins⟩

atone·ment \ə-ˈtōn-mənt\ *n* **1** : the reconciliation of God and mankind through the death of Jesus Christ **2** : reparation for an offense : SATISFACTION

¹atop \ə-ˈtäp\ *adv or adj* : on, to, or at the top

²atop *prep* : on top of

ATP \ˌā-ˌtē-ˈpē\ *n* [*a*denosine *tri*phosphate] : a compound that occurs widely in living tissue and supplies energy for many cellular processes by undergoing enzymatic hydrolysis

atri·um \ˈā-trē-əm\ *n, pl* **atria** \-trē-ə\ *also* **atri·ums** **1** : the central room of a Roman house; *also* : an open patio or court in the center of a building (as a hotel) **2** : an anatomical cavity or passage; *esp* : one of the chambers of the heart that receives blood from the veins — **atri·al** \-əl\ *adj*

atro·cious \ə-ˈtrō-shəs\ *adj* **1** : savagely brutal, cruel, or wicked **2** : very bad : ABOMINABLE — **atro·cious·ly** *adv* — **atro·cious·ness** *n*

atroc·i·ty \ə-ˈträ-sə-tē\ *n, pl* **-ties** **1** : ATROCIOUSNESS **2** : an atrocious act or object ⟨the *atrocities* of war⟩

at·ro·phy \ˈa-trə-fē\ *n, pl* **-phies** : decrease in size or wasting away of a bodily part or tissue — **atrophy** *vb*

at·ro·pine \ˈa-trə-ˌpēn\ *n* : a drug from belladonna and related plants used esp. to relieve spasms and to dilate the pupil of the eye

¹att *var of* AT

²att *abbr* **1** attached **2** attention **3** attorney

at·tach \ə-ˈtach\ *vb* **1** : to seize legally in order to force payment of a debt **2** : to bind by personal ties **3** : FASTEN, CONNECT **4** : to be fastened or connected

at·ta·ché \ˌa-tə-ˈshā, ˌa-ˌta-, ə-ˌta-\ *n* [F] : a technical expert on the diplomatic staff of an ambassador

at·ta·ché case \ə-ˈta-shā-, ˌa-tə-ˈshā-\ *n* : a small thin suitcase used esp. for carrying papers; *also* : BRIEFCASE

at·tach·ment \ə-ˈtach-mənt\ *n* **1** : legal seizure of property **2** : connection by ties of affection and regard **3** : a device attached to a machine or implement **4** : a connection by which one thing is attached to another **5** : a document or image included with an electronic message

¹at·tack \ə-ˈtak\ *vb* **1** : to set upon with force or words : ASSAIL, ASSAULT **2** : to set to work on — **at·tack·er** *n*

²attack *n* **1** : an offensive action **2** : a fit of sickness **3** : a scoring action in a game

³attack *adj* : designed, planned, or used for a military attack

at·tain \ə-ˈtān\ *vb* **1** : ACHIEVE, ACCOMPLISH **2** : to arrive at : REACH — **at·tain·abil·i·ty** \-ˌtā-nə-ˈbi-lə-tē\ *n* — **at·tain·able** *adj*

at·tain·der \ə-ˈtān-dər\ *n* : extinction of the civil rights of a person upon sentence of death or outlawry

at·tain·ment \ə-ˈtān-mənt\ *n* **1** : the act of attaining **2** : ACCOMPLISHMENT

at·tar \ˈa-tər\ *n* [Pers *ʿaṭir* perfumed, fr. Ar, fr. *ʿiṭr* perfume] : a fragrant floral oil

at·tempt \ə-ˈtempt\ *vb* : to make an effort toward : TRY — **attempt** *n*

at·tend \ə-ˈtend\ *vb* **1** : to look after : TEND **2** : to be present with **3** : to be present at **4** : to apply oneself **5** : to pay attention **6** : to direct one's attention

at·ten·dance \ə-ˈten-dəns\ *n* **1** : the act or fact of attending **2** : the number of persons present; *also* : the number of times a person attends

¹at·ten·dant \ə-ˈten-dənt\ *n* : one that attends another to render a service

²attendant *adj* : ACCOMPANYING ⟨~ circumstances⟩

at·ten·tion \ə-ˈten-chən\ *n* **1** : the act or state of applying the mind to an object **2** : CONSIDERATION **3** : an act of courtesy **4** : a position of readiness assumed on command by a soldier — **at·ten·tive** \-ˈten-tiv\ *adj* — **at·ten·tive·ly** *adv* — **at·ten·tive·ness** *n*

attention deficit disorder *n* : a behavioral syndrome esp. of children that is marked by hyperactivity, impulsive behavior, and inattention

attention–deficit/hyperactivity disorder *n* : ATTENTION DEFICIT DISORDER

attention span *n* : the length of time during which one is able to concentrate or remain interested

at·ten·u·ate \ə-ˈten-yə-ˌwāt\ *vb* **-at·ed; -at·ing 1** : to make or become thin **2** : WEAKEN ⟨sorrows ~ with time⟩ — **attenuate** \-wət\ *adj* — **at·ten·u·a·tion** \-ˌten-yə-ˈwā-shən\ *n*

at·test \ə-ˈtest\ *vb* **1** : to certify as genuine by signing as a witness **2** : MANIFEST ⟨her record ~*s* her integrity⟩ **3** : TESTIFY ⟨~ to a belief⟩ — **at·tes·ta·tion** \ˌa-ˌtes-ˈtā-shən\ *n*

at·tic \ˈa-tik\ *n* : the space or room in a building immediately below the roof

[1]**at·tire** \ə-ˈtī(-ə)r\ *vb* **at·tired; at·tir·ing** : to put garments on : DRESS, ARRAY

[2]**attire** *n* : DRESS, CLOTHES

at·ti·tude \ˈa-tə-ˌtüd, -ˌtyüd\ *n* **1** : POSTURE **2** : a mental position or feeling with regard to a fact or state **3** : the position of something in relation to something else **4** : a negative or hostile state of mind **5** : a cocky or arrogant manner

at·ti·tu·di·nise *Brit var of* ATTITUDINIZE

at·ti·tu·di·nize \ˌa-tə-ˈtü-də-ˌnīz, -ˈtyü-\ *vb* **-nized; -niz·ing** : to assume an affected mental attitude : POSE

attn *abbr* attention

at·tor·ney \ə-ˈtər-nē\ *n, pl* **-neys** : a legal agent qualified to act for persons in legal proceedings

attorney general *n, pl* **attorneys general** *or* **attorney generals** : the chief legal representative and adviser of a nation or state

at·tract \ə-ˈtrakt\ *vb* **1** : to draw to or toward oneself : cause to approach **2** : to draw by emotional or aesthetic appeal ♦ ***Synonyms*** CHARM, FASCINATE, ALLURE, CAPTIVATE, ENCHANT — **at·trac·tive** \-ˈtrak-tiv\ *adj* — **at·trac·tive·ly** *adv* — **at·trac·tive·ness** *n*

at·trac·tant \ə-ˈtrak-tənt\ *n* : a substance (as a pheromone) that attracts specific animals (as insects)

at·trac·tion \ə-ˈtrak-shən\ *n* **1** : the act or power of attracting; *esp* : personal charm **2** : an attractive quality, object, or feature **3** : a force tending to draw particles together

attrib *abbr* attributive

[1]**at·tri·bute** \ˈa-trə-ˌbyüt\ *n* **1** : an inherent characteristic **2** : a word ascribing a quality; *esp* : ADJECTIVE

[2]**at·trib·ute** \ə-ˈtri-ˌbyüt, -byət\ *vb* **-ut·ed; -ut·ing 1** : to explain as to cause or origin ⟨~ the illness to fatigue⟩ **2** : to regard as a characteristic ♦ ***Synonyms*** ASCRIBE, CREDIT, CHARGE, IMPUTE — **at·trib·ut·able** *adj* — **at·tri·bu·tion** \ˌa-trə-ˈbyü-shən\ *n*

at·trib·u·tive \ə-ˈtrib-yə-tiv\ *adj* : joined directly to a modified noun without a linking verb ⟨*red* in *red hair* is an ~ adjective⟩ — **attributive** *n* — **at·trib·u·tive·ly** *adv*

at·tri·tion \ə-ˈtri-shən\ *n* **1** : the act of wearing away by or as if by rubbing **2** : a reduction in numbers as a result of resignation, retirement, or death

at·tune \ə-ˈtün, -ˈtyün\ *vb* : to bring into harmony : TUNE — **at·tune·ment** *n*

atty *abbr* attorney

ATV \ˌā-ˌtē-ˈvē\ *n* : ALL-TERRAIN VEHICLE

atyp·i·cal \ā-ˈti-pi-kəl\ *adj* : not typical : IRREGULAR — **atyp·i·cal·ly** \-k(ə-)lē\ *adv*

Au *symbol* [L *aurum*] gold

au·burn \ˈȯ-bərn\ *adj* : reddish brown — **auburn** *n*

au cou·rant \ˌō-kü-ˈrä^n\ *adj* [F, lit., in the current] : UP-TO-DATE, STYLISH

[1]**auc·tion** \ˈȯk-shən\ *n* [L *auction-, auctio,* fr. *augēre* to increase] : public sale of property to the highest bidder

[2]**auction** *vb* **auc·tioned; auc·tion·ing** \-shə-niŋ\ : to sell at auction

auc·tion·eer \ˌȯk-shə-ˈnir\ *n* : an agent who conducts an auction

aud *abbr* audit; auditor

au·da·cious \ȯ-ˈdā-shəs\ *adj* **1** : DARING, BOLD **2** : INSOLENT — **au·da·cious·ly** *adv* — **au·da·cious·ness** *n* — **au·dac·i·ty** \-ˈda-sə-tē\ *n*

[1]**au·di·ble** \ˈȯ-də-bəl\ *adj* : capable of being heard — **au·di·bil·i·ty** \ˌȯ-də-ˈbi-lə-tē\ *n* — **au·di·bly** \ˈȯ-də-blē\ *adv*

[2]**audible** *n* : a play called at the line of scrimmage — **audible** *vb*

au·di·ence \ˈȯ-dē-əns\ *n* **1** : a formal interview **2** : an opportunity of being heard **3** : an assembly of listeners or spectators

[1]**au·dio** \ˈȯ-dē-ˌō\ *adj* **1** : of or relating to frequencies (as of radio waves) corresponding to those of audible sound waves **2** : of or relating to sound or its reproduction and esp. high-fidelity reproduction **3** : relating to or used in the transmission or reception of sound

[2]**audio** *n* **1** : the transmission, reception, or reproduction of sound **2** : the section of television or motion-picture equipment that deals with sound

au·dio·book \ˈȯ-dē-ō-bu̇k\ *n* : a recording of a book or magazine being read aloud

au·di·ol·o·gy \ˌȯ-dē-ˈä-lə-jē\ *n* : a branch of science dealing with hearing and esp. with the treatment of individuals having trouble with hearing — **au·di·o·log·i·cal** \-ə-ˈlä-ji-kəl\ *adj* — **au·di·ol·o·gist** \-ˈä-lə-jist\ *n*

au·dio·phile \ˈȯ-dē-ō-ˌfī(-ə)l\ *n* : one who is enthusiastic about high-fidelity sound reproduction

au·dio·tape \ˈȯ-dē-ō-ˌtāp\ *n* : a tape recording of sound

au·dio·vi·su·al \ˌȯ-dē-ō-ˈvi-zhə-wəl\ *adj* : of, relating to, or making use of both hearing and sight

au·dio·vi·su·als \-wəlz\ *n pl* : audiovisual teaching materials (as videotapes)

[1]**au·dit** \ˈȯ-dət\ *n* : a formal examination and verification of financial accounts

[2]**audit** *vb* **1** : to perform an audit on or for **2** : to attend (a course) without expecting formal credit

[1]**au·di·tion** \ȯ-ˈdi-shən\ *n* **1** : HEARING **2** : a trial performance to appraise an entertainer's merits

[2]**audition** *vb* **-tioned; -tion·ing** \-ˈdi-shə-

niŋ\ : to give an audition to; *also* : to give a trial performance

au·di·tor \ˈȯ-də-tər\ *n* **1** : LISTENER **2** : a person who audits

au·di·to·ri·um \ˌȯ-də-ˈtȯr-ē-əm\ *n, pl* **-ri·ums** *or* **-ria** \-rē-ə\ **1** : the part of a public building where an audience sits **2** : a hall or building used for public gatherings

au·di·to·ry \ˈȯ-də-ˌtȯr-ē\ *adj* : of or relating to hearing or to the sense or organs of hearing ⟨~ stimuli⟩

auditory tube *n* : EUSTACHIAN TUBE

auf Wie·der·seh·en \au̇f-ˈvē-dər-ˌzān\ *interj* [G] — used to express farewell

Aug *abbr* August

au·ger \ˈȯ-gər\ *n* : a tool for boring

aught \ˈȯt, ˈät\ *n* : ZERO, CIPHER

aug·ment \ȯg-ˈment\ *vb* : ENLARGE, INCREASE — **aug·men·ta·tion** \ˌȯg-mən-ˈtā-shən\ *n*

au gra·tin \ō-ˈgra-tᵊn, ȯ-, -ˈgrä-\ *adj* [F, lit., with the burnt scrapings from the pan] : covered with bread crumbs or grated cheese and browned

¹**au·gur** \ˈȯ-gər\ *n* : DIVINER, SOOTHSAYER

²**augur** *vb* **1** : to foretell esp. from omens **2** : to give promise of ⟨the decision doesn't ~ well⟩

au·gu·ry \ˈȯ-gyə-rē, -gə-\ *n, pl* **-ries** **1** : divination from omens **2** : OMEN, PORTENT

au·gust \ȯ-ˈgəst\ *adj* : marked by majestic dignity or grandeur — **au·gust·ly** *adv* — **au·gust·ness** *n*

Au·gust \ˈȯ-gəst\ *n* [ME, fr. OE, fr. L *Augustus,* fr. *Augustus* Caesar] : the 8th month of the year

au jus \ō-ˈzhü, -ˈzhüs, -ˈjüs; ō-zhue\ *adj* [F] : served in the juice obtained from roasting

auk \ˈȯk\ *n* : any of several stocky black-and-white diving seabirds that breed in colder parts of the northern hemisphere

auld \ˈȯl, ˈȯld, ˈäl, ˈäld\ *adj, chiefly Scot* : OLD

aunt \ˈant, ˈänt\ *n* **1** : the sister of one's father or mother **2** : the wife of one's uncle or aunt

aunt·ie \ˈan-tē, ˈän-\ *n* : AUNT

au pair \ˈō-ˈper\ *n* [F, on even terms] : a usu. young foreign person who does domestic work for a family in return for room and board and to learn the family's language

au·ra \ˈȯr-ə\ *n* **1** : a distinctive atmosphere surrounding a given source **2** : a luminous radiation

au·ral \ˈȯr-əl\ *adj* : of or relating to the ear or to the sense of hearing

aurar *pl of* EYRIR

au·re·ole \ˈȯr-ē-ˌōl\ *or* **au·re·o·la** \ȯ-ˈrē-ə-lə\ *n* : HALO, NIMBUS

au re·voir \ˌō-rə-ˈvwär\ *n* [F, lit., till seeing again] : GOOD-BYE

au·ri·cle \ˈȯr-i-kəl\ *n* : an atrium of the heart

au·ric·u·lar \ȯ-ˈri-kyə-lər\ *adj* **1** : told privately ⟨~ confession⟩ **2** : known or recognized by the sense of hearing

au·ro·ra \ə-ˈrȯr-ə\ *n, pl* **auroras** *or* **au·ro·rae** \-(ˌ)ē\ : a luminous phenomenon of streamers or arches of light appearing in the upper atmosphere esp. of a planet's polar regions — **au·ro·ral** \-əl\ *adj*

aurora aus·tra·lis \-ȯ-ˈstrā-ləs\ *n* : an aurora that occurs in earth's southern hemisphere

aurora bo·re·al·is \-ˌbȯr-ē-ˈa-ləs\ *n* : an aurora that occurs in earth's northern hemisphere

AUS *abbr* Army of the United States

aus·pice \ˈȯ-spəs\ *n, pl* **aus·pic·es** \-spə-səz, -ˌsēz\ [L *auspicium,* fr. *auspic-, auspex* diviner by birds, fr. *avis* bird + *specere* to look, look at] **1** : observation of birds by an augur **2** *pl* : kindly patronage and protection **3** : a prophetic sign or omen

aus·pi·cious \ȯ-ˈspi-shəs\ *adj* **1** : promising success : PROPITIOUS **2** : FORTUNATE, PROSPEROUS ⟨an ~ year⟩ — **aus·pi·cious·ly** *adv* — **aus·pi·cious·ness** *n*

aus·tere \ȯ-ˈstir\ *adj* **1** : STERN, SEVERE, STRICT ⟨~ Puritans⟩ **2** : markedly simple ⟨an ~ lifestyle⟩ **3** : UNADORNED ⟨~ furnishings⟩ — **aus·tere·ly** *adv* — **aus·ter·i·ty** \-ˈster-ə-tē\ *n*

aus·tral \ˈȯs-trəl\ *adj* : SOUTHERN

Aus·tro·ne·sian \ˌȯs-trə-ˈnē-zhən\ *adj* : of, relating to, or constituting a family of languages spoken in the area extending from Madagascar eastward through the Malay Peninsula to Hawaii and Easter Island

auth *abbr* **1** authentic **2** author **3** authorized

au·then·tic \ə-ˈthen-tik, ȯ-\ *adj* : GENUINE, REAL — **au·then·ti·cal·ly** \-ti-k(ə-)lē\ *adv* — **au·then·tic·i·ty** \ˌȯ-ˌthen-ˈti-sə-tē\ *n*

au·then·ti·cate \ə-ˈthen-ti-ˌkāt, ȯ-\ *vb* **-cat·ed**; **-cat·ing** : to prove genuine — **au·then·ti·ca·tion** \-ˌthen-ti-ˈkā-shən\ *n*

au·thor \ˈȯ-thər\ *n* [ME *auctour,* fr. AF *auctor, autor,* fr. L *auctor* originator, author, fr. *augēre* to increase] **1** : one that originates or creates **2** : one that writes or composes a literary work

au·thor·ess \ˈȯ-thə-rəs\ *n* : a woman or girl who is an author

au·tho·ri·sa·tion, au·tho·rise *Brit var of* AUTHORIZATION, AUTHORIZE

au·thor·i·tar·i·an \ȯ-ˌthär-ə-ˈter-ē-ən, ə-, -ˌthȯr-\ *adj* **1** : characterized by or favoring the principle of blind obedience to authority **2** : characterized by or favoring concentration of political power in an authority not responsible to the people — **authoritarian** *n*

au·thor·i·ta·tive \ə-ˈthär-ə-ˌtā-tiv, ȯ-, -ˈthȯr-\ *adj* : supported by, proceeding from, or being an authority — **au·thor·i·ta·tive·ly** *adv* — **au·thor·i·ta·tive·ness** *n*

au·thor·i·ty \ə-ˈthär-ə-tē, ȯ-, -ˈthȯr-\ *n, pl* **-ties** **1** : a citation used in support of a statement or in defense of an action; *also* : the source of such a citation **2** : one appealed to as an expert **3** : power to influence thought or behavior **4** : freedom granted : RIGHT **5** : persons in command; *esp* : GOVERNMENT **6** : convincing force

au·tho·rize \'ȯ-thə-ˌrīz\ *vb* **-rized**; **-riz·ing** **1** : SANCTION ⟨custom *authorized* by time⟩ **2** : to give legal power to — **au·tho·ri·za·tion** \ˌȯ-thə-rə-'zā-shən\ *n*

au·thor·ship \'ȯ-thər-ˌship\ *n* **1** : the state of being an author **2** : the source of a piece of writing, music, or art

au·tism \'ȯ-ˌti-zəm\ *n* : a disorder that appears by age three and is characterized esp. by impaired ability to communicate with others and form normal social relationships and by repetitive patterns of behavior — **au·tis·tic** \ȯ-'tis-tik\ *adj or n*

[1]**au·to** \'ȯ-tō\ *n, pl* **autos** : AUTOMOBILE

[2]**auto** *abbr* automatic

au·to·bahn \'ȯ-tō-ˌbän, 'au̇-\ *n* : a German, Swiss, or Austrian expressway

au·to·bi·og·ra·phy \ˌȯ-tə-bī-'ä-grə-fē\ *n* : the biography of a person narrated by that person — **au·to·bi·og·ra·pher** \-fər\ *n* — **au·to·bi·o·graph·i·cal** \-ˌbī-ə-'gra-fi-kəl\ *adj* — **au·to·bi·o·graph·i·cal·ly** \-k(ə-)lē\ *adv*

au·toch·tho·nous \ȯ-'täk-thə-nəs\ *adj* : INDIGENOUS, NATIVE ⟨an ~ people⟩

au·to·clave \'ȯ-tō-ˌklāv\ *n* : an apparatus (as for sterilizing) using superheated high-pressure steam

au·to–com·plete \'ȯ-tō-kəm-'plēt\ *n* : a software feature that attempts to predict and automatically complete a word or phrase being entered by a user — **auto-complete** *vb*

au·toc·ra·cy \ȯ-'tä-krə-sē\ *n, pl* **-cies** : government by one person having unlimited power — **au·to·crat** \'ȯ-tə-ˌkrat\ *n* — **au·to·crat·ic** \ˌȯ-tə-'kra-tik\ *adj* — **au·to·crat·i·cal·ly** \-ti-k(ə-)lē\ *adv*

au·to·ex·po·sure \ˌȯ-tō-ik-'spō-zhər\ *n* : a camera system that automatically adjusts the exposure according to ambient light

au·to·fill \'ȯ-tō-ˌfil\ *n* a software feature that automatically enters previously stored information into a data field — **autofill** *vb*

[1]**au·to·graph** \'ȯ-tə-ˌgraf\ *n* **1** : an original manuscript **2** : a person's signature written by hand

[2]**autograph** *vb* : to write one's signature on

au·to·im·mune \ˌȯ-tō-i-'myün\ *adj* : of, relating to, or caused by antibodies or lymphocytes that attack molecules, cells, or tissues of the organism producing them ⟨~ diseases⟩ — **au·to·im·mu·ni·ty** \-i-'myü-nə-tē\ *n*

au·to·mate \'ȯ-tə-ˌmāt\ *vb* **-mat·ed**; **-mat·ing** **1** : to operate automatically using mechanical or electronic devices **2** : to convert to automatic operation — **au·to·ma·tion** \ȯ-tə-'mā-shən\ *n*

automated teller machine *n* : ATM

[1]**au·to·mat·ic** \ˌȯ-tə-'ma-tik\ *adj* **1** : INVOLUNTARY **2** : made so that certain parts act in a desired manner at the proper time : SELF-ACTING ⟨an ~ transmission⟩ — **au·to·mat·i·cal·ly** \-ti-k(ə-)lē\ *adv*

[2]**automatic** *n* **1** : an automatic firearm **2** : an automobile with an automatic transmission

automatic teller *n* : ATM

automatic teller machine *n* : ATM

au·tom·a·ton \ȯ-'tä-mə-tən, -ˌtän\ *n, pl* **-atons** *or* **-a·ta** \-ə-tə, -ə-ˌtä\ **1** : an automatic machine; *esp* : ROBOT **2** : an individual who acts mechanically

au·to·mo·bile \'ȯ-tə-mō-ˌbēl, ˌȯ-tə-mə-'bēl\ *n* : a usu. 4-wheeled automotive vehicle for conveying passengers

au·to·mo·tive \ˌȯ-tə-'mō-tiv\ *adj* **1** : of or relating to automobiles, trucks, or buses **2** : SELF-PROPELLED

au·to·nom·ic nervous system \ˌȯ-tə-'nä-mik-\ *n* : a part of the vertebrate nervous system that governs involuntary actions and that consists of the sympathetic nervous system and the parasympathetic nervous system

au·ton·o·mous \ȯ-'tä-nə-məs\ *adj* : having the right or power of self-government — **au·ton·o·mous·ly** *adv* — **au·ton·o·my** \-mē\ *n*

au·top·sy \'ȯ-ˌtäp-sē, 'ȯ-təp-\ *n, pl* **-sies** [Gk *autopsia* act of seeing with one's own eyes, fr. *autos* self + *opsis* sight] : examination of a dead body usu. with dissection sufficient to determine the cause of death or extent of change produced by disease — **autopsy** *vb*

au·tumn \'ȯ-təm\ *n* : the season between summer and winter — **au·tum·nal** \ȯ-'təm-nəl\ *adj*

aux *abbr* auxiliary

[1]**aux·il·ia·ry** \ȯg-'zil-yə-rē, -'zi-lə-rē\ *adj* **1** : providing help **2** : functioning in a subsidiary capacity **3** : accompanying a verb form to express person, number, mood, or tense ⟨~ verbs⟩

[2]**auxiliary** *n, pl* **-ries** **1** : an auxiliary person, group, or device **2** : an auxiliary verb

aux·in \'ȯk-sən\ *n* : a plant hormone that stimulates growth in length

av *abbr* **1** avenue **2** average **3** avoirdupois

AV *abbr* **1** ad valorem **2** audiovisual **3** Authorized Version

[1]**avail** \ə-'vāl\ *vb* : to be of use or advantage : HELP, BENEFIT

[2]**avail** *n* : USE ⟨effort was of no ~⟩

avail·able \ə-'vā-lə-bəl\ *adj* **1** : USABLE ⟨~ resources⟩ **2** : ACCESSIBLE ⟨~ in any drugstore⟩ — **avail·abil·i·ty** \-ˌvā-lə-'bi-lə-tē\ *n*

av·a·lanche \'a-və-ˌlanch\ *n* : a mass of snow, ice, earth, or rock sliding down a mountainside

avant–garde \ˌä-ˌvän-'gärd, -ˌvänt-\ *n* [F, vanguard] : those esp. in the arts who create or apply new or experimental ideas and techniques — **avant–garde** *adj*

av·a·rice \'a-və-rəs\ *n* : excessive desire for wealth : GREED — **av·a·ri·cious** \ˌa-və-'ri-shəs\ *adj*

avast \ə-'vast\ *vb imper* — a nautical command to stop or cease

av·a·tar \'a-və-ˌtär\ *n* [Skt *avatāra* descent] : INCARNATION

avaunt \ə-ˈvȯnt\ *adv* : AWAY, HENCE

avdp *abbr* avoirdupois

ave *abbr* avenue

Ave Ma·ria \ˌä-ˌvā-mə-ˈrē-ə\ *n* : HAIL MARY 1

avenge \ə-ˈvenj\ *vb* **avenged; aveng·ing** : to take vengeance for — **aveng·er** *n*

av·e·nue \ˈa-və-ˌnü, -ˌnyü\ *n* **1** : a way or route to a place or goal : PATH **2** : a broad street

aver \ə-ˈvər\ *vb* **averred; aver·ring** : ALLEGE, ASSERT; *also* : DECLARE

[1]**av·er·age** \ˈa-və-rij, ˈa-vrij\ *n* [earlier, proportionally distributed charge for damage at sea, modif. of MF *avarie* damage to ship or cargo, fr. It *avaria,* fr. Ar *ʽawārīyah* damaged merchandise] **1** : ARITHMETIC MEAN **2** : a ratio of successful tries to total tries esp. in athletics ⟨batting ~ of .303⟩

[2]**average** *adj* **1** : equaling or approximating an arithmetic mean **2** : being about midway between extremes **3** : not out of the ordinary : COMMON

[3]**average** *vb* **av·er·aged; av·er·ag·ing** **1** : to be at or come to an average **2** : to be, do, or get usually **3** : to find the average of

averse \ə-ˈvərs\ *adj* : having an active feeling of dislike or reluctance ⟨~ to exercise⟩

aver·sion \ə-ˈvər-zhən\ *n* **1** : a feeling of repugnance for something with a desire to avoid it **2** : something decidedly disliked

avert \ə-ˈvərt\ *vb* **1** : to turn aside or away ⟨~ the eyes⟩ **2** : to ward off

avg *abbr* average

avi·an \ˈā-vē-ən\ *adj* [L *avis* bird] : of, relating to, or derived from birds

avi·ary \ˈā-vē-ˌer-ē\ *n, pl* **-ar·ies** : a place for keeping birds confined

avi·a·tion \ˌā-vē-ˈā-shən, ˌa-\ *n* **1** : the operation of heavier-than-air aircraft **2** : aircraft manufacture, development, and design

avi·a·tor \ˈā-vē-ˌā-tər, ˈa-\ *n* : an airplane pilot

avi·a·trix \ˌā-vē-ˈā-triks, ˌa-\ *n, pl* **-trix·es** \-trik-səz\ *or* **-tri·ces** \-trə-ˌsēz\ : a woman who is an aviator

av·id \ˈa-vəd\ *adj* **1** : craving eagerly : GREEDY **2** : enthusiastic in pursuit of an interest — **avid·i·ty** \ə-ˈvi-də-tē, a-\ *n* — **av·id·ly** *adv* — **av·id·ness** *n*

avi·on·ics \ˌā-vē-ˈä-niks, ˌa-\ *n pl* : electronics designed for use in aerospace vehicles — **avi·on·ic** \-nik\ *adj*

avo \ˈa-(ˌ)vü\ *n, pl* **avos** — see *pataca* at MONEY table

av·o·ca·do \ˌa-və-ˈkä-dō, ˌä-\ *n, pl* **-dos** *also* **-does** [modif. of Sp *aguacate,* fr. Nahuatl *āhuacatl,* avocado, testicle] : a pulpy green- to purple-skinned nutty-flavored fruit of a tropical American tree; *also* : this tree

av·o·ca·tion \ˌa-və-ˈkā-shən\ *n* : HOBBY

av·o·cet \ˈa-və-ˌset\ *n* : any of several long-legged shorebirds with webbed feet and slender upward-curving bills

avoid \ə-ˈvȯid\ *vb* **1** : to keep away from : SHUN **2** : to prevent the occurrence of **3** : to refrain from — **avoid·able** *adj* — **avoid·ably** *adv* — **avoid·ance** \ə-ˈvȯi-dəns\ *n*

av·oir·du·pois \ˌa-vər-də-ˈpȯiz\ *n* [ME *avoir de pois* goods sold by weight, fr. AF, lit., goods of weight] **1** : AVOIRDUPOIS WEIGHT **2** : WEIGHT, HEAVINESS; *esp* : personal weight

avoirdupois weight *n* : a system of weights based on a pound of 16 ounces and an ounce of 16 drams (28 grams) — see WEIGHT table

avouch \ə-ˈvau̇ch\ *vb* **1** : to declare positively : AVER **2** : to vouch for

avow \ə-ˈvau̇\ *vb* : to declare openly — **avow·al** \-ˈvau̇(-ə)l\ *n*

avun·cu·lar \ə-ˈvəŋ-kyə-lər\ *adj* : of, relating to, or resembling an uncle

await \ə-ˈwāt\ *vb* : to wait for : EXPECT

[1]**awake** \ə-ˈwāk\ *vb* **awoke** \-ˈwōk\ *also* **awaked** \-ˈwākt\; **awo·ken** \-ˈwō-kən\ *or* **awaked** *also* **awoke; awak·ing** : to bring back to consciousness : wake up

[2]**awake** *adj* : not asleep; *also* : ALERT

awak·en \ə-ˈwā-kən\ *vb* **awak·ened; awak·en·ing** \-ˈwā-kə-niŋ\ : AWAKE

[1]**award** \ə-ˈwȯrd\ *vb* **1** : to give by judicial decision ⟨~ damages⟩ **2** : to give in recognition of merit or achievement

[2]**award** *n* **1** : a final decision : JUDGMENT **2** : something awarded : PRIZE

aware \ə-ˈwer\ *adj* : having perception or knowledge : CONSCIOUS, INFORMED — **aware·ness** *n*

awash \ə-ˈwȯsh, -ˈwäsh\ *adj* **1** : washed by waves or tide **2** : AFLOAT **3** : FLOODED ⟨the street was ~ after the storm⟩

[1]**away** \ə-ˈwā\ *adv* **1** : from this or that place ⟨go ~⟩ **2** : out of the way **3** : in another direction ⟨turn ~⟩ **4** : out of existence ⟨fade ~⟩ **5** : from one's possession ⟨give ~⟩ **6** : without interruption ⟨chatter ~⟩ **7** : at a distance in space or time ⟨far ~⟩ ⟨~ back in 1910⟩

[2]**away** *adj* **1** : ABSENT **2** : distant in space or time ⟨a lake 10 miles ~⟩

[1]**awe** \ˈȯ\ *n* **1** : profound and reverent dread of the supernatural **2** : respectful fear inspired by authority

[2]**awe** *vb* **awed; aw·ing** : to inspire with awe

aweigh \ə-ˈwā\ *adj* : just clear of the bottom ⟨anchors ~⟩

awe·some \ˈȯ-səm\ *adj* **1** : expressive of awe ⟨~ tribute⟩ **2** : inspiring awe

awe·struck \-ˌstrək\ *also* **awe·strick·en** \-ˌstri-kən\ *adj* : filled with awe

aw·ful \ˈȯ-fəl\ *adj* **1** : inspiring awe **2** : extremely disagreeable **3** : very great ⟨an ~ lot of money⟩ — **aw·ful·ly** *adv*

awhile \ə-ˈhwī(-ə)l\ *adv* : for a while

awhirl \ə-ˈhwərl\ *adj* : being in a whirl

awk·ward \ˈȯ-kwərd\ *adj* **1** : CLUMSY ⟨~ with needle and thread⟩ **2** : UNGRACEFUL ⟨~ writing⟩ **3** : difficult to explain : EMBARRASSING **4** : difficult to deal with — **awk·ward·ly** *adv* — **awk·ward·ness** *n*

awl \ˈȯl\ *n* : a pointed instrument for making small holes

aw·ning \ˈȯ-niŋ\ *n* : a rooflike cover (as of canvas) extended over or in front of a place as a shelter

AWOL \ˈā-ˌwȯl, ˌā-ˌdə-bəl-yü-ˌō-ˈel\ *n* : a person who is absent without leave — **AWOL** *adj or adv*

awry \ə-ˈrī\ *adv or adj* **1** : ASKEW ⟨with hair ~⟩ **2** : AMISS ⟨their plans went ~⟩

ax *or* **axe** \ˈaks\ *n* : a chopping or cutting tool with an edged head fitted parallel to a handle

ax·i·al \ˈak-sē-əl\ *adj* **1** : of, relating to, or functioning as an axis **2** : situated around, in the direction of, on, or along an axis — **ax·i·al·ly** *adv*

ax·i·om \ˈak-sē-əm\ *n* [L *axioma,* fr. Gk *axiōma,* lit., something worthy, fr. *axioun* to think worthy, fr. *axios* worth, worthy] **1** : a statement generally accepted as true : MAXIM **2** : a proposition regarded as a self-evident truth — **ax·i·om·at·ic** \ˌak-sē-ə-ˈma-tik\ *adj* — **ax·i·om·at·i·cal·ly** \-ti-k(ə-)lē\ *adv*

ax·is \ˈak-səs\ *n, pl* **ax·es** \-ˌsēz\ **1** : a straight line around which a body rotates **2** : a straight line or structure with respect to which a body or figure is symmetrical **3** : one of the reference lines of a system of coordinates **4** : an alliance between major powers

ax·le \ˈak-səl\ *n* : a shaft on which a wheel revolves

ax·on \ˈak-ˌsän\ *n* : the long thin usu. unbranched part of a nerve cell that usu. conducts impulses away from the cell body

ayah \ˈī-ə\ *n* [Hindi & Urdu *āyā,* fr. Pg *aia,* fr. L *avia* grandmother] : a nurse or maid native to India

aya·tol·lah \ˌī-ə-ˈtō-lə\ *n* [Pers *āyatollāh,* lit., sign of God, fr. Ar *aya* sign, miracle + *allāh* God] : an Islamic religious leader — used as a title of respect

[1]**aye** *also* **ay** \ˈā\ *adv* : ALWAYS, EVER

[2]**aye** *also* **ay** \ˈī\ *adv* : YES

[3]**aye** *also* **ay** \ˈī\ *n, pl* **ayes** : an affirmative vote

AZ *abbr* Arizona

aza·lea \ə-ˈzāl-yə\ *n* : any of numerous rhododendrons with funnel-shaped blossoms and usu. deciduous leaves

az·i·do·thy·mi·dine \ə-ˌzi-dō-ˈthī-mə-ˌdēn\ *n* : AZT

az·i·muth \ˈa-zə-məth\ *n* : horizontal direction expressed as an angular distance from a fixed point

AZT \ˌā-(ˌ)zē-ˈtē\ *n* : an antiviral drug used to treat AIDS

Az·tec \ˈaz-ˌtek\ *n* : a member of a Nahuatl-speaking people that ruled a large empire in Mexico in the 15th–16th centuries — **Az·tec·an** *adj*

azure \ˈa-zhər\ *n* : the blue of the clear sky — **azure** *adj*

B

[1]**b** \ˈbē\ *n, pl* **b's** *or* **bs** \ˈbēz\ *often cap* **1** : the 2d letter of the English alphabet **2** : a grade rating a student's work as good

[2]**b** *abbr, often cap* **1** bachelor **2** bass **3** bishop **4** book **5** born

B *symbol* boron

Ba *symbol* barium

BA *abbr* **1** bachelor of arts **2** batting average

bab·ble \ˈba-bəl\ *vb* **bab·bled; bab·bling** **1** : to talk enthusiastically or excessively **2** : to utter meaningless sounds — **babble** *n* — **bab·bler** \-b(ə-)lər\ *n*

babe \ˈbāb\ *n* **1** : BABY **2** *slang* : GIRL, WOMAN **3** *slang* : a person who is physically attractive

ba·bel \ˈbā-bəl, ˈba-\ *n, often cap* [fr. the Tower of *Babel,* Gen 11:4–9] : a place or scene of noise and confusion; *also* : a confused sound ♦ ***Synonyms*** HUBBUB, RACKET, DIN, UPROAR, CLAMOR

ba·boon \ba-ˈbün\ *n* [ME *babewin,* fr. MF *babouin,* fr. *baboue* grimace] : any of several large apes of Asia and Africa with doglike muzzles

ba·bush·ka \bə-ˈbüsh-kə, -ˈbu̇sh-\ *n* [Russ, grandmother, dim. of *baba* old woman] : a kerchief for the head

[1]**ba·by** \ˈbā-bē\ *n, pl* **babies** **1** : a very young child : INFANT **2** : the youngest or smallest of a group **3** : a childish person — **baby** *adj* — **ba·by·hood** *n* — **ba·by·ish** *adj*

[2]**baby** *vb* **ba·bied; ba·by·ing** : to tend or treat often with excessive care

baby boom *n* : a marked rise in birthrate — **baby boom·er** \-ˈbü-mər\ *n*

baby's breath *n* : any of a genus of herbs that are related to the pinks and have small delicate flowers

ba·by–sit \ˈbā-bē-ˌsit\ *vb* **-sat** \-ˌsat\; **-sit·ting** : to care for children usu. during a short absence of the parents — **ba·by·sit·ter** *n*

bac·ca·lau·re·ate \ˌba-kə-ˈlȯr-ē-ət\ *n* **1** : the degree of bachelor conferred by colleges and universities **2** : a sermon delivered to a graduating class

bac·ca·rat \ˌbä-kə-ˈrä, ˌba-\ *n* : a card game in which three hands are dealt and players may bet either or both hands against the dealer's

bac·cha·nal \ˈba-kə-nᵊl, ˌba-kə-ˈnal, ˌbä-kə-ˈnäl\ *n* **1** : ORGY **2** : REVELER

bac·cha·na·lia \ˌba-kə-ˈnāl-yə\ *n, pl* **bacchanalia** : a drunken orgy — **bac·cha·na·lian** \-ˈnāl-yən\ *adj or n*

bach·e·lor \ˈbach-lər, ˈba-chə-lər\ *n* **1** : a person who has received the usu. lowest degree conferred by a 4-year college **2** : an unmarried man — **bach·e·lor·hood** *n*

bach·e·lor·ette \ˌbach-lə-ˈret, ˌba-chə-\ *n* : a young unmarried woman

bachelor's button *n* : a European plant related to the daisies and having usu. blue, pink, or white flower heads

ba·cil·lus \bə-ˈsi-ləs\ *n, pl* **-li** \-ˌlī\ [NL, fr. ML, small staff, dim. of L *baculus* staff] : any of a genus of rod-shaped bacteria; *also* : a disease-producing bacterium — **bac·il·lary** \ˈba-sə-ˌler-ē\ *adj*

[1]**back** \ˈbak\ *n* **1** : the rear or dorsal part of the human body; *also* : the corresponding part of a lower animal **2** : the part or surface opposite the front **3** : a player in the backfield in football — **back·less** \-ləs\ *adj*

[2]**back** *adv* **1** : to, toward, or at the rear **2** : AGO **3** : so as to be restrained or delayed **4** : to, toward, or in a former place or state **5** : in return or reply

[3]**back** *adj* **1** : located at or in the back; *also* : REMOTE **2** : OVERDUE ⟨~ rent⟩ **3** : moving or operating backward **4** : not current ⟨~ issues of a magazine⟩

[4]**back** *vb* **1** : SUPPORT, UPHOLD **2** : to go or cause to go backward or in reverse **3** : to furnish with a back : form the back of — **back·er** *n*

back·ache \ˈbak-ˌāk\ *n* : a pain in the lower back

back–bench·er \-ˈben-chər\ *n* : a rank-and-file member of a British legislature

back·bite \-ˌbīt\ *vb* **-bit** \-ˌbit\; **-bit·ten** \-ˌbi-tᵊn\; **-bit·ing** \-ˌbī-tiŋ\ : to say mean or spiteful things about someone who is absent — **back·bit·er** *n*

back·board \-ˌbȯrd\ *n* : a board placed at or serving as the back of something

back·bone \-ˌbōn\ *n* **1** : the bony column in the back of a vertebrate that is the chief support of the trunk and consists of a jointed series of vertebrae enclosing and protecting the spinal cord **2** : firm resolute character **3** : the primary high-speed hardware and transmission lines of a telecommunication network

back·drop \ˈbak-ˌdräp\ *n* : a painted cloth hung across the rear of a stage

back·field \-ˌfēld\ *n* : the football players whose positions are behind the line

[1]**back·fire** \-ˌfī(-ə)r\ *n* : a loud noise caused by the improperly timed explosion of fuel in the cylinder of an internal combustion engine

[2]**backfire** *vb* **1** : to make or undergo a backfire **2** : to have a result opposite to what was intended

back·flip \-ˌflip\ *n* : a backward somersault esp. in the air

back·gam·mon \ˈbak-ˌga-mən\ *n* : a game played with pieces on a double board in which the moves are determined by throwing dice

back·ground \ˈbak-ˌgrau̇nd\ *n* **1** : the scenery behind something **2** : the setting within which something takes place; *also* : the sum of a person's experience, training, and understanding

back·hand \ˈbak-ˌhand\ *n* : a stroke (as in tennis) made with the back of the hand turned in the direction of movement; *also* : the side on which such a stroke is made — **back·hand** *vb*

back·hand·ed \ˈbak-ˈhan-dəd\ *adj* **1** : INDIRECT, DEVIOUS; *esp* : SARCASTIC ⟨a ~ compliment⟩ **2** : using or made with a backhand ⟨a ~ catch⟩

back·hoe \ˈbak-ˌhō\ *n* : an excavating machine having a bucket that is drawn toward the machine

back·ing \ˈba-kiŋ\ *n* **1** : something forming a back **2** : SUPPORT, AID ⟨needed financial ~⟩; *also* : a body of supporters

back·lash \ˈbak-ˌlash\ *n* **1** : a sudden violent backward movement or reaction **2** : a strong adverse reaction

[1]**back·log** \-ˌlȯg, -ˌläg\ *n* **1** : a large log at the back of a hearth fire **2** : an accumulation of tasks unperformed or materials not processed

[2]**backlog** *vb* : to accumulate in reserve

back of *prep* : BEHIND

back order *n* : a business order yet to be fulfilled because stock is unavailable — **back–order** *vb*

back out *vb* : to withdraw esp. from a commitment or contest

[1]**back·pack** \ˈbak-ˌpak\ *n* **1** : a bag that usu. has two shoulder straps, is carried on the back, and is used for holding personal belongings or supplies **2** : a piece of equipment designed for use while being carried on the back

[2]**backpack** *vb* : to hike with a backpack — **back·pack·er** *n*

back·ped·al \ˈbak-ˌpe-dᵊl\ *vb* : RETREAT

back·rest \-ˌrest\ *n* : a rest for the back

back·side \-ˌsīd\ *n* : BUTTOCKS

back·slap \-ˌslap\ *vb* : to display excessive cordiality — **back·slap·per** *n*

back·slide \-ˌslīd\ *vb* **-slid** \-ˌslid\; **-slid** *or* **-slid·den** \-ˌsli-dᵊn\; **-slid·ing** \-ˌslī-diŋ\ : to lapse morally or in religious practice — **back·slid·er** *n*

back·space \-ˌspās\ *vb* : to move back a space in a text with the press of a key — **backspace** *n*

back·spin \-ˌspin\ *n* : a backward rotary motion of a ball

[1]**back·stage** \ˈbak-ˌstāj\ *adj* **1** : relating to or occurring in the area behind a stage **2** : of or relating to the private lives of theater people **3** : of or relating to the inner working or operation

[2]**back·stage** \ˈbak-ˈstāj\ *adv* **1** : in or to a backstage area **2** : SECRETLY

back·stairs \-ˌsterz\ *adj* : SECRET, FURTIVE; *also* : SORDID, SCANDALOUS

[1]**back·stop** \-ˌstäp\ *n* : something serving as a stop behind something else; *esp* : a screen or fence to keep a ball from leaving the field of play

[2]**backstop** *vb* **1** : SUPPORT **2** : to serve as a backstop to

back·story \-ˌstȯr-ē\ *n* : a story that tells what led up to the main story or plot

back·stretch \ˈbak-ˈstrech\ *n* : the side opposite the homestretch on a racecourse

back·stroke \-ˌstrōk\ *n* : a swimming stroke executed on the back — **back·strok·er** \-ˌstrō-kər\ *n*

back talk *n* : impudent, insolent, or argumentative replies

back·track \ˈbak-ˌtrak\ *vb* **1** : to retrace one's course **2** : to reverse a position or stand

back·up \-ˌəp\ *n* **1** : one that serves as a substitute or alternative **2** : a copy of computer data — **back up** *vb*

[1]**back·ward** \ˈbak-wərd\ *or* **back·wards** \-wərdz\ *adv* **1** : toward the back **2** : with the back foremost ⟨ride ~⟩ **3** : in a reverse or contrary direction or way ⟨count ~⟩ **4** : toward the past; *also* : toward a worse state

[2]**backward** *adj* **1** : directed, turned, or done backward **2** : DIFFIDENT, SHY **3** : slow in development or learning — **back·ward·ly** *adv* — **back·ward·ness** *n*

back·wash \ˈbak-ˌwȯsh, -ˌwäsh\ *n* : a backward flow or movement (as of water or air) produced by a propelling force (as the motion of oars)

back·wa·ter \-ˌwȯ-tər, -ˌwä-\ *n* **1** : water held or turned back in its course **2** : an isolated or backward place or condition

back·woods \-ˈwu̇dz\ *n pl* **1** : wooded or partly cleared areas far from cities **2** : a remote or isolated place

ba·con \ˈbā-kən\ *n* : salted and smoked meat from the sides or back of a pig

bacteria *pl of* BACTERIUM

bac·te·ri·cid·al \bak-ˌtir-ə-ˈsī-dᵊl\ *adj* : destroying bacteria — **bac·te·ri·cide** \-ˈtir-ə-ˌsīd\ *n*

bac·te·ri·ol·o·gy \bak-ˌtir-ē-ˈä-lə-jē\ *n* **1** : a science dealing with bacteria **2** : bacterial life and phenomena — **bac·te·ri·o·log·ic** \-ə-ˈlä-jik\ *or* **bac·te·ri·o·log·i·cal** \-ə-ˈlä-ji-kəl\ *adj* — **bac·te·ri·ol·o·gist** \-ˈä-lə-jist\ *n*

bac·te·rio·phage \bak-ˈtir-ē-ə-ˌfāj\ *n* : any of various viruses that attack specific bacteria

bac·te·ri·um \bak-ˈtir-ē-əm\ *n, pl* **-ria** \-ē-ə\ [NL, fr. Gk *baktērion* staff] : any of a group of single-celled microorganisms including some that cause disease and others that are valued esp. for their chemical effects (as fermentation) — **bac·te·ri·al** \-ē-əl\ *adj*

bad \ˈbad\ *adj* **worse** \ˈwərs\; **worst** \ˈwərst\ **1** : below standard : POOR; *also* : UNFAVORABLE ⟨a ~ report⟩ **2** : SPOILED, DECAYED **3** : WICKED; *also* : not well-behaved : NAUGHTY **4** : DISAGREEABLE ⟨a ~ taste⟩; *also* : HARMFUL **5** : DEFECTIVE, FAULTY ⟨~ wiring⟩; *also* : not valid ⟨a ~ check⟩ **6** : UNWELL, ILL **7** : SORRY, REGRETFUL ⟨feels ~ about forgetting to call⟩ ♦ ***Synonyms*** EVIL, WRONG, IMMORAL, INIQUITOUS — **bad·ly** *adv* — **bad·ness** *n*

bade *past and past part of* BID

badge \ˈbaj\ *n* : a device or token usu. worn as a sign of status

[1]**bad·ger** \ˈba-jər\ *n* : any of several sturdy burrowing mammals with long claws on their forefeet

[2]**badger** *vb* : to harass or annoy persistently

ba·di·nage \ˌba-də-ˈnäzh\ *n* [F] : playful talk back and forth : BANTER

bad·land \ˈbad-ˌland\ *n* : a region marked by intricate erosional sculpturing and scanty vegetation — usu. used in pl.

bad·min·ton \ˈbad-ˌmi-tᵊn, -ˌmin-tᵊn\ *n* : a court game played with light rackets and a shuttlecock volleyed over a net

bad–mouth \ˈbad-ˌmau̇th\ *vb* : to criticize severely

Bae·de·ker \ˈbā-di-kər, ˈbe-\ *n* : GUIDEBOOK

[1]**baf·fle** \ˈba-fəl\ *vb* **baf·fled**; **baf·fling** \-fə-liŋ\ : FRUSTRATE, THWART, FOIL; *also* : PERPLEX — **baf·fle·ment** *n*

[2]**baffle** *n* : a device (as a wall or screen) to deflect, check, or regulate flow (as of liquid or sound) — **baf·fled** \ˈba-fəld\ *adj*

[1]**bag** \ˈbag\ *n* **1** : a flexible usu. closable container (as for storing or carrying) **2** : something that bulges and sags like a bag ⟨~*s* under the eyes⟩

[2]**bag** *vb* **bagged**; **bag·ging** **1** : DISTEND, BULGE **2** : to put in a bag **3** : to get possession of; *esp* : to take in hunting ♦ ***Synonyms*** TRAP, SNARE, CATCH, CAPTURE, COLLAR

ba·gasse \bə-ˈgas\ *n* [F] : plant residue (as of sugarcane) left after a product (as juice) has been extracted

bag·a·telle \ˌba-gə-ˈtel\ *n* [F] : TRIFLE 1

ba·gel \ˈbā-gəl\ *n* [Yiddish *beygl*] : a firm doughnut-shaped roll usu. made by boiling and then baking

bag·gage \ˈba-gij\ *n* **1** : the traveling bags and personal belongings of a traveler : LUGGAGE **2** : intangible things that get in the way ⟨emotional ~⟩

bag·gie \ˈba-gē\ *n* : a usu. small clear plastic bag

bag·gies \ˈba-gēz\ *n pl* : baggy pants or shorts

bag·gy \ˈba-gē\ *adj* **bag·gi·er**; **-est** : puffed out or hanging like a bag ⟨a ~ sweater⟩ — **bag·gi·ly** \-gə-lē\ *adv* — **bag·gi·ness** \-gē-nəs\ *n*

bag·man \ˈbag-mən\ *n* : a person who collects or distributes illicitly gained money on behalf of another

ba·gnio \ˈban-yō\ *n, pl* **bagnios** [It *bagno,* lit., public bath] : BROTHEL

bag of waters : a double-walled fluid-filled sac that encloses and protects the fetus in the womb and that breaks releasing its fluid during the process of birth

bag·pipe \ˈbag-ˌpīp\ *n* : a musical wind instrument consisting of a bag, a tube with valves, and sounding pipes — often used in pl. — **bag·pip·er** \-ˌpī-pər\ *n*

ba·guette \ba-ˈget\ *n* [F, lit., rod] **1** : a gem having the shape of a narrow rectangle; *also* : the shape itself **2** : a long thin loaf of French bread

baht \ˈbät\ *n, pl* **baht** *also* **bahts** — see MONEY table

[1]**bail** \ˈbāl\ *n* : a container for ladling water out of a boat

[2]**bail** *vb* : to dip and throw water from a boat — **bail·er** *n*

[3]**bail** *n* : security given to guarantee a prisoner's appearance when legally required;

also : one giving such security or the release secured

4**bail** *vb* : to release under bail; *also* : to procure the release of by giving bail — **bail·able** \ˈbā-lə-bəl\ *adj*

5**bail** *n* : the arched handle (as of a pail or kettle)

bai·liff \ˈbā-ləf\ *n* **1** : an aide of a British sheriff who serves writs and makes arrests; *also* : a minor officer of a U.S. court **2** : an estate or farm manager esp. in Britain : STEWARD

bai·li·wick \ˈbā-li-ˌwik\ *n* : one's special province or domain ♦ ***Synonyms*** TERRITORY, FIELD, SPHERE

bail·out \ˈbā-ˌlau̇t\ *n* : a rescue from financial distress

bairn \ˈbern\ *n, chiefly Scot* : CHILD

1**bait** \ˈbāt\ *vb* **1** : to persecute by continued attacks **2** : to harass with dogs usu. for sport ⟨~ a bear⟩ **3** : to furnish (as a hook) with bait **4** : ALLURE, ENTICE **5** : to give food and drink to (as an animal) ♦ ***Synonyms*** BADGER, HECKLE, HOUND

2**bait** *n* **1** : a lure for catching animals (as fish) **2** : LURE, TEMPTATION ♦ ***Synonyms*** SNARE, TRAP, DECOY, COME-ON, ENTICEMENT

bait·fish \ˈbāt-ˌfish\ *n* : a small fish that attracts and is a food source for a larger fish; *also* : a fish used for bait

bai·za \ˈbī-(ˌ)zä\ *n, pl* **baiza** *or* **baizas** — see *rial* at MONEY table

baize \ˈbāz\ *n* : a coarse feltlike fabric

1**bake** \ˈbāk\ *vb* **baked**; **bak·ing** **1** : to cook or become cooked in dry heat esp. in an oven **2** : to dry and harden by heat ⟨~ bricks⟩ — **bak·er** *n*

2**bake** *n* : a social gathering featuring baked food

baker's dozen *n* : THIRTEEN

bak·ery \ˈbā-k(ə-)rē\ *n, pl* **-er·ies** : a place for baking or selling baked goods

bake sale *n* : a fund-raising event at which usu. homemade foods are sold

bake·shop \ˈbāk-ˌshäp\ *n* : BAKERY

bake·ware \-ˌwer\ *n* : dishes used for baking and serving food

baking powder *n* : a powder that consists of a carbonate, an acid, and a starch and that makes the dough rise in baking cakes and biscuits

baking soda *n* : SODIUM BICARBONATE

bak·sheesh \ˈbak-ˌshēsh\ *n* : payment (as a tip or bribe) to expedite service

bal *abbr* balance

bal·a·lai·ka \ˌba-lə-ˈlī-kə\ *n* [Russ] : a triangular 3-stringed instrument of Russian origin played by plucking or strumming

1**bal·ance** \ˈba-ləns\ *n* [ME, fr. AF, fr. VL **bilancia*, fr. LL *bilanc-, bilanx* having two scalepans, fr. L *bi* two + *lanc-, lanx* plate] **1** : a weighing device : SCALE **2** : a weight, force, or influence counteracting the effect of another **3** : an oscillating wheel used to regulate a timepiece **4** : a state of equilibrium **5** : REMAINDER, REST; *esp* : an amount in excess esp. on the credit side of an account — **bal·anced** \-lənst\ *adj*

2**balance** *vb* **bal·anced**; **bal·anc·ing** **1** : to compute the balance of an account **2** : to arrange so that one set of elements equals another; *also* : to equal or equalize in weight, number, or proportions **3** : WEIGH **4** : to bring or come to a state or position of balance; *also* : to bring into harmony or proportion

bal·boa \bal-ˈbō-ə\ *n* — see MONEY table

bal·co·ny \ˈbal-kə-nē\ *n, pl* **-nies** **1** : a platform projecting from the side of a building and enclosed by a railing **2** : a gallery inside a building

bald \ˈbȯld\ *adj* **1** : lacking a natural or usual covering (as of hair) **2** : UNADORNED, PLAIN ⟨the ~ truth⟩ **3** : having little or no tread ⟨~ tires⟩ **4** : not disguised ⟨~ hate⟩ ♦ ***Synonyms*** BARE, BARREN, NAKED, NUDE — **bald·ly** *adv* — **bald·ness** *n*

bal·da·chin \ˈbȯl-də-kən, ˈbal-\ *or* **bal·da·chi·no** \ˌbal-də-ˈkē-nō\ *n, pl* **-chins** *or* **-chinos** : a canopylike structure over an altar

bald cypress *n* : either of two coniferous trees of southern U.S. swamps; *also* : their hard red wood

bald eagle *n* : a large brown eagle of No. America that when mature has white head and neck feathers and a white tail

bal·der·dash \ˈbȯl-dər-ˌdash\ *n* : NONSENSE

bald·ing \ˈbȯl-diŋ\ *adj* : becoming bald

bal·dric \ˈbȯl-drik\ *n* : a belt worn over the shoulder to carry a sword or bugle

1**bale** \ˈbāl\ *n* : a large or closely packed bundle

2**bale** *vb* **baled**; **bal·ing** : to pack in a bale — **bal·er** *n*

ba·leen \bə-ˈlēn\ *n* : a horny substance attached in plates to the upper jaw of some large whales (**baleen whales**)

bale·ful \ˈbāl-fəl\ *adj* : DEADLY, HARMFUL; *also* : OMINOUS ♦ ***Synonyms*** SINISTER, MALEFIC, MALEFICENT, MALIGN

1**balk** \ˈbȯk\ *n* **1** : HINDRANCE, CHECK, SETBACK **2** : an illegal motion of the pitcher in baseball while in position

2**balk** *vb* **1** : BLOCK, THWART **2** : to stop short and refuse to go on **3** : to commit a balk in sports ♦ ***Synonyms*** FRUSTRATE, BAFFLE, FOIL, THWART — **balky** \ˈbȯ-kē\ *adj*

1**ball** \ˈbȯl\ *n* **1** : a rounded body or mass (as an object used in a game or as a missile); *also* : a roundish protuberant part of the body ⟨the ~ of the foot⟩ **2** : a game played with a ball **3** : a pitched baseball that misses the strike zone and is not swung at by the batter **4** : a hit or thrown ball in various games ⟨foul ~⟩ — **on the ball** : COMPETENT, ALERT

2**ball** *vb* : to form into a ball

3**ball** *n* : a large formal dance

bal·lad \ˈba-ləd\ *n* **1** : a narrative poem of strongly marked rhythm suitable for singing **2** : a simple song : AIR **3** : a slow romantic song

bal·lad·eer \ˌba-lə-ˈdir\ *n* : a singer of ballads

1**bal·last** \ˈba-ləst\ *n* **1** : heavy material used to stabilize a ship or control a balloon's ascent **2** : crushed stone laid in a railroad bed or used in making concrete

[2]**ballast** *vb* : to provide with ballast **♦ *Synonyms*** BALANCE, STABILIZE, STEADY

ball bearing *n* : a bearing in which the revolving part turns upon steel balls that roll easily in a groove; *also* : one of the balls in such a bearing

ball·car·ri·er \ˈbȯl-ˌker-ē-ər\ *n* : the football player carrying the ball in an offensive play

ball·er \ˈbȯ-lər\ *n* : an implement for shaping food into a ball ⟨melon ~⟩

bal·le·ri·na \ˌba-lə-ˈrē-nə\ *n* : a female ballet dancer

bal·let \ˈba-ˌlā, ba-ˈlā\ *n* **1** : dancing in which fixed poses and steps are combined with light flowing movements often to convey a story; *also* : a theatrical art form using ballet dancing **2** : a company of ballet dancers

bal·let·o·mane \ba-ˈle-tə-ˌmān\ *n* : a devotee of ballet

bal·lis·tic missile \bə-ˈlis-tik-\ *n* : a missile that is guided during ascent and that falls freely during descent

bal·lis·tics \-tiks\ *n sing or pl* **1** : the science of the motion of projectiles (as bullets) in flight **2** : the flight characteristics of a projectile — **ballistic** *adj*

ball of fire : an unusually energetic person

[1]**bal·loon** \bə-ˈlün\ *n* **1** : a bag filled with gas or heated air so as to rise and float in the atmosphere usu. carrying a suspended load **2** : an inflatable bag used as a toy or decoration — **bal·loon·ist** *n*

[2]**balloon** *vb* **1** : to swell or puff out **2** : to travel in a balloon **3** : to increase rapidly

[1]**bal·lot** \ˈba-lət\ *n* [It *ballotta* small ball used in secret voting, fr. It dial., dim. of *balla* ball] **1** : a piece of paper used to cast a vote **2** : the action or a system of voting; *also* : the right to vote

[2]**ballot** *vb* : to decide by ballot : VOTE

[1]**ball·park** \ˈbȯl-ˌpärk\ *n* : a park in which ball games are played

[2]**ballpark** *adj* : approximately correct ⟨~ estimate⟩

ball·point \ˈbȯl-ˌpȯint\ *n* : a pen whose writing point is a small rotating metal ball that inks itself from an inner container

ball·room \ˈbȯl-ˌrüm, -ˌrům\ *n* : a large room for dances

ballroom dance *n* : any of various dances (as the tango, two-step, and waltz) in which couples perform set moves

bal·ly·hoo \ˈba-lē-ˌhü\ *n, pl* **-hoos** : extravagant statements and claims made for publicity — **ballyhoo** *vb*

balm \ˈbäm, ˈbälm\ *n* **1** : a fragrant healing or soothing lotion or ointment **2** : any of several spicy fragrant herbs of the mint family **3** : something that comforts or soothes

balmy \ˈbä-mē, ˈbäl-\ *adj* **balm·i·er**; **-est** **1** : gently soothing : MILD **2** : FOOLISH, ABSURD **♦ *Synonyms*** SOFT, BLAND, MILD, GENTLE — **balm·i·ness** *n*

ba·lo·ney \bə-ˈlō-nē\ *n* : NONSENSE

bal·sa \ˈbȯl-sə\ *n* : the extremely light strong wood of a tropical American tree; *also* : the tree

bal·sam \ˈbȯl-səm\ *n* **1** : a fragrant aromatic and usu. resinous substance oozing from various plants; *also* : a preparation containing or smelling like balsam **2** : a balsam-yielding tree (as balsam fir) **3** : a common garden ornamental plant — **bal·sam·ic** \bȯl-ˈsa-mik\ *adj*

balsam fir *n* : a resinous No. American evergreen tree that is widely used for pulpwood and as a Christmas tree

balsamic vinegar *n* : an aged Italian vinegar made from white grapes

Balt \ˈbȯlt\ *n* : a native or inhabitant of Lithuania, Latvia, or Estonia

Bal·ti·more oriole \ˈbȯl-tə-ˌmȯr-\ *n* : a common American oriole in which the male is brightly colored with orange, black, and white

bal·us·ter \ˈba-lə-stər\ *n* [F *balustre,* fr. It *balaustro,* fr. *balaustra* wild pomegranate flower, fr. L *balaustium;* fr. its shape] : an upright support for a rail

bal·us·trade \ˈba-lə-ˌstrād\ *n* : a row of balusters topped by a rail

bam·boo \bam-ˈbü\ *n, pl* **bamboos** : any of various woody mostly tall tropical grasses including some with strong hollow stems used for building, furniture, or utensils

bamboo curtain *n, often cap B&C* : a political, military, and ideological barrier in eastern Asia

bam·boo·zle \bam-ˈbü-zəl\ *vb* **-boo·zled**; **-boo·zling** : TRICK, HOODWINK

[1]**ban** \ˈban\ *vb* **banned**; **ban·ning** : PROHIBIT, FORBID

[2]**ban** *n* **1** : CURSE **2** : a legal or formal prohibition ⟨a ~ on beef imports⟩

[3]**ban** \ˈbän\ *n, pl* **ba·ni** \ˈbä-nē\ — see *leu* at MONEY table

ba·nal \bə-ˈnäl, -ˈnal; ˈbā-nᵊl\ *adj* [F] : COMMONPLACE, TRITE ⟨~ remarks⟩ — **ba·nal·i·ty** \bā-ˈna-lə-tē\ *n*

ba·nana \bə-ˈna-nə\ *n* : a treelike tropical plant bearing thick clusters of yellow or reddish finger-shaped fruit; *also* : this fruit

[1]**band** \ˈband\ *n* **1** : something that binds, ties, or goes around **2** : a strip or stripe that can be distinguished (as by color or texture) from nearby matter **3** : a range of wavelengths (as in radio)

[2]**band** *vb* **1** : to tie up, finish, or enclose with a band **2** : to gather together or unite esp. for some common end — **band·er** *n*

[3]**band** *n* : a group of persons, animals, or things; *esp* : a group of musicians organized for playing together

[1]**ban·dage** \ˈban-dij\ *n* : a strip of material used esp. in dressing wounds

[2]**bandage** *vb* **ban·daged**; **ban·dag·ing** : to dress or cover with a bandage

Band–Aid \ˈban-ˈdād\ *adj* : offering, making use of, or serving as a temporary or expedient remedy or solution

ban·dan·na *or* **ban·dana** \ban-ˈda-nə\ *n* : a large colored figured handkerchief

B and B *abbr* bed-and-breakfast
band•box \ˈband-ˌbäks\ *n* : a usu. cylindrical box for carrying clothing
band•ed \ˈban-dəd\ *adj* : having or marked with bands
ban•de•role *or* **ban•de•rol** \ˈban-də-ˌrōl\ *n* : a long narrow forked flag or streamer
ban•dit \ˈban-dət\ *n* [It *bandito,* fr. *bandire* to banish] **1** *pl also* **ban•dit•ti** \ban-ˈdi-tē\ : an outlaw who lives by plunder; *esp* : a member of a band of marauders **2** : ROBBER — **ban•dit•ry** \ˈban-də-trē\ *n*
band•lead•er \ˈband-ˌlē-dər\ *n* : the conductor of a band
ban•do•lier *or* **ban•do•leer** \ˌban-də-ˈlir\ *n* : a belt slung over the shoulder esp. to carry ammunition
band saw *n* : a saw in the form of an endless steel belt running over pulleys
band•stand \ˈband-ˌstand\ *n* : a usu. roofed platform on which a band or orchestra performs outdoors
b and w *abbr* black and white
band•wag•on \ˈband-ˌwa-gən\ *n* **1** : a wagon carrying musicians in a parade **2** : a movement that attracts growing support ⟨a political ~⟩
band•width \-ˈwidth\ *n* : the capacity for data transfer of an electronic communication system
¹ban•dy \ˈban-dē\ *vb* **ban•died; ban•dy•ing** **1** : to exchange (as blows or quips) esp. in rapid succession **2** : to use in a glib or offhand way
²bandy *adj* : curved outward ⟨~ legs⟩
bane \ˈbān\ *n* **1** : POISON **2** : WOE, HARM; *also* : a source of this — **bane•ful** *adj*
¹bang \ˈbaŋ\ *vb* **1** : BUMP ⟨fell and ~*ed* his knee⟩ **2** : to strike, thrust, or move usu. with a loud noise
²bang *n* **1** : a resounding blow **2** : a sudden loud noise
³bang *adv* : DIRECTLY, RIGHT ⟨ran ~ up against more trouble⟩
⁴bang *n* : a fringe of hair cut short (as across the forehead) — usu. used in pl.
⁵bang *vb* : to cut (as hair) to produce bangs
ban•gle \ˈbaŋ-gəl\ *n* **1** : BRACELET **2** : a loose-hanging ornament
bang–up \ˈbaŋ-ˌəp\ *adj* : FIRST-RATE, EXCELLENT ⟨a ~ job⟩
bani *pl of* ³BAN
ban•ish \ˈba-nish\ *vb* **1** : to require by authority to leave a country **2** : to drive out : EXPEL ♦ ***Synonyms*** EXILE, OSTRACIZE, DEPORT, RELEGATE — **ban•ish•ment** *n*
ban•is•ter \ˈba-nə-stər\ *n* **1** : a handrail with its supporting posts **2** : HANDRAIL **3** : BALUSTER
ban•jo \ˈban-ˌjō\ *n, pl* **banjos** *also* **banjoes** : a musical instrument with a long neck, a drumlike body, and usu. five strings — **ban•jo•ist** \-ist\ *n*
¹bank \ˈbaŋk\ *n* **1** : a piled-up mass (as of cloud or earth) **2** : an undersea elevation **3** : rising ground bordering a lake, river, or sea **4** : the sideways slope of a surface along a curve or of a vehicle as it rounds a curve
²bank *vb* **1** : to form a bank about **2** : to cover (as a fire) with fuel to keep inactive **3** : to build (a curve) with the roadbed or track inclined laterally upward from the inside edge **4** : to pile or heap in a bank; *also* : to arrange in a tier **5** : to incline (an airplane) laterally
³bank *n* [ME, fr. MF or It; MF *banque,* fr. It *banca,* lit., bench, of Gmc origin] **1** : an establishment concerned esp. with the custody, loan, exchange, or issue of money, the extension of credit, and the transmission of funds **2** : a stock of or a place for holding something in reserve ⟨a blood ~⟩
⁴bank *vb* **1** : to conduct the business of a bank **2** : to deposit money or have an account in a bank — **bank•er** *n* — **bank•ing** *n*
⁵bank *n* : a group of objects arranged close together (as in a row or tier) ⟨a ~ of file drawers⟩
bank•book \ˈbaŋk-ˌbu̇k\ *n* : the depositor's book in which a bank records deposits and withdrawals
bank•card \-ˌkärd\ *n* : a card (as a credit card or an ATM card) issued by a bank
bank•note \-ˌnōt\ *n* : a promissory note issued by a bank and circulating as money
bank•roll \-ˌrōl\ *n* : supply of money : FUNDS
¹bank•rupt \ˈbaŋk-(ˌ)rəpt\ *n* [modif. of MF *banquerote* bankruptcy, fr. It *bancarotta,* fr. *banca* bank + *rotta* broken] : an insolvent person; *esp* : one whose property is turned over by court action to a trustee to be handled for the benefit of his creditors — **bankrupt** *vb*
²bankrupt *adj* **1** : reduced to financial ruin; *esp* : legally declared bankrupt **2** : wholly lacking in or deprived of some essential ⟨morally ~⟩ — **bank•rupt•cy** \ˈbaŋk-(ˌ)rəpt-sē\ *n*
¹ban•ner \ˈba-nər\ *n* **1** : a piece of cloth attached to a staff and used by a leader as his standard **2** : FLAG **3** : an advertisement that runs usu. across the top of a Web page
²banner *adj* : distinguished from all others esp. in excellence ⟨a ~ year⟩
ban•nock \ˈba-nək\ *n* : a flat oatmeal or barley cake usu. cooked on a griddle
banns \ˈbanz\ *n pl* : public announcement esp. in church of a proposed marriage
ban•quet \ˈbaŋ-kwət\ *n* [MF, fr. It *banchetto,* fr. dim. of *banca* bench] : a ceremonial dinner — **banquet** *vb*
ban•quette \baŋ-ˈket\ *n* : a long upholstered bench esp. along a wall
ban•shee \ˈban-shē\ *n* [Ir *bean sídhe* & ScGael *bean sìth,* lit., woman of fairyland] : a female spirit in Gaelic folklore whose wailing warns a family that one of them will soon die
ban•tam \ˈban-təm\ *n* **1** : any of numerous small domestic fowls that are often miniatures of standard breeds **2** : a small but pugnacious person
¹ban•ter \ˈban-tər\ *vb* : to speak to in a witty and teasing manner

[2]**banter** *n* : good-natured witty joking

Ban·tu \ˈban-ˌtü\ *n, pl* **Bantu** *or* **Bantus** **1** : a group of languages spoken in central and southern Africa **2** : a member of a group of African peoples who speak Bantu

ban·yan \ˈban-yən\ *n* : a large tropical Asian tree whose aerial roots grow downward to the ground and form new trunks

ban·zai \bän-ˈzī\ *n* : a Japanese cheer or cry of triumph

bao·bab \ˈbau̇-ˌbab, ˈbā-ə-\ *n* : a tropical African tree with short swollen trunk and sour edible fruits resembling gourds

bap·tism \ˈbap-ˌti-zəm\ *n* **1** : a Christian sacrament signifying spiritual rebirth and symbolized by the ritual use of water **2** : an act of baptizing — **bap·tis·mal** \bap-ˈtiz-məl\ *adj*

baptismal name *n* : GIVEN NAME

Bap·tist \ˈbap-tist\ *n* : a member of any of several Protestant denominations emphasizing baptism by immersion of believers only

bap·tis·tery *or* **bap·tis·try** \ˈbap-tə-strē\ *n, pl* **-ter·ies** *or* **-tries** : a place esp. in a church used for baptism

bap·tize \bap-ˈtīz, ˈbap-ˌtīz\ *vb* **bap·tized**; **bap·tiz·ing** [ME, fr. AF *baptiser,* fr. L *baptizare,* fr. Gk *baptizein* to dip, baptize, fr. *baptein* to dip] **1** : to administer baptism to; *also* : CHRISTEN **2** : to purify esp. by an ordeal

[1]**bar** \ˈbär\ *n* **1** : a long narrow piece of material (as wood or metal) used esp. for a lever, fastening, or support **2** : BARRIER, OBSTACLE **3** : the railing in a law court at which prisoners are stationed; *also* : the legal profession or the whole body of lawyers **4** : a stripe, band, or line much longer than wide **5** : a counter at which food or esp. drink is served; *also* : BARROOM **6** : a vertical line across the musical staff

[2]**bar** *vb* **barred**; **bar·ring** **1** : to fasten, confine, or obstruct with or as if with a bar or bars **2** : to mark with bars : STRIPE **3** : to shut or keep out : EXCLUDE **4** : FORBID, PREVENT

[3]**bar** *prep* : EXCEPT ⟨the best, ~ none⟩

[4]**bar** *abbr* barometer; barometric

Bar *abbr* Baruch

barb \ˈbärb\ *n* **1** : a sharp projection extending backward (as from the point of an arrow) **2** : a biting critical remark — **barbed** \ˈbärbd\ *adj* — **barb·less** \ˈbärb-ləs\ *adj*

bar·bar·ian \bär-ˈber-ē-ən\ *adj* **1** : of, relating to, or being a land, culture, or people alien to and usu. believed to be inferior to another's **2** : lacking refinement, learning, or artistic or literary culture — **barbarian** *n* — **bar·bar·i·an·ism** \-ē-ə-ˌni-zəm\ *n*

bar·bar·ic \bär-ˈber-ik\ *adj* **1** : BARBARIAN ⟨~ tribes⟩ **2** : marked by a lack of restraint : WILD ⟨~ attacks⟩ **3** : PRIMITIVE, UNSOPHISTICATED

bar·ba·rism \ˈbär-bə-ˌri-zəm\ *n* **1** : the social condition of barbarians; *also* : the use or display of barbarian or barbarous acts, attitudes, or ideas **2** : a word or expression that offends standards of correctness or purity

bar·ba·rous \ˈbär-bə-rəs\ *adj* **1** : lacking culture or refinement **2** : using linguistic barbarisms **3** : mercilessly harsh or cruel — **bar·bar·i·ty** \bär-ˈber-ə-tē\ *n* — **bar·ba·rous·ly** *adv* — **bar·ba·rous·ness** *n*

[1]**bar·be·cue** \ˈbär-bi-ˌkyü\ *vb* **-cued**; **-cu·ing** **1** : to cook on a rack or revolving spit over or before a source of heat **2** : to prepare (food, such as meat) by seasoning and cooking usu. slowly and with exposure to low heat and smoke

[2]**barbecue** *n* **1** : a social gathering at which barbecued food is served **2** : an often portable grill or fireplace used for roasting meat and fish

bar·bell \ˈbär-ˌbel\ *n* : a bar with adjustable weights attached to each end used for exercise and in weight lifting

bar·ber \ˈbär-bər\ *n* [ME, fr. AF *barboor,* fr. *barbe* beard, fr. L *barba*] : one whose business is cutting and dressing hair and shaving and trimming beards

bar·ber·ry \ˈbär-ˌber-ē\ *n* : any of a genus of spiny shrubs bearing yellow flowers and oblong red berries

bar·bi·tu·rate \bär-ˈbi-chə-rət\ *n* : any of various compounds (as a salt or ester) formed from an organic acid (**bar·bi·tu·ric acid** \ˌbär-bə-ˈtu̇r-ik-, -ˈtyu̇r-\); *esp* : one used as a sedative or hypnotic

bar·ca·role *or* **bar·ca·rolle** \ˈbär-kə-ˌrōl\ *n* : a Venetian boat song characterized by a beat suggesting a rowing rhythm; *also* : a piece of music imitating this

bar chart *n* : BAR GRAPH

bar·code \ˈbär-ˌkōd\ *n* : a set of printed and variously spaced bars and sometimes numerals that is designed to be scanned to provide information about the object it labels — **bar–cod·ed** \ˈbär-ˌkō-dəd\ *adj* — **bar coding** *n*

bard \ˈbärd\ *n* : POET

[1]**bare** \ˈber\ *adj* **bar·er**; **bar·est** **1** : NAKED **2** : UNCONCEALED, EXPOSED **3** : EMPTY ⟨the cupboard was ~⟩ **4** : leaving nothing to spare : MERE **5** : PLAIN, UNADORNED ⟨the ~ facts⟩ ♦ ***Synonyms*** NUDE, BALD — **bare·ness** *n*

[2]**bare** *vb* **bared**; **bar·ing** : to make or lay bare : UNCOVER

bare·back \-ˌbak\ *or* **bare·backed** \-ˈbakt\ *adv or adj* : without a saddle

bare·faced \-ˈfāst\ *adj* **1** : having the face uncovered; *esp* : BEARDLESS **2** : not concealed : OPEN ⟨a ~ lie⟩ — **bare·faced·ly** \-ˈfā-səd-lē, -ˈfāst-lē\ *adv*

bare·foot \-ˌfu̇t\ *or* **bare·foot·ed** \-ˈfu̇-təd\ *adv or adj* : with bare feet

bare–hand·ed \-ˈhan-dəd\ *adv or adj* **1** : without gloves **2** : without tools or weapons ⟨~ fighting⟩

bare·head·ed \-ˈhe-dəd\ *adv or adj* : without a hat

bare·ly \ˈber-lē\ *adv* **1** : PLAINLY, MEAGERLY ⟨a ~ furnished room⟩ **2** : by a narrow margin : only just ⟨~ enough money⟩

bar·fly \ˈbär-ˌflī\ *n* : a drinker who frequents bars

[1]**bar·gain** \ˈbär-gən\ *n* **1** : AGREEMENT **2**

: an advantageous purchase **3** : a transaction, situation, or event regarded in the light of its results

²**bargain** *vb* **1** : to negotiate over the terms of an agreement; *also* : to come to terms **2** : BARTER

bar·gain–base·ment \ˈbär-gən-ˈbās-mənt\ *adj* : markedly inexpensive

¹**barge** \ˈbärj\ *n* **1** : a broad flat-bottomed boat usu. moved by towing **2** : a motorboat supplied to a flagship (as for an admiral) **3** : a ceremonial boat elegantly furnished — **barge·man** \-mən\ *n*

²**barge** *vb* **barged; barg·ing** **1** : to carry by barge **2** : to move or thrust oneself clumsily or rudely

bar graph *n* : a graphic technique for comparing amounts by rectangles whose lengths are proportional to the amounts they represent

bar·iat·rics \ˌber-ē-ˈa-triks\ *n* : a branch of medicine that deals with the treatment of obesity — **bar·iat·ric** \-trik\ *adj*

ba·ris·ta \bə-ˈrēs-tə\ *n* : a person who makes and serves coffee to the public

bari·tone \ˈber-ə-ˌtōn\ *n* [F *baryton* or It *baritono,* fr. Gk *barytonos* deep sounding, fr. *barys* heavy + *tonos* tone] : a male singing voice between bass and tenor; *also* : a person having this voice

bar·i·um \ˈber-ē-əm\ *n* : a silver-white metallic chemical element that occurs only in combination

¹**bark** \ˈbärk\ *vb* **1** : to make the short loud cry of a dog **2** : to speak or utter in a curt loud tone : SNAP

²**bark** *n* : the sound made by a barking dog

³**bark** *n* : the tough corky outer covering of a woody stem or root

⁴**bark** *vb* **1** : to strip the bark from **2** : to rub the skin from : ABRADE

⁵**bark** *n* : a ship of three or more masts with the aft mast fore-and-aft rigged and the others square-rigged

bar·keep \ˈbär-ˌkēp\ *also* **bar·keep·er** \-ˌkē-pər\ *n* : BARTENDER

bark·er \ˈbär-kər\ *n* : a person who stands at the entrance esp. to a show and tries to attract customers to it

bar·ley \ˈbär-lē\ *n* : a cereal grass with seeds used as food and in making malt liquors; *also* : its seed

bar mitz·vah \bär-ˈmits-və\ *n, often cap B&M* [Heb *bar miṣwāh,* lit., son of the (divine) law] **1** : a Jewish boy who reaches his 13th birthday and assumes religious responsibilities **2** : the ceremony recognizing a boy as a bar mitzvah

barn \ˈbärn\ *n* [ME *bern,* fr. OE *bereærn,* fr. *bere* barley + *ærn* house, store] : a building used esp. for storing hay and grain and for housing livestock or farm equipment

bar·na·cle \ˈbär-ni-kəl\ *n* : any of numerous small marine crustaceans free-swimming when young but permanently fixed (as to rocks or ships) when adult

barn·storm \ˈbärn-ˌstȯrm\ *vb* : to travel through the country making brief stops to entertain (as with shows or flying stunts) or to campaign for political office

barn·yard \-ˌyärd\ *n* : a usu. fenced area adjoining a barn

baro·graph \ˈber-ə-ˌgraf\ *n* : a recording barometer

ba·rom·e·ter \bə-ˈräm-ə-tər\ *n* : an instrument for measuring atmospheric pressure — **baro·met·ric** \ˌbar-ə-ˈme-trik\ *adj*

bar·on \ˈber-ən\ *n* : a member of the lowest grade of the British peerage — **ba·ro·ni·al** \bə-ˈrō-nē-əl\ *adj* — **bar·ony** \ˈber-ə-nē\ *n*

bar·on·age \ˈber-ə-nij\ *n* : PEERAGE

bar·on·ess \ˈber-ə-nəs\ *n* **1** : the wife or widow of a baron **2** : a woman holding a baronial title in her own right

bar·on·et \ˈber-ə-nət\ *n* : the holder of a rank of honor below a baron but above a knight — **bar·on·et·cy** \-sē\ *n*

ba·roque \bə-ˈrōk, -ˈräk\ *adj* : marked by the use of complex forms, bold ornamentation, and the juxtapositioning of contrasting elements

ba·rouche \bə-ˈrüsh\ *n* [G *Barutsche,* fr. It *biroccio,* ultim. fr. LL *birotus* two-wheeled, fr. L *bi-* two + *rota* wheel] : a 4-wheeled carriage with a high driver's seat in front and a folding top

bar·racks \ˈber-əks\ *n sing or pl* : a building or group of buildings for lodging soldiers

bar·ra·cu·da \ˌber-ə-ˈkü-də\ *n, pl* **-da** *or* **-das** : any of several large slender predaceous sea fishes including some used for food

bar·rage \bə-ˈräzh, -ˈräj\ *n* : a heavy concentration of fire (as of artillery)

barred \ˈbärd\ *adj* : STRIPED

¹**bar·rel** \ˈber-əl\ *n* **1** : a round bulging cask with flat ends of equal diameter **2** : the amount contained in a barrel **3** : a cylindrical or tubular part ⟨gun ~⟩ — **bar·reled** \-əld\ *adj*

²**barrel** *vb* **-reled** *or* **-relled; -rel·ing** *or* **-rel·ling** **1** : to pack in a barrel **2** : to travel at high speed

bar·rel·head \-ˌhed\ *n* : the flat end of a barrel — **on the barrelhead** : asking for or granting no credit ⟨paid cash *on the barrelhead*⟩

barrel roll *n* : an airplane maneuver in which a complete revolution about the longitudinal axis is made

¹**bar·ren** \ˈber-ən\ *adj* **1** : STERILE, UNFRUITFUL **2** : unproductive of results ⟨a ~ scheme⟩ **3** : lacking interest or charm **4** : lacking inspiration or ideas — **bar·ren·ness** \-nəs\ *n*

²**barren** *n* : a tract of barren land

bar·rette \bä-ˈret, bə-\ *n* : a clasp or bar for holding the hair in place

¹**bar·ri·cade** \ˈber-ə-ˌkād, ˌber-ə-ˈkād\ *vb* **-cad·ed; -cad·ing** : to block, obstruct, or fortify with a barricade

²**barricade** *n* [F, fr. MF, fr. *barriquer* to barricade, fr. *barrique* barrel] **1** : a hastily thrown-up obstruction or fortification **2** : BARRIER, OBSTACLE

bar·ri·er \ˈber-ē-ər\ *n* : something that separates, demarcates, or serves as a barricade ⟨concrete ~*s*⟩

barrier island *n* : a long broad sandy island lying parallel to a shore
barrier reef *n* : a coral reef roughly parallel to a shore and separated from it usu. by a lagoon
bar·ring \'bär-iŋ\ *prep* : excluding by exception : EXCEPTING
bar·rio \'bär-ē-ˌō, 'ber-\ *n, pl* **-ri·os** **1** : a district of a city or town in a Spanish-speaking country **2** : a Spanish-speaking quarter in a U.S. city
bar·ris·ter \'ber-ə-stər\ *n* : a British counselor admitted to plead in the higher courts
bar·room \'bär-ˌrüm, -ˌru̇m\ *n* : a room or establishment whose main feature is a bar for the sale of liquor
[1]**bar·row** \'ber-ō\ *n* : a large burial mound of earth and stones
[2]**barrow** *n* **1** : WHEELBARROW **2** : a cart with a boxlike body and two shafts for pushing it
Bart *abbr* baronet
bar·tend·er \'bär-ˌten-dər\ *n* : a person who serves liquor at a bar
bar·ter \'bär-tər\ *vb* : to trade by exchange of goods — **barter** *n* — **bar·ter·er** *n*
Ba·ruch \'bär-ˌük, bə-'rük\ *n* — see BIBLE table
bas·al \'bā-səl\ *adj* **1** : situated at or forming the base **2** : BASIC
basal metabolism *n* : the turnover of energy in a fasting and resting organism using energy solely to maintain vital cellular activity, respiration, and circulation as measured by the rate at which heat is given off
ba·salt \bə-'sȯlt, 'bā-ˌsȯlt\ *n* : a dark fine-grained igneous rock — **ba·sal·tic** \bə-'sȯl-tik\ *adj*
[1]**base** \'bās\ *n, pl* **bas·es** \'bā-səz\ **1** : BOTTOM, FOUNDATION **2** : a side or face on which a geometrical figure stands; *also* : the length of a base **3** : a main ingredient or fundamental part **4** : the point of beginning an act or operation **5** : a place on which a force depends for supplies **6** : a number (as 5 in 5^7) that is raised to a power; *esp* : a number that when raised to a power equal to the logarithm of a number yields the number itself ⟨the logarithm of 100 to ~ 10 is 2 since $10^2 = 100$⟩ **7** : the number of units in a given digit's place of a number system that is required to give the numeral 1 in the next higher place ⟨the decimal system uses a ~ of 10⟩; *also* : such a system using an indicated base ⟨convert from ~ 10 to ~ 2⟩ **8** : any of the four stations at the corners of a baseball diamond **9** : a chemical compound (as lime or ammonia) that reacts with an acid to form a salt, has a bitter taste, and turns litmus blue ♦ ***Synonyms*** BASIS, GROUND, GROUNDWORK, FOOTING, FOUNDATION — **base·less** *adj*
[2]**base** *vb* **based**; **bas·ing** **1** : to form or serve as a base for **2** : ESTABLISH
[3]**base** *adj* **1** : of low value and inferior quality : DEBASED, ALLOYED **2** : CONTEMPTIBLE, IGNOBLE ⟨~ motives⟩ **3** : MENIAL, DEGRADING ♦ ***Synonyms*** LOW, VILE, DESPICABLE, WRETCHED — **base·ly** *adv* — **base·ness** *n*
base·ball \'bās-ˌbȯl\ *n* : a game played with a bat and ball by two teams on a field with four bases arranged in a diamond; *also* : the ball used in this game
baseball cap *n* : a cap of the kind worn by baseball players that has a rounded crown and a long visor
base·board \-ˌbōrd\ *n* : a line of boards or molding covering the joint of a wall and the adjoining floor
base·born \-'bȯrn\ *adj* **1** : MEAN, IGNOBLE **2** : of humble birth **3** : born to parents who are not married to each other
base exchange *n* : a post exchange at a naval or air force base
base hit *n* : a hit in baseball that enables the batter to reach base safely with no error made and no base runner forced out
BASE jumping \'bās-\ *n* [*b*uilding, *a*ntenna, *s*pan, *e*arth] : the activity of parachuting from a high structure or cliff
base·line \'bās-ˌlīn\ *n* **1** : a line serving as a basis esp. to calculate or locate something **2** : the area within which a baseball player must keep when running between bases
base·ment \-mənt\ *n* **1** : the part of a building that is wholly or partly below ground level **2** : the lowest or fundamental part of something
base on balls : an advance to first base given to a baseball player who receives four balls
base runner *n* : a baseball player who is on base or is attempting to reach a base
[1]**bash** \'bash\ *vb* **1** : to strike violently : HIT **2** : to smash by a blow **3** : to attack physically or verbally
[2]**bash** *n* **1** : a heavy blow **2** : a festive social gathering : PARTY
bash·ful \'bash-fəl\ *adj* : inclined to shrink from public attention — **bash·ful·ly** \-fə-lē\ *adv* — **bash·ful·ness** *n*
ba·sic \'bā-sik\ *adj* **1** : of, relating to, or forming the base or essence : FUNDAMENTAL **2** : concerned with fundamental scientific principles : not applied **3** : of, relating to, or having the character of a chemical base ♦ ***Synonyms*** UNDERLYING, BASAL, PRIMARY — **ba·sic·i·ty** \bā-'si-sə-tē\ *n*
BA·SIC \'bā-sik\ *n* [*B*eginner's *A*ll-purpose *S*ymbolic *I*nstruction *C*ode] : a simplified language for programming a computer
ba·si·cal·ly \'bā-si-k(ə-)lē\ *adv* **1** : at a basic level **2** : for the most part **3** : in a basic manner
ba·sil \'bā-zəl, 'ba-, -səl\ *n* : any of several mints with fragrant leaves used in cooking; *also* : the leaves
ba·sil·i·ca \bə-'si-li-kə, -'zi-\ *n* [L, fr. Gk *basilikē*, fr. fem. of *basilikos* royal, fr. *basileus* king] **1** : an early Christian church building consisting of nave and aisles with clerestory and apse **2** : a Ro-

man Catholic church given ceremonial privileges

bas·i·lisk \'ba-sə-ˌlisk, 'ba-zə-\ *n* [ME, fr. L *basiliscus,* fr. Gk *basiliskos,* fr. dim. of *basileus* king] : a legendary reptile with fatal breath and glance

ba·sin \'bā-sᵊn\ *n* **1** : an open usu. circular vessel with sloping sides for holding liquid (as water) **2** : a hollow or enclosed place containing water; *also* : the region drained by a river

ba·sis \'bā-səs\ *n, pl* **ba·ses** \-ˌsēz\ **1** : FOUNDATION, BASE **2** : a fundamental principle

bask \'bask\ *vb* **1** : to expose oneself to comfortable heat **2** : to enjoy something warmly comforting

bas·ket \'bas-kət\ *n* : a container made of woven material (as twigs or grasses); *also* : any of various lightweight usu. wood containers — **bas·ket·ful** *n*

bas·ket·ball \-ˌbȯl\ *n* : a game played on a court by two teams who try to throw an inflated ball through a raised goal; *also* : the ball used in this game — **bas·ket·ball·er** \-ˌbȯ-lər\ *n*

basket case *n* **1** : a person who has all four limbs amputated **2** : a person who is mentally incapacitated or worn out (as from nervous tension)

basket weave *n* : a textile weave resembling the checkered pattern of a plaited basket

bas·ma·ti rice \ˌbäz-'mä-tē-\ *n* : an aromatic long-grain rice originating in southern Asia

bas mitzvah *var of* BAT MITZVAH

Basque \'bask\ *n* **1** : a member of a people inhabiting a region bordering on the Bay of Biscay in northern Spain and southwestern France **2** : the language of the Basque people — **Basque** *adj*

bas–re·lief \ˌbä-ri-'lēf\ *n* [F] : a sculpture in relief with the design raised very slightly from the background

¹**bass** \'bas\ *n, pl* **bass** *or* **bass·es** : any of numerous sport and food bony fishes (as a striped bass)

²**bass** \'bās\ *adj* : of low pitch

³**bass** \'bās\ *n* **1** : a deep sound or tone **2** : the lower half of the musical pitch range **3** : the lowest part in a 4-part chorus; *also* : a singer having this voice or part

bas·set hound \'ba-sət-\ *n* : any of an old breed of short-legged hunting dogs of French origin having long ears and a short smooth coat

bas·si·net \ˌba-sə-'net\ *n* : a baby's bed that resembles a basket and often has a hood over one end

bas·so \'ba-sō, 'bä-\ *n, pl* **bassos** *or* **bas·si** \'bä-ˌsē\ [It] : a bass singer

bas·soon \bə-'sün\ *n* : a musical wind instrument lower in pitch than the oboe

bass·wood \'bas-ˌwu̇d\ *n* : any of several New World lindens or their wood

bast \'bast\ *n* : BAST FIBER

¹**bas·tard** \'bas-tərd\ *n* **1** *usu offensive* : a child born to parents who are not married to each other **2** : an offensive or disagreeable person

²**bastard** *adj* **1** : ILLEGITIMATE **2** : of an inferior or nontypical kind, size, or form; *also* : SPURIOUS — **bas·tardy** *n*

bas·tard·ise *Brit var of* BASTARDIZE

bas·tard·ize \'bas-tər-ˌdīz\ *vb* **-ized; -iz·ing** : to reduce from a higher to a lower state : DEBASE

¹**baste** \'bāst\ *vb* **bast·ed; bast·ing** : to sew with long stitches so as to keep temporarily in place

²**baste** *vb* **bast·ed; bast·ing** : to moisten (as meat) at intervals with liquid while cooking

bast fiber *n* : a strong woody plant fiber obtained chiefly from phloem and used esp. in making ropes

bas·ti·na·do \ˌbas-tə-'nā-dō, -'nä-\ *or* **bas·ti·nade** \ˌbas-tə-'nād, -'näd\ *n, pl* **-na·does** *or* **-nades** **1** : a blow or beating esp. with a stick **2** : a punishment consisting of beating the soles of the feet

bas·tion \'bas-chən\ *n* : a projecting part of a fortification; *also* : a fortified position

¹**bat** \'bat\ *n* **1** : a stout stick : CLUB **2** : a sharp blow **3** : an implement (as of wood) used to hit a ball (as in baseball) **4** : a turn at batting — usu. used in the phrase *at bat*

²**bat** *vb* **bat·ted; bat·ting** : to hit with or as if with a bat

³**bat** *n* : any of an order of night-flying mammals with forelimbs modified to form wings

⁴**bat** *vb* **bat·ted; bat·ting** : WINK, BLINK

batch \'bach\ *n* **1** : a quantity (as of bread) baked at one time **2** : a quantity of material for use at one time or produced at one operation

bate \'bāt\ *vb* **bat·ed; bat·ing** : MODERATE, REDUCE ⟨he *bated* his breath⟩

bath \'bath, 'bäth\ *n, pl* **baths** \'ba<u>th</u>z, 'baths, 'bä<u>th</u>z, 'bäths\ **1** : a washing of the body **2** : water for washing the body **3** : a liquid in which objects are immersed so that it can act on them **4** : BATHROOM **5** : a financial loss ⟨took a ~ in the market⟩

bathe \'bā<u>th</u>\ *vb* **bathed; bath·ing** **1** : to wash in liquid and esp. water; *also* : to apply water or a medicated liquid to ⟨*bathed* her eyes⟩ **2** : to take a bath; *also* : to take a swim **3** : to wash along, over, or against so as to wet **4** : to suffuse with or as if with light — **bath·er** *n*

bath·house \'bath-ˌhau̇s, 'bäth-\ *n* **1** : a building equipped for bathing **2** : a building containing dressing rooms for bathers

bathing suit *n* : SWIMSUIT

ba·thos \'bā-ˌthäs\ *n* [Gk, lit., depth] **1** : the sudden appearance of the commonplace in otherwise elevated matter or style **2** : insincere or overdone pathos — **ba·thet·ic** \bə-'the-tik\ *adj*

bath·robe \'bath-ˌrōb, 'bäth-\ *n* : a loose often absorbent robe worn before and after bathing or as a dressing gown

bath·room \-ˌrüm, -ˌru̇m\ *n* : a room containing a bathtub or shower and usu. a sink and toilet

bathroom tissue *n* : TOILET PAPER
bath•tub \-ˌtəb\ *n* : a usu. fixed tub for bathing
ba•tik \bə-ˈtēk, ˈba-tik\ *n* [Javanese *baṭik*] **1** : an Indonesian method of hand-printing textiles by coating with wax the parts not to be dyed; *also* : a design so executed **2** : a fabric printed by batik
ba•tiste \bə-ˈtēst\ *n* : a fine sheer fabric of plain weave
bat•man \ˈbat-mən\ *n* : an orderly of a British military officer
bat mitz•vah \bät-ˈmits-və\ *also* **bas mitzvah** \bäs-\ *n, often cap B&M* [Heb *bath miṣwāh,* lit., daughter of the (divine) law] **1** : a Jewish girl who at 12 or more years of age assumes religious responsibilities **2** : the ceremony recognizing a girl as a bat mitzvah
ba•ton \bə-ˈtän\ *n* : STAFF, ROD; *esp* : a stick with which the leader directs an orchestra or band
bats•man \ˈbats-mən\ *n* : a batter esp. in cricket
bat•tal•ion \bə-ˈtal-yən\ *n* **1** : a large body of troops organized to act together : ARMY **2** : a military unit composed of a headquarters and two or more units (as companies)
¹bat•ten \ˈba-tᵊn\ *vb* **1** : to grow or make fat **2** : THRIVE
²batten *n* : a strip of wood used esp. to seal or strengthen a joint
³batten *vb* : to fasten with or as if with battens
¹bat•ter \ˈba-tər\ *vb* : to beat or damage with repeated blows
²batter *n* : a soft mixture (as for cake) basically of flour and liquid
³batter *n* : one that bats; *esp* : the player whose turn it is to bat
battering ram *n* **1** : an ancient military machine for battering down walls **2** : a heavy metal bar with handles used to batter down doors
bat•tery \ˈba-tə-rē\ *n, pl* **-ter•ies** **1** : BEATING; *esp* : unlawful beating or use of force on a person **2** : a grouping of artillery pieces for tactical purposes; *also* : the guns of a warship **3** : a group of electric cells for furnishing electric current; *also* : a single electric cell ⟨a flashlight ~⟩ **4** : a number of similar items grouped or used as a unit ⟨a ~ of tests⟩ **5** : the pitcher and catcher of a baseball team
bat•ting \ˈba-tiŋ\ *n* : layers or sheets of cotton or wool (as for lining quilts)
batting cage *n* : a screen around the back and sides of the home plate area to stop baseballs during practice
¹bat•tle \ˈba-tᵊl\ *n* [ME *batel,* fr. AF *bataille* battle, battalion, fr. LL *battalia* combat, alter. of *battualia* fencing exercises, fr. L *battuere* to beat] : a general military engagement; *also* : an extended contest or controversy
²battle *vb* **bat•tled**; **bat•tling** : to engage in battle : CONTEND, FIGHT
bat•tle–ax *or* **battle–axe** \ˈba-tᵊl-ˌaks\ *n* **1** : a long-handled ax formerly used as a weapon **2** : a usu. older woman who is harsh, domineering, or combative
battle fatigue *n* : COMBAT FATIGUE
bat•tle•field \ˈba-tᵊl-ˌfēld\ *n* : a place where a battle is fought
bat•tle•ment \-mənt\ *n* : a decorative or defensive parapet on top of a wall
bat•tle•ship \-ˌship\ *n* : a warship of the most heavily armed and armored class
bat•tle•wag•on \-ˌwa-gən\ *n* : BATTLESHIP
bat•ty \ˈba-tē\ *adj* **bat•ti•er**; **-est** *informal* : CRAZY, FOOLISH
bau•ble \ˈbȯ-bəl\ *n* : TRINKET
baud \ˈbȯd, *Brit* ˈbōd\ *n, pl* **baud** *also* **bauds** : a unit of data transmission speed
baulk *chiefly Brit var of* BALK
baux•ite \ˈbȯk-ˌsīt\ *n* : a clayey mixture that is the chief ore of aluminum
bawd \ˈbȯd\ *n* **1** : MADAM 2 **2** : PROSTITUTE
bawdy \ˈbȯ-dē\ *adj* **bawd•i•er**; **-est** : OBSCENE, LEWD — **bawd•i•ly** \ˈbȯ-də-lē\ *adv* — **bawd•i•ness** \-dē-nəs\ *n*
¹bawl \ˈbȯl\ *vb* : to cry or cry out loudly; *also* : to scold harshly
²bawl *n* : a long loud cry : BELLOW
¹bay \ˈbā\ *adj* : reddish brown
²bay *n* **1** : a bay-colored animal **2** : a reddish brown color
³bay *n* **1** : a section or compartment of a building or vehicle **2** : a compartment projecting outward from the wall of a building and containing a window (**bay window**)
⁴bay *vb* : to bark with deep long tones
⁵bay *n* **1** : the position of one unable to escape and forced to face danger **2** : a baying of dogs
⁶bay *n* : an inlet of a body of water (as the sea) usu. smaller than a gulf
⁷bay *n* : LAUREL; *also* : a shrub or tree resembling the laurel
bay•ber•ry \ˈbā-ˌber-ē\ *n* : a hardy deciduous shrub of coastal eastern No. America bearing small hard berries coated with a white wax used for candles; *also* : its fruit
bay leaf *n* : the dried leaf of the European laurel used in cooking
¹bay•o•net \ˈbā-ə-nət, ˌbā-ə-ˈnet\ *n* : a daggerlike weapon made to fit on the muzzle end of a rifle
²bayonet *vb* **-net•ed** *also* **-net•ted**; **-net•ing** *also* **-net•ting** : to use or stab with a bayonet
bay•ou \ˈbī-yü, -ō\ *n* [Louisiana F, fr. Choctaw *bayuk*] : a marshy or sluggish body of water
bay rum *n* : a fragrant liquid used esp. as a cologne or after-shave lotion
ba•zaar \bə-ˈzär\ *n* **1** : a group of shops : MARKETPLACE **2** : a fair for the sale of articles usu. for charity
ba•zoo•ka \bə-ˈzü-kə\ *n* [*bazooka* (a crude musical instrument made of pipes and a funnel)] : a weapon consisting of a tube that launches a rocket able to pierce armor
¹BB \ˈbē-(ˌ)bē\ *n* : a small round shot pellet
²BB *abbr* base on balls
BBB *abbr* Better Business Bureau

BBC *abbr* British Broadcasting Corporation
bbl *abbr* barrel; barrels
BC *abbr* **1** before Christ — often printed in small capitals and often punctuated **2** British Columbia
[1]**bcc** \ˌbē-ˌsē-ˈsē\ *vb* **bcc'd; bcc'ing** **1** : to send a blind carbon copy to **2** : to send as a blind carbon copy
[2]**bcc** *abbr* blind carbon copy
B cell *n* [*b*one-marrow-derived *cell*] : any of the lymphocytes that secrete antibodies when mature
B complex *n* : VITAMIN B COMPLEX
bd *abbr* **1** board **2** bound
bdl *or* **bdle** *abbr* bundle
bdrm *abbr* bedroom
be \ˈbē\ *vb, past 1st & 3d sing* **was** \ˈwəz, ˈwäz\; *2d sing* **were** \ˈwər\; *pl* **were**; *past subjunctive* **were**; *past part* **been** \ˈbin, ˈben\; *pres part* **be•ing** \ˈbē-iŋ\; *pres 1st sing* **am** \əm, ˈam\; *2d sing* **are** \ər, ˈär\; *3d sing* **is** \ˈiz, əz\; *pl* **are**; *pres subjunctive* **be** **1** : to equal in meaning or symbolically ⟨God *is* love⟩; *also* : to have a specified qualification or relationship ⟨leaves *are* green⟩ ⟨this fish *is* a trout⟩ **2** : to have objective existence ⟨I think, therefore I *am*⟩; *also* : to have or occupy a particular place ⟨here *is* your pen⟩ **3** : to take place : OCCUR ⟨the meeting *is* tonight⟩ **4** — used with the past participle of transitive verbs as a passive voice auxiliary ⟨the door *was* opened⟩ **5** — used as the auxiliary of the present participle in expressing continuous action ⟨he *is* sleeping⟩ **6** — used as an auxiliary with the past participle of some intransitive verbs to form archaic perfect tenses **7** — used as an auxiliary with *to* and the infinitive to express futurity, prearrangement, or obligation ⟨you *are* to wait here⟩
Be *symbol* beryllium
[1]**beach** \ˈbēch\ *n* : a sandy or gravelly part of the shore of an ocean or lake
[2]**beach** *vb* : to run or drive ashore
beach buggy *n* : DUNE BUGGY
beach•comb•er \ˈbēch-ˌkō-mər\ *n* : a person who searches along a shore for something of use or value
beach•head \ˈbēch-ˌhed\ *n* : a small area on an enemy-held shore occupied in the initial stages of an invasion
bea•con \ˈbē-kən\ *n* **1** : a signal fire **2** : a guiding or warning signal (as a lighthouse) **3** : a radio transmitter emitting signals for guidance of aircraft
[1]**bead** \ˈbēd\ *n* [ME *bede* prayer, prayer bead, fr. OE *bed, gebed* prayer] **1** *pl* : a series of prayers and meditations made with a rosary **2** : a small piece of material pierced for threading on a line (as in a rosary) **3** : a small globular body **4** : a narrow projecting rim or band — **bead•ing** *n* — **beady** *adj*
[2]**bead** *vb* : to form into a bead
bea•dle \ˈbē-dᵊl\ *n* : a usu. English parish officer whose duties include keeping order in church
bea•gle \ˈbē-gəl\ *n* : a small short-legged smooth-coated hound
beak \ˈbēk\ *n* : the bill of a bird and esp. of a bird of prey; *also* : a pointed projecting part — **beaked** \ˈbēkt\ *adj*
bea•ker \ˈbē-kər\ *n* **1** : a large widemouthed drinking cup **2** : a widemouthed thin-walled laboratory vessel
[1]**beam** \ˈbēm\ *n* **1** : a large long piece of timber or metal **2** : the bar of a balance from which the scales hang **3** : the breadth of a ship at its widest part **4** : a ray or shaft of light **5** : a collection of nearly parallel rays (as X-rays) or particles (as electrons) **6** : a constant radio signal transmitted for the guidance of pilots; *also* : the course indicated by this signal
[2]**beam** *vb* **1** : to send out light **2** : BROADCAST **3** : to transmit (data) electronically **4** : to smile with joy
[1]**bean** \ˈbēn\ *n* : the edible seed borne in pods by some leguminous plants; *also* : a plant or a pod bearing beans
[2]**bean** *vb* : to strike on the head with an object
bean•bag \ˈbēn-ˌbag\ *n* : a cloth bag partially filled typically with dried beans and used as a toy
bean•ball \ˈbēn-ˌbȯl\ *n* : a pitch thrown at a batter's head
bean curd *n* : TOFU
bean•ie \ˈbē-nē\ *n* : a small round tight-fitting skullcap
beano \ˈbē-nō\ *n, pl* **beanos** : BINGO
[1]**bear** \ˈber\ *n, pl* **bears** **1** *or pl* **bear** : any of a family of large heavy mammals with shaggy hair and small tails **2** : a gruff or sullen person **3** : one who sells (as securities) in expectation of a price decline — **bear•ish** *adj*
[2]**bear** *vb* **bore** \ˈbȯr\; **borne** \ˈbȯrn\ *also* **born** \ˈbȯrn\; **bear•ing** **1** : CARRY **2** : to be equipped with **3** : to give as testimony ⟨~ witness to the facts⟩ **4** : to give birth to; *also* : PRODUCE, YIELD ⟨a tree that ~*s* regularly⟩ **5** : ENDURE, SUSTAIN ⟨~ pain⟩ ⟨*bore* the weight on piles⟩; *also* : to exert pressure or influence **6** : to go in an indicated direction ⟨~ right⟩ — **bear•able** *adj* — **bear•er** *n*
[1]**beard** \ˈbird\ *n* **1** : the hair that grows on the face of a man **2** : a growth of bristly hairs (as on a goat's chin) — **beard•ed** \ˈbir-dəd\ *adj* — **beard•less** *adj*
[2]**beard** *vb* : to confront boldly
bearing *n* **1** : manner of carrying oneself : COMPORTMENT **2** : a supporting object, purpose, or point **3** : a machine part in which another part (as an axle or pin) turns **4** : an emblem in a coat of arms **5** : the position or direction of one point with respect to another or to the compass; *also* : a determination of position **6** *pl* : comprehension of one's situation **7** : connection with or influence on something; *also* : SIGNIFICANCE
bear market *n* : a market in which securities or commodities are persistently declining in value
bear•skin \ˈber-ˌskin\ *n* : an article (as a hat) made of the skin of a bear
beast \ˈbēst\ *n* **1** : ANIMAL 1; *esp* : a

4-footed mammal **2** : a contemptible person

[1]**beast·ly** \ˈbēst-lē\ *adj* **beast·li·er; -est** **1** : BESTIAL **2** : ABOMINABLE, DISAGREEABLE — **beast·li·ness** \-nəs\ *n*

[2]**beastly** *adv* : VERY ⟨a ∼ cold day⟩

[1]**beat** \ˈbēt\ *vb* **beat; beat·en** \ˈbē-tᵊn\ *or* **beat; beat·ing** **1** : to strike repeatedly **2** : TREAD **3** : to affect or alter by beating ⟨∼ metal into sheets⟩ **4** : to sound (as an alarm) on a drum **5** : OVERCOME ⟨∼ his opponent⟩; *also* : SURPASS ⟨a meal hard to ∼⟩ **6** : to act or arrive before ⟨∼ his brother home⟩ **7** : THROB — **beat·er** *n*

[2]**beat** *n* **1** : a single stroke or blow esp. of a series; *also* : PULSATION **2** : a rhythmic stress in poetry or music or the rhythmic effect of these **3** : a regularly traversed course

[3]**beat** *adj* **1** : EXHAUSTED **2** : of or relating to beatniks

[4]**beat** *n* : BEATNIK

be·atif·ic \ˌbē-ə-ˈti-fik\ *adj* : giving or indicative of great joy or bliss

be·at·i·fy \bē-ˈa-tə-ˌfī\ *vb* **-fied; -fy·ing** **1** : to make supremely happy **2** : to declare to have attained the blessedness of heaven and authorize the title "Blessed" for — **be·at·i·fi·ca·tion** \-ˌa-tə-fə-ˈkā-shən\ *n*

be·at·i·tude \bē-ˈa-tə-ˌtüd, -ˌtyüd\ *n* **1** : a state of utmost bliss **2** : any of the declarations made in the Sermon on the Mount (Matthew 5:3–12) beginning "Blessed are"

beat·nik \ˈbēt-nik\ *n* : a usu. young and artistic person who rejects the mores of established society

beau \ˈbō\ *n, pl* **beaux** \ˈbōz\ *or* **beaus** [F, fr. *beau* beautiful, fr. L *bellus* pretty] **1** : a man of fashion : DANDY **2** : BOYFRIEND 2

beau geste \bō-ˈzhest\ *n, pl* **beaux gestes** *or* **beau gestes** \bō-ˈzhest\ [F] : a graceful or magnanimous gesture

beau ide·al \ˌbō-ī-ˈdē(-ə)l\ *n, pl* **beau ideals** [F] : the perfect type or model

Beau·jo·lais \ˌbō-zhō-ˈlā\ *n* : a light fruity red wine

beau monde \bō-ˈmänd, -ˈmōⁿd\ *n, pl* **beau mondes** \-ˈmänz, -ˈmändz\ *or* **beaux mondes** \bō-ˈmōⁿd\ [F] : the world of high society and fashion

beau·te·ous \ˈbyü-tē-əs\ *adj* : BEAUTIFUL — **beau·te·ous·ly** *adv*

beau·ti·cian \byü-ˈti-shən\ *n* : COSMETOLOGIST

beau·ti·ful \ˈbyü-ti-fəl\ *adj* : characterized by beauty : LOVELY ♦ *Synonyms* PRETTY, FAIR, COMELY — **beau·ti·ful·ly** \-f(ə-)lē\ *adv*

beautiful people *n pl, often cap B&P* : wealthy or famous people whose lifestyle is usu. expensive and well-publicized

beau·ti·fy \ˈbyü-tə-ˌfī\ *vb* **-fied; -fy·ing** : to make more beautiful — **beau·ti·fi·ca·tion** \ˌbyü-tə-fə-ˈkā-shən\ *n* — **beau·ti·fi·er** *n*

beau·ty \ˈbyü-tē\ *n, pl* **beauties** : qualities that give pleasure to the senses or exalt the mind : LOVELINESS; *also* : something having such qualities

beauty shop *n* : an establishment where hairdressing, facials, and manicures are done

beaux arts \bō-ˈzär\ *n pl* [F] : FINE ARTS

bea·ver \ˈbē-vər\ *n, pl* **beavers** : a large fur-bearing herbivorous rodent that builds dams and underwater houses of mud and sticks; *also* : its fur

be·calm \bi-ˈkäm, -ˈkälm\ *vb* : to keep (as a ship) motionless by lack of wind

be·cause \bi-ˈkȯz, -ˈkəz\ *conj* : for the reason that ⟨rested ∼ he was tired⟩

because of *prep* : by reason of

beck \ˈbek\ *n* : a beckoning gesture; *also* : SUMMONS

beck·on \ˈbe-kən\ *vb* : to summon or signal esp. by a nod or gesture; *also* : ATTRACT

be·cloud \bi-ˈklau̇d\ *vb* : OBSCURE

be·come \bi-ˈkəm\ *vb* **-came** \-ˈkām\; **-come; -com·ing** **1** : to come to be ⟨∼ tired⟩ **2** : to suit or be suitable to ⟨her dress ∼*s* her⟩

becoming *adj* : SUITABLE, FIT; *also* : ATTRACTIVE — **be·com·ing·ly** *adv*

[1]**bed** \ˈbed\ *n* **1** : an article of furniture to sleep on **2** : a plot of ground prepared for plants **3** : FOUNDATION, BOTTOM ⟨the ocean ∼⟩ **4** : LAYER, STRATUM ⟨a ∼ of rice⟩

[2]**bed** *vb* **bed·ded; bed·ding** **1** : to put or go to bed **2** : to fix in a foundation : EMBED **3** : to plant in beds **4** : to lay or lie flat or in layers

bed–and–breakfast *n* : an establishment offering lodging and breakfast

be·daub \bi-ˈdȯb\ *vb* : SMEAR

be·daz·zle \bi-ˈda-zəl\ *vb* : to confuse by or as if by a strong light; *also* : FASCINATE — **be·daz·zle·ment** *n*

bed·bug \ˈbed-ˌbəg\ *n* : a wingless bloodsucking bug infesting houses and esp. beds

bed·clothes \ˈbed-ˌklōthz\ *n pl* : materials for making up a bed

bed·ding \ˈbe-diŋ\ *n* **1** : BEDCLOTHES **2** : FOUNDATION ⟨straw ∼⟩

be·deck \bi-ˈdek\ *vb* : ADORN

be·dev·il \bi-ˈde-vəl\ *vb* **1** : HARASS, TORMENT **2** : CONFUSE, MUDDLE

be·dew \bi-ˈdü, -ˈdyü\ *vb* : to wet with or as if with dew

bed·fast \ˈbed-ˌfast\ *adj* : BEDRIDDEN

bed·fel·low \-ˌfe-lō\ *n* **1** : one sharing the bed of another **2** : a close associate : ALLY ⟨politics makes strange ∼*s*⟩

be·di·zen \bi-ˈdī-zᵊn, -ˈdi-\ *vb* : to dress or adorn with showy or vulgar finery

bed·lam \ˈbed-ləm\ *n* [*Bedlam,* popular name for the Hospital of St. Mary of Bethlehem, London, an insane asylum, fr. ME *Bedlem* Bethlehem] **1** *often cap* : an insane asylum **2** : a scene of uproar and confusion ⟨∼ in the court⟩

bed·ou·in *also* **bed·u·in** \ˈbe-də-wən\ *n, pl* **bedouin** *or* **bedouins** *also* **beduin** *or* **beduins** *often cap* [ME *Bedoyne,* fr. MF *bedoïn,* fr. Ar *badawī* desert dweller] : a nomadic Arab of the Arabian, Syrian, or northern African deserts

bed·pan \ˈbed-ˌpan\ *n* : a shallow vessel

used by a bedridden person for urination or defecation

bed·post \-ˌpōst\ *n* : the post of a bed

be·drag·gled \bi-ˈdra-gəld\ *adj* : soiled and disordered as if by being drenched

bed·rid·den \ˈbed-ˌri-dᵊn\ *adj* : kept in bed by illness or weakness

¹**bed·rock** \-ˈräk\ *n* : the solid rock underlying surface materials (as soil)

²**bedrock** *adj* : solidly fundamental, basic, or reliable ⟨traditional ~ values⟩

bed·roll \ˈbed-ˌrōl\ *n* : bedding rolled up for carrying

bed·room \-ˌrüm, -ˌru̇m\ *n* : a room containing a bed and used esp. for sleeping

bed·side \-ˌsīd\ *n* : the place beside a bed esp. of a sick or dying person

bed·sore \-ˌsȯr\ *n* : an ulceration of tissue deprived of adequate blood supply by prolonged pressure

bed·spread \-ˌspred\ *n* : a usu. ornamental cloth cover for a bed

bed·stead \-ˌsted\ *n* : the framework of a bed

bed·time \-ˌtīm\ *n* : time for going to bed

bed–wet·ting \-ˌwe-tiŋ\ *n* : involuntary discharge of urine esp. in bed during sleep — **bed–wet·ter** *n*

¹**bee** \ˈbē\ *n* : any of numerous 4-winged insects (as honeybees or bumblebees) that feed on nectar and pollen and that sometimes produce honey or have a painful sting

²**bee** *n* : a gathering of people for a specific purpose ⟨a quilting ~⟩

beech \ˈbēch\ *n, pl* **beech·es** *or* **beech** : any of a genus of hardwood trees with smooth gray bark and small sweet triangular nuts; *also* : its wood — **beech·en** \ˈbē-chən\ *adj*

beech·nut \ˈbēch-ˌnət\ *n* : the nut of a beech

¹**beef** \ˈbēf\ *n, pl* **beefs** \ˈbēfs\ *or* **beeves** \ˈbēvz\ **1** : the flesh of a steer, cow, or bull; *also* : the dressed carcass of a beef animal **2** : a steer, cow, or bull esp. when fattened for food **3** : MUSCLE, BRAWN **4** *pl beefs* : COMPLAINT

²**beef** *vb* **1** : STRENGTHEN — usu. used with *up* ⟨~*ed* up security⟩ **2** : COMPLAIN

beef·eat·er \ˈbē-ˌfē-tər\ *n* : a yeoman of the guard of an English monarch

beef·steak \-ˌstāk\ *n* : a slice of beef suitable for broiling or frying

beefy \ˈbē-fē\ *adj* **beef·i·er**; **-est** : THICKSET, BRAWNY ⟨a ~ wrestler⟩

bee·hive \ˈbē-ˌhīv\ *n* : HIVE 1, HIVE 3

bee·keep·er \-ˌkē-pər\ *n* : a person who raises bees — **bee·keep·ing** *n*

bee·line \-ˌlīn\ *n* : a straight direct course

been *past part of* BE

beep·er \ˈbē-pər\ *n* : PAGER; *esp* : one that beeps

beer \ˈbir\ *n* : an alcoholic beverage brewed from malt and hops — **beery** *adj*

beer belly *n* : POTBELLY

bees·wax \ˈbēz-ˌwaks\ *n* : WAX 1

beet \ˈbēt\ *n* : a garden plant with edible leaves and a thick sweet root used as a vegetable, as a source of sugar, or as forage; *also* : its root

¹**bee·tle** \ˈbē-tᵊl\ *n* : any of an order of insects having four wings of which the stiff outer pair covers the membranous inner pair when not in flight

²**beetle** *vb* **bee·tled**; **bee·tling** : to jut out : PROJECT

be·fall \bi-ˈfȯl\ *vb* **-fell** \-ˈfel\; **-fall·en** \-ˈfȯ-lən\ : to happen to : OCCUR

be·fit \bi-ˈfit\ *vb* : to be suitable to

be·fog \bi-ˈfȯg, -ˈfäg\ *vb* : OBSCURE; *also* : CONFUSE ⟨drink *befogged* his senses⟩

¹**be·fore** \bi-ˈfȯr\ *adv or adj* **1** : in front **2** : EARLIER

²**before** *prep* **1** : in front of ⟨stood ~ him⟩ **2** : earlier than ⟨got there ~ me⟩ **3** : in a more important category than ⟨put quality ~ quantity⟩

³**before** *conj* **1** : earlier than the time that ⟨she started ~ I did⟩ **2** : more willingly than ⟨he'd starve ~ he'd steal⟩

be·fore·hand \bi-ˈfȯr-ˌhand\ *adv or adj* : in advance

be·foul \bi-ˈfau̇(-ə)l\ *vb* : SOIL

be·friend \bi-ˈfrend\ *vb* : to act as friend to

be·fud·dle \bi-ˈfə-dᵊl\ *vb* : MUDDLE, CONFUSE

beg \ˈbeg\ *vb* **begged**; **beg·ging** **1** : to ask as a charity; *also* : ENTREAT **2** : EVADE; *also* : assume as established, settled, or proved ⟨~ the question⟩

be·get \bi-ˈget\ *vb* **-got** \-ˈgät\; **-got·ten** \-ˈgä-tᵊn\ *or* **-got**; **-get·ting** : to become the father of : SIRE

¹**beg·gar** \ˈbe-gər\ *n* : one that begs; *esp* : a person who begs as a way of life

²**beggar** *vb* : IMPOVERISH

beg·gar·ly \ˈbe-gər-lē\ *adj* **1** : contemptibly mean or inadequate **2** : marked by unrelieved poverty ⟨a ~ life⟩

beg·gary \ˈbe-gə-rē\ *n* : extreme poverty

be·gin \bi-ˈgin\ *vb* **be·gan** \-ˈgan\; **be·gun** \-ˈgən\; **be·gin·ning** **1** : to do the first part of an action : COMMENCE **2** : to come into being : ARISE; *also* : FOUND ⟨he *began* the movement⟩ **3** : ORIGINATE, INVENT — **be·gin·ner** *n*

beg off *vb* : to ask to be excused from something

be·gone \bi-ˈgȯn\ *vb* : to go away : DEPART — used esp. in the imperative

be·go·nia \bi-ˈgō-nyə\ *n* : any of a genus of tropical herbs widely grown for their showy leaves and waxy flowers

be·grime \bi-ˈgrīm\ *vb* **be·grimed**; **be·grim·ing** : to make dirty

be·grudge \bi-ˈgrəj\ *vb* **1** : to give or concede reluctantly **2** : to be reluctant to grant or allow — **be·grudg·ing·ly** \-ˈgrə-jiŋ-lē\ *adv*

be·guile \-ˈgī(-ə)l\ *vb* **be·guiled**; **be·guil·ing** **1** : DECEIVE **2** : to while away ⟨*beguiled* sorrow with music⟩ **3** : to engage the interest of by guile

be·guine \bi-ˈgēn\ *n* [AmerF *béguine,* fr. F *béguin* flirtation] : a vigorous popular dance of the islands of Saint Lucia and Martinique

be·gum \ˈbā-gəm, ˈbē-\ *n* : a Muslim woman of high rank

be·half \bi-ˈhaf, -ˈhäf\ *n* : BENEFIT, SUPPORT, DEFENSE ⟨argued in their ~⟩

be·have \bi-ˈhāv\ *vb* **be·haved; be·hav·ing** **1** : to bear, comport, or conduct oneself in a particular and esp. a proper way **2** : to act, function, or react in a particular way

be·hav·ior \bi-ˈhā-vyər\ *n* : way of behaving; *esp* : personal conduct — **be·hav·ior·al** \-vyə-rəl\ *adj* — **be·hav·ior·al·ly** \-rə-lē\ *adv*

be·hav·ior·ism \bi-ˈhā-vyə-ˌri-zəm\ *n* : a school of psychology concerned with the objective evidence of behavior without reference to conscious experience

be·hav·ior·ist \-vyə-rist\ *n* **1** : a person who supports behaviorism **2** : a person who studies behavior

be·hav·iour, be·hav·iour·ism *chiefly Brit var of* BEHAVIOR, BEHAVIORISM

be·head \bi-ˈhed\ *vb* : to cut off the head of

be·he·moth \bi-ˈhē-məth, ˈbē-ə-ˌmäth\ *n* : a huge powerful animal described in Job 40:15–24; *also* : something of monstrous size or power

be·hest \bi-ˈhest\ *n* **1** : COMMAND **2** : an urgent prompting

[1]**be·hind** \bi-ˈhīnd\ *adv or adj* **1** : BACK, BACKWARD ⟨look ~⟩ **2** : LATE, SLOW

[2]**behind** *prep* **1** : in or to a place or situation in back of or to the rear of ⟨look ~ you⟩ ⟨the staff stayed ~ the troops⟩ **2** : inferior to (as in rank) : BELOW ⟨three games ~ the first-place team⟩ **3** : in support of : SUPPORTING ⟨we're ~ you all the way⟩

be·hind·hand \bi-ˈhīnd-ˌhand\ *adj* : being in arrears ♦ ***Synonyms*** TARDY, LATE, OVERDUE, BELATED

be·hold \bi-ˈhōld\ *vb* **-held** \-ˈheld\; **-hold·ing** **1** : to have in sight : SEE **2** — used imperatively to direct the attention ♦ ***Synonyms*** VIEW, OBSERVE, NOTICE, ESPY — **be·hold·er** *n*

be·hold·en \bi-ˈhōl-dən\ *adj* : OBLIGATED, INDEBTED

be·hoove \bi-ˈhüv\ *vb* **be·hooved; be·hoov·ing** : to be necessary, proper, or advantageous for

be·hove *chiefly Brit var of* BEHOOVE

beige \ˈbāzh\ *n* : a pale dull yellowish brown — **beige** *adj*

be·ing \ˈbē-iŋ\ *n* **1** : EXISTENCE; *also* : LIFE **2** : the qualities or constitution of an existent thing **3** : a living thing; *esp* : PERSON

be·la·bor \bi-ˈlā-bər\ *vb* : to assail (as with words) tiresomely or at length

be·la·bour *chiefly Brit var of* BELABOR

be·lat·ed \bi-ˈlā-təd\ *adj* : DELAYED, LATE ⟨~ birthday wishes⟩

be·lay \bi-ˈlā\ *vb* **1** : to wind (a rope) around a pin or cleat in order to hold secure **2** : QUIT, STOP — used in the imperative

belch \ˈbelch\ *vb* **1** : to expel (gas) from the stomach through the mouth **2** : to gush forth ⟨a volcano *~ing* lava⟩ — **belch** *n*

bel·dam *or* **bel·dame** \ˈbel-dəm\ *n* [ME *beldam* grandmother, fr. AF *bel* beautiful + ME *dam* lady, mother] : an old woman

be·lea·guer \bi-ˈlē-gər\ *vb* **1** : BESIEGE **2** : HARASS ⟨*~ed* parents⟩

bel·fry \ˈbel-frē\ *n, pl* **belfries** : a tower for a bell (as on a church); *also* : the part of the tower in which the bell hangs

Belg *abbr* Belgian; Belgium

Bel·gian endive \ˈbel-jən\ *n* : the blanched shoot of chicory

Belgian waffle *n* : a waffle having large depressions and usu. topped with fruit and whipped cream

be·lie \bi-ˈlī\ *vb* **-lied; -ly·ing** **1** : MISREPRESENT **2** : to show (something) to be false **3** : to run counter to

be·lief \bə-ˈlēf\ *n* **1** : CONFIDENCE, TRUST **2** : something (as a tenet or creed) believed ♦ ***Synonyms*** CONVICTION, OPINION, PERSUASION, SENTIMENT

be·lieve \bə-ˈlēv\ *vb* **be·lieved; be·liev·ing** **1** : to have religious convictions **2** : to have a firm conviction about something : accept as true **3** : to hold as an opinion : SUPPOSE — **be·liev·able** \-ˈlē-və-bəl\ *adj* — **be·liev·ably** \-blē\ *adv* — **be·liev·er** *n*

be·like \bi-ˈlīk\ *adv, archaic* : PROBABLY

be·lit·tle \bi-ˈli-tᵊl\ *vb* **-lit·tled; -lit·tling** : to make seem little or less; *also* : DISPARAGE ⟨*belittled* his opponent⟩

[1]**bell** \ˈbel\ *n* **1** : a hollow metallic device that makes a ringing sound when struck **2** : the sounding or stroke of a bell (as on shipboard to tell the time); *also* : time so indicated **3** : something with the flared form of a bell

[2]**bell** *vb* : to provide with a bell

bel·la·don·na \ˌbe-lə-ˈdä-nə\ *n* [It, lit., beautiful lady] : a medicinal extract (as atropine) from a poisonous European herb related to the potato; *also* : this herb

bell–bot·toms \ˈbel-ˈbä-təmz\ *n pl* : pants with wide flaring bottoms — **bell–bottom** *adj*

bell·boy \ˈbel-ˌbȯi\ *n* : BELLHOP

belle \ˈbel\ *n* : an attractive and popular girl or woman

belles let·tres \bel-ˈletrᵊ\ *n pl* [F] : literature that is an end in itself and not practical or purely informative — **bel·le·tris·tic** \ˌbe-lə-ˈtris-tik\ *adj*

bell·hop \ˈbel-ˌhäp\ *n* : a hotel or club employee who takes guests to rooms, carries luggage, and runs errands

bel·li·cose \ˈbe-li-ˌkōs\ *adj* : WARLIKE, PUGNACIOUS ♦ ***Synonyms*** BELLIGERENT, QUARRELSOME, COMBATIVE, CONTENTIOUS — **bel·li·cos·i·ty** \ˌbe-li-ˈkä-sə-tē\ *n*

bel·lig·er·en·cy \bə-ˈli-jə-rən-sē\ *n* **1** : the status of a nation engaged in war **2** : BELLIGERENCE, TRUCULENCE

bel·lig·er·ent \-rənt\ *adj* **1** : waging war **2** : aggressively self-assertive ♦ ***Synonyms*** BELLICOSE, PUGNACIOUS, COMBATIVE, CONTENTIOUS, WARLIKE — **bel·lig·er·ence** \-rəns\ *n* — **belligerent** *n* — **bel·lig·er·ent·ly** *adv*

bel·low \ˈbe-lō\ *vb* **1** : to make the deep hollow sound characteristic of a bull **2** : to shout in a deep voice — **bellow** *n*

bel·lows \-lōz, -ləz\ *n sing or pl* : a closed

device with sides that can be spread apart and then pressed together to draw in air and expel it through a tube

bell·weth·er \ˈbel-ˈwe-thər, -ˌwe-\ *n* : one that takes the lead or initiative; *also* : an indicator of trends

[1]**bel·ly** \ˈbe-lē\ *n, pl* **bellies** [ME *bely* bellows, belly, fr. OE *belg* bag, skin] **1** : ABDOMEN 1; *also* : POTBELLY **2** : the underpart of an animal's body

[2]**belly** *vb* **bel·lied; bel·ly·ing** : BULGE

[1]**bel·ly·ache** \ˈbe-lē-ˌāk\ *n* : pain in the abdomen : STOMACHACHE

[2]**bellyache** *vb* : COMPLAIN

belly button *n* : the human navel

belly dance *n* : a usu. solo dance emphasizing movement of the belly — **belly dance** *vb* — **belly dancer** *n*

belly laugh *n* : a deep hearty laugh

be·long \bi-ˈlȯŋ\ *vb* **1** : to be suitable or appropriate; *also* : to be properly situated ⟨shoes ~ in the closet⟩ **2** : to be the property ⟨this ~*s* to me⟩; *also* : to be attached (as through birth or membership) ⟨~ to a club⟩ **3** : to form an attribute or part ⟨this wheel ~*s* to the cart⟩ **4** : to be classified ⟨whales ~ among the mammals⟩

be·long·ings \-ˈlȯŋ-iŋz\ *n pl* : GOODS, EFFECTS, POSSESSIONS

be·loved \bi-ˈləvd, -ˈlə-vəd\ *adj* : dearly loved — **beloved** *n*

[1]**be·low** \bi-ˈlō\ *adv* **1** : in or to a lower place or rank **2** : on earth **3** : in hell

[2]**below** *prep* **1** : lower than ⟨~ sea level⟩ **2** : inferior to (as in rank)

be·low·decks \bi-ˌlō-ˈdeks, -ˈlō-ˌdeks\ *adv* : inside the superstructure of a boat or down to a lower deck

[1]**belt** \ˈbelt\ *n* **1** : a strip (as of leather) worn about the waist **2** : a flexible continuous band to communicate motion or convey material **3** : a region marked by some distinctive feature; *esp* : one suited to a particular crop

[2]**belt** *vb* **1** : to encircle or secure with a belt **2** : to beat with or as if with a belt **3** : to mark with an encircling band **4** : to sing loudly

[3]**belt** *n* **1** : a jarring blow : WHACK **2** : DRINK ⟨a ~ of whiskey⟩

belt·er \ˈbel-tər\ *n* : a singer with a powerful voice

belt–tightening *n* : a reduction in spending

belt·way \ˈbelt-ˌwā\ *n* : a highway around a city

be·lu·ga \bə-ˈlü-gə\ *n* [Russ] **1** : a large white sturgeon of the Black Sea, Caspian Sea, and their tributaries that is a source of caviar; *also* : caviar from beluga roe **2** : a whale of arctic and subarctic waters that is white when mature

bel·ve·dere \ˈbel-və-ˌdir\ *n* [It, lit., beautiful view] : a structure (as a summerhouse) designed to command a view

be·mire \bi-ˈmī(-ə)r\ *vb* : to cover or soil with or sink in mire

be·moan \bi-ˈmōn\ *vb* : LAMENT, DEPLORE ♦ ***Synonyms*** BEWAIL, GRIEVE, MOAN, WEEP

be·muse \bi-ˈmyüz\ *vb* : BEWILDER, CONFUSE

[1]**bench** \ˈbench\ *n* **1** : a long seat for two or more persons **2** : the seat of a judge in court; *also* : the office or dignity of a judge **3** : COURT; *also* : JUDGES **4** : a table for holding work and tools ⟨a carpenter's ~⟩

[2]**bench** *vb* **1** : to furnish with benches **2** : to seat on a bench **3** : to remove from or keep out of a game

[1]**bench·mark** \ˈbench-ˌmärk\ *n* **1** *usu* **bench mark** : a mark on a permanent object serving as an elevation reference in topographical surveys **2** : a point of reference for measurement; *also* : STANDARD

[2]**benchmark** *vb* : to study (as a competitor's business practices) in order to improve one's own performance

bench press *n* : an exercise in which a weight is raised by a person lying on a bench — **bench–press** *vb*

bench warrant *n* : a warrant issued by a presiding judge or by a court against a person guilty of contempt or indicted for a crime

[1]**bend** \ˈbend\ *vb* **bent** \ˈbent\; **bend·ing** **1** : to draw (as a bow) taut **2** : to curve or cause a change of shape in ⟨~ a bar⟩ **3** : to make fast : SECURE **4** : DEFLECT **5** : to turn in a certain direction ⟨*bent* his steps toward town⟩ **6** : APPLY ⟨*bent* themselves to the task⟩ **7** : SUBDUE **8** : to curve downward **9** : YIELD, SUBMIT

[2]**bend** *n* **1** : an act or process of bending **2** : something bent; *esp* : CURVE **3** *pl* : a painful and sometimes fatal disorder caused by release of gas bubbles in the tissues upon too rapid decrease in air pressure after a stay in a compressed atmosphere

[3]**bend** *n* : a knot by which a rope is fastened (as to another rope)

bend·er \ˈben-dər\ *n* : SPREE ⟨hungover after a weekend ~⟩

[1]**be·neath** \bi-ˈnēth\ *adv* : BELOW ⟨the mountains and the town ~⟩ ♦ ***Synonyms*** UNDER, UNDERNEATH

[2]**beneath** *prep* **1** : BELOW, UNDER ⟨stood ~ a tree⟩ **2** : unworthy of ⟨considered such behavior ~ her⟩ **3** : concealed by ⟨a warm heart ~ a gruff manner⟩

bene·dic·tion \ˌbe-nə-ˈdik-shən\ *n* : the invocation of a blessing esp. at the close of a public worship service

ben·e·fac·tion \-ˈfak-shən\ *n* : a charitable donation ♦ ***Synonyms*** CONTRIBUTION, ALMS, BENEFICENCE, OFFERING

ben·e·fac·tor \ˈben-ə-ˌfak-tər\ *n* : one that confers a benefit and esp. a benefaction

ben·e·fac·tress \-ˌfak-trəs\ *n* : a woman who is a benefactor

ben·e·fice \ˈbe-nə-fəs\ *n* : an ecclesiastical office to which the revenue from an endowment is attached

be·nef·i·cence \bə-ˈne-fə-səns\ *n* **1** : beneficent quality **2** : BENEFACTION

be·nef·i·cent \-sənt\ *adj* : doing or producing good (as by acts of kindness or charity); *also* : BENEFICIAL

ben·e·fi·cial \ˌbe-nə-ˈfi-shəl\ *adj* : being of benefit or help : HELPFUL ♦ ***Synonyms*** ADVANTAGEOUS, PROFITABLE, FAVORABLE, PROPITIOUS — **ben·e·fi·cial·ly** *adv*

ben·e·fi·cia·ry \ˌbe-nə-ˈfi-shē-ˌer-ē, -ˈfi-shə-rē\ *n, pl* **-ries** : one that receives a benefit (as the income of a trust or the proceeds of an insurance)

[1]**ben·e·fit** \ˈbe-nə-ˌfit\ *n* **1** : ADVANTAGE ⟨the ~*s* of exercise⟩ **2** : useful aid : HELP; *also* : material aid or service provided or due (as in sickness or unemployment) as a right in addition to regular pay **3** : a performance or event to raise funds

[2]**benefit** *vb* **-fit·ed** \-ˌfi-təd\ *also* **-fit·ted**; **-fit·ing** *also* **-fit·ting** **1** : to be useful or profitable to **2** : to receive benefit

be·nev·o·lence \bə-ˈne-və-ləns\ *n* **1** : charitable nature **2** : an act of kindness : CHARITY — **be·nev·o·lent** \-lənt\ *adj* — **be·nev·o·lent·ly** *adv*

be·night·ed \bi-ˈnī-təd\ *adj* **1** : overtaken by darkness or night **2** : living in ignorance

be·nign \bi-ˈnīn\ *adj* [ME *benigne,* fr. AF, fr. L *benignus*] **1** : of a gentle disposition; *also* : showing kindness **2** : of a mild kind; *esp* : not malignant ⟨~ tumors⟩ ♦ ***Synonyms*** BENIGNANT, KIND, KINDLY, GOOD-HEARTED — **be·nig·ni·ty** \-ˈnig-nə-tē\ *n* — **be·nign·ly** *adv*

be·nig·nant \-ˈnig-nənt\ *adj* : BENIGN 1 ♦ ***Synonyms*** KIND, KINDLY, GOOD-HEARTED

ben·i·son \ˈbe-nə-sən, -zən\ *n* : BLESSING, BENEDICTION

[1]**bent** \ˈbent\ *n* **1** : strong inclination or interest; *also* : TALENT **2** : power of endurance ♦ ***Synonyms*** TALENT, APTITUDE, GIFT, FLAIR, KNACK, GENIUS

[2]**bent** *adj* **1** : changed by bending : CROOKED ⟨~ branches⟩ **2** : strongly inclined : DETERMINED ⟨~ on going⟩

bent grass *n* : any of a genus of stiff velvety grasses used esp. for lawns and pastures

ben·thic \ˈben-thik\ *adj* : of, relating to, or occurring at the bottom of a body of water

ben·ton·ite \ˈben-tə-ˌnīt\ *n* : an absorptive clay used esp. as a filler (as in paper)

bent·wood \ˈbent-ˌwu̇d\ *adj* : made of wood bent into shape ⟨a ~ rocker⟩

be·numb \bi-ˈnəm\ *vb* **1** : DULL, DEADEN **2** : to make numb esp. by cold

ben·zene \ˈben-ˌzēn\ *n* : a colorless volatile flammable liquid hydrocarbon used in organic synthesis and as a solvent — **ben·ze·noid** \-zə-ˌnȯid\ *adj or n*

ben·zine \ˈben-ˌzēn\ *n* : any of various flammable petroleum distillates used as solvents or as motor fuels

ben·zo·ate \ˈben-zə-ˌwāt\ *n* : a salt or ester of benzoic acid

ben·zo·ic acid \ben-ˈzō-ik-\ *n* : a white crystalline acid used as a preservative and antiseptic and in synthesizing chemicals

ben·zo·in \ˈben-zə-wən, -ˌzȯin\ *n* : a balsamic resin from trees of southern Asia used esp. in medicine and perfumes

be·queath \bi-ˈkwēth, -ˈkwēth\ *vb* [ME *bequethen,* fr. OE *becwethan,* fr. *be-* + *cwethan* to say] **1** : to leave by will **2** : to hand down

be·quest \bi-ˈkwest\ *n* **1** : the action of bequeathing **2** : something bequeathed : LEGACY

be·rate \-ˈrāt\ *vb* : to scold harshly

Ber·ber \ˈbər-bər\ *n* : a member of any of various peoples living in northern Africa west of Tripoli

ber·ceuse \ber-ˈsœz, -ˈsüz\ *n, pl* **ber·ceuses** *same or* -ˈsü-zəz\ [F, fr. *bercer* to rock] **1** : LULLABY **2** : a musical composition that resembles a lullaby

[1]**be·reaved** \bi-ˈrēvd\ *adj* : suffering the death of a loved one ⟨her ~ parents⟩ — **be·reave·ment** *n*

[2]**bereaved** *n, pl* **bereaved** : one who is bereaved

be·reft \-ˈreft\ *adj* **1** : deprived of or lacking something — usu. used with *of* **2** : BEREAVED ⟨a ~ mother⟩

be·ret \bə-ˈrā\ *n* : a round soft cap with no visor

berg \ˈbərg\ *n* : ICEBERG

beri·beri \ˌber-ē-ˈber-ē\ *n* : a deficiency disease marked by weakness, wasting, and nerve damage and caused by lack of thiamine

berke·li·um \ˈbər-klē-əm\ *n* : an artificially produced radioactive chemical element

berm \ˈbərm\ *n* : a narrow shelf or path at the top or bottom of a slope; *also* : a mound or bank of earth

Bermuda grass *n* : a creeping grass often used for lawns and pastures

Ber·mu·das \bər-ˈmyü-dəz\ *n pl* : BERMUDA SHORTS

Bermuda shorts *n pl* : knee-length walking shorts

ber·ry \ˈber-ē\ *n, pl* **berries** **1** : a small pulpy fruit (as a strawberry) **2** : a simple fruit (as a grape, tomato, or cucumber) with the wall of the ripened ovary thick and pulpy **3** : the dry seed of some plants (as coffee)

ber·serk \bər-ˈsərk, -ˈzərk\ *adj* [ON *berserkr* warrior frenzied in battle, prob. fr. *ber-* bear + *serkr* shirt] : FRENZIED, CRAZED ⟨~ behavior⟩ — **berserk** *adv*

[1]**berth** \ˈbərth\ *n* **1** : adequate distance esp. for a ship to maneuver **2** : the place where a ship is anchored or a vehicle rests **3** : ACCOMMODATIONS **4** : JOB, POSITION ♦ ***Synonyms*** POST, SITUATION, OFFICE, APPOINTMENT

[2]**berth** *vb* **1** : to bring or come into a berth **2** : to allot a berth to

ber·yl \ˈber-əl\ *n* : a hard silicate mineral occurring as colorless hexagonal crystals when pure

be·ryl·li·um \bə-ˈri-lē-əm\ *n* : a light strong metallic chemical element used as a hardener in alloys

be·seech \bi-ˈsēch\ *vb* **-sought** \-ˈsȯt\ *or* **-seeched**; **-seech·ing** : to beg urgently : ENTREAT ♦ ***Synonyms*** IMPLORE, PLEAD, SUPPLICATE, IMPORTUNE

be·seem \bi-ˈsēm\ *vb, archaic* : BEFIT

be·set \-ˈset\ *vb* **-set; -set·ting** **1** : TROUBLE, HARASS ⟨the ills that ~ humanity⟩ **2** : ASSAIL ⟨~ by wild dogs⟩; *also* : SURROUND
be·set·ting *adj* : persistently present
¹**be·side** \bi-ˈsīd\ *prep* **1** : by the side of ⟨sit ~ me⟩ **2** : BESIDES **3** : not relevant to ⟨~ the point⟩
²**beside** *adv, archaic* : BESIDES
¹**be·sides** \bi-ˈsīdz\ *prep* **1** : other than ⟨no one ~ us⟩ **2** : together with
²**besides** *adv* **1** : as well : ALSO **2** : MOREOVER
be·siege \bi-ˈsēj\ *vb* : to lay siege to; *also* : to press with requests — **be·sieg·er** *n*
be·smear \-ˈsmir\ *vb* : SMEAR
be·smirch \-ˈsmərch\ *vb* : SMIRCH, SOIL
be·som \ˈbē-zəm\ *n* : BROOM
be·sot \bi-ˈsät\ *vb* **be·sot·ted; be·sot·ting** **1** : INFATUATE ⟨*besotted* lovers⟩ **2** : to make dull esp. by drinking
be·spat·ter \-ˈspa-tər\ *vb* : SPATTER
be·speak \bi-ˈspēk\ *vb* **-spoke** \-ˈspōk\; **-spo·ken** \-ˈspō-kən\; **-speak·ing** **1** : PREARRANGE **2** : ADDRESS **3** : REQUEST **4** : INDICATE, SIGNIFY ⟨her new album ~*s* her talent⟩ **5** : FORETELL
be·sprin·kle \-ˈspriŋ-kəl\ *vb* : SPRINKLE
¹**best** \ˈbest\ *adj, superlative of* GOOD **1** : excelling all others **2** : most productive (as of good or satisfaction) ⟨the ~ thing to do⟩ **3** : LARGEST, MOST
²**best** *adv, superlative of* WELL **1** : in the best way **2** : MOST
³**best** *n* : something that is best
⁴**best** *vb* : to get the better of : OUTDO
best friend *n* : one's closest and dearest friend
bes·tial \ˈbes-chəl\ *adj* **1** : of or relating to beasts **2** : resembling a beast esp. in brutality or lack of intelligence
bes·ti·al·i·ty \ˌbes-chē-ˈa-lə-tē, ˌbēs-\ *n, pl* **-ties** **1** : the condition or status of a lower animal **2** : display or gratification of bestial traits or impulses **3** : sexual relations between a human being and a lower animal
bes·ti·ary \ˈbes-chē-ˌer-ē\ *n, pl* **-ar·ies** : a medieval allegorical or moralizing work on the appearance and habits of animals
best·ie \ˈbe-stē\ *n* : BEST FRIEND
be·stir \bi-ˈstər\ *vb* : to rouse to action
best man *n* : the principal groomsman at a wedding
be·stow \bi-ˈstō\ *vb* **1** : PUT, PLACE, STOW **2** : to present as a gift — **be·stow·al** *n* — **be·stow·er** *n*
be·stride \bi-ˈstrīd\ *vb* **-strode** \-ˈstrōd\; **-strid·den** \-ˈstri-dᵊn\; **-strid·ing** : to ride, sit, or stand astride
¹**bet** \ˈbet\ *n* **1** : something that is wagered, risked, or pledged usu. between two parties on the outcome of a contest; *also* : the making of such a bet **2** : OPTION ⟨the back road is your best ~⟩
²**bet** *vb* **bet** *also* **bet·ted; bet·ting** **1** : to stake on the outcome of an issue or a contest ⟨~ $2 on the race⟩ **2** : to make a bet with **3** : to lay a bet
³**bet** *abbr* between
be·ta \ˈbā-tə\ *n* **1** : the 2d letter of the Greek alphabet — Β or β **2** : a nearly complete form of a new product (as software)
beta–block·er \-ˌblä-kər\ *n* : any of a group of drugs that decrease the rate and force of heart contractions and lower high blood pressure
be·ta–car·o·tene \-ˈker-ə-ˌtēn\ *n* : an isomer of carotene found in dark green and dark yellow vegetables and fruits
be·take \bi-ˈtāk\ *vb* **-took** \-ˈtu̇k\; **-tak·en** \-ˈtā-kən\; **-tak·ing** : to cause (oneself) to go
beta particle *n* : a high-speed electron; *esp* : one emitted by a radioactive nucleus
beta ray *n* **1** : BETA PARTICLE **2** : a stream of beta particles
beta test *n* : a field test of the beta version of a product esp. by outside testers and prior to commercial release — **beta test** *vb*
be·tel \ˈbē-tᵊl\ *n* : a climbing pepper of southern Asia whose leaves are chewed together with lime and betel nut as a stimulant
betel nut *n* : the astringent seed of an Asian palm that is chewed with betel leaves
bête noire \ˌbet-ˈnwär, ˌbāt-\ *n, pl* **bêtes noires** *same or* -ˈnwärz\ [F, lit., black beast] : a person or thing strongly disliked or avoided
beth·el \ˈbe-thəl\ *n* [Heb *bēth'ēl* house of God] : a place of worship esp. for seamen
be·tide \bi-ˈtīd\ *vb* : to happen to
be·times \bi-ˈtīmz\ *adv* : in good time : EARLY ♦ ***Synonyms*** SOON, SEASONABLY, TIMELY
be·to·ken \bi-ˈtō-kən\ *vb* **1** : PRESAGE **2** : to give evidence of ♦ ***Synonyms*** INDICATE, ATTEST, BESPEAK, TESTIFY
be·tray \bi-ˈtrā\ *vb* **1** : to lead astray; *esp* : SEDUCE **2** : to deliver to an enemy **3** : ABANDON **4** : to prove unfaithful to **5** : to reveal unintentionally; *also* : SHOW, INDICATE ♦ ***Synonyms*** MISLEAD, DELUDE, DECEIVE, BEGUILE — **be·tray·al** *n* — **be·tray·er** *n*
be·troth \bi-ˈtrōth, -ˈtrȯth\ *vb* : to promise to marry — **be·troth·al** *n*
be·trothed *n* : the person to whom one is betrothed
¹**bet·ter** \ˈbe-tər\ *adj, comparative of* GOOD **1** : greater than half **2** : improved in health **3** : more attractive, favorable, or commendable **4** : more advantageous or effective ⟨a ~ solution⟩ **5** : improved in accuracy or performance
²**better** *vb* **1** : to make or become better **2** : SURPASS, EXCEL
³**better** *adv, comparative of* WELL **1** : in a superior manner **2** : to a higher or greater degree; *also* : MORE
⁴**better** *n* **1** : something better; *also* : a superior esp. in merit or rank **2** : ADVANTAGE ⟨got the ~ of his opponent⟩
⁵**better** *verbal auxiliary* : had better ⟨you ~ hurry⟩
better half *n* : SPOUSE
bet·ter·ment \ˈbe-tər-mənt\ *n* : IMPROVEMENT
bet·tor *or* **bet·ter** \ˈbe-tər\ *n* : one that bets

[1]**be·tween** \bi-ˈtwēn\ *prep* **1** : by the common action of ⟨earned $10,000 ~ the two of them⟩ **2** : in the interval separating ⟨an alley ~ two buildings⟩; *also* : in intermediate relation to **3** : in point of comparison of ⟨choose ~ two cars⟩

[2]**between** *adv* : in an intervening space or interval

be·twixt \bi-ˈtwikst\ *adv or prep* : BETWEEN

[1]**bev·el** \ˈbe-vəl\ *n* **1** : a device for adjusting the slant of the surfaces of a piece of work **2** : the angle or slant that one surface or line makes with another when not at right angles

[2]**bevel** *vb* **-eled** *or* **-elled**; **-el·ing** *or* **-el·ling** **1** : to cut or shape to a bevel **2** : INCLINE, SLANT

bev·er·age \ˈbev-rij\ *n* : a drinkable liquid

bevy \ˈbe-vē\ *n, pl* **bev·ies** **1** : a large group or collection **2** : a group of animals and esp. quail

be·wail \bi-ˈwāl\ *vb* : LAMENT ♦ ***Synonyms*** DEPLORE, BEMOAN, GRIEVE, MOAN, WEEP

be·ware \-ˈwer\ *vb* : to be on one's guard : be wary of

be·wil·der \bi-ˈwil-dər\ *vb* : PERPLEX, CONFUSE ♦ ***Synonyms*** MYSTIFY, DISTRACT, PUZZLE — **be·wil·der·ment** *n*

be·witch \-ˈwich\ *vb* **1** : to affect by witchcraft **2** : CHARM, FASCINATE ♦ ***Synonyms*** ENCHANT, ATTRACT, CAPTIVATE — **be·witch·ment** *n*

bey \ˈbā\ *n* **1** : a provincial governor in the Ottoman Empire **2** : the former native ruler of Tunis or Tunisia

[1]**be·yond** \bē-ˈänd\ *adv* **1** : FARTHER ⟨extends to the river and ~⟩ **2** : BESIDES

[2]**beyond** *prep* **1** : on or to the farther side of **2** : out of the reach or sphere of **3** : BESIDES

be·zel \ˈbē-zəl, ˈbe-\ *n* **1** : a rim that holds a transparent covering (as on a watch) **2** : the faceted part of a cut gem that rises above the setting

bf *abbr* boldface

BFF *abbr* best friends forever

BG *or* **B Gen** *abbr* brigadier general

Bh *symbol* bohrium

bhang \ˈbaŋ\ *n* [Hindi *bhāṅg*] : HEMP; *also* : a mildly intoxicating preparation made from hemp leaves

Bi *symbol* bismuth

BIA *abbr* Bureau of Indian Affairs

bi·an·nu·al \(ˌ)bī-ˈan-yə-wəl\ *adj* : occurring twice a year — **bi·an·nu·al·ly** *adv*

[1]**bi·as** \ˈbī-əs\ *n* **1** : a line diagonal to the grain of a fabric **2** : an inclination of temperament or outlook; *esp* : a personal and sometimes unreasoned judgment : PREJUDICE

[2]**bias** *adv* : on the bias : DIAGONALLY

[3]**bias** *vb* **bi·ased** *or* **bi·assed**; **bi·as·ing** *or* **bi·as·sing** : PREJUDICE

bi·ath·lon \bī-ˈath-lən, -ˌlän\ *n* : a composite athletic contest consisting of cross-country skiing and target shooting with a rifle

[1]**bib** \ˈbib\ *n* : a cloth or plastic shield tied under the chin to protect the clothes while eating

[2]**bib** *abbr* Bible; biblical

bi·be·lot \ˈbē-bə-ˌlō\ *n, pl* **bibelots** *same or* -ˌlōz\ : a small household ornament or decorative object

bi·ble \ˈbī-bəl\ *n* [ME, fr. OF, fr. ML *biblia,* fr. Gk, pl. of *biblion* book, dim. of *byblos* papyrus, book, fr. *Byblos,* ancient Phoenician city from which papyrus was exported] **1** *cap* : the sacred scriptures of Christians comprising the Old and New Testaments **2** *cap* : the sacred scriptures of Judaism; *also* : those of some other religion **3** : a publication that is considered authoritative for its subject — **bib·li·cal** \ˈbi-bli-kəl\ *adj*

bib·li·og·ra·phy \ˌbi-blē-ˈä-grə-fē\ *n, pl* **-phies** **1** : the history or description of writings or publications **2** : a list of writings (as on a subject or of an author) — **bib·li·og·ra·pher** \-fər\ *n* — **bib·li·o·graph·ic** \-ə-ˈgra-fik\ *also* **bib·li·o·graph·i·cal** \-fi-kəl\ *adj*

bib·lio·phile \ˈbi-blē-ə-ˌfī(-ə)l\ *n* : a lover of books

bib·u·lous \ˈbi-byə-ləs\ *adj* **1** : highly absorbent **2** : fond of alcoholic beverages

bi·cam·er·al \ˈbī-ˈka-mə-rəl\ *adj* : having or consisting of two legislative branches

bicarb \(ˌ)bī-ˈkärb, ˈbī-ˌ\ *n* : SODIUM BICARBONATE

bi·car·bon·ate \(ˌ)bī-ˈkär-bə-ˌnāt, -nət\ *n* : an acid carbonate

bicarbonate of soda : SODIUM BICARBONATE

bi·cen·te·na·ry \ˌbī-sen-ˈte-nə-rē, bī-ˈsen-tᵊn-ˌer-ē\ *n* : BICENTENNIAL — **bicentenary** *adj*

bi·cen·ten·ni·al \ˌbī-sen-ˈte-nē-əl\ *n* : a 200th anniversary or its celebration — **bicentennial** *adj*

bi·ceps \ˈbī-ˌseps\ *n, pl* **biceps** *also* **bi·ceps·es** [NL, fr. L, two-headed, fr. *bi-* two + *caput* head] : a muscle (as in the front of the upper arm) having two points of origin

[1]**bick·er** \ˈbi-kər\ *n* : ALTERCATION

[2]**bicker** *vb* : to engage in a petty quarrel

bi·coast·al \bī-ˈkōs-tᵊl\ *adj* : living or working on both the east and west coasts of the U.S.

bi·con·cave \ˌbī-(ˌ)kän-ˈkāv, (ˌ)bī-ˈkän-ˌkāv\ *adj* : concave on both sides

bi·con·vex \ˌbī-(ˌ)kän-ˈveks, (ˌ)bī-ˈkän-ˌveks\ *adj* : convex on both sides

bi·cus·pid \bī-ˈkəs-pəd\ *n* : PREMOLAR

[1]**bi·cy·cle** \ˈbī-ˌsi-kəl\ *n* : a light 2-wheeled vehicle with a saddle, pedals, and handlebars for steering

[2]**bicycle** *vb* **-cy·cled**; **-cy·cling** \-ˌsi-k(ə-)liŋ, -ˌsī-\ : to ride a bicycle — **bi·cy·cler** \-k(ə-)lər\ *n* — **bi·cy·clist** \-k(ə-)list\ *n*

[1]**bid** \ˈbid\ *vb* **bade** \ˈbad, ˈbād\ *or* **bid**; **bid·den** \ˈbi-dᵊn\ *or* **bid** *also* **bade**; **bid·ding** **1** : COMMAND, ORDER **2** : INVITE **3** : to give expression to ⟨*bade* a tearful farewell⟩ **4** : to make a bid : OFFER — **bid·der** *n*

[2]**bid** *n* **1** : the act of one who bids; *also* : an offer for something **2** : INVITATION **3** : an announcement in a card game of

BOOKS OF THE BIBLE

JEWISH SCRIPTURE

LAW	*PROPHETS*		*WRITINGS*
Genesis	Joshua	Obadiah	Psalms
Exodus	Judges	Jonah	Proverbs
Leviticus	1 & 2 Samuel	Micah	Job
Numbers	1 & 2 Kings	Nahum	Song of Songs
Deuteronomy	Isaiah	Habakkuk	Ruth
	Jeremiah	Zephaniah	Lamentations
	Ezekiel	Haggai	Ecclesiastes
	Hosea	Zechariah	Esther
	Joel	Malachi	Daniel
	Amos		Ezra
			Nehemiah
			1 & 2 Chronicles

CHRISTIAN CANON—OLD TESTAMENT

ROMAN CATHOLIC	*PROTESTANT*	*ROMAN CATHOLIC*	*PROTESTANT*
Genesis	Genesis	Wisdom	
Exodus	Exodus	Sirach	
Leviticus	Leviticus	Isaiah	Isaiah
Numbers	Numbers	Jeremiah	Jeremiah
Deuteronomy	Deuteronomy	Lamentations	Lamentations
Joshua	Joshua	Baruch	
Judges	Judges	Ezekiel	Ezekiel
Ruth	Ruth	Daniel	Daniel
1 & 2 Samuel	1 & 2 Samuel	Hosea	Hosea
1 & 2 Kings	1 & 2 Kings	Joel	Joel
1 & 2 Chronicles	1 & 2 Chronicles	Amos	Amos
Ezra	Ezra	Obadiah	Obadiah
Nehemiah	Nehemiah	Jonah	Jonah
Tobit		Micah	Micah
Judith		Nahum	Nahum
Esther	Esther	Habakkuk	Habakkuk
Job	Job	Zephaniah	Zephaniah
Psalms	Psalms	Haggai	Haggai
Proverbs	Proverbs	Zechariah	Zechariah
Ecclesiastes	Ecclesiastes	Malachi	Malachi
Song of Songs	Song of Solomon	1 & 2 Maccabees	

PROTESTANT APOCRYPHA

1 & 2 Esdras	Baruch
Tobit	Prayer of Azariah and the Song of the Three Holy Children
Judith	Susanna
Additions to Esther	Bel and the Dragon
Wisdom of Solomon	The Prayer of Manasses
Ecclesiasticus or the Wisdom of Jesus Son of Sirach	1 & 2 Maccabees

CHRISTIAN CANON—NEW TESTAMENT

Matthew	Ephesians	James
Mark	Philippians	1 & 2 Peter
Luke	Colossians	1, 2, 3 John
John	1 & 2 Thessalonians	Jude
Acts of the Apostles	1 & 2 Timothy	Revelation *or* Apocalypse
Romans	Titus	
1 & 2 Corinthians	Philemon	
Galatians	Hebrews	

what a player proposes to accomplish **4** : an attempt to win or gain
bid·da·ble \ˈbi-də-bəl\ *adj* **1** : OBEDIENT, DOCILE **2** : capable of being bid
bid·dy \ˈbi-dē\ *n, pl* **biddies** : HEN; *also* : a young chicken
bide \ˈbīd\ *vb* **bode** \ˈbōd\ *or* **bid·ed**; **bided**; **bid·ing** **1** : to wait for **2** : WAIT, TARRY **3** : DWELL
bi·det \bi-ˈdā\ *n* : a bathroom fixture used esp. for bathing the external genitals and the anal region
bi·di·rec·tion·al \ˌbī-də-ˈrek-sh(ə-)nəl\ *adj* : involving, moving, or taking place in two usu. opposite directions — **bi·di·rec·tion·al·ly** *adv*
bi·en·ni·al \bī-ˈe-nē-əl\ *adj* **1** : taking place once in two years **2** : lasting two years **3** : producing leaves the first year and fruiting and dying the second year — **biennial** *n* — **bi·en·ni·al·ly** *adv*
bi·en·ni·um \bī-ˈe-nē-əm\ *n, pl* **-niums** *or* **-nia** \-ə\ [L, fr. *bi-* two + *annus* year] : a period of two years
bier \ˈbir\ *n* : a stand bearing a coffin or corpse
bi·fo·cal \ˈbī-ˌfō-kəl\ *adj* : having two focal lengths
bifocals \-kəlz\ *n pl* : eyeglasses with lenses that have one part that corrects for near vision and one for distant vision
bi·fold \ˈbī-ˌfōld\ *adj* : designed to fold twice ⟨∼ doors⟩
bi·fur·cate \ˈbī-fər-ˌkāt, bī-ˈfər-\ *vb* **-cat·ed**; **-cat·ing** : to divide into two branches or parts — **bi·fur·ca·tion** \ˌbī-fər-ˈkā-shən\ *n*
big \ˈbig\ *adj* **big·ger**; **big·gest** **1** : large in size, amount, or scope **2** : PREGNANT; *also* : SWELLING **3** : IMPORTANT, IMPOSING **4** : NOBLE, GENEROUS **5** : POPULAR — **big·ness** *n* — **big on** : strongly favoring or liking
big·a·my \ˈbi-gə-mē\ *n* : the act of marrying one person while still legally married to another — **big·a·mist** \-mist\ *n* — **big·a·mous** \-məs\ *adj*
big bang theory *n* : a theory in astronomy: the universe originated in a rapid expansion (**big bang**) from a single point of nearly infinite energy density
big brother *n* **1** : an older brother **2** : a man who serves as a companion, father figure, and role model for a boy **3** *cap both Bs* : the leader of an authoritarian state or movement **4** : a powerful government or organization that watches and controls people's actions
big cheese *n* : ³BOSS
big crunch *n* : a hypothetical event in which all matter in the universe collapses to a single point of nearly infinite energy density
Big Dipper *n* : the seven principal stars of Ursa Major in a form resembling a dipper
big·foot \ˈbig-ˌfu̇t\ *n* : SASQUATCH
big·horn sheep \ˈbig-ˌhȯrn\ *n* : a wild sheep of mountainous western No. America
bight \ˈbīt\ *n* **1** : a curve in a coast; *also* : the bay formed by such a curve **2** : a slack part in a rope
big–name \ˈbig-ˈnām\ *adj* : widely popular ⟨a ∼ performer⟩ — **big name** *n*
big·ot \ˈbi-gət\ *n* : one who regards or treats members of a group with hatred and intolerance ♦ *Synonyms* FANATIC, ENTHUSIAST, ZEALOT — **big·ot·ed** \-gə-təd\ *adj* — **big·ot·ry** \-trē\ *n*
big screen *n* : the motion picture medium as contrasted to television
big shot \ˈbig-ˌshät\ *n* : an important person
big sister *n* **1** : an older sister **2** : a woman who serves as a companion, mother figure, and role model for a girl
big time \-ˌtīm\ *n* **1** : a high-paying vaudeville circuit requiring only two performances a day **2** : the top rank of an activity or enterprise — **big–tim·er** *n*
big top *n* **1** : the main tent of a circus **2** : CIRCUS
big·wig \ˈbig-ˌwig\ *n* : BIG SHOT
bike \ˈbīk\ *n* **1** : BICYCLE **2** : MOTORCYCLE
bik·er *n* **1** : one who rides a bicycle : BICYCLIST **2** : one who rides a motorcycle : MOTORCYCLIST; *esp* : one who is a member of a motorcycling group
bike·way \ˈbīk-ˌwā\ *n* : a thoroughfare for bicycles
bi·ki·ni \bə-ˈkē-nē\ *n* [F, fr. *Bikini,* atoll in the Marshall Islands] : a woman's brief 2-piece bathing suit
bi·lat·er·al \bī-ˈla-tə-rəl\ *adj* **1** : having or involving two sides **2** : affecting reciprocally two sides or parties — **bi·lat·er·al·ism** \-tə-rə-ˌli-zəm\ *n* — **bi·lat·er·al·ly** *adv*
bile \ˈbī(-ə)l\ *n* **1** : a bitter greenish fluid secreted by the liver that aids in the digestion of fats **2** : an ill-humored mood
bilge \ˈbilj\ *n* **1** : the part of a ship that lies between the bottom and the point where the sides go straight up **2** : stale or worthless remarks or ideas
bi·lin·gual \bī-ˈliŋ-gwəl\ *adj* : expressed in, knowing, or using two languages
bil·ious \ˈbil-yəs\ *adj* **1** : marked by or suffering from disordered liver function **2** : IRRITABLE, ILL-TEMPERED ⟨a ∼ disposition⟩ — **bil·ious·ness** *n*
bilk \ˈbilk\ *vb* : CHEAT, SWINDLE
¹**bill** \ˈbil\ *n* : the jaws of a bird together with their horny covering; *also* : a mouthpart (as of a turtle) resembling these — **billed** \ˈbild\ *adj*
²**bill** *vb* : to caress fondly
³**bill** *n* **1** : an itemized statement of particulars; *also* : INVOICE **2** : a written document or note **3** : a printed advertisement (as a poster) announcing an event **4** : a draft of a law presented to a legislature for enactment **5** : a written statement of a legal wrong suffered or of some breach of law **6** : a piece of paper money
⁴**bill** *vb* **1** : to enter in or prepare a bill; *also* : to submit a bill or account to **2** : to advertise by bills or posters
bill·board \-ˌbȯrd\ *n* : a flat surface on which advertising bills are posted
¹**bil·let** \ˈbi-lət\ *n* **1** : an order requiring a person to provide lodging for a soldier;

also : quarters assigned by or as if by such an order **2** : POSITION, APPOINTMENT

²**billet** *vb* : to assign lodging to by billet

bil·let–doux \ˌbi-lā-ˈdü\ *n, pl* **billets–doux** *same or* -ˈdüz\ [F *billet doux,* lit., sweet letter] : a love letter

bill·fold \ˈbil-ˌfōld\ *n* : WALLET

bil·liards \ˈbil-yərdz\ *n* : any of several games played on an oblong table by driving balls against each other or into pockets with a cue

bil·lings·gate \ˈbi-liŋz-ˌgāt, *Brit usu* -git\ *n* [*Billingsgate,* old gate and fish market, London, England] : coarsely abusive language

bil·lion \ˈbil-yən\ *n* **1** : a thousand millions **2** *Brit* : a million millions — **billion** *adj* — **bil·lionth** \-yənth\ *adj or n*

bill of attainder : a legislative act that imposes punishment without a trial

bill of health : a usu. favorable report following an examination

bill of sale : a legal document transferring ownership of goods

¹**bil·low** \ˈbi-lō\ *n* **1** : WAVE; *esp* : a great wave **2** : a rolling mass (as of fog or flame) like a great wave — **bil·lowy** \ˈbi-lə-wē\ *adj*

²**billow** *vb* : to rise and roll in waves; *also* : to swell out ⟨~*ing* sails⟩

bil·ly \ˈbi-lē\ *n, pl* **billies** : BILLY CLUB

billy club *n* : a heavy usu. wooden club; *esp* : a police officer's club

bil·ly goat \ˈbi-lē-\ *n* : a male goat

bi·met·al \ˈbī-ˌme-tᵊl\ *adj* : BIMETALLIC — **bimetal** *n*

bi·me·tal·lic \ˌbī-mə-ˈta-lik\ *adj* : made of two different metals — often used of devices having a bonded expansive part — **bimetallic** *n*

bi·met·al·lism \bī-ˈme-tᵊl-ˌi-zəm\ *n* : the use of two metals at fixed ratios to form a standard of value for a monetary system

¹**bi·month·ly** \bī-ˈmənth-lē\ *adj* **1** : occurring every two months **2** : occurring twice a month : SEMIMONTHLY — **bimonthly** *adv*

²**bimonthly** *n* : a bimonthly publication

bin \ˈbin\ *n* : a box, crib, or enclosure used for storage

bi·na·ry \ˈbī-nə-rē, -ˌner-ē\ *adj* **1** : consisting of two things or parts **2** : relating to, being, or belonging to a system of numbers having 2 as its base ⟨the ~ digits 0 and 1⟩ **3** : involving a choice between or condition of two alternatives only (as on-off, yes-no) — **binary** *n*

binary star *n* : a system of two stars revolving around each other

binary system *n* : BINARY STAR

bin·au·ral \bī-ˈnȯr-əl\ *adj* : of or relating to sound reproduction involving the use of two separated microphones and two transmission channels to achieve a stereophonic effect

bind \ˈbīnd\ *vb* **bound** \ˈbau̇nd\; **binding** **1** : TIE; *also* : to restrain as if by tying **2** : to put under an obligation; *also* : to constrain with legal authority **3** : BANDAGE **4** : to unite into a mass **5** : to compel as if by a pledge ⟨a handshake ~*s* the deal⟩ **6** : to strengthen or decorate with a band **7** : to fasten together and enclose in a cover ⟨~ books⟩ **8** : to exert a tying, restraining, or compelling effect — **bind·er** *n*

bin·di \ˈbin-dē\ *n* : a mark or ornament worn on the middle of the forehead esp. by Hindu women

bind·ing \ˈbīn-diŋ\ *n* : something (as a ski fastening, a cover, or an edging fabric) used to bind

bin·dle \ˈbin-dᵊl\ *n* : a bundle of clothes or bedding

¹**binge** \ˈbinj\ *n* **1** : SPREE **2** : an act of excessive consumption (as of food)

²**binge** *vb* **binged**; **binge·ing** *or* **bing·ing** : to go on a binge — **bing·er** *n*

bin·go \ˈbiŋ-gō\ *n, pl* **bingos** : a game of chance played with cards having numbered squares corresponding to numbered balls drawn at random and won by covering five squares in a row

bin·na·cle \ˈbi-ni-kəl\ *n* [alter. of ME *bitakle,* fr. Pg or Sp; Pg *bitácola* & Sp *bitácula,* fr. L *habitaculum* dwelling place, fr. *habitare* to inhabit] : a container holding a ship's compass

¹**bin·oc·u·lar** \bī-ˈnä-kyə-lər, bə-\ *adj* : of, relating to, or adapted to the use of both eyes — **bin·oc·u·lar·ly** *adv*

²**bin·oc·u·lar** \bə-ˈnä-kyə-lər, bī-\ *n* **1** : a binocular optical instrument (as a microscope) **2** : a hand-held optical instrument composed of two telescopes and a focusing device — usu. used in pl.

bi·no·mi·al \bī-ˈnō-mē-əl\ *n* **1** : a mathematical expression consisting of two terms connected by the sign plus (+) or minus (–) **2** : a biological species name consisting of two terms — **binomial** *adj*

bio·chem·is·try \ˌbī-ō-ˈke-mə-strē\ *n* : chemistry that deals with the chemical compounds and processes occurring in living things — **bio·chem·i·cal** \-mi-kəl\ *adj or n* — **bio·chem·ic·al·ly** \-k(ə-)lē\ *adv* — **bio·chem·ist** \-mist\ *n*

bio·de·grad·able \-di-ˈgrā-də-bəl\ *adj* : capable of being broken down esp. into innocuous products by the actions of living things (as microorganisms) ⟨a ~ detergent⟩ — **bio·de·grad·abil·i·ty** \-ˌgrā-də-ˈbi-lə-tē\ *n* — **bio·deg·ra·da·tion** \-ˌde-grə-ˈdā-shən\ *n* — **bio·de·grade** \-di-ˈgrād\ *vb*

bio·di·ver·si·ty \-də-ˈvər-sə-tē, -dī-\ *n* : biological diversity in an environment as indicated by numbers of different species of plants and animals

bio·en·gi·neer·ing \-ˌen-jə-ˈnir-iŋ\ *n* **1** : the application of engineering principles to medicine and biology **2** : GENETIC ENGINEERING

bio·eth·ics \-ˈe-thiks\ *n* : the ethics of biological research and its applications esp. in medicine — **bio·eth·i·cal** \-ˈe-thi-kəl\ *adj* — **bio·eth·i·cist** \-ˈe-thə-sist\ *n*

bio·feed·back \-ˈfēd-ˌbak\ *n* : the technique of making unconscious or involuntary bodily processes (as heartbeats or brain waves) perceptible to the senses (as by use of an oscilloscope) in order to manipulate them by conscious mental control

biog *abbr* biographer; biographical; biography

bio·ge·og·ra·phy \ˌbī-ō-jē-ˈä-grə-fē\ *n* : a science that deals with the geographical distribution of plants and animals — **bio·ge·og·ra·pher** *n*

bi·og·ra·phy \bī-ˈä-grə-fē, bē-\ *n, pl* **-phies** : a written history of a person's life; *also* : such writings in general — **bi·og·ra·pher** *n* — **bi·o·graph·i·cal** \ˌbī-ə-ˈgra-fi-kəl\ *also* **bi·o·graph·ic** \-fik\ *adj*

bio·in·for·mat·ics \ˌbī-ō-in-fər-ˈma-tiks\ *n* : the storage, classification, and analysis of biological information using computers

biol *abbr* biologic; biological; biologist; biology

bi·o·log·i·cal \ˌbī-ə-ˈlä-ji-kəl\ *also* **bi·o·log·ic** \-jik\ *adj* **1** : of, relating to, or produced by biology or life and living processes **2** : connected by direct genetic relationship rather than by adoption or marriage ⟨her ~ father⟩ — **bi·o·log·i·cal·ly** \-ji-k(ə-)lē\ *adv*

biological clock *n* : an inherent timing mechanism in a living system that is inferred to exist in order to explain the timing of various physiological and behavioral states and processes

biological warfare *n* : warfare in which harmful living organisms (**biological weapons**) are used against an enemy esp. to cause large-scale death or disease

bi·ol·o·gy \bī-ˈä-lə-jē\ *n* [G *Biologie,* fr. Gk *bios* mode of life + *logos* word, discourse] **1** : a science that deals with living beings and life processes **2** : the life processes of an organism or group — **bi·ol·o·gist** \bī-ˈä-lə-jist\ *n*

bio·mass \ˈbī-ō-ˌmas\ *n* **1** : the amount of living matter (as in a unit area) **2** : plant materials and animal waste used esp. as fuel

bio·med·i·cal \ˌbī-ō-ˈme-di-kəl\ *adj* : of, relating to, or involving biological, medical, and physical science

bi·on·ic \bī-ˈä-nik\ *adj* : having normal biological capability or performance enhanced by or as if by electronic or mechanical devices

bio·phys·ics \ˌbī-ō-ˈfi-ziks\ *n* : a branch of science concerned with the application of physical principles and methods to biological problems — **bio·phys·i·cal** \-zi-kəl\ *adj* — **bio·phys·i·cist** \-ˈfi-zə-sist\ *n*

bio·pic \ˈbī-ō-ˌpik\ *n* : a biographical movie

bi·op·sy \ˈbī-ˌäp-sē\ *n, pl* **-sies** : the removal of tissue, cells, or fluids from the living body for examination

bio·rhythm \ˈbī-ō-ˌri-t͟həm\ *n* : an innately determined rhythmic biological process (as sleep); *also* : the internal mechanism controlling such a process

bio·sci·ence \-ˈsī-əns\ *n* : BIOLOGY 1; *also* : LIFE SCIENCE

bio·sphere \ˈbī-ə-ˌsfir\ *n* **1** : the part of the world in which life can exist **2** : living organisms together with their environment

bio·tech \ˈbī-ō-ˌtek\ *n* : BIOTECHNOLOGY

bio·tech·nol·ogy \ˌbī-ō-tek-ˈnä-lə-jē\ *n* : the manipulation (as through genetic engineering) of living organisms to produce useful products; *also* : biological science so applied

bio·ter·ror·ism \-ˈter-ər-ˌi-zəm\ *n* : terrorism involving the use of biological weapons — **bio·ter·ror·ist** \-ist\ *adj or n*

bi·ot·ic \bī-ˈä-tik\ *adj* : of, relating to, or caused by living organisms

bi·o·tin \ˈbī-ə-tən\ *n* : a vitamin of the vitamin B complex found esp. in yeast, liver, and egg yolk and active in growth promotion

bi·o·tite \ˈbī-ə-ˌtīt\ *n* : a dark mica containing iron, magnesium, potassium, and aluminum

bi·par·ti·san \bī-ˈpär-tə-zən\ *adj* : marked by or involving cooperation, agreement, and compromise between two major political parties — **bi·par·ti·san·ship** \-ˌship\

bi·par·tite \-ˈpär-ˌtīt\ *adj* **1** : being in two parts **2** : shared by two ⟨~ treaty⟩

bi·ped \ˈbī-ˌped\ *n* : a 2-footed animal — **bi·ped·al** \(ˌ)bī-ˈpe-dᵊl\ *adj*

bi·plane \ˈbī-ˌplān\ *n* : an aircraft with two wings placed one above the other

BIPOC *abbr* : Black, Indigenous, (and) People of Color

bi·po·lar \bī-ˈpō-lər\ *adj* : having or involving the use of two poles — **bi·po·lar·i·ty** \ˌbī-pō-ˈler-ə-tē\ *n*

bipolar disorder *n* : any of several psychological disorders of mood characterized usu. by alternating episodes of depression and mania

bi·ra·cial \bī-ˈrā-shəl\ *adj* : of, relating to, or involving members of two races; *also* : having parents of two races

¹birch \ˈbərch\ *n* **1** : any of a genus of mostly short-lived deciduous shrubs and trees with membranous outer bark and pale close-grained wood; *also* : this wood **2** : a birch rod or bundle of twigs for flogging — **birch** *or* **birch·en** \ˈbər-chən\ *adj*

²birch *vb* : WHIP, FLOG

¹bird \ˈbərd\ *n* : any of a class of warm-blooded egg-laying vertebrates having the body feathered and the forelimbs modified to form wings

²bird *vb* : to observe or identify wild birds in their native habitat — **bird·er** *n*

bird·bath \ˈbərd-ˌbath, -ˌbäth\ *n* : a usu. ornamental basin set up for birds to bathe in

bird·house \-ˌhau̇s\ *n* : an artificial nesting place for birds; *also* : AVIARY

bird·ie \ˈbər-dē\ *n* : a score of one under par on a hole in golf

bird·lime \-ˌlīm\ *n* : a sticky substance smeared on twigs to snare small birds

bird of paradise : any of numerous brilliantly colored plumed birds of the New Guinea area

bird of prey : a carnivorous bird that feeds wholly or chiefly on carrion or on meat taken by hunting

bird·seed \ˈbərd-ˌsēd\ *n* : a mixture of small seeds (as of hemp or millet) used for feeding birds

bird's–eye \ˈbərdz-ˌī\ *adj* **1** : marked

with spots resembling birds' eyes ⟨~ maple⟩ **2** : seen from above as if by a flying bird ⟨~ view⟩; *also* : CURSORY

bi·ret·ta \bə-ˈre-tə\ *n* : a square cap with three ridges on top worn esp. by Roman Catholic clergymen

birr \ˈbir, ˈbər\ *n, pl* **birr** — see MONEY table

[1]**birth** \ˈbərth\ *n* **1** : the act or fact of being born or of bringing forth young **2** : LINEAGE, DESCENT **3** : ORIGIN, BEGINNING — **birth** *vb*

[2]**birth** *adj* : BIOLOGICAL 2 ⟨~ parents⟩

birth canal *n* : the channel formed by the cervix, vagina, and vulva through which the fetus passes during birth

birth control *n* : control of the number of children born esp. by preventing or lessening the frequency of conception

birth·day \ˈbərth-ˌdā\ *n* : the day or anniversary of one's birth

birth defect *n* : a physical or biochemical defect present at birth and inherited or environmentally induced

birth·er \ˈbərth-ər\ *n* : a person who believes in or endorses any of various discredited claims that former U.S. president Barack Obama is not a natural-born U.S. citizen

birth·mark \ˈbərth-ˌmärk\ *n* : an unusual mark or blemish on the skin at birth

birth·place \-ˌplās\ *n* : place of birth or origin

birth·rate \-ˌrāt\ *n* : the number of births per number of individuals in a given area or group during a given time

birth·right \-ˌrīt\ *n* : a right, privilege, or possession to which one is entitled by birth ♦ ***Synonyms*** LEGACY, PATRIMONY, HERITAGE, INHERITANCE

birth·stone \-ˌstōn\ *n* : a gemstone associated symbolically with the month of one's birth

bis·cuit \ˈbis-kət\ *n* [ME *bisquite,* fr. AF *besquit,* fr. (*pain*) *besquit* twice-cooked bread] **1** : a small flat cake; *esp, Brit* : COOKIE **2** : a small quick bread made from dough that has been rolled and cut or dropped from a spoon

bi·sect \ˈbī-ˌsekt\ *vb* : to divide into two usu. equal parts; *also* : CROSS, INTERSECT — **bi·sec·tion** \ˈbī-ˌsek-shən\ *n* — **bi·sec·tor** \-tər\ *n*

bi·sex·u·al \bī-ˈsek-shə-wəl\ *adj* **1** : possessing characters of both sexes ⟨~ flowers⟩ **2** : having sexual or romantic attraction to both sexes **3** : of, relating to, or involving both sexes — **bisexual** *n* — **bi·sex·u·al·i·ty** \ˌbī-ˌsek-shə-ˈwal-ə-tē\ *n*

bish·op \ˈbi-shəp\ *n* [ME *bisshop,* fr. OE *bisceop,* fr. LL *episcopus,* fr. Gk *episkopos,* lit., overseer, fr. *epi-* on, over + *skeptesthai* to look] **1** : a member of the clergy ranking above a priest and typically governing a diocese **2** : any of various Protestant church officials who superintend other clergy **3** : a chess piece that can move diagonally across any number of adjoining unoccupied squares

bish·op·ric \ˈbi-shə-prik\ *n* **1** : DIOCESE **2** : the office of bishop

bis·muth \ˈbiz-məth\ *n* : a heavy brittle grayish white metallic chemical element used in alloys and medicine

bi·son \ˈbī-sᵊn, -zᵊn\ *n, pl* **bison** : any of several large bovine mammals with a long broad head, short horns, a large muscular hump across the shoulders, and a shaggy mane on the head and lower neck; *esp* : one formerly abundant in No. America but now reduced to small populations of plains and prairies

bisque \ˈbisk\ *n* : a thick cream soup

bis·tro \ˈbēs-trō, ˈbis-\ *n, pl* **bistros** [F] **1** : a small or unpretentious restaurant **2** : BAR; *also* : NIGHTCLUB

[1]**bit** \ˈbit\ *n* **1** : the biting or cutting edge or part of a tool **2** : the part of a bridle that is placed in a horse's mouth

[2]**bit** *n* **1** : a morsel of food; *also* : a small piece or quantity of something **2** : a small coin; *also* : a unit of value equal to 12½ cents **3** : something small or trivial **4** : an indefinite usu. small degree or extent ⟨a ~ tired⟩

[3]**bit** *n* [*bi*nary digi*t*] : a unit of computer information equivalent to the result of a choice between two alternatives; *also* : its physical representation

[1]**bitch** \ˈbich\ *n* **1** : a female canine; *esp* : a female dog **2** *often offensive* : a malicious, spiteful, or overbearing woman **3** : something difficult or unpleasant

[2]**bitch** *vb* : COMPLAIN

Bit·coin \ˈbit-ˌkȯin\ *n* : a digital currency created for use in online transactions

[1]**bite** \ˈbīt\ *vb* **bit** \ˈbit\; **bit·ten** \ˈbi-tᵊn\ *also* **bit**; **bit·ing** \ˈbī-tiŋ\ **1** : to grip with teeth or jaws; *also* : to wound or sting with or as if with fangs **2** : to cut or pierce with or as if with an edged instrument **3** : to cause to smart or sting **4** : CORRODE **5** : to take bait

[2]**bite** *n* **1** : the act or manner of biting **2** : FOOD **3** : a wound made by biting; *also* : a penetrating effect

bite–size \ˈbīt-ˌsīz\ *adj* **1** : of a size that can be eaten in one bite **2** : being or made small or brief esp. so as to be easily manageable

biting *adj* : SHARP, CUTTING

bit·map \ˈbit-ˌmap\ *n* : an array of binary data representing a bitmapped image or display

bit·mapped \ˈbit-ˌmapt\ *adj* : of, relating to, or being a digital image or display for which an array of binary data specifies the value of each pixel

bit·ter \ˈbi-tər\ *adj* **1** : being or inducing the one of the basic taste sensations that is acrid, astringent, or disagreeable and is suggestive of hops **2** : marked by intensity or severity (as of distress or hatred) **3** : extremely harsh or cruel — **bit·ter·ly** *adv* — **bit·ter·ness** *n*

bit·tern \ˈbi-tərn\ *n* : any of various small or medium-sized herons

bit·ters \ˈbi-tərz\ *n sing or pl* : a usu. alcoholic solution of bitter and often aromatic plant products used in mixing drinks and as a mild tonic

[1]**bit·ter·sweet** \ˈbi-tər-ˌswēt\ *n* **1** : a poisonous nightshade with purple flowers

and reddish berries **2** : a woody vine with yellow capsules that open when ripe to show scarlet seed covers

²bittersweet *adj* : being at once both bitter and sweet

bi·tu·mi·nous coal \bə-ˈtü-mə-nəs-, bī-, -ˈtyü-\ *n* : a coal that when heated yields considerable volatile waste matter

bi·valve \ˈbī-ˌvalv\ *n* : any of a class of mollusks (as clams or scallops) of two separate parts that open and shut — **bivalve** *adj*

¹biv·ouac \ˈbi-və-ˌwak\ *n* [F, fr. Low G *biwacht,* fr. *bi* at + *wacht* guard] : a temporary encampment or shelter

²bivouac *vb* **-ouacked; -ouack·ing** : to form a bivouac : CAMP

¹bi·week·ly \ˌbī-ˈwē-klē\ *adj* **1** : occurring twice a week **2** : occurring every two weeks : FORTNIGHTLY — **biweekly** *adv*

²biweekly *n* : a biweekly publication

bi·year·ly \-ˈyir-lē\ *adj* **1** : BIANNUAL **2** : BIENNIAL

bi·zarre \bə-ˈzär\ *adj* : ODD, ECCENTRIC, FANTASTIC — **bi·zarre·ly** *adv*

bi·zar·ro \bə-ˈzär-ō\ *adj* : characterized by a bizarre, fantastic, or unconventional approach ⟨~ horror movies⟩

bk *abbr* **1** bank **2** book

Bk *symbol* berkelium

bkg *abbr* banking

bkgd *abbr* background

bks *abbr* barracks

bkt *abbr* **1** basket **2** bracket

bl *abbr* **1** bale **2** barrel **3** blue

blab \ˈblab\ *vb* **blabbed; blab·bing** : TATTLE, GOSSIP

¹black \ˈblak\ *adj* **1** : of the color black; *also* : very dark **2** : SWARTHY **3** *cap* : of or relating to any of various population groups often considered to have dark pigmentation of the skin but in fact having a wide range of skin colors **4** *cap* : of or relating to Black people and esp. to African American people or their culture **5** : wearing black **6** : SOILED, DIRTY **7** : lacking light ⟨a ~ night⟩ **8** : WICKED, EVIL ⟨~ magic⟩ **9** : DISMAL, GLOOMY ⟨a ~ outlook⟩ **10** : SULLEN ⟨a ~ mood⟩ — **black·ish** *adj* — **black·ly** *adv* — **black·ness** *n*

²black *n* **1** : a black pigment or dye; *also* : something (as clothing) that is black **2** : the characteristic color of soot or coal **3** *cap* : a person belonging to any of various population groups considered to have dark pigmentation of the skin but in fact having a wide range of skin colors **4** *cap* : AFRICAN AMERICAN

³black *vb* : BLACKEN

black–and–blue \ˌbla-kən-ˈblü\ *adj* : darkly discolored from blood effused by bruising

black–and–white \ˌbla-kən-ˈhwīt\ *n* : SQUAD CAR

black·ball \ˈblak-ˌbȯl\ *vb* **1** : to vote against; *esp* : to exclude from membership by casting a negative vote **2** : OSTRACIZE — **black·ball** *n*

black bass *n* : any of several freshwater sunfishes native to eastern and central No. America

black bear *n* : a usu. black-furred bear of No. American forests

¹black belt \ˈblak-ˌbelt\ *n, often cap both Bs* : an area densely populated by Black people

²black belt \-ˈbelt\ *n* : one who holds the rating of expert (as in judo or karate); *also* : the rating itself

black·ber·ry \-ˌber-ē\ *n* : the usu. black or purple juicy but seedy edible fruit of various brambles; *also* : a plant bearing this fruit

black·bird \-ˌbərd\ *n* : any of various birds (as the red-winged blackbird) of which the male is largely or wholly black

black·board \-ˌbȯrd\ *n* : a smooth usu. dark surface used for writing or drawing on with chalk

black·body \-ˈbä-dē\ *n* : a body or surface that completely absorbs incident radiation with no reflection

black box *n* **1** : a usu. complicated electronic device whose components and workings are unknown or mysterious to the user **2** : a device used in aircraft to record cockpit conversations and flight data

black death *n* : an epidemic of bacterial plague and esp. bubonic plague that spread rapidly in Europe and Asia in the 14th century

black·en \ˈbla-kən\ *vb* **black·ened; black·en·ing** **1** : to make or become black **2** : DEFAME, SULLY

black·ened *adj* : coated with spices and quickly seared in a very hot skillet ⟨~ swordfish⟩

black eye *n* : a discoloration of the skin around the eye from bruising

black–eyed Su·san \ˌblak-ˌīd-ˈsü-zᵊn\ *n* : a No. American coneflower that has deep yellow to orange flower heads with dark conical centers

black·face \ˈblak-ˌfās\ *n* : dark makeup worn to mimic the appearance of a Black person and esp. to mock or ridicule Black people

Black·foot \ˈblak-ˌfu̇t\ *n, pl* **Black·feet** *or* **Blackfoot** : a member of an Indigenous people of Montana, Alberta, and Saskatchewan; *also* : their language

black·guard \ˈbla-gərd, -ˌgärd\ *n* : SCOUNDREL, RASCAL

black·head \ˈblak-ˌhed\ *n* : a small usu. dark oily mass plugging the outlet of a skin gland

black hole *n* : a celestial object with a gravitational field so strong that light cannot escape from it

black ice *n* : a thin layer of ice on a paved road that is very difficult to see

black·ing \ˈbla-kiŋ\ *n* : a substance applied to something to make it black

¹black·jack \ˈblak-ˌjak\ *n* **1** : a leather-covered club with a flexible handle **2** : a card game in which the object is to be dealt cards having a higher count than the dealer but not exceeding 21

²blackjack *vb* : to hit with or as if with a blackjack

black light *n* : invisible ultraviolet light

black·list \ˈblak-ˌlist\ *n* : a list of persons who are disapproved of and are to be punished or boycotted — **blacklist** *vb*

Black Lives Matter *n* : a movement founded in 2013 to end white supremacy and support Black communities

black·mail \ˈblak-ˌmāl\ *n* : extortion by threats esp. of public exposure; *also* : something so extorted — **blackmail** *vb* — **black·mail·er** *n*

black market *n* : illicit trade in goods; *also* : a place where such trade is carried on

Black Mass *n* : a travesty of the Christian Mass ascribed to worshipers of Satan

Black Muslim *n* : a member of a chiefly Black group that professes Islamic religious belief

black nationalist *n, often cap B&N* : a member of a Black advocacy group in the U.S. esp. in the 1960s and 1970s that sought to empower Black people financially, promote a sense of Black community and identity, and form a separate self-governing Black nation — **black nationalism** *n, often cap B&N*

black–on–black *adj* : involving a Black person against another Black person ⟨~ crime⟩

black·out \ˈblak-ˌau̇t\ *n* **1** : a period of darkness due to electrical power failure **2** : a transitory loss or dulling of vision or consciousness **3** : the prohibition or restriction of the telecasting of a sports event — **black out** *vb*

black pepper *n* : a spice that consists of the dried berry of a pepper plant ground with the black husk still on

black power *n often cap B&P* : the mobilization of the political and economic power of Black Americans esp. to compel respect for their rights and improve their condition

black sheep *n* : a member of a group who is disreputable or not regarded favorably

black·smith \ˈblak-ˌsmith\ *n* : a smith who forges iron — **black·smith·ing** *n*

black·strap molasses \ˈblak-ˌstrap-\ *n* : a thick dark molasses obtained from successive processing of raw sugar

black·thorn \-ˌthȯrn\ *n* : a European thorny plum

black–tie \ˈblak-ˈtī\ *adj* : characterized by or requiring semiformal evening clothes consisting of a usu. black tie and tuxedo for men and a formal dress for women

black·top \ˈblak-ˌtäp\ *n* : a dark tarry material (as asphalt) used esp. for surfacing roads — **blacktop** *vb*

black widow *n* : a venomous New World spider having the female black with an hourglass-shaped red mark on the underside of the abdomen

blad·der \ˈbla-dər\ *n* : a sac in which liquid or gas is stored; *esp* : one in a vertebrate into which urine passes from the kidneys

¹**blade** \ˈblād\ *n* **1** : a leaf of a plant and esp. of a grass; *also* : the flat part of a leaf as distinguished from its stalk **2** : something (as the flat part of an oar or an arm of a propeller) resembling the blade of a leaf **3** : the cutting part of an instrument or tool **4** : SWORD; *also* : SWORDSMAN **5** : a dashing man **6** : the runner of an ice skate — **blad·ed** \ˈblā-dəd\ *adj*

²**blade** *vb* **blad·ed**; **blad·ing** : to skate on in-line skates — **blad·er** \ˈblā-dər\ *n*

blain \ˈblān\ *n* : an inflammatory swelling or sore

¹**blame** \ˈblām\ *vb* **blamed**; **blam·ing** [ME, fr. AF *blamer, blasmer,* fr. L *blasphemare* to blaspheme, fr. Gk *blasphēmein*] **1** : to find fault with **2** : to hold responsible or responsible for ♦ ***Synonyms*** CENSURE, DENOUNCE, CONDEMN, CRITICIZE — **blam·able** *adj*

²**blame** *n* **1** : CENSURE, REPROOF **2** : responsibility for fault or error ♦ ***Synonyms*** GUILT, FAULT, CULPABILITY, ONUS — **blame·less** *adj* — **blame·less·ly** *adv* — **blame·less·ness** *n*

blame·wor·thy \-ˌwər-t͟hē\ *adj* : deserving blame — **blame·wor·thi·ness** *n*

blanch \ˈblanch\ *vb* : to make or become white or pale ⟨fear ~*ed* her cheeks⟩

blanc·mange \blə-ˈmänj, -ˈmänzh\ *n* : a dessert made from gelatin or a starchy substance and milk usu. sweetened and flavored

bland \ˈbland\ *adj* **1** : smooth in manner : SUAVE ⟨a ~ smile⟩ **2** : gently soothing ⟨a ~ diet⟩; *also* : INSIPID ♦ ***Synonyms*** GENTLE, MILD, SOFT, BALMY — **bland·ly** *adv* — **bland·ness** *n*

blan·dish·ment \ˈblan-dish-mənt\ *n* : flattering or coaxing speech or action : CAJOLERY

¹**blank** \ˈblaŋk\ *adj* **1** : showing or causing an appearance of dazed dismay; *also* : EXPRESSIONLESS **2** : free from writing or marks; *also* : having spaces to be filled in **3** : DULL, EMPTY ⟨~ moments⟩ **4** : ABSOLUTE, DOWNRIGHT ⟨a ~ refusal⟩ **5** : not shaped in final form — **blank·ly** *adv* — **blank·ness** *n*

²**blank** *n* **1** : an empty space **2** : a form with spaces for the entry of data **3** : an unfinished form (as of a key) **4** : a cartridge with propellant and a seal but no projectile

³**blank** *vb* **1** : to cover or close up : OBSCURE **2** : to keep from scoring

blank check *n* **1** : a signed check with the amount unspecified **2** : complete freedom of action

¹**blan·ket** \ˈblaŋ-kət\ *n* **1** : a heavy woven often woolen covering **2** : a covering layer ⟨a ~ of snow⟩

²**blanket** *vb* : to cover with a blanket

³**blanket** *adj* : covering a group or class ⟨~ insurance⟩; *also* : applicable in all instances ⟨~ rules⟩

blank verse *n* : unrhymed iambic pentameter

blare \ˈbler\ *vb* **blared**; **blar·ing** : to sound loud and harsh; *also* : to proclaim loudly — **blare** *n*

blar·ney \ˈblär-nē\ *n* [*Blarney stone,* a stone in Blarney Castle, near Cork, Ireland, held to bestow skill in flattery on those who kiss it] : skillful flattery : BLANDISHMENT

bla·sé \blä-ˈzā\ *adj* [F] : apathetic to pleasure or excitement as a result of excessive indulgence; *also* : SOPHISTICATED

blas·pheme \blas-ˈfēm, ˈblas-ˌ\ *vb* **blas·phemed; blas·phem·ing** **1** : to speak of or address with irreverence **2** : to utter blasphemy — **blas·phem·er** *n*

blas·phe·my \ˈblas-fə-mē\ *n, pl* **-mies** **1** : the act of expressing lack of reverence for God **2** : irreverence toward something considered sacred — **blas·phe·mous** \-məs\ *adj*

¹**blast** \ˈblast\ *n* **1** : a violent gust of wind; *also* : its effect **2** : sound made by a wind instrument **3** : a current of air forced at high pressure through a hole in a furnace (**blast furnace**) **4** : a sudden withering esp. of plants : BLIGHT **5** : EXPLOSION; *also* : the shock wave of an explosion

²**blast** *vb* : to shatter by or as if by an explosive

blast off *vb* : TAKE OFF 4 — used esp. of rocket-propelled vehicles — **blast·off** \ˈblast-ˌȯf\ *n*

bla·tant \ˈblā-tᵊnt\ *adj* : offensively obtrusive : vulgarly showy ♦ ***Synonyms*** VOCIFEROUS, BOISTEROUS, CLAMOROUS, OBSTREPEROUS — **bla·tan·cy** \-tᵊn-sē\ *n* — **bla·tant·ly** *adv*

blath·er \ˈbla-t͟hər\ *vb* : to talk foolishly at length — **blather** *n*

blath·er·skite \ˈbla-t͟hər-ˌskīt\ *n* : a person who blathers

blax·ploi·ta·tion \ˌblak-ˌsplȯi-ˈtā-shən\ *n* : the exploitation of Black people by producers of Black-oriented films

¹**blaze** \ˈblāz\ *n* **1** : FIRE **2** : intense direct light accompanied by heat **3** : something (as a dazzling display or sudden outburst) suggesting fire ⟨a ~ of autumn leaves⟩ ♦ ***Synonyms*** GLARE, GLOW, FLAME

²**blaze** *vb* **blazed; blaz·ing** **1** : to burn brightly; *also* : to flare up **2** : to be conspicuously bright : GLITTER

³**blaze** *vb* **blazed; blaz·ing** : to make public or conspicuous

⁴**blaze** *n* **1** : a usu. white stripe on the face of an animal **2** : a trail marker; *esp* : one made on a tree

⁵**blaze** *vb* **blazed; blaz·ing** : to mark (as a tree or trail) with blazes

blaze orange *n* : a very bright orange used in clothing for visibility

blaz·er \ˈblā-zər\ *n* : a sports jacket often with notched collar and pockets that are stitched on

¹**bla·zon** \ˈblā-zᵊn\ *n* **1** : COAT OF ARMS **2** : ostentatious display

²**blazon** *vb* **1** : to publish widely : PROCLAIM **2** : DECK, ADORN

bldg *abbr* building

bldr *abbr* builder

¹**bleach** \ˈblēch\ *vb* : WHITEN, BLANCH

²**bleach** *n* : a preparation used in bleaching

bleach·ers \ˈblē-chərz\ *n sing or pl* : a usu. uncovered stand of tiered seats for spectators

bleak \ˈblēk\ *adj* **1** : desolately barren and often windswept **2** : lacking warm or cheering qualities ⟨the future looks ~⟩ — **bleak·ly** *adv* — **bleak·ness** *n*

blear \ˈblir\ *adj* : dim with water or tears ⟨~ eyes⟩

bleary \ˈblir-ē\ *adj* **1** : dull or dimmed esp. from fatigue or sleep **2** : poorly outlined or defined ⟨a ~ view⟩

bleat \ˈblēt\ *n* : the cry of a sheep or goat or a sound like it — **bleat** *vb*

bleed \ˈblēd\ *vb* **bled** \ˈbled\; **bleed·ing** **1** : to lose or shed blood **2** : to be wounded; *also* : to feel pain or distress **3** : to flow or ooze from a wounded surface; *also* : to draw fluid from ⟨~ a tire⟩ **4** : to extort money from

bleed·er \ˈblē-dər\ *n* : one that bleeds; *esp* : HEMOPHILIAC

bleeding heart *n* **1** : a garden plant related to the poppies that has usu. deep pink or white drooping heart-shaped flowers **2** *disparaging* : a person who shows extravagant sympathy esp. for an object of alleged persecution

¹**blem·ish** \ˈble-mish\ *vb* : to spoil by a flaw : MAR

²**blemish** *n* : a noticeable flaw

¹**blench** \ˈblench\ *vb* [ME, to deceive, blench, fr. OE *blencan* to deceive] : FLINCH, QUAIL ♦ ***Synonyms*** SHRINK, RECOIL, WINCE, START

²**blench** *vb* : to grow or make pale

¹**blend** \ˈblend\ *vb* **blend·ed; blend·ing** **1** : to mix thoroughly **2** : to prepare (as coffee) by mixing different varieties **3** : to combine into an integrated whole **4** : HARMONIZE ♦ ***Synonyms*** FUSE, MERGE, MINGLE, COALESCE — **blend·er** *n*

²**blend** *n* : a product of blending ♦ ***Synonyms*** COMPOUND, COMPOSITE, ALLOY, MIXTURE

blended family *n* : a family that includes children of a previous marriage of one spouse or both

bless \ˈbles\ *vb* **blessed** \ˈblest\ *also* **blest** \ˈblest\; **bless·ing** [ME, fr. OE *blētsian*, fr. *blōd* blood; fr. the use of blood in consecration] **1** : to consecrate by religious rite or word **2** : to sanctify with the sign of the cross **3** : to invoke divine care for **4** : PRAISE, GLORIFY **5** : to confer happiness upon

bless·ed \ˈble-səd\ *also* **blest** \ˈblest\ *adj* **1** : HOLY **2** : BEATIFIED **3** : DELIGHTFUL ⟨~ relief from the heat⟩ — **bless·ed·ly** *adv* — **bless·ed·ness** *n*

bless·ing \ˈble-siŋ\ *n* **1** : the act or words of one who blesses; *also* : APPROVAL **2** : a thing conducive to happiness ⟨count your ~*s*⟩ **3** : grace said at a meal

blew *past of* BLOW

¹**blight** \ˈblīt\ *n* **1** : a plant disease or injury marked esp. by withering and death of parts; *also* : an organism causing blight **2** : an impairing or frustrating influence; *also* : a deteriorated condition ⟨urban ~⟩

²**blight** *vb* : to affect with or suffer from blight

blimp \ˈblimp\ *n* : an airship that maintains its form by pressure of contained gas

¹**blind** \ˈblīnd\ *adj* **1** : lacking or grossly

deficient in ability to see; *also* : intended for blind persons **2** : not based on reason, evidence, or knowledge ⟨~ faith⟩ **3** : not intelligently controlled or directed ⟨~ chance⟩ **4** : performed solely by using aircraft instruments ⟨a ~ landing⟩ **5** : hard to discern or make out : HIDDEN ⟨a ~ seam⟩ **6** : lacking an opening or outlet ⟨a ~ alley⟩ — **blind·ly** *adv* — **blind·ness** \ˈblīnd-nəs\ *n*

[2]**blind** *vb* **1** : to make blind **2** : DAZZLE **3** : DARKEN; *also* : HIDE

[3]**blind** *n* **1** : something (as a shutter) to hinder vision or keep out light **2** : a place of concealment **3** : SUBTERFUGE

blind carbon copy *n* : a copy of a message (such as an email) that is sent without the knowledge of the other recipients

blind date *n* : a date between persons who have not previously met; *also* : either of these persons

blind·er \ˈblīn-dər\ *n* : either of two flaps on a horse's bridle to prevent it from seeing to the side

blind·fold \ˈblīnd-ˌfōld\ *vb* : to cover the eyes of with or as if with a bandage — **blindfold** *n*

[1]**blink** \ˈbliŋk\ *vb* **1** : WINK **2** : TWINKLE **3** : EVADE, IGNORE **4** : YIELD, GIVE IN

[2]**blink** *n* **1** : GLIMMER, SPARKLE **2** : a usu. involuntary shutting and opening of the eye

blink·er \ˈbliŋ-kər\ *n* : a blinking light used as a signal

blin·tze \ˈblint-sə\ *or* **blintz** \ˈblints\ *n* [Yiddish *blintse*] : a thin rolled pancake with a filling usu. of cream cheese

blip \ˈblip\ *n* **1** : a spot on a radar screen **2** : ABERRATION 1

bliss \ˈblis\ *n* : complete happiness : JOY ♦ ***Synonyms*** BEATITUDE, BLESSEDNESS — **bliss·ful** \-fəl\ *adj* — **bliss·ful·ly** *adv*

[1]**blis·ter** \ˈblis-tər\ *n* **1** : a raised area of skin containing watery fluid; *also* : an agent that causes blisters **2** : something (as a raised spot in paint) suggesting a blister **3** : a disease of plants marked by large raised patches on the leaves

[2]**blister** *vb* : to develop a blister; *also* : to cause blisters

blithe \ˈblīth, ˈblīth\ *adj* **blith·er; blith·est** : happily lighthearted ♦ ***Synonyms*** MERRY, JOVIAL, JOLLY, JOCUND — **blithe·ly** *adv* — **blithe·some** \-səm\ *adj*

blitz \ˈblits\ *n* **1** : an intensive series of air raids **2** : a fast intensive campaign **3** : a rush of the passer by the defensive linebackers in football — **blitz** *vb*

blitz·krieg \-ˌkrēg\ *n* [G, fr. *Blitz* lightning + *Krieg* war] : a sudden violent enemy attack

bliz·zard \ˈbli-zərd\ *n* : a long severe snowstorm

blk *abbr* **1** black **2** block

BLM *abbr* **1** Black Lives Matter **2** Bureau of Land Management

bloat \ˈblōt\ *vb* : to swell by or as if by filling with water or air

blob \ˈbläb\ *n* : a small lump or drop of a thick consistency

bloc \ˈbläk\ *n* [F, lit., block] : a combination of individuals or groups (as nations) working for a common purpose

[1]**block** \ˈbläk\ *n* **1** : a solid piece of substantial material (as wood or stone) **2** : HINDRANCE, OBSTRUCTION; *also* : interruption of normal function of body or mind ⟨heart ~⟩ **3** : a frame enclosing one or more pulleys and having a hook or strap by which it may be attached **4** : a piece of material with a hand-cut design on its surface from which copies are to be made **5** : a large building divided into separate units (as apartments or offices) **6** : a row of houses or shops **7** : a city square; *also* : the distance along one of the sides of such a square **8** : a quantity of things considered as a unit

[2]**block** *vb* **1** : OBSTRUCT, CHECK **2** : to outline roughly ⟨~ out a design⟩ **3** : to provide or support with a block ♦ ***Synonyms*** BAR, IMPEDE, HINDER, OBSTRUCT — **block·er** *n*

block·ade \blä-ˈkād\ *n* : the isolation of a place usu. by troops or ships — **blockade** *vb* — **block·ad·er** *n*

block·age \ˈblä-kij\ *n* : an act or instance of obstructing : the state of being blocked

block·bust·er \ˈbläk-ˌbəs-tər\ *n* : one that is very large, successful, expensive, or extravagant ⟨a ~ movie⟩

block·chain \ˈbläk-ˌchān\ *n* : a digital database (as of financial transactions) that can be publicly used and shared within a large network; *also* : the technology used for such a database

block·head \ˈbläk-ˌhed\ *n* : DOLT, DUNCE

block·house \-ˌhau̇s\ *n* : a small strong building used as a shelter (as from enemy fire) or observation post

blog \ˈblȯg, ˈbläg\ *n* [short for *Weblog*] : a website containing one's reflections, opinions, and comments; *also* : the contents of such a site — **blog** *vb* — **blog·ger** *n* — **blog·ging** \ˈblȯ-giŋ, ˈblä-\ *n*

[1]**blond** *or* **blonde** \ˈbländ\ *adj* : fair in complexion; *also* : of a light or bleached color ⟨~ mahogany⟩ — **blond·ish** \ˈblän-dish\ *adj*

[2]**blond** *or* **blonde** *n* : a person having blond hair

blood \ˈbləd\ *n* **1** : a usu. red liquid that circulates in the heart, arteries, and veins of animals **2** : LIFEBLOOD; *also* : LIFE **3** : LINEAGE, STOCK **4** : KINSHIP; *also* : KINDRED **5** : the taking of life **6** : TEMPER, PASSION **7** : DANDY 1 **8** : members of a group — **blood·less** *adj* — **bloody** *adj*

blood·bath \ˈbləd-ˌbath, -ˌbäth\ *n* : MASSACRE

blood count *n* : the determination of the number of blood cells in a specific volume of blood; *also* : the number of cells so determined

blood·cur·dling \ˈbləd-kərd-liŋ, -ˌkər-dᵊl-iŋ\ *adj* : arousing fright or horror

blood·ed \ˈblə-dəd\ *adj* **1** : having blood of a specified kind ⟨warm-*blooded* animals⟩ **2** : entirely or largely purebred ⟨~ horses⟩

blood group *n* : one of the classes into which human beings can be separated by the presence or absence in their blood of specific antigens

blood·hound \'bləd-ˌhau̇nd\ *n* : any of a breed of large powerful hounds with long drooping ears, a wrinkled face, and keen sense of smell

blood·let·ting \-ˌle-tiŋ\ *n* **1** : PHLEBOTOMY **2** : BLOODSHED

blood·line \-ˌlīn\ *n* : a sequence of direct ancestors esp. in a pedigree

blood·lust \-ˌləst\ *n* : desire for bloodshed

blood·mo·bile \-mō-ˌbēl\ *n* : a motor vehicle equipped for collecting blood from donors

blood poisoning *n* : invasion of the bloodstream by virulent microorganisms from a focus of infection accompanied esp. by chills, fever, and prostration

blood pressure *n* : pressure of the blood on the walls of blood vessels and esp. arteries

blood·root \'bləd-ˌrüt, -ˌru̇t\ *n* : a plant related to the poppy that has a red root and sap, a solitary leaf, and a white flower in early spring

blood·shed \-ˌshed\ *n* : wounding or taking of life : CARNAGE, SLAUGHTER

blood·shot \-ˌshät\ *adj* : inflamed to redness ⟨~ eyes⟩

blood·stain \-ˌstān\ *n* : a discoloration caused by blood — **blood·stained** \-ˌstānd\ *adj*

blood·stone \-ˌstōn\ *n* : a green quartz sprinkled with red spots

blood·stream \-ˌstrēm\ *n* : the flowing blood in a circulatory system

blood·suck·er \-ˌsə-kər\ *n* : an animal that sucks blood; *esp* : LEECH — **blood·suck·ing** *adj*

blood test *n* : a test of the blood (as to detect disease-causing agents)

blood thinner *n* : a drug used to prevent the clotting of blood

blood·thirsty \'bləd-ˌthər-stē\ *adj* : eager to shed blood — **blood·thirst·i·ly** \-ˌthər-stə-lē\ *adv* — **blood·thirst·i·ness** \-stē-nəs\ *n*

blood type *n* : BLOOD GROUP — **blood–typ·ing** *n*

blood vessel *n* : a vessel (as a vein or artery) in which blood circulates in the body

Bloody Mary \-'mer-ē\ *n, pl* **Bloody Marys** : a drink made essentially of vodka and tomato juice

[1]**bloom** \'blüm\ *n* **1** : FLOWER 1; *also* : flowers or amount of flowers (as of a plant) **2** : the period or state of flowering **3** : a state or time of beauty and vigor **4** : a powdery coating esp. on fruits and leaves **5** : rosy color; *also* : an appearance of freshness or health — **bloomy** *adj*

[2]**bloom** *vb* **1** : to produce or yield flowers **2** : MATURE **3** : to glow esp. with healthy color ♦ ***Synonyms*** FLOWER, BLOSSOM

bloo·mers \'blü-mərz\ *n pl* [Amelia *Bloomer* †1894 Am. reformer] : a woman's garment of short loose pants gathered at the knee

bloop·er \'blü-pər\ *n* **1** : a fly ball hit barely beyond a baseball infield **2** : an embarrassing public blunder

[1]**blos·som** \'blä-səm\ *n* **1** : the flower of a plant **2** : the period or state of flowering

[2]**blossom** *vb* : FLOWER, BLOOM

[1]**blot** \'blät\ *n* **1** : SPOT, STAIN ⟨ink ~*s*⟩ **2** : BLEMISH ♦ ***Synonyms*** STIGMA, BRAND, SLUR

[2]**blot** *vb* **blot·ted**; **blot·ting** **1** : SPOT, STAIN **2** : OBSCURE, ECLIPSE ⟨~ out the sun⟩ **3** *obs* : MAR; *esp* : DISGRACE **4** : to dry or remove with or as if with an absorbing material **5** : to make a blot

blotch \'bläch\ *n* : a usu. large and irregular spot or mark (as of ink or color) — **blotch** *vb* — **blotchy** *adj*

blot·ter \'blä-tər\ *n* **1** : a piece of blotting paper **2** : a book for preliminary records (as of sales or arrests)

blot·ting paper *n* : a spongy paper used to absorb ink

blouse \'blau̇s, 'blau̇z\ *n* **1** : a loose outer garment like a smock **2** : a usu. loose garment reaching from the neck to about the waist

[1]**blow** \'blō\ *vb* **blew** \'blü\; **blown** \'blōn\; **blow·ing** **1** : to be in motion; *esp* : to move forcibly ⟨the wind *blew*⟩ **2** : to send forth a current of gas (as air) **3** : to act on with a current of gas or vapor; *esp* : to drive with such a current **4** : to clear with a current of air **5** : to sound or cause to sound ⟨~ a horn⟩ **6** : PANT, GASP; *also* : to expel moist air in breathing ⟨the whale *blew*⟩ **7** : BOAST; *also* : BLUSTER **8** : ERUPT, EXPLODE **9** : MELT — used of an electrical fuse **10** : to shape or form by blown or injected air ⟨~ glass⟩ **11** : to shatter or destroy by or as if by explosion **12** : to make breathless by exertion **13** : to spend recklessly **14** : BOTCH ⟨*blew* her lines⟩ — **blow·er** *n*

[2]**blow** *n* **1** : a usu. strong blowing of air : GALE **2** : BOASTING, BRAG **3** : an act or instance of blowing

[3]**blow** *vb* **blew** \'blü\; **blown** \'blōn\; **blow·ing** : FLOWER, BLOOM

[4]**blow** *n* **1** : a forcible stroke ⟨a ~ to the head⟩ **2** : COMBAT ⟨come to ~*s*⟩ **3** : a severe and usu. unexpected calamity

blow–by–blow *adj* : minutely detailed ⟨~ account⟩

blow–dry \-ˌdrī\ *vb* : to dry and usu. style hair with a blow-dryer

blow–dryer \-ˌdrī(-ə)r\ *n* : a hand-held hair dryer

blow·fly \'blō-ˌflī\ *n* : any of a family of dipteran flies (as a bluebottle) that deposit their eggs or maggots on meat or in wounds

blow·gun \-ˌgən\ *n* : a tube from which an arrow or a dart may be shot by the force of the breath

blow·out \'blō-ˌau̇t\ *n* **1** : a bursting of something (as a tire) because of pressure of the contents (as air) **2** : a depression created by the wind in sand or soil

blow·sy *also* **blow·zy** \ˈblau̇-zē\ *adj* : DISHEVELED, SLOVENLY

blow·torch \ˈblō-ˌtȯrch\ *n* : a small portable burner whose flame is made hotter by a blast of air or oxygen

blow·up \ˈblō-ˌəp\ *n* **1** : EXPLOSION **2** : an outburst of temper **3** : a photographic enlargement

blowy \ˈblō-ē\ *adj* : WINDY

BLT \ˌbē-ˌel-ˈtē\ *n* : a bacon, lettuce, and tomato sandwich

[1]**blub·ber** \ˈblə-bər\ *vb* : to cry noisily

[2]**blubber** *n* **1** : the fat of large sea mammals (as whales) **2** : a noisy crying

[1]**blud·geon** \ˈblə-jən\ *n* : a short often loaded club

[2]**bludgeon** *vb* : to strike with or as if with a bludgeon

[1]**blue** \ˈblü\ *adj* **blu·er**; **blu·est** [ME, fr. AF *blef, blew,* of Gmc origin] **1** : of the color blue; *also* : BLUISH **2** : MELANCHOLY; *also* : DEPRESSING **3** : PURITANICAL **4** : INDECENT **5** : tending to support Democratic candidates or policies ⟨~ states⟩ — **blue·ness** *n*

[2]**blue** *n* **1** : a color between green and violet in the spectrum : the color of the clear daytime sky **2** : something (as clothing or the sky) that is blue

blue baby *n* : a baby with bluish skin due to faulty circulation caused by a heart defect

blue·bell \-ˌbel\ *n* : any of various plants with blue bell-shaped flowers

blue·ber·ry \ˈblü-ˌber-ē, -bə-rē\ *n* : the edible blue or blackish berry of various shrubs of the heath family; *also* : one of these shrubs

blue·bird \-ˌbərd\ *n* : any of three small No. American thrushes that are blue above and reddish-brown or pale blue below

blue·bon·net \ˈblü-ˌbä-nət\ *n* : either of two low-growing annual lupines of Texas with silky foliage and blue flowers

blue·bot·tle \ˈblü-ˌbä-tᵊl\ *n* : any of several blowflies with iridescent blue bodies or abdomens

blue cheese *n* : cheese having veins of greenish-blue mold

blue–col·lar \ˈblü-ˈkä-lər\ *adj* : of, relating to, or being the class of workers whose duties call for work clothes

blue·fish \-ˌfish\ *n* : a marine sport and food fish that is bluish above and silvery below

blue·grass \-ˌgras\ *n* **1** : KENTUCKY BLUEGRASS **2** : country music played on stringed instruments having free improvisation and close harmonies

blue jay \-ˌjā\ *n* : a crested bright blue No. American jay

blue jeans *n pl* : pants usu. made of blue denim

blue·nose \ˈblü-ˌnōz\ *n* : a person who advocates a rigorous moral code

blue·point \-ˌpȯint\ *n* : a small oyster typically from the south shore of Long Island, New York

blue·print \-ˌprint\ *n* **1** : a photographic print in white on a blue ground used esp. for copying mechanical drawings and architects' plans **2** : a detailed plan of action — **blueprint** *vb*

blues \ˈblüz\ *n pl* **1** : MELANCHOLY **2** : music in a style marked by recurrent minor intervals and melancholy lyrics

blue screen *n* : a technique in which a subject is filmed in front of a blue background so as to allow the creation of a composite with other footage

blue·stock·ing \ˈblü-ˌstä-kiŋ\ *n* : a woman having intellectual interests

blu·et \ˈblü-ət\ *n* : a low No. American herb with dainty bluish flowers

blue whale *n* : a very large baleen whale that may reach a weight of 150 tons (135 metric tons) and a length of 100 feet (30 meters)

[1]**bluff** \ˈbləf\ *adj* **1** : having a broad flattened front **2** : rising steeply with a broad flat front **3** : OUTSPOKEN, FRANK ♦ ***Synonyms*** ABRUPT, BLUNT, BRUSQUE, CURT, GRUFF

[2]**bluff** *n* : a high steep bank : CLIFF

[3]**bluff** *vb* : to frighten or deceive by pretense or a mere show of strength

[4]**bluff** *n* : an act or instance of bluffing; *also* : one who bluffs

blu·ing *or* **blue·ing** \ˈblü-iŋ\ *n* : a preparation used in laundering to counteract yellowing of white fabrics

blu·ish \ˈblü-ish\ *adj* : somewhat blue

[1]**blun·der** \ˈblən-dər\ *vb* **1** : to move clumsily or unsteadily **2** : to make a stupid or needless mistake

[2]**blunder** *n* : an avoidable and usu. serious mistake

blun·der·buss \ˈblən-dər-ˌbəs\ *n* [obs. D *donderbus,* fr. D *donder* thunder + obs. D *bus* gun] : an obsolete short-barreled firearm with a flaring muzzle

[1]**blunt** \ˈblənt\ *adj* **1** : not sharp : DULL **2** : lacking in tact : BLUFF ⟨~ criticism⟩ ♦ ***Synonyms*** BRUSQUE, CURT, GRUFF, ABRUPT, CRUSTY — **blunt·ly** *adv* — **blunt·ness** *n*

[2]**blunt** *vb* : to make or become dull

[1]**blur** \ˈblər\ *n* **1** : a smear or stain that obscures **2** : something vaguely perceived; *esp* : something moving too quickly to be clearly perceived — **blur·ry** \-ē\ *adj*

[2]**blur** *vb* **blurred**; **blur·ring** : DIM, CLOUD, OBSCURE ⟨*blurred* vision⟩

blurb \ˈblərb\ *n* : a short publicity notice (as on a book jacket)

blurt \ˈblərt\ *vb* : to utter suddenly and impulsively

blush \ˈbləsh\ *n* **1** : a reddening of the face (as from modesty or confusion) : FLUSH **2** : a cosmetic used to tint the face pink — **blush** *vb* — **blush·ful** *adj*

blus·ter \ˈbləs-tər\ *vb* **1** : to blow in stormy noisy gusts **2** : to talk or act with noisy swaggering threats — **bluster** *n* — **blus·tery** \-tə-rē\ *adj*

blvd *abbr* boulevard

B lymphocyte *n* : B CELL

BM *abbr* bowel movement

B movie *n* : a cheaply produced motion picture

BO *abbr* **1** best offer **2** body odor **3** box office **4** branch office

boa \ˈbō-ə\ *n* **1** : a large snake (as the **boa con·stric·tor** \-kən-ˈstrik-tər\ or the related anaconda) that suffocates and kills its prey by constriction **2** : a fluffy scarf usu. of fur or feathers

boar \ˈbȯr\ *n* : a male swine; *also* : WILD BOAR

[1]**board** \ˈbȯrd\ *n* **1** : the side of a ship **2** : a thin flat length of sawed lumber; *also* : material (as cardboard) or a piece of material formed as a thin flat firm sheet **3** *pl* : STAGE 1 **4** : a table spread with a meal; *also* : daily meals esp. when furnished for pay **5** : a table at which a council or magistrates sit **6** : a group or association of persons organized for a special responsibility (as the management of a business or institution); *also* : an organized commercial exchange **7** : a sheet of insulating material carrying circuit elements and inserted in an electronic device **8** : BULLETIN BOARD

[2]**board** *vb* **1** : to go or put aboard ⟨~ a boat⟩ **2** : to cover with boards **3** : to provide or be provided with meals and often lodging — **board·er** *n*

board game *n* : a game of strategy (as checkers or chess) played by placing or moving pieces on a board

board·ing·house \ˈbȯr-diŋ-ˌhau̇s\ *n* : a house at which persons are boarded

board·walk \ˈbȯrd-ˌwȯk\ *n* : a promenade (as of planking) along a beach

boast \ˈbōst\ *vb* **1** : to praise oneself **2** : to mention or assert with excessive pride **3** : to prize as a possession; *also* : HAVE ⟨the house ~*s* a fireplace⟩ — **boast** *n* — **boast·ful** \-fəl\ *adj* — **boast·ful·ly** *adv* — **boast·ful·ness** *n*

boat \ˈbōt\ *n* : a small vessel for travel on water; *also* : SHIP — **boat** *vb*

boat·er \ˈbō-tər\ *n* **1** : one that travels in a boat **2** : a stiff straw hat

boat·man \ˈbōt-mən\ *n* : a man who operates, works on, or deals in boats

boat people *n pl* : refugees fleeing by boat

boat·swain *or* **bo·sun** \ˈbō-sᵊn\ *n* : a subordinate officer of a ship in charge of the hull and related equipment

[1]**bob** \ˈbäb\ *vb* **bobbed**; **bob·bing** **1** : to move up and down jerkily or repeatedly **2** : to emerge, arise, or appear suddenly or unexpectedly

[2]**bob** *n* : a bobbing movement

[3]**bob** *n* **1** : a knob, knot, twist, or curl esp. of ribbons, yarn, or hair **2** : a short haircut of a woman or child **3** : FLOAT 2 **4** : a weight hanging from a line

[4]**bob** *vb* **bobbed**; **bob·bing** : to cut hair in a bob

[5]**bob** *n, pl* **bob** *slang Brit* : SHILLING

bob·bin \ˈbä-bən\ *n* : a cylinder or spindle for holding or dispensing thread (as in a sewing machine)

bob·ble \ˈbä-bəl\ *vb* **bob·bled**; **bob·bling** **1** : to move up and down quickly or repeatedly **2** : FUMBLE ⟨the catcher *bobbled* the ball⟩ — **bobble** *n*

bob·by \ˈbä-bē\ *n, pl* **bobbies** [*Bobby,* nickname for Sir *Robert* Peel, who organized the London police force] *Brit* : a police officer

bobby pin *n* : a flat wire hairpin with prongs that press close together

bob·cat \ˈbäb-ˌkat\ *n* : a small usu. rusty-colored No. American lynx

bob·o·link \ˈbä-bə-ˌliŋk\ *n* : an American migratory songbird related to the meadowlarks

bob·sled \ˈbäb-ˌsled\ *n* **1** : a short sled usu. used as one of a joined pair **2** : a racing sled with two pairs of runners, a steering wheel, and a hand brake — **bobsled** *vb*

bob·white \(ˌ)bäb-ˈhwīt\ *n* : any of a genus of quail; *esp* : a popular game bird of eastern and central No. America

boc·cie *or* **boc·ci** *or* **boc·ce** \ˈbä-chē\ *n* : Italian lawn bowling played on a long narrow court

bock \ˈbäk\ *n* : a dark malty beer usu. sold in winter or early spring

bod \ˈbäd\ *n* : BODY

[1]**bode** \ˈbōd\ *vb* **bod·ed**; **bod·ing** : to indicate by signs : PRESAGE

[2]**bode** *past of* BIDE

bo·de·ga \bō-ˈdā-gə\ *n* [Sp, fr. L *apotheca* storehouse] : a usu. small store specializing in Hispanic groceries

bod·ice \ˈbä-dəs\ *n* [alter. of *bodies,* pl. of *body*] : the usu. close-fitting part of a dress above the waist

bodi·less \ˈbä-di-ləs\ *adj* : lacking a body or material form

[1]**bodi·ly** \ˈbä-dᵊl-ē\ *adj* : of or relating to the body ⟨~ contact⟩ ⟨~ organs⟩

[2]**bodily** *adv* **1** : in the flesh **2** : as a whole ⟨lifted the crate up ~⟩

bod·kin \ˈbäd-kən\ *n* **1** : DAGGER **2** : a pointed implement for punching holes in cloth **3** : a blunt needle for drawing tape or ribbon through a loop or hem

body \ˈbä-dē\ *n, pl* **bod·ies** **1** : the physical whole of a living or dead organism; *also* : the trunk or main mass of an organism as distinguished from its appendages **2** : a human being : PERSON **3** : the main part of something **4** : a mass of matter distinct from other masses **5** : GROUP ⟨the student ~⟩ **6** : VISCOSITY, FIRMNESS **7** : richness of flavor — used esp. of wines — **bod·ied** \ˈbä-dēd\ *adj*

body·build·ing \ˈbä-dē-ˌbil-diŋ\ *n* : the developing of the body through exercise and diet — **body·build·er** \-dər\ *n*

body English *n* : bodily motions made in a usu. unconscious effort to influence the movement of a propelled object

body·guard \ˈbä-dē-ˌgärd\ *n* : a personal guard; *also* : RETINUE

body language *n* : movements (as with the hands) or posture used as a means of communication

body stocking *n* : a sheer close-fitting one-piece garment for the torso that often has sleeves and legs

body·work \ˈbä-dē-ˌwərk\ *n* : the making or repairing of vehicle bodies

Boer \ˈbȯr, ˈbu̇r\ *n* [D, lit., farmer] : a

South African of Dutch or Huguenot descent

[1]**bog** \ˈbäg, ˈbȯg\ *n* : wet, spongy, poorly drained, and usu. acid ground — **bog·gy** *adj*

[2]**bog** *vb* **bogged**; **bog·ging** : to sink into or as if into a bog

bo·gey *also* **bo·gie** *or* **bo·gy** \ˈbu̇-gē, ˈbō- *for 1*; ˈbō- *for 2*\ *n, pl* **bogeys** *also* **bogies** **1** : SPECTER, HOBGOBLIN; *also* : a source of fear or annoyance **2** : a score of one over par on a hole in golf

bo·gey·man \ˈbu̇-gē-ˌman, ˈbō-, ˈbü-\ *n* : an imaginary monster used in threatening children

bog·gle \ˈbä-gəl\ *vb* **bog·gled**; **bog·gling** : to overwhelm or be overwhelmed with fright or amazement

bo·gus \ˈbō-gəs\ *adj* : SPURIOUS, SHAM

Bo·he·mi·an \bō-ˈhē-mē-ən\ *n* **1** : a native or inhabitant of Bohemia **2** *often not cap* : VAGABOND, WANDERER **3** *often not cap* : a person (as a writer or artist) living an unconventional life — **bohemian** *adj, often cap*

bohr·i·um \ˈbȯr-ē-əm\ *n* : an artificially produced radioactive chemical element

[1]**boil** \ˈbȯi(-ə)l\ *n* : an inflamed swelling on the skin containing pus

[2]**boil** *vb* **1** : to heat or become heated to a temperature (**boil·ing point**) at which vapor is formed and rises in bubbles ⟨water ~*s* and changes to steam⟩; *also* : to act on or be acted on by a boiling liquid ⟨~ eggs⟩ **2** : to be in a state of seething agitation

[3]**boil** *n* **1** : the act or state of boiling **2** : a boiled dish (as of seafood) **3** : a gathering where boiled food is served

boil·er \ˈbȯi-lər\ *n* **1** : a container in which something is boiled **2** : a strong vessel used in making steam **3** : a tank holding hot water

boil·er·mak·er \ˈbȯi-lər-ˌmā-kər\ *n* : whiskey with a beer chaser

bois·ter·ous \ˈbȯi-st(ə-)rəs\ *adj* : noisily turbulent or exuberant — **bois·ter·ous·ly** *adv*

bok choy \ˈbäk-ˈchȯi\ *n* : a Chinese vegetable related to the mustards that forms a loose head of green leaves with long thick white stalks

bo·la \ˈbō-lə\ *or* **bo·las** \-ləs\ *n, pl* **bolas** \-ləz\ *also* **bo·las·es** [AmerSp *bolas,* fr. Sp *bola* ball] : a cord with weights attached to the ends for hurling at and entangling an animal

bold \ˈbōld\ *adj* **1** : COURAGEOUS, INTREPID **2** : IMPUDENT **3** : STEEP ⟨~ cliffs⟩ **4** : ADVENTUROUS, FREE ⟨a ~ thinker⟩ ♦ ***Synonyms*** DAUNTLESS, BRAVE, VALIANT — **bold·ly** *adv* — **boldness** \ˈbōld-nəs\ *n*

bold·face \ˈbōld-ˌfās\ *n* : a heavy-faced type; *also* : printing in boldface — **bold–faced** \-ˈfāst\ *adj*

bole \ˈbōl\ *n* : the trunk of a tree

bo·le·ro \bə-ˈler-ō\ *n, pl* **-ros** **1** : a Spanish dance or its music **2** : a short loose jacket open at the front

bo·li·var \bə-ˈlē-ˌvär, ˈbä-lə-vər\ *n, pl* **-va·res** \ˌbä-lə-ˈvär-ˌās, ˌbō-\ *or* **-vars** — see MONEY table

Bo·liv·i·an \bə-ˈli-vē-ən\ *n* : a native or inhabitant of Bolivia — **Bolivian** *adj*

bo·li·vi·a·no \bə-ˈli-vē-ˈä-(ˌ)nō\ *n, pl* **-nos** — see MONEY table

boll \ˈbōl\ *n* : a seed pod (as of cotton)

boll weevil *n* : a small usu. grayish or brown weevil that infests the cotton plant both as a larva and as an adult

boll·worm \ˈbōl-ˌwərm\ *n* : any of several moths and esp. the corn earworm whose larvae feed on cotton bolls

bo·lo·gna \bə-ˈlō-nē\ *n* [short for *Bologna sausage,* fr. *Bologna,* Italy] : a large smoked sausage of beef, veal, and pork

Bol·she·vik \ˈbōl-shə-ˌvik\ *n, pl* **Bolsheviks** *also* **Bol·she·vi·ki** \ˌbōl-shə-ˈvi-kē\ [Russ *bol'shevik,* fr. *bol'shiĭ* larger] **1** : a member of the party that seized power in Russia in the revolution of November 1917 **2** : COMMUNIST — **Bolshevik** *adj*

bol·she·vism \ˈbōl-shə-ˌvi-zəm\ *n, often cap* : the doctrine or program of the Bolsheviks advocating violent overthrow of capitalism

[1]**bol·ster** \ˈbōl-stər\ *n* : a long pillow or cushion

[2]**bolster** *vb* : to support with or as if with a bolster; *also* : REINFORCE

[1]**bolt** \ˈbōlt\ *n* **1** : a missile (as an arrow) for a crossbow or catapult **2** : a flash of lightning : THUNDERBOLT **3** : a sliding bar used to fasten a door **4** : a roll of cloth or wallpaper of specified length **5** : a rod with a head at one end and a screw thread at the other used with a nut to fasten objects together **6** : a metal cylinder that drives the cartridge into the chamber of a firearm

[2]**bolt** *vb* **1** : to move suddenly (as in fright or hurry) : START, DASH **2** : to break away (as from association) ⟨~ from a political platform⟩ **3** : to produce seed prematurely **4** : to secure or fasten with a bolt **5** : to swallow hastily or without chewing

[3]**bolt** *n* : an act of bolting

bo·lus \ˈbō-ləs\ *n, pl* **bo·lus·es** **1** : a large pill **2** : a soft mass of chewed food

[1]**bomb** \ˈbäm\ *n* **1** : a fused explosive device designed to detonate under specified conditions (as impact) **2** : an aerosol or foam dispenser (as of insecticide) : SPRAY CAN **3** : FAILURE, FLOP **4** : a long pass, shot, or hit

[2]**bomb** *vb* **1** : to attack with bombs **2** : FAIL ⟨~*ed* at the audition⟩

bom·bard \bäm-ˈbärd\ *vb* **1** : to attack esp. with artillery or bombers **2** : to assail persistently **3** : to subject to the impact of rapidly moving particles (as electrons) — **bom·bard·ment** *n*

bom·bar·dier \ˌbäm-bər-ˈdir\ *n* : a bomber-crew member who releases the bombs

bom·bast \ˈbäm-ˌbast\ *n* [ME, cotton padding, fr. MF *bombace,* fr. ML *bombax* cotton, alter. of L *bombyx* silkworm, silk, fr. Gk] : pretentious wordy speech or writing — **bom·bas·tic** \bäm-ˈbas-tik\ *adj* — **bom·bas·ti·cal·ly** \-ti-k(ə-)lē\ *adv*

bom·ba·zine \ˌbäm-bə-ˈzēn\ *n* **1** : a twilled fabric with silk warp and worsted filling **2** : a silk fabric in twill weave dyed black

bomb cyclone *n* : a powerful, rapidly intensifying storm associated with a sudden and significant drop in atmospheric pressure

bomb·er \ˈbä-mər\ *n* : one that bombs; *esp* : an airplane for dropping bombs

bomb·proof \ˈbäm-ˌprüf\ *adj* : safe against the explosive force of bombs

bomb·shell \ˈbäm-ˌshel\ *n* **1** : BOMB 1 **2** : one that stuns, amazes, or completely upsets

bona fide \ˈbō-nə-ˌfīd, ˈbä-; ˌbō-nə-ˈfī-dē, -də\ *adj* [L, in good faith] **1** : made in good faith ⟨a *bona fide* agreement⟩ **2** : GENUINE, REAL ⟨a *bona fide* bargain⟩

bo·nan·za \bə-ˈnan-zə\ *n* [Sp, lit., calm sea, fr. ML *bonacia,* alter. of L *malacia,* fr. Gk *malakia,* lit., softness, fr. *malakos* soft] **1** : something yielding a rich return **2** : a spectacular event

bon·bon \ˈbän-ˌbän\ *n* : a candy with a creamy center and a soft covering (as of chocolate)

[1]**bond** \ˈbänd\ *n* **1** : FETTER **2** : a binding or uniting force or tie ⟨~*s* of friendship⟩ **3** : an agreement or obligation often made binding by a pledge of money or goods **4** : a person who acts as surety for another **5** : an interest-bearing certificate of public or private indebtedness **6** : the state of goods subject to supervision pending payment of taxes or duties due

[2]**bond** *vb* **1** : to assure payment of duties or taxes on (goods) by giving a bond **2** : to insure against losses caused by the acts of ⟨~ a bank teller⟩ **3** : to make or become firmly united as if by bonds ⟨~ iron to copper⟩ **4** : to form a close relationship ⟨~*ed* with her stepmother⟩

bond·age \ˈbän-dij\ *n* **1** : SLAVERY, SERVITUDE **2** : sexual practices involving the physical restraint of one partner

bond·hold·er \ˈbänd-ˌhōl-dər\ *n* : one that owns a government or corporation bond

bond·ing \ˈbän-diŋ\ *n* **1** : the formation of a close personal relationship esp. through frequent or constant association **2** : the attaching of a material (as porcelain) to a tooth surface esp. for cosmetic purposes

bond·man \ˈbänd-mən\ *n* : an enslaved person : SLAVE, SERF

[1]**bonds·man** \ˈbändz-mən\ *n* : SURETY 3

[2]**bondsman** *var of* BONDMAN

bond·wom·an \ˈbänd-ˌwu̇-mən\ *n* : a woman who is a slave or serf

[1]**bone** \ˈbōn\ *n* **1** : a hard largely calcareous tissue forming most of the skeleton of a vertebrate animal; *also* : one of the pieces of bone making up a vertebrate skeleton **2** : a hard animal substance (as ivory or baleen) similar to true bone **3** : something made of bone — **bone·less** *adj* — **bony** *also* **bon·ey** \ˈbō-nē\ *adj*

[2]**bone** *vb* **boned**; **bon·ing** : to free from bones ⟨~ a chicken⟩

bone black *n* : the black carbon residue from calcined bones used esp. as a pigment

bone marrow *n* : MARROW

bone·meal \ˈbōn-ˌmēl\ *n* : crushed or ground bone used esp. as fertilizer or feed

bon·er \ˈbō-nər\ *n* : a stupid and ridiculous blunder

bone up *vb* **1** : CRAM 3 **2** : to refresh one's memory ⟨*boned up* on the speech before giving it⟩

bon·fire \ˈbän-ˌfī(-ə)r\ *n* [ME *bonefire* a fire of bones, fr. *bon* bone + *fire*] : a large fire built in the open air

bon·go \ˈbäŋ-gō\ *n, pl* **bongos** *also* **bongoes** [AmerSp *bongó*] : one of a pair of small tuned drums played with the hands

bon·ho·mie \ˌbä-nə-ˈmē\ *n* [F *bonhomie,* fr. *bonhomme* good-natured man, fr. *bon* good + *homme* man] : good-natured easy friendliness

bo·ni·to \bə-ˈnē-tō\ *n, pl* **-tos** *or* **-to** : any of several medium-sized tunas

bon mot \bō^{n}-ˈmō\ *n, pl* **bons mots** *same*\ *or* **bon mots** *same*\ [F, lit., good word] : a clever remark

bon·net \ˈbä-nət\ *n* : a covering (as a cap) for the head; *esp* : a hat for a woman or infant tied under the chin

bon·ny \ˈbä-nē\ *adj* **bon·ni·er**; **-est** *chiefly Brit* : ATTRACTIVE, FAIR; *also* : FINE, EXCELLENT

bon·sai \bōn-ˈsī, ˈbän-ˌ\ *n, pl* **bonsai** [Jp] : a potted plant (as a tree) dwarfed and trained to an artistic shape; *also* : the art of growing such a plant

bo·nus \ˈbō-nəs\ *n* : something in addition to what is expected

bon vi·vant \ˌbän-vē-ˈvänt, ˌbō^{n}-vē-ˈvä^{n}\ *n, pl* **bons vivants** \ˌbän-vē-ˈvänts, ˌbō^{n}-vē-ˈvä^{n}\ *or* **bon vivants** *same*\ [F, lit., good liver] : a person having cultivated, refined, and sociable tastes esp. in food and drink

bon voy·age \ˌbō^{n}-ˌvȯi-ˈäzh, ˌbän-; ˌbō^{n}-ˌvwä-ˈyäzh\ *n* : FAREWELL — often used as an interjection

bony fish *n* : any of a class of fishes (as eels or sturgeons) with a bony rather than a cartilaginous skeleton

bonze \ˈbänz\ *n* : a Buddhist monk

boo \ˈbü\ *n, pl* **boos** : a shout of disapproval or contempt — **boo** *vb*

boo·by \ˈbü-bē\ *n, pl* **boobies** : an awkward foolish person : DOPE

booby hatch *n* : a psychiatric hospital

booby prize *n* : an award for the poorest performance in a contest

booby trap *n* : a trap for the unwary; *esp* : a concealed explosive device set to go off when some harmless-looking object is touched — **booby–trap** *vb*

boo·dle \ˈbü-d^{ə}l\ *n* **1** : bribe money **2** : a large amount of money

[1]**book** \ˈbu̇k\ *n* **1** : a set of sheets bound into a volume **2** : a long written or printed narrative or record **3** : a major division of a long literary work **4** *cap* : BIBLE — **in one's book** : in one's own opinion

[2]**book** *vb* **1** : to engage, reserve, or sched-

ule by or as if by writing in a book ⟨~ seats on a plane⟩ **2** : to enter charges against in a police register
book·case \-ˌkās\ *n* : a piece of furniture consisting of shelves to hold books
book·end \-ˌend\ *n* : a support to hold up a row of books
book·ie \ˈbu̇-kē\ *n* : BOOKMAKER
book·ish \ˈbu̇-kish\ *adj* **1** : fond of books and reading **2** : inclined to rely unduly on book knowledge
book·keep·er \ˈbu̇k-ˌkē-pər\ *n* : a person who records the accounts or transactions of a business — **book·keep·ing** *n*
book·let \ˈbu̇k-lət\ *n* : PAMPHLET
book·mak·er \ˈbu̇k-ˌmā-kər\ *n* : a person who determines odds and receives and pays off bets — **book·mak·ing** *n*
book·mark \-ˌmärk\ *or* **book·mark·er** \-ˌmär-kər\ *n* **1** : a marker for finding a place in a book **2** : a shortcut to a previously viewed location (as a website) on a computer — **bookmark** *vb*
book·mo·bile \ˈbu̇k-mō-ˌbēl\ *n* : a truck that serves as a traveling library
book·plate \ˈbu̇k-ˌplāt\ *n* : a label pasted in a book to show who owns it
book·sell·er \ˈbu̇k-ˌse-lər\ *n* : one that sells books; *esp* : the proprietor of a bookstore
book·shelf \-ˌshelf\ *n* : a shelf for books
book·worm \ˈbu̇k-ˌwərm\ *n* : a person unusually devoted to reading and study
[1]**boom** \ˈbüm\ *vb* **1** : to make a deep hollow sound : RESOUND **2** : to grow or cause to grow rapidly esp. in number, value, esteem, or importance
[2]**boom** *n* **1** : a booming sound or cry **2** : a rapid expansion or increase esp. of economic activity
[3]**boom** *n* [D, tree, beam] **1** : a long spar used to extend the bottom of a sail **2** : a line of floating timbers used to obstruct passage or catch floating objects **3** : a beam projecting from the upright pole of a derrick to support or guide the object lifted **4** : a long usu. horizontal supporting arm (as for a microphone)
boom box *n* : a large portable radio and often tape or CD player
boo·mer·ang \ˈbü-mə-ˌraŋ\ *n* [Dharuk (an Australian aboriginal language) *bumarin*ʸ] : a bent or angular club that can be so thrown as to return near the starting point
boom·ing \ˈbü-miŋ\ *adj* **1** : making a loud deep sound ⟨a ~ voice⟩ **2** : powerfully executed ⟨hit a ~ serve⟩
[1]**boon** \ˈbün\ *n* [ME *bone* prayer, request, the favor requested, fr. ON *bōn* request] : BENEFIT, BLESSING ♦ ***Synonyms*** FAVOR, GIFT, LARGESS, PRESENT
[2]**boon** *adj* [ME *bon*, fr. AF, good] : CONVIVIAL ⟨a ~ companion⟩
boon·docks \ˈbün-ˌdäks\ *n pl* [Tagalog (language of the Philippines) *bundok* mountain] **1** : rough country filled with dense brush **2** : a remote and thinly settled rural area
boon·dog·gle \ˈbün-ˌdä-gəl, -ˌdȯ-\ *n* : a useless or wasteful project or activity
boor \ˈbu̇r\ *n* **1** : YOKEL **2** : a rude or insensitive person ♦ ***Synonyms*** CHURL, LOUT, CLOWN, CLODHOPPER — **boor·ish** *adj*
boost \ˈbüst\ *vb* **1** : to push up from below **2** : INCREASE, RAISE ⟨~ prices⟩ **3** : AID, PROMOTE ⟨voted a bonus to ~ morale⟩ — **boost** *n* — **boost·er** *n*
[1]**boot** \ˈbüt\ *n* : something to equalize a trade — **to boot** : BESIDES
[2]**boot** *vb, archaic* : AVAIL, PROFIT
[3]**boot** *n* **1** : a covering for the foot and leg **2** : a protective sheath (as of a flower) **3** *Brit* : an automobile trunk **4** : KICK; *also* : a discharge from employment **5** : a navy or marine corps trainee
[4]**boot** *vb* **1** : KICK **2** : to eject or discharge summarily **3** : to load or become loaded into a computer from a disk **4** : to start or become ready for use esp. by booting a program ⟨~ up the computer⟩
boot·black \ˈbüt-ˌblak\ *n* : a person who shines shoes
boot camp *n* **1** : a navy or marine corps training camp **2** : a facility with a rigorous disciplinary program for young offenders
boo·tee *or* **boo·tie** \ˈbü-tē\ *n* : an infant's knitted or crocheted sock
booth \ˈbüth\ *n, pl* **booths** \ˈbü*th*z, ˈbüths\ **1** : a small enclosed stall (as at a fair) **2** : a small enclosure giving privacy for a person ⟨voting ~⟩ ⟨telephone ~⟩ **3** : a restaurant accommodation having a table between backed benches
boot·leg \ˈbüt-ˌleg\ *vb* : to make, transport, or sell (as liquor) illegally — **boot·leg** *adj or n* — **boot·leg·ger** *n*
boot·less \ˈbüt-ləs\ *adj* : USELESS ⟨their efforts were ~⟩ ♦ ***Synonyms*** FUTILE, VAIN, ABORTIVE, FRUITLESS — **boot·less·ly** *adv* — **boot·less·ness** *n*
[1]**boo·ty** \ˈbü-tē\ *n, pl* **booties** : PLUNDER, SPOIL
[2]**booty** *also* **boo·tie** \ˈbü-tē\ *n, pl* **booties** *slang* : BUTTOCKS
[1]**booze** \ˈbüz\ *vb* **boozed**; **booz·ing** : to drink liquor to excess — **booz·er** *n*
[2]**booze** *n* : intoxicating liquor — **boozy** *adj*
bop \ˈbäp\ *vb* **bopped**; **bop·ping** : HIT, SOCK — **bop** *n*
BOQ *abbr* bachelor officers' quarters
bor *abbr* borough
bo·rate \ˈbȯr-ˌāt\ *n* : a salt or ester of boric acid
bo·rax \ˈbȯr-ˌaks\ *n* : a crystalline borate of sodium that occurs as a mineral and is used as a flux and cleanser
bor·del·lo \bȯr-ˈde-lō\ *n, pl* **-los** [It] : BROTHEL
[1]**bor·der** \ˈbȯr-dər\ *n* **1** : EDGE, MARGIN **2** : BOUNDARY, FRONTIER ♦ ***Synonyms*** RIM, BRIM, BRINK, FRINGE, PERIMETER
[2]**border** *vb* **bor·dered**; **bor·der·ing** **1** : to put a border on **2** : ADJOIN **3** : VERGE
border collie *n, often cap B* : any of a British breed of medium-sized long-haired sheepdogs
bor·der·land \ˈbȯr-dər-ˌland\ *n* **1** : terri-

tory at or near a border **2** : an outlying or intermediate region often not clearly defined

bor·der·line \-ˌlīn\ *adj* : being in an intermediate position or state; *esp* : not quite up to what is standard or expected ⟨~ intelligence⟩

[1]**bore** \ˈbȯr\ *vb* **bored; bor·ing 1** : to make a hole in with or as if with a drill **2** : to make (as a well) by boring or digging away material ♦ ***Synonyms*** PERFORATE, DRILL, PRICK, PUNCTURE — **bor·er** *n*

[2]**bore** *n* **1** : a hole made by or as if by boring **2** : a cylindrical cavity **3** : the diameter of a hole or tube; *esp* : the interior diameter of a gun barrel or engine cylinder

[3]**bore** *past of* BEAR

[4]**bore** *n* : a tidal flood with a high abrupt front

[5]**bore** *n* : one that causes boredom

[6]**bore** *vb* **bored; bor·ing** : to weary with tedious dullness

bo·re·al \ˈbȯr-ē-əl\ *adj* : of, relating to, or located in northern regions

bore·dom \ˈbȯr-dəm\ *n* : the condition of being bored

bo·ric acid \ˈbȯr-ik-\ *n* : a white crystalline weak acid that contains boron and is used esp. as an antiseptic

born \ˈbȯrn\ *adj* **1** : brought into life by birth **2** : NATIVE ⟨American-*born*⟩ **3** : having special natural abilities or character from birth ⟨a ~ leader⟩

born–again *adj* : having experienced a revival of a personal faith or conviction ⟨a ~ believer⟩ ⟨a ~ liberal⟩

borne *past part of* BEAR

bo·ron \ˈbȯr-ˌän\ *n* : a chemical element that occurs in nature only in combination (as in borax)

bor·ough \ˈbər-ō\ *n* [ME *burgh,* fr. OE *burg* fortified town] **1** : a British town that sends one or more members to Parliament; *also* : an incorporated British urban area **2** : an incorporated town or village in some U.S. states; *also* : any of the five political divisions of New York City **3** : a civil division of the state of Alaska corresponding to a county in most other states

bor·row \ˈbär-ō\ *vb* **1** : to take or receive (something) temporarily and with intent to return ⟨~*ed* my car⟩ **2** : to take into possession or use from another source : DERIVE, APPROPRIATE ⟨~ a metaphor⟩

borscht \ˈbȯrsht\ *or* **borsch** \ˈbȯrsh\ *n* [Yiddish *borsht* & Ukrainian & Russ *borshch*] : a soup made mainly from beets

bosh \ˈbäsh\ *n* [Turk *boş* empty] : foolish talk or action : NONSENSE

bosky \ˈbäs-kē\ *adj* : covered with trees or shrubs

[1]**bos·om** \ˈbu̇-zəm, ˈbü-\ *n* **1** : the front of the human chest; *esp* : the female breasts **2** : the seat of secret thoughts and feelings **3** : the part of a garment covering the breast — **bos·omed** \-zəmd\ *adj*

[2]**bosom** *adj* : CLOSE, INTIMATE

[1]**boss** \ˈbäs, ˈbȯs\ *n* : a knoblike ornament : STUD

[2]**boss** *vb* : to ornament with bosses

[3]**boss** \ˈbȯs\ *n* **1** : one (as a foreman or manager) exercising control or supervision **2** : a politician who controls votes or dictates policies — **bossy** *adj*

[4]**boss** \ˈbȯs\ *vb* : to act as or in the manner of a boss

bosun *var of* BOATSWAIN

[1]**bot** \ˈbät\ *n* **1** : ROBOT **2** : a computer program that performs automatic, repetitive, and sometimes harmful tasks **3** : a computer program or character that mimics human actions

[2]**bot** *abbr* botanical; botanist; botany

bot·a·ny \ˈbä-tə-nē, ˈbät-nē\ *n, pl* **-nies 1** : a branch of biology dealing with plants and plant life **2** : plant life (as of a given region); *also* : the biology of a plant or plant group — **bo·tan·i·cal** \bə-ˈta-ni-kəl\ *adj or n* — **bo·tan·i·cal·ly** \-k(ə-)lē\ *adv* — **bot·a·nist** *n* — **bot·a·nize** \ˈbät-ə-ˌnīz\ *vb*

botch \ˈbäch\ *vb* : to foul up hopelessly : BUNGLE — **botch** *n*

[1]**both** \ˈbōth\ *pron* : both ones : the one as well as the other

[2]**both** *conj* — used as a function word to indicate and stress the inclusion of each of two or more things specified by coordinated words, phrases, or clauses ⟨~ New York and London⟩

[3]**both** *adj* : being the two : including the one and the other ⟨went to ~ museums⟩

both·er \ˈbä-thər\ *vb* **1** : PESTER, TROUBLE ⟨was ~*ed* by bees⟩ **2** : to concern oneself : make an effort ⟨didn't ~ asking⟩ ♦ ***Synonyms*** VEX, ANNOY, IRK, PROVOKE — **bother** *n* — **both·er·some** \-səm\ *adj*

[1]**bot·tle** \ˈbä-tᵊl\ *n* **1** : a container (as of glass) with a narrow neck and usu. no handles **2** : the quantity held by a bottle **3** : intoxicating liquor

[2]**bottle** *vb* **bot·tled; bot·tling 1** : to confine as if in a bottle : RESTRAIN ⟨*bottled* up his anger⟩ **2** : to put into a bottle

bot·tle·neck \ˈbä-tᵊl-ˌnek\ *n* **1** : a narrow passage or point of congestion **2** : something that obstructs or impedes

[1]**bot·tom** \ˈbä-təm\ *n* **1** : an under or supporting surface; *also* : BUTTOCKS **2** : the surface on which a body of water lies **3** : the lowest part or place; *also* : an inferior position ⟨start at the ~⟩ **4** : BOTTOMLAND **5** : BASIS, SOURCE ⟨get to the ~ of this mystery⟩ **6** : a quark with a charge of -⅓ and a measured energy of approximately 5 billion electron volts — **bottom** *adj* — **bot·tom·less** *adj*

[2]**bottom** *vb* **1** : to furnish with a bottom **2** : to reach the bottom **3** : to reach a point where a decline is halted or reversed — usu. used with *out*

bot·tom·land \ˈbä-təm-ˌland\ *n* : low land along a river

bottom line *n* **1** : the essential point : CRUX **2** : the final result : OUTCOME

bot·u·lism \ˈbä-chə-ˌli-zəm\ *n* : an acute paralytic disease caused by a bacterial toxin (**bot·u·li·num toxin** \ˌbä-chə-ˈlī-nəm-\) esp. in tainted food

bou·doir \ˈbü-ˌdwär, ˈbu̇-, ˌbü-ˈ, ˌbu̇-ˈ\ *n* [F, fr. *bouder* to pout] : a woman's dressing room or bedroom

bouf·fant \bü-ˈfänt, ˈbü-ˌfänt\ *adj* [F] : puffed out ⟨~ hairdos⟩

bough \ˈbau̇\ *n* : a usu. large or main branch of a tree

bought *past and past part of* BUY

bouil·la·baisse \ˌbü-yə-ˈbās\ *n* [F] : a highly seasoned fish stew made with at least two kinds of fish

bouil·lon \ˈbü-ˌyän; ˈbu̇l-ˌyän, -yən\ *n* : a clear soup made usu. from beef

boul·der *also* **bowl·der** \ˈbōl-dər\ *n* : a large detached rounded or worn mass of rock — **boul·dered** \-dərd\ *adj*

bou·le·vard \ˈbu̇-lə-ˌvärd, ˈbü-\ *n* [F, modif. of MD *bolwerc* bulwark] : a broad often landscaped thoroughfare

bounce \ˈbau̇ns\ *vb* **bounced**; **bounc·ing 1** : to cause to rebound ⟨~ a ball⟩ **2** : to rebound after striking **3** : to issue (a check) from an account with insufficient funds — **bounce** *n* — **bouncy** \ˈbau̇n-sē\ *adj*

bounc·er \ˈbau̇n-sər\ *n* : a person employed in a public place to remove disorderly persons

[1]**bound** \ˈbau̇nd\ *adj* : intending to go ⟨homeward ~⟩

[2]**bound** *n* : LIMIT, BOUNDARY — **boundless** *adj* — **bound·less·ness** *n*

[3]**bound** *vb* **1** : to set limits to **2** : to form the boundary of **3** : to name the boundaries of

[4]**bound** *past and past part of* BIND

[5]**bound** *adj* **1** : constrained by or as if by bonds : CONFINED, OBLIGED ⟨was duty ~ to help⟩ **2** : enclosed in a binding or cover **3** : RESOLVED, DETERMINED; *also* : SURE

[6]**bound** *n* **1** : LEAP, JUMP **2** : REBOUND, BOUNCE

[7]**bound** *vb* : SPRING, BOUNCE

bound·ary \ˈbau̇n-drē\ *n, pl* **-aries** : something that marks or fixes a limit or extent (as of territory) ♦ ***Synonyms*** BORDER, FRONTIER, MARCH

bound·en \ˈbau̇n-dən\ *adj* : BINDING ⟨our ~ duty⟩

boun·te·ous \ˈbau̇n-tē-əs\ *adj* **1** : GENEROUS **2** : ABUNDANT — **boun·te·ous·ly** *adv* — **boun·te·ous·ness** *n*

boun·ti·ful \ˈbau̇n-ti-fəl\ *adj* **1** : giving freely **2** : PLENTIFUL — **boun·ti·ful·ly** *adv* — **boun·ti·ful·ness** *n*

boun·ty \ˈbau̇n-tē\ *n, pl* **bounties** [ME *bounte* goodness, fr. AF *bunté,* fr. L *bonitas,* fr. *bonus* good] **1** : GENEROSITY **2** : something given liberally **3** : a reward, premium, or subsidy given usu. for doing something

bou·quet \bō-ˈkā, bü-\ *n* [F, fr. MF, thicket, bunch of flowers, fr. OF (dial. of Normandy and Picardy) *bosquet* thicket, fr. *bosc* forest] **1** : flowers picked and fastened together in a bunch **2** : a distinctive aroma (as of wine) ♦ ***Synonyms*** SCENT, FRAGRANCE, PERFUME, REDOLENCE

bour·bon \ˈbər-bən\ *n* : a whiskey distilled from a corn mash

bour·geois \ˈbu̇rzh-ˌwä, bu̇rzh-ˈwä\ *n, pl* **bourgeois** *same or* -ˌwäz, -ˈwäz\ [MF, fr. OF *burgeis* townsman, fr. *burc, borg* town, fr. L *burgus* fortified place, of Gmc origin] : a middle-class person — **bourgeois** *adj*

bour·geoi·sie \ˌbu̇rzh-ˌwä-ˈzē\ *n* : a social order dominated by bourgeois

bourne *also* **bourn** \ˈbōrn, ˈbu̇rn\ *n* : BOUNDARY; *also* : DESTINATION

bourse \ˈbu̇rs\ *n* : a European stock exchange

bout \ˈbau̇t\ *n* **1** : CONTEST, MATCH **2** : OUTBREAK, ATTACK ⟨a ~ of measles⟩

bou·tique \bü-ˈtēk\ *n* : a small fashionable specialty shop

bou·ton·niere \ˌbü-tᵊn-ˈiər\ *n* : a flower or bouquet worn in a buttonhole

[1]**bo·vine** \ˈbō-ˌvīn, -ˌvēn\ *adj* **1** : of or relating to bovines **2** : having qualities (as placidity or dullness) characteristic of oxen or cows

[2]**bovine** *n* : any of a group of mammals including oxen, bison, and their close relatives

bovine spon·gi·form encephalopathy \-ˈspən-ji-ˌfōrm-\ *n* : MAD COW DISEASE

[1]**bow** \ˈbau̇\ *vb* **1** : SUBMIT, YIELD **2** : to bend the head or body (as in submission, courtesy, or assent) **3** : DEBUT ⟨the play ~*s* next month⟩

[2]**bow** *n* : an act or posture of bowing

[3]**bow** \ˈbō\ *n* **1** : BEND, ARCH; *esp* : RAINBOW **2** : a weapon for shooting arrows; *also* : ARCHER **3** : a knot formed by doubling a line into two or more loops **4** : a wooden rod strung with horsehairs for playing an instrument of the violin family

[4]**bow** \ˈbō\ *vb* **1** : BEND, CURVE **2** : to play (an instrument) with a bow

[5]**bow** \ˈbau̇\ *n* : the forward part of a ship — **bow** *adj*

bowd·ler·ise *Brit var of* BOWDLERIZE

bowd·ler·ize \ˈbōd-lə-ˌrīz, ˈbau̇d-\ *vb* **-ized**; **-iz·ing** : to expurgate by omitting parts considered vulgar

bow·el \ˈbau̇(-ə)l\ *n* **1** : INTESTINE; *also* : one of the divisions of the intestine — usu. used in pl. **2** *pl* : the inmost parts ⟨the ~*s* of the earth⟩

bowel movement *n* : an act of passing usu. solid waste through the rectum and anus; *also* : STOOL 4

bow·er \ˈbau̇(-ə)r\ *n* : a shelter of boughs or vines : ARBOR

[1]**bowl** \ˈbōl\ *n* **1** : a concave vessel used to hold liquids **2** : a drinking vessel **3** : a bowl-shaped part or structure — **bowlful** \-ˌfu̇l\ *n*

[2]**bowl** *n* **1** : a ball for rolling on a level surface in bowling **2** : a cast of the ball in bowling

[3]**bowl** *vb* **1** : to play a game of bowling; *also* : to roll a ball in bowling **2** : to travel (as in a vehicle) rapidly and smoothly **3** : to strike or knock down with a moving object

bowlder *var of* BOULDER

bow·legged \ˈbō-ˌle-gəd\ *adj* : having legs

that bow outward at or below the knee — **bow·leg** \'bō-ˌleg\ *n*

[1]**bowl·er** \'bō-lər\ *n* : a person who bowls

[2]**bow·ler** \'bō-lər\ *n* : DERBY 3

bow·line \'bō-lən, -ˌlīn\ *n* : a knot used to form a loop that neither slips nor jams

bowl·ing \'bō-liŋ\ *n* : any of various games in which balls are rolled on a green or alley at an object or a group of objects

bow·man \'bō-mən\ *n* : ARCHER

bow·sprit \'bau̇-ˌsprit\ *n* : a spar projecting forward from the prow of a ship

bow·string \'bō-ˌstriŋ\ *n* : the cord connecting the two ends of a shooting bow

[1]**box** \'bäks\ *n, pl* **box** *or* **box·es** : an evergreen shrub or small tree used esp. for hedges

[2]**box** *n* **1** : a rigid typically rectangular receptacle often with a cover; *also* : the quantity held by a box **2** : a small compartment (as for a group of theater patrons); *also* : a boxlike receptacle or division **3** : a usu. rectangular space demarcated for a particular purpose ⟨the batter's ~⟩ **4** : a difficult situation : PREDICAMENT — **boxy** \'bäk-sē\ *adj*

[3]**box** *vb* : to enclose in or as if in a box

[4]**box** *n* : a punch or slap esp. on the ear

[5]**box** *vb* **1** : to strike with the hand **2** : to engage in boxing with

box·car \'bäks-ˌkär\ *n* : a roofed freight car usu. with sliding doors in the sides

box cutter *n* : a small cutting tool with a retractable razor blade

[1]**box·er** \'bäk-sər\ *n* **1** : a person who engages in boxing **2** *pl* : BOXER SHORTS

[2]**boxer** *n* : any of a German breed of compact medium-sized dogs with a short usu. fawn or brindled coat

boxer shorts *n pl* : men's loose-fitting shorts worn as underwear

box·ing \'bäk-siŋ\ *n* : the sport of fighting with the fists

box office *n* : an office (as in a theater) where admission tickets are sold

box turtle *n* : any of several No. American land turtles able to withdraw completely into their shell

box·wood \'bäks-ˌwu̇d\ *n* : the tough hard wood of the box; *also* : a box tree or shrub

boy \'bȯi\ *n* **1** : a male child : YOUTH **2** : SON — **boy·hood** \-ˌhu̇d\ *n* — **boy·ish** *adj* — **boy·ish·ly** *adv* — **boy·ish·ness** *n*

boy·cott \'bȯi-ˌkät\ *vb* [Charles C. *Boycott* †1897 Eng. land agent in Ireland who was ostracized for refusing to reduce rents] : to refrain from having any dealings with — **boycott** *n*

boy·friend \'bȯi-ˌfrend\ *n* **1** : a male friend **2** : a frequent or regular male companion in a romantic relationship

Boy Scout *n* : a member of any of various national scouting programs (as the Boy Scouts of America)

boy·sen·ber·ry \'bȯi-zᵊn-ˌber-ē, 'bȯis-\ *n* : a large reddish-black fruit with a raspberry flavor; *also* : the hybrid bramble bearing it developed by crossing blackberries and raspberries

bo·zo \'bō-ˌzō\ *n, pl* **bozos** : a foolish or incompetent person

bp *abbr* **1** bishop **2** birthplace

BP *abbr* **1** batting practice **2** blood pressure **3** boiling point

bpl *abbr* birthplace

BPOE *abbr* Benevolent and Protective Order of Elks

br *abbr* **1** branch **2** brass **3** brown

[1]**Br** *abbr* Britain; British

[2]**Br** *symbol* bromine

BR *abbr* bedroom

bra \'brä\ *n* : BRASSIERE

[1]**brace** \'brās\ *vb* **braced**; **brac·ing** **1** *archaic* : to make fast : BIND **2** : to tighten preparatory to use; *also* : to get ready for : prepare oneself **3** : INVIGORATE **4** : to furnish or support with a brace; *also* : STRENGTHEN **5** : to set firmly **6** : to gain courage or confidence

[2]**brace** *n, pl* **brac·es** **1** *or pl* **brace** : two of a kind ⟨a ~ of dogs⟩ **2** : a crank-shaped device for turning a bit **3** : something (as a tie, prop, or clamp) that distributes, directs, or resists pressure or weight **4** *pl* : SUSPENDERS **5** : an appliance for supporting a body part (as the shoulders) **6** *pl* : a dental appliance used to exert pressure to straighten misaligned teeth **7** : one of two marks { } used to connect words or items to be considered together

brace·let \'brā-slət\ *n* [ME, fr. MF, dim. of *bras* arm, fr. L *bracchium,* fr. Gk *brachiōn*] : an ornamental band or chain worn around the wrist

bra·ce·ro \brä-'ser-ō\ *n, pl* **-ros** : a Mexican laborer admitted to the U.S. esp. for seasonal farm work

brack·en \'bra-kən\ *n* : a large coarse fern; *also* : a growth of such ferns

[1]**brack·et** \'bra-kət\ *n* **1** : a projecting framework or arm designed to support weight; *also* : a shelf on such framework **2** : one of a pair of punctuation marks [ ] used esp. to enclose interpolated matter **3** : a continuous section of a series; *esp* : one of a graded series of income groups

[2]**bracket** *vb* **1** : to furnish or fasten with brackets **2** : to place within brackets; *also* : to separate or group with or as if with brackets

brack·ish \'bra-kish\ *adj* : somewhat salty — **brack·ish·ness** *n*

bract \'brakt\ *n* : an often modified leaf on or at the base of a flower stalk

brad \'brad\ *n* : a slender nail with a small head

brae \'brā\ *n, chiefly Scot* : a hillside esp. along a river

brag \'brag\ *vb* **bragged**; **brag·ging** : to talk or assert boastfully — **brag** *n* — **brag·ger** *n*

brag·ga·do·cio \ˌbra-gə-'dō-shē-ˌō, -sē-, -chē-\ *n, pl* **-cios** **1** : BRAGGART, BOASTER **2** : empty boasting **3** : arrogant pretension : COCKINESS

brag·gart \'bra-gərt\ *n* : one who brags

Brah·man *or* **Brah·min** \'brä-mən *for 1;* 'brā-, 'brä-, 'bra- *for 2*\ *n* **1** : a Hindu of the highest caste traditionally assigned to the priesthood **2 :** any of a breed of large vigorous humped cattle developed in the southern U.S. from Indian stock **3** *usu* *Brahmin* **:** a person of high social standing and cultivated intellect and taste

Brah·man·ism \ˈbrä-mə-ˌni-zəm\ *n* **:** orthodox Hinduism

[1]**braid** \ˈbrād\ *vb* **1 :** to form (strands) into a braid **:** PLAIT; *also* **:** to make from braids **2 :** to ornament with braid

[2]**braid** *n* **1 :** a length of braided hair **2 :** a cord or ribbon of three or more interwoven strands; *esp* **:** a narrow ornamental one

braille \ˈbrāl\ *n, often cap* **:** a system of writing for the blind that uses characters made up of raised dots

[1]**brain** \ˈbrān\ *n* **1 :** the part of the vertebrate central nervous system enclosed in the skull and continuous with the spinal cord that is composed of neurons and supporting structures and is the center of thought and nervous system control; *also* **:** a centralized mass of nerve tissue in an invertebrate **2 :** INTELLECT, INTELLIGENCE — often used in pl. — **brained** \ˈbrānd\ *adj* — **brain·less** *adj* — **brainy** *adj*

[2]**brain** *vb* **1 :** to kill by smashing the skull **2 :** to hit on the head

brain·child \ˈbrān-ˌchī(-ə)ld\ *n* **:** a product of one's creative imagination

brain death *n* **:** final cessation of activity in the central nervous system esp. as indicated by a flat electroencephalogram — **brain–dead** \-ˌded\ *adj*

brain drain *n* **:** the departure of educated or professional people from one country, sector, or field to another usu. for better pay or living conditions

brain·storm \-ˌstȯrm\ *n* **:** a sudden inspiration or idea — **brainstorm** *vb*

brain·teas·er \-ˌtē-zər\ *n* **:** a challenging puzzle

brain·wash·ing \ˈbrān-ˌwȯ-shiŋ, -ˌwä-\ *n* **1 :** a forcible indoctrination to induce someone to give up basic political, social, or religious beliefs and attitudes and to accept contrasting regimented ideas **2 :** persuasion by propaganda or salesmanship — **brain·wash** *vb*

brain wave *n* **1 :** BRAINSTORM **2 :** rhythmic fluctuations of voltage between parts of the brain; *also* **:** a current produced by brain waves

braise \ˈbrāz\ *vb* **braised; brais·ing :** to cook slowly in fat and little moisture in a closed pot

[1]**brake** \ˈbrāk\ *n* **:** a common bracken fern

[2]**brake** *n* **:** rough or wet land heavily overgrown (as with thickets or reeds)

[3]**brake** *n* **:** a device for slowing or stopping motion esp. by friction — **brake·less** *adj*

[4]**brake** *vb* **braked; brak·ing 1 :** to slow or stop by or as if by a brake **2 :** to apply a brake

brake·man \ˈbrāk-mən\ *n* **:** a train crew member who inspects the train and assists the conductor

bram·ble \ˈbram-bəl\ *n* **:** any of a large genus of prickly shrubs (as a blackberry) related to the roses; *also* **:** any rough prickly shrub or vine — **bram·bly** \-b(ə-)lē\ *adj*

bran \ˈbran\ *n* **:** the edible broken husks of cereal grain sifted from flour or meal

[1]**branch** \ˈbranch\ *n* [ME, fr. AF *branche,* fr. LL *branca* paw] **1 :** a natural subdivision (as a bough or twig) of a plant stem **2 :** a division (as of an antler or a river) related to a whole like a plant branch to its stem **3 :** a discrete element of a complex system ⟨the executive ~⟩; *esp* **:** a division of a family descended from one ancestor — **branched** \ˈbrancht\ *adj*

[2]**branch** *vb* **1 :** to develop branches **2 :** DIVERGE **3 :** to extend activities ⟨the business is *~ing* out⟩

[1]**brand** \ˈbrand\ *n* **1 :** a piece of charred or burning wood **2 :** a mark made (as by burning) usu. to identify; *also* **:** a mark of disgrace **:** STIGMA **3 :** a class of goods identified as the product of a particular firm or producer **4 :** a distinctive kind ⟨my own ~ of humor⟩

[2]**brand** *vb* **1 :** to mark with a brand **2 :** STIGMATIZE ⟨was *~ed* a traitor⟩

bran·dish \ˈbran-dish\ *vb* **:** to shake or wave menacingly ⟨~ a knife⟩ ♦ ***Synonyms*** FLOURISH, FLASH, FLAUNT

brand–new \ˈbran-ˈnü, -ˈnyü\ *adj* **:** conspicuously new and unused

bran·dy \ˈbran-dē\ *n, pl* **brandies** [short for *brandywine,* fr. D *brandewijn,* fr. MD *brantwijn,* fr. *brant* distilled + *wijn* wine] **:** a liquor distilled from wine or fermented fruit juice — **brandy** *vb*

brash \ˈbrash\ *adj* **1 :** IMPETUOUS, AUDACIOUS **2 :** aggressively self-assertive — **brash·ly** *adv* — **brash·ness** *n*

brass \ˈbras\ *n* **1 :** an alloy of copper and zinc; *also* **:** an object of brass **2 :** brazen self-assurance **3 :** persons of high rank (as in the military) — **brassy** *adj*

bras·siere \brə-ˈzir\ *n* **:** a woman's close-fitting undergarment designed to support the breasts

brat \ˈbrat\ *n, disparaging* **:** an ill-behaved child — **brat·ti·ness** *n* — **brat·ty** *adj*

bra·va·do \brə-ˈvä-dō\ *n, pl* **-does** *or* **-dos 1 :** blustering swaggering conduct **2 :** a show of bravery

[1]**brave** \ˈbrāv\ *adj* **brav·er; brav·est** [MF, fr. It & Sp *bravo* courageous, wild, prob. fr. L *barbarus* barbarous] **1 :** showing courage **2 :** EXCELLENT, SPLENDID ♦ ***Synonyms*** BOLD, INTREPID, COURAGEOUS, VALIANT — **brave·ly** *adv*

[2]**brave** *vb* **braved; brav·ing :** to face or endure bravely

[3]**brave** *n* **:** a warrior of an Indigenous people of No. America

brav·ery \ˈbrā-və-rē\ *n, pl* **-er·ies :** COURAGE

bra·vo \ˈbrä-vō\ *n, pl* **bravos :** a shout of approval — often used as an interjection in applauding

bra·vu·ra \brə-ˈvyu̇r-ə, -ˈvu̇r-\ *n* **1 :** a florid brilliant musical style **2 :** self-assured brilliant performance — **bravura** *adj*

brawl \ˈbrȯl\ *n* : a noisy quarrel ♦ ***Synonyms*** FRACAS, ROW, RUMPUS, SCRAP, FRAY, MELEE — **brawl** *vb* — **brawl·er** *n*

brawn \ˈbrȯn\ *n* : strong muscles; *also* : muscular strength — **brawn·i·ness** *n* — **brawny** *adj*

bray \ˈbrā\ *n* : the characteristic harsh cry of a donkey — **bray** *vb*

braze \ˈbrāz\ *vb* **brazed**; **braz·ing** : to solder with an alloy (as brass) that melts at a lower temperature than the metals being joined — **braz·er** *n*

[1]**bra·zen** \ˈbrā-zᵊn\ *adj* **1** : made of brass **2** : sounding harsh and loud **3** : of the color of brass **4** : marked by contemptuous boldness ⟨a ~ rebuff⟩ — **bra·zen·ly** *adv* — **bra·zen·ness** *n*

[2]**brazen** *vb* : to face boldly or defiantly

[1]**bra·zier** \ˈbrā-zhər\ *n* : a worker in brass

[2]**brazier** *n* **1** : a vessel holding burning coals (as for heating) **2** : a device on which food is grilled

Bra·zil nut \brə-ˈzil-\ *n* : a triangular oily edible nut borne in large capsules by a tall So. American tree; *also* : the tree

[1]**breach** \ˈbrēch\ *n* **1** : a breaking of a law, obligation, tie (as of friendship), or standard (as of conduct) **2** : an interruption or opening made by or as if by breaking through ♦ ***Synonyms*** VIOLATION, TRANSGRESSION, INFRINGEMENT, TRESPASS

[2]**breach** *vb* **1** : to make a breach in ⟨the army *~ed* the castle wall⟩ **2** : to leap out of water ⟨whales *~ing*⟩

[1]**bread** \ˈbred\ *n* **1** : baked food made basically of flour or meal **2** : FOOD

[2]**bread** *vb* : to cover with bread crumbs

bread·bas·ket \ˈbred-ˌbas-kət\ *n* : a major cereal-producing region

bread·fruit \-ˌfrüt\ *n* : a round usu. seedless fruit resembling bread in color and texture when baked; *also* : a tall tropical tree related to the mulberry and bearing breadfruit

bread·stuff \-ˌstəf\ *n* : GRAIN, FLOUR

breadth \ˈbredth, ˈbretth\ *n* **1** : WIDTH **2** : comprehensive quality : SCOPE ⟨her ~ of knowledge⟩

bread·win·ner \ˈbred-ˌwi-nər\ *n* : a member of a family whose wages supply its livelihood

[1]**break** \ˈbrāk\ *vb* **broke** \ˈbrōk\; **bro·ken** \ˈbrō-kən\; **break·ing** **1** : to separate into parts usu. suddenly or violently; *also* : to render inoperable ⟨*broke* his watch⟩ **2** : TRANSGRESS ⟨~ a law⟩ **3** : to force a way into, out of, or through **4** : to disrupt the order or unity of ⟨~ ranks⟩ ⟨~ up a gang⟩; *also* : to bring to submission or helplessness **5** : EXCEED, SURPASS ⟨~ a record⟩ **6** : RUIN **7** : to make known ⟨~ the bad news⟩ **8** : HALT, INTERRUPT; *also* : to act or change abruptly (as a course or activity) **9** : to come esp. suddenly into being or notice ⟨as day *~s*⟩ **10** : to fail under stress **11** : HAPPEN, DEVELOP ⟨report news as it *~s*⟩ — **break·able** *adj or n* — **break into** **1** : to begin with a sudden throwing off of restraint ⟨*broke into* tears⟩ **2** : to make entry or entrance into ⟨*break into* show business⟩

[2]**break** *n* **1** : an act of breaking **2** : a result of breaking; *esp* : an interruption of continuity ⟨coffee ~⟩ ⟨a ~ for the commercial⟩ **3** : a stroke of luck

break·age \ˈbrā-kij\ *n* **1** : loss due to things broken **2** : the action of breaking **3** : articles or amount broken

break·down \ˈbrāk-ˌdau̇n\ *n* **1** : functional failure; *esp* : a physical, mental, or nervous collapse **2** : DISINTEGRATION **3** : the process of decomposing **4** : ANALYSIS, CLASSIFICATION — **break down** *vb*

break·er \ˈbrā-kər\ *n* **1** : one that breaks **2** : a wave that breaks into foam (as against the shore)

break·fast \ˈbrek-fəst\ *n* : the first meal of the day — **breakfast** *vb*

break in *vb* **1** : to enter a building by force **2** : INTERRUPT; *also* : INTRUDE **3** : TRAIN ⟨*break in* new employees⟩ — **break–in** \ˈbrāk-ˌin\ *n*

break·neck \ˈbrāk-ˈnek\ *adj* : very fast or dangerous ⟨~ speed⟩

break out *vb* **1** : to develop or erupt suddenly or with force **2** : to develop a skin rash

break·through \ˈbrāk-ˌthrü\ *n* **1** : an act or instance of breaking through an obstruction or defensive line **2** : a sudden advance in knowledge or technique ⟨a scientific ~⟩

break·up \-ˌəp\ *n* **1** : DISSOLUTION **2** : a division into smaller units — **break up** *vb*

break·wa·ter \ˈbrāk-ˌwȯ-tər, -ˌwä-\ *n* : a structure protecting a harbor or beach from the force of waves

bream \ˈbrim, ˈbrēm\ *n, pl* **bream** *or* **breams** : any of various small freshwater sunfishes

breast \ˈbrest\ *n* **1** : either of the pair of mammary glands extending from the front of the chest esp. in pubescent and adult human females **2** : the front part of the body between the neck and the abdomen **3** : the seat of emotion and thought

breast·bone \ˈbrest-ˌbōn\ *n* : STERNUM

breast–feed \-ˌfēd\ *vb* : to feed (a baby) from a mother's breast

breast·plate \-ˌplāt\ *n* : a metal plate of armor for the breast

breast·stroke \-ˌstrōk\ *n* : a swimming stroke executed by extending both arms forward and then sweeping them back with palms out while kicking backward and outward with both legs

breast·work \-ˌwərk\ *n* : a temporary fortification

breath \ˈbreth\ *n* **1** : the act or power of breathing **2** : a slight breeze **3** : air inhaled or exhaled in breathing **4** : spoken sound **5** : SPIRIT — **breath·less** *adj* — **breath·less·ly** *adv* — **breath·less·ness** *n* — **breathy** \ˈbre-thē\ *adj*

breathe \ˈbrēth\ *vb* **breathed**; **breath·ing** **1** : to inhale and exhale **2** : LIVE **3** : to halt for rest **4** : to utter softly or secretly — **breath·able** *adj*

breath·er \ˈbrē-thər\ *n* **1** : one that breathes **2** : a short rest

breath·tak·ing \ˈbreth-ˌtā-kiŋ\ *adj* **1** : making one out of breath **2** : EXCITING, THRILLING ⟨~ beauty⟩ — **breath·tak·ing·ly** *adv*

brec·cia \ˈbre-chē-ə, -chə\ *n* : a rock composed of sharp fragments held in fine-grained material

breech \ˈbrēch\ *n* **1** *pl* *usu* ˈbri-chəz\ : pants ending near the knee **2** : BUTTOCKS, RUMP **3** : the part of a firearm at the rear of the barrel

[1]**breed** \ˈbrēd\ *vb* **bred** \ˈbred\; **breed·ing** **1** : BEGET; *also* : ORIGINATE **2** : to propagate sexually; *also* : MATE **3** : BRING UP, NURTURE **4** : to produce (fissionable material) from material that is not fissionable ♦ ***Synonyms*** GENERATE, REPRODUCE, PROCREATE, PROPAGATE — **breed·er** *n*

[2]**breed** *n* **1** : a strain of similar and presumably related plants or animals usu. developed in domestication **2** : KIND, SORT, CLASS

breeding *n* **1** : ANCESTRY **2** : training in polite social interaction **3** : sexual propagation of plants or animals

[1]**breeze** \ˈbrēz\ *n* **1** : a light wind **2** : CINCH, SNAP — **breeze·less** *adj*

[2]**breeze** *vb* **breezed**; **breez·ing** : to progress quickly and easily

breeze·way \ˈbrēz-ˌwā\ *n* : a roofed open passage connecting two buildings (as a house and garage)

breezy \ˈbrē-zē\ *adj* **1** : swept by breezes **2** : briskly informal ⟨~ prose⟩ — **breez·i·ly** \ˈbrē-zə-lē\ *adv* — **breez·i·ness** \-zē-nəs\ *n*

breth·ren \ˈbreth-rən, ˈbre-thə-; ˈbre-thərn\ *pl of* BROTHER — used esp. in formal or solemn address

Brethren *n pl* : members of one of several Protestant denominations originating chiefly in a German religious movement and stressing personal religious experience

bre·via·ry \ˈbrē-vyə-rē, -vē-ˌer-ē\ *n, pl* **-ries** *often cap* : a book of prayers, hymns, psalms, and readings used by Roman Catholic priests

brev·i·ty \ˈbre-və-tē\ *n, pl* **-ties** **1** : shortness or conciseness of expression **2** : shortness of duration

brew \ˈbrü\ *vb* **1** : to prepare (as beer) by steeping, boiling, and fermenting **2** : to prepare (as tea) by steeping in hot water — **brew** *n* — **brew·er** *n* — **brew·ery** \ˈbrü-ə-rē, ˈbrů(-ə)r-ē\ *n*

[1]**bri·ar** *also* **bri·er** \ˈbrī-ər\ *n* : a plant (as a bramble or rose) with a thorny or prickly usu. woody stem; *also* : a mass or twig of these — **bri·ary** \ˈbrī-ər-ē\ *adj*

[2]**briar** *n* : a tobacco pipe made from the root or stem of a European heath

[1]**bribe** \ˈbrīb\ *n* [ME, morsel given to a beggar, bribe, fr. AF, morsel] : something (as money or a favor) given or promised to a person to influence conduct

[2]**bribe** *vb* **bribed**; **brib·ing** : to influence by offering a bribe — **brib·able** *adj* — **brib·er** *n* — **brib·ery** \ˈbrī-bə-rē\ *n*

bric–a–brac \ˈbri-kə-ˌbrak\ *n pl* [F] : small ornamental articles

[1]**brick** \ˈbrik\ *n* : a block molded from moist clay and hardened by heat used esp. for building

[2]**brick** *vb* : to close, cover, or pave with bricks

brick·bat \ˈbrik-ˌbat\ *n* **1** : a piece of a hard material (as a brick) esp. when thrown as a missile **2** : an uncomplimentary remark

brick·lay·er \ˈbrik-ˌlā-ər\ *n* : a person who builds or paves with bricks — **brick·lay·ing** *n*

[1]**brid·al** \ˈbrī-dᵊl\ *n* [ME *bridale,* fr. OE *brȳdealu,* fr. *brȳd* bride + *ealu* ale] : MARRIAGE, WEDDING

[2]**bridal** *adj* : of or relating to a bride or a wedding

bride \ˈbrīd\ *n* : a woman just married or about to be married

bride·groom \ˈbrīd-ˌgrüm, -ˌgrům\ *n* : a man just married or about to be married

brides·maid \ˈbrīdz-ˌmād\ *n* : a woman who attends a bride at her wedding

[1]**bridge** \ˈbrij\ *n* **1** : a structure built over a depression or obstacle for use as a passageway **2** : something (as the upper part of the nose) resembling a bridge in form or function **3** : a curved piece raising the strings of a musical instrument **4** : the forward part of a ship's superstructure from which it is navigated **5** : an artificial replacement for missing teeth

[2]**bridge** *vb* **bridged**; **bridg·ing** : to build a bridge over — **bridge·able** *adj*

[3]**bridge** *n* : a card game for four players developed from whist

bridge·head \-ˌhed\ *n* : an advanced position seized in enemy territory

bridge·work \-ˌwərk\ *n* : dental bridges

[1]**bri·dle** \ˈbrī-dᵊl\ *n* **1** : headgear with which a horse is controlled **2** : CURB, RESTRAINT

[2]**bridle** *vb* **bri·dled**; **bri·dling** **1** : to put a bridle on; *also* : to restrain with or as if with a bridle **2** : to show hostility or scorn usu. by tossing the head

Brie \ˈbrē\ *n* : a soft cheese with a whitish rind and a pale yellow interior

[1]**brief** \ˈbrēf\ *adj* **1** : short in duration or extent **2** : CONCISE; *also* : CURT — **brief·ly** *adv* — **brief·ness** *n*

[2]**brief** *n* **1** : a concise statement or document; *esp* : one summarizing a law client's case or a legal argument **2** *pl* : short snug underpants

[3]**brief** *vb* : to give instructions or information to

brief·case \ˈbrēf-ˌkās\ *n* : a flat flexible case for carrying papers

brier *var of* BRIAR

[1]**brig** \ˈbrig\ *n* : a 2-masted square-rigged sailing ship

[2]**brig** *n* : the place of confinement for offenders on a naval ship

[3]**brig** *abbr* brigade

bri·gade \bri-ˈgād\ *n* **1** : a military unit composed of a headquarters, one or more units of infantry or armored forces, and supporting units **2** : a group organized for a particular purpose (as fire fighting)

brig·a·dier general \ˈbri-gə-ˌdir-\ *n* : a commissioned officer (as in the army) ranking next below a major general
brig·and \ˈbri-gənd\ *n* : BANDIT — **brig·and·age** \-gən-dij\ *n*
brig·an·tine \ˈbri-gən-ˌtēn\ *n* : a 2-masted square-rigged ship with a fore-and-aft mainsail
Brig Gen *abbr* brigadier general
bright \ˈbrīt\ *adj* **1** : SHINING, RADIANT **2** : ILLUSTRIOUS, GLORIOUS **3** : INTELLIGENT, CLEVER; *also* : LIVELY, CHEERFUL ⟨a ~ smile⟩ ♦ ***Synonyms*** BRILLIANT, LUSTROUS, BEAMING — **bright** *adv* — **bright·ly** *adv* — **bright·ness** *n*
bright·en \ˈbrī-tᵊn\ *vb* : to make or become bright or brighter ⟨the good news ~*ed* her mood⟩ — **bright·en·er** *n*
[1]**bril·liant** \ˈbril-yənt\ *adj* [F *brillant,* prp. of *briller* to shine, fr. It *brillare*] **1** : very bright **2** : STRIKING, DISTINCTIVE **3** : very intelligent ⟨a ~ idea⟩ ♦ ***Synonyms*** RADIANT, LUSTROUS, BEAMING, LUCID, BRIGHT, LAMBENT — **bril·liance** \-yəns\ *n* — **bril·lian·cy** \-yən-sē\ *n* — **bril·liant·ly** *adv*
[2]**brilliant** *n* : a gem cut in a particular form with many facets
[1]**brim** \ˈbrim\ *n* : EDGE, RIM ♦ ***Synonyms*** BRINK, BORDER, VERGE, FRINGE — **brim·less** *adj*
[2]**brim** *vb* **brimmed**; **brim·ming** : to be or become full often to overflowing
brim·ful \-ˈfu̇l\ *adj* : full to the brim
brim·stone \ˈbrim-ˌstōn\ *n* : SULFUR
brin·dled \ˈbrin-dᵊld\ *adj* : having dark streaks or flecks on a gray or tawny ground ⟨a ~ Great Dane⟩
brine \ˈbrīn\ *n* **1** : water saturated with salt **2** : OCEAN — **brin·i·ness** *n* — **briny** \ˈbrī-nē\ *adj*
bring \ˈbriŋ\ *vb* **brought** \ˈbrȯt\; **bring·ing** \ˈbriŋ-iŋ\ **1** : to cause to come with one **2** : INDUCE, PERSUADE, LEAD **3** : PRODUCE, EFFECT **4** : to sell for ⟨~ a good price⟩ — **bring·er** *n*
bring about *vb* : to cause to take place
bring up *vb* **1** : to give a parent's fostering care to **2** : to come or bring to a sudden halt **3** : to call to notice
brink \ˈbriŋk\ *n* **1** : an edge at the top of a steep place **2** : the point of onset
brio \ˈbrē-ō\ *n* : VIVACITY, SPIRIT
bri·quette *or* **bri·quet** \bri-ˈket\ *n* : a compacted often brick-shaped mass of fine material ⟨a charcoal ~⟩
bris *also* **briss** \ˈbris\ *n* : the Jewish rite of circumcision
brisk \ˈbrisk\ *adj* **1** : ALERT, LIVELY **2** : INVIGORATING ⟨~ weather⟩ **3** : highly active ⟨a ~ business⟩ ♦ ***Synonyms*** AGILE, SPRY, NIMBLE — **brisk·ly** *adv* — **brisk·ness** *n*
bris·ket \ˈbris-kət\ *n* : the breast or lower chest of a quadruped; *also* : a cut of beef from the brisket
bris·ling \ˈbriz-liŋ, ˈbris-\ *n* : SPRAT 1
[1]**bris·tle** \ˈbri-səl\ *n* : a short stiff coarse hair — **bris·tle·like** \ˈbri-səl-ˌlīk\ *adj* — **bris·tly** *adj*
[2]**bristle** *vb* **bris·tled**; **bris·tling** **1** : to stand stiffly erect **2** : to show angry defiance ⟨*bristled* at the charges⟩ **3** : to appear as if covered with bristles
Brit *abbr* Britain; British
Bri·tan·nic \bri-ˈta-nik\ *adj* : BRITISH
britch·es \ˈbri-chəz\ *n pl* : BREECHES, TROUSERS
Brit·ish \ˈbri-tish\ *n pl* : the people of Great Britain or the Commonwealth — **British** *adj* — **Brit·ish·ness** *n*
British thermal unit *n* : the quantity of heat needed to raise the temperature of one pound of water one degree Fahrenheit
Brit·on \ˈbri-tᵊn\ *n* **1** : a member of a people inhabiting Britain before the Anglo-Saxon invasion **2** : a native or inhabitant of Great Britain
brit·tle \ˈbri-tᵊl\ *adj* **brit·tler**; **brit·tlest** : easily broken : FRAGILE ♦ ***Synonyms*** CRISP, CRUMBLY, FRIABLE — **brit·tle·ness** *n*
bro \ˈbrō\ *n, pl* **bros** **1** : BROTHER 1 **2** : SOUL BROTHER
[1]**broach** \ˈbrōch\ *n* : a pointed tool
[2]**broach** *vb* **1** : to pierce (as a cask) in order to draw the contents **2** : to open up (a subject) for discussion
broad \ˈbrȯd\ *adj* **1** : WIDE **2** : SPACIOUS ⟨the ~ plains⟩ **3** : CLEAR, OPEN ⟨~ daylight⟩ **4** : OBVIOUS ⟨a ~ hint⟩ **5** : COARSE, CRUDE ⟨~ stories⟩ **6** : tolerant in outlook **7** : GENERAL ⟨a ~ rule⟩ **8** : dealing with essential points — **broad·ly** *adv* — **broad·ness** *n*
broad·band \ˈbrȯd-ˌband\ *n* : a system of high-speed telecommunication in which a frequency range is divided into multiple independent channels for simultaneous transmission of signals
[1]**broad·cast** \ˈbrȯd-ˌkast\ *vb* **broadcast** *also* **broad·cast·ed**; **broad·cast·ing** **1** : to scatter or sow broadcast **2** : to make widely known **3** : to transmit a broadcast — **broad·cast·er** *n*
[2]**broadcast** *adv* : to or over a wide area
[3]**broadcast** *n* **1** : the transmission of sound or images by radio or television **2** : a single radio or television program
broad·cloth \-ˌklȯth\ *n* **1** : a smooth dense woolen cloth **2** : a fine soft cloth of cotton, silk, or synthetic fiber
broad·en \ˈbrȯ-dᵊn\ *vb* : WIDEN
broad·loom \-ˌlüm\ *adj* : woven on a wide loom esp. in a solid color
broad–mind·ed \-ˈmīn-dəd\ *adj* : tolerant of varied opinions — **broad–mind·ed·ly** *adv* — **broad–mind·ed·ness** *n*
[1]**broad·side** \-ˌsīd\ *n* **1** : a sheet of paper printed usu. on one side (as an advertisement) **2** : all of the guns on one side of a ship; *also* : their simultaneous firing **3** : a volley of abuse or denunciation
[2]**broadside** *adv* **1** : with one side forward : SIDEWAYS **2** : from the side ⟨the car was hit ~⟩
broad–spectrum *adj* : effective against a wide range of organisms ⟨~ antibiotics⟩
broad·sword \ˈbrȯd-ˌsȯrd\ *n* : a broad-bladed sword

broad·tail \-ˌtāl\ *n* : a karakul esp. with flat and wavy fur

bro·cade \brō-ˈkād\ *n* : a usu. silk fabric with a raised design

broc·co·li \ˈbrä-kə-lē\ *n* [It, pl. of *broccolo* flowering top of a cabbage, dim. of *brocco* small nail, sprout, fr. L *broccus* projecting] : the stems and immature usu. green or purple flower heads of either of two garden vegetable plants closely related to the cabbage; *also* : either of the plants

bro·chette \brō-ˈshet\ *n* : SKEWER

bro·chure \brō-ˈshu̇r\ *n* [F, fr. *brocher* to sew, fr. MF, to prick, fr. OF *brochier,* fr. *broche* pointed tool] : PAMPHLET, BOOKLET

bro·gan \ˈbrō-gən, brō-ˈgan\ *n* : a heavy shoe

brogue \ˈbrōg\ *n* : a dialect or regional pronunciation; *esp* : an Irish accent

broil \ˈbrȯi(-ə)l\ *vb* : to cook by exposure to radiant heat : GRILL — **broil** *n*

broil·er \ˈbrȯi-lər\ *n* **1** : a utensil for broiling **2** : a young chicken fit for broiling

broil·ing \ˈbrȯi(-ə)-liŋ\ *adj* : extremely hot ⟨a ~ sun⟩

[1]**broke** \ˈbrōk\ *past of* BREAK

[2]**broke** *adj* : PENNILESS

[1]**bro·ken** \ˈbrō-kən\ *past part of* BREAK

[2]**broken** *adj* **1** : SHATTERED ⟨~ glass⟩ **2** : having gaps or breaks : INTERRUPTED, DISRUPTED **3** : SUBDUED, CRUSHED ⟨a ~ spirit⟩ **4** : BANKRUPT **5** : imperfectly spoken ⟨~ English⟩ — **bro·ken·ly** *adv*

bro·ken·heart·ed \ˌbrō-kən-ˈhär-təd\ *adj* : overcome by grief or despair

bro·ker \ˈbrō-kər\ *n* : an agent who negotiates contracts of purchase and sale — **broker** *vb*

bro·ker·age \ˈbrō-kə-rij\ *n* **1** : the business of a broker **2** : the fee or commission charged by a broker

bro·mance \ˈbrō-ˌman(t)s\ *n* [blend of *bro* and *romance*] : a close nonsexual friendship between men — **bro·man·tic** \brō-ˈman-tik\ *adj*

bro·me·li·ad \brō-ˈmē-lē-ˌad\ *n* : any of several tropical American ornamental plants related to the pineapple that usu. grow on trees

bro·mide \ˈbrō-ˌmīd\ *n* : a compound of bromine and another element or chemical group including some (as potassium bromide) used as sedatives

bro·mid·ic \brō-ˈmi-dik\ *adj* : TRITE, UNORIGINAL

bro·mine \ˈbrō-ˌmēn\ *n* [F *brome* bromine, fr. Gk *brōmos* stink] : a deep red liquid corrosive chemical element that gives off an irritating vapor

bronc \ˈbräŋk\ *n* : an unbroken or partly broken range horse of western No. America; *also* : MUSTANG

bron·chi·al \ˈbräŋ-kē-əl\ *adj* : of, relating to, or affecting the bronchi or their branches

bron·chi·tis \brän-ˈkī-təs, bräŋ-\ *n* : inflammation of the bronchi and their branches — **bron·chit·ic** \-ˈki-tik\ *adj*

bron·chus \ˈbräŋ-kəs\ *n, pl* **bron·chi** \ˈbräŋ-ˌkī, -ˌkē\ : either of the main divisions of the trachea each leading to a lung

bron·co \ˈbräŋ-kō\ *n, pl* **broncos** [MexSp, fr. Sp, rough, wild] : BRONC

bron·to·sau·rus \ˌbrän-tə-ˈsȯr-əs\ *also* **bron·to·saur** \ˈbrän-tə-ˌsȯr\ *n* [NL, fr. Gk *brontē* thunder + *sauros* lizard] : any of a genus of large 4-footed sauropod dinosaurs of the Jurassic : APATOSAURUS

Bronx cheer \ˈbräŋks-\ *n* : RASPBERRY 2

[1]**bronze** \ˈbränz\ *vb* **bronzed**; **bronz·ing** : to give the appearance of bronze to

[2]**bronze** *n* **1** : an alloy of copper and tin and sometimes other elements; *also* : something made of bronze **2** : a yellowish brown color — **bronzy** \ˈbrän-zē\ *adj*

brooch \ˈbrōch, ˈbrüch\ *n* : an ornamental clasp or pin

[1]**brood** \ˈbrüd\ *n* : a family of young animals or children and esp. of birds

[2]**brood** *adj* : kept for breeding ⟨a ~ mare⟩

[3]**brood** *vb* **1** : to sit on eggs to hatch them; *also* : to shelter (hatched young) with the wings **2** : to think anxiously or gloomily about something — **brood·ing·ly** *adv*

brood·er \ˈbrü-dər\ *n* **1** : one that broods **2** : a heated structure for raising young birds

[1]**brook** \ˈbru̇k\ *n* : a small natural stream

[2]**brook** *vb* : TOLERATE, BEAR ⟨would ~ no nonsense⟩

brook·let \ˈbru̇-klət\ *n* : a small brook

brook trout *n* : a common speckled cold-water char of No. America

broom \ˈbrüm, ˈbru̇m\ *n* **1** : any of several shrubs of the legume family with long slender branches and usu. yellow flowers **2** : an implement with a long handle (**broom·stick** \-ˌstik\) used for sweeping

broth \ˈbrȯth\ *n, pl* **broths** \ˈbrȯths, ˈbrȯt͟hz\ **1** : liquid in which meat or sometimes vegetable food has been cooked **2** : a fluid culture medium

broth·el \ˈbrä-thəl, ˈbrȯ-\ *n* : a house of prostitution

broth·er \ˈbrə-t͟hər\ *n, pl* **brothers** *also* **breth·ren** \ˈbret͟h-rən, ˈbre-t͟hə-; ˈbre-t͟hərn\ **1** : a male having one or both parents in common with another individual **2** : a man who is a religious but not a priest **3** : KINSMAN; *also* : SOUL BROTHER — **broth·er·li·ness** \-lē-nəs\ *n* — **broth·er·ly** *adj*

broth·er·hood \ˈbrə-t͟hər-ˌhu̇d\ *n* **1** : the state of being brothers or a brother **2** : ASSOCIATION, FRATERNITY **3** : the whole body of persons in a business or profession ⟨the medical ~⟩

broth·er–in–law \ˈbrə-t͟hə-rən-ˌlȯ, ˈbrə-t͟hərn-ˌlȯ\ *n, pl* **brothers–in–law** \ˈbrə-t͟hər-zən-\ : the brother of one's spouse; *also* : the husband of one's sibling or of one's spouse's sibling

brougham \ˈbrü(-ə)m, ˈbrō(-ə)m\ *n* : a light closed horse-drawn carriage with the driver outside in front

brought *past and past part of* BRING

brou·ha·ha \ˈbrü-ˌhä-ˌhä\ *n* : HUBBUB, UPROAR

brow \ˈbrau̇\ *n* **1** : the eyebrow or the

ridge on which it grows; *also* : FOREHEAD **2** : the projecting upper part of a steep place

brow·beat \ˈbrau̇-ˌbēt\ *vb* **-beat**; **-beat·en** \-ˈbē-tᵊn\ *or* **-beat**; **-beat·ing** : to intimidate by sternness or arrogance

[1]**brown** \ˈbrau̇n\ *adj* **1** : of the color brown; *also* : having dark or tanned skin **2** : of or relating to any of various population groups considered as having medium pigmentation of the skin

[2]**brown** *n* : a color like that of coffee or chocolate that is a blend of red and yellow darkened by black — **brown·ish** *adj*

[3]**brown** *vb* : to make or become brown

brown bag·ging \-ˈba-giŋ\ *n* : the practice of carrying one's lunch usu. in a brown bag — **brown bag·ger** *n*

brown bear *n* : any of various large typically brown-furred bears including the grizzly bear

brown·ie \ˈbrau̇-nē\ *n* **1** : a legendary cheerful elf who performs good deeds at night **2** *cap* : a member of a program of the Girl Scouts for girls in the first through third grades **3** : a small square or rectangle of rich chocolate cake

brown·nose \ˈbrau̇n-ˌnōz\ *vb, disparaging* : to ingratiate oneself with — **brown-nose** *n* — **brownnoser** *n*

brown·out \ˈbrau̇-ˌnau̇t\ *n* : a period of reduced voltage of electricity caused esp. by high demand and resulting in reduced illumination

brown rice *n* : hulled but unpolished rice that retains most of the bran layers

brown·stone \ˈbrau̇n-ˌstōn\ *n* : a dwelling faced with reddish-brown sandstone

[1]**browse** \ˈbrau̇z\ *vb* **browsed**; **brows·ing** **1** : to feed on browse; *also* : GRAZE **2** : to read or look over something in a casual way **3** : to access (a network) with a browser

[2]**browse** *n* : tender shoots, twigs, and leaves fit for food for cattle

brows·er \ˈbrau̇-zər\ *n* : a computer program for accessing sites or information on a network (as the World Wide Web)

bru·in \ˈbrü-ən\ *n* : BEAR

[1]**bruise** \ˈbrüz\ *vb* **bruised**; **bruis·ing** **1** : to inflict a bruise on; *also* : to become bruised **2** : to break down (as leaves or berries) by pounding

[2]**bruise** *n* : a surface injury to flesh : CONTUSION

bruis·er \ˈbrü-zər\ *n* : a big husky man

bruit \ˈbrüt\ *vb* : to make widely known by common report ⟨word of his dismissal was ~*ed* about⟩

brunch \ˈbrənch\ *n* : a meal that combines a late breakfast and an early lunch

bru·net *or* **bru·nette** \brü-ˈnet\ *adj* [F *brunet,* masc., *brunette,* fem., brownish, fr. OF, fr. *brun* brown, of Gmc origin] : having brown or black hair — **brunet** *or* **brunette** *n*

brunt \ˈbrənt\ *n* : the main shock, force, or stress esp. of an attack; *also* : the greater burden

bru·schet·ta \brü-ˈshe-tə, -ˈske-\ *n* : an appetizer of grilled bread with toppings

[1]**brush** \ˈbrəsh\ *n* **1** : BRUSHWOOD **2** : scrub vegetation or land covered with it

[2]**brush** *n* **1** : a device composed of bristles set in a handle and used esp. for cleaning or painting **2** : a bushy tail (as of a fox) **3** : an electrical conductor that makes contact between a stationary and a moving part (as of a motor) **4** : a quick light touch in passing

[3]**brush** *vb* **1** : to treat (as in cleaning or painting) with a brush **2** : to remove with or as if with a brush; *also* : to dismiss in an offhand manner **3** : to touch gently in passing

[4]**brush** *n* : SKIRMISH ⟨a ~ with the law⟩ ♦ ***Synonyms*** ENCOUNTER, RUN-IN

brush fire *n* **1** : a fire involving low-growing plants **2** : a minor conflict or crisis

brush–off \ˈbrəsh-ˌȯf\ *n* : a curt offhand dismissal

brush up *vb* : to renew one's skill

brush·wood \ˈbrəsh-ˌwu̇d\ *n* **1** : small branches of wood esp. when cut **2** : a thicket of shrubs and small trees

brusque \ˈbrəsk\ *adj* [F *brusque,* fr. It *brusco,* fr. ML *bruscus* a plant with stiff twigs used for brooms] : CURT, BLUNT, ABRUPT ⟨a ~ answer⟩ ♦ ***Synonyms*** GRUFF, BLUFF, CRUSTY, SHORT — **brusque·ly** *adv*

brus·sels sprout \ˈbrəs-əlz-\ *n, often cap B* : one of the edible green heads borne on the stalk of a plant closely related to the cabbage; *also, pl* : this plant

bru·tal \ˈbrü-tᵊl\ *adj* **1** : befitting a brute : UNFEELING, CRUEL **2** : HARSH, SEVERE ⟨~ weather⟩ **3** : unpleasantly accurate ⟨a ~ depiction of war⟩ — **bru·tal·i·ty** \brü-ˈta-lə-tē\ *n* — **bru·tal·ly** *adv*

bru·tal·ise *Brit var of* BRUTALIZE

bru·tal·ize \ˈbrü-tᵊl-ˌīz\ *vb* **-ized**; **-iz·ing** **1** : to make brutal **2** : to treat brutally

[1]**brute** \ˈbrüt\ *adj* [ME, fr. MF *brut* rough, fr. L *brutus* brutish, lit., heavy] **1** : of or relating to beasts **2** : BRUTAL **3** : UNREASONING; *also* : purely physical ⟨~ strength⟩

[2]**brute** *n* **1** : BEAST 1 **2** : a brutal person

brut·ish \ˈbrü-tish\ *adj* **1** : BRUTE 1 **2** : strongly sensual; *also* : showing little intelligence

BS *abbr* bachelor of science

BSA *abbr* Boy Scouts of America

bskt *abbr* basket

Bt *abbr* baronet

btry *abbr* battery

Btu *abbr* British thermal unit

bu *abbr* bushel

[1]**bub·ble** \ˈbə-bəl\ *n* **1** : a globule of gas in a liquid **2** : a thin film of liquid filled with gas **3** : something lacking firmness or solidity **4** : a state of booming economic activity that often ends in a sudden collapse **5 a** : an enclosed or isolated sphere of experience or activity **b** : a small group of people who regularly interact with each other but with few or no others — **bub·bly** *adj*

[2]**bubble** *vb* **bub·bled**; **bub·bling** : to form, rise in, or give off bubbles

bub·kes \ˈbəp-kəs, ˈbu̇p-\ *n pl* [Yiddish] : the least amount ⟨didn't win ~⟩

bu·bo \ˈbü-bō, ˈbyü-\ *n, pl* **buboes** : an inflammatory swelling of a lymph gland

bu·bon·ic plague \bü-ˈbä-nik-, byü-\ *n* : plague caused by a bacterium transmitted to human beings by flea bites and marked esp. by chills and fever and by buboes usu. in the groin

buc·ca·neer \ˌbə-kə-ˈnir\ *n* : PIRATE

1buck \ˈbək\ *n, pl* **bucks** **1** *or pl* **buck** : a male animal (as a deer or antelope) **2** : DANDY **3** : DOLLAR

2buck *vb* **1** : to spring with an arching leap ⟨a ~*ing* horse⟩ **2** : to charge against something; *also* : to strive for advancement sometimes without regard to ethical behavior

buck·board \-ˌbȯrd\ *n* : a 4-wheeled horse-drawn wagon with a floor of long springy boards

buck·et \ˈbə-kət\ *n* **1** : PAIL **2** : an object resembling a bucket in collecting, scooping, or carrying something ⟨a tractor's ~⟩ — **buck·et·ful** *n*

bucket list *n* [from *kick the bucket* (to die)] : a list of things one has not done before but wants to do before dying

bucket seat *n* : a low separate seat for one person (as in an automobile)

buck·eye \ˈbə-ˌkī\ *n* : any of various trees or shrubs related to the horse chestnut; *also* : the large nutlike seed of such a shrub or tree

buck fever *n* : nervous excitement of an inexperienced hunter at the sight of game

1buck·le \ˈbə-kəl\ *n* : a clasp (as on a belt) for two loose ends

2buckle *vb* **buck·led**; **buck·ling** **1** : to fasten with a buckle **2** : to apply oneself with vigor **3** : to crumple up : BEND, COLLAPSE

3buckle *n* : BEND, FOLD, KINK

buck·ler \ˈbə-klər\ *n* : SHIELD

buck·ram \ˈbə-krəm\ *n* : a coarse stiff cloth used esp. for binding books

buck·saw \ˈbək-ˌsȯ\ *n* : a saw set in a usu. H-shaped frame for sawing wood

buck·shot \ˈbək-ˌshät\ *n* : lead shot that is from .24 to .33 inch (about 6.1 to 8.4 millimeters) in diameter

buck·skin \-ˌskin\ *n* **1** : the skin of a buck **2** : a soft usu. suede-finished leather — **buckskin** *adj*

buck·tooth \-ˈtüth\ *n* : a large protruding front tooth — **buck–toothed** \-ˈtütht\ *adj*

buck·wheat \-ˌhwēt\ *n* : either of two plants grown for their triangular seeds which are used as a cereal grain; *also* : these seeds

bu·col·ic \byü-ˈkä-lik\ *adj* [L *bucolicus,* fr. Gk *boukolikos,* fr. *boukolos* cowherd] : PASTORAL, RURAL ⟨a ~ countryside⟩

1bud \ˈbəd\ *n* **1** : an undeveloped plant shoot (as of a leaf or a flower); *also* : a partly opened flower **2** : an asexual reproductive structure that detaches from the parent and forms a new individual **3** : something not yet fully developed ⟨nipped in the ~⟩

2bud *vb* **bud·ded**; **bud·ding** **1** : to form or put forth buds; *also* : to reproduce by asexual buds **2** : to be or develop like a bud **3** : to reproduce a desired variety (as of peach) by inserting a bud in a plant of a different variety

Bud·dhism \ˈbü-ˌdi-zəm, ˈbu̇-\ *n* : a religion of eastern and central Asia growing out of the teachings of Gautama Buddha — **Bud·dhist** \ˈbü-dist, ˈbu̇-\ *n or adj*

bud·dy \ˈbə-dē\ *n, pl* **buddies** **1** : COMPANION; *also* : FRIEND **2** : FELLOW

budge \ˈbəj\ *vb* **budged**; **budg·ing** : MOVE, SHIFT; *also* : YIELD

bud·ger·i·gar \ˈbə-jə-rē-ˌgär\ *n* : a small brightly colored Australian parrot often kept as a pet

1bud·get \ˈbə-jət\ *n* [ME *bowgette,* fr. MF *bougette,* dim. of *bouge* leather bag, fr. L *bulga*] **1** : STOCK, SUPPLY **2** : a financial report containing estimates of income and expenses; *also* : a plan for coordinating income and expenses **3** : the amount of money available for a particular use — **bud·get·ary** \ˈbə-jə-ˌter-ē\ *adj*

2budget *vb* **1** : to allow for in a budget **2** : to draw up a budget

3budget *adj* : INEXPENSIVE

bud·gie \ˈbə-jē\ *n* : BUDGERIGAR

1buff \ˈbəf\ *n* **1** : a yellow to orange yellow color **2** : FAN, ENTHUSIAST

2buff *adj* : of the color buff

3buff *vb* : POLISH, SHINE

buf·fa·lo \ˈbə-fə-ˌlō\ *n, pl* **-lo** *or* **-loes** *also* **-los** **1** : WATER BUFFALO **2** : BISON

buffalo soldier *n* : an African American soldier serving in the western U.S. after the Civil War

1buf·fer \ˈbə-fər\ *n* : something or someone that protects or shields (as from physical damage or a financial blow)

2buffer *n* : one that buffs

1buf·fet \ˈbə-fət\ *n* : BLOW, SLAP

2buffet *vb* **1** : to strike with the hand; *also* : to pound repeatedly **2** : to struggle against or on ♦ ***Synonyms*** BEAT, BATTER, DRUB, PUMMEL, THRASH

3buf·fet \(ˌ)bə-ˈfā, bü-\ *n* **1** : SIDEBOARD **2** : a counter for refreshments; *also* : a meal at which people serve themselves informally

buff leather *n* : a strong supple oil-tanned leather

buf·foon \(ˌ)bə-ˈfün\ *n* [MF *bouffon,* fr. It *buffone*] : CLOWN 2 — **buf·foon·ery** \-ˈfü-nə-rē\ *n* — **buf·foon·ish** \-ˈfü-nish\ *adj*

1bug \ˈbəg\ *n* **1** : an insect or other creeping or crawling invertebrate animal; *esp* : an insect pest (as the cockroach or bedbug) **2** : any of an order of insects with sucking mouthparts and incomplete metamorphosis that includes many plant pests **3** : an unexpected flaw or imperfection ⟨a ~ in a computer program⟩ **4** : a disease-producing germ; *also* : a disease caused by it **5** : a concealed listening device — **bug·gy** \ˈbə-gē\ *adj*

2bug *vb* **bugged**; **bug·ging** **1** : BOTHER, ANNOY **2** : to plant a concealed microphone in

[3]**bug** *vb* **bugged**; **bug·ging** *of the eyes* : PROTRUDE, BULGE

bug·a·boo \ˈbə-gə-ˌbü\ *n, pl* **-boos** : BOGEY 1

bug·bear \ˈbəg-ˌber\ *n* : BOGEY 1; *also* : a source of dread

bug·gy \ˈbə-gē\ *n, pl* **buggies** : a light horse-drawn carriage; *also* : a carriage for a baby

bu·gle \ˈbyü-gəl\ *n* [ME, wild ox, instrument made from the horn of an ox, bugle, fr. AF, fr. L *buculus,* dim. of *bos* head of cattle] : a valveless brass instrument resembling a trumpet and used esp. for military calls — **bu·gler** *n*

bug out *vb* **1** : to flee in panic **2** : to depart in a hurry

[1]**build** \ˈbild\ *vb* **built** \ˈbilt\; **build·ing** **1** : to form or have formed by ordering and uniting materials ⟨~ a house⟩; *also* : to bring into being or develop **2** : to produce or create gradually ⟨~ an argument on facts⟩ **3** : INCREASE, ENLARGE; *also* : ENHANCE **4** : to engage in building — **build·er** *n*

[2]**build** *n* : form or mode of structure; *esp* : PHYSIQUE

build·ing \ˈbil-diŋ\ *n* **1** : a usu. roofed and walled structure (as a house) for permanent use **2** : the art or business of constructing buildings

build·up \ˈbild-ˌəp\ *n* : the act or process of building up; *also* : something produced by this

built–in \ˈbilt-ˈin\ *adj* **1** : forming an integral part of a structure **2** : INHERENT

bulb \ˈbəlb\ *n* **1** : an underground resting stage of a plant (as a lily or an onion) consisting of a short stem base bearing one or more buds enclosed in overlapping leaves; *also* : a fleshy plant structure (as a tuber) resembling a bulb **2** : a plant having or growing from a bulb **3** : a rounded more or less bulb-shaped object or part (as for an electric lamp) — **bul·bous** \ˈbəl-bəs\ *adj*

[1]**bulge** \ˈbəlj\ *vb* **bulged**; **bulg·ing** : to become or cause to become protuberant

[2]**bulge** *n* : a swelling projecting part

bu·li·mia \bü-ˈlē-mē-ə, byü-, -ˈli-\ *n* **1** : an abnormal and constant craving for food **2** : a serious eating disorder chiefly of females that is characterized by compulsive overeating usu. followed by self-induced vomiting or laxative or diuretic abuse — **bu·lim·ic** \-ˈlē-mik, -ˈli-\ *adj or n*

[1]**bulk** \ˈbəlk\ *n* **1** : MAGNITUDE, VOLUME **2** : material that forms a mass in the intestine; *esp* : FIBER 2 **3** : a large mass **4** : the major portion

[2]**bulk** *vb* **1** : to cause to swell or bulge **2** : to appear as a factor : LOOM

bulk·head \ˈbəlk-ˌhed\ *n* **1** : a partition separating compartments **2** : a structure built to cover a shaft or a cellar stairway

bulky \ˈbəl-kē\ *adj* **bulk·i·er**; **-est** : having bulk; *esp* : being large and unwieldy

[1]**bull** \ˈbu̇l\ *n* **1** : a male bovine animal; *also* : a usu. adult male of various large animals (as the moose, elephant, or whale) **2** : one who buys securities or commodities in expectation of a price increase — **bull·ish** *adj*

[2]**bull** *adj* **1** : of, relating to, or suggestive of a bull : MALE **2** : large of its kind ⟨a ~ lathe⟩

[3]**bull** *n* [ME *bulle,* fr. ML *bulla,* fr. L, bubble, amulet] **1** : a papal letter **2** : DECREE

[4]**bull** *n, slang* : NONSENSE

[5]**bull** *abbr* bulletin

[1]**bull·dog** \ˈbu̇l-ˌdȯg\ *n* : any of a breed of compact muscular short-haired dogs of English origin

[2]**bulldog** *vb* : to throw (a steer) by seizing the horns and twisting the neck

bull·doze \-ˌdōz\ *vb* **1** : to move, clear, or level with a tractor-driven machine (**bull·doz·er**) having a broad blade for pushing **2** : to force as if by using a bulldozer

bul·let \ˈbu̇-lət\ *n* [MF *boulette* small ball & *boulet* missile, dims. of *boule* ball, fr. L *bulla* bubble] : a missile to be shot from a firearm

bul·le·tin \ˈbu̇-lə-tᵊn\ *n* **1** : a brief public report intended for immediate release on a matter of public interest **2** : a periodical publication (as of a college)

bulletin board *n* **1** : a board for posting notices **2** : a public forum on a computer network in which users write or read messages or download files

bul·let·proof \ˈbu̇-lət-ˌprüf\ *adj* **1** : impenetrable to bullets **2** : not subject to correction, alteration, or modification **3** : INVINCIBLE

bull·fight \ˈbu̇l-ˌfīt\ *n* : an event in which people ceremonially fight with and usu. kill bulls in an arena — **bull·fight·er** *n*

bull·frog \-ˌfrȯg, -ˌfräg\ *n* : a large deep-voiced frog

bull·head \-ˌhed\ *n* : any of several common large-headed freshwater catfishes of the U.S.

bull·head·ed \-ˈhe-dəd\ *adj* : stupidly stubborn : HEADSTRONG

bul·lion \ˈbu̇l-yən\ *n* : gold or silver esp. in bars or ingots

bull market *n* : a market in which securities or commodities are persistently rising in value

bull·ock \ˈbu̇-lək\ *n* : a young bull; *also* : STEER

bull pen *n* : a place on a baseball field where pitchers warm up; *also* : the relief pitchers of a baseball team

bull session *n* : an informal discussion

bull's–eye \ˈbu̇lz-ˌī\ *n, pl* **bull's–eyes** : the center of a target; *also* : a shot that hits the bull's-eye

[1]**bul·ly** \ˈbu̇-lē\ *n, pl* **bul·lies** : a person habitually cruel to others who are weaker

[2]**bully** *adj* : EXCELLENT, FIRST-RATE — often used interjectionally ⟨~ for you⟩

[3]**bully** *vb* **bul·lied**; **bul·ly·ing** : to behave as a bully toward : DOMINEER ◆ ***Synonyms*** BROWBEAT, INTIMIDATE, HECTOR — **bul·ly·ing** *n*

bul·rush \ˈbu̇l-ˌrəsh\ *n* : any of several large rushes or sedges of wetlands

bul·wark \ˈbu̇l-(ˌ)wərk, -ˌwȯrk; ˈbəl-(ˌ)wərk\ *n* **1** : a wall-like defensive structure **2** : a strong support or protection

[1]**bum** \ˈbəm\ *adj* **1** : of poor quality ⟨~ advice⟩ **2** : disabled by damage or injury ⟨a ~ knee⟩

[2]**bum** *vb* **bummed**; **bum·ming** **1** : to spend time unemployed and wandering; *also* : LOAF **2** : to obtain by begging

[3]**bum** *n* **1** : LOAFER **2** : one whose time is devoted to a recreational activity ⟨a ski ~⟩ **3** : TRAMP 1

bum·ble \ˈbəm-bəl\ *vb* **bum·bled**; **bum·bling** **1** : to speak in a stuttering and faltering manner **2** : to proceed unsteadily **3** : BUNGLE

bum·ble·bee \ˈbəm-bəl-ˌbē\ *n* : any of numerous large hairy social bees

bum·mer \ˈbə-mər\ *n* **1** : an unpleasant experience **2** : FAILURE

[1]**bump** \ˈbəmp\ *n* **1** : a local bulge; *esp* : a swelling of tissue **2** : a sudden forceful blow or impact — **bumpy** *adj*

[2]**bump** *vb* **1** : to strike or knock forcibly; *also* : to move by or as if by bumping **2** : to collide with

[1]**bum·per** \ˈbəm-pər\ *n* **1** : a cup or glass filled to the brim **2** : something unusually large — **bumper** *adj*

[2]**bump·er** \ˈbəm-pər\ *n* : a device for absorbing shock or preventing damage; *esp* : a usu. metal bar at either end of an automobile

bump·kin \ˈbəmp-kən\ *n* : an awkward and unsophisticated country person

bump·tious \ˈbəmp-shəs\ *adj* : obtusely and often noisily self-assertive

bun \ˈbən\ *n* : a sweet or plain round roll

[1]**bunch** \ˈbənch\ *n* **1** : SWELLING **2** : CLUSTER, GROUP — **bunchy** *adj*

[2]**bunch** *vb* : to form into a group or bunch

bun·co *or* **bun·ko** \ˈbəŋ-kō\ *n, pl* **buncos** *or* **bunkos** : a swindling scheme — **bunco** *vb*

[1]**bun·dle** \ˈbən-dᵊl\ *n* **1** : several items bunched and fastened together; *also* : something wrapped for carrying **2** : a considerable amount : LOT **3** : a small band of mostly parallel nerve or muscle fibers **4** : a package offering related products or services at a single price

[2]**bundle** *vb* **bun·dled**; **bun·dling** : to gather or tie in a bundle

bundling *n* : a former custom of a courting couple's occupying the same bed without undressing

bung \ˈbəŋ\ *n* : the stopper in the bunghole of a cask

bun·ga·low \ˈbəŋ-gə-ˌlō\ *n* [Hindi & Urdu *banglā,* lit., (house) in the Bengal style] : a one-storied house with a low-pitched roof

bun·gee cord \ˈbən-jē-\ *n* : a long elastic cord used esp. as a fastening or shock-absorbing device

bungee jump *vb* : to jump from a height while attached to a bungee cord — **bungee jumper** *n*

bung·hole \ˈbəŋ-ˌhōl\ *n* : a hole for emptying or filling a cask

bun·gle \ˈbəŋ-gəl\ *vb* **bun·gled**; **bun·gling** : to do badly : BOTCH — **bungle** *n* — **bun·gler** *n*

bun·ion \ˈbən-yən\ *n* : an inflamed swelling of the first joint of the big toe

[1]**bunk** \ˈbəŋk\ *n* : BED; *esp* : a built-in bed that is often one of a tier

[2]**bunk** *n* : BUNKUM, NONSENSE

bunk bed *n* : one of two single beds usu. placed one above the other

bun·ker \ˈbəŋ-kər\ *n* **1** : a bin or compartment for storage (as for coal on a ship) **2** : a protective embankment or dugout **3** : a sand trap or embankment constituting a hazard on a golf course

bun·kum *or* **bun·combe** \ˈbəŋ-kəm\ *n* [*Buncombe* County, N.C.; fr. a remark made by its congressman, who defended an irrelevant speech by claiming that he was speaking to Buncombe] : insincere or foolish talk

bun·ny \ˈbə-nē\ *n, pl* **-nies** : RABBIT

bunny slope *n* : a gentle incline used by novice skiers

Bun·sen burner \ˈbən-sən-\ *n* : a gas burner usu. consisting of a straight tube with air holes at the bottom

[1]**bunt** \ˈbənt\ *vb* **1** : [1]BUTT **2** : to push or tap a baseball lightly without swinging the bat

[2]**bunt** *n* : an act or instance of bunting; *also* : a bunted ball

[1]**bun·ting** \ˈbən-tiŋ\ *n* : any of numerous small stout-billed finches

[2]**bunting** *n* : a thin fabric used esp. for flags; *also* : FLAGS

[1]**buoy** \ˈbü-ē, ˈbȯi\ *n* **1** : a floating object anchored in water to mark something (as a channel) **2** : a float consisting of a ring of buoyant material to support a person who has fallen into the water

[2]**buoy** *vb* **1** : to mark by a buoy **2** : to keep afloat **3** : to raise the spirits of

buoy·an·cy \ˈbȯi-ən-sē, ˈbü-yən-\ *n* **1** : the tendency of a body to float or rise when submerged in a fluid **2** : the power of a fluid to exert an upward force on a body placed in it **3** : resilience of spirit — **buoy·ant** \-ənt, -yənt\ *adj*

[1]**bur** *var of* BURR

[2]**bur** *abbr* bureau

burbs \ˈbərbz\ *n pl* : SUBURBS

[1]**bur·den** \ˈbər-dᵊn\ *n* **1** : LOAD; *also* : CARE, RESPONSIBILITY **2** : something oppressive : ENCUMBRANCE ⟨the tax ~⟩ **3** : CARGO; *also* : capacity for cargo

[2]**burden** *vb* : LOAD, OPPRESS ⟨~*ed* with guilt⟩ — **bur·den·some** \-səm\ *adj*

[3]**burden** *n* **1** : REFRAIN, CHORUS **2** : a main theme or idea : GIST

bur·dock \ˈbər-ˌdäk\ *n* : any of a genus of coarse composite herbs with globe-shaped flower heads surrounded by prickly bracts

bu·reau \ˈbyu̇r-ō\ *n, pl* **bureaus** *also* **bu·reaux** \-ōz\ [F, desk, cloth covering for desks, fr. OF *burel* woolen cloth, ultim. fr. L *burra* shaggy cloth] **1** : a chest of drawers **2** : an administrative unit (as of a government department) **3** : a branch of a publication or wire service in an important news center

bu·reau·cra·cy \byu̇-ˈrä-krə-sē\ *n, pl* **-cies** **1** : a body of appointive government officials **2** : government marked by specialization of functions under fixed rules and a hierarchy of authority; *also* : an unwieldy administrative system burdened with excessive complexity and lack of flexibility — **bu·reau·crat** \ˈbyu̇r-ə-ˌkrat\ *n* — **bu·reau·crat·ic** \ˌbyu̇r-ə-ˈkra-tik\ *adj*

bur·geon \ˈbər-jən\ *vb* : to put forth fresh growth (as from buds) : grow vigorously : FLOURISH

burgh \ˈbər-ō\ *n* : a Scottish town

bur·gher \ˈbər-gər\ *n* **1** : TOWNSMAN **2** : a prosperous solid citizen

bur·glary \ˈbər-glə-rē\ *n, pl* **-glar·ies** : forcible entry into a building esp. at night with the intent to commit a crime (as theft) — **bur·glar** \-glər\ *n* — **bur·glar·ize** \ˈbər-glə-ˌrīz\ *vb*

bur·gle \ˈbər-gəl\ *vb* **bur·gled**; **bur·gling** : to commit burglary on

bur·go·mas·ter \ˈbər-gə-ˌmas-tər\ *n* : the chief magistrate of a town in some European countries

bur·gun·dy \ˈbər-gən-dē\ *n, pl* **-dies** *often cap* **1** : a red or white table wine from the Burgundy region of France **2** : a blended red wine **3** : a reddish-purple color

buri·al \ˈber-ē-əl\ *n* : the act or process of burying

bur·ka *or* **bur·qa** \ˈbu̇r-kə\ *n* : a loose garment that covers the face and body and is worn in public by certain Muslim women

burl \ˈbərl\ *n* : a hard woody often flattened hemispherical outgrowth on a tree

bur·lap \ˈbər-ˌlap\ *n* : a coarse fabric usu. of jute or hemp used esp. for bags

[1]**bur·lesque** \(ˌ)bər-ˈlesk\ *n* [*burlesque,* adj., comic, droll, fr. F, fr. It *burlesco,* fr. *burla* joke, fr. Sp] **1** : a witty or derisive literary or dramatic imitative work **2** : broadly humorous theatrical entertainment consisting of several items (as songs, skits, or dances)

[2]**burlesque** *vb* **bur·lesqued**; **bur·lesqu·ing** : to make ludicrous by burlesque ♦ ***Synonyms*** CARICATURE, PARODY, TRAVESTY

bur·ly \ˈbər-lē\ *adj* **bur·li·er**; **-est** : strongly and heavily built : HUSKY ♦ ***Synonyms*** MUSCULAR, BRAWNY, BEEFY, HEFTY

[1]**burn** \ˈbərn\ *vb* **burned** \ˈbərnd, ˈbərnt\ *or* **burnt** \ˈbərnt\; **burn·ing** **1** : to be on fire **2** : to feel or look as if on fire **3** : to alter or become altered by or as if by the action of fire or heat **4** : to use as fuel ⟨∼ coal⟩; *also* : to destroy by fire ⟨∼ trash⟩ **5** : to cause or make by fire ⟨∼ a hole⟩; *also* : to affect as if by heat **6** : to record digital data or music on (an optical disk) using a laser ⟨∼ a CD⟩

[2]**burn** *n* : an injury or effect produced by or as if by burning

burn·er \ˈbər-nər\ *n* : the part of a fuel-burning or heat-producing device where the flame or heat is produced

bur·nish \ˈbər-nish\ *vb* : to make shiny esp. by rubbing : POLISH — **bur·nish·er** *n* — **bur·nish·ing** *adj or n*

bur·noose *or* **bur·nous** \(ˌ)bər-ˈnüs\ *n* : a hooded cloak worn esp. by Arabs

burn·out \ˈbərn-ˌau̇t\ *n* **1** : the cessation of operation of a jet or rocket engine **2** : exhaustion of one's physical or emotional strength; *also* : a person suffering from burnout

burp \ˈbərp\ *n* : an act of belching — **burp** *vb*

burp gun *n* : a small submachine gun

burr \ˈbər\ *n* **1** *usu* **bur** : a rough or prickly envelope of a fruit; *also* : a plant that bears burs **2** : roughness left in cutting or shaping metal **3** : a trilled \r\ as used by some speakers in northern England and Scotland **4** : WHIR — **bur·ry** *adj*

bur·ri·to \bə-ˈrē-tō\ *n* [AmerSp, fr. Sp, little donkey, dim. of *burro*] : a flour tortilla rolled around a filling and baked

bur·ro \ˈbər-ō, ˈbu̇r-\ *n, pl* **burros** [Sp] : a usu. small donkey

[1]**bur·row** \ˈbər-ō\ *n* : a hole in the ground made by an animal (as a rabbit)

[2]**burrow** *vb* **1** : to form by tunneling; *also* : to make a burrow **2** : to progress by or as if by digging — **bur·row·er** *n*

bur·sar \ˈbər-sər\ *n* : a treasurer esp. of a college

bur·si·tis \(ˌ)bər-ˈsī-təs\ *n* : inflammation of the serous sac (**bur·sa** \ˈbər-sə\) of a joint (as the elbow or shoulder)

[1]**burst** \ˈbərst\ *vb* **burst** *or* **burst·ed**; **burst·ing** **1** : to fly apart or into pieces **2** : to show one's feelings suddenly; *also* : PLUNGE ⟨∼ into song⟩ **3** : to enter or emerge suddenly : SPRING **4** : to be filled to the breaking point

[2]**burst** *n* **1** : a sudden outbreak : SPURT **2** : EXPLOSION **3** : result of bursting

bury \ˈber-ē\ *vb* **bur·ied**; **bury·ing** **1** : to deposit in the earth; *also* : to inter with funeral ceremonies **2** : CONCEAL, HIDE **3** : SUBMERGE, ENGROSS — usu. used with *in* ⟨*buried* himself in work⟩

[1]**bus** \ˈbəs\ *n, pl* **bus·es** *also* **bus·ses** [short for *omnibus,* fr. F, fr. L, for all, dative pl. of *omnis* all] : a large motor vehicle for carrying passengers

[2]**bus** *vb* **bused** *or* **bussed**; **bus·ing** *or* **bus·sing** **1** : to travel or transport by bus **2** : to work as a busboy

[3]**bus** *abbr* business

bus·boy \ˈbəs-ˌbȯi\ *n* : a waiter's helper

bus·by \ˈbəz-bē\ *n, pl* **busbies** : a military full-dress fur hat

bush \ˈbu̇sh\ *n* **1** : SHRUB **2** : rough uncleared country **3** : a thick tuft ⟨a ∼ of hair⟩ — **bushy** *adj*

bushed \ˈbu̇sht\ *adj* : TIRED, EXHAUSTED

bush·el \ˈbu̇-shəl\ *n* — see WEIGHT table

bush·ing \ˈbu̇-shiŋ\ *n* : a usu. removable cylindrical lining for an opening of a mechanical part to limit the size of the opening, resist wear, or serve as a guide

bush·mas·ter \ˈbu̇sh-ˌmas-tər\ *n* : a large venomous pit viper of Central and So. America

bush·whack \-ˌhwak\ *vb* **1** : AMBUSH **2** : to clear a path through esp. by chopping down bushes and branches — **bush·whack·er** *n*

busi·ness \ˈbiz-nəs, -nəz\ *n* **1** : OCCUPATION; *also* : TASK, MISSION **2** : a commercial or industrial enterprise; *also* : TRADE ⟨~ is good⟩ **3** : AFFAIR, MATTER **4** : personal concern

busi·ness·man \-ˌman\ *n* : a man engaged in business esp. as an executive

busi·ness·per·son \-ˌpər-sᵊn\ *n* : a businessman or businesswoman

busi·ness·wom·an \-ˌwu̇-mən\ *n* : a woman engaged in business esp. as an executive

bus·kin \ˈbəs-kən\ *n* **1** : a laced boot reaching halfway to the knee **2** : tragic drama

buss \ˈbəs\ *n* : KISS — **buss** *vb*

[1]**bust** \ˈbəst\ *n* [F *buste,* fr. It *busto,* fr. L *bustum* tomb] **1** : sculpture representing the upper part of the human figure **2** : the part of the human torso between the neck and the waist; *esp* : the breasts of a woman

[2]**bust** *vb* **bust·ed** *also* **bust**; **bust·ing** **1** : BREAK, SMASH; *also* : BURST **2** : to ruin financially **3** : TAME **4** : DEMOTE **5** *slang* : ARREST; *also* : RAID

[3]**bust** *n* **1** : a drinking session **2** : a complete failure : FLOP **3** : a business depression **4** : PUNCH, SOCK **5** *slang* : a police raid; *also* : ARREST

[1]**bus·tle** \ˈbə-səl\ *vb* **bus·tled**; **bus·tling** : to move or work in a brisk busy manner

[2]**bustle** *n* : briskly energetic activity

[3]**bustle** *n* : a pad or frame worn to support the fullness at the back of a woman's skirt

[1]**busy** \ˈbi-zē\ *adj* **busi·er**; **-est** **1** : engaged in action : not idle **2** : being in use ⟨~ telephones⟩ **3** : full of activity ⟨~ streets⟩ **4** : full of distracting detail ⟨a ~ design⟩ — **busi·ly** \ˈbi-zə-lē\ *adv*

[2]**busy** *vb* **bus·ied**; **busy·ing** : to make or keep busy : OCCUPY

busy·body \ˈbi-zē-ˌbä-dē\ *n* : MEDDLER

busy·work \-ˌwərk\ *n* : work that appears productive but only keeps one occupied

[1]**but** \ˈbət\ *conj* **1** : except for the fact ⟨would have protested ~ that he was afraid⟩ **2** : THAT ⟨there's no doubt ~ he won⟩ **3** : without the certainty that ⟨never rains ~ it pours⟩ **4** : on the contrary ⟨not one, ~ two job offers⟩ **5** : YET ⟨poor ~ proud⟩ **6** : with the exception of ⟨none ~ the strongest attempt it⟩

[2]**but** *prep* : other than : EXCEPT ⟨this letter is nothing ~ an insult⟩; *also* : with the exception of ⟨no one here ~ me⟩

bu·tane \ˈbyü-ˌtān\ *n* : either of two gaseous hydrocarbons used as a fuel

butch \ˈbu̇ch\ *adj* : notably masculine in appearance or manner

[1]**butch·er** \ˈbu̇-chər\ *n* [ME *bocher,* fr. AF, fr. *buc* he-goat] **1** : one who slaughters animals or dresses their flesh; *also* : a dealer in meat **2** : one that kills brutally or needlessly **3** : one that botches — **butch·ery** \-chə-rē\ *n*

[2]**butcher** *vb* **1** : to slaughter and dress for meat ⟨~ hogs⟩ **2** : to kill barbarously **3** : BOTCH ⟨the band ~*ed* my favorite song⟩

but·ler \ˈbət-lər\ *n* [ME *buteler,* fr. AF *butiller,* † fr. OF *botele* bottle] : the chief male servant of a household

[1]**butt** \ˈbət\ *vb* : to strike with the head or horns

[2]**butt** *n* : a blow or thrust with the head or horns

[3]**butt** *n* : a large cask

[4]**butt** *n* **1** : TARGET **2** : an object of abuse or ridicule ⟨the ~ of everyone's jokes⟩

[5]**butt** *n* **1** : BUTTOCKS **2** : a large, thicker, or bottom end of something

[6]**butt** *vb* **1** : ABUT — used with *on* or *against* **2** : to place or join edge to edge without overlapping

butte \ˈbyüt\ *n* : an isolated steep hill

[1]**but·ter** \ˈbə-tər\ *n* [ME, fr. OE *butere,* fr. L *butyrum* butter, fr. Gk *boutyron,* fr. *bous* cow + *tyros* cheese] **1** : a solid edible emulsion of fat obtained from cream by churning **2** : a substance resembling butter — **but·tery** *adj*

[2]**butter** *vb* : to spread with or as if with butter ⟨~*ed* toast⟩

but·ter–and–eggs \ˌbə-tər-ᵊn-ˈegz\ *n sing or pl* : a common perennial herb related to the snapdragon that has showy yellow and orange flowers

butter bean *n* **1** : LIMA BEAN **2** : WAX BEAN **3** : a green shell bean

but·ter·cream \ˈbə-tər-ˌkrēm\ *n* : a sweet butter-based mixture used esp. as a filling or frosting

but·ter·cup \ˈbə-tər-ˌkəp\ *n* : any of a genus of herbs having usu. yellow flowers with five petals and sepals

but·ter·fat \-ˌfat\ *n* : the natural fat of milk and chief constituent of butter

but·ter·fin·gered \-ˌfiŋ-gərd\ *adj* : likely to let things fall or slip through the fingers — **but·ter·fin·gers** \-gərz\ *n sing or pl*

but·ter·fly \-ˌflī\ *n* : any of a group of slender day-flying insects with broad often brightly-colored wings

but·ter·milk \-ˌmilk\ *n* : the liquid remaining after butter is churned

but·ter·nut \-ˌnət\ *n* : the sweet egg-shaped nut of an American tree related to the walnut; *also* : this tree

butternut squash *n* : a smooth buff-colored cylindrical winter squash

but·ter·scotch \-ˌskäch\ *n* : a candy made from brown sugar, corn syrup, and water; *also* : the flavor of such candy

but·tock \ˈbə-tək\ *n* **1** : the back of a hip that forms one of the fleshy parts on which a person sits **2** *pl* : the seat of the body : RUMP

[1]**but·ton** \ˈbə-tᵊn\ *n* **1** : a small knob secured to an article (as of clothing) and used as a fastener by passing it through a buttonhole or loop **2** : something that resembles a button **3** : PUSH BUTTON **4** : a hidden sensitivity that can be manipulated to produce a desired response **5** : a usu. box-shaped computer icon that initiates a software function

[2]**button** *vb* : to close or fasten with or as if with buttons

[1]**but·ton·hole** \ˈbə-tᵊn-ˌhōl\ *n* : a slit or loop for a button to pass through

[2]**buttonhole** *vb* : to detain in conversation by or as if by holding on to the outer garments of

[1]**but·tress** \'bə-trəs\ *n* [ME *butres,* fr. AF (*arche*) *boteraz* thrusting (arch), ultim. fr. *buter* to thrust] **1** : a projecting structure to support a wall **2** : PROP, SUPPORT

[2]**buttress** *vb* : PROP, SUPPORT

bu·tut \bu̇-'tüt\ *n, pl* **bututs** *or* **butut** — see *dalasi* at MONEY table

bux·om \'bək-səm\ *adj* : healthily plump; *esp* : full-bosomed

[1]**buy** \'bī\ *vb* **bought** \'bȯt\; **buy·ing** **1** : to obtain for a price : PURCHASE; *also* : BRIBE **2** : to accept as true — **buy·er** *n*

[2]**buy** *n* **1** : PURCHASE 1, 2 **2** : an exceptional value : BARGAIN

[1]**buzz** \'bəz\ *vb* **1** : to make a buzz **2** : to fly fast and close to

[2]**buzz** *n* **1** : a low humming sound **2** : RUMOR, GOSSIP

buz·zard \'bə-zərd\ *n* : any of various usu. large birds of prey and esp. the turkey vulture

buzz·er \'bə-zər\ *n* : a device that signals with a buzzing sound

buzz saw *n* : CIRCULAR SAW

buzz·word \'bəz-ˌwərd\ *n* : a voguish word or phrase often from technical jargon

BVM *abbr* Blessed Virgin Mary

BWI *abbr* British West Indies

bx *abbr* box

BX *abbr* base exchange

[1]**by** \'bī, bə\ *prep* **1** : NEAR ⟨stood ~ the window⟩ **2** : through or through the medium of : VIA ⟨left ~ the door⟩ **3** : PAST ⟨drove ~ the house⟩ **4** : DURING, AT ⟨studied ~ night⟩ **5** : no later than ⟨get here ~ 3 p.m.⟩ **6** : through the means or direct agency of ⟨~ force⟩ **7** : in conformity with; *also* : ACCORDING TO ⟨did it ~ the book⟩ **8** : with respect to ⟨a doctor ~ profession⟩ **9** : to the amount or extent of ⟨won ~ a nose⟩ **10** — used to express relationship in multiplication, in division, and in measurements ⟨divide *a* ~ *b*⟩ ⟨multiply ~ 6⟩ ⟨15 feet ~ 20 feet⟩

[2]**by** \'bī\ *adv* **1** : near at hand; *also* : IN ⟨stop ~⟩ **2** : PAST ⟨saw him go ~⟩ **3** : ASIDE, APART ⟨put some money ~⟩

bye \'bī\ *n* : a position of a participant in a tournament who advances to the next round without playing

by–elec·tion *also* **bye–election** \'bī-ə-ˌlek-shən\ *n* : a special election held between regular elections in order to fill a vacancy

by·gone \'bī-ˌgȯn\ *adj* : gone by : PAST — **bygone** *n*

by·law *also* **bye·law** \'bī-ˌlȯ\ *n* : a rule adopted by an organization for managing its internal affairs

by–line \'bī-ˌlīn\ *n* : a line at the beginning of a news story or magazine article giving the writer's name

BYO *abbr* bring your own

BYOB *abbr* bring your own beer; bring your own booze; bring your own bottle

[1]**by·pass** \'bī-ˌpas\ *n* : a passage to one side or around a blocked or congested area; *also* : a surgical procedure establishing this ⟨a coronary ~⟩

[2]**bypass** *vb* : to avoid by means of a bypass

by·path \-ˌpath, -ˌpäth\ *n* : BYWAY

by·play \'bī-ˌplā\ *n* : action engaged in on the side (as of a stage) while the main action proceeds

by–prod·uct \-ˌprä-(ˌ)dəkt\ *n* : a sometimes unexpected product or result produced in addition to the main product or result

by·stand·er \-ˌstan-dər\ *n* : one present but not participating ♦ ***Synonyms*** ONLOOKER, WITNESS, SPECTATOR, EYEWITNESS

byte \'bīt\ *n* : a unit of computer information consisting of a group of 8 bits

by·way \'bī-ˌwā\ *n* **1** : a little-traveled side road **2** : a secondary aspect

by·word \-ˌwərd\ *n* **1** : PROVERB **2** : one that is noteworthy or notorious

Byz·an·tine \'biz-ᵊn-ˌtēn, 'bī-, -ˌtīn; bə-'zan-, bī-\ *adj* **1** : of, relating to, or characteristic of the ancient city of Byzantium or the Byzantine Empire **2** *often not cap* : intricately involved and often devious

C

[1]**c** \'sē\ *n, pl* **c's** *or* **cs** \'sēz\ *often cap* **1** : the 3d letter of the English alphabet **2** *slang* : a sum of $100 **3** : a grade rating a student's work as fair

[2]**c** *abbr, often cap* **1** calorie **2** carat **3** Celsius **4** cent **5** centigrade **6** centimeter **7** century **8** chapter **9** circa **10** cocaine **11** copyright

C *symbol* carbon

ca *abbr* circa

Ca *symbol* calcium

CA *abbr* **1** California **2** chartered accountant **3** chief accountant **4** chronological age

cab \'kab\ *n* **1** : a light closed horse-drawn carriage **2** : TAXICAB **3** : the covered compartment for the engineer and controls of a locomotive; *also* : a similar compartment (as on a truck) — **cab** *vb*

CAB *abbr* Civil Aeronautics Board

ca·bal \kə-'bäl, -'bal\ *n* [F *cabale,* fr. ML *cabbala* cabala, fr. Heb *qabbālāh,* lit., received (lore)] **1** : a secret group of plotters or political conspirators **2** : CLUB, GROUP ⟨a ~ of artists⟩

cabala *var of* KABBALAH

ca·bana \kə-'ban-yə, -'ba-nə\ *n* : a shelter at a beach or swimming pool

cab·a·ret \ˌka-bə-'rā\ *n* : NIGHTCLUB

cab·bage \'ka-bij\ *n* [ME *caboche,* fr. MF

dial., lit., head, noggin] : a vegetable related to the mustard with a dense head of leaves

cab•bie *or* **cab•by** \'ka-bē\ *n, pl* **cabbies** : a driver of a cab

cab•er•net sau•vi•gnon \ˌka-bər-'nā-sō-vē-'nyōⁿ\ *n* : a dry red wine made from a single variety of black grape

cab•in \'ka-bən\ *n* **1** : a private room on a ship; *also* : a compartment below deck on a boat for passengers or crew **2** : an aircraft or spacecraft compartment for passengers, crew, or cargo **3** : a small simple one-story house

cabin boy *n* : a boy working as a servant on a ship

cabin class *n* : a class of accommodations on a passenger ship superior to tourist class and inferior to first class

cabin cruiser *n* : CRUISER 3

cab•i•net \'kab-nit\ *n* **1** : a case or cupboard for holding or displaying articles **2** : the advisory council of a head of state (as a president or sovereign)

cab•i•net•mak•er \-ˌmā-kər\ *n* : a woodworker who makes fine furniture — **cab•i•net•mak•ing** *n*

cab•i•net•work \-ˌwərk\ *n* : the finished work of a cabinetmaker

¹**ca•ble** \'kā-bəl\ *n* **1** : a very strong rope, wire, or chain **2** : a bundle of insulated wires usu. twisted around a central core **3** : CABLEGRAM **4** : CABLE TELEVISION

²**cable** *vb* **ca•bled**; **ca•bling** : to telegraph by cable

cable car *n* : a vehicle moved by an endless cable

ca•ble•cast \'kā-bəl-ˌkast\ *n* : a cable television transmission — **cablecast** *vb*

ca•ble•gram \'kā-bəl-ˌgram\ *n* : a message sent by a submarine telegraph cable

cable modem *n* : a modem for connecting a computer to a network over a cable television line

cable television *n* : a system of television reception in which signals from distant stations are sent by cable to the receivers of paying subscribers

cab•o•chon \'ka-bə-ˌshän\ *n* : a gem or bead cut in convex form and highly polished but not given facets; *also* : this style of cutting — **cabochon** *adv*

ca•boose \kə-'büs\ *n* : a car usu. at the rear of a freight train for the use of the train crew and railroad workers

cab•ri•o•let \ˌka-brē-ə-'lā\ *n* [F] **1** : a light 2-wheeled one-horse carriage **2** : a convertible coupe

cab•stand \'kab-ˌstand\ *n* : a place where cabs wait for passengers

ca•cao \kə-'kau̇, -'kā-ō\ *n, pl* **cacaos** [Sp, fr. Nahuatl *cacahuatl*] : a So. American tree whose seeds (**cacao beans**) are the source of cocoa and chocolate; *also* : its dried fatty seeds

cac•cia•to•re \ˌkä-chə-'tōr-ē\ *adj* [It] : cooked with tomatoes and herbs

cache \'kash\ *n* [F] : a hiding place esp. for preserving provisions; *also* : something hidden or stored in a cache — **cache** *vb*

ca•chet \ka-'shā\ *n* [F] **1** : a seal used esp. as a mark of official approval **2** : a feature or quality conferring prestige; *also* : PRESTIGE **3** : a design, inscription, or advertisement printed or stamped on mail

cack•le \'ka-kəl\ *vb* **cack•led**; **cack•ling** **1** : to make the sharp broken cry characteristic of a hen **2** : to laugh or chatter noisily — **cackle** *n* — **cack•ler** *n*

ca•coph•o•ny \ka-'kä-fə-nē\ *n, pl* **-nies** : harsh or discordant sound — **ca•coph•o•nous** \-nəs\ *adj*

cac•tus \'kak-təs\ *n, pl* **cac•ti** \-ˌtī\ *or* **cac•tus•es** *also* **cactus** : any of a large family of drought-resistant flowering plants with succulent stems and with leaves replaced by scales or prickles

cad \'kad\ *n* : a man who deliberately disregards another's feelings — **cad•dish** \'ka-dish\ *adj* — **cad•dish•ly** *adv* — **cad•dish•ness** *n*

ca•dav•er \kə-'da-vər\ *n* : a dead body

ca•dav•er•ous \kə-'da-və-rəs\ *adj* : suggesting a corpse esp. in gauntness or pallor ♦ ***Synonyms*** WASTED, EMACIATED, GAUNT — **ca•dav•er•ous•ly** *adv*

cad•die *or* **cad•dy** \'ka-dē\ *n, pl* **caddies** [Sc, errand boy, modif. of F *cadet* military cadet] : a person who assists a golfer esp. by carrying the clubs — **caddie** *or* **caddy** *vb*

cad•dy \'ka-dē\ *n, pl* **caddies** [Malay *kati* a unit of weight] : a small box, can, or chest; *esp* : one to keep tea in

ca•dence \'kād-ᵊns\ *n* : the measure or beat of a rhythmical flow : RHYTHM — **ca•denced** \-ᵊnst\ *adj*

ca•den•za \kə-'den-zə\ *n* [It] : a brilliant sometimes improvised passage usu. toward the close of a musical composition

ca•det \kə-'det\ *n* [F, fr. Occitan (Gascony) *capdet* chief, fr. L *capitellum,* fr. L *caput* head] **1** : a younger son or brother **2** : a student in a service academy

Ca•dette \kə-'det\ *n* : a member of a Girl Scout program for girls in sixth through ninth grades

cadge \'kaj\ *vb* **cadged**; **cadg•ing** : SPONGE, BEG — **cadg•er** *n*

cad•mi•um \'kad-mē-əm\ *n* : a bluish-white metallic chemical element used esp. in protective platings

cad•re \'ka-ˌdrā, 'kä-, -drē\ *n* [F] **1** : FRAMEWORK **2** : a central unit esp. of trained personnel able to assume control and train others **3** : a group of indoctrinated leaders active in promoting the interests of a revolutionary party

ca•du•ceus \kə-'dü-sē-əs, -'dyü-, -shəs\ *n, pl* **-cei** \-sē-ˌī\ [L] **1** : the staff of a herald; *esp* : a representation of a staff with two entwined snakes and two wings at the top **2** : an insignia bearing a caduceus and symbolizing a physician

cae•cum *var of* CECUM

Cae•sar \'sē-zər\ *n* **1** : any of the Roman emperors succeeding Augustus Caesar — used as a title **2** *often not cap* : a powerful ruler : AUTOCRAT, DICTATOR; *also* : the civil or temporal power

caesarean *also* **caesarian** *var of* CESAREAN
cae·si·um *chiefly Brit var of* CESIUM
cae·sura \si-ˈzhu̇r-ə\ *n, pl* **-suras** *or* **-su·rae** \-ˈzhu̇r-(ˌ)ē\ : a break in the flow of sound usu. in the middle of a line of verse
ca·fé \ka-ˈfā\ *n* [F, lit., coffee] **1** : RESTAURANT **2** : BARROOM **3** : NIGHTCLUB
ca·fé au lait \(ˌ)ka-ˌfā-ō-ˈlā\ *n* : coffee with hot milk in about equal parts
caf·e·te·ria \ˌka-fə-ˈtir-ē-ə\ *n* [AmerSp *cafetería* coffeehouse] : a restaurant in which the customers serve themselves or are served at a counter
caf·fein·at·ed \ˈka-fə-ˌnā-təd\ *adj* **1** : stimulated by or as if by caffeine **2** : containing caffeine
caf·feine \ka-ˈfēn, ˈka-ˌfēn\ *n* : a stimulating alkaloid found esp. in coffee and tea
caf·fe lat·te \ˈkä-fā-ˈlä-tā\ *n* [It] : espresso mixed with hot or steamed milk
caf·tan \kaf-ˈtan, ˈkaf-ˌtan\ *n* [Russ *kaftan,* fr. Turk, fr. Pers *qaftān*] : an ankle-length garment with long sleeves worn in countries of the eastern Mediterranean
[1]**cage** \ˈkāj\ *n* **1** : an openwork enclosure for confining an animal **2** : something resembling a cage
[2]**cage** *vb* **caged; cag·ing** : to put or keep in or as if in a cage
ca·gey *also* **ca·gy** \ˈkā-jē\ *adj* **ca·gi·er; -est** : wary of being trapped or deceived : SHREWD ⟨a ~ dealer⟩ — **ca·gi·ly** \-jə-lē\ *adv* — **ca·gi·ness** \-jē-nəs\ *n*
CAGS *abbr* Certificate of Advanced Graduate Study
ca·hoot \kə-ˈhüt\ *n* : PARTNERSHIP, LEAGUE — usu. used in pl. ⟨officials in ~*s* with the underworld⟩
cai·man *also* **cayman** \ˈkā-mən; kā-ˈman, kī-\ *n* : any of several Central and So. American reptiles closely related to alligators and crocodiles
cairn \ˈkarn\ *n* : a heap of stones serving as a memorial or a landmark
cais·son \ˈkā-ˌsän, ˈkās-ᵊn\ *n* **1** : a usu. 2-wheeled vehicle for artillery ammunition **2** : a watertight chamber used in underwater construction work or as a foundation
caisson disease *n* : [2]BEND 3
cai·tiff \ˈkā-təf\ *adj* [ME *caitif,* fr. AF *caitif, chaitif* wretched, despicable, fr. L *captivus* captive] : being base, cowardly, or despicable — **caitiff** *n*
ca·jole \kə-ˈjōl\ *vb* **ca·joled; ca·jol·ing** [F *cajoler*] : to persuade or coax esp. with flattery or false promises — **ca·jole·ment** *n* — **ca·jol·ery** \-ˈjō-lə-rē\ *n*
Ca·jun \ˈkā-jən\ *n* : a Louisianian descended from French-speaking immigrants from Acadia (Nova Scotia) — **Cajun** *adj*
[1]**cake** \ˈkāk\ *n* **1** : a baked or fried breadlike food usu. in a small flat shape **2** : a sweet baked food made from batter or dough usu. containing flour, sugar, shortening, and a leaven (as baking powder) **3** : a hardened or compacted substance ⟨a ~ of soap⟩ **4** : something easily done
[2]**cake** *vb* **caked; cak·ing** **1** : ENCRUST **2** : to form or harden into a cake
cake·walk \ˈkāk-ˌwȯk\ *n* **1** : a stage dance typically involving a high prance with backward tilt **2** : a one-sided contest or an easy task
cal *abbr* **1** calendar **2** caliber
Cal *abbr* **1** California **2** calorie
cal·a·bash \ˈka-lə-ˌbash\ *n* : the fruit of a gourd; *also* : a utensil made from its hard shell
cal·a·boose \ˈka-lə-ˌbüs\ *n* [Sp *calabozo* dungeon] : JAIL
ca·la·di·um \kə-ˈlā-dē-əm\ *n* : any of a genus of tropical American ornamental plants related to the arums
cal·a·mari \ˌkä-lə-ˈmär-ē\ *n* [It] : squid used as food
cal·a·mine \ˈka-lə-ˌmīn\ *n* : a lotion of oxides of zinc and iron
ca·lam·i·ty \kə-ˈla-mə-tē\ *n, pl* **-ties** **1** : great distress or misfortune **2** : an event causing great harm or loss and affliction : DISASTER ⟨an economic ~⟩ — **ca·lam·i·tous** \-təs\ *adj* — **ca·lam·i·tous·ly** *adv* — **ca·lam·i·tous·ness** *n*
calc *abbr* calculate; calculated
cal·car·e·ous \kal-ˈkar-ē-əs\ *adj* : resembling calcium carbonate in hardness; *also* : containing calcium or calcium carbonate
cal·cif·er·ous \kal-ˈsi-fə-rəs\ *adj* : producing or containing calcium carbonate
cal·ci·fy \ˈkal-sə-ˌfī\ *vb* **-fied; -fy·ing** : to make or become calcareous — **cal·ci·fi·ca·tion** \ˌkal-sə-fə-ˈkā-shən\ *n*
cal·ci·mine \ˈkal-sə-ˌmīn\ *n* : a thin water paint used esp. on plastered surfaces — **calcimine** *vb*
cal·cine \kal-ˈsīn\ *vb* **cal·cined; cal·cin·ing** : to heat to a high temperature but without fusing to drive off volatile matter and often to reduce to powder — **cal·ci·na·tion** \ˌkal-sə-ˈnā-shən\ *n*
cal·cite \ˈkal-ˌsīt\ *n* : a crystalline mineral consisting of calcium carbonate — **cal·cit·ic** \kal-ˈsi-tik\ *adj*
cal·ci·um \ˈkal-sē-əm\ *n* : a silver-white soft metallic chemical element occurring only in combination
calcium carbonate *n* : a substance found in nature as limestone and marble and in plant ashes, bones, and shells
cal·cu·late \ˈkal-kyə-ˌlāt\ *vb* **-lat·ed; -lat·ing** [L *calculare,* fr. *calculus* pebble (used in reckoning)] **1** : to determine by mathematical processes **2** : to reckon by exercise of practical judgment : ESTIMATE **3** : to design or adapt for a purpose **4** : COUNT, RELY — **cal·cu·la·ble** \-lə-bəl\ *adj* — **cal·cu·la·tor** \-ˌlā-tər\ *n*
cal·cu·lat·ed \-ˌlā-təd\ *adj* **1** : undertaken after estimating the chance of success or failure ⟨a ~ risk⟩ **2** : planned purposefully : DELIBERATE ⟨a ~ strategy⟩
cal·cu·lat·ing \-ˌlā-tiŋ\ *adj* : marked by shrewd consideration esp. of self-interest — **cal·cu·lat·ing·ly** *adv*
cal·cu·la·tion \ˌkal-kyə-ˈlā-shən\ *n* **1** : the process or an act of calculating **2** : the result of an act of calculating **3**

: studied care; *also* : cold heartless planning to promote self-interest

cal·cu·lus \ˈkal-kyə-ləs\ *n, pl* **-li** \-ˌlī\ *also* **-lus·es** [L, pebble (used in reckoning)] **1** : a method of computation or calculation in a special notation (as of logic) **2** : a branch of mathematics concerned with the rate of change of functions and with methods of finding lengths, areas, and volumes **3** : a concretion usu. of mineral salts esp. in hollow organs or ducts

cal·de·ra \kal-ˈder-ə, kȯl-, -ˈdir-\ *n* [Sp, lit., cauldron] : a large crater usu. formed by the collapse of a volcanic cone

cal·dron *var of* CAULDRON

[1]**cal·en·dar** \ˈka-lən-dər\ *n* **1** : an arrangement of time into days, weeks, months, and years; *also* : a sheet or folder containing such an arrangement for a period **2** : an orderly list

[2]**calendar** *vb* : to enter in a calendar

[1]**cal·en·der** \ˈka-lən-dər\ *vb* : to press (as cloth or paper) between rollers or plates so as to make smooth or glossy or to thin into sheets

[2]**calender** *n* : a machine for calendering

ca·lends \ˈka-ləndz, ˈkā-\ *n sing or pl* : the first day of the ancient Roman month

ca·len·du·la \kə-ˈlen-jə-lə\ *n* : any of a genus of yellow-flowered herbs related to the daisies

[1]**calf** \ˈkaf, ˈkȧf\ *n, pl* **calves** \ˈkavz, ˈkȧvz\ **1** : the young of the domestic cow; *also* : the young of various large mammals (as the elephant or whale) **2** : CALFSKIN

[2]**calf** *n, pl* **calves** \ˈkavz, ˈkȧvz\ : the fleshy back of the leg below the knee

calf·skin \ˈkaf-ˌskin, ˈkȧf-\ *n* : leather made of the skin of a calf

cal·i·ber *or* **cal·i·bre** \ˈka-lə-bər\ *n* [MF *calibre,* fr. It *calibro,* fr. Ar *qālib* shoemaker's last] **1** : degree of mental capacity, excellence, or importance **2** : the diameter of a projectile **3** : the diameter of the bore of a gun

cal·i·brate \ˈka-lə-ˌbrāt\ *vb* **-brat·ed**; **-brat·ing** : to adjust precisely

cal·i·bra·tion \ˌka-lə-ˈbrā-shən\ *n* : a set of graduated marks indicating values or positions — usu. used in pl.

cal·i·co \ˈka-li-ˌkō\ *n, pl* **-coes** *or* **-cos** **1** : printed cotton fabric **2** : a mottled or spotted animal — **calico** *adj*

Calif *abbr* California

Cal·i·for·nia poppy \ˌka-lə-ˈfȯr-nyə-\ *n* : a widely cultivated herb with usu. yellow or orange flowers that is related to the poppies

cal·i·for·ni·um \ˌka-lə-ˈfȯr-nē-əm\ *n* : an artificially prepared radioactive chemical element

cal·i·per \ˈka-lə-pər\ *n* **1** : any of various instruments having two arms, legs, or jaws used esp. to measure diameter or thickness — usu. used in pl. **2** : a device for pressing a frictional material against the sides of a rotating wheel or disk

ca·liph \ˈkā-ləf, ˈka-\ *n* : a successor of Muhammad as head of Islam — used as a title — **ca·liph·ate** \-lə-ˌfāt, -fət\ *n*

cal·is·then·ics \ˌka-ləs-ˈthe-niks\ *n sing or pl* [Gk *kalos* beautiful + *sthenos* strength] : bodily exercises usu. done without apparatus — **cal·is·then·ic** *adj*

calk \ˈkȯk\ *var of* CAULK

[1]**call** \ˈkȯl\ *vb* **1** : SHOUT, CRY; *also* : to utter a characteristic note or cry **2** : to utter in a loud clear voice ⟨~*ed* out my name⟩ **3** : to announce authoritatively **4** : SUMMON ⟨was ~*ed* to testify⟩ **5** : to make a request or demand ⟨~ for an investigation⟩ **6** : to halt (as a baseball game) because of unsuitable conditions **7** : to demand payment of (a loan); *also* : to demand surrender of (as a bond) for redemption **8** : to get or try to get in communication by telephone or by a similar communication service **9** : to make a brief visit **10** : to speak of or address by name : give a name to **11** : to estimate or consider for practical purposes ⟨~ it ten miles⟩ **12** : to temporarily transfer control of computer processing to (as a subroutine or procedure) — **call·er** *n*

[2]**call** *n* **1** : SHOUT **2** : the cry of an animal (as a bird) **3** : a request or a command to come or assemble : INVITATION, SUMMONS **4** : DEMAND, CLAIM; *also* : REQUEST **5** : a brief usu. formal visit **6** : an act of calling by telephone or by a similar communication service **7** : DECISION ⟨a tough ~⟩ **8** : a temporary transfer of control of computer processing to a particular set of instructions

cal·la lily \ˈka-lə-\ *n* : a plant related to the arums and grown for its large white lilylike bract that surrounds a fleshy spike of small yellow flowers

call·back \ˈkȯl-ˌbak\ *n* : a calling back; *esp* : RECALL 5

call–board \-ˌbōrd\ *n* : a board for posting notices (as of rehearsal calls)

call down *vb* : REPRIMAND

call girl *n* : a prostitute with whom appointments are made by phone

cal·lig·ra·phy \kə-ˈli-grə-fē\ *n* : artistic or elegant handwriting; *also* : the art of producing such writing — **cal·lig·ra·pher** \-fər\ *n* — **cal·li·graph·ic** \ˌka-lə-ˈgraf-ik\ *adj*

call–in \ˈkȯl-ˌin\ *adj* : allowing listeners to engage in broadcast telephone conversations ⟨a ~ show⟩

call in *vb* **1** : to order to return or be returned **2** : to summon to one's aid **3** : to report by telephone

call·ing \ˈkȯ-liŋ\ *n* **1** : a strong inner impulse toward a particular course of action **2** : the activity in which one customarily engages as an occupation

cal·li·ope \kə-ˈlī-ə-(ˌ)pē, ˈka-lē-ˌōp\ *n* [fr. *Calliope,* chief of the Muses, fr. L, fr. Gk *Kalliopē*] : a keyboard musical instrument similar to an organ and made up of a series of whistles

cal·li·per *chiefly Brit var of* CALIPER

call number *n* : a combination of characters assigned to a library book to indicate its place on a shelf

call off *vb* : CANCEL ⟨*called off* the trip⟩

cal•los•i•ty \ka-ˈlä-sə-tē\ *n, pl* **-ties** **1** : the quality or state of being callous **2** : CALLUS 1

[1]**cal•lous** \ˈka-ləs\ *adj* **1** : being thickened and hardened ⟨~ skin⟩ **2** : feeling no emotion or sympathy — **cal•lous•ly** *adv* — **cal•lous•ness** *n*

[2]**callous** *vb* : to make callous

cal•low \ˈka-lō\ *adj* [ME *calu* bald, fr. OE] : lacking adult sophistication ⟨a ~ youth⟩ — **cal•low•ness** *n*

call–up \ˈkȯ-ˌləp\ *n* : an order to report for active military service

call up *vb* : to summon for active military duty

cal•lus \ˈka-ləs\ *n* **1** : a callous area on skin or bark **2** : tissue that is converted into bone in the healing of a bone fracture — **callus** *vb*

call–waiting *n* : a telephone service by which during a call in progress an incoming call is signaled (as by a click)

[1]**calm** \ˈkäm, ˈkälm\ *n* **1** : a period or a condition free from storms, high winds, or rough water **2** : complete or almost complete absence of wind **3** : a state of tranquillity

[2]**calm** *vb* : to make or become calm

[3]**calm** *adj* : marked by calm : STILL, UNRUFFLED — **calm•ly** *adv* — **calm•ness** *n*

cal•o•mel \ˈka-lə-məl, -ˌmel\ *n* : a chloride of mercury used esp. as a fungicide

ca•lor•ic \kə-ˈlȯr-ik\ *adj* **1** : of or relating to heat **2** : of, relating to, or containing calories — **ca•lo•ric•al•ly** \-i-k(ə-)lē\ *adv*

cal•o•rie *also* **cal•o•ry** \ˈka-lə-rē\ *n, pl* **-ries** : a unit for measuring heat; *esp* : one for measuring the value of foods for producing heat and energy in the human body equivalent to the amount of heat required to raise the temperature of one kilogram of water one degree Celsius

cal•o•rim•e•ter \ˌka-lə-ˈri-mə-tər\ *n* : an apparatus for measuring quantities of heat — **cal•o•rim•e•try** \-trē\ *n*

cal•u•met \ˈkal-yə-ˌmet, -mət\ *n* : a ceremonial pipe used by some Indigenous American people

ca•lum•ni•ate \kə-ˈləm-nē-ˌāt\ *vb* **-at•ed**; **-at•ing** : to make false and malicious statements about ♦ ***Synonyms*** DEFAME, MALIGN, LIBEL, SLANDER, TRADUCE — **ca•lum•ni•a•tion** \-ˌləm-nē-ˈā-shən\ *n* — **ca•lum•ni•a•tor** \-ˈləm-nē-ˌā-tər\ *n*

cal•um•ny \ˈka-ləm-nē\ *n, pl* **-nies** : false and malicious accusation — **ca•lum•ni•ous** \kə-ˈləm-nē-əs\ *adj*

calve \ˈkav, ˈkȧv\ *vb* **calved**; **calv•ing** : to give birth to a calf

calves *pl of* CALF

Cal•vin•ism \ˈkal-və-ˌni-zəm\ *n* : the theological system of John Calvin and his followers — **Cal•vin•ist** \-nist\ *n or adj* — **Cal•vin•is•tic** \ˌkal-və-ˈnis-tik\ *adj*

ca•lyp•so \kə-ˈlip-sō\ *n, pl* **-sos** : a style of music originating in the British West Indies and having lyrics that usu. satirize local personalities and events

ca•lyx \ˈkā-liks, ˈka-\ *n, pl* **ca•lyx•es** *or* **ca•ly•ces** \ˈkā-lə-ˌsēz, ˈka-\ : the usu. green or leaflike outer part of a flower consisting of sepals

cal•zo•ne \kal-ˈzōn, -ˈzō-nē\ *n* : a baked or fried turnover of pizza dough stuffed with cheese and various fillings

[1]**cam** \ˈkam\ *n* : a rotating or sliding piece in a mechanical linkage by which rotary motion is transformed into linear motion or vice versa

[2]**cam** *n* : CAMERA

ca•ma•ra•de•rie \ˌkäm-ˈrä-də-rē, ˌkam-, -ˈra-\ *n* [F] : friendly feeling and goodwill among comrades

cam•bi•um \ˈkam-bē-əm\ *n, pl* **-bi•ums** *or* **-bia** \-bē-ə\ : a thin cellular layer between xylem and phloem of most higher plants from which new tissues develop — **cam•bi•al** \-əl\ *adj*

Cam•bri•an \ˈkam-brē-ən, ˈkām-\ *adj* : of, relating to, or being the earliest period of the Paleozoic era — **Cambrian** *n*

cam•bric \ˈkām-brik\ *n* : a fine thin white linen or cotton fabric

cam•cord•er \ˈkam-ˌkȯr-dər\ *n* : a small portable combined camera and VCR

came *past of* COME

cam•el \ˈka-məl\ *n* : either of two large cud-chewing mammals that have one or two fatty humps on their backs and are used esp. in desert regions for carrying and riding

camel hair *also* **camel's hair** *n* **1** : the hair of a camel or a substitute for it **2** : cloth made of camel hair or of camel hair and wool

ca•mel•lia \kə-ˈmēl-yə\ *n* : any of a genus of shrubs and trees related to the tea plant and grown in warm regions and greenhouses for their showy roselike flowers

Cam•em•bert \ˈka-məm-ˌber\ *n* : a soft cheese with a grayish rind and yellow interior

cam•eo \ˈka-mē-ˌō\ *n, pl* **-eos** **1** : a gem carved in relief; *also* : a small medallion with a profiled head in relief **2** : a brief appearance esp. by a well-known actor in a play or movie

cam•era \ˈkam-rə, ˈka-mə-rə\ *n* : a device with a lightproof chamber fitted with a lens through which the image of an object is projected onto a surface for recording (as on film) or for conversion into electrical signals (as for broadcast on television or the Internet) — **cam•era•man** \-ˌman, -mən\ *n* — **cam•era•per•son** *n* — **cam•era•wom•an** *n*

cam•i•sole \ˈka-mə-ˌsōl\ *n* : a short sleeveless garment for women

camomile *var of* CHAMOMILE

cam•ou•flage \ˈka-mə-ˌfläzh, -ˌfläj\ *n* [F] **1** : the disguising of military equipment with paint, nets, or foliage; *also* : the disguise itself **2** : deceptive behavior — **camouflage** *vb*

[1]**camp** \ˈkamp\ *n* **1** : a place where tents or buildings are erected for usu. temporary shelter **2** : a collection of tents or other shelters **3** : a program offering recreational activities (as boating and hiking) for a limited time ⟨summer ~⟩ **4** : a

body of persons encamped **5 :** a training session for athletes outside of the regular season — **camp·ground** \-ˌgraůnd\ *n* — **camp·site** \-ˌsīt\ *n*

²**camp** *vb* **1 :** to make or occupy a camp **2 :** to live in a camp or outdoors

³**camp** *n* **1 :** exaggerated effeminate mannerisms **2 :** something so outrageous, inappropriate, or theatrical as to be considered amusing — **camp** *adj* — **camp·i·ly** \ˈkam-pə-lē\ *adv* — **camp·i·ness** \-pē-nəs\ *n* — **campy** \-pē\ *adj*

⁴**camp** *vb* **:** to engage in camp : exhibit the qualities of camp

cam·paign \kam-ˈpān\ *n* **1 :** a series of military operations forming one distinct stage in a war **2 :** a series of activities designed to bring about a particular result ⟨advertising ~⟩ — **campaign** *vb* — **cam·paign·er** *n*

cam·pa·ni·le \ˌkam-pə-ˈnē-lē\ *n, pl* **-ni·les** *or* **-ni·li** \-ˈnē-lē\ **:** a usu. freestanding bell tower

cam·pa·nol·o·gy \ˌkam-pə-ˈnä-lə-jē\ *n* **:** the art of bell ringing — **cam·pa·nol·o·gist** \-jist\ *n*

camp·er \ˈkam-pər\ *n* **1 :** one who camps **2 :** a portable dwelling (as a specially equipped vehicle) for use during casual travel and camping

Camp Fire Girl *n* **:** a girl who is a member of a national organization of young people from ages 5 to 18

camp follower *n* **1 :** a civilian (as a prostitute) who follows a military unit to attend or exploit its personnel **2 :** a follower of a group who is not an adherent; *esp* **:** a politician who joins a movement solely for personal gain

cam·phor \ˈkam-fər\ *n* **:** a gummy volatile aromatic compound obtained from an evergreen Asian tree (**camphor tree**) and used esp. in medicine

camp meeting *n* **:** a series of evangelistic meetings usu. held outdoors

camp·o·ree \ˌkam-pə-ˈrē\ *n* **:** a gathering of Boy Scouts or Girl Scouts from a given geographic area

cam·pus \ˈkam-pəs\ *n* [L, plain] **:** the grounds and buildings of a college or school; *also* **:** grounds resembling a campus ⟨hospital ~⟩

cam·shaft \ˈkam-ˌshaft\ *n* **:** a shaft to which a cam is fastened

¹**can** \kən, ˈkan\ *vb, past* **could** \kəd, ˈkůd\; *pres sing & pl* **can 1 :** be able to **2 :** may perhaps ⟨~ he still be alive⟩ **3 :** be permitted by conscience or feeling to ⟨you ~ hardly blame her⟩ **4 :** have permission to ⟨you ~ go now⟩

²**can** \ˈkan\ *n* **1 :** a usu. cylindrical container or receptacle ⟨garbage ~⟩ ⟨coffee ~⟩ **2 :** JAIL **3 :** TOILET

³**can** \ˈkan\ *vb* **canned; can·ning 1 :** to put in a can : preserve by sealing in airtight cans or jars **2** *slang* **:** to discharge from employment **3** *slang* **:** to put a stop or an end to — **can·ner** *n*

Can *or* **Canad** *abbr* Canada; Canadian

Can·a·da goose \ˈka-nə-də-\ *n* **:** a common wild goose of No. America

ca·naille \kə-ˈnī, -ˈnāl\ *n* [F, fr. It *canaglia,* fr. *cane* dog] **:** RABBLE, RIFFRAFF

ca·nal \kə-ˈnal\ *n* **1 :** a tubular passage in the body : DUCT **2 :** an artificial waterway (as for boats or irrigation)

can·a·lize \ˈkan-ᵊl-ˌīz\ *vb* **-lized; -liz·ing 1 :** to provide with a canal or make into or like a channel **2 :** to provide with an outlet; *esp* **:** to direct into preferred channels — **ca·nal·i·za·tion** \ˌkan-ᵊl-ə-ˈzā-shən\ *n*

can·a·pé \ˈka-nə-pē, -ˌpā\ *n* [F, lit., sofa, fr. ML *canopeum, canapeum* mosquito net] **:** a piece of bread or toast or a cracker topped with a savory food

ca·nard \kə-ˈnärd\ *n* **:** a false or unfounded report, story or belief

ca·nary \kə-ˈner-ē\ *n, pl* **ca·nar·ies** [fr. the *Canary* islands] **1 :** a usu. sweet wine similar to Madeira **2 :** a usu. yellow or greenish finch often kept in a cage as a pet

ca·nas·ta \kə-ˈnas-tə\ *n* [Sp, lit., basket] **:** rummy played with two full decks of cards plus four jokers

canc *abbr* canceled

can·can \ˈkan-ˌkan\ *n* **:** a woman's dance of French origin characterized by high kicking

¹**can·cel** \ˈkan-səl\ *vb* **-celed** *or* **-celled; -cel·ing** *or* **-cel·ling** [ME *cancellen,* fr. AF *canceller, chanceller,* fr. LL *cancellare,* fr. L, to make like a lattice, fr. *cancelli* lattice] **1 :** to destroy the force or validity of : ANNUL **2 :** to match in force or effect : OFFSET **3 :** to cross out : DELETE **4 :** to remove (a common divisor) from a numerator and denominator; *also* **:** to remove (equivalents) on opposite sides of an equation or account **5 :** to mark (a postage stamp or check) so that it cannot be reused **6 :** to neutralize each other's strength or effect — **can·cel·la·tion** \ˌkan-sə-ˈlā-shən\ *n* — **can·cel·er** *or* **can·cel·ler** *n*

²**cancel** *n* **1 :** CANCELLATION **2 :** a deleted part

can·cer \ˈkan-sər\ *n* [L, lit., crab] **1** *cap* **:** a zodiacal constellation between Gemini and Leo usu. pictured as a crab **2** *cap* **:** the 4th sign of the zodiac in astrology; *also* **:** one born under this sign **3 :** a malignant tumor that tends to spread in the body; *also* **:** an abnormal state marked by such tumors **4 :** a malignant evil that spreads destructively — **can·cer·ous** \-sə-rəs\ *adj* — **can·cer·ous·ly** *adv*

can·de·la·bra \ˌkan-də-ˈlä-brə, -ˈla-\ *n* **:** an ornamental branched candlestick or lamp with several lights

can·de·la·brum \-brəm\ *n, pl* **-bra** *also* **-brums :** CANDELABRA

can·did \ˈkan-dəd\ *adj* **1 :** FRANK, STRAIGHTFORWARD **2 :** relating to photography of subjects acting naturally or spontaneously without being posed — **can·did·ly** *adv* — **can·did·ness** *n*

can·di·da·cy \ˈkan-də-də-sē\ *n, pl* **-cies :** the state of being a candidate

can·di·date \ˈkan-də-ˌdāt, ˈka-nə-, -dət\ *n* [L *candidatus,* fr. *candidatus* clothed in white, fr. *candidus* white; fr. the white toga worn by office seekers in ancient Rome] : one who seeks or is proposed for an office, honor, or membership ⟨a ~ for governor⟩

can•di•da•ture \ˈkan-də-də-ˌchu̇r, ˈka-nə-\ *n, chiefly Brit* : CANDIDACY

can•died \ˈkan-dēd\ *adj* : preserved in or encrusted with sugar

[1]**can•dle** \ˈkan-dᵊl\ *n* : a usu. slender mass of tallow or wax molded around a wick that is burned to give light

[2]**candle** *vb* **can•dled; can•dling** : to examine (as eggs) by holding between the eye and a light — **can•dler** *n*

can•dle•light \ˈkan-dᵊl-ˌlīt\ *n* **1** : the light of a candle; *also* : any soft artificial light **2** : the time when candles are lit : TWILIGHT

can•dle•lit \-ˌlit\ *adj* : illuminated by candlelight ⟨a ~ dinner⟩

Can•dle•mas \ˈkan-dᵊl-məs\ *n* : February 2 observed as a church festival in commemoration of the presentation of Christ in the temple

can•dle•stick \-ˌstik\ *n* : a holder with a socket for a candle

can•dle•wick \-ˌwik\ *n* : a soft cotton yarn; *also* : embroidery made with this yarn usu. in tufts

can•dor \ˈkan-dər\ *n* : FRANKNESS, OUTSPOKENNESS

can•dour *chiefly Brit var of* CANDOR

C and W *abbr* country and western

[1]**can•dy** \ˈkan-dē\ *n, pl* **candies** [ME *sugre candy,* fr. MF *sucre candi,* fr. OF *sucre* sugar + Ar *qandī* candied, fr. *qand* crystallized sugar] **1** : a confection made from sugar often with flavoring and filling **2** : something that appeals in a light or frivolous way

[2]**candy** *vb* **can•died; can•dy•ing** : to encrust in sugar often by cooking in a syrup

candy strip•er \-ˈstrī-pər\ *n* : a teenage volunteer worker at a hospital

[1]**cane** \ˈkān\ *n* **1** : a slender hollow or pithy stem (as of a reed or bramble) **2** : a tall woody grass or reed (as sugarcane or sorghum) **3** : a walking stick; *also* : a rod for flogging

[2]**cane** *vb* **caned; can•ing** **1** : to beat with a cane **2** : to weave or make with cane — **can•er** *n*

cane•brake \ˈkān-ˌbrāk\ *n* : a thicket of cane

[1]**ca•nine** \ˈkā-ˌnīn\ *n* **1** : a pointed tooth between the outer incisor and the first premolar **2** : a canine mammal (as a domestic dog)

[2]**canine** *adj* [L *caninus,* fr. *canis* dog] : of or relating to dogs or to the family to which they belong

can•is•ter \ˈka-nə-stər\ *n* : an often cylindrical container

can•ker \ˈkaŋ-kər\ *n* : a spreading sore that eats into tissue — **can•ker•ous** \-kə-rəs\ *adj*

can•ker•worm \-ˌwərm\ *n* : either of two moths and esp. their larvae that are pests of fruit and shade trees

can•na \ˈka-nə\ *n* : any of a genus of tropical herbs with large leaves and racemes of bright-colored flowers

can•na•bis \ˈka-nə-bəs\ *n* : any of the psychoactive preparations (as marijuana) or chemicals (as THC) derived from hemp; *also* : HEMP

canned \ˈkand\ *adj* : prepared in standardized form for general use or wide distribution ⟨~ music⟩

can•nery \ˈka-nə-rē\ *n, pl* **-ner•ies** : a factory for the canning of foods

can•ni•bal \ˈka-nə-bəl\ *n* [NL *Canibalis* a member of an Indigenous people of the Caribbean, fr. Sp *Caníbal*] : one that eats the flesh of its own kind — **can•ni•bal•ism** \-bə-ˌli-zəm\ *n* — **can•ni•bal•is•tic** \-bə-ˈlis-tik\ *adj*

can•ni•bal•ise *Brit var of* CANNIBALIZE

can•ni•bal•ize \ˈka-nə-bə-ˌlīz\ *vb* **-ized; -iz•ing** **1** : to take usable parts from (as an inoperative machine) to construct or repair another machine **2** : to practice cannibalism

can•non \ˈka-nən\ *n, pl* **cannons** *or* **cannon** [ME *canon,* fr. AF, fr. It *cannone,* lit., large tube, fr. *canna* reed, tube, fr. L, cane, reed] : a large heavy gun; *esp* : one mounted on a carriage

can•non•ade \ˌka-nə-ˈnād\ *n* : a heavy fire of artillery — **cannonade** *vb*

can•non•ball \ˈka-nən-ˌbȯl\ *n* : a usu. round solid missile for a cannon

can•non•eer \ˌka-nə-ˈnir\ *n* : an artillery gunner

can•not \ˈka-ˌnät; kə-ˈnät\ : can not — **cannot but** : to be unable to do otherwise than ⟨we *cannot but* wonder why⟩

can•nu•la \ˈkan-yə-lə\ *n, pl* **-las** *or* **-lae** \-ˌlē\ : a small tube for insertion into a body cavity or into a duct or vessel

can•ny \ˈka-nē\ *adj* **can•ni•er; -est** : PRUDENT, SHREWD — **can•ni•ly** \ˈkan-ᵊl-ē\ *adv* — **can•ni•ness** \ˈka-nē-nəs\ *n*

ca•noe \kə-ˈnü\ *n* : a light narrow boat with sharp ends and curved sides that is usu. propelled by paddles — **canoe** *vb* — **ca•noe•ist** *n*

ca•no•la \kə-ˈnō-lə\ *n* : a rape plant producing seeds that are low in a toxic acid and yield an edible oil (**canola oil**) high in monounsaturated fatty acids; *also* : this oil

[1]**can•on** \ˈka-nən\ *n* **1** : a regulation decreed by a church council; *also* : a provision of canon law **2** : an official or authoritative list (as of works of literature) **3** : an accepted principle

[2]**canon** *n* : a member of the clergy on the staff of a cathedral

ca•non•i•cal \kə-ˈnä-ni-kəl\ *adj* **1** : of, relating to, or forming a canon **2** : conforming to a general rule or acceptable procedure : ORTHODOX **3** : of or relating to a canon of a cathedral — **ca•non•i•cal•ly** \-k(ə-)lē\ *adv*

can•on•ize \ˈka-nə-ˌnīz\ *vb* **can•on•ized** \-ˌnīzd\; **can•on•iz•ing** **1** : to declare (a deceased person) an officially recognized saint **2** : GLORIFY, EXALT — **can•on•i•za•tion** \ˌka-nə-nə-ˈzā-shən\ *n*

canon law *n* : the law governing a church

can·o·py \ˈka-nə-pē\ *n, pl* **-pies** [ME *canope,* fr. ML *canopeum* mosquito net, fr. L *conopeum,* fr. Gk *kōnōpion,* fr. *kōnōps* mosquito] **1** : an overhanging cover, shelter, or shade **2** : the uppermost spreading layer of a forest **3** : a transparent cover for an airplane cockpit **4** : the fabric part of a parachute — **canopy** *vb*

[1]**cant** \ˈkant\ *vb* : to give a slant to

[2]**cant** *n* **1** : an oblique or slanting surface **2** : TILT, SLANT

[3]**cant** *vb* **1** : to beg in a whining manner **2** : to talk hypocritically

[4]**cant** *n* **1** : the special idiom of a profession or trade : JARGON **2** : insincere speech; *esp* : insincerely pious words or statements

Cant *abbr* Canticle of Canticles

can·ta·bi·le \kän-ˈtä-bə-ˌlā\ *adv or adj* [It] : in a singing manner — used as a direction in music

can·ta·loupe *also* **can·ta·loup** \ˈkant-ᵊl-ˌōp\ *n* : MUSKMELON; *esp* : one with orange flesh and rough skin

can·tan·ker·ous \kan-ˈtaŋ-kə-rəs\ *adj* : difficult to deal with : ILL-NATURED ⟨a ~ mule⟩ — **can·tan·ker·ous·ly** *adv* — **can·tan·ker·ous·ness** *n*

can·ta·ta \kən-ˈtä-tə\ *n* [It] : a choral composition usu. sung to instrumental accompaniment

can·teen \kan-ˈtēn\ *n* [F *cantine* bottle case, canteen (store), fr. It *cantina* wine cellar] **1** : a flask for carrying liquids **2** : a place of recreation and entertainment for military personnel **3** : a small cafeteria or counter at which snacks are served

can·ter \ˈkan-tər\ *n* : a horse's 3-beat gait resembling but smoother and slower than a gallop — **canter** *vb*

Can·ter·bury bell \ˈkant-ər-ˌber-ē-\ *n* : any of several plants related to the bluebell that are cultivated for their showy flowers

can·ti·cle \ˈkan-ti-kəl\ *n* : SONG; *esp* : any of several liturgical songs taken from the Bible

Canticle of Canticles *n* : SONG OF SONGS

[1]**can·ti·le·ver** \ˈkant-ᵊl-ˌē-vər\ *n* : a projecting beam or structure supported only at one end; *also* : either of a pair of such structures projecting toward each other so that when joined they form a bridge

[2]**cantilever** *vb* **1** : to support by a cantilever ⟨a ~*ed* shelf⟩ **2** : to build as a cantilever **3** : to project as a cantilever

can·tle \ˈkant-ᵊl\ *n* : the upwardly projecting rear part of a saddle

can·to \ˈkan-ˌtō\ *n, pl* **cantos** [It, fr. L *cantus* song] : one of the major divisions of a long poem

can·ton \ˈkant-ᵊn, ˈkan-ˌtän\ *n* : a small territorial division of a country; *esp* : one of the political divisions of Switzerland — **can·ton·al** \ˈkant-ᵊn-əl, kan-ˈtän-ᵊl\ *adj*

can·ton·ment \kan-ˈtōn-mənt, -ˈtän-\ *n* : usu. temporary quarters for troops

can·tor \ˈkan-tər\ *n* **1** : a choir leader **2** : a synagogue official who sings liturgical music and leads the congregation in prayer

can·vas *also* **can·vass** \ˈkan-vəs\ *n* **1** : a strong cloth formerly much used for making tents and sails **2** : a set of sails **3** : a group of tents **4** : a piece of cloth prepared as a surface for a painting; *also* : a painting on this surface **5** : the canvas-covered floor of a boxing or wrestling ring

can·vas·back \ˈkan-vəs-ˌbak\ *n* : a No. American wild duck with red head and gray back

[1]**can·vass** *also* **can·vas** \ˈkan-vəs\ *vb* **can·vassed**; **can·vas·sing** : to go through (a district) or to (persons) to solicit votes or orders for goods or to determine public opinion or sentiment — **can·vass·er** *n*

[2]**canvass** *n* : an act or instance of canvassing

can·yon \ˈkan-yən\ *n* : a deep narrow valley with high steep sides

[1]**cap** \ˈkap\ *n* **1** : a covering for the head esp. with a visor and no brim; *also* : something resembling such a covering esp. on a tip, knob or end ⟨a bottle ~⟩ **2** : a container holding an explosive charge (as for a toy gun) **3** : an upper limit (as on expenditures)

[2]**cap** *vb* **capped**; **cap·ping** **1** : to provide or protect with a cap **2** : to form a cap over : CROWN ⟨snow-*capped* mountains⟩ **3** : OUTDO, SURPASS **4** : to bring to a conclusion ⟨~ off dinner with coffee⟩

[3]**cap** *abbr* **1** capacity **2** capital **3** capitalize; capitalized

CAP *abbr* Civil Air Patrol

ca·pa·ble \ˈkā-pə-bəl\ *adj* : having ability, capacity, or power to do something : ABLE, COMPETENT — **ca·pa·bil·i·ty** \ˌkā-pə-ˈbi-lə-tē\ *n* — **ca·pa·bly** *adv*

ca·pa·cious \kə-ˈpā-shəs\ *adj* : able to contain much — **ca·pa·cious·ly** *adv* — **ca·pa·cious·ness** *n*

ca·pac·i·tance \kə-ˈpa-sə-təns\ *n* : the property of an electric nonconductor that permits the storage of energy

ca·pac·i·tor \kə-ˈpa-sə-tər\ *n* : an electronic circuit device for temporary storage of electrical energy

[1]**ca·pac·i·ty** \kə-ˈpa-sə-tē\ *n, pl* **-ties** **1** : legal qualification or fitness ⟨~ to stand trial⟩ **2** : the ability to contain, receive, or accommodate ⟨seating ~⟩ **3** : the maximum amount or number that can be contained — see METRIC SYSTEM table, WEIGHT table **4** : ABILITY **5** : position or character assigned or assumed

[2]**capacity** *adj* : equaling maximum capacity ⟨a ~ crowd⟩

cap–a–pie *or* **cap–à–pie** \ˌka-pə-ˈpē\ *adv* [MF] : from head to foot : at all points

ca·par·i·son \kə-ˈpar-ə-sən\ *n* **1** : an ornamental covering for a horse **2** : TRAPPINGS, ADORNMENT — **caparison** *vb*

[1]**cape** \ˈkāp\ *n* **1** : a point of land jutting out into water **2** *often cap* : CAPE COD COTTAGE

[2]**cape** *n* : a sleeveless garment hanging

from the neck over the shoulders — **caped** *adj*

Cape Cod cottage \ˈkāp-ˈkäd-\ *n* : a compact rectangular dwelling of one or one-and-a-half stories usu. with a steep gable roof

[1]**ca·per** \ˈkā-pər\ *n* : the greenish flower bud or young berry of a Mediterranean shrub pickled for use as a relish; *also* : this shrub

[2]**caper** *vb* **ca·pered**; **ca·per·ing** : to leap about in a playful manner

[3]**caper** *n* **1** : a frolicsome leap **2** : a capricious escapade **3** : an illegal or questionable act

cape·skin \ˈkāp-ˌskin\ *n* : a light flexible leather made from sheepskins

cap·ful \ˈkap-ˌfu̇l\ *n, pl* **cap·fuls** *also* **caps·ful** \ˈkaps-\ : as much as a cap will hold

cap·il·lar·i·ty \ˌka-pə-ˈlar-ə-tē\ *n, pl* **-ties** : the action by which the surface of a liquid where it is in contact with a solid (as in a slender tube) is raised or lowered depending on the relative attraction of the molecules of the liquid for each other and for those of the solid

[1]**cap·il·lary** \ˈka-pə-ˌler-ē\ *adj* **1** : resembling a hair **2** : having a very small bore ⟨~ tube⟩ **3** : of or relating to capillaries or to capillarity

[2]**capillary** *n, pl* **-lar·ies** : any of the tiny thin-walled blood vessels that carry blood between the smallest arteries and their corresponding veins

[1]**cap·i·tal** \ˈka-pət-ᵊl\ *n* : the top part or piece of an architectural column

[2]**capital** *adj* **1** : conforming to the series A, B, C rather than a, b, c ⟨~ letters⟩ ⟨~ G⟩ **2** : punishable by death ⟨a ~ crime⟩ **3** : most serious ⟨a ~ error⟩ **4** : first in importance or position : CHIEF; *also* : being the seat of government ⟨the ~ city⟩ **5** : of or relating to capital ⟨~ expenditures⟩; *esp* : relating to or being assets that add to the long-term net worth of a corporation **6** : FIRST-RATE, EXCELLENT

[3]**capital** *n* **1** : accumulated wealth esp. as used to produce more wealth **2** : the total face value of shares of stock issued by a company **3** : persons holding capital **4** : ADVANTAGE, GAIN **5** : a letter larger than the ordinary small letter and often different in form **6** : the capital city of a state, province, or country; *also* : a city preeminent in some activity

capital gain *n* : the increase in value of an asset (as stock or real estate) between the time it is bought and the time it is sold

capital goods *n pl* : machinery, tools, factories, and commodities used in the production of goods

cap·i·tal·ise *Brit var of* CAPITALIZE

cap·i·tal·ism \ˈka-pət-ᵊl-ˌi-zəm\ *n* : an economic system characterized by private or corporate ownership of capital goods and by prices, production, and distribution of goods that are determined mainly by competition in a free market

[1]**cap·i·tal·ist** \-ist\ *n* **1** : a person who has capital esp. invested in business **2** : a person of great wealth : PLUTOCRAT **3** : a believer in capitalism

[2]**capitalist** *or* **cap·i·tal·is·tic** \ˌka-pət-ᵊl-ˈis-tik\ *adj* **1** : owning capital **2** : practicing or advocating capitalism **3** : marked by capitalism — **cap·i·tal·is·ti·cal·ly** \-ti-k(ə-)lē\ *adv*

cap·i·tal·iza·tion \ˌka-pət-ᵊl-ə-ˈzā-shən\ *n* **1** : the act or process of capitalizing **2** : the total amount of money used as capital in a business

cap·i·tal·ize \ˈka-pət-ᵊl-ˌīz\ *vb* **-ized**; **-iz·ing** **1** : to write or print with an initial capital or in capitals **2** : to convert into or use as capital **3** : to supply capital for **4** : to gain by turning something to advantage : PROFIT

cap·i·tal·ly \ˈka-pət-ᵊl-ē\ *adv* : ADMIRABLY, EXCELLENTLY

cap·i·ta·tion \ˌka-pə-ˈtā-shən\ *n* : a direct uniform tax levied on each person

cap·i·tol \ˈka-pət-ᵊl\ *n* : the building in which a legislature holds its sessions

ca·pit·u·late \kə-ˈpi-chə-ˌlāt\ *vb* **-lat·ed**; **-lat·ing** **1** : to surrender esp. on conditions agreed upon **2** : to cease resisting : ACQUIESCE ♦ ***Synonyms*** SUBMIT, YIELD, SUCCUMB, CAVE, DEFER — **ca·pit·u·la·tion** \-ˌpi-chə-ˈlā-shən\ *n*

cap·let \ˈka-plət\ *n* : a capsule-shaped medicinal tablet

ca·pon \ˈkā-ˌpän, -pən\ *n* : a castrated male chicken

cap·puc·ci·no \ˌka-pə-ˈchē-nō, ˌkä-\ *n* [It, lit., Capuchin; fr. the likeness of its color to that of a Capuchin's habit] : espresso mixed with foamy hot milk or cream and often flavored with cinnamon

ca·pric·cio \kə-ˈprē-chē-ˌō, -chō\ *n, pl* **-cios** [It, lit., whim, prank] : an instrumental piece in free form usu. lively in tempo and brilliant in style

ca·price \kə-ˈprēs\ *n* [F, fr. It *capriccio*] **1** : a sudden whim or fancy **2** : an inclination to do things impulsively **3** : CAPRICCIO — **ca·pri·cious** \-ˈpri-shəs\ *adj* — **ca·pri·cious·ly** *adv* — **ca·pri·cious·ness** *n*

Cap·ri·corn \ˈka-pri-ˌkȯrn\ *n* **1** : a zodiacal constellation between Sagittarius and Aquarius usu. pictured as a goat **2** : the 10th sign of the zodiac in astrology; *also* : one born under this sign

cap·ri·ole \ˈka-prē-ˌōl\ *n* : [3]CAPER 1; *also* : an upward leap of a horse with a backward kick at the height of the leap — **capriole** *vb*

caps *abbr* **1** capitals **2** capsule

cap·sa·i·cin \kap-ˈsā-ə-sən\ *n* : a colorless compound found in various capsicums that gives hot peppers their hotness

cap·si·cum \ˈkap-si-kəm\ *n* : PEPPER 2

cap·size \ˈkap-ˌsīz, kap-ˈsīz\ *vb* **cap·sized**; **cap·siz·ing** : UPSET, OVERTURN

cap·stan \ˈkap-stən, -ˌstan\ *n* **1** : a machine for moving or raising heavy weights that consists of a vertical drum which can be rotated and around which cable is turned **2** : a rotating shaft that drives recorder tape

cap·su·lar \ˈkap-sə-lər\ *adj* : of, relating to, or resembling a capsule

cap•su•lat•ed \-ˌlā-təd\ *adj* : enclosed in a capsule

[1]**cap•sule** \ˈkap-səl, -sül\ *n* **1** : a membrane or sac enclosing a body part (as of a joint) **2** : a case bearing spores or seeds **3** : a shell usu. of gelatin that is used for packaging something (as a drug); *also* : such a shell together with its contents **4** : a small pressurized compartment or vehicle (as for space flight)

[2]**capsule** *adj* **1** : very brief ⟨a ~ biography⟩ **2** : very compact ⟨a ~ camera⟩

Capt *abbr* captain

[1]**cap•tain** \ˈkap-tən\ *n* **1** : a commander of a body of troops **2** : a commissioned officer in the army, air force, or marine corps ranking next below a major **3** : an officer in charge of a ship **4** : a commissioned officer in the navy ranking next below a rear admiral or a commodore **5** : a leader of a side or team **6** : a dominant figure — **cap•tain•cy** *n*

[2]**captain** *vb* : to be captain of : LEAD

cap•tion \ˈkap-shən\ *n* **1** : a heading esp. of an article or document : TITLE **2** : the explanatory matter accompanying an illustration **3** : a motion-picture subtitle — **caption** *vb*

cap•tious \ˈkap-shəs\ *adj* : marked by an inclination to find fault — **cap•tious•ly** *adv* — **cap•tious•ness** *n*

cap•ti•vate \ˈkap-tə-ˌvāt\ *vb* **-vat•ed**; **-vat•ing** : to attract and hold irresistibly by some special charm or art — **cap•ti•va•tion** \ˌkap-tə-ˈvā-shən\ *n* — **cap•ti•va•tor** \ˈkap-tə-ˌvā-tər\ *n*

cap•tive \ˈkap-tiv\ *adj* **1** : made prisoner esp. in war **2** : kept within bounds : CONFINED **3** : held under control — **captive** *n* — **cap•tiv•i•ty** \kap-ˈti-və-tē\ *n*

cap•tor \ˈkap-tər\ *n* : one that captures

[1]**cap•ture** \ˈkap-chər\ *n* **1** : the act of capturing **2** : one that has been captured

[2]**capture** *vb* **cap•tured**; **cap•tur•ing** **1** : to take captive : WIN, GAIN ⟨~ the crown⟩ **2** : to preserve in a relatively permanent form ⟨~ the moment on film⟩

Ca•pu•chin \ˈka-pyə-shən\ *n* : a member of an austere branch of the order of St. Francis of Assisi engaged in missionary work and preaching

car \ˈkär\ *n* **1** : a vehicle moving on wheels **2** : the compartment of an elevator **3** : the part of a balloon or airship that carries passengers or equipment

car•a•cole \ˈkar-ə-ˌkōl\ *n* : a half turn to right or left executed by a mounted horse — **caracole** *vb*

car•a•cul \ˈkar-ə-ˌkəl\ *n* : the pelt of a karakul lamb after the curl begins to loosen

ca•rafe \kə-ˈraf, -ˈräf\ *n* **1** : a bottle with a flaring lip used esp. to hold wine **2** : a usu. glass pitcher for pouring coffee

car•am•bo•la \ˌkar-əm-ˈbō-lə\ *n* **1** : a 5-angled green to yellow edible tropical fruit of star-shaped cross section **2** : a tropical Asian tree widely cultivated for carambolas

car•a•mel \ˈkar-ə-məl, ˈkär-məl\ *n* **1** : an amorphous substance obtained by heating sugar and used for flavoring and coloring **2** : a firm chewy candy

car•a•pace \ˈkar-ə-ˌpās\ *n* : a protective case or shell on the back of some animals (as turtles or crabs)

[1]**carat** *var of* KARAT

[2]**car•at** \ˈkar-ət\ *n* : a unit of weight for precious stones equal to 200 milligrams

car•a•van \ˈkar-ə-ˌvan\ *n* **1** : a group of travelers journeying together through desert or hostile regions **2** : a group of vehicles traveling in a file

car•a•van•sa•ry \ˌkar-ə-ˈvan-sə-rē\ *or* **car•a•van•se•rai** \-sə-ˌrī\ *n, pl* **-ries** *or* **-rais** *or* **-rai** [Pers *kārvānsarāī*, fr. *kārvān* caravan + *sarāī* palace, inn] **1** : an inn in eastern countries where caravans rest at night **2** : HOTEL, INN

car•a•vel \ˈkar-ə-ˌvel\ *n* : a small 15th and 16th century ship with a broad bow, high narrow poop, and usu. three masts

car•a•way \ˈkar-ə-ˌwā\ *n* : an aromatic herb related to the carrot with fruits (**caraway seed**) used in seasoning and medicine; *also* : its fruit

car•bide \ˈkär-ˌbīd\ *n* : a compound of carbon with another element

car•bine \ˈkär-ˌbēn, -ˌbīn\ *n* : a short-barreled lightweight rifle

car•bo•hy•drate \ˌkär-bō-ˈhī-ˌdrāt, -drət\ *n* : any of various compounds composed of carbon, hydrogen, and oxygen (as sugars and starches)

car•bol•ic acid \ˌkär-ˈbä-lik-\ *n* : PHENOL

car•bon \ˈkär-bən\ *n* **1** : a nonmetallic chemical element occurring in nature esp. as diamond and graphite and as a constituent of coal, petroleum, and limestone **2** : a sheet of carbon paper; *also* : CARBON COPY 1 — **car•bon•less** \-ləs\ *adj*

car•bo•na•ceous \ˌkär-bə-ˈnā-shəs\ *adj* : relating to, containing, or composed of carbon

[1]**car•bon•ate** \ˈkär-bə-ˌnāt, -nət\ *n* : a salt or ester of carbonic acid

[2]**car•bon•ate** \-ˌnāt\ *vb* **-at•ed**; **-at•ing** : to combine or infuse with carbon dioxide ⟨*carbonated* beverages⟩ — **car•bon•ation** \ˌkär-bə-ˈnā-shən\ *n*

carbon black *n* : any of various black substances consisting chiefly of carbon and used esp. as pigments

carbon copy *n* **1** : a copy made by carbon paper **2** : DUPLICATE

carbon dating *n* : the determination of the age of old material (as an archaeological specimen) by its content of carbon 14

carbon di•ox•ide \(ˌ)dī-ˈäk-ˌsīd\ *n* : a heavy colorless gas that does not support combustion and is formed in animal respiration and in the combustion and decomposition of organic substances

carbon footprint *n* : the amount of carbon dioxide emitted by something in a given period

carbon 14 *n* : a heavy radioactive form of carbon used esp. in dating old materials (as archaeological specimens)

car•bon•ic acid \kär-ˈbä-nik-\ *n* : a weak

acid that decomposes readily into water and carbon dioxide
car·bon·if·er·ous \ˌkär-bə-ˈni-fə-rəs\ *adj* **1** : producing or containing carbon or coal **2** *cap* : of, relating to, or being the period of the Paleozoic era between the Devonian and the Permian — **Carboniferous** *n*
carbon monoxide *n* : a colorless odorless very poisonous gas formed by the incomplete burning of carbon
carbon paper *n* : a thin paper coated with a pigment and used for making copies
carbon tet·ra·chlo·ride \-ˌte-trə-ˈklōr-ˌīd\ *n* : a colorless nonflammable toxic liquid used esp. as a solvent
carbon 12 *n* : the most abundant isotope of carbon having a nucleus of 6 protons and 6 neutrons and used as a standard for measurements of atomic weight
car·boy \ˈkär-ˌbȯi\ *n* [Pers *qarāba,* fr. Ar *qarrāba* demijohn] : a large container for liquids
car·bun·cle \ˈkär-ˌbəŋ-kəl\ *n* : a painful inflammation of the skin and underlying tissue that discharges pus from several openings
car·bu·re·tor \ˈkär-bə-ˌrā-tər, -byə-\ *n* : an apparatus for premixing vaporized fuel and air and supplying the mixture to an internal combustion engine
car·bu·ret·tor *also* **car·bu·ret·ter** \ˌkär-byə-ˈre-tər, ˈkär-byə-ˌ\ *chiefly Brit var of* CARBURETOR
car·case *Brit var of* CARCASS
car·cass \ˈkär-kəs\ *n* : a dead body; *esp* : one of an animal dressed for food
car·cin·o·gen \kär-ˈsi-nə-jən\ *n* : a substance or agent causing cancer — **car·ci·no·gen·ic** \ˌkärs-ᵊn-ō-ˈje-nik\ *adj* — **car·ci·no·ge·nic·i·ty** \-jə-ˈni-sə-tē\ *n*
car·ci·no·ma \ˌkärs-ᵊn-ˈō-mə\ *n, pl* **-mas** *also* **-ma·ta** \-tə\ : a malignant tumor of epithelial origin — **car·ci·no·ma·tous** \-təs\ *adj*
[1]**card** \ˈkärd\ *vb* : to comb with a card : cleanse and untangle before spinning ⟨~*ed* cotton⟩ — **card·er** *n*
[2]**card** *n* : an instrument for combing fibers (as wool or cotton)
[3]**card** *n* **1** : PLAYING CARD **2** *pl* : a game played with playing cards; *also* : card playing **3** : an emotional issue used to one's advantage (as in a political campaign) **4** : a usu. clownishly amusing person : WAG **5** : a flat stiff usu. small piece of paper, cardboard, or plastic often bearing pictures or information **6** : PROGRAM; *esp* : a sports program — **in the cards** : INEVITABLE
[4]**card** *vb* **1** : to list or schedule on a card **2** : SCORE **3** : to ask for identification (as at a bar)
[5]**card** *abbr* cardinal
car·da·mom \ˈkär-də-məm\ *n* : the aromatic capsular fruit of an Indian herb related to the ginger whose seeds are used as a spice or condiment and in medicine; *also* : this plant
card·board \ˈkärd-ˌbōrd\ *n* : a material thicker than paper and made from cellulose fiber
card–car·ry·ing \ˈkärd-ˌkar-ē-iŋ\ *adj* : being a regularly enrolled member of an organization (as a political party)
card catalog *n* : a catalog (as of books) in which the entries are arranged systematically on cards
car·di·ac \ˈkär-dē-ˌak\ *adj* [L *cardiacus,* fr. Gk *kardiakos,* fr. *kardia* heart] **1** : of, relating to, or located near the heart **2** : of, relating to, or affected with heart disease ⟨~ patients⟩
car·di·gan \ˈkär-di-gən\ *n* : a sweater or jacket usu. without a collar and with a full-length opening in the front
[1]**car·di·nal** \ˈkärd-nəl, ˈkär-dᵊn-əl\ *n* **1** : an ecclesiastical official of the Roman Catholic Church ranking next below the pope **2** : a crested No. American finch that is nearly completely red in the male
[2]**cardinal** *adj* [ME, fr. LL *cardinalis,* fr. L serving as a hinge, fr. *cardo* hinge] **1** : of basic importance : CHIEF, MAIN, PRIMARY ⟨a ~ principle⟩ **2** : very serious ⟨a ~ sin⟩ — **car·di·nal·ly** *adv*
car·di·nal·ate \ˈkärd-nə-lət, -ˈkär-dᵊn-ə-let, -ˌlāt\ *n* : the office, rank, or dignity of a cardinal
cardinal flower *n* : a No. American plant that bears a spike of brilliant red flowers
cardinal number *n* : a number (as 1, 5, 82, 357) that is used in simple counting and answers the question "how many?" — compare ORDINAL NUMBER
cardinal point *n* : one of the four principal compass points north, south, east, and west
car·dio \ˈkär-dē-ō\ *adj* : CARDIOVASCULAR 2
car·di·ol·o·gy \ˌkär-dē-ˈä-lə-jē\ *n* : the study of the heart and its action and diseases — **car·di·ol·o·gist** \-jist\ *n*
car·dio·pul·mo·nary resuscitation \ˌkär-dē-ō-ˈpu̇l-mə-ˌner-ē-\ *n* : a procedure to restore normal breathing after cardiac arrest that includes the clearance of air passages to the lungs, mouth-to-mouth method of artificial respiration, and heart massage by the exertion of pressure on the chest
car·dio·vas·cu·lar \-ˈvas-kyə-lər\ *adj* **1** : of or relating to the heart and blood vessels **2** : causing a temporary increase in heart rate ⟨a ~ workout⟩
card·sharp \-ˌshärp\ *or* **card·sharp·er** \ˈkärd-ˌshär-pər\ *n* : a cheater at cards
[1]**care** \ˈker\ *n* **1** : a disquieted state of uncertainty and responsibility : ANXIETY **2** : watchful attention : HEED **3** : CHARGE, SUPERVISION ⟨under a doctor's ~⟩ **4** : a person or thing that is an object of anxiety or solicitude
[2]**care** *vb* **cared; car·ing** **1** : to feel anxiety **2** : to feel interest **3** : to give care **4** : to have a liking, fondness, taste, or inclination **5** : to be concerned about ⟨~ what happens⟩
CARE *abbr* Cooperative for American Relief to Everywhere
ca·reen \kə-ˈrēn\ *vb* **1** : to put (a ship or

boat) on a beach esp. in order to clean or repair its hull **2** : to sway from side to side **3** : CAREER

[1]**ca·reer** \kə-ˈrir\ *n* [MF *carrière,* fr. Old Occitan *carriera* street, fr. ML *carraria* road for vehicles, fr. L *carrus* car] **1** : COURSE, PASSAGE; *also* : speed in a course ⟨ran at full ~⟩ **2** : an occupation or profession followed as a life's work

[2]**career** *vb* : to go at top speed esp. in a headlong manner

care·free \ˈker-ˌfrē\ *adj* : free from care or worry

care·ful \-fəl\ *adj* **care·ful·ler; care·ful·lest** **1** : using or taking care : VIGILANT **2** : marked by solicitude, caution, or prudence — **care·ful·ly** *adv* — **care·ful·ness** *n*

care·giv·er \-ˌgi-vər\ *n* : a person who provides direct care (as for children, elderly people, or the chronically ill)

care·less \-ləs\ *adj* **1** : free from care : UNTROUBLED **2** : UNCONCERNED, INDIFFERENT ⟨~ of the consequences⟩ **3** : not taking care **4** : not showing or receiving care — **care·less·ly** *adv* — **care·less·ness** *n*

care package *n* : a package of useful or pleasurable items given as a gift to another

[1]**ca·ress** \kə-ˈres\ *vb* : to touch or stroke tenderly or lovingly — **ca·ress·er** *n*

[2]**caress** *n* : a tender or loving touch or embrace

car·et \ˈker-ət\ *n* [L, there is lacking, fr. *carēre* to lack, be without] : a mark ^ used to indicate the place where something is to be inserted

care·tak·er \ˈker-ˌtā-kər\ *n* **1** : one in charge usu. as occupant in place of an absent owner **2** : one temporarily fulfilling the functions of an office

care·worn \-ˌwōrn\ *adj* : showing the effects of grief or anxiety

car·fare \ˈkär-ˌfer\ *n* : passenger fare (as on a streetcar or bus)

car·go \ˈkär-gō\ *n, pl* **cargoes** *or* **cargos** : the goods carried in a ship, airplane, or vehicle : FREIGHT

Ca·rib·be·an \ˌker-ə-ˈbē-ən, kə-ˈri-bē-ən\ *adj* : of or relating to the eastern and southern West Indies or the Caribbean Sea

car·i·bou \ˈker-ə-ˌbü\ *n, pl* **caribou** *or* **caribous** : a large circumpolar gregarious deer of northern taiga and tundra that usu. has large branched antlers usu. in both sexes — used esp. for one of the New World

car·i·ca·ture \ˈker-i-kə-ˌchu̇r\ *n* **1** : distorted representation to produce a ridiculous effect **2** : a representation esp. in literature or art having the qualities of caricature — **caricature** *vb* — **car·i·ca·tur·ist** \-ist\ *n*

car·ies \ˈker-ēz\ *n, pl* **caries** : tooth decay

car·il·lon \ˈker-ə-ˌlän\ *n* : a set of tuned bells sounded by hammers controlled from a keyboard

car·i·ous \ˈker-ē-əs\ *adj* : affected with caries

car·jack·ing \ˈkär-ˌja-kiŋ\ *n* : the theft of an automobile by force or intimidation — **car·jack·er** *n*

car·load \ˈkär-ˌlōd\ *n* : a load that fills a car

car·mi·na·tive \kär-ˈmi-nə-tiv\ *adj* : expelling gas from the stomach or intestines — **carminative** *n*

car·mine \ˈkär-mən, -ˌmīn\ *n* : a vivid red

car·nage \ˈkär-nij\ *n* : great destruction of life : SLAUGHTER

car·nal \ˈkär-nᵊl\ *adj* [ME, fr. LL *carnalis,* fr. L *carn-, caro* flesh] **1** : of or relating to the body **2** : relating to or given to sensual pleasures and appetites — **car·nal·i·ty** \kär-ˈna-lə-tē\ *n* — **car·nal·ly** *adv*

car·na·tion \kär-ˈnā-shən\ *n* : a cultivated pink of any of numerous usu. double-flowered varieties derived from an Old World species

car·nau·ba wax \kär-ˈnȯ-bə-, -ˈnau̇-; ˌkär-nə-ˈü-bə-\ *n* : a brittle yellowish wax from a Brazilian palm that is used esp. in polishes

car·ne·lian \kär-ˈnēl-yən\ *n* : a hard red chalcedony used as a gem

car·ni·val \ˈkär-nə-vəl\ *n* [It *carnevale,* alter. of *carnelevare,* lit., removal of meat] **1** : a festival of merrymaking just before Lent **2** : a boisterous merrymaking **3** : a traveling enterprise offering amusements **4** : an organized program of entertainment

car·ni·val·esque \ˌkär-nə-və-ˈlesk\ *adj* : suggestive of a carnival

car·niv·o·ra \kär-ˈni-və-rə\ *n pl* : carnivorous mammals

car·ni·vore \ˈkär-nə-ˌvȯr\ *n* : a flesh-eating animal; *esp* : any of an order of mammals (as dogs, cats, bears, minks, and seals) feeding mostly on animal flesh

car·niv·o·rous \kär-ˈni-və-rəs\ *adj* **1** : feeding on animal tissues **2** : of or relating to the carnivores — **car·niv·o·rous·ly** *adv* — **car·niv·o·rous·ness** *n*

car·ny *or* **car·ney** *or* **car·nie** \ˈkär-nē\ *n, pl* **carnies** *or* **carneys** **1** : CARNIVAL 3 **2** : one who works with a carnival

car·ol \ˈker-əl\ *n* : a song of joy or devotion — **carol** *vb* — **car·ol·er** *or* **car·ol·ler** *n*

car·om \ˈker-əm\ *n* **1** : a shot in billiards in which the cue ball strikes two other balls **2** : a rebounding esp. at an angle — **carom** *vb*

car·o·tene \ˈker-ə-ˌtēn\ *n* : any of several orange to red pigments (as beta-carotene) formed esp. in plants and used as a source of vitamin A

ca·rot·en·oid \kə-ˈrä-tə-ˌnȯid\ *n* : any of various usu. yellow to red pigments (as carotenes) found widely in plants and animals

ca·rot·id \kə-ˈrä-təd\ *adj* : of, relating to, or being the chief artery or pair of arteries that pass up the neck and supply the head — **carotid** *n*

ca·rous·al \kə-ˈrau̇-zəl\ *n* : CAROUSE

ca·rouse \kə-ˈrau̇z\ *n* [MF *carrousse,* fr. *carous,* adv., all out (in *boire carous* to

empty the cup), fr. G *garaus*] : a drunken revel — **carouse** *vb* — **ca·rous·er** *n*
car·ou·sel *also* **car·rou·sel** \ˌker-ə-ˈsel, ˈkar-ə-ˌsel\ *n* **1** : MERRY-GO-ROUND **2** : a circular conveyor ⟨a baggage ~⟩
[1]**carp** \ˈkärp\ *vb* : to find fault : CAVIL, COMPLAIN — **carp** *n* — **carp·er** *n*
[2]**carp** *n, pl* **carp** *or* **carps** : a large variable Asian freshwater fish of sluggish waters often raised for food
[1]**car·pal** \ˈkär-pəl\ *adj* : of or relating to the wrist or the bones of the wrist
[2]**carpal** *n* : a carpal element or bone
carpal tunnel syndrome *n* : a condition characterized esp. by weakness, pain, and disturbances of sensation (as numbness) in the hand and fingers and caused by compression of a nerve in the wrist
car·pe di·em \ˈkär-pe-ˈdē-ˌem, -ˈdī-\ *n* [L, lit., pluck the day] : enjoyment of the present without concern for the future
car·pel \ˈkär-pəl\ *n* : one of the highly modified leaves that together form the ovary of a flower of a seed plant
car·pen·ter \ˈkär-pən-tər\ *n* : one who builds or repairs wooden structures — **carpenter** *vb* — **car·pen·try** \-trē\ *n*
car·pet \ˈkär-pət\ *n* : a heavy fabric used as a floor covering — **carpet** *vb*
car·pet·bag \-ˌbag\ *n* : a traveling bag common in the 19th century
car·pet·bag·ger \-ˌba-gər\ *n* **1** : a Northerner in the South after the American Civil War usu. seeking private gain under the reconstruction governments **2** : outsider
car·pet·ing \ˈkär-pə-tiŋ\ *n* : material for carpets; *also* : CARPETS
car pool *n* : an arrangement in which a group of people commute together by car; *also* : a group having this arrangement — **car·pool** \-ˌpül\ *vb*
car·port \ˈkär-ˌpȯrt\ *n* : an open-sided automobile shelter
car·pus \ˈkär-pəs\ *n* : the wrist or its bones
car·ra·geen·an *or* **car·ra·geen·in** \ˌker-ə-ˈgē-nən\ *n* : a colloid extracted esp. from a dark purple branching seaweed and used in foods esp. to stabilize and thicken them
car·rel \ˈker-əl\ *n* : a table often partitioned or enclosed for individual study in a library
car·riage \ˈker-ij\ *n* **1** : the act of carrying **2** : manner of holding the body **3** : a wheeled vehicle **4** *Brit* : a railway passenger coach **5** : a movable part of a machine for supporting some other moving part ⟨a typewriter ~⟩
carriage trade *n* : trade from well-to-do or upper-class people
car·ri·er \ˈker-ē-ər\ *n* **1** : one that carries **2** : a person or organization in the transportation business **3** : AIRCRAFT CARRIER **4** : one whose system carries the causative agents of a disease but who is immune to the disease **5** : an individual having a gene for a trait or condition that is not expressed outwardly **6** : an electromagnetic wave whose amplitude or frequency is varied in order to convey a radio or television signal
carrier pigeon *n* : a pigeon used esp. to carry messages
car·ri·on \ˈker-ē-ən\ *n* : dead and decaying flesh
car·rot \ˈker-ət\ *n* : the elongated usu. orange root of a common garden plant that is eaten as a vegetable; *also* : this plant
carrousel *var of* CAROUSEL
[1]**car·ry** \ˈka-rē, ˈker-ē\ *vb* **car·ried**; **car·ry·ing** [ME *carien,* fr. AF *carier,* fr. *carre* vehicle, fr. L *carrus*] **1** : to move while supporting : TRANSPORT, CONVEY, TAKE **2** : to influence by mental or emotional appeal **3** : to get possession or control of : CAPTURE, WIN **4** : to transfer from one place (as a column) to another ⟨~ a number in adding⟩ **5** : to have or wear on one's person; *also* : to bear within one **6** : INVOLVE, IMPLY **7** : to hold or bear (oneself) in a specified way **8** : to keep in stock for sale **9** : to sustain the weight or burden of : SUPPORT **10** : to prolong in space, time, or degree **11** : to keep on one's books as a debtor **12** : to succeed in (an election) **13** : to win adoption (as in a legislature) **14** : PUBLISH, PRINT **15** : to reach or penetrate to a distance ⟨voices ~ well over water⟩
[2]**carry** *n* **1** : the range of a gun or projectile or of a struck or thrown ball **2** : PORTAGE **3** : an act or method of carrying ⟨fireman's ~⟩
car·ry·all \-ˌȯl\ *n* : a capacious bag or case
carry away *vb* : to arouse to a high and often excessive degree of emotion
carrying charge *n* : a charge added to the price of merchandise sold on the installment plan
car·ry–on \-ˌȯn, -ˌän\ *n* : a piece of luggage suitable for being carried aboard an airplane by a passenger — **carry–on** *adj*
carry on *vb* **1** : CONDUCT, MANAGE **2** : to behave in a foolish, excited, or improper manner **3** : to continue in spite of hindrance or discouragement
carry out *vb* **1** : to bring to a successful conclusion **2** : to put into execution
car·sick \ˈkär-ˌsik\ *adj* : affected with motion sickness esp. in an automobile — **car sickness** *n*
[1]**cart** \ˈkärt\ *n* **1** : a heavy 2-wheeled wagon **2** : a small wheeled vehicle
[2]**cart** *vb* : to convey in or as if in a cart — **cart·er** *n*
cart·age \ˈkär-tij\ *n* : the act of or rate charged for carting
carte blanche \ˈkärt-ˈblä^{n}sh\ *n, pl* **cartes blanches** *same or* -ˈblä^{n}-shəz\ [F, lit., blank document] : full discretionary power
car·tel \kär-ˈtel\ *n* : a combination of independent business enterprises designed to limit competition ♦ ***Synonyms*** POOL, SYNDICATE, MONOPOLY, TRUST
car·ti·lage \ˈkär-tə-lij\ *n* : a usu. translucent somewhat elastic tissue that composes most of the skeleton of young vertebrate embryos and later is mostly converted to bone in higher vertebrates

— **car·ti·lag·i·nous** \ˌkär-tə-ˈla-jə-nəs\ *adj*
cartilaginous fish *n* : any of a class of fishes (as a shark or ray) having the skeleton wholly or largely composed of cartilage
car·tog·ra·phy \kär-ˈtä-grə-fē\ *n* : the making of maps — **car·tog·ra·pher** *n* — **car·to·graph·ic** \ˌkär-tə-ˈgra-fik\ *adj*
car·ton \ˈkär-tᵊn\ *n* : a cardboard box or container
car·toon \kär-ˈtün\ *n* **1** : a preparatory sketch (as for a painting) **2** : a drawing intended as humor, caricature, or satire **3** : COMIC STRIP — **cartoon** *vb* — **car·toon·ist** *n*
car·tridge \ˈkär-trij\ *n* **1** : a tube containing a complete charge for a firearm **2** : a container of material for insertion into an apparatus **3** : a small case containing a phonograph needle and transducer that is attached to a tonearm **4** : a case containing a magnetic tape or disk **5** : a case for holding integrated circuits containing a computer program
cart·wheel \ˈkärt-ˌhwēl\ *n* **1** : a large coin (as a silver dollar) **2** : a lateral handspring with arms and legs extended
carve \kärv\ *vb* **carved**; **carv·ing** **1** : to cut with care or precision : shape by cutting **2** : to cut into pieces or slices **3** : to slice and serve meat at table — **carv·er** *n*
cary·at·id \ˌker-ē-ˈa-təd\ *n, pl* **-ids** *or* **-i·des** \-ˈa-tə-ˌdēz\ : a sculptured draped female figure used as an architectural column
CAS *abbr* certificate of advanced study
ca·sa·ba \kə-ˈsä-bə\ *n* : any of several muskmelons with a yellow rind and sweet flesh
[1]**cas·cade** \ˌkas-ˈkād\ *n* **1** : a steep usu. small waterfall **2** : something arranged in a series or succession of stages so that each stage derives from or acts upon the product of the preceding
[2]**cas·cade** *vb* **cas·cad·ed**; **cas·cad·ing** : to fall, pass, or connect in or as if in a cascade ⟨water *cascaded* over the rocks⟩
cas·cara \ka-ˈska-rə\ *n* : the dried bark of a small Pacific coastal tree of the U.S. and southern Canada used as a laxative; *also* : this tree
[1]**case** \ˈkās\ *n* [ME *cas,* fr. AF, fr. L *casus* fall, chance, fr. *cadere* to fall] **1** : a particular instance or situation **2** : an inflectional form of a noun, pronoun, or adjective indicating its grammatical relation to other words; *also* : such a relation whether indicated by inflection or not **3** : what actually exists or happens : FACT **4** : a suit or action in law : CAUSE **5** : a convincing argument **6** : an instance of disease or injury; *also* : PATIENT **7** : INSTANCE, EXAMPLE — **in case** : as a precaution — **in case of** : in the event of
[2]**case** *n* [ME *cas,* fr. AF *case, chase,* fr. L *capsa*] **1** : a box or container for holding something; *also* : a box with its contents **2** : an outer covering **3** : a divided tray for holding printing type **4** : CASING 2
[3]**case** *vb* **cased**; **cas·ing** **1** : to enclose in or cover with a case **2** : to inspect esp. with intent to rob
ca·sein \ˈkā-ˌsēn, kā-ˈ\ *n* : any of several phosphorus-containing proteins occurring in or produced from milk
case·ment \ˈkās-mənt\ *n* : a window that opens like a door
case·work \-ˌwərk\ *n* : social work that involves the individual person or family — **case·work·er** *n*
[1]**cash** \ˈkash\ *n* [MF or It; MF *casse* money box, fr. It *cassa,* fr. L *capsa* chest, case] **1** : ready money **2** : money or its equivalent paid at the time of purchase or delivery
[2]**cash** *vb* : to pay or obtain cash for
ca·shew \ˈka-shü, kə-ˈshü\ *n* : an edible kidney-shaped nut of a tropical American tree related to the sumacs; *also* : this tree
[1]**ca·shier** \ka-ˈshir\ *vb* : to dismiss from service; *esp* : to dismiss in disgrace
[2]**cash·ier** \ka-ˈshir\ *n* **1** : a bank official responsible for moneys received and paid out **2** : a person who receives and records payments
cashier's check *n* : a check drawn by a bank upon its own funds and signed by its cashier
cash in *vb* **1** : to convert into cash ⟨*cash in* bonds⟩ **2** : to settle accounts and withdraw from a gambling game or business deal **3** : to obtain financial profit or advantage
cash·less \ˈkash-ləs\ *adj* : relying on monetary transactions that use electronic means rather than cash
cash·mere \ˈkazh-ˌmir, ˈkash-\ *n* : fine wool from the undercoat of an Indian goat (**cashmere goat**) or a yarn spun of this; *also* : a soft twilled fabric orig. woven from this yarn
cash out *vb* : to convert noncash assets into cash
cash register *n* : a business machine that usu. has a money drawer, indicates each sale, and records the money received
cash–strapped \ˈkash-ˌstrapt\ *adj* : lacking sufficient money
cas·ing \ˈkā-siŋ\ *n* **1** : something that encases **2** : the frame of a door or window
ca·si·no \kə-ˈsē-nō\ *n, pl* **-nos** [It, fr. *casa* house] **1** : a building or room for social amusements; *esp* : one used for gambling **2** *also* **cas·si·no** : a card game in which players win cards by matching those on the table
cask \ˈkask\ *n* : a barrel-shaped container usu. for liquids; *also* : the quantity held by such a container
cas·ket \ˈkas-kət\ *n* **1** : a small box (as for jewels) **2** : COFFIN
casque \ˈkask\ *n* : HELMET
cas·sa·va \kə-ˈsä-və\ *n* : any of several tropical spurges with rootstocks yielding a nutritious starch from which tapioca is prepared; *also* : the rootstock or its starch
cas·se·role \ˈka-sə-ˌrōl\ *n* **1** : a dish in which food may be baked and served **2** : food cooked and served in a casserole

cas•sette *also* **ca•sette** \kə-ˈset\ *n* **1** : a lightproof container for photographic plates or film **2** : a plastic case containing magnetic tape

cas•sia \ˈka-shə\ *n* **1** : a dried coarse cinnamon bark **2** : any of a genus of leguminous herbs, shrubs, and trees of warm regions including several which yield senna

cas•sit•er•ite \kə-ˈsi-tə-ˌrīt\ *n* : a dark mineral that is the chief tin ore

cas•sock \ˈka-sək\ *n* : an ankle-length garment worn esp. by Roman Catholic and Anglican clergy

cas•so•wary \ˈka-sə-ˌwer-ē\ *n, pl* **-war•ies** : any of a genus of large flightless birds closely related to the emu

[1]**cast** \ˈkast\ *vb* **cast**; **cast•ing** **1** : THROW, FLING **2** : DIRECT ⟨~ a glance⟩ **3** : to deposit (a ballot) formally **4** : to throw off, out, or away : DISCARD, SHED **5** : COMPUTE; *esp* : to add up **6** : to assign the parts of (a play) to actors; *also* : to assign to a role or part **7** : to shape (a substance) by pouring in liquid or plastic form into a mold and letting harden without pressure **8** : to make (as a knot or stitch) by looping or catching up

[2]**cast** *n* **1** : THROW, FLING **2** : a throw of dice **3** : the set of actors in a dramatic production **4** : something formed in or as if in a mold; *also* : a rigid surgical casing (as for protecting and supporting a fractured bone) **5** : TINGE, HUE **6** : APPEARANCE, LOOK ⟨features of delicate ~⟩ **7** : something thrown out or off, shed, or expelled ⟨worm ~*s*⟩

cas•ta•net \ˌkas-tə-ˈnet\ *n* [Sp *castañeta*, fr. *castaña* chestnut, fr. L *castanea*] : a rhythm instrument consisting of two small wooden, ivory, or plastic shells held in the hand and clicked together

cast•away \ˈkas-tə-ˌwā\ *adj* **1** : thrown away : REJECTED **2** : cast adrift or ashore as a survivor of a shipwreck — **castaway** *n*

caste \ˈkast\ *n* [Pg *casta*, lit., race, lineage, fr. fem. of *casto* pure, chaste, fr. L *castus*] **1** : one of the hereditary social classes in Hinduism **2** : a division of a society based on wealth, inherited rank, or occupation **3** : social position : PRESTIGE **4** : a system of rigid social stratification

cas•tel•lat•ed \ˈkas-tə-ˌlā-təd\ *adj* : having battlements like a castle

cast•er \ˈkas-tər\ *n* **1** *or* **cas•tor** : a small container to hold salt or pepper at the table **2** : a small wheel that turns freely and is used to support and move furniture, trucks, and equipment

cas•ti•gate \ˈkas-tə-ˌgāt\ *vb* **-gat•ed**; **-gat•ing** : to punish or criticize severely — **cas•ti•ga•tion** \ˌkas-tə-ˈgā-shən\ *n* — **cas•ti•ga•tor** \ˈkas-tə-ˌgā-tər\ *n*

cast•ing \ˈkas-tiŋ\ *n* **1** : CAST 7 **2** : something cast in a mold

casting vote *n* : a deciding vote cast by a presiding officer to break a tie

cast iron *n* : a hard brittle alloy of iron, carbon, and silicon cast in a mold

cas•tle \ˈka-səl\ *n* **1** : a large fortified building or set of buildings **2** : a large or imposing house **3** : [3]ROOK

castle in the air : an impracticable project

cast–off \ˈkast-ˌȯf\ *adj* : thrown away or aside — **cast•off** *n*

cas•tor oil \ˈkas-tər-\ *n* : a thick yellowish oil extracted from the poisonous seeds of an herb (**castor–oil plant**) and used as a lubricant and purgative

cas•trate \ˈkas-ˌtrāt\ *vb* **cas•trat•ed**; **cas•trat•ing** : to deprive of sex glands and esp. testes — **cas•tra•tion** \kas-ˈtrā-shən\ *n* — **cas•tra•tor** \-ər\ *n*

ca•su•al \ˈka-zhə-wəl\ *adj* **1** : resulting from or occurring by chance **2** : OCCASIONAL, INCIDENTAL ⟨~ employment⟩ **3** : OFFHAND, NONCHALANT ⟨a ~ approach to cooking⟩ **4** : designed for informal use ⟨~ clothing⟩ — **ca•su•al•ly** *adv* — **ca•su•al•ness** *n*

ca•su•al•ty \ˈka-zhəl-tē, ˈka-zhə-wəl-\ *n, pl* **-ties** **1** : serious or fatal accident **2** : a military person lost through death, injury, sickness, or capture or through being missing in action **3** : a person or thing injured, lost, or destroyed

ca•su•ist•ry \ˈka-zhə-wə-strē\ *n, pl* **-ries** : specious argument : RATIONALIZATION — **ca•su•ist** \-wist\ *n* — **ca•su•is•tic** \ˌka-zhə-ˈwis-tik\ *or* **ca•su•is•ti•cal** \-ti-kəl\ *adj*

ca•sus bel•li \ˌkä-səs-ˈbe-ˌlē, ˌkā-səs-ˈbe-ˌlī\ *n, pl* **ca•sus belli** \ˌkä-ˌsüs-, ˌkā-\ [NL, occasion of war] : a cause or pretext for a declaration of war

[1]**cat** \ˈkat\ *n* **1** : a carnivorous mammal long domesticated as a pet and for catching rats and mice **2** : any of a family of animals (as the lion, lynx, or leopard) including the domestic cat **3** : a malicious woman **4** : GUY

[2]**cat** *abbr* catalog

ca•tab•o•lism \kə-ˈta-bə-ˌli-zəm\ *n* : destructive metabolism involving the release of energy and resulting in the breakdown of complex materials — **cat•a•bol•ic** \ˌka-tə-ˈbä-lik\ *adj*

cat•a•clysm \ˈka-tə-ˌkli-zəm\ *n* : a violent change or upheaval — **cat•a•clys•mal** \ˌka-tə-ˈkliz-məl\ *or* **cat•a•clys•mic** \-ˈkliz-mik\ *adj*

cat•a•comb \ˈka-tə-ˌkōm\ *n* : an underground burial place with galleries and recesses for tombs

cat•a•falque \ˈka-tə-ˌfalk, -ˌfȯlk, -ˌfȯk\ *n* : an ornamental structure sometimes used in solemn funerals to hold the body

cat•a•lep•sy \ˈka-tə-ˌlep-sē\ *n, pl* **-sies** : a trancelike state characterized esp. by loss of voluntary motion — **cat•a•lep•tic** \ˌka-tə-ˈlep-tik\ *adj or n*

[1]**cat•a•log** *or* **cat•a•logue** \ˈka-tə-ˌlȯg\ *n* **1** : LIST, REGISTER **2** : a systematic list of items with descriptive details; *also* : a book containing such a list

[2]**catalog** *or* **catalogue** *vb* **-loged** *or* **-logued**; **-log•ing** *or* **-logu•ing** **1** : to make a catalog of **2** : to enter in a catalog — **cat•a•log•er** *or* **cat•a•logu•er** *n*

ca·tal·pa \kə-ˈtal-pə\ *n* : any of a genus of broad-leaved trees with showy flowers and long slim pods
ca·tal·y·sis \kə-ˈta-lə-səs\ *n, pl* **-y·ses** \-ˌsēz\ : a change and esp. increase in the rate of a chemical reaction brought about by a substance (**cat·a·lyst** \ˈka-tə-list\) that is itself unchanged at the end of the reaction — **cat·a·lyt·ic** \ˌka-tə-ˈli-tik\ *adj* — **cat·a·lyt·i·cal·ly** \-ti-k(ə-)lē\ *adv*
catalytic converter *n* : an automobile exhaust-system component in which a catalyst changes harmful gases into mostly harmless products
cat·a·lyze \ˈka-tə-ˌlīz\ *vb* **-lyzed**; **-lyz·ing** : to bring about the catalysis of (a chemical reaction)
cat·a·ma·ran \ˌka-tə-mə-ˈran\ *n* [Tamil (a language of southern India) *kaṭṭumaram,* fr. *kaṭṭu* to tie + *maram* tree] : a boat with twin hulls
cat·a·mount \ˈka-tə-ˌmau̇nt\ *n* : COUGAR; *also* : LYNX
cat·a·pult \ˈka-tə-ˌpəlt, -ˌpu̇lt\ *n* **1** : an ancient military machine for hurling missiles **2** : a device for launching an airplane (as from an aircraft carrier) — **catapult** *vb*
cat·a·ract \ˈka-tə-ˌrakt\ *n* **1** : a cloudiness of the lens of the eye obstructing vision **2** : a large waterfall; *also* : steep rapids in a river
ca·tarrh \kə-ˈtär\ *n* : inflammation of a mucous membrane esp. of the nose and throat — **ca·tarrh·al** \-əl\ *adj*
ca·tas·tro·phe \kə-ˈtas-trə-(ˌ)fē\ *n* [Gk *katastrophē,* fr. *katastrephein* to overturn, fr. *kata-* down + *strephein* to turn] **1** : a great disaster or misfortune **2** : utter failure — **cat·a·stroph·ic** \ˌka-tə-ˈsträ-fik\ *adj* — **cat·a·stroph·i·cal·ly** \-fi-k(ə-)lē\ *adv*
cat·a·ton·ic \ˌka-tə-ˈtä-nik\ *adj* : of, relating to, or marked by schizophrenia characterized esp. by stupor, negativism, rigidity, purposeless excitement, and bizarre posturing — **catatonic** *n*
cat·bird \ˈkat-ˌbərd\ *n* : an American songbird with a catlike mewing call
cat·boat \ˈkat-ˌbōt\ *n* : a single-masted sailboat with a single large sail extended by a long boom
cat·call \-ˌkȯl\ *n* : a loud cry made esp. to express disapproval — **catcall** *vb*
[1]**catch** \ˈkach, ˈkech\ *vb* **caught** \ˈkȯt\; **catch·ing** [ME *cacchen,* fr. AF *cacher, chacher, chacer* to hunt, ultim. fr. L *captare* to chase] **1** : to capture esp. after pursuit **2** : TRAP **3** : to discover unexpectedly ⟨*caught* in the act⟩ **4** : to become suddenly aware of **5** : to take hold of : SNATCH ⟨~ at a straw⟩ **6** : INTERCEPT **7** : to get entangled **8** : to become affected with or by ⟨~ fire⟩ ⟨~ cold⟩ **9** : to seize and hold firmly; *also* : FASTEN **10** : OVERTAKE **11** : to be in time for ⟨~ a train⟩ **12** : to take in and retain **13** : to watch or see ⟨~ a TV show⟩
[2]**catch** *n* **1** : something caught **2** : the act of catching; *also* : a game consisting of throwing and catching a ball **3** : something that catches or checks or holds immovable **4** : one worth catching esp. as a mate **5** : FRAGMENT, SNATCH **6** : a concealed difficulty or complication
catch·all \ˈkach-ˌȯl, ˈkech-\ *n* : something to hold a variety of odds and ends
catch–as–catch–can *adj* : using any means available
catch·er \ˈka-chər, ˈke-\ *n* : one that catches; *esp* : a player positioned behind home plate in baseball
catch·ing *adj* **1** : INFECTIOUS, CONTAGIOUS **2** : ALLURING, CATCHY
catch·ment \ˈkach-mənt, ˈkech-\ *n* **1** : something that catches water **2** : the action of catching water
catch on *vb* **1** : UNDERSTAND **2** : to become popular
catch·pen·ny \ˈkach-ˌpe-nē, ˈkech-\ *adj* : using sensationalism or cheapness for appeal ⟨a ~ newspaper⟩
catch·phrase \-ˌfrāz\ *n* : a word or expression frequently used to represent or characterize a person, group, idea, or point of view
catch–22 \-ˌtwen-tē-ˈtü\ *n, pl* **catch–22's** *or* **catch–22s** *often cap C* [fr. *Catch-22,* a paradoxical rule found in the novel *Catch-22* (1961) by Joseph Heller] : a problematic situation for which the only solution is denied by a circumstance inherent in the problem or by a rule; *also* : the circumstance or rule that denies a solution
catchup *var of* KETCHUP
catch up *vb* : to travel or work fast enough to overtake or complete
catch·word \ˈkach-ˌwərd, ˈkech-\ *n* **1** : GUIDE WORD **2** : CATCHPHRASE
catchy \ˈka-chē, ˈke-\ *adj* **catch·i·er**; **-est** **1** : likely to catch the interest or attention **2** : TRICKY ⟨a ~ question⟩
cat·e·chism \ˈka-tə-ˌki-zəm\ *n* : a summary or test (as of religious doctrine) usu. in the form of questions and answers — **cat·e·chist** \-ˌkist\ *n* — **cat·e·chize** \-ˌkīz\ *vb*
cat·e·chu·men \ˌka-tə-ˈkyü-mən\ *n* : a religious convert receiving training before baptism
cat·e·gor·i·cal \ˌka-tə-ˈgȯr-i-kəl\ *adj* **1** : ABSOLUTE, UNQUALIFIED ⟨a ~ denial⟩ **2** : of, relating to, or constituting a category — **cat·e·gor·i·cal·ly** \-i-k(ə-)lē\ *adv*
cat·e·go·rise *Brit var of* CATEGORIZE
cat·e·go·rize \ˈka-ti-gə-ˌrīz\ *vb* **-rized**; **-riz·ing** : to put into a category : CLASSIFY — **cat·e·go·ri·za·tion** \ˌka-ti-gə-rə-ˈzā-shən\ *n*
cat·e·go·ry \ˈka-tə-ˌgȯr-ē\ *n, pl* **-ries** : a division used in classification; *also* : CLASS, GROUP, KIND
ca·ter \ˈkā-tər\ *vb* [obs. *cater* buyer of provisions, fr. ME *catour,* short for *acatour,* fr. AF, fr. *acater, achater* to buy] **1** : to provide a supply of food **2** : to supply what is wanted — **ca·ter·er** *n*
catercorner *or* **cater–cornered** *var of* KITTY-CORNER
cat·er·pil·lar \ˈka-tər-ˌpi-lər\ *n* [ME *catyr-*

pel, fr. OF *catepelose,* lit., hairy cat] : a wormlike often hairy insect larva esp. of a butterfly or moth

cat·er·waul \ˈka-tər-ˌwȯl\ *vb* : to make a harsh cry — **caterwaul** *n*

cat·fish \ˈkat-ˌfish\ *n* : any of an order of chiefly freshwater stout-bodied fishes with slender tactile processes around the mouth

cat·gut \-ˌgət\ *n* : a tough cord made usu. from sheep intestines

ca·thar·sis \kə-ˈthär-səs\ *n, pl* **ca·thar·ses** \-ˌsēz\ **1** : an act of purging or purification **2** : elimination of a complex by bringing it to consciousness and affording it expression

[1]**ca·thar·tic** \kə-ˈthär-tik\ *adj* : of, relating to, or producing catharsis

[2]**cathartic** *n* : PURGATIVE

ca·the·dral \kə-ˈthē-drəl\ *n* : the principal church of a diocese

cath·e·ter \ˈka-thə-tər\ *n* : a tube for insertion into a bodily passage or cavity usu. for injecting or drawing off material or for keeping a passage open

cath·e·ter·i·za·tion \ˌka-thə-tə-rə-ˈzā-shən\ *n* : the use of or introduction of a catheter — **cath·e·ter·ize** \ˈka-thə-tə-ˌrīz\ *vb*

cath·ode \ˈka-ˌthōd\ *n* **1** : the negative electrode of an electrolytic cell **2** : the positive terminal of a battery **3** : the electron-emitting electrode of an electron tube — **cath·od·al** \ˈka-ˌthō-dᵊl\ *adj* — **ca·thod·ic** \ka-ˈthä-dik\ *adj*

cathode–ray tube *n* : a vacuum tube in which a beam of electrons is projected on a phosphor-coated screen to produce a luminous spot

cath·o·lic \ˈkath-lik, ˈka-thə-\ *adj* [ME *catholik* relating to the church universal, ultim. fr. Gk *katholikos* universal, general, fr. *katholou* in general] **1** *cap* : of or relating to Catholics and esp. Roman Catholics **2** : GENERAL, UNIVERSAL

Cath·o·lic \ˈkath-lik, ˈka-thə-\ *n* : a member of a church claiming historical continuity from the ancient undivided Christian church; *esp* : a member of the Roman Catholic Church — **Ca·thol·i·cism** \kə-ˈthä-lə-ˌsi-zəm\ *n*

cath·o·lic·i·ty \ˌka-thə-ˈli-sə-tē\ *n, pl* **-ties** **1** *cap* : the character of being in conformity with a Catholic church **2** : liberality of sentiments or views **3** : comprehensive range

cat·ion \ˈkat-ˌī-ən\ *n* : the ion in an electrolyte that migrates to the cathode; *also* : a positively charged ion

cat·kin \ˈkat-kən\ *n* : a long flower cluster (as of a willow) bearing crowded flowers and prominent bracts

cat·like \-ˌlīk\ *adj* : resembling a cat or its behavior; *esp* : STEALTHY

cat·nap \-ˌnap\ *n* : a very short light nap — **catnap** *vb*

cat·nip \-ˌnip\ *n* : an aromatic mint that is esp. attractive to cats

cat–o'–nine–tails \ˌka-tə-ˈnīn-ˌtālz\ *n, pl* **cat–o'–nine–tails** : a whip made of usu. nine knotted cords fastened to a handle

CAT scan \ˈkat-\ *n* [computerized *a*xial *t*omography] : an image made by computed tomography

CAT scanner *n* : a medical instrument consisting of integrated X-ray and computing equipment that is used to make CAT scans

cat's cradle *n* : a game played with a string looped on the fingers in such a way as to resemble a small cradle

cat's–eye \ˈkats-ˌī\ *n, pl* **cat's–eyes** : any of various iridescent gems

cat's–paw \-ˌpȯ\ *n, pl* **cat's–paws** : a person used by another as a tool

cat·suit \ˈkat-ˌsüt\ *n* : a close-fitting one-piece garment that covers the torso and the legs

catsup *var of* KETCHUP

cat·tail \ˈkat-ˌtāl\ *n* : any of a genus of tall reedlike marsh plants with furry brown spikes of tiny flowers

cat·tle \ˈka-tᵊl\ *n pl* : LIVESTOCK; *esp* : domestic bovines (as cows, bulls, or calves) — **cat·tle·man** \-mən, -ˌman\ *n*

cat·ty \ˈka-tē\ *adj* **cat·ti·er**; **-est** : slyly spiteful ⟨~ comments⟩ — **cat·ti·ly** \ˈka-tə-lē\ *adv* — **cat·ti·ness** *n*

catty–corner *or* **catty–cornered** *var of* KITTY-CORNER

CATV *abbr* community antenna television

cat·walk \ˈkat-ˌwȯk\ *n* : a narrow walk (as along a bridge)

Cau·ca·sian \kȯ-ˈkā-zhən\ *adj* : of or relating to the white racial group of humankind — **Caucasian** *n* — **Cau·ca·soid** \ˈkȯ-kə-ˌsȯid\ *adj or n*

cau·cus \ˈkȯ-kəs\ *n* : a meeting of a group of persons belonging to the same political party or faction usu. to decide on policies and candidates — **caucus** *vb*

cau·dal \ˈkȯ-dᵊl\ *adj* : of, relating to, or located near the tail or the hind end of the body — **cau·dal·ly** *adv*

cau·di·llo \kau̇-ˈthē-(ˌ)yō, -ˈthēl-\ *n, pl* **-llos** : a Spanish or Latin-American military dictator

caught \ˈkȯt\ *past and past part of* CATCH

caul \ˈkȯl\ *n* : the inner fetal membrane of higher vertebrates esp. when covering the head at birth

caul·dron \ˈkȯl-drən\ *n* : a large kettle

cau·li·flow·er \ˈkȯ-li-ˌflau̇(-ə)r\ *n* [It *cavolfiore,* fr. *cavolo* cabbage + *fiore* flower] : a garden plant closely related to cabbage and grown for its compact edible head of undeveloped flowers; *also* : this head used as a vegetable

cauliflower ear *n* : an ear deformed from injury and excessive growth of scar tissue

[1]**caulk** *or* **calk** \ˈkȯk\ *vb* [ME, fr. AF *cauker, calcher* to trample, fr. L *calcare,* fr. *calx* heel] : to stop up and make tight against leakage (as a boat or its seams) — **caulk·er** *n*

[2]**caulk** *or* **calk** *also* **caulk·ing** *or* **calk·ing** *n* : material used to caulk

caus·al \ˈkȯ-zəl\ *adj* **1** : expressing or indicating cause **2** : relating to or acting as a cause — **cau·sal·i·ty** \kȯ-ˈza-lə-tē\ *n* — **caus·al·ly** *adv*

cau·sa·tion \kȯ-ˈzā-shən\ *n* **1** : the act or

process of causing **2 :** the means by which an effect is produced

[1]**cause** \ˈkȯz\ *n* **1 :** REASON, MOTIVE **2 :** something that brings about a result; *esp* **:** a person or thing that is the agent of bringing something about **3 :** a suit or action in court **:** CASE **4 :** a question or matter to be decided **5 :** a principle or movement earnestly supported — **cause·less** *adj*

[2]**cause** *vb* **caused; caus·ing :** to be the cause or occasion of — **caus·a·tive** \ˈkȯ-zə-tiv\ *adj* — **caus·er** *n*

cause cé·lè·bre \ˌkōz-sā-ˈlebrᵊ, ˌkȯz-\ *n, pl* **causes célèbres** *same*\ [F, lit., celebrated case] **1 :** a legal case that excites widespread interest **2 :** a notorious person, thing, incident, or episode

cau·se·rie \ˌkōz-ˈrē, ˌkō-zə-\ *n* [F] **1 :** an informal conversation **:** CHAT **2 :** a short informal essay

cause·way \ˈkȯz-ˌwā\ *n* **:** a raised way or road across wet ground or water

[1]**caus·tic** \ˈkȯ-stik\ *adj* **1 :** CORROSIVE **2 :** SHARP, INCISIVE ⟨~ wit⟩

[2]**caustic** *n* **1 :** a substance that burns or destroys organic tissue by chemical action **2 :** SODIUM HYDROXIDE

cau·ter·ize \ˈkȯ-tə-ˌrīz\ *vb* **-ized; -iz·ing :** to burn or sear usu. to prevent infection or bleeding — **cau·ter·i·za·tion** \ˌkȯ-tə-rə-ˈzā-shən\ *n*

[1]**cau·tion** \ˈkȯ-shən\ *n* **1 :** ADMONITION, WARNING **2 :** prudent forethought to minimize risk **3 :** one that astonishes — **cau·tion·ary** \-shə-ˌner-ē\ *adj*

[2]**caution** *vb* **:** to advise caution to

cau·tious \ˈkȯ-shəs\ *adj* **:** marked by or given to caution **:** CAREFUL — **cau·tious·ly** *adv* — **cau·tious·ness** *n*

cav *abbr* **1** cavalry **2** cavity

cav·al·cade \ˌka-vəl-ˈkād\ *n* **1 :** a procession of riders or carriages; *also* **:** a procession of vehicles **2 :** a dramatic sequence or procession ⟨a ~ of films⟩

[1]**cav·a·lier** \ˌka-və-ˈlir\ *n* [MF, fr. It *cavaliere,* fr. Old Occitan *cavalier,* fr. LL *caballarius* horseman, fr. L *caballus* horse] **1 :** a mounted soldier **:** KNIGHT **2** *cap* **:** an adherent of Charles I of England **3 :** GALLANT

[2]**cavalier** *adj* **1 :** DEBONAIR **2 :** DISDAINFUL, HAUGHTY ⟨a ~ attitude toward money⟩ — **cav·a·lier·ly** *adv*

cav·al·ry \ˈka-vəl-rē\ *n, pl* **-ries :** troops mounted on horseback or moving in motor vehicles — **cav·al·ry·man** \-mən, -ˌman\ *n*

[1]**cave** \ˈkāv\ *n* **:** a natural underground chamber open to the surface

[2]**cave** *vb* **caved; cav·ing 1 :** to collapse or cause to collapse **2 :** to cease to resist **:** SUBMIT — usu. used with *in*

ca·ve·at \ˈka-vē-ˌät, -ˌat; ˈkä-vē-ˌät\ *n* [L, let him beware] **:** WARNING

caveat emp·tor \-ˈemp-tər, -ˌtȯr\ *n* [NL, let the buyer beware] **:** a principle in commerce: without a warranty the buyer takes a risk

cave–in \ˈkā-ˌvin\ *n* **1 :** the action of caving in **2 :** a place where earth has caved in

cave·man \ˈkāv-ˌman\ *n* **1 :** a cave dweller esp. of the Stone Age **2 :** a man who acts in a rough or crude manner

cav·ern \ˈka-vərn\ *n* **:** CAVE; *esp* **:** one of large or unknown size — **cav·ern·ous** *adj* — **cav·ern·ous·ly** *adv*

cav·i·ar *also* **cav·i·are** \ˈka-vē-ˌär, ˈkä-\ *n* **:** the salted roe of a large fish (as sturgeon) used as an appetizer

cav·il \ˈka-vəl\ *vb* **-iled** *or* **-illed; -il·ing** *or* **-il·ling :** to make frivolous objections or raise trivial objections to — **cavil** *n* — **cav·il·er** *or* **cav·il·ler** *n*

cav·ing \ˈkā-viŋ\ *n* **:** the sport of exploring caves **:** SPELUNKING

cav·i·ta·tion \ˌka-və-ˈtā-shən\ *n* **:** the formation of partial vacuums in a liquid by a swiftly moving solid body (as a propeller) or by high-intensity sound waves

cav·i·ty \ˈka-və-tē\ *n, pl* **-ties 1 :** an unfilled space within a mass **:** a hollow place **2 :** an area of decay in a tooth

ca·vort \kə-ˈvȯrt\ *vb* **:** PRANCE, CAPER

ca·vy \ˈkā-vē\ *n, pl* **cavies :** GUINEA PIG 1

caw \ˈkȯ\ *vb* **:** to utter the harsh call of the crow or a similar cry — **caw** *n*

cay \ˈkē, ˈkā\ *n* **:** [4]KEY

cay·enne pepper \ˌkī-ˈen-, ˌkā-\ *n* **:** a condiment consisting of ground dried fruits or seeds of a hot pepper

cayman *var of* CAIMAN

Ca·yu·ga \kā-ˈü-gə, kī-\ *n, pl* **Cayuga** *or* **Cayugas :** a member of an Indigenous people of central New York; *also* **:** their language

Cay·use \ˈkī-ˌyüs, kī-ˈ\ *n* **1** *pl* **Cayuse** *or* **Cayuses :** a member of a once-nomadic Indigenous people of Oregon and Washington **2** *pl cayuses, not cap, West* **:** a native range horse

Cb *symbol* columbium

CB \ˈsē-ˈbē\ *n* **:** CITIZENS BAND; *also* **:** the radio set used for citizens-band communications

CBC *abbr* Canadian Broadcasting Corporation

CBD *abbr* cash before delivery

CBS *abbr* Columbia Broadcasting System

CBW *abbr* chemical and biological warfare

[1]**cc** \ˌsē-ˈsē\ *vb* **cc'd; cc'ing :** to send a copy of an email, letter, etc., to someone ⟨~ an email to a coworker⟩ ⟨~ me on your reply⟩

[2]**cc** *abbr* **1** carbon copy **2** cubic centimeter

CC *abbr* **1** community college **2** country club

CCD \ˌsē-ˌsē-ˈdē\ *n* **:** CHARGE-COUPLED DEVICE

CCTV *abbr* closed-circuit television

CCU *abbr* **1** cardiac care unit **2** coronary care unit **3** critical care unit

ccw *abbr* counterclockwise

cd *abbr* cord

Cd *symbol* cadmium

[1]**CD** \ˌsē-ˈdē\ *n* **:** CERTIFICATE OF DEPOSIT

[2]**CD** *n* **:** a small optical disk usu. containing recorded music or computer data; *also* **:** the content of a CD

[3]**CD** *abbr* Civil Defense

CDR *abbr* commander
CD–ROM \ˌsē-ˌdē-ˈräm\ *n* : a CD containing computer data that cannot be altered
CDT *abbr* central daylight (saving) time
Ce *symbol* cerium
CE *abbr* **1** chemical engineer **2** civil engineer **3** Corps of Engineers
cease \ˈsēs\ *vb* **ceased; ceas•ing** : to come or bring to an end : STOP
cease–fire \ˈsēs-ˈfī(-ə)r\ *n* : a suspension of active hostilities
cease•less \ˈsēs-ləs\ *adj* : being without pause or stop : CONTINUOUS — **cease•less•ly** *adv* — **cease•less•ness** *n*
ce•cum *also* **cae•cum** \ˈsē-kəm\ *n, pl* **ce•ca** \-kə\ : the blind pouch at the beginning of the large intestine into which the small intestine opens — **ce•cal** *also* **cae•cal** \-kəl\ *adj*
ce•dar \ˈsē-dər\ *n* : any of numerous coniferous trees (as a juniper) noted for their fragrant durable wood; *also* : this wood
cede \ˈsēd\ *vb* **ced•ed; ced•ing** **1** : to yield or give up esp. by treaty **2** : ASSIGN, TRANSFER — **ced•er** *n*
ce•di \ˈsā-dē\ *n* — see MONEY table
ce•dil•la \si-ˈdi-lə\ *n* : a mark placed under the letter *c* (as ç) to show that the *c* is to be pronounced like *s*
ceil•ing \ˈsē-liŋ\ *n* **1** : the overhead inside lining of a room **2** : the height above the ground of the base of the lowest layer of clouds when over half of the sky is obscured **3** : the greatest height at which an airplane can operate efficiently **4** : a prescribed upper limit ⟨price ~⟩
cel•an•dine \ˈse-lən-ˌdīn, -ˌdēn\ *n* : a yellow-flowered herb related to the poppies
cel•e•brant \ˈse-lə-brənt\ *n* : one who celebrates; *esp* : a priest officiating at the Eucharist
cel•e•brate \ˈse-lə-ˌbrāt\ *vb* **-brat•ed; -brat•ing** **1** : to perform (as a sacrament) with appropriate rites **2** : to honor (as a holiday) by solemn ceremonies or by refraining from ordinary business **3** : to observe a notable occasion with festivities **4** : EXTOL — **cel•e•bra•tion** \ˌse-lə-ˈbrā-shən\ *n* — **cel•e•bra•tor** \ˈse-lə-brā-tər\ *n* — **cel•e•bra•to•ry** \-brə-ˌtȯr-ē, ˌse-lə-ˈbrā-tə-rē\ *adj*
celebrated *adj* : widely known and often referred to ⟨a ~ author⟩ ♦ ***Synonyms*** DISTINGUISHED, RENOWNED, NOTED, FAMOUS, ILLUSTRIOUS, NOTORIOUS
ce•leb•ri•ty \sə-ˈle-brə-tē\ *n, pl* **-ties** **1** : the state of being celebrated : RENOWN **2** : a celebrated person
ce•ler•i•ty \sə-ˈler-ə-tē\ *n* : SPEED, RAPIDITY
cel•ery \ˈse-lə-rē\ *n, pl* **-er•ies** : a European herb related to the carrot and widely grown for the crisp edible stems of its leaves
celery cabbage *n* : CHINESE CABBAGE 2
ce•les•ta \sə-ˈles-tə\ *or* **ce•leste** \sə-ˈlest\ *n* : a keyboard instrument with hammers that strike steel plates
ce•les•tial \sə-ˈles-chəl\ *adj* **1** : HEAVENLY, DIVINE **2** : of or relating to the sky ⟨~ bodies⟩ — **ce•les•tial•ly** *adv*
celestial navigation *n* : navigation by observation of the positions of stars
celestial sphere *n* : an imaginary sphere of infinite radius against which the celestial bodies appear to be projected
cel•i•ba•cy \ˈse-lə-bə-sē\ *n* **1** : the state of being unmarried; *esp* : abstention by vow from marriage **2** : abstention from sexual intercourse
cel•i•bate \ˈse-lə-bət\ *n* : one who lives in celibacy — **celibate** *adj*
cell \ˈsel\ *n* **1** : a small room (as in a convent or prison) usu. for one person; *also* : a small compartment, cavity, or bounded space **2** : a tiny mass of protoplasm that usu. contains a nucleus, is enclosed by a membrane, and forms the smallest structural unit of living matter capable of functioning independently **3** : a container holding an electrolyte either for generating electricity or for use in electrolysis **4** : a single unit in a device for converting radiant energy into electrical energy — **celled** \ˈseld\ *adj*
cel•lar \ˈse-lər\ *n* **1** : BASEMENT 1 **2** : the lowest place in the standings (as in an athletic league) **3** : a stock of wines
cel•lar•ette *or* **cel•lar•et** \ˌse-lə-ˈret\ *n* : a case or cabinet for a few bottles of wine or liquor
cell body *n* : the nucleus-containing central part of a neuron exclusive of its processes
cel•lo \ˈche-lō\ *n, pl* **cellos** : a bass member of the violin family tuned an octave below the viola — **cel•list** \-list\ *n*
cel•lo•phane \ˈse-lə-ˌfān\ *n* : a thin transparent material made from cellulose and used as a wrapping
cell phone *n* : a portable cordless telephone for use in a cellular system
cel•lu•lar \ˈsel-yə-lər\ *adj* **1** : of, relating to, or consisting of cells ⟨~ proteins⟩ **2** : of, relating to, or being a radiotelephone system in which a geographical area is divided into small sections each served by a transmitter of limited range
cel•lu•lite \ˈsel-yə-ˌlīt\ *n* : deposits of lumpy fat within connective tissue (as in the thighs, hips, and buttocks)
cel•lu•lose \ˈsel-yə-ˌlōs\ *n* : a complex carbohydrate of the cell walls of plants used esp. in making paper or rayon — **cel•lu•los•ic** \ˌsel-yə-ˈlō-sik\ *adj or n*
Cel•si•us \ˈsel-sē-əs\ *adj* : relating to or having a scale for measuring temperature on which the interval between the triple point and the boiling point of water is divided into 99.99 degrees with 0.01° being the triple point and 100.00° the boiling point; *also* : CENTIGRADE
Celt \ˈkelt, ˈselt\ *n* : a member of any of a group of peoples (as the Irish or Welsh) of western Europe — **Celt•ic** *adj*
cem•ba•lo \ˈchem-bə-ˌlō\ *n, pl* **-ba•li** \-ˌlē\ *or* **-balos** [It] : HARPSICHORD
[1]**ce•ment** \si-ˈment\ *n* **1** : CONCRETE; *also* : a powder that is produced from a burned mixture chiefly of clay and limestone and that is used in mortar and concrete **2** : a binding element or agency **3**

: CEMENTUM; *also* : a substance for filling cavities in teeth

²**cement** *vb* **1** : to unite by or as if by cement **2** : to cover with concrete — **ce•ment•er** *n*

ce•men•tum \si-ˈmen-təm\ *n* : a specialized external bony layer covering the dentin of the part of a tooth normally within the gum

cem•e•tery \ˈse-mə-ˌter-ē\ *n, pl* **-ter•ies** [ME *cimitery,* fr. AF *cimiterie,* fr. LL *coemeterium,* fr. Gk *koimētērion* sleeping chamber, burial place, fr. *koiman* to put to sleep] : a burial ground : GRAVEYARD

cen•o•bite \ˈse-nə-ˌbīt\ *n* : a member of a religious group living together in a monastic community — **cen•o•bit•ic** \ˌse-nə-ˈbi-tik\ *adj*

ceno•taph \ˈse-nə-ˌtaf\ *n* [F *cénotaphe,* fr. L *cenotaphium,* fr. Gk *kenotaphion,* fr. *kenos* empty + *taphos* tomb] : a tomb or a monument erected in honor of a person whose body is elsewhere

Ce•no•zo•ic \ˌsē-nə-ˈzō-ik, ˌse-\ *adj* : of, relating to, or being the era of geologic history that extends from about 65 million years ago to the present — **Cenozoic** *n*

cen•ser \ˈsen-sər\ *n* : a vessel for burning incense (as in a religious ritual)

¹**cen•sor** \ˈsen-sər\ *n* **1** : a person who inspects printed matter or films with power to suppress anything objectionable **2** : one of two early Roman magistrates whose duties included taking the census — **cen•so•ri•al** \sen-ˈsȯr-ē-əl\ *adj*

²**censor** *vb* : to subject to censorship

cen•so•ri•ous \sen-ˈsōr-ē-əs\ *adj* : marked by or given to censure : CRITICAL — **cen•so•ri•ous•ly** *adv* — **cen•so•ri•ous•ness** *n*

cen•sor•ship \ˈsen-sər-ˌship\ *n* **1** : the action of a censor esp. in stopping the transmission or publication of matter considered objectionable **2** : the office of a Roman censor

¹**cen•sure** \ˈsen-chər\ *n* **1** : the act of blaming or condemning sternly **2** : an official reprimand

²**censure** *vb* **cen•sured**; **cen•sur•ing** : to find fault with and criticize as blameworthy — **cen•sur•able** *adj* — **cen•sur•er** *n*

cen•sus \ˈsen-səs\ *n* **1** : a periodic governmental count of population **2** : COUNT, TALLY — **census** *vb*

¹**cent** \ˈsent\ *n* [F, hundred, fr. L *centum*] **1** — see *birr, dollar, euro, leone, lilangeni, nakfa, rand, rupee, shilling* at MONEY table **2** : a coin, token, or note representing one cent **3** : a monetary unit formerly used in Suriname ($\frac{1}{100}$ gulden), Malta ($\frac{1}{100}$ lira), and Cyprus ($\frac{1}{100}$ pound)

²**cent** *abbr* **1** centigrade **2** central **3** century

cen•tas \ˈsen-ˌtäs\ *n, pl* **cen•tai** \-ˌtī\ *or* **cen•tu** \-ˌtü\ : a monetary unit equal to $\frac{1}{100}$ litas formerly used in Lithuania

cen•taur \ˈsen-ˌtȯr\ *n* : any of a race of creatures in Greek mythology half human and half horse

¹**cen•ta•vo** \sen-ˈtä-(ˌ)vō\ *n, pl* **-vos** **1** — see *boliviano, cordoba, lempira, peso, quetzal* at MONEY table **2** : a monetary unit equal to $\frac{1}{100}$ sucre formerly used in Ecuador

²**cen•ta•vo** \-ˈtä-(ˌ)vü, -(ˌ)vō\ *n, pl* **-vos** **1** — see *escudo, metical, real* at MONEY table **2** : a former monetary unit equal to $\frac{1}{100}$ Portuguese escudo

cen•te•nar•i•an \ˌsen-tə-ˈner-ē-ən\ *n* : a person who is 100 or more years old

cen•te•na•ry \sen-ˈte-nə-rē, ˈsen-tə-ˌner-ē\ *n, pl* **-ries** : CENTENNIAL — **centenary** *adj*

cen•ten•ni•al \sen-ˈte-nē-əl\ *n* : a 100th anniversary or its celebration — **centennial** *adj*

¹**cen•ter** \ˈsen-tər\ *n* **1** : the point that is equally distant from all points on the circumference of a circle or surface of a sphere; *also* : MIDDLE 1 **2** : the point about which an activity concentrates or from which something originates **3** : a region of concentrated population **4** : a middle part **5** *often cap* : political figures holding moderate views esp. between those of conservatives and liberals **6** : a player occupying a middle position (as in football or basketball)

²**center** *vb* **1** : to place or fix at or around a center or central area **2** : to give a central focus or basis : CONCENTRATE **3** : to have a center : FOCUS

cen•ter•board \ˈsen-tər-ˌbȯrd\ *n* : a retractable keel used esp. in sailboats

cen•ter•piece \-ˌpēs\ *n* **1** : an object in a central position; *esp* : an adornment in the center of a table **2** : one that is of central importance or interest in a larger whole ⟨the ~ of his speech⟩

cen•tes•i•mal \sen-ˈte-sə-məl\ *adj* : marked by or relating to division into hundredths

¹**cen•tes•i•mo** \chen-ˈte-zə-ˌmō\ *n, pl* **-mi** \-(ˌ)mē\ : a former monetary unit equal to $\frac{1}{100}$ Italian lira

²**cen•tes•i•mo** \sen-ˈte-sə-ˌmō\ *n, pl* **-mos** — see *balboa, peso* at MONEY table

cen•ti•grade \ˈsen-tə-ˌgrād, ˈsän-\ *adj* : relating to, conforming to, or having a thermometer scale on which the interval between the freezing and boiling points of water is divided into 100 degrees with 0° representing the freezing point and 100° the boiling point ⟨10° ~⟩ — compare CELSIUS

cen•ti•gram \-ˌgram\ *n* — see METRIC SYSTEM table

cen•ti•li•ter \ˈsen-ti-ˌlē-tər\ *n* — see METRIC SYSTEM table

cen•time \ˈsän-ˌtēm\ *n* **1** : a former monetary unit of any of several countries (as Belgium, France, and Luxembourg) equal to $\frac{1}{100}$ franc **2** — see *dinar, dirham, franc, gourde* at MONEY table

cen•ti•me•ter \ˈsen-tə-ˌmē-tər, ˈsän-\ *n* — see METRIC SYSTEM table

centimeter–gram–second *adj* : of, relating to, or being a system of units based on the centimeter as the unit of length, the gram as the unit of mass, and the second as the unit of time

cen·ti·mo \ˈsen-tə-ˌmō\ *n, pl* **-mos** **1** — see *bolivar, colón, dobra, guarani, sol* at MONEY table **2** : a former monetary unit equal to ⅟₁₀₀ peseta

cên·ti·mo \ˈsen-tə-ˌmō\ *n, plural* **-mos** — see *kwanza* at MONEY table

cen·ti·pede \ˈsen-tə-ˌpēd\ *n* [L *centipeda,* fr. *centum* hundred + *pes* foot] : any of a class of long flattened segmented arthropods with one pair of legs on each segment except the first which has a pair of poison fangs

[1]**cen·tral** \ˈsen-trəl\ *adj* **1** : constituting a center **2** : ESSENTIAL, PRINCIPAL ⟨the novel's ~ character⟩ **3** : situated at, in, or near the center **4** : centrally placed and superseding separate units ⟨~ heating⟩ — **cen·tral·ly** *adv*

[2]**central** *n* : a central controlling office

cen·tral·ise *Brit var of* CENTRALIZE

cen·tral·ize \ˈsen-trə-ˌlīz\ *vb* **-ized; -iz·ing** : to bring to a central point or under central control — **cen·tral·i·za·tion** \ˌsen-trə-lə-ˈzā-shən\ *n* — **cen·tral·iz·er** \ˈsen-trə-ˌlī-zər\ *n*

central nervous system *n* : the part of the nervous system which integrates nervous function and activity and which in vertebrates consists of the brain and spinal cord

cen·tre *chiefly Brit var of* CENTER

cen·trif·u·gal \sen-ˈtri-fyə-gəl, -fi-\ *adj* [NL *centrifugus,* fr. *centr-* center + L *fugere* to flee] **1** : proceeding or acting in a direction away from a center or axis **2** : using or acting by centrifugal force

centrifugal force *n* : the apparent force felt by an object moving in a curved path and acting outward from a center of rotation

cen·tri·fuge \ˈsen-trə-ˌfyüj\ *n* : a machine using centrifugal force (as for separating substances of different densities or for removing moisture)

cen·trip·e·tal \sen-ˈtri-pə-tᵊl\ *adj* [NL *centripetus,* fr. *centr-* center + L *petere* to seek] : proceeding or acting in a direction toward a center or axis

centripetal force *n* : the force needed to keep an object revolving about a point moving in a circular path

cen·trist \ˈsen-trist\ *n* **1** *often cap* : a member of a center party **2** : one who holds moderate views

cen·tu·ri·on \sen-ˈtu̇r-ē-ən, -ˈtyu̇r-\ *n* : an officer commanding a Roman century

cen·tu·ry \ˈsen-chə-rē\ *n, pl* **-ries** **1** : a subdivision of a Roman legion **2** : a group or sequence of 100 like things **3** : a period of 100 years

century plant *n* : a Mexican agave maturing and flowering only once in many years and then dying

CEO \ˌsē-(ˌ)ē-ˈō\ *n* : the executive with the chief decision-making authority in an organization or business

ce·phal·ic \sə-ˈfa-lik\ *adj* **1** : of or relating to the head **2** : directed toward or situated on or in or near the head

ce·ram·ic \sə-ˈra-mik\ *n* **1** *pl* : the art or process of making articles from a nonmetallic mineral (as clay) by firing **2** : a product produced by ceramics — **ceramic** *adj*

ce·ra·mist \sə-ˈra-mist\ *or* **ce·ram·i·cist** \sə-ˈra-mə-sist\ *n* : one who engages in ceramics

[1]**ce·re·al** \ˈsir-ē-əl\ *adj* [L *cerealis,* fr. *Ceres,* the Roman goddess of agriculture] : relating to grain or to the plants that produce it; *also* : made of grain

[2]**cereal** *n* **1** : a grass (as wheat) yielding grain suitable for food; *also* : its grain **2** : a food and esp. a breakfast food prepared from the grain of a cereal

cer·e·bel·lum \ˌser-ə-ˈbe-ləm\ *n, pl* **-bel·lums** *or* **-bel·la** \-lə\ [ML, fr. L, dim. of *cerebrum* brain] : a part of the brain that projects over the medulla and is concerned esp. with coordination of muscular action and with bodily balance — **cer·e·bel·lar** \-lər\ *adj*

ce·re·bral \sə-ˈrē-brəl, ˈser-ə-\ *adj* **1** : of or relating to the brain, intellect, or cerebrum **2** : appealing to or involving the intellect — **ce·re·bral·ly** *adv*

cerebral cortex *n* : the surface layer of gray matter of the cerebrum that functions chiefly in coordination of sensory and motor information

cerebral palsy *n* : a disorder caused by brain damage usu. before, during, or shortly after birth and marked esp. by defective muscle control

cer·e·brate \ˈser-ə-ˌbrāt\ *vb* **-brat·ed; -brat·ing** : THINK — **cer·e·bra·tion** \ˌser-ə-ˈbrā-shən\ *n*

ce·re·brum \sə-ˈrē-brəm, ˈser-ə-\ *n, pl* **-brums** *or* **-bra** \-brə\ [L, brain] : the enlarged front and upper part of the brain that contains the higher nervous centers

cere·ment \ˈser-ə-mənt, ˈsir-mənt\ *n* : a shroud for the dead

[1]**cer·e·mo·ni·al** \ˌser-ə-ˈmō-nē-əl\ *adj* : of, relating to, or forming a ceremony; *also* : stressing careful attention to form and detail — **cer·e·mo·ni·al·ly** *adv*

[2]**ceremonial** *n* : a ceremonial act or system : RITUAL, FORM

cer·e·mo·ni·ous \ˌser-ə-ˈmō-nē-əs\ *adj* **1** : devoted to forms and ceremony **2** : CEREMONIAL **3** : according to formal usage or procedure **4** : marked by ceremony — **cer·e·mo·ni·ous·ly** *adv* — **cer·e·mo·ni·ous·ness** *n*

cer·e·mo·ny \ˈser-ə-ˌmō-nē\ *n, pl* **-nies** **1** : a formal act or series of acts prescribed by law, ritual, or convention **2** : a conventional act of politeness **3** : a mere outward form with no deeper significance **4** : FORMALITY

ce·re·us \ˈsir-ē-əs\ *n* : any of various cacti of the western U.S. and tropical America

ce·rise \sə-ˈrēs\ *n* [F, lit., cherry] : a moderate red color

ce·ri·um \ˈsir-ē-əm\ *n* : a malleable metallic chemical element used esp. in alloys

cer·met \ˈsər-ˌmet\ *n* : a strong alloy of a heat-resistant compound and a metal used esp. for turbine blades

cert *abbr* certificate; certification; certified; certify

[1]**cer·tain** \ˈsər-tᵊn\ *adj* **1 :** FIXED, SETTLED **2 :** of a specific but unspecified character ⟨~ people in authority⟩ **3 :** DEPENDABLE, RELIABLE **4 :** INDISPUTABLE, UNDENIABLE ⟨it is ~ that we exist⟩ **5 :** assured in mind or action ⟨I am ~ that they are right⟩ — **cer·tain·ly** *adv*
[2]**certain** *pron* **:** certain ones
cer·tain·ty \-tē\ *n, pl* **-ties 1 :** something that is certain **2 :** the quality or state of being certain
cer·tif·i·cate \sər-ˈti-fi-kət\ *n* **1 :** a document testifying to the truth of a fact **2 :** a document testifying that one has fulfilled certain requirements (as of a course) **3 :** a document giving evidence of ownership or debt ⟨a stock ~⟩
certificate of deposit : a money-market bond redeemable without penalty only on maturity
cer·ti·fi·ca·tion \ˌsər-tə-fə-ˈkā-shən\ *n* **1 :** the act of certifying **:** the state of being certified **2 :** a certified statement
certified mail *n* **:** first class mail for which proof of delivery may be secured but no indemnity value is claimed
certified public accountant *n* **:** an accountant who has met the requirements of a state law and has been granted a certificate
cer·ti·fy \ˈsər-tə-ˌfī\ *vb* **-fied; -fy·ing 1 :** VERIFY, CONFIRM **2 :** to endorse officially **3 :** to guarantee (a bank check) as good by a statement to that effect stamped on its face **4 :** to recognize as having met specific qualifications within a field ⟨*certified* teachers⟩ ♦ ***Synonyms*** ACCREDIT, APPROVE, SANCTION, ENDORSE — **cer·ti·fi·able** \-ə-bəl\ *adj* — **cer·ti·fi·ably** \-blē\ *adv* — **cer·ti·fi·er** *n*
cer·ti·tude \ˈsər-tə-ˌtüd, -ˌtyüd\ *n* **:** the state of being or feeling certain
ce·ru·le·an \sə-ˈrü-lē-ən\ *adj* **:** AZURE
ce·ru·men \sə-ˈrü-mən\ *n* **:** EARWAX
cer·vi·cal \ˈsər-vi-kəl\ *adj* **:** of or relating to a neck or cervix
cervical cap *n* **:** a contraceptive device in the form of a thimble-shaped molded cap that fits snugly over the uterine cervix and blocks sperm from entering the uterus
cer·vix \ˈsər-viks\ *n, pl* **cer·vi·ces** \-və-ˌsēz\ *or* **cer·vix·es 1 :** NECK; *esp* **:** the back part of the neck **2 :** a constricted portion of an organ or part; *esp* **:** the narrow outer end of the uterus
ce·sar·e·an *or* **cae·sar·e·an** *also* **ce·sar·i·an** *or* **cae·sar·i·an** \si-ˈzer-ē-ən\ *n, often cap* **:** CESAREAN SECTION — **cesarean** *or* **caesarean** *also* **cesarian** *or* **caesarian** *adj*
cesarean section *also* **caesarean section** *n, often cap C* [fr. the legendary association of such a delivery with the Roman cognomen *Caesar*] **:** surgical incision of the walls of the abdomen and uterus for delivery of offspring
ce·si·um \ˈsē-zē-əm\ *n* **:** a silver-white soft ductile chemical element
ces·sa·tion \se-ˈsā-shən\ *n* **:** a temporary or final ceasing (as of action)
ces·sion \ˈse-shən\ *n* **:** a yielding (as of rights) to another
cess·pool \ˈses-ˌpül\ *n* **1 :** an underground pit or tank for receiving household sewage **2 :** a filthy or corrupt situation
ce·ta·cean \si-ˈtā-shən\ *n* **:** any of an order of aquatic mostly marine mammals that includes whales, porpoises, dolphins, and related forms — **cetacean** *adj*
cf *abbr* [L *confer*] compare
Cf *symbol* californium
CF *abbr* cystic fibrosis
CFC *abbr* chlorofluorocarbon
CFL *abbr* compact fluorescent lamp; compact fluorescent light bulb
CFO *abbr* chief financial officer
cg *abbr* centigram
CG *abbr* **1** coast guard **2** commanding general
cgs *abbr* centimeter-gram-second
ch *abbr* **1** chain **2** champion **3** chapter **4** church
CH *abbr* **1** clearinghouse **2** courthouse **3** customhouse
Cha·blis \sha-ˈblē, shə-, shä-; ˈsha-ˌblē\ *n, pl* **Cha·blis** \-ˈblēz, -(ˌ)blēz\ **1 :** a dry sharp white Burgundy wine **2 :** a white California wine
cha–cha \ˈchä-ˌchä\ *n* **:** a fast rhythmic ballroom dance of Latin American origin
chafe \ˈchāf\ *vb* **chafed; chaf·ing 1 :** IRRITATE, VEX **2 :** FRET **3 :** to warm by rubbing **4 :** to rub so as to wear away; *also* **:** to make sore by rubbing
cha·fer \ˈchā-fər\ *n* **:** any of various scarab beetles
[1]**chaff** \ˈchaf\ *n* **1 :** debris separated from grain in threshing **2 :** something relatively worthless — **chaffy** *adj*
[2]**chaff** *n* **:** light jesting talk **:** BANTER
[3]**chaff** *vb* **:** to tease good-naturedly
chaf·fer \ˈcha-fər\ *vb* **:** BARGAIN, HAGGLE — **chaf·fer·er** *n*
chaf·finch \ˈcha-ˌfinch\ *n* **:** a common European finch with a cheerful song
chaf·ing dish \ˈchā-fiŋ-\ *n* **:** a utensil for cooking food at the table
[1]**cha·grin** \shə-ˈgrin\ *n* **:** mental uneasiness or annoyance caused by failure, disappointment, or humiliation
[2]**chagrin** *vb* **cha·grined** \-ˈgrind\; **cha·grin·ing :** to cause to feel chagrin
chai \ˈchī\ *n* **:** a beverage that is a blend of black tea, honey, spices, and milk
[1]**chain** \ˈchān\ *n* [ME *cheyne,* fr. AF *chaene,* fr. L *catena*] **1 :** a flexible series of connected links **2 :** a chainlike surveying instrument; *also* **:** a unit of length equal to 66 feet (about 20 meters) **3** *pl* **:** BONDS, FETTERS **4 :** a series of things linked together ⟨mountain ~*s*⟩; *also* **:** a group of usu. identical enterprises with a single owner ⟨fast-food ~*s*⟩ ♦ ***Synonyms*** TRAIN, STRING, SEQUENCE, SUCCESSION, SERIES
[2]**chain** *vb* **:** to fasten, bind, or connect with a chain; *also* **:** FETTER
chain gang *n* **:** a gang of convicts chained together
chain letter *n* **:** a letter sent to several per-

sons with a request that each send copies to an equal number of persons
chain mail *n* : flexible armor of interlocking metal rings
chain reaction *n* **1** : a series of events in which each event initiates the succeeding one **2** : a chemical or nuclear reaction yielding products that cause further reactions of the same kind
chain saw *n* : a portable power saw that has teeth linked together to form an endless chain — **chain•saw** \ˈchān-ˌsȯ\ *vb*
chain–smoke \ˈchān-ˈsmōk\ *vb* : to smoke esp. cigarettes continuously
[1]**chair** \ˈcher\ *n* [ME *chaiere,* fr. AF, fr. L *cathedra,* fr. Gk *kathedra,* fr. *kata-* down + *hedra* seat] **1** : a seat with a back for one person **2** : ELECTRIC CHAIR **3** : an official seat; *also* : an office or position of authority or dignity **4** : CHAIRMAN
[2]**chair** *vb* : to act as chairman of
chair•lift \ˈcher-ˌlift\ *n* : a motor-driven conveyor for skiers consisting of seats hung from a moving cable
chair•man \-mən\ *n* : the presiding officer of a meeting, committee, or event — **chair•man•ship** *n*
chair•per•son \-ˌpər-sən\ *n* : CHAIRMAN
chair•wom•an \-ˌwu̇-mən\ *n* : a woman who serves as chairman
chaise \ˈshāz\ *n* : a 2-wheeled horse-drawn carriage with a folding top
chaise longue \ˈshāz-ˈlȯŋ\ *n, pl* **chaise longues** *same or* -ˈlȯŋz\ [F, lit., long chair] : a long reclining chair
chaise lounge \-ˈlau̇nj\ *n* : CHAISE LONGUE
chal•ced•o•ny \kal-ˈse-dᵊn-ē\ *n, pl* **-nies** : a translucent quartz of various colors
chal•co•py•rite \ˌkal-kə-ˈpī-ˌrīt\ *n* : a yellow mineral constituting an important copper ore
cha•let \sha-ˈlā\ *n* **1** : a herdsman's cabin in the Swiss mountains **2** : a building in the style of a Swiss cottage with a wide roof overhang
chal•ice \ˈcha-ləs\ *n* : a drinking cup; *esp* : the eucharistic cup
[1]**chalk** \ˈchȯk\ *n* **1** : a soft limestone **2** : chalk or chalky material esp. when used as a crayon — **chalky** *adj*
[2]**chalk** *vb* **1** : to rub or mark with chalk **2** : to record with or as if with chalk — usu. used with *up*
chalk•board \ˈchȯk-ˌbȯrd\ *n* : BLACKBOARD
chalk up *vb* **1** : ASCRIBE, CREDIT **2** : ATTAIN, ACHIEVE ⟨*chalk up* a victory⟩
[1]**chal•lenge** \ˈcha-lənj\ *vb* **chal•lenged**; **chal•leng•ing** [ME *chalengen* to accuse, fr. AF *chalenger,* fr. L *calumniari* to accuse falsely, fr. *calumnia* calumny] **1** : to order to halt and prove identity **2** : to take exception to : DISPUTE ⟨∼ a ruling⟩ **3** : to issue an invitation to compete ⟨*challenged* me to another game⟩ **4** : to stimulate by presenting difficulties ⟨a job that ∼*s* her⟩ — **chal•leng•er** *n*
[2]**challenge** *n* **1** : a summons to a duel **2** : an invitation to compete in a sport **3** : a calling into question **4** : an exception taken to a juror **5** : a sentry's command to halt and prove identity **6** : a stimulating or interesting task or problem
challenged *adj* : presented with difficulties (as by a disability)
chal•lis \ˈsha-lē\ *n, pl* **chal•lises** \-lēz\ : a lightweight clothing fabric of wool, cotton, or synthetic yarns
cham•ber \ˈchām-bər\ *n* **1** : ROOM; *esp* : BEDROOM **2** : an enclosed space or cavity **3** : a hall for meetings of a legislative body **4** : a judge's consultation room — usu. used in pl. **5** : a legislative or judicial body; *also* : a council for a business purpose **6** : the part of a firearm that holds the cartridge or powder charge during firing — **cham•bered** \-bərd\ *adj*
cham•ber•lain \ˈchām-bər-lən\ *n* **1** : a chief officer in the household of a king or nobleman **2** : TREASURER
cham•ber•maid \-ˌmād\ *n* : a maid who takes care of bedrooms
chamber music *n* : music intended for performance by a few musicians before a small audience
chamber of commerce : an association of businesspeople for promoting commercial and industrial interests in the community
cham•bray \ˈsham-ˌbrā\ *n* : a lightweight clothing fabric of white and colored threads
cha•me•leon \kə-ˈmēl-yən\ *n* [ME *camelion,* fr. MF, fr. L *chamaeleon,* fr. Gk *chamaileōn,* fr. *chamai* on the ground + *leōn* lion] : a small lizard whose skin changes color esp. according to its surroundings
[1]**cham•fer** \ˈcham-fər\ *vb* **1** : to cut a furrow in (as a column) : GROOVE **2** : to make a chamfer on : BEVEL
[2]**chamfer** *n* : a beveled edge
cham•ois \ˈsha-mē\ *n, pl* **cham•ois** *same or* -mēz\ **1** : a small goatlike ruminant mammal of Europe and the Caucasus region of Russia **2** *also* **cham•my** \ˈsha-mē\ : a soft leather made esp. from the skin of the sheep or goat **3** : a cotton fabric made in imitation of chamois leather
cham•o•mile *or* **cam•o•mile** \ˈka-mə-ˌmī(-ə)l, -ˌmēl\ *n* : any of a genus of strong-scented herbs related to the daisies and having flower heads that yield a bitter substance used esp. in tonics and teas
[1]**champ** \ˈchamp, ˈchämp\ *vb* **1** : to chew noisily **2** : to show impatience of delay or restraint
[2]**champ** \ˈchamp\ *n* : CHAMPION
cham•pagne \sham-ˈpān\ *n* : a white effervescent wine
[1]**cham•pi•on** \ˈcham-pē-ən\ *n* **1** : a militant advocate or defender **2** : one that wins first prize or place in a contest **3** : one that is acknowledged to be better than all others
[2]**champion** *vb* : to protect or fight for as a champion ♦ ***Synonyms*** BACK, ADVOCATE, UPHOLD, SUPPORT
cham•pi•on•ship \-ˌship\ *n* **1** : the position or title of a champion **2** : the act of

championing : DEFENSE **3** : a contest held to determine a champion

[1]**chance** \ˈchans\ *n* **1** : something that happens without apparent cause **2** : the unpredictable element in existence : LUCK, FORTUNE **3** : OPPORTUNITY **4** : the likelihood of a particular outcome in an uncertain situation : PROBABILITY **5** : RISK **6** : a raffle ticket — **chance** *adj* — **by chance** : in the haphazard course of events

[2]**chance** *vb* **chanced**; **chanc·ing** **1** : to take place by chance : HAPPEN **2** : to come casually and unexpectedly — used with *upon* **3** : to leave to chance **4** : to accept the risk of

chan·cel \ˈchan-səl\ *n* : the part of a church including the altar and choir

chan·cel·lery *or* **chan·cel·lory** \ˈchan-sə-lə-rē\ *n, pl* **-ler·ies** *or* **-lor·ies** **1** : the position or office of a chancellor **2** : the building or room where a chancellor works **3** : the office or staff of an embassy or consulate

chan·cel·lor \ˈchan-sə-lər\ *n* **1** : a high state official in various countries **2** : the head of a university **3** : a judge in the equity court in various states of the U.S. **4** : the chief minister of state in some European countries — **chan·cel·lor·ship** *n*

chan·cery \ˈchan-sə-rē\ *n, pl* **-cer·ies** **1** : a record office for public or diplomatic archives **2** : any of various courts of equity in the U.S. and Britain **3** : a chancellor's court or office **4** : the office of an embassy **5** : the business office of a diocese

chan·cre \ˈshaŋ-kər\ *n* [F, fr. OF, fr. L *cancer*] : a primary sore or ulcer at the site of entry of an infective agent

chan·croid \ˈchaŋ-ˌkrȯid\ *n* : a sexually transmitted disease caused by a bacterium and characterized by chancres that differ from those of syphilis in lacking hardened margins

chancy \ˈchan-sē\ *adj* **chanc·i·er**; **-est** **1** *Scot* : AUSPICIOUS **2** : RISKY

chan·de·lier \ˌshan-də-ˈlir\ *n* : a branched lighting fixture suspended from a ceiling

chan·dler \ˈchand-lər\ *n* [ME *chandeler* a maker or seller of candles, fr. AF, fr. *chandele* candle, fr. L *candela*] : a dealer in provisions and supplies of a specified kind ⟨ship's ~⟩ — **chan·dlery** *n*

[1]**change** \ˈchānj\ *vb* **changed**; **chang·ing** **1** : to make or become different : ALTER **2** : to replace with another **3** : to give or receive an equivalent sum in notes or coins of usu. smaller denominations or of another currency **4** : to put fresh clothes or covering on ⟨~ a bed⟩ **5** : to put on different clothes **6** : EXCHANGE — **change·able** *adj* — **chang·er** *n*

[2]**change** *n* **1** : the act, process, or result of changing **2** : a fresh set of clothes **3** : money given in exchange for other money of higher denomination **4** : money returned when a payment exceeds the sum due **5** : coins esp. of small denominations — **change·ful** *adj*

change·ling \ˈchānj-liŋ\ *n* : a child secretly exchanged for another in infancy

change of life : MENOPAUSE

change·over \ˈchānj-ˌō-vər\ *n* : CONVERSION, TRANSITION

change ringing *n* : the art or practice of ringing a set of tuned bells in continually varying order

[1]**chan·nel** \ˈcha-nᵊl\ *n* **1** : the bed of a stream **2** : the deeper part of a waterway **3** : STRAIT **4** : a means of passage or transmission **5 a** : a range of frequencies of sufficient width for a single radio or television transmission **b** : an account on an online media sharing or streaming service used to make media content (such as videos) available to others **6** : a usu. tubular enclosed passage : CONDUIT **7** : a long gutter, groove, or furrow

[2]**channel** *vb* **-neled** *or* **-nelled**; **-neling** *or* **-nel·ling** **1** : to make a channel in **2** : to direct into or through a channel

chan·nel·ize \ˈcha-nə-ˌlīz\ *vb* **-ized**; **-iz·ing** : CHANNEL — **chan·nel·i·za·tion** \ˌcha-nə-lə-ˈzā-shən\ *n*

chan·son \shäⁿ-ˈsōⁿ\ *n, pl* **chan·sons** *same or* -ˈsōⁿz\ : SONG; *esp* : a cabaret song

[1]**chant** \ˈchant\ *vb* **1** : SING; *esp* : to sing a chant **2** : to utter or recite in the manner of a chant **3** : to celebrate or praise in song — **chant·er** *n*

[2]**chant** *n* **1** : a repetitive melody in which several words are sung to one tone : SONG; *esp* : a liturgical melody **2** : a manner of singing or speaking in musical monotones

chan·te·relle \ˌshan-tə-ˈrel\ *n* : a fragrant edible mushroom

chan·teuse \shäⁿ-ˈtərz, shan-ˈtüz\ *n, pl* **chan·teuses** *same or* -ˈtər-zəz, -ˈtü-zəz\ [F] : a woman who is a concert or nightclub singer

chan·tey *or* **chan·ty** \ˈshan-tē, ˈchan-\ *n, pl* **chanteys** *or* **chanties** : a song sung by sailors in rhythm with their work

chan·ti·cleer \ˌchan-tə-ˈklir, ˌshan-\ *n* : ROOSTER

Chanukah *var of* HANUKKAH

cha·os \ˈkā-ˌäs\ *n* **1** *often cap* : the confused unorganized state existing before the creation of distinct forms **2** : the inherent unpredictability in the behavior of a complex natural system (as the atmosphere or the beating heart) **3** : complete disorder ♦ ***Synonyms*** CONFUSION, JUMBLE, SNARL, MUDDLE, DISARRAY — **cha·ot·ic** \kā-ˈä-tik\ *adj* — **cha·ot·i·cal·ly** \-ti-k(ə-)lē\ *adv*

chaos theory *n* : a branch of mathematical and physical theory concerned with chaotic systems

[1]**chap** \ˈchap\ *vb* **chapped**; **chap·ping** : to dry and crack open usu. from wind and cold ⟨*chapped* lips⟩

[2]**chap** *n* : a jaw with its fleshy covering — usu. used in pl.

[3]**chap** *n, chiefly Brit* : FELLOW

[4]**chap** *abbr* chapter

chap·ar·ral \ˌsha-pə-ˈral\ *n* **1** : a dense impenetrable thicket of shrubs or dwarf trees **2** : an ecological community esp. of southern California composed of shrubby plants

chap·book \'chap-ˌbu̇k\ *n* : a small book of ballads, tales, or tracts

cha·peau \sha-'pō\ *n, pl* **cha·peaus** \-'pōz\ *or* **cha·peaux** \-'pō, -'pōz\ [MF] : HAT

cha·pel \'cha-pəl\ *n* [ME, fr. AF *chapele,* fr. ML *cappella,* fr. LL *cappa* cloak; fr. the cloak of St. Martin of Tours preserved as a sacred relic in a chapel built for that purpose] **1** : a private or subordinate place of worship **2** : an assembly at an educational institution usu. including devotional exercises **3** : a place of worship used by a Christian group other than an established church

[1]**chap·er·one** *or* **chap·er·on** \'sha-pə-ˌrōn\ *n* [F *chaperon,* lit., hood, fr. MF, head covering, fr. *chape* cape, fr. LL *cappa*] **1** : a person (as a matron) who accompanies young unmarried women in public for propriety **2** : an older person who accompanies young people at a social gathering to ensure proper behavior

[2]**chaperone** *or* **chaperon** *vb* **-oned**; **-on·ing** **1** : ESCORT, GUIDE **2** : to act as a chaperone to or for ⟨~ a dance⟩ ⟨~ teens⟩ — **chap·er·on·age** \-ˌrō-nij\ *n*

chap·fall·en \'chap-ˌfo̊-lən, 'chäp-\ *adj* **1** : having the lower jaw hanging loosely **2** : DEJECTED, DEPRESSED

chap·lain \'cha-plən\ *n* **1** : a member of the clergy officially attached to a special group (as the army) **2** : a person chosen to conduct religious exercises (as for a club) — **chap·lain·cy** \-sē\ *n*

chap·let \'cha-plət\ *n* **1** : a wreath for the head **2** : a string of beads : NECKLACE

chap·man \'chap-mən\ *n, Brit* : an itinerant dealer : PEDDLER

chaps \'shaps, 'chaps\ *n pl* [MexSp *chaparreras*] : leather leggings resembling pants without a seat that are worn esp. by western ranch hands

chap·ter \'chap-tər\ *n* **1** : a main division of a book **2** : a body of canons (as of a cathedral) **3** : a local branch of a society or fraternity

[1]**char** \'chär\ *n, pl* **char** *or* **chars** : any of a genus of trouts (as the common brook trout) with small scales

[2]**char** *vb* **charred**; **char·ring** **1** : to burn or become burned to charcoal **2** : SCORCH

[3]**char** *vb* **charred**; **char·ring** : to work as a cleaning woman

char·ac·ter \'ker-ik-tər\ *n* [ME *caracter,* fr. L *character* mark, distinctive quality, fr. Gk *charaktēr,* fr. *charassein* to scratch, engrave] **1** : a graphic symbol (as a letter) used in writing or printing **2** : a symbol that represents information; *also* : a representation of such a character that may be accepted by a computer **3** : a distinguishing feature : ATTRIBUTE **4** : the complex of mental and ethical traits marking a person or a group **5** : a person marked by conspicuous often peculiar traits **6** : one of the persons in a novel or play **7** : REPUTATION ⟨an attack on his ~⟩ **8** : moral excellence

[1]**char·ac·ter·is·tic** \ˌker-ik-tə-'ris-tik\ *n* : a distinguishing trait, quality, or property

[2]**characteristic** *adj* : serving to mark individual character ♦ ***Synonyms*** INDIVIDUAL, PECULIAR, DISTINCTIVE — **char·ac·ter·is·ti·cal·ly** \-ti-k(ə-)lē\ *adv*

char·ac·ter·ize \'ker-ik-tə-ˌrīz\ *vb* **-ized**; **-iz·ing** **1** : to describe the character of **2** : to be characteristic of — **char·ac·ter·i·za·tion** \ˌker-ik-tə-rə-'zā-shən\ *n*

cha·rades \shə-'rādz\ *n sing or pl* : a game in which some of the players try to guess a word or phrase from the actions of another player who may not speak

char·coal \'chär-ˌkōl\ *n* **1** : a porous carbon prepared from vegetable or animal substances **2** : a piece of fine charcoal used in drawing; *also* : a drawing made with charcoal

chard \'chärd\ *n* : SWISS CHARD

char·don·nay \ˌshar-dᵊn-'ā\ *n, often cap* [F] : a dry white wine made from a single variety of white grape

[1]**charge** \'chärj\ *n* **1** : a quantity (as of fuel or ammunition) required to fill something to capacity **2** : a store or accumulation of force **3** : an excess or deficiency of electrons in a body **4** : THRILL, KICK **5** : a task or duty imposed **6** : CARE, RESPONSIBILITY **7** : one given into another's care **8** : instructions from a judge to a jury **9** : COST, EXPENSE, PRICE; *also* : a debit to an account **10** : ACCUSATION, INDICTMENT **11** : ATTACK, ASSAULT

[2]**charge** *vb* **charged**; **charg·ing** **1** : to load or fill to capacity **2** : to give an electric charge to; *also* : to restore the activity of (a storage battery) by means of an electric current **3** : to impose a task or responsibility on **4** : COMMAND, ORDER **5** : ACCUSE **6** : to rush against : rush forward in assault **7** : to make liable for payment; *also* : to record a debt or liability against **8** : to fix as a price — **charge·able** *adj*

charge–coupled device *n* : a semiconductor device used esp. as an optical sensor

char·gé d'af·faires \shär-ˌzhā-də-'fer\ *n, pl* **chargés d'affaires** \-ˌzhā-, -ˌzhāz-\ [F] : a diplomat who substitutes for an ambassador or minister

[1]**char·ger** \'chär-jər\ *n* : a large platter

[2]**charg·er** *n* **1** : a device or a worker that charges something **2** : WARHORSE 1

char·i·ot \'cher-ē-ət\ *n* : a 2-wheeled horse-drawn vehicle of ancient times used esp. in war and in races — **char·i·o·teer** \ˌcher-ē-ə-'tir\ *n*

cha·ris·ma \kə-'riz-mə\ *n* : a personal quality of leadership arousing popular loyalty or enthusiasm — **char·is·mat·ic** \ˌkar-əz-'ma-tik\ *adj*

char·i·ta·ble \'cher-ə-tə-bəl\ *adj* **1** : liberal in giving to needy people **2** : merciful or lenient in judging others ♦ ***Synonyms*** BENEVOLENT, PHILANTHROPIC, ALTRUISTIC, HUMANITARIAN — **char-**

i·ta·ble·ness *n* — **char·i·ta·bly** \-blē\ *adv*

char·i·ty \ˈcher-ə-tē\ *n, pl* **-ties** **1** : goodwill toward or love of humanity **2** : an act or feeling of generosity **3** : the giving of aid to the poor; *also* : ALMS **4** : an institution engaged in relief of the poor **5** : leniency in judging others ♦ ***Synonyms*** MERCY, CLEMENCY, LENITY

char·la·tan \ˈshär-lə-tən\ *n* : a person making usu. showy pretenses to knowledge or ability : FRAUD, FAKER

Charles·ton \ˈchärl-stən\ *n* : a lively dance in which the knees are swung in and out and the heels are turned sharply outward on each step

char·ley horse \ˈchär-lē-ˌhȯrs\ *n* : a muscular pain, cramping, or stiffness from a strain or bruise

[1]**charm** \ˈchärm\ *n* [ME *charme,* fr. AF, fr. L *carmen* song, fr. *canere* to sing] **1** : a practice or expression believed to have magic power **2** : something worn about the person to ward off evil or bring good fortune : AMULET **3** : a trait that fascinates or allures **4** : physical grace or attraction **5** : a small ornament worn on a bracelet or chain **6** : a quark with a charge of +⅔ and a measured energy of approximately 1.5 billion electron volts

[2]**charm** *vb* **1** : to affect by or as if by a magic spell **2** : to protect by or as if by charms **3** : FASCINATE, ENCHANT ♦ ***Synonyms*** ALLURE, CAPTIVATE, BEWITCH, ATTRACT — **charm·er** *n*

charmed \ˈchärmd\ *adj* : extremely lucky or prosperous ⟨a ~ life⟩

charm·ing \ˈchär-miŋ\ *adj* : PLEASING, DELIGHTFUL — **charm·ing·ly** *adv*

char·nel house \ˈchär-nᵊl-\ *n* : a building or chamber in which bodies or bones are deposited

[1]**chart** \ˈchärt\ *n* **1** : MAP **2** : a sheet giving information in the form of a table, list, or diagram; *also* : GRAPH

[2]**chart** *vb* **1** : PLAN ⟨~ a course⟩ **2** : to make a chart of **3** : CHRONICLE ⟨~*ed* his adventures⟩

[1]**char·ter** \ˈchär-tər\ *n* **1** : an official document granting rights or privileges (as to a colony, town, or college) from a sovereign or a governing body **2** : CONSTITUTION **3** : a written instrument from a society creating a branch **4** : a mercantile lease of a ship

[2]**charter** *vb* **1** : to grant a charter to **2** *Brit* : CERTIFY ⟨~*ed* engineer⟩ **3** : to hire, rent, or lease for temporary use ⟨~ a bus⟩ — **char·ter·er** *n*

charter member *n* : an original member of an organization

char·treuse \shär-ˈtrüz, -ˈtrüs\ *n* : a brilliant yellow green

char·wom·an \ˈchär-ˌwu̇-mən\ *n* : a cleaning woman esp. in large buildings

chary \ˈcher-ē\ *adj* **chari·er; -est** [ME, sorrowful, dear, fr. OE *cearig* sorrowful, fr. *caru* sorrow] **1** : CAUTIOUS, CIRCUMSPECT **2** : SPARING — **char·i·ly** \-ə-lē\ *adv*

[1]**chase** \ˈchās\ *n* **1** : PURSUIT; *also* : HUNTING **2** : QUARRY **3** : a tract of unenclosed land used as a game preserve

[2]**chase** *vb* **chased; chas·ing** **1** : to follow rapidly : PURSUE **2** : HUNT **3** : to seek out ⟨*chasing* down clues⟩ **4** : to cause to depart or flee : drive away **5** : RUSH, HASTEN

[3]**chase** *vb* **chased; chas·ing** : to decorate (a metal surface) by embossing or engraving

[4]**chase** *n* : FURROW, GROOVE

chas·er \ˈchā-sər\ *n* **1** : one that chases **2** : a mild drink (as beer) taken after hard liquor

chasm \ˈka-zəm\ *n* : GORGE 2

chas·sis \ˈcha-sē, ˈsha-sē\ *n, pl* **chas·sis** \-sēz\ : the supporting frame of a structure (as an automobile or television set)

chaste \ˈchāst\ *adj* **chast·er; chast·est** **1** : innocent of unlawful sexual intercourse : VIRTUOUS, PURE **2** : CELIBATE **3** : pure in thought : MODEST **4** : severe or simple in design — **chaste·ly** *adv* — **chaste·ness** *n*

chas·ten \ˈchā-sᵊn\ *vb* : to correct through punishment or suffering : DISCIPLINE; *also* : PURIFY — **chas·ten·er** *n*

chas·tise \chas-ˈtīz\ *vb* **chas·tised; chas·tis·ing** [ME *chastisen,* alter. of *chasten*] **1** : to punish esp. bodily **2** : to censure severely : CASTIGATE — **chas·tise·ment** \-mənt, ˈchas-təz-\ *n*

chas·ti·ty \ˈchas-tə-tē\ *n* : the quality or state of being chaste; *esp* : sexual purity

cha·su·ble \ˈcha-zə-bəl, -sə-\ *n* : the outer vestment of the priest at mass

chat \ˈchat\ *n* **1** : light familiar informal talk **2** : online discussion in a chat room — **chat** *vb*

châ·teau \sha-ˈtō\ *n, pl* **châ·teaus** \-ˈtōz\ *or* **châ·teaux** \-ˈtō, -ˈtōz\ [F, fr. OF *chastel,* fr. L *castellum* castle, dim. of *castra* camp] **1** : a feudal castle in France **2** : a large country house **3** : a French vineyard estate

chat·e·laine \ˈshat-ə-ˈlān\ *n* **1** : the mistress of a chateau **2** : a clasp or hook for a watch, purse, or keys

chat room *n* : a real-time online interactive discussion group

chat·tel \ˈcha-tᵊl\ *n* **1** : an item of tangible property other than real estate **2** : SLAVE, BONDMAN

chat·ter \ˈcha-tər\ *vb* **1** : to utter speechlike but meaningless sounds **2** : to talk idly, incessantly, or fast **3** : to click repeatedly or uncontrollably — **chatter** *n* — **chat·ter·er** *n*

chat·ter·box \ˈcha-tər-ˌbäks\ *n* : one who talks incessantly

chat·ty \ˈcha-tē\ *adj* **chat·ti·er; -est** : TALKATIVE — **chat·ti·ly** \-tə-lē\ *adv* — **chat·ti·ness** \-tē-nəs\ *n*

[1]**chauf·feur** \ˈshō-fər, shō-ˈfər\ *n* [F, lit., stoker, fr. *chauffer* to heat] : a person employed to drive an automobile

[2]**chauffeur** *vb* **1** : to do the work of a chauffeur **2** : to transport in the manner of a chauffeur ⟨~*ed* the kids to school⟩

chaunt *var of* CHANT

chau·vin·ism \ˈshō-və-ˌni-zəm\ *n* [F

chauvinisme, fr. Nicolas *Chauvin,* fictional soldier of excessive patriotism and devotion to Napoleon] **1** : excessive or blind patriotism **2** : an attitude of superiority toward members of the opposite sex — **chau·vin·ist** \-nist\ *n or adj* — **chau·vin·is·tic** \ˌshō-və-ˈnis-tik\ *adj* — **chau·vin·is·ti·cal·ly** \-ti-k(ə-)lē\ *adv*

cheap \ˈchēp\ *adj* **1** : INEXPENSIVE **2** : costing little effort to obtain ⟨~ tickets⟩ **3** : worth little : SHODDY, TAWDRY ⟨~ workmanship⟩ **4** : worthy of scorn **5** : STINGY — **cheap** *adv* — **cheap·ly** *adv* — **cheap·ness** *n*

cheap·en \ˈchē-pən\ *vb* **1** : to make or become cheap or cheaper in price or value **2** : to make tawdry

cheap·skate \ˈchēp-ˌskāt\ *n* : a miserly or stingy person; *esp* : one who tries to avoid paying a fair share of costs

¹cheat \ˈchēt\ *vb* **1** : to deprive of something through fraud or deceit ⟨~*ed* workers of their pay⟩ **2** : to practice fraud or trickery **3** : to violate rules dishonestly ⟨~ at cards⟩ **4** : to be sexually unfaithful — **cheat·er** *n*

²cheat *n* **1** : the act of deceiving : FRAUD, DECEPTION **2** : one that cheats : a dishonest person

¹check \ˈchek\ *n* **1** : exposure of a chess king to an attack **2** : a sudden stoppage of progress **3** : a sudden pause or break **4** : something that stops or restrains **5** : a standard for testing or evaluation **6** : EXAMINATION, INVESTIGATION **7** : the act of testing or verifying **8** : a written order to a bank to pay money **9** : a ticket or token showing ownership or identity **10** : a slip indicating an amount due **11** : a pattern in squares; *also* : a fabric in such a pattern **12** : a mark typically ✓ placed beside an item to show that it has been noted **13** : CRACK, SPLIT

²check *vb* **1** : to put (a chess king) in check **2** : to slow down or stop : BRAKE **3** : to restrain the action or force of : CURB **4** : to compare with a source, original, or authority : VERIFY **5** : to inspect or test for satisfactory condition **6** : to mark with a check as examined **7** : to consign for shipment for one holding a passenger ticket **8** : to mark into squares **9** : to leave or accept for safekeeping in a checkroom **10** : to prove to be consistent or truthful **11** : CRACK, SPLIT

check·book \ˈchek-ˌbu̇k\ *n* : a book containing blank checks

¹check·er \ˈche-kər\ *n* : a piece in the game of checkers

²checker *vb* **1** : to variegate with different colors or shades **2** : to vary with contrasting elements ⟨a ~*ed* career⟩ **3** : to mark into squares

³checker *n* : one that checks; *esp* : an employee who checks out purchases in a store

check·er·ber·ry \ˈche-kər-ˌber-ē\ *n* : WINTERGREEN 1; *also* : the spicy red fruit of this plant

check·er·board \-ˌbōrd\ *n* : a board of 64 squares of alternate colors used in various games

check·ered \ˈche-kərd\ *adj* : marked by inconsistent fortune or recurring problems ⟨his ~ past⟩

check·ers \ˈche-kərz\ *n* : a checkerboard game for 2 players each with 12 pieces

check in *vb* : to report one's presence or arrival (as at a hotel)

check·list \ˈchek-ˌlist\ *n* : a list of things to be checked or done; *also* : a comprehensive list

check·mate \ˈchek-ˌmāt\ *vb* [ME *chekmaten,* fr. *chekmate,* interj. used to announce checkmate, fr. AF *eschec mat,* fr. Ar *shāh māt,* fr. Pers, lit., the king is left unable to escape] **1** : to thwart completely : DEFEAT, FRUSTRATE **2** : to attack (an opponent's king) in chess so that escape is impossible — **checkmate** *n*

check·off \ˈchek-ˌȯf\ *n* : the deduction of union dues from a worker's paycheck by the employer

check·out \ˈchek-ˌau̇t\ *n* **1** : the action or an instance of checking out **2** : a counter at which checking out is done **3** : the process of examining and testing something as to readiness for intended use

check out *vb* **1** : to settle one's account (as at a hotel) and leave **2** : to total or have totaled the cost of purchases in a store and to make or receive payment for them

check·point \ˈchek-ˌpȯint\ *n* : a point at which a check is performed

check·room \-ˌrüm, -ˌru̇m\ *n* : a room at which baggage, parcels, or clothing is left for safekeeping

checks and balances *n pl* : a system allowing each branch of a government to restrict the actions of another branch (as by a veto)

check·up \ˈchek-ˌəp\ *n* : EXAMINATION; *esp* : a general physical examination

ched·dar \ˈche-dər\ *n, often cap* : a hard mild to sharp white or yellow cheese of smooth texture

cheek \ˈchēk\ *n* **1** : the fleshy side part of the face **2** : IMPUDENCE, BOLDNESS, AUDACITY **3** : BUTTOCK 1 — **cheeked** \ˈchēkt\ *adj*

cheek·bone \ˈchēk-ˌbōn\ *n* : the bone or bony ridge below the eye

cheeky \ˈchē-kē\ *adj* **cheek·i·er**; **-est** : IMPUDENT, SAUCY — **cheek·i·ly** \-kə-lē\ *adv* — **cheek·i·ness** \-kē-nəs\ *n*

cheep \ˈchēp\ *vb* : to utter faint shrill sounds : PEEP — **cheep** *n*

¹cheer \ˈchir\ *n* [ME *chere* face, cheer, fr. AF, face, fr. ML *cara,* prob. fr. Gk *kara* head, face] **1** : state of mind or heart : SPIRIT **2** : ANIMATION, GAIETY **3** : hospitable entertainment : WELCOME **4** : food and drink for a feast **5** : something that gladdens **6** : a shout of applause or encouragement

²cheer *vb* **1** : to give hope or courage to : COMFORT **2** : to make glad **3** : to urge on esp. by shouts **4** : to applaud with shouts **5** : to grow or be cheerful — usu. used with *up* — **cheer·er** *n*

cheer•ful \ˈchir-fəl\ *adj* **1** : having or showing good spirits **2** : conducive to good spirits : pleasant and bright — **cheer•ful•ly** *adv* — **cheer•ful•ness** *n*
cheer•lead•er \ˈchir-ˌlē-dər\ *n* : a person who directs organized cheering esp. at a sports event — **cheer•lead•ing** *n*
cheer•less \ˈchir-ləs\ *adj* : BLEAK, DISPIRITING ⟨a ~ office⟩ — **cheer•less•ly** *adv* — **cheer•less•ness** *n*
cheery \ˈchir-ē\ *adj* **cheer•i•er**; **-est** : CHEERFUL ⟨~ music⟩ — **cheer•i•ly** \-ə-lē\ *adv* — **cheer•i•ness** \-ē-nəs\ *n*
cheese \ˈchēz\ *n* : the curd of milk usu. pressed into cakes and cured for use as food
cheese•burg•er \-ˌbər-gər\ *n* : a hamburger topped with cheese
cheese•cake \-ˌkāk\ *n* **1** : a dessert consisting of a creamy filling usu. containing cheese baked in a shell **2** : photographs of shapely scantily clad women
cheese•cloth \-ˌklȯth\ *n* : a lightweight coarse cotton gauze
cheese•par•ing \-ˌper-iŋ\ *n* : miserly economizing — **cheeseparing** *adj*
cheese•steak \-ˌstāk\ *n* : a sandwich of thinly sliced beef topped with melted cheese
cheesy \ˈchē-zē\ *adj* **chees•i•er**; **-est** **1** : resembling, suggesting, or containing cheese **2** : CHEAP 3 ⟨~ motels⟩
chee•tah \ˈchē-tə\ *n* [Hindi *cītā* leopard, fr. Skt *citraka,* fr. *citra* bright, variegated] : a large long-legged swift-moving spotted cat of Africa and formerly Asia
chef \ˈshef\ *n* : COOK; *esp* : one who manages a kitchen (as of a restaurant)
chef d'oeu•vre \shā-ˈdœvrᵊ\ *n, pl* **chefs d'oeuvre** *same*\ : MASTERPIECE
chem *abbr* chemical; chemist; chemistry
¹**chem•i•cal** \ˈke-mi-kəl\ *adj* **1** : of, relating to, used in, or produced by chemistry ⟨~ reactions⟩ **2** : acting or operated or produced by chemicals — **chem•i•cal•ly** \-k(ə-)lē\ *adv*
²**chemical** *n* **1** : a substance obtained by a chemical process or producing a chemical effect **2** : DRUG
chemical engineering *n* : engineering dealing with the industrial application of chemistry — **chemical engineer** *n*
chemical warfare *n* : warfare using incendiary mixtures, smokes, or irritant, burning, or asphyxiating gases
chemical weapon *n* : a weapon used in chemical warfare
che•mise \shə-ˈmēz\ *n* **1** : a woman's one-piece undergarment **2** : a loose straight-hanging dress
chem•ist \ˈke-mist\ *n* **1** : one trained in chemistry **2** *Brit* : PHARMACIST
chem•is•try \ˈke-mə-strē\ *n, pl* **-tries** **1** : the science that deals with the composition, structure, and properties of substances and of the changes they undergo **2** : chemical composition or properties ⟨the ~ of gasoline⟩ **3** : a strong mutual attraction; *also* : harmonious interaction among people (as on a team)
che•mo \ˈkē-mō\ *n* : CHEMOTHERAPY
che•mo•ther•a•py \ˌkē-mō-ˈther-ə-pē\ *n* : the use of chemicals in the treatment or control of disease — **che•mo•ther•a•peu•tic** \-ˌther-ə-ˈpyü-tik\ *adj*
che•nille \shə-ˈnēl\ *n* [F, lit., caterpillar, fr. OF, fr. L *canicula,* dim. of *canis* dog] : a fabric with a deep fuzzy pile often used for bedspreads and rugs
cheque *chiefly Brit var of* ¹CHECK 7
che•quer *chiefly Brit var of* CHECKER
cher•ish \ˈcher-ish\ *vb* **1** : to hold dear : treat with care and affection **2** : to keep deeply in mind ⟨~ a memory⟩ — **cher•ish•able** *adj* — **cher•ish•er** *n*
Cher•o•kee \ˈcher-ə-(ˌ)kē\ *n, pl* **Cherokee** *or* **Cherokees** : a member of an Indigenous people orig. of Tennessee and No. Carolina; *also* : their language
che•root \shə-ˈrüt\ *n* : a cigar cut square at both ends
cher•ry \ˈcher-ē\ *n, pl* **cherries** [ME *chery,* fr. AF *cherise, cirice* (taken as a plural), fr. LL *ceresia,* fr. L *cerasus* cherry tree, fr. Gk *kerasos*] **1** : the small fleshy pale yellow to deep blackish red fruit of a tree related to the roses; *also* : the tree or its wood **2** : a moderate red
chert \ˈchərt, ˈchat\ *n* : a rock resembling flint and consisting essentially of fine crystalline quartz and fibrous chalcedony — **cherty** *adj*
cher•ub \ˈcher-əb\ *n* **1** *pl* **cher•u•bim** \ˈcher-ə-ˌbim\ : an angel of the 2d highest rank **2** *pl* **cherubs** : a chubby rosy person — **che•ru•bic** \chə-ˈrü-bik\ *adj*
chess \ˈches\ *n* : a game for 2 played on a chessboard with each player having 16 pieces — **chess•man** \-ˌman, -mən\ *n*
chess•board \ˈches-ˌbȯrd\ *n* : a checkerboard used in the game of chess
chest \ˈchest\ *n* **1** : a box, case, or boxlike receptacle for storage or shipping **2** : the part of the body enclosed by the ribs and sternum — **chest•ed** \ˈches-təd\ *adj* — **chest•ful** \ˈchest-ˌfu̇l\ *n*
ches•ter•field \ˈches-tər-ˌfēld\ *n* : an overcoat with a velvet collar
chest•nut \ˈches-(ˌ)nət\ *n* **1** : the edible nut of any of a genus of trees related to the beeches and oaks; *also* : this tree or its wood **2** : a grayish to reddish brown **3** : an old joke or story
chet•rum \ˈche-trəm\ *n, pl* **chetrums** *or* **chetrum** — see *ngultrum* at MONEY table
che•val glass \shə-ˈval-\ *n* : a full-length mirror that may be tilted in a frame
che•va•lier \ˌshe-və-ˈlir, shə-ˈval-ˌyā\ *n* : a member of one of various orders of knighthood or of merit
chev•i•ot \ˈshe-vē-ət\ *n, often cap* **1** : a twilled fabric with a rough nap **2** : a sturdy soft-finished cotton fabric
chev•ron \ˈshe-vrən\ *n* : a sleeve badge of one or more V-shaped or inverted V-shaped stripes worn to indicate rank or service (as in the armed forces)
¹**chew** \ˈchü\ *vb* : to crush or grind with the teeth — **chew•able** *adj* — **chew•er** *n* — **chewy** \ˈchü-ē\ *adj* — **chew on** : to think about : PONDER ⟨*chew on* the proposals⟩ — **chew the fat** : to make conversation : CHAT

²**chew** *n* **1** : an act of chewing **2** : something for chewing

Chey•enne \shī-ˈan, -ˈen\ *n, pl* **Cheyenne** *or* **Cheyennes** [AmerF, fr. Dakota *šahíyena*] : a member of an Indigenous people of the western Great Plains of the U.S.; *also* : their language

chg *abbr* **1** change **2** charge

chi \ˈkī\ *n* : the 22d letter of the Greek alphabet — X or χ

Chi•an•ti \kē-ˈän-tē, -ˈan-\ *n* : a dry usu. red wine

chiar•oscu•ro \kē-ˌär-ə-ˈskůr-ō, -ˈskyůr-\ *n, pl* **-ros** [It, fr. *chiaro* clear, light + *oscuro* obscure, dark] **1** : pictorial representation in terms of light and shade without regard to color **2** : the arrangement or treatment of light and dark parts in a pictorial work of art

¹**chic** \ˈshēk\ *n* : STYLISHNESS

²**chic** *adj* : cleverly stylish : SMART; *also* : currently fashionable

Chi•ca•na \chi-ˈkä-nə *also* shi-\ *n* : an American woman or girl of Mexican descent — **Chicana** *adj*

chi•cane \shi-ˈkān\ *n* : CHICANERY

chi•ca•nery \-ˈka-nə-rē\ *n, pl* **-ner•ies** : TRICKERY, DECEPTION

Chi•ca•no \chi-ˈkä-nō\ *n, pl* **-nos** : a usu. male American of Mexican descent — **Chicano** *adj*

chi•chi \ˈshē-(ˌ)shē, ˈchē-(ˌ)chē\ *adj* [F] **1** : SHOWY, FRILLY **2** : ARTY, PRECIOUS ⟨~ poetry⟩ **3** : CHIC — **chichi** *n*

chick \ˈchik\ *n* **1** : a young chicken; *also* : a young bird **2** *sometimes offensive* : GIRL, WOMAN

chick•a•dee \ˈchi-kə-(ˌ)dē\ *n* : any of several small grayish American birds with black or brown caps

Chick•a•saw \ˈchi-kə-ˌsȯ\ *n, pl* **Chickasaw** *or* **Chickasaws** : a member of an Indigenous people orig. of western Tennessee and parts of adjacent states; *also* : their language

¹**chick•en** \ˈchi-kən\ *n* **1** : a common domestic fowl esp. when young; *also* : its flesh used as food **2** : COWARD

²**chicken** *adj* **1** : COWARDLY **2** *slang* : insistent on petty esp. military discipline

chicken feed *n, slang* : an insignificant sum of money

chick•en•heart•ed \ˌchi-kən-ˈhär-təd\ *adj* : TIMID, COWARDLY

chicken out *vb* : to lose one's courage

chicken pox *n* : an acute contagious viral disease esp. of children characterized by a low fever and blisters

chicken wire *n* : a light wire netting of hexagonal mesh

chick•pea \ˈchik-ˌpē\ *n* : an Asian herb of the legume family cultivated for its short pods with one or two edible seeds; *also* : its seed

chick•weed \ˈchik-ˌwēd\ *n* : any of several low-growing small-leaved weeds related to the pinks

chi•cle \ˈchi-kəl\ *n* : a gum from the latex of a tropical tree used as the chief ingredient of chewing gum

chic•o•ry \ˈchi-kə-rē\ *n, pl* **-ries** : a usu. blue-flowered herb related to the daisies and grown for its root and for use in salads; *also* : its dried ground root used to flavor or adulterate coffee

chide \ˈchīd\ *vb* **chid** \ˈchid\ *or* **chid•ed** \ˈchī-dəd\; **chid** *or* **chid•den** \ˈchid-ᵊn\ *or* **chided**; **chid•ing** : to speak disapprovingly to ♦ ***Synonyms*** REPROACH, REPROVE, REPRIMAND, ADMONISH, SCOLD, REBUKE

¹**chief** \ˈchēf\ *adj* **1** : highest in rank ⟨the ~ executive⟩ **2** : most important ⟨the ~ complaint⟩ ♦ ***Synonyms*** PRINCIPAL, MAIN, LEADING, MAJOR — **chief•ly** *adv*

²**chief** *n* **1** : the leader of a body or organization : HEAD **2** : the principal or most valuable part — **chief•dom** *n*

chief master sergeant *n* : a noncommissioned officer of the highest rank in the air force

chief of staff **1** : the ranking officer of a staff in the armed forces **2** : the ranking office of the army or air force

chief of state : the formal head of a national state as distinguished from the head of the government

chief petty officer *n* : an enlisted person in the navy ranking next below a senior chief petty officer

chief•tain \ˈchēf-tən\ *n* : a chief esp. of a band, tribe, or clan — **chief•tain•cy** \-sē\ *n* — **chief•tain•ship** *n*

chief warrant officer *n* : a warrant officer of senior rank

chif•fon \shi-ˈfän, ˈshi-ˌ\ *n* [F, lit., rag, fr. *chiffe* old rag] : a sheer fabric esp. of silk

chif•fo•nier \ˌshi-fə-ˈnir\ *n* : a high narrow chest of drawers

chig•ger \ˈchi-gər\ *n* : a bloodsucking larval mite that causes intense itching

chi•gnon \ˈshēn-ˌyän\ *n* [F, fr. MF *chaignon* chain, collar, nape] : a knot of hair worn at the back of the head

Chi•hua•hua \chə-ˈwä-ˌwä\ *n* : any of a breed of very small large-eared dogs that originated in Mexico

chil•blain \ˈchil-ˌblān\ *n* : a sore or inflamed swelling (as on the feet or hands) caused by exposure to cold

child \ˈchī(-ə)ld\ *n, pl* **chil•dren** \ˈchil-drən\ **1** : an unborn or recently born person **2 a** : a young person esp. between infancy and puberty **b** : a person not yet of the age of majority **3** : a male or female offspring : SON, DAUGHTER **4** : one strongly influenced by another or by a place or state of affairs — **child•ish** *adj* — **child•ish•ly** *adv* — **child•ish•ness** *n* — **child•less** *adj* — **child•less•ness** *n* — **child•like** *adj*

child•bear•ing \ˈchīld-ˌber-iŋ\ *n* : CHILDBIRTH — **childbearing** *adj*

child•birth \-ˌbərth\ *n* : the act or process of giving birth to offspring

child•hood \-ˌhůd\ *n* : the state or time of being a child

¹**child•proof** \-ˌprüf\ *adj* **1** : made to prevent opening or use by children ⟨~ lighters⟩ **2** : made safe for children

²**childproof** *vb* : to make childproof ⟨~ a house⟩

child's play *n* : a simple task or act
chili *also* **chile** *or* **chil·li** \'chi-lē\ *n, pl* **chil·ies** *also* **chil·es** *or* **chilis** *or* **chil·lies** **1** : any of various pungent peppers related to the tomato **2** : a thick sauce of meat and chilies **3** : CHILI CON CARNE
chili con car·ne \ˌchi-lē-kän-'kär-nē\ *n* [AmerSp *chile con carne* chili with meat] : a spiced stew of ground beef and chili peppers or chili powder usu. with beans
chili powder *n* : a seasoning made of ground chili peppers and other spices
chili sauce *n* : a spiced tomato sauce usu. made with red and green peppers
[1]**chill** \'chil\ *n* **1** : a feeling of coldness accompanied by shivering **2** : moderate coldness **3** : a check to enthusiasm or warmth of feeling
[2]**chill** *adj* **1** : moderately cold **2** : COLD, RAW **3** : DISTANT, FORMAL ⟨a ~ reception⟩ **4** : DEPRESSING, DISPIRITING **5** : LAID-BACK, RELAXED
[3]**chill** *vb* **1** : to make or become cold or chilly **2** : to make cool esp. without freezing **3** : RELAX — **chill·er** *n*
chill·ing \'chi-liŋ\ *adj* : gravely disturbing or frightening ⟨a ~ scene⟩
chilly \'chi-lē\ *adj* **chill·i·er**; **-est** **1** : noticeably cold **2** : unpleasantly affected by cold **3** : lacking warmth of feeling ⟨a ~ reception⟩ — **chill·i·ness** *n*
chimaera *chiefly Brit var of* CHIMERA
[1]**chime** \'chīm\ *n* **1** : a set of bells musically tuned **2** : the sound of a set of bells — usu. used in pl. **3** : a musical sound suggesting bells
[2]**chime** *vb* **chimed**; **chim·ing** **1** : to make bell-like sounds **2** : to indicate (as the time of day) by chiming **3** : to be or act in accord : be in harmony
chime in *vb* : to break into or join in a conversation
chi·me·ra \kī-'mir-ə, kə-\ *n* [L *chimaera,* fr. Gk *chimaira* she-goat, chimera] **1** : an imaginary monster made up of incongruous parts **2** : an illusion or fabrication of the mind; *esp* : an impossible dream
chi·me·ri·cal \ki-'mer-i-kəl\ *also* **chi·me·ric** \-ik\ *adj* **1** : FANTASTIC, IMAGINARY **2** : inclined to fantastic schemes
chim·ney \'chim-nē\ *n, pl* **chimneys** **1** : a vertical structure extending above the roof of a building for carrying off smoke **2** : a glass tube around a lamp flame
chimp \'chimp\ *n* : CHIMPANZEE
chim·pan·zee \ˌchim-ˌpan-'zē, chim-'pan-zē\ *n* : an African ape related to the much larger gorilla
[1]**chin** \'chin\ *n* : the part of the face below the lower lip including the prominence of the lower jaw — **chin·less** *adj*
[2]**chin** *vb* **chinned**; **chin·ning** : to raise (oneself) while hanging by the hands until the chin is level with the support
chi·na \'chī-nə\ *n* : porcelain ware; *also* : domestic pottery in general
Chi·na·town \-ˌtau̇n\ *n* : the Chinese quarter of a city
chinch bug \'chinch-\ *n* : a small black and white bug destructive to cereal grasses
chin·chil·la \chin-'chi-lə\ *n* **1** : either of two small So. American rodents with soft pearl-gray fur; *also* : this fur **2** : a heavy long-napped woolen cloth
chine \'chīn\ *n* : BACKBONE, SPINE; *also* : a cut of meat including all or part of the backbone
Chi·nese \chī-'nēz, -'nēs\ *n, pl* **Chinese** **1** : a native or inhabitant of China **2** : any of a group of related languages of China — **Chinese** *adj*
Chinese cabbage *n* **1** : BOK CHOY **2** : an Asian garden plant related to the cabbage and widely grown in the U.S. for its tight elongate cylindrical heads of pale green to cream-colored leaves
Chinese checkers *n* : a game in which each player in turn transfers a set of marbles from a home point to the opposite point of a pitted 6-pointed star
Chinese gooseberry *n* : a subtropical vine that bears kiwifruit; *also* : KIWIFRUIT
Chinese lantern *n* : a collapsible translucent cover for a light
[1]**chink** \'chiŋk\ *n* : a small crack or fissure
[2]**chink** *vb* : to fill the chinks of : stop up
[3]**chink** *n* : a slight sharp metallic sound
[4]**chink** *vb* : to make a slight sharp metallic sound
chi·no \'chē-nō\ *n, pl* **chinos** **1** : a usu. khaki cotton twill **2** *pl* : an article of clothing made of chino
Chi·nook \shə-'nu̇k, chə-, -'nük\ *n, pl* **Chinook** *or* **Chinooks** : a member of an Indigenous people of Oregon; *also* : their language
chintz \'chints\ *n* : a usu. glazed printed cotton cloth
chintzy \'chint-sē\ *adj* **chintz·i·er**; **-est** **1** : decorated with or as if with chintz **2** : GAUDY, CHEAP ⟨a ~ low-budget film⟩ **3** : STINGY — **chintz·i·ness** *n*
chin–up \'chin-ˌəp\ *n* : the act of chinning oneself
[1]**chip** \'chip\ *n* **1** : a small usu. thin and flat piece (as of wood) cut or broken off **2** : a thin crisp morsel of food **3** : a counter used in games (as poker) **4** *pl, slang* : MONEY **5** : a flaw left after a chip is broken off **6** : INTEGRATED CIRCUIT **7** : a very small slice of silicon containing electronic circuits — **chip off the old block** : a child that resembles his or her parent
[2]**chip** *vb* **chipped**; **chip·ping** **1** : to cut or break chips from **2** : to break off in small pieces at the edges **3** : to play a chip shot
chip in *vb* : CONTRIBUTE 1
chip·munk \'chip-ˌməŋk\ *n* [earlier *chitmunk,* prob. fr. Ojibwa *ačitamo·n?* red squirrel] : any of a genus of small striped No. American and Asian rodents closely related to the squirrels and marmots
chi·pot·le \chə-'pōt-lā\ *n* : a smoked and usu. dried jalapeño pepper
chipped beef \'chipt-\ *n* : smoked dried beef sliced thin
[1]**chip·per** \'chi-pər\ *n* : one that chips
[2]**chipper** *adj* : LIVELY, CHEERFUL
Chip·pe·wa \'chi-pə-ˌwȯ, -ˌwä, -ˌwā, -wə\ *n, pl* **Chippewa** *or* **Chippewas** : OJIBWA

chip shot *n* : a short usu. low shot to the green in golf

chi·rog·ra·phy \kī-ˈrä-grə-fē\ *n* : HANDWRITING, PENMANSHIP — **chi·ro·graph·ic** \ˌkī-rə-ˈgra-fik\ *adj*

chi·rop·o·dy \kə-ˈrä-pə-dē, shə-\ *n* : PODIATRY — **chi·rop·o·dist** \-dist\ *n*

chi·ro·prac·tic \ˈkī-rə-ˌprak-tik\ *n* : a system of therapy based esp. on manipulation of body structures — **chi·ro·prac·tor** \-tər\ *n*

chirp \ˈchərp\ *n* : a short sharp sound characteristic of a small bird or cricket — **chirp** *vb* — **chirpy** \ˈchər-pē\ *adj*

[1]**chis·el** \ˈchi-zəl\ *n* : a metal tool with a sharpened edge at one end used to chip, carve, or cut into a solid material (as wood or stone)

[2]**chisel** *vb* **-eled** *or* **-elled**; **-el·ing** *or* **-el·ling 1** : to work with or as if with a chisel **2** : to obtain by shrewd often unfair methods; *also* : CHEAT — **chis·el·er** *n*

[1]**chit** \ˈchit\ *n* [ME *chitte* kitten, cub] **1** : CHILD **2** : a pert young woman

[2]**chit** *n* [Hindi *ciṭṭhī* letter, note] : a signed voucher for a small debt

chit·chat \ˈchit-ˌchat\ *n* : casual or trifling conversation — **chitchat** *vb*

chi·tin \ˈkī-tᵊn\ *n* : a sugar polymer that forms part of the hard outer integument esp. of insects — **chi·tin·ous** *adj*

chit·ter·lings *or* **chit·lins** \ˈchit-lənz\ *n pl* : the intestines of hogs esp. when prepared as food

chi·val·ric \shə-ˈval-rik\ *adj* : relating to chivalry : CHIVALROUS

chiv·al·rous \ˈshi-vəl-rəs\ *adj* **1** : of or relating to chivalry **2** : marked by honor, courtesy, and generosity **3** : marked by courtesy esp. to women — **chiv·al·rous·ly** *adv* — **chiv·al·rous·ness** *n*

chiv·al·ry \ˈshi-vəl-rē\ *n, pl* **-ries 1** : mounted men-at-arms **2** : the system or practices of knighthood **3** : the spirit or character of the ideal knight

chive \ˈchīv\ *n* : an herb related to the onion that has slender leaves used for flavoring; *also* : its leaves

chla·myd·ia \klə-ˈmi-dē-ə\ *n, pl* **-i·ae** \-dē-ˌē\ **1** : any of a genus of bacteria that cause various diseases of the eye and urogenital tract **2** : a disease or infection caused by chlamydiae

chlo·ral hydrate \ˈklȯr-əl-\ *n* : a white crystalline compound used as a hypnotic and sedative

chlor·dane \ˈklȯr-ˌdān\ *n* : a highly chlorinated persistent insecticide

chlo·ride \ˈklȯr-ˌīd\ *n* : a compound of chlorine with another element or group

chlo·ri·nate \ˈklȯr-ə-ˌnāt\ *vb* **-nat·ed**; **-nat·ing** : to treat or combine with chlorine or a chlorine compound — **chlo·ri·na·tion** \ˌklȯr-ə-ˈnā-shən\ *n* — **chlo·ri·na·tor** \ˈklȯr-ə-ˌnā-tər\ *n*

chlo·rine \ˈklȯr-ˌēn\ *n* : a nonmetallic chemical element that is found alone as a strong-smelling greenish-yellow irritating gas and is used as a bleach, oxidizing agent, and disinfectant

chlorine monoxide *n* : a reactive radical that plays a major role in stratospheric ozone depletion

chlo·rite \ˈklȯr-ˌīt\ *n* : a usu. green mineral found with and resembling mica

chlo·ro·flu·o·ro·car·bon \ˌklȯr-ə-ˈflȯr-ə-ˌkär-bən, -ˈflu̇r-\ *n* : any of several gaseous compounds that contain carbon, chlorine, fluorine, and sometimes hydrogen and are used esp. as solvents, refrigerants, and aerosol propellants

[1]**chlo·ro·form** \ˈklȯr-ə-ˌfȯrm\ *n* : a colorless heavy fluid with etherlike odor used as a solvent

[2]**chloroform** *vb* : to treat with chloroform to produce anesthesia or death

chlo·ro·phyll \-ˌfil\ *n* : the green coloring matter of plants that functions in photosynthesis

chlo·ro·plast \ˈklȯr-ə-ˌplast\ *n* : a cytoplasmic organelle that contains chlorophyll and is the site of photosynthesis

chm *abbr* chairman

chock \ˈchäk\ *n* : a wedge for steadying something or for blocking the movement of a wheel — **chock** *vb*

chock·a·block \ˈchä-kə-ˌbläk\ *adj* : very full : CROWDED

chock–full \ˈchək-ˈfu̇l, ˈchäk-\ *adj* : full to the limit : CRAMMED

choc·o·late \ˈchä-k(ə-)lət, ˈchȯ-\ *n* [Sp, fr. Nahuatl *chocolātl*] **1** : a food prepared from ground roasted cacao beans; *also* : a drink prepared from this **2** : a candy made of or with a coating of chocolate **3** : a dark brown color — **choc·o·laty** *or* **choc·o·lat·ey** \-k(ə-)lə-tē\ *adj*

Choc·taw \ˈchäk-ˌtȯ\ *n, pl* **Choctaw** *or* **Choctaws** : a member of an Indigenous people orig. of Mississippi and Alabama; *also* : their language

[1]**choice** \ˈchȯis\ *n* **1** : the act of choosing : SELECTION **2** : the power or opportunity of choosing : OPTION **3** : the best part **4** : a person or thing selected **5** : a variety offered for selection

[2]**choice** *adj* **choic·er**; **choic·est 1** : worthy of being chosen **2** : selected with care **3** : of high quality

choir \ˈkwī(-ə)r\ *n* **1** : an organized company of singers (as in a church service) **2** : the part of a church occupied by the singers or by the clergy

choir·boy \ˈkwī(-ə)r-ˌbȯi\ *n* : a boy member of a choir

choir·mas·ter \-ˌmas-tər\ *n* : the director of a choir (as in a church)

[1]**choke** \ˈchōk\ *vb* **choked**; **chok·ing 1** : to hinder breathing (as by obstructing the trachea) : STRANGLE **2** : to check the growth or action of **3** : CLOG, OBSTRUCT **4** : to enrich the fuel mixture of (a motor) by restricting the carburetor air intake **5** : to perform badly in a critical situation

[2]**choke** *n* **1** : the act of choking **2** : a narrowing in size toward the muzzle in the bore of a gun **3** : a valve for choking a gasoline engine

choke hold *n* **1** : a hold that involves strong choking pressure **2** : absolute control

chok·er \ˈchō-kər\ *n* : something (as a necklace) worn tightly around the neck

cho·ler \ˈkä-lər, ˈkō-\ *n* : a tendency toward anger : IRASCIBILITY

chol·era \ˈkä-lə-rə\ *n* : any of several bacterial diseases usu. marked by severe vomiting and dysentery

cho·ler·ic \ˈkä-lə-rik, kə-ˈler-ik\ *adj* **1** : IRASCIBLE **2** : ANGRY, IRATE

cho·les·ter·ol \kə-ˈles-tə-ˌrȯl\ *n* : a physiologically important waxy steroid alcohol found in animal tissues and in high concentrations implicated as a cause of arteriosclerosis

chomp \ˈchämp, ˈchȯmp\ *vb* : to chew or bite on something heavily

chon \ˈchän\ *n, pl* **chon** **1** — see *won* at MONEY table **2** : the jeon of South Korea

choose \ˈchüz\ *vb* **chose** \chōz\; **cho·sen** \ˈchō-zᵊn\; **choos·ing** \chü-ziŋ\ **1** : to select esp. after consideration **2** : DECIDE **3** : to have a preference for — **choos·er** *n*

choosy *or* **choos·ey** \ˈchü-zē\ *adj* **choos·i·er**; **-est** : very particular in making choices

[1]**chop** \ˈchäp\ *vb* **chopped**; **chop·ping** **1** : to cut by repeated blows **2** : to cut into small pieces : MINCE **3** : to strike (a ball) with a short quick downward stroke

[2]**chop** *n* **1** : a sharp downward blow or stroke **2** : a small cut of meat often including part of a rib **3** : a short abrupt motion (as of a wave)

[3]**chop** *n* **1** : an official seal or stamp **2** : a mark on goods to indicate quality or kind; *also* : QUALITY, GRADE

chop·house \ˈchäp-ˌhau̇s\ *n* : RESTAURANT

chop·per \ˈchä-pər\ *n* **1** : one that chops **2** *pl, slang* : TEETH **3** : HELICOPTER

chop·pi·ness \ˈchä-pē-nəs\ *n* : the quality or state of being choppy

[1]**chop·py** \ˈchä-pē\ *adj* **chop·pi·er**; **-est** **1** : rough with small waves ⟨a ~ sea⟩ **2** : JERKY, DISCONNECTED ⟨short ~ sentences⟩ — **chop·pi·ly** \-pə-lē\ *adv*

[2]**choppy** *adj* **chop·pi·er**; **-est** : CHANGEABLE, VARIABLE ⟨a ~ wind⟩

chops \ˈchäps\ *n pl* **1** : the fleshy covering of the jaws **2** : expertise in a particular field or activity ⟨acting ~⟩

chop·stick \ˈchäp-ˌstik\ *n* : one of a pair of sticks used chiefly in Asian countries for lifting food to the mouth

chop su·ey \chäp-ˈsü-ē\ *n, pl* **chop su·eys** : a dish made of vegetables (as bean sprouts, bamboo shoots, water chestnuts, onions, mushrooms) and meat or fish and served with rice

cho·ral \ˈkȯr-əl\ *adj* : of, relating to, or sung by a choir or chorus or in chorus — **cho·ral·ly** *adv*

cho·rale \kə-ˈral, -ˈräl\ *n* **1** : a hymn or psalm sung in church; *also* : a harmonization of a traditional melody **2** : CHORUS, CHOIR

[1]**chord** \ˈkȯrd\ *n* [alter. of ME *cord*, short for *accord*] : three or more musical tones sounded simultaneously

[2]**chord** *n* **1** : CORD 2 **2** : a straight line joining two points on a curve

chore \ˈchȯr\ *n* [ME *char* turn, piece of work, fr. OE *chierr*] **1** *pl* : the daily light work of a household or farm **2** : a routine task or job **3** : a difficult or disagreeable task

cho·rea \kə-ˈrē-ə\ *n* : any of various nervous disorders marked by spasmodic uncontrolled movements

cho·re·og·ra·phy \ˌkȯr-ē-ˈä-grə-fē\ *n, pl* **-phies** : the art of composing and arranging dances and esp. ballets — **cho·reo·graph** \ˈkȯr-ē-ə-ˌgraf\ *vb* — **cho·re·og·ra·pher** \ˌkȯr-ē-ˈä-grə-fər\ *n* — **cho·reo·graph·ic** \ˌkȯr-ē-ə-ˈgra-fik\ *adj* — **cho·reo·graph·i·cal·ly** \-fi-k(ə-)lē\ *adv*

cho·ris·ter \ˈkȯr-ə-stər\ *n* : a singer in a choir

cho·ri·zo \chə-ˈrē-zō, -sō\ *n* : a spicy pork sausage

chor·tle \ˈchȯr-tᵊl\ *vb* **chor·tled**; **chor·tling** : to laugh or chuckle esp. in satisfaction or exultation — **chortle** *n*

[1]**chorus** \ˈkȯr-əs\ *n* **1** : an organized company of singers : CHOIR **2** : a group of dancers and singers (as in a musical comedy) **3** : a part of a song repeated at intervals **4** : a composition to be sung by a chorus; *also* : group singing **5** : sounds uttered by a number of persons or animals together ⟨a ~ of boos⟩

[2]**chorus** *vb* : to sing or utter in chorus

chose *past of* CHOOSE

cho·sen \ˈchō-zᵊn\ *adj* : selected or marked for special favor or privilege

chou·croute \shü-ˈkrüt\ *n* **1** : SAUERKRAUT **2** *or* **choucroute gar·nie** \-gär-ˈnē\ : sauerkraut cooked and served with meat

[1]**chow** \ˈchau̇\ *n* : FOOD

[2]**chow** *vb* : EAT — often used with *down*

[3]**chow** *n* : CHOW CHOW

chow·chow \ˈchau̇-ˌchau̇\ *n* : chopped mixed pickles in mustard sauce

chow chow \ˈchau̇-ˌchau̇\ *n* : any of a breed of thick-coated muscular dogs of Chinese origin with a blue-black tongue and a short tail curled close to the back

chow·der \ˈchau̇-dər\ *n* : a soup or stew made from seafood or vegetables and containing milk or tomatoes

chow mein \ˈchau̇-ˈmān\ *n* : a seasoned stew of shredded or diced meat, mushrooms, and vegetables that is usu. served with fried noodles

chrism \ˈkri-zəm\ *n* : consecrated oil used esp. in baptism, confirmation, and ordination

Christ \ˈkrīst\ *n* [ME *Crist*, fr. OE, fr. L *Christus*, fr. Gk *Christos*, lit., anointed] : Jesus esp. as the Messiah — **Christ·like** *adj* — **Christ·ly** *adj*

chris·ten \ˈkri-sᵊn\ *vb* **1** : BAPTIZE **2** : to name at baptism **3** : to name or dedicate (as a ship) by a ceremony suggestive of baptism — **chris·ten·ing** *n*

Chris·ten·dom \ˈkri-sᵊn-dəm\ *n* **1** : CHRISTIANITY **2** : the part of the world in which Christianity prevails

[1]**Chris·tian** \ˈkris-chən\ *n* : an adherent of Christianity

[2]**Christian** *adj* **1** : of or relating to Christianity **2** : based on or conforming with Christianity **3** : of or relating to a Christian **4** : professing Christianity
Chris·ti·an·i·ty \ˌkris-chē-ˈa-nə-tē\ *n* : the religion derived from Jesus Christ, based on the Bible as sacred scripture, and professed by Christians
Chris·tian·ize \ˈkris-chə-ˌnīz\ *vb* **-ized; -iz·ing** : to make Christian
Christian name *n* : GIVEN NAME
Christian Science *n* : a religion and system of healing founded by Mary Baker Eddy and taught by the Church of Christ, Scientist — **Christian Scientist** *n*
chris·tie *or* **chris·ty** \ˈkris-tē\ *n, pl* **christies** : a skiing turn made by shifting body weight forward and skidding into a turn with parallel skis
Christ·mas \ˈkris-məs\ *n* : December 25 celebrated as a church festival in commemoration of the birth of Christ and observed as a legal holiday
Christmas club *n* : a savings account in which regular deposits are made to provide money for Christmas shopping
Christ·mas·tide \ˈkris-məs-ˌtīd\ *n* : the season of Christmas
chro·mat·ic \krō-ˈma-tik\ *adj* **1** : of or relating to color **2** : proceeding by half steps of the musical scale — **chro·mat·i·cism** \-tə-ˌsi-zəm\ *n*
chro·mato·graph \krō-ˈma-tə-ˌgraf\ *n* : an instrument used in chromatography
chro·ma·tog·ra·phy \ˌkrō-mə-ˈtä-grə-fē\ *n* : the separation of a complex mixture into its component compounds as a result of the different rates at which the compounds travel through or over a stationary substance due to differing affinities for the substance — **chro·mato·graph·ic** \krō-ˌma-tə-ˈgra-fik\ *adj* — **chro·mato·graph·i·cal·ly** \-fi-k(ə-)lē\ *adv*
chrome \ˈkrōm\ *n* **1** : CHROMIUM **2** : a chromium pigment **3** : something plated with an alloy of chromium
chro·mi·um \ˈkrō-mē-əm\ *n* : a bluish white metallic element used esp. in alloys and chrome plating
chro·mo·some \ˈkrō-mə-ˌsōm, -ˌzōm\ *n* [G *Chromosom,* fr. Gk *chrōma* color, pigment + *sōma* body] : any of the rod-shaped or threadlike DNA-containing structures of cellular organisms that contain most or all of the genes of the organism — **chro·mo·som·al** \ˌkrō-mə-ˈsō-məl, -ˈzō-\ *adj*
chro·mo·sphere \ˈkrō-mə-ˌsfir\ *n* : the lower part of a star's atmosphere
chron *abbr* **1** chronicle **2** chronological; chronology
Chron *abbr* Chronicles
chron·ic \ˈkrä-nik\ *adj* : marked by long duration or frequent recurrence ⟨a ~ disease⟩; *also* : HABITUAL ⟨a ~ grumbler⟩ — **chron·i·cal·ly** \-ni-k(ə-)lē\ *adv*
chronic fatigue syndrome *n* : a disorder of unknown cause that is characterized by persistent profound fatigue
[1]**chron·i·cle** \ˈkrä-ni-kəl\ *n* : HISTORY, NARRATIVE
[2]**chronicle** *vb* **-cled; -cling** : to record in or as if in a chronicle — **chron·i·cler** *n*
Chronicles *n* — see BIBLE table
chronic traumatic encephalopathy *n* : a progressive neurological disease esp. of athletes (as boxers or football players) who have experienced repetitive mild injury to the brain
chro·no·graph \ˈkrä-nə-ˌgraf\ *n* : an instrument for measuring and recording time intervals with accuracy — **chro·no·graph·ic** \ˌkrä-nə-ˈgra-fik\ *adj* — **chro·nog·ra·phy** \krə-ˈnä-grə-fē\ *n*
chro·nol·o·gy \krə-ˈnä-lə-jē\ *n, pl* **-gies** **1** : the science that deals with measuring time and dating events **2** : a chronological list or table **3** : arrangement of events in the order of their occurrence — **chron·o·log·i·cal** \ˌkrän-ᵊl-ˈä-ji-kəl\ *adj* — **chron·o·log·i·cal·ly** \-k(ə-)lē\ *adv* — **chro·nol·o·gist** \krə-ˈnä-lə-jist\ *n*
chro·nom·e·ter \krə-ˈnä-mə-tər\ *n* : a very accurate timepiece
chrys·a·lid \ˈkri-sə-ləd\ *n* : CHRYSALIS
chrys·a·lis \ˈkri-sə-ləs\ *n, pl* **chry·sal·i·des** \kri-ˈsa-lə-ˌdēz\ *or* **chrys·a·lis·es** : an insect pupa in a firm case without a cocoon
chry·san·the·mum \kri-ˈsan-thə-məm\ *n* [L, fr. Gk *chrysanthemon,* fr. *chrysos* gold + *anthemon* flower] : any of various plants related to the daisies including some grown for their showy brightly colored flowers or for medicinal products or insecticides; *also* : a flower of a chrysanthemum
chub \ˈchəb\ *n, pl* **chub** *or* **chubs** : any of various small freshwater fishes related to the carp
chub·by \ˈchə-bē\ *adj* **chub·bi·er; -est** : PLUMP ⟨a ~ child⟩ — **chub·bi·ness** *n*
[1]**chuck** \ˈchək\ *vb* **1** : to give a pat or tap **2** : TOSS **3** : DISCARD; *also* : EJECT **4** : to have done with ⟨~*ed* his job⟩
[2]**chuck** *n* **1** : a light pat under the chin **2** : TOSS
[3]**chuck** *n* **1** : a cut of beef including most of the neck and the parts around the shoulder blade and the first three ribs **2** : a device for holding work or a tool in a machine (as a lathe)
chuck·hole \ˈchək-ˌhōl\ *n* : POTHOLE
chuck·le \ˈchə-kəl\ *vb* **chuck·led; chuck·ling** : to laugh in a quiet hardly audible manner — **chuckle** *n*
chuck wagon *n* : a wagon equipped with a stove and food supplies
[1]**chug** \ˈchəg\ *n* : a dull explosive sound made by or as if by a laboring engine
[2]**chug** *vb* **chugged; chug·ging** : to move or go with chugs
chuk·ka \ˈchə-kə\ *n* : a usu. ankle-length leather boot
chuk·ker \ˈchə-kər\ *also* **chuk·ka** \ˈchə-kə\ *n* : a playing period of a polo game
[1]**chum** \ˈchəm\ *n* : a close friend
[2]**chum** *vb* **chummed; chum·ming** **1** : to room together **2** : to be a close friend
chum·my \ˈchə-mē\ *adj* **chum·mi·er; -est** : quite friendly — **chum·mi·ly** \-mə-lē\ *adv* — **chum·mi·ness** \-mē-nəs\ *n*

chump \ˈchəmp\ *n* : FOOL, BLOCKHEAD
chunk \ˈchəŋk\ *n* **1** : a short thick piece ⟨a ~ of meat⟩ **2** : a sizable amount
chunky \ˈchəŋ-kē\ *adj* **chunk·i·er**; **-est 1** : STOCKY **2** : containing chunks
church \ˈchərch\ *n* [ME *chirche,* fr. OE *cirice,* ultim. fr. LGk *kyriakon,* fr. Gk, neut. of *kyriakos* of the lord, fr. *kyrios* lord, master] **1** : a building esp. for Christian public worship **2** *often cap* : the whole body of Christians **3** : DENOMINATION **4** : CONGREGATION **5** : public divine worship
church·go·er \ˈchərch-ˌgō-ər\ *n* : one who habitually attends church — **church·go·ing** *adj or n*
church·less \ˈchərch-ləs\ *adj* : not affiliated with a church
church·man \ˈchərch-mən\ *n* **1** : CLERGYMAN **2** : a member of a church
church·war·den \ˈchərch-ˌwȯr-dᵊn\ *n* : WARDEN 5
church·yard \-ˌyärd\ *n* : a yard that belongs to a church and is often used as a burial ground
churl \ˈchərl\ *n* **1** : a medieval peasant **2** : RUSTIC **3** : a rude ill-bred person — **churl·ish** *adj* — **churl·ish·ly** *adv* — **churl·ish·ness** *n*
¹**churn** \ˈchərn\ *n* : a container in which milk or cream is agitated in making butter
²**churn** *vb* **1** : to stir in a churn; *also* : to make (butter) by such stirring **2** : to shake around violently
churn out *vb* : to produce mechanically or in large quantity
chute \ˈshüt\ *n* **1** : an inclined surface, trough, or passage down or through which something may pass ⟨a coal ~⟩ ⟨a mail ~⟩ **2** : PARACHUTE
chut·ney \ˈchət-nē\ *n, pl* **chutneys** : a thick sauce containing fruits, vinegar, sugar, and spices
chutz·pah \ˈhu̇t-spə, ˈk̲u̇t-, -(ˌ)spä\ *n* : supreme self-confidence
CIA *abbr* Central Intelligence Agency
cía *abbr* [Sp *compañía*] company
cia·bat·ta \chə-ˈbä-tə\ *n* [It, lit., slipper] : a flat bread with a moist interior and a crispy crust
ciao \ˈchau̇\ *interj* — used to express greeting or farewell
ci·ca·da \sə-ˈkā-də\ *n* : any of a family of stout-bodied insects related to the aphids and having wide blunt heads and large transparent wings
ci·ca·trix \ˈsi-kə-ˌtriks\ *n, pl* **ci·ca·tri·ces** \ˌsi-kə-ˈtrī-ˌsēz\ [L] : a scar resulting from formation and contraction of fibrous tissue in a wound
ci·ce·ro·ne \ˌsi-sə-ˈrō-nē, ˌchē-chə-\ *n, pl* **-ni** \-(ˌ)nē\ : a guide who conducts sightseers
CID *abbr* Criminal Investigation Department
ci·der \ˈsī-dər\ *n* : juice pressed from fruit (as apples) and used as a beverage, vinegar, or flavoring
cie *abbr* [F *compagnie*] company
ci·gar \si-ˈgär\ *n* [Sp *cigarro*] : a roll of tobacco for smoking
cig·a·rette \ˌsi-gə-ˈret, ˈsi-gə-ˌret\ *n* [F, dim. of *cigare* cigar] : a slender roll of cut tobacco enclosed in paper for smoking
cig·a·ril·lo \ˌsi-gə-ˈri-lō, -ˈrē-ō\ *n, pl* **-los** [Sp] **1** : a very small cigar **2** : a cigarette wrapped in tobacco rather than paper
ci·lan·tro \si-ˈlän-trō, -ˈlan-\ *n* : leaves of coriander used as a flavoring or garnish; *also* : the coriander plant
cil·i·ate \ˈsi-lē-ˌāt\ *n* : any of a group of protozoans characterized by cilia
cil·i·um \ˈsi-lē-əm\ *n, pl* **cil·ia** \-lē-ə\ **1** : a minute short hairlike process; *esp* : one of a cell **2** : EYELASH
C in C *abbr* commander in chief
cinch \ˈsinch\ *n* **1** : a girth for a pack or saddle **2** : a sure or an easy thing — **cinch** *vb*
cin·cho·na \siŋ-ˈkō-nə\ *n* : any of a genus of So. American trees related to the madder; *also* : the bitter quinine-containing bark of a cinchona
cinc·ture \ˈsiŋk-chər\ *n* : BELT, SASH
cin·der \ˈsin-dər\ *n* **1** : SLAG **2** *pl* : ASHES **3** : a hot piece of partly burned wood or coal **4** : a fragment of lava from an erupting volcano — **cin·dery** *adj*
cinder block *n* : a building block made of cement and coal cinders
cin·e·ma \ˈsi-nə-mə\ *n* **1** : a motion-picture theater **2** : MOVIES — **cin·e·mat·ic** \ˌsi-nə-ˈma-tik\ *adj*
cin·e·ma·theque \ˌsi-nə-mə-ˈtek\ *n* : a small movie house specializing in avant-garde films
cin·e·ma·tog·ra·phy \ˌsi-nə-mə-ˈtä-grə-fē\ *n* : motion-picture photography — **cin·e·ma·tog·ra·pher** *n* — **cin·e·mat·o·graph·ic** \-ˌma-tə-ˈgra-fik\ *adj*
cine·phile \ˈsi-nə-ˌfī(-ə)l\ *n* : a lover of motion pictures
cin·e·plex \ˈsi-nə-ˌpleks\ *n* : a complex that houses several movie theaters
cin·er·ar·i·um \ˌsi-nə-ˈrer-ē-əm\ *n, pl* **-ia** \-ē-ə\ : a place to receive the ashes of the cremated dead — **cin·er·ary** \ˈsi-nə-ˌrer-ē\ *adj*
cin·na·bar \ˈsi-nə-ˌbär\ *n* **1** : a red mineral that is the only important ore of mercury **2** : a deep vivid red
cin·na·mon \ˈsi-nə-mən\ *n* : a spice prepared from the highly aromatic bark of any of several Asian trees related to the true laurel; *also* : a tree that yields cinnamon
cinque·foil \ˈsiŋk-ˌfȯi(-ə)l, ˈsaŋk-\ *n* : any of a genus of plants related to the roses with leaves having five lobes
¹**ci·pher** \ˈsī-fər\ *n* [ME, fr. ML *cifra,* fr. Ar *ṣifr* empty, zero] **1** : ZERO, NAUGHT **2** : a method of secret writing
²**cipher** *vb* : to compute arithmetically
cir *or* **circ** *abbr* circular
cir·ca \ˈsər-kə\ *prep* : ABOUT ⟨~ 1600⟩
cir·ca·di·an \sər-ˈkā-dē-ən\ *adj* : being, having, characterized by, or occurring in approximately 24-hour intervals (as of biological activity)
¹**cir·cle** \ˈsər-kəl\ *n* **1** : a closed curve every point of which is equally distant from a fixed point within it **2** : something cir-

cular **3** : an area of action or influence **4** : CYCLE **5** : a group bound by a common tie ⟨sewing ~⟩

²circle *vb* **cir·cled**; **cir·cling** **1** : to enclose in a circle **2** : to move or revolve around; *also* : to move in a circle

cir·clet \ˈsər-klət\ *n* : a small circle; *esp* : a circular ornament

cir·cuit \ˈsər-kət\ *n* **1** : a boundary around an enclosed space **2** : a course around a periphery **3** : a regular tour (as by a judge) around an assigned territory **4** : the complete path of an electric current; *also* : an assemblage of electronic components **5** : LEAGUE; *also* : a chain of theaters

circuit board *n* : BOARD 7

circuit breaker *n* : a switch that automatically interrupts the current of an overloaded circuit

circuit court *n* : a court that sits at two or more places within one judicial district

cir·cu·i·tous \ˌsər-ˈkyü-ə-təs\ *adj* **1** : having a circular or winding course ⟨a ~ route⟩ **2** : not being forthright or direct in language or action ⟨a ~ explanation⟩

cir·cuit·ry \ˈsər-kə-trē\ *n, pl* **-ries** : the plan or the components of an electric circuit

cir·cu·ity \ˌsər-ˈkyü-ə-tē\ *n, pl* **-ities** : INDIRECTION

¹cir·cu·lar \ˈsər-kyə-lər\ *adj* **1** : having the form of a circle : ROUND **2** : moving in or around a circle **3** : CIRCUITOUS **4** : intended for circulation ⟨a ~ letter⟩ — **cir·cu·lar·i·ty** \ˈsər-kyə-ˈler-ə-tē\ *n*

²circular *n* : a paper (as a leaflet) intended for wide distribution

cir·cu·lar·ise *Brit var of* CIRCULARIZE

cir·cu·lar·ize \ˈsər-kyə-lə-ˌrīz\ *vb* **-ized**; **-iz·ing** **1** : to send circulars to **2** : to poll by questionnaire **3** : to make circular

circular saw *n* : a power saw with a round cutting blade

cir·cu·late \ˈsər-kyə-ˌlāt\ *vb* **-lat·ed**; **-lat·ing** **1** : to move or cause to move in a circle, circuit, or orbit **2** : to pass from place to place or from person to person — **cir·cu·la·tion** \ˌsər-kyə-ˈlā-shən\ *n*

cir·cu·la·to·ry \ˈsər-kyə-lə-ˌtȯr-ē\ *adj* : of or relating to circulation or the circulatory system

circulatory system *n* : the system of blood, blood vessels, lymphatic vessels, and heart concerned with the circulation of the blood and lymph

cir·cum·am·bu·late \ˌsər-kəm-ˈam-byə-ˌlāt\ *vb* **-lat·ed**; **-lat·ing** : to circle on foot esp. as part of a ritual

cir·cum·cise \ˈsər-kəm-ˌsīz\ *vb* **-cised**; **-cis·ing** [ME, fr. L *circumcisus,* pp. of *circumcidere,* lit., to cut around, fr. *circum* around + *caedere* to cut] : to cut off the foreskin of — **cir·cum·ci·sion** \ˌsər-kəm-ˈsi-zhən\ *n*

cir·cum·fer·ence \sər-ˈkəm-f(ə-)rəns\ *n* **1** : the perimeter of a circle **2** : the external boundary or surface of a figure or object

cir·cum·flex \ˈsər-kəm-ˌfleks\ *n* : the mark ˆ over a vowel

cir·cum·lo·cu·tion \ˌsər-kəm-lō-ˈkyü-shən\ *n* : the use of unnecessary words in expressing an idea

cir·cum·lu·nar \-ˈlü-nər\ *adj* : revolving about or surrounding the moon

cir·cum·nav·i·gate \-ˈna-və-ˌgāt\ *vb* : to go completely around (as the earth) esp. by water — **cir·cum·nav·i·ga·tion** \-ˌna-və-ˈgā-shən\ *n*

cir·cum·po·lar \-ˈpō-lər\ *adj* **1** : continually visible above the horizon ⟨a ~ star⟩ **2** : surrounding or found near a pole of the earth ⟨a ~ current⟩

cir·cum·scribe \ˈsər-kəm-ˌskrīb\ *vb* **1** : to constrict the range or activity of **2** : to draw a line around — **cir·cum·scrip·tion** \ˌsər-kəm-ˈskrip-shən\ *n*

cir·cum·spect \ˈsər-kəm-ˌspekt\ *adj* : careful to consider all circumstances and consequences : PRUDENT — **cir·cum·spec·tion** \ˌsər-kəm-ˈspek-shən\ *n*

cir·cum·stance \ˈsər-kəm-ˌstans\ *n* **1** : a fact or event that must be considered along with another fact or event **2** : surrounding conditions **3** : CHANCE, FATE **4** *pl* : situation with regard to wealth **5** : CEREMONY ⟨pomp and ~⟩

cir·cum·stan·tial \ˌsər-kəm-ˈstan-chəl\ *adj* **1** : consisting of or depending on circumstances **2** : INCIDENTAL **3** : containing full details — **cir·cum·stan·tial·ly** *adv*

cir·cum·vent \ˌsər-kəm-ˈvent\ *vb* : to check or defeat esp. by stratagem — **cir·cum·ven·tion** \ˈvent-shən\ *n*

cir·cus \ˈsər-kəs\ *n* **1** : a usu. traveling show that features feats of physical skill, wild animal acts, and performances by clowns **2** : a circus performance; *also* : the equipment, livestock, and personnel of a circus

cirque \ˈsərk\ *n* : a deep steep-walled mountain basin usu. forming the blunt end of a valley

cir·rho·sis \sə-ˈrō-səs\ *n, pl* **-rho·ses** \-ˌsēz\ [NL, fr. Gk *kirrhos* orange-colored] : fibrosis of the liver — **cir·rhot·ic** \-ˈrä-tik\ *adj or n*

cir·rus \ˈsir-əs\ *n, pl* **cir·ri** \ˈsir-ˌī\ : a wispy white cloud usu. of minute ice crystals at high altitudes

cis \ˈsis\ *adj* : CISGENDER

cis·gen·der \(ˌ)sis-ˈjen-dər\ *also* **cis·gen·dered** \-dərd\ *adj* : of, relating to, or being a person whose gender identity corresponds with the sex the person had or was identified as having at birth

cis·lu·nar \(ˌ)sis-ˈlü-nər\ *adj* : lying between the earth and the moon or the moon's orbit

cis·sy *Brit var of* SISSY

cis·tern \ˈsis-tərn\ *n* : an often underground tank for storing water

cit *abbr* **1** citation; cited **2** citizen

cit·a·del \ˈsi-tə-dəl, -ˌdel\ *n* **1** : a fortress commanding a city **2** : STRONGHOLD

ci·ta·tion \sī-ˈtā-shən\ *n* **1** : an official summons to appear (as before a court) **2** : QUOTATION **3** : a formal statement of the achievements of a person; *also* : a specific reference in a military dispatch to meritorious performance of duty

cite \ˈsīt\ *vb* **cit·ed; cit·ing** **1** : to summon to appear before a court **2** : QUOTE **3** : to refer to esp. in commendation or praise
cit·i·fied \ˈsi-ti-ˌfīd\ *adj* : of, relating to, or characterized by an urban style of living
cit·i·zen \ˈsi-tə-zən\ *n* **1** : an inhabitant of a city or town **2** : a person who owes allegiance to a government and is entitled to its protection — **cit·i·zen·ship** *n*
cit·i·zen·ry \-rē\ *n, pl* **-ries** : a whole body of citizens
citizens band *n* : a range of radio frequencies set aside for private radio communications
cit·ric acid \ˈsi-trik-\ *n* : a sour organic acid obtained from lemon and lime juices or by fermentation of sugars and used chiefly as a flavoring
cit·ron \ˈsi-trən\ *n* **1** : the oval lemonlike fruit of a citrus tree; *also* : the tree **2** : a small hard-fleshed watermelon used esp. in pickles and preserves
cit·ro·nel·la \ˌsi-trə-ˈne-lə\ *n* : a lemon-scented oil obtained from a fragrant grass of southern Asia and used in perfumes and as an insect repellent
cit·rus \ˈsi-trəs\ *n, pl* **citrus** *or* **cit·rus·es** : any of a genus of often thorny evergreen trees or shrubs grown in warm regions for their fruits (as the orange, lemon, lime, and grapefruit); *also* : the fruit
city \ˈsi-tē\ *n, pl* **cit·ies** [ME *citie* large or small town, fr. AF *cité*, fr. ML *civitas*, fr. L, citizenship, state, city of Rome, fr. *civis* citizen] **1** : an inhabited place larger or more important than a town **2** : a municipality in the U.S. governed under a charter granted by the state; *also* : an incorporated municipal unit of the highest class in Canada
city manager *n* : an official employed by an elected council to direct the administration of a city government
city–state \ˈsi-tē-ˌstāt\ *n* : an autonomous state consisting of a city and surrounding territory
civ *abbr* **1** civil; civilian **2** civilization
civ·et \ˈsi-vət\ *n* : a yellowish strong-smelling substance obtained from a catlike Old World mammal (**civet cat**) and used in making perfumes
civ·ic \ˈsi-vik\ *adj* : of or relating to a city, citizenship, or civil affairs
civ·ics \-viks\ *n* : a social science dealing with the rights and duties of citizens
civ·il \ˈsi-vəl\ *adj* **1** : of or relating to citizens or to the state as a political body **2** : COURTEOUS, POLITE **3** : of or relating to legal proceedings in connection with private rights and obligations ⟨the ~ code⟩ **4** : of or relating to the general population : not military or ecclesiastical
civil defense *n* : protective measures and emergency relief activities conducted by civilians in case of enemy attack or natural disaster
civil disobedience *n* : refusal to obey governmental commands esp. as a nonviolent means of protest
civil engineer *n* : an engineer whose training or occupation is in the design and construction esp. of public works (as roads or harbors) — **civil engineering** *n*
ci·vil·ian \sə-ˈvil-yən\ *n* : a person not on active duty in a military, police, or fire-fighting force
civ·i·li·sa·tion, civ·i·lise *chiefly Brit var of* CIVILIZATION, CIVILIZE
ci·vil·i·ty \sə-ˈvi-lə-tē\ *n, pl* **-ties** **1** : POLITENESS, COURTESY **2** : a polite act or expression
civ·i·li·za·tion \ˌsi-və-lə-ˈzā-shən\ *n* **1** : a relatively high level of cultural and technological development **2** : the culture characteristic of a time or place — **civ·i·li·za·tion·al** \-shə-nᵊl\ *adj*
civ·i·lize \ˈsi-və-ˌlīz\ *vb* **-lized; -liz·ing** **1** : to raise from a primitive state to an advanced and ordered stage of cultural development **2** : REFINE — **civ·i·lized** *adj*
civil liberty *n* : freedom from arbitrary governmental interference specifically by denial of governmental power — usu. used in pl.
civ·il·ly \ˈsi-vəl-lē\ *adv* **1** : in terms of civil rights, matters, or law ⟨~ dead⟩ **2** : in a civil manner : POLITELY
civil rights *n pl* : the nonpolitical rights of a citizen; *esp* : those guaranteed by the 13th and 14th amendments to the Constitution and by acts of Congress
civil servant *n* : a member of a civil service
civil service *n* : the administrative service of a government
civil war *n* : a war between opposing groups of citizens of the same country
civ·vies \ˈsi-vēz\ *n pl* : civilian clothes as distinguished from a military uniform
CJ *abbr* chief justice
ck *abbr* **1** cask **2** check
cl *abbr* **1** centiliter **2** class
Cl *symbol* chlorine
¹**clack** \ˈklak\ *vb* **1** : CHATTER, PRATTLE **2** : to make or cause to make a clatter
²**clack** *n* **1** : rapid continuous talk : CHATTER **2** : a sound of clacking ⟨the ~ of a typewriter⟩
clad \ˈklad\ *adj* **1** : CLOTHED, COVERED **2** : being or consisting of coins made of outer layers of one metal bonded to a core of a different metal
¹**claim** \ˈklām\ *vb* [ME, fr. AF *claimer, clamer*, fr. L *clamare* to cry out, shout] **1** : to ask for as one's own; *also* : to take as the rightful owner **2** : to call for : REQUIRE **3** : to state as a fact : MAINTAIN
²**claim** *n* **1** : a demand for something due ⟨an insurance ~⟩ **2** : a right to something usu. in another's possession **3** : an assertion open to challenge **4** : something claimed (as a tract of land)
claim·ant \ˈklā-mənt\ *n* : a person making a claim
clair·voy·ant \klar-ˈvȯi-ənt\ *adj* [F, fr. *clair* clear + *voyant* seeing] **1** : able to see beyond the range of ordinary perception **2** : having the power of discerning objects not present to the senses — **clair·voy·ance** \-əns\ *n* — **clairvoyant** *n*
clam \ˈklam\ *n* **1** : any of numerous bi-

valve mollusks including many that are edible **2** : DOLLAR

clam·bake \-ˌbāk\ *n* : a party or gathering (as at the seashore) at which food is cooked usu. on heated rocks covered by seaweed

clam·ber \ˈklam-bər\ *vb* : to climb awkwardly — **clam·ber·er** *n*

clam·my \ˈkla-mē\ *adj* **clam·mi·er**; **-est** : being damp, soft, sticky, and usu. cool — **clam·mi·ness** *n*

clam·or \ˈkla-mər\ *n* **1** : a noisy shouting **2** : a loud continuous noise **3** : insistent public expression (as of support or protest) — **clamor** *vb* — **clam·or·ous** *adj*

clam·our *chiefly Brit var of* CLAMOR

[1]**clamp** \ˈklamp\ *n* : a device that holds or presses parts together firmly

[2]**clamp** *vb* : to fasten with or as if with a clamp

clamp down *vb* : to impose restrictions : become repressive — **clamp·down** \ˈklamp-ˌdau̇n\ *n*

clam·shell \ˈklam-ˌshel\ *n* **1** : the shell of a clam **2** : a bucket or grapnel (as on a dredge) having two hinged jaws

clam up *vb* : to become silent

clan \ˈklan\ *n* [ME, fr. ScGael *clann* offspring, clan, fr. Old Irish *cland* plant, offspring, fr. L *planta* plant] : a group (as in the Scottish Highlands) made up of households whose heads claim descent from a common ancestor — **clan·nish** *adj* — **clan·nish·ness** *n*

clan·des·tine \klan-ˈdes-tən\ *adj* : held in or conducted with secrecy

clang \ˈklaŋ\ *n* : a loud metallic ringing sound — **clang** *vb*

clan·gor \ˈklaŋ-ər, -gər\ *n* : a resounding clang or medley of clangs

clan·gour *chiefly Brit var of* CLANGOR

clank \ˈklaŋk\ *n* : a sharp brief metallic ringing sound — **clank** *vb*

[1]**clap** \ˈklap\ *vb* **clapped**; **clap·ping** **1** : to strike noisily **2** : APPLAUD

[2]**clap** *n* **1** : a loud noisy crash **2** : the noise made by clapping the hands

[3]**clap** *n* : GONORRHEA

clap·board \ˈkla-bərd, -ˌbȯrd; ˈklap-ˌbȯrd\ *n* : a narrow board thicker at one edge than the other used for siding — **clap·board** *vb*

clap·per \ˈkla-pər\ *n* : one that claps; *esp* : the tongue of a bell

clap·trap \ˈklap-ˌtrap\ *n* : pretentious nonsense

claque \ˈklak\ *n* [F, fr. *claquer* to clap] **1** : a group hired to applaud at a performance **2** : a group of sycophants

clar·et \ˈkler-ət\ *n* [ME, fr. AF (*vin*) *claret* clear wine] : a dry red wine

clar·i·fy \ˈkler-ə-ˌfī\ *vb* **-fied**; **-fy·ing** : to make or become clear — **clar·i·fi·ca·tion** \ˌkler-ə-fə-ˈkā-shən\ *n*

clar·i·net \ˌkler-ə-ˈnet\ *n* : a single-reed woodwind instrument in the form of a cylindrical tube with a moderately flaring end — **clar·i·net·ist** *or* **clar·i·net·tist** \-ˈne-tist\ *n*

clar·i·on \ˈkler-ē-ən\ *adj* : brilliantly clear ⟨a ~ call⟩

clar·i·ty \ˈkler-ə-tē\ *n* : CLEARNESS

[1]**clash** \ˈklash\ *vb* **1** : to make or cause to make a clash **2** : CONFLICT, COLLIDE

[2]**clash** *n* **1** : a noisy usu. metallic sound of collision **2** : a hostile encounter **3** : a sharp conflict ⟨a ~ of opinions⟩

clasp \ˈklasp\ *n* **1** : a device (as a hook) for holding objects or parts together **2** : EMBRACE, GRASP — **clasp** *vb*

[1]**class** \ˈklas\ *n* [F *classe,* fr. L *classis* group called to military service, fleet, class] **1** : a group of students meeting regularly in a course; *also* : a group graduating together **2** : a course of instruction; *also* : the period when such a course is taught **3** : social rank; *also* : high quality **4** : a group of the same general status or nature; *esp* : a major category in biological classification that is above the order and below the phylum **5** : a division or rating based on grade or quality — **class·less** *adj*

[2]**class** *vb* : CLASSIFY

class action *n* : a legal action undertaken in behalf of the plaintiffs and all others having an identical interest in the alleged wrong

[1]**clas·sic** \ˈkla-sik\ *adj* **1** : serving as a standard of excellence ⟨a ~ novel⟩; *also* : TRADITIONAL **2** : CLASSICAL 2 **3** : notable esp. as the best example ⟨his winning goal was ~⟩ **4** : AUTHENTIC ⟨a ~ folk dance⟩

[2]**classic** *n* **1** : a work of enduring excellence and esp. of ancient Greece or Rome; *also* : its author **2** : a traditional event ⟨a football ~⟩

clas·si·cal \ˈkla-si-kəl\ *adj* **1** : CLASSIC **2** : of or relating to the ancient Greek and Roman classics **3** : of or relating to a form or system of primary significance before modern times ⟨~ economics⟩ **4** : concerned with a general study of the arts and sciences — **clas·si·cal·ly** \-k(ə-)lē\ *adv*

clas·si·cism \ˈkla-sə-ˌsi-zəm\ *n* **1** : the principles or style of the literature or art of ancient Greece and Rome **2** : adherence to traditional standards believed to be universally valid — **clas·si·cist** \-sist\ *n*

clas·si·fied \ˈkla-sə-ˌfīd\ *adj* : withheld from general circulation for reasons of national security

clas·si·fieds \-ˌfīdz\ *n pl* : advertisements grouped by subject

clas·si·fy \ˈkla-sə-ˌfī\ *vb* **-fied**; **-fy·ing** : to arrange in or assign to classes — **clas·si·fi·able** *adj* — **clas·si·fi·ca·tion** \ˌkla-sə-fə-ˈkā-shən\ *n* — **clas·si·fi·er** *n*

class·ism \ˈkla-ˌsi-zəm\ *n* **1** : a belief that a person's social or economic station determines their value in society; *also* : prejudice or discrimination based on class **2** : the systemic oppression of the lower and middle classes to benefit the upper class

class·mate \ˈklas-ˌmāt\ *n* : a member of the same class (as in a college)

class·room \-ˌrüm-, -ˌru̇m\ *n* : a place where classes meet

classy \ˈkla-sē\ *adj* **class·i·er; -est** : ELEGANT, STYLISH ⟨a ~ clientele⟩ — **class·i·ness** *n*

clat·ter \ˈkla-tər\ *n* : a rattling sound — **clatter** *vb*

clause \ˈklȯz\ *n* **1** : a group of words having its own subject and predicate but forming only part of a compound or complex sentence **2** : a separate part of an article or document

claus·tro·pho·bia \ˌklȯ-strə-ˈfō-bē-ə\ *n* : abnormal dread of being in closed or narrow spaces — **claus·tro·pho·bic** \-bik\ *adj*

clav·i·chord \ˈkla-və-ˌkȯrd\ *n* : an early keyboard instrument in use before the piano

clav·i·cle \ˈkla-vi-kəl\ *n* [F *clavicule,* fr. NL *clavicula,* fr. L, dim. of L *clavis* key] : COLLARBONE

cla·vier \klə-ˈvir; ˈklā-vē-ər\ *n* **1** : the keyboard of a musical instrument **2** : an early keyboard instrument

¹**claw** \ˈklȯ\ *n* **1** : a sharp usu. curved nail on the toe of an animal **2** : a sharp curved process (as on the foot of an insect); *also* : a pincerlike organ at the end of a limb of some arthropods (as a lobster) — **clawed** \ˈklȯd\ *adj*

²**claw** *vb* : to rake, seize, or dig with or as if with claws

clay \ˈklā\ *n* **1** : an earthy material that is plastic when moist but hard when fired and is used in making pottery; *also* : finely divided soil consisting largely of such clay **2** : EARTH, MUD **3** : a plastic substance used for modeling **4** : the mortal human body — **clay·ey** \ˈklā-ē\ *adj*

clay·more \ˈklā-ˌmȯr\ *n* : a large 2-edged sword formerly used by Scottish Highlanders

clay pigeon *n* : a saucer-shaped target thrown from a trap in trapshooting

¹**clean** \ˈklēn\ *adj* **1** : free from dirt, disease, or pollution ⟨~ air⟩ **2** : PURE ⟨the ~ thrill of one's first flight⟩; *also* : HONORABLE **3** : THOROUGH ⟨made a ~ sweep⟩ **4** : TRIM ⟨a ~ edge⟩ ⟨a ship with ~ lines⟩; *also* : EVEN **5** : habitually neat — **clean** *adv* — **clean·ly** \ˈklēn-lē\ *adv* — **clean·ness** \ˈklēn-nəs\ *n*

²**clean** *vb* : to make or become clean — **clean·able** \ˈklē-nə-bəl\ *adj* — **clean·er** *n*

clean–cut \ˈklēn-ˈkət\ *adj* **1** : cut so that the surface or edge is smooth and even **2** : sharply defined or outlined **3** : giving an effect of wholesomeness

clean·ly \ˈklen-lē\ *adj* **clean·li·er; -est** **1** : careful to keep clean **2** : habitually kept clean — **clean·li·ness** *n*

clean room \ˈklēn-ˌrüm, -ˌru̇m\ *n* : an uncontaminated room maintained for the manufacture or assembly of objects (as precision parts)

cleanse \ˈklenz\ *vb* **cleansed; cleans·ing** : to make clean — **cleans·er** *n*

¹**clean·up** \ˈklēn-ˌəp\ *n* **1** : an act or instance of cleaning **2** : a very large profit

²**cleanup** *adj* : being 4th in the batting order of a baseball team — **cleanup** *adv*

clean up *vb* : to make a spectacular business profit

¹**clear** \ˈklir\ *adj* [ME *clere,* fr. AF *cler,* fr. L *clarus*] **1** : BRIGHT, LUMINOUS; *also* : UNTROUBLED, SERENE **2** : CLOUDLESS **3** : CLEAN, PURE; *also* : TRANSPARENT **4** : easily heard, seen, or understood **5** : capable of sharp discernment; *also* : free from doubt **6** : INNOCENT ⟨a ~ conscience⟩ **7** : free from restriction, obstruction, or entanglement — **clear** *adv* — **clear·ness** *n*

²**clear** *vb* **1** : to make or become clear **2** : to go away : DISPERSE **3** : to free from accusation or blame; *also* : to certify as trustworthy **4** : EXPLAIN **5** : to get free from obstruction **6** : SETTLE ⟨~ a debt⟩ **7** : NET ⟨~*ed* a profit⟩ **8** : to get rid of : REMOVE ⟨~ snow off the road⟩ **9** : to jump or go by without touching; *also* : PASS ⟨the bill ~*ed* the legislature⟩

³**clear** *n* : a clear space or part

clear·ance \ˈklir-əns\ *n* **1** : an act or process of clearing **2** : the distance by which one object clears another **3** : AUTHORIZATION

clear–cut \ˈklir-ˈkət\ *adj* **1** : sharply outlined **2** : DEFINITE, UNEQUIVOCAL ⟨a ~ victory⟩

clear–cut·ting \-ˌkə-tiŋ\ *n* : removal of all the trees in a stand of timber — **clear–cut** \-ˌkət\ *vb*

clear·head·ed \-ˈhe-dəd\ *adj* : having a clear understanding : PERCEPTIVE

clear·ing \ˈklir-iŋ\ *n* **1** : a tract of land cleared of wood and brush **2** : the passage of checks and claims through a clearinghouse

clear·ing·house \-ˌhau̇s\ *n* : an institution maintained by banks for making an exchange of checks and claims held by each bank against other banks; *also* : an informal channel for information or assistance

clear·ly \ˈklir-lē\ *adv* **1** : in a clear manner **2** : it is clear

cleat \ˈklēt\ *n* : a piece of wood or metal fastened on or projecting from something to give strength, provide a grip, or prevent slipping

cleav·age \ˈklē-vij\ *n* **1** : a splitting apart : SPLIT **2** : the depression between a woman's breasts esp. when exposed by a low-cut neckline

¹**cleave** \ˈklēv\ *vb* **cleaved** \ˈklēvd\ *or* **clove** \ˈklōv\; **cleaved; cleav·ing** : ADHERE, CLING ⟨the child *cleaved* to her mother⟩

²**cleave** *vb* **cleaved** \ˈklēvd\ *also* **cleft** \ˈkleft\ *or* **clove** \ˈklōv\; **cleaved** *also* **cleft** *or* **clo·ven** \ˈklō-vən\; **cleav·ing** **1** : to divide by force : split asunder ⟨~ logs⟩ **2** : DIVIDE

cleav·er \ˈklē-vər\ *n* : a heavy chopping knife for cutting meat

clef \ˈklef\ *n* : a sign placed on the staff in music to show what pitch is represented by each line and space

cleft \ˈkleft\ *n* : FISSURE, CRACK
cleft lip *n* : a birth defect in which the upper lip is vertically split
cleft palate *n* : a split in the roof of the mouth that appears as a birth defect
clem•a•tis \ˈkle-mə-təs; kli-ˈma-təs\ *n* : any of a genus of vines or herbs related to the buttercups that have showy usu. white or purple flowers
clem•en•cy \ˈkle-mən-sē\ *n, pl* **-cies** **1** : disposition to be merciful **2** : mildness of weather
clem•ent \ˈkle-mənt\ *adj* **1** : MERCIFUL, LENIENT ⟨a ~ judge⟩ **2** : TEMPERATE, MILD ⟨~ weather for this time of year⟩
clem•en•tine \ˈkle-mən-ˌtēn\ : a small citrus fruit that is probably a hybrid between a tangerine and an orange
clench \ˈklench\ *vb* **1** : CLINCH 1 **2** : to hold fast **3** : to set or close tightly
clere•sto•ry \ˈklir-ˌstȯr-ē\ *n* : an outside wall of a room or building that rises above an adjoining roof and contains windows
cler•gy \ˈklər-jē\ *n* : a body of religious officials authorized to conduct services
cler•gy•man \-mən\ *n* : a member of the clergy
cler•gy•per•son \-ˌpər-sᵊn\ *n* : a member of the clergy
cler•ic \ˈkler-ik\ *n* : a member of the clergy
cler•i•cal \ˈkler-i-kəl\ *adj* **1** : of or relating to the clergy ⟨~ vestments⟩ **2** : of or relating to a clerk
cler•i•cal•ism \ˈkler-i-kə-ˌli-zəm\ *n* : a policy of maintaining or increasing the power of a religious hierarchy
clerk \ˈklərk, *Brit* ˈklärk\ *n* **1** : CLERIC **2** : an official responsible for correspondence, records, and accounts; *also* : a person employed to perform general office work **3** : a store salesperson — **clerk** *vb* — **clerk•ship** *n*
clev•er \ˈkle-vər\ *adj* **1** : showing skill or resourcefulness **2** : marked by wit or ingenuity — **clev•er•ly** *adv* — **clev•er•ness** *n*
clev•is \ˈkle-vəs\ *n* : a U-shaped shackle used for fastening
¹**clew** \ˈklü\ *n* **1** : CLUE **2** : a metal loop on a lower corner of a sail
²**clew** *vb* : to haul (a sail) up or down by ropes through the clews
cli•ché \kli-ˈshā\ *n* [F] : a trite phrase or expression — **cli•chéd** \-ˈshād\ *adj*
¹**click** \ˈklik\ *vb* **1** : to make or cause to make a click **2** : to fit or work together smoothly **3** : to select or make a selection on a computer by pressing a button on a control device (as a mouse) — **click•able** \ˈkli-kə-bəl\ *adj*
²**click** *n* **1** : a slight sharp noise **2** : an instance of clicking ⟨a mouse ~⟩
click•er \ˈkli-kər\ *n* : REMOTE CONTROL 2
cli•ent \ˈklī-ənt\ *n* **1** : DEPENDENT **2** : a person who engages the professional services of another; *also* : PATRON, CUSTOMER **3** : a computer in a network that uses the services (as access to files) provided by a server
cli•en•tele \ˌklī-ən-ˈtel, ˌklē-\ *n* : a body of clients and esp. customers
cliff \ˈklif\ *n* : a high steep face of rock, earth, or ice
cliff–hang•er \-ˌhaŋ-ər\ *n* **1** : an adventure serial or melodrama usu. presented in installments each of which ends in suspense **2** : a contest whose outcome is in doubt up to the very end
cli•mac•ter•ic \klī-ˈmak-tə-rik\ *n* **1** : a major turning point or critical stage **2** : MENOPAUSE; *also* : a corresponding period in the male
cli•mate \ˈklī-mət\ *n* [ME *climat,* fr. MF, fr. LL *clima,* fr. Gk *klima* inclination, latitude, climate, fr. *klinein* to lean] **1** : a region having specific climatic conditions **2** : the average weather conditions at a place over a period of years **3** : the prevailing set of conditions (as temperature and humidity) indoors **4** : a prevailing atmosphere or environment ⟨the ~ of opinion⟩ — **cli•mat•ic** \klī-ˈma-tik\ *adj* — **cli•mat•i•cal•ly** \-ti-k(ə-)lē\ *adv*
climate change *n* : significant and long-lasting change in the earth's climate and weather patterns; *esp* : such change associated with global warming
cli•ma•tol•o•gy \ˌklī-mə-ˈtä-lə-jē\ *n* : the science that deals with climates — **cli•ma•to•log•i•cal** \-mə-tə-ˈlä-ji-kəl\ *adj* — **cli•ma•to•log•i•cal•ly** \-k(ə-)lē\ *adv* — **cli•ma•tol•o•gist** \-mə-ˈtä-lə-jist\ *n*
¹**cli•max** \ˈklī-ˌmaks\ *n* [L, fr. Gk *klimax,* lit., ladder, fr. *klinein* to lean] **1** : a series of ideas or statements so arranged that they increase in force and power from the first to the last; *also* : the last member of such a series **2** : the highest point ⟨the ~ of her career⟩ **3** : ORGASM — **cli•mac•tic** \klī-ˈmak-tik\ *adj*
²**climax** *vb* : to come or bring to a climax
¹**climb** \ˈklīm\ *vb* **1** : to rise to a higher point **2** : to go up or down esp. by use of hands and feet; *also* : to ascend in growing — **climb•er** *n*
²**climb** *n* **1** : a place where climbing is necessary **2** : the act of climbing : ascent by climbing
clime \ˈklīm\ *n* : CLIMATE ⟨warmer ~*s*⟩
¹**clinch** \ˈklinch\ *vb* **1** : to turn over or flatten the end of something sticking out ⟨~ a nail⟩; *also* : to fasten by clinching **2** : to make final : SETTLE ⟨~ a deal⟩ **3** : to hold a boxing opponent **4** : to hold fast or firmly
²**clinch** *n* **1** : a fastening by means of a clinched nail, rivet, or bolt **2** : an act or instance of clinching in boxing
clinch•er \ˈklin-chər\ *n* : one that clinches; *esp* : a decisive fact, argument, act, or remark
cling \ˈkliŋ\ *vb* **clung** \ˈkləŋ\; **cling•ing** **1** : to adhere as if glued; *also* : to hold or hold on tightly **2** : to have a strong emotional attachment — **clingy** \ˈkliŋ-ē\ *adj*
cling•stone \ˈkliŋ-ˌstōn\ *n* : any of various fruits (as some peaches) whose flesh adheres strongly to the pit
clin•ic \ˈkli-nik\ *n* **1** : a medical class in which patients are examined and dis-

cussed **2** : a group meeting for teaching a certain skill and working on individual problems **3** : a facility (as of a hospital) for diagnosis and treatment of outpatients

clin•i•cal \ˈkli-ni-kəl\ *adj* **1** : of, relating to, or typical of a clinic; *esp* : involving direct observation of the patient ⟨~ studies⟩ **2** : scientifically dispassionate — **clin•i•cal•ly** \-k(ə-)lē\ *adv*

cli•ni•cian \kli-ˈni-shən\ *n* : a person qualified in the clinical practice of medicine, psychiatry, or psychology as distinguished from one specializing in laboratory or research techniques or in theory

[1]**clink** \ˈkliŋk\ *vb* : to make or cause to make a sharp short metallic sound

[2]**clink** *n* : a clinking sound

clin•ker \ˈkliŋ-kər\ *n* : stony matter fused together : SLAG

[1]**clip** \ˈklip\ *vb* **clipped**; **clip•ping** : to fasten with a clip

[2]**clip** *n* **1** : a device that grips, clasps, or hooks **2** : a cartridge holder for a rifle

[3]**clip** *vb* **clipped**; **clip•ping** **1** : to cut or cut off with shears ⟨*clipped* a recipe from the magazine⟩ **2** : CURTAIL, DIMINISH **3** : HIT, PUNCH **4** : to illegally block (an opponent) in football

[4]**clip** *n* **1** : a 2-bladed instrument for cutting esp. the nails **2** : a sharp blow **3** : a rapid pace ⟨moving at a good ~⟩

clip art *n* : ready-made usu. copyright-free illustrations

clip•board \ˈklip-ˌbȯrd\ *n* **1** : a small writing board with a spring clip at the top for holding papers **2** : a section of computer memory that temporarily stores data esp. to facilitate its movement or duplication

clip joint *n, slang* : an establishment (as a nightclub) that makes a practice of defrauding its customers

clip•per \ˈkli-pər\ *n* **1** : an implement for clipping esp. the hair or nails — usu. used in pl. **2** : a fast sailing ship

clip•ping \ˈkli-piŋ\ *n* : a piece clipped from something (as a newspaper)

clique \ˈklēk, ˈklik\ *n* [F] : a small exclusive group of people : COTERIE ⟨high school ~*s*⟩ — **cliqu•ey** \ˈklē-kē, ˈkli-\ *adj* — **cliqu•ish** \-kish\ *adj*

cli•to•ris \ˈkli-tə-rəs\ *n, pl* **cli•to•ris•es** : a small erectile organ at the anterior or ventral part of the vulva homologous to the penis — **cli•to•ral** \-rəl\ *adj*

clk *abbr* clerk

clo *abbr* clothing

[1]**cloak** \ˈklōk\ *n* **1** : a loose outer garment **2** : something that conceals

[2]**cloak** *vb* : to cover or hide with a cloak

cloak–and–dagger *adj* : involving or suggestive of espionage

clob•ber \ˈklä-bər\ *vb* **1** : to pound mercilessly; *also* : to hit with force : SMASH **2** : to defeat overwhelmingly

cloche \ˈklōsh\ *n* [F, lit., bell] : a woman's small close-fitting hat

[1]**clock** \ˈkläk\ *n* : a timepiece not intended to be carried on the person

[2]**clock** *vb* **1** : to time (a person or a performance) by a timing device **2** : to register (as speed) on a mechanical recording device — **clock•er** *n*

[3]**clock** *n* : an ornamental figure on a stocking or sock

clock•wise \ˈkläk-ˌwīz\ *adv* : in the direction in which the hands of a clock move — **clockwise** *adj*

clock•work \-ˌwərk\ *n* **1** : the machinery that runs a mechanical device (as a clock or toy) **2** : the precision or regularity associated with a clock

clod \ˈkläd\ *n* **1** : a lump esp. of earth or clay **2** : a dull or insensitive person

clod•hop•per \-ˌhä-pər\ *n* **1** : an uncouth rustic **2** : a large heavy shoe

[1]**clog** \ˈkläg\ *n* **1** : a weight attached esp. to an animal to impede motion **2** : a thick-soled shoe

[2]**clog** *vb* **clogged**; **clog•ging** **1** : to impede with a clog : HINDER **2** : to obstruct passage through **3** : to become filled with extraneous matter

cloi•son•né \ˌklȯi-zə-ˈnā\ *adj* : a colored decoration made of enamels poured into the divided areas in a design outlined with wire or metal strips

[1]**clois•ter** \ˈklȯi-stər\ *n* [ME *cloistre,* fr. AF, fr. ML *claustrum,* fr. L, bar, bolt, fr. *claudere* to close] **1** : a monastic establishment **2** : a covered usu. colonnaded passage on the side of a court — **clois•tral** \-strəl\ *adj*

[2]**cloister** *vb* : to shut away from the world

clone \ˈklōn\ *n* [Gk *klōn* twig, slip] **1** : the collection of genetically identical cells or organisms produced asexually from a single ancestral cell or organism; *also* : an individual grown from a single cell and genetically identical to it ⟨a sheep ~⟩ **2** : a group of replicas of a biological molecule (as DNA) **3** : one that appears to be a copy of an original form — **clon•al** \ˈklō-nᵊl\ *adj* — **clone** *vb*

clop \ˈkläp\ *n* : a sound made by or as if by a hoof or wooden shoe against pavement — **clop** *vb*

[1]**close** \ˈklōz\ *vb* **closed**; **clos•ing** **1** : to bar passage through : SHUT **2** : to suspend the operations (as of a school) **3** : END, TERMINATE **4** : to bring together the parts or edges of; *also* : to fill up **5** : GRAPPLE ⟨~ with the enemy⟩ **6** : to enter into an agreement — **clos•able** *or* **close•able** *adj*

[2]**close** \ˈklōz\ *n* : CONCLUSION, END

[3]**close** \ˈklōs\ *adj* **clos•er**; **clos•est** **1** : having no openings **2** : narrowly restricting or restricted **3** : limited to a privileged class **4** : SECLUDED; *also* : SECRETIVE **5** : RIGOROUS ⟨keep ~ watch⟩ **6** : SULTRY, STUFFY **7** : STINGY **8** : having little space between items or units **9** : fitting tightly; *also* : SHORT ⟨~ haircut⟩ **10** : NEAR ⟨at ~ range⟩ **11** : INTIMATE ⟨~ friends⟩ **12** : ACCURATE **13** : decided by a narrow margin ⟨a ~ game⟩ — **close** *adv* — **close•ly** *adv* — **close•ness** *n*

closed–circuit \ˈklōzd-ˈsər-kət\ *adj* : used in, shown on, or being a television installation in which the signal is transmitted by wire to a limited number of receivers

closed shop *n* : an establishment having only members of a labor union on the payroll

close·fist·ed \ˈklōz-ˈfis-təd, ˈklōs-\ *adj* : STINGY

close–knit \ˈklōs-ˈnit\ *adj* : closely bound together by social, cultural, economic, or political ties

close·mouthed \ˈklōz-ˈmau̇t͟hd, ˈklōs-ˈmau̇tht\ *adj* : cautious or reticent in speaking

close·out \ˈklōz-ˌau̇t\ *n* : a sale of a business's entire stock at low prices

close out *vb* **1** : to dispose of by a closeout **2** : to dispose of a business : SELL OUT

clos·er \ˈklō-zər\ *n* : one that closes; *esp* : a relief pitcher who specializes in finishing games

[1]**clos·et** \ˈklä-zət, ˈklȯ-\ *n* **1** : a small room for privacy **2** : a small compartment for household utensils or clothing **3** : a state or condition of secrecy ⟨came out of the ~⟩

[2]**closet** *vb* : to take into a private room for an interview

close–up \ˈklōs-ˌəp\ *n* **1** : a photograph or movie shot taken at close range **2** : an intimate view or examination

clo·sure \ˈklō-zhər\ *n* **1** : an act of closing : the condition of being closed **2** : something that closes **3** : CLOTURE

clot \ˈklät\ *n* : a mass formed by a portion of liquid (as blood) thickening and sticking together — **clot** *vb*

cloth \ˈklȯth\ *n, pl* **cloths** \ˈklȯt͟hz, ˈklȯths\ **1** : a pliable fabric made usu. by weaving or knitting natural or synthetic fibers and filaments **2** : TABLECLOTH **3** : distinctive dress of the clergy; *also* : CLERGY

clothe \ˈklōt͟h\ *vb* **clothed** *or* **clad** \ˈklad\; **cloth·ing** **1** : DRESS; *also* : to provide with clothes **2** : to express by suitably significant language ⟨policies *clothed* in rhetoric⟩

clothes \ˈklōt͟hz, ˈklōz\ *n pl* **1** : CLOTHING **2** : BEDCLOTHES

clothes·horse \-ˌhȯrs\ *n* **1** : a frame on which to hang clothes **2** : a conspicuously dressy person

[1]**clothes·line** \-ˌlīn\ *n* : a rope or cord on which clothes are hung to dry

[2]**clothesline** *vb* : to knock down by catching by the neck with one's outstretched arm

clothes moth *n* : any of several small pale moths whose larvae eat wool, fur, and feathers

clothes·pin \ˈklōt͟hz-ˌpin, ˈklōz-\ *n* : a device for fastening clothes on a line

clothes·press \-ˌpres\ *n* : a receptacle for clothes

cloth·ier \ˈklōt͟h-yər, ˈklō-t͟hē-ər\ *n* : a maker or seller of clothing

cloth·ing \ˈklō-t͟hiŋ\ *n* : garments in general

clo·ture \ˈklō-chər\ *n* : the closing or limitation (as by calling for a vote) of debate in a legislative body

[1]**cloud** \ˈklau̇d\ *n* [ME, rock, cloud, fr. OE *clūd*] **1** : a visible mass of particles of condensed vapor (as water or ice) suspended in the atmosphere **2** : a usu. visible mass of minute airborne particles; *also* : a mass of obscuring matter in interstellar space **3** : CROWD, SWARM ⟨a ~ of mosquitoes⟩ **4** : something having a dark or threatening aspect ⟨a ~ of suspicion⟩ **5** : something that obscures or blemishes ⟨a ~ of ambiguity⟩ **6** : the computers and networks that support cloud computing — **cloud·i·ness** \ˈklau̇-dē-nəs\ *n* — **cloud·less** *adj* — **cloud·like** \ˈklau̇d-ˌlīk\ *adj* — **cloudy** *adj*

[2]**cloud** *vb* **1** : to darken or hide with or as if with a cloud **2** : OBSCURE ⟨~*ed* in mystery⟩ **3** : TAINT, SULLY ⟨a ~*ed* reputation⟩

cloud·burst \-ˌbərst\ *n* : a sudden heavy rainfall

cloud computing *n* : the practice of storing regularly used computer data on multiple servers that can be accessed through the Internet

cloud·let \-lət\ *n* : a small cloud

cloud nine *n* : a feeling of extreme well-being or elation — usu. used with *on*

[1]**clout** \ˈklau̇t\ *n* **1** : a blow esp. with the hand **2** : PULL, INFLUENCE

[2]**clout** *vb* : to hit forcefully

[1]**clove** \ˈklōv\ *n* : one of the small bulbs that grows at the base of the scales of a large bulb ⟨a ~ of garlic⟩

[2]**clove** *past of* CLEAVE

[3]**clove** *n* [ME *clowe*, fr. AF *clou* (*de girofle*), lit., nail of clove, fr. L *clavus* nail] : the dried flower bud of a tropical tree used esp. as a spice

clo·ven \ˈklō-vən\ *past part of* CLEAVE

cloven foot *n* : CLOVEN HOOF — **cloven–foot·ed** \-ˈfu̇-təd\ *adj*

cloven hoof *n* : a foot (as of a sheep) with the front part divided into two parts — **cloven–hoofed** \-ˈhu̇ft, -ˈhu̇vd\ *adj*

clo·ver \ˈklō-vər\ *n* : any of a genus of leguminous herbs with usu. 3-parted leaves and dense flower heads

clo·ver·leaf \-ˌlēf\ *n, pl* **cloverleafs** \-ˌlēfs\ *or* **clo·ver·leaves** \-ˌlēvz\ : an interchange between two major highways that from above resembles a 4-leaf clover

[1]**clown** \ˈklau̇n\ *n* **1** : BOOR **2** : a fool or comedian in an entertainment (as a circus) **3** : a person given to joking and buffoonery — **clown·ish** *adj* — **clown·ish·ly** *adv* — **clown·ish·ness** *n*

[2]**clown** *vb* : to act like a clown

cloy \ˈklȯi\ *vb* : to disgust or nauseate with excess of something orig. pleasing — **cloy·ing·ly** *adv*

clr *abbr* clear

[1]**club** \ˈkləb\ *n* **1** : a heavy wooden stick or staff used as a weapon; *also* : BAT **2** : any of a suit of playing cards marked with a black figure resembling a clover leaf **3** : a group of persons associated for a common purpose; *also* : the meeting place of such a group **4** : CLUB SANDWICH

[2]**club** *vb* **clubbed**; **club·bing** **1** : to strike with a club **2** : to unite or combine for a common cause **3** : to patronize nightclubs

club·foot \'kləb-'fu̇t\ *n* : a misshapen foot twisted out of position from birth; *also* : this deformed condition — **club·foot·ed** \-'fu̇-təd\ *adj*

club·house \'kləb-ˌhau̇s\ *n* **1** : a house occupied by a club **2** : locker rooms used by an athletic team **3** : a building at a golf course with locker rooms and usu. a pro shop and a restaurant

club sandwich *n* : a sandwich of three slices of bread with two layers of meat (as turkey) and lettuce, tomato, and mayonnaise

club soda *n* : SODA WATER

cluck \'klək\ *n* : the call of a hen esp. to her chicks — **cluck** *vb*

[1]**clue** \'klü\ *n* **1** : something that guides through an intricate procedure or maze; *esp* : a piece of evidence leading to the solution of a problem **2** : IDEA, NOTION ⟨has no ~ what he's doing⟩

[2]**clue** *vb* **clued**; **clue·ing** *or* **clu·ing** : to provide with a clue; *also* : to give information to ⟨~ me in⟩

[1]**clump** \'kləmp\ *n* **1** : a group of things clustered together **2** : a heavy tramping sound

[2]**clump** *vb* : to tread clumsily and noisily

clum·sy \'kləm-zē\ *adj* **clum·si·er**; **-est** **1** : lacking dexterity, nimbleness, or grace **2** : not tactful or subtle ⟨a ~ attempt at a joke⟩ — **clum·si·ly** \-zə-lē\ *adv* — **clum·si·ness** \-zē-nəs\ *n*

clung *past and past part of* CLING

clunk·er \'kləŋ-kər\ *n* **1** : a dilapidated automobile **2** : a notable failure

[1]**clus·ter** \'kləs-tər\ *n* : GROUP, BUNCH

[2]**cluster** *vb* : to grow or gather in a cluster

[1]**clutch** \'kləch\ *vb* : to grasp with or as if with the hand

[2]**clutch** *n* **1** : the claws or a hand in the act of grasping; *also* : CONTROL, POWER **2** : a device for gripping an object **3** : a coupling used to connect and disconnect a driving and a driven part of a mechanism; *also* : a lever or pedal operating such a coupling **4** : a crucial situation

[3]**clutch** *adj* : made, done, or successful in a crucial situation

[4]**clutch** *n* **1** : a nest or batch of eggs; *also* : a brood of chicks **2** : GROUP, BUNCH

[1]**clut·ter** \'klə-tər\ *vb* : to fill or cover with a disorderly scattering of things

[2]**clutter** *n* : a crowded mass

cm *abbr* centimeter

Cm *symbol* curium

CM *abbr* [Commonwealth of the Northern Mariana Islands] Northern Mariana Islands

cmdr *abbr* commander

cml *abbr* commercial

CMSgt *abbr* chief master sergeant

Cn *symbol* copernicium

CNO *abbr* chief of naval operations

CNS *abbr* central nervous system

co *abbr* **1** company **2** county

Co *symbol* cobalt

CO *abbr* **1** Colorado **2** commanding officer **3** conscientious objector

c/o *abbr* care of

[1]**coach** \'kōch\ *n* [MF *coche,* ultim. fr. Hung *kocsi (szekér),* lit., (wagon) of Kocs (town in Hungary)] **1** : a large closed 4-wheeled carriage with an elevated outside front seat for the driver **2** : a railroad passenger car esp. for day travel **3** : BUS **4** : a private tutor; *also* : one who instructs or trains ⟨a soccer ~⟩

[2]**coach** *vb* : to instruct, direct, or prompt as a coach

coach·man \-mən\ *n* : a man who drives a coach or carriage

co·ad·ju·tor \ˌkō-ə-'jü-tər, kō-'a-jə-tər\ *n* : ASSISTANT; *esp* : an assistant bishop having the right of succession

co·ag·u·lant \kō-'a-gyə-lənt\ *n* : something that produces coagulation

co·ag·u·late \-ˌlāt\ *vb* **-lat·ed**; **-lat·ing** : CLOT — **co·ag·u·la·tion** \kō-ˌa-gyə-'lā-shən\ *n*

[1]**coal** \'kōl\ *n* **1** : EMBER **2** : a black solid combustible mineral used as fuel

[2]**coal** *vb* **1** : to supply with coal **2** : to take in coal

co·a·lesce \ˌkō-ə-'les\ *vb* **co·a·lesced**; **co·a·lesc·ing** : to grow together; *also* : FUSE ♦ ***Synonyms*** MERGE, BLEND, MINGLE, MIX — **co·a·les·cence** \-ᵊns\ *n*

coal·field \'kōl-ˌfēld\ *n* : a region rich in coal deposits

coal gas *n* : gas from coal; *esp* : gas distilled from bituminous coal and used for heating

co·a·li·tion \ˌkō-ə-'li-shən\ *n* : UNION; *esp* : a temporary union for a common purpose — **co·a·li·tion·ist** *n*

coal oil *n* : KEROSENE

coal tar *n* : tar distilled from bituminous coal and used in dyes and drugs

co·an·chor \'kō-'aŋ-kər\ *n* : a newscaster who shares the duties of head broadcaster

coarse \'kȯrs\ *adj* **coars·er**; **coars·est** **1** : of ordinary or inferior quality **2** : composed of large parts or particles ⟨~ sand⟩ **3** : CRUDE ⟨~ manners⟩ **4** : ROUGH, HARSH — **coarse·ly** *adv* — **coarse·ness** *n*

coars·en \'kȯr-sᵊn\ *vb* : to make or become coarse

[1]**coast** \'kōst\ *n* [ME *cost,* fr. AF *coste,* fr. L *costa* rib, side] **1** : SEASHORE **2** : a slide down a slope **3** : the immediate area of view — used in the phrase *the coast is clear* — **coast·al** *adj*

[2]**coast** *vb* **1** : to sail along the shore **2** : to move (as downhill on a sled) without effort

coast·er *n* **1** : one that coasts **2** : a shallow container or a plate or mat to protect a surface

coaster brake *n* : a brake in the hub of the rear wheel of a bicycle

coast guard *n* : a military force employed in guarding or patrolling a coast — **coast·guards·man** \'kōst-ˌgärdz-mən\ *n*

coast·line \'kōst-ˌlīn\ *n* : the outline or shape of a coast

[1]**coat** \ˈkōt\ *n* **1** : an outer garment for the upper part of the body **2** : an external growth (as of fur or feathers) on an animal **3** : a covering layer ⟨a ~ of paint⟩ — **coat·ed** \ˈkō-təd\ *adj*

[2]**coat** *vb* : to cover usu. with a finishing or protective coat

coat·ing \ˈkō-tiŋ\ *n* : COAT, COVERING

coat of arms : the heraldic bearings (as of a person) usu. depicted on an escutcheon

coat of mail : a garment of metal scales or rings worn as armor

co·au·thor \ˈkō-ˈȯ-thər\ *n* : a joint or associate author — **coauthor** *vb*

coax \ˈkōks\ *vb* : WHEEDLE; *also* : to gain by gentle urging or flattery

co·ax·i·al \ˈkō-ˈak-sē-əl\ *adj* : having coincident axes — **co·ax·i·al·ly** *adv*

coaxial cable *n* : a cable that consists of a tube of electrically conducting material surrounding a central conductor

cob \ˈkäb\ *n* **1** : a male swan **2** : CORNCOB **3** : a short-legged stocky horse

co·balt \ˈkō-ˌbȯlt\ *n* [G *Kobalt,* alter. of *Kobold,* lit., goblin; fr. its occurrence in silver ore, believed to be due to goblins] : a tough shiny silver-white magnetic metallic chemical element found with iron and nickel

cob·ble \ˈkä-bəl\ *vb* **cob·bled**; **cob·bling** : to make or put together roughly or hastily ⟨~ together a solution⟩

cob·bler \ˈkä-blər\ *n* **1** : a mender or maker of shoes **2** : a deep-dish fruit pie with a thick crust

cob·ble·stone \ˈkä-bəl-ˌstōn\ *n* : a naturally rounded stone larger than a pebble and smaller than a boulder

co·bra \ˈkō-brə\ *n* [Pg *cobra* (*de capello*), lit., hooded snake] : any of several venomous snakes of Asia and Africa that when excited expand the skin of the neck into a broad hood

cob·web \ˈkäb-ˌweb\ *n* [ME *coppeweb,* fr. *coppe* spider, fr. OE ātor*coppe*] **1** : SPIDERWEB; *also* : a thread spun by a spider or insect larva **2** : something flimsy or entangling — **cob·web·by** \-ˌwe-bē\ *adj*

co·caine \kō-ˈkān, ˈkō-ˌkān\ *n* : a drug obtained from the leaves of a So. American shrub (**co·ca** \ˈkō-kə\) that can result in severe psychological dependence and is sometimes used in medicine as a local anesthetic and illegally as a stimulant of the central nervous system

coc·cus \ˈkä-kəs\ *n, pl* **coc·ci** \ˈkäk-ˌsī\ : a spherical bacterium

coc·cyx \ˈkäk-siks\ *n, pl* **coc·cy·ges** \ˈkäk-sə-ˌjēz\ *also* **coc·cyx·es** \ˈkäk-sik-səz\ : the end of the spinal column beyond the sacrum esp. in humans

co·chi·neal \ˈkä-chə-ˌnēl\ *n* : a red dye made from the dried bodies of females of a tropical American insect (**cochineal insect**)

co·chlea \ˈkō-klē-ə, ˈkä-\ *n, pl* **co·chle·as** *or* **co·chle·ae** \-klē-ˌē, -ˌī\ : the usu. spiral part of the inner ear containing nerve endings which carry information about sound to the brain — **co·chle·ar** \-klē-ər\ *adj*

[1]**cock** \ˈkäk\ *n* **1** : the adult male of a bird and esp. of the common domestic chicken **2** : VALVE, FAUCET **3** : LEADER **4** : the hammer of a firearm; *also* : the position of the hammer when ready for firing

[2]**cock** *vb* **1** : to draw back the hammer of a firearm **2** : to set or draw back in readiness for some action ⟨~ your arm to throw⟩ **3** : to turn or tilt usu. to one side ⟨~ one's head⟩

[3]**cock** *n* : a small pile (as of hay)

cock·ade \kä-ˈkād\ *n* : an ornament worn on the hat as a badge

cock·a·tiel \ˌkä-kə-ˈtēl\ *n* : a small crested gray parrot often kept as a cage bird

cock·a·too \ˈkä-kə-ˌtü\ *n, pl* **-toos** [D *kaketoe,* fr. Malay *kakatua*] : any of various large noisy crested parrots chiefly of Australia

cock·a·trice \ˈkä-kə-trəs, -ˌtrīs\ *n* : a legendary serpent with a deadly glance

cock·crow \ˈkäk-ˌkrō\ *n* : DAWN

cocked hat \ˈkäkt-\ *n* : a hat with the brim turned up on two or three sides

cock·er·el \ˈkä-kə-rəl\ *n* : a young male domestic chicken

cock·er spaniel \ˈkä-kər-\ *n* [*cocking* woodcock hunting] : any of a breed of small spaniels with long ears, square muzzle, and silky coat

cock·eyed \ˈkä-ˈkīd\ *adj* **1** : turned or tilted to one side **2** : slightly crazy : FOOLISH

cock·fight \ˈkäk-ˌfīt\ *n* : a contest of gamecocks usu. fitted with metal spurs

[1]**cock·le** \ˈkä-kəl\ *n* : any of several weedy plants related to the pinks

[2]**cockle** *n* : a bivalve mollusk with a heart-shaped shell

cock·le·shell \-ˌshel\ *n* **1** : the shell of a cockle **2** : a light flimsy boat

cock·ney \ˈkäk-nē\ *n, pl* **cockneys** : a native of London and esp. of the East End of London; *also* : the dialect of a cockney

cock·pit \ˈkäk-ˌpit\ *n* **1** : a pit for cockfights **2** : a space or compartment in a vehicle from which it is steered, piloted, or driven

cock·roach \ˈkäk-ˌrōch\ *n* [Sp *cucaracha*] : any of an order or suborder of active nocturnal insects including some which infest houses and ships

cock·sure \ˈkäk-ˈshu̇r\ *adj* **1** : perfectly sure : CERTAIN **2** : COCKY

cock·tail \ˈkäk-ˌtāl\ *n* **1** : an iced drink made of liquor and flavoring ingredients **2** : an appetizer (as tomato juice) served as a first course of a meal

cocky \ˈkä-kē\ *adj* **cock·i·er**; **-est** : marked by overconfidence : PERT, CONCEITED — **cock·i·ly** \-kə-lē\ *adv* — **cock·i·ness** \-kē-nəs\ *n*

co·coa \ˈkō-kō\ *n* **1** : CACAO **2** : chocolate deprived of some of its fat and powdered; *also* : a drink made of this heated with water or milk

cocoa butter *n* : a pale vegetable fat obtained from cacao beans

co·co·nut \ˈkō-kə-(ˌ)nət\ *n* : a large edible hard-shelled fruit produced by a tall tropical palm (**coconut palm**)

co·coon \kə-ˈkün\ *n* **1** : a case usu. of silk formed by some insect larvae for protection during the pupal stage **2** : something that offers protection or isolation

cod \ˈkäd\ *n, pl* **cod** *also* **cods** : a bottom-dwelling bony fish of the North Atlantic that is an important food fish; *also* : a related fish of the Pacific Ocean

COD *abbr* **1** cash on delivery **2** collect on delivery

co·da \ˈkō-də\ *n* : a closing section in a musical composition that is formally distinct from the main structure

cod·dle \ˈkä-dᵊl\ *vb* **cod·dled; cod·dling** **1** : to cook slowly in water below the boiling point **2** : PAMPER

[1]**code** \ˈkōd\ *n* [ME, fr. MF, fr. L *caudex, codex* trunk of a tree, document formed orig. from wooden tablets] **1** : a systematic statement of a body of law **2** : a system of principles or rules ⟨moral ~⟩ **3** : a system of signals **4** : a system of symbols (as in secret communication) with special meanings **5** : GENETIC CODE **6** : instructions for a computer (as within a piece of software)

[2]**code** *vb* **cod·ed; cod·ing** : to put into the form or symbols of a code

co·deine \ˈkō-ˌdēn\ *n* : a narcotic drug obtained from opium and used esp. as an analgesic and cough suppressant

co·dex \ˈkō-ˌdeks\ *n, pl* **co·di·ces** \ˈkō-də-ˌsēz, ˈkä-\ : a manuscript book (as of the Scriptures or classics)

cod·fish \ˈkäd-ˌfish\ *n* : COD

cod·ger \ˈkä-jər\ *n* : an odd or cranky and usu. elderly fellow

cod·i·cil \ˈkä-də-səl, -ˌsil\ *n* : a legal instrument modifying an earlier will

cod·i·fy \ˈkä-də-ˌfī, ˈkō-\ *vb* **-fied; -fy·ing** : to arrange in a systematic form — **cod·i·fi·ca·tion** \ˌkä-də-fə-ˈkā-shən, ˌkō-\ *n*

co·ed \ˈkō-ˌed\ *n* : a female student in a coeducational institution — **coed** *adj*

co·ed·u·ca·tion \ˌkō-ˌe-jə-ˈkā-shən\ *n* : the education of male and female students at the same institution — **co·ed·u·ca·tion·al** \-shə-nəl\ *adj* — **co·ed·u·ca·tion·al·ly** *adv*

co·ef·fi·cient \ˌkō-ə-ˈfi-shənt\ *n* **1** : a constant factor as distinguished from a variable in a mathematical term **2** : a number that serves as a measure of some property (as of a substance, device, or process)

coe·len·ter·ate \si-ˈlen-tə-ˌrāt, -rət\ *n* : any of a phylum of radially symmetrical invertebrate animals including the corals, sea anemones, and jellyfishes

co·equal \kō-ˈē-kwəl\ *adj* : equal with another — **coequal** *n* — **co·equal·i·ty** \ˌkō-ē-ˈkwä-lə-tē\ *n* — **co·equal·ly** *adv*

co·erce \kō-ˈərs\ *vb* **co·erced; co·erc·ing** **1** : RESTRAIN, REPRESS **2** : COMPEL **3** : ENFORCE — **co·er·cion** \-ˈər-zhən, -shən\ *n* — **co·er·cive** \-ˈər-siv\ *adj*

co·e·val \kō-ˈē-vəl\ *adj* : of the same age — **coeval** *n*

co·ex·ist \ˌkō-ig-ˈzist\ *vb* **1** : to exist together or at the same time **2** : to live in peace with each other — **co·ex·is·tence** \-ˈzis-təns\ *n*

co·ex·ten·sive \ˌkō-ik-ˈsten-siv\ *adj* : having the same scope or extent in space or time

C of C *abbr* Chamber of Commerce

cof·fee \ˈkȯ-fē\ *n* [It & Turk; It *caffè,* fr. Turk *kahve,* fr. Ar *qahwa*] : a drink made from the roasted and ground seeds of a fruit of a tropical shrub or tree; *also* : these seeds (**coffee beans**) or a plant producing them

cof·fee·house \-ˌhau̇s\ *n* : a place where refreshments (as coffee) are sold

coffee klatch \-ˌklach\ *n* : KAFFEEKLATSCH

cof·fee·pot \-ˌpät\ *n* : a pot for brewing or serving coffee

coffee shop *n* : a small restaurant

coffee table *n* : a low table customarily placed in front of a sofa

cof·fer \ˈkȯ-fər\ *n* : a chest or box used esp. for valuables

cof·fer·dam \-ˌdam\ *n* : a watertight enclosure from which water is pumped to expose the bottom of a body of water and permit construction

cof·fin \ˈkȯ-fən\ *n* : a box or chest for burying a corpse

C of S *abbr* chief of staff

[1]**cog** \ˈkäg\ *n* : a tooth on the rim of a wheel or gear — **cogged** \ˈkägd\ *adj*

[2]**cog** *abbr* cognate

co·gen·er·a·tion \ˌkō-ˌje-nə-ˈrā-shən\ *n* : the simultaneous generation of electricity and heat from the same fuel

co·gent \ˈkō-jənt\ *adj* : having power to compel or constrain : CONVINCING ⟨a ~ argument⟩ — **co·gen·cy** \-jən-sē\ *n*

cog·i·tate \ˈkä-jə-ˌtāt\ *vb* **-tat·ed; -tat·ing** : THINK, PONDER ⟨*cogitated* about his future⟩ — **cog·i·ta·tion** \ˌkä-jə-ˈtā-shən\ *n* — **cog·i·ta·tive** \ˈkä-jə-ˌtā-tiv\ *adj*

co·gnac \ˈkōn-ˌyak\ *n* : a French brandy

cog·nate \ˈkäg-ˌnāt\ *adj* **1** : of the same or similar nature **2** : RELATED; *esp* : related by descent from the same ancestral language — **cognate** *n*

cog·ni·tive \ˈkäg-nə-tiv\ *adj* : of, relating to, or being conscious intellectual activity (as thinking, remembering, reasoning, or using language) — **cog·ni·tion** \käg-ˈni-shən\ *n* — **cog·ni·tive·ly** *adv*

cog·ni·zance \ˈkäg-nə-zəns\ *n* **1** : apprehension by the mind : AWARENESS ⟨had no ~ of the crime⟩ **2** : NOTICE, HEED — **cog·ni·zant** \ˈkäg-nə-zənt\ *adj*

cog·no·men \käg-ˈnō-mən, ˈkäg-nə-\ *n, pl* **cognomens** *or* **cog·no·mi·na** \käg-ˈnä-mə-nə, -ˈnō-\ : NAME; *esp* : NICKNAME

co·gno·scen·te \ˌkän-yə-ˈshen-tē\ *n, pl* **-scen·ti** \-tē\ [obs. It] : CONNOISSEUR

cog·wheel \ˈkäg-ˌhwēl\ *n* : a wheel with cogs or teeth

co·hab·it \kō-ˈha-bət\ *vb* : to live together as a couple — **co·hab·i·ta·tion** \-ˌha-bə-ˈtā-shən\ *n*

co·here \kō-ˈhir\ *vb* **co·hered; co·her·ing** : to stick together

co·her·ent \kō-ˈhir-ənt\ *adj* **1** : having the quality of cohering **2** : logically consistent ⟨a ~ explanation⟩ — **co·her·ence** \-əns\ *n* — **co·her·ent·ly** *adv*

co·he·sion \kō-ˈhē-zhən\ *n* **1** : a sticking together **2** : molecular attraction by which the particles of a body are united — **co·he·sive** \-siv\ *adj* — **co·he·sive·ly** *adv* — **co·he·sive·ness** *n*

co·ho \ˈkō-ˌhō\ *n, pl* **cohos** *or* **coho** : a rather small Pacific salmon with light-colored flesh

co·hort \ˈkō-ˌhȯrt\ *n* **1** : a group of warriors or followers **2** : COMPANION, ACCOMPLICE

coif \ˈkȯif; *2 usu* ˈkwäf\ *n* **1** : a close-fitting hat **2** : COIFFURE

coif·feur \kwä-ˈfər\ *n* [F] : HAIRDRESSER

coif·feuse \kwä-ˈfərz, -ˈfəz, -ˈfüz, -ˈfyüz\ *n* : a female hairdresser

coif·fure \kwä-ˈfyu̇r\ *n* : a manner of arranging the hair

[1]**coil** \ˈkȯi(-ə)l\ *vb* : to wind in a spiral shape

[2]**coil** *n* : a series of rings or loops (as of coiled rope, wire, or pipe) : RING, LOOP

[1]**coin** \ˈkȯin\ *n* [ME, wedge, corner, image on a coin, fr. AF *coing,* fr. L *cuneus* wedge] **1** : a piece of metal issued by government authority as money **2** : metal money

[2]**coin** *vb* **1** : to make (a coin) esp. by stamping : MINT **2** : CREATE, INVENT ⟨~ a phrase⟩ — **coin·er** *n*

coin·age \ˈkȯi-nij\ *n* **1** : the act or process of coining **2** : COINS

co·in·cide \ˌkō-ən-ˈsīd, ˈkō-ən-ˌsīd\ *vb* **-cid·ed; -cid·ing** **1** : to occupy the same place in space or time **2** : to correspond or agree exactly

co·in·ci·dence \kō-ˈin-sə-dəns\ *n* **1** : exact agreement **2** : occurrence together apparently without reason; *also* : an event that so occurs

co·in·ci·dent \-sə-dənt\ *adj* **1** : of similar nature **2** : occupying the same space or time — **co·in·ci·den·tal** \kō-ˌin-sə-ˈden-tᵊl\ *adj*

co·i·tus \ˈkō-ə-təs\ *n* [L, fr. *coire* to come together] : SEXUAL INTERCOURSE 1 — **co·i·tal** \-tᵊl\ *adj*

[1]**coke** \ˈkōk\ *n* : a hard gray porous fuel made by heating soft coal to drive off most of its volatile material

[2]**coke** *n* : COCAINE

[1]**col** *abbr* **1** colonial; colony **2** column

[2]**col** *or* **coll** *abbr* **1** collect; collected; collection **2** college; collegiate

Col *abbr* **1** colonel **2** Colorado **3** Colossians

COL *abbr* **1** colonel **2** cost of living

co·la \ˈkō-lə\ *n* : a carbonated soft drink usu. containing sugar, caffeine, caramel, and special flavoring

col·an·der \ˈkə-lən-dər, ˈkä-\ *n* : a perforated utensil for draining food

[1]**cold** \ˈkōld\ *adj* **1** : having a low or decidedly subnormal temperature **2** : lacking warmth of feeling **3** : suffering or uncomfortable from lack of warmth — **cold·ly** *adv* — **cold·ness** *n* — **in cold blood** : with premeditation : DELIBERATELY ⟨murdered her *in cold blood*⟩

[2]**cold** *n* **1** : a condition marked by low temperature; *also* : cold weather **2** : a chilly feeling **3** : a bodily disorder popularly associated with chilling; *esp* : COMMON COLD

[3]**cold** *adv* **1** : TOTALLY, FINALLY ⟨stopped them ~⟩ **2** : without notice or preparation ⟨performed the song ~⟩

cold–blood·ed \ˈkōld-ˈblə-dəd\ *adj* **1** : lacking normal human feelings **2** : having a body temperature not internally regulated but close to that of the environment **3** : sensitive to cold

cold cuts *n pl* : sliced assorted cold cooked meats

cold feet *n pl* : doubt or fear that prevents action

cold front *n* : an advancing edge of a cold air mass

cold shoulder *n* : cold or unsympathetic behavior — **cold–shoul·der** *vb*

cold sore *n* : a group of fluid-filled blisters appearing in or about the mouth in the oral form of herpes simplex

cold sweat *n* : concurrent perspiration and chill usu. associated with fear, pain, or shock

[1]**cold turkey** *n* : abrupt complete cessation of the use of an addictive drug

[2]**cold turkey** *adv* **1** : without a period of adjustment **2** : without preparation

cold war *n* : a conflict characterized by the use of means short of sustained overt military action

cole·slaw \ˈkōl-ˌslȯ\ *n* [D *koolsla,* fr. *kool* cabbage + *sla* salad] : a salad made of raw cabbage

col·ic \ˈkä-lik\ *n* **1** : sharp sudden abdominal pain **2** : a condition marked by recurrent episodes of crying and irritability in an otherwise healthy infant — **col·icky** \ˈkä-li-kē\ *adj*

col·i·se·um \ˌkä-lə-ˈsē-əm\ *n* : a large structure esp. for athletic contests

co·li·tis \kō-ˈlī-təs\ *n* : inflammation of the colon

col·lab·o·rate \kə-ˈla-bə-ˌrāt\ *vb* **-rat·ed; -rat·ing** **1** : to work jointly with others (as in writing a book) **2** : to cooperate with an enemy force occupying one's country — **col·lab·o·ra·tion** \-ˌla-bə-ˈrā-shən\ *n* — **col·lab·o·ra·tive** \-ˈla-bə-ˌrā-tiv, -b(ə-)rə-\ *adj* — **col·lab·o·ra·tor** \-ˈla-bə-ˌrā-tər\ *n*

col·lage \kə-ˈläzh\ *n* [F, lit., gluing] : an artistic composition of fragments (as of printed matter) pasted on a surface; *also* : a work that combines various elements into a cohesive whole

col·la·gen \ˈkä-lə-jən\ *n* : any of a group of fibrous proteins widely found in vertebrate connective tissue

[1]**col·lapse** \kə-ˈlaps\ *vb* **col·lapsed; col·laps·ing** **1** : to shrink together abruptly **2** : DISINTEGRATE; *also* : to fall in : give way **3** : to break down physically or mentally; *esp* : to fall helpless or unconscious **4** : to fold down compactly — **col·laps·ible** *adj*

[2]**collapse** *n* : BREAKDOWN
[1]**col·lar** \ˈkä-lər\ *n* **1** : a band, strip, or chain worn around the neck or the neckline of a garment **2** : something resembling a collar — **col·lar·less** *adj*
[2]**collar** *vb* : to seize by the collar; *also* : ARREST, GRAB ⟨~ a fugitive⟩
col·lar·bone \-ˌbōn\ *n* : the bone of the shoulder that joins the breastbone and the shoulder blade
col·lard \ˈkä-lərd\ *n* : a stalked smooth-leaved kale — usu. used in pl.
col·late \kə-ˈlāt; ˈkä-ˌlāt, ˈkō-\ *vb* **col·lat·ed; col·lat·ing 1** : to compare (as two texts) carefully and critically **2** : to assemble in proper order
[1]**col·lat·er·al** \kə-ˈla-tə-rəl\ *adj* **1** : associated but of secondary importance **2** : descended from the same ancestors but not in the same line **3** : PARALLEL **4** : of, relating to, or being collateral used as security; *also* : secured by collateral
[2]**collateral** *n* : property (as stocks) used as security for the repayment of a loan
col·la·tion \kä-ˈlā-shən, kō-\ *n* **1** : a light meal **2** : the act, process, or result of collating
col·league \ˈkä-ˌlēg\ *n* : an associate esp. in a profession
[1]**col·lect** \ˈkä-likt, -ˌlekt\ *n* : a short prayer comprising an invocation, petition, and conclusion
[2]**col·lect** \kə-ˈlekt\ *vb* **1** : to bring or come together into one body or place : GATHER **2** : to accumulate (as coins) as a hobby **3** : to gain control of ⟨~ his thoughts⟩ **4** : to receive payment of — **col·lect·ible** *or* **col·lect·able** *adj or n* — **col·lec·tor** \-ˈlek-tər\ *n*
[3]**col·lect** \kə-ˈlekt\ *adv or adj* : to be paid for by the receiver
col·lect·ed \kə-ˈlek-təd\ *adj* **1** : gathered together ⟨his ~ poems⟩ **2** : SELF-POSSESSED, CALM
col·lec·tion \kə-ˈlek-shən\ *n* **1** : the act or process of collecting ⟨garbage ~⟩ **2** : something collected ⟨a stamp ~⟩ **3** : GROUP, AGGREGATE
[1]**col·lec·tive** \kə-ˈlek-tiv\ *adj* **1** : of, relating to, or denoting a group of individuals considered as a whole **2** : involving all members of a group as distinct from its individuals ⟨~ action⟩ **3** : shared or assumed by all members of the group ⟨a ~ groan⟩ — **col·lec·tive·ly** *adv*
[2]**collective** *n* **1** : GROUP **2** : a cooperative unit or organization
collective bargaining *n* : negotiation between an employer and a labor union
col·lec·tiv·ise *chiefly Brit var of* COLLECTIVIZE
col·lec·tiv·ism \kə-ˈlek-ti-ˌvi-zəm\ *n* : a political or economic theory advocating collective control esp. over production and distribution
col·lec·tiv·ize \-ˌvīz\ *vb* **-ized; -iz·ing** : to organize under collective control — **col·lec·tiv·i·za·tion** \-ˌlek-ti-və-ˈzā-shən\ *n*
col·leen \kä-ˈlēn, ˈkä-ˌlēn\ *n* : an Irish girl
col·lege \ˈkä-lij\ *n* [ME, endowed body of clergy or scholars, fr. AF, fr. L *collegium* society, fr. *collega* colleague, fr. *com-* with + *legare* to depute] **1** : a building used for an educational or religious purpose **2** : an institution of higher learning or division of a university granting a bachelor's degree; *also* : an institution offering instruction esp. in a vocational or technical field ⟨barber ~⟩ **3** : an organized body of persons having common interests or duties ⟨~ of cardinals⟩ — **col·le·giate** \kə-ˈlē-jət\ *adj*
col·le·gi·al·i·ty \kə-ˌlē-jē-ˈa-lə-tē\ *n* : the relationship of colleagues
col·le·gian \kə-ˈlē-jən\ *n* : a college student or recent college graduate
col·le·gi·um \kə-ˈle-gē-əm, -ˈlā-\ *n, pl* **-gia** \-gē-ə\ *or* **-giums** : a group in which each member has approximately equal power
col·lide \kə-ˈlīd\ *vb* **col·lid·ed; col·lid·ing 1** : to come together with solid impact **2** : to come into conflict : CLASH
col·lid·er \kə-ˈlī-dər\ *n* : a particle accelerator in which two beams of particles are made to collide
col·lie \ˈkä-lē\ *n* : any of a breed of large dogs developed in Scotland for herding sheep that occur in rough-coated and smooth-coated varieties
col·lier \ˈkäl-yər\ *n* **1** : a coal miner **2** : a ship for carrying coal
col·liery \ˈkäl-yə-rē\ *n, pl* **-lier·ies** : a coal mine and its associated buildings
col·li·mate \ˈkä-lə-ˌmāt\ *vb* **-mat·ed; -mat·ing** : to make (as light rays) parallel
col·li·sion \kə-ˈli-zhən\ *n* : an act or instance of colliding
col·lo·ca·tion \ˌkä-lə-ˈkā-shən\ *n* : the act or result of placing or arranging together; *esp* : a noticeable arrangement or conjoining of linguistic elements (as words)
col·loid \ˈkä-ˌlȯid\ *n* : a substance in the form of submicroscopic particles that when in solution or suspension do not settle out; *also* : such a substance together with the medium in which it is dispersed — **col·loi·dal** \kə-ˈlȯi-dᵊl\ *adj*
colloq *abbr* colloquial
col·lo·qui·al \kə-ˈlō-kwē-əl\ *adj* : of, relating to, or characteristic of conversation and esp. of familiar and informal conversation
col·lo·qui·al·ism \-ˈlō-kwē-ə-ˌli-zəm\ *n* : a colloquial expression
col·lo·qui·um \kə-ˈlō-kwē-əm\ *n, pl* **-qui·ums** *or* **-quia** \-ə\ : CONFERENCE, SEMINAR
col·lo·quy \ˈkä-lə-kwē\ *n, pl* **-quies** : a usu. formal conversation or conference
col·lu·sion \kə-ˈlü-zhən\ *n* : secret agreement or cooperation for an illegal or deceitful purpose — **col·lu·sive** \-siv\ *adj*
Colo *abbr* Colorado
co·logne \kə-ˈlōn\ *n* [*Cologne,* Germany] : a perfumed liquid — **co·logned** \-ˈlōnd\ *adj*
Co·lom·bi·an \kə-ˈləm-bē-ən\ *n* : a native or inhabitant of Colombia — **Colombian** *adj*
[1]**co·lon** \ˈkō-lən\ *n, pl* **colons** *or* **co·la** \-lə\ : the part of the large intestine ex-

tending from the cecum to the rectum — **co·lon·ic** \kō-ˈlä-nik\ *adj*

[2]**colon** *n, pl* **colons** : a punctuation mark : used esp. to direct attention to following matter (as a list)

co·lón *also* **co·lone** \kə-ˈlōn\ *n, pl* **co·lo·nes** \-ˈlō-ˌnās\ — see MONEY table

col·o·nel \ˈkər-nᵊl\ *n* [alter. of *coronel,* fr. MF, fr. It *colonnello* column of soldiers, colonel, ultim. fr. L *columna* column] : a commissioned officer (as in the army) ranking next below a brigadier general

[1]**co·lo·nial** \kə-ˈlō-nē-əl\ *adj* **1** : of, relating to, or characteristic of a colony; *also* : possessing or composed of colonies **2** *often cap* : of or relating to the original 13 colonies forming the U.S.

[2]**colonial** *n* **1** : a member or inhabitant of a colony **2** : a house built in the style of the American colonial period

co·lo·nial·ism \-ə-ˌli-zəm\ *n* : control by one power over a dependent area or people; *also* : a policy advocating or based on such control — **co·lo·nial·ist** \-list\ *n or adj*

col·o·nise *Brit var of* COLONIZE

col·o·nist \ˈkä-lə-nist\ *n* **1** : COLONIAL **2** : one that colonizes or settles in a new country

col·o·nize \ˈkä-lə-ˌnīz\ *vb* **-nized; -niz·ing** **1** : to establish a colony in or on **2** : SETTLE — **col·o·ni·za·tion** \ˌkä-lə-nə-ˈzā-shən\ *n* — **col·o·niz·er** *n*

col·on·nade \ˌkä-lə-ˈnād\ *n* : an evenly spaced row of columns usu. supporting the base of a roof structure

co·lo·nos·co·py \ˌkō-lə-ˈnäs-kə-pē\ *n, pl* **-pies** : endoscopic examination of the colon — **co·lon·o·scope** \kō-ˈlä-nə-ˌskōp\ *n*

col·o·ny \ˈkä-lə-nē\ *n, pl* **-nies** **1** : a body of people living in a new territory; *also* : the territory inhabited by these people **2** : a localized population of organisms ⟨a ~ of bees⟩ **3** : a group with common interests situated in close association ⟨a writers' ~⟩; *also* : the area occupied by such a group

col·o·phon \ˈkä-lə-fən, -ˌfän\ *n* **1** : an inscription placed at the end of a book with facts relative to its production **2** : an identifying mark used by a printer or publisher

[1]**col·or** \ˈkə-lər\ *n* **1** : a phenomenon of light (as red or blue) or visual perception that enables one to differentiate otherwise identical objects; *also* : a hue as contrasted with black, white, or gray **2** : APPEARANCE **3** : skin pigmentation other than what is considered characteristic of people typically identified as white ⟨a person of ~⟩ **4** : complexion tint **5** *pl* : FLAG; *also* : military service ⟨a call to the ~*s*⟩ **6** : VIVIDNESS, INTEREST — **col·or·ful** *adj* — **col·or·less** *adj*

[2]**color** *vb* **1** : to give color to; *also* : to change the color of **2** : BLUSH

Col·o·ra·do potato beetle \ˌkä-lə-ˈra-dō-, -ˈrä-\ *n* : a black-and-yellow striped beetle that feeds on the leaves of the potato

col·or·ation \ˌkə-lə-ˈrā-shən\ *n* : use or arrangement of colors

col·or·a·tu·ra \ˌkə-lə-rə-ˈtu̇r-ə, -ˈtyu̇r-\ *n* **1** : elaborate ornamentation in vocal music **2** : a soprano specializing in coloratura

col·or–blind \ˈkə-lər-ˌblīnd\ *adj* **1** : partially or totally unable to distinguish one or more chromatic colors **2** : not influenced by differences of race — **color blindness** *n*

co·lo·rec·tal \ˌkō-lō-ˈrek-tᵊl\ *adj* : relating to or affecting the colon and rectum ⟨~ cancer⟩

col·ored \ˈkə-lərd\ *adj* **1** : having color **2** : SLANTED, BIASED

col·or·fast \ˈkə-lər-ˌfast\ *adj* : having color that does not fade or run — **col·or·fast·ness** *n*

col·or·ize \ˈkə-lə-ˌrīz\ *vb* **-ized; -iz·ing** : to add color to by means of a computer — **col·or·i·za·tion** \ˌkə-lə-rə-ˈzā-shən\ *n*

co·los·sal \kə-ˈlä-səl\ *adj* : of very great size or degree ⟨a ~ feat⟩

Co·los·sians \kə-ˈlä-shənz\ *n* — see BIBLE table

co·los·sus \kə-ˈlä-səs\ *n, pl* **co·los·si** \-ˌsī\ [L] : a gigantic statue; *also* : something of immense size or power

col·our *chiefly Brit var of* COLOR

col·por·teur \ˈkäl-ˌpȯr-tər\ *n* [F] : a peddler of religious books

colt \ˈkōlt\ *n* : FOAL; *also* : a young male horse, ass, or zebra — **colt·ish** *adj*

col·um·bine \ˈkä-ləm-ˌbīn\ *n* [ME, fr. AF, fr. ML *columbina,* fr. L, fem. of *columbinus* dovelike, fr. *columba* dove] : any of a genus of plants with showy spurred flowers that are related to the buttercups

co·lum·bi·um \kə-ˈləm-bē-əm\ *n* : NIOBIUM

Columbus Day \kə-ˈləm-bəs-\ *n* : the 2d Monday in October or formerly October 12 observed as a legal holiday in many states in commemoration of the landing of Columbus in the Bahamas in 1492

col·umn \ˈkä-ləm\ *n* **1** : one of two or more vertical sections of a printed page; *also* : one in a usu. regular series of articles (as in a newspaper) **2** : a supporting pillar; *esp* : one consisting of a usu. round shaft, a capital, and a base **3** : something resembling a column ⟨a ~ of water⟩ **4** : a long row (as of soldiers) **5** : a statistical category tracked vertically (as on a spreadsheet) — **co·lum·nar** \kə-ˈləm-nər\ *adj*

col·um·nist \ˈkä-ləm-nist\ *n* : a person who writes a newspaper or magazine column

com *abbr* **1** comedy; comic **2** comma **3** commercial organization

co·ma \ˈkō-mə\ *n* : a state of deep unconsciousness caused by disease, injury, or poison — **co·ma·tose** \ˈkō-mə-ˌtōs, ˈkä-\ *adj*

Co·man·che \kə-ˈman-chē\ *n, pl* **Comanche** *or* **Comanches** : a member of an Indigenous people of the southern High Plains of the U.S.; *also* their language

[1]**comb** \ˈkōm\ *n* **1** : a toothed instrument

for arranging the hair or for separating and cleaning textile fibers **2** : a fleshy crest on the head of a fowl **3** : HONEYCOMB

[2]**comb** *vb* **1** : to pass a comb through **2** : to search through systematically

[3]**comb** *abbr* combination; combining

com•bat \kəm-ˈbat, ˈkäm-ˌbat\ *vb* **-bat•ed** *or* **-bat•ted; -bat•ing** *or* **-bat•ting** **1** : FIGHT, CONTEND **2** : to struggle against : OPPOSE — **com•bat** \ˈkäm-ˌbat\ *n* — **com•bat•ant** \kəm-ˈba-tᵊnt, ˈkäm-bə-tənt\ *n* — **com•bat•ive** \kəm-ˈba-tiv\ *adj*

combat fatigue *n* : a traumatic psychological reaction occurring under wartime conditions (as combat) that cause intense stress

comb•er \ˈkō-mər\ *n* **1** : one that combs **2** : a long curling wave of the sea

com•bi•na•tion \ˌkäm-bə-ˈnā-shən\ *n* **1** : a result or product of combining **2** : a sequence of letters or numbers chosen in setting a lock **3** : the act or process of combining; *also* : the quality or state of being combined

[1]**com•bine** \kəm-ˈbīn\ *vb* **com•bined; com•bin•ing** : to become one : UNITE

[2]**com•bine** \ˈkäm-ˌbīn\ *n* **1** : a combination esp. of business or political interests **2** : a machine that harvests and threshes grain while moving over a field

comb•ings \ˈkō-miŋz\ *n pl* : loose hairs or fibers removed by a comb

combining form *n* : a linguistic form that occurs only in compounds or derivatives

com•bo \ˈkäm-bō\ *n, pl* **combos** : a small jazz or dance band

comb–over \ˈkōm-ˌō-vər\ *n* : a hairstyle in which hair from the side of the head is combed over a bald spot

com•bus•ti•ble \kəm-ˈbəs-tə-bəl\ *adj* **1** : capable of being burned **2** : easily excited — **com•bus•ti•bil•i•ty** \-ˌbəs-tə-ˈbi-lə-tē\ *n* — **combustible** *n*

com•bus•tion \kəm-ˈbəs-chən\ *n* **1** : an act or instance of burning **2** : slow oxidation (as in the animal body)

comdg *abbr* commanding

comdr *abbr* commander

comdt *abbr* commandant

come \ˈkəm\ *vb* **came** \ˈkām\; **come; com•ing** \ˈkə-miŋ\ **1** : APPROACH **2** : ARRIVE **3** : to reach the point of being or becoming ⟨∼ to a boil⟩ **4** : AMOUNT ⟨the bill *came* to $10⟩ **5** : to take place **6** : ORIGINATE, ARISE ⟨wine ∼*s* from grapes⟩ **7** : to be available ⟨∼*s* in three sizes⟩ **8** : REACH, EXTEND ⟨grass that ∼*s* to our knees⟩ — **come across** **1** : to make a specified impression ⟨*came across* as rude⟩ **2** : to find esp. by chance ⟨*came across* an intriguing story⟩ — **come clean** : CONFESS — **come into** : ACQUIRE, ACHIEVE — **come of age** : MATURE — **come to grips with** : to meet or deal with frankly — **come to pass** : HAPPEN — **come to terms** : to reach an agreement

come•back \ˈkəm-ˌbak\ *n* **1** : RETORT **2** : a return to a former position or condition — **come back** *vb*

co•me•di•an \kə-ˈmē-dē-ən\ *n* **1** : an actor in comedy **2** : a comic person; *esp* : an entertainer specializing in comedy

co•me•di•enne \-ˌmē-dē-ˈen\ *n* : a woman who is a comedian

come•down \ˈkəm-ˌdaůn\ *n* : a descent in rank or dignity

com•e•dy \ˈkä-mə-dē\ *n, pl* **-dies** [ME, narrative that ends happily, fr. ML *comoedia,* fr. L, play with a happy ending, fr. Gk *kōmōidia,* fr. *kōmos* revel + *aeidein* to sing] **1** : a light amusing play with a happy ending **2** : a literary work treating a comic theme or written in a comic style **3** : humorous entertainment — **co•me•dic** \kə-ˈmē-dik\ *adj*

come•ly \ˈkəm-lē\ *adj* **come•li•er; -est** : ATTRACTIVE, HANDSOME — **come•li•ness** *n*

come off *vb* **1** : APPEAR, SEEM ⟨*comes off* as crass⟩ **2** : SUCCEED **3** : to have recently ended ⟨is *coming off* surgery⟩

come–on \ˈkə-ˌmȯn, -ˌmän\ *n* : INDUCEMENT, LURE

come out *vb* **1** : to come into public view **2** : to declare oneself **3** : TURN OUT 6 ⟨everything *came out* all right⟩ **4** : to openly declare one's sexual orientation or gender identity — **come out with** : SAY 1

com•er \ˈkə-mər\ *n* **1** : one that comes ⟨all ∼*s*⟩ **2** : a promising beginner

[1]**co•mes•ti•ble** \kə-ˈmes-tə-bəl\ *adj* : EDIBLE

[2]**comestible** *n* : FOOD — usu. used in pl.

com•et \ˈkä-mət\ *n* [ME *comete,* fr. OE *cometa,* fr. L, fr. Gk *komētēs,* lit., long-haired, fr. *komē* hair] : a small bright celestial body that develops a long tail when near the sun

come to *vb* : to regain consciousness

come•up•pance \kə-ˈmə-pəns\ *n* : a deserved rebuke or penalty

com•fit \ˈkəm-fət\ *n* : a candied fruit or nut

[1]**com•fort** \ˈkəm-fərt\ *vb* **1** : to give strength and hope to **2** : CONSOLE

[2]**comfort** *n* **1** : CONSOLATION **2** : freedom from pain, trouble, or anxiety; *also* : something that gives such freedom

com•fort•able \ˈkəm-fər-tə-bəl, ˈkəmf-tər-\ *adj* **1** : providing comfort or security **2** : feeling at ease — **com•fort•ably** \-blē\ *adv*

com•fort•er \ˈkəm-fər-tər\ *n* **1** : one that comforts **2** : QUILT

com•frey \ˈkəm-frē\ *n, pl* **comfreys** : any of a genus of perennial herbs that have coarse hairy leaves and are often used in herbal remedies

com•fy \ˈkəm-fē\ *adj* : COMFORTABLE

[1]**com•ic** \ˈkä-mik\ *adj* **1** : relating to comedy or comic strips **2** : provoking laughter or amusement ♦ ***Synonyms*** LAUGHABLE, FUNNY, FARCICAL — **com•i•cal** *adj*

[2]**comic** *n* **1** : COMEDIAN **2** *pl* : the part of a newspaper devoted to comic strips

comic book *n* : a magazine containing sequences of comic strips

comic strip *n* : a group of cartoons in narrative sequence

coming *adj* **1** : APPROACHING, NEXT **2** : gaining importance ⟨the ∼ trend⟩

co·mi·ty \ˈkä-mə-tē, ˈkō-\ *n, pl* **-ties** : friendly civility : COURTESY

coml *abbr* commercial

comm *abbr* **1** command; commander **2** commerce; commercial **3** commission; commissioner **4** committee **5** common **6** commonwealth

com·ma \ˈkä-mə\ *n* : a punctuation mark , used esp. as a mark of separation within the sentence

[1]**com·mand** \kə-ˈmand\ *vb* **1** : to direct authoritatively : ORDER **2** : DOMINATE, CONTROL, GOVERN **3** : to overlook from a strategic position

[2]**command** *n* **1** : an order given **2** : ability to control : MASTERY **3** : the act of commanding **4** : a signal that actuates a device (as a computer); *also* : the activation of a device by means of a signal **5** : a body of troops under a commander; *also* : an area or position that one commands **6** : a position of highest authority

com·man·dant \ˈkä-mən-ˌdant, -ˌdänt\ *n* : an officer in command

com·man·deer \ˌkä-mən-ˈdir\ *vb* : to take possession of by force

com·mand·er \kə-ˈman-dər\ *n* **1** : LEADER, CHIEF; *esp* : an officer commanding an army or subdivision of an army **2** : a commissioned officer in the navy ranking next below a captain

commander in chief : the supreme commander of the armed forces

com·mand·ment \kə-ˈmand-mənt\ *n* : COMMAND, ORDER; *esp* : any of the Ten Commandments

command module *n* : a space vehicle module designed to carry the crew and reentry equipment

com·man·do \kə-ˈman-dō\ *n, pl* **-dos** *or* **-does** : a member of a military unit trained for surprise raids

command sergeant major *n* : a noncommissioned officer in the army ranking above a sergeant major

com·mem·o·rate \kə-ˈme-mə-ˌrāt\ *vb* **-rat·ed**; **-rat·ing** **1** : to call or recall to mind **2** : to serve as a memorial of — **com·mem·o·ra·tion** \-ˌme-mə-ˈrā-shən\ *n*

com·mem·o·ra·tive \kə-ˈmem-rə-tiv, -ˈme-mə-ˌrā-tiv\ *adj* : intended to commemorate an event ⟨a ~ stamp⟩

com·mence \kə-ˈmens\ *vb* **com·menced**; **com·menc·ing** : BEGIN, START ⟨~ the festivities⟩

com·mence·ment \-mənt\ *n* **1** : the act or time of a beginning **2** : the graduation exercises of a school or college

com·mend \kə-ˈmend\ *vb* **1** : to commit to one's care **2** : RECOMMEND **3** : PRAISE — **com·mend·able** \-ˈmen-də-bəl\ *adj* — **com·mend·ably** \-blē\ *adv* — **com·men·da·tion** \ˌkä-mən-ˈdā-shən, -ˌmen-\ *n* — **com·mend·er** *n*

com·men·su·ra·ble \kə-ˈmen-sə-rə-bəl\ *adj* : having a common measure or a common divisor

com·men·su·rate \kə-ˈmen-sə-rət, -ˈmen-chə-\ *adj* : equal in measure or extent; *also* : PROPORTIONAL, CORRESPONDING ⟨a job ~ with her abilities⟩

com·ment \ˈkä-ˌment\ *n* **1** : an expression of opinion **2** : an explanatory, illustrative, or critical note or observation : REMARK — **comment** *vb*

com·men·tary \ˈkä-mən-ˌter-ē\ *n, pl* **-tar·ies** : a systematic series of comments

com·men·ta·tor \-ˌtā-tər\ *n* : one who comments; *esp* : a person who discusses news events on radio or television

com·merce \ˈkä-(ˌ)mərs\ *n* : the buying and selling of commodities : TRADE

[1]**com·mer·cial** \kə-ˈmər-shəl\ *adj* : having to do with commerce; *also* : designed for profit or for mass appeal — **com·mer·cial·ly** *adv*

[2]**commercial** *n* : an advertisement included with another broadcast (as on radio, television, or a podcast)

com·mer·cial·ise *Brit var of* COMMERCIALIZE

com·mer·cial·ism \kə-ˈmər-shə-ˌli-zəm\ *n* **1** : a spirit, method, or practice characteristic of business **2** : excessive emphasis on profit

com·mer·cial·ize \-ˌlīz\ *vb* **-ized**; **-iz·ing** **1** : to manage on a business basis for profit **2** : to exploit for profit

com·mi·na·tion \ˌkä-mə-ˈnā-shən\ *n* : DENUNCIATION — **com·mi·na·to·ry** \ˈkä-mə-nə-ˌtȯr-ē\ *adj*

com·min·gle \kə-ˈmiŋ-gəl\ *vb* : MINGLE, BLEND

com·mis·er·ate \kə-ˈmi-zə-ˌrāt\ *vb* **-at·ed**; **-at·ing** : to feel or express pity : SYMPATHIZE — **com·mis·er·a·tion** \-ˌmi-zə-ˈrā-shən\ *n*

com·mis·sar \ˈkä-mə-ˌsär\ *n* [Russ *komissar*] : a Communist party official

com·mis·sar·i·at \ˌkä-mə-ˈser-ē-ət\ *n* **1** : a system for supplying troops with food **2** : a department headed by a commissar

com·mis·sary \ˈkä-mə-ˌser-ē\ *n, pl* **-sar·ies** : a store for equipment and provisions esp. for military personnel

[1]**com·mis·sion** \kə-ˈmi-shən\ *n* **1** : a warrant granting certain powers and imposing certain duties **2** : a certificate conferring military rank and authority **3** : authority to act as agent for another; *also* : something to be done by an agent **4** : a body of persons charged with performing a duty **5** : the doing of some act ⟨~ of a crime⟩; *also* : the thing done **6** : the allowance made to an agent for transacting business for another **7** : a formal request to produce something (as an artistic work) in exchange for payment; *also* : a work produced by such a request

[2]**commission** *vb* **1** : to give a commission to **2** : to order to be made ⟨~ a portrait⟩ **3** : to put (a ship) into a state of readiness for service

commissioned officer *n* : an officer of the armed forces holding rank by a commission from the president

com·mis·sion·er \kə-ˈmi-shə-nər\ *n* **1** : a member of a commission **2** : an official in charge of a department of public service ⟨a police ~⟩ **3** : the administrative head of a professional sport — **com·mis·sion·er·ship** *n*

com·mit \kə-ˈmit\ *vb* **com·mit·ted; com·mit·ting** **1** : to put into charge or trust : ENTRUST **2** : to put in a prison or mental institution **3** : TRANSFER, CONSIGN **4** : to carry into action : PERPETRATE ⟨~ a crime⟩ **5** : to pledge or assign to some particular course or use — **com·mit·ment** *n* — **com·mit·tal** *n*

com·mit·tee \kə-ˈmi-tē\ *n* : a body of persons selected to consider and act or report on some matter — **com·mit·tee·man** \-mən\ *n* — **com·mit·tee·wom·an** \-ˌwu̇-mən\ *n*

commo *abbr* commodore

com·mode \kə-ˈmōd\ *n* [F, fr. *commode,* adj., suitable, convenient, fr. L *commodus,* fr. *com-* with + *modus* measure] **1** : a movable washstand with cupboard below **2** : TOILET 3

com·mo·di·ous \kə-ˈmō-dē-əs\ *adj* : comfortably spacious : ROOMY

com·mod·i·ty \kə-ˈmä-də-tē\ *n, pl* **-ties** **1** : a product of agriculture or mining **2** : an article of commerce **3** : something useful or valued ⟨that valuable ~ patience⟩

com·mo·dore \ˈkä-mə-ˌdȯr\ *n* **1** : a commissioned officer in the navy ranking next below a rear admiral **2** : an officer commanding a group of merchant ships **3** : the chief officer of a yacht club

[1]**com·mon** \ˈkä-mən\ *adj* **1** : belonging to or serving the community : PUBLIC **2** : shared by a number in a group **3** : widely or generally known, found, or observed : FAMILIAR ⟨~ knowledge⟩ **4** : VERNACULAR 3 ⟨~ names of plants⟩ **5** : not above the average esp. in social status ♦ ***Synonyms*** UNIVERSAL, GENERAL, GENERIC — **com·mon·ly** *adv*

[2]**common** *n* **1** *pl* : the common people **2** *pl* : a dining hall **3** *pl, cap* : the lower house of the British and Canadian parliaments **4** : a piece of land subject to common use — **in common** : shared together

com·mon·al·ty \ˈkä-mə-nᵊl-tē\ *n, pl* **-ties** : the common people

common cold *n* : a contagious respiratory disease caused by a virus and characterized by a sore, swollen, and inflamed nose and throat, usu. by much mucus, and by coughing and sneezing

common denominator *n* **1** : a common multiple of the denominators of a group of fractions **2** : a common trait or theme

common divisor *n* : a number or expression that divides two or more numbers or expressions without remainder

com·mon·er \ˈkä-mə-nər\ *n* : one of the common people : a person having no rank of nobility

common fraction *n* : a fraction (as ½ or ¾) in which the numerator and denominator are both integers and are separated by a horizontal or slanted line

common law *n* : a group of legal practices and traditions based on judges' decisions and social customs and usu. having the same force as laws passed by legislative bodies

common logarithm *n* : a logarithm whose base is 10

common market *n* : an economic association formed to remove trade barriers among members

common multiple *n* : a multiple of each of two or more numbers or expressions

[1]**com·mon·place** \ˈkä-mən-ˌplās\ *n* : something that is ordinary or trite

[2]**commonplace** *adj* : ORDINARY

common sense *n* : ordinary good sense and judgment — **com·mon·sen·si·cal** \ˈkä-mən-ˈsen-si-kəl\ *adj*

com·mon·weal \ˈkä-mən-ˌwēl\ *n* **1** *archaic* : COMMONWEALTH **2** : the general welfare

com·mon·wealth \-ˌwelth\ *n* **1** : the body of people politically organized into a state **2** : STATE; *also* : an association or federation of autonomous states

com·mo·tion \kə-ˈmō-shən\ *n* **1** : DISTURBANCE, UPRISING **2** : AGITATION

com·mu·nal \kə-ˈmyü-nᵊl, ˈkäm-yə-nᵊl\ *adj* **1** : of or relating to a commune or community **2** : marked by collective ownership and use of property **3** : shared or used in common

[1]**com·mune** \kə-ˈmyün\ *vb* **com·muned; com·mun·ing** : to communicate intimately ⟨~ with nature⟩

[2]**com·mune** \ˈkäm-ˌyün; kə-ˈmyün\ *n* **1** : the smallest administrative district in some European countries **2** : a community organized on a communal basis

com·mu·ni·ca·ble \kə-ˈmyü-ni-kə-bəl\ *adj* : capable of being communicated ⟨~ diseases⟩ — **com·mu·ni·ca·bil·i·ty** \-ˌmyü-ni-kə-ˈbi-lə-tē\ *n*

com·mu·ni·cant \-ˈmyü-ni-kənt\ *n* **1** : a church member entitled to receive Communion **2** : one that communicates; *esp* : INFORMANT

com·mu·ni·cate \kə-ˈmyü-nə-ˌkāt\ *vb* **-cat·ed; -cat·ing** **1** : to make known **2** : to pass from one to another : TRANSMIT **3** : to receive Communion **4** : to be in communication **5** : JOIN, CONNECT — **com·mu·ni·cat·or** \-ˌkā-tər\ *n*

com·mu·ni·ca·tion \kə-ˌmyü-nə-ˈkā-shən\ *n* **1** : an act of transmitting **2** : MESSAGE **3** : exchange of information or opinions **4** : a means of communicating — **com·mu·ni·ca·tive** \-ˈmyü-nə-ˌkā-tiv, -ni-kə-tiv\ *adj*

com·mu·nion \kə-ˈmyü-nyən\ *n* **1** : a sharing of something with others **2** *cap* : a Christian sacrament in which bread and wine are consumed as the substance or symbols of Christ's body and blood in commemoration of the death of Christ **3** : intimate fellowship or rapport **4** : a body of Christians having a common faith and discipline ⟨the Anglican ~⟩

com·mu·ni·qué \kə-ˈmyü-nə-ˌkā, -ˌmyü-nə-ˈkā\ *n* : BULLETIN 1

com·mu·nism \ˈkäm-yə-ˌni-zəm\ *n* **1** : social organization in which goods are held in common **2** : a theory of social organization advocating common ownership of means of production and a distribution of products of industry based on need **3** *cap* : a political doctrine based on revolutionary Marxist socialism that was the official ideology of the U.S.S.R. and some other countries; *also* : a system of government in which one party controls state-owned means of production — **com·mu·nist** \-nist\ *n or adj, often cap* — **com·mu·nis·tic** \ˌkäm-yə-ˈnis-tik\ *adj, often cap*

com·mu·ni·ty \kə-ˈmyü-nə-tē\ *n, pl* **-ties** **1** : a body of people living in the same place under the same laws; *also* : a natural population of plants and animals that interact ecologically and live in one place (as a pond) **2** : society at large **3** : joint ownership ⟨~ of goods⟩ **4** : SIMILARITY, LIKENESS ⟨~ of interests⟩

community college *n* : a 2-year government-supported college that offers an associate degree

community property *n* : property held jointly by a married couple

com·mu·ta·tion \ˌkäm-yə-ˈtā-shən\ *n* : substitution of one form of payment or penalty for another

com·mu·ta·tive \ˈkäm-yə-ˌtā-tiv, kə-ˈmyü-tə-\ *adj* : of, having, or being the property that the result obtained using a mathematical operation on any two elements of a set does not differ with the order in which the elements are used ⟨*a* x *b* = *b* x *a* because multiplication is ~⟩ — **com·mu·ta·tiv·i·ty** \kə-ˌmyü-tə-ˈti-və-tē, ˌkäm-yə-tə-\ *n*

com·mu·ta·tor \ˈkäm-yə-ˌtā-tər\ *n* : a device (as on a generator or motor) for changing the direction of electric current

¹com·mute \kə-ˈmyüt\ *vb* **com·mut·ed**; **com·mut·ing** **1** : EXCHANGE **2** : to revoke (a sentence) and impose a milder penalty **3** : to travel back and forth regularly — **com·mut·er** *n*

²commute *n* : a trip made in commuting

comp *abbr* **1** comparative; compare **2** compensation **3** compiled; compiler **4** composition; compositor **5** compound **6** comprehensive **7** comptroller

¹com·pact \kəm-ˈpakt, ˈkäm-ˌpakt\ *adj* **1** : SOLID, DENSE **2** : BRIEF, SUCCINCT **3** : occupying a small volume by efficient use of space ⟨~ camera⟩ — **com·pact·ly** *adv* — **com·pact·ness** *n*

²compact *vb* : to pack together : COMPRESS — **com·pac·tor** \kəm-ˈpak-tər, ˈkäm-ˌpak-\ *n*

³com·pact \ˈkäm-ˌpakt\ *n* **1** : a small case for cosmetics **2** : a small automobile

⁴com·pact \ˈkäm-ˌpakt\ *n* : AGREEMENT, COVENANT

com·pact disc \ˈkäm-ˌpakt-\ *n* : CD

com·pa·dre \kəm-ˈpä-drā\ *n* : a close friend : BUDDY

¹com·pan·ion \kəm-ˈpan-yən\ *n* [ME *compainoun*, fr. AF *cumpaing, cumpaignun*, fr. LL *companion-, companio*, fr. L *com-* together + *panis* bread] **1** : an intimate friend or associate : COMRADE **2** : one that is closely connected with something similar **3** : a celestial body that appears close to another but that may not be associated with it in space — **com·pan·ion·able** *adj* — **com·pan·ion·ship** *n*

²companion *n* : COMPANIONWAY

com·pan·ion·way \-ˌwā\ *n* : a ship's stairway from one deck to another

com·pa·ny \ˈkəm-pə-nē\ *n, pl* **-nies** **1** : association with others : FELLOWSHIP; *also* : COMPANIONS **2** : GUESTS **3** : a group of persons or things **4** : an infantry unit consisting of two or more platoons and normally commanded by a captain **5** : a group of musical or dramatic performers **6** : the officers and crew of a ship **7** : an association of persons for carrying on a business ♦ ***Synonyms*** PARTY, BAND, TROOP, TROUPE, CORPS, OUTFIT

com·pa·ra·ble \ˈkäm-pə-rə-bəl, -prə-\ *adj* : capable of being compared ⟨singers of ~ talent⟩ ♦ ***Synonyms*** PARALLEL, SIMILAR, LIKE, ALIKE, CORRESPONDING — **com·pa·ra·bil·i·ty** \ˌkäm-pə-rə-ˈbi-lə-tē\ *n*

¹com·par·a·tive \kəm-ˈper-ə-tiv\ *adj* **1** : of, relating to, or constituting the degree of grammatical comparison that denotes increase in quality, quantity, or relation **2** : RELATIVE ⟨a ~ stranger⟩ — **com·par·a·tive·ly** *adv*

²comparative *n* : the comparative degree or form in a language

¹com·pare \kəm-ˈper\ *vb* **com·pared**; **com·par·ing** **1** : to represent as similar : LIKEN **2** : to examine for likenesses and differences **3** : to inflect or modify (an adjective or adverb) according to the degrees of comparison

²compare *n* : the possibility of comparing ⟨beauty beyond ~⟩

com·par·i·son \kəm-ˈper-ə-sən\ *n* **1** : the act of comparing **2** : change in the form of an adjective or adverb to show different levels of quality, quantity, or relation

com·part·ment \kəm-ˈpärt-mənt\ *n* **1** : a separate division **2** : a section of an enclosed space : ROOM

com·part·men·tal·ise *Brit var of* COMPARTMENTALIZE

com·part·men·tal·ize \kəm-ˌpärt-ˈmen-tᵊl-ˌīz\ *vb* **-ized**; **-iz·ing** : to separate into compartments

¹com·pass \ˈkəm-pəs, ˈkäm-\ *vb* [ME, fr. AF *cumpasser* to measure, fr. VL **compassare* to pace off, fr. L *com-* + *passus* pace] **1** : CONTRIVE, PLOT **2** : ENCIRCLE, ENCOMPASS **3** : BRING ABOUT, ACHIEVE

²compass *n* **1** : BOUNDARY, CIRCUMFERENCE **2** : an enclosed space **3** : RANGE, SCOPE **4** : a device for determining direction by means of a magnetic needle swinging freely and pointing to the magnetic north; *also* : a nonmagnetic device that indicates direction **5** : an instrument for drawing circles or transferring measurements consisting of two legs joined by a pivot

com·pas·sion \kəm-ˈpa-shən\ *n* : sympathetic feeling : PITY, MERCY — **com·pas·sion·ate** \-shə-nət\ *adj* — **com·pas·sion·ate·ly** *adv*

com·pat·i·ble \kəm-ˈpa-tə-bəl\ *adj* : able

to exist or act together harmoniously ⟨~ colors⟩ ⟨~ drugs⟩ ♦ ***Synonyms*** CONSONANT, CONGENIAL, SYMPATHETIC — **com·pat·i·bil·i·ty** \-ˌpa-tə-ˈbi-lə-tē\ *n*
com·pa·tri·ot \kəm-ˈpā-trē-ət, -ˌät\ *n* : a fellow countryman
com·peer \ˈkäm-ˌpir\ *n* : EQUAL, PEER
com·pel \kəm-ˈpel\ *vb* **com·pelled; com·pel·ling** : to drive or urge with force
com·pen·di·ous \kəm-ˈpen-dē-əs\ *adj* : concise and comprehensive; *also* : COMPREHENSIVE ⟨a ~ almanac⟩
com·pen·di·um \kəm-ˈpen-dē-əm\ *n, pl* **-di·ums** *or* **-dia** \-ə\ **1** : a brief summary of a larger work or of a field of knowledge **2** : COLLECTION
com·pen·sate \ˈkäm-pən-ˌsāt\ *vb* **-sat·ed; -sat·ing** **1** : to be equivalent to : make up for **2** : PAY, REMUNERATE ♦ ***Synonyms*** BALANCE, OFFSET, COUNTERBALANCE, COUNTERPOISE — **com·pen·sa·tion** \ˌkäm-pən-ˈsā-shən\ *n* — **com·pen·sa·to·ry** \kəm-ˈpen-sə-ˌtȯr-ē\ *adj*
com·pete \kəm-ˈpēt\ *vb* **com·pet·ed; com·pet·ing** : CONTEND, VIE ⟨~ for the title⟩ ⟨~ for customers⟩
com·pe·tence \ˈkäm-pə-təns\ *n* **1** : adequate means for subsistence **2** : FITNESS, ABILITY ⟨trusted his doctor's ~⟩
com·pe·ten·cy \-tən-sē\ *n, pl* **-cies** : COMPETENCE
com·pe·tent \-tənt\ *adj* : CAPABLE, FIT, QUALIFIED ⟨a ~ mechanic⟩ ⟨a ~ juror⟩
com·pe·ti·tion \ˌkäm-pə-ˈti-shən\ *n* **1** : the act of competing : RIVALRY **2** : CONTEST, MATCH; *also* : one's competitors — **com·pet·i·tive** \kəm-ˈpe-tə-tiv\ *adj* — **com·pet·i·tive·ly** *adv* — **com·pet·i·tive·ness** *n*
com·pet·i·tor \kəm-ˈpe-tə-tər\ *n* : one that competes : RIVAL
com·pile \kəm-ˈpī(-ə)l\ *vb* **com·piled; com·pil·ing** [ME, fr. AF *compiler,* fr. L *compilare* to plunder] **1** : to compose out of materials from other documents **2** : to collect and edit into a volume **3** : to translate (a computer program) with a compiler **4** : to build up gradually ⟨~ a record of four wins and two losses⟩ — **com·pi·la·tion** \ˌkäm-pə-ˈlā-shən\ *n*
com·pil·er \kəm-ˈpī-lər\ *n* **1** : one that compiles **2** : a computer program that translates any program correctly written in a specific programming language into machine language
com·pla·cence \kəm-ˈplā-sᵊns\ *n* : COMPLACENCY — **com·pla·cent** \-sᵊnt\ *adj* — **com·pla·cent·ly** *adv*
com·pla·cen·cy \-sᵊn-sē\ *n, pl* **-cies** : SATISFACTION; *esp* : SELF-SATISFACTION
com·plain \kəm-ˈplān\ *vb* **1** : to express grief, pain, or discontent **2** : to make a formal accusation — **com·plain·ant** *n* — **com·plain·er** *n*
com·plaint \kəm-ˈplānt\ *n* **1** : expression of grief, pain, or dissatisfaction **2** : a bodily ailment or disease **3** : a formal accusation against a person
com·plai·sance \kəm-ˈplā-sᵊns, ˌkäm-plā-ˈzans\ *n* [F] : disposition to please — **com·plai·sant** \-sᵊnt, -ˈzant\ *adj* — **com·plai·sant·ly** *adv*
com·pleat \kəm-ˈplēt\ *adj* : PROFICIENT
com·plect·ed \kəm-ˈplek-təd\ *adj* : having a specified facial complexion ⟨dark-*complected*⟩
¹**com·ple·ment** \ˈkäm-plə-mənt\ *n* **1** : something that fills up or completes; *also* : the full quantity, number, or amount that makes a thing complete **2** : an added word by which a predicate is made complete **3** : a group of proteins in blood that combines with antibodies to destroy antigens — **com·ple·men·ta·ry** \ˌkäm-plə-ˈmen-t(ə-)rē\ *adj*
²**com·ple·ment** \-ˌment\ *vb* : to be complementary to : fill out
complementary medicine *n* : ALTERNATIVE MEDICINE
¹**com·plete** \kəm-ˈplēt\ *adj* **com·plet·er; -est** **1** : having all parts or elements **2** : brought to an end **3** : fully carried out; *also* : ABSOLUTE 2 ⟨~ silence⟩ — **com·plete·ly** *adv* — **com·plete·ness** *n* — **com·ple·tion** \-ˈplē-shən\ *n*
²**complete** *vb* **com·plet·ed; com·plet·ing** **1** : FINISH, CONCLUDE **2** : to make whole or perfect ⟨the hat ~*s* the outfit⟩
com·plet·ist \kəm-ˈplē-tist\ *n* : one who wants to make something (as a collection) complete
¹**com·plex** \ˈkäm-ˌpleks\ *n* **1** : a whole made up of or involving intricately interrelated elements **2** : a group of repressed desires and memories that exert a dominating influence on one's personality and behavior ⟨a guilt ~⟩
²**com·plex** \käm-ˈpleks, ˈkäm-ˌpleks\ *adj* **1** : composed of two or more parts **2** : consisting of a main clause and one or more subordinate clauses ⟨~ sentence⟩ **3** : hard to separate, analyze, or solve — **com·plex·i·ty** \käm-ˈplek-sə-tē\ *n* — **com·plex·ly** *adv*
complex fraction *n* : a fraction with a fraction or mixed number in the numerator or denominator or both
com·plex·ion \kəm-ˈplek-shən\ *n* **1** : the hue or appearance of the skin esp. of the face **2** : overall appearance — **com·plex·ioned** \-shənd\ *adj*
complex number *n* : a number of the form $a + b\sqrt{-1}$ where *a* and *b* are real numbers
com·pli·ance \kəm-ˈplī-əns\ *n* **1** : the act of complying to a demand or proposal **2** : a disposition to yield — **com·pli·ant** \-ənt\ *adj*
com·pli·cate \ˈkäm-plə-ˌkāt\ *vb* **-cat·ed; -cat·ing** : to make or become complex or intricate
com·pli·cat·ed \ˈkäm-plə-ˌkā-təd\ *adj* **1** : consisting of parts intricately combined **2** : difficult to analyze, understand, or explain ⟨a ~ issue⟩ — **com·pli·cat·ed·ly** *adv*
com·pli·ca·tion \ˌkäm-plə-ˈkā-shən\ *n* **1** : the quality or state of being complicated; *also* : a complex feature **2** : a disease or condition that develops during and af-

fects the course of a primary disease or condition

com·plic·i·ty \kəm-ˈpli-sə-tē\ *n, pl* **-ties** : the state of being an accomplice

¹**com·pli·ment** \ˈkäm-plə-ment\ *n* **1** : an expression of approval or admiration; *esp* : a flattering remark **2** *pl* : best wishes : REGARDS

²**com·pli·ment** \-ˌment\ *vb* : to pay a compliment to

com·pli·men·ta·ry \ˌkäm-plə-ˈmen-t(ə-)rē\ *adj* **1** : containing or expressing a compliment **2** : given free as a courtesy ⟨~ ticket⟩

com·ply \kəm-ˈplī\ *vb* **com·plied**; **com·ply·ing** : CONFORM, YIELD

¹**com·po·nent** \kəm-ˈpō-nənt, ˈkäm-ˌpō-\ *n* : a component part ♦ ***Synonyms*** INGREDIENT, ELEMENT, FACTOR, CONSTITUENT

²**component** *adj* : serving to form a part of : CONSTITUENT

com·port \kəm-ˈpȯrt\ *vb* **1** : AGREE, ACCORD ⟨actions that ~ with policy⟩ **2** : CONDUCT ⟨~ oneself with dignity⟩ ♦ ***Synonyms*** BEHAVE, ACQUIT, DEPORT — **com·port·ment** *n*

com·pose \kəm-ˈpōz\ *vb* **com·posed**; **com·pos·ing** **1** : to form by putting together : FASHION **2** : to produce (as pages of type) by composition **3** : ADJUST, ARRANGE **4** : CALM, QUIET ⟨~ yourself before acting⟩ **5** : to practice composition ⟨~ music⟩ — **com·pos·er** *n*

¹**com·pos·ite** \käm-ˈpä-zət\ *adj* **1** : made up of distinct parts or elements **2** : of, relating to, or being a large family of flowering plants (as a daisy or aster) that bear many small flowers united into compact heads resembling single flowers

²**composite** *n* **1** : something composite **2** : a plant of the composite family ♦ ***Synonyms*** BLEND, COMPOUND, MIXTURE, AMALGAMATION

com·po·si·tion \ˌkäm-pə-ˈzi-shən\ *n* **1** : the act or process of composing; *esp* : arrangement esp. in artistic form **2** : the arrangement or production of type for printing **3** : general makeup **4** : a product of mixing various elements or ingredients **5** : a literary, musical, or artistic product; *esp* : ESSAY

com·po·si·tion·ist \-ˈzi-shə-nist\ *n* : a teacher of writing

com·pos·i·tor \kəm-ˈpä-zə-tər\ *n* : one who sets type

com·post \ˈkäm-ˌpōst\ *n* : a fertilizing material consisting largely of decayed organic matter — **compost** *vb*

com·po·sure \kəm-ˈpō-zhər\ *n* : CALMNESS, SELF-POSSESSION

com·pote \ˈkäm-ˌpōt\ *n* **1** : fruits cooked in syrup **2** : a bowl (as of glass) usu. with a base and stem for serving esp. fruit or compote

¹**com·pound** \käm-ˈpaund, ˈkäm-ˌ\ *vb* [ME *compounen,* fr. AF **cumpundre,* fr. L *componere,* fr. *com-* together + *ponere* to put] **1** : COMBINE **2** : to form by combining parts ⟨~ a medicine⟩ **3** : SETTLE ⟨~ a dispute⟩; *also* : to refrain from prosecuting (an offense) in return for a consideration **4** : to increase (as interest) by an amount that can itself vary; *also* : to add to

²**com·pound** \ˈkäm-ˌpau̇nd\ *adj* **1** : made up of individual parts **2** : composed of united similar parts esp. of a kind usu. independent ⟨a ~ plant ovary⟩ **3** : formed by the combination of two or more otherwise independent elements ⟨~ sentence⟩

³**com·pound** \ˈkäm-ˌpau̇nd\ *n* **1** : a word consisting of parts that are words **2** : something formed from a union of elements or parts; *esp* : a distinct substance formed by the union of two or more chemical elements ♦ ***Synonyms*** MIXTURE, COMPOSITE, BLEND, ADMIXTURE, ALLOY

⁴**com·pound** \ˈkäm-ˌpau̇nd\ *n* [by folk etymology fr. Malay *kampung* group of buildings, village] : an enclosure containing buildings

compound interest *n* : interest computed on the sum of an original principal and accrued interest

com·pre·hend \ˌkäm-pri-ˈhend\ *vb* **1** : UNDERSTAND **2** : INCLUDE — **com·pre·hen·si·ble** \-ˈhen-sə-bəl\ *adj* — **com·pre·hen·sion** \-ˈhen-chən\ *n*

com·pre·hen·sive \ˌkäm-pri-ˈhen-siv\ *adj* : covering completely or broadly ⟨~ insurance⟩ — **com·pre·hen·sive·ly** *adv* — **com·pre·hen·sive·ness** *n*

¹**com·press** \kəm-ˈpres\ *vb* **1** : to squeeze together **2** : to reduce in size as if by squeezing ♦ ***Synonyms*** CONSTRICT, CONTRACT, SHRINK — **com·pres·sor** \-ˈpre-sər\ *n*

²**com·press** \ˈkäm-ˌpres\ *n* : a folded pad or cloth used to press upon a body part

compressed air *n* : air under pressure greater than that of the atmosphere

com·pres·sion \kəm-ˈpre-shən\ *n* **1** : the act or process of compressing **2** : the process of compressing the fuel mixture in an internal combustion engine **3** : conversion (as of data) in order to reduce the space occupied or the bandwidth required

com·prise \kəm-ˈprīz\ *vb* **com·prised**; **com·pris·ing** **1** : INCLUDE, CONTAIN **2** : to be made up of ⟨the play ~*s* three acts⟩ **3** : COMPOSE, CONSTITUTE

¹**com·pro·mise** \ˈkäm-prə-ˌmīz\ *n* : a settlement of differences reached by mutual concessions

²**compromise** *vb* **-mised**; **-mis·ing** **1** : to settle by compromise **2** : to expose to suspicion or loss of reputation **3** : to cause the impairment of ⟨drugs that can ~ the immune system⟩

comp·trol·ler \kən-ˈtrō-lər, ˈkämp-ˌtrō-\ *n* : an official who audits and supervises expenditures and accounts

com·pul·sion \kəm-ˈpəl-shən\ *n* **1** : an act of compelling **2** : a force that compels **3** : an irresistible persistent impulse to perform an act ♦ ***Synonyms*** CONSTRAINT, FORCE, VIOLENCE, DURESS — **com·pul·sive** \-siv\ *adj* — **com·pul-**

sive·ly *adv* — **com·pul·so·ry** \-sə-rē\ *adj*

com·punc·tion \kəm-ˈpəŋk-shən\ *n* : anxiety arising from guilt : REMORSE

com·pute \kəm-ˈpyüt\ *vb* **com·put·ed; com·put·ing** : CALCULATE, RECKON — **com·pu·ta·tion** \ˌkäm-pyu̇-ˈtā-shən\ *n* — **com·pu·ta·tion·al** *adj*

computed tomography *n* : radiography in which a three-dimensional image of a body structure is constructed by computer from a series of plane cross-sectional images made along an axis

com·put·er \kəm-ˈpyü-tər\ *n* : a programmable electronic device that can store, retrieve, and process data

com·put·er·ise *chiefly Brit var of* COMPUTERIZE

com·put·er·ize \kəm-ˈpyü-tə-ˌrīz\ *vb* **-ized; -iz·ing 1** : to carry out, control, or produce by means of a computer **2** : to provide with computers **3** : to store in a computer; *also* : put into a form that a computer can use — **com·put·er·i·za·tion** \-ˌpyü-tə-rə-ˈzā-shən\ *n*

computerized axial tomography *n* : COMPUTED TOMOGRAPHY

com·rade \ˈkäm-ˌrad\ *n* [MF *camarade* group sleeping in one room, roommate, companion, fr. Sp *camarada,* fr. *cámara* room, fr. LL *camera*] : COMPANION, ASSOCIATE — **com·rade·ly** *adj* — **com·rade·ship** *n*

com·rad·ery \ˈkäm-ˌra-də-rē, -ˌrā-\ *n* : CAMARADERIE

¹**con** \ˈkän\ *vb* **conned; con·ning 1** : MEMORIZE **2** : STUDY

²**con** *adv* : in opposition : AGAINST

³**con** *n* : an opposing argument, person, or position ⟨pros and ∼*s*⟩

⁴**con** *vb* **conned; con·ning 1** : SWINDLE **2** : PERSUADE, CAJOLE

⁵**con** *n* : CONVICT

⁶**con** *n* : CONVENTION, 3

conc *abbr* concentrated

con·cat·e·nate \kän-ˈka-tə-ˌnāt\ *vb* **-nat·ed; -nat·ing** : to link together in a series or chain — **con·cat·e·na·tion** \(ˌ)kän-ˌka-tə-ˈnā-shən\ *n*

con·cave \kän-ˈkāv, ˈkän-ˌ\ *adj* : curved or rounded inward like the inside of a bowl — **con·cav·i·ty** \kän-ˈka-və-tē\ *n*

con·ceal \kən-ˈsēl\ *vb* : to place out of sight : HIDE ⟨∼ evidence⟩ — **con·ceal·er** *n* — **con·ceal·ment** *n*

con·cede \kən-ˈsēd\ *vb* **con·ced·ed; con·ced·ing 1** : to admit to be true **2** : GRANT, YIELD ♦ ***Synonyms*** ALLOW, ACKNOWLEDGE, AVOW, CONFESS

con·ceit \kən-ˈsēt\ *n* **1** : excessively high opinion of one's self or ability : VANITY **2** : an elaborate or strained metaphor — **con·ceit·ed** *adj* — **con·ceit·ed·ly** *adv* — **con·ceit·ed·ness** *n*

con·ceive \kən-ˈsēv\ *vb* **con·ceived; con·ceiv·ing 1** : to become pregnant or pregnant with ⟨∼ a child⟩ **2** : to form an idea of : THINK, IMAGINE ⟨∼ a plan⟩ — **con·ceiv·able** \-ˈsē-və-bəl\ *adj* — **con·ceiv·ably** \-blē\ *adv*

con·cel·e·brant \kən-ˈse-lə-brənt\ *n* : one that jointly participates in celebrating the Eucharist

¹**con·cen·trate** \ˈkän-sən-ˌtrāt\ *vb* **-trat·ed; -trat·ing 1** : to gather into one body, mass, or force **2** : to make less dilute **3** : to fix one's powers, efforts, or attentions

²**concentrate** *n* : something concentrated

con·cen·tra·tion \ˌkän-sən-ˈtrā-shən\ *n* **1** : the act or process of concentrating : the state of being concentrated; *esp* : direction of attention on a single object **2** : the amount of a component in a given area or volume

concentration camp *n* : a place where large numbers of people (as prisoners of war, refugees, or members of an ethnic or religious minority) are confined

con·cen·tric \kən-ˈsen-trik\ *adj* **1** : having a common center ⟨∼ circles⟩ **2** : COAXIAL

¹**con·cept** \ˈkän-ˌsept\ *n* : THOUGHT, NOTION, IDEA — **con·cep·tu·al** \kən-ˈsep-chə-wəl\ *adj* — **con·cep·tu·al·ly** *adv*

²**concept** *adj* **1** : organized around a main idea or theme ⟨a ∼ album⟩ **2** : created to illustrate a concept ⟨a ∼ car⟩

con·cep·tion \kən-ˈsep-shən\ *n* **1** : the process of conceiving or being conceived **2** : the power to form or understand ideas or concepts **3** : IDEA, CONCEPT **4** : the originating of something

con·cep·tu·al·ise *Brit var of* CONCEPTUALIZE

con·cep·tu·al·ize \-ˈsep-chə-wə-ˌlīz\ *vb* **-ized; -iz·ing** : to form a conception of

¹**con·cern** \kən-ˈsərn\ *vb* **1** : to relate to **2** : to be the business of : INVOLVE **3** : ENGAGE, OCCUPY

²**concern** *n* **1** : INTEREST, ANXIETY **2** : AFFAIR, MATTER **3** : a business organization ♦ ***Synonyms*** CARE, WORRY, DISQUIET, UNEASE

con·cerned \-ˈsərnd\ *adj* **1** : ANXIOUS, UNEASY ⟨∼ for their safety⟩ **2** : INVOLVED ⟨is ∼*ed* with films⟩

con·cern·ing \-ˈsər-niŋ\ *prep* : relating to : REGARDING ⟨news ∼ his business⟩

con·cern·ment \kən-ˈsərn-mənt\ *n* **1** : something in which one is concerned **2** : IMPORTANCE, CONSEQUENCE

¹**con·cert** \ˈkän-(ˌ)sərt\ *n* **1** : agreement in a plan or design **2** : a public performance (as of music)

²**con·cert** \kən-ˈsərt\ *vb* : to plan together

con·cert·ed \kən-ˈsər-təd\ *adj* : mutually agreed on; *also* : performed in unison

con·cer·ti·na \ˌkän-sər-ˈtē-nə\ *n* : an instrument of the accordion family

concertina wire *n* : a coiled wire with sharp points for use as an obstacle

con·cert·mas·ter \ˈkän-sərt-ˌmas-tər\ *or* **con·cert·meis·ter** \-ˌmī-stər\ *n* : the leader of the first violins of an orchestra and assistant to the conductor

con·cer·to \kən-ˈcher-tō\ *n, pl* **-ti** \-(ˌ)tē\ *or* **-tos** [It] : a piece for one or more solo instruments and orchestra in three movements

con·ces·sion \kən-ˈse-shən\ *n* **1** : an act of conceding or yielding **2** : something yielded **3** : a grant by a government of land or of a right to use it **4** : a grant of a portion of premises for some specific purpose; *also* : the activities or enterprise carried on **5** : a small business where things (as food or souvenirs) are sold in a public place; *also* : things sold at such a business — **con·ces·sion·ary** \-ˈse-shə-ˌner-ē\ *adj*

con·ces·sion·aire \kən-ˌse-shə-ˈner\ *n* : one that owns or operates a concession

conch \ˈkäŋk, ˈkänch\ *n, pl* **conchs** \ˈkäŋks\ *or* **conch·es** \ˈkän-chəz\ : a large spiral-shelled marine gastropod mollusk; *also* : its shell

con·cierge \kōⁿ-ˈsyerzh\ *n, pl* **con·cierg·es** *same or* -ˈsyer-zhəz\ [F] **1** : a resident in an apartment building who performs services for the tenants **2 a** : a usu. multilingual hotel staff member who provides help and information to hotel guests **b** : a person or service that provides assistance with personal business

con·cil·i·ate \kən-ˈsi-lē-ˌāt\ *vb* **-at·ed; -at·ing 1** : to bring into agreement : RECONCILE **2** : to gain the goodwill of — **con·cil·i·a·tion** \-ˌsi-lē-ˈā-shən\ *n* — **con·cil·i·a·tor** \-ˈsi-lē-ˌā-tər\ *n* — **con·cil·ia·to·ry** \-ˈsi-lē-ə-ˌtȯr-ē\ *adj*

con·cise \kən-ˈsīs\ *adj* : expressing much in few words : BRIEF ⟨a ~ history⟩ — **con·cise·ly** *adv* — **con·cise·ness** *n*

con·clave \ˈkän-ˌklāv\ *n* [ME, fr. ML, fr. L, room that can be locked, fr. *com-* together + *clavis* key] : a private gathering; *also* : CONVENTION

con·clude \kən-ˈklüd\ *vb* **con·clud·ed; con·clud·ing 1** : to bring to a close : END **2** : DECIDE, JUDGE **3** : to bring about as a result ♦ ***Synonyms*** CLOSE, FINISH, TERMINATE, COMPLETE, HALT

con·clu·sion \kən-ˈklü-zhən\ *n* **1** : the logical consequence of a reasoning process **2** : TERMINATION, END **3** : OUTCOME, RESULT — **con·clu·sive** \-siv\ *adj* — **con·clu·sive·ly** *adv* — **con·clu·sive·ness** *n*

con·coct \kən-ˈkäkt, kän-\ *vb* **1** : to prepare by combining raw materials **2** : DEVISE — **con·coc·tion** \-ˈkäk-shən\ *n*

con·com·i·tant \-ˈkä-mə-tənt\ *adj* : ACCOMPANYING, ATTENDING — **concomitant** *n*

con·cord \ˈkän-ˌkȯrd, ˈkäŋ-\ *n* : AGREEMENT, HARMONY

con·cor·dance \kən-ˈkȯr-dᵊns\ *n* **1** : an alphabetical index of words in a book or in an author's works with the passages in which they occur **2** : AGREEMENT, COVENANT

con·cor·dant \-dᵊnt\ *adj* : HARMONIOUS, AGREEING

con·cor·dat \kən-ˈkȯr-ˌdat\ *n* : CONCORDANCE 2

con·course \ˈkän-ˌkȯrs\ *n* **1** : a spontaneous coming together : GATHERING **2** : an open space or hall (as in a bus terminal) where crowds gather

¹**con·crete** \kän-ˈkrēt, ˈkän-ˌkrēt\ *adj* **1** : naming a real thing or class of things : not abstract **2** : not theoretical : ACTUAL **3** : made of or relating to concrete

²**con·crete** \ˈkän-ˌkrēt, kän-ˈkrēt\ *vb* **con·cret·ed; con·cret·ing 1** : SOLIDIFY **2** : to cover with concrete

³**con·crete** \ˈkän-ˌkrēt, kän-ˈkrēt\ *n* : a hard building material made by mixing cement, sand, and gravel with water

con·cre·tion \kän-ˈkrē-shən\ *n* : a hard mass esp. when formed abnormally in the body

con·cu·bine \ˈkäŋ-kyu̇-ˌbīn\ *n* [ME, fr. AF, fr. L *concubina,* fr. *com-* with + *cubare* to lie] : a woman who is not legally a wife but lives with a man and sometimes has a recognized position in his household; *also* : MISTRESS — **con·cu·bi·nage** \kän-ˈkyü-bə-nij\ *n*

con·cu·pis·cence \kän-ˈkyü-pə-səns\ *n* : ardent sexual desire : LUST

con·cur \kən-ˈkər\ *vb* **con·curred; con·cur·ring 1** : to act together **2** : AGREE **3** : COINCIDE ♦ ***Synonyms*** UNITE, COMBINE, COOPERATE, BAND, JOIN

con·cur·rence \-ˈkər-əns\ *n* **1** : agreement in action or opinion **2** : occurrence together : CONJUNCTION

con·cur·rent \-ˈkər-ənt\ *adj* **1** : happening or operating at the same time **2** : joint and equal in authority

con·cus·sion \kən-ˈkə-shən\ *n* **1** : a hard blow or collision; *also* : bodily injury (as to the brain) resulting from a sudden jar **2** : AGITATION, SHAKING

con·demn \kən-ˈdem\ *vb* **1** : to declare to be wrong **2** : to convict of guilt **3** : to sentence judicially **4** : to pronounce unfit for use ⟨~ a building⟩ **5** : to declare forfeited or taken for public use ♦ ***Synonyms*** DENOUNCE, CENSURE, BLAME, CRITICIZE, REPREHEND — **con·dem·na·tion** \ˌkän-ˌdem-ˈnā-shən\ *n* — **con·dem·na·to·ry** \kən-ˈdem-nə-ˌtȯr-ē\ *adj*

con·den·sate \ˈkän-dən-ˌsāt, kən-ˈden-\ *n* : a product of condensation

con·dense \kən-ˈdens\ *vb* **con·densed; con·dens·ing 1** : to make or become more compact or dense : CONCENTRATE **2** : to change from vapor to liquid ♦ ***Synonyms*** CONTRACT, SHRINK, COMPRESS, CONSTRICT — **con·den·sa·tion** \ˌkän-den-ˈsā-shən\ *n*

con·dens·er \kən-ˈden-sər\ *n* **1** : one that condenses **2** : CAPACITOR

con·de·scend \ˌkän-di-ˈsend\ *vb* : to assume an air of superiority — **con·de·scend·ing·ly** \-ˈsen-diŋ-lē\ *adv* — **con·de·scen·sion** \-ˈsen-chən\ *n*

con·dign \kən-ˈdīn, ˈkän-ˌdīn\ *adj* : DESERVED, APPROPRIATE ⟨~ punishment⟩

con·di·ment \ˈkän-də-mənt\ *n* : something used to make food savory; *esp* : a pungent seasoning (as pepper)

¹**con·di·tion** \kən-ˈdi-shən\ *n* **1** : something essential to the occurrence of some other thing **2** : state of being **3** : social status **4** *pl* : state of affairs : CIRCUMSTANCES **5** : a bodily state in which something is wrong ⟨a heart ~⟩ **6** : a state of health, fitness, or working order

²**condition** *vb* **1** : to put into proper condition for action or use **2** : to adapt, modi-

fy, or mold to respond in a particular way **3** : to modify so that an act or response previously associated with one stimulus becomes associated with another

con·di·tion·al \kən-ˈdi-shə-nəl\ *adj* : containing, implying, or depending on a condition — **con·di·tion·al·ly** *adv*

con·di·tioned \-ˈdi-shənd\ *adj* : determined or established by conditioning

con·di·tion·er \-ˈdi-shə-nər\ *n* : a preparation used to improve the condition of hair

con·do \ˈkän-(ˌ)dō\ *n* : CONDOMINIUM 3

con·dole \kən-ˈdōl\ *vb* **con·doled**; **con·dol·ing** : to express sympathetic sorrow — **con·do·lence** \kən-ˈdō-ləns\ *n*

con·dom \ˈkän-dəm, ˈkən-\ *n* : a usu. rubber sheath worn over the penis (as to prevent pregnancy or venereal infection during sexual intercourse)

con·do·min·i·um \ˌkän-də-ˈmi-nē-əm\ *n, pl* **-ums** **1** : joint sovereignty (as by two or more nations) **2** : a politically dependent territory under condominium **3** : individual ownership of a unit (as an apartment) in a multiunit structure; *also* : a unit so owned

con·done \kən-ˈdōn\ *vb* **con·doned**; **con·don·ing** : to overlook or forgive esp. by treating (an offense) as harmless or trivial ♦ ***Synonyms*** EXCUSE, PARDON, FORGIVE, REMIT — **con·do·na·tion** \ˌkän-də-ˈnā-shən\ *n*

con·dor \ˈkän-dər, -ˌdȯr\ *n* [Sp *cóndor,* fr. Quechua *kuntur*] : a very large American vulture of the high Andes; *also* : a related nearly extinct vulture of southern California now resident only in captivity

con·duce \kən-ˈdüs, -ˈdyüs\ *vb* **con·duced**; **con·duc·ing** : to lead or contribute to a particular result — **con·du·cive** *adj*

¹**con·duct** \ˈkän-(ˌ)dəkt\ *n* **1** : MANAGEMENT, DIRECTION **2** : BEHAVIOR

²**con·duct** \kən-ˈdəkt\ *vb* **1** : GUIDE, ESCORT **2** : MANAGE, DIRECT **3** : to act as a medium for conveying or transmitting **4** : BEHAVE — **con·duc·tion** \-ˈdək-shən\ *n*

con·duc·tance \kən-ˈdək-təns\ *n* : the readiness with which a conductor transmits an electric current

con·duc·tive \kən-ˈdək-tiv\ *adj* : having the power to conduct (as heat or electricity) — **con·duc·tiv·i·ty** \ˌkän-ˌdək-ˈti-və-tē\ *n*

con·duc·tor \kən-ˈdək-tər\ *n* **1** : one that conducts; *esp* : a material that permits an electric current to flow easily **2** : a collector of fares in a public conveyance **3** : the leader of a musical ensemble

con·duit \ˈkän-ˌdü-ət, ˌdyü-, -dwət\ *n* **1** : a channel for conveying fluid **2** : a tube or trough for protecting electric wires or cables **3** : a means of transmitting or distributing

con·dyle \ˈkän-ˌdī(-ə)l, -dᵊl\ *n* : an articular prominence of a bone — **con·dy·lar** \-də-lər\ *adj*

cone \ˈkōn\ *n* **1** : the scaly usu. ovate fruit of trees of most conifers **2** : a solid figure formed by rotating a right triangle about one of its legs **3** : a solid figure that slopes evenly to a point from a usu. circular base **4** : any of the conical light-sensitive receptor cells of the retina that function in color vision **5** : something shaped like a cone

cone·flow·er \ˈkōn-ˌflau̇(-ə)r\ *n* : any of several composite plants having cone-shaped flower disks

Con·es·to·ga wagon \ˌkä-nə-ˈstō-gə-\ *n* : a broad-wheeled covered wagon used esp. for transporting freight across the prairies

co·ney *or* **co·ny** \ˈkō-nē\ *n, pl* **coneys** *or* **conies** **1** : RABBIT; *also* : its fur **2** : PIKA

conf *abbr* **1** conference **2** confidential

con·fab \ˈkän-ˌfab, kən-ˈfab\ *n* : CONFABULATION 1

con·fab·u·la·tion \kən-ˌfab-yə-ˈlā-shən\ *n* **1** : CHAT; *also* : CONFERENCE **2** : a filling in of gaps in memory by fabrication — **con·fab·u·late** \-ˈfa-byə-ˌlāt\ *vb*

con·fec·tion \kən-ˈfek-shən\ *n* **1** : something put together from varied material **2** : a fancy dish or sweet; *also* : CANDY — **con·fect** \kən-ˈfekt\ *vb*

con·fec·tion·er \-sh(ə-)nər\ *n* : a maker of or dealer in confections

con·fec·tion·ery \-shə-ˌner-ē\ *n, pl* **-er·ies** **1** : sweet foods **2** : a confectioner's place of business

Confed *abbr* Confederate

con·fed·er·a·cy \kən-ˈfe-də-rə-sē\ *n, pl* **-cies** **1** : LEAGUE, ALLIANCE **2** *cap* : the 11 southern states that seceded from the U.S. in 1860 and 1861

¹**con·fed·er·ate** \kən-ˈfe-də-rət\ *adj* **1** : united in a league : ALLIED **2** *cap* : of or relating to the Confederacy

²**confederate** *n* **1** : ALLY, ACCOMPLICE **2** *cap* : an adherent of the Confederacy

³**con·fed·er·ate** \-ˈfe-də-ˌrāt\ *vb* **-at·ed**; **-at·ing** : to unite in a confederacy

con·fed·er·a·tion \kən-ˌfe-də-ˈrā-shən\ *n* **1** : an act of confederating : ALLIANCE **2** : LEAGUE

con·fer \kən-ˈfər\ *vb* **con·ferred**; **con·fer·ring** **1** : GRANT, BESTOW 〈~ an award〉 **2** : to exchange views : CONSULT — **con·fer·ee** \ˌkän-fə-ˈrē\ *n*

con·fer·ence \ˈkän-f(ə-)rəns\ *n* **1** : an interchange of views; *also* : a meeting for this purpose **2** : an association of athletic teams

con·fer·enc·ing \ˈkän-f(ə-)rən-siŋ\ *n* : the holding of conferences esp. by means of electronic devices

con·fess \kən-ˈfes\ *vb* **1** : to acknowledge or disclose one's misdeed, fault, or sin **2** : to acknowledge one's sins to God or to a priest **3** : to receive the confession of (a penitent) ♦ ***Synonyms*** ADMIT, OWN, AVOW, CONCEDE, GRANT

con·fessed·ly \-ˈfe-səd-lē\ *adv* : by confession : ADMITTEDLY

con·fes·sion \-ˈfe-shən\ *n* **1** : an act of confessing (as in the sacrament of penance) **2** : an acknowledgment of guilt **3** : a formal statement of religious beliefs **4**

: a religious body having a common creed — **con·fes·sion·al** *adj*
con·fes·sion·al \-ˈfe-shə-nəl\ *n* : a place where a priest hears confessions
con·fes·sor \kən-ˈfe-sər\ *n* **1** : one that confesses **2** : a priest who hears confessions
con·fet·ti \kən-ˈfe-tē\ *n* [It, pl. of *confetto* sweetmeat, fr. ML *confectum*, fr. L, neut. of *confectus*, pp. of *conficere* to prepare] : bits of colored paper or ribbon for throwing (as at weddings)
con·fi·dant \ˈkän-fə-ˌdänt, -ˌdant\ *n* : one to whom secrets are confided
con·fi·dante \-ˌdänt, -ˌdant\ *n* : CONFIDANT; *esp* : one who is a woman
con·fide \kən-ˈfīd\ *vb* **con·fid·ed**; **con·fid·ing** **1** : to have or show faith : TRUST ⟨~ in a friend⟩ **2** : to tell confidentially ⟨~ a secret⟩ **3** : ENTRUST
[1]**con·fi·dence** \ˈkän-fə-dəns\ *n* **1** : TRUST, RELIANCE **2** : SELF-ASSURANCE, BOLDNESS **3** : a state of trust or intimacy **4** : SECRET 2 — **con·fi·dent** \-dənt\ *adj* — **con·fi·dent·ly** *adv*
[2]**confidence** *adj* : of or relating to swindling by false promises ⟨a ~ game⟩
con·fi·den·tial \ˌkän-fə-ˈden-shəl\ *adj* **1** : SECRET, PRIVATE ⟨~ information⟩ **2** : entrusted with confidences ⟨~ clerk⟩ — **con·fi·den·ti·al·i·ty** \-ˌden-shē-ˈa-lə-tē\ *n* — **con·fi·den·tial·ly** \-ˈden-shə-lē\ *adv*
con·fig·u·ra·tion \kən-ˌfi-gyə-ˈrā-shən\ *n* : structural arrangement of parts : SHAPE
con·fig·ure \kən-ˈfi-gyər\ *vb* **-ured**; **-ur·ing** : to set up for operation esp. in a particular way
con·fine \kən-ˈfīn\ *vb* **con·fined**; **con·fin·ing** **1** : to hold within a location; *also* : IMPRISON **2** : to keep within limits ⟨will ~ my remarks to one subject⟩ — **con·fine·ment** *n* — **con·fin·er** *n*
con·fines \ˈkän-ˌfīnz\ *n pl* : BOUNDS, BORDERS
con·firm \kən-ˈfərm\ *vb* **1** : to give approval to : RATIFY **2** : to make firm or firmer **3** : to administer the rite of confirmation to **4** : VERIFY, CORROBORATE — **con·fir·ma·to·ry** \-ˈfər-mə-ˌtȯr-ē\ *adj*
con·fir·ma·tion \ˌkän-fər-ˈmā-shən\ *n* **1** : a religious ceremony admitting a person to full membership in a church or synagogue **2** : an act of ratifying or corroborating; *also* : PROOF
con·fis·cate \ˈkän-fə-ˌskāt\ *vb* **-cat·ed**; **-cat·ing** [L *confiscare*, fr. *com-* with + *fiscus* treasury] : to take possession of by or as if by public authority — **con·fis·ca·tion** \ˌkän-fə-ˈskā-shən\ *n* — **con·fis·ca·to·ry** \kən-ˈfis-kə-ˌtȯr-ē\ *adj*
con·fit \kōn-ˈfē\ *n* : a garnish of fruit or vegetables cooked in a seasoned liquid
con·fla·gra·tion \ˌkän-flə-ˈgrā-shən\ *n* : FIRE; *esp* : a large disastrous fire
[1]**con·flict** \ˈkän-ˌflikt\ *n* **1** : WAR **2** : a clash between hostile or opposing elements, ideas, or forces
[2]**con·flict** \kən-ˈflikt\ *vb* : to show opposition or irreconcilability : CLASH
con·flu·ence \ˈkän-ˌflü-əns, kən-ˈflü-\ *n* **1** : a coming together at one point **2** : the meeting or place of meeting of two or more streams — **con·flu·ent** \-ənt\ *adj*
con·flux \ˈkän-ˌfləks\ *n* : CONFLUENCE
con·form \kən-ˈfȯrm\ *vb* **1** : to be similar or identical; *also* : AGREE **2** : to obey customs or standards; *also* : COMPLY ⟨~ to regulations⟩ — **con·form·able** *adj* — **con·form·ist** \-ˈfȯr-mist\ *adj*
con·for·mance \kən-ˈfȯr-məns\ *n* : CONFORMITY
con·for·ma·tion \ˌkän-fȯr-ˈmā-shən\ *n* : a forming into a whole by arranging parts
con·for·mi·ty \kən-ˈfȯr-mə-tē\ *n, pl* **-ties** **1** : HARMONY, AGREEMENT **2** : COMPLIANCE, OBEDIENCE
con·found \kən-ˈfau̇nd, kän-\ *vb* **1** : to throw into disorder or confusion **2** : CONFUSE 2 ♦ ***Synonyms*** BEWILDER, PUZZLE, PERPLEX, BEFOG
con·fra·ter·ni·ty \ˌkän-frə-ˈtər-nə-tē\ *n* : a society devoted esp. to a religious or charitable cause
con·frere \ˈkän-ˌfrer, ˈkōⁿ-\ *n* : COLLEAGUE, COMRADE
con·front \kən-ˈfrənt\ *vb* **1** : to face esp. in challenge : OPPOSE; *also* : to deal unflinchingly with ⟨~*ed* the issue⟩ **2** : to cause to face or meet — **con·fron·ta·tion** \ˌkän-frən-ˈtā-shən\ *n* — **con·fron·ta·tion·al** \-shə-nᵊl\ *adj*
Con·fu·cian \kən-ˈfyü-shən\ *adj* : of or relating to the Chinese philosopher Confucius or his teachings — **Con·fu·cian·ism** \-shə-ˌni-zəm\ *n*
con·fuse \kən-ˈfyüz\ *vb* **con·fused**; **con·fus·ing** **1** : to make mentally unclear or uncertain; *also* : to disturb the composure of **2** : to mix up : JUMBLE ♦ ***Synonyms*** MUDDLE, BEFUDDLE, ADDLE, FLUSTER — **con·fus·ed·ly** \-ˈfyü-zəd-lē\ *adv* — **con·fus·ing·ly** \-ˈfyü-ziŋ-lē\ *adv*
con·fu·sion \-ˈfyü-zhən\ *n* **1** : an act or instance of confusing **2** : the quality or state of being confused
con·fute \kən-ˈfyüt\ *vb* **con·fut·ed**; **con·fut·ing** : to overwhelm by argument : REFUTE ⟨~ a proposition⟩ — **con·fu·ta·tion** \ˌkän-fyu̇-ˈtā-shən\ *n*
cong *abbr* congress; congressional
con·ga \ˈkäŋ-gə\ *n* : a Cuban dance of African origin performed by a group usu. in single file
con·geal \kən-ˈjēl\ *vb* **1** : FREEZE **2** : to make or become hard or thick
con·gee \ˈkän-jē\ *n* : porridge made from rice
con·ge·ner \ˈkän-jə-nər\ *n* : one related to another; *esp* : a plant or animal of the same taxonomic genus as another — **con·ge·ner·ic** \ˌkän-jə-ˈner-ik\ *adj*
con·ge·nial \kən-ˈjē-nyəl\ *adj* **1** : KINDRED, SYMPATHETIC ⟨~ companions⟩ **2** : suited to one's taste or nature : AGREEABLE — **con·ge·ni·al·i·ty** \-ˌjē-nē-ˈa-lə-tē\ *n* — **con·ge·nial·ly** *adv*
con·gen·i·tal \kən-ˈje-nə-tᵊl\ *adj* : existing at or dating from birth ⟨~ deafness⟩ ♦ ***Synonyms*** INBORN, INNATE, NATURAL
con·ger eel \ˈkäŋ-gər-\ *n* : a large edible marine eel of the Atlantic

con·ge·ries \ˈkän-jə-(ˌ)rēz\ *n, pl* **congeries** : AGGREGATION, COLLECTION

con·gest \kən-ˈjest\ *vb* **1** : to cause excessive accumulation of blood or mucus in (an organ or part) **2** : to obstruct by overcrowding — **con·ges·tion** \-ˈjes-chən\ *n* — **con·ges·tive** \-ˈjes-tiv\ *adj*

congestive heart failure *n* : heart failure in which the heart is unable to keep enough blood circulating in the tissues or is unable to pump out the blood returned to it by the veins

[1]**con·glom·er·ate** \kən-ˈglä-mə-rət\ *adj* [L *conglomerare* to roll together, fr. *com-* together + *glomerare* to wind into a ball, fr. *glomer-, glomus* ball] : made up of parts from various sources

[2]**con·glom·er·ate** \-ˌrāt\ *vb* **-at·ed; -at·ing** : to form into a mass — **con·glom·er·a·tion** \-ˌglä-mə-ˈrā-shən\ *n*

[3]**con·glom·er·ate** \-rət\ *n* **1** : a mass formed of fragments from various sources; *esp* : a rock composed of fragments varying from pebbles to boulders held together by a cementing material **2** : a widely diversified corporation

con·grat·u·late \kən-ˈgra-chə-ˌlāt\ *vb* **-lat·ed; -lat·ing** : to express pleasure to on account of success or good fortune — **con·grat·u·la·tion** \-ˌgra-chə-ˈlā-shən\ *n* — **con·grat·u·la·to·ry** \-ˈgra-chə-lə-ˌtōr-ē\ *adj*

con·gre·gate \ˈkäŋ-gri-ˌgāt\ *vb* **-gat·ed; -gat·ing** [ME, fr. L *congregatus,* pp. of *congregare,* fr. *com-* together + *greg-, grex* flock] : ASSEMBLE

con·gre·ga·tion \ˌkäŋ-gri-ˈgā-shən\ *n* **1** : an assembly of persons met esp. for worship; *also* : a group that habitually so meets **2** : a religious community or order **3** : the act or an instance of congregating

con·gre·ga·tion·al \-shə-nəl\ *adj* **1** : of or relating to a congregation **2** *cap* : observing the faith and practice of certain Protestant churches which recognize the independence of each congregation in church matters — **con·gre·ga·tion·al·ism** \-nə-ˌli-zəm\ *n, often cap* — **con·gre·ga·tion·al·ist** \-list\ *n, often cap*

con·gress \ˈkäŋ-grəs\ *n* **1** : an assembly esp. of delegates for discussion and usu. action on some question **2** : the body of senators and representatives constituting a nation's legislature — **con·gres·sio·nal** \kən-ˈgre-shə-nəl\ *adj*

con·gress·man \ˈkäŋ-grəs-mən\ *n* : a member of a congress

con·gress·wom·an \-ˌwu̇-mən\ *n* : a woman who is a member of a congress

con·gru·ence \kən-ˈgrü-əns, ˈkäŋ-grü-\ *n* : the quality of agreeing or coinciding : CONGRUITY — **con·gru·ent** \kən-ˈgrü-ənt, ˈkäŋ-grü-\ *adj*

con·gru·en·cy \-sē\ *n, pl* **-cies** : CONGRUENCE

con·gru·ity \kän-ˈgrü-ə-tē\ *n, pl* **-ities** : correspondence between things — **con·gru·ous** \ˈkäŋ-grü-əs\ *adj*

con·ic \ˈkä-nik\ *adj* **1** : of or relating to a cone **2** : CONICAL

con·i·cal \ˈkä-ni-kəl\ *adj* : resembling a cone esp. in shape

co·ni·fer \ˈkä-nə-fər, ˈkō-\ *n* : any of an order of shrubs or trees (as the pines) that usu. are evergreen and bear cones — **co·nif·er·ous** \kō-ˈni-fə-rəs\ *adj*

conj *abbr* conjunction

con·jec·ture \kən-ˈjek-chər\ *n* : GUESS, SURMISE — **con·jec·tur·al** \-chə-rəl\ *adj* — **conjecture** *vb*

con·join \kən-ˈjȯin\ *vb* : to join together — **con·joint** \-ˈjȯint\ *adj*

con·ju·gal \ˈkän-ji-gəl\ *adj* : of or relating to marriage : MATRIMONIAL

[1]**con·ju·gate** \ˈkän-ji-gət, -jə-ˌgāt\ *adj* **1** : united esp. in pairs : COUPLED **2** : of kindred origin and meaning ⟨*sing* and *song* are ~⟩ — **con·ju·gate·ly** *adv*

[2]**con·ju·gate** \-jə-ˌgāt\ *vb* **-gat·ed; -gat·ing** **1** : INFLECT ⟨~ a verb⟩ **2** : to join together : COUPLE

con·ju·ga·tion \ˌkän-jə-ˈgā-shən\ *n* **1** : an arrangement of the inflectional forms of a verb **2** : the act of conjugating : the state of being conjugated

con·junct \kän-ˈjəŋkt\ *adj* : JOINED, UNITED

con·junc·tion \kən-ˈjəŋk-shən\ *n* **1** : COMBINATION **2** : occurrence at the same time **3** : a word that joins together sentences, clauses, phrases, or words

con·junc·ti·va \ˌkän-ˌjəŋk-ˈtī-və\ *n, pl* **-vas** *or* **-vae** \-(ˌ)vē\ : the mucous membrane lining the inner surface of the eyelids and continuing over the forepart of the eyeball

con·junc·tive \kən-ˈjəŋk-tiv\ *adj* **1** : CONNECTIVE **2** : CONJUNCT ⟨the ~ operation of different factors⟩ **3** : being or functioning like a conjunction

con·junc·ti·vi·tis \kən-ˌjəŋk-ti-ˈvī-təs\ *n* : inflammation of the conjunctiva

con·junc·ture \kən-ˈjəŋk-chər\ *n* **1** : CONJUNCTION, UNION **2** : JUNCTURE 3

con·jun·to \kōn-ˈhün-tō\ *n* : Mexican-American music influenced by the music of German immigrants to Texas

con·jure \ˈkän-jər, ˈkən- *for 1, 2;* kən-ˈju̇r *for 3*\ *vb* **con·jured; con·jur·ing** **1** : to implore earnestly or solemnly **2** : to practice magic; *esp* : to summon (as a devil) by sorcery **3** : to practice sleight of hand — **con·ju·ra·tion** \ˌkän-ju̇-ˈrā-shən, ˌkən-\ *n* — **con·jur·er** *or* **con·ju·ror** \ˈkän-jər-ər, ˈkən-\ *n*

conk \ˈkäŋk\ *vb* : BREAK DOWN; *esp* : STALL ⟨the motor ~*ed* out⟩

Conn *abbr* Connecticut

con·nect \kə-ˈnekt\ *vb* **1** : JOIN, LINK **2** : to associate in one's mind **3** : to establish a communications connection ⟨~ to the Internet⟩ — **con·nect·able** *adj* — **con·nec·tor** *n*

con·nec·tion \kə-ˈnek-shən\ *n* **1** : JUNCTION, UNION **2** : logical relationship : COHERENCE; *esp* : relation of a word to other words in a sentence **3** : family relationship **4** : BOND, LINK **5** : a person related by blood or marriage **6** : relationship in social affairs or in business **7** : an association of persons; *esp* : a religious denomination **8** : a means of communication or transport ⟨a telephone ~⟩

[1]**con·nec·tive** \kə-ˈnek-tiv\ *adj* : serving to connect — **con·nec·tiv·i·ty** \ˌkä-ˌnek-ˈti-və-tē\ *n*

[2]**connective** *n* : a word (as a conjunction) that connects words or word groups

connective tissue *n* : a tissue (as bone or cartilage) that forms a supporting framework for the body or its parts

con·nex·ion *chiefly Brit var of* CONNECTION

con·ning tower \ˈkä-niŋ-\ *n* : a raised structure on the deck of a submarine

con·nip·tion \kə-ˈnip-shən\ *n* : a fit of rage, hysteria, or alarm

con·nive \kə-ˈnīv\ *vb* **con·nived**; **con·niv·ing** [F or L; F *conniver,* fr. L *conivēre* to close the eyes, connive] **1** : to pretend ignorance of something one ought to oppose as wrong **2** : to cooperate secretly : give secret aid — **con·niv·ance** *n* — **con·niv·er** *n*

con·nois·seur \ˌkä-nə-ˈsər\ *n* : a critical judge in matters of art or taste

con·no·ta·tion \ˌkä-nə-ˈtā-shən\ *n* : a meaning in addition to or apart from the thing explicitly named or described by a word

con·no·ta·tive \ˈkä-nə-ˌtā-tiv, kə-ˈnō-tə-\ *adj* **1** : connoting or tending to connote **2** : relating to connotation

con·note \kə-ˈnōt\ *vb* **con·not·ed**; **con·not·ing** : to suggest or mean as a connotation

con·nu·bi·al \kə-ˈnü-bē-əl, -ˈnyü-\ *adj* : of or relating to marriage : CONJUGAL

con·quer \ˈkäŋ-kər\ *vb* **1** : to gain by force of arms : WIN **2** : to get the better of : OVERCOME ♦ ***Synonyms*** DEFEAT, SUBJUGATE, SUBDUE, OVERTHROW, VANQUISH — **con·quer·or** \-ər\ *n*

con·quest \ˈkän-ˌkwest, ˈkäŋ-\ *n* **1** : an act of conquering : VICTORY **2** : something conquered

con·quis·ta·dor \kȯŋ-ˈkēs-tə-ˌdȯr, kän-ˈkwis-\ *n, pl* **-do·res** \-ˌkēs-tə-ˈdȯr-ēz, -ˌkwis-\ *or* **-dors** : CONQUEROR; *esp* : a leader in the Spanish conquest of the Americas in the 16th century

cons *abbr* consonant

con·san·guin·i·ty \ˌkän-ˌsan-ˈgwi-nə-tē, -ˌsaŋ-\ *n, pl* **-ties** : blood relationship — **con·san·guin·e·ous** \-nē-əs\ *adj*

con·science \ˈkän-chəns\ *n* : consciousness of the moral right and wrong of one's own acts or motives — **con·science·less** *adj*

con·sci·en·tious \ˌkän-chē-ˈen-chəs\ *adj* : guided by one's own sense of right and wrong ♦ ***Synonyms*** SCRUPULOUS, HONORABLE, HONEST, UPRIGHT, JUST — **con·sci·en·tious·ly** *adv*

conscientious objector *n* : a person who refuses to serve in the armed forces or to bear arms on moral or religious grounds

[1]**con·scious** \ˈkän-chəs\ *adj* **1** : AWARE **2** : known or felt by one's inner self **3** : mentally awake or alert : not asleep or unconscious **4** : done with awareness or purpose ⟨a ~ decision⟩ — **con·scious·ly** *adv* — **con·scious·ness** *n*

[2]**conscious** *n* : the upper level of mental life of which a person is aware : CONSCIOUSNESS

con·script \kən-ˈskript\ *vb* : to enroll by compulsion for military or naval service — **conscript** \ˈkän-ˌskript\ *n* — **con·scrip·tion** \kən-ˈskrip-shən\ *n*

con·se·crate \ˈkän-sə-ˌkrāt\ *vb* **-crat·ed**; **-crat·ing** [ME, fr. L *consecratus,* pp. of *consecrare,* fr. *com-* together + *sacrare* to set aside as sacred, fr. *sacer* sacred] **1** : to induct (as a bishop) into an office with a religious rite **2** : to make or declare sacred ⟨~ a church⟩ **3** : to devote solemnly to a purpose — **con·se·cra·tion** \ˌkän-sə-ˈkrā-shən\ *n*

con·sec·u·tive \kən-ˈse-kyə-tiv\ *adj* : following in regular order : SUCCESSIVE — **con·sec·u·tive·ly** *adv*

con·sen·su·al \kən-ˈsen-chə-wəl\ *adj* : involving or based on mutual consent

con·sen·sus \kən-ˈsen-səs\ *n* **1** : agreement in opinion, testimony, or belief **2** : collective opinion

[1]**con·sent** \kən-ˈsent\ *vb* : to give assent or approval ⟨~*ed* to the marriage⟩

[2]**consent** *n* : approval or acceptance of something done or proposed by another

con·se·quence \ˈkän-sə-ˌkwens\ *n* **1** : RESULT **2** : IMPORTANCE ♦ ***Synonyms*** EFFECT, OUTCOME, AFTERMATH, UPSHOT

con·se·quent \-kwənt, -ˌkwent\ *adj* : following as a result or effect

con·se·quen·tial \ˌkän-sə-ˈkwen-chəl\ *adj* **1** : having significant consequences **2** : showing self-importance

con·se·quent·ly \ˈkän-sə-ˌkwent-lē, -kwənt-\ *adv* : as a result : ACCORDINGLY

con·ser·van·cy \kən-ˈsər-vən-sē\ *n, pl* **-cies** : an organization or area designated to conserve natural resources

con·ser·va·tion \ˌkän-sər-ˈvā-shən\ *n* : PRESERVATION; *esp* : planned management of natural resources

con·ser·va·tion·ist \-shə-nist\ *n* : a person who advocates conservation esp. of natural resources

con·ser·va·tism \kən-ˈsər-və-ˌti-zəm\ *n* : disposition to keep to established ways : opposition to change

[1]**con·ser·va·tive** \kən-ˈsər-və-tiv\ *adj* **1** : PRESERVATIVE **2** : disposed to maintain existing views, conditions, or institutions **3** : MODERATE, CAUTIOUS ⟨a ~ investment⟩ — **con·ser·va·tive·ly** *adv*

[2]**conservative** *n* : a person who is conservative esp. in politics

con·ser·va·tor \kən-ˈsər-və-tər, ˈkän-sər-ˌvā-\ *n* **1** : PROTECTOR, GUARDIAN **2** : one named by a court to protect the interests of an incompetent (as a child)

con·ser·va·to·ry \kən-ˈsər-və-ˌtȯr-ē\ *n, pl* **-ries** **1** : GREENHOUSE **2** : a place of instruction in one of the fine arts (as music)

[1]**con·serve** \kən-ˈsərv\ *vb* **con·served**; **con·serv·ing** : to keep from losing or wasting : PRESERVE ⟨~ energy⟩

[2]**con·serve** \ˈkän-ˌsərv\ *n* **1** : CONFEC-

TION 2; *esp* : a candied fruit **2** : PRESERVE; *esp* : one prepared from a mixture of fruits

con·sid·er \kən-ˈsi-dər\ *vb* [ME, fr. AF *considerer,* fr. L *considerare* to observe, think about, fr. *com-* together + *sider-, sidus* heavenly body] **1** : THINK, PONDER **2** : HEED, REGARD **3** : JUDGE, BELIEVE — **con·sid·ered** *adj*

con·sid·er·able \-ˈsi-dər-ə-bəl, -ˈsi-drə-bəl\ *adj* **1** : IMPORTANT **2** : large in extent, amount, or degree — **con·sid·er·ably** \-blē\ *adv*

con·sid·er·ate \kən-ˈsi-də-rət\ *adj* : observant of the rights and feelings of others ♦ ***Synonyms*** THOUGHTFUL, ATTENTIVE

con·sid·er·ation \kən-ˌsi-də-ˈrā-shən\ *n* **1** : careful thought : DELIBERATION **2** : a matter taken into account **3** : thoughtful attention **4** : JUDGMENT, OPINION **5** : RECOMPENSE

con·sid·er·ing \-ˈsi-d(ə-)riŋ\ *prep* : in view of : taking into account ⟨did well ~ his limitations⟩

con·sign \kən-ˈsīn\ *vb* **1** : ENTRUST, COMMIT **2** : to deliver formally **3** : to send (goods) to an agent for sale — **con·sign·ee** \ˌkän-sə-ˈnē, -ˌsī-; kən-ˌsī-\ *n* — **con·sign·or** \ˌkän-sə-ˈnȯr, -ˌsī-; kən-ˌsī-\ *n*

con·sign·ment \kən-ˈsīn-mənt\ *n* : something consigned esp. in a single shipment

con·sil·ience \kən-ˈsil-yəns\ *n* : the linking together of principles from different disciplines when forming a comprehensive theory

con·sist \kən-ˈsist\ *vb* **1** : to be inherent : LIE — usu. used with *in* **2** : to be composed or made up — usu. used with *of*

con·sis·tence \kən-ˈsis-təns\ *n* : CONSISTENCY

con·sis·ten·cy \-tən-sē\ *n, pl* **-cies** **1** : COHESIVENESS, FIRMNESS **2** : agreement or harmony in parts or of different things **3** : UNIFORMITY ⟨~ of behavior⟩ — **con·sis·tent** \-tənt\ *adj* — **con·sis·tent·ly** *adv*

con·sis·to·ry \kən-ˈsis-tə-rē\ *n, pl* **-ries** : a solemn assembly (as of Roman Catholic cardinals)

consol *abbr* consolidated

[1]**con·sole** \ˈkän-ˌsōl\ *n* [F] **1** : the desklike part of an organ at which the organist sits **2** : the combination of displays and controls of a device or system **3** : a cabinet for a radio or television set resting directly on the floor **4** : a small storage cabinet between bucket seats in an automobile

[2]**con·sole** \kən-ˈsōl\ *vb* **con·soled; con·sol·ing** : to soothe the grief of : COMFORT, SOLACE — **con·so·la·tion** \ˌkän-sə-ˈlā-shən\ *n* — **con·so·la·to·ry** \kən-ˈsō-lə-ˌtȯr-ē, -ˈsä-\ *adj*

con·sol·i·date \kən-ˈsä-lə-ˌdāt\ *vb* **-dat·ed; -dat·ing** **1** : to unite or become united into one whole : COMBINE **2** : to make firm or secure **3** : to form into a compact mass — **con·sol·i·da·tion** \-ˌsä-lə-ˈdā-shən\ *n* — **con·sol·i·da·tor** \-ˈsä-lə-ˌdā-tər\ *n*

con·som·mé \ˌkän-sə-ˈmā\ *n* [F] : a clear soup made from well-seasoned stock

con·so·nance \ˈkän-sə-nəns\ *n* **1** : AGREEMENT, HARMONY **2** : repetition of consonants esp. as an alternative to rhyme in verse

[1]**con·so·nant** \-nənt\ *adj* : having consonance, harmony, or agreement ♦ ***Synonyms*** CONSISTENT, COMPATIBLE, CONGRUOUS, CONGENIAL, SYMPATHETIC — **con·so·nant·ly** *adv*

[2]**consonant** *n* **1** : a speech sound (as \p\, \g\, \n\, \l\, \s\, \r\) characterized by constriction or closure at one or more points in the breath channel **2** : a letter other than *a, e, i, o,* and *u* — **con·so·nan·tal** \ˌkän-sə-ˈnan-tᵊl\ *adj*

[1]**con·sort** \ˈkän-ˌsȯrt\ *n* **1** : a ship accompanying another **2** : SPOUSE, MATE

[2]**con·sort** \kən-ˈsȯrt\ *vb* **1** : to keep company **2** : ACCORD, HARMONIZE

con·sor·tium \kən-ˈsȯr-shəm; -shē-əm, -tē-\ *n, pl* **-sor·tia** \-shə-; -shē-ə, -tē-\ [L, fellowship] : an agreement or combination (as of companies) formed to undertake a large enterprise

con·spec·tus \kən-ˈspek-təs\ *n* **1** : a brief survey or summary **2** : SUMMARY

con·spic·u·ous \kən-ˈspi-kyə-wəs\ *adj* : attracting attention : PROMINENT, STRIKING ♦ ***Synonyms*** NOTICEABLE, REMARKABLE, OUTSTANDING — **con·spic·u·ous·ly** *adv*

con·spir·a·cy \kən-ˈspir-ə-sē\ *n, pl* **-cies** : an agreement among conspirators : PLOT

con·spir·a·tor \kən-ˈspir-ə-tər\ *n* : one who conspires — **con·spir·a·to·ri·al** \-ˌspir-ə-ˈtȯr-ē-əl\ *adj*

con·spire \kən-ˈspī(-ə)r\ *vb* **conspired; con·spir·ing** [ME, fr. AF *conspirer,* fr. L *conspirare* to be in harmony, conspire, fr. *com-* together + *spirare* to breathe] : to plan secretly an unlawful act : PLOT

const *abbr* **1** constant **2** constitution; constitutional

con·sta·ble \ˈkän-stə-bəl, ˈkən-\ *n* [ME *conestable,* fr. AF, fr. LL *comes stabuli,* lit., officer of the stable] : a public officer responsible for keeping the peace

con·stab·u·lary \kən-ˈsta-byə-ˌler-ē\ *n, pl* **-lar·ies** **1** : the police of a particular district or country **2** : a police force organized like the military

con·stan·cy \ˈkän-stən-sē\ *n, pl* **-cies** **1** : firmness of mind **2** : STABILITY

[1]**con·stant** \-stənt\ *adj* **1** : STEADFAST, FAITHFUL ⟨~ friends⟩ **2** : FIXED, UNCHANGING ⟨a ~ flow⟩ **3** : continually recurring : REGULAR ⟨a ~ annoyance⟩ — **con·stant·ly** *adv*

[2]**constant** *n* : something unchanging

con·stel·la·tion \ˌkän-stə-ˈlā-shən\ *n* **1** : any of 88 groups of stars forming patterns **2** : a group of usu. related persons, qualities, or things

con·ster·na·tion \ˌkän-stər-ˈnā-shən\ *n* : amazed dismay and confusion

con·sti·pa·tion \ˌkän-stə-ˈpā-shən\ *n* : abnormally difficult or infrequent bowel movements — **con·sti·pate** \ˈkän-stə-ˌpāt\ *vb*

con·stit·u·en·cy \kən-ˈsti-chə-wən-sē\ *n, pl* **-cies** : a body of constituents; *also* : an electoral district

[1]**con·stit·u·ent** \-wənt\ *n* **1** : a person entitled to vote for a representative for a district **2** : a component part

[2]**constituent** *adj* **1** : COMPONENT ⟨~ parts⟩ **2** : having power to create a government or frame or amend a constitution

con·sti·tute \ˈkän-stə-ˌtüt, -ˌtyüt\ *vb* **-tut·ed; -tut·ing** **1** : to appoint to an office or duty **2** : SET UP, ESTABLISH ⟨~ a law⟩ **3** : MAKE UP, COMPOSE

con·sti·tu·tion \ˌkän-stə-ˈtü-shən, -ˈtyü-\ *n* **1** : an established law or custom **2** : the physical makeup of the individual **3** : the structure, composition, or makeup of something ⟨~ of the sun⟩ **4** : the basic law in a politically organized body; *also* : a document containing such law

[1]**con·sti·tu·tion·al** \-shə-nəl\ *adj* **1** : of or relating to the constitution of body or mind **2** : being in accord with the constitution of a state or society; *also* : of or relating to such a constitution — **con·sti·tu·tion·al·ly** *adv*

[2]**constitutional** *n* : a walk taken for one's health

con·sti·tu·tion·al·i·ty \-ˌtü-shə-ˈna-lə-tē, -ˌtyü-\ *n* : the quality or state of being constitutional

con·sti·tu·tive \ˈkän-stə-ˌtü-tiv, -tyü-, kən-ˈsti-chə-tiv\ *adj* **1** : CONSTRUCTIVE **2** : CONSTITUENT, ESSENTIAL

constr *abbr* construction

con·strain \kən-ˈstrān\ *vb* **1** : COMPEL, FORCE **2** : CONFINE **3** : RESTRAIN

con·straint \-ˈstrānt\ *n* **1** : COMPULSION; *also* : RESTRAINT **2** : repression of one's natural feelings

con·strict \kən-ˈstrikt\ *vb* : to draw together : SQUEEZE — **con·stric·tion** \-ˈstrik-shən\ *n* — **con·stric·tive** \-ˈstrik-tiv\ *adj*

con·stric·tor \kən-ˈstrik-tər\ *n* : a snake that coils around and compresses its prey

con·struct \kən-ˈstrəkt\ *vb* : BUILD, MAKE — **con·struc·tor** \-ˈstrək-tər\ *n*

con·struc·tion \kən-ˈstrək-shən\ *n* **1** : INTERPRETATION **2** : the art, process, or manner of building; *also* : something built, created, or established : STRUCTURE **3** : syntactical arrangement of words in a sentence — **con·struc·tive** \-tiv\ *adj*

con·struc·tion·ist \-shə-nist\ *n* : a person who construes a legal document (as the U.S. Constitution) in a specific way ⟨a strict ~⟩

con·strue \kən-ˈstrü\ *vb* **con·strued; con·stru·ing** **1** : to analyze the mutual relations of words in a sentence; *also* : TRANSLATE **2** : EXPLAIN, INTERPRET ⟨*construed* the act as hostile⟩ — **con·stru·able** *adj* — **con·stru·al** \-ˈstrü-əl\ *n*

con·sub·stan·ti·a·tion \ˌkän-səb-ˌstan-chē-ˈā-shən\ *n* : the actual substantial presence and combination of the body and blood of Christ with the eucharistic bread and wine

con·sul \ˈkän-səl\ *n* **1** : a chief magistrate of the Roman republic **2** : a government official who resides in a foreign country to care for the commercial interests of the appointing government's citizens — **con·sul·ar** \-sə-lər\ *adj* — **con·sul·ate** \-lət\ *n* — **con·sul·ship** *n*

con·sult \kən-ˈsəlt\ *vb* **1** : to ask the advice or opinion of **2** : CONFER — **con·sul·tant** \-ˈsəl-tᵊnt\ *n* — **con·sul·ta·tion** \ˌkän-səl-ˈtā-shən\ *n*

con·sume \kən-ˈsüm\ *vb* **con·sumed; con·sum·ing** **1** : DESTROY ⟨*consumed* by fire⟩ **2** : to spend wastefully **3** : to eat up : DEVOUR **4** : to absorb the attention of : ENGROSS ⟨*consumed* with jealousy⟩ **5** : to utilize as a customer — **con·sum·able** *adj* — **con·sum·er** *n*

con·sum·er·ism \kən-ˈsü-mə-ˌri-zəm\ *n* : the promotion of consumers' interests (as against false advertising)

consumer price index *n* : an index measuring the change in the cost of widely purchased goods and services from the cost in some base period

[1]**con·sum·mate** \ˈkän-sə-mət, kən-ˈsə\ *adj* : PERFECT ⟨a ~ team player⟩ ♦ ***Synonyms*** FINISHED, ACCOMPLISHED

[2]**con·sum·mate** \ˈkän-sə-ˌmāt\ *vb* **-mat·ed; -mat·ing** : to make complete : FINISH, ACHIEVE — **con·sum·ma·tion** \ˌkän-sə-ˈmā-shən\ *n*

con·sump·tion \kən-ˈsəmp-shən\ *n* **1** : progressive bodily wasting away; *also* : TUBERCULOSIS **2** : the act of consuming or using up **3** : the use of economic goods

[1]**con·sump·tive** \-ˈsəmp-tiv\ *adj* **1** : tending to consume **2** : relating to or affected with consumption

[2]**consumptive** *n* : a person who has consumption

cont *abbr* **1** containing **2** contents **3** continent; continental **4** continued **5** control

[1]**con·tact** \ˈkän-ˌtakt\ *n* **1** : a touching or meeting of bodies **2** : ASSOCIATION, RELATIONSHIP; *also* : CONNECTION, COMMUNICATION **3** : a person serving as a go-between or source of information **4** : CONTACT LENS — **con·tact·less** *adj*

[2]**contact** *vb* **1** : to come or bring into contact : TOUCH **2** : to get in communication with ⟨~*ed* his lawyer⟩

contact lens *n* : a thin lens fitting over the cornea usu. to correct vision

con·ta·gion \kən-ˈtā-jən\ *n* [ME, fr. L *contagio*, fr. *contingere* to have contact with, pollute, fr. *com-* together + *tangere* to touch] **1** : a contagious disease; *also* : the transmission of such a disease **2** : a disease-producing agent (as a virus) **3** : transmission of an influence on the mind or emotions

con·ta·gious \-jəs\ *adj* **1** : able to be passed by contact between individuals ⟨colds are ~⟩ ⟨~ disease⟩; *also* : capable of passing on a contagious disease **2** : communicated or transmitted like a contagious disease; *esp* : exciting similar emotion or conduct in others

con·tain \kən-ˈtān\ *vb* **1** : RESTRAIN **2** : to have within : HOLD **3** : COMPRISE, INCLUDE — **con·tain·able** \-ˈtā-nə-bəl\ *adj* — **con·tain·ment** \-ˈtān-mənt\ *n*

con·tain·er \kən-ˈtā-nər\ *n* : RECEPTACLE

con·tam·i·nant \kən-ˈta-mə-nənt\ *n* : something that contaminates

con·tam·i·nate \kən-ˈta-mə-ˌnāt\ *vb* **-nat·ed; -nat·ing** : to soil, stain, or infect by contact or association — **con·tam·i·na·tion** \-ˌta-mə-ˈnā-shən\ *n*

contd *abbr* continued

con·temn \kən-ˈtem\ *vb* : to view or treat with contempt : DESPISE

con·tem·plate \ˈkän-təm-ˌplāt\ *vb* **-plat·ed; -plat·ing** [L *contemplari,* fr. *com-* with + *templum* space marked out for observation of auguries] **1** : to view or consider with continued attention **2** : INTEND — **con·tem·pla·tion** \ˌkän-təm-ˈplā-shən\ *n* — **con·tem·pla·tive** \kən-ˈtem-plə-tiv, ˈkän-təm-ˌplā-\ *adj*

con·tem·po·ra·ne·ous \kən-ˌtem-pə-ˈrā-nē-əs\ *adj* : CONTEMPORARY 1

con·tem·po·rary \kən-ˈtem-pə-ˌrer-ē\ *adj* **1** : occurring or existing at the same time **2** : marked by characteristics of the present period — **contemporary** *n*

con·tempt \kən-ˈtempt\ *n* **1** : the act of despising : the state of mind of one who despises **2** : the state of being despised **3** : disobedience to or open disrespect of a court or legislature

con·tempt·ible \kən-ˈtemp-tə-bəl\ *adj* : deserving contempt : DESPICABLE — **con·tempt·ibly** \-blē\ *adv*

con·temp·tu·ous \-ˈtemp-chə-wəs\ *adj* : feeling or expressing contempt — **con·temp·tu·ous·ly** *adv*

con·tend \kən-ˈtend\ *vb* **1** : to strive against rivals or difficulties **2** : ARGUE **3** : MAINTAIN, ASSERT — **con·tend·er** *n*

[1]**con·tent** \kən-ˈtent\ *adj* : SATISFIED

[2]**content** *vb* : SATISFY; *esp* : to limit (oneself) in requirements or actions

[3]**content** *n* : CONTENTMENT ⟨ate to his heart's ~⟩

[4]**con·tent** \ˈkän-ˌtent\ *n* **1** : something contained ⟨~*s* of a room⟩ **2** : subject matter or topics treated (as in a book) **3** : material (as text or music) offered by a website **4** : MEANING, SIGNIFICANCE **5** : the amount of material contained

con·tent·ed \kən-ˈten-təd\ *adj* : SATISFIED — **con·tent·ed·ly** *adv* — **con·tent·ed·ness** *n*

con·ten·tion \kən-ˈten-chən\ *n* **1** : CONTEST, STRIFE **2** : an idea or point for which a person argues — **con·ten·tious** \-chəs\ *adj* — **con·ten·tious·ly** *adv*

con·tent·ment \kən-ˈtent-mənt\ *n* : ease of mind : SATISFACTION

con·ter·mi·nous \kän-ˈtər-mə-nəs\ *adj* : having the same or a common boundary — **con·ter·mi·nous·ly** *adv*

[1]**con·test** \kən-ˈtest\ *vb* **1** : to engage in a struggle or competition : COMPETE, VIE **2** : CHALLENGE, DISPUTE ⟨~ the accusations⟩ — **con·tes·tant** \-ˈtes-tənt\ *n*

[2]**con·test** \ˈkän-ˌtest\ *n* : STRUGGLE, COMPETITION

con·text \ˈkän-ˌtekst\ *n* [ME, fr. L *contextus* connection of words, coherence, fr. *contexere* to weave together] : the parts of a discourse that surround a word or passage and help to explain its meaning; *also* : the circumstances surrounding an act or event ⟨the ~ of the war⟩ — **con·tex·tu·al·ly** *adv*

con·tig·u·ous \kən-ˈti-gyə-wəs\ *adj* : being in contact : TOUCHING ⟨the 48 ~ states⟩; *also* : NEXT, ADJOINING — **con·ti·gu·i·ty** \ˌkän-tə-ˈgyü-ə-tē\ *n*

con·ti·nence \ˈkän-tə-nəns\ *n* **1** : SELF-RESTRAINT; *esp* : a refraining from sexual intercourse **2** : the ability to retain urine or feces voluntarily

[1]**con·ti·nent** \ˈkän-tə-nənt\ *adj* : exercising continence

[2]**continent** *n* **1** : any of the great divisions of land on the globe **2** *cap* : the continent of Europe

[1]**con·ti·nen·tal** \ˌkän-tə-ˈnen-tᵊl\ *adj* **1** : of or relating to a continent; *esp, often cap* : of or relating to the continent of Europe **2** *often cap* : of or relating to the colonies later forming the U.S. **3** : of or relating to cuisine based on classical European cooking

[2]**continental** *n* **1** *often cap* : a soldier in the Continental army **2** : EUROPEAN

continental drift *n* : a slow movement of the continents over a fluid layer deep within the earth

continental shelf *n* : a shallow submarine plain forming a border to a continent

continental slope *n* : a comparatively steep slope from a continental shelf to the ocean floor

con·tin·gen·cy \kən-ˈtin-jən-sē\ *n, pl* **-cies** : a chance or possible event

[1]**con·tin·gent** \-jənt\ *adj* **1** : liable but not certain to happen : POSSIBLE **2** : happening by chance : not planned **3** : dependent on something that may or may not occur **4** : CONDITIONAL ♦ ***Synonyms*** ACCIDENTAL, CASUAL, INCIDENTAL, ODD

[2]**contingent** *n* : a quota (as of troops) supplied from an area or group

con·tin·u·al \kən-ˈtin-yə-wəl\ *adj* **1** : CONTINUOUS, UNBROKEN **2** : steadily recurring — **con·tin·u·al·ly** *adv*

con·tin·u·ance \-yə-wəns\ *n* **1** : unbroken succession **2** : the extent of continuing : DURATION **3** : adjournment of legal proceedings

con·tin·u·a·tion \kən-ˌtin-yə-ˈwā-shən\ *n* **1** : extension or prolongation of a state or activity **2** : resumption after an interruption; *also* : something that carries on after a pause or break

con·tin·ue \kən-ˈtin-yü\ *vb* **-tin·ued; -tinu·ing** **1** : to maintain without interruption **2** : ENDURE, LAST ⟨the tradition ~*s*⟩ **3** : to remain in a place or condition ⟨~ at this job⟩ **4** : to resume (as a story) after an intermission **5** : EXTEND ⟨~ a subscription⟩; *also* : to persist in ⟨will ~ to remind you⟩ **6** : to allow to remain **7** : to keep (a legal case) on the calendar or undecided

con·ti·nu·i·ty \ˌkän-tə-ˈnü-ə-tē, -ˈnyü-\ *n, pl* **-ties** **1** : the state of being continuous **2** : something (as a film script) that has or provides continuity

con·tin·u·ous \kən-ˈtin-yə-wəs\ *adj* : continuing without interruption — **con·tin·u·ous·ly** *adv*

con·tin·u·um \-yə-wəm\ *n, pl* **-ua** \-yə-wə\ *also* **-u·ums** : something that is the same throughout or consists of a series of variations or of a sequence of things in regular order

con·tort \kən-ˈtȯrt\ *vb* : to twist out of shape ⟨a ~*ed* face⟩ ⟨~ the truth⟩ — **con·tor·tion** \-ˈtȯr-shən\ *n*

con·tor·tion·ist \-ˈtȯr-shə-nist\ *n* : an acrobat able to twist the body into unusual postures

con·tour \ˈkän-ˌtu̇r\ *n* [F, fr. It *contorno* fr. *contornare* to round off, fr. ML, to turn around, fr. L *com-* together + *tornare* to turn on a lathe, fr. *tornus* lathe] **1** : OUTLINE **2** : SHAPE, FORM — often used in pl. ⟨the ~*s* of a statue⟩

contr *abbr* contract; contraction

con·tra·band \ˈkän-trə-ˌband\ *n* : goods legally prohibited in trade; *also* : smuggled goods

con·tra·cep·tion \ˌkän-trə-ˈsep-shən\ *n* : intentional prevention of conception and pregnancy — **con·tra·cep·tive** \-ˈsep-tive\ *adj or n*

1**con·tract** \ˈkän-ˌtrakt\ *n* **1** : a binding agreement; *also* : a document stating its terms **2** : an undertaking to win a specified number of tricks in bridge — **contract** *adj* — **con·trac·tu·al** \kən-ˈtrak-chə-wəl\ *adj* — **con·trac·tu·al·ly** *adv*

2**con·tract** \kən-ˈtrakt, *2 usu* ˈkän-ˌtrakt\ *vb* **1** : to become affected with ⟨~ a disease⟩ **2** : to establish or undertake by contract **3** : SHRINK, LESSEN; *esp* : to draw together esp. so as to shorten ⟨~ a muscle⟩ **4** : to shorten (a word) by omitting letters or sounds in the middle — **con·tract·ible** \kən-ˈtrak-tə-bəl, ˈkän-ˌ\ *adj* — **con·trac·tion** \kən-ˈtrak-shən\ *n* — **con·trac·tor** \ˈkän-ˌtrak-tər, kən-ˈtrak-\ *n*

con·trac·tile \kən-ˈtrak-t^{ə}l\ *adj* : able to contract — **con·trac·til·i·ty** \ˌkän-ˌtrak-ˈti-lə-tē\ *n*

con·tra·dict \ˌkän-trə-ˈdikt\ *vb* : to assert the contrary of : deny the truth of ⟨~ a rumor⟩ — **con·tra·dic·tion** \-ˈdik-shən\ *n* — **con·tra·dic·to·ry** \-ˈdik-tə-rē\ *adj*

con·tra·dis·tinc·tion \ˌkän-trə-dis-ˈtiŋk-shən\ *n* : distinction by contrast

con·trail \ˈkän-ˌtrāl\ *n* : a streak of condensed water vapor created by an airplane or rocket at high altitudes

con·tra·in·di·cate \ˌkän-trə-ˈin-də-ˌkāt\ *vb* : to make (a treatment or procedure) inadvisable — **con·tra·in·di·ca·tion** \-ˌin-də-ˈkā-shən\ *n*

con·tral·to \kən-ˈtral-tō\ *n, pl* **-tos** : the lowest female voice; *also* : a singer having such a voice

con·trap·tion \kən-ˈtrap-shən\ *n* : CONTRIVANCE, DEVICE

con·tra·pun·tal \ˌkän-trə-ˈpən-t^{ə}l\ *adj* : of or relating to counterpoint

con·tra·ri·ety \ˌkän-trə-ˈrī-ə-tē\ *n, pl* **-eties** : the state of being contrary : DISAGREEMENT, INCONSISTENCY

con·trari·wise \ˈkän-ˌtrer-ē-ˌwīz, kən-ˈtrer-\ *adv* **1** : on the contrary **2** : VICE VERSA

con·trary \ˈkän-ˌtrer-ē; *4 often* kən-ˈtrer-ē\ *adj* **1** : opposite in nature or position **2** : COUNTER, OPPOSED **3** : UNFAVORABLE — used of wind or weather **4** : unwilling to accept control or advice — **con·trar·i·an** \kən-ˈtrer-ē-ən, kän-\ *n or adj* — **con·trari·ly** \ˈkän-ˌtrer-ə-lē, kən-ˈtrer-\ *adv* — **con·trary** *n is* ˈkän-ˌtrer-ē, *adv is like adj*\ *n or adv*

1**con·trast** \kən-ˈtrast\ *vb* [F *contraster,* fr. MF, to oppose, resist, fr. VL **contrastare,* fr. L *contra-* against + *stare* to stand] **1** : to show differences when compared **2** : to compare in such a way as to show differences

2**con·trast** \ˈkän-ˌtrast\ *n* **1** : diversity of adjacent parts in color, emotion, tone, or brightness **2** : unlikeness as shown when things are compared : DIFFERENCE

con·tra·vene \ˌkän-trə-ˈvēn\ *vb* **-vened; -ven·ing** **1** : to go or act contrary to ⟨~ a law⟩ **2** : CONTRADICT ⟨~ a claim⟩

con·tre·temps \ˈkän-trə-ˌtä^{n}, kō^{n}-trə-ˈtä^{n}\ *n, pl* **con·tre·temps** \-ˌtä^{n}, -ˌtä^{n}z\ [F] : an inopportune or embarrassing occurrence

contrib *abbr* contribution; contributor

con·trib·ute \kən-ˈtri-byət\ *vb* **-ut·ed; -ut·ing** **1** : to give along with others (as to a fund); *also* : HELP, ASSIST **2** : to supply (something, as an article) for a publication — **con·tri·bu·tion** \ˌkän-trə-ˈbyü-shən\ *n* — **con·trib·u·tor** \kən-ˈtri-byə-tər\ *n* — **con·trib·u·to·ry** \-byə-ˌtȯr-ē\ *adj*

con·trite \ˈkän-ˌtrīt, kən-ˈtrīt\ *adj* : PENITENT, REPENTANT — **con·trite·ly** *adv* — **con·tri·tion** \kən-ˈtri-shən\ *n*

con·triv·ance \kən-ˈtrī-vəns\ *n* **1** : a mechanical device **2** : SCHEME, PLAN

con·trive \kən-ˈtrīv\ *vb* **con·trived; con·triv·ing** **1** : PLAN, DEVISE **2** : FRAME, MAKE **3** : to bring about with difficulty — **con·triv·er** *n*

con·trived \-ˈtrīvd\ *adj* : lacking in natural quality ⟨a ~ plot⟩

1**con·trol** \kən-ˈtrōl\ *vb* **con·trolled; con·trol·ling** [ME *countrollen* to verify, fr. AF *countrerouler,* fr. *countreroule* copy of an account, audit, fr. ML *contrarotulus,* fr. L *contra* against + ML *rotulus* roll] **1** : to exercise restraining or directing influence over : REGULATE **2** : DOMINATE, RULE — **con·trol·la·ble** \-ˈtrō-lə-bəl\ *adj*

2**control** *n* **1** : power to direct or regulate **2** : RESERVE, RESTRAINT **3** : a device for regulating a mechanism

con·trol·ler \kən-ˈtrō-lər, ˈkän-ˌtrō-lər\ *n* **1** : COMPTROLLER **2** : a person or thing that controls ⟨an air traffic ~⟩ ⟨a game ~⟩

con·tro·ver·sy \ˈkän-trə-ˌvər-sē\ *n, pl* **-sies** : a clash of opposing views : DISPUTE — **con·tro·ver·sial** \ˌkän-trə-ˈvər-shəl, -sē-əl\ *adj*

con·tro·vert \ˈkän-trə-ˌvərt, ˌkän-trə-ˈvərt\ *vb* : DENY, CONTRADICT ⟨~ an allegation⟩ — **con·tro·vert·ible** *adj*
con·tu·ma·cious \ˌkän-tü-ˈmā-shəs, -tyü-\ *adj* : stubbornly disobedient ♦ ***Synonyms*** REBELLIOUS, INSUBORDINATE, SEDITIOUS — **con·tu·ma·cy** \kən-ˈtü-mə-sē, -ˈtyü-; ˈkän-tyə-\ *n* — **con·tu·ma·cious·ly** *adv*
con·tu·me·ly \kən-ˈtü-mə-lē, -ˈtyü-; ˈkän-tə-ˌmē-lē, -tyə-\ *n, pl* **-lies** : contemptuous treatment : INSULT
con·tu·sion \kən-ˈtü-zhən, -ˈtyü-\ *n* : BRUISE — **con·tuse** \-ˈtüz, -ˈtyüz\ *vb*
co·nun·drum \kə-ˈnən-drəm\ *n* : RIDDLE
conv *abbr* **1** convention **2** convertible
con·va·lesce \ˌkän-və-ˈles\ *vb* **-lesced; -lesc·ing** : to recover health gradually — **con·va·les·cence** \-ˈle-sᵊns\ *n* — **con·va·les·cent** \-sᵊnt\ *adj or n*
con·vec·tion \kən-ˈvek-shən\ *n* : circulatory motion in a fluid due to warmer portions rising and cooler denser portions sinking; *also* : the transfer of heat by such motion — **con·vec·tion·al** \-shə-nəl\ *adj* — **con·vec·tive** \-ˈvek-tiv\ *adj*
convection oven *n* : an oven with a fan that circulates hot air uniformly and continuously around the food
con·vene \kən-ˈvēn\ *vb* **con·vened; con·ven·ing** : ASSEMBLE, MEET
con·ve·nience \kən-ˈvē-nyəns\ *n* **1** : SUITABLENESS **2** : a laborsaving device **3** : a suitable time ⟨at your ~⟩ **4** : personal comfort : EASE
convenience store *n* : a small market that is open long hours
con·ve·nient \-nyənt\ *adj* **1** : suited to personal comfort or ease **2** : placed near at hand — **con·ve·nient·ly** *adv*
con·vent \ˈkän-vənt, -ˌvent\ *n* [ME *covent,* fr. AF, fr. ML *conventus,* fr. L, assembly, fr. *convenire* to come together] : a local community or house of a religious order esp. of nuns — **con·ven·tu·al** \kän-ˈven-chə-wəl\ *adj*
con·ven·ti·cle \kən-ˈven-ti-kəl\ *n* : MEETING; *esp* : a secret meeting for worship
con·ven·tion \kən-ˈven-chən\ *n* **1** : an agreement esp. between states on a matter of common concern **2** : MEETING, ASSEMBLY **3** : an assembly of persons convened for some purpose **4** : generally accepted custom, practice, or belief
con·ven·tion·al \-chə-nəl\ *adj* **1** : sanctioned by general custom **2** : COMMONPLACE, ORDINARY — **con·ven·tion·al·i·ty** \-ˌven-chə-ˈna-lə-tē\ *n* — **con·ven·tion·al·ize** \-ˈven-chə-nə-ˌlīz\ *vb* — **con·ven·tion·al·ly** *adv*
con·verge \kən-ˈvərj\ *vb* **con·verged; con·verg·ing** : to approach one common center or single point ⟨*converging* paths⟩ — **con·ver·gence** \kən-ˈvər-jəns\ *n* — **con·ver·gent** \-jənt\ *adj*
con·ver·sant \kən-ˈvər-sᵊnt\ *adj* : having knowledge and experience — used with *with*
con·ver·sa·tion \ˌkän-vər-ˈsā-shən\ *n* : an informal talking together — **con·ver·sa·tion·al** \-shə-nᵊl\ *adj* — **con·ver·sa·tion·al·ly** *adv*
con·ver·sa·tion·al·ist \-shə-nᵊl-ist\ *n* : a person who converses a great deal or who excels in conversation
¹con·verse \ˈkän-ˌvərs\ *n* : CONVERSATION
²con·verse \kən-ˈvərs\ *vb* **con·versed; con·vers·ing** : to engage in conversation
³con·verse \ˈkän-ˌvərs\ *n* : a statement related to another statement by having its hypothesis and conclusion or its subject and predicate reversed or interchanged
⁴con·verse \kən-ˈvərs, ˈkän-ˌvers\ *adj* : reversed in order or relation — **con·verse·ly** *adv*
con·ver·sion \kən-ˈvər-zhən\ *n* **1** : a change in nature or form **2** : an experience associated with a decisive adoption of religion
¹con·vert \kən-ˈvərt\ *vb* **1** : to turn from one belief or party to another **2** : TRANSFORM, CHANGE **3** : MISAPPROPRIATE **4** : EXCHANGE — **con·vert·er** *or* **con·ver·tor** \-ˈvər-tər\ *n*
²con·vert \ˈkän-ˌvərt\ *n* : a person who has undergone religious conversion
¹con·vert·ible \kən-ˈvər-tə-bəl\ *adj* : capable of being converted
²convertible *n* : an automobile with a top that may be lowered or removed
con·vex \kän-ˈveks, ˈkän-ˌveks\ *adj* : curved or rounded outward like the exterior of a sphere or circle — **con·vex·i·ty** \kän-ˈvek-sə-tē\ *n*
con·vey \kən-ˈvā\ *vb* **1** : CARRY, TRANSPORT ⟨a river ~*ing* logs⟩ **2** : TRANSFER, COMMUNICATE ⟨~ a message⟩ — **con·vey·or** *also* **con·vey·er** \-ər\ *n*
con·vey·ance \-ˈvā-əns\ *n* **1** : the act of conveying **2** : a legal paper transferring ownership of property **3** : VEHICLE
¹con·vict \kən-ˈvikt\ *vb* : to prove or find guilty
²con·vict \ˈkän-ˌvikt\ *n* : a person serving a prison sentence
con·vic·tion \kən-ˈvik-shən\ *n* **1** : the act of convicting esp. in a court **2** : the state of being convinced : BELIEF
con·vince \kən-ˈvins\ *vb* **con·vinced; con·vinc·ing** : to bring (as by argument) to belief or action — **con·vinc·ing** *adj* — **con·vinc·ing·ly** *adv*
con·viv·ial \kən-ˈvi-vē-əl\ *adj* [LL *convivialis,* fr. L *convivium* banquet, fr. *com-* together + *vivere* to live] : enjoying companionship and the pleasures of feasting and drinking : JOVIAL, FESTIVE ⟨a ~ gathering⟩ — **con·viv·i·al·i·ty** \-ˌvi-vē-ˈa-lə-tē\ *n* — **con·viv·ial·ly** *adv*
con·vo·ca·tion \ˌkän-və-ˈkā-shən\ *n* **1** : a ceremonial assembly (as of the clergy) **2** : the act of convoking
con·voke \kən-ˈvōk\ *vb* **con·voked; con·vok·ing** : to call together to a meeting ⟨*convoked* a meeting of the delegates⟩
con·vo·lut·ed \ˈkän-və-ˌlü-təd\ *adj* **1** : folded in curved or tortuous windings **2** : INVOLVED, INTRICATE ⟨~ logic⟩
con·vo·lu·tion \ˌkän-və-ˈlü-shən\ *n* : a tortuous or winding structure; *esp* : one of the ridges of the brain
¹con·voy \ˈkän-ˌvȯi, kən-ˈvȯi\ *vb* : to accompany for protection

[2]**con•voy** \ˈkän-ˌvȯi\ *n* **1** : one that convoys; *esp* : a protective escort (as for ships) **2** : the act of convoying **3** : a group of moving vehicles

con•vulse \kən-ˈvəls\ *vb* **con•vulsed**; **con•vuls•ing** : to agitate violently

con•vul•sion \kən-ˈvəl-shən\ *n* **1** : an abnormal and violent involuntary contraction or series of contractions of muscle **2** : a violent disturbance — **con•vul•sive** \-siv\ *adj* — **con•vul•sive•ly** *adv*

cony *var of* CONEY

coo \ˈkü\ *n* : a soft low sound made by doves or pigeons; *also* : a sound like this — **coo** *vb*

COO *abbr* chief operating officer

[1]**cook** \ˈku̇k\ *n* : a person who prepares food for eating

[2]**cook** *vb* **1** : to prepare food for eating **2** : to subject to heat or fire **3** : CONCOCT, FABRICATE — usu. used with *up* ⟨~ up a scheme⟩ — **cook•er** *n* — **cook•ware** \-ˌwer\ *n*

cook•book \-ˌbu̇k\ *n* : a book of cooking directions and recipes

cook•ery \ˈku̇-kə-rē\ *n, pl* **-er•ies** : the art or practice of cooking

cook•ie *or* **cooky** \ˈku̇-kē\ *n, pl* **cook•ies** [D *koekje,* dim. of *koek* cake] **1** : a small sweet flat cake **2** *cookie* : a file containing information about a website user created and read by a website server and stored on the user's computer

cookie–cutter *adj* : marked by a lack of originality or distinction ⟨~ malls⟩

cook•out \ˈku̇k-ˌau̇t\ *n* : an outing at which a meal is cooked and served in the open

[1]**cool** \ˈkül\ *adj* **1** : moderately cold **2** : not excited : CALM **3** : not friendly **4** : IMPUDENT **5** : protecting from heat **6** *slang* : very good **7** *slang* : FASHIONABLE ♦ ***Synonyms*** UNFLAPPABLE, COMPOSED, COLLECTED, UNRUFFLED, NONCHALANT — **cool•ly** *adv* — **cool•ness** *n*

[2]**cool** *vb* : to make or become cool

[3]**cool** *n* **1** : a cool time or place **2** : INDIFFERENCE; *also* : SELF-ASSURANCE, COMPOSURE ⟨kept his ~⟩

cool•ant \ˈkü-lənt\ *n* : a usu. fluid cooling agent

cool•er \ˈkü-lər\ *n* **1** : a container for keeping food or drink cool **2** : JAIL, PRISON **3** : a tall iced drink

coo•lie \ˈkü-lē\ *n* [Hindi & Urdu *qulī*] *usu offensive* : an unskilled laborer usu. in or from the Far East

coon \ˈkün\ *n* : RACCOON

coon•hound \-ˌhau̇nd\ *n* : a sporting dog trained to hunt raccoons

coon•skin \-ˌskin\ *n* : the pelt of a raccoon; *also* : something (as a cap) made of this

[1]**coop** \ˈküp, ˈku̇p\ *n* : a small enclosure or building usu. for poultry

[2]**coop** *vb* : to confine in or as if in a coop — usu. used with *up*

co–op \ˈkō-ˌäp\ *n* : COOPERATIVE

coo•per \ˈkü-pər, ˈku̇-\ *n* : one who makes or repairs barrels or casks — **cooper** *vb* — **coo•per•age** \-pə-rij\ *n*

co•op•er•ate \kō-ˈä-pə-ˌrāt\ *vb* : to act jointly or in compliance with others — **co•op•er•a•tion** \-ˌä-pə-ˈrā-shən\ *n* — **co•op•er•a•tor** \-ˈä-pə-ˌrā-tər\ *n*

[1]**co•op•er•a•tive** \kō-ˈä-prə-tiv, -ˈä-pə-ˌrā-\ *adj* **1** : willing to work with others **2** : of or relating to an association formed to enable its members to buy or sell to better advantage by eliminating middlemen's profits

[2]**cooperative** *n* : a cooperative association

co–opt \kō-ˈäpt\ *vb* **1** : to choose or elect as a colleague **2** : ABSORB, ASSIMILATE; *also* : TAKE OVER ⟨a style ~*ed* by advertisers⟩

[1]**co•or•di•nate** \kō-ˈȯr-də-nət\ *adj* **1** : equal in rank or order **2** : of equal rank in a compound sentence ⟨~ clause⟩ **3** : joining words or word groups of the same rank — **co•or•di•nate•ly** *adv*

[2]**co•or•di•nate** \-ˈȯr-də-ˌnāt\ *vb* **-nat•ed**; **-nat•ing** **1** : to make or become coordinate ⟨~ our schedules⟩ **2** : to work or act together harmoniously ⟨a *coordinated* wardrobe⟩ — **co•or•di•na•tion** \-ˌȯr-də-ˈnā-shən\ *n* — **co•or•di•na•tor** \-ˈȯr-də-ˈnā-tər\ *n*

[3]**co•or•di•nate** \-ˈȯr-də-nət\ *n* **1** : one of a set of numbers used in specifying the location of a point on a surface or in space **2** *pl* : articles (as of clothing) designed to be used together and to attain their effect through pleasing contrast

coot \ˈküt\ *n* **1** : a dark-colored ducklike bird related to the rails **2** : any of several No. American sea ducks **3** : a harmless simple person

coo•tie \ˈkü-tē\ *n* : a body louse

[1]**cop** \ˈkäp\ *n* : POLICE OFFICER

[2]**cop** *vb* **1** *slang* : STEAL ⟨~ a glance⟩ **2** *slang* : ADMIT — used with *to* ⟨~ to the charges⟩ **3** : ADOPT ⟨~ an attitude⟩

co–pay \ˈkō-ˈpā\ *n* : CO-PAYMENT

co–pay•ment \ˈkō-ˌpā-mənt, ˌkō-ˈ\ *n* : a fixed fee required of a patient by a health insurer (as an HMO) at the time of each outpatient service or filling of a prescription

[1]**cope** \ˈkōp\ *n* : a long cloaklike ecclesiastical vestment

[2]**cope** *vb* **coped**; **cop•ing** : to struggle to overcome problems or difficulties ⟨~ with tragedy⟩

co•per•nic•i•um \ˌkō-pər-ˈni-sē-əm\ *n* [NL, fr. Nikolaus *Copernicus*] : a short-lived artificially produced radioactive element

copi•er \ˈkä-pē-ər\ *n* : one that copies; *esp* : a machine for making copies

co•pi•lot \ˈkō-ˌpī-lət\ *n* : an assistant pilot of an aircraft or spacecraft

cop•ing \ˈkō-piŋ\ *n* : the top layer of a wall

co•pi•ous \ˈkō-pē-əs\ *adj* : LAVISH, ABUNDANT ⟨a ~ harvest⟩ — **co•pi•ous•ly** *adv* — **co•pi•ous•ness** *n*

cop–out \ˈkäp-ˌau̇t\ *n* : an excuse for copping out; *also* : an act of copping out

cop out *vb* : to back out (as of an unwanted responsibility)

cop•per \ˈkä-pər\ *n* **1** : a malleable reddish metallic chemical element that is one of the best conductors of heat and electricity **2 :** a coin or token made of copper — **cop·pery** *adj*

cop·per·head \ˈkä-pər-ˌhed\ *n* **:** a largely coppery brown pit viper esp. of the eastern and central U.S.

cop·pice \ˈkä-pəs\ *n* **:** THICKET

co·pra \ˈkō-prə\ *n* **:** dried coconut meat yielding coconut oil

copse \ˈkäps\ *n* **:** THICKET

cop·ter \ˈkäp-tər\ *n* **:** HELICOPTER

cop·u·la \ˈkä-pyə-lə\ *n* **:** LINKING VERB — **cop·u·la·tive** \-lə-tiv, -ˌlā-\ *adj*

cop·u·late \ˈkä-pyə-ˌlāt\ *vb* **-lat·ed; -lat·ing :** to engage in sexual intercourse — **cop·u·la·tion** \ˌkä-pyə-ˈlā-shən\ *n* — **cop·u·la·to·ry** \ˈkä-pyə-lə-ˌtȯr-ē\ *adj*

[1]**copy** \ˈkä-pē\ *n, pl* **cop·ies** **1 :** an imitation or reproduction of an original work **2 :** material to be set in type **3 :** DUPLICATE ♦ ***Synonyms*** DUPLICATE, REPRODUCTION, FACSIMILE, REPLICA

[2]**copy** *vb* **cop·ied; copy·ing** **1 :** to make a copy of **2 :** IMITATE — **copy·ist** *n*

copy·book \ˈkä-pē-ˌbu̇k\ *n* **:** a book formerly used to teach handwriting containing examples to be copied

copy·boy \-ˌbȯi\ *n* **:** a person who carries copy and runs errands (as in a newspaper office)

copy·cat \-ˌkat\ *n* **:** one who imitates another

copy·desk \-ˌdesk\ *n* **:** the desk at which newspaper copy is edited

copy editor *n* **:** one who edits or prepares copy (as headlines) esp. for a newspaper

copy·read·er \-ˌrē-dər\ *n* **:** COPY EDITOR

[1]**copy·right** \-ˌrīt\ *n* **:** the sole right to reproduce, publish, sell, or distribute a literary or artistic work

[2]**copyright** *vb* **:** to secure a copyright on

copy·writ·er \ˈkä-pē-ˌrī-tər\ *n* **:** a writer of advertising copy

co·quet *or* **co·quette** \kō-ˈket\ *vb* **co·quet·ted; co·quet·ting :** FLIRT — **co·quet·ry** \ˈkō-kə-trē, kō-ˈke-trē\ *n*

co·quette \kō-ˈket\ *n* [F, fem. of *coquet,* flirtatious man, dim. of *coq* cock] **:** FLIRT — **co·quett·ish** *adj*

cor *abbr* corner

Cor *abbr* Corinthians

cor·a·cle \ˈkȯr-ə-kəl\ *n* [W *corwgl*] **:** a boat made of a frame covered usu. with hide or tarpaulin

cor·al \ˈkȯr-əl\ *n* **1 :** a stony or horny material that forms the skeleton of colonies of tiny sea polyps and includes a red form used in jewelry; *also* **:** a coral-forming polyp or polyp colony **2 :** a deep pink color — **coral** *adj*

coral snake *n* **:** any of several venomous chiefly tropical New World snakes brilliantly banded in red, black, and yellow or white

cor·bel \ˈkȯr-bəl\ *n* **:** a bracket-shaped architectural member that projects from a wall and supports a weight

[1]**cord** \ˈkȯrd\ *n* **1 :** a usu. heavy string consisting of several strands woven or twisted together **2 :** a long slender anatomical structure (as a tendon or nerve) **3 :** a small flexible insulated electrical cable used to connect an appliance with a receptacle **4 :** a cubic measure used esp. for firewood and equal to a stack 4×4×8 feet **5 :** a rib or ridge on cloth

[2]**cord** *vb* **1 :** to tie or furnish with a cord **2 :** to pile (wood) in cords

cord·age \ˈkȯr-dij\ *n* **:** ROPES, CORDS; *esp* **:** ropes in the rigging of a ship

[1]**cor·dial** \ˈkȯr-jəl\ *adj* [ME, fr. ML *cordialis,* fr. L *cord-, cor* heart] **:** warmly receptive or welcoming **:** HEARTFELT, HEARTY — **cor·di·al·i·ty** \ˌkȯr-jē-ˈa-lə-tē, kȯr-ˈja-\ *n* — **cor·dial·ly** *adv*

[2]**cordial** *n* **1 :** a stimulating medicine or drink **2 :** LIQUEUR

cor·dil·le·ra \ˌkȯr-dəl-ˈyer-ə, -də-ˈler-\ *n* [Sp] **:** a series of parallel mountain ranges

cord·less \ˈkȯrd-ləs\ *adj* **:** having no cord; *esp* **:** powered by a battery ⟨a ~ phone⟩ — **cord·less** *n*

cór·do·ba \ˈkȯr-də-bə, -və\ *n* — see MONEY table

cor·don \ˈkȯr-dᵊn\ *n* **1 :** an ornamental cord or ribbon **2 :** an encircling line (as of troops or police) — **cordon** *vb*

cor·do·van \ˈkȯr-də-vən\ *n* **:** a soft fine-grained leather

cor·du·roy \ˈkȯr-də-ˌrȯi\ *n, pl* **-roys :** a heavy ribbed fabric; *also, pl* **:** pants of this material

cord·wain·er \ˈkȯrd-ˌwā-nər\ *n* **:** SHOEMAKER

[1]**core** \ˈkȯr\ *n* **1 :** the central usu. inedible part of some fruits (as the apple); *also* **:** an inmost part of something **2 :** GIST, ESSENCE

[2]**core** *vb* **cored; cor·ing :** to take out the core of — **cor·er** *n*

CORE \ˈkȯr\ *abbr* Congress of Racial Equality

co·re·op·sis \ˌkȯr-ē-ˈäp-səs\ *n, pl* **coreopsis :** any of a genus of widely cultivated composite herbs with showy often yellow flower heads

co·re·spon·dent \ˌkō-ri-ˈspän-dənt\ *n* **:** a person named as guilty of adultery with the defendant in a divorce suit

co·ri·an·der \ˈkȯr-ē-ˌan-dər\ *n* **:** an herb related to the carrot; *also* **:** its aromatic dried fruit used as a flavoring

Cor·in·thi·ans \kə-ˈrin-thē-ənz\ *n* — see BIBLE table

[1]**cork** \ˈkȯrk\ *n* **1 :** the tough elastic bark of a European oak (**cork oak**) used esp. for stoppers and insulation; *also* **:** a stopper of this **2 :** a tissue of a woody plant making up most of the bark — **corky** *adj*

[2]**cork** *vb* **:** to furnish with or stop up with cork or a cork ⟨~ a bottle⟩

cork·screw \ˈkȯrk-ˌskrü\ *n* **:** a device for drawing corks from bottles

corm \ˈkȯrm\ *n* **:** a solid bulblike underground part of a stem (as of the crocus or gladiolus)

cor·mo·rant \ˈkȯr-mə-rənt, -ˌrant\ *n* [ME *cormeraunt,* fr. MF *cormorant,* fr. OF *cormareng,* fr. *corp* raven + *marenc* of the sea, fr. L *marinus*] **:** any of various dark-colored water birds with a long neck, hooked bill, and distensible throat pouch

[1]**corn** \ˈkȯrn\ *n* **1** *Brit* : the seeds of a cereal grass and esp. of the chief cereal crop of a region (as wheat in Britain); *also* : a cereal grass **2** : a tall widely cultivated cereal grass grown for its large ears of starchy seeds **3** : the typically yellow or whitish seeds of corn used esp. as a food **4** : an ear of corn

[2]**corn** *vb* : to salt (as beef) in brine and preservatives

[3]**corn** *n* : a local hardening and thickening of skin (as on a toe)

[1]**corn•ball** \ˈkȯrn-ˌbȯl\ *n* : an unsophisticated person; *also* : something corny

[2]**cornball** *adj* : CORNY ⟨~ humor⟩

corn bread *n* : bread made with cornmeal

corn•cob \-ˌkäb\ *n* : the woody core on which the kernels of corn are arranged

corn•crib \-ˌkrib\ *n* : a crib for storing ears of corn

cor•nea \ˈkȯr-nē-ə\ *n* : the transparent part of the coat of the eyeball covering the iris and the pupil — **cor•ne•al** *adj*

corn ear•worm \-ˈir-ˌwərm\ *n* : a moth whose larva is destructive esp. to corn

[1]**cor•ner** \ˈkȯr-nər\ *n* [ME, fr. AF *cornere,* fr. *corne* horn, corner, fr. L *cornu* horn, point] **1** : the point or angle formed by the meeting of lines, edges, or sides **2** : the place where two streets come together **3** : a quiet secluded place **4** : a position from which retreat or escape is impossible **5** : control of enough of the available supply (as of a commodity) to permit manipulation of the price — **cor•nered** *adj* — **around the corner** : IMMINENT ⟨has a birthday just *around the corner*⟩

[2]**cor•ner** *vb* **1** : to drive into a corner **2** : to get a corner on ⟨~ the wheat market⟩ **3** : to turn a corner

cor•ner•stone \ˈkȯr-nər-ˌstōn\ *n* **1** : a stone forming part of a corner in a wall; *esp* : such a stone laid at a formal ceremony **2** : something of basic importance

cor•net \kȯr-ˈnet\ *n* : a brass band instrument resembling the trumpet

corn flour *n, Brit* : CORNSTARCH

corn•flow•er \ˈkȯrn-ˌflau̇(-ə)r\ *n* : BACHELOR'S BUTTON

cor•nice \ˈkȯr-nəs\ *n* : the horizontal projecting part crowning the wall of a building

corn•meal \ˈkȯrn-ˌmēl\ *n* : meal ground from corn

corn•row \-ˌrō\ *n* : a section of hair braided flat to the scalp in rows — **cornrow** *vb*

corn•stalk \-ˌstȯk\ *n* : a stalk of corn

corn•starch \-ˌstärch\ *n* : a starch made from corn and used in cookery as a thickening agent

corn syrup *n* : a sweet syrup obtained from cornstarch

cor•nu•co•pia \ˌkȯr-nə-ˈkō-pē-ə, -nyə-\ *n* [LL, fr. L *cornu copiae* horn of plenty] **1** : a horn-shaped container filled with fruits and grain emblematic of abundance **2** : ABUNDANCE

corny \ˈkȯr-nē\ *adj* **corn•i•er; -est** : tiresomely simple or sentimental

co•rol•la \kə-ˈrä-lə, -ˈrō-\ *n* : the petals of a flower

cor•ol•lary \ˈkȯr-ə-ˌler-ē\ *n, pl* **-lar•ies** **1** : a deduction from a proposition already proved true **2** : CONSEQUENCE, RESULT

co•ro•na \kə-ˈrō-nə\ *n* **1** : a colored circle often seen around and close to a luminous body (as the sun or moon) **2** : the outermost part of the atmosphere of a star (as the sun) — **co•ro•nal** \ˈkȯr-ə-nᵊl, kə-ˈrō-\ *adj*

cor•o•nal \ˈkȯr-ə-nᵊl\ *n* : a circlet for the head

[1]**cor•o•nary** \ˈkȯr-ə-ˌner-ē\ *adj* : of or relating to the heart or its blood vessels

[2]**coronary** *n, pl* **-nar•ies** **1** : a coronary blood vessel **2** : CORONARY THROMBOSIS; *also* : HEART ATTACK

coronary thrombosis *n* : the blocking by a thrombus of one of the arteries supplying the heart tissues

cor•o•na•tion \ˌkȯr-ə-ˈnā-shən\ *n* : the act or ceremony of crowning a monarch

co•ro•na•vi•rus \kə-ˈrō-nə-ˌvī-rəs\ *n* **1** : any of a family of viruses that infect birds and many mammals including humans and include the causative agent of COVID-19 **2** : an illness caused by a coronavirus; *esp* : COVID-19

cor•o•ner \ˈkȯr-ə-nər\ *n* [ME, an officer of the crown, fr. AF, fr. *corone* crown, fr. L *corona*] : a public official who investigates causes of deaths possibly not due to natural causes

cor•o•net \ˌkȯr-ə-ˈnet\ *n* **1** : a small crown **2** : an ornamental band worn around the temples

corp *abbr* **1** corporal **2** corporation

[1]**cor•po•ral** \ˈkȯr-p(ə-)rəl\ *adj* : of or relating to the body ⟨~ punishment⟩

[2]**corporal** *n* : a noncommissioned officer (as in the army) ranking next below a sergeant

cor•po•rate \ˈkȯr-p(ə-)rət\ *adj* **1** : INCORPORATED; *also* : belonging to an incorporated body **2** : of or relating to large-scale business ⟨~ mergers⟩ **3** : combined into one body

cor•po•ra•tion \ˌkȯr-pə-ˈrā-shən\ *n* **1** : the municipal authorities of a town or city **2** : a legal creation authorized to act with the rights and liabilities of a person; *also* : COMPANY

cor•po•rat•ize \ˈkȯr-pə-rə-ˌtīz\ *vb* **-ized; -iz•ing** : to subject to corporate control

cor•po•re•al \kȯr-ˈpȯr-ē-əl\ *adj* **1** : PHYSICAL, MATERIAL **2** *archaic* : BODILY — **cor•po•re•al•i•ty** \kȯr-ˌpȯr-ē-ˈa-lə-tē\ *n* — **cor•po•re•al•ly** *adv*

corps \ˈkȯr\ *n, pl* **corps** \ˈkȯrz\ [F, fr. OF *cors,* fr. L *corpus* body] **1** : an organized subdivision of a country's military forces **2** : a group acting under common direction

corpse \ˈkȯrps\ *n* : a dead body

corps•man \ˈkȯr-mən, ˈkȯrz-\ *n* : an enlisted person trained to give first aid

cor•pu•lence \ˈkȯr-pyə-ləns\ *n* : excessive fatness : OBESITY

cor•pu•lent \-lənt\ *adj* : OBESE

cor•pus \ˈkȯr-pəs\ *n, pl* **cor•po•ra** \-pə-rə\ [ME, fr. L] **1** : BODY; *esp* : CORPSE **2** : a body of writings or works

cor·pus·cle \ˈkȯr-pə-səl, -ˌpə-\ *n* **1** : a minute particle **2** : a living cell (as in blood or cartilage) not aggregated into continuous tissues — **cor·pus·cu·lar** \kȯr-ˈpəs-kyə-lər\ *adj*

cor·pus de·lic·ti \ˌkȯr-pəs-di-ˈlik-ˌtī, -tē\ *n, pl* **corpora delicti** [NL, lit., body of the crime] **1** : the substantial fact proving that a crime has been committed **2** : the body of a victim of murder

corr *abbr* **1** correct; corrected; correction **2** correspondence; correspondent; corresponding

cor·ral \kə-ˈral\ *n* [Sp] : an enclosure for confining or capturing animals; *also* : an enclosure of wagons for defending a camp — **corral** *vb*

[1]**cor·rect** \kə-ˈrekt\ *vb* **1** : to make right ⟨~ an error⟩ **2** : REPROVE, CHASTISE ⟨~*ed* the child⟩ — **cor·rect·able** \-ˈrek-tə-bəl\ *adj* — **cor·rec·tion** \-ˈrek-shən\ *n* — **cor·rec·tion·al** \-ˈrek-sh(ə-)nəl\ *adj* — **cor·rec·tive** \-ˈrek-tiv\ *adj*

[2]**correct** *adj* **1** : conforming to a conventional standard ⟨~ behavior⟩ **2** : agreeing with fact or truth ⟨a ~ answer⟩ **3** : conforming to the standards of a specific ideology ⟨environmentally ~⟩ — **cor·rect·ly** *adv* — **cor·rect·ness** *n*

cor·re·late \ˈkȯr-ə-ˌlāt\ *vb* **-lat·ed**; **-lat·ing** : to connect in a systematic way : establish the mutual relations of — **cor·re·late** \-lət, -ˌlāt\ *n* — **cor·re·la·tion** \ˌkȯr-ə-ˈlā-shən\ *n*

cor·rel·a·tive \kə-ˈre-lə-tiv\ *adj* **1** : reciprocally related **2** : regularly used together (as *either* and *or*) — **correlative** *n* — **cor·rel·a·tive·ly** *adv*

cor·re·spond \ˌkȯr-ə-ˈspänd\ *vb* **1** : to be in agreement : SUIT, MATCH **2** : to communicate by letter — **cor·re·spond·ing·ly** *adv*

cor·re·spon·dence \-ˈspän-dəns\ *n* **1** : agreement between particular things **2** : communication by letters; *also* : the letters exchanged

[1]**cor·re·spon·dent** \-dənt\ *adj* **1** : SIMILAR **2** : FITTING, CONFORMING

[2]**correspondent** *n* **1** : something that corresponds **2** : a person with whom one communicates by letter **3** : a person employed to contribute news regularly from a place ⟨a war ~⟩

cor·ri·dor \ˈkȯr-ə-dər, -ˌdȯr\ *n* **1** : a passageway into which compartments or rooms open (as in a hotel or school) **2** : a narrow strip of land esp. through foreign-held territory **3** : a densely populated strip of land including two or more major cities **4** : an area identified by a common characteristic or purpose ⟨a ~ of liberalism⟩

cor·ri·gen·dum \ˌkȯr-ə-ˈjen-dəm\ *n, pl* **-da** \-də\ [L] : an error in a printed work discovered after printing and shown with its correction on a separate sheet

cor·ri·gi·ble \ˈkȯr-ə-jə-bəl\ *adj* : CORRECTABLE

cor·rob·o·rate \kə-ˈrä-bə-ˌrāt\ *vb* **-rat·ed**; **-rat·ing** [L *corroborare,* fr. *robur* strength] : to support with evidence : CONFIRM — **cor·rob·o·ra·tion** \-ˌrä-bə-ˈrā-shən\ *n* — **cor·rob·o·ra·tive** \-ˈrä-bə-ˌrā-tiv, -ˈrä-brə-\ *adj* — **cor·rob·o·ra·to·ry** \-ˈrä-bə-rə-ˌtȯr-ē\ *adj*

cor·rode \kə-ˈrōd\ *vb* **cor·rod·ed**; **cor·rod·ing** : to wear or be worn away gradually (as by chemical action) — **cor·ro·sion** \-ˈrō-zhən\ *n* — **cor·ro·sive** \-ˈrō-siv\ *adj or n*

cor·ru·gate \ˈkȯr-ə-ˌgāt\ *vb* **-gat·ed**; **-gat·ing** : to form into wrinkles or ridges and grooves — **cor·ru·gat·ed** *adj* — **cor·ru·ga·tion** \ˌkȯr-ə-ˈgā-shən\ *n*

[1]**cor·rupt** \kə-ˈrəpt\ *vb* **1** : to make evil : DEPRAVE; *esp* : BRIBE **2** : ROT, SPOIL — **cor·rupt·ible** *adj* — **cor·rup·tion** \-ˈrəp-shən\ *n*

[2]**corrupt** *adj* : morally degenerate; *also* : characterized by improper conduct ⟨~ officials⟩

cor·sage \kȯr-ˈsäzh, -ˈsäj\ *n* [F, bust, bodice, fr. OF, bust, fr. *cors* body, fr. L *corpus*] **1** : the waist or bodice of a dress **2** : a bouquet to be worn or carried

cor·sair \ˈkȯr-ˌser\ *n* : PIRATE

cor·set \ˈkȯr-sət\ *n* : a stiffened undergarment worn for support or to give shape to the waist and hips

cor·tege *also* **cor·tège** \kȯr-ˈtezh, ˈkȯr-ˌtezh\ *n* [F] : PROCESSION; *esp* : a funeral procession

cor·tex \ˈkȯr-ˌteks\ *n, pl* **cor·ti·ces** \ˈkȯr-tə-ˌsēz\ *or* **cor·tex·es** : an outer or covering layer of an organism or one of its parts ⟨the adrenal ~⟩ ⟨~ of a plant stem⟩; *esp* : CEREBRAL CORTEX — **cor·ti·cal** \ˈkȯr-ti-kəl\ *adj*

cor·ti·co·ste·roid \ˌkȯr-ti-kō-ˈstir-ˌȯid, -ˈster-\ *n* : any of various steroids made in the adrenal cortex and used medically as anti-inflammatory agents

cor·ti·sone \ˈkȯr-tə-ˌsōn, -ˌzōn\ *n* : a corticosteroid used esp. in treating rheumatoid arthritis

co·run·dum \kə-ˈrən-dəm\ *n* : a very hard aluminum-containing mineral used as an abrasive or as a gem

cor·us·cate \ˈkȯr-ə-ˌskāt\ *vb* **-cat·ed**; **-cat·ing** : FLASH, SPARKLE — **cor·us·ca·tion** \ˌkȯr-ə-ˈskā-shən\ *n*

cor·vette \kȯr-ˈvet\ *n* **1** : a naval sailing ship smaller than a frigate **2** : an armed escort ship smaller than a destroyer

co·ry·za \kə-ˈrī-zə\ *n* : an inflammatory disorder of the upper respiratory tract; *esp* : COMMON COLD

cos *abbr* cosine

COS *abbr* **1** cash on shipment **2** chief of staff

co·sig·na·to·ry \kō-ˈsig-nə-ˌtȯr-ē\ *n* : a joint signer

co·sign·er \ˈkō-ˌsī-nər\ *n* : COSIGNATORY; *esp* : a joint signer of a promissory note

co·sine \ˈkō-ˌsīn\ *n* : the trigonometric function that is the ratio between the side next to an acute angle in a right triangle and the hypotenuse

[1]**cos·met·ic** \käz-ˈme-tik\ *adj* [Gk *kosmē-*

tikos skilled in adornment, fr. *kosmein* to arrange, adorn, fr. *kosmos* order, ornament, universe] **1** : intended to beautify the hair or complexion **2** : correcting physical defects esp. to improve appearance ⟨~ dentistry⟩ **3** : SUPERFICIAL ⟨~ changes⟩ — **cos·met·i·cal·ly** \-ti-k(ə-)lē\ *adv*

²**cosmetic** *n* : a cosmetic preparation

cos·me·tol·o·gist \ˌkäz-mə-ˈtä-lə-jist\ *n* : one who gives beauty treatments — **cos·me·tol·o·gy** \-jē\ *n*

cos·mic \ˈkäz-mik\ *also* **cos·mi·cal** \-mi-kəl\ *adj* **1** : of or relating to the cosmos **2** : VAST, GRAND **3** : of or relating to spiritual or metaphysical ideas ⟨a ~ thinker⟩ — **cos·mi·cal·ly** *adv*

cosmic ray *n* : a stream of very penetrating atomic nuclei that enter the earth's atmosphere from outer space

cos·mog·o·ny \käz-ˈmä-gə-nē\ *n, pl* **-nies** : the origin or creation of the world or universe

cos·mol·o·gy \-ˈmä-lə-jē\ *n, pl* **-gies** : a branch of astronomy dealing with the origin and structure of the universe — **cos·mo·log·i·cal** \ˌkäz-mə-ˈlä-ji-kəl\ *adj* — **cos·mol·o·gist** \käz-ˈmä-lə-jist\ *n*

cos·mo·naut \ˈkäz-mə-ˌnȯt\ *n* : a Soviet or Russian astronaut

cos·mo·pol·i·tan \ˌkäz-mə-ˈpä-lə-tən\ *adj* : belonging to all the world : not local ♦ ***Synonyms*** UNIVERSAL, GLOBAL, CATHOLIC — **cosmopolitan** *n*

cos·mos \ˈkäz-məs, *1 also* -ˌmōs, -ˌmäs\ *n* **1** : UNIVERSE **2** : a tall garden herb related to the daisies

cos·play \ˈkäz-ˌplā, ˈkäs-\ *n* : the activity or practice of dressing up as a character from a work of fiction (such as a comic book or television show)

co·spon·sor \ˈkō-ˌspän-sər, -ˈspän-\ *n* : a joint sponsor — **cosponsor** *vb*

Cos·sack \ˈkä-ˌsak, -sək\ *n* [Polish & Ukrainian *kozak,* of Turkic origin] : a member of one of several autonomous communities drawn from various ethnic groups in southern Russia; *also* : a mounted soldier from one of these communities

¹**cost** \ˈkȯst\ *n* **1** : the amount paid or charged for something : PRICE **2** : the loss or penalty incurred in gaining something **3** *pl* : expenses incurred in a lawsuit — **at all costs** : regardless of consequences ⟨win *at all costs*⟩

²**cost** *vb* **cost; cost·ing** **1** : to require a specified amount in payment **2** : to cause to pay, suffer, or lose

co–star \ˈkō-ˌstär\ *n* : one of two leading players in a motion picture or play — **co–star** *vb*

cos·tive \ˈkäs-tiv\ *adj* : affected with or causing constipation

cost·ly \ˈkȯst-lē\ *adj* **cost·li·er; -est** **1** : of great cost or value ⟨~ gems⟩ **2** : done at great expense or sacrifice ⟨a ~ error⟩ ♦ ***Synonyms*** DEAR, VALUABLE, EXPENSIVE — **cost·li·ness** *n*

cos·tume \ˈkäs-ˌtüm, -ˌtyüm\ *n* [F, fr. It, custom, dress, fr. L *consuetudo* custom] **1** : the style of attire characteristic of a period or country **2** : a special or fancy dress ⟨Halloween ~*s*⟩ — **cos·tum·er** \ˈkäs-ˌtü-mər, -ˌtyü-\ *n*

costume jewelry *n* : inexpensive jewelry

cosy *chiefly Brit var of* COZY

¹**cot** \ˈkät\ *n* : a small house : COTTAGE

²**cot** *n* : a small often collapsible bed

cote \ˈkōt, ˈkät\ *n* : a small shed or coop (as for sheep or doves)

co·te·rie \ˈkō-tə-ˌrē, ˌkō-tə-ˈrē\ *n* [F] : an intimate often exclusive group of persons with a common interest

co·ter·mi·nous \ˌkō-ˈtər-mə-nəs\ *adj* : having the same scope or duration

co·til·lion \kō-ˈtil-yən, kə-\ *n* : a formal ball

cot·tage \ˈkä-tij\ *n* : a small house — **cot·tag·er** *n*

cottage cheese *n* : a soft uncured cheese made from soured skim milk

cot·tar *or* **cot·ter** \ˈkä-tər\ *n* : a peasant or farm laborer occupying a cottage and often a small holding

cotter pin *n* : a metal strip bent into a pin whose ends can be spread apart after insertion through a hole or slot

cot·ton \ˈkä-tᵊn\ *n* [ME *coton,* fr. AF *cotun,* fr. Ar *quṭun*] **1** : a soft fibrous usu. white substance composed of hairs attached to the seeds of various tropical plants related to the mallow; *also* : this plant **2** : thread or cloth made of cotton — **cot·tony** *adj*

cotton candy *n* : a candy made of spun sugar

cot·ton·mouth \ˈkä-tᵊn-ˌmau̇th\ *n* : WATER MOCCASIN

cot·ton·seed \-ˌsēd\ *n* : the seed of the cotton plant yielding a protein-rich meal and a fatty oil (**cottonseed oil**) used esp. in cooking

cot·ton·tail \-ˌtāl\ *n* : a No. American rabbit with a white-tufted tail

cot·ton·wood \-ˌwu̇d\ *n* : a poplar having seeds with cottony hairs

cot·y·le·don \ˌkä-tə-ˈlē-dᵊn\ *n* : the first leaf or one of the first pair or whorl of leaves developed by a seed plant

¹**couch** \ˈkau̇ch\ *vb* **1** : to lie or place on a couch **2** : to phrase in a specified manner ⟨proposals ~*ed* in jargon⟩

²**couch** *n* : a piece of furniture (as a bed or sofa) that one can sit or lie on

couch·ant \ˈkau̇-chənt\ *adj* : lying down with the head raised ⟨coat of arms with lion ~⟩

couch potato *n* : one who spends a great deal of time watching television

cou·gar \ˈkü-gər\ *n, pl* **cougars** *also* **cougar** [F *couguar,* fr. NL *cuguacuarana,* modif. of Tupi (an Indigenous language of Brazil) *sɨwasuarána,* fr. *sɨwásu* deer + *-ran* resembling] : a large powerful tawny brown wild American cat

cough \ˈkȯf\ *vb* : to force air from the lungs with short sharp noises; *also* : to expel by coughing — **cough** *n*

could \kəd, ˈku̇d\ *past of* CAN — used as an auxiliary in the past or as a polite or less forceful alternative to *can* in the present

cou·lee \ˈkü-lē\ *n* **1** : a small stream **2** : a dry streambed **3** : GULLY
cou·lomb \ˈkü-ˌläm, -ˌlōm\ *n* : a unit of electric charge equal to the electricity transferred by a current of one ampere in one second
coun·cil \ˈkau̇n-səl\ *n* **1** : ASSEMBLY, MEETING **2** : an official body of lawmakers ⟨city ~⟩ — **coun·cil·lor** *or* **coun·cil·or** \-sə-lər\ *n* — **coun·cil·man** \-səl-mən\ *n* — **coun·cil·wom·an** \-ˌwu̇-mən\ *n*
¹**coun·sel** \ˈkau̇n-səl\ *n* **1** : ADVICE **2** : a plan of action **3** : deliberation together **4** *pl* **counsel** : LAWYER
²**counsel** *vb* **-seled** *or* **-selled**; **-sel·ing** *or* **-sel·ling** **1** : ADVISE **2** : CONSULT
coun·sel·or *or* **coun·sel·lor** \ˈkau̇n-sə-lər\ *n* **1** : ADVISER **2** : LAWYER **3** : one who has supervisory duties at a summer camp
¹**count** \ˈkau̇nt\ *vb* [ME, fr. AF *cunter, counter,* fr. L *computare,* fr. *com-* with + *putare* to consider] **1** : to name or indicate one by one in order to find the total number **2** : to recite numbers in order **3** : CONSIDER, ACCOUNT **4** : RELY ⟨you can ~ on me⟩ **5** : to be of value or account ⟨~*s* toward your grade⟩ — **count·able** *adj*
²**count** *n* **1** : the act of counting; *also* : the total obtained by counting **2** : a particular charge in an indictment or legal declaration ⟨two ~*s* of murder⟩
³**count** *n* [ME, fr. AF *cunte,* fr. LL *comes,* fr. L, companion, one of the imperial court, fr. *com-* with + *ire* to go] : a European nobleman whose rank corresponds to that of a British earl
count·down \ˈkau̇nt-ˌdau̇n\ *n* : a backward counting in fixed units (as seconds) to indicate the time remaining before an event (as the launching of a rocket) — **count down** *vb*
¹**coun·te·nance** \ˈkau̇n-tᵊn-əns\ *n* **1** : the human face **2** : FAVOR, APPROVAL
²**countenance** *vb* **-nanced**; **-nanc·ing** : SANCTION, TOLERATE
¹**count·er** \ˈkau̇n-tər\ *n* **1** : a piece (as of metal or plastic) used in reckoning or in games **2** : a level surface over which business is transacted, food is served, or work is conducted
²**count·er** *n* : a device for recording a number or amount
³**coun·ter** *vb* : to act in opposition to
⁴**coun·ter** *adv* : in an opposite direction : CONTRARY
⁵**coun·ter** *n* **1** : OPPOSITE, CONTRARY **2** : an answering or offsetting force or blow
⁶**coun·ter** *adj* : CONTRARY, OPPOSITE
coun·ter·act \ˌkau̇n-tər-ˈakt\ *vb* : to lessen the force of : OFFSET — **coun·ter·ac·tive** \-ˈak-tiv\ *adj*
coun·ter·at·tack \ˈkau̇n-tər-ə-ˌtak\ *n* : an attack made to oppose an enemy's attack — **counterattack** *vb*
¹**coun·ter·bal·ance** \ˈkau̇n-tər-ˌba-ləns\ *n* : a weight or influence that balances another
²**counterbalance** \ˌkau̇n-tər-ˈba-ləns\ *vb* : to oppose with equal weight or influence
coun·ter·claim \ˈkau̇n-tər-ˌklām\ *n* : an opposing claim esp. in law
coun·ter·clock·wise \ˌkau̇n-tər-ˈkläk-ˌwīz\ *adv* : in a direction opposite to that in which the hands of a clock rotate — **counterclockwise** *adj*
coun·ter·cul·ture \ˈkau̇n-tər-ˌkəl-chər\ *n* : a culture with values and mores that run counter to those of established society
coun·ter·es·pi·o·nage \ˌkau̇n-tər-ˈes-pē-ə-ˌnäzh, -nij\ *n* : activities intended to discover and defeat enemy espionage
¹**coun·ter·feit** \ˈkau̇n-tər-ˌfit\ *adj* : SHAM, SPURIOUS; *also* : FORGED ⟨~ money⟩
²**counterfeit** *vb* **1** : to copy or imitate in order to deceive **2** : PRETEND, FEIGN — **coun·ter·feit·er** *n*
³**counterfeit** *n* : something counterfeit : FORGERY ♦ ***Synonyms*** FRAUD, SHAM, FAKE, IMPOSTURE, DECEIT, DECEPTION
coun·ter·in·sur·gen·cy \ˌkau̇n-tər-in-ˈsər-jən-sē\ *n* : military activity designed to deal with insurgents
coun·ter·in·tel·li·gence \-in-ˈte-lə-jəns\ *n* : organized activities of an intelligence service designed to counter the activities of an enemy's intelligence service
coun·ter·in·tu·i·tive \-in-ˈtü-ə-tiv, -ˈtyü-\ *adj* : contrary to what would intuitively be expected
count·er·man \ˈkau̇n-tər-ˌman, -mən\ *n* : one who tends a counter
coun·ter·mand \ˈkau̇nt-ər-ˌmand\ *vb* : to withdraw (an order already given) by a contrary order
coun·ter·mea·sure \-ˌme-zhər\ *n* : an action or device designed to counter another
coun·ter·of·fen·sive \-ə-ˌfen-siv\ *n* : a large-scale counterattack
coun·ter·pane \-ˌpān\ *n* : BEDSPREAD
coun·ter·part \-ˌpärt\ *n* : a person or thing very closely like or corresponding to another person or thing
coun·ter·point \-ˌpȯint\ *n* : music in which one melody is accompanied by one or more other melodies all woven into a harmonious whole
coun·ter·poise \-ˌpȯiz\ *n* : COUNTERBALANCE
coun·ter·rev·o·lu·tion \ˌkau̇n-tər-ˌre-və-ˈlü-shən\ *n* : a revolution opposed to a current or earlier one — **coun·ter·rev·o·lu·tion·ary** \-shə-ˌner-ē\ *adj or n*
coun·ter·sign \ˈkau̇n-tər-ˌsīn\ *n* **1** : a confirmatory signature added to a writing already signed by another person **2** : a military secret signal that must be given by a person who wishes to pass a guard — **countersign** *vb*
coun·ter·sink \-ˌsiŋk\ *vb* **-sunk** \-ˌsəŋk\; **-sink·ing** **1** : to form a funnel-shaped enlargement at the outer end of a drilled hole **2** : to set the head of (as a screw) at or below the surface — **countersink** *n*
coun·ter·spy \-ˌspī\ *n* : a spy engaged in counterespionage
coun·ter·ten·or \-ˌte-nər\ *n* : a tenor with an unusually high range

coun·ter·vail \ˌkau̇n-tər-ˈvāl\ *vb* : COUNTERACT

coun·ter·weight \ˈkau̇n-tər-ˌwāt\ *n* : COUNTERBALANCE

count·ess \ˈkau̇n-təs\ *n* **1** : the wife or widow of a count or an earl **2** : a woman holding the rank of a count or an earl in her own right

count·ing·house \ˈkau̇n-tiŋ-ˌhau̇s\ *n* : a building or office for keeping books and conducting business

count·less \ˈkau̇nt-ləs\ *adj* : INNUMERABLE

coun·tri·fied *also* **coun·try·fied** \ˈkən-tri-ˌfīd\ *adj* **1** : RURAL, RUSTIC **2** : UNSOPHISTICATED **3** : played or sung in the manner of country music

[1]**coun·try** \ˈkən-trē\ *n, pl* **countries** [ME *contree,* fr. AF *cuntree, contré,* fr. ML *contrata,* fr. L *contra* against, on the opposite side] **1** : REGION, DISTRICT **2** : FATHERLAND **3** : a nation or its territory **4** : rural regions as opposed to towns and cities **5** : COUNTRY MUSIC

[2]**country** *adj* **1** : RURAL **2** : of or relating to country music ⟨a ~ singer⟩

country and western *n* : COUNTRY MUSIC

country club *n* : a suburban club for social life and recreation; *esp* : one having a golf course — **country–club** *adj*

coun·try–dance \ˈkən-trē-ˌdans\ *n* : an English dance in which partners face each other esp. in rows

coun·try·man \ˈkən-trē-mən, *2 often* -ˌman\ *n* **1** : an inhabitant of a specified country **2** : COMPATRIOT **3** : one raised or living in the country : RUSTIC

country music *n* : music derived from or imitating the folk style of the southern U.S. or of the Western cowboy

coun·try·side \ˈkən-trē-ˌsīd\ *n* : a rural area or its people

coun·ty \ˈkau̇n-tē\ *n, pl* **counties** **1** : the domain of a count **2** : a territorial division of a country or state for purposes of local government

coup \ˈkü\ *n, pl* **coups** \ˈküz\ [F, blow, stroke] **1** : a brilliant sudden stroke or stratagem **2** : COUP D'ÉTAT

coup de grace \ˌkü-də-ˈgräs\ *n, pl* **coups de grace** *same*\ [F *coup de grâce,* lit., stroke of mercy] : DEATHBLOW; *also* : a final decisive stroke or event

coup d'état \ˌkü-də-ˈtä\ *n, pl* **coups d'état** *same*\ [F, lit., stroke of state] : a sudden violent overthrow of a government by a small group

cou·pé *or* **coupe** \kü-ˈpā, *2 often* ˈküp\ *n* [F *coupé,* fr. *couper* to cut] **1** : a closed horse-drawn carriage for two persons inside with an outside seat for the driver **2** *usu coupe* : a 2-door automobile with an enclosed body

[1]**cou·ple** \ˈkə-pəl\ *n* **1** : two persons married, engaged, or otherwise romantically paired **2** : PAIR **3** : BOND, TIE **4** : an indefinite small number : FEW ⟨a ~ of days ago⟩

[2]**couple** *vb* **cou·pled**; **cou·pling** : to link together

cou·plet \ˈkə-plət\ *n* : two successive rhyming lines of verse

cou·pling \ˈkə-pliŋ (*usual for 2*), -pə-liŋ\ *n* **1** : CONNECTION **2** : a device for connecting two parts or things

cou·pon \ˈkü-ˌpän, ˈkyü-\ *n* **1** : a statement attached to a bond showing interest due and designed to be cut off and presented for payment **2** : a form surrendered in order to obtain an article, service, or accommodation **3** : a printed document or slip used to submit orders or inquiries or to obtain a discount on merchandise or services

cour·age \ˈkər-ij\ *n* : ability to conquer fear or despair : BRAVERY, VALOR — **cou·ra·geous** \kə-ˈrā-jəs\ *adj* — **cou·ra·geous·ly** *adv*

cou·ri·er \ˈku̇r-ē-ər, ˈkər-ē-\ *n* : one who bears messages or information esp. for the diplomatic or military services

[1]**course** \ˈkȯrs\ *n* **1** : PROGRESS, PASSAGE; *also* : direction of progress **2** : the ground or path over which something moves **3** : method of procedure : CONDUCT, BEHAVIOR **4** : an ordered series of acts or proceedings : sequence of events **5** : a series of instruction periods dealing with a subject **6** : the series of studies leading to graduation from a school or college **7** : the part of a meal served at one time — **of course** : as might be expected

[2]**course** *vb* **coursed**; **cours·ing** **1** : to hunt with dogs **2** : to run or go speedily

cours·er \ˈkȯr-sər\ *n* : a swift or spirited horse

[1]**court** \ˈkȯrt\ *n* [ME, fr. AF, fr. L *cohort-, cohors* enclosure, group, retinue, cohort] **1** : the residence of a sovereign or similar dignitary **2** : a sovereign's formal assembly of officials and advisers as a governing power **3** : an assembly of the retinue of a sovereign **4** : an open space enclosed by a building or buildings **5** : a space walled or marked off for playing a game (as tennis or basketball) **6** : the place where justice is administered; *also* : a judicial body or a meeting of a judicial body **7** : attention intended to win favor

[2]**court** *vb* **1** : to try to gain the favor of **2** : WOO **3** : ATTRACT, TEMPT

cour·te·ous \ˈkər-tē-əs\ *adj* : marked by respect for others : CIVIL, POLITE — **cour·te·ous·ly** *adv*

cour·te·san \ˈkȯr-tə-zən, -ˌzan\ *n* : PROSTITUTE

cour·te·sy \ˈkər-tə-sē\ *n, pl* **-sies** **1** : courteous behavior : POLITENESS **2** : a favor courteously performed

court·house \ˈkȯrt-ˌhau̇s\ *n* : a building in which courts of law are held or county offices are located

court·ier \ˈkȯr-tē-ər\ *n* : a person in attendance at a royal court

court·ly \ˈkȯrt-lē\ *adj* **court·li·er**; **-est** : REFINED, ELEGANT, POLITE ♦ ***Synonyms*** GALLANT, GRACIOUS — **court·li·ness** *n*

court–mar·tial \ˈkȯrt-ˌmär-shəl\ *n, pl* **courts–martial** : a military or naval court for trial of offenses against military or naval law; *also* : a trial by this court — **court–martial** *vb*

court•room \-ˌrüm, -ˌru̇m\ *n* : a room in which a court of law is held

court•ship \-ˌship\ *n* : the act of courting : WOOING

court•yard \-ˌyärd\ *n* : an enclosure next to a building

cous•cous \ˈküs-ˌküs\ *n* : a No. African dish of steamed semolina usu. served with meat or vegetables; *also* : the semolina itself

cous•in \ˈkə-zən\ *n* [ME *cosin,* fr. AF, fr. L *consobrinus,* fr. *com-* with + *sobrinus* second cousin, fr. *soror* sister] : a child of one's uncle or aunt

cou•ture \kü-ˈtu̇r, -ˈtœr\ *n* [F] : the business of designing fashionable custom-made clothing; *also* : the designers and establishments in this business

cou•tu•ri•er \kü-ˈtu̇r-ē-ər, -ē-ˌā\ *n* [F, dressmaker] : the owner of an establishment engaged in couture

cove \ˈkōv\ *n* : a small sheltered inlet or bay

co•ven \ˈkə-vən\ *n* : an assembly or band of witches

cov•e•nant \ˈkə-və-nənt\ *n* : a formal binding agreement : COMPACT — **cov•e•nant** \-nənt, -ˌnant\ *vb*

[1]**cov•er** \ˈkə-vər\ *vb* **1** : to bring or hold within range of a firearm **2** : PROTECT, GUARD ⟨~*ed* by insurance⟩ ⟨~ third base⟩ **3** : HIDE, CONCEAL ⟨~ up a crime⟩ **4** : to place something over or upon **5** : INCLUDE, COMPRISE **6** : to have as one's field of activity ⟨one salesman ~*s* the state⟩ **7** : to buy (stocks) in order to have them for delivery on a previous short sale

[2]**cover** *n* **1** : something that protects or shelters **2** : LID, TOP **3** : CASE, BINDING **4** : TABLECLOTH **5** : a cloth used on a bed **6** : SCREEN, DISGUISE **7** : an envelope or wrapper for mail

cov•er•age \ˈkə-və-rij\ *n* **1** : the act or fact of covering **2** : the total group covered : SCOPE

cov•er•all \ˈkə-vər-ˌȯl\ *n* : a one-piece outer garment worn to protect one's clothes — usu. used in pl.

cover charge *n* : a charge made by a restaurant or nightclub in addition to the charge for food and drink

cover crop *n* : a crop planted to prevent soil erosion and to provide humus

cov•er•let \ˈkə-vər-lət\ *n* : BEDSPREAD

[1]**co•vert** \ˈkō-ˌvərt, ˈkə-vərt\ *adj* **1** : HIDDEN, SECRET ⟨a ~ operation⟩ **2** : SHELTERED — **co•vert•ly** *adv*

[2]**co•vert** \ˈkə-vərt, ˈkō-\ *n* **1** : a secret or sheltered place; *esp* : a thicket sheltering game **2** : a feather covering the bases of the quills of the wings and tail of a bird

cov•er–up \ˈkə-vər-ˌəp\ *n* **1** : a device for masking or concealing **2** : a usu. concerted effort to keep an illegal or unethical act or situation from being made public

cov•et \ˈkə-vət\ *vb* : to desire enviously (what belongs to another) — **cov•et•ous** *adj* — **cov•et•ous•ness** *n*

cov•ey \ˈkə-vē\ *n, pl* **coveys** [ME, fr. AF *covee* sitting (of a hen), fr. *cover* to sit on, brood over, fr. L *cubare* to lie] **1** : a bird with her brood of young **2** : a small flock (as of quail) **3** : GROUP 1

COVID–19 \ˈkō-vid-nīn-ˈtēn\ *also* **Covid–19** *or* **COVID** \ˈkō-vid\ *or* **Co•vid** *n* **1** : a mild to severe respiratory illness that is caused by a coronavirus, is transmitted chiefly by contact with infected material (as respiratory droplets), and is characterized esp. by fever, cough, and shortness of breath and may progress to pneumonia and respiratory failure **2** : the coronavirus that causes COVID-19

[1]**cow** \ˈkau̇\ *n* **1** : the mature female of cattle or of an animal (as the moose, elephant, or whale) of which the male is called *bull* **2** : any domestic bovine animal irrespective of sex or age

[2]**cow** *vb* : INTIMIDATE, DAUNT, OVERAWE

cow•ard \ˈkau̇(-ə)rd\ *n* [ME, fr. AF *cuard,* fr. *cue, coe* tail, fr. L *cauda*] : one who lacks courage or shows shameful fear or timidity — **coward** *adj* — **cow•ard•ice** \ˈkau̇-ər-dəs\ *n* — **cow•ard•ly** *adv or adj*

cow•bird \ˈkau̇-ˌbərd\ *n* : a small No. American blackbird that lays its eggs in the nests of other birds

cow•boy \-ˌbȯi\ *n* : one (as a mounted ranch hand) who tends cattle or horses

cow•er \ˈkau̇(-ə)r\ *vb* : to shrink or crouch down from fear or cold : QUAIL

cow•girl \ˈkau̇-ˌgərl\ *n* : a girl or woman who tends cattle or horses

cow•hand \ˈkau̇-ˌhand\ *n* : COWBOY

cow•herd \-ˌhərd\ *n* : one who tends cows

cow•hide \-ˌhīd\ *n* **1** : the hide of a cow; *also* : leather made from it **2** : a coarse whip of braided rawhide

cowl \ˈkau̇(-ə)l\ *n* : a monk's hood

cow•lick \ˈkau̇-ˌlik\ *n* : a turned-up tuft of hair that resists control

cowl•ing \ˈkau̇-liŋ\ *n* : a usu. metal covering for the engine or another part of an airplane

cow•man \ˈkau̇-mən, -ˌman\ *n* : COWBOY; *also* : a cattle owner or rancher

co•work•er \ˈkō-ˌwər-kər\ *n* : a fellow worker

cow•poke \ˈkau̇-ˌpōk\ *n* : COWBOY

cow pony *n* : a strong and agile horse trained for herding cattle

cow•pox \ˈkau̇-ˌpäks\ *n* : a mild disease of the cow that when communicated to humans protects against smallpox

cow•punch•er \-ˌpən-chər\ *n* : COWBOY

cow•slip \ˈkau̇-ˌslip\ *n* **1** : a yellow-flowered European primrose **2** : MARSH MARIGOLD

cox•comb \ˈkäks-ˌkōm\ *n* : a conceited foolish person : FOP

cox•swain \ˈkäk-sən, -ˌswān\ *n* : the steersman of a ship's boat or a racing shell

coy \ˈkȯi\ *adj* [ME, quiet, shy, fr. AF *quei, quoi, koi* quiet, fr. L *quietus*] **1** : BASHFUL, SHY **2** : marked by artful playfulness : COQUETTISH — **coy•ly** *adv* — **coy•ness** *n*

coy•ote \ˈkī-ˌōt, kī-ˈō-tē\ *n, pl* **coyotes** *or*

coyote : a mammal of No. America smaller than the related wolves
coy·pu \ˈkȯi-pü\ *n* : NUTRIA 2
coz·en \ˈkə-zᵊn\ *vb* : CHEAT, DEFRAUD — **coz·en·age** \-ij\ *n* — **coz·en·er** *n*
¹**co·zy** \ˈkō-zē\ *adj* **co·zi·er**; **-est** : SNUG, COMFORTABLE ⟨a ~ cabin⟩ — **co·zi·ly** \-zə-lē\ *adv* — **co·zi·ness** \-zē-nəs\ *n*
²**cozy** *n, pl* **co·zies** : a padded covering for a vessel (as a teapot) to keep the contents hot
cp *abbr* **1** compare **2** coupon
CP *abbr* **1** cerebral palsy **2** chemically pure **3** command post **4** communist party
CPA *abbr* certified public accountant
CPB *abbr* Corporation for Public Broadcasting
cpd *abbr* compound
CPI *abbr* consumer price index
Cpl *abbr* corporal
CPO *abbr* chief petty officer
CPOM *abbr* master chief petty officer
CPOS *abbr* senior chief petty officer
CPR *abbr* cardiopulmonary resuscitation
CPT *abbr* captain
CPU \ˌsē-ˌpē-ˈyü\ *n* [central *p*rocessing *u*nit] : the part of a computer that performs its basic operations, manages its components, and exchanges data with memory or peripherals
CQ *abbr* charge of quarters
cr *abbr* credit; creditor
Cr *symbol* chromium
¹**crab** \ˈkrab\ *n, pl* **crabs** *also* **crab** : any of various crustaceans with a short broad shell and small abdomen
²**crab** *n* : an ill-natured person
³**crab** *vb* **crabbed**; **crab·bing** : COMPLAIN, GROUSE
crab apple *n* : a small often highly colored sour apple; *also* : a tree that produces crab apples
crab·bed \ˈkra-bəd\ *adj* **1** : MOROSE, PEEVISH ⟨a ~ view of life⟩ **2** : CRAMPED, IRREGULAR ⟨~ handwriting⟩
crab·by \ˈkra-bē\ *adj* **crab·bi·er**; **-est** : CROSS, ILL-NATURED
crab·grass \ˈkrab-ˌgras\ *n* : a weedy grass with creeping or sprawling stems that root freely at the nodes
crab louse *n* : a louse infesting the pubic region in humans
¹**crack** \ˈkrak\ *vb* **1** : to break with a sharp sudden sound **2** : to break with or without completely separating into parts **3** : to fail in tone or become harsh ⟨her voice *~ed*⟩ **4** : to subject (as a petroleum oil) to heat for breaking down into lighter products (as gasoline)
²**crack** *n* **1** : a sudden sharp noise **2** : a witty or sharp remark **3** : a narrow break or opening : FISSURE **4** : a sharp blow **5** : ATTEMPT, TRY **6** : a potent form of cocaine in small chips used illicitly for smoking
³**crack** *adj* : extremely proficient
crack·down \ˈkrak-ˌdau̇n\ *n* : an act or instance of taking positive disciplinary action ⟨a ~ on gambling⟩ — **crack down** *vb*
crack·er \ˈkra-kər\ *n* **1** : FIRECRACKER **2** : a dry thin crispy baked bread product made of flour and water
crack·er·jack \-ˌjak\ *adj* : EXCELLENT, GREAT ⟨a ~ salesperson⟩ — **crackerjack** *n*
crack·le \ˈkra-kəl\ *vb* **crack·led**; **crack·ling** **1** : to make small sharp snapping noises **2** : to develop fine cracks in a surface — **crackle** *n* — **crack·ly** \-k(ə-)lē\ *adj*
crack·pot \ˈkrak-ˌpät\ *n* : an eccentric person
crack–up \ˈkrak-ˌəp\ *n* : CRASH, WRECK; *also* : BREAKDOWN
crack up *vb* **1** : PRAISE ⟨isn't all it's *cracked up* to be⟩ **2** : to laugh or cause to laugh out loud **3** : to crash a vehicle
¹**cra·dle** \ˈkrā-dᵊl\ *n* **1** : a baby's bed or cot **2** : a framework or support (as for a telephone receiver) **3** : INFANCY ⟨from ~ to the grave⟩ **4** : a place of origin
²**cradle** *vb* **cra·dled**; **cra·dling** **1** : to place in or as if in a cradle **2** : SHELTER, REAR
craft \ˈkraft\ *n* **1** : ART, SKILL; *also* : an occupation requiring special skill **2** : CUNNING, GUILE ⟨used ~ to close the deal⟩ **3** *pl usu* **craft** : a boat esp. of small size; *also* : AIRCRAFT, SPACECRAFT
crafts·man \ˈkrafts-mən\ *n* : a skilled artisan — **crafts·man·ship** *n*
crafty \ˈkraf-tē\ *adj* **craft·i·er**; **-est** : CUNNING, DECEITFUL, SUBTLE — **craft·i·ly** \-tə-lē\ *adv* — **craft·i·ness** \-tē-nəs\ *n*
crag \ˈkrag\ *n* : a steep rugged cliff or rock — **crag·gy** *adj*
cram \ˈkram\ *vb* **crammed**; **cram·ming** **1** : to pack in tight : JAM **2** : to eat greedily **3** : to study rapidly under pressure for an examination
¹**cramp** \ˈkramp\ *n* **1** : a sudden painful contraction of muscle **2** : sharp abdominal pain — usu. used in pl.
²**cramp** *vb* **1** : to affect with a cramp or cramps **2** : to restrain from free action : HAMPER
cran·ber·ry \ˈkran-ˌber-ē, -bə-rē\ *n* : the red acid berry of any of several trailing plants related to the heaths; *also* : one of these plants
¹**crane** \ˈkrān\ *n* **1** : any of a family of tall wading birds related to the rails; *also* : any of several herons **2** : a machine for lifting and carrying heavy objects
²**crane** *vb* **craned**; **cran·ing** : to stretch one's neck to see better
crane fly *n* : any of a family of long-legged slender dipteran flies that resemble large mosquitoes but do not bite
cranial nerve *n* : any of the nerves that arise in pairs from the lower surface of the brain and pass through openings in the skull to the periphery of the body
cra·ni·um \ˈkrā-nē-əm\ *n, pl* **-ni·ums** *or* **-nia** \-ə\ : SKULL; *esp* : the part enclosing the brain — **cra·ni·al** \-əl\ *adj*
¹**crank** \ˈkraŋk\ *n* **1** : a bent part of an axle or shaft or an arm at right angles to the end of a shaft by which circular motion is imparted to or received from it **2**

: an eccentric person **3** : a bad-tempered person : GROUCH

²crank *vb* : to start or operate by or as if by turning a crank

crank•case \ˈkraŋk-ˌkās\ *n* : the housing of a crankshaft

crank out *vb* : to produce in a mechanical manner

crank•shaft \ˈkraŋk-ˌshaft\ *n* : a shaft turning or driven by a crank

cranky \ˈkraŋ-kē\ *adj* **crank•i•er; -est 1** : IRRITABLE **2** : operating uncertainly or imperfectly ⟨a ~ old tractor⟩

cran•ny \ˈkra-nē\ *n, pl* **crannies** : CREVICE, CHINK

craps \ˈkraps\ *n* : a gambling game played with two dice

crap•shoot•er \ˈkrap-ˌshü-tər\ *n* : a person who plays craps

¹crash \ˈkrash\ *vb* **1** : to break noisily : SMASH **2** : to damage an airplane in landing **3** : to enter or attend without invitation or without paying ⟨~ a party⟩ **4** : to suffer a sudden major failure usu. with loss of data ⟨my computer ~*ed*⟩

²crash *n* **1** : a loud sound (as of things smashing) **2** : an instance of crashing ⟨a plane ~⟩; *also* : COLLISION **3** : a sudden failure (as of a business)

³crash *adj* : marked by concentrated effort over the shortest possible time ⟨a ~ diet⟩

⁴crash *n* : coarse linen fabric used for towels and draperies

crash–land \ˈkrash-ˈland\ *vb* : to land an aircraft or spacecraft under emergency conditions usu. with damage to the craft — **crash landing** *n*

crass \ˈkras\ *adj* : GROSS, INSENSITIVE ⟨~ ignorance⟩ — **crass•ly** *adv* — **crass•ness** *n*

crate \ˈkrāt\ *n* : a container often of wooden slats — **crate** *vb*

cra•ter \ˈkrā-tər\ *n* [L, mixing bowl, crater, fr. Gk *kratēr,* fr. *kerannynai* to mix] **1** : the depression around the opening of a volcano **2** : a depression formed by the impact of a meteorite or by the explosion of a bomb or shell

cra•vat \krə-ˈvat\ *n* : NECKTIE

crave \ˈkrāv\ *vb* **craved; crav•ing 1** : to ask for earnestly : BEG **2** : to long for : DESIRE

cra•ven \ˈkrā-vən\ *adj* : COWARDLY — **craven** *n* — **cra•ven•ly** *adv*

crav•ing \ˈkrā-viŋ\ *n* : an urgent or abnormal desire

craw•fish \ˈkrȯ-ˌfish\ *n* **1** : CRAYFISH 1 **2** : SPINY LOBSTER

¹crawl \ˈkrȯl\ *vb* **1** : to move slowly by drawing the body along the ground **2** : to advance feebly, cautiously, or slowly **3** : to be swarming with or feel as if swarming with creeping things ⟨a place ~*ing* with ants⟩ ⟨her flesh ~*ed*⟩

²crawl *n* **1** : a very slow pace **2** : a prone speed swimming stroke

cray•fish \ˈkrā-ˌfish\ *n* **1** : any of numerous freshwater crustaceans usu. much smaller than the related lobsters **2** : SPINY LOBSTER

cray•on \ˈkrā-ˌän, -ən\ *n* : a stick of chalk or wax used for writing, drawing, or coloring; *also* : a drawing made with such material — **crayon** *vb*

¹craze \ˈkrāz\ *vb* **crazed; craz•ing** [ME *crasen* to crush, craze, of Scandinavian origin] : to make or become insane

²craze *n* : FAD, MANIA

cra•zy \ˈkrā-zē\ *adj* **cra•zi•er; -est 1** : mentally disordered : INSANE — not used technically **2** : wildly impractical ⟨a ~ plan⟩; *also* : ERRATIC — **cra•zi•ly** \-zə-lē\ *adv* — **cra•zi•ness** \-zē-nəs\ *n*

CRC *abbr* Civil Rights Commission

creak \ˈkrēk\ *vb* : to make a prolonged squeaking or grating sound — **creak** *n* — **creaky** *adj*

¹cream \ˈkrēm\ *n* **1** : the yellowish fat-rich part of milk **2** : a thick smooth sauce, confection, or cosmetic **3** : the choicest part **4** : a pale yellow color — **creamy** *adj*

²cream *vb* **1** : to prepare with a cream sauce **2** : to beat or blend into creamy consistency **3** : to defeat decisively

cream cheese *n* : a cheese made from whole milk enriched with cream

cream•ery \ˈkrē-mə-rē\ *n, pl* **-er•ies** : an establishment where butter and cheese are made or milk and cream are prepared for sale

crease \ˈkrēs\ *n* : a mark or line made by or as if by folding — **crease** *vb*

cre•ate \krē-ˈāt\ *vb* **cre•at•ed; cre•at•ing** : to bring into being : cause to exist : MAKE, PRODUCE — **cre•a•tive** \-ˈā-tiv\ *adj* — **cre•a•tive•ness** *n* — **cre•a•tiv•i•ty** \ˌkrē-(ˌ)ā-ˈti-və-tē\ *n*

cre•a•tion \krē-ˈā-shən\ *n* **1** : the act of creating or producing ⟨~ of the world⟩ **2** : something that is created **3** : all created things : WORLD

cre•a•tion•ism \krē-ˈā-shə-ˌni-zəm\ *n* : a doctrine or theory holding that matter, the various forms of life, and the world were created by God out of nothing — **cre•a•tion•ist** \-nist\ *n or adj*

cre•a•tor \krē-ˈā-tər\ *n* **1** : one that creates : MAKER, AUTHOR **2** *cap* : GOD 1

crea•ture \ˈkrē-chər\ *n* : a lower animal; *also* : a human being

crèche \ˈkresh\ *n* [F, manger, crib, fr. OF *creche,* of Gmc origin] : a representation of the Nativity scene

cre•dence \ˈkrē-dᵊns\ *n* : mental acceptance as true or real

cre•den•tial \kri-ˈden-chəl\ *n* : something that gives a basis for credit or confidence

cre•den•za \kri-ˈden-zə\ *n* [It, lit., belief, confidence] : a sideboard, buffet, or bookcase usu. without legs

cred•i•ble \ˈkre-də-bəl\ *adj* : TRUSTWORTHY, BELIEVABLE — **cred•i•bil•i•ty** \ˌkre-də-ˈbi-lə-tē\ *n* — **cred•i•bly** \ˈkre-də-blē\ *adv*

¹cre•dit \ˈkre-dət\ *n* [MF, fr. It *credito,* fr. L *creditum* something entrusted to another, loan, fr. *credere* to believe, entrust] **1** : the balance (as in a bank) in a person's favor **2** : time given for payment for goods sold on trust **3** : an accounting entry of payment received **4** : BELIEF, FAITH **5** : financial trustworthiness **6** : ESTEEM **7** : a source of honor or distinction **8** : a unit of academic work

²**credit** *vb* **1** : BELIEVE **2** : to give credit to ⟨the players all ~*ed* their coach⟩

cred·it·able \ˈkre-də-tə-bəl\ *adj* : worthy of esteem or praise ⟨did a ~ job⟩ — **cred·it·ably** \-blē\ *adv*

credit card *n* : a card authorizing purchases on credit

cred·i·tor \ˈkre-də-tər\ *n* : a person to whom money is owed

cre·do \ˈkrē-dō, ˈkrā-\ *n, pl* **credos** [ME, fr. L, I believe] : CREED

cred·u·lous \ˈkre-jə-ləs\ *adj* : inclined to believe esp. on slight evidence — **cre·du·li·ty** \kri-ˈdü-lə-tē, -ˈdyü-\ *n* — **cred·u·lous·ly** *adv*

Cree \ˈkrē\ *n, pl* **Cree** *or* **Crees** : a member of a First Nations people of Quebec, Ontario, Manitoba, and Saskatchewan; *also* : their language

creed \ˈkrēd\ *n* [ME *crede,* fr. OE *crēda,* fr. L *credo* I believe, first word of the Apostles' and Nicene Creeds] : a statement of the essential beliefs of a religious faith

creek \ˈkrēk, ˈkrik\ *n* **1** *chiefly Brit* : a small inlet **2** : a stream smaller than a river and larger than a brook

Creek \ˈkrēk\ *n* : a member of an Indigenous people orig. of Alabama, Georgia, and Florida; *also* : their language

creel \ˈkrēl\ *n* : a wicker basket esp. for carrying fish

creep \ˈkrēp\ *vb* **crept** \ˈkrept\; **creep·ing** **1** : CRAWL **2** : to feel as though insects were crawling on the skin **3** : to spread or grow over a surface like ivy — **creep** *n* — **creep·er** *n*

creep·ing \ˈkrē-piŋ\ *adj* : developing or advancing by imperceptible degrees

creepy \ˈkrē-pē\ *adj* **creep·i·er**; **-est** : having or producing a nervous shivery fear

cre·mate \ˈkrē-ˌmāt\ *vb* **cre·mat·ed**; **cre·mat·ing** : to reduce (a dead body) to ashes with fire — **cre·ma·tion** \kri-ˈmā-shən\ *n*

cre·ma·to·ri·um \ˌkrē-mə-ˈtȯr-ē-əm, ˌkre-\ *n, pl* **-ria** \-ə\ *or* **-ri·ums** : a place where the bodies of the dead are cremated

cre·ma·to·ry \ˈkrē-mə-ˌtȯr-ē, ˈkre-\ *n, pl* **-ries** : CREMATORIUM

crème *or* **creme** \ˈkrem, ˈkrēm\ *n, pl* **crèmes** *or* **cremes** *same or* ˈkremz, ˈkrēmz\ [F, lit., cream] : a sweet liqueur

cren·el·lat·ed *or* **cren·el·at·ed** \ˈkre-nə-lā-təd\ *adj* : having battlements — **cren·el·la·tion** \ˌkre-nə-ˈlā-shən\ *n*

Cre·ole \ˈkrē-ˌōl\ *n* **1** : a descendant of early French or Spanish settlers of the U.S. Gulf states preserving their speech and culture; *also* : a person of mixed French or Spanish and Black descent speaking a dialect of French or Spanish **2** *not cap* : a language that has evolved from a pidgin but serves as the native language of a speech community

cre·o·sote \ˈkrē-ə-ˌsōt\ *n* : an oily liquid obtained by distillation of coal tar and used in preserving wood

crepe *or* **crêpe** \ˈkrāp\ *n* : a light crinkled fabric of any of various fibers

crêpe su·zette \ˌkrāp-sü-ˈzet\ *n, pl* **crêpes suzette** *same or* ˌkrāps-\ *or* **crêpe suzettes** \-sü-ˈzets\ *often cap S* : a thin folded or rolled pancake in a hot orange-butter sauce that is sprinkled with a liqueur and set ablaze for serving

cre·pus·cu·lar \kri-ˈpəs-kyə-lər\ *adj* **1** : of, relating to, or resembling twilight **2** : occurring or active during twilight

cre·scen·do \krə-ˈshen-dō\ *adv or adj* [It] : increasing in loudness — used as a direction in music — **crescendo** *n*

cres·cent \ˈkre-sᵊnt\ *n* [ME *cressant,* fr. AF fr. prp. of *crestre* to grow, increase, fr. L *crescere*] : the moon at any stage between new moon and first quarter and between last quarter and new moon; *also* : something shaped like the figure of the crescent moon with a convex and a concave edge — **cres·cen·tic** \kre-ˈsen-tik\ *adj*

cress \ˈkres\ *n* : any of several salad plants related to the mustards

¹**crest** \ˈkrest\ *n* **1** : a tuft or process on the head of an animal (as a bird) **2** : a heraldic device **3** : an upper part, edge, or limit ⟨the ~ of a hill⟩ — **crest·ed** \ˈkres-təd\ *adj* — **crest·less** *adj*

²**crest** *vb* **1** : CROWN **2** : to reach the crest of **3** : to rise to a crest

crest·fall·en \ˈkrest-ˌfȯ-lən\ *adj* : DISPIRITED, DEJECTED

Cre·ta·ceous \kri-ˈtā-shəs\ *adj* : of, relating to, or being the latest period of the Mesozoic era marked by great increase in flowering plants, diversification of mammals, and extinction of the dinosaurs — **Cretaceous** *n*

cre·tin \ˈkrē-tᵊn\ *n* [F *crétin,* fr. F dial. *cretin,* lit., wretch, innocent victim, fr. L *christianus* Christian] **1** : one affected with cretinism **2** : a stupid person

cre·tin·ism \-ˌi-zəm\ *n* : a usu. congenital condition characterized by physical stunting and intellectual disability

cre·tonne \ˈkrē-ˌtän\ *n* : a strong unglazed cotton cloth for curtains and upholstery

cre·vasse \kri-ˈvas\ *n* : a deep fissure esp. in a glacier

crev·ice \ˈkre-vəs\ *n* : a narrow fissure

¹**crew** \ˈkrü\ *chiefly Brit past of* CROW

²**crew** *n* [ME *crue,* fr. MF, a reinforcement, lit., increase, fr. *croistre* to grow, fr. L *crescere*] **1** : a body of people trained to work together for certain purposes **2** : a group of people who operate a ship, train, aircraft, or spacecraft **3** : the rowers and coxswain of a racing shell; *also* : the sport of rowing engaged in by a crew — **crewed** \ˈkrü-\ *adj* — **crew·man** \ˈkrümən\ *n*

crew cut *n* : a very short bristly haircut

crew·el \ˈkrü-əl\ *n* : slackly twisted worsted yarn used for embroidery — **crew·el·work** \-ˌwərk\ *n*

¹**crib** \ˈkrib\ *n* **1** : a manger for feeding

animals **2 :** a child's bedstead with high sides **3 :** a building or bin for storage (as of grain) **4 :** something used for cheating in an exam

²**crib** *vb* **cribbed; crib·bing 1 :** to put in a crib **2 :** STEAL, PLAGIARIZE — **crib·ber** *n*

crib·bage \ˈkri-bij\ *n* **:** a card game usu. played by two players and scored on a board (**cribbage board**)

crib death *n* **:** SUDDEN INFANT DEATH SYNDROME

crick \ˈkrik\ *n* **:** a painful spasm of muscles (as of the neck)

¹**crick·et** \ˈkri-kət\ *n* [ME *criket,* fr. AF, of imitative origin] **:** any of a family of leaping insects related to the grasshoppers and noted for the chirping noises of the male

²**cricket** *n* [MF *criquet* goal stake in a bowling game] **:** a game played with a bat and ball by two teams on a field centering upon two wickets each defended by a batsman

cri·er \ˈkrī(-ə)r\ *n* **:** one who calls out proclamations and announcements

crime \ˈkrīm\ *n* **:** a serious offense against the public law

¹**crim·i·nal** \ˈkri-mə-nᵊl\ *adj* **1 :** involving or being a crime **2 :** relating to crime or its punishment — **crim·i·nal·i·ty** \ˌkri-mə-ˈna-lə-tē\ *n* — **crim·i·nal·ly** *adv*

²**criminal** *n* **:** one who has committed a crime

crim·i·nol·o·gy \ˌkri-mə-ˈnä-lə-jē\ *n* **:** the scientific study of crime and criminals — **crim·i·no·log·i·cal** \-mə-nə-ˈlä-ji-kəl\ *adj* — **crim·i·nol·o·gist** \ˌkri-mə-ˈnä-lə-jist\ *n*

¹**crimp** \ˈkrimp\ *vb* **:** to cause to become crinkled, wavy, or bent

²**crimp** *n* **:** something (as a curl in hair) produced by or as if by crimping

crim·son \ˈkrim-zən\ *n* **:** a deep purplish red color — **crimson** *adj*

cringe \ˈkrinj\ *vb* **cringed; cring·ing :** to shrink in fear **:** WINCE, COWER

crin·kle \ˈkriŋ-kəl\ *vb* **crin·kled; crin·kling :** to form many short bends or curves; *also* **:** WRINKLE — **crinkle** *n* — **crin·kly** \-kə-lē\ *adj*

crin·o·line \ˈkri-nə-lən\ *n* **1 :** an open-weave cloth used for stiffening and lining **2 :** a full stiff skirt or underskirt made of crinoline

¹**crip·ple** \ˈkri-pəl\ *n* **:** one that is disabled or deficient in a specified manner

²**cripple** *vb* **crip·pled; crip·pling 1 :** to make lame **2 :** to make useless or imperfect — **crip·pler** \ˈkri-p(ə-)lər\ *n*

cri·sis \ˈkrī-səs\ *n, pl* **cri·ses** \-ˌsēz\ [ME, fr. L, fr. Gk *krisis,* lit., decision, fr. *krinein* to decide] **1 :** the turning point for better or worse in an acute disease or fever **2 :** a decisive or critical moment

crisp \ˈkrisp\ *adj* **1 :** CURLY, WAVY **2 :** BRITTLE ⟨a ~ potato chip⟩ **3 :** FIRM, FRESH ⟨~ lettuce⟩ **4 :** being sharp and clear ⟨a ~ photo⟩ **5 :** LIVELY, SPARKLING **6 :** FROSTY, SNAPPY; *also* **:** INVIGORATING — **crisp** *vb* — **crisp·ly** *adv* — **crisp·ness** *n* — **crispy** *adj*

¹**criss·cross** \ˈkris-ˌkrȯs\ *vb* **1 :** to mark with crossed lines **2 :** to go or pass back and forth

²**crisscross** *adj* **:** marked or characterized by crisscrossing — **crisscross** *adv*

³**crisscross** *n* **:** a pattern formed by crossed lines

crit *abbr* critical; criticism

cri·te·ri·on \krī-ˈtir-ē-ən\ *n, pl* **-ria** \-ē-ə\ **:** a standard on which a judgment may be based

crit·ic \ˈkri-tik\ *n* **1 :** a person who judges literary or artistic works **2 :** one inclined to find fault

crit·i·cal \ˈkri-ti-kəl\ *adj* **1 :** being or relating to a condition or disease involving danger of death ⟨~ care⟩ **2 :** being a crisis **3 :** inclined to criticize **4 :** relating to criticism or critics **5 :** requiring careful judgment ⟨~ thinking⟩ — **crit·i·cal·ly** \-k(ə-)lē\ *adv*

critical care *n* **:** INTENSIVE CARE

crit·i·cise *Brit var of* CRITICIZE

crit·i·cism \ˈkri-tə-ˌsi-zəm\ *n* **1 :** the act of criticizing; *esp* **:** CENSURE **2 :** a judgment or review **3 :** the art of judging works of literature or art

crit·i·cize \ˈkri-tə-ˌsīz\ *vb* **-cized; -ciz·ing 1 :** to judge as a critic **:** EVALUATE **2 :** to find fault **:** express criticism ♦ ***Synonyms*** BLAME, CENSURE, CONDEMN

cri·tique \krə-ˈtēk\ *n* **:** a critical estimate or discussion

crit·ter \ˈkri-tər\ *n* **:** CREATURE

croak \ˈkrōk\ *n* **:** a hoarse harsh cry (as of a frog) — **croak** *vb*

croak·er \ˈkrō-kər\ *n* **1 :** an animal that croaks **2 :** a fish that produces croaking or grunting noises

Croat \ˈkrō-ˌat\ *n* **:** CROATIAN

Cro·atian \krō-ˈā-shən\ *n* **1 :** a native or inhabitant of Croatia **2 :** a Slavic language spoken by Croatians — **Croatian** *adj*

cro·chet \krō-ˈshā\ *n* **:** needlework done with a single thread and hooked needle — **crochet** *vb*

crock \ˈkräk\ *n* **:** a thick earthenware pot or jar

crock·ery \ˈkrä-kə-rē\ *n* **:** EARTHENWARE

croc·o·dile \ˈkrä-kə-ˌdī(-ə)l\ *n* [ME & L; ME *cocodrille,* fr. AF, fr. ML *cocodrillus,* alter. of L *crocodilus,* fr. Gk *krokodilos* lizard, crocodile, fr. *krokē* shingle, pebble + *drilos* worm] **:** any of several thick-skinned long-bodied carnivorous reptiles of tropical and subtropical waters

cro·cus \ˈkrō-kəs\ *n, pl* **cro·cus·es** *also* **crocus** *or* **cro·ci** \-ˌkī\ **:** any of a large genus of low herbs related to the irises and having brightly colored flowers borne singly in early spring

Crohn's disease \ˈkrōnz\ *n* **:** a chronic inflammatory disease of the gastrointestinal tract and esp. the ileum

crois·sant \krə-ˈsänt, krwä-ˈsäⁿ\ *n, pl* **croissants** *same or* -ˈsänts, -ˈsäⁿz\ **:** a rich crescent-shaped roll

Cro–Ma·gnon \krō-ˈmag-nən, -ˈman-yən\ *n* **:** a hominid of a tall erect race known from skeletal remains found in southern

France and usu. classified as the same species as present-day humans — **Cro–Magnon** *adj*

crone \'krōn\ *n* : HAG

cro•ny \'krō-nē\ *n, pl* **cronies** : a close friend esp. of long standing

[1]**crook** \'krůk\ *vb* : to curve or bend sharply

[2]**crook** *n* **1** : a bent or curved implement **2** : a bent or curved part; *also* : BEND, CURVE **3** : SWINDLER, THIEF

crook•ed \'krů-kəd\ *adj* **1** : having a crook : BENT, CURVED **2** : DISHONEST — **crook•ed•ly** *adv* — **crook•ed•ness** *n*

croon \'krün\ *vb* : to sing or hum in a gentle murmuring voice — **croon•er** *n*

[1]**crop** \'kräp\ *n* **1** : the handle of a whip; *also* : a short riding whip **2** : a pouch in the throat of many birds and insects where food is received **3** : something (as a plant product) that can be harvested; *also* : the yield at harvest

[2]**crop** *vb* **cropped**; **crop•ping** **1** : to remove the tips of : cut off short; *also* : TRIM **2** : to feed on by cropping **3** : to devote (land) to crops **4** : to appear unexpectedly ⟨a problem *cropped* up⟩

crop duster *n* : a person who uses an airplane to spray crops with insecticidal dusts; *also* : an airplane so used

crop•land \-ˌland\ *n* : land devoted to the production of plant crops

crop•per \'krä-pər\ *n* : a raiser of crops; *esp* : SHARECROPPER

cro•quet \krō-'kā\ *n* : a game in which mallets are used to drive wooden balls through a series of wickets set out on a lawn

cro•quette \krō-'ket\ *n* [F] : a small often rounded mass of minced meat, fish, or vegetables fried in deep fat

cro•sier *or* **cro•zier** \'krō-zhər\ *n* : a staff carried by bishops and abbots

[1]**cross** \'kròs\ *n* **1** : a structure consisting of an upright beam and a crossbar used esp. by the ancient Romans for execution **2** : a figure of the cross on which Christ was crucified used as a Christian symbol **3** : a hybridizing of unlike individuals or strains; *also* : a product of this **4** : a punch delivered with a circular motion over an opponent's lead

[2]**cross** *vb* **1** : to lie or place across; *also* : INTERSECT **2** : to cancel by marking a cross on or by lining through **3** : THWART, OBSTRUCT **4** : to go or extend across : TRAVERSE **5** : HYBRIDIZE **6** : to meet and pass on the way ⟨our letters ~*ed* in the mail⟩

[3]**cross** *adj* **1** : lying across **2** : CONTRARY, OPPOSED **3** : marked by bad temper **4** : HYBRID — **cross•ly** *adv*

cross•bar \'kròs-ˌbär\ *n* : a transverse bar or piece

cross•bow \-ˌbō\ *n* : a short bow mounted crosswise at the end of a wooden stock that shoots short arrows

cross•breed \'kròs-ˌbrēd, -'brēd\ *vb* **-bred** \-'bred\; **-breed•ing** : HYBRIDIZE

cross–coun•try \-'kən-trē\ *adj* **1** : extending or moving across a country **2** : proceeding over the countryside (as fields and woods) and not by roads **3** : of or relating to racing or skiing over the countryside instead of over a track or run — **cross–country** *adv*

cross•cur•rent \-'kər-ənt\ *n* **1** : a current running counter to another **2** : a conflicting tendency — usu. used in pl.

[1]**cross•cut** \-ˌkət\ *vb* : to cut or saw crosswise esp. of the grain of wood

[2]**crosscut** *adj* **1** : made or used for crosscutting **2** : cut across the grain

[3]**crosscut** *n* : something that cuts through transversely

cross–ex•am•ine \ˌkrò-sig-'za-mən\ *vb* : to examine with questions to check the answers to previous questions — **cross–ex•am•i•na•tion** \-ˌza-mə-'nā-shən\ *n* — **cross–ex•am•in•er** *n*

cross–eyed \'krò-ˌsīd\ *adj* : having one or both eyes turned inward toward the nose

cross–fer•til•i•za•tion \-ˌfər-tə-lə-'zā-shən\ *n* **1** : fertilization between sex cells produced by separate individuals or sometimes by individuals of different kinds; *also* : CROSS-POLLINATION **2** : a broadening or productive interchange (as between cultures) — **cross–fer•til•ize** \-'fərt-tə-ˌlīz\ *vb*

cross fire *n* **1** : crossing lines of fire in combat **2** : rapid or angry interchange

cross•hair \'kròs-ˌher\ *n* : a fine wire or thread in the eyepiece of an optical instrument used as a reference line

cross•hatch \'kròs-ˌhach\ *vb* : to mark with two series of parallel lines that intersect — **cross–hatch•ing** *n*

cross•ing \'krò-siŋ\ *n* **1** : a place or structure for crossing something (as a river) **2** : a point of intersection (as of a street and a railroad track)

cross•over \'kròs-ˌō-vər\ *n* **1** : CROSSING **2** : a member of a political party who votes in the primary of the other party **3** : a broadening of the popular appeal of an artist (as a musician) by a change in the artist's style, genre, or medium **4** : an instance of breaking into another category **5** : a basketball maneuver in which a player dribbles the ball quickly from one hand to the other **6** *or* **crossover SUV** : an automotive vehicle similar to an SUV but built on a car chassis

cross over *vb* : to achieve broader popularity by a change of medium or style

cross•piece \'kròs-ˌpēs\ *n* : a horizontal member

cross–pol•li•na•tion \ˌkròs-ˌpä-lə-'nā-shən\ *n* : transfer of pollen from one flower to the stigma of another — **cross–pol•li•nate** \'kròs-'pä-lə-ˌnāt\ *vb*

cross–pur•pose \'kròs-'pər-pəs\ *n* : a purpose contrary to another purpose

cross–ques•tion \-'kwes-chən\ *vb* : CROSS-EXAMINE — **cross–question** *n*

cross–re•fer \ˌkròs-ri-'fər\ *vb* : to refer by a notation or direction from one place to another (as in a book or list) — **cross–ref•er•ence** \'kròs-'re-frəns\ *n*

cross•road \ˈkrȯs-ˌrōd\ *n* **1 :** a road that crosses a main road or runs between main roads **2 :** a place where roads meet — usu. used in pl. **3 :** a crucial point where a decision must be made — usu. used in pl.

cross section *n* **1 :** a section cut across something; *also* **:** a representation made by or as if by such cutting **2 :** a number of persons or things selected from a group that show the general nature of the whole group — **cross–sec•tion•al** *adj*

cross–sell \ˈkrȯs-ˈsel\ *vb* **:** to sell or promote (a different or related product or service) to an existing customer

cross•walk \ˈkrȯs-ˌwȯk\ *n* **:** a marked path for pedestrians crossing a street

cross•ways \-ˌwāz\ *adv* **:** CROSSWISE

cross•wind \-ˌwind\ *n* **:** a wind not parallel to a course (as of an airplane)

cross•wise \-ˌwīz\ *adv* **:** so as to cross something **:** ACROSS — **crosswise** *adj*

cross•word \ˈkrȯs-ˌwərd\ *n* **:** a puzzle in which words are put into a pattern of numbered squares in answer to clues

cros•ti•ni \krȯ-ˈstē-nē\ *n pl* **:** small slices of toasted bread served with a topping

crotch \ˈkräch\ *n* **:** an angle or area formed by the parting of two legs, branches, or members

crotch•et \ˈkrä-chət\ *n* **:** an odd notion **:** WHIM — **crotch•ety** *adj*

crouch \ˈkrau̇ch\ *vb* **1 :** to stoop or bend low **2 :** CRINGE, COWER — **crouch** *n*

croup \ˈkrüp\ *n* **:** laryngitis esp. of infants marked by a hoarse ringing cough and difficult breathing — **croupy** *adj*

crou•pi•er \ˈkrü-pē-ər, -pē-ˌā\ *n* [F, lit., rider on the rump of a horse, fr. *croupe* rump] **:** an employee of a gambling casino who collects and pays bets at a gaming table

crou•ton \ˈkrü-ˌtän\ *n* [F *croûton,* dim. of *croûte* crust] **:** a small cube of bread toasted or fried crisp

[1]**crow** \ˈkrō\ *n* **1 :** any of various large glossy black birds related to the jays **2** *cap* **:** a member of an Indigenous people of the Great Plains; *also* **:** their language

[2]**crow** *vb* **1 :** to make the loud shrill sound characteristic of the cock **2 :** to utter a sound expressive of pleasure **3 :** EXULT, GLOAT; *also* **:** BRAG, BOAST

[3]**crow** *n* **:** the cry of the cock

crow•bar \ˈkrō-ˌbär\ *n* **:** a metal bar usu. wedge-shaped at the end for use as a pry or lever

[1]**crowd** \ˈkrau̇d\ *vb* **1 :** to press close **2 :** to collect in numbers **:** THRONG **3 :** CRAM, STUFF ⟨a box ~*ed* with toys⟩

[2]**crowd** *n* **:** a large number of people gathered together at random **:** THRONG

crowd•fund \-ˌfənd\ *vb* **:** to obtain funding for (something, such as a new business) by soliciting contributions from a large number of people esp. from the online community

[1]**crown** \ˈkrau̇n\ *n* **1 :** a mark of victory or honor; *esp* **:** the title of a champion in a sport **2 :** a royal headdress **3 :** the top of the head; *also* **:** the part of a hat that covers the top of the head **4 :** the highest part (as of a tree or tooth) **5** *often cap* **:** sovereign power; *also* **:** MONARCH **6 :** a formerly used British silver coin — **crowned** \ˈkrau̇nd\ *adj*

[2]**crown** *vb* **1 :** to place a crown on **2 :** HONOR **3 :** TOP, SURMOUNT **4 :** to fit (a tooth) with an artificial crown

crown vetch *n* **:** a Eurasian leguminous herb with umbels of pink-and-white flowers and sharp-angled pods

crow's–foot \ˈkrōz-ˌfu̇t\ *n, pl* **crow's–feet** \-ˌfēt\ **:** any of the wrinkles around the outer corners of the eyes — usu. used in pl.

crow's nest *n* **:** a partly enclosed platform high on a ship's mast for use as a lookout

crozier *var of* CROSIER

[1]**CRT** \ˌsē-(ˌ)är-ˈtē\ *n, pl* **CRTs** *or* **CRT's** **:** CATHODE-RAY TUBE; *also* **:** a display device incorporating a cathode-ray tube

[2]**CRT** *abbr* carrier route

cru•cial \ˈkrü-shəl\ *adj* **:** DECISIVE ⟨a ~ step⟩; *also* **:** IMPORTANT, SIGNIFICANT ⟨a ~ question⟩

cru•ci•ate \ˈkrü-shē-ˌāt\ *adj* **:** CRUCIFORM

cru•ci•ble \ˈkrü-sə-bəl\ *n* **:** a heat-resistant container in which material can be subjected to great heat

cru•ci•fix \ˈkrü-sə-ˌfiks\ *n* **:** a representation of Christ on the cross

cru•ci•fix•ion \ˌkrü-sə-ˈfik-shən\ *n* **1** *cap* **:** the crucifying of Christ **2 :** the act of crucifying

cru•ci•form \ˈkrü-sə-ˌfȯrm\ *adj* **:** shaped like a cross

cru•ci•fy \ˈkrü-sə-ˌfī\ *vb* **-fied; -fy•ing 1 :** to put to death by nailing or binding the hands and feet to a cross **2 :** MORTIFY 1 **3 :** TORTURE, PERSECUTE

[1]**crude** \ˈkrüd\ *adj* **crud•er; crud•est 1 :** not refined **:** RAW ⟨~ oil⟩ ⟨~ statistics⟩ **2 :** lacking grace, taste, tact, or polish **:** RUDE — **crude•ly** *adv* — **crude•ness** *n* — **cru•di•ty** \ˈkrü-də-tē\ *n*

[2]**crude** *n* **:** unrefined petroleum

cru•el \ˈkrü-əl\ *adj* **cru•el•er** *or* **cru•el•ler; cru•el•est** *or* **cru•el•lest** [ME, fr. AF, fr. L *crudelis,* fr. *crudus* crude] **:** causing pain and suffering to others **:** MERCILESS — **cru•el•ly** *adv* — **cru•el•ty** \-tē\ *n*

cru•et \ˈkrü-ət\ *n* **:** a small usu. glass bottle for vinegar, oil, or sauce

cruise \ˈkrüz\ *vb* **cruised; cruis•ing** [D *kruisen* to make a cross, cruise] **1 :** to sail about touching at a series of ports **2 :** to travel for pleasure **3 :** to travel about the streets at random **4 :** to travel at the most efficient operating speed ⟨the plane's *cruising* speed⟩ **5 :** SURF 2 — **cruise** *n*

cruis•er \ˈkrü-zər\ *n* **1 :** SQUAD CAR **2 :** a large fast moderately armored and gunned warship **3 :** a motorboat equipped for living aboard

cruis•er•weight \-ˌwāt\ *n* **:** a boxer weighing no more than 190 pounds

crul•ler \ˈkrə-lər\ *n* **1 :** a small sweet cake in the form of a twisted strip fried in deep fat **2** *Northern & Midland* **:** an unraised doughnut

[1]**crumb** \ˈkrəm\ *n* : a small fragment
[2]**crumb** *vb* **1** : to break into crumbs **2** : to cover with crumbs
crum·ble \ˈkrəm-bəl\ *vb* **crum·bled**; **crum·bling** : to break into small pieces : DISINTEGRATE — **crum·bly** *adj*
crum·my *also* **crumby** \ˈkrə-mē\ *adj* **crum·mi·er** *also* **crumb·i·er**; **-est** : very poor or inferior : LOUSY
crum·pet \ˈkrəm-pət\ *n* : a small round unsweetened bread cooked on a griddle
crum·ple \ˈkrəm-pəl\ *vb* **crum·pled**; **crum·pling** **1** : to crush together : RUMPLE **2** : COLLAPSE
[1]**crunch** \ˈkrənch\ *vb* : to chew with a grinding noise; *also* : to grind or press with a crushing noise
[2]**crunch** *n* **1** : an act of or a sound made by crunching **2** : a tight or critical situation — **crunchy** *adj*
cru·sade \krü-ˈsād\ *n* **1** *cap* : any of the expeditions in the 11th, 12th, and 13th centuries undertaken by Christian countries to take the Holy Land from the Muslims **2** : a reforming enterprise undertaken with zeal — **crusade** *vb* — **cru·sad·er** *n*
cruse \ˈkrüz, ˈkrüs\ *n* : a jar for water or oil
[1]**crush** \ˈkrəsh\ *vb* **1** : to squeeze out of shape **2** : HUG, EMBRACE **3** : to grind or pound to small bits **4** : OVERWHELM, SUPPRESS **5** : to experience an intense and usu. passing infatuation
[2]**crush** *n* **1** : an act of crushing **2** : a violent crowding **3** : INFATUATION
crust \ˈkrəst\ *n* **1** : the outside part of bread; *also* : a piece of old dry bread **2** : the cover of a pie **3** : a hard or brittle surface layer — **crust·al** *adj*
crus·ta·cean \ˌkrəs-ˈtā-shən\ *n* : any of a large class of mostly aquatic arthropods (as lobsters or crabs) having a firm crustlike shell — **crustacean** *adj*
crusty \ˈkrəs-tē\ *adj* **crust·i·er**; **-est** **1** : having or being a crust **2** : CROSS, GRUMPY
crutch \ˈkrəch\ *n* : a supporting device; *esp* : a support fitting under the armpit for use by the disabled in walking
crux \ˈkrəks, ˈkrüks\ *n, pl* **crux·es** [L, cross, torture] **1** : a puzzling or difficult problem **2** : a crucial point
[1]**cry** \ˈkrī\ *vb* **cried**; **cry·ing** **1** : to call out : SHOUT **2** : to proclaim publicly : ADVERTISE **3** : WEEP
[2]**cry** *n, pl* **cries** **1** : a loud outcry **2** : APPEAL, ENTREATY **3** : a fit of weeping **4** : the characteristic sound uttered by an animal **5** : DISTANCE — usu. used in the phrase *a far cry*
cry·ba·by \ˈkrī-ˌbā-bē\ *n* : one who cries easily or often
cryo·gen·ic \ˌkrī-ə-ˈje-nik\ *adj* : of or relating to the production of very low temperatures; *also* : involving the use of a very low temperature — **cryo·gen·i·cal·ly** \-ni-k(ə-)lē\ *adv*
cryo·gen·ics \-niks\ *n* : a branch of physics that relates to the production and effects of very low temperatures
cryo·lite \ˈkrī-ə-ˌlīt\ *n* : a usu. white mineral formerly used in making aluminum
cryo·sphere \ˈkrī-ō-ˌsfir\ *n* : the part of the earth's surface characterized by the presence of frozen water
crypt \ˈkript\ *n* : a chamber wholly or partly underground
cryp·tic \ˈkrip-tik\ *adj* : meant to be puzzling or mysterious ⟨~ messages⟩
cryp·to·cur·ren·cy \ˌkrip-tōˈkər-ən-sē\ *n* : a digital currency that usu. has no central issuing or regulating authority, uses a blockchain to record transactions, and relies on cryptography to prevent fraud
cryp·to·gram \ˈkrip-tə-ˌgram\ *n* : a communication in cipher or code
cryp·tog·ra·phy \krip-ˈtä-grə-fē\ *n* **1** : the coding and decoding of secret messages **2** : computerized encoding and decoding of information — **cryp·tog·ra·pher** \-fər\ *n*
cryp·to·sys·tem \ˌkrip-tō-ˈsis-təm\ *n* : a method for coding and decoding messages
crys·tal \ˈkris-tᵊl\ *n* [ME *cristal*, fr. AF, fr. L *crystallum*, fr. Gk *krystallos* ice, crystal] **1** : transparent quartz **2** : something resembling crystal (as in transparency); *esp* : a clear colorless glass of superior quality **3** : a body that is formed by solidification of a substance and has a regular repeating arrangement of atoms and often of external plane faces ⟨a salt ~⟩ **4** : the transparent cover of a watch dial
crystal clear *adj* : perfectly or transparently clear
crys·tal·line \ˈkris-tə-lən\ *adj* **1** : made of or resembling crystal **2** : very clear or sparkling
crys·tal·lise *Brit var of* CRYSTALLIZE
crys·tal·lize \ˈkris-tə-ˌlīz\ *vb* **-lized**; **-liz·ing** **1** : to assume or cause to assume a crystalline form **2** : to take or cause to take a definite form ⟨publicity can ~ public opinion⟩ — **crys·tal·li·za·tion** \ˌkris-tə-lə-ˈzā-shən\ *n*
crys·tal·log·ra·phy \ˌkris-tə-ˈlä-grə-fē\ *n* : the science dealing with the forms and structures of crystals — **crys·tal·log·ra·pher** *n*
cs *abbr* case; cases
Cs *symbol* cesium
CS *abbr* **1** civil service **2** county seat
CSA *abbr* Confederate States of America
C–section \ˈsē-ˌsek-shən\ *n* : CESAREAN SECTION
CSM *abbr* command sergeant major
CST *abbr* central standard time
ct *abbr* **1** carat **2** cent **3** count **4** county **5** court
CT *abbr* **1** central time **2** Connecticut
CTE *abbr* chronic traumatic encephalopathy
ctn *abbr* carton
ctr *abbr* **1** center **2** counter
CT scan \ˌsē-ˈtē-\ *n* : CAT SCAN
cu *abbr* cubic
Cu *symbol* [L *cuprum*] copper
cub \ˈkəb\ *n* : a young individual of some animals (as a fox, bear, or lion)

Cu·ban sandwich \ˈkyü-bən-\ *n* : a usu. grilled and pressed sandwich served on a long split roll

cub·by·hole \ˈkə-bē-ˌhōl\ *n* : a snug place (as for storing things)

[1]**cube** \ˈkyüb\ *n* **1** : a solid having 6 equal square sides **2** : the result of raising a number to the third power ⟨the ~ of 3 is 27⟩

[2]**cube** *vb* **cubed**; **cub·ing 1** : to raise to the third power **2** : to form into a cube **3** : to cut into cubes

cube root *n* : a number whose cube is a given number

cu·bic \ˈkyü-bik\ *also* **cu·bi·cal** *adj* **1** : having the form of a cube **2** : being the volume of a cube whose edge is a specified unit **3** : having length, width, and height

cu·bi·cle \ˈkyü-bi-kəl\ *n* : a small separate space (as for sleeping, studying, or working)

cubic measure *n* : a unit (as cubic inch) for measuring volume — see METRIC SYSTEM table, WEIGHT table

cubic zir·co·nia \-ˌzər-ˈkō-nē-ə\ *also* **cubic zirconium** *n* : a synthetic gemstone resembling a diamond made from an oxide of zirconium

cub·ism \ˈkyü-ˌbi-zəm\ *n* : a style of art characterized by the abstraction of natural forms into fragmented geometric shapes — **cub·ist** \-bist\ *n or adj*

cu·bit \ˈkyü-bət\ *n* : an ancient unit of length equal to about 18 inches (46 centimeters)

Cub Scout *n* : a member of the program of the Boy Scouts for boys in the first through fifth grades in school

cuck·old \ˈkə-kəld, ˈku̇-\ *n* : a man whose wife is unfaithful — **cuckold** *vb*

[1]**cuck·oo** \ˈkü-kü, ˈku̇-\ *n, pl* **cuckoos** : a largely grayish brown European bird that lays its eggs in the nests of other birds for them to hatch

[2]**cuckoo** *adj* : SILLY, FOOLISH

cu·cum·ber \ˈkyü-(ˌ)kəm-bər\ *n* : the long fleshy many-seeded fruit of a vine of the gourd family that is grown as a garden vegetable; *also* : this vine

cud \ˈkəd\ *n* : food brought up into the mouth by some animals (as cows) from the rumen to be chewed again

cud·dle \ˈkə-dᵊl\ *vb* **cud·dled**; **cud·dling** : to lie close : SNUGGLE

cud·gel \ˈkə-jəl\ *n* : a short heavy club — **cudgel** *vb*

[1]**cue** \ˈkyü\ *n* **1** : a word, phrase, or action in a play serving as a signal for the next actor to speak or act **2** : HINT — **cue** *vb*

[2]**cue** *n* : a tapered rod for striking the balls in billiards or pool

cue ball *n* : the ball a player strikes with a cue in billiards or pool

[1]**cuff** \ˈkəf\ *n* **1** : a part (as of a sleeve or glove) encircling the wrist **2** : the folded hem of a trouser leg

[2]**cuff** *vb* : to strike esp. with the open hand : SLAP

[3]**cuff** *n* : a blow with the hand esp. when open

cui·sine \kwi-ˈzēn\ *n* : style of cooking; *also* : the food prepared

cuke \ˈkyük\ *n* : CUCUMBER

cul–de–sac \ˌkəl-di-ˈsak, ˌku̇l-\ *n, pl* **cul–de–sacs** \ˌkəl-də-ˈsaks, ˌku̇l-\ *also* **culs–de–sac** *same or* ˌkəlz-, ˌku̇lz-\ [F, lit., bottom of the bag] : a street or passage closed at one end

cu·li·nary \ˈkə-lə-ˌner-ē, ˈkyü-\ *adj* : of or relating to the kitchen or cookery

[1]**cull** \ˈkəl\ *vb* **1** : to pick out from a group **2** : to reduce or control the size of (as a herd of animals) by removal (as by hunting or slaughter) of individuals

[2]**cull** *n* : something rejected from a group or lot as worthless or inferior

cul·mi·nate \ˈkəl-mə-ˌnāt\ *vb* **-nat·ed**; **-nat·ing** : to reach the highest point — **cul·mi·na·tion** \ˌkəl-mə-ˈnā-shən\ *n*

cu·lotte \ˈkü-ˌlät, ˌkyü-, ku̇-ˌlät, kyu̇-\ *n* [F, breeches, fr. dim. of *cul* backside] : a divided skirt; *also* : a garment having a divided skirt — often used in pl.

cul·pa·ble \ˈkəl-pə-bəl\ *adj* : deserving blame — **cul·pa·bil·i·ty** \ˌkəl-pə-ˈbi-lə-tē\ *n*

cul·prit \ˈkəl-prət\ *n* [AF *cul.* (abbr. of *culpable* guilty) + *prest, prit* ready (i.e., to prove it), fr. L *praestus*] : one accused or guilty of a crime

cult \ˈkəlt\ *n* **1** : formal religious veneration **2** : a religious system; *also* : its adherents **3** : faddish devotion; *also* : a group of persons showing such devotion — **cult·ish** \ˈkəl-tish\ *adj* — **cult·ist** \-tist\ *n*

cul·ti·va·ble \ˈkəl-tə-və-bəl\ *adj* : capable of being cultivated

cul·ti·var \ˈkəl-tə-ˌvär, -ver\ *n* : a plant variety originating and persisting under cultivation

cul·ti·vate \ˈkəl-tə-ˌvāt\ *vb* **-vat·ed**; **-vat·ing 1** : to prepare for the raising of crops **2** : to foster the growth of by tilling or by labor and care ⟨~ vegetables⟩ **3** : REFINE, IMPROVE ⟨~ the mind⟩ **4** : ENCOURAGE, FURTHER ⟨~ the arts⟩ **5** : to seek the friendship of — **cul·ti·va·tion** \ˌkəl-tə-ˈvā-shən\ *n* — **cul·ti·va·tor** \ˈkəl-tə-ˌvā-tər\ *n*

cul·ture \ˈkəl-chər\ *n* **1** : TILLAGE, CULTIVATION **2** : the act of developing by education and training **3** : refinement of intellectual and artistic taste **4** : the customary beliefs, social forms, and material traits of a racial, religious, or social group — **cul·tur·al** \ˈkəl-chə-rəl\ *adj* — **cul·tur·al·ly** *adv* — **cul·tured** \-chərd\ *adj*

cul·vert \ˈkəl-vərt\ *n* : a drain crossing under a road or railroad

cum *abbr* cumulative

cum·ber \ˈkəm-bər\ *vb* : to weigh down : BURDEN, HINDER

cum·ber·some \ˈkəm-bər-səm\ *adj* : hard to handle or manage because of size or weight — **cum·ber·some·ly** *adv*

cum·brous \ˈkəm-brəs\ *adj* : CUMBERSOME — **cum·brous·ly** *adv* — **cum·brous·ness** *n*

cum·in \ˈkə-mən, ˈkyü-\ *n* : the seedlike

fruit of a small annual herb related to the carrot that is used as a spice; *also* : this herb

cum·mer·bund \ˈkə-mər-ˌbənd, ˈkəm-bər-\ *n* [Hindi & Urdu *kamarband*, fr. Pers, fr. *kamar* waist + *band* band] : a broad sash worn as a waistband

cu·mu·la·tive \ˈkyü-myə-lə-tiv, -ˌlā-\ *adj* : increasing in force or value by successive additions

cu·mu·lo·nim·bus \ˌkyü-myə-lō-ˈnim-bəs\ *n* : an anvil-shaped cumulus cloud extending to great heights

cu·mu·lus \ˈkyü-myə-ləs\ *n, pl* **-li** \-ˌlī, -ˌlē\ : a dense puffy cloud having a flat base and rounded outlines

cu·ne·i·form \kyü-ˈnē-ə-ˌfȯrm\ *adj* **1** : wedge-shaped **2** : composed of wedge-shaped characters

cun·ni·lin·gus \ˌkə-ni-ˈliŋ-gəs\ *also* **cun·ni·linc·tus** \-ˈliŋk-təs\ *n* : oral stimulation of the vulva or clitoris

¹cun·ning \ˈkə-niŋ\ *adj* **1** : SKILLFUL, DEXTEROUS **2** : marked by wiliness and trickery ‹~ schemes› **3** : CUTE ‹a ~ kitten› — **cun·ning·ly** *adv*

²cunning *n* **1** : SKILL **2** : SLYNESS

¹cup \ˈkəp\ *n* **1** : a small bowl-shaped drinking vessel **2** : the contents of a cup **3** : the consecrated wine of the Communion **4** : something resembling a cup : a small bowl or hollow **5** : a half pint — **cup·ful** *n* — **cup·like** \-ˌlīk\ *adj*

²cup *vb* **cupped**; **cup·ping** : to curve into the shape of a cup

cup·board \ˈkə-bərd\ *n* : a small closet with shelves for food or dishes

cup·cake \ˈkəp-ˌkāk\ *n* : a small cake baked in a cuplike mold

cu·pid \ˈkyü-pəd\ *n* : a winged naked figure of an infant often with a bow and arrow that represents the god Cupid

cu·pid·i·ty \kyü-ˈpi-də-tē\ *n, pl* **-ties** : excessive desire for money

cu·po·la \ˈkyü-pə-lə, -ˌlō\ *n* : a small structure on top of a roof or building

¹cur \ˈkər\ *n* : a mongrel dog

²cur *abbr* **1** currency **2** current

¹cu·rate \ˈkyu̇r-ət\ *n* **1** : a member of the clergy who is in charge of a parish **2** : a member of the clergy who assists a rector or vicar — **cu·ra·cy** \-ə-sē\ *n*

²cu·rate \ˈkyu̇r-ˌāt\ *vb* **cu·rat·ed cu·rat·ing** : to act as a curator of ‹~ a museum exhibit›

cu·rat·ed \-ˌā-təd\ *adj* : carefully chosen and thoughtfully organized or presented

cu·ra·tive \-ə-tiv\ *adj* **1** : relating to or used in the cure of diseases ‹~ therapy› ‹~ powers› **2** : serving to correct or negate ‹a ~ amendment› — **curative** *n*

cu·ra·tor \ˈkyu̇r-ˈā-tər, kyu̇-ˈrā-\ *n* : CUSTODIAN; *esp* : one in charge of a place of exhibit (as a museum or zoo)

¹curb \ˈkərb\ *n* **1** : a bit that exerts pressure on a horse's jaws **2** : CHECK, RESTRAINT **3** : a raised edging (as of stone or concrete) along a paved street

²curb *vb* : to hold in or back : RESTRAIN

curb·ing \ˈkər-biŋ\ *n* **1** : the material for a curb **2** : CURB

curd \ˈkərd\ *n* : the thick protein-rich part of coagulated milk

cur·dle \ˈkər-dᵊl\ *vb* **cur·dled**; **cur·dling** : to form curds; *also* : SPOIL, SOUR

¹cure \ˈkyu̇r\ *n* **1** : spiritual care **2** : recovery or relief from disease **3** : a curative agent : REMEDY **4** : a course or period of treatment

²cure *vb* **cured**; **cur·ing** **1** : to restore to health : HEAL, REMEDY; *also* : to become cured **2** : to process for storage or use ‹~ bacon› — **cur·able** *adj*

cu·ré \kyu̇-ˈrā\ *n* [F] : a parish priest

cure–all \ˈkyu̇r-ˌȯl\ *n* : a remedy for all ills : PANACEA

cu·ret·tage \ˌkyu̇r-ə-ˈtäzh\ *n* : a surgical scraping or cleaning of a body part (as the uterus)

cur·few \ˈkər-ˌfyü\ *n* [ME, fr. AF *covrefeu*, signal given to bank the hearth fire, curfew, fr. *coverir* to cover + *fu, feu* fire, fr. L *focus* hearth] : a regulation or requirement that specified persons (as children) be off the streets or at home at a stated time; *also* : the sounding of a signal (as a bell) at this time

cu·ria \ˈkyu̇r-ē-ə, ˈku̇r-\ *n, pl* **cu·ri·ae** \ˈkyu̇r-ē-ˌē, ˈku̇r-ē-ˌī\ *often cap* : the body of congregations, tribunals, and offices through which the pope governs the Roman Catholic Church

cu·rie \ˈkyu̇r-ē\ *n* : a unit of radioactivity equal to 37 billion disintegrations per second

cu·rio \ˈkyu̇r-ē-ˌō\ *n, pl* **cu·ri·os** : an object or article valued because it is strange or rare

cu·ri·ous \ˈkyu̇r-ē-əs\ *adj* **1** : having a desire to investigate and learn **2** : STRANGE, UNUSUAL, ODD ‹a ~ coincidence› — **cu·ri·os·i·ty** \ˌkyu̇r-ē-ˈä-sə-tē\ *n* — **cu·ri·ous·ness**

cu·ri·ous·ly *adv* **1** : in a curious manner **2** : as is curious

cu·ri·um \ˈkyu̇r-ē-əm\ *n* : a metallic radioactive element produced artificially

¹curl \ˈkərl\ *vb* **1** : to form into ringlets **2** : CURVE, COIL — **curl·er** *n*

²curl *n* **1** : a lock of hair that coils : RINGLET **2** : something having a spiral or twisted form — **curly** *adj*

cur·lew \ˈkər-lü, ˈkərl-yü\ *n, pl* **curlews** *or* **curlew** : any of various long-legged brownish birds that have a down-curved bill and are related to the sandpipers and snipes

curli·cue \ˈkər-li-ˌkyü\ *n* : a fancifully curved or spiral figure

cur·rant \ˈkər-ənt\ *n* **1** : a small seedless raisin **2** : the acid berry of various shrubs related to the gooseberry; *also* : this plant

cur·ren·cy \ˈkər-ən-sē\ *n, pl* **-cies** **1** : general use or acceptance **2** : something that is in circulation as a medium of exchange : MONEY

¹cur·rent \ˈkər-ənt\ *adj* **1** : occurring in or belonging to the present ‹the ~ crisis› **2** : used as a medium of exchange **3** : generally accepted or practiced

²current *n* **1** : the part of a body of fluid moving continuously in a certain direction; *also* : the swiftest part of a stream **2**

: a flow of electric charge; *also* : the rate of such flow

cur·ric·u·lum \kə-ˈri-kyə-ləm\ *n, pl* **-la** \-lə\ *also* **-lums** [L, running, course, fr. *currere* to run] : the courses offered by an educational institution

¹**cur·ry** \ˈkər-ē\ *vb* **cur·ried; cur·ry·ing** **1** : to clean the coat of (a horse) with a currycomb **2** : to treat (tanned leather) esp. by incorporating oil or grease — **curry favor** : to seek to gain favor by flattery or attention

²**cur·ry** *n, pl* **cur·ries** : a powder of pungent spices used in cooking; *also* : a food seasoned with curry

cur·ry·comb \-ˌkōm\ *n* : a comb used esp. to curry horses — **currycomb** *vb*

¹**curse** \ˈkərs\ *n* **1** : a prayer for harm to come upon one **2** : something that is cursed **3** : evil or misfortune coming as if in response to a curse

²**curse** *vb* **cursed; curs·ing** **1** : to call on divine power to send injury upon **2** : BLASPHEME **3** : AFFLICT ♦ ***Synonyms*** EXECRATE, DAMN, ANATHEMATIZE, OBJURGATE

cur·sive \ˈkər-siv\ *adj* : written with the strokes of the letters joined together and the angles rounded

cur·sor \ˈkər-sər\ *n* : a visual cue (as a pointer) on a computer screen that indicates position (as for data entry)

cur·so·ry \ˈkər-sə-rē\ *adj* : rapidly and often superficially done : HASTY ⟨a ~ reading⟩ — **cur·so·ri·ly** \-rə-lē\ *adj*

curt \ˈkərt\ *adj* : rudely short or abrupt — **curt·ly** *adv* — **curt·ness** *n*

cur·tail \(ˌ)kər-ˈtāl\ *vb* : to cut off the end of : SHORTEN — **cur·tail·ment** *n*

cur·tain \ˈkər-tᵊn\ *n* **1** : a hanging screen that can be drawn back esp. at a window **2** : the screen between the stage and auditorium of a theater — **curtain** *vb*

curt·sy *also* **curt·sey** \ˈkərt-sē\ *n, pl* **curtsies** *or* **curtseys** : a courteous bow made by women chiefly by bending the knees — **curtsy** *also* **curtsey** *vb*

cur·va·ceous *also* **cur·va·cious** \ˌkər-ˈvā-shəs\ *adj* : having curves suggestive of a well-proportioned feminine figure

cur·va·ture \ˈkər-və-ˌchu̇r\ *n* : a measure or amount of curving : BEND

¹**curve** \ˈkərv\ *vb* **curved; curv·ing** : to bend from a straight line or course

²**curve** *n* **1** : a line esp. when curved **2** : something that bends or curves without angles ⟨a ~ in the road⟩ **3** : a baseball pitch thrown so that it swerves esp. downward and to one side **4** : a representation of the way a single variable changes over time ⟨a learning ~⟩ **5** : TREND — **curvy** \ˈkər-vē\ *adj*

cur·vet \(ˌ)kər-ˈvet\ *n* : a prancing leap of a horse — **curvet** *vb*

¹**cush·ion** \ˈku̇-shən\ *n* [ME *cusshin,* fr. AF *cussin, quissin,* fr. VL **coxinus,* fr. L *coxa* hip] **1** : a soft pillow or pad to rest on or against **2** : the springy pad inside the rim of a billiard table **3** : something soft that prevents discomfort or protects against injury

²**cushion** *vb* **1** : to provide (as a seat) with a cushion **2** : to soften or lessen the force or shock of

cusp \ˈkəsp\ *n* : a pointed end or part (as of a tooth)

cus·pid \ˈkəs-pəd\ *n* : a canine tooth

cus·pi·dor \ˈkəs-pə-ˌdȯr\ *n* : SPITTOON

cus·tard \ˈkəs-tərd\ *n* : a sweetened cooked mixture of milk and eggs

cus·to·di·al \ˌkəs-ˈtō-dē-əl\ *adj* : marked by watching and protecting rather than seeking to cure ⟨~ care⟩

cus·to·di·an \ˌkəs-ˈtō-dē-ən\ *n* : one who has custody (as of a building)

cus·to·dy \ˈkəs-tə-dē\ *n, pl* **-dies** : immediate charge and control

¹**cus·tom** \ˈkəs-təm\ *n* **1** : habitual course of action : recognized usage **2** *pl* : taxes levied on imports **3** : business patronage

²**custom** *adj* **1** : made to personal order **2** : doing work only on order

cus·tom·ary \ˈkəs-tə-ˌmer-ē\ *adj* **1** : based on or established by custom **2** : commonly practiced or observed : HABITUAL — **cus·tom·ar·i·ly** *adv*

cus·tom–built \ˈkəs-təm-ˈbilt\ *adj* : built to individual order

cus·tom·er \ˈkəs-tə-mər\ *n* : BUYER, PURCHASER; *esp* : a regular or frequent buyer

cus·tom·house \ˈkəs-təm-ˌhau̇s\ *n* : the building where customs are paid

cus·tom·ise *Brit var of* CUSTOMIZE

cus·tom·ize \ˈkəs-tə-ˌmīz\ *vb* **-ized; -iz·ing** : to build, fit, or alter according to individual specifications

cus·tom–made \ˈkəs-təm-ˈmād\ *adj* : made to individual order

¹**cut** \ˈkət\ *vb* **cut; cut·ting** **1** : to penetrate or divide with a sharp edge : CLEAVE, GASH; *also* : to experience the growth of (a tooth) through the gum **2** : to hurt the feelings of **3** : to strike sharply **4** : SHORTEN, REDUCE **5** : to remove by severing or paring **6** : INTERSECT, CROSS **7** : to divide into parts **8** : to go quickly or change direction abruptly **9** : to cause to stop **10** : to remove (text, etc.) from a computer document for pasting elsewhere

²**cut** *n* **1** : something made by cutting : GASH, CLEFT **2** : SHARE **3** : a segment or section of a meat carcass **4** : an excavated channel or roadway **5** : BAND 4 **6** : a sharp stroke or blow **7** : REDUCTION ⟨a ~ in wages⟩ **8** : the shape or manner in which a thing is cut

cut–and–dried \ˌkət-ᵊn-ˈdrīd\ *also* **cut–and–dry** \-ˈdrī\ *adj* : according to a plan, set procedure, or formula

cu·ta·ne·ous \kyu̇-ˈtā-nē-əs\ *adj* : of, relating to, or affecting the skin

cut·back \ˈkət-ˌbak\ *n* **1** : something cut back **2** : REDUCTION

cute \ˈkyüt\ *adj* **cut·er; cut·est** [short for *acute*] **1** : CLEVER, SHREWD **2** : daintily attractive : PRETTY

cu·ti·cle \ˈkyü-ti-kəl\ *n* **1** : an outer layer (as of skin or a leaf) **2** : dead or horny epidermis esp. around a fingernail — **cu·tic·u·lar** \kyu̇-ˈti-kyə-lər\ *adj*

cut in *vb* **1** : to thrust oneself between

others **2** : to interrupt a dancing couple and take one as one's partner

cut·lass \ˈkət-ləs\ *n* : a short heavy curved sword

cut·ler \ˈkət-lər\ *n* [ME, fr. AF *cuteler,* fr. LL *cultellarius,* fr. L *cultellus* knife] : one who makes, deals in, or repairs cutlery

cut·lery \ˈkət-lə-rē\ *n* : edged or cutting tools; *esp* : implements for cutting and eating food

cut·let \ˈkət-lət\ *n* : a slice of meat (as veal) for broiling or frying

cut·off \ˈkət-ˌȯf\ *n* **1** : the channel formed when a stream cuts through the neck of an oxbow; *also* : SHORTCUT **2** : a device for cutting off **3** *pl* : shorts orig. made from jeans with the legs cut off at the knees or higher

cut·out \ˈkət-ˌau̇t\ *n* : something cut out or prepared for cutting out from something else

cut out *vb* **1** : to determine or assign through necessity ⟨had her work *cut out* for her⟩ **2** : DISCONNECT **3** : to cease operating ⟨the engine *cut out*⟩ **4** : ELIMINATE ⟨*cut out* unnecessary expense⟩

cut–rate \ˈkət-ˈrāt\ *adj* : relating to or dealing in goods sold at reduced rates

cut·ter \ˈkə-tər\ *n* **1** : a tool or a machine for cutting **2** : a ship's boat for carrying stores and passengers **3** : a small armed vessel in government service **4** : a light sleigh

[1]**cut·throat** \ˈkət-ˌthrōt\ *n* : MURDERER

[2]**cutthroat** *adj* **1** : MURDEROUS, CRUEL **2** : RUTHLESS ⟨~ competition⟩

cutthroat trout *n* : a large American trout with a red mark under the jaw

[1]**cut·ting** \ˈkə-tiŋ\ *n* : a piece of a plant able to grow into a new plant

[2]**cutting** *adj* **1** : SHARP, EDGED **2** : marked by piercing cold **3** : likely to hurt the feelings : SARCASTIC ⟨a ~ remark⟩

cut·tle·fish \ˈkə-tᵊl-ˌfish\ *n* : any of various marine mollusks having eight arms and two usu. longer tentacles and an internal shell (**cut·tle·bone** \-ˌbōn\) composed of calcium compounds

cut·up \ˈkət-ˌəp\ *n* : a person who clowns or acts boisterously — **cut up** *vb*

cut·worm \-ˌwərm\ *n* : any of various smooth-bodied moth larvae that feed on plants at night

cw *abbr* clockwise

CWO *abbr* **1** cash with order **2** chief warrant officer

cwt *abbr* hundredweight

-cy \sē\ *n suffix* **1** : action : practice ⟨mendican*cy*⟩ **2** : rank : office ⟨chaplain*cy*⟩ **3** : body : class ⟨constituen*cy*⟩ **4** : state : quality ⟨accura*cy*⟩

cy·an \ˈsī-ˌan, -ən\ *n* : a greenish blue color

cy·a·nide \ˈsī-ə-ˌnīd, -nəd\ *n* : a poisonous compound of carbon and nitrogen with another element (as potassium)

cy·ber \ˈsī-bər\ *adj* : of, relating to, or involving computers or computer networks

cyber- *comb form* : computer : computer network

cy·ber·at·tack \ˈsī-bər-ə-ˌtak\ *n* : an attempt to gain illegal access to a computer or computer system for the purpose of causing damage or harm

cy·ber·bul·ly·ing \ˈsī-bər-ˌbu̇-lē-iŋ, -ˌbə-\ *n* : the electronic posting of mean-spirited messages about a person

cy·ber·ca·fe \ˈsī-bər-ka-ˈfā\ *n* : a small restaurant offering use of computers with Internet access

cy·ber·net·ics \ˌsī-bər-ˈne-tiks\ *n* : the science of communication and control theory that is concerned esp. with the comparative study of automatic control systems — **cy·ber·net·ic** *adj*

cy·ber·punk \ˈsī-bər-ˌpəŋk\ *n* **1** : science fiction dealing with computer-dominated future societies **2** : HACKER 3

cy·ber·sex \ˈsī-bər-ˌseks\ *n* **1** : online sex-oriented conversations **2** : sex-oriented material available on a computer

cy·ber·space \ˈsī-bər-ˌspās\ *n* : the online world of the Internet

cy·ber·ter·ror·ism \-ˌter-ər-ˌi-zəm\ *n* : terrorist activities intended to damage or disrupt computer systems

cy·cla·men \ˈsī-klə-mən\ *n* : any of a genus of plants related to the primroses and having showy nodding flowers

[1]**cy·cle** \ˈsī-kəl\ *n* **1** : a period of time occupied by a series of events that repeat themselves regularly and in the same order **2** : a recurring round of operations or events **3** : one complete occurrence of a periodic process (as a vibration or current alternation) **4** : a circular or spiral arrangement **5** : a long period of time : AGE **6** : BICYCLE **7** : MOTORCYCLE — **cy·clic** \ˈsī-klik, ˈsi-\ *or* **cy·cli·cal** \-kli-kəl\ *adj* — **cy·cli·cal·ly** \-k(ə-)lē\ *also* **cy·clic·ly** *adv*

[2]**cycle** *vb* **cy·cled**; **cy·cling** : to ride a cycle — **cy·clist** \ˈsī-klist, -kə-list\ *n*

cy·clone \ˈsī-ˌklōn\ *n* **1** : a storm or system of winds that rotates about a center of low atmospheric pressure and advances at 20 to 30 miles (about 30 to 50 kilometers) an hour **2** : TORNADO — **cy·clon·ic** \sī-ˈklä-nik\ *adj*

cy·clo·pe·dia *also* **cy·clo·pae·dia** \ˌsī-klə-ˈpē-dē-ə\ *n* : ENCYCLOPEDIA

cy·clo·tron \ˈsī-klə-ˌträn\ *n* : a device for giving high speed to charged particles by magnetic and electric fields

cy·der *Brit var of* CIDER

cyg·net \ˈsig-nət\ *n* : a young swan

cyl *abbr* cylinder

cyl·in·der \ˈsi-lən-dər\ *n* : the solid figure formed by turning a rectangle about one side as an axis; *also* : a body or space of this form ⟨an engine ~⟩ ⟨a bullet in the ~ of a revolver⟩ — **cy·lin·dri·cal** \sə-ˈlin-dri-kəl\ *adj*

cym·bal \ˈsim-bəl\ *n* : a concave brass plate that produces a brilliant clashing sound

cyn·ic \ˈsi-nik\ *n* : one who attributes all actions to selfish motives — **cyn·i·cal** \-ni-kəl\ *adj* — **cyn·i·cal·ly** \-k(ə-)lē\ *adv* — **cyn·i·cism** \si-nə-ˌsi-zəm\ *n*

cy·no·sure \ˈsī-nə-ˌshu̇r, ˈsi-\ *n* [MF & L;

MF, Ursa Minor, guide, fr. L *cynosura* Ursa Minor, fr. Gk *kynosoura,* fr. *kynos oura,* lit., dog's tail] : a center of attraction

CYO *abbr* Catholic Youth Organization

cy·pher *chiefly Brit var of* CIPHER

cy·press \ˈsī-prəs\ *n* **1 :** any of a genus of scaly-leaved evergreen trees and shrubs **2 :** BALD CYPRESS **3 :** the wood of a cypress

cyst \ˈsist\ *n* **:** an abnormal closed bodily sac usu. containing liquid — **cys·tic** \ˈsis-tik\ *adj*

cystic fibrosis *n* **:** a hereditary disease marked esp. by thick sticky mucus in the lungs and pancreas, respiratory symptoms (as persistent cough or infection), and excess sodium and chloride in the sweat

cy·tol·o·gy \sī-ˈtä-lə-jē\ *n* **:** a branch of biology dealing with cells — **cy·to·log·i·cal** \ˌsī-tə-ˈlä-ji-kəl\ *or* **cy·to·log·ic** \-jik\ *adj* — **cy·tol·o·gist** \sī-ˈtä-lə-jist\ *n*

cy·to·plasm \ˈsī-tə-ˌpla-zəm\ *n* **:** the protoplasm of a cell that lies external to the nucleus — **cy·to·plas·mic** \ˌsī-tə-ˈplaz-mik\ *adj*

cy·to·sine \ˈsī-tə-ˌsēn\ *n* **:** a chemical base that is a pyrimidine coding genetic information in DNA and RNA

CZ *abbr* **1** Canal Zone **2** cubic zirconia

czar *also* **tsar** *or* **tzar** \ˈzär, ˈtsär\ *n* [NL, fr. Russ *tsar',* ultim. fr. L *Caesar* Caesar] **:** the ruler of Russia until 1917; *also* **:** one having great authority — **czar·ist** *also* **tsar·ist** *or* **tzarist** \-ist\ *n or adj*

cza·ri·na \zä-ˈrē-nə\ *n* **:** the wife of a czar

Czech \ˈchek\ *n* **1 :** a native or inhabitant of Czechoslovakia or the Czech Republic **2 :** the language of the Czechs — **Czech** *adj*

D

¹d \ˈdē\ *n, pl* **d's** *or* **ds** \ˈdēz\ *often cap* **1 :** the 4th letter of the English alphabet **2 :** a grade rating a student's work as poor **3 :** DEFENSE

²d *abbr, often cap* **1** date **2** daughter **3** day **4** dead **5** deceased **6** degree **7** Democrat **8** L *denarius, denarii* penny; pence **9** depart; departure **10** diameter

D *symbol* deuterium

DA *abbr* **1** deposit account **2** district attorney **3** don't answer

¹dab \ˈdab\ *n* **1 :** a sudden blow or thrust **:** POKE; *also* **:** PECK **2 :** a gentle touch or stroke **:** PAT

²dab *vb* **dabbed; dab·bing 1 :** to strike or touch gently **:** PAT **2 :** to apply lightly or irregularly **:** DAUB — **dab·ber** *n*

³dab *n* **1 :** DAUB **2 :** a small amount

dab·ble \ˈda-bəl\ *vb* **dab·bled; dab·bling 1 :** to wet by splashing **:** SPATTER **2 :** to paddle or play in or as if in water **3 :** to work or involve oneself without serious effort — **dab·bler** *n*

da ca·po \dä-ˈkä-(ˌ)pō\ *adv or adj* [It] **:** from the beginning — used as a direction in music to repeat

dace \ˈdās\ *n, pl* **dace :** any of various small No. American freshwater fishes related to the carp

da·cha \ˈdä-chə\ *n* [Russ] **:** a Russian country house

dachs·hund \ˈdäks-ˌhu̇nt\ *n* [G, fr. *Dachs* badger + *Hund* dog] **:** any of a breed of long-bodied short-legged dogs of German origin

dac·tyl \ˈdak-tᵊl\ *n* [ME *dactile,* fr. L *dactylus,* fr. Gk *daktylos,* lit., finger; fr. the fact that the three syllables have the first one longest like the joints of the finger] **:** a metrical foot of one accented syllable followed by two unaccented syllables — **dac·tyl·ic** \dak-ˈti-lik\ *adj or n*

dad \ˈdad\ *n* **:** FATHER 1

Da·da \ˈdä-(ˌ)dä\ *n* **:** a movement in art and literature based on deliberate irrationality and negation of traditional artistic values — **da·da·ism** \-ˌi-zəm\ *n, often cap* — **da·da·ist** \-ˌist\ *n or adj, often cap*

dad·dy \ˈda-dē\ *n, pl* **daddies :** FATHER 1

dad·dy long·legs \ˌda-dē-ˈlȯŋ-ˌlegz\ *n, pl* **daddy longlegs :** any of an order of arachnids resembling the true spiders but having small rounded bodies and long slender legs

daemon *var of* DEMON

daf·fo·dil \ˈda-fə-ˌdil\ *n* **:** any of various bulbous herbs with usu. large flowers having a trumpetlike center

daf·fy \ˈda-fē\ *adj* **daf·fi·er; -est :** DAFT

daft \ˈdaft\ *adj* **1 :** FOOLISH **2** *chiefly Brit, informal* **:** INSANE — **daft·ness** *n*

dag *abbr* dekagram

dag·ger \ˈda-gər\ *n* **1 :** a sharp pointed knife for stabbing **2 :** a character † used as a reference mark or to indicate a death date

da·guerre·o·type \də-ˈger-(ē-)ə-ˌtīp\ *n* **:** an early photograph produced on a silver or a silver-covered copper plate

dahl·ia \ˈdal-yə, ˈdäl-\ *n* **:** any of a genus of tuberous herbs related to the daisies and having showy flowers

¹dai·ly \ˈdā-lē\ *adj* **1 :** occurring, done, or used every day or every weekday **2 :** of or relating to every day ⟨~ visitors⟩ **3 :** computed in terms of one day ⟨~ wages⟩ ♦ ***Synonyms*** DIURNAL, QUOTIDIAN — **dai·li·ness** \-lē-nəs\ *n* — **daily** *adv*

²daily *n, pl* **dailies :** a newspaper published every weekday

daily double *n* **:** a system of betting on races in which the bettor must pick the winners of two stipulated races in order to win

¹dain·ty \ˈdān-tē\ *n, pl* **dainties** [ME *deinte* high esteem, delight, fr. AF *deinté,* fr. L *dignitas* dignity, worth] **:** something delicious or pleasing to the taste **:** DELICACY

[2]**dainty** *adj* **dain·ti·er; -est** **1** : pleasing to the taste **2** : delicately pretty **3** : having or showing delicate taste; *also* : FASTIDIOUS ♦ ***Synonyms*** CHOICE, DELICATE, EXQUISITE, RARE, RECHERCHÉ — **dain·ti·ly** \-ti-lē\ *adv* — **dain·ti·ness** \-tē-nəs\ *n*

dai·qui·ri \ˈda-kə-rē, ˈdī-\ *n* [*Daiquirí*, Cuba] : a cocktail made usu. of rum, lime juice, and sugar

dairy \ˈder-ē\ *n, pl* **dair·ies** [ME *deyerie*, fr. *deye* dairymaid, fr. OE *dǣge* kneader of bread] **1** : CREAMERY **2** : a farm specializing in milk production **3** : food made primarily of or from milk

dairy·ing \ˈder-ē-iŋ\ *n* : the business of operating a dairy

dairy·maid \-ˌmād\ *n* : a woman employed in a dairy

dairy·man \-mən, -ˌman\ *n* : a person who operates a dairy farm or works in a dairy

da·is \ˈdā-əs\ *n* : a raised platform usu. above the floor of a hall or large room

dai·sy \ˈdā-zē\ *n, pl* **daisies** [ME *dayeseye*, fr. OE *dægesēage*, fr. *dæg* day + *ēage* eye] : any of numerous composite plants having flower heads in which the marginal flowers resemble petals

dai·sy–chain \-ˌchān\ *vb* : to link (as computer components) together in series — **daisy chain** *n*

daisy wheel *n* : a disk with spokes bearing type that serves as the printing element of an electric typewriter or printer; *also* : a printer that uses such a disk

Da·ko·ta \də-ˈkō-tə\ *n, pl* **Dakotas** *also* **Dakota** : a member of an Indigenous people of the northern Mississippi valley; *also* : their language

dal *abbr* dekaliter

da·la·si \dä-ˈlä-sē\ *n, pl* **dalasi** *or* **dalasis** — see MONEY table

dale \ˈdāl\ *n* : VALLEY

dal·ly \ˈda-lē\ *vb* **dal·lied; dal·ly·ing** **1** : to act playfully; *esp* : to play amorously **2** : to waste time **3** : LINGER, DAWDLE ♦ ***Synonyms*** FLIRT, COQUET, TOY, TRIFLE — **dal·li·ance** \-lē-əns\ *n*

dal·ma·tian \dal-ˈmā-shən\ *n, often cap* : any of a breed of medium-sized dogs having a white short-haired coat with many black or brown spots

[1]**dam** \ˈdam\ *n* : the female parent of an animal and esp. of a domestic animal

[2]**dam** *n* : a barrier (as across a stream) to stop the flow of water — **dam** *vb*

[3]**dam** *abbr* dekameter

[1]**dam·age** \ˈda-mij\ *n* **1** : loss or harm due to injury to persons, property, or reputation **2** *pl* : compensation in money imposed by law for loss or injury ⟨bring a suit for ~*s*⟩

[2]**damage** *vb* **dam·aged; dam·ag·ing** : to cause damage to ⟨~ the furniture⟩

dam·a·scene \ˈda-mə-ˌsēn\ *vb* **-scened; -scen·ing** : to ornament (as iron or steel) with wavy patterns or with inlaid work of precious metals

dam·ask \ˈda-məsk\ *n* **1** : a firm lustrous reversible figured fabric used for household linen **2** : a tough steel having decorative wavy lines

dame \ˈdām\ *n* **1** : a woman of rank, station, or authority **2** : an elderly woman **3** : WOMAN

damn \ˈdam\ *vb* [ME *dampnen*, fr. AF *dampner*, fr. L *damnare*, fr. *damnum* damage, loss, fine] **1** : to condemn esp. to hell **2** : CURSE — **damned** *adj*

dam·na·ble \ˈdam-nə-bəl\ *adj* **1** : liable to or deserving punishment **2** : DETESTABLE ⟨~ weather⟩ — **dam·na·bly** \-blē\ *adv*

dam·na·tion \dam-ˈnā-shən\ *n* **1** : the act of damning **2** : the state of being damned

[1]**damp** \ˈdamp\ *n* **1** : a noxious gas **2** : MOISTURE

[2]**damp** *vb* : DAMPEN

[3]**damp** *adj* : MOIST — **damp·ness** *n*

damp·en \ˈdam-pən\ *vb* **1** : to check or diminish in activity or vigor ⟨~ enthusiasm⟩ **2** : to make or become damp

damp·er \ˈdam-pər\ *n* **1** : a dulling or deadening influence ⟨put a ~ on the party⟩ **2** : one that damps; *esp* : a valve or movable plate (as in the flue of a stove, furnace, or fireplace) to regulate the draft

dam·sel \ˈdam-zəl\ *n* : MAIDEN, GIRL

dam·sel·fly \-ˌflī\ *n* : any of a group of insects that are closely related to the dragonflies but fold their wings above the body when at rest

dam·son \ˈdam-zən\ *n* : a plum with acid purple fruit; *also* : its fruit

Dan *abbr* Daniel

[1]**dance** \ˈdans\ *vb* **danced; danc·ing** **1** : to glide, step, or move through a set series of movements usu. to music **2** : to move quickly up and down or about **3** : to perform or take part in as a dancer — **danc·er** *n*

[2]**dance** *n* **1** : an act or instance of dancing **2** : a social gathering for dancing **3** : a piece of music (as a waltz) by which dancing may be guided **4** : the art of dancing

D & C *n* [*d*ilation *and* *c*urettage] : a surgical procedure that involves stretching the cervix and scraping the inside walls of the uterus (as to test for cancer or to perform an abortion)

dan·de·li·on \ˈdan-də-ˌlī-ən, -dē-\ *n* [ME *dendelyoun*, fr. AF *dent de lion*, lit., lion's tooth] : any of a genus of common yellow-flowered composite herbs

dan·der \ˈdan-dər\ *n* : ANGER, TEMPER

dan·di·fy \ˈdan-di-ˌfī\ *vb* **-fied; -fy·ing** : to cause to resemble a dandy

dan·dle \ˈdan-dᵊl\ *vb* **dan·dled; dan·dling** : to move up and down in one's arms or on one's knee in affectionate play ♦ ***Synonyms*** CARESS, FONDLE, LOVE, PET

dan·druff \ˈdan-drəf\ *n* : scaly white or grayish flakes of dead skin cells that come off the scalp — **dan·druffy** \-drə-fē\ *adj*

[1]**dan·dy** \ˈdan-dē\ *n, pl* **dandies** **1** : a man unduly attentive to personal appearance **2** : something excellent in its class ♦ ***Synonyms*** FOP, COXCOMB, POPINJAY

[2]**dandy** *adj* **dan·di·er; -est** : very good : FIRST-RATE

Dane \ˈdān\ *n* **1** : a native or inhabitant of Denmark **2** : GREAT DANE

dan·ger \ˈdān-jər\ *n* [ME *daunger* control, resistance, peril, fr. AF *dangier,* fr. VL **dominiarium,* fr. L *dominium* ownership] **1** : exposure or liability to injury, harm, or evil **2** : something that may cause injury or harm ♦ ***Synonyms*** PERIL, HAZARD, RISK, JEOPARDY

dan·ger·ous \ˈdān-jə-rəs\ *adj* **1** : HAZARDOUS, PERILOUS ⟨a ~ slope⟩ **2** : able or likely to inflict injury ⟨a ~ man⟩ — **dan·ger·ous·ly** *adv*

dan·gle \ˈdaŋ-gəl\ *vb* **dan·gled; dan·gling** **1** : to hang loosely esp. with a swinging motion : SWING **2** : to be a hanger-on or dependent **3** : to be left without proper grammatical connection in a sentence ⟨a *dangling* participle⟩ **4** : to keep hanging uncertainly **5** : to offer as an inducement

Dan·iel \ˈdan-yəl\ *n* — see BIBLE table

Dan·ish \ˈdā-nish\ *n* : the language of the Danes — **Danish** *adj*

Danish pastry *n* : a pastry made of a rich yeast-raised dough

dank \ˈdaŋk\ *adj* : disagreeably wet or moist : DAMP — **dank·ness** *n*

dan·seuse \dä^n-ˈsərz, -ˈsəz; dän-ˈsüz\ *n* [F] : a female ballet dancer

dap·per \ˈda-pər\ *adj* **1** : SPRUCE, TRIM **2** : being alert and lively in movement and manners : JAUNTY

dap·ple \ˈda-pəl\ *vb* **dap·pled; dap·pling** : to mark with different-colored spots

DAR *abbr* Daughters of the American Revolution

[1]**dare** \ˈder\ *vb* **dared; dar·ing** **1** : to have sufficient courage : be bold enough to **2** : CHALLENGE ⟨*dared* him to jump⟩ **3** : to confront boldly

[2]**dare** *n* : an act or instance of daring : CHALLENGE

dare·dev·il \-ˌde-vəl\ *n* : a recklessly bold person — **daredevil** *adj*

dar·ing \ˈder-iŋ\ *n* : venturesome boldness — **daring** *adj* — **dar·ing·ly** *adv*

[1]**dark** \ˈdärk\ *adj* **1** : being without light or without much light **2** : not light in color ⟨a ~ suit⟩ **3** : GLOOMY ⟨a ~ outlook⟩ **4** *often cap* : being a period of stagnation or decline ⟨the *Dark* Ages⟩ **5** : SECRETIVE ⟨~ dealings⟩ ♦ ***Synonyms*** DIM, DUSKY, MURKY, TENEBROUS — **dark·ly** *adv* — **dark·ness** *n*

[2]**dark** *n* **1** : absence of light : DARKNESS; *esp* : NIGHT **2** : a dark or deep color — **in the dark** **1** : in secrecy **2** : in ignorance ⟨kept *in the dark* about the plans⟩

dark·en \ˈdär-kən\ *vb* **1** : to make or grow dark or darker **2** : DIM **3** : BESMIRCH, TARNISH **4** : to make or become gloomy or forbidding

dark horse *n* : a contestant or a political figure whose abilities and chances as a contender are not known

dark·ling \ˈdär-kliŋ\ *adj* **1** : DARK ⟨a ~ plain⟩ **2** : MYSTERIOUS

dark·room \ˈdärk-ˌrüm, -ˌrum\ *n* : a lightproof room in which photographic materials are processed

[1]**dar·ling** \ˈdär-liŋ\ *n* **1** : a dearly loved person **2** : FAVORITE

[2]**darling** *adj* **1** : dearly loved : FAVORITE **2** : very pleasing : CHARMING

darm·stadt·i·um \ˌdärm-ˈsta-tē-əm\ *n* : a short-lived radioactive chemical element produced artificially

[1]**darn** \ˈdärn\ *vb* : to mend with interlacing stitches — **darn·er** *n*

[2]**darn** *or* **darned** \ˈdärnd\ *adv* : VERY, EXTREMELY ⟨a ~ good job⟩

darning needle *n* **1** : a needle for darning **2** : DRAGONFLY

[1]**dart** \ˈdärt\ *n* **1** : a small missile with a point on one end and feathers on the other; *also, pl* : a game in which darts are thrown at a target **2** : something causing a sudden pain **3** : a stitched tapering fold in a garment **4** : a quick movement

[2]**dart** *vb* **1** : to throw with a sudden movement **2** : to thrust or move suddenly or rapidly ⟨~*ed* across the street⟩ **3** : to shoot with a dart containing a usu. tranquilizing drug

dart·er \ˈdär-tər\ *n* : any of numerous small No. American freshwater fishes related to the perches

Dar·win·ism \ˈdär-wə-ˌni-zəm\ *n* : a theory explaining the origin and continued existence of new species of plants and animals by means of natural selection acting on chance variations — **Dar·win·ist** \-nist\ *n or adj*

[1]**dash** \ˈdash\ *vb* **1** : SMASH **2** : to knock, hurl, or thrust violently **3** : SPLASH, SPATTER **4** : RUIN **5** : DEPRESS, SADDEN **6** : to perform or finish hastily ⟨~ off a letter⟩ **7** : to move with sudden speed ⟨~*ed* down the hall⟩

[2]**dash** *n* **1** : a sudden burst or splash **2** : a stroke of a pen **3** : a punctuation mark — that is used esp. to indicate a break in the thought or structure of a sentence **4** : a small addition ⟨a ~ of salt⟩ **5** : flashy showiness **6** : animation in style and action **7** : a sudden rush or attempt ⟨made a ~ for the door⟩ **8** : a short foot race **9** : DASHBOARD 1

dash·board \-ˌbȯrd\ *n* **1** : a panel in an automobile or aircraft below the windshield usu. containing dials and controls **2** : a graphical report (as on a website) of various data relevant to a particular business or group

dash·er \ˈda-shər\ *n* : a device (as in a churn) for agitating something

da·shi·ki \də-ˈshē-kē\ *also* **dai·shi·ki** \dī-\ *n* [modif. of Yoruba (an African language) *dàńṣíkí*] : a usu. brightly colored loose-fitting pullover garment

dash·ing \ˈda-shiŋ\ *adj* **1** : marked by vigorous action **2** : marked by smartness esp. in dress and manners ♦ ***Synonyms*** STYLISH, CHIC, FASHIONABLE, MODISH, SMART, SWANK

das·tard \ˈdas-tərd\ *n* **1** : COWARD **2** : a person who acts treacherously — **das·tard·ly** *adj*

dat *abbr* dative

da·ta \ˈdā-tə, ˈda-, ˈdä-\ *n sing or pl* [L, pl. of *datum*] : factual information (as measurements or statistics) used as a basis for reasoning, discussion, or calculation

da·ta·base \-ˌbās\ *n* : a usu. large collection of data organized esp. for rapid search and retrieval (as by a computer) — **database** *vb*

data file *n* : a digital file on which data is stored

data processing *n* : the action or process of supplying a computer with information and having the computer use it to produce a desired result

[1]**date** \ˈdāt\ *n* [ME, fr. AF, ultim. fr. L *dactylus,* fr. Gk *daktylos,* lit., finger] : the oblong edible fruit of a tall palm; *also* : this palm

[2]**date** *n* [ME, fr. AF, fr. LL *data,* fr. *data* (as in *data Romae* given at Rome), fem. of L *datus,* pp. of *dare* to give] **1** : the day, month, or year of an event **2** : a statement giving the time of execution or making (as of a coin or check) **3** : the period to which something belongs **4** : APPOINTMENT; *esp* : a social engagement between two persons that often has a romantic character **5** : a person with whom one has a usu. romantic date — **to date** : up to the present moment

[3]**date** *vb* **dat·ed; dat·ing** **1** : to record the date of or on **2** : to determine, mark, or reveal the date, age, or period of **3** : go on a date or dates with ⟨~*ed* her for a year⟩ **4** : ORIGINATE ⟨~*s* from ancient times⟩ **5** : EXTEND ⟨*dating* back to childhood⟩ **6** : to show qualities typical of a past period

dat·ed \ˈdā-təd\ *adj* **1** : provided with a date **2** : OLD-FASHIONED ⟨a ~ custom⟩ ♦ ***Synonyms*** ANTIQUATED, ARCHAIC, OLD HAT, OUTDATED, OUTMODED, PASSÉ

date·less \ˈdāt-ləs\ *adj* **1** : ENDLESS **2** : having no date **3** : too ancient to be dated **4** : TIMELESS

date·line \ˈdāt-ˌlīn\ *n* : a line in a publication giving the date and place of composition or issue — **dateline** *vb*

date rape *n* : rape committed by the victim's date

da·tive \ˈdā-tiv\ *adj* : of, relating to, or constituting a grammatical case marking typically the indirect object of a verb — **dative** *n*

da·tum \ˈdā-təm, ˈda-, ˈdä-\ *n, pl* **da·ta** \-tə\ *or* **datums** : a single piece of data : FACT

dau *abbr* daughter

[1]**daub** \ˈdȯb\ *vb* **1** : to cover with soft adhesive matter **2** : SMEAR, SMUDGE **3** : to paint crudely — **daub·er** *n*

[2]**daub** *n* **1** : something daubed on : SMEAR **2** : a crude picture

daugh·ter \ˈdȯ-tər\ *n* **1** : a female offspring esp. of human beings **2** : a female adopted child **3** : a human female descendant — **daughter** *adj* — **daugh·ter·less** \-ləs\ *adj*

daugh·ter–in–law \ˈdȯ-tə-rən-ˌlȯ\ *n, pl* **daugh·ters–in–law** \-tər-zən-\ : the wife of one's son or daughter

daunt \ˈdȯnt\ *vb* [ME, fr. AF *danter, daunter,* fr. L *domitare* to tame] : to lessen the courage of : INTIMIDATE, OVERWHELM

daunt·ing \ˈdȯn-tiŋ\ *adj* : tending to overwhelm or intimidate ⟨a ~ task⟩

daunt·less \-ləs\ *adj* : FEARLESS, UNDAUNTED ♦ ***Synonyms*** BRAVE, BOLD, COURAGEOUS, LIONHEARTED — **daunt·less·ly** *adv*

dau·phin \ˈdȯ-fən\ *n, often cap* : the eldest son of a king of France

DAV *abbr* Disabled American Veterans

dav·en·port \ˈda-vən-ˌpȯrt\ *n* : a large upholstered sofa

da·vit \ˈdā-vət, ˈda-\ *n* : a small crane on a ship used in pairs esp. to raise or lower boats

daw·dle \ˈdȯ-dᵊl\ *vb* **daw·dled; daw·dling** **1** : to spend time wastefully or idly **2** : LOITER — **daw·dler** *n*

[1]**dawn** \ˈdȯn\ *vb* **1** : to begin to grow light as the sun rises **2** : to begin to appear or develop **3** : to begin to be understood ⟨the solution ~*ed* on him⟩

[2]**dawn** *n* **1** : the first appearance of light in the morning **2** : a first appearance : BEGINNING ⟨the ~ of a new era⟩

day \ˈdā\ *n* **1** : the period of light between one night and the next; *also* : DAYLIGHT, DAYTIME **2** : the period of rotation of a planet (as earth) or a moon on its axis **3** : a period of 24 hours beginning at midnight **4** : a specified day or date ⟨wedding ~⟩ **5** : a specified time or period : AGE ⟨in olden ~*s*⟩ **6** : the conflict or contention of the day **7** : the time set apart by usage or law for work ⟨the 8-hour ~⟩

day·bed \ˈdā-ˌbed\ *n* : a couch that can be converted into a bed

day·book \-ˌbu̇k\ *n* : DIARY, JOURNAL

day·break \-ˌbrāk\ *n* : DAWN

day care *n* : supervision of and care for children or disabled adults provided during the day; *also* : a program offering day care

day·dream \ˈdā-ˌdrēm\ *n* : a pleasant reverie — **daydream** *vb*

day·light \ˈdā-ˌlīt\ *n* **1** : the light of day **2** : DAYTIME **3** : DAWN **4** : understanding of something that has been obscure **5** *pl* : CONSCIOUSNESS; *also* : WITS **6** : a perceptible space, gap, or difference

daylight saving time *n* : time usu. one hour ahead of standard time

Day of Atonement : YOM KIPPUR

day school *n* : a private school without boarding facilities

day student *n* : a student who attends regular classes at a college or preparatory school but does not live there

day·time \ˈdā-ˌtīm\ *n* : the period of daylight

daze \ˈdāz\ *vb* **dazed; daz·ing** **1** : to stupefy esp. by a blow **2** : DAZZLE — **daze** *n* — **da·zed·ly** \ˈdā-zəd-lē\ *adv*

daz·zle \ˈda-zəl\ *vb* **daz·zled; daz·zling** **1** : to overpower with light **2** : to impress greatly or confound with brilliance ⟨*dazzled* by her wit⟩ — **dazzle** *n*

dB *abbr* decibel
Db *symbol* dubnium
d/b/a *abbr* doing business as
dbl *or* **dble** *abbr* double
DC *abbr* **1** It *da capo* from the beginning **2** direct current **3** District of Columbia **4** doctor of chiropractic
DD *abbr* **1** days after date **2** demand draft **3** dishonorable discharge **4** doctor of divinity
D–day *n* [*D,* abbr. for *day*] : a day set for launching an operation (as an invasion)
DDS *abbr* doctor of dental surgery
DDT \ˌdē-(ˌ)dē-ˈtē\ *n* : a persistent insecticide poisonous to many higher animals
DE *abbr* Delaware
dea•con \ˈdē-kən\ *n* [ME *dekene,* fr. OE *dēacon,* fr. LL *diaconus,* fr. Gk *diakonos,* lit., servant] : a subordinate officer in a Christian church
dea•con•ess \ˈdē-kə-nəs\ *n* : a woman chosen to assist in the church ministry
de•ac•ti•vate \dē-ˈak-tə-ˌvāt\ *vb* : to make inactive or ineffective
[1]**dead** \ˈded\ *adj* **1** : LIFELESS **2** : DEATHLIKE, DEADLY ⟨in a ~ faint⟩ **3** : NUMB **4** : very tired **5** : UNRESPONSIVE **6** : EXTINGUISHED ⟨~ coals⟩ **7** : INANIMATE, INERT **8** : no longer active or functioning ⟨a ~ battery⟩ **9** : lacking power, significance, or effect ⟨a ~ custom⟩ **10** : OBSOLETE ⟨a ~ language⟩ **11** : lacking in merriment or animation ⟨a ~ party⟩ **12** : QUIET, IDLE, UNPRODUCTIVE ⟨~ capital⟩ **13** : lacking elasticity ⟨a ~ tennis ball⟩ **14** : not circulating : STAGNANT ⟨~ air⟩ **15** : lacking warmth, vigor, or taste ⟨~ wine⟩ **16** : absolutely uniform ⟨~ level⟩ **17** : UNERRING, EXACT ⟨a ~ shot⟩ **18** : ABRUPT ⟨a ~ stop⟩ **19** : COMPLETE ⟨a ~ loss⟩
[2]**dead** *n, pl* **dead** **1** : one that is dead — usu. used collectively ⟨the living and the ~⟩ **2** : the time of greatest quiet ⟨the ~ of the night⟩
[3]**dead** *adv* **1** : UTTERLY ⟨~ right⟩ **2** : in a sudden and complete manner ⟨stopped ~⟩ **3** : DIRECTLY ⟨~ ahead⟩
dead•beat \-ˌbēt\ *n* : a person who persistently fails to pay personal debts or expenses
dead duck *n* : GONER
dead•en \ˈde-dᵊn\ *vb* **1** : to impair in vigor or sensation : BLUNT ⟨~ pain⟩ **2** : to lessen the luster or spirit of **3** : to make (as a wall) soundproof
dead end *n* **1** : an end (as of a street) without an exit **2** : a position, situation, or course of action that leads to nothing further — **dead–end** \ˌded-ˌend\ *adj*
dead heat *n* : a contest in which two or more contestants tie (as by crossing the finish line simultaneously)
dead horse *n* : an exhausted topic or issue
dead letter *n* **1** : something that has lost its force or authority without being formally abolished **2** : a letter that cannot be delivered or returned
dead•line \ˈded-ˌlīn\ *n* : a date or time before which something must be done
dead•lock \ˈded-ˌläk\ *n* **1** : a stoppage of action because neither faction in a struggle will give in **2** : a tie score — **deadlock** *vb*
[1]**dead•ly** \ˈded-lē\ *adj* **dead•li•er; -est** **1** : likely to cause or capable of causing death **2** : HOSTILE, IMPLACABLE **3** : very accurate : UNERRING **4** : tending to deprive of force or vitality ⟨a ~ habit⟩ **5** : suggestive of death **6** : very great : EXTREME — **dead•li•ness** *n*
[2]**deadly** *adv* **1** : suggesting death ⟨~ pale⟩ **2** : EXTREMELY ⟨~ dull⟩
deadly sin *n* : one of seven sins of pride, covetousness, lust, anger, gluttony, envy, and sloth held to be fatal to spiritual progress
dead meat *n* : one that is doomed
[1]**dead•pan** \ˈded-ˌpan\ *adj* : marked by an impassive manner or expression ⟨~ humor⟩ — **deadpan** *vb* — **deadpan** *adv*
[2]**deadpan** *n* : a completely expressionless face
dead reckoning *n* : the determination of the position of a ship or aircraft solely from the record of the direction and distance of its course
dead•weight \ˈded-ˈwāt\ *n* **1** : the unrelieved weight of an inert mass **2** : a ship's load including the weight of cargo, fuel, crew, and passengers
dead•wood \-ˌwu̇d\ *n* **1** : wood dead on the tree **2** : useless personnel or material
deaf \ˈdef\ *adj* **1** : totally or partially unable to hear **2** : unwilling to hear or listen ⟨~ to reason⟩ — **deaf•ness** *n*
deaf•en \ˈde-fən\ *vb* : to make deaf
[1]**deal** \ˈdēl\ *n* **1** : a usu. large or indefinite quantity or degree ⟨a great ~ of support⟩ **2** : the act or right of distributing cards to players in a card game; *also* : HAND
[2]**deal** *vb* **dealt** \ˈdelt\; **deal•ing** **1** : DISTRIBUTE; *esp* : to distribute playing cards to players in a game **2** : ADMINISTER, DELIVER ⟨*dealt* him a blow⟩ **3** : to concern itself : TREAT ⟨the book ~*s* with crime⟩ **4** : to take action in regard to something ⟨~ with offenders⟩ **5** : TRADE; *also* : to sell or distribute something as a business ⟨~ in used cars⟩ **6** : to reach a state of acceptance ⟨~ with her mother's death⟩ — **deal•er** *n*
[3]**deal** *n* **1** : BARGAINING, NEGOTIATION **2** : TRANSACTION; *esp* : an agreement by contract **3** : treatment received ⟨a raw ~⟩ **4** : an often secret agreement or arrangement for mutual advantage **5** : BARGAIN
[4]**deal** *n* : wood or a board of fir or pine
deal•er•ship \ˈdē-lər-ˌship\ *n* : an authorized sales agency ⟨an auto ~⟩
deal•ing \ˈdē-liŋ\ *n* **1** : a way of acting or of doing business **2** *pl* : friendly or business transactions
dean \ˈdēn\ *n* [ME *deen,* fr. AF *deien,* fr. LL *decanus,* lit., chief of ten, fr. Gk *dekanos,* fr. *deka* ten] **1** : a clergyman who is head of a group of canons or of joint pastors of a church **2** : the head of a division, faculty, college, or school of a

university **3** : a college or secondary school administrator in charge of counseling and disciplining students **4** : DOYEN ⟨the ~ of a diplomatic corps⟩ — **dean·ship** *n*

dean·ery \ˈdē-nə-rē\ *n, pl* **-er·ies** : the office, jurisdiction, or official residence of a clerical dean

¹dear \ˈdir\ *adj* **1** : highly valued : PRECIOUS **2** : AFFECTIONATE, FOND **3** : EXPENSIVE **4** : HEARTFELT — **dear·ly** *adv* — **dear·ness** *n*

²dear *n* : a loved one : DARLING

Dear John \-ˈjän\ *n* : a letter (as to a soldier) in which a woman breaks off a marital or romantic relationship

dearth \ˈdərth\ *n* **1** : SCARCITY, FAMINE **2** : an inadequate supply : LACK ⟨a ~ of jobs⟩

death \ˈdeth\ *n* **1** : the end of life **2** : the cause of loss of life **3** : a cause of ruin **4** : the state of being dead **5** : DESTRUCTION, EXTINCTION **6** : SLAUGHTER — **death·like** *adj*

death·bed \-ˌbed\ *n* **1** : the bed in which a person dies **2** : the last hours of life

death·blow \-ˌblō\ *n* : a destructive or killing stroke or event

death grip *n* : an extremely tight grip or hold

death·less \-ləs\ *adj* : IMMORTAL, IMPERISHABLE ⟨~ fame⟩

death·ly \-lē\ *adj* **1** : FATAL **2** : of, relating to, or suggestive of death ⟨a ~ pallor⟩ — **deathly** *adv*

death rattle *n* : a sound produced by air passing through mucus in the lungs and air passages of a dying person

death's–head \ˈdeths-ˌhed\ *n* : a human skull emblematic of death

death·watch \ˈdeth-ˌwäch\ *n* : a vigil kept over the dead or dying

deb \ˈdeb\ *n* : DEBUTANTE

de·ba·cle \di-ˈbä-kəl, -ˈba-\ *also* **dé·bâ·cle** *same or* dā-ˈbäk\ *n* [F *débâcle*] : DISASTER, FAILURE, ROUT ⟨a financial ~⟩

de·bar \di-ˈbär\ *vb* : to bar from having or doing something : PRECLUDE

de·bark \di-ˈbärk\ *vb* : DISEMBARK — **de·bar·ka·tion** \ˌdē-ˌbär-ˈkā-shən\ *n*

de·base \di-ˈbās\ *vb* : to lower in character, quality, or value ♦ ***Synonyms*** DEGRADE, CORRUPT, DEPRAVE — **de·base·ment** *n*

de·bate \di-ˈbāt\ *vb* **de·bat·ed; de·bat·ing 1** : to discuss a question by considering opposed arguments **2** : to take part in a debate — **de·bat·able** *adj* — **debate** *n* — **de·bat·er** *n*

de·bauch \di-ˈbȯch\ *vb* : SEDUCE, CORRUPT ♦ ***Synonyms*** DEBASE, DEMORALIZE, DEPRAVE, PERVERT — **de·bauch·ery** \-ˈbȯ-chə-rē\ *n*

de·ben·ture \di-ˈben-chər\ *n* : BOND; *esp* : one secured by the general credit of the issuer rather than a lien on particular assets

de·bil·i·tate \di-ˈbi-lə-ˌtāt\ *vb* **-tat·ed; -tat·ing** : to impair the health or strength of ♦ ***Synonyms*** WEAKEN, DISABLE, ENFEEBLE, UNDERMINE

de·bil·i·ty \di-ˈbi-lə-tē\ *n, pl* **-ties** : an infirm or weakened state

¹deb·it \ˈde-bət\ *vb* : to enter as a debit : charge with or as a debit

²debit *n* **1** : an entry in an account showing money paid out or owed **2** : DISADVANTAGE, SHORTCOMING

debit card *n* : a card by which money may be withdrawn or the cost of purchases paid directly from the holder's bank account

deb·o·nair \ˌde-bə-ˈner\ *adj* [ME *debonere*, fr. AF *deboneire*, fr. *de bon aire* of good family or nature] : SUAVE, URBANE; *also* : LIGHTHEARTED

de·bouch \di-ˈbau̇ch, -ˈbüsh\ *vb* [F *déboucher*, fr. *dé-* out of + *bouche* mouth] : to come out into an open area : EMERGE

de·brief \di-ˈbrēf\ *vb* **1** : to question (as a pilot back from a mission) in order to obtain useful information **2** : to review carefully upon completion

de·bris \də-ˈbrē, dā-; ˈdā-ˌbrē\ *n, pl* **de·bris** \-ˈbrēz, -ˌbrēz\ **1** : the remains of something broken down or destroyed **2** : an accumulation of rock fragments **3** : RUBBISH

debt \ˈdet\ *n* **1** : SIN, TRESPASS **2** : something owed : OBLIGATION **3** : a condition of owing

debt·or \ˈde-tər\ *n* **1** : one guilty of neglect or violation of duty **2** : one that owes a debt

de·bug \(ˌ)dē-ˈbəg\ *vb* : to eliminate errors in ⟨~ a computer program⟩

de·bunk \dē-ˈbəŋk\ *vb* : to expose the sham or falseness of ⟨~ a legend⟩

¹de·but \ˈdā-ˌbyü, dā-ˈbyü\ *n* **1** : a first appearance **2** : a formal entrance into society

²debut *vb* : to make a debut; *also* : INTRODUCE

deb·u·tante \ˈde-byu̇-ˌtänt\ *n* : a young woman making her formal entrance into society

dec *abbr* **1** deceased **2** decrease

Dec *abbr* December

de·cade \ˈde-ˌkād, de-ˈkād\ *n* : a period of 10 years

dec·a·dence \ˈde-kə-dəns, di-ˈkā-dᵊns\ *n* : DETERIORATION, DECLINE — **dec·a·dent** \ˈde-kə-dənt, di-ˈkā-dᵊnt\ *adj or n*

de·caf \ˈdē-ˌkaf\ *n* : decaffeinated coffee

de·caf·fein·at·ed \(ˌ)dē-ˈka-fə-nā-təd\ *adj* : having the caffeine removed ⟨~ coffee⟩

deca·gon \ˈde-kə-ˌgän\ *n* : a plane polygon of 10 angles and 10 sides

de·cal \ˈdē-ˌkal\ *n* : a picture, design, or label made to be transferred (as to glass) from specially prepared paper

de·cal·co·ma·nia \di-ˌkal-kə-ˈmā-nē-ə\ *n* [F *décalcomanie*, fr. *décalquer* to copy by tracing (fr. *calquer* to trace, fr. It *calcare*, lit., to tread, fr. L) + *manie* mania, fr. LL *mania*] : the process of making decals; *also* : DECAL

Deca·logue \ˈde-kə-ˌlȯg\ *n* : TEN COMMANDMENTS

de·camp \di-ˈkamp\ *vb* **1** : to break up a camp **2** : to depart suddenly ♦ ***Synonyms*** ESCAPE, ABSCOND, FLEE

de·cant \di-ˈkant\ *vb* : to pour (as wine) from one vessel into another
de·cant·er \di-ˈkan-tər\ *n* : an ornamental glass bottle for serving wine
de·cap·i·tate \di-ˈka-pə-ˌtāt\ *vb* **-tat·ed; -tat·ing** : BEHEAD — **de·cap·i·ta·tion** \-ˌka-pə-ˈtā-shən\ *n* — **de·cap·i·ta·tor** \-ˈka-pə-ˌtā-tər\ *n*
deca·syl·lab·ic \ˌde-kə-sə-ˈla-bik\ *adj* : having or composed of verses having 10 syllables — **decasyllabic** *n*
de·cath·lon \di-ˈkath-lən, -ˌlän\ *n* : a 10-event athletic contest
de·cay \di-ˈkā\ *vb* **1** : to decline from a sound or prosperous condition ⟨a ~*ing* town⟩ **2** : to cause or undergo decomposition ⟨radium ~*s* slowly⟩; *esp* : to break down while spoiling : ROT ⟨~*ing* teeth⟩ — **decay** *n*
decd *abbr* deceased
de·cease \di-ˈsēs\ *n* : DEATH
¹**de·ceased** \-ˈsēst\ *adj* : no longer living; *esp* : recently dead
²**deceased** *n, pl* **deceased** : a dead person
de·ce·dent \di-ˈsē-dᵊnt\ *n* : a deceased person
de·ceit \di-ˈsēt\ *n* **1** : DECEPTION **2** : TRICK **3** : DECEITFULNESS ♦ ***Synonyms*** DISSIMULATION, DUPLICITY, GUILE
de·ceit·ful \-fəl\ *adj* **1** : practicing or tending to practice deceit **2** : MISLEADING, DECEPTIVE ⟨a ~ answer⟩ — **de·ceit·ful·ly** *adv* — **de·ceit·ful·ness** *n*
de·ceive \di-ˈsēv\ *vb* **de·ceived; de·ceiv·ing** **1** : to cause to believe an untruth **2** : to use or practice deceit ♦ ***Synonyms*** BEGUILE, BETRAY, DELUDE, MISLEAD — **de·ceiv·er** *n*
de·cel·er·ate \dē-ˈse-lə-ˌrāt\ *vb* **-at·ed; -at·ing** : to slow down
De·cem·ber \di-ˈsem-bər\ *n* [ME *Decembre,* fr. OE or AF, both fr. L *December* (tenth month), fr. *decem* ten] : the 12th month of the year
de·cen·cy \ˈdē-sᵊn-sē\ *n, pl* **-cies** **1** : PROPRIETY **2** : conformity to standards of taste, propriety, or quality **3** : standard of propriety — usu. used in pl.
de·cen·ni·al \di-ˈse-nē-əl\ *adj* **1** : consisting of 10 years **2** : happening every 10 years ⟨~ census⟩
de·cent \ˈdē-sᵊnt\ *adj* **1** : conforming to standards of propriety, good taste, or morality **2** : modestly clothed **3** : free from immodesty or obscenity **4** : ADEQUATE ⟨~ housing⟩ — **de·cent·ly** *adv*
de·cen·tral·i·za·tion \dē-ˌsen-trə-lə-ˈzā-shən\ *n* **1** : the distribution of powers from a central authority to regional and local authorities **2** : the redistribution of population and industry from urban centers to outlying areas — **de·cen·tral·ize** \-ˈsen-trə-ˌlīz\ *vb*
de·cep·tion \di-ˈsep-shən\ *n* **1** : the act of deceiving **2** : the fact or condition of being deceived **3** : FRAUD, TRICK — **de·cep·tive** \-ˈsep-tiv\ *adj* — **de·cep·tive·ly** *adv* — **de·cep·tive·ness** *n*
deci·bel \ˈde-sə-ˌbel, -bəl\ *n* : a unit for measuring the relative loudness of sounds
de·cide \di-ˈsīd\ *vb* **de·cid·ed; de·cid·ing** [ME, fr. L *decidere,* lit., to cut off, fr. *de-* off + *caedere* to cut] **1** : make a final choice or judgment **2** : to bring to a definitive end ⟨one blow *decided* the fight⟩ **3** : to induce to come to a choice
de·cid·ed \di-ˈsī-dəd\ *adj* **1** : UNQUESTIONABLE ⟨a ~ advantage⟩ **2** : FIRM, DETERMINED — **de·cid·ed·ly** *adv*
de·cid·u·ous \di-ˈsi-jə-wəs\ *adj* **1** : falling off or out usu. at the end of a period of growth or function ⟨~ leaves⟩ ⟨a ~ tooth⟩ **2** : having deciduous parts ⟨~ trees⟩
deci·gram \ˈde-sə-ˌgram\ *n* — see METRIC SYSTEM table
deci·li·ter \-ˌlē-tər\ *n* — see METRIC SYSTEM table
¹**dec·i·mal** \ˈde-sə-məl\ *adj* : based on the number 10 : reckoning by tens
²**decimal** *n* : any number expressed in base 10; *esp* : DECIMAL FRACTION
decimal fraction *n* : a fraction or mixed number in which the denominator is a power of 10 and that is usu. expressed with a decimal point ⟨the *decimal fraction* .25 is equivalent to the common fraction $^{25}/_{100}$⟩
decimal place *n* : the position of a digit as counted to the right of the decimal point in a decimal fraction
decimal point *n* : a period, centered dot, or in some countries a comma at the left of a decimal fraction (as .678) less than one or between a whole number and a decimal fraction in a mixed number (as 3.678)
dec·i·mate \ˈde-sə-ˌmāt\ *vb* **-mat·ed; -mat·ing** **1** : to take or destroy the 10th part of **2** : to cause great destruction or harm to ⟨factories *decimated* by fire⟩
dec·i·me·ter \ˈde-sə-ˌmē-tər\ *n* — see METRIC SYSTEM table
de·ci·pher \di-ˈsī-fər\ *vb* **1** : DECODE **2** : to make out the meaning of despite indistinctness — **de·ci·pher·able** *adj*
de·ci·sion \di-ˈsi-zhən\ *n* **1** : the act or result of deciding **2** : promptness and firmness in deciding : DETERMINATION
de·ci·sive \-ˈsī-siv\ *adj* **1** : having the power to decide ⟨the ~ vote⟩ **2** : RESOLUTE, DETERMINED **3** : CONCLUSIVE ⟨a ~ victory⟩ — **de·ci·sive·ly** *adv* — **de·ci·sive·ness** *n*
¹**deck** \ˈdek\ *n* **1** : a floorlike platform of a ship; *also* : something resembling the deck of a ship **2** : a pack of playing cards **3** : a collection of slides presented one after another
²**deck** *vb* **1** : ARRAY ⟨men ~*ed* out in suits⟩ **2** : DECORATE **3** : to furnish with a deck **4** : KNOCK DOWN, FLOOR
deck·hand \ˈdek-ˌhand\ *n* : a sailor who performs manual duties
de·claim \di-ˈklām\ *vb* : to speak or deliver in the manner of a formal speech ⟨an actor ~*ing* his lines⟩ — **dec·la·ma·tion** \ˌde-klə-ˈmā-shən\ *n* — **de·clam·a·to·ry** \di-ˈkla-mə-ˌtȯr-ē\ *adj*
de·clar·a·tive \di-ˈkler-ə-tiv\ *adj* : making a declaration ⟨~ sentence⟩

de·clare \di-ˈkler\ *vb* **de·clared; de·clar·ing** **1** : to make known formally, officially, or explicitly : ANNOUNCE ⟨~ war⟩ **2** : to state emphatically : AFFIRM **3** : to make a full statement of ♦ ***Synonyms*** BLAZON, BROADCAST, PROCLAIM, PUBLISH — **dec·la·ra·tion** \ˌde-klə-ˈrā-shən\ *n* — **de·clar·a·to·ry** \di-ˈkler-ə-ˌtȯr-ē\ *adj* — **de·clar·er** *n*

de·clas·si·fy \dē-ˈkla-sə-ˌfī\ *vb* : to remove the security classification of ⟨~ documents⟩ — **de·clas·si·fi·ca·tion** \-ˌkla-sə-fə-ˈkā-shən\ *n*

de·clen·sion \di-ˈklen-chən\ *n* **1** : the inflectional forms of a noun, pronoun, or adjective **2** : DECLINE, DETERIORATION **3** : DESCENT, SLOPE

[1]**de·cline** \di-ˈklīn\ *vb* **de·clined; de·clin·ing** **1** : to slope downward : DESCEND **2** : DROOP **3** : RECEDE ⟨morale *declined*⟩ **4** : WANE **5** : to withhold consent; *also* : REFUSE, REJECT ⟨~ an invitation⟩ ⟨~ to answer⟩ **6** : INFLECT 2 ⟨~ a noun⟩ — **de·clin·able** *adj* — **dec·li·na·tion** \ˌde-klə-ˈnā-shən\ *n*

[2]**decline** *n* **1** : a gradual sinking and wasting away **2** : a change to a lower state or level **3** : the time when something is approaching its end ⟨an empire in ~⟩ **4** : a descending slope

de·cliv·i·ty \di-ˈkli-və-tē\ *n, pl* **-ties** : a steep downward slope

de·code \dē-ˈkōd\ *vb* : to convert (a coded message) into ordinary language — **de·cod·er** *n*

dé·col·le·tage \dā-ˌkä-lə-ˈtäzh\ *n* : the low-cut neckline of a dress

dé·col·le·té \dā-ˌkäl-ˈtā\ *adj* [F] **1** : wearing a strapless or low-necked gown **2** : having a low-cut neckline

de·com·mis·sion \ˌdē-kə-ˈmi-shən\ *vb* : to remove from service

de·com·pose \ˌdē-kəm-ˈpōz\ *vb* **1** : to separate into constituent parts **2** : to break down in decay : ROT — **de·com·po·si·tion** \dē-ˌkäm-pə-ˈzi-shən\ *n*

de·com·press \ˌdē-kəm-ˈpres\ *vb* : to release from pressure or compression — **de·com·pres·sion** \-ˈpre-shən\ *n*

decompression sickness *n* : [2]BEND 3

de·con·ges·tant \ˌdē-kən-ˈjes-tənt\ *n* : an agent that relieves congestion (as of mucous membranes)

de·con·struc·tion \ˌdē-kən-ˈstrək-shən\ *n* : the analysis of something (as language or literature) by the separation and individual examination of its basic elements — **de·con·struct** \-ˈstrəkt\ *vb*

de·con·tam·i·nate \ˌdē-kən-ˈta-mə-ˌnāt\ *vb* : to rid of contamination (as radioactive material) — **de·con·tam·i·na·tion** \-ˌta-mə-ˈnā-shən\ *n*

de·con·trol \ˌdē-kən-ˈtrōl\ *vb* : to end control of ⟨~ prices⟩ — **decontrol** *n*

de·cor *or* **dé·cor** \dā-ˈkȯr, ˈdā-ˌkȯr\ *n* : DECORATION; *esp* : the style and layout of interior furnishings

dec·o·rate \ˈde-kə-ˌrāt\ *vb* **-rat·ed; -rat·ing** **1** : to furnish with something ornamental ⟨~ a room⟩ **2** : to award a mark of honor (as a medal) to ⟨*decorated* soldiers⟩ ♦ ***Synonyms*** ADORN, BEAUTIFY, BEDECK, GARNISH, ORNAMENT

dec·o·ra·tion \ˌde-kə-ˈrā-shən\ *n* **1** : the act or process of decorating **2** : ORNAMENT **3** : a badge of honor

dec·o·ra·tive \ˈde-kə-rə-tiv\ *adj* : ORNAMENTAL

dec·o·ra·tor \ˈde-kə-ˌrā-tər\ *n* : one that decorates; *esp* : a person who designs or executes interiors and their furnishings

dec·o·rous \ˈde-kə-rəs, di-ˈkȯr-əs\ *adj* : PROPER, SEEMLY, CORRECT

de·co·rum \di-ˈkōr-əm\ *n* [L] **1** : conformity to accepted standards of conduct **2** : ORDERLINESS, PROPRIETY

[1]**de·coy** \ˈdē-ˌkȯi, di-ˈkȯi\ *n* [prob. fr. D *de kooi,* lit., the cage] **1** : something that lures or entices; *esp* : an artificial bird used to attract live birds within shot **2** : something used to draw attention away from another

[2]**de·coy** \di-ˈkȯi, ˈdē-ˌkȯi\ *vb* : to lure by or as if by a decoy : ENTICE

[1]**de·crease** \di-ˈkrēs\ *vb* **de·creased; de·creas·ing** : to grow or cause to grow less : DIMINISH

[2]**de·crease** \ˈdē-ˌkrēs\ *n* **1** : the process of decreasing **2** : REDUCTION

[1]**de·cree** \di-ˈkrē\ *n* **1** : ORDER, EDICT **2** : a judicial decision

[2]**decree** *vb* **de·creed; de·cree·ing** **1** : COMMAND **2** : to determine or order judicially ♦ ***Synonyms*** DICTATE, ORDAIN, PRESCRIBE

dec·re·ment \ˈde-krə-mənt\ *n* **1** : gradual decrease **2** : the quantity lost by diminution or waste

de·crep·it \di-ˈkre-pət\ *adj* : broken down with age : WORN-OUT — **de·crep·i·tude** \-pə-ˌtüd, -ˌtyüd\ *n*

de·cre·scen·do \ˌdā-krə-ˈshen-dō\ *adv or adj* : with a decrease in volume — used as a direction in music

de·crim·i·nal·ize \dē-ˈkri-mə-nə-ˌlīz\ *vb* : to remove or reduce the criminal status of

de·cry \di-ˈkrī\ *vb* : to express strong disapproval of ⟨~ welfare policies⟩

ded·i·cate \ˈde-di-ˌkāt\ *vb* **-cat·ed; -cat·ing** **1** : to devote to the worship of a divine being esp. with sacred rites **2** : to set apart for a definite purpose **3** : to inscribe or address as a compliment ⟨~ a novel⟩ — **ded·i·ca·tion** \ˌde-di-ˈkā-shən\ *n* — **ded·i·ca·tor** \ˈde-di-ˌkā-tər\ *n* — **ded·i·ca·to·ry** \-kə-ˌtȯr-ē\ *adj*

de·duce \di-ˈdüs, -ˈdyüs\ *vb* **de·duced; de·duc·ing** **1** : to derive by reasoning : INFER **2** : to trace the course of — **de·duc·ible** *adj*

de·duct \di-ˈdəkt\ *vb* : SUBTRACT — **de·duct·ible** *adj*

de·duc·tion \di-ˈdək-shən\ *n* **1** : SUBTRACTION **2** : something that is or may be subtracted **3** : the deriving of a conclusion by reasoning : the conclusion so reached — **de·duc·tive** \-ˈdək-tiv\ *adj* — **de·duc·tive·ly** *adv*

[1]**deed** \ˈdēd\ *n* **1** : something done **2** : FEAT, EXPLOIT **3** : a document containing some legal transfer, bargain, or contract

[2]**deed** *vb* : to convey or transfer by deed

dee·jay \ˈdē-ˌjā\ *n* : DISC JOCKEY

deem \ˈdēm\ *vb* : THINK, JUDGE ♦ ***Synonyms*** CONSIDER, ACCOUNT, RECKON, REGARD, VIEW

de–em·pha·size \dē-ˈem-fə-ˌsīz\ *vb* : to reduce in relative importance; *also* : to attach little importance to — **de–em·pha·sis** \-səs\ *n*

[1]**deep** \ˈdēp\ *adj* **1** : extending far down, back, within, or outward ⟨a ∼ well⟩ **2** : having a specified extension downward or backward ⟨3 feet ∼⟩ **3** : difficult to understand; *also* : MYSTERIOUS, OBSCURE ⟨a ∼ dark secret⟩ **4** : WISE **5** : ENGROSSED, INVOLVED ⟨∼ in thought⟩ **6** : INTENSE, PROFOUND ⟨∼ sleep⟩ **7** : dark and rich in color ⟨a ∼ red⟩ **8** : having a low musical pitch or range ⟨a ∼ voice⟩ **9** : situated well within **10** : covered, enclosed, or filled often to a specified degree — **deep·ly** *adv*

[2]**deep** *adv* **1** : DEEPLY **2** : far on : LATE ⟨∼ in the night⟩

[3]**deep** *n* **1** : an extremely deep place or part; *esp* : OCEAN **2** : the middle or most intense part ⟨the ∼ of winter⟩

deep·en \ˈdē-pən\ *vb* : to make or become deep or deeper

deep–freeze \ˈdēp-ˈfrēz\ *vb* **-froze** \-ˈfrōz\; **-fro·zen** \-ˈfrō-zᵊn\ : QUICK-FREEZE

deep–fry *vb* : to cook in enough oil to cover the food being fried

deep pocket *n* **1** : one having substantial financial resources **2** *pl* : substantial financial resources

deep–root·ed \ˈdēp-ˈrü-təd, -ˈru̇-\ *adj* : deeply implanted or established

deep–sea \ˈdēp-ˈsē\ *adj* : of, relating to, or occurring in the deeper parts of the sea ⟨∼ fishing⟩

deep–seat·ed \ˈdēp-ˈsē-təd\ *adj* **1** : situated far below the surface **2** : firmly established ⟨∼ convictions⟩

deer \ˈdir\ *n, pl* **deer** [ME, deer, animal, fr. OE *dēor* beast] : any of numerous ruminant mammals with cloven hoofs and usu. antlers esp. in the males

deer·fly \-ˌflī\ *n* : any of numerous small horseflies

deer·skin \-ˌskin\ *n* : leather made from the skin of a deer; *also* : a garment of such leather

deer tick *n* : a tick that transmits the bacterium causing Lyme disease

de–es·ca·late \dē-ˈes-kə-ˌlāt\ *vb* : to decrease in extent, volume, or scope : LIMIT — **de–es·ca·la·tion** \-ˌes-kə-ˈlā-shən\ *n*

deet \ˈdēt\ *n, often all cap* : a colorless oily liquid insect and tick repellent

[1]**def** \ˈdef\ *adj* **def·fer; def·fest** *slang* : very good : COOL

[2]**def** *abbr* **1** defendant **2** definite **3** definition

de·face \di-ˈfās\ *vb* : to destroy or mar the face or surface of ⟨∼ a desk⟩ — **de·face·ment** *n* — **de·fac·er** *n*

de fac·to \di-ˈfak-tō, dā-\ *adj or adv* **1** : existing though not formally recognized ⟨a *de facto* recession⟩ **2** : actually exercising power ⟨*de facto* government⟩

de·fal·ca·tion \ˌdē-ˌfal-ˈkā-shən, -ˌfȯl-; ˌde-fəl-\ *n* : EMBEZZLEMENT

de·fame \di-ˈfām\ *vb* **de·famed; de·fam·ing** : to injure or destroy the reputation of by libel or slander ♦ ***Synonyms*** CALUMNIATE, DENIGRATE, LIBEL, MALIGN, SLANDER, VILIFY — **def·a·ma·tion** \ˌde-fə-ˈmā-shən\ *n* — **de·fam·a·to·ry** \di-ˈfa-mə-ˌtȯr-ē\ *adj*

de·fault \di-ˈfȯlt\ *n* **1** : failure to do something required by duty or law; *also* : failure to appear for a legal proceeding **2** : failure to compete in or to finish an appointed contest ⟨lose a race by ∼⟩ **3** : a choice made without active consideration due to lack of viable alternatives **4** : a selection made automatically by a computer in the absence of a choice by the user — **default** *vb* — **de·fault·er** *n*

[1]**de·feat** \di-ˈfēt\ *vb* **1** : FRUSTRATE, NULLIFY **2** : to win victory over : BEAT — **de·feat·able** \-ˈfē-tə-bəl\ *adj*

[2]**defeat** *n* **1** : FRUSTRATION **2** : an overthrow of an army in battle **3** : loss of a contest

de·feat·ism \-ˈfē-ˌti-zəm\ *n* : acceptance of or resignation to defeat — **de·feat·ist** \-tist\ *n or adj*

def·e·cate \ˈde-fi-ˌkāt\ *vb* **-cat·ed; -cat·ing** **1** : to free from impurity or corruption **2** : to discharge feces from the bowels — **def·e·ca·tion** \ˌde-fi-ˈkā-shən\ *n*

[1]**de·fect** \ˈdē-ˌfekt, di-ˈfekt\ *n* : BLEMISH, FAULT, IMPERFECTION

[2]**de·fect** \di-ˈfekt\ *vb* : to desert a cause, party, or nation esp. in order to espouse another — **de·fec·tion** \-ˈfek-shən\ *n* — **de·fec·tor** \-ˈfek-tər\ *n*

de·fec·tive \di-ˈfek-tiv\ *adj* : FAULTY, DEFICIENT — **defective** *n*

de·fence *chiefly Brit var of* DEFENSE

de·fend \di-ˈfend\ *vb* [ME, fr. AF *defendre,* fr. L *defendere,* fr. *de-* from + *-fendere* to strike] **1** : to repel danger or attack from ⟨∼ the fort⟩ **2** : to act as attorney for **3** : to oppose the claim of another in a lawsuit : CONTEST **4** : to maintain against opposition ⟨∼ an idea⟩ **5** : to try to retain against a challenge ⟨∼*ed* his title⟩ — **de·fend·er** *n*

de·fen·dant \di-ˈfen-dənt\ *n* : someone who is being sued or accused of a crime

de·fense \di-ˈfens\ *n* **1** : the act of defending : resistance against attack **2** : means, method, or capability of defending **3** : an argument in support **4** : the answer made by the defendant in a legal action **5** : a defending party, group, or team — **de·fense·less** *adj* — **de·fen·si·ble** *adj*

defense mechanism *n* : an often unconscious mental process (as repression) that assists in reaching compromise solutions to personal problems

[1]**de·fen·sive** \di-ˈfen-siv\ *adj* **1** : serving or intended to defend or protect **2** : of or relating to the attempt to keep an opponent from scoring (as in a game) — **de·fen·sive·ly** *adv* — **de·fen·sive·ness** *n*

[2]**defensive** *n* : a defensive position

[1]**de·fer** \di-ˈfər\ *vb* **de·ferred; de·fer·ring** [ME *deferren, differren,* fr. MF *differer,* fr. L *differre* to postpone, be different] : POSTPONE, PUT OFF

[2]**defer** *vb* **deferred; deferring** [ME *deferren, differren,* fr. MF *deferer, defferer,* fr. LL *deferre,* fr. L, to bring down, bring, fr. *de-* down + *ferre* to carry] : to submit or yield to the opinion or wishes of another — **de·fer·ral** \-əl\ *n*

def·er·ence \ˈde-fər-əns\ *n* : courteous, respectful, or ingratiating regard for another's wishes ♦ ***Synonyms*** HONOR, HOMAGE, OBEISANCE, REVERENCE — **def·er·en·tial** \ˌde-fə-ˈren-chəl\ *adj*

de·fer·ment \di-ˈfər-mənt\ *n* : the act of delaying; *esp* : official postponement of military service

de·fi·ance \di-ˈfī-əns\ *n* **1** : CHALLENGE **2** : disposition to resist or contend

de·fi·ant \-ənt\ *adj* : full of defiance : BOLD, IMPUDENT — **de·fi·ant·ly** *adv*

de·fi·bril·la·tor \dē-ˈfi-brə-ˌlā-tər\ *n* : an electronic device that applies an electric shock to restore the rhythm of a fibrillating heart — **de·fi·bril·late** \-ˌlāt\ *vb* — **de·fi·bril·la·tion** \-ˌfi-brə-ˈlā-shən\ *n*

deficiency disease *n* : a disease (as scurvy or beriberi) caused by a lack of essential dietary elements and esp. a vitamin or mineral

de·fi·cient \di-ˈfi-shənt\ *adj* : lacking in something necessary; *also* : not up to a normal standard — **de·fi·cien·cy** \-shən-sē\ *n*

def·i·cit \ˈde-fə-sət\ *n* : a deficiency in amount; *esp* : an excess of expenditures over revenue

[1]**de·file** \di-ˈfī(-ə)l\ *vb* **de·filed; de·fil·ing** **1** : to make filthy **2** : CORRUPT **3** : to violate the chastity of **4** : to violate the sanctity of : DESECRATE **5** : DISHONOR ♦ ***Synonyms*** CONTAMINATE, POLLUTE, SOIL, TAINT — **de·file·ment** *n*

[2]**de·file** \di-ˈfī(-ə)l, ˈdē-ˌfī(-ə)l\ *n* : a narrow passage or gorge

de·fine \di-ˈfīn\ *vb* **de·fined; de·fin·ing** **1** : to set forth the meaning of ⟨~ a word⟩ **2** : to fix or mark the limits of **3** : to clarify in outline or character — **de·fin·able** *adj* — **de·fin·er** *n*

def·i·nite \ˈde-fə-nət\ *adj* **1** : having distinct limits : FIXED **2** : clear in meaning **3** : typically designating an identified or immediately identifiable person or thing ⟨a ~ article⟩ — **def·i·nite·ly** *adv* — **def·i·nite·ness** *n*

def·i·ni·tion \ˌde-fə-ˈni-shən\ *n* **1** : an act of determining or settling **2** : a statement of the meaning of a word or word group; *also* : the action or process of defining **3** : the action or the power of making definite and clear : CLARITY, DISTINCTNESS

de·fin·i·tive \di-ˈfi-nə-tiv\ *adj* **1** : DECISIVE, CONCLUSIVE **2** : authoritative and apparently exhaustive ⟨a ~ edition⟩ **3** : serving to define or specify precisely ⟨~ laws⟩

de·flate \di-ˈflāt\ *vb* **de·flat·ed; de·flat·ing** **1** : to release air or gas from **2** : to reduce in size, importance, or effectiveness; *also* : to reduce from a state of inflation **3** : to become deflated

de·fla·tion \-ˈflā-shən\ *n* **1** : an act or instance of deflating : the state of being deflated **2** : reduction in the volume of available money or credit resulting in a decline of the general price level

de·flect \di-ˈflekt\ *vb* : to turn aside — **de·flec·tion** \-ˈflek-shən\ *n*

de·flo·ra·tion \ˌde-flə-ˈrā-shən\ *n* : rupture of the hymen

de·flow·er \dē-ˈflau̇(-ə)r\ *vb* : to deprive of virginity

de·fog \dē-ˈfȯg, -ˈfäg\ *vb* : to remove fog or condensed moisture from ⟨~ a windshield⟩ — **de·fog·ger** *n*

de·fo·li·ant \dē-ˈfō-lē-ənt\ *n* : a chemical spray or dust used to defoliate plants

de·fo·li·ate \-ˌāt\ *vb* : to deprive of leaves esp. prematurely — **de·fo·li·a·tion** \dē-ˌfō-lē-ˈā-shən\ *n* — **de·fo·li·a·tor** \dē-ˈfō-lē-ˌā-tər\ *n*

de·for·es·ta·tion \dē-ˌfȯr-ə-ˈstā-shən\ *n* : the action or process of clearing an area of forests; *also* : the state of having been cleared of forests — **de·for·est** \(ˌ)dē-ˈfȯr-əst, -ˈfär-\ *vb*

de·form \di-ˈfȯrm\ *vb* **1** : DISFIGURE, DEFACE **2** : to make or become misshapen or changed in shape — **de·for·ma·tion** \ˌdē-ˌfȯr-ˈmā-shən, ˌde-fər-\ *n*

de·for·mi·ty \di-ˈfȯr-mə-tē\ *n, pl* **-ties** **1** : the state of being deformed **2** : a physical blemish or distortion

de·fraud \di-ˈfrȯd\ *vb* : CHEAT

de·fray \di-ˈfrā\ *vb* : to provide for the payment of : PAY — **de·fray·al** *n*

de·frock \(ˌ)dē-ˈfräk\ *vb* : to deprive (as a priest) of the right to exercise the functions of office

de·frost \di-ˈfrȯst\ *vb* **1** : to thaw out **2** : to free from ice — **de·frost·er** *n*

deft \ˈdeft\ *adj* : quick and neat in action — **deft·ly** *adv* — **deft·ness** *n*

de·funct \di-ˈfəŋkt\ *adj* : DEAD, EXTINCT ⟨a ~ language⟩

de·fuse \dē-ˈfyüz\ *vb* **1** : to remove the fuse from (as a bomb) **2** : to make less harmful, potent, or tense

de·fy \di-ˈfī\ *vb* **de·fied; de·fy·ing** [ME, to renounce faith in, challenge, fr. AF *desfier, defier,* fr. *de-* from + *fier* to entrust, ultim. fr. L *fidere* to trust] **1** : CHALLENGE, DARE **2** : to refuse boldly to obey or to yield to : DISREGARD ⟨~ the law⟩ **3** : WITHSTAND, BAFFLE ⟨a scene that *defies* description⟩

deg *abbr* degree

de·gas \dē-ˈgas\ *vb* : to remove gas from

de·gen·er·a·cy \di-ˈje-nə-rə-sē\ *n, pl* **-cies** **1** : the state of being degenerate **2** : the process of becoming degenerate **3** : PERVERSION

[1]**de·gen·er·ate** \di-ˈje-nə-rət\ *adj* : fallen or deteriorated from a former, higher, or normal condition — **de·gen·er·a·tion** \-ˌje-nə-ˈrā-shən\ *n* — **de·gen·er·a·tive** \-ˈje-nə-ˌrā-tiv\ *adj*

[2]**de·gen·er·ate** \di-ˈje-nə-ˌrāt\ *vb* : to un-

dergo deterioration (as in morality, intelligence, structure, or function)

³**de·gen·er·ate** \-rət\ *n* : a degenerate person; *esp* : a sexual pervert

de·grad·able \di-ˈgrā-də-bəl\ *adj* : capable of being chemically degraded

de·grade \di-ˈgrād\ *vb* **1** : to reduce from a higher to a lower rank or degree **2** : DEBASE, CORRUPT **3** : DECOMPOSE — **deg·ra·da·tion** \ˌde-grə-ˈdā-shən\ *n*

de·gree \di-ˈgrē\ *n* [ME, fr. AF *degré,* fr. VL **degradus,* fr. L *de-* down + *gradus* step, grade] **1** : a step in a series **2** : a rank or grade of official, ecclesiastical, or social position; *also* : the civil condition of a person **3** : the extent, intensity, or scope of something esp. as measured by a graded series **4** : one of the forms or sets of forms used in the comparison of an adjective or adverb **5** : a title conferred upon students by a college, university, or professional school on completion of a program of study **6** : a line or space of the musical staff; *also* : a note or tone of a musical scale **7** : a unit of measure for angles that is equal to an angle with its vertex at the center of a circle and its sides cutting off $\frac{1}{360}$ of the circumference; *also* : a unit of measure for arcs of a circle that is equal to the amount of arc extending $\frac{1}{360}$ of the circumference **8** : any of various units for measuring temperature

de·horn \dē-ˈhȯrn\ *vb* : to deprive of horns

de·hu·man·ize \dē-ˈhyü-mə-ˌnīz\ *vb* : to deprive of human qualities, personality, or spirit — **de·hu·man·i·za·tion** \ˌdē-ˌhyü-mə-nə-ˈzā-shən\ *n*

de·hu·mid·i·fy \ˌdē-hyü-ˈmi-də-ˌfī\ *vb* : to remove moisture from (as the air) — **de·hu·mid·i·fi·er** *n*

de·hy·drate \dē-ˈhī-ˌdrāt\ *vb* : to remove water from; *also* : to lose liquid — **de·hy·dra·tion** \ˌdē-hī-ˈdrā-shən\ *n*

de·hy·dro·ge·na·tion \ˌdē-(ˌ)hī-ˌdrä-jə-ˈnā-shən, -drə-\ *n* : the removal of hydrogen from a chemical compound — **de·hy·dro·ge·nate** \ˌdē-(ˌ)hī-ˈdrä-jə-ˌnāt, dē-ˈhī-drə-jə-\ *vb*

de·ice \dē-ˈīs\ *vb* : to keep free or rid of ice ⟨~ a plane⟩ — **de·ic·er** *n*

de·i·fy \ˈdē-ə-ˌfī, ˈdā-\ *vb* **-fied; -fy·ing** **1** : to make a god of **2** : WORSHIP, GLORIFY — **de·i·fi·ca·tion** \ˌdē-ə-fə-ˈkā-shən, ˌdā-\ *n*

deign \ˈdān\ *vb* [ME, fr. AF *deigner,* fr. L *dignare, dignari,* fr. *dignus* worthy] : CONDESCEND

de·ion·ize \dē-ˈī-ə-ˌnīz\ *vb* : to remove ions from

de·ism \ˈdē-ˌi-zəm, ˈdā-\ *n, often cap* : a system of thought advocating natural religion based on human morality and reason rather than divine revelation — **de·ist** \-ist\ *n, often cap* — **de·is·tic** \dē-ˈis-tik, dā-\ *adj*

de·i·ty \ˈdē-ə-tē, ˈdā-\ *n, pl* **-ties** **1** : DIVINITY 2 **2** *cap* : GOD 1 **3** : a god or goddess

dé·jà vu \ˌdā-ˌzhä-ˈvü\ *n* [F, adj., already seen] : the feeling that one has seen or heard something before

de·ject·ed \di-ˈjek-təd\ *adj* : low in spirits : SAD — **de·ject·ed·ly** *adv*

de·jec·tion \di-ˈjek-shən\ *n* : lowness of spirits

de ju·re \dē-ˈju̇r-ē\ *adv or adj* [ML] : by legal right

deka·gram \ˈde-kə-ˌgram\ *n* — see METRIC SYSTEM table

deka·li·ter \-ˌlē-tər\ *n* — see METRIC SYSTEM table

deka·me·ter \-ˌmē-tər\ *n* — see METRIC SYSTEM table

del *abbr* delegate; delegation

Del *abbr* Delaware

Del·a·ware \ˈde-lə-ˌwer\ *n, pl* **Delaware** *or* **Delawares** : a member of an Indigenous people orig. of the Delaware valley; *also* : the Algonquian language of the Delaware people

¹**de·lay** \di-ˈlā\ *n* **1** : the act of delaying : the state of being delayed **2** : the time for which something is delayed

²**delay** *vb* **1** : POSTPONE, PUT OFF **2** : to stop, detain, or hinder for a time **3** : to move or act slowly

de·lec·ta·ble \di-ˈlek-tə-bəl\ *adj* **1** : highly pleasing : DELIGHTFUL **2** : DELICIOUS

de·lec·ta·tion \ˌdē-ˌlek-ˈtā-shən\ *n* : DELIGHT, PLEASURE, DIVERSION

¹**del·e·gate** \ˈde-li-gət, -ˌgāt\ *n* **1** : DEPUTY, REPRESENTATIVE **2** : a member of the lower house of the legislature of Maryland, Virginia, or West Virginia

²**del·e·gate** \-ˌgāt\ *vb* **-gat·ed; -gat·ing** **1** : to entrust to another ⟨~ authority⟩ **2** : to appoint as one's delegate

del·e·ga·tion \ˌde-li-ˈgā-shən\ *n* **1** : the act of delegating **2** : one or more persons chosen to represent others

de·le·git·i·mize \ˌdē-lə-ˈji-tə-ˌmīz\ *vb* : to diminish or destroy the legitimacy, prestige, or authority of

de·lete \di-ˈlēt\ *vb* **de·let·ed; de·let·ing** [L *deletus,* pp. of *delēre* to wipe out, destroy] : to eliminate esp. by blotting out, cutting out, or erasing ⟨~ a computer file⟩ — **de·le·tion** \-ˈlē-shən\ *n*

del·e·te·ri·ous \ˌde-lə-ˈtir-ē-əs\ *adj* : HARMFUL, NOXIOUS

delft \ˈdelft\ *n* **1** : a Dutch pottery with an opaque white glaze and predominantly blue decoration **2** : glazed pottery esp. when blue and white

delft·ware \-ˌwer\ *n* : DELFT

deli \ˈde-lē\ *n, pl* **del·is** : DELICATESSEN

¹**de·lib·er·ate** \di-ˈli-bə-ˌrāt\ *vb* **-at·ed; -at·ing** : to consider carefully — **de·lib·er·a·tion** \-ˌli-bə-ˈrā-shən\ *n* — **de·lib·er·a·tive** \-ˈli-bə-ˌrā-tiv, -brə-tiv\ *adj* — **de·lib·er·a·tive·ly** *adv*

²**de·lib·er·ate** \di-ˈli-bə-rət, -ˈli-brət\ *adj* **1** : determined after careful thought **2** : done or said intentionally **3** : UNHURRIED, SLOW — **de·lib·er·ate·ly** *adv* — **de·lib·er·ate·ness** *n*

del·i·ca·cy \ˈde-li-kə-sē\ *n, pl* **-cies** **1** : something pleasing to eat and considered rare or luxurious **2** : FINENESS, DAINTINESS; *also* : FRAILTY **3** : nicety or expressiveness of touch **4** : precise perception and discrimination : SENSITIVITY **5** : sensibility in feeling or conduct; *also* : SQUEAMISHNESS **6** : the quality or state of requiring delicate handling

del•i•cate \ˈde-li-kət\ *adj* **1** : pleasing to the senses of taste or smell esp. in a mild or subtle way **2** : marked by daintiness or charm : EXQUISITE **3** : FASTIDIOUS, SQUEAMISH ⟨a person of ~ tastes⟩ **4** : easily damaged : FRAGILE; *also* : SICKLY **5** : requiring skill or tact **6** : marked by care, skill, or tact **7** : marked by minute precision : very sensitive ⟨a ~ instrument⟩ — **del•i•cate•ly** *adv*

del•i•ca•tes•sen \ˌde-li-kə-ˈte-sᵊn\ *n pl* [G, pl. of *Delicatesse* delicacy, fr. F *délicatesse*] **1** : ready-to-eat food products (as cooked meats and prepared salads) **2** *sing, pl* **delicatessens** : a store where delicatessen are sold

de•li•cious \di-ˈli-shəs\ *adj* : affording great pleasure : DELIGHTFUL; *esp* : very pleasing to the taste or smell — **de•li•cious•ly** *adv* — **de•li•cious•ness** *n*

[1]**de•light** \di-ˈlīt\ *n* **1** : great pleasure or satisfaction : JOY **2** : something that gives great pleasure — **de•light•ful** \-fəl\ *adj* — **de•light•ful•ly** *adv*

[2]**delight** *vb* **1** : to take great pleasure **2** : to satisfy greatly : PLEASE

de•light•ed *adj* : highly pleased : GRATIFIED — **de•light•ed•ly** *adv*

de•lim•it \di-ˈli-mət\ *vb* : to fix the limits of

de•lin•eate \di-ˈli-nē-ˌāt\ *vb* **-eat•ed; -eat•ing** **1** : SKETCH, PORTRAY **2** : to picture in words : DESCRIBE — **de•lin•ea•tion** \-ˌli-nē-ˈā-shən\ *n*

de•lin•quen•cy \di-ˈliŋ-kwən-sē\ *n, pl* **-cies** : the quality or state of being delinquent

[1]**de•lin•quent** \-kwənt\ *n* : a delinquent person

[2]**delinquent** *adj* **1** : offending by neglect or violation of duty or of law **2** : being overdue in payment

del•i•quesce \ˌde-li-ˈkwes\ *vb* **-quesced; -quesc•ing** : MELT, DISSOLVE — **del•i•ques•cent** \-ˈkwe-sᵊnt\ *adj*

de•lir•i•um \di-ˈlir-ē-əm\ *n* [L, fr. *delirare* to be crazy, lit., to leave the furrow (in plowing), fr. *de-* from + *lira* furrow] : mental disturbance marked by confusion, disordered speech, and hallucinations; *also* : frenzied excitement — **de•lir•i•ous** \-ē-əs\ *adj* — **de•lir•i•ous•ly** *adv*

delirium tre•mens \-ˈtrē-mənz, -ˈtre-\ *n* : a violent delirium with tremors that is induced by excessive and prolonged use of alcoholic liquors

de•liv•er \di-ˈli-vər\ *vb* **-ered; -er•ing** **1** : to set free **2** : CONVEY, TRANSFER ⟨~ a letter⟩ **3** : to assist in giving birth or at the birth of; *also* : to give birth to **4** : UTTER, COMMUNICATE **5** : to send to an intended target or destination — **de•liv•er•able** \-ˈli-v(ə-)rə-bəl\ *adj* — **de•liv•er•ance** \-v(ə-)rəns\ *n* — **de•liv•er•er** *n*

de•liv•ery \di-ˈli-və-rē\ *n, pl* **-er•ies** : the act of delivering something; *also* : something delivered — **de•liv•ery•man** \-ˌman\ *n*

dell \ˈdel\ *n* : a small secluded valley

de•louse \dē-ˈlau̇s\ *vb* : to remove lice from

del•phin•i•um \del-ˈfi-nē-əm\ *n* : any of a genus of mostly perennial herbs related to the buttercups with tall branching spikes of irregular flowers

del•ta \ˈdel-tə\ *n* **1** : the 4th letter of the Greek alphabet — Δ or δ **2** : something shaped like a capital Δ; *esp* : the triangular silt-formed land at the mouth of a river — **del•ta•ic** \del-ˈtā-ik\ *adj*

del•toid \ˈdel-ˌtȯid\ *n* : a large triangular muscle that covers the shoulder joint and raises the arm laterally

de•lude \di-ˈlüd\ *vb* **de•lud•ed; de•lud•ing** : MISLEAD, DECEIVE, TRICK

[1]**del•uge** \ˈdel-yüj\ *n* **1** : a flooding of land by water **2** : a drenching rain **3** : a great amount or number ⟨a ~ of mail⟩

[2]**deluge** *vb* **del•uged; del•ug•ing** **1** : INUNDATE, FLOOD **2** : to overwhelm as if with a deluge ⟨*deluged* with emails⟩

de•lu•sion \di-ˈlü-zhən\ *n* : a deluding or being deluded; *esp* : a persistent false psychotic belief — **de•lu•sion•al** \-ˈlü-zhə-nəl\ *adj* — **de•lu•sive** \-ˈlü-siv\ *adj*

de•luxe \di-ˈlu̇ks, -ˈləks, -ˈlüks\ *adj* : notably luxurious or elegant

delve \ˈdelv\ *vb* **delved; delv•ing** **1** : DIG **2** : to seek laboriously for information

dely *abbr* delivery

Dem *abbr* Democrat; Democratic

de•mag•ne•tize \dē-ˈmag-nə-ˌtīz\ *vb* : to cause to lose magnetic properties — **de•mag•ne•ti•za•tion** \dē-ˌmag-nə-tə-ˈzā-shən\ *n*

dem•a•gogue *also* **dem•a•gog** \ˈde-mə-ˌgäg\ *n* [Gk *dēmagōgos,* fr. *dēmos* people + *agōgos* leading, fr. *agein* to lead] : a person who appeals to the emotions and prejudices of people esp. in order to gain political power — **dem•a•gogu•ery** \-ˌgä-gə-rē\ *n* — **dem•a•gogy** \-ˌgä-gē, -ˌgä-jē\ *n*

[1]**de•mand** \di-ˈmand\ *n* **1** : an act of demanding; *also* : something claimed as due or just **2** : the ability and desire to buy goods or services; *also* : the quantity of goods wanted at a stated price **3** : a seeking or being sought after : urgent need **4** : a pressing need or requirement

[2]**demand** *vb* **1** : to ask for with authority : claim as due or just **2** : to ask earnestly or in the manner of a command **3** : REQUIRE, NEED ⟨~*s* constant care⟩

de•mar•cate \di-ˈmär-ˌkāt, ˈdē-ˌmär-\ *vb* **-cat•ed; -cat•ing** **1** : DELIMIT **2** : to set apart : DISTINGUISH — **de•mar•ca•tion** \ˌdē-ˌmär-ˈkā-shən\ *n*

dé•marche *or* **de•marche** \dā-ˈmärsh\ *n* : a course of action : MANEUVER

[1]**de•mean** \di-ˈmēn\ *vb* **de•meaned; de•mean•ing** : to behave or conduct (oneself) usu. in a proper manner

[2]**demean** *vb* **de•meaned; de•mean•ing** : DEGRADE, DEBASE

de·mean·or \di-ˈmē-nər\ *n* : CONDUCT, BEARING
de·mean·our *Brit var of* DEMEANOR
de·ment·ed \di-ˈmen-təd\ *adj* **1** *informal* : MAD, INSANE **2** : exhibiting cognitive dementia — **de·ment·ed·ly** *adv*
de·men·tia \di-ˈmen-chə\ *n* **1** : deterioration of cognitive functioning (as in Alzheimer's disease) **2** : INSANITY ⟨fanaticism bordering on ~⟩
de·mer·it \di-ˈmer-ət\ *n* **1** : FAULT **2** : a mark placed against a person's record for some fault or offense
de·mesne \di-ˈmān, -ˈmēn\ *n* **1** : REALM **2** : manorial land actually possessed by the lord and not held by free tenants **3** : ESTATE **4** : REGION
demi·god \ˈde-mi-ˌgäd\ *n* : a mythological being with more power than a mortal but less than a god
demi·john \ˈde-mi-ˌjän\ *n* [F *dame-jeanne,* lit., Lady Jane] : a large narrow-necked bottle usu. enclosed in wickerwork
de·mil·i·ta·rize \dē-ˈmi-lə-tə-ˌrīz\ *vb* : to strip of military forces, weapons, or fortifications — **de·mil·i·tar·i·za·tion** \dē-ˌmi-lə-tə-rə-ˈzā-shən\ *n*
demi·mon·daine \ˌde-mi-ˌmän-ˈdān\ *n* : a woman of the demimonde
demi·monde \ˈde-mi-ˌmänd\ *n* [F *demi-monde,* fr. *demi-* half + *monde* world] **1** : a class of women on the fringes of respectable society supported by wealthy lovers **2** : a distinct isolated group having low reputation or prestige
de·min·er·al·ize \dē-ˈmi-nə-rə-ˌlīz\ *vb* : to remove the mineral matter from — **de·min·er·al·i·za·tion** \-ˌmi-nə-rə-lə-ˈzā-shən\ *n*
de·mise \di-ˈmīz\ *n* **1** : LEASE **2** : transfer of sovereignty to a successor ⟨~ of the crown⟩ **3** : DEATH **4** : loss of status
demi·tasse \ˈde-mi-ˌtas\ *n* : a small cup of black coffee; *also* : the cup used to serve it
demo \ˈde-mō\ *n, pl* **dem·os** **1** : DEMONSTRATION **2** : a product used to show performance or merits to prospective buyers **3** : a recording used to show off a song or performer
de·mo·bi·lize \di-ˈmō-bə-ˌlīz, dē-\ *vb* **1** : DISBAND **2** : to discharge from military service — **de·mo·bi·li·za·tion** \di-ˌmō-bə-lə-ˈzā-shən, dē-\ *n*
de·moc·ra·cy \di-ˈmä-krə-sē\ *n, pl* **-cies** [MF *democratie,* fr. LL *democratia,* fr. Gk *dēmokratia,* fr. *dēmos* people + *kratos* strength, power] **1** : government by the people; *esp* : rule of the majority **2** : a government in which the supreme power is held by the people **3** : a political unit that has a democratic government **4** *cap* : the principles and policies of the Democratic party in the U.S. **5** : the common people esp. when constituting the source of political authority **6** : the absence of hereditary or arbitrary class distinctions or privileges
dem·o·crat \ˈde-mə-ˌkrat\ *n* **1** : one who believes in or practices democracy **2** *cap* : a member of the Democratic party of the U.S.
dem·o·crat·ic \ˌde-mə-ˈkra-tik\ *adj* **1** : of, relating to, or favoring democracy **2** *often cap* : of or relating to one of the two major political parties in the U.S. associated in modern times with policies of broad social reform and internationalism **3** : relating to or appealing to the common people ⟨~ art⟩ **4** : not snobbish — **dem·o·crat·i·cal·ly** \-ti-k(ə-)lē\ *adv*
de·moc·ra·tize \di-ˈmä-krə-ˌtīz\ *vb* **-tized; -tiz·ing** : to make democratic
dé·mo·dé \ˌdā-mō-ˈdā\ *adj* [F] : no longer fashionable : OUT-OF-DATE
de·mo·graph·ics \ˌde-mə-ˈgra-fiks, ˌdē-\ *n pl* : the statistical characteristics of human populations
de·mog·ra·phy \di-ˈmä-grə-fē\ *n* : the statistical study of human populations and esp. their size and distribution and the number of births and deaths — **de·mog·ra·pher** \-fər\ *n* — **de·mo·graph·ic** \ˌde-mə-ˈgra-fik, ˌdē-\ *adj* — **de·mo·graph·i·cal·ly** \-fi-k(ə-)lē\ *adv*
dem·oi·selle \ˌdem-wə-ˈzel\ *n* [F] : a young woman
de·mol·ish \di-ˈmä-lish\ *vb* **1** : to destroy by breaking apart : RAZE **2** : SMASH **3** : to put an end to ⟨~ a theory⟩
de·mo·li·tion \ˌde-mə-ˈli-shən, ˌdē-\ *n* : the act of demolishing; *esp* : destruction by means of explosives
de·mon *or* **dae·mon** \ˈdē-mən\ *n* **1** : an evil spirit : DEVIL **2** *usu daemon* : an attendant power or spirit **3** : one that has unusual drive or effectiveness ⟨a ~ for work⟩
de·mon·e·tize \dē-ˈmä-nə-ˌtīz, -ˈmə-\ *vb* : to stop using as money or as a monetary standard ⟨~ silver⟩ — **de·mon·e·ti·za·tion** \dē-ˌmä-nə-tə-ˈzā-shən, -ˌmə-\ *n*
de·mo·ni·ac \di-ˈmō-nē-ˌak\ *also* **de·mo·ni·a·cal** \ˌdē-mə-ˈnī-ə-kəl\ *adj* **1** : possessed or influenced by a demon **2** : DEMONIC
de·mon·ic \di-ˈmä-nik\ *also* **de·mon·i·cal** \-ni-kəl\ *adj* : DEVILISH, FIENDISH ⟨~ cruelty⟩
de·mon·ize \ˈdē-mə-ˌnīz\ *vb* **-ized; -iz·ing** **1** : to convert into a demon **2** : to characterize or treat as evil or harmful
de·mon·ol·o·gy \ˌdē-mə-ˈnä-lə-jē\ *n* **1** : the study of demons **2** : belief in demons
de·mon·stra·ble \di-ˈmän-strə-bəl\ *adj* **1** : capable of being demonstrated **2** : APPARENT, EVIDENT — **de·mon·stra·bly** \-blē\ *adv*
dem·on·strate \ˈde-mən-ˌstrāt\ *vb* **-strat·ed; -strat·ing** **1** : to show clearly **2** : to prove or make clear by reasoning or evidence **3** : to explain esp. with many examples **4** : to show publicly ⟨~ a new car⟩ **5** : to make a public display ⟨~ in protest⟩ — **dem·on·stra·tion** \ˌde-mən-ˈstrā-shən\ *n* — **dem·on·stra·tor** \ˈde-mən-ˌstrā-tər\ *n*
[1]**de·mon·stra·tive** \di-ˈmän-strə-tiv\ *adj* **1** : demonstrating as real or true **2** : charac-

terized by demonstration **3** : pointing out the one referred to and distinguishing it from others of the same class ⟨~ pronoun⟩ **4** : marked by display of feeling : EFFUSIVE — **de•mon•stra•tive•ly** *adv* — **de•mon•stra•tive•ness** *n*

[2]**demonstrative** *n* : a demonstrative word and esp. a pronoun

de•mor•al•ize \di-ˈmȯr-ə-ˌlīz\ *vb* **1** : to corrupt in morals **2** : to weaken in discipline or spirit : DISORGANIZE — **de•mor•al•i•za•tion** \di-ˌmȯr-ə-lə-ˈzā-shən\ *n*

de•mote \di-ˈmōt\ *vb* **de•mot•ed; de•mot•ing** : to reduce to a lower grade or rank — **de•mo•tion** \-ˈmō-shən\ *n*

de•mot•ic \di-ˈmä-tik\ *adj* : COMMON, POPULAR ⟨~ idiom⟩

de•mur \di-ˈmər\ *vb* **de•murred; de•mur•ring** [ME *demuren, demeren* to linger, fr. AF *demurer, demoerer,* fr. L *demorari,* fr. *morari* to linger, fr. *mora* delay] : to take exception : OBJECT — **de•mur** *n*

de•mure \di-ˈmyu̇r\ *adj* **1** : quietly modest : DECOROUS **2** : affectedly modest, reserved, or serious : PRIM ♦ ***Synonyms*** SHY, BASHFUL, COY, DIFFICULT, RETIRING, UNASSERTIVE — **de•mure•ly** *adv*

de•mur•rer \di-ˈmər-ər\ *n* : a claim by the defendant in a legal action that the plaintiff does not have sufficient grounds to proceed

den \ˈden\ *n* **1** : LAIR 1 **2** : HIDEOUT ⟨a robber's ~⟩; *also* : a place like a hideout or a center of secret activity ⟨opium ~⟩ ⟨a ~ of iniquity⟩ **3** : a cozy private room

Den *abbr* Denmark

de•nar \ˈde-ˌnär, ˈdā-\ — see MONEY table

de•na•ture \dē-ˈnā-chər\ *vb* **de•na•tured; de•na•tur•ing** : to remove or change the natural qualities of; *esp* : to make (alcohol) unfit for drinking

den•drol•o•gy \den-ˈdrä-lə-jē\ *n* : the study of trees — **den•drol•o•gist** \-jist\ *n*

den•gue \ˈdeŋ-gē, -ˌgā\ *n* [Sp] : an acute infectious disease characterized by headache, severe joint pain, and rash

de•ni \ˈde-ˌnē, ˈdā-\ *n pl* — see *denar* at MONEY table

de•ni•al \di-ˈnī(-ə)l\ *n* **1** : rejection of a request **2** : refusal to admit the truth of a statement or charge; *also* : assertion that something alleged is false **3** : DISAVOWAL **4** : restriction on one's own activity or desires

de•nier \ˈden-yər\ *n* : a unit of fineness for yarn

den•i•grate \ˈde-ni-ˌgrāt\ *vb* **-grat•ed; -grat•ing** [L *denigrare,* fr. *nigrare* to blacken, fr. *niger* black] : to cast aspersions on : DEFAME — **den•i•gra•tion** \ˌde-ni-ˈgrā-shən\ *n*

den•im \ˈde-nəm\ *n* [F *(serge) de Nîmes* serge of Nîmes, France] **1** : a firm durable twilled usu. cotton fabric woven with colored warp and white filling threads **2** *pl* : overalls or pants of usu. blue denim

den•i•zen \ˈde-nə-zən\ *n* : INHABITANT

de•nom•i•nate \di-ˈnä-mə-ˌnāt\ *vb* : to give a name to : DESIGNATE

de•nom•i•na•tion \di-ˌnä-mə-ˈnā-shən\ *n* **1** : an act of denominating **2** : a value or size of a series of related values (as of money) **3** : NAME, DESIGNATION; *esp* : a general name for a category **4** : a religious organization uniting local congregations in a single body — **de•nom•i•na•tion•al** \-shə-nəl\ *adj*

de•nom•i•na•tor \di-ˈnä-mə-ˌnā-tər\ *n* : the part of a fraction that is below the line indicating division

de•no•ta•tive \ˈdē-nō-ˌtā-tiv, di-ˈnō-tə-tiv\ *adj* **1** : denoting or tending to denote **2** : relating to denotation

de•note \di-ˈnōt\ *vb* **1** : to mark out plainly : INDICATE **2** : to make known **3** : MEAN, NAME — **de•no•ta•tion** \ˌdē-nō-ˈtā-shən\ *n*

de•noue•ment \ˌdā-ˌnü-ˈmäⁿ\ *n* [F *dénouement,* lit., untying] : the final outcome of the dramatic complications in a literary work

de•nounce \di-ˈnau̇ns\ *vb* **de•nounced; de•nounc•ing** **1** : to pronounce esp. publicly to be blameworthy or evil **2** : to inform against : ACCUSE **3** : to announce formally the termination of (as a treaty) — **de•nounce•ment** *n*

de no•vo \di-ˈnō-vō\ *adv or adj* [L] : over again : ANEW ⟨a case tried ~⟩

dense \ˈdens\ *adj* **dens•er; dens•est** **1** : marked by compactness or crowding together of parts : THICK ⟨~ forest⟩ ⟨a ~ fog⟩ **2** : DULL, STUPID — **dense•ly** *adv* — **dense•ness** *n*

den•si•ty \ˈden-sə-tē\ *n, pl* **-ties** **1** : the quality or state of being dense **2** : the quantity of something per unit volume, unit area, or unit length

dent \ˈdent\ *n* **1** : a small depressed place made by a blow or by pressure **2** : an impression or weakening effect made usu. against resistance **3** : initial progress — **dent** *vb*

den•tal \ˈden-tᵊl\ *adj* : of or relating to teeth or dentistry — **den•tal•ly** *adv*

dental floss *n* : a thread used to clean between the teeth

dental hygienist *n* : a person licensed to clean and examine teeth

den•tate \ˈden-ˌtāt\ *adj* : having pointed projections : NOTCHED

den•ti•frice \ˈden-tə-frəs\ *n* [ME *dentifricie,* fr. L *dentifricium,* fr. *dent-, dens* tooth + *fricare* to rub] : a powder, paste, or liquid for cleaning the teeth

den•tin \ˈden-tᵊn\ *or* **den•tine** \ˈden-ˌtēn, den-ˈtēn\ *n* : a calcareous material like bone but harder and denser that composes the principal mass of a tooth

den•tist \ˈden-tist\ *n* : a person licensed in the care, treatment, and replacement of teeth — **den•tist•ry** *n*

den•ti•tion \den-ˈti-shən\ *n* : the number, kind, and arrangement of teeth (as of a person or animal); *also* : TEETH

den•ture \ˈden-chər\ *n* : a set of teeth; *esp* : a partial or complete set of false teeth

de•nude \di-ˈnüd, -ˈnyüd\ *vb* **de•nud•ed; de•nud•ing** : to strip the covering from — **de•nu•da•tion** \ˌdē-nü-ˈdā-shən, -nyü-\ *n*

de·nun·ci·a·tion \di-ˌnən-sē-ˈā-shən\ *n* : the act of denouncing; *esp* : a public condemnation — **de·nun·ci·a·to·ry** \-ˈnən-sē-ə-ˌtȯr-ē\ *adj*

de·ny \di-ˈnī\ *vb* **de·nied; de·ny·ing** **1** : to declare untrue **2** : to refuse to recognize or acknowledge : DISAVOW **3** : to refuse to grant ⟨~ a request⟩ **4** : to reject as false ⟨~ a theory⟩

de·o·dar \ˈdē-ə-ˌdär\ *n* [Hindi & Urdu *devadār, deodār,* fr. Skt *devadāru,* fr. *deva* god + *dāru* wood] : a Himalayan cedar

de·odor·ant \dē-ˈō-də-rənt\ *n* : a preparation that destroys or masks unpleasant odors

de·odor·ize \dē-ˈō-də-ˌrīz\ *vb* : to eliminate the offensive odor of

de·ox·i·dize \dē-ˈäk-sə-ˌdīz\ *vb* : to remove esp. elemental oxygen from

de·oxy·ri·bo·nu·cle·ic acid \dē-ˈäk-si-ˌrī-bō-nu̇-ˌklē-ik-, -nyu̇-\ *n* : DNA

de·oxy·ri·bose \dē-ˌäk-si-ˈrī-ˌbōs\ *n* : a sugar with five carbon and four oxygen atoms in each molecule that is part of DNA

dep *abbr* **1** depart; departure **2** deposit **3** deputy

de·part \di-ˈpärt\ *vb* **1** : to go away : go away from : LEAVE **2** : DIE **3** : to turn aside : DEVIATE

de·part·ee \di-pär-ˈtē\ *n* : a person who is departing or who has departed

de·part·ment \di-ˈpärt-mənt\ *n* **1** : a distinct sphere or category esp. of an activity or attribute **2** : a functional or territorial division (as of a government, business, or college) — **de·part·men·tal** \di-ˌpärt-ˈmen-tᵊl, ˌdē-\ *adj* — **de·part·men·tal·ly** *adv*

department store *n* : a store having separate sections for a wide variety of goods

de·par·ture \di-ˈpär-chər\ *n* **1** : the act of going away **2** : a starting out (as on a journey) **3** : DIVERGENCE ⟨a ~ from tradition⟩

de·pend \di-ˈpend\ *vb* **1** : to be determined, based, or contingent ⟨life ~*s* on food⟩ **2** : TRUST, RELY ⟨you can ~ on me⟩ **3** : to be dependent esp. for financial support **4** : to hang down ⟨a vine ~*ing* from a tree⟩

de·pend·able \di-ˈpen-də-bəl\ *adj* : TRUSTWORTHY, RELIABLE — **de·pend·abil·i·ty** \-ˌpen-də-ˈbi-lə-tē\ *n*

de·pen·dence *also* **de·pen·dance** \di-ˈpen-dəns\ *n* **1** : the quality or state of being dependent; *esp* : the quality or state of being influenced by or subject to another **2** : RELIANCE, TRUST **3** : something on which one relies **4** : drug addiction; *also* : HABITUATION 2

de·pen·den·cy \-dən-sē\ *n, pl* **-cies** **1** : DEPENDENCE **2** : a territory under the jurisdiction of a nation but not formally annexed by it

¹**de·pen·dent** \-dənt\ *adj* **1** : hanging down **2** : determined or conditioned by another; *also* : affected with drug dependence **3** : relying on another for support **4** : subject to another's jurisdiction **5** : SUBORDINATE 4 ⟨~ clauses⟩

²**dependent** *also* **de·pen·dant** \-dənt\ *n* : one that is dependent; *esp* : a person who relies on another for support

dependent variable *n* : a variable whose value is determined by that of one or more other variables in a function

de·pict \di-ˈpikt\ *vb* **1** : to represent by a picture **2** : to describe in words — **de·pic·tion** \-ˈpik-shən\ *n*

de·pil·a·to·ry \di-ˈpi-lə-ˌtȯr-ē\ *n, pl* **-ries** : a preparation for removing hair, wool, or bristles

de·plane \dē-ˈplān\ *vb* : to get out of an airplane

de·plete \di-ˈplēt\ *vb* **de·plet·ed; de·plet·ing** : to exhaust esp. of strength or resources — **de·ple·tion** \-ˈplē-shən\ *n*

de·plor·able \di-ˈplȯr-ə-bəl\ *adj* **1** : LAMENTABLE ⟨a ~ death⟩ **2** : WRETCHED — **de·plor·ably** *adv*

de·plore \-ˈplȯr\ *vb* **de·plored; de·plor·ing** **1** : to feel or express grief for **2** : to regret strongly **3** : to consider unfortunate or deserving of disapproval

de·ploy \di-ˈplȯi\ *vb* : to spread out (as troops or ships) in order for battle — **de·ploy·ment** \-mənt\ *n*

de·po·nent \di-ˈpō-nənt\ *n* : one who gives evidence

de·pop·u·late \dē-ˈpä-pyə-ˌlāt\ *vb* : to reduce greatly the population of — **de·pop·u·la·tion** \-ˌpä-pyə-ˈlā-shən\ *n*

de·port \di-ˈpȯrt\ *vb* **1** : CONDUCT, BEHAVE **2** : BANISH, EXILE — **de·por·ta·tion** \ˌdē-ˌpȯr-ˈtā-shən\ *n*

de·port·ment \di-ˈpȯrt-mənt\ *n* : BEHAVIOR, BEARING

de·pose \di-ˈpōz\ *vb* **de·posed; de·pos·ing** **1** : to remove from high office (as of king) **2** : to testify under oath or by affidavit

¹**de·pos·it** \di-ˈpä-zət\ *vb* **de·pos·it·ed** \-zə-təd\; **de·pos·it·ing** **1** : to place for safekeeping or as a pledge; *esp* : to put money in a bank **2** : to lay down : PLACE **3** : to let fall or sink ⟨silt ~*ed* by a flood⟩ — **de·pos·i·tor** \-zə-tər\ *n*

²**deposit** *n* **1** : the state of being deposited ⟨money on ~⟩ **2** : something placed for safekeeping; *esp* : money deposited in a bank **3** : money given as a pledge **4** : an act of depositing **5** : something laid down ⟨a ~ of silt⟩ **6** : a natural accumulation (as of a mineral)

de·po·si·tion \ˌde-pə-ˈzi-shən, ˌdē-\ *n* **1** : an act of removing from a position of authority **2** : TESTIMONY **3** : the process of depositing **4** : DEPOSIT

de·pos·i·to·ry \di-ˈpä-zə-ˌtȯr-ē\ *n, pl* **-ries** : a place where something is deposited esp. for safekeeping

de·pot *1, 2 usu* ˈde-pō, *3 usu* ˈdē-\ *n* **1** : a place for storing goods or vehicles **2** : a place where military supplies or replacements are kept or assembled **3** : a building for railroad or bus passengers

depr *abbr* depreciation

de·prave \di-ˈprāv\ *vb* **de·praved; de·prav·ing** [ME, fr. AF *depraver,* fr. L *depravare* to pervert, fr. *pravus* crooked, bad] : CORRUPT, PERVERT — **de·praved** *adj* — **de·prav·i·ty** \-ˈpra-və-tē\ *n*

dep·re·cate \ˈde-pri-ˌkāt\ *vb* **-cat·ed; -cat·ing** [L *deprecari* to avert by prayer, fr. *precari* to pray] **1** : to express disapproval of **2** : BELITTLE — **dep·re·ca·tion** \ˌde-pri-ˈkā-shən\ *n*
dep·re·ca·to·ry \ˈde-pri-kə-ˌtȯr-ē\ *adj* **1** : APOLOGETIC **2** : serving to deprecate : DISAPPROVING
de·pre·ci·ate \di-ˈprē-shē-ˌāt\ *vb* **-at·ed; -at·ing** [ME, fr. LL *depreciatus,* pp. of *depretiare,* fr. L *pretium* price] **1** : BELITTLE, DISPARAGE **2** : to lessen in price or value — **de·pre·cia·ble** \-shə-bəl\ *adj* — **de·pre·ci·a·tion** \-ˌprē-shē-ˈā-shən\ *n*
dep·re·da·tion \ˌde-prə-ˈdā-shən\ *n* : a laying waste or plundering — **dep·re·date** \ˈde-prə-ˌdāt\ *vb*
de·press \di-ˈpres\ *vb* **1** : to press down : cause to sink to a lower position **2** : to lessen the activity or force of **3** : SADDEN, DISCOURAGE **4** : to lessen in price or value — **de·pres·sor** \-ˈpre-sər\ *n*
de·pres·sant \di-ˈpre-sᵊnt\ *n* : one that depresses; *esp* : a chemical substance (as a drug) that reduces bodily functional activity — **depressant** *adj*
de·pressed \-ˈprest\ *adj* **1** : low in spirits; *also* : affected with psychological depression **2** : suffering from economic depression
de·pres·sion \di-ˈpre-shən\ *n* **1** : an act of depressing : a state of being depressed **2** : a pressing down : LOWERING **3** : a state of feeling sad **4** : a psychological disorder marked esp. by sadness, inactivity, difficulty in thinking and concentration, and feelings of dejection **5** : a depressed area or part **6** : a period of low general economic activity with widespread unemployment
¹**de·pres·sive** \di-ˈpre-siv\ *adj* **1** : tending to depress **2** : characterized or affected by psychological depression
²**depressive** *n* : a person affected with or prone to psychological depression
de·pres·sur·ize \(ˌ)dē-ˈpre-shə-ˌrīz\ *vb* : to release pressure from
dep·ri·va·tion \ˌde-prə-ˈvā-shən\ *n* **1** : an act or instance of depriving : LOSS **2** : PRIVATION 2
de·prive \di-ˈprīv\ *vb* **de·prived; de·priv·ing** **1** : to take something away from **2** : to stop from having something
deprived *adj* : marked by deprivation esp. of the necessities of life
de·pro·gram \(ˌ)dē-ˈprō-ˌgram, -grəm\ *vb* : to dissuade from convictions usu. of a religious nature often by coercive means
dept *abbr* department
depth \ˈdepth\ *n, pl* **depths** \ˈdepths\ **1** : something that is deep; *esp* : the deep part of a body of water **2** : a part that is far from the outside or surface; *also* : the middle or innermost part **3** : ABYSS **4** : a profound or intense state ⟨the ∼*s* of reflection⟩; *also* : the worst part ⟨during the ∼*s* of the depression⟩ **5** : a reprehensibly low condition **6** : the distance from top to bottom or from front to back **7** : the quality of being deep **8** : the degree of intensity
depth charge *n* : an explosive device for use underwater esp. against submarines
dep·u·ta·tion \ˌde-pyə-ˈtā-shən\ *n* **1** : the act of appointing a deputy **2** : DELEGATION
de·pute \di-ˈpyüt\ *vb* **de·put·ed; de·put·ing** : DELEGATE
dep·u·tize \ˈde-pyə-ˌtīz\ *vb* **-tized; -tiz·ing** : to appoint or act as deputy
dep·u·ty \ˈde-pyə-tē\ *n, pl* **-ties** **1** : a person appointed to act for or in place of another **2** : an assistant empowered to act as a substitute in the absence of a superior **3** : a member of a lower house of a legislative assembly
der *or* **deriv** *abbr* derivation; derivative
de·rail \di-ˈrāl\ *vb* : to leave or cause to leave the rails — **de·rail·ment** *n*
de·rail·leur \di-ˈrā-lər\ *n* [F *dérailleur*] : a device for shifting gears on a bicycle by moving the chain from one set of exposed gears to another
de·range \di-ˈrānj\ *vb* **de·ranged; de·rang·ing** **1** : DISARRANGE, UPSET **2** : to make insane — **de·range·ment** *n*
der·by \ˈdər-bē, *Brit* ˈdär-\ *n, pl* **derbies** **1** : a horse race usu. for three-year-olds held annually **2** : a race or contest open to all **3** : a stiff felt hat with dome-shaped crown and narrow brim
de·re·cho \də-ˈrā-(ˌ)chō\ *n, pl* **-chos** [Sp, straight (contrasted with *tornado,* taken to mean "turned")] : a complex of thunderstorms with powerful winds
de·reg·u·la·tion \(ˌ)dē-ˌre-gyu̇-ˈlā-shən\ *n* : the act of removing restrictions or regulations — **de·reg·u·late** \-ˈre-gyu̇-ˌlāt\ *vb*
¹**der·e·lict** \ˈder-ə-ˌlikt\ *adj* **1** : abandoned by the owner or occupant **2** : NEGLIGENT ⟨∼ in his duty⟩
²**derelict** *n* **1** : something voluntarily abandoned; *esp* : a ship abandoned on the high seas **2** : a destitute homeless social misfit : VAGRANT, BUM
der·e·lic·tion \ˌder-ə-ˈlik-shən\ *n* **1** : the act of abandoning : the state of being abandoned **2** : intentional neglect ⟨∼ of duty⟩
de·ride \di-ˈrīd\ *vb* **de·rid·ed; de·rid·ing** [L *deridēre,* fr. *ridēre* to laugh] : to laugh at scornfully : RIDICULE
de ri·gueur \də-rē-ˈgər\ *adj* [F] : prescribed or required by fashion, etiquette, or custom : PROPER
de·ri·sion \də-ˈri-zhən\ *n* : RIDICULE — **de·ri·sive** \-ˈrī-siv\ *adj* — **de·ri·sive·ly** *adv* — **de·ri·sive·ness** *n* — **de·ri·so·ry** \-ˈrī-sə-rē\ *adj*
der·i·va·tion \ˌder-ə-ˈvā-shən\ *n* **1** : the formation of a word from an earlier word or root; *also* : an act of ascertaining or stating the derivation of a word **2** : ETYMOLOGY **3** : SOURCE, ORIGIN; *also* : DESCENT **4** : an act or process of deriving
de·riv·a·tive \di-ˈri-və-tiv\ *n* **1** : a word formed by derivation **2** : something derived **3** : the limit of the ratio of the change of a function's value to the change in its independent variable as the latter change approaches zero — **derivative** *adj*

de•rive \di-ˈrīv\ *vb* **de•rived; de•riv•ing** [ME, fr. AF *deriver,* fr. L *derivare,* lit., to draw off (water), fr. *de-* from + *rivus* stream] **1** : to receive or obtain from a source **2** : to obtain from a parent substance **3** : INFER, DEDUCE **4** : to trace the derivation of **5** : to come from a certain source

der•mal \ˈdər-məl\ *adj* : of or relating to the skin : CUTANEOUS

der•ma•ti•tis \ˌdər-mə-ˈtī-təs\ *n, pl* **-tit•i•des** \-ˈti-tə-ˌdēz\ *or* **-ti•tis•es** : inflammation of the skin

der•ma•tol•o•gy \-ˈtä-lə-jē\ *n* : a branch of medical science dealing with the structure, functions, and diseases of the skin — **der•ma•tol•o•gist** \-jist\ *n*

der•mis \ˈdər-məs\ *n* : the sensitive vascular inner layer of the skin

der•o•gate \ˈder-ə-ˌgāt\ *vb* **-gat•ed; -gat•ing** **1** : to cause to seem inferior : DISPARAGE **2** : DETRACT — **der•o•ga•tion** \ˌder-ə-ˈgā-shən\ *n* — **de•ro•ga•tive** \di-ˈrä-gə-tiv\ *adj*

de•rog•a•to•ry \di-ˈrä-gə-ˌtȯr-ē\ *adj* : intended to lower the reputation of a person or thing : DISPARAGING — **de•rog•a•to•ri•ly** \-ˌrä-gə-ˈtȯr-ə-lē\ *adv*

der•rick \ˈder-ik\ *n* [obs. *derrick* hangman, gallows, fr. *Derick,* name of 17th cent. Eng. hangman] **1** : a hoisting apparatus : CRANE **2** : a framework over a drill hole (as for oil) for supporting machinery

der•ri•ere *or* **der•ri•ère** \ˌder-ē-ˈer\ *n* : BUTTOCKS

der•ring–do \ˌder-iŋ-ˈdü\ *n* : DARING

der•rin•ger \ˈder-ən-jər\ *n* : a short-barreled pocket pistol

der•vish \ˈdər-vish\ *n* [Turk *derviş,* lit., beggar, fr. Pers *darvīsh*] : a member of a Muslim religious order noted for devotional exercises (as bodily movements leading to a trance)

de•sal•i•nate \dē-ˈsa-lə-ˌnāt\ *vb* **-nat•ed; -nat•ing** : DESALT — **de•sal•i•na•tion** \-ˌsa-lə-ˈnā-shən\ *n*

de•sal•i•nize \dē-ˈsa-lə-ˌnīz\ *vb* **-nized; -niz•ing** : DESALT — **de•sal•i•ni•za•tion** \-ˌsa-lə-nə-ˈzā-shən\ *n*

de•salt \dē-ˈsȯlt\ *vb* : to remove salt from ⟨~ seawater⟩ — **de•salt•er** *n*

des•cant \ˈdes-ˌkant\ *vb* **1** : to sing or play part music : SING **2** : to discourse or write at length

de•scend \di-ˈsend\ *vb* **1** : to pass from a higher to a lower place or level : pass, move, or climb down or down along **2** : DERIVE ⟨~*ed* from royalty⟩ **3** : to pass by inheritance or transmission **4** : to incline, lead, or extend downward **5** : to swoop down or appear suddenly (as in an attack)

¹**de•scen•dant** *also* **de•scen•dent** \di-ˈsen-dənt\ *adj* **1** : DESCENDING **2** : proceeding from an ancestor or source

²**descendant** *also* **descendent** *n* **1** : one descended from another or from a common stock **2** : one deriving directly from a precursor or prototype

de•scent \di-ˈsent\ *n* **1** : ANCESTRY, BIRTH, LINEAGE **2** : the act or process of descending **3** : SLOPE **4** : a descending way (as a downgrade) **5** : a sudden hostile raid or assault **6** : a downward step (as in station or value) : DECLINE

de•scram•ble \dē-ˈskram-bəl\ *vb* : UNSCRAMBLE 2 ⟨~ satellite transmissions⟩ — **de•scram•bler** \-b(ə-)lər\ *n*

de•scribe \di-ˈskrīb\ *vb* **de•scribed; de•scrib•ing** **1** : to represent or give an account of in words **2** : to trace the outline of — **de•scrib•able** *adj*

de•scrip•tion \di-ˈskrip-shən\ *n* **1** : an account of something; *esp* : an account that presents a picture to a person who reads or hears it **2** : KIND, SORT — **de•scrip•tive** \-ˈskrip-tiv\ *adj*

de•scry \di-ˈskrī\ *vb* **de•scried; de•scry•ing** **1** : to catch sight of **2** : to discover by observation or investigation

des•e•crate \ˈde-si-ˌkrāt\ *vb* **-crat•ed; -crat•ing** : PROFANE — **des•e•cra•tion** \ˌde-si-ˈkrā-shən\ *n*

de•seg•re•gate \dē-ˈse-gri-ˌgāt\ *vb* : to eliminate segregation in; *esp* : to free of any law or practice requiring isolation on the basis of race — **de•seg•re•ga•tion** \-ˌse-gri-ˈgā-shən\ *n*

de•sen•si•tize \dē-ˈsen-sə-ˌtīz\ *vb* : to make (a sensitized or hypersensitive individual) insensitive or nonreactive to a sensitizing agent — **de•sen•si•ti•za•tion** \-ˌsen-sə-tə-ˈzā-shən\ *n*

¹**des•ert** \ˈde-zərt\ *n* : dry land with few plants and little rainfall

²**des•ert** \ˈde-zərt\ *adj* : of, relating to, or resembling a desert; *esp* : being barren and without life ⟨a ~ island⟩

³**de•sert** \di-ˈzərt\ *n* **1** : the quality or fact of deserving reward or punishment **2** : a just reward or punishment

⁴**de•sert** \di-ˈzərt\ *vb* **1** : to withdraw from **2** : ABANDON, FORSAKE — **de•sert•er** *n* — **de•ser•tion** \-ˈzər-shən\ *n*

de•serve \di-ˈzərv\ *vb* **de•served; de•serv•ing** : to be worthy of : MERIT — **de•serv•ing** *adj*

de•serv•ed•ly \-ˈzər-vəd-lē\ *adv* : according to merit : JUSTLY

deshabille *var of* DISHABILLE

des•ic•cate \ˈde-si-ˌkāt\ *vb* **-cat•ed; -cat•ing** : DRY, DEHYDRATE — **des•ic•ca•tion** \ˌde-si-ˈkā-shən\ *n* — **des•ic•ca•tor** \ˈde-si-ˌkā-tər\ *n*

de•sid•er•a•tum \di-ˌsi-də-ˈrä-təm, -ˌzi-, -ˈrā-\ *n, pl* **-ta** \-tə\ [L] : something desired as essential

¹**de•sign** \di-ˈzīn\ *vb* **1** : to conceive and plan out in the mind **2** : INTEND **3** : to devise for a specific function or end **4** : to make a pattern or sketch of **5** : to conceive and draw the plans for

²**design** *n* **1** : a particular purpose : deliberate planning **2** : a mental project or scheme : PLAN **3** : a secret project or scheme : PLOT **4** *pl* : aggressive or evil intent — used with *on* or *against* **5** : a preliminary sketch or plan **6** : an underlying scheme that governs functioning, developing, or unfolding : MOTIF ⟨the general ~ of the epic⟩ **7** : the arrange-

ment of elements or details in a product or a work of art **8** : a decorative pattern ⟨a floral ~⟩ **9** : the art of executing designs

[1]**des·ig·nate** \ˈde-zig-ˌnāt, -nət\ *adj* : chosen but not yet installed ⟨ambassador ~⟩

[2]**des·ig·nate** \-ˌnāt\ *vb* **-nat·ed; -nat·ing** **1** : to appoint and set apart for a special purpose **2** : to mark or point out : INDICATE; *also* : SPECIFY, STIPULATE **3** : to call by a name or title — **des·ig·na·tion** \ˌde-zig-ˈnā-shən\ *n*

designated driver *n* : a person chosen to abstain from alcohol so as to transport others safely

designated hitter *n* : a baseball player designated at the start of the game to bat in place of the pitcher without causing the pitcher to be removed from the game

de·sign·er \di-ˈzī-nər\ *n* **1** : one who creates plans for a project or structure **2** : one who designs and manufactures high-fashion clothing — **designer** *adj*

designer drug *n* : a synthetic version of an illicit drug that has been chemically altered to avoid its prohibition

de·sign·ing \di-ˈzī-niŋ\ *adj* : CRAFTY, SCHEMING

de·sir·able \di-ˈzī-rə-bəl\ *adj* **1** : PLEASING, ATTRACTIVE **2** : ADVISABLE ⟨~ legislation⟩ — **de·sir·abil·i·ty** \-ˌzī-rə-ˈbi-lə-tē\ *n* — **de·sir·able·ness** *n* — **de·sir·ably** \-ˈzī-rə-blē\ *adv*

[1]**de·sire** \di-ˈzī(-ə)r\ *vb* **de·sired; de·sir·ing** [ME, fr. AF *desirer,* fr. L *desiderare,* fr. *sider-, sidus* heavenly body] **1** : to long or hope for : exhibit or feel desire for **2** : REQUEST

[2]**desire** *n* **1** : a strong wish : LONGING, CRAVING **2** : sexual urge or appetite **3** : a usu. formal request for action **4** : something desired

de·sir·ous \di-ˈzī(-ə)r-əs\ *adj* : eagerly wishing : DESIRING ⟨~ of fame⟩

de·sist \di-ˈzist, -ˈsist\ *vb* : to cease to proceed or act

desk \ˈdesk\ *n* [ME *deske,* fr. ML *desca,* fr. It *desco* table, fr. L *discus* dish, disc] **1** : a table, frame, or case esp. for writing and reading **2** : a counter, stand, or booth at which a person performs duties **3** : a specialized division of an organization (as a newspaper) ⟨city ~⟩

desk·top publishing \ˈdesk-ˌtäp-\ *n* : the production of printed matter by means of a microcomputer

[1]**des·o·late** \ˈde-sə-lət, -zə-\ *adj* **1** : DESERTED, ABANDONED **2** : FORSAKEN, LONELY **3** : DILAPIDATED **4** : BARREN, LIFELESS ⟨a ~ landscape⟩ **5** : CHEERLESS, GLOOMY ⟨~ memories⟩ — **des·o·late·ly** *adv* — **des·o·late·ness** *n*

[2]**des·o·late** \-ˌlāt\ *vb* **-lat·ed; -lat·ing** : to make desolate : lay waste : make wretched

des·o·la·tion \ˌde-sə-ˈlā-shən, -zə-\ *n* **1** : the action of desolating **2** : GRIEF, SADNESS **3** : LONELINESS **4** : DEVASTATION, RUIN **5** : barren wasteland

des·oxy·ri·bo·nu·cle·ic acid \de-ˌzäk-sē-ˈrī-bō-nu̇-ˌklē-ik-, -nyu̇-\ *n* : DNA

[1]**de·spair** \di-ˈsper\ *vb* : to lose all hope or confidence — **de·spair·ing** \-iŋ\ *adj* — **de·spair·ing·ly** *adv*

[2]**despair** *n* **1** : utter loss of hope **2** : a cause of hopelessness

des·patch *chiefly Brit var of* DISPATCH

des·per·a·do \ˌdes-pə-ˈrä-dō, -ˈrā-\ *n, pl* **-does** *or* **-dos** : a bold or reckless criminal

des·per·ate \ˈdes-pə-rət, -prət\ *adj* **1** : being beyond or almost beyond hope : causing despair **2** : RASH ⟨a ~ attempt⟩ **3** : extremely intense — **des·per·ate·ly** *adv* — **des·per·ate·ness** *n*

des·per·a·tion \ˌdes-pə-ˈrā-shən\ *n* **1** : a loss of hope and surrender to despair **2** : a state of hopelessness leading to rashness

de·spi·ca·ble \di-ˈspi-kə-bəl, ˈdes-pi-\ *adj* : deserving to be despised — **de·spi·ca·bly** \-blē\ *adv*

de·spise \di-ˈspīz\ *vb* **de·spised; de·spis·ing** **1** : to look down on with contempt or aversion : DISDAIN, DETEST **2** : to regard as negligible, worthless, or distasteful

de·spite \di-ˈspīt\ *prep* : in spite of

de·spoil \di-ˈspȯi(-ə)l\ *vb* : to strip of belongings, possessions, or value — **de·spoil·er** *n* — **de·spoil·ment** *n*

de·spo·li·a·tion \di-ˌspō-lē-ˈā-shən\ *n* : the act of plundering : the state of being despoiled

[1]**de·spond** \di-ˈspänd\ *vb* : to become discouraged or disheartened

[2]**despond** *n* : DESPONDENCY

de·spon·den·cy \-ˈspän-dən-sē\ *n* : DEJECTION, HOPELESSNESS — **de·spon·dent** \-dənt\ *adj* — **de·spon·dent·ly** *adv*

des·pot \ˈdes-pət, -ˌpät\ *n* [MF *despote,* fr. Gk *despotēs* master, lord, autocrat] **1** : a ruler with absolute power and authority **2** : a person exercising power tyrannically — **des·pot·ic** \des-ˈpä-tik\ *adj* — **des·po·tism** \ˈdes-pə-ˌti-zəm\ *n*

des·sert \di-ˈzərt\ *n* : a course of sweet food, fruit, or cheese served at the close of a meal

de·stig·ma·tize \dē-ˈstig-mə-ˌtīz\ *vb* : to remove associations of shame or disgrace from

des·ti·na·tion \ˌdes-tə-ˈnā-shən\ *n* **1** : a purpose for which something is destined **2** : an act of appointing, setting aside for a purpose, or predetermining **3** : a place to which one is journeying or to which something is sent

des·tine \ˈdes-tən\ *vb* **des·tined; des·tin·ing** **1** : to settle in advance **2** : to designate, assign, or dedicate in advance **3** : to direct or set apart for a specific purpose or place

des·ti·ny \ˈdes-tə-nē\ *n, pl* **-nies** **1** : something to which a person or thing is destined : FATE, FORTUNE **2** : a predetermined course of events

des·ti·tute \ˈdes-tə-ˌtüt, -ˌtyüt\ *adj* **1** : lacking something needed or desirable **2** : suffering extreme poverty — **des·ti·tu·tion** \ˌdes-tə-ˈtü-shən, -ˈtyü-\ *n*

de·stroy \di-ˈstrȯi\ *vb* **1** : to put an end to : RUIN **2** : KILL

de·stroy·er \di-ˈstrȯi-ər\ *n* **1** : one that destroys **2** : a small speedy warship
de·struc·ti·ble \di-ˈstrək-tə-bəl\ *adj* : capable of being destroyed — **de·struc·ti·bil·i·ty** \-ˌstrək-tə-ˈbi-lə-tē\ *n*
de·struc·tion \di-ˈstrək-shən\ *n* **1** : RUIN **2** : the action or process of destroying something **3** : a destroying agency
de·struc·tive \di-ˈstrək-tiv\ *adj* **1** : causing destruction : RUINOUS **2** : designed or tending to hurt or destroy — **de·struc·tive·ly** *adv* — **de·struc·tive·ness** *n*
de·sue·tude \ˈde-swi-ˌtüd, -ˌtyüd\ *n* : DISUSE
des·ul·to·ry \ˈde-səl-ˌtȯr-ē\ *adj* : passing aimlessly from one thing or subject to another : DISCONNECTED
det *abbr* **1** detached; detachment **2** detail
de·tach \di-ˈtach\ *vb* **1** : to separate esp. from a larger mass **2** : DISENGAGE, WITHDRAW — **de·tach·able** *adj*
de·tached \di-ˈtacht\ *adj* **1** : not joined or connected : SEPARATE **2** : ALOOF, IMPARTIAL ⟨a ~ attitude⟩
de·tach·ment \di-ˈtach-mənt\ *n* **1** : SEPARATION **2** : the dispatching of a body of troops or part of a fleet from the main body for special service; *also* : the portion so dispatched **3** : a small permanent military unit of special composition **4** : indifference to worldly concerns : ALOOFNESS **5** : IMPARTIALITY
[1]**de·tail** \di-ˈtāl, ˈdē-ˌtāl\ *n* [F *détail,* fr. OF *detail* slice, piece, fr. *detaillier* to cut in pieces, fr. *taillier* to cut] **1** : a dealing with something item by item ⟨go into ~⟩; *also* : ITEM, PARTICULAR ⟨the ~*s* of a story⟩ **2** : selection (as of soldiers) for special duty; *also* : the persons thus selected
[2]**detail** *vb* **1** : to report in particulars : SPECIFY **2** : to assign to a special duty
de·tailed \di-ˈtāld, ˈdē-ˌtāld\ *adj* : marked by abundant detail
de·tail·ing \ˈdē-ˌtāl-iŋ\ *n* : the meticulous cleaning and refurbishing of an automobile
de·tain \di-ˈtān\ *vb* **1** : to hold in or as if in custody **2** : STOP, DELAY
de·tect \di-ˈtekt\ *vb* : to discover the nature, existence, presence, or fact of — **de·tect·able** *adj* — **de·tec·tion** \-ˈtek-shən\ *n* — **de·tec·tor** \-ˈtek-tər\ *n*
[1]**de·tec·tive** \di-ˈtek-tiv\ *adj* **1** : fitted or used for detection **2** : of or relating to detectives
[2]**detective** *n* : a person employed or engaged in detecting lawbreakers or getting information that is not readily accessible
dé·tente *or* **de·tente** \dā-ˈtänt\ *n* [F] : a relaxation of strained relations or tensions (as between nations)
de·ten·tion \di-ˈten-chən\ *n* **1** : the act or fact of detaining : CONFINEMENT; *esp* : a period of temporary custody prior to disposition by a court **2** : a forced delay
de·ter \di-ˈtər\ *vb* **de·terred; de·ter·ring** [L *deterrēre,* fr. *terrēre* to frighten] **1** : to turn aside, discourage, or prevent from acting (as by fear) **2** : INHIBIT
de·ter·gent \di-ˈtər-jənt\ *n* : a cleansing agent; *esp* : a chemical product similar to soap in its cleaning ability
de·te·ri·o·rate \di-ˈtir-ē-ə-ˌrāt\ *vb* **-rat·ed; -rat·ing** : to make or become worse in quality or condition — **de·te·ri·o·ra·tion** \-ˌtir-ē-ə-ˈrā-shən\ *n*
de·ter·min·able \-ˈtər-mə-nə-bəl\ *adj* : capable of being determined; *esp* : ASCERTAINABLE
de·ter·mi·nant \-mə-nənt\ *n* **1** : something that determines or conditions **2** : GENE
de·ter·mi·nate \di-ˈtər-mə-nət\ *adj* **1** : having fixed limits : DEFINITE ⟨a ~ period of time⟩ **2** : definitely settled ⟨in ~ order⟩ — **de·ter·mi·nate·ness** *n*
de·ter·mi·na·tion \di-ˌtər-mə-ˈnā-shən\ *n* **1** : the act of coming to a decision; *also* : the decision or conclusion reached **2** : a fixing of the extent, position, or character of something **3** : accurate measurement (as of length or volume) **4** : firm or fixed purpose — **de·ter·mi·na·tive** \-ˈtər-mə-ˌnā-tiv, -ˈtər-mə-nə-\ *adj*
de·ter·mine \di-ˈtər-mən\ *vb* **-mined; -min·ing** **1** : to fix conclusively or authoritatively **2** : to come to a decision : SETTLE, RESOLVE **3** : to fix the form or character of beforehand : ORDAIN; *also* : REGULATE **4** : to find out the limits, nature, dimensions, or scope of ⟨~ a position at sea⟩ **5** : to bring about as a result
de·ter·mined \-ˈtər-mənd\ *adj* **1** : firmly resolved **2** : characterized by or showing determination — **de·ter·mined·ly** \-mənd-lē, -mə-nəd-lē\ *adv* — **de·ter·mined·ness** *n*
de·ter·min·ism \di-ˈtər-mə-ˌni-zəm\ *n* : a doctrine that acts of the will, natural events, or social changes are determined by preceding events or natural causes — **de·ter·min·ist** \-nist\ *n or adj*
de·ter·rence \di-ˈtər-əns\ *n* : the inhibition of criminal behavior by fear esp. of punishment
de·ter·rent \-ənt\ *adj* **1** : serving to deter ⟨the law's ~ effect⟩ **2** : relating to deterrence — **deterrent** *n*
de·test \di-ˈtest\ *vb* [L *detestari,* lit., to curse while calling a deity to witness, fr. *de-* from + *testari* to call to witness, fr. *testis* witness] : LOATHE, HATE — **de·test·able** *adj* — **de·tes·ta·tion** \ˌdē-ˌtes-ˈtā-shən\ *n*
de·throne \di-ˈthrōn\ *vb* : to remove from a throne : DEPOSE — **de·throne·ment** *n*
det·o·nate \ˈde-tᵊn-ˌāt\ *vb* **-nat·ed; -nat·ing** : to explode or cause to explode with violence — **det·o·na·tion** \ˌde-tᵊn-ˈā-shən\ *n*
det·o·na·tor \ˈde-tᵊn-ˌā-tər\ *n* : a device for detonating an explosive
[1]**de·tour** \ˈdē-ˌtu̇r\ *n* : an indirect way replacing part of a route
[2]**detour** *vb* : to go by detour
de·tox \ˈdē-ˌtäks, di-ˈtäks\ *n* : detoxification from an intoxicating or addictive substance — **detox** *vb*

de·tox·i·fy \dē-ˈtäk-sə-ˌfī\ *vb* **-fied; -fy·ing** **1 :** to remove a poison or toxin or the effect of such from **2 :** to free (someone) from an intoxicating or addictive substance or from dependence on it — **de·tox·i·fi·ca·tion** \dē-ˌtäk-sə-fə-ˈkā-shən\ *n*

de·tract \di-ˈtrakt\ *vb* **1 :** to take away or diminish the value or effect of something **2 :** DIVERT ⟨~*s* attention from the real issue⟩ — **de·trac·tion** \-ˈtrak-shən\ *n* — **de·trac·tor** \-ˈtrak-tər\ *n*

de·train \dē-ˈtrān\ *vb* **:** to leave or cause to leave a railroad train

det·ri·ment \ˈde-trə-mənt\ *n* **:** INJURY, DAMAGE; *also* **:** a cause of injury or damage — **det·ri·men·tal** \ˌde-trə-ˈment-ᵊl\ *adj* — **det·ri·men·tal·ly** *adv*

de·tri·tus \di-ˈtrī-təs\ *n, pl* **de·tri·tus** **:** fragments resulting from disintegration (as of rocks) **:** DEBRIS

deuce \ˈdüs, ˈdyüs\ *n* **1 :** a two in cards or dice **2 :** a tie in a tennis game with both sides at 40 **3 :** DEVIL — used chiefly as a mild oath

Deut *abbr* Deuteronomy

deu·te·ri·um \dü-ˈtir-ē-əm, dyü-\ *n* **:** an isotope of hydrogen that has twice the mass of ordinary hydrogen

Deu·ter·on·o·my \ˌdü-tə-ˈrä-nə-mē, ˌdyü-\ *n* — see BIBLE table

deut·sche mark \ˈdȯi-chə-ˌmärk\ *n* **:** a former basic monetary unit of Germany

dev *abbr* deviation

de·val·ue \dē-ˈval-yü\ *vb* **:** to reduce the international exchange value of ⟨~ a currency⟩ — **de·val·u·a·tion** \-ˌval-yə-ˈwā-shən\ *n*

dev·as·tate \ˈde-və-ˌstāt\ *vb* **-tat·ed; -tat·ing** **1 :** to bring to ruin **2 :** to reduce to chaos or helplessness — **dev·as·tat·ing·ly** *adv* — **dev·as·ta·tion** \ˌde-və-ˈstā-shən\ *n*

de·vel·op \di-ˈve-ləp\ *vb* **1 :** to unfold gradually or in detail **2 :** to place (exposed photographic material) in chemicals to produce a visible image **3 :** to bring out the possibilities of **4 :** to make more available or usable ⟨~ land⟩ **5 :** to acquire gradually ⟨~ a taste for olives⟩ **6 :** to go through a natural process of growth, differentiation, or evolution **7 :** to come into being gradually — **de·vel·op·er** *n* — **de·vel·op·ment** *n* — **de·vel·op·men·tal** \-ˌve-ləp-ˈment-ᵊl\ *adj* — **de·vel·op·men·tal·ly** \-tᵊl-ē\ *adv*

de·vi·ant \ˈdē-vē-ənt\ *adj* **:** deviating esp. from some accepted norm ⟨~ behavior⟩ — **de·vi·ance** \-əns\ *n* — **de·vi·an·cy** \-ən-sē\ *n* — **deviant** *n*

de·vi·ate \ˈdē-vē-ˌāt\ *vb* **-at·ed; -at·ing** [LL *deviare,* fr. L *de-* from + *via* way] **:** to turn aside from a course, standard, principle, or topic — **de·vi·ate** \-vē-ət, -vē-ˌāt\ *n* — **de·vi·a·tion** \ˌdē-vē-ˈā-shən\ *n*

de·vice \di-ˈvīs\ *n* **1 :** SCHEME, STRATAGEM **2 :** a piece of equipment or a mechanism for a special purpose **3 :** DESIRE, INCLINATION ⟨left to my own ~*s*⟩ **4 :** an emblematic design

[1]**dev·il** \ˈde-vəl\ *n* [ME *devel,* fr. OE *dēofol,* fr. LL *diabolus,* fr. Gk *diabolos,* lit., slanderer, fr. *diaballein* to throw across, slander, fr. *dia-* across + *ballein* to throw] **1** *often cap* **:** the personal supreme spirit of evil **2 :** DEMON **3 :** a wicked person **4 :** an energetic, reckless, or dashing person **5 :** FELLOW ⟨poor ~⟩ ⟨lucky ~⟩

[2]**devil** *vb* **-iled** *or* **-illed; -il·ing** *or* **-il·ling** **1 :** to season highly ⟨~*ed* eggs⟩ **2 :** TEASE, ANNOY

dev·il·ish \ˈde-və-lish\ *adj* **1 :** befitting a devil **:** EVIL; *also* **:** MISCHIEVOUS **2 :** EXTREME ⟨in a ~ hurry⟩ — **dev·il·ish·ly** *adv* — **dev·il·ish·ness** *n*

dev·il·ment \ˈde-vəl-mənt, -ˌment\ *n* **:** MISCHIEF

dev·il·ry \-rē\ *or* **dev·il·try** \-trē\ *n, pl* **-il·ries** *or* **-il·tries** **1 :** action performed with the help of the devil **2 :** MISCHIEF

de·vi·ous \ˈdē-vē-əs\ *adj* **1 :** deviating from a straight line **:** ROUNDABOUT **2 :** ERRANT 3 **3 :** TRICKY, CUNNING

[1]**de·vise** \di-ˈvīz\ *vb* **de·vised; de·vis·ing** [ME, fr. AF *deviser* to divide, distinguish, invent, fr. VL **divisare,* fr. L *dividere* to divide] **1 :** INVENT **2 :** PLOT **3 :** to give (real estate) by will

[2]**devise** *n* **1 :** a disposing of real property by will **2 :** a will or clause of a will disposing of real property **3 :** property given by will

de·vi·tal·ize \dē-ˈvī-tə-ˌlīz\ *vb* **:** to deprive of life or vitality

de·void \di-ˈvȯid\ *adj* **:** being without **:** VOID ⟨a book ~ of interest⟩

de·voir \də-ˈvwär\ *n* **1 :** DUTY **2 :** a formal act of civility or respect

de·volve \di-ˈvälv\ *vb* **de·volved; de·volv·ing** **:** to pass (as rights or responsibility) from one to another usu. by succession or transmission — **dev·o·lu·tion** \ˌde-və-ˈlü-shən, ˌdē-\ *n*

De·vo·ni·an \di-ˈvō-nē-ən\ *adj* **:** of, relating to, or being the period of the Paleozoic era between the Silurian and the Mississippian — **Devonian** *n*

de·vote \di-ˈvōt\ *vb* **de·vot·ed; de·vot·ing** **1 :** to commit to wholly or chiefly ⟨~*s* herself to serving the poor⟩ **2 :** to set apart for a special purpose **:** DEDICATE

de·vot·ed \-ˈvō-təd\ *adj* **:** characterized by loyalty and devotion **:** FAITHFUL

dev·o·tee \ˌde-və-ˈtē, -ˈtā\ *n* **:** an ardent follower, supporter, or enthusiast

de·vo·tion \di-ˈvō-shən\ *n* **1 :** religious fervor **2 :** an act of prayer or private worship — usu. used in pl. **3 :** a religious exercise for private use **4 :** the fact or state of being dedicated and loyal ⟨~ to music⟩; *also* **:** the act of devoting — **de·vo·tion·al** \-shə-nəl\ *adj*

de·vour \di-ˈvau̇(-ə)r\ *vb* **1 :** to eat up greedily or ravenously **2 :** WASTE, ANNIHILATE ⟨a forest ~*ed* by fire⟩ **3 :** to enjoy avidly ⟨~ a book⟩ — **de·vour·er** *n*

de·vout \di-ˈvau̇t\ *adj* **1 :** devoted to religion **:** PIOUS **2 :** expressing devotion or piety **3 :** EARNEST, SERIOUS ⟨a ~ baseball fan⟩ — **de·vout·ly** *adv* — **de·vout·ness** *n*

dew \ˈdü, ˈdyü\ *n* : moisture that condenses on the surfaces of cool bodies at night — **dewy** *adj*
dew·ber·ry \ˈdü-ˌber-ē, ˈdyü-\ *n* : any of several sweet edible berries related to and resembling blackberries; *also* : a trailing bramble bearing these
dew·claw \-ˌklȯ\ *n* : a digit on the foot of a mammal that does not reach the ground; *also* : its claw or hoof
dew·lap \-ˌlap\ *n* : loose skin hanging under the neck of an animal
dew point *n* : the temperature at which the moisture in the air begins to condense
dex·ter·i·ty \dek-ˈster-ə-tē\ *n, pl* **-ties** **1** : mental skill or quickness **2** : readiness and grace in physical activity; *esp* : skill and ease in using the hands
dex·ter·ous \ˈdek-strəs\ *adj* **1** : CLEVER **2** : done with skillfulness **3** : skillful and competent with the hands — **dex·ter·ous·ly** *adv*
dex·trose \ˈdek-ˌstrōs\ *n* : the naturally occurring form of glucose found in plants and blood
DFC *abbr* Distinguished Flying Cross
dg *abbr* decigram
DG *abbr* **1** LL *Dei gratia* by the grace of God **2** director general
DH \ˌdē-ˈāch\ *n* : DESIGNATED HITTER
dhow \ˈdau̇\ *n* : an Arab sailing ship usu. having a long overhang forward and a high poop
DI *abbr* drill instructor
dia *abbr* diameter
di·a·be·tes \ˌdī-ə-ˈbē-tēz, -təs\ *n* : an abnormal state marked by passage of excessive amounts of urine; *esp* : one (**diabetes mel·li·tus** \-ˈme-lə-təs\) characterized by deficient insulin, by excess sugar in the blood and urine, and by thirst, hunger, and loss of weight — **di·a·bet·ic** \-ˈbe-tik\ *adj or n*
di·a·bol·i·cal \ˌdī-ə-ˈbä-li-kəl\ *or* **di·a·bol·ic** \-lik\ *adj* : DEVILISH ⟨a ~ plot⟩ — **di·a·bol·i·cal·ly** \-k(ə-)lē\ *adv*
di·a·crit·ic \ˌdī-ə-ˈkri-tik\ *n* : a mark accompanying a letter and indicating a sound value different from that of the same letter when unmarked — **di·a·crit·i·cal** \-ti-kəl\ *adj*
di·a·dem \ˈdī-ə-ˌdem\ *n* : CROWN; *esp* : a royal headband
di·aer·e·sis *or* **di·er·e·sis** \dī-ˈer-ə-səs\ *n, pl* **-e·ses** \-ˌsēz\ : a mark ¨ placed over a vowel to show that it is pronounced in a separate syllable (as in *naïve*)
diag *abbr* **1** diagonal **2** diagram
di·ag·no·sis \ˌdī-ig-ˈnō-səs\ *n, pl* **-no·ses** \-ˌsēz\ : the art or act of identifying a disease from its signs and symptoms; *also* : the decision reached by diagnosis — **di·ag·nose** \ˈdī-ig-ˌnōs\ *vb* — **di·ag·nos·tic** \ˌdī-ig-ˈnäs-tik\ *adj* — **di·ag·nos·ti·cian** \-ˌnäs-ˈti-shən\ *n*
[1]**di·ag·o·nal** \dī-ˈa-gə-nəl\ *adj* **1** : extending from one corner to the opposite corner in a 4-sided figure **2** : running in a slanting direction ⟨~ stripes⟩ **3** : having slanting markings or parts ⟨a ~ weave⟩ — **di·ag·o·nal·ly** *adv*
[2]**diagonal** *n* **1** : a diagonal line **2** : a diagonal row, pattern, or direction **3** : SLASH 3
[1]**di·a·gram** \ˈdī-ə-ˌgram\ *n* : a design and esp. a drawing that makes something easier to understand — **di·a·gram·ma·ble** \-ˌgra-mə-bəl\ *adj* — **di·a·gram·mat·ic** \ˌdī-ə-grə-ˈma-tik\ *adj* — **di·a·gram·mat·i·cal·ly** \-ti-k(ə-)lē\ *adv*
[2]**diagram** *vb* **-grammed** *or* **-gramed** \-ˌgramd\; **-gram·ming** *or* **-gram·ing** : to represent by a diagram
[1]**di·al** \ˈdī(-ə)l\ *n* [ME *dyal,* fr. ML *dialis* clock wheel revolving daily, fr. L *dies* day] **1** : the face of a sundial **2** : the face of a timepiece **3** : a face with a pointer and numbers that indicate something ⟨the ~ of a gauge⟩ **4** : a device used for making electrical connections or for regulating operation (as of a radio)
[2]**dial** *vb* **di·aled** *or* **di·alled; di·al·ing** *or* **di·al·ling** **1** : to manipulate a dial so as to operate or select **2** : to make a telephone call or connection
[3]**dial** *abbr* dialect
di·a·lect \ˈdī-ə-ˌlekt\ *n* : a regional variety of a language
di·a·lec·tic \ˌdī-ə-ˈlek-tik\ *n* : the process or art of reasoning by discussion of conflicting ideas; *also* : the tension between opposing elements — **di·a·lec·ti·cal** \-ti-kəl\ *adj*
dialog box *n* : a window on a computer screen for choosing options or inputting information
di·a·logue \ˈdī-ə-ˌlȯg\ *n* **1** : a conversation between two or more parties **2** : the parts of a literary or dramatic work that represent conversation
di·al·y·sis \dī-ˈa-lə-səs\ *n, pl* **-y·ses** \-ˌsēz\ **1** : the separation of substances from solution by means of their unequal diffusion through semipermeable membranes **2** : the medical procedure of removing blood from an artery, purifying it by dialysis, and returning it to a vein
diam *abbr* diameter
di·am·e·ter \dī-ˈa-mə-tər\ *n* [ME *diametre,* fr. MF, fr. L *diametros,* fr. Gk, fr. *dia-* through + *metron* measure] **1** : a straight line passing through the center of a figure or body; *esp* : one that divides a circle in half **2** : the length of a diameter
di·a·met·ric \ˌdī-ə-ˈme-trik\ *or* **di·a·met·ri·cal** \-tri-kəl\ *adj* **1** : of, relating to, or constituting a diameter **2** : completely opposed or opposite — **di·a·met·ri·cal·ly** \-k(ə-)lē\ *adv*
di·a·mond \ˈdī-mənd, ˈdī-ə-\ *n* **1** : a hard brilliant mineral that consists of crystalline carbon and is used as a gem **2** : a flat figure having four equal sides, two acute angles, and two obtuse angles **3** : any of a suit of playing cards marked with a red diamond **4** : INFIELD; *also* : the entire playing field in baseball
di·a·mond·back rattlesnake \-ˌbak-\ *n* : either of two large and deadly rattlesnakes of the southern U.S.
di·an·thus \dī-ˈan-thəs\ *n* : [1]PINK 1
di·a·pa·son \ˌdī-ə-ˈpā-zᵊn, -sᵊn\ *n* **1** : the organ stop governing the flue pipes that

form the primary basis of organ tone **2** : the entire range of musical tones

[1]**di·a·per** \ˈdī-pər, ˈdī-ə-\ *n* **1** : a cotton or linen fabric woven in a simple geometric pattern **2** : a garment for a baby drawn up between the legs and fastened about the waist

[2]**diaper** *vb* **1** : to ornament with diaper designs **2** : to put a diaper on

di·aph·a·nous \dī-ˈa-fə-nəs\ *adj* : of so fine a texture as to be transparent

di·a·pho·ret·ic \ˌdī-ə-fə-ˈre-tik\ *adj* : having the power to increase perspiration — **diaphoretic** *n*

di·a·phragm \ˈdī-ə-ˌfram\ *n* **1** : a sheet of muscle between the chest and abdominal cavities of a mammal **2** : a vibrating disk (as in a microphone) **3** : a cup-shaped device usu. of thin rubber fitted over the uterine cervix to act as a mechanical contraceptive barrier — **di·a·phrag·mat·ic** \ˌdī-ə-frəg-ˈma-tik, -ˌfrag-\ *adj*

di·a·rist \ˈdī-ə-rist\ *n* : one who keeps a diary

di·a·ris·tic \ˌdī-ə-ˈris-tik\ *adj* : of, relating to, or characteristic of a diary

di·ar·rhea \ˌdī-ə-ˈrē-ə\ *n* [ME *diaria,* fr. LL *diarrhoea,* fr. Gk *diarrhoia,* fr. *diarrhein* to flow through, fr. *dia-* through + *rhein* to flow] : abnormally frequent and watery bowel movements — **di·ar·rhe·al** \-ˈrē-əl\ *adj*

di·ar·rhoea *chiefly Brit var of* DIARRHEA

di·a·ry \ˈdī-ə-rē\ *n, pl* **-ries** : a daily record esp. of personal experiences; *also* : a book used as a diary

di·as·po·ra \dī-ˈas-pə-rə\ *n* **1** *cap* : the settling of scattered colonies of Jews outside Palestine after the Babylonian exile **2** *cap* : the Jews living outside Palestine or modern Israel **3** : the migration or scattering of a people away from an ancestral homeland

di·as·to·le \dī-ˈas-tə-(ˌ)lē\ *n* : the stretching of the chambers of the heart during which they fill with blood — **di·a·stol·ic** \ˌdī-ə-ˈstä-lik\ *adj*

dia·ther·my \ˈdī-ə-ˌthər-mē\ *n* : the generation of heat in tissue by electric currents for medical purposes

di·a·tom \ˈdī-ə-ˌtäm\ *n* : any of a class of planktonic one-celled or colonial algae with skeletons of silica

di·atom·ic \ˌdī-ə-ˈtä-mik\ *adj* : having two atoms in the molecule

di·a·tribe \ˈdī-ə-ˌtrīb\ *n* : biting or abusive speech or writing

di·az·e·pam \dī-ˈa-zə-ˌpam\ *n* : a tranquilizer used esp. to relieve anxiety, tension, and muscle spasms

dib·ble \ˈdi-bəl\ *n* : a pointed hand tool for making holes (as for planting bulbs) in the ground — **dibble** *vb*

[1]**dice** \ˈdīs\ *n, pl* **dice** : DIE 1

[2]**dice** *vb* **diced; dic·ing** **1** : to cut into small cubes ⟨~ carrots⟩ **2** : to play games with dice

di·chot·o·my \dī-ˈkä-tə-mē\ *n, pl* **-mies** : a division or the process of dividing into two esp. mutually exclusive or contradictory groups — **di·chot·o·mous** \-məs\ *adj*

dick·er \ˈdi-kər\ *vb* : BARGAIN, HAGGLE

dick·ey *or* **dicky** \ˈdi-kē\ *n, pl* **dickeys** *or* **dick·ies** : a small fabric insert worn to fill in the neckline

di·cot·y·le·don \ˌdī-ˌkä-tə-ˈlēd-ᵊn\ *n* : any of a group of seed plants having an embryo with two cotyledons — **di·cot·y·le·don·ous** *adj*

dict *abbr* dictionary

[1]**dic·tate** \ˈdik-ˌtāt\ *vb* **dic·tat·ed; dic·tat·ing** **1** : to speak or read for a person to transcribe or for a machine to record **2** : COMMAND, ORDER — **dic·ta·tion** \dik-ˈtā-shən\ *n*

[2]**dic·tate** \ˈdik-ˌtāt\ *n* : an authoritative rule, prescription, or injunction : COMMAND ⟨the ~*s* of conscience⟩

dic·ta·tor \ˈdik-ˌtā-tər\ *n* **1** : a person ruling absolutely and often brutally and oppressively **2** : one that dictates

dic·ta·to·ri·al \ˌdik-tə-ˈtȯr-ē-əl\ *adj* : of, relating to, or characteristic of a dictator or a dictatorship

dic·ta·tor·ship \dik-ˈtā-tər-ˌship, ˈdik-ˌtā-\ *n* **1** : the office of a dictator **2** : autocratic rule, control, or leadership **3** : a government or country in which absolute power is held by a dictator or a small clique

dic·tion \ˈdik-shən\ *n* **1** : choice of words esp. with regard to correctness, clearness, or effectiveness : WORDING **2** : ENUNCIATION

dic·tio·nary \ˈdik-shə-ˌner-ē\ *n, pl* **-nar·ies** : a reference book containing words usu. alphabetically arranged along with information about their forms, pronunciations, functions, etymologies, meanings, and syntactical and idiomatic uses

dic·tum \ˈdik-təm\ *n, pl* **dic·ta** \-tə\ *also* **dictums** : a noteworthy, formal, or authoritative statement or observation

did *past of* DO

di·dac·tic \dī-ˈdak-tik\ *adj* **1** : intended to instruct, inform, or teach a moral lesson **2** : making moral observations

di·do \ˈdī-dō\ *n, pl* **didoes** *or* **didos** : a mischievous act : PRANK

[1]**die** \ˈdī\ *vb* **died; dy·ing** \ˈdī-iŋ\ [ME *dien,* fr. or akin to ON *deyja* to die] **1** : to stop living : EXPIRE **2** : to pass out of existence ⟨a *dying* language⟩ **3** : SUBSIDE 4 ⟨the wind *died* down⟩ **4** : to long keenly ⟨*dying* to go⟩ **5** : STOP ⟨the motor *died*⟩

[2]**die** \ˈdī\ *n* [ME *dee,* fr. AF *dé*] **1** *pl* **dice** \ˈdīs\ : a small cube marked on each face with one to six spots and used usu. in pairs in games and gambling **2** *pl* **dies** \ˈdīz\ : a device used to shape, finish, or impress an object

die·hard \ˈdī-ˌhärd\ *n* : one who is strongly devoted or determined — **die–hard** *adj*

dieresis *var of* DIAERESIS

die·sel \ˈdē-zəl, -səl\ *n* **1** : DIESEL ENGINE **2** : a vehicle driven by a diesel engine **3** : DIESEL FUEL

diesel engine *n* : an internal combustion engine in whose cylinders air is compressed to a temperature sufficiently high to ignite the fuel

diesel fuel *n* : a heavy mineral oil used as fuel in diesel engines

die·sel·ing \ˈdē-zə-liŋ\ *n* : the continued operation of an internal combustion engine after the ignition has been turned off

[1]**di·et** \ˈdī-ət\ *n* [ME *diete,* fr. AF, fr. L *diaeta,* fr. Gk *diaita,* lit., manner of living, fr. *diaitasthai* to lead one's life] **1** : food and drink regularly consumed : FARE **2** : an allowance of food prescribed for a special reason (as to lose weight) — **di·e·tary** \-ə-ˌter-ē\ *adj or n*

[2]**diet** *vb* : to eat or cause to eat or drink less or according to a prescribed rule — **di·et·er** *n*

dietary supplement *n* : a product taken orally that contains ingredients (as vitamins or amino acids) intended to supplement one's diet

di·e·tet·ics \ˌdī-ə-ˈte-tiks\ *n sing or pl* : the science or art of applying the principles of nutrition to diet — **di·e·tet·ic** *adj*

di·e·ti·tian *or* **di·e·ti·cian** \ˌdī-ə-ˈti-shən\ *n* : a specialist in dietetics

dif *or* **diff** *abbr* difference

dif·fer \ˈdi-fər\ *vb* **dif·fered; dif·fer·ing** **1** : to be unlike **2** : VARY **3** : DISAGREE

dif·fer·ence \ˈdi-frəns, ˈdi-fə-rəns\ *n* **1** : UNLIKENESS ⟨~ in their looks⟩ **2** : distinction or discrimination in preference **3** : DISAGREEMENT; *also* : an instance or cause of disagreement ⟨unable to settle their ~*s*⟩ **4** : the amount by which one number or quantity differs from another

dif·fer·ent \ˈdi-frənt, ˈdi-fə-rənt\ *adj* **1** : unlike in nature or quality **2** : DISTINCT ⟨~ age groups⟩; *also* : VARIOUS ⟨~ members of the club⟩ **3** : ANOTHER ⟨try a ~ channel⟩ **4** : UNUSUAL, SPECIAL ⟨a quite ~ style⟩ — **dif·fer·ent·ly** *adv*

[1]**dif·fer·en·tial** \ˌdi-fə-ˈren-chəl\ *adj* : showing, creating, or relating to a difference

[2]**differential** *n* **1** : the amount or degree by which things differ **2** : an arrangement of gears in an automobile that allows one wheel to turn faster than another (as in rounding curves)

differential gear *n* : DIFFERENTIAL 2

dif·fer·en·ti·ate \ˌdi-fə-ˈren-chē-ˌāt\ *vb* **-at·ed; -at·ing** **1** : to make or become different **2** : to attain a specialized adult form and function during development **3** : to recognize or state the difference ⟨~ between them⟩ — **dif·fer·en·ti·a·tion** \-ˌren-chē-ˈā-shən\ *n*

dif·fi·cult \ˈdi-fi-(ˌ)kəlt\ *adj* **1** : hard to do or make ⟨a ~ climb⟩ **2** : hard to understand or deal with ⟨~ reading⟩ ⟨a ~ child⟩

dif·fi·cul·ty \-(ˌ)kəl-tē\ *n, pl* **-ties** [ME *difficulte,* fr. AF *difficulté,* fr. L *difficilis* not easy, fr. *dis-* not + *facilis* easy] **1** : difficult nature ⟨the ~ of a task⟩ **2** : DISAGREEMENT ⟨settled their *difficulties*⟩ **3** : OBSTACLE ⟨overcome *difficulties*⟩ **4** : TROUBLE ⟨in financial *difficulties*⟩ ♦ ***Synonyms*** HARDSHIP, RIGOR, VICISSITUDE

dif·fi·dent \ˈdi-fə-dənt\ *adj* **1** : lacking confidence **2** : RESERVED 1 — **dif·fi·dence** \-dəns\ *n* — **dif·fi·dent·ly** *adv*

dif·frac·tion \di-ˈfrak-shən\ *n* : the bending or spreading of waves (as of light) esp. when passing through narrow slits

[1]**dif·fuse** \di-ˈfyüs\ *adj* **1** : VERBOSE, WORDY ⟨~ writing⟩ **2** : not concentrated or localized ⟨~ light⟩

[2]**dif·fuse** \di-ˈfyüz\ *vb* **dif·fused; dif·fus·ing** **1** : to pour out or spread widely **2** : to undergo or cause to undergo diffusion **3** : to break up light by diffusion

dif·fu·sion \di-ˈfyü-zhən\ *n* **1** : a diffusing or a being diffused **2** : movement of particles (as of a gas) from a region of high to one of lower concentration **3** : the reflection of light from a rough surface or the passage of light through a translucent material

[1]**dig** \ˈdig\ *vb* **dug** \ˈdəg\; **dig·ging** **1** : to turn up the soil (as with a spade) **2** : to hollow out or form by removing earth ⟨~ a hole⟩ **3** : to uncover or seek by turning up earth ⟨~ potatoes⟩ **4** : DISCOVER ⟨~ up information⟩ **5** : POKE, THRUST ⟨~ a person in the ribs⟩ **6** : to work hard **7** : UNDERSTAND, APPRECIATE; *also* : LIKE, ADMIRE

[2]**dig** *n* **1** : THRUST, POKE; *also* : a cutting remark : GIBE **2** *pl* : living or working accommodations

[3]**dig** *abbr* digest

[1]**di·gest** \ˈdī-ˌjest\ *n* : a summarized or shortened version esp. of a literary work

[2]**di·gest** \dī-ˈjest, də-\ *vb* **1** : to think over and arrange in the mind **2** : to convert (food) into simpler forms that can be absorbed by the body **3** : to compress into a short summary — **di·gest·ibil·i·ty** \-ˌjes-tə-ˈbi-lə-tē\ *n* — **di·gest·ible** *adj* — **di·ges·tion** \-ˈjes-chən\ *n* — **di·ges·tive** \-ˈjes-tiv\ *adj*

di·ges·tif \ˌdē-zhes-ˈtēf\ *n* : an alcoholic drink taken after a meal

dig in *vb* **1** : to take a defensive stand esp. by digging trenches **2** : to firmly set to work **3** : to begin eating

dig·it \ˈdi-jət\ *n* [ME, fr. L *digitus* finger, toe] **1** : any of the Arabic numerals 1 to 9 and usu. the symbol 0 **2** : FINGER, TOE

dig·i·tal \ˈdi-jə-tᵊl\ *adj* **1** : of, relating to, or done with a finger or toe **2** : of, relating to, or using calculation by numerical methods or by discrete units **3** : relating to or employing communications signals in the form of binary digits ⟨a ~ broadcast⟩ **4** : providing a readout in numerical digits ⟨a ~ watch⟩ **5** : ELECTRONIC; *also* : characterized by computerized technology ⟨the ~ age⟩ — **dig·i·tal·ly** *adv*

digital camera *n* : a camera that records images as digital data instead of on film

dig·i·tal·is \ˌdi-jə-ˈta-ləs\ *n* : a drug from the common foxglove that is a powerful heart stimulant; *also* : FOXGLOVE

digital video disc *n* : DVD

dig·ni·fied \ˈdig-nə-ˌfīd\ *adj* : showing or expressing dignity

dig·ni·fy \-ˌfī\ *vb* **-fied; -fy·ing** : to give dignity, distinction, or attention to

dig·ni·tary \ˈdig-nə-ˌter-ē\ *n, pl* **-tar·ies** : a person of high position or honor

dig·ni·ty \ˈdig-nə-tē\ *n, pl* **-ties** **1** : the quality or state of being worthy, honored, or esteemed **2** : high rank, office, or position **3** : formal reserve of manner, language, or appearance

di·graph \ˈdī-ˌgraf\ *n* : a group of two successive letters whose phonetic value is a single sound (as *ea* in *bread*)

di·gress \dī-ˈgres, də-\ *vb* : to turn aside esp. from the main subject or argument — **di·gres·sion** \-ˈgre-shən\ *n* — **di·gres·sive** \-ˈgre-siv\ *adj*

Di·jon mustard \ˈdē-ˌzhän-, di-ˈzhän-\ *n* : a mustard made from dark mustard seeds, white wine, and spices

dike \ˈdīk\ *n* : a bank of earth constructed to control water : LEVEE

dil *abbr* dilute

di·lap·i·dat·ed \də-ˈla-pə-ˌdā-təd\ *adj* : fallen into partial ruin or decay — **di·lap·i·da·tion** \-ˌla-pə-ˈdā-shən\ *n*

di·late \dī-ˈlāt, ˈdī-ˌlāt\ *vb* **di·lat·ed; di·lat·ing** : SWELL, DISTEND, EXPAND ⟨her pupils were *dilated*⟩ — **dil·a·ta·tion** \ˌdi-lə-ˈtā-shən\ *n* — **di·la·tion** \dī-ˈlā-shən\ *n*

dil·a·to·ry \ˈdi-lə-ˌtȯr-ē\ *adj* **1** : DELAYING **2** : TARDY, SLOW

di·lem·ma \də-ˈle-mə\ *n* **1** : a usu. undesirable or unpleasant choice; *also* : a situation involving such a choice **2** : PREDICAMENT

dil·et·tante \ˌdi-lə-ˈtänt, -ˈtant\ *n, pl* **-tantes** *or* **-tan·ti** \-ˈtän-tē, -ˈtan-\ [It, fr. prp. of *dilettare* to delight, fr. L *dilectare*] : a person having a superficial interest in an art or a branch of knowledge

dil·i·gent \ˈdi-lə-jənt\ *adj* : characterized by steady, earnest, and energetic effort : PAINSTAKING — **dil·i·gence** \-jəns\ *n* — **dil·i·gent·ly** *adv*

dill \ˈdil\ *n* : an herb related to the carrot with aromatic leaves and seeds used as a seasoning and in pickles

dil·ly \ˈdi-lē\ *n, pl* **dil·lies** : one that is remarkable or outstanding

dil·ly·dal·ly \ˈdi-lē-ˌda-lē\ *vb* : to waste time by loitering or delaying

[1]**di·lute** \dī-ˈlüt, də-\ *vb* **di·lut·ed; di·lut·ing** : to lessen the consistency or strength of by mixing with something else — **di·lu·tion** \-ˈlü-shən\ *n*

[2]**dilute** *adj* : DILUTED, WEAK

[1]**dim** \ˈdim\ *adj* **dim·mer; dim·mest** **1** : LUSTERLESS, DULL ⟨~ colors⟩ **2** : not bright or distinct : OBSCURE, FAINT **3** : not seeing or understanding clearly — **dim·ly** *adv* — **dim·ness** *n*

[2]**dim** *vb* **dimmed; dim·ming** **1** : to make or become dim or lusterless **2** : to reduce the light from

[3]**dim** *abbr* **1** dimension **2** diminished **3** diminutive

dime \ˈdīm\ *n* [ME, tenth part, tithe, fr. AF *disme, dime,* fr. L *decima,* fr. fem. of *decimus* tenth, fr. *decem* ten] : a U.S. coin worth 1/10 dollar

di·men·sion \də-ˈmen-chən, dī-\ *n* **1** : the physical property of length, breadth, or thickness; *also* : a measure of this **2** : EXTENT, SCOPE, PROPORTIONS — usu. used in pl. ⟨the ~*s* of this problem⟩ — **di·men·sion·al** \-ˈmen-chə-nəl\ *adj* — **di·men·sion·al·i·ty** \-ˌmen-chə-ˈna-lə-tē\ *n*

di·min·ish \də-ˈmi-nish\ *vb* **1** : to make less or cause to appear less **2** : BELITTLE **3** : DWINDLE **4** : TAPER — **dim·i·nu·tion** \ˌdi-mə-ˈnü-shən, -ˈnyü-\ *n*

di·min·u·en·do \də-ˌmin-yə-ˈwen-dō\ *adv or adj* : DECRESCENDO

[1]**di·min·u·tive** \də-ˈmin-yə-tiv\ *n* **1** : a diminutive word or affix ⟨the word "kitchenette" is a ~⟩ **2** : a diminutive individual

[2]**diminutive** *adj* **1** : indicating small size and sometimes the state or quality of being lovable, pitiable, or contemptible ⟨the ~ suffixes *-ette* and *-ling*⟩ **2** : extremely small : TINY

dim·i·ty \ˈdi-mə-tē\ *n, pl* **-ties** : a thin usu. corded cotton fabric

dim·mer \ˈdi-mər\ *n* : a device for controlling the amount of light from an electric lighting unit

di·mor·phic \(ˌ)dī-ˈmȯr-fik\ *adj* : occurring in two distinct forms — **di·mor·phism** \-ˌfi-zəm\ *n*

[1]**dim·ple** \ˈdim-pəl\ *n* : a small depression esp. in the cheek or chin

[2]**dimple** *vb* **dim·pled; dim·pling** : to form dimples (as in smiling)

din \ˈdin\ *n* : a loud confused mixture of noises

di·nar \di-ˈnär\ *n* **1** — see MONEY table **2** — see *rial* at MONEY table

dine \ˈdīn\ *vb* **dined; din·ing** [ME, fr. AF *disner, diner* to eat, have a meal, fr. VL **disjejunare* to break one's fast, ultim. fr. L *jejunus* fasting] **1** : to eat dinner **2** : to give a dinner to

din·er \ˈdī-nər\ *n* **1** : one that dines **2** : a railroad dining car **3** : a restaurant usu. resembling a dining car

di·nette \dī-ˈnet\ *n* : an alcove or small room used for dining

ding \ˈdiŋ\ *vb* : to cause minor damage to a surface — **ding** *n*

din·ghy \ˈdiŋ-ē\ *n, pl* **dinghies** **1** : a small boat **2** : LIFE RAFT

din·gle \ˈdiŋ-gəl\ *n* : a small wooded valley

din·go \ˈdiŋ-gō\ *n, pl* **dingoes** : a reddish brown wild dog of Australia

din·gus \ˈdiŋ-gəs, -əs\ *n* : DOODAD

din·gy \ˈdin-jē\ *adj* **din·gi·er; -est** : DIRTY, UNCLEAN; *also* : SHABBY — **din·gi·ness** *n*

dink \ˈdiŋk\ *n, often all cap* [*d*ouble *in*come, *no k*ids] : a couple with two incomes and no children; *also* : a member of such a couple

din·ky \ˈdiŋ-kē\ *adj* **din·ki·er; -est** : overly small ⟨a ~ apartment⟩

din·ner \ˈdi-nər\ *n* : the main meal of the day; *also* : a formal banquet

din·ner·ware \ˈdi-nər-ˌwer\ *n* : tableware other than flatware

di·no \ˈdī-nō\ *n, pl* **dinos** : DINOSAUR

di·no·fla·gel·late \ˌdī-nō-ˈfla-jə-lət, -ˌlāt\ *n* : any of an order of planktonic plantlike unicellular flagellates of which some cause red tide

di•no•saur \'dī-nə-ˌsȯr\ *n* [ultim. fr. Gk *deinos* terrifying + *sauros* lizard] : any of a group of extinct long-tailed Mesozoic reptiles often of huge size

dint \'dint\ *n* **1** : FORCE ⟨by ~ of sheer grit⟩ **2** : DENT

di•o•cese \'dī-ə-səs, -ˌsēz, -ˌsēs\ *n, pl* **-ces•es** \-sə-səz, -ˌsē-zəz, -ˌsē-səz\ : the territorial jurisdiction of a bishop — **di•oc•e•san** \dī-'ä-sə-sən, ˌdī-ə-'sē-zᵊn\ *adj or n*

di•ode \'dī-ˌōd\ *n* : an electronic device with two electrodes or terminals used esp. as a rectifier

di•ox•in \dī-'äk-sən\ *n* : a persistent toxic hydrocarbon that occurs esp. as a by-product of industrial processes and waste incineration

¹dip \'dip\ *vb* **dipped; dip•ping** **1** : to plunge temporarily or partially under the surface (as of a liquid) **2** : to thrust in a way to suggest immersion **3** : to scoop up or out : LADLE **4** : to lower and then raise quickly ⟨~ a flag in salute⟩ **5** : to drop or slope down esp. suddenly ⟨the moon *dipped* below the crest⟩ **6** : to decrease moderately and usu. temporarily ⟨prices *dipped*⟩ **7** : to reach inside or as if inside or below a surface ⟨*dipped* into their savings⟩ **8** : to delve casually into something; *esp* : to read superficially ⟨~ into a book⟩

²dip *n* **1** : an act of dipping; *esp* : a short swim **2** : inclination downward : DROP **3** : something obtained by or used in dipping **4** : a sauce or soft mixture into which food may be dipped **5** : a liquid into which something may be dipped (as for cleansing or coloring)

diph•the•ria \dif-'thir-ē-ə\ *n* : an acute contagious bacterial disease marked by fever and by coating of the air passages with a membrane that interferes with breathing

diph•thong \'dif-ˌthȯŋ, 'dip-\ *n* : two vowel sounds joined in one syllable to form one speech sound (as *ou* in *out*)

dip•loid \'di-ˌplȯid\ *adj* : having two haploid sets of chromosomes ⟨~ somatic cells⟩ — **diploid** *n*

di•plo•ma \də-'plō-mə\ *n* : an official record of graduation from or of a degree conferred by a school

di•plo•ma•cy \də-'plō-mə-sē\ *n* **1** : the art and practice of conducting negotiations between nations **2** : TACT

dip•lo•mat \'di-plə-ˌmat\ *n* : one employed or skilled in diplomacy — **dip•lo•mat•ic** \ˌdi-plə-'ma-tik\ *adj*

di•plo•ma•tist \də-'plō-mə-tist\ *n* : DIPLOMAT

dip•per \'di-pər\ *n* **1** : any of a genus of birds that are related to the thrushes and are skilled in diving **2** : something (as a ladle or scoop) that dips or is used for dipping **3** *cap* : BIG DIPPER **4** *cap* : LITTLE DIPPER

dip•so•ma•nia \ˌdip-sə-'mā-nē-ə\ *n* : an uncontrollable craving for alcoholic liquors — **dip•so•ma•ni•ac** \-nē-ˌak\ *n*

dip•stick \'dip-ˌstik\ *n* : a graduated rod for indicating depth

dip•ter•an \'dip-tə-rən\ *adj* : of, relating to, or being a fly (sense 2) — **dipteran** *n* — **dip•ter•ous** \-rəs\ *adj*

dir *abbr* **1** direction **2** director

di•ram \dē-'ram\ *n* — see *somoni* at MONEY table

dire \'dī(-ə)r\ *adj* **dir•er; dir•est** **1** : very horrible : DREADFUL ⟨~ suffering⟩ **2** : warning of disaster **3** : EXTREME ⟨~ poverty⟩

¹di•rect \də-'rekt, dī-\ *vb* **1** : ADDRESS ⟨~ a letter⟩; *also* : to impart orally : AIM ⟨~ a remark to the gallery⟩ **2** : to regulate the activities or course of : guide the supervision, organizing, or performance of **3** : to cause to turn, move, or point or to follow a certain course **4** : to point, extend, or project in a specified line or course **5** : to request or instruct with authority **6** : to show or point out the way

²direct *adj* **1** : stemming immediately from a source ⟨~ result⟩ **2** : being or passing in a straight line of descent : LINEAL ⟨~ ancestor⟩ **3** : leading from one point to another in time or space without turn or stop : STRAIGHT **4** : NATURAL, STRAIGHTFORWARD ⟨a ~ manner⟩ **5** : operating without an intervening agency or step ⟨~ action⟩ **6** : effected by the action of the people or the electorate and not by representatives ⟨~ democracy⟩ **7** : consisting of or reproducing the exact words of a speaker or writer — **direct** *adv* — **di•rect•ly** *adv* — **di•rect•ness** *n*

direct broadcast satellite *n* : a television broadcasting system in which satellite transmissions are received at the viewing location

direct current *n* : an electric current flowing in one direction only

direct deposit *n* : a method of payment in which money is transferred to the payee's account without the use of checks or cash

di•rec•tion \də-'rek-shən, dī-\ *n* **1** : MANAGEMENT, GUIDANCE **2** : COMMAND, ORDER, INSTRUCTION **3** : the course or line along which something moves, lies, or points **4** : TENDENCY, TREND — **di•rec•tion•al** \-shə-nəl\ *adj*

di•rec•tive \də-'rek-tiv, dī-\ *n* : something that directs and usu. impels toward an action or goal; *esp* : an order issued by a high-level body or official

direct mail *n* : printed matter used for soliciting business or contributions and mailed direct to individuals

di•rec•tor \də-'rek-tər, dī-\ *n* **1** : one that directs : MANAGER, SUPERVISOR, CONDUCTOR **2** : one of a group of persons who direct the affairs of an organized body — **di•rec•to•ri•al** \-ˌrek-'tȯr-ē-əl\ *adj* — **di•rec•tor•ship** *n*

di•rec•tor•ate \-tə-rət\ *n* **1** : the office or position of director **2** : a board of directors; *also* : membership on such a board **3** : an executive staff

director's cut *n* : a version of a motion picture that is edited according to the director's wishes

di·rec·to·ry \-tə-rē\ *n, pl* **-ries** **1** : an alphabetical or classified list esp. of names and addresses **2** : FOLDER 4

dire·ful \ˈdī(-ə)r-fəl\ *adj* : DREADFUL ⟨a ~ disease⟩; *also* : OMINOUS

dirge \ˈdərj\ *n* [ME *dirige* church service for the dead, fr. the first word of a LL anthem, fr. L, imper. of *dirigere* to direct] : a song of lamentation; *also* : a slow mournful piece of music

dir·ham \ˈdir-həm\ *n* **1** — see MONEY table **2** — see *dinar, riyal* at MONEY table

di·ri·gi·ble \ˈdir-ə-jə-bəl, də-ˈri-jə-\ *n* : AIRSHIP

dirk \ˈdərk\ *n* : DAGGER 1

dirndl \ˈdərn-dᵊl\ *n* [short for G *Dirndlkleid,* fr. G dial. *Dirndl* girl + G *Kleid* dress] : a full skirt with a tight waistband

dirt \ˈdərt\ *n* **1** : a filthy or soiling substance (as mud, dust, or grime) **2** : loose or packed earth : SOIL **3** : moral uncleanness **4** : scandalous gossip **5** : embarrassing or incriminating information

[1]**dirty** \ˈdər-tē\ *adj* **dirt·i·er; -est** **1** : SOILED, FILTHY **2** : INDECENT, SMUTTY ⟨~ jokes⟩ **3** : BASE, UNFAIR ⟨a ~ trick⟩ **4** : STORMY, FOGGY ⟨~ weather⟩ **5** : not clear in color : DULL ⟨a ~ red⟩ — **dirt·i·ness** *n* — **dirty** *adv*

[2]**dirty** *vb* **dirt·ied; dirty·ing** : to make or become dirty

dis·able \di-ˈsā-bəl\ *vb* **dis·abled; dis·abling** **1** : to disqualify legally **2** : to make unable to perform by or as if by illness, injury, or malfunction — **dis·abil·i·ty** \ˌdi-sə-ˈbi-lə-tē\ *n*

dis·abled *adj* : incapacitated by illness or injury; *also* : physically or mentally impaired

dis·abuse \ˌdi-sə-ˈbyüz\ *vb* : to free from error, fallacy, or misconception

dis·ad·van·tage \ˌdi-səd-ˈvan-tij\ *n* **1** : loss or damage esp. to reputation or finances **2** : an unfavorable, inferior, or prejudicial condition, quality, or circumstance — **dis·ad·van·ta·geous** \di-ˌsad-ˌvan-ˈtā-jəs, -vən-\ *adj*

dis·ad·van·taged \-tijd\ *adj* : lacking in basic resources or conditions believed necessary for an equal position in society

dis·af·fect \ˌdi-sə-ˈfekt\ *vb* : to alienate the affection or loyalty of — **dis·af·fec·tion** \-ˈfek-shən\ *n*

dis·agree \ˌdi-sə-ˈgrē\ *vb* **1** : to fail to agree **2** : to differ in opinion **3** : to cause discomfort or distress ⟨fried foods ~ with her⟩ — **dis·agree·ment** *n*

dis·agree·able \-ə-bəl\ *adj* **1** : causing discomfort : UNPLEASANT, OFFENSIVE ⟨a ~ odor⟩ **2** : ILL-TEMPERED, PEEVISH — **dis·agree·able·ness** *n* — **dis·agree·ably** \-blē\ *adv*

dis·al·low \ˌdis-ə-ˈlau̇\ *vb* : to refuse to admit or recognize : REJECT ⟨~ a claim⟩ — **dis·al·low·ance** *n*

dis·ap·pear \ˌdis-ə-ˈpir\ *vb* **1** : to pass out of sight **2** : to cease to be : become lost — **dis·ap·pear·ance** *n*

dis·ap·point \ˌdis-ə-ˈpȯint\ *vb* : to fail to fulfill the expectation or hope of — **dis·ap·point·ment** *n*

dis·ap·pro·ba·tion \dis-ˌa-prə-ˈbā-shən\ *n* : DISAPPROVAL

dis·ap·prov·al \ˌdis-ə-ˈprü-vəl\ *n* : adverse judgment : CENSURE

dis·ap·prove \-ˈprüv\ *vb* **1** : CONDEMN **2** : to feel or express disapproval ⟨~*s* of smoking⟩ **3** : REJECT — **dis·ap·prov·ing·ly** \-ˈprü-viŋ-lē\ *adv*

dis·arm \dis-ˈärm\ *vb* **1** : to take arms or weapons from **2** : to reduce the size and strength of the armed forces of a country **3** : to make harmless, peaceable, or friendly : win over ⟨a ~*ing* smile⟩ — **dis·ar·ma·ment** \-ˈär-mə-mənt\ *n*

dis·ar·range \ˌdis-ə-ˈrānj\ *vb* : to disturb the arrangement or order of — **dis·ar·range·ment** *n*

dis·ar·ray \-ˈrā\ *n* **1** : DISORDER, CONFUSION **2** : disorderly or careless dress

dis·as·sem·ble \ˌdis-ə-ˈsem-bəl\ *vb* : to take apart

dis·as·so·ci·ate \-ˈsō-shē-ˌāt, -sē-\ *vb* : to detach from association

di·sas·ter \di-ˈzas-tər, -ˈsas-\ *n* [MF *desastre,* fr. It *disastro,* fr. *astro* star, fr. L *astrum*] : a sudden or great misfortune — **di·sas·trous** \-ˈzas-trəs\ *adj* — **di·sas·trous·ly** *adv*

dis·avow \ˌdis-ə-ˈvau̇\ *vb* : to deny responsibility for : REPUDIATE — **dis·avow·al** \-ˈvau̇(-ə)l\ *n*

dis·band \dis-ˈband\ *vb* : to break up the organization of : DISPERSE

dis·bar \dis-ˈbär\ *vb* : to expel from the legal profession — **dis·bar·ment** *n*

dis·be·lieve \ˌdis-bə-ˈlēv\ *vb* **1** : to hold not worthy of belief : not believe **2** : to withhold or reject belief — **dis·be·lief** \-ˈlēf\ *n* — **dis·be·liev·er** *n*

dis·bur·den \dis-ˈbər-dᵊn\ *vb* : to rid of a burden

dis·burse \dis-ˈbərs\ *vb* **dis·bursed; dis·burs·ing** **1** : to pay out : EXPEND **2** : DISTRIBUTE — **dis·burse·ment** *n*

[1]**disc** *var of* DISK

[2]**disc** *abbr* discount

dis·card \dis-ˈkärd, ˈdis-ˌkärd\ *vb* **1** : to let go a playing card from one's hand; *also* : to play (a card) from a suit other than a trump but different from the one led **2** : to get rid of as unwanted — **discard** \ˈdis-ˌkärd\ *n*

disc brake *n* : a brake that operates by the friction of a pair of plates pressing against the sides of a rotating disc

dis·cern \di-ˈsərn, -ˈzərn\ *vb* **1** : to detect with the eyes : DISTINGUISH **2** : DISCRIMINATE **3** : to come to know or recognize mentally ⟨~ right from wrong⟩ — **dis·cern·ible** *adj* — **dis·cern·ment** *n*

dis·cern·ing *adj* : revealing insight and understanding ⟨a ~ critic⟩

[1]**dis·charge** \dis-ˈchärj, ˈdis-ˌchärj\ *vb* **1** : to relieve of a charge, load, or burden : UNLOAD; *esp* : to remove the electrical energy from ⟨~ a storage battery⟩ **2** : to let or put off ⟨~ passengers⟩ **3** : SHOOT ⟨~ an arrow⟩ **4** : to set free ⟨~ a prisoner⟩ **5** : to dismiss from service or em-

ployment ⟨~ a soldier⟩ **6 :** to get rid of by paying or doing ⟨~ a debt⟩ **7 :** to give forth fluid ⟨the river ~*s* into the ocean⟩

[2]**dis·charge** \ˈdis-ˌchärj, dis-ˈchärj\ *n* **1 :** the act of discharging, unloading, or releasing **2 :** something that discharges; *esp* **:** a certification of release or payment **3 :** a firing off (as of a gun) **4 :** a flowing out (as of blood from a wound); *also* **:** something that is emitted ⟨a purulent ~⟩ **5 :** release or dismissal esp. from an office or employment; *also* **:** complete separation from military service **6 :** a flow of electricity (as through a gas)

dis·ci·ple \di-ˈsī-pəl\ *n* [ultim. fr. LL *discipulus* follower of Jesus in his lifetime, fr. L, pupil] **1 :** one who accepts and helps to spread the teachings of another; *also* **:** a convinced adherent **2** *cap* **:** a member of the Disciples of Christ

dis·ci·pli·nar·i·an \ˌdi-sə-plə-ˈner-ē-ən\ *n* **:** one who enforces order

dis·ci·plin·ary \ˈdi-sə-plə-ˌner-ē\ *adj* **:** of or relating to discipline; *also* **:** CORRECTIVE ⟨take ~ action⟩

[1]**dis·ci·pline** \ˈdi-sə-plən\ *n* **1 :** PUNISHMENT **2 :** a field of study **:** SUBJECT **3 :** training that corrects, molds, or perfects **4 :** control gained by obedience or training **:** orderly conduct **5 :** a system of rules governing conduct

[2]**discipline** *vb* **-plined; -plin·ing 1 :** PUNISH **2 :** to train or develop by instruction and exercise esp. in self-control **3 :** to bring under control ⟨~ troops⟩; *also* **:** to impose order upon

disc jockey *or* **disk jockey** *n* **:** an announcer of a radio show of popular recorded music

dis·claim \dis-ˈklām\ *vb* **:** DENY, DISAVOW — **dis·claim·er** *n*

dis·close \dis-ˈklōz\ *vb* **:** to expose to view — **dis·clo·sure** \-ˈklō-zhər\ *n*

dis·co \ˈdis-kō\ *n, pl* **discos 1 :** a nightclub for dancing to live or recorded music **2 :** popular dance music characterized by hypnotic rhythm, repetitive lyrics, and electronically produced sounds

dis·col·or \dis-ˈkə-lər\ *vb* **:** to alter or change in hue or color esp. for the worse — **dis·col·or·ation** \-ˌkə-lə-ˈrā-shən\ *n*

dis·com·bob·u·late \ˌdis-kəm-ˈbä-byü-ˌlāt\ *vb* **-lat·ed; -lat·ing :** UPSET, CONFUSE

dis·com·fit \dis-ˈkəm-fət, *esp Southern* ˌdis-kəm-ˈfit\ *vb* **:** UPSET, FRUSTRATE — **dis·com·fi·ture** \dis-ˈkəm-fə-ˌchu̇r\ *n*

[1]**dis·com·fort** \dis-ˈkəm-fərt\ *vb* **:** to make uncomfortable or uneasy

[2]**discomfort** *n* **:** mental or physical uneasiness

dis·com·mode \ˌdis-kə-ˈmōd\ *vb* **-mod·ed; -mod·ing :** INCONVENIENCE, TROUBLE

dis·com·pose \-kəm-ˈpōz\ *vb* **1 :** to destroy the calmness or peace of **2 :** DISARRANGE — **dis·com·po·sure** \-ˈpō-zhər\ *n*

dis·con·cert \ˌdis-kən-ˈsərt\ *vb* **:** CONFUSE, UPSET ⟨the bad news ~*ed* her⟩

dis·con·nect \ˌdis-kə-ˈnekt\ *vb* **:** to undo the connection of — **dis·con·nec·tion** \-ˈnek-shən\ *n*

dis·con·nect·ed *adj* **:** not connected; *also* **:** INCOHERENT — **dis·con·nect·ed·ly** *adv* — **dis·con·nect·ed·ness** *n*

dis·con·so·late \dis-ˈkän-sə-lət\ *adj* **1 :** CHEERLESS **2 :** hopelessly sad — **dis·con·so·late·ly** *adv*

dis·con·tent \ˌdis-kən-ˈtent\ *n* **:** uneasiness of mind **:** DISSATISFACTION — **dis·con·tent·ed** *adj*

dis·con·tin·ue \ˌdis-kən-ˈtin-yü\ *vb* **1 :** to break the continuity of **:** cease to operate, use, or take **2 :** END — **dis·con·tin·u·ance** \-yə-wəns\ *n* — **dis·con·ti·nu·i·ty** \dis-ˌkän-tə-ˈnü-ə-tē, -ˈnyü-\ *n* — **dis·con·tin·u·ous** \ˌdis-kən-ˈtin-yə-wəs\ *adj*

dis·cord \ˈdis-ˌkȯrd\ *n* **1 :** lack of agreement or harmony **:** DISSENSION, CONFLICT **2 :** a harsh combination of musical sounds **3 :** a harsh or unpleasant sound — **dis·cor·dant** \dis-ˈkȯr-dᵊnt\ *adj* — **dis·cor·dant·ly** *adv*

dis·co·theque *or* **discothèque** \ˈdis-kə-ˌtek\ *n* **:** DISCO 1

[1]**dis·count** \ˈdis-ˌkau̇nt\ *n* **1 :** a reduction made from a regular or list price **2 :** a deduction of interest in advance when lending money

[2]**dis·count** \ˈdis-ˌkau̇nt, dis-ˈkau̇nt\ *vb* **1 :** to deduct from the amount of a bill, debt, or charge usu. for cash or prompt payment; *also* **:** to sell or offer for sale at a discount **2 :** to lend money after deducting the discount ⟨~ a note⟩ **3 :** DISREGARD; *also* **:** MINIMIZE **4 :** to make allowance for bias or exaggeration **5 :** to take into account (as a future event) in present calculations — **dis·count·able** *adj* — **dis·count·er** *n*

[3]**dis·count** \ˈdis-ˌkau̇nt\ *adj* **:** selling goods or services at a discount; *also* **:** sold at or reflecting a discount

dis·coun·te·nance \dis-ˈkau̇n-tə-nənts\ *vb* **1 :** EMBARRASS, DISCONCERT **2 :** to look with disfavor on

dis·cour·age \dis-ˈkər-ij\ *vb* **-aged; -ag·ing 1 :** to deprive of courage or confidence **:** DISHEARTEN **2 :** to hinder by disfavoring **3 :** to attempt to dissuade — **dis·cour·age·ment** *n* — **dis·cour·ag·ing·ly** *adv*

[1]**dis·course** \ˈdis-ˌkȯrs\ *n* [ME *discours,* fr. ML & LL *discursus;* ML, argument, fr. LL, conversation, fr. L, act of running about, fr. *discurrere* to run about, fr. *currere* to run] **1 :** CONVERSATION **2 :** formal and usu. extended expression of thought on a subject

[2]**dis·course** \dis-ˈkȯrs\ *vb* **dis·coursed; dis·cours·ing 1 :** to express oneself in esp. oral discourse **2 :** TALK, CONVERSE

dis·cour·te·ous \(ˌ)dis-ˈkər-tē-əs\ *adj* **:** lacking courtesy **:** UNCIVIL, RUDE — **dis·cour·te·ous·ly** *adv*

dis·cour·te·sy \-ˈkər-tə-sē\ *n* **:** RUDENESS; *also* **:** a rude act

dis·cov·er \dis-ˈkə-vər\ *vb* **1 :** to make known or visible **2 :** to obtain sight or

knowledge of for the first time; *also* : FIND OUT — **dis·cov·er·er** *n*
dis·cov·ery \dis-ˈkə-və-rē\ *n, pl* **-er·ies** **1** : the act or process of discovering **2** : something discovered **3** : the disclosure usu. before a civil trial of pertinent facts or documents
¹**dis·cred·it** \(ˌ)dis-ˈkre-dət\ *vb* **1** : DISBELIEVE **2** : to cause disbelief in the accuracy or authority of **3** : DISGRACE — **dis·cred·it·able** *adj*
²**discredit** *n* **1** : loss of reputation **2** : lack or loss of belief or confidence
dis·creet \dis-ˈkrēt\ *adj* : showing good judgment; *esp* : capable of observing prudent silence — **dis·creet·ly** *adv*
dis·crep·an·cy \dis-ˈkre-pən-sē\ *n, pl* **-cies** **1** : DIFFERENCE, DISAGREEMENT **2** : an instance of being discrepant
dis·crep·ant \-pənt\ *adj* [ME *discrepaunt,* fr. L *discrepans,* prp. of *discrepare* to sound discordantly, fr. *crepare* to rattle, creak] : being at variance : DISAGREEING ⟨~ conclusions⟩
dis·crete \dis-ˈkrēt, ˈdis-ˌkrēt\ *adj* **1** : individually distinct ⟨several ~ sections⟩ **2** : NONCONTINUOUS
dis·cre·tion \dis-ˈkre-shən\ *n* **1** : the quality of being discreet : PRUDENCE **2** : individual choice or judgment ⟨left the decision to his ~⟩ **3** : power of free decision or latitude of choice — **dis·cre·tion·ary** *adj*
dis·crim·i·nate \dis-ˈkri-mə-ˌnāt\ *vb* **-nat·ed; -nat·ing** **1** : DISTINGUISH, DIFFERENTIATE **2** : to make a difference in treatment on a basis other than individual merit — **dis·crim·i·na·tion** \-ˌkri-mə-ˈnā-shən\ *n*
dis·crim·i·nat·ing *adj* : marked by discrimination; *esp* : DISCERNING, JUDICIOUS — **dis·crim·i·nat·ing·ly** *adv*
dis·crim·i·na·to·ry \dis-ˈkri-mə-nə-ˌtȯr-ē\ *adj* : marked by esp. unjust discrimination ⟨~ treatment⟩
dis·cur·sive \dis-ˈkər-siv\ *adj* : passing from one topic to another : RAMBLING ⟨a ~ speech⟩ — **dis·cur·sive·ly** *adv* — **dis·cur·sive·ness** *n*
dis·cus \ˈdis-kəs\ *n, pl* **dis·cus·es** : a heavy disk that is hurled for distance in a track-and-field contest
dis·cuss \di-ˈskəs\ *vb* [ME, fr. AF *discusser,* fr. L *discussus,* pp. of *discutere* to disperse, fr. *dis-* apart + *quatere* to shake] **1** : to argue or consider carefully by presenting the various sides **2** : to talk about — **dis·cus·sion** \-ˈskə-shən\ *n*
dis·cus·sant \di-ˈskə-sᵊnt\ *n* : one who takes part in a formal discussion
¹**dis·dain** \dis-ˈdān\ *n* : CONTEMPT, SCORN ⟨a look of ~⟩ — **dis·dain·ful** \-fəl\ *adj* — **dis·dain·ful·ly** *adv*
²**disdain** *vb* **1** : to look on with scorn **2** : to reject or refrain from because of disdain ⟨~*ed* gambling⟩
dis·ease \di-ˈzēz\ *n* : an abnormal bodily condition that impairs normal functioning and can usu. be recognized by signs and symptoms : SICKNESS — **dis·eased** \-ˈzēzd\ *adj*
dis·em·bark \ˌdi-səm-ˈbärk\ *vb* : to go or put ashore from a ship — **dis·em·bar·ka·tion** \di-ˌsem-ˌbär-ˈkā-shən\ *n*
dis·em·body \ˌdi-səm-ˈbä-dē\ *vb* : to deprive of bodily existence
dis·em·bow·el \-ˈbau̇(-ə)l\ *vb* : EVISCERATE 1 — **dis·em·bow·el·ment** *n*
dis·em·power \ˌdis-im-ˈpau̇(-ə)r\ *vb* : to deprive of power, authority, or influence
dis·en·chant \ˌdis-in-ˈchant\ *vb* : DISILLUSION — **dis·en·chant·ment** \-mənt\ *n*
dis·en·chant·ed \-ˈchan-təd\ *adj* : DISAPPOINTED, DISSATISFIED
dis·en·cum·ber \ˌdis-ᵊn-ˈkəm-bər\ *vb* : to free from something that burdens
dis·en·fran·chise \ˌdis-in-ˈfran-ˌchīz\ *vb* : to deprive of a franchise, a legal right, or a privilege; *esp* : to deprive of the right to vote — **dis·en·fran·chise·ment** *n*
dis·en·gage \ˌdis-ᵊn-ˈgāj\ *vb* : RELEASE, EXTRICATE, DISENTANGLE ⟨~ from a harness⟩ — **dis·en·gage·ment** *n*
dis·en·gaged \-ˈgājd\ *adj* : IMPARTIAL, DETACHED ⟨a ~ observer⟩
dis·en·tan·gle \ˌdis-in-ˈtaŋ-gəl\ *vb* : to free from entanglement : UNRAVEL
dis·equi·lib·ri·um \dis-ˌē-kwə-ˈli-brē-əm\ *n* : loss or lack of equilibrium
dis·es·tab·lish \ˌdis-ə-ˈsta-blish\ *vb* : to end the establishment of; *esp* : to deprive of the status of an established church — **dis·es·tab·lish·ment** *n*
dis·es·teem \ˌdis-ə-ˈstēm\ *n* : lack of esteem : DISFAVOR, DISREPUTE
dis·fa·vor \(ˌ)dis-ˈfā-vər\ *n* **1** : DISAPPROVAL, DISLIKE **2** : the state or fact of being no longer favored
dis·fig·ure \dis-ˈfi-gyər\ *vb* : to spoil the appearance of ⟨*disfigured* by a scar⟩ — **dis·fig·ure·ment** *n*
dis·fran·chise \dis-ˈfran-ˌchīz\ *vb* : DISENFRANCHISE — **dis·fran·chise·ment** *n*
disfunction *var of* DYSFUNCTION
dis·gorge \-ˈgȯrj\ *vb* : VOMIT; *also* : to discharge forcefully or confusedly
¹**dis·grace** \di-ˈskrās, dis-ˈgrās\ *vb* : to bring reproach or shame to
²**disgrace** *n* **1** : SHAME, DISHONOR; *also* : a cause of shame **2** : the condition of being out of favor : loss of respect — **dis·grace·ful** \-fəl\ *adj* — **dis·grace·ful·ly** *adv*
dis·grun·tle \dis-ˈgrən-tᵊl\ *vb* **dis·grun·tled; dis·grun·tling** : to put in bad humor ⟨*disgruntled* employees⟩
¹**dis·guise** \dis-ˈgīz\ *vb* **dis·guised; dis·guis·ing** **1** : to change the appearance of so as to conceal the identity or to resemble another **2** : HIDE, CONCEAL
²**disguise** *n* **1** : clothing put on to conceal one's identity or counterfeit another's **2** : an outward appearance that hides what something really is
¹**dis·gust** \dis-ˈgəst\ *n* : AVERSION, REPUGNANCE — **dis·gust·ful** \-fəl\ *adj*
²**disgust** *vb* : to provoke to loathing, repugnance, or aversion : be offensive to — **dis·gust·ed·ly** *adv* — **dis·gust·ing** \-ˈgəs-tiŋ\ *adj* — **dis·gust·ing·ly** *adv*
¹**dish** \ˈdish\ *n* [ME, fr. OE *disc* plate, fr. L *discus* quoit, disk, dish, fr. Gk *diskos,* fr.

dikein to throw] **1** : a vessel used for serving food **2** : the food served in a dish ⟨a ~ of berries⟩ **3** : food prepared in a particular way **4** : something resembling a dish esp. in being shallow and concave **5** : SATELLITE DISH **6** : GOSSIP 2

[2]**dish** *vb* **1** : to put into a dish **2** : to make concave like a dish **3** : GOSSIP

dis·ha·bille \ˌdi-sə-ˈbēl\ *or* **des·ha·bille** \ˌde-\ *n* [F *déshabillé*] : the state of being dressed in a casual or careless manner

dis·har·mo·ny \(ˌ)dis-ˈhär-mə-nē\ *n* : lack of harmony — **dis·har·mo·ni·ous** \ˌdis-(ˌ)här-ˈmō-nē-əs\ *adj*

dish·cloth \ˈdish-ˌklȯth\ *n* : a cloth for washing dishes

dis·heart·en \dis-ˈhär-tᵊn\ *vb* : DISCOURAGE, DEJECT

dished \ˈdisht\ *adj* : CONCAVE

di·shev·el \di-ˈshe-vəl\ *vb* **-shev·eled** *or* **-shev·elled; -shev·el·ing** *or* **-shev·el·ling** [ME *discheveled* bareheaded, with disordered hair, fr. AF *deschevelé,* fr. *des-* apart + *chevoil* hair, fr. L *capillus*] : to throw into disorder or disarray — **di·shev·eled** *or* **di·shev·elled** *adj* — **di·shev·el·ment** \-mənt\ *n*

dis·hon·est \di-ˈsä-nəst\ *adj* : not honest : UNTRUSTWORTHY, DECEITFUL — **dis·hon·est·ly** *adv* — **dis·hon·es·ty** \-nə-stē\ *n*

[1]**dis·hon·or** \dis-ˈä-nər\ *n* **1** : lack or loss of honor **2** : SHAME, DISGRACE **3** : a cause of disgrace **4** : the act of dishonoring a negotiable instrument when presented for payment — **dis·hon·or·able** \dis-ˈä-nə-rə-bəl\ *adj* — **dis·hon·or·ably** \-blē\ *adv*

[2]**dishonor** *vb* **1** : DISGRACE **2** : to refuse to accept or pay ⟨~ a check⟩

dish out *vb* : to give freely

dish·rag \ˈdish-ˌrag\ *n* : DISHCLOTH

dish·wash·er \-ˌwȯ-shər, -ˌwä-\ *n* : a person or machine that washes dishes

dish·wa·ter \-ˌwȯ-tər, -ˌwä-\ *n* : water used for washing dishes

dis·il·lu·sion \ˌdis-ə-ˈlü-zhən\ *vb* : to free from illusion — **dis·il·lu·sion·ment** *n*

dis·il·lu·sioned *adj* : DISAPPOINTED, DISSATISFIED

dis·in·cli·na·tion \dis-ˌin-klə-ˈnā-shən\ *n* : a preference for avoiding something : slight aversion

dis·in·cline \ˌdis-in-ˈklīn\ *vb* : to make unwilling

dis·in·clined *adj* : unwilling because of dislike or disapproval

dis·in·fect \ˌdis-in-ˈfekt\ *vb* : to cleanse of infection-causing germs — **dis·in·fec·tant** \-ˈfek-tənt\ *n* — **dis·in·fec·tion** \-ˈfek-shən\ *n*

dis·in·for·ma·tion \-ˌin-fər-ˈmā-shən\ *n* : false information deliberately and often covertly spread

dis·in·gen·u·ous \ˌdis-in-ˈjen-yə-wəs\ *adj* : lacking in candor; *also* : giving a false appearance of simple frankness

dis·in·her·it \ˌdis-in-ˈher-ət\ *vb* : to deprive of the right to inherit

dis·in·te·grate \dis-ˈin-tə-ˌgrāt\ *vb* **1** : to break or decompose into constituent parts or small particles **2** : to destroy the unity or integrity of — **dis·in·te·gra·tion** \-ˌin-tə-ˈgrā-shən\ *n*

dis·in·ter \ˌdis-in-ˈtər\ *vb* **1** : to take from the grave or tomb **2** : UNEARTH

dis·in·ter·est·ed \(ˌ)dis-ˈin-tə-rəs-təd, -ˌres-\ *adj* **1** : not interested **2** : free from selfish motive or interest : UNBIASED — **dis·in·ter·est·ed·ness** *n*

dis·join \(ˌ)dis-ˈjȯin\ *vb* : SEPARATE

dis·joint \(ˌ)dis-ˈjȯint\ *vb* : to disturb the orderly arrangement of; *also* : to separate at the joints

dis·joint·ed *adj* **1** : INCOHERENT ⟨~ conversation⟩ **2** : separated at or as if at the joint

disk *or* **disc** \ˈdisk\ *n* **1** : something round and flat; *esp* : a flat rounded anatomical structure (as the central part of the flower head of a composite plant or a pad of cartilage between vertebrae) **2** *usu disc* : a phonograph record **3** : a round flat plate coated with a magnetic substance on which data for a computer is stored **4** *usu disc* : OPTICAL DISK

disk drive *n* : a device for accessing or storing data on a magnetic disk

disk jockey *var of* DISC JOCKEY

[1]**dis·like** \(ˌ)dis-ˈlīk\ *n* : a feeling of aversion or disapproval

[2]**dislike** *vb* : to regard with dislike : DISAPPROVE

dis·lo·cate \ˈdis-lō-ˌkāt, dis-ˈlō-\ *vb* **1** : to put out of place; *esp* : to displace (a bone or joint) from normal connections ⟨~ a shoulder⟩ **2** : DISRUPT — **dis·lo·ca·tion** \ˌdis-(ˌ)lō-ˈkā-shən\ *n*

dis·lodge \(ˌ)dis-ˈläj\ *vb* : to force out of a place esp. of rest, hiding, or defense

dis·loy·al \(ˌ)dis-ˈlȯi(-ə)l\ *adj* : lacking in loyalty — **dis·loy·al·ty** *n*

dis·mal \ˈdiz-məl\ *adj* [ME, fr. *dismal,* n., days marked as unlucky in medieval calendars, fr. AF, fr. ML *dies mali,* lit., evil days] **1** : showing or causing gloom or depression **2** : lacking merit ⟨a ~ performance⟩ — **dis·mal·ly** *adv*

dis·man·tle \(ˌ)dis-ˈman-tᵊl\ *vb* **-tled; -tling** **1** : to take apart **2** : to strip of furniture and equipment — **dis·man·tle·ment** *n*

dis·may \dis-ˈmā\ *vb* : to cause to lose courage or resolution from alarm or fear : DAUNT — **dismay** *n* — **dis·may·ing·ly** *adv*

dis·mem·ber \dis-ˈmem-bər\ *vb* **1** : to cut off or separate the limbs or parts of **2** : to break up or tear into pieces — **dis·mem·ber·ment** *n*

dis·miss \dis-ˈmis\ *vb* **1** : to send away **2** : DISCHARGE 5 **3** : to put aside or out of mind **4** : to put out of judicial consideration ⟨~*ed* all charges⟩ — **dis·miss·al** *n* — **dis·mis·sive** \-ˈmi-siv\ *adj* — **dis·mis·sive·ly** *adv*

dis·mount \dis-ˈmau̇nt\ *vb* **1** : to get down from something (as a horse or bicycle) **2** : UNHORSE **3** : DISASSEMBLE

dis·obe·di·ence \ˌdis-ə-ˈbē-dē-əns\ *n* : neglect or refusal to obey — **dis·obe·di·ent** \-ənt\ *adj*

dis·obey \ˌdis-ə-ˈbā\ *vb* : to fail to obey : be disobedient
dis·oblige \ˌdis-ə-ˈblīj\ *vb* **1** : to go counter to the wishes of **2** : INCONVENIENCE
[1]**dis·or·der** \dis-ˈȯr-dər\ *vb* **1** : to disturb the order of **2** : to disturb the regular or normal functions of
[2]**disorder** *n* **1** : lack of order : CONFUSION **2** : breach of the peace or public order : TUMULT **3** : an abnormal physical or mental condition : AILMENT
dis·or·der·ly \-lē\ *adj* **1** : offensive to public order **2** : marked by disorder ⟨a ~ desk⟩ — **dis·or·der·li·ness** *n*
dis·or·ga·nize \dis-ˈȯr-gə-ˌnīz\ *vb* : to break up the regular system of : throw into disorder — **dis·or·ga·ni·za·tion** \dis-ˌȯr-gə-nə-ˈzā-shən\ *n*
dis·ori·ent \dis-ˈȯr-ē-ˌent\ *vb* : to cause to be confused or lost — **dis·ori·en·ta·tion** \dis-ˌȯr-ē-ən-ˈtā-shən\ *n*
dis·own \dis-ˈōn\ *vb* : REPUDIATE, RENOUNCE, DISCLAIM ⟨her parents ~*ed* her⟩
dis·par·age \di-ˈsper-ij\ *vb* **-aged; -aging** [ME, to degrade by marriage below one's class, disparage, fr. AF *desparager* to marry below one's class, fr. *parage* equality, lineage, fr. *per* peer] **1** : to lower in rank or reputation : DEGRADE **2** : BELITTLE — **dis·par·age·ment** *n* — **dis·par·ag·ing·ly** *adv*
dis·pa·rate \ˈdis-pə-rət, di-ˈsper-ət\ *adj* : distinct in quality or character — **dis·par·i·ty** \di-ˈsper-ə-tē\ *n*
dis·pas·sion·ate \(ˌ)dis-ˈpa-shə-nət\ *adj* : not influenced by strong feeling : CALM, IMPARTIAL — **dis·pas·sion** \-ˈpa-shən\ *n* — **dis·pas·sion·ate·ly** *adv*
[1]**dis·patch** \di-ˈspach\ *vb* **1** : to send off or away with promptness or speed esp. on official business **2** : to put to death **3** : to attend to rapidly or efficiently **4** : DEFEAT — **dis·patch·er** *n*
[2]**dis·patch** \di-ˈspach, ˈdis-ˌpach\ *n* **1** : MESSAGE **2** : a news item sent in by a correspondent to a newspaper **3** : the act of dispatching; *esp* : SHIPMENT **4** : the act of putting to death **5** : promptness and efficiency in performing a task
dis·pel \di-ˈspel\ *vb* **dis·pelled; dis·pel·ling** : to drive away by scattering : DISSIPATE ⟨~ a rumor⟩
dis·pens·able \di-ˈspen-sə-bəl\ *adj* : capable of being dispensed with
dis·pen·sa·ry \di-ˈspen-sə-rē\ *n, pl* **-ries** : a place where medicine or medical or dental aid is dispensed
dis·pen·sa·tion \ˌdis-pən-ˈsā-shən\ *n* **1** : a system of rules for ordering affairs **2** : a particular arrangement or provision esp. of nature **3** : an exemption from a rule or from a vow or oath **4** : the act of dispensing **5** : something dispensed or distributed
dis·pense \di-ˈspens\ *vb* **dis·pensed; dis·pens·ing** **1** : to portion out **2** : ADMINISTER ⟨~ justice⟩ **3** : EXEMPT **4** : to make up and give out (remedies) — **dis·pens·er** *n* — **dispense with** **1** : SUSPEND **2** : to do without
dis·perse \di-ˈspərs\ *vb* **dis·persed; dis·pers·ing** : to break up and scatter about : SPREAD — **dis·per·sal** \-ˈspər-səl\ *n* — **dis·per·sion** \-ˈspər-zhən\ *n*
dis·pir·it \dis-ˈpir-ət\ *vb* : DEPRESS, DISCOURAGE, DISHEARTEN
dis·place \dis-ˈplās\ *vb* **1** : to remove from the usual or proper place; *esp* : to expel or force to flee from home or native land ⟨*displaced* persons⟩ **2** : to move out of position ⟨water *displaced* by a floating object⟩ **3** : to take the place of : REPLACE
dis·place·ment \-mənt\ *n* **1** : the act of displacing : the state of being displaced **2** : the volume or weight of a fluid (as water) displaced by a floating body (as a ship) **3** : the difference between the initial position of an object and a later position
[1]**dis·play** \di-ˈsplā\ *vb* [ME, fr. AF *desplaier, desploier,* lit., to unfold, fr. *des-* un- + *ploier, plier* to fold, fr. L *plicare*] : to present to view : make evident
[2]**display** *n* **1** : a displaying of something **2** : an electronic device (as a cathode-ray tube) that gives information in visual form; *also* : the visual information
dis·please \(ˌ)dis-ˈplēz\ *vb* **1** : to arouse the disapproval and dislike of **2** : to be offensive to : give displeasure
dis·plea·sure \-ˈple-zhər\ *n* : a feeling of dislike and irritation
dis·port \di-ˈspȯrt\ *vb* **1** : DIVERT, AMUSE **2** : FROLIC **3** : DISPLAY
dis·pos·able \di-ˈspō-zə-bəl\ *adj* **1** : remaining after deduction of taxes ⟨~ income⟩ **2** : designed to be used once and then thrown away ⟨~ diapers⟩ — **disposable** *n*
dis·pos·al \di-ˈspō-zəl\ *n* **1** : CONTROL, COMMAND **2** : an orderly arrangement **3** : a getting rid of **4** : MANAGEMENT, ADMINISTRATION **5** : presenting or bestowing something ⟨~ of favors⟩ **6** : a device used to reduce waste matter (as by grinding)
dis·pose \di-ˈspōz\ *vb* **dis·posed; dis·pos·ing** **1** : to give a tendency to : INCLINE ⟨*disposed* to accept⟩ **2** : to put in place : ARRANGE ⟨troops *disposed* for withdrawal⟩ **3** : SETTLE — **dis·pos·er** *n* — **dispose of** **1** : to transfer to the control of another **2** : to get rid of **3** : to deal with conclusively
dis·po·si·tion \ˌdis-pə-ˈzi-shən\ *n* **1** : the act or power of disposing : DISPOSAL **2** : RELINQUISHMENT **3** : ARRANGEMENT **4** : TENDENCY, INCLINATION **5** : natural attitude toward things ⟨a cheerful ~⟩
dis·pos·sess \ˌdis-pə-ˈzes\ *vb* : to put out of possession or occupancy — **dis·pos·ses·sion** \-ˈze-shən\ *n*
dis·praise \(ˌ)dis-ˈprāz\ *vb* : DISPARAGE — **dispraise** *n* — **dis·prais·er** *n*
dis·pro·por·tion \ˌdis-prə-ˈpȯr-shən\ *n* : lack of proportion, symmetry, or proper relation — **dis·pro·por·tion·ate** \-shə-nət\ *adj*
dis·prove \(ˌ)dis-ˈprüv\ *vb* : to prove to be false — **dis·proof** \-ˈprüf\ *n*

dis·pu·tant \di-ˈspyü-tᵊnt, ˈdis-pyə-tənt\ *n* : one that is engaged in a dispute

dis·pu·ta·tion \ˌdis-pyu̇-ˈtā-shən\ *n* **1** : DEBATE **2** : an oral defense of an academic thesis

dis·pu·ta·tious \-shəs\ *adj* : inclined to dispute : ARGUMENTATIVE

¹**dis·pute** \di-ˈspyüt\ *vb* **dis·put·ed; dis·put·ing** **1** : ARGUE, DEBATE **2** : WRANGLE **3** : to deny the truth or rightness of **4** : to struggle against or over : OPPOSE — **dis·put·able** \di-ˈspyü-tə-bəl, ˈdis-pyə-tə-bəl\ *adj* — **dis·put·er** *n*

²**dispute** *n* **1** : DEBATE **2** : QUARREL

dis·qual·i·fy \(ˌ)dis-ˈkwä-lə-ˌfī\ *vb* : to make or declare unfit or not qualified — **dis·qual·i·fi·ca·tion** \-ˌkwä-lə-fə-ˈkā-shən\ *n*

¹**dis·qui·et** \(ˌ)dis-ˈkwī-ət\ *vb* : to make uneasy or restless : DISTURB ⟨was ~*ed* by the news⟩ — **dis·qui·et·ing** *adj*

²**disquiet** *n* : lack of peace or tranquillity : ANXIETY

dis·qui·etude \(ˌ)dis-ˈkwī-ə-ˌtüd, -ˌtyüd\ *n* : AGITATION, ANXIETY

dis·qui·si·tion \ˌdis-kwə-ˈzi-shən\ *n* : a formal inquiry or discussion

¹**dis·re·gard** \ˌdis-ri-ˈgärd\ *vb* : to pay no attention to : treat as unworthy of notice or regard

²**disregard** *n* : the act of disregarding : the state of being disregarded : NEGLECT — **dis·re·gard·ful** *adj*

dis·re·pair \ˌdis-ri-ˈper\ *n* : the state of being in need of repair

dis·rep·u·ta·ble \dis-ˈre-pyu̇-tə-bəl\ *adj* : having a bad reputation

dis·re·pute \ˌdis-ri-ˈpyüt\ *n* : lack or decline of reputation : low esteem

dis·re·spect \ˌdis-ri-ˈspekt\ *n* : DISCOURTESY — **dis·re·spect·ful** *adj*

dis·robe \dis-ˈrōb\ *vb* : UNDRESS

dis·rupt \dis-ˈrəpt\ *vb* **1** : to break apart **2** : to throw into disorder **3** : INTERRUPT — **dis·rup·tion** \-ˈrəp-shən\ *n* — **dis·rup·tive** \-ˈrəp-tiv\ *adj*

dis·sat·is·fac·tion \di-ˌsa-təs-ˈfak-shən\ *n* : DISCONTENT

dis·sat·is·fy \di-ˈsa-təs-ˌfī\ *vb* : to fail to satisfy : DISPLEASE

dis·sect \dī-ˈsekt, di-\ *vb* **1** : to divide into parts esp. for examination and study **2** : ANALYZE — **dis·sec·tion** \-ˈsek-shən\ *n* — **dis·sec·tor** \-ˈsek-tər\ *n*

dis·sect·ed *adj* : cut deeply into narrow lobes ⟨a ~ leaf⟩

dis·sem·ble \di-ˈsem-bəl\ *vb* **-bled; -bling** **1** : to hide under or put on a false appearance : conceal facts, intentions, or feelings under some pretense **2** : SIMULATE — **dis·sem·bler** *n*

dis·sem·i·nate \di-ˈse-mə-ˌnāt\ *vb* **-nat·ed; -nat·ing** : to spread abroad as if sowing seed ⟨~ ideas⟩ — **dis·sem·i·na·tion** \-ˌse-mə-ˈnā-shən\ *n*

dis·sen·sion \di-ˈsen-chən\ *n* : disagreement in opinion : DISCORD

¹**dis·sent** \di-ˈsent\ *vb* **1** : to withhold assent **2** : to differ in opinion

²**dissent** *n* **1** : difference of opinion; *esp* : religious nonconformity **2** : a written statement in which a justice disagrees with the opinion of the majority

dis·sent·er \di-ˈsen-tər\ *n* **1** : one that dissents **2** *cap* : an English Nonconformist

dis·ser·ta·tion \ˌdi-sər-ˈtā-shən\ *n* : an extended usu. written treatment of a subject; *esp* : one submitted for a doctorate

dis·ser·vice \di-ˈsər-vəs\ *n* : INJURY, HARM, MISCHIEF

dis·sev·er \di-ˈse-vər\ *vb* : SEPARATE, DISUNITE

dis·si·dent \ˈdi-sə-dənt\ *adj* [L *dissidens*, prp. of *dissidēre* to sit apart, disagree, fr. *dis-* apart + *sedēre* to sit] : disagreeing esp. with an established religious or political system, organization, or belief — **dis·si·dence** \-dəns\ *n* — **dissident** *n*

dis·sim·i·lar \di-ˈsi-mə-lər\ *adj* : UNLIKE — **dis·sim·i·lar·i·ty** \di-ˌsi-mə-ˈler-ə-tē\ *n*

dis·sim·u·late \di-ˈsi-myə-ˌlāt\ *vb* : to hide under a false appearance : DISSEMBLE — **dis·sim·u·la·tion** \di-ˌsi-myə-ˈlā-shən\ *n*

dis·si·pate \ˈdi-sə-ˌpāt\ *vb* **-pat·ed; -pat·ing** **1** : to break up and drive off : DISPERSE, SCATTER ⟨the breeze *dissipated* the fog⟩ **2** : SQUANDER **3** : to break up and vanish **4** : to be dissolute; *esp* : to drink alcoholic beverages to excess — **dis·si·pat·ed** *adj* — **dis·si·pa·tion** \di-sə-ˈpā-shən\ *n*

dis·so·ci·ate \di-ˈsō-shē-ˌāt\ *vb* **-at·ed; -at·ing** : DISCONNECT, DISUNITE — **dis·so·ci·a·tion** \di-ˌsō-shē-ˈā-shən\ *n* — **dis·so·cia·tive** \di-ˈsō-shē-ˌā-tiv\ *adj*

dis·so·lute \ˈdi-sə-ˌlüt\ *adj* : loose in morals or conduct — **dis·so·lute·ly** *adv* — **dis·so·lute·ness** *n*

dis·so·lu·tion \ˌdi-sə-ˈlü-shən\ *n* **1** : the action or process of dissolving **2** : separation of a thing into its parts **3** : DECAY; *also* : DEATH **4** : the termination or breaking up of (as an assembly)

dis·solve \di-ˈzälv\ *vb* **1** : to separate into component parts **2** : to pass or cause to pass into solution ⟨sugar ~*s* in water⟩ **3** : TERMINATE, DISPERSE ⟨~ parliament⟩ **4** : to waste or fade away ⟨his courage *dissolved*⟩ **5** : to be overcome emotionally ⟨~ in tears⟩ **6** : to resolve itself as if by dissolution

dis·so·nance \ˈdi-sə-nəns\ *n* : DISCORD — **dis·so·nant** \-nənt\ *adj*

dis·suade \di-ˈswād\ *vb* **dis·suad·ed; dis·suad·ing** : to advise against a course of action : persuade or try to persuade not to do something — **dis·sua·sion** \-ˈswā-zhən\ *n* — **dis·sua·sive** \-ˈswā-siv\ *adj*

dist *abbr* **1** distance **2** district

¹**dis·taff** \ˈdis-ˌtaf\ *n, pl* **distaffs** \-ˌtafs, -ˌtavz\ [ME *distaf*, fr. OE *distæf*, fr. *dis-* bunch of flax + *stæf* stick, staff] **1** : a staff for holding the flax, tow, or wool in spinning **2** : a woman's work or domain **3** : the female branch or side of a family

²**distaff** *adj* **1** : MATERNAL 2 ⟨the ~ side of the family⟩ **2** : FEMALE 1 ⟨~ executives⟩

dis·tal \ˈdis-tᵊl\ *adj* **1** : situated away

from the point of attachment or origin esp. on the body **2** : of, relating to, or being the surface of a tooth that is farthest from the middle of the front of the jaw — **dis·tal·ly** *adv*

[1]**dis·tance** \ˈdis-təns\ *n* **1** : measure of separation in space or time **2** : EXPANSE **3** : the full length ⟨go the ~⟩ **4** : spatial remoteness **5** : COLDNESS, RESERVE **6** : DIFFERENCE, DISPARITY **7** : a distant point

[2]**distance** *vb* **dis·tanced; dis·tanc·ing** : to leave far behind : OUTSTRIP

[3]**distance** *adj* : taking place via electronic media linking instructors and students ⟨~ learning⟩

dis·tant \ˈdis-tənt\ *adj* **1** : separate in space : AWAY **2** : FAR-OFF ⟨a ~ galaxy⟩ **3** : far apart or behind **4** : not close in relationship ⟨a ~ cousin⟩ **5** : different in kind **6** : RESERVED, ALOOF, COLD ⟨~ politeness⟩ **7** : going a long distance ⟨~ voyages⟩ — **dis·tant·ly** *adv* — **dis·tant·ness** *n*

dis·taste \(ˌ)dis-ˈtāst\ *n* : DISINCLINATION, DISLIKE — **dis·taste·ful** *adj*

dis·tem·per \(ˌ)dis-ˈtem-pər\ *n* : a bodily disorder usu. of a domestic animal; *esp* : a contagious often fatal virus disease of dogs

dis·tend \di-ˈstend\ *vb* : EXPAND, SWELL — **dis·ten·si·ble** \-ˈsten-sə-bəl\ *adj* — **dis·ten·sion** *or* **dis·ten·tion** \-chən\ *n*

dis·tich \ˈdis-(ˌ)tik\ *n* : a unit of two lines of poetry

dis·till *also* **dis·til** \di-ˈstil\ *vb* **dis·tilled; dis·till·ing** **1** : to fall or let fall in drops **2** : to obtain or purify by distillation — **dis·till·er** *n* — **dis·till·ery** \-ˈsti-lə-rē\ *n*

dis·til·late \ˈdis-tə-ˌlāt, -lət\ *n* : a liquid product condensed from vapor during distillation

dis·til·la·tion \ˌdis-tə-ˈlā-shən\ *n* : the process of purifying a liquid by successive evaporation and condensation

dis·tinct \di-ˈstiŋkt\ *adj* **1** : SEPARATE, INDIVIDUAL ⟨a ~ cultural group⟩ **2** : presenting a clear unmistakable impression — **dis·tinct·ly** *adv* — **dis·tinct·ness** *n*

dis·tinc·tion \di-ˈstiŋk-shən\ *n* **1** : the distinguishing of a difference; *also* : the difference distinguished **2** : something that distinguishes **3** : special honor or recognition

dis·tinc·tive \di-ˈstiŋk-tiv\ *adj* **1** : serving to distinguish ⟨the ~ flight of the crane⟩ **2** : having or giving style or distinction — **dis·tinc·tive·ly** *adv* — **dis·tinc·tive·ness** *n*

dis·tin·guish \di-ˈstiŋ-gwish\ *vb* [alter. of ME *distinguen,* fr. AF *distinguer,* fr. L *distinguere,* lit., to separate by pricking] **1** : to recognize by some mark or characteristic **2** : to hear or see clearly : DISCERN **3** : to make distinctions ⟨~ between right and wrong⟩ **4** : to give prominence or distinction to; *also* : to take special notice of — **dis·tin·guish·able** *adj*

dis·tin·guished \-gwisht\ *adj* **1** : marked by eminence or excellence **2** : befitting an eminent person

dis·tort \di-ˈstȯrt\ *vb* **1** : to twist out of the true meaning **2** : to twist out of a natural, normal, or original shape or condition **3** : to cause to be perceived unnaturally — **dis·tor·tion** \-ˈstȯr-shən\ *n*

distr *abbr* distribute; distribution

dis·tract \di-ˈstrakt\ *vb* **1** : to draw (the attention or mind) to a different object : DIVERT **2** : to stir up or confuse with conflicting emotions or motives — **dis·trac·tion** \-ˈstrak-shən\ *n*

dis·trait \di-ˈstrā\ *adj* : DISTRAUGHT 1

dis·traught \di-ˈstrȯt\ *adj* **1** : agitated with doubt or mental conflict or pain **2** : driven mad

[1]**dis·tress** \di-ˈstres\ *n* **1** : suffering of body or mind : PAIN, ANGUISH **2** : TROUBLE, MISFORTUNE **3** : a condition of danger or desperate need — **dis·tress·ful** *adj*

[2]**distress** *vb* **1** : to subject to great strain or difficulties **2** : UPSET

dis·tress·ed \-ˈstrest\ *adj* : experiencing economic decline or difficulty

dis·trib·ute \di-ˈstri-byüt\ *vb* **-ut·ed; -ut·ing** **1** : to divide among several or many **2** : to spread out : SCATTER; *also* : DELIVER **3** : CLASSIFY — **dis·tri·bu·tion** \ˌdis-trə-ˈbyü-shən\ *n*

dis·trib·u·tive \di-ˈstri-byu̇-tiv\ *adj* **1** : of or relating to distribution **2** : of, having, or being the property of producing the same value when an operation is carried out on a whole expression and when it is carried out on each part of an expression with the results then collected together ⟨$a(b + c) = ab + ac$ because multiplication is ~⟩ — **dis·trib·u·tive·ly** *adv*

dis·trib·u·tor \di-ˈstri-byu̇-tər\ *n* **1** : one that distributes **2** : one that markets goods **3** : a device for directing current to the spark plugs of an engine

dis·trict \ˈdis-(ˌ)trikt\ *n* **1** : a fixed territorial division (as for administrative or electoral purposes) **2** : an area, region, or section with a distinguishing character

district attorney *n* : the prosecuting attorney of a judicial district

[1]**dis·trust** \dis-ˈtrəst\ *n* : a lack or absence of trust — **dis·trust·ful** \-fəl\ *adj* — **dis·trust·ful·ly** *adv*

[2]**distrust** *vb* : to have no trust or confidence in

dis·turb \di-ˈstərb\ *vb* **1** : to interfere with : INTERRUPT **2** : to alter the position or arrangement of; *also* : to upset the natural and esp. the ecological balance of **3** : to destroy the tranquillity or composure of : make uneasy **4** : to throw into disorder **5** : INCONVENIENCE — **dis·tur·bance** \-ˈstər-bəns\ *n* — **dis·turb·er** *n* — **dis·turb·ing·ly** \-ˈstər-biŋ-lē\ *adv*

dis·turbed \-ˈstərbd\ *adj* : showing symptoms of emotional illness

dis·unite \ˌdis-yü-ˈnīt\ *vb* : DIVIDE, SEPARATE

dis·uni·ty \dis-ˈyü-nə-tē\ *n* : lack of unity; *esp* : DISSENSION

dis·use \-ˈyüs\ *n* : a cessation of use or practice
dis·used \-ˈyüzd\ *adj* : no longer used or occupied
[1]**ditch** \ˈdich\ *n* : a long narrow channel or trench dug in the earth
[2]**ditch** *vb* **1** : to enclose with a ditch; *also* : to dig a ditch in **2** : to get rid of : DISCARD **3** : to make a forced landing of an airplane on water
dith·er \ˈdi-thər\ *n* : a highly nervous, excited, or agitated state
dit·to \ˈdi-tō\ *n, pl* **dittos** [It *ditto, detto,* pp. of *dire* to say, fr. L *dicere*] **1** : a thing mentioned previously or above — used to avoid repeating a word **2** : a mark " or " used as a symbol for the word *ditto*
dit·ty \ˈdi-tē\ *n, pl* **ditties** : a short simple song
dit·zy *or* **dit·sy** \ˈdit-sē\ *adj* **ditz·i·er** *or* **dits·i·er; -est** : eccentrically silly, giddy, or inane
di·uret·ic \ˌdī-yə-ˈre-tik\ *adj* : tending to increase urine flow — **diuretic** *n*
di·ur·nal \dī-ˈər-nᵊl\ *adj* **1** : DAILY ⟨a ~ chore⟩ **2** : of, relating to, occurring, or active in the daytime ⟨~ animals⟩
div *abbr* **1** divided **2** dividend **3** division **4** divorced
di·va \ˈdē-və\ *n, pl* **divas** *or* **di·ve** \-ˌvā\ [It, lit., goddess, fr. L, fem. of *divus* divine, god] **1** : PRIMA DONNA **2** : a usu. glamorous and successful female performer or personality
di·va·gate \ˈdī-və-ˌgāt\ *vb* **-gat·ed; -gat·ing** : to wander or stray from a course or subject : DIVERGE — **di·va·ga·tion** \ˌdī-və-ˈgā-shən\ *n*
di·van \ˈdī-ˌvan, di-ˈvan\ *n* : COUCH, SOFA
[1]**dive** \ˈdīv\ *vb* **dived** \ˈdīvd\ *or* **dove** \ˈdōv\; **dived; div·ing 1** : to plunge into water headfirst **2** : SUBMERGE **3** : to come or drop down precipitously **4** : to descend in an airplane at a steep angle **5** : to plunge into some matter or activity **6** : DART, LUNGE — **div·er** *n*
[2]**dive** *n* **1** : the act or an instance of diving **2** : a sharp decline **3** : a disreputable bar or place of amusement
di·verge \də-ˈvərj, dī-\ *vb* **di·verged; di·verg·ing 1** : to move or extend in different directions from a common point : draw apart **2** : to differ in character, form, or opinion **3** : DEVIATE **4** : DEFLECT — **di·ver·gence** \-ˈvər-jəns\ *n* — **di·ver·gent** \-jənt\ *adj*
di·vers \ˈdī-vərz\ *adj* : VARIOUS
di·verse \dī-ˈvərs, də-, ˈdī-ˌvərs\ *adj* **1** : UNLIKE **2** : composed of distinct forms or qualities — **di·verse·ly** *adv*
di·ver·si·fy \də-ˈvər-sə-ˌfī, dī-\ *vb* **-fied; -fy·ing** : to make different or various in form or quality — **di·ver·si·fi·ca·tion** \-ˌvər-sə-fə-ˈkā-shən\ *n*
di·ver·sion \də-ˈvər-zhən, dī-\ *n* **1** : a turning aside from a course, activity, or use : DEVIATION **2** : something that diverts or amuses : PASTIME
di·ver·si·ty \də-ˈvər-sə-tē, dī-\ *n, pl* **-ties 1** : the condition of being diverse : VARIETY **2** : an instance of being diverse
di·vert \də-ˈvərt, dī-\ *vb* **1** : to turn from a course or purpose : DEFLECT **2** : DISTRACT **3** : ENTERTAIN, AMUSE
di·vert·ing \-ˈvər-tiŋ\ *adj* : providing amusement or entertainment
di·vest \dī-ˈvest, də-\ *vb* **1** : to deprive or dispossess esp. of property, authority, or rights **2** : to strip esp. of clothing, ornament, or equipment
[1]**di·vide** \də-ˈvīd\ *vb* **di·vid·ed; di·vid·ing 1** : SEPARATE; *also* : CLASSIFY **2** : CLEAVE, PART ⟨a ship *dividing* the waves⟩ **3** : DISTRIBUTE, APPORTION **4** : to possess or make use of in common : share in **5** : to cause to be separate, distinct, or apart from one another **6** : to separate into opposing sides or parties **7** : to mark divisions on **8** : to subject to or use in mathematical division; *also* : to be used as a divisor with respect to **9** : to branch out
[2]**divide** *n* : WATERSHED 1
div·i·dend \ˈdi-və-ˌdend\ *n* **1** : an individual share of something distributed **2** : BONUS **3** : a number to be divided **4** : a sum or fund to be divided or distributed
di·vid·er \də-ˈvī-dər\ *n* **1** : one that divides (as a partition) ⟨room ~⟩ **2** *pl* : COMPASS 5
div·i·na·tion \ˌdi-və-ˈnā-shən\ *n* **1** : the art or practice of using omens or magic powers to foretell the future **2** : unusual insight or intuitive perception
[1]**di·vine** \də-ˈvīn\ *adj* **di·vin·er; -est 1** : of, relating to, or being God or a god **2** : supremely good : SUPERB; *also* : HEAVENLY — **di·vine·ly** *adv*
[2]**divine** *n* **1** : CLERGYMAN **2** : THEOLOGIAN
[3]**divine** *vb* **di·vined; di·vin·ing 1** : INFER, CONJECTURE **2** : PROPHESY **3** : DOWSE — **di·vin·er** *n*
divining rod *n* : a forked rod believed to reveal the presence of water or minerals by dipping downward when held over a vein
di·vin·i·ty \də-ˈvi-nə-tē\ *n, pl* **-ties 1** : THEOLOGY **2** : the quality or state of being divine **3** : a divine being; *esp* : GOD 1
di·vis·i·ble \də-ˈvi-zə-bəl\ *adj* : capable of being divided ⟨9 is ~ by 3⟩ — **di·vis·i·bil·i·ty** \-ˌvi-zə-ˈbi-lə-tē\ *n*
di·vi·sion \də-ˈvi-zhən\ *n* **1** : DISTRIBUTION, SEPARATION **2** : one of the parts or groupings into which a whole is divided **3** : DISAGREEMENT, DISUNITY **4** : something that divides or separates **5** : the mathematical operation of finding how many times one number is contained in another **6** : a large self-contained military unit **7** : an administrative or operating unit of a governmental, business, or educational organization — **di·vi·sion·al** \-ˈvi-zhə-nəl\ *adj*
di·vi·sive \də-ˈvī-siv, -ˈvi-ziv\ *adj* : creating disunity or dissension — **di·vi·sive·ly** *adv* — **di·vi·sive·ness** *n*
di·vi·sor \də-ˈvī-zər\ *n* : the number by which a dividend is divided
di·vorce \də-ˈvȯrs\ *n* **1** : an act or in-

stance of legally dissolving a marriage **2** : SEPARATION, SEVERANCE — **divorce** *vb* — **di·vorce·ment** *n*

di·vor·cé \də-ˌvȯr-ˈsā\ *n* [F] : a divorced man

di·vor·cée \də-ˌvȯr-ˈsā, -ˈsē\ *n* : a divorced woman

div·ot \ˈdi-vət\ *n* : a piece of turf dug from a golf fairway in making a stroke

di·vulge \də-ˈvəlj, dī-\ *vb* **di·vulged; di·vulg·ing** : REVEAL, DISCLOSE

Di·wa·li \də-ˈwä-lē, -ˈvä-\ *also* **Di·va·li** *or* **De·wa·li** *n* : a Hindu festival of lights held in late October

Dix·ie·land \ˈdik-sē-ˌland\ *n* : jazz music in duple time played in a style developed in New Orleans

DIY \ˌdē-ˌī-ˈwī\ *n* : do-it-yourself

diz·zy \ˈdi-zē\ *adj* **diz·zi·er; -est** [ME *disy,* fr. OE *dysig* stupid] **1** : FOOLISH, SILLY **2** : having a sensation of whirling : GIDDY **3** : causing or caused by giddiness — **diz·zi·ly** \-zə-lē\ *adv* — **diz·zi·ness** \-zē-nəs\ *n*

DJ *n, often not cap* : DISC JOCKEY

dk *abbr* **1** dark **2** deck **3** dock

dl *abbr* deciliter

DLitt *or* **DLit** *abbr* [NL *doctor litterarum*] doctor of letters; doctor of literature

DLO *abbr* dead letter office

dm *abbr* decimeter

DMD *abbr* [NL *dentariae medicinae doctor*] doctor of dental medicine

DMZ *abbr* demilitarized zone

dn *abbr* down

DNA \ˌdē-(ˌ)en-ˈā\ *n* : any of various nucleic acids that are usu. the molecular basis of heredity and are localized esp. in cell nuclei

DNR *abbr* do not resuscitate

[1]**do** \ˈdü\ *vb* **did** \ˈdid\; **done** \ˈdən\; **do·ing; does** \ˈdəz\ **1** : to bring to pass : ACCOMPLISH **2** : ACT, BEHAVE ⟨~ as I say⟩ **3** : to be active or busy ⟨up and ~*ing*⟩ **4** : HAPPEN ⟨what's ~*ing*?⟩ **5** : to be engaged in the study or practice of : work at ⟨he *does* tailoring⟩ **6** : COOK ⟨steak *done* rare⟩ **7** : to put in order (as by cleaning or arranging) ⟨~ the dishes⟩ **8** : DECORATE ⟨*did* the hall in blue⟩ **9** : GET ALONG ⟨~ well in school⟩ **10** : CARRY ON, MANAGE **11** : RENDER ⟨sleep will ~ you good⟩ **12** : FINISH ⟨when he had *done*⟩ **13** : EXERT ⟨*did* my best⟩ **14** : PRODUCE ⟨*did* a poem⟩ **15** : to play the part of **16** : CHEAT ⟨*did* him out of his share⟩ **17** : TRAVERSE, TOUR **18** : TRAVEL **19** : to spend or serve out a period of time ⟨*did* ten years in prison⟩ **20** : SUFFICE, SUIT **21** : to be fitting or proper **22** : USE ⟨doesn't ~ drugs⟩ **23** — used as an auxiliary verb (1) before the subject in an interrogative sentence ⟨*does* he work?⟩ and after some adverbs ⟨never *did* she say so⟩, (2) in a negative statement ⟨I *don't* know⟩, (3) for emphasis ⟨you ~ know⟩, and (4) as a substitute for a preceding predicate ⟨he works harder than I ~⟩ — **do·able** \ˈdü-ə-bəl\ *adj* — **do away with 1** : to put an end to **2** : DESTROY, KILL — **do by** : to deal with : TREAT ⟨*did* right *by* her⟩ — **do for** *chiefly Brit* : to bring about the death or ruin of — **do the trick** : to produce a desired result

[2]**do** *n* **1** : AFFAIR, PARTY **2** : a command or entreaty to do something ⟨list of ~*s* and don'ts⟩ **3** : HAIRSTYLE

[3]**do** *abbr* ditto

DOA *abbr* dead on arrival

DOB *abbr* date of birth

dob·bin \ˈdä-bən\ *n* [*Dobbin,* nickname for *Robert*] **1** : a farm horse **2** : a quiet plodding horse

Do·ber·man pin·scher \ˈdō-bər-mən-ˈpin-chər\ *n* : any of a German breed of short-haired medium-sized dogs

do·bra \ˈdō-brə\ *n* — see MONEY table

[1]**doc** \ˈdäk\ *n* : DOCTOR

[2]**doc** *abbr* document

do·cent \ˈdō-sᵊnt, dōt-ˈsent\ *n* [obs. G (now *Dozent*), fr. L *docens,* prp. of *docēre* to teach] : TEACHER, LECTURER; *also* : a person who leads a guided tour

doc·ile \ˈdä-səl\ *adj* [L *docilis,* fr. *docēre* to teach] : easily taught, led, or managed : TRACTABLE — **do·cil·i·ty** \dä-ˈsi-lə-tē\ *n*

[1]**dock** \ˈdäk\ *n* : any of a genus of coarse weedy herbs related to buckwheat

[2]**dock** *vb* **1** : to cut off the end of : cut short **2** : to take away a part of : deduct from ⟨~ a worker's wages⟩

[3]**dock** *n* **1** : an artificial basin to receive ships **2** : [2]SLIP 2 **3** : a wharf or platform for loading or unloading materials or for mooring a boat **4** : a device in which an electronic device (as a smartphone) is placed for charging or connecting

[4]**dock** *vb* **1** : to bring or come into dock **2** : to join (as two spacecraft) mechanically in space

[5]**dock** *n* : the place in a court where a prisoner stands or sits during trial

dock·age \ˈdä-kij\ *n* : docking facilities

dock·et \ˈdä-kət\ *n* **1** : a formal abridged record of the proceedings in a legal action; *also* : a register of such records **2** : a list of legal causes to be tried **3** : a calendar of matters to be acted on : AGENDA **4** : a label attached to a document containing identification or directions — **docket** *vb*

dock·hand \ˈdäk-ˌhand\ *n* : LONGSHOREMAN

dock·work·er \-ˌwər-kər\ *n* : LONGSHOREMAN

dock·yard \-ˌyärd\ *n* : SHIPYARD

[1]**doc·tor** \ˈdäk-tər\ *n* [ME *doctour* teacher, doctor, fr. AF & ML; AF, fr. ML *doctor,* fr. L, teacher, fr. *docēre* to teach] **1** : a person holding one of the highest academic degrees (as a PhD) conferred by a university **2** : a person skilled in healing arts; *esp* : one (as a physician, dentist, or veterinarian) academically and legally qualified to practice **3** : a person who restores or repairs things — **doc·tor·al** \-tə-rəl\ *adj*

[2]**doctor** *vb* **1** : to give medical treatment to **2** : to practice medicine **3** : REPAIR **4** : to adapt or modify for a desired end **5** : to alter deceptively

doc·tor·ate \ˈdäk-tə-rət\ *n* : the degree, title, or rank of a doctor

doc·tri·naire \ˌdäk-trə-ˈner\ *n* [F] : one who attempts to put an abstract theory into effect without regard to practical difficulties — **doctrinaire** *adj*

doc·trine \ˈdäk-trən\ *n* **1** : something that is taught **2** : DOGMA, TENET — **doc·tri·nal** \-trə-nᵊl\ *adj*

docu·dra·ma \ˈdä-kyə-ˌdrä-mə, -ˌdra-\ *n* : a drama made for television, motion pictures, or theater that deals freely with historical events

doc·u·ment \ˈdä-kyə-mənt\ *n* **1** : a paper that furnishes information, proof, or support of something else **2** : a computer file containing information input by a computer user usu. via a word processor — **doc·u·ment** \-ˌment\ *vb* — **doc·u·men·ta·tion** \ˌdä-kyə-mən-ˈtā-shən\ *n* — **doc·u·ment·er** *n*

doc·u·men·ta·ry \ˌdä-kyə-ˈmen-tə-rē\ *adj* **1** : consisting of documents; *also* : being in writing ⟨~ proof⟩ **2** : giving a factual presentation in artistic form ⟨a ~ movie⟩ — **documentary** *n*

DOD *abbr* Department of Defense

[1]**dod·der** \ˈdä-dər\ *n* : any of a genus of leafless parasitic twining vines that are highly deficient in chlorophyll

[2]**dodder** *vb* **dod·dered; dod·der·ing** **1** : to tremble or shake usu. from age **2** : to progress feebly and unsteadily

[1]**dodge** \ˈdäj\ *n* **1** : an act of evading by sudden bodily movement **2** : an artful device to evade, deceive, or trick **3** : EXPEDIENT

[2]**dodge** *vb* **dodged; dodg·ing** **1** : to evade usu. by trickery **2** : to move suddenly aside; *also* : to avoid or evade by so doing — **dodg·er** *n*

do·do \ˈdō-dō\ *n, pl* **dodoes** *or* **dodos** [Pg *doudo,* fr. *doudo* silly, stupid] **1** : an extinct heavy flightless bird of the island of Mauritius related to the pigeons and larger than a turkey **2** : one hopelessly behind the times; *also* : a stupid person

doe \ˈdō\ *n, pl* **does** *or* **doe** : an adult female of various mammals (as a deer, rabbit, or kangaroo) of which the male is called *buck*

DOE *abbr* Department of Energy

do·er \ˈdü-ər\ *n* : one that does

does *pres 3d sing of* DO *pl of* DOE

doff \ˈdäf\ *vb* [ME, fr. *don* to do + *of* off] **1** : to take off (the hat) in greeting or as a sign of respect **2** : to rid oneself of

[1]**dog** \ˈdȯg\ *n* **1** : a flesh-eating domestic mammal related to the wolves; *esp* : a male of this animal **2** : a worthless or contemptible person **3** : FELLOW, CHAP ⟨you lucky ~⟩ **4** : a mechanical device for holding something **5** : uncharacteristic or affected stylishness or dignity ⟨put on the ~⟩ **6** *pl* : RUIN ⟨gone to the ~*s*⟩

[2]**dog** *vb* **dogged; dog·ging** **1** : to hunt or track like a hound **2** : to worry as if by pursuit with dogs : PLAGUE

dog·bane \ˈdȯg-ˌbān\ *n* : any of a genus of mostly poisonous herbs with milky juice and often showy flowers

dog·cart \-ˌkärt\ *n* : a light one-horse carriage with two seats back to back

dog·catch·er \-ˌka-chər, -ˌke-\ *n* : a community official assigned to catch and dispose of stray dogs

dog–ear \ˈdȯg-ˌir\ *n* : the turned-down corner of a leaf of a book — **dog–ear** *vb* — **dog–eared** \-ˌird\ *adj*

dog·fight \ˈdȯg-ˌfīt\ *n* : a fight between fighter planes at close range

dog·fish \-ˌfish\ *n* : any of various small usu. bottom-dwelling sharks

dog·ged \ˈdȯ-gəd\ *adj* : stubbornly determined : TENACIOUS — **dog·ged·ly** *adv* — **dog·ged·ness** *n*

dog·ger·el \ˈdȯ-gə-rəl\ *n* : verse that is loosely styled and irregular in measure esp. for comic effect

dog·gie bag *or* **doggy bag** \ˈdȯ-gē-\ *n* : a container for carrying home leftover food from a restaurant meal

[1]**dog·gy** *or* **dog·gie** \ˈdȯ-gē\ *n, pl* **doggies** : a small dog

[2]**dog·gy** *adj* **dog·gi·er; -est** : of or resembling a dog ⟨a ~ odor⟩

dog·house \ˈdȯg-ˌhau̇s\ *n* : a shelter for a dog — **in the doghouse** : in a state of disfavor

do·gie \ˈdō-gē\ *n, chiefly West* : a motherless calf in a range herd

dog·leg \ˈdȯg-ˌleg\ *n* : a sharp bend or angle (as in a road or golf fairway) — **dogleg** *vb*

dog·ma \ˈdȯg-mə\ *n, pl* **dogmas** *also* **dog·ma·ta** \-mə-tə\ [L, fr. Gk, fr. *dokein* to think, have an opinion] **1** : a tenet or code of tenets **2** : a doctrine or body of doctrines formally proclaimed by a church

dog·ma·tism \ˈdȯg-mə-ˌti-zəm\ *n* : positiveness in stating matters of opinion esp. when unwarranted or arrogant — **dog·mat·ic** \dȯg-ˈma-tik\ *adj* — **dog·mat·i·cal·ly** \-ti-k(ə-)lē\ *adv*

do–good·er \ˈdü-ˌgu̇-dər\ *n* : an earnest often naive humanitarian or reformer

dog·tooth violet \ˈdȯg-ˌtüth-\ *n* : any of a genus of small spring-flowering bulbous herbs related to the lilies

dog·trot \ˈdȯg-ˌträt\ *n* : a gentle trot — **dogtrot** *vb*

dog·wood \ˈdȯg-ˌwu̇d\ *n* : any of a genus of trees and shrubs having heads of small flowers often with showy white, pink, or red bracts

doi·ly \ˈdȯi-lē\ *n, pl* **doilies** : a small often decorative mat

do in *vb* **1** : RUIN **2** : KILL **3** : TIRE, EXHAUST ⟨the climb *did* him *in*⟩ **4** : CHEAT

do·ings \ˈdü-iŋz\ *n pl* : GOINGS-ON

do–it–yourself *n* : the activity of doing or making something without professional training or help — **do–it–your·self·er** *n*

dol *abbr* dollar

dol·drums \ˈdōl-drəmz, ˈdäl-\ *n pl* **1** : a spell of listlessness or despondency **2** *often cap* : a part of the ocean near the equator known for calms **3** : a state or period of inactivity, stagnation, or slump

[1]**dole** \ˈdōl\ *n* **1** : a distribution esp. of food, money, or clothing to the needy;

also : something so distributed **2** : a grant of government funds to the unemployed

²dole *vb* **doled; dol·ing** : to give or distribute as a charity — usu. used with *out*

dole·ful \ˈdōl-fəl\ *adj* : full of grief : SAD — **dole·ful·ly** *adv*

dole out *vb* **1** : to give or deliver in small portions **2** : DISH OUT

doll \ˈdäl, ˈdȯl\ *n* **1** : a small figure of a human being used esp. as a child's plaything **2** : a pretty woman **3** : an attractive person — **doll·ish** \ˈdä-lish, ˈdȯ-\ *adj*

dol·lar \ˈdä-lər\ *n* [D or Low G *daler,* fr. G *Taler,* short for *Joachimstaler,* fr. Sankt *Joachimsthal,* Bohemia, where talers were first made] **1** : any of various basic monetary units (as in the U.S. and Canada) — see MONEY table **2** : a coin, note, or token representing one dollar **3** : RINGGIT

dol·lop \ˈdä-ləp\ *n* **1** : LUMP, GLOB **2** : PORTION 1 — **dollop** *vb*

doll up *vb* **1** : to dress elegantly or extravagantly **2** : to make more attractive **3** : to get dolled up

dol·ly \ˈdä-lē\ *n, pl* **dollies** : a small cart or wheeled platform (as for a television or movie camera)

dol·men \ˈdōl-mən, ˈdäl-\ *n* : a prehistoric monument consisting of two or more upright stones supporting a horizontal stone slab

do·lo·mite \ˈdō-lə-ˌmīt, ˈdä-\ *n* : a mineral found in broad layers as a compact limestone

do·lor \ˈdō-lər, ˈdä-\ *n* : mental suffering or anguish : SORROW — **do·lor·ous** *adj* — **do·lor·ous·ly** *adv*

do·lour *chiefly Brit var of* DOLOR

dol·phin \ˈdäl-fən\ *n* **1** : any of various small whales with conical teeth and an elongated beaklike snout **2** : either of two active food fishes of tropical and temperate seas

dolt \ˈdōlt\ *n* : a stupid person — **dolt·ish** \ˈdōl-tish\ *adj* — **dolt·ish·ness** *n*

dom *abbr* **1** domestic **2** dominant **3** dominion

-dom *n suffix* **1** : dignity : office ⟨duke*dom*⟩ **2** : realm : jurisdiction ⟨king*dom*⟩ **3** : state or fact of being ⟨free*dom*⟩ **4** : those having a (specified) office, occupation, interest, or character ⟨official*dom*⟩

do·main \dō-ˈmān\ *n* **1** : complete and absolute ownership of land **2** : land completely owned **3** : a territory over which dominion is exercised **4** : a sphere of knowledge, influence, or activity ⟨the ~ of science⟩ **5** : a subdivision of the Internet made up of computers whose URLs share a characteristic abbreviation (as *com* or *gov*)

domain name *n* : a sequence of characters (as Merriam-Webster.com) that specifies a group of online resources and forms part of its URL

dome \ˈdōm\ *n* **1** : a large hemispherical roof or ceiling **2** : a structure or natural formation that resembles the dome of a building **3** : a roofed sports stadium — **dome** *vb*

¹do·mes·tic \də-ˈmes-tik\ *adj* **1** : living near or about human habitations **2** : TAME, DOMESTICATED **3** : relating and limited to one's own country or the country under consideration **4** : of or relating to the household or the family **5** : devoted to home duties and pleasures **6** : INDIGENOUS 1 ⟨a ~ species⟩ — **do·mes·ti·cal·ly** \-ti-k(ə-)lē\ *adv*

²domestic *n* : a household servant

do·mes·ti·cate \də-ˈmes-ti-ˌkāt\ *vb* **-cat·ed; -cat·ing** : to adapt to life in association with and to the use of humans — **do·mes·ti·ca·tion** \-ˌmes-ti-ˈkā-shən\ *n*

do·mes·tic·i·ty \ˌdō-ˌmes-ˈti-sə-tē, də-\ *n, pl* **-ties** **1** : the quality or state of being domestic or domesticated **2** : domestic activities or life

domestic partner *n* : either member of an unmarried cohabiting couple

domestic violence *n* : the inflicting of injury by one family or household member on another

do·mi·cile \ˈdä-mə-ˌsī(-ə)l, ˈdō-; ˈdä-mə-səl\ *n* : a dwelling place : HOME — **domicile** *vb* — **dom·i·cil·i·ary** \ˌdä-mə-ˈsi-lē-ˌer-ē, ˌdō-\ *adj*

dom·i·nance \ˈdä-mə-nəns\ *n* **1** : AUTHORITY, CONTROL **2** : the property of one of a pair of alleles or traits that suppresses expression of the other when both are present

¹dom·i·nant \-nənt\ *adj* **1** : controlling or prevailing over all others **2** : overlooking from a high position **3** : exhibiting genetic dominance

²dominant *n* : a dominant gene or trait

dom·i·nate \ˈdä-mə-ˌnāt\ *vb* **-nat·ed; -nat·ing** **1** : RULE, CONTROL **2** : to have a commanding position or controlling power over **3** : to rise high above in a position suggesting power to dominate — **dom·i·na·tor** \-ˌnā-tər\ *n*

dom·i·na·tion \ˌdä-mə-ˈnā-shən\ *n* **1** : supremacy or preeminence over another **2** : exercise of mastery, ruling power, or preponderant influence

do·mi·na·trix \ˌdä-mə-ˈnā-triks\ *n, pl* **-tri·ces** \-ˈnā-trə-ˌsēz, -nə-ˈtrī-sēz\ : a woman who dominates her partner in a sadomasochistic encounter; *broadly* : a dominating woman

dom·i·neer \ˌdä-mə-ˈnir\ *vb* **1** : to rule in an arrogant manner **2** : to be overbearing

do·mi·nie *1 usu* ˈdä-mə-nē, *2 usu* ˈdō-\ *n* **1** *chiefly Scot* : SCHOOLMASTER **2** : CLERGYMAN

do·min·ion \də-ˈmin-yən\ *n* **1** : DOMAIN **2** : supreme authority : SOVEREIGNTY **3** *often cap* : a self-governing nation of the Commonwealth

dom·i·no \ˈdä-mə-ˌnō\ *n, pl* **-noes** *or* **-nos** **1** : a long loose hooded cloak usu. worn with a half mask as a masquerade costume **2** : a flat rectangular block used as a piece in a game (**dominoes**)

¹don \ˈdän\ *vb* **donned; don·ning** [ME, fr. *don* to do + *on*] : to put on (as clothes)

²don *n* [Sp, fr. L *dominus* lord, master] **1** : a Spanish nobleman or gentleman —

used as a title prefixed to the Christian name **2** : a head, tutor, or fellow in an English university

do·ña \'dō-nyə\ *n* : a Spanish woman of rank — used as a title prefixed to the Christian name

do·nate \'dō-ˌnāt\ *vb* **do·nat·ed; do·nat·ing 1** : to make a gift of : CONTRIBUTE **2** : to make a donation

do·na·tion \dō-'nā-shən\ *n* **1** : the making of a gift esp. to a charity **2** : a free contribution : GIFT

[1]**done** \'dən\ *past part of* DO

[2]**done** *adj* **1** : doomed to failure, defeat, or death **2** : gone by : OVER ⟨when day is ~⟩ **3** : cooked sufficiently **4** : conformable to social convention

done deal *n* : FAIT ACCOMPLI

dong \'dȯŋ, 'däŋ\ *n* — see MONEY table

don·key \'däŋ-kē, 'dəŋ-\ *n, pl* **donkeys 1** : a sturdy and patient domestic mammal classified with the asses **2** : a stupid or obstinate person

don·ny·brook \'dä-nē-ˌbru̇k\ *n, often cap* [*Donnybrook* Fair, annual Irish event known for its brawls] : an uproarious brawl

do·nor \'dō-nər\ *n* : one that gives, donates, or presents

donut *var of* DOUGHNUT

doo·dad \'dü-ˌdad\ *n* : an often small article whose common name is unknown or forgotten

doo·dle \'dü-dᵊl\ *vb* **doo·dled; doo·dling** : to draw or scribble aimlessly while occupied with something else — **doodle** *n* — **doo·dler** *n*

doom \'düm\ *n* **1** : JUDGMENT; *esp* : a judicial condemnation or sentence **2** : DESTINY **3** : RUIN, DEATH — **doom** *vb*

dooms·day \'dümz-ˌdā\ *n* : JUDGMENT DAY

door \'dōr\ *n* **1** : a barrier by which an entry is closed and opened; *also* : a similar part of a piece of furniture **2** : DOORWAY **3** : a means of access or participation : OPPORTUNITY

door·keep·er \-ˌkē-pər\ *n* : a person who tends a door

door·knob \-ˌnäb\ *n* : a knob that when turned releases a door latch

door·man \-ˌman, -mən\ *n* : a usu. uniformed attendant at the door of a building (as a hotel)

door·mat \-ˌmat\ *n* : a mat placed before or inside a door for wiping dirt from the shoes

door·plate \-ˌplāt\ *n* : a nameplate on a door

door·step \-ˌstep\ *n* : a step or series of steps before an outer door

door·way \-ˌwā\ *n* **1** : the opening that a door closes **2** : DOOR 3

do·pa \'dō-pə\ *n* : a form of an amino acid that is used esp. in the treatment of Parkinson's disease

do·pa·mine \'dō-pə-ˌmēn\ *n* : an organic compound that occurs esp. as a neurotransmitter in the brain

[1]**dope** \'dōp\ *n* **1** : a preparation for giving a desired quality **2** : an illicit, habit-forming, or narcotic drug; *esp* : MARIJUANA **3** : a stupid person **4** : INFORMATION

[2]**dope** *vb* **doped; dop·ing 1** : to treat with dope; *esp* : to give a narcotic to **2** : FIGURE OUT — usu. used with *out* **3** : to take dope — **dop·er** *n*

dop·ey *also* **dopy** \'dō-pē\ *adj* **dop·i·er; -est 1** : dulled by alcohol or a narcotic **2** : SLUGGISH **3** : STUPID — **dop·i·ness** *n*

doping *n* : the use of a substance or technique to illegally improve athletic performance

Dopp·ler effect \'dä-plər-\ *n* : a change in the frequency at which waves (as of sound) reach an observer from a source in motion with respect to the observer

do–rag \'dü-ˌrag\ *n* : a close-fitting usu. stretchable piece of cloth worn to cover the hair

dork \'dȯrk\ *n, informal* : NERD; *also* : JERK 2

dorm \'dȯrm\ *n* : DORMITORY

dor·mant \'dȯr-mənt\ *adj* : INACTIVE; *esp* : not actively growing or functioning ⟨~ buds⟩ — **dor·man·cy** \-mən-sē\ *n*

dor·mer \'dȯr-mər\ *n* [MF *dormeor* dormitory, fr. L *dormitorium,* fr. *dormire* to sleep] : a window built upright in a sloping roof; *also* : the roofed structure containing such a window

dor·mi·to·ry \'dȯr-mə-ˌtȯr-ē\ *n, pl* **-ries 1** : a room for sleeping; *esp* : a large room containing a number of beds **2** : a residence hall providing sleeping rooms

dor·mouse \'dȯr-ˌmau̇s\ *n* : any of numerous Old World rodents that resemble small squirrels

dor·sal \'dȯr-səl\ *adj* : of, relating to, or located near or on the surface of the body that in humans is the back but in most other animals is the upper surface — **dor·sal·ly** *adv*

do·ry \'dȯr-ē\ *n, pl* **dories** : a flat-bottomed boat with high flaring sides and a sharp bow

DOS *abbr* disk operating system

[1]**dose** \'dōs\ *n* [ME, fr. MF, fr. LL *dosis,* fr. Gk, lit., act of giving, fr. *didonai* to give] **1** : a measured quantity (as of medicine) to be taken or administered at one time **2** : the quantity of radiation administered or absorbed — **dos·age** \'dō-sij\ *n*

[2]**dose** *vb* **dosed; dos·ing 1** : to give in doses **2** : to give medicine to

do·sim·e·ter \dō-'si-mə-tər\ *n* : a device for measuring doses of radiations (as X-rays) — **do·sim·e·try** \-mə-trē\ *n*

dos·sier \'dȯs-ˌyā, 'dȯ-sē-ˌā\ *n* [F, bundle of documents labeled on the back, dossier, fr. *dos* back, fr. OF, fr. L *dorsum*] : a file containing detailed records on a particular person or subject

[1]**dot** \'dät\ *n* **1** : a small spot : SPECK **2** : a small round mark **3** : a precise point esp. in time ⟨be here on the ~⟩

[2]**dot** *vb* **dot·ted; dot·ting 1** : to mark with a dot ⟨~ an *i*⟩ **2** : to cover with or as if with dots — **dot·ter** *n*

DOT *abbr* Department of Transportation

dot·age \'dō-tij\ *n* : feebleness of mind esp. in old age : SENILITY

dot·ard \-tərd\ *n* : a person in dotage

dot–com \'dät-ˌkäm\ *n* : a company that markets its products or services usu. exclusively via a website

dote \'dōt\ *vb* **dot·ed; dot·ing** **1** : to exhibit mental decline esp. from old age **2** : to be lavish or excessive in one's attention, affection, or fondness ⟨*doted* on her niece⟩

dot matrix *n* : a rectangular arrangement of dots from which alphanumeric characters can be formed (as by a computer printer)

Dou·ay Version \dü-'ā-\ *n* : an English translation of the Vulgate used by Roman Catholics

[1]**dou·ble** \'də-bəl\ *adj* [ME, fr. AF, fr. L *duplus,* fr. *duo* two + *-plus* multiplied by] **1** : TWOFOLD, DUAL ⟨serving a ~ function⟩ **2** : consisting of two members or parts **3** : being twice as great or as many **4** : folded in two **5** : having more than one whorl of petals ⟨~ roses⟩

[2]**double** *vb* **dou·bled; dou·bling** **1** : to make, be, or become twice as great or as many **2** : to make a call in bridge that increases the trick values and penalties of (an opponent's bid) **3** : FOLD **4** : CLENCH **5** : to be or cause to be bent over **6** : to take the place of another **7** : to hit a double **8** : to turn sharply and suddenly; *esp* : to turn back on one's course

[3]**double** *adv* **1** : DOUBLY **2** : two together ⟨sleep ~⟩

[4]**double** *n* **1** : something twice another in size, strength, speed, quantity, or value **2** : a base hit that enables the batter to reach second base **3** : COUNTERPART, DUPLICATE; *esp* : a person who closely resembles another **4** : UNDERSTUDY, SUBSTITUTE **5** : a sharp turn : REVERSAL **6** : FOLD **7** : a combined bet placed on two different contests **8** *pl* : a game between two pairs of players **9** : an act of doubling in a card game

double bond *n* : a chemical bond in which two atoms in a molecule share two pairs of electrons

double cross *n* : an act of betraying or cheating esp. an associate — **dou·ble–cross** \ˌdə-bəl-'krȯs\ *vb* — **dou·ble–cross·er** *n*

dou·ble–deal·ing \ˌdə-bəl-'dē-liŋ\ *n* : DUPLICITY — **dou·ble–deal·er** \-'dē-lər\ *n* — **double–dealing** *adj*

dou·ble–deck·er \-'de-kər\ *n* : something having two decks, levels, or layers — **dou·ble–deck** \-ˌdek\ *or* **dou·ble–decked** \-ˌdekt\ *adj*

dou·ble–dig·it \ˌdə-bəl-'di-jət\ *adj* : amounting to 10 percent or more

double down *vb* : to become more tenacious, zealous, or resolute

dou·ble en·ten·dre \ˌdüb-əl-äⁿ-'täⁿd, ˌdə-bəl-, -'tänd-rə\ *n, pl* **double entendres** *same or* -'tän-drəz\ [obs. F, lit., double meaning] : a word or expression capable of two interpretations with one usu. risqué

dou·ble·head·er \ˌdə-bəl-'he-dər\ *n* : two games played consecutively on the same day

double helix *n* : a helix or spiral consisting of two strands (as of DNA) in the surface of a cylinder which coil around its axis

dou·ble–hung \ˌdə-bəl-'həŋ\ *adj, of a window* : having an upper and a lower sash that can slide past each other

dou·ble–joint·ed \-'jȯin-təd\ *adj* : having a joint that permits an exceptional degree of freedom of motion of the parts joined ⟨a ~ finger⟩

dou·ble–park \ˌdə-bəl-'pärk\ *vb* : to park a vehicle beside a row of vehicles already parked parallel to the curb

double play *n* : a play in baseball by which two players are put out

double pneumonia *n* : pneumonia affecting both lungs

double standard *n* : a set of principles that applies differently and usu. more rigorously to one group of people or circumstances than to another

dou·blet \'də-blət\ *n* **1** : a man's close-fitting jacket worn in Europe esp. in the 16th century **2** : one of two similar or identical things

dou·ble take \'də-bəl-ˌtāk\ *n* : a delayed reaction to a surprising or significant situation after an initial failure to notice anything unusual

dou·ble–talk \-ˌtȯk\ *n* : language that appears to be meaningful but in fact is a mixture of sense and nonsense

double up *vb* : to share accommodations designed for one

double whammy *n* : a combination of two usu. adverse forces, circumstances, or effects

dou·bloon \ˌdə-'blün\ *n* : a former gold coin of Spain and Spanish America

dou·bly \'də-blē\ *adv* **1** : in a twofold manner **2** : to twice the degree ⟨~ glad⟩

[1]**doubt** \'dau̇t\ *vb* **1** : to be uncertain about **2** : to lack confidence in : DISTRUST **3** : to consider unlikely — **doubt·able** *adj* — **doubt·er** *n*

[2]**doubt** *n* **1** : uncertainty of belief or opinion **2** : a condition causing uncertainty, hesitation, or suspense ⟨the outcome was in ~⟩ **3** : DISTRUST **4** : an inclination not to believe or accept

doubt·ful \'dau̇t-fəl\ *adj* **1** : QUESTIONABLE ⟨~ they knew what happened⟩ **2** : UNDECIDED ⟨the outcome of the election is ~⟩ — **doubt·ful·ly** *adv* — **doubt·ful·ness** *n*

[1]**doubt·less** \'dau̇t-ləs\ *adv* **1** : without doubt **2** : PROBABLY

[2]**doubtless** *adj* : free from doubt : CERTAIN — **doubt·less·ly** *adv*

douche \'düsh\ *n* [F] **1** : a jet of fluid (as water) directed against a part or into a cavity of the body; *also* : a cleansing with a douche **2** : a device for giving douches — **douche** *vb*

dough \'dō\ *n* **1** : a mixture that consists of flour or meal and a liquid (as milk or water) and is stiff enough to knead or roll **2** : something resembling dough esp. in consistency **3** : MONEY — **doughy** \ˈdō-ē\ *adj*

dough·boy \-ˌbȯi\ *n* : an American infantryman esp. in World War I

dough·nut *also* **do·nut** \-(ˌ)nət\ *n* : a small usu. ring-shaped cake fried in fat

dough·ty \ˈdau̇-tē\ *adj* **dough·ti·er; -est** : ABLE, VALIANT ⟨a ~ warrior⟩

Doug·las fir \ˈdə-gləs-\ *n* : a tall evergreen timber tree of the western U.S.

dou·la \ˈdü-lə\ *n* : a woman who provides assistance to a mother before, during, and just after childbirth

do up *vb* **1** : to prepare (as by cleaning) for use **2** : to wrap up **3** : CLOTHE, DECORATE **4** : FASTEN

dour \ˈdau̇(-ə)r, ˈdu̇r\ *adj* [ME, fr. L *durus* hard] **1** : STERN, HARSH **2** : OBSTINATE **3** : SULLEN — **dour·ly** *adv*

douse \ˈdau̇s, ˈdau̇z\ *vb* **doused; dous·ing** **1** : to plunge into water **2** : DRENCH **3** : EXTINGUISH ⟨~ a match⟩

[1]**dove** \ˈdəv\ *n* **1** : any of numerous pigeons; *esp* : a small wild pigeon **2** : an advocate of peace or of a peaceful policy — **dov·ish** \ˈdə-vish\ *adj*

[2]**dove** \ˈdōv\ *past of* DIVE

[1]**dove·tail** \ˈdəv-ˌtāl\ *n* : something that resembles a dove's tail; *esp* : a flaring tenon and a mortise into which it fits tightly

[2]**dovetail** *vb* **1** : to join by means of dovetails **2** : to fit skillfully together to form a whole ⟨our plans ~ nicely⟩

dow·a·ger \ˈdau̇-i-jər\ *n* **1** : a widow owning property or a title from her deceased husband **2** : a dignified elderly woman

dowdy \ˈdau̇-dē\ *adj* **dowd·i·er; -est** : lacking neatness and charm : SHABBY, UNTIDY; *also* : lacking smartness

dow·el \ˈdau̇(-ə)l\ *n* **1** : a pin used for fastening together two pieces of wood **2** : a round rod (as of wood) — **dowel** *vb*

[1]**dow·er** \ˈdau̇(-ə)r\ *n* [ME *dowere,* fr. AF *dower, douaire,* fr. ML *dotarium,* fr. L *dot-, dos* gift, marriage portion] **1** : the part of a deceased husband's real estate which the law gives for life to his widow **2** : DOWRY

[2]**dower** *vb* : to supply with a dower or dowry : ENDOW

dow·itch·er \ˈdau̇-i-chər\ *n* : any of several long-billed wading birds related to the sandpipers

[1]**down** \ˈdau̇n\ *adv* [ME *doun,* fr. OE *dūne,* short for *adūne,* of *dūne,* lit., from (the) hill] **1** : toward or in a lower physical position **2** : to a lying or sitting position **3** : toward or to the ground, floor, or bottom **4** : as a down payment ⟨paid $5 ~⟩ **5** : on paper ⟨put ~ what he says⟩ **6** : in a direction that is the opposite of up **7** : SOUTH **8** : to or in a lower or worse condition or status **9** : from a past time **10** : to or in a state of less activity **11** : into defeat ⟨voted the motion ~⟩

[2]**down** *prep* : down in, on, along, or through : toward the bottom of ⟨fell ~ a hole⟩ ⟨lives ~ the road⟩

[3]**down** *vb* **1** : to go or cause to go or come down ⟨~*ed* a warplane⟩ **2** : DEFEAT **3** : to cause (a football) to be out of play **4** : CONSUME 3 ⟨~*ed* two beers⟩

[4]**down** *adj* **1** : occupying a low position; *esp* : lying on the ground **2** : directed or going downward **3** : being in a state of reduced or low activity **4** : not operating or able to function **5** : DEPRESSED, DEJECTED **6** : SICK ⟨~ with a cold⟩ **7** : FINISHED, DONE **8** : completely mastered ⟨got her lines ~⟩ **9** : being on record ⟨you're ~ for two tickets⟩

[5]**down** *n* **1** : a low or falling period (as in activity, emotional life, or fortunes) **2** : one of a series of attempts to advance a football **3** : a quark with a charge of -⅓ that is one of the constituents of the proton and neutron

[6]**down** *n* : a rolling usu. treeless upland with sparse soil — usu. used in pl.

[7]**down** *n* **1** : a covering of soft fluffy feathers; *also* : such feathers **2** : a downlike covering or material

down·beat \ˈdau̇n-ˌbēt\ *n* : the downward stroke of a conductor indicating the principally accented note of a measure of music; *also* : the first beat of a measure

down·burst \-ˌbərst\ *n* : a powerful downdraft usu. associated with a thunderstorm that is a hazard for low-flying aircraft; *also* : MICROBURST

down·cast \-ˌkast\ *adj* **1** : DEJECTED **2** : directed down ⟨a ~ glance⟩

down·draft \-ˌdraft\ *n* : a downward current of gas (as air)

down·er \ˈdau̇-nər\ *n* **1** : a depressant drug; *esp* : BARBITURATE **2** : someone or something depressing

down·fall \ˈdau̇n-ˌfȯl\ *n* **1** : a sudden fall (as from high rank) **2** : something that causes a downfall — **down·fall·en** \-ˌfȯ-lən\ *adj*

[1]**down·grade** \ˈdau̇n-ˌgrād\ *n* **1** : a downward slope (as of a road) **2** : a decline toward a worse condition

[2]**downgrade** *vb* : to lower in quality, value, extent, or status

down·heart·ed \-ˈhär-təd\ *adj* : DEJECTED

[1]**down·hill** \ˈdau̇n-ˈhil\ *adv* : toward the bottom of a hill — **downhill** \-ˌhil\ *adj*

[2]**down·hill** \-ˌhil\ *n* : the sport of skiing downhill usu. in a race against time

[1]**down·load** \ˈdau̇n-ˌlōd\ *n* : an act or instance of downloading something; *also* : the item downloaded

[2]**download** *vb* : to transfer (data) from a computer to another device — **download·able** \-ˌlō-də-bəl\ *adj*

down payment *n* : a part of the full price paid at the time of purchase or delivery with the balance to be paid later

down·play \ˈdau̇n-ˌplā\ *vb* : DE-EMPHASIZE ⟨~*ed* the allegations⟩

down·pour \ˈdau̇n-ˌpȯr\ *n* : a heavy rain

down·range \-ˈrānj\ *adv* : away from a launching site

[1]**down·right** \-ˌrīt\ *adv* : THOROUGHLY

[2]**downright** *adj* **1** : ABSOLUTE, UTTER ⟨a ~ lie⟩ **2** : PLAIN, BLUNT ⟨a ~ man⟩

down·shift \-ˌshift\ *vb* : to shift an automotive vehicle into a lower gear

down·size \ˌ-ˌsīz\ *vb* : to reduce or undergo reduction in size or numbers
down·spout \-ˌspau̇t\ *n* : a vertical pipe used to drain rainwater from a roof
Down syndrome \ˈdau̇n-\ *or* **Down's syndrome** \ˈdau̇nz-\ *n* : a congenital condition characterized esp. by developmental delays, usu. mild to moderate cognitive impairment, slanting eyes, short stature, broad hands with short fingers, and the presence of an extra chromosome
down·stage \ˈdau̇n-ˈstāj\ *adv or adj* : toward or at the front of a theatrical stage — **down·stage** \-ˌstāj\ *n*
down·stairs \-ˈsterz\ *adv* : on or to a lower floor and esp. the main or ground floor — **down·stairs** \-ˌsterz\ *adj or n*
down·stream \-ˈstrēm\ *adv or adj* : in the direction of flow of a stream
down·stroke \-ˌstrōk\ *n* : a downward stroke
down·swing \-ˌswiŋ\ *n* **1** : a swing downward **2** : DOWNTURN
down–to–earth *adj* : PRACTICAL, REALISTIC
down·town \ˈdau̇n-ˌtau̇n\ *n* : the main business district of a town or city — **downtown** \ˈdau̇n-ˈtau̇n\ *adj or adv*
down·trod·den \ˈdau̇n-ˈträ-d^{ə}n\ *adj* : suffering oppression
down·turn \-ˌtərn\ *n* : a downward turn esp. in economic activity
[1]**down·ward** \ˈdau̇n-wərd\ *or* **down·wards** \-wərdz\ *adv* **1** : from a higher to a lower place or condition **2** : from an earlier time **3** : from an ancestor or predecessor
[2]**downward** *adj* : directed toward or situated in a lower place or condition
down·wind \ˈdau̇n-ˈwind\ *adv or adj* : in the direction that the wind is blowing
downy \ˈdau̇-nē\ *adj* **down·i·er; -est** : resembling or covered with down
downy mildew *n* : any of various parasitic fungi producing whitish masses esp. on the underside of plant leaves; *also* : a plant disease caused by downy mildew
downy woodpecker *n* : a small black-and-white woodpecker of No. America
dow·ry \ˈdau̇(-ə)r-ē\ *n, pl* **dowries** [ME *dowarie,* fr. AF, alter. of *dower, douaire* dower] : the property that a woman brings to her husband in marriage
dowse \ˈdau̇z\ *vb* **dowsed; dows·ing** : to use a divining rod esp. to find water — **dows·er** *n*
dox·ol·o·gy \däk-ˈsä-lə-jē\ *n, pl* **-gies** : a usu. short hymn of praise to God
doy·en \ˈdȯi-ən, ˈdwä-ˌya^{n}\ *n* : the senior or most experienced person in a group
doy·enne \dȯi-ˈyen, dwä-ˈyen\ *n* : a woman who is a doyen
doy·ley *chiefly Brit var of* DOILY
doz *abbr* dozen
doze \ˈdōz\ *vb* **dozed; doz·ing** : to sleep lightly — **doze** *n*
doz·en \ˈdə-z^{ə}n\ *n, pl* **dozens** *or* **dozen** [ME *dozeine,* fr. AF *duzeine,* fr. *duze* twelve, fr. L *duodecim,* fr. *duo* two + *decem* ten] : a group of twelve — **doz·enth** \-z^{ə}nth\ *adj*
[1]**DP** \ˌdē-ˈpē\ *n, pl* **DP's** *or* **DPs** **1** : a displaced person **2** : DOUBLE PLAY
[2]**DP** *abbr* data processing
dpt *abbr* department
DPT *abbr* diphtheria-pertussis-tetanus (vaccines)
dr *abbr* **1** debtor **2** dram **3** drive **4** drum
Dr *abbr* doctor
DR *abbr* **1** dead reckoning **2** dining room
drab \ˈdrab\ *adj* **drab·ber; drab·best** **1** : being of a light olive-brown color **2** : DULL, MONOTONOUS, CHEERLESS — **drab·ly** *adv* — **drab·ness** *n*
drach·ma \ˈdrak-mə\ *n, pl* **drach·mas** *or* **drach·mai** \-ˌmī\ *or* **drach·mae** \-(ˌ)mē\ : the former basic monetary unit of Greece
dra·co·ni·an \drā-ˈkō-nē-ən, drə-\ *adj, often cap* : CRUEL; *also* : SEVERE
[1]**draft** \ˈdraft, ˈdräft\ *n* **1** : the act of drawing or hauling **2** : the act or an instance of drinking or inhaling; *also* : the portion drunk or inhaled in one such act **3** : DOSE, POTION **4** : DELINEATION, PLAN, DESIGN; *also* : a preliminary sketch, outline, or version ⟨a rough ~ of a speech⟩ **5** : the act of drawing (as from a cask); *also* : a portion of liquid so drawn **6** : the depth of water a ship draws esp. when loaded **7** : a system for or act of selecting persons (as for sports teams or compulsory military service); *also* : the persons so selected **8** : an order for the payment of money drawn by one person or bank on another **9** : a heavy demand : STRAIN **10** : a current of air; *also* : a device to regulate air supply (as in a stove) — **on draft** : ready to be drawn from a receptacle ⟨beer *on draft*⟩
[2]**draft** *adj* **1** : used or adapted for drawing loads ⟨~ horses⟩ **2** : being or having been on draft ⟨~ beer⟩
[3]**draft** *vb* **1** : to select usu. on a compulsory basis; *esp* : to conscript for military service **2** : to draw the preliminary sketch, version, or plan of **3** : COMPOSE, PREPARE **4** : to draw off or away
draft·ee \draf-ˈtē, ˈdräf-\ *n* : a person who is drafted
drafts·man \ˈdraft-smən, ˈdräft-\ *n* : a person who draws plans (as for buildings or machinery) — **drafts·man·ly** \-lē\ *adj*
drafty \ˈdraf-tē, ˈdräf-\ *adj* **draft·i·er; -est** : exposed to or abounding in drafts of air ⟨a ~ room⟩
[1]**drag** \ˈdrag\ *n* **1** : a device pulled along under water for detecting or gathering **2** : something (as a harrow or sledge) that is dragged along over a surface **3** : the act or an instance of dragging **4** : something that hinders progress; *also* : something boring ⟨thinks school is a ~⟩ **5** : STREET ⟨the main ~⟩ **6** : clothing typical of one sex worn by a member of the opposite sex
[2]**drag** *vb* **dragged; drag·ging** **1** : HAUL **2** : to move or proceed with slowness or difficulty ⟨*dragged* himself out of bed⟩ ⟨the lecture *dragged* on⟩ **3** : to force into

or out of some situation, condition, or course of action **4** : PROTRACT ⟨~ a story out⟩ **5** : to hang or lag behind **6** : to explore, search, or fish with a drag **7** : to trail along on the ground **8** : DRAW, PUFF ⟨~ on a cigarette⟩ **9** : to move (items on a computer screen) esp. by using a mouse — **drag·ger** *n* — **drag one's feet** *also* **drag one's heels** : to act slowly or with hesitation

drag·net \\-ˌnet\\ *n* **1** : NET, TRAWL **2** : a network of planned actions for pursuing and catching ⟨a police ~⟩

drag·o·man \\ˈdra-gə-mən\\ *n, pl* **-mans** *or* **-men** \\-mən\\ : an interpreter employed esp. in the Near East

drag·on \\ˈdra-gən\\ *n* [ME, fr. AF *dragun,* fr. L *dracon-, draco* serpent, dragon, fr. Gk *drakōn* serpent] : a mythical animal usu. represented as a huge winged scaly reptile with a crested head and large claws

drag·on·fly \\-ˌflī\\ *n* : any of a group of large harmless 4-winged insects that hold the wings horizontal and unfolded in repose

[1]**dra·goon** \\drə-ˈgün, dra-\\ *n* [F *dragon* dragon, dragoon, fr. MF] **1** : a heavily armed mounted soldier **2** : CAVALRYMAN

[2]**dragoon** *vb* : to force or attempt to force into submission : COERCE

drag race *n* : an acceleration contest between vehicles — **drag racer** *n*

drag·ster \\ˈdrag-stər\\ *n* : a usu. high-powered vehicle used in a drag race

drag strip *n* : a site for drag races

[1]**drain** \\ˈdrān\\ *vb* **1** : to draw off or flow off gradually or completely **2** : to exhaust physically or emotionally ⟨~*ed* by the work⟩ **3** : to make or become gradually dry or empty ⟨~ a swamp⟩ **4** : to carry away the surface water of : discharge surface or surplus water **5** : EMPTY, EXHAUST ⟨~*ed* our savings⟩ — **drain·er** *n*

[2]**drain** *n* **1** : a means (as a channel or sewer) of draining **2** : the act of draining **3** : a gradual outflow; *also* : something causing an outflow ⟨a ~ on our savings⟩

drain·age \\ˈdrā-nij\\ *n* **1** : the act or process of draining; *also* : something that is drained off **2** : a means for draining : DRAIN, SEWER **3** : an area drained

drain·pipe \\ˈdrān-ˌpīp\\ *n* : a pipe for drainage

drake \\ˈdrāk\\ *n* : a male duck

[1]**dram** \\ˈdram\\ *n* **1** — see WEIGHT table **2** : FLUID DRAM **3** : a small drink

[2]**dram** \\ˈdräm\\ *n* — see MONEY table

dra·ma \\ˈdrä-mə, ˈdra-\\ *n* [LL, fr. Gk, deed, drama, fr. *dran* to do, act] **1** : a literary composition designed for theatrical presentation; *also* : a production (as a film) with a serious tone or subject **2** : dramatic art, literature, or affairs **3** : a series of events involving conflicting forces — **dra·mat·ic** \\drə-ˈma-tik\\ *adj* — **dra·mat·i·cal·ly** \\-ti-k(ə-)lē\\ *adv* — **dra·ma·tist** \\ˈdra-mə-tist, ˈdrä-\\ *n*

dram·a·ti·sa·tion, dra·ma·tise *Brit var of* DRAMATIZATION, DRAMATIZE

dra·ma·tize \\ˈdra-mə-ˌtīz, ˈdrä-\\ *vb* **-tized; -tiz·ing** **1** : to adapt for or be suitable for theatrical presentation **2** : to present or represent in a dramatic manner — **dram·a·ti·za·tion** \\ˌdra-mə-tə-ˈzā-shən, ˌdrä-\\ *n*

dra·me·dy \\ˈdrä-mə-ˌdē, ˈdra-\\ *n* : a comedy having dramatic moments

drank *past and past part of* DRINK

[1]**drape** \\ˈdrāp\\ *vb* **draped; drap·ing** **1** : to cover or adorn with or as if with folds of cloth ⟨kings *draped* in robes⟩ **2** : to cause to hang or stretch out loosely or carelessly **3** : to arrange or become arranged in flowing lines or folds

[2]**drape** *n* **1** : CURTAIN **2** : arrangement in or of folds **3** : the cut or hang of clothing

drap·er \\ˈdrā-pər\\ *n, chiefly Brit* : a dealer in cloth and sometimes in clothing and dry goods

drap·ery \\ˈdrā-pə-rē\\ *n, pl* **-er·ies** **1** *Brit* : DRY GOODS **2** : a decorative fabric esp. hung in loose folds; *also* : hangings of heavy fabric used as a curtain

dras·tic \\ˈdras-tik\\ *adj* : HARSH, RIGOROUS, SEVERE ⟨~ punishment⟩ — **dras·ti·cal·ly** \\-ti-k(ə-)lē\\ *adv*

draught \\ˈdräft\\, **draughty** \\ˈdräf-tē\\ *chiefly Brit var of* DRAFT, DRAFTY

draughts \\ˈdräfts\\ *n, Brit* : CHECKERS

draughts·man *chiefly Brit var of* DRAFTSMAN

Dra·vid·i·an \\drə-ˈvi-dē-ən\\ *n* : a language family of south Asia that includes the major literary languages of southern India

[1]**draw** \\ˈdrȯ\\ *vb* **drew** \\ˈdrü\\; **drawn** \\ˈdrȯn\\; **draw·ing** **1** : to cause to move toward a force exerted **2** : to cause to go in a certain direction ⟨*drew* him aside⟩ **3** : to move or go steadily or gradually ⟨night ~*s* near⟩ **4** : ATTRACT, ENTICE **5** : PROVOKE, ROUSE ⟨*drew* enemy fire⟩ **6** : INHALE ⟨~ a deep breath⟩ **7** : to bring or pull out ⟨*drew* a gun⟩ **8** : to cause to come out of a container or source ⟨~ blood⟩ ⟨~ water for a bath⟩ **9** : EVISCERATE **10** : to require (a specified depth) to float in **11** : ACCUMULATE, GAIN ⟨~*ing* interest⟩ **12** : to take money from a place of deposit : WITHDRAW **13** : to receive regularly ⟨~ a salary⟩ **14** : to take (cards) from a stack or the dealer **15** : to receive or take at random ⟨~ a winning number⟩ **16** : to bend (a bow) by pulling back the string **17** : WRINKLE, SHRINK **18** : to change shape by or as if by pulling or stretching ⟨a face *drawn* with sorrow⟩ **19** : to leave (a contest) undecided : TIE **20** : DELINEATE, SKETCH **21** : to write out in due form : DRAFT ⟨~ up a will⟩ **22** : FORMULATE ⟨~ comparisons⟩ **23** : INFER ⟨~ a conclusion⟩ **24** : to spread or elongate (metal) by hammering or by pulling through dies **25** : to produce or allow a draft or current of air ⟨the chimney ~*s* well⟩ **26** : to swell out in a wind ⟨all sails ~*ing*⟩— **draw a blank** : to be unable to think of something — **draw the line** *or* **draw a line** : to fix an arbitrary boundary usu. between two things

[2]**draw** *n* **1** : the act, process, or result of drawing **2** : a lot or chance drawn at random **3** : a contest left undecided or deadlocked : TIE **4** : one that draws attention or patronage : ATTRACTION

draw·back \ˈdrȯ-ˌbak\ *n* : DISADVANTAGE 2 ⟨the ~*s* of rural living⟩

draw·bridge \-ˌbrij\ *n* : a bridge made to be raised, lowered, or turned to permit or deny passage

draw·er \ˈdrȯr, ˈdrȯ-ər\ *n* **1** : one that draws **2** *pl* : an undergarment for the lower part of the body **3** : a sliding boxlike compartment (as in a table or desk)

draw·ing \ˈdrȯ-iŋ\ *n* **1** : an act or instance of drawing; *esp* : an occasion when something is decided by drawing lots ⟨tonight's lottery ~⟩ **2** : the act or art of making a figure, plan, or sketch by means of lines **3** : a representation made by drawing : SKETCH

drawing card *n* : DRAW 4

drawing room *n* : a formal reception room

drawl \ˈdrȯl\ *vb* : to speak or utter slowly with vowels greatly prolonged — **drawl** *n*

draw on *vb* : APPROACH ⟨night *draws on*⟩

draw out *vb* **1** : PROLONG **2** : to cause to speak freely

draw·string \ˈdrȯ-ˌstriŋ\ *n* : a string, cord, or tape for use in closing a bag or controlling fullness in garments or curtains

draw up *vb* **1** : to prepare a draft or version of **2** : to pull oneself erect **3** : to bring or come to a stop

dray \ˈdrā\ *n* : a strong low cart for carrying heavy loads

[1]**dread** \ˈdred\ *vb* **1** : to fear greatly **2** : to feel extreme reluctance to meet or face

[2]**dread** *n* : great fear esp. of some harm to come

[3]**dread** *adj* **1** : causing great fear or anxiety ⟨a ~ disease⟩ **2** : inspiring awe

dread·ful \ˈdred-fəl\ *adj* **1** : inspiring dread or awe : FRIGHTENING **2** : extremely distasteful, unpleasant, or shocking ⟨a ~ accident⟩ — **dread·ful·ly** *adv*

dread·locks \ˈdred-ˌläks\ *n pl* : long braids of hair over the entire head

dread·nought \ˈdred-ˌnȯt\ *n* : BATTLESHIP

[1]**dream** \ˈdrēm\ *n* [ME *dreem,* fr. OE *drēam* noise, joy, and ON *draumr* dream] **1** : a series of thoughts, images, or emotions occurring during sleep **2** : a dreamlike vision : DAYDREAM, REVERIE **3** : something notable for its beauty, excellence, or enjoyable quality **4** : IDEAL — **dream·like** \-ˌlīk\ *adj* — **dreamy** *adj*

[2]**dream** \ˈdrēm\ *vb* **dreamed** \ˈdremt, ˈdrēmd\ *or* **dreamt** \ˈdremt\; **dream·ing** **1** : to have a dream of **2** : to indulge in daydreams or fantasies : pass (time) in reverie or inaction **3** : IMAGINE — **dream·er** *n*

dream·boat \ˈdrēm-ˌbōt\ *n, slang* : something highly desirable; *esp* : a very attractive person

dream·land \ˈdrēm-ˌland\ *n* : an unreal delightful country that exists in imagination or in dreams

dream up *vb* : INVENT, CONCOCT

dream·world \-ˌwərld\ *n* : a world of illusion or fantasy

drear \ˈdrir\ *adj* : DREARY

drea·ry \ˈdrir-ē\ *adj* **drea·ri·er; -est** [ME *drery,* fr. OE *drēorig* sad, bloody, fr. *drēor* gore] **1** : DOLEFUL, SAD **2** : DISMAL, GLOOMY — **drea·ri·ly** \-ə-lē\ *adv*

[1]**dredge** \ˈdrej\ *vb* **dredged; dredg·ing** : to gather or search with or as if with a dredge — **dredg·er** *n*

[2]**dredge** *n* : a machine or barge for removing earth or silt

[3]**dredge** *vb* **dredged; dredg·ing** : to coat (food) by sprinkling (as with flour)

dregs \ˈdregz\ *n pl* **1** : SEDIMENT 1 **2** : the most undesirable part ⟨the ~ of humanity⟩

drench \ˈdrench\ *vb* : to wet thoroughly

[1]**dress** \ˈdres\ *vb* [ME, fr. AF *drescer* to direct, put right, fr. VL **directiare,* fr. L *directus* direct] **1** : to make or set straight : ALIGN **2** : to prepare for use; *esp* : BUTCHER **3** : TRIM, EMBELLISH ⟨~ a store window⟩ **4** : to put clothes on : CLOTHE; *also* : to put on or wear formal or fancy clothes **5** : to apply dressings or medicine to ⟨~ a wound⟩ **6** : to arrange (the hair) by combing, brushing, or curling **7** : to apply fertilizer to ⟨~ a field⟩ **8** : SMOOTH, FINISH ⟨~ leather⟩

[2]**dress** *n* **1** : APPAREL, CLOTHING ⟨casual ~⟩ **2** : a garment usu. consisting of a one-piece bodice and skirt — **dress·mak·er** \-ˌmā-kər\ *n* — **dress·mak·ing** \-ˌmā-kiŋ\ *n*

[3]**dress** *adj* : suitable for a formal occasion; *also* : requiring formal dress

dres·sage \drə-ˈsäzh\ *n* [F] : the execution by a trained horse of complex movements in response to barely perceptible signals from its rider

dress down *vb* : to scold severely

[1]**dress·er** \ˈdre-sər\ *n* : a chest of drawers or bureau with a mirror

[2]**dresser** *n* : one that dresses

dress·ing \ˈdre-siŋ\ *n* **1** : the act or process of one who dresses **2** : a sauce for adding to a dish (as a salad) **3** : a seasoned mixture usu. used as stuffing **4** : material used to cover an injury (as a wound)

dressing gown *n* : a loose robe worn esp. while dressing or resting

dressy \ˈdre-sē\ *adj* **dress·i·er; -est** **1** : showy in dress **2** : STYLISH, SMART

drew *past of* DRAW

[1]**drib·ble** \ˈdri-bəl\ *vb* **drib·bled; drib·bling** **1** : to fall or flow in drops : TRICKLE **2** : DROOL **3** : to propel by successive slight taps or bounces

[2]**dribble** *n* **1** : a small trickling stream or flow **2** : a drizzling shower **3** : the dribbling of a ball or puck

drib·let \ˈdri-blət\ *n* **1** : a trifling amount **2** : a drop of liquid

dri·er *or* **dry·er** \ˈdrī-ər\ *n* **1** : a substance that speeds drying (as of paint or ink) **2** *usu dryer* : a device for drying

[1]**drift** \ˈdrift\ *n* **1** : the motion or course of something drifting; *also* : a gradual shift

of position **2 :** a mass of matter (as snow or sand) piled up esp. by wind **3 :** earth, gravel, and rock deposited by a glacier **4 :** a general underlying design or tendency : MEANING ⟨catch my ~⟩

²drift *vb* **1 :** to float or be driven along by or as if by a current of water or air ⟨~*ing* logs⟩ **2 :** to become piled up by wind or water ⟨~*ing* snow⟩

drift·er \ˈdrif-tər\ *n* **:** a person who moves about aimlessly

drift net *n* **:** a fishing net often miles in extent arranged to drift with the tide or current

drift·wood \ˈdrift-ˌwu̇d\ *n* **:** wood drifted or floated by water

¹drill \ˈdril\ *n* **1 :** a tool for boring holes **2 :** the training of soldiers in marching and the handling of arms **3 :** a regularly practiced exercise ⟨a shooting ~⟩

²drill *vb* **1 :** to instruct and exercise by repetition **2 :** to train in or practice military drill **3 :** to bore with a drill ⟨~ a hole⟩ — **drill·er** *n*

³drill *n* **1 :** a shallow furrow or trench in which seed is sown **2 :** an agricultural implement for making furrows and dropping seed into them

⁴drill *n* **:** a firm cotton twilled fabric

drill·mas·ter \ˈdril-ˌmas-tər\ *n* **:** an instructor in military drill

drill press *n* **:** an upright drilling machine in which the drill is pressed to the work usu. by a hand lever

drily *var of* DRYLY

¹drink \ˈdriŋk\ *vb* **drank** \ˈdraŋk\; **drunk** \ˈdrəŋk\ *or* **drank; drink·ing 1 :** to swallow liquid : IMBIBE **2 :** ABSORB **3 :** to take in through the senses ⟨~ in the beautiful scenery⟩ **4 :** to give or join in a toast **5 :** to drink alcoholic beverages esp. to excess — **drink·able** *adj* — **drink·er** *n*

²drink *n* **1 :** BEVERAGE; *also* **:** an alcoholic beverage **2 :** a draft or portion of liquid **3 :** excessive consumption of alcoholic beverages

¹drip \ˈdrip\ *vb* **dripped; drip·ping 1 :** to fall or let fall in drops **2 :** to let fall drops of moisture or liquid ⟨a *dripping* faucet⟩ **3 :** to overflow with or as if with moisture ⟨clothes *dripping* with sweat⟩ ⟨stories *dripping* with irony⟩

²drip *n* **1 :** a falling in drops **2 :** liquid that falls, overflows, or is extruded in drops **3 :** the sound made by or as if by falling drops

¹drive \ˈdrīv\ *vb* **drove** \ˈdrōv\; **driv·en** \ˈdri-vən\; **driv·ing 1 :** to urge, push, or force onward **2 :** to carry through strongly ⟨~ a bargain⟩ **3 :** to set or keep in motion or operation **4 :** to direct the movement or course of **5 :** to convey in a vehicle ⟨*drove* her to school⟩ **6 :** to bring into a specified condition ⟨the noise ~*s* me crazy⟩ **7 :** FORCE, COMPEL ⟨*driven* by hunger to steal⟩ **8 :** to project, inject, or impress forcefully ⟨*drove* the lesson home⟩ **9 :** to produce by opening a way ⟨~ a well⟩ **10 :** to progress with strong momentum ⟨a *driving* rain⟩ **11 :** to propel an object of play (as a golf ball) by a hard blow — **driv·er** *n*

²drive *n* **1 :** a trip in a carriage or automobile **2 :** a driving or collecting of animals ⟨a cattle ~⟩ **3 :** the guiding of logs downstream to a mill **4 :** the act of driving a ball; *also* **:** the flight of a ball **5 :** DRIVEWAY **6 :** a public road for driving (as in a park) **7 :** the state of being hurried and under pressure **8 :** an intensive campaign ⟨membership ~⟩ **9 :** the apparatus by which motion is imparted to a machine **10 :** an offensive or aggressive move : a military attack **11 :** NEED, LONGING ⟨the ~ to succeed⟩ **12 :** dynamic quality **13 :** a device for reading and writing on magnetic media (as magnetic tape or disks)

drive–in \ˈdrī-ˌvin\ *adj* **:** accommodating patrons while they remain in their automobiles — **drive–in** *n*

¹driv·el \ˈdri-vəl\ *vb* **-eled** *or* **-elled; -el·ing** *or* **-el·ling 1 :** DROOL, SLAVER **2 :** to talk or utter stupidly, carelessly, or in an infantile way — **driv·el·er** *n*

²drivel *n* **:** NONSENSE

drive·shaft \ˈdrīv-ˌshaft\ *n* **:** a shaft that transmits mechanical power

drive–through *also* **drive–thru** \ˈdrīv-ˌthrü\ *adj* **:** designed for the service of patrons remaining in their automobiles — **drive–through** *also* **drive–thru** *n*

drive·way \-ˌwā\ *n* **:** a short private road leading from the street to a house, garage, or parking lot

¹driz·zle \ˈdri-zəl\ *n* **:** a fine misty rain

²drizzle *vb* **driz·zled; driz·zling :** to rain in very small drops

drogue \ˈdrōg\ *n* **:** a small parachute for slowing down or stabilizing something (as a space capsule)

droid \ˈdrȯid\ *n* **:** ANDROID

droll \ˈdrōl\ *adj* [F *drôle,* fr. *drôle* scamp, fr. MF *drolle,* fr. MD, imp] **:** having a humorous, whimsical, or odd quality ⟨a ~ expression⟩ — **droll·ery** \ˈdrō-lə-rē\ *n* — **drol·ly** *adv*

drom·e·dary \ˈdrä-mə-ˌder-ē\ *n, pl* **-dar·ies** [ME *dromedarie,* fr. MF *dromedaire,* fr. LL *dromedarius,* fr. L *dromad-, dromas,* fr. Gk, running] **:** CAMEL; *esp* **:** a domesticated one-humped camel of western Asia and northern Africa

¹drone \ˈdrōn\ *n* **1 :** a male honeybee **2 :** one that lives on the labors of others : PARASITE **3 :** an uncrewed aircraft or ship guided by remote control **4 :** one whose work is menial or monotonous

²drone *vb* **droned; dron·ing :** to sound with a low dull monotonous murmuring sound : speak monotonously

³drone *n* **:** a deep monotonous sound ⟨the ~ of engines⟩

drool \ˈdrül\ *vb* **1 :** to let liquid flow from the mouth **2 :** to talk foolishly — **drool** *n*

droop \ˈdrüp\ *vb* **1 :** to hang or incline downward **2 :** to sink gradually **3 :** LANGUISH — **droop** *n* — **droopy** *adj*

¹drop \ˈdräp\ *n* **1 :** the quantity of fluid that falls in one spherical mass **2** *pl* **:** a dose of medicine measured by drops **3** : a small quantity of drink **4** : the smallest practical unit of liquid measure **5** : something (as a pendant or a small round candy) that resembles a liquid drop **6** : FALL **7** : a decline in quantity or quality **8** : a descent by parachute **9** : the distance through which something drops **10** : a slot into which something is to be dropped **11** : something that drops or has dropped

²**drop** *vb* **dropped; drop·ping 1** : to fall or let fall in drops **2** : to let fall : LOWER ⟨~ a glove⟩ ⟨*dropped* his voice⟩ **3** : SEND ⟨~ me a note⟩ **4** : to let go : DISMISS ⟨~ the subject⟩ **5** : MENTION ⟨~ a suggestion⟩ **6** : to knock down : cause to fall **7** : to go lower : become less ⟨prices *dropped*⟩ **8** : SPEND, LOSE ⟨~ $20⟩ ⟨*dropped* ten pounds⟩ **9** : to come or go unexpectedly or informally ⟨a friend *dropped* in⟩ **10** : to pass from one state into a less active one ⟨~ off to sleep⟩ **11** : to move downward or with a current **12** : QUIT ⟨*dropped* out of the race⟩ — **drop back** : to move toward the rear — **drop behind** : to fail to keep up

drop–down \ˈdräp-ˌdau̇n\ *adj* : PULL-DOWN

drop·kick \-ˈkik\ *n* : a kick made by dropping a ball to the ground and kicking it at the moment it starts to rebound — **drop–kick** *vb*

drop·let \ˈdrä-plət\ *n* : a tiny drop

drop–off \ˈdräp-ˌȯf\ *n* **1** : a steep or perpendicular descent **2** : a marked decline ⟨a ~ in attendance⟩ **3** : an act or instance of delivering or depositing something ⟨~ points along the route⟩

drop off *vb* : to fall asleep

drop out *vb* : to withdraw from participation or membership; *esp* : to leave school before graduation — **drop·out** \ˈdräp-ˌau̇t\ *n*

drop·per \ˈdrä-pər\ *n* **1** : one that drops **2** : a short glass tube with a rubber bulb used to measure out liquids by drops

drop·pings *n pl* : MANURE, DUNG

drop·sy \ˈdräp-sē\ *n* [ME *dropesie,* short for *ydropesie,* fr. AF, fr. L *hydropisis,* fr. Gk *hydrōps,* fr. *hydōr* water] : EDEMA — **drop·si·cal** \-si-kəl\ *adj*

drop–top \ˈdräp-ˌtäp\ *n* : CONVERTIBLE

dross \ˈdräs\ *n* **1** : the scum that forms on the surface of a molten metal **2** : waste matter : REFUSE

drought \ˈdrau̇t\ *also* **drouth** \ˈdrau̇th\ *n* : a long spell of dry weather

¹**drove** \ˈdrōv\ *n* **1** : a group of animals driven or moving in a body **2** : a large number : CROWD — usu. used in pl. ⟨tourists arriving in ~*s*⟩

²**drove** *past of* DRIVE

drov·er \ˈdrō-vər\ *n* : one who drives domestic animals usu. to market

drown \ˈdrau̇n\ *vb* **drowned** \ˈdrau̇nd\; **drown·ing 1** : to suffocate by submersion esp. in water **2** : to become drowned **3** : to cover with water **4** : to cause to be muted (as a sound) by a loud noise **5** : OVERPOWER, OVERWHELM

drowse \ˈdrau̇z\ *vb* **drowsed; drows·ing** : DOZE — **drowse** *n*

drowsy \ˈdrau̇-zē\ *adj* **drows·i·er; -est 1** : ready to fall asleep **2** : making one sleepy ⟨~ music⟩ — **drows·i·ly** \-zə-lē\ *adv* — **drows·i·ness** \-zē-nəs\ *n*

drub \ˈdrəb\ *vb* **drubbed; drub·bing 1** : to beat severely **2** : to berate critically **3** : to defeat decisively

drudge \ˈdrəj\ *vb* **drudged; drudg·ing** : to do hard, menial, or monotonous work — **drudge** *n* — **drudg·ery** \ˈdrə-jə-rē\ *n*

¹**drug** \ˈdrəg\ *n* **1** : a substance used as a medicine or in making medicine **2** : a substance (as heroin or marijuana) that can cause addiction, habituation, or a marked change in mental status

²**drug** *vb* **drugged; drug·ging** : to affect with or as if with drugs; *esp* : to stupefy with a narcotic

drug·gist \ˈdrə-gist\ *n* : a dealer in drugs and medicines; *also* : PHARMACIST

drug·store \ˈdrəg-ˌstȯr\ *n* : a retail shop where medicines and miscellaneous articles are sold

dru·id \ˈdrü-əd\ *n, often cap* : one of an ancient Celtic priesthood appearing in Irish, Welsh, and Christian legends as magicians and wizards

¹**drum** \ˈdrəm\ *n* **1** : a percussion instrument usu. consisting of a hollow cylinder with a skin or plastic head stretched over one or both ends that is beaten with the hands or with a stick **2** : the sound of a drum; *also* : a similar sound **3** : a drum-shaped object (as a structure or container)

²**drum** *vb* **drummed; drum·ming 1** : to beat a drum **2** : to sound rhythmically : THROB, BEAT **3** : to summon or enlist by or as if by beating a drum ⟨*drummed* into service⟩ **4** : EXPEL — usu. used with *out* **5** : to drive or force by steady effort ⟨~ the facts into memory⟩ **6** : to strike or tap repeatedly so as to produce rhythmic sounds

drum·beat \ˈdrəm-ˌbēt\ *n* : a stroke on a drum or its sound

drum major *n* : the leader of a marching band

drum ma·jor·ette \-ˌmā-jə-ˈret\ *n* : a girl or woman who leads a marching band; *also* : a baton twirler who accompanies a marching band

drum·mer \ˈdrə-mər\ *n* **1** : one that plays a drum **2** : a traveling salesman

drum·stick \ˈdrəm-ˌstik\ *n* **1** : a stick for beating a drum **2** : the lower segment of a fowl's leg

drum up *vb* **1** : to bring about by persistent effort ⟨*drum up* business⟩ **2** : INVENT, ORIGINATE ⟨*drum up* an excuse⟩

¹**drunk** *past part of* DRINK

²**drunk** \ˈdrəŋk\ *adj* **1** : having the faculties impaired by alcohol ⟨~ drivers⟩ **2** : dominated by an intense feeling ⟨~ with power⟩ **3** : of, relating to, caused by, or characterized by intoxication

³**drunk** *n* **1** : a period of excessive drinking **2** : a drunken person

drunk·ard \ˈdrəŋ-kərd\ *n* : one who is habitually drunk
drunk·en \ˈdrəŋ-kən\ *adj* **1** : DRUNK **2** : given to habitual excessive use of alcohol **3** : of, relating to, or resulting from intoxication ⟨a ~ brawl⟩ **4** : unsteady or lurching as if from intoxication ⟨walked with a ~ shuffle⟩ — **drunk·en·ly** *adv* — **drunk·en·ness** *n*
drupe \ˈdrüp\ *n* : a partly fleshy fruit (as a plum or cherry) having one seed enclosed in a hard inner shell
¹**dry** \ˈdrī\ *adj* **dri·er** \ˈdrī-ər\; **dri·est** \-əst\ **1** : free or freed from water or liquid ⟨~ fruits⟩; *also* : not being in or under water **2** : characterized by lack of water or moisture ⟨~ climate⟩ **3** : lacking freshness : STALE **4** : devoid of natural moisture; *also* : THIRSTY **5** : no longer liquid or sticky ⟨the ink is ~⟩ **6** : not giving milk ⟨a ~ cow⟩ **7** : marked by the absence of alcoholic beverages ⟨a ~ dormitory⟩ **8** : prohibiting the making or distributing of alcoholic beverages **9** : not sweet ⟨~ wine⟩ **10** : solid as opposed to liquid ⟨~ groceries⟩ **11** : containing or employing no liquid **12** : SEVERE; *also* : UNINTERESTING, WEARISOME **13** : not productive ⟨a writer's ~ spell⟩ **14** : marked by a matter-of-fact, ironic, or terse manner of expression ⟨~ humor⟩ — **dri·ly** *or* **dry·ly** *adv* — **dry·ness** *n*
²**dry** *vb* **dried**; **dry·ing** : to make or become dry
³**dry** *n, pl* **drys** : PROHIBITIONIST
dry·ad \ˈdrī-əd, -ˌad\ *n* : WOOD NYMPH
dry cell *n* : a battery whose contents are not spillable
dry–clean \ˈdrī-ˌklēn\ *vb* : to clean (fabrics) chiefly with solvents other than water — **dry cleaning** *n*
dry dock \ˈdrī-ˌdäk\ *n* : a dock that can be kept dry during ship construction or repair
dryer *var of* DRIER
dry farm·ing *n* : farming without irrigation in areas of limited rainfall — **dry–farm** *vb* — **dry farm·er** *n*
dry goods \ˈdrī-ˌgu̇dz\ *n pl* : cloth goods (as fabrics, ribbon, and ready-to-wear clothing)
dry ice *n* : solid carbon dioxide
dry measure *n* : a series of units of capacity for dry commodities — see METRIC SYSTEM table, WEIGHT table
dry rot *n* : decay of timber in which fungi consume the wood's cellulose
dry run *n* : REHEARSAL, TRIAL
dry·wall \ˈdrī-ˌwȯl\ *n* : a wallboard consisting of fiberboard, paper, or felt over a plaster core
Ds *symbol* darmstadtium
DSC *abbr* **1** Distinguished Service Cross **2** doctor of surgical chiropody
DSM *abbr* Distinguished Service Medal
DST *abbr* daylight saving time
DTP *abbr* diphtheria, tetanus, pertussis (vaccines)
d.t.'s \ˌdē-ˈtēz\ *n pl, often cap D&T* : DELIRIUM TREMENS
du·al \ˈdü-əl, ˈdyü-\ *adj* **1** : TWOFOLD, DOUBLE **2** : having a double character or nature — **du·al·ism** \-ə-ˌli-zəm\ *n* — **du·al·i·ty** \dü-ˈa-lə-tē, dyü-\ *n*
du·ath·lon \dü-ˈath-lən, -ˌlän\ *n* : a long-distance race involving running and bicycling — **du·ath·lete** *n*
¹**dub** \ˈdəb\ *vb* **dubbed**; **dub·bing** **1** : to confer knighthood upon **2** : NAME, NICKNAME
²**dub** *n* : a clumsy person : DUFFER
³**dub** *vb* **dubbed**; **dub·bing** : to add (sound effects) to a motion picture or to a radio or television production
du·bi·ety \dü-ˈbī-ə-tē, dyü-\ *n, pl* **-eties** **1** : UNCERTAINTY **2** : a matter of doubt
du·bi·ous \ˈdü-bē-əs, ˈdyü-\ *adj* **1** : UNCERTAIN **2** : QUESTIONABLE ⟨a ~ choice⟩ **3** : feeling doubt : UNDECIDED — **du·bi·ous·ly** *adv* — **du·bi·ous·ness** *n*
dub·ni·um \ˈdüb-nē-əm, ˈdəb-\ *n* : a short-lived radioactive chemical element produced artificially
du·cal \ˈdü-kəl, ˈdyü-\ *adj* : of or relating to a duke or dukedom
duc·at \ˈdə-kət\ *n* : a gold coin formerly used in various European countries
duch·ess \ˈdə-chəs\ *n* **1** : the wife or widow of a duke **2** : a woman holding the rank of duke in her own right
duchy \ˈdə-chē\ *n, pl* **duch·ies** : the territory of a duke or duchess : DUKEDOM
¹**duck** \ˈdək\ *n, pl* **ducks** : any of various swimming birds related to but smaller than geese and swans
²**duck** *vb* **1** : to thrust or plunge under water **2** : to lower the head or body suddenly : BOW; *also* : DODGE **3** : to evade a duty, question, or responsibility
³**duck** *n* **1** : a durable closely woven usu. cotton fabric **2** *pl* : light clothes made of duck
duck·bill \ˈdək-ˌbil\ *n* : PLATYPUS
duck·ling \-liŋ\ *n* : a young duck
duck·pin \-ˌpin\ *n* **1** : a small bowling pin shorter and wider in the middle than a tenpin **2** *pl but sing in constr* : a bowling game using duckpins
duck sauce *n* : a thick sweet sauce made with fruits and seasonings and used in Chinese cuisine
duct \ˈdəkt\ *n* **1** : a tube or canal for conveying a bodily fluid **2** : a pipe or tube through which a fluid (as air) flows — **duct·less** *adj*
duc·tile \ˈdək-tᵊl\ *adj* **1** : capable of being drawn out into wire or thread **2** : easily led : DOCILE — **duc·til·i·ty** \ˌdək-ˈti-lə-tē\ *n*
ductless gland *n* : an endocrine gland
duct tape *n* : a cloth adhesive tape orig. designed for sealing certain ducts and joints — **duct–tape** *vb*
dud \ˈdəd\ *n* **1** *pl* : CLOTHING **2** : one that fails completely; *also* : a bomb or missile that fails to explode
dude \ˈdüd, ˈdyüd\ *n* **1** : DANDY 1 **2** : a city dweller; *esp* : an Easterner in the West **3** : FELLOW, GUY — sometimes used as an informal form of address

dude ranch *n* : a vacation resort offering activities (as horseback riding) typical of western ranches

dud·geon \ˈdə-jən\ *n* : a fit or state of indignation ⟨in high ~⟩

[1]**due** \ˈdü, ˈdyü\ *adj* [ME, fr. AF *deu*, pp. of *dever* to owe, fr. L *debēre*] **1** : owed or owing as a debt **2** : owed or owing as a right ⟨is ~ a fair trial⟩ **3** : APPROPRIATE, FITTING ⟨with all ~ respect⟩ **4** : SUFFICIENT, ADEQUATE **5** : REGULAR, LAWFUL ⟨~ process of law⟩ **6** : ATTRIBUTABLE, ASCRIBABLE ⟨~ to negligence⟩ **7** : PAYABLE ⟨a bill ~ today⟩ **8** : SCHEDULED ⟨~ to arrive soon⟩

[2]**due** *n* **1** : something that rightfully belongs to one ⟨give everyone their ~⟩ **2** : DEBT **3** *pl* : FEES, CHARGES

[3]**due** *adv* : DIRECTLY, EXACTLY ⟨~ north⟩

du·el \ˈdü-əl, ˈdyü-\ *n* : a combat between two persons; *esp* : one fought with weapons in front of witnesses — **duel** *vb* — **du·el·ist** \-ə-list\ *n*

du·en·de \dü-ˈen-dā\ *n* [Sp dial., charm, fr. Sp, ghost, goblin, fr. *duen de casa*, prob. fr. *dueño de casa* owner of a house] : the power to attract through personal magnetism and charm

du·en·na \dü-ˈe-nə, dyü-\ *n* **1** : an elderly woman in charge of the younger ladies in a Spanish or Portuguese family **2** : CHAPERONE

du·et \dü-ˈet, dyü-\ *n* : a musical composition for two performers

due to *prep* : BECAUSE OF

duf·fel bag \ˈdə-fəl-\ *n* : a soft oblong bag for personal belongings

duf·fer \ˈdə-fər\ *n* : an incompetent or clumsy person

dug *past and past part of* DIG

dug·out \ˈdəg-ˌau̇t\ *n* **1** : a boat made by hollowing out a log **2** : a shelter dug in the ground **3** : a low shelter facing a baseball diamond that contains the players' bench

DUI *n* : the act or crime of driving while under the influence of alcohol

duke \ˈdük, ˈdyük\ *n* **1** : a sovereign ruler of a continental European duchy **2** : a nobleman of the highest rank; *esp* : a member of the highest grade of the British peerage **3** *slang* : FIST 1 ⟨put up your ~*s*⟩ — **duke·dom** *n*

dul·cet \ˈdəl-sət\ *adj* **1** : pleasing to the ear **2** : AGREEABLE, SOOTHING

dul·ci·mer \ˈdəl-sə-mər\ *n* **1** : a stringed instrument of trapezoidal shape played with light hammers held in the hands **2** *or* **dul·ci·more** \-ˌmōr\ : an American folk instrument with three or four strings that is held on the lap and played by plucking or strumming

[1]**dull** \ˈdəl\ *adj* **1** : mentally slow : STUPID **2** : slow in perception or sensibility **3** : LISTLESS **4** : slow in action : SLUGGISH ⟨a ~ market⟩ **5** : lacking intensity ⟨a ~ pain⟩; *also* : not resonant or ringing **6** : BLUNT **7** : lacking brilliance or luster ⟨a ~ finish⟩ **8** : low in saturation and lightness ⟨~ color⟩ **9** : CLOUDY, OVERCAST ⟨~ weather⟩ **10** : TEDIOUS, UNINTERESTING ⟨a ~ lecture⟩ — **dull·ness** *also* **dul·ness** *n* — **dul·ly** *adv*

[2]**dull** *vb* : to make or become dull

dull·ard \ˈdə-lərd\ *n* : a stupid person

du·ly \ˈdü-lē, ˈdyü-\ *adv* : in a due manner or time

dumb \ˈdəm\ *adj* **1** *dated, offensive* : lacking the power of speech **2** : SILENT **3** : STUPID — **dumb·ly** *adv*

dumb·bell \ˈdəm-ˌbel\ *n* **1** : a bar with weights at the end used for exercise **2** : one who is stupid

dumb down *vb* : to lower the level of intelligence or intellectual content of

dumb·found *also* **dum·found** \ˌdəm-ˈfau̇nd\ *vb* : ASTONISH, AMAZE — **dumb·found·ing·ly** \-ˈfau̇n-diŋ-lē\ *adv*

dumb·wait·er \ˈdəm-ˌwā-tər\ *n* : a small elevator for conveying food and dishes from one floor to another

dum·my \ˈdə-mē\ *n, pl* **dummies** **1** : a stupid person **2** *dated, offensive* : a person who cannot speak **3** : the exposed hand in bridge played by the declarer in addition to that player's own hand; *also* : a bridge player whose hand is a dummy **4** : an imitative substitute for something; *also* : MANNEQUIN **5** : one seeming to act alone but really acting for another **6** : a mock-up of matter to be reproduced esp. by printing

[1]**dump** \ˈdəmp\ *vb* : to let fall in a pile ⟨~ laundry on the floor⟩; *also* : to get rid of carelessly ⟨~*ed* her boyfriend⟩

[2]**dump** *n* **1** : a place for dumping something (as refuse) **2** : a reserve supply; *also* : a place where such supplies are kept ⟨an ammunition ~⟩ **3** : a messy or objectionable place

dump·ing \ˈdəm-piŋ\ *n* : the selling of goods in quantity at below market price

dump·ling \ˈdəm-pliŋ\ *n* **1** : a small mass of boiled or steamed dough **2** : a dessert of fruit baked in biscuit dough

dumps \ˈdəmps\ *n pl* : a gloomy state of mind : low spirits ⟨in the ~⟩

dump·ster \ˈdəm(p)-stər\ *n, often cap* : a large trash receptacle

dump truck *n* : a truck for transporting and dumping bulk material

dumpy \ˈdəm-pē\ *adj* **dump·i·er; -est** **1** : short and thick in build **2** : SHABBY

[1]**dun** \ˈdən\ *n* : a brownish dark gray

[2]**dun** *vb* **dunned; dun·ning** **1** : to make persistent demands for payment **2** : PLAGUE, PESTER — **dun** *n*

dunce \ˈdəns\ *n* [John *Duns* Scotus, whose once accepted writings were ridiculed in the 16th cent.] : a slow stupid person

dun·der·head \ˈdən-dər-ˌhed\ *n* : DUNCE, BLOCKHEAD

dune \ˈdün, ˈdyün\ *n* : a hill or ridge of sand piled up by the wind

dune buggy *n* : a motor vehicle with oversize tires for use on sand

[1]**dung** \ˈdəŋ\ *n* : MANURE

[2]**dung** *vb* : to fertilize (land) with dung

dun·ga·ree \ˌdəŋ-gə-ˈrē\ *n* **1** : a heavy coarse cotton twill; *esp* : blue denim **2** *pl* : clothes made of blue denim

dun·geon \ˈdən-jən\ *n* [ME *dongeoun* fortress, prison, fr. AF *donjun,* fr. VL **domnion-, *domnio* keep, mastery, fr. L *dominus* lord] : a dark prison commonly underground
dung·hill \ˈdəŋ-ˌhil\ *n* : a manure pile
dunk \ˈdəŋk\ *vb* **1** : to dip or submerge temporarily in liquid **2** : to submerge oneself in water **3** : to shoot a basketball into the basket from above the rim
duo \ˈdü-(ˌ)ō, ˈdyü-\ *n, pl* **du·os** **1** : DUET **2** : PAIR 3
duo·dec·i·mal \ˌdü-ə-ˈde-sə-məl, ˌdyü-\ *adj* : of, relating to, or being a system of numbers with a base of 12
du·o·de·num \ˌdü-ə-ˈdē-nəm, ˌdyü-, dü-ˈä-də-nəm, dyü-\ *n, pl* **-de·na** \-ˈdē-nə, -də-nə\ *or* **-denums** : the first part of the small intestine extending from the stomach to the jejunum — **du·o·de·nal** \-ˈdē-nᵊl, -də-nəl\ *adj*
dup *abbr* **1** duplex **2** duplicate
[1]**dupe** \ˈdüp, ˈdyüp\ *n* : one who is easily deceived or cheated : FOOL
[2]**dupe** *vb* **duped; dup·ing** : to make a dupe of : DECEIVE, FOOL
du·ple \ˈdü-pəl, ˈdyü-\ *adj* : having two beats or a multiple of two beats to the measure ⟨~ time⟩
[1]**du·plex** \ˈdü-ˌpleks, ˈdyü-\ *adj* : DOUBLE
[2]**duplex** *n* : something duplex; *esp* : a 2-family house
[1]**du·pli·cate** \ˈdü-pli-kət, ˈdyü-\ *adj* **1** : consisting of or existing in two corresponding or identical parts or examples **2** : being the same as another
[2]**du·pli·cate** \ˈdü-pli-ˌkāt, ˈdyü-\ *vb* **-cat·ed; -cat·ing** **1** : to make double or twofold **2** : to make a copy of — **du·pli·ca·tion** \ˌdü-pli-ˈkā-shən, ˌdyü-\ *n*
[3]**du·pli·cate** \-kət\ *n* : a thing that exactly resembles another in appearance, pattern, or content : COPY
du·pli·ca·tor \ˈdü-pli-ˌkā-tər, ˈdyü-\ *n* : COPIER
du·plic·i·ty \dụ-ˈpli-sə-tē, dyụ-\ *n, pl* **-ties** : the disguising of true intentions by deceptive words or action — **du·plic·i·tous** \-təs\ *adj* — **du·plic·i·tous·ly** *adv*
du·ra·ble \ˈdụr-ə-bəl, ˈdyụr-\ *adj* : able to exist for a long time without significant deterioration ⟨~ goods⟩ — **du·ra·bil·i·ty** \ˌdụr-ə-ˈbi-lə-tē, ˌdyụr-\ *n*
du·rance \ˈdụr-əns, ˈdyụr-\ *n* : restraint by or as if by physical force ⟨held in ~ vile⟩
du·ra·tion \dụ-ˈrā-shən, dyụ-\ *n* : the time during which something exists or lasts
du·ress \dụ-ˈres, dyụ-\ *n* : compulsion by threat ⟨confession made under ~⟩
dur·ing \ˈdụr-iŋ, ˈdyụr-\ *prep* **1** : THROUGHOUT ⟨swims every day ~ the summer⟩ **2** : at some point in ⟨broke in ~ the night⟩
dusk \ˈdəsk\ *n* **1** : the darker part of twilight esp. at night **2** : partial darkness
dusky \ˈdəs-kē\ *adj* **dusk·i·er; -est** **1** : somewhat dark in color **2** : SHADOWY — **dusk·i·ly** \-kə-lē\ *adv* — **dusk·i·ness** *n*
[1]**dust** \ˈdəst\ *n* **1** : fine particles of matter **2** : the particles into which something disintegrates **3** : something worthless **4** : the surface of the ground — **dust·less** *adj* — **dusty** *adj*
[2]**dust** *vb* **1** : to make free of or remove dust ⟨~ the furniture⟩ **2** : to sprinkle with fine particles ⟨popcorn *~ed* with salt⟩ **3** : to sprinkle in the form of dust **4** : to defeat badly
dust bowl *n* : a region suffering from long droughts and dust storms
dust devil *n* : a small whirlwind containing sand or dust
dust·er \ˈdəs-tər\ *n* **1** : one that removes dust **2** : a dress-length housecoat **3** : one that scatters fine particles; *esp* : a device for applying insecticides to crops
dust·pan \ˈdəst-ˌpan\ *n* : a flat-ended pan for sweepings
dust storm *n* : a violent wind carrying dust across a dry region
dutch \ˈdəch\ *adv, often cap* : with each person paying his or her own way ⟨go ~⟩
Dutch \ˈdəch\ *n* **1 Dutch** *pl* : the people of the Netherlands **2** : the language of the Netherlands — **Dutch** *adj* — **Dutch·man** \-mən\ *n*
Dutch elm disease *n* : a fungus disease of elms characterized by yellowing of the foliage, defoliation, and death
dutch treat *n, often cap D* : an entertainment (as a meal) for which each person pays his or her own way — **dutch treat** *adv, often cap D*
du·te·ous \ˈdü-tē-əs, ˈdyü-\ *adj* : DUTIFUL, OBEDIENT
du·ti·able \ˈdü-tē-ə-bəl, ˈdyü-\ *adj* : subject to a duty ⟨~ imports⟩
du·ti·ful \ˈdü-ti-fəl, ˈdyü-\ *adj* **1** : motivated by a sense of duty ⟨a ~ son⟩ **2** : coming from or showing a sense of duty ⟨~ affection⟩ — **du·ti·ful·ly** *adv* — **du·ti·ful·ness** *n*
du·ty \ˈdü-tē, ˈdyü-\ *n, pl* **duties** **1** : conduct or action required by one's occupation or position **2** : assigned service or business; *esp* : active military service **3** : a moral or legal obligation **4** : TAX **5** : the service required (as of a machine) : USE ⟨a heavy-*duty* tire⟩
DV *abbr* **1** L *Deo volente* God willing **2** Douay Version
DVD \ˌdē-ˌvē-ˈdē\ *n* [*d*igital *v*ideo *d*isc] : a high-capacity optical disk format; *also* : an optical disk using such a format
DVM *abbr* doctor of veterinary medicine
DVR \ˌdē-ˌvē-ˈär\ *n* [*d*igital *v*ideo *r*ecorder] : a device that records and plays back television programs
[1]**dwarf** \ˈdwȯrf\ *n, pl* **dwarfs** \ˈdwȯrfs\ *also* **dwarves** \ˈdwȯrvz\ **1** *sometimes offensive* : a person of unusually small stature **2** : an animal or plant that is much below normal size **3** : a small legendary humanlike being **4** : a celestial object of relatively small mass or size — **dwarf·ish** *adj* — **dwarf·ism** \ˈdwȯr-ˌfi-zəm\ *n*
[2]**dwarf** *vb* **1** : to restrict the growth or development of : STUNT **2** : to cause to appear smaller ⟨*dwarfed* by comparison⟩
dwarf planet *n* : a spherical celestial body

that orbits the sun but is too small to disturb other objects from its orbit

dwell \'dwel\ *vb* **dwelt** \'dwelt\ *or* **dwelled** \'dweld, 'dwelt\; **dwell·ing** [ME, fr. OE *dwellan* to go astray, hinder] **1** : ABIDE, REMAIN **2** : RESIDE, EXIST **3** : to keep the attention directed **4** : to write or speak insistently — used with *on* or *upon* — **dwell·er** *n*

dwell·ing \'dwe-liŋ\ *n* : RESIDENCE

DWI \ˌdē-ˌdəb-əl-(ˌ)yü-'ī\ *n* [*d*riving *w*hile *i*ntoxicated] : DUI

dwin·dle \'dwin-dᵊl\ *vb* **dwin·dled; dwin·dling** : to make or become steadily less : DIMINISH

dwt *abbr* pennyweight

Dy *symbol* dysprosium

dyb·buk \'di-bək\ *n, pl* **dyb·bu·kim** \ˌdi-bu̇-'kēm\ *also* **dybbuks** : a wandering soul believed in Jewish folklore to enter and possess a person

[1]**dye** \'dī\ *n* **1** : color produced by dyeing **2** : material used for coloring or staining

[2]**dye** *vb* **dyed; dye·ing** **1** : to impart a new color to esp. by impregnating with a dye **2** : to take up or impart color in dyeing — **dy·er** \'dī(-ə)r\ *n*

dye·stuff \'dī-ˌstəf\ *n* : DYE 2

dying *pres part of* DIE

dyke *chiefly Brit var of* DIKE

dy·nam·ic \dī-'na-mik\ *also* **dy·nam·i·cal** \-mi-kəl\ *adj* : of or relating to physical force producing motion : ENERGETIC, FORCEFUL

[1]**dy·na·mite** \'dī-nə-ˌmīt\ *n* : an explosive made of nitroglycerin absorbed in a porous material; *also* : an explosive made without nitroglycerin

[2]**dynamite** *vb* **-mit·ed; -mit·ing** : to blow up with dynamite

[3]**dynamite** *adj* : TERRIFIC, WONDERFUL

dy·na·mo \'dī-nə-ˌmō\ *n, pl* **-mos** **1** : an electrical generator **2** : a forceful energetic individual

dy·na·mom·e·ter \ˌdī-nə-'mä-mə-tər\ *n* : an instrument for measuring mechanical power (as of an engine)

dy·nas·ty \'dī-nəs-tē, -ˌnas-\ *n, pl* **-ties** **1** : a succession of rulers of the same family **2** : a powerful group or family that maintains its position for a long time — **dy·nas·tic** \dī-'nas-tik\ *adj*

dys·en·tery \'di-sᵊn-ˌter-ē\ *n, pl* **-ter·ies** : a disease marked by diarrhea with blood and mucus in the feces; *also* : DIARRHEA

dys·func·tion *also* **dis·func·tion** \dis-'fəŋk-shən\ *n* **1** : impaired or abnormal functioning ⟨liver ~⟩ **2** : abnormal or unhealthy behavior within a group ⟨family ~⟩ — **dys·func·tion·al** \-shə-nəl\ *adj*

dys·lex·ia \dis-'lek-sē-ə\ *n* : a learning disability marked by difficulty in reading, writing, and spelling — **dys·lex·ic** \-sik\ *adj or n*

dys·pep·sia \dis-'pep-shə, -sē-ə\ *n* : INDIGESTION — **dys·pep·tic** \-'pep-tik\ *adj or n*

dys·pla·sia \dis-'plā-zh(ē-)ə\ *n* : abnormal growth or development

dys·pro·si·um \dis-'prō-zē-əm\ *n* : a metallic chemical element that forms highly magnetic compounds

dys·to·pia \dis-'tō)-pē-ə\ *n* **1** : an imagined world in which people lead wretched fearful lives **2** : a work describing a dystopia — **dys·to·pi·an** \-ən\ *adj*

dys·tro·phy \'dis-trə-fē\ *n, pl* **-phies** : a disorder involving atrophy of muscular tissue; *esp* : MUSCULAR DYSTROPHY

dz *abbr* dozen

E

[1]**e** \'ē\ *n, pl* **e's** *or* **es** \'ēz\ *often cap* **1** : the 5th letter of the English alphabet **2** : the base of the system of natural logarithms having the approximate value 2.71828 **3** : a grade rating a student's work as poor or failing

[2]**e** *abbr, often cap* **1** east; eastern **2** error **3** excellent

e- *comb form* : electronic ⟨*e*-commerce⟩

ea *abbr* each

[1]**each** \'ēch\ *adj* : being one of the class named ⟨~ player⟩

[2]**each** *pron* : every individual one

[3]**each** *adv* : APIECE ⟨cost five cents ~⟩

each other *pron* : each of two or more in reciprocal action or relation ⟨looked at *each other*⟩

ea·ger \'ē-gər\ *adj* : marked by urgent or enthusiastic desire or interest ⟨~ to learn⟩ ♦ ***Synonyms*** AVID, ANXIOUS, ARDENT, KEEN — **ea·ger·ly** *adv* — **ea·ger·ness** *n*

[1]**ea·gle** \'ē-gəl\ *n* **1** : a large bird of prey related to the hawks **2** : a score of two under par on a hole in golf

[2]**eagle** *vb* **ea·gled; ea·gling** : to score an eagle on a golf hole

ea·glet \'ē-glət\ *n* : a young eagle

-ean — see -AN

E and OE *abbr* errors and omissions excepted

[1]**ear** \'ir\ *n* **1** : the organ of hearing; *also* : the outer part of this in a vertebrate **2** : something resembling a mammal's ear in shape, position, or function **3** : an ability to understand and appreciate something heard ⟨a good ~ for music⟩ **4** : sympathetic attention

[2]**ear** *n* : the fruiting spike of a cereal (as wheat or corn)

ear·ache \-ˌāk\ *n* : an ache or pain in the ear

ear·drum \-ˌdrəm\ *n* : a thin membrane that receives and transmits sound waves in the ear

eared \'ird\ *adj* : having ears esp. of a

specified kind or number ⟨a long-*eared* dog⟩

ear·ful \ˈir-ˌfu̇l\ *n* : a verbal outpouring (as of news, gossip, or complaint)

earl \ˈərl\ *n* [ME *erl,* fr. OE *eorl* warrior, nobleman] : a member of the British peerage ranking below a marquess and above a viscount — **earl·dom** \-dəm\ *n*

ear·lobe \ˈir-ˌlōb\ *n* : the pendent part of the ear

[1]**ear·ly** \ˈər-lē\ *adv* **ear·li·er; -est** : at an early time (as in a period or series)

[2]**early** *adj* **ear·li·er; -est 1** : of, relating to, or occurring near the beginning **2** : ANCIENT, PRIMITIVE ⟨~ tools⟩ **3** : occurring before the usual time ⟨an ~ breakfast⟩; *also* : occurring in the near future

[1]**ear·mark** \ˈir-ˌmärk\ *n* : an identification mark (as on the ear of an animal); *also* : a distinguishing mark ⟨~*s* of poverty⟩

[2]**earmark** *vb* **1** : to mark with an earmark **2** : to designate for a specific purpose ⟨money ~*ed* for education⟩

ear·muff \-ˌməf\ *n* : one of a pair of ear coverings worn to protect against cold

earn \ˈərn\ *vb* **1** : to receive as a return for service **2** : DESERVE, MERIT ♦ ***Synonyms*** GAIN, SECURE, GET, OBTAIN, ACQUIRE, WIN — **earn·er** *n*

earned run *n* : a run in baseball that scores without benefit of an error before the fielding team has had a chance to make the third putout of the inning

earned run average *n* : the average number of earned runs per game scored against a pitcher in baseball

[1]**ear·nest** \ˈər-nəst\ *n* : an intensely serious state of mind ⟨spoke in ~⟩

[2]**earnest** *adj* **1** : seriously intent and sober ⟨an ~ face⟩ ⟨an ~ attempt⟩ **2** : GRAVE, IMPORTANT ♦ ***Synonyms*** SOLEMN, SEDATE, STAID — **ear·nest·ly** *adv* — **ear·nest·ness** *n*

[3]**earnest** *n* **1** : something of value given by a buyer to a seller to bind a bargain **2** : PLEDGE

earn·ings \ˈər-niŋz\ *n pl* **1** : something (as wages) earned **2** : the balance of revenue after deduction of costs and expenses

ear·phone \ˈir-ˌfōn\ *n* : a device that reproduces sound and is worn over or in the ear

ear·piece \-ˌpēs\ *n* : a part of an instrument which is placed against or in the ear; *esp* : EARPHONE

ear·plug \-ˌpləg\ *n* : a protective device for insertion into the opening of the ear

ear·ring \-ˌriŋ\ *n* : an ornament for the earlobe

ear·shot \-ˌshät\ *n* : range of hearing

ear·split·ting \-ˌspli-tiŋ\ *adj* : intolerably loud or shrill

earth \ˈərth\ *n* **1** : SOIL, DIRT **2** : LAND, GROUND **3** *often cap* : the planet on which we live that is 3d in order from the sun

earth·en \ˈər-thən\ *adj* : made of earth or baked clay

earth·en·ware \-ˌwer\ *n* : slightly porous opaque pottery fired at low heat

earth·ling \ˈərth-liŋ\ *n* : an inhabitant of the earth

earth·ly \ˈərth-lē\ *adj* : having to do with the earth esp. as distinguished from heaven — **earth·li·ness** *n*

earth·quake \-ˌkwāk\ *n* : a shaking or trembling of a portion of the earth

earth science *n* : any of the sciences (as geology or meteorology) that deal with the earth or one of its parts

earth·shak·ing \ˈərth-ˌshā-kiŋ\ *adj* : of great importance : MOMENTOUS

earth·ward \-wərd\ *also* **earth·wards** \-wərdz\ *adv* : toward the earth

earth·work \ˈərth-ˌwərk\ *n* : an embankment or fortification of earth

earth·worm \-ˌwərm\ *n* : a long segmented worm found in damp soil

earthy \ˈər-thē\ *adj* **earth·i·er; -est 1** : of, relating to, or consisting of earth; *also* : suggesting earth ⟨~ flavors⟩ **2** : PRACTICAL 4 **3** : COARSE, GROSS ⟨~ humor⟩ — **earth·i·ness** *n*

ear·wax \ˈir-ˌwaks\ *n* : the yellow waxy secretion from the ear

ear·wig \-ˌwig\ *n* : any of numerous insects with slender antennae and a pair of appendages resembling forceps at the end of the body

[1]**ease** \ˈēz\ *n* **1** : comfort of body or mind **2** : naturalness of manner **3** : freedom from difficulty or effort ♦ ***Synonyms*** RELAXATION, REST, REPOSE, LEISURE

[2]**ease** *vb* **eased; eas·ing 1** : to relieve from distress **2** : to lessen the pressure or tension of **3** : to make or become less difficult ⟨~ credit⟩

ea·sel \ˈē-zəl\ *n* [D *ezel,* lit., ass] : a frame for supporting something (as an artist's canvas)

[1]**east** \ˈēst\ *adv* : to or toward the east

[2]**east** *adj* **1** : situated toward or at the east ⟨an ~ window⟩ **2** : coming from the east ⟨an ~ wind⟩

[3]**east** *n* **1** : the general direction of sunrise **2** : the compass point directly opposite to west **3** *cap* : regions or countries east of a specified or implied point — **east·er·ly** \ˈē-stər-lē\ *adv or adj* — **east·ward** *adv or adj* — **east·wards** *adv*

Eas·ter \ˈē-stər\ *n* : a church feast observed on a Sunday in March or April in commemoration of Christ's resurrection

east·ern \ˈē-stərn\ *adj* **1** *often cap* : of, relating to, or characteristic of a region designated East **2** *cap* : of, relating to, or being the Christian churches originating in the Church of the Eastern Roman Empire **3** : lying toward or coming from the east — **East·ern·er** *n*

easy \ˈē-zē\ *adj* **eas·i·er; -est 1** : marked by ease ⟨an ~ life⟩; *esp* : not causing distress or difficulty ⟨~ tasks⟩ **2** : MILD, LENIENT ⟨be ~ on him⟩ **3** : GRADUAL ⟨an ~ slope⟩ **4** : LEISURELY ⟨an ~ pace⟩ **5** : free from pain, trouble, or worry **6** : COMFORTABLE ⟨an ~ chair⟩ **7** : showing ease : NATURAL ⟨an ~ manner⟩ — **eas·i·ly** \ˈē-zə-lē\ *adv* — **eas·i·ness** \-zē-nəs\ *n*

easy·go·ing \ˌē-zē-ˈgō-iŋ\ *adj* : relaxed and casual in style or manner

eat \ˈēt\ *vb* **ate** \ˈāt\; **eat·en** \ˈēt-ᵊn\; **eat·ing** 1 : to take in as food : take food 2 : to use up : DEVOUR 3 : CORRODE — **eat·able** *adj or n* — **eat·er** *n*

eat·ery \ˈē-tə-rē\ *n, pl* **-er·ies** : LUNCHEONETTE, RESTAURANT

eaves \ˈēvz\ *n pl* : the overhanging lower edge of a roof

eaves·drop \ˈēvz-ˌdräp\ *vb* : to listen secretly — **eaves·drop·per** *n*

[1]**ebb** \ˈeb\ *n* 1 : the flowing back from shore of water brought in by the tide 2 : a point or state of decline

[2]**ebb** *vb* 1 : to recede from the flood 2 : DECLINE ⟨his fortunes ~*ed*⟩

EBCDIC \ˈeb-sə-ˌdik\ *n* [*e*xtended *b*inary *c*oded *d*ecimal *i*nterchange *c*ode] : a computer code for representing alphanumeric information

Ebo·la \ē-ˈbō-lə\ *n* : an often fatal hemorrhagic fever caused by a virus (**Ebola virus**) of African origin

[1]**eb·o·ny** \ˈe-bə-nē\ *n, pl* **-nies** : a hard heavy blackish wood of various tropical trees related to the persimmon

[2]**ebony** *adj* 1 : made of or resembling ebony 2 : BLACK, DARK

e–book \ˈē-ˌbu̇k\ *n* : a book in digital form for display on a computer screen or a handheld device

ebul·lient \i-ˈbu̇l-yənt, -ˈbəl-\ *adj* 1 : BOILING, AGITATED 2 : EXUBERANT — **ebul·lience** \-yəns\ *n*

EC *abbr* European Community

ec·cen·tric \ik-ˈsen-trik\ *adj* 1 : deviating from a usual or accepted pattern 2 : deviating from a circular path ⟨~ orbits⟩ 3 : set with axis or support off center ⟨an ~ cam⟩; *also* : being off center ♦ ***Synonyms*** ERRATIC, SINGULAR, CURIOUS, ODD — **eccentric** *n* — **ec·cen·tri·cal·ly** \-tri-k(ə-)lē\ *adv* — **ec·cen·tric·i·ty** \ˌek-ˌsen-ˈtri-sə-tē\ *n*

Eccles *abbr* Ecclesiastes

Ec·cle·si·as·tes \i-ˌklē-zē-ˈas-tēz\ *n* — see BIBLE table

ec·cle·si·as·tic \i-ˌklē-zē-ˈas-tik\ *n* : CLERGYMAN

ec·cle·si·as·ti·cal \-ti-kəl\ *or* **ec·cle·si·as·tic** \-tik\ *adj* : of or relating to a church esp. as an institution ⟨~ art⟩ — **ec·cle·si·as·ti·cal·ly** \-ti-k(ə-)lē\ *adv*

Ec·cle·si·as·ti·cus \i-ˌklē-zē-ˈas-ti-kəs\ *n* — see BIBLE table

Ecclus *abbr* Ecclesiasticus

ECG *abbr* electrocardiogram

ech·e·lon \ˈe-shə-ˌlän\ *n* [F *échelon,* lit., rung of a ladder] 1 : a steplike arrangement (as of troops or airplanes) 2 : a level (as of authority or responsibility) within an organization

ech·i·na·cea \ˌe-ki-ˈnā-sē-ə, -shə\ *n* : the dried root of three composite herbs that is used primarily in herbal remedies to boost the immune system; *also* : any of these herbs

echi·no·derm \i-ˈkī-nə-ˌdərm\ *n* : any of a phylum of marine animals (as starfishes and sea urchins) having similar body parts (as the arms of a starfish) arranged around a central axis and often having a calcium-containing outer skeleton

echo \ˈe-kō\ *n, pl* **ech·oes** *also* **ech·os** : repetition of a sound caused by a reflection of the sound waves; *also* : the reflection of a radar signal by an object — **echo** *vb* — **echo·ic** \e-ˈkō-ik\ *adj*

echo·lo·ca·tion \ˌe-kō-lō-ˈkā-shən\ *n* : a process for locating distant or invisible objects by sound waves reflected back to the sender (as a bat) from the objects

echt \ˈekt\ *adj* [G] : TRUE, GENUINE ⟨an ~ New Yorker⟩

éclair \ā-ˈkler\ *n* [F, lit., lightning] : an oblong shell of light pastry with whipped cream or custard filling

e–cig·a·rette \ˈē-ˌsi-gə-ˈret, -ˈsi-gə-ˌret\ *n* : ELECTRONIC CIGARETTE

éclat \ā-ˈklä\ *n* [F] 1 : a dazzling effect or success 2 : ACCLAIM

eclec·tic \e-ˈklek-tik\ *adj* : selecting or made up of what seems best of varied sources — **eclectic** *n* — **eclec·ti·cism** \-ˈklek-tə-ˌsi-zəm\ *n*

[1]**eclipse** \i-ˈklips\ *n* 1 : the total or partial obscuring of one heavenly body by another; *also* : a passing into the shadow of a heavenly body 2 : a falling into obscurity or decline ⟨a career in ~⟩

[2]**eclipse** *vb* **eclipsed; eclips·ing** : to cause an eclipse of; *also* : SURPASS

eclip·tic \i-ˈklip-tik\ *n* : the great circle of the celestial sphere that is the apparent path of the sun

ec·logue \ˈek-ˌlȯg, -ˌläg\ *n* : a pastoral poem

ECM *abbr* European Common Market

ecol *abbr* ecological; ecology

E. coli \ˌē-ˈkō-ˌlī\ *n, pl* **E. coli** : a rod-shaped bacterium that sometimes causes intestinal illness

ecol·o·gy \i-ˈkä-lə-jē, e-\ *n, pl* **-gies** [G *Ökologie,* fr. Gk *oikos* house + *logos* word] 1 : a branch of science concerned with the relationships between organisms and their environment 2 : the pattern of relations between one or more organisms and the environment — **eco·log·i·cal** \ˌē-kə-ˈlä-ji-kəl, ˌe-\ *also* **eco·log·ic** \-jik\ *adj* — **eco·log·i·cal·ly** \-ji-k(ə-)lē\ *adv* — **ecol·o·gist** \i-ˈkä-lə-jist, e-\ *n*

e–com·merce \ˈē-ˌkä-(ˌ)mərs\ *n* : commerce conducted via the Internet

econ *abbr* economics; economist; economy

eco·nom·ic \ˌe-kə-ˈnä-mik, ˌē-\ *adj* : of or relating to the production, distribution, and consumption of goods and services

eco·nom·i·cal \-ˈnä-mi-kəl\ *adj* 1 : THRIFTY 2 : operating with little waste or at a saving ♦ ***Synonyms*** FRUGAL, SPARING, PROVIDENT — **ec·o·nom·i·cal·ly** \-k(ə-)lē\ *adv*

eco·nom·ics \ˌe-kə-ˈnä-miks, ˌē-\ *n sing or pl* : a social science dealing with the production, distribution, and consumption of goods and services — **econ·o·mist** \i-ˈkä-nə-mist\ *n*

econ·o·mise *Brit var of* ECONOMIZE

econ·o·mize \i-ˈkä-nə-ˌmīz\ *vb* **-mized;**

-miz·ing : to practice economy : be frugal — **econ·o·miz·er** *n*

[1]**econ·o·my** \i-ˈkä-nə-mē\ *n, pl* **-mies** [MF *yconomie,* fr. ML *oeconomia,* fr. Gk *oikonomia,* fr. *oikonomos* household manager, fr. *oikos* house + *nemein* to manage] **1** : thrifty and efficient use of resources; *also* : an instance of this **2** : manner of arrangement or functioning : ORGANIZATION **3** : an economic system ⟨a money ~⟩

[2]**economy** *adj* : ECONOMICAL ⟨~ cars⟩

eco·sys·tem \ˈē-kō-ˌsis-təm, ˈe-\ *n* : the complex of an ecological community and its environment functioning as a unit in nature

eco·tour·ism \ˌē-kō-ˈtu̇r-ˌi-zəm, ˌe-\ *n* : the touring of natural habitats in a manner meant to minimize ecological impact — **eco·tour·ist** \-ˈtu̇r-ist\ *n*

ecru \ˈe-krü, ˈā-\ *n* [F *écru,* lit., unbleached] : BEIGE — **ecru** *adj*

ec·sta·sy \ˈek-stə-sē\ *n, pl* **-sies** **1** : extreme and usu. rapturous emotional excitement **2** *often cap* : an illicit drug with hallucinogenic properties that is chemically related to amphetamine — **ec·stat·ic** \ek-ˈsta-tik, ik-\ *adj* — **ec·stat·i·cal·ly** \-ti-k(ə-)lē\ *adv*

Ecua *abbr* Ecuador

ec·u·men·i·cal \ˌe-kyu̇-ˈme-ni-kəl\ *adj* **1** : general in extent or influence **2** : promoting or tending toward worldwide Christian unity — **ec·u·men·i·cal·ly** \-k(ə-)lē\ *adv*

ec·ze·ma \ig-ˈzē-mə, ˈeg-zə-mə, ˈek-sə-\ *n* : an itching skin inflammation with oozing and then crusted lesions — **ec·zem·a·tous** \ig-ˈze-mə-təs\ *adj*

ed *abbr* **1** edited; edition; editor **2** education

[1]**-ed** \d *after a vowel or* b, g, j, l, m, n, ŋ, r, th, v, z, zh; əd, id *after* d, t; t *after other sounds*\ *vb suffix or adj suffix* **1** — used to form the past participle of regular weak verbs ⟨end*ed*⟩ ⟨fad*ed*⟩ ⟨tri*ed*⟩ ⟨patt*ed*⟩ **2** : having : characterized by ⟨cultur*ed*⟩ ⟨2-legg*ed*⟩; *also* : having the characteristics of ⟨bigot*ed*⟩

[2]**-ed** *vb suffix* — used to form the past tense of regular weak verbs ⟨judg*ed*⟩ ⟨deni*ed*⟩ ⟨dropp*ed*⟩

Edam \ˈē-dəm, -ˌdam\ *n* : a yellow Dutch pressed cheese made in balls

ed·a·ma·me \ˌe-də-ˈmä-mā\ *n* [Jp, fr. *eda* branch + *mame* beans] : immature green soybeans usu. in the pod

ed·dy \ˈe-dē\ *n, pl* **eddies** : WHIRLPOOL — **eddy** *vb*

edel·weiss \ˈā-dᵊl-ˌwīs, -ˌvīs\ *n* [G, fr. *edel* noble + *weiss* white] : a small perennial woolly composite herb that grows high in the Alps

ede·ma \i-ˈdē-mə\ *n* : abnormal accumulation of watery fluid in connective tissue or in a serous cavity — **edem·a·tous** \-ˈde-mə-təs\ *adj*

Eden \ˈē-dᵊn\ *n* : PARADISE 2

[1]**edge** \ˈej\ *n* **1** : the cutting side of a blade **2** : SHARPNESS; *also* : FORCE, EFFECTIVENESS **3** : the line where something begins or ends; *also* : the area adjoining such an edge **4** : ADVANTAGE ⟨has an ~ on the competition⟩ — **edged** \ˈejd\ *adj*

[2]**edge** *vb* **edged; edg·ing** **1** : to give or form an edge **2** : to move or force gradually ⟨~ into a crowd⟩ **3** : to defeat by a small margin — **edg·er** *n*

edge·wise \ˈej-ˌwīz\ *adv* : SIDEWAYS

edg·ing \ˈe-jiŋ\ *n* : something that forms an edge or border ⟨a lace ~⟩

edgy \ˈe-jē\ *adj* **edg·i·er; -est** **1** : SHARP ⟨an ~ tone⟩ **2** : TENSE, NERVOUS **3** : having a bold, provocative, or unconventional quality — **edg·i·ness** *n*

ed·i·ble \ˈe-də-bəl\ *adj* : fit or safe to be eaten — **ed·i·bil·i·ty** \ˌe-də-ˈbi-lə-tē\ *n* — **edible** *n*

edict \ˈē-ˌdikt\ *n* : ORDER, DECREE

ed·i·fi·ca·tion \ˌe-də-fə-ˈkā-shən\ *n* : instruction and improvement esp. in morality — **ed·i·fy** \ˈe-də-ˌfī\ *vb*

ed·i·fice \ˈe-də-fəs\ *n* : a usu. large building

ed·it \ˈe-dət\ *vb* **1** : to revise, assemble, or prepare for publication or release (as a motion picture) **2** : to direct the publication and policies of (as a newspaper) **3** : DELETE — **ed·i·tor** \ˈe-də-tər\ *n* — **ed·i·tor·ship** *n* — **ed·i·tress** \-trəs\ *n*

edi·tion \i-ˈdi-shən\ *n* **1** : the form in which a text is published **2** : the total number of copies (as of a book) published at one time **3** : VERSION

[1]**ed·i·to·ri·al** \ˌe-də-ˈtȯr-ē-əl\ *adj* **1** : of or relating to an editor or editing **2** : being or resembling an editorial — **ed·i·to·ri·al·ly** *adv*

[2]**editorial** *n* : an article (as in a newspaper) giving the views of the editors or publishers; *also* : an expression of opinion resembling an editorial ⟨a television ~⟩

ed·i·to·ri·al·ize \ˌe-də-ˈtȯr-ē-ə-ˌlīz\ *vb* **-ized; -iz·ing** **1** : to express an opinion in an editorial **2** : to introduce opinions into factual reporting **3** : to express an opinion — **ed·i·to·ri·al·i·za·tion** \-ˌtȯr-ē-ə-lə-ˈzā-shən\ *n* — **ed·i·to·ri·al·iz·er** *n*

EDP *abbr* electronic data processing

EDT *abbr* Eastern daylight (saving) time

educ *abbr* education; educational

ed·u·ca·ble \ˈe-jə-kə-bəl\ *adj* : capable of being educated

ed·u·cate \ˈe-jə-ˌkāt\ *vb* **-cat·ed; -cat·ing** [ME, to rear, fr. L *educatus*, pp. of *educare*, fr. *educere* to lead forth, draw out] **1** : to provide with schooling **2** : to develop mentally and morally; *also* : to provide with information ♦ ***Synonyms*** TRAIN, DISCIPLINE, SCHOOL, INSTRUCT, TEACH — **ed·u·ca·tor** \-ˌkā-tər\ *n*

ed·u·ca·tion \ˌe-jə-ˈkā-shən\ *n* **1** : the action or process of educating or being educated **2** : a field of study dealing with methods of teaching and learning — **ed·u·ca·tion·al** \-shə-nəl\ *adj* — **ed·u·ca·tion·al·ly** *adv*

educational television *n* **1** : television that provides educational programming (as for students) **2** : television (as public television) that receives support from contributions rather than from commercials

educe \i-ˈdüs, -ˈdyüs\ *vb* **educed; educing** **1** : ELICIT, EVOKE **2** : DEDUCE ♦ *Synonyms* EXTRACT, EVINCE, EXTORT

ed•u•tain•ment \ˌe-jə-ˈtān-mənt\ *n* : entertainment that is designed to be educational

[1]**-ee** \ˈē, (ˌ)ē\ *n suffix* **1** : one that receives or benefits from (a specified action or thing) ⟨grant*ee*⟩ ⟨patent*ee*⟩ **2** : a person who does (a specified action) ⟨escap*ee*⟩

[2]**-ee** *n suffix* **1** : a particular esp. small kind of ⟨boot*ee*⟩ **2** : one resembling or suggestive of ⟨goat*ee*⟩

EE *abbr* electrical engineer

EEC *abbr* European Economic Community

EEG *abbr* **1** electroencephalogram **2** electroencephalograph

eel \ˈēl\ *n* : any of numerous snakelike bony fishes with a smooth slimy skin

EEO *abbr* equal employment opportunity

ee•rie *also* **ee•ry** \ˈir-ē\ *adj* **ee•ri•er; -est** : WEIRD, UNCANNY — **ee•ri•ly** \ˈir-ə-lē\ *adv*

eff *abbr* efficiency

ef•face \i-ˈfās, e-\ *vb* **ef•faced; ef•fac•ing** : to obliterate or obscure by or as if by rubbing out ♦ *Synonyms* ERASE, DELETE, ANNUL, CANCEL, EXPUNGE — **ef•face•able** *adj* — **ef•face•ment** *n*

[1]**ef•fect** \i-ˈfekt\ *n* **1** : MEANING, INTENT **2** : RESULT **3** : APPEARANCE **4** : INFLUENCE **5** *pl* : GOODS, POSSESSIONS **6** : the quality or state of being operative : OPERATION ♦ *Synonyms* CONSEQUENCE, OUTCOME, UPSHOT, AFTERMATH, ISSUE

[2]**effect** *vb* : to cause to happen ⟨~ repairs⟩ ⟨~ changes⟩

ef•fec•tive \i-ˈfek-tiv\ *adj* **1** : producing a decisive or desired effect **2** : IMPRESSIVE, STRIKING **3** : ready for service or action ⟨~ manpower⟩ **4** : being in effect — **ef•fec•tive•ly** *adv* — **ef•fec•tive•ness** *n*

ef•fec•tu•al \i-ˈfek-chə-wəl\ *adj* : producing an intended effect : ADEQUATE — **ef•fec•tu•al•ly** *adv*

ef•fec•tu•ate \i-ˈfek-chə-ˌwāt\ *vb* **-at•ed; -at•ing** : BRING ABOUT, EFFECT

ef•fem•i•nate \ə-ˈfe-mə-nət\ *adj* : marked by qualities more typical of women than men — **ef•fem•i•na•cy** \-nə-sē\ *n*

ef•fen•di \e-ˈfen-dē\ *n* [Turk *efendi* master, fr. ModGk *authentēs*] : a man of property, authority, or education in an eastern Mediterranean country

ef•fer•ent \ˈe-fə-rənt\ *adj* : bearing or conducting outward from a more central part ⟨~ nerves⟩

ef•fer•vesce \ˌe-fər-ˈves\ *vb* **-vesced; -vesc•ing** **1** : to bubble and hiss as gas escapes **2** : to show liveliness or exhilaration — **ef•fer•ves•cence** \-ˈve-sᵊns\ *n* — **ef•fer•ves•cent** \-sᵊnt\ *adj* — **ef•fer•ves•cent•ly** *adv*

ef•fete \e-ˈfēt\ *adj* **1** : having lost character, vitality, or strength; *also* : DECADENT **2** : EFFEMINATE

ef•fi•ca•cious \ˌe-fə-ˈkā-shəs\ *adj* : producing an intended effect ⟨~ remedies⟩ ♦ *Synonyms* EFFECTUAL, EFFECTIVE, EFFICIENT — **ef•fi•ca•cy** \ˈe-fi-kə-sē\ *n*

ef•fi•cient \i-ˈfi-shənt\ *adj* : productive of desired effects esp. without waste — **ef•fi•cien•cy** \-shən-sē\ *n* — **ef•fi•cient•ly** *adv*

ef•fi•gy \ˈe-fə-jē\ *n, pl* **-gies** : IMAGE; *esp* : a crude figure of a hated person

ef•flo•res•cence \ˌe-flə-ˈre-sᵊns\ *n* **1** : the period or state of flowering **2** : the action or process of developing **3** : fullness of development : FLOWERING

ef•flu•ence \ˈe-ˌflü-əns\ *n* : something that flows out

ef•flu•ent \ˈe-ˌflü-ənt\ *n* : something that flows out; *esp* : a fluid (as sewage) discharged as waste — **effluent** *adj*

ef•flu•vi•um \e-ˈflü-vē-əm\ *n, pl* **-via** \-vē-ə\ *also* **-vi•ums** [L, outflow] **1** : a usu. unpleasant emanation **2** : a by-product usu. in the form of waste

ef•fort \ˈe-fərt\ *n* **1** : EXERTION, ENDEAVOR; *also* : a product of effort **2** : active or applied force — **ef•fort•less** *adj* — **ef•fort•less•ly** *adv*

ef•fron•tery \i-ˈfrən-tə-rē\ *n, pl* **-ter•ies** : shameless boldness : IMPUDENCE ♦ *Synonyms* TEMERITY, AUDACITY, BRASS, GALL, NERVE, CHUTZPAH

ef•ful•gence \i-ˈfu̇l-jəns, -ˈfəl-\ *n* : radiant splendor : BRILLIANCE ⟨the ~ of its golden age⟩ — **ef•ful•gent** \-jənt\ *adj*

ef•fu•sion \i-ˈfyü-zhən, e-\ *n* : a gushing forth; *also* : unrestrained utterance — **ef•fuse** \-ˈfyüz, e-\ *vb* — **ef•fu•sive** \i-ˈfyü-siv, e-\ *adj* — **ef•fu•sive•ly** *adv*

eft \ˈeft\ *n* : NEWT

EFT *or* **EFTS** *abbr* electronic funds transfer (system)

e.g. *abbr* [L *exempli gratia*] for example

Eg *abbr* Egypt; Egyptian

egal•i•tar•i•an•ism \i-ˌga-lə-ˈter-ē-ə-ˌni-zəm\ *n* : a belief in human equality esp. in social, political, and economic affairs — **egal•i•tar•i•an** *adj or n*

[1]**egg** \ˈeg\ *vb* [ME, fr. ON *eggja;* akin to OE *ecg* edge] : to urge to action — usu. used with *on*

[2]**egg** *n* [ME *egge,* fr. ON *egg;* akin to OE *ǣg* egg, L *ovum*] **1** : a rounded usu. hard-shelled reproductive body esp. of birds and reptiles from which the young hatches; *also* : the egg of the common domestic chicken as an article of food **2** : a germ cell produced by a female

egg•beat•er \ˈeg-ˌbē-tər\ *n* : a hand-operated kitchen utensil for beating, stirring, or whipping

egg cell *n* : EGG 2

egg foo yong *or* **egg foo young** *or* **egg foo yung** \-ˈfü-ˈyəŋ\ : a fried egg patty

egg•head \-ˌhed\ *n, often disparaging* : INTELLECTUAL, HIGHBROW

egg•nog \-ˌnäg\ *n* : a drink consisting of eggs beaten with sugar, milk or cream, and often alcoholic liquor

egg•plant \-ˌplant\ *n* : the edible usu. large and dark purplish fruit of a plant related to the potato; *also* : the plant

egg roll *n* : a thin egg-dough casing filled with minced vegetables and often bits of meat and usu. deep-fried

egg·shell \ˈeg-ˌshel\ *n* : the hard exterior covering of an egg

egis *var of* AEGIS

eg·lan·tine \ˈe-glən-ˌtīn, -ˌtēn\ *n* : SWEETBRIAR

ego \ˈē-gō\ *n, pl* **egos** [L, I] **1** : the self as distinguished from others **2** : the one of the three divisions of the psyche in psychoanalytic theory that is the organized conscious mediator between the person and reality

ego·cen·tric \ˌē-gō-ˈsen-trik\ *adj* : concerned or overly concerned with the self; *esp* : SELF-CENTERED

ego·ism \ˈē-gō-ˌi-zəm\ *n* **1** : a doctrine holding self-interest to be the motive or the valid end of action **2** : excessive concern for oneself with or without exaggerated feelings of self-importance — **ego·ist** \-ist\ *n* — **ego·is·tic** \ˌē-gō-ˈis-tik\ *adj* — **ego·is·ti·cal·ly** *adv*

ego·tism \ˈē-gə-ˌti-zəm\ *n* **1** : the practice of talking about oneself too much **2** : an exaggerated sense of self-importance : CONCEIT — **ego·tist** \-tist\ *n* — **ego·tis·tic** \ˌē-gə-ˈtis-tik\ *or* **ego·tis·ti·cal** \-ti-kəl\ *adj* — **ego·tis·ti·cal·ly** *adv*

ego trip *n* : an act that enhances and satisfies one's ego

egre·gious \i-ˈgrē-jəs\ *adj* [L *egregius* outstanding, fr. *ex, e* out of + *greg-, grex* flock, herd] : notably bad : FLAGRANT ⟨~ errors⟩ — **egre·gious·ly** *adv* — **egre·gious·ness** *n*

egress \ˈē-ˌgres\ *n* : a way out : EXIT

egret \ˈē-grət, i-ˈgret\ *n* : any of various herons that bear long plumes during the breeding season

Egyp·tian \i-ˈjip-shən\ *n* **1** : a native or inhabitant of Egypt **2** : the language of the ancient Egyptians from earliest times to about the 3d century A.D. — **Egyptian** *adj*

ei·der \ˈī-dər\ *n* : any of several northern sea ducks that yield a soft down

ei·der·down \-ˌdau̇n\ *n* **1** : the down of the eider **2** : a comforter filled with eiderdown

ei·do·lon \ī-ˈdō-lən\ *n, pl* **-lons** *or* **-la** \-lə\ **1** : PHANTOM **2** : IDEAL

eight \ˈāt\ *n* **1** : one more than seven **2** : the 8th in a set or series **3** : something having eight units — **eight** *adj or pron* — **eighth** \ˈātth\ *adj or adv or n*

eight ball *n* : a black pool ball numbered 8 — **behind the eight ball** : in a highly disadvantageous position

eigh·teen \āt-ˈtēn\ *n* : one more than 17 — **eighteen** *adj or pron* — **eigh·teenth** \-ˈtēnth\ *adj or n*

eighty \ˈā-tē\ *n, pl* **eight·ies** : eight times 10 — **eight·i·eth** \ˈā-tē-əth\ *adj or n* — **eighty** *adj or pron*

ein·stei·ni·um \īn-ˈstī-nē-əm\ *n* : an artificially produced radioactive element

ei·re·nic *chiefly Brit var of* IRENIC

[1]**ei·ther** \ˈē-t͟hər, ˈī-\ *adj* **1** : being the one and the other of two : EACH ⟨trees on ~ side⟩ **2** : being the one or the other of two ⟨take ~ road⟩

[2]**either** *pron* : the one or the other

[3]**either** *conj* — used as a function word before the first of two or more words or word groups of which the last is preceded by *or* to indicate that they represent alternatives ⟨a statement is ~ true or false⟩

ejac·u·late \i-ˈja-kyə-ˌlāt\ *vb* **-lat·ed; -lat·ing** **1** : to eject a fluid (as semen) **2** : to utter suddenly : EXCLAIM — **ejac·u·la·tion** \-ˌja-kyə-ˈlā-shən\ *n* — **ejac·u·la·to·ry** \-ˈja-kyə-lə-ˌtȯr-ē\ *adj*

eject \i-ˈjekt\ *vb* : to drive or throw out or off ♦ ***Synonyms*** EXPEL, OUST, EVICT, DISMISS — **ejec·tion** \-ˈjek-shən\ *n*

eke \ˈēk\ *vb* **eked; ek·ing** : to gain, supplement, or extend usu. with effort — usu. used with *out* ⟨~ out a living⟩

EKG *abbr* [G *Elektrokardiogramm*] electrocardiogram; electrocardiograph

el *abbr* elevation

[1]**elab·o·rate** \i-ˈla-bə-rət, -ˈla-brət\ *adj* **1** : planned or carried out with great care **2** : being complex and usu. ornate — **elab·o·rate·ly** *adv* — **elab·o·rate·ness** *n*

[2]**elab·o·rate** \i-ˈla-bə-ˌrāt\ *vb* **-rat·ed; -rat·ing** **1** : to build up from simpler ingredients **2** : to work out in detail : DEVELOP — **elab·o·ra·tion** \-ˌla-bə-ˈrā-shən\ *n*

élan \ā-ˈläⁿ\ *n* [F] : ARDOR, SPIRIT

eland \ˈē-lənd, -ˌland\ *n, pl* **eland** *also* **elands** [Afrikaans] : either of two large African antelopes with spirally twisted horns in both sexes

elapse \i-ˈlaps\ *vb* **elapsed; elaps·ing** : to slip by : PASS

[1]**elas·tic** \i-ˈlas-tik\ *adj* **1** : SPRINGY **2** : FLEXIBLE, PLIABLE ⟨an ~ bandage⟩ **3** : ADAPTABLE ⟨an ~ plan⟩ ♦ ***Synonyms*** RESILIENT, SUPPLE, STRETCH — **elas·tic·i·ty** \-ˌlas-ˈti-sə-tē, ˌē-ˌlas-\ *n*

[2]**elastic** *n* **1** : elastic material **2** : a rubber band

elate \i-ˈlāt\ *vb* **elat·ed; elat·ing** : to fill with joy — **ela·tion** \-ˈlā-shən\ *n*

[1]**el·bow** \ˈel-ˌbō\ *n* [ME *elbowe*, fr. OE *elboga*, fr. *el-* (akin to *eln* ell) + *boga* bow] **1** : the joint of the arm; *also* : the outer curve of the bent arm **2** : a bend or joint resembling an elbow in shape

[2]**elbow** *vb* : to push aside with the elbow; *also* : to make one's way by elbowing

elbow bump *n* : a gesture in which two people bump their elbows together

elbow grease *n* : hard esp. physical work

el·bow room \ˈel-ˌbō-ˌrüm, -ˌru̇m\ *n* : enough space for work or operation

[1]**el·der** \ˈel-dər\ *n* : ELDERBERRY 2

[2]**elder** *adj* **1** : OLDER **2** : EARLIER, FORMER **3** : of higher rank : SENIOR

[3]**elder** *n* **1** : an older individual : SENIOR **2** : one having authority by reason of age and experience **3** : a church officer

el·der·ber·ry \ˈel-dər-ˌber-ē\ *n* **1** : the edible black or red fruit of a shrub or tree related to the honeysuckle and bearing flat clusters of small white or pink flowers **2** : a tree or shrub bearing elderberries

el·der·ly \ˈel-dər-lē\ *adj* **1** : rather old; *esp* : past middle age **2** : of, relating to, or characteristic of later life

el·dest \ˈel-dəst\ *adj* : of the greatest age

El Do·ra·do \ˌel-də-ˈrä-dō, -ˈrā-\ *n* [Sp, lit., the gilded one] : a place of vast riches, abundance, or opportunity

elec *abbr* electric; electrical; electricity

[1]**elect** \i-ˈlekt\ *adj* **1** : CHOSEN, SELECT **2** : elected but not yet installed in office ⟨the president-*elect*⟩

[2]**elect** *n, pl* **elect** **1** : a selected person **2** *pl* : a select or exclusive group

[3]**elect** *vb* **1** : to select by vote (as for office or membership) **2** : CHOOSE, PICK

elec·tion \i-ˈlek-shən\ *n* **1** : an act or process of electing **2** : the fact of being elected

elec·tion·eer \i-ˌlek-shə-ˈnir\ *vb* : to work for the election of a candidate or party

[1]**elec·tive** \i-ˈlek-tiv\ *adj* **1** : chosen or filled by election **2** : permitting a choice : OPTIONAL

[2]**elective** *n* : an elective course or subject of study

elec·tor \i-ˈlek-tər\ *n* **1** : one qualified to vote in an election **2** : one elected to an electoral college — **elec·tor·al** \i-ˈlek-tə-rəl\ *adj*

electoral college *n* : a body of electors who elect the president and vice president of the U.S.

elec·tor·ate \i-ˈlek-tə-rət\ *n* : a body of persons entitled to vote

elec·tric \i-ˈlek-trik\ *adj* [NL *electricus* produced from amber by friction, electric, fr. ML, of amber, fr. L *electrum* amber, fr. Gk *ēlektron*] **1** *or* **elec·tri·cal** \-tri-kəl\ : of, relating to, operated by, or produced by electricity **2** : ELECTRIFYING, THRILLING ⟨an ~ performance⟩ — **elec·tri·cal·ly** *adv*

electrical storm *n* : THUNDERSTORM

electric chair *n* : a chair used to carry out the death penalty by electrocution

electric eye *n* : PHOTOELECTRIC CELL

elec·tri·cian \i-ˌlek-ˈtri-shən\ *n* : a person who installs, operates, or repairs electrical equipment

elec·tric·i·ty \i-ˌlek-ˈtri-sə-tē\ *n, pl* **-ties** **1** : a form of energy that occurs naturally (as in lightning) or is produced (as in a generator) and that is expressed in terms of the movement and interaction of electrons **2** : electric current

elec·tri·fy \i-ˈlek-trə-ˌfī\ *vb* **-fied; -fy·ing** **1** : to charge with electricity **2** : to equip for use of electric power **3** : THRILL — **elec·tri·fi·ca·tion** \i-ˌlek-trə-fə-ˈkā-shən\ *n*

elec·tro·car·dio·gram \i-ˌlek-trō-ˈkär-dē-ə-ˌgram\ *n* : the tracing made by an electrocardiograph

elec·tro·car·dio·graph \-ˌgraf\ *n* : a device for recording the changes of electrical potential occurring during the heartbeat — **elec·tro·car·dio·graph·ic** \-ˌkär-dē-ə-ˈgra-fik\ *adj* — **elec·tro·car·di·og·ra·phy** \-dē-ˈä-grə-fē\ *n*

elec·tro·chem·is·try \-ˈke-mə-strē\ *n* : a branch of chemistry that deals with the relation of electricity to chemical changes — **elec·tro·chem·i·cal** \-ˈke-mi-kəl\ *adj*

elec·tro·cute \i-ˈlek-trə-ˌkyüt\ *vb* **-cut·ed; -cut·ing** **1** : to kill (a criminal) by electricity **2** : to kill by electric shock — **elec·tro·cu·tion** \-ˌlek-trə-ˈkyü-shən\ *n*

elec·trode \i-ˈlek-ˌtrōd\ *n* : a conductor used to establish electrical contact with a nonmetallic part of a circuit

elec·tro·en·ceph·a·lo·gram \i-ˌlek-trō-in-ˈse-fə-lə-ˌgram\ *n* : the tracing made by an electroencephalograph

elec·tro·en·ceph·a·lo·graph \-ˌgraf\ *n* : an apparatus for detecting and recording brain waves — **elec·tro·en·ceph·a·lo·graph·ic** \-ˌse-fə-lə-ˈgra-fik\ *adj* — **ele c·tro·en·ceph·a·log·ra·phy** \-ˈlä-grə-fē\ *n*

elec·trol·o·gist \i-ˌlek-ˈträ-lə-jist\ *n* : one that uses electrical means to remove hair, warts, moles, and birthmarks from the body

elec·trol·y·sis \i-ˌlek-ˈträ-lə-səs\ *n* **1** : the production of chemical changes by passage of an electric current through an electrolyte **2** : the destruction of hair roots with an electric current — **elec·tro·lyt·ic** \-trə-ˈli-tik\ *adj*

elec·tro·lyte \i-ˈlek-trə-ˌlīt\ *n* : a nonmetallic electric conductor in which current is carried by the movement of ions; *also* : a substance whose solution or molten form is such a conductor

elec·tro·mag·net \i-ˌlek-trō-ˈmag-nət\ *n* : a core of magnetic material (as iron) surrounded by a coil of wire through which an electric current is passed to magnetize the core

elec·tro·mag·net·ic \-mag-ˈne-tik\ *adj* : of, relating to, or produced by electromagnetism — **elec·tro·mag·net·i·cal·ly** *adv*

electromagnetic radiation *n* : energy in the form of electromagnetic waves; *also* : a series of electromagnetic waves

electromagnetic wave *n* : a wave (as a radio wave, an X-ray, or a wave of visible light) that consists of associated electric and magnetic effects and that travels at the speed of light

elec·tro·mag·ne·tism \i-ˌlek-trō-ˈmag-nə-ˌti-zəm\ *n* **1** : magnetism developed by a current of electricity **2** : a natural force responsible for interactions between charged particles which result from their charge

elec·tro·mo·tive force \i-ˌlek-trə-ˈmō-tiv-\ *n* : the potential difference derived from an electrical source per unit quantity of electricity passing through the source

elec·tron \i-ˈlek-ˌträn\ *n* : a negatively charged elementary particle

elec·tron·ic \i-ˌlek-ˈträ-nik\ *adj* **1** : of or relating to electrons or electronics **2** : involving a computer — **elec·tron·i·cal·ly** \-ni-k(ə-)lē\ *adv*

electronic cigarette *n* : a battery-operated device designed to resemble a cigarette and used to inhale a usu. nicotine-containing vapor

electronic mail *n* : EMAIL

elec·tron·ics \i-ˌlek-ˈträ-niks\ *n* **1** : the physics of electrons and electronic devices **2** : electronic components, devices, or equipment

electron microscope *n* : an instrument in which a beam of electrons is used to produce an enlarged image of a minute object

electron tube *n* : a device in which electrical conduction by electrons takes place within a sealed container and which is used for the controlled flow of electrons

electron volt *n* : a unit of energy equal to 1.60×10^{-19} joule

elec·tro·pho·re·sis \i-ˌlek-trə-fə-ˈrē-səs\ *n* : the movement of suspended particles through a medium (as paper or gel) by an electromotive force — **elec·tro·pho·ret·ic** \-ˈrē-tik\ *adj*

elec·tro·plate \i-ˈlek-trə-ˌplāt\ *vb* : to coat (as with metal) by electrolysis

elec·tro·shock therapy \i-ˈlek-trō-ˌshäk-\ *n* : the treatment of mental illness by applying electric current to the head and inducing convulsions

elec·tro·stat·ics \i-ˌlek-trə-ˈsta-tiks\ *n* : physics dealing with the interactions of stationary electric charges

el·ee·mos·y·nary \ˌe-li-ˈmäs-sə-ˌner-ē\ *adj* : CHARITABLE

el·e·gance \ˈe-li-gəns\ *n* **1** : refined gracefulness; *also* : tasteful richness (as of design) **2** : something marked by elegance — **el·e·gant** \-gənt\ *adj* — **el·e·gant·ly** *adv*

ele·giac \ˌe-lə-ˈjī-ək, -ˌak\ *adj* : of or relating to an elegy

el·e·gy \ˈe-lə-jē\ *n, pl* **-gies** : a song, poem, or speech expressing grief for one who is dead; *also* : a reflective poem usu. melancholy in tone

elem *abbr* elementary

el·e·ment \ˈe-lə-mənt\ *n* **1** *pl* : weather conditions; *esp* : severe weather ⟨boards exposed to the ~*s*⟩ **2** : natural environment ⟨in her ~⟩ **3** : a constituent part **4** *pl* : the simplest principles (as of an art or science) : RUDIMENTS **5** : a member of a mathematical set **6** : any of the fundamental substances that consist of atoms of only one kind ♦ ***Synonyms*** COMPONENT, INGREDIENT, CONSTITUENT — **el·e·men·tal** \ˌe-lə-ˈment-ᵊl\ *adj*

☞ the ELEMENT table is on page 236

el·e·men·ta·ry \ˌe-lə-ˈmen-trē, -tə-rē\ *adj* : SIMPLE, RUDIMENTARY; *also* : of, relating to, or teaching the basic subjects of education

elementary particle *n* : a subatomic particle of matter and energy that does not appear to be made up of other smaller particles

elementary school *n* : a school usu. including the first six or the first eight grades

el·e·phant \ˈe-lə-fənt\ *n, pl* **elephants** *also* **elephant** : any of a family of huge thickset nearly hairless mammals that have the snout lengthened into a trunk and two long curving pointed ivory tusks

el·e·phan·ti·a·sis \ˌe-lə-fən-ˈtī-ə-səs\ *n, pl* **-a·ses** \-ˌsēz\ : enlargement and thickening of tissues in response esp. to infection by minute parasitic worms

el·e·phan·tine \ˌe-lə-ˈfan-ˌtēn, -ˌtīn, ˈe-lə-fən-\ *adj* **1** : of great size or strength **2** : CLUMSY, PONDEROUS ⟨~ verse⟩

elev *abbr* elevation

el·e·vate \ˈe-lə-ˌvāt\ *vb* **-vat·ed; -vat·ing** **1** : to lift up : RAISE **2** : EXALT, ENNOBLE ⟨great books that ~ their readers⟩ **3** : ELATE

el·e·va·tion \ˌe-lə-ˈvā-shən\ *n* **1** : the height to which something is raised (as above sea level) **2** : a lifting up **3** : something (as a hill) that is elevated

el·e·va·tor \ˈe-lə-ˌvā-tər\ *n* **1** : a cage or platform for conveying people or things from one level to another **2** : a building for storing and discharging grain **3** : a movable surface on an airplane to produce motion up or down

elev·en \i-ˈle-vən\ *n* **1** : one more than 10 **2** : the 11th in a set or series **3** : something having 11 units; *esp* : a football team — **eleven** *adj or pron* — **elev·enth** \-vənth\ *adj or n*

elf \ˈelf\ *n, pl* **elves** \ˈelvz\ : a mischievous fairy — **elf·ish** \ˈel-fish\ *adj*

ELF *abbr* extremely low frequency

elf·in \ˈel-fən\ *adj* : of, relating to, or resembling an elf

elic·it \i-ˈli-sət\ *vb* : to draw out or forth ♦ ***Synonyms*** EVOKE, EDUCE, EXTRACT, EXTORT

elide \i-ˈlīd\ *vb* **elid·ed; elid·ing** : to suppress or alter by elision

el·i·gi·ble \ˈe-lə-jə-bəl\ *adj* : qualified to participate or to be chosen — **el·i·gi·bil·i·ty** \ˌe-lə-jə-ˈbi-lə-tē\ *n* — **eligible** *n*

elim·i·nate \i-ˈli-mə-ˌnāt\ *vb* **-nat·ed; -nat·ing** [L *eliminatus,* pp. of *eliminare,* fr. *limen* threshold] **1** : REMOVE, ERADICATE **2** : to pass (wastes) from the body **3** : to leave out : IGNORE — **elim·i·na·tion** \-ˌli-mə-ˈnā-shən\ *n*

eli·sion \i-ˈli-zhən\ *n* : the omission of a final or initial sound or of a word; *esp* : the omission of an unstressed vowel or syllable in a verse to achieve a uniform rhythm

elite \ā-ˈlēt, ē-\ *n* [F *élite*] **1** : the choice part; *also* : a superior group **2** : a typewriter type providing 12 characters to the inch — **elite** *adj*

elit·ism \-ˈlē-ˌti-zəm\ *n* : leadership or rule by an elite; *also* : advocacy of such elitism — **elit·ist** \-tist\ *n or adj*

elix·ir \i-ˈlik-sər\ *n* [ME, fr. ML, fr. Ar *al-iksīr* the elixir, fr. *al* the + *iksīr* elixir] **1** : a substance held capable of prolonging life indefinitely; *also* : PANACEA **2** : a sweetened alcoholic medicinal solution

Eliz·a·be·than \i-ˌli-zə-ˈbē-thən\ *adj* : of, relating to, or characteristic of Elizabeth I of England or her times

elk \ˈelk\ *n, pl* **elk** *or* **elks** **1** : MOOSE —

CHEMICAL ELEMENTS

ELEMENT NAME	SYMBOL & ATOMIC NUMBER	ATOMIC WEIGHT[1]	ELEMENT NAME	SYMBOL & ATOMIC NUMBER	ATOMIC WEIGHT[1]
actinium	(Ac = 89)	(227)	mendelevium	(Md = 101)	(258)
aluminum	(Al = 13)	26.98154	mercury	(Hg = 80)	200.59
americium	(Am = 95)	(243)	molybdenum	(Mo = 42)	95.94
antimony	(Sb = 51)	121.760	moscovium	(Mc = 115)	(289)
argon	(Ar = 18)	39.948	neodymium	(Nd = 60)	144.242
arsenic	(As = 33)	74.92160	neon	(Ne = 10)	20.180
astatine	(At = 85)	(210)	neptunium	(Np = 93)	(237)
barium	(Ba = 56)	137.33	nickel	(Ni = 28)	58.6934
berkelium	(Bk = 97)	(247)	nihonium	(Nh = 113)	(286)
beryllium	(Be = 4)	9.012182	niobium	(Nb = 41)	92.90638
bismuth	(Bi = 83)	208.98040	nitrogen	(N = 7)	14.0067
bohrium	(Bh = 107)	(264)	nobelium	(No = 102)	(259)
boron	(B = 5)	10.81	oganesson	(Og = 118)	(294)
bromine	(Br = 35)	79.904	osmium	(Os = 76)	190.23
cadmium	(Cd = 48)	112.41	oxygen	(O = 8)	15.9994
calcium	(Ca = 20)	40.078	palladium	(Pd = 46)	106.42
californium	(Cf = 98)	(251)	phosphorus	(P = 15)	30.973762
carbon	(C = 6)	12.011	platinum	(Pt = 78)	195.084
cerium	(Ce = 58)	140.116	plutonium	(Pu = 94)	(244)
cesium	(Cs = 55)	132.90545	polonium	(Po = 84)	(209)
chlorine	(Cl = 17)	35.453	potassium	(K = 19)	39.0983
chromium	(Cr = 24)	51.996	praseodymium	(Pr = 59)	140.90765
cobalt	(Co = 27)	58.93320	promethium	(Pm = 61)	(145)
copernicium	(Cn = 112)	(285)	protactinium	(Pa = 91)	(231)
copper	(Cu = 29)	63.546	radium	(Ra = 88)	(226)
curium	(Cm = 96)	(247)	radon	(Rn = 86)	(222)
darmstadtium	(Ds = 110)	(269)	rhenium	(Re = 75)	186.207
dubnium	(Db = 105)	(262)	rhodium	(Rh = 45)	102.90550
dysprosium	(Dy = 66)	162.50	roentgenium	(Rg = 111)	(280)
einsteinium	(Es = 99)	(252)	rubidium	(Rb = 37)	85.4678
erbium	(Er = 68)	167.259	ruthenium	(Ru = 44)	101.07
europium	(Eu = 63)	151.964	rutherfordium	(Rf = 104)	(261)
fermium	(Fm = 100)	(257)	samarium	(Sm = 62)	150.36
flerovium	(Fl = 114)	(289)	scandium	(Sc = 21)	44.95591
fluorine	(F = 9)	18.998403	seaborgium	(Sg = 106)	(266)
francium	(Fr = 87)	(223)	selenium	(Se = 34)	78.96
gadolinium	(Gd = 64)	157.25	silicon	(Si = 14)	28.0855
gallium	(Ga = 31)	69.723	silver	(Ag = 47)	107.8682
germanium	(Ge = 32)	72.64	sodium	(Na = 11)	22.989769
gold	(Au = 79)	196.96657	strontium	(Sr = 38)	87.62
hafnium	(Hf = 72)	178.49	sulfur	(S = 16)	32.07
hassium	(Hs = 108)	(277)	tantalum	(Ta = 73)	180.9479
helium	(He = 2)	4.002602	technetium	(Tc = 43)	(98)
holmium	(Ho = 67)	164.93032	tellurium	(Te = 52)	127.60
hydrogen	(H = 1)	1.0079	tennessine	(Ts = 117)	(293)
indium	(In = 49)	114.818	terbium	(Tb = 65)	158.92535
iodine	(I = 53)	126.90447	thallium	(Tl = 81)	204.3833
iridium	(Ir = 77)	192.217	thorium	(Th = 90)	(232)
iron	(Fe = 26)	55.845	thulium	(Tm = 69)	168.93421
krypton	(Kr = 36)	83.80	tin	(Sn = 50)	118.71
lanthanum	(La = 57)	138.90547	titanium	(Ti = 22)	47.867
lawrencium	(Lr = 103)	(262)	tungsten	(W = 74)	183.84
lead	(Pb = 82)	207.2	uranium	(U = 92)	(238)
lithium	(Li = 3)	6.941	vanadium	(V = 23)	50.9415
livermorium	(Lv = 116)	(293)	xenon	(Xe = 54)	131.29
lutetium	(Lu = 71)	174.967	ytterbium	(Yb = 70)	173.04
magnesium	(Mg = 12)	24.305	yttrium	(Y = 39)	88.90585
manganese	(Mn = 25)	54.93805	zinc	(Zn = 30)	65.39
meitnerium	(Mt = 109)	(268)	zirconium	(Zr = 40)	91.224

[1]Weights are based on the naturally occurring isotope compositions and scaled to $^{12}C = 12$. For elements lacking stable isotopes, the mass number of the longest-lived one is shown in parentheses.

used for one of the Old World **2** : a large gregarious deer of No. America, Europe, Asia, and northwestern Africa with curved antlers having many branches

[1]ell \ˈel\ *n* [ME *eln*, fr. OE; akin to L *ulna* forearm, Gk *ōlenē* elbow] : a former English cloth measure of 45 inches

[2]ell *n* : an extension at right angles to a building

el·lipse \i-ˈlips, e-\ *n* : a closed curve of oval shape

el·lip·sis \i-ˈlip-səs, e-\ *n, pl* **el·lip·ses** \-ˌsēz\ **1** : omission from an expression of a word clearly implied **2** : marks (as . . .) to show omission

el·lip·soid \i-ˈlip-ˌsȯid, e-\ *n* : a surface all plane sections of which are circles or ellipses — **el·lip·soi·dal** \-ˌlip-ˈsȯi-dᵊl\ *also* **ellipsoid** *adj*

el·lip·ti·cal \i-ˈlip-ti-kəl, e-\ *or* **el·lip·tic** \-tik\ *adj* **1** : of, relating to, or shaped like an ellipse **2** : of, relating to, or marked by ellipsis — **el·lip·ti·cal·ly** \-ti-k(ə-)lē\ *adv*

elm \ˈelm\ *n* : any of a genus of large trees that have toothed leaves and nearly circular one-seeded winged fruits and are often grown as shade trees; *also* : the wood of an elm

El Ni·ño \el-ˈnē-nyō\ *n* : a flow of unusually warm Pacific Ocean water moving toward and along the west coast of So. America

el·o·cu·tion \ˌe-lə-ˈkyü-shən\ *n* : the art of effective public speaking — **el·o·cu·tion·ist** \-shə-nist\ *n*

elon·gate \i-ˈlȯŋ-ˌgāt\ *vb* **-gat·ed; -gat·ing** : to make or grow longer ♦ ***Synonyms*** EXTEND, LENGTHEN, PROLONG, PROTRACT — **elon·ga·tion** \(ˌ)ē-ˌlȯŋ-ˈgā-shən\ *n*

elope \i-ˈlōp\ *vb* **eloped; elop·ing** : to run away esp. to be married — **elope·ment** *n* — **elop·er** *n*

el·o·quent \ˈe-lə-kwənt\ *adj* **1** : having or showing clear and forceful expression ⟨an ~ speaker⟩ **2** : clearly showing some feeling or meaning — **el·o·quence** \-kwəns\ *n* — **el·o·quent·ly** *adv*

[1]else \ˈels\ *adv* **1** : in a different or additional manner or place or at a different or additional time ⟨where ~ can we meet⟩ **2** : OTHERWISE ⟨obey or ~ you'll be sorry⟩

[2]else *adj* : OTHER; *esp* : being in addition ⟨what ~ do you want⟩

else·where \-ˌhwer\ *adv* : in or to another place ⟨took my business ~⟩

elu·ci·date \i-ˈlü-sə-ˌdāt\ *vb* **-dat·ed; -dat·ing** : to make clear usu. by explanation ♦ ***Synonyms*** CLARIFY, EXPLAIN, ILLUMINATE — **elu·ci·da·tion** \-ˌlü-sə-ˈdā-shən\ *n*

elude \ē-ˈlüd\ *vb* **elud·ed; elud·ing** **1** : EVADE **2** : to escape the notice of

elu·sive \ē-ˈlü-siv\ *adj* : tending to elude : EVASIVE ⟨the solution remains ~⟩ — **elu·sive·ly** *adv* — **elu·sive·ness** *n*

el·ver \ˈel-vər\ *n* [alter. of *eelfare* migration of eels] : a young eel

elves *pl of* ELF

Ely·si·um \i-ˈli-zhē-əm, -zē-\ *n, pl* **-si·ums** *or* **-sia** \-zhē-ə, -zē-\ : PARADISE 2 — **Ely·sian** \-ˈli-zhən\ *adj*

em \ˈem\ *n* : a length approximately the width of the letter *M*

EM *abbr* **1** electromagnetic **2** electron microscope **3** enlisted man

ema·ci·ate \i-ˈmā-shē-ˌāt\ *vb* **-at·ed; -at·ing** : to become or cause to become very thin — **ema·ci·a·tion** \-ˌmā-shē-ˈā-shən, -sē-\ *n*

email *or* **e–mail** \ˈē-ˌmāl\ *n* **1** : a system for transmitting messages between computers on a network **2** : a message or messages sent and received through an email system — **email** *or* **e–mail** *vb* — **email·er** *n*

emalangeni *pl of* LILANGENI

em·a·nate \ˈe-mə-ˌnāt\ *vb* **-nat·ed; -nat·ing** : to come out from a source ♦ ***Synonyms*** PROCEED, SPRING, RISE, ARISE, ORIGINATE — **em·a·na·tion** \ˌe-mə-ˈnā-shən\ *n*

eman·ci·pate \i-ˈman-sə-ˌpāt\ *vb* **-pat·ed; -pat·ing** : to set free ♦ ***Synonyms*** LIBERATE, RELEASE, DELIVER, DISCHARGE — **eman·ci·pa·tion** \-ˌman-sə-ˈpā-shən\ *n* — **eman·ci·pa·tor** \-ˈman-sə-ˌpā-tər\ *n*

emas·cu·late \i-ˈmas-kyu̇-ˌlāt\ *vb* **-lat·ed; -lat·ing** : to deprive of virility : CASTRATE; *also* : WEAKEN — **emas·cu·la·tion** \-ˌmas-kyu̇-ˈlā-shən\ *n*

em·balm \im-ˈbäm, -ˈbälm\ *vb* : to treat (a corpse) so as to protect from decay — **em·balm·er** *n*

em·bank·ment \im-ˈbaŋk-mənt\ *n* : a raised structure (as of earth) to hold back water or carry a roadway

em·bar·go \im-ˈbär-gō\ *n, pl* **-goes** [Sp, fr. *embargar* to bar] : a prohibition on commerce — **embargo** *vb*

em·bark \im-ˈbärk\ *vb* **1** : to put or go on board a ship or airplane **2** : to make a start — **em·bar·ka·tion** \ˌem-ˌbär-ˈkā-shən\ *n*

em·bar·rass \im-ˈber-əs\ *vb* **1** : CONFUSE, DISCONCERT **2** : to involve in financial difficulties **3** : to cause to experience self-conscious distress **4** : HINDER, IMPEDE — **em·bar·rass·ing·ly** *adv* — **em·bar·rass·ment** *n*

em·bas·sy \ˈem-bə-sē\ *n, pl* **-sies** **1** : a group of representatives headed by an ambassador **2** : the function, position, or mission of an ambassador **3** : the official residence and offices of an ambassador

em·bat·tle \im-ˈba-tᵊl\ *vb* : to arrange in order for battle; *also* : FORTIFY

em·bat·tled *adj* **1** : engaged in battle, conflict, or controversy **2** : being a site of battle, conflict, or controversy **3** : characterized by conflict or controversy ⟨an ~ presidency⟩

em·bed \im-ˈbed\ *vb* **em·bed·ded; em·bed·ding** **1** : to enclose closely in a surrounding mass **2** : to make something an integral part of

em·bel·lish \im-ˈbe-lish\ *vb* **1** : ADORN, DECORATE **2** : to add ornamental details to ♦ ***Synonyms*** BEAUTIFY, DECK, BE-

DECK, GARNISH, ORNAMENT, DRESS — **em·bel·lish·er** *n* — **em·bel·lish·ment** *n*
em·ber \'em-bər\ *n* **1** : a glowing or smoldering fragment from a fire **2** *pl* : the smoldering remains of a fire
em·bez·zle \im-'be-zəl\ *vb* **-zled; -zling** : to steal (as money) by falsifying records — **em·bez·zle·ment** *n* — **em·bez·zler** *n*
em·bit·ter \im-'bi-tər\ *vb* **1** : to arouse bitter feelings in **2** : to make bitter
em·bla·zon \im-'blā-zᵊn\ *vb* **1** : to adorn with heraldic devices **2** : to display conspicuously
em·blem \'em-bləm\ *n* : something (as an object or picture) suggesting another object or an idea : SYMBOL — **em·blem·at·ic** \ˌem-blə-'ma-tik\ *also* **em·blem·at·i·cal** \-ti-kəl\ *adj*
em·body \im-'bä-dē\ *vb* **em·bod·ied; em·body·ing** **1** : INCARNATE **2** : to express in definite form **3** : to incorporate into a system or body **4** : PERSONIFY ♦ ***Synonyms*** COMBINE, INTEGRATE — **em·bodi·ment** \-di-mənt\ *n*
em·bold·en \im-'bōl-dən\ *vb* : to inspire with courage ⟨his speech ~*ed* the soldiers⟩
em·bo·lism \'em-bə-ˌli-zəm\ *n* : the obstruction of a blood vessel by a foreign or abnormal particle
em·bon·point \äⁿ-bōⁿ-'pwaⁿ\ *n* [F] : plumpness of person : STOUTNESS
em·boss \im-'bäs, -'bȯs\ *vb* : to ornament with raised work
em·bou·chure \'äm-bu̇-ˌshu̇r, ˌäm-bu̇-'shu̇r\ *n* [F, ultim. fr. *bouche* mouth] : the position and use of the lips, tongue, and teeth in playing a wind instrument
em·bow·er \im-'bau̇(-ə)r\ *vb* : to shelter or enclose in a bower
[1]**em·brace** \im-'brās\ *vb* **em·braced; em·brac·ing** **1** : to clasp in the arms; *also* : CHERISH, LOVE **2** : ENCIRCLE **3** : TAKE UP, ADOPT ⟨*embraced* the cause⟩; *also* : WELCOME ⟨*embraced* the opportunity⟩ **4** : INCLUDE **5** : to participate in an embrace ♦ ***Synonyms*** COMPREHEND, INVOLVE, ENCOMPASS, EMBODY
[2]**embrace** *n* : an encircling with the arms
em·bra·sure \im-'brā-zhər\ *n* **1** : an opening in a wall through which a cannon is fired **2** : a recess of a door or window
em·bro·ca·tion \ˌem-brə-'kā-shən\ *n* : LINIMENT
em·broi·der \im-'brȯi-dər\ *vb* **1** : to ornament with or do needlework **2** : to elaborate with exaggerated detail
em·broi·dery \im-'brȯi-də-rē\ *n, pl* **-der·ies** **1** : the forming of decorative designs with needlework **2** : something embroidered
em·broil \im-'brȯi(-ə)l\ *vb* **1** : to throw into confusion or disorder **2** : to involve in conflict or difficulties ⟨~*ed* in a dispute⟩ — **em·broil·ment** *n*
em·bryo \'em-brē-ˌō\ *n, pl* **embryos** : a living thing in its earliest stages of development — **em·bry·on·ic** \ˌem-brē-'ä-nik\ *adj*
em·bry·ol·o·gy \ˌem-brē-'ä-lə-jē\ *n* : a branch of biology dealing with embryos and their development — **em·bry·o·log·i·cal** \-brē-ə-'lä-ji-kəl\ *adj* — **em·bry·ol·o·gist** \-brē-'ä-lə-jist\ *n*
em·cee \ˌem-'sē\ *n* : MASTER OF CEREMONIES — **emcee** *vb*
EMEA *abbr* Europe, Middle East, Africa
emend \ē-'mend\ *vb* : to correct usu. by altering the text of ♦ ***Synonyms*** RECTIFY, REVISE, AMEND — **emen·da·tion** \ˌē-ˌmen-'dā-shən\ *n*
emer *abbr* emeritus
[1]**em·er·ald** \'em-rəld, 'e-mə-\ *n* : a green beryl prized as a gem
[2]**emerald** *adj* : brightly or richly green
emerge \i-'mərj\ *vb* **emerged; emerg·ing** : to rise, come forth, or come out into view — **emer·gence** \-'mər-jəns\ *n* — **emer·gent** \-jənt\ *adj*
emer·gen·cy \i-'mər-jən-sē\ *n, pl* **-cies** : an unforeseen event or condition requiring prompt action ♦ ***Synonyms*** EXIGENCY, CONTINGENCY, CRISIS, JUNCTURE
emergency room *n* : a hospital room for receiving and treating persons needing immediate medical care
emer·i·ta \i-'mer-ə-tə\ *adj* : EMERITUS — used of a woman
emer·i·tus \i-'mer-ə-təs\ *adj* [L] : retired from active duty ⟨professor ~⟩
em·ery \'e-mə-rē\ *n, pl* **em·er·ies** : a dark granular mineral consisting primarily of corundum and used as an abrasive
emet·ic \i-'me-tik\ *n* : an agent that induces vomiting — **emetic** *adj*
emf *n* [electro*m*otive *f*orce] : POTENTIAL DIFFERENCE
em·i·grate \'e-mə-ˌgrāt\ *vb* **-grat·ed; -grat·ing** : to leave a place (as a country) to settle elsewhere — **em·i·grant** \-mi-grənt\ *n* — **em·i·gra·tion** \ˌe-mə-'grā-shən\ *n*
émi·gré *also* **emi·gré** \'e-mi-ˌgrā, ˌe-mi-'grā\ *n* [F] : a person who emigrates esp. because of political conditions
em·i·nence \'e-mə-nəns\ *n* **1** : high rank or position; *also* : a person of high rank or attainment **2** : a lofty place
em·i·nent \'e-mə-nənt\ *adj* **1** : CONSPICUOUS, EVIDENT **2** : DISTINGUISHED, PROMINENT ⟨an ~ physician⟩ — **em·i·nent·ly** *adv*
eminent domain *n* : a right of a government to take private property for public use
emir *or* **amir** \ə-'mir, ā-\ *n* [Ar *amīr* commander] : a ruler, chief, or commander in Islamic countries — **emir·ate** \'e-mər-ət\ *n*
em·is·sary \'e-mə-ˌser-ē\ *n, pl* **-sar·ies** : AGENT; *esp* : a secret agent
emis·sion \ē-'mi-shən\ *n* : something emitted; *esp* : substances discharged into the air
emit \ē-'mit\ *vb* **emit·ted; emit·ting** **1** : to give off or out ⟨~ light⟩; *also* : EJECT **2** : EXPRESS, UTTER ⟨*emitted* a groan⟩ — **emit·ter** *n*
emo·ji \ē-'mō-jē\ *n, pl* **emoji** *or* **emo·jis** [Jp, fr. *e-* picture, drawing + *moji* charac-

ter] : any of various small images, symbols, or icons used in text fields in electronic communications to express something (as an emotion) without using words

emol·lient \i-ˈmäl-yənt\ *adj* : making soft or supple; *also* : soothing esp. to the skin or mucous membrane ⟨an ~ hand lotion⟩ — **emol·lient** *n*

emol·u·ment \i-ˈmäl-yə-mənt\ *n* [ME, fr. L *emolumentum* advantage, fr. *emolere* to produce by grinding] : the product (as salary or fees) of an employment

emote \i-ˈmōt\ *vb* **emot·ed; emot·ing** : to give expression to emotion in or as if in a play

emo·ti·con \i-ˈmō-ti-ˌkän\ *n* : a group of keyboard characters (as :)) that often represents a facial expression and that is used esp. in electronic communications

emo·tion \i-ˈmō-shən\ *n* : a usu. intense feeling (as of love, hate, or despair) — **emo·tion·al** \-shə-nəl\ *adj* — **emo·tion·al·ly** *adv*

emot·ive \i-ˈmō-tiv\ *adj* **1** : of or relating to the emotions **2** : appealing to or expressing emotion

emp *abbr* emperor; empress

empanel *var of* IMPANEL

em·pa·thy \ˈem-pə-thē\ *n* : the experiencing as one's own of the feelings of another; *also* : the capacity for this — **em·path·ic** \em-ˈpa-thik\ *adj*

em·pen·nage \ˌäm-pə-ˈnäzh, ˌem-\ *n* [F] : the tail assembly of an airplane

em·per·or \ˈem-pər-ər\ *n* : the sovereign male ruler of an empire

em·pha·sis \ˈem-fə-səs\ *n, pl* **-pha·ses** \-ˌsēz\ : particular prominence given (as to a syllable in speaking or to a phase of action)

em·pha·sise *Brit var of* EMPHASIZE

em·pha·size \-ˌsīz\ *vb* **-sized; -siz·ing** : to place emphasis on : STRESS

em·phat·ic \im-ˈfa-tik, em-\ *adj* : uttered with emphasis : STRESSED ⟨an ~ refusal⟩ — **em·phat·i·cal·ly** \-ˈti-k(ə-)lē\ *adv*

em·phy·se·ma \ˌem-fə-ˈzē-mə, -ˈsē-\ *n* : a condition marked esp. by abnormal expansion of the air spaces of the lungs resulting in severe breathlessness

em·pire \ˈem-ˌpī(-ə)r\ *n* **1** : a large state or a group of states under a single sovereign who is usu. an emperor; *also* : something resembling a political empire **2** : imperial sovereignty or dominion

em·pir·i·cal \im-ˈpir-i-kəl\ *also* **em·pir·ic** \-ik\ *adj* : based on observation; *also* : subject to verification by observation or experiment ⟨~ laws⟩ — **em·pir·i·cal·ly** \-i-k(ə-)lē\ *adv*

em·pir·i·cism \im-ˈpir-ə-ˌsi-zəm, em-\ *n* : the practice of relying on observation and experiment esp. in the natural sciences — **em·pir·i·cist** \-sist\ *n*

em·place·ment \im-ˈplās-mənt\ *n* **1** : a prepared position for weapons or military equipment **2** : PLACEMENT

¹em·ploy \im-ˈplȯi\ *vb* **1** : to make use of **2** : to use the services of **3** : OCCUPY, DEVOTE — **em·ploy·er** *n*

²em·ploy \im-ˈplȯi; ˈim-ˌplȯi, ˈem-\ *n* : EMPLOYMENT

em·ploy·ee *also* **em·ploye** \im-ˌplȯi-ˈē, ˌem-; im-ˈplȯi-ˌē, em-\ *n* : a person who works for another

em·ploy·ment \im-ˈplȯi-mənt\ *n* **1** : OCCUPATION, ACTIVITY **2** : the act of employing : the condition of being employed

em·po·ri·um \im-ˈpȯr-ē-əm, em-\ *n, pl* **-ri·ums** *also* **-ria** \-ē-ə\ [L, fr. Gk *emporion,* fr. *emporos* traveler, trader] : a commercial center; *esp* : a store carrying varied articles

em·pow·er \im-ˈpau̇(-ə)r\ *vb* : to give authority or power to; *also* : ENABLE — **em·pow·er·ment** \-mənt\ *n*

em·press \ˈem-prəs\ *n* **1** : the wife or widow of an emperor **2** : a woman who is the sovereign ruler of an empire

¹emp·ty \ˈemp-tē\ *adj* **emp·ti·er; -est** [ME, fr. OE *ǣmettig* unoccupied, fr. *ǣmetta* leisure] **1** : containing nothing ⟨~ shelves⟩ **2** : UNOCCUPIED, UNINHABITED ⟨an ~ building⟩ **3** : lacking value, force, sense, or purpose ♦ ***Synonyms*** VACANT, BLANK, VOID, STARK, VACUOUS — **emp·ti·ness** *n*

²empty *vb* **emp·tied; emp·ty·ing** **1** : to make or become empty **2** : to discharge contents; *also* : to remove from what holds or encloses

³empty *n, pl* **empties** : an empty bottle or can

emp·ty–hand·ed \ˌemp-tē-ˈhan-dəd\ *adj* **1** : having or bringing nothing **2** : having acquired or gained nothing

em·py·re·an \ˌem-ˌpī-ˈrē-ən, -pə-\ *n* **1** : the highest heaven; *also* : FIRMAMENT **2** : an ideal place or state

EMT \ˌē-(ˌ)em-ˈtē\ *n* [*e*mergency *m*edical *t*echnician] : a specially trained medical technician certified to provide basic medical services before and during transport to a hospital

¹emu \ˈē-myü, -mü\ *n* : a swift-running flightless Australian bird smaller than the related ostrich

²emu *abbr* electromagnetic unit

em·u·late \ˈem-yu̇-ˌlāt\ *vb* **-lat·ed; -lat·ing** : to strive to equal or excel : IMITATE — **em·u·la·tion** \ˌem-yu̇-ˈlā-shən\ *n* — **em·u·lous** \ˈem-yu̇-ləs\ *adj*

emul·si·fi·er \i-ˈməl-sə-ˌfī(-ə)r\ *n* : a substance (as a soap) that helps to form and stabilize an emulsion

emul·si·fy \-ˌfī\ *vb* **-fied; -fy·ing** : to disperse (as an oil) in an emulsion — **emul·si·fi·ca·tion** \i-ˌməl-sə-fə-ˈkā-shən\ *n*

emul·sion \i-ˈməl-shən\ *n* **1** : a mixture of mutually insoluble liquids in which one is dispersed in droplets throughout the other ⟨an ~ of oil in water⟩ **2** : a light-sensitive coating on photographic film or paper

en \ˈen\ *n* : a length approximately half the width of the letter *M*

¹-en *also* **-n** *adj suffix* : made of : consisting of ⟨earth*en*⟩

²-en *vb suffix* **1** : become or cause to be ⟨sharp*en*⟩ **2** : cause or come to have ⟨length*en*⟩

en·able \i-ˈnā-bəl\ *vb* **en·abled; en·abling** **1** : to make able or feasible ⟨wings that ~ one to fly⟩ **2** : to give legal power, capacity, or sanction to

en·act \i-ˈnakt\ *vb* **1** : to make into law **2** : to act out — **en·act·ment** *n*

enam·el \i-ˈna-məl\ *n* **1** : a glasslike substance used to coat the surface of metal or pottery **2** : the hard outer layer of a tooth **3** : a usu. glossy paint that forms a hard coat — **enamel** *vb*

enam·el·ware \-ˌwer\ *n* : metal utensils coated with enamel

en·am·or \i-ˈna-mər\ *vb* : to inflame with love

en·am·our *chiefly Brit var of* ENAMOR

en bloc \äⁿ-ˈbläk\ *adv or adj* : as a whole : in a mass

enc *or* **encl** *abbr* enclosure

en·camp \in-ˈkamp\ *vb* : to make camp — **en·camp·ment** *n*

en·cap·su·late \in-ˈkap-sə-ˌlāt\ *vb* **-lat·ed; -lat·ing** **1** : to encase or become encased in a capsule **2** : SUMMARIZE — **en·cap·su·la·tion** \-ˌkap-sə-ˈlā-shən\ *n*

en·case \in-ˈkās\ *vb* : to enclose in or as if in a case — **en·case·ment** \-ˈkā-smənt\ *n*

-ence *n suffix* **1** : action or process ⟨emerg*ence*⟩ : instance of an action or process ⟨refer*ence*⟩ **2** : quality or state ⟨depend*ence*⟩

en·ceinte \äⁿn-ˈsant\ *adj* : PREGNANT 1

en·ceph·a·li·tis \in-ˌse-fə-ˈlī-təs\ *n, pl* **-lit·i·des** \-ˈli-tə-ˌdēz\ : inflammation of the brain — **en·ceph·a·lit·ic** \-ˈli-tik\ *adj*

en·ceph·a·lop·a·thy \in-ˌse-fə-ˈlä-pə-thē\ *n, pl* **-thies** : a disease of the brain

en·chain \in-ˈchān\ *vb* : FETTER, CHAIN

en·chant \in-ˈchant\ *vb* **1** : BEWITCH **2** : ENRAPTURE, FASCINATE ⟨was ~*ed* by his poetry⟩ — **en·chant·er** *n* — **en·chant·ing·ly** *adv* — **en·chant·ment** *n* — **en·chant·ress** \-ˈchan-trəs\ *n*

en·chi·la·da \ˌen-chə-ˈlä-də\ *n* : a tortilla rolled around a filling, covered with chili sauce, and usu. baked

en·ci·pher \in-ˈsī-fər, en-\ *vb* : ENCODE

en·cir·cle \in-ˈsər-kəl\ *vb* : to pass completely around : SURROUND — **en·cir·cle·ment** *n*

en·clave \ˈen-ˌklāv; ˈän-ˌkläv\ *n* : a distinct territorial, cultural, or social unit enclosed within or as if within foreign territory

en·close \in-ˈklōz\ *vb* **1** : to shut up or in; *esp* : to surround with a fence **2** : to include along with something else in a parcel or envelope ⟨~ a check⟩ — **en·clo·sure** \-ˈklō-zhər\ *n*

en·code \in-ˈkōd, en-\ *vb* : to convert (a message) into code

en·co·mi·um \en-ˈkō-mē-əm\ *n, pl* **-mi·ums** *also* **-mia** \-mē-ə\ : high or glowing praise

en·com·pass \in-ˈkəm-pəs\ *vb* **1** : ENCIRCLE **2** : ENVELOP, INCLUDE

en·core \ˈän-ˌkȯr\ *n* **1** : a demand for repetition or reappearance **2** : a further performance or appearance demanded by an audience **3** : a second achievement that usu. surpasses the first — **encore** *vb*

[1]**en·coun·ter** \in-ˈkau̇n-tər\ *vb* **1** : to meet as an enemy : FIGHT **2** : to meet usu. unexpectedly ⟨~ problems⟩

[2]**encounter** *n* **1** : a hostile usu. violent meeting **2** : a chance meeting **3** : an experience shared with another ⟨a romantic ~⟩

en·cour·age \in-ˈkər-ij\ *vb* **-aged; -ag·ing** **1** : to inspire with courage and hope **2** : STIMULATE, INCITE ⟨tax cuts to ~ spending⟩ **3** : FOSTER — **en·cour·age·ment** *n* — **en·cour·ag·ing·ly** *adv*

en·croach \in-ˈkrōch\ *vb* [ME *encrochen* to seize, fr. AF *encrocher,* fr. *croche* hook] : to enter gradually or stealthily upon another's property or rights — **en·croach·er** *n* — **en·croach·ment** *n*

en·crust *also* **in·crust** \in-ˈkrəst\ *vb* : to provide with or form a crust

en·crus·ta·tion \(ˌ)in-ˌkrəs-ˈtā-shən, ˌen-\ *var of* INCRUSTATION

en·crypt \in-ˈkript, en-\ *vb* : to change (information) from one form to another esp. to hide its meaning — **en·cryp·tion** \-ˈkrip-shən\ *n*

en·cum·ber \in-ˈkəm-bər\ *vb* **1** : to weigh down : BURDEN **2** : to hinder the function or activity of ⟨relations ~*ed* by mistrust⟩ — **en·cum·brance** \-brəns\ *n*

ency *or* **encyc** *abbr* encyclopedia

-en·cy *n suffix* : quality or state ⟨despon*dency*⟩

[1]**en·cyc·li·cal** \in-ˈsi-kli-kəl, en-\ *adj* : addressed to all the individuals of a group

[2]**encyclical** *n* : an encyclical letter; *esp* : a papal letter to the bishops of the church

en·cy·clo·pae·dia, en·cy·clo·pae·dic *chiefly Brit var of* ENCYCLOPEDIA, ENCYCLOPEDIC

en·cy·clo·pe·dia \in-ˌsī-klə-ˈpē-dē-ə\ *n* [ML *encyclopaedia* course of general education, fr. Gk *enkyklios paideia* general education] : a work treating the various branches of learning — **en·cy·clo·pe·dic** \-ˈpē-dik\ *adj*

en·cyst \in-ˈsist, en-\ *vb* : to form or become enclosed in a cyst — **en·cyst·ment** *n*

[1]**end** \ˈend\ *n* **1** : the part of an area that lies at the boundary; *also* : a point which marks the extent or limit of something or at which something ceases to exist **2** : a ceasing of a course (as of action or activity); *also* : DEATH **3** : the ultimate state; *also* : RESULT, ISSUE **4** : REMNANT **5** : PURPOSE, OBJECTIVE **6** : a player stationed at the extremity of a line (as in football) **7** : a share, operation, or aspect of an undertaking

[2]**end** *vb* **1** : to bring or come to an end **2** : DESTROY; *also* : DIE **3** : to form or be at the end of ♦ ***Synonyms*** CLOSE, CONCLUDE, TERMINATE, FINISH, COMPLETE

en·dan·ger \in-ˈdān-jər\ *vb* : to bring into danger; *also* : to create danger

en·dan·gered *adj* : being or relating to an endangered species

endangered species *n* : a species threatened with extinction

en·dear \in-ˈdir\ *vb* : to cause to become beloved or admired

en·dear·ment \-mənt\ *n* : a word or an act expressing affection : CARESS
en·deav·or \in-ˈde-vər\ *vb* : TRY, ATTEMPT — **endeavor** *n*
en·deav·our *chiefly Brit var of* ENDEAVOR
en·dem·ic \en-ˈde-mik, in-\ *adj* : restricted to a particular place ⟨~ plants⟩ ⟨an ~ disease⟩ — **endemic** *n*
end·ing \ˈen-diŋ\ *n* : something that forms an end; *esp* : SUFFIX
en·dive \ˈen-ˌdīv\ *n* **1** : an herb related to chicory and grown as a salad plant **2** : the blanched shoot of chicory
end·less \ˈend-ləs\ *adj* **1** : having or seeming to have no end : ETERNAL ⟨~ debates⟩ **2** : united at the ends : CONTINUOUS ⟨an ~ belt⟩ ♦ ***Synonyms*** INTERMINABLE, EVERLASTING, UNCEASING, CEASELESS, UNENDING — **end·less·ly** *adv*
end·most \-ˌmōst\ *adj* : situated at the very end
end·note \-ˌnōt\ *n* : a note placed at the end of a text
en·do·crine \ˈen-də-krən, -ˌkrīn, -ˌkrēn\ *adj* : producing secretions that are distributed by way of the bloodstream ⟨~ glands⟩ — **endocrine** *n* — **en·do·cri·nol·o·gist** \-kri-ˈnä-lə-jist\ *n* — **en·do·cri·nol·o·gy** \-jē\ *n*
en·dog·e·nous \en-ˈdä-jə-nəs\ *adj* : caused or produced by factors inside the organism or system ⟨~ depression⟩ — **en·dog·e·nous·ly** *adv*
en·do·me·tri·um \ˌen-dō-ˈmē-trē-əm\ *n, pl* **-tria** \-trē-ə\ : the mucous membrane lining the uterus — **en·do·me·tri·al** \-trē-əl\ *adj*
en·dor·phin \en-ˈdȯr-fən\ *n* : any of a group of endogenous morphinelike proteins found esp. in the brain
en·dorse *also* **in·dorse** \in-ˈdȯrs\ *vb* **en·dorsed; en·dors·ing** [ME *endosen*, fr. AF *endosser* to put on, don, write on the back of, fr. *dos* back, fr. L *dorsum*] **1** : to sign one's name on the back of (as a check) **2** : to approve openly : SANCTION ⟨~ an idea⟩ **3** : to recommend (as a product) usu. for financial compensation — **en·dorse·ment** *also* **in·dorse·ment** *n*
en·do·scope \ˈen-də-ˌskōp\ *n* : an illuminated usu. fiber-optic instrument for visualizing the interior of a hollow organ or part (as the colon or esophagus) — **en·do·scop·ic** \ˌen-də-ˈskä-pik\ *adj* — **en·dos·co·py** \en-ˈdäs-kə-pē\ *n*
en·do·ther·mic \ˌen-də-ˈthər-mik\ *adj* : characterized by or formed with absorption of heat
en·dow \in-ˈdau̇\ *vb* **1** : to furnish with funds for support ⟨~ a school⟩ **2** : to furnish with something freely or naturally ⟨~*ed* with intellect⟩ — **en·dow·ment** *n*
en·due \in-ˈdü, -ˈdyü\ *vb* **en·dued; en·du·ing** : PROVIDE, ENDOW
en·dur·ance \in-ˈdu̇r-əns, -ˈdyu̇r-\ *n* **1** : DURATION **2** : the ability to withstand hardship or stress : FORTITUDE
en·dure \in-ˈdu̇r, -ˈdyu̇r\ *vb* **en·dured; en·dur·ing** **1** : LAST, PERSIST **2** : to suffer firmly or patiently : BEAR **3** : TOLERATE — **en·dur·able** *adj*
end·ways \ˈend-ˌwāz\ *adv or adj* **1** : LENGTHWISE **2** : with the end forward **3** : on end
end·wise \-ˌwīz\ *adv or adj* : ENDWAYS
ENE *abbr* east-northeast
en·e·ma \ˈe-nə-mə\ *n, pl* **enemas** *also* **ene·ma·ta** \ˌe-nə-ˈmä-tə, ˈe-nə-mə-tə\ : injection of liquid into the rectum; *also* : material so injected
en·e·my \ˈe-nə-mē\ *n, pl* **-mies** [ME *enemi*, fr. AF, fr. L *inimicus*, fr. *in-* not + *amicus* friend] : one that attacks or tries to harm another : FOE; *esp* : a military opponent
en·er·get·ic \ˌe-nər-ˈje-tik\ *adj* : marked by energy : ACTIVE, VIGOROUS ♦ ***Synonyms*** STRENUOUS, LUSTY, DYNAMIC, VITAL — **en·er·get·i·cal·ly** \-ti-k(ə-)lē\ *adv*
en·er·gise *Brit var of* ENERGIZE
en·er·gize \ˈe-nər-ˌjīz\ *vb* **-gized; -giz·ing** : to give energy to
en·er·gy \ˈe-nər-jē\ *n, pl* **-gies** **1** : vigorous action : EFFORT **2** : capacity for action **3** : a fundamental entity of nature usu. regarded as the capacity for performing work **4** : usable power (as heat or electricity); *also* : the resources for producing such power
energy level *n* : one of the stable states of constant energy that may be assumed by a physical system (as the electrons in an atom)
en·er·vate \ˈe-nər-ˌvāt\ *vb* **-vat·ed; -vat·ing** : to lessen the strength or vigor of : weaken in mind or body ⟨*enervated* by work⟩ — **en·er·vat·ing·ly** \-ˌvā-tiŋ-lē\ *adv* — **en·er·va·tion** \ˌe-nər-ˈvā-shən\ *n*
en·fee·ble \in-ˈfē-bəl\ *vb* **-bled; -bling** : to make feeble ♦ ***Synonyms*** WEAKEN, DEBILITATE, SAP, UNDERMINE, CRIPPLE — **en·fee·ble·ment** *n*
en·fi·lade \ˈen-fə-ˌlād, -ˌläd\ *n* : gunfire directed along the length of an enemy battle line — **enfilade** *vb*
en·fold \in-ˈfōld\ *vb* **1** : ENVELOP ⟨darkness ~*ed* the city⟩ **2** : EMBRACE
en·force \in-ˈfȯrs\ *vb* **1** : COMPEL ⟨~ obedience by threats⟩ **2** : to execute effectively ⟨~ the law⟩ — **en·force·able** *adj* — **en·force·ment** *n*
en·forc·er \in-ˈfȯr-sər\ *n* : one that enforces; *esp* : a player (as in ice hockey) known for rough play
en·fran·chise \in-ˈfran-ˌchīz\ *vb* **-chised; -chis·ing** **1** : to set free (as from slavery) **2** : to admit to citizenship; *also* : to grant the vote to — **en·fran·chise·ment** \-ˌchīz-mənt, -chəz-\ *n*
eng *abbr* engine; engineer; engineering
Eng *abbr* England; English
en·gage \in-ˈgāj\ *vb* **en·gaged; en·gag·ing** **1** : PLEDGE; *esp* : to bind by a pledge to marry **2** : EMPLOY, HIRE **3** : to attract and hold esp. by interesting; *also* : to cause to participate **4** : to commence or take part in a venture ⟨*engaged* in shady deals⟩ **5** : to bring or enter into

conflict ⟨~ the enemy⟩ **6** : to connect or interlock with : MESH; *also* : to cause to mesh
en•gage•ment \in-ˈgāj-mənt\ *n* **1** : APPOINTMENT **2** : EMPLOYMENT **3** : a mutual promise to marry : BETROTHAL **4** : a hostile encounter
en•gag•ing *adj* : ATTRACTIVE ⟨an ~ smile⟩ — **en•gag•ing•ly** *adv*
en•gen•der \in-ˈjen-dər\ *vb* **1** : BEGET **2** : BRING ABOUT, CREATE ⟨~ controversy⟩ ♦ *Synonyms* GENERATE, BREED, OCCASION, PRODUCE
en•gine \ˈen-jən\ *n* [ME *engin,* fr. AF, fr. L *ingenium* natural disposition, talent] **1** : a mechanical device **2** : a machine for converting energy into mechanical motion **3** : LOCOMOTIVE **4** : software that performs a fundamental function esp. of a larger program — **en•gine•less** *adj*
[1]**en•gi•neer** \ˌen-jə-ˈnir\ *n* **1** : a member of a military unit specializing in engineering work **2** : a designer or builder of engines **3** : one trained in engineering **4** : one that operates an engine
[2]**engineer** *vb* **1** : to lay out or manage as an engineer **2** : to guide the course of ⟨~ a rally⟩ ♦ *Synonyms* PILOT, LEAD, STEER
en•gi•neer•ing *n* : the practical applications of scientific and mathematical principles
En•glish \ˈiŋ-glish\ *n* **1** : the language of England, the U.S., and many areas now or formerly under British rule **2 English** *pl* : the people of England **3** : spin imparted to a ball that is driven or rolled — **English** *adj* — **En•glish•man** \-mən\ *n* — **En•glish•wom•an** \-ˌwu̇-mən\ *n*
English horn *n* : a woodwind instrument longer than and having a range lower than the oboe
English setter *n* : any of a breed of hunting dogs with a flat silky coat of white or white with color
English sparrow *n* : HOUSE SPARROW
English system *n* : a system of weights and measures in which the foot is the principal unit of length and the pound is the principal unit of weight
engr *abbr* **1** engineer **2** engraved
en•gram \ˈen-ˌgram\ *n* : a hypothetical change in neural tissue postulated in order to account for persistence of memory
en•grave \in-ˈgrāv\ *vb* **en•graved; en•grav•ing** **1** : to produce (as letters or lines) by incising a surface **2** : to cut figures, letters, or designs on for printing; *also* : to print from an engraved plate ⟨~ an invitation⟩ **3** : PHOTOENGRAVE — **en•grav•er** *n*
en•grav•ing \in-ˈgrā-viŋ\ *n* **1** : the art of one who engraves **2** : an engraved plate; *also* : a print made from it
en•gross \in-ˈgrōs\ *vb* : to take up the whole interest or attention of ♦ *Synonyms* MONOPOLIZE, ABSORB, CONSUME
en•gulf \in-ˈgəlf\ *vb* : to flow over and enclose : OVERWHELM ⟨~*ed* in flames⟩
en•hance \in-ˈhans\ *vb* **en•hanced; en•hanc•ing** : to increase or improve (as in value or desirability) ♦ *Synonyms* HEIGHTEN, INTENSIFY, MAGNIFY — **en•hance•ment** *n*
enig•ma \i-ˈnig-mə\ *n* [L *aenigma,* fr. Gk *ainigma,* fr. *ainissesthai* to speak in riddles, fr. *ainos* fable] : something obscure or hard to understand
enig•mat•ic \ˌen-ig-ˈma-tik\ *adj* : resembling an enigma ♦ *Synonyms* OBSCURE, CRYPTIC, MYSTIFYING — **en•ig•mat•i•cal•ly** \-ti-k(ə-)lē\ *adv*
en•join \in-ˈjȯin\ *vb* **1** : COMMAND, ORDER ⟨~*ed* us to desist⟩ **2** : FORBID ♦ *Synonyms* DIRECT, BID, CHARGE, COMMAND, INSTRUCT
en•joy \in-ˈjȯi\ *vb* **1** : to have for one's benefit or use ⟨~ good health⟩ **2** : to take pleasure or satisfaction in ⟨~*ed* the concert⟩ — **en•joy•able** *adj* — **en•joy•ment** *n*
enl *abbr* **1** enlarged **2** enlisted
en•large \in-ˈlärj\ *vb* **en•larged; en•larg•ing** **1** : to make or grow larger **2** : ELABORATE ♦ *Synonyms* INCREASE, AUGMENT, MULTIPLY, EXPAND — **en•large•ment** *n*
en•light•en \in-ˈlī-tᵊn\ *vb* **1** : INSTRUCT, INFORM **2** : to give spiritual insight to — **en•light•en•ment** *n*
en•list \in-ˈlist\ *vb* **1** : to secure the aid or support of **2** : to engage for service in the armed forces — **en•list•ee** \-ˌlis-ˈtē\ *n* — **en•list•ment** \-ˈlist-mənt\ *n*
en•list•ed \in-ˈlis-təd\ *adj* : of, relating to, or forming the part of a military force below commissioned or warrant officers
enlisted man *n* : a man or woman in the armed forces ranking below a commissioned or warrant officer
en•liv•en \in-ˈlī-vən\ *vb* : to give life, action, or spirit to : ANIMATE
en masse \äⁿ-ˈmas\ *adv* [F] : in a body : as a whole
en•mesh \in-ˈmesh\ *vb* : to catch or entangle in or as if in meshes
en•mi•ty \ˈen-mə-tē\ *n, pl* **-ties** : ILL WILL; *esp* : mutual hatred ♦ *Synonyms* HOSTILITY, ANTIPATHY, ANIMOSITY, RANCOR, ANTAGONISM
en•no•ble \i-ˈnō-bəl\ *vb* **-bled; -bling** : EXALT, ELEVATE; *esp* : to raise to noble rank — **en•no•ble•ment** *n*
en•nui \ˌän-ˈwē\ *n* [F] : BOREDOM
enor•mi•ty \i-ˈnȯr-mə-tē\ *n, pl* **-ties** **1** : an outrageous, vicious, or immoral act **2** : great wickedness **3** : IMMENSITY
enor•mous \i-ˈnȯr-məs\ *adj* [L *enormis,* fr. *e, ex* out of + *norma* rule] **1** : exceedingly wicked **2** : great in size, number, or degree : HUGE ♦ *Synonyms* IMMENSE, VAST, GIGANTIC, COLOSSAL, MAMMOTH, ELEPHANTINE — **enor•mous•ly** *adv*
[1]**enough** \i-ˈnəf\ *adj* : SUFFICIENT
[2]**enough** *adv* **1** : SUFFICIENTLY **2** : FULLY, QUITE **3** : TOLERABLY
[3]**enough** *pron* : a sufficient number, quantity, or amount
en•quire \in-ˈkwī(-ə)r\, **en•qui•ry** \ˈin-ˌkwī(-ə)r-ē, in-ˈ; ˈin-kwə-rē, ˈiŋ-\ *chiefly Brit var of* INQUIRE, INQUIRY

en·rage \in-ˈrāj\ *vb* : to fill with rage

en·rap·ture \in-ˈrap-chər\ *vb* **en·rap·tured; en·rap·tur·ing** : DELIGHT

en·rich \in-ˈrich\ *vb* **1** : to make rich or richer **2** : ORNAMENT, ADORN — **en·rich·ment** *n*

en·roll *also* **en·rol** \in-ˈrōl\ *vb* **en·rolled; en·roll·ing** **1** : to enter or register on a roll or list **2** : to offer (oneself) for enrolling — **en·roll·ment** *n*

en route \än-ˈrüt, en-\ *adv or adj* : on or along the way ⟨while *en route* to work⟩

ENS *abbr* ensign

en·sconce \in-ˈskäns\ *vb* **en·sconced; en·sconc·ing** **1** : SHELTER, CONCEAL **2** : to settle snugly or securely ♦ ***Synonyms*** SECRETE, HIDE, CACHE, STASH

en·sem·ble \än-ˈsäm-bəl\ *n* [F, fr. *ensemble* together, fr. L *insimul* at the same time] : a group (as of singers, dancers, or players) or a set (as of clothes) producing a single effect

en·sheathe \in-ˈshēth\ *vb* : to cover with or as if with a sheath

en·shrine \in-ˈshrīn\ *vb* **1** : to enclose in or as if in a shrine **2** : to cherish as sacred — **en·shrine·ment** \-mənt\ *n*

en·shroud \in-ˈshrau̇d\ *vb* : SHROUD, OBSCURE

en·sign \ˈen-sən, *1 also* ˈen-ˌsīn\ *n* **1** : FLAG; *also* : BADGE, EMBLEM **2** : a commissioned officer in the navy ranking next below a lieutenant junior grade

en·slave \in-ˈslāv\ *vb* : to reduce to or as if to slavery — **en·slave·ment** *n*

en·snare \in-ˈsner\ *vb* : SNARE, TRAP ♦ ***Synonyms*** ENTRAP, BAG, CATCH, CAPTURE

en·sue \in-ˈsü\ *vb* **en·sued; en·su·ing** : to follow in time or as a result ⟨the birds escaped and chaos *ensued*⟩

en·sure \in-ˈshu̇r\ *vb* **en·sured; en·sur·ing** : INSURE, GUARANTEE

ENT \ˌē-ˌen-ˈtē\ *n* : a physician specializing in otolaryngology

en·tail \in-ˈtāl\ *vb* **1** : to limit the inheritance of (property) to the owner's lineal descendants or to a class thereof **2** : to include or involve as a necessary step or result ⟨the sacrifices that parenting ~*s*⟩ — **en·tail·ment** *n*

en·tan·gle \in-ˈtaŋ-gəl\ *vb* : TANGLE, CONFUSE — **en·tan·gle·ment** *n*

en·tente \än-ˈtänt\ *n* [F] : an understanding providing for joint action; *also* : parties linked by such an entente

en·ter \ˈen-tər\ *vb* **1** : to go or come in or into **2** : to become a member of : JOIN ⟨~ the ministry⟩ **3** : BEGIN **4** : to take part in : CONTRIBUTE **5** : to go into or upon and take possession **6** : to set down (as in a list) : REGISTER ⟨~ the data⟩ **7** : to place (a complaint) before a court; *also* : to put on record ⟨~ a complaint⟩

en·ter·i·tis \ˌen-tə-ˈrī-təs\ *n* : intestinal inflammation; *also* : a disease marked by this

en·ter·prise \ˈen-tər-ˌprīz\ *n* **1** : UNDERTAKING, PROJECT **2** : readiness for daring action : INITIATIVE **3** : a business organization

en·ter·pris·ing \-ˌprī-ziŋ\ *adj* : bold and vigorous in action : ENERGETIC

en·ter·tain \ˌen-tər-ˈtān\ *vb* **1** : to treat or receive as a guest **2** : AMUSE, DIVERT ⟨~*ed* us with jokes⟩ **3** : to hold in mind ⟨~*ed* thoughts of retirement⟩ ♦ ***Synonyms*** HARBOR, SHELTER, LODGE, HOUSE, BILLET — **en·ter·tain·er** *n* — **en·ter·tain·ment** *n*

en·thrall *or* **en·thral** \in-ˈthrȯl\ *vb* **en·thralled; en·thrall·ing** **1** : ENSLAVE **2** : to hold spellbound

en·throne \in-ˈthrōn\ *vb* **1** : to seat on or as if on a throne **2** : EXALT

en·thuse \in-ˈthüz, -ˈthyüz\ *vb* **en·thused; en·thus·ing** **1** : to make enthusiastic **2** : to show enthusiasm

en·thu·si·asm \in-ˈthü-zē-ˌa-zəm, -ˈthyü-\ *n* [Gk *enthousiasmos,* fr. *enthousiazein* to be inspired, irreg. fr. *entheos* inspired, fr. *theos* god] **1** : strong warmth of feeling : keen interest : FERVOR **2** : a cause of fervor — **en·thu·si·ast** \-ˌast, -əst\ *n* — **en·thu·si·as·tic** \in-ˌthü-zē-ˈas-tik, -ˌthyü-\ *adj* — **en·thu·si·as·ti·cal·ly** \-ti-k(ə-)lē\ *adv*

en·tice \in-ˈtīs\ *vb* **en·ticed; en·tic·ing** : ALLURE, TEMPT — **en·tice·ment** *n*

en·tire \in-ˈtī(-ə)r\ *adj* : COMPLETE, WHOLE ♦ ***Synonyms*** SOUND, PERFECT, INTACT, UNDAMAGED — **en·tire·ly** *adv*

en·tire·ty \in-ˈtī-rə-tē, -ˈtī(-ə)r-tē\ *n, pl* **-ties** **1** : COMPLETENESS **2** : WHOLE, TOTALITY

en·ti·tle \in-ˈtī-tᵊl\ *vb* **en·ti·tled; en·ti·tling** **1** : NAME, DESIGNATE **2** : to give a right or claim to ⟨*entitled* to a fair trial⟩

en·ti·tle·ment \in-ˈtī-tᵊl-mənt\ *n* : a government program providing benefits to members of a specified group

en·ti·ty \ˈen-tə-tē\ *n, pl* **-ties** **1** : EXISTENCE, BEING **2** : something with separate and real existence

en·tomb \in-ˈtüm\ *vb* : to place in a tomb : BURY — **en·tomb·ment** *n*

en·to·mol·o·gy \ˌen-tə-ˈmä-lə-jē\ *n* : a branch of zoology that deals with insects — **en·to·mo·log·i·cal** \-mə-ˈlä-ji-kəl\ *adj* — **en·to·mol·o·gist** \-jist\ *n*

en·tou·rage \ˌän-tü-ˈräzh\ *n* [F] : RETINUE

en·tr'acte \ˈä^{n}n-ˌtrakt\ *n* [F] **1** : something (as a dance) performed between two acts of a play **2** : the interval between two acts of a play

en·trails \ˈen-ˌtrālz\ *n pl* : VISCERA; *esp* : INTESTINES

1**en·trance** \ˈen-trəns\ *n* **1** : permission or right to enter **2** : the act of entering **3** : a means or place of entry

2**en·trance** \in-ˈtrans\ *vb* **en·tranced; en·tranc·ing** : CHARM, DELIGHT

en·trant \ˈen-trənt\ *n* : one that enters esp. as a competitor

en·trap \in-ˈtrap\ *vb* : ENSNARE, TRAP — **en·trap·ment** *n*

en·treat \in-ˈtrēt\ *vb* : to ask urgently : BESEECH ♦ ***Synonyms*** BEG, IMPLORE, PLEAD, SUPPLICATE — **en·treaty** \-ˈtrē-tē\ *n*

en·trée *or* **en·tree** \ˈän-ˌtrā\ *n* [F *entrée*]

1 : freedom of entry or access 2 : the main course of a meal in the U.S. ♦ *Synonyms* ADMISSION, ADMITTANCE, ENTRANCE

en·trench \in-ˈtrench\ *vb* 1 : to place within or surround with a trench esp. for defense; *also* : to establish solidly ⟨~*ed* customs⟩ 2 : ENCROACH, TRESPASS — **en·trench·ment** *n*

en·tre·pre·neur \ˌän-trə-prə-ˈnər, -ˈnu̇r, -ˈnyu̇r\ *n* [F, fr. OF, fr. *entreprendre* to undertake] : one who organizes and assumes the risk of a business or enterprise — **en·tre·pre·neur·ial** \-ˈnu̇r-ē-əl, -ˈnyu̇r-, -ˈnər-\ *adj* — **en·tre·pre·neur·ship** \-ˌship\ *n*

en·tro·py \ˈen-trə-pē\ *n, pl* **-pies** 1 : the degree of disorder in a system 2 : an ultimate state of inert uniformity

en·trust \in-ˈtrəst\ *vb* 1 : to commit something to as a trust 2 : to commit to another with confidence ♦ *Synonyms* CONFIDE, CONSIGN, RELEGATE, COMMEND

en·try \ˈen-trē\ *n, pl* **entries** 1 : ENTRANCE 2 2 : ENTRANCE 3; *also* : VESTIBULE 1 3 : an entering in a record; *also* : an item so entered 4 : a headword with its definition or identification; *also* : VOCABULARY ENTRY 5 : one entered in something (as a contest or market)

en·twine \in-ˈtwīn\ *vb* : to twine together or around

enu·mer·ate \i-ˈnü-mə-ˌrāt, -ˈnyü-\ *vb* **-at·ed; -at·ing** 1 : to determine the number of : COUNT 2 : LIST — **enu·mer·a·tion** \-ˌnü-mə-ˈrā-shən, -ˌnyü-\ *n*

enun·ci·ate \ē-ˈnən-sē-ˌāt\ *vb* **-at·ed; -at·ing** 1 : to state definitely; *also* : ANNOUNCE, PROCLAIM 2 : PRONOUNCE, ARTICULATE ⟨~ every syllable⟩ — **enun·ci·a·tion** \-ˌnən-sē-ˈā-shən\ *n*

en·ure·sis \ˌen-yu̇-ˈrē-səs\ *n* : involuntary discharge of urine : BED-WETTING

env *abbr* envelope

en·vel·op \in-ˈve-ləp\ *vb* : to enclose completely with or as if with a covering — **en·vel·op·ment** *n*

en·ve·lope \ˈen-və-ˌlōp, ˈän-\ *n* 1 : a usu. paper container for a letter 2 : WRAPPER, COVERING 3 : a conventionally accepted limit ⟨fashions that push the ~⟩

en·ven·om \in-ˈve-nəm\ *vb* 1 : to make poisonous 2 : EMBITTER

en·vi·able \ˈen-vē-ə-bəl\ *adj* : highly desirable — **en·vi·ably** \-blē\ *adv*

en·vi·ous \ˈen-vē-əs\ *adj* : feeling or showing envy — **en·vi·ous·ly** *adv* — **en·vi·ous·ness** *n*

en·vi·ron·ment \in-ˈvī-rən-mənt, -ˈvī(-ə)rn-\ *n* 1 : SURROUNDINGS 2 : the whole complex of factors (as soil, climate, and living things) that influence the form and the ability to survive of a plant or animal or ecological community — **en·vi·ron·men·tal** \-ˌvī-rən-ˈmen-tᵊl, -ˌvīrn-\ *adj* — **en·vi·ron·men·tal·ly** \-tᵊl-ē\ *adv*

en·vi·ron·men·tal·ist \-ˌvī-rən-ˈmen-təl-ist, -ˌvīr(-ə)n-\ *n* : a person concerned about environmental quality esp. with respect to control of pollution — **en·vi·ron·men·tal·ism** \-ˌvī-rən-ˈmen-tə-ˌli-zəm, -ˌvī(-ə)rn-\

en·vi·rons \in-ˈvī-rənz\ *n pl* 1 : SUBURBS 2 : SURROUNDINGS; *also* : VICINITY

en·vis·age \in-ˈvi-zij\ *vb* **-aged; -ag·ing** : to have a mental picture of

en·vi·sion \in-ˈvi-zhən, en-\ *vb* : to picture to oneself ⟨~*s* world peace⟩

en·voy \ˈen-ˌvȯi, ˈän-\ *n* 1 : a diplomatic agent 2 : REPRESENTATIVE, MESSENGER

¹**en·vy** \ˈen-vē\ *n, pl* **envies** [ME *envie,* fr. AF, fr. L *invidia,* fr. *invidus* envious, fr. *invidēre* to look askance at, envy, fr. *vidēre* to see] : painful or resentful awareness of another's advantages; *also* : an object of envy

²**envy** *vb* **en·vied; en·vy·ing** : to feel envy toward or on account of

en·zyme \ˈen-ˌzīm\ *n* : any of various complex proteins produced by living cells that catalyze specific biochemical reactions at body temperatures — **en·zy·mat·ic** \ˌen-zə-ˈma-tik\ *adj*

Eo·cene \ˈē-ə-ˌsēn\ *adj* : of, relating to, or being the epoch of the Tertiary between the Paleocene and the Oligocene — **Eocene** *n*

EOE *abbr* equal opportunity employer

eo·lian \ē-ˈō-lē-ən\ *adj* : borne, deposited, or produced by the wind

EOM *abbr* end of month

eon \ˈē-ən, -ˌän\ *n* : an indefinitely long time : AGE

EP *abbr* European plan

EPA *abbr* Environmental Protection Agency

ep·au·let *also* **ep·au·lette** \ˌe-pə-ˈlet\ *n* [F *épaulette,* dim. of *épaule* shoulder] : a shoulder ornament esp. on a coat or military uniform

épée \ˈe-ˌpā, ā-ˈpā\ *n* [F] : a fencing or dueling sword

Eph *or* **Ephes** *abbr* Ephesians

ephed·rine \i-ˈfe-drən\ *n* : a stimulant drug used to treat asthma and nasal congestion

ephem·era \i-ˈfe-mər-ə\ *n pl* : paper items (as posters or tickets) of little original value collected usu. as a hobby

ephem·er·al \i-ˈfe-mə-rəl\ *adj* [Gk *ephēmeros* lasting a day, daily, fr. *epi-* on + *hēmera* day] : SHORT-LIVED, TRANSITORY ♦ *Synonyms* PASSING, FLEETING, TRANSIENT, EVANESCENT — **ephem·er·al·i·ty** \i-ˌfe-mə-ˈra-lə-tē\ *n*

Ephe·sians \i-ˈfē-zhənz\ *n* — see BIBLE table

ep·ic \ˈe-pik\ *n* : a long poem in elevated style narrating the deeds of a hero — **epic** *adj*

epi·cen·ter \ˈe-pi-ˌsen-tər\ *n* : the point on the earth's surface directly above the point of origin of an earthquake

ep·i·cure \ˈe-pi-ˌkyu̇r\ *n* : a person with sensitive and discriminating tastes esp. in food and wine

ep·i·cu·re·an \ˌe-pi-kyu̇-ˈrē-ən, -ˈkyu̇r-ē-\ *n* : EPICURE — **epicurean** *adj*

¹**ep·i·dem·ic** \ˌe-pə-ˈde-mik\ *adj* : affecting many persons at one time ⟨~ disease⟩; *also* : excessively prevalent

²**epidemic** *n* : an epidemic outbreak esp. of disease

ep·i·de·mi·ol·o·gy \ˌep-ə-ˌdē-mē-ˈä-lə-jē\ *n* : the study of the incidence, distribution, and control of disease in a population — **ep·i·de·mi·o·log·i·cal** \-ˌdē-mē-ə-ˈlä-ji-kəl\ *also* **ep·i·de·mi·o·log·ic** \-jik\ *adj* — **ep·i·de·mi·ol·o·gist** \-ˈä-lə-jist\ *n*

epi·der·mis \ˌe-pə-ˈdər-məs\ *n* : an outer layer esp. of skin — **epi·der·mal** \-məl\ *adj*

epi·du·ral \ˌe-pi-ˈd(y)u̇r-əl\ *adj* : administered into the space outside the membrane that envelops the spinal cord ⟨~ anesthesia⟩ — **epidural** *n*

epi·glot·tis \ˌe-pə-ˈglä-təs\ *n* : a thin plate of flexible tissue protecting the tracheal opening during swallowing

ep·i·gram \ˈe-pə-ˌgram\ *n* : a short witty poem or saying — **ep·i·gram·mat·ic** \ˌe-pə-grə-ˈma-tik\ *adj*

ep·i·lep·sy \ˈe-pə-ˌlep-sē\ *n, pl* **-sies** [ultim. fr. Gk *epilēpsia*, fr. *epilambanein* to seize] : a disorder marked by abnormal electrical discharges in the brain and typically manifested by sudden periods of diminished consciousness or by convulsions — **ep·i·lep·tic** \ˌe-pə-ˈlep-tik\ *adj or n*

ep·i·logue *also* **ep·i·log** \ˈe-pə-ˌlȯg, -ˌläg\ *n* **1** : a concluding section of a literary work **2** : a speech addressed to the spectators by an actor at the end of a play

epi·neph·rine \ˌe-pə-ˈne-frən\ *n* : an adrenal hormone used medicinally esp. as a heart stimulant, a muscle relaxant, and a vasoconstrictor

epiph·a·ny \i-ˈpi-fə-nē\ *n, pl* **-nies** **1** *cap* : January 6 observed as a church festival in commemoration of the coming of the Magi to Jesus at Bethlehem **2** : a sudden striking understanding of something

epis·co·pa·cy \i-ˈpis-kə-pə-sē\ *n, pl* **-cies** **1** : government of a church by bishops **2** : EPISCOPATE

epis·co·pal \i-ˈpis-kə-pəl\ *adj* **1** : of or relating to a bishop or episcopacy **2** *cap* : of or relating to the Protestant Episcopal Church

Epis·co·pa·lian \i-ˌpis-kə-ˈpāl-yən\ *n* : a member of the Protestant Episcopal Church

epis·co·pate \i-ˈpis-kə-pət, -ˌpāt\ *n* **1** : the rank, office, or term of a bishop **2** : a body of bishops

ep·i·sode \ˈe-pə-ˌsōd\ *n* [Gk *epeisodion*, fr. *epeisodios* coming in besides, fr. *eisodios* coming in, fr. *eis* into + *hodos* road, journey] **1** : a unit of action in a dramatic or literary work **2** : an incident in a course of events : OCCURRENCE ⟨a feverish ~⟩ — **ep·i·sod·ic** \ˌe-pə-ˈsä-dik\ *adj*

epis·tle \i-ˈpi-səl\ *n* **1** *cap* : one of the letters of the New Testament **2** : LETTER — **epis·to·lary** \i-ˈpis-tə-ˌler-ē\ *adj*

ep·i·taph \ˈe-pə-ˌtaf\ *n* : an inscription in memory of a dead person

ep·i·tha·la·mi·um \ˌe-pə-thə-ˈlā-mē-əm\ *or* **ep·i·tha·la·mi·on** \-mē-ən\ *n, pl* **-mi·ums** *or* **-mia** \-mē-ə\ : a song or poem in honor of a bride and bridegroom

ep·i·the·li·um \ˌe-pə-ˈthē-lē-əm\ *n, pl* **-lia** \-lē-ə\ : a cellular membrane covering a bodily surface or lining a cavity — **ep·i·the·li·al** \-lē-əl\ *adj*

ep·i·thet \ˈe-pə-ˌthet, -thət\ *n* : a characterizing and often abusive word or phrase

epit·o·me \i-ˈpi-tə-mē\ *n* **1** : ABSTRACT, SUMMARY **2** : EMBODIMENT ⟨the ~ of elegance⟩ — **epit·o·mize** \-ˌmīz\ *vb*

ep·och \ˈe-pək, -ˌpäk\ *n* : a usu. extended period : ERA, AGE — **ep·och·al** \-pə-kəl, -ˌpä-\ *adj*

ep·onym \ˈe-pə-ˌnim\ *n* **1** : one for whom something is or is believed to be named **2** : a name (as of a disease) based on or derived from an eponym — **epon·y·mous** \i-ˈpä-nə-məs\ *adj*

ep·oxy \i-ˈpäk-sē\ *vb* **ep·ox·ied** *or* **ep·oxyed; ep·oxy·ing** : to glue, fill, or coat with epoxy resin

epoxy resin *n* : a synthetic resin used in coatings and adhesives

ep·si·lon \ˈep-sə-län, -lən\ *n* : the 5th letter of the Greek alphabet — Ε or ϵ

Ep·som salts \ˈep-səm-\ *n* : a bitter colorless or white magnesium salt with cathartic properties

eq *abbr* **1** equal **2** equation

equa·ble \ˈe-kwə-bəl, ˈē-\ *adj* : UNIFORM, EVEN; *esp* : free from unpleasant extremes — **eq·ua·bil·i·ty** \ˌe-kwə-ˈbi-lə-tē, ˌē-\ *n* — **eq·ua·bly** \ˈe-kwə-blē, ˈē-\ *adv*

¹equal \ˈē-kwəl\ *adj* **1** : of the same measure, quantity, value, quality, number, degree, or status as another ⟨~ opportunity⟩ **2** : IMPARTIAL ⟨~ justice⟩ **3** : free from extremes **4** : able to cope with a situation or task — **equal·i·ty** \i-ˈkwä-lə-tē\ *n* — **equal·ly** *adv*

²equal *vb* **equaled** *or* **equalled; equal·ing** *or* **equal·ling** : to be or become equal to; *also* : to be identical in value to

³equal *n* : one that is equal

equal·ise, equal·is·er *Brit var of* EQUALIZE, EQUALIZER

equal·ize \ˈē-kwə-ˌlīz\ *vb* **-ized; -iz·ing** : to make equal, uniform, or constant — **equal·i·za·tion** \ˌē-kwə-lə-ˈzā-shən\ *n* — **equal·iz·er** *n*

equals sign *or* **equal sign** *n* : a sign = indicating equivalence

equa·nim·i·ty \ˌē-kwə-ˈni-mə-tē, ˌe-\ *n, pl* **-ties** : COMPOSURE

equate \i-ˈkwāt\ *vb* **equat·ed; equat·ing** : to make, treat, or regard as equal or comparable ⟨~*s* liars with thieves⟩

equa·tion \i-ˈkwā-zhən\ *n* **1** : an act of equating : the state of being equated **2** : a usu. formal statement of equivalence esp. of mathematical expressions

equa·tor \i-ˈkwā-tər, ˈē-ˌ\ *n* : an imaginary circle around the earth that is everywhere equally distant from the two poles — **equa·to·ri·al** \ˌē-kwə-ˈtȯr-ē-əl, ˌe-\ *adj*

equer·ry \ˈe-kwə-rē, i-ˈkwer-ē\ *n, pl* **-ries** **1** : an officer in charge of the horses of a prince or noble **2** : a personal attendant of a member of the British royal family

¹eques·tri·an \i-ˈkwes-trē-ən\ *adj* : of or relating to horseback riding ⟨~ competition⟩; *also* : representing a person on horseback ⟨an ~ statue⟩

[2]**equestrian** *n* : one who rides a horse
eques·tri·enne \i-ˌkwes-trē-ˈen\ *n* : a female rider on horseback
equi·dis·tant \ˌē-kwə-ˈdis-tənt\ *adj* : equally distant
equi·lat·er·al \ˌē-kwə-ˈla-tə-rəl\ *adj* : having all sides or faces equal ⟨~ triangles⟩
equi·lib·ri·um \ˌē-kwə-ˈli-brē-əm, ˌe-\ *n, pl* **-ri·ums** *or* **-ria** \-brē-ə\ : a state of intellectual or emotional balance; *also* : a state of balance between opposing forces or actions ♦ ***Synonyms*** POISE, BALANCE, EQUIPOISE
equine \ˈē-ˌkwīn, ˈe-\ *adj* [L *equinus,* fr. *equus* horse] : of or relating to the horse — **equine** *n*
equi·noc·tial \ˌē-kwə-ˈnäk-shəl, ˌe-\ *adj* : relating to an equinox
equi·nox \ˈē-kwə-ˌnäks, ˈe-\ *n* : either of the two times each year when the sun appears directly overhead at the equator and day and night are everywhere on earth of equal length
equip \i-ˈkwip\ *vb* **equipped; equip·ping** [AF *eskiper* to load on board a ship, outfit, man, of Gmc origin] **1** : to supply with needed resources **2** : to make ready : PREPARE ⟨*equipped* for the challenge⟩
eq·ui·page \ˈe-kwə-pij\ *n* : a horse-drawn carriage usu. with its servants
equip·ment \i-ˈkwip-mənt\ *n* **1** : things used in equipping : SUPPLIES, OUTFIT **2** : the equipping of a person or thing : the state of being equipped
equi·poise \ˈe-kwə-ˌpȯiz, ˈē-\ *n* **1** : BALANCE, EQUILIBRIUM **2** : COUNTERBALANCE
eq·ui·ta·ble \ˈe-kwə-tə-bəl\ *adj* : JUST, FAIR — **eq·ui·ta·bly** \-blē\ *adv*
eq·ui·ta·tion \ˌe-kwə-ˈtā-shən\ *n* : the act or art of riding on horseback
eq·ui·ty \ˈe-kwə-tē\ *n, pl* **-ties** **1** : JUSTNESS, IMPARTIALITY **2** : value of a property or of an interest in it in excess of claims against it
equiv *abbr* equivalent
equiv·a·lent \i-ˈkwi-və-lənt\ *adj* : EQUAL; *also* : virtually identical — **equiv·a·lence** \-ləns\ *n* — **equivalent** *n*
equiv·o·cal \i-ˈkwi-və-kəl\ *adj* **1** : AMBIGUOUS ⟨~ answers⟩ **2** : UNCERTAIN, UNDECIDED **3** : SUSPICIOUS, DUBIOUS ⟨~ behavior⟩ ♦ ***Synonyms*** OBSCURE, DARK, VAGUE, ENIGMATIC — **equiv·o·cal·ly** *adv*
equiv·o·cate \i-ˈkwi-və-ˌkāt\ *vb* **-cat·ed; -cat·ing** **1** : to use misleading language **2** : to avoid giving a definite answer — **equiv·o·ca·tion** \-ˌkwi-və-ˈkā-shən\ *n*
[1]**-er** \ər\ *adj suffix or adv suffix* — used to form the comparative degree of adjectives and adverbs of one or two syllables ⟨hott*er*⟩ ⟨dri*er*⟩ ⟨silli*er*⟩ and sometimes of longer ones
[2]**-er** \ər\ *also* **-ier** \ē-ər, yər\ *or* **-yer** \yər\ *n suffix* **1** : a person occupationally connected with ⟨furri*er*⟩ ⟨law*yer*⟩ **2** : a person or thing belonging to or associated with ⟨old-tim*er*⟩ **3** : a native of : resident of ⟨island*er*⟩ **4** : one that has ⟨double-deck*er*⟩ **5** : one that produces or yields ⟨pork*er*⟩ **6** : one that does or performs (a specified action) ⟨batt*er*⟩ **7** : one that is a suitable object of (a specified action) ⟨broil*er*⟩ **8** : one that is ⟨foreign*er*⟩
Er *symbol* erbium
ER *abbr* emergency room
era \ˈer-ə, ˈe-rə, ˈir-ə\ *n* [LL *aera,* fr. L, counters, pl. of *aes* copper, money] **1** : a chronological order or system of notation reckoned from a given date as basis **2** : a period identified by some special feature ⟨the ~ of industrialization⟩ **3** : any of the four major divisions of geologic time ♦ ***Synonyms*** AGE, EPOCH, PERIOD, TIME
ERA *abbr* **1** earned run average **2** Equal Rights Amendment
erad·i·cate \i-ˈra-də-ˌkāt\ *vb* **-cat·ed; -cat·ing** [L *eradicatus,* pp. of *eradicare,* fr. *e-* out + *radix* root] : UPROOT, ELIMINATE ♦ ***Synonyms*** EXTERMINATE, ANNIHILATE, ABOLISH, EXTINGUISH — **erad·i·ca·ble** \-di-kə-bəl\ *adj* — **erad·i·ca·tion** \-ˌra-də-ˈkā-shən\ *n*
erase \i-ˈrās\ *vb* **erased; eras·ing** : to rub or scratch out (as written words); *also* : OBLITERATE ♦ ***Synonyms*** CANCEL, EFFACE, DELETE, EXPUNGE — **eras·er** *n* — **era·sure** \i-ˈrā-shər\ *n*
er·bi·um \ˈər-bē-əm\ *n* : a rare metallic element found with yttrium
[1]**ere** \ˈer\ *prep* : BEFORE
[2]**ere** *conj* : BEFORE
e–read·er \ˈē-ˌrē-dər\ *n* : a handheld electronic device used esp. for reading e-books
[1]**erect** \i-ˈrekt\ *adj* **1** : not leaning or lying down : UPRIGHT **2** : being in a state of physiological erection
[2]**erect** *vb* **1** : BUILD **2** : to fix or set in an upright position ⟨~ an antenna⟩ **3** : SET UP; *also* : ESTABLISH, DEVELOP
erec·tile \i-ˈrek-tᵊl, -ˈrek-ˌtī(-ə)l\ *adj* : capable of becoming erect ⟨~ tissue⟩ ⟨~ feathers of a bird⟩
erec·tion \i-ˈrek-shən\ *n* **1** : the turgid state of a previously flaccid bodily part when it becomes dilated with blood **2** : CONSTRUCTION ⟨the ~ of a building⟩
ere·long \er-ˈlȯŋ\ *adv, archaic* : before long
er·e·mite \ˈer-ə-ˌmīt\ *n* : HERMIT
er·go \ˈer-gō, ˈər-\ *adv* [L] : THEREFORE
er·go·nom·ics \ˌər-gə-ˈnä-miks\ *n sing or pl* : an applied science concerned with designing and arranging things people use in order to improve efficiency and safety — **er·go·nom·ic** \-mik\ *adj*
er·got \ˈər-gət, -ˌgät\ *n* **1** : a disease of rye and other cereals caused by a fungus; *also* : this fungus **2** : a medicinal compound or preparation derived from an ergot fungus
er·mine \ˈər-mən\ *n, pl* **ermines** **1** : any of several weasels with winter fur mostly white; *also* : this white fur **2** : a rank or office whose official robe is ornamented with ermine
erode \i-ˈrōd\ *vb* **erod·ed; erod·ing** : to diminish or destroy by degrees; *esp* : to gradually eat into or wear away ⟨soil

eroded by wind and water⟩ — **erod·ible** *also* **erod·able** \-ˈrō-də-bəl\ *adj*

erog·e·nous \i-ˈrä-jə-nəs\ *adj* **1** : sexually sensitive ⟨~ zones⟩ **2** : of, relating to, or arousing sexual feelings

ero·sion \i-ˈrō-zhən\ *n* : the process or state of being eroded — **ero·sion·al** \-ˈrō-zhə-nəl\ *adj* — **ero·sion·al·ly** *adv*

ero·sive \i-ˈrō-siv\ *adj* : tending to erode — **ero·sive·ness** *n*

erot·ic \i-ˈrä-tik\ *adj* : relating to or dealing with sexual love : AMATORY ⟨~ art⟩ — **erot·i·cal·ly** \-ti-k(ə-)lē\ *adv* — **erot·i·cism** \-tə-ˌsi-zəm\ *n*

err \ˈer, ˈər\ *vb* : to be or do wrong

er·rand \ˈer-ənd\ *n* : a short trip taken to do something; *also* : the object or purpose of such a trip

er·rant \ˈer-ənt\ *adj* **1** : WANDERING ⟨an ~ knight⟩ **2** : straying outside proper bounds ⟨an ~ throw⟩ **3** : behaving wrongly ⟨an ~ child⟩

er·ra·ta \e-ˈrä-tə\ *n* : a list of corrigenda

er·rat·ic \i-ˈra-tik\ *adj* **1** : having no fixed course **2** : INCONSISTENT ⟨~ dieting⟩; *also* : ECCENTRIC ⟨~ behavior⟩ — **er·rat·i·cal·ly** \-ti-k(ə-)lē\ *adv*

er·ra·tum \e-ˈrä-təm\ *n, pl* **-ta** \-tə\ : CORRIGENDUM

er·ro·ne·ous \i-ˈrō-nē-əs, e-ˈrō-\ *adj* : INCORRECT — **er·ro·ne·ous·ly** *adv*

er·ror \ˈer-ər\ *n* **1** : a usu. ignorant or unintentional deviating from accuracy or truth ⟨made an ~ in adding⟩ **2** : a defensive misplay in baseball **3** : the state of one that errs ⟨to be in ~⟩ **4** : a product of mistake ⟨a typographical ~⟩ — **er·ror·less** *adj*

er·satz \ˈer-ˌzäts\ *adj* [G *ersatz-,* fr. *Ersatz,* n., substitute] : being usu. an artificial and inferior substitute ⟨~ diamonds⟩

erst \ˈərst\ *adv, archaic* : ERSTWHILE

[1]**erst·while** \-ˌhwī(-ə)l\ *adv* : in the past : FORMERLY

[2]**erstwhile** *adj* : FORMER, PREVIOUS ⟨~ friends⟩

er·u·di·tion \ˌer-ə-ˈdi-shən, ˌer-yə-\ *n* : SCHOLARSHIP, LEARNING — **er·u·dite** \ˈer-ə-ˌdīt, ˈer-yə-\ *adj*

erupt \i-ˈrəpt\ *vb* **1** : to burst forth or cause to burst forth : EXPLODE **2** : to break through a surface ⟨teeth ~*ing* through the gum⟩ **3** : to break out with or as if with a skin rash — **erup·tion** \-ˈrəp-shən\ *n* — **erup·tive** \-tiv\ *adj*

-ery *n suffix* **1** : qualities collectively : character : -NESS ⟨snobb*ery*⟩ **2** : art : practice ⟨cook*ery*⟩ **3** : place of doing, keeping, producing, or selling (the thing specified) ⟨fish*ery*⟩ ⟨bak*ery*⟩ **4** : collection : aggregate ⟨fin*ery*⟩ **5** : state or condition ⟨slav*ery*⟩

ery·sip·e·las \ˌer-ə-ˈsi-pə-ləs, ˌir-\ *n* : an acute bacterial disease marked by fever and severe skin inflammation

er·y·the·ma \ˌer-ə-ˈthē-mə\ *n* : abnormal redness of the skin due to capillary congestion (as in inflammation)

eryth·ro·cyte \i-ˈri-thrə-ˌsīt\ *n* : RED BLOOD CELL

Es *symbol* einsteinium

[1]**-es** \əz, iz *after* s, z, sh, ch; z *after* v *or a vowel*\ *n pl suffix* — used to form the plural of most nouns that end in *s* ⟨glass*es*⟩, *z* ⟨fuzz*es*⟩, *sh* ⟨bush*es*⟩, *ch* ⟨peach*es*⟩, or a final *y* that changes to *i* ⟨ladi*es*⟩ and of some nouns ending in *f* that changes to *v* ⟨loav*es*⟩

[2]**-es** *vb suffix* — used to form the third person singular present of most verbs that end in *s* ⟨bless*es*⟩, *z* ⟨fizz*es*⟩, *sh* ⟨hush*es*⟩, *ch* ⟨catch*es*⟩, or a final *y* that changes to *i* ⟨defi*es*⟩

es·ca·late \ˈes-kə-ˌlāt\ *vb* **-lat·ed; -lat·ing** : to increase in extent, volume, number, intensity, or scope ⟨the violence *escalated*⟩ — **es·ca·la·tion** \ˌes-kə-ˈlā-shən\ *n*

es·ca·la·tor \ˈes-kə-ˌlā-tər\ *n* : a moving set of stairs

escallop *var of* SCALLOP

es·ca·pade \ˈes-kə-ˌpād\ *n* [F, action of escaping] : a mischievous adventure

[1]**es·cape** \is-ˈkāp\ *vb* **es·caped; es·cap·ing** [ME, fr. AF *escaper, eschaper,* fr. VL **excappare,* fr. L *ex-* out + LL *cappa* head covering, cloak] **1** : to get free or away **2** : to avoid a threatening evil **3** : AVOID 2 ⟨~ injury⟩ **4** : ELUDE ⟨his name ~*s* me⟩ **5** : to be produced or uttered involuntarily by ⟨let a sob ~ him⟩

[2]**escape** *n* **1** : flight from or avoidance of something unpleasant **2** : LEAKAGE **3** : a means of escape

[3]**escape** *adj* : providing a means or way of escape

es·cap·ee \is-ˌkā-ˈpē, ˌes-(ˌ)kā-\ *n* : one that has escaped esp. from prison

escape room *n* : a game in which players confined to a room attempt to escape by discovering hidden clues and solving puzzles or riddles

escape velocity *n* : the minimum velocity needed by a body (as a rocket) to escape from the gravitational field of a celestial body (as the earth)

es·cap·ism \is-ˈkā-ˌpi-zəm\ *n* : diversion of the mind to imaginative activity as an escape from routine — **es·cap·ist** \-pist\ *adj or n*

es·car·got \ˌes-ˌkär-ˈgō\ *n, pl* **-gots** \-ˈgō(z)\ : a snail prepared for use as food

es·ca·role \ˈes-kə-ˌrōl\ *n* : ENDIVE 1

es·carp·ment \es-ˈkärp-mənt\ *n* **1** : a steep slope in front of a fortification **2** : a long cliff

es·chew \is-ˈchü\ *vb* : SHUN, AVOID

[1]**es·cort** \ˈes-ˌkȯrt\ *n* : one (as a person or warship) accompanying another esp. as a protection or courtesy

[2]**es·cort** \is-ˈkȯrt, es-\ *vb* : to accompany as an escort

es·crow \ˈes-ˌkrō\ *n* [AF *escrowe* scroll, strip of parchment] : something (as a deed or a sum of money) delivered by one person to another to be delivered to a third party only upon the fulfillment of a condition; *also* : a fund or deposit serving as an escrow

es·cu·do \is-ˈkü-dō\ *n, pl* **-dos** **1** : the former basic monetary unit of Portugal **2** — see MONEY table

es·cutch·eon \is-ˈkə-chən\ *n* : the usu.

shield-shaped surface on which a coat of arms is shown

Esd *abbr* Esdras

Es·dras \ˈez-drəs\ *n* — see BIBLE table

ESE *abbr* east-southeast

Es·ki·mo \ˈes-kə-ˌmō\ *n* **1** *now sometimes offensive* : a member of a group of Indigenous peoples of southwestern and northern Alaska, arctic Canada, Greenland, and eastern Siberia **2** : any of the languages of the Eskimo peoples

Eskimo dog *n* : a sled dog of American origin

ESL *abbr* English as a second language

esoph·a·gus \i-ˈsä-fə-gəs\ *n, pl* **-gi** \-ˌgī, -ˌjī\ : a muscular tube that leads from the cavity behind the mouth to the stomach — **esoph·a·geal** \-ˌsä-fə-ˈjē-əl\ *adj*

es·o·ter·ic \ˌe-sə-ˈter-ik\ *adj* **1** : designed for or understood only by the specially initiated **2** : PRIVATE, SECRET

esp *abbr* especially

ESP \ˌē-(ˌ)es-ˈpē\ *n* : EXTRASENSORY PERCEPTION

es·pa·drille \ˈes-pə-ˌdril\ *n* [F] : a flat sandal usu. having a fabric upper and a flexible sole

es·pal·ier \is-ˈpal-yər, -ˌyā\ *n* : a plant (as a fruit tree) trained to grow flat against a support — **espalier** *vb*

es·pe·cial \is-ˈpe-shəl\ *adj* : SPECIAL, PARTICULAR — **es·pe·cial·ly** *adv*

Es·pe·ran·to \ˌes-pə-ˈran-tō, -ˈrän-\ *n* : an artificial international language based esp. on words common to the chief European languages

es·pi·o·nage \ˈes-pē-ə-ˌnäzh, -nij\ *n* [F *espionnage*] : the practice of spying

es·pla·nade \ˈes-plə-ˌnäd\ *n* : a level open stretch or area; *esp* : one for walking or driving along a shore

es·pous·al \i-ˈspau̇-zəl\ *n* **1** : BETROTHAL; *also* : WEDDING **2** : a taking up (as of a cause) as a supporter ⟨~ of human rights⟩ — **es·pouse** \-ˈspau̇z\ *vb*

espres·so \e-ˈspre-sō\ *n, pl* **-sos** : coffee brewed by forcing steam or hot water through finely ground darkly roasted coffee beans

es·prit \i-ˈsprē\ *n* : sprightly wit

es·prit de corps \i-ˌsprē-də-ˈkȯr\ *n* [F] : the common spirit existing in the members of a group

es·py \i-ˈspī\ *vb* **es·pied; es·py·ing** : to catch sight of ♦ ***Synonyms*** BEHOLD, SEE, VIEW, DESCRY

Esq *or* **Esqr** *abbr* esquire

es·quire \ˈes-ˌkwī(-ə)r\ *n* [ME, fr. AF *esquier* squire, fr. LL *scutarius,* fr. L *scutum* shield] **1** : a man of the English gentry ranking next below a knight **2** : a candidate for knighthood serving as attendant to a knight **3** — used as a title of courtesy

-ess \əs, ˌes\ *n suffix* : female ⟨author*ess*⟩

[1]**es·say** \e-ˈsā, ˈe-ˌsā\ *vb* : ATTEMPT, TRY

[2]**es·say** *n* **1** ˈe-ˌsā, e-ˈsā : ATTEMPT **2** ˈe-ˌsā : a literary composition usu. dealing with a subject from a limited or personal point of view — **es·say·ist** \ˈe-ˌsā-ist\ *n*

es·sence \ˈe-sᵊns\ *n* **1** : fundamental nature or quality **2** : a substance distilled or extracted from another substance (as a plant or drug) and having the special qualities of the original substance **3** : PERFUME **4** : the most significant element or aspect of something ⟨the ~ of the issue⟩

[1]**es·sen·tial** \i-ˈsen-chəl\ *adj* **1** : of, relating to, or constituting an essence ⟨voting is an ~ right of citizenship⟩ ⟨~ oils⟩ **2** : of the utmost importance : INDISPENSABLE ⟨water is ~ for life⟩ **3** : being a substance that must be obtained from the diet because it is not sufficiently produced by the body ⟨~ amino acids⟩ ♦ ***Synonyms*** IMPERATIVE, NECESSARY, NECESSITOUS — **es·sen·tial·ly** *adv*

[2]**essential** *n* : something essential

est *abbr* **1** established **2** estimate; estimated

EST *abbr* eastern standard time

[1]**-est** \əst, ist\ *adj suffix or adv suffix* — used to form the superlative degree of adjectives and adverbs of one or two syllables ⟨fatt*est*⟩ ⟨lat*est*⟩ ⟨lucki*est*⟩ ⟨often*est*⟩ and less often of longer ones

[2]**-est** \əst, ist\ *or* **-st** \st\ *vb suffix* — used to form the archaic second person singular of English verbs (with *thou*) ⟨did*st*⟩

es·tab·lish \i-ˈsta-blish\ *vb* **1** : to institute permanently ⟨~ a law⟩ **2** : FOUND ⟨~ a settlement⟩; *also* : EFFECT **3** : to make firm or stable **4** : to put on a firm basis : SET UP ⟨~ a son in business⟩ **5** : to gain acceptance or recognition of ⟨the movie ~*ed* her as a star⟩; *also* : PROVE ⟨~*ed* his innocence⟩

es·tab·lish·ment \-mənt\ *n* **1** : something established **2** : a place of residence or business with its furnishings and staff **3** : an established ruling or controlling group ⟨the literary ~⟩ **4** : the act or state of establishing or being established

es·tate \i-ˈstāt\ *n* **1** : STATE, CONDITION; *also* : social standing : STATUS **2** : a social or political class ⟨the three ~*s* of nobility, clergy, and commons⟩ **3** : a person's possessions : FORTUNE **4** : a landed property

[1]**es·teem** \i-ˈstēm\ *n* : high regard

[2]**esteem** *vb* **1** : REGARD ⟨was highly ~*ed*⟩ **2** : to set a high value on ♦ ***Synonyms*** RESPECT, ADMIRE, REVERE

es·ter \ˈes-tər\ *n* : an often fragrant organic compound formed by the reaction of an acid and an alcohol

Esth *abbr* Esther

Es·ther \ˈes-tər\ *n* — see BIBLE table

esthete, esthetic, esthetically, esthetics *var of* AESTHETE, AESTHETIC, AESTHETICALLY, AESTHETICS

es·ti·ma·ble \ˈes-tə-mə-bəl\ *adj* : worthy of esteem ⟨an ~ adversary⟩

[1]**es·ti·mate** \ˈes-tə-ˌmāt\ *vb* **-mat·ed; -mat·ing 1** : to give or form an approximation (as of value, size, or cost) **2** : JUDGE, CONCLUDE ♦ ***Synonyms*** EVALUATE, VALUE, RATE, APPRAISE, ASSAY, ASSESS — **es·ti·ma·tor** \-ˌmā-tər\ *n*

[2]**es·ti·mate** \ˈes-tə-mət\ *n* **1** : OPINION,

JUDGMENT **2 :** a rough or approximate calculation **3 :** a statement of the cost of work to be done

es·ti·ma·tion \ˌes-tə-ˈmā-shən\ *n* **1 :** JUDGMENT, OPINION **2 :** ESTIMATE **3 :** ESTEEM, HONOR

es·ti·vate \ˈes-tə-ˌvāt\ *vb* **-vat·ed; -vat·ing :** to pass the summer in an inactive or resting state ⟨creatures *estivating* in the cool mud⟩ — **es·ti·va·tion** \ˌes-tə-ˈvā-shən\ *n*

es·trange \i-ˈstrānj\ *vb* **es·tranged; es·trang·ing :** to alienate the affections or confidence of — **es·trange·ment** *n*

es·tro·gen \ˈes-trə-jən\ *n* **:** a steroid (as a sex hormone) that tends to cause estrus and the development of female secondary sex characteristics — **es·tro·gen·ic** \ˌes-trə-ˈje-nik\ *adj*

estrous cycle *n* **:** the cycle of changes in the endocrine and reproductive systems of a female mammal from the beginning of one period of estrus to the beginning of the next

es·trus \ˈes-trəs\ *n* **:** a periodic state of sexual excitability during which the female of most mammals is willing to mate with the male and is capable of becoming pregnant **:** HEAT — **es·trous** \-trəs\ *adj*

es·tu·ary \ˈes-chə-ˌwer-ē\ *n, pl* **-ar·ies :** an arm of the sea at the mouth of a river — **es·tu·a·rine** \-wə-ˌrīn, -ˌrēn, -rin\ *adj*

ET *abbr* eastern time

eta \ˈā-tə\ *n* **:** the 7th letter of the Greek alphabet — H or η

ETA *abbr* estimated time of arrival

et al. \et-ˈal\ *abbr* [L *et alii* (masc.), *et aliae* (fem.), or *et alia* (neut.)] and others

etc. *abbr* et cetera

et cet·era \et-ˈse-tə-rə, -ˈse-trə\ [L] and others esp. of the same kind

etch \ˈech\ *vb* [D *etsen,* fr. G *ätzen* to etch, corrode, fr. OHG *azzen* to feed] **1 :** to produce (as a design) on a hard material by corroding its surface (as by acid) **2 :** to delineate clearly — **etch·er** *n*

etch·ing *n* **1 :** the action, process, or art of etching **2 :** a design produced on or print made from an etched plate

ETD *abbr* estimated time of departure

eter·nal \i-ˈtər-nᵊl\ *adj* **:** EVERLASTING, PERPETUAL — **eter·nal·ly** *adv*

eter·ni·ty \i-ˈtər-nə-tē\ *n, pl* **-ties 1 :** infinite duration **2 :** IMMORTALITY

[1]**-eth** \əth, ith\ *or* **-th** \th\ *vb suffix* — used to form the archaic third person singular present of verbs ⟨do*th*⟩

[2]**-eth** — see [2]-TH

eth·ane \ˈe-ˌthān\ *n* **:** a colorless odorless gaseous hydrocarbon found in natural gas and used esp. as a fuel

eth·a·nol \ˈe-thə-ˌnȯl\ *n* **:** ALCOHOL 1

ether \ˈē-thər\ *n* **1 :** the upper regions of space; *also* **:** the gaseous element formerly held to fill these regions **2 :** a light flammable liquid used as an anesthetic and solvent

ethe·re·al \i-ˈthir-ē-əl\ *adj* **1 :** CELESTIAL, HEAVENLY **2 :** exceptionally delicate **:** AIRY, DAINTY ⟨~ flaky pastry⟩ — **ethe·re·al·ly** *adv* — **ethe·re·al·ness** *n*

Ether·net \ˈē-thər-ˌnet\ *n* **:** a computer network architecture for local area networks

eth·i·cal \ˈe-thi-kəl\ *adj* **1 :** of or relating to ethics **2 :** conforming to accepted and esp. professional standards of conduct ♦ ***Synonyms*** VIRTUOUS, MORAL, PRINCIPLED — **eth·i·cal·ly** *adv*

eth·ics \ˈe-thiks\ *n sing or pl* **1 :** a discipline dealing with good and evil and with moral duty **2 :** moral principles or practice

[1]**eth·nic** \ˈeth-nik\ *adj* [ME, pagan, fr. LL *ethnicus,* fr. Gk *ethnikos* national, gentile, fr. *ethnos* nation, people] **:** of or relating to large groups of people classed according to common traits and customs — **eth·ni·cal·ly** *adv*

[2]**ethnic** *n* **:** a member of a minority ethnic group who retains its customs, language, or social views

eth·nol·o·gy \eth-ˈnä-lə-jē\ *n* **:** anthropology dealing chiefly with the comparative and analytic study of cultures — **eth·no·log·i·cal** \ˌeth-nə-ˈlä-ji-kəl\ *adj* — **eth·nol·o·gist** \eth-ˈnä-lə-jist\ *n*

ethol·o·gy \ē-ˈthä-lə-jē\ *n* **:** the scientific and objective study of animal behavior — **etho·log·i·cal** \ˌē-thə-ˈlä-ji-kəl, ˌe-\ *adj* — **ethol·o·gist** \ē-ˈthä-lə-jist\ *n*

ethos \ˈē-ˌthäs\ *n* **:** the distinguishing character, sentiment, moral nature, or guiding beliefs of a person, group, or institution

ethyl alcohol *n* **:** ALCOHOL 1

eth·yl·ene \ˈe-thə-ˌlēn\ *n* **:** a colorless flammable gas found in coal gas or obtained from petroleum

eti·ol·o·gy \ˌē-tē-ˈä-lə-jē\ *n* **:** the causes of a disease or abnormal condition; *also* **:** a branch of medicine concerned with the causes and origins of diseases — **eti·o·log·ic** \ˌē-tē-ə-ˈlä-jik\ *or* **eti·o·log·i·cal** \-ji-kəl\ *adj*

et·i·quette \ˈe-ti-kət, -ˌket\ *n* [F *étiquette,* lit., label, list] **:** the forms prescribed by custom or authority to be observed in social, official, or professional life ♦ ***Synonyms*** PROPRIETY, DECORUM, DECENCY, DIGNITY

Etrus·can \i-ˈtrəs-kən\ *n* **1 :** the language of the Etruscans **2 :** an inhabitant of ancient Etruria — **Etruscan** *adj*

et seq *abbr* [L *et sequens*] and the following one; L *et sequentes* (masc. & fem. pl.) or *et sequentia* (neut. pl.) and the following ones

-ette \ˈet, ˌet, ət, it\ *n suffix* **1 :** little one ⟨din*ette*⟩ **2 :** female ⟨usher*ette*⟩

étude \ˈā-ˌtüd, -ˌtyüd\ *n* [F, lit., study] **:** a musical composition for practice to develop technical skill

et·y·mol·o·gy \ˌe-tə-ˈmä-lə-jē\ *n, pl* **-gies 1 :** the history of a linguistic form (as a word) shown by tracing its development and relationships **2 :** a branch of linguistics dealing with etymologies — **et·y·mo·log·i·cal** \-mə-ˈlä-ji-kəl\ *adj* — **et·y·mol·o·gist** \-ˈmä-lə-jist\ *n*

Eu *symbol* europium

EU *abbr* European Union

eu·ca·lyp·tus \ˌyü-kə-ˈlip-təs\ *n, pl* **-ti** \-ˌtī\ *or* **-tus·es** : any of a genus of mostly Australian evergreen trees widely grown for shade or their wood, oils, resins, and gums

Eu·cha·rist \ˈyü-kə-rəst\ *n* : COMMUNION 2 — **eu·cha·ris·tic** \ˌyü-kə-ˈris-tik\ *adj, often cap*

[1]**eu·chre** \ˈyü-kər\ *n* : a card game in which the side naming the trump must take three of five tricks to win

[2]**euchre** *vb* **eu·chred; eu·chring** : CHEAT, TRICK

eu·clid·e·an *also* **eu·clid·i·an** \yü-ˈkli-dē-ən\ *adj, often cap* : of or relating to the geometry of Euclid or a geometry based on similar axioms

eu·gen·ics \yü-ˈje-niks\ *n* : a science dealing with the improvement (as by selective breeding) of hereditary qualities esp. of human beings — **eu·gen·ic** \-nik\ *adj*

eu·lo·gy \ˈyü-lə-jē\ *n, pl* **-gies** **1** : a speech in praise of some person or thing esp. in honor of a deceased person **2** : high praise — **eu·lo·gis·tic** \ˌyü-lə-ˈjis-tik\ *adj* — **eu·lo·gize** \ˈyü-lə-ˌjīz\ *vb*

eu·nuch \ˈyü-nək\ *n* : a castrated man

eu·phe·mism \ˈyü-fə-ˌmi-zəm\ *n* [Gk *euphēmismos,* fr. *euphēmos* auspicious, sounding good, fr. *eu-* good + *phēmē* speech] : the substitution of a mild or pleasant expression for one offensive or unpleasant; *also* : the expression substituted — **eu·phe·mis·tic** \ˌyü-fə-ˈmis-tik\ *adj* — **eu·phe·mis·ti·cal·ly** \-ti-k(ə-)lē\ *adv*

eu·pho·ni·ous \yü-ˈfō-nē-əs\ *adj* : pleasing to the ear — **eu·pho·ni·ous·ly** *adv*

eu·pho·ny \ˈyü-fə-nē\ *n, pl* **-nies** : the effect produced by words so combined as to please the ear

eu·pho·ria \yü-ˈfȯr-ē-ə\ *n* : a marked feeling of well-being or elation — **eu·phor·ic** \-ˈfȯr-ik\ *adj*

Eur *abbr* Europe; European

Eur·asian \yü-ˈrā-zhən, -shən\ *adj* **1** : of mixed European and Asian origin **2** : of or relating to Europe and Asia — **Eurasian** *n*

eu·re·ka \yü-ˈrē-kə\ *interj* [Gk *heurēka* I have found, fr. *heuriskein* to find; fr. the exclamation attributed to Archimedes on discovering a method for determining the purity of gold] — used to express triumph on a discovery

eu·ro \ˈyür-ō\ *n, pl* **euros** : the common basic monetary unit of most countries of the European Union — see MONEY table

Eu·ro–Amer·i·can \ˌyür-ō-ə-ˈmer-ə-kən\ *n* **1** : a person of both European and American ancestry **2** : an American of European and esp. white European descent

Eu·ro·bond \ˈyür-ō-ˌbänd\ *n* : a bond of a U.S. corporation that is sold outside the U.S. but that is valued and paid for in dollars and yields interest in dollars

Eu·ro·cur·ren·cy \ˌyür-ō-ˈkər-ən-sē\ *n* : moneys (as of the U.S. and Japan) held outside their countries of origin and used in the money markets of Europe

Eu·ro·dol·lar \ˈyür-ō-ˌdä-lər\ *n* : a U.S. dollar held as Eurocurrency

Eu·ro·pe·an \ˌyür-ə-ˈpē-ən\ *n* **1** : a native or inhabitant of Europe **2** : a person of European descent — **European** *adj* — **Eu·ro·pe·an·ize** \-ə-ˌnīz\ *vb*

European–American *n* : EURO-AMERICAN

Eu·ro·pe·an·ism \yür-ˌō-ˈpē-ə-ni-zəm\ *n* **1** : allegiance to the traditions, interests, or ideals of Europeans **2** : advocacy of political and economic integration of Europe — **eu·ro·pe·an·ist** \-nist\ *n*

European plan *n* : a hotel plan whereby the daily rates cover only the cost of the room

eu·ro·pi·um \yü-ˈrō-pē-əm\ *n* : a rare metallic chemical element

eu·sta·chian tube \yü-ˈstā-shən-\ *n, often cap E* : a tube connecting the inner cavity of the ear with the throat and equalizing air pressure on both sides of the eardrum

eu·tha·na·sia \ˌyü-thə-ˈnā-zhə\ *n* [Gk, easy death, fr. *eu-* good + *thanatos* death] : the act or practice of killing or permitting the death of hopelessly sick or injured persons or animals with as little pain as possible for reasons of mercy

EVA *abbr* extravehicular activity

evac·u·ate \i-ˈva-kyə-ˌwāt\ *vb* **-at·ed; -at·ing** **1** : EMPTY **2** : to discharge wastes from the body **3** : to remove or withdraw from : VACATE — **evac·u·a·tion** \-ˌva-kyə-ˈwā-shən\ *n*

evac·u·ee \i-ˌva-kyə-ˈwē\ *n* : a person removed from a dangerous place

evade \i-ˈvād\ *vb* **evad·ed; evad·ing** : to manage to avoid esp. by dexterity or slyness : ELUDE, ESCAPE ⟨*evaded* capture⟩

eval·u·ate \i-ˈval-yü-ˌwāt\ *vb* **-at·ed; -at·ing** : APPRAISE, VALUE ⟨~ the candidates⟩ — **eval·u·a·tion** \-ˌval-yü-ˈwā-shən\ *n*

ev·a·nes·cent \ˌe-və-ˈne-sᵊnt\ *adj* : tending to vanish like vapor ⟨~ pleasures⟩ ♦ ***Synonyms*** PASSING, TRANSIENT, TRANSITORY, MOMENTARY — **ev·a·nes·cence** \-sᵊns\ *n*

evan·gel·i·cal \ˌē-ˌvan-ˈje-li-kəl, ˌe-vən-\ *adj* [LL *evangelium* gospel, fr. Gk *evangelion,* fr. *euangelos* bringing good news, fr. *eu-* good + *angelos* messenger] **1** : of or relating to the Christian gospel esp. as presented in the four Gospels **2** : of or relating to certain Protestant churches emphasizing the authority of Scripture and the importance of preaching as contrasted with ritual **3** : ZEALOUS ⟨~ fervor⟩ — **Evangelical** *n* — **Evan·gel·i·cal·ism** \-kə-ˌli-zəm\ *n* — **evan·gel·i·cal·ly** *adv*

evan·ge·lism \i-ˈvan-jə-ˌli-zəm\ *n* **1** : the winning or revival of personal commitments to Christ **2** : militant or crusading zeal — **evan·ge·lis·tic** \-ˌvan-jə-ˈlis-tik\ *adj* — **evan·ge·lis·ti·cal·ly** *adv*

evan·ge·list \i-ˈvan-jə-list\ *n* **1** *often cap* : the writer of any of the four Gospels **2** : a person who evangelizes; *esp* : a Protestant minister or layman who preaches at special services

evan·ge·lize \i-ˈvan-jə-ˌlīz\ *vb* **-lized; -liz·ing** **1** : to preach the gospel **2** : to convert to Christianity
evap *abbr* evaporate
evap·o·rate \i-ˈva-pə-ˌrāt\ *vb* **-rat·ed; -rat·ing** **1** : to pass off or cause to pass off in vapor **2** : to disappear quickly **3** : to drive out the moisture from (as by heat) — **evap·o·ra·tion** \-ˌva-pə-ˈrā-shən\ *n* — **evap·o·ra·tor** \-ˌrā-tər\ *n*
evap·o·rite \i-ˈva-pə-ˌrīt\ *n* : a sedimentary rock that originates by the evaporation of seawater in an enclosed basin
eva·sion \i-ˈvā-zhən\ *n* **1** : a means of evading **2** : an act or instance of evading ⟨arrested for tax ~⟩ — **eva·sive** \i-ˈvā-siv\ *adj* — **eva·sive·ness** *n*
eve \ˈēv\ *n* **1** : EVENING **2** : the period just before some important event
¹even \ˈē-vən\ *adj* **1** : LEVEL, FLAT ⟨~ ground⟩ **2** : REGULAR, SMOOTH **3** : EQUAL, FAIR ⟨an ~ exchange⟩ **4** : BALANCED; *also* : fully revenged **5** : divisible by two **6** : EXACT ⟨an ~ dollar⟩ — **even·ly** *adv* — **even·ness** *n*
²even *adv* **1** : EXACTLY, PRECISELY **2** : FULLY, QUITE **3** : at the very time **4** — used as an intensive to stress identity ⟨~ I know that⟩ **5** — used as an intensive to emphasize something extreme or highly unlikely ⟨so simple ~ a child can do it⟩ **6** — used as an intensive to stress the comparative degree ⟨did ~ better⟩ **7** — used as an intensive to indicate a small or minimum degree ⟨didn't ~ try⟩
³even *vb* : to make or become even
even·hand·ed \ˌē-vən-ˈhan-dəd\ *adj* : FAIR, IMPARTIAL ⟨an ~ assessment⟩ — **even·hand·ed·ly** *adv*
eve·ning \ˈēv-niŋ\ *n* **1** : the end of the day and early part of the night **2** *chiefly Southern & Midland* : AFTERNOON
evening primrose *n* : a coarse biennial herb with yellow flowers that open in the evening
evening star *n* : a bright planet (as Venus) seen esp. in the western sky at or after sunset
even·song \ˈē-vən-ˌsȯŋ\ *n, often cap* **1** : VESPERS **2** : evening prayer esp. when sung
event \i-ˈvent\ *n* [MF or L; MF, fr. L *eventus,* fr. *evenire* to happen, fr. *venire* to come] **1** : OCCURRENCE **2** : a noteworthy happening **3** : CONTINGENCY ⟨in the ~ of rain⟩ **4** : a contest in a program of sports — **event·ful** *adj*
even·tide \ˈē-vən-ˌtīd\ *n* : EVENING
even·tu·al \i-ˈven-chü-wəl\ *adj* : coming at some later time : ULTIMATE — **even·tu·al·ly** *adv*
even·tu·al·i·ty \i-ˌven-chü-ˈwa-lə-tē\ *n, pl* **-ties** : a possible event or outcome
even·tu·ate \i-ˈven-chü-ˌwāt\ *vb* **-at·ed; -at·ing** : to result finally
ev·er \ˈe-vər\ *adv* **1** : ALWAYS ⟨~ faithful⟩ **2** : at any time **3** : in any way : AT ALL ⟨how can I ~ thank you⟩
ev·er·glade \ˈe-vər-ˌglād\ *n* : a low-lying tract of swampy or marshy land
ev·er·green \-ˌgrēn\ *adj* : having foliage that remains green ⟨most coniferous trees are ~⟩ — **evergreen** *n*
¹ev·er·last·ing \ˌe-vər-ˈlas-tiŋ\ *adj* **1** : enduring forever : ETERNAL **2** : having or being flowers or foliage that retain form or color for a long time when dried — **ev·er·last·ing·ly** *adv*
²everlasting *n* **1** : ETERNITY ⟨from ~⟩ **2** : a plant with everlasting flowers; *also* : its flower
ev·er·more \ˌe-vər-ˈmȯr\ *adv* : FOREVER
ev·ery \ˈev-rē\ *adj* [ME *everich, every,* fr. OE *ǣfre ǣlc,* fr. *ǣfre* ever + *ǣlc* each] **1** : being each one of a group **2** : all possible ⟨given ~ chance⟩; *also* : COMPLETE ⟨have ~ confidence⟩
ev·ery·body \ˈev-ri-ˌbä-dē, -bə-\ *pron* : every person
ev·ery·day \ˈev-rē-ˌdā\ *adj* : encountered or used routinely : ORDINARY
ev·ery·one \-(ˌ)wən\ *pron* : EVERYBODY
ev·ery·thing \ˈev-rē-ˌthiŋ\ *pron* **1** : all that exists **2** : all that is relevant
ev·ery·where \ˈev-rē-ˌhwer\ *adv* : in every place or part
evg *abbr* evening
evict \i-ˈvikt\ *vb* **1** : to put (a person) out from a property by legal process **2** : EXPEL ♦ ***Synonyms*** EJECT, OUST, DISMISS — **evic·tion** \-ˈvik-shən\ *n*
¹ev·i·dence \ˈe-və-dəns\ *n* **1** : an outward sign **2** : PROOF, TESTIMONY; *esp* : matter submitted in court to determine the truth of alleged facts
²evidence *vb* : PROVE, EVINCE
ev·i·dent \-dənt\ *adj* : clear to the vision and understanding ♦ ***Synonyms*** MANIFEST, DISTINCT, OBVIOUS, APPARENT, PLAIN
ev·i·dent·ly \ˈe-və-dənt-lē, ˌe-və-ˈdent-\ *adv* **1** : in an evident manner **2** : on the basis of available evidence
¹evil \ˈē-vəl\ *adj* **evil·er** *or* **evil·ler; evil·est** *or* **evil·lest** **1** : WICKED **2** : causing or threatening distress or harm : PERNICIOUS — **evil·ly** *adv*
²evil *n* **1** : the fact of suffering, misfortune, and wrongdoing **2** : a source of sorrow, distress, or calamity
evil·do·er \ˌē-vəl-ˈdü-ər\ *n* : one who does evil
evil–mind·ed \-ˈmīn-dəd\ *adj* : having an evil disposition or evil thoughts — **evil–mind·ed·ly** *adv*
evince \i-ˈvins\ *vb* **evinced; evinc·ing** : SHOW, REVEAL ⟨*evinced* an interest in art⟩
evis·cer·ate \i-ˈvi-sə-ˌrāt\ *vb* **-at·ed; -at·ing** **1** : to remove the entrails of **2** : to deprive of vital content or force — **evis·cer·a·tion** \-ˌvi-sə-ˈrā-shən\ *n*
evoke \i-ˈvōk\ *vb* **evoked; evok·ing** : to call forth or up — **evo·ca·tion** \ˌē-vō-ˈkā-shən, ˌe-və-\ *n* — **evoc·a·tive** \i-ˈvä-kə-tiv\ *adj*
evo·lu·tion \ˌe-və-ˈlü-shən\ *n* **1** : one of a set of prescribed movements (as in a dance) **2** : a process of change in a particular direction **3** : a theory that the various kinds of plants and animals are

descended from other kinds that lived in earlier times and that the differences are due to inherited changes that occurred over many generations — **evo·lu·tion·ary** \-shə-ˌner-ē\ *adj* — **evo·lu·tion·ist** \-shə-nist\ *n*

evolve \i-ˈvälv\ *vb* **evolved; evolv·ing** [L *evolvere* to unroll] : to develop or change by or as if by evolution

EW *abbr* enlisted woman

e–waste \ˈē-ˌwāst\ *n* : waste consisting of discarded electronic products

ewe \ˈyü\ *n* : a female sheep

ew·er \ˈyü-ər\ *n* : a water pitcher

[1]**ex** \ˈeks\ *prep* [L] : out of : FROM

[2]**ex** *n* : a former spouse

[3]**ex** *abbr* **1** example **2** express **3** extra

Ex *abbr* Exodus

ex- \e *also occurs in this prefix where only* i *is shown below (as in* "express") and *ks* sometimes occurs where only gz is shown (as in "exact")\ *prefix* **1** : out of : outside **2** : former ⟨*ex*-president⟩

ex·ac·er·bate \ig-ˈza-sər-ˌbāt\ *vb* **-bat·ed; -bat·ing** : to make more violent, bitter, or severe ⟨comments that ~ the dispute⟩ — **ex·ac·er·ba·tion** \-ˌza-sər-ˈbā-shən\ *n*

[1]**ex·act** \ig-ˈzakt\ *vb* **1** : to compel to furnish **2** : to call for as suitable or necessary — **ex·ac·tion** \-ˈzak-shən\ *n*

[2]**exact** *adj* : precisely accurate or correct — **ex·act·ly** *adv* — **ex·act·ness** *n*

ex·act·ing \ig-ˈzak-tiŋ\ *adj* **1** : greatly demanding ⟨an ~ taskmaster⟩ **2** : requiring close attention and precision

ex·ac·ti·tude \ig-ˈzak-tə-ˌtüd, -ˌtyüd\ *n* : the quality or state of being exact

ex·ag·ger·ate \ig-ˈza-jə-ˌrāt\ *vb* **-at·ed; -at·ing** [L *exaggeratus*, pp. of *exaggerare*, lit., to heap up, fr. *agger* heap] : to enlarge (as a statement) beyond normal : OVERSTATE — **ex·ag·ger·at·ed·ly** *adv* — **ex·ag·ger·a·tion** \-ˌza-jə-ˈrā-shən\ *n* — **ex·ag·ger·a·tor** \-ˈza-jə-ˌrā-tər\ *n*

ex·alt \ig-ˈzȯlt\ *vb* **1** : to raise up esp. in rank, power, or dignity **2** : GLORIFY ⟨the poem ~*s* her beauty⟩ — **ex·al·ta·tion** \ˌeg-ˌzȯl-ˈtā-shən, ˌek-ˌsȯl-\ *n*

ex·am \ig-ˈzam\ *n* : EXAMINATION

ex·am·ine \ig-ˈza-mən\ *vb* **ex·am·ined; ex·am·in·ing** **1** : to inspect closely **2** : QUESTION; *esp* : to test by questioning ♦ ***Synonyms*** INTERROGATE, QUERY, QUIZ, CATECHIZE — **ex·am·i·na·tion** \-ˌza-mə-ˈnā-shən\ *n*

ex·am·ple \ig-ˈzam-pəl\ *n* **1** : something forming a model to be followed or avoided **2** : a representative sample **3** : a problem to be solved in order to show the application of some rule

ex·as·per·ate \ig-ˈzas-pə-ˌrāt\ *vb* **-at·ed; -at·ing** : VEX, IRRITATE — **ex·as·per·a·tion** \ig-ˌzas-pə-ˈrā-shən\ *n*

exc *abbr* **1** excellent **2** except

ex·ca·vate \ˈek-skə-ˌvāt\ *vb* **-vat·ed; -vat·ing** **1** : to hollow out; *also* : to form by hollowing out **2** : to dig out and remove (as earth) **3** : to reveal to view by digging away a covering — **ex·ca·va·tion** \ˌek-skə-ˈvā-shən\ *n* — **ex·ca·va·tor** \ˈek-skə-ˌvā-tər\ *n*

ex·ceed \ik-ˈsēd\ *vb* **1** : to go or be beyond the limit of **2** : SURPASS ⟨~*ed* our expectations⟩ — **ex·ceed·ance** \-ˈsē-dᵊns\ *n*

ex·ceed·ing·ly \-ˈsē-diŋ-lē\ *also* **ex·ceed·ing** *adv* : EXTREMELY, VERY

ex·cel \ik-ˈsel\ *vb* **ex·celled; ex·cel·ling** : SURPASS, OUTDO

ex·cel·lence \ˈek-sə-ləns\ *n* **1** : the quality of being excellent **2** : an excellent or valuable quality : VIRTUE **3** : EXCELLENCY 2

ex·cel·len·cy \-lən-sē\ *n, pl* **-cies** **1** : EXCELLENCE **2** — used as a title of honor

ex·cel·lent \-lənt\ *adj* : very good of its kind : FIRST-CLASS — **ex·cel·lent·ly** *adv*

ex·cel·si·or \ik-ˈsel-sē-ər\ *n* : fine curled wood shavings used esp. for packing fragile items

[1]**ex·cept** \ik-ˈsept\ *also* **ex·cept·ing** *prep* : with the exclusion or exception of ⟨daily ~ Sundays⟩

[2]**except** *vb* **1** : to take or leave out ⟨children were ~*ed* from the study⟩ **2** : OBJECT

[3]**except** *also* **excepting** *conj* **1** : UNLESS ⟨~ you repent⟩ **2** : ONLY ⟨I'd go, ~ it's too far⟩

ex·cep·tion \ik-ˈsep-shən\ *n* **1** : the act of excepting **2** : something excepted ⟨an ~ to the rule⟩ **3** : OBJECTION

ex·cep·tion·able \ik-ˈsep-shə-nə-bəl\ *adj* : OBJECTIONABLE

ex·cep·tion·al \ik-ˈsep-shə-nəl\ *adj* **1** : UNUSUAL ⟨an ~ number of rainy days⟩ **2** : SUPERIOR ⟨~ skill⟩ — **ex·cep·tion·al·ly** *adv*

ex·cerpt \ˈek-ˌsərpt, ˈeg-ˌzərpt\ *n* : a passage selected or copied : EXTRACT — **ex·cerpt** \ek-ˈsərpt, eg-ˈzərpt; ˈek-ˌsərpt, ˈeg-ˌzərpt\ *vb*

ex·cess \ik-ˈses, ˈek-ˌses\ *n* **1** : SUPERFLUITY, SURPLUS **2** : the amount by which one quantity exceeds another **3** : INTEMPERANCE; *also* : an instance of intemperance ⟨the dictator's ~*es*⟩ — **excess** *adj* — **ex·ces·sive** \ik-ˈse-siv\ *adj* — **ex·ces·sive·ly** *adv*

exch *abbr* exchange; exchanged

[1]**ex·change** \iks-ˈchānj\ *n* **1** : the giving or taking of one thing in return for another : TRADE **2** : a substituting of one thing for another **3** : interchange of valuables and esp. of bills of exchange or money of different countries **4** : a place where things and services are exchanged; *esp* : a marketplace for securities **5** : a central office in which telephone lines are connected for communication

[2]**exchange** *vb* **ex·changed; ex·chang·ing** : to transfer in return for some equivalent : BARTER, SWAP — **ex·change·able** \iks-ˈchān-jə-bəl\ *adj*

ex·che·quer \ˈeks-ˌche-kər\ *n* [ME *escheker*, fr. AF, chessboard, counting table, office charged with revenue collection, fr. *eschec* check (in chess), chess] : TREASURY; *esp* : a national treasury

ex·cise \ˈek-ˌsīz\ *n* : a tax on the manufacture, sale, or consumption of a commodity

ex·ci·sion \ik-ˈsi-zhən\ *n* : removal by or as if by cutting out esp. by surgical means — **ex·cise** \ik-ˈsīz\ *vb*
ex·cit·able \ik-ˈsī-tə-bəl\ *adj* : easily excited — **ex·cit·abil·i·ty** \-ˌsī-tə-ˈbi-lə-tē\ *n*
ex·cite \ik-ˈsīt\ *vb* **ex·cit·ed; ex·cit·ing** **1** : to stir up the emotions of : ROUSE **2** : to increase the activity of : STIMULATE ♦ ***Synonyms*** PROVOKE, PIQUE, QUICKEN — **ex·ci·ta·tion** \ˌek-ˌsī-ˈtā-shən, ˌek-sə-\ *n* — **ex·cit·ed·ly** *adv* — **ex·cit·ing·ly** *adv*
ex·cite·ment \ik-ˈsīt-mənt\ *n* : AGITATION, STIR
ex·claim \iks-ˈklām\ *vb* : to cry out, speak, or utter sharply or vehemently — **ex·cla·ma·tion** \ˌeks-klə-ˈmā-shən\ *n* — **ex·clam·a·to·ry** \iks-ˈkla-mə-ˌtōr-ē\ *adj*
exclamation point *n* : a punctuation mark ! used esp. after an interjection or exclamation
ex·clude \iks-ˈklüd\ *vb* **ex·clud·ed; ex·clud·ing** **1** : to prevent from using or participating : BAR **2** : to put out : EXPEL — **ex·clu·sion** \-ˈklü-zhən\ *n* — **ex·clu·sion·ary** \-zhə-ˌner-ē\ *adj*
ex·clu·sive \iks-ˈklü-siv\ *adj* **1** : reserved for particular persons **2** : snobbishly aloof; *also* : STYLISH **3** : SOLE ⟨~ rights⟩; *also* : UNDIVIDED ⟨my ~ attention⟩ ♦ ***Synonyms*** CHIC, MODISH, SMART, SWANK, FASHIONABLE — **exclusive** *n* — **ex·clu·sive·ly** *adv* — **ex·clu·sive·ness** *n* — **ex·clu·siv·i·ty** \ˌeks-ˌklü-si-və-tē, iks-, -zi-\ *n*
exclusive of *prep* : not taking into account
ex·cog·i·tate \ek-ˈskä-jə-ˌtāt\ *vb* : to think out : DEVISE
ex·com·mu·ni·cate \ˌek-skə-ˈmyü-nə-ˌkāt\ *vb* : to cut off officially from the rites of the church — **ex·com·mu·ni·ca·tion** \-ˌmyü-nə-ˈkā-shən\ *n*
ex·co·ri·ate \ek-ˈskōr-ē-ˌāt\ *vb* **-at·ed; -at·ing** : to criticize severely — **ex·co·ri·a·tion** \(ˌ)ek-ˌskōr-ē-ˈā-shən\ *n*
ex·cre·ment \ˈek-skrə-mənt\ *n* : waste discharged from the body; *esp* : FECES — **ex·cre·men·tal** \ˌek-skrə-ˈmen-tᵊl\ *adj*
ex·cres·cence \ik-ˈskre-sᵊns\ *n* : OUTGROWTH; *esp* : an abnormal outgrowth (as a wart)
ex·cre·ta \ik-ˈskrē-tə\ *n pl* : waste matter (as feces) separated or eliminated from the body
ex·crete \ik-ˈskrēt\ *vb* **ex·cret·ed; ex·cret·ing** : to separate and eliminate wastes from the body esp. in urine or sweat — **ex·cre·tion** \-ˈskrē-shən\ *n* — **ex·cre·to·ry** \ˈek-skrə-ˌtōr-ē\ *adj*
ex·cru·ci·at·ing \ik-ˈskrü-shē-ˌā-tiŋ\ *adj* [L *excruciare* to torture, fr. *cruciare* to crucify, fr. *crux* cross] : intensely painful or distressing ♦ ***Synonyms*** AGONIZING, HARROWING, TORTUROUS — **ex·cru·ci·at·ing·ly** *adv*
ex·cul·pate \ˈek-(ˌ)skəl-ˌpāt\ *vb* **-pat·ed; -pat·ing** : to clear from alleged fault or guilt ♦ ***Synonyms*** ABSOLVE, EXONERATE, ACQUIT, VINDICATE, CLEAR
ex·cur·sion \ik-ˈskər-zhən\ *n* **1** : EXPEDITION; *esp* : a pleasure trip **2** : DIGRESSION — **ex·cur·sion·ist** \-zhə-nist\ *n*
ex·cur·sive \-ˈskər-siv\ *adj* : constituting or characterized by digression
¹**ex·cuse** \ik-ˈskyüz\ *vb* **ex·cused; ex·cus·ing** [ME, fr. AF *excuser*, fr. L *excusare*, fr. *causa* cause, explanation] **1** : to make apology for **2** : PARDON **3** : to release from an obligation **4** : JUSTIFY — **ex·cus·able** *adj*
²**excuse** \ik-ˈskyüs\ *n* **1** : an act of excusing **2** : something that excuses or is a reason for excusing : JUSTIFICATION
exec *n* : EXECUTIVE
ex·e·cra·ble \ˈek-si-krə-bəl\ *adj* **1** : DETESTABLE ⟨~ crimes⟩ **2** : very bad ⟨~ spelling⟩
ex·e·crate \ˈek-sə-ˌkrāt\ *vb* **-crat·ed; -crat·ing** [L *exsecratus*, pp. of *exsecrari* to put under a curse, fr. *ex-* out of + *sacer* sacred] : to denounce as evil or detestable; *also* : DETEST — **ex·e·cra·tion** \ˌek-sə-ˈkrā-shən\ *n*
ex·e·cute \ˈek-si-ˌkyüt\ *vb* **-cut·ed; -cut·ing** **1** : to carry out fully : put completely into effect **2** : to do what is called for (as by a law) **3** : to put to death in accordance with a legal sentence **4** : to produce by carrying out a design **5** : to do what is needed to give validity to ⟨~ a deed⟩ — **ex·e·cu·tion** \ˌek-si-ˈkyü-shən\ *n* — **ex·e·cu·tion·er** *n*
¹**ex·ec·u·tive** \ig-ˈze-kyə-tiv\ *adj* **1** : of or relating to the enforcement of laws and the conduct of affairs **2** : designed for or related to carrying out plans or purposes
²**executive** *n* **1** : the branch of government with executive duties **2** : one having administrative or managerial responsibility
executive chef *n* : the head chef of a professional kitchen
ex·ec·u·tor \ig-ˈze-kyə-tər\ *n* : the person named in a will to execute it
ex·ec·u·trix \ig-ˈze-kyə-ˌtriks\ *n, pl* **ex·ec·u·tri·ces** \-ˌze-kyə-ˈtrī-ˌsēz\ *or* **ex·ec·u·trix·es** \-ˈze-kyə-ˌtrik-səz\ : a woman who is an executor
ex·e·ge·sis \ˌek-sə-ˈjē-səs\ *n, pl* **-ge·ses** \-ˈjē-ˌsēz\ : explanation or critical interpretation of a text
ex·e·gete \ˈek-sə-ˌjēt\ *n* : one who practices exegesis — **ex·e·get·i·cal** \ˌek-sə-ˈje-ti-kəl\ *adj*
ex·em·plar \ig-ˈzem-ˌplär, -plər\ *n* **1** : one that serves as a model or example; *esp* : an ideal model ⟨an ~ of courage⟩ **2** : a typical instance or example
ex·em·pla·ry \ig-ˈzem-plə-rē\ *adj* : serving as a pattern; *also* : COMMENDABLE ⟨~ courage⟩
ex·em·pli·fy \ig-ˈzem-plə-ˌfī\ *vb* **-fied; -fy·ing** : to illustrate by example : serve as an example of — **ex·em·pli·fi·ca·tion** \-ˌzem-plə-fə-ˈkā-shən\ *n*
¹**ex·empt** \ig-ˈzempt\ *adj* : free from some liability to which others are subject ⟨~ from taxation⟩
²**exempt** *vb* : to make exempt : EXCUSE — **ex·emp·tion** \ig-ˈzemp-shən\ *n*
¹**ex·er·cise** \ˈek-sər-ˌsīz\ *n* **1** : EMPLOY-

MENT, USE ⟨~ of authority⟩ **2** : exertion made for the sake of training or physical fitness **3** : a task or problem done to develop skill **4** *pl* : a public exhibition or ceremony

[2]**exercise** *vb* **-cised; -cis·ing** **1** : EXERT ⟨~ control⟩ **2** : to train by or engage in exercise **3** : WORRY, DISTRESS ⟨issues that ~ voters⟩ — **ex·er·cis·er** *n*

ex·ert \ig-ˈzərt\ *vb* : to bring or put into action ⟨~ influence⟩ ⟨~*ed* himself⟩ — **ex·er·tion** \-ˈzər-shən\ *n*

ex·fo·li·ate \eks-ˈfō-lē-ˌāt\ *vb* **-at·ed; -at·ing** : to cast off in scales, layers, or splinters — **ex·fo·lia·tion** \-ˌfō-lē-ˈā-shən\ *n*

ex·hale \eks-ˈhāl\ *vb* **ex·haled; ex·hal·ing** **1** : to breathe out **2** : to give or pass off in the form of vapor — **ex·ha·la·tion** \ˌeks-hə-ˈlā-shən\ *n*

[1]**ex·haust** \ig-ˈzȯst\ *vb* **1** : to use up wholly **2** : to tire or wear out **3** : to draw off or let out completely; *also* : EMPTY **4** : to develop (a subject) completely

[2]**exhaust** *n* **1** : the escape of used vapor or gas from an engine; *also* : the gas that escapes **2** : a system of pipes through which exhaust escapes

ex·haus·tion \ig-ˈzȯs-chən\ *n* : extreme weariness : FATIGUE

ex·haus·tive \ig-ˈzȯ-stiv\ *adj* : covering all possibilities : THOROUGH ⟨an ~ investigation⟩ — **ex·haus·tive·ly** *adv*

[1]**ex·hib·it** \ig-ˈzi-bət\ *vb* **1** : to display esp. publicly **2** : to present to a court in legal form ♦ ***Synonyms*** DISPLAY, SHOW, PARADE, FLAUNT — **ex·hi·bi·tion** \ˌek-sə-ˈbi-shən\ *n* — **ex·hib·i·tor** \ig-ˈzi-bə-tər\ *n*

[2]**exhibit** *n* **1** : an act or instance of exhibiting; *also* : something exhibited **2** : something produced and identified in court for use as evidence

ex·hi·bi·tion·ism \ˌek-sə-ˈbi-shə-ˌni-zəm\ *n* **1** : a perversion marked by a tendency to indecently expose one's genitals **2** : the act or practice of behaving so as to attract attention to oneself — **ex·hi·bi·tion·ist** \-nist\ *n or adj*

ex·hil·a·rate \ig-ˈzi-lə-ˌrāt\ *vb* **-rat·ed; -rat·ing** : ENLIVEN, STIMULATE — **ex·hil·a·ra·tion** \-ˌzi-lə-ˈrā-shən\ *n*

ex·hort \ig-ˈzȯrt\ *vb* : to urge, advise, or warn earnestly — **ex·hor·ta·tion** \ˌek-ˌsȯr-tā-shən, ˌeg-ˌzȯr-, -zər-\ *n*

ex·hume \ig-ˈzüm, iks-ˈhyüm\ *vb* **ex·humed; ex·hum·ing** [ME fr. ML *exhumare,* fr. L *ex* out of + *humus* earth] : DISINTER — **ex·hu·ma·tion** \ˌeks-hyü-ˈmā-shən, ˌeg-zü-\ *n*

ex·i·gen·cy \ˈek-sə-jən-sē, ig-ˈzi-jən-\ *n, pl* **-cies** **1** *pl* : REQUIREMENTS **2** : urgent need — **ex·i·gent** \ˈek-sə-jənt\ *adj*

ex·ig·u·ous \ig-ˈzi-gyə-wəs\ *adj* : scanty in amount — **ex·i·gu·i·ty** \ˌeg-zi-ˈgyü-ə-tē\ *n*

[1]**ex·ile** \ˈeg-ˌzī(-ə)l, ˈek-ˌsī(-ə)l\ *n* **1** : BANISHMENT; *also* : voluntary absence from one's country or home **2** : a person driven from his or her native place

[2]**exile** *vb* **ex·iled; ex·il·ing** : BANISH, EXPEL ♦ ***Synonyms*** EXPATRIATE, DEPORT, OSTRACIZE

ex·ist \ig-ˈzist\ *vb* **1** : to have being **2** : to continue to be : LIVE

ex·is·tence \ig-ˈzis-təns\ *n* **1** : continuance in living **2** : actual or present occurrence ⟨~ of a state of war⟩ — **ex·is·tent** \-tənt\ *adj*

ex·is·ten·tial \ˌeg-zis-ˈten-chəl, ˌek-sis-\ *adj* **1** : of or relating to existence **2** : EMPIRICAL **3** : having being in time and space **4** : of or relating to existentialism or existentialists

ex·is·ten·tial·ism \ˌeg-zis-ˈten-chə-ˌli-zəm\ *n* : a philosophy centered on individual existence and personal responsibility for acts of free will in the absence of certain knowledge of what is right or wrong — **ex·is·ten·tial·ist** \-list\ *adj or n*

ex·it \ˈeg-zət, ˈek-sət\ *n* **1** : a departure from a stage **2** : a going out or away; *also* : DEATH **3** : a way out of an enclosed space **4** : a point of departure from an expressway — **exit** *vb*

exo·bi·ol·o·gy \ˌek-sō-bī-ˈä-lə-jē\ *n* : biology concerned with life originating or existing outside the earth or its atmosphere — **exo·bi·ol·o·gist** \-jist\ *n*

exo·crine gland \ˈek-sə-krən-, -ˌkrīn-, -ˌkrēn-\ *n* : a gland (as a salivary gland) that releases a secretion externally by means of a canal or duct

Exod *abbr* Exodus

ex·o·dus \ˈek-sə-dəs\ *n* **1** *cap* — see BIBLE table **2** : a mass departure : EMIGRATION

ex of·fi·cio \ˌek-sə-ˈfi-shē-ˌō\ *adv or adj* : by virtue of or because of an office ⟨*ex officio* chairman⟩

ex·og·e·nous \ek-ˈsä-jə-nəs\ *adj* : caused or produced by factors outside the organism or system — **ex·og·e·nous·ly** *adv*

ex·on·er·ate \ig-ˈzä-nə-ˌrāt\ *vb* **-at·ed; -at·ing** [ME, fr. L *exoneratus,* pp. of *exonerare* to unburden, fr. *ex-* out + *onus* load] : to free from blame ♦ ***Synonyms*** ACQUIT, ABSOLVE, EXCULPATE, VINDICATE — **ex·on·er·a·tion** \-ˌzä-nə-ˈrā-shən\ *n*

exo·plan·et \ˈek-sō-ˌpla-nət\ *n* : a planet orbiting a star that is not our sun

ex·or·bi·tant \ig-ˈzȯr-bə-tənt\ *adj* : exceeding what is usual or proper

ex·or·cise \ˈek-ˌsȯr-ˌsīz, -sər-\ *vb* **-cised; -cis·ing** **1** : to get rid of by or as if by solemn command **2** : to free of an evil spirit — **ex·or·cism** \-ˌsi-zəm\ *n* — **ex·or·cist** \-ˌsist\ *n*

exo·sphere \ˈek-sō-ˌsfir\ *n* : the outermost region of the atmosphere

exo·ther·mic \ˌek-sō-ˈthər-mik\ *adj* : characterized by or formed with evolution of heat

ex·ot·ic \ig-ˈzä-tik\ *adj* **1** : introduced from another country ⟨~ plants⟩ **2** : strikingly, excitingly, or mysteriously different or unusual ⟨~ flavors⟩ — **exotic** *n* — **ex·ot·i·cal·ly** \-ti-k(ə-)lē\ *adv* — **ex·ot·i·cism** \-tə-ˌsi-zəm\ *n*

exp *abbr* **1** expense **2** experiment **3** export **4** express

ex·pand \ik-ˈspand\ *vb* **1** : to open up : UNFOLD **2** : ENLARGE **3** : to develop in detail ♦ *Synonyms* AMPLIFY, SWELL, DISTEND, INFLATE, DILATE — **ex·pand·able** \-ˈspan-də-bəl\ *adj* — **ex·pand·er** *n*

ex·panse \ik-ˈspans\ *n* : a broad extent (as of land or sea)

ex·pan·sion \ik-ˈspan-chən\ *n* **1** : the act or process of expanding **2** : the quality or state of being expanded **3** : an expanded part or thing

expansion slot *n* : a socket on a motherboard for a circuit board (**expansion card**) offering additional capabilities

ex·pan·sive \ik-ˈspan-siv\ *adj* **1** : tending to expand or to cause expansion **2** : warmly benevolent, generous, or ready to talk **3** : of large extent or scope — **ex·pan·sive·ly** *adv* — **ex·pan·sive·ness** *n*

ex par·te \eks-ˈpär-tē\ *adv or adj* [ML] : from a one-sided point of view

ex·pa·ti·ate \ek-ˈspā-shē-ˌāt\ *vb* **-at·ed; -at·ing** : to talk or write at length — **ex·pa·ti·a·tion** \ek-ˌspā-shē-ˈā-shən\ *n*

[1]**ex·pa·tri·ate** \ek-ˈspā-trē-ˌāt\ *vb* **-at·ed; -at·ing** : EXILE — **ex·pa·tri·a·tion** \ek-ˌspā-trē-ˈā-shən\ *n*

[2]**ex·pa·tri·ate** \ek-ˈspā-trē-ˌāt, -trē-ət\ *adj* : living in a foreign country — **expatriate** *n*

ex·pect \ik-ˈspekt\ *vb* **1** : SUPPOSE, THINK **2** : to look forward to : ANTICIPATE **3** : to consider reasonable, due, or necessary **4** : to consider to be obliged

ex·pec·tan·cy \-ˈspek-tən-sē\ *n, pl* **-cies** **1** : EXPECTATION **2** : the expected amount (as of years of life)

ex·pec·tant \-tənt\ *adj* : marked by expectation; *esp* : expecting the birth of a child ⟨~ parents⟩ — **ex·pec·tant·ly** *adv*

ex·pec·ta·tion \ˌek-ˌspek-ˈtā-shən\ *n* **1** : the act or state of expecting **2** : prospect of inheritance — usu. used in pl. **3** : something expected

ex·pec·to·rant \ik-ˈspek-tə-rənt\ *n* : an agent that promotes the discharge or expulsion of mucus from the respiratory tract — **expectorant** *adj*

ex·pec·to·rate \-ˌrāt\ *vb* **-rat·ed; -rat·ing** : SPIT — **ex·pec·to·ra·tion** \-ˌspek-tə-ˈrā-shən\ *n*

ex·pe·di·ence \ik-ˈspē-dē-əns\ *n* : EXPEDIENCY

ex·pe·di·en·cy \-ən-sē\ *n, pl* **-cies** **1** : fitness to some end **2** : use of expedient means and methods; *also* : something expedient

[1]**ex·pe·di·ent** \-ənt\ *adj* [ME, fr. AF or L; AF, fr. L *expediens,* prp. of *expedire* to extricate, prepare, be useful, fr. *ex-* out + *ped-, pes* foot] **1** : adapted for achieving a particular end **2** : marked by concern with what is advantageous; *esp* : governed by self-interest

[2]**expedient** *n* : something expedient; *esp* : a temporary means to an end

ex·pe·dite \ˈek-spə-ˌdīt\ *vb* **-dit·ed; -dit·ing** : to carry out promptly; *also* : to speed up ⟨~ a lawsuit⟩

ex·pe·dit·er \-ˌdī-tər\ *n* : one that expedites; *esp* : one employed to ensure efficient movement of goods or supplies in a business

ex·pe·di·tion \ˌek-spə-ˈdi-shən\ *n* **1** : a journey for a particular purpose; *also* : the persons making it **2** : efficient promptness

ex·pe·di·tion·ary \-ˈdi-shə-ˌner-ē\ *adj* : of, relating to, or constituting an expedition; *also* : sent on military service abroad

ex·pe·di·tious \-ˈdi-shəs\ *adj* : marked by or acting with prompt efficiency ♦ *Synonyms* SWIFT, FAST, RAPID, SPEEDY

ex·pel \ik-ˈspel\ *vb* **ex·pelled; ex·pel·ling** : to drive or force out : EJECT

ex·pend \ik-ˈspend\ *vb* **1** : to pay out : SPEND **2** : UTILIZE ⟨~ resources⟩; *also* : USE UP — **ex·pend·able** *adj*

ex·pen·di·ture \ik-ˈspen-di-chər, -ˌchu̇r\ *n* **1** : the act or process of expending **2** : something expended

ex·pense \ik-ˈspens\ *n* **1** : EXPENDITURE **2** : COST **3** : a cause of expenditure **4** : SACRIFICE ⟨had a laugh at my ~⟩

ex·pen·sive \ik-ˈspen-siv\ *adj* : COSTLY, DEAR — **ex·pen·sive·ly** *adv*

[1]**ex·pe·ri·ence** \ik-ˈspir-ē-əns\ *n* **1** : observation of or participation in events resulting in or tending toward knowledge **2** : knowledge, practice, or skill derived from observation or participation in events; *also* : the length of such participation **3** : something encountered, undergone, or lived through (as by a person or community)

[2]**experience** *vb* **-enced; -enc·ing** **1** : FIND OUT, DISCOVER **2** : to have experience of : UNDERGO ⟨~ the loss of a pet⟩

ex·pe·ri·enced *adj* : made capable through experience ⟨an ~ pilot⟩

[1]**ex·per·i·ment** \ik-ˈsper-ə-mənt\ *n* : a controlled procedure carried out to discover, test, or demonstrate something; *also* : the process of testing — **ex·per·i·men·tal** \-ˌsper-ə-ˈmen-tᵊl\ *adj* — **ex·per·i·men·tal·ly** \-ˈmen-tᵊl-ē\ *adv*

[2]**ex·per·i·ment** \-ˌment\ *vb* : to make experiments — **ex·per·i·men·ta·tion** \ik-ˌsper-ə-mən-ˈtā-shən\ *n* — **ex·per·i·men·ter** *n*

[1]**ex·pert** \ˈek-ˌspərt\ *adj* : showing special skill or knowledge — **ex·pert·ly** *adv* — **ex·pert·ness** *n*

[2]**ex·pert** \ˈek-ˌspərt\ *n* : an expert person : SPECIALIST ⟨a computer ~⟩

ex·per·tise \ˌek-(ˌ)spər-ˈtēz\ *n* : the skill of an expert ⟨~ in legal matters⟩

expert system *n* : computer software that attempts to mimic the reasoning of a human specialist

ex·pi·ate \ˈek-spē-ˌāt\ *vb* **-at·ed; -at·ing** : to give satisfaction for : ATONE ⟨~ sin⟩ — **ex·pi·a·tion** \ˌek-spē-ˈā-shən\ *n*

ex·pi·a·to·ry \ˈek-spē-ə-ˌtȯr-ē\ *adj* : serving to expiate

expiration date *n* **1** : the date after which something is no longer in effect **2** : the date after which a product is expected to decline in quality or effectiveness

ex·pire \ik-ˈspī(-ə)r, ek-\ *vb* **ex·pired; ex·pir·ing** **1** : to breathe one's last breath : DIE **2** : to come to an end **3** : to breathe out from or as if from the lungs — **ex·pi·ra·tion** \ˌek-spə-ˈrā-shən\ *n*

ex·plain \ik-ˈsplān\ *vb* [ME *explanen,* fr. L *explanare,* lit., to make level, fr. *planus* level, flat] **1** : to make clear **2** : to give the reason for — **ex·pla·na·tion** \ˌek-splə-ˈnā-shən\ *n* — **ex·plan·a·to·ry** \ik-ˈspla-nə-ˌtȯr-ē\ *adj*
ex·ple·tive \ˈek-splə-tiv\ *n* : a usu. profane exclamation
ex·pli·ca·ble \ek-ˈspli-kə-bəl, ˈek-(ˌ)spli-\ *adj* : capable of being explained
ex·pli·cate \ˈek-splə-ˌkāt\ *vb* **-cat·ed; -cat·ing** : to give a detailed explanation of — **ex·pli·ca·tion** \ˌek-spli-ˈkā-shən\ *n*
ex·plic·it \ik-ˈspli-sət\ *adj* : clearly and precisely expressed ⟨~ directions⟩ — **ex·plic·it·ly** *adv* — **ex·plic·it·ness** *n*
ex·plode \ik-ˈsplōd\ *vb* **ex·plod·ed; ex·plod·ing** [L *explodere* to drive off the stage by clapping, fr. *ex-* out + *plaudere* to clap] **1** : DISCREDIT ⟨~ a belief⟩ **2** : to burst or cause to burst violently and noisily ⟨~ a bomb⟩ ⟨the boiler *exploded*⟩ **3** : to undergo a rapid chemical or nuclear reaction with production of heat and violent expansion of gas ⟨dynamite ~*s*⟩ **4** : to give forth a sudden strong and noisy outburst of emotion **5** : to increase rapidly ⟨the city's population *exploded*⟩
exploded *adj* : showing the parts separated but in correct relationship to each other ⟨an ~ view of a carburetor⟩
[1]**ex·ploit** \ˈek-ˌsplȯit\ *n* : DEED; *esp* : a notable or heroic act
[2]**ex·ploit** \ik-ˈsplȯit\ *vb* **1** : to make productive use of : UTILIZE ⟨~ natural resources⟩ **2** : to use unfairly for one's own advantage ⟨~ migrant workers⟩ — **ex·ploi·ta·tion** \ˌek-ˌsplȯi-ˈtā-shən\ *n*
ex·plore \ik-ˈsplȯr\ *vb* **ex·plored; ex·plor·ing** **1** : to look into or travel over thoroughly **2** : to examine carefully ⟨~ a wound⟩ — **ex·plo·ra·tion** \ˌek-splə-ˈrā-shən\ *n* — **ex·plor·ato·ry** \ik-ˈsplōr-ə-ˌtȯr-ē\ *adj* — **ex·plor·er** *n*
ex·plo·sion \ik-ˈsplō-zhən\ *n* : the act or an instance of exploding
ex·plo·sive \ik-ˈsplō-siv\ *adj* **1** : relating to or able to cause explosion **2** : tending to explode ⟨an ~ temper⟩ — **explosive** *n* — **ex·plo·sive·ly** *adv*
ex·po \ˈek-ˌspō\ *n, pl* **expos** : EXPOSITION 2
ex·po·nent \ik-ˈspō-nənt, ˈek-ˌspō-\ *n* **1** : a symbol written above and to the right of a mathematical expression (as ^{3} in a^3) to signify how many times it is to be used as a factor **2** : INTERPRETER, EXPOUNDER **3** : ADVOCATE, CHAMPION — **ex·po·nen·tial** \ˌek-spə-ˈnen-chəl\ *adj* — **ex·po·nen·tial·ly** *adv*
ex·po·nen·ti·a·tion \ˌek-spə-ˌnen-chē-ˈā-shən\ *n* : the mathematical operation of raising a quantity to a power
[1]**ex·port** \ek-ˈspȯrt, ˈek-ˌspȯrt\ *vb* : to send (as merchandise) to foreign countries — **ex·por·ta·tion** \ˌek-ˌspōr-ˈtā-shən, -spər-\ *n* — **ex·port·er** *n*
[2]**ex·port** \ˈek-ˌspȯrt\ *n* **1** : something exported esp. for trade **2** : the act of exporting
ex·pose \ik-ˈspōz\ *vb* **ex·posed; ex·pos·ing** **1** : to deprive of shelter or protection **2** : to submit or subject to an action or influence; *esp* : to subject (as photographic film) to radiant energy (as light) **3** : to bring to light : DISCLOSE ⟨~ a scam⟩ **4** : to cause to be open to view
ex·po·sé \ˌek-spō-ˈzā\ *n* : an exposure of something discreditable
ex·po·si·tion \ˌek-spə-ˈzi-shən\ *n* **1** : a setting forth of the meaning or purpose (as of a writing); *also* : discourse designed to convey information **2** : a public exhibition
ex·pos·i·tor \ik-ˈspä-zə-tər\ *n* : one who explains : COMMENTATOR
ex post fac·to \ˌeks-ˈpōst-ˌfak-tō\ *adv or adj* : after the fact
ex·pos·tu·late \ik-ˈspäs-chə-ˌlāt\ *vb* : to reason earnestly with a person esp. in dissuading : REMONSTRATE — **ex·pos·tu·la·tion** \-ˌspäs-chə-ˈlā-shən\ *n*
ex·po·sure \ik-ˈspō-zhər\ *n* **1** : the fact or condition of being exposed **2** : the act or an instance of exposing **3** : the length of time for which a film is exposed **4** : a section of a photographic film for one picture
ex·pound \ik-ˈspau̇nd\ *vb* **1** : STATE **2** : INTERPRET, EXPLAIN — **ex·pound·er** *n*
[1]**ex·press** \ik-ˈspres\ *adj* **1** : EXPLICIT; *also* : EXACT, PRECISE **2** : SPECIFIC ⟨this ~ purpose⟩ **3** : traveling at high speed and esp. with few stops ⟨an ~ train⟩; *also* : adapted to high-speed use ⟨~ roads⟩ — **ex·press·ly** *adv*
[2]**express** *adv* : by express ⟨ship it ~⟩
[3]**express** *n* **1** : a system for the prompt transportation of goods; *also* : a company operating such a service or the shipments so transported **2** : an express vehicle
[4]**express** *vb* **1** : to make known : SHOW, STATE ⟨~ regret⟩; *also* : SYMBOLIZE **2** : to squeeze out : extract by pressing **3** : to send by express **4** : to manifest or produce by a genetic process
ex·pres·sion \ik-ˈspre-shən\ *n* **1** : UTTERANCE **2** : something that represents or symbolizes : SIGN; *esp* : a mathematical symbol or combination of signs and symbols representing a quantity or operation **3** : the detectable effect of a gene **4** : a significant word or phrase; *also* : manner of expressing (as in writing or music) **5** : facial aspect or vocal intonation indicative of feeling — **ex·pres·sion·less** *adj*
ex·pres·sion·ism \ik-ˈspre-shə-ˌni-zəm\ *n* : a theory or practice in art of seeking to depict the artist's subjective responses to objects and events — **ex·pres·sion·ist** \-nist\ *n or adj* — **ex·pres·sion·is·tic** \-ˌspre-shə-ˈnis-tik\ *adj*
ex·pres·sive \ik-ˈspre-siv\ *adj* **1** : of or relating to expression **2** : serving to express ⟨an ~ gesture⟩ — **ex·pres·sive·ly** *adv* — **ex·pres·sive·ness** *n*
ex·press·way \ik-ˈspres-ˌwā\ *n* : a divided superhighway with limited access
ex·pro·pri·ate \ek-ˈsprō-prē-ˌāt\ *vb* **-at·ed; -at·ing** : to deprive of possession or

the right to own — **ex·pro·pri·a·tion** \(ˌ)ek-ˌsprō-prē-ˈā-shən\ *n*

expt *abbr* experiment

ex·pul·sion \ik-ˈspəl-shən\ *n* : an expelling or being expelled : EJECTION

ex·punge \ik-ˈspənj\ *vb* **ex·punged; ex·pung·ing** [L *expungere* to mark for deletion by dots, fr. *ex-* out + *pungere* to prick] : OBLITERATE, ERASE

ex·pur·gate \ˈek-spər-ˌgāt\ *vb* **-gat·ed; -gat·ing** : to clear (as a book) of objectionable passages — **ex·pur·ga·tion** \ˌek-spər-ˈgā-shən\ *n*

ex·qui·site \ek-ˈskwi-zət, ˈek-(ˌ)skwi-\ *adj* [ME *exquisit,* fr. L *exquisitus,* pp. of *exquirere* to search out, fr. *ex* out + *quaerere* to seek] **1** : marked by flawless form or workmanship **2** : keenly appreciative or sensitive **3** : pleasingly beautiful or delicate **4** : INTENSE ⟨~ pain⟩

ext *abbr* **1** extension **2** exterior **3** external **4** extra **5** extract

ex·tant \ˈek-stənt; ek-ˈstant\ *adj* : EXISTENT; *esp* : not lost or destroyed

ex·tem·po·ra·ne·ous \ek-ˌstem-pə-ˈrā-nē-əs\ *adj* : not planned beforehand : IMPROMPTU — **ex·tem·po·ra·ne·ous·ly** *adv*

ex·tem·po·rary \ik-ˈstem-pə-ˌrer-ē\ *adj* : EXTEMPORANEOUS

ex·tem·po·re \ik-ˈstem-pə-(ˌ)rē\ *adv* : EXTEMPORANEOUSLY

ex·tem·po·rise *Brit var of* EXTEMPORIZE

ex·tem·po·rize \ik-ˈstem-pə-ˌrīz\ *vb* **-rized; -riz·ing** : to do something extemporaneously ⟨~ a speech⟩

ex·tend \ik-ˈstend\ *vb* **1** : to spread or stretch forth or out (as in reaching) **2** : to exert or cause to exert to full capacity **3** : PROFFER ⟨~ credit⟩ **4** : PROLONG ⟨~ a note⟩ **5** : to make greater or broader ⟨~ knowledge⟩ ⟨~ a business⟩ **6** : to stretch out or reach across a distance, space, or time ♦ ***Synonyms*** LENGTHEN, ELONGATE, PROTRACT — **ex·tend·able** *also* **ex·tend·ible** \-ˈsten-də-bəl\ *adj*

ex·ten·sion \ik-ˈsten-chən\ *n* **1** : an extending or being extended **2** : a program that geographically extends the educational resources of an institution **3** : an additional part; *also* : an extra telephone connected to a line

ex·ten·sive \ik-ˈsten-siv\ *adj* : of considerable extent : FAR-REACHING, BROAD ⟨~ training⟩ — **ex·ten·sive·ly** *adv*

ex·tent \ik-ˈstent\ *n* **1** : the range or space over which something extends ⟨a property of large ~⟩ **2** : the point or degree to which something extends ⟨to the fullest ~ of the law⟩

ex·ten·u·ate \ik-ˈsten-yü-ˌwāt\ *vb* **-at·ed; -at·ing** : to lessen the seriousness of — **ex·ten·u·a·tion** \-ˌsten-yü-ˈwā-shən\ *n*

[1]**ex·te·ri·or** \ek-ˈstir-ē-ər\ *adj* **1** : EXTERNAL **2** : suitable for use on an outside surface ⟨~ paint⟩

[2]**exterior** *n* : an exterior part or surface

ex·ter·mi·nate \ik-ˈstər-mə-ˌnāt\ *vb* **-nat·ed; -nat·ing** : to get rid of completely usu. by killing off ♦ ***Synonyms*** EXTIRPATE, ERADICATE, ABOLISH, ANNIHILATE — **ex·ter·mi·na·tion** \-ˌstər-mə-ˈnā-shən\ *n* — **ex·ter·mi·na·tor** \-ˈstər-mə-ˌnā-tər\ *n*

[1]**ex·ter·nal** \ek-ˈstər-nᵊl\ *adj* **1** : outwardly perceivable; *also* : SUPERFICIAL **2** : of, relating to, or located on the outside or an outer part **3** : arising or acting from without; *also* : FOREIGN ⟨~ affairs⟩ — **ex·ter·nal·ly** *adv*

[2]**external** *n* : an external feature

ex·tinct \ik-ˈstiŋkt\ *adj* **1** : EXTINGUISHED; *also* : no longer active ⟨an ~ volcano⟩ **2** : no longer existing or in use ⟨dinosaurs are ~⟩ ⟨~ languages⟩ — **ex·tinc·tion** \ik-ˈstiŋk-shən\ *n*

ex·tin·guish \ik-ˈstiŋ-gwish\ *vb* : to cause to stop burning; *also* : to bring to an end (as by destroying) — **ex·tin·guish·able** *adj* — **ex·tin·guish·er** *n*

ex·tir·pate \ˈek-stər-ˌpāt\ *vb* **-pat·ed; -pat·ing** [L *exstirpatus,* pp. of *exstirpare,* fr. *ex-* out + *stirps* trunk, root] **1** : to destroy completely ⟨~ a heresy⟩ **2** : UPROOT ♦ ***Synonyms*** EXTERMINATE, ERADICATE, ABOLISH, ANNIHILATE — **ex·tir·pa·tion** \ˌek-stər-ˈpā-shən\ *n*

ex·tol *also* **ex·toll** \ik-ˈstōl\ *vb* **ex·tolled; ex·tol·ling** : to praise highly : GLORIFY

ex·tort \ik-ˈstȯrt\ *vb* [L *extortus,* pp. of *extorquēre* to wrench out, extort, fr. *ex-* out + *torquēre* to twist] : to obtain by force or improper pressure ⟨~ a bribe⟩ — **ex·tor·tion** \-ˈstȯr-shən\ *n* — **ex·tor·tion·er** *n* — **ex·tor·tion·ist** *n*

ex·tor·tion·ate \ik-ˈstȯr-shə-nət\ *adj* : EXCESSIVE, EXORBITANT ⟨~ prices⟩ — **ex·tor·tion·ate·ly** *adv*

[1]**ex·tra** \ˈek-strə\ *adj* **1** : ADDITIONAL ⟨~ work⟩ **2** : SUPERIOR ⟨~ quality⟩

[2]**extra** *n* **1** : a special edition of a newspaper **2** : an added charge **3** : an additional worker or performer (as in a motion picture)

[3]**extra** *adv* : beyond what is usual ⟨~ large⟩

[1]**ex·tract** \ik-ˈstrakt, *esp for 3* ˈek-ˌstrakt\ *vb* **1** : to draw out; *esp* : to pull out forcibly ⟨~ a tooth⟩ **2** : to withdraw (as a juice or a constituent) by a physical or chemical process **3** : to select for citation : QUOTE — **ex·tract·able** *adj* — **ex·trac·tion** \ik-ˈstrak-shən\ *n* — **ex·trac·tor** \-tər\ *n*

[2]**ex·tract** \ˈek-ˌstrakt\ *n* **1** : EXCERPT, CITATION **2** : a product (as a juice or concentrate) obtained by extracting

ex·tra·cur·ric·u·lar \ˌek-strə-kə-ˈri-kyə-lər\ *adj* : lying outside the regular curriculum; *esp* : of or relating to school-connected activities (as sports) usu. carrying no academic credit

ex·tra·dite \ˈek-strə-ˌdīt\ *vb* **-dit·ed; -dit·ing** : to obtain by or deliver up to extradition

ex·tra·di·tion \ˌek-strə-ˈdi-shən\ *n* : the surrender of an alleged criminal to a different jurisdiction for trial

ex·tra·mar·i·tal \ˌek-strə-ˈma-rə-tᵊl\ *adj* : of or relating to sexual intercourse by a married person with someone other than his or her spouse

ex·tra·mu·ral \-ˈmyu̇r-əl\ *adj* : existing or functioning beyond the bounds of an organized unit

ex·tra·ne·ous \ek-ˈstrā-nē-əs\ *adj* **1** : coming from without ⟨~ light⟩ **2** : not forming a vital part; *also* : IRRELEVANT — **ex·tra·ne·ous·ly** *adv*

ex·tra·net \ˈek-strə-ˌnet\ *n* : a network like an intranet but also allowing access by certain outside parties

ex·traor·di·nary \ik-ˈstrȯr-də-ˌner-ē, ˌek-strə-ˈȯr-\ *adj* **1** : notably unusual or exceptional **2** : employed on special service ⟨an ambassador ~⟩ — **ex·traor·di·nari·ly** \-ˌstrȯr-də-ˈner-ə-lē, ˌek-strə-ˌȯr-\ *adv*

ex·trap·o·late \ik-ˈstra-pə-ˌlāt\ *vb* **-lat·ed; -lat·ing** : to infer (unknown data) from known data — **ex·trap·o·la·tion** \-ˌstra-pə-ˈlā-shən\ *n*

ex·tra·sen·so·ry \ˌek-strə-ˈsen-sə-rē\ *adj* : not acting or occurring through the known senses

extrasensory perception *n* : perception (as in telepathy) of events external to the self not gained through the senses and not deducible from previous experience

ex·tra·solar \-ˈsō-lər\ *adj* : originating or existing outside the solar system

ex·tra·ter·res·tri·al \-tə-ˈres-trē-əl\ *adj* : originating or existing outside the earth or its atmosphere ⟨~ life⟩ — **extraterrestrial** *n*

ex·tra·ter·ri·to·ri·al \-ˌter-ə-ˈtȯr-ē-əl\ *adj* : existing or taking place outside the territorial limits of a jurisdiction

ex·tra·ter·ri·to·ri·al·i·ty \-ˌtȯr-ē-ˈa-lə-tē\ *n* : exemption from the application or jurisdiction of local law or tribunals ⟨diplomats enjoy ~⟩

ex·trav·a·gant \ik-ˈstra-vi-gənt\ *adj* **1** : EXCESSIVE ⟨~ claims⟩ **2** : unduly lavish : WASTEFUL **3** : too costly ♦ ***Synonyms*** IMMODERATE, EXORBITANT, EXTREME, INORDINATE, UNDUE — **ex·trav·a·gance** \-gəns\ *n* — **ex·trav·a·gant·ly** *adv*

ex·trav·a·gan·za \ik-ˌstra-və-ˈgan-zə\ *n* **1** : a literary or musical work marked by extreme freedom of style and structure **2** : a spectacular show

ex·tra·ve·hic·u·lar \ˌek-strə-vē-ˈhi-kyə-lər\ *adj* : taking place outside a vehicle (as a spacecraft) ⟨~ activity⟩

[1]**ex·treme** \ik-ˈstrēm\ *adj* **1** : very great or intense ⟨~ cold⟩ **2** : very severe or radical ⟨~ measures⟩ **3** : going to great lengths or beyond normal limits ⟨politically ~⟩ **4** : most remote ⟨the ~ end⟩ **5** : UTMOST; *also* : MAXIMUM — **ex·treme·ly** *adv*

[2]**extreme** *n* **1** : something located at one end or the other of a range or series **2** : EXTREMITY 4

extremely low frequency *n* : a radio frequency in the lowest range of the radio spectrum

ex·trem·ism \ik-ˈstrē-ˌmi-zəm\ *n* : the quality or state of being extreme; *esp* : advocacy of extreme political measures — **ex·trem·ist** \-mist\ *n or adj*

ex·trem·i·ty \ik-ˈstre-mə-tē\ *n, pl* **-ties** **1** : the most remote part or point **2** : a limb of the body; *esp* : a human hand or foot **3** : the greatest need or danger **4** : the utmost degree ⟨the *extremities* of suffering⟩ **5** : a drastic or desperate measure

ex·tri·cate \ˈek-strə-ˌkāt\ *vb* **-cat·ed; -cat·ing** [L *extricatus,* pp. of *extricare,* fr. *ex-* out + *tricae* trifles, perplexities] : to free from an entanglement or difficulty ♦ ***Synonyms*** DISENTANGLE, UNTANGLE, DISENCUMBER — **ex·tri·ca·ble** \ik-ˈstri-kə-bəl, ek-; ˈek-(ˌ)stri-\ *adj* — **ex·tri·ca·tion** \ˌek-strə-ˈkā-shən\ *n*

ex·trin·sic \ek-ˈstrin-zik, -sik\ *adj* **1** : not forming part of or belonging to a thing **2** : EXTERNAL — **ex·trin·si·cal·ly** \-zi-k(ə-)lē, -si-\ *adv*

ex·tro·vert *also* **ex·tra·vert** \ˈek-strə-ˌvərt\ *n* : a gregarious and unreserved person — **ex·tro·ver·sion** *or* **ex·tra·ver·sion** \ˌek-strə-ˈvər-zhən\ *n* — **ex·tro·vert·ed** *also* **ex·tra·vert·ed** *adj*

ex·trude \ik-ˈstrüd\ *vb* **ex·trud·ed; ex·trud·ing** **1** : to force, press, or push out **2** : to shape (as plastic) by forcing through a die — **ex·tru·sion** \-ˈstrü-zhən\ *n* — **ex·trud·er** *n*

ex·u·ber·ant \ig-ˈzü-bə-rənt\ *adj* **1** : unrestrained in enthusiasm or style **2** : PROFUSE ⟨~ vegetation⟩ — **ex·u·ber·ance** \-rəns\ *n* — **ex·u·ber·ant·ly** *adv*

ex·ude \ig-ˈzüd\ *vb* **ex·ud·ed; ex·ud·ing** [L *exsudare,* fr. *ex-* out + *sudare* to sweat] **1** : to discharge slowly through pores or cuts : OOZE **2** : to display conspicuously or abundantly ⟨~*s* charm⟩ — **ex·u·date** \ˈek-su̇-ˌdāt, -syu̇-\ *n* — **ex·u·da·tion** \ˌek-su̇-ˈdā-shən, -syu̇-\ *n*

ex·ult \ig-ˈzəlt\ *vb* : REJOICE, GLORY ⟨~*ed* in their victory⟩ — **ex·ul·tant** \-ˈzəl-tᵊnt\ *adj* — **ex·ul·tant·ly** *adv* — **ex·ul·ta·tion** \ˌek-(ˌ)səl-ˈtā-shən, ˌeg-(ˌ)zəl-\ *n*

ex·urb \ˈek-ˌsərb, ˈeg-ˌzərb\ *n* : a region outside a city and its suburbs inhabited chiefly by well-to-do families — **ex·ur·ban** \ek-ˈsər-bən, eg-ˈzər-\ *adj*

ex·ur·ban·ite \ek-ˈsər-bə-ˌnīt; eg-ˈzər-\ *n* : one who lives in an exurb

ex·ur·bia \ek-ˈsər-bē-ə, eg-ˈzər-\ *n* : the generalized region of exurbs

-ey — see -Y

[1]**eye** \ˈī\ *n* **1** : an organ of sight typically consisting in vertebrates of a globular structure that is located in a socket of the skull, is lined with a sensitive retina, and is normally paired **2** : VISION, PERCEPTION; *also* : faculty of discrimination ⟨an ~ for bargains⟩ **3** : POINT OF VIEW, JUDGMENT — often used in pl. ⟨in the ~*s* of the law⟩ **4** : something suggesting an eye (as the hole of a needle or the bud of a potato) **5** : the calm center of a cyclone — **eyed** \ˈīd\ *adj*

[2]**eye** *vb* **eyed; eye·ing** *or* **ey·ing** : to look at : WATCH

[1]**eye·ball** \ˈī-ˌbȯl\ *n* : the globular capsule of the vertebrate eye

[2]**eyeball** *vb* : to look at intently

eye·brow \-ˌbrau̇\ *n* : the ridge over the eye or the hair growing on it

eye·drop·per \-ˌdrä-pər\ *n* : DROPPER 2
eye·glass \-ˌglas\ *n* : a lens worn to aid vision; *also, pl* : GLASSES
eye·lash \-ˌlash\ *n* **1** : the fringe of hair edging the eyelid — usu. used in pl. **2** : a single hair of the eyelashes
eye·let \-lət\ *n* **1** : a small hole intended for ornament or for passage of a cord or lace **2** : a typically metal ring for reinforcing an eyelet : GROMMET
eye·lid \-ˌlid\ *n* : either of the movable folds of skin and muscle that can be closed over the eyeball
eye·lin·er \-ˌlī-nər\ *n* : makeup used to emphasize the contour of the eyes
eye–open·er \-ˌō-pə-nər\ *n* : something startling or surprising — **eye–open·ing** *adj*
eye·piece \-ˌpēs\ *n* : the lens or combination of lenses at the eye end of an optical instrument
eye roll *n* : an upward turning of the eyes esp. as an expression of annoyance, frustration, disbelief, etc.
eye shadow *n* : a colored cosmetic applied to the eyelids to accent the eyes
eye·sight \-ˌsīt\ *n* : SIGHT, VISION
eye·sore \-ˌsȯr\ *n* : something offensive to view
eye·strain \-ˌstrān\ *n* : weariness or a strained state of the eye
eye·tooth \-ˈtüth\ *n* : a canine tooth of the upper jaw
eye·wash \-ˌwȯsh, -ˌwäsh\ *n* **1** : an eye lotion **2** : misleading or deceptive statements, actions, or procedures
eye·wit·ness \-ˈwit-nəs\ *n* : a person who actually sees something happen
ey·rie *chiefly Brit var of* AERIE
ey·rir \ˈā-ˌrir\ *n, pl* **au·rar** \ˈau̇-ˌrär\ — see *krona* at MONEY table
Ez *or* **Ezr** *abbr* Ezra
Ezech *abbr* Ezechiel
Eze·chiel \i-ˈzē-kyəl\ *n* — see BIBLE table
Ezek *abbr* Ezekiel
Eze·kiel \i-ˈzē-kyəl\ *n* — see BIBLE table
e–zine \ˈē-ˌzēn\ *n* : an online magazine
Ez·ra \ˈez-rə\ *n* — see BIBLE table

F

[1]**f** \ˈef\ *n, pl* **f's** *or* **fs** \ˈefs\ *often cap* **1** : the 6th letter of the English alphabet **2** : a grade rating a student's work as failing
[2]**f** *abbr, often cap* **1** Fahrenheit **2** false **3** family **4** farad **5** female **6** feminine **7** forte **8** French **9** frequency **10** Friday
[3]**f** *symbol* focal length
F *symbol* fluorine
FAA *abbr* Federal Aviation Administration
fab \ˈfab\ *adj* : FABULOUS
Fa·bi·an \ˈfā-bē-ən\ *adj* : of, relating to, or being a society of socialists organized in England in 1884 to spread socialist principles gradually — **Fabian** *n* — **Fa·bi·an·ism** *n*
fa·ble \ˈfā-bəl\ *n* **1** : a legendary story of supernatural happenings **2** : a narration intended to teach a lesson; *esp* : one in which animals speak and act like people **3** : FALSEHOOD
fa·bled \ˈfā-bəld\ *adj* **1** : FICTITIOUS **2** : told or celebrated in fable ⟨~ deeds⟩
fab·ric \ˈfa-brik\ *n* [MF *fabrique,* fr. L *fabrica* workshop, structure] **1** : STRUCTURE, FRAMEWORK **2** : CLOTH; *also* : a material that resembles cloth
fab·ri·cate \ˈfa-bri-ˌkāt\ *vb* **-cat·ed; -cat·ing** **1** : INVENT, CREATE **2** : to make up for the sake of deception ⟨reporters *fabricating* news stories⟩ **3** : CONSTRUCT, MANUFACTURE ⟨~ tools⟩ — **fab·ri·ca·tion** \ˌfa-bri-ˈkā-shən\ *n*
fab·u·lous \ˈfa-byə-ləs\ *adj* **1** : resembling a fable; *also* : INCREDIBLE, MARVELOUS ⟨had a ~ time⟩ **2** : told in or based on fable — **fab·u·lous·ly** *adv*
fac *abbr* **1** facsimile **2** faculty
fa·cade *also* **fa·çade** \fə-ˈsäd\ *n* [F *façade,* fr. It *facciata,* fr. *faccia* face] **1** : the principal face or front of a building **2** : a false, superficial, or artificial appearance ♦ ***Synonyms*** MASK, DISGUISE, FRONT, GUISE, PRETENSE, VENEER
[1]**face** \ˈfās\ *n* **1** : the front part of the head **2** : PRESENCE ⟨in the ~ of danger⟩ **3** : facial expression : LOOK ⟨put a sad ~ on⟩ **4** : GRIMACE ⟨made a ~⟩ **5** : outward appearance ⟨looks easy on the ~ of it⟩ **6** : CONFIDENCE; *also* : BOLDNESS **7** : DIGNITY, PRESTIGE ⟨afraid to lose ~⟩ **8** : SURFACE; *esp* : a front, principal, bounding, or contacting surface ⟨~ of a cliff⟩ ⟨the ~*s* of a cube⟩ ⟨the ~ of a golf club⟩ — **faced** \ˈfāst, ˈfā-səd\ *adj*
[2]**face** *vb* **faced; fac·ing** **1** : to confront brazenly **2** : to line near the edge esp. with a different material; *also* : to cover the front or surface of ⟨~ a building with marble⟩ **3** : to meet or bring in direct contact or confrontation ⟨*faced* the problem⟩ **4** : to stand or sit with the face toward ⟨~ the sun⟩ **5** : to have the front oriented toward ⟨a house *facing* the park⟩ **6** : to have as or be a prospect ⟨~ a grim future⟩ **7** : to turn the face or body in a specified direction — **face the music** : to meet the unpleasant consequences of one's actions
face·down \ˌfās-ˈdau̇n\ *adv* : with the face downward ⟨cards turned ~⟩
face·less \-ləs\ *n* **1** : lacking character or individuality **2** : lacking a face
face–lift \ˈfās-ˌlift\ *n* **1** : plastic surgery on the face and neck to remove defects (as wrinkles) typical of aging **2** : MODERNIZATION — **face–lift** *vb*

face mask *n* : a mask or protective covering for the face

face–off \ˈfās-ˌȯf\ *n* **1** : a method of beginning play by dropping a puck or ball (as in hockey) between two opposing players each of whom attempts to control it **2** : CONFRONTATION — **face off** *vb*

fac•et \ˈfa-sət\ *n* [F *facette,* dim. of *face*] **1** : a small plane surface of a cut gem **2** : ASPECT, PHASE

fa•ce•tious \fə-ˈsē-shəs\ *adj* **1** : joking often inappropriately ⟨~ remarks⟩ **2** : JOCULAR, JOCOSE ♦ ***Synonyms*** WITTY, HUMOROUS — **fa•ce•tious•ly** *adv* — **fa•ce•tious•ness** *n*

¹fa•cial \ˈfā-shəl\ *adj* **1** : of or relating to the face **2** : used to improve the appearance of the face

²facial *n* : a facial treatment

fac•ile \ˈfa-səl\ *adj* **1** : easily accomplished, handled, or attained **2** : SIMPLISTIC **3** : readily manifested and often insincere ⟨~ prose⟩ **4** : READY, FLUENT ⟨a ~ writer⟩

fa•cil•i•tate \fə-ˈsi-lə-ˌtāt\ *vb* **-tat•ed; -tat•ing** : to make easier — **fa•cil•i•ta•tion** \-ˌsi-lə-ˈtā-shən\ *n* — **fa•cil•i•ta•tor** \-ˈsi-lə-ˌtā-tər\ *n*

fa•cil•i•ty \fə-ˈsi-lə-tē\ *n, pl* **-ties** **1** : the quality of being easily performed **2** : ease in performance : APTITUDE **3** : PLIANCY **4** : something that makes easier an action, operation, or course of conduct; *also* : REST ROOM — often used in pl. **5** : something (as a hospital) built or installed for a particular purpose

fac•ing \ˈfā-siŋ\ *n* **1** : a lining at the edge esp. of a garment **2** *pl* : the collar, cuffs, and trimmings of a uniform coat **3** : an ornamental or protective layer **4** : material for facing

fac•sim•i•le \fak-ˈsi-mə-lē\ *n* [L *fac simile* make similar] **1** : an exact copy **2** : a system of transmitting and reproducing printed matter or pictures by means of signals sent over telephone lines

fact \ˈfakt\ *n* **1** : DEED; *esp* : CRIME ⟨accessory after the ~⟩ **2** : the quality of being actual **3** : something that exists or occurs **4** : a piece of information— **in fact** : in truth

fac•tion \ˈfak-shən\ *n* : a group or combination (as in a government) acting together within and usu. against a larger body : CLIQUE — **fac•tion•al•ism** \-shə-nə-ˌli-zəm\ *n*

fac•tious \ˈfak-shəs\ *adj* **1** : of, relating to, or caused by faction **2** : inclined to faction or the formation of factions : causing dissension ♦ ***Synonyms*** INSUBORDINATE, CONTUMACIOUS, INSURGENT, SEDITIOUS, REBELLIOUS

fac•ti•tious \fak-ˈti-shəs\ *adj* : ARTIFICIAL, SHAM ⟨a ~ display of grief⟩

fac•toid \ˈfak-ˌtȯid\ *n* **1** : an invented fact believed to be true because of its appearance in print **2** : a brief usu. trivial fact

¹fac•tor \ˈfak-tər\ *n* **1** : AGENT **2** : something that actively contributes to a result ⟨a ~ in her decision⟩ **3** : GENE **4** : any of the numbers or symbols in mathematics that when multiplied together form a product; *esp* : any of the integers that divide a given integer without a remainder

²factor *vb* **1** : to work as a factor **2** : to find the mathematical factors of and esp. the prime mathematical factors of

¹fac•to•ri•al \fak-ˈtȯr-ē-əl\ *adj* : of, relating to, or being a factor

²factorial *n* : the product of all the positive integers from 1 to a given integer *n*

fac•to•ry \ˈfak-trē, -tə-rē\ *n, pl* **-ries** **1** : a trading post where resident brokers trade **2** : a building or group of buildings used for manufacturing

fac•to•tum \fak-ˈtō-təm\ *n* [NL, lit., do everything, fr. L *fac* do + *totum* everything] : a person (as a servant) having numerous or varied duties

facts of life : the physiological processes and behavior involved in sex and reproduction

fac•tu•al \ˈfak-chə-wəl\ *adj* : of or relating to facts; *also* : based on fact — **fac•tu•al•ly** *adv*

fac•ul•ty \ˈfa-kəl-tē\ *n, pl* **-ties** **1** : ability to act or do : POWER; *also* : natural aptitude **2** : one of the powers of the mind or body ⟨the ~ of hearing⟩ **3** : the teachers in a school or college or one of its divisions

fad \ˈfad\ *n* : a practice or interest followed for a time with exaggerated zeal : CRAZE — **fad•dish** *adj* — **fad•dish•ly** *adv* — **fad•dist** *n*

¹fade \ˈfād\ *vb* **fad•ed; fad•ing** **1** : WITHER **2** : to lose or cause to lose freshness or brilliance of color **3** : VANISH ⟨a *fading* memory⟩ **4** : to grow dim or faint

²fade *n* : a short haircut in which hair on top of the head stands high

FADM *abbr* fleet admiral

fae•cal, fae•ces *chiefly Brit var of* FECAL, FECES

fa•er•ie *also* **fa•ery** \ˈfā-rē, ˈfer-ē\ *n, pl* **fa•er•ies** **1** : FAIRYLAND **2** : FAIRY

¹fag \ˈfag\ *vb* **fagged; fag•ging** **1** : DRUDGE **2** : TIRE, EXHAUST ⟨*fagged* by the work⟩

²fag *n* : MENIAL, DRUDGE

³fag *n* : an English public-school boy who acts as servant to another

⁴fag *vb* : to act as a fag

⁵fag *n* : CIGARETTE

fag end *n* **1** : REMNANT **2** : the extreme end **3** : the last part or coarser end of a web of cloth **4** : the untwisted end of a rope

fag•ot *or* **fag•got** \ˈfa-gət\ *n* : a bundle of sticks or twigs

fag•ot•ing *or* **fag•got•ing** *n* : an embroidery produced by tying threads in hourglass-shaped clusters

Fah *or* **Fahr** *abbr* Fahrenheit

Fahr•en•heit \ˈfer-ən-ˌhīt\ *adj* : relating to, conforming to, or having a thermometer scale with the boiling point of water at 212 degrees and the freezing point at 32 degrees above zero

fa•ience *or* **fa•ïence** \fā-ˈäns\ *n* [F] : earthenware decorated with opaque colored glazes

[1]fail \ˈfāl\ *vb* **1** : to become feeble; *esp* : to decline in health **2** : to die away **3** : to stop functioning **4** : to fall short ⟨~*ed* in his duty⟩ **5** : to be or become absent or inadequate **6** : to be unsuccessful esp. in achieving a passing grade **7** : to become bankrupt **8** : DISAPPOINT **9** : NEGLECT ⟨~*ed* to lock the door⟩
[2]fail *n* : FAILURE ⟨without ~⟩
[1]fail·ing \ˈfā-liŋ\ *n* : WEAKNESS, SHORTCOMING
[2]failing *prep* : in the absence or lack of
faille \ˈfī(-ə)l\ *n* : a somewhat shiny closely woven ribbed fabric (as silk)
fail–safe \ˈfāl-ˌsāf\ *adj* **1** : incorporating a counteractive feature for a possible source of failure **2** : having no chance of failure — **fail–safe** *n*
fail·ure \ˈfāl-yər\ *n* **1** : a failing to do or perform **2** : a state of inability to perform a normal function adequately ⟨heart ~⟩; *also* : an abrupt cessation of functioning ⟨a power ~⟩ **3** : a fracturing or giving way under stress **4** : a lack of success **5** : BANKRUPTCY **6** : DEFICIENCY ⟨crop ~⟩ **7** : DETERIORATION, DECAY **8** : one that has failed
[1]fain \ˈfān\ *adj* **1** *archaic* : GLAD; *also* : INCLINED **2** : being obliged or compelled
[2]fain *adv* **1** : with pleasure **2** : by preference
[1]faint \ˈfānt\ *adj* [ME *faint, feint,* fr. AF, fr. *faindre, feindre* to feign, lose heart] **1** : COWARDLY, SPIRITLESS ⟨~ of heart⟩ **2** : weak, dizzy, and likely to faint **3** : lacking vigor or strength : FEEBLE ⟨~ praise⟩ **4** : hardly perceptible ⟨~ handwriting⟩ — **faint·ly** *adv* — **faint·ness** *n*
[2]faint *vb* : to lose consciousness
[3]faint *n* : the action of fainting; *also* : the resulting condition
faint·heart·ed \ˌfānt-ˈhär-təd\ *adj* : lacking courage : TIMID
[1]fair \ˈfer\ *adj* **1** : pleasing in appearance : BEAUTIFUL **2** : superficially pleasing : SPECIOUS **3** : CLEAN, PURE **4** : CLEAR, LEGIBLE **5** : not stormy or cloudy **6** : JUST **7** : conforming with the rules : ALLOWED; *also* : being within the foul lines ⟨~ ball⟩ **8** : open to legitimate pursuit or attack ⟨~ game⟩ **9** : PROMISING, LIKELY ⟨a ~ chance of winning⟩ **10** : favorable to a ship's course ⟨a ~ wind⟩ **11** : light in complexion : BLOND **12** : ADEQUATE **13** : significant in size ⟨a ~ amount of traffic⟩ — **fairness** *n*
[2]fair *adv* **1** : in a fair manner ⟨play ~⟩ **2** *chiefly Brit* : FAIRLY 4
[3]fair *n* **1** : a gathering of buyers and sellers at a stated time and place for trade **2** : a competitive exhibition (as of farm products) **3** : a sale of assorted articles usu. for a charitable purpose ⟨a book ~⟩ **4** : an exhibition that promotes available services ⟨a job ~⟩
fair·ground \-ˌgrau̇nd\ *n* : an area where outdoor fairs, circuses, or exhibitions are held
fair·ing \ˈfer-iŋ\ *n* : a structure for producing a smooth outline and reducing drag (as on an airplane)
fair·ly \ˈfer-lē\ *adv* **1** : HANDSOMELY **2** : in a manner of speaking ⟨~ bursting with pride⟩ **3** : without bias **4** : to a full degree or extent : PLAINLY, DISTINCTLY **5** : SOMEWHAT, RATHER ⟨a ~ easy job⟩
fair–spo·ken \ˈfer-ˈspō-kən\ *adj* : pleasant and courteous in speech
fair–trade \-ˈtrād\ *adj* : of, relating to, or being an agreement between a producer and a seller that branded merchandise will be sold at or above a specified price — **fair–trade** *vb*
fair·way \-ˌwā\ *n* : the mowed part of a golf course between tee and green
fairy \ˈfer-ē\ *n, pl* **fair·ies** [ME *fairie* fairyland, enchantment, fr. AF *faerie,* fr. *fee* fairy, fr. L *Fata,* goddess of fate, fr. *fatum* fate] : an imaginary being of folklore and romance usu. having diminutive human form and magic powers — **fairy** *adj*
fairy·land \-ˌland\ *n* **1** : the land of fairies **2** : a beautiful or charming place
fairy tale *n* **1** : a children's story usu. about mythical beings (as fairies) **2** : FIB
fait ac·com·pli \ˈfāt-ˌa-ˌkōⁿ-ˈplē\ *n, pl* **faits accomplis** *same or* -ˈplēz\ [F, accomplished fact] : a thing accomplished and presumably irreversible
faith \ˈfāth\ *n, pl* **faiths** \ˈfāths, ˈfāthz\ [ME *feith,* fr. AF *feid, fei,* fr. L *fides*] **1** : allegiance to duty or a person : LOYALTY **2** : belief and trust in God **3** : complete trust **4** : a system of religious beliefs — **faith·ful** \-fəl\ *adj* — **faith·ful·ly** *adv* — **faith·ful·ness** *n*
faith·less \ˈfāth-ləs\ *adj* **1** : DISLOYAL **2** : not to be relied on ♦ ***Synonyms*** FALSE, TRAITOROUS, TREACHEROUS, UNFAITHFUL — **faith·less·ly** *adv* — **faith·less·ness** *n*
fa·ji·ta \fə-ˈhē-tə\ *n* : a marinated strip usu. of beef or chicken grilled or broiled and served usu. with a flour tortilla and savory fillings
[1]fake \ˈfāk\ *adj* : COUNTERFEIT, SHAM
[2]fake *n* **1** : IMITATION, FRAUD; *also* : IMPOSTOR **2** : a simulated move in sports (as a pretended pass)
[3]fake *vb* **faked; fak·ing** **1** : to treat so as to falsify **2** : COUNTERFEIT **3** : to deceive (an opponent) in a sports contest by making a fake — **fak·er** *n*
fa·kir \fə-ˈkir\ *n* [Ar *faqīr,* lit., poor man] **1** : a Muslim mendicant : DERVISH **2** : a wandering Hindu ascetic
fal·con \ˈfal-kən, ˈfȯl-\ *n* **1** : a hawk trained for use in falconry **2** : any of various swift long-winged long-tailed hawks having a notched beak and usu. inhabiting open areas
fal·con·ry \ˈfal-kən-rē, ˈfȯl-\ *n* **1** : the art of training hawks to hunt in cooperation with a person **2** : the sport of hunting with hawks — **fal·con·er** *n*
[1]fall \ˈfȯl\ *vb* **fell** \ˈfel\; **fall·en** \ˈfȯ-lən\; **fall·ing** **1** : to descend freely by the force of gravity **2** : to hang freely **3** : to come or go as if by falling ⟨darkness *fell*⟩ **4** : to become uttered **5** : to lower or become lowered : DROP ⟨her eyes *fell*⟩ **6** : to

leave an erect position suddenly and involuntarily **7** : STUMBLE, STRAY **8** : to drop down wounded or dead esp. in battle **9** : to become captured ⟨the city *fell* to the enemy⟩ **10** : to suffer ruin, defeat, or failure **11** : to commit an immoral act **12** : to move or extend in a downward direction **13** : SUBSIDE, ABATE **14** : to decline in quality, activity, quantity, or value **15** : to assume a look of shame or dejection ⟨her face *fell*⟩ **16** : to occur at a certain time **17** : to come by chance **18** : DEVOLVE ⟨the duties *fell* to him⟩ **19** : to have the proper place or station ⟨the accent *~s* on the first syllable⟩ **20** : to come within the scope of something **21** : to pass from one condition to another ⟨*fell* ill⟩ **22** : to set about heartily or actively ⟨~ to work⟩ — **fall all over oneself** *or* **fall over backward** : to display excessive eagerness — **fall flat** : to produce no response or result — **fall for 1** : to fall in love with **2** : to become a victim of — **fall from grace** : BACKSLIDE — **fall into line** : to comply with a certain course of action — **fall short 1** : to be deficient **2** : to fail to attain

²fall *n* **1** : the act of falling **2** : a falling out, off, or away : DROPPING **3** : AUTUMN **4** : a thing or quantity that falls ⟨a light ~ of snow⟩ **5** : COLLAPSE, DOWNFALL **6** : the surrender or capture of a besieged place **7** : departure from virtue or goodness **8** : SLOPE **9** : WATERFALL — usu. used in pl. **10** : a decrease in size, quantity, degree, or value ⟨a ~ in price⟩ **11** : the distance which something falls **12** : an act of forcing a wrestler's shoulders to the mat; *also* : a bout of wrestling

fal·la·cious \fə-ˈlā-shəs\ *adj* **1** : embodying a fallacy ⟨a ~ argument⟩ **2** : MISLEADING, DECEPTIVE

fal·la·cy \ˈfa-lə-sē\ *n, pl* **-cies 1** : a false or mistaken idea **2** : an often plausible argument using false or illogical reasoning

fall back *vb* : RETREAT, RECEDE

fall guy *n* : SCAPEGOAT

fal·li·ble \ˈfa-lə-bəl\ *adj* **1** : liable to be erroneous **2** : capable of making a mistake — **fal·li·bly** \-blē\ *adv*

fall·ing–out \ˌfȯ-liŋ-ˈau̇t\ *n, pl* **falling–s–out** *or* **falling–outs** : QUARREL

falling star *n* : METEOR

fal·lo·pi·an tube \fə-ˈlō-pē-ən-\ *n, often cap F* : either of the pair of anatomical tubes that carry the eggs from the ovary to the uterus

fall·out \ˈfȯl-ˌau̇t\ *n* **1** : the often radioactive particles that result from a nuclear explosion and descend through the air **2** : a secondary and often lingering effect or result

fall out *vb* : QUARREL

¹fal·low \ˈfa-(ˌ)lō\ *n* : fallow land; *also* : the state or period of being fallow — **fallow** *vb*

²fallow *adj* **1** : left without tilling or sowing after plowing **2** : DORMANT, INACTIVE ⟨a writer's ~ period⟩

false \ˈfȯls\ *adj* **fals·er; fals·est 1** : not genuine : ARTIFICIAL ⟨~ teeth⟩ **2** : intentionally untrue **3** : adjusted or made so as to deceive ⟨~ scales⟩ **4** : tending to mislead : DECEPTIVE ⟨~ promises⟩ **5** : not true ⟨~ concepts⟩ **6** : not faithful or loyal : TREACHEROUS **7** : not essential or permanent ⟨~ front⟩ **8** : inaccurate in pitch **9** : based on mistaken ideas — **false·ly** *adv* — **false·ness** *n* — **fal·si·ty** \ˈfȯl-sə-tē\ *n*

false flag *n* **1** : a deliberate misrepresentation of motives or identity; *also* : something used for such misrepresentation **2** : a hostile or harmful action (as an attack) designed to look like it was carried out by someone other than the person or group responsible for it

false·hood \ˈfȯls-ˌhu̇d\ *n* **1** : LIE **2** : absence of truth or accuracy **3** : the practice of lying

fal·set·to \fȯl-ˈse-tō\ *n, pl* **-tos** [It, fr. dim. of *falso* false] : an artificially high voice; *esp* : an artificial singing voice that overlaps and extends above the range of the full voice esp. of a tenor

fal·si·fy \ˈfȯl-sə-ˌfī\ *vb* **-fied; -fy·ing 1** : to prove to be false **2** : to alter so as to deceive **3** : LIE; *also* : MISREPRESENT — **fal·si·fi·able** \ˌfȯl-sə-ˈfī-ə-bəl\ *adj* — **fal·si·fi·ca·tion** \ˌfȯl-sə-fə-ˈkā-shən\ *n*

fal·ter \ˈfȯl-tər\ *vb* **1** : to move unsteadily : STUMBLE, TOTTER **2** : to hesitate in speech : STAMMER **3** : to hesitate in purpose or action : WAVER, FLINCH **4** : to lose effectiveness ⟨a *~ing* business⟩ — **fal·ter·ing·ly** *adv*

fam *abbr* **1** familiar **2** family

fame \ˈfām\ *n* : public reputation : RENOWN — **famed** \ˈfāmd\ *adj*

fa·mil·ial \fə-ˈmil-yəl\ *adj* **1** : of, relating to, or suggestive of a family **2** : tending to occur in more members of a family than expected by chance alone ⟨a ~ disorder⟩

¹fa·mil·iar \fə-ˈmil-yər\ *n* **1** : COMPANION **2** : a spirit held to attend and serve or guard a person **3** : one who frequents a place

²familiar *adj* **1** : closely acquainted : INTIMATE **2** : of or relating to a family **3** : INFORMAL ⟨a ~ style⟩ **4** : FORWARD, PRESUMPTUOUS **5** : frequently seen or experienced ⟨a ~ face⟩ **6** : of everyday occurrence — **fa·mil·iar·ly** *adv*

fa·mil·iar·ise *Brit var of* FAMILIARIZE

fa·mil·iar·i·ty \fə-ˌmil-ˈyer-ə-tē, -ˌmi-lē-ˈer-\ *n, pl* **-ties 1** : close friendship : INTIMACY **2** : INFORMALITY **3** : an unduly bold or forward act or expression : IMPROPRIETY **4** : close acquaintance with something ⟨~ with current software⟩

fa·mil·iar·ize \fə-ˈmil-yə-ˌrīz\ *vb* **-ized; -iz·ing 1** : to make known or familiar **2** : to make thoroughly acquainted

fam·i·ly \ˈfam-lē, ˈfa-mə-\ *n, pl* **-lies** [ME *familie,* fr. L *familia* household, fr. *famulus* servant] **1** : a group of individuals living under one roof and under one head : HOUSEHOLD **2** : a group of persons of common ancestry : CLAN **3** : a group of things having common characteristics;

esp : a group of related plants or animals ranking in biological classification above a genus and below an order **4** : a social unit usu. consisting of one or two parents and their children

family planning *n* : planning intended to determine the number and spacing of one's children by using birth control

family tree *n* : GENEALOGY; *also* : a genealogical diagram

fam•ine \'fa-mən\ *n* **1** : an extreme scarcity of food **2** : a great shortage

fam•ish \'fa-mish\ *vb* **1** : STARVE **2** : to suffer for lack of something necessary

fa•mous \'fā-məs\ *adj* **1** : widely known **2** : honored for achievement **3** : EXCELLENT, FIRST-RATE ♦ ***Synonyms*** RENOWNED, CELEBRATED, NOTED, NOTORIOUS, DISTINGUISHED, EMINENT, ILLUSTRIOUS

fa•mous•ly *adv* : SPLENDIDLY, EXCELLENTLY ⟨got along ~⟩

[1]**fan** \'fan\ *n* : a device (as a hand-waved triangular piece or a mechanism with blades) for producing a current of air

[2]**fan** *vb* **fanned; fan•ning** **1** : to drive away the chaff from grain by winnowing **2** : to move (air) with or as if with a fan **3** : to direct a current of air upon ⟨~ a fire⟩ **4** : to stir up to activity : STIMULATE **5** : to spread like a fan **6** : to strike out in baseball

[3]**fan** *n* : an enthusiastic follower or admirer

fa•nat•ic \fə-'na-tik\ *or* **fa•nat•i•cal** \-ti-kəl\ *adj* [L *fanaticus* inspired by a deity, frenzied, fr. *fanum* temple] : marked by excessive enthusiasm and often intense uncritical devotion — **fanatic** *n* — **fa•nat•i•cism** \-tə-ˌsi-zəm\ *n*

fan•ci•er \'fan-sē-ər\ *n* **1** : one that has a special liking or interest **2** : a person who breeds or grows some kind of animal or plant for points of excellence

fan•ci•ful \'fan-si-fəl\ *adj* **1** : marked by, existing in, or given to unrestrained imagination or whim rather than reason **2** : curiously made or shaped ⟨a ~ design⟩ — **fan•ci•ful•ly** *adv*

[1]**fan•cy** \'fan-sē\ *vb* **fan•cied; fan•cy•ing** **1** : LIKE **2** : IMAGINE **3** : to believe without evidence or certainty **4** : to visualize or interpret as

[2]**fancy** *n, pl* **fancies** [ME *fantasie, fantsy* imagination, image, preference, fr. AF *fantasie* illusion, fr. L *phantasia,* fr. Gk, appearance, imagination] **1** : LIKING, INCLINATION; *also* : LOVE **2** : WHIM, NOTION, IDEA ⟨a passing ~⟩ **3** : IMAGINATION **4** : TASTE, JUDGMENT ♦ ***Synonyms*** CAPRICE, CROTCHET, VAGARY

[3]**fancy** *adj* **fan•ci•er; -est** **1** : WHIMSICAL **2** : not plain : ORNAMENTAL, POSH **3** : of particular excellence **4** : bred esp. for a showy appearance **5** : EXCESSIVE **6** : executed with technical skill and style — **fan•ci•ly** \'fan-sə-lē\ *adv*

fancy dress *n* : a costume (as for a masquerade) chosen to suit a fancy

fan•cy–free \ˌfan-sē-'frē\ *adj* : free from amorous attachment; *also* : free to imagine

fan•cy•work \'fan-sē-ˌwərk\ *n* : ornamental needlework (as embroidery)

fan•dan•go \fan-'daŋ-gō\ *n, pl* **-gos** **1** : a lively Spanish or Spanish-American dance **2** : TOMFOOLERY

fane \'fān\ *n* **1** : TEMPLE **2** : CHURCH

fan•fare \'fan-ˌfer\ *n* **1** : a flourish of trumpets **2** : a showy display

fan fiction *n* : stories involving fictional characters that are written by fans

fang \'faŋ\ *n* : a long sharp tooth; *esp* : a grooved or hollow tooth of a venomous snake — **fanged** \'faŋd\ *adj*

fan•light \'fan-ˌlīt\ *n* : a semicircular window with radiating bars like a fan that is set over a door or window

fan•ny \'fa-nē\ *n, pl* **fannies** : BUTTOCKS

fan•tail \'fan-ˌtāl\ *n* **1** : a fan-shaped tail or end **2** : an overhang at the stern of a ship

fan•ta•sia \fan-'tā-zhə, -zhē-ə, -zē-ə; ˌfan-tə-'zē-ə\ *n* : a musical composition free and fanciful in form

fan•ta•sise *Brit var of* FANTASIZE

fan•ta•size \'fan-tə-ˌsīz\ *vb* **-sized; -siz•ing** : IMAGINE, DAYDREAM

fan•tas•tic \fan-'tas-tik\ *also* **fan•tas•ti•cal** \-ti-kəl\ *adj* **1** : IMAGINARY, UNREAL **2** : conceived by unrestrained fancy **3** : exceedingly or unbelievably great **4** : ECCENTRIC ♦ ***Synonyms*** CHIMERICAL, FANCIFUL, IMAGINARY — **fan•tas•ti•cal•ly** \-ti-k(ə-)lē\ *adv*

fan•ta•sy *also* **phan•ta•sy** \'fan-tə-sē\ *n, pl* **-sies** **1** : IMAGINATION, FANCY **2** : a product of the imagination : ILLUSION **3** : FANTASIA — **fantasy** *vb*

FAQ \'fak, ˌef-ˌā-'kyü\ *n* : a document (as on a website) that provides answers to a list of typical user questions

[1]**far** \'fär\ *adv* **far•ther** \-t͟hər\ *or* **fur•ther** \'fər-\; **far•thest** *or* **fur•thest** \-t͟həst\ **1** : at or to a considerable distance in space or time ⟨~ from home⟩ **2** : by a broad interval : WIDELY, MUCH ⟨~ better⟩ **3** : to or at a definite distance, point, or degree ⟨as ~ as I know⟩ **4** : to an advanced point or extent ⟨go ~ in his field⟩ — **by far** : by a considerable margin — **far and away** : DECIDEDLY — **so far** : until now

[2]**far** *adj* **farther** *or* **further; farthest** *or* **furthest** **1** : remote in space or time **2** : DIFFERENT **3** : LONG ⟨a ~ journey⟩ **4** : being the more distant of two ⟨on the ~ side of the lake⟩

far•ad \'fer-ˌad, -əd\ *n* : a unit of capacitance equal to the capacitance of a capacitor having a potential difference of one volt between its plates when it is charged with one coulomb of electricity

far•away \'fär-ə-ˌwā\ *adj* **1** : DISTANT, REMOTE ⟨~ lands⟩ **2** : DREAMY

farce \'färs\ *n* **1** : a broadly satirical comedy with an improbable plot **2** : the humor characteristic of farce or pretense **3** : a ridiculous or empty display — **far•ci•cal** \'fär-si-kəl\ *adj*

far cry *n* **1** : a long distance **2** : something notably different ⟨a *far cry* from what we expected⟩

[1]**fare** \'fer\ *vb* **fared; far•ing** **1** : GO, TRAV-

EL **2** : GET ALONG, SUCCEED ⟨*fared* well in math⟩ **3** : EAT, DINE

[2]**fare** *n* **1** : range of food : DIET; *also* : material provided for use, consumption, or enjoyment **2** : the price charged to transport a person **3** : a person paying a fare : PASSENGER

[1]**fare·well** \fer-ˈwel\ *vb imper* : get along well — used interjectionally to or by one departing

[2]**farewell** *n* **1** : a wish of well-being at parting : GOOD-BYE **2** : LEAVE-TAKING

[3]**fare·well** \ˈfer-ˌwel\ *adj* : PARTING, FINAL ⟨a ~ concert⟩

far–fetched \ˈfär-ˈfecht\ *adj* : not easily or naturally deduced or introduced : IMPROBABLE ⟨a ~ story⟩

far–flung \-ˈfləŋ\ *adj* : widely spread or distributed ⟨a ~ empire⟩

fa·ri·na \fə-ˈrē-nə\ *n* [L, meal, flour] : a fine meal (as of wheat) used in puddings or as a breakfast cereal

far·i·na·ceous \ˌfer-ə-ˈnā-shəs\ *adj* **1** : having a mealy texture or surface **2** : containing or rich in starch

[1]**farm** \ˈfärm\ *n* [ME *ferme* rent, lease, fr. AF, fr. *fermer* to fix, rent, fr. L *firmare* to make firm, fr. *firmus* firm] **1** : a tract of land used for raising crops or livestock **2** : a minor-league subsidiary of a major-league team

[2]**farm** *vb* : to use (land) as a farm ⟨~*ed* 200 acres⟩; *also* : to raise crops or livestock — **farm·er** *n*

farm·hand \ˈfärm-ˌhand\ *n* : a farm laborer

farm·house \-ˌhau̇s\ *n* : a dwelling on a farm

farm·ing \ˈfär-miŋ\ *n* : the occupation or business of a person who farms

farm·land \ˈfärm-ˌland\ *n* : land used or suitable for farming

farm out *vb* : to turn over (as a task) to another

farm·stead \ˈfärm-ˌsted\ *n* : a farm with its buildings

farm·yard \-ˌyärd\ *n* : land around or enclosed by farm buildings

far–off \ˈfär-ˈȯf\ *adj* : remote in time or space : DISTANT

fa·rouche \fə-ˈrüsh\ *adj* [F] **1** : WILD **2** : marked by shyness and lack of polish

far–out \ˈfär-ˈau̇t\ *adj* : very unconventional ⟨~ clothes⟩

far·ra·go \fə-ˈrä-gō, -ˈrā-\ *n, pl* **-goes** [L, mixed fodder, mixture] : a confused collection : MIXTURE

far–reach·ing \ˈfär-ˈrē-chiŋ\ *adj* : having a wide range or effect

far·ri·er \ˈfer-ē-ər\ *n* [alter. of ME *ferrour,* fr. AF, blacksmith, fr. *ferrer* to shoe (horses)] : a person who shoes horses

[1]**far·row** \ˈfer-ō\ *vb* : to give birth to a litter of pigs

[2]**farrow** *n* : a litter of pigs

far·see·ing \ˈfär-ˌsē-iŋ\ *adj* **1** : FARSIGHTED 1 **2** : FARSIGHTED 2

far·sight·ed \ˈfär-ˌsī-təd\ *adj* **1** : seeing or able to see to a great distance **2** : JUDICIOUS, WISE, SHREWD **3** : affected with an eye condition in which vision is better for distant than near objects — **far·sight·ed·ness** *n*

[1]**far·ther** \ˈfär-t͟hər\ *adv* **1** : at or to a greater distance or more advanced point **2** : to a greater degree or extent

[2]**farther** *adj* **1** : more distant **2** : ADDITIONAL

far·ther·most \-ˌmōst\ *adj* : FARTHEST

[1]**far·thest** \ˈfär-t͟həst\ *adj* : most distant

[2]**farthest** *adv* **1** : to or at the greatest distance : REMOTEST ⟨hit the ball ~⟩ **2** : to the most advanced point **3** : by the greatest degree or extent : MOST

far·thing \ˈfär-t͟hiŋ\ *n* **1** : a former British monetary unit equal to $^{1}/_{4}$ of a penny; *also* : a coin representing this unit **2** : something of small value

fas·cia *1 is usu* ˈfā-sh(ē-)ə, *2 is usu* ˈfa-\ *n, pl* **-ci·ae** \-shē-ˌē\ *or* **-cias** **1** : a flat usu. horizontal part (as a band or board) of or on a building **2** : a sheet of connective tissue covering body structures (as muscles)

fas·ci·cle \ˈfa-si-kəl\ *n* **1** : a small or slender bundle (as of pine needles or nerve fibers) **2** : one of the divisions of a book published in parts — **fas·ci·cled** \-kəld\ *adj*

fas·ci·nate \ˈfa-sə-ˌnāt\ *vb* **-nat·ed; -nat·ing** [L *fascinare,* fr. *fascinum* evil spell] **1** : to transfix and hold spellbound by an irresistible power **2** : ALLURE **3** : to be irresistibly attractive — **fas·ci·na·tion** \ˌfa-sə-ˈnā-shən\ *n*

fas·cism \ˈfa-ˌshi-zəm\ *n, often cap* : a political philosophy, movement, or regime that exalts nation and often race and stands for a centralized autocratic often militaristic government — **fas·cist** \-shist\ *n or adj, often cap* — **fas·cis·tic** \fa-ˈshis-tik\ *adj, often cap*

[1]**fash·ion** \ˈfa-shən\ *n* **1** : the make or form of something **2** : MANNER, WAY **3** : a prevailing custom, usage, or style **4** : the prevailing style (as in dress) ♦ ***Synonyms*** MODE, VOGUE, RAGE, TREND

[2]**fashion** *vb* **1** : MOLD, CONSTRUCT ⟨~ a vase out of clay⟩ **2** : FIT, ADAPT

fash·ion·able \ˈfa-shə-nə-bəl\ *adj* **1** : dressing or behaving according to fashion : STYLISH **2** : of or relating to the world of fashion ⟨~ resorts⟩ ♦ ***Synonyms*** CHIC, MODISH, SMART, SWANK — **fash·ion·ably** \-blē\ *adv*

fashion–forward *adj* : stylishly up-to-date : very fashionable ⟨~ clothing⟩

[1]**fast** \ˈfast\ *adj* **1** : firmly fixed **2** : tightly shut **3** : adhering firmly **4** : STUCK **5** : STAUNCH ⟨~ friends⟩ **6** : characterized by quick motion, operation, or effect ⟨a ~ trip⟩ ⟨a ~ track⟩ **7** : indicating ahead of the correct time ⟨the clock is ~⟩ **8** : not easily disturbed : SOUND ⟨a ~ sleep⟩ **9** : permanently dyed; *also* : being proof against fading ⟨colors ~ to sunlight⟩ **10** : DISSIPATED, WILD ⟨a ~ crowd⟩ **11** : sexually promiscuous ♦ ***Synonyms*** RAPID, SWIFT, FLEET, QUICK, SPEEDY, HASTY

[2]**fast** *adv* **1** : in a firm or fixed manner ⟨stuck ~ in the mud⟩ **2** : SOUNDLY,

DEEPLY ⟨~ asleep⟩ **3** : SWIFTLY **4** : RECKLESSLY

³fast *vb* **1** : to abstain from food **2** : to eat sparingly or abstain from some foods

⁴fast *n* **1** : the act or practice of fasting **2** : a time of fasting

fast·back \ˈfast-ˌbak\ *n* : an automobile having a roof with a long slope to the rear

fast·ball \-ˌbȯl\ *n* : a baseball pitch thrown at full speed

fas·ten \ˈfa-sᵊn\ *vb* **1** : to attach or join by or as if by pinning, tying, or nailing **2** : to make fast : fix securely **3** : to become fixed or joined **4** : to focus attention ⟨~*ed* onto the newest trends⟩ — **fas·ten·er** *n*

fas·ten·ing *n* : something that fastens : FASTENER

fast–food \ˌfast-ˈfüd\ *adj* : specializing in food that is prepared and served quickly ⟨a ~ restaurant⟩

fast–for·ward \-ˈfȯr-wərd\ *n* **1** : a function of an electronic device that advances a recording rapidly **2** : a state of rapid advancement — **fast–forward** *vb*

fas·tid·i·ous \fa-ˈsti-dē-əs\ *adj* **1** : overly difficult to please **2** : showing a meticulous or demanding attitude ⟨~ workmanship⟩ ♦ ***Synonyms*** NICE, FINICKY, FUSSY, PARTICULAR, PERSNICKETY, SQUEAMISH — **fas·tid·i·ous·ly** *adv* — **fas·tid·i·ous·ness** *n*

fast·ness \ˈfast-nəs\ *n* **1** : the quality or state of being fast **2** : a fortified or secure place : STRONGHOLD

fast–talk \ˈfast-ˌtȯk\ *vb* : to influence by persuasive and usu. deceptive talk

fast–track \ˈfast-ˌtrak\ *vb* : to speed up the processing or production of

fast track *n* : a course leading to rapid advancement or success

¹fat \ˈfat\ *adj* **fat·ter; fat·test** **1** : notable for having an unusual amount of fat : PLUMP, OBESE **2** : OILY, GREASY **3** : well filled out : BIG **4** : well stocked : ABUNDANT **5** : richly rewarding — **fat·ness** *n*

²fat *n* **1** : animal tissue rich in greasy or oily matter **2** : any of various energy-rich esters that occur naturally in animal fats and in plants and are soluble in organic solvents (as ether) but not in water **3** : the best or richest portion ⟨lived on the ~ of the land⟩ **4** : OBESITY **5** : excess matter ⟨trim the ~ from the budget⟩

fa·tal \ˈfāt-ᵊl\ *adj* **1** : FATEFUL ⟨that ~ day⟩ **2** : causing death or ruin ⟨a ~ mistake⟩ — **fa·tal·ly** *adv*

fa·tal·ism \-ˌi-zəm\ *n* : the belief that events are determined by fate — **fa·tal·ist** \-ist\ *n* — **fa·tal·is·tic** \ˌfāt-ᵊl-ˈis-tik\ *adj* — **fa·tal·is·ti·cal·ly** \-ti-k(ə-)lē\ *adv*

fa·tal·i·ty \fā-ˈta-lə-tē, fə-\ *n, pl* **-ties** **1** : DEADLINESS **2** : FATE **3** : death resulting from a disaster or accident; *also* : one who suffers such a death

fat·back \ˈfat-ˌbak\ *n* : a fatty strip from the back of the hog usu. cured by salting and drying

fat·berg \-ˌbərg\ *n* : a large mass of fat and solid waste that collects in a sewer system

fat cat *n* **1** : a wealthy contributor to a political campaign **2** : a wealthy privileged person

fate \ˈfāt\ *n* [ME, fr. MF or L; MF, fr. L *fatum,* lit., what has been spoken, fr. *fari* to speak] **1** : the cause or will that is held to determine events : DESTINY **2** : LOT, FORTUNE **3** : DISASTER; *esp* : DEATH **4** : END, OUTCOME **5** *pl, cap* : the three goddesses of classical mythology who determine the course of human life

fat·ed \ˈfā-təd\ *adj* : decreed, controlled, or marked by fate

fate·ful \ˈfāt-fəl\ *adj* **1** : OMINOUS, PROPHETIC **2** : IMPORTANT, DECISIVE **3** : DEADLY, DESTRUCTIVE **4** : determined by fate — **fate·ful·ly** *adv*

fath *abbr* fathom

fat·head \ˈfat-ˌhed\ *n* : a stupid person — **fat·head·ed** \-ˈhe-dəd\ *adj*

¹fa·ther \ˈfä-t͟hər\ *n* **1** : a male parent **2** *cap* : God esp. as the first person of the Trinity **3** : FOREFATHER **4** : one deserving the respect and love given to a father **5** *often cap* : an early Christian writer accepted by the church as an authoritative witness to its teaching and practice **6** : ORIGINATOR ⟨the ~ of modern radio⟩; *also* : SOURCE **7** : PRIEST — used esp. as a title **8** : one of the leading men ⟨city ~*s*⟩ — **fa·ther·hood** \-ˌhu̇d\ *n* — **fa·ther·less** *adj* — **fa·ther·ly** *adj*

²father *vb* **1** : BEGET **2** : to be the founder, producer, or author of **3** : to treat or care for as a father

father–in–law \ˈfä-t͟hə-rən-ˌlȯ\ *n, pl* **fa·thers–in–law** \-t͟hər-zən-\ : the father of one's spouse

fa·ther·land \ˈfä-t͟hər-ˌland\ *n* **1** : the native land or country of one's ancestors **2** : one's native land or country

¹fath·om \ˈfa-t͟həm\ *n* [ME *fadme,* fr. OE *fæthm* length of the outstretched arms] : a unit of length equal to 6 feet (about 1.8 meters) used esp. for measuring the depth of water

²fathom *vb* **1** : to measure by a sounding line **2** : PROBE **3** : to penetrate and come to understand ⟨~ the problem⟩ — **fath·om·able** \ˈfa-t͟hə-mə-bəl\ *adj*

fath·om·less \ˈfa-t͟həm-ləs\ *adj* : incapable of being fathomed

¹fa·tigue \fə-ˈtēg\ *n* [F] **1** : manual or menial work performed by military personnel **2** *pl* : the uniform or work clothing worn on fatigue and in the field **3** : weariness from labor or stress **4** : the tendency of a material to break under repeated stress

²fatigue *vb* **fa·tigued; fa·tigu·ing** : WEARY, TIRE

fat–shame \ˈfat-ˌshām\ *vb* : to subject to criticism or mockery for being fat or overweight ⟨*fat-shamed* a classmate⟩

fat·ten \ˈfa-tᵊn\ *vb* : to make or grow fat

Fat Tuesday *n* : MARDI GRAS

¹fat·ty \ˈfa-tē\ *adj* **fat·ti·er; -est** **1** : containing fat esp. in unusual amounts **2** : GREASY

²fatty *n, pl* **fat·ties** *offensive* : an overweight person

fatty acid *n* : any of numerous acids that contain only carbon, hydrogen, and oxygen and that occur naturally in fats and various oils
fa·tu·ity \fə-ˈtü-ə-tē, -ˈtyü-\ *n, pl* **-ities** : FOOLISHNESS, STUPIDITY
fat·u·ous \ˈfa-chü-wəs\ *adj* : FOOLISH, INANE, SILLY — **fat·u·ous·ly** *adv*
fau·bourg \fō-ˈbu̇r\ *n* **1** : a suburb esp. of a French city **2** : a city quarter
fau·ces \ˈfȯ-ˌsēz\ *n pl* [L, throat] : the narrow passage located between the soft palate and the base of the tongue that joins the mouth to the pharynx
fau·cet \ˈfȯ-sət, ˈfä-\ *n* : a fixture for drawing off a liquid (as from a pipe)
[1]**fault** \ˈfȯlt\ *n* **1** : a weakness in character : FAILING **2** : IMPERFECTION, IMPAIRMENT, DEFECT **3** : an error esp. in service in a net or racket game **4** : MISDEMEANOR; *also* : MISTAKE **5** : responsibility for something wrong **6** : a fracture in the earth's crust accompanied by a displacement of one side relative to the other — **fault·i·ly** \ˈfȯl-tə-lē\ *adv* — **fault·less** *adj* — **fault·less·ly** *adv* — **faulty** *adj*
[2]**fault** *vb* **1** : to commit a fault : ERR **2** : to fracture so as to produce a geologic fault **3** : to find a fault in **4** : BLAME, CRITICIZE
fault·find·er \ˈfȯlt-ˌfīn-dər\ *n* : a person who tends to find fault or complain ♦ ***Synonyms*** CRITIC, CARPER, CAVILER, COMPLAINER — **fault·find·ing** *n or adj*
faun \ˈfȯn\ *n* : a Roman god similar to but gentler than a satyr
fau·na \ˈfȯ-nə\ *n, pl* **faunas** *also* **fau·nae** \-ˌnē, -ˌnī\ [NL, fr. L *Fauna,* sister of Faunus (the Roman god of animals)] : animals or animal life esp. of a region, period, or environment — **fau·nal** \-nəl\ *adj*
fau·vism \ˈfō-ˌvi-zəm\ *n, often cap* : a movement in painting characterized by vivid colors, free treatment of form, and a vibrant and decorative effect — **fau·vist** \-vist\ *n, often cap*
faux \ˈfō\ *adj* : not real or genuine ⟨~ fur⟩ ⟨a ~ apology⟩
faux pas \ˈfō-ˌpä, fo-ˈ\ *n, pl* **faux pas** *same or* -ˌpäz, -ˈpäz\ [F, lit., false step] : BLUNDER; *esp* : a social blunder
fa·va bean \ˈfä-və-\ *n* : the large flat edible seed of an Old World vetch; *also* : this plant
[1]**fa·vor** \ˈfā-vər\ *n* **1** : friendly regard shown toward another esp. by a superior **2** : APPROVAL **3** : PARTIALITY **4** : POPULARITY **5** : gracious kindness; *also* : an act of such kindness **6** *pl* : effort in one's behalf : ATTENTION **7** : a token of love (as a ribbon) usu. worn conspicuously **8** : a small gift or decorative item given out at a party **9** : a special privilege **10** : sexual privileges — usu. used in pl. **11** *archaic* : LETTER **12** : BEHALF, INTEREST ⟨acted in his own ~⟩
[2]**favor** *vb* **1** : to regard or treat with favor **2** : OBLIGE **3** : ENDOW ⟨~*ed* by nature⟩ **4** : to treat gently or carefully : SPARE ⟨~ a lame leg⟩ **5** : PREFER **6** : SUPPORT, SUSTAIN ⟨~*ed* the tax reform⟩ **7** : FACILITATE ⟨darkness ~*s* attack⟩ **8** : RESEMBLE ⟨he ~*s* his father⟩
fa·vor·able \ˈfā-və-rə-bəl\ *adj* **1** : APPROVING ⟨a ~ response⟩ **2** : HELPFUL, PROMISING, ADVANTAGEOUS ⟨~ weather⟩ — **fa·vor·ably** \-blē\ *adv*
fa·vor·ite \ˈfā-və-rət, -vrət\ *n* **1** : a person or a thing that is favored above others **2** : a competitor regarded as most likely to win — **favorite** *adj*
favorite son *n* : a candidate supported by the delegates of his state at a presidential nominating convention
fa·vor·it·ism \ˈfā-və-rə-ˌti-zəm\ *n* : PARTIALITY, BIAS
fa·vour *chiefly Brit var of* FAVOR
[1]**fawn** \ˈfȯn, ˈfän\ *vb* **1** : to show affection ⟨a dog ~*ing* on its master⟩ **2** : to court favor by a cringing or flattering manner ♦ ***Synonyms*** GROVEL, KOWTOW, TOADY, TRUCKLE
[2]**fawn** *n* **1** : a young deer **2** : a light grayish brown — **fawny** \ˈfȯ-nē, ˈfä-\ *adj*
fax \ˈfaks\ *n* **1** : FACSIMILE 2 **2** : a device used to send or receive facsimile communications; *also* : such a communication — **fax** *vb*
fay \ˈfā\ *n* : FAIRY, ELF — **fay** *adj*
faze \ˈfāz\ *vb* **fazed; faz·ing** : to disturb the composure or courage of : DAUNT
FBI *abbr* Federal Bureau of Investigation
FCC *abbr* Federal Communications Commission
FD *abbr* fire department
FDA *abbr* Food and Drug Administration
FDIC *abbr* Federal Deposit Insurance Corporation
Fe *symbol* [L *ferrum*] iron
fe·al·ty \ˈfē(-ə)l-tē\ *n, pl* **-ties** : LOYALTY, ALLEGIANCE ♦ ***Synonyms*** FIDELITY, DEVOTION, FAITHFULNESS, PIETY
[1]**fear** \ˈfir\ *vb* **1** : to have a reverent awe of ⟨~ God⟩ **2** : to be afraid of ⟨~*s* spiders⟩ **3** : to be apprehensive
[2]**fear** *n* **1** : an unpleasant often strong emotion caused by expectation or awareness of danger; *also* : an instance of or a state marked by this emotion **2** : anxious concern **3** : profound reverence esp. toward God ♦ ***Synonyms*** DREAD, FRIGHT, ALARM, PANIC, TERROR, TREPIDATION
fear·ful \-fəl\ *adj* **1** : causing fear **2** : filled with fear **3** : showing or caused by fear **4** : extremely bad, intense, or large ⟨paid a ~ price⟩ — **fear·ful·ly** *adv*
fear·less \-ləs\ *adj* : free from fear : BRAVE — **fear·less·ly** *adv* — **fear·less·ness** *n*
fear·some \-səm\ *adj* **1** : causing fear **2** : TIMID **3** : INTENSE ⟨~ determination⟩
fea·si·ble \ˈfē-zə-bəl\ *adj* [ME *faisible,* fr. AF *faisable,* fr. *fais-,* stem of *faire* to make, do] **1** : capable of being done or carried out ⟨a ~ plan⟩ **2** : SUITABLE **3** : REASONABLE, LIKELY ♦ ***Synonyms*** POSSIBLE, PRACTICABLE, VIABLE, WORKABLE — **fea·si·bil·i·ty** \ˌfē-zə-ˈbi-lə-tē\ *n* — **fea·si·bly** \ˈfē-zə-blē\ *adv*
[1]**feast** \ˈfēst\ *n* **1** : an elaborate meal

: BANQUET **2** : ABUNDANCE ⟨a ~ of good books⟩ **3** : FESTIVAL 1

²feast *vb* **1** : to take part in a feast; *also* : to give a feast for **2** : to enjoy some unusual pleasure or delight **3** : DELIGHT, GRATIFY

feat \ˈfēt\ *n* : DEED, EXPLOIT, ACHIEVEMENT; *esp* : an act notable for courage, skill, endurance, or ingenuity

¹feath•er \ˈfe-thər\ *n* **1** : any of the light horny outgrowths that form the external covering of the body of a bird **2** : the vane of an arrow **3** : PLUMAGE **4** : KIND, NATURE ⟨birds of a ~⟩ **5** : ATTIRE, DRESS ⟨in full ~⟩ **6** : CONDITION, MOOD ⟨in fine ~⟩ — **feath•ered** \-thərd\ *adj* — **feath•er•less** *adj* — **feath•ery** *adj* — **a feather in one's cap** : a mark of distinction : HONOR

²feather *vb* **1** : to furnish with a feather ⟨~ an arrow⟩ **2** : to cover, clothe, line, or adorn with or as if with feathers — **feather one's nest** : to provide for oneself financially esp. while exploiting a position of trust

feath•er•bed•ding \ˈfe-thər-ˌbe-diŋ\ *n* : the requiring of an employer usu. under a union rule or safety statute to employ more workers than are needed

feath•er•edge \-ˌej\ *n* : a very thin sharp edge

feath•er•weight \-ˌwāt\ *n* : one that is very light in weight; *esp* : a boxer weighing more than 118 but not over 126 pounds

¹fea•ture \ˈfē-chər\ *n* [ME *feture,* fr. AF, fr. L *factura* act of making, fr. *facere* to make] **1** : the shape or appearance of the face or its parts **2** : a part of the face ⟨her eyes are her best ~⟩ **3** : a prominent part or characteristic **4** : a special attraction (as in a newspaper) **5** : something offered to the public or advertised as particularly attractive ⟨a new car's ~*s*⟩ — **fea•ture•less** *adj*

²feature *vb* **1** : to picture in the mind : IMAGINE **2** : to give special prominence to ⟨the show ~*s* new artists⟩ **3** : to play an important part

Feb *abbr* February

fe•brile \ˈfe-ˌbrī(-ə)l\ *adj* : FEVERISH

Feb•ru•ary \ˈfe-b(y)ə-ˌwer-ē, ˈfe-brə-\ *n* [ME *Februarie,* fr. L *Februarius,* fr. *Februa,* pl., feast of purification] : the 2d month of the year

fe•ces \ˈfē-ˌsēz\ *n pl* : bodily waste discharged from the intestine : EXCREMENT — **fe•cal** \-kəl\ *adj*

feck•less \ˈfek-ləs\ *adj* **1** : WEAK, INEFFECTIVE **2** : WORTHLESS, IRRESPONSIBLE ⟨~ drifters⟩

fe•cund \ˈfe-kənd, ˈfē-\ *adj* : FRUITFUL, PROLIFIC ⟨~ fields⟩ — **fe•cun•di•ty** \fi-ˈkən-də-tē, fe-\ *n*

fed *abbr* federal; federation

fed•er•al \ˈfe-də-rəl, -drəl\ *adj* **1** : formed by a compact between political units that surrender individual sovereignty to a central authority but retain certain limited powers **2** : of or constituting a form of government in which power is distributed between a central authority and constituent territorial units **3** : of or relating to the central government of a federation **4** *cap* : FEDERALIST **5** *often cap* : of, relating to, or loyal to the federal government or the Union armies of the U.S. in the American Civil War — **fed•er•al•ly** *adv*

Federal *n* : a supporter of the U.S. government in the Civil War; *esp* : a soldier in the federal armies

federal district *n* : a district (as the District of Columbia) set apart as the seat of the central government of a federation

fed•er•al•ism \ˈfe-də-rə-li-zəm, -drə-\ *n* **1** *often cap* : the distribution of power in an organization (as a government) between a central authority and the constituent units **2** : support or advocacy of federalism **3** *cap* : the principles of the Federalists

fed•er•al•ist \-list\ *n* **1** : an advocate of federalism **2** *often cap* : an advocate of a federal union between the American colonies after the Revolution and of adoption of the U.S. Constitution **3** *cap* : a member of a major political party in the early years of the U.S. favoring a strong centralized national government — **federalist** *adj, often cap*

fed•er•al•ize \ˈfe-də-rə-ˌlīz, -drə-\ *vb* **-ized; -iz•ing** **1** : to unite in or under a federal system **2** : to bring under the jurisdiction of a federal government

fed•er•ate \ˈfe-də-ˌrāt\ *vb* **-at•ed; -at•ing** : to join in a federation

fed•er•a•tion \ˌfe-də-ˈrā-shən\ *n* **1** : a political or societal entity formed by uniting smaller entities **2** : a federal government **3** : a union of organizations **4** : the forming of a federal union

fedn *abbr* federation

fe•do•ra \fi-ˈdȯr-ə\ *n* : a low soft felt hat with the crown creased lengthwise

fed up *adj* : utterly sated, tired, or disgusted ⟨*fed up* with bureaucracy⟩

fee \ˈfē\ *n* [ME, fr. AF *fé, fief,* of Gmc origin; akin to OE *feoh* cattle, property] **1** : an estate in land held from a feudal lord **2** : an inherited or heritable estate in land **3** : a fixed charge; *also* : a charge for a service

fee•ble \ˈfē-bəl\ *adj* **fee•bler** \-bə-lər\; **fee•blest** \-bə-ləst\ [ME *feble,* fr. AF, fr. L *flebilis* lamentable, wretched, fr. *flēre* to weep] **1** : DECREPIT, FRAIL **2** : INEFFECTIVE, INADEQUATE ⟨a ~ protest⟩ — **fee•ble•ness** *n* — **fee•bly** \-blē\ *adv*

fee•ble•mind•ed \ˌfē-bəl-ˈmīn-dəd\ *adj, dated, offensive* : lacking normal intelligence — **fee•ble•mind•ed•ness** *n*

¹feed \ˈfēd\ *vb* **fed** \ˈfed\; **feed•ing** **1** : to give food to; *also* : to give as food **2** : EAT 1; *also* : PREY **3** : to furnish what is necessary to the development or function of ⟨used wood to ~ the fire⟩ **4** : to supply for another to use ⟨~ a pass⟩ ⟨*fed* the actor his lines⟩ — **feed•er** *n*

²feed *n* **1** : a usu. large meal **2** : food for livestock **3** : a mechanism for feeding material to a machine **4** : a continuous

series of electronic information updates (as to a blog or social media account)
feed·back \ˈfēd-ˌbak\ *n* **1** : the return to the input of a part of the output of a machine, system, or process **2** : response esp. to one in authority about an activity or policy **3** : sound (as whistling) resulting from the retransmission of an amplified or broadcast signal
feed·lot \ˈfēd-ˌlät\ *n* : land on which cattle are fattened for market
feed·stuff \-ˌstəf\ *n* : FEED 2
[1]**feel** \ˈfēl\ *vb* **felt** \ˈfelt\; **feel·ing** **1** : to perceive or examine through physical contact : TOUCH, HANDLE **2** : EXPERIENCE; *also* : to suffer from **3** : to ascertain by cautious trial ⟨~ out public sentiment⟩ **4** : to be aware of **5** : to be conscious of an inward impression, state of mind, or physical condition **6** : BELIEVE, THINK **7** : to search for something with the fingers : GROPE **8** : SEEM ⟨it ~*s* like spring⟩ **9** : to have sympathy or pity
[2]**feel** *n* **1** : the sense of touch **2** : SENSATION, FEELING **3** : the quality of a thing as imparted through touch
feel·er \ˈfē-lər\ *n* **1** : one that feels; *esp* : a tactile organ (as on the head of an insect) **2** : a proposal or remark made to find out the views of other people
[1]**feel·ing** \ˈfē-liŋ\ *n* **1** : the sense of touch; *also* : a sensation perceived by this **2** : a state of mind ⟨a ~ of loneliness⟩ **3** *pl* : general emotional condition : SENSIBILITIES ⟨hurt their ~*s*⟩ **4** : OPINION, BELIEF **5** : capacity to respond emotionally
[2]**feeling** *adj* **1** : SENSITIVE; *esp* : easily moved emotionally **2** : expressing emotion or sensitivity — **feel·ing·ly** *adv*
feet *pl of* FOOT
feign \ˈfān\ *vb* **1** : to give a false appearance of : SHAM ⟨~ illness⟩ **2** : to assert as if true : PRETEND
feint \ˈfānt\ *n* : something feigned; *esp* : a mock blow or attack intended to distract attention from the real point of attack — **feint** *vb*
feisty \ˈfī-stē\ *adj* **feist·i·er**; **-est** : having or showing a lively aggressiveness
feld·spar \ˈfeld-ˌspär\ *n* : any of a group of crystalline minerals consisting of silicates of aluminum with another element (as potassium or sodium)
fe·lic·i·tate \fi-ˈli-sə-ˌtāt\ *vb* **-tat·ed**; **-tat·ing** : CONGRATULATE — **fe·lic·i·ta·tion** \-ˌli-sə-ˈtā-shən\ *n*
fe·lic·i·tous \fi-ˈli-sə-təs\ *adj* **1** : well chosen : APT **2** : PLEASANT, DELIGHTFUL — **fe·lic·i·tous·ly** *adv*
fe·lic·i·ty \fi-ˈli-sə-tē\ *n, pl* **-ties** **1** : the quality or state of being happy; *esp* : great happiness **2** : something that causes happiness **3** : a pleasing manner or quality esp. in art or language ⟨her ~ with words⟩ **4** : an apt expression
fe·line \ˈfē-ˌlīn\ *adj* [L *felinus,* fr. *felis* cat] **1** : of or relating to cats or their kin **2** : sleekly graceful **3** : SLY, TREACHEROUS **4** : STEALTHY — **feline** *n*
[1]**fell** \ˈfel\ *n* : SKIN, HIDE, PELT
[2]**fell** *vb* **1** : to cut, beat, or knock down; *also* : KILL **2** : to sew (a seam) by folding one raw edge under the other
[3]**fell** *past of* FALL
[4]**fell** *adj* : CRUEL, FIERCE; *also* : DEADLY— **in one fell swoop** *also* **at one fell swoop** : all at once : with a single effort
fel·lah \ˈfe-lə, fə-ˈlä\ *n, pl* **fel·la·hin** *or* **fel·la·heen** \ˌfe-lə-ˈhēn\ : a peasant or agricultural laborer in Arab countries (as Egypt or Syria)
fel·la·tio \fə-ˈlā-shē-ˌō\ *also* **fel·la·tion** \-shən\ *n* : oral stimulation of the penis
fel·low \ˈfe-lō\ *n* [ME *felawe,* fr. OE *fēolaga,* fr. ON *fēlagi,* fr. *fēlag* partnership (fr. *fē* cattle, money) + *lag* act of laying] **1** : COMRADE, ASSOCIATE **2** : EQUAL, PEER **3** : one of a pair : MATE **4** : a member of an incorporated literary or scientific society **5** : MAN, BOY **6** : BOYFRIEND **7** : a person granted a stipend for advanced study
fellow man *n* : a kindred human being
fel·low·ship \ˈfe-lō-ˌship\ *n* **1** : the condition of friendly relationship existing among persons : COMRADESHIP **2** : a community of interest or feeling **3** : a group with similar interests **4** : the position of a fellow (as of a university) **5** : the stipend granted a fellow
fellow traveler *n* : a sympathetic supporter of another's cause; *esp* : a person who sympathizes with and often furthers the ideals and program of an organized group (as the Communist party) without joining it
fel·on \ˈfe-lən\ *n* **1** : one who has committed a felony **2** : WHITLOW
fel·o·ny \ˈfe-lə-nē\ *n, pl* **-nies** : a serious crime punishable by a heavy sentence — **fe·lo·ni·ous** \fə-ˈlō-nē-əs\ *adj*
fel·spar *chiefly Brit var of* FELDSPAR
[1]**felt** \ˈfelt\ *n* **1** : a cloth made of wool and fur often mixed with natural or synthetic fibers **2** : a material resembling felt
[2]**felt** *past and past part of* FEEL
fem *abbr* **1** female **2** feminine
FEMA *abbr* Federal Emergency Management Agency
fe·male \ˈfē-ˌmāl\ *adj* [ME, alter. of *femel,* fr. AF *femele,* fr. ML *femella,* fr. L, girl, dim. of *femina* woman] **1** : of, relating to, or being the sex that typically bears young; *also* : PISTILLATE **2** : characteristic of girls or women ⟨~ voices⟩ **3** : having a gender identity that is the opposite of male ♦ ***Synonyms*** FEMININE, WOMANLY, WOMANLIKE, WOMANISH, EFFEMINATE — **female** *n*
fem·i·cide \ˈfe-mə-ˌsīd\ *n* : the murder of a woman or girl by a man
[1]**fem·i·nine** \ˈfe-mə-nən\ *adj* **1** : of the female sex; *also* : characteristic of or appropriate or unique to women **2** : of, relating to, or constituting the gender that includes most words or grammatical forms referring to females — **fem·i·nin·i·ty** \ˌfe-mə-ˈni-nə-tē\ *n*
[2]**feminine** *n* : a noun, pronoun, adjective, or inflectional form or class of the feminine gender; *also* : the feminine gender
fem·i·nism \ˈfe-mə-ˌni-zəm\ *n* : belief in

and advocacy of the political, economic, and social equality of the sexes expressed esp. through organized activity on behalf of women's rights and interests — **fem·i·nist** \-nist\ *n or adj*

femme fa·tale \ˌfem-fə-ˈtal\ *n, pl* **femmes fa·tales** *same or* -ˈtalz\ [F, lit., disastrous woman] : a seductive woman

fe·mur \ˈfē-mər\ *n, pl* **fe·murs** *or* **fem·o·ra** \ˈfe-mə-rə\ : the long leg bone extending from the hip to the knee — **fem·o·ral** \ˈfe-mə-rəl\ *adj*

[1]**fen** \ˈfen\ *n* : low swampy land

[2]**fen** \ˈfən\ *n, pl* **fen** — see *yuan* at MONEY table

[1]**fence** \ˈfens\ *n* [ME *fens,* short for *defens* defense] **1** : a barrier to prevent escape or entry or to mark a boundary **2** : a person who receives stolen goods; *also* : a place where stolen goods are disposed of — **on the fence** : in a position of neutrality or indecision

[2]**fence** *vb* **fenced; fenc·ing** **1** : to enclose with a fence **2** : to keep in or out with a fence **3** : to practice fencing **4** : to use tactics of attack and defense esp. in debate — **fenc·er** *n*

fenc·ing *n* **1** : the art or practice of attack and defense with the foil, épée, or saber **2** : the fences of a property or region **3** : material used for building fences

fend \ˈfend\ *vb* **1** : to keep or ward off : REPEL **2** : SHIFT ⟨~ for yourself⟩

fend·er \ˈfen-dər\ *n* : a protective device (as a guard over the wheel of an automobile)

fen·es·tra·tion \ˌfe-nə-ˈstrā-shən\ *n* : the arrangement and design of windows and doors in a building

Fe·ni·an \ˈfē-nē-ən\ *n* : a member of a secret 19th century Irish and Irish-American organization dedicated to overthrowing British rule in Ireland

fen·ing \ˈfe-niŋ\ *n, pl* **fen·inga** \ˈfe-niŋ-ə\ *also* **fen·ing** \ˈfe-niŋ\ *or* **fen·ings** — see *marka* at MONEY table

fen·nel \ˈfe-nᵊl\ *n* : a garden plant related to the carrot and grown for its aromatic foliage and seeds

FEPC *abbr* Fair Employment Practices Commission

fe·ral \ˈfir-əl, ˈfer-\ *adj* **1** : of, relating to, or suggestive of a wild beast **2** : WILD 1 **3** : having escaped from domestication and become wild

fer–de–lance \ˈfer-də-ˈlans\ *n, pl* **fer–de–lance** [F, lit., lance iron, spearhead] : a large venomous pit viper of Central and So. America

[1]**fer·ment** \fər-ˈment\ *vb* **1** : to cause or undergo fermentation **2** : to be or cause to be in a state of agitation or intense activity

[2]**fer·ment** \ˈfər-ˌment\ *n* **1** : a living organism (as a yeast) causing fermentation by its enzymes; *also* : ENZYME **2** : AGITATION, TUMULT

fer·men·ta·tion \ˌfər-mən-ˈtā-shən, -ˌmen-\ *n* **1** : chemical decomposition of an organic substance (as in the souring of milk or the formation of alcohol from sugar) by enzymatic action in the absence of oxygen often with formation of gas **2** : FERMENT 2

fer·mi·um \ˈfer-mē-əm, ˈfər-\ *n* : an artificially produced radioactive metallic chemical element

fern \ˈfərn\ *n* : any of an order of vascular plants resembling seed plants in having roots, stems, and leaflike fronds but reproducing by spores instead of by flowers and seeds

fern·ery \ˈfər-nə-rē\ *n, pl* **-er·ies** **1** : a place for growing ferns **2** : a collection of growing ferns

fe·ro·cious \fə-ˈrō-shəs\ *adj* **1** : FIERCE, SAVAGE **2** : extremely intense — **fe·ro·cious·ly** *adv* — **fe·ro·cious·ness** *n*

fe·roc·i·ty \fə-ˈrä-sə-tē\ *n* : the quality or state of being ferocious

[1]**fer·ret** \ˈfer-ət\ *n* : a partially domesticated usu. white European mammal related to the weasels

[2]**ferret** *vb* **1** : to hunt game with ferrets **2** : to drive out of a hiding place **3** : to find and bring to light by searching ⟨~ out the truth⟩

fer·ric \ˈfer-ik\ *adj* : of, relating to, or containing iron

ferric oxide *n* : an oxide of iron found in nature as hematite and as rust and used esp. as a pigment, for polishing, and in magnetic materials

Fer·ris wheel \ˈfer-əs-\ *n* : an amusement device consisting of a large upright power-driven wheel with seats that remain horizontal around its rim

fer·ro·mag·net·ic \ˌfer-ō-mag-ˈne-tik\ *adj* : of or relating to substances that are easily magnetized

fer·rous \ˈfer-əs\ *adj* : of, relating to, or containing iron

fer·rule \ˈfer-əl\ *n* : a metal ring or cap around a slender wooden shaft to prevent splitting

[1]**fer·ry** \ˈfer-ē\ *vb* **fer·ried; fer·ry·ing** [ME *ferien,* fr. OE *ferian* to carry, convey] **1** : to carry by boat across a body of water **2** : to cross by a ferry **3** : to convey from one place to another

[2]**ferry** *n, pl* **ferries** **1** : a place where persons or things are ferried **2** : FERRYBOAT

fer·ry·boat \ˈfer-ē-ˌbōt\ *n* : a boat used in ferrying

fer·tile \ˈfər-tᵊl\ *adj* **1** : producing plentifully : PRODUCTIVE ⟨~ soils⟩ ⟨a ~ mind⟩ **2** : capable of developing or reproducing ⟨~ seed⟩ ⟨a ~ bull⟩ ♦ ***Synonyms*** FRUITFUL, PROLIFIC, FECUND, PRODUCTIVE — **fer·til·i·ty** \(ˌ)fər-ˈti-lə-tē\ *n*

fer·til·ize \ˈfər-tə-ˌlīz\ *vb* **-ized; -iz·ing** **1** : to unite with in the process of fertilization ⟨a sperm ~*s* an egg⟩ **2** : to apply fertilizer to — **fer·til·i·za·tion** \ˌfər-tə-lə-ˈzā-shən\ *n*

fer·til·iz·er \ˈfər-tə-ˌlī-zər\ *n* : material (as manure or a chemical mixture) for enriching land

fer·ule \ˈfer-əl\ *n* : a rod or ruler used to punish children

fer·ven·cy \ˈfər-vən-sē\ *n, pl* **-cies** : FERVOR

fer·vent \ˈfər-vənt\ *adj* **1** : very hot : GLOWING **2** : marked by great intensity of feeling ♦ ***Synonyms*** IMPASSIONED, ARDENT, FERVID, FIERY, PASSIONATE — **fer·vent·ly** *adv*

fer·vid \-vəd\ *adj* **1** : very hot **2** : ARDENT, ZEALOUS — **fer·vid·ly** *adv*

fer·vor \ˈfər-vər\ *n* **1** : intense heat **2** : intensity of feeling or expression

fer·vour *chiefly Brit var of* FERVOR

fes·cue \ˈfes-kyü\ *n* : any of a genus of tufted perennial grasses

fes·tal \ˈfes-tᵊl\ *adj* : FESTIVE

fester \ˈfes-tər\ *vb* **1** : to form pus **2** : PUTREFY, ROT **3** : RANKLE

fes·ti·val \ˈfes-tə-vəl\ *n* **1** : a time of celebration marked by special observances; *esp* : an occasion marked with religious ceremonies **2** : a periodic season or program of cultural events or entertainment

fes·tive \ˈfes-tiv\ *adj* **1** : of, relating to, or suitable for a feast or festival **2** : JOYFUL, MERRY — **fes·tive·ly** *adv*

fes·tiv·i·ty \fes-ˈti-və-tē\ *n, pl* **-ties** **1** : FESTIVAL 1 **2** : the quality or state of being festive **3** : festive activity

[1]**fes·toon** \fes-ˈtün\ *n* [F *feston,* fr. It *festone,* fr. *festa* festival] **1** : a decorative chain or strip hanging between two points **2** : a carved, molded, or painted ornament representing a decorative chain

[2]**festoon** *vb* **1** : to hang or form festoons on **2** : to shape into festoons

fe·ta \ˈfe-tə\ *n* : a white crumbly Greek cheese made from sheep's or goat's milk

fe·tal \ˈfē-tᵊl\ *adj* : of, relating to, or being a fetus

fetch \ˈfech\ *vb* **1** : to go or come after and bring or take back ⟨teach a dog to ~ a stick⟩ **2** : to bring in (as a price) **3** : to cause to come : bring out ⟨~*ed* tears from the eyes⟩ **4** : to give by striking ⟨~ him a blow⟩

fetch·ing *adj* : ATTRACTIVE, PLEASING ⟨a ~ smile⟩ — **fetch·ing·ly** *adv*

[1]**fete** *or* **fête** \ˈfāt, ˈfet\ *n* [F *fête,* fr. OF *feste*] **1** : FESTIVAL **2** : a large elaborate entertainment or party

[2]**fete** *or* **fête** *vb* **fet·ed** *or* **fêt·ed; fet·ing** *or* **fêt·ing** **1** : to honor or commemorate with a fete **2** : to pay high honor to

fet·id \ˈfe-təd\ *adj* : having an offensive smell : STINKING

fe·tish *also* **fe·tich** \ˈfe-tish\ *n* [F & Pg; F *fétiche,* fr. Pg *feitiço,* fr. *feitiço* artificial, false, fr. L *facticius* factitious] **1** : an object (as an idol or image) believed to have magical powers (as in curing disease) **2** : an object of unreasoning devotion or concern **3** : an object whose real or fantasied presence is psychologically necessary for sexual gratification

fe·tish·ism \-ti-ˌshi-zəm\ *n* **1** : belief in or devotion to fetishes **2** : the pathological transfer of sexual interest and gratification to a fetish — **fe·tish·ist** \-shist\ *n* — **fe·tish·is·tic** \ˌfe-ti-ˈshis-tik\ *adj*

fe·tish·ize \-ti-ˌshīz\ *vb* **-ized -iz·ing** : to make a fetish of

fet·lock \ˈfet-ˌläk\ *n* : a projection on the back of a horse's leg above the hoof; *also* : a tuft of hair on this

fet·ter \ˈfe-tər\ *n* **1** : a chain or shackle for the feet **2** : something that confines : RESTRAINT — **fetter** *vb*

fet·tle \ˈfe-tᵊl\ *n* : a state of fitness or order : CONDITION ⟨in fine ~⟩

fe·tus \ˈfē-təs\ *n* : an unborn or unhatched vertebrate esp. after its basic structure is laid down; *esp* : a developing human in the uterus from usu. three months after conception to birth

feud \ˈfyüd\ *n* : a prolonged quarrel; *esp* : a lasting conflict between families or clans marked by violent attacks made for revenge — **feud** *vb*

feu·dal \ˈfyü-dᵊl\ *adj* **1** : of, relating to, or having the characteristics of a medieval fee **2** : of, relating to, or characteristic of feudalism

feu·dal·ism \ˈfyü-də-ˌli-zəm\ *n* : a system of political organization prevailing in medieval Europe in which a vassal renders service to a lord and receives protection and land in return; *also* : a similar political or social system — **feu·dal·is·tic** \ˌfyü-dᵊl-ˈis-tik\ *adj*

[1]**feu·da·to·ry** \ˈfyü-də-ˌtȯr-ē\ *adj* : owing feudal allegiance

[2]**feudatory** *n, pl* **-ries** **1** : FIEF **2** : a person who holds lands by feudal law or usage

fe·ver \ˈfē-vər\ *n* **1** : a rise in body temperature above the normal; *also* : a disease of which this is a chief symptom **2** : a state of heightened emotion or activity **3** : CRAZE ⟨football ~⟩ — **fe·ver·ish** *adj* — **fe·ver·ish·ly** *adv*

[1]**few** \ˈfyü\ *pron* : not many : a small number

[2]**few** *adj* **1** : consisting of or amounting to a small number **2** : not many but some ⟨caught a ~ fish⟩ — **few·ness** *n* — **few and far between** : RARE 3

[3]**few** *n* **1** : a small number of units or individuals ⟨a ~ of them⟩ **2** : a special limited number ⟨among the ~⟩

few·er \ˈfyü-ər\ *pron* : a smaller number of persons or things

fey \ˈfā\ *adj* **1** *chiefly Scot* : fated to die; *also* : marked by a foreboding of death or calamity **2** : able to see into the future : VISIONARY **3** : marked by an otherworldly air or attitude **4** : CRAZY, TOUCHED

fez \ˈfez\ *n, pl* **fez·zes** *also* **fez·es** : a round red felt hat that has a flat top and a tassel but no brim

ff *abbr* **1** folios **2** *f*ollowing and the following ones **3** fortissimo

FHA *abbr* Federal Housing Administration

fi·an·cé \ˌfē-ˌän-ˈsā\ *n* [F, fr. MF, fr. pp. of *fiancer* to promise, betroth, fr. OF *fiancier,* fr. *fiance* promise, trust, fr. *fier* to trust, ultim. fr. L *fidere*] : a man engaged to be married

fi·an·cée \ˌfē-ˌän-ˈsā\ *n* : a woman engaged to be married

fi·as·co \fē-ˈas-kō\ *n, pl* **-coes** [F] : a complete failure

fi·at \'fē-ət, -ˌat, -ˌät; 'fī-ət, -ˌat\ *n* [L, let it be done] : an authoritative and often arbitrary order or decree

¹fib \'fib\ *n* : a trivial or childish lie

²fib *vb* **fibbed; fib·bing** : to tell a fib — **fib·ber** *n*

fi·ber \'fī-bər\ *n* **1** : a threadlike substance or structure (as a muscle cell or fine root); *esp* : a natural (as wool or flax) or artificial (as rayon) filament capable of being spun or woven **2** : indigestible material in food that stimulates the intestine to move its contents along **3** : an element that gives texture or substance **4** : basic toughness : STRENGTH ⟨moral ~⟩ — **fi·brous** \-brəs\ *adj*

fi·ber·board \'fī-bər-ˌbȯrd\ *n* : a material made by compressing fibers (as of wood) into stiff sheets

fi·ber·fill \-ˌfil\ *n* : synthetic fibers used as a filling material (as for cushions)

fi·ber·glass \-ˌglas\ *n* : glass in fibrous form used in making various products (as insulation)

fiber optics *n* **1** *pl* : thin transparent fibers of glass or plastic that are enclosed by a less refractive material and that transmit light by internal reflection; *also* : a bundle of such fibers used in an instrument **2** : the technique of the use of fiber optics — **fiber–optic** *adj*

fibre *chiefly Brit var of* FIBER

fi·bril \'fī-brəl, 'fi-\ *n* : a small fiber

fi·bril·la·tion \ˌfi-brə-'lā-shən, ˌfī-\ *n* : rapid irregular contractions of the heart muscle fibers resulting in a lack of synchronism between heartbeat and pulse — **fib·ril·late** \'fi-brə-ˌlāt, 'fī-\ *vb*

fi·brin \'fī-brən\ *n* : a white insoluble fibrous protein formed in the clotting of blood

¹fi·broid \'fī-brȯid, 'fi-\ *adj* : resembling, forming, or consisting of fibrous tissue ⟨~ tumors⟩

²fibroid *n* : a benign tumor of the uterus

fi·bro·my·al·gia \ˌfī-ˌbrō-ˌmī-'al-jə\ *n* : any of a group of rheumatic disorders affecting soft tissues

fi·bro·sis \fī-'brō-səs\ *n* : a condition marked by abnormal increase of fiber-containing tissue

fib·u·la \'fi-byə-lə\ *n, pl* **-lae** \-lē, -lī\ *or* **-las** : the outer and usu. the smaller of the two bones between the knee and ankle — **fib·u·lar** \-lər\ *adj*

FICA *abbr* Federal Insurance Contributions Act

-fication *n comb form* : making : production ⟨simpli*fication*⟩

fiche \'fēsh\ *n, pl* **fiche** : MICROFICHE

fi·chu \'fi-shü\ *n* [F] : a woman's light triangular scarf draped over the shoulders and fastened in front

fick·le \'fi-kəl\ *adj* : not firm or steadfast in disposition or character : INCONSTANT ⟨~ friends⟩ — **fick·le·ness** *n*

fic·tion \'fik-shən\ *n* **1** : something (as a story) invented by the imagination **2** : fictitious literature (as novels) — **fic·tion·al** \-shə-nəl\ *adj* — **fic·tion·al·ly** *adv*

fic·ti·tious \fik-'ti-shəs\ *adj* **1** : of, relating to, or characteristic of fiction : IMAGINARY **2** : FALSE, ASSUMED ⟨a ~ name⟩ **3** : FEIGNED ♦ ***Synonyms*** CHIMERICAL, FANCIFUL, FANTASTIC, UNREAL

¹fid·dle \'fi-dᵊl\ *n* : VIOLIN

²fiddle *vb* **fid·dled; fid·dling** **1** : to play on a fiddle **2** : to move the hands or fingers restlessly **3** : PUTTER **4** : MEDDLE, TAMPER — **fid·dler** *n*

fid·dle·head \'fi-dᵊl-ˌhed\ *n* : one of the young unfurling fronds of some ferns that are often eaten as greens

fiddler crab *n* : any of a genus of burrowing crabs with one claw much enlarged in the male

fid·dle·stick \'fi-dᵊl-ˌstik\ *n* **1** : a violin bow **2** *pl* : NONSENSE — used as an interjection

fi·del·i·ty \fə-'de-lə-tē, fī-\ *n, pl* **-ties** **1** : the quality or state of being faithful **2** : ACCURACY ⟨~ in sound reproduction⟩ ♦ ***Synonyms*** ALLEGIANCE, LOYALTY, DEVOTION, FEALTY

¹fidg·et \'fi-jət\ *n* **1** : uneasiness or restlessness as shown by nervous movements — usu. used in pl. **2** : one that fidgets — **fidg·ety** *adj*

²fidget *vb* : to move or cause to move or act restlessly or nervously

fi·du·cia·ry \fə-'dü-shē-ˌer-ē, -'dyü-, -shə-rē\ *adj* **1** : involving a confidence or trust **2** : held or holding in trust for another ⟨~ accounts⟩ — **fiduciary** *n*

fie \'fī\ *interj* — used to express disgust or disapproval

fief \'fēf\ *n* [F, fr. OF] : a feudal estate : FEE

¹field \'fēld\ *n* **1** : open country **2** : a piece of cleared land for cultivation or pasture **3** : a piece of land yielding some special product **4** : the place where a battle is fought; *also* : BATTLE **5** : an area, division, or sphere of activity ⟨the ~ of science⟩ ⟨salesmen in the ~⟩ **6** : an area for military exercises **7** : an area for sports **8** : a background on which something is drawn or projected ⟨a flag with white stars on a ~ of blue⟩ **9** : a region or space in which a given effect (as magnetism) exists **10** : a particular area (as of a record in a database) in which the same type of information is regularly recorded — **field** *adj*

²field *vb* **1** : to handle a batted or thrown baseball while on defense **2** : to put into the field **3** : to answer satisfactorily ⟨~ a tough question⟩ — **field·er** *n*

field day *n* **1** : a day devoted to outdoor sports and athletic competition **2** : a time of extraordinary pleasure or opportunity

field event *n* : a track-and-field event (as weight-throwing) other than a race

field glass *n* : a hand-held binocular telescope — usu. used in pl.

field guide *n* : a manual for identifying natural objects, plants, or animals

field hockey *n* : a field game played between two teams of 11 players each whose object is to knock a ball into the opponent's goal with a curved stick

field marshal *n* : an officer (as in the British army) of the highest rank
field–test \-ˌtest\ *vb* : to test (as a new product) in actual situations reflecting intended use — **field test** *n*
fiend \ˈfēnd\ *n* **1** : DEVIL 1 **2** : DEMON **3** : an extremely wicked or cruel person **4** : a person excessively devoted to a pursuit ⟨a golf ~⟩ **5** : ADDICT ⟨a dope ~⟩ — **fiend·ish** *adj* — **fiend·ish·ly** *adv*
fierce \ˈfirs\ *adj* **fierc·er; fierc·est** **1** : violently hostile or aggressive in temperament **2** : PUGNACIOUS **3** : INTENSE ⟨~ pain⟩ **4** : furiously active or determined **5** : wild or menacing in appearance ♦ ***Synonyms*** FEROCIOUS, BARBAROUS, SAVAGE, CRUEL — **fierce·ly** *adv* — **fierce·ness** *n*
fi·ery \ˈfī-ə-rē\ *adj* **fi·er·i·er; -est** **1** : consisting of fire **2** : BURNING, BLAZING **3** : FLAMMABLE **4** : hot like a fire : INFLAMED, FEVERISH **5** : RED ⟨a ~ sunset⟩ **6** : full of emotion or spirit **7** : IRRITABLE — **fi·eri·ness** \-rē-nəs\ *n*
fi·es·ta \fē-ˈes-tə\ *n* [Sp] : FESTIVAL
fife \ˈfīf\ *n* [G *Pfeife* pipe, fife] : a small flute
FIFO *abbr* first in, first out
fif·teen \fif-ˈtēn\ *n* : one more than 14 — **fifteen** *adj or pron* — **fif·teenth** \-ˈtēnth\ *adj or n*
fifth \ˈfifth\ *n* **1** : one that is number five in a countable series **2** : one of five equal parts of something **3** : a unit of measure for liquor equal to $^1/_5$ U.S. gallon (0.757 liter) — **fifth** *adj or adv*
fifth column *n* : a group of secret supporters of a nation's enemy that engage in espionage or sabotage within the country — **fifth columnist** *n*
fifth wheel *n* : one that is unnecessary and often burdensome
fif·ty \ˈfif-tē\ *n, pl* **fifties** : five times 10 — **fif·ti·eth** \-tē-əth\ *adj or n* — **fifty** *adj or pron*
fif·ty–fif·ty \ˌfif-tē-ˈfif-tē\ *adj* **1** : shared equally ⟨a ~ proposition⟩ **2** : half favorable and half unfavorable
[1]**fig** \ˈfig\ *n* : a soft usu. pear-shaped edible fruit of a tree related to the mulberry; *also* : a tree bearing figs
[2]**fig** *abbr* **1** figurative; figuratively **2** figure
[1]**fight** \ˈfīt\ *vb* **fought** \ˈfȯt\; **fight·ing** **1** : to contend against another in battle or physical combat **2** : BOX **3** : to put forth a determined effort **4** : STRUGGLE, CONTEND **5** : to attempt to prevent the success or effectiveness of **6** : WAGE ⟨~ a war⟩ **7** : to gain by struggle
[2]**fight** *n* **1** : a hostile encounter : BATTLE **2** : a boxing match **3** : a verbal disagreement **4** : a struggle for a goal or an objective **5** : strength or disposition for fighting ⟨full of ~⟩
fight·er \ˈfī-tər\ *n* **1** : one that fights; *esp* : WARRIOR **2** : BOXER 1 **3** : a fast maneuverable warplane for destroying enemy aircraft
fig·ment \ˈfig-mənt\ *n* : something imagined or made up
fig·u·ra·tion \ˌfi-gyə-ˈrā-shən, -gə-\ *n* **1** : FORM, OUTLINE **2** : an act or instance of representation in figures and shapes
fig·u·ra·tive \ˈfi-gyə-rə-tiv, -gə-\ *adj* **1** : EMBLEMATIC **2** : SYMBOLIC, METAPHORICAL ⟨~ language⟩ — **fig·u·ra·tive·ly** *adv*
[1]**fig·ure** \ˈfi-gyər, -gər\ *n* [ME, fr. AF, fr. L *figura,* fr. *fingere* to shape] **1** : NUMERAL **2** *pl* : arithmetical calculations **3** : a written or printed character **4** : PRICE, SUM ⟨sold at a low ~⟩ **5** : a combination of points, lines, or surfaces in geometry ⟨a circle is a closed plane ~⟩ **6** : SHAPE, FORM, OUTLINE **7** : the graphic representation of a form esp. of a person **8** : a diagram or pictorial illustration of textual matter **9** : PATTERN, DESIGN **10** : appearance made or impression produced ⟨they cut quite a ~⟩ **11** : a series of movements (as in a dance) **12** : PERSONAGE ⟨a well-known sports ~⟩
[2]**figure** *vb* **fig·ured; fig·ur·ing** **1** : to represent by or as if by a figure or outline **2** : to decorate with a pattern **3** : to indicate or represent by numerals **4** : REGARD, CONSIDER **5** : to be or appear important or conspicuous **6** : COMPUTE, CALCULATE ⟨*figured* the cost⟩
fig·ure·head \ˈfi-gyər-ˌhed, -gər-\ *n* **1** : a figure on the bow of a ship **2** : a head or chief in name only
figure of speech : a form of expression (as a simile or metaphor) that often compares or identifies one thing with another to convey meaning or heighten effect
figure out *vb* **1** : FIND OUT, DISCOVER **2** : SOLVE ⟨*figure out* a math problem⟩
figure skating *n* : skating that includes various jumps, spins, and dance movements
fig·u·rine \ˌfi-gyə-ˈrēn, -gə-\ *n* : a small carved or molded figure
fil·a·ment \ˈfi-lə-mənt\ *n* : a fine thread or threadlike object, part, or process — **fil·a·men·tous** \ˌfi-lə-ˈmen-təs\ *adj*
fil·bert \ˈfil-bərt\ *n* : the sweet thick-shelled nut of either of two European hazels; *also* : a shrub or small tree bearing filberts
filch \ˈfilch\ *vb* : to steal furtively
[1]**file** \ˈfī(-ə)l\ *n* : a usu. steel tool with a ridged or toothed surface used esp. for smoothing a hard substance
[2]**file** *vb* **filed; fil·ing** : to rub, smooth, or cut away with a file
[3]**file** *vb* **filed; fil·ing** [ME, fr. ML *filare* to string documents on a string or wire, fr. *filum* file of documents, lit., thread, fr. L] **1** : to arrange in order **2** : to enter or record officially or as prescribed by law ⟨~ a lawsuit⟩ **3** : to send (copy) to a newspaper
[4]**file** *n* **1** : a device (as a folder or cabinet) by means of which papers may be kept in order **2** : a collection of papers or publications usu. arranged or classified **3** : a collection of data (as text) treated by a computer as a unit
[5]**file** *n* : a row of persons, animals, or things arranged one behind the other

[6]**file** *vb* **filed; fil·ing** : to march or proceed in file

fi·let mi·gnon \ˌfi-(ˌ)lā-mēn-ˈyōⁿ, fi-ˌlā-\ *n, pl* **filets mignons** \-(ˌ)lā-mēn-ˈyōⁿz, -ˌlā-\ [F, lit., dainty fillet] : a thick slice of beef cut from the narrow end of a beef tenderloin

fil·ial \ˈfi-lē-əl, ˈfil-yəl\ *adj* : of, relating to, or befitting a son or daughter

fil·i·bus·ter \ˈfi-lə-ˌbəs-tər\ *n* [Sp *filibustero,* lit., freebooter] **1** : a military adventurer; *esp* : an American engaged in fomenting 19th century Latin American uprisings **2** : the use of delaying tactics (as extremely long speeches) esp. in a legislative assembly; *also* : an instance of this practice — **filibuster** *vb* — **fil·i·bus·ter·er** *n*

fil·i·cide \ˈfi-lə-ˌsīd\ *n* : the murder of one's own daughter or son

fil·i·gree \ˈfi-lə-ˌgrē\ *n* [F *filigrane*] : ornamental openwork (as of fine wire) — **fil·i·greed** \-ˌgrēd\ *adj*

fil·ing \ˈfī-liŋ\ *n* **1** : the act or instance of using a file **2** : a small piece scraped off by a file ⟨iron ~*s*⟩

Fil·i·pi·no \ˌfi-lə-ˈpē-nō\ *n, pl* **Filipinos** : a native or inhabitant of the Philippines — **Filipino** *adj*

[1]**fill** \ˈfil\ *vb* **1** : to make or become full **2** : to stop up : PLUG ⟨~ a cavity⟩ **3** : FEED, SATIATE **4** : SATISFY, FULFILL ⟨~ all requirements⟩ **5** : to occupy fully **6** : to spread through ⟨laughter ~*ed* the room⟩ **7** : OCCUPY ⟨~ the office of president⟩ **8** : to put a person in ⟨~ a vacancy⟩ **9** : to supply as directed ⟨~ a prescription⟩

[2]**fill** *n* **1** : a full supply; *esp* : a quantity that satisfies or satiates **2** : material used esp. for filling a low place

[1]**fill·er** \ˈfi-lər\ *n* **1** : one that fills **2** : a substance added to another substance (as to increase bulk or weight) **3** : a material used for filling cracks and pores in wood before painting

[2]**fil·ler** \ˈfi-ˌler\ *n, pl* **fillers** *or* **filler** — see *forint* at MONEY table

[1]**fil·let** \ˈfi-lət, *in sense 2* fi-ˈlā, ˈfi-(ˌ)lā\ *also* **fi·let** \fi-ˈlā, ˈfi-(ˌ)lā\ *n* [ME *filet,* fr. AF, dim. of *fil* thread] **1** : a narrow band, strip, or ribbon **2** : a piece or slice of boneless meat or fish; *esp* : the tenderloin of beef

[2]**fil·let** \ˈfi-lət, *in sense 2 also* fi-ˈlā, ˈfi-(ˌ)lā\ *vb* **1** : to bind or adorn with or as if with a fillet **2** : to cut into fillets

fill in *vb* **1** : to provide necessary or recent information **2** : to serve as a temporary substitute

fill·ing \ˈfi-liŋ\ *n* **1** : material used to fill something ⟨a ~ for a tooth⟩ **2** : the yarn interlacing the warp in a fabric **3** : a food mixture used to fill pastry or sandwiches

filling station *n* : GAS STATION

fil·lip \ˈfi-ləp\ *n* **1** : a blow or gesture made by a flick or snap of the finger across the thumb **2** : something that serves to arouse or excite — **fillip** *vb*

fill–up \ˈfil-ˌəp\ *n* : an act or instance of filling something

fil·ly \ˈfi-lē\ *n, pl* **fillies** : a young female horse usu. less than four years old

[1]**film** \ˈfilm\ *n* **1** : a thin skin or membrane **2** : a thin coating or layer **3** : a flexible strip of chemically treated material used in taking pictures **4** : MOTION PICTURE — **filmy** *adj*

[2]**film** *vb* **1** : to cover with a film **2** : to make a motion picture of

film·dom \ˈfilm-dəm\ *n* : the motion-picture industry

film·og·ra·phy \fil-ˈmä-grə-fē\ *n, pl* **-phies** : a list of motion pictures featuring the work of a film figure or a particular topic

film·strip \ˈfilm-ˌstrip\ *n* : a strip of film bearing a sequence of images for projection as still pictures

[1]**fils** \ˈfēs\ *n* [F] : SON — used after a family name to distinguish a son from his father

[2]**fils** \ˈfils\ *n, pl* **fils** — see *dinar, dirham, rial* at MONEY table

[1]**fil·ter** \ˈfil-tər\ *n* **1** : a porous material through which a fluid is passed to separate out matter in suspension; *also* : a device containing such material **2** : a device for suppressing waves of certain frequencies; *esp* : one (as for a camera) that absorbs light of certain colors **3** : software for sorting or blocking certain online material

[2]**filter** *vb* **1** : to remove by means of a filter **2** : to pass through a filter — **fil·ter·able** *also* **fil·tra·ble** \-tə-rə-bəl, -trə-\ *adj* — **fil·tra·tion** \fil-ˈtrā-shən\ *n*

filth \ˈfilth\ *n* [ME, fr. OE *fȳlth,* fr. *fūl* foul] **1** : foul matter; *esp* : loathsome dirt or refuse **2** : moral corruption **3** : OBSCENITY — **filth·i·ness** *n* — **filthy** \ˈfil-thē\ *adj*

filthy *adv* : VERY, EXTREMELY ⟨~ dirty⟩ ⟨~ rich⟩

fil·trate \ˈfil-ˌtrāt\ *n* : fluid that has passed through a filter

[1]**fin** \ˈfin\ *n* **1** : a thin external process by which an aquatic animal (as a fish) moves through water **2** : a fin-shaped part (as on an airplane) **3** : FLIPPER 2 — **finned** \ˈfind\ *adj*

[2]**fin** *abbr* **1** finance; financial **2** finish

fi·na·gle \fə-ˈnā-gəl\ *vb* **-gled; -gling** **1** : to obtain by indirect or dishonest means : WANGLE **2** : to use devious dishonest methods to achieve one's ends — **fi·na·gler** *n*

[1]**fi·nal** \ˈfī-nᵊl\ *adj* **1** : not to be altered or undone ⟨all sales are ~⟩ **2** : ULTIMATE **3** : relating to or occurring at the end or conclusion ⟨the ~ results⟩ — **fi·nal·i·ty** \fī-ˈna-lə-tē, fə-\ *n* — **fi·nal·ly** *adv*

[2]**final** *n* **1** : a deciding match or game — usu. used in pl. **2** : the last examination in a course — often used in pl.

fi·na·le \fə-ˈna-lē, fi-ˈnä-\ *n* : the close or end of something; *esp* : the last section of a musical composition

fi·nal·ise *Brit var of* FINALIZE

fi·nal·ist \ˈfī-nə-list\ *n* : a contestant in the finals of a competition

fi•nal•ize \'fī-nə-ˌlīz\ *vb* **-ized; -iz•ing** : to put in final or finished form

[1]**fi•nance** \fə-'nans, 'fī-ˌnans\ *n* [ME, ending, payment, fr. AF, fr. *finer* to end, pay, fr. *fin* end, fr. L *finis* boundary, end] **1** *pl* : money resources available esp. to a government or business **2** : management of money affairs

[2]**finance** *vb* **fi•nanced; fi•nanc•ing** **1** : to raise or provide funds for **2** : to furnish with necessary funds **3** : to sell or supply on credit

finance company *n* : a company that makes usu. small short-term loans usu. to individuals

fi•nan•cial \fə-'nan-chəl, fī-\ *adj* : relating to finance or financiers ⟨~ problems⟩ — **fi•nan•cial•ly** *adv*

fi•nan•cials \-shəlz\ *n pl* : financial statistics

fi•nan•cier \ˌfi-nən-'sir, ˌfī-ˌnan-\ *n* **1** : a person skilled in managing public moneys **2** : a person who deals with large-scale finance and investment

finch \'finch\ *n* : any of numerous songbirds with strong conical bills

[1]**find** \'fīnd\ *vb* **found** \'faůnd\; **find•ing** **1** : to meet with either by chance or by searching or study : ENCOUNTER, DISCOVER **2** : to obtain by effort or management ⟨~ time to read⟩ **3** : to arrive at : REACH ⟨the bullet *found* its mark⟩ **4** : EXPERIENCE, FEEL ⟨*found* happiness⟩ **5** : to gain or regain the use of ⟨*found* his voice again⟩ **6** : to determine and make a statement about ⟨~ a verdict⟩

[2]**find** *n* **1** : an act or instance of finding **2** : something found; *esp* : a valuable item of discovery

find•er \'fīn-dər\ *n* : one that finds; *esp* : VIEWFINDER

fin de siè•cle \ˌfaⁿ-də-sē-'eklᵊ\ *adj* [F, end of century] **1** : of, relating to, or characteristic of the close of the 19th century **2** : of or relating to the end of a century

find•ing \'fīn-diŋ\ *n* **1** : the act of finding **2** : FIND 2 **3** : the result of a judicial proceeding or inquiry

find out *vb* : to learn by study, observation, or search : DISCOVER

[1]**fine** \'fīn\ *n* : money exacted as a penalty for an offense

[2]**fine** *vb* **fined; fin•ing** : to impose a fine on : punish by a fine

[3]**fine** *adj* **fin•er; fin•est** **1** : free from impurity **2** : very thin in gauge or texture **3** : not coarse ⟨~ sand⟩ **4** : SUBTLE, SENSITIVE ⟨a ~ distinction⟩ **5** : superior in quality or appearance **6** : ELEGANT, REFINED ⟨~ manners⟩ — **fine•ly** *adv* — **fine•ness** *n*

[4]**fine** *adv* **1** : very well **2** — used to express agreement

fine art *n* : art (as painting, sculpture, or music) concerned esp. with the creation of beautiful objects — usu. used in pl.

fin•ery \'fī-nə-rē\ *n, pl* **-er•ies** : ORNAMENT, DECORATION; *esp* : showy clothing and jewels

fine•spun \'fīn-'spən\ *adj* : developed with extremely or excessively fine delicacy or detail

fi•nesse \fə-'nes\ *n* **1** : refinement or delicacy of workmanship, structure, or texture **2** : CUNNING, SUBTLETY ⟨handling questions with ~⟩ — **finesse** *vb*

fine–tune \'fīn-'tün\ *vb* : to adjust so as to bring to the highest level of performance or effectiveness

fin•fish \'fin-ˌfish\ *n* : FISH 2

[1]**fin•ger** \'fiŋ-gər\ *n* **1** : any of the five divisions at the end of the hand; *esp* : one other than the thumb **2** : something that resembles or does the work of a finger **3** : a part of a glove into which a finger is inserted

[2]**finger** *vb* **fin•gered; fin•ger•ing** **1** : to touch or feel with the fingers : HANDLE **2** : to perform with the fingers or with a certain fingering **3** : to mark the notes of a piece of music as a guide in playing **4** : to point out ⟨was ~*ed* as a suspect⟩

fin•ger•board \'fiŋ-gər-ˌbȯrd\ *n* : the part of a stringed instrument against which the fingers press the strings to vary the pitch

finger bowl *n* : a small water bowl for rinsing the fingers at the table

fin•ger•ing \'fiŋ-gə-riŋ\ *n* **1** : handling or touching with the fingers **2** : the act or method of using the fingers in playing an instrument **3** : the marking of the method of fingering

fin•ger•ling \'fiŋ-gər-liŋ\ *n* : a small fish

fin•ger•nail \'fiŋ-gər-ˌnāl\ *n* : the nail of a finger

fin•ger•print \-ˌprint\ *n* : the pattern of marks made by pressing the tip of a finger or thumb on a surface; *esp* : an ink impression of such a pattern taken for the purpose of identification — **fingerprint** *vb*

fin•ger•tip \-ˌtip\ *n* : the tip of a finger

fin•i•al \'fi-nē-əl\ *n* : an ornamental projection or end (as on a spire)

fin•ick•ing \'fi-ni-kiŋ\ *adj* : FINICKY

fin•icky \'fi-ni-kē\ *adj* : excessively particular in taste or standards ⟨a ~ eater⟩

fi•nis \'fi-nəs\ *n* : END, CONCLUSION

[1]**fin•ish** \'fi-nish\ *vb* **1** : TERMINATE **2** : to use or dispose of entirely **3** : to bring to completion : ACCOMPLISH **4** : to put a final coat or surface on **5** : to come to the end of a course or undertaking ⟨my horse ~*ed* third⟩ — **fin•ish•er** *n*

[2]**finish** *n* **1** : END, CONCLUSION **2** : something that completes or perfects **3** : the final treatment or coating of a surface

fi•nite \'fī-ˌnīt\ *adj* **1** : having definite or definable limits; *also* : having a limited nature or existence **2** : being less than some positive integer in number or measure and greater than its negative **3** : showing distinction of grammatical person and number ⟨a ~ verb⟩

fink \'fiŋk\ *n* **1** : a contemptible person **2** : STRIKEBREAKER **3** : INFORMER

Finn \'fin\ *n* : a native or inhabitant of Finland

fin•nan had•die \ˌfi-nən-'ha-dē\ *n* : smoked haddock

[1]Finn·ish \ˈfi-nish\ *adj* : of or relating to Finland, the Finns, or Finnish
[2]Finnish *n* : the language of the Finns
fin·ny \ˈfi-nē\ *adj* **1** : having or characterized by fins **2** : relating to or being fish
fiord *var of* FJORD
fir \ˈfər\ *n* : any of a genus of usu. large evergreen trees related to the pines; *also* : the light soft wood of a fir
[1]fire \ˈfī(-ə)r\ *n* **1** : the light or heat and esp. the flame of something burning **2** : ENTHUSIASM, ZEAL **3** : fuel that is burning (as in a stove or fireplace) **4** : destructive burning (as of a house) **5** : the firing of weapons — **fire·less** *adj*
[2]fire *vb* **fired; fir·ing** **1** : KINDLE, IGNITE ⟨~ a house⟩ **2** : STIR, ENLIVEN ⟨~ the imagination⟩ **3** : to dismiss from employment **4** : SHOOT ⟨~ a gun⟩ ⟨~ an arrow⟩ **5** : BAKE ⟨*firing* pottery in a kiln⟩ **6** : to apply fire or fuel to something ⟨~ a furnace⟩
fire ant *n* : either of two small fiercely stinging So. American ants introduced into the southeastern U.S. where they are agricultural pests
fire·arm \ˈfī(-ə)r-ˌärm\ *n* : a weapon (as a pistol) from which a shot is discharged by gunpowder
fire·ball \-ˌbȯl\ *n* **1** : a ball of fire **2** : a very bright meteor **3** : the highly luminous cloud of vapor and dust created by a nuclear explosion **4** : a highly energetic person
fire·boat \-ˌbōt\ *n* : a boat equipped for fighting fires
fire·bomb \-ˌbäm\ *n* : an incendiary bomb — **firebomb** *vb*
fire·box \-ˌbäks\ *n* **1** : a chamber (as of a furnace) that contains a fire **2** : a box containing a fire alarm
fire·brand \-ˌbrand\ *n* **1** : a piece of burning wood **2** : a person who creates unrest or strife : AGITATOR
fire·break \-ˌbrāk\ *n* : a barrier of cleared or plowed land intended to check a forest or grass fire
fire·bug \-ˌbəg\ *n* : a person who deliberately sets destructive fires
fire·crack·er \-ˌkra-kər\ *n* : a usu. paper tube containing an explosive and a fuse and set off to make a noise
fire department *n* : an organization for preventing or extinguishing fires; *also* : its members
fire engine *n* : a motor vehicle with equipment for extinguishing fires
fire escape *n* : a stairway or ladder for escape from a burning building
fire·fight·er \ˈfī(-ə)r-ˌfī-tər\ *n* : a person who fights fires; *esp* : a member of a fire department
fire·fly \-ˌflī\ *n* : any of various small night-flying beetles that produce flashes of light for courtship purposes
fire·house \-ˌhau̇s\ *n* : FIRE STATION
fire irons *n pl* : tools for tending a fire esp. in a fireplace
fire·man \ˈfī(-ə)r-mən\ *n* **1** : STOKER **2** : FIREFIGHTER
fire off *vb* : to write and send
fire·place \-ˌplās\ *n* **1** : a framed opening made in a chimney to hold an open fire **2** : an outdoor structure of brick or stone for an open fire
fire·plug \-ˌpləg\ *n* : HYDRANT
fire·pow·er \-ˌpau̇(-ə)r\ *n* : the ability to deliver gunfire or warheads on a target
[1]fire·proof \-ˈprüf\ *adj* : resistant to fire
[2]fireproof *vb* : to make fireproof
fire–sale \-ˌsāl\ *adj* : heavily discounted ⟨~ prices⟩
fire screen *n* : a protective screen before a fireplace
[1]fire·side \ˈfī(-ə)r-ˌsīd\ *n* **1** : a place near the fire or hearth **2** : HOME
[2]fireside *adj* : having an informal or intimate quality
fire station *n* : a building housing fire engines and usu. firefighters
fire·storm \ˈfī(-ə)r-ˌstȯrm\ *n* **1** : a large destructive very hot fire **2** : a sudden or violent outburst ⟨~ of criticism⟩
fire tower *n* : a tower (as in a forest) from which a watch for fires is kept
fire·trap \ˈfī(-ə)r-ˌtrap\ *n* : a building or place apt to catch on fire or difficult to escape from in case of fire
fire truck *n* : FIRE ENGINE
fire·wall \-ˌwȯl\ *n* : computer hardware or software for preventing unauthorized access to data
fire·wa·ter \ˈfī(-ə)r-ˌwȯ-tər, -ˌwä-\ *n* : intoxicating liquor
fire·wood \-ˌwu̇d\ *n* : wood used for fuel
fire·work \-ˌwərk\ *n* : a device designed to produce a striking display by the burning of explosive or flammable materials
firing line *n* **1** : a line from which fire is delivered against a target **2** : the forefront of an activity
[1]firm \ˈfərm\ *adj* **1** : securely fixed in place **2** : SOLID, VIGOROUS ⟨a ~ handshake⟩ **3** : having a solid or compact texture **4** : not subject to change or fluctuation : STEADY ⟨~ prices⟩ **5** : STEADFAST **6** : indicating firmness or resolution — **firm·ly** *adv* — **firm·ness** *n*
[2]firm *vb* : to make or become firm
[3]firm *n* [G *Firma,* fr. It, signature, ultim. fr. L *firmare* to make firm, confirm] **1** : the name under which a company transacts business **2** : a business partnership of two or more persons **3** : a business enterprise
fir·ma·ment \ˈfər-mə-mənt\ *n* : the arch of the sky : HEAVENS
firm·ware \ˈfirm-ˌwer\ *n* : computer programs contained permanently in a hardware device
[1]first \ˈfərst\ *adj* : preceding all others as in time, order, or importance
[2]first *adv* **1** : before any other **2** : for the first time **3** : in preference to something else
[3]first *n* **1** : number one in a countable series **2** : something that is first **3** : the lowest forward gear in an automotive vehicle **4** : the winning or highest place in a competition or examination
first aid *n* : emergency care or treatment given an injured or ill person

first·born \ˈfərst-ˈbȯrn\ *adj* : ELDEST — **firstborn** *n*
first class *n* : the best or highest group in a classification — **first–class** *adj or adv*
first gentleman *n, often cap F&G* : the husband or male partner of the chief executive of a country or jurisdiction
first·hand \ˈfərst-ˈhand\ *adj* : coming from direct personal observation or experience — **firsthand** *adv*
first lady *n, often cap F&L* : the wife, female partner, or hostess of the chief executive of a country or jurisdiction
first lieutenant *n* : a commissioned officer (as in the army) ranking next below a captain
first·ling \ˈfərst-liŋ\ *n* : one that comes or is produced first
first·ly \-lē\ *adv* : in the first place : FIRST
First Nation *n* : any of a number of peoples esp. of Canada who are indigenous to No. America
¹**first–rate** \-ˈrāt\ *adj* : of the first order of size, importance, or quality
²**first–rate** *adv* : very well
first sergeant *n* **1** : a noncommissioned officer serving as the chief assistant to the commander of a military unit **2** : a rank in the army below a sergeant major and in the marine corps below a master gunnery sergeant
first strike *n* : a preemptive nuclear attack
first–string \ˈfərst-ˈstriŋ\ *adj* : being a regular as distinguished from a substitute — **first–string·er** \-ˌstriŋ-ər\ *n*
first–year \-ˌyir\ *n* : a student in the first year (as at a high school or college)
firth \ˈfərth\ *n* [ME, fr. ON *fjǫrthr*] : ESTUARY
fis·cal \ˈfis-kəl\ *adj* [L *fiscalis,* fr. *fiscus* basket, treasury] **1** : of or relating to taxation, public revenues, or public debt **2** : of or relating to financial matters — **fis·cal·ly** *adv*
¹**fish** \ˈfish\ *n, pl* **fish** *or* **fish·es** **1** : a water-dwelling animal — usu. used in combination ⟨star*fish*⟩ ⟨shell*fish*⟩ **2** : any of numerous cold-blooded water-breathing vertebrates with fins, gills, and usu. scales that include the bony fishes and usu. the cartilaginous and jawless fishes **3** : the flesh of fish used as food
²**fish** *vb* **1** : to attempt to catch fish **2** : to seek something by roundabout means ⟨∼ for praise⟩ **3** : to search for something underwater **4** : to engage in a search by groping **5** : to draw forth
fish–and–chips *n pl* : fried fish and french fried potatoes
fish·bowl \ˈfish-ˌbōl\ *n* **1** : a bowl for the keeping of live fish **2** : a place or condition that affords no privacy
fish·er \ˈfi-shər\ *n* **1** : one that fishes **2** : a dark brown No. American carnivorous mammal related to the weasels
fish·er·man \-mən\ *n* **1** : a person engaged in fishing **2** : a fishing boat
fish·ery \ˈfi-shə-rē\ *n, pl* **-er·ies** **1** : the business of catching fish **2** : a place for catching fish
fish·hook \ˈfish-ˌhu̇k\ *n* : a usu. barbed hook for catching fish
fish ladder *n* : an arrangement of pools in steps by which fish can pass over a dam in going upstream
fish·net \ˈfish-ˌnet\ *n* **1** : netting for catching fish **2** : a coarse open-mesh fabric
fish·tail \-ˌtāl\ *vb* : to have the rear end slide from side to side out of control while moving forward
fish·wife \-ˌwīf\ *n* **1** : a woman who sells fish **2** : a vulgar abusive woman
fishy \ˈfi-shē\ *adj* **fish·i·er; -est** **1** : of or resembling fish **2** : QUESTIONABLE ⟨the story sounds ∼ to me⟩
fis·sion \ˈfi-shən, -zhən\ *n* [L *fissio,* fr. *findere* to split] **1** : a cleaving into parts **2** : a method of reproduction in which a living cell or body divides into two or more parts each of which grows into a whole new individual **3** : the splitting of an atomic nucleus resulting in the release of large amounts of energy — **fis·sion·able** \ˈfi-shə-nə-bəl, -zhə-\ *adj*
fis·sure \ˈfi-shər\ *n* : a narrow opening or crack
fist \ˈfist\ *n* **1** : the hand with fingers folded into the palm **2** : INDEX 6
fist bump *n* : a gesture in which two people bump their fists together — **fist–bump** *vb*
fist·ful \ˈfist-ˌfu̇l\ *n* : HANDFUL
fist·i·cuffs \ˈfis-ti-ˌkəfs\ *n pl* : a fight with the fists
fist pump *n* : a celebratory gesture in which the fist is raised and lowered quickly and vigorously — **fist–pump** *vb*
fis·tu·la \ˈfis-chə-lə\ *n, pl* **-las** *or* **-lae** : an abnormal passage leading from an abscess or hollow organ — **fis·tu·lous** \-ləs\ *adj*
¹**fit** \ˈfit\ *adj* **fit·ter; fit·test** **1** : adapted to a purpose : APPROPRIATE **2** : PROPER, RIGHT ⟨a movie ∼ for children⟩ **3** : PREPARED, READY **4** : physically and mentally sound — **fit·ly** *adv* — **fit·ness** *n*
²**fit** *n* **1** : a sudden violent attack (as in epilepsy) **2** : a sudden outburst
³**fit** *vb* **fit·ted** *also* **fit; fit·ting** **1** : to be suitable for or to **2** : to be correctly adjusted to or shaped for **3** : to insert or adjust until correctly in place **4** : to make a place or room for **5** : to be in agreement or accord with **6** : PREPARE **7** : ADJUST **8** : SUPPLY, EQUIP ⟨*fitted* out with gear⟩ **9** : BELONG — **fit·ter** *n*
⁴**fit** *n* : the fact, condition, or manner of fitting or being fitted
fit·ful \ˈfit-fəl\ *adj* : not regular : INTERMITTENT ⟨∼ sleep⟩ — **fit·ful·ly** *adv*
¹**fit·ting** \ˈfi-tiŋ\ *adj* : APPROPRIATE, SUITABLE ⟨a ∼ tribute⟩ — **fit·ting·ly** *adv*
²**fitting** *n* **1** : the action or act of one that fits; *esp* : a trying on of clothes being made or altered **2** : a small often standardized part ⟨a plumbing ∼⟩
five \ˈfīv\ *n* **1** : one more than four **2** : the 5th in a set or series **3** : something having five units; *esp* : a basketball team **4** : a 5-dollar bill — **five** *adj or pron*

[1]fix \ˈfiks\ *vb* **1** : to make firm, stable, or fast **2** : to give a permanent or final form to **3** : AFFIX, ATTACH **4** : to hold or direct steadily ⟨~*es* his eyes on the horizon⟩ **5** : ESTABLISH, SET **6** : ASSIGN ⟨~ the blame⟩ **7** : to set in order : ADJUST **8** : PREPARE **9** : to make whole or sound again **10** : to get even with **11** : to influence by improper or illegal methods ⟨~ a race⟩ — **fix·er** *n*

[2]fix *n* **1** : PREDICAMENT **2** : a determination of position (as of a ship) **3** : an accurate determination or understanding **4** : an act of improper influence **5** : a supply or dose of something (as an addictive drug) strongly desired or craved **6** : something that fixes or restores

fix·a·tion \fik-ˈsā-shən\ *n* : an obsessive or unhealthy preoccupation or attachment — **fix·ate** \ˈfik-ˌsāt\ *vb*

fix·a·tive \ˈfik-sə-tiv\ *n* : something that stabilizes or sets

fixed \ˈfikst\ *adj* **1** : securely placed or fastened : STATIONARY **2** : not volatile **3** : SETTLED, FINAL **4** : INTENT, CONCENTRATED ⟨a ~ stare⟩ **5** : supplied with a definite amount of something needed (as money) — **fixed·ly** \ˈfik-səd-lē\ *adv* — **fixed·ness** \ˈfik-səd-nəs\ *n*

fix·i·ty \ˈfik-sə-tē\ *n, pl* **-ties** : the quality or state of being fixed or stable

fix·ture \ˈfiks-chər\ *n* **1** : something firmly attached as a permanent part of some other thing **2** : a familiar feature in a particular setting; *esp* : a person associated with a place or activity

[1]fizz \ˈfiz\ *vb* : to make a hissing or sputtering sound

[2]fizz *n* : an effervescent beverage

[1]fiz·zle \ˈfi-zəl\ *vb* **fiz·zled; fiz·zling** **1** : FIZZ **2** : to fail after a good start — often used with *out*

[2]fizzle *n* : FAILURE

fjord \fē-ˈȯrd\ *n* [Norwegian] : a narrow inlet of the sea between cliffs or steep slopes

fl *abbr* **1** L *floruit* flourished **2** fluid

Fl *symbol* flerovium

FL *or* **Fla** *abbr* Florida

flab \ˈflab\ *n* : soft flabby body tissue

flab·ber·gast \ˈfla-bər-ˌgast\ *vb* : ASTOUND

flab·by \ˈfla-bē\ *adj* **flab·bi·er; -est** : lacking firmness : FLACCID ⟨~ muscles⟩ — **flab·bi·ness** \-bē-nəs\ *n*

flac·cid \ˈfla-səd\ *adj* : lacking firmness ⟨~ muscles⟩

[1]flag \ˈflag\ *n* : any of various irises; *esp* : a wild iris

[2]flag *n* **1** : a usu. rectangular piece of fabric of distinctive design that is used as a symbol (as of a nation) or as a signaling device **2** : something used like a flag to signal or attract attention **3** : one of the cross strokes of a musical note less than a quarter note in value

[3]flag *vb* **flagged; flag·ging** **1** : to signal with or as if with a flag; *esp* : to signal to stop ⟨~ a taxi⟩ **2** : to mark or identify with or as if with a flag **3** : to call a penalty on ⟨~ a football player⟩

[4]flag *vb* **flagged; flag·ging** **1** : to hang loose or limp **2** : to become unsteady, feeble, or spiritless **3** : to decline in interest or attraction ⟨the topic *flagged*⟩

[5]flag *n* : a hard flat stone suitable for paving

flag·el·late \ˈfla-jə-ˌlāt\ *vb* **-lat·ed; -lat·ing** : to punish by whipping — **flag·el·la·tion** \ˌfla-jə-ˈlā-shən\ *n*

fla·gel·lum \flə-ˈje-ləm\ *n, pl* **-la** \-lə\ *also* **-lums** : a long whiplike process that is the primary organ of motion of many microorganisms — **fla·gel·lar** \-lər\ *adj*

fla·geo·let \ˌfla-jə-ˈlet, -ˈlā\ *n* [F] : a small woodwind instrument belonging to the flute class

fla·gi·tious \flə-ˈji-shəs\ *adj* : grossly wicked : VILLAINOUS

flag·on \ˈfla-gən\ *n* : a container for liquids usu. with a handle, spout, and lid

flag·pole \ˈflag-ˌpōl\ *n* : a pole on which to raise a flag

fla·grant \ˈflā-grənt\ *adj* [L *flagrans,* prp. of *flagrare* to burn] : conspicuously bad ⟨~ abuse of power⟩ — **fla·grant·ly** *adv*

fla·gran·te de·lic·to \flə-ˌgran-tē-di-ˈlik-tō\ *adv* : IN FLAGRANTE DELICTO

flag·ship \ˈflag-ˌship\ *n* **1** : the ship that carries the commander of a fleet or subdivision thereof and flies his flag **2** : the most important one of a group

flag·staff \-ˌstaf\ *n* : FLAGPOLE

flag·stone \-ˌstōn\ *n* : [5]FLAG

[1]flail \ˈflāl\ *n* : a tool for threshing grain by hand

[2]flail *vb* : to strike or swing with or as if with a flail

flair \ˈfler\ *n* [F, lit., sense of smell, fr. OF, odor, fr. *flairier* to give off an odor, fr. VL **flagrare,* alter. of L *fragrare*] **1** : ability to appreciate or make good use of something : BENT, TALENT **2** : a unique style

flak \ˈflak\ *n, pl* **flak** [G, fr. *Fl*ieger*a*bweh*rk*anonen, fr. *Flieger* flyer + *Abwehr* defense + *Kanonen* cannons] **1** : antiaircraft guns or bursting shells fired from them **2** : CRITICISM, OPPOSITION

[1]flake \ˈflāk\ *n* **1** : a small loose mass or bit **2** : a thin flattened piece or layer : CHIP — **flaky** *adj*

[2]flake *vb* **flaked; flak·ing** : to form or separate into flakes

[3]flake *n* : a markedly eccentric person : ODDBALL — **flak·i·ness** \ˈflā-kē-nəs\ *n* — **flaky** *adj*

flam·beau \ˈflam-ˌbō\ *n, pl* **flambeaux** \-ˌbōz\ *or* **flambeaus** [F, fr. MF, fr. *flambe* flame] : a flaming torch

flam·boy·ant \flam-ˈbȯi-ənt\ *adj* : marked by or given to strikingly elaborate or colorful display or behavior — **flam·boy·ance** \-əns\ *n* — **flam·boy·an·cy** \-ən-sē\ *n* — **flam·boy·ant·ly** *adv*

flame \ˈflām\ *n* **1** : the glowing gaseous part of a fire **2** : a state of blazing combustion **3** : a flamelike condition **4** : burning zeal or passion **5** : BRILLIANCE **6** : SWEETHEART **7** : an angry, hostile, or abusive electronic message — **flame** *vb*

fla·men·co \flə-ˈmeŋ-kō\ *n, pl* **-cos** : a

vigorous rhythmic dance style of southern Spain

flame•throw•er \ˈflām-ˌthrō-ər\ *n* : a device that expels from a nozzle a burning stream of liquid or semiliquid fuel under pressure

fla•min•go \flə-ˈmiŋ-gō\ *n, pl* **-gos** *also* **-goes** : any of several long-legged long-necked tropical water birds with scarlet wings and a broad bill bent downward

flam•ma•ble \ˈfla-mə-bəl\ *adj* : easily ignited and quick-burning — **flam•ma•bil•i•ty** \ˌfla-mə-ˈbi-lə-tē\ *n* — **flammable** *n*

flan \ˈflan, ˈflän\ *n* **1** : an open pie with a sweet or savory filling **2** : custard baked with a caramel glaze

flange \ˈflanj\ *n* : a rim used for strengthening or guiding something or for attachment to another object

[1]**flank** \ˈflaŋk\ *n* **1** : the fleshy part of the side between the ribs and the hip; *also* : the side of a quadruped **2** : SIDE **3** : the right or left of a formation

[2]**flank** *vb* **1** : to be situated on the side of : BORDER **2** : to attack or threaten the flank of

flank•er \ˈflaŋ-kər\ *n* : a football player stationed wide of the formation slightly behind the line of scrimmage as a pass receiver

flan•nel \ˈfla-nᵊl\ *n* **1** : a soft twilled wool or worsted fabric with a napped surface **2** : a stout cotton fabric napped on one side **3** *pl* : flannel underwear or pants

[1]**flap** \ˈflap\ *n* **1** : a stroke with something broad : SLAP **2** : something broad, limber, or flat and usu. thin that hangs loose **3** : the motion or sound of something broad and limber as it swings to and fro **4** : a state of excitement or confusion

[2]**flap** *vb* **flapped; flap•ping** **1** : to beat with something broad and flat **2** : FLING **3** : to move (as wings) with a beating motion **4** : to sway loosely usu. with a noise of striking

flap•jack \ˈflap-ˌjak\ *n* : PANCAKE

flap•per \ˈfla-pər\ *n* **1** : one that flaps **2** : a young woman of the 1920s who showed freedom from conventions (as in conduct)

[1]**flare** \ˈfler\ *n* **1** : a blaze of light used esp. to signal or illuminate; *also* : a device for producing such a blaze **2** : an unsteady glaring light

[2]**flare** *vb* **flared; flar•ing** **1** : to flame with a sudden unsteady light **2** : to become suddenly excited or angry **3** : to spread outward

flare–up \-ˌəp\ *n* : a sudden outburst or intensification

[1]**flash** \ˈflash\ *vb* **1** : to break forth in or like a sudden flame **2** : to appear or pass suddenly or with great speed **3** : to send out in or as if in flashes ⟨~ a message⟩ **4** : to make a sudden display (as of brilliance or feeling) **5** : to gleam or glow intermittently **6** : to fill by a sudden rush of water **7** : to expose to view very briefly ⟨~ a badge⟩ ♦ ***Synonyms*** GLANCE, GLINT, SPARKLE, TWINKLE — **flash•er** *n*

[2]**flash** *n* **1** : a sudden burst of light **2** : a movement of a flag or light in signaling **3** : a sudden and brilliant burst (as of wit) **4** : a brief time **5** : SHOW, DISPLAY; *esp* : ostentatious display **6** : one that attracts notice; *esp* : an outstanding athlete **7** : GLIMPSE, LOOK **8** : a first brief news report **9** : FLASHLIGHT **10** : a device for producing a brief and very bright flash of light for taking photographs **11** : a quick-spreading flame or momentary intense outburst of radiant heat

[3]**flash** *adj* : of sudden origin and short duration ⟨a ~ fire⟩ ⟨a ~ flood⟩

[4]**flash** *adv* : by very brief exposure to an intense agent (as heat or cold) ⟨~ fry⟩ ⟨~ freeze⟩

flash•back \ˈflash-ˌbak\ *n* **1** : interruption of the chronological sequence (as of a film or literary work) by an event of earlier occurrence **2** : a past event remembered vividly

flash back *vb* **1** : to vividly remember a past incident **2** : to employ a flashback

flash–bang \ˈflash-ˌbaŋ\ *n* : an explosive device that produces a blinding flash of light and a sudden loud noise intended to temporarily stun, distract, and disperse people — called also flash-bang grenade

flash•bulb \-ˌbəlb\ *n* : an electric bulb that can be used only once to produce a brief and very bright flash of light for taking photographs

flash card *n* : a card bearing words, numbers, or pictures briefly displayed usu. as a learning aid

flash drive *n* : a data storage device that uses flash memory

flash•gun \-ˌgən\ *n* : a device for producing a bright flash of light for photography

flash•ing \ˈfla-shiŋ\ *n* : sheet metal used in waterproofing (as at the angle between a chimney and a roof)

flash•light \ˈflash-ˌlīt\ *n* : a battery-operated portable electric light

flash memory *n* : a computer memory chip not requiring connection to a power source to retain its data

flashy \ˈfla-shē\ *adj* **flash•i•er; -est** **1** : momentarily dazzling **2** : superficially attractive or impressive : SHOWY ⟨~ clothes⟩ — **flash•i•ly** \-shə-lē\ *adv* — **flash•i•ness** \-shē-nəs\ *n*

flask \ˈflask\ *n* : a flattened bottle-shaped container ⟨a whiskey ~⟩

[1]**flat** \ˈflat\ *adj* **flat•ter; flat•test** **1** : spread out along a surface; *also* : being or characterized by a horizontal line **2** : having a smooth, level, or even surface **3** : having a broad smooth surface and little thickness **4** : DOWNRIGHT, POSITIVE ⟨a ~ refusal⟩ **5** : FIXED, UNCHANGING ⟨a ~ fee⟩ **6** : EXACT, PRECISE ⟨in four minutes ~⟩ **7** : DULL, UNINTERESTING; *also* : INSIPID **8** : DEFLATED ⟨a ~ tire⟩ **9** : lower than the true pitch; *also* : lower by a half step **10** : free from gloss ⟨a ~ paint⟩ **11** : lacking depth of characterization — **flat•ly** *adv* — **flat•ness** *n*

[2]**flat** *n* **1** : a level surface of land : PLAIN **2** : a flat part or surface **3** : a character ♭

that indicates that a specified note is to be lowered by a half step; *also* : the resulting note **4** : something flat **5** : an apartment on one floor **6** : a deflated tire

[3]**flat** *adv* **1** : FLATLY **2** : COMPLETELY ⟨~ broke⟩ **3** : below the true musical pitch

[4]**flat** *vb* **flat·ted; flat·ting 1** : FLATTEN **2** : to lower in pitch esp. by a half step

flat·bed \ˈflat-ˌbed\ *n* : a truck or trailer with a body in the form of a platform or shallow box

flat·boat \-ˌbōt\ *n* : a flat-bottomed boat used esp. for carrying bulky freight

flat·car \-ˌkär\ *n* : a railroad freight car without sides or roof

flat·fish \-ˌfish\ *n* : any of an order of flattened marine bony fishes with both eyes on the upper side

flat·foot \-ˌfu̇t, -ˈfu̇t\ *n, pl* **flat·feet** \-ˌfēt, -ˈfēt\ : a condition in which the arch of the foot is flattened so that the entire sole rests upon the ground — **flat–foot·ed** \-ˈfu̇-təd\ *adj*

Flat·head \-ˌhed\ *n, pl* **Flatheads** *or* **Flathead** : a member of an Indigenous people of Montana

flat·iron \-ˌī(-ə)rn\ *n* : IRON 3

flat·land \-ˌland\ *n* : land lacking significant variation in elevation

flat–out \ˈflat-ˌau̇t\ *adj* **1** : being or going at maximum effort or speed **2** : OUT-AND-OUT, DOWNRIGHT ⟨it was a ~ lie⟩

flat out *adv* **1** : BLUNTLY, DIRECTLY **2** : at top speed **3** *usu* **flat–out** : to the greatest degree : COMPLETELY ⟨is just *flat-out* confusing⟩

flat–pan·el \-ˈpa-nᵊl\ *adj* : relating to or being a thin flat video display

flat·ten \ˈfla-tᵊn\ *vb* : to make or become flat

flat·ter \ˈfla-tər\ *vb* [ME *flateren,* fr. AF *flater* to lap, flatter] **1** : to praise too much or without sincerity **2** : to represent too favorably ⟨the portrait ~*s* him⟩ **3** : to display to advantage **4** : to judge (oneself) favorably or too favorably — **flat·ter·er** *n*

flat·tery \ˈfla-tə-rē\ *n, pl* **-ter·ies** : flattering speech or attentions : insincere or excessive praise

flat·top \ˈflat-ˌtäp\ *n* **1** : AIRCRAFT CARRIER **2** : CREW CUT

flat·u·lent \ˈfla-chə-lənt\ *adj* **1** : full of gas ⟨a ~ stomach⟩ **2** : INFLATED, POMPOUS — **flat·u·lence** \-ləns\ *n*

fla·tus \ˈflā-təs\ *n* : gas formed in the intestine or stomach

flat·ware \ˈflat-ˌwer\ *n* : eating and serving utensils

flat·worm \-ˌwu̇rm\ *n* : any of a phylum of flattened mostly parasitic segmented worms (as trematodes and tapeworms)

flaunt \ˈflȯnt\ *vb* **1** : to display oneself to public notice **2** : to wave or flutter showily **3** : to display ostentatiously or impudently : PARADE — **flaunt** *n*

flau·ta \ˈflau̇-tə\ *n* : a tortilla rolled around a filling and deep-fried

flau·tist \ˈflȯ-tist, ˈflau̇-\ *n* [It *flautista*] : FLUTIST

[1]**fla·vor** \ˈflā-vər\ *n* **1** : the quality of something that affects the sense of taste or of taste and smell **2** : a substance that adds flavor **3** : characteristic or predominant quality — **fla·vored** \-vərd\ *adj* — **fla·vor·ful** *adj* — **fla·vor·less** *adj* — **fla·vor·some** *adj*

[2]**flavor** *vb* : to give or add flavor to

fla·vor·ing *n* : FLAVOR 2

fla·vour *chiefly Brit var of* FLAVOR

flaw \ˈflȯ\ *n* : a small often hidden defect — **flaw·less** *adj* — **flaw·less·ly** *adv* — **flaw·less·ness** *n*

flax \ˈflaks\ *n* : a fiber that is the source of linen; *also* : a blue-flowered plant grown for this fiber and its oily seeds

flax·en \ˈflak-sən\ *adj* **1** : made of flax **2** : resembling flax esp. in pale soft straw color

flay \ˈflā\ *vb* **1** : to strip off the skin or surface of **2** : to criticize harshly

fl dr *abbr* fluid dram

flea \ˈflē\ *n* : any of an order of small wingless leaping bloodsucking insects

flea·bane \ˈflē-ˌbān\ *n* : any of various plants of the daisy family once believed to drive away fleas

flea–bit·ten \-ˌbi-tᵊn\ *adj* : bitten by or infested with fleas

flea market *n* : a usu. open-air market for secondhand articles and antiques

[1]**fleck** \ˈflek\ *vb* : STREAK, SPOT

[2]**fleck** *n* **1** : SPOT, MARK **2** : FLAKE, PARTICLE

fledge \ˈflej\ *vb* **fledged; fledg·ing** : to develop the feathers necessary for flying or independent activity

fledg·ling \ˈflej-liŋ\ *n* **1** : a young bird just fledged **2** : an immature or inexperienced person

flee \ˈflē\ *vb* **fled** \ˈfled\; **flee·ing 1** : to run away often from danger or evil **2** : VANISH **3** : to run away from : SHUN

[1]**fleece** \ˈflēs\ *n* **1** : the woolly coat of an animal and esp. a sheep **2** : a soft or woolly covering — **fleecy** *adj*

[2]**fleece** *vb* **fleeced; fleec·ing 1** : to strip of money or property by fraud or extortion **2** : SHEAR

[1]**fleet** \ˈflēt\ *vb* : to pass rapidly

[2]**fleet** *n* [ME *flete,* fr. OE *flēot* ship, fr. *flēotan* to float] **1** : a group of warships under one command **2** : a group (as of trucks) under one management

[3]**fleet** *adj* **1** : SWIFT, NIMBLE **2** : not enduring : FLEETING — **fleet·ness** *n*

fleet admiral *n* : an admiral of the highest rank in the navy

fleet·ing \ˈflē-tiŋ\ *adj* : passing swiftly

Flem·ing \ˈfle-miŋ\ *n* : a member of a Germanic people inhabiting chiefly northern Belgium

Flem·ish \ˈfle-mish\ *n* **1** : the Dutch language as spoken by the Flemings **2** **Flemish** *pl* : FLEMINGS — **Flemish** *adj*

fle·ro·vi·um \flə-ˈrō-vē-əm\ *n* a short-lived artificially produced radioactive chemical element

[1]**flesh** \ˈflesh\ *n* **1** : the soft parts of an animal's body; *esp* : muscular tissue **2** : MEAT **3** : the physical nature of humans as distinguished from the soul **4** : human

beings; *also* : living beings 5 : STOCK, KINDRED 6 : fleshy plant tissue (as fruit pulp) — **fleshed** \ˈflesht\ *adj*

²flesh *vb* : to make fuller or more nearly complete — usu. used with *out* ⟨*flesh out* a schedule⟩

flesh fly *n* : a dipteran fly whose maggots feed on flesh

flesh·ly \ˈflesh-lē\ *adj* 1 : CORPOREAL, BODILY 2 : not spiritual : WORLDLY 3 : CARNAL, SENSUAL ⟨~ appetites⟩

flesh·pot \ˈflesh-ˌpät\ *n* 1 *pl* : bodily comfort : LUXURY 2 : a place of lascivious entertainment — usu. used in pl.

fleshy \ˈfle-shē\ *adj* **flesh·i·er; -est** 1 : consisting of or resembling animal flesh 2 : PLUMP, FAT

flew *past of* ¹FLY

flex \ˈfleks\ *vb* : to bend esp. repeatedly — **flex** *n*

flex·i·ble \ˈflek-sə-bəl\ *adj* 1 : capable of being flexed : PLIANT 2 : yielding to influence : TRACTABLE 3 : readily changed or changing : ADAPTABLE ♦ ***Synonyms*** ELASTIC, SUPPLE, RESILIENT, SPRINGY — **flex·i·bil·i·ty** \ˌflek-sə-ˈbi-lə-tē\ *n*

flex·or \ˈflek-sər, -ˌsȯr\ *n* : a muscle serving to bend a body part

flex·ure \ˈflek-shər\ *n* : TURN, FOLD

flib·ber·ti·gib·bet \ˌfli-bər-tē-ˈji-bət\ *n* : a silly flighty person

¹flick \ˈflik\ *n* 1 : a light sharp jerky stroke or movement 2 : a sound produced by a flick 3 : ²FLICKER

²flick *vb* 1 : to strike lightly with a quick sharp motion 2 : FLUTTER, FLIT

³flick *n* : MOVIE

¹flick·er \ˈfli-kər\ *vb* 1 : to move irregularly or unsteadily : FLUTTER 2 : to burn fitfully or with a fluctuating light — **flick·er·ing·ly** *adv*

²flicker *n* 1 : an act of flickering 2 : a sudden brief movement 3 : a momentary stirring 4 : a slight indication : HINT 5 : a wavering light

³flicker *n* : a large barred and spotted No. American woodpecker with a brown back that occurs as an eastern form with yellow on the underside of the wings and tail and a western form with red in these areas

flied *past and past part of* ³FLY

fli·er \ˈflī(-ə)r\ *n* 1 : one that flies; *esp* : PILOT 2 : a reckless or speculative undertaking 3 *usu* **fly·er** : an advertising circular

¹flight \ˈflīt\ *n* 1 : an act or instance of flying 2 : the ability to fly 3 : a passing through air or space 4 : the distance covered in a flight 5 : swift movement 6 : a trip made by or in an airplane or spacecraft 7 : a group of similar individuals (as birds or airplanes) flying as a unit 8 : a passing (as of the imagination) beyond ordinary limits 9 : a series of stairs from one landing to another — **flight·less** *adj*

²flight *n* : an act or instance of running away

flight bag *n* 1 : a lightweight traveling bag with zippered outside pockets 2 : a small canvas satchel

flight line *n* : a parking and servicing area for airplanes

flighty \ˈflī-tē\ *adj* **flight·i·er; -est** 1 : easily upset : VOLATILE 2 : easily excited : SKITTISH 3 : CAPRICIOUS, SILLY — **flight·i·ness** \-tē-nəs\ *n*

flim·flam \ˈflim-ˌflam\ *n* : DECEPTION, FRAUD — **flim·flam·mery** \-ˌfla-mə-re\ *n*

flim·sy \ˈflim-zē\ *adj* **flim·si·er; -est** 1 : lacking strength or substance 2 : of inferior materials and workmanship 3 : having little worth or plausibility ⟨a ~ excuse⟩ — **flim·si·ly** \-zə-lē\ *adv* — **flim·si·ness** \-zē-nəs\ *n*

flinch \ˈflinch\ *vb* [MF *flenchir* to bend] : to shrink from or as if from pain : WINCE — **flinch** *n*

¹fling \ˈfliŋ\ *vb* **flung** \ˈfləŋ\; **fling·ing** 1 : to move hastily, brusquely, or violently ⟨*flung* out of the room⟩ 2 : to kick or plunge vigorously 3 : to throw with force or recklessness; *also* : to cast as if by throwing 4 : to put suddenly into a state or condition

²fling *n* 1 : an act or instance of flinging 2 : a casual try : ATTEMPT 3 : a period of self-indulgence

flint \ˈflint\ *n* 1 : a hard dark quartz that produces a spark when struck by steel 2 : an alloy used for producing a spark in lighters — **flinty** *adj*

flint glass *n* : heavy glass containing an oxide of lead and used in lenses and prisms

flint·lock \ˈflint-ˌläk\ *n* 1 : a lock for a gun using a flint to ignite the charge 2 : a firearm fitted with a flintlock

¹flip \ˈflip\ *vb* **flipped; flip·ping** 1 : to turn by tossing ⟨~ a coin⟩ 2 : to turn over; *also* : to leaf through 3 : FLICK, JERK ⟨~ a light switch⟩ 4 : to lose self-control — **flip** *n*

²flip *adj* : FLIPPANT, IMPERTINENT

flip·pant \ˈfli-pənt\ *adj* : lacking proper respect or seriousness — **flip·pan·cy** \ˈfli-pən-sē\ *n*

flip·per \ˈfli-pər\ *n* 1 : a broad flat limb (as of a seal) adapted for swimming 2 : a paddlelike shoe used in skin diving

flip side *n* : the reverse and usu. less popular side of a phonograph record

¹flirt \ˈflərt\ *vb* 1 : to move erratically : FLIT 2 : to behave amorously without serious intent 3 : to show casual interest ⟨~*ed* with the idea⟩; *also* : to come close to ⟨~ with danger⟩ — **flir·ta·tion** \ˌflər-ˈtā-shən\ *n* — **flir·ta·tious** \-shəs\ *adj*

²flirt *n* 1 : an act or instance of flirting 2 : a person who flirts

flit \ˈflit\ *vb* **flit·ted; flit·ting** : to pass or move quickly or abruptly from place to place : DART — **flit** *n*

flitch \ˈflich\ *n* : a side of cured meat; *esp* : a side of bacon

fliv·ver \ˈfli-vər\ *n* : a small cheap usu. old automobile

¹float \ˈflōt\ *n* 1 : something (as a raft) that floats 2 : a cork buoying up the baited end of a fishing line 3 : a hollow ball that floats at the end of a lever in a cistern or tank and regulates the liquid level **4 :** a vehicle with a platform to carry an exhibit **5 :** a soft drink with ice cream floating in it

²float *vb* **1 :** to rest on the surface of or be suspended in a fluid **2 :** to move gently on or through a fluid **3 :** to cause to float **4 :** WANDER **5 :** to offer (securities) in order to finance an enterprise **6 :** to finance by floating an issue of stocks or bonds **7 :** to arrange for ⟨∼ a loan⟩ — **float·er** *n*

floaty \ˈflō-tē\ *adj* **float·i·er; -est** **1 :** tending to float : BUOYANT **2 :** light and billowy ⟨a ∼ skirt⟩

¹flock \ˈfläk\ *n* **1 :** a group of animals assembled or herded together **2 :** a group of people under the guidance of a leader; *esp* : CONGREGATION **3 :** a large number ⟨a ∼ of tourists⟩

²flock *vb* **:** to gather or move in a flock ⟨people ∼*ed* to the beach⟩

floe \ˈflō\ *n* **:** a flat mass of floating ice

flog \ˈfläg\ *vb* **flogged; flog·ging** **1 :** to beat with or as if with a rod or whip **2 :** SELL ⟨∼ encyclopedias⟩ — **flog·ger** *n*

¹flood \ˈfləd\ *n* **1 :** a great flow of water over the land **2 :** the flowing in of the tide **3 :** an overwhelming volume

²flood *vb* **1 :** to cover or become filled with a flood **2 :** to fill abundantly or excessively; *esp* : to supply an excess of fuel to **3 :** to pour forth in a flood — **flood·er** *n*

flood·gate \ˈfləd-ˌgāt\ *n* **:** a gate for controlling a body of water : SLUICE

flood·light \-ˌlīt\ *n* **:** a lamp that throws a broad beam of light; *also* : the beam itself — **floodlight** *vb*

flood·plain \-ˌplān\ *n* **:** a plain along a river or stream subject to periodic flooding

flood tide *n* **1 :** a rising tide **2 :** an overwhelming quantity **3 :** a high point

flood·wa·ter \ˈfləd-ˌwȯ-tər, -ˌwä-\ *n* **:** the water of a flood

¹floor \ˈflȯr\ *n* **1 :** the bottom of a room on which one stands **2 :** a ground surface **3 :** a story of a building **4 :** a main level space (as in a legislative chamber) distinguished from a platform or gallery **5 :** AUDIENCE **6 :** the right to address an assembly **7 :** a lower limit ⟨put a ∼ under wheat prices⟩ — **floor·ing** *n*

²floor *vb* **1 :** to furnish with a floor **2 :** to knock down **3 :** AMAZE, DUMBFOUND ⟨was ∼*ed* by the news⟩ **4 :** to press (a vehicle's accelerator) to the floorboard esp. rapidly

floor·board \-ˌbȯrd\ *n* **1 :** a board in a floor **2 :** the floor of an automobile

floor leader *n* **:** a member of a legislative body who has charge of a party's organization and strategy on the floor

floor show *n* **:** a series of acts presented in a nightclub

floor·walk·er \ˈflȯr-ˌwȯ-kər\ *n* **:** a person employed in a retail store to oversee the sales force and aid customers

floo·zy *or* **floo·zie** \ˈflü-zē\ *n, pl* **floozies** **:** a usu. young woman of loose morals

flop \ˈfläp\ *vb* **flopped; flop·ping** **1 :** FLAP **2 :** to throw oneself down heavily, clumsily, or in a relaxed manner ⟨*flopped* into a chair⟩ **3 :** FAIL ⟨the show *flopped*⟩ — **flop** *n* — **flop** *adv* — **flop·per** *n*

flop·house \ˈfläp-ˌhau̇s\ *n* **:** a cheap hotel

¹flop·py \ˈflä-pē\ *adj* **flop·pi·er; -est** **:** tending to flop; *esp* : soft and flexible — **flop·pi·ly** \-pə-lē\ *adv*

²floppy *n, pl* **flop·pies** **:** FLOPPY DISK

floppy disk *n* **:** a thin plastic disk with a magnetic coating on which computer data can be stored

flop sweat *n* **:** sweat caused by the fear of failing

flo·ra \ˈflȯr-ə\ *n, pl* **floras** *also* **flo·rae** \-ˌē, -ˌī\ [L *Flora,* Roman goddess of flowers] **:** plants or plant life esp. of a region or period

flo·ral \ˈflȯr-əl\ *adj* **:** of, relating to, or depicting flowers ⟨a ∼ design⟩

flo·res·cence \flȯ-ˈre-sᵊns, flə-\ *n* **:** a state or period of being in bloom or flourishing — **flo·res·cent** \-ᵊnt\ *adj*

flor·id \ˈflȯr-əd\ *adj* **1 :** very flowery in style : ORNATE ⟨∼ prose⟩ **2 :** tinged with red : RUDDY **3 :** marked by emotional or sexual fervor ⟨∼ love letters⟩

flo·rin \ˈflȯr-ən\ *n* **1 :** an old gold coin first struck at Florence, Italy, in 1252 **2 :** a gold coin of a European country patterned after the florin of Florence **3 :** any of several modern silver coins issued in Commonwealth countries **4 :** GULDEN

flo·rist \ˈflȯr-ist\ *n* **:** a person who sells flowers or ornamental plants

¹floss \ˈfläs\ *n* **1 :** soft thread of silk or mercerized cotton for embroidery **2 :** DENTAL FLOSS **3 :** fluffy fibrous material

²floss *vb* **:** to use dental floss on (one's teeth)

flossy \ˈflä-sē\ *adj* **floss·i·er; -est** **1 :** of, relating to, or having the characteristics of floss **2 :** STYLISH, GLAMOROUS ⟨∼ hotels⟩ — **floss·i·ly** \-sə-lē\ *adv*

flo·ta·tion \flō-ˈtā-shən\ *n* **:** the process or an instance of floating

flo·til·la \flō-ˈti-lə\ *n* [Sp, dim. of *flota* fleet] **:** a fleet esp. of small ships

flot·sam \ˈflät-səm\ *n* **:** floating wreckage of a ship or its cargo

¹flounce \ˈflau̇ns\ *vb* **flounced; flounc·ing** **1 :** to move with exaggerated jerky or bouncy motions **2 :** to go with sudden determination

²flounce *n* **:** an act or instance of flouncing — **flouncy** \ˈflau̇n-sē\ *adj*

³flounce *n* **:** a strip of fabric attached by one edge; *also* : a wide ruffle

¹floun·der \ˈflau̇n-dər\ *n, pl* **flounder** *or* **flounders** **:** FLATFISH; *esp* : any of various important marine food fishes

²flounder *vb* **1 :** to struggle to move or obtain footing **2 :** to proceed clumsily ⟨∼*ed* through the speech⟩

¹flour \ˈflau̇(-ə)r\ *n* [ME, flower, best of anything, flour, fr. AF *flur* flower] **:** finely ground and sifted meal of a grain (as wheat); *also* : a fine soft powder — **floury** *adj*

[2]**flour** *vb* : to coat with or as if with flour

[1]**flour·ish** \ˈflər-ish\ *vb* **1** : THRIVE, PROSPER **2** : to be in a state of activity or production ⟨~*ed* about 1850⟩ **3** : to reach a height of development or influence **4** : to make bold and sweeping gestures **5** : BRANDISH ⟨~*ed* his sword⟩

[2]**flourish** *n* **1** : a florid bit of speech or writing; *also* : an ornamental touch or decorative detail **2** : FANFARE ⟨a ~ of trumpets⟩ **3** : WAVE ⟨with a ~ of his cane⟩ **4** : showiness in doing something

[1]**flout** \ˈflau̇t\ *vb* : to treat with contemptuous disregard ⟨~ the law⟩ — **flout·er** *n*

[2]**flout** *n* : TAUNT

[1]**flow** \ˈflō\ *vb* **1** : to issue or move in a stream **2** : RISE ⟨the tide ebbs and ~*s*⟩ **3** : ABOUND **4** : to proceed smoothly and readily **5** : to have a smooth continuity **6** : to hang loose and billowing **7** : COME, ARISE **8** : MENSTRUATE

[2]**flow** *n* **1** : an act of flowing **2** : FLOOD 1, 2 **3** : a smooth uninterrupted movement **4** : STREAM; *also* : a mass of material that has flowed when molten **5** : the quantity that flows in a certain time **6** : MENSTRUATION **7** : a continuous transfer of energy — **flow·age** \ˈflō-ij\ *n*

flow·chart \ˈflō-ˌchärt\ *n* : a symbolic diagram showing step-by-step progression through a procedure

flow diagram *n* : FLOWCHART

[1]**flow·er** \ˈflau̇(-ə)r\ *n* [ME *flour,* fr. AF *flur, flour,* fr. L *flor-, flos*] **1** : a plant shoot modified for reproduction and bearing leaves specialized into floral organs; *esp* : one of a seed plant consisting of a calyx, corolla, stamens, and carpels **2** : a plant cultivated for its blossoms **3** : the best part or example **4** : the finest most vigorous period **5** : a state of blooming or flourishing — **flow·ered** \ˈflau̇(-ə)rd\ *adj* — **flow·er·less** *adj* — **flow·er·like** \-ˌlīk\ *adj*

[2]**flower** *vb* **1** : DEVELOP; *also* : FLOURISH **2** : to produce flowers : BLOOM

flower girl *n* : a little girl who carries flowers at a wedding

flower head *n* : a compact cluster of small flowers without stems suggesting a single flower

flowering plant *n* : any of a major group of vascular plants (as magnolias, grasses, or roses) that produce flowers and fruit and have the seeds enclosed in an ovary

flow·er·pot \ˈflau̇(-ə)r-ˌpät\ *n* : a pot in which to grow plants

flow·ery \ˈflau̇(-ə)r-ē\ *adj* **1** : of, relating to, or resembling flowers **2** : full of fine words or phrases ⟨a ~ speech⟩ — **flow·er·i·ness** \-ē-nəs\ *n*

flown \ˈflōn\ *past part of* [1]FLY

fl oz *abbr* fluid ounce

flu \ˈflü\ *n* **1** : INFLUENZA **2** : any of several virus diseases marked esp. by respiratory or intestinal symptoms — **flu–like** \-ˌlīk\ *adj*

flub \ˈfləb\ *vb* **flubbed; flub·bing** : BOTCH, BLUNDER — **flub** *n*

fluc·tu·ate \ˈflək-chə-ˌwāt\ *vb* **-at·ed; -at·ing** **1** : WAVER **2** : to move up and down or back and forth — **fluc·tu·a·tion** \ˌflək-chə-ˈwā-shən\ *n*

flue \ˈflü\ *n* : a passage (as in a chimney) for directing a current (as of smoke or gases)

flu·ent \ˈflü-ənt\ *adj* **1** : capable of flowing : FLUID **2** : ready or facile in speech ⟨~ in French⟩; *also* : having or showing mastery in a subject or skill **3** : effortlessly smooth and rapid ⟨~ speech⟩ — **flu·en·cy** \-ən-sē\ *n* — **flu·ent·ly** *adv*

flue pipe *n* : an organ pipe whose tone is produced by an air current striking the beveled opening of the pipe

[1]**fluff** \ˈfləf\ *n* **1** : [7]DOWN 1 ⟨~ from a pillow⟩ **2** : something fluffy **3** : something inconsequential **4** : BLUNDER; *esp* : an actor's lapse of memory

[2]**fluff** *vb* **1** : to make or become fluffy ⟨~ up a pillow⟩ **2** : to make a mistake

fluffy \ˈflə-fē\ *adj* **fluff·i·er; -est** **1** : covered with or resembling fluff **2** : being light and soft or airy ⟨a ~ omelet⟩ **3** : lacking in meaning or substance — **fluff·i·ly** \-fə-lē\ *adv*

[1]**flu·id** \ˈflü-əd\ *adj* **1** : capable of flowing **2** : subject to change or movement **3** : showing a smooth easy style ⟨~ movements⟩ **4** : available for a different use; *esp* : LIQUID 5 ⟨~ assets⟩ — **flu·id·i·ty** \flü-ˈi-də-tē\ *n* — **flu·id·ly** *adv*

[2]**fluid** *n* : a substance (as a liquid or gas) tending to flow or take the shape of its container

fluid dram *or* **flu·i·dram** \ˌflü-ə-ˈdram\ *n* — see WEIGHT table

fluid ounce *n* — see WEIGHT table

[1]**fluke** \ˈflük\ *n* : any of various trematode flatworms

[2]**fluke** *n* **1** : the part of an anchor that fastens in the ground **2** : a lobe of a whale's tail

[3]**fluke** *n* : a stroke of luck — **fluky** *also* **fluk·ey** \ˈflü-kē\ *adj*

flume \ˈflüm\ *n* **1** : an inclined channel for carrying water **2** : a ravine or gorge with a stream running through it

flung *past and past part of* FLING

flunk \ˈfləŋk\ *vb* : to fail esp. in an examination or course — **flunk** *n*

flun·ky *also* **flun·key** *or* **flun·kie** \ˈfləŋ-kē\ *n, pl* **flunkies** *also* **flunkeys** **1** : a liveried servant; *also* : one performing menial or miscellaneous duties **2** : YES-MAN

fluo·res·cence \flȯ-ˈre-sᵊns\ *n* : luminescence caused by radiation absorption that ceases almost immediately after the incident radiation has stopped; *also* : the emitted radiation — **fluo·resce** \-ˈres\ *vb* — **fluo·res·cent** \-ˈre-sᵊnt\ *adj*

fluorescent lamp *n* : a tubular electric lamp in which light is produced by the action of ultraviolet light on a fluorescent material that coats the inner surface of the lamp

fluo·ri·date \ˈflȯr-ə-ˌdāt\ *vb* **-dat·ed; -dat·ing** : to add a fluoride to (as drinking water) to reduce tooth decay — **fluo·ri·da·tion** \ˌflȯr-ə-ˈdā-shən\ *n*

fluo·ride \ˈflȯr-ˌīd\ *n* : a compound of fluorine

fluo·ri·nate \ˈflȯr-ə-ˌnāt\ *vb* **-nat·ed; -nat·ing** : to treat or cause to combine with fluorine or a compound of fluorine — **fluo·ri·na·tion** \ˌflȯr-ə-ˈnā-shən\ *n*

fluo·rine \ˈflȯr-ˌēn, -ən\ *n* : a pale yellowish flammable irritating toxic gaseous chemical element

fluo·rite \ˈflȯr-ˌīt\ *n* : a mineral that consists of the fluoride of calcium used as a flux and in making glass

fluo·ro·car·bon \ˌflȯr-ō-ˈkär-bən\ *n* : a compound containing fluorine and carbon used chiefly as a lubricant, refrigerant, or nonstick coating; *also* : CHLOROFLUOROCARBON

fluo·ro·scope \ˈflȯr-ə-ˌskōp\ *n* : an instrument for observing the internal structure of an opaque object (as the living body) by means of X-rays — **fluo·ro·scop·ic** \ˌflȯr-ə-ˈskä-pik\ *adj* — **fluo·ros·co·py** \-ˈä-skə-pē\ *n*

fluo·ro·sis \ˌflü-ˈrō-səs, ˌflȯ-\ *n* : an abnormal condition (as spotting of the teeth) caused by fluorine or its compounds

flu·ox·e·tine \flü-ˈäk-sə-ˌtēn\ *n* : an antidepressant drug that enhances serotonin activity

flur·ry \ˈflər-ē\ *n, pl* **flurries** **1** : a gust of wind **2** : a brief light snowfall **3** : COMMOTION, BUSTLE **4** : a brief outburst of activity ⟨a ~ of trading⟩ — **flurry** *vb*

¹flush \ˈfləsh\ *vb* : to cause (a bird) to fly away suddenly

²flush *n* : a hand of cards all of the same suit

³flush *n* **1** : a sudden flow (as of water) **2** : a surge esp. of emotion ⟨a ~ of triumph⟩ **3** : a tinge of red : BLUSH **4** : a fresh and vigorous state **5** : a passing sensation of extreme heat

⁴flush *vb* **1** : to flow and spread suddenly and freely **2** : to glow brightly **3** : BLUSH **4** : to wash out with a rush of fluid **5** : INFLAME, EXCITE ⟨was ~*ed* with anger⟩ **6** : to cause to blush

⁵flush *adj* **1** : of a ruddy healthy color **2** : full of life and vigor **3** : filled to overflowing **4** : AFFLUENT **5** : readily available : ABUNDANT **6** : having an unbroken or even surface **7** : directly abutting : immediately adjacent **8** : set even with an edge of a type page or column — **flush·ness** *n*

⁶flush *adv* **1** : in a flush manner **2** : SQUARELY ⟨a blow ~ on the chin⟩

⁷flush *vb* : to make flush

flus·ter \ˈfləs-tər\ *vb* : to put into a state of agitated confusion — **fluster** *n*

flute \ˈflüt\ *n* **1** : a hollow pipelike musical instrument **2** : a grooved pleat **3** : GROOVE — **flute** *vb* — **flut·ed** *adj*

flut·ing *n* : fluted decoration

flut·ist \ˈflü-tist\ *n* : a flute player

¹flut·ter \ˈflə-tər\ *vb* [ME *floteren* to float, flutter, fr. OE *floterian,* fr. *flotian* to float] **1** : to flap the wings rapidly **2** : to move with quick wavering or flapping motions **3** : to vibrate in irregular spasms **4** : to move about or behave in an agitated aimless manner — **flut·tery** \-tə-rē\ *adj*

²flutter *n* **1** : an act of fluttering **2** : a state of nervous confusion **3** : FLURRY

¹flux \ˈfləks\ *n* **1** : an act of flowing **2** : a state of continuous change **3** : a substance used to aid in fusing metals

²flux *vb* : ¹FUSE

¹fly \ˈflī\ *vb* **flew** \ˈflü\; **flown** \ˈflōn\; **fly·ing** **1** : to move in or pass through the air with wings **2** : to move through the air or before the wind **3** : to float or cause to float, wave, or soar in the air **4** : FLEE **5** : to fade and disappear : VANISH **6** : to move or pass swiftly ⟨time *flies*⟩ **7** : to become expended or dissipated rapidly **8** : to operate or travel in an aircraft or spacecraft **9** : to journey over by flying **10** : AVOID, SHUN **11** : to transport by flying

²fly *n, pl* **flies** **1** : the action or process of flying : FLIGHT **2** *pl* : the space over a theater stage **3** : a garment closing concealed by a fold of cloth **4** : the length of an extended flag from its staff or support **5** : a baseball hit high into the air **6** : the outer canvas of a tent with a double top — **on the fly** : while still in the air

³fly *vb* **flied; fly·ing** : to hit a fly in baseball

⁴fly *n, pl* **flies** **1** : a winged insect — usu. used in combination ⟨butter*fly*⟩ **2** : any of a large order of insects mostly with one pair of functional wings and another pair that if present are reduced to balancing organs and often with larvae without a head, eyes, or legs; *esp* : one (as a housefly) that is large and stout-bodied **3** : a fishhook dressed to suggest an insect

fly·able \ˈflī-ə-bəl\ *adj* : suitable for flying or being flown

fly ball *n* : ²FLY 5

fly·blown \ˈflī-ˌblōn\ *adj* : not pure : TAINTED, CORRUPT

fly·by \-ˌbī\ *n, pl* **flybys** **1** : a usu. low-altitude flight by an aircraft over a public gathering **2** : a flight of a spacecraft past a heavenly body (as Jupiter) close enough to obtain scientific data

fly–by–night \-bī-ˌnīt\ *adj* **1** : seeking a quick profit usu. by shady acts **2** : TRANSITORY, PASSING ⟨~ fashions⟩

fly casting *n* : the casting of artificial flies in fly-fishing or as a competitive sport

fly·catch·er \-ˌka-chər, -ˌke-\ *n* : any of various passerine birds that feed on insects caught in flight

flyer *var of* FLIER

fly–fish·ing \ˈflī-ˌfi-shiŋ\ *n* : a method of fishing in which an artificial fly is used for bait

flying boat *n* : a seaplane with a hull designed for floating

flying buttress *n* : a projecting arched structure to support a wall or building

flying fish *n* : any of numerous marine bony fishes capable of long gliding flights out of water by spreading their large fins like wings

flying saucer *n* : an unidentified flying object reported to be saucer-shaped or disk-shaped

flying squirrel *n* : either of two small nocturnal No. American squirrels with folds of skin connecting the forelegs and hind legs that enable them to make long gliding leaps

fly·leaf \ˈflī-ˌlēf\ *n, pl* **fly·leaves** \-ˌlēvz\ : a blank leaf at the beginning or end of a book

fly·pa·per \-ˌpā-pər\ *n* : paper poisoned or coated with a sticky substance for killing or catching flies

fly·speck \-ˌspek\ *n* **1** : a speck of fly dung **2** : something small and insignificant

fly·way \-ˌwā\ *n* : an established air route of migratory birds

fly·wheel \-ˌhwēl\ *n* : a heavy wheel for regulating the speed of machinery

fm *abbr* fathom

Fm *symbol* fermium

FM \ˈef-ˌem\ *n* : a broadcasting system using frequency modulation; *also* : a radio receiver of such a system

fn *abbr* footnote

fo *or* **fol** *abbr* folio

FO *abbr* foreign office

[1]**foal** \ˈfōl\ *n* : a young horse or related animal; *esp* : one under one year

[2]**foal** *vb* : to give birth to a foal

[1]**foam** \ˈfōm\ *n* **1** : a mass of bubbles formed on the surface of a liquid **2** : material (as rubber) in a lightweight cellular form — **foamy** *adj*

[2]**foam** *vb* : to form foam : FROTH

fob \ˈfäb\ *n* **1** : a short strap, ribbon, or chain attached esp. to a pocket watch **2** : a small ornament worn on a fob

FOB *abbr* free on board

fob off *vb* **1** : to put off with a trick, excuse, or inferior substitute **2** : to pass or offer as genuine **3** : to put aside

FOC *abbr* free of charge

focal length *n* : the distance of a focus from a lens or curved mirror

fo'c'sle *var of* FORECASTLE

[1]**fo·cus** \ˈfō-kəs\ *n, pl* **fo·ci** \-ˌsī\ *also* **fo·cus·es** [NL, fr. L, hearth] **1** : a point at which rays (as of light, heat, or sound) meet or diverge or appear to diverge; *esp* : the point at which an image is formed by a mirror, lens, or optical system **2** : FOCAL LENGTH **3** : adjustment (as of eyes or eyeglasses) that gives clear vision **4** : central point : CENTER — **fo·cal** \ˈfō-kəl\ *adj* — **fo·cal·ly** *adv*

[2]**focus** *vb* **-cused** *also* **-cussed; -cus·ing** *also* **-cus·sing** **1** : to bring or come to a focus ⟨~ rays of light⟩ **2** : CENTER ⟨~ attention on a problem⟩ **3** : to adjust the focus of

fod·der \ˈfä-dər\ *n* **1** : coarse dry food (as cornstalks) for livestock **2** : available material used to supply a heavy demand

foe \ˈfō\ *n* [ME *fo,* fr. OE *fāh,* fr. *fāh* hostile] : ENEMY

FOE *abbr* Fraternal Order of Eagles

foehn *or* **föhn** \ˈfərn, ˈfœn, ˈfān\ *n* [G *Föhn*] : a warm dry wind blowing down a mountainside

foe·man \ˈfō-mən\ *n* : FOE

foe·tal, foe·tus *chiefly Brit var of* FETAL, FETUS

[1]**fog** \ˈfȯg, ˈfäg\ *n* **1** : fine particles of water suspended in the lower atmosphere **2** : mental confusion ⟨was in a ~ as what to do next⟩ — **fog·gy** *adj*

[2]**fog** *vb* **fogged; fog·ging** : to obscure or be obscured with or as if with fog

fog·horn \ˈfȯg-ˌhȯrn, ˈfäg-\ *n* : a horn sounded in a fog to give warning

fo·gy *also* **fo·gey** \ˈfō-gē\ *n, pl* **fogies** *also* **fogeys** : a person with old-fashioned ideas ⟨an old ~⟩

foi·ble \ˈfȯi-bəl\ *n* : a minor failing or weakness in character or behavior

foie gras \ˈfwä-ˈgrä\ *n* [F, lit., fat liver] : the fattened liver of an animal and esp. of a goose usu. served as a pâté

[1]**foil** \ˈfȯi(-ə)l\ *vb* [ME, alter. of *fullen* to full cloth, fr. AF *foller*] **1** : to prevent from attaining an end : DEFEAT **2** : to bring to naught : THWART

[2]**foil** *n* [ME, leaf, fr. AF *fuille, foille,* fr. L *folia,* pl. of *folium* leaf] **1** : a very thin sheet of metal ⟨aluminum ~⟩ **2** : one that serves as a contrast to another ⟨acted as a ~ for a comedian⟩

[3]**foil** *n* : a light fencing sword with a flexible blade tapering to a blunt point

foist \ˈfȯist\ *vb* : to pass off (something false or worthless) as genuine

[1]**fold** \ˈfōld\ *n* **1** : an enclosure for sheep **2** : a group of people with a common faith, belief, or interest

[2]**fold** *vb* : to house (sheep) in a fold

[3]**fold** *vb* **1** : to lay one part over or against another part **2** : to clasp together **3** : EMBRACE **4** : to bend (as a layer of rock) into folds **5** : to incorporate into a mixture by overturning repeatedly without stirring or beating **6** : to become doubled or pleated **7** : FAIL, COLLAPSE ⟨the business ~*ed*⟩

[4]**fold** *n* **1** : a doubling or folding over **2** : a part doubled or laid over another part

fold·away \ˈfōld-ə-ˌwā\ *adj* : designed to fold out of the way or out of sight

fold·er \ˈfōl-dər\ *n* **1** : one that folds **2** : a folded printed circular **3** : a folded cover or large envelope for loose papers **4** : an object in a computer operating system used to organize files or other folders

fol·de·rol \ˈfäl-də-ˌräl\ *n* **1** : a useless trifle **2** : NONSENSE

fold·out \ˈfōld-ˌau̇t\ *n* : a folded leaf (as in a magazine) larger in some dimension than the page

fo·liage \ˈfō-lē-ij\ *n* : a mass of leaves (as of a plant or forest)

fo·li·at·ed \ˈfō-lē-ˌā-təd\ *adj* : composed of or separable into layers

fo·lic acid \ˌfō-lik-\ *n* : a vitamin of the vitamin B complex used esp. to treat nutritional anemias

fo·lio \ˈfō-lē-ˌō\ *n, pl* **fo·li·os** **1** : a leaf of a book; *also* : a page number **2** : the size of a piece of paper cut two from a sheet **3** : a book printed on folio pages

[1]**folk** \ˈfōk\ *n, pl* **folk** *or* **folks** **1** : the largest number or most characteristic part of a group of people forming a tribe or nation **2** *pl* : PEOPLE, PERSONS ⟨country ~⟩ ⟨old ~*s*⟩ **3** *folks pl* : the persons of one's own family

²folk *adj* : of, relating to, or originating among the common people ⟨~ music⟩
folk art *n* : the traditional anonymous art of usu. untrained people
folk·lore \ˈfōk-ˌlȯr\ *n* : customs, beliefs, stories, and sayings of a people handed down from generation to generation — **folk·lor·ic** \-ˌlȯr-ik\ *adj* — **folk·lor·ist** \-ist\ *n*
folk mass *n* : a mass in which traditional liturgical music is replaced by folk music
folk·sing·er \ˈfōk-ˌsiŋ-ər\ *n* : a singer of folk songs — **folk·sing·ing** *n*
folksy \ˈfōk-sē\ *adj* **folks·i·er; -est** **1** : SOCIABLE, FRIENDLY **2** : informal, casual, or familiar in manner or style ⟨~ humor⟩
folk·way \ˈfōk-ˌwā\ *n* : a way of thinking, feeling, or acting common to a given group of people; *esp* : a traditional social custom
fol·li·cle \ˈfä-li-kəl\ *n* **1** : a small anatomical cavity or gland ⟨a hair ~⟩ **2** : a small fluid-filled cavity in the ovary of a mammal enclosing a developing egg — **fol·lic·u·lar** \fə-ˈli-kyə-lər\ *adj*
fol·low \ˈfä-lō\ *vb* **1** : to go or come after **2** : to proceed along ⟨~ the path⟩ **3** : to engage in as a way of life ⟨~ the sea⟩ ⟨~ a profession⟩ **4** : OBEY ⟨~ instructions⟩ **5** : PURSUE **6** : to come after in order or rank or natural sequence **7** : to keep one's attention fixed on **8** : to result from **9** : to subscribe to the social media feed of ♦ ***Synonyms*** SUCCEED, ENSUE, SUPERVENE — **fol·low·er** *n* — **follow suit** **1** : to play a card of the same suit as the card led **2** : to follow an example set
¹fol·low·ing \ˈfä-lə-wiŋ\ *adj* **1** : next after : SUCCEEDING ⟨the ~ day⟩ **2** : that immediately follows ⟨trains will leave at the ~ times⟩
²following *n* : a group of followers, adherents, or partisans
³following *prep* : subsequent to : AFTER ⟨~ the lecture tea was served⟩
follow–up \ˈfä-lō-ˌəp\ *n* : a system or instance of pursuing an initial effort by supplementary action
fol·ly \ˈfä-lē\ *n, pl* **follies** [ME *folie,* fr. AF, fr. *fol* fool] **1** : lack of good sense **2** : a foolish act or idea **3** : an excessively costly or unprofitable undertaking
fo·ment \fō-ˈment\ *vb* : INCITE
fo·men·ta·tion \ˌfō-mən-ˈtā-shən, -ˌmen-\ *n* **1** : a hot moist material (as a damp cloth) applied to the body to ease pain **2** : the act of fomenting : INSTIGATION
FOMO \ˈfō-ˌmō\ *n* : fear of missing out : fear of not being included in something that others are enjoying
fond \ˈfänd\ *adj* [ME, fr. *fonne* fool] **1** : FOOLISH, SILLY ⟨~ pride⟩ **2** : prizing highly : DESIROUS ⟨~ of praise⟩ **3** : strongly attracted or predisposed ⟨~ of music⟩ **4** : foolishly tender : INDULGENT; *also* : LOVING, AFFECTIONATE **5** : CHERISHED, DEAR ⟨his ~*est* hopes⟩ — **fond·ly** *adv* — **fond·ness** *n*
fon·dant \ˈfän-dənt\ *n* : a creamy preparation of sugar used as a basis for candies or icings
fon·dle \ˈfän-dᵊl\ *vb* **fon·dled; fon·dling** **1** : to touch or handle lovingly : CARESS **2** : to touch sexually
fon·due *also* **fon·du** \fän-ˈdü, -ˈdyü\ *n* [F] : a preparation of melted cheese often flavored with white wine
¹font \ˈfänt\ *n* **1** : a receptacle for baptismal or holy water **2** : FOUNTAIN, SOURCE ⟨a ~ of information⟩
²font *n* : an assortment of printing type of one style and sometimes one size
food \ˈfüd\ *n* **1** : material taken into an organism and used for growth, repair, and vital processes and as a source of energy; *also* : organic material produced by green plants and used by them as food **2** : nourishment in solid form **3** : something that nourishes, sustains, or supplies ⟨~ for thought⟩
food chain *n* **1** : a hierarchical arrangement of organisms in an ecological community such that each uses the next usu. lower member as a food source **2** : a hierarchy based on power or importance
food court *n* : an area (as within a shopping mall) set apart for food concessions
food poisoning *n* : a digestive illness caused by bacteria or by chemicals in food
food·stuff \ˈfüd-ˌstəf\ *n* : a substance with food value; *esp* : a specific nutrient (as fat or protein)
¹fool \ˈfül\ *n* [ME, fr. AF *fol,* fr. LL *follis,* fr. L, bellows, bag] **1** : a person who lacks sense or judgment **2** : JESTER **3** : DUPE **4** : IDIOT
²fool *vb* **1** : to spend time idly or aimlessly **2** : to meddle or tamper thoughtlessly or ignorantly **3** : JOKE **4** : DECEIVE **5** : FRITTER ⟨~*ed* away his time⟩
fool·ery \ˈfü-lə-rē\ *n, pl* **-er·ies** **1** : a foolish act, utterance, or belief **2** : foolish behavior
fool·har·dy \ˈfül-ˌhär-dē\ *adj* : foolishly daring : RASH — **fool·har·di·ness** \-dē-nəs\ *n*
fool·ish \ˈfü-lish\ *adj* **1** : showing or arising from folly or lack of judgment **2** : ABSURD, RIDICULOUS **3** : ABASHED — **fool·ish·ly** *adv* — **fool·ish·ness** *n*
fool·proof \ˈfül-ˌprüf\ *adj* : so simple or reliable as to leave no opportunity for error, misuse, or failure ⟨a ~ plan⟩
fools·cap \ˈfül-ˌskap\ *n* [fr. the watermark of a fool's cap formerly applied to such paper] : a size of paper typically 16×13 inches
fool's gold *n* : PYRITE
¹foot \ˈfu̇t\ *n, pl* **feet** \ˈfēt\ *also* **foot** **1** : the end part of a leg below the ankle of a vertebrate animal **2** — see WEIGHT table **3** : a group of syllables forming the basic unit of verse meter **4** : something resembling an animal's foot in position or use **5** : the lowest part : BOTTOM **6** : the part at the opposite end from the head **7** : the part (as of a stocking) that covers the foot
²foot *vb* **1** : DANCE **2** : to go on foot **3** : to add up **4** : to pay or provide for paying
foot·age \ˈfu̇-tij\ *n* **1** : length expressed in

feet **2** : the length of film used for a recording **3** : material recorded on film or video
foot–and–mouth disease *n* : an acute contagious viral disease esp. of cattle
foot·ball \ˈfu̇t-ˌbȯl\ *n* **1** : any of several games played by two teams on a rectangular field with goalposts at each end in which the object is to get the ball over the goal line or between goalposts by running, passing, or kicking **2** : the ball used in football
foot·board \-ˌbȯrd\ *n* **1** : a narrow platform on which to stand or brace the feet **2** : a board forming the foot of a bed
foot·bridge \-ˌbrij\ *n* : a bridge for pedestrians
foot·ed \ˈfu̇-təd\ *adj* : having a foot or feet of a specified kind or number ⟨flat-*footed*⟩ ⟨four-*footed*⟩
-foot·er \ˈfu̇-tər\ *comb form* : one that is a specified number of feet in height, length, or breadth ⟨a six-*footer*⟩
foot·fall \ˈfu̇t-ˌfȯl\ *n* : the sound of a footstep
foot·hill \-ˌhil\ *n* : a hill at the foot of higher hills or mountains
foot·hold \-ˌhōld\ *n* **1** : a hold for the feet : FOOTING **2** : a position usable as a base for further advance
foot·ing *n* **1** : the placing of one's feet in a stable position **2** : the act of moving on foot **3** : a place or space for standing : FOOTHOLD **4** : position with respect to one another : STATUS **5** : BASIS
foot·less \ˈfu̇t-ləs\ *adj* **1** : having no feet ⟨~ tights⟩ **2** : INEPT, INEFFECTUAL
foot·lights \-ˌlīts\ *n pl* **1** : a row of lights along the front of a stage floor **2** : the stage as a profession
foo·tling \ˈfüt-liŋ\ *adj* **1** : INEPT ⟨~ amateurs⟩ **2** : TRIVIAL
foot·lock·er \ˈfu̇t-ˌlä-kər\ *n* : a small trunk designed to be placed at the foot of a bed (as in a barracks)
foot·loose \-ˌlüs\ *adj* : having no ties : FREE, UNTRAMMELED
foot·man \-mən\ *n* : a male servant who attends a carriage or waits on table, admits visitors, and runs errands
foot·note \-ˌnōt\ *n* **1** : a note of reference, explanation, or comment placed usu. at the bottom of a page **2** : COMMENTARY
foot·pad \-ˌpad\ *n* : a round somewhat flat foot on the leg of a spacecraft for distributing weight to minimize sinking into a surface
foot·path \-ˌpath, -ˌpäth\ *n* : a narrow path for pedestrians
foot·print \-ˌprint\ *n* **1** : an impression of the foot **2** : the area on a surface covered by something ⟨a tire with a wide ~⟩
foot·race \-ˌrās\ *n* : a race run on foot
foot·rest \-ˌrest\ *n* : a support for the feet
foot·sore \-ˌsȯr\ *adj* : having sore or tender feet (as from much walking)
foot·step \-ˌstep\ *n* **1** : the mark of the foot : TRACK **2** : TREAD **3** : distance covered by a step : PACE **4** : a step on which to ascend or descend **5** : a way of life, conduct, or action
foot·stool \-ˌstül\ *n* : a low stool to support the feet
foot·wear \-ˌwer\ *n* : apparel (as shoes or boots) for the feet
foot·work \-ˌwərk\ *n* : the management of the feet (as in boxing)
fop \ˈfäp\ *n* : DANDY 1 — **fop·pery** \ˈfä-pə-rē\ *n* — **fop·pish** *adj*
[1]**for** \fər, ˈfȯr\ *prep* **1** : as a preparation toward ⟨dress ~ dinner⟩ **2** : toward the purpose or goal of ⟨need time ~ study⟩ ⟨money ~ a trip⟩ **3** : so as to reach or attain ⟨run ~ cover⟩ **4** : as being ⟨took him ~ a fool⟩ **5** : because of ⟨cry ~ joy⟩ **6** — used to indicate a recipient ⟨a letter ~ you⟩ **7** : in support of ⟨fought ~ his country⟩ **8** : directed at : AFFECTING ⟨a cure ~ what ails you⟩ **9** — used with a noun or pronoun followed by an infinitive to form the equivalent of a noun clause ⟨~ you to go would be silly⟩ **10** : in exchange as equal to : so as to return the value of ⟨a lot of trouble ~ nothing⟩ ⟨pay $10 ~ a hat⟩ **11** : CONCERNING ⟨a stickler ~ detail⟩ **12** : CONSIDERING ⟨tall ~ her age⟩ **13** : through the period of ⟨served ~ three years⟩ **14** : in honor of ⟨named ~ her grandmother⟩
[2]**for** *conj* : BECAUSE
[3]**for** *abbr* **1** foreign **2** forestry
fora *pl of* FORUM
[1]**for·age** \ˈfȯr-ij\ *n* [ME, fr. AF, fr. *fuerre, foer* fodder, straw, of Gmc origin] **1** : food for animals esp. when taken by browsing or grazing **2** : a search for food or supplies
[2]**forage** *vb* **for·aged; for·ag·ing** **1** : to collect forage from **2** : to search for food or supplies **3** : to get by foraging **4** : to make a search : RUMMAGE
for·ay \ˈfȯr-ˌā, fȯ-ˈrā\ *vb* : to raid esp. in search of plunder : PILLAGE — **foray** *n*
[1]**for·bear** \fȯr-ˈber\ *vb* **-bore** \-ˈbȯr\; **-borne** \-ˈbȯrn\; **-bear·ing** **1** : to refrain from : ABSTAIN **2** : to be patient — **for·bear·ance** \-ˈber-əns\ *n*
[2]**forbear** *var of* FOREBEAR
for·bid \fər-ˈbid\ *vb* **-bade** \-ˈbad, -ˈbād\ *also* **-bad** \-ˈbad\; **-bid·den** \-ˈbi-dᵊn\; **-bid·ding** **1** : to command against : PROHIBIT **2** : HINDER, PREVENT ♦ ***Synonyms*** ENJOIN, INTERDICT, INHIBIT, BAN
forbidding *adj* : DISAGREEABLE, REPELLENT ⟨a ~ task⟩
[1]**force** \ˈfȯrs\ *n* **1** : strength or energy esp. of an exceptional degree : active power **2** : capacity to persuade or convince **3** : military strength; *also, pl* : the whole military strength (as of a nation) **4** : a body (as of persons or ships) available for a particular purpose **5** : VIOLENCE, COMPULSION **6** : an influence (as a push or pull) that causes motion or a change of motion — **force·ful** \-fəl\ *adj* — **force·ful·ly** *adv* — **in force** **1** : in great numbers **2** : VALID, OPERATIVE ⟨the ban remains *in force*⟩
[2]**force** *vb* **forced; forc·ing** **1** : COMPEL, COERCE **2** : to cause through necessity

⟨*forced* to admit defeat⟩ **3** : to press, attain to, or effect against resistance or inertia ⟨~ your way through⟩ **4** : to raise or accelerate to the utmost ⟨~ the pace⟩ **5** : to produce with unnatural or unwilling effort ⟨*forced* a smile⟩ **6** : to hasten (as in growth) by artificial means

for·ceps \ˈfȯr-səps\ *n, pl* **forceps** [L] : a handheld instrument for grasping, holding, or pulling objects esp. for delicate operations (as by a surgeon)

forc·ible \ˈfȯr-sə-bəl\ *adj* **1** : obtained or done by force **2** : showing force or energy : POWERFUL — **forc·i·bly** \-blē\ *adv*

[1]**ford** \ˈfȯrd\ *n* : a place where a stream may be crossed by wading

[2]**ford** *vb* : to cross (a body of water) by wading

[1]**fore** \ˈfȯr\ *adv* : in, toward, or adjacent to the front : FORWARD

[2]**fore** *adj* : being or coming before in time, order, or space

[3]**fore** *n* : something that occupies a front position

[4]**fore** *interj* — used by a golfer to warn anyone within range of the probable line of flight of the ball

fore–and–aft \ˌfȯr-ə-ˈnaft\ *adj* : lying, running, or acting along the length of a structure (as a ship)

[1]**fore·arm** \(ˌ)fȯr-ˈärm\ *vb* : to arm in advance : PREPARE

[2]**fore·arm** \ˈfȯr-ˌärm\ *n* : the part of the arm between the elbow and the wrist

fore·bear \-ˌber\ *n* : ANCESTOR, FOREFATHER

fore·bode *also* **for·bode** \fȯr-ˈbōd\ *vb* **1** : to have a premonition esp. of misfortune **2** : FORETELL, PREDICT ♦ ***Synonyms*** AUGUR, BODE, FORESHADOW, PORTEND, PROMISE — **fore·bod·ing** *n or adj* — **fore·bod·ing·ly** *adv*

fore·cast \ˈfȯr-ˌkast\ *vb* **-cast** *also* **-cast·ed; -cast·ing** **1** : PREDICT, CALCULATE ⟨~ weather conditions⟩ **2** : to indicate as likely to occur — **forecast** *n* — **fore·cast·er** *n*

fore·cas·tle *or* **fo'·c'sle** \ˈfōk-səl\ *n* **1** : the forward part of the upper deck of a ship **2** : the crew's quarters usu. in a ship's bow

fore·close \fȯr-ˈklōz\ *vb* **1** : to shut out : PRECLUDE **2** : to take legal measures to terminate a mortgage and take possession of the mortgaged property

fore·clo·sure \-ˈklō-zhər\ *n* : the act of foreclosing; *esp* : the legal procedure of foreclosing a mortgage

fore·doom \fȯr-ˈdüm\ *vb* : to doom beforehand

fore·fa·ther \ˈfȯr-ˌfä-t͟hər\ *n* **1** : ANCESTOR **2** : a person of an earlier period and common heritage

forefend *var of* FORFEND

fore·fin·ger \-ˌfiŋ-gər\ *n* : INDEX FINGER

fore·foot \-ˌfu̇t\ *n* : either of the front feet of a quadruped; *also* : the front part of the human foot

fore·front \-ˌfrənt\ *n* : the foremost part or place

foregather *var of* FORGATHER

[1]**fore·go** \fȯr-ˈgō\ *vb* **-went** \-ˈwent\; **-gone** \-ˈgȯn\; **-go·ing** : PRECEDE

[2]**forego** *var of* FORGO

foregoing *adj* : PRECEDING ⟨the ~ statement can be proven⟩

fore·gone \ˈfȯr-ˌgȯn\ *adj* : determined in advance ⟨a ~ conclusion⟩

fore·ground \-ˌgrau̇nd\ *n* **1** : the part of a scene or representation that appears nearest to and in front of the spectator **2** : a position of prominence

fore·hand \-ˌhand\ *n* : a stroke (as in tennis) made with the palm of the hand turned in the direction in which the hand is moving; *also* : the side on which such a stroke is made — **forehand** *adj*

fore·hand·ed \(ˌ)fȯr-ˈhan-dəd\ *adj* : mindful of the future : PRUDENT

fore·head \ˈfȯr-əd, ˈfȯr-ˌhed\ *n* : the part of the face above the eyes

for·eign \ˈfȯr-ən\ *adj* [ME *forein,* fr. AF, fr. LL *foranus* on the outside, fr. L *foris* outside] **1** : situated outside a place or country and esp. one's own country **2** : born in, belonging to, or characteristic of some place or country other than the one under consideration ⟨~ language⟩ **3** : not connected, pertinent, or characteristically present **4** : related to or dealing with other nations ⟨~ affairs⟩ **5** : occurring in an abnormal situation in the living body ⟨a ~ body in the eye⟩

for·eign·er \ˈfȯr-ə-nər\ *n* : a person belonging to or owing allegiance to a foreign country

foreign minister *n* : a governmental minister for foreign affairs

fore·know \fȯr-ˈnō\ *vb* **-knew** \-ˈnü, -ˈnyü\; **-known** \-ˈnōn\; **-know·ing** : to have previous knowledge of — **fore·knowl·edge** \ˈfȯr-ˌnä-lij, fȯr-ˈnä-\ *n*

fore·la·dy \ˈfȯr-ˌlā-dē\ *n* : FOREWOMAN

fore·leg \-ˌleg\ *n* : a front leg

fore·limb \-ˌlim\ *n* : a front or upper limb (as a wing, arm, fin, or leg)

fore·lock \-ˌläk\ *n* : a lock of hair growing from the front part of the head

fore·man \-mən\ *n* **1** : a spokesperson of a jury **2** : a person in charge of a group of workers

fore·mast \-ˌmast\ *n* : the mast nearest the bow of a ship

fore·most \-ˌmōst\ *adj* : first in time, place, or order : most important : PREEMINENT — **foremost** *adv*

fore·name \-ˌnām\ *n* : a first name

fore·named \-ˌnāmd\ *adj* : previously named : AFORESAID

fore·noon \-ˌnün\ *n* : MORNING

[1]**fo·ren·sic** \fə-ˈren-sik\ *adj* [L *forensis* public, forensic, fr. *forum* forum] **1** : belonging to, used in, or suitable to courts of law or to public speaking or debate **2** : relating to the application of scientific knowledge to legal problems ⟨~ medicine⟩

[2]**forensic** *n* **1** : an argumentative exercise **2** *pl* : the art or study of argumentative discourse **3** *pl* : scientific analysis of physical evidence (as from a crime scene)

fore·or·dain \ˌfōr-ōr-ˈdān\ *vb* : to ordain or decree beforehand : PREDESTINE
fore·part \ˈfōr-ˌpärt\ *n* **1** : the anterior part of something **2** : the earlier part of a period of time
fore·quar·ter \-ˌkwȯr-tər\ *n* : the front half of a lateral half of the body or carcass of a quadruped ‹a ~ of beef›
fore·run·ner \-ˌrə-nər\ *n* **1** : one that goes before to give notice of the approach of others : HARBINGER **2** : PREDECESSOR, ANCESTOR ♦ ***Synonyms*** PRECURSOR, HERALD
fore·sail \-ˌsāl, -səl\ *n* **1** : the lowest sail on the foremast of a square-rigged ship or schooner **2** : the principal sail forward of the foremast (as of a sloop)
fore·see \fōr-ˈsē\ *vb* **-saw** \-ˈsȯ\; **-seen** \-ˈsēn\; **-see·ing** : to see or realize beforehand : EXPECT ♦ ***Synonyms*** FOREKNOW, DIVINE, APPREHEND, ANTICIPATE — **fore·see·able** *adj*
fore·shad·ow \-ˈsha-dō\ *vb* : to give a hint or suggestion of beforehand
fore·short·en \fōr-ˈshȯr-tᵊn\ *vb* : to shorten (a detail) in a drawing or painting so that it appears to have depth
fore·sight \ˈfōr-ˌsīt\ *n* **1** : the act or power of foreseeing **2** : care or provision for the future : PRUDENCE **3** : an act of looking forward; *also* : a view forward — **fore·sight·ed** \-ˌsī-təd\ *adj* — **fore·sight·ed·ly** *adv* — **fore·sight·ed·ness** *n*
fore·skin \-ˌskin\ *n* : a fold of skin enclosing the end of the penis
for·est \ˈfȯr-əst\ *n* [ME, fr. AF, fr. LL *forestis* (*silva*) unenclosed (woodland), fr. L *foris* outside] : a large thick growth of trees and underbrush — **for·est·ed** \ˈfȯr-ə-stəd\ *adj* — **for·est·land** \ˈfȯr-əst-ˌland\ *n*
fore·stall \fōr-ˈstȯl\ *vb* : to counter, hinder, or prevent by measures taken in advance ‹~ a conflict›
forest ranger *n* : a person in charge of the management and protection of a portion of a forest
for·est·ry \ˈfȯr-ə-strē\ *n* : the science of growing and caring for forests — **for·est·er** \ˈfȯr-ə-stər\ *n*
foreswear *var of* FORSWEAR
¹**fore·taste** \ˈfōr-ˌtāst\ *n* : an advance indication, warning, or notion
²**fore·taste** \fōr-ˈtāst\ *vb* : to taste beforehand : ANTICIPATE
fore·tell \fōr-ˈtel\ *vb* **-told** \-ˈtōld\; **-tell·ing** : to tell of beforehand : PREDICT ♦ ***Synonyms*** FORECAST, PROPHESY, PROGNOSTICATE
fore·thought \ˈfōr-ˌthȯt\ *n* **1** : PREMEDITATION **2** : consideration for the future
fore·to·ken \fōr-ˈtō-kən\ *vb* : to indicate in advance
fore·top \ˈfōr-ˌtäp\ *n* : a platform near the top of a ship's foremast
for·ev·er \fōr-ˈe-vər\ *adv* **1** : for a limitless time **2** : at all times : ALWAYS
for·ev·er·more \-ˌe-vər-ˈmōr\ *adv* : FOREVER
fore·warn \fōr-ˈwȯrn\ *vb* : to warn beforehand — **fore·warn·ing** \-ˈwȯr-niŋ\ *n*
forewent *past of* FOREGO
fore·wing \ˈfōr-ˌwiŋ\ *n* : either of the anterior wings of a 4-winged insect
fore·wom·an \ˈfōr-ˌwu̇-mən\ *n* : a woman who is a foreman
fore·word \-ˌwərd\ *n* : PREFACE
¹**for·feit** \ˈfȯr-fət\ *n* [ME *forfait,* fr. AF, fr. pp. of *forfaire, forsfaire* to commit a crime, forfeit, fr. *fors* outside + *faire* to do] **1** : something forfeited : PENALTY, FINE **2** : FORFEITURE **3** : something deposited and then redeemed on payment of a fine **4** *pl* : a game in which forfeits are exacted
²**forfeit** *vb* : to lose or lose the right to esp. by some error, offense, or crime
for·fei·ture \ˈfȯr-fə-ˌchu̇r\ *n* **1** : the act of forfeiting **2** : something forfeited : PENALTY
for·fend \fȯr-ˈfend\ *vb* **1** : PREVENT **2** : PROTECT, PRESERVE
for·gath·er *or* **fore·gath·er** \fōr-ˈga-t͟hər\ *vb* **1** : to come together : ASSEMBLE **2** : to meet someone usu. by chance
¹**forge** \ˈfōrj\ *n* [ME, fr. AF, fr. L *fabrica,* fr. *faber* smith] : a furnace or shop with its furnace where metal is heated and worked
²**forge** *vb* **forged; forg·ing** **1** : to form (metal) by heating and hammering **2** : FASHION, SHAPE ‹~ an agreement› **3** : to make or imitate falsely esp. with intent to defraud ‹~ a signature› — **forg·er** *n* — **forg·ery** \ˈfōr-jə-rē\ *n*
³**forge** *vb* **forged; forg·ing** : to move ahead steadily but gradually
for·get \fər-ˈget\ *vb* **-got** \-ˈgät\; **-got·ten** \-ˈgät-ᵊn\ *or* **-got; -get·ting** **1** : to be unable to think of or recall **2** : to fail to become mindful of at the proper time **3** : NEGLECT, DISREGARD ‹*forgot* their old friends› **4** : to give up hope for or expectation of — **for·get·ful** \-ˈget-fəl\ *adj* — **for·get·ful·ly** *adv* — **for·get·ful·ness** *n*
for·get–me–not \fər-ˈget-mē-ˌnät\ *n* : any of a genus of small herbs with bright blue or white flowers
forg·ing *n* : a piece of forged work
for·give \fər-ˈgiv\ *vb* **-gave** \-ˈgāv\; **-giv·en** \-ˈgi-vən\; **-giv·ing** **1** : to give up resentment of **2** : PARDON, ABSOLVE **3** : to grant relief from payment of ‹~ a debt› — **for·giv·able** *adj* — **for·give·ness** *n* — **for·giv·er** *n*
forgiving *adj* **1** : willing or able to forgive **2** : allowing room for error or weakness ‹a ~ recipe›
for·go \fōr-ˈgō\ *vb* **-went** \-ˈwent\; **-gone** \-ˈgȯn\; **-go·ing** : to give up the enjoyment or advantage of : do without
fo·rint \ˈfȯr-int\ *n, pl* **forints** *also* **forint** — see MONEY table
¹**fork** \ˈfȯrk\ *n* **1** : an implement with two or more prongs for taking up (as in eating), pitching, or digging **2** : a forked part, tool, or piece of equipment **3** : a dividing into branches or a place where something branches; *also* : a branch of such a fork
²**fork** *vb* **1** : to divide into two or more branches **2** : to give the form of a fork to

⟨∼*ing* her fingers⟩ **3** : to raise or pitch with a fork ⟨∼ hay⟩ **4** : PAY, CONTRIBUTE — used with *over, out,* or *up*

forked \ˈfȯrkt, ˈfȯr-kəd\ *adj* : having a fork : shaped like a fork ⟨∼ lightning⟩

fork·lift \ˈfōrk-ˌlift\ *n* : a machine for lifting heavy objects by means of steel fingers inserted under the load

for·lorn \fər-ˈlȯrn, fȯr-\ *adj* **1** : sad and lonely because of isolation or desertion **2** : WRETCHED **3** : nearly hopeless — **for·lorn·ly** *adv* — **for·lorn·ness** *n*

[1]**form** \ˈfȯrm\ *n* **1** : SHAPE, STRUCTURE **2** : a body esp. of a person : FIGURE **3** : the essential nature of a thing **4** : established manner of doing or saying something **5** : FORMULA **6** : a document with blank spaces for insertion of information ⟨tax ∼⟩ **7** : CEREMONY **8** : manner of performing according to recognized standards **9** : a long seat : BENCH **10** : a model of the human figure used for displaying clothes **11** : MOLD ⟨a ∼ for concrete⟩ **12** : type or plates in a frame ready for printing **13** : MODE, KIND, VARIETY **14** : orderly method of arrangement; *also* : a particular kind or instance of such arrangement **15** : the structural element, plan, or design of a work of art **16** : a bounded surface or volume **17** : a grade in a British school or in some American private schools **18** : RACING FORM **19** : known ability to perform; *also* : condition (as of an athlete) suitable for performing **20** : one of the ways in which a word is changed to show difference in use ⟨the plural ∼ of a noun⟩ — **form·less** *adj*

[2]**form** *vb* **1** : to give form or shape to : FASHION, MAKE **2** : TRAIN, INSTRUCT **3** : CONSTITUTE, COMPOSE **4** : DEVELOP, ACQUIRE ⟨∼ a habit⟩ **5** : to arrange in order ⟨∼ a battle line⟩ **6** : to take form : ARISE ⟨clouds are ∼*ing*⟩ **7** : to take a definite form, shape, or arrangement

[1]**for·mal** \ˈfȯr-məl\ *adj* **1** : according with conventional forms and rules ⟨a ∼ dinner party⟩ **2** : done in due or lawful form ⟨a ∼ contract⟩ **3** : CEREMONIOUS, PRIM ⟨a ∼ manner⟩ **4** : NOMINAL — **for·mal·ly** *adv*

[2]**formal** *n* : something (as a social event) formal in character

form·al·de·hyde \fȯr-ˈmal-də-ˌhīd\ *n* : a colorless pungent gas used in water solution as a preservative and disinfectant

for·mal·ise *Brit var of* FORMALIZE

for·mal·ism \ˈfȯr-mə-ˌli-zəm\ *n* : strict adherence to set forms

for·mal·i·ty \fȯr-ˈma-lə-tē\ *n, pl* **-ties** **1** : compliance with formal or conventional rules **2** : the quality or state of being formal **3** : an established form that is required or conventional

for·mal·ize \ˈfȯr-mə-ˌlīz\ *vb* **-ized; -iz·ing** **1** : to give a certain or definite form to **2** : to make formal; *also* : to give formal status or approval to

[1]**for·mat** \ˈfȯr-ˌmat\ *n* **1** : the general composition or style of a publication **2** : the general plan or arrangement of something **3** : a method of organizing data ⟨various file ∼*s*⟩

[2]**format** *vb* **for·mat·ted; for·mat·ting** : to arrange (as material to be printed) in a particular format — **for·mat·ter** *n*

for·ma·tion \fȯr-ˈmā-shən\ *n* **1** : an act of giving form to something : DEVELOPMENT **2** : something that is formed **3** : STRUCTURE, SHAPE **4** : an arrangement of persons or things in a prescribed manner or for a certain purpose

for·ma·tive \ˈfȯr-mə-tiv\ *adj* **1** : giving or capable of giving form : CONSTRUCTIVE **2** : of, relating to, or characterized by important growth or formation ⟨a child's ∼ years⟩

for·mer \ˈfȯr-mər\ *adj* **1** : PREVIOUS, EARLIER **2** : FOREGOING ⟨the ∼ part of the chapter⟩ **3** : being first mentioned or in order of two or more things

for·mer·ly \-lē\ *adv* : in time past : PREVIOUSLY

form·fit·ting \ˈfȯrm-ˌfi-tiŋ\ *adj* : conforming to the outline of the body ⟨a ∼ sweater⟩

for·mi·da·ble \ˈfȯr-mə-də-bəl, fȯr-ˈmi-\ *adj* **1** : exciting fear, dread, or awe ⟨a ∼ foe⟩ **2** : imposing serious difficulties ⟨a ∼ barrier⟩ — **for·mi·da·bly** \-blē\ *adv*

form letter *n* **1** : a letter on a frequently recurring topic that can be sent to different people at different times **2** : a letter for mass circulation sent out in many printed copies

for·mu·la \ˈfȯr-myə-lə\ *n, pl* **-las** *or* **-lae** \-ˌlē, -ˌlī\ **1** : a set form of words for ceremonial use **2** : RECIPE, PRESCRIPTION **3** : a milk mixture or substitute for a baby **4** : a group of symbols or figures joined to express information concisely **5** : a customary or set form or method

for·mu·late \-ˌlāt\ *vb* **-lat·ed; -lat·ing** **1** : to express in a formula **2** : DESIGN, DEVISE ⟨∼ a policy⟩ **3** : to prepare according to a formula — **for·mu·la·tion** \ˌfȯr-myə-ˈlā-shən\ *n*

for·ni·ca·tion \ˌfȯr-nə-ˈkā-shən\ *n* : consensual sexual intercourse between two persons not married to each other — **for·ni·cate** \ˈfȯr-nə-ˌkāt\ *vb* — **for·ni·ca·tor** \-ˌkā-tər\ *n*

for·sake \fər-ˈsāk, fȯr-\ *vb* **for·sook** \-ˈsu̇k\; **for·sak·en** \-ˈsā-kən\; **for·sak·ing** [ME, fr. OE *forsacan,* fr. *sacan* to dispute] : to give up or leave entirely ⟨*forsook* teaching for politics⟩

for·sooth \fər-ˈsüth\ *adv* : in truth : INDEED

for·swear \fȯr-ˈswer\ *vb* **-swore** \-ˈswȯr\; **-sworn** \-ˈswȯrn\; **-swear·ing** **1** : to swear falsely : commit perjury **2** : to renounce earnestly or under oath **3** : to deny under oath

for·syth·ia \fər-ˈsi-thē-ə\ *n, pl* **-ias** *also* **-ia** : any of a genus of shrubs related to the olive and having yellow bell-shaped flowers appearing before the leaves in early spring

fort \ˈfȯrt\ *n* [ME *forte,* fr. AF *fort,* fr. *fort* strong, fr. L *fortis*] **1** : a fortified place **2** : a permanent army post

[1]**forte** \ˈfȯrt, ˈfȯr-ˌtā\ *n* [F *fort,* fr. *fort,* adj., strong] : one's strong point
[2]**for·te** \ˈfȯr-ˌtā\ *adv or adj* [It, fr. *forte* strong] : LOUD — used as a direction in music
forth \ˈfȯrth\ *adv* **1** : FORWARD, ONWARD ⟨from that day ~⟩ **2** : out into view ⟨plants putting ~ leaves⟩
forth·com·ing \fȯrth-ˈkə-miŋ\ *adj* **1** : coming or available soon ⟨the ~ holidays⟩ **2** : marked by openness and candor : OUTGOING
forth·right \ˈfȯrth-ˌrīt\ *adj* : free from ambiguity or evasiveness : going straight to the point ⟨a ~ answer⟩ — **forth·right·ly** *adv* — **forth·right·ness** *n*
forth·with \ˌfȯrth-ˈwith\ *adv* : IMMEDIATELY
for·ti·fy \ˈfȯr-tə-ˌfī\ *vb* **-fied; -fy·ing** **1** : to strengthen by military defenses **2** : to give physical strength or endurance to **3** : ENCOURAGE **4** : to strengthen or enrich with a material ⟨~ bread with vitamins⟩ — **for·ti·fi·ca·tion** \ˌfȯr-tə-fə-ˈkā-shən\ *n*
for·tis·si·mo \fȯr-ˈti-sə-ˌmō\ *adv or adj* : very loud — used as a direction in music
for·ti·tude \ˈfȯr-tə-ˌtüd, -ˌtyüd\ *n* : strength of mind that enables one to meet danger or bear pain or adversity with courage ♦ ***Synonyms*** GRIT, BACKBONE, PLUCK, GUTS
fort·night \ˈfȯrt-ˌnīt\ *n* [ME *fourtenight,* alter. of *fourtene night* fourteen nights] : two weeks — **fort·night·ly** \-lē\ *adj or adv*
for·tress \ˈfȯr-trəs\ *n* : FORT 1
for·tu·itous \fȯr-ˈtü-ə-təs, -ˈtyü-\ *adj* **1** : happening by chance ⟨a ~ discovery⟩ **2** : FORTUNATE — **for·tu·itous·ly** *adv*
for·tu·ity \-ə-tē\ *n, pl* **-ities** **1** : the quality or state of being fortuitous **2** : a chance event or occurrence
for·tu·nate \ˈfȯr-chə-nət\ *adj* **1** : bringing some good thing not foreseen **2** : LUCKY
for·tu·nate·ly \-lē\ *adv* **1** : in a fortunate manner **2** : it is fortunate that
for·tune \ˈfȯr-chən\ *n* **1** : prosperity attained partly through luck; *also* : CHANCE, LUCK **2** : what happens to a person : good or bad luck **3** : FATE, DESTINY **4** : RICHES, WEALTH
fortune hunter *n* : a person who seeks wealth esp. by marriage
for·tune–tell·er \-ˌte-lər\ *n* : a person who professes to foretell future events — **for·tune–tell·ing** *n or adj*
for·ty \ˈfȯr-tē\ *n, pl* **forties** : four times 10 — **for·ti·eth** \ˈfȯr-tē-əth\ *adj or n* — **forty** *adj or pron*
for·ty–five \ˌfȯr-tē-ˈfīv\ *n* **1** : a .45 caliber handgun — usu. written .45 **2** : a phonograph record designed to be played at 45 revolutions per minute — usu. written 45
for·ty–nin·er \-ˈnī-nər\ *n* : a person in the rush to California for gold in 1849
forty winks *n sing or pl* : a short sleep
fo·rum \ˈfȯr-əm\ *n, pl* **forums** *also* **fo·ra** \-ə\ [L] **1** : the marketplace or central meeting place of an ancient Roman city **2** : a medium (as a publication or online service) of open discussion **3** : COURT **4** : a public assembly, lecture, or program involving audience or panel discussion
[1]**for·ward** \ˈfȯr-wərd\ *adj* **1** : being near or at or belonging to the front **2** : EAGER, READY **3** : BRASH, BOLD **4** : notably advanced or developed : PRECOCIOUS **5** : moving, tending, or leading toward a position in front **6** : EXTREME, RADICAL **7** : of, relating to, or getting ready for the future — **for·ward·ness** *n*
[2]**forward** *adv* : to or toward what is ahead or in front
[3]**forward** *vb* **1** : to help onward : ADVANCE **2** : to send forward : TRANSMIT **3** : to send or ship onward
[4]**forward** *n* : a player who plays at the front of a team's offensive formation near the opponent's goal
for·ward·er \-wər-dər\ *n* : one that forwards; *esp* : an agent who forwards goods
for·wards \ˈfȯr-wərdz\ *adv* : FORWARD
forwent *past of* FORGO
[1]**fos·sil** \ˈfä-səl\ *adj* [L *fossilis* obtained by digging, fr. *fodere* to dig] **1** : preserved from a past geologic age ⟨~ plants⟩ **2** : of or relating to fossil fuels
[2]**fossil** *n* **1** : a trace or impression or the remains of a plant or animal of a past geologic age preserved in the earth's crust **2** : a person whose ideas are out-of-date — **fos·sil·ize** \ˈfä-sə-ˌlīz\ *vb*
fossil fuel *n* : a fuel (as coal or oil) that is formed in the earth from plant or animal remains
[1]**fos·ter** \ˈfȯs-tər\ *adj* [ME, fr. OE *fōstor-,* fr. *fōstor* food, feeding] : affording, receiving, or sharing nourishment or parental care though not related by blood or legal ties ⟨~ parent⟩ ⟨~ child⟩
[2]**foster** *vb* **1** : to give parental care to : NURTURE **2** : to promote the growth or development of : ENCOURAGE
foster home *n* : a household in which an orphaned, neglected, or delinquent child is placed for care
fos·ter·ling \-tər-liŋ\ *n* : a foster child
Fou·cault pendulum \ˌfü-ˈkō-\ *n* : a device that consists of a heavy weight hung by a long wire and that swings in a constant direction which appears to change showing that the earth rotates
fought *past and past part of* FIGHT
[1]**foul** \ˈfau̇(-ə)l\ *adj* **1** : offensive to the senses : LOATHSOME; *also* : clogged with dirt **2** : ODIOUS, DETESTABLE ⟨a ~ crime⟩ **3** : OBSCENE, ABUSIVE ⟨~ language⟩ **4** : DISAGREEABLE, STORMY ⟨~ weather⟩ **5** : TREACHEROUS, DISHONORABLE, UNFAIR ⟨by fair means or ~⟩ **6** : marking the bounds of a playing field ⟨~ lines⟩; *also* : being outside the foul line ⟨~ ball⟩ ⟨~ territory⟩ **7** : containing marked-up corrections **8** : ENTANGLED — **foul·ly** *adv* — **foul·ness** *n*
[2]**foul** *n* **1** : an entanglement or collision in fishing or sailing **2** : an infraction of the rules in a game or sport; *also* : a baseball hit outside the foul line

³foul *vb* **1** : to make or become foul or filthy **2** : to entangle or become entangled **3** : OBSTRUCT, BLOCK **4** : to collide with **5** : to make or hit a foul
⁴foul *adv* : in a foul manner
fou·lard \fü-ˈlärd\ *n* : a lightweight silk of plain or twill weave usu. decorated with a printed pattern
foul·mouthed \ˈfau̇(-ə)l-ˈmau̇t͟hd, -ˈmau̇tht\ *adj* : given to the use of obscene, profane, or abusive language
foul of *prep* : AFOUL OF
foul play *n* : VIOLENCE; *esp* : MURDER
foul–up \ˈfau̇(-ə)l-ˌəp\ *n* **1** : a state of being fouled up **2** : a mechanical difficulty
foul up *vb* **1** : to spoil by mistakes or poor judgment **2** : to cause a foul-up : BUNGLE
¹found \ˈfau̇nd\ *past and past part of* FIND
²found *vb* [ME, fr. AF *funder, fonder,* fr. L *fundare,* fr. *fundus* bottom] **1** : to take the first steps in building **2** : to set or ground on something solid : BASE **3** : to establish (as an institution) often with provision for future maintenance — **found·er** *n*
foun·da·tion \fau̇n-ˈdā-shən\ *n* **1** : the act of founding **2** : a basis upon which something stands or is supported ⟨suspicions without ~⟩ **3** : funds given for the permanent support of an institution : ENDOWMENT; *also* : an institution so endowed **4** : supporting structure : BASE **5** : CORSET — **foun·da·tion·al** \-shə-nəl\ *adj*
foun·der \ˈfau̇n-dər\ *vb* **1** : to make or become lame ⟨the horse ~*ed*⟩ **2** : COLLAPSE **3** : SINK ⟨a ~*ing* ship⟩ **4** : FAIL
found·ling \ˈfau̇nd-liŋ\ *n* : an infant found after its unknown parents have abandoned it
found·ry \ˈfau̇n-drē\ *n, pl* **foundries** : a building or works where metal is cast
fount \ˈfau̇nt\ *n* : SOURCE, FOUNTAIN
foun·tain \ˈfau̇n-tᵊn\ *n* **1** : a spring of water **2** : SOURCE **3** : an artificial jet of water **4** : a container for liquid that can be drawn off as needed
foun·tain·head \-ˌhed\ *n* : SOURCE
fountain pen *n* : a pen with a reservoir that feeds the writing point with ink
four \ˈfȯr\ *n* **1** : one more than three **2** : the 4th in a set or series **3** : something having four units — **four** *adj or pron*
4x4 *also* **four–by–four** \ˈfȯr-bī-ˌfȯr\ *n* : a four-wheel automobile with four-wheel drive
four–flush \-ˌfləsh\ *vb* : to make a false claim : BLUFF — **four–flush·er** *n*
four·fold \-ˌfōld, -ˈfōld\ *adj* **1** : being four times as great or as many **2** : having four units or members — **four·fold** \-ˈfōld\ *adv*
4–H \ˈfȯr-ˈāch\ *adj* [fr. the fourfold aim of improving the head, heart, hands, and health] : of or relating to a program set up by the U.S. Department of Agriculture to help young people become productive citizens — **4–H'·er** *n*
Four Hundred *or* **400** *n* : the exclusive social set of a community — used with *the*
four–in–hand \ˈfȯr-ən-ˌhand\ *n* **1** : a team of four horses driven by one person; *also* : a vehicle drawn by such a team **2** : a necktie tied in a slipknot with long ends overlapping vertically in front
four–o'clock \ˈfȯr-ə-ˌkläk\ *n* : a garden plant with fragrant yellow, red, or white flowers without petals that open late in the afternoon
four–post·er \ˌfȯr-ˈpō-stər\ *n* : a bed with tall corner posts orig. designed to support curtains or a canopy
four·score \ˈfȯr-ˈskȯr\ *adj* : being four times twenty : EIGHTY
four·some \ˈfȯr-səm\ *n* **1** : a group of four persons or things **2** : a golf match between two pairs of partners
four·square \-ˈskwer\ *adj* **1** : SQUARE **2** : marked by boldness and conviction : FORTHRIGHT — **foursquare** *adv*
four·teen \fȯr-ˈtēn\ *n* : one more than 13 — **fourteen** *adj or pron* — **four·teenth** \-ˈtēnth\ *adj or n*
fourth \ˈfȯrth\ *n* **1** : one that is number four in a countable series **2** : one of four equal parts of something — **fourth** *adj or adv*
fourth estate *n, often cap F&E* : the public press
fourth wall *n* : an imaginary wall that keeps performers from recognizing or directly addressing their audience
4WD *abbr* four-wheel drive
four–wheel \ˈfȯr-ˌhwēl\ *or* **four–wheeled** \-ˌhwēld\ *adj* : acting on or by means of four wheels of a motor vehicle ⟨~ disc brakes⟩
four–wheel drive *n* : an automotive drive mechanism that acts on all four wheels of the vehicle; *also* : a vehicle with such a drive
¹fowl \ˈfau̇(-ə)l\ *n, pl* **fowl** *or* **fowls** **1** : BIRD **2** : a cock or hen of the domestic chicken; *also* : the flesh of these used as food
²fowl *vb* : to hunt wildfowl
¹fox \ˈfäks\ *n, pl* **fox·es** *also* **fox** **1** : any of various flesh-eating mammals related to the wolves but smaller and with shorter legs and a more pointed muzzle; *also* : the fur of a fox **2** : a clever crafty person **3** *cap* : a member of an Indigenous people formerly living in what is now Wisconsin
²fox *vb* : TRICK, OUTWIT
fox·glove \ˈfäks-ˌgləv\ *n* : a common plant related to the snapdragons that is grown for its showy spikes of dotted white or purple tubular flowers and as a source of digitalis
fox·hole \-ˌhōl\ *n* : a pit dug for protection against enemy fire
fox·hound \-ˌhau̇nd\ *n* : any of various large swift powerful hounds used in hunting foxes
fox·ing \ˈfäk-siŋ\ *n* : brownish spots on old paper
fox terrier *n* : a small lively terrier that occurs in varieties with smooth dense coats or with harsh wiry coats
fox·trot \ˈfäks-ˌträt\ *n* **1** : a short broken slow trotting gait **2** : a ballroom dance in duple time
foxy \ˈfäk-sē\ *adj* **fox·i·er; -est** **1** : resem-

bling or suggestive of a fox **2** : WILY **3** : physically attractive

foy·er \'fȯi(-ə)r, 'fȯi-ˌyā\ *n* [F, lit., fireplace, fr. OF *foier,* fr. VL **focarium,* fr. L *focus* hearth] : LOBBY; *also* : an entrance hallway

fpm *abbr* feet per minute

FPO *abbr* fleet post office

fps *abbr* feet per second

fr *abbr* **1** father **2** franc **3** friar **4** from

¹Fr *abbr* **1** France; French **2** Friday

²Fr *symbol* francium

fra·cas \'frā-kəs, 'fra-\ *n, pl* **fra·cas·es** \-kə-səz\ [F, din, row, fr. It *fracasso,* fr. *fracassare* to shatter] : BRAWL

frack·ing \'fra-kiŋ\ *n* [by shortening & alter. fr. *(hydraulic) fracturing*] : the injection of fluid into shale beds so as to free up petroleum — **frack** \'frak\ *vb*

frac·tal \'frak-tᵊl\ *n* : an irregular curve or shape that repeats itself at any scale on which it is examined — **fractal** *adj*

frac·tion \'frak-shən\ *n* **1** : a numerical representation (as $^1/_2$, $^3/_4$, or 3.323) indicating the quotient of two numbers **2** : FRAGMENT **3** : PORTION ⟨a small ~ of voters⟩ — **frac·tion·al** \-shə-nəl\ *adj* — **frac·tion·al·ly** *adv*

frac·tious \'frak-shəs\ *adj* **1** : tending to be troublesome : hard to handle or control **2** : QUARRELSOME, IRRITABLE

frac·ture \'frak-chər\ *n* **1** : a breaking of something and esp. a bone **2** : CRACK, CLEFT — **fracture** *vb*

frag·ile \'fra-jəl, -ˌjī(-ə)l\ *adj* : easily broken — **fra·gil·i·ty** \frə-'ji-lə-tē\ *n*

¹frag·ment \'frag-mənt\ *n* : a part broken off, detached, or incomplete

²frag·ment \-ˌment\ *vb* : to break into fragments — **frag·men·ta·tion** \ˌfrag-mən-'tā-shən, -ˌmən-\ *n*

frag·men·tary \'frag-mən-ˌter-ē\ *adj* : made up of fragments : INCOMPLETE ⟨a ~ account⟩

fra·grant \'frā-grənt\ *adj* : sweet or agreeable in smell — **fra·grance** \-grəns\ *n* — **fra·grant·ly** *adv*

frail \'frāl\ *adj* [ME, fr. AF *fraile,* fr. L *fragilis* fragile, fr. *frangere* to break] **1** : morally or physically weak **2** : FRAGILE, DELICATE

frail·ty \'frāl-tē\ *n, pl* **frailties** **1** : the quality or state of being frail **2** : a fault due to weakness

¹frame \'frām\ *vb* **framed; fram·ing** **1** : PLAN, CONTRIVE **2** : SHAPE, CONSTRUCT **3** : FORMULATE **4** : DRAW UP ⟨~ a constitution⟩ **5** : to make appear guilty **6** : to fit or adjust for a purpose : ARRANGE **7** : to provide with or enclose in a frame — **fram·er** *n*

²frame *n* **1** : something made of parts fitted and joined together **2** : the physical makeup of the body **3** : an arrangement of structural parts that gives form or support **4** : a supporting or enclosing border or open case (as for a window or picture) **5** : one picture of a series (as on a length of film) **6** : FRAME-UP

³frame *adj* : having a wood frame ⟨~ houses⟩

frame of mind *n* : mental attitude or outlook : MOOD

frame–up \'frā-ˌməp\ *n* **1** : an act or series of actions in which someone is framed **2** : an action that is planned, contrived, or formulated

frame·work \'frām-ˌwərk\ *n* : a basic supporting part or structure

franc \'fraŋk\ *n* **1** : any of various former basic monetary units (as of Belgium, France, and Luxembourg) **2** — see MONEY table

fran·chise \'fran-ˌchīz\ *n* [ME, fr. AF, fr. *franchir* to free, fr. *franc* free] **1** : a right or license granted to an individual or group ⟨a ~ to operate a ferry⟩ **2** : a constitutional or statutory right or privilege; *esp* : the right to vote **3** : the right of membership in a professional sports league; *also* : a team having such membership **4** : a series of related works (as novels or films) set in the same fictional universe and usu. featuring some of the same characters

fran·chi·see \ˌfran-ˌchī-'zē, -chə-\ *n* : one granted a franchise

fran·chis·er \'fran-ˌchī-zər\ *n* **1** : FRANCHISEE **2** : FRANCHISOR

fran·chi·sor \ˌfran-ˌchī-'zȯr, -chə-\ *n* : one that grants a franchise

fran·ci·um \'fran-sē-əm\ *n* : a radioactive metallic chemical element

Fran·co–Amer·i·can \ˌfraŋ-kō-ə-'mer-ə-kən\ *n* : an American of French or esp. French-Canadian descent — **Franco–American** *adj*

fran·gi·ble \'fran-jə-bəl\ *adj* : BREAKABLE — **fran·gi·bil·i·ty** \ˌfran-jə-'bi-lə-tē\ *n*

¹frank \'fraŋk\ *adj* : marked by free, forthright, and sincere expression — **frank·ness** *n*

²frank *vb* : to mark (a piece of mail) with an official sign so that it can be mailed free; *also* : to mail free

³frank *n* **1** : the signature or mark on a piece of mail indicating free or paid postage **2** : the privilege of sending mail free

⁴frank *n* : FRANKFURTER

Fran·ken·stein \'fraŋ-kən-ˌstīn\ *n* **1** : a monstrous creation that usu. ruins its originator **2** : a monster in the shape of a man

frank·furt·er \'fraŋk-fər-tər, -ˌfər-\ *or* **frank·furt** \-fərt\ *n* : a seasoned sausage (as of beef or beef and pork)

frank·in·cense \'fraŋ-kən-ˌsens\ *n* : a fragrant resin burned as incense

frank·ly \'fraŋ-klē\ *adv* **1** : in a frank manner **2** : in truth : INDEED ⟨~, I don't know⟩

fran·tic \'fran-tik\ *adj* : marked by uncontrolled emotion or disordered anxious activity — **fran·ti·cal·ly** \-ti-k(ə-)lē\ *adv*

frap·pé \fra-'pā\ *or* **frappe** *same or* 'frap\ *n* [F *frappé,* fr. pp. of *frapper* to strike, chill] **1** : an iced or frozen drink **2** : a thick milk shake — **frap·pé** \fra-'pā\ *adj*

fra·ter·nal \frə-'tər-nᵊl\ *adj* **1** : of, relating to, or involving brothers **2** : of, relating to, or being a fraternity or society 3 : derived from two ova ⟨~ twins⟩ 4 : FRIENDLY, BROTHERLY — **fra·ter·nal·ly** *adv*

fra·ter·ni·ty \frə-ˈtər-nə-tē\ *n, pl* **-ties** 1 : a social, honorary, or professional group; *esp* : a men's student organization 2 : BROTHERLINESS, BROTHERHOOD 3 : persons of the same class, profession, or tastes

frat·er·nize \ˈfra-tər-ˌnīz\ *vb* **-nized; -niz·ing** 1 : to mingle as friends 2 : to associate on close terms with members of a hostile group — **frat·er·ni·za·tion** \ˌfra-tər-nə-ˈzā-shən\ *n*

frat·ri·cide \ˈfra-trə-ˌsīd\ *n* 1 : one that kills a sibling or countryman 2 : the act of a fratricide — **frat·ri·cid·al** \ˌfra-trə-ˈsī-dᵊl\ *adj*

fraud \ˈfrȯd\ *n* 1 : DECEIT, TRICKERY 2 : TRICK 3 : IMPOSTOR, CHEAT

fraud·ster \ˈfrȯd-stər\ *n, chiefly Brit* : a person who engages in fraud

fraud·u·lent \ˈfrȯ-jə-lənt\ *adj* : characterized by, based on, or done by fraud : DECEITFUL — **fraud·u·lence** \-ləns\ *n* — **fraud·u·lent·ly** *adv*

fraught \ˈfrȯt\ *adj* : full of or accompanied by something specified ⟨~ with danger⟩

¹**fray** \ˈfrā\ *n* : FIGHT, STRUGGLE; *also* : QUARREL, DISPUTE

²**fray** *vb* 1 : to wear (as an edge of cloth) by rubbing 2 : to separate the threads at the edge of 3 : STRAIN, IRRITATE ⟨~*ed* nerves⟩

fraz·zle \ˈfra-zəl\ *vb* **fraz·zled; fraz·zling** 1 : FRAY 2 : to put in a state of extreme physical or nervous fatigue — **frazzle** *n*

¹**freak** \ˈfrēk\ *n* 1 : WHIM, CAPRICE 2 : a strange, abnormal, or unusual person or thing 3 *slang* : a person who uses an illicit drug 4 : an ardent enthusiast — **freak·ish** *adj* — **freaky** \ˈfrē-kē\ *adj*

²**freak** *vb* 1 : to experience the effects (as hallucinations) of taking illicit drugs — often used with *out* 2 : to distress or become distressed — often used with *out* — **freak–out** \ˈfrē-ˌkau̇t\ *n*

freck·le \ˈfre-kəl\ *n* : a small brownish spot on the skin — **freckle** *vb*

¹**free** \ˈfrē\ *adj* **fre·er; fre·est** 1 : having liberty 2 : enjoying political or personal independence; *also* : not subject to or allowing slavery 3 : made or done voluntarily : SPONTANEOUS 4 : relieved from or lacking something unpleasant 5 : not subject to a duty, tax, or charge 6 : not obstructed : CLEAR 7 : not being used or occupied ⟨waved with my ~ hand⟩ 8 : not fastened ⟨the ~ end of the rope⟩ 9 : LAVISH 10 : OPEN, FRANK ⟨a ~ exchange of ideas⟩ 11 : given without charge 12 : not literal or exact ⟨~ translation⟩ 13 : not restricted by conventional forms ⟨~ skating⟩ — **free·ly** *adv*

²**free** *vb* **freed; free·ing** 1 : to set free 2 : RELIEVE, RID 3 : DISENTANGLE, CLEAR ♦ ***Synonyms*** RELEASE, LIBERATE, DISCHARGE, EMANCIPATE, LOOSE

³**free** *adv* 1 : FREELY 2 : without charge

free·base \ˈfrē-ˌbās\ *n* : purified cocaine smoked as crack or heated to produce vapors for inhalation — **freebase** *vb*

free·bie *or* **free·bee** \ˈfrē-bē\ *n* : something given without charge

free·board \ˈfrē-ˌbȯrd\ *n* : the vertical distance between the waterline and the upper edge of the side of a boat

free·boo·ter \-ˌbü-tər\ *n* [D *vrijbuiter,* fr. *vrijbuit* plunder, fr. *vrij* free + *buit* booty] : PLUNDERER, PIRATE

free·born \-ˈbȯrn\ *adj* 1 : not born in vassalage or slavery 2 : of, relating to, or befitting one that is freeborn

freed·man \ˈfrēd-mən, -ˌman\ *n* : a person freed from slavery

free·dom \ˈfrē-dəm\ *n* 1 : the quality or state of being free : INDEPENDENCE 2 : EXEMPTION, RELEASE 3 : EASE, FACILITY 4 : FRANKNESS 5 : unrestricted use 6 : a political right; *also* : FRANCHISE, PRIVILEGE

freedom fighter *n* : a person who takes part in a resistance movement against an oppressive political or social establishment

free enterprise *n* : freedom of private business to operate with little regulation by the government

free–for–all \ˈfrē-fə-ˌrȯl\ *n* : a competition or fight open to all comers and usu. with no rules : BRAWL — **free–for–all** *adj*

free·hand \-ˌhand\ *adj* : done without mechanical aids or devices ⟨~ drawing⟩

free·hold \ˈfrē-ˌhōld\ *n* : ownership of an estate for life usu. with the right to bequeath it to one's heirs; *also* : an estate thus owned — **free·hold·er** *n*

free·lance \-ˌlans\ *n* : one who pursues a profession (as writing) without a long-term commitment to any one employer — **free·lance** *adj or vb*

free–living \ˈfrē-ˈli-viŋ\ *adj* 1 : unrestricted in pursuing personal pleasures 2 : being neither parasitic nor symbiotic ⟨~ organisms⟩

free·load \ˈfrē-ˌlōd\ *vb* : to impose upon another's hospitality — **free·load·er** *n*

free love *n* 1 : the practice of living openly with one of the opposite sex without marriage 2 : sexual relations without any commitments by either partner

free·man \ˈfrē-mən, -ˌman\ *n* 1 : one who has civil or political liberty 2 : one having the full rights of a citizen

Free·ma·son \-ˌmā-sᵊn\ *n* : a member of a secret fraternal society called Free and Accepted Masons — **Free·ma·son·ry** \-rē\ *n*

free radical *n* : an esp. reactive atom or group of atoms with one or more unpaired electrons; *esp* : one that can cause bodily damage (as by altering the chemical structure of cells)

free–range \ˈfrē-ˌrānj\ *adj* : allowed to range and forage with relative freedom ⟨~ chickens⟩; *also* : produced by free-range animals ⟨~ eggs⟩

free speech *n* : speech that is protected

by the First Amendment to the U.S. Constitution

free spirit *n* : NONCONFORMIST

free•stand•ing \ˈfrē-ˈstan-diŋ\ *adj* : standing alone or on its own foundation free of support

free•stone \ˈfrē-ˌstōn\ *n* **1** : a stone that may be cut freely without splitting **2** : a fruit stone to which the flesh does not cling; *also* : a fruit (as a peach or cherry) having such a stone

free•think•er \-ˈthiŋ-kər\ *n* : one who forms opinions on the basis of reason independently of authority; *esp* : one who doubts or denies religious dogma — **free•think•ing** *n or adj*

free trade *n* : trade between nations without restrictions (as high taxes on imports)

free verse *n* : verse whose meter is irregular or whose rhythm is not metrical

free•ware \ˈfrē-ˌwer\ *n* : software that is free or that has a small usu. optional cost

free•way \ˈfrē-ˌwā\ *n* : an expressway without tolls

free•wheel \-ˈhwēl\ *vb* : to move, live, or play freely or irresponsibly

free•will \ˈfrē-ˌwil\ *adj* : VOLUNTARY

free will *n* : voluntary choice or decision

[1]**freeze** \ˈfrēz\ *vb* **froze** \ˈfrōz\; **fro•zen** \ˈfrō-zᵊn\; **freez•ing** **1** : to harden or cause to harden into a solid (as ice) by loss of heat **2** : to withstand freezing **3** : to chill or become chilled with cold **4** : to damage by frost **5** : to adhere solidly by or as if by freezing **6** : to become fixed, motionless, or incapable of speech **7** : to cause to grip tightly **8** : to become clogged with ice **9** : to fix at a certain stage or level ⟨~ wages⟩

[2]**freeze** *n* **1** : an act or instance of freezing **2** : the state of being frozen **3** : a state of weather marked by low temperature

freeze–dry \ˈfrēz-ˈdrī\ *vb* : to dry in a frozen state under vacuum esp. for preservation — **freeze–dried** *adj*

freez•er \ˈfrē-zər\ *n* : a compartment, device, or room for freezing food or keeping it frozen

[1]**freight** \ˈfrāt\ *n* **1** : payment for carrying goods **2** : CARGO **3** : BURDEN **4** : the carrying of goods by a common carrier **5** : a train that carries freight

[2]**freight** *vb* **1** : to load with goods for transportation **2** : BURDEN, CHARGE **3** : to ship or transport by freight

freight•er \ˈfrā-tər\ *n* : a ship or airplane used chiefly to carry freight

French \ˈfrench\ *n* **1** : the language of France **2 French** *pl* : the people of France **3** : strong language ⟨pardon my ~⟩ — **French** *adj* — **French•man** \-mən\ *n* — **French•wom•an** \-ˌwu̇-mən\ *n*

French door *n* : a door with small panes of glass extending the full length

French dressing *n* **1** : a thin salad dressing usu. made of vinegar and oil with spices **2** : a creamy salad dressing flavored with tomatoes

french fry *n, often cap 1st F* : a strip of potato fried in deep fat until brown — **french fry** *vb, often cap 1st F*

French horn *n* : a curved brass instrument with a funnel-shaped mouthpiece and a flaring bell

French press *n* : a coffeepot in which ground beans are infused and then pressed by a plunger

French toast *n* : bread dipped in a mixture of eggs and milk and fried at a low heat

French twist *n* : a woman's hairstyle in which the hair is coiled at the rear and secured in place

fren•e•my \ˈfre-nə-mē\ *n, pl* **-mies** : one who pretends to be a friend but is actually an enemy

fre•net•ic \fri-ˈne-tik\ *adj* : FRANTIC — **fre•net•i•cal•ly** \-ti-k(ə-)lē\ *adv*

fren•zy \ˈfren-zē\ *n, pl* **frenzies** **1** : temporary madness or a violently agitated state **2** : intense often disordered activity — **fren•zied** \-zēd\ *adj*

freq *abbr* frequency; frequent; frequently

fre•quen•cy \ˈfrē-kwən-sē\ *n, pl* **-cies** **1** : the fact or condition of occurring frequently **2** : rate of occurrence **3** : the number of cycles per second of an alternating current **4** : the number of waves (as of sound or electromagnetic energy) that pass a fixed point each second

frequency modulation *n* : variation of the frequency of a carrier wave according to another signal; *also* : FM

[1]**fre•quent** \frē-ˈkwent, ˈfrē-kwənt\ *vb* : to associate with, be in, or resort to habitually — **fre•quent•er** *n*

[2]**fre•quent** \ˈfrē-kwənt\ *adj* **1** : happening often or at short intervals ⟨making ~ stops⟩ **2** : HABITUAL ⟨a ~ visitor⟩ — **fre•quent•ly** *adv*

fre•quent–fli•er \ˈfrē-kwənt-ˈflī-ər\ *adj* : of, relating to, or being an airline program offering awards for specified numbers of air miles traveled

fres•co \ˈfres-kō\ *n, pl* **frescoes** [It, fr. *fresco* fresh] : the art of painting on fresh plaster; *also* : a painting done by this method

fresh \ˈfresh\ *adj* **1** : VIGOROUS, REFRESHED **2** : not stale, sour, or decayed **3** : not faded **4** : not worn or rumpled **5** : not altered by processing (as freezing or canning) **6** : not containing salt **7** : free from taint : PURE ⟨~ air⟩ **8** : fairly strong : BRISK ⟨~ breeze⟩ **9** : experienced, made, or received newly or anew **10** : ADDITIONAL, ANOTHER ⟨a ~ start⟩ **11** : ORIGINAL, VIVID **12** : INEXPERIENCED **13** : newly come or arrived ⟨~ from school⟩ **14** : IMPUDENT — **fresh•ly** *adv* — **fresh•ness** *n*

fresh•en \ˈfre-shən\ *vb* : to make, grow, or become fresh

fresh•et \ˈfre-shət\ *n* : an overflowing of a stream (as by heavy rains)

fresh•man \ˈfresh-mən\ *n* **1** : a 1st-year student in high school or college **2** : BEGINNER, NEWCOMER

fresh•wa•ter \-ˌwȯ-tər, -ˌwä-\ *n* : water that is not salty — **freshwater** *adj*

[1]**fret** \ˈfret\ *vb* **fret•ted; fret•ting** [ME, to devour, fret, fr. OE *fretan* to devour] **1**

: WEAR, CORRODE; *also* : FRAY **2** : RUB, CHAFE **3** : to make by wearing away **4** : to become irritated : WORRY, VEX ⟨*fretted* over his taxes⟩ **5** : GRATE; *also* : AGITATE

²**fret** *n* : an irritated or worried state ⟨in a ~ about the interview⟩

³**fret** *n* : ornamental work esp. of straight lines in symmetrical patterns

⁴**fret** *n* : one of a series of ridges across the fingerboard of a stringed musical instrument — **fret·ted** *adj*

fret·ful \ˈfret-fəl\ *adj* : IRRITABLE — **fret·ful·ly** *adv* — **fret·ful·ness** *n*

fret·saw \-ˌsȯ\ *n* : a narrow-bladed handsaw used for cutting curved outlines

fret·work \-ˌwərk\ *n* **1** : decoration consisting of frets **2** : ornamental openwork or work in relief

Fri *abbr* Friday

fri·a·ble \ˈfrī-ə-bəl\ *adj* : easily crumbled or pulverized ⟨~ soil⟩

fri·ar \ˈfrī(-ə)r\ *n* [ME *frere, fryer,* fr. AF *frere, friere,* lit., brother, fr. L *frater*] : a member of a religious order that orig. lived by alms

fri·ary \ˈfrī(-ə)r-ē\ *n, pl* **-ar·ies** : a monastery of friars

¹**fric·as·see** \ˈfri-kə-ˌsē, ˌfri-kə-ˈsē\ *n* : a dish made of meat (as chicken) cut into pieces, stewed in stock, and served in sauce

²**fricassee** *vb* **-seed; -see·ing** : to cook as a fricassee

fric·tion \ˈfrik-shən\ *n* **1** : the rubbing of one body against another **2** : the force that resists motion between bodies in contact **3** : clash in opinions between persons or groups : DISAGREEMENT — **fric·tion·al** *adj*

friction tape *n* : a usu. cloth adhesive tape impregnated with insulating material and used esp. to protect and insulate electrical conductors

Fri·day \ˈfrī-dē, -(ˌ)dā\ *n* : the sixth day of the week

fridge \ˈfrij\ *n* : REFRIGERATOR

fried·cake \ˈfrīd-ˌkāk\ *n* : DOUGHNUT, CRULLER

fried rice *n* : a dish of boiled or steamed rice that is stir-fried with soy sauce and typically includes egg, meat, and vegetables

¹**friend** \ˈfrend\ *n* **1** : one attached to another by respect or affection **2** : ACQUAINTANCE **3** : one who is not hostile **4** : one who supports or favors something ⟨a ~ of art⟩ **5** *cap* : a member of the Society of Friends : QUAKER — **friend·less** *adj* — **friend·li·ness** \-lē-nəs\ *n* — **friend·ly** *adj* — **friend·ship** \-ˌship\ *n*

²**friend** *vb* **1** : BEFRIEND **2** : to include (someone) in a list of designated friends on a person's social networking site

frieze \ˈfrēz\ *n* : an ornamental often sculptured band extending around something (as a building or room)

frig·ate \ˈfri-gət\ *n* **1** : a square-rigged warship **2** : a warship smaller than a destroyer

fright \ˈfrīt\ *n* **1** : sudden terror : ALARM **2** : something that is ugly or shocking

fright·en \ˈfrī-tᵊn\ *vb* **1** : to make afraid **2** : to drive away or out by frightening **3** : to become frightened — **fright·en·ing·ly** *adv*

fright·ful \ˈfrīt-fəl\ *adj* **1** : TERRIFYING **2** : STARTLING **3** : EXTREME ⟨~ thirst⟩ — **fright·ful·ly** *adv* — **fright·ful·ness** *n*

frig·id \ˈfri-jəd\ *adj* **1** : intensely cold **2** : lacking warmth or ardor : INDIFFERENT **3** : abnormally averse to or unable to achieve orgasm during sexual intercourse — used esp. of women — **fri·gid·i·ty** \fri-ˈji-də-tē\ *n*

frigid zone *n* : the area or region between the arctic circle and the north pole or between the antarctic circle and the south pole

frill \ˈfril\ *n* **1** : a gathered, pleated, or ruffled edging **2** : something unessential — **frilly** *adj*

fringe \ˈfrinj\ *n* [ME *frenge,* fr. AF, fr. VL **frimbia,* alter. of L *fimbriae* (pl.)] **1** : an ornamental border consisting of short threads or strips hanging from an edge or band **2** : something that resembles a fringe : EDGE ⟨operated on the ~*s* of the law⟩ **3** : something that is additional or secondary to an activity, process, or subject — **fringe** *vb*

fringe benefit *n* **1** : an employment benefit paid for by an employer without affecting basic wage rates **2** : any additional benefit

frip·pery \ˈfri-pə-rē\ *n, pl* **-per·ies** [MF *friperie*] **1** : FINERY **2** : pretentious display

frisk \ˈfrisk\ *vb* **1** : to leap, skip, or dance in a lively or playful way : GAMBOL **2** : to search (a person) esp. for concealed weapons by running the hand rapidly over the clothing

frisky \ˈfris-kē\ *adj* **frisk·i·er; -est** : PLAYFUL — **frisk·i·ly** \-kə-lē\ *adv* — **frisk·i·ness** \-kē-nəs\ *n*

¹**frit·ter** \ˈfri-tər\ *n* : a small lump of fried batter often containing fruit or meat

²**fritter** *vb* **1** : to reduce or waste piecemeal **2** : to break into small fragments

fritz \ˈfrits\ *n* : a state of disorder or disrepair — used in the phrase *on the fritz*

friv·o·lous \ˈfri-və-ləs\ *adj* **1** : of little importance : TRIVIAL **2** : lacking in seriousness — **fri·vol·i·ty** \fri-ˈvä-lə-tē\ *n* — **friv·o·lous·ly** *adv*

frizz \ˈfriz\ *vb* : to form into small tight curls — **frizz** *n* — **frizzy** *adj*

friz·zies \ˈfri-zēz\ *n pl* : hair which has become difficult to manage (as due to humidity)

¹**friz·zle** \ˈfri-zəl\ *vb* **friz·zled; friz·zling** : FRIZZ, CURL — **frizzle** *n*

²**frizzle** *vb* **friz·zled; friz·zling** **1** : to fry until crisp and curled **2** : to cook with a sizzling noise

fro \ˈfrō\ *adv* : BACK, AWAY — used in the phrase *to and fro*

frock \ˈfräk\ *n* **1** : an outer garment worn by monks and friars **2** : an outer garment worn esp. by men **3 :** a woman's or girl's dress

frock coat *n* **:** a man's knee-length usu. double-breasted coat

frog \ˈfrȯg, ˈfräg\ *n* **1 :** any of various largely aquatic smooth-skinned tailless leaping amphibians **2 :** an ornamental braiding for fastening the front of a garment by a loop through which a button passes **3 :** a condition in the throat causing hoarseness **4 :** a small holder (as of metal, glass, or plastic) with perforations or spikes that is placed in a bowl or vase to keep cut flowers in position

frog·man \ˈfrȯg-ˌman, ˈfräg-, -mən\ *n* **:** a swimmer equipped to work underwater for long periods of time

[1]**frol·ic** \ˈfrä-lik\ *vb* **frol·icked; frol·ick·ing 1 :** to make merry **2 :** to play about happily **:** ROMP

[2]**frolic** *n* **1 :** a playful or mischievous action **2 :** FUN, MERRIMENT — **frol·ic·some** \-səm\ *adj*

from \ˈfrəm, ˈfräm\ *prep* **1** — used to show a starting point ⟨a letter ~ home⟩ **2** — used to show removal or separation ⟨subtract 3 ~ 9⟩ **3** — used to show a material, source, or cause ⟨suffering ~ a cold⟩

frond \ˈfränd\ *n* **:** a usu. large divided leaf esp. of a fern or palm tree

[1]**front** \ˈfrənt\ *n* **1 :** FOREHEAD; *also* **:** the whole face **2 :** external and often feigned appearance **3 :** a region of active fighting; *also* **:** a sphere of activity **4 :** a political coalition **5 :** the side of a building containing the main entrance **6 :** the forward part or surface **7 :** FRONTAGE **8 :** a boundary between two dissimilar air masses **9 :** a position directly before or ahead of something else **10 :** a person, group, or thing used to mask the identity of the actual controlling agent

[2]**front** *vb* **1 :** to have the principal side adjacent to something **2 :** to serve as a front **3 :** CONFRONT

front·age \ˈfrən-tij\ *n* **1 :** a piece of land lying adjacent (as to a street or the ocean) **2 :** the length of a frontage **3 :** the front side of a building

front·al \ˈfrən-t^{ə}l\ *adj* **1 :** of, relating to, or next to the forehead **2 :** of, relating to, or directed at the front ⟨a ~ attack⟩ — **fron·tal·ly** *adv*

fron·tier \ˌfrən-ˈtir\ *n* **1 :** a border between two countries **2 :** a region that forms the margin of settled territory **3 :** the outer limits of knowledge or achievement ⟨the ~*s* of science⟩ — **fron·tiers·man** \-ˈtirz-mən\ *n*

fron·tis·piece \ˈfrən-tə-ˌspēs\ *n* **:** an illustration preceding and usu. facing the title page of a book

front man *n* **:** a person serving as a front or figurehead

front·ward \ˈfrənt-wərd\ *or* **front·wards** \-wərdz\ *adv or adj* **:** toward the front

[1]**frost** \ˈfrȯst\ *n* **1 :** freezing temperature **2 :** a covering of tiny ice crystals on a cold surface — **frosty** *adj*

[2]**frost** *vb* **1 :** to cover with frost **2 :** to put icing on (as a cake) **3 :** to produce a slightly roughened surface on (as glass) **4 :** to injure or kill by frost

[1]**frost·bite** \ˈfrȯst-ˌbīt\ *vb* **-bit** \-ˌbit\; **-bit·ten** \-ˌbi-t^{ə}n\; **-bit·ing :** to injure by frost or frostbite

[2]**frostbite** *n* **:** the freezing or the local effect of a partial freezing of some part of the body

frost heave *n* **:** an upthrust of pavement caused by freezing of moist soil

frost·ing \ˈfrȯs-tiŋ\ *n* **1 :** ICING **2 :** dull finish on metal or glass

froth \ˈfrȯth\ *n, pl* **froths** \ˈfrȯths, ˈfrȯthz\ [ME, fr. ON *frotha*] **1 :** bubbles formed in or on a liquid **2 :** something light or worthless — **frothy** *adj*

frou·frou \ˈfrü-ˌfrü\ *n* [F] **1 :** a rustling esp. of a woman's skirts **2 :** showy or frilly ornamentation

fro·ward \ˈfrō-wərd\ *adj* **:** DISOBEDIENT, WILLFUL

frown \ˈfrau̇n\ *vb* **1 :** to wrinkle the forehead (as in displeasure or thought) **2 :** to look with disapproval **3 :** to express with a frown — **frown** *n*

frow·sy *or* **frow·zy** \ˈfrau̇-zē\ *adj* **frow·si·er** *or* **frow·zi·er; -est :** having a slovenly or uncared-for appearance

froze *past of* FREEZE

fro·zen \ˈfrō-z^{ə}n\ *adj* **1 :** treated, affected, or crusted over by freezing **2 :** subject to long and severe cold **3 :** incapable of being changed, moved, or undone **:** FIXED ⟨~ wages⟩ **4 :** not available for present use ⟨~ capital⟩ **5 :** expressing or characterized by cold unfriendliness

FRS *abbr* Federal Reserve System

frt *abbr* freight

fruc·ti·fy \ˈfrək-tə-ˌfī, ˈfru̇k-\ *vb* **-fied; -fy·ing 1 :** to bear fruit **2 :** to make fruitful or productive

fruc·tose \ˈfrək-ˌtōs, ˈfru̇k-\ *n* **:** a very sweet soluble sugar that occurs esp. in fruit juices and honey

fru·gal \ˈfrü-gəl\ *adj* **:** ECONOMICAL, THRIFTY — **fru·gal·i·ty** \frü-ˈga-lə-tē\ *n* — **fru·gal·ly** *adv*

[1]**fruit** \ˈfrüt\ *n* [ME, fr. AF *frut, fruit,* fr. L *fructus* fruit, use, fr. *frui* to enjoy, have the use of] **1 :** a product of plant growth; *esp* **:** a usu. edible and sweet reproductive body of a seed plant **2 :** a product of fertilization in a plant; *esp* **:** the ripe ovary of a seed plant with its contents and appendages **3 :** CONSEQUENCE, RESULT — **fruit·ed** \ˈfrü-təd\ *adj*

[2]**fruit** *vb* **:** to bear or cause to bear fruit

fruit·cake \ˈfrüt-ˌkāk\ *n* **:** a rich cake containing nuts, dried or candied fruits, and spices

fruit fly *n* **:** any of various small dipteran flies whose larvae feed on fruit or decaying vegetable matter

fruit·ful \ˈfrüt-fəl\ *adj* **1 :** yielding or producing fruit **2 :** very productive; *also* **:** bringing results ⟨a ~ idea⟩ — **fruit·ful·ly** *adv* — **fruit·ful·ness** *n*

fru·ition \frü-ˈi-shən\ *n* **1 :** ENJOYMENT **2 :** the state of bearing fruit **3**

: REALIZATION, ACCOMPLISHMENT ⟨guided the project to ~⟩
fruit·less \ˈfrüt-ləs\ *adj* **1** : not bearing fruit **2** : UNSUCCESSFUL ⟨a ~ attempt⟩ — **fruit·less·ly** *adv*
fruity \ˈfrü-tē\ *adj* **fruit·i·er; -est** : resembling a fruit esp. in flavor
frumpy \ˈfrəm-pē\ *adj* **frump·i·er; -est** : DOWDY, DRAB ⟨a ~ dress⟩
frus·trate \ˈfrəs-ˌtrāt\ *vb* **frus·trat·ed; frus·trat·ing 1** : to balk or defeat in an endeavor **2** : to induce feelings of insecurity, discouragement, or dissatisfaction in **3** : to bring to nothing — **frus·trat·ing·ly** *adv* — **frus·tra·tion** \ˌfrəs-ˈtrā-shən\ *n*
frus·tum \ˈfrəs-təm\ *n, pl* **frustums** *or* **frus·ta** \-tə\ : the part of a cone or pyramid formed by cutting off the top by a plane parallel to the base
frwy *abbr* freeway
[1]**fry** \ˈfrī\ *vb* **fried; fry·ing** [ME *frien,* fr. AF *frire,* fr. L *frigere* to roast] **1** : to cook in a pan or on a griddle over heat esp. with the use of fat **2** : to undergo frying **3** : to damage or destroy by overheating esp. by high voltage
[2]**fry** *n, pl* **fries 1** : a social gathering where fried food is eaten **2** : a dish of something fried; *esp, pl* : FRENCH FRIES
[3]**fry** *n, pl* **fry** [ME, fr. AF *frie,* fr. *freier, frier* to rub, spawn, fr. L *fricare* to rub] **1** : recently hatched fishes; *also* : very small adult fishes **2** : members of a group or class ⟨small ~⟩
fry·er \ˈfrī(-ə)r\ *n* **1** : something (as a young chicken) suitable for frying **2** : a deep utensil for frying foods
FSLIC *abbr* Federal Savings and Loan Insurance Corporation
ft *abbr* **1** feet; foot **2** fort
FTC *abbr* Federal Trade Commission
FTP \ˌef-ˌtē-ˈpē\ *n* [*f*ile *t*ransfer *p*rotocol] : a system for transferring computer files esp. via the Internet — **FTP** *vb*
fuch·sia \ˈfyü-shə\ *n* **1** : any of a genus of shrubs related to the evening primrose and grown for their showy nodding often red or purple flowers **2** : a vivid reddish purple color
fud·dle \ˈfə-dᵊl\ *vb* **fud·dled; fud·dling** : MUDDLE, CONFUSE
fud·dy–dud·dy \ˈfə-dē-ˌdə-dē\ *n, pl* **-dies** : one that is old-fashioned, unimaginative, or conservative
[1]**fudge** \ˈfəj\ *vb* **fudged; fudg·ing 1** : to exceed the proper bounds of something **2** : CHEAT; *also* : FALSIFY ⟨*fudged* their data⟩ **3** : to fail to come to grips with
[2]**fudge** *n* **1** : NONSENSE **2** : a soft candy of milk, sugar, butter, and flavoring
[1]**fu·el** \ˈfyü-əl, ˈfyül\ *n* : a material used to produce heat or power by burning; *also* : a material from which nuclear energy can be liberated
[2]**fuel** *vb* **-eled** *or* **-elled; -el·ing** *or* **-el·ling** : to provide with or take in fuel
fuel cell *n* : a device that continuously changes the chemical energy of a fuel directly into electrical energy
fuel injection *n* : a system for injecting a precise amount of atomized fuel into an internal combustion engine — **fuel–in·ject·ed** \ˈfyül-in-ˈjek-təd\ *adj*
[1]**fu·gi·tive** \ˈfyü-jə-tiv\ *adj* **1** : running away or trying to escape **2** : likely to vanish suddenly : not fixed or lasting
[2]**fugitive** *n* **1** : one who flees or tries to escape **2** : something elusive or hard to find
fugue \ˈfyüg\ *n* **1** : a musical composition in which different parts successively repeat the theme **2** : a disturbed state of consciousness characterized by acts that are not recalled upon recovery
füh·rer *or* **fueh·rer** \ˈfyu̇r-ər, ˈfir-\ *n* [G] : LEADER; *esp* : TYRANT
[1]**-ful** \fəl\ *adj suffix, sometimes* **-ful·ler;** *sometimes* **-ful·lest 1** : full of ⟨pride*ful*⟩ **2** : characterized by ⟨peace*ful*⟩ **3** : having the qualities of ⟨master*ful*⟩ **4** : tending, given, or liable to ⟨help*ful*⟩
[2]**-ful** \ˌfu̇l\ *n suffix* : number or quantity that fills or would fill ⟨room*ful*⟩
ful·crum \ˈfu̇l-krəm, ˈfəl-\ *n, pl* **ful·crums** *or* **ful·cra** \-krə\ [LL, fr. L, bedpost] : the support on which a lever turns
ful·fill *or* **ful·fil** \fu̇l-ˈfil\ *vb* **ful·filled; ful·fill·ing 1** : to put into effect **2** : to bring to an end **3** : SATISFY ⟨~*ed* expectations⟩ — **ful·fill·ment** *or* **ful·fil·ment** *n*
[1]**full** \ˈfu̇l\ *adj* **1** : FILLED **2** : complete esp. in detail, number, or duration **3** : having all the distinguishing characteristics ⟨a ~ member⟩ **4** : MAXIMUM ⟨~ strength⟩ **5** : rounded in outline ⟨a ~ figure⟩ **6** : possessing or containing an abundance ⟨~ of wrinkles⟩ **7** : having an abundance of material ⟨a ~ skirt⟩ **8** : satisfied esp. with food or drink **9** : having volume or depth of sound **10** : completely occupied with a thought or plan — **full·ness** *also* **ful·ness** *n*
[2]**full** *adv* **1** : VERY, EXTREMELY **2** : ENTIRELY ⟨fill a glass ~⟩ **3** : STRAIGHT, SQUARELY ⟨hit him ~ in the face⟩
[3]**full** *n* **1** : the highest or fullest state or degree **2** : the utmost extent— **in full** : to the requisite or complete amount
[4]**full** *vb* : to shrink and thicken (woolen cloth) by moistening, heating, and pressing — **full·er** *n*
full·back \ˈfu̇l-ˌbak\ *n* : a football back stationed between the halfbacks
full–blood·ed \ˈfu̇l-ˈblə-dəd\ *adj* : of unmixed ancestry : PUREBRED
full–blown \-ˈblōn\ *adj* **1** : being at the height of bloom **2** : fully mature or developed
full–bod·ied \-ˈbä-dēd\ *adj* : marked by richness and fullness
full dress *n* : the style of dress worn for ceremonial or formal occasions
full–fledged \ˈfu̇l-ˈflejd\ *adj* **1** : fully developed **2** : having attained complete status ⟨a ~ lawyer⟩
full house *n* : a poker hand containing three of a kind and a pair
full moon *n* : the moon with its whole disk illuminated
full–on \-ˌȯn, -ˌän\ *adj* : COMPLETE, FULL-FLEDGED

full–scale \ˈfu̇l-ˈskāl\ *adj* **1** : identical to an original in proportion and size ⟨~ drawing⟩ **2** : involving full use of available resources ⟨a ~ revolt⟩
full–term \-ˌtərm\ *adj* : retained in the uterus for the normal period of gestation before birth ⟨a ~ baby⟩
full–throat·ed \-ˈthrō-təd\ *adj* : loudly and powerfully voiced ⟨a ~ cry⟩; *also* : having a loud and powerful voice **2** : expressed with or marked by unreserved enthusiasm or conviction
full tilt *adv* : at high speed
full–time \ˈfu̇l-ˈtīm\ *adj or adv* : involving or working a normal or standard schedule
ful·ly \ˈfu̇-lē\ *adv* **1** : in a full manner or degree : COMPLETELY **2** : at least
ful·mi·nate \ˈfu̇l-mə-ˌnāt, ˈfəl-\ *vb* **-nat·ed; -nat·ing** [ME, fr. ML *fulminatus,* pp. of *fulminare,* fr. L, to strike (of lightning), fr. *fulmen* lightning] : to utter or send out censure or invective : condemn severely ⟨*fulminated* against the tax increase⟩ — **ful·mi·na·tion** \ˌfu̇l-mə-ˈnā-shən, ˌfəl-\ *n*
ful·some \ˈfu̇l-səm\ *adj* **1** : COPIOUS, ABUNDANT ⟨~ detail⟩ **2** : generous in amount or extent ⟨a ~ victory⟩ **3** : excessively flattering ⟨~ praise⟩
fu·ma·role \ˈfyü-mə-ˌrōl\ *n* : a hole in a volcanic region from which hot gases issue
fum·ble \ˈfəm-bəl\ *vb* **fum·bled; fum·bling** **1** : to grope about clumsily **2** : to fail to hold, catch, or handle properly — **fumble** *n*
[1]**fume** \ˈfyüm\ *n* : a usu. irritating smoke, vapor, or gas
[2]**fume** *vb* **fumed; fum·ing** **1** : to treat with fumes **2** : to give off fumes **3** : to express anger or annoyance
fu·mi·gant \ˈfyü-mi-gənt\ *n* : a substance used for fumigation
fu·mi·gate \ˈfyü-mə-ˌgāt\ *vb* **-gat·ed; -gat·ing** : to treat with fumes to disinfect or destroy pests — **fu·mi·ga·tion** \ˌfyü-mə-ˈgā-shən\ *n* — **fu·mi·ga·tor** \ˈfyü-mə-ˌgā-tər\ *n*
[1]**fun** \ˈfən\ *n* [E dial. *fun* to hoax] **1** : something that provides amusement or enjoyment **2** : ENJOYMENT
[2]**fun** *adj* : full of fun ⟨a ~ person⟩ ⟨had a ~ time⟩
[1]**func·tion** \ˈfəŋk-shən\ *n* **1** : OCCUPATION **2** : special purpose **3** : the particular purpose for which a person or thing is specially fitted or used or for which a thing exists ⟨the ~ of a hammer⟩; *also* : the natural or proper action of a bodily part in a living thing ⟨the ~ of the heart⟩ **4** : a formal ceremony or social affair **5** : a mathematical relationship that assigns to each element of a set one and only one element of the same or another set **6** : a variable (as a quality, trait, or measurement) that depends on and varies with another ⟨height is a ~ of age in children⟩ **7** : a computer subroutine that performs a calculation with variables provided by a program — **func·tion·al** \-shə-nəl\ *adj* — **func·tion·al·ly** *adv*
[2]**function** *vb* : to have or carry on a function ⟨the computer ~*s* well⟩
func·tion·ary \ˈfəŋk-shə-ˌner-ē\ *n, pl* **-ar·ies** : one who performs a certain function; *esp* : OFFICIAL
function word *n* : a word (as a preposition, auxiliary verb, or conjunction) expressing the grammatical relationship between other words
[1]**fund** \ˈfənd\ *n* [L *fundus* bottom, country estate] **1** : a sum of money or resources intended for a special purpose **2** : STORE, SUPPLY **3** *pl* : available money **4** : an organization administering a special fund
[2]**fund** *vb* **1** : to provide funds for ⟨~*ed* cancer research⟩ **2** : to convert (a short-term obligation) into a long-term interest-bearing debt — **fund·er** *n*
fun·da·men·tal \ˌfən-də-ˈmen-tᵊl\ *adj* **1** : serving as an origin : PRIMARY **2** : BASIC, ESSENTIAL **3** : RADICAL ⟨~ change⟩ **4** : of central importance : PRINCIPAL ⟨~ purpose⟩ — **fundamental** *n* — **fun·da·men·tal·ly** *adv*
fun·da·men·tal·ism \-tə-ˌli-zəm\ *n* **1** *often cap* : a Protestant movement emphasizing the literal infallibility of the Bible **2** : a movement or attitude stressing strict adherence to a set of basic principles — **fun·da·men·tal·ist** \-list\ *adj or n*
[1]**fu·ner·al** \ˈfyü-nə-rəl\ *adj* **1** : of, relating to, or constituting a funeral **2** : FUNEREAL 2
[2]**funeral** *n* : the ceremonies held for a dead person usu. before burial
fu·ner·ary \ˈfyü-nə-ˌrer-ē\ *adj* : of, used for, or associated with burial ⟨~ rites⟩
fu·ne·re·al \fyu̇-ˈnir-ē-əl\ *adj* **1** : of or relating to a funeral **2** : suggesting a funeral ⟨a ~ mood⟩
fun·gi·ble \ˈfən-jə-bəl\ *adj* **1** : having such a nature that one part or quantity may be replaced by another part or quantity in satisfaction of an obligation ⟨~ goods⟩ **2** : capable of mutual substitution : INTERCHANGEABLE **3** : FLEXIBLE 3
fun·gi·cide \ˈfən-jə-ˌsīd, ˈfəŋ-gə-\ *n* : an agent that kills or checks the growth of fungi — **fun·gi·cid·al** \ˌfən-jə-ˈsī-dᵊl, ˌfəŋ-gə-\ *adj*
fun·gus \ˈfəŋ-gəs\ *n, pl* **fun·gi** \ˈfən-ˌjī, ˈfəŋ-ˌgī\ *also* **fun·gus·es** \ˈfəŋ-gə-səz\ : any of a kingdom of parasitic spore-producing organisms (as molds and mushrooms) formerly classified as plants — **fun·gal** \-gəl\ *adj* — **fun·gous** \-gəs\ *adj*
fu·nic·u·lar \fyu̇-ˈni-kyə-lər, fə-\ *n* : a cable railway ascending a mountain
[1]**funk** \ˈfəŋk\ *n* : a strong offensive smell
[2]**funk** *n* : a depressed state of mind
[3]**funk** *n* : music that combines forms of blues, gospel, or soul and is marked by a strong downbeat
funky \ˈfəŋ-kē\ *adj* **funk·i·er; -est** **1** : having an offensive smell **2** : having an earthy unsophisticated style and feeling; *esp* : having the style and feeling of older African American music or funk **3** : odd or quaint in appearance or style ⟨a ~ little restaurant⟩ — **funk·i·ness** *n*
[1]**fun·nel** \ˈfə-nᵊl\ *n* **1** : a cone-shaped uten-

sil with a tube used for catching and directing a downward flow (as of liquid) **2** : FLUE, SMOKESTACK

[2]**funnel** *vb* **-neled** *also* **-nelled; -nel·ing** *also* **-nel·ling** **1** : to pass through or as if through a funnel **2** : to move to a central point or into a central channel

fun·nies \ˈfə-nēz\ *n pl* : a comic strip or a comic section (as of a newspaper) — used with *the*

fun·ny \ˈfə-nē\ *adj* **fun·ni·er; -est** **1** : AMUSING **2** : FACETIOUS **3** : PECULIAR 3 **4** : UNDERHANDED — **funny** *adv*

funny bone *n* : a place at the back of the elbow where a blow easily compresses a nerve and causes a painful tingling sensation

fun·plex \ˈfən-ˌpleks\ *n* : a center containing various entertainment facilities

[1]**fur** \ˈfər\ *n* **1** : an article of clothing made of or with fur **2** : the hairy coat of a mammal esp. when fine, soft, and thick; *also* : this coat dressed for use — **fur** *adj* — **furred** \ˈfərd\ *adj*

[2]**fur** *abbr* furlong

fur·be·low \ˈfər-bə-ˌlō\ *n* **1** : FLOUNCE, RUFFLE **2** : showy trimming

fur·bish \ˈfər-bish\ *vb* **1** : to make lustrous : POLISH **2** : to give a new look to : RENOVATE

fu·ri·ous \ˈfyu̇r-ē-əs\ *adj* **1** : FIERCE, ANGRY, VIOLENT **2** : BOISTEROUS **3** : INTENSE ⟨∼ growth⟩ — **fu·ri·ous·ly** *adv*

furl \ˈfərl\ *vb* **1** : to wrap or roll (as a sail or a flag) close to or around something **2** : to curl in furls — **furl** *n*

fur·long \ˈfər-ˌlȯŋ\ *n* [ME, fr. OE *furlang,* fr. *furh* furrow + *lang* long] : a unit of distance equal to 220 yards (about 201 meters)

fur·lough \ˈfər-lō\ *n* [D *verlof,* lit., permission] : a leave of absence from duty granted esp. to a soldier — **furlough** *vb*

fur·nace \ˈfər-nəs\ *n* : an enclosed structure in which heat is produced

fur·nish \ˈfər-nish\ *vb* **1** : to provide with what is needed : EQUIP **2** : SUPPLY, GIVE ⟨∼*ed* them with food⟩

fur·nish·ings \-ni-shiŋz\ *n pl* **1** : articles or accessories of dress **2** : FURNITURE

fur·ni·ture \ˈfər-ni-chər\ *n* : equipment that is necessary or desirable; *esp* : movable articles (as chairs or beds) for a room

fu·ror \ˈfyu̇r-ˌȯr\ *n* **1** : ANGER, RAGE **2** : a contagious excitement; *esp* : a fashionable craze **3** : UPROAR

fu·rore \-ˌȯr\ *n* [It] : FUROR 2, 3

fur·ri·er \ˈfər-ē-ər\ *n* : one who prepares or deals in fur

fur·ring \ˈfər-iŋ\ *n* : wood or metal strips applied to a wall or ceiling to form a level surface or an air space

fur·row \ˈfər-ō\ *n* **1** : a trench in the earth made by a plow **2** : a narrow groove or wrinkle — **furrow** *vb*

fur·ry \ˈfər-ē\ *adj* **fur·ri·er; -est** **1** : resembling or consisting of fur **2** : covered with fur

[1]**fur·ther** \ˈfər-t͟hər\ *adv* **1** : FARTHER 1 **2** : in addition : MOREOVER **3** : to a greater extent or degree

[2]**further** *vb* : to help forward — **fur·ther·ance** \ˈfər-t͟hə-rəns\ *n*

[3]**further** *adj* **1** : FARTHER 1 **2** : ADDITIONAL ⟨∼ education⟩

fur·ther·more \ˈfər-t͟hər-ˌmȯr\ *adv* : in addition to what precedes : BESIDES

fur·ther·most \-ˌmōst\ *adj* : most distant : FARTHEST

fur·thest \ˈfər-t͟həst\ *adv or adj* : FARTHEST

fur·tive \ˈfər-tiv\ *adj* [F or L; F *furtif,* fr. L *furtivus,* fr. *furtum* theft, fr. *fur* thief] : done by stealth : SLY ⟨a ∼ glance⟩ — **fur·tive·ly** *adv* — **fur·tive·ness** *n*

fu·ry \ˈfyu̇r-ē\ *n, pl* **furies** **1** : intense and often destructive rage **2** : extreme fierceness or violence **3** : FRENZY

furze \ˈfərz\ *n* : GORSE

[1]**fuse** \ˈfyüz\ *vb* **fused; fus·ing** **1** : MELT **2** : to unite by or as if by melting together — **fus·ible** *adj*

[2]**fuse** *n* : an electrical safety device having a metal wire or strip that melts and interrupts the circuit when the current becomes too strong

[3]**fuse** *n* **1** : a cord or cable that is set afire to ignite an explosive charge **2** *usu* **fuze** : a mechanical or electrical device for setting off the explosive charge of a projectile, bomb, or torpedo

[4]**fuse** *also* **fuze** \ˈfyüz\ *vb* **fused** *also* **fuzed; fus·ing** *also* **fuz·ing** : to equip with a fuse

fu·se·lage \ˈfyü-sə-ˌläzh, -zə-\ *n* : the central body portion of an aircraft

fu·sil·lade \ˈfyü-sə-ˌläd, -ˌlād\ *n* : a number of shots fired simultaneously or in rapid succession

fu·sion \ˈfyü-zhən\ *n* **1** : the act or process of melting or making plastic by heat **2** : union by or as if by melting **3** : the union of light atomic nuclei to form heavier nuclei with the release of huge quantities of energy

[1]**fuss** \ˈfəs\ *n* **1** : needless bustle or excitement : COMMOTION **2** : effusive praise **3** : a state of agitation **4** : OBJECTION, PROTEST **5** : DISPUTE

[2]**fuss** *vb* : to make a fuss

fuss·bud·get \ˈfəs-ˌbə-jət\ *n* : one who fusses or is fussy about trifles

fussy \ˈfə-sē\ *adj* **fuss·i·er; -est** **1** : IRRITABLE **2** : overly decorative ⟨a ∼ wallpaper pattern⟩ **3** : requiring or giving close attention or concern to details or niceties — **fuss·i·ly** \-sə-lē\ *adv* — **fuss·i·ness** \-sē-nəs\ *n*

fus·tian \ˈfəs-chən\ *n* **1** : a strong usu. cotton fabric **2** : pretentious writing or speech — **fustian** *adj*

fus·ty \ˈfəs-tē\ *adj* **fus·ti·er; -est** [prob. alter. of ME *foisted, foist* musty, fr. *foist* wine cask, fr. AF *fust, fuist* wood, tree trunk, cask] **1** : MUSTY **2** : OLD-FASHIONED ⟨∼ notions⟩

fut *abbr* future

fu·tile \ˈfyü-tᵊl, ˈfyü-ˌtī(-ə)l\ *adj* **1** : USELESS, VAIN **2** : FRIVOLOUS, TRIVIAL — **fu·tile·ly** *adv* — **fu·til·i·ty** \fyü-ˈti-lə-tē\ *n*

fu·ton \ˈfü-ˌtän\ *n* [Jp] : a usu. cotton-filled mattress used on the floor or in a frame as a bed, couch, or chair

[1]**fu·ture** \ˈfyü-chər\ *adj* **1** : of, relating to,

or constituting a verb tense that expresses time yet to come **2** : coming after the present

[2]**future** *n* **1** : time that is to come **2** : what is going to happen **3** : an expectation of advancement or progressive development **4** : the future tense; *also* : a verb form in it

fu·tur·ism \ˈfyü-chə-ˌri-zəm\ *n* : a modern movement in art, music, and literature that tries esp. to express the energy and activity of mechanical processes — **fu·tur·ist** \ˈfyü-chə-rist\ *n*

fu·tur·is·tic \ˌfyü-chə-ˈris-tik\ *adj* : of or relating to the future or to futurism; *also* : very modern

fu·tu·ri·ty \fyu̇-ˈtu̇r-ə-tē, -ˈtyu̇r-\ *n, pl* **-ties** **1** : FUTURE **2** : the quality or state of being future **3** *pl* : future events or prospects

fuze *var of* FUSE

fuzz \ˈfəz\ *n* : fine light particles or fibers (as of down or fluff)

fuzzy \ˈfə-zē\ *adj* **fuzz·i·er; -est** **1** : having or resembling fuzz **2** : INDISTINCT ⟨~ photos⟩ **3** : being or relating to pleasant usu. sentimental emotions ⟨~ feelings⟩ — **fuzz·i·ness** \-zē-nəs\ *n*

fuzzy logic *n* : a system of logic in which a statement can be true, false, or any of a continuum of values in between

fwd *abbr* forward

FWD *abbr* front-wheel drive

FY *abbr* fiscal year

-fy *vb suffix* : make : form into ⟨dandi*fy*⟩

FYI *abbr* for your information

G

[1]**g** \ˈjē\ *n, pl* **g's** *or* **gs** \ˈjēz\ *often cap* **1** : the 7th letter of the English alphabet **2** : a unit of force equal to the force exerted by gravity on a body at rest and used to indicate the force to which a body is subjected when accelerated **3** *slang* : a sum of $1000

[2]**g** *abbr, often cap* **1** game **2** gauge **3** good **4** gram **5** gravity

ga *abbr* gauge

[1]**Ga** *abbr* Georgia

[2]**Ga** *symbol* gallium

GA *abbr* **1** general assembly **2** general average **3** general of the army **4** Georgia

gab \ˈgab\ *vb* **gabbed; gab·bing** : to talk in a rapid or thoughtless manner : CHATTER — **gab** *n*

gab·ar·dine \ˈga-bər-ˌdēn\ *n* **1** : GABERDINE 1 **2** : a firm durable twilled fabric having diagonal ribs and made of various fibers; *also* : a garment of gabardine

gab·ble \ˈga-bəl\ *vb* **gab·bled; gab·bling** : JABBER, BABBLE

gab·by \ˈga-bē\ *adj* **gab·bi·er; -est** : TALKATIVE, GARRULOUS

gab·er·dine \ˈga-bər-ˌdēn\ *n* **1** : a long loose outer garment worn in medieval times and associated esp. with Jews **2** : GABARDINE 2

gab·fest \ˈgab-ˌfest\ *n* **1** : an informal gathering for general talk **2** : an extended conversation

ga·ble \ˈgā-bəl\ *n* : the vertical triangular end of a building formed by the sides of the roof sloping from the ridge down to the eaves — **ga·bled** \-bəld\ *adj*

gad \ˈgad\ *vb* **gad·ded; gad·ding** : to be constantly active without specific purpose — usu. used with *about* ⟨*gadded* about Europe for a year⟩ — **gad·der** *n*

gad·about \ˈga-də-ˌbau̇t\ *n* : a person who flits about in social activity

gad·fly \ˈgad-ˌflī\ *n* **1** : a fly that bites or harasses livestock **2** : a person who annoys esp. by persistent criticism

gad·get \ˈga-jət\ *n* : DEVICE, CONTRIVANCE — **gad·get·ry** \ˈga-jə-trē\ *n*

gad·o·lin·i·um \ˌga-də-ˈli-nē-əm\ *n* : a magnetic metallic chemical element

[1]**Gael** \ˈgāl\ *n* : a Celtic inhabitant of Ireland or Scotland

[2]**Gael** *abbr* Gaelic

Gael·ic \ˈgā-lik\ *adj* : of or relating to the Gaels or their languages — **Gaelic** *n*

gaff \ˈgaf\ *n* **1** : a spear used in taking fish or turtles; *also* : a metal hook for holding or lifting heavy fish **2** : the spar supporting the top of a fore-and-aft sail **3** : rough treatment : ABUSE — **gaff** *vb*

gaffe \ˈgaf\ *n* : a usu. social blunder

gaf·fer \ˈga-fər\ *n* **1** : an old man **2** : a lighting electrician on a motion-picture or television set

[1]**gag** \ˈgag\ *vb* **gagged; gag·ging** **1** : to restrict use of the mouth of with a gag **2** : to prevent from speaking freely **3** : to retch or cause to retch **4** : OBSTRUCT, CHOKE **5** : BALK **6** : to make quips — **gag·ger** *n*

[2]**gag** *n* **1** : something thrust into the mouth esp. to prevent speech or outcry **2** : an official check or restraint on free speech **3** : a laugh-provoking remark or act **4** : PRANK, TRICK

[1]**gage** \ˈgāj\ *n* **1** : a token of defiance; *esp* : a glove or cap cast on the ground as a pledge of combat **2** : SECURITY

[2]**gage** *var of* GAUGE

gag·gle \ˈga-gəl\ *n* [ME *gagyll,* fr. *gagelen* to cackle] **1** : a flock of geese **2** : an unorganized group

gai·ety *also* **gay·ety** \ˈgā-ə-tē\ *n, pl* **-eties** **1** : festive activity : MERRYMAKING **2** : MERRIMENT **3** : FINERY ♦ ***Synonyms*** MIRTH, FESTIVITY, GLEE, HILARITY, JOLLITY

gai·ly *also* **gay·ly** \ˈgā-lē\ *adv* : in a gay manner ⟨chatting ~⟩

[1]**gain** \ˈgān\ *n* **1** : PROFIT **2** : ACQUISITION, ACCUMULATION **3** : INCREASE

[2]**gain** *vb* **1** : to get possession of : EARN **2** : WIN ⟨~ a victory⟩ **3** : to increase in ⟨~ momentum⟩ **4** : PERSUADE **5** : to arrive at **6** : ACHIEVE ⟨~ strength⟩ **7** : to run fast ⟨the watch ~*s* a minute a day⟩ **8** : PROFIT **9** : INCREASE **10** : to improve in health ♦ ***Synonyms*** ACCOMPLISH, ATTAIN, REALIZE — **gain·er** *n*

gain·ful \ˈgān-fəl\ *adj* : PROFITABLE ⟨~ employment⟩ — **gain·ful·ly** *adv*

gain·say \ˌgān-ˈsā\ *vb* **-said** \-ˈsād, -ˈsed\; **-say·ing; -says** \-ˈsāz, -ˈsez\ [ME *gainsayen,* fr. *gain-* against + *sayen* to say] **1** : DENY, DISPUTE **2** : to speak against ♦ ***Synonyms*** CONTRADICT, CONTRAVENE, IMPUGN, NEGATE — **gain·say·er** *n*

gait \ˈgāt\ *n* : manner of moving on foot; *also* : a particular pattern or style of such moving — **gait·ed** *adj*

gai·ter \ˈgā-tər\ *n* **1** : a leg covering reaching from the instep to ankle, mid-calf, or knee **2** : an overshoe with a fabric upper **3** : an ankle-high shoe with elastic gores in the sides

[1]**gal** \ˈgal\ *n* : GIRL

[2]**gal** *abbr* gallon

Gal *abbr* Galatians

ga·la \ˈgā-lə, ˈga-, ˈgä-\ *n* : a festive celebration : FESTIVITY — **gala** *adj*

ga·lac·tic \gə-ˈlak-tik\ *adj* : of or relating to a galaxy

Ga·la·tians \gə-ˈlā-shənz\ *n* — see BIBLE table

gal·axy \ˈga-lək-sē\ *n, pl* **-ax·ies** [ME *galaxie, galaxias,* fr. LL *galaxias,* fr. Gk, fr. *galakt-, gala* milk] **1** *often cap* : MILKY WAY GALAXY — used with *the* **2** : a very large group of stars **3** : an assemblage of brilliant or famous persons or things

gale \ˈgāl\ *n* **1** : a strong wind **2** : an emotional outburst ⟨~*s* of laughter⟩

ga·le·na \gə-ˈlē-nə\ *n* : a lustrous bluish gray mineral that consists of the sulfide of lead and is the chief ore of lead

[1]**gall** \ˈgȯl\ *n* **1** : BILE **2** : something bitter to endure **3** : RANCOR **4** : IMPUDENCE ♦ ***Synonyms*** EFFRONTERY, BRASS, CHEEK, CHUTZPAH, AUDACITY, PRESUMPTION

[2]**gall** *n* : a skin sore caused by chafing

[3]**gall** *vb* **1** : CHAFE; *esp* : to become sore or worn by rubbing **2** : VEX, HARASS

[4]**gall** *n* : an abnormal outgrowth of plant tissue usu. due to parasites

[1]**gal·lant** \gə-ˈlant, -ˈlänt; ˈga-lənt\ *n* **1** : a young man of fashion **2** : a man who shows a marked fondness for the company of women and who is esp. attentive to them **3** : SUITOR

[2]**gal·lant** \ˈga-lənt *(usual for 2, 3, 4);* gə-ˈlant, -ˈlänt *(usual for 5)*\ *adj* **1** : showy in dress or bearing : SMART **2** : SPLENDID, STATELY **3** : SPIRITED, BRAVE **4** : CHIVALROUS, NOBLE **5** : polite and attentive to women — **gal·lant·ly** *adv*

gal·lant·ry \ˈga-lən-trē\ *n, pl* **-ries** **1** *archaic* : gallant appearance **2** : an act of marked courtesy **3** : courteous attention to a woman **4** : conspicuous bravery ♦ ***Synonyms*** HEROISM, VALOR, PROWESS

gall·blad·der \ˈgȯl-ˌbla-dər\ *n* : a membranous muscular sac attached to the liver and serving to store bile

gal·le·on \ˈga-lē-ən\ *n* : a large square-rigged sailing ship formerly used esp. by the Spanish

gal·le·ria \ˌga-lə-ˈrē-ə\ *n* [It] : a roofed and usu. glass-enclosed promenade or court

gal·lery \ˈga-lə-rē\ *n, pl* **-ler·ies** **1** : an outdoor balcony; *also* : PORCH, VERANDA **2** : a long narrow passage, apartment, or hall **3** : a narrow passage (as one made underground by a miner or through wood by an insect) **4** : a room where works of art are exhibited; *also* : an organization dealing in works of art **5** : a balcony in a theater, auditorium, or church; *esp* : the highest one in a theater **6** : the spectators at a sporting event (as a tennis or golf match) **7** : a photographer's studio — **gal·ler·ied** \-rēd\ *adj*

gal·ley \ˈga-lē\ *n, pl* **galleys** **1** : a long low ship propelled esp. by oars and formerly used esp. in the Mediterranean Sea **2** : the kitchen esp. of a ship or airplane **3** : a proof of typeset matter esp. in a single column

Gal·lic \ˈga-lik\ *adj* : of or relating to Gaul or France

gal·li·mau·fry \ˌga-lə-ˈmȯ-frē\ *n, pl* **-fries** [MF *galimafree* stew] : HODGEPODGE

gal·li·nule \ˈga-lə-ˌnül, -ˌnyül\ *n* : any of several aquatic birds related to the rails

gal·li·um \ˈga-lē-əm\ *n* : a bluish-white metallic chemical element used esp. in semiconductors

gal·li·vant \ˈga-lə-ˌvant\ *vb* : to travel, roam, or move about for pleasure

gal·lon \ˈga-lən\ *n* — see WEIGHT table

[1]**gal·lop** \ˈga-ləp\ *vb* **1** : to go or cause to go at a gallop **2** : to run fast — **gal·lop·er** *n*

[2]**gallop** *n* **1** : a bounding gait of a quadruped; *esp* : a fast 3-beat gait of a horse **2** : a ride or run at a gallop

gal·lows \ˈga-lōz\ *n, pl* **gallows** *or* **gal·lows·es** : a frame usu. of two upright posts and a crosspiece from which criminals are hanged; *also* : the punishment of hanging

gall·stone \ˈgȯl-ˌstōn\ *n* : an abnormal concretion occurring in the gallbladder or bile passages

gal·lus·es \ˈga-lə-səz\ *n pl* : SUSPENDERS

ga·lore \gə-ˈlȯr\ *adj* [Ir *go leor* enough] : ABUNDANT, PLENTIFUL

ga·losh \gə-ˈläsh\ *n* : a high overshoe

galv *abbr* galvanized

gal·va·nise *Brit var of* GALVANIZE

gal·va·nize \ˈgal-və-ˌnīz\ *vb* **-nized; -niz·ing** **1** : to stimulate as if by an electric shock ⟨~ public opinion⟩ **2** : to coat (iron or steel) with zinc — **gal·va·ni·za·tion** \ˌgal-və-nə-ˈzā-shən\ *n* — **gal·va·niz·er** *n*

gal·va·nom·e·ter \ˌgal-və-ˈnä-mə-tər\ *n* : an instrument for detecting or measuring a small electric current

gam·bit \ˈgam-bət\ *n* [It *gambetto,* lit., act of tripping someone, fr. *gamba* leg] **1** : a chess opening in which a player risks one or more minor pieces to gain an advantage in position **2** : a calculated move : STRATAGEM ♦ ***Synonyms*** TRICK, ARTIFICE, GIMMICK, MANEUVER, PLAY, RUSE

[1]**gam·ble** \ˈgam-bəl\ *vb* **gam·bled; gam·bling** **1** : to play a game for money or property **2** : BET, WAGER **3** : VENTURE, HAZARD — **gam·bler** *n*

[2]**gamble** *n* : a risky undertaking

gam·bol \ˈgam-bəl\ *vb* **-boled** *or* **-bolled; -bol·ing** *or* **-bol·ling** : to skip about in play : FRISK — **gambol** *n*

gam·brel roof \ˈgam-brəl-\ *n* : a roof with a lower steeper slope and an upper flatter one on each side

[1]**game** \ˈgām\ *n* **1** : AMUSEMENT, DIVERSION **2** : SPORT, FUN ⟨made ~ of the strange boy⟩ **3** : SCHEME, PROJECT **4** : a line of work : PROFESSION **5** : CONTEST **6** : animals hunted for sport or food; *also* : the flesh of a game animal

[2]**game** *vb* **gamed; gam·ing** **1** : to play for a stake **2** : to take dishonest advantage of ⟨~ the tax system⟩

[3]**game** *adj* : PLUCKY, RESOLUTE — **game·ly** *adv* — **game·ness** *n*

[4]**game** *adj* : LAME ⟨a ~ leg⟩

game·cock \ˈgām-ˌkäk\ *n* : a rooster trained for fighting

game fish *n* : SPORT FISH

game·keep·er \ˈgām-ˌkē-pər\ *n* : a person in charge of the breeding and protection of game animals or birds on a private preserve

game show *n* : a television program on which contestants compete usu. for prizes in a game

game·some \ˈgām-səm\ *adj* : MERRY ♦ ***Synonyms*** PLAYFUL, FROLICSOME, SPORTIVE, ANTIC

game·ster \ˈgām-stər\ *n* : GAMBLER

gam·ete \ˈga-ˌmēt\ *n* : a mature germ cell — **ga·met·ic** \gə-ˈme-tik\ *adj*

game theory *n* : the analysis of a situation involving conflicting interests (as in business) in terms of gains and losses among opposing players

gam·in \ˈga-mən\ *n* [F] **1** : a boy who loiters on the streets **2** : GAMINE 2

ga·mine \ga-ˈmēn\ *n* **1** : a girl who loiters on the streets **2** : a small playfully mischievous girl

gam·ma \ˈga-mə\ *n* : the 3d letter of the Greek alphabet — Γ or γ

gamma globulin *n* : a blood protein fraction rich in antibodies; *also* : a solution of this from human blood donors that is given to provide immunity against some infectious diseases (as measles)

gamma ray *n* : a photon emitted by a radioactive substance; *also* : a photon of higher energy than that of an X-ray — usu. used in pl.

gam·mon \ˈga-mən\ *n, chiefly Brit* : a cured ham or side of bacon

gam·ut \ˈga-mət\ *n* : an entire range or series ♦ ***Synonyms*** SCALE, SPECTRUM

gamy *or* **gam·ey** \ˈgā-mē\ *adj* **gam·i·er; -est** **1** : GAME, PLUCKY **2** : having the flavor of game esp. when near tainting ⟨~ meat⟩ **3** : SCANDALOUS; *also* : DISREPUTABLE — **gam·i·ness** \-mē-nəs\ *n*

[1]**gan·der** \ˈgan-dər\ *n* : a male goose

[2]**gander** *n* : LOOK, GLANCE

[1]**gang** \ˈgaŋ\ *n* **1** : a set of implements or devices arranged to operate together **2** : a group of persons working or associated together; *esp* : a group of criminals or young delinquents

[2]**gang** *vb* **1** : to attack in a gang — usu. used with *up* **2** : to form into or move or act as a gang

gang·land \ˈgaŋ-ˌland\ *n* : the world of organized crime

gan·gling \ˈgaŋ-gliŋ\ *adj* : loosely and awkwardly built : LANKY

gan·gli·on \ˈgaŋ-glē-ən\ *n, pl* **-glia** \-ə\ *also* **-gli·ons** : a mass of nerve tissue containing cell bodies of neurons outside the central nervous tissue; *also* : NUCLEUS 3 — **gan·gli·on·ic** \ˌgaŋ-glē-ˈä-nik\ *adj*

gan·gly \ˈgaŋ-glē\ *adj* : GANGLING

gang·plank \ˈgaŋ-ˌplaŋk\ *n* : a movable bridge from a ship to the shore

gang·plow \-ˌplau̇\ *n* : a plow that turns two or more furrows at one time

gan·grene \ˈgaŋ-ˌgrēn, gaŋ-ˈgrēn\ *n* : the death of soft tissues in a local area of the body due to loss of the blood supply — **gangrene** *vb* — **gan·gre·nous** \ˈgaŋ-grə-nəs\ *adj*

gang·sta \ˈgaŋ-stə\ *n* : a member of an urban street gang

gangsta rap *n* : rap music with lyrics explicitly portraying urban gang life

gang·ster \ˈgaŋ-stər\ *n* : a member of a gang of criminals : RACKETEER

gang·way \ˈgaŋ-ˌwā\ *n* **1** : PASSAGEWAY; *also* : GANGPLANK **2** : clear passage through a crowd

gan·net \ˈga-nət\ *n, pl* **gannets** *also* **gannet** : any of several large fish-eating usu. white and black seabirds that breed chiefly on offshore islands

gantlet *var of* GAUNTLET

gan·try \ˈgan-trē\ *n, pl* **gantries** : a frame structure on side supports over or around something

GAO *abbr* General Accounting Office

gaol \ˈjāl\, **gaol·er** \ˈjā-lər\ *chiefly Brit var of* JAIL, JAILER

gap \ˈgap\ *n* **1** : BREACH, CLEFT **2** : a mountain pass **3** : a blank space; *also* : an incomplete or deficient area **4** : a wide difference in character or attitude **5** : a problem caused by a disparity ⟨credibility ~⟩

gape \ˈgāp\ *vb* **gaped; gap·ing** **1** : to open the mouth wide **2** : to open or part widely **3** : to stare with mouth open **4** : YAWN — **gape** *n*

[1]**gar** \ˈgär\ *n* : any of several fishes that have a long body resembling that of a pike and long narrow jaws

[2]**gar** *abbr* garage

GAR *abbr* Grand Army of the Republic

[1]**ga·rage** \gə-ˈräzh, -ˈräj\ *n* [F, act of docking, garage, fr. *garer* to dock, fr. MF *garrer,* prob. ultim. fr. ON *vara* to beware, take care] : a shelter or repair shop for automobiles

[2]**garage** *vb* **ga·raged; ga·rag·ing** : to keep or put in a garage

garage sale *n* : a sale of used household or personal articles held on the seller's own premises

garb \ˈgärb\ *n* **1** : style of dress **2** : outward form : APPEARANCE — **garb** *vb*

gar•bage \ˈgär-bij\ *n* **1** : food waste **2** : unwanted or useless material

gar•bage•man \-ˌman\ *n* : a person who collects and removes garbage

gar•ble \ˈgär-bəl\ *vb* **gar•bled; gar•bling** : to distort the meaning of ⟨~ a story⟩

gar•çon \gär-ˈsōⁿ\ *n, pl* **garçons** *same or* gär-ˈsoⁿz\ [F, boy, servant] : WAITER

[1]**gar•den** \ˈgär-dᵊn\ *n* **1** : a plot for growing fruits, flowers, or vegetables **2** : a public recreation area; *esp* : one for displaying plants or animals

[2]**garden** *vb* : to lay out or work in a garden — **gar•den•er** *n*

gar•de•nia \gär-ˈdē-nyə\ *n* [NL, genus name, fr. Alexander *Garden* †1791 Scot. naturalist] : any of a genus of tropical trees or shrubs that are related to the madder and have fragrant white or yellow flowers

garden–variety *adj* : COMMONPLACE, ORDINARY ⟨~ police dramas⟩

gar•fish \ˈgär-ˌfish\ *n* : GAR

gar•gan•tuan \gär-ˈgan-chə-wən\ *adj, often cap* : tremendous in size, volume, or degree ⟨~ waterfalls⟩ ♦ ***Synonyms*** HUGE, COLOSSAL, GIGANTIC, MAMMOTH, MONSTROUS, TITANIC

gar•gle \ˈgär-gəl\ *vb* **gar•gled; gar•gling** : to rinse the throat with liquid agitated by air forced through it from the lungs — **gargle** *n*

gar•goyle \ˈgär-ˌgȯi(-ə)l\ *n* **1** : a waterspout in the form of a grotesque human or animal figure projecting from the roof or eaves of a building **2** : a grotesquely carved figure

gar•ish \ˈger-ish\ *adj* : FLASHY, GLARING, SHOWY, GAUDY ⟨a ~ wardrobe⟩

[1]**gar•land** \ˈgär-lənd\ *n* : a decorative wreath or rope (as of leaves)

[2]**garland** *vb* : to form into or deck with a garland

gar•lic \ˈgär-lik\ *n* [ME *garlek,* fr. OE *gārlēac,* fr. *gār* spear + *lēac* leek] : an herb related to the lilies and grown for its pungent bulbs used in cooking; *also* : its bulb — **gar•licky** \-li-kē\ *adj*

gar•ment \ˈgär-mənt\ *n* : an article of clothing

gar•ner \ˈgär-nər\ *vb* **1** : to gather into storage **2** : to acquire by effort ⟨~ evidence⟩ **3** : ACCUMULATE, COLLECT

gar•net \ˈgär-nət\ *n* [ME *gernet,* fr. AF *gernete,* fr. *gernet* dark red, fr. *pume gernete* pomegranate] : a transparent deep red mineral sometimes used as a gem

gar•nish \ˈgär-nish\ *vb* **1** : DECORATE, EMBELLISH **2** : to add decorative or savory touches to (food) **3** : GARNISHEE — **garnish** *n*

gar•nish•ee \ˌgär-nə-ˈshē\ *vb* **-eed; -ee•ing** **1** : to serve with a garnishment **2** : to take (as a debtor's wages) by legal authority

gar•nish•ment \ˈgär-nish-mənt\ *n* **1** : GARNISH **2** : a legal warning concerning the attachment of property to satisfy a debt; *also* : the attachment of such property

gar•ni•ture \-ni-chər, -ˌchu̇r\ *n* : EMBELLISHMENT, TRIMMING

gar•ret \ˈger-ət\ *n* : the part of a house just under the roof : ATTIC

gar•ri•son \ˈger-ə-sən\ *n* [ME *garisoun* protection, fr. AF *garisun* healing, protection, fr. *garir* to heal, protect, of Gmc origin] **1** : a military post; *esp* : a permanent military installation **2** : the troops stationed at a garrison — **garrison** *vb*

garrison state *n* : a state organized on a primarily military basis

gar•rote *or* **ga•rotte** \gə-ˈrät, -ˈrōt\ *n* [Sp *garrote*] **1** : a method of execution by strangulation; *also* : the apparatus used **2** : an implement (as a wire with handles) for strangulation — **garrote** *or* **garotte** *vb*

gar•ru•lous \ˈger-ə-ləs\ *adj* : TALKATIVE — **gar•ru•li•ty** \gə-ˈrü-lə-tē\ *n* — **gar•ru•lous•ly** *adv* — **gar•ru•lous•ness** *n*

gar•ter \ˈgär-tər\ *n* : a band or strap worn to hold up a stocking or sock

garter snake *n* : any of a genus of harmless American snakes with longitudinal stripes on the back

[1]**gas** \ˈgas\ *n, pl* **gas•es** *also* **gas•ses** [NL, alter. of L *chaos* space, chaos] **1** : a fluid (as hydrogen or air) that tends to expand indefinitely **2** : a gas or mixture of gases used as a fuel or anesthetic **3** : a substance that can be used to produce a poisonous, asphyxiating, or irritant atmosphere **4** : GASOLINE — **gas•eous** \ˈga-sē-əs, -shəs\ *adj*

[2]**gas** *vb* **gassed; gas•sing** **1** : to treat with gas; *also* : to poison with gas **2** : to fill with gasoline ⟨~ up the car⟩

gash \ˈgash\ *n* : a deep long cut — **gash** *vb*

gas•ket \ˈgas-kət\ *n* : material (as rubber) or a part used to seal a joint

gas•light \ˈgas-ˌlīt\ *n* **1** : light made by burning illuminating gas **2** : a gas flame; *also* : a gas lighting fixture

gas mask *n* : a mask with a chemical air filter used to protect the face and lungs against poison gas

gas•o•line \ˈga-sə-ˌlēn, ˌga-sə-ˈlēn\ *n* : a flammable liquid mixture made from petroleum and used esp. as a motor fuel

gasp \ˈgasp\ *vb* **1** : to catch the breath audibly (as with shock) **2** : to breathe laboriously : PANT **3** : to utter in a gasping manner — **gasp** *n*

gas station *n* : a retail station for servicing and fueling motor vehicles

gas•tric \ˈgas-trik\ *adj* : of or relating to the stomach

gastric juice *n* : the acid digestive secretion of the stomach

gas•tri•tis \gas-ˈtrī-təs\ *n* : inflammation of the lining of the stomach

gas•tro•en•ter•i•tis \ˌgas-trō-ˌen-tə-ˈrī-təs\ *n* : inflammation of the lining membrane of the stomach and intestines

gas•tro•en•ter•ol•o•gy \ˌgas-trō-ˌen-tə-

ˈrä-lə-jē\ *n* : a branch of medicine concerned with the structure, functions, and diseases of the stomach and intestines — **gas·tro·en·ter·ol·o·gist** \-jist\ *n*

gas·tro·in·tes·ti·nal \ˌgas-trō-in-ˈtes-tə-nᵊl\ *adj* : of, relating to, affecting, or including both the stomach and intestine ⟨~ tract⟩ ⟨~ distress⟩

gas·tron·o·my \gas-ˈträ-nə-mē\ *n* [F *gastronomie,* fr. Gk *Gastronomia,* title of a 4th cent. B.C. poem, fr. *gastēr* belly + *-nomia* system of laws] : the art of good eating — **gas·tro·nom·ic** \ˌgas-trə-ˈnä-mik\ *also* **gas·tro·nom·i·cal** \-mi-kəl\ *adj* — **gas·tro·nom·i·cal·ly** \-k(ə-)lē\ *adv*

gas·tro·pod \ˈgas-trə-ˌpäd\ *n* : any of a large class of mollusks (as snails and slugs) with a muscular foot and a spiral shell or none — **gastropod** *adj*

gas·works \ˈgas-ˌwərks\ *n sing or pl* : a plant for manufacturing gas

gate \ˈgāt\ *n* **1** : an opening for passage in a wall or fence **2** : a city or castle entrance often with defensive structures **3** : the frame or door that closes a gate **4** : a device (as a valve) for controlling the passage of a fluid or signal **5** : the total admission receipts or the number of people at an event

-gate \ˌgāt\ *n comb form* [Water*gate,* scandal that resulted in the resignation of President Richard Nixon in 1974] : usu. political scandal often involving the concealment of wrongdoing

gate–crash·er \ˈgāt-ˌkra-shər\ *n* : a person who enters without paying admission or attends without invitation

gate·keep·er \-ˌkē-pər\ *n* : a person who tends or guards a gate

gate·post \-ˌpōst\ *n* : the post to which a gate is hung or against which it closes

gate·way \-ˌwā\ *n* **1** : an opening for a gate **2** : a means of entrance or exit

¹**gath·er** \ˈga-t͟hər\ *vb* **1** : to bring together : COLLECT **2** : PICK, HARVEST **3** : to pick up little by little **4** : to scoop up from a resting place ⟨~*ed* up the child⟩ **5** : to gain or win by gradual increase **6** : ATTRACT, ACCUMULATE ⟨~ dust⟩ **7** : to summon up ⟨~ courage to dive⟩ **8** : to gain control of ⟨~*ed* his wits⟩ **9** : to draw about or close to something **10** : to pull (fabric) along a line of stitching into puckers **11** : GUESS, DEDUCE, INFER **12** : ASSEMBLE **13** : to swell out and fill with pus **14** : GROW, INCREASE ♦ ***Synonyms*** CONGREGATE, FORGATHER — **gath·er·er** *n*

²**gather** *n* : a puckering in cloth made by gathering

GATT \ˈgat\ *abbr* General Agreement on Tariffs and Trade

gauche \ˈgōsh\ *adj* [F, lit., left] **1** : lacking social experience or grace; *also* : not tactful **2** : crudely made or done ♦ ***Synonyms*** CLUMSY, HEAVY-HANDED, INEPT, MALADROIT

gau·che·rie \ˌgō-shə-ˈrē\ *n* : a tactless or awkward action

gau·cho \ˈgau̇-chō\ *n, pl* **gauchos** : a cowboy of the So. American pampas

gaud \ˈgȯd\ *n* : ORNAMENT, TRINKET

gaudy \ˈgȯ-dē\ *adj* **gaud·i·er; -est 1** : ostentatiously or tastelessly ornamented **2** : marked by showiness or extravagance : OUTLANDISH **3** : EXCEPTIONAL ⟨a ~ batting average⟩ ♦ ***Synonyms*** GARISH, FLASHY, GLARING, TAWDRY — **gaud·i·ly** \-də-lē\ *adv* — **gaud·i·ness** \-dē-nəs\ *n*

¹**gauge** *also* **gage** \ˈgāj\ *n* **1** : measurement according to some standard or system **2** : DIMENSIONS, SIZE **3** *usu gage* : an instrument for measuring, testing, or registering

²**gauge** *also* **gage** *vb* **gauged** *also* **gaged; gaug·ing** *also* **gag·ing 1** : MEASURE **2** : to determine the capacity or contents of **3** : ESTIMATE, JUDGE

gaunt \ˈgȯnt\ *adj* **1** : excessively thin and angular ⟨a ~ face⟩ **2** : BARREN, DESOLATE ♦ ***Synonyms*** BONY, LANK, LANKY, LEAN, RAWBONED, SKINNY — **gaunt·ness** *n*

¹**gaunt·let** *also* **gant·let** \ˈgȯnt-lət\ *n* **1** : a protective glove **2** : an open challenge (as to combat) **3** : a dress glove extending above the wrist

²**gauntlet** *also* **gantlet** *n* **1** : a double file of men armed with weapons (as clubs) with which to strike at an individual who is made to run between them **2** : ORDEAL **3** : a line or series of something to be greeted or managed

gauss \ˈgau̇s\ *n* : the centimeter-gram-second unit of magnetic flux density that is equal to 1×10^{-4} tesla

gauze \ˈgȯz\ *n* : a very thin often transparent fabric used esp. for draperies and surgical dressings

gauzy \ˈgȯ-zē\ *adj* **gauz·i·er; -est 1** : made of or resembling gauze **2** : not clear : HAZY ⟨a ~ memory⟩

gave *past of* GIVE

gav·el \ˈga-vəl\ *n* : a mallet used by a presiding officer or auctioneer

ga·votte \gə-ˈvät\ *n* : a dance of French peasant origin marked by the raising rather than sliding of the feet

gawk \ˈgȯk\ *vb* : to gape or stare stupidly — **gawk·er** *n*

gawky \ˈgȯ-kē\ *adj* **gawk·i·er; -est** : AWKWARD, CLUMSY — **gawk·i·ly** \-kə-lē\ *adv* — **gawk·i·ness** *n*

gay \ˈgā\ *adj* **1** : MERRY **2** : BRIGHT, LIVELY **3** : brilliant in color **4** : given to social pleasures; *also* : LICENTIOUS **5** : of, relating to, or characterized by sexual or romantic attraction to people of one's same sex — often used to refer to men only ⟨~ and lesbian students⟩; *also* : of, relating to, or intended for people who are gay, lesbian, bisexual, or transgender ⟨a ~ bar⟩

gayety, gayly *var of* GAIETY, GAILY

gaz *abbr* gazette

gaze \ˈgāz\ *vb* **gazed; gaz·ing** : to fix the eyes in a steady intent look ♦ ***Synonyms*** GAPE, GAWK, GLARE, GOGGLE, PEER, STARE — **gaze** *n* — **gaz·er** *n*

ga·ze·bo \gə-ˈzē-bō\ *n, pl* **-bos 1** : BELVEDERE **2** : a freestanding roofed structure usu. open on the sides

ga·zelle \gə-ˈzel\ *n, pl* **gazelles** *also* **gazelle** : any of numerous small swift graceful antelopes

ga·zette \gə-ˈzet\ *n* **1** : NEWSPAPER **2** : an official journal

gaz·et·teer \ˌga-zə-ˈtir\ *n* : a geographical dictionary

ga·zil·lion \gə-ˈzil-yən\ *n* : ZILLION — **gazillion** *adj* — **ga·zil·lionth** \-yənth\ *adj*

gaz·pa·cho \gəz-ˈpä-(ˌ)chō, gə-ˈspä-\ *n, pl* **-chos** [Sp] : a spicy soup usu. made from raw vegetables and served cold

GB *abbr* Great Britain

GCA *abbr* ground-controlled approach

gd *abbr* good

Gd *symbol* gadolinium

GDR *abbr* German Democratic Republic

Ge *symbol* germanium

gear \ˈgir\ *n* **1** : CLOTHING **2** : movable property : GOODS **3** : EQUIPMENT ⟨fishing ~⟩ **4** : a mechanism that performs a specific function ⟨steering ~⟩ **5** : a toothed wheel **6** : working order or adjustment ⟨got her career in ~⟩ **7** : an adjustment of transmission gears (as of an automobile or bicycle) that determines speed and direction of travel — **gear** *vb*

gear·box \ˈgir-ˌbäks\ *n* : TRANSMISSION 3

gear·shift \-ˌshift\ *n* : a mechanism by which transmission gears are shifted

gear·wheel \-ˌhwēl\ *n* : GEAR 5

gecko \ˈge-kō\ *n, pl* **geck·os** *also* **geck·oes** : any of numerous small chiefly tropical insect-eating lizards

GED *abbr* general equivalency diploma

geek \ˈgēk\ *n* : a person of an intellectual bent who is often disliked — **geek·i·ness** *n* — **geeky** *adj*

geese *pl of* GOOSE

gee·zer \ˈgē-zər\ *n* : an odd or eccentric person usu. of old age

Gei·ger counter \ˈgī-gər-\ *n* : an electronic instrument for detecting the presence of cosmic rays or radioactive substances

gei·sha \ˈgā-shə, ˈgē-\ *n, pl* **geisha** *or* **geishas** [Jp, fr. *gei* art + *-sha* person] : a Japanese girl or woman who is trained to provide entertaining company for men

gel \ˈjel\ *n* : a solid jellylike colloid (as gelatin dessert) — **gel** *vb*

gel·a·tin *also* **gel·a·tine** \ˈje-lə-tən\ *n* : glutinous material and esp. protein obtained from animal tissues by boiling and used as a food, in dyeing, and in photography; *also* : an edible jelly formed with gelatin — **ge·lat·i·nous** \jə-ˈla-tə-nəs\ *adj*

geld \ˈgeld\ *vb* : CASTRATE

geld·ing *n* : a castrated male horse

gel·id \ˈje-ləd\ *adj* : extremely cold

gem \ˈjem\ *n* **1** : JEWEL **2** : a usu. valuable stone cut and polished for ornament **3** : something valued for beauty or perfection ⟨a ~ of colonial architecture⟩

Gem·i·ni \ˈje-mə-(ˌ)nē, -ˌnī; ˈge-mə-ˌnē\ *n* **1** : a zodiacal constellation between Taurus and Cancer usu. pictured as twins sitting together **2** : the 3d sign of the zodiac in astrology; *also* : one born under this sign

gem·ol·o·gy *or* **gem·mol·o·gy** \je-ˈmä-lə-jē, jə-\ *n* : the science of gems — **gem·olog·i·cal** \ˌje-mə-ˈlä-ji-kəl\ *adj* — **gem·ol·o·gist** *also* **gem·mol·o·gist** \-jist\ *n*

gem·stone \ˈjem-ˌstōn\ *n* : a mineral or petrified material that when cut and polished can be used in jewelry

gen *abbr* **1** general **2** genitive

Gen *abbr* Genesis

Gen AF *abbr* general of the air force

gen·darme \ˈzhän-ˌdärm, ˈjän-\ *n* [F, intended as sing. of *gensdarmes,* pl. of *gent d'armes,* lit., armed people] : a member of a body of soldiers esp. in France serving as an armed police force

gen·der \ˈjen-dər\ *n* [ME *gendre,* fr. AF *genre, gendre,* fr. L *gener-, genus* birth, race, kind, gender] **1** : any of two or more divisions within a grammatical class that determine agreement with and selection of other words or grammatical forms **2 a** : SEX 1 **b** : GENDER IDENTITY — **gen·der·less** *adj*

gender expression *n* : the physical and behavioral manifestations of one's gender identity

gender identity *n* : a person's internal sense of being male, female, a combination of male and female, or neither male nor female

gender nonconforming *adj* : exhibiting behavioral, cultural, or psychological traits that do not correspond with the traits typically associated with one's sex — **gender nonconformity** *n*

gene \ˈjēn\ *n* : a part of DNA or RNA that contains chemical information needed to make a particular protein (as an enzyme) controlling or influencing an inherited bodily trait (as eye color) or activity (as metabolism) or that influences or controls the activity of another gene or genes — **gen·ic** \ˈjē-nik, ˈje-\ *adj*

ge·ne·al·o·gy \ˌjē-nē-ˈä-lə-jē, ˌje-, -ˈa-\ *n, pl* **-gies** : PEDIGREE, LINEAGE; *also* : the study of family pedigrees — **ge·ne·a·log·i·cal** \ˌjē-nē-ə-ˈlä-ji-kəl, ˌje-\ *adj* — **ge·ne·a·log·i·cal·ly** \-k(ə-)lē\ *adv* — **ge·ne·al·o·gist** \ˌjē-nē-ˈä-lə-jist, ˌje-; -ˈa-\ *n*

gene pool *n* : the total genetic information contained in a population of interbreeding organisms

genera *pl of* GENUS

[1]**gen·er·al** \ˈje-nə-rəl, ˈjen-rəl\ *adj* **1** : of or relating to the whole **2** : taken as a whole **3** : relating to or covering all instances **4** : not special or specialized **5** : common to many ⟨a ~ custom⟩ **6** : not limited in meaning : not specific **7** : holding superior rank ⟨inspector ~⟩ ♦ ***Synonyms*** GENERIC, UNIVERSAL

[2]**general** *n* **1** : something that involves or is applicable to the whole **2** : a commissioned officer ranking next below a general of the army or a general of the air force **3** : a commissioned officer of the highest rank in the marine corps — **in general** : for the most part

general assembly *n* **1** : a legislative

assembly; *esp* : a U.S. state legislature **2** *cap G&A* : the supreme deliberative body of the United Nations
gen·er·al·i·sa·tion, gen·er·al·ise, gen·er·al·ised *Brit var of* GENERALIZATION, GENERALIZE, GENERALIZED
gen·er·a·lis·si·mo \ˌje-nə-rə-ˈli-sə-ˌmō\ *n, pl* **-mos** [It, fr. *generale* general] : the chief commander of an army
gen·er·al·i·ty \ˌje-nə-ˈra-lə-tē\ *n, pl* **-ties** **1** : the quality or state of being general **2** : GENERALIZATION 2 **3** : a vague or inadequate statement **4** : the greatest part : BULK
gen·er·al·i·za·tion \ˌje-nə-rə-lə-ˈzā-shən, ˌjen-rə-\ *n* **1** : the act or process of generalizing **2** : a general statement, law, principle, or proposition
gen·er·al·ize \ˈje-nə-rə-ˌlīz, ˈjen-rə-\ *vb* **-ized; -iz·ing** **1** : to make general **2** : to draw general conclusions from **3** : to reach a general conclusion esp. on the basis of particular instances **4** : to extend throughout the body
gen·er·al·ly \ˈjen-rə-lē, ˈje-nə-\ *adv* **1** : in a general manner **2** : as a rule
general of the air force : a commissioned officer of the highest rank in the air force
general of the army : a commissioned officer of the highest rank in the army
general practitioner *n* : a physician or veterinarian whose practice is not limited to a specialty
gen·er·al·ship \ˈje-nə-rəl-ˌship, ˈjen-rəl-\ *n* **1** : office or tenure of office of a general **2** : LEADERSHIP **3** : military skill as a high commander
general store *n* : a retail store that carries a wide variety of goods but is not divided into departments
gen·er·ate \ˈje-nə-ˌrāt\ *vb* **-at·ed; -at·ing** : to bring into existence : PRODUCE ⟨~ electricity⟩ ♦ ***Synonyms*** CREATE, ORIGINATE, PROCREATE, SPAWN
gen·er·a·tion \ˌje-nə-ˈrā-shən\ *n* **1** : a body of living beings constituting a single step in the line of descent from an ancestor; *also* : the average period between generations **2** : PRODUCTION
Generation X *n* : the generation of Americans born in the 1960s and 1970s
gen·er·a·tive \ˈje-nə-rə-tiv, -ˌrā-tiv\ *adj* : having the power or function of generating, originating, producing, or reproducing ⟨~ organs⟩
gen·er·a·tor \ˈje-nə-ˌrā-tər\ *n* : one that generates; *esp* : a machine by which mechanical energy is changed into electrical energy
ge·ner·ic \jə-ˈner-ik\ *adj* **1** : not specific : GENERAL **2** : not protected by a trademark ⟨a ~ drug⟩ **3** : of or relating to a biological genus **4** : having no particularly distinctive quality ⟨~ towns⟩ — **generic** *n* — **ge·ner·i·cal·ly** \-i-k(ə-)lē\ *adv*
gen·er·ous \ˈje-nə-rəs\ *adj* **1** : free in giving or sharing ⟨~ donors⟩ **2** : HIGH-MINDED, NOBLE **3** : ABUNDANT, AMPLE, COPIOUS ⟨a ~ salary⟩ ♦ ***Synonyms*** LIBERAL, BOUNTIFUL, MUNIFICENT, OPENHANDED — **gen·er·os·i·ty** \ˌje-nə-ˈrä-sə-tē\ *n* — **gen·er·ous·ly** \ˈje-nə-rəs-lē\ *adv* — **gen·er·ous·ness** *n*
gen·e·sis \ˈje-nə-səs\ *n, pl* **-e·ses** \-ˌsēz\ : the origin or coming into existence of something
Genesis *n* — see BIBLE table
gene–splic·ing \-ˌsplī-siŋ\ *n* : the process of preparing recombinant DNA
gene therapy *n* : the insertion of normal or altered genes into cells esp. to replace defective genes in the treatment of genetic disorders or to provide a specialized disease-fighting function
ge·net·ic \jə-ˈne-tik\ *adj* : of or relating to the origin, development, or causes of something; *also* : of, relating to, or caused by genes or genetics ⟨~ research⟩ — **ge·net·i·cal·ly** \-ti-k(ə-)lē\ *adv*
genetic code *n* : the chemical code that is the basis of genetic inheritance and consists of units of three linked chemical groups in DNA and RNA which specify particular amino acids used to make proteins or which start or stop the process of making proteins
genetic engineering *n* : the alteration of genetic material esp. by cutting up and joining together DNA from one or more species of organism and inserting the result into an organism — **genetically engineered** *adj*
ge·net·ics \jə-ˈne-tiks\ *n* : a branch of biology dealing with heredity and variation — **ge·net·i·cist** \-tə-sist\ *n*
ge·nial \ˈjē-nyəl, ˈjē-nē-əl\ *adj* **1** : favorable to growth or comfort ⟨~ sunshine⟩ **2** : CHEERFUL, KINDLY ⟨a ~ host⟩ ♦ ***Synonyms*** AFFABLE, CONGENIAL, CORDIAL, GRACIOUS, SOCIABLE — **ge·nial·i·ty** \ˌjē-nē-ˈa-lə-tē, jēn-ˈya-\ *n* — **ge·nial·ly** *adv*
-gen·ic \ˈje-nik\ *adj comb form* **1** : producing : forming **2** : produced by : formed from **3** : suitable for production or reproduction by (such) a medium
ge·nie \ˈjē-nē\ *n, pl* **ge·nies** *also* **ge·nii** \-nē-ˌī\ [F *génie,* fr. Ar *jinnī*] : a supernatural spirit that often takes human form usu. serving the person who calls on it
gen·i·tal \ˈje-nə-tᵊl\ *adj* **1** : concerned with reproduction ⟨~ organs⟩ **2** : of, relating to, or characterized by the stage of psychosexual development in psychoanalytic theory in which oral and anal impulses are subordinated to adaptive interpersonal mechanisms — **gen·i·tal·ly** *adv*
gen·i·ta·lia \ˌje-nə-ˈtāl-yə\ *n pl* : reproductive organs; *esp* : the external genital organs — **gen·i·ta·lic** \-ˈta-lik, -ˈtā-\ *adj*
gen·i·tals \ˈje-nə-tᵊlz\ *n pl* : GENITALIA
gen·i·tive \ˈje-nə-tiv\ *adj* : of, relating to, or constituting a grammatical case marking typically a relationship of possessor or source — **genitive** *n*
gen·i·to·uri·nary \ˌje-nə-tō-ˈyu̇r-ə-ˌner-ē\ *adj* : of or relating to the genital and urinary organs or functions
ge·nius \ˈjē-nyəs\ *n, pl* **ge·nius·es** *or* **ge·nii** \-nē-ˌī\ [L, tutelary spirit, natural

inclinations, fr. *gignere* to beget] **1** *pl genii* : an attendant spirit of a person or place; *also* : a person who influences another for good or evil **2** : a strong leaning or inclination **3** : a peculiar or distinctive character or spirit (as of a nation or a language) **4** *pl usu genii* : SPIRIT, GENIE **5** *pl usu geniuses* : a single strongly marked capacity or aptitude **6** : extraordinary intellectual power; *also* : a person having such power ♦ ***Synonyms*** GIFT, FACULTY, FLAIR, KNACK, TALENT

genl *abbr* general

geno·cide \ˈje-nə-ˌsīd\ *n* : the deliberate and systematic destruction of a racial, political, or cultural group

ge·nome \ˈjē-ˌnōm\ *n* **1** : one haploid set of chromosomes **2** : the genetic material of an organism

ge·no·mics \jē-ˈnō-miks\ *n* : a branch of biotechnology concerned esp. with investigating and collecting data about the structure and function of all or part of an organism's genome

-genous \jə-nəs\ *adj comb form* **1** : producing : yielding ⟨ero*genous*⟩ **2** : having (such) an origin ⟨endo*genous*⟩

genre \ˈzhän-rə, ˈzhäⁿ-; ˈzhäⁿr; ˈjän-rə\ *n* **1** : a distinctive type or category esp. of literary composition **2** : a style of painting in which everyday subjects are treated realistically

gens \ˈjenz, ˈgens\ *n, pl* **gen·tes** \ˈjen-ˌtēz, ˈgen-ˌtās\ [L] : a Roman clan embracing the families of the same stock in the male line

gent *n* : GENTLEMAN

gen·teel \jen-ˈtēl\ *adj* **1** : ARISTOCRATIC **2** : ELEGANT, STYLISH **3** : POLITE, REFINED **4** : maintaining the appearance of superior social status **5** : marked by false delicacy, prudery, or affectation — **gen·teel·ly** *adv* — **gen·teel·ness** *n*

gen·tian \ˈjen-chən\ *n* : any of numerous herbs with opposite leaves and showy usu. blue flowers in the fall

gen·tile \ˈjen-ˌtī(-ə)l\ *n* [ME, fr. LL *gentilis* pagan, fr. L *gent-, gens* clan, nation] **1** *often cap* : a person who is not Jewish; *esp* : a Christian as distinguished from a Jew **2** : PAGAN — **gentile** *adj, often cap*

gen·til·i·ty \jen-ˈti-lə-tē\ *n, pl* **-ties** **1** : good birth and family **2** : the qualities characteristic of a well-bred person **3** : good manners **4** : superior social status shown in manners or mode of life

¹**gen·tle** \ˈjen-tᵊl\ *adj* **gen·tler** \ˈjent-lər, -tᵊl-ər\; **gen·tlest** \ˈjent-ləst, -tᵊl-əst\ **1** : belonging to a family of high social station **2** : of, relating to, or characteristic of a gentleman **3** : KIND, AMIABLE ⟨a ~ pastor⟩ **4** : TRACTABLE, DOCILE ⟨a ~ dog⟩ **5** : not harsh, stern, or violent **6** : SOFT, DELICATE **7** : MODERATE — **gen·tle·ness** *n* — **gen·tly** *adv*

²**gentle** *vb* **gen·tled**; **gen·tling** **1** : to make or become mild, docile, soft, or moderate **2** : MOLLIFY, PLACATE

gen·tle·folk \ˈjen-tᵊl-ˌfōk\ *also* **gen·tle·folks** \-ˌfōks\ *n* : persons of good family and breeding

gen·tle·man \-mən\ *n* **1** : a man of good family **2** : a well-bred man **3** : MAN — used in pl. as a form of address — **gen·tle·man·ly** *adj*

gen·tle·wom·an \-ˌwu̇-mən\ *n* **1** : a woman of good family **2** : a woman attending a lady of rank **3** : a woman with very good manners : LADY

gen·tri·fi·ca·tion \ˌjen-trə-fə-ˈkā-shən\ *n* : the process of renewal accompanying the influx of middle-class people into deteriorating areas that often displaces earlier usu. poorer residents — **gen·tri·fy** \ˈjen-trə-ˌfī\ *vb*

gen·try \ˈjen-trē\ *n, pl* **gentries** **1** : people of good birth, breeding, and education : ARISTOCRACY **2** : the class of English people between the nobility and the yeomanry **3** : persons of a designated class

gen·u·flect \ˈjen-yu̇-ˌflekt\ *vb* : to bend the knee esp. in worship — **gen·u·flec·tion** \ˌjen-yu̇-ˈflek-shən\ *n*

gen·u·ine \ˈjen-yə-wən\ *adj* **1** : actually having the reputed qualities : REAL, AUTHENTIC ⟨a ~ signature⟩ **2** : SINCERE, HONEST ⟨their love is ~⟩ ♦ ***Synonyms*** BONA FIDE, TRUE, VERITABLE — **gen·u·ine·ly** *adv* — **gen·u·ine·ness** *n*

ge·nus \ˈjē-nəs\ *n, pl* **gen·era** \ˈje-nə-rə\ [L, birth, race, kind] : a category of biological classification that ranks between the family and the species and contains related species

geo·cen·tric \ˌjē-ō-ˈsen-trik\ *adj* **1** : relating to or measured from the earth's center **2** : having or relating to the earth as a center

geo·chem·is·try \-ˈke-mə-strē\ *n* : a branch of geology that deals with the chemical composition of and chemical changes in the earth — **geo·chem·i·cal** \-mi-kəl\ *adj* — **geo·chem·ist** \-mist\ *n*

ge·ode \ˈjē-ˌōd\ *n* : a nodule of stone having a cavity lined with mineral matter

¹**geo·de·sic** \ˌjē-ə-ˈde-sik\ *adj* : made of light straight structural elements ⟨a ~ dome⟩

²**geodesic** *n* : the shortest line between two points on a surface

geo·det·ic \ˌjē-ə-ˈde-tik\ *adj* : of, relating to, or being precise measurement of the earth and its features ⟨a ~ survey⟩

geog *abbr* geographic; geographical; geography

ge·og·ra·phy \jē-ˈä-grə-fē\ *n, pl* **-phies** **1** : a science that deals with the natural features of the earth and its climate, products, and inhabitants **2** : the natural features of a region — **ge·og·ra·pher** \-fər\ *n* — **geo·graph·ic** \ˌjē-ə-ˈgra-fik\ *or* **geo·graph·i·cal** \-fi-kəl\ *adj* — **geo·graph·i·cal·ly** \-fi-k(ə-)lē\ *adv*

geol *abbr* geologic; geological; geology

ge·ol·o·gy \jē-ˈä-lə-jē\ *n, pl* **-gies** **1** : a science that deals with the history of the earth and its life esp. as recorded in rocks; *also* : a study of the features of a celestial body (as the moon) **2** : the geologic features of an area — **geo·log·ic** \ˌjē-ə-ˈlä-jik\ *or* **geo·log·i·cal** \-ji-kəl\ *adj*

— **geo·log·i·cal·ly** \-ji-k(ə-)lē\ *adv* — **ge·ol·o·gist** \jē-ˈä-lə-jist\ *n*

geom *abbr* geometric; geometrical; geometry

geo·mag·net·ic \ˌjē-ō-mag-ˈne-tik\ *adj* : of or relating to the magnetism of the earth — **geo·mag·ne·tism** \-ˈmag-nə-ˌti-zəm\ *n*

geometric mean *n* : the *n*th root of the product of *n* numbers; *esp* : a number that is the second term of three consecutive terms of a geometric progression ⟨the *geometric mean* of 9 and 4 is 6⟩

geometric progression *n* : a progression (as 1, $^1/_2$, $^1/_4$) in which the ratio of a term to its predecessor is always the same

ge·om·e·try \jē-ˈä-mə-trē\ *n, pl* **-tries** [ultim. fr. Gk *geōmetria,* fr. *gēometrein* to measure the earth, fr. *gē* earth + *metron* measure] : a branch of mathematics dealing with the relations, properties, and measurements of solids, surfaces, lines, points, and angles — **ge·om·e·ter** \-tər\ *n* — **geo·met·ric** \ˌjē-ə-ˈme-trik\ *or* **geo·met·ri·cal** \-tri-kəl\ *adj*

geo·phys·ics \ˌjē-ō-ˈfi-ziks\ *n* : the physics of the earth — **geo·phys·i·cal** \-zi-kəl\ *adj* — **geo·phys·i·cist** \-zə-sist\ *n*

geo·pol·i·tics \-ˈpä-lə-ˌtiks\ *n* : a combination of political and geographic factors relating to a state — **geo·po·lit·i·cal** \-pə-ˈli-ti-kəl\ *adj*

geo·ther·mal \ˌjē-ō-ˈthər-məl\ *adj* : of, relating to, or using the heat of the earth's interior ⟨~ energy⟩

ger *abbr* gerund

Ger *abbr* German; Germany

ge·ra·ni·um \jə-ˈrā-nē-əm\ *n* [L, fr. Gk *geranion,* fr. *geranos* crane] : any of a genus of herbs with usu. deeply cut leaves and typically pink, purple, or white flowers; *also* : any of a related genus of herbs that are native to southern Africa and are widely grown for their clusters of showy usu. red, pink, or white flowers

ger·bil *also* **ger·bile** \ˈjər-bəl\ *n* : any of numerous Old World burrowing desert rodents with long hind legs

ge·ri·at·ric \ˌjer-ē-ˈa-trik\ *adj* **1** : of or relating to geriatrics or the process of aging **2** : of, relating to, or appropriate for elderly people **3** : OLD

ge·ri·at·rics \-triks\ *n* : a branch of medicine dealing with the problems and diseases of old age and aging

germ \ˈjərm\ *n* **1** : a bit of living matter capable of growth and development (as into an organism) **2** : SOURCE, RUDIMENTS **3** : MICROORGANISM; *esp* : one causing disease

Ger·man \ˈjər-mən\ *n* **1** : a native or inhabitant of Germany **2** : the language of Germany, Austria, and parts of Switzerland — **German** *adj* — **Ger·man·ic** \jər-ˈma-nik\ *adj*

ger·mane \jər-ˈmān\ *adj* [ME *germain,* lit., having the same parents, fr. AF, fr. L *germanus,* fr. *germen* sprout, bud] : RELEVANT, APPROPRIATE ♦ ***Synonyms*** APPLICABLE, MATERIAL, PERTINENT

ger·ma·ni·um \jər-ˈmā-nē-əm\ *n* : a grayish white hard chemical element used esp. in semiconductor and optical materials and as a catalyst

German measles *n sing or pl* : an acute contagious virus disease milder than typical measles but damaging to the fetus when occurring early in pregnancy

German shepherd *n* : any of a breed of intelligent responsive working dogs of German origin often used in police work and as guide dogs for the blind

germ cell *n* : an egg or sperm or one of their antecedent cells

ger·mi·cide \ˈjər-mə-ˌsīd\ *n* : an agent that destroys germs — **ger·mi·cid·al** \ˌjər-mə-ˈsī-dᵊl\ *adj*

ger·mi·nal \ˈjər-mə-nəl\ *adj* : of or relating to a germ or germ cell; *also* : EMBRYONIC

ger·mi·nate \ˈjər-mə-ˌnāt\ *vb* **-nat·ed; -nat·ing** **1** : to cause to develop : begin to develop : SPROUT **2** : to come into being : EVOLVE — **ger·mi·na·tion** \ˌjər-mə-ˈnā-shən\ *n*

ger·on·tol·o·gy \ˌjer-ən-ˈtä-lə-jē\ *n* : a scientific study of aging and the problems of the aged — **ge·ron·to·log·i·cal** \jə-ˌrän-tə-ˈlä-ji-kəl\ *adj* — **ger·on·tol·o·gist** \ˌjer-ən-ˈtä-lə-jist\ *n*

ger·ry·man·der \ˈjer-ē-ˌman-dər\ *vb* : to divide into election districts so as to give one political party an advantage — **gerrymander** *n*

ger·und \ˈjer-ənd\ *n* : a word having the characteristics of both verb and noun

ge·sta·po \gə-ˈstä-pō\ *n, pl* **-pos** [G, fr. *Ge*heime *Sta*ats*po*lizei, lit., secret state police] : a usu. terrorist secret-police organization operating against persons suspected of disloyalty

ges·ta·tion \je-ˈstā-shən\ *n* : PREGNANCY, INCUBATION — **ges·tate** \ˈjes-ˌtāt\ *vb*

ges·tic·u·late \je-ˈsti-kyə-ˌlāt\ *vb* **-lat·ed; -lat·ing** : to make gestures esp. when speaking — **ges·tic·u·la·tion** \-ˌsti-kyə-ˈlā-shən\ *n*

ges·ture \ˈjes-chər\ *n* **1** : a movement usu. of the body or limbs that expresses or emphasizes an idea, sentiment, or attitude **2** : something said or done by way of formality or courtesy, as a symbol or token, or for its effect on the attitudes of others — **ges·tur·al** \-chə-rəl\ *adj* — **gesture** *vb*

ge·sund·heit \gə-ˈzu̇nt-ˌhīt\ *interj* [G, lit., health] — used to wish good health esp. to one who has just sneezed

¹get \ˈget\ *vb* **got** \ˈgät\; **got** *or* **got·ten** \ˈgä-tᵊn\; **get·ting** **1** : to gain possession of (as by receiving, acquiring, earning, buying, or winning) : PROCURE, OBTAIN, FETCH **2** : to succeed in coming or going ⟨*got* away to the lake⟩ **3** : to cause to come or go ⟨*got* the car to the station⟩ **4** : BEGET **5** : to cause to be in a certain condition or position ⟨don't ~ wet⟩ **6** : BECOME ⟨~ sick⟩ **7** : PREPARE **8** : SEIZE **9** : to move emotionally; *also* : IRRITATE **10** : BAFFLE, PUZZLE **11** : KILL **12** : HIT **13** : to be subjected to ⟨~ the measles⟩ **14** : to receive as punishment **15** : to find out by calculation **16** : HEAR; *also* : UNDERSTAND ⟨*got* the joke⟩ **17** : PERSUADE, INDUCE **18** : HAVE ⟨he's *got* no money⟩ **19** : to have as an obligation or necessity ⟨you have *got* to come⟩ **20** : to establish communication with **21** : to be able ⟨finally *got* to go to med school⟩ **22** : to come to be ⟨*got* talking about old times⟩ **23** : to leave at once— **get ahead** : to achieve success — **get a move on** : HURRY — **get away with** : to avoid punishment for (as a crime) — **get into** : to become strongly involved or interested in ⟨*got into* music⟩ — **get over** : to reconcile oneself to ⟨*got over* the breakup⟩

[2]**get** \ˈget\ *n* : OFFSPRING, PROGENY

get along *vb* **1** : GET BY **2** : to be on friendly terms

get·away \ˈge-tə-ˌwā\ *n* **1** : ESCAPE **2** : START **3** : a usu. brief vacation

get by *vb* : to meet one's needs

get–to·geth·er \ˈget-tə-ˌge-t͟hər\ *n* : an informal social gathering

get·up \ˈget-ˌəp\ *n* **1** : OUTFIT, COSTUME **2** : general composition or structure

get up *vb* **1** : to arise from bed **2** : to rise to one's feet **3** : PREPARE, ORGANIZE ⟨*get up* a petition⟩ **4** : to produce in oneself by effort ⟨*get up* the courage⟩

gew·gaw \ˈgü-ˌgȯ, ˈgyü-\ *n* : a showy trifle : BAUBLE, TRINKET

gey·ser \ˈgī-zər\ *n* [Icelandic *Geysir,* hot spring in Iceland] : a spring that intermittently shoots up hot water and steam

g–force \ˈjē-ˌfȯrs\ *n* : the force of gravity or acceleration on a body

ghast·ly \ˈgast-lē\ *adj* **ghast·li·er; -est** **1** : HORRIBLE, SHOCKING **2** : resembling a ghost : DEATHLIKE, PALE ♦ ***Synonyms*** GRUESOME, GRIM, LURID, GRISLY, MACABRE

ghat \ˈgȯt\ *n* [Hindi & Urdu *ghāṭ*] : a broad flight of steps on an Indian riverbank that provides access to the water

gher·kin \ˈgər-kən\ *n* **1** : a small prickly fruit of a vine related to the cucumber used to make pickles **2** : an immature cucumber

ghet·to \ˈge-tō\ *n, pl* **ghettos** *or* **ghettoes** : a quarter of a city in which members of a minority group live because of social, legal, or economic pressure

[1]**ghost** \ˈgōst\ *n* **1** : the seat of life : SOUL **2** : a disembodied soul; *esp* : the soul of a dead person believed to be an inhabitant of the unseen world or to appear in bodily form to living people **3** : SPIRIT, DEMON **4** : a faint trace ⟨a ~ of a smile⟩ **5** : a false image in a photographic negative or on a television screen — **ghost·ly** *adv*

[2]**ghost** *vb* **1** : GHOSTWRITE **2** : to abruptly cut off all contact with (someone) usu. without explanation

ghost·write \-ˌrīt\ *vb* **-wrote** \-ˌrōt\; **-writ·ten** \-ˌri-tᵊn\ : to write for and in the name of another — **ghost·writ·er** *n*

ghoul \ˈgül\ *n* [Ar *ghūl*] : a legendary evil being that robs graves and feeds on corpses — **ghoul·ish** *adj*

GHQ *abbr* general headquarters

gi *abbr* gill

[1]**GI** \ˌjē-ˈī\ *adj* [galvanized iron; fr. abbr. used in listing such articles as garbage cans, but taken as abbr. for *government issue*] **1** : provided by an official U.S. military supply department ⟨~ shoes⟩ **2** : of, relating to, or characteristic of U.S. military personnel **3** : conforming to military regulations or customs ⟨a ~ haircut⟩

[2]**GI** *n, pl* **GIs** *or* **GI's** \-ˈīz\ : a member or former member of the U.S. armed forces; *esp* : an enlisted person

[3]**GI** *abbr* **1** galvanized iron **2** gastrointestinal **3** general issue **4** government issue

gi·ant \ˈjī-ənt\ *n* **1** : a legendary humanlike being of great size and strength **2** : a living being or thing of extraordinary size or powers — **giant** *adj*

gi·ant·ess \ˈjī-ən-təs\ *n* : a female giant

giant panda *n* : PANDA 2

gib·ber \ˈji-bər\ *vb* : to speak rapidly, inarticulately, and often foolishly

gib·ber·ish \ˈji-bə-rish\ *n* : unintelligible or confused speech or language

[1]**gib·bet** \ˈji-bət\ *n* : GALLOWS

[2]**gibbet** *vb* **1** : to hang on a gibbet **2** : to expose to public scorn **3** : to execute by hanging

gib·bon \ˈgi-bən\ *n* : any of several tailless apes of southeastern Asia

gib·bous \ˈji-bəs, ˈgi-\ *adj* **1** : rounded like the exterior of a sphere or circle **2** : seen with more than half but not all of the apparent disk illuminated ⟨~ moon⟩ **3** : having a hump

gibe *or* **jibe** \ˈjīb\ *vb* **gibed** *or* **jibed; gib·ing** *or* **jib·ing** : to utter taunting words : SNEER — **gibe** *or* **jibe** *n*

gib·lets \ˈjib-ləts\ *n pl* : the edible viscera of a fowl

Gib·son girl \ˈgib-sən-\ *adj* : of or relating to a style in women's clothing characterized by high necks, full sleeves, and slender waistlines

gid·dy \ˈgi-dē\ *adj* **gid·di·er; -est** **1** : DIZZY **2** : causing dizziness ⟨a ~ height⟩ **3** : not serious : FRIVOLOUS, SILLY — **gid·di·ness** \-dē-nəs\ *n*

gid·dy·ap \ˌgi-dē-ˈap, -ˈəp\ *or* **gid·dy·up** \-ˈəp\ *vb imper* — a command (as to a horse) to go ahead or go faster

GIF \ˈgif, ˈjif\ *n* [graphic *i*nterchange *f*ormat] : a computer file format for digital images; *also* : the image itself

gift \ˈgift\ *n* **1** : a special ability : TALENT **2** : something given : PRESENT **3** : the act or power of giving

gift card *n* : a card entitling the recipient to goods or services of a specified value from the issuer

gift·ed \ˈgif-təd\ *adj* : TALENTED

[1]**gig** \ˈgig\ *n* **1** : a long light ship's boat **2** : a light 2-wheeled one-horse carriage

[2]**gig** *n* : a pronged spear for catching fish — **gig** *vb*

[3]**gig** *n* : a job for a specified time; *esp* : an entertainer's engagement

[4]**gig** *n* : a military demerit — **gig** *vb*

giga·byte \ˈji-gə-ˌbīt, ˈgi-\ *n* : 1024

megabytes or 1,073,741,824 bytes; *also* : one billion bytes

gi·gan·tic \jī-ˈgan-tik\ *adj* : exceeding the usual (as in size or force)

gig economy *n* : economic activity that involves the use of temporary or freelance workers to perform jobs

gig·gle \ˈgi-gəl\ *vb* **gig·gled; gig·gling** : to laugh with repeated short catches of the breath — **giggle** *n* — **gig·gly** \-gə-lē\ *adj*

GIGO *abbr* garbage in, garbage out

gig·o·lo \ˈji-gə-ˌlō\ *n, pl* **-los** **1** : a man supported by a woman usu. in return for his attentions **2** : a professional dancing partner or male escort

gig worker *n* : a worker in the gig economy

Gi·la monster \ˈhē-lə-\ *n* : a large orange and black venomous lizard of the southwestern U.S.

¹gild \ˈgild\ *vb* **gild·ed** *or* **gilt** \ˈgilt\; **gild·ing** **1** : to overlay with or as if with a thin covering of gold **2** : to give an attractive but often deceptive appearance to

²gild *var of* GUILD

¹gill \ˈjil\ *n* — see WEIGHT table

²gill \ˈgil\ *n* : an organ (as of a fish) for obtaining oxygen from water

¹gilt \ˈgilt\ *adj* : of the color of gold

²gilt *n* : gold or a substance resembling gold laid on the surface of an object

³gilt *n* : a young female swine

¹gim·crack \ˈjim-ˌkrak\ *n* : a showy object of little use or value

²gimcrack *adj* : CHEAP, SHODDY

gim·let \ˈgim-lət\ *n* : a small tool with screw point and cross handle for boring holes

gim·me cap \ˈgi-mē-\ *n* : an adjustable visored cap featuring a corporate logo or slogan

gim·mick \ˈgi-mik\ *n* **1** : CONTRIVANCE, GADGET **2** : an important feature that is not immediately apparent : CATCH **3** : a new and ingenious scheme **4** : a device used to attract business or attention — **gim·micky** \-mi-kē\ *adj*

gim·mick·ry \ˈgi-mi-krē\ *n, pl* **-ries** : an array of or the use of gimmicks

gimpy \ˈgim-pē\ *adj* : LAME 1

¹gin \ˈjin\ *n* [ME *gin,* fr. AF, short for *engin* engine] **1** : TRAP, SNARE **2** : a machine to separate seeds from cotton — **gin** *vb*

²gin *n* [by shortening & alter. fr. *geneva,* kind of gin] : a liquor distilled from a grain mash and flavored with juniper berries

gin·ger \ˈjin-jər\ *n* : the pungent aromatic rootstock of a tropical plant used esp. as a spice and in medicine; *also* : the spice or the plant

ginger ale *n* : a carbonated soft drink flavored with ginger

gin·ger·bread \ˈjin-jər-ˌbred\ *n* **1** : a cake made with molasses and flavored with ginger **2** : lavish or superfluous ornament esp. in architecture

gin·ger·ly \ˈjin-jər-lē\ *adj* : very cautious or careful — **gingerly** *adv*

gin·ger·snap \-ˌsnap\ *n* : a thin brittle molasses cookie flavored with ginger

ging·ham \ˈgiŋ-əm\ *n* : a cotton cloth that is often marked with a pattern of colored squares

gin·gi·vi·tis \ˌjin-jə-ˈvī-təs\ *n* : inflammation of the gums

gink·go *also* **ging·ko** \ˈgiŋ-(ˌ)kō\ *n, pl* **ginkgoes** *or* **ginkgos** *also* **gingkos** *or* **gingkoes** **1** : a tree of eastern China with fan-shaped leaves often grown as a shade tree **2** : GINKGO BILOBA

ginkgo bi·lo·ba \-ˌbī-ˈlō-bə\ *n* : an extract of the leaves of ginkgo that is held to enhance mental functioning

gin·seng \ˈjin-ˌseŋ\ *n* : an aromatic root of a Chinese or No. American herb used esp. in Chinese medicine; *also* : one of these herbs

Gip·sy *chiefly Brit var of* GYPSY

gi·raffe \jə-ˈraf\ *n, pl* **giraffes** [It *giraffa,* fr. Ar *zirāfa*] : an African ruminant mammal with a very long neck and a short coat with dark blotches

gird \ˈgərd\ *vb* **gird·ed** *or* **girt** \ˈgərt\; **gird·ing** **1** : to encircle or fasten (as a sword) with or as if with a belt **2** : to invest esp. with power or authority **3** : PREPARE, BRACE

gird·er \ˈgər-dər\ *n* : a horizontal main supporting beam

gir·dle \ˈgər-dᵊl\ *n* **1** : something (as a belt or sash) that encircles or confines **2** : a woman's supporting undergarment that extends from the waist to below the hips — **girdle** *vb*

girl \ˈgərl\ *n* **1** : a female child **2** : a young woman **3** : SWEETHEART — **girl·hood** \-ˌhu̇d\ *n* — **girl·ish** *adj*

girl Friday *n* : a female assistant (as in an office) entrusted with a wide variety of tasks

girl·friend \ˈgərl-ˌfrend\ *n* **1** : a female friend **2** : a regular female companion in a romantic or sexual relationship

Girl Scout *n* : a member of any of the scouting programs of the Girl Scouts of the United States of America

girth \ˈgərth\ *n* **1** : a band around an animal by which something (as a saddle) may be fastened on its back **2** : a measure around something

gist \ˈjist\ *n* [AF, it lies, fr. *gesir* to lie, ultim. fr. L *jacēre*] : the main point or part ⟨the ~ of his speech⟩

git *dial var of* GET

¹give \ˈgiv\ *vb* **gave** \ˈgāv\; **giv·en** \ˈgi-vən\; **giv·ing** **1** : to make a present of **2** : to bestow by formal action **3** : to accord or yield to another **4** : to yield to force, strain, or pressure **5** : to put into the possession or keeping of another **6** : PROFFER ⟨*gave* her his hand⟩ **7** : DELIVER ⟨*gave* the bride away⟩ **8** : to present in public performance or to view **9** : PROVIDE ⟨~ a party⟩ **10** : ATTRIBUTE **11** : to make, form, or yield as a product or result ⟨cows ~ milk⟩ **12** : PAY **13** : to deliver by some bodily action ⟨*gave* me a push⟩ **14** : to offer as a pledge ⟨I ~ you my word⟩ **15** : DEVOTE **16** : to cause to have or receive ⟨~ me time⟩

²give *n* **1** : capacity or tendency to yield to force or strain **2** : the quality or state of being springy

give–and–take \ˌgiv-ən-ˈtāk\ *n* **1** : COMPROMISE **2** : a usu. good-natured exchange (as of remarks or ideas)
give·away \ˈgi-və-ˌwā\ *n* **1** : an unintentional revelation or betrayal **2** : something given away free; *esp* : PREMIUM
give in *vb* : SUBMIT, SURRENDER
[1]**giv·en** \ˈgi-vən\ *adj* **1** : DISPOSED, INCLINED ⟨~ to swearing⟩ **2** : SPECIFIED, PARTICULAR ⟨at a ~ time⟩
[2]**given** *n* : something taken for granted : a basic condition or assumption
[3]**given** *prep* : CONSIDERING
given name *n* : a name that precedes one's surname
give out *vb* **1** : EMIT **2** : BREAK DOWN **3** : to become exhausted : COLLAPSE
give up *vb* **1** : SURRENDER **2** : to abandon (oneself) to a feeling, influence, or activity **3** : QUIT ⟨*gave up* his job⟩
giz·mo *also* **gis·mo** \ˈgiz-mō\ *n, pl* **gizmos** *also* **gismos** : GADGET
giz·zard \ˈgi-zərd\ *n* : the muscular usu. horny-lined enlargement of the alimentary canal of a bird used for churning and grinding up food
gla·cial \ˈglā-shəl\ *adj* **1** : extremely cold **2** : of or relating to glaciers **3** : being or relating to a past period of time when a large part of the earth was covered by glaciers **4** *cap* : PLEISTOCENE **5** : very slow ⟨a ~ pace⟩ — **gla·cial·ly** *adv*
gla·ci·ate \ˈglā-shē-ˌāt\ *vb* **-at·ed; -at·ing** **1** : to subject to glacial action **2** : to produce glacial effects in or on — **gla·ci·a·tion** \ˌglā-shē-ˈā-shən, -sē-\ *n*
gla·cier \ˈglā-shər\ *n* [F, fr. MF dial. (Savoy), fr. *glace* ice, fr. L *glacies*] : a large body of ice moving slowly down a slope or spreading outward on a land surface
[1]**glad** \ˈglad\ *adj* **glad·der; glad·dest** **1** : experiencing pleasure, joy, or delight **2** : PLEASED **3** : very willing ⟨was ~ to help⟩ **4** : PLEASANT, JOYFUL **5** : CHEERFUL ⟨a ~ morning⟩ — **glad·ly** *adv* — **glad·ness** *n*
[2]**glad** *n* : GLADIOLUS
glad·den \ˈgla-dᵊn\ *vb* : to make glad
glade \ˈglād\ *n* : a grassy open space surrounded by woods
glad·i·a·tor \ˈgla-dē-ˌā-tər\ *n* **1** : a person engaged in a fight to the death for public entertainment in ancient Rome **2** : a person engaging in a public fight or controversy; *also* : PRIZEFIGHTER — **glad·i·a·to·ri·al** \ˌgla-dē-ə-ˈtȯr-ē-əl\ *adj*
glad·i·o·lus \ˌgla-dē-ˈō-ləs\ *n, pl* **-oli** \-ˈō-(ˌ)lē, -ˌlī\ *or* **-olus** *also* **-o·lus·es** [L, fr. dim. of *gladius* sword] : any of a genus of chiefly African plants related to the irises and having erect sword-shaped leaves and stalks of bright-colored flowers
glad·some \ˈglad-səm\ *adj* : giving or showing joy : CHEERFUL
glam \ˈglam\ *n* : extravagantly showy glamour — **glam** *adj*
glam·or·ise *Brit var of* GLAMORIZE
glam·or·ize *also* **glam·our·ize** \ˈgla-mə-ˌrīz\ *vb* **-ized; -iz·ing** : to make or look upon as glamorous
glam·our *also* **glam·or** \ˈgla-mər\ *n* [Sc *glamour* magic spell, alter. of E *grammar;* fr. the popular association of erudition with occult practices] : an exciting and often illusory and romantic attractiveness; *esp* : alluring personal attraction — **glam·or·ous** *also* **glam·our·ous** \-mə-rəs\ *adj*
[1]**glance** \ˈglans\ *vb* **glanced; glanc·ing** **1** : to strike and fly off to one side **2** : GLEAM **3** : to give a quick look
[2]**glance** *n* **1** : a quick intermittent flash or gleam **2** : a deflected impact or blow **3** : a quick look
gland \ˈgland\ *n* : a cell or group of cells that prepares and secretes a substance (as saliva or sweat) for further use in or discharge from the body
glan·du·lar \ˈglan-jə-lər\ *adj* : of, relating to, or involving glands
glans \ˈglanz\ *n, pl* **glan·des** \ˈglan-ˌdēz\ [L, lit., acorn] : a conical vascular body forming the extremity of the penis or clitoris
[1]**glare** \ˈgler\ *vb* **glared; glar·ing** **1** : to shine with a harsh dazzling light **2** : to stare fiercely or angrily
[2]**glare** *n* **1** : a harsh dazzling light **2** : an angry or fierce stare
glaring *adj* : very conspicuous ⟨a ~ error⟩ — **glar·ing·ly** *adv*
glass \ˈglas\ *n* **1** : a hard brittle amorphous usu. transparent or translucent material consisting typically of silica **2** : something made of glass; *esp* : TUMBLER 2 **3** *pl* : a pair of lenses used to correct defects of vision : SPECTACLES **4** : the quantity held by a glass container — **glass** *adj* — **glass·ful** \-ˌfu̇l\ *n* — **glassy** *adj*
glass·blow·ing \-ˌblō-iŋ\ *n* : the art of shaping a mass of glass that has been softened by heat by blowing air into it through a tube — **glass·blow·er** *n*
glass·ware \-ˌwer\ *n* : articles made of glass
glau·co·ma \glau̇-ˈkō-mə, glȯ-\ *n* : a disease of the eye marked by increased pressure within the eyeball resulting in damage to the retina and gradual loss of vision
[1]**glaze** \ˈglāz\ *vb* **glazed; glaz·ing** **1** : to furnish (as a window frame) with glass **2** : to apply glaze to
[2]**glaze** *n* : a glassy coating or surface
gla·zier \ˈglā-zhər\ *n* : a person who sets glass in window frames
[1]**gleam** \ˈglēm\ *n* **1** : a transient subdued or partly obscured light **2** : GLINT **3** : a faint trace ⟨a ~ of hope⟩
[2]**gleam** *vb* **1** : to shine with subdued light or moderate brightness **2** : to appear briefly or faintly ♦ ***Synonyms*** FLASH, GLIMMER, GLISTEN, GLITTER, SHIMMER, SPARKLE
glean \ˈglēn\ *vb* **1** : to gather grain left by reapers **2** : to collect little by little or with patient effort ⟨antiques ~*ed* from flea markets⟩ — **glean·able** *adj* — **glean·er** *n*
glean·ings \ˈglē-niŋz\ *n pl* : things acquired by gleaning

glee \ˈglē\ *n* [ME, fr. OE *glēo* entertainment, music] **1** : JOY, HILARITY **2** : a part-song for three usu. male voices — **glee·ful** *adj* — **glee·ful·ly** *adv*
glee club *n* : a chorus organized for singing usu. short choral pieces
glen \ˈglen\ *n* : a narrow hidden valley
glen·gar·ry \glen-ˈga-rē\ *n, pl* **-ries** *often cap* : a woolen cap of Scottish origin
glib \ˈglib\ *adj* **glib·ber; glib·best** : speaking or spoken with careless ease — **glib·ly** *adv*
glide \ˈglīd\ *vb* **glid·ed; glid·ing** **1** : to move smoothly and effortlessly **2** : to descend gradually without engine power ⟨∼ in an airplane⟩ — **glide** *n*
glid·er \ˈglī-dər\ *n* **1** : one that glides **2** : an aircraft resembling an airplane but having no engine **3** : a porch seat suspended from an upright frame
[1]**glim·mer** \ˈgli-mər\ *vb* : to shine faintly or unsteadily
[2]**glimmer** *n* **1** : a faint unsteady light **2** : INKLING **3** : a small amount : HINT
[1]**glimpse** \ˈglimps\ *vb* **glimpsed; glimps·ing** : to take a brief look : see momentarily or incompletely
[2]**glimpse** *n* **1** : a faint idea : GLIMMER **2** : a short hurried look
glint \ˈglint\ *vb* **1** : to shine by reflection : SPARKLE, GLITTER, GLEAM **2** : to appear briefly or faintly — **glint** *n*
glis·san·do \gli-ˈsän-(ˌ)dō\ *n, pl* **-di** \-(ˌ)dē\ *or* **-dos** : a rapid sliding up or down the musical scale
[1]**glis·ten** \ˈgli-sᵊn\ *vb* : to shine by reflection with a soft luster or sparkle
[2]**glisten** *n* : GLITTER, SPARKLE
glis·ter \ˈglis-tər\ *vb* : GLITTER
glitch \ˈglich\ *n* : MALFUNCTION; *also* : SNAG 2
[1]**glit·ter** \ˈgli-tər\ *vb* **1** : to shine with brilliant or metallic luster : SPARKLE **2** : to shine with strong emotion : FLASH ⟨eyes ∼*ing* in anger⟩ **3** : to be brilliantly attractive esp. in a superficial way
[2]**glitter** *n* **1** : sparkling brilliancy, showiness, or attractiveness **2** : small glittering objects used for ornamentation — **glit·tery** \ˈgli-tə-rē\ *adj*
[1]**glitz** \ˈglits\ *n* : extravagant showiness — **glitzy** \ˈglit-sē\ *adj*
[2]**glitz** *vb* : to make flashy or extravagant in appearance — often used with *up*
gloam·ing \ˈglō-miŋ\ *n* : TWILIGHT, DUSK
gloat \ˈglōt\ *vb* : to think about something with triumphant and often malicious delight ⟨∼*ing* over their victory⟩
glob \ˈgläb\ *n* **1** : a small drop **2** : a large rounded mass
glob·al \ˈglō-bəl\ *adj* **1** : WORLDWIDE **2** : COMPREHENSIVE, GENERAL — **glob·al·ly** *adv*
glob·al·i·za·tion \ˌglō-bə-lə-ˈzā-shən\ *n* : the development of an increasingly integrated global economy
Global Positioning System *n* : GPS
global warming *n* : an increase in the earth's atmospheric and oceanic temperatures due to an increase in the greenhouse effect
globe \ˈglōb\ *n* **1** : BALL, SPHERE **2** : EARTH; *also* : a spherical representation of the earth
globe–trot·ter \ˈglōb-ˌträ-tər\ *n* : a person who travels widely — **globe–trot·ting** *n or adj*
glob·u·lar \ˈglä-byə-lər\ *adj* : having the shape of a globe or globule
glob·ule \ˈglä-(ˌ)byül\ *n* : a tiny globe or ball esp. of a liquid
glob·u·lin \ˈglä-byə-lən\ *n* : any of a class of simple proteins insoluble in pure water but soluble in dilute salt solutions that occur widely in plant and animal tissues
glock·en·spiel \ˈglä-kən-ˌshpēl, -ˌspēl\ *n* [G, fr. *Glocke* bell + *Spiel* play] : a percussion musical instrument consisting of a series of metal bars played with two hammers
gloom \ˈglüm\ *n* **1** : partial or total darkness **2** : lowness of spirits : DEJECTION **3** : an atmosphere of despondency ⟨a ∼ fell over the household⟩ — **gloom·i·ly** \ˈglü-mə-lē\ *adv* — **gloom·i·ness** \-mē-nəs\ *n* — **gloomy** \ˈglü-mē\ *adj*
Gloomy Gus \-ˈgəs\ *n, pl* **Gloomy Gus·es** : a person who is habitually gloomy
glop \ˈgläp\ *n* : a messy mass or mixture
glo·ri·fy \ˈglȯr-ə-ˌfī\ *vb* **-fied; -fy·ing** **1** : to raise to heavenly glory **2** : to light up brilliantly **3** : EXTOL **4** : to give glory to (as in worship) — **glo·ri·fi·ca·tion** \ˌglȯr-ə-fə-ˈkā-shən\ *n*
glo·ri·ous \ˈglȯr-ē-əs\ *adj* **1** : possessing or deserving glory : PRAISEWORTHY **2** : conferring glory **3** : RESPLENDENT, MAGNIFICENT ⟨a ∼ sunset⟩ **4** : DELIGHTFUL, WONDERFUL ⟨had a ∼ weekend⟩ — **glo·ri·ous·ly** *adv*
[1]**glo·ry** \ˈglȯr-ē\ *n, pl* **glories** **1** : RENOWN **2** : honor and praise rendered in worship **3** : something that secures praise or renown **4** : a distinguishing quality or asset **5** : RESPLENDENCE, MAGNIFICENCE **6** : heavenly bliss **7** : a height of prosperity or achievement
[2]**glory** *vb* **glo·ried; glo·ry·ing** : to rejoice proudly : EXULT
[1]**gloss** \ˈgläs, ˈglȯs\ *n* **1** : LUSTER, SHEEN, BRIGHTNESS **2** : outward show
[2]**gloss** *vb* **1** : to give a false appearance of acceptableness to ⟨∼ over inadequacies⟩ **2** : to deal with too lightly or not at all ⟨∼*ed* over the problem⟩
[3]**gloss** *n* [alter. of *gloze,* fr. ME *glose,* fr. AF, fr. ML *glosa, glossa,* fr. Gk *glōssa, glōtta* tongue, language, unusual word] **1** : an explanatory note (as in the margin of a text) **2** : GLOSSARY **3** : an interlinear translation **4** : a continuous commentary accompanying a text
[4]**gloss** *vb* : to furnish glosses for
glos·sa·ry \ˈglä-sə-rē, ˈglȯ-\ *n, pl* **-ries** : a collection of difficult or specialized terms with their meanings — **glos·sar·i·al** \glä-ˈser-ē-əl, glȯ-\ *adj*
glos·so·la·lia \ˌglä-sə-ˈlā-lē-ə, ˌglȯ-\ *n* [ultim. fr. Gk *glōssa* tongue, language + *lalia* chatter] : TONGUE 6
[1]**glossy** \ˈglä-sē, ˈglȯ-\ *adj* **gloss·i·er; -est**

: having a surface luster or brightness — **gloss·i·ly** \-sə-lē\ *adv* — **gloss·i·ness** \-sē-nəs\ *n*

[2]**glossy** *n, pl* **gloss·ies** : a photograph printed on smooth shiny paper

glot·tis \ˈglä-təs\ *n, pl* **glot·tis·es** *or* **glot·ti·des** \-tə-ˌdēz\ : the slitlike opening between the vocal cords in the larynx — **glot·tal** \ˈglä-tᵊl\ *adj*

glove \ˈgləv\ *n* **1** : a covering for the hand having separate sections for each finger **2** : a padded leather covering for the hand for use in a sport

[1]**glow** \ˈglō\ *vb* **1** : to shine with or as if with intense heat **2** : to have a rich warm usu. ruddy color : FLUSH, BLUSH **3** : to feel hot **4** : to show exuberance or elation ⟨~ with pride⟩

[2]**glow** *n* **1** : brightness or warmth of color; *esp* : REDNESS **2** : warmth of feeling or emotion **3** : a sensation of warmth **4** : light such as is emitted from a heated substance

glow·er \ˈglaů(-ə)r\ *vb* : to stare angrily : SCOWL — **glower** *n*

glow·worm \ˈglō-ˌwərm\ *n* : any of various insect larvae or adults that give off light

glox·in·ia \gläk-ˈsi-nē-ə\ *n* : any of a genus of tropical herbs related to the African violets; *esp* : one with showy bell-shaped or slipper-shaped flowers

gloze \ˈglōz\ *vb* **glozed; gloz·ing** : to make appear right or acceptable : GLOSS

glu·cose \ˈglü-ˌkōs\ *n* **1** : a form of crystalline sugar; *esp* : DEXTROSE **2** : a sweet light-colored syrup made from cornstarch

glue \ˈglü\ *n* : a jellylike protein substance made from animal materials and used for sticking things together; *also* : any of various other strong adhesives — **glue** *vb* — **glu·ey** \ˈglü-ē\ *adj*

glum \ˈgləm\ *adj* **glum·mer; glum·mest 1** : broodingly morose : SULLEN **2** : DREARY, GLOOMY ⟨a ~ countenance⟩

♦ ***Synonyms*** CRABBED, DOUR, SATURNINE, SULKY

[1]**glut** \ˈglət\ *vb* **glut·ted; glut·ting 1** : OVERSUPPLY **2** : to fill esp. with food to satiety : SATIATE

[2]**glut** *n* : an excessive supply

glu·ten \ˈglü-tᵊn\ *n* : a gluey protein substance that causes dough to be sticky

glu·ti·nous \ˈglü-tə-nəs\ *adj* : STICKY

glut·ton \ˈglə-tᵊn\ *n* : one that eats to excess — **glut·ton·ous** \ˈglə-tə-nəs\ *adj* — **glut·tony** \ˈglə-tə-nē\ *n*

glyc·er·in *or* **glyc·er·ine** \ˈgli-sə-rən\ *n* : GLYCEROL

glyc·er·ol \ˈgli-sə-ˌrȯl, -ˌrōl\ *n* : a sweet syrupy alcohol usu. obtained from fats and used esp. as a solvent

gly·co·gen \ˈglī-kə-jən\ *n* : a white tasteless substance that is the chief storage carbohydrate of animals

gm *abbr* gram

GM *abbr* **1** general manager **2** guided missile

G–man \ˈjē-ˌman\ *n* : a special agent of the Federal Bureau of Investigation

GMT *abbr* Greenwich mean time

gnarled \ˈnärld\ *adj* **1** : KNOTTY ⟨~ hands⟩ **2** : GLOOMY, SULLEN

gnash \ˈnash\ *vb* : to grind (as teeth) together

gnat \ˈnat\ *n* : any of various small usu. biting dipteran flies

gnaw \ˈnȯ\ *vb* **1** : to consume, wear away, or make by persistent biting or nibbling **2** : to affect as if by gnawing — **gnaw·er** *n*

gneiss \ˈnīs\ *n* : a layered rock similar in composition to granite

gnome \ˈnōm\ *n* : a dwarf of folklore who lives inside the earth and guards precious ore or treasure — **gnome·like** \-ˌlīk\ *adj* — **gnom·ish** *adj*

GNP *abbr* gross national product

gnu \ˈnü\ *n, pl* **gnu** *or* **gnus** : WILDEBEEST

[1]**go** \ˈgō\ *vb* **went** \ˈwent\; **gone** \ˈgȯn, ˈgän\; **go·ing; goes** \ˈgōz\ **1** : to move on a course : PROCEED ⟨~ slow⟩ **2** : LEAVE, DEPART **3** : to take a certain course or follow a certain procedure ⟨reports ~ through department channels⟩ **4** : EXTEND, RUN ⟨his land *~es* to the river⟩; *also* : LEAD ⟨that door *~es* to the cellar⟩ **5** : to be habitually in a certain state ⟨*~es* barefoot⟩ **6** : to become lost, consumed, or spent; *also* : DIE **7** : ELAPSE, PASS **8** : to pass by sale ⟨*went* for a good price⟩ **9** : to become impaired or weakened ⟨his hearing started to ~⟩ **10** : to give way under force or pressure : BREAK **11** : to move along in a specified manner ⟨it *went* well⟩ **12** : to be in general or on an average ⟨cheap, as yachts ~⟩ **13** : to become esp. as the result of a contest ⟨the decision *went* against him⟩ **14** : to put or subject oneself ⟨~ to great expense⟩ **15** : RESORT ⟨*went* to court to recover damages⟩ **16** : to begin or maintain an action or motion **17** : to function properly ⟨the clock doesn't ~⟩ **18** : to be known ⟨*~es* by an alias⟩ **19** : to be or act in accordance ⟨a good rule to ~ by⟩ **20** : to come to be applied **21** : to pass by award, assignment, or lot **22** : to contribute to a result ⟨qualities that ~ to make a hero⟩ **23** : to be about, intending, or expecting something ⟨is *~ing* to leave town⟩ **24** : to arrive at a certain state or condition ⟨~ to sleep⟩ **25** : to come to be ⟨the tire *went* flat⟩ **26** : to be capable of being sung or played ⟨the tune *~es* like this⟩ **27** : to be suitable or becoming : HARMONIZE **28** : to be capable of passing, extending, or being contained or inserted ⟨this coat will ~ in the trunk⟩ **29** : to have a usual or proper place or position : BELONG ⟨these books ~ on the top shelf⟩ **30** : to be capable of being divided ⟨3 *~es* into 6 twice⟩ **31** : to have a tendency ⟨that *~es* to show that he is honest⟩ **32** : to be acceptable, satisfactory, or adequate ⟨any color will ~ with black⟩ **33** : to empty the bladder or bowels **34** : to proceed along or according to : FOLLOW **35** : TRAVERSE **36** : BET, BID

⟨willing to ~ $50⟩ **37** : to assume the function or obligation of ⟨~ bail for a friend⟩ **38** : to participate to the extent of ⟨~ halves⟩ **39** : WEIGH **40** : ENDURE, TOLERATE **41** : AFFORD ⟨can't ~ the price⟩ **42** : SAY — used chiefly in oral narration of speech **43** : to engage in ⟨don't ~ telling everyone⟩ — **go at 1** : ATTACK, ATTEMPT **2** : UNDERTAKE — **go back on 1** : ABANDON **2** : BETRAY **3** : FAIL — **go by the board** : to be discarded — **go for 1** : to pass for or serve as **2** : to try to secure **3** : FAVOR — **go one better** : OUTDO, SURPASS — **go over 1** : EXAMINE **2** : REPEAT **3** : STUDY, REVIEW — **go places** : to be on the way to success — **go steady** : to date one person exclusively — **go to bat for** : DEFEND, CHAMPION — **go to town 1** : to work or act efficiently **2** : to be very successful

²**go** *n, pl* **goes 1** : the act or manner of going **2** : the height of fashion ⟨boots are all the ~⟩ **3** : a turn of affairs : OCCURRENCE **4** : ENERGY, VIGOR **5** : ATTEMPT, TRY ⟨give it a ~⟩ **6** : a spell of activity ⟨finished the job at one ~⟩ — **no go** : USELESS, HOPELESS — **on the go** : constantly active

³**go** *adj* : functioning properly ⟨declared all systems ~⟩

goad \ˈgōd\ *n* [ME *gode,* fr. OE *gād* spear, goad] **1** : a pointed rod used to urge on an animal **2** : something that urges ♦ ***Synonyms*** STIMULUS, IMPETUS, INCENTIVE, SPUR, STIMULANT — **goad** *vb*

go–ahead \ˈgō-ə-ˌhed\ *n* : authority to proceed ⟨got the ~ for the project⟩

goal \ˈgōl\ *n* **1** : the mark set as limit to a race; *also* : an area to be reached safely in children's games **2** : AIM, PURPOSE **3** : an area or object toward which play is directed to score; *also* : a successful attempt to score

goal•ie \ˈgō-lē\ *n* : GOALKEEPER

goal•keep•er \ˈgōl-ˌkē-pər\ *n* : a player who defends the goal in various games

goal•post \-ˌpōst\ *n* : one of the two vertical posts with a crossbar that constitute the goal in various games

goat \ˈgōt\ *n, pl* **goats** *or* **goat** : any of various hollow-horned ruminant mammals related to the sheep that have backward-curving horns, a short tail, and usu. straight hair

goa•tee \gō-ˈtē\ *n* : a small trim pointed or tufted beard on a man's chin

goat•herd \ˈgōt-ˌhərd\ *n* : a person who tends goats

goat•skin \-ˌskin\ *n* : the skin of a goat or a leather made from it

¹**gob** \ˈgäb\ *n* : LUMP, MASS

²**gob** *n* : SAILOR

gob•bet \ˈgä-bət\ *n* : LUMP, MASS

¹**gob•ble** \ˈgä-bəl\ *vb* **gob•bled; gob•bling 1** : to swallow or eat greedily **2** : to take eagerly : GRAB

²**gobble** *vb* **gob•bled; gob•bling** : to make the natural guttural noise of a male turkey

gob•ble•dy•gook *also* **gob•ble•de•gook** \ˈgä-bəl-dē-ˌgu̇k, -ˌgük\ *n* : generally unintelligible jargon

gob•bler \ˈgä-blər\ *n* : a male turkey

go–be•tween \ˈgō-bə-ˌtwēn\ *n* : an intermediate agent : BROKER

gob•let \ˈgä-blət\ *n* : a drinking glass with a foot and stem

gob•lin \ˈgä-blən\ *n* : an ugly or grotesque sprite that is mischievous and sometimes evil and malicious

go•by \ˈgō-bē\ *n, pl* **gobies** *also* **goby** : any of numerous spiny-finned fishes usu. having the pelvic fins united to form a ventral sucking disk

god \ˈgäd, ˈgȯd\ *n* **1** *cap* : the supreme reality; *esp* : the Being worshiped as the creator and ruler of the universe **2** : a being or object believed to have supernatural attributes and powers and to require worship **3** : a thing of supreme value **4** : an extraordinarily attractive person

god•child \ˈgäd-ˌchī(-ə)ld, ˈgȯd-\ *n* : a person for whom another person stands as sponsor at baptism

god•daugh•ter \-ˌdȯ-tər\ *n* : a female godchild

god•dess \ˈgä-dəs, ˈgȯ-\ *n* **1** : a female god **2** : a woman whose charm or beauty arouses adoration

god•fa•ther \ˈgäd-ˌfä-t͟hər, ˈgȯd-\ *n* **1** : a man who sponsors a person at baptism **2** : the leader of an organized crime syndicate

god•head \-ˌhed\ *n* **1** : divine nature or essence **2** *cap* : GOD 1; *also* : the nature of God esp. as existing in three persons

god•hood \-ˌhu̇d\ *n* : DIVINITY

god•less \-ləs\ *adj* : not acknowledging a deity or divine law — **god•less•ness** *n*

god•like \-ˌlīk\ *adj* : resembling or having the qualities of God or a god

god•ly \-lē\ *adj* **god•li•er; -est 1** : DIVINE **2** : PIOUS, DEVOUT — **god•li•ness** *n*

god•moth•er \-ˌmə-t͟hər\ *n* : a woman who sponsors a person at baptism

god•par•ent \-ˌper-ənt\ *n* : a sponsor at baptism

god•send \-ˌsend\ *n* : a desirable or needed thing or event that comes unexpectedly

god•son \-ˌsən\ *n* : a male godchild

God•speed \-ˈspēd\ *n* : a prosperous journey : SUCCESS ⟨bade him ~⟩

go•fer *or* **go•pher** \ˈgō-fər\ *n* [alter. of *go for*] : an employee whose duties include running errands

go–get•ter \ˈgō-ˌge-tər\ *n* : an aggressively enterprising person — **go–get•ting** *adj or n*

gog•gle \ˈgä-gəl\ *vb* **gog•gled; gog•gling** : to stare with wide or protuberant eyes

gog•gles \ˈgä-gəlz\ *n pl* : protective glasses set in a flexible frame that fits snugly against the face

go–go \ˈgō-ˌgō\ *adj* **1** : related to, being, or employed to entertain in a disco ⟨~ dancers⟩ **2** : aggressively enterprising and energetic ⟨~ entrepreneurs⟩

go•ings–on \ˌgō-iŋ-ˈzȯn, -ˈzän\ *n pl* : ACTIONS, EVENTS

goi·ter \'gȯi-tər\ *n* : an abnormally enlarged thyroid gland visible as a swelling at the base of the neck — **goi·trous** \-trəs, -tə-rəs\ *adj*
goi·tre *chiefly Brit var of* GOITER
go–kart \'gō-ˌkärt\ *n* : a small motorized vehicle used esp. for racing
gold \'gōld\ *n* **1** : a malleable yellow metallic chemical element used esp. for coins and jewelry **2** : gold coins; *also* : MONEY **3** : a yellow color
gold·brick \'gōld-ˌbrik\ *n* : a person who shirks assigned work — **goldbrick** *vb*
gold coast *n, often cap G&C* : an exclusive residential district
gold digger *n* : a person who uses charm to extract money or gifts from others
gold·en \'gōl-dən\ *adj* **1** : made of or relating to gold **2** : having the color of gold; *also* : BLOND **3** : SHINING, LUSTROUS **4** : SUPERB **5** : FLOURISHING, PROSPEROUS **6** : radiantly youthful and vigorous **7** : FAVORABLE, ADVANTAGEOUS ⟨a ~ opportunity⟩ **8** : MELLOW, RESONANT ⟨a ~ tenor⟩
gold·en–ag·er \'gōl-dən-'ā-jər\ *n* : an elderly and often retired person usu. engaging in club activities
golden eagle *n* : a large dark brown eagle with gold-colored feathers on the back of the head and neck
golden hamster *n* : a small tawny hamster often kept as a pet
golden handcuffs *n pl* : special benefits offered to an employee as an inducement to continue service
golden handshake *n* : a generous severance agreement given esp. as an inducement to early retirement
golden retriever *n* : any of a breed of retrievers with a flat golden coat
gold·en·rod \'gōl-dən-ˌräd\ *n* : any of numerous herbs related to the daisies that have tall slender stalks with many tiny usu. yellow flower heads
golden years *n pl* : the advanced years in a lifetime
gold·finch \-ˌfinch\ *n* **1** : a small largely red, black, and yellow Old World finch often kept in a cage **2** : any of three small related American finches of which the males usu. become bright yellow and black in summer
gold·fish \-ˌfish\ *n* : a small usu. golden-orange carp often kept as an aquarium or pond fish
gold·smith \-ˌsmith\ *n* : a person who makes or deals in articles of gold
golf \'gälf, 'gȯlf\ *n* : a game played with a small ball and various clubs on a course having 9 or 18 holes — **golf** *vb* — **golf·er** *n*
-gon \ˌgän\ *n comb form* : figure having (so many) angles ⟨hexa*gon*⟩
go·nad \'gō-ˌnad\ *n* : a sperm- or egg-producing gland : OVARY, TESTIS — **go·nad·al** \gō-'na-dᵊl\ *adj*
go·nad·o·trop·ic \gō-ˌna-də-'trä-pik\ *also* **go·nad·o·tro·phic** \-'trō-fik, -'trä-\ *adj* : acting on or stimulating the gonads
go·nad·o·tro·pin \-'trō-pən\ *also* **go·nad·o·tro·phin** \-fən\ *n* : a gonadotropic hormone
gon·do·la \'gän-də-lə (*usual for 1*), gän-'dō-\ *n* [It. dial. (Venice), prob. fr. MGk *kontoura* small vessel] **1** : a long narrow boat used on the canals of Venice **2** : a railroad car used for hauling loose freight (as coal) **3** : an enclosure beneath an airship or balloon **4** : an enclosed car suspended from a cable and used esp. for transporting skiers
gon·do·lier \ˌgän-də-'lir\ *n* : a person who propels a gondola
¹**gone** \'gȯn\ *past part of* GO
²**gone** *adj* **1** : LOST, RUINED **2** : DEAD **3** : SINKING, WEAK **4** : INVOLVED, ABSORBED **5** : INFATUATED **6** : PREGNANT **7** : PAST
gon·er \'gȯ-nər\ *n* : one whose case is hopeless
gong \'gäŋ, 'gȯŋ\ *n* : a metallic disk that produces a resounding tone when struck
gono·coc·cus \ˌgä-nə-'kä-kəs\ *n, pl* **-coc·ci** \-'käk-ˌsī, -(ˌ)sē, -'kä-ˌkī, -(ˌ)kē\ : a pus-producing bacterium causing gonorrhea — **gono·coc·cal** \-'kä-kəl\ *adj*
gon·or·rhea \ˌgä-nə-'rē-ə\ *n* : a contagious sexually transmitted inflammation of the genital tract caused by the gonococcus — **gon·or·rhe·al** \-'rē-əl\ *adj*
goo \'gü\ *n* **1** : a viscid or sticky substance **2** : sentimental tripe — **goo·ey** \-ē\ *adj*
goo·ber \'gü-bər, 'gu̇-\ *n, Southern & Midland* : PEANUT
¹**good** \'gu̇d\ *adj* **bet·ter** \'be-tər\; **best** \'best\ **1** : of a favorable character or tendency **2** : BOUNTIFUL, FERTILE ⟨~ land⟩ **3** : COMELY, ATTRACTIVE **4** : SUITABLE, FIT **5** : SOUND, WHOLE ⟨only one ~ arm⟩ **6** : AGREEABLE, PLEASANT ⟨had a ~ time⟩ **7** : SALUTARY, WHOLESOME **8** : CONSIDERABLE, AMPLE ⟨a ~ bit of time⟩ **9** : FULL ⟨waited a ~ hour⟩ **10** : WELL-FOUNDED **11** : TRUE ⟨holds ~ for everybody⟩ **12** : legally valid or effectual **13** : ADEQUATE, SATISFACTORY **14** : conforming to a standard ⟨~ English⟩ **15** : DISCRIMINATING **16** : COMMENDABLE, VIRTUOUS **17** : KIND **18** : UPPER-CLASS **19** : COMPETENT **20** : LOYAL, CLOSE ⟨a ~ friend⟩ — **good·ish** *adj*
²**good** *n* **1** : something good **2** : GOODNESS **3** : BENEFIT, WELFARE ⟨for the ~ of mankind⟩ **4** : something that has economic utility **5** *pl* : personal property **6** *pl* : CLOTH **7** *pl* : WARES, MERCHANDISE ⟨canned ~*s*⟩ **8** : good persons ⟨the ~ die young⟩ **9** *pl* : proof of wrongdoing — **for good** : FOREVER, PERMANENTLY — **to the good** : in a position of net gain or profit ⟨$10 *to the good*⟩
³**good** *adv* : WELL
good–bye *or* **good–by** \gu̇d-'bī, gə-\ *n* : a concluding remark at parting
good cholesterol *n* : HDL
good–for–noth·ing \'gu̇d-fər-ˌnə-thiŋ\ *adj* : of no use or value — **good–for–nothing** *n*
Good Friday *n* : the Friday before Easter

observed as the anniversary of the crucifixion of Christ
good–heart·ed \ˈgu̇d-ˈhär-təd\ *adj* : having a kindly generous disposition — **good–heart·ed·ly** *adv* — **good–heart·ed·ness** *n*
good–look·ing \ˈgu̇d-ˈlu̇-kiŋ\ *adj* : having an attractive appearance
good·ly \ˈgu̇d-lē\ *adj* **good·li·er; -est** **1** : of pleasing appearance **2** : LARGE, CONSIDERABLE ⟨a ~ sum of money⟩
good·man \ˈgu̇d-mən\ *n, archaic* : MR.
good–na·tured \ˈgu̇d-ˈnā-chərd\ *adj* : of a cheerful disposition — **good–na·tured·ly** \-chərd-lē\ *adv*
good·ness \-nəs\ *n* : EXCELLENCE, VIRTUE
good·wife \-ˌwīf\ *n, archaic* : MRS.
good·will \-ˈwil\ *n* **1** : BENEVOLENCE **2** : the value of the trade a business has built up over time **3** : cheerful consent **4** : willing effort
goody *or* **good·ie** \ˈgu̇-dē\ *n, pl* **good·ies** : something that is good esp. to eat
goody–goody \ˌgu̇-dē-ˈgu̇-dē\ *adj* : affectedly good — **goody–goody** *n*
goof \ˈgüf\ *vb* **1** : to spend time idly or foolishly — usu. used with *off* **2** : BLUNDER — usu. used with *up* — **goof** *n*
goof·ball \ˈgüf-ˌbȯl\ *n* **1** *slang* : a barbiturate sleeping pill **2** : a goofy person
go off *vb* **1** : EXPLODE **2** : to follow a course ⟨the party *went off* well⟩
goof–off \ˈgüf-ˌȯf\ *n* : one who evades work or responsibility
goofy \ˈgü-fē\ *adj* **goof·i·er; -est** : CRAZY, SILLY — **goof·i·ness** \-fē-nəs\ *n*
goo·gle \ˈgü-gəl\ *vb* **goo·gled; goo·gling** [*Google*, trademark for a search engine] : to use the Google search engine to obtain information on the World Wide Web
goon \ˈgün\ *n* : a man hired to terrorize or kill opponents
go on *vb* **1** : to continue in a course of action **2** : to take place : HAPPEN
goose \ˈgüs\ *n, pl* **geese** \ˈgēs\ **1** : any of numerous long-necked web-footed birds related to the swans and ducks; *also* : a female goose as distinguished from a gander **2** : a foolish person **3** *pl* **goos·es** : a tailor's smoothing iron
goose·ber·ry \ˈgüs-ˌber-ē, ˈgüz-, -bə-rē\ *n* : the acid berry of any of several shrubs related to the currant and used esp. in jams and pies
goose bumps *n pl* : roughening of the skin caused usu. by cold, fear, or a sudden feeling of excitement
goose·flesh \-ˌflesh\ *n* : GOOSE BUMPS
goose pimples *n pl* : GOOSE BUMPS
go out *vb* **1** : to become extinguished **2** : to become a candidate ⟨*went out* for the football team⟩
go over *vb* : SUCCEED
GOP *abbr* Grand Old Party (Republican)
[1]**go·pher** \ˈgō-fər\ *n* **1** : a burrowing American land tortoise **2** : any of a family of No. American burrowing rodents with large cheek pouches opening beside the mouth **3** : any of several small ground squirrels of the prairie region of No. America
[2]**gopher** *var of* GOFER
go·pik \gō-ˈpēk, -ˈpik\ *n, pl* **gopik** — see *manat* at MONEY table
[1]**gore** \ˈgȯr\ *n* : a tapering or triangular piece (as of cloth in a skirt)
[2]**gore** *vb* **gored; gor·ing** : to pierce or wound with something pointed
[3]**gore** *n* **1** : BLOOD **2** : gruesomeness depicted in vivid detail
[1]**gorge** \ˈgȯrj\ *n* **1** : THROAT **2** : a narrow ravine **3** : a mass of matter that chokes up a passage
[2]**gorge** *vb* **gorged; gorg·ing** : to eat greedily : stuff to capacity : GLUT
gor·geous \ˈgȯr-jəs\ *adj* : resplendently beautiful
Gor·gon·zo·la \ˌgȯr-gən-ˈzō-lə\ *n* : a pungent blue cheese of Italian origin
go·ril·la \gə-ˈri-lə\ *n* [NL, fr. Gk *Gorillai*, a tribe of hairy women in an account of a voyage around Africa] : an African anthropoid ape related to but much larger than the chimpanzee
gor·man·dise *chiefly Brit var of* GORMANDIZE
gor·man·dize \ˈgȯr-mən-ˌdīz\ *vb* **-dized; -diz·ing** : to eat ravenously — **gor·man·diz·er** *n*
gorp \ˈgȯrp\ *n* : a snack consisting of high-calorie food (as raisins and nuts)
gorse \ˈgȯrs\ *n* : a spiny yellow-flowered European evergreen shrub of the legume family
gory \ˈgȯr-ē\ *adj* **gor·i·er; -est** **1** : BLOODSTAINED **2** : HORRIBLE, SENSATIONAL ⟨the ~ details⟩
gos·hawk \ˈgäs-ˌhȯk\ *n* : any of several long-tailed hawks with short rounded wings
gos·ling \ˈgäz-liŋ, ˈgȯz-\ *n* : a young goose
[1]**gos·pel** \ˈgäs-pəl\ *n* [ME, fr. OE *gōdspel*, fr. *gōd* good + *spell* message, news] **1** : the teachings of Christ and the apostles **2** *cap* : any of the first four books of the New Testament **3** : something accepted or promoted as infallible truth **4** : American religious songs associated with evangelism
[2]**gospel** *adj* **1** : of, relating to, or emphasizing the gospel **2** : relating to or being American religious songs associated with evangelism
gos·sa·mer \ˈgä-sə-mər\ *n* [ME *gossomer*, fr. *gos* goose + *somer* summer] **1** : a film of cobwebs floating in the air **2** : something light, delicate, or tenuous
[1]**gos·sip** \ˈgä-səp\ *n* **1** : a person who habitually reveals personal or sensational facts **2** : rumor or report of an intimate nature **3** : an informal conversation — **gos·sipy** *adj*
[2]**gossip** *vb* : to spread gossip
got *past and past part of* GET
Goth \ˈgäth\ *n* : a member of a Germanic people that early in the Christian era overran the Roman Empire
[1]**Goth·ic** \ˈgä-thik\ *adj* **1** : of or relating to the Goths **2** : of or relating to a style of architecture prevalent in western Europe from the middle 12th to the early 16th century

[2]**Gothic** *n* **1** : the Germanic language of the Goths **2** : the Gothic architectural style or decoration

gotten *past part of* GET

Gou·da \ˈgü-də\ *n* : a mild Dutch milk cheese shaped in balls

[1]**gouge** \ˈgau̇j\ *n* **1** : a rounded troughlike chisel **2** : a hole or groove made with or as if with a gouge

[2]**gouge** *vb* **gouged; goug·ing** **1** : to cut holes or grooves in with or as if with a gouge **2** : DEFRAUD, CHEAT

gou·lash \ˈgü-ˌläsh, -ˌlash\ *n* [Hungarian *gulyás*] : a stew made with meat, assorted vegetables, and paprika

go under *vb* : to be overwhelmed, defeated, or destroyed : FAIL

gourd \ˈgȯrd, ˈgu̇rd\ *n* **1** : any of a family of tendril-bearing vines including the cucumber, squash, and melon **2** : the fruit of a gourd; *esp* : any of various inedible hard-shelled fruits used esp. for ornament or implements

gourde \ˈgu̇rd\ *n* — see MONEY table

gour·mand \ˈgu̇r-ˌmänd\ *n* **1** : one who is excessively fond of eating and drinking **2** : GOURMET

gour·met \ˈgu̇r-ˌmā, gu̇r-ˈmā\ *n* [F, fr. MF, alter. of *gromet* boy servant, vintner's assistant] : a connoisseur of food and drink

gout \ˈgau̇t\ *n* : a metabolic disease marked by painful inflammation and swelling of the joints — **gouty** *adj*

gov *abbr* **1** government **2** governor **3** governmental institution — used in World Wide Web addresses

gov·ern \ˈgə-vərn\ *vb* [ME, fr. AF *governer*, fr. L *gubernare* to steer, govern, fr. Gk *kybernan*] **1** : to control and direct the making and administration of policy in : RULE **2** : CONTROL, DIRECT, INFLUENCE **3** : DETERMINE, REGULATE **4** : RESTRAIN — **gov·ern·able** \-vər-nə-bəl\ *adj* — **gov·er·nance** \-vər-nəns\ *n*

gov·ern·ess \ˈgə-vər-nəs\ *n* : a woman who teaches and trains a child esp. in a private home

gov·ern·ment \ˈgə-vərn-mənt\ *n* **1** : authoritative direction or control : RULE **2** : the making of policy **3** : the organization or agency through which a political unit exercises authority **4** : the complex of institutions, laws, and customs through which a political unit is governed **5** : the governing body — **gov·ern·men·tal** \ˌgə-vərn-ˈmen-tᵊl\ *adj* — **gov·ern·men·tal·ly** \-tᵊl-ē\ *adv*

gov·er·nor \ˈgə-vər-nər\ *n* **1** : one that governs; *esp* : a ruler, chief executive, or head of a political unit (as a state) **2** : an attachment to a machine for automatic control of speed — **gov·er·nor·ship** *n*

govt *abbr* government

gown \ˈgau̇n\ *n* **1** : a loose flowing outer garment **2** : an official robe worn esp. by a judge, clergyman, or teacher **3** : a woman's dress ⟨evening ~*s*⟩ **4** : a loose robe **5** : an academic community within a town or city — **gown** *vb*

gp *abbr* group

GP *abbr* general practitioner

GPO *abbr* **1** general post office **2** Government Printing Office

GPS \ˌjē-ˌpē-ˈes\ *n* [*G*lobal *P*ositioning *S*ystem] : a navigation system that uses satellite signals to fix location; *also* : the signal receiver itself

GQ *abbr* general quarters

gr *abbr* **1** grade **2** grain **3** gram **4** gravity **5** gross

grab \ˈgrab\ *vb* **grabbed; grab·bing** : to take hastily : SNATCH — **grab** *n*

[1]**grace** \ˈgrās\ *n* **1** : unmerited help given to people by God (as in overcoming temptation) **2** : freedom from sin through divine grace **3** : a virtue coming from God **4** — used as a title for a duke, a duchess, or an archbishop **5** : a short prayer at a meal **6** : a temporary respite (as from the payment of a debt) **7** : APPROVAL, ACCEPTANCE ⟨in his good ~*s*⟩ **8** : CHARM **9** : ATTRACTIVENESS, BEAUTY **10** : fitness or proportion of line or expression **11** : ease of movement **12** : a musical trill or ornament — **grace·ful** \-fəl\ *adj* — **grace·ful·ly** *adv* — **grace·ful·ness** *n* — **grace·less** *adj*

[2]**grace** *vb* **graced; grac·ing** **1** : HONOR **2** : ADORN, EMBELLISH

gra·cious \ˈgrā-shəs\ *adj* **1** : marked by kindness and courtesy ⟨a ~ host⟩ **2** : GRACEFUL **3** : characterized by charm and good taste **4** : MERCIFUL — **gra·cious·ly** *adv* — **gra·cious·ness** *n*

grack·le \ˈgra-kəl\ *n* : any of several large American blackbirds with glossy iridescent plumage

grad *abbr* graduate; graduated

gra·da·tion \grā-ˈdā-shən, grə-\ *n* **1** : a series forming successive stages **2** : a step, degree, or stage in a series **3** : an advance by regular degrees **4** : the act or process of grading

[1]**grade** \ˈgrād\ *n* [L *gradus* step, degree, fr. *gradi* to step, go] **1** : a position in a scale of rank, quality, or order **2** : a stage in a process or ranking **3** : a level of study in an elementary, middle, or high school that is completed during one year; *also* : the pupils in such a level **4** : a class of persons or things of the same rank or quality **5** : a mark or rating esp. of accomplishment in school **6** : the degree of slope (as of a road); *also* : SLOPE **7** *pl* : the elementary school system

[2]**grade** *vb* **grad·ed; grad·ing** **1** : to arrange in grades : SORT **2** : to make level or evenly sloping ⟨~ a highway⟩ **3** : to give a grade to ⟨~ a pupil in history⟩ **4** : to assign to a grade

grade inflation *n* : the assigning of grades higher than previously assigned for given levels of achievement

grad·er \ˈgrā-dər\ *n* **1** : a machine for leveling earth **2** : a pupil in a school grade

grade school *n* : ELEMENTARY SCHOOL

gra·di·ent \ˈgrā-dē-ənt\ *n* : SLOPE, GRADE

grad·u·al \ˈgra-jə-wəl\ *adj* : proceeding or changing by steps or degrees ⟨~ improvements⟩ — **grad·u·al·ly** *adv*

grad·u·al·ism \-wə-ˌli-zəm\ *n* : the policy of approaching a desired end gradually

[1]**grad·u·ate** \ˈgra-jə-wət\ *n* **1** : a holder of an academic degree or diploma **2** : a graduated container for measuring contents

[2]**graduate** *adj* **1** : holding an academic degree or diploma **2** : of or relating to studies beyond the first or bachelor's degree ⟨~ school⟩

[3]**grad·u·ate** \ˈgra-jə-ˌwāt\ *vb* **-at·ed; -at·ing** **1** : to grant or receive an academic degree or diploma **2** : to divide into grades, classes, or intervals **3** : to admit to a particular standing or grade

grad·u·a·tion \ˌgra-jə-ˈwā-shən\ *n* **1** : a mark that graduates something **2** : an act or process of graduating **3** : COMMENCEMENT 2

graf·fi·ti \grə-ˈfē-(ˌ)tē\ *n* : unauthorized writing or drawing on a public surface

graf·fi·to \gra-ˈfē-tō, grə-\ *n, pl* **-ti** \-(ˌ)tē\ : an inscription or drawing made on a public surface (as a wall)

[1]**graft** \ˈgraft\ *n* **1** : a grafted plant; *also* : the point of union in this **2** : material (as skin) used in grafting **3** : the getting of money or advantage dishonestly; *also* : the money or advantage so gained

[2]**graft** *vb* **1** : to insert a shoot from one plant into another so that they join and grow; *also* : to join one thing to another as in plant grafting ⟨~ skin over a burn⟩ **2** : to get (as money) dishonestly — **graft·er** *n*

gra·ham cracker \ˈgrā-əm-, ˈgram-\ *n* : a slightly sweet cracker made chiefly of whole wheat flour

Grail \ˈgrāl\ *n* **1** : the cup or platter used according to medieval legend by Christ at the Last Supper and thereafter the object of knightly quests **2** *not cap* : the object of an extended or difficult quest

grain \ˈgrān\ *n* **1** : a seed or fruit of a cereal grass **2** : seeds or fruits of various food plants and esp. cereal grasses; *also* : a plant (as wheat) producing grain **3** : a small hard particle **4** : a unit of weight based on the weight of a grain of wheat — see WEIGHT table **5** : TEXTURE; *also* : the arrangement of fibers in wood **6** : natural disposition ⟨lying goes against my ~⟩ — **grained** \ˈgrānd\ *adj*

grain alcohol *n* : ALCOHOL 1

grainy \ˈgrā-nē\ *adj* **grain·i·er; -est** **1** : resembling or having some characteristic of grain : not smooth or fine **2** *of a photograph* : appearing to be composed of grain-like particles

[1]**gram** \ˈgram\ *n* [F *gramme,* fr. LL *gramma,* a small weight, fr. Gk *gramma* letter, writing, a small weight, fr. *graphein* to write] : a metric unit of mass and weight equal to $^1/_{1000}$ kilogram — see METRIC SYSTEM table

[2]**gram** *abbr* grammar; grammatical

-gram \ˌgram\ *n comb form* : drawing : writing : record ⟨tele*gram*⟩

gram·mar \ˈgra-mər\ *n* **1** : the study of the classes of words, their inflections, and their functions and relations in the sentence **2** : a study of what is to be preferred and what avoided in inflection and syntax **3** : speech or writing evaluated according to its conformity to grammatical rules — **gram·mar·i·an** \grə-ˈmer-ē-ən, -ˈmar-\ *n* — **gram·mat·i·cal** \-ˈma-ti-kəl\ *adj* — **gram·mat·i·cal·ly** \-k(ə-)lē\ *adv*

grammar school *n* **1** : a secondary school emphasizing Latin and Greek in preparation for college; *also* : a British college preparatory school **2** : a school intermediate between the primary grades and high school **3** : ELEMENTARY SCHOOL

gramme \ˈgram\ *chiefly Brit var of* GRAM

gram·o·phone \ˈgra-mə-ˌfōn\ *n* : PHONOGRAPH

gra·na·ry \ˈgrā-nə-rē, ˈgra-\ *n, pl* **-ries** **1** : a storehouse for grain **2** : a region producing grain in abundance

[1]**grand** \ˈgrand\ *adj* **1** : higher in rank or importance : FOREMOST, CHIEF **2** : great in size **3** : INCLUSIVE, COMPLETE ⟨a ~ total⟩ **4** : MAGNIFICENT, SPLENDID **5** : showing wealth or high social standing **6** : IMPRESSIVE, STATELY **7** : very good : FINE ⟨had a ~ time⟩ — **grand·ly** *adv* — **grand·ness** *n*

[2]**grand** *n, pl* **grand** *slang* : a thousand dollars

gran·dam \ˈgran-ˌdam, -dəm\ *or* **gran·dame** \-ˌdām, -dəm\ *n* : an old woman

grand·child \ˈgrand-ˌchī(-ə)ld\ *n* : a child of one's son or daughter

grand·daugh·ter \ˈgran-ˌdȯ-tər\ *n* : a daughter of one's son or daughter

grande dame \ˈgrän-ˈdäm\ *n, pl* **grandes dames** : a usu. elderly woman of great prestige or ability

gran·dee \gran-ˈdē\ *n* : a high-ranking Spanish or Portuguese nobleman

gran·deur \ˈgran-jər\ *n* **1** : the quality or state of being grand : MAGNIFICENCE **2** : something that is grand

grand·fa·ther \ˈgrand-ˌfä-t͟hər\ *n* : the father of one's father or mother; *also* : ANCESTOR

grandfather clock *n* : a tall clock that stands on the floor

gran·dil·o·quence \gran-ˈdi-lə-kwəns\ *n* : pompous eloquence — **gran·dil·o·quent** \-kwənt\ *adj*

gran·di·ose \ˈgran-dē-ˌōs, ˌgran-dē-ˈōs\ *adj* : IMPRESSIVE, IMPOSING; *also* : affectedly splendid — **gran·di·ose·ly** *adv* — **gran·di·os·i·ty** \ˌgran-dē-ˈä-sə-tē\ *n*

grand jury *n* : a jury that examines accusations of crime against persons and makes formal charges on which the persons are later tried

grand mal \ˈgrän-ˌmäl; ˈgrand-ˌmal\ *n* [F, lit., great illness] : severe epilepsy

grand·moth·er \ˈgrand-ˌmə-t͟hər\ *n* : the mother of one's father or mother; *also* : a female ancestor

grand·par·ent \-ˌper-ənt\ *n* : a parent of one's father or mother

grand piano *n* : a piano with horizontal frame and strings

grand prix \ˈgräⁿ-ˈprē\ *n, pl* **grand prix** *same or* -ˈprēz\ *often cap G&P* : a long-distance auto race over a road course;

also : a high-level competition in another sport (as sailing)

grand slam *n* **1** : a total victory or success **2** : a home run hit with three runners on base

grand·son \ˈgrand-ˌsən\ *n* : a son of one's son or daughter

grand·stand \-ˌstand\ *n* : a usu. roofed stand for spectators at a racecourse or stadium

grange \ˈgrānj\ *n* **1** : a farm or farmhouse with its various buildings **2** *cap* : one of the lodges of a national association originally made up of farmers; *also* : the association itself — **Grang·er** \ˈgrān-jər\ *n*

gran·ite \ˈgra-nət\ *n* : a hard granular igneous rock used esp. for building — **gra·nit·ic** \gra-ˈni-tik\ *adj*

gran·ite·ware \ˈgra-nət-ˌwer\ *n* : ironware with mottled enamel

gra·no·la \grə-ˈnō-lə\ *n* : a cereal made of rolled oats and usu. raisins and nuts

[1]**grant** \ˈgrant\ *vb* **1** : to consent to : ALLOW, PERMIT **2** : GIVE, BESTOW ⟨~*ed* land to settlers⟩ **3** : to admit as true — **grant·er** *n* — **grant·or** \ˈgran-tər, -ˌtȯr\ *n*

[2]**grant** *n* **1** : the act of granting **2** : something granted; *esp* : a gift for a particular purpose ⟨a ~ for study abroad⟩ **3** : a transfer of property by deed or writing; *also* : the instrument by which such a transfer is made **4** : the property transferred by grant — **grant·ee** \gran-ˈtē\ *n*

gran·u·lar \ˈgra-nyə-lər\ *adj* : consisting of or appearing to consist of granules — **gran·u·lar·i·ty** \ˌgra-nyə-ˈlar-ə-tē\ *n*

gran·u·late \ˈgra-nyə-ˌlāt\ *vb* **-lat·ed; -lat·ing** : to form into grains or crystals — **gran·u·la·tion** \ˌgra-nyə-ˈlā-shən\ *n*

gran·ule \ˈgra-nyül\ *n* : a small grain or particle

grape \ˈgrāp\ *n* [ME, fr. AF, grape stalk, bunch of grapes, grape, of Gmc origin] **1** : a smooth-skinned juicy edible greenish white, deep red, or purple berry that is the chief source of wine **2** : any of numerous woody vines widely grown for their bunches of grapes

grape·fruit \ˈgrāp-ˌfrüt\ *n* **1** *pl* **grapefruit** *or* **grapefruits** : a large edible yellow-skinned citrus fruit **2** : a tree bearing grapefruit

grape hyacinth *n* : any of several small bulbous herbs related to the lilies that produce clusters of usu. blue flowers in the spring

grape·shot \ˈgrāp-ˌshät\ *n* : a cluster of small iron balls formerly fired at people from short range by a cannon

grape·vine \-ˌvīn\ *n* **1** : GRAPE 2 **2** : RUMOR; *also* : an informal means of circulating information or gossip

graph \ˈgraf\ *n* : a diagram that usu. by means of dots and lines shows change in one variable factor in comparison with one or more other factors — **graph** *vb*

-graph \ˌgraf\ *n comb form* **1** : something written ⟨auto*graph*⟩ **2** : instrument for making or transmitting records ⟨seismo*graph*⟩

[1]**graph·ic** \ˈgra-fik\ *also* **graph·i·cal** \-fi-kəl\ *adj* **1** : of or relating to the arts (**graphic arts**) of representation, decoration, and printing on flat surfaces **2** : being written, drawn, or engraved **3** : vividly described ⟨~ details⟩ — **graph·i·cal·ly** \-fi-k(ə-)lē\ *adv*

[2]**graphic** *n* **1** : a picture, map, or graph used for illustration **2** : a pictorial image displayed on a computer screen

graphical user interface *n* : a computer program designed to allow easy user interaction esp. by having graphic menus or icons

graph·ics tablet \-fiks-\ *n* : a computer input device for entering pictorial information by drawing or tracing

graph·ite \ˈgra-ˌfīt\ *n* [G *Graphit,* fr. Gk *graphein* to write] : a soft black form of carbon used esp. for lead pencils and lubricants

grap·nel \ˈgrap-nəl\ *n* : a small anchor used esp. to recover a sunken object or to anchor a small boat

[1]**grap·ple** \ˈgra-pəl\ *n* : the act of grappling

[2]**grapple** *vb* **grap·pled; grap·pling** **1** : to seize or hold with or as if with a hooked implement **2** : to come to grips with : WRESTLE

[1]**grasp** \ˈgrasp\ *vb* **1** : to make the motion of seizing **2** : to take or seize firmly **3** : to enclose and hold with the fingers or arms **4** : COMPREHEND

[2]**grasp** *n* **1** : HANDLE **2** : EMBRACE **3** : HOLD, CONTROL **4** : the reach of the arms **5** : the power of seizing and holding or attaining **6** : COMPREHENSION

grasp·ing *adj* : GREEDY, AVARICIOUS

grass \ˈgras\ *n* **1** : herbage for grazing animals **2** : any of a large family of plants (as wheat, bamboo, or sugarcane) with jointed stems and narrow leaves **3** : grass-covered land **4** : MARIJUANA — **grass·like** \-ˌlīk\ *adj* — **grassy** *adj*

grass·hop·per \-ˌhä-pər\ *n* : any of numerous leaping plant-eating insects

grass·land \-ˌland\ *n* : land covered naturally or under cultivation with grasses and low-growing herbs

grass roots *n pl* : society at the local level as distinguished from the centers of political leadership

[1]**grate** \ˈgrāt\ *vb* **grat·ed; grat·ing** **1** : to pulverize by rubbing against something rough **2** : to grind or rub against with a rasping noise **3** : IRRITATE — **grat·er** *n* — **grat·ing·ly** *adv*

[2]**grate** *n* **1** : GRATING **2** : a frame of iron bars for holding fuel while it burns

grate·ful \ˈgrāt-fəl\ *adj* **1** : THANKFUL, APPRECIATIVE; *also* : expressing gratitude **2** : PLEASING — **grate·ful·ly** *adv* — **grate·ful·ness** *n*

grat·i·fy \ˈgra-tə-ˌfī\ *vb* **-fied; -fy·ing** : to afford pleasure to — **grat·i·fi·ca·tion** \ˌgra-tə-fə-ˈkā-shən\ *n*

grat·ing \ˈgrā-tiŋ\ *n* : a framework with parallel bars or crossbars

gra·tis \ˈgra-təs, ˈgrā-\ *adv or adj* : without charge or recompense : FREE

grat·i·tude \ˈgra-tə-ˌtüd, -ˌtyüd\ *n* : THANKFULNESS

gra·tu·itous \grə-ˈtü-ə-təs, -ˈtyü-\ *adj* **1** : done or provided without recompense : FREE **2** : UNWARRANTED ⟨a ~ assumption⟩ ⟨~ violence in movies⟩
gra·tu·ity \-ə-tē\ *n, pl* **-ities** : [10]TIP
gra·va·men \grə-ˈvā-mən\ *n, pl* **-va·mens** *or* **-vam·i·na** \-ˈva-mə-nə\ [LL, burden] : the basic or significant part of a grievance or complaint
[1]**grave** \ˈgrāv\ *vb* **graved; grav·en** \ˈgrā-vən\ *or* **graved; grav·ing** : SCULPTURE, ENGRAVE
[2]**grave** *n* : an excavation in the earth as a place of burial; *also* : TOMB
[3]**grave** \ˈgrāv; *5 also* ˈgräv\ *adj* **1** : IMPORTANT **2** : threatening great harm or danger **3** : DIGNIFIED, SOLEMN **4** : drab in color : SOMBER **5** : of, marked by, or being an accent mark having the form ` — **grave·ly** *adv* — **grave·ness** *n*
grav·el \ˈgra-vəl\ *n* : pebbles and small pieces of rock larger than grains of sand — **grav·el·ly** *adj*
Graves' disease \ˈgrāvz-\ *n* : hyperthyroidism characterized by goiter and often protrusion of the eyeballs
grave·stone \ˈgrāv-ˌstōn\ *n* : a burial monument
grave·yard \-ˌyärd\ *n* : CEMETERY
grav·id \ˈgra-vəd\ *adj* [L *gravidus,* fr. *gravis* heavy] : PREGNANT
gra·vi·me·ter \gra-ˈvi-mə-tər, ˈgra-və-ˌmē-\ *n* : a device for measuring variations in a gravitational field
grav·i·tate \ˈgra-və-ˌtāt\ *vb* **-tat·ed; -tat·ing** : to move or tend to move toward something
grav·i·ta·tion \ˌgra-və-ˈtā-shən\ *n* **1** : a natural force of attraction that tends to draw bodies together and that occurs because of the mass of the bodies **2** : the action or process of gravitating — **grav·i·ta·tion·al** \-shə-nəl\ *adj* — **grav·i·ta·tion·al·ly** *adv*
grav·i·ty \ˈgra-və-tē\ *n, pl* **-ties** **1** : IMPORTANCE; *esp* : SERIOUSNESS **2** : [2]MASS 5 **3** : the gravitational attraction of the mass of a celestial object (as earth) for bodies close to it; *also* : GRAVITATION 1
gra·vure \grə-ˈvyu̇r\ *n* [F] : PHOTOGRAVURE
gra·vy \ˈgrā-vē\ *n, pl* **gravies** **1** : a sauce made from the thickened and seasoned juices of cooked meat **2** : unearned or illicit gain : GRAFT
[1]**gray** *also* **grey** \ˈgrā\ *adj* **1** : of the color gray; *also* : dull in color **2** : having gray hair **3** : CHEERLESS, DISMAL ⟨a ~ day⟩ **4** : intermediate in position or character ⟨an ethically ~ area⟩ — **gray·ish** *adj* — **gray·ness** *n*
[2]**gray** *also* **grey** *n* **1** : something of a gray color **2** : a neutral color ranging between black and white
[3]**gray** *also* **grey** *vb* : to make or become gray
gray·beard \ˈgrā-ˌbird\ *n* : an old man
gray·ling \ˈgrā-liŋ\ *n, pl* **grayling** *also* **graylings** : any of several slender freshwater food and sport fishes related to the trouts
gray matter *n* **1** : the grayish part of nervous tissue consisting mostly of the cell bodies of neurons **2** : INTELLIGENCE
gray wolf *n* : a large wolf of northern No. America and Asia that is usu. gray
[1]**graze** \ˈgrāz\ *vb* **grazed; graz·ing** [ME *grasen,* fr. OE *grasian,* fr. *græs* grass] **1** : to feed on herbage or pasture **2** : to feed (livestock) on grass or pasture — **graz·er** *n*
[2]**graze** *vb* **grazed; graz·ing** **1** : to touch lightly in passing **2** : SCRATCH, ABRADE
[1]**grease** \ˈgrēs\ *n* **1** : rendered animal fat **2** : oily material **3** : a thick lubricant — **greasy** \ˈgrē-sē, -zē\ *adj*
[2]**grease** \ˈgrēs, ˈgrēz\ *vb* **greased; greas·ing** : to smear or lubricate with grease
grease·paint \ˈgrēs-ˌpānt\ *n* : theater makeup
great \ˈgrāt\ *adj* **1** : large in size : BIG **2** : ELABORATE, AMPLE ⟨in ~ detail⟩ **3** : large in number : NUMEROUS **4** : being beyond the average : MIGHTY, INTENSE ⟨a ~ weight⟩ ⟨in ~ pain⟩ **5** : EMINENT, GRAND **6** : long continued ⟨a ~ while⟩ **7** : MAIN, PRINCIPAL ⟨a reception in the ~ hall⟩ **8** : more distant in a family relationship by one generation ⟨a *great*-grandfather⟩ **9** : markedly superior in character, quality, or skill ⟨~ at bridge⟩ **10** : EXCELLENT, FINE ⟨had a ~ time⟩ — **great·ly** *adv* — **great·ness** *n*
great ape *n* : any of a family of primates including the gorilla, orangutan, and chimpanzees
great blue heron *n* : a large crested grayish-blue American heron
great circle *n* : a circle on the surface of a sphere that has the same center as the sphere; *esp* : one on the surface of the earth an arc of which is the shortest travel distance between two points
great·coat \ˈgrāt-ˌkōt\ *n* : a heavy overcoat
Great Dane *n* : any of a breed of very tall powerful smooth-coated dogs
great·er *adj, often cap* : consisting of a central city together with adjacent areas ⟨~ London⟩
great·heart·ed \ˈgrāt-ˈhär-təd\ *adj* **1** : COURAGEOUS **2** : MAGNANIMOUS
great power *n, often cap G&P* : one of the nations that figure most decisively in international affairs
great white shark *n* : a large and dangerous shark of warm seas that has large saw-edged teeth and is whitish below and bluish or brownish above
grebe \ˈgrēb\ *n* : any of a family of lobe-toed diving birds related to the loons
Gre·cian \ˈgrē-shən\ *adj* : GREEK
greed \ˈgrēd\ *n* : acquisitive or selfish desire beyond reason — **greed·i·ly** \ˈgrē-də-lē\ *adv* — **greed·i·ness** \-dē-nəs\ *n* — **greedy** \ˈgrē-dē\ *adj*
[1]**Greek** \ˈgrēk\ *n* **1** : a native or inhabitant of Greece **2** : the ancient or modern language of Greece
[2]**Greek** *adj* **1** : of, relating to, or characteristic of Greece, the Greeks, or Greek **2** : ORTHODOX 3

[1]**green** \ˈgrēn\ *adj* **1** : of the color green **2** : covered with verdure; *also* : consisting of green plants or of the leafy parts of plants ⟨a ~ salad⟩ **3** : UNRIPE; *also* : IMMATURE **4** : having a sickly appearance **5** : not fully processed or treated ⟨~ liquor⟩ ⟨~ hides⟩ **6** : INEXPERIENCED; *also* : NAIVE **7** : concerned with or supporting environmentalism ⟨~ companies⟩ — **green·ish** *adj* — **green·ness** *n*

[2]**green** *vb* : to make or become green

[3]**green** *n* **1** : a color between blue and yellow in the spectrum : the color of growing fresh grass or of the emerald **2** : something of a green color **3** : green vegetation; *esp, pl* : leafy herbs or leafy parts of a vegetable ⟨collard ~*s*⟩ ⟨beet ~*s*⟩ **4** : a grassy plot; *esp* : a smooth grassy area around the hole into which the ball must be played in golf

green·back \ˈgrēn-ˌbak\ *n* : a U.S. legal-tender note

green bean *n* : a kidney bean that is used as a snap bean when the pods are colored green

green·belt \ˈgrēn-ˌbelt\ *n* : a belt of parks or farmlands around a community

green card *n* : an identity card attesting the permanent resident status of an alien in the U.S.

green·ery \ˈgrē-nə-rē\ *n, pl* **-er·ies** : green foliage or plants

green–eyed \ˈgrē-ˈnīd\ *adj* : JEALOUS

green·gro·cer \ˈgrēn-ˌgrō-sər\ *n, chiefly Brit* : a retailer of fresh vegetables and fruit

green·horn \-ˌhȯrn\ *n* : an inexperienced person; *also* : NEWCOMER

green·house \-ˌhau̇s\ *n* : a glass structure for the growing of tender plants

greenhouse effect *n* : warming of a planet's atmosphere that occurs when the sun's radiation passes through the atmosphere, is absorbed by the planet, and is reradiated as radiation of longer wavelength that can be absorbed by atmospheric gases

green manure *n* : an herbaceous crop (as clover) plowed under when green to enrich the soil

green onion *n* : a young onion pulled before the bulb has enlarged and used esp. in salads : SCALLION

green pepper *n* : a sweet pepper before it turns red at maturity

green·room \ˈgrēn-ˌrüm, -ˌru̇m\ *n* : a room (as in a theater or studio) where performers can relax before, between, or after appearances

green·sward \-ˌswȯrd\ *n* : turf that is green with growing grass

green tea *n* : light-colored tea made from leaves that have not been oxidized before drying

green thumb *n* : an unusual ability to make plants grow

green·wash·ing \ˈgrēn-ˌwȯ-shiŋ, -ˌwä-\ *n* : expressions of environmentalist concerns as a cover for products, policies, or activities deleterious to the environment

Green·wich mean time \ˈgri-nij-, ˈgre-, -nich-\ *n* [*Greenwich,* England] : the time of the meridian of Greenwich used historically as the basis of worldwide standard time

Greenwich time *n* : GREENWICH MEAN TIME

green·wood \ˈgrēn-ˌwu̇d\ *n* : a forest that is green with foliage

greet \ˈgrēt\ *vb* **1** : to address with expressions of kind wishes **2** : to meet or react to in a specified manner **3** : to be perceived by — **greet·er** *n*

greet·ing *n* **1** : a salutation on meeting **2** *pl* : best wishes : REGARDS

greeting card *n* : a card that bears a message usu. sent on a special occasion

gre·gar·i·ous \gri-ˈger-ē-əs\ *adj* [L *gregarius* of a flock or herd, fr. *greg-, grex* flock, herd] **1** : SOCIAL, COMPANIONABLE **2** : tending to flock together — **gre·gar·i·ous·ly** *adv* — **gre·gar·i·ous·ness** *n*

grem·lin \ˈgrem-lən\ *n* : a cause of error or equipment malfunction conceived of as a small gnome

gre·nade \grə-ˈnād\ *n* [MF, lit., pomegranate, fr. LL *granata,* fr. L, fem. of *granatus* seedy, fr. *granum* grain] : a small bomb that is thrown by hand or launched (as by a rifle)

gren·a·dier \ˌgre-nə-ˈdir\ *n* : a member of a European regiment formerly armed with grenades

gren·a·dine \ˌgre-nə-ˈdēn, ˈgre-nə-ˌdēn\ *n* : a syrup flavored with pomegranates and used in mixed drinks

grew *past of* GROW

grey *var of* GRAY

grey·hound \ˈgrā-ˌhau̇nd\ *n* : any of a breed of tall slender dogs noted for speed and keen sight

grid \ˈgrid\ *n* **1** : GRATING **2** : a network of conductors for distributing electric power **3** : a network of horizontal and perpendicular lines (as for locating points on a map) **4** : GRIDIRON 2; *also* : FOOTBALL

grid·dle \ˈgri-dᵊl\ *n* : a flat usu. metal surface for cooking food

griddle cake *n* : PANCAKE

grid·iron \ˈgrid-ˌī(-ə)rn\ *n* **1** : a grate for broiling food **2** : a football field

grid·lock \-ˌläk\ *n* : a traffic jam in which an intersection is so blocked that vehicles cannot move

grief \ˈgrēf\ *n* **1** : emotional distress caused by or as if by bereavement; *also* : a cause of such distress **2** : DISASTER ⟨the ship came to ~⟩; *also* : MISHAP

griev·ance \ˈgrē-vəns\ *n* **1** : a cause of distress affording reason for complaint or resistance **2** : COMPLAINT

grieve \ˈgrēv\ *vb* **grieved; griev·ing** [ME *greven,* fr. AF *grever,* fr. L *gravare* to burden, fr. *gravis* heavy, grave] **1** : to cause grief or sorrow to : DISTRESS **2** : to feel grief : SORROW

griev·ous \ˈgrē-vəs\ *adj* **1** : causing suffering, grief, or sorrow : SEVERE ⟨a ~ wound⟩ **2** : OPPRESSIVE, ONEROUS ⟨~ costs of war⟩ **3** : SERIOUS, GRAVE ⟨a ~ fault⟩ — **griev·ous·ly** *adv*

[1]**grill** \'gril\ *vb* **1** : to broil on a grill; *also* : to fry or toast on a griddle **2** : to question intensely ⟨~ a suspect⟩

[2]**grill** *n* **1** : a cooking utensil of parallel bars on which food is grilled **2** : a usu. informal restaurant

grille *or* **grill** \'gril\ *n* : a grating that forms a barrier or screen

grill·work \'gril-ˌwərk\ *n* : work constituting or resembling a grille

grim \'grim\ *adj* **grim·mer; grim·mest** **1** : CRUEL, FIERCE **2** : harsh and forbidding in appearance **3** : ghastly or repellent in character **4** : RELENTLESS — **grim·ly** *adv* — **grim·ness** *n*

gri·mace \'gri-məs, gri-'mās\ *n* : a facial expression usu. of disgust or disapproval — **grimace** *vb*

grime \'grīm\ *n* : soot, smut, or dirt adhering to or embedded in a surface; *also* : accumulated dirtiness and disorder — **grimy** *adj*

grin \'grin\ *vb* **grinned; grin·ning** : to draw back the lips so as to show the teeth esp. in amusement — **grin** *n*

[1]**grind** \'grīnd\ *vb* **ground** \'graủnd\; **grind·ing** **1** : to reduce to small particles **2** : to wear down, polish, or sharpen by friction **3** : OPPRESS **4** : to press with a grating noise : GRIT ⟨~ the teeth⟩ **5** : to operate or produce by turning a crank **6** : DRUDGE; *esp* : to study hard **7** : to move with difficulty or friction ⟨gears ~*ing*⟩

[2]**grind** *n* **1** : dreary monotonous labor, routine, or study **2** : one who works or studies excessively

grind·er \'grīn-dər\ *n* **1** : MOLAR **2** *pl* : TEETH **3** : one that grinds **4** : SUBMARINE 2 **5** : an athlete who succeeds through hard work and determination

grind·stone \'grīnd-ˌstōn\ *n* : a flat circular stone of natural sandstone that revolves on an axle and is used for grinding, shaping, or smoothing

[1]**grip** \'grip\ *vb* **gripped; grip·ping** **1** : to seize or hold firmly **2** : to hold the interest of strongly ⟨*gripped* by the story⟩

[2]**grip** *n* **1** : GRASP; *also* : strength in gripping **2** : a firm tenacious hold **3** : UNDERSTANDING **4** : a device for gripping **5** : TRAVELING BAG

gripe \'grīp\ *vb* **griped; grip·ing** **1** : IRRITATE, VEX **2** : to cause or experience spasmodic pains in the bowels **3** : COMPLAIN — **gripe** *n*

grippe \'grip\ *n* : INFLUENZA

gris–gris \'grē-ˌgrē\ *n, pl* **gris–gris** \-ˌgrēz\ [F] : an amulet or incantation used chiefly by people of Black African ancestry

gris·ly \'griz-lē\ *adj* **gris·li·er; -est** : HORRIBLE, GRUESOME

grist \'grist\ *n* : grain to be ground or already ground

gris·tle \'gri-səl\ *n* : CARTILAGE — **gris·tly** \'gris-lē\ *adj*

grist·mill \'grist-ˌmil\ *n* : a mill for grinding grain

[1]**grit** \'grit\ *n* **1** : a hard sharp granule (as of sand); *also* : material composed of such granules **2** : unyielding courage ⟨the pioneers' ~⟩ — **grit·ty** *adj*

[2]**grit** *vb* **grit·ted; grit·ting** : GRIND, GRATE

grits \'grits\ *n pl* : coarsely ground hulled grain ⟨hominy ~⟩

griz·zled \'gri-zəld\ *adj* : streaked or mixed with gray; *also* : having gray hair

griz·zly \'griz-lē\ *adj* **griz·zli·er; -est** : GRIZZLED

grizzly bear *n* : a large powerful brownish bear of western No. America

gro *abbr* gross

groan \'grōn\ *vb* **1** : MOAN **2** : to make a harsh sound under sudden or prolonged strain ⟨the chair ~*ed* under his weight⟩ — **groan** *n*

groat \'grōt\ *n* : an old British coin worth four pennies

gro·cer \'grō-sər\ *n* [ME, fr. AF *groser* wholesaler, fr. *gros* coarse, wholesale, fr. L *grossus* coarse] : a dealer esp. in staple foodstuffs — **gro·cery** \'grōs-rē, 'grōsh-, 'grō-sə-\ *n*

grog \'gräg\ *n* [*Old Grog,* nickname of Edward Vernon †1757 Eng. admiral responsible for diluting the sailors' rum] : alcoholic liquor; *esp* : liquor (as rum) mixed with water

grog·gy \'grä-gē\ *adj* **grog·gi·er; -est** : weak and unsteady on the feet or in action — **grog·gi·ly** \-gə-lē\ *adv* — **grog·gi·ness** \-gē-nəs\ *n*

groin \'grȯin\ *n* **1** : the juncture of the lower abdomen and inner part of the thigh; *also* : the region of this juncture **2** : the curved line or rib on a ceiling along which two vaults meet

grok \'gräk\ *vb* **grokked; grok·king** : to understand profoundly and intuitively

grom·met \'grä-mət, 'grə-\ *n* **1** : a ring of rope **2** : an eyelet of firm material to strengthen or protect an opening

[1]**groom** \'grüm, 'grủm\ *n* **1** : a person responsible for the care of horses **2** : BRIDEGROOM

[2]**groom** *vb* **1** : to clean and care for (an animal) **2** : to make neat or attractive **3** : PREPARE

grooms·man \'grümz-mən, 'grủmz-\ *n* : a male friend who attends a bridegroom at his wedding

groove \'grüv\ *n* **1** : a long narrow channel **2** : a fixed routine — **groove** *vb*

groovy \'grü-vē\ *adj* **groov·i·er; -est** **1** : EXCELLENT **2** : HIP

grope \'grōp\ *vb* **groped; grop·ing** **1** : to feel about or search for blindly or uncertainly ⟨~ for the right word⟩ **2** : to feel one's way by groping

gros·beak \'grōs-ˌbēk\ *n* : any of several finches of Europe or America with large stout conical bills

gro·schen \'grō-shən\ *n, pl* **groschen** : a former Austrian monetary unit equal to $^{1}/_{100}$ schilling

gros·grain \'grō-ˌgrān\ *n* [F *gros grain* coarse texture] : a silk or rayon fabric with crosswise cotton ribs

[1]**gross** \'grōs\ *adj* **1** : glaringly noticeable **2** : OUT-AND-OUT, UTTER **3** : BIG, BULKY; *esp* : excessively fat **4** : GENER-

AL, BROAD **5** : consisting of an overall total exclusive of deductions ⟨~ earnings⟩ **6** : CARNAL, EARTHY ⟨~ pleasures⟩ **7** : UNREFINED; *also* : crudely vulgar **8** : lacking knowledge — **gross·ly** *adv* — **gross·ness** *n*

²**gross** *n* : an overall total exclusive of deductions — **gross** *vb*

³**gross** *n, pl* **gross** : a total of 12 dozen things ⟨a ~ of pencils⟩

gross domestic product *n* : the gross national product excluding the value of net income earned abroad

gross national product *n* : the total value of the goods and services produced in a nation during a year

gro·szy \ˈgrȯ-shē\ *n, pl* **groszy** — see *zloty* at MONEY table

grot \ˈgrät\ *n* : GROTTO

gro·tesque \grō-ˈtesk\ *adj* **1** : FANCIFUL, BIZARRE **2** : absurdly incongruous **3** : ECCENTRIC — **gro·tesque·ly** *adv*

grot·to \ˈgrä-tō\ *n, pl* **grottoes** *also* **grottos** **1** : CAVE **2** : an artificial cavelike structure

grouch \ˈgrau̇ch\ *n* **1** : a fit of bad temper **2** : a habitually irritable or complaining person — **grouch** *vb* — **grouchy** *adj*

¹**ground** \ˈgrau̇nd\ *n* **1** : the bottom of a body of water **2** *pl* : sediment at the bottom of a liquid **3** : a basis for belief, action, or argument **4** : BACKGROUND **5** : the surface of the earth; *also* : SOIL **6** : an area with a particular use ⟨fishing ~*s*⟩ **7** *pl* : the area about and belonging to a building **8** : a conductor that makes electrical connection with the earth — **ground·less** *adj*

²**ground** *vb* **1** : to bring to or place on the ground **2** : to run or cause to run aground **3** : to provide a reason or justification for **4** : to furnish with a foundation of knowledge **5** : to connect electrically with a ground **6** : to restrict to the ground; *also* : prohibit from some activity ⟨~*ed* the boy for a week⟩

³**ground** *past and past part of* GRIND

ground ball *n* : a batted baseball that rolls or bounces along the ground

ground cover *n* : low plants that grow over and cover the soil; *also* : a plant suitable for use as ground cover

ground·ed \ˈgrau̇n-dəd\ *adj* : mentally and emotionally stable

ground·er \ˈgrau̇n-dər\ *n* : GROUND BALL

ground·hog \ˈgrau̇nd-ˌhȯg, -ˌhäg\ *n* : WOODCHUCK

ground·ling \ˈgrau̇nd-liŋ\ *n* : a spectator in the pit of an Elizabethan theater

ground rule *n* **1** : a sports rule adopted to modify play on a particular field, court, or course **2** : a rule of procedure

ground squirrel *n* : any of various burrowing squirrels of No. America and Eurasia that often live in colonies in open areas

ground swell *n* **1** : a broad deep ocean swell caused by an often distant gale or earthquake **2** *usu* **ground·swell** : a rapid spontaneous growth (as of political opinion)

ground·wa·ter \ˈgrau̇nd-ˌwȯ-tər, -ˌwä-\ *n* : water within the earth that supplies wells and springs

ground·work \-ˌwərk\ *n* : FOUNDATION, BASIS

ground zero *n* **1** : the point above, below, or at which a nuclear explosion occurs **2** : the center or origin of rapid, intense, or violent activity

¹**group** \ˈgrüp\ *n* **1** : a number of individuals related by a common factor (as physical association, community of interests, or blood) **2** : a combination of atoms commonly found together in a molecule ⟨a methyl ~⟩

²**group** *vb* : to associate in groups : CLUSTER, AGGREGATE

grou·per \ˈgrü-pər\ *n, pl* **groupers** *also* **grouper** : any of numerous large solitary bottom fishes of warm seas

group home *n* : a residence for persons requiring care or supervision

group·ie \ˈgrü-pē\ *n* : a fan of a rock group who usu. follows the group around on concert tours; *also* : ENTHUSIAST, FAN

group therapy *n* : therapy in the presence of a therapist in which several patients discuss their personal problems

groupware \ˈgrüp-ˌwer\ *n* : software that enables users to work jointly via a network on projects or files

¹**grouse** \ˈgrau̇s\ *n, pl* **grouse** *or* **grouses** : any of various chiefly ground-dwelling game birds that have feathered legs and are usu. of reddish brown or other protective color

²**grouse** *vb* **groused; grous·ing** : COMPLAIN, GRUMBLE

grout \ˈgrau̇t\ *n* : material (as mortar) used for filling spaces — **grout** *vb*

grove \ˈgrōv\ *n* : a small wood usu. without underbrush

grov·el \ˈgrä-vəl, ˈgrə-\ *vb* **-eled** *or* **-elled; -el·ing** *or* **-el·ling** **1** : to creep or lie with the body prostrate in fear or humility **2** : to abase oneself

grow \ˈgrō\ *vb* **grew** \ˈgrü\; **grown** \ˈgrōn\; **grow·ing** **1** : to spring up and develop to maturity **2** : to be able to grow : THRIVE **3** : to take on some relation through or as if through growth ⟨tree limbs *grown* together⟩ **4** : INCREASE, EXPAND **5** : to develop from a parent source **6** : BECOME **7** : to have an increasing influence **8** : to cause to grow ⟨~ a business⟩ — **grow·er** *n*

growing pains *n pl* **1** : pains in the legs of growing children having no known relation to growth **2** : the stresses and strains attending a new project or development

growl \ˈgrau̇(-ə)l\ *vb* **1** : RUMBLE **2** : to utter a deep throaty sound **3** : GRUMBLE — **growl** *n*

grown–up \ˈgrō-ˌnəp\ *adj* : not childish : ADULT — **grown–up** *n*

growth \ˈgrōth\ *n* **1** : stage or condition attained in growing **2** : a process of growing esp. through progressive development or increase **3** : a result or product of growing ⟨a fine ~ of hair⟩; *also* : an abnormal mass of tissue (as a tumor)

growth hormone *n* : a vertebrate hormone that is secreted by the pituitary gland and regulates growth

growth industry *n* : a business, interest, or activity that is increasingly popular, profitable, or trendy

[1]**grub** \'grəb\ *vb* **grubbed; grub•bing** **1** : to clear or root out by digging **2** : to dig in the ground usu. for a hidden object **3** : to search about

[2]**grub** *n* **1** : a soft thick wormlike insect larva ⟨beetle ~*s*⟩ **2** : DRUDGE; *also* : a slovenly person **3** : FOOD

grub•by \'grə-bē\ *adj* **grub•bi•er; -est** : DIRTY, SLOVENLY ⟨~ clothes⟩ — **grub•bi•ness** \-bē-nəs\ *n*

grub•stake \'grəb-ˌstāk\ *n* : supplies or funds furnished a mining prospector in return for a share in his finds

[1]**grudge** \'grəj\ *vb* **grudged; grudg•ing** : to be reluctant to give : BEGRUDGE

[2]**grudge** *n* : a feeling of deep-seated resentment or ill will

gru•el \'grü-əl\ *n* : a thin porridge

gru•el•ing *or* **gru•el•ling** \'grü-liŋ, 'grü-ə-\ *adj* : requiring extreme effort : EXHAUSTING ⟨a ~ race⟩

grue•some \'grü-səm\ *adj* [fr. earlier *growsome,* fr. E dial. *grow, grue* to shiver] : inspiring horror or repulsion — **grue•some•ly** *adv* — **grue•some•ness** *n*

gruff \'grəf\ *adj* **1** : rough in speech or manner **2** : being deep and harsh : HOARSE — **gruff•ly** *adv*

grum•ble \'grəm-bəl\ *vb* **grum•bled; grum•bling** **1** : to mutter in discontent **2** : GROWL, RUMBLE — **grum•bler** *n*

grumpy \'grəm-pē\ *adj* **grump•i•er; -est** : moodily cross : SURLY — **grump•i•ly** \-pə-lē\ *adv* — **grump•i•ness** \-pē-nəs\ *n*

grunge \'grənj\ *n* **1** : one that is grungy **2** : heavy metal rock music expressing alienation and discontent **3** : untidy or tattered clothing typically worn by grunge fans

grun•gy \'grən-jē\ *adj* **grun•gi•er; -est** : shabby or dirty in character or condition

grun•ion \'grən-yən\ *n* : a fish of the California coast which comes inshore to spawn at nearly full moon

grunt \'grənt\ *n* : a deep throaty sound (as that of a hog) — **grunt** *vb*

GSA *abbr* **1** General Services Administration **2** Girl Scouts of America

G suit *n* [gravity] : a suit for a pilot or astronaut designed to counteract the physiological effects of acceleration

GSUSA *abbr* Girl Scouts of the United States of America

gt *abbr* great

Gt Brit *abbr* Great Britain

gtd *abbr* guaranteed

GU *abbr* Guam

gua•ca•mo•le \ˌgwä-kə-'mō-lē\ *n* [MexSp, fr. Nahuatl *āhuacamōlli,* fr. *āhuacatl* avocado + *mōlli* sauce] : mashed and seasoned avocado

gua•nine \'gwä-ˌnēn\ *n* : a purine base that codes genetic information in the molecular chain of DNA and RNA

gua•no \'gwä-nō\ *n* [Sp, fr. Quechua *wanu* fertilizer, dung] : excrement esp. of seabirds or bats; *also* : a fertilizer composed chiefly of this excrement

gua•ra•ni \ˌgwär-ə-'nē\ *n, pl* **guaranies** *also* **guaranis** — see MONEY table

[1]**guar•an•tee** \ˌger-ən-'tē\ *n* **1** : GUARANTOR **2** : GUARANTY 1 **3** : an agreement by which one person undertakes to secure another in the possession or enjoyment of something **4** : an assurance of the quality of or of the length of use to be expected from a product offered for sale **5** : GUARANTY 4

[2]**guarantee** *vb* **-teed; -tee•ing** **1** : to undertake to answer for the debt, failure to perform, or faulty performance of (another) **2** : to undertake an obligation to establish, perform, or continue **3** : to give security to

guar•an•tor \ˌger-ən-'tȯr\ *n* : one who gives a guarantee

[1]**guar•an•ty** \'ger-ən-tē\ *n, pl* **-ties** **1** : an undertaking to answer for another's failure to pay a debt or perform a duty **2** : GUARANTEE 3 **3** : GUARANTOR **4** : PLEDGE, SECURITY

[2]**guaranty** *vb* **-tied; -ty•ing** : GUARANTEE

[1]**guard** \'gärd\ *n* **1** : a person or a body of persons on sentinel duty **2** *pl* : troops assigned to protect a sovereign **3** : a defensive position (as in boxing) **4** : the act or duty of protecting or defending **5** : PROTECTION **6** : a protective or safety device **7** : a football lineman playing between center and tackle; *also* : a basketball player stationed farthest from the goal — **on guard** : WATCHFUL, ALERT

[2]**guard** *vb* **1** : PROTECT, DEFEND **2** : to watch over **3** : to be on guard

guard•house \'gärd-ˌhau̇s\ *n* **1** : a building occupied by a guard or used as a headquarters by soldiers on guard duty **2** : a military jail

guard•ian \'gär-dē-ən\ *n* **1** : CUSTODIAN **2** : one who has the care of the person or property of another — **guard•ian•ship** *n*

guard•room \'gärd-ˌrüm\ *n* **1** : a room used by a military guard while on duty **2** : a room where military prisoners are confined

guards•man \'gärdz-mən\ *n* : a member of a military body called *guard* or *guards*

gua•va \'gwä-və\ *n* : the sweet yellow or pink acid fruit of a shrubby tropical American tree used esp. for making jam and jelly; *also* : the tree

gu•ber•na•to•ri•al \ˌgü-bər-nə-'tȯr-ē-əl\ *adj* : of or relating to a governor

guer•don \'gər-dᵊn\ *n* : REWARD, RECOMPENSE

Guern•sey \'gərn-zē\ *n, pl* **Guernseys** : any of a breed of usu. reddish-brown and white dairy cattle that produce rich yellowish milk

guer•ril•la *or* **gue•ril•la** \gə-'ri-lə\ *n* [Sp *guerrilla,* fr. dim. of *guerra* war, of Gmc origin] : one who engages in irregular warfare esp. as a member of an independent unit

guess \ˈges\ *vb* **1 :** to form an opinion from little or no evidence **2 :** BELIEVE, SUPPOSE **3 :** to conjecture correctly about : DISCOVER — **guess** *n*

guest \ˈgest\ *n* **1 :** a person to whom hospitality (as of a house or a club) is extended **2 :** a patron of a commercial establishment (as a hotel) **3 :** a person not a regular member of a cast who appears on a program

guest·house \ˈgest-ˌhau̇s\ *n* **:** a house run as a boarding house or bed-and-breakfast

guf·faw \(ˌ)gə-ˈfȯ\ *n* **:** a loud burst of laughter — **guf·faw** *vb*

guid·ance \ˈgī-dᵊns\ *n* **1 :** the act or process of guiding **2 :** ADVICE, DIRECTION

¹guide \ˈgīd\ *n* **1 :** one who leads or directs another's course **2 :** one who shows and explains points of interest **3 :** something that provides guiding information; *also* : SIGNPOST 1 **4 :** a device to direct the motion of something

²guide *vb* **guid·ed; guid·ing 1 :** to act as a guide to **2 :** MANAGE, DIRECT **3 :** to superintend the training of — **guid·able** \ˈgī-də-bəl\ *adj*

guide·book \ˈgīd-ˌbu̇k\ *n* **:** a book of information for travelers

guided missile *n* **:** a missile whose course may be altered during flight

guide dog *n* **:** a dog trained to lead the blind

guide·line \ˈgīd-ˌlīn\ *n* **:** an indication or outline of policy or conduct

guide word *n* **:** a term at the head of a page of an alphabetical reference work that indicates the alphabetically first or last word on that page

gui·don \ˈgī-ˌdän, -dᵊn\ *n* **:** a small flag (as of a military unit)

guild \ˈgild\ *n* **:** an association of people with common aims and interests; *esp* **:** a medieval association of merchants or craftsmen — **guild·hall** \-ˌhȯl\ *n*

guil·der \ˈgil-dər\ *n* **:** GULDEN

guile \ˈgī(-ə)l\ *n* **:** deceitful cunning : DUPLICITY — **guile·ful** *adj* — **guile·less** *adj* — **guile·less·ness** *n*

guil·lo·tine \ˈgi-lə-ˌtēn, ˌgē-ə-ˈtēn\ *n* [F, fr. Joseph *Guillotin* †1814 Fr. physician] **:** a machine for beheading persons — **guillotine** *vb*

guilt \ˈgilt\ *n* **1 :** the fact of having committed an offense esp. against the law **2 :** BLAMEWORTHINESS **3 :** a feeling of responsibility for wrongdoing — **guilt·less** *adj*

guilt–trip \ˈgilt-ˌtrip\ *vb* **:** to cause feelings of guilt in

guilty \ˈgil-tē\ *adj* **guilt·i·er; -est 1 :** having committed a breach of conduct or a crime **2 :** suggesting or involving guilt **3 :** aware of or suffering from guilt — **guilt·i·ly** \-tə-lē\ *adv* — **guilt·i·ness** \-tē-nəs\ *n*

guin·ea \ˈgi-nē\ *n* **1 :** a British gold coin no longer issued worth 21 shillings **2 :** a unit of value equal to 21 shillings

guinea fowl *n* **:** a gray and white spotted West African bird related to the pheasants and widely raised for food; *also* **:** any of several related birds

guinea hen *n* **:** a female guinea fowl; *also* **:** GUINEA FOWL

guinea pig *n* **1 :** a small stocky short-eared and nearly tailless So. American rodent often kept as a pet or used in lab research **2 :** a subject of research or testing

guise \ˈgīz\ *n* **1 :** a form or style of dress **:** COSTUME **2 :** external appearance **:** SEMBLANCE

gui·tar \gi-ˈtär\ *n* **:** a musical instrument with usu. six strings plucked with a pick or with the fingers

gulch \ˈgəlch\ *n* **:** RAVINE

gul·den \ˈgül-dən, ˈgu̇l-\ *n, pl* **guldens** *or* **gulden 1 :** the basic monetary unit of the Netherlands until 2002 **2 :** the basic monetary unit of Suriname until 2004

gulf \ˈgəlf\ *n* [ME *goulf,* fr. MF *golfe,* fr. It *golfo,* fr. LL *colpus,* fr. Gk *kolpos* bosom, gulf] **1 :** a part of an ocean or sea partly or mostly surrounded by land **2 :** ABYSS, CHASM **3 :** a wide separation ⟨the ∼ between generations⟩

¹gull \ˈgəl\ *n* **:** any of numerous mostly white or gray long-winged web-footed seabirds

²gull *vb* **:** to make a dupe of : DECEIVE

³gull *n* **:** DUPE

gul·let \ˈgə-lət\ *n* **:** ESOPHAGUS; *also* **:** THROAT

gull·ible \ˈgə-lə-bəl\ *adj* **:** easily duped or cheated

gul·ly \ˈgə-lē\ *n, pl* **gullies :** a trench worn in the earth by and often filled with running water after rains

gulp \ˈgəlp\ *vb* **1 :** to swallow hurriedly or greedily **2 :** SUPPRESS ⟨∼ down a sob⟩ **3 :** to catch the breath as if in taking a long drink — **gulp** *n*

¹gum \ˈgəm\ *n* **:** the oral tissue that surrounds the necks of the teeth

²gum *n* [ME *gomme,* fr. MF, fr. L *cummi, gummi,* fr. Gk *kommi,* fr. Egyptian *qmy.t*] **1 :** a sticky plant exudate; *esp* **:** one that hardens on drying **2 :** a sticky substance **3 :** a preparation usu. of a plant gum sweetened and flavored and used for chewing — **gum·my** *adj*

gum arabic *n* **:** a water-soluble gum obtained from several acacias and used esp. in making inks, adhesives, confections, and pharmaceuticals

gum·bo \ˈgəm-bō\ *n* [AmerF *gombo,* of Bantu origin] **:** a rich thick soup usu. thickened with okra

gum·drop \ˈgəm-ˌdräp\ *n* **:** a candy made usu. from corn syrup with gelatin and coated with sugar crystals

gump·tion \ˈgəmp-shən\ *n* **1** *chiefly dial* **:** shrewd common sense **2 :** ENTERPRISE, INITIATIVE ⟨lacked the ∼ to try⟩

gum·shoe \ˈgəm-ˌshü\ *n* **:** DETECTIVE — **gumshoe** *vb*

¹gun \ˈgən\ *n* **1 :** CANNON **2 :** a portable firearm **3 :** a discharge of a gun **4 :** something suggesting a gun in shape or function **5 :** THROTTLE — **gunned** \ˈgənd\ *adj*

²gun *vb* **gunned; gun·ning 1 :** to hunt with a gun **2 :** SHOOT **3 :** to open up the throttle of so as to increase speed

gun·boat \ˈgən-ˌbōt\ *n* : a small lightly armed ship for use in shallow waters

gun·fight \-ˌfīt\ *n* : a duel with guns — **gun·fight·er** *n*

gun·fire \-ˌfī(-ə)r\ *n* : the firing of guns

gung ho \ˈgəŋ-ˈhō\ *adj* : extremely zealous or enthusiastic

gun·man \-mən\ *n* : a man armed with a gun; *esp* : a professional killer

gun·ner \ˈgə-nər\ *n* **1** : a soldier or airman who operates or aims a gun **2** : one who hunts with a gun

gun·nery \ˈgə-nə-rē\ *n* : the use of guns; *esp* : the science of the flight of projectiles and effective use of guns

gunnery sergeant *n* : a noncommissioned officer in the marine corps ranking next below a master sergeant

gun·ny·sack \ˈgə-nē-ˌsak\ *n* : a sack made of a coarse heavy fabric (as burlap)

gun·point \ˈgən-ˌpȯint\ *n* : the muzzle of a gun — **at gunpoint** : under a threat of death by being shot

gun·pow·der \-ˌpau̇-dər\ *n* : an explosive powder used in guns and blasting

gun·shot \-ˌshät\ *n* **1** : shot fired from a gun **2** : the range of a gun ⟨within ~⟩

gun–shy \-ˌshī\ *adj* **1** : afraid of a loud noise **2** : markedly distrustful

gun·sling·er \-ˌsliŋ-ər\ *n* : a skilled gunman esp. in the American West

gun·smith \-ˌsmith\ *n* : one who designs, makes, or repairs firearms

gun·wale *also* **gun·nel** \ˈgə-nᵊl\ *n* : the upper edge of a ship's or boat's side

gup·py \ˈgə-pē\ *n, pl* **guppies** [R.J.L. *Guppy* †1916 Trinidadian naturalist] : a small brightly colored tropical fish

gur·gle \ˈgər-gəl\ *vb* **gur·gled; gur·gling** : to make a sound like that of an irregularly flowing or gently splashing liquid — **gurgle** *n*

Gur·kha \ˈgu̇r-kə, ˈgər-\ *n* : a soldier from Nepal in the British or Indian army

gur·ney \ˈgər-nē\ *n, pl* **gurneys** : a wheeled cot or stretcher

gu·ru \ˈgu̇r-ü\ *n, pl* **gurus** [ultim. fr. Sanskrit *guru,* fr. *guru,* adj., heavy, venerable] **1** : a personal religious and spiritual teacher in Hinduism **2** : a teacher in matters of fundamental concern **3** : EXPERT ⟨a fitness ~⟩

gush \ˈgəsh\ *vb* **1** : to issue or pour forth copiously or violently : SPOUT **2** : to make an effusive display of affection or enthusiasm

gush·er \ˈgə-shər\ *n* : one that gushes; *esp* : an oil well with a large natural flow

gushy \ˈgə-shē\ *adj* **gush·i·er; -est** : marked by effusive sentimentality

gus·set \ˈgə-sət\ *n* : a triangular insert (as in a seam of a sleeve) to give width or strength — **gusset** *vb*

gus·sy up \ˈgə-sē-\ *vb* **gus·sied up; gus·sy·ing up** **1** : to dress in best or formal clothes **2** : to make more attractive, glamorous, or fancy

¹gust \ˈgəst\ *n* **1** : a sudden brief rush of wind **2** : a sudden outburst : SURGE ⟨a ~ of emotion⟩ — **gusty** *adj*

²gust *vb* : to blow in gusts

gus·ta·to·ry \ˈgəs-tə-ˌtȯr-ē\ *adj* : relating to or associated with the sense of taste

gus·to \ˈgəs-tō\ *n, pl* **gustoes** : enthusiastic enjoyment; *also* : VITALITY 4

¹gut \ˈgət\ *n* **1** *pl* : BOWELS, ENTRAILS **2** : the alimentary canal or a part of it (as the intestine); *also* : BELLY, ABDOMEN **3** *pl* : the inner essential parts ⟨a car's ~*s*⟩ **4** *pl* : COURAGE, PLUCK

²gut *vb* **gut·ted; gut·ting** **1** : EVISCERATE **2** : to destroy the inside of ⟨fire *gutted* the building⟩

gut check *n* : a test of courage, character, or determination

gutsy \ˈgət-sē\ *adj* **guts·i·er; -est** : marked by courage and determination

gut·ter \ˈgə-tər\ *n* : a groove or channel for carrying off esp. rainwater

gut·ter·snipe \-ˌsnīp\ *n* : a street urchin

gut·tur·al \ˈgə-tə-rəl\ *adj* **1** : sounded in the throat **2** : being or marked by an utterance that is strange, unpleasant, or disagreeable — **guttural** *n*

gut·ty \ˈgə-tē\ *adj* **gut·ti·er; -est** **1** : GUTSY **2** : having a vigorous challenging quality ⟨a ~ role in a play⟩

gut–wrench·ing \ˈgət-ˌren-chiŋ\ *adj* : causing emotional anguish

¹guy \ˈgī\ *n* : a rope, chain, or rod attached to something as a brace or guide

²guy *vb* : to steady or reinforce with a guy

³guy *n* : MAN, FELLOW; *also, pl* : PERSONS

⁴guy *vb* : to make fun of : RIDICULE

guz·zle \ˈgə-zəl\ *vb* **guz·zled; guz·zling** : to drink greedily

gym \ˈjim\ *n* : GYMNASIUM

gym·kha·na \jim-ˈkä-nə\ *n* : a meet featuring sports contests; *esp* : a contest of automobile-driving skill

gym·na·si·um *for 1* jim-ˈnā-zē-əm, -zhəm, *for 2* gim-ˈnä-zē-əm\ *n, pl* **-na·si·ums** *or* **-na·sia** \-ˈnā-zē-ə, -ˈnā-zhə; -ˈnä-zē-ə\ [L, exercise ground, school, fr. Gk *gymnasion,* fr. *gymnazein* to exercise naked, fr. *gymnos* naked] **1** : a room or building for indoor sports **2** : a European secondary school that prepares students for the university

gym·nas·tics \jim-ˈnas-tiks\ *n* : a competitive sport developed from physical exercises designed to demonstrate strength, balance, and body control — **gym·nast** \ˈjim-ˌnast\ *n* — **gym·nas·tic** *adj*

gym·no·sperm \ˈjim-nə-ˌspərm\ *n* : any of a group of woody vascular seed plants (as conifers) that produce naked seeds not enclosed in an ovary

gyn *or* **gynecol** *abbr* gynecology

gy·nae·col·o·gy *chiefly Brit var of* GYNECOLOGY

gy·ne·col·o·gy \ˌgī-nə-ˈkä-lə-jē\ *n* : a branch of medicine that deals with the diseases and routine care of the reproductive system of women — **gy·ne·co·log·ic** \-ni-kə-ˈlä-jik\ *or* **gy·ne·co·log·i·cal** \-ji-kəl\ *adj* — **gy·ne·col·o·gist** \-nə-ˈkä-lə-jist\ *n*

gy·no·cen·tric \ˌgī-nə-ˈsen-trik\ *adj* : emphasizing feminine interests or a feminine point of view

gyp \ˈjip\ *n, offensive* **1** : CHEAT, SWINDLER **2** : FRAUD, SWINDLE — **gyp** *vb, offensive*
gyp·sum \ˈjip-səm\ *n* : a calcium-containing mineral used in making plaster of paris
Gyp·sy \ˈjip-sē\ *n, pl* **Gypsies** [by shortening & alter. fr. *Egyptian*] **1** *usu offensive* : ROMANI
gypsy moth *n* : an Old World moth that was introduced into the U.S. where its caterpillar is a destructive defoliator of many trees
gy·rate \ˈjī-ˌrāt\ *vb* **gy·rat·ed; gy·rat·ing** **1** : to revolve around a point or axis **2** : to oscillate with or as if with a circular or spiral motion — **gy·ra·tion** \jī-ˈrā-shən\ *n*
gyr·fal·con \ˈjər-ˌfal-kən, -ˌfȯl-\ *n* : an arctic falcon with several color forms that is the largest of all falcons
[1]**gy·ro** \ˈjī-rō\ *n, pl* **gyros** : GYROSCOPE
[2]**gy·ro** \ˈyē-ˌrō, ˈzhir-ō\ *n, pl* **gyros** : a sandwich esp. of lamb and beef, tomato, onion, and yogurt sauce on pita bread
gy·ro·scope \ˈjī-rō-ˌskōp\ *n* : a wheel or disk mounted to spin rapidly about an axis that is free to turn in various directions
Gy Sgt *abbr* gunnery sergeant
gyve \ˈjīv, ˈgīv\ *n* : FETTER — **gyve** *vb*

H

[1]**h** \ˈāch\ *n, pl* **h's** *or* **hs** \ˈā-chəz\ *often cap* : the 8th letter of the English alphabet
[2]**h** *abbr, often cap* **1** hard; hardness **2** heroin **3** hit **4** husband
H *symbol* hydrogen
[1]**ha** \ˈhä\ *interj* — used esp. to express surprise or joy
[2]**ha** *abbr* hectare
Hab *abbr* Habacuc; Habakkuk
Ha·ba·cuc \ˈha-bə-ˌkək, hə-ˈba-kək\ *n* : HABAKKUK
Ha·bak·kuk \ˈha-bə-ˌkək, hə-ˈba-kək\ *n* — see BIBLE table
ha·ba·ne·ra \ˌhä-bə-ˈner-ə\ *n* [Sp *(danza) habanera,* lit., dance of Havana] : a Cuban dance in slow time; *also* : the music for this dance
ha·ba·ne·ro *also* **ha·ba·ñe·ro** \ˌ(h)ä-bə-ˈn(y)er-ō\ *n* : a very hot chili pepper that is usu. orange when mature
ha·be·as cor·pus \ˈhā-bē-əs-ˈkȯr-pəs\ *n* [ME, fr. ML, lit., you should have the body (the opening words of the writ)] : a writ issued to bring a party before a court
hab·er·dash·er \ˈha-bər-ˌda-shər\ *n* : a dealer in men's clothing and accessories
hab·er·dash·ery \-ˌda-shə-rē\ *n, pl* **-er·ies** **1** : goods sold by a haberdasher **2** : a haberdasher's shop
ha·bil·i·ment \hə-ˈbi-lə-mənt\ *n* **1** *pl* : TRAPPINGS, EQUIPMENT **2** : DRESS; *esp* : the dress characteristic of an occupation or occasion — usu. used in pl.
hab·it \ˈha-bət\ *n* **1** : DRESS, GARB **2** : BEARING, CONDUCT **3** : PHYSIQUE **4** : mental makeup **5** : a usual manner of behavior : CUSTOM **6** : a behavior pattern acquired by frequent repetition ⟨has a ~ of swearing⟩ **7** : ADDICTION ⟨a drug ~⟩ **8** : mode of growth or occurrence ⟨trees with a spreading ~⟩
hab·it·able \ˈha-bə-tə-bəl\ *adj* : capable of being lived in — **hab·it·abil·i·ty** \ˌha-bə-tə-ˈbi-lə-tē\ *n*
hab·i·tat \ˈha-bə-ˌtat\ *n* [L, it inhabits] : the place or environment where a plant or animal naturally occurs
hab·i·ta·tion \ˌha-bə-ˈtā-shən\ *n* **1** : OCCUPANCY **2** : a dwelling place : RESIDENCE **3** : SETTLEMENT
hab·it–form·ing \ˈha-bət-ˌfȯr-miŋ\ *adj* : causing addiction : ADDICTIVE
ha·bit·u·al \hə-ˈbi-chə-wəl\ *adj* **1** : CUSTOMARY **2** : doing, practicing, or acting by force of habit **3** : inherent in an individual ⟨~ grace⟩ — **ha·bit·u·al·ly** *adv* — **ha·bit·u·al·ness** *n*
ha·bit·u·ate \hə-ˈbi-chə-ˌwāt\ *vb* **-at·ed; -at·ing** **1** : ACCUSTOM **2** : to cause or undergo habituation
ha·bit·u·a·tion \hə-ˌbi-chə-ˈwā-shən\ *n* **1** : the process of making habitual **2** : psychological dependence on a drug after a period of use
ha·bi·tué *also* **ha·bi·tue** \hə-ˈbi-chə-ˌwā\ *n* [F] **1** : one who may be regularly found in or at (as a place of entertainment) **2** : DEVOTEE
ha·ci·en·da \ˌhä-sē-ˈen-də\ *n* **1** : a large estate in a Spanish-speaking country **2** : the main building of a farm or ranch
[1]**hack** \ˈhak\ *vb* **1** : to cut or sever with repeated irregular blows **2** : to cough in a short dry manner **3** : to manage successfully; *also* : TOLERATE ⟨can't ~ the pressure⟩ **4** : to gain access to a computer or computer system illegally
[2]**hack** *n* **1** : an implement for hacking **2** : a short dry cough **3** : a hacking blow **4** : an act or instance of gaining access to a computer or computer system illegally
[3]**hack** *n* **1** : a horse hired or used for varied work **2** : a horse worn out in service **3** : a light easy often 3-gaited saddle horse **4** : HACKNEY, TAXICAB **5** : a person who works solely for mercenary reasons; *esp* : a writer working solely for commercial success — **hack** *adj*
[4]**hack** *vb* : to operate a taxicab
hack·er \ˈha-kər\ *n* **1** : one that hacks; *also* : a person unskilled at something **2** : an expert at using a computer **3** : a person who illegally gains access to and sometimes tampers with information in a computer system
hack·ie \ˈha-kē\ *n* : a taxicab driver

hack·le \ˈha-kəl\ *n* **1** : one of the long feathers on the neck or back of a bird **2** *pl* : hairs (as on a dog's neck) that can be erected **3** *pl* : TEMPER, DANDER
hack·man \ˈhak-mən\ *n* : HACKIE
[1]**hack·ney** \ˈhak-nē\ *n, pl* **hackneys** **1** : a horse for riding or driving **2** : a carriage or automobile kept for hire
[2]**hackney** *vb* : to make trite
hack·neyed \ˈhak-nēd\ *adj* : lacking in freshness or originality ⟨~ slogans⟩
hack·saw \ˈhak-ˌsȯ\ *n* : a fine-tooth saw in a frame for cutting metal
hack·work \-ˌwərk\ *n* : work done on order usu. according to a formula
had *past and past part of* HAVE
had·dock \ˈha-dək\ *n, pl* **haddock** *also* **haddocks** : an Atlantic food fish usu. smaller than the related cod
Ha·des \ˈhā-(ˌ)dēz\ *n* **1** : the abode of the dead in Greek mythology **2** *often not cap* : HELL
haem *chiefly Brit var of* HEME
hae·ma·tite *Brit var of* HEMATITE
haf·ni·um \ˈhaf-nē-əm\ *n* : a gray metallic chemical element
haft \ˈhaft\ *n* : the handle of a weapon or tool
hag \ˈhag\ *n* **1** : an ugly or evil-looking old woman **2** : WITCH 1
Hag *abbr* Haggai
Hag·gai \ˈha-gē-ˌī, ˈha-ˌgī\ *n* — see BIBLE table
hag·gard \ˈha-gərd\ *adj* : having a worn or emaciated appearance ⟨~ faces⟩ ♦ ***Synonyms*** CAREWORN, WASTED, DRAWN — **hag·gard·ly** *adv* — **hag·gard·ness** *n*
hag·gis \ˈha-gəs\ *n* : a traditionally Scottish dish made of the heart, liver, and lungs of a sheep or a calf minced with suet, onions, oatmeal, and seasonings
hag·gle \ˈha-gəl\ *vb* **hag·gled; hag·gling** : to argue in bargaining — **hag·gler** *n*
Ha·gi·og·ra·pha \ˌha-gē-ˈä-grə-fə, ˌhā-jē-\ *n pl* — see WRITINGS
ha·gio·graph·ic \ˌha-gē-ə-ˈgra-fik, ˌhā-, -jē-\ *adj* : of or relating to hagiography; *esp* : excessively flattering
ha·gi·og·ra·phy \ˌha-gē-ˈä-grə-fē, ˌhā-jē-\ *n* **1** : biography of saints or venerated persons **2** : idealizing or idolizing biography — **ha·gi·og·ra·pher** \-fər\ *n*
hai·ku \ˈhī-(ˌ)kü\ *n, pl* **haiku** [Jp] : an unrhymed Japanese verse form of three lines containing usu. five, seven, and five syllables respectively; *also* : a poem in this form
[1]**hail** \ˈhāl\ *n* **1** : precipitation in the form of small lumps of ice **2** : something that gives the effect of falling hail
[2]**hail** *vb* **1** : to precipitate hail **2** : to pour down and strike like hail
[3]**hail** *interj* [ME, fr. ON *heill,* fr. *heill* healthy] — used to express acclamation
[4]**hail** *vb* **1** : SALUTE, GREET **2** : SUMMON
[5]**hail** *n* **1** : an expression of greeting, approval, or praise **2** : hearing distance
Hail Mary *n* **1** : a salutation and prayer to the Virgin Mary **2** : a long forward pass in football thrown as a final attempt to score
hail·stone \ˈhāl-ˌstōn\ *n* : a pellet of hail
hail·storm \-ˌstȯrm\ *n* : a storm accompanied by hail
hair \ˈher\ *n* : a threadlike outgrowth esp. from the skin of a mammal; *also* : a covering or growth of hairs of an animal or a body part — **haired** \ˈherd\ *adj* — **hair·less** *adj*
hair·breadth \ˈher-ˌbredth\ *or* **hairs·breadth** \ˈherz-\ *n* : a very small distance or margin
hair·brush \-ˌbrəsh\ *n* : a brush for the hair
hair·cloth \-ˌklȯth\ *n* : a stiff wiry fabric used esp. for upholstery
hair·cut \-ˌkət\ *n* : the act, process, or style of cutting and shaping the hair
hair·do \-ˌdü\ *n, pl* **hairdos** : HAIRSTYLE
hair·dress·er \-ˌdre-sər\ *n* : a person who dresses or cuts hair — **hair·dress·ing** *n*
hair·line \-ˌlīn\ *n* **1** : a very thin line **2** : the outline of the hair on the head
hair·piece \-ˌpēs\ *n* **1** : supplementary hair (as an extension) used in some hairstyles **2** : TOUPEE
hair·pin \-ˌpin\ *n* **1** : a U-shaped pin to hold the hair in place **2** : a sharp U-shaped turn in a road — **hairpin** *adj*
hair–rais·ing \ˈher-ˌrā-ziŋ\ *adj* : causing terror or astonishment
hair·split·ter \-ˌspli-tər\ *n* : one who makes excessively fine distinctions in reasoning — **hair·split·ting** \-ˌspli-tiŋ\ *adj or n*
hair·spray \ˈher-ˌsprā\ *n* : a liquid sprayed onto the hair to hold it in place
hair·style \-ˌstī(-ə)l\ *n* : a way of wearing the hair — **hair·styl·ing** *n*
hair·styl·ist \-ˌstī-list\ *n* : HAIRDRESSER
hair–trigger *adj* : immediately responsive to the slightest stimulus
hairy \ˈher-ē\ *adj* **hair·i·er; -est** **1** : covered with or as if with hair **2** : tending to cause nervous tension ⟨a few ~ moments⟩ **3** : difficult to deal with — **hair·i·ness** \-ē-nəs\ *n*
hairy woodpecker *n* : a common No. American woodpecker with a white back that is larger than the similarly marked downy woodpecker
hajj \ˈhaj\ *n* : a pilgrimage to Mecca prescribed as a religious duty for Muslims
hajji \ˈha-jē\ *n* : one who has made a pilgrimage to Mecca — often used as a title
hake \ˈhāk\ *n* : any of several marine food fishes related to the cod
ha·la·la \hə-ˈlä-lə\ *n, pl* **halala** *or* **halalas** — see *riyal* at MONEY table
hal·berd \ˈhal-bərd, ˈhȯl-\ *also* **hal·bert** \-bərt\ *n* : a weapon esp. of the 15th and 16th centuries consisting of a battle-ax and pike on a long handle
hal·cy·on \ˈhal-sē-ən\ *adj* [Gk *halkyōn, alkyōn*, a mythical bird believed to nest at sea and to calm the waves] **1** : CALM, PEACEFUL ⟨a ~ lake⟩ **2** : being a time of happiness, success, or prosperity
[1]**hale** \ˈhāl\ *adj* : free from defect, disease, or infirmity ♦ ***Synonyms*** HEALTHY, SOUND, ROBUST, WELL
[2]**hale** *vb* **haled; hal·ing** **1** : HAUL, PULL **2** : to compel to go

ha·ler \ˈhä-lər\ *n, pl* **ha·le·ru** \ˈhä-lə-ˌrü\ — see *koruna* at MONEY table

[1]**half** \ˈhaf, ˈhäf\ *n, pl* **halves** \ˈhavz, ˈhävz\ **1** : either of two equal parts into which something is divisible **2** : one of a pair

[2]**half** *adj* **1** : being one of two equal parts **2** : amounting to nearly half **3** : PARTIAL, INCOMPLETE — **half** *adv*

half–and–half \ˌhaf-ᵊn-ˈhaf, ˌhäf-ᵊn-ˈhäf\ *n* : something that is half one thing and half another

half–ass \ˈhaf-ˈas, ˈhäf-ˈäs\ *vb, slang, often vulgar* : to do (something) poorly due to lack of care or effort — **half–assed** *adj*

half·back \ˈhaf-ˌbak, ˈhäf-\ *n* **1** : a football back stationed on or near the flank **2** : a player stationed immediately behind the forward line

half–baked \-ˈbākt\ *adj* **1** : poorly planned **2** : lacking common sense **3** : not thoroughly baked

half–breed \-ˌbrēd\ *n, offensive* : one of mixed racial descent — **half–breed** *adj, offensive*

half brother *n* : a brother related through one parent only

half–caste \ˈhaf-ˌkast, ˈhäf-\ *n, offensive* : HALF-BREED — **half–caste** *adj, often offensive*

half–cocked \ˈhaf-ˈkäkt, ˈhäf-\ *adj* : lacking adequate preparation

half–dol·lar \-ˈdä-lər\ *n* **1** : a coin representing one half of a dollar **2** : the sum of fifty cents

half·heart·ed \-ˈhär-təd\ *adj* : lacking spirit or interest — **half·heart·ed·ly** *adv* — **half·heart·ed·ness** *n*

half–life \-ˌlīf\ *n* : the time required for half of something (as atoms or a drug) to undergo a process

half–mast \-ˈmast\ *n* : a point about halfway down from the top of a mast or staff

half note *n* : a musical note equal in time to one half that of a whole note

half·pen·ny \ˈhāp-nē\ *n, pl* **half·pence** \ˈhā-pəns\ *or* **halfpennies** : a formerly used British coin representing one half of a penny

half–pint \ˈhaf-ˌpīnt, ˈhäf-\ *adj* : of less than average size — **half–pint** *n*

half sister *n* : a sister related through one parent only

half sole *n* : a shoe sole extending from the shank forward — **half–sole** *vb*

half–staff \ˈhaf-ˈstaf, ˈhäf-\ *n* : HALF-MAST

half step *n* : a musical interval equivalent to one twelfth of an octave

half·time \ˈhaf-ˌtīm, ˈhäf-\ *n* : an intermission between halves of a game

half–track \-ˌtrak\ *n* : a motor vehicle propelled by an endless chain-track drive system; *esp* : such a vehicle lightly armored for military use

half–truth \-ˌtrüth\ *n* : a statement that is only partially true; *esp* : one that deliberately mixes truth and falsehood

half·way \-ˈwā\ *adj* **1** : midway between two points **2** : PARTIAL 1 — **halfway** *adv*

half–wit \-ˌwit\ *n* : a foolish or imbecilic person — **half–wit·ted** \-ˈwi-təd\ *adj* — **half–wit·ted·ness** *n*

hal·i·but \ˈha-lə-bət\ *n, pl* **halibut** *also* **halibuts** [ME *halybutte,* fr. *haly, holy* holy + *butte* flatfish; fr. its being eaten on holy days] : any of several large edible marine flatfishes

ha·lite \ˈha-ˌlīt, ˈhā-\ *n* : ROCK SALT

hal·i·to·sis \ˌha-lə-ˈtō-səs\ *n* : the condition of having fetid breath

hall \ˈhȯl\ *n* **1** : the residence of a medieval king or noble; *also* : the house of a landed proprietor **2** : a large public building **3** : a college or university building; *also* : DORMITORY **4** : LOBBY; *also* : CORRIDOR **5** : AUDITORIUM

hal·le·lu·jah \ˌha-lə-ˈlü-yə\ *interj* [Heb *hallĕlūyāh* praise (ye) the Lord] — used to express praise, joy, or thanks

hall·mark \ˈhȯl-ˌmärk\ *n* **1** : a mark put on an article to indicate origin, purity, or genuineness **2** : a distinguishing characteristic

hal·low \ˈha-lō\ *vb* **1** : CONSECRATE **2** : REVERE, VENERATE ⟨our ~*ed* leader⟩ — **hal·lowed** \-lōd, -lə-wəd\ *adj*

Hal·low·een *also* **Hal·low·e'en** \ˌha-lə-ˈwēn, ˌhä-\ *n* : the evening of October 31 observed esp. by children in merrymaking and masquerading

hal·lu·ci·nate \hə-ˈlü-sə-ˌnāt\ *vb* **-nat·ed; -nat·ing** : to have hallucinations or experience as a hallucination

hal·lu·ci·na·tion \hə-ˌlü-sə-ˈnā-shən\ *n* : perception of objects with no reality due usu. to use of drugs (as LSD) or to disorder of the nervous system; *also* : something so perceived ♦ ***Synonyms*** DELUSION, ILLUSION, MIRAGE — **hal·lu·ci·na·to·ry** \-ˈlü-sə-nə-ˌtȯr-ē\ *adj*

hal·lu·ci·no·gen \hə-ˈlü-sə-nə-jən\ *n* : a substance that induces hallucinations — **hal·lu·ci·no·gen·ic** \-ˌlü-sə-nə-ˈje-nik\ *adj or n*

hall·way \ˈhȯl-ˌwā\ *n* **1** : an entrance hall **2** : CORRIDOR

ha·lo \ˈhā-lō\ *n, pl* **halos** *or* **haloes** [L *halos,* fr. Gk *halōs* threshing floor, disk, halo] **1** : a circle of light appearing to surround a shining body (as the sun) **2** : the aura of glory surrounding an idealized person or thing

[1]**hal·o·gen** \ˈha-lə-jən\ *n* : any of the five elements fluorine, chlorine, bromine, iodine, and astatine

[2]**halogen** *adj* : containing, using, or being a halogen ⟨a ~ lamp⟩

[1]**halt** \ˈhȯlt\ *adj* : LAME 1

[2]**halt** *n* : STOP

[3]**halt** *vb* **1** : to stop marching or traveling **2** : DISCONTINUE, END ⟨~ protests⟩

[1]**hal·ter** \ˈhȯl-tər\ *n* **1** : a rope or strap for leading or tying an animal; *also* : HEADSTALL **2** : NOOSE **3** : a brief blouse held in place by straps around the neck and across the back

[2]**halter** *vb* **hal·tered; hal·ter·ing** **1** : to catch with or as if with a halter; *also* : to put a halter on (as a horse) **2** : HANG **3** : IMPEDE, RESTRAIN

halt·ing \ˈhȯl-tiŋ\ *adj* : UNCERTAIN, FALTERING — **halt·ing·ly** *adv*
halve \ˈhav, ˈhäv\ *vb* **halved; halv·ing 1** : to divide into two equal parts **2** : to reduce to one half
halv·ers \ˈha-vərz, ˈhä-\ *n pl* : half shares : HALVES
halves *pl of* HALF
hal·yard \ˈhal-yərd\ *n* : a rope or tackle for hoisting and lowering (as sails)
¹ham \ˈham\ *n* **1** : a buttock with its associated thigh — usu. used in pl. **2** : a cut of meat and esp. pork from the thigh **3** : a showy performer **4** : an operator of an amateur radio station — **ham** *adj*
²ham *vb* **hammed; ham·ming** : to overplay a part : OVERACT
ham·burg·er \ˈham-ˌbər-gər\ *or* **hamburg** \-ˌbərg\ *n* [G *Hamburger* of Hamburg, Germany] **1** : ground beef **2** : a sandwich consisting of a ground-beef patty in a round roll
ham·let \ˈham-lət\ *n* : a small village
¹ham·mer \ˈha-mər\ *n* **1** : a hand tool used for pounding; *also* : something resembling a hammer in form or function **2** : the part of a gun whose striking action causes explosion of the charge **3** : a metal sphere hurled by a flexible handle for distance in a track-and-field event (**hammer throw**) **4** : ACCELERATOR 2
²hammer *vb* **1** : to beat, drive, or shape with repeated blows of a hammer : POUND **2** : to produce or bring about as if by repeated blows — usu. used with *out* **3** : to criticize severely
ham·mer·head \ˈha-mər-ˌhed\ *n* **1** : the striking part of a hammer **2** : any of a family of medium-sized sharks with eyes at the ends of lateral extensions of the flattened head
ham·mer·lock \-ˌläk\ *n* : a wrestling hold in which an opponent's arm is held bent behind the back
ham·mer·toe \-ˌtō\ *n* : a toe deformed by having one or more joints permanently flexed
¹ham·mock \ˈha-mək\ *n* [Sp *hamaca,* fr. Taino, an Indigenous language of the Greater Antilles] : a swinging couch hung by cords at each end
²hammock *n* : a fertile elevated area of the southern U.S. and esp. Florida with hardwood vegetation and soil rich in humus
¹ham·per \ˈham-pər\ *vb* : IMPEDE; *also* : RESTRAIN ♦ ***Synonyms*** TRAMMEL, CLOG, FETTER, SHACKLE
²hamper *n* : a large usu. lidded basket
ham·ster \ˈham-stər\ *n* [G, fr. OHG *hamustro,* of Slavic origin] : any of a subfamily of small Old World rodents with large cheek pouches
¹ham·string \ˈham-ˌstriŋ\ *n* : any of several muscles at the back of the thigh or tendons at the back of the knee
²hamstring *vb* **-strung** \-ˌstrəŋ\; **-string·ing 1** : to make ineffective or powerless ⟨*hamstrung* by guilt⟩ **2** : to cripple by cutting the leg tendons
¹hand \ˈhand\ *n* **1** : the end of a front limb when modified (as in humans) for grasping **2** : an indicator or pointer on a dial **3** : personal possession — usu. used in pl.; *also* : CONTROL **4** : SIDE 5 **5** : a pledge esp. of betrothal **6** : HANDWRITING **7** : SKILL, ABILITY; *also* : a significant part ⟨had a ~ in the victory⟩ **8** : ASSISTANCE; *also* : PARTICIPATION ⟨had no ~ in the affair⟩ **9** : an outburst of applause **10** : a single round in a card game; *also* : the cards held by a player after a deal **11** : WORKER, EMPLOYEE; *also* : a member of a ship's crew — **hand·less** *adj* — **at hand** : near in time or place — **on hand** : in present possession or readily available — **out of hand** : out of control
²hand *vb* **1** : to lead, guide, or assist with the hand **2** : to give, pass, or transmit with the hand ⟨~*ed* her the letter⟩
hand·bag \ˈhand-ˌbag\ *n* : a bag for carrying small personal articles and money
hand·ball \-ˌbȯl\ *n* : a game played by striking a small rubber ball against a wall with the hand
hand·bill \-ˌbil\ *n* : a small printed sheet for distribution by hand
hand·book \-ˌbu̇k\ *n* : a concise reference book : MANUAL
hand·car \-ˌkär\ *n* : a small 4-wheeled railroad car propelled by hand or by a small motor
hand·clasp \-ˌklasp\ *n* : HANDSHAKE
hand·craft \-ˌkraft\ *vb* : to fashion by manual skill
¹hand·cuff \-ˌkəf\ *n* : a metal fastening that can be locked around a wrist and is usu. connected with another such fastening — usu. used in pl.
²handcuff *vb* : MANACLE
hand·ed \ˈhan-dəd\ *adj* : having or using such or so many hands ⟨a left-*handed* person⟩ — **hand·ed·ness** *n*
hand·ful \ˈhand-ˌfu̇l\ *n, pl* **hand·fuls** \-ˌfu̇lz\ *also* **hands·ful** \ˈhandz-ˌfu̇l\ **1** : as much or as many as the hand will grasp **2** : a small number **3** : as much as one can manage
hand·gun \-ˌgən\ *n* : a firearm held and fired with one hand
hand·held \-ˌheld\ *adj* : designed for use while being held in the hand — **handheld** *n*
¹hand·i·cap \ˈhan-di-ˌkap\ *n* [obs. E *handicap,* a game in which forfeit money was held in a cap, fr. *hand in cap*] **1** : a contest in which an artificial advantage is given or disadvantage imposed on a contestant to equalize chances of winning; *also* : the advantage given or disadvantage imposed **2** : a disadvantage that makes achievement difficult
²handicap *vb* **-capped; -cap·ping 1** : to give a handicap to **2** : to put at a disadvantage
hand·i·capped *adj, sometimes offensive* : having a physical or mental disability; *also* : of or for disabled persons
hand·i·cap·per \-ˌka-pər\ *n* : a person who predicts the winners in a contest
hand·i·craft \ˈhan-di-ˌkraft\ *n* **1** : manual

skill **2** : an occupation requiring manual skill **3** : the articles fashioned by those engaged in handicraft — **hand·i·craft·er** \-ˌkraf-tər\ *n* — **hand·i·crafts·man** \-ˌkrafts-mən\ *n*

hand in glove *or* **hand and glove** *adv* : in an extremely close relationship

hand·i·work \ˈhan-di-ˌwərk\ *n* : work done personally or by the hands

hand·ker·chief \ˈhaŋ-kər-chəf, -ˌchēf\ *n, pl* **-chiefs** \-chəfs, -ˌchēfs\ *also* **-chieves** \-ˌchēvz\ : a small piece of cloth used for various personal purposes (as the wiping of the face)

¹**han·dle** \ˈhan-dᵊl\ *n* **1** : a part (as of a tool) designed to be grasped by the hand **2** : NAME; *also* : NICKNAME — **han·dled** \-dᵊld\ *adj* — **off the handle** : into a state of sudden and violent anger — usu. used with *fly*

²**handle** *vb* **han·dled; han·dling** **1** : to touch, hold, or manage with the hands **2** : to have responsibility for **3** : to deal or trade in **4** : to behave in a certain way when managed or directed ⟨a car that ~*s* well⟩ — **han·dler** *n*

han·dle·bar \ˈhan-dᵊl-bär\ *n* : a usu. bent bar with a grip at each end (as for steering a bicycle) — usu. used in pl.

hand·made \ˈhand-ˈmād\ *adj* : made by hand or by a hand process

hand·maid·en \-ˌmā-dᵊn\ *also* **hand·maid** \-ˌmād\ *n* : a female attendant

hand–me–down \-me-ˌdau̇n\ *adj* : used by one person after having been used by another — **hand–me–down** *n*

hand·out \ˈhand-ˌau̇t\ *n* **1** : a portion (as of food) given to a beggar **2** : a piece of printed information for free distribution; *also* : a prepared statement released to the press

hand over *vb* : to yield control of

hand·pick \ˈhand-ˈpik\ *vb* : to select personally ⟨a ~*ed* candidate⟩

hand·rail \-ˌrāl\ *n* : a narrow rail for grasping as a support

hand·saw \-ˌsȯ\ *n* : a saw designed to be used with one hand

hands down *adv* **1** : with little effort **2** : without question

hand·sel \ˈhan-səl\ *n* **1** : a gift made as a token of good luck **2** : a first installment : earnest money

hand·set \ˈhand-ˌset\ *n* : a combined telephone transmitter and receiver mounted on a handheld device

hand·shake \-ˌshāk\ *n* : a clasping usu. of right hands by two people

hands–off \ˈhandz-ˈȯf\ *adj* : characterized by noninterference

hand·some \ˈhan-səm\ *adj* **hand·som·er; -est** [ME *handsom* easy to manipulate] **1** : SIZABLE, AMPLE ⟨a ~ profit⟩ **2** : GENEROUS, LIBERAL **3** : pleasing and usu. impressive in appearance ♦ ***Synonyms*** BEAUTIFUL, LOVELY, PRETTY, COMELY, FAIR — **hand·some·ly** *adv* — **hand·some·ness** *n*

hands–on \ˈhandz-ˈȯn, -ˈän\ *adj* **1** : being or providing direct practical experience in the operation of something **2** : characterized by active personal involvement ⟨~ management⟩

hand·spring \ˈhand-ˌspriŋ\ *n* : an acrobatic feat in which the body turns in a full circle from a standing position and lands first on the hands and then on the feet

hand·stand \-ˌstand\ *n* : an act of supporting the body on the hands with the trunk and legs balanced in the air

hand–to–hand *adj* : involving physical contact or very close range ⟨~ fighting⟩ — **hand to hand** *adv*

hand–to–mouth *adj* : having or providing nothing to spare ⟨lived a ~ existence⟩ — **hand to mouth** *adv*

hand·wo·ven \ˈhand-ˌwō-vən\ *adj* : produced on a hand-operated loom

hand·writ·ing \-ˌrī-tiŋ\ *n* : writing done by hand; *also* : the form of writing peculiar to a person — **hand·writ·ten** \-ˌri-tᵊn\ *adj*

handy \ˈhan-dē\ *adj* **hand·i·er; -est** **1** : conveniently near **2** : easily used ⟨a ~ tool⟩ **3** : DEXTEROUS — **hand·i·ly** \-də-lē\ *adv* — **hand·i·ness** \-dē-nəs\ *n*

handy·man \-ˌman\ *n* **1** : one who does odd jobs **2** : one competent in a variety of small skills or repair work

¹**hang** \ˈhaŋ\ *vb* **hung** \ˈhəŋ\ *also* **hanged; hang·ing** **1** : to fasten or remain fastened to an elevated point without support from below; *also* : to fasten or be fastened so as to allow free motion on the point of suspension ⟨~ a door⟩ **2** : to suspend by the neck until dead; *also* : to die by hanging **3** : DROOP ⟨*hung* his head in shame⟩ **4** : to fasten to a wall ⟨~ wallpaper⟩ **5** : to prevent (a jury) from coming to a decision **6** : to display (pictures) in a gallery **7** : to remain stationary in the air **8** : to be imminent **9** : DEPEND **10** : to take hold for support **11** : to be burdensome **12** : to undergo delay **13** : to incline downward; *also* : to fit or fall from the figure in easy lines **14** : to be raptly attentive **15** : to pass time idly by relaxing or socializing ⟨~*ing* at the mall⟩ — often used with *around* or *out* — **hang out to dry** : to subject to ruin by abandonment

²**hang** *n* **1** : the manner in which a thing hangs **2** : an understanding of something ⟨got the ~ of skiing⟩

han·gar \ˈhaŋ-ər\ *n* [F] : a covered and usu. enclosed area for housing and repairing aircraft

hang·dog \ˈhaŋ-ˌdȯg\ *adj* **1** : SAD, DEJECTED ⟨a ~ look on his face⟩ **2** : SHEEPISH

hang·er \ˈhaŋ-ər\ *n* **1** : one that hangs **2** : a device that fits inside or around a garment for hanging from a hook or rod

hang·er–on \ˈhaŋ-ər-ˈȯn, -ˈän\ *n, pl* **hangers–on** : one who hangs around a person or place esp. for personal gain

hang in *vb* : to persist tenaciously

hang·ing *n* **1** : an execution by strangling or snapping the neck by a suspended noose **2** : something hung

hang·man \ˈhaŋ-mən\ *n* **1** : a public

executioner **2** : a game in which players must identify an unknown word by guessing the letters that comprise it within a designated number of chances

hang·nail \-ˌnāl\ *n* : a bit of skin hanging loose at the edge of a fingernail

hang on *vb* **1** : to keep hold onto something **2** : HANG IN **3** : to await something desired

hang·out \ˈhaŋ-ˌau̇t\ *n* : a favorite place for spending time

hang·over \-ˌō-vər\ *n* **1** : something that remains from what is past **2** : disagreeable physical effects following heavy drinking or the use of drugs

hang–up \ˈhaŋ-ˌəp\ *n* : a source of mental or emotional difficulty

hang up *vb* **1** : to place on a hook or hanger **2** : to end a telephone conversation by breaking the connection **3** : to keep delayed or suspended

hank \ˈhaŋk\ *n* : COIL, LOOP ⟨a ~ of rope⟩

han·ker \ˈhaŋ-kər\ *vb* : to desire strongly or persistently — **han·ker·ing** *n*

han·kie *or* **han·ky** \ˈhaŋ-kē\ *n, pl* **hankies** : HANDKERCHIEF

han·ky–pan·ky \ˌhaŋ-kē-ˈpaŋ-kē\ *n* **1** : questionable or underhanded activity **2** : sexual dalliance

hansel *var of* HANDSEL

han·som \ˈhan-səm\ *n* : a 2-wheeled covered carriage with the driver's seat elevated at the rear

han·ta·virus \ˈhän-tə-ˌvī-rəs, ˈhən-, ˈhan-\ *n* : any of a genus of viruses including some transmitted by rodents that cause pneumonia or hemorrhagic fevers

Ha·nuk·kah *also* **Cha·nu·kah** \ˈkä-nə-kə, ˈhä-\ *n* [Heb *ḥănukkāh* dedication] : an 8-day Jewish holiday commemorating the rededication of the Temple of Jerusalem after its defilement by Antiochus of Syria

hap \ˈhap\ *n* **1** : HAPPENING **2** : CHANCE, FORTUNE

¹hap·haz·ard \hap-ˈha-zərd\ *n* : CHANCE

²haphazard *adj* : marked by lack of plan or order — **hap·haz·ard·ly** *adv* — **hap·haz·ard·ness** *n*

hap·less \ˈhap-ləs\ *adj* : UNFORTUNATE — **hap·less·ly** *adv* — **hap·less·ness** *n*

hap·loid \ˈhap-ˌlȯid\ *adj* : having the number of chromosomes characteristic of gametic cells — **haploid** *n*

hap·ly \ˈhap-lē\ *adv* : by chance

hap·pen \ˈha-pən\ *vb* **1** : to occur by chance **2** : to take place **3** : CHANCE 2

¹hap·pen·ing *n* **1** : OCCURRENCE **2** : an event that is especially interesting, entertaining, or important

²happening *adj* **1** : very fashionable **2** : offering much stimulating activity ⟨a ~ nightclub⟩

hap·pi·ly \ˈha-pə-lē\ *adv* **1** : LUCKILY **2** : in a happy manner or state ⟨lived ~ ever after⟩ **3** : APTLY, SUCCESSFULLY

hap·pi·ness \ˈha-pē-nəs\ *n* **1** : a state of well-being and contentment; *also* : a pleasurable satisfaction **2** : APTNESS

hap·py \ˈha-pē\ *adj* **hap·pi·er; -est** **1** : FORTUNATE **2** : APT, FELICITOUS **3** : enjoying well-being and contentment ⟨a ~ childhood⟩ **4** : PLEASANT ⟨a ~ ending⟩; *also* : PLEASED, GRATIFIED ⟨~ to meet you⟩ **5** : quick or enthusiastic to use or do something ⟨trigger-*happy*⟩ ⟨a cliché-*happy* writer⟩ ♦ ***Synonyms*** GLAD, CHEERFUL, LIGHTHEARTED, JOYFUL, JOYOUS

hap·py–go–lucky \ˌha-pē-gō-ˈlə-kē\ *adj* : CAREFREE

happy hour *n* : a period of time when the price of drinks at a bar is reduced

hara–kiri \ˌha-ri-ˈkir-ē, -ˈka-rē\ *n* [Jp *harakiri,* fr. *hara* belly + *kiri* cutting] : ritual suicide by disembowelment

ha·rangue \hə-ˈraŋ\ *n* **1** : a ranting speech or writing **2** : LECTURE — **harangue** *vb* — **ha·rangu·er** *n*

ha·rass \hə-ˈras, ˈha-rəs\ *vb* [F *harasser,* fr. MF, fr. *harer* to set a dog on, fr. OF *hare,* interj. used to incite dogs, of Gmc origin] **1** : EXHAUST, FATIGUE **2** : to worry and impede by repeated raids **3** : to annoy continually **4** : to create an unpleasant or hostile situation for esp. by one's verbal or physical conduct ♦ ***Synonyms*** HARRY, PLAGUE, PESTER, TEASE, BEDEVIL — **ha·rass·ment** *n*

har·bin·ger \ˈhär-bən-jər\ *n* : one that announces or foreshadows what is coming : PRECURSOR; *also* : PORTENT

¹har·bor \ˈhär-bər\ *n* **1** : a place of security and comfort **2** : a part of a body of water protected and deep enough to furnish anchorage : PORT

²harbor *vb* **1** : to give or take refuge : SHELTER ⟨~ a fugitive⟩ ⟨~*ed* in the barn⟩ **2** : to be the home or habitat of; *also* : LIVE **3** : to hold a thought or feeling ⟨~ a grudge⟩

har·bor·age \ˈhär-bə-rij\ *n* : HARBOR

har·bour *chiefly Brit var of* HARBOR

hard \ˈhärd\ *adj* **1** : not easily penetrated : not easily yielding to pressure **2** : high in alcoholic content **3** : containing salts that prevent lathering with soap ⟨~ water⟩ **4** : stable in value ⟨~ currency⟩ **5** : physically fit **6** : FIRM, DEFINITE ⟨~ agreement⟩; *also* : based on clear fact ⟨~ evidence⟩ **7** : CLOSE, SEARCHING ⟨a ~ look⟩ **8** : REALISTIC ⟨good ~ sense⟩ **9** : OBDURATE, UNFEELING ⟨a ~ heart⟩ **10** : difficult to bear ⟨~ times⟩; *also* : HARSH, SEVERE **11** : RESENTFUL ⟨~ feelings⟩ **12** : STRICT, UNRELENTING ⟨a ~ bargain⟩ **13** : INCLEMENT ⟨a ~ winter⟩ **14** : intense in force or manner ⟨a ~ gust of wind⟩ **15** : ARDUOUS, STRENUOUS ⟨~ work⟩ **16** : sounding as in *arcing* and *geese* respectively — used of *c* and *g* **17** : TROUBLESOME ⟨a ~ problem⟩ **18** : having difficulty in doing something ⟨~ of hearing⟩ **19** : addictive and gravely detrimental to health ⟨~ drugs⟩ **20** : of or relating to the natural sciences and esp. the physical sciences — **hard** *adv* — **hard·ness** *n*

hard–and–fast *adj* : rigidly binding : STRICT ⟨a ~ rule⟩

hard·back \ˈhärd-ˌbak\ *n* : a hardcover book

hard·ball \-ˌbȯl\ *n* **1** : BASEBALL **2** : forceful uncompromising methods
hard–bit·ten \-ˈbi-tᵊn\ *adj* : SEASONED, TOUGH ⟨~ campaigners⟩
hard·board \-ˌbȯrd\ *n* : a very dense fiberboard
hard–boiled \-ˈbȯi(-ə)ld\ *adj* **1** *of an egg* : boiled until both white and yolk have solidified **2** : lacking sentiment : TOUGH; *also* : HARDHEADED 2
hard·bound \-ˌbau̇nd\ *adj* : HARDCOVER
hard copy *n* : a copy of textual or graphic information (as from computer storage) produced on paper
hard–core \ˈhärd-ˈkȯr\ *adj* **1** : extremely resistant to solution or improvement **2** : being the most determined or dedicated members of a specified group **3** : containing explicit depictions of sex acts — **hard core** *n*
hard·cov·er \-ˈkə-vər\ *adj* : having rigid boards on the sides covered in cloth or paper ⟨~ books⟩
hard disk *n* : a sealed rigid metal disk used as a computer storage device; *also* : HARD DRIVE
hard drive *n* : a data-storage device consisting of a drive and one or more hard disks
hard·en \ˈhär-dᵊn\ *vb* **1** : to make or become hard or harder **2** : to confirm or become confirmed in disposition or action — **hard·en·er** *n*
hard·hack \ˈhärd-ˌhak\ *n* : an American spirea with dense clusters of pink or white flowers and leaves having a hairy rusty yellow underside
hard hat *n* **1** : a protective hat worn esp. by construction workers **2** : a construction worker
hard·head·ed \ˈhärd-ˈhe-dəd\ *adj* **1** : STUBBORN, WILLFUL **2** : SOBER, REALISTIC ⟨some ~ advice⟩ — **hard·head·ed·ly** *adv* — **hard·head·ed·ness** *n*
hard–heart·ed \-ˈhär-təd\ *adj* : PITILESS, CRUEL — **hard–heart·ed·ly** *adv* — **hard–heart·ed·ness** *n*
har·di·hood \ˈhär-dē-ˌhu̇d\ *n* **1** : resolute courage and fortitude **2** : VIGOR, ROBUSTNESS
hard–line \ˈhärd-ˈlīn\ *adj* : advocating or involving a rigidly uncompromising course of action ⟨a ~ conservative⟩ — **hard–lin·er** \-ˈlī-nər\ *n*
hard–luck \-ˌlək\ *adj* : marked by or relating to bad luck ⟨~ losing teams⟩
hard·ly \ˈhärd-lē\ *adv* **1** : with force **2** : SEVERELY **3** : with difficulty **4** : only just : BARELY ⟨can ~ tell the difference⟩ **5** : certainly not ⟨is ~ a friend of mine⟩
hard–nosed \ˈhärd-ˈnōzd\ *adj* : TOUGH, UNCOMPROMISING; *also* : HARDHEADED 2
hard palate *n* : the bony anterior part of the palate forming the roof of the mouth
hard·pan \ˈhärd-ˌpan\ *n* : a compact layer in soil that is impenetrable by roots
hard–pressed \-ˈprest\ *adj* : HARD PUT; *esp* : being under financial strain
hard put *adj* **1** : barely able **2** : faced with difficulty or perplexity
hard rock *n* : rock music marked by a heavy beat, high amplification, and usu. frenzied performances
hard–shell \ˈhärd-ˌshel\ *or* **hard–shelled** \-ˌsheld\ *adj* **1** : having a hard shell **2** : HIDEBOUND, UNCOMPROMISING ⟨a ~ conservative⟩
hard·ship \-ˌship\ *n* **1** : SUFFERING, PRIVATION **2** : something that causes suffering or privation
hard·tack \-ˌtak\ *n* : a saltless hard biscuit, bread, or cracker
hard·top \-ˌtäp\ *n* : an automobile having a permanent rigid top
hard·ware \-ˌwer\ *n* **1** : ware (as cutlery or tools) made of metal **2** : the physical components (as electronic devices) of a vehicle (as a spacecraft) or an apparatus (as a computer)
hard·wired \-ˌwī(-ə)rd\ *adj* **1** : connected or incorporated by or as if by permanent electrical connections **2** : genetically or innately determined or predisposed ⟨~ reactions⟩ ⟨is ~ to avoid change⟩
hard·wood \-ˌwu̇d\ *n* : the wood of a broad-leaved usu. deciduous tree as distinguished from that of a conifer; *also* : such a tree — **hardwood** *adj*
hard·work·ing \-ˈwər-kiŋ\ *adj* : INDUSTRIOUS, DILIGENT
har·dy \ˈhär-dē\ *adj* **har·di·er; -est** **1** : BOLD, BRAVE ⟨~ pioneers⟩ **2** : AUDACIOUS, BRAZEN **3** : ROBUST; *also* : able to withstand adverse conditions (as of weather) ⟨~ shrubs⟩ — **har·di·ly** \-də-lē\ *adv* — **har·di·ness** \-dē-nəs\ *n*
hare \ˈher\ *n, pl* **hare** *or* **hares** : any of various swift timid long-eared mammals like the related rabbits but born with open eyes and fur
hare·bell \ˈher-ˌbel\ *n* : a slender herb with bright blue bell-shaped flowers
hare·brained \-ˈbrānd\ *adj* : FOOLISH, ABSURD ⟨~ notions⟩
hare·lip \-ˈlip\ *n, sometimes offensive* : CLEFT LIP
ha·rem \ˈher-əm\ *n* [Ar *ḥarīm,* lit., something forbidden & *ḥaram,* lit., sanctuary] **1** : a house or part of a house allotted to women in a Muslim household **2** : the women and servants occupying a harem **3** : a group of females associated with one male
hark \ˈhärk\ *vb* : LISTEN
harken *var of* HEARKEN
har·le·quin \ˈhär-li-kən, -kwən\ *n* **1** *cap* : a character (as in comedy) with a shaved head, masked face, variegated tights, and wooden sword **2** : CLOWN 2
har·lot \ˈhär-lət\ *n, disparaging* : PROSTITUTE
¹harm \ˈhärm\ *n* **1** : physical or mental damage : INJURY **2** : MISCHIEF, HURT — **harm·ful** \-fəl\ *adj* — **harm·ful·ly** *adv* — **harm·ful·ness** *n* — **harm·less** *adj* — **harm·less·ly** *adv* — **harm·less·ness** *n*
²harm *vb* : to cause harm to : INJURE
¹har·mon·ic \här-ˈmä-nik\ *adj* **1** : of or relating to musical harmony or harmonics **2** : pleasing to the ear — **har·mon·i·cal·ly** \-ni-k(ə-)lē\ *adv*

²**harmonic** *n* : a musical overtone
har·mon·i·ca \här-ˈmä-ni-kə\ *n* : a small wind instrument in which the sound is produced by metal reeds
har·mo·ni·ous \här-ˈmō-nē-əs\ *adj* **1** : musically concordant **2** : CONGRUOUS **3** : marked by accord in sentiment or action ⟨a ~ relationship⟩ — **har·mo·ni·ous·ly** *adv* — **har·mo·ni·ous·ness** *n*
har·mo·nise *Brit var of* HARMONIZE
har·mo·ni·um \här-ˈmō-nē-əm\ *n* : a keyboard wind instrument in which the wind acts on a set of metal reeds
har·mo·nize \ˈhär-mə-ˌnīz\ *vb* **-nized; -niz·ing** **1** : to play or sing in harmony **2** : to be in harmony **3** : to bring into consonance or accord — **har·mo·ni·za·tion** \ˌhär-mə-nə-ˈzā-shən\ *n*
har·mo·ny \ˈhär-mə-nē\ *n, pl* **-nies** [ME *armony,* fr. AF *armonie,* fr. L *harmonia,* fr. Gk, joint, harmony, fr. *harmos* joint] **1** : musical agreement of sounds; *esp* : the combination of tones into chords and progressions of chords **2** : a pleasing arrangement of parts; *also* : ACCORD **3** : internal calm
¹**har·ness** \ˈhär-nəs\ *n* **1** : the gear other than a yoke of a draft animal **2** : something that resembles a harness
²**harness** *vb* **1** : to put a harness on; *also* : YOKE **2** : UTILIZE ⟨~ one's potential⟩
¹**harp** \ˈhärp\ *n* : a musical instrument consisting of a triangular frame set with strings plucked by the fingers — **harp·ist** \ˈhär-pist\ *n*
²**harp** *vb* **1** : to play on a harp **2** : to dwell on a subject tiresomely — **harp·er** *n*
har·poon \här-ˈpün\ *n* : a barbed spear used esp. in hunting whales — **harpoon** *vb* — **har·poon·er** *n*
harp·si·chord \ˈhärp-si-ˌkȯrd\ *n* : a keyboard instrument producing tones by the plucking of its strings with quills or with leather or plastic points
har·py \ˈhär-pē\ *n, pl* **harpies** [L *Harpyia,* a malign creature of myth having a woman's head and a bird's body, fr. Gk] **1** : a predatory person : LEECH **2** : a shrewish woman
har·ri·dan \ˈher-ə-dən\ *n* : SHREW 2
¹**har·ri·er** \ˈher-ē-ər\ *n* **1** : any of a breed of medium-sized foxhounds **2** : a runner on a cross-country team
²**harrier** *n* : a slender long-legged hawk
¹**har·row** \ˈher-ō\ *n* : a cultivating tool that has spikes, spring teeth, or disks and is used esp. to pulverize and smooth the soil
²**harrow** *vb* **1** : to cultivate with a harrow **2** : TORMENT, VEX
har·rumph \hə-ˈrəmf\ *vb* : to comment disapprovingly as though clearing the throat
har·ry \ˈher-ē\ *vb* **har·ried; har·ry·ing** **1** : RAID, PILLAGE **2** : to torment by or as if by constant attack ♦ ***Synonyms*** WORRY, ANNOY, PLAGUE, PESTER
harsh \ˈhärsh\ *adj* **1** : disagreeably rough **2** : causing discomfort or pain **3** : unduly exacting : SEVERE — **harsh·ly** *adv* — **harsh·ness** *n*
harsh·en \ˈhär-shən\ *vb* : to make or become harsh ⟨~*ed* his voice⟩
hart \ˈhärt\ *n, chiefly Brit* : STAG
har·um–scar·um \ˌhar-əm-ˈskar-əm\ *adj* : RECKLESS, IRRESPONSIBLE
¹**har·vest** \ˈhär-vəst\ *n* **1** : the season for gathering in crops; *also* : the act of gathering in a crop **2** : a mature crop **3** : the product or reward of effort
²**harvest** *vb* **1** : to gather in a crop : REAP **2** : to gather, hunt, or kill (as deer) for human use or population control **3** : to remove cells, tissues, or organs from a living or recently deceased body esp. for transplanting — **har·vest·er** *n*
has *pres 3d sing of* HAVE
has–been \ˈhaz-ˌbin\ *n* : one that has passed the peak of ability, power, effectiveness, or popularity
¹**hash** \ˈhash\ *vb* [F *hacher,* fr. OF *hachier,* fr. *hache* battle-ax, of Gmc origin] **1** : to chop into small pieces **2** : to talk about — often used with *over* or *out*
²**hash** *n* **1** : chopped meat mixed with potatoes and browned **2** : HODGEPODGE, JUMBLE
³**hash** *n* : HASHISH
hash browns *n pl* : boiled potatoes that have been diced, mixed with chopped onions and shortening, and fried
hash·ish \ˈha-ˌshēsh, ha-ˈshēsh\ *n* [Ar *ḥashīsh*] : the intoxicating concentrated resin from the flowering tops of the female hemp plant
hash·tag \ˈhash-ˌtag\ *n* : a word or phrase preceded by the symbol # that classifies the accompanying text
hasp \ˈhasp\ *n* : a fastener (as for a door) consisting of a hinged metal strap that fits over a staple and is secured by a pin or padlock
has·si·um \ˈha-sē-əm\ *n* : an artificially produced radioactive metallic chemical element
has·sle \ˈha-səl\ *n* **1** : WRANGLE; *also* : FIGHT **2** : an annoying or troublesome concern — **hassle** *vb*
has·sock \ˈha-sək\ *n* : a cushion that serves as a seat or leg rest; *also* : a cushion to kneel on in prayer
haste \ˈhāst\ *n* **1** : rapidity of motion or action : SPEED **2** : rash or headlong action **3** : excessive eagerness — **hast·i·ly** \ˈhā-stə-lē\ *adv* — **hast·i·ness** \-stē-nəs\ *n* — **hasty** \ˈhā-stē\ *adj*
has·ten \ˈhā-sᵊn\ *vb* **1** : to urge on **2** : to move or act quickly : HURRY ♦ ***Synonyms*** SPEED, ACCELERATE, QUICKEN
hat \ˈhat\ *n* : a covering for the head usu. having a shaped crown and brim— **under one's hat** : SECRET ⟨kept the plans *under his hat*⟩
hat·box \ˈhat-ˌbäks\ *n* : a round piece of luggage esp. for carrying hats
¹**hatch** \ˈhach\ *n* **1** : a small door or opening **2** : a door or cover for access down into a compartment of a ship
²**hatch** *vb* **1** : to produce by incubation; *also* : INCUBATE **2** : to emerge from an egg or pupa; *also* : to give forth young **3** : ORIGINATE ⟨~ a scheme⟩ — **hatch·ery** \ˈha-chə-rē\ *n*
hatch·back \ˈhach-ˌbak\ *n* : an automobile with a rear hatch that opens upward

hatch·et \ˈha-chət\ *n* **1 :** a short-handled ax with a hammerlike part opposite the blade **2 :** TOMAHAWK

hatchet man *n* **:** a person hired for murder, coercion, or unscrupulous attack

hatch·ing \ˈha-chiŋ\ *n* **:** the engraving or drawing of closely spaced fine lines chiefly to give an effect of shading; *also* **:** the pattern so created

hatch·way \ˈhach-ˌwā\ *n* **:** a hatch giving access usu. by a ladder or stairs

[1]**hate** \ˈhāt\ *n* **1 :** intense hostility and aversion **2 :** an object of hatred — **hate·ful** \-fəl\ *adj* — **hate·ful·ly** *adv* — **hate·ful·ness** *n*

[2]**hate** *vb* **hat·ed; hat·ing 1 :** to express or feel extreme enmity **2 :** to find distasteful ♦ ***Synonyms*** DETEST, ABHOR, ABOMINATE, LOATHE — **hat·er** *n*

ha·tred \ˈhā-trəd\ *n* **:** HATE; *also* **:** prejudiced hostility or animosity

hat·ter \ˈha-tər\ *n* **:** one that makes, sells, or cleans and repairs hats

hau·berk \ˈhȯ-bərk\ *n* **:** a coat of mail

haugh·ty \ˈhȯ-tē\ *adj* **haugh·ti·er; -est** [obs. *haught,* fr. ME *haute,* fr. AF *halt, haut,* lit., high, fr. L *altus*] **:** disdainfully proud ♦ ***Synonyms*** INSOLENT, LORDLY, OVERBEARING, ARROGANT — **haugh·ti·ly** \-tə-lē\ *adv* — **haugh·ti·ness** \-tē-nəs\ *n*

[1]**haul** \ˈhȯl\ *vb* **1 :** to exert traction on **:** DRAW, PULL **2 :** to furnish transportation **:** CART — **haul·er** *n*

[2]**haul** *n* **1 :** PULL, TUG **2 :** the result of an effort to obtain, collect, or win **3 :** the length or course of a transportation route; *also* **:** LOAD

haul·age \ˈhȯ-lij\ *n* **1 :** the act or process of hauling **2 :** a charge for hauling

haunch \ˈhȯnch\ *n* **1 :** [2]HIP 1 **2 :** HINDQUARTER 2 — usu. used in pl. **3 :** HINDQUARTER 1

[1]**haunt** \ˈhȯnt\ *vb* **1 :** to visit often **:** FREQUENT **2 :** to have a disquieting effect on ⟨was ~*ed* by his past⟩; *also* **:** to reappear continually in **3 :** to visit or inhabit as a ghost — **haunt·er** *n* — **haunt·ing·ly** *adv*

[2]**haunt** \ˈhȯnt, *2 is usu* ˈhant\ *n* **1 :** a place habitually frequented **2** *chiefly dial* **:** GHOST

haute cou·ture \ˌōt-kü-ˈtu̇r\ *n* [F] **:** the establishments or designers that create exclusive and often trend-setting fashions for women; *also* **:** the fashions created

haute cui·sine \-kwi-ˈzēn\ *n* **:** artful or elaborate cuisine

hau·teur \hȯ-ˈtər, ō-, hō-\ *n* **:** ARROGANCE, HAUGHTINESS

[1]**have** \ˈhav, həv, v; *in sense 2 before "to" usu* ˈhaf\ *vb* **had** \ˈhad, həd\; **hav·ing; has** \ˈhaz, həz, *in sense 2 before "to" usu* ˈhas\ **1 :** to hold in possession; *also* **:** to hold in one's use, service, or regard ⟨*has* a good job⟩ **2 :** to be compelled or forced ⟨~ to go now⟩ **3 :** to stand in relationship to ⟨*has* many enemies⟩ **4 :** OBTAIN; *also* **:** RECEIVE, ACCEPT **5 :** to be marked by ⟨*has* red hair⟩ **6 :** SHOW; *also* **:** USE, EXERCISE ⟨~ mercy⟩ **7 :** EXPERIENCE; *also* **:** TAKE ⟨~ a look⟩ **8 :** to entertain in the mind ⟨~ an idea⟩ **9 :** to cause to **10 :** ALLOW **11 :** to be competent in **12 :** to hold in a disadvantageous position; *also* **:** TRICK **13 :** BEGET **14 :** to partake of **15** — used as an auxiliary with the past participle to form the present perfect, past perfect, or future perfect — **have at :** ATTACK — **have coming :** DESERVE — **have done with :** to be finished with — **have had it :** to have endured all one will permit or can stand — **have to do with :** to have in the way of relation with or effect on

[2]**have** \ˈhav\ *n* **:** one that has material wealth

ha·ven \ˈhā-vən\ *n* **1 :** HARBOR, PORT **2 :** a place of safety **3 :** a place offering favorable conditions ⟨an artist's ~⟩

have–not \ˈhav-ˌnät, -ˈnät\ *n* **:** one that is poor in material wealth

hav·er·sack \ˈha-vər-ˌsak\ *n* [F *havresac,* fr. G *Habersack* bag for oats] **:** a bag similar to a knapsack but worn over one shoulder

hav·oc \ˈha-vək\ *n* **1 :** wide and general destruction **2 :** great confusion and disorder

haw \ˈhȯ\ *n* **:** a hawthorn berry; *also* **:** HAWTHORN

Ha·wai·ian \hə-ˈwä-yən\ *n* **1 :** a native or resident of Hawaii; *esp* **:** one of Polynesian ancestry **2 :** a native or resident of Hawaii not of Polynesian ancestry — considered an error **3 :** the Polynesian language of Hawaii — **Hawaiian** *adj*

[1]**hawk** \ˈhȯk\ *n* **1 :** any of numerous mostly small or medium-sized day-flying birds of prey (as a falcon or kite) **2 :** a supporter of a war or a warlike policy — **hawk·ish** *adj*

[2]**hawk** *vb* **:** to make a harsh coughing sound in or as if in clearing the throat; *also* **:** to raise by hawking

[3]**hawk** *vb* **:** to offer goods for sale by calling out in the street — **hawk·er** *n*

hawk·weed \ˈhȯk-ˌwēd\ *n* **:** any of several plants related to the daisies usu. having yellow flowers

haw·ser \ˈhȯ-zər\ *n* **:** a large rope for towing, mooring, or securing a ship

haw·thorn \ˈhȯ-ˌthȯrn\ *n* **:** any of a genus of spiny spring-flowering shrubs or small trees related to the apple

[1]**hay** \ˈhā\ *n* **1 :** herbage (as grass) mowed and cured for fodder **2 :** REWARD **3** *slang* **:** BED ⟨hit the ~⟩ **4 :** a small amount of money

[2]**hay** *vb* **:** to cut, cure, and store for hay

hay·cock \ˈhā-ˌkäk\ *n* **:** a small conical pile of hay

hay fever *n* **:** an acute allergic reaction esp. to plant pollen that resembles a cold

hay·loft \ˈhā-ˌlȯft\ *n* **:** a loft for hay

hay·mow \-ˌmau̇\ *n* **:** a mow of or for hay

hay·rick \-ˌrik\ *n* **:** a large sometimes thatched outdoor stack of hay

hay·seed \-ˌsēd\ *n, pl* **hayseed** *or* **hayseeds 1 :** clinging bits of straw or chaff from hay **2 :** BUMPKIN, YOKEL

hay·stack \-ˌstak\ *n* **:** a stack of hay

hay·wire \-ˌwī(-ə)r\ *adj* **:** being out of order or control **:** CRAZY ⟨things went ~⟩

[1]**haz·ard** \ˈha-zərd\ *n* [ME, a dice game, fr. AF *hasard,* fr. Sp *azar,* Ar *al-zahr* the die] **1** : a source of danger **2** : CHANCE; *also* : ACCIDENT **3** : an obstacle on a golf course — **haz·ard·ous** *adj*

[2]**hazard** *vb* : VENTURE, RISK ⟨~ a guess⟩

[1]**haze** \ˈhāz\ *n* **1** : fine dust, smoke, or light vapor causing lack of transparency in the air **2** : vagueness of mind or perception

[2]**haze** *vb* **hazed; haz·ing** : to harass by abusive and humiliating tricks usu. by way of initiation

ha·zel \ˈhā-zəl\ *n* **1** : any of a genus of shrubs or small trees related to the birches and bearing edible brown nuts (**ha·zel·nuts** \-ˌnəts\) **2** : a light brown color

hazy \ˈhā-zē\ *adj* **haz·i·er; -est** **1** : obscured or darkened by haze **2** : VAGUE, INDEFINITE ⟨a ~ memory⟩; *also* : UNCERTAIN — **haz·i·ly** \-zə-lē\ *adv* — **haz·i·ness** \-zē-nəs\ *n*

Hb *abbr* hemoglobin

[1]**HBCU** \ˌāch-ˌbē-ˌsē-ˈyü\ *n* : a college or university in the U.S. established before 1964 for African American students

[2]**HBCU** *abbr* : historically Black colleges and universities

HBM *abbr* Her Britannic Majesty; His Britannic Majesty

H–bomb \ˈāch-ˌbäm\ *n* : HYDROGEN BOMB

HC *abbr* **1** Holy Communion **2** House of Commons

hd *abbr* head

HD *abbr* **1** heavy-duty **2** high definition

hdbk *abbr* handbook

hdkf *abbr* handkerchief

HDL \ˌāch-(ˌ)dē-ˈel\ *n* [*h*igh-*d*ensity *l*ipoprotein] : a cholesterol-poor protein-rich lipoprotein of blood plasma correlated with reduced risk of atherosclerosis

hdwe *abbr* hardware

he \ˈhē\ *pron* **1** : that male one **2** : a person : the person ⟨~ who hesitates is lost⟩

He *symbol* helium

HE *abbr* **1** Her Excellency **2** His Eminence **3** His Excellency

[1]**head** \ˈhed\ *n* **1** : the front or upper part of the body containing the brain, the chief sense organs, and the mouth **2** : MIND; *also* : natural aptitude ⟨has a ~ for math⟩ **3** : POISE ⟨a level ~⟩ **4** : the obverse of a coin **5** : INDIVIDUAL; *also, pl* **head** : one of a number (as of cattle) **6** : the end that is upper or higher or opposite the foot; *also* : either end of something (as a drum) whose two ends need not be distinguished **7** : a compact mass of plant parts (as leaves or flowers) **8** : the source of a stream **9** : DIRECTOR, LEADER; *also* : a leading element (as of a procession) **10** : a projecting part; *also* : the striking part of a weapon **11** : the place of leadership or honor **12** : a separate part or topic **13** : the foam on a fermenting or effervescing liquid **14** : a critical point ⟨events came to a ~⟩ — **head·ed** \ˈhe-dəd\ *adj* — **head·less** *adj* — **over one's head** : beyond one's comprehension or competence

[2]**head** *adj* : PRINCIPAL, CHIEF ⟨~ chef⟩

[3]**head** *vb* **1** : to provide with or form a head; *also* : to form the head of **2** : LEAD, CONDUCT ⟨~*ed* the search⟩ **3** : to get in front of esp. so as to stop; *also* : SURPASS **4** : to put or stand at the head **5** : to point or proceed in a certain direction ⟨~*ed* west⟩

head·ache \ˈhe-ˌdāk\ *n* **1** : pain in the head **2** : a baffling situation or problem — **head·achy** *also* **head·achey** \-ˌā-kē\ *adj*

head·band \ˈhed-ˌband\ *n* : a band worn on or around the head

head·bang·er \-ˌbaŋ-ər\ *n* : one who performs or enjoys hard rock

head·board \-ˌbȯrd\ *n* : a board forming the head (as of a bed)

head cold *n* : a common cold centered in the nasal passages and adjacent mucous tissues

head·dress \ˈhed-ˌdres\ *n* : an often elaborate covering for the head

head·first \-ˈfərst\ *adv* : HEADLONG 1 ⟨dove ~ into the pool⟩ — **headfirst** *adj*

head·gear \-ˌgir\ *n* : a covering or protective device for the head

head·hunt·er \-ˌhən-tər\ *n* **1** : one that engages in head-hunting **2** : a recruiter of esp. executive personnel

head–hunt·ing \-ˌhən-tiŋ\ *n* : the practice of seeking out and decapitating enemies and preserving their heads as trophies

head·ing \ˈhe-diŋ\ *n* **1** : the compass direction in which the longitudinal axis of a ship or airplane points **2** : something that appears at the top or beginning of something else (as a document)

head·land \ˈhed-lənd, -ˌland\ *n* : PROMONTORY

head·light \-ˌlīt\ *n* : a light mounted on the front of a vehicle to illuminate the road ahead

[1]**head·line** \-ˌlīn\ *n* : a head of a newspaper story or article usu. printed in large type

[2]**headline** *vb* **1** : to provide with a headline **2** : to publicize highly **3** : to be a leading performer in

head·lock \-ˌläk\ *n* : a wrestling hold in which one encircles the opponent's head with one arm

[1]**head·long** \-ˈlȯŋ\ *adv* **1** : with the head foremost **2** : RECKLESSLY **3** : without delay

[2]**head·long** \-ˌlȯŋ\ *adj* **1** : PRECIPITATE, RASH ⟨~ flight⟩ **2** : plunging with the head foremost

head·man \ˈhed-ˈman, -ˌman\ *n* : one who is a leader : CHIEF

head·mas·ter \-ˌmas-tər\ *n* : a man who is head of a private school

head·mis·tress \-ˌmis-trəs\ *n* : a woman who is head of a private school

head of steam : strong driving force : MOMENTUM

head–on \ˈhed-ˈȯn, -ˈän\ *adj* : having the front facing in the direction of initial contact or line of sight ⟨~ collision⟩ — **head–on** *adv*

head·phone \-ˌfōn\ *n* : an earphone held

on by a band over the head; *also* : a small earphone inserted into the ear

head·piece \-ˌpēs\ *n* : a covering for the head

head·pin \-ˌpin\ *n* : a bowling pin that stands foremost in the arrangement of pins

head·quar·ters \-ˌkwȯr-tərz\ *n sing or pl* **1** : a place from which a commander exercises command **2** : the administrative center of an enterprise

head·rest \-ˌrest\ *n* **1** : a support for the head **2** : a pad at the top of the back of an automobile seat

head·room \-ˌrüm, -ˌru̇m\ *n* : vertical space in which to stand, sit, or move

head–scratcher \-ˌskra-chər\ *n* : PUZZLE, MYSTERY

head·set \-ˌset\ *n* : an earphone or pair of earphones held on the head by a band and usu. with an attached microphone

head·ship \-ˌship\ *n* : the position, office, or dignity of a head

heads·man \ˈhedz-mən\ *n* : EXECUTIONER

head·stall \ˈhed-ˌstȯl\ *n* : a part of a bridle or halter that encircles the head

head·stone \-ˌstōn\ *n* : a memorial stone at the head of a grave

head·strong \ˈhed-ˌstrȯŋ\ *adj* **1** : not easily restrained **2** : directed by ungovernable will ♦ ***Synonyms*** UNRULY, INTRACTABLE, WILLFUL, PERTINACIOUS, REFRACTORY, STUBBORN

heads–up \ˈhedz-ˈəp\ *n* : WARNING

head·wait·er \-ˈwā-tər\ *n* : the head of the dining-room staff of a restaurant or hotel

head·wa·ter \-ˌwȯ-tər, -ˌwä-\ *n* : the source of a stream — usu. used in pl.

head·way \-ˌwā\ *n* : forward motion; *also* : PROGRESS

head·wind \-ˌwind\ *n* : a wind blowing in a direction opposite to a course esp. of a ship or aircraft

head·word \ˈhed-ˌwərd\ *n* **1** : a word or term placed at the beginning **2** : a word qualified by a modifier

head·work \-ˌwərk\ *n* : mental work or effort : THINKING

heady \ˈhe-dē\ *adj* **head·i·er; -est** **1** : WILLFUL, RASH; *also* : IMPETUOUS **2** : INTOXICATING ⟨a ~ wine⟩ **3** : SHREWD

heal \ˈhēl\ *vb* **1** : to make or become healthy, sound, or whole **2** : CURE, REMEDY — **heal·er** *n*

health \ˈhelth\ *n* **1** : sound physical or mental condition; *also* : overall condition of the body ⟨in poor ~⟩ **2** : WELL-BEING **3** : a toast to someone's health or prosperity

health care *n* : efforts made to maintain or restore health — usu. hyphenated when used attributively

health club *n* : a commercial establishment providing health and fitness facilities and equipment for members

health·ful \ˈhelth-fəl\ *adj* **1** : beneficial to health **2** : HEALTHY — **health·ful·ly** *adv* — **health·ful·ness** *n*

health maintenance organization *n* : HMO

healthy \ˈhel-thē\ *adj* **health·i·er; -est** **1** : enjoying or typical of good health : WELL **2** : evincing or conducive to health **3** : PROSPEROUS ⟨a ~ economy⟩; *also* : CONSIDERABLE 2 ⟨a ~ savings⟩ — **health·i·ly** \-thə-lē\ *adv* — **health·i·ness** \-thē-nəs\ *n*

[1]**heap** \ˈhēp\ *n* : PILE ⟨rubbish ~⟩; *also* : LOT 5 ⟨a ~ of fun⟩

[2]**heap** *vb* **1** : to throw or lay in a heap **2** : to give in large quantities; *also* : to load heavily

hear \ˈhir\ *vb* **heard** \ˈhərd\; **hear·ing** **1** : to perceive by the ear **2** : to gain knowledge of by hearing : LEARN **3** : HEED; *also* : ATTEND **4** : to give a legal hearing to or take testimony from — **hear·er** *n*

hear·ing *n* **1** : the process, function, or power of perceiving sound; *esp* : the special sense by which noises and tones are received as stimuli **2** : EARSHOT **3** : opportunity to be heard **4** : a listening to arguments (as in a court); *also* : a session (as of a legislative committee) in which testimony is taken from witnesses

hear·ken \ˈhär-kən\ *vb* : to give attention : LISTEN ♦ ***Synonyms*** HEAR, HARK, HEED

hear·say \ˈhir-ˌsā\ *n* : RUMOR

hearse \ˈhərs\ *n* : a vehicle for carrying the dead to the grave

heart \ˈhärt\ *n* **1** : a hollow muscular organ that by rhythmic contraction keeps up the circulation of the blood in the body; *also* : something resembling a heart in shape **2** : any of a suit of playing cards marked with a red figure of a heart; *also, pl* : a card game in which the object is to avoid taking tricks containing hearts **3** : the whole personality; *also* : the emotional or moral as distinguished from the intellectual nature **4** : COURAGE **5** : one's innermost being ⟨knew it in his ~⟩ **6** : CENTER; *also* : the essential part **7** : the younger central part of a compact leafy cluster (as of lettuce) — **heart·ed** \ˈhär-təd\ *adj* — **by heart** : by rote or from memory

heart·ache \-ˌāk\ *n* : anguish of mind

heart attack *n* : an acute episode of heart disease due to insufficient blood supply to the heart muscle

heart·beat \ˈhärt-ˌbēt\ *n* : one complete pulsation of the heart

heart·break \-ˌbrāk\ *n* : crushing grief

heart·break·ing \-ˌbrā-kiŋ\ *adj* : causing extreme sorrow or distress — **heart·break·er** \-ˌbrā-kər\ *n* — **heart·break·ing·ly** *adv*

heart·bro·ken \-ˌbrō-kən\ *adj* : overcome by sorrow

heart·burn \-ˌbərn\ *n* : a burning distress behind the sternum due esp. to the backward flow of acid from the stomach to the esophagus

heart disease *n* : an abnormal organic condition of the heart or of the heart and circulation

heart·en \ˈhär-tᵊn\ *vb* : ENCOURAGE, CHEER ⟨were ~*ed* by the victory⟩

heart·felt \ˈhärt-ˌfelt\ *adj* : deeply felt : SINCERE ⟨~ thanks⟩

hearth \ˈhärth\ *n* **1** : an area (as of brick) in front of a fireplace; *also* : the floor of a fireplace **2** : HOME
hearth·stone \ˈhärth-ˌstōn\ *n* **1** : stone forming a hearth **2** : HOME
heart·less \ˈhärt-ləs\ *adj* : CRUEL
heart·rend·ing \-ˌren-diŋ\ *adj* : HEARTBREAKING
heart·sick \-ˌsik\ *adj* : very despondent — **heart·sick·ness** *n*
heart–stop·ping \-ˌstä-piŋ\ *adj* : extremely shocking or exciting
heart·strings \-ˌstriŋz\ *n pl* : the deepest emotions or affections
heart·throb \-ˌthräb\ *n* **1** : the throb of a heart **2** : sentimental emotion **3** : SWEETHEART **4** : an entertainer noted for his sex appeal
heart–to–heart *adj* : SINCERE, FRANK
heart·warm·ing \ˈhärt-ˌwȯr-miŋ\ *adj* : inspiring sympathetic feeling
heart·wood \-ˌwu̇d\ *n* : the older harder nonliving and usu. darker wood of the central part of a tree trunk
¹**hearty** \ˈhär-tē\ *adj* **heart·i·er; -est** **1** : giving full support; *also* : JOVIAL **2** : vigorously healthy **3** : ABUNDANT; *also* : NOURISHING ⟨~ soups⟩ ♦ ***Synonyms*** SINCERE, WHOLEHEARTED, UNFEIGNED, HEARTFELT — **heart·i·ly** \-tə-lē\ *adv* — **heart·i·ness** \-tē-nəs\ *n*
²**hearty** *n, pl* **heart·ies** : an enthusiastic jovial fellow; *also* : SAILOR
¹**heat** \ˈhēt\ *vb* **1** : to make or become warm or hot **2** : EXCITE ⟨a ~*ed* discussion⟩ — **heat·ed·ly** *adv* — **heat·er** *n*
²**heat** *n* **1** : a condition of being hot : WARMTH **2** : a form of energy that when added to a body causes the body to rise in temperature, to fuse, to evaporate, or to expand **3** : high temperature **4** : intensity of feeling; *also* : sexual excitement esp. in a female mammal **5** : a preliminary race for narrowing the competition **6** : pungency of flavor **7** *slang* : POLICE **8** : PRESSURE, COERCION; *also* : ABUSE, CRITICISM ⟨took ~ for my mistakes⟩
heat exchanger *n* : a device (as an automobile radiator) for transferring heat from one fluid to another without allowing them to mix
heat exhaustion *n* : a condition marked by weakness, nausea, dizziness, and profuse sweating resulting from physical exertion in a hot environment
heath \ˈhēth\ *n* **1** : a tract of wasteland **2** : any of a family of often evergreen shrubby plants (as a blueberry or heather) of wet acid soils — **heathy** *adj*
hea·then \ˈhē-t͟hən\ *n, pl* **heathens** *or* **heathen** **1** *often disparaging* : PAGAN **2** : an uncivilized or irreligious person — **heathen** *adj* — **hea·then·dom** *n* — **hea·then·ish** *adj* — **hea·then·ism** *n*
heath·er \ˈhe-t͟hər\ *n* : a northern and alpine evergreen heath with usu. lavender flowers — **heath·ery** *adj*
heat lightning *n* : flashes of light without thunder ascribed to distant lightning reflected by high clouds
heat·stroke \ˈhēt-ˌstrōk\ *n* : a disorder marked esp. by high body temperature without sweating and by collapse that follows prolonged exposure to excessive heat
¹**heave** \ˈhēv\ *vb* **heaved** *or* **hove** \ˈhōv\; **heav·ing** **1** : to rise or lift upward **2** : THROW **3** : to rise and fall rhythmically; *also* : PANT **4** : RETCH **5** : PULL, PUSH — **heav·er** *n*
²**heave** *n* **1** : an effort to lift or raise **2** : THROW, CAST **3** : an upward motion **4** *pl* : a chronic lung disease of horses marked by difficult breathing and persistent cough
heav·en \ˈhe-vən\ *n* **1** : FIRMAMENT — usu. used in pl. **2** *often cap* : the abode of the Deity and of the blessed dead; *also* : a spiritual state of everlasting communion with God **3** *cap* : GOD 1 **4** : a place of supreme happiness — **heav·en·ly** *adj* — **heav·en·ward** *adv or adj*
¹**heavy** \ˈhe-vē\ *adj* **heavi·er; -est** **1** : having great weight **2** : hard to bear **3** : SERIOUS **4** : DEEP, PROFOUND ⟨a ~ silence⟩ **5** : burdened with something oppressive; *also* : PREGNANT **6** : SLUGGISH **7** : DRAB; *also* : DOLEFUL **8** : DROWSY **9** : greater than the average of its kind or class **10** : very rich and hard to digest; *also* : not properly raised or leavened **11** : producing goods (as steel) used in the production of other goods — **heavi·ly** \-və-lē\ *adv* — **heavi·ness** \-vē-nəs\ *n*
²**heavy** *n, pl* **heav·ies** : a theatrical role representing a dignified or imposing person; *also* : a villain esp. in a story
heavy–du·ty \ˌhe-vē-ˈdü-tē, -ˈdyü-\ *adj* : able to withstand unusual strain
heavy–hand·ed \-ˈhan-dəd\ *adj* **1** : CLUMSY **2** : OPPRESSIVE, HARSH
heavy·heart·ed \-ˈhär-təd\ *adj* : SADDENED, DESPONDENT
heavy lifting *n* : a burdensome or laborious duty
heavy metal *n* : energetic and highly amplified electronic rock music
heavy·set \ˌhe-vē-ˈset\ *adj* : stocky and compact in build
heavy water *n* : water enriched in deuterium
heavy·weight \ˈhe-vē-ˌwāt\ *n* : one above average in weight; *esp* : a boxer in an unlimited weight division
Heb *abbr* Hebrews
He·bra·ism \ˈhē-brā-ˌi-zəm\ *n* : the thought, spirit, or practice characteristic of the Hebrews — **He·bra·ic** \hi-ˈbrā-ik\ *adj*
He·bra·ist \ˈhē-ˌbrā-ist\ *n* : a specialist in Hebrew and Hebraic studies
He·brew \ˈhē-brü\ *n* **1** : the language of the Hebrews **2** : a member of or descendant from a group of Semitic peoples; *esp* : ISRAELITE — **Hebrew** *adj*
He·brews \ˈhē-(ˌ)brüz\ *n* — see BIBLE table
hec·a·tomb \ˈhe-kə-ˌtōm\ *n* : an ancient Greek and Roman sacrifice of 100 oxen or cattle
heck·le \ˈhe-kəl\ *vb* **heck·led; heck·ling**

: to harass with questions or gibes : BADGER — **heck·ler** *n*

hect·are \ˈhek-ˌter\ *n* — see METRIC SYSTEM table

hec·tic \ˈhek-tik\ *adj* **1** : being hot and flushed **2** : filled with excitement, activity, or confusion — **hec·ti·cal·ly** \-ti-k(ə-)lē\ *adv*

hec·to·gram \ˈhek-tə-ˌgram\ *n* — see METRIC SYSTEM table

hec·to·li·ter \ˈhek-tə-ˌlē-tər\ *n* — see METRIC SYSTEM table

hec·to·me·ter \ˈhek-tə-ˌmē-tər, hek-ˈtä-mə-tər\ *n* — see METRIC SYSTEM table

hec·tor \ˈhek-tər\ *vb* [*hector* bully, fr. *Hector,* champion of Troy in Greek legend] **1** : SWAGGER **2** : to intimidate by bluster or personal pressure

¹**hedge** \ˈhej\ *n* **1** : a fence or boundary formed of shrubs or small trees **2** : BARRIER **3** : a means of protection (as against financial loss)

²**hedge** *vb* **hedged; hedg·ing** **1** : ENCIRCLE **2** : HINDER **3** : to protect oneself financially by a counterbalancing action **4** : to evade the risk of commitment — **hedg·er** *n*

hedge·hog \ˈhej-ˌhȯg, -ˌhäg\ *n* : a small Old World insect-eating mammal covered with spines; *also* : PORCUPINE

hedge·hop \-ˌhäp\ *vb* : to fly an airplane very close to the ground

hedge·row \-ˌrō\ *n* : a row of shrubs or trees bounding or separating fields

he·do·nism \ˈhē-də-ˌni-zəm\ *n* [Gk *hēdonē* pleasure] : the doctrine that pleasure is the chief good in life; *also* : a way of life based on this — **he·do·nist** \-nist\ *n* — **he·do·nis·tic** \ˌhē-də-ˈni-stik\ *adj*

¹**heed** \ˈhēd\ *vb* : to pay attention

²**heed** *n* : ATTENTION, NOTICE — **heed·ful** \-fəl\ *adj* — **heed·ful·ly** *adv* — **heed·ful·ness** *n* — **heed·less** *adj* — **heed·less·ly** *adv* — **heed·less·ness** *n*

¹**heel** \ˈhēl\ *n* **1** : the hind part of the foot **2** : one of the crusty ends of a loaf of bread **3** : a solid attachment forming the back of the sole of a shoe **4** : a rear, low, or bottom part **5** : a contemptible person

²**heel** *vb* : to tilt to one side : LIST

¹**heft** \ˈheft\ *n* : WEIGHT, HEAVINESS

²**heft** *vb* : to test the weight of by lifting

hefty \ˈhef-tē\ *adj* **heft·i·er; -est** **1** : marked by bigness, bulk, and usu. strength **2** : impressively large ⟨got a ~ raise⟩

he·ge·mo·ny \hi-ˈje-mə-nē\ *n* : preponderant influence or authority over others : DOMINATION

he·gi·ra \hi-ˈjī-rə\ *n* [the *Hegira,* flight of Muhammad from Mecca in A.D. 622, fr. ML, fr. Ar *hijra,* lit., departure] : a journey esp. when undertaken to escape a dangerous or undesirable environment

heif·er \ˈhe-fər\ *n* : a young cow; *esp* : one that has not had a calf

height \ˈhīt\ *n* **1** : the highest part or point **2** : the distance from the bottom to the top of something standing upright **3** : ALTITUDE

height·en \ˈhī-tᵊn\ *vb* **1** : to increase in amount or degree **2** : to make or become high or higher ♦ ***Synonyms*** ENHANCE, INTENSIFY, AGGRAVATE, MAGNIFY

Heim·lich maneuver \ˈhīm-lik-\ *n* [Henry J. *Heimlich* *b*1920 Am. surgeon] : the manual application of sudden upward pressure on the upper abdomen of a choking victim to force a foreign object from the trachea

hei·nous \ˈhā-nəs\ *adj* [ME, fr. AF *hainus, heinous,* fr. *haine* hate, fr. *hair* to hate] : hatefully or shockingly evil — **hei·nous·ly** *adv* — **hei·nous·ness** *n*

heir \ˈer\ *n* : one who inherits or is entitled to inherit property, rank, title, or office — **heir·ship** *n*

heir apparent *n, pl* **heirs apparent** : an heir whose right to succeed (as to a title) cannot be taken away if he or she survives the present holder

heir·ess \ˈer-əs\ *n* : a female heir esp. to great wealth

heir·loom \ˈer-ˌlüm\ *n* **1** : a piece of personal property that descends by inheritance **2** : something handed on from one generation to another

heir presumptive *n, pl* **heirs presumptive** : an heir whose present right to inherit could be lost through the birth of a nearer relative

heist \ˈhīst\ *vb* : to commit armed robbery on; *also* : STEAL — **heist** *n*

held *past and past part of* HOLD

he·li·cal \ˈhe-li-kəl, ˈhē-\ *adj* : SPIRAL

he·li·cop·ter \ˈhe-lə-ˌkäp-tər, ˈhē-\ *n* [F *hélicoptère,* fr. Gk *helik-, helix* spiral + *pteron* wing] : an aircraft that is supported in the air by one or more rotors revolving on substantially vertical axes

he·lio·cen·tric \ˌhē-lē-ō-ˈsen-trik\ *adj* : having or relating to the sun as center

he·li·o·sphere \ˈhē-lē-ə-ˌsfir, -ō-\ *n* : the region in space influenced by the sun or solar wind

he·lio·trope \ˈhē-lē-ə-ˌtrōp\ *n* [L *heliotropium,* fr. Gk *hēliotropion,* fr. *hēlios* sun + *tropos* turn; fr. its flowers' turning toward the sun] : any of a genus of herbs or shrubs related to the forget-me-nots that have small white or purple flowers

he·li·port \ˈhe-lə-ˌpȯrt\ *n* : a landing and takeoff place for a helicopter

he·li·um \ˈhē-lē-əm\ *n* [NL, fr. Gk *hēlios* sun] : a very light inert gaseous chemical element occurring in various natural gases

he·lix \ˈhē-liks\ *n, pl* **he·li·ces** \ˈhe-lə-ˌsēz, ˈhē-\ *also* **he·lix·es** \ˈhē-lik-səz\ : something spiral in form

hell \ˈhel\ *n* **1** : a nether world in which the dead continue to exist **2** : the realm of the devil in which the damned suffer everlasting punishment **3** : a place or state of torment or destruction — **hell·ish** *adj*

hel·la·cious \ˌhe-ˈlā-shəs\ *adj* **1** : exceptionally powerful or violent ⟨~ winds⟩ **2** : remarkably good **3** : extremely difficult ⟨a ~ schedule⟩ **4** : extraordinarily large

hell–bent \ˈhel-ˌbent\ *adj* : stubbornly determined ⟨~ on revenge⟩

hell·cat \-ˌkat\ *n* **1** : WITCH 2 **2** : a violently temperamental person; *esp* : an ill-tempered woman
hel·le·bore \ˈhe-lə-ˌbȯr\ *n* **1** : any of a genus of poisonous herbs related to the buttercups; *also* : the dried root of a hellebore **2** : a poisonous plant related to the lilies; *also* : its dried roots used in medicine and insecticides
Hel·lene \ˈhe-ˌlēn\ *n* : GREEK
Hel·le·nism \ˈhe-lə-ˌni-zəm\ *n* : a body of humanistic and classical ideals associated with ancient Greece — **Hel·len·ic** \he-ˈle-nik\ *adj* — **Hel·le·nist** \ˈhe-lə-nist\ *n*
Hel·le·nis·tic \ˌhe-lə-ˈnis-tik\ *adj* : of or relating to Greek history, culture, or art after Alexander the Great
hell–for–leather *adv* : at full speed
hell·gram·mite \ˈhel-grə-ˌmīt\ *n* : an aquatic insect larva that is used as bait in fishing
hell·hole \ˈhel-ˌhōl\ *n* : a place of extreme misery or squalor
hel·lion \ˈhel-yən\ *n* : a troublesome or mischievous person
hel·lo \hə-ˈlō, he-\ *n, pl* **hellos** : an expression of greeting — used interjectionally
helm \ˈhelm\ *n* **1** : a lever or wheel for steering a ship **2** : a position of control
hel·met \ˈhel-mət\ *n* : a protective covering for the head
helms·man \ˈhelmz-mən\ *n* : the person at the helm : STEERSMAN
helms·per·son \-ˌpər-sᵊn\ *n* : HELMSMAN
hel·ot \ˈhe-lət\ *n* : an enslaved person or serf
[1]**help** \ˈhelp\ *vb* **1** : AID, ASSIST **2** : IMPROVE, RELIEVE **3** : to be of use; *also* : PROMOTE **4** : to change for the better **5** : to refrain from; *also* : PREVENT **6** : to serve with food or drink ⟨~ yourself⟩ — **help·er** *n*
[2]**help** *n* **1** : AID, ASSISTANCE; *also* : a source of aid **2** : REMEDY, RELIEF **3** : one who assists another **4** : EMPLOYEE — **help·ful** \-fəl\ *adj* — **help·ful·ly** *adv* — **help·ful·ness** *n* — **help·less** *adj* — **help·less·ly** *adv* — **help·less·ness** *n*
helper T cell *n* : a T cell that participates in the immune response by recognizing foreign antigens and has a protein on its surface to which HIV attaches
help·ing *n* : a portion of food
help·mate \ˈhelp-ˌmāt\ *n* **1** : HELPER **2** : WIFE
help·meet \-ˌmēt\ *n* : HELPMATE
hel·ter–skel·ter \ˌhel-tər-ˈskel-tər\ *adv* **1** : in undue haste or disorder **2** : HAPHAZARDLY
helve \ˈhelv\ *n* : a handle of a tool or weapon
Hel·ve·tian \hel-ˈvē-shən\ *adj* : SWISS — **Helvetian** *n*
[1]**hem** \ˈhem\ *n* **1** : a border of an article (as of cloth) doubled back and stitched down **2** : RIM, MARGIN
[2]**hem** *vb* **hemmed; hem·ming** **1** : to make a hem in sewing; *also* : BORDER, EDGE **2** : to surround restrictively
he–man \ˈhē-ˌman\ *n* : a strong virile man
he·ma·tite \ˈhē-mə-ˌtīt\ *n* : a mineral that consists of an oxide of iron and that constitutes an important iron ore
he·ma·tol·o·gy \ˌhē-mə-ˈtä-lə-jē\ *n* : a branch of biology that deals with the blood and blood-forming organs — **he·ma·to·log·ic** \-tə-ˈlä-jik\ *also* **he·ma·to·log·i·cal** \-ji-kəl\ *adj* — **he·ma·tol·o·gist** \-ˈtä-lə-jist\ *n*
he·ma·to·ma \-ˈtō-mə\ *n, pl* **-mas** *also* **-ma·ta** \-mə-tə\ : a usu. clotted mass of blood forming as a result of a broken blood vessel
heme \ˈhēm\ *n* : the deep red iron-containing part of hemoglobin
hemi·sphere \ˈhe-mə-ˌsfir\ *n* **1** : one of the halves of the earth as divided by the equator into northern and southern parts or by a meridian into eastern and western parts **2** : either of two half spheres formed by a plane through the sphere's center — **hemi·spher·ic** \ˌhe-mə-ˈsfir-ik, -ˈsfer-\ *or* **hemi·spher·i·cal** \-ˈsfir-i-kəl, -ˈsfer-\ *adj*
hem·line \ˈhem-ˌlīn\ *n* : the line formed by the lower edge of a garment
hem·lock \ˈhem-ˌläk\ *n* **1** : any of several poisonous herbs related to the carrot **2** : an evergreen tree related to the pines; *also* : its soft light wood
he·mo·glo·bin \ˈhē-mə-ˌglō-bən\ *n* : an iron-containing compound found in red blood cells that carries oxygen from the lungs to the body tissues
he·mo·phil·ia \ˌhē-mə-ˈfi-lē-ə\ *n* : a hereditary blood defect usu. of males that slows blood clotting with resulting difficulty in stopping bleeding — **he·mo·phil·i·ac** \-lē-ˌak\ *adj or n*
hem·or·rhage \ˈhem-rij, ˈhe-mə-\ *n* : a large discharge of blood from the blood vessels — **hemorrhage** *vb* — **hem·or·rhag·ic** \ˌhe-mə-ˈra-jik\ *adj*
hemorrhagic fever *n* : any of a group of virus diseases characterized chiefly by sudden onset, fever, aching, and bleeding in the internal organs
hem·or·rhoid \ˈhem-ˌrȯid, ˈhe-mə-\ *n* : a swollen mass of dilated veins at or just within the anus — usu. used in pl.
hemp \ˈhemp\ *n* : a tall widely grown Asian herb that is the source of a tough fiber used in rope and of marijuana and hashish from its flowers and leaves; *also* : the fiber — **hemp·en** \ˈhem-pən\ *adj*
hem·stitch \ˈhem-ˌstich\ *vb* : to embroider (fabric) by drawing out parallel threads and stitching the exposed threads in groups to form designs
hen \ˈhen\ *n* : a female chicken esp. over a year old; *also* : a female bird
hence \ˈhens\ *adv* **1** : AWAY **2** : from this time ⟨four years ~⟩ **3** : CONSEQUENTLY **4** : from this source or origin
hence·forth \hens-ˌfȯrth\ *adv* : from this point on
hence·for·ward \-ˈfȯr-wərd\ *adv* : HENCEFORTH
hench·man \ˈhench-mən\ *n* [ME *hengestman* groom, fr. *hengest* stallion] : a trusted follower or supporter
hen·na \ˈhe-nə\ *n* **1** : an Old World tropi-

cal shrub with fragrant white flowers; *also* : a reddish brown dye obtained from its leaves and used esp. on hair **2** : the color of henna dye

hen•peck \ˈhen-ˌpek\ *vb* : to nag and boss one's husband

hep \ˈhep\ *adj* : HIP

hep•a•rin \ˈhe-pə-rən\ *n* : a compound found esp. in liver that slows the clotting of blood and is used medically

he•pat•ic \hi-ˈpa-tik\ *adj* : of, relating to, or associated with the liver

he•pat•i•ca \hi-ˈpa-ti-kə\ *n* : any of a genus of herbs related to the buttercups that have lobed leaves and delicate white, pink, or bluish flowers

hep•a•ti•tis \ˌhe-pə-ˈtī-təs\ *n, pl* **-tit•i•des** \-ˈti-tə-ˌdēz\ : inflammation of the liver; *also* : a virus disease of which this is a feature

hep•tam•e•ter \hep-ˈta-mə-tər\ *n* : a line of verse containing seven metrical feet

hep•tath•lon \hep-ˈtath-lən, -ˌlän\ *n* : a 7-event athletic contest for women

[1]**her** \ˈhər\ *adj* : of or relating to her or herself

[2]**her** *pron, objective case of* SHE

[1]**her•ald** \ˈher-əld\ *n* **1** : an official crier or messenger **2** : HARBINGER **3** : ANNOUNCER **4** : ADVOCATE

[2]**herald** *vb* **1** : to give notice of **2** : HAIL, GREET; *also* : PUBLICIZE

he•ral•dic \he-ˈral-dik, hə-\ *adj* : of or relating to heralds or heraldry

her•ald•ry \ˈher-əl-drē\ *n, pl* **-ries** **1** : the practice of devising and granting armorial insignia and of tracing genealogies **2** : INSIGNIA **3** : PAGEANTRY

herb \ˈərb, ˈhərb\ *n* **1** : a seed plant that lacks woody tissue and dies to the ground at the end of a growing season **2** : a plant or plant part valued for medicinal or savory qualities — **her•ba•ceous** \ˌər-ˈbā-shəs, ˌhər-\ *adj*

herb•age \ˈər-bij, ˈhər-\ *n* : green plants esp. when used or fit for grazing

her•bal \ˈər-bəl, ˈhər-\ *adj* : of, relating to, utilizing, or made of herbs

herb•al•ist \ˈər-bə-list, ˈhər-\ *n* **1** : a person who practices healing by the use of herbs **2** : a person who collects or grows herbs

her•bar•i•um \ˌər-ˈber-ē-əm, ˌhər-\ *n, pl* **-ia** \-ē-ə\ **1** : a collection of dried plant specimens **2** : a place that houses an herbarium

her•bi•cide \ˈər-bə-ˌsīd, ˈhər-\ *n* : an agent used to destroy or inhibit plant growth — **her•bi•cid•al** \ˌər-bə-ˈsī-dᵊl, ˌhər-\ *adj*

her•biv•o•rous \ˌər-ˈbi-və-rəs, ˌhər-\ *adj* : feeding on plants — **her•bi•vore** \ˈər-bə-ˌvȯr, ˈhər-\ *n*

her•cu•le•an \ˌhər-kyə-ˈlē-ən, ˌhər-ˈkyü-lē-\ *adj, often cap* [*Hercules,* hero of Greek myth renowned for his strength] : of extraordinary power, size, or difficulty ⟨a ~ task⟩

[1]**herd** \ˈhərd\ *n* **1** : a group of animals of one kind kept or living together **2** : a group of people with a common bond ⟨a ~ of tourists⟩ **3** : MOB

[2]**herd** *vb* : to assemble or move in a herd — **herd•er** *n*

herd immunity *n* : a reduction in the risk of infection with a specific communicable disease (such as influenza) that occurs when a significant proportion of the population has become immune to infection (as because of exposure or vaccination)

herds•man \ˈhərdz-mən\ *n* : one who manages, breeds, or tends livestock

[1]**here** \ˈhir\ *adv* **1** : in or at this place; *also* : NOW **2** : at or in this point, particular, or case **3** : in the present life or state **4** : to this place ⟨come ~⟩

[2]**here** *n* : this place ⟨get away from ~⟩

here•abouts \ˈhir-ə-ˌbau̇ts\ *or* **here•about** \-ˌbau̇t\ *adv* : in this vicinity

[1]**here•af•ter** \hir-ˈaf-tər\ *adv* **1** : after this in sequence or in time **2** : in some future time or state

[2]**hereafter** *n, often cap* **1** : FUTURE **2** : an existence beyond earthly life

here•by \hir-ˈbī\ *adv* : by means of this

he•red•i•tary \hə-ˈre-də-ˌter-ē\ *adj* **1** : genetically passed or passable from parent to offspring **2** : passing by inheritance; *also* : having title or possession through inheritance **3** : of a kind established by tradition

he•red•i•ty \-də-tē\ *n* : the characteristics and potentialities genetically derived from one's ancestors; *also* : the passing of these from ancestor to descendant

Her•e•ford \ˈhər-fərd\ *n* : any of a breed of red-coated beef cattle with white faces and markings

here•in \hir-ˈin\ *adv* : in this

here•of \-ˈəv, -ˈäv\ *adv* : of this

here•on \-ˈȯn, -ˈän\ *adv* : on this

her•e•sy \ˈher-ə-sē\ *n, pl* **-sies** [ME *heresie,* fr. AF, fr. LL *haeresis,* fr. LGk *hairesis,* fr. Gk, action of taking, choice, sect, fr. *hairein* to take] **1** : adherence to a religious opinion contrary to church dogma **2** : an opinion or doctrine contrary to church dogma **3** : dissent from a dominant theory, opinion, or practice — **her•e•tic** \-ˌtik\ *n* — **he•ret•i•cal** \hə-ˈre-ti-kəl\ *adj*

here•to \hir-ˈtü\ *adv* : to this document

here•to•fore \ˈhir-tə-ˌfȯr\ *adv* : up to this time

here•un•der \hir-ˈən-dər\ *adv* : under this or according to this writing

here•un•to \hir-ˈən-tü\ *adv* : to this

here•up•on \ˈhir-ə-ˌpȯn, -ˌpän\ *adv* : on this or immediately after this

here•with \ˈhir-ˈwith, -ˈwith\ *adv* **1** : with this **2** : HEREBY

her•i•ta•ble \ˈher-ə-tə-bəl\ *adj* : capable of being inherited

her•i•tage \ˈher-ə-tij\ *n* **1** : property that descends to an heir **2** : LEGACY **3** : BIRTHRIGHT

her•maph•ro•dite \(ˌ)hər-ˈma-frə-ˌdīt\ *n* : an animal or plant having both male and female reproductive organs — **hermaphrodite** *adj* — **her•maph•ro•dit•ic** \(ˌ)hər-ˌma-frə-ˈdi-tik\ *adj*

her•met•ic \hər-ˈme-tik\ *also* **her•met-**

i·cal \-ti-kəl\ *adj* : AIRTIGHT — **her·met·i·cal·ly** \-ti-k(ə-)lē\ *adv*
her·mit \ˈhər-mət\ *n* [ME *heremite, eremite,* fr. AF, fr. LL *eremita,* fr. LGk *erēmitēs,* fr. Gk, adj., living in the desert, fr. *erēmia* desert, fr. *erēmos* desolate] : one who lives in solitude esp. for religious reasons
her·mit·age \-mə-tij\ *n* **1** : the dwelling of a hermit **2** : a secluded dwelling
hermit crab *n* : any of numerous crabs that occupy empty mollusk shells
her·nia \ˈhər-nē-ə\ *n, pl* **-ni·as** *or* **-ni·ae** \-nē-ˌē, -nē-ˌī\ : a protrusion of a bodily part (as a loop of intestine) into a pouch of the weakened wall of a cavity in which it is normally enclosed — **her·ni·ate** \-nē-ˌāt\ *vb* — **her·ni·a·tion** \ˌhər-nē-ˈā-shən\ *n*
he·ro \ˈhē-rō\ *n, pl* **heroes** **1** : a mythological or legendary figure of great strength or ability **2** : a man admired for his achievements and qualities **3** : the chief male character in a literary or dramatic work **4** *pl usu* **heros** : SUBMARINE 2 — **he·ro·ic** \hi-ˈrō-ik\ *adj* — **he·ro·i·cal·ly** \-i-k(ə-)lē\ *adv*
heroic couplet *n* : a rhyming couplet in iambic pentameter
he·ro·ics \hi-ˈrō-iks\ *n pl* : heroic or showy behavior
her·o·in \ˈher-ə-wən\ *n* : an illicit addictive narcotic drug made from morphine
her·o·ine \ˈher-ə-wən\ *n* **1** : a woman admired for her achievements and qualities **2** : the chief female character in a literary or dramatic work
her·o·ism \ˈher-ə-ˌwi-zəm\ *n* **1** : heroic conduct **2** : the qualities of a hero ♦ ***Synonyms*** VALOR, PROWESS, GALLANTRY
her·on \ˈher-ən\ *n, pl* **herons** *also* **heron** : any of various long-legged long-billed wading birds with soft plumage
her·pes \ˈhər-pēz\ *n* : any of several virus diseases characterized by the formation of blisters on the skin or mucous membranes
herpes sim·plex \-ˈsim-ˌpleks\ *n* : either of two virus diseases marked in one by watery blisters above the waist (as on the mouth and lips) and in the other on the sex organs
herpes zos·ter \-ˈzäs-tər\ *n* : SHINGLES
her·pe·tol·o·gy \ˌhər-pə-ˈtä-lə-jē\ *n* : a branch of zoology dealing with reptiles and amphibians — **her·pe·tol·o·gist** \ˌhər-pə-ˈtä-lə-jist\ *n*
her·ring \ˈher-iŋ\ *n, pl* **herring** *or* **herrings** : a valuable narrow-bodied food fish of the No. Atlantic; *also* : a related fish of the No. Pacific harvested esp. for its roe
her·ring·bone \ˈher-iŋ-ˌbōn\ *n* : a pattern made up of rows of parallel lines with adjacent rows slanting in reverse directions; *also* : a twilled fabric with this pattern
hers \ˈhərz\ *pron* : one or the ones belonging to her
her·self \hər-ˈself\ *pron* : SHE, HER — used reflexively, for emphasis, or in absolute constructions
hertz \ˈhərts, ˈherts\ *n, pl* **hertz** : a unit of frequency equal to one cycle per second
hes·i·tant \ˈhe-zə-tənt\ *adj* : tending to hesitate — **hes·i·tance** \-təns\ *n* — **hes·i·tan·cy** \-tən-sē\ *n* — **hes·i·tant·ly** *adv*
hes·i·tate \ˈhe-zə-ˌtāt\ *vb* **-tat·ed; -tat·ing** **1** : to hold back (as in doubt) **2** : PAUSE ♦ ***Synonyms*** WAVER, VACILLATE, FALTER, SHILLY-SHALLY — **hes·i·ta·tion** \ˌhe-zə-ˈtā-shən\ *n*
het·ero·dox \ˈhe-tə-rə-ˌdäks\ *adj* **1** : differing from an acknowledged standard **2** : holding unorthodox opinions — **het·er·o·doxy** \-ˌdäk-sē\ *n*
het·er·o·ge·neous \ˌhe-tə-rə-ˈjē-nē-əs, -nyəs\ *adj* : consisting of dissimilar ingredients or constituents : MIXED — **het·er·o·ge·ne·ity** \-jə-ˈnē-ə-tē\ *n* — **het·er·o·ge·neous·ly** *adv*
het·ero·glos·sia \ˌhe-tə-rō-ˈglä-sē-ə, -ˈglȯ-\ *n* : a diversity of voices, styles of discourse, or points of view in a literary work
het·ero·sex·ism \ˌhe-tə-rō-ˈsek-si-zəm\ *n* : discrimination or prejudice against people who are not heterosexual
het·ero·sex·u·al \ˌhe-tə-rō-ˌsek-shə-wəl\ *adj* **1** : of, relating to, or characterized by sexual or romantic attraction to or between people of the opposite sex; *also* : of, relating to, or involving sexual activity between individuals of the opposite sex **2** : of or relating to different sexes — **heterosexual** *n* — **het·ero·sex·u·al·i·ty** \-ˌsek-shə-ˈwa-lə-tē\ *n*
hew \ˈhyü\ *vb* **hewed; hewed** *or* **hewn** \ˈhyün\; **hew·ing** **1** : to cut or fell with blows (as of an ax) **2** : to give shape to with or as if with an ax **3** : to conform strictly ⟨~*ed* to the rules⟩ — **hew·er** *n*
HEW *abbr* Department of Health, Education, and Welfare
¹hex \ˈheks\ *vb* **1** : to practice witchcraft **2** : JINX
²hex *n* : SPELL, JINX
³hex *adj* : HEXAGONAL
⁴hex *abbr* hexagon
hexa·gon \ˈhek-sə-ˌgän\ *n* [ultim. fr. Gk *hex* six + *gōnia* angle] : a polygon having six angles and six sides — **hex·ag·o·nal** \hek-ˈsa-gən-ᵊl\ *adj*
hex·am·e·ter \hek-ˈsa-mə-tər\ *n* : a line of verse containing six metrical feet
hey \ˈhā\ *interj* **1** — used esp. to call attention or to express doubt, surprise, or joy **2** — used as an informal greeting
hey·day \ˈhā-ˌdā\ *n* : a period of greatest strength, vigor, or prosperity
hf *abbr* half
Hf *symbol* hafnium
HF *abbr* high frequency
hg *abbr* hectogram
Hg *symbol* [NL *hydrargyrum,* lit., water silver] mercury
hgt *abbr* height
hgwy *abbr* highway
HH *abbr* **1** Her Highness **2** His Highness **3** His Holiness
HHS *abbr* Department of Health and Human Services

HI *abbr* **1** Hawaii **2** humidity index
hi·a·tus \hī-ˈā-təs\ *n* [L, fr. *hiare* to yawn] **1** : a break in an object : GAP **2** : a period when something is suspended or interrupted
hi·ba·chi \hi-ˈbä-chē\ *n* [Jp] : a charcoal brazier
hi·ber·nate \ˈhī-bər-ˌnāt\ *vb* **-nat·ed; -nat·ing** : to pass the winter in a torpid or resting state — **hi·ber·na·tion** \ˌhī-bər-ˈnā-shən\ *n* — **hi·ber·na·tor** \ˈhī-bər-ˌnā-tər\ *n*
hi·bis·cus \hī-ˈbis-kəs, hə-\ *n* : any of a genus of herbs, shrubs, and trees related to the mallows and noted for large showy flowers
hic·cup *also* **hic·cough** \ˈhi-(ˌ)kəp\ *n* **1** : a spasmodic breathing movement checked by sudden closing of the glottis accompanied by a peculiar sound; *also, pl* : an attack of hiccuping **2** : a slight irregularity, error, or malfunction **3** : a brief minor interruption or change — **hiccup** *vb*
hick \ˈhik\ *n* [*Hick,* nickname for *Richard*] : an unsophisticated provincial person — **hick** *adj*
hick·o·ry \ˈhi-kə-rē\ *n, pl* **-ries** : any of a genus of No. American hardwood trees related to the walnuts; *also* : the wood of a hickory — **hickory** *adj*
hi·dal·go \hi-ˈdal-gō\ *n, pl* **-gos** *often cap* [Sp, fr. earlier *fijo dalgo,* lit., son of something] : a member of the lower nobility of Spain
hidden tax *n* **1** : a tax ultimately paid by someone other than the person on whom it is formally levied **2** : an economic injustice that reduces one's income or buying power
[1]**hide** \ˈhīd\ *vb* **hid** \ˈhid\; **hid·den** \ˈhid-ᵊn\ *or* **hid; hid·ing** **1** : to put or remain out of sight **2** : to conceal for shelter or protection; *also* : to seek protection **3** : to keep secret **4** : to turn away in shame or anger — **hid·er** *n*
[2]**hide** *n* : the skin of an animal
hide–and–seek \ˌhīd-ᵊn-ˈsēk\ *n* : a children's game in which everyone hides from one player who tries to find them
hide·away \ˈhī-də-ˌwā\ *n* : HIDEOUT
hide·bound \ˈhīd-ˌbaund\ *adj* : being inflexible or conservative
hid·eous \ˈhi-dē-əs\ *adj* [ME *hidous,* fr. AF *hidus, hisdos,* fr. *hisde, hide* terror] **1** : offensive to one of the senses : UGLY **2** : morally offensive : SHOCKING ♦ ***Synonyms*** GHASTLY, GRISLY, GRUESOME, HORRIBLE, LURID, MACABRE — **hid·eous·ly** *adv* — **hid·eous·ness** *n*
hide·out \ˈhīd-ˌaut\ *n* : a place of refuge or concealment
hie \ˈhī\ *vb* **hied; hy·ing** *or* **hie·ing** : HASTEN
hi·er·ar·chy \ˈhī-ə-ˌrär-kē\ *n, pl* **-chies** **1** : a ruling body of clergy organized into ranks **2** : persons or things arranged in a graded series — **hi·er·ar·chi·cal** \ˌhī-ə-ˈrär-ki-kəl\ *adj* — **hi·er·ar·chi·cal·ly** \-k(ə-)lē\ *adv*
hi·er·o·glyph·ic \ˌhī-ə-rə-ˈgli-fik\ *n* [MF *hieroglyphique,* adj., ultim. fr. Gk *hieroglyphikos,* fr. *hieros* sacred + *glyphein* to carve] **1** : a character in a system of picture writing (as of the ancient Egyptians) **2** : a symbol or sign difficult to decipher
hi–fi \ˈhī-ˈfī\ *n* **1** : HIGH FIDELITY **2** : equipment for reproduction of sound with high fidelity
hig·gle·dy–pig·gle·dy \ˌhi-gəl-dē-ˈpi-gəl-dē\ *adv* : in confusion
[1]**high** \ˈhī\ *adj* **1** : ELEVATED; *also* : TALL **2** : advanced toward fullness or culmination; *also* : slightly tainted **3** : advanced esp. in complexity ⟨~*er* mathematics⟩ **4** : long past **5** : SHRILL, SHARP **6** : far from the equator ⟨~ latitudes⟩ **7** : exalted in character **8** : of greater degree, size, or amount than average ⟨~ in cholesterol⟩ **9** : of relatively great importance **10** : FORCIBLE, STRONG ⟨~ winds⟩ **11** : showing elation or excitement **12** : INTOXICATED; *also* : excited or stupefied by or as if by a drug — **high·ly** *adv*
[2]**high** *adv* **1** : at or to a high place or degree **2** : LUXURIOUSLY ⟨living ~⟩
[3]**high** *n* **1** : an elevated place **2** : a region of high barometric pressure **3** : a high point or level **4** : the gear of a vehicle giving the highest speed **5** : an excited or stupefied state produced by or as if by a drug
high·ball \ˈhī-ˌbȯl\ *n* : a usu. tall drink of liquor mixed with water or a carbonated beverage
high beam *n* : a vehicle headlight with a long-range focus
high·born \ˈhī-ˈbȯrn\ *adj* : of noble birth
high·boy \-ˌbȯi\ *n* : a high chest of drawers mounted on a base with legs
high·bred \-ˈbred\ *adj* : coming from superior stock
high·brow \-ˌbrau̇\ *n* : a person of superior learning or culture — **highbrow** *adj* — **high·brow·ism** \-ˌbrau̇-ˌi-zəm\ *n*
high–definition *adj* : being or relating to a television system with twice as many scan lines per frame as a conventional system — **high definition** *n*
high–density li·po·pro·tein \-ˌlī-pō-ˈprō-tēn, -ˌli-\ *n* : HDL
high·er–up \ˌhī-ər-ˈəp\ *n* : a superior officer or official
high·fa·lu·tin \ˌhī-fə-ˈlü-tᵊn\ *adj* : PRETENTIOUS, POMPOUS
high fashion *n* **1** : HIGH STYLE **2** : HAUTE COUTURE
high fidelity *n* : the reproduction of sound or image with a high degree of faithfulness to the original
high five *n* : a slapping of upraised right hands by two people (as in celebration) — **high–five** *vb*
high–flown \ˈhī-ˈflōn\ *adj* **1** : EXALTED **2** : BOMBASTIC
high frequency *n* : a radio frequency between 3 and 30 megahertz
high gear *n* **1** : HIGH 4 **2** : a state of intense or maximum activity
high–hand·ed \ˈhī-ˈhan-dəd\ *adj* : OVER-

BEARING — **high–hand·ed·ly** *adv* — **high–hand·ed·ness** *n*
high–hat \-'hat\ *adj* : SUPERCILIOUS, SNOBBISH — **high–hat** *vb*
high·land \'hī-lənd\ *n* : elevated or mountainous land
high·land·er \-lən-dər\ *n* **1** : an inhabitant of a highland **2** *cap* : an inhabitant of the Scottish Highlands
high–lev·el \'hī-'le-vəl\ *adj* **1** : being of high importance or rank **2** : being or relating to highly concentrated and environmentally hazardous nuclear waste
[1]**high·light** \-ˌlīt\ *n* : an event or detail of major importance
[2]**highlight** *vb* **1** : EMPHASIZE **2** : to constitute a highlight of **3** : to mark (text) with a highlighter **4** : to cause to be displayed in a way that stands out on a computer screen
high·light·er \-ˌlīt-ər\ *n* **1** : a pen with transparent ink used for marking text passages **2** : a cosmetic for making facial features (such as the cheekbones) appear lighter or brighter
high–mind·ed \-'mīn-dəd\ *adj* : marked by elevated principles and feelings — **high–mind·ed·ness** *n*
high·ness \'hī-nəs\ *n* **1** : the quality or state of being high **2** — used as a title (as for kings)
high–pres·sure \-'pre-shər\ *adj* : using or involving aggressive and insistent sales techniques
high–rise \-'rīz\ *adj* **1** : having several stories and being equipped with elevators ⟨~ apartments⟩ **2** : of or relating to high-rise buildings
high road *n* : HIGHWAY
high school *n* : a school usu. including grades 9 to 12 or 10 to 12
high sea *n* : the open sea outside territorial waters — usu. used in pl.
high–sound·ing \'hī-'saůn-diŋ\ *adj* : POMPOUS, IMPOSING ⟨~ rhetoric⟩
high–spir·it·ed \-'spir-ə-təd\ *adj* : characterized by a bold or energetic spirit
high–strung \-'strəŋ\ *adj* : having an extremely nervous or sensitive temperament
high style *n* : the newest in fashion or design
high·tail \'hī-ˌtāl\ *vb* : to retreat at full speed
high tech \-'tek\ *n* : HIGH TECHNOLOGY
high technology *n* : technology involving the use of advanced devices
high–ten·sion \'hī-'ten-chən\ *adj* : having or using a high voltage
high–test \-'test\ *adj* : having a high octane number
high–tick·et \-'ti-kət\ *adj* : EXPENSIVE
high–toned \-'tōnd\ *adj* **1** : high in social, moral, or intellectual quality **2** : PRETENTIOUS, POMPOUS
high·way \'hī-ˌwā\ *n* : a main direct road
high·way·man \'hī-ˌwā-mən\ *n* : a thief who robs travelers on a road
hi·jab \hē-'jäb, -'jab\ *n* [Ar *ḥijāb* cover, screen, veil] : the covering for the hair and neck that is worn by Muslim women
hi·jack *also* **high·jack** \'hī-ˌjak\ *vb* : to steal esp. by stopping a vehicle on the highway; *also* : to commandeer a flying airplane — **hijack** *n* — **hi·jack·er** *n*
[1]**hike** \'hīk\ *vb* **hiked; hik·ing** **1** : to move or raise with a sudden motion **2** : to take a long walk — **hik·er** *n*
[2]**hike** *n* **1** : a long walk **2** : RISE, INCREASE ⟨price ~⟩
hi·lar·i·ous \hi-'ler-ē-əs, hī-\ *adj* : marked by or providing boisterous merriment — **hi·lar·i·ous·ly** *adv* — **hi·lar·i·ty** \-ə-tē\ *n*
hill \'hil\ *n* **1** : a usu. rounded elevation of land **2** : a little heap or mound (as of earth) — **hilly** *adj*
hill·bil·ly \'hil-ˌbi-lē\ *n, pl* **-lies** *often offensive* : a person from a backwoods area
hill·ock \'hi-lək\ *n* : a small hill
hill·side \'hil-ˌsīd\ *n* : the part of a hill between the summit and the foot
hill·top \-ˌtäp\ *n* : the top of a hill
hilt \'hilt\ *n* : a handle esp. of a sword or dagger
him \'him\ *pron, objective case of* HE
him·self \him-'self\ *pron* : HE, HIM — used reflexively, for emphasis, or in absolute constructions
[1]**hind** \'hīnd\ *n, pl* **hinds** *also* **hind** : a female of a common Eurasian deer
[2]**hind** *adj* : REAR ⟨the dog's ~ legs⟩
[1]**hin·der** \'hin-dər\ *vb* **1** : to impede the progress of **2** : to hold back ♦ ***Synonyms*** OBSTRUCT, BLOCK, BAR, IMPEDE
[2]**hind·er** \'hīn-dər\ *adj* : HIND
Hin·di \'hin-dē\ *n* : a literary and official language of northern India
hind·most \'hīnd-ˌmōst\ *adj* : farthest to the rear
hind·quar·ter \-ˌkwȯr-tər\ *n* **1** : one side of the back half of the carcass of a quadruped **2** *pl* : the part of the body of a quadruped behind the junction of hind limbs and trunk
hin·drance \'hin-drəns\ *n* **1** : the state of being hindered **2** : IMPEDIMENT 1 **3** : the action of hindering
hind·sight \'hīnd-ˌsīt\ *n* : understanding of an event after it has happened
Hindu–Arabic *adj* : relating to, being, or composed of Arabic numerals
Hin·du·ism \'hin-dü-ˌi-zəm\ *n* : a body of religious beliefs and practices native to India — **Hin·du** *n or adj*
hind wing *n* : either of the posterior wings of a 4-winged insect
[1]**hinge** \'hinj\ *n* : a jointed device on which a swinging part (as a door or lid) turns
[2]**hinge** *vb* **hinged; hing·ing** **1** : to attach by or furnish with hinges **2** : to be contingent on a single consideration
hint \'hint\ *n* **1** : an indirect or summary suggestion **2** : CLUE **3** : a very small amount ♦ ***Synonyms*** DASH, SOUPÇON, SUSPICION, TINCTURE, TOUCH — **hint** *vb*
hin·ter·land \'hin-tər-ˌland\ *n* **1** : a region behind a coast **2** : a region remote from cities
[1]**hip** \'hip\ *n* : the fruit of a rose
[2]**hip** *n* **1** : the part of the body on either side below the waist consisting of the side of the pelvis and the upper thigh **2** : HIP JOINT

³hip *adj* **hip·per; hip·pest** : keenly aware of or interested in the newest developments or styles — **hip·ness** *n*

⁴hip *vb* **hipped; hip·ping** : TELL, INFORM

hip·bone \ˈhip-ˈbōn, -ˌbōn\ *n* : the large flaring bone that makes a lateral half of the pelvis in mammals

hip–hop \ˈhip-ˌhäp\ *n* **1** : a subculture esp. of inner-city youths who are devotees of rap music **2** : the stylized rhythmic music that accompanies rap — **hip–hop** *adj*

hip–hug·gers \ˈhip-ˌhə-gərz\ *n pl* : low-slung close-fitting pants that rest on the hips

hip joint *n* : the articulation between the femur and the hipbone

hipped \ˈhipt\ *adj* : having hips esp. of a specified kind ⟨broad-*hipped*⟩

hip·pie *or* **hip·py** \ˈhi-pē\ *n, pl* **hippies** : a usu. young person who rejects established mores and advocates nonviolence; *also* : a long-haired unconventionally dressed young person

hip·po \ˈhi-pō\ *n, pl* **hippos** : HIPPOPOTAMUS

hip·po·drome \ˈhi-pə-ˌdrōm\ *n* : an arena for equestrian performances

hip·po·pot·a·mus \ˌhi-pə-ˈpä-tə-məs\ *n, pl* **-mus·es** *or* **-mi** \-ˌmī\ [L, fr. Gk *hippopotamos,* alter. of *hippos potamios,* lit., river horse] : a large thick-skinned aquatic mammal of sub-Saharan Africa that is related to the swine

¹hire \ˈhī(-ə)r\ *n* **1** : payment for labor or personal services : WAGES **2** : EMPLOYMENT **3** : one who is hired

²hire *vb* **hired; hir·ing** **1** : to employ for pay **2** : to engage the temporary use of for pay **3** : to take employment

hire·ling \ˈhī(-ə)r-liŋ\ *n* : a hired person; *esp* : one with mercenary motives

hir·sute \ˈhər-ˌsüt, ˈhir-\ *adj* : HAIRY

¹his \ˈhiz\ *adj* : of or relating to him or himself

²his *pron* : one or the ones belonging to him

His·pan·ic \hi-ˈspa-nik\ *adj* : of, relating to, or being a person of Latin-American descent living in the U.S. — **Hispanic** *n*

hiss \ˈhis\ *vb* : to make a sharp sibilant sound; *also* : to express disapproval of by hissing — **hiss** *n*

hissy fit \ˈhi-sē-\ *n* : TANTRUM

hist *abbr* historian; historical; history

his·ta·mine \ˈhis-tə-ˌmēn, -mən\ *n* : a compound widespread in animal tissues that plays a major role in allergic reactions (as hay fever)

his·to·gram \ˈhis-tə-ˌgram\ *n* : a representation of statistical data by rectangles whose widths represent class intervals and whose heights usu. represent corresponding frequencies

his·tol·og·y \his-ˈtä-lə-jē\ *n, pl* **-gies** **1** : a branch of anatomy dealing with tissue structure **2** : tissue structure or organization — **his·to·log·i·cal** \ˌhis-tə-ˈlä-ji-kəl\ *or* **his·to·log·ic** \-ˈlä-jik\ *adj* — **his·tol·o·gist** \-ˈtä-lə-jist\ *n*

his·to·ri·an \hi-ˈstȯr-ē-ən\ *n* : a student or writer of history

his·to·ric·i·ty \ˌhis-tə-ˈri-sə-tē\ *n* : historical actuality

his·to·ri·og·ra·pher \hi-ˌstȯr-ē-ˈä-grə-fər\ *n* : HISTORIAN

his·to·ry \ˈhis-tə-rē\ *n, pl* **-ries** [ultim. fr. L *historia,* fr. Gk, inquiry, history, fr. *histōr, istōr* knowing, learned] **1** : a chronological record of significant events often with an explanation of their causes **2** : a branch of knowledge that records and explains past events **3** : events that form the subject matter of history **4** : an established record ⟨a convict's ~ of violence⟩ — **his·tor·ic** \hi-ˈstȯr-ik\ *adj* — **his·tor·i·cal** \-i-kəl\ *adj* — **his·tor·i·cal·ly** \-k(ə-)lē\ *adv*

his·tri·on·ic \ˌhis-trē-ˈä-nik\ *adj* [LL *histrionicus,* fr. L *histrio* actor] **1** : deliberately affected **2** : of or relating to actors, acting, or the theater — **his·tri·on·i·cal·ly** \-ni-k(ə-)lē\ *adv*

his·tri·on·ics \-niks\ *n pl* **1** : theatrical performances **2** : deliberate display of emotion for effect

¹hit \ˈhit\ *vb* **hit; hit·ting** **1** : to reach with a blow : STRIKE; *also* : to arrive with a force like a blow ⟨the storm ~⟩ **2** : to make or bring into contact : COLLIDE **3** : to affect detrimentally ⟨was ~ by the flu⟩ **4** : to make a request of **5** : to come upon **6** : to accord with : SUIT **7** : REACH, ATTAIN **8** : to indulge in often to excess — **hit·ter** *n*

²hit *n* **1** : an act or instance of hitting or being hit **2** : a great success **3** : BASE HIT **4** : a dose of a drug **5** : a murder committed by a gangster **6** : an instance of connecting to a particular website **7** : a successful match in a search (as of the Internet)

¹hitch \ˈhich\ *vb* **1** : to move by jerks **2** : to catch or fasten esp. by a hook or knot **3** : HITCHHIKE

²hitch *n* **1** : JERK, PULL **2** : a sudden halt **3** : a connection between something towed and its mover **4** : KNOT

hitch·hike \ˈhich-ˌhīk\ *vb* : to travel by securing free rides from passing vehicles — **hitch·hik·er** *n*

¹hith·er \ˈhi-t͟hər\ *adv* : to this place

²hither *adj* : being on the near or adjacent side

hith·er·to \-ˌtü\ *adv* : up to this time

HIV \ˌāch-(ˌ)ī-ˈvē\ *n* [*h*uman *i*mmunodeficiency *v*irus] : any of several retroviruses that infect and destroy helper T cells causing the great reduction in their numbers that is diagnostic of AIDS

hive \ˈhīv\ *n* **1** : a container for housing honeybees **2** : a colony of bees **3** : a place swarming with busy occupants — **hive** *vb*

hives \ˈhīvz\ *n sing or pl* : an allergic disorder marked by raised itching patches on the skin or mucous membranes

hl *abbr* hectoliter

HL *abbr* House of Lords

hm *abbr* hectometer

HM *abbr* **1** Her Majesty; Her Majesty's **2** His Majesty; His Majesty's

HMO \ˌāch-(ˌ)em-ˈō\ *n* [*h*ealth *m*aintenance organization] : a comprehensive health-care organization financed by periodic fixed payments by voluntarily enrolled individuals and families

HMS *abbr* **1** Her Majesty's ship **2** His Majesty's ship

Ho *symbol* holmium

hoa·gie *also* **hoa·gy** \ˈhō-gē\ *n, pl* **hoagies** : SUBMARINE 2

hoard \ˈhȯrd\ *n* : a hidden accumulation — **hoard** *vb* — **hoard·er** *n*

hoar·frost \ˈhȯr-ˌfrȯst\ *n* : FROST 2

hoarse \ˈhȯrs\ *adj* **hoars·er; hoars·est** **1** : rough and harsh in sound **2** : having a grating voice — **hoarse·ly** *adv* — **hoarse·ness** *n*

hoary \ˈhȯr-ē\ *adj* **hoar·i·er; -est** **1** : gray or white with or as if with age **2** : ANCIENT — **hoar·i·ness** \ˈhōr-ē-nəs\ *n*

hoax \ˈhōks\ *n* : an act intended to trick or dupe; *also* : something accepted or established by fraud — **hoax** *vb* — **hoax·er** *n*

hob \ˈhäb\ *n* : MISCHIEF, TROUBLE ⟨raising ~⟩

[1]**hob·ble** \ˈhä-bəl\ *vb* **hob·bled, hob·bling** **1** : to limp along; *also* : to make lame **2** : FETTER

[2]**hobble** *n* **1** : a hobbling movement **2** : something used to hobble an animal

hob·by \ˈhä-bē\ *n, pl* **hobbies** : a pursuit or interest engaged in for relaxation — **hob·by·ist** \-ist\ *n*

hob·by·horse \ˈhä-bē-ˌhȯrs\ *n* **1** : a stick with a horse's head on which children pretend to ride **2** : a toy horse mounted on rockers **3** : a topic to which one constantly reverts

hob·gob·lin \ˈhäb-ˌgäb-lən\ *n* **1** : a mischievous goblin **2** : BOGEY 1

hob·nail \-ˌnāl\ *n* : a short large-headed nail for studding shoe soles — **hob·nailed** \-ˌnāld\ *adj*

hob·nob \-ˌnäb\ *vb* **hob·nobbed; hob·nob·bing** : to associate familiarly

ho·bo \ˈhō-bō\ *n, pl* **hoboes** *also* **hobos** : TRAMP 2

[1]**hock** \ˈhäk\ *n* : a joint or region in the hind limb of a quadruped just above the foot and corresponding to the human ankle

[2]**hock** *n* [D *hok* pen, prison] : [2]PAWN 2 ⟨got his watch out of ~⟩; *also* : DEBT 3 ⟨trying to get out of ~⟩ — **hock** *vb*

hock·ey \ˈhä-kē\ *n* **1** : FIELD HOCKEY **2** : ICE HOCKEY

ho·cus–po·cus \ˌhō-kəs-ˈpō-kəs\ *n* **1** : SLEIGHT OF HAND **2** : nonsense or sham used to conceal deception

hod \ˈhäd\ *n* : a long-handled carrier for mortar or bricks

hodge·podge \ˈhäj-ˌpäj\ *n* : a heterogeneous mixture : JUMBLE

Hodgkin's disease \ˈhäj-kinz-\ *n* : a neoplastic disease of lymphoid tissue characterized esp. by enlargement of lymph nodes, spleen, and liver

hoe \ˈhō\ *n* : a long-handled implement with a thin flat blade used esp. for cultivating, weeding, or loosening the earth around plants — **hoe** *vb*

hoe·cake \ˈhō-ˌkāk\ *n* : a small cornmeal cake

hoe·down \-ˌdau̇n\ *n* **1** : SQUARE DANCE **2** : a gathering featuring hoedowns

[1]**hog** \ˈhȯg, ˈhäg\ *n, pl* **hogs** *also* **hog** **1** : a domestic swine esp. when grown **2** : a selfish, gluttonous, or filthy person — **hog·gish** *adj*

[2]**hog** *vb* **hogged; hog·ging** : to take or hold selfishly ⟨*hogged* the limelight⟩

ho·gan \ˈhō-ˌgän\ *n* : a Navajo Indian dwelling usu. made of logs and mud

hog·back \ˈhȯg-ˌbak, ˈhäg-\ *n* : a ridge with a sharp summit and steep sides

hog·nose snake \ˈhȯg-ˌnōz-, ˈhäg-\ *or* **hog·nosed snake** \-ˌnōzd-\ *n* : any of a genus of rather small harmless stout-bodied No. American snakes that seldom bite but hiss wildly and often play dead when disturbed

hogs·head \ˈhȯgz-ˌhed, ˈhägz-\ *n* **1** : a large cask or barrel **2** : a liquid measure equal to 63 U.S. gallons

hog–tie \ˈhȯg-ˌtī, ˈhäg-\ *vb* **1** : to tie together the feet of ⟨~ a calf⟩ **2** : to make helpless

hog·wash \-ˌwȯsh, -ˌwäsh\ *n* **1** : SWILL, SLOP **2** : NONSENSE, BALONEY

hog wild *adj* : lacking in restraint

hoi pol·loi \ˌhȯi-pə-ˈlȯi\ *n pl* [Gk, the many] : the general populace

hoi·sin sauce \ˈhȯi-ˌsin-\ *n* : a thick reddish sauce of soybeans, spices, and garlic used in Asian cookery

[1]**hoist** \ˈhȯist\ *vb* : RAISE, LIFT

[2]**hoist** *n* **1** : LIFT **2** : an apparatus for hoisting

hoke \ˈhōk\ *vb* **hoked; hok·ing** : FAKE — usu. used with *up*

hok·ey \ˈhō-kē\ *adj* **hok·i·er; -est** **1** : CORNY ⟨~ songs⟩ **2** : PHONY ⟨a ~ excuse⟩

ho·kum \ˈhō-kəm\ *n* : NONSENSE

[1]**hold** \ˈhōld\ *vb* **held** \ˈheld\; **hold·ing** **1** : POSSESS; *also* : KEEP **2** : RESTRAIN **3** : to have a grasp on **4** : to support, remain, or keep in a particular situation or position **5** : SUSTAIN; *also* : RESERVE **6** : BEAR, COMPORT **7** : to maintain in being or action : PERSIST **8** : CONTAIN, ACCOMMODATE **9** : HARBOR, ENTERTAIN; *also* : CONSIDER, REGARD **10** : to carry on by concerted action; *also* : CONVOKE **11** : to occupy esp. by appointment or election **12** : to be valid **13** : HALT, PAUSE — **hold·er** *n* — **hold forth** : to speak at length — **hold to** : to adhere to : MAINTAIN — **hold with** : to agree with or approve of

[2]**hold** *n* **1** : STRONGHOLD **2** : CONFINEMENT; *also* : PRISON **3** : the act or manner of holding : GRIP **4** : a restraining, dominating, or controlling influence **5** : something that may be grasped as a support **6** : an order or indication that something is to be reserved or delayed — **on hold** : in a temporary state of waiting (as during a phone call); *also* : in a state of postponement ⟨plans *on hold*⟩

[3]**hold** *n* **1** : the interior of a ship below

decks; *esp* : a ship's cargo deck **2** : an airplane's cargo compartment

hold·ing *n* **1** : land or other property owned **2** : a ruling of a court esp. on an issue of law

holding pattern *n* : a course flown by an aircraft waiting to land

hold out *vb* **1** : to continue to fight or work **2** : to refuse to come to an agreement — **hold·out** \ˈhōl-ˌdau̇t\ *n*

hold·over \ˈhōl-ˌdō-vər\ *n* : one that is held over

hold·up \ˈhōl-ˌdəp\ *n* **1** : DELAY **2** : robbery at the point of a gun

hole \ˈhōl\ *n* **1** : an opening into or through something **2** : a hollow place (as a pit or cave) **3** : DEN, BURROW **4** : a wretched or dingy place **5** : a unit of play from tee to cup in golf **6** : an awkward position — **hole** *vb*

hol·i·day \ˈhä-lə-ˌdā\ *n* [ME, fr. OE *hālig-dæg,* fr. *hālig* holy + *dæg* day] **1** : a day set aside for special religious observance **2** : a day of freedom from work; *esp* : one in commemoration of an event **3** : VACATION — **holiday** *vb*

ho·li·ness \ˈhō-lē-nəs\ *n* : the quality or state of being holy — used as a title for various high religious officials

ho·lis·tic \hō-ˈlis-tik\ *adj* : relating to or concerned with integrated wholes or complete systems rather than with the analysis or treatment of separate parts ⟨~ medicine⟩ ⟨~ ecology⟩

hol·lan·daise \ˌhä-lən-ˈdāz\ *n* : a rich sauce made basically of butter, egg yolks, and lemon juice or vinegar

hol·ler \ˈhä-lər\ *vb* : to cry out : SHOUT — **holler** *n*

¹**hol·low** \ˈhä-lō\ *n* **1** : CAVITY, HOLE **2** : a surface depression

²**hollow** *adj* **hol·low·er** \ˈhä-lə-wər\; **hol·low·est** \-lə-wəst\ **1** : CONCAVE, SUNKEN **2** : having a cavity within **3** : lacking in real value, sincerity, or substance; *also* : FALSE **4** : MUFFLED ⟨a ~ sound⟩ — **hol·low·ness** *n*

³**hollow** *vb* : to make or become hollow

hol·low·ware *or* **hol·lo·ware** \ˈhä-lə-ˌwar\ *n* : vessels (as bowls or cups) with a significant depth and volume

hol·ly \ˈhä-lē\ *n, pl* **hollies** : either of two trees or shrubs with branches of usu. evergreen glossy spiny-margined leaves and red berries

hol·ly·hock \ˈhä-lē-ˌhäk, -ˌhȯk\ *n* [ME *holihoc,* fr. *holi* holy + *hoc* mallow] : a biennial or perennial herb related to the mallows that is widely grown for its tall stalks of showy flowers

hol·mi·um \ˈhōl-mē-əm\ *n* : a metallic chemical element

ho·lo·caust \ˈhä-lə-ˌkȯst, ˈhō-\ *n* **1** : a thorough destruction esp. by fire **2** *often cap* : the killing of European Jews by the Nazis during World War II; *also* : GENOCIDE

Ho·lo·cene \ˈhō-lə-ˌsēn\ *adj* : of, relating to, or being the present geologic epoch — **Holocene** *n*

ho·lo·gram \ˈhō-lə-ˌgram, ˈhä-\ *n* : a three-dimensional image produced by an interference pattern of light (as laser light)

ho·lo·graph \ˈhō-lə-ˌgraf, ˈhä-\ *n* : a document wholly in the handwriting of its author

ho·log·ra·phy \hō-ˈlä-grə-fē\ *n* : the process of making a hologram — **ho·lo·graph·ic** \ˌhō-lə-ˈgra-fik, ˌhä-\ *adj*

Hol·stein \ˈhōl-ˌstēn, -ˌstīn\ *n* : any of a breed of large black-and-white dairy cattle that produce large quantities of comparatively low-fat milk

Hol·stein–Frie·sian \-ˈfrē-zhən\ *n* : HOLSTEIN

hol·ster \ˈhōl-stər\ *n* [D] : a usu. leather case for a firearm

ho·ly \ˈhō-lē\ *adj* **ho·li·er; -est** **1** : worthy of absolute devotion **2** : SACRED **3** : having a divine quality ♦ ***Synonyms*** HALLOWED, BLESSED, SANCTIFIED, CONSECRATED — **ho·li·ly** \-lə-lē\ *adv*

Holy Spirit *n* : the third person of the Christian Trinity

ho·ly·stone \ˈhō-lē-ˌstōn\ *n* : a soft sandstone used to scrub a ship's wooden decks — **holystone** *vb*

hom·age \ˈä-mij, ˈhä-\ *n* [ME, fr. AF *homage, omage,* fr. *home* man, vassal, fr. L *homo* human being] : expression of high regard; *also* : TRIBUTE 3

hom·bre \ˈäm-ˈbrā, ˈəm-, -brē\ *n* : GUY, FELLOW

hom·burg \ˈhäm-ˌbərg\ *n* [*Homburg,* Germany] : a man's felt hat with a stiff curled brim and a high crown creased lengthwise

¹**home** \ˈhōm\ *n* **1** : one's residence; *also* : HOUSE **2** : the social unit formed by a family living together **3** : a congenial environment; *also* : HABITAT **4** : a place of origin **5** : the objective in various games

²**home** *vb* **homed; hom·ing** **1** : to go or return home **2** : to proceed to or toward a source of radiated energy used as a guide

home·body \ˈhōm-ˌbä-dē\ *n* : one whose life centers on home

home·boy \-ˌbȯi\ *n* **1** : a boy or man from one's neighborhood, hometown, or region **2** : a fellow member of a youth gang **3** : an inner-city youth

home·bred \-ˈbred\ *adj* : produced at home : INDIGENOUS

home·com·ing \-ˌkə-miŋ\ *n* **1** : a return home **2** : an annual celebration for alumni at a college or university

home computer *n* : a small inexpensive microcomputer

home economics *n* : a class that teaches skills which are useful in the home

home·girl \ˈhōm-gərl\ *n* **1** : a girl or woman from one's neighborhood, hometown, or region **2** : a girl or woman who is a member of one's peer group **3** : an inner-city girl or woman

home·grown \ˈhōm-ˈgrōn\ *adj* **1** : grown domestically ⟨~ peaches⟩ **2** : LOCAL, INDIGENOUS ⟨a ~ artist⟩

home·land \-ˌland\ *n* **1** : native land **2** : an area set aside to be a state for a people of a particular national, cultural, or racial origin

home·less \-ləs\ *adj* : having no home or permanent residence — **home·less·ness** *n*

home·ly \ˈhōm-lē\ *adj* **home·li·er; -est 1** : FAMILIAR **2** : unaffectedly natural **3** : lacking beauty or proportion — **home·li·ness** \-lē-nəs\ *n*

home·made \ˈhōm-ˌmād\ *adj* : made in the home, on the premises, or by one's own efforts

home·mak·er \-ˌmā-kər\ *n* : one who manages a household esp. as a wife and mother — **home·mak·ing** \-kiŋ\ *n*

ho·me·op·a·thy \ˌhō-mē-ˈä-pə-thē\ *n* : a system of medical practice that treats disease esp. with minute doses of a remedy that would in larger amounts produce symptoms in healthy persons similar to those of the disease — **ho·meo·path** \ˈhō-mē-ə-ˌpath\ *n* — **ho·meo·path·ic** \ˌhō-mē-ə-ˈpa-thik\ *adj*

ho·meo·sta·sis \ˌhō-mē-ō-ˈstā-səs\ *n* : the maintenance of a relatively stable state of equilibrium between interrelated physiological, psychological, or social factors characteristic of an individual or group — **ho·meo·stat·ic** \-ˈsta-tik\ *adj*

home page *n* : the page usu. encountered first at a website that usu. contains hyperlinks to the other pages of the site

home plate *n* : a slab at the apex of a baseball diamond that a base runner must touch in order to score

hom·er \ˈhō-mər\ *n* : HOME RUN — **homer** *vb*

home·room \ˈhōm-ˌrüm, -ˌru̇m\ *n* : a classroom where pupils report at the beginning of each school day

home run *n* : a hit in baseball that enables the batter to go around all the bases and score a run

home·school \ˈhōm-ˌskül\ *vb* : to teach school subjects to one's children at home — **home·school·er** \-ˌskü-lər\ *n*

home·sick \ˈhōm-ˌsik\ *adj* : longing for home and family while absent from them — **home·sick·ness** *n*

home·spun \-ˌspən\ *adj* **1** : spun or made at home; *also* : made of a loosely woven usu. woolen or linen fabric **2** : SIMPLE, HOMELY

[1]**home·stead** \-ˌsted\ *n* : the home and land occupied by a family

[2]**homestead** *vb* : to acquire or settle on public land — **home·stead·er** *n*

home·stretch \-ˈstrech\ *n* **1** : the part of a racecourse between the last curve and the winning post **2** : a final stage (as of a project)

home theater *n* : an entertainment system (as a television with surround sound and a DVD player) for the home

home video *n* : prerecorded videocassettes or videodiscs for home viewing

[1]**home·ward** \-wərd\ *or* **home·wards** \-wərdz\ *adv* : toward home

[2]**homeward** *adj* : being or going toward home

home·work \-ˌwərk\ *n* **1** : an assignment given a student to be completed outside the classroom **2** : preparatory reading or research

[1]**hom·ey** \ˈhō-mē\ *adj* **hom·i·er; -est** : characteristic of home

[2]**homey** *or* **hom·ie** \ˈhō-mē\ *n, pl* **homeys** *or* **homies** : HOMEBOY

ho·mi·cide \ˈhä-mə-ˌsīd, ˈhō-\ *n* [L *homicida* murderer & *homicidium* manslaughter; both fr. *homo* human being + *caedere* to cut, kill] **1** : a person who kills another **2** : a killing of one human being by another — **hom·i·cid·al** \ˌhä-mə-ˈsī-dᵊl\ *adj*

hom·i·ly \ˈhä-mə-lē\ *n, pl* **-lies** : SERMON — **hom·i·let·ic** \ˌhä-mə-ˈle-tik\ *adj*

homing pigeon *n* : a racing pigeon trained to return home

hom·i·nid \ˈhä-mə-nəd, -ˌnid\ *n* : any of a family of primate mammals that comprise all living humans and extinct ancestral and related forms — **hominid** *adj*

hom·i·ny \ˈhä-mə-nē\ *n* : hulled corn with the germ removed

ho·mo·cys·te·ine \ˌhō-mō-ˈsis-tə-ˌēn\ *n* : an amino acid associated with an increased risk of heart disease when occurring at high levels in the blood

ho·mo·erot·ic \ˌhō-mō-i-ˈrä-tik\ *adj* : marked by or portraying sexual desire between people of the same sex — **ho·mo·erot·i·cism** \-ˈrä-tə-ˌsi-zəm\ *n*

ho·mo·ge·neous \ˌhō-mə-ˈjē-nē-əs, -nyəs\ *adj* : of the same or a similar kind; *also* : of uniform structure — **ho·mo·ge·ne·i·ty** \-jə-ˈnē-ə-tē\ *n* — **ho·mo·ge·neous·ly** *adv*

ho·mog·e·ni·sa·tion, ho·mog·e·nise *Brit var of* HOMOGENIZATION, HOMOGENIZE

ho·mog·e·nize \hō-ˈmä-jə-ˌnīz, hə-\ *vb* **-nized; -niz·ing 1** : to make homogeneous **2** : to reduce the particles in (as milk) to uniform size and distribute them evenly throughout the liquid — **ho·mog·e·ni·za·tion** \-ˌmä-jə-nə-ˈzā-shən\ *n* — **ho·mog·e·niz·er** *n*

ho·mo·graph \ˈhä-mə-ˌgraf, ˈhō-\ *n* : one of two or more words spelled alike but different in origin, meaning, or pronunciation (as the *bow* of a ship, a *bow* and arrow)

ho·mol·o·gy \hō-ˈmä-lə-jē, hə-\ *n, pl* **-gies 1** : structural likeness between corresponding parts of different plants or animals due to evolution from a common ancestor **2** : structural likeness between different parts of the same individual — **ho·mol·o·gous** \-ˈmä-lə-gəs\ *adj*

hom·onym \ˈhä-mə-ˌnim, ˈhō-\ *n* **1** : HOMOPHONE, HOMOGRAPH **2** : one of two or more words spelled and pronounced alike but different in meaning (as *pool* of water and *pool* the game)

ho·mo·pho·bia \ˈhō-mə-ˈfō-bē-ə\ *n* : irrational fear of, aversion to, or discrimination against homosexuality or gay people — **ho·mo·phobe** \ˈhō-mə-ˌfōb\ *n* — **ho·mo·pho·bic** \-ˈfō-bik\ *adj*

ho·mo·phone \ˈhä-mə-ˌfōn, ˈhō-\ *n* : one of two or more words (as *to, too, two*) pronounced alike but different in meaning or derivation or spelling

Ho•mo sa•pi•ens \ˌhō-mō-ˈsā-pē-ənz, -ˈsa-\ *n* : HUMANKIND

ho•mo•sex•u•al \ˌhō-mō-ˈsek-shə-wəl\ *adj, now sometimes disparaging and offensive* : of, relating to, or characterized by sexual or romantic attraction to people of one's same sex : GAY; *also* : of, relating to, or involving sexual activity between people of the same sex — **homosexual** *n* — **ho•mo•sex•u•al•i•ty** \-ˌsek-shə-ˈwa-lə-tē\ *n*

hon *abbr* honor; honorable; honorary

hone \ˈhōn\ *n* : WHETSTONE — **hone** *vb* — **hon•er** *n*

hone in *vb* : to move toward or direct attention to an objective

[1]**hon•est** \ˈä-nəst\ *adj* [ME, fr. AF, fr. L *honestus* honorable, fr. *honos, honor* honor] **1** : free from deception : TRUTHFUL; *also* : GENUINE, REAL **2** : REPUTABLE **3** : CREDITABLE ⟨an ~ day's work⟩ **4** : marked by integrity **5** : FRANK ♦ ***Synonyms*** UPRIGHT, JUST, CONSCIENTIOUS, HONORABLE — **hon•est•ly** *adv* — **hon•es•ty** \-nə-stē\ *n*

[2]**honest** *adv* : HONESTLY; *also* : with all sincerity ⟨I didn't do it, ~⟩

hon•ey \ˈhə-nē\ *n, pl* **honeys** : a sweet sticky substance made by honeybees from the nectar of flowers — **hon•eyed** \-nēd\ *adj*

hon•ey•bee \ˈhə-nē-ˌbē\ *n* : a honey-producing bee often kept in hives

[1]**hon•ey•comb** \-ˌkōm\ *n* : a mass of 6-sided wax cells built by honeybees; *also* : something of similar structure or appearance

[2]**honeycomb** *vb* : to make or become full of cavities like a honeycomb

hon•ey•dew \-ˌdü, -ˌdyü\ *n* : a sweetish deposit secreted on plants by aphids, scale insects, or fungi

honeydew melon *n* : a smooth-skinned muskmelon with sweet green flesh

honey locust *n* : a tall usu. spiny No. American leguminous tree with hard durable wood and long twisted pods

hon•ey•moon \ˈhə-nē-ˌmün\ *n* **1** : a period of harmony esp. just after marriage **2** : a holiday taken by a newly married couple — **honeymoon** *vb* — **hon•ey•moon•er** *n*

hon•ey•suck•le \ˈhə-nē-ˌsə-kəl\ *n* : any of a genus of shrubs with fragrant tube-shaped flowers rich in nectar

honk \ˈhäŋk, ˈhȯŋk\ *n* : the cry of a goose; *also* : a similar sound (as of a horn) — **honk** *vb* — **honk•er** *n*

hon•ky–tonk \ˈhäŋ-kē-ˌtäŋk, ˈhȯŋ-kē-ˌtȯŋk\ *n* : a tawdry nightclub or dance hall — **honky–tonk** *adj*

[1]**hon•or** \ˈä-nər\ *n* **1** : good name : REPUTATION; *also* : outward respect **2** : PRIVILEGE **3** : a person of superior standing — used esp. as a title **4** : one who brings respect or fame ⟨an ~ to the class⟩ **5** : an evidence or symbol of distinction **6** : CHASTITY, PURITY **7** : INTEGRITY ♦ ***Synonyms*** HOMAGE, REVERENCE, DEFERENCE, OBEISANCE

[2]**honor** *vb* **1** : to regard or treat with honor **2** : to confer honor on **3** : to fulfill the terms of; *also* : to accept as payment — **hon•or•ee** \ˌä-nə-ˈrē\ *n* — **hon•or•er** *n*

hon•or•able \ˈä-nə-rə-bəl\ *adj* **1** : deserving of honor **2** : of great renown **3** : accompanied with marks of honor **4** : doing credit to the possessor **5** : characterized by integrity — **hon•or•able•ness** *n* — **hon•or•ably** \-blē\ *adv*

hon•o•rar•i•um \ˌä-nə-ˈrer-ē-əm\ *n, pl* **-ia** \-ē-ə\ *also* **-i•ums** : a reward usu. for services on which custom or propriety forbids a price to be set

hon•or•ary \ˈä-nə-ˌrer-ē\ *adj* **1** : having or conferring distinction **2** : conferred in recognition of achievement without the usual prerequisites ⟨~ degree⟩ **3** : UNPAID, VOLUNTARY ⟨an ~ chairman⟩ — **hon•or•ari•ly** \ˌä-nə-ˈrer-ə-lē\ *adv*

hon•or•if•ic \ˌä-nə-ˈri-fik\ *adj* : conferring or conveying honor ⟨~ titles⟩

hon•our, hon•our•able *chiefly Brit var of* HONOR, HONORABLE

[1]**hood** \ˈhu̇d\ *n* **1** : a covering for the head and neck and sometimes the face **2** : an ornamental fold (as at the back of an ecclesiastical vestment) **3** : a cover for parts of mechanisms; *esp* : the covering over an automobile engine — **hood•ed** \ˈhu̇-dəd\ *adj*

[2]**hood** \ˈhu̇d, ˈhüd\ *n* : HOODLUM

[3]**hood** \ˈhu̇d\ *n* : an inner-city neighborhood; *also* : INNER CITY

-hood \ˌhu̇d\ *n suffix* **1** : state : condition : quality : character ⟨boy*hood*⟩ ⟨hardi*hood*⟩ **2** : instance of a (specified) state or quality ⟨false*hood*⟩ **3** : individuals sharing a (specified) state or character ⟨brother*hood*⟩

hood•ie \ˈhu̇-dē\ *n* : a hooded sweatshirt

hood•lum \ˈhüd-ləm, ˈhu̇d-\ *n* **1** : THUG **2** : a young ruffian

hoo•doo \ˈhü-dü\ *n, pl* **hoodoos** **1** : a body of magical practices traditional esp. among Black people in the southern U.S. **2** : something that brings bad luck — **hoodoo** *vb*

hood•wink \ˈhu̇d-ˌwiŋk\ *vb* : to deceive by false appearance

hoo•ey \ˈhü-ē\ *n* : NONSENSE

hoof \ˈhu̇f, ˈhüf\ *n, pl* **hooves** \ˈhu̇vz, ˈhüvz\ *also* **hoofs** : a horny covering that protects the ends of the toes of ungulate mammals (as horses or cattle); *also* : a hoofed foot — **hoofed** \ˈhu̇ft, ˈhüft\ *adj*

[1]**hook** \ˈhu̇k\ *n* **1** : a curved or bent device for catching, holding, or pulling **2** : something curved or bent like a hook **3** : a flight of a ball (as in golf) that curves in a direction opposite to the dominant hand of the player propelling it **4** : a short punch delivered with a circular motion and with the elbow bent and rigid

[2]**hook** *vb* **1** : CURVE, CROOK **2** : to seize or make fast with a hook **3** : STEAL **4** : to work as a prostitute

hoo•kah \ˈhu̇-kə, ˈhü-\ *n* [Ar *ḥuqqa* bottle of a water pipe] : WATER PIPE

hook•er \ˈhu̇-kər\ *n* **1** : one that hooks **2** : PROSTITUTE

hook·up \ˈhu̇-ˌkəp\ *n* : an assemblage (as of apparatus or circuits) used for a specific purpose (as in radio)
hook up *vb* : to become involved in a working, social, or sexual relationship
hook·worm \ˈhu̇k-ˌwərm\ *n* : any of several parasitic intestinal nematode worms having hooks or plates around the mouth; *also* : infestation with or disease caused by hookworms
hoo·li·gan \ˈhü-li-gən\ *n* : RUFFIAN, HOODLUM — **hoo·li·gan·ism** \-gə-ˌni-zəm\ *n*
hoop \ˈhu̇p, ˈhüp\ *n* **1** : a circular strip used esp. for holding together the staves of a barrel **2** : a circular figure or object : RING **3** : a circle of flexible material for expanding a woman's skirt **4** : BASKETBALL — usu. used in pl.
hoop·la \ˈhüp-ˌlä, ˈhu̇p-\ *n* [F *houp-là,* interj.] : TO-DO; *also* : BALLYHOO
hoop·ster \ˈhüp-stər\ *n* : a basketball player
hoo·ray \hu̇-ˈrā\ *interj* — used to express joy, approval, or encouragement
hoose·gow \ˈhüs-ˌgau̇\ *n* [Sp *juzgado* panel of judges, courtroom] : JAIL
[1]**hoot** \ˈhüt\ *vb* **1** : to shout or laugh usu. in contempt **2** : to make the natural throat noise of an owl — **hoot·er** *n*
[2]**hoot** *n* **1** : a sound of hooting **2** : the least bit ⟨don't give a ~⟩ **3** : something or someone amusing ⟨the play is a real ~⟩
hoo·te·nan·ny \ˈhü-tə-ˌna-nē\ *n, pl* **-nies** : a gathering at which folksingers entertain often with the audience joining in
[1]**hop** \ˈhäp\ *vb* **hopped; hop·ping 1** : to move by quick springy leaps **2** : to make a quick trip **3** : to ride on esp. surreptitiously and without authorization
[2]**hop** *n* **1** : a short brisk leap esp. on one leg **2** : DANCE **3** : a short trip by air
[3]**hop** *n* : a vine related to the hemp plant whose ripe dried pistillate catkins are used esp. in flavoring malt liquors; *also, pl* : its pistillate catkins
[1]**hope** \ˈhōp\ *vb* **hoped; hop·ing** : to desire with expectation of fulfillment
[2]**hope** *n* **1** : TRUST, RELIANCE **2** : desire accompanied by expectation of fulfillment; *also* : something hoped for **3** : one that gives promise for the future — **hope·ful** \-fəl\ *adj* — **hope·ful·ness** *n* — **hope·less** *adj* — **hope·less·ly** *adv* — **hope·less·ness** *n*
HOPE *abbr* Health Opportunity for People Everywhere
hope·ful·ly \ˈhōp-fə-lē\ *adv* **1** : in a hopeful manner **2** : it is hoped
Ho·pi \ˈhō-pē\ *n, pl* **Hopi** *or* **Hopis** : a member of an Indigenous people of Arizona; *also* : the language of the Hopi people
hopped–up \ˈhäpt-ˈəp\ *adj* **1** : being under the influence of a narcotic; *also* : full of enthusiasm or excitement **2** : having more than usual power ⟨a ~ engine⟩
hop·per \ˈhä-pər\ *n* **1** : a usu. immature hopping insect (as a grasshopper) **2** : a usu. funnel-shaped container for delivering material (as grain) **3** : a freight car with hinged doors in a sloping bottom **4** : a box into which a bill to be considered by a legislative body is dropped **5** : a tank holding a liquid and having a device for releasing its contents through a pipe
hop·scotch \ˈhäp-ˌskäch\ *n* : a child's game in which a player tosses an object (as a stone) into areas of a figure drawn on the ground and hops through the figure to pick up the object
hor *abbr* horizontal
horde \ˈhȯrd\ *n* : THRONG, SWARM
ho·ri·zon \hə-ˈrī-zᵊn\ *n* [ME, fr. LL, fr. Gk *horizont-, horizōn,* fr. prp. of *horizein* to bound, fr. *horos* limit, boundary] **1** : the apparent junction of earth and sky **2** : range of outlook or experience
hor·i·zon·tal \ˌhȯr-ə-ˈzän-tᵊl\ *adj* : parallel to the horizon : LEVEL — **horizontal** *n* — **hor·i·zon·tal·ly** *adv*
hor·mon·al \hȯr-ˈmō-nᵊl\ *adj* : of, relating to, or effected by hormones — **hor·mon·al·ly** \-nᵊl-ē\ *adv*
hor·mone \ˈhȯr-ˌmōn\ *n* [Gk *hormōn,* prp. of *horman* to stir up, fr. *hormē* impulse, assault] : a product of living cells that circulates in body fluids and has a specific effect on the activity of cells remote from its point of origin
horn \ˈhȯrn\ *n* **1** : one of the hard projections of bone or keratin on the head of many hoofed mammals **2** : something resembling or suggesting a horn **3** : a brass wind instrument **4** : a usu. electrical device that makes a noise ⟨an automobile ~⟩ — **horned** \ˈhȯrnd\ *adj* — **horn·less** *adj*
horn·book \ˈhȯrn-ˌbu̇k\ *n* **1** : a child's primer consisting of a sheet of parchment or paper protected by a sheet of transparent horn **2** : a rudimentary treatise
horned toad *n* : any of several small harmless insect-eating lizards with spines on the head resembling horns and spiny scales on the body
hor·net \ˈhȯr-nət\ *n* : any of the larger social wasps
horn in *vb* : to participate without invitation : INTRUDE
horn·pipe \ˈhȯrn-ˌpīp\ *n* : a lively folk dance of the British Isles
horny \ˈhȯr-nē\ *adj* **horn·i·er; -est 1** : of or made of horn; *also* : HARD, CALLOUS **2** : having horns **3** : desiring sexual gratification; *also* : excited sexually
ho·rol·o·gy \hə-ˈrä-lə-jē\ *n* : the science of measuring time or constructing time-indicating instruments — **hor·o·log·i·cal** \ˌhȯr-ə-ˈlä-ji-kəl\ *adj* — **ho·rol·o·gist** \hə-ˈrä-lə-jist\ *n*
horo·scope \ˈhȯr-ə-ˌskōp\ *n* [ME *horoscopum,* fr. L *horoscopus,* fr. Gk *hōroskopos,* fr. *hōra* hour + *skopos* watcher] **1** : a diagram of the relative positions of planets and signs of the zodiac at a particular time for use by astrologers to foretell events of a person's life **2** : an astrological forecast
hor·ren·dous \hȯ-ˈren-dəs\ *adj* : DREADFUL, HORRIBLE
hor·ri·ble \ˈhȯr-ə-bəl\ *adj* **1** : marked by

or conducive to horror **2 :** highly disagreeable ⟨a ~ mistake⟩ — **hor·ri·ble·ness** *n* — **hor·ri·bly** \-blē\ *adv*

hor·rid \ˈhȯr-əd\ *adj* **1 :** HIDEOUS **2 :** REPULSIVE — **hor·rid·ly** *adv*

hor·rif·ic \hȯ-ˈri-fik\ *adj* **:** having the power to horrify ⟨a ~ crime⟩ — **hor·rif·i·cal·ly** \-fi-k(ə-)lē\ *adv*

hor·ri·fy \ˈhȯr-ə-ˌfī\ *vb* **-fied; -fy·ing :** to cause to feel horror ♦ ***Synonyms*** APPALL, DAUNT, DISMAY

hor·ror \ˈhȯr-ər\ *n* **1 :** painful and intense fear, dread, or dismay **2 :** intense repugnance **3 :** something that horrifies

horror story *n* **:** an account of an unsettling or unfortunate occurrence

hors de com·bat \ˌȯr-də-kōⁿ-ˈbä\ *adv or adj* **:** in a disabled condition

hors d'oeuvre \ȯr-ˈdərv\ *n, pl* **hors d'oeuvres** *same or* -ˈdərvz\ *also* **hors d'oeuvre** [F *hors-d'oeuvre,* lit., outside of the work] **:** any of various savory foods usu. served as appetizers

horse \ˈhȯrs\ *n, pl* **hors·es** *also* **horse 1 :** a large solid-hoofed herbivorous mammal domesticated as a draft and saddle animal **2 :** a supporting framework usu. with legs — **horse·less** *adj*

¹horse·back \ˈhȯrs-ˌbak\ *n* **:** the back of a horse

²horseback *adv* **:** on horseback

horse chestnut *n* **:** a large tree with palmate leaves, erect conical clusters of showy flowers, and large glossy brown seeds enclosed in a prickly bur; *also* **:** its seed

horse·flesh \ˈhȯrs-ˌflesh\ *n* **:** horses for riding, driving, or racing

horse·fly \-ˌflī\ *n* **:** any of a family of large dipteran flies with bloodsucking females

horse·hair \-ˌher\ *n* **1 :** the hair of a horse esp. from the mane or tail **2 :** cloth made from horsehair

horse·hide \-ˌhīd\ *n* **1 :** the dressed or raw hide of a horse **2 :** the ball used in baseball

horse latitudes *n pl* **:** either of two calm regions near 30°N and 30°S latitude

horse·laugh \ˈhȯrs-ˌlaf, -ˌläf\ *n* **:** a loud boisterous laugh

horse·man \-mən\ *n* **1 :** one who rides horseback; *also* **:** one skilled in managing horses **2 :** a breeder or raiser of horses — **horse·man·ship** *n*

horse·play \-ˌplā\ *n* **:** rough boisterous play

horse·play·er \-ər\ *n* **:** a bettor on horse races

horse·pow·er \ˈhȯrs-ˌpau̇(-ə)r\ *n* **:** a unit of power equal in the U.S. to 746 watts

horse·rad·ish \-ˌra-dish\ *n* **:** a tall white-flowered herb related to the mustards whose pungent root is used as a condiment; *also* **:** the pungent condiment

horse·shoe \ˈhȯrs-ˌshü\ *n* **1 :** a usu. U-shaped protective metal plate fitted to the rim of a horse's hoof **2** *pl* **:** a game in which horseshoes are pitched at a fixed object — **horse·shoe** *vb* — **horse·sho·er** *n*

horseshoe crab *n* **:** any of several marine arthropods with a broad crescent-shaped combined head and thorax

horse·tail \ˈhȯrs-ˌtāl\ *n* **:** any of a genus of primitive spore-producing plants with hollow jointed stems and leaves reduced to sheaths about the joints

horse·whip \-ˌhwip\ *vb* **:** to flog with a whip made to be used on a horse

horse·wom·an \-ˌwu̇-mən\ *n* **1 :** a woman skilled in riding horseback or in caring for or managing horses **2 :** a woman who breeds or raises horses

hors·ey *also* **horsy** \ˈhȯr-sē\ *adj* **hors·i·er; -est 1 :** of, relating to, or suggesting a horse **2 :** having to do with horses or horse racing

hort *abbr* horticultural; horticulture

hor·ta·tive \ˈhȯr-tə-tiv\ *adj* **:** giving exhortation ⟨a ~ appeal⟩

hor·ta·to·ry \ˈhȯr-tə-ˌtȯr-ē\ *adj* **:** HORTATIVE

hor·ti·cul·ture \ˈhȯr-tə-ˌkəl-chər\ *n* **:** the science and art of growing fruits, vegetables, flowers, and ornamental plants — **hor·ti·cul·tur·al** \ˌhȯr-tə-ˈkəl-chə-rəl\ *adj* — **hor·ti·cul·tur·ist** \-rist\ *n*

Hos *abbr* Hosea

ho·san·na \hō-ˈza-nə, -ˈzä-\ *interj* [Gk *hōsanna,* fr. Heb *hōshīʿāh-nnā* pray, save (us)!] — used as a cry of acclamation and adoration — **hosanna** *n*

¹hose \ˈhōz\ *n, pl* **hose** *or* **hos·es 1** *pl hose* **:** STOCKING, SOCK; *also* **:** a close-fitting garment covering the legs and waist **2 :** a flexible tube for conveying fluids (as from a faucet)

²hose *vb* **hosed; hos·ing :** to spray, water, or wash with a hose

Ho·sea \hō-ˈzā-ə, -ˈzē-\ *n* — see BIBLE table

ho·siery \ˈhō-zhə-rē, -zə-\ *n* **:** STOCKINGS, SOCKS

hosp *abbr* hospital

hos·pice \ˈhäs-pəs\ *n* **1 :** a lodging for travelers or for young persons or the underprivileged **2 :** a facility or program for caring for dying persons

hos·pi·ta·ble \hä-ˈspi-tə-bəl, ˈhäs-(ˌ)pi-\ *adj* **1 :** given to generous and cordial reception of guests **2 :** readily receptive — **hos·pi·ta·bly** \-blē\ *adv*

hos·pi·tal \ˈhäs-ˌpi-tᵊl\ *n* [ME, fr. AF, fr. ML *hospitale* hospice, guest house, fr. neut. of L *hospitalis* of a guest, fr. *hospit-, hospes* guest, host] **:** an institution where the sick or injured receive medical or surgical care

hos·pi·tal·ise *Brit var of* HOSPITALIZE

hos·pi·tal·i·ty \ˌhäs-pə-ˈta-lə-tē\ *n, pl* **-ties :** hospitable treatment, reception, or disposition

hos·pi·tal·ize \ˈhäs-ˌpi-tə-ˌlīz\ *vb* **-ized; -iz·ing :** to place in a hospital as a patient — **hos·pi·tal·i·za·tion** \ˌhäs-ˌpi-tᵊl-ə-ˈzā-shən\ *n*

¹host \ˈhōst\ *n* [ME, fr. AF *ost,* fr. LL *hostis,* fr. L, stranger, enemy] **1 :** ARMY **2 :** MULTITUDE ⟨a ~ of options⟩

²host *n* [ME *hoste* host, guest, fr. AF, fr. L *hospit-, hospes*] **1 :** one who receives or entertains guests **2 :** one who talks to guests on a show **3 :** an animal or plant on or in which a parasite lives **4 :** one into which something (as an organ) is transplanted **5 :** SERVER 2 — **host** *vb*

[3]**host** *n, often cap* [ultim. fr. L *hostia* sacrifice] : the eucharistic bread

hos·tage \ˈhäs-tij\ *n* **1 :** a person kept as a pledge pending the fulfillment of an agreement **2 :** a person taken by force to secure the taker's demands

hos·tel \ˈhäs-tᵊl\ *n* [ME, fr. AF, fr. ML *hospitale* hospice] **1 :** INN **2 :** a supervised lodging for youth — **hos·tel·er** *or* **hos·tel·ler** *n*

hos·tel·ry \-rē\ *n, pl* **-ries :** INN, HOTEL

host·ess \ˈhō-stəs\ *n* **1 :** a woman who receives or entertains guests **2 :** a woman who talks to guests on a show

hos·tile \ˈhäs-tᵊl, -ˌtī(-ə)l\ *adj* **:** marked by usu. overt antagonism : UNFRIENDLY — **hostile** *n* — **hos·tile·ly** *adv*

hos·til·i·ty \hä-ˈsti-lə-tē\ *n, pl* **-ties 1 :** an unfriendly state or action **2** *pl* **:** overt acts of war

hos·tler \ˈhäs-lər, ˈäs-\ *n* **:** one who takes care of horses or mules

hot \ˈhät\ *adj* **hot·ter; hot·test 1 :** marked by a high temperature or an uncomfortable degree of body heat **2 :** giving a sensation of heat or of burning **3 :** ARDENT, FIERY **4 :** sexually excited **5 :** EAGER **6 :** newly made or received **7 :** PUNGENT **8 :** unusually lucky or favorable ⟨∼ dice⟩ **9 :** recently and illegally obtained ⟨∼ jewels⟩ — **hot** *adv* — **hot·ly** *adv* — **hot·ness** *n*

hot·bed \-ˌbed\ *n* **1 :** a glass-covered bed of soil heated (as by fermenting manure) and used esp. for raising seedlings **2 :** an environment that favors rapid growth or development

hot–blood·ed \-ˈblə-dəd\ *adj* **:** easily roused or excited ⟨∼ rebels⟩

hot·box \-ˌbäks\ *n* **:** a bearing (as of a railroad car) overheated by friction

hot button *n* **:** an emotional issue or concern that triggers immediate intense reaction

hot·cake \-ˌkāk\ *n* **:** PANCAKE

hot dog *n* **:** a cooked frankfurter usu. served in a long split roll

ho·tel \hō-ˈtel\ *n* [F *hôtel,* fr. OF *hostel,* fr. ML *hospitale* hospice] **:** a building where lodging and usu. meals, entertainment, and various personal services are provided for the public

hot flash *n* **:** a sudden brief flushing and sensation of heat usu. associated with menopausal endocrine imbalance

hot·head·ed \ˈhät-ˈhe-dəd\ *adj* **:** FIERY, IMPETUOUS ⟨a ∼ troublemaker⟩ — **hot·head** \-ˌhed\ *n* — **hot·head·ed·ly** *adv* — **hot·head·ed·ness** *n*

hot·house \-ˌhau̇s\ *n* **:** a heated greenhouse esp. for raising tropical plants

hotline *n* **:** a telephone line for emergency use (as between governments or to a counseling service)

hot mess *n* **1** *archaic* **a :** a hot mixture of ingredients cooked or eaten together **b :** a hot dish of soft food **2 :** something or someone that is emphatically a mess

hot pants *n pl* **:** very short shorts

hot pepper *n* **:** a small usu. thin-walled pepper with a pungent taste; *also* **:** a plant bearing hot peppers

hot plate *n* **:** a simple portable appliance for heating or for cooking

hot potato *n* **:** an embarrassing or controversial issue

hot rod *n* **:** an automobile modified for high speed and fast acceleration — **hot–rod·der** \-ˈrä-dər\ *n*

hots \ˈhäts\ *n pl* **:** strong sexual desire — usu. used with *the*

hot seat *n* **:** a position of anxiety or embarrassment

hot·shot \ˈhät-ˌshät\ *n* **:** a showily skillful person ⟨a ∼ lawyer⟩

hot spot *n* **1 a :** an area of political, military, or civil unrest **b :** a place where there is an increased transmission risk of a disease **2 :** a place of more than usual interest or activity **3 :** a place in the upper mantle of the earth at which hot magma upwells through the crust to form a volcanic feature **4 :** a place where a wireless Internet connection is available **5 :** an inflamed patch of moist infected skin on a domestic animal

hot tub *n* **:** a large tub of hot water for one or more bathers

hot water *n* **:** TROUBLE, DIFFICULTY

hot–wire \ˈhät-ˌwī(-ə)r\ *vb* **:** to start (an automobile) by short-circuiting the ignition system

[1]**hound** \ˈhau̇nd\ *n* **1 :** any of various hunting dogs that track prey by scent or sight **2 :** FAN, ADDICT ⟨autograph ∼*s*⟩

[2]**hound** *vb* **:** to pursue relentlessly

hour \ˈau̇(-ə)r\ *n* **1 :** the 24th part of a day : 60 minutes **2 :** the time of day **3 :** a particular or customary time **4 :** a class session — **hour·ly** *adv or adj*

hour·glass \ˈau̇(-ə)r-ˌglas\ *n* **:** a glass vessel for measuring time in which sand runs from an upper compartment to a lower compartment in an hour

hou·ri \ˈhu̇r-ē\ *n* [F, fr. Pers *hūri,* fr. Ar *ḥūrīya*] **:** one of the beautiful maidens of the Muslim paradise

[1]**house** \ˈhau̇s\ *n, pl* **hous·es** \ˈhau̇-zəz\ **1 :** a building for human habitation **2 :** an animal shelter (as a den or nest) **3 :** a building in which something is stored **4 :** HOUSEHOLD; *also* **:** FAMILY **5 :** a residence for a religious community or for students; *also* **:** those in residence **6 :** a legislative body **7 :** a place of business or entertainment **8 :** a business organization **9 :** the audience in a theater or concert hall — **house·ful** *n*

[2]**house** \ˈhau̇z\ *vb* **housed; hous·ing 1 :** to provide with or take shelter : LODGE **2 :** STORE ⟨paintings *housed* in a gallery⟩

house·boat \ˈhau̇s-ˌbōt\ *n* **:** a pleasure boat fitted for use as a dwelling or for leisurely cruising

house·boy \-ˌbȯi\ *n* **:** a boy or man hired to act as a household servant

house·break \-ˌbrāk\ *vb* **-broke; -brok·en; -break·ing** : to train (a pet) in excretory habits acceptable in indoor living
house·break·ing \-ˌbrā-kiŋ\ *n* : the act of breaking into a dwelling with the intent of committing a felony
house·clean \-ˌklēn\ *vb* : to clean a house and its furniture — **house·clean·ing** *n*
house·coat \-ˌkōt\ *n* : a woman's often long-skirted informal garment for wear around the house
house·fly \-ˌflī\ *n* : a dipteran fly that is common about human habitations
[1]**house·hold** \-ˌhōld\ *n* : those who dwell as a family under the same roof — **house·hold·er** *n*
[2]**household** *adj* **1** : DOMESTIC **2** : FAMILIAR, COMMON ⟨a ~ name⟩
house·keep·er \-ˌkē-pər\ *n* : a person employed to take care of a house
house·keep·ing \-ˌkē-piŋ\ *n* : the care and management of a house or institutional property
house·lights \-ˌlīts\ *n pl* : the lights that illuminate the auditorium of a theater
house·maid \-ˌmād\ *n* : a girl or woman who is a servant employed to do housework
house·moth·er \-ˌmə-t͟hər\ *n* : a woman acting as hostess, chaperone, and often housekeeper in a group residence
house·plant \-ˌplant\ *n* : a plant grown or kept indoors
house sparrow *n* : a Eurasian sparrow widely introduced in urban and agricultural areas
house·top \ˈhau̇s-ˌtäp\ *n* : ROOF
house·wares \-ˌwerz\ *n pl* : small articles of household equipment
house·warm·ing \-ˌwȯr-miŋ\ *n* : a party to celebrate the taking possession of a house or premises
house·wife \-ˌwīf\ *n* : a married woman in charge of a household — **house·wife·ly** *adj* — **house·wif·ery** \-ˌwī-fə-rē\ *n*
house·work \-ˌwərk\ *n* : the work of housekeeping
[1]**hous·ing** \ˈhau̇-ziŋ\ *n* **1** : SHELTER; *also* : dwellings provided for people **2** : something that covers or protects
[2]**housing** *n* : CAPARISON 1
HOV *abbr* high-occupancy vehicle
hove *past and past part of* HEAVE
hov·el \ˈhə-vəl, ˈhä-\ *n* : a small, wretched, and often dirty house : HUT
hov·er \ˈhə-vər, ˈhä-\ *vb* **hov·ered; hov·er·ing** **1** : FLUTTER; *also* : to move to and fro **2** : to be in an uncertain state
hov·er·craft \-ˌkraft\ *n* : a vehicle that rides on a cushion of air over a surface
[1]**how** \ˈhau̇\ *adv* **1** : in what way or manner ⟨~ was it done⟩ **2** : with what meaning ⟨~ do we interpret such behavior⟩ **3** : for what reason ⟨~ could you have done such a thing⟩ **4** : to what extent or degree ⟨~ deep is it⟩ **5** : in what state or condition ⟨~ are you⟩ — **how about** : what do you say to or think of ⟨*how about* coming with me⟩ — **how come** : why is it that
[2]**how** *conj* **1** : the way or manner in which ⟨remember ~ they fought⟩ **2** : HOWEVER ⟨do it ~ you like⟩
[1]**how·be·it** \hau̇-ˈbē-ət\ *conj* : ALTHOUGH
[2]**howbeit** *adv* : NEVERTHELESS
how·dah \ˈhau̇-də\ *n* [Hindi & Urdu *hau-da,* fr. Ar *haudaj*] : a seat or covered pavilion on the back of an elephant or camel
[1]**how·ev·er** \hau̇-ˈe-vər\ *conj* : in whatever manner that
[2]**however** *adv* **1** : in whatever manner; *also* : to whatever degree **2** : in spite of that
how·it·zer \ˈhau̇-ət-sər\ *n* : a short cannon that shoots shells at a high angle
howl \ˈhau̇(-ə)l\ *vb* **1** : to emit a loud long doleful sound characteristic of dogs **2** : to cry loudly — **howl** *n*
howl·er \ˈhau̇-lər\ *n* **1** : one that howls **2** : a humorous and ridiculous blunder
howl·ing *adj* **1** : DESOLATE, WILD **2** : very great ⟨a ~ success⟩
how·so·ev·er \ˌhau̇-sə-ˈwe-vər\ *adv* : HOWEVER 1
hoy·den \ˈhȯi-dᵊn\ *n* : a girl or woman of saucy, boisterous, or carefree behavior — **hoy·den·ish** *adj*
hp *abbr* horsepower
HP *abbr* high pressure
HPF *abbr* highest possible frequency
HQ *abbr* headquarters
hr *abbr* **1** here **2** hour
HR *abbr* House of Representatives
HRH *abbr* **1** Her Royal Highness **2** His Royal Highness
hryv·nia \ˈ(h)riv-nē-ə\ *n, pl* **hryvnia** *or* **hryvnias** — see MONEY table
hrzn *abbr* horizon
Hs *symbol* hassium
HS *abbr* high school
HST *abbr* Hawaiian standard time
ht *abbr* height
HT *abbr* **1** Hawaii time **2** high-tension
HTML \ˌāch-ˌtē-ˌem-ˈel\ *n* [*h*yper*t*ext *m*ark-up *l*anguage] : a computer language used to create World Wide Web documents
http *abbr* hypertext transfer protocol
hua·ra·che \wə-ˈrä-chē\ *n* [MexSp] : a sandal with an upper made of interwoven leather strips
hub \ˈhəb\ *n* **1** : the central part of a circular object (as a wheel) **2** : a center of activity; *esp* : an airport or city through which an airline routes most of its traffic
hub·bub \ˈhə-bəb\ *n* : UPROAR ⟨the ~ in the stadium⟩; *also* : TURMOIL ⟨the ~ following the war⟩
hub·cap \ˈhəb-ˌkap\ *n* : a removable metal cap over the end of an axle
hu·bris \ˈhyü-brəs\ *n* : exaggerated pride or self-confidence
huck·le·ber·ry \ˈhə-kəl-ˌber-ē\ *n* **1** : any of a genus of American shrubs of the heath family; *also* : its edible dark blue berry **2** : BLUEBERRY
huck·ster \ˈhək-stər\ *n* : PEDDLER, HAWKER — **huck·ster·ism** \-stə-ˌri-zəm\ *n*
HUD *abbr* Department of Housing and Urban Development

[1]hud·dle \ˈhə-dᵊl\ *vb* **hud·dled; hud·dling** **1** : to crowd together **2** : CONFER

[2]huddle *n* **1** : a closely packed group **2** : MEETING, CONFERENCE

hue \ˈhyü\ *n* **1** : COLOR; *also* : gradation of color **2** : the attribute of colors that permits them to be classed as red, yellow, green, blue, or an intermediate color — **hued** \ˈhyüd\ *adj*

hue and cry *n* : a clamor of pursuit or protest

huff \ˈhəf\ *n* : a fit of anger or pique — **huff** *vb* — **huff·i·ly** \ˈhə-fə-lē\ *adv* — **huffy** \ˈhə-fē\ *adj*

hug \ˈhəg\ *vb* **hugged; hug·ging** **1** : EMBRACE **2** : to stay close to — **hug** *n*

huge \ˈhyüj\ *adj* **hug·er; hug·est** : very large or extensive — **huge·ly** *adv* — **huge·ness** *n*

hug·ger–mug·ger \ˈhə-gər-ˌmə-gər\ *n* **1** : SECRECY **2** : CONFUSION, MUDDLE

Hu·gue·not \ˈhyü-gə-ˌnät\ *n* : a French Protestant of the 16th and 17th centuries

hu·la \ˈhü-lə\ *n* : a sinuous Polynesian dance usu. accompanied by chants

hulk \ˈhəlk\ *n* **1** : a heavy clumsy ship **2** : an old ship unfit for service **3** : a bulky or unwieldy person or thing

hulk·ing \ˈhəl-kiŋ\ *adj* : BURLY, MASSIVE

[1]hull \ˈhəl\ *n* **1** : the outer covering of a fruit or seed **2** : the frame or body esp. of a ship or boat

[2]hull *vb* : to remove the hulls of — **hull·er** *n*

hul·la·ba·loo \ˈhə-lə-bə-ˌlü\ *n, pl* **-loos** : a confused noise : UPROAR

hul·lo \ˌhə-ˈlō\ *chiefly Brit var of* HELLO

hum \ˈhəm\ *vb* **hummed; hum·ming** **1** : to utter a sound like that of the speech sound \m\ prolonged **2** : DRONE **3** : to be busily active **4** : to run smoothly **5** : to sing with closed lips — **hum** *n* — **hum·mer** *n*

[1]hu·man \ˈhyü-mən, ˈyü-\ *adj* **1** : of, relating to, being, or characteristic of humans **2** : having human form or attributes — **hu·man·ly** *adv* — **hu·man·ness** *n*

[2]human *n* : any of a species of bipedal primate mammals comprising all living persons and their recent ancestors; *also* : HOMINID — **hu·man·like** \-ˌlīk\ *adj*

hu·mane \hyü-ˈmān, yü-\ *adj* **1** : marked by compassion, sympathy, or consideration for others **2** : HUMANISTIC — **hu·mane·ly** *adv* — **hu·mane·ness** *n*

human immunodeficiency virus *n* : HIV

hu·man·ism \ˈhyü-mə-ˌni-zəm, ˈyü-\ *n* **1** : devotion to the humanities; *also* : the revival of classical letters characteristic of the Renaissance **2** : a doctrine or way of life centered on human interests or values — **hu·man·ist** \-nist\ *n or adj* — **hu·man·is·tic** \ˌhyü-mə-ˈnis-tik, ˌyü-\ *adj*

hu·man·i·tar·i·an \hyü-ˌma-nə-ˈter-ē-ən, yü-\ *n* : one who practices philanthropy — **humanitarian** *adj* — **hu·man·i·tar·i·an·ism** *n*

hu·man·i·ty \hyü-ˈma-nə-tē, yü-\ *n, pl* **-ties** **1** : the quality or state of being human or humane **2** *pl* : the branches of learning dealing with human concerns (as philosophy) as opposed to natural processes (as physics) **3** : the human race

hu·man·ize \ˈhyü-mə-ˌnīz, ˈyü-\ *vb* **-ized; -iz·ing** : to make human or humane — **hu·man·i·za·tion** \ˌhyü-mə-nə-ˈzā-shən, ˌyü-\ *n* — **hu·man·iz·er** *n*

hu·man·kind \ˈhyü-mən-ˌkīnd, ˈyü-\ *n* : the human race

hu·man·oid \ˈhyü-mə-ˌnȯid, ˈyü-\ *adj* : having human form or characteristics — **humanoid** *n*

human pap·il·lo·ma·virus \-ˌpa-pə-ˈlō-mə-ˌvī-rəs\ *n* : any of numerous DNA-containing viruses that cause various human warts

[1]hum·ble \ˈhəm-bəl\ *adj* **hum·bler** \-bə-lər\; **hum·blest** \-bə-ləst\ [ME, fr. AF, fr. L *humilis* low, humble, fr. *humus* earth] **1** : not proud or haughty **2** : not pretentious : UNASSUMING **3** : INSIGNIFICANT ♦ ***Synonyms*** MEEK, MODEST, LOWLY — **hum·ble·ness** *n* — **hum·bly** *adv*

[2]humble *vb* **hum·bled; hum·bling** **1** : to make humble **2** : to destroy the power or prestige of — **hum·bler** *n*

[1]hum·bug \ˈhəm-ˌbəg\ *n* **1** : HOAX, FRAUD **2** : NONSENSE

[2]humbug *vb* **hum·bugged; hum·bug·ging** : DECEIVE

hum·ding·er \ˈhəm-ˈdiŋ-ər\ *n* : a person or thing of striking excellence

hum·drum \ˈhəm-ˌdrəm\ *adj* : MONOTONOUS, DULL — **humdrum** *n*

hu·mer·us \ˈhyü-mə-rəs\ *n, pl* **hu·meri** \ˈhyü-mə-ˌrī, -ˌrē\ : the long bone extending from shoulder to elbow

hu·mid \ˈhyü-məd, ˈyü-\ *adj* : containing or characterized by perceptible moisture : DAMP — **hu·mid·ly** *adv*

hu·mid·i·fy \hyü-ˈmi-də-ˌfī\ *vb* **-fied; -fy·ing** : to make humid — **hu·mid·i·fi·ca·tion** \-ˌmi-də-fə-ˈkā-shən\ *n* — **hu·mid·i·fi·er** \-ˈmi-də-ˌfī-ər\ *n*

hu·mid·i·ty \hyü-ˈmi-də-tē, yü-\ *n, pl* **-ties** : the amount of atmospheric moisture

hu·mi·dor \ˈhyü-mə-ˌdȯr, ˈyü-\ *n* : a case (as for storing cigars) in which the air is kept properly humidified

hu·mil·i·ate \hyü-ˈmi-lē-ˌāt, yü-\ *vb* **-at·ed; -at·ing** : to injure the self-respect of : MORTIFY — **hu·mil·i·at·ing·ly** *adv* — **hu·mil·i·a·tion** \-ˌmi-lē-ˈā-shən\ *n*

hu·mil·i·ty \hyü-ˈmi-lə-tē, yü-\ *n* : the quality or state of being humble

hum·ming·bird \ˈhə-miŋ-ˌbərd\ *n* : any of a family of tiny brightly colored American birds related to the swifts

hum·mock \ˈhə-mək\ *n* : a rounded mound : KNOLL — **hum·mocky** \-mə-kē\ *adj*

hum·mus \ˈhə-məs, ˈhu̇-\ *n* [Ar *ḥummuṣ* chickpeas] : a paste of pureed chickpeas usu. mixed with sesame oil or paste

hu·mon·gous \hyü-ˈməŋ-gəs, -ˈmäŋ-\ *adj* [perh. alter. of *huge* + *monstrous*] : extremely large ⟨a ~ stadium⟩

[1]hu·mor \ˈhyü-mər, ˈyü-\ *n* **1** : TEMPERAMENT **2** : MOOD **3** : WHIM **4** : a quality that appeals to a sense of the ludicrous or incongruous; *also* : a keen perception of the ludicrous or incongruous **5** : comical or amusing entertainment — **hu·mor·ist** \ˈhyü-mə-rist, ˈyü-\ *n* — **hu·mor·less** \ˈhyü-mər-ləs, ˈyü-\ *adj* — **hu·mor·less·ly** *adv* — **hu·mor·less·ness** *n* — **hu·mor·ous** \ˈhyü-mə-rəs, ˈyü-\ *adj* — **hu·mor·ous·ly** *adv* — **hu·mor·ous·ness** *n*

²**humor** *vb* : to comply with the wishes or mood of ⟨~*ed* his boss⟩

hu·mour *chiefly Brit var of* HUMOR

hump \ˈhəmp\ *n* **1** : a rounded protuberance (as on the back of a camel) **2** : a difficult phase or obstacle ⟨over the ~⟩ — **humped** *adj*

hump·back \ˈhəmp-ˌbak; *1 also* -ˈbak\ *n* **1** *dated, often offensive* : HUNCHBACK **2** : HUMPBACK WHALE — **humpbacked** *adj*

humpback whale *n* : a large baleen whale having very long flippers

hu·mus \ˈhyü-məs, ˈyü-\ *n* : the dark organic part of soil formed from decaying matter

Hun \ˈhən\ *n* : a member of an Asian people that invaded Europe about A.D. 450

¹**hunch** \ˈhənch\ *vb* **1** : to thrust oneself forward **2** : to assume or cause to assume a bent or crooked posture

²**hunch** *n* **1** : PUSH **2** : a strong intuitive feeling about what will happen

hunch·back \ˈhənch-ˌbak\ *n, often offensive* : a person with a crooked back; *also* : a back with a hump — **hunch·backed** *adj*

hun·dred \ˈhən-drəd\ *n, pl* **hundreds** *or* **hundred** : 10 times 10 — **hundred** *adj* — **hun·dredth** \-drədth\ *adj or n*

hun·dred·weight \-ˌwāt\ *n, pl* **hundredweight** *or* **hundredweights** — see WEIGHT table

¹**hung** *past and past part of* HANG

²**hung** *adj* : unable to reach a decision or verdict ⟨a ~ jury⟩

Hung *abbr* Hungarian; Hungary

Hun·gar·i·an \ˌhəŋ-ˈger-ē-ən\ *n* **1** : a native or inhabitant of Hungary **2** : the language of the Hungarians — **Hungarian** *adj*

hun·ger \ˈhəŋ-gər\ *n* **1** : a craving or urgent need for food **2** : a strong desire — **hunger** *vb* — **hun·gri·ly** *adv* — **hun·gry** *adj*

hung·over \ˈhəŋ-ˈō-vər\ *adj* : having a hangover

hung up *adj* **1** : DELAYED **2** : ENTHUSIASTIC; *also* : PREOCCUPIED — usu. used with *on* ⟨*hung up* on winning⟩

hunk \ˈhəŋk\ *n* **1** : a large piece **2** : an attractive well-built man — **hunky** *adj*

hun·ker \ˈhəŋ-kər\ *vb* **1** : CROUCH, SQUAT — usu. used with *down* **2** : to settle in for a sustained period — used with *down*

hun·ky–do·ry \ˌhəŋ-kē-ˈdȯr-ē\ *adj* : quite satisfactory : FINE

¹**hunt** \ˈhənt\ *vb* **1** : to pursue for food or in sport; *also* : to take part in a hunt **2** : to try to find : SEEK **3** : to drive or chase esp. by harrying **4** : to traverse in search of prey — **hunt·er** *n*

²**hunt** *n* : an act, practice, or instance of hunting

Hun·ting·ton's disease \ˈhən-tiŋ-tənz-\ *n* : a chorea that usu. begins in middle age and leads to dementia

hunt·ress \ˈhən-trəs\ *n* : a woman who hunts game

hunts·man \ˈhənts-mən\ *n* **1** : HUNTER **2** : a person who manages a hunt and looks after the hounds

hur·dle \ˈhər-dᵊl\ *n* **1** : a barrier to leap over in a race **2** : OBSTACLE — **hurdle** *vb* — **hur·dler** *n*

hur·dy–gur·dy \ˌhər-dē-ˈgər-dē, ˈhər-dē-ˌgər-dē\ *n, pl* **-gur·dies** : a musical instrument in which the sound is produced by turning a crank

hurl \ˈhərl\ *vb* **1** : to move or cause to move vigorously **2** : to throw down with violence **3** : FLING; *also* : PITCH — **hurl** *n* — **hurl·er** *n*

hur·ly–bur·ly \ˌhər-lē-ˈbər-lē\ *n* : UPROAR, TUMULT

Hu·ron \ˈhyu̇r-ən, ˈhyu̇r-ˌän\ *n, pl* **Hurons** *or* **Huron** : a member of a confederacy of Indigenous peoples formerly living between Georgian Bay and Lake Ontario; *also* : the language of the Huron people

hur·rah \hu̇-ˈrȯ, -ˈrä\ *also* **hur·ray** \hu̇-ˈrā\ *interj* — used to express joy, approval, or encouragement

hur·ri·cane \ˈhər-ə-ˌkān\ *n* [Sp *huracán*, fr. Taino, an Indigenous language of the Greater Antilles] : a tropical cyclone with winds of 74 miles (118 kilometers) per hour or greater that is usu. accompanied by rain, thunder, and lightning

¹**hur·ry** \ˈhər-ē\ *vb* **hur·ried; hur·ry·ing 1** : to carry or cause to go with haste **2** : to impel to a greater speed **3** : to move or act with haste — **hurried** *adj* — **hur·ried·ly** *adv*

²**hurry** *n* : extreme haste or eagerness

¹**hurt** \ˈhərt\ *vb* **hurt; hurt·ing 1** : to feel or cause to feel physical or emotional pain **2** : to do harm to : DAMAGE **3** : OFFEND **4** : HAMPER **5** : to be in need — usu. used with *for* — **hurt** *adj*

²**hurt** *n* **1** : a bodily injury or wound **2** : SUFFERING **3** : HARM, WRONG — **hurt·ful** *adj* — **hurt·ful·ness** *n*

hur·tle \ˈhər-tᵊl\ *vb* **hur·tled; hur·tling 1** : to move rapidly or forcefully **2** : HURL, FLING

¹**hus·band** \ˈhəz-bənd\ *n* [ME *husbonde*, fr. OE *hūsbonda* master of a house, fr. ON *hūsbōndi*, fr. *hūs* house + *bōndi* householder] : a male partner in a marriage

²**husband** *vb* : to manage prudently

hus·band·man \ˈhəz-bənd-mən\ *n* : FARMER

hus·band·ry \ˈhəz-bən-drē\ *n* **1** : the control or judicious use of resources **2** : AGRICULTURE **3** : the production and care of domestic animals

¹**hush** \ˈhəsh\ *vb* **1** : to make or become quiet or calm **2** : SUPPRESS

²**hush** *n* : SILENCE, QUIET

hush–hush \ˈhəsh-ˌhəsh\ *adj* : SECRET, CONFIDENTIAL

[1]**husk** \ˈhəsk\ *n* **1** : a usu. thin dry outer covering of a seed or fruit **2** : an outer layer : SHELL
[2]**husk** *vb* : to strip the husk from — **husk·er** *n*
[1]**hus·ky** \ˈhəs-kē\ *adj* **hus·ki·er; -est** : HOARSE — **hus·ki·ly** \-kə-lē\ *adv* — **hus·ki·ness** \-kē-nəs\ *n*
[2]**husky** *n, pl* **huskies** **1** : a heavy-coated working dog of the New World Arctic **2** : SIBERIAN HUSKY
[3]**husky** *adj* **1** : BURLY, ROBUST **2** : LARGE
hus·sar \(ˌ)hə-ˈzär\ *n* [Hungarian *huszár*] : a member of any of various European cavalry units
hus·sy \ˈhə-zē, -sē\ *n, pl* **hussies** [alter. of *housewife*] **1** *dated, offensive* : a promiscuous or rudely bold woman **2** : a pert or mischievous girl
hus·tings \ˈhəs-tiŋz\ *n pl* : a place where political campaign speeches are made; *also* : the proceedings in an election campaign
hus·tle \ˈhə-səl\ *vb* **hus·tled; hus·tling** **1** : JOSTLE, SHOVE **2** : HASTEN, HURRY **3** : to work energetically — **hustle** *n* — **hus·tler** \ˈhəs-lər\ *n*
hut \ˈhət\ *n* : a small and often temporary dwelling : SHACK
hutch \ˈhəch\ *n* **1** : a chest or compartment for storage **2** : a cupboard usu. surmounted with open shelves **3** : a pen or coop for an animal **4** : HUT
huz·zah *or* **huz·za** \(ˌ)hə-ˈzä\ *n* : a shout of acclaim — often used interjectionally to express joy or approbation
HV *abbr* **1** high velocity **2** high voltage
HVAC *abbr* heating, ventilating and air-conditioning
hvy *abbr* heavy
HW *abbr* hot water
hwy *abbr* highway
hy·a·cinth \ˈhī-ə-(ˌ)sinth\ *n* : a bulbous Mediterranean herb related to the lilies that is widely grown for its spikes of fragrant bell-shaped flowers
hy·brid \ˈhī-brəd\ *n* **1** : an offspring of genetically differing parents (as members of different breeds or species) **2** : one of mixed origin or composition — **hybrid** *adj* — **hy·brid·i·za·tion** \ˌhī-brə-də-ˈzā-shən\ *n* — **hy·brid·ize** \ˈhī-brə-ˌdīz\ *vb* — **hy·brid·iz·er** *n*
hy·dra \ˈhī-drə\ *n* : any of numerous small tubular freshwater coelenterates that are polyps having at one end a mouth surrounded by tentacles
hy·dran·gea \hī-ˈdrān-jə\ *n* : any of a genus of shrubs related to the currants and grown for their showy clusters of white, pink, or bluish flowers
hy·drant \ˈhī-drənt\ *n* : a pipe with a valve and spout at which water may be drawn from a main pipe
hy·drate \ˈhī-ˌdrāt\ *n* : a compound formed by union of water with some other substance — **hydrate** *vb*
hy·drau·lic \hī-ˈdrȯ-lik\ *adj* [ultim. fr. Gk *hydraulis* pipe organ using water pressure, fr. *hydōr* water + *aulos* reed instrument] **1** : operated, moved, or effected by means of water **2** : of or relating to hydraulics **3** : operated by the resistance offered or the pressure transmitted when a quantity of liquid is forced through a small orifice or through a tube **4** : hardening or setting under water
hy·drau·lics \-liks\ *n* : a science that deals with practical applications of liquid (as water) in motion
hydro \ˈhī-drō\ *n* : HYDROPOWER
hy·dro·car·bon \ˈhī-drō-ˌkär-bən\ *n* : an organic compound containing only carbon and hydrogen
hy·dro·ceph·a·lus \ˌhī-drō-ˈse-fə-ləs\ *n* : abnormal increase in the amount of fluid in the cranial cavity accompanied by enlargement of the skull and atrophy of the brain
hy·dro·chlo·ric acid \ˌhī-drə-ˈklȯr-ik-\ *n* : a sharp-smelling corrosive acid used in the laboratory and in industry and present in dilute form in gastric juice
hy·dro·dy·nam·ics \ˌhī-drō-dī-ˈna-miks\ *n* : a science that deals with the motion of fluids and the forces acting on moving bodies immersed in fluids — **hy·dro·dy·nam·ic** *adj*
hy·dro·elec·tric \ˌhī-drō-i-ˈlek-trik\ *adj* : of or relating to production of electricity by waterpower — **hy·dro·elec·tric·i·ty** \-ˌlek-ˈtri-sə-tē\ *n*
hy·dro·foil \ˈhī-drə-ˌfȯi(-ə)l\ *n* : a boat that has fins attached to the bottom by struts for lifting the hull clear of the water to allow faster speeds
hy·dro·gen \ˈhī-drə-jən\ *n* [F *hydrogène*, fr. Gk *hydōr* water + *-genēs* born; fr. the fact that water is generated by its combustion] : a gaseous colorless odorless highly flammable chemical element that is the lightest of the elements — **hy·drog·e·nous** \hī-ˈdrä-jə-nəs\ *adj*
hy·dro·ge·nate \hī-ˈdrä-jə-ˌnāt, ˈhī-drə-\ *vb* **-nat·ed; -nat·ing** : to combine or treat with hydrogen; *esp* : to add hydrogen to the molecule of — **hy·dro·ge·na·tion** \hī-ˌdrä-jə-ˈnā-shən, ˌhī-drə-\ *n*
hydrogen bomb *n* : a bomb whose violent explosive power is due to the sudden release of atomic energy resulting from the fusion of light nuclei (as of hydrogen atoms)
hydrogen peroxide *n* : an unstable compound of hydrogen and oxygen used esp. as an oxidizing and bleaching agent, an antiseptic, and a propellant
hy·dro·graph·ic \ˌhī-drə-ˈgra-fik\ *adj* : of or relating to the description and study of bodies of water — **hy·drog·ra·pher** *n* — **hy·drog·ra·phy** \hī-ˈdrä-grə-fē\ *n*
hy·drol·o·gy \hī-ˈdrä-lə-jē\ *n* : a science dealing with the properties, distribution, and circulation of water — **hy·dro·log·ic** \ˌhī-drə-ˈlä-jik\ *or* **hy·dro·log·i·cal** \-ji-kəl\ *adj* — **hy·drol·o·gist** \hī-ˈdrä-lə-jist\ *n*
hy·dro·ly·sis \hī-ˈdrä-lə-səs\ *n* : a chemical decomposition involving the addition of the elements of water
hy·drom·e·ter \hī-ˈdrä-mə-tər\ *n* : a floating instrument for determining specific

gravities of liquids and hence the strength (as of alcoholic liquors)
hy·dro·pho·bia \ˌhī-drə-ˈfō-bē-ə\ *n* [LL, fr. Gk, fr. *hydōr* water + *phobos* fear] : RABIES
hy·dro·phone \ˈhī-drə-ˌfōn\ *n* : an underwater listening device
[1]**hy·dro·plane** \ˈhī-drə-ˌplān\ *n* **1** : a powerboat designed for racing that skims the surface of the water **2** : SEAPLANE
[2]**hydroplane** *vb* : to skid on a wet road due to loss of contact between the tires and road
hy·dro·pon·ics \ˌhī-drə-ˈpä-niks\ *n* : the growing of plants in nutrient solutions — **hy·dro·pon·ic** *adj*
hy·dro·pow·er \ˈhī-drə-ˌpau̇(-ə)r\ *n* : hydroelectric power
hy·dro·sphere \ˈhī-drə-ˌsfir\ *n* : the water (as vapor or lakes) of the earth
hy·dro·stat·ic \ˌhī-drə-ˈsta-tik\ *adj* : of or relating to fluids at rest or to the pressures they exert or transmit
hy·dro·ther·a·py \ˌhī-drə-ˈther-ə-pē\ *n* : the use of water esp. externally in the treatment of disease or disability
hy·dro·ther·mal \ˌhī-drə-ˈthər-məl\ *adj* : of or relating to hot water
hy·drous \ˈhī-drəs\ *adj* : containing water
hy·drox·ide \hī-ˈdräk-ˌsīd\ *n* **1** : a negatively charged ion consisting of one atom of oxygen and one atom of hydrogen **2** : a compound of hydroxide with an element or group
hy·e·na \hī-ˈē-nə\ *n* [ME *hyene,* fr. L *hyaena,* fr. Gk *hyaina,* fr. *hys* hog] : any of several large doglike carnivorous mammals of Asia and Africa
hyg·ge \ˈhyü-gə, ˈhü-, ˈhu̇-\ *n* [Danish] : a cozy quality that makes one feel content
hy·giene \ˈhī-ˌjēn\ *n* **1** : a science concerned with establishing and maintaining good health **2** : conditions or practices conducive to health — **hy·gien·ic** \hī-ˈjenik, -ˈjē-\ *adj* — **hy·gien·i·cal·ly** \-ni-k(ə-)lē\ *adv* — **hy·gien·ist** \hī-ˈjē-nist, ˈhī-ˌjē-, hī-ˈje-\ *n*
hy·grom·e·ter \hī-ˈgrä-mə-tər\ *n* : any of several instruments for measuring the humidity of the atmosphere
hy·gro·scop·ic \ˌhī-grə-ˈskä-pik\ *adj* : readily taking up and retaining moisture
hying *pres part of* HIE
hy·men \ˈhī-mən\ *n* : a fold of mucous membrane partly closing the opening of the vagina
hy·me·ne·al \ˌhī-mə-ˈnē-əl\ *adj* : NUPTIAL
hymn \ˈhim\ *n* : a song of praise esp. to God — **hymn** *vb*
hym·nal \ˈhim-nəl\ *n* : a book of hymns
hyp *abbr* hypothesis; hypothetical
[1]**hype** \ˈhīp\ *vb* **hyped; hyp·ing** **1** : STIMULATE — usu. used with *up* **2** : INCREASE — **hyped–up** *adj*
[2]**hype** *vb* **hyped; hyping** **1** : DECEIVE **2** : PUBLICIZE
[3]**hype** *n* **1** : DECEPTION, PUT-ON **2** : PUBLICITY
hy·per \ˈhī-pər\ *adj* **1** : HIGH-STRUNG, EXCITABLE **2** : extremely active
hy·per·acid·i·ty \ˌhī-pər-ə-ˈsi-də-tē\ *n* : the condition of containing excessive acid esp. in the stomach — **hy·per·ac·id** \-ˈa-səd\ *adj*
hy·per·ac·tive \-ˈak-tiv\ *adj* : excessively or pathologically active — **hy·per·ac·tiv·i·ty** \-ˌak-ˈti-və-tē\ *n*
hy·per·bar·ic \ˌhī-pər-ˈber-ik\ *adj* : of, relating to, or utilizing greater than normal pressure (as of oxygen)
hy·per·bo·la \hī-ˈpər-bə-lə\ *n, pl* **-las** *or* **-lae** \-(ˌ)lē\ : a curve formed by the intersection of a double right circular cone with a plane that cuts both halves of the cone — **hy·per·bol·ic** \ˌhī-pər-ˈbä-lik\ *adj*
hy·per·bo·le \hī-ˈpər-bə-(ˌ)lē\ *n* : extravagant exaggeration used as a figure of speech
hy·per·crit·i·cal \ˌhī-pər-ˈkri-ti-kəl\ *adj* : excessively critical — **hy·per·crit·i·cal·ly** \-k(ə-)lē\ *adv*
hy·per·drive \ˈhī-pər-ˌdrīv\ *n* : a state of extremely heightened activity
hy·per·ex·tend \ˌhī-pər-ik-ˈstend\ *vb* : to extend beyond the normal range of motion — **hy·per·ex·ten·sion** \-ˈsten-shən\ *n*
hy·per·gly·ce·mia \ˌhī-pər-glī-ˈsē-mē-ə\ *n* : excess of sugar in the blood — **hy·per·gly·ce·mic** \-mik\ *adj*
hy·per·ki·net·ic \-kə-ˈne-tik\ *adj* : characterized by fast-paced or frenetic activity
hy·per·link \ˈhī-pər-ˌliŋk\ *n* : a connecting element (as highlighted text) between one place in a hypertext or hypermedia document and another
hy·per·me·dia \ˈhī-pər-ˌmē-dē-ə\ *n* : a database format offering direct access to text, sound, or images related to that on display
hy·per·opia \ˌhī-pə-ˈrō-pē-ə\ *n* : a condition in which visual images come to focus behind the retina resulting esp. in defective vision for near objects — **hy·per·opic** \-ˈrō-pik, -ˈrä-\ *adj*
hy·per·sen·si·tive \-ˈsen-sə-tiv\ *adj* **1** : excessively or abnormally sensitive **2** : abnormally susceptible physiologically to a specific agent (as a drug) — **hy·per·sen·si·tive·ness** *n* — **hy·per·sen·si·tiv·i·ty** \-ˌsen-sə-ˈti-və-tē\ *n*
hy·per·ten·sion \ˈhī-pər-ˌten-chən\ *n* : high blood pressure — **hy·per·ten·sive** \ˌhī-pər-ˈten-siv\ *adj or n*
hy·per·text \ˈhī-pər-ˌtekst\ *n* : a database format in which information related to that on display can be accessed directly from the display
hy·per·thy·roid·ism \ˌhī-pər-ˈthī-ˌrȯi-ˌdi-zəm\ *n* : excessive activity of the thyroid gland; *also* : the resulting bodily condition — **hy·per·thy·roid** \-ˈthī-ˌrȯid\ *adj*
hy·per·tro·phy \hī-ˈpər-trə-fē\ *n, pl* **-phies** : excessive development of a body part — **hy·per·tro·phic** \ˌhī-pər-ˈtrō-fik\ *adj* — **hypertrophy** *vb*
hy·per·ven·ti·late \ˌhī-pər-ˈven-tə-ˌlāt\ *vb* : to breathe rapidly and deeply esp. to the point of losing an abnormal amount of carbon dioxide from the blood —

hy·per·ven·ti·la·tion \-ˌven-tə-ˈlā-shən\ *n*
hy·phen \ˈhī-fən\ *n* : a punctuation mark - used esp. to divide or to compound words or word parts — **hyphen** *vb*
hy·phen·ate \ˈhī-fə-ˌnāt\ *vb* **-at·ed; -at·ing** : to connect or divide with a hyphen — **hy·phen·ation** \ˌhī-fə-ˈnā-shən\ *n*
hyp·no·sis \hip-ˈnō-səs\ *n, pl* **-no·ses** \-ˌsēz\ : an induced state that resembles sleep and in which the subject is responsive to suggestions of the inducer (**hyp·no·tist** \ˈhip-nə-tist\) — **hyp·no·tism** \ˈhip-nə-ˌti-zəm\ *n* — **hyp·no·tiz·able** \ˈhip-nə-ˌtī-zə-bəl\ *adj* — **hyp·no·tize** \-ˌtīz\ *vb*
¹**hyp·not·ic** \hip-ˈnä-tik\ *adj* **1** : inducing sleep : SOPORIFIC **2** : of or relating to hypnosis or hypnotism **3** : readily holding the attention — **hyp·not·i·cal·ly** \-ti-k(ə-)lē\ *adv*
²**hypnotic** *n* : a sleep-inducing drug
hy·po \ˈhī-pō\ *n, pl* **hypos** : SODIUM THIOSULFATE; *also* : a solution of sodium thiosulfate
hy·po·al·ler·gen·ic \ˌhī-pō-ˌa-lər-ˈje-nik\ *adj* : having little likelihood of causing an allergic response
hy·po·cen·ter \ˈhī-pə-ˌsen-tər\ *n* : the point of origin of an earthquake
hy·po·chon·dria \ˌhī-pə-ˈkän-drē-ə\ *n* [NL, fr. LL, pl., upper abdomen (formerly regarded as the seat of hypochondria), fr. Gk, lit., the parts under the cartilage (of the breastbone), fr. *hypo-* under + *chondros* cartilage] : excessive concern about one's health esp. accompanied by imagined physical ailments — **hy·po·chon·dri·ac** \-drē-ˌak\ *adj or n*
hy·poc·ri·sy \hi-ˈpä-krə-sē\ *n, pl* **-sies** : a feigning to be what one is not or to believe what one does not; *esp* : the false assumption of an appearance of virtue or religion — **hyp·o·crite** \ˈhi-pə-ˌkrit\ *n* — **hyp·o·crit·i·cal** \ˌhi-pə-ˈkri-ti-kəl\ *adj* — **hyp·o·crit·i·cal·ly** \-k(ə-)lē\ *adv*
¹**hy·po·der·mic** \ˌhī-pə-ˈdər-mik\ *adj* : administered by or used in making an injection beneath the skin
²**hypodermic** *n* : HYPODERMIC SYRINGE; *also* : an injection made with this
hypodermic needle *n* : NEEDLE 3; *also* : HYPODERMIC SYRINGE
hypodermic syringe *n* : a small syringe with a hollow needle for injecting material into or through the skin
hy·po·gly·ce·mia \ˌhī-pō-glī-ˈsē-mē-ə\ *n* : abnormal decrease of sugar in the blood — **hy·po·gly·ce·mic** \-mik\ *adj*
hy·pot·e·nuse \hī-ˈpä-tə-ˌnüs, -ˌnyüs, -ˌnüz, -ˌnyüz\ *n* : the side of a right triangle that is opposite the right angle; *also* : its length
hy·po·thal·a·mus \ˌhī-pō-ˈtha-lə-məs\ *n* : a part of the brain that lies beneath the thalamus and is a control center for the autonomic nervous system
hy·poth·e·sis \hī-ˈpä-thə-səs\ *n, pl* **-e·ses** \-ˌsēz\ : an assumption made esp. in order to test its logical or empirical consequences — **hy·po·thet·i·cal** \ˌhī-pə-ˈthe-ti-kəl\ *adj* — **hy·po·thet·i·cal·ly** \-k(ə-)lē\ *adv*
hy·poth·e·size \-ˌsīz\ *vb* **-sized; -siz·ing** : to adopt as a hypothesis
hy·po·thy·roid·ism \ˌhī-pō-ˈthī-ˌrȯi-ˌdi-zəm\ *n* : deficient activity of the thyroid gland; *also* : a resultant lowered metabolic rate and general loss of vigor — **hy·po·thy·roid** *adj*
hys·sop \ˈhi-səp\ *n* : a European mint sometimes used as a potherb
hys·ter·ec·to·my \ˌhis-tə-ˈrek-tə-mē\ *n, pl* **-mies** : surgical removal of the uterus
hys·te·ria \hi-ˈster-ē-ə, -ˈstir-\ *n* [NL, fr. E *hysteric,* adj., fr. L *hystericus,* fr. Gk *hysterikos,* fr. *hystera* womb; fr. the Greek notion that hysteria was peculiar to women and caused by disturbances in the uterus] **1** : a nervous disorder marked esp. by defective emotional control **2** : unmanageable fear or outburst of emotion — **hys·ter·ic** \-ˈster-ik\ *n* — **hys·ter·i·cal** \-ˈster-i-kəl\ *also* **hysteric** *adj* — **hys·ter·i·cal·ly** \-k(ə-)lē\ *adv*
hys·ter·ics \-ˈster-iks\ *n pl* : a fit of uncontrollable laughter or crying
Hz *abbr* hertz

I

¹**i** \ˈī\ *n, pl* **i's** *or* **is** \ˈīz\ *often cap* : the 9th letter of the English alphabet
²**i** *abbr, often cap* island; isle
³**i** *symbol* imaginary unit
¹**I** \ˈī, ə\ *pron* : the one speaking or writing
²**I** *abbr* interstate
³**I** *symbol* iodine
Ia *or* **IA** *abbr* Iowa
-ial *adj suffix* : ¹-AL ⟨manorial⟩
iamb \ˈī-ˌam\ *or* **iam·bus** \ī-ˈam-bəs\ *n, pl* **iambs** \ˈī-ˌamz\ *or* **iam·bus·es** : a metrical foot of one unaccented syllable followed by one accented syllable — **iam·bic** \ī-ˈam-bik\ *adj or n*
-ian — see -AN
-iatric *also* **-iatrical** *adj comb form* : of or relating to (such) medical treatment or healing ⟨ped*iatric*⟩
-iatrics *n pl comb form* : medical treatment ⟨ped*iatrics*⟩
ib *or* **ibid** *abbr* ibidem
ibex \ˈī-ˌbeks\ *n, pl* **ibex** *or* **ibex·es** [L] : any of several Old World wild goats with large curved horns
ibi·dem \ˈi-bə-ˌdem, i-ˈbī-dəm\ *adv* [L] : in the same place
-ibility — see -ABILITY
ibis \ˈī-bəs\ *n, pl* **ibis** *or* **ibis·es** [L, fr. Gk,

fr. Egyptian *hbw*] : any of various wading birds related to the herons but having a downwardly curved bill

-ible — see -ABLE

ibu·pro·fen \ˌī-byu̇-ˈprō-fən\ *n* : a nonsteroidal anti-inflammatory drug used to relieve pain and fever

IC \ˌī-ˈsē\ *n* : INTEGRATED CIRCUIT

[1]**-ic** *adj suffix* **1** : of, relating to, or having the form of : being ⟨panoram*ic*⟩ **2** : related to, derived from, or containing ⟨alcohol*ic*⟩ **3** : in the manner of : like that of : characteristic of **4** : associated or dealing with : utilizing ⟨electron*ic*⟩ **5** : characterized by : exhibiting ⟨nostalg*ic*⟩ : affected with ⟨aller*gic*⟩ **6** : caused by **7** : tending to produce ⟨analges*ic*⟩

[2]**-ic** *n suffix* : one having the character or nature of : one belonging to or associated with : one exhibiting or affected by : one that produces

-ical *adj suffix* : -IC ⟨symmetr*ical*⟩ ⟨geolog*ical*⟩ — **-ically** *adv suffix*

ICBM \ˌī-ˌsē-(ˌ)bē-ˈem\ *n, pl* **ICBM's** *or* **ICBMs** \-ˈemz\ : an intercontinental ballistic missile

ICC *abbr* Interstate Commerce Commission

[1]**ice** \ˈīs\ *n* **1** : frozen water **2** : a substance resembling ice **3** : a state of coldness (as from formality or reserve) **4** : a flavored frozen dessert; *esp* : one containing no milk or cream

[2]**ice** *vb* **iced; ic·ing 1** : FREEZE **2** : CHILL **3** : to cover with or as if with icing

ice age *n* : a time of widespread glaciation

ice bag *n* : a waterproof bag to hold ice for local application of cold to the body

ice·berg \ˈīs-ˌbərg\ *n* : a large floating mass of ice broken off from a glacier

iceberg lettuce *n* : any of various crisp light green lettuces that form a compact head like a cabbage

ice·boat \ˈīs-ˌbōt\ *n* : a boatlike frame on runners propelled on ice by sails

ice·bound \-ˌbau̇nd\ *adj* : surrounded, obstructed, or covered by ice

ice·box \-ˌbäks\ *n* : REFRIGERATOR

ice·break·er \-ˌbrā-kər\ *n* : a ship equipped (as with a reinforced bow) to make a channel through ice

ice cap *n* : a glacier forming on relatively level land and flowing outward from its center

ice cream *n* : a frozen food containing sweetened or flavored cream or butterfat

ice hockey *n* : a game in which two teams of ice-skating players try to shoot a puck into the opponent's goal

ice·house \ˈīs-ˌhau̇s\ *n* : a building in which ice is made or stored

[1]**Ice·lan·dic** \īs-ˈlan-dik\ *adj* : of, relating to, or characteristic of Iceland, the Icelanders, or their language

[2]**Icelandic** *n* : the language of Iceland

ice·man \ˈīs-ˌman\ *n* : one who sells or delivers ice

ice milk *n* : a sweetened frozen food made of skim milk

ice pick *n* : a hand tool ending in a spike for chipping ice

ice–skate \ˈīs-ˌskāt\ *vb* : to skate on ice — **ice–skater** *n*

ice storm *n* : a storm in which falling rain freezes on contact

ice water *n* : chilled or iced water esp. for drinking

ich·thy·ol·o·gy \ˌik-thē-ˈä-lə-jē\ *n* : a branch of zoology dealing with fishes — **ich·thy·ol·o·gist** \-jist\ *n*

ici·cle \ˈī-ˌsi-kəl\ *n* [ME *isikel,* fr. *is* ice + *ikel* icicle, fr. OE *gicel*] : a hanging mass of ice formed by the freezing of dripping water

ic·ing \ˈī-siŋ\ *n* : a sweet usu. creamy mixture used to coat baked goods

ICJ *abbr* International Court of Justice

icky \ˈi-kē\ *adj* **ick·i·er; -est** : OFFENSIVE, DISTASTEFUL — **ick·i·ness** *n*

icon *also* **ikon** \ˈī-ˌkän\ *n* **1** : IMAGE; *esp* : a religious image painted on a wood panel **2** : a widely admired person or thing **3** : a small picture on a computer display that suggests the purpose of an available function — **icon·ic** \ī-ˈkä-nik\ *adj*

icon·o·clasm \ī-ˈkä-nə-ˌkla-zəm\ *n* : the doctrine, practice, or attitude of an iconoclast

icon·o·clast \-ˌklast\ *n* [ML *iconoclastes,* fr. MGk *eikonoklastēs,* lit., image destroyer, fr. Gk *eikōn* image + *klan* to break] **1** : one who destroys religious images or opposes their veneration **2** : one who attacks cherished beliefs or institutions

-ics \iks\ *n sing or pl suffix* **1** : study : knowledge : skill : practice ⟨linguist*ics*⟩ ⟨electron*ics*⟩ **2** : characteristic actions or activities ⟨acrobat*ics*⟩ **3** : characteristic qualities, operations, or phenomena ⟨mechan*ics*⟩

ic·tus \ˈik-təs\ *n* : the recurring stress or beat in a rhythmic or metrical series of sounds

ICU *abbr* intensive care unit

icy \ˈī-sē\ *adj* **ic·i·er; -est 1** : covered with, abounding in, or consisting of ice **2** : intensely cold **3** : being cold and unfriendly — **ic·i·ly** \ˈī-sə-lē\ *adv* — **ic·i·ness** \-sē-nəs\ *n*

[1]**id** \ˈid\ *n* [L, it] : the part of the psyche in psychoanalytic theory that is completely unconscious and concerned with instinctual needs and drives

[2]**id** *abbr* idem

[1]**ID** \ˈī-ˈdē\ *n* : a document with identifying information about an individual whose name appears on it

[2]**ID** *vb* **ID'd** *or* **IDed; ID'ing** *or* **IDing** : IDENTIFY

[3]**ID** *abbr* **1** Idaho **2** identification

idea \ī-ˈdē-ə\ *n* **1** : a plan for action : DESIGN **2** : something imagined or pictured in the mind **3** : a central meaning or purpose ♦ ***Synonyms*** CONCEPT, CONCEPTION, NOTION, IMPRESSION

[1]**ide·al** \ī-ˈdēl\ *adj* **1** : existing only in the mind : IMAGINARY; *also* : lacking practicality **2** : of or relating to an ideal or to perfection : PERFECT

[2]**ideal** *n* 1 : a standard of excellence 2 : one regarded as a model worthy of imitation 3 : GOAL ♦ ***Synonyms*** ARCHETYPE, EXAMPLE, EXEMPLAR, PARADIGM, PATTERN
ide·al·ise *Brit var of* IDEALIZE
ide·al·ism \ī-ˈdē-ə-ˌli-zəm\ *n* : the practice of forming ideals or living under their influence; *also* : an idealized representation — **ide·al·ist** \-list\ *n* — **ide·al·is·tic** \ī-ˌdē-ə-ˈlis-tik\ *adj* — **ide·al·is·ti·cal·ly** \-ti-k(ə-)lē\ *adv*
ide·al·ize \ī-ˈdē-ə-ˌlīz\ *vb* **-ized; -iz·ing** : to think of or represent as ideal — **ide·al·i·za·tion** \-ˌdē-ə-lə-ˈzā-shən\ *n*
ide·al·ly \ī-ˈdē-lē, -ˈdē-ə-lē\ *adv* 1 : in idea or imagination : MENTALLY 2 : in agreement with an ideal : PERFECTLY
ide·a·tion \ˌī-dē-ˈā-shən\ *n* : the forming or entertaining of ideas — **ide·ate** \ˈī-dē-ˌāt\ *vb* — **ide·a·tion·al** \ˌī-dē-ˈā-shə-nəl\ *adj*
idem \ˈī-ˌdem, ˈē-, ˈi-\ *pron* [L, same] : the same as something previously mentioned
iden·ti·cal \ī-ˈden-ti-kəl\ *adj* 1 : being the same 2 : essentially alike ♦ ***Synonyms*** EQUIVALENT, EQUAL, TANTAMOUNT
iden·ti·fi·ca·tion \ī-ˌden-tə-fə-ˈkā-shən\ *n* 1 : an act of identifying : the state of being identified 2 : evidence of identity 3 : an unconscious psychological process by which an individual models thoughts, feelings, and actions after another person or an object
iden·ti·fy \ī-ˈden-tə-ˌfī\ *vb* **-fied; -fy·ing** 1 : to regard as identical 2 : ASSOCIATE 3 : to establish the identity of 4 : to practice psychological identification — **iden·ti·fi·able** \-ˌden-tə-ˈfī-ə-bəl\ *adj* — **iden·ti·fi·ably** \-blē\ *adv* — **iden·ti·fi·er** \-ˌfī(-ə)r\ *n*
iden·ti·ty \ī-ˈden-tə-tē\ *n, pl* **-ties** 1 : sameness of essential character 2 : INDIVIDUALITY 3 : the fact of being the same person or thing as claimed
identity crisis *n* : psychological conflict esp. in adolescence involving confusion about one's social role and one's personality
identity theft *n* : the illegal use of someone else's personal information to obtain money or credit
ideo·gram \ˈī-dē-ə-ˌgram, ˈi-\ *n* 1 : a picture or symbol used in a system of writing to represent a thing or an idea 2 : a character or symbol used in a system of writing to represent an entire word
ideo·logue *also* **idea·logue** \ˈī-dē-ə-ˌlȯg\ *n* : a partisan advocate or adherent of a particular ideology
ide·ol·o·gy \ˌī-dē-ˈä-lə-jē, ˌi-\ *also* **ide·al·o·gy** \-ˈä-lə-jē, -ˈa-\ *n, pl* **-gies** 1 : the body of ideas characteristic of a particular individual, group, or culture 2 : the assertions, theories, and aims that constitute a political, social, and economic program — **ide·o·log·i·cal** \ˌī-dē-ə-ˈlä-ji-kəl, ˌi-\ *adj* — **ideo·log·i·cal·ly** \-ˈlä-ji-k(ə-)lē\ *adv* — **ide·ol·o·gist** \-dē-ˈä-lə-jist\ *n*
ides \ˈīdz\ *n sing or pl* : the 15th day of March, May, July, or October or the 13th day of any other month in the ancient Roman calendar
id·i·o·cy \ˈi-dē-ə-sē\ *n, pl* **-cies** 1 : something notably stupid or foolish 2 *dated, now offensive* : extreme intellectual disability
id·i·om \ˈi-dē-əm\ *n* 1 : the language peculiar to a person or group 2 : the characteristic form or structure of a language 3 : an expression that cannot be understood from the meanings of its separate words (as *give way*) — **id·i·o·mat·ic** \ˌi-dē-ə-ˈma-tik\ *adj* — **id·i·o·mat·i·cal·ly** \-ti-k(ə-)lē\ *adv*
id·i·o·path·ic \ˌi-dē-ə-ˈpa-thik\ *adj* : arising spontaneously or from an obscure or unknown cause ⟨an ~ disease⟩
id·i·o·syn·cra·sy \ˌi-dē-ə-ˈsiŋ-krə-sē\ *n, pl* **-sies** : personal peculiarity — **id·i·o·syn·crat·ic** \ˌi-dē-ō-sin-ˈkra-tik\ *adj* — **id·i·o·syn·crat·i·cal·ly** \-ˈkra-ti-k(ə-)lē\ *adv*
id·i·ot \ˈi-dē-ət\ *n* [ME, fr. AF *ydiote,* fr. L *idiota* ignorant person, fr. Gk *idiōtēs* one in a private station, layman, ignorant person, fr. *idios* one's own, private] 1 : a foolish or stupid person 2 *dated, now offensive* : a person affected with extreme intellectual disability — **id·i·ot·ic** \ˌi-dē-ˈä-tik\ *adj* — **id·i·ot·i·cal·ly** \-ti-k(ə-)lē\ *adv*
id·i·ot·proof \ˈi-dē-ət-ˌprüf\ *adj* : extremely easy to operate or maintain
IDK *abbr* I don't know
[1]**idle** \ˈī-dᵊl\ *adj* **idler** \ˈī-də-lər\; **idlest** \ˈī-də-ləst\ 1 : GROUNDLESS, WORTHLESS, USELESS ⟨~ talk⟩ 2 : not occupied or employed : INACTIVE 3 : LAZY — **idleness** *n* — **idly** \ˈīd-lē\ *adv*
[2]**idle** *vb* **idled; idling** 1 : to spend time doing nothing 2 : to make idle 3 : to run without being connected so that power is not used for useful work — **idler** *n*
idol \ˈī-dᵊl\ *n* 1 : an image worshipped as a god; *also* : a false god 2 : an object of passionate devotion ⟨a sports ~⟩
idol·a·ter *or* **idol·a·tor** \ī-ˈdä-lə-tər\ *n* : a worshiper of idols
idol·a·try \-trē\ *n, pl* **-tries** 1 : the worship of a physical object as a god 2 : excessive devotion — **idol·a·trous** \-trəs\ *adj*
idol·ize \ˈī-də-ˌlīz\ *vb* **-ized; -iz·ing** : to make an idol of ⟨*idolized* his father⟩ — **idol·i·za·tion** \ˌī-də-lə-ˈzā-shən\ *n*
idyll \ˈī-dᵊl\ *n* 1 : a simple work of writing or poetry that describes country life or suggests a peaceful setting 2 : a fit subject for an idyll — **idyl·lic** \ī-ˈdi-lik\ *adj*
i.e. \ˈī-ˈē\ *abbr* [L *id est*] that is
IE *abbr* industrial engineer
IED *abbr* improvised explosive device
-ier — see -ER
if \ˈif\ *conj* 1 : in the event that ⟨~ he stays, I leave⟩ 2 : WHETHER ⟨ask ~ he left⟩ 3 — used as a function word to introduce an exclamation expressing a wish ⟨~ it would only rain⟩ 4 : even though ⟨an interesting ~ untenable argument⟩ 5 : and perhaps not even ⟨few ~ any changes are expected⟩
IF *abbr* intermediate frequency

if·fy \ˈi-fē\ *adj* : full of contingencies or unknown conditions

-i·fy \ə-ˌfī\ *vb suffix* : -FY

IG *abbr* inspector general

ig·loo \ˈi-glü\ *n, pl* **igloos** [Inuit *iglu* house] : a house or hut that is often made of snow blocks and in the shape of a dome and that is associated esp. with indigenous peoples of arctic regions

ig·ne·ous \ˈig-nē-əs\ *adj* **1** : FIERY **2** : formed by solidification of molten rock

ig·nite \ig-ˈnīt\ *vb* **ig·nit·ed; ig·nit·ing** : to set afire or catch fire — **ig·nit·able** \-ˈnī-tə-bəl\ *adj*

ig·ni·tion \ig-ˈni-shən\ *n* **1** : a setting on fire **2** : the process or means (as an electric spark) of igniting the fuel mixture in an engine **3** : a device that activates an ignition system

ig·no·ble \ig-ˈnō-bəl\ *adj* **1** : of common birth **2** : not honorable : BASE, MEAN ♦ ***Synonyms*** DESPICABLE, SCURVY, SORDID, VILE, WRETCHED — **ig·no·bly** *adv*

ig·no·min·i·ous \ˌig-nə-ˈmi-nē-əs\ *adj* **1** : DISHONORABLE **2** : DESPICABLE **3** : HUMILIATING, DEGRADING ♦ ***Synonyms*** DISREPUTABLE, DISCREDITABLE, DISGRACEFUL, INGLORIOUS — **ig·no·min·i·ous·ly** *adv* — **ig·no·mi·ny** \ˈig-nə-ˌmi-nē, ig-ˈnä-mə-nē\ *n*

ig·no·ra·mus \ˌig-nə-ˈrā-məs\ *n, pl* **-mus·es** *also* **-mi** \-mē\ [*Ignoramus,* ignorant lawyer in *Ignoramus* (1615), play by George Ruggle] : an utterly ignorant person

ig·no·rance \ˈig-nə-rəns\ *n* : the state of being ignorant

ig·no·rant \ˈig-nə-rənt\ *adj* **1** : lacking knowledge **2** : resulting from or showing lack of knowledge or intelligence **3** : UNAWARE, UNINFORMED ♦ ***Synonyms*** BENIGHTED, ILLITERATE, UNEDUCATED, UNLETTERED, UNTUTORED — **ig·no·rant·ly** *adv*

ig·nore \ig-ˈnōr\ *vb* **ig·nored; ig·nor·ing** : to refuse to take notice of ♦ ***Synonyms*** OVERLOOK, SLIGHT, NEGLECT

igua·na \i-ˈgwä-nə\ *n* : any of various large tropical American lizards

ihp *abbr* indicated horsepower

IHS \ˌī-ˌāch-ˈes\ [LL, part transliteration of Gk ΙΗΣ, abbr. for ΙΗΣΟΥΣ *Iēsous* Jesus] — used as a Christian symbol and monogram for *Jesus*

ikon *var of* ICON

IL *abbr* Illinois

il·e·itis \ˌi-lē-ˈī-təs\ *n* : inflammation of the ileum

il·e·um \ˈi-lē-əm\ *n, pl* **il·ea** \-lē-ə\ : the part of the small intestine between the jejunum and the large intestine

il·i·ac \ˈi-lē-ˌak\ *adj* : of, relating to, or located near the ilium

il·i·um \ˈi-lē-əm\ *n, pl* **il·ia** \-lē-ə\ : the uppermost and largest of the three bones making up either side of the pelvis

ilk \ˈilk\ *n* : SORT, KIND

[1]**ill** \ˈil\ *adj* **worse** \ˈwərs\; **worst** \ˈwərst\ **1** : attended or caused by an evil intent ⟨~ deeds⟩ **2** : not normal or sound ⟨~ health⟩; *also* : not in good health : SICK **3** : BAD, UNLUCKY ⟨an ~ omen⟩ **4** : not right or proper ⟨~ manners⟩ **5** : UNFRIENDLY, HOSTILE ⟨~ feeling⟩

[2]**ill** *adv* **worse; worst** **1** : with displeasure **2** : in a harsh manner **3** : HARDLY, SCARCELY ⟨can ~ afford it⟩ **4** : BADLY, UNLUCKILY **5** : in a faulty way

[3]**ill** *n* **1** : EVIL **2** : MISFORTUNE, DISTRESS **3** : AILMENT, SICKNESS; *also* : TROUBLE

[4]**ill** *abbr* illustrated; illustration; illustrator

Ill *abbr* Illinois

ill–ad·vised \ˌil-əd-ˈvīzd\ *adj* : not well counseled ⟨~ efforts⟩ — **ill–ad·vis·ed·ly** \-ˈvī-zəd-lē\ *adv*

ill–bred \-ˈbred\ *adj* : badly brought up : IMPOLITE ⟨an ~ child⟩

il·le·gal \il-ˈlē-gəl\ *adj* : not lawful; *also* : not sanctioned by official rules ♦ ***Synonyms*** UNLAWFUL, CRIMINAL, ILLEGITIMATE, ILLICIT, WRONGFUL — **il·le·gal·i·ty** \ˌi-li-ˈga-lə-tē\ *n* — **il·le·gal·ly** *adv*

il·leg·i·ble \il-ˈle-jə-bəl\ *adj* : not legible — **il·leg·i·bil·i·ty** \il-ˌle-jə-ˈbi-lə-tē\ *n* — **il·leg·i·bly** \il-ˈle-jə-blē\ *adv*

il·le·git·i·mate \ˌi-li-ˈji-tə-mət\ *adj* **1** : born of unmarried parents **2** : ILLOGICAL **3** : ILLEGAL — **il·le·git·i·ma·cy** \-ˈji-tə-mə-sē\ *n* — **il·le·git·i·mate·ly** *adv*

ill–fat·ed \ˈil-ˈfā-təd\ *adj* : UNFORTUNATE ⟨an ~ expedition⟩

ill–fa·vored \-ˈfā-vərd\ *adj* : UGLY, UNATTRACTIVE

ill–got·ten \-ˈgä-tᵊn\ *adj* : acquired by improper means ⟨~ gains⟩

ill–hu·mored \-ˈhyü-mərd, -ˈyü-\ *adj* : SURLY, IRRITABLE

il·lib·er·al \il-ˈli-bə-rəl\ *adj* : not liberal : NARROW, BIGOTED

il·lic·it \il-ˈli-sət\ *adj* : not permitted : UNLAWFUL — **il·lic·it·ly** *adv*

il·lim·it·able \il-ˈli-mə-tə-bəl\ *adj* : BOUNDLESS, MEASURELESS — **il·lim·it·ably** \-blē\ *adv*

Il·li·nois \ˌi-lə-ˈnȯi *also* -ˈnȯiz\ *n, pl* **Illinois** : a member of a confederation of Indigenous people of Illinois, Iowa, and Wisconsin; *also* : their language

il·lit·er·ate \il-ˈli-tə-rət\ *adj* **1** : having little or no education; *esp* : unable to read or write **2** : showing a lack of familiarity with the fundamentals of a particular field of knowledge — **il·lit·er·a·cy** \-ˈli-tə-rə-sē\ *n* — **illiterate** *n*

ill–man·nered \ˈil-ˈma-nərd\ *adj* : marked by bad manners : RUDE

ill–na·tured \-ˈnā-chərd\ *adj* : CROSS, SURLY — **ill–na·tured·ly** *adv*

ill·ness \ˈil-nəs\ *n* : SICKNESS

il·log·i·cal \il-ˈlä-ji-kəl\ *adj* : lacking sound reasoning; *also* : SENSELESS — **il·log·i·cal·ly** \-ji-k(ə-)lē\ *adv*

ill–starred \ˈil-ˈstärd\ *adj* : UNLUCKY 1

ill–tem·pered \-ˈtem-pərd\ *adj* : CROSS

ill–treat \-ˈtrēt\ *vb* : to treat cruelly or improperly : MALTREAT — **ill–treat·ment** *n*

il·lu·mi·nate \i-ˈlü-mə-ˌnāt\ *vb* **-nat·ed; -nat·ing** **1** : to supply or brighten with light : light up **2** : to make clear : ELUCI-

DATE; *also* : to bring to the fore **3** : to decorate (as a manuscript) with designs or pictures in gold or colors — **il·lu·mi·nat·ing·ly** *adv* — **il·lu·mi·na·tion** \-ˌlü-mə-ˈnā-shən\ *n* — **il·lu·mi·na·tor** \-ˈlü-mə-ˌnā-tər\ *n*

il·lu·mine \i-ˈlü-mən\ *vb* **-mined; -min·ing** : ILLUMINATE

ill–us·age \ˈil-ˈyü-sij\ *n* : harsh, unkind, or abusive treatment

ill–use \-ˈyüz\ *vb* : MALTREAT, ABUSE

il·lu·sion \i-ˈlü-zhən\ *n* [ME, fr. AF, fr. LL *illusio,* fr. L, action of mocking, fr. *illudere* to mock at, fr. *ludere* to play, mock] **1** : a mistaken idea : MISCONCEPTION **2** : a misleading visual image; *also* : HALLUCINATION

il·lu·sion·ist \i-ˈlü-zhə-nist\ *n* : one that produces illusions; *esp* : a sleight-of-hand performer

il·lu·sive \i-ˈlü-siv\ *adj* : DECEPTIVE

il·lu·so·ry \i-ˈlü-sə-rē, -zə-\ *adj* : DECEPTIVE ⟨~ hopes⟩

illust *or* **illus** *abbr* illustrated; illustration

il·lus·trate \ˈi-ləs-ˌtrāt\ *vb* **-trat·ed; -trat·ing** [L *illustrare,* fr. *lustrare* to purify, make bright] **1** : to explain by use of examples : CLARIFY; *also* : DEMONSTRATE **2** : to provide with pictures or figures that explain or decorate **3** : to serve to explain or decorate — **il·lus·tra·tor** \ˈi-lə-ˌstrā-tər\ *n*

il·lus·tra·tion \ˌi-lə-ˈstrā-shən\ *n* **1** : the act of illustrating : the condition of being illustrated **2** : an example or instance that helps make something clear **3** : a picture or diagram that explains or decorates

il·lus·tra·tive \i-ˈləs-trə-tiv, ˈi-lə-ˌstrā-\ *adj* : serving, tending, or designed to illustrate — **il·lus·tra·tive·ly** *adv*

il·lus·tri·ous \i-ˈləs-trē-əs\ *adj* : notably outstanding because of rank or achievement ♦ ***Synonyms*** DISTINGUISHED, EMINENT, FAMOUS, GREAT, NOTABLE, PROMINENT — **il·lus·tri·ous·ness** *n*

ill will *n* : unfriendly feeling

ILS *abbr* instrument landing system

¹**IM** \ˈī-ˈem\ *vb* **IM'd; IM'ing** **1** : to send an instant message to **2** : to communicate by instant message

²**IM** *abbr* instant message

¹**im·age** \ˈi-mij\ *n* **1** : a likeness or imitation of a person or thing; *esp* : STATUE **2** : a picture of an object formed by a device (as a mirror or lens) **3** : a visual representation of something ⟨a computer ~⟩ **4** a person strikingly like another person ⟨he is the ~ of his father⟩ **5** : a mental picture or conception : IMPRESSION, IDEA, CONCEPT **6** : a vivid representation or description

²**image** *vb* **im·aged; im·ag·ing** **1** : to call up a mental picture of **2** : to describe or portray in words **3** : to create a representation of **4** : REFLECT, MIRROR **5** : to make appear : PROJECT

im·ag·ery \ˈi-mij-rē\ *n, pl* **-er·ies** **1** : IMAGES; *also* : the art of making images **2** : figurative language **3** : mental images; *esp* : the products of imagination

imag·in·able \i-ˈma-jə-nə-bəl\ *adj* : capable of being imagined : CONCEIVABLE — **imag·in·ably** *adv*

imag·i·nary \i-ˈma-jə-ˌner-ē\ *adj* **1** : existing only in the imagination **2** : containing or relating to a quantity (**imaginary unit**) that is the positive square root of minus 1 ($\sqrt{-1}$)

imaginary number *n* : a complex number (as 2 + 3*i*) with a nonzero term (**imaginary part**) containing the imaginary unit as a factor

imag·i·na·tion \i-ˌma-jə-ˈnā-shən\ *n* **1** : the act or power of forming a mental image of something not present to the senses or not previously known or experienced **2** : creative ability **3** : RESOURCEFULNESS **4** : a mental image : a creation of the mind — **imag·i·na·tive** \i-ˈma-jə-nə-tiv, -ˌnā-\ *adj* — **imag·i·na·tive·ly** *adv*

imag·ine \i-ˈma-jən\ *vb* **imag·ined; imag·in·ing** **1** : to form a mental picture of something not present **2** : THINK, GUESS ⟨I ~ it will rain⟩

imag·in·ings \-ˈmaj-niŋz, -ˈma-jə-\ *n pl* : products of the imagination

im·ag·ism \ˈi-mi-ˌji-zəm\ *n, often cap* : a movement in poetry advocating free verse and the expression of ideas and emotions through clear precise images — **im·ag·ist** \-jist\ *n*

ima·go \i-ˈmā-gō, -ˈmä-\ *n, pl* **imagoes** *or* **ima·gi·nes** \-ˈmā-gə-ˌnēz, -ˈmä-\ [NL, fr. L, image] : an insect in its final adult stage — **ima·gi·nal** \i-ˈmā-gə-nᵊl, -ˈmä-\ *adj*

im·bal·ance \ˈim-ˈba-ləns\ *n* : lack of balance : the state of being out of equilibrium or out of proportion

im·be·cile \ˈim-bə-səl, -ˌsil\ *n* **1** : FOOL, IDIOT **2** *dated, now offensive* : a person affected with moderate intellectual disability — **imbecile** *or* **im·be·cil·ic** \ˌim-bə-ˈsi-lik\ *adj* — **im·be·cil·i·ty** \ˌim-bə-ˈsi-lə-tē\ *n*

imbed *var of* EMBED

im·bibe \im-ˈbīb\ *vb* **im·bibed; im·bib·ing** **1** : to receive and retain in the mind **2** : to drink alcoholic beverages **3** : to take in or up : ABSORB — **im·bib·er** *n*

im·bri·ca·tion \ˌim-brə-ˈkā-shən\ *n* **1** : an overlapping of edges (as of tiles) **2** : a pattern showing imbrication — **im·bri·cate** \ˈim-bri-kət\ *adj*

im·bro·glio \im-ˈbrōl-yō\ *n, pl* **-glios** [It, fr. *imbrogliare* to entangle] **1** : a confused mass **2** : a complicated situation; *also* : a serious or embarrassing misunderstanding

im·brue \im-ˈbrü\ *vb* **im·brued; im·bru·ing** : STAIN ⟨hands *imbrued* with blood⟩

im·bue \-ˈbyü\ *vb* **im·bued; im·bu·ing** **1** : to permeate or influence as if by dyeing **2** : to tinge or dye deeply

IMF *abbr* International Monetary Fund

imit *abbr* imitative

im·i·ta·ble \ˈi-mə-tə-bəl\ *adj* : capable or worthy of being imitated or copied

im·i·tate \ˈi-mə-ˌtāt\ *vb* **-tat·ed; -tat·ing** **1** : to follow as a model : COPY **2** : RESEM-

BLE **3** : REPRODUCE **4** : MIMIC, COUNTERFEIT — **im·i·ta·tor** \-ˌtā-tər\ *n*

im·i·ta·tion \ˌi-mə-ˈtā-shən\ *n* **1** : an act of imitating **2** : COPY, COUNTERFEIT **3** : a literary work that reproduces the style of another author — **imitation** *adj*

im·i·ta·tive \ˈi-mə-ˌtā-tiv\ *adj* **1** : marked by imitation **2** : inclined to imitate **3** : COUNTERFEIT

im·mac·u·late \i-ˈma-kyə-lət\ *adj* **1** : being without stain or blemish : PURE **2** : spotlessly clean ⟨~ linen⟩ — **im·mac·u·late·ly** *adv*

im·ma·nent \ˈi-mə-nənt\ *adj* **1** INHERENT **2** : being within the limits of experience or knowledge — **im·ma·nence** \-nəns\ *n* — **im·ma·nen·cy** \-nən-sē\ *n*

im·ma·te·ri·al \ˌi-mə-ˈtir-ē-əl\ *adj* **1** : not consisting of matter : SPIRITUAL **2** : UNIMPORTANT, TRIFLING ♦ ***Synonyms*** BODILESS, DISEMBODIED, INCORPOREAL, INSUBSTANTIAL, NONPHYSICAL — **im·ma·te·ri·al·i·ty** \-ˌtir-ē-ˈa-lə-tē\ *n*

im·ma·ture \ˌi-mə-ˈtu̇r, -ˈtyu̇r\ *adj* : lacking complete development : not yet mature ⟨~ behavior⟩ — **im·ma·tu·ri·ty** \-ˈtu̇r-ə-tē, -ˈtyu̇r-\ *n*

im·mea·sur·able \(ˌ)i-ˈme-zhə-rə-bəl\ *adj* : not capable of being measured : indefinitely extensive : ILLIMITABLE — **im·mea·sur·ably** \-blē\ *adv*

im·me·di·a·cy \i-ˈmē-dē-ə-sē\ *n, pl* **-cies** **1** : the quality or state of being immediate **2** : something that is of immediate importance

im·me·di·ate \i-ˈmē-dē-ət\ *adj* **1** : acting directly and alone : DIRECT ⟨the ~ cause of death⟩ **2** : being next in line or relation ⟨members of the ~ family⟩ **3** : not distant : CLOSE **4** : made or done at once ⟨an ~ response⟩ **5** : near to or related to the present time ⟨the ~ future⟩ — **im·me·di·ate·ly** *adv*

im·me·mo·ri·al \ˌi-mə-ˈmȯr-ē-əl\ *adj* : extending beyond the reach of memory, record, or tradition ⟨from time ~⟩

im·mense \i-ˈmens\ *adj* [ME, fr. MF, fr. L *immensus* immeasurable, fr. *mensus,* pp. of *metiri* to measure] **1** : very great in size or degree : VAST, HUGE **2** : EXCELLENT — **im·mense·ly** *adv* — **im·men·si·ty** \-ˈmen-sə-tē\ *n*

im·merse \i-ˈmərs\ *vb* **im·mersed; im·mers·ing** **1** : to plunge or dip esp. into a fluid **2** : ENGROSS, ABSORB **3** : to baptize by immersing — **im·mer·sion** \-ˈmər-zhən\ *n*

im·mi·grant \ˈi-mi-grənt\ *n* **1** : a person who immigrates **2** : a plant or animal that becomes established where it did not previously occur

im·mi·grate \ˈi-mə-ˌgrāt\ *vb* **-grat·ed; -grat·ing** : to come into a foreign country and take up residence — **im·mi·gra·tion** \ˌi-mə-ˈgrā-shən\ *n*

im·mi·nent \ˈi-mə-nənt\ *adj* : ready to take place; *esp* : hanging threateningly over one's head ⟨in ~ danger⟩ — **im·mi·nence** \-nəns\ *n* — **im·mi·nent·ly** *adv*

im·mis·ci·ble \(ˌ)i-ˈmi-sə-bəl\ *adj* : incapable of mixing

im·mis·er·a·tion \(ˌ)i-ˌmi-zə-ˈrā-shən\ *n* : IMPOVERISHMENT

im·mo·bile \(ˌ)i-ˈmō-bəl\ *adj* : incapable of being moved : FIXED — **im·mo·bil·i·ty** \ˌi-mō-ˈbi-lə-tē\ *n*

im·mo·bi·lize \i-ˈmō-bə-ˌlīz\ *vb* : to make immobile — **im·mo·bi·li·za·tion** \i-ˌmō-bə-lə-ˈzā-shən\ *n*

im·mod·er·ate \(ˌ)i-ˈmä-də-rət\ *adj* : lacking in moderation : EXCESSIVE ⟨~ drinking⟩ — **im·mod·er·a·cy** \-rə-sē\ *n* — **im·mod·er·ate·ly** *adv*

im·mod·est \(ˌ)i-ˈmä-dəst\ *adj* : not modest : BRAZEN, INDECENT ⟨an ~ dress⟩ ⟨~ conduct⟩ — **im·mod·est·ly** *adv* — **im·mod·es·ty** \-də-stē\ *n*

im·mo·late \ˈi-mə-ˌlāt\ *vb* **-lat·ed; -lat·ing** [L *immolare,* to sprinkle with meal before sacrificing, sacrifice, fr. *mola* sacrificial barley cake, lit., millstone] : to offer in sacrifice; *esp* : to kill as a sacrificial victim — **im·mo·la·tion** \ˌi-mə-ˈlā-shən\ *n*

im·mor·al \(ˌ)i-ˈmȯr-əl\ *adj* : not moral — **im·mor·al·ly** *adv*

im·mo·ral·i·ty \ˌi-mȯ-ˈra-lə-tē, ˌi-mə-\ *n* **1** : WICKEDNESS; *esp* : UNCHASTITY **2** : an immoral act or practice

[1]**im·mor·tal** \(ˌ)i-ˈmȯr-tᵊl\ *adj* **1** : not mortal : exempt from death ⟨~ gods⟩ **2** : destined to be remembered forever ⟨those ~ words⟩ — **im·mor·tal·ly** *adv*

[2]**immortal** *n* **1** : one exempt from death **2** *pl, often cap* : the gods in Greek and Roman mythology **3** : a person whose fame is lasting ⟨an ~ of baseball⟩

im·mor·tal·ise *Brit var of* IMMORTALIZE

im·mor·tal·i·ty \ˌi-ˌmȯr-ˈta-lə-tē\ *n* : the quality or state of being immortal; *esp* : unending existence

im·mor·tal·ize \i-ˈmȯr-tə-ˌlīz\ *vb* **-ized; -iz·ing** : to make immortal

im·mov·able \(ˌ)i-ˈmü-və-bəl\ *adj* **1** : firmly fixed, settled, or fastened : FAST, STATIONARY ⟨~ mountains⟩ **2** : STEADFAST, UNYIELDING **3** : IMPASSIVE — **im·mov·abil·ity** \-ˌmü-və-ˈbi-lə-tē\ *n* — **im·mov·ably** \-blē\ *adv*

im·mune \i-ˈmyün\ *adj* **1** : EXEMPT **2** : having a special capacity for resistance (as to a disease) **3** : containing or producing antibodies — **im·mu·ni·ty** \-ˈmyü-nə-tē\ *n*

immune response *n* : a response of the body to an antigen resulting in the formation of antibodies and cells designed to react with the antigen and render it harmless

immune system *n* : the bodily system that protects the body from foreign substances, cells, and tissues by producing the immune response and that includes esp. the thymus, spleen, lymph nodes, and lymphocytes

im·mu·nize \ˈi-myə-ˌnīz\ *vb* **-nized; -niz·ing** : to make immune — **im·mu·ni·za·tion** \ˌi-myə-nə-ˈzā-shən\ *n*

im·mu·no·com·pro·mised \ˌi-myə-nō-ˈkäm-prə-ˌmīzd\ *adj* : having a weakened immune system

im·mu·no·de·fi·cien·cy \ˌi-myə-nō-di-ˈfi-shən-sē\ *n* : inability to produce the normal number of antibodies or immunologically sensitized cells esp. in response to specific antigens — **im•mu•no•de•fi•cient** \-ˈfi-shənt\ *adj*

im•mu•no•glob•u•lin \ˌi-myə-nō-ˈglä-byə-lən\ *n* : ANTIBODY

im•mu•nol•o•gy \ˌi-myə-ˈnä-lə-jē\ *n* : a science that deals with the immune system, immunity, and the immune response — **im•mu•no•log•ic** \-nə-ˈlä-jik\ *or* **im•mu•no•log•i•cal** \-ji-kəl\ *adj* — **im•mu•no•log•i•cal•ly** \-ji-k(ə-)lē\ *adv* — **im•mu•nol•o•gist** \-ˈnä-lə-jist\ *n*

im•mu•no•sup•pres•sion \ˌi-myə-nō-sə-ˈpre-shən\ *n* : suppression (as by drugs) of natural immune responses — **im•mu•no•sup•press** \-ˈpres\ *vb* — **im•mu•no•sup•pres•sant** \-ˈpre-sᵊnt\ *n or adj* — **im•mu•no•sup•pres•sive** \-ˈpre-siv\ *adj*

im•mu•no•ther•a•py \-ˈther-ə-pē\ *n* : the treatment or prevention of disease by attempting to induce immunity

im•mure \i-ˈmyu̇r\ *vb* **im•mured; im•mur•ing** **1** : to enclose within or as if within walls **2** : to build into a wall; *esp* : to entomb in a wall

im•mu•ta•ble \(ˌ)i-ˈmyü-tə-bəl\ *adj* : UNCHANGEABLE, UNCHANGING — **im•mu•ta•bil•i•ty** \-ˌmyü-tə-ˈbi-lə-tē\ *n* — **im•mu•ta•bly** \-ˈmyü-tə-blē\ *adv*

IMO *abbr* in my opinion

¹imp \ˈimp\ *n* **1** : a small demon : FIEND **2** : a mischievous child

²imp *abbr* **1** imperative **2** imperfect **3** imperial **4** import; imported

¹im•pact \im-ˈpakt\ *vb* **1** : to press together **2** : to have an impact on

²im•pact \ˈim-ˌpakt\ *n* **1** : a forceful contact, collision, or onset; *also* : the impetus communicated in or as if in a collision **2** : EFFECT

im•pact•ed \im-ˈpak-təd\ *adj* **1** : packed or wedged in **2** : wedged between the jawbone and another tooth

im•pair \im-ˈper\ *vb* : to diminish in quantity, value, excellence, or strength : DAMAGE, LESSEN — **im•pair•ment** *n*

im•paired \-ˈpard\ *adj* : being in a less than perfect or whole condition; *esp* : disabled or functionally defective — often used in combination ⟨hearing-*impaired*⟩

im•pa•la \im-ˈpa-lə\ *n, pl* **impalas** *or* **impala** : a large brownish African antelope that in the male has slender curved horns with ridges

im•pale \im-ˈpāl\ *vb* **im•paled; im•pal•ing** : to pierce with or as if with something pointed — **im•pale•ment** *n*

im•pal•pa•ble \(ˌ)im-ˈpal-pə-bəl\ *adj* **1** : unable to be felt by touch : INTANGIBLE **2** : not easily seen or understood — **im•pal•pa•bly** \-blē\ *adv*

im•pan•el *or* **em•pan•el** \im-ˈpan-ᵊl\ *vb* : to enter in or on a panel : ENROLL ⟨~ a jury⟩

im•part \im-ˈpärt\ *vb* **1** : to give from one's store or abundance ⟨the sun ~*s* warmth⟩ **2** : to make known

im•par•tial \(ˌ)im-ˈpär-shəl\ *adj* : not partial : UNBIASED, JUST — **im•par•tial•i•ty** \-ˌpär-shē-ˈa-lə-tē\ *n* — **im•par•tial•ly** *adv*

im•pass•able \(ˌ)im-ˈpa-sə-bəl\ *adj* : incapable of being passed, traversed, or crossed ⟨~ roads⟩ — **im•pass•ably** \-blē\ *adv*

im•passe \ˈim-ˌpas\ *n* **1** : a predicament from which there is no obvious escape **2** : an impassable road or way

im•pas•si•ble \(ˌ)im-ˈpa-sə-bəl\ *adj* : incapable of feeling : IMPASSIVE

im•pas•sioned \im-ˈpa-shənd\ *adj* : filled with passion or zeal : showing great warmth or intensity of feeling ♦ ***Synonyms*** PASSIONATE, ARDENT, FERVENT, FERVID

im•pas•sive \(ˌ)im-ˈpa-siv\ *adj* : showing no signs of feeling, emotion, or interest : EXPRESSIONLESS, INDIFFERENT ♦ ***Synonyms*** STOIC, PHLEGMATIC, APATHETIC, STOLID — **im•pas•sive•ly** *adv* — **im•pas•siv•i•ty** \ˌim-ˌpa-ˈsi-və-tē\ *n*

im•pas•to \im-ˈpas-tō, -ˈpäs-\ *n* : the thick application of a pigment to a canvas or panel in painting; *also* : the body of pigment so applied

im•pa•tiens \im-ˈpā-shənz, -shəns\ *n* : any of a genus of herbs with usu. spurred flowers and seed capsules that readily split open

im•pa•tient \(ˌ)im-ˈpā-shənt\ *adj* **1** : not patient : restless or short of temper esp. under irritation, delay, or opposition **2** : INTOLERANT ⟨~ of poverty⟩ **3** : prompted or marked by impatience ⟨an ~ reply⟩ **4** : ANXIOUS — **im•pa•tience** \-shəns\ *n* — **im•pa•tient•ly** *adv*

im•peach \im-ˈpēch\ *vb* [ME *empechen* to accuse, fr. AF *empecher, enpechier* to ensnare, impede, prosecute, fr. LL *impedicare* to fetter, fr. L *pedica* fetter, fr. *ped-, pes* foot] **1** : to charge (a public official) before an authorized tribunal with misconduct in office **2** : to challenge the credibility or validity of **3** : to remove from public office for misconduct — **im•peach•ment** *n*

im•pec•ca•ble \(ˌ)im-ˈpe-kə-bəl\ *adj* **1** : not capable of sinning or wrongdoing **2** : FAULTLESS, IRREPROACHABLE ⟨a man of ~ character⟩ — **im•pec•ca•bil•i•ty** \-ˌpe-kə-ˈbi-lə-tē\ *n* — **im•pec•ca•bly** \-ˈpe-kə-blē\ *adv*

im•pe•cu•nious \ˌim-pi-ˈkyü-nyəs, -nē-əs\ *adj* : having little or no money — **im•pe•cu•nious•ness** *n*

im•ped•ance \im-ˈpē-dᵊns\ *n* : the opposition in an electrical circuit to the flow of an alternating current

im•pede \im-ˈpēd\ *vb* **im•ped•ed; im•ped•ing** [L *impedire,* fr. *ped-, pes* foot] : to interfere with the progress of

im•ped•i•ment \im-ˈpe-də-mənt\ *n* **1** : something that impedes, hinders, or obstructs **2** : a speech defect

im•ped•i•men•ta \im-ˌpe-də-ˈmen-tə\ *n pl* : things that impede

im•pel \im-ˈpel\ *vb* **im•pelled; im•pel•ling** : to urge or drive forward or on : FORCE; *also* : PROPEL

im•pel•ler *also* **im•pel•lor** \im-ˈpe-lər\ *n* : a rotor esp. in a pump

im•pend \im-ˈpend\ *vb* **1** : to hover or

hang over threateningly : MENACE **2** : to be about to occur

im·pen·e·tra·ble \(ˌ)im-ˈpe-nə-trə-bəl\ *adj* **1** : incapable of being penetrated or pierced ⟨an ~ jungle⟩ **2** : incapable of being comprehended : INSCRUTABLE ⟨an ~ mystery⟩ — **im·pen·e·tra·bil·i·ty** \-ˌpe-nə-trə-ˈbi-lə-tē\ *n* — **im·pen·e·tra·bly** \-ˈpe-nə-trə-blē\ *adv*

im·pen·i·tent \(ˌ)im-ˈpe-nə-tənt\ *adj* : not penitent : not repenting of sin — **im·pen·i·tence** \-təns\ *n*

im·per·a·tive \im-ˈper-ə-tiv\ *adj* **1** : expressing a command, request, or encouragement ⟨~ sentence⟩ **2** : having power to restrain, control, or direct **3** : NECESSARY ⟨an ~ duty⟩ — **imperative** *n* — **im·per·a·tive·ly** *adv*

im·per·cep·ti·ble \ˌim-pər-ˈsep-tə-bəl\ *adj* : not perceptible; *esp* : too slight to be perceived ⟨~ changes⟩ — **im·per·cep·ti·bly** \-blē\ *adv*

im·per·cep·tive \ˌim-pər-ˈsep-tiv\ *adj* : not perceptive ⟨an ~ reader⟩

imperf *abbr* imperfect

[1]**im·per·fect** \(ˌ)im-ˈpər-fikt\ *adj* **1** : not perfect : DEFECTIVE, INCOMPLETE **2** : of, relating to, or being a verb tense used to designate a continuing state or an incomplete action esp. in the past — **im·per·fect·ly** *adv*

[2]**imperfect** *n* : the imperfect tense; *also* : a verb form in it

im·per·fec·tion \ˌim-pər-ˈfek-shən\ *n* : the quality or state of being imperfect; *also* : FAULT, BLEMISH

im·pe·ri·al \im-ˈpir-ē-əl\ *adj* **1** : of, relating to, or befitting an empire or an emperor; *also* : of or relating to the United Kingdom or to the Commonwealth or British Empire **2** : ROYAL, SOVEREIGN; *also* : REGAL, IMPERIOUS **3** : of unusual size or excellence

im·pe·ri·al·ism \im-ˈpir-ē-ə-ˌli-zəm\ *n* : the policy of seeking to extend the power, dominion, or territories of a nation — **im·pe·ri·al·ist** \-list\ *n or adj* — **im·pe·ri·al·is·tic** \-ˌpir-ē-ə-ˈlis-tik\ *adj* — **im·pe·ri·al·is·ti·cal·ly** \-ti-k(ə-)lē\ *adv*

im·per·il \im-ˈper-əl\ *vb* **-iled** *or* **-illed; -il·ing** *or* **-il·ling** : ENDANGER

im·pe·ri·ous \im-ˈpir-ē-əs\ *adj* **1** : COMMANDING, LORDLY **2** : ARROGANT, DOMINEERING **3** : IMPERATIVE, URGENT ⟨~ problems⟩ — **im·pe·ri·ous·ly** *adv*

im·per·ish·able \(ˌ)im-ˈper-i-shə-bəl\ *adj* : not perishable or subject to decay

im·per·ma·nent \(ˌ)im-ˈpər-mə-nənt\ *adj* : not permanent : TRANSIENT — **im·per·ma·nent·ly** *adv*

im·per·me·able \(ˌ)im-ˈpər-mē-ə-bəl\ *adj* : not permitting passage (as of a fluid) through its substance

im·per·mis·si·ble \ˌim-pər-ˈmi-sə-bəl\ *adj* : not permissible ⟨~ by law⟩

im·per·son·al \(ˌ)im-ˈpər-sə-nəl\ *adj* **1** : not referring to any particular person or thing **2** : not involving human emotions — **im·per·son·al·i·ty** \-ˌpər-sə-ˈna-lə-tē\ *n* — **im·per·son·al·ly** *adv*

im·per·son·ate \im-ˈpər-sə-ˌnāt\ *vb* **-at·ed; -at·ing** : to assume or act the character of — **im·per·son·a·tion** \-ˌpər-sə-ˈnā-shən\ *n* — **im·per·son·a·tor** \-ˈpər-sə-ˌnā-tər\ *n*

im·per·ti·nent \(ˌ)im-ˈpər-tə-nənt\ *adj* **1** : IRRELEVANT **2** : not restrained within due or proper bounds : RUDE, INSOLENT, SAUCY ⟨an ~ reply⟩ — **im·per·ti·nence** \-nəns\ *n* — **im·per·ti·nent·ly** *adv*

im·per·turb·able \ˌim-pər-ˈtər-bə-bəl\ *adj* : marked by extreme calm, impassivity, and steadiness : SERENE

im·per·vi·ous \(ˌ)im-ˈpər-vē-əs\ *adj* **1** : incapable of being penetrated (as by moisture) **2** : not capable of being affected or disturbed ⟨~ to criticism⟩

im·pe·ti·go \ˌim-pə-ˈtē-gō, -ˈtī-\ *n* : a contagious skin disease characterized by vesicles, pustules, and yellowish crusts

im·pet·u·ous \im-ˈpe-chə-wəs\ *adj* **1** : marked by impulsive vehemence ⟨~ temper⟩ **2** : marked by force and violence ⟨with ~ speed⟩ — **im·pet·u·os·i·ty** \(ˌ)im-ˌpe-chə-ˈwä-sə-tē\ *n* — **im·pet·u·ous·ly** *adv*

im·pe·tus \ˈim-pə-təs\ *n* [L, assault, impetus, fr. *impetere* to attack, fr. *petere* to go to, seek] **1** : a driving force : IMPULSE; *also* : INCENTIVE **2** : MOMENTUM

im·pi·e·ty \(ˌ)im-ˈpī-ə-tē\ *n, pl* **-ties** **1** : the quality or state of being impious **2** : an impious act

im·pinge \im-ˈpinj\ *vb* **im·pinged; im·ping·ing** **1** : to strike or dash esp. with a sharp collision **2** : ENCROACH, INFRINGE — **im·pinge·ment** *n*

im·pi·ous \ˈim-pē-əs, (ˌ)im-ˈpī-\ *adj* : not pious : IRREVERENT, PROFANE

imp·ish \ˈim-pish\ *adj* : of, relating to, or befitting an imp; *esp* : MISCHIEVOUS — **imp·ish·ly** *adv* — **imp·ish·ness** *n*

im·pla·ca·ble \(ˌ)im-ˈpla-kə-bəl, -ˈplā-\ *adj* : not capable of being appeased, pacified, mitigated, or changed ⟨an ~ enemy⟩ — **im·pla·ca·bil·i·ty** \-ˌpla-kə-ˈbi-lə-tē, -ˌplā-\ *n* — **im·pla·ca·bly** \-ˈpla-kə-blē\ *adv*

im·plant \im-ˈplant\ *vb* **1** : to set firmly or deeply **2** : to fix in the mind or spirit **3** : to insert in living tissue (as for growth or absorption) — **im·plant** \ˈim-ˌplant\ *n* — **im·plan·ta·tion** \ˌim-ˌplan-ˈtā-shən\ *n*

im·plau·si·ble \(ˌ)im-ˈplȯ-zə-bəl\ *adj* : not plausible — **im·plau·si·bil·i·ty** \-ˌplȯ-zə-ˈbi-lə-tē\ *n* — **im·plau·si·bly** \-ˈplȯ-zə-blē\ *adv*

[1]**im·ple·ment** \ˈim-plə-mənt\ *n* [ME, fr. AF, fr. ML *implementum* item making a full complement, appurtenance, tool, fr. LL, act of filling up, fr. L *implēre* to fill up] : TOOL, UTENSIL, INSTRUMENT

[2]**im·ple·ment** \-ˌment\ *vb* **1** : CARRY OUT; *esp* : to put into practice ⟨~ a plan⟩ **2** : to provide implements for — **im·ple·men·ta·tion** \ˌim-plə-mən-ˈtā-shən\ *n*

im·pli·cate \ˈim-plə-ˌkāt\ *vb* **-cat·ed; -cat·ing** **1** : IMPLY **2** : INVOLVE — **im·pli·ca·tion** \ˌim-plə-ˈkā-shən\ *n*

im·plic·it \im-ˈpli-sət\ *adj* **1** : understood though not directly stated or expressed : IMPLIED; *also* : POTENTIAL **2** : COM-

PLETE, UNQUESTIONING, ABSOLUTE ⟨~ faith⟩ — **im·plic·it·ly** *adv*

implicit bias *n* : a bias or prejudice that is present but not consciously held or recognized

im·plode \im-ˈplōd\ *vb* **im·plod·ed; im·plod·ing** **1** : to burst or collapse inward **2** : SELF-DESTRUCT — **im·plo·sion** \-ˈplō-zhən\ *n* — **im·plo·sive** \-siv\ *adj*

im·plore \im-ˈplȯr\ *vb* **im·plored; im·plor·ing** : BESEECH, ENTREAT ⟨*implored* him not to go⟩ ♦ ***Synonyms*** SUPPLICATE, BEG, IMPORTUNE, PLEAD

im·ply \im-ˈplī\ *vb* **im·plied; im·ply·ing** **1** : to involve or indicate by inference, association, or necessary consequence rather than by direct statement ⟨war *implies* fighting⟩ **2** : to express indirectly : hint at : SUGGEST

im·po·lite \ˌim-pə-ˈlīt\ *adj* : not polite : RUDE, DISCOURTEOUS

im·pol·i·tic \(ˌ)im-ˈpä-lə-ˌtik\ *adj* : not politic : UNWISE

im·pon·der·a·ble \(ˌ)im-ˈpän-də-rə-bəl\ *adj* : incapable of being weighed or evaluated with exactness — **imponderable** *n*

[1]im·port \im-ˈpȯrt\ *vb* **1** : MEAN, SIGNIFY **2** : to bring (as merchandise) into a place or country from a foreign or external source — **im·port·er** *n*

[2]im·port \ˈim-ˌpȯrt\ *n* **1** : IMPORTANCE, SIGNIFICANCE **2** : MEANING, SIGNIFICATION **3** : something (as merchandise) brought in from another country

im·por·tance \im-ˈpȯr-tᵊns\ *n* : the quality or state of being important : MOMENT, SIGNIFICANCE ♦ ***Synonyms*** CONSEQUENCE, IMPORT, WEIGHT

im·por·tant \im-ˈpȯr-tᵊnt\ *adj* **1** : marked by importance : SIGNIFICANT **2** : giving an impression of importance — **im·por·tant·ly** *adv*

im·por·ta·tion \ˌim-ˌpȯr-ˈtā-shən, -pər-\ *n* **1** : the act or practice of importing **2** : something imported

im·por·tu·nate \im-ˈpȯr-chə-nət\ *adj* **1** : troublesomely urgent or persistent **2** : BURDENSOME, TROUBLESOME

im·por·tune \ˌim-pər-ˈtün, -ˈtyün; im-ˈpȯr-chən\ *vb* **-tuned; -tun·ing** : to urge or beg with troublesome persistence — **im·por·tu·ni·ty** \-pər-ˈtü-nə-tē, -ˈtyü-\ *n*

im·pose \im-ˈpōz\ *vb* **im·posed; im·pos·ing** **1** : to establish or apply by authority ⟨~ a tax⟩; *also* : to establish by force ⟨*imposed* a government⟩ **2** : OBTRUDE ⟨*imposed* herself on others⟩ **3** : to take unwarranted advantage of something ⟨~ on her good nature⟩ — **im·po·si·tion** \ˌim-pə-ˈzi-shən\ *n*

im·pos·ing *adj* : impressive because of size, bearing, dignity, or grandeur — **im·pos·ing·ly** *adv*

im·pos·si·ble \(ˌ)im-ˈpä-sə-bəl\ *adj* **1** : incapable of being or of occurring **2** : enormously difficult **3** : extremely undesirable : UNACCEPTABLE — **im·pos·si·bil·i·ty** \-ˌpä-sə-ˈbi-lə-tē\ *n* — **im·pos·si·bly** \-ˈpä-sə-blē\ *adv*

[1]im·post \ˈim-ˌpōst\ *n* : TAX, DUTY

[2]impost *n* : a block, capital, or molding from which an arch springs

im·pos·tor *or* **im·pos·ter** \im-ˈpäs-tər\ *n* : one that assumes an identity or title not one's own in order to deceive

im·pos·ture \im-ˈpäs-chər\ *n* : DECEPTION; *esp* : fraudulent impersonation

im·po·tent \ˈim-pə-tənt\ *adj* **1** : lacking in power or strength : HELPLESS **2** : unable to copulate; *also* : STERILE — **im·po·tence** \-təns\ *n* — **im·po·ten·cy** \-tən-sē\ *n* — **im·po·tent·ly** *adv*

im·pound \im-ˈpau̇nd\ *vb* **1** : CONFINE, ENCLOSE ⟨~ strays⟩ **2** : to seize and hold in legal custody **3** : to collect in a reservoir ⟨~ water⟩ — **im·pound·ment** *n*

im·pov·er·ish \im-ˈpä-və-rish\ *vb* : to make poor; *also* : to deprive of strength, richness, or fertility — **im·pov·er·ish·ment** *n*

im·prac·ti·ca·ble \(ˌ)im-ˈprak-ti-kə-bəl\ *adj* : not practicable : incapable of being put into practice or use ⟨an ~ plan⟩

im·prac·ti·cal \(ˌ)im-ˈprak-ti-kəl\ *adj* **1** : not practical **2** : IMPRACTICABLE

im·pre·cate \ˈim-pri-ˌkāt\ *vb* **-cat·ed; -cat·ing** : CURSE — **im·pre·ca·tion** \ˌim-pri-ˈkā-shən\ *n*

im·pre·cise \ˌim-pri-ˈsīs\ *adj* : not precise — **im·pre·cise·ly** *adv* — **im·pre·cise·ness** *n* — **im·pre·ci·sion** \-ˈsi-zhən\ *n*

im·preg·na·ble \im-ˈpreg-nə-bəl\ *adj* : incapable of being taken by assault : UNCONQUERABLE, UNASSAILABLE — **im·preg·na·bil·i·ty** \(ˌ)im-ˌpreg-nə-ˈbi-lə-tē\ *n*

im·preg·nate \im-ˈpreg-ˌnāt\ *vb* **-nat·ed; -nat·ing** **1** : to fertilize or make pregnant **2** : to cause to be filled, permeated, or saturated — **im·preg·na·tion** \ˌim-ˌpreg-ˈnā-shən\ *n*

im·pre·sa·rio \ˌim-prə-ˈsär-ē-ˌō\ *n, pl* **-ri·os** [It, fr. *impresa* undertaking, fr. *imprendere* to undertake] **1** : the manager or conductor of an opera or concert company **2** : one who puts on an entertainment **3** : MANAGER, PRODUCER

[1]im·press \im-ˈpres\ *vb* **1** : to apply with or produce (as a mark) by pressure : IMPRINT **2** : to press, stamp, or print in or upon **3** : to produce a vivid impression of **4** : to affect esp. forcibly or deeply — **im·press·ible** *adj*

[2]im·press \ˈim-ˌpres\ *n* **1** : a characteristic or distinctive mark **2** : IMPRESSION, EFFECT **3** : an impression or image of something formed by or as if by pressure; *also* : a product of pressure or influence

[3]im·press \im-ˈpres\ *vb* **1** : to force into naval service **2** : to get the aid or services of by forcible argument or persuasion — **im·press·ment** *n*

im·pres·sion \im-ˈpre-shən\ *n* **1** : a characteristic trait or feature resulting from influence : IMPRESS **2** : a stamp, form, or figure made by impressing : IMPRINT **3** : an esp. marked influence or effect on feeling, sense, or mind **4** : a single print or copy (as from type or from an engraved plate or book) **5** : all the copies of a publication (as a book) printed for one issue : PRINTING **6** : a usu. vague notion or remembrance **7** : an imitation in caricature of a noted personality as a form of entertainment

im·pres·sion·able \im-ˈpre-shə-nə-bəl\ *adj* : capable of being easily impressed : easily molded or influenced

im·pres·sion·ism \im-ˈpre-shə-ˌni-zəm\ *n, often cap* : a theory or practice in modern art of depicting the natural appearances of objects by dabs or strokes of primary unmixed colors in order to simulate actual reflected light — **im·pres·sion·is·tic** \-ˌpre-shə-ˈnis-tik\ *adj*

im·pres·sion·ist \im-ˈpre-shə-nist\ *n* **1** *often cap* : a painter who practices impressionism **2** : an entertainer who does impressions

im·pres·sive \im-ˈpre-siv\ *adj* : making or tending to make a marked impression ⟨an ~ speech⟩ — **im·pres·sive·ly** *adv* — **im·pres·sive·ness** *n*

im·pri·ma·tur \ˌim-prə-ˈmä-ˌtu̇r\ *n* [NL, let it be printed] **1** : a license to print or publish; *also* : official approval of a publication by a censor **2** : SANCTION, APPROVAL

¹**im·print** \im-ˈprint, ˈim-ˌprint\ *vb* **1** : to stamp or mark by or as if by pressure : IMPRESS **2** : to fix firmly (as on the memory)

²**im·print** \ˈim-ˌprint\ *n* **1** : something imprinted or printed **2** : a publisher's name printed at the foot of a title page **3** : an indelible distinguishing effect or influence ⟨put her ~ on the company⟩

im·pris·on \im-ˈpri-zᵊn\ *vb* : to put in or as if in prison : CONFINE — **im·pris·on·ment** *n*

im·prob·a·ble \(ˌ)im-ˈprä-bə-bəl\ *adj* : unlikely to be true or to occur — **im·prob·a·bil·i·ty** \-ˌprä-bə-ˈbi-lə-tē\ *n* — **im·prob·a·bly** \-ˈprä-bə-blē\ *adv*

im·promp·tu \im-ˈprämp-tü, -tyü\ *adj* [F, fr. *impromptu* extemporaneously, fr. L *in promptu* in readiness] **1** : made or done on or as if on the spur of the moment **2** : EXTEMPORANEOUS, UNREHEARSED ⟨an ~ speech⟩ — **impromptu** *adv or n*

im·prop·er \(ˌ)im-ˈprä-pər\ *adj* **1** : not proper, fit, or suitable **2** : INCORRECT, INACCURATE **3** : not in accord with propriety, modesty, or good manners — **im·prop·er·ly** *adv*

improper fraction *n* : a fraction whose numerator is equal to or larger than the denominator

im·pro·pri·e·ty \ˌim-prə-ˈprī-ə-tē\ *n, pl* **-ties** **1** : an improper act or remark; *esp* : an unacceptable use of a word or of language **2** : the quality or state of being improper

im·prov \ˈim-ˌpräv\ *adj* : of, relating to, or being an improvised comedy routine — **improv** *n*

im·prove \im-ˈprüv\ *vb* **im·proved; im·prov·ing** **1** : to enhance or increase in value or quality **2** : to grow or become better ⟨your work is *improving*⟩ **3** : to make good use of ⟨~ the time by reading⟩ — **im·prov·able** \-ˈprü-və-bəl\ *adj*

im·prove·ment \im-ˈprüv-mənt\ *n* **1** : the act or process of improving **2** : increased value or excellence of something **3** : something that adds to the value or appearance of a thing

im·prov·i·dent \(ˌ)im-ˈprä-və-dənt\ *adj* : not providing for the future — **im·prov·i·dence** \-dəns\ *n*

im·pro·vise \ˈim-prə-ˌvīz\ *vb* **-vised; -vis·ing** [F *improviser,* fr. It *improvvisare,* fr. *improvviso* sudden, fr. L *improvisus,* lit., unforeseen] **1** : to compose, recite, play, or sing on the spur of the moment : EXTEMPORIZE ⟨~ on the piano⟩ **2** : to make, invent, or arrange offhand ⟨~ a sail out of shirts⟩ — **im·pro·vi·sa·tion** \im-ˌprä-və-ˈzā-shən, ˌim-prə-və-\ *n* — **im·pro·vis·er** *or* **im·pro·vi·sor** \ˌim-prə-ˈvī-zər, ˈim-prə-ˌvī-\ *n*

im·pru·dent \(ˌ)im-ˈprü-dᵊnt\ *adj* : not prudent : lacking discretion, wisdom, or good judgment — **im·pru·dence** \-dᵊns\ *n* — **im·pru·dent·ly** *adv*

im·pu·dent \ˈim-pyu̇-dənt\ *adj* : marked by contemptuous boldness or disregard of others — **im·pu·dence** \-dəns\ *n* — **im·pu·dent·ly** *adv*

im·pugn \im-ˈpyün\ *vb* [ME, to assail, fr. AF *empugner,* fr. L *inpugnare,* fr. *pugnare* to fight] : to attack by words or arguments : oppose or attack as false or as lacking integrity ⟨~*ed* his rival's character⟩

im·pulse \ˈim-ˌpəls\ *n* **1** : a force that starts a body into motion; *also* : the motion produced by such a force **2** : an arousing of the mind and spirit to some usu. unpremeditated action **3** : NERVE IMPULSE

im·pul·sion \im-ˈpəl-shən\ *n* **1** : the act of impelling : the state of being impelled **2** : a force that impels **3** : IMPULSE 2; *also* : COMPULSION 3

im·pul·sive \im-ˈpəl-siv\ *adj* **1** : having the power of or actually driving or impelling **2** : arising from or prone to act on impulse — **im·pul·sive·ly** *adv* — **im·pul·sive·ness** *n*

im·pu·ni·ty \im-ˈpyü-nə-tē\ *n* [MF or L; MF *impunité,* fr. L *impunitas,* fr. *impune* without punishment, fr. *poena* penalty, punishment] : exemption from punishment, harm, or loss

im·pure \(ˌ)im-ˈpyu̇r\ *adj* **1** : not pure : UNCHASTE, OBSCENE **2** : DIRTY, FOUL ⟨~ water⟩ **3** : ADULTERATED, MIXED — **im·pu·ri·ty** \-ˈpyu̇r-ə-tē\ *n*

im·pute \im-ˈpyüt\ *vb* **im·put·ed; im·put·ing** **1** : to lay the responsibility or blame for often falsely or unjustly **2** : to credit to a person or a cause : ATTRIBUTE — **im·put·able** \-ˈpyü-tə-bəl\ *adj* — **im·pu·ta·tion** \ˌim-pyu̇-ˈtā-shən\ *n*

¹**in** \ˈin\ *prep* **1** — used to indicate physical surroundings ⟨swim ~ the lake⟩ **2** : INTO 1 ⟨ran ~ the house⟩ **3** : DURING ⟨~ the summer⟩ **4** : WITH ⟨written ~ pencil⟩ **5** — used to indicate one's situation or state of being ⟨~ luck⟩ ⟨~ love⟩ **6** — used to indicate manner or purpose ⟨~ a hurry⟩ ⟨said ~ reply⟩ **7** : INTO 2 ⟨broke ~ pieces⟩

[2]**in** *adv* **1 :** to or toward the inside ⟨come ~⟩; *also* **:** to or toward some destination or place ⟨flew ~ from the South⟩ **2 :** at close quarters **:** NEAR ⟨the enemy closed ~⟩ **3 :** into the midst of something ⟨mix ~ the flour⟩ **4 :** to or at its proper place ⟨fit a piece ~⟩ **5 :** WITHIN ⟨locked ~⟩ **6 :** in vogue or season **7 :** in one's presence, possession, or control ⟨the results are ~⟩

[3]**in** *adj* **1 :** located inside or within **2 :** that is in position, operation, or power ⟨the ~ party⟩ **3 :** directed inward **:** INCOMING ⟨the ~ train⟩ **4 :** keenly aware of and responsive to what is new and fashionable ⟨the ~ crowd⟩; *also* **:** extremely fashionable ⟨the ~ thing to do⟩

[4]**in** *n* **1 :** one who is in office or power or on the inside **2 :** INFLUENCE, PULL ⟨he has an ~ with the owner⟩

[5]**in** *abbr* **1** inch **2** inlet

In *symbol* indium

IN *abbr* Indiana

in- \(ˌ)in\ *prefix* **:** not **:** absence of **:** NON-, UN-

in·abil·i·ty \ˌi-nə-ˈbi-lə-tē\ *n* **:** the quality or state of being unable

in ab·sen·tia \ˌin-ab-ˈsen-chə, -chē-ə\ *adv* **:** in one's absence

in·ac·ti·vate \(ˌ)i-ˈnak-tə-ˌvāt\ *vb* **:** to make inactive — **in·ac·ti·va·tion** \(ˌ)i-ˌnak-tə-ˈvā-shən\ *n*

in·ad·e·quate \(ˌ)i-ˈna-di-kwət\ *adj* **:** not adequate **:** INSUFFICIENT — **in·ad·e·qua·cy** \-kwə-sē\ *n* — **in·ad·e·quate·ly** *adv* — **in·ad·e·quate·ness** *n*

in·ad·ver·tent \ˌi-nəd-ˈvər-tᵊnt\ *adj* **1 :** HEEDLESS, INATTENTIVE **2 :** UNINTENTIONAL ⟨an ~ omission⟩ — **in·ad·ver·tence** \-tᵊns\ *n* — **in·ad·ver·ten·cy** \-tᵊn-sē\ *n* — **in·ad·ver·tent·ly** *adv*

in·alien·able \(ˌ)i-ˈnāl-yə-nə-bəl, -ˈnā-lē-ə-\ *adj* **:** incapable of being alienated, surrendered, or transferred ⟨~ rights⟩ — **in·alien·abil·i·ty** \(ˌ)i-ˌnāl-yə-nə-ˈbi-lə-tē, -ˌnā-lē-ə-\ *n* — **in·alien·ably** *adv*

in·amo·ra·ta \i-ˌnä-mə-ˈrä-tə\ *n* **:** a woman with whom one is in love

inane \i-ˈnān\ *adj* **inan·er; -est :** EMPTY, INSUBSTANTIAL; *also* **:** SHALLOW, SILLY ⟨~ comments⟩ — **inane·ly** *adv* — **inan·i·ty** \i-ˈna-nə-tē\ *n*

in·an·i·mate \(ˌ)i-ˈna-nə-mət\ *adj* **:** not animate or animated **:** lacking the qualities of living things — **in·an·i·mate·ly** *adv* — **in·an·i·mate·ness** *n*

in·ap·pre·cia·ble \ˌi-nə-ˈprē-shə-bəl\ *adj* **:** too small to be perceived — **in·ap·pre·cia·bly** \-blē\ *adv*

in·apt \(ˌ)i-ˈnapt\ *adj* **1 :** not suitable ⟨an ~ analogy⟩ **2 :** INEPT — **in·apt·ly** *adv* — **in·apt·ness** *n*

in·ar·tic·u·late \ˌi-när-ˈti-kyə-lət\ *adj* **1 :** not understandable as spoken words **2 :** MUTE **3 :** incapable of being expressed by speech ⟨~ fear⟩; *also* **:** UNSPOKEN **4 :** not having the power of distinct utterance or effective expression — **in·ar·tic·u·late·ly** *adv*

in·as·much as \ˌi-nəz-ˈməch-\ *conj* **:** seeing that **:** SINCE

in·at·ten·tion \ˌi-nə-ˈten-chən\ *n* **:** failure to pay attention **:** DISREGARD — **in·at·ten·tive** \-ˈten-tiv\ *adj*

[1]**in·au·gu·ral** \i-ˈnȯ-gyə-rəl, -gə-\ *adj* **1 :** of or relating to an inauguration **2 :** marking a beginning

[2]**inaugural** *n* **1 :** an inaugural address **2 :** INAUGURATION

in·au·gu·rate \i-ˈnȯ-gyə-ˌrāt, -gə-\ *vb* **-rat·ed; -rat·ing 1 :** to introduce into an office with suitable ceremonies **:** INSTALL **2 :** to dedicate ceremoniously **3 :** BEGIN, INITIATE — **in·au·gu·ra·tion** \-ˌnȯ-gyə-ˈrā-shən, -gə-\ *n*

in·board \ˈin-ˌbȯrd\ *adv* **1 :** inside the hull of a ship **2 :** close or closest to the center line of a vehicle or craft — **inboard** *adj*

in·born \ˈin-ˈbȯrn\ *adj* **1 :** present from or as if from birth **2 :** HEREDITARY, INHERITED ♦ ***Synonyms*** INNATE, CONGENITAL, NATIVE

in·bound \ˈin-ˌbau̇nd\ *adj* **:** inward bound ⟨~ traffic⟩

in–box \ˈin-ˌbäks\ *n* **:** a receptacle for incoming interoffice letters; *also* **:** a computer folder for incoming email

in·bred \ˈin-ˈbred\ *adj* **1 :** ingrained in one's nature as deeply as if by heredity **2 :** subjected to or produced by inbreeding

in·breed·ing \ˈin-ˌbrē-diŋ\ *n* **1 :** the interbreeding of closely related individuals esp. to preserve and fix desirable characters of and to eliminate unfavorable characters from a stock **2 :** confinement to a narrow range or a local or limited field of choice — **in·breed** \-ˈbrēd\ *vb*

inc *abbr* **1** incomplete **2** incorporated **3** increase

In·ca \ˈiŋ-kə\ *n* [Sp, fr. Quechua *inka* ruler of the Inca empire] **1 :** a noble or a member of the Quechuan peoples of Peru maintaining an empire until the Spanish conquest **2 :** a member of any people under Inca influence

in·cal·cu·la·ble \(ˌ)in-ˈkal-kyə-lə-bəl\ *adj* **1 :** not capable of being calculated; *esp* **:** very great **2 :** not predictable ⟨~ consequences⟩ — **in·cal·cu·la·bly** \-blē\ *adv*

in·can·des·cent \ˌin-kən-ˈde-sᵊnt\ *adj* **1 :** glowing with heat **2 :** SHINING, BRILLIANT — **in·can·des·cence** \-sᵊns\ *n*

incandescent lamp *n* **:** LIGHT BULB 1

in·can·ta·tion \ˌin-ˌkan-ˈtā-shən\ *n* **:** a use of spells or verbal charms spoken or sung as a part of a ritual of magic; *also* **:** a formula of words used in or as if in such a ritual

---

inaccessibility
inaccessible
inaccuracy
inaccurate
inaction
inactive
inactivity
inadmissibility
inadmissible
inadvisability
inadvisable
inapparent
inapplicable
inapposite
inapproachable
inappropriate
inaptitude
inarguable
inartistic
inattentive
inaudible
inaudibly
inauspicious
inauthentic
incautious

in•ca•pa•ble \(ˌ)in-ˈkā-pə-bəl\ *adj* : lacking ability or qualification for a particular purpose; *also* : UNQUALIFIED — **in•ca•pa•bil•i•ty** \-ˌkā-pə-ˈbi-lə-tē\ *n*
in•ca•pac•i•tate \ˌin-kə-ˈpa-sə-ˌtāt\ *vb* **-tat•ed; -tat•ing** : to make incapable or unfit
in•ca•pac•i•ty \ˌin-kə-ˈpa-sə-tē\ *n, pl* **-ties** : the quality or state of being incapable
in•car•cer•ate \in-ˈkär-sə-ˌrāt\ *vb* **-at•ed; -at•ing** : IMPRISON, CONFINE — **in•car•cer•a•tion** \(ˌ)in-ˌkär-sə-ˈrā-shən\ *n*
in•car•na•dine \in-ˈkär-nə-ˌdīn, -ˌdēn\ *vb* **-dined; -din•ing** : REDDEN
in•car•nate \in-ˈkär-nət, -ˌnāt\ *adj* **1** : having bodily and esp. human form and substance **2** : PERSONIFIED — **in•car•nate** \-ˌnāt\ *vb*
in•car•na•tion \ˌin-ˌkär-ˈnā-shən\ *n* **1** : the embodiment of a deity or spirit in an earthly form **2** *cap* : the union of divine and human natures in Jesus Christ **3** : a person showing a trait or typical character to a marked degree **4** : the act of incarnating : the state of being incarnate
in•cen•di•ary \in-ˈsen-dē-ˌer-ē\ *adj* **1** : of or relating to a deliberate burning of property **2** : tending to excite or inflame **3** : designed to start fires ⟨an ~ bomb⟩ — **incendiary** *n*
¹**in•cense** \ˈin-ˌsens\ *n* **1** : material used to produce a fragrant odor when burned **2** : the perfume or smoke from some spices and gums when burned
²**in•cense** \in-ˈsens\ *vb* **in•censed; in•cens•ing** : to make extremely angry
in•cen•tive \in-ˈsen-tiv\ *n* [ME, fr. LL *incentivum,* fr. *incentivus* stimulating, fr. L, setting the tune, fr. *incinere* to play (a tune), fr. *canere* to sing] : something that incites or is likely to incite to determination or action
in•cep•tion \in-ˈsep-shən\ *n* : BEGINNING, COMMENCEMENT
in•cer•ti•tude \(ˌ)in-ˈsər-tə-ˌtüd, -ˌtyüd\ *n* **1** : UNCERTAINTY, DOUBT, INDECISION **2** : INSECURITY, INSTABILITY
in•ces•sant \(ˌ)in-ˈse-sᵊnt\ *adj* : continuing or flowing without interruption ⟨~ rains⟩ — **in•ces•sant•ly** *adv*
in•cest \ˈin-ˌsest\ *n* [ME, fr. L *incestus* sexual impurity, fr. *incestus* impure, fr. *castus* pure] : sexual intercourse between persons so closely related that marriage is illegal — **in•ces•tu•ous** \in-ˈses-chü-wəs\ *adj*
¹**inch** \ˈinch\ *n* [ME, fr. OE *ynce,* fr. L *uncia* twelfth part, inch, ounce] — see WEIGHT table
²**inch** *vb* : to move by small degrees
in•cho•ate \in-ˈkō-ət, ˈin-kə-ˌwāt\ *adj* : being only partly in existence or operation : INCOMPLETE ⟨~ yearnings⟩
inch•worm \ˈinch-ˌwərm\ *n* : LOOPER
in•ci•dence \ˈin-sə-dəns\ *n* : rate of occurrence or effect
¹**in•ci•dent** \-dənt\ *n* **1** : OCCURRENCE, HAPPENING **2** : an action likely to lead to grave consequences esp. in diplomatic matters
²**incident** *adj* **1** : occurring or likely to occur esp. in connection with some other happening **2** : falling or striking on something ⟨~ light rays⟩
¹**in•ci•den•tal** \ˌin-sə-ˈden-tᵊl\ *adj* **1** : subordinate, nonessential, or attendant in position or significance ⟨~ expenses⟩ **2** : CASUAL, CHANCE
²**incidental** *n* **1** *pl* : minor items (as of expense) that are not individually accounted for **2** : something incidental
in•ci•den•tal•ly \ˌin-sə-ˈden-tə-lē, -ˈdent-lē\ *adv* **1** : in an incidental manner **2** : by the way
in•cin•er•ate \in-ˈsi-nə-ˌrāt\ *vb* **-at•ed; -at•ing** : to burn to ashes — **in•cin•er•a•tion** \-ˌsi-nə-ˈrā-shən\ *n*
in•cin•er•a•tor \in-ˈsi-nə-ˌrā-tər\ *n* : a furnace for burning waste
in•cip•i•ent \in-ˈsi-pē-ənt\ *adj* : beginning to be or become apparent
in•cise \in-ˈsīz\ *vb* **in•cised; in•cis•ing** **1** : to cut into **2** : CARVE, ENGRAVE
in•ci•sion \in-ˈsi-zhən\ *n* : CUT, GASH; *esp* : a surgical cut
in•ci•sive \in-ˈsī-siv\ *adj* : impressively direct and decisive — **in•ci•sive•ly** *adv*
in•ci•sor \in-ˈsī-zər\ *n* : a front tooth typically adapted for cutting
in•cite \in-ˈsīt\ *vb* **in•cit•ed; in•cit•ing** : to arouse to action : stir up — **in•cite•ment** *n* — **in•cit•er** *n*
in•ci•vil•i•ty \ˌin-sə-ˈvi-lə-tē\ *n* **1** : RUDENESS, DISCOURTESY **2** : a rude or discourteous act
incl *abbr* include; included; including; inclusive
in•clem•ent \(ˌ)in-ˈkle-mənt\ *adj* : SEVERE, STORMY ⟨~ weather⟩ — **in•clem•en•cy** \-mən-sē\ *n*
in•cli•na•tion \ˌin-klə-ˈnā-shən\ *n* **1** : a tendency to a particular aspect, state, character, or action; *esp* : LIKING **2** : BOW, NOD ⟨an ~ of the head⟩ **3** : a tilting of something **4** : SLANT, SLOPE
¹**in•cline** \in-ˈklīn\ *vb* **in•clined; in•clin•ing** **1** : BOW, BEND **2** : to be drawn toward an opinion or course of action **3** : to deviate from the vertical or horizontal : SLOPE **4** : INFLUENCE, PERSUADE — **in•clin•er** *n*
²**in•cline** \ˈin-ˌklīn\ *n* : SLOPE
inclose, inclosure *var of* ENCLOSE, ENCLOSURE
in•clude \in-ˈklüd\ *vb* **in•clud•ed; in•clud•ing** : to take in or comprise as a part of a whole ⟨the price ~*s* tax⟩ — **in•clu•sion** \in-ˈklü-zhən\ *n*
in•clu•sive \in-ˈklü-siv\ *adj* **1** : including stated limits or extremes ⟨from Monday to Friday ~⟩ **2** : broad in scope; *esp* : covering all items, costs, or services **3** : including everyone; *esp* : allowing and accommodating people who have historically been excluded — **in•clu•sive•ly** *adj* — **in•clu•sive•ness** *n*
incog *abbr* incognito
¹**in•cog•ni•to** \ˌin-ˌkäg-ˈnē-tō, in-ˈkäg-nə-ˌtō\ *adv or adj* [It, fr. L *incognitus* unknown, fr. *cognoscere* to know] : with one's identity concealed
²**incognito** *n, pl* **-tos** **1** : one appearing or

living incognito **2** : the state or disguise of an incognito
in·co·her·ent \ˌin-kō-ˈhir-ənt, -ˈher-\ *adj* **1** : not sticking closely or compactly together : LOOSE **2** : lacking normal clarity or intelligibility in speech or thought ⟨an ~ patient⟩ — **in·co·her·ence** \-əns\ *n* — **in·co·her·ent·ly** *adv*
in·come \ˈin-ˌkəm\ *n* : a gain usu. measured in money that derives from labor, business, or property
income tax *n* : a tax on the net income of an individual or business concern
in·com·ing \ˈin-ˌkə-miŋ\ *adj* : coming in ⟨the ~ tide⟩ ⟨~ freshmen⟩
in·com·men·su·rate \ˌin-kə-ˈmen-sə-rət, -ˈmen-chə-\ *adj* : not commensurate; *esp* : INADEQUATE
in·com·mode \ˌin-kə-ˈmōd\ *vb* **-mod·ed; -mod·ing** : INCONVENIENCE, DISTURB
in·com·mu·ni·ca·ble \ˌin-kə-ˈmyü-ni-kə-bəl\ *adj* : not communicable : not capable of being communicated or imparted; *also* : UNCOMMUNICATIVE
in·com·mu·ni·ca·do \ˌin-kə-ˌmyü-nə-ˈkä-dō\ *adv or adj* : without means of communication; *also* : in solitary confinement ⟨a prisoner held ~⟩
in·com·pa·ra·ble \(ˌ)in-ˈkäm-pə-rə-bəl, -prə-\ *adj* **1** : eminent beyond comparison : MATCHLESS **2** : not suitable for comparison — **in·com·pa·ra·bly** \-blē\ *adv*
in·com·pat·i·ble \ˌin-kəm-ˈpa-tə-bəl\ *adj* : incapable of or unsuitable for association or use together ⟨~ colors⟩ ⟨temperamentally ~⟩ — **in·com·pat·i·bil·i·ty** \ˌin-kəm-ˌpa-tə-ˈbi-lə-tē\ *n*
in·com·pe·tent \(ˌ)in-ˈkäm-pə-tənt\ *adj* **1** : not legally qualified **2** : not competent : lacking sufficient knowledge, skill, or ability — **in·com·pe·tence** \-təns\ *n* — **in·com·pe·ten·cy** \-tən-sē\ *n* — **incompetent** *n*
in·com·plete \ˌin-kəm-ˈplēt\ *adj* : lacking a part or parts : UNFINISHED, IMPERFECT — **in·com·plete·ly** *adv* — **in·com·plete·ness** *n*
in·com·pre·hen·si·ble \ˌin-ˌkäm-prē-ˈhen-sə-bəl\ *adj* : impossible to comprehend : UNINTELLIGIBLE ⟨~ muttering⟩
in·con·ceiv·able \ˌin-kən-ˈsē-və-bəl\ *adj* **1** : impossible to comprehend **2** : UNBELIEVABLE
in·con·gru·ous \(ˌ)in-ˈkäŋ-grü-wəs\ *adj* : not consistent with or suitable to the surroundings or associations — **in·con·gru·i·ty** \ˌin-kən-ˈgrü-ə-tē, -ˌkän-\ *n* — **in·con·gru·ous·ly** *adv*
in·con·se·quen·tial \ˌin-ˌkän-sə-ˈkwen-chəl\ *adj* **1** : ILLOGICAL; *also* : IRRELEVANT **2** : of no significance : UNIMPORTANT — **in·con·se·quence** \(ˌ)in-ˈkän-sə-ˌkwens\ *n* — **in·con·se·quen·tial·ly** *adv*
in·con·sid·er·able \ˌin-kən-ˈsi-də-rə-bəl\ *adj* : SLIGHT, TRIVIAL ⟨the cost was not ~⟩
in·con·sid·er·ate \ˌin-kən-ˈsi-də-rət\ *adj* : HEEDLESS, THOUGHTLESS; *esp* : not respecting the rights or feelings of others — **in·con·sid·er·ate·ly** *adv* — **in·con·sid·er·ate·ness** *n*
in·con·sol·able \ˌin-kən-ˈsō-lə-bəl\ *adj* : incapable of being consoled — **in·con·sol·ably** \-blē\ *adv*
in·con·spic·u·ous \ˌin-kən-ˈspi-kyə-wəs\ *adj* : not readily noticeable — **in·con·spic·u·ous·ly** *adv*
in·con·stant \(ˌ)in-ˈkän-stənt\ *adj* : not constant : CHANGEABLE ♦ ***Synonyms*** FICKLE, CAPRICIOUS, MERCURIAL, UNSTABLE, VOLATILE — **in·con·stan·cy** \-stən-sē\ *n* — **in·con·stant·ly** *adv*
in·con·test·able \ˌin-kən-ˈtes-tə-bəl\ *adj* : not contestable : INDISPUTABLE — **in·con·test·ably** \-ˈtes-tə-blē\ *adv*
in·con·ti·nent \(ˌ)in-ˈkänt-ᵊn-ənt\ *adj* **1** : lacking self-restraint **2** : unable to retain urine or feces voluntarily — **in·con·ti·nence** \-əns\ *n*
in·con·tro·vert·ible \ˌin-ˌkän-trə-ˈvər-tə-bəl\ *adj* : not open to question : INDISPUTABLE ⟨~ evidence⟩ — **in·con·tro·vert·ibly** \-blē\ *adv*
¹in·con·ve·nience \ˌin-kən-ˈvē-nyəns\ *n* **1** : something that is inconvenient **2** : the quality or state of being inconvenient
²inconvenience *vb* **-nienced; -nienc·ing** : to subject to inconvenience
in·con·ve·nient \ˌin-kən-ˈvē-nyənt\ *adj* : not convenient : causing trouble or annoyance : INOPPORTUNE — **in·con·ve·nient·ly** *adv*
in·cor·po·rate \in-ˈkȯr-pə-ˌrāt\ *vb* **-rat·ed; -rat·ing** **1** : to unite closely or so as to form one body : BLEND **2** : to form, form into, or become a corporation **3** : to give material form to : EMBODY — **in·cor·po·ra·tion** \-ˌkȯr-pə-ˈrā-shən\ *n*
in·cor·po·re·al \ˌin-kȯr-ˈpȯr-ē-əl\ *adj* : having no material body or form
in·cor·rect \ˌin-kə-ˈrekt\ *adj* **1** : INACCURATE, FAULTY ⟨an ~ transcription⟩ **2** : not true : WRONG **3** : UNBECOMING, IMPROPER — **in·cor·rect·ly** *adv* — **in·cor·rect·ness** *n*
in·cor·ri·gi·ble \(ˌ)in-ˈkȯr-ə-jə-bəl\ *adj* : incapable of being corrected, amended, or reformed — **in·cor·ri·gi·bil·i·ty** \(ˌ)in-ˌkȯr-ə-jə-ˈbi-lə-tē\ *n* — **in·cor·ri·gi·bly** \-ˈkȯr-ə-jə-blē\ *adv*
in·cor·rupt·ible \ˌin-kə-ˈrəp-tə-bəl\ *adj* **1** : not subject to decay or dissolution **2** : incapable of being bribed or morally corrupted — **in·cor·rupt·ibil·i·ty** \-ˌrəp-tə-ˈbi-lə-tē\ *n* — **in·cor·rupt·ibly** \-ˈrəp-tə-blē\ *adv*
incr *abbr* increase; increased
¹in·crease \in-ˈkrēs, ˈin-ˌkrēs\ *vb* **in·creased; in·creas·ing** [ME *encresen*, fr. AF *encreistre*, fr. L. *increscere*, fr. *crescere* to grow] **1** : to become greater : GROW **2** : to multiply by the production of young ⟨rabbits ~ rapidly⟩ **3** : to make greater

incombustible **incomprehension** **inconclusive** **incongruent** **inconsistency** **inconsistent** **incoordination**

— **increased** *adj* — **in·creas·ing·ly** \-ˈkrē-siŋ-lē\ *adv*

[2]**in·crease** \ˈin-ˌkrēs, in-ˈkrēs\ *n* **1** : addition or enlargement in size, extent, or quantity : GROWTH **2** : something that is added to an original stock or amount (as by growth)

in·cred·i·ble \(ˌ)in-ˈkre-də-bəl\ *adj* : too extraordinary and improbable to be believed; *also* : hard to believe — **in·cred·i·bil·i·ty** \(ˌ)in-ˌkre-də-ˈbi-lə-tē\ *n* — **in·cred·i·bly** \-ˈkre-də-blē\ *adv*

in·cred·u·lous \-ˈkre-jə-ləs\ *adj* **1** : SKEPTICAL **2** : expressing disbelief — **in·cre·du·li·ty** \ˌin-kri-ˈdü-lə-tē, -ˈdyü-\ *n* — **in·cred·u·lous·ly** *adv*

in·cre·ment \ˈiŋ-krə-mənt, ˈin-\ *n* **1** : the action or process of increasing esp. in quantity or value : ENLARGEMENT **2** : something gained or added; *esp* : one of a series of regular consecutive additions — **in·cre·men·tal** \ˌiŋ-krə-ˈmen-tᵊl, ˌin-\ *adj* — **in·cre·men·tal·ly** *adv*

in·crim·i·nate \in-ˈkri-mə-ˌnāt\ *vb* **-nat·ed; -nat·ing** : to charge with or prove involvement in a crime or fault : ACCUSE — **in·crim·i·na·tion** \-ˌkri-mə-ˈnā-shən\ *n* — **in·crim·i·na·to·ry** \-ˈkri-mə-nə-ˌtōr-ē\ *adj*

incrust *var of* ENCRUST

in·crus·ta·tion *also* **en·crus·ta·tion** \ˌin-ˌkrəs-ˈtā-shən\ *n* **1** : CRUST; *also* : an accumulation (as of habits, opinions, or customs) resembling a crust **2** : the act of encrusting : the state of being encrusted

in·cu·bate \ˈiŋ-kyü-ˌbāt, ˈin-\ *vb* **-bat·ed; -bat·ing** : to sit on (eggs) to hatch by the warmth of the body; *also* : to keep (as an embryo) under conditions favorable for development — **in·cu·ba·tion** \ˌiŋ-kyü-ˈbā-shən, ˌin-\ *n*

in·cu·ba·tor \ˈiŋ-kyü-ˌbāt-ər, ˈin-\ *n* : one that incubates; *esp* : an apparatus providing suitable conditions (as of warmth and moisture) for incubating something (as a premature baby)

in·cu·bus \ˈiŋ-kyə-bəs, ˈin-\ *n, pl* **-bi** \-ˌbī, -ˌbē\ *also* **-bus·es** [ME, fr. LL, fr. L *incubare* to lie on] **1** : a spirit supposed to work evil on persons in their sleep **2** : NIGHTMARE 1 **3** : one that oppresses like a nightmare

in·cul·cate \in-ˈkəl-ˌkāt, ˈin-(ˌ)kəl-\ *vb* **-cat·ed; -cat·ing** [L *inculcare,* lit., to tread on, fr. *calcare* to trample, fr. *calx* heel] : to teach and impress by frequent repetitions or admonitions — **in·cul·ca·tion** \ˌin-(ˌ)kəl-ˈkā-shən\ *n*

in·cul·pa·ble \(ˌ)in-ˈkəl-pə-bəl\ *adj* : free from guilt : INNOCENT

in·cul·pate \in-ˈkəl-ˌpāt, ˈin-(ˌ)kəl-\ *vb* **-pat·ed; -pat·ing** : INCRIMINATE

in·cum·ben·cy \in-ˈkəm-bən-sē\ *n, pl* **-cies** **1** : something that is incumbent **2** : the quality or state of being incumbent **3** : the office or period of office of an incumbent

[1]**in·cum·bent** \in-ˈkəm-bənt\ *n* : the holder of an office or position

[2]**incumbent** *adj* **1** : imposed as a duty **2** : occupying a specified office **3** : lying or resting on something else

in·cu·nab·u·lum \ˌin-kyə-ˈna-byə-ləm, iŋ-\ *n, pl* **-la** \-lə\ [NL, fr. L *incunabula,* pl., bands holding the baby in a cradle, fr. *cunae* cradle] : a book printed before 1501

in·cur \in-ˈkər\ *vb* **in·curred; in·cur·ring** : to become liable or subject to : bring down upon oneself

in·cur·able \(ˌ)in-ˈkyu̇r-ə-bəl\ *adj* **1** : not curable **2** : not likely to be changed — **incurable** *n* — **in·cur·ably** \(ˌ)in-ˈkyu̇r-ə-blē\ *adv*

in·cur·sion \in-ˈkər-zhən\ *n* **1** : a sudden hostile invasion : RAID **2** : an entering in or into (as an activity)

in·cus \ˈiŋ-kəs\ *n, pl* **in·cu·des** \iŋ-ˈkyü-(ˌ)dēz\ [NL, fr. L, anvil] : the middle bone of a chain of three small bones in the middle ear of a mammal

ind *abbr* **1** independent **2** index **3** industrial; industry

Ind *abbr* **1** Indian **2** Indiana

in·debt·ed \in-ˈde-təd\ *adj* **1** : owing gratitude or recognition to another **2** : owing money — **in·debt·ed·ness** *n*

in·de·cent \(ˌ)in-ˈdē-sᵊnt\ *adj* : not decent; *esp* : grossly improper or offensive — **in·de·cen·cy** \-sᵊn-sē\ *n* — **in·de·cent·ly** *adv*

in·de·ci·sion \ˌin-di-ˈsi-zhən\ *n* : a wavering between two or more possible courses of action : IRRESOLUTION

in·de·ci·sive \ˌin-di-ˈsī-siv\ *adj* **1** : INCONCLUSIVE ⟨an ~ battle⟩ **2** : marked by or prone to indecision **3** : INDEFINITE — **in·de·ci·sive·ly** *adv* — **in·de·ci·sive·ness** *n*

in·de·co·rous \(ˌ)in-ˈde-kə-rəs; ˌin-di-ˈkōr-əs\ *adj* : conflicting with accepted standards of good conduct or good taste ♦ ***Synonyms*** IMPROPER, UNSEEMLY, INDECENT, UNBECOMING, INDELICATE — **in·de·co·rous·ly** *adv* — **in·de·co·rous·ness** *n*

in·deed \in-ˈdēd\ *adv* **1** : without any question : TRULY — often used interjectionally to express irony, disbelief, or surprise **2** : in reality **3** : all things considered

in·de·fat·i·ga·ble \ˌin-di-ˈfa-ti-gə-bəl\ *adj* : UNTIRING ⟨an ~ worker⟩ — **in·de·fat·i·ga·bly** \-blē\ *adv*

in·de·fea·si·ble \-ˈfē-zə-bəl\ *adj* : not capable of being annulled or voided — **in·de·fea·si·bly** \-blē\ *adv*

in·de·fen·si·ble \-ˈfen-sə-bəl\ *adj* **1** : incapable of being maintained as right or valid **2** : INEXCUSABLE ⟨~ comments⟩ **3** : incapable of being protected against physical attack

in·de·fin·able \-ˈfī-nə-bəl\ *adj* : incapable of being precisely described or analyzed — **in·de·fin·ably** \-blē\ *adv*

in·def·i·nite \(ˌ)in-ˈde-fə-nət\ *adj* **1** : not defining or identifying ⟨*an* is an ~ article⟩ **2** : not precise : VAGUE **3** : having no fixed limits — **in•def•i•nite•ly** *adv* — **in•def•i•nite•ness** *n*

in•del•i•ble \in-ˈde-lə-bəl\ *adj* [ME, fr. ML *indelibilis,* alter. of L *indelebilis,* fr. *delēre* to delete, destroy] **1 :** not capable of being removed or erased **2 :** making marks that cannot be erased **3 :** LASTING, UNFORGETTABLE ⟨an ~ performance⟩ — **in•del•i•bly** \in-ˈde-lə-blē\ *adv*

in•del•i•cate \(ˌ)in-ˈde-li-kət\ *adj* **:** not delicate; *esp* **:** IMPROPER, COARSE, TACTLESS ♦ ***Synonyms*** INDECENT, UNSEEMLY, INDECOROUS, UNBECOMING — **in•del•i•ca•cy** \in-ˈde-lə-kə-sē\ *n*

in•dem•ni•fy \in-ˈdem-nə-ˌfī\ *vb* **-fied; -fy•ing** [L *indemnis* unharmed, fr. *in-* not + *damnum* damage] **1 :** to secure against hurt, loss, or damage **2 :** to make compensation to for hurt, loss, or damage — **in•dem•ni•fi•ca•tion** \-ˌdem-nə-fə-ˈkā-shən\ *n*

in•dem•ni•ty \in-ˈdem-nə-tē\ *n, pl* **-ties 1 :** security against hurt, loss, or damage; *also* **:** exemption from incurred penalties or liabilities **2 :** something that indemnifies

[1]**in•dent** \in-ˈdent\ *vb* [ME, fr. AF *endenter,* fr. *dent* tooth, fr. L *dent-, dens*] **1 :** to notch the edge of **2 :** INDENTURE **3 :** to set (as a line of a paragraph) in from the margin

[2]**indent** *vb* **1 :** to force inward so as to form a depression **2 :** to form a dent in

in•den•ta•tion \ˌin-ˌden-ˈtā-shən\ *n* **1 :** NOTCH; *also* **:** a recess in a surface **2 :** the action of indenting **:** the condition of being indented **3 :** DENT **4 :** INDENTION 2

in•den•tion \in-ˈden-chən\ *n* **1 :** INDENTATION 2 **2 :** the blank space produced by indenting

[1]**in•den•ture** \in-ˈden-chər\ *n* **1 :** a written certificate or agreement; *esp* **:** a contract binding one person (as an apprentice) to work for another for a given period of time — often used in pl. **2 :** INDENTATION 1 **3 :** DENT

[2]**indenture** *vb* **in•den•tured; in•den•tur•ing :** to bind (as an apprentice) by indentures

in•de•pen•dence \ˌin-də-ˈpen-dəns\ *n* **:** the quality or state of being independent **:** FREEDOM

Independence Day *n* **:** July 4 observed as a legal holiday in the U.S. in commemoration of the adoption of the Declaration of Independence in 1776

in•de•pen•dent \ˌin-də-ˈpen-dənt\ *adj* **1 :** SELF-GOVERNING; *also* **:** not affiliated with a larger controlling unit **2 :** not requiring or relying on something else or somebody else ⟨an ~ conclusion⟩ ⟨~ of her parents⟩ **3 :** not easily influenced **:** showing self-reliance and personal freedom ⟨an ~ mind⟩ **4 :** not committed to a political party ⟨an ~ voter⟩ **5 :** MAIN ⟨an ~ clause⟩ — **independent** *n* — **in•de•pen•dent•ly** *adv*

independent variable *n* **:** a variable whose value is not determined by that of any other variable in a function

in•de•scrib•able \ˌin-di-ˈskrī-bə-bəl\ *adj* **1 :** that cannot be described **2 :** being too intense or great for description — **in•de•scrib•ably** \-blē\ *adv*

in•de•ter•mi•nate \ˌin-di-ˈtər-mə-nət\ *adj* **1 :** VAGUE; *also* **:** not known in advance **2 :** not limited in advance; *also* **:** not leading to a definite end or result — **in•de•ter•mi•na•cy** \-nə-sē\ *n* — **in•de•ter•mi•nate•ly** *adv*

[1]**in•dex** \ˈin-ˌdeks\ *n, pl* **in•dex•es** *or* **in•di•ces** \-də-ˌsēz\ **1 :** POINTER **2 :** SIGN, INDICATION ⟨an ~ of character⟩ **3 :** a guide for facilitating references; *esp* **:** an alphabetical list of items treated in a printed work with the page number where each item may be found **4 :** a list of restricted or prohibited material **5** *pl usu indices* **:** a number or symbol or expression (as an exponent) associated with another to indicate a mathematical operation or use or position in an arrangement or expansion **6 :** a character ☞ used to direct attention (as to a note) **7 :** INDEX NUMBER

[2]**index** *vb* **1 :** to provide with or put into an index **2 :** to serve as an index of **3 :** to regulate by indexation

in•dex•ation \ˌin-ˌdek-ˈsā-shən\ *n* **:** a system of economic control in which a body of variables (as wages and interest) rise or fall at the same rate as an index of the cost of living

index finger *n* **:** the finger next to the thumb

in•dex•ing *n* **:** INDEXATION

index number *n* **:** a number used to indicate change in magnitude (as of cost) as compared with the magnitude at some specified time

index of refraction : REFRACTIVE INDEX

in•dia ink \ˈin-dē-ə-\ *n, often cap 1st I* **1 :** a solid black pigment used in drawing **2 :** a fluid made from india ink

In•di•an \ˈin-dē-ən\ *n* **1 :** a native or inhabitant of India or of the East Indies; *also* **:** a person of Indian descent **2 :** AMERICAN INDIAN — **Indian** *adj*

Indian corn *n* **1 :** CORN 2 **2 :** corn having hard kernels of various colors (as reddish-brown or purple) used esp. for ornament

Indian meal *n* **:** CORNMEAL

Indian paintbrush *n* **:** any of a genus of herbaceous plants related to the snapdragons that have brightly colored bracts

Indian pipe *n* **:** a waxy white leafless saprophytic herb of Asia and the U.S.

Indian summer *n* **:** a period of mild weather in late autumn or early winter

In•dia paper \ˈin-dē-ə-\ *n* **1 :** a thin absorbent paper used esp. for taking impressions (as of steel engravings) **2 :** a thin tough opaque printing paper

in•di•cate \ˈin-də-ˌkāt\ *vb* **-cat•ed; -cat•ing 1 :** to point out or to **2 :** to show indirectly **3 :** to state briefly —

indemonstrable indestructible indeterminable

in·di·ca·tion \ˌin-də-ˈkā-shən\ *n* — **in·di·ca·tor** \ˈin-də-ˌkā-tər\ *n*

[1]**in·dic·a·tive** \in-ˈdi-kə-tiv\ *adj* **1** : of, relating to, or being a verb form that represents an act or state as a fact ⟨~ mood⟩ **2** : serving to indicate ⟨actions ~ of fear⟩

[2]**indicative** *n* **1** : the indicative mood of a language **2** : a form in the indicative mood

in·di·cia \in-ˈdi-shə, -shē-ə\ *n pl* **1** : distinctive marks **2** : postal markings often imprinted on mail or mailing labels

in·dict \in-ˈdīt\ *vb* [alter. of earlier *indite,* fr. ME, fr. AF *enditer* to write, point out, indict, ultim. fr. L *indicere* to make known formally, fr. *dicere* to say] **1** : to charge with a fault or offense **2** : to charge with a crime by the finding of a jury — **in·dict·able** *adj* — **in·dict·ment** *n*

in·die \ˈin-dē\ *n* **1** : one that is independent; *esp* : an unaffiliated record or motion-picture production company **2** something produced by an indie — **indie** *adj*

in·dif·fer·ent \in-ˈdi-frənt, -fə-rənt\ *adj* **1** : UNBIASED, UNPREJUDICED **2** : of no importance one way or the other **3** : marked by no special liking for or dislike of something **4** : being neither excessive nor inadequate **5** : PASSABLE, MEDIOCRE **6** : being neither right nor wrong — **in·dif·fer·ence** \-frəns, -fə-rəns\ *n* — **in·dif·fer·ent·ly** *adv*

in·dig·e·nous \in-ˈdi-jə-nəs\ *adj* **1** : produced, growing, or living naturally in a particular region **2** *usu cap* : of or relating to the earliest known inhabitants of a place and esp. of a place that was colonized

in·di·gent \ˈin-di-jənt\ *adj* : IMPOVERISHED, NEEDY — **in·di·gence** \-jəns\ *n*

in·di·gest·ible \ˌin-dī-ˈjes-tə-bəl, -də-\ *adj* : not readily digested

in·di·ges·tion \-ˈjes-chən\ *n* : inadequate or difficult digestion : DYSPEPSIA

in·dig·nant \in-ˈdig-nənt\ *adj* : filled with or marked by indignation — **in·dig·nant·ly** *adv*

in·dig·na·tion \ˌin-dig-ˈnā-shən\ *n* : anger aroused by something unjust, unworthy, or mean

in·dig·ni·ty \in-ˈdig-nə-tē\ *n, pl* **-ties** : an offense against personal dignity or self-respect; *also* : humiliating treatment

in·di·go \ˈin-di-ˌgō\ *n, pl* **-gos** *or* **-goes** [It dial., fr. L *indicum,* fr. Gk *indikon,* fr. *indikos* Indic, fr. *Indos* India] **1** : a blue dye obtained from plants or synthesized **2** : a deep reddish blue color

in·di·rect \ˌin-də-ˈrekt, -dī-\ *adj* **1** : not straight ⟨an ~ route⟩ **2** : not straightforward and open ⟨~ methods⟩ **3** : not having a plainly seen connection ⟨an ~ cause⟩ **4** : not directly to the point ⟨an ~ answer⟩ — **in·di·rec·tion** \-ˈrek-shən\ *n* — **in·di·rect·ly** *adv* — **in·di·rect·ness** *n*

in·dis·creet \ˌin-di-ˈskrēt\ *adj* : not discreet : IMPRUDENT — **in·dis·creet·ly** *adv*

in·dis·cre·tion \ˌin-di-ˈskre-shən\ *n* **1** : IMPRUDENCE ⟨dietary ~⟩ **2** : something marked by lack of discretion; *esp* : an act deviating from accepted morality

in·dis·crim·i·nate \ˌin-di-ˈskri-mə-nət\ *adj* **1** : not careful in making choices **2** : HAPHAZARD, RANDOM ⟨an ~ application of a law⟩ **3** : UNRESTRAINED **4** : MOTLEY — **in·dis·crim·i·nate·ly** *adv*

in·dis·pens·able \ˌin-di-ˈspen-sə-bəl\ *adj* : absolutely essential : REQUISITE — **in·dis·pens·abil·i·ty** \-ˌspen-sə-ˈbi-lə-tē\ *n* — **indispensable** *n* — **in·dis·pens·ably** \-ˈspen-sə-blē\ *adv*

in·dis·posed \-ˈspōzd\ *adj* **1** : slightly ill **2** : AVERSE — **in·dis·po·si·tion** \(ˌ)in-ˌdis-pə-ˈzi-shən\ *n*

in·dis·put·able \ˌin-di-ˈspyü-tə-bəl, (ˌ)in-ˈdis-pyə-\ *adj* : not disputable : UNQUESTIONABLE ⟨~ proof⟩ — **in·dis·put·ably** \-blē\ *adv*

in·dis·sol·u·ble \ˌin-di-ˈsäl-yə-bəl\ *adj* : not capable of being dissolved, undone, or broken : PERMANENT ⟨an ~ contract⟩

in·dis·tinct \ˌin-di-ˈstiŋkt\ *adj* **1** : not sharply outlined or separable : BLURRED, FAINT, DIM **2** : not readily distinguishable : UNCERTAIN — **in·dis·tinct·ly** *adv* — **in·dis·tinct·ness** *n*

in·dite \in-ˈdīt\ *vb* **in·dit·ed; in·dit·ing** : COMPOSE ⟨~ a poem⟩; *also* : to put in writing ⟨~ a letter⟩

in·di·um \ˈin-dē-əm\ *n* : a malleable silvery metallic chemical element

indiv *abbr* individual

[1]**in·di·vid·u·al** \ˌin-də-ˈvi-jə-wəl\ *adj* **1** : of, relating to, or associated with an individual ⟨~ traits⟩ **2** : being an individual : existing as an indivisible whole **3** : intended for one person **4** : SEPARATE ⟨~ copies⟩ **5** : having marked individuality ⟨an ~ style⟩ — **in·di·vid·u·al·ly** *adv*

[2]**individual** *n* **1** : a single member of a category : a particular person, animal, or thing **2** : PERSON ⟨a disagreeable ~⟩

in·di·vid·u·al·ise *Brit var of* INDIVIDUALIZE

in·di·vid·u·al·ism \ˌin-də-ˈvi-jə-wə-ˌli-zəm\ *n* **1** : a doctrine that the interests of the individual are primary **2** : a doctrine holding that the individual has political or economic rights with which the state must not interfere **3** : INDIVIDUALITY

in·di·vid·u·al·ist \-list\ *n* **1** : one that pursues a markedly independent course in thought or action **2** : one that advocates or practices individualism — **individualist** *or* **in·di·vid·u·al·is·tic** \-ˌvi-jə-wə-ˈlis-tik\ *adj*

in·di·vid·u·al·i·ty \-ˌvi-jə-ˈwa-lə-tē\ *n, pl* **-ties** **1** : the sum of qualities that characterize and distinguish an individual from all others; *also* : PERSONALITY **2** : separate or distinct existence **3** : INDIVIDUAL, PERSON

in·di·vid·u·al·ize \-ˈvi-jə-wə-ˌlīz\ *vb* **-ized;**

-iz·ing **1** : to make individual in character **2** : to treat or notice individually : PARTICULARIZE **3** : to adapt to the needs of an individual

individual retirement account *n* : IRA

in·di·vid·u·ate \ˌin-də-ˈvi-jə-ˌwāt\ *vb* **-at·ed; -at·ing** : to give individuality to : form into an individual — **in·di·vid·u·a·tion** \-ˌvi-jə-ˈwā-shən\ *n*

in·di·vis·i·ble \ˌin-də-ˈvi-zə-bəl\ *adj* : impossible to divide or separate — **in·di·vis·i·bil·i·ty** \-ˌvi-zə-ˈbi-lə-tē\ *n* — **in·di·vis·i·bly** *adv*

In·do–Ar·y·an \ˌin-dō-ˈer-ē-ən\ *n* : a branch of the Indo-European language family that includes Hindi and other languages of south Asia

in·doc·tri·nate \in-ˈdäk-trə-ˌnāt\ *vb* **-nat·ed; -nat·ing** **1** : to instruct esp. in fundamentals or rudiments : TEACH **2** : to teach the beliefs and doctrines of a particular group — **in·doc·tri·na·tion** \(ˌ)in-ˌdäk-trə-ˈnā-shən\ *n* — **in·doc·tri·na·tor** *n*

In·do–Eu·ro·pe·an \ˌin-dō-ˌyu̇r-ə-ˈpē-ən\ *adj* : of, relating to, or constituting a family of languages comprising those spoken in most of Europe and in the parts of the world colonized by Europeans since 1500 and also in Persia, the subcontinent of India, and some other parts of Asia

in·do·lent \ˈin-də-lənt\ *adj* [LL *indolens* insensitive to pain, fr. L *dolēre* to feel pain] **1** : slow to develop or heal ⟨~ ulcers⟩ **2** : LAZY — **in·do·lence** \-ləns\ *n* — **in·do·lent·ly** *adv*

in·dom·i·ta·ble \in-ˈdä-mə-tə-bəl\ *adj* : UNCONQUERABLE ⟨~ courage⟩ — **in·dom·i·ta·bly** \-blē\ *adv*

in·door \ˈin-ˈdȯr\ *adj* **1** : of or relating to the inside of a building **2** : living, located, or carried on within a building

in·doors \in-ˈdȯrz\ *adv* : in or into a building

indorse, indorsement *var of* ENDORSE, ENDORSEMENT

in·du·bi·ta·ble \(ˌ)in-ˈdü-bə-tə-bəl, -ˈdyü-\ *adj* : UNQUESTIONABLE ⟨~ truths⟩ — **in·du·bi·ta·bly** \-blē\ *adv*

in·duce \in-ˈdüs, -ˈdyüs\ *vb* **in·duced; in·duc·ing** **1** : PERSUADE, INFLUENCE **2** : BRING ABOUT **3** : to produce (as an electric current) by induction **4** : to determine by induction; *esp* : to infer from particulars — **in·duc·er** *n*

in·duce·ment \-mənt\ *n* **1** : something that induces : MOTIVE **2** : the act or process of inducing

in·duct \in-ˈdəkt\ *vb* **1** : to place in office **2** : to admit as a member **3** : to enroll for military training or service — **in·duct·ee** \-ˌdək-ˈtē\ *n*

in·duc·tance \in-ˈdək-təns\ *n* : a property of an electric circuit by which a varying current produces an electromotive force in that circuit or in a nearby circuit; *also* : the measure of this property

in·duc·tion \in-ˈdək-shən\ *n* **1** : the act or process of inducting; *also* : INITIATION **2** : the formality by which a civilian is inducted into military service **3** : inference of a generalized conclusion from particular instances; *also* : a conclusion so reached **4** : the act of causing or bringing on or about **5** : the process by which an electric current, an electric charge, or magnetism is produced in a body by the proximity of an electric or magnetic field

in·duc·tive \in-ˈdək-tiv\ *adj* : of, relating to, or employing induction

in·duc·tor \in-ˈdək-tər\ *n* : an electrical component that acts upon another or is itself acted upon by induction

in·dulge \in-ˈdəlj\ *vb* **in·dulged; in·dulg·ing** **1** : to give free rein to : GRATIFY **2** : HUMOR **3** : to gratify one's taste or desire for ⟨~ in alcohol⟩

in·dul·gence \in-ˈdəl-jəns\ *n* **1** : remission of temporal punishment due in Roman Catholic doctrine for sins whose eternal punishment has been remitted by reception of the sacrifice of penance **2** : the act of indulging : the state of being indulgent **3** : an indulgent act **4** : the thing indulged in **5** : SELF-INDULGENCE — **in·dul·gent** \-jənt\ *adj* — **in·dul·gent·ly** *adv*

in·du·rat·ed \ˈin-dyu̇-ˌrā-təd, -du̇-\ *adj* : physically or emotionally hardened — **in·du·ra·tion** \ˌin-dyu̇-ˈrā-shən, -du̇-\ *n*

in·dus·tri·al \in-ˈdəs-trē-əl\ *adj* **1** : of or relating to industry **2** : HEAVY-DUTY ⟨an ~ zipper⟩ **3** : characterized by highly developed industries — **in·dus·tri·al·ly** *adv*

in·dus·tri·al·ise *Brit var of* INDUSTRIALIZE

in·dus·tri·al·ist \-ə-list\ *n* : a person owning or engaged in the management of an industry

in·dus·tri·al·ize \in-ˈdəs-trē-ə-ˌlīz\ *vb* **-ized; -iz·ing** : to make or become industrial — **in·dus·tri·al·i·za·tion** \-ˌdəs-trē-ə-lə-ˈzā-shən\ *n*

in·dus·tri·ous \in-ˈdəs-trē-əs\ *adj* : DILIGENT, BUSY — **in·dus·tri·ous·ly** *adv* — **in·dus·tri·ous·ness** *n*

in·dus·try \ˈin-(ˌ)dəs-trē\ *n, pl* **-tries** **1** : DILIGENCE **2** : a department or branch of a craft, art, business, or manufacture; *esp* : one that employs a large personnel and capital **3** : a distinct group of productive enterprises **4** : manufacturing activity as a whole

in·dwell \(ˌ)in-ˈdwel\ *vb* : to exist within as an activating spirit or force

In·dy car \ˈin-dē-\ *n* : a single-seat, open-cockpit racing car with the engine in the rear

[1]**in·ebri·ate** \i-ˈnē-brē-ˌāt\ *vb* **-at·ed; -at·ing** : to make drunk : INTOXICATE — **in·ebri·a·tion** \-ˌnē-brē-ˈā-shən\ *n*

[2]**in·ebri·ate** \-ət\ *n* : one that is drunk; *esp* : DRUNKARD

in·ef·fa·ble \(ˌ)in-ˈe-fə-bəl\ *adj* **1** : incapable of being expressed in words : INDESCRIBABLE ⟨~ joy⟩ **2** : UNSPEAKABLE ⟨~ disgust⟩ **3** : not to be uttered : TABOO — **in·ef·fa·bly** \-blē\ *adv*

in·ef·fec·tive \ˌi-nə-ˈfek-tiv\ *adj* **1** : INEF-

FECTUAL **2** : not able to perform efficiently or as expected : INCAPABLE — **in·ef·fec·tive·ly** *adv* — **in·ef·fec·tive·ness** *n*
in·ef·fec·tu·al \-ˈfek-chə-wəl\ *adj* **1** : not producing the proper or usual effect **2** : INEFFECTIVE 2 — **in·ef·fec·tu·al·ly** *adv*
in·ef·fi·cient \ˌi-nə-ˈfi-shənt\ *adj* **1** : not producing the desired effect **2** : wasteful of time or energy **3** : INCAPABLE, INCOMPETENT — **in·ef·fi·cien·cy** \-ˈfi-shən-sē\ *n* — **in·ef·fi·cient·ly** *adv*
in·el·e·gant \(ˌ)i-ˈne-li-gənt\ *adj* : lacking in refinement, grace, or good taste — **in·el·e·gance** \-gəns\ *n* — **in·el·e·gant·ly** *adv*
in·el·i·gi·ble \(ˌ)i-ˈne-lə-jə-bəl\ *adj* : not qualified for an office or position — **in·el·i·gi·bil·i·ty** \(ˌ)i-ˌne-lə-jə-ˈbi-lə-tē\ *n*
in·eluc·ta·ble \ˌi-ni-ˈlək-tə-bəl\ *adj* : not to be avoided, changed, or resisted ⟨an ~ conclusion⟩ — **in·eluc·ta·bly** \-blē\ *adv*
in·ept \i-ˈnept\ *adj* **1** : lacking in fitness or aptitude : UNFIT **2** : FOOLISH **3** : being out of place : INAPPROPRIATE **4** : generally incompetent : BUNGLING — **in·ept·ly** *adv* — **in·ept·ness** *n*
in·ep·ti·tude \(ˌ)i-ˈnep-ti-ˌtüd, -ˌtyüd\ *n* : the quality or state of being inept; *esp* : INCOMPETENCE
in·equal·i·ty \ˌi-ni-ˈkwä-lə-tē\ *n* **1** : the quality of being unequal or uneven; *esp* : UNEVENNESS, DISPARITY **2** : an instance of being unequal
in·ert \i-ˈnərt\ *adj* [L *inert-, iners* unskilled, idle, fr. *art-, ars* skill] **1** : powerless to move **2** : SLUGGISH **3** : lacking in active properties ⟨chemically ~⟩ — **in·ert·ly** *adv* — **in·ert·ness** *n*
in·er·tia \i-ˈnər-shə, -shē-ə\ *n* **1** : a property of matter whereby it remains at rest or continues in uniform motion unless acted upon by some outside force **2** : INERTNESS, SLUGGISHNESS — **in·er·tial** \-shəl\ *adj*
in·es·cap·able \ˌi-nə-ˈskā-pə-bəl\ *adj* : incapable of being escaped : INEVITABLE — **in·es·cap·ably** \-blē\ *adv*
in·es·ti·ma·ble \(ˌ)i-ˈnes-tə-mə-bəl\ *adj* **1** : incapable of being estimated or computed ⟨~ errors⟩ **2** : too valuable or excellent to be fully appreciated — **in·es·ti·ma·bly** \-blē\ *adv*
in·ev·i·ta·ble \i-ˈne-və-tə-bəl\ *adj* : incapable of being avoided or evaded : bound to happen ⟨the ~ result⟩ — **in·ev·i·ta·bil·i·ty** \(ˌ)i-ˌne-və-tə-ˈbi-lə-tē\ *n*
in·ev·i·ta·bly \-blē\ *adv* **1** : in an inevitable way **2** : as is to be expected
in·ex·act \ˌi-nig-ˈzakt\ *adj* **1** : not precisely correct or true : INACCURATE **2** : not rigorous and careful — **in·ex·act·ly** *adv* — **in·ex·act·ness** *n*
in·ex·cus·able \ˌi-nik-ˈskyü-zə-bəl\ *adj* : impossible to excuse or justify ⟨~ rudeness⟩ — **in·ex·cus·ably** \-blē\ *adv*
in·ex·haust·ible \ˌi-nig-ˈzȯ-stə-bəl\ *adj* **1** : incapable of being used up ⟨an ~ supply⟩ **2** : UNTIRING ⟨an ~ hiker⟩ — **in·ex·haust·ibly** \-blē\ *adv*
in·ex·o·ra·ble \(ˌ)i-ˈnek-sə-rə-bəl\ *adj* : not to be persuaded, moved, or stopped : RELENTLESS — **in·ex·o·ra·bly** *adv*
in·ex·pe·ri·ence \ˌi-nik-ˈspir-ē-əns\ *n* : lack of experience or of knowledge gained by experience — **in·ex·pe·ri·enced** \-ənst\ *adj*
in·ex·pert \(ˌ)i-ˈnek-ˌspərt\ *adj* : not expert : UNSKILLED — **in·ex·pert·ly** *adv*
in·ex·pi·a·ble \(ˌ)i-ˈnek-spē-ə-bəl\ *adj* : not capable of being atoned for
in·ex·pli·ca·ble \ˌi-nik-ˈspli-kə-bəl, (ˌ)i-ˈnek-(ˌ)spli-\ *adj* : incapable of being explained or accounted for ⟨an ~ mistake⟩ — **in·ex·pli·ca·bly** \-blē\ *adv*
in·ex·press·ible \-ˈspre-sə-bəl\ *adj* : not capable of being expressed ⟨~ joy⟩ — **in·ex·press·ibly** \-blē\ *adv*
in ex·tre·mis \ˌin-ik-ˈstrā-məs, -ˈstrē-\ *adv* : in extreme circumstances; *esp* : at the point of death
in·ex·tri·ca·ble \ˌi-nik-ˈstri-kə-bəl, (ˌ)i-ˈnek-(ˌ)stri-\ *adj* **1** : forming a maze or tangle from which it is impossible to get free **2** : incapable of being disentangled or untied — **in·ex·tri·ca·bly** \-blē\ *adv*
inf *abbr* **1** infantry **2** infinitive
in·fal·li·ble \(ˌ)in-ˈfa-lə-bəl\ *adj* **1** : incapable of error : UNERRING ⟨an ~ marksman⟩ **2** : SURE, CERTAIN ⟨an ~ remedy⟩ — **in·fal·li·bil·i·ty** \(ˌ)in-ˌfa-lə-ˈbi-lə-tē\ *n* — **in·fal·li·bly** \(ˌ)in-ˈfa-lə-blē\ *adv*
in·fa·mous \ˈin-fə-məs\ *adj* **1** : having a reputation of the worst kind **2** : DISGRACEFUL — **in·fa·mous·ly** *adv*
in·fa·my \-mē\ *n, pl* **-mies** **1** : evil reputation brought about by something grossly criminal, shocking, or brutal **2** : an extreme and publicly known criminal or evil act **3** : the state of being infamous
in·fan·cy \ˈin-fən-sē\ *n, pl* **-cies** **1** : early childhood **2** : a beginning or early period of existence
in·fant \ˈin-fənt\ *n* [ME *enfaunt,* fr. AF *enfant,* fr. L *infant-, infans,* adj., incapable of speech, young, fr. *fant-, fans,* prp. of *fari* to speak] : BABY; *also* : a person who is a legal minor
in·fan·ti·cide \in-ˈfan-tə-ˌsīd\ *n* : the killing of an infant
in·fan·tile \ˈin-fən-ˌtī(-ə)l, -tᵊl, -ˌtēl\ *adj* : of or relating to infants; *also* : CHILDISH
infantile paralysis *n* : POLIOMYELITIS
in·fan·try \ˈin-fən-trē\ *n, pl* **-tries** [MF & It; MF *infanterie,* fr. It *infanteria,* fr. *infante* boy, foot soldier] : soldiers trained, armed, and equipped to fight on foot — **in·fan·try·man** \-mən\ *n*
in·farct \ˈin-ˌfärkt\ *n* [L *infarctus,* pp. of *infarcire* to stuff] : an area of dead tissue (as of the heart wall) caused by blocking of local blood circulation — **in·farc·tion** \in-ˈfärk-shən\ *n*
in·fat·u·ate \in-ˈfa-chə-ˌwāt\ *vb* **-at·ed; -at·ing** : to inspire with a foolish or ex-

inefficacious
inefficacy
inelastic
inelasticity
inequitable
inequity
ineradicable
inerrant
inexpedient
inexpensive
inexpressive
inextinguishable

travagant love or admiration — **in·fat·u·a·tion** \-ˌfa-chə-ˈwā-shən\ *n*

in·fect \in-ˈfekt\ *vb* **1** : to contaminate with disease-producing matter **2** : to communicate a pathogen or disease to **3** : to cause to share one's feelings ⟨~*ed* us with his enthusiasm⟩

in·fec·tion \in-ˈfek-shən\ *n* **1** : a disease or condition caused by a germ or parasite; *also* : such a germ or parasite **2** : an act or process of infecting — **in·fec·tious** \-shəs\ *adj* — **in·fec·tive** \-ˈfek-tiv\ *adj*

infectious mononucleosis *n* : an acute infectious disease characterized by fever, swelling of lymph glands, and increased numbers of lymph cells in the blood

in·fe·lic·i·tous \ˌin-fi-ˈli-sə-təs\ *adj* : not appropriate in application or expression ⟨~ comments⟩ — **in·fe·lic·i·ty** \-sə-tē\ *n*

in·fer \in-ˈfər\ *vb* **in·ferred; in·fer·ring** **1** : to derive as a conclusion from facts or premises **2** : GUESS, SURMISE **3** : to lead to as a conclusion or consequence **4** : HINT, SUGGEST ♦ ***Synonyms*** DEDUCE, CONCLUDE, JUDGE, GATHER — **in·fer·ence** \ˈin-frəns, -fə-rəns\ *n* — **in·fer·en·tial** \ˌin-fə-ˈren-chəl\ *adj*

in·fe·ri·or \in-ˈfir-ē-ər\ *adj* **1** : situated lower down **2** : of low or lower degree or rank **3** : of lesser quality **4** : of little or less importance, value, or merit ⟨an ~ opponent⟩ — **inferior** *n* — **in·fe·ri·or·i·ty** \(ˌ)in-ˌfir-ē-ˈȯr-ə-tē\ *n*

in·fer·nal \in-ˈfər-nᵊl\ *adj* **1** : of or relating to hell **2** : HELLISH, FIENDISH ⟨~ schemes⟩ **3** : DAMNABLE ⟨an ~ pest⟩ — **in·fer·nal·ly** *adv*

in·fer·no \in-ˈfər-nō\ *n, pl* **-nos** [It, hell, fr. LL *infernus,* fr. L, lower] : a place or a state that resembles or suggests hell; *also* : intense heat

in·fer·tile \(ˌ)in-ˈfər-tᵊl\ *adj* : not fertile or productive : BARREN — **in·fer·til·i·ty** \ˌin-fər-ˈti-lə-tē\ *n*

in·fest \in-ˈfest\ *vb* : to trouble by spreading or swarming in or over; *also* : to live in or on as a parasite — **in·fes·ta·tion** \ˌin-ˌfes-ˈtā-shən\ *n*

in·fi·del \ˈin-fə-dᵊl, -fə-ˌdel\ *n* **1** : one who is not a Christian or opposes Christianity **2** : an unbeliever esp. with respect to a particular religion

in·fi·del·i·ty \ˌin-fə-ˈde-lə-tē, -fī-\ *n, pl* **-ties** **1** : lack of belief in a religion **2** : unfaithfulness or an instance of it esp. in marriage

in·field \ˈin-ˌfēld\ *n* : the part of a baseball field inside the baselines — **in·field·er** *n*

in·fight·ing \ˈin-ˌfī-tiŋ\ *n* **1** : fighting at close quarters **2** : dissension or rivalry among members of a group

in·fil·trate \in-ˈfil-ˌtrāt, ˈin-(ˌ)fil-\ *vb* **-trat·ed; -trat·ing** **1** : to enter or filter into or through something **2** : to pass into or through by or as if by filtering or permeating — **in·fil·tra·tion** \ˌin-(ˌ)fil-ˈtrā-shən\ *n* — **in·fil·tra·tor** *n*

in·fi·nite \ˈin-fə-nət\ *adj* **1** : LIMITLESS, BOUNDLESS, ENDLESS ⟨~ space⟩ ⟨~ patience⟩ **2** : VAST, IMMENSE; *also* : INEXHAUSTIBLE ⟨~ wealth⟩ **3** : greater than any preassigned finite value however large ⟨~ number of positive integers⟩; *also* : extending to infinity ⟨~ plane surface⟩ — **infinite** *n* — **in·fi·nite·ly** *adv*

in·fin·i·tes·i·mal \(ˌ)in-ˌfi-nə-ˈte-sə-məl\ *adj* : immeasurably or incalculably small — **in·fin·i·tes·i·mal·ly** *adv*

in·fin·i·tive \in-ˈfi-nə-tiv\ *n* : a verb form having the characteristics of both verb and noun and in English usu. being used with *to*

in·fin·i·tude \in-ˈfi-nə-ˌtüd, -ˌtyüd\ *n* **1** : the quality or state of being infinite **2** : something that is infinite esp. in extent

in·fin·i·ty \in-ˈfi-nə-tē\ *n, pl* **-ties** **1** : the quality of being infinite **2** : unlimited extent of time, space, or quantity **3** : an indefinitely great number or amount

in·firm \in-ˈfərm\ *adj* **1** : deficient in vitality; *esp* : feeble from age **2** : weak of mind, will, or character : IRRESOLUTE **3** : not solid or stable : INSECURE

in·fir·ma·ry \in-ˈfər-mə-rē\ *n, pl* **-ries** : a place for the care of the infirm or sick

in·fir·mi·ty \in-ˈfər-mə-tē\ *n, pl* **-ties** **1** : FEEBLENESS **2** : DISEASE, AILMENT **3** : a personal failing : FOIBLE

infl *abbr* influenced

in fla·gran·te de·lic·to \ˌin-flə-ˈgrän-tē-di-ˈlik-tō, -ˈgran-\ *adv* **1** : in the very act of committing a misdeed **2** : in the midst of sexual activity

in·flame \in-ˈflām\ *vb* **in·flamed; in·flam·ing** **1** : KINDLE **2** : to excite to excessive or uncontrollable action or feeling; *also* : INTENSIFY **3** : to affect or become affected with inflammation

in·flam·ma·ble \in-ˈfla-mə-bəl\ *adj* **1** : FLAMMABLE **2** : easily inflamed, excited, or angered : IRASCIBLE

in·flam·ma·tion \ˌin-flə-ˈmā-shən\ *n* : a bodily response to injury in which an affected area becomes red, hot, and painful and congested with blood

in·flam·ma·to·ry \in-ˈfla-mə-ˌtȯr-ē\ *adj* **1** : tending to excite the senses or to arouse anger, disorder, or tumult : SEDITIOUS **2** : causing or accompanied by inflammation ⟨an ~ disease⟩

in·flate \in-ˈflāt\ *vb* **in·flat·ed; in·flat·ing** **1** : to swell with air or gas ⟨~ a balloon⟩ **2** : to puff up : ELATE ⟨~ one's ego⟩ **3** : to expand or increase abnormally ⟨~ prices⟩ — **in·flat·able** *adj*

in·fla·tion \in-ˈflā-shən\ *n* **1** : an act of inflating : the state of being inflated **2** : empty pretentiousness : POMPOSITY **3** : a continuing rise in the general price level usu. attributed to an increase in the volume of money and credit

in·fla·tion·ary \-shə-ˌner-ē\ *adj* : of, characterized by, or productive of inflation

in·flect \in-ˈflekt\ *vb* **1** : to turn from a direct line or course : CURVE **2** : to vary a word by inflection **3** : to change or vary the pitch of the voice

in·flec·tion \in-ˈflek-shən\ *n* **1** : the act or result of curving or bending **2** : a change

infeasible

in pitch or loudness of the voice **3** : the change of form that words undergo to mark case, gender, number, tense, person, mood, or voice — **in·flec·tion·al** \-shə-nəl\ *adj*

in·flex·i·ble \(ˌ)in-ˈflek-sə-bəl\ *adj* **1** : UNYIELDING **2** : RIGID **3** : incapable of change ⟨an ~ deadline⟩ — **in·flex·i·bil·i·ty** \-ˌflek-sə-ˈbi-lə-tē\ *n* — **in·flex·i·bly** \-ˈflek-sə-blē\ *adv*

in·flex·ion \in-ˈflek-shən\ *chiefly Brit var of* INFLECTION

in·flict \in-ˈflikt\ *vb* : AFFLICT; *also* : to give by or as if by striking ⟨~ pain⟩ — **in·flic·tion** \-ˈflik-shən\ *n*

in·flo·res·cence \ˌin-flə-ˈre-sᵊn(t)s\ *n* : the manner of development and arrangement of flowers on a stem; *also* : a flowering stem with its appendages : a flower cluster

in·flow \ˈin-ˌflō\ *n* : a flowing in

¹in·flu·ence \ˈin-ˌflü-əns\ *n* **1** : the act or power of producing an effect without apparent force or direct authority **2** : the power or capacity of causing an effect in indirect or intangible ways **3** : one that exerts influence — **in·flu·en·tial** \ˌin-flü-ˈen-chəl\ *adj* — **under the influence** : affected by alcohol

²influence *vb* **-enced; -enc·ing** **1** : to affect or alter by influence : SWAY **2** : to have an effect on the condition or development of : MODIFY

in·flu·en·za \ˌin-flü-ˈen-zə\ *n* [It, lit., influence, fr. ML *influentia;* fr. the belief that epidemics were due to the influence of the stars] : an acute and highly contagious virus disease marked by fever, prostration, aches and pains, and respiratory inflammation; *also* : any of various feverish usu. virus diseases typically with respiratory symptoms

in·flux \ˈin-ˌfləks\ *n* : a coming in

in·fo \ˈin-(ˌ)fō\ *n* : INFORMATION

in·fold \in-ˈfōld\ *vb* **1** : ENFOLD **2** : to fold inward or toward one another

in·fo·mer·cial \ˈin-fō-ˌmər-shəl\ *n* : a television program that is an extended advertisement often including a discussion or demonstration

in·form \in-ˈfȯrm\ *vb* **1** : to communicate knowledge to : TELL **2** : to give information or knowledge **3** : to act as an informer ♦ ***Synonyms*** ACQUAINT, APPRISE, ADVISE, NOTIFY

in·for·mal \(ˌ)in-ˈfȯr-məl\ *adj* **1** : conducted or carried out without formality or ceremony ⟨an ~ party⟩ **2** : characteristic of or appropriate to ordinary, casual, or familiar use ⟨~ clothes⟩ — **in·for·mal·i·ty** \ˌin-fȯr-ˈma-lə-tē, -fər-\ *n* — **in·for·mal·ly** \(ˌ)in-ˈfȯr-mə-lē\ *adv*

in·for·mant \in-ˈfȯr-mənt\ *n* : a person who gives information : INFORMER

in·for·ma·tion \ˌin-fər-ˈmā-shən\ *n* **1** : the communication or reception of knowledge or intelligence **2** : knowledge obtained from investigation, study, or instruction : FACTS, DATA **3** : the attribute communicated by one of two or more alternative sequences of something (as nucleotides in DNA or binary digits in a computer program) — **in·for·ma·tion·al** \-shə-nəl\ *adj*

information superhighway *n* : INTERNET

information technology *n* : technology involving computer systems and networks for the processing and distribution of data

in·for·ma·tive \in-ˈfȯr-mə-tiv\ *adj* : imparting knowledge : INSTRUCTIVE

in·formed \in-ˈfȯrmd\ *adj* **1** : having or based on information ⟨an ~ decision⟩ **2** : EDUCATED, KNOWLEDGEABLE

informed consent *n* : consent to a medical procedure by someone who understands what is involved

in·form·er \-ˈfor-mər\ *n* : one that informs; *esp* : a person who informs against others for illegalities esp. for financial gain

in·fo·tain·ment \ˌin-fō-ˈtān-mənt\ *n* : a television program that presents information (as news) in a manner intended to be entertaining

in·frac·tion \in-ˈfrak-shən\ *n* [ME, fr. ML *infractio,* fr. L, subduing, fr. *infringere* to break, crush] : the act of infringing : VIOLATION

in·fra dig \ˌin-frə-ˈdig\ *adj* [short for L *infra dignitatem*] : being beneath one's dignity

in·fra·red \ˌin-frə-ˈred\ *adj* : being, relating to, or using radiation having wavelengths longer than those of red light — **infrared** *n*

in·fra·struc·ture \ˈin-frə-ˌstrək-chər\ *n* **1** : the underlying foundation or basic framework (as of a system or organization) **2** : the system of public works of a country, state, or region; *also* : the resources (as buildings or equipment) required for an activity

in·fre·quent \(ˌ)in-ˈfrē-kwənt\ *adj* **1** : seldom happening : RARE **2** : placed or occurring at wide intervals in space or time ♦ ***Synonyms*** UNCOMMON, SCARCE, SPORADIC — **in·fre·quent·ly** *adv*

in·fringe \in-ˈfrinj\ *vb* **in·fringed; in·fring·ing** **1** : VIOLATE, TRANSGRESS ⟨~ a patent⟩ **2** : ENCROACH, TRESPASS ⟨~ on our rights⟩ — **in·fringe·ment** *n*

in·fu·ri·ate \in-ˈfyu̇r-ē-ˌāt\ *vb* **-at·ed; -at·ing** : to make furious : ENRAGE — **in·fu·ri·at·ing·ly** *adv*

in·fuse \in-ˈfyüz\ *vb* **in·fused; in·fus·ing** **1** : to instill a principle or quality in ⟨*infused* the team with confidence⟩ **2** : INSPIRE, ANIMATE **3** : to steep (as tea) without boiling — **in·fu·sion** \-ˈfyü-zhən\ *n*

¹-ing \iŋ\ *n suffix* **1** : action or process ⟨sleep*ing*⟩ : instance of an action or process ⟨a meet*ing*⟩ **2** : product or result of an action or process ⟨an engrav*ing*⟩ ⟨earn*ings*⟩ **3** : something used in an action or process ⟨a bed cover*ing*⟩ **4** : something connected with, consisting of, or used in making (a specified thing) ⟨scaffold*ing*⟩ **5** : something related to (a specified concept) ⟨off*ing*⟩

²-ing *n suffix* : one of a (specified) kind

³-ing *vb suffix or adj suffix* — used to form the present participle ⟨sail*ing*⟩ and sometimes to form an adjective resembling a present participle but not derived from a verb ⟨swashbuck*ling*⟩

in·ga·ther \ˈin-ˌga-t͟hər\ *vb* : to gather in : ASSEMBLE

in·ge·nious \in-ˈjēn-yəs\ *adj* **1** : marked by special aptitude at discovering, inventing, or contriving **2** : marked by originality, resourcefulness, and cleverness in conception or execution — **in·ge·nious·ly** *adv* — **in·ge·nious·ness** *n*

in·ge·nue *or* **in·gé·nue** \ˈan-jə-ˌnü, ˈän-; ˈaⁿ-zhə-, ˈäⁿ-\ *n* : a naive girl or young woman; *esp* : an actress portraying such a person

in·ge·nu·i·ty \ˌin-jə-ˈnü-ə-tē, -ˈnyü-\ *n, pl* **-ties** : skill or cleverness in planning or inventing : INVENTIVENESS

in·gen·u·ous \in-ˈjen-yə-wəs\ *adj* [L *ingenuus* native, freeborn, fr. *gignere* to beget] **1** : innocently straightforward ⟨her ~ curiosity⟩ **2** : lacking craft or subtlety ⟨~ comments⟩ — **in·gen·u·ous·ly** *adv* — **in·gen·u·ous·ness** *n*

in·gest \in-ˈjest\ *vb* : to take in for or as if for digestion — **in·ges·tion** \-ˈjes-chən\ *n*

in·gle·nook \ˈiŋ-gəl-ˌnu̇k\ *n* : a nook by a large open fireplace; *also* : a bench occupying this nook

in·glo·ri·ous \(ˌ)in-ˈglȯr-ē-əs\ *adj* **1** : SHAMEFUL **2** : not glorious : lacking fame or honor — **in·glo·ri·ous·ly** *adv*

in·got \ˈiŋ-gət\ *n* : a mass of metal cast in a form convenient for storage or transportation

¹**in·grain** \(ˌ)in-ˈgrān\ *vb* : to work indelibly into the natural texture or mental or moral constitution — **in·grained** *adj*

²**in·grain** \ˈin-ˌgrān\ *adj* **1** : made of fiber that is dyed before being spun into yarn **2** : made of yarn that is dyed before being woven or knitted **3** : INNATE — **in·grain** *n*

in·grate \ˈin-ˌgrāt\ *n* : an ungrateful person

in·gra·ti·ate \in-ˈgrā-shē-ˌāt\ *vb* **-at·ed; -at·ing** : to gain favor by deliberate effort

in·gra·ti·at·ing *adj* **1** : capable of winning favor : PLEASING ⟨an ~ smile⟩ **2** : FLATTERING ⟨an ~ manner⟩

in·grat·i·tude \(ˌ)in-ˈgra-tə-ˌtüd, -ˌtyüd\ *n* : lack of gratitude : UNGRATEFULNESS

in·gre·di·ent \in-ˈgrē-dē-ənt\ *n* : one of the substances that make up a mixture or compound : CONSTITUENT

in·gress \ˈin-ˌgres\ *n* : ENTRANCE, ACCESS — **in·gres·sion** \in-ˈgre-shən\ *n*

in·grow·ing \ˈin-ˌgrō-iŋ\ *adj* : growing or tending inward

in·grown \-ˌgrōn\ *adj* : grown in; *esp* : having the free tip or edge embedded in the flesh ⟨an ~ toenail⟩

in·gui·nal \ˈiŋ-gwə-nᵊl\ *adj* : of, relating to, or situated in or near the region of the groin ⟨an ~ hernia⟩

in·hab·it \in-ˈha-bət\ *vb* : to live or dwell in ⟨spiders that ~ caves⟩ — **in·hab·it·able** *adj* — **in·hab·i·ta·tion** \in-ˌha-bə-ˈtā-shən\ *n*

in·hab·i·tant \in-ˈha-bə-tənt\ *n* : a permanent resident in a place

in·hal·ant \in-ˈhā-lənt\ *n* : something (as a medicine) that is inhaled

in·ha·la·tor \ˈin-hə-ˌlā-tər\ *n* : a device that provides a mixture of carbon dioxide and oxygen for breathing

in·hale \in-ˈhāl\ *vb* **in·haled; in·hal·ing** : to breathe in — **in·ha·la·tion** \ˌin-hə-ˈlā-shən\ *n*

in·hal·er \in-ˈhā-lər\ *n* : a device by means of which medicinal material is inhaled

in·here \in-ˈhir\ *vb* **in·hered; in·her·ing** : to be inherent

in·her·ent \in-ˈhir-ənt, -ˈher-\ *adj* : established as an essential part of something : INTRINSIC ⟨risks ~ in the venture⟩ — **in·her·ent·ly** *adv*

in·her·it \in-ˈher-ət\ *vb* **1** : to receive esp. from one's ancestors **2** : to receive by genetic transmission — **in·her·it·able** \-ə-tə-bəl\ *adj* — **in·her·i·tance** \-ə-təns\ *n* — **in·her·i·tor** \-ə-tər\ *n*

in·hib·it \in-ˈhi-bət\ *vb* **1** : PROHIBIT, FORBID **2** : to hold in check : RESTRAIN ⟨~*ed* by fear⟩ — **in·hib·i·tor** \-bə-tər\ *n* — **in·hib·i·to·ry** \-bə-ˌtȯr-ē\ *adj*

in·hi·bi·tion \ˌin-hə-ˈbi-shən\ *n* **1** : PROHIBITION, RESTRAINT **2** : a usu. inner check on free activity, expression, or functioning

in–house \ˈin-ˌhau̇s, -ˈhau̇s\ *adj* : existing, originating, or carried on within a group or organization

in·hu·man \(ˌ)in-ˈhyü-mən, -ˈyü-\ *adj* **1** : lacking pity, kindness, or mercy : SAVAGE ⟨an ~ tyrant⟩ **2** : COLD, IMPERSONAL **3** : not worthy of or conforming to the needs of human beings ⟨~ living conditions⟩ **4** : of or suggesting a nonhuman class of beings — **in·hu·man·ly** *adv* — **in·hu·man·ness** *n*

in·hu·mane \ˌin-hyü-ˈmān, -yü-\ *adj* : not humane : INHUMAN 1

in·hu·man·i·ty \-ˈma-nə-tē\ *n, pl* **-ties** **1** : the quality or state of being cruel or barbarous **2** : a cruel or barbarous act

in·im·i·cal \i-ˈni-mi-kəl\ *adj* **1** : being adverse often by reason of hostility ⟨forces ~ to change⟩ **2** : HOSTILE, UNFRIENDLY ⟨~ factions⟩ — **in·im·i·cal·ly** *adv*

in·im·i·ta·ble \(ˌ)i-ˈni-mə-tə-bəl\ *adj* : not capable of being imitated

in·iq·ui·ty \i-ˈni-kwə-tē\ *n, pl* **-ties** [ME *iniquite,* fr. AF *iniquité,* fr. L *iniquitas,* fr. *iniquus* uneven, fr. *aequus* equal] **1** : WICKEDNESS **2** : a wicked act — **in·iq·ui·tous** \-təs\ *adj*

¹**ini·tial** \i-ˈni-shəl\ *adj* **1** : of or relating to the beginning : INCIPIENT ⟨my ~ reaction⟩ **2** : being at the beginning — **ini·tial·ly** *adv*

²**initial** *n* : the first letter of a word or name

³**initial** *vb* **-tialed** *or* **-tialled; -tial·ing** *or* **-tial·ling** : to affix an initial to

¹**ini·ti·ate** \i-ˈni-shē-ˌāt\ *vb* **-at·ed; -at·ing** **1** : START, BEGIN **2** : to induct into membership by or as if by special ceremonies **3** : to instruct in the rudi-

ments or principles of something — **ini·ti·a·tion** \-ˌni-shē-ˈā-shən\ *n*

[2]**ini·tiate** \i-ˈni-shē-ət\ *n* **1** : a person who is undergoing or has passed an initiation **2** : a person who is instructed or adept in some special field

ini·tia·tive \i-ˈni-shə-tiv\ *n* **1** : an introductory step **2** : self-reliant enterprise ⟨showed great ~⟩ **3** : a process by which laws may be introduced or enacted directly by vote of the people

ini·tia·to·ry \i-ˈni-shē-ə-ˌtȯr-ē\ *adj* **1** : INTRODUCTORY **2** : tending or serving to initiate ⟨~ rites⟩

in·ject \in-ˈjekt\ *vb* **1** : to force into something ⟨~ serum with a needle⟩ **2** : to introduce as an element into some situation or subject ⟨~ a note of suspicion⟩ — **in·jec·tion** \-ˈjek-shən\ *n*

in·junc·tion \in-ˈjəŋk-shən\ *n* **1** : ORDER, ADMONITION **2** : a court writ whereby one is required to do or to refrain from doing a specified act

in·jure \ˈin-jər\ *vb* **in·jured; in·jur·ing** **1** : WRONG **2** : to damage or hurt esp. physically ♦ ***Synonyms*** HARM, IMPAIR, MAR, SPOIL

in·ju·ry \ˈin-jə-rē\ *n, pl* **-ries** **1** : an act that damages or hurts : WRONG **2** : hurt, damage, or loss sustained — **in·ju·ri·ous** \in-ˈju̇r-ē-əs\ *adj*

in·jus·tice \(ˌ)in-ˈjəs-təs\ *n* **1** : violation of a person's rights : UNFAIRNESS **2** : an unjust act or deed : WRONG

[1]**ink** \ˈiŋk\ *n* [ME *enke,* fr. AF *encre, enke,* fr. LL *encaustum,* fr. L *encaustus* burned in, fr. Gk *enkaustos,* fr. *enkaiein* to burn in] : a usu. liquid and colored material for writing and printing — **inky** *adj*

[2]**ink** *vb* : to put ink on; *esp* : SIGN

ink·blot test \ˈiŋk-ˌblät-\ *n* : any of several psychological tests based on the interpretation of irregular figures

ink·horn \-ˌhȯrn\ *n* : a small bottle (as of horn) for holding ink

in–kind \ˈin-ˈkīnd\ *adj* : consisting of something (as goods) other than money

ink–jet *n* : a computer printer that sprays electrically charged droplets of ink onto paper — **inkjet** *adj*

in·kling \ˈiŋ-kliŋ\ *n* **1** : HINT, INTIMATION **2** : a vague idea

ink·stand \ˈiŋk-ˌstand\ *n* : INKWELL; *also* : a pen and ink stand

ink·well \-ˌwel\ *n* : a container for ink

in·laid \ˈin-ˈlād\ *adj* : decorated with material set into a surface

[1]**in·land** \ˈin-ˌland, -lənd\ *adj* **1** *chiefly Brit* : not foreign : DOMESTIC ⟨~ revenue⟩ **2** : of or relating to the interior of a country ⟨the ~ states⟩

[2]**inland** *n* : the interior of a country

[3]**inland** *adv* : into or toward the interior

in–law \ˈin-ˌlȯ\ *n* : a relative by marriage

[1]**in·lay** \(ˌ)in-ˈlā, ˈin-ˌlā\ *vb* **in·laid** \-ˈlād\; **in·lay·ing** : to set (a material) into a surface or ground material esp. for decoration

[2]**in·lay** \ˈin-ˌlā\ *n* **1** : inlaid work **2** : a shaped filling cemented into a tooth

in·let \ˈin-ˌlet, -lət\ *n* **1** : a small or narrow bay **2** : an opening for intake esp. of a fluid

in–line skate *n* : a roller skate whose four wheels are set in a straight line — **in–line skater** *n* — **in–line skating** *n*

in·mate \ˈin-ˌmāt\ *n* : any of a group occupying a single place of residence; *esp* : a person confined (as in a hospital or prison)

in me·di·as res \in-ˌmā-dē-əs-ˈrās\ *adv* [L, lit., into the midst of things] : in or into the middle of a narrative or plot

in me·mo·ri·am \ˌin-mə-ˈmȯr-ē-əm\ *prep* [L] : in memory of

in·most \ˈin-ˌmōst\ *adj* : deepest within : INNERMOST

inn \ˈin\ *n* : HOTEL, TAVERN

in·nards \ˈi-nərdz\ *n pl* [alter. of *inwards*] **1** : the internal organs of a human being or animal; *esp* : VISCERA **2** : the internal parts of a structure or mechanism

in·nate \i-ˈnāt\ *adj* **1** : existing in, belonging to, or determined by factors present in an individual from birth : NATIVE **2** : INHERENT, INTRINSIC ⟨the ~ defects of a plan⟩ — **in·nate·ly** *adv*

in·ner \ˈi-nər\ *adj* **1** : situated farther in ⟨the ~ bark⟩ **2** : near a center esp. of influence ⟨the ~ circle⟩ **3** : of or relating to the mind or spirit ⟨an ~ voice⟩ **4** : being a usu. repressed part of one's psychological makeup ⟨the ~ child⟩

inner city *n* : the usu. older, poorer, and more densely populated section of a city — **inner–city** *adj*

in·ner–di·rect·ed \ˌi-nər-də-ˈrek-təd, -(ˌ)dī-\ *adj* : directed in thought and action by one's own scale of values as opposed to external norms

inner ear *n* : the part of the ear that is most important for hearing, is located in a cavity in the temporal bone, and contains sense organs of hearing and of awareness of position in space

in·ner·most \ˈi-nər-ˌmōst\ *adj* : farthest inward : INMOST

in·ner·sole \ˈi-nər-ˈsōl\ *n* : INSOLE

in·ner·spring \ˈi-nər-ˈspriŋ\ *adj* : having coil springs inside a padded casing ⟨an ~ mattress⟩

inner tube *n* : an airtight rubber tube inside a tire to hold air under pressure

in·ning \ˈi-niŋ\ *n* **1** *sing or pl* : a division of a cricket match **2** : a baseball team's turn at bat; *also* : a division of a baseball game consisting of a turn at bat for each team

inn·keep·er \ˈin-ˈkē-pər\ *n* **1** : a proprietor of an inn **2** : a hotel manager

in·no·cence \ˈi-nə-səns\ *n* **1** : BLAMELESSNESS; *also* : freedom from legal guilt **2** : GUILELESSNESS, SIMPLICITY; *also* : IGNORANCE

in·no·cent \-sənt\ *adj* [ME, fr. AF, fr. L *innocens,* fr. *nocens* wicked, fr. *nocēre* to harm] **1** : free from guilt or sin : BLAMELESS **2** : harmless in effect or intention; *also* : CANDID ⟨an ~ remark⟩ **3** : free from legal guilt or fault : LAWFUL **4** : INGENUOUS ⟨an ~ question⟩ **5** : UNAWARE — **innocent** *n* — **in·no·cent·ly** *adv*

in·noc·u·ous \i-ˈnä-kyə-wəs\ *adj* **1** : HARMLESS **2** : not offensive; *also* : INSIPID ⟨~ jokes⟩
in·nom·i·nate \i-ˈnä-mə-nət\ *adj* : having no name; *also* : ANONYMOUS
in·no·vate \ˈi-nə-ˌvāt\ *vb* **-vat·ed; -vat·ing** : to introduce as or as if new : make changes — **in·no·va·tive** \-ˌvā-tiv\ *adj* — **in·no·va·tor** \-ˌvā-tər\ *n*
in·no·va·tion \ˌi-nə-ˈvā-shən\ *n* **1** : the introduction of something new **2** : a new idea, method, or device
in·nu·en·do \ˌin-yə-ˈwen-dō\ *n, pl* **-dos** *or* **-does** [L, by nodding, fr. *innuere* to nod to, make a sign to, fr. *nuere* to nod] : HINT, INSINUATION; *esp* : a veiled reflection on character or reputation
in·nu·mer·a·ble \i-ˈnü-mə-rə-bəl, -ˈnyü-\ *adj* : too many to be numbered
in·oc·u·late \i-ˈnä-kyə-lāt\ *vb* **-lat·ed; -lat·ing** [ME, to insert a bud in a plant, fr. L *inoculare,* fr. *oculus* eye, bud] : to introduce something into; *esp* : to introduce a serum or antibody into (an organism) to treat or prevent a disease — **in·oc·u·la·tion** \-ˌnä-kyə-ˈlā-shən\ *n*
in·op·er·a·ble \(ˌ)in-ˈä-pə-rə-bəl\ *adj* **1** : not suitable for surgery ⟨an ~ tumor⟩ **2** : not operable ⟨~ vehicles⟩
in·op·er·a·tive \-ˈä-pə-rə-tiv, -ˈä-pə-ˌrā-\ *adj* : not functioning
in·op·por·tune \(ˌ)in-ˌä-pər-ˈtün, -ˈtyün\ *adj* : INCONVENIENT, INAPPROPRIATE — **in·op·por·tune·ly** *adv*
in·or·di·nate \in-ˈór-dᵊn-ət\ *adj* : exceeding reasonable limits : IMMODERATE ⟨an ~ amount⟩ — **in·or·di·nate·ly** *adv*
in·or·gan·ic \ˌin-ˌór-ˈga-nik\ *adj* : being or composed of matter of other than plant or animal origin : MINERAL
in·pa·tient \ˈin-ˌpā-shənt\ *n* : a hospital patient who receives lodging and food as well as treatment
in·put \ˈin-ˌpu̇t\ *n* **1** : something put in **2** : power or energy put into a machine or system **3** : information fed into a computer or data processing system **4** : ADVICE, OPINION — **input** *vb*
in·quest \ˈin-ˌkwest\ *n* **1** : an official inquiry or examination esp. before a jury **2** : INQUIRY, INVESTIGATION
in·qui·etude \(ˌ)in-ˈkwī-ə-ˌtüd, -ˌtyüd\ *n* : UNEASINESS, RESTLESSNESS
in·quire \in-ˈkwī(-ə)r\ *vb* **in·quired; in·quir·ing** **1** : to ask about : ASK **2** : INVESTIGATE, EXAMINE — **in·quir·er** *n* — **in·quir·ing·ly** *adv*
in·qui·ry \ˈin-ˌkwī(-ə)r-ē, in-ˈkwī(-ə)r-ē; ˈin-kwə-rē, ˈiŋ-\ *n, pl* **-ries** **1** : a request for information; *also* : RESEARCH **2** : a systematic investigation of a matter of public interest
in·qui·si·tion \ˌin-kwə-ˈzi-shən, ˌiŋ-\ *n* **1** : a judicial or official inquiry usu. before a jury **2** *cap* : a former Roman Catholic tribunal for the discovery and punishment of heresy **3** : a severe questioning — **in·quis·i·tor** \in-ˈkwi-zə-tər\ *n* — **in·quis·i·to·ri·al** \-ˌkwi-zə-ˈtór-ē-əl\ *adj*
in·quis·i·tive \in-ˈkwi-zə-tiv\ *adj* **1** : given to examination or investigation ⟨an ~ mind⟩ **2** : unduly curious — **in·quis·i·tive·ly** *adv* — **in·quis·i·tive·ness** *n*
in re \in-ˈrā, -ˈrē\ *prep* : in the matter of
INRI *abbr* [L *Iesus Nazarenus Rex Iudaeorum*] Jesus of Nazareth, King of the Jews
in·road \ˈin-ˌrōd\ *n* **1** : INVASION, RAID **2** : an advance made usu. at the expense of another ⟨made ~*s* in the industry⟩
in·rush \ˈin-ˌrəsh\ *n* : a crowding or flooding in
ins *abbr* **1** inches **2** insurance
INS *abbr* Immigration and Naturalization Service
in·sa·lu·bri·ous \ˌin-sə-ˈlü-brē-əs\ *adj* : UNWHOLESOME, NOXIOUS ⟨~ air⟩
ins and outs *n pl* **1** : characteristic peculiarities **2** : RAMIFICATIONS
in·sane \(ˌ)in-ˈsān\ *adj* **1** : exhibiting a severely disordered state of mind; *also* : used by or for people having a severely disordered state of mind **2** : ABSURD **3** : greatly exceeding the ordinary, usual, or expected — **in·sane·ly** *adv* — **in·san·i·ty** \in-ˈsa-nə-tē\ *n*
in·sa·tia·ble \(ˌ)in-ˈsā-shə-bəl\ *adj* : incapable of being satisfied ⟨an ~ thirst⟩ — **in·sa·tia·bil·i·ty** \(ˌ)in-ˌsā-shə-ˈbi-lə-tē\ *n* — **in·sa·tia·bly** *adv*
in·sa·tiate \(ˌ)in-ˈsā-shē-ət, -shət\ *adj* : INSATIABLE — **in·sa·tiate·ly** *adv*
in·scribe \in-ˈskrīb\ *vb* **1** : to write, engrave, or print as a lasting record **2** : ENROLL **3** : to write, engrave, or print characters upon **4** : to dedicate to someone **5** : to draw within a figure so as to touch in as many places as possible — **in·scrip·tion** \-ˈskrip-shən\ *n*
in·scru·ta·ble \in-ˈskrü-tə-bəl\ *adj* : not readily comprehensible : MYSTERIOUS ⟨an ~ smile⟩ — **in·scru·ta·bly** \-blē\ *adv*
in·seam \ˈin-ˌsēm\ *n* : the seam on the inside of the leg of a pair of pants; *also* : the length of this seam
in·sect \ˈin-ˌsekt\ *n* [L *insectum,* fr. *insectus,* pp. of *insecare* to cut into, fr. *secare* to cut] : any of a class of small usu. winged arthropod animals (as flies, bees, beetles, and moths) with usu. three pairs of legs as adults
in·sec·ti·cide \in-ˈsek-tə-ˌsīd\ *n* : an agent for destroying insects — **in·sec·ti·cid·al** \(ˌ)in-ˌsek-tə-ˈsī-dᵊl\ *adj*
in·sec·tiv·o·rous \ˌin-ˌsek-ˈti-və-rəs\ *adj* : feeding on insects
in·se·cure \ˌin-si-ˈkyu̇r\ *adj* **1** : UNCERTAIN **2** : not protected : UNSAFE ⟨an ~ investment⟩ **3** : LOOSE, SHAKY ⟨an ~ hinge⟩ **4** : not highly stable ⟨an ~ marriage⟩; *also* : lacking assurance : ANXIOUS, FEARFUL — **in·se·cure·ly** *adv* — **in·se·cu·ri·ty** \-ˈkyu̇r-ə-tē\ *n*
in·sem·i·nate \in-ˈse-mə-ˌnāt\ *vb* **-nat·ed; -nat·ing** : to introduce semen into the genital tract of (a female) — **in·sem·i·na·tion** \-ˌse-mə-ˈnā-shən\ *n*
in·sen·sate \(ˌ)in-ˈsen-ˌsāt, -sət\ *adj* **1** : lacking sense or understanding; *also*

: FOOLISH **2** : INANIMATE **3** : BRUTAL, INHUMAN ⟨~ rage⟩

in·sen·si·ble \(ˌ)in-ˈsen-sə-bəl\ *adj* **1** : IMPERCEPTIBLE; *also* : SLIGHT, GRADUAL **2** : INANIMATE **3** : UNCONSCIOUS **4** : lacking sensory perception or ability to react ⟨~ to pain⟩ **5** : APATHETIC, INDIFFERENT; *also* : UNAWARE ⟨~ of their danger⟩ **6** : MEANINGLESS **7** : lacking delicacy or refinement — **in·sen·si·bil·i·ty** \-ˌsen-sə-ˈbi-lə-tē\ *n* — **in·sen·si·bly** \-ˈsen-sə-blē\ *adv*

in·sen·tient \(ˌ)in-ˈsen-chē-ənt\ *adj* : lacking perception, consciousness, or animation — **in·sen·tience** \-chē-əns\ *n*

in·sep·a·ra·ble \(ˌ)in-ˈse-prə-bəl, -pə-rə-\ *adj* **1** : incapable of being separated or disjoined **2** : very close or intimate ⟨~ friends⟩ — **in·sep·a·ra·bil·i·ty** \-ˌse-prə-ˈbi-lə-tē, -pə-rə-\ *n* — **inseparable** *n* — **in·sep·a·ra·bly** \-ˈse-prə-blē, -pə-rə-\ *adv*

[1]**in·sert** \in-ˈsərt\ *vb* **1** : to put or thrust in ⟨~ a key in a lock⟩ ⟨~ a comma⟩ **2** : INTERPOLATE **3** : to set in (as a piece of fabric) and make fast

[2]**in·sert** \ˈin-ˌsərt\ *n* : something that is inserted or is for insertion; *esp* : written or printed material inserted (as between the leaves of a book)

in·ser·tion \in-ˈsər-shən\ *n* **1** : something that is inserted **2** : the act or process of inserting

in·set \ˈin-ˌset\ *vb* **inset** *or* **in·set·ted; in·set·ting** : to set in : INSERT — **inset** *n*

[1]**in·shore** \ˈin-ˈshȯr\ *adj* **1** : situated, living, or carried on near shore **2** : moving toward shore ⟨an ~ current⟩

[2]**inshore** *adv* : to or toward shore

[1]**in·side** \in-ˈsīd, ˈin-ˌsīd\ *n* **1** : an inner side or surface : INTERIOR **2** : inward nature, thoughts, or feeling **3** *pl* : VISCERA, ENTRAILS **4** : a position of power, trust, or familiarity — **inside** *adj*

[2]**inside** *adv* **1** : on the inner side **2** : in or into the interior

[3]**inside** *prep* **1** : in or into the inside of ⟨~ the house⟩ **2** : WITHIN ⟨~ an hour⟩

inside of *prep* : INSIDE

inside out *adv* **1** : in such a manner that the inner surface becomes the outer ⟨turned the shirt *inside out*⟩ **2** : in a state of disarray or reorganization ⟨turned her life *inside out*⟩

in·sid·er \in-ˈsī-dər\ *n* : a person who is in a position of power or has access to confidential information

in·sid·i·ous \in-ˈsi-dē-əs\ *adj* [L *insidiosus*, fr. *insidiae* ambush, fr. *insidēre* to sit in, sit on, fr. *sedēre* to sit] **1** : SLY, TREACHEROUS **2** : SEDUCTIVE **3** : having a gradual and cumulative effect : SUBTLE — **in·sid·i·ous·ly** *adv* — **in·sid·i·ous·ness** *n*

in·sight \ˈin-ˌsīt\ *n* : the power, act, or result of seeing into a situation : UNDERSTANDING ⟨a leader of great ~⟩ — **in·sight·ful** \ˈin-ˌsīt-fəl, in-ˈsīt-\ *adj*

in·sig·nia \in-ˈsig-nē-ə\ *also* **in·sig·ne** \-(ˌ)nē\ *n, pl* **-nia** *or* **-ni·as** : a distinguishing mark esp. of authority or honor : BADGE

in·sin·cere \ˌin-sin-ˈsir\ *adj* : not sincere : HYPOCRITICAL — **in·sin·cere·ly** *adv* — **in·sin·cer·i·ty** \-ˈser-ə-tē\ *n*

in·sin·u·ate \in-ˈsin-yə-ˌwāt\ *vb* **-at·ed; -at·ing** [L *insinuare*, fr. *sinuare* to bend, curve, fr. *sinus* curve] **1** : to introduce gradually or in a subtle, indirect, or artful way **2** : to imply in a subtle or devious way — **in·sin·u·a·tion** \(ˌ)in-ˌsin-yə-ˈwā-shən\ *n*

in·sin·u·at·ing *adj* **1** : winning favor and confidence by imperceptible degrees **2** : tending gradually to cause doubt, distrust, or change of outlook

in·sip·id \in-ˈsi-pəd\ *adj* **1** : lacking taste or savor **2** : DULL, FLAT ⟨an ~ movie⟩ — **in·si·pid·i·ty** \ˌin-sə-ˈpi-də-tē\ *n*

in·sist \in-ˈsist\ *vb* [MF or L; MF *insister*, fr. L *insistere* to stand upon, persist, fr. *sistere* to take a stand] : to take a resolute stand ⟨~*ed* on paying⟩

in·sis·tence \in-ˈsis-təns\ *n* : the act of insisting; *also* : an insistent attitude or quality : URGENCY

in·sis·tent \in-ˈsis-tənt\ *adj* : disposed to insist — **in·sis·tent·ly** *adv*

in si·tu \in-ˈsī-tü, -ˈsē-\ *adv or adj* [L, in position] : in the natural or original position ⟨an *in situ* cancer⟩

in·so·far as \ˌin-sə-ˈfär-\ *conj* : to the extent or degree that

insol *abbr* insoluble

in·so·la·tion \ˌin-(ˌ)sō-ˈlā-shən\ *n* : solar radiation that has been received

in·sole \ˈin-ˌsōl\ *n* **1** : an inside sole of a shoe **2** : a loose thin strip placed inside a shoe for warmth or comfort

in·so·lent \ˈin-sə-lənt\ *adj* : contemptuous, rude, disrespectful, or bold in behavior or language — **in·so·lence** \-ləns\ *n*

in·sol·u·ble \(ˌ)in-ˈsäl-yə-bəl\ *adj* **1** : having or admitting of no solution or explanation **2** : difficult or impossible to dissolve — **in·sol·u·bil·i·ty** \-ˌsäl-yə-ˈbi-lə-tē\ *n*

in·sol·vent \(ˌ)in-ˈsäl-vənt\ *adj* **1** : unable or insufficient to pay all debts ⟨an ~ estate⟩ **2** : IMPOVERISHED, DEFICIENT — **in·sol·ven·cy** \-vən-sē\ *n*

in·som·nia \in-ˈsäm-nē-ə\ *n* : prolonged and usu. abnormal sleeplessness — **in·som·ni·ac** \-nē-ˌak\ *n*

in·so·much as \ˌin-sə-ˈməch-\ *conj* : INASMUCH AS

insomuch that *conj* : to such a degree that : SO

in·sou·ci·ance \in-ˈsü-sē-əns, a^{n}-süs-ˈyä^{n}s\ *n* [F] : lighthearted unconcern ⟨youthful ~⟩ — **in·sou·ci·ant** \in-ˈsü-sē-ənt, a^{n}-süs-ˈyä^{n}\ *adj*

insp *abbr* inspector

in·spect \in-ˈspekt\ *vb* : to view closely and critically : EXAMINE ⟨~ the gem for flaws⟩ — **in·spec·tion** \-ˈspek-shən\ *n* — **in·spec·tor** \-tər\ *n*

inspector general *n* : the head of a system of inspection (as of an army)

in·spi·ra·tion \ˌin-spə-ˈrā-shən\ *n* **1** : the act or power of moving the intellect or emotions **2** : INHALATION **3** : the quality or state of being inspired; *also* : something that is inspired **4** : an inspiring agent or influence — **in·spi·ra·tion·al** \-shə-nəl\ *adj*

in·spire \in-ˈspīr\ *vb* **in·spired; in·spir·ing** **1** : to influence, move, or guide by divine or supernatural inspiration **2** : to exert an animating, enlivening, or exalting influence upon ⟨a painter *inspired* by cubism⟩; *also* : AFFECT **3** : to communicate to an agent supernaturally; *also* : bring out or about **4** : INHALE **5** : INCITE **6** : to spread by indirect means — **in·spir·er** *n*

in·spir·it \in-ˈspir-ət\ *vb* : ENCOURAGE, HEARTEN ⟨~*ed* the team⟩

in·spo \ˈin-spō\ *n, slang* : INSPIRATION

inst *abbr* **1** instant **2** institute; institution; institutional

in·sta·bil·i·ty \ˌin-stə-ˈbi-lə-tē\ *n* : lack of steadiness; *esp* : lack of emotional or mental stability

in·stal *chiefly Brit var of* INSTALL

in·stall \in-ˈstȯl\ *vb* **1** : to place formally in office : induct into an office, rank, or order **2** : to establish in an indicated place, condition, or status **3** : to set up for use or service — **in·stal·la·tion** \ˌin-stə-ˈlā-shən\ *n*

¹in·stall·ment *also* **in·stal·ment** \in-ˈstȯl-mənt\ *n* : INSTALLATION

²installment *also* **instalment** *n* **1** : one of the parts into which a debt or sum is divided for payment **2** : one of several parts presented at intervals

¹in·stance \ˈin-stəns\ *n* **1** : INSTIGATION, REQUEST **2** : EXAMPLE ⟨for ~⟩ **3** : an event or step that is part of a process or series ♦ ***Synonyms*** CASE, ILLUSTRATION, SAMPLE, SPECIMEN

²instance *vb* **in·stanced; in·stanc·ing** : to mention as a case or example

¹in·stant \ˈin-stənt\ *n* **1** : MOMENT ⟨the ~ we met⟩ **2** : the present or current month

²instant *adj* **1** : URGENT **2** : PRESENT, CURRENT **3** : IMMEDIATE ⟨~ relief⟩ **4** : premixed or precooked for easy final preparation ⟨~ cake mix⟩; *also* : immediately soluble in water ⟨~ coffee⟩

in·stan·ta·neous \ˌin-stən-ˈtā-nē-əs\ *adj* : done or occurring in an instant or without delay ⟨an ~ chemical reaction⟩ — **in·stan·ta·neous·ly** *adv*

in·stan·ter \in-ˈstan-tər\ *adv* : at once

in·stan·ti·ate \in-ˈstan-chē-ˌāt\ *vb* **-at·ed; -at·ing** : to represent (an abstraction) by a concrete example — **in·stan·ti·a·tion** \-ˌstan-chē-ˈā-shən\ *n*

in·stant·ly \ˈin-stənt-lē\ *adv* : at once : IMMEDIATELY

instant messaging *n* : a means or system for transmitting electronic messages instantly — **instant message** *n or vb*

in·state \in-ˈstāt\ *vb* : to establish in a rank or office : INSTALL

in·stead \in-ˈsted\ *adv* **1** : as a substitute or equivalent **2** : as an alternative

instead of *prep* : as a substitute for or alternative to ⟨use glue *instead of* paste⟩

in·step \ˈin-ˌstep\ *n* : the arched part of the human foot in front of the ankle joint; *esp* : its upper surface

in·sti·gate \ˈin-stə-ˌgāt\ *vb* **-gat·ed; -gat·ing** : to goad or urge forward : PROVOKE, INCITE ⟨~ a revolt⟩ — **in·sti·ga·tion** \ˌin-stə-ˈgā-shən\ *n* — **in·sti·ga·tor** \ˈin-stə-ˌgā-tər\ *n*

in·stil *chiefly Brit var of* INSTILL

in·still \in-ˈstil\ *vb* **1** : to cause to enter drop by drop **2** : to impart gradually

¹in·stinct \ˈin-ˌstiŋkt\ *n* **1** : a natural aptitude **2** : a largely inheritable and unalterable tendency of an organism to make a complex and specific response to environmental stimuli without involving reason; *also* : behavior originating below the conscious level — **in·stinc·tive** \in-ˈstiŋk-tiv\ *adj* — **in·stinc·tive·ly** *adv*

²in·stinct \in-ˈstiŋkt, ˈin-ˌstiŋkt\ *adj* : IMBUED, INFUSED

in·stinc·tu·al \in-ˈstiŋk-chə-wəl\ *adj* : of, relating to, or based on instinct

¹in·sti·tute \ˈin-stə-ˌtüt, -ˌtyüt\ *vb* **-tut·ed; -tut·ing** **1** : to establish in a position or office **2** : ORGANIZE **3** : INAUGURATE, INITIATE ⟨~ a new policy⟩

²institute *n* **1** : an elementary principle recognized as authoritative; *also, pl* : a collection of such principles and precepts **2** : an organization for the promotion of a cause : ASSOCIATION **3** : an educational institution **4** : a brief course of instruction on a particular field

in·sti·tu·tion \ˌin-stə-ˈtü-shən, -ˈtyü-\ *n* **1** : an act of originating, setting up, or founding **2** : an established practice, law, or custom **3** : a society or corporation esp. of a public character ⟨a charitable ~⟩; *also* : ASYLUM 3 — **in·sti·tu·tion·al** \-ˈtü-shə-nəl, -ˈtyü-\ *adj* — **in·sti·tu·tion·al·ize** \-nə-ˌlīz\ *vb* — **in·sti·tu·tion·al·ly** *adv*

instr *abbr* **1** instructor **2** instrument; instrumental

in·struct \in-ˈstrəkt\ *vb* [ME, fr. L *instructus,* pp. of *instruere,* fr. *struere* to build] **1** : TEACH **2** : INFORM **3** : to give an order or a command to

in·struc·tion \in-ˈstrək-shən\ *n* **1** : LESSON, PRECEPT **2** : COMMAND, ORDER **3** *pl* : DIRECTIONS **4** : the action, practice, or profession of a teacher — **in·struc·tion·al** \-shə-nəl\ *adj*

in·struc·tive \in-ˈstrək-tiv\ *adj* : carrying a lesson : ENLIGHTENING ⟨an ~ book⟩

in·struc·tor \in-ˈstrək-tər\ *n* : one that instructs; *esp* : a college teacher below professorial rank — **in·struc·tor·ship** *n*

in·stru·ment \ˈin-strə-mənt\ *n* **1** : a device used to produce music **2** : a means by which something is done **3** : a device for doing work and esp. precision work ⟨a drafting ~⟩ **4** : a legal document (as a deed) **5** : a device used in navigating an airplane — **in·stru·ment** \-ˌment\ *vb*

in·stru·men·tal \ˌin-strə-ˈmen-tᵊl\ *adj* **1** : acting as a crucial agent or means ⟨was ~ in arranging the deal⟩ **2** : of, relating to, or done with an instrument **3** : relating to, composed for, or performed on a musical instrument

in·stru·men·tal·ist \-ˈmen-tə-list\ *n* : a player on a musical instrument

in·stru·men·tal·i·ty \ˌin-strə-mən-ˈta-lə-tē, -ˌmen-\ *n, pl* **-ties** **1** : the quality or state of being instrumental **2** : MEANS, AGENCY

in·stru·men·ta·tion \ˌin-strə-mən-ˈtā-shən, -ˌmen-\ *n* **1** : ORCHESTRATION **2** : instruments for a particular purpose

instrument panel *n* : DASHBOARD 1

in·sub·or·di·nate \ˌin-sə-ˈbȯr-də-nət\ *adj* : disobedient to authority — **in·sub·or·di·na·tion** \-ˌbȯr-də-ˈnā-shən\ *n*

in·sub·stan·tial \ˌin-səb-ˈstan-chəl\ *adj* **1** : lacking substance or reality **2** : lacking firmness or solidity

in·suf·fer·able \(ˌ)in-ˈsə-fə-rə-bəl\ *adj* : not to be endured : INTOLERABLE ⟨an ~ bore⟩ — **in·suf·fer·ably** \-blē\ *adv*

in·suf·fi·cient \ˌin-sə-ˈfi-shənt\ *adj* : not sufficient ⟨~ funds⟩; *also* : lacking capacity — **in·suf·fi·cien·cy** \-shən-sē\ *n* — **in·suf·fi·cient·ly** *adv*

in·su·lar \ˈin-sə-lər, -syə-\ *adj* **1** : of, relating to, or forming an island **2** : dwelling or situated on an island **3** : NARROW-MINDED ⟨an ~ perspective⟩ — **in·su·lar·i·ty** \ˌin-sə-ˈlar-ə-tē, -syə-\ *n*

in·su·late \ˈin-sə-ˌlāt\ *vb* **-lat·ed; -lat·ing** [L *insula* island] : ISOLATE; *esp* : to separate a conductor of electricity, heat, or sound from other conducting bodies by means of a nonconductor — **in·su·la·tion** \ˌin-sə-ˈlā-shən\ *n* — **in·su·la·tor** \ˈin-sə-ˌlā-tər\ *n*

in·su·lin \ˈin-sə-lən\ *n* : a pancreatic hormone essential esp. for the metabolism of carbohydrates and the regulation of glucose levels in the blood

¹**in·sult** \in-ˈsəlt\ *vb* [MF or L; MF *insulter,* fr. L *insultare,* lit., to spring upon, fr. *saltare* to leap] : to treat with insolence or contempt : AFFRONT ⟨were ~*ed* by his rudeness⟩ — **in·sult·ing·ly** *adv*

²**in·sult** \ˈin-ˌsəlt\ *n* : a gross indignity

in·su·per·a·ble \(ˌ)in-ˈsü-pə-rə-bəl\ *adj* : incapable of being surmounted, overcome, passed over, or solved — **in·su·per·a·bly** \-blē\ *adv*

in·sup·port·able \ˌin-sə-ˈpȯr-tə-bəl\ *adj* **1** : UNENDURABLE **2** : UNJUSTIFIABLE

in·sur·able \in-ˈshu̇r-ə-bəl\ *adj* : capable of being or proper to be insured

in·sur·ance \in-ˈshu̇r-əns\ *n* **1** : the business of insuring persons or property **2** : coverage by contract whereby one party agrees to guarantee another against a specified loss **3** : the sum for which something is insured **4** : a means of guaranteeing protection or safety

in·sure \in-ˈshu̇r\ *vb* **in·sured; in·sur·ing** **1** : to provide or obtain insurance on or for : UNDERWRITE **2** : to make certain : ENSURE

in·sured \in-ˈshu̇rd\ *n* : a person whose life or property is insured

in·sur·er \in-ˈshu̇r-ər\ *n* : one that insures; *esp* : an insurance company

in·sur·gent \in-ˈsər-jənt\ *n* **1** : a person who revolts against civil authority or an established government : REBEL **2** : a member of a political party who rebels against it — **in·sur·gence** \-jəns\ *n* — **in·sur·gen·cy** \-jən-sē\ *n* — **in·sur·gent** *adj*

in·sur·mount·able \ˌin-sər-ˈmau̇n-tə-bəl\ *adj* : INSUPERABLE ⟨~ problems⟩ — **in·sur·mount·ably** \-blē\ *adv*

in·sur·rec·tion \ˌin-sə-ˈrek-shən\ *n* : an act or instance of revolting against civil authority or an established government — **in·sur·rec·tion·ist** \-shə-nist\ *n*

int *abbr* **1** interest **2** interior **3** intermediate **4** internal **5** international **6** intransitive

in·tact \in-ˈtakt\ *adj* : untouched esp. by anything that harms or diminishes

in·ta·glio \in-ˈtal-yō\ *n, pl* **-glios** [It] : an engraving cut deeply into the surface of a hard material (as stone)

in·take \ˈin-ˌtāk\ *n* **1** : an opening through which fluid enters **2** : the act of taking in **3** : something taken in

¹**in·tan·gi·ble** \(ˌ)in-ˈtan-jə-bəl\ *adj* : incapable of being touched : IMPALPABLE ⟨~ benefits⟩ — **in·tan·gi·bly** \-blē\ *adv*

²**intangible** *n* **1** : an incorporeal asset **2** : an abstract quality or attribute

in·te·ger \ˈin-ti-jər\ *n* [L, adj., whole, entire] : a number (as 1, 2, 3, 12, 432) that is not a fraction and does not include a fraction, is the negative of such a number, or is 0

¹**in·te·gral** \ˈin-ti-grəl\ *adj* **1** : essential to completeness ⟨~ to the company⟩ **2** : formed as a unit with another part **3** : composed of parts that make up a whole **4** : ENTIRE

²**integral** *n* : the result of a mathematical integration

in·te·grate \ˈin-tə-ˌgrāt\ *vb* **-grat·ed; -grat·ing** **1** : to find a function that has a given derivative **2** : to form, coordinate, or blend into a functioning whole : UNITE **3** : to incorporate into a larger unit **4** : to end the segregation of and bring into equal membership in society or an organization; *also* : DESEGREGATE — **in·te·gra·tion** \ˌin-tə-ˈgrā-shən\ *n*

integrated circuit *n* : a group of tiny electronic components and their connections that is produced in or on a small slice of material (as silicon)

in·teg·ri·ty \in-ˈte-grə-tē\ *n* **1** : adherence to a code of values : INCORRUPTIBILITY **2** : SOUNDNESS **3** : COMPLETENESS

in·teg·u·ment \in-ˈte-gyə-mənt\ *n* : a covering layer (as a skin or cuticle) of an organism or one of its parts

in·tel·lect \ˈin-tə-ˌlekt\ *n* **1** : the power of knowing : the capacity for knowledge **2** : the capacity for rational or intelligent thought esp. when highly developed **3** : a person with great intellectual powers

in·tel·lec·tu·al \ˌin-tə-ˈlek-chə-wəl\ *adj* **1** : of, relating to, or performed by the intellect : RATIONAL **2** : given to study, reflection, and speculation ⟨~ games⟩ 3 : engaged in activity requiring the creative use of the intellect — **intellectual** *n* — **in·tel·lec·tu·al·ly** *adv*

intellectual disability *n* : mild to severe impairment in intellectual ability accompanied by deficits in skills (as in interpersonal communication, reasoning, or self-care) necessary for independent daily functioning

in·tel·lec·tu·al·ism \-chə-wə-ˌli-zəm\ *n* : devotion to the exercise of intellect or to intellectual pursuits

in·tel·li·gence \in-ˈte-lə-jəns\ *n* **1** : ability to learn and understand or to deal with new or trying situations **2** : mental acuteness **3** : INFORMATION, NEWS **4** : an agency engaged in obtaining information esp. concerning an enemy or possible enemy; *also* : the information so gained

intelligence quotient *n* : IQ

in·tel·li·gent \in-ˈte-lə-jənt\ *adj* [L *intelligens,* fr. *intelligere* to understand, fr. *inter* between + *legere* to select] : having or showing intelligence or intellect ⟨an ~ decision⟩ — **in·tel·li·gent·ly** *adv*

in·tel·li·gen·tsia \in-ˌte-lə-ˈjent-sē-ə, -ˈgent-\ *n* [Russ *intelligentsiya,* fr. L *intelligentia* intelligence] : intellectuals forming a vanguard or elite

in·tel·li·gi·ble \in-ˈte-lə-jə-bəl\ *adj* : capable of being understood or comprehended ⟨a very ~ plan⟩ — **in·tel·li·gi·bil·i·ty** \-ˌte-lə-jə-ˈbi-lə-tē\ *n* — **in·tel·li·gi·bly** \-ˈte-lə-jə-blē\ *adv*

in·tem·per·ance \(ˌ)in-ˈtem-pə-rəns\ *n* : lack of moderation; *esp* : habitual or excessive drinking of intoxicants — **in·tem·per·ate** \-pə-rət\ *adj* — **in·tem·per·ate·ness** *n*

in·tend \in-ˈtend\ *vb* [ME *entenden, intenden,* fr. AF *entendre,* fr. L *intendere* to stretch out, direct, aim at, fr. *tendere* to stretch] **1** : to have in mind as a purpose or aim ⟨~*s* to retire⟩ **2** : to design for a specified use or future ⟨programs ~*ed* to help students⟩

in·ten·dant \in-ˈten-dənt\ *n* : an official (as a governor) esp. under the French, Spanish, or Portuguese monarchies

[1]**in·tend·ed** *adj* **1** : expected to be such in the future; *esp* : BETROTHED **2** : INTENTIONAL ⟨an ~ pun⟩

[2]**intended** *n* : an engaged person

in·tense \in-ˈtens\ *adj* **1** : existing in an extreme degree ⟨~ pain⟩ **2** : marked by great zeal, energy, or eagerness ⟨~ effort⟩ **3** : showing strong feeling; *also* : deeply felt — **in·tense·ly** *adv*

in·ten·si·fy \in-ˈten-sə-ˌfī\ *vb* **-fied; -fy·ing 1** : to make or become intense or more intensive **2** : to make more acute : SHARPEN ♦ ***Synonyms*** AGGRAVATE, HEIGHTEN, ENHANCE, MAGNIFY — **in·ten·si·fi·ca·tion** \-ˌten-sə-fə-ˈkā-shən\ *n*

in·ten·si·ty \in-ˈten-sə-tē\ *n, pl* **-ties 1** : the quality or state of being intense; *esp* : degree of strength, energy, or force

[1]**in·ten·sive** \in-ˈten-siv\ *adj* **1** : highly concentrated **2** : serving to give emphasis — **in·ten·sive·ly** *adv*

[2]**intensive** *n* : an intensive word, particle, or prefix ⟨the word "very" is an ~⟩

intensive care *n* : continuous monitoring and treatment of seriously ill patients; *also* : an area of a hospital providing this treatment

[1]**in·tent** \in-ˈtent\ *n* **1** : the state of mind with which an act is done : VOLITION **2** : PURPOSE, AIM ⟨the artist's ~⟩ **3** : MEANING, SIGNIFICANCE

[2]**intent** *adj* **1** : directed with keen attention ⟨an ~ gaze⟩ **2** : ENGROSSED; *also* : DETERMINED ⟨~ on winning⟩ — **in·tent·ly** *adv* — **in·tent·ness** *n*

in·ten·tion \in-ˈten-chən\ *n* **1** : a determination to act in a certain way **2** : PURPOSE, AIM, END ♦ ***Synonyms*** INTENT, DESIGN, OBJECT, OBJECTIVE, GOAL

in·ten·tion·al \in-ˈten-chə-nəl\ *adj* : done by intention or design : INTENDED — **in·ten·tion·al·ly** *adv*

in·ter \in-ˈtər\ *vb* **in·terred; in·ter·ring** : BURY

in·ter·ac·tion \ˌin-tər-ˈak-shən\ *n* : mutual or reciprocal action or influence — **in·ter·act** \-ˈakt\ *vb*

in·ter·ac·tive \-ˈak-tiv\ *adj* **1** : mutually or reciprocally active **2** : involving the actions or input of a user ⟨~ exhibits⟩ **3** : allowing two-way electronic communications (as between a person and a computer) — **in·ter·ac·tive·ly** *adv* — **in·ter·ac·tiv·i·ty** \-ak-ˈti-və-tē\ *n*

in·ter alia \ˌin-tər-ˈā-lē-ə, -ˈä-\ *adv* : among other things

in·ter·atom·ic \ˌin-tər-ə-ˈtä-mik\ *adj* : existing or acting between atoms

in·ter·breed \-ˈbrēd\ *vb* **-bred** \-ˈbred\; **-breed·ing** : to breed together

in·ter·ca·la·ry \in-ˈtər-kə-ˌler-ē\ *adj* **1** : INTERCALATED ⟨February 29 is an ~ day⟩ **2** : INTERPOLATED

in·ter·ca·late \-ˌlāt\ *vb* **-lat·ed; -lat·ing 1** : to insert (as a day) in a calendar **2** : to insert between or among existing elements or layers — **in·ter·ca·la·tion** \-ˌtər-kə-ˈlā-shən\ *n*

in·ter·cede \ˌin-tər-ˈsēd\ *vb* **-ced·ed; -ced·ing** : to act between parties with a view to reconciling differences

[1]**in·ter·cept** \ˌin-tər-ˈsept\ *vb* **1** : to stop or interrupt the progress or course of **2** : to include (as part of a curve or solid) between two points, curves, or surfaces **3** : to gain possession of (an opponent's pass) — **in·ter·cep·tion** \-ˈsep-shən\ *n*

[2]**in·ter·cept** \ˈin-tər-ˌsept\ *n* : INTERCEPTION; *esp* : the interception of a target by an interceptor or missile

in·ter·cep·tor \ˌin-tər-ˈsep-tər\ *n* : a fighter plane designed for defense against attacking bombers

in·ter·ces·sion \ˌin-tər-ˈse-shən\ *n* **1** : MEDIATION **2** : prayer or petition in favor of another — **in·ter·ces·sor** \-ˈse-sər\ *n* — **in·ter·ces·so·ry** \-ˈse-sə-rē\ *adj*

[1]**in·ter·change** \ˌin-tər-ˈchānj\ *vb* **1** : to put each in the place of the other **2** : EXCHANGE **3** : to change places mutually — **in·ter·change·able** \-ˈchān-jə-bəl\ *adj* — **in·ter·change·ably** \-blē\ *adv*

²in·ter·change \ˈin-tər-ˌchānj\ *n* **1** : EXCHANGE **2** : a highway junction that by separated levels permits passage between highways without crossing traffic streams

in·ter·col·le·giate \ˌin-tər-kə-ˈlē-jət\ *adj* : existing or carried on between colleges ⟨~ sports⟩

in·ter·com \ˈin-tər-ˌkäm\ *n* : a two-way system for localized communication

in·ter·con·nect \ˌin-tər-kə-ˈnekt\ *vb* : to connect with one another — **in·ter·con·nec·tion** \-ˈnek-shən\ *n*

in·ter·con·ti·nen·tal \-ˌkän-tə-ˈnen-tᵊl\ *adj* **1** : extending among or carried on between continents ⟨~ trade⟩ **2** : capable of traveling between continents ⟨~ ballistic missiles⟩

in·ter·course \ˈin-tər-ˌkȯrs\ *n* **1** : connection or dealings between persons or nations **2** : physical sexual contact between individuals that involves the genitalia of at least one person ⟨anal ~⟩; *esp* : SEXUAL INTERCOURSE

in·ter·de·nom·i·na·tion·al \ˌin-tər-di-ˌnä-mə-ˈnā-shə-nəl\ *adj* : involving different denominations

in·ter·de·part·men·tal \ˌin-tər-di-ˌpärt-ˈmen-tᵊl, -ˌdē-\ *adj* : carried on between or involving different departments (as of a college)

in·ter·de·pen·dent \ˌin-tər-di-ˈpen-dənt\ *adj* : dependent upon one another — **in·ter·de·pen·dence** \-dəns\ *n*

in·ter·dict \ˌin-tər-ˈdikt\ *vb* **1** : to prohibit by decree **2** : to destroy, cut off, or damage (as an enemy line of supply) **3** : INTERCEPT ⟨~*ed* drug shipments⟩ — **in·ter·dic·tion** \-ˈdik-shən\ *n*

in·ter·dis·ci·plin·ary \-ˈdi-sə-plə-ˌner-ē\ *adj* : involving two or more academic, scientific, or artistic disciplines

¹in·ter·est \ˈin-trəst; ˈin-tə-rəst, -ˌrest\ *n* **1** : right, title, or legal share in something **2** : a charge for borrowed money that is generally a percentage of the amount borrowed; *also* : the return received by capital on its investment **3** : WELFARE, BENEFIT; *also* : SELF-INTEREST **4** : CURIOSITY, CONCERN **5** : readiness to be concerned with or moved by an object or class of objects **6** : a quality in a thing that arouses interest

²interest *vb* **1** : to persuade to participate or engage **2** : to engage the attention of

in·ter·est·ing *adj* : holding the attention — **in·ter·est·ing·ly** *adv*

¹in·ter·face \ˈin-tər-ˌfās\ *n* **1** : a surface forming a common boundary of two bodies, spaces, or phases ⟨an oil-water ~⟩ **2** : the place at which two independent systems meet and act on or communicate with each other ⟨the man-machine ~⟩ **3** : the means by which interaction or communication is achieved at an interface — **in·ter·fa·cial** \ˌin-tər-ˈfā-shəl\ *adj*

²interface *vb* **-faced; -fac·ing** **1** : to connect by means of an interface **2** : to serve as an interface

in·ter·faith \ˌin-tər-ˈfāth\ *adj* : involving persons of different religious faiths

in·ter·fere \ˌin-tər-ˈfir\ *vb* **-fered; -fer·ing** [ME *enterferen,* fr. AF *(s')entreferir* to strike one another, fr. *entre* between, among + *ferir* to strike, fr. L *ferire*] **1** : to come in collision or be in opposition : CLASH **2** : to enter into the affairs of others **3** : to affect one another

in·ter·fer·ence \-ˈfir-əns\ *n* **1** : the act or process of interfering **2** : something that interferes : OBSTRUCTION **3** : the mutual effect on meeting of two waves resulting in areas of increased and decreased amplitude **4** : the blocking of an opponent in football to make way for the ballcarrier **5** : the illegal hindering of an opponent in sports

in·ter·fer·om·e·ter \ˌin-tər-fə-ˈrä-mə-tər\ *n* : an apparatus that uses the interference of waves (as of light) for making precise measurements — **in·ter·fer·om·e·try** \-fə-ˈrä-mə-trē\ *n*

in·ter·fer·on \ˌin-tər-ˈfir-ˌän\ *n* : any of a group of antiviral proteins of low molecular weight produced usu. by animal cells in response to a virus, a parasite in the cell, or a chemical

in·ter·ga·lac·tic \ˌin-tər-gə-ˈlak-tik\ *adj* : relating to or situated in the spaces between galaxies

in·ter·gen·er·a·tion·al \-ˌje-nə-ˈrā-shə-nəl\ *adj* : existing or occurring between generations ⟨~ conflicts⟩

in·ter·gla·cial \-ˈglā-shəl\ *n* : a warm period between successive glaciations

in·ter·gov·ern·men·tal \-ˌgə-vərn-ˈmen-tᵊl\ *adj* : existing or occurring between two governments or levels of government

in·ter·im \ˈin-tə-rəm\ *n* [L, adv., meanwhile, fr. *inter* between] : a time intervening : INTERVAL — **interim** *adj*

¹in·te·ri·or \in-ˈtir-ē-ər\ *adj* **1** : lying, occurring, or functioning within the limiting boundaries : INSIDE, INNER **2** : remote from the surface, border, or shore : INLAND

²interior *n* **1** : the inland part (as of a country) **2** : INSIDE **3** : the internal affairs of a state or nation **4** : a scene or view of the interior of a building

interior decoration *n* : INTERIOR DESIGN — **interior decorator** *n*

interior design *n* : the art or practice of planning and supervising the design and execution of architectural interiors and their furnishings — **interior designer** *n*

interj *abbr* interjection

in·ter·ject \ˌin-tər-ˈjekt\ *vb* : to throw in between or among other things

in·ter·jec·tion \ˌin-tər-ˈjek-shən\ *n* : an exclamatory word (as *ouch*) — **in·ter·jec·tion·al·ly** \-shə-nə-lē\ *adv*

in·ter·lace \ˌin-tər-ˈlās\ *vb* **1** : to unite by or as if by lacing together : INTERWEAVE **2** : INTERSPERSE

in·ter·lard \ˌin-tər-ˈlärd\ *vb* : to vary by inserting or interjecting something ⟨a speech ~*ed* with anecdotes⟩

in·ter·leave \ˌin-tər-ˈlēv\ *vb* **-leaved; -leav·ing** : to arrange in alternate layers

in·ter·leu·kin \ˌin-tər-ˈlü-kən\ *n* : any of several proteins of low molecular weight that are produced by cells of the body and regulate the immune system and immune responses

1in·ter·line \ˌin-tər-ˈlīn\ *vb* : to insert between lines already written or printed

2interline *vb* : to provide (as a coat) with an interlining

in·ter·lin·ear \ˌin-tər-ˈli-nē-ər\ *adj* : inserted between lines already written or printed ⟨an ~ translation of a text⟩

in·ter·lin·gual \ˌin-tər-ˈliŋ-gwəl\ *adj* : of, relating to, or existing between two or more languages

in·ter·lin·ing \ˈin-tər-ˌlī-niŋ\ *n* : a lining (as of a coat) between the ordinary lining and the outside fabric

in·ter·link \ˌin-tər-ˈliŋk\ *vb* : to link together

in·ter·lock \ˌin-tər-ˈläk\ *vb* **1** : to engage or interlace together : lock together : UNITE **2** : to connect so that action of one part affects action of another part — **in·ter·lock** \ˈin-tər-ˌläk\ *n*

in·ter·loc·u·tor \ˌin-tər-ˈlä-kyə-tər\ *n* : one who takes part in dialogue or conversation

in·ter·loc·u·to·ry \-ˌtȯr-ē\ *adj* : made during the progress of a legal action and not final or definite ⟨an ~ decree⟩

in·ter·lope \ˌin-tər-ˈlōp\ *vb* **-loped; -lop·ing 1** : to encroach on the rights (as in trade) of others **2** : INTRUDE, INTERFERE — **in·ter·lop·er** *n*

in·ter·lude \ˈin-tər-ˌlüd\ *n* **1** : a usu. short simple play or dramatic entertainment **2** : an intervening period, space, or event **3** : a piece of music inserted between the parts of a longer composition or a religious service

in·ter·mar·riage \ˌin-tər-ˈmer-ij\ *n* **1** : marriage within one's own group as required by custom **2** : marriage between members of different groups

in·ter·mar·ry \-ˈmer-ē\ *vb* **1** : to marry each other **2** : to marry within a group **3** : to become connected by intermarriage

1in·ter·me·di·ary \ˌin-tər-ˈmē-dē-ˌer-ē\ *adj* **1** : INTERMEDIATE **2** : acting as a mediator

2intermediary *n, pl* **-ar·ies** : MEDIATOR, GO-BETWEEN

1in·ter·me·di·ate \ˌin-tər-ˈmē-dē-ət\ *adj* : being or occurring at the middle place or degree or between extremes

2intermediate *n* **1** : one that is intermediate **2** : INTERMEDIARY

intermediate school *n* **1** : JUNIOR HIGH SCHOOL **2** : a school usu. comprising grades 4–6

in·ter·ment \in-ˈtər-mənt\ *n* : BURIAL

in·ter·mez·zo \ˌin-tər-ˈmet-sō, -ˈmed-zō\ *n, pl* **-zi** \-sē, -zē\ *or* **-zos** [It, ultim. fr. L *intermedius* intermediate] : a short movement connecting major sections of an extended musical work (as a symphony); *also* : a short independent instrumental composition

in·ter·mi·na·ble \(ˌ)in-ˈtər-mə-nə-bəl\ *adj* : ENDLESS; *esp* : wearisomely protracted — **in·ter·mi·na·bly** \-blē\ *adv*

in·ter·min·gle \ˌin-tər-ˈmiŋ-gəl\ *vb* : to mingle or mix together

in·ter·mis·sion \ˌin-tər-ˈmi-shən\ *n* **1** : INTERRUPTION, BREAK **2** : a temporary halt esp. in a public performance

in·ter·mit \-ˈmit\ *vb* **-mit·ted; -mit·ting** : DISCONTINUE; *also* : to be intermittent

in·ter·mit·tent \-ˈmi-tᵊnt\ *adj* : coming and going at intervals ⟨~ rain⟩ ♦ ***Synonyms*** RECURRENT, PERIODIC, ALTERNATE — **in·ter·mit·tent·ly** *adv*

in·ter·mix \ˌin-tər-ˈmiks\ *vb* : to mix together : INTERMINGLE — **in·ter·mix·ture** \-ˈmiks-chər\ *n*

in·ter·mo·lec·u·lar \-mə-ˈle-kyə-lər\ *adj* : existing or acting between molecules

1in·tern \ˈin-ˌtərn, in-ˈtərn\ *vb* : to confine or impound esp. during a war — **in·tern·ee** \(ˌ)in-ˌtər-ˈnē\ *n* — **in·tern·ment** \in-ˈtərn-mənt\ *n*

2in·tern *also* **in·terne** \ˈin-ˌtərn\ *n* : an advanced student or recent graduate (as in medicine) gaining supervised practical experience — **in·tern·ship** *n*

3in·tern \ˈin-ˌtərn\ *vb* : to work as an intern

in·ter·nal \in-ˈtər-nᵊl\ *adj* **1** : INWARD, INTERIOR **2** : relating to or located in the inside of the body ⟨~ pain⟩ **3** : of, relating to, or occurring within the confines of an organized structure ⟨~ affairs⟩ **4** : of, relating to, or existing within the mind **5** : INTRINSIC, INHERENT ⟨~ evidence⟩ — **in·ter·nal·ly** *adv*

internal combustion engine *n* : an engine in which the fuel is ignited within the engine cylinder

in·ter·nal·ise *Brit var of* INTERNALIZE

in·ter·nal·ize \in-ˈtər-nə-ˌlīz\ *vb* **-ized; -iz·ing** : to incorporate (as values) within the self through learning or socialization ⟨*internalized* their parents' values⟩ — **in·ter·nal·i·za·tion** \-ˌtər-nə-lə-ˈzā-shən\ *n*

internal medicine *n* : a branch of medicine that deals with the diagnosis and treatment of diseases not requiring surgery

1in·ter·na·tion·al \ˌin-tər-ˈna-shə-nəl\ *adj* **1** : common to or affecting two or more nations ⟨~ trade⟩ **2** : of, relating to, or constituting a group having members in two or more nations — **in·ter·na·tion·al·ly** *adv*

2international *n* : one that is international; *esp* : an organization of international scope

in·ter·na·tion·al·ise *Brit var of* INTERNATIONALIZE

in·ter·na·tion·al·ism \-ˈna-shə-nə-ˌli-zəm\ *n* : a policy of cooperation among nations; *also* : an attitude favoring such a policy — **in·ter·na·tion·al·ist** \-ˌlist\ *n or adj*

in·ter·na·tion·al·ize \-ˈna-shə-nə-ˌlīz\ *vb* : to make international; *esp* : to place under international control

International System of Units *n* : a system of units based on the metric system and used by international convention esp. for scientific work

in·ter·ne·cine \ˌin-tər-ˈne-ˌsēn, -ˈnē-ˌsīn\ *adj* [L *internecinus,* fr. *internecare* to destroy, kill, fr. *necare* to kill, fr. *nec-, nex* violent death] **1** : DEADLY; *esp* : mutually destructive **2** : of, relating to, or involving conflict within a group ⟨~ feuds⟩

In·ter·net \ˈin-tər-ˌnet\ *n, often not cap* : an electronic communications network that connects computer networks worldwide

Internet service provider *n* : a company that provides its customers with Internet access and related services

in·ter·nist \ˈin-ˌtər-nist\ *n* : a physician who specializes in internal medicine

in·ter·nun·cio \ˌin-tər-ˈnən-sē-ˌō, -ˈnu̇n-\ *n* [It *internunzio*] : a papal legate of lower rank than a nuncio

in·ter·of·fice \-ˈȯ-fəs\ *adj* : functioning or communicating between the offices of an organization

in·ter·per·son·al \-ˈpər-sə-nəl\ *adj* : being, relating to, or involving relations between persons ⟨~ communication⟩ — **in·ter·per·son·al·ly** *adv*

in·ter·plan·e·tary \ˌin-tər-ˈpla-nə-ˌter-ē\ *adj* : existing, carried on, or operating between planets ⟨~ space⟩

in·ter·play \ˈin-tər-ˌplā\ *n* : INTERACTION

in·ter·po·late \in-ˈtər-pə-ˌlāt\ *vb* **-lat·ed; -lat·ing** **1** : to change (as a text) by inserting new or foreign matter **2** : to insert (as words) into a text or into a conversation **3** : to estimate values of (data or a function) between two known values — **in·ter·po·la·tion** \-ˌtər-pə-ˈlā-shən\ *n*

in·ter·pose \ˌin-tər-ˈpōz\ *vb* **-posed; -pos·ing** **1** : to place between **2** : to thrust in : INTRUDE, INTERRUPT **3** : to inject between parts of a conversation or argument **4** : to come or be between ♦ ***Synonyms*** INTERFERE, INTERCEDE, INTERMEDIATE, INTERVENE — **in·ter·po·si·tion** \-pə-ˈzi-shən\ *n*

in·ter·pret \in-ˈtər-prət\ *vb* **1** : to explain the meaning of; *also* : to act as an interpreter : TRANSLATE **2** : to understand according to individual belief, judgment, or interest **3** : to represent artistically — **in·ter·pret·er** *n* — **in·ter·pre·tive** \-ˈtər-prə-tiv\ *adj*

in·ter·pre·ta·tion \in-ˌtər-prə-ˈtā-shən\ *n* **1** : EXPLANATION ⟨~ of the law⟩ **2** : an instance of artistic interpretation in performance or adaptation — **in·ter·pre·ta·tive** \-ˈtər-prə-ˌtā-tiv\ *adj*

in·ter·ra·cial \-ˈrā-shəl\ *adj* : of, involving, or designed for members of different races

in·ter·reg·num \ˌin-tə-ˈreg-nəm\ *n, pl* **-nums** *or* **-na** \-nə\ **1** : the time during which a throne is vacant between two successive reigns or regimes **2** : a pause in a continuous series

in·ter·re·late \ˌin-tər-ri-ˈlāt\ *vb* : to bring into or have a mutual relationship — **in·ter·re·lat·ed·ness** \-lā-təd-nəs\ *n* — **in·ter·re·la·tion** \-ˈlā-shən\ *n* — **in·ter·re·la·tion·ship** *n*

interrog *abbr* interrogative

in·ter·ro·gate \in-ˈter-ə-ˌgāt\ *vb* **-gat·ed; -gat·ing** : to question esp. formally and systematically ⟨~ a suspect⟩ — **in·ter·ro·ga·tion** \-ˌter-ə-ˈgā-shən\ *n* — **in·ter·ro·ga·tor** \-ˈter-ə-ˌgā-tər\ *n*

in·ter·rog·a·tive \ˌin-tə-ˈrä-gə-tiv\ *adj* : asking a question ⟨~ sentence⟩ — **interrogative** *n* — **in·ter·rog·a·tive·ly** *adv*

in·ter·rog·a·to·ry \ˌin-tə-ˈrä-gə-ˌtȯr-ē\ *adj* : INTERROGATIVE

in·ter·rupt \ˌin-tə-ˈrəpt\ *vb* **1** : to stop or hinder by breaking in **2** : to break the uniformity or continuity of **3** : to break in by speaking while another is speaking — **in·ter·rupt·er** *n* — **in·ter·rup·tion** \-ˈrəp-shən\ *n* — **in·ter·rup·tive** \-ˈrəp-tiv\ *adv*

in·ter·scho·las·tic \ˌin-tər-skə-ˈlas-tik\ *adj* : existing or carried on between schools ⟨~ sports⟩

in·ter·sect \ˌin-tər-ˈsekt\ *vb* **1** : to divide by passing through or across **2** : to meet and cross (as at a point); *also* : OVERLAP — **in·ter·sec·tion** \-ˈsek-shən\ *n*

in·ter·sperse \ˌin-tər-ˈspərs\ *vb* **-spersed; -spers·ing** **1** : to place something at intervals in or among **2** : to insert at intervals among other things — **in·ter·sper·sion** \-ˈspər-zhən\ *n*

[1]**in·ter·state** \ˌin-tər-ˈstāt\ *adj* : relating to, including, or connecting two or more states esp. of the U.S. ⟨~ commerce⟩

[2]**in·ter·state** \ˈin-tər-ˌstāt\ *n* : an interstate highway

in·ter·stel·lar \ˌin-tər-ˈste-lər\ *adj* : located or taking place among the stars

in·ter·stice \in-ˈtər-stəs\ *n, pl* **-stic·es** \-stə-ˌsēz, -stə-səz\ : a space that intervenes between things : CHINK — **in·ter·sti·tial** \ˌin-tər-ˈsti-shəl\ *adj*

in·ter·tid·al \ˌin-tər-ˈtī-dᵊl\ *adj* : of, relating to, or being the area that is above low-tide mark but exposed to tidal flooding ⟨life in the ~ mud⟩

in·ter·twine \-ˈtwīn\ *vb* : to twine or cause to twine about one another : INTERLACE

in·ter·twist \-ˈtwist\ *vb* : INTERTWINE

in·ter·ur·ban \-ˈər-bən\ *adj* : connecting cities or towns

in·ter·val \ˈin-tər-vəl\ *n* [ME *intervalle,* fr. AF & L; AF *entreval,* fr. L *intervallum* space between ramparts, interval, fr. *inter-* between + *vallum* rampart] **1** : a space of time between events or states : PAUSE **2** : a space between objects, units, or states **3** : the difference in pitch between two tones

in·ter·vene \ˌin-tər-ˈvēn\ *vb* **-vened; -ven·ing** **1** : to occur, fall, or come between points of time or between events **2** : to enter or appear as an unrelated feature or circumstance ⟨rain *intervened* and we postponed the trip⟩ **3** : to come in or between in order to stop, settle, or modify ⟨~ in a quarrel⟩ **4** : to occur or lie between two things — **in·ter·ven·tion** \-ˈven-chən\ *n*

in·ter·ven·tion·ism \-ˈven-chə-ˌni-zəm\ *n* : interference by one country in the political affairs of another — **in·ter·ven·tion·ist** \-ˈven-chə-nist\ *n or adj*

in·ter·view \ˈin-tər-ˌvyü\ *n* **1** : a formal consultation usu. to evaluate qualifications **2** : a meeting at which a writer or reporter obtains information from a person; *also* : the recorded or written account of such a meeting — **interview** *vb* — **in·ter·view·ee** \ˌin-tər-(ˌ)vyü-ˈē\ *n* — **in·ter·view·er** *n*

in·ter·vo·cal·ic \ˌin-tər-vō-ˈka-lik\ *adj* : immediately preceded and immediately followed by a vowel ⟨an ~ consonant⟩

in·ter·weave \ˌin-tər-ˈwēv\ *vb* **-wove** \-ˈwōv\ *also* **-weaved; -wo·ven** \-ˈwō-vən\ *also* **-weaved; -weav·ing** : to weave or blend together : INTERTWINE, INTERMINGLE — **interwoven** *adj*

in·tes·tate \in-ˈtes-ˌtāt, -tət\ *adj* **1** : having made no valid will ⟨died ~⟩ **2** : not disposed of by will ⟨~ estate⟩

in·tes·tine \in-ˈtes-tən\ *n* : the tubular part of the alimentary canal that extends from stomach to anus and consists of a long narrow upper part (**small intestine**) followed by a broader shorter lower part (**large intestine**) — **in·tes·ti·nal** \-tə-nᵊl\ *adj*

in·ti·fa·da \ˌin-tə-ˈfä-də\ *n* : an armed uprising of Palestinians against Israeli occupation of the West Bank and Gaza Strip

¹in·ti·mate \ˈin-tə-ˌmāt\ *vb* **-mat·ed; -mat·ing** [LL *intimare* to put in, announce, fr. L *intimus* innermost] **1** : ANNOUNCE, NOTIFY **2** : to communicate indirectly : HINT — **in·ti·ma·tion** \ˌin-tə-mā-shən\ *n*

²in·ti·mate \ˈin-tə-mət\ *adj* **1** : INTRINSIC; *also* : INNERMOST **2** : marked by very close association, contact, or familiarity **3** : marked by a warm friendship ⟨~ friends⟩ **4** : suggesting informal warmth or privacy **5** : of a very personal or private nature ⟨~ feelings⟩ — **in·ti·ma·cy** \ˈin-tə-mə-sē\ *n* — **in·ti·mate·ly** *adv*

³in·ti·mate \ˈin-tə-mət\ *n* : an intimate friend, associate, or confidant

in·tim·i·date \in-ˈti-mə-ˌdāt\ *vb* **-dat·ed; -dat·ing** : to make timid or fearful : FRIGHTEN; *esp* : to compel or deter by or as if by threats ♦ ***Synonyms*** COW, BULLDOZE, BULLY, BROWBEAT — **in·tim·i·dat·ing·ly** *adv* — **in·tim·i·da·tion** \-ˌti-mə-ˈdā-shən\ *n*

intl *or* **intnl** *abbr* international

in·to \ˈin-tü\ *prep* **1** : to the inside of ⟨ran ~ the house⟩ **2** : to the state, condition, or form of ⟨got ~ trouble⟩ **3** : AGAINST ⟨ran ~ a wall⟩

in·tol·er·a·ble \(ˌ)in-ˈtä-lə-rə-bəl\ *adj* **1** : UNBEARABLE ⟨~ pain⟩ **2** : EXCESSIVE — **in·tol·er·a·bly** \-blē\ *adv*

in·tol·er·ant \(ˌ)in-ˈtä-lə-rənt\ *adj* **1** : unable or unwilling to endure ⟨is lactose ~⟩ **2** : unwilling to grant equality, freedom, or other social rights : BIGOTED — **in·tol·er·ance** \-rəns\ *n*

in·to·na·tion \ˌin-tō-ˈnā-shən\ *n* **1** : something that is intoned **2** : the act of intoning and esp. of chanting **3** : the manner of singing, playing, or uttering tones; *esp* : the rise and fall in pitch of the voice in speech

in·tone \in-ˈtōn\ *vb* **in·toned; in·ton·ing** : to utter in musical or prolonged tones : CHANT ⟨~ a prayer⟩

in to·to \in-ˈtō-tō\ *adv* [L, on the whole] : TOTALLY, ENTIRELY

in·tox·i·cant \in-ˈtäk-si-kənt\ *n* : something that intoxicates; *esp* : an alcoholic drink — **intoxicant** *adj*

in·tox·i·cate \-sə-ˌkāt\ *vb* **-cat·ed; -cat·ing** **1** : to affect by a drug (as alcohol or cocaine) esp. to the point of physical or mental impairment **2** : to excite to enthusiasm or frenzy ⟨*intoxicated* by his power⟩ — **in·tox·i·ca·tion** \-ˌtäk-sə-ˈkā-shən\ *n*

in·trac·ta·ble \(ˌ)in-ˈtrak-tə-bəl\ *adj* : not easily controlled

in·tra·mu·ral \-ˈmyu̇r-əl\ *adj* : being or occurring within the walls or limits (as of a city or college) ⟨~ sports⟩

in·tra·mus·cu·lar \-ˈməs-kyə-lər\ *adj* : situated within, occurring in, or administered by entering a muscle — **in·tra·mus·cu·lar·ly** *adv*

in·tra·net \ˈin-trə-ˌnet\ *n* a network similar to the World Wide Web but having access limited to certain authorized users

intrans *abbr* intransitive

in·tran·si·gent \-jənt\ *adj* : UNCOMPROMISING ⟨an ~ attitude⟩ — **in·tran·si·gence** \-jəns\ *n* — **intransigent** *n*

in·tran·si·tive \(ˌ)in-ˈtran-sə-tiv, -zə-\ *adj* : not transitive; *esp* : not having or containing an object ⟨an ~ verb⟩ — **in·tran·si·tive·ly** *adv* — **in·tran·si·tive·ness** *n*

in·tra·state \ˌin-trə-ˈstāt\ *adj* : existing or occurring within a state ⟨~ rivals⟩

in·tra·uter·ine device \-ˈyü-tə-rən-, -ˌrīn-\ *n* : a device inserted into and left in the uterus to prevent pregnancy

in·tra·ve·nous \ˌin-trə-ˈvē-nəs\ *adj* : being within or entering by way of the veins ⟨~ feeding⟩; *also* : used in or using intravenous procedures ⟨~ needles⟩ — **in·tra·ve·nous·ly** *adv*

intrench *var of* ENTRENCH

in·trep·id \in-ˈtre-pəd\ *adj* : characterized by resolute fearlessness, fortitude, and endurance ⟨an ~ explorer⟩ — **in·tre·pid·i·ty** \ˌin-trə-ˈpi-də-tē\ *n*

in·tri·cate \ˈin-tri-kət\ *adj* [ME, fr. L *intricatus,* pp. of *intricare* to entangle, fr. *tricae* trifles, complications] **1** : having many complexly interrelated parts : COMPLICATED **2** : difficult to follow, understand, or solve — **in·tri·ca·cy** \-tri-kə-sē\ *n* — **in·tri·cate·ly** *adv*

¹in·trigue \ˈin-ˌtrēg, in-ˈtrēg\ *n* **1** : a secret scheme : PLOT **2** : a clandestine love affair

²in·trigue \in-ˈtrēg\ *vb* **in·trigued; in·trigu·ing** **1** : to accomplish by intrigue **2** : to carry on an intrigue; *esp* : PLOT, SCHEME **3** : to arouse the interest, desire, or curiosity of — **in·trigu·ing·ly** *adv*

in·trin·sic \in-ˈtrin-zik, -sik\ *adj* : belonging to the essential nature or constitution of a thing — **in·trin·si·cal·ly** \-zi-k(ə-)lē, -si-\ *adv*

introd *abbr* introduction

in·tro·duce \ˌin-trə-ˈdüs, -ˈdyüs\ *vb* **-duced; -duc·ing** **1** : to lead or bring in esp. for the first time **2** : to bring into practice or use **3** : to cause to be acquainted **4** : to present for discussion **5**

: PLACE, INSERT ♦ *Synonyms* INSINUATE, INTERPOLATE, INTERPOSE, INTERJECT — **in·tro·duc·tion** \-ˈdək-shən\ *n* — **in·tro·duc·to·ry** \-ˈdək-tə-rē\ *adj*

in·troit \ˈin-ˌtrȯit, -ˌtrō-ət\ *n* **1** *often cap* : the first part of the traditional proper of the Mass **2** : a piece of music sung or played at the beginning of a worship service

in·tro·spec·tion \-ˈspek-shən\ *n* : a reflective looking inward : an examination of one's own thoughts or feelings — **in·tro·spect** \ˌin-trə-ˈspekt\ *vb* — **in·tro·spec·tive** \-ˈspek-tiv\ *adj* — **in·tro·spec·tive·ly** *adv*

in·tro·vert \ˈin-trə-ˌvərt\ *n* : a typically reserved or quiet person who tends to be introspective and enjoys spending time alone — **in·tro·ver·sion** \ˌin-trə-ˈvər-zhən\ *n* — **introvert** *adj* — **in·tro·vert·ed** \ˈin-trə-ˌvər-təd\ *adj*

in·trude \in-ˈtrüd\ *vb* **in·trud·ed; in·trud·ing** **1** : to thrust, enter, or force in or upon **2** : ENCROACH, TRESPASS — **in·trud·er** *n* — **in·tru·sion** \-ˈtrü-zhən\ *n* — **in·tru·sive** \-ˈtrü-siv\ *adj* — **in·tru·sive·ness** *n*

intrust *var of* ENTRUST

in·tu·it \in-ˈtü-ət, -ˈtyü-\ *vb* : to know, sense, or understand by intuition

in·tu·ition \ˌin-tu̇-ˈwi-shən, -tyu̇-\ *n* **1** : quick and ready insight **2** : the power or faculty of knowing things without conscious reasoning — **in·tu·i·tive** \in-ˈtü-ə-tiv, -ˈtyü-\ *adj* — **in·tu·i·tive·ly** *adv*

In·u·it \ˈi-nu̇-wət, ˈin-yu̇-\ *n* [Inuit *inuit,* pl. of *inuk* person] **1** *pl* **Inuit** *or* **Inuits** : a member of an Indigenous people of northern Alaska, arctic Canada, and Greenland **2** : the language of the Inuit people

in·un·date \ˈi-nən-ˌdāt\ *vb* **-dat·ed; -dat·ing** : to cover with or as if with a flood : OVERFLOW — **in·un·da·tion** \ˌi-nən-ˈdā-shən\ *n*

in·ure \i-ˈnu̇r, -ˈnyu̇r\ *vb* **in·ured; in·ur·ing** [ME *enuren,* fr. *in ure* customary, fr. *putten in ure* to use, put into practice, part trans. of AF *mettre en ovre, en uevre*] **1** : to accustom to accept something undesirable ⟨*inured* to violence⟩ **2** : to become of advantage

in utero \in-ˈyü-tə-ˌrō\ *adv or adj* [L] : in the uterus : before birth

inv *abbr* **1** inventor **2** invoice

in vac·uo \in-ˈva-kyu̇-ˌwō\ *adv* [L] : in a vacuum

in·vade \in-ˈvād\ *vb* **in·vad·ed; in·vad·ing** **1** : to enter for conquest or plunder **2** : to encroach upon **3** : to spread through and usu. harm ⟨germs ~ the tissues⟩ — **in·vad·er** *n*

¹in·val·id \(ˌ)in-ˈva-ləd\ *adj* : being without foundation or force in fact, reason, or law — **in·va·lid·i·ty** \ˌin-və-ˈli-də-tē\ *n* — **in·val·id·ly** *adv*

²in·va·lid \ˈin-və-ləd\ *adj* : being in ill health : SICKLY

³invalid \ˈin-və-ləd\ *n* : a person in usu. chronic ill health — **in·va·lid·ism** \-lə-ˌdi-zəm\ *n*

⁴in·va·lid \ˈin-və-ləd, -ˌlid\ *vb* **1** : to remove from active duty by reason of sickness or disability **2** : to make sickly or disabled

in·val·i·date \(ˌ)in-ˈva-lə-ˌdāt\ *vb* : to make invalid ⟨*invalidate* a contract⟩; *esp* : to weaken or make valueless — **in·val·i·da·tion** \in-ˌva-lə-ˈdā-shən\ *n*

in·valu·able \-ˈval-yə-bəl, -yə-wə-bəl\ *adj* : valuable beyond estimation

in·vari·able \-ˈver-ē-ə-bəl\ *adj* : not changing or capable of change : CONSTANT — **in·vari·ably** \-blē\ *adv*

in·va·sion \in-ˈvā-zhən\ *n* : an act or instance of invading; *esp* : entry of an army into a country for conquest

in·va·sive \in-ˈvā-siv, -ziv\ *adj* **1** : tending to spread ⟨~ cancer cells⟩ **2** : involving entry into the living body (as by surgery)

in·vec·tive \in-ˈvek-tiv\ *n* **1** : an abusive expression or speech **2** : abusive language — **invective** *adj*

in·veigh \in-ˈvā\ *vb* : to protest or complain bitterly or vehemently : RAIL

in·vei·gle \in-ˈvā-gəl, -ˈvē-\ *vb* **in·vei·gled; in·vei·gling** [AF *enveegler, aveogler* to blind, hoodwink, fr. *avogle, enveugle* blind, fr. ML *ab oculis,* lit., lacking eyes] **1** : to win over by flattery : ENTICE **2** : to acquire by ingenuity or flattery ⟨*inveigled* his way into her confidence⟩

in·vent \in-ˈvent\ *vb* **1** : to think up **2** : to create or produce for the first time — **in·ven·tor** \-ˈven-tər\ *n*

in·ven·tion \in-ˈven-chən\ *n* **1** : INVENTIVENESS **2** : a creation of the imagination; *esp* : a false conception **3** : a device, contrivance, or process originated after study and experiment **4** : the act or process of inventing

in·ven·tive \in-ˈven-tiv\ *adj* **1** : CREATIVE, INGENIOUS ⟨an ~ composer⟩ **2** : characterized by invention ⟨an ~ turn of mind⟩ — **in·ven·tive·ness** *n*

in·ven·to·ry \ˈin-vən-ˌtȯr-ē\ *n, pl* **-ries** **1** : an itemized list of current goods or assets **2** : SURVEY, SUMMARY **3** : STOCK, SUPPLY **4** : the act or process of taking an inventory — **inventory** *vb*

¹in·verse \(ˌ)in-ˈvərs, ˈin-ˌvərs\ *adj* : opposite in order, nature, or effect : REVERSED — **in·verse·ly** *adv*

²inverse *n* : something inverse or resulting in or from inversion : OPPOSITE

in·ver·sion \in-ˈvər-zhən\ *n* **1** : a reversal of position, order, or relationship; *esp* : an increase of temperature with altitude through a layer of air **2** : the act or process of inverting

in·vert \in-ˈvərt\ *vb* **1** : to reverse in position, order, or relationship **2** : to turn upside down or inside out **3** : to turn inward

in·ver·te·brate \(ˌ)in-ˈvər-tə-brət, -ˌbrāt\ *adj* : lacking a backbone; *also* : of or relating to invertebrate animals — **invertebrate** *n*

¹in·vest \in-ˈvest\ *vb* **1** : to install formally in an office or honor **2** : to furnish with power or authority : VEST **3** : to cover completely : ENVELOP **4** : CLOTHE, ADORN **5** : BESIEGE **6** : to endow with a quality or characteristic

²**invest** *vb* **1** : to commit (money) in order to earn a financial return ⟨~*ed* in real estate⟩ **2** : to expend for future benefits or advantages **3** : to make an investment — **in·ves·tor** \-ˈves-tər\ *n*

in·ves·ti·gate \in-ˈves-tə-ˌgāt\ *vb* **-gat·ed; -gat·ing** [L *investigare* to track, investigate, fr. *vestigium* footprint, track] : to study by close examination and systematic inquiry — **in·ves·ti·ga·tion** \-ˌves-tə-ˈgā-shən\ *n* — **in·ves·ti·ga·tive** \-ˈves-tə-ˌgā-tiv\ *adj* — **in·ves·ti·ga·tor** \-ˌgā-tər\ *n*

in·ves·ti·ture \in-ˈves-tə-ˌchu̇r, -chər\ *n* **1** : the act of ratifying or establishing in office **2** : something that covers or adorns

¹**in·vest·ment** \in-ˈvest-mənt\ *n* **1** : an outer layer : ENVELOPE **2** : INVESTITURE 1 **3** : BLOCKADE, SIEGE

²**investment** *n* : the outlay of money for income or profit; *also* : the sum invested or the property purchased

in·vet·er·ate \in-ˈve-tə-rət\ *adj* **1** : firmly established by age or long persistence **2** : confirmed in a habit ⟨an ~ liar⟩

in·vi·a·ble \(ˌ)in-ˈvī-ə-bəl\ *adj* : incapable of surviving

in·vid·i·ous \in-ˈvi-dē-əs\ *adj* **1** : tending to cause discontent, animosity, or envy ⟨an ~ rule⟩ **2** : ENVIOUS **3** : OBNOXIOUS ⟨~ remarks⟩ — **in·vid·i·ous·ly** *adv*

in·vig·o·rate \in-ˈvi-gə-ˌrāt\ *vb* **-rat·ed; -rat·ing** : to give life and energy to : ANIMATE ⟨~ the economy⟩ — **in·vig·o·ra·tion** \-ˌvi-gə-ˈrā-shən\ *n*

in·vin·ci·ble \(ˌ)in-ˈvin-sə-bəl\ *adj* : incapable of being conquered, overcome, or subdued — **in·vin·ci·bil·i·ty** \-ˌvin-sə-ˈbi-lə-tē\ *n* — **in·vin·ci·bly** \-ˈvin-sə-blē\ *adv*

in·vi·o·la·ble \-ˈvī-ə-lə-bəl\ *adj* **1** : safe from violation or profanation **2** : UNASSAILABLE ⟨~ borders⟩ — **in·vi·o·la·bil·i·ty** \-ˌvī-ə-lə-ˈbi-lə-tē\ *n*

in·vi·o·late \-ˈvī-ə-lət\ *adj* : not violated or profaned : PURE ⟨an ~ principle⟩

in·vis·i·ble \-ˈvi-zə-bəl\ *adj* **1** : incapable of being seen ⟨~ to the naked eye⟩ **2** : HIDDEN **3** : IMPERCEPTIBLE, INCONSPICUOUS — **in·vis·i·bil·i·ty** \-ˌvi-zə-ˈbi-lə-tē\ *n* — **in·vis·i·bly** \-ˈvi-zə-blē\ *adv*

invisible hand *n* : a hypothetical economic force that works for the benefit of all

in·vi·ta·tion·al \ˌin-və-ˈtā-shə-nəl\ *adj* : limited to invited participants ⟨an ~ tournament⟩ — **invitational** *n*

in·vite \in-ˈvīt\ *vb* **in·vit·ed; in·vit·ing** **1** : ENTICE, TEMPT **2** : to increase the likelihood of ⟨~ trouble⟩ **3** : to request the presence or participation of : ASK **4** : to request formally **5** : ENCOURAGE ⟨~ suggestions⟩ — **in·vi·ta·tion** \ˌin-və-ˈtā-shən\ *n*

in·vit·ing *adj* : ATTRACTIVE, TEMPTING

in vi·tro \in-ˈvē-trō, -ˈvī-, -ˈvi-\ *adv or adj* [NL, lit., in glass] : outside the living body and in an artificial environment ⟨*in vitro* fertilization⟩

in·vo·ca·tion \ˌin-və-ˈkā-shən\ *n* **1** : SUPPLICATION; *esp* : a prayer at the beginning of a service **2** : a formula for conjuring : INCANTATION

¹**in·voice** \ˈin-ˌvȯis\ *n* [modif. of MF *envois,* pl. of *envoi* message] : an itemized list of goods shipped usu. specifying the price and the terms of sale : BILL

²**invoice** *vb* **in·voiced; in·voic·ing** : to send an invoice to or for : BILL

in·voke \in-ˈvōk\ *vb* **in·voked; in·vok·ing** **1** : to petition for help or support **2** : to appeal to or cite as authority ⟨~ a law⟩ **3** : to call forth by incantation : CONJURE ⟨~ spirits⟩ **4** : to make an earnest request for : SOLICIT ⟨*invoked* mercy⟩ **5** : to put into effect or operation **6** : to bring about : CAUSE

in·vol·un·tary \(ˌ)in-ˈvä-lən-ˌter-ē\ *adj* **1** : done contrary to or without choice **2** : COMPULSORY ⟨~ servitude⟩ **3** : not controlled by the will : REFLEX ⟨~ contractions⟩ — **in·vol·un·tari·ly** \-ˌvä-lən-ˈter-ə-lē\ *adv*

in·vo·lute \ˈin-və-ˌlüt\ *adj* : INVOLVED, INTRICATE ⟨an ~ maneuver⟩

in·vo·lu·tion \ˌin-və-ˈlü-shən\ *n* **1** : the act or an instance of enfolding or entangling **2** : COMPLEXITY, INTRICACY

in·volve \in-ˈvälv\ *vb* **in·volved; in·volv·ing** **1** : to draw in as a participant **2** : ENVELOP **3** : to occupy (as oneself) absorbingly; *esp* : to commit oneself emotionally **4** : to relate closely : CONNECT **5** : to have as part of itself : INCLUDE **6** : ENTAIL, IMPLY ⟨the job ~*s* traveling⟩ **7** : ²AFFECT — **in·volve·ment** *n*

in·volved \-ˈvälvd\ *adj* : INTRICATE, COMPLEX ⟨an ~ plot⟩

in·vul·ner·a·ble \(ˌ)in-ˈvəl-nə-rə-bəl\ *adj* **1** : incapable of being wounded, injured, or damaged **2** : immune to or proof against attack — **in·vul·ner·a·bil·i·ty** \-ˌvəl-nə-rə-ˈbi-lə-tē\ *n* — **in·vul·ner·a·bly** \-ˈvəl-nə-rə-blē\ *adv*

¹**in·ward** \ˈin-wərd\ *adj* **1** : situated on the inside **2** : MENTAL; *also* : SPIRITUAL **3** : directed toward the interior

²**inward** *or* **in·wards** \-wərdz\ *adv* **1** : toward the inside, center, or interior **2** : toward the inner being ⟨turned his thoughts ~⟩

in·ward·ly \ˈin-wərd-lē\ *adv* **1** : MENTALLY, SPIRITUALLY **2** : INTERNALLY ⟨bled ~⟩ **3** : to oneself ⟨cursed ~⟩

IOC *abbr* International Olympic Committee

io·dide \ˈī-ə-ˌdīd\ *n* : a compound of iodine with another element or group

io·dine \ˈī-ə-ˌdīn, -dᵊn\ *n* **1** : a nonmetallic chemical element used esp. in medicine and photography **2** : a solution of iodine used as a local antiseptic

io·dise *Brit var of* IODIZE

io·dize \ˈī-ə-ˌdīz\ *vb* **io·dized; io·diz·ing** : to treat with iodine or an iodide

ion \ˈī-ən, ˈī-ˌän\ *n* [Gk, neut. of *iōn,* prp.

of *ienai* to go; so called because in electrolysis it goes to one of the two poles] : an electrically charged particle, atom, or group of atoms — **ion·ic** \ī-ˈä-nik\ *adj*

-ion *n suffix* : act, process, state, or condition ⟨validat*ion*⟩

ion·ise *Brit var of* IONIZE

ion·ize \ˈī-ə-ˌnīz\ *vb* **ion·ized; ion·iz·ing** **1** : to convert wholly or partly into ions **2** : to become ionized — **ion·iz·able** \ˌī-ə-ˈnī-zə-bəl\ *adj* — **ion·i·za·tion** \ˌī-ə-nə-ˈzā-shən\ *n* — **ion·iz·er** \ˈī-ə-ˌnī-zər\ *n*

ion·o·sphere \ī-ˈä-nə-ˌsfir\ *n* : the part of the earth's atmosphere extending from about 30 miles (50 kilometers) to the exosphere that contains ionized atmospheric gases — **ion·o·spher·ic** \ī-ˌä-nə-ˈsfir-ik, -ˈsfer-\ *adj*

IOOF *abbr* Independent Order of Odd Fellows

io·ta \ī-ˈō-tə\ *n* [L, fr. Gk *iōta*] **1** : the 9th letter of the Greek alphabet — Ι or ι **2** : a very small quantity : JOT

IOU \ˌī-(ˌ)ō-ˈyü\ *n* : an acknowledgement of a debt

IP *abbr* innings pitched

IP address \ˈī-ˈpē-\ *n* [*I*nternet *p*rotocol] : the numeric address of a computer on the Internet

ip·e·cac \ˈi-pi-ˌkak\ *n* [Pg *ipecacuanha*] : an emetic and expectorant drug used esp. as a syrup in treating accidental poisoning; *also* : either of two tropical American plants or their rhizomes and roots used to make ipecac

IPO \ˌī-ˌpē-ˈō\ *n, pl* **IPOs** : an initial public offering of a company's stock

ip·so fac·to \ˌip-sō-ˈfak-tō\ *adv* [NL, lit., by the fact itself] : by the very nature of the case

iq *abbr* [L *idem quod*] the same as

IQ \ˈī-ˈkyü\ *n* : a number used to express a person's relative intelligence as determined by a standardized test

[1]**Ir** *abbr* Irish

[2]**Ir** *symbol* iridium

IR *abbr* infrared

[1]**IRA** \ˌī-(ˌ)är-ˈā; ˈī-rə\ *n* [*i*ndividual *r*etirement *a*ccount] : a retirement savings account in which income taxes are deferred until withdrawals are made

[2]**IRA** *abbr* Irish Republican Army

irai·mbi·lan·ja \ē-ˌrīm-bē-ˈlän(d)-zə\ *n, pl* **iraimbilanja** — see *ariary* at MONEY table

iras·ci·ble \i-ˈra-sə-bəl\ *adj* : marked by hot temper and easily provoked anger ♦ ***Synonyms*** CHOLERIC, TESTY, TOUCHY, CRANKY, CROSS — **iras·ci·bil·i·ty** \-ˌra-sə-ˈbi-lə-tē\ *n*

irate \ī-ˈrāt\ *adj* **1** : roused to ire ⟨an ∼ customer⟩ **2** : arising from anger — **irate·ly** *adv*

ire \ˈī(-ə)r\ *n* : ANGER, WRATH — **ire·ful** *adj*

Ire *abbr* Ireland

ire·nic \ī-ˈre-nik\ *adj* : favoring, conducive to, or operating toward peace or conciliation ⟨∼ measures⟩

ir·i·des·cence \ˌir-ə-ˈde-sᵊns\ *n* : a rainbowlike play of colors — **ir·i·des·cent** \-sᵊnt\ *adj*

irid·i·um \ir-ˈi-dē-əm\ *n* : a hard brittle heavy metallic chemical element

iris \ˈī-rəs\ *n, pl* **iris·es** *also* **iri·des** \ˈī-rə-ˌdēz, ˈir-ə-\ [ME, fr. L *iris* rainbow, iris plant, fr. Gk, rainbow, iris plant, iris of the eye] **1** : the colored part around the pupil of the eye **2** : any of a large genus of plants with linear basal leaves and large showy flowers

Irish \ˈī-rish\ *n* **1 Irish** *pl* : the people of Ireland **2** : the Celtic language of Ireland — **Irish** *adj* — **Irish·man** \-mən\ *n* — **Irish·wom·an** \-ˌwu̇-mən\ *n*

Irish bull *n* : an incongruous statement (as "it was hereditary in his family to have no children")

Irish coffee *n* : hot sugared coffee with Irish whiskey and whipped cream

Irish moss *n* : the dried and bleached plants of a red alga that is a source of carrageenan; *also* : this red alga

Irish setter *n* : any of a breed of hunting dogs with a mahogany-red coat

irk \ˈərk\ *vb* : to make weary, irritated, or bored : ANNOY

irk·some \ˈərk-səm\ *adj* : tending to irk : ANNOYING — **irk·some·ly** *adv*

[1]**iron** \ˈī(-ə)rn\ *n* [ME, fr. OE *īsern, īren*] **1** : a heavy malleable magnetic metallic chemical element that rusts easily and is vital to biological processes **2** : something made of metal and esp. iron; *also* : something (as handcuffs) used to bind or restrain ⟨put them in ∼*s*⟩ **3** : a household device with a flat base that is heated and used for pressing cloth **4** : STRENGTH, HARDNESS

[2]**iron** *vb* **1** : to press or smooth with or as if with a heated iron **2** : to remove (as wrinkles) by ironing — **iron·er** *n*

[1]**iron·clad** \-ˈklad\ *adj* **1** : sheathed in iron armor **2** : so firm or secure as to be unbreakable

[2]**iron·clad** \-ˌklad\ *n* : an armored naval vessel esp. of the 19th century

iron curtain *n* : a political, military, and ideological barrier that isolates an area; *esp, often cap* : one formerly isolating an area under Soviet control

iron·ic \ī-ˈrä-nik\ *also* **iron·i·cal** \-ni-kəl\ *adj* **1** : of, relating to, or marked by irony **2** : given to irony

iron·i·cal·ly \-ni-k(ə-)lē\ *adv* **1** : in an ironic manner **2** : it is ironic

iron·ing *n* : clothes ironed or to be ironed

iron lung *n* : a device for artificial respiration that encloses the chest in a chamber in which changes of pressure force air into and out of the lungs

iron out *vb* : to remove or lessen difficulties in or extremes of

iron oxide *n* : FERRIC OXIDE

iron·stone \ˈī(-ə)rn-ˌstōn\ *n* **1** : a hard iron-rich sedimentary rock **2** : a hard heavy durable pottery developed in England in the 19th century

iron·ware \-ˌwer\ *n* : articles made of iron

iron·weed \-ˌwēd\ *n* : any of a genus of mostly weedy plants related to the asters that have terminal heads of red, purple, or white flowers

iron•wood \-ˌwu̇d\ *n* : any of numerous trees or shrubs with exceptionally hard wood; *also* : the wood
iron•work \-ˌwərk\ *n* **1** : work in iron **2** *pl* : a mill or building where iron or steel is smelted or heavy iron or steel products are made — **iron•work•er** *n*
iro•ny \ˈī-rə-nē\ *n, pl* **-nies** [L *ironia,* fr. Gk *eirōnia,* fr. *eirōn* dissembler] **1** : the use of words to express the opposite of what one really means **2** : incongruity between the actual result of a sequence of events and the expected result
Ir•o•quois \ˈir-ə-ˌkwȯi\ *n, pl* **Iroquois** *same or* -ˌkwȯiz\ **1** *pl* : a confederacy of Indigenous peoples orig. of New York that consisted of the Cayuga, Mohawk, Oneida, Onondaga, and Seneca and later included the Tuscarora **2** : a member of any of the Iroquois peoples
ir•ra•di•ate \i-ˈrā-dē-ˌāt\ *vb* **-at•ed; -at•ing 1** : ILLUMINATE **2** : ENLIGHTEN **3** : to treat by exposure to radiation **4** : RADIATE — **ir•ra•di•a•tion** \-ˌrā-dē-ˈā-shən\ *n*
[1]**ir•ra•tio•nal** \(ˌ)i-ˈra-shə-nəl\ *adj* **1** : incapable of reasoning ⟨~ beasts⟩; *also* : defective in mental power ⟨~ with fever⟩ **2** : not based on reason ⟨~ fears⟩ **3** : being or numerically equal to an irrational number — **ir•ra•tio•nal•i•ty** \(ˌ)i-ˌra-shə-ˈna-lə-tē\ *n* — **ir•ra•tio•nal•ly** *adv*
[2]**irrational** *n* : IRRATIONAL NUMBER
irrational number *n* : a real number that cannot be expressed as the quotient of two integers
ir•rec•on•cil•able \(ˌ)i-ˌre-kən-ˈsī-lə-bəl, -ˈre-kən-ˌsī-\ *adj* : impossible to reconcile, adjust, or harmonize — **ir•rec•on•cil•abil•i•ty** \(ˌ)i-ˌre-kən-ˌsī-lə-ˈbi-lə-tē\ *n*
ir•re•cov•er•able \ˌir-i-ˈkə-və-rə-bəl\ *adj* : not capable of being recovered or rectified : IRREPARABLE ⟨an ~ loss⟩ — **ir•re•cov•er•ably** \-blē\ *adv*
ir•re•deem•able \ˌir-i-ˈdē-mə-bəl\ *adj* **1** : not redeemable; *esp* : not terminable by payment of the principal ⟨an ~ bond⟩ **2** : not convertible into gold or silver at the will of the holder **3** : being beyond remedy : HOPELESS ⟨~ villains⟩
ir•re•den•tism \-ˈden-ˌti-zəm\ *n* : a principle or policy directed toward the incorporation of a territory historically or ethnically part of another into that other — **ir•re•den•tist** \-tist\ *n or adj*
ir•re•duc•ible \ˌir-i-ˈdü-sə-bəl, -ˈdyü-\ *adj* : not reducible ⟨an ~ fraction⟩ — **ir•re•duc•ibly** \-blē\ *adv*
ir•re•fut•able \ˌir-i-ˈfyü-tə-bəl, (ˌ)i-ˈre-fyət-\ *adj* : impossible to refute
irreg *abbr* irregular
ir•reg•u•lar \(ˌ)i-ˈre-gyə-lər\ *adj* **1** : not regular : not natural or uniform **2** : not conforming to the normal or usual manner of inflection ⟨~ verbs⟩ **3** : not belonging to a regular or organized army ⟨~ troops⟩ — **irregular** *n* — **ir•reg•u•lar•ly** *adv*
ir•reg•u•lar•i•ty \i-ˌre-gyə-ˈla-rə-tē\ *n, pl* **-ties 1** : something that is irregular **2** : the quality or state of being irregular **3** : occasional constipation
ir•rel•e•vant \(ˌ)i-ˈre-lə-vənt\ *adj* : not relevant — **ir•rel•e•vance** \-vəns\ *n*
ir•re•li•gious \ˌir-i-ˈli-jəs\ *adj* : lacking religious emotions, doctrines, or practices
ir•re•me•di•a•ble \ˌir-i-ˈmē-dē-ə-bəl\ *adj* : impossible to remedy or correct
ir•re•mov•able \-ˈmü-və-bəl\ *adj* : not removable
ir•rep•a•ra•ble \(ˌ)i-ˈre-pə-rə-bəl\ *adj* : impossible to make good, undo, repair, or remedy ⟨~ damage⟩
ir•re•place•able \ˌir-i-ˈplā-sə-bəl\ *adj* : not replaceable ⟨~ antiques⟩
ir•re•press•ible \-ˈpre-sə-bəl\ *adj* : impossible to repress or control ⟨~ curiosity⟩
ir•re•proach•able \-ˈprō-chə-bəl\ *adj* : not reproachable : BLAMELESS
ir•re•sist•ible \ˌir-i-ˈzis-tə-bəl\ *adj* : impossible to successfully resist ⟨an ~ craving⟩ — **ir•re•sist•ibly** \-blē\ *adv*
ir•res•o•lute \(ˌ)i-ˈre-zə-ˌlüt\ *adj* : uncertain how to act or proceed : VACILLATING — **ir•res•o•lute•ly** \-ˌlüt-lē; (ˌ)i-ˌre-zə-ˈlüt-\ *adv* — **ir•res•o•lu•tion** \(ˌ)i-ˌre-zə-ˈlü-shən\ *n*
ir•re•spec•tive of \ˌir-i-ˈspek-tiv-\ *prep* : without regard to
ir•re•spon•si•ble \-ˈspän-sə-bəl\ *adj* : not responsible ⟨~ wastrels⟩ — **ir•re•spon•si•bil•i•ty** \-ˌspän-sə-ˈbi-lə-tē\ *n* — **ir•re•spon•si•bly** \-ˈspän-sə-blē\ *adv*
ir•re•triev•able \ˌir-i-ˈtrē-və-bəl\ *adj* : not retrievable : IRRECOVERABLE
ir•rev•er•ence \(ˌ)i-ˈre-və-rəns\ *n* **1** : lack of reverence **2** : an irreverent act or utterance — **ir•rev•er•ent** \-rənt\ *adj* — **ir•rev•er•ent•ly** *adv*
ir•re•vers•ible \ˌir-i-ˈvər-sə-bəl\ *adj* : incapable of being reversed ⟨an ~ loss⟩
ir•rev•o•ca•ble \(ˌ)i-ˈre-və-kə-bəl\ *adj* : incapable of being revoked or recalled ⟨~ change⟩ — **ir•rev•o•ca•bly** \-blē\ *adv*
ir•ri•gate \ˈir-ə-ˌgāt\ *vb* **-gat•ed; -gat•ing** : to supply (as land) with water by artificial means; *also* : to flush with liquid — **ir•ri•ga•tion** \ˌir-ə-ˈgā-shən\ *n*
ir•ri•ta•bil•i•ty \ˌir-ə-tə-ˈbi-lə-tē\ *n* **1** : the property of living things and of protoplasm that enables reaction to stimuli **2** : the quality or state of being irritable; *esp* : readiness to become annoyed or angry
ir•ri•ta•ble \ˈir-ə-tə-bəl\ *adj* : capable of being irritated; *esp* : readily or easily irritated — **ir•ri•ta•bly** \-blē\ *adv*
ir•ri•tate \ˈir-ə-ˌtāt\ *vb* **-tat•ed; -tat•ing 1** : to excite to anger : EXASPERATE **2** : to make sore or inflamed — **ir•ri•tant** \ˈir-ə-tənt\ *adj or n* — **ir•ri•tat•ing•ly** *adv* — **ir•ri•ta•tion** \ˌir-ə-ˈtā-shən\ *n*
ir•rupt \(ˌ)i-ˈrəpt\ *vb* **1** : to rush in forcibly or violently **2** : to increase suddenly in numbers ⟨rabbits ~ in cycles⟩ — **ir•rup•tion** \-ˈrəp-shən\ *n*
IRS *abbr* Internal Revenue Service
is *pres 3d sing of* BE
Isa *or* **Is** *abbr* Isaiah
Isa•iah \ī-ˈzā-ə\ *n* — see BIBLE table
Isa•ias \ī-ˈzā-əs\ *n* : ISAIAH
ISBN *abbr* International Standard Book Number
is•che•mia \is-ˈkē-mē-ə\ *n* : deficient sup-

ply of blood to a body part (as the brain) — **is•che•mic** \-mik\ *adj*

-ish *adj suffix* **1** : of, relating to, or being ⟨Finn*ish*⟩ **2** : characteristic of ⟨boy*ish*⟩ ⟨mul*ish*⟩ **3** : inclined or liable to ⟨book*ish*⟩ **4** : having a touch or trace of : somewhat ⟨purpl*ish*⟩ **5** : having the approximate age of ⟨forty*ish*⟩

isin•glass \ˈī-zᵊn-ˌglas, ˈī-ziŋ-\ *n* **1** : a gelatin obtained from various fish **2** : mica esp. in thin sheets

isl *abbr* island

Is•lam \is-ˈläm, iz-, -ˈlam, ˈis-ˌ, ˈiz-ˌ\ *n* [Ar *islām* submission (to the will of God)] : the religious faith of Muslims including belief in Allah as the sole deity and in Muhammad as his prophet; *also* : the civilization built on this faith — **Is•lam•ic** \is-ˈlä-mik, iz-, -ˈla-\ *adj*

is•land \ˈī-lənd\ *n* [ME *iland,* fr. OE *īgland,* fr. *īg* island + *land* land] **1** : a body of land smaller than a continent surrounded by water **2** : something resembling an island in its isolation

is•land•er \ˈī-lən-dər\ *n* : a native or inhabitant of an island

isle \ˈī(-ə)l\ *n* : ISLAND; *esp* : a small island

is•let \ˈī-lət\ *n* : a small island

ism \ˌi-zəm\ *n* : a distinctive doctrine, cause, or theory

-ism *n suffix* **1** : act : practice : process ⟨critic*ism*⟩ **2** : manner of action or behavior characteristic of a (specified) person or thing ⟨fanatic*ism*⟩ **3** : state : condition : property ⟨dual*ism*⟩ **4** : abnormal state or condition ⟨alcohol*ism*⟩ **5** : doctrine : theory : cult ⟨Buddh*ism*⟩ **6** : adherence to a set of principles ⟨stoic*ism*⟩ **7** : prejudice or discrimination on the basis of a (specified) attribute ⟨rac*ism*⟩ ⟨sex*ism*⟩ **8** : characteristic or peculiar feature or trait ⟨colloquial*ism*⟩

iso•bar \ˈī-sə-ˌbär\ *n* : a line on a map connecting places of equal barometric pressure — **iso•bar•ic** \ˌī-sə-ˈbär-ik, -ˈber-\ *adj*

iso•late \ˈī-sə-ˌlāt\ *vb* **-lat•ed; -lat•ing** [fr. *isolated* set apart, fr. F *isolé,* fr. It *isolato,* fr. *isola* island, fr. L *insula*] : to place or keep by itself : separate from others — **iso•la•tion** \ˌī-sə-ˈlā-shən\ *n*

isolated *adj* **1** : occurring alone or once : UNIQUE **2** : SPORADIC ⟨~ outbreaks⟩

iso•la•tion•ism \ˌī-sə-ˈlā-shə-ˌni-zəm\ *n* : a policy of national isolation by abstention from international political and economic relations — **iso•la•tion•ist** \-shə-nist\ *n or adj*

iso•mer \ˈī-sə-mər\ *n* : any of two or more chemical compounds that contain the same numbers of atoms of the same elements but differ in structural arrangement and properties — **iso•mer•ic** \ˌī-sə-ˈmer-ik\ *adj* — **isom•er•ism** \ī-ˈsä-mə-ˌri-zəm\ *n*

iso•met•rics \ˌī-sə-ˈme-triks\ *n sing or pl* : exercise involving a series of brief and intense contractions of muscles against each other or against an immovable resistance — **iso•met•ric** *adj*

iso•prene \ˈī-sə-ˌprēn\ *n* : a hydrocarbon used esp. in making synthetic rubber

isos•ce•les \ī-ˈsä-sə-ˌlēz\ *adj* : having two equal sides ⟨an ~ triangle⟩

iso•therm \ˈī-sə-ˌthərm\ *n* : a line on a map connecting points having the same temperature

iso•ther•mal \ˌī-sə-ˈthər-məl\ *adj* : of, relating to, or marked by equality of temperature

iso•tope \ˈī-sə-ˌtōp\ *n* [Gk *isos* equal + *topos* place] : any of the forms of a chemical element that differ chiefly in the number of neutrons in an atom — **iso•to•pic** \ˌī-sə-ˈtä-pik, -ˈtō-\ *adj* — **iso•to•pi•cal•ly** \-ˈtä-pi-k(ə-)lē, -ˈtō-\ *adv*

ISP *abbr* Internet service provider

Isr *abbr* Israel; Israeli

Is•ra•el•ite \ˈiz-rē-ə-ˌlīt\ *n* : a member of the Hebrew people descended from Jacob

is•su•ance \ˈi-shü-wəns\ *n* : the act of issuing or giving out esp. officially

¹is•sue \ˈi-shü\ *n* [ME, exit, proceeds, fr. AF, fr. *issir* to come out, go out, fr. L. *exire,* fr. *ire* to go] **1** : the action of going, coming, or flowing out : EGRESS, EMERGENCE **2** : EXIT, OUTLET, VENT **3** : OFFSPRING, PROGENY **4** : OUTCOME, RESULT **5** : a point of debate or controversy; *also* : the point at which an unsettled matter is ready for a decision **6** : a discharge (as of blood) from the body **7** : something coming forth from a specified source **8** : the act of officially giving out or printing : PUBLICATION; *also* : the quantity of things given out at one time

²issue *vb* **is•sued; is•su•ing** **1** : to go, come, or flow out **2** : to come forth or cause to come forth : EMERGE, DISCHARGE, EMIT **3** : ACCRUE **4** : to descend from a specified parent or ancestor **5** : to result in **6** : to put forth or distribute officially **7** : PUBLISH **8** : EMANATE, RESULT — **is•su•er** *n*

¹-ist *n suffix* **1** : one that performs a (specified) action ⟨cycl*ist*⟩ : one that makes or produces ⟨novel*ist*⟩ **2** : one that plays a (specified) musical instrument ⟨harp*ist*⟩ **3** : one that operates a (specified) mechanical instrument or contrivance ⟨machin*ist*⟩ **4** : one that specializes in a (specified) art or science or skill ⟨geolog*ist*⟩ **5** : one that adheres to or advocates a (specified) doctrine or system or code of behavior ⟨social*ist*⟩ or that of a (specified) individual ⟨Darwin*ist*⟩

²-ist *adj suffix* : -ISTIC

isth•mus \ˈis-məs\ *n* : a narrow strip of land connecting two larger land areas

¹it \ˈit, ət\ *pron* **1** : that one — used of a lifeless thing, a plant, a person or animal, or an abstract entity ⟨~'s a big building⟩ ⟨~'s a shade tree⟩ ⟨who is ~⟩ ⟨beauty is everywhere and ~ is a source of joy⟩ **2** — used as a subject of an impersonal verb that expresses a condition or action without reference to an agent ⟨~ is raining⟩ **3** — used as an anticipatory subject or object ⟨~'s good to see you⟩

²it \ˈit\ *n* : the player in a game who performs the principal action of the game (as trying to find others in hide-and-seek)

It *abbr* Italian; Italy
ital *abbr* italic; italicized
Ital *abbr* Italian
Ital•ian \i-ˈtal-yən\ *n* **1** : a native or inhabitant of Italy **2** : the language of Italy — **Italian** *adj*
ital•ic \i-ˈta-lik, ī-\ *adj* : relating to type in which the letters slope up toward the right (as in *"italic"*) — **italic** *n*
ital•i•cise *Brit var of* ITALICIZE
ital•i•cize \i-ˈta-lə-ˌsīz, ī-\ *vb* **-cized; -cizing** : to print in italics — **ital•i•ci•za•tion** \-ˌta-lə-sə-ˈzā-shən\ *n*
itch \ˈich\ *n* **1** : an uneasy irritating skin sensation that evokes a desire to scratch the affected area **2** : a skin disorder accompanied by an itch **3** : a persistent desire — **itch** *vb* — **itchy** *adj*
-ite *n suffix* **1** : native : resident ⟨suburban*ite*⟩ **2** : adherent : follower ⟨Lenin*ite*⟩ **3** : product ⟨metabol*ite*⟩ **4** : mineral : rock ⟨quartz*ite*⟩
item \ˈī-təm\ *n* [L, likewise, also] **1** : a separate particular in a list, account, or series : ARTICLE **2** : a separate piece of news (as in a newspaper)
item•ise *Brit var of* ITEMIZE
item•ize \ˈī-tə-ˌmīz\ *vb* **-ized; -iz•ing** : to set down in detail : LIST — **item•i•za•tion** \ˌī-tə-mə-ˈzā-shən\ *n*
it•er•ate \ˈi-tə-ˌrāt\ *vb* **-at•ed; -at•ing** : REITERATE ⟨*iterated* his innocence⟩
it•er•a•tion \ˌi-tə-ˈrā-shən\ *n* **1** : REPETITION; *esp* : a computational process in which a series of operations is repeated until a condition is met **2** : one repetition of the series of operations in iteration **3** : VERSION
itin•er•ant \ī-ˈti-nə-rənt, ə-\ *adj* : traveling from place to place; *esp* : covering a circuit ⟨an ~ preacher⟩
itin•er•ary \ī-ˈti-nə-ˌrer-ē, ə-\ *n, pl* **-ar•ies 1** : the route of a journey or the proposed outline of one **2** : a travel diary **3** : GUIDEBOOK
its \ˈits\ *adj* : of or relating to it or itself
it•self \it-ˈself\ *pron* : that identical one — used reflexively, for emphasis, or in absolute constructions
-ity *n suffix* : quality : state : degree ⟨alkal*inity*⟩
IUD \ˌī-(ˌ)yü-ˈdē\ *n* : INTRAUTERINE DEVICE
IV \ˌī-ˈvē\ *n, pl* **IVs** [*i*ntra*v*enous] : an apparatus used to administer a fluid (as of nutrients) intravenously; *also* : a fluid administered by IV
-ive *adj suffix* : that performs or tends toward an (indicated) action ⟨correct*ive*⟩
ivo•ry \ˈī-vrē, -və-rē\ *n, pl* **-ries** [ME *ivorie,* fr. AF *ivoire, ivurie,* fr. L *eboreus* of ivory, fr. *ebur* ivory] **1** : the hard creamy-white material composing the tusks of an elephant or walrus **2** : a pale yellow color **3** : something made of ivory or of a similar substance
ivory tower *n* **1** : an impractical lack of concern with urgent problems **2** : a place of learning
ivy \ˈī-vē\ *n, pl* **ivies** : a trailing woody evergreen vine with small black berries that is related to ginseng
IWW *abbr* Industrial Workers of the World
-ize *vb suffix* **1** : cause to be or conform to or resemble ⟨American*ize*⟩ : cause to be formed into ⟨union*ize*⟩ **2** : subject to a (specified) action ⟨satir*ize*⟩ **3** : saturate, treat, or combine with ⟨macadam*ize*⟩ **4** : treat like ⟨idol*ize*⟩ **5** : become : become like ⟨crystall*ize*⟩ **6** : be productive in or of : engage in a (specified) activity ⟨philosoph*ize*⟩ **7** : adopt or spread the manner of activity or the teaching of ⟨Christian*ize*⟩

J

[1]**j** \ˈjā\ *n, pl* **j's** *or* **js** \ˈjāz\ *often cap* : the 10th letter of the English alphabet
[2]**j** *abbr, often cap* **1** jack **2** journal **3** judge **4** justice
[1]**jab** \ˈjab\ *vb* **jabbed; jab•bing** : to thrust quickly or abruptly : POKE
[2]**jab** *n* : a usu. short straight punch
jab•ber \ˈja-bər\ *vb* : to talk rapidly, indistinctly, or unintelligibly : CHATTER — **jabber** *n* — **jab•ber•er** *n*
jab•ber•wocky \ˈja-bər-ˌwä-kē\ *n* : meaningless speech or writing
ja•bot \zha-ˈbō, ˈja-ˌbō\ *n* : a ruffle worn down the front of a dress or shirt
jac•a•ran•da \ˌja-kə-ˈran-də\ *n* : any of a genus of pinnate-leaved tropical American trees with clusters of showy blue flowers
[1]**jack** \ˈjak\ *n* **1** : a mechanical device; *esp* : one used to raise a heavy body a short distance **2** : a male donkey **3** : a small target ball in lawn bowling **4** : a small national flag flown by a ship **5** : a small 6-pointed metal object used in a game **(jacks) 6** : a playing card bearing the figure of a soldier or servant **7** : a socket into which a plug is inserted for connecting electric circuits
[2]**jack** *vb* **1** : to raise by means of a jack **2** : INCREASE ⟨~ up prices⟩
jack•al \ˈja-kəl\ *n* [Turk *çakal,* fr. Pers *shaqāl*] : any of several mammals of Asia and Africa related to the wolves
jack•a•napes \ˈja-kə-ˌnāps\ *n* **1** : MONKEY, APE **2** : an impudent or conceited person
jack•ass \ˈjak-ˌas\ *n* **1** : DONKEY; *esp* : a male donkey **2** : a stupid person : FOOL
jack•boot \-ˌbüt\ *n* **1** : a heavy military boot of glossy black leather extending above the knee **2** : a laceless military boot reaching to the calf

jack·daw \ˈjak-ˌdȯ\ *n* : a black and gray Old World crowlike bird

jack·et \ˈja-kət\ *n* [ME *jaket,* fr. AF *jackés,* pl., dim. of MF *jaque* short jacket, fr. *jacques* peasant, fr. the name *Jacques* James] **1** : a garment for the upper body usu. having a front opening, collar, and sleeves **2** : an outer covering or casing ⟨a book ~⟩

Jack Frost *n* : frost or frosty weather personified

jack·ham·mer \ˈjak-ˌha-mər\ *n* : a pneumatic percussion tool for drilling rock or breaking pavement

jack–in–the–box *n, pl* **jack–in–the–boxes** *or* **jacks–in–the–box** : a toy consisting of a small box out of which a figure springs when the lid is raised

jack–in–the–pulpit *n, pl* **jack–in–the–pulpits** *also* **jacks–in–the–pulpit** : a No. American spring-flowering woodland herb having an upright club-shaped spadix arched over by a green and purple spathe

[1]**jack·knife** \ˈjak-ˌnīf\ *n* **1** : a large pocketknife **2** : a dive in which the diver bends from the waist and touches the ankles before straightening out

[2]**jackknife** *vb* : to fold like a jackknife ⟨the trailer truck *jackknifed*⟩

jack·leg \ˈjak-ˌleg\ *adj* **1** : lacking skill or training **2** : MAKESHIFT

jack–of–all–trades *n, pl* **jacks–of–all–trades** : one who is able to do passable work at various tasks

jack–o'–lan·tern \ˈja-kə-ˌlan-tərn\ *n* : a lantern made of a pumpkin cut to look like a human face

jack·pot \ˈjak-ˌpät\ *n* **1** : a large sum of money formed by the accumulation of stakes from previous play (as in poker) **2** : an impressive and often unexpected success or reward

jack·rab·bit \-ˌra-bət\ *n* : any of several large hares of western No. America with very long ears and hind legs

Jack Russell terrier \ˈjak-ˈrə-səl-\ *n* : any of a breed of small terriers having a white coat with dark markings

jack·straw \-ˌstrȯ\ *n* **1** *pl* : a game in which straws or thin sticks are let fall in a heap and each player in turn tries to remove them one at a time without disturbing the rest **2** : one of the pieces used in jackstraws

jack–tar \-ˈtär\ *n, often cap* : SAILOR

Ja·cob's ladder \ˈjā-kəbz-\ *n* : any of several perennial herbs related to phlox that have pinnate leaves and blue or white bell-shaped flowers

jac·quard \ˈja-ˌkärd\ *n, often cap* : a fabric of intricate variegated weave or pattern

[1]**jade** \ˈjād\ *n* **1** : a broken-down, vicious, or worthless horse **2** : a disreputable woman

[2]**jade** *vb* **jad·ed; jad·ing** **1** : to wear out by overwork or abuse **2** : to become weary
♦ ***Synonyms*** EXHAUST, FATIGUE, TIRE

[3]**jade** *n* [F, fr. obs. Sp (*piedra de la*) *ijada,* lit., loin stone; fr. the belief that jade cures renal colic] : a usu. green gemstone that takes a high polish

jad·ed *adj* : made dull, apathetic, or cynical by experience or by surfeit

[1]**jag** \ˈjag\ *n* : a sharp projecting part

[2]**jag** *n* : SPREE ⟨a crying ~⟩

jag·ged \ˈja-gəd\ *adj* : sharply notched

jag·uar \ˈja-ˌgwär\ *n* : a black-spotted tropical American cat that is larger and stockier than the Old World leopard

jai alai \ˈhī-ˌlī\ *n* [Sp, fr. Basque, fr. *jai* festival + *alai* merry] : a court game played by usu. two or four players with a ball and a curved wicker basket strapped to the wrist

jail \ˈjāl\ *n* [ME *jaiole,* fr. AF *gaiole, jaiole,* fr. LL *caveola,* dim. of L *cavea* cage] : PRISON; *esp* : one for persons held in lawful custody — **jail** *vb*

jail·bird \-ˌbərd\ *n* : a habitual criminal

jail·break \-ˌbrāk\ *n* : a forcible escape from jail

jail·er *also* **jail·or** \ˈjā-lər\ *n* : a keeper of a jail

jal·ap \ˈja-ləp, ˈjä-\ *n* : a powdered purgative drug from the root of a Mexican plant related to the morning glory; *also* : this root or plant

ja·la·pe·ño \ˌhä-lə-ˈpān-(ˌ)yō\ *n* : a small plump dark green chili pepper

ja·lopy \jə-ˈlä-pē\ *n, pl* **ja·lop·ies** : a dilapidated vehicle (as an automobile)

jal·ou·sie \ˈja-lə-sē\ *n* [F, lit., jealousy] : a blind, window, or door with adjustable horizontal slats or louvers

[1]**jam** \ˈjam\ *vb* **jammed; jam·ming** **1** : to press into a close or tight position **2** : to cause to become wedged so as to be unworkable; *also* : to make or become unworkable through the jamming of a movable part **3** : to push forcibly ⟨~ on the brakes⟩ **4** : CRUSH, BRUISE ⟨*jammed* a finger in the door⟩ **5** : to make unintelligible by sending out interfering signals or messages **6** : to take part in a jam session — **jam·mer** *n*

[2]**jam** *n* **1** : a crowded mass that impedes or blocks ⟨traffic ~⟩ **2** : a difficult state of affairs

[3]**jam** *n* : a food made by boiling fruit and sugar to a thick consistency

Jam *abbr* Jamaica

jamb \ˈjam\ *n* [ME *jambe,* fr. AF *jambe, gambe,* lit., leg] : an upright piece forming the side of an opening (as of a door)

jam·ba·laya \ˌjəm-bə-ˈlī-ə\ *n* [Louisiana F] : rice cooked with ham, sausage, chicken, shrimp, or oysters and seasoned with herbs

jam·bo·ree \ˌjam-bə-ˈrē\ *n* : a large festive gathering

James \ˈjāmz\ *n* — see BIBLE table

jam–pack \ˈjam-ˈpak\ *vb* : to pack tightly or to excess

jam session *n* : an impromptu performance esp. by jazz musicians

Jan *abbr* January

jan·gle \ˈjaŋ-gəl\ *vb* **jan·gled; jan·gling** : to make a harsh or discordant sound — **jangle** *n*

jan·i·tor \ˈja-nə-tər\ *n* [L, doorkeeper, fr.

janus arch, gate] : a person who has the care of a building — **jan·i·to·ri·al** \ˌja-nə-ˈtȯr-ē-əl\ *adj*

Jan·u·ary \ˈja-nyə-ˌwer-ē\ *n* [ME *Januarie,* fr. L *Januarius,* first month of the ancient Roman year, fr. *Janus,* two-faced god of gates and beginnings] : the 1st month of the year

[1]**ja·pan** \jə-ˈpan\ *n* : a varnish giving a hard brilliant finish

[2]**japan** *vb* **ja·panned; ja·pan·ning** : to cover with a coat of japan

Jap·a·nese \ˌja-pə-ˈnēz, -ˈnēs\ *n, pl* **Japanese** **1** : a native or inhabitant of Japan **2** : the language of Japan — **Japanese** *adj*

Japanese beetle *n* : a small metallic green and brown scarab beetle introduced from Japan that is a pest on the roots of grasses as a grub and on foliage and fruits as an adult

[1]**jape** \ˈjāp\ *vb* **japed; jap·ing** **1** : JOKE **2** : MOCK

[2]**jape** *n* : JEST, GIBE

[1]**jar** \ˈjär\ *vb* **jarred; jar·ring** **1** : to make a harsh or discordant sound **2** : to have a harsh or disagreeable effect **3** : VIBRATE, SHAKE ⟨tremors *jarred* the house⟩

[2]**jar** *n* **1** : a state of conflict **2** : a harsh discordant sound **3** : JOLT **4** : a painful effect : SHOCK

[3]**jar** *n* : a widemouthed container usu. of glass or earthenware

jar·di·niere \ˌjär-də-ˈnir\ *n* : an ornamental stand for plants or flowers

jar·gon \ˈjär-gən\ *n* **1** : confused unintelligible language **2** : the special vocabulary of a particular group or activity **3** : obscure and often pretentious language

Jas *abbr* James

jas·mine \ˈjaz-mən\ *also* **jes·sa·mine** \ˈjes-mən, ˈje-sə-\ *n* [MF *jasmin,* fr. Ar *yāsamīn,* fr. Pers] : any of various climbing shrubs with fragrant flowers

jas·per \ˈjas-pər\ *n* : a usu. red, yellow, or brown opaque quartz

jaun·dice \ˈjȯn-dəs\ *n* : yellowish discoloration of skin, tissues, and body fluids by bile pigments; *also* : an abnormal condition marked by jaundice

jaun·diced \-dəst\ *adj* **1** : affected with or as if with jaundice **2** : exhibiting envy, distaste, or hostility ⟨a ~ critic⟩

jaunt \ˈjȯnt\ *n* : a short trip usu. for pleasure

jaun·ty \ˈjȯn-tē\ *adj* **jaun·ti·er; -est** : sprightly in manner or appearance : LIVELY ⟨~ tunes⟩ — **jaun·ti·ly** \-tə-lē\ *adv* — **jaun·ti·ness** \-tē-nəs\ *n*

jav·e·lin \ˈja-və-lən\ *n* **1** : a light spear **2** : a slender shaft thrown for distance in a track-and-field contest

[1]**jaw** \ˈjȯ\ *n* **1** : either of the bony or cartilaginous structures that support the soft tissues enclosing the mouth and that usu. bear teeth **2** : the parts forming the walls of the mouth and serving to open and close it — usu. used in pl. **3** : one of a pair of movable parts for holding or crushing something — **jawed** \ˈjȯd\ *adj*

[2]**jaw** *vb* : to talk abusively, indignantly, or at length ⟨~*ing* with her sister⟩

[1]**jaw·bone** \-ˌbōn\ *n* : JAW 1

[2]**jawbone** *vb* : to talk forcefully and persuasively

jaw·break·er \-ˌbrā-kər\ *n* **1** : a word difficult to pronounce **2** : a round hard candy

jaw–drop·ping \ˈjȯ-ˌdra-piŋ\ *adj* : causing great surprise or astonishment

jaw·less fish \ˈjȯ-ləs-\ *n* : any of a group of primitive vertebrates (as lampreys) without jaws

jay \ˈjā\ *n* : any of various noisy brightly colored often largely blue birds smaller than the related crows

jay·bird \ˈjā-ˌbərd\ *n* : JAY

jay·vee \ˌjā-ˈvē\ *n* **1** : JUNIOR VARSITY **2** : a member of a junior varsity team

jay·walk \ˈjā-ˌwȯk\ *vb* : to cross a street carelessly without regard for traffic regulations — **jay·walk·er** *n*

[1]**jazz** \ˈjaz\ *n* **1** : American music characterized by improvisation, syncopated rhythms, and contrapuntal ensemble playing **2** : empty talk **3** : similar but unspecified things : STUFF

[2]**jazz** *vb* : ENLIVEN ⟨~ things up⟩

jazzy \ˈja-zē\ *adj* **jazz·i·er; -est** **1** : having the characteristics of jazz **2** : marked by unrestraint, animation, or flashiness

JCS *abbr* joint chiefs of staff

jct *abbr* junction

JD *abbr* **1** L *juris doctor* doctor of jurisprudence; doctor of law **2** L *jurum doctor* doctor of laws **3** justice department **4** juvenile delinquent

jeal·ous \ˈje-ləs\ *adj* **1** : demanding complete devotion **2** : suspicious of a rival or of one believed to enjoy an advantage ⟨~ of his rich friends⟩ **3** : VIGILANT — **jeal·ous·ly** *adv* — **jeal·ou·sy** \-lə-sē\ *n*

jeans \ˈjēnz\ *n pl* [pl. of *jean* twilled cloth, short for *jean fustian,* fr. ME *Gene* Genoa, Italy] : pants made of durable twilled cotton cloth

jeep \ˈjēp\ *n* : a small four-wheel drive general-purpose motor vehicle used in World War II

[1]**jeer** \ˈjir\ *vb* : to speak or cry out in derision : MOCK ⟨~*ed* the umpire⟩

[2]**jeer** *n* : TAUNT

jeg·ging \ˈje-giŋ\ *n* : a legging resembling tight-fitting denim jeans and made of stretchy fabric — usu. used in pl.

Je·ho·vah \ji-ˈhō-və\ *n* : GOD 1

je·hu \ˈjē-hü, -hyü\ *n* : a driver of a coach or cab

je·june \ji-ˈjün\ *adj* [L *jejunus* empty of food, hungry, meager] : lacking interest or significance : DULL

je·ju·num \ji-ˈjü-nəm\ *n* [L] : the section of the small intestine between the duodenum and the ileum — **je·ju·nal** \-ˈjü-nᵊl\ *adj*

jell \ˈjel\ *vb* **1** : to come to the consistency of jelly **2** : to take shape ⟨my idea began to ~⟩

jel·ly \ˈje-lē\ *n, pl* **jellies** **1** : a food with a soft elastic consistency due usu. to the presence of gelatin or pectin; *esp* : a fruit product made by boiling sugar and the juice of a fruit **2** : a substance resembling jelly — **jelly** *vb* — **jel·ly·like** *adj*

jelly bean *n* : a bean-shaped candy
jel·ly·fish \ˈje-lē-ˌfish\ *n* : a marine coelenterate with a nearly transparent jellylike body and stinging tentacles
jen·net \ˈje-nət\ *n* **1** : a small Spanish horse **2** : a female donkey
jen·ny \ˈje-nē\ *n, pl* **jennies** : a female bird or donkey
je·on \(ˌ)jā-ˈȯn\ *n, pl* **jeon** — see *won* at MONEY table
jeop·ar·dy \ˈje-pər-dē\ *n* [ME *jeopardie,* fr. AF *juparti, jeuparti* alternative, lit., divided game] : exposure to death, loss, or injury ♦ ***Synonyms*** PERIL, HAZARD, RISK, DANGER — **jeop·ar·dize** \-ˌdīz\ *vb*
Jer *abbr* Jeremiah; Jeremias
jer·e·mi·ad \ˌjer-ə-ˈmī-əd, -ˌad\ *n* : a prolonged lamentation or complaint; *also* : a cautionary or angry harangue
Jer·e·mi·ah \ˌjer-ə-ˈmī-ə\ *n* — see BIBLE table
Jer·e·mi·as \ˌjer-ə-ˈmī-əs\ *n* : JEREMIAH
¹**jerk** \ˈjərk\ *n* **1** : a short quick pull or twist : TWITCH **2** : an annoyingly stupid or foolish person — **jerk·i·ly** \ˈjər-kə-lē\ *adv* — **jerky** \ˈjər-kē\ *adj*
²**jerk** *vb* **1** : to give a sharp quick push, pull, or twist **2** : to move in short abrupt motions
jer·kin \ˈjər-kən\ *n* : a close-fitting usu. sleeveless jacket
jerk·wa·ter \ˈjərk-ˌwȯ-tər, -ˌwä-\ *adj* [fr. *jerkwater* rural train] : of minor importance : INSIGNIFICANT ⟨~ towns⟩
jer·ry–built \ˈjer-ē-ˌbilt\ *adj* : built cheaply and flimsily
jer·ry–rigged \-ˌrigd\ *adj* : organized or constructed in a crude or improvised manner
jer·sey \ˈjər-zē\ *n, pl* **jerseys** [*Jersey,* one of the Channel islands] **1** : a plain weft-knitted fabric **2** : a close-fitting knitted shirt **3** *often cap* : any of a breed of small usu. fawn-colored dairy cattle
Jersey barrier *n* : a concrete slab that is used with others to block or reroute traffic or to divide a highway
Je·ru·sa·lem artichoke \jə-ˈrü-sə-ləm-\ *n* : a No. American sunflower widely grown for its edible tubers that are used as a vegetable; *also* : its tubers
jess \ˈjes\ *n* : a leg strap by which a captive bird of prey may be controlled
jessamine *var of* JASMINE
jest \ˈjest\ *n* **1** : an act intended to provoke laughter **2** : a witty remark **3** : a frivolous mood ⟨said in ~⟩ — **jest** *vb*
jest·er \ˈjes-tər\ *n* : a retainer formerly kept to provide casual entertainment
¹**jet** \ˈjet\ *n* : a velvet-black coal that takes a good polish and is often used for jewelry
²**jet** *vb* **jet·ted; jet·ting** : to spout or emit in a stream
³**jet** *n* **1** : a forceful rush (as of liquid or gas) through a narrow opening; *also* : a nozzle for a jet of fluid **2** : a jet-propelled airplane
⁴**jet** *vb* **jet·ted; jet·ting** : to travel by jet
jet lag *n* : a condition that is marked esp. by fatigue and irritability and occurs following a long flight through several time zones — **jet–lagged** *adj*
jet·lin·er \ˈjet-ˌlī-nər\ *n* : a jet-propelled airliner
jet·port \-ˌpȯrt\ *n* : an airport designed to handle jets
jet–pro·pelled \ˌjet-prə-ˈpeld\ *adj* : driven by an engine (**jet engine**) that produces propulsion (**jet propulsion**) by the rearward discharge of a jet of fluid (as heated air and exhaust gases)
jet·sam \ˈjet-səm\ *n* : jettisoned goods; *esp* : such goods washed ashore
jet set *n* : an international group of wealthy people who frequent fashionable resorts
jet stream *n* : a long narrow high-altitude current of high-speed winds blowing generally from the west
jet·ti·son \ˈje-tə-sən\ *vb* **1** : to throw (goods) overboard to lighten a ship or aircraft in distress **2** : DISCARD ⟨~*ed* their old computers⟩ — **jettison** *n*
jet·ty \ˈje-tē\ *n, pl* **jetties** **1** : a pier built to influence the current or to protect a harbor **2** : a landing wharf
jeu d'es·prit \zhœ-des-ˈprē\ *n, pl* **jeux d'esprit** *same*\ [F, lit., play of the mind] : a witty comment or composition
Jew \ˈjü\ *n* **1** : ISRAELITE **2** : one whose religion is Judaism — **Jew·ish** *adj*
¹**jew·el** \ˈjü-əl\ *n* [ME *juel,* fr. AF, dim. of *ju, jeu* game, play, fr. L *jocus* game, joke] **1** : an ornament of precious metal **2** : GEMSTONE, GEM
²**jewel** *vb* **-eled** *or* **-elled; -el·ing** *or* **-el·ling** : to adorn or equip with jewels
jewel box *n* : a thin plastic case for a CD or DVD
jew·el·er *or* **jew·el·ler** \ˈjü-ə-lər\ *n* : a person who makes or deals in jewelry and related articles
jew·el·lery *chiefly Brit var of* JEWELRY
jew·el·ry \ˈjü-əl-rē\ *n* : JEWELS; *esp* : objects of precious metal set with gems and worn for personal adornment
Jew·ry \ˈju̇r-ē, ˈju̇-ər-ē, ˈjü-rē\ *n* : the Jewish people
jg *abbr* junior grade
¹**jib** \ˈjib\ *n* : a triangular sail set on a line running from the bow to the mast
²**jib** *vb* **jibbed; jib·bing** : to refuse to proceed further
¹**jibe** *var of* GIBE
²**jibe** \ˈjīb\ *vb* **jibed; jib·ing** : to be in accord : AGREE ⟨his conclusion does not ~ with theirs⟩
ji·ca·ma \ˈhē-kə-mə\ *n* : an edible starchy tuber of a tropical American vine of the legume family
jif·fy \ˈji-fē\ *n, pl* **jiffies** : MOMENT, INSTANT ⟨I'll be ready in a ~⟩
¹**jig** \ˈjig\ *n* **1** : a lively dance in triple rhythm **2** : TRICK, GAME ⟨the ~ is up⟩ **3** : a device used to hold work during manufacture or assembly
²**jig** *vb* **jigged; jig·ging** : to dance a jig
jig·ger \ˈji-gər\ *n* : a measure usu. holding 1 to 2 ounces (30 to 60 milliliters) used in mixing drinks
jig·gle \ˈji-gəl\ *vb* **jig·gled; jig·gling** : to move with quick little jerks — **jiggle** *n*

jig·saw \ˈjig-ˌsȯ\ *n* : SCROLL SAW 2
jigsaw puzzle *n* : a puzzle consisting of small irregularly cut pieces to be fitted together to form a picture
ji·had \ji-ˈhäd, -ˈhad\ *n* **1** : a Muslim holy war **2** : CRUSADE 2
ji·had·ist \ji-ˈhä-dist, -ˈha-\ *n* : a Muslim who advocates or participates in a jihad
¹**jilt** \ˈjilt\ *vb* : to drop (as a lover) capriciously or unfeelingly
²**jilt** *n* : one who jilts a lover
jim crow \ˈjim-ˈkrō\ *n, often cap J&C* : discrimination against Black people esp. by legal enforcement or traditional sanctions — **jim crow** *adj, often cap J&C* — **jim crow·ism** \-ˈkrō-ˌi-zəm\ *n, often cap J&C*
jim–dan·dy \ˈjim-ˈdan-dē\ *n* : something excellent of its kind — **jim–dandy** *adj*
jim·mies \ˈji-mēz\ *n pl* : tiny rod-shaped bits of usu. chocolate-flavored candy often sprinkled on ice cream
¹**jim·my** \ˈji-mē\ *n, pl* **jimmies** : a small crowbar
²**jimmy** *vb* **jim·mied; jim·my·ing** : to force open with a jimmy
jim·son·weed \ˈjim-sən-ˌwēd\ *n, often cap* : a coarse poisonous weed related to the tomato that has large trumpet-shaped white or violet flowers
¹**jin·gle** \ˈjiŋ-gəl\ *vb* **jin·gled; jin·gling** : to make a light clinking or tinkling sound
²**jingle** *n* **1** : a light clinking or tinkling sound **2** : a short verse or song with catchy repetition
jin·go·ism \ˈjiŋ-gō-ˌi-zəm\ *n* : extreme chauvinism or nationalism marked esp. by a belligerent foreign policy — **jin·go·ist** \-ist\ *n* — **jin·go·is·tic** \ˌjiŋ-gō-ˈis-tik\ *adj*
jin·rik·sha \jin-ˈrik-ˌshȯ\ *n* : RICKSHAW
¹**jinx** \ˈjiŋks\ *n* : one that brings bad luck
²**jinx** *vb* : to foredoom to failure or misfortune
jit·ney \ˈjit-nē\ *n, pl* **jitneys** : a small bus that serves a regular route on a flexible schedule
jit·ter·bug \ˈji-tər-ˌbəg\ *n* : a dance in which couples two-step, balance, and twirl vigorously in standardized patterns — **jitterbug** *vb*
jit·ters \ˈji-tərz\ *n pl* : extreme nervousness — **jit·tery** \-tə-rē\ *adj*
¹**jive** \ˈjīv\ *n* **1** : swing music or dancing performed to it **2** : glib, deceptive, or foolish talk **3** : the jargon of jazz enthusiasts
²**jive** *vb* **jived; jiv·ing** **1** : KID, TEASE **2** : to dance to or play jive
Jn *or* **Jno** *abbr* John
Jo *abbr* Joel
¹**job** \ˈjäb\ *n* **1** : a piece of work **2** : something that has to be done : TASK **3** : a regular remunerative position — **job·less** *adj*
²**job** *vb* **jobbed; job·bing** **1** : to do occasional pieces of work for hire **2** : to hire or let by the job
Job \ˈjōb\ *n* — see BIBLE table
job action *n* : a protest action by workers to force compliance with demands
job·ber \ˈjä-bər\ *n* **1** : a person who buys goods and then sells them to other dealers : MIDDLEMAN **2** : a person who does work by the job
job·hold·er \ˈjäb-ˌhōl-dər\ *n* : one having a regular job
jock \ˈjäk\ *n* [*jockstrap*] : ATHLETE; *esp* : a school or college athlete
¹**jock·ey** \ˈjä-kē\ *n, pl* **jockeys** : one who rides a horse esp. as a professional in a race
²**jockey** *vb* **jock·eyed; jock·ey·ing** : to maneuver or manipulate by adroit or devious means ⟨rivals ~*ed* for power⟩
jock·strap \ˈjäk-ˌstrap\ *n* [E slang *jock* penis] : ATHLETIC SUPPORTER
jo·cose \jō-ˈkōs\ *adj* **1** : MERRY ⟨~ partygoers⟩ **2** : HUMOROUS ♦ ***Synonyms*** JOCULAR, FACETIOUS, WITTY
joc·u·lar \ˈjä-kyə-lər\ *adj* : marked by jesting : PLAYFUL — **joc·u·lar·i·ty** \ˌjäk-yə-ˈlar-ə-tē\ *n* — **joc·u·lar·ly** *adv*
jo·cund \ˈjä-kənd\ *adj* : marked by mirth or cheerfulness ⟨a ~ celebration⟩
jodh·pur \ˈjäd-pər\ *n* **1** *pl* : riding breeches loose above the knee and tight-fitting below **2** : an ankle-high boot fastened with a strap
Joe Blow \ˈjō-\ *n* : an average or ordinary man
Jo·el \ˈjō-əl\ *n* — see BIBLE table
Joe Six–Pack \ˈjō-\ *n* : a blue-collar worker
¹**jog** \ˈjäg\ *vb* **jogged; jog·ging** **1** : to give a slight shake or push to **2** : to go at a slow monotonous pace **3** : to run or ride at a slow trot — **jog·ger** *n*
²**jog** *n* **1** : a slight shake **2** : a jogging movement or pace
³**jog** *n* **1** : a projecting or retreating part of a line or surface **2** : a brief abrupt change in direction
jog·gle \ˈjä-gəl\ *vb* **jog·gled; jog·gling** : to shake slightly — **joggle** *n*
john \ˈjän\ *n* **1** : TOILET **2** : a prostitute's client
John \ˈjän\ *n* — see BIBLE table
john·ny \ˈjä-nē\ *n, pl* **johnnies** : a short-sleeved gown opening in the back that is worn by hospital patients
John·ny–jump–up \ˌjä-nē-ˈjəmp-ˌəp\ *n* : any of various small-flowered cultivated pansies
joie de vi·vre \ˌzhwä-də-ˈvēvrᵊ\ *n* [F] : keen enjoyment of life
join \ˈjȯin\ *vb* **1** : to come or bring together so as to form a unit **2** : to come or bring into close association **3** : to become a member of **4** : ADJOIN **5** : to take part in a collective activity
join·er \ˈjȯi-nər\ *n* **1** : a worker who constructs articles by joining pieces of wood **2** : a gregarious person who joins many organizations
¹**joint** \ˈjȯint\ *n* **1** : the point of contact between bones of an animal skeleton with the parts that surround and support it **2** : a cut of meat suitable for roasting **3** : a place where two things or parts are connected **4** : ESTABLISHMENT; *esp* : a shabby or disreputable establish-

ment **5** : a marijuana cigarette — **joint·ed** *adj*

²joint *adj* **1** : UNITED **2** : common to two or more — **joint·ly** *adv*

³joint *vb* **1** : to unite by or provide with a joint **2** : to separate the joints of

joist \ˈjȯist\ *n* : any of the small beams ranged parallel from wall to wall in a building to support a floor or ceiling

¹joke \ˈjōk\ *n* : something said or done to provoke laughter; *esp* : a brief narrative with a humorous climax

²joke *vb* **joked; jok·ing** : to make jokes — **jok·ing·ly** *adv*

jok·er \ˈjō-kər\ *n* **1** : a person who jokes **2** : an extra card used in some card games **3** : a misleading part of an agreement that works to one party's disadvantage

jol·li·fi·ca·tion \ˌjä-li-fə-ˈkā-shən\ *n* : a festive celebration

jol·li·ty \ˈjä-lə-tē\ *n, pl* **-ties** : GAIETY, MERRIMENT

jol·ly \ˈjä-lē\ *adj* **jol·li·er; -est** : full of high spirits : MERRY

¹jolt \ˈjōlt\ *vb* **1** : to give a quick hard knock or blow to **2** : to move with a sudden jerky motion — **jolt·er** *n*

²jolt *n* **1** : an abrupt jerky blow or movement **2** : a sudden shock

Jon *abbr* Jonah; Jonas

Jo·nah \ˈjō-nə\ *n* — see BIBLE table

Jo·nas \ˈjō-nəs\ *n* : JONAH

¹jones \ˈjōnz\ *n* **1** *slang* : addiction to heroin **2** *slang* : HEROIN **3** *slang* : a craving for something

²jones *vb, slang* : to have a craving for something

jon·gleur \zhōⁿ-ˈglər\ *n* : an itinerant medieval minstrel

jon·quil \ˈjän-kwəl\ *n* [F *jonquille,* fr. Sp *junquillo,* dim. of *junco* reed, fr. L *juncus*] : a narcissus with fragrant clustered white or yellow flowers

josh \ˈjäsh\ *vb* : TEASE, JOKE

Josh *abbr* Joshua

Josh·ua \ˈjä-shə-wə\ *n* — see BIBLE table

Joshua tree *n* : a tall branched yucca of the southwestern U.S.

jos·tle \ˈjä-səl\ *vb* **jos·tled; jos·tling** **1** : to come in contact or into collision **2** : to make one's way by pushing and shoving ⟨*jostled* his way onto the bus⟩

Jos·ue \ˈjä-shü-ē\ *n* : JOSHUA

¹jot \ˈjät\ *n* : the least bit : IOTA

²jot *vb* **jot·ted; jot·ting** : to write briefly and hurriedly

jot·ting \ˈjä-tiŋ\ *n* : a brief note

joule \ˈjül\ *n* : a unit of work or energy equal to the work done by a force of one newton acting through a distance of one meter

jounce \ˈjau̇ns\ *vb* **jounced; jounc·ing** : JOLT — **jounce** *n*

jour *abbr* **1** journal **2** journeyman

jour·nal \ˈjər-nᵊl\ *n* [ME, service book containing the day hours, fr. AF *jurnal,* fr. *jurnal* daily, fr. L *diurnalis,* fr. *dies* day] **1** : a brief account of daily events **2** : a record of proceedings (as of a legislative body) **3** : a periodical (as a newspaper) dealing esp. with current events **4** : the part of a rotating axle or spindle that turns in a bearing

jour·nal·ese \ˌjər-nə-ˈlēz, -ˈlēs\ *n* : a style of writing held to be characteristic of newspapers

jour·nal·ism \ˈjər-nə-ˌli-zəm\ *n* **1** : the business of writing for, editing, or publishing periodicals (as newspapers) **2** : writing designed for or characteristic of newspapers — **jour·nal·ist** \-list\ *n* — **jour·nal·is·tic** \ˌjər-nə-ˈlis-tik\ *adj*

¹jour·ney \ˈjər-nē\ *n, pl* **journeys** [ME, fr. OF *journee* day's journey, fr. *jour* day] : a traveling from one place to another

²journey *vb* **jour·neyed; jour·ney·ing** : to go on a journey : TRAVEL

jour·ney·man \-mən\ *n* **1** : a worker who has learned a trade and works for another person **2** : an experienced reliable worker

¹joust \ˈjau̇st\ *vb* : to engage in a joust

²joust *n* : a combat on horseback between two knights with lances esp. as part of a tournament

jo·vial \ˈjō-vē-əl\ *adj* : marked by good humor ⟨in a ~ mood⟩ — **jo·vi·al·i·ty** \ˌjō-vē-ˈa-lə-tē\ *n* — **jo·vi·al·ly** *adv*

¹jowl \ˈjau̇(-ə)l\ *n* : loose flesh about the lower jaw or throat

²jowl *n* **1** : the lower jaw **2** : CHEEK

¹joy \ˈjȯi\ *n* [ME, fr. AF *joie,* fr. L *gaudia*] **1** : a feeling of happiness that comes from success, good fortune, or a sense of well-being **2** : a source of happiness ♦ ***Synonyms*** BLISS, DELIGHT, ENJOYMENT, PLEASURE — **joy·less** *adj*

²joy *vb* : REJOICE

joy·ful \-fəl\ *adj* : experiencing, causing, or showing joy ⟨~ news⟩ — **joy·ful·ly** *adv*

joy·ous \ˈjȯi-əs\ *adj* : JOYFUL — **joy·ous·ly** *adv* — **joy·ous·ness** *n*

joy·ride \ˈjȯi-ˌrīd\ *n* : a ride for pleasure often marked by reckless driving — **joyride** *vb* — **joy·rid·er** *n* — **joy·rid·ing** *n*

joy·stick \-ˌstik\ *n* : a control device (as for a computer) consisting of a lever capable of motion in two or more directions

JP *abbr* **1** jet propulsion **2** justice of the peace

JPEG \ˈjā-ˌpeg\ *n* [*J*oint *P*hotographic *E*xperts *G*roup] : a computer file format for usu. high-quality digital images

Jr *abbr* junior

jt *or* **jnt** *abbr* joint

ju·bi·lant \ˈjü-bə-lənt\ *adj* [L *jubilans,* prp. of *jubilare* to rejoice] : EXULTANT ⟨~ winners⟩ — **ju·bi·lant·ly** *adv*

ju·bi·la·tion \ˌjü-bə-ˈlā-shən\ *n* : EXULTATION

ju·bi·lee \ˈjü-bə-ˌlē, ˌjü-bə-ˈlē\ *n* [ME, fr. AF & LL; AF *jubilé,* fr. LL *jubilaeus,* fr. LGk *iōbēlaios,* fr. Heb *yōbhēl* ram's horn, trumpet, jubilee] **1** : a 50th anniversary **2** : a season or occasion of celebration

ju·co \ˈjü-ˌkō\ *n, pl* **jucos** : JUNIOR COLLEGE; *also* : an athlete at a junior college

Jud *abbr* Judith

Ju·da·ic \jü-ˈdā-ik\ *also* **Ju·da·ical** \-ˈdā-ə-kəl\ *adj* : of, relating to, or characteristic of Jews or Judaism

Ju·da·ism \ˈjü-də-ˌi-zəm, -dā-, -dē-\ *n* : a religion developed among the ancient Hebrews and marked by belief in one God and by the moral and ceremonial laws of the Old Testament and the rabbinic tradition

Jude \ˈjüd\ *n* — see BIBLE table

Judg *abbr* Judges

[1]**judge** \ˈjəj\ *vb* **judged; judg·ing** **1** : to form an authoritative opinion **2** : to decide as a judge : TRY **3** : to form an estimate or evaluation about something : THINK ♦ ***Synonyms*** CONCLUDE, DEDUCE, GATHER, INFER

[2]**judge** *n* **1** : a public official authorized to decide questions brought before a court **2** : UMPIRE **3** : one who gives an authoritative opinion : CRITIC — **judgeship** *n*

Judges *n* — see BIBLE table

judg·ment *or* **judge·ment** \ˈjəj-mənt\ *n* **1** : a decision or opinion given after judging; *esp* : a formal decision given by a court **2** *cap* : the final judging of mankind by God **3** : the process of forming an opinion by discerning and comparing **4** : the capacity for judging : DISCERNMENT

judg·men·tal \ˌjəj-ˈmen-təl\ *adj* **1** : of, relating to, or involving judgment **2** : characterized by a tendency to judge harshly — **judg·men·tal·ly** *adv*

judgment call *n* : a subjective decision, ruling, or opinion

Judgment Day *n* : the day of the final judging of all human beings by God

ju·di·ca·ture \ˈjü-di-kə-ˌchu̇r\ *n* **1** : the administration of justice **2** : JUDICIARY 1

ju·di·cial \ju̇-ˈdi-shəl\ *adj* **1** : of or relating to the administration of justice or the judiciary **2** : ordered or enforced by a court **3** : CRITICAL — **ju·di·cial·ly** *adv*

ju·di·cia·ry \ju̇-ˈdi-shē-ˌer-ē, -shə-rē\ *n* **1** : a system of courts of law; *also* : the judges of these courts **2** : a branch of government in which judicial power is vested — **judiciary** *adj*

ju·di·cious \ju̇-ˈdi-shəs\ *adj* : having, exercising, or characterized by sound judgment ⟨a ~ decision⟩ ♦ ***Synonyms*** PRUDENT, SAGE, SANE, SENSIBLE, WISE — **ju·di·cious·ly** *adv*

Ju·dith \ˈjü-dəth\ *n* — see BIBLE table

ju·do \ˈjü-dō\ *n* [Jp, fr. *jū* weakness, gentleness + *dō* art] : a sport derived from jujitsu that emphasizes the use of quick movement and leverage to throw an opponent — **ju·do·ist** \-ist\ *n*

ju·do·ka \ˈjü-dō-ˌkä\ *n, pl* **judoka** *or* **judokas** : one who participates in judo

[1]**jug** \ˈjəg\ *n* **1** : a large deep container with a narrow mouth and a handle **2** : JAIL, PRISON

[2]**jug** *vb* **jugged; jug·ging** : JAIL, IMPRISON

jug–eared \ˈjəg-ˌird\ *adj* : having protuberant ears

jug·ger·naut \ˈjə-gər-ˌnȯt\ *n* [Hindi *Jagannāth,* title of Vishnu (a Hindu god), lit., lord of the world] : a massive inexorable force or object that crushes everything in its path

jug·gle \ˈjə-gəl\ *vb* **jug·gled; jug·gling** **1** : to keep several objects in motion in the air at the same time **2** : to manipulate esp. in order to achieve a desired and often fraudulent end — **jug·gler** \ˈjə-glər\ *n*

jug·u·lar \ˈjə-gyə-lər\ *adj* : of, relating to, or situated in or on the throat or neck ⟨the ~ veins⟩

juice \ˈjüs\ *n* **1** : the extractable fluid contents of cells or tissues **2** *pl* : the natural fluids of an animal body **3** : something that supplies power; *esp* : ELECTRICITY 2

juic·er \ˈjü-sər\ *n* : an appliance for extracting juice (as from fruit)

juice up *vb* : to give life, energy, or spirit to ⟨*juice up* the music⟩

juicy \ˈjü-sē\ *adj* **juic·i·er; -est** **1** : SUCCULENT **2** : rich in interest; *also* : RACY ⟨~ gossip⟩ — **juic·i·ly** \-sə-lē\ *adv* — **juic·i·ness** \-sē-nəs\ *n*

ju·jit·su *also* **ju·jut·su** *or* **jiu·jit·su** \jü-ˈjit-sü\ *n* : an art of fighting employing holds, throws, and paralyzing blows

ju·ju \ˈjü-jü\ *n* : a style of African music characterized by a rapid beat, use of percussion instruments, and vocal harmonies

ju·jube \ˈjü-ˌjüb, ˈjü-ju̇-ˌbē\ *n* : a fruit-flavored gumdrop or lozenge

juke·box \ˈjük-ˌbäks\ *n* : a coin-operated machine that automatically plays selected recordings

Jul *abbr* July

ju·lep \ˈjü-ləp\ *n* [ME, sweetened water, fr. MF, fr. Ar *julāb,* fr. Pers *gulāb,* fr. *gul* rose + *āb* water] : a drink made of bourbon, sugar, and mint served over crushed ice

Ju·ly \ju̇-ˈlī\ *n* [ME *Julie,* fr. OE *Julius,* fr. L, fr. Gaius *Julius* Caesar] : the 7th month of the year

[1]**jum·ble** \ˈjəm-bəl\ *vb* **jum·bled; jum·bling** : to mix in a confused mass

[2]**jumble** *n* : a disorderly mass or pile

jum·bo \ˈjəm-bō\ *n, pl* **jumbos** [*Jumbo,* a huge elephant exhibited by P.T. Barnum] : a very large specimen of its kind ⟨a ~ TV screen⟩ — **jumbo** *adj*

[1]**jump** \ˈjəmp\ *vb* **1** : to spring into the air : leap over **2** : to give a start **3** : to rise or increase suddenly or sharply **4** : to make a sudden attack **5** : to leave hurriedly and often furtively ⟨~ town⟩ **6** : to act or move before (as a signal) — **jump bail** : to abscond after being released from custody on bail — **jump ship** **1** : to leave the company of a ship without authority **2** : to desert a cause — **jump the gun** : to begin something before the proper time

[2]**jump** *n* **1** : a spring into the air; *esp* : one made for height or distance in a track meet **2** : a sharp sudden increase **3** : an initial advantage ⟨got the ~ on his rival⟩

[1]**jump·er** \ˈjəm-pər\ *n* : one that jumps

[2]**jumper** *n* **1** : a loose blouse **2** : a sleeveless one-piece dress worn usu. with a blouse **3** *pl* : a child's sleeveless coverall

jumping bean *n* : a seed of any of several

Mexican shrubs that tumbles about because of the movements of a small moth larva inside it
jumping–off place *n* **1 :** a remote or isolated place **2 :** a place from which an enterprise is launched
jump·mas·ter \ˈjəmp-ˌmas-tər\ *n* **:** a person who supervises parachutists
jump–start \ˈjəmp-ˌstärt\ *vb* **:** to start (an engine or vehicle) by connection to an external power source
jump·suit \ˈjəmp-ˌsüt\ *n* **1 :** a coverall worn by parachutists in jumping **2 :** a one-piece garment consisting of a blouse or shirt with attached pants or shorts
jumpy \ˈjəm-pē\ *adj* **jump·i·er; -est :** NERVOUS, JITTERY
jun *abbr* junior
Jun *abbr* June
junc *abbr* junction
jun·co \ˈjəŋ-kō\ *n, pl* **juncos** *or* **juncoes :** any of a genus of small common pink-billed No. American finches that are largely gray with conspicuous white tail feathers
junc·tion \ˈjəŋk-shən\ *n* **1 :** an act of joining **2 :** a place or point of meeting
junc·ture \ˈjəŋk-chər\ *n* **1 :** JOINT, CONNECTION **2 :** UNION **3 :** a critical time or state of affairs
June \ˈjün\ *n* [ME, fr. L *Junius*] **:** the 6th month of the year
June·teenth \ˌjün-ˈtēnth\ *n* **:** June 19 celebrated esp. in Texas to commemorate the belated announcement there of the Emancipation Proclamation in 1865
jun·gle \ˈjəŋ-gəl\ *n* [Hindi & Urdu *jangal* forest] **1 :** a thick tangled mass of tropical vegetation; *also* **:** a tract overgrown with vegetation **2 :** a place of ruthless struggle for survival
[1]**ju·nior** \ˈjü-nyər\ *adj* **1 :** YOUNGER **2 :** lower in rank ⟨a ~ partner⟩ **3 :** of or relating to juniors
[2]**junior** *n* **1 :** a person who is younger or of lower rank than another **2 :** a student in the next-to-last year before graduating
junior college *n* **:** a school that offers studies corresponding to those of the 1st two years of college
junior high school *n* **:** a school usu. including grades 7–9
junior varsity *n* **:** a team whose members lack the experience or qualifications required for the varsity
ju·ni·per \ˈjü-nə-pər\ *n* **:** any of numerous coniferous shrubs or trees with leaves like needles or scales and female cones like berries
[1]**junk** \ˈjəŋk\ *n* **1 :** old iron, glass, paper, or waste; *also* **:** discarded articles **2 :** a shoddy product **3 :** something of little meaning, worth, or significance **4** *slang* **:** NARCOTICS; *esp* **:** HEROIN — **junky** *adj*
[2]**junk** *vb* **:** DISCARD, SCRAP
[3]**junk** *n* **:** a ship of eastern Asia with a high stern and 4-cornered sails
junk·er \ˈjəŋ-kər\ *n* **:** something (as an old automobile) ready for scrapping
Jun·ker \ˈyůŋ-kər\ *n* [G] **:** a member of the Prussian landed aristocracy
jun·ket \ˈjəŋ-kət\ *n* **1 :** a pudding of sweetened flavored milk set by rennet **2 :** a trip made by an official at public expense
junk food *n* **:** food that is high in calories but low in nutritional content
junk·ie *also* **junky** \ˈjəŋ-kē\ *n, pl* **junkies 1** *offensive* **:** a narcotics peddler or addict **2 :** one that derives inordinate pleasure from or is dependent on something ⟨a sugar ~⟩
jun·ta \ˈhůn-tə, ˈjən-, ˈhən-\ *n* [Sp, fr. *junto* joined, fr. L *junctus,* pp. of *jungere* to join] **:** a group of persons controlling a government esp. after a revolutionary seizure of power
Ju·pi·ter \ˈjü-pə-tər\ *n* **:** the largest of the planets and the one 5th in order of distance from the sun
Ju·ras·sic \jů-ˈra-sik\ *adj* **:** of, relating to, or being the period of the Mesozoic era between the Triassic and the Cretaceous that is marked esp. by the presence of dinosaurs — **Jurassic** *n*
ju·rid·i·cal \jů-ˈri-di-kəl\ *also* **ju·rid·ic** \-dik\ *adj* **1 :** of or relating to the administration of justice **2 :** LEGAL — **ju·rid·i·cal·ly** \-di-k(ə-)lē\ *adv*
ju·ris·dic·tion \ˌjůr-əs-ˈdik-shən\ *n* **1 :** the power, right, or authority to interpret and apply the law **2 :** the authority of a sovereign power **3 :** the limits or territory within which authority may be exercised — **ju·ris·dic·tion·al** \-shə-nəl\ *adj*
ju·ris·pru·dence \-ˈprü-dᵊns\ *n* **1 :** the science or philosophy of law **2 :** a system of laws
ju·rist \ˈjůr-ist\ *n* **:** one having a thorough knowledge of law; *esp* **:** JUDGE
ju·ris·tic \jů-ˈris-tik\ *adj* **1 :** of or relating to a jurist or jurisprudence **2 :** of, relating to, or recognized in law
ju·ror \ˈjůr-ər, -ˌór\ *n* **:** a member of a jury
[1]**ju·ry** \ˈjůr-ē\ *n, pl* **juries 1 :** a body of persons sworn to inquire into a matter submitted to them and to give their verdict **2 :** a committee for judging and awarding prizes
[2]**jury** *adj* **:** improvised for temporary use esp. in an emergency ⟨a ~ mast⟩
jury nullification *n* **:** the acquitting of a defendant by a jury in disregard of the judge's instructions and contrary to the jury's findings of fact
jury–rig \ˈjůr-ē-ˌrig\ *vb* **:** to construct or arrange in a makeshift fashion
[1]**just** \ˈjəst\ *adj* **1 :** having a basis in or conforming to fact or reason **:** REASONABLE ⟨~ comment⟩ **2 :** CORRECT, PROPER ⟨~ proportions⟩ **3 :** morally or legally right ⟨a ~ title⟩ **4 :** DESERVED, MERITED ⟨~ punishment⟩ ♦ ***Synonyms*** UPRIGHT, HONORABLE, CONSCIENTIOUS, HONEST — **just·ly** *adv* — **just·ness** *n*
[2]**just** \ˈjəst, ˈjist\ *adv* **1 :** EXACTLY ⟨~ right⟩ **2 :** very recently ⟨has ~ left⟩ **3 :** BARELY ⟨~ too late⟩ **4 :** DIRECTLY ⟨~ west of here⟩ **5 :** ONLY ⟨~ last year⟩ **6 :** QUITE ⟨~ wonderful⟩ **7 :** POSSIBLY ⟨it ~ might work⟩

jus·tice \ˈjəs-təs\ *n* **1** : the administration of what is just (as by assigning merited rewards or punishments) **2** : JUDGE **3** : the administration of law **4** : FAIRNESS; *also* : RIGHTEOUSNESS

justice of the peace : a local magistrate empowered chiefly to try minor cases, to administer oaths, and to perform marriages

jus·ti·fy \ˈjəs-tə-ˌfī\ *vb* **-fied; -fy·ing** **1** : to prove to be just, right, or reasonable **2** : to pronounce free from guilt or blame **3** : to adjust spaces in a line of printed text so the margins are even — **jus·ti·fi·able** *adj* — **jus·ti·fi·ca·tion** \ˌjəs-tə-fə-ˈkā-shən\ *n*

jut \ˈjət\ *vb* **jut·ted; jut·ting** : PROJECT, PROTRUDE

jute \ˈjüt\ *n* : a strong glossy fiber from either of two tropical plants used esp. for making sacks and twine

juv *abbr* juvenile

[1]**ju·ve·nile** \ˈjü-və-ˌnī(-ə)l, -nəl\ *adj* **1** : showing incomplete development **2** : of, relating to, or characteristic of children or young people

[2]**juvenile** *n* **1** : a young person; *esp* : one below the legally established age of adulthood **2** : a young animal (as a fish or a bird) or plant **3** : an actor or actress who plays youthful parts

juvenile delinquency *n* : violation of the law or antisocial behavior by a juvenile — **juvenile delinquent** *n*

jux·ta·pose \ˈjək-stə-ˌpōz\ *vb* **-posed; -pos·ing** : to place side by side — **jux·ta·po·si·tion** \ˌjək-stə-pə-ˈzi-shən\ *n*

JV *abbr* junior varsity

K

[1]**k** \ˈkā\ *n, pl* **k's** *or* **ks** \ˈkāz\ **1** *often cap* : the 11th letter of the English alphabet **2** *cap* : STRIKEOUT

[2]**k** *abbr* **1** karat **2** kitchen **3** knit **4** kosher — often enclosed in a circle

[1]**K** *abbr* **1** Kelvin **2** kindergarten

[2]**K** *symbol* [NL *kalium*] potassium

kab·ba·lah *also* **kab·ba·la** *or* **ka·ba·la** *or* **ca·ba·la** \kə-ˈbä-lə, ˈka-bə-lə\ *n, often cap* **1** : a medieval Jewish mysticism marked by belief in creation through emanation and a cipher method of interpreting Scripture **2** : esoteric or mysterious doctrine

kabob *var of* KEBAB

Ka·bu·ki \kə-ˈbü-kē\ *n* : traditional Japanese popular drama with highly stylized singing and dancing

kad·dish \ˈkä-dish\ *n, often cap* : a Jewish prayer recited in the daily synagogue ritual and by mourners at public services after the death of a close relative

kaf·fee·klatsch \ˈkȯ-fē-ˌklach, ˈkä-\ *n, often cap* [G] : an informal social gathering for coffee and conversation

kai·ser \ˈkī-zər\ *n* : EMPEROR; *esp* : the ruler of Germany from 1871 to 1918

Ka·lash·ni·kov \kə-ˈlash-nə-ˌkȯf\ *n* [M. T. *Kalashnikov* †2013 Soviet weapons designer] : a Soviet-designed assault rifle

kale \ˈkāl\ *n* : a hardy cabbage with curled leaves that do not form a head

ka·lei·do·scope \kə-ˈlī-də-ˌskōp\ *n* : a tube containing loose bits of colored material (as glass) and two mirrors at one end that shows many different patterns as it is turned — **ka·lei·do·scop·ic** \-ˌlī-də-ˈskä-pik\ *adj* — **ka·lei·do·scop·i·cal·ly** \-pi-k(ə-)lē\ *adv*

ka·ma·ai·na \ˌkä-mə-ˈī-nə\ *n* [Hawaiian *kama'āina,* fr. *kama* child + *'āina* land] : one who has lived in Hawaii for a long time

kame \ˈkām\ *n* [Sc, lit., comb] : a short ridge or mound of material deposited by water from a melting glacier

ka·mi·ka·ze \ˌkä-mi-ˈkä-zē\ *n* [Jp, lit., divine wind] : a member of a corps of Japanese pilots assigned to make a suicidal crash on a target; *also* : an airplane flown in such an attack

Kan *or* **Kans** *abbr* Kansas

kan·ga·roo \ˌkaŋ-gə-ˈrü\ *n, pl* **-roos** : any of various large leaping marsupial mammals of Australia and adjacent islands with powerful hind legs and a long thick tail used as a support

kangaroo court *n* : a court or an illegal self-appointed tribunal characterized by irresponsible, perverted, or irregular procedures

ka·o·lin \ˈkā-ə-lən\ *n* : a fine usu. white clay used in ceramics and refractories and for the treatment of diarrhea

ka·pey·ka \kä-ˈpā-kä\ *n, pl* **ka·pe·ek** \kä-ˈpā-ək\ — see *rubel* at MONEY table

ka·pok \ˈkā-ˌpäk\ *n* : silky fiber from the seeds of a tropical tree used esp. as a filling (as for life preservers)

Kap·o·si's sar·co·ma \ˈka-pə-sēz-sär-ˈkō-mə\ *n* : a neoplastic disease associated esp. with AIDS that affects esp. the skin and mucous membranes and is characterized usu. by the formation of pink to reddish-brown or bluish plaques

kap·pa \ˈka-pə\ *n* : the 10th letter of the Greek alphabet — K or κ

ka·put *also* **ka·putt** \kä-ˈpu̇t, kə-, -ˈpüt\ *adj* [G, fr. F *capot* not having made a trick at piquet] **1** : utterly defeated or destroyed **2** : unable to function : USELESS

kar·a·kul \ˈker-ə-kəl\ *n* : the usu. curly glossy black coat of a very young lamb of a hardy Asian breed of sheep

kar·a·o·ke \ˌker-ē-ˈō-kē\ *n* [Jp] : a device that plays instrumental accompaniments for songs to which the user sings along

kar·at \ˈker-ət\ *n* : a unit for expressing proportion of gold in an alloy equal to $^1/_{24}$ part of pure gold

ka·ra·te \kə-ˈrä-tē\ *n* [Jp, lit., empty hand] : an art of self-defense in which an attacker is disabled by crippling kicks and punches

kar·ma \ˈkär-mə\ *n, often cap* [Skt] : the force generated by a person's actions held in Hinduism and Buddhism to perpetuate reincarnation and to determine the nature of the person's next existence — **kar·mic** \-mik\ *adj*

karst \ˈkärst\ *n* [G] : an irregular limestone region with sinks, underground streams, and caverns

ka·ty·did \ˈkā-tē-ˌdid\ *n* : any of several large green tree-dwelling American grasshoppers with long antennae

kay·ak \ˈkī-ˌak\ *n* : a canoe that is made of a skin-covered frame with a small opening and propelled by a double-bladed paddle and that is associated esp. with Indigenous peoples of arctic regions; *also* : a similar portable boat — **kay·ak·er** *n*

kayo \(ˌ)kā-ˈō, ˈkā-ō\ *n* : KNOCKOUT — **kayo** *vb*

ka·zoo \kə-ˈzü\ *n, pl* **kazoos** : a toy musical instrument consisting of a tube with a membrane sealing one end and a side hole to sing or hum into

KB *abbr* kilobyte

kc *abbr* kilocycle

KC *abbr* **1** Kansas City **2** King's Counsel **3** Knights of Columbus

kc/s *abbr* kilocycles per second

KD *abbr* knocked down

ke·bab *or* **ke·bob** *also* **ka·bob** \kə-ˈbäb\ *n* : cubes of meat cooked with vegetables usu. on a skewer

kedge \ˈkej\ *n* : a small anchor

[1]**keel** \ˈkēl\ *n* **1** : the chief structural member of a ship running lengthwise along the center of its bottom **2** : something (as a bird's breastbone) like a ship's keel in form or use — **keeled** \ˈkēld\ *adj*

[2]**keel** *vb* : FAINT, SWOON — usu. used with *over* ⟨~*ed* over from the heat⟩

keel·boat \ˈkēl-ˌbōt\ *n* : a shallow covered keeled riverboat for freight that is usu. rowed, poled, or towed

keel·haul \-ˌhȯl\ *vb* : to haul under the keel of a ship as punishment

[1]**keen** \ˈkēn\ *adj* **1** : SHARP ⟨a ~ knife⟩ **2** : SEVERE ⟨a ~ wind⟩ **3** : ENTHUSIASTIC ⟨~ about swimming⟩ **4** : mentally alert ⟨a ~ mind⟩ **5** : STRONG, ACUTE ⟨~ eyesight⟩ **6** : WONDERFUL, EXCELLENT — **keen·ly** *adv* — **keen·ness** *n*

[2]**keen** *n* : a lamentation for the dead uttered in a loud wailing voice or in a wordless cry — **keen** *vb*

[1]**keep** \ˈkēp\ *vb* **kept** \ˈkept\; **keep·ing** **1** : FULFILL, OBSERVE ⟨~ a promise⟩ ⟨~ a holiday⟩ **2** : GUARD ⟨~ us from harm⟩; *also* : to take care of ⟨~ a neighbor's children⟩ **3** : MAINTAIN ⟨~ silence⟩ **4** : to have in one's service or at one's disposal ⟨~ a horse⟩ **5** : to preserve a record in ⟨~ a diary⟩ **6** : to have in stock for sale **7** : to retain in one's possession ⟨~ what you find⟩ **8** : to carry on (as a business) : CONDUCT **9** : HOLD, DETAIN ⟨~ him in jail⟩ **10** : to refrain from revealing ⟨~ a secret⟩ **11** : to continue in good condition ⟨meat will ~ in a freezer⟩ **12** : ABSTAIN, REFRAIN — **keep·er** *n*

[2]**keep** *n* **1** : FORTRESS **2** : the means or provisions by which one is kept — **for keeps 1** : with the provision that one keep what one has won ⟨play marbles *for keeps*⟩ **2** : PERMANENTLY ⟨came home *for keeps*⟩

keep–away \ˈkēp-ə-ˌwā\ *n* : a game in which players try to keep an object from one or more other players

keeping *n* : CONFORMITY ⟨in ~ with good taste⟩

keeping room *n* : a common room used for multiple purposes

keep·sake \ˈkēp-ˌsāk\ *n* : MEMENTO

keep up *vb* **1** : to persevere in **2** : MAINTAIN, SUSTAIN **3** : to keep informed **4** : to continue without interruption

keg \ˈkeg\ *n* : a small cask or barrel

keg·ger \ˈke-gər\ *n* : a party featuring one or more kegs of beer

keg·ler \ˈke-glər\ *n* : [1]BOWLER

kelp \ˈkelp\ *n* : any of various coarse brown seaweeds; *also* : a mass of these or their ashes often used as fertilizer

kel·vin \ˈkel-vən\ *n* : a unit of temperature equal to $^1/_{273.16}$ of the Kelvin scale temperature of the triple point of water

Kelvin *adj* : relating to, conforming to, or being a temperature scale according to which absolute zero is 0 K, the equivalent of −273.15°C

ken \ˈken\ *n* **1** : range of vision : SIGHT **2** : range of understanding

ken·nel \ˈke-nᵊl\ *n* : a shelter for a dog or cat; *also* : an establishment for the breeding or boarding of dogs or cats — **kennel** *vb*

ke·no \ˈkē-nō\ *n* : a game resembling bingo

ke·no·sis \kə-ˈnō-səs\ *n* : the relinquishment of divine attributes by Jesus Christ in becoming human — **ke·not·ic** \-ˈnä-tik\ *adj*

ken·te cloth \ˈken-ˌtā-\ *n* : colorfully patterned cloth traditionally woven by hand in Ghana

Ken·tucky bluegrass \kən-ˈtə-kē-\ *n* : a valuable pasture and meadow grass of both Europe and America

ke·pi \ˈkā-pē, ˈke-\ *n* [F] : a military cap with a round flat top and a visor

ker·a·tin \ˈker-ə-tən\ *n* : any of various sulfur-containing proteins that make up hair and horny tissues

kerb \ˈkərb\ *n, Brit* : CURB 3

ker·chief \ˈkər-chəf, -ˌchēf\ *n, pl* **ker·chiefs** \-chəfs, -ˌchēfs\ *also* **kerchieves** \-ˌchēvz\ [ME *courchef,* fr. AF *coverchef, cuerchief,* fr. *coverir* to cover + *chef* head] **1** : a square of cloth worn esp. as a head covering **2** : HANDKERCHIEF

kerf \ˈkərf\ *n* : a slit or notch made by a saw or cutting torch

ker·nel \ˈkər-nᵊl\ *n* **1** : the inner softer

part of a seed, fruit stone, or nut **2** : a whole seed of a cereal ⟨a ~ of corn⟩ **3** : a central or essential part : CORE

ker·o·sene *also* **ker·o·sine** \ˈker-ə-ˌsēn, ˌker-ə-ˈsēn\ *n* : a flammable oil produced from petroleum and used for a fuel and as a solvent

kes·trel \ˈkes-trəl\ *n* : any of various small falcons that usu. hover in the air while searching for prey

ketch \ˈkech\ *n* : a large fore-and-aft rigged boat with two masts

ketch·up *also* **catch·up** \ˈke-chəp, ˈka-\ *or* **cat·sup** \ˈke-chəp, ˈka-; ˈkat-səp\ *n* : a seasoned tomato puree

ke·to·gen·ic \ˌkē-tō-je-nik\ *adj* **1** : producing or involved in the formation of ketone bodies; *also* : marked by the presence of ketone bodies **2** : of, relating to, or caused by a ketogenic diet ⟨~ weight loss⟩

ketogenic diet *or* **ke·to diet** \ˈkē-tō-\ *n* : a diet usu. for weight loss that is high in fats and low in carbohydrates

ketone body \ˈkē-ˌtōn-\ *n* : a compound that is a normal intermediate in the breakdown of fat and accumulates in the blood and urine in conditions of impaired metabolism

ket·tle \ˈke-tᵊl\ *n* : a metallic vessel for boiling liquids

ket·tle·drum \-ˌdrəm\ *n* : a brass, copper, or fiberglass drum with calfskin or plastic stretched across the top

[1]**key** \ˈkē\ *n* **1** : a usu. metal instrument by which the bolt of a lock is turned; *also* : a device having the form or function of a key **2** : a means of gaining or preventing entrance, possession, or control **3** : EXPLANATION, SOLUTION **4** : one of the levers pressed by a finger in operating or playing an instrument **5** : a leading individual or principle **6** : a system of seven tones based on their relationship to a tonic; *also* : the tone or pitch of a voice **7** : a small switch for opening or closing an electric circuit ⟨a telegraph ~⟩

[2]**key** *vb* **1** : SECURE, FASTEN **2** : to regulate the musical pitch of **3** : to bring into harmony or conformity **4** : to make nervous — usu. used with *up*

[3]**key** *adj* : BASIC, CENTRAL ⟨~ issues⟩

[4]**key** *n* : a low island or reef (as off the southern coast of Florida)

[5]**key** *n, slang* : a kilogram esp. of marijuana or heroin

key·board \-ˌbȯrd\ *n* **1** : a row of keys (as on a piano) **2** : an assemblage of keys for operating a machine

key club *n* : a private club serving liquor and providing entertainment

key·hole \ˈkē-ˌhōl\ *n* : a hole for receiving a key

[1]**key·note** \-ˌnōt\ *n* **1** : the first and harmonically fundamental tone of a scale **2** : the central fact, idea, or mood

[2]**keynote** *vb* **1** : to set the keynote of **2** : to deliver the major address (as at a convention) — **key·not·er** *n*

key·punch \ˈkē-ˌpənch\ *n* : a machine with a keyboard used to cut holes or notches in punch cards — **keypunch** *vb* — **key·punch·er** *n*

key·stone \-ˌstōn\ *n* : the wedge-shaped piece at the crown of an arch that locks the other pieces in place

key·stroke \-ˌstrōk\ *n* : an act or instance of depressing a key on a keyboard

key word *n* : a word that is a key; *esp, usu* **key·word** : a significant word from a title or document used esp. as an indication of the content

kg *abbr* kilogram

KGB *abbr* [Russ *Komitet gosudarstvennoĭ bezopasnosti*] (Soviet) State Security Committee

kha·ki \ˈka-kē, ˈkä-\ *n* [Hindi & Urdu *khākī* dust-colored, fr. *khāk* dust, fr. Pers] **1** : a light yellowish brown color **2** : a khaki-colored cloth; *also* : a military uniform of this cloth

khan \ˈkän, ˈkan\ *n* : a Mongol leader; *esp* : a successor of Genghis Khan

khe·dive \kə-ˈdēv\ *n* : a ruler of Egypt from 1867 to 1914 governing as a viceroy of the sultan of Turkey

khoum \ˈküm\ *n* — see *ouguiya* at MONEY table

kHz *abbr* kilohertz

KIA *abbr* killed in action

kib·ble \ˈki-bəl\ *vb* **kib·bled; kib·bling** : to grind coarsely — **kibble** *n*

kib·butz \ki-ˈbu̇ts, -ˈbüts\ *n, pl* **kib·but·zim** \-ˌbu̇t-ˈsēm, -ˌbüt-\ [ModHeb *qibbūṣ*] : a communal farm or settlement in Israel

ki·bitz·er \ˈki-bət-sər, kə-ˈbit-\ *n* : one who looks on and usu. offers unwanted advice — **kib·itz** \ˈki-bəts\ *vb*

ki·bosh \ˈkī-ˌbäsh\ *n* : something that serves as a check or stop ⟨put the ~ on his plan⟩

[1]**kick** \ˈkik\ *vb* **1** : to strike out or hit with the foot; *also* : to score by kicking a ball **2** : to object strongly **3** : to recoil when fired — **kick·er** *n*

[2]**kick** *n* **1** : a blow or thrust with the foot; *esp* : a propelling of a ball with the foot **2** : the recoil of a gun **3** : a feeling or expression of objection **4** : stimulating effect esp. of pleasure

kick·back \ˈkik-ˌbak\ *n* **1** : a sharp violent reaction **2** : a secret return of a part of a sum received

kick back *vb* : to assume a relaxed position or attitude

kick·box·ing \ˈkik-ˌbäk-siŋ\ *n* : boxing in which boxers are permitted to kick with bare feet — **kick·box·er** \-sər\ *n*

kick in *vb* **1** : CONTRIBUTE 1 **2** *slang* : DIE **3** : to begin operating or having an effect ⟨the caffeine started to *kick in*⟩

kick·off \ˈkik-ˌȯf\ *n* **1** : a kick that puts the ball in play (as in football) **2** : COMMENCEMENT ⟨campaign ~⟩

kick off *vb* **1** : to start or resume play with a placekick **2** : to begin proceedings ⟨*kick off* a campaign⟩ **3** *slang* : DIE

kick over *vb* : to begin or cause to begin to fire — used of an internal combustion engine

kick·shaw \ˈkik-ˌshȯ\ *n* [modif. of F

quelque chose something] **1** : DELICACY **2** : TRINKET

kick•stand \ˈkik-ˌstand\ *n* : a swiveling metal bar attached to a 2-wheeled vehicle for holding it up when not in use

kick–start \ˈkik-ˌstärt\ *vb* : JUMP-START

kicky \ˈki-kē\ *adj* : providing a kick or thrill : EXCITING; *also* : excitingly fashionable

[1]**kid** \ˈkid\ *n* **1** : a young goat **2** : the flesh, fur, or skin of a young goat; *also* : something made of kid **3** : CHILD, YOUNGSTER — **kid•dish** *adj*

[2]**kid** *vb* **kid•ded; kid•ding** **1** : FOOL **2** : TEASE — **kid•der** *n* — **kid•ding•ly** *adv*

kid•do \ˈki-dō\ *n, pl* **kiddos** **1** — used as a familiar form of address ⟨you're okay, ~⟩ **2** : CHILD, KID

kid•nap \ˈkid-ˌnap\ *vb* **kid•napped** *also* **kid•naped** \-ˌnapt\; **kid•nap•ping** *also* **kid•nap•ing** \-ˌna-piŋ\ : to hold or carry a person away by unlawful force or by fraud and against one's will — **kid•nap•per** *also* **kid•nap•er** \-ˌna-pər\ *n*

kid•ney \ˈkid-nē\ *n, pl* **kidneys** : either of a pair of organs lying near the backbone that excrete waste products of the body in the form of urine

kidney bean *n* **1** : an edible seed of the common cultivated bean; *esp* : one that is large and dark red **2** : a plant bearing kidney beans

kid•skin \ˈkid-ˌskin\ *n* : the skin of a young goat used for leather

kiel•ba•sa \kēl-ˈbä-sə, kil-\ *n, pl* **-basas** *also* **-ba•sy** \-ˈbä-sē\ [Polish *kiełbasa*] : a smoked sausage of Polish origin

[1]**kill** \ˈkil\ *vb* **1** : to deprive of life **2** : to put an end to ⟨~ competition⟩; *also* : DEFEAT ⟨~ a proposed amendment⟩ **3** : USE UP ⟨~ time⟩ **4** : to mark for omission ♦ ***Synonyms*** SLAY, MURDER, ASSASSINATE, EXECUTE — **kill•er** *n*

[2]**kill** *n* **1** : an act of killing **2** : an animal or animals killed (as in a hunt); *also* : an aircraft, ship, or vehicle destroyed by military action

kill•deer \ˈkil-ˌdir\ *n, pl* **killdeers** *or* **killdeer** [imitative] : an American plover with a plaintive penetrating cry

killer app \-ˈap\ *n* : a component (as a computer application) that in itself makes something worth having or using

killer bee *n* : AFRICANIZED BEE

killer whale *n* : a small gregarious black and white flesh-eating whale with a white oval patch behind each eye

kill•ing *n* : a sudden notable gain or profit

killing field *n* : a scene of mass killing

kill•joy \ˈkil-ˌjȯi\ *n* : one who spoils the pleasures of others

kiln \ˈkil, ˈkiln\ *n* [ME *kilne,* fr. OE *cyln,* fr. L *culina* kitchen] : a heated enclosure (as an oven) for processing a substance by burning, firing, or drying — **kiln** *vb*

ki•lo \ˈkē-lō\ *n, pl* **kilos** : KILOGRAM

ki•lo•byte \ˈki-lə-ˌbīt, ˈkē-\ *n* : 1024 bytes

kilo•cy•cle \ˈki-lə-ˌsī-kəl\ *n* : KILOHERTZ

ki•lo•gram \ˈkē-lə-ˌgram, ˈki-\ *n* **1** : the basic metric unit of mass that is nearly equal to the mass of 1000 cubic centimeters of water at its maximum density — see METRIC SYSTEM table **2** : the weight of a kilogram mass under earth's gravity

ki•lo•hertz \ˈki-lə-ˌhərts, ˈkē-, -ˌherts\ *n* : 1000 hertz

kilo•li•ter \ˈki-lə-ˌlē-tər\ *n* — see METRIC SYSTEM table

ki•lo•me•ter \ki-ˈlä-mə-tər, ˈki-lə-ˌmē-\ *n* : a metric unit of length equal to 1000 meters — see METRIC SYSTEM table

ki•lo•ton \ˈki-lə-ˌtən, ˈkē-lō-\ *n* **1** : 1000 tons **2** : an explosive force equivalent to that of 1000 tons of TNT

ki•lo•volt \-ˌvōlt\ *n* : 1000 volts

kilo•watt \ˈki-lə-ˌwät\ *n* : 1000 watts

kilowatt–hour *n* : a unit of energy equal to that expended by one kilowatt in one hour

kilt \ˈkilt\ *n* : a knee-length pleated skirt usu. of tartan worn by men in Scotland

kil•ter \ˈkil-tər\ *n* : proper condition ⟨out of ~⟩

ki•mo•no \kə-ˈmō-nə\ *n, pl* **-nos** **1** : a loose robe with wide sleeves traditionally worn with a wide sash as an outer garment by the Japanese **2** : a loose dressing gown or jacket

kin \ˈkin\ *n* **1** : an individual's relatives **2** : KINSMAN

ki•na \ˈkē-nə\ *n, pl* **kina** — see MONEY table

ki•na•ra \kē-ˈnä-rə\ *n* : a candelabra with seven candlesticks used during Kwanzaa

[1]**kind** \ˈkīnd\ *n* **1** : essential quality or character **2** : a group united by common traits or interests : CATEGORY; *also* : VARIETY **3** : goods or commodities as distinguished from money

[2]**kind** *adj* **1** : of a sympathetic, forbearing, or pleasant nature **2** : arising from sympathy or forbearance ⟨~ deeds⟩ ♦ ***Synonyms*** BENEVOLENT, BENIGN, BENIGNANT, KINDLY — **kind•ness** *n*

kin•der•gar•ten \ˈkin-dər-ˌgär-tᵊn\ *n* [G, lit., children's garden] : a school or class for children usu. from four to six years old

kin•der•gart•ner \-ˌgärt-nər\ *n* **1** : a kindergarten teacher **2** : a kindergarten pupil

kind•heart•ed \ˌkīnd-ˈhär-təd\ *adj* : marked by a sympathetic nature

kin•dle \ˈkin-dᵊl\ *vb* **kin•dled; kin•dling** **1** : to set on fire : start burning **2** : to stir up : AROUSE **3** : ILLUMINATE, GLOW

kin•dling \ˈkind-liŋ, ˈkin-lən\ *n* : easily combustible material for starting a fire

[1]**kind•ly** \ˈkīnd-lē\ *adj* **kind•li•er; -est** **1** : of an agreeable or beneficial nature **2** : of a sympathetic or generous nature — **kind•li•ness** *n*

[2]**kindly** *adv* **1** : READILY ⟨does not take ~ to criticism⟩ **2** : SYMPATHETICALLY **3** : COURTEOUSLY, OBLIGINGLY

kind of *adv* : to a moderate degree ⟨it's *kind of* late to begin⟩

[1]**kin•dred** \ˈkin-drəd\ *n* **1** : a group of related individuals **2** : one's relatives

[2]**kindred** *adj* : of a like nature or character

kine \ˈkīn\ *archaic pl of* COW

kin·e·ma \'ki-nə-mə\ *Brit var of* CINEMA
ki·ne·mat·ics \,ki-nə-'ma-tiks\ *n* : a science that deals with motion apart from considerations of mass and force — **ki·ne·mat·ic** \-tik\ *or* **ki·ne·mat·i·cal** \-ti-kəl\ *adj*
kin·es·the·sia \,ki-nəs-'thē-zhə, -zhē-ə\ *or* **kin·es·the·sis** \-'thē-səs\ *n, pl* **-the·sias** *or* **-the·ses** \-,sēz\ : a sense that perceives bodily movement, position, and weight and is mediated by nervous receptors in tendons, muscles, and joints; *also* : sensory experience derived from this sense — **kin·es·thet·ic** \-'the-tik\ *adj*
ki·net·ic \kə-'ne-tik\ *adj* : of or relating to the motion of material bodies and the forces and energy (**kinetic energy**) associated with them
ki·net·ics \-tiks\ *n sing or pl* : a science that deals with the effects of forces upon the motions of material bodies or with changes in a physical or chemical system
kin·folk \'kin-,fōk\ *or* **kinfolks** *n pl* : RELATIVES
king \'kiŋ\ *n* **1** : a male monarch **2** : a chief among competitors ⟨home-run ~⟩ **3** : the principal piece in the game of chess **4** : a playing card bearing the figure of a king **5** : a checker that has been crowned — **king·less** *adj* — **king·ly** *adj* — **king·ship** *n*
king crab *n* **1** : HORSESHOE CRAB **2** : a large crab of the No. Pacific caught commercially for food
king·dom \'kiŋ-dəm\ *n* **1** : a country whose head is a king or queen **2** : a realm or region in which something or someone is dominant ⟨a cattle ~⟩ **3** : one of the three primary divisions of lifeless material, plants, and animals into which natural objects are grouped; *also* : a biological category that ranks above the phylum
king·fish·er \-,fi-shər\ *n* : any of numerous usu. bright-colored crested birds that feed chiefly on fish
king·pin \'kiŋ-,pin\ *n* **1** : HEADPIN **2** : the leader in a group or undertaking
Kings *n* — see BIBLE table
king-size \'kiŋ-,sīz\ *or* **king-sized** \-,sīzd\ *adj* **1** : longer than the regular or standard size **2** : unusually large **3** : having dimensions of about 76 by 80 inches (1.9 by 2.0 meters) ⟨a ~ bed⟩; *also* : of a size that fits a king-size bed
kink \'kiŋk\ *n* **1** : a short tight twist or curl **2** : a mental peculiarity : QUIRK **3** : CRAMP ⟨a ~ in the back⟩ **4** : an imperfection likely to cause difficulties in operation — **kinky** *adj*
kin·ship \'kin-,ship\ *n* : RELATIONSHIP
kins·man \'kinz-mən\ *n* : RELATIVE; *esp* : a male relative
kins·wom·an \-,wu̇-mən\ *n* : a female relative
ki·osk \'kē-,äsk\ *n* **1** : a small structure with one or more open sides **2** : a stand-alone device providing information and services on a computer screen ⟨interactive ~*s* at the museum⟩
Ki·o·wa \'kī-ə-,wȯ, -,wä, -,wā\ *n, pl* **Kiowa** *or* **Kiowas** : a member of an Indigenous people of the southern Great Plains; *also* : the language of the Kiowa
kip \'kip, 'gip\ *n, pl* **kip** *or* **kips** — see MONEY table
kip·pah *or* **kip·pa** \'kē-pə\ *n* : YARMULKE
kip·per \'ki-pər\ *n* : a fish (as a herring) preserved by salting and drying or smoking — **kipper** *vb*
kirk \'kərk, 'kirk\ *n, chiefly Scot* : CHURCH
kir·tle \'kər-tᵊl\ *n* : a long gown or dress worn by women
kis·met \'kiz-,met, -mət\ *n, often cap* [Turk, fr. Ar *qisma* portion, lot] : FATE
[1]**kiss** \'kis\ *vb* **1** : to touch or caress with the lips as a mark of affection or greeting **2** : to touch gently or lightly
[2]**kiss** *n* **1** : a caress with the lips **2** : a gentle touch or contact **3** : a bite-size candy
kiss·er \'ki-sər\ *n* **1** : one that kisses **2** *slang* : MOUTH **3** *slang* : FACE
kit \'kit\ *n* **1** : a set of articles for personal use; *also* : a set of tools or implements or of parts to be assembled **2** : a container (as a case) for a kit
kitch·en \'ki-chən\ *n* **1** : a room with cooking facilities **2** : the personnel that prepares, cooks, and serves food
kitch·en·ette \,ki-chə-'net\ *n* : a small kitchen or an alcove containing cooking facilities
kitchen police *n* **1** : KP **2** : the work of KPs
kitch·en·ware \'ki-chən-,wer\ *n* : utensils and appliances for kitchen use
kite \'kīt\ *n* **1** : any of various long-winged hawks often with deeply forked tails **2** : a light frame covered with paper or cloth and designed to be flown in the air at the end of a long string
kith \'kith\ *n* [ME, fr. OE *cȳthth,* fr. *cūth* known] : familiar friends, neighbors, or relatives ⟨~ and kin⟩
kitsch \'kich\ *n* [G] : something often of poor quality that appeals to popular or lowbrow taste — **kitschy** \'ki-chē\ *adj*
kit·ten \'ki-tᵊn\ *n* : a young cat — **kit·ten·ish** *adj*
[1]**kit·ty** \'ki-tē\ *n, pl* **kitties** : CAT; *esp* : KITTEN
[2]**kitty** *n, pl* **kitties** : a fund in a poker game made up of contributions from each pot; *also* : POOL
kit·ty-cor·ner *also* **cat·ty-cor·ner** *or* **cat·er·cor·ner** \'ki-tē-,kȯr-nər, 'ka-; 'ka-tə-\ *or* **kit·ty-cor·nered** *or* **cat·ty-cor·nered** *or* **cat·er·cornered** \-nərd\ *adv or adj* : in a diagonal or oblique position
ki·wi \'kē-(,)wē\ *n* **1** : any of a small genus of flightless New Zealand birds **2** : KIWIFRUIT
ki·wi·fruit \-,früt\ *n* : a brownish hairy egg-shaped fruit of a subtropical vine that has sweet bright green flesh and small edible black seeds
KJV *abbr* King James Version
KKK *abbr* Ku Klux Klan
kl *abbr* kiloliter
klatch *also* **klatsch** \'klach\ *n* [G *Klatsch* gossip] : a gathering marked by informal conversation

klep·toc·ra·cy \klep-ˈtä-krə-sē\ *n, pl* **-cies** : government by those who seek chiefly status and personal gain at the expense of the governed

klep·to·ma·nia \ˌklep-tə-ˈmā-nē-ə\ *n* : a persistent neurotic impulse to steal esp. without economic motive — **klep·to·ma·ni·ac** \-nē-ˌak\ *n*

klieg light *or* **kleig light** \ˈklēg-\ *n* : a very bright lamp used in making motion pictures

klutz \ˈkləts\ *n* [Yiddish *klots,* lit., wooden beam] : a clumsy person — **klutzy** *adj*

km *abbr* kilometer

kn *abbr* knot

knack \ˈnak\ *n* **1** : a clever way of doing something **2** : natural aptitude

knap·sack \ˈnap-ˌsak\ *n* : a bag (as of canvas) strapped on the back and used esp. for carrying supplies

knave \ˈnāv\ *n* **1** : ROGUE **2** : JACK 6 — **knav·ery** \ˈnā-və-rē\ *n* — **knav·ish** \ˈnā-vish\ *adj*

knead \ˈnēd\ *vb* : to work and press into a mass with the hands; *also* : MASSAGE — **knead·er** *n*

knee \ˈnē\ *n* : the joint in the middle part of the leg — **kneed** \ˈnēd\ *adj*

knee·cap \ˈnē-ˌkap\ *n* : a thick flat triangular movable bone forming the front of the knee

knee·hole \-ˌhōl\ *n* : a space (as under a desk) for the knees

knee–jerk \ˈnē-ˌjərk\ *adj* : readily predictable ⟨a ~ reaction⟩

kneel \ˈnēl\ *vb* **knelt** \ˈnelt\ *or* **kneeled; kneel·ing** : to bend the knee : fall or rest on the knees

¹**knell** \ˈnel\ *vb* **1** : to ring esp. for a death or disaster **2** : to summon, announce, or proclaim by a knell

²**knell** *n* **1** : a stroke of a bell esp. when tolled (as for a funeral) **2** : an indication of the end or failure of something

knew *past of* KNOW

knick·ers \ˈni-kərz\ *n pl* : loose-fitting short pants gathered at the knee

knick·knack \ˈnik-ˌnak\ *n* : a small trivial article intended for ornament

¹**knife** \ˈnīf\ *n, pl* **knives** \ˈnīvz\ **1** : a cutting instrument consisting of a sharp blade fastened to a handle **2** : a sharp cutting tool in a machine

²**knife** *vb* **knifed; knif·ing** : to stab, slash, or wound with a knife

¹**knight** \ˈnīt\ *n* **1** : a mounted warrior of feudal times serving a king **2** : a man honored by a sovereign for merit and in Great Britain ranking below a baronet **3** : a man devoted to the service of a lady **4** : a member of an order or society **5** : a chess piece having an L-shaped move — **knight·ly** *adj*

²**knight** *vb* : to make a knight of

knight·hood \ˈnīt-ˌhu̇d\ *n* **1** : the rank, dignity, or profession of a knight **2** : CHIVALRY **3** : knights as a class or body

knish \kə-ˈnish\ *n* [Yiddish] : a small round or square of dough stuffed with a filling (as of meat or fruit) and baked or fried

¹**knit** \ˈnit\ *vb* **knit** *or* **knit·ted; knit·ting** **1** : to link firmly or closely **2** : WRINKLE ⟨~ her brows⟩ **3** : to form a fabric by interlacing yarn or thread in connected loops with needles **4** : to grow together ⟨the fractured bone *knitted* slowly⟩ — **knit·ter** *n*

²**knit** *n* **1** : a basic knitting stitch **2** : a knitted garment or fabric

knit·wear \-ˌwer\ *n* : knitted clothing

knob \ˈnäb\ *n* **1** : a rounded protuberance; *also* : a small rounded ornament or handle **2** : a rounded usu. isolated hill — **knobbed** \ˈnäbd\ *adj* — **knob·by** \ˈnä-bē\ *adj*

¹**knock** \ˈnäk\ *vb* **1** : to strike with a sharp blow **2** : BUMP, COLLIDE **3** : to make a pounding noise; *esp* : to have engine knock **4** : to find fault with

²**knock** *n* **1** : a sharp blow **2** : a pounding noise; *esp* : one caused by abnormal ignition in an automobile engine

knock·down \ˈnäk-ˌdau̇n\ *n* **1** : the action of knocking down **2** : something (as a blow) that knocks down **3** : something that can be easily assembled or disassembled

knock down *vb* **1** : to strike to the ground with or as if with a sharp blow **2** : to take apart : DISASSEMBLE **3** : to receive as income or salary : EARN **4** : to make a reduction in

knock·er \ˈnä-kər\ *n* : one that knocks; *esp* : a device hinged to a door for use in knocking

knock–knee \ˈnäk-ˌnē\ *n* : a condition in which the legs curve inward at the knees — **knock–kneed** \-ˌnēd\ *adj*

knock·off \ˈnäk-ˌȯf\ *n* : a copy or imitation of someone or something popular

knock off *vb* **1** : to stop doing something **2** : to do quickly, carelessly, or routinely **3** : to deduct from a price **4** : KILL **5** : ROB **6** : COPY, IMITATE

knock·out \ˈnäk-ˌau̇t\ *n* **1** : a blow that fells and immobilizes an opponent (as in boxing) **2** : something sensationally striking or attractive

knock out *vb* **1** : to defeat by a knockout **2** : to make unconscious or inoperative **3** : to tire out : EXHAUST

knock·wurst *also* **knack·wurst** \ˈnäk-ˌwərst, -ˌvu̇rst\ *n* : a short thick heavily seasoned sausage

knoll \ˈnōl\ *n* : a small round hill

¹**knot** \ˈnät\ *n* **1** : an interlacing (as of string) forming a lump or knob and often used for fastening or tying together **2** : PROBLEM **3** : a bond of union; *esp* : the marriage bond **4** : a protuberant lump or swelling in tissue **5** : a rounded cross-grained area in lumber that is a section through the junction of a tree branch with the trunk; *also* : the woody tissue forming this junction in a tree **6** : GROUP, CLUSTER **7** : an ornamental bow of ribbon **8** : one nautical mile per hour; *also* : one nautical mile — **knot·ty** *adj*

²**knot** *vb* **knot·ted; knot·ting** **1** : to tie in or with a knot **2** : ENTANGLE

knot·hole \-ˌhōl\ *n* : a hole in a board or tree trunk where a knot has come out

knout \ˈnau̇t, ˈnüt\ *n* : a whip used for flogging

know \ˈnō\ *vb* **knew** \ˈnü, ˈnyü\; **known** \ˈnōn\; **know·ing** **1** : to perceive directly : have understanding or direct cognition of; *also* : to recognize the nature of **2** : to be acquainted or familiar with **3** : to be aware of the truth of **4** : to have a practical understanding of — **know·able** *adj* — **know·er** *n* — **in the know** : possessing confidential information

know–how \ˈnō-ˌhau̇\ *n* : knowledge of how to do something smoothly and efficiently

knowing *adj* **1** : having or reflecting knowledge, intelligence, or information **2** : shrewdly and keenly alert **3** : DELIBERATE ⟨~ interference⟩ ♦ ***Synonyms*** CLEVER, BRIGHT, SMART — **know·ing·ly** *adv*

knowl·edge \ˈnä-lij\ *n* **1** : understanding gained by actual experience ⟨a ~ of carpentry⟩ **2** : range of information ⟨to the best of my ~⟩ **3** : clear perception of truth **4** : something learned and kept in the mind

knowl·edge·able \ˈnä-li-jə-bəl\ *adj* : having or showing knowledge or intelligence

knuck·le \ˈnə-kəl\ *n* : the rounded knob at a joint and esp. at a finger joint

knuckle down *vb* : to apply oneself earnestly ⟨*knuckled down* to the task⟩

knuckle under *vb* : SUBMIT, SURRENDER

knurl \ˈnərl\ *n* **1** : KNOB **2** : one of a series of small ridges on a metal surface to aid in gripping — **knurled** \ˈnərld\ *adj* — **knurly** *adj*

[1]**KO** \(ˌ)kā-ˈō, ˈkā-ō\ *n* : KNOCKOUT

[2]**KO** *vb* **KO'd; KO'·ing** : to knock out in boxing

ko·ala \kō-ˈä-lə\ *n* : a gray furry Australian marsupial that has large hairy ears and feeds on eucalyptus leaves

ko·bo \ˈkō-(ˌ)bō\ *n, pl* **kobo** — see *naira* at MONEY table

K of C *abbr* Knights of Columbus

kohl·ra·bi \kōl-ˈrä-bē\ *n, pl* **-bies** [G, fr. It *cavolo rapa,* lit., cabbage turnip] : a cabbage that forms no head but has a swollen fleshy edible stem

koi \ˈkȯi\ *n, pl* **koi** [Jp] : a carp bred for large size and a variety of colors and often stocked in ornamental ponds

ko·lin·sky \kə-ˈlin-skē\ *n, pl* **-skies** : the fur of various Asian minks

Ko·mo·do dragon \kə-ˈmō-dō-\ *n* [*Komodo* Island, Indonesia] : a carnivorous lizard of Indonesia that is the largest of all known lizards

kook \ˈkük\ *n* : SCREWBALL 2

kooky *also* **kook·ie** \ˈkü-kē\ *adj* **kook·i·er; -est** : having the characteristics of a kook : CRAZY, ECCENTRIC ⟨a ~ radical⟩ — **kook·i·ness** *n*

Koo·te·nai *or* **Ku·te·nai** \ˈkü-tə-ˌnā\ *n, pl* **-nai** *or* **-nais** : a member of an Indigenous people of the Rocky Mountains in both the U.S. and Canada; *also* : their language

ko·peck *or* **ko·pek** \ˈkō-ˌpek\ *n* [Russ *kopeĭka*] — see *ruble* at MONEY table

ko·piy·ka \ˌkō-ˈpē-kə\ *n* — see *hryvnia* at MONEY table

ko·ra \ˈkȯr-ə\ *n* : a 21-stringed African musical instrument

Ko·ran *or* **Qur·an** *also* **Qur·'an** \kə-ˈran, -ˈrän\ *n* [Ar *qur'ān*] : a sacred book of Islam that contains revelations made to Muhammad by Allah

ko·ru·na \ˈkȯr-ə-ˌnä\ *n, pl* **ko·ru·ny** \-ə-nē\ *or* **korunas** *or* **ko·run** \-ən\ **1** — see MONEY table **2** : the basic monetary unit of Slovakia from 1992 to 2009

ko·sher \ˈkō-shər\ *adj* [Yiddish, fr. Heb *kāshēr* fit, proper] **1** : ritually fit for use according to Jewish law **2** : selling or serving kosher food

kow·tow \kau̇-ˈtau̇, ˈkau̇-ˌtau̇\ *vb* [Chin *kòutóu,* fr. *kòu* to knock + *tóu* head] **1** : to show obsequious deference **2** : to kneel and touch the forehead to the ground as a sign of homage or deep respect

KP \ˌkā-ˈpē\ *n* **1** : an enlisted person detailed to help the cooks in a military mess **2** : the work of KPs

kph *abbr* kilometers per hour

Kr *symbol* krypton

kraal \ˈkräl, ˈkrȯl\ *n* **1** : a native village in southern Africa **2** : an enclosure for domestic animals in southern Africa

kraut \ˈkrau̇t\ *n* : SAUERKRAUT

Krem·lin \ˈkrem-lən\ *n* : the Russian government

Krem·lin·ol·o·gist \ˌkrem-lə-ˈnä-lə-jist\ *n* : a specialist in the policies and practices of the government of the Soviet Union

[1]**kro·na** \ˈkrō-nə\ *n, pl* **kro·nor** \-ˌnȯr\ [Swedish] — see MONEY table

[2]**kro·na** \ˈkrō-nə\ *n, pl* **kro·nur** \-nər\ [Icelandic] — see MONEY table

kro·ne \ˈkrō-nə\ *n, pl* **kro·ner** \-nər\ — see MONEY table

kroon \ˈkrōn\ *n, pl* **kroo·ni** \ˈkrō-nē\ *or* **kroons** : the basic monetary unit of Estonia from 1928 to 1940 and from 1991 to 2011

Kru·ger·rand \ˈkrü-gər-ˌrand, -ˌränd\ *n* : a 1-ounce gold coin of the Republic of South Africa

kryp·ton \ˈkrip-ˌtän\ *n* : a gaseous chemical element used esp. in electric lamps

KS *abbr* Kansas

kt *abbr* **1** karat **2** knight

ku·do \ˈkü-dō, ˈkyü-\ *n, pl* **kudos** [fr. *kudos* (taken as pl.)] **1** : AWARD, HONOR **2** : COMPLIMENT, PRAISE

ku·dos \ˈkü-ˌdäs, ˈkyü-\ *n* : fame and renown resulting from achievement

kud·zu \ˈku̇d-zü, ˈkəd-\ *n* [Jp *kuzu*] : a fast-growing weedy leguminous vine used for forage and erosion control

ku·lak \kü-ˈlak, kyü-, -ˈläk\ *n* [Russ, lit., fist] **1** : a wealthy peasant farmer in 19th century Russia **2** : a farmer characterized by Communists as too wealthy

kum·quat \ˈkəm-ˌkwät\ *n* : any of several small citrus fruits with sweet spongy rind and acid pulp

ku·na \ˈkü-ˌnä\ *n, pl* **kuna** *or* **ku·ne** \-nā\ — see MONEY table

kung fu \ˌkəŋ-ˈfü, ˌku̇ŋ-\ *n* : a Chinese art of self-defense resembling karate

kung pao \ˈkəŋ-ˈpau̇, ˈküŋ-, ˈku̇ŋ-\ *adj*

: being stir-fried or deep-fried and served in a spicy hot sauce usu. with peanuts
kur·ta \ˈkər-tə\ *n* : a long loose-fitting collarless shirt
ku·rus \kə-ˈrüsh\ *n, pl* **kurus** — see *lira* at MONEY table
kV *abbr* kilovolt
kvell \ˈkvel\ *vb* : to be extraordinarily proud
kvetch \ˈkvech, ˈkfech\ *vb* : to complain habitually — **kvetch** *n*
kW *abbr* kilowatt
kwa·cha \ˈkwä-chə\ *n, pl* **kwacha** — see MONEY table
kwan·za \ˈkwän-zə\ *n, pl* **kwanzas** *or* **kwanza** — see MONEY table
Kwan·zaa *also* **Kwan·za** \ˈkwän-zə\ *n* [Swahili *kwanza* first] : an African American cultural festival held from December 26 to January 1
kwash·i·or·kor \ˌkwä-shē-ˈór-kór, -ór-ˈkór\ *n* : a disease of young children caused by deficient intake of protein
kWh *abbr* kilowatt-hour
Ky *or* **KY** *abbr* Kentucky
kyat \ˈchät\ *n, pl* **kyats** *or* **kyat** — see MONEY table
ky·bosh *chiefly Brit var of* KIBOSH

L

[1]**l** \ˈel\ *n, pl* **l's** *or* **ls** \ˈelz\ *often cap* : the 12th letter of the English alphabet
[2]**l** *abbr, often cap* **1** lake **2** large **3** left **4** L *libra* pound **5** line **6** liter
[1]**La** *abbr* Louisiana
[2]**La** *symbol* lanthanum
LA *abbr* **1** law agent **2** Los Angeles **3** Louisiana
laa·ri \ˈlä-rē\ *n, pl* **laari** — see *rufiyaa* at MONEY table
lab \ˈlab\ *n* : LABORATORY
Lab *n* : LABRADOR RETRIEVER
[1]**la·bel** \ˈlā-bəl\ *n* **1** : a slip attached to something for identification or description **2** : a descriptive or identifying word or phrase **3** : BRAND 3
[2]**label** *vb* **-beled** *or* **-belled; -bel·ing** *or* **-bel·ling** **1** : to affix a label to **2** : to describe or name with a label
la·bi·al \ˈlā-bē-əl\ *adj* : of, relating to, or situated near the lips or labia
la·bia ma·jo·ra \ˈlā-bē-ə-mə-ˈjór-ə\ *n pl* : the outer fatty folds of the vulva
labia mi·no·ra \-mə-ˈnór-ə\ *n pl* : the inner highly vascular folds of the vulva
la·bile \ˈlā-ˌbī(-ə)l, -bəl\ *adj* **1** : UNSTABLE ⟨a ~ mineral⟩ **2** : ADAPTABLE
la·bi·um \ˈlā-bē-əm\ *n, pl* **la·bia** \-ə\ [NL, fr. L, lip] : any of the folds at the margin of the vulva
[1]**la·bor** \ˈlā-bər\ *n* **1** : physical or mental effort; *also* : human activity that provides the goods or services in an economy **2** : the physical efforts of giving birth; *also* : the period of such labor **3** : TASK **4** : those who do manual labor or work for wages; *also* : labor unions or their officials
[2]**labor** *vb* **1** : WORK **2** : to move with great effort **3** : to be in the labor of giving birth **4** : to suffer from some disadvantage or distress ⟨~ under a delusion⟩ **5** : to treat or work out laboriously — **la·bor·er** *n*
lab·o·ra·to·ry \ˈla-brə-ˌtór-ē, -bə-rə-\ *n, pl* **-ries** : a place equipped for making scientific experiments or tests
Labor Day *n* : the 1st Monday in September observed as a legal holiday in recognition of the working people
la·bored \ˈlā-bərd\ *adj* : not freely or easily done ⟨~ breathing⟩
la·bo·ri·ous \lə-ˈbór-ē-əs\ *adj* **1** : INDUSTRIOUS **2** : requiring great effort — **la·bo·ri·ous·ly** *adv*
la·bor·sav·ing \ˈlā-bər-ˌsā-viŋ\ *adj* : designed to replace or decrease labor
labor union *n* : an organization of workers formed to advance its members' interest in respect to wages and working conditions
la·bour *chiefly Brit var of* LABOR
lab·ra·dor·ite \ˈla-brə-ˌdór-ˌīt\ *n* : an iridescent feldspar used in jewelry
Lab·ra·dor retriever \ˈla-brə-ˌdór-\ *n* : any of a breed of strongly built retrievers having a short dense black, yellow, or chocolate coat
la·bur·num \lə-ˈbər-nəm\ *n* : any of a genus of leguminous shrubs or trees with hanging clusters of yellow flowers
lab·y·rinth \ˈla-bə-ˌrinth\ *n* : a place constructed of or filled with confusing intricate passageways : MAZE
lab·y·rin·thine \ˌla-bə-ˈrin-thən, -ˌthīn, -ˌthēn\ *adj* : INTRICATE, INVOLVED ⟨a ~ plot⟩ ⟨~ hallways⟩
lac \ˈlak\ *n* : a resinous substance secreted by a scale insect and used chiefly in the form of shellac
[1]**lace** \ˈlās\ *vb* **laced; lac·ing** **1** : TIE **2** : to adorn with lace **3** : INTERTWINE **4** : BEAT, LASH **5** : to add something that taints (as a drug) or enhances flavor (as a spice) **6** : to criticize sharply — used with *into* ⟨*laced* into his opponent⟩
[2]**lace** *n* [ME, fr. AF *lace, laz,* fr. L *laqueus* snare] **1** : a cord or string used for drawing together two edges **2** : an ornamental braid **3** : a fine openwork usu. figured fabric made of thread — **lacy** \ˈlā-sē\ *adj*
lac·er·ate \ˈla-sə-ˌrāt\ *vb* **-at·ed; -at·ing** : to tear roughly — **lac·er·a·tion** \ˌla-sə-ˈrā-shən\ *n*
lace·wing \ˈlās-ˌwiŋ\ *n* : any of various insects with delicate wing veins, long antennae, and often brilliant eyes
lach·ry·mal *or* **lac·ri·mal** \ˈla-krə-məl\ *adj* **1** *usu lacrimal* : of, relating to, or be-

ing glands that produce tears **2** : of, relating to, or marked by tears

lach•ry•mose \ˈla-krə-ˌmōs\ *adj* **1** : TEARFUL **2** : MOURNFUL ⟨~ songs⟩

[1]**lack** \ˈlak\ *vb* **1** : to be wanting or missing **2** : to be deficient in ⟨~*s* experience⟩

[2]**lack** *n* : the fact or state of being wanting or deficient : NEED

lack•a•dai•si•cal \ˌla-kə-ˈdā-zi-kəl\ *adj* : lacking life, spirit, or zest — **lack•a•dai•si•cal•ly** \-k(ə-)lē\ *adv*

lack•ey \ˈla-kē\ *n, pl* **lackeys** **1** : FOOTMAN, SERVANT **2** : TOADY

lack•lus•ter \ˈlak-ˌləs-tər\ *adj* : DULL

la•con•ic \lə-ˈkä-nik\ *adj* [L *laconicus* Spartan, fr. Gk *lakōnikos;* fr. the Spartan reputation for terseness of speech] : sparing of words : TERSE ♦ ***Synonyms*** CONCISE, CURT, SHORT, SUCCINCT, BRUSQUE — **la•con•i•cal•ly** \-ni-k(ə-)lē\ *adv*

lac•quer \ˈla-kər\ *n* : a clear or colored usu. glossy and quick-drying surface coating — **lacquer** *vb*

lac•ri•ma•tion \ˌla-krə-ˈmā-shən\ *n* : secretion of tears

la•crosse \lə-ˈkrós\ *n* [CanF *la crosse,* lit., the crooked stick] : a goal game in which players use a long-handled triangular-headed stick having a mesh pouch for catching, carrying, and throwing the ball

lac•tate \ˈlak-ˌtāt\ *vb* **lac•tat•ed; lac•tat•ing** : to secrete milk — **lac•ta•tion** \lak-ˈtā-shən\ *n*

lac•tic \ˈlak-tik\ *adj* **1** : of or relating to milk **2** : obtained from sour milk or whey

lactic acid *n* : a syrupy acid present in blood and muscle tissue and used esp. in food and medicine

lac•tose \ˈlak-ˌtōs\ *n* : a sugar present in milk

la•cu•na \lə-ˈkü-nə, -ˈkyü-\ *n, pl* **la•cu•nae** \-nē\ *also* **la•cu•nas** [L, pool, pit, gap, fr. *lacus* lake] : a blank space or missing part : GAP, DEFICIENCY

lad \ˈlad\ *n* : YOUTH; *also* : FELLOW

lad•der \ˈla-dər\ *n* **1** : a structure for climbing that consists of two parallel sidepieces joined at intervals by crosspieces **2** : something resembling a ladder in having ascending steps or stages ⟨a tournament ~⟩

lad•die \ˈla-dē\ *n* : a young lad

lad•en \ˈlā-dᵊn\ *adj* : LOADED, BURDENED

lad•ing \ˈlā-diŋ\ *n* : CARGO, FREIGHT

la•dle \ˈlā-dᵊl\ *n* : a deep-bowled long-handled spoon used in taking up and conveying liquids — **ladle** *vb*

la•dy \ˈlā-dē\ *n, pl* **ladies** [ME, fr. OE *hlǣfdīge,* fr. *hlāf* bread + *-dīge* (akin to *dǣge* kneader of bread)] **1** : a woman of property, rank, or authority; *also* : a woman of superior social position or of refinement **2** : WOMAN **3** : WIFE

lady beetle *n* : LADYBUG

la•dy•bird \ˈlā-dē-ˌbərd\ *n* : LADYBUG

la•dy•bug \-ˌbəg\ *n* : any of various small nearly hemispherical and usu. brightly colored beetles that feed mostly on other insects

la•dy•fin•ger \-ˌfiŋ-gər\ *n* : a small finger-shaped sponge cake

lady–in–waiting *n, pl* **ladies–in–waiting** : a lady appointed to attend or wait on a queen or princess

la•dy•like \ˈlā-dē-ˌlīk\ *adj* : WELL-BRED

la•dy•ship \-ˌship\ *n* : the condition of being a lady : rank of lady

lady's slipper *also* **lady slipper** *n* : any of several No. American orchids with slipper-shaped flowers

[1]**lag** \ˈlag\ *n* **1** : a slowing up or falling behind; *also* : the amount by which one lags **2** : INTERVAL

[2]**lag** *vb* **lagged; lag•ging** **1** : to fail to keep up : stay behind **2** : to slacken gradually ♦ ***Synonyms*** DAWDLE, DALLY, TARRY, LOITER

la•ger \ˈlä-gər\ *n* : a usu. dry beer slowly brewed and matured under refrigeration

lag•gard \ˈla-gərd\ *adj* : tending to lag ⟨~ workers⟩ — **laggard** *n* — **lag•gard•ly** *adv or adj* — **lag•gard•ness** *n*

la•gniappe \ˈlan-ˌyap\ *n* : something given free esp. with a purchase

la•goon \lə-ˈgün\ *n* : a shallow sound, channel, or pond near or connected to a larger body of water

laid *past and past part of* LAY

laid–back \ˈlād-ˈbak\ *adj* : having a relaxed style or character ⟨~ music⟩

lain *past part of* [1]LIE

lair \ˈler\ *n* **1** : the resting or living place of a wild animal : DEN **2** : a usu. hidden refuge

laird \ˈlerd\ *n, chiefly Scot* : a landed proprietor

lais•ser–faire *chiefly Brit var of* LAISSEZ-FAIRE

lais•sez–faire \ˌle-ˌsā-ˈfer, ˌlā-, -ˌzā-\ *n* [F *laissez faire* let do] : a doctrine opposing governmental control of economic affairs beyond that necessary to maintain peace and property rights

la•ity \ˈlā-ə-tē\ *n* **1** : the people of a religious faith as distinct from its clergy **2** : the mass of people as distinct from those of a particular field

lake \ˈlāk\ *n* : an inland body of standing water of considerable size; *also* : a pool of liquid (as lava or pitch)

La•ko•ta \lə-ˈkō-tə\ *n, pl* **Lakota** *also* **Lakotas** : a member of a western division of the Dakota peoples; *also* : their language

[1]**lam** \ˈlam\ *vb* **lammed; lam•ming** : to flee hastily — **lam** *n*

[2]**lam** *abbr* laminated

Lam *abbr* Lamentations

la•ma \ˈlä-mə\ *n* : a Buddhist monk of Tibet or Mongolia

la•ma•sery \ˈlä-mə-ˌser-ē\ *n, pl* **-ser•ies** : a monastery for lamas

[1]**lamb** \ˈlam\ *n* **1** : a young sheep; *also* : its flesh used as food **2** : an innocent or gentle person

[2]**lamb** *vb* : to bring forth a lamb

lam•baste *or* **lam•bast** \lam-ˈbāst, -ˈbast\ *vb* **1** : BEAT **2** : EXCORIATE ♦ ***Synonyms*** CASTIGATE, FLAY, LASH

lamb•da \ˈlam-də\ *n* : the 11th letter of the Greek alphabet — Λ or λ

lam·bent \ˈlam-bənt\ *adj* [L *lambens,* prp. of *lambere* to lick] **1** : FLICKERING ⟨a ~ flame⟩ **2** : softly radiant ⟨~ eyes⟩ **3** : marked by lightness or brilliance ⟨~ humor⟩ ♦ ***Synonyms*** EFFULGENT, INCANDESCENT, LUCENT, LUMINOUS — **lam·ben·cy** \-bən-sē\ *n* — **lam·bent·ly** *adv*

lamb·skin \ˈlam-ˌskin\ *n* : a lamb's skin or a small fine-grade sheepskin or the leather made from either

[1]**lame** \ˈlām\ *adj* **lam·er; lam·est** **1** : having a body part and esp. a limb so disabled as to impair freedom of movement; *also* : marked by stiffness and soreness **2** : lacking substance : WEAK ⟨~ excuses⟩ **3** : INFERIOR, PITIFUL ⟨a ~ school⟩ — **lame·ly** *adv* — **lame·ness** *n*

[2]**lame** *vb* **lamed; lam·ing** : to make lame : DISABLE ⟨was *lamed* by a broken leg⟩

la·mé \lä-ˈmā, la-\ *n* [F] : a brocaded clothing fabric with tinsel filling threads (as of gold or silver)

lame·brain \ˈlām-ˌbrān\ *n* : DOLT

lame duck *n* : an elected official continuing to hold office between an election and the inauguration of a successor — **lame–duck** *adj*

[1]**la·ment** \lə-ˈment\ *vb* **1** : to mourn aloud : WAIL **2** : to express sorrow or regret for : BEWAIL — **lam·en·ta·ble** \ˈla-mən-tə-bəl, lə-ˈmen-tə-\ *adj* — **lam·en·ta·bly** \-blē\ *adv* — **lam·en·ta·tion** \ˌla-mən-ˈtā-shən\ *n*

[2]**lament** *n* **1** : a crying out in grief : WAIL **2** : DIRGE, ELEGY **3** : COMPLAINT

Lamentations *n* — see BIBLE table

la·mia \ˈlā-mē-ə\ *n* : a female demon

lam·i·na \ˈla-mə-nə\ *n, pl* **-nae** \-ˌnē\ *or* **-nas** : a thin plate or scale

[1]**lam·i·nate** \ˈla-mə-ˌnāt\ *vb* **-nat·ed; -nat·ing** : to make by uniting layers of one or more materials — **lam·i·na·tion** \ˌla-mə-ˈnā-shən\ *n*

[2]**lam·i·nate** \-nət\ *n* : a product manufactured by laminating

lamp \ˈlamp\ *n* **1** : a vessel with a wick for burning a flammable liquid (as oil) to produce light **2** : a device for producing light or heat

lamp·black \-ˌblak\ *n* : black soot used esp. as a pigment

lamp·light·er \-ˌlī-tər\ *n* : one that lights a lamp

lam·poon \lam-ˈpün\ *n* : SATIRE; *esp* : a harsh satire directed against an individual — **lampoon** *vb*

lam·prey \ˈlam-prē\ *n, pl* **lampreys** : any of a family of eel-shaped jawless fishes that have well-developed eyes and a large disk-shaped sucking mouth armed with horny teeth

LAN \ˈlan, ˌel-ˌā-ˈen\ *n* : LOCAL AREA NETWORK

la·nai \lə-ˈnī\ *n* [Hawaiian *lānai*] : PORCH, VERANDA

[1]**lance** \ˈlans\ *n* **1** : a spear carried by mounted soldiers **2** : any of various sharp-pointed implements; *esp* : LANCET

[2]**lance** *vb* **lanced; lanc·ing** : to pierce or open with a lance ⟨~ a boil⟩

lance corporal *n* : an enlisted person in the marine corps ranking above a private first class and below a corporal

lanc·er \ˈlan-sər\ *n* : a cavalryman of a unit formerly armed with lances

lan·cet \ˈlan-sət\ *n* : a sharp-pointed and usu. 2-edged surgical instrument

[1]**land** \ˈland\ *n* **1** : the solid part of the surface of the earth; *also* : a part of the earth's surface ⟨fenced ~⟩ ⟨marshy ~⟩ **2** : NATION **3** : REALM, DOMAIN ⟨the ~ of the living⟩ — **land·less** *adj*

[2]**land** *vb* **1** : DISEMBARK; *also* : to touch at a place on shore **2** : to alight or cause to alight on a surface ⟨~ a punch⟩ **3** : to bring to or arrive at a destination **4** : to catch and bring in ⟨~ a fish⟩; *also* : GAIN, SECURE ⟨~ a job⟩

lan·dau \ˈlan-ˌdau̇\ *n* : a 4-wheeled carriage with a top divided into two sections that can be lowered, thrown back, or removed

land·ed *adj* : having an estate in land ⟨~ gentry⟩

land·er \ˈlan-dər\ *n* : a space vehicle designed to land on a celestial body

land·fall \ˈland-ˌfȯl\ *n* : a sighting or making of land (as after a voyage); *also* : the land first sighted

land·fill \-ˌfil\ *n* : a low-lying area on which refuse is buried between layers of earth — **landfill** *vb*

land·form \-ˌfȯrm\ *n* : a natural feature of a land surface

land·hold·er \-ˌhōl-dər\ *n* : a holder or owner of land — **land·hold·ing** \-diŋ\ *adj or n*

land·ing \ˈlan-diŋ\ *n* **1** : the action of one that lands **2** : a place for discharging or taking on passengers and cargo **3** : a level part of a staircase

landing gear *n* : the part that supports the weight of an aircraft when it is on the ground

land·la·dy \ˈland-ˌlā-dē\ *n* : a woman who is a landlord

land·locked \-ˌläkt\ *adj* **1** : enclosed or nearly enclosed by land ⟨a ~ country⟩ **2** : confined to fresh water by some barrier ⟨~ salmon⟩

land·lord \-ˌlȯrd\ *n* **1** : the owner of property leased or rented to another **2** : a person who rents lodgings : INNKEEPER

land·lub·ber \-ˌlə-bər\ *n* : one who knows little of the sea or seamanship

land·mark \-ˌmärk\ *n* **1** : an object that marks a course or boundary or serves as a guide **2** : an event that marks a turning point **3** : a structure of unusual historical and usu. aesthetic interest

land·mass \-ˌmas\ *n* : a large area of land

land mine *n* **1** : a mine placed on or just below the surface of the ground and designed to be exploded by the weight of someone or something passing over it **2** : a trap for the unwary

land·own·er \-ˌō-nər\ *n* : an owner of land

[1]**land·scape** \-ˌskāp\ *n* **1** : a picture of natural inland scenery **2** : a portion of land that can be seen in one glance

²landscape *vb* **land·scaped; land·scap·ing** : to modify (a natural landscape) by grading, clearing, or decorative planting

land·slide \-ˌslīd\ *n* **1** : the slipping down of a mass of rocks or earth on a steep slope; *also* : the mass of material that slides **2** : an overwhelming victory esp. in a political contest

lands·man \ˈlandz-mən\ *n* : a person who lives on land; *esp* : LANDLUBBER

land·ward \ˈland-wərd\ *adv or adj* : to or toward the land

lane \ˈlān\ *n* **1** : a narrow passageway (as between fences) **2** : a relatively narrow way or track ⟨traffic ~⟩

lang *abbr* language

lan·guage \ˈlaŋ-gwij\ *n* [ME, fr. AF *langage*, fr. *langue* tongue, language, fr. L *lingua*] **1** : the words, their pronunciation, and the methods of combining them used and understood by a community **2** : form or style of verbal expression ⟨legal ~⟩ **3** : a system of signs and symbols and rules for using them that is used to carry information

lan·guid \ˈlaŋ-gwəd\ *adj* **1** : WEAK **2** : sluggish in character or disposition : LISTLESS ⟨a ~ summer day⟩ **3** : SLOW — **lan·guid·ly** *adv* — **lan·guid·ness** *n*

lan·guish \ˈlaŋ-gwish\ *vb* **1** : to become languid **2** : to become dispirited : PINE **3** : to appeal for sympathy by assuming an expression of grief

lan·guor \ˈlaŋ-gər\ *n* **1** : a languid feeling **2** : listless indolence or inertia ♦ ***Synonyms*** LETHARGY, LASSITUDE, TORPIDITY, TORPOR — **lan·guor·ous** *adj* — **lan·guor·ous·ly** *adv*

La Ni·ña \lä-ˈnē-nyə\ *n* : an upwelling of unusually cold ocean water along the west coast of So. America that often follows an El Niño

lank \ˈlaŋk\ *adj* **1** : not well filled out **2** : hanging straight and limp ⟨~ hair⟩

lanky \ˈlaŋ-kē\ *adj* **lank·i·er; -est** : ungracefully tall and thin

lan·o·lin \ˈlan-ᵊl-ən\ *n* : the fatty coating of sheep's wool esp. when refined for use in ointments and cosmetics

lan·ta·na \lan-ˈtä-nə\ *n* : any of a genus of tropical shrubs related to the vervains with showy heads of small bright flowers

lan·tern \ˈlan-tərn\ *n* [ME *lanterne*, fr. AF, fr. L *lanterna*, fr. Gk *lamptēr*, fr. *lampein* to shine] **1** : a usu. portable light with a protective covering **2** : the chamber in a lighthouse containing the light **3** : a projector for slides

lan·tha·num \ˈlan-thə-nəm\ *n* : a soft malleable metallic chemical element

lan·yard \ˈlan-yərd\ *n* : a piece of rope for fastening something in ships; *also* : any of various cords

¹lap \ˈlap\ *n* **1** : a loose panel of a garment **2** : the clothing that lies on the knees, thighs, and lower part of the trunk when one sits; *also* : the front part of the lower trunk and thighs of a seated person **3** : an environment of nurture ⟨the ~ of luxury⟩ **4** : CHARGE, CONTROL ⟨in the ~ of the gods⟩

²lap *vb* **lapped; lap·ping** **1** : FOLD **2** : WRAP **3** : to lay over or near so as to partly cover

³lap *n* **1** : the amount by which an object overlaps another; *also* : the part of an object that overlaps another **2** : an act or instance of going over a course (as a track or swimming pool)

⁴lap *vb* **lapped; lap·ping** **1** : to scoop up food or drink with the tip of the tongue; *also* : DEVOUR — usu. used with *up* **2** : to splash gently ⟨*lapping* waves⟩

⁵lap *n* **1** : an act or instance of lapping **2** : a gentle splashing sound

lap·a·ros·co·py \ˌla-pə-ˈräs-kə-pē\ *n, pl* **-pies** **1** : visual examination of the abdomen by means of an endoscope; *also* : surgery using laparoscopy — **lap·a·ro·scope** \ˈla-pə-rə-ˌskōp\ *n* — **lap·a·ro·scop·ic** \ˌla-pə-rə-ˈskä-pik\ *adj*

lap·dog \ˈlap-ˌdȯg\ *n* : a small dog that may be held in the lap

la·pel \lə-ˈpel\ *n* : the fold of the front of a coat that is usu. a continuation of the collar

¹lap·i·dary \ˈla-pə-ˌder-ē\ *n, pl* **-dar·ies** : a person who cuts, polishes, or engraves precious stones

²lapidary *adj* **1** : of, relating to, or suitable for engraved inscriptions **2** : of, relating to, or suggestive of precious stones or the art of cutting them

lap·in \ˈla-pən\ *n* : rabbit fur usu. sheared and dyed

la·pis la·zu·li \ˌla-pəs-ˈla-zə-lē, -zhə-\ *n* : a usu. blue semiprecious stone often having sparkling bits of pyrite

lap·pet \ˈla-pət\ *n* : a fold or flap on a garment

¹lapse \ˈlaps\ *n* [L *lapsus*, fr. *labi* to slip] **1** : a slight error ⟨a mental ~⟩ **2** : a fall from a higher to a lower state **3** : the termination of a right or privilege through failure to meet requirements **4** : INTERRUPTION **5** : APOSTASY **6** : a passage of time; *also* : INTERVAL ♦ ***Synonyms*** BLOOPER, BLUNDER, BONER, GOOF, MISTAKE, SLIP

²lapse *vb* **lapsed; laps·ing** **1** : to commit apostasy **2** : SINK, SLIP ⟨*lapsed* into a coma⟩ **3** : CEASE

lap·top \ˈlap-ˌtäp\ *adj* : of a size that can be used conveniently on one's lap ⟨a ~ computer⟩ — **laptop** *n*

lap·wing \ˈlap-ˌwiŋ\ *n* : an Old World crested plover

lar·board \ˈlär-bərd\ *n* : ⁵PORT

lar·ce·ny \ˈlär-sə-nē\ *n, pl* **-nies** [ME, fr. AF *larecin* theft, fr. L *latrocinium* robbery, fr. *latro* mercenary soldier] : THEFT — **lar·ce·nous** \-nəs\ *adj*

larch \ˈlärch\ *n* : any of a genus of trees related to the pines that shed their needles in the fall

¹lard \ˈlärd\ *vb* **1** : to insert strips of usu. pork fat into (meat) before cooking; *also* : GREASE **2** *obs* : ENRICH

²lard *n* : a soft white fat obtained by rendering fatty tissue of the hog

lar·der \ˈlär-dər\ *n* : a place where foods (as meat) are kept

large \ˈlärj\ *adj* **larg·er; larg·est** **1** : having more than usual power, capacity, or scope **2** : exceeding most other things of like kind in quantity or size ♦ *Synonyms* BIG, GREAT, OVERSIZE — **large** *adv* — **large·ness** *n* — **at large** **1** : UNCONFINED **2** : as a whole

large·ly \ˈlärj-lē\ *adv* : to a large extent

lar·gesse *or* **lar·gess** \lär-ˈzhes, -ˈjes\ *n* **1** : liberal giving **2** : a generous gift

¹**lar·go** \ˈlär-gō\ *adv or adj* [It, slow, broad, fr. L *largus* abundant] : at a very slow tempo — used as a direction in music

²**largo** *n, pl* **largos** : a largo movement

lari \ˈlä-rē\ *n, pl* **lari** — see MONEY table

lar·i·at \ˈlar-ē-ət\ *n* [AmerSp *la reata* the lasso, fr. Sp *la* the + AmerSp *reata* lasso, fr. Sp *reatar* to tie again] : a long rope used to catch or tether livestock : LASSO

¹**lark** \ˈlärk\ *n* : any of a family of small songbirds; *esp* : SKYLARK

²**lark** *n* : a source of or quest for fun or adventure

³**lark** *vb* : to engage in harmless fun or mischief — often used with *about*

lark·spur \ˈlärk-ˌspər\ *n* : DELPHINIUM; *esp* : any of the widely cultivated annual delphiniums

lar·va \ˈlär-və\ *n, pl* **lar·vae** \-(ˌ)vē\ *also* **larvas** [NL, fr. L, specter, mask] : the wingless often wormlike form in which insects hatch from the egg; *also* : any young animal (as a tadpole) that is fundamentally unlike its parent — **lar·val** \-vəl\ *adj*

lar·yn·gi·tis \ˌlar-ən-ˈjī-təs\ *n* : inflammation of the larynx

lar·ynx \ˈlar-iŋks\ *n, pl* **la·ryn·ges** \lə-ˈrin-ˌjēz\ *or* **lar·ynx·es** : the upper part of the trachea containing the vocal cords — **la·ryn·ge·al** \lə-ˈrin-jəl\ *adj*

la·sa·gna \lə-ˈzän-yə\ *n* [It] : boiled broad flat noodles baked with a sauce usu. of tomatoes, cheese, and meat

las·car \ˈlas-kər\ *n* : an Indian sailor

las·civ·i·ous \lə-ˈsi-vē-əs\ *adj* : LUSTFUL, LEWD ♦ *Synonyms* LICENTIOUS, LECHEROUS, LIBIDINOUS, SALACIOUS — **las·civ·i·ous·ness** *n*

la·ser \ˈlā-zər\ *n* [*l*ight *a*mplification by *s*timulated *e*mission of *r*adiation] **1** : a device that produces an intense monochromatic beam of light **2** : something thrown or directed straight with high speed or intensity ⟨threw a ~ into the end zone⟩

laser disc *n* : OPTICAL DISK; *esp* : one containing a video recording

¹**lash** \ˈlash\ *vb* **1** : to move violently or suddenly **2** : WHIP **3** : to attack verbally

²**lash** *n* **1** : a stroke esp. with a whip; *also* : WHIP **2** : a stinging rebuke **3** : EYELASH

³**lash** *vb* : to bind with or as if with a line

lass \ˈlas\ *n* : GIRL

lass·ie \ˈla-sē\ *n* : LASS

las·si·tude \ˈla-sə-ˌtüd, -ˌtyüd\ *n* **1** : WEARINESS, FATIGUE **2** : LANGUOR

las·so \ˈla-sō, la-ˈsü\ *n, pl* **lassos** *or* **lassoes** [Sp *lazo*] : a rope or long leather thong with a noose used for catching livestock — **lasso** *vb*

¹**last** \ˈlast\ *vb* **1** : to continue in existence or operation **2** : to remain fresh or unimpaired : ENDURE **3** : to manage to continue **4** : to be enough for the needs of

²**last** *n* : a foot-shaped form on which a shoe is shaped or repaired

³**last** *vb* : to shape with a last

⁴**last** *adv* **1** : at the end **2** : most recently **3** : in conclusion

⁵**last** *adj* **1** : following all the rest : FINAL **2** : next before the present ⟨~ week⟩ **3** : most up-to-date **4** : farthest from a specified quality, attitude, or likelihood ⟨the ~ thing we want⟩ **5** : CONCLUSIVE; *also* : SUPREME — **last·ly** *adv*

⁶**last** *n* : something that is last ⟨the ~ of them⟩ — **at last** : FINALLY

last–ditch \ˈlast-ˌdich\ *adj* : made as a final effort esp. to avert disaster

last laugh *n* : an ultimate satisfaction or triumph despite previous doubt or criticism

Last Supper *n* : the supper eaten by Jesus and his disciples on the night of his betrayal

lat *abbr* latitude

Lat *abbr* Latin

¹**latch** \ˈlach\ *vb* : to catch or get hold

²**latch** *n* : a catch that holds a door or gate closed

³**latch** *vb* : to make fast with a latch

latch·et \ˈla-chət\ *n* : a strap, thong, or lace for fastening a shoe or sandal

latch·key \ˈlach-ˌkē\ *n* : a key for opening a door latch esp. from the outside

latch·string \-ˌstriŋ\ *n* : a string on a latch that may be left hanging outside the door for raising the latch

¹**late** \ˈlāt\ *adj* **lat·er; lat·est** **1** : coming or remaining after the due, usual, or proper time **2** : far advanced toward the close or end **3** : recently deceased **4** : made, appearing, or happening just previous to the present : RECENT ⟨~ news⟩ — **late·ly** *adv* — **late·ness** *n*

²**late** *adv* **lat·er; lat·est** **1** : after the usual or proper time; *also* : at or to an advanced point in time **2** : RECENTLY

late·com·er \ˈlāt-ˌkə-mər\ *n* : one who arrives late

la·teen \lə-ˈtēn\ *adj* : relating to or being a triangular sail extended by a long spar slung to a low mast

la·tent \ˈlāt-ᵊnt\ *adj* : present but not visible or active ♦ *Synonyms* DORMANT, QUIESCENT, POTENTIAL — **la·ten·cy** \-ᵊn-sē\ *n*

¹**lat·er·al** \ˈla-tə-rəl\ *adj* : situated on, directed toward, or coming from the side ⟨a ~ view⟩ — **lat·er·al·ly** *adv*

²**lateral** *n* **1** : a branch from the main part **2** : a football pass thrown parallel to the line of scrimmage or away from the opponent's goal

la·tex \ˈlā-ˌteks\ *n, pl* **la·ti·ces** \ˈlā-tə-ˌsēz, ˈla-\ *or* **la·tex·es** **1** : a milky juice produced by various plant cells (as of milkweeds, poppies, and the rubber tree) **2** : a water emulsion of a synthetic rubber or plastic used esp. in paint

lath \ˈlath, ˈla*th*\ *n, pl* **laths** *or* **lath** : a thin narrow strip of wood used esp. as a base for plaster; *also* : a building material in sheets used for the same purpose — **lath** *vb*

lathe \ˈlāth\ *n* : a machine in which a piece of material is held and turned while being shaped by a tool

¹lath·er \ˈla-thər\ *n* **1** : a foam or froth formed when a detergent is agitated in water; *also* : foam from profuse sweating (as by a horse) **2** : DITHER

²lather *vb* : to spread lather over ⟨~*ed* his face before shaving⟩; *also* : to form a lather

Lat·in \ˈlat-ᵊn\ *n* **1** : the language of ancient Rome **2** : a member of any of the peoples whose languages derive from Latin — **Latin** *adj*

La·ti·na \lə-tē-nə\ *n* : a woman or girl who is a native or inhabitant of Latin America; *also* : a woman or girl of Latin-American origin living in the U.S.

Latin American *n* : a native or inhabitant of any of the countries of No., Central, or So. America whose official language is Spanish or Portuguese — **Latin–American** *adj*

La·ti·no \lə-ˈtē-nō\ *n, pl* **-nos** : a native or inhabitant of Latin America; *also* : a person of Latin-American origin living in the U.S. — **Latino** *adj*

La·tinx \lə-ˈtē-ˌneks\ *adj* : of or relating to Latin American heritage — used as a gender-neutral alternative to *Latino* or *Latina* — **Latinx** *n*

lat·i·tude \ˈla-tə-ˌtüd, -ˌtyüd\ *n* **1** : angular distance north or south from the earth's equator measured in degrees **2** : a region marked by its latitude **3** : freedom of action or choice

lat·i·tu·di·nar·i·an \ˌla-tə-ˌtü-də-ˈner-ē-ən, -ˌtyü-\ *n* : a person who is liberal in religious belief and conduct

la·trine \lə-ˈtrēn\ *n* : TOILET

lats \ˈläts\ *n, pl* **la·ti** \ˈlä-tē\ *or* **la·tu** \ˈlä-tü\ : the basic monetary unit of Latvia from 1922 to 1940 and from 1991 through 2013

lat·ter \ˈla-tər\ *adj* **1** : more recent; *also* : FINAL **2** : of, relating to, or being the second of two things referred to

lat·ter–day *adj* **1** : of present or recent times **2** : of a later or subsequent time

Latter–day Saint *n* : a member of a religious body founded by Joseph Smith in 1830 and accepting the Book of Mormon as divine revelation : MORMON

lat·ter·ly \ˈla-tər-lē\ *adv* **1** : LATER **2** : of late : RECENTLY

lat·tice \ˈla-təs\ *n* **1** : a framework of crossed wood or metal strips; *also* : a window, door, or gate having a lattice **2** : a regular geometrical arrangement

lat·tice·work \-ˌwərk\ *n* : LATTICE; *also* : work made of lattices

Lat·vi·an \ˈlat-vē-ən\ *n* **1** : a native or inhabitant of Latvia **2** : the language of the Latvians — **Latvian** *adj*

¹laud \ˈlȯd\ *n* : PRAISE, ACCLAIM

²laud *vb* : PRAISE, EXTOL ♦ ***Synonyms*** CELEBRATE, EULOGIZE, GLORIFY, MAGNIFY — **laud·able** *adj* — **laud·ably** *adv*

lau·da·num \ˈlȯd-ᵊn-əm\ *n* : a tincture of opium

lau·da·to·ry \ˈlȯ-də-ˌtōr-ē\ *adj* : of, relating to, or expressive of praise

¹laugh \ˈlaf, ˈlȧf\ *vb* [ME, fr. OE *hliehhan*] : to show mirth, joy, or scorn with a chuckle or explosive vocal sound; *also* : to become amused or derisive — **laugh·able** *adj* — **laugh·ing·ly** *adv*

²laugh *n* **1** : the act of laughing **2** : JOKE; *also* : JEER **3** *pl* : SPORT 1

laughing gas *n* : NITROUS OXIDE

laugh·ing·stock \ˈla-fiŋ-ˌstäk, ˈlȧ-\ *n* : an object of ridicule

laugh·ter \ˈlaf-tər, ˈlȧf-\ *n* : the action or sound of laughing

¹launch \ˈlȯnch\ *vb* **1** : THROW, HURL; *also* : to send off ⟨~ a rocket⟩ **2** : to set afloat **3** : to set in operation : START ⟨~ a business⟩ — **launch·er** *n*

²launch *n* : an act or instance of launching

³launch *n* : a small open or half-decked motorboat

launch·pad \ˈlȯnch-ˌpad\ *n* : a platform from which a rocket is launched

laun·der \ˈlȯn-dər\ *vb* **1** : to wash or wash and iron clothing and household linens **2** : to transfer (as money of an illegal origin) through an outside party to conceal the true source — **laun·der·er** *n*

laun·dress \ˈlȯn-drəs\ *n* : a woman who is a laundry worker

laun·dry \ˈlȯn-drē\ *n, pl* **laundries** [fr. obs. *launder* launderer, fr. AF *lavandere,* fr. ML *lavandarius,* fr. L *lavandus* needing to be washed, fr. *lavare* to wash] **1** : a place where laundering is done **2** : clothes or linens that have been or are to be laundered — **laun·dry·man** \-mən\ *n*

lau·re·ate \ˈlȯr-ē-ət\ *n* : the recipient of honor for achievement in an art or science — **lau·re·ate·ship** *n*

lau·rel \ˈlȯ-rəl\ *n* **1** : an evergreen tree or shrub of southern Europe that is related to the sassafras and cinnamon and has glossy aromatic leaves **2** : MOUNTAIN LAUREL **3** : a crown of laurel awarded as an honor — usu. used in pl.

lav *abbr* lavatory

la·va \ˈlä-və, ˈla-\ *n* [It] : melted rock coming from a volcano; *also* : such rock that has cooled and hardened

la·vage \lə-ˈväzh\ *n* [F] : WASHING; *esp* : the washing out (as of an organ) esp. for medicinal reasons

lav·a·to·ry \ˈla-və-ˌtōr-ē\ *n, pl* **-ries** **1** : a fixed washbowl with running water and drainpipe **2** : BATHROOM

lave \ˈlāv\ *vb* **laved; lav·ing** : WASH

lav·en·der \ˈla-vən-dər\ *n* **1** : a Mediterranean mint or its dried leaves and flowers used to perfume clothing and bed linen **2** : a pale purple color

¹lav·ish \ˈla-vish\ *adj* [ME *laves, lavage,* prob. fr. MF *lavasse, lavache* downpour, fr. *laver* to wash] **1** : expending or bestowing profusely **2** : expended or produced in abundance ⟨~ gifts⟩ **3** : marked by excess ⟨~ decor⟩ — **lav·ish·ly** *adv* — **lav·ish·ness** *n*

²**lavish** *vb* : to expend or give freely
law \'lȯ\ *n* **1** : a rule of conduct or action established by custom or laid down and enforced by a governing authority; *also* : the whole body of such rules **2** : the control brought about by enforcing rules **3** *cap* : the revelation of the divine will set forth in the Old Testament; *also* : the first part of the Jewish scriptures — see BIBLE table **4** : a rule or principle of construction or procedure **5** : the science that deals with laws and their interpretation and application **6** : the profession of a lawyer **7** : a rule or principle stating something that always works in the same way under the same conditions
law·break·er \'lȯ-ˌbrā-kər\ *n* : a person who violates the law
law·ful \'lȯ-fəl\ *adj* **1** : permitted by law **2** : RIGHTFUL — **law·ful·ly** *adv*
law·giv·er \-ˌgi-vər\ *n* : LEGISLATOR
law·less \'lȯ-ləs\ *adj* **1** : having no laws **2** : UNRULY, DISORDERLY ⟨a ~ mob⟩ — **law·less·ly** *adv* — **law·less·ness** *n*
law·mak·er \-ˌmā-kər\ *n* : LEGISLATOR
law·man \'lȯ-mən\ *n* : a law enforcement official (as a sheriff or marshal)
¹**lawn** \'lȯn\ *n* : ground (as around a house) covered with mowed grass
²**lawn** *n* : a fine sheer linen or cotton fabric
lawn bowling *n* : a bowling game played on a green with wooden balls which are rolled at a jack
law·ren·ci·um \lȯ-'ren-sē-əm\ *n* : a short-lived radioactive element
law·suit \'lȯ-ˌsüt\ *n* : a suit in law
law·yer \'lȯ-yər\ *n* : one who conducts lawsuits for clients or advises as to legal rights and obligations in other matters — **law·yer·ly** *adj*
lax \'laks\ *adj* **1** : not strict ⟨~ discipline⟩ **2** : not tense or rigid ♦ ***Synonyms*** REMISS, NEGLIGENT, NEGLECTFUL, DELINQUENT, DERELICT — **lax·i·ty** \'lak-sə-tē\ *n* — **lax·ly** *adv* — **lax·ness** *n*
¹**lax·a·tive** \'lak-sə-tiv\ *adj* : relieving constipation
²**laxative** *n* : a usu. mild laxative drug
¹**lay** \'lā\ *vb* **laid** \'lād\; **lay·ing** **1** : to beat or strike down **2** : to put on or set down : PLACE **3** : to produce and deposit eggs **4** : SETTLE; *also* : ALLAY **5** : SPREAD **6** : PREPARE, CONTRIVE **7** : WAGER **8** : to impose esp. as a duty or burden **9** : to set in order or position **10** : to bring to a specified condition ⟨*laid* waste the land⟩ **11** : to put forward : SUBMIT
²**lay** *n* : the way in which something lies or is laid in relation to something else
³**lay** *past of* ¹LIE
⁴**lay** *n* **1** : a simple narrative poem **2** : SONG
⁵**lay** *adj* **1** : of or relating to the laity **2** : not of a particular profession; *also* : lacking extensive knowledge of a particular subject
lay·away \'lā-ə-ˌwā\ *n* : a purchasing agreement by which a retailer agrees to hold merchandise secured by a deposit until the price is paid in full
lay·er \'lā-ər\ *n* **1** : one that lays **2** : one thickness, course, or fold laid or lying over or under another
lay·ette \lā-'et\ *n* [F, fr. MF, dim. of *laye* box] : an outfit of clothing and equipment for a newborn infant
lay·man \'lā-mən\ *n* : a person who is a member of the laity
lay·off \'lā-ˌȯf\ *n* **1** : a period of inactivity **2** : the act of laying off an employee
lay off *vb* **1** : to cease to employ (a worker) often temporarily **2** : to leave undisturbed **3** : to stop doing something
lay·out \'lā-ˌau̇t\ *n* : the final arrangement, plan, or design of something
lay·over \-ˌō-vər\ *n* : STOPOVER
lay·per·son \-ˌpər-sən\ *n* : a member of the laity
lay·wom·an \'lā-ˌwu̇-mən\ *n* : a woman who is a member of the laity
la·zar \'la-zər, 'lā-\ *n* : LEPER
laze \'lāz\ *vb* **lazed; laz·ing** : to pass time in idleness or relaxation
la·zy \'lā-zē\ *adj* **la·zi·er; -est** **1** : disliking activity or exertion **2** : encouraging idleness ⟨a ~ day⟩ **3** : SLUGGISH **4** : DROOPY, LAX **5** : not rigorous or strict ⟨~ work habits⟩ — **la·zi·ly** \-zə-lē\ *adv* — **la·zi·ness** \-zē-nəs\ *n*
la·zy·bones \-ˌbōnz\ *n sing or pl* : a lazy person
lazy Su·san \ˌlā-zē-'süz-ᵊn\ *n* : a revolving tray used for serving food
lb *abbr* [L *libra*] pound
lc *abbr* lowercase
LC *abbr* Library of Congress
¹**LCD** \ˌel-(ˌ)sē-'dē\ *n* [*l*iquid *c*rystal *d*isplay] : a display (as of the time in a digital watch) that consists of segments of a liquid crystal whose reflectivity varies with the voltage applied to them
²**LCD** *abbr* least common denominator; lowest common denominator
LCDR *abbr* lieutenant commander
LCM *abbr* least common multiple; lowest common multiple
LCpl *abbr* lance corporal
LCS *abbr* League Championship Series
ld *abbr* **1** load **2** lord
LD *abbr* learning disabled; learning disability
LDC *abbr* less developed country
ldg *abbr* **1** landing **2** loading
LDL \ˌel-(ˌ)dē-'el\ *n* [*l*ow-*d*ensity *l*ipoprotein] : a cholesterol-rich protein-poor lipoprotein of blood plasma correlated with increased probability of developing atherosclerosis
L–do·pa \'el-'dō-pə\ *n* : an isomer of dopa used esp. in the treatment of Parkinson's disease
LDS *abbr* Latter-day Saints
lea \'lē, 'lā\ *n* : PASTURE, MEADOW
leach \'lēch\ *vb* : to pass a liquid (as water) through to carry off the soluble components; *also* : to dissolve out by such means ⟨~ alkali from ashes⟩
¹**lead** \'lēd\ *vb* **led** \'led\; **lead·ing** **1** : to guide on a way **2** : LIVE ⟨~ a quiet life⟩ **3** : to direct the operations, activity, or performance of ⟨~ an orchestra⟩ **4**

: to go at the head of : be first ⟨~ a parade⟩ **5** : to begin play with; *also* : BEGIN, OPEN **6** : to tend toward a definite result ⟨study ~*ing* to a degree⟩ — **lead·er** *n* — **lead·er·less** *adj* — **lead·er·ship** *n*

²**lead** \ˈlēd\ *n* **1** : a position at the front; *also* : a margin by which one leads **2** : the privilege of leading in cards; *also* : the card or suit led **3** : EXAMPLE **4** : one that leads **5** : a principal role (as in a play); *also* : one who plays such a role **6** : INDICATION, CLUE **7** : an insulated electrical conductor

³**lead** \ˈled\ *n* **1** : a heavy malleable bluish white chemical element **2** : an article made of lead; *esp* : a weight for sounding at sea **3** : a thin strip of metal used to separate lines of type in printing **4** : a thin stick of marking substance in or for a pencil

⁴**lead** \ˈled\ *vb* **1** : to cover, line, or weight with lead **2** : to fix (glass) in position with lead **3** : to treat or mix with lead or a lead compound

lead·en \ˈled-ᵊn\ *adj* **1** : made of lead; *also* : of the color of lead **2** : SLUGGISH, DULL ⟨a ~ lecture⟩

lead off *vb* : OPEN, BEGIN; *esp* : to bat first in an inning — **lead·off** \ˈlēd-ˌȯf\ *n or adj*

¹**leaf** \ˈlēf\ *n, pl* **leaves** \ˈlēvz\ **1** : a usu. flat and green outgrowth of a plant stem that is a unit of foliage and functions esp. in photosynthesis; *also* : FOLIAGE **2** : something (as a page or a flat moving part) that is suggestive of a leaf — **leaf·less** *adj* — **leafy** *adj*

²**leaf** *vb* **1** : to produce leaves **2** : to turn the pages of a book

leaf·age \ˈlē-fij\ *n* : FOLIAGE

leafed \ˈlēft\ *adj* : LEAVED

leaf·hop·per \ˈlēf-ˌhä-pər\ *n* : any of a family of small leaping insects related to the cicadas that suck the juices of plants

leaf·let \ˈlē-flət\ *n* **1** : a division of a compound leaf **2** : PAMPHLET, FOLDER

leaf mold *n* : a compost or layer composed chiefly of decayed leaves

leaf·stalk \ˈlēf-ˌstȯk\ *n* : PETIOLE

¹**league** \ˈlēg\ *n* : a unit of distance equal to about three miles (five kilometers)

²**league** *n* **1** : an association or alliance (as of nations or sports teams) for a common purpose **2** : CLASS, CATEGORY — **league** *vb* — **leagu·er** \ˈlē-gər\ *n*

¹**leak** \ˈlēk\ *vb* **1** : to enter or escape through a leak **2** : to let a substance in or out through an opening **3** : to become or make known ⟨~*ed* the news⟩

²**leak** *n* **1** : a crack or hole that accidentally admits a fluid or light or lets it escape; *also* : something that secretly or accidentally permits the admission or escape of something else **2** : LEAKAGE — **leaky** *adj*

leak·age \ˈlē-kij\ *n* **1** : the act of leaking **2** : the thing or amount that leaks

¹**lean** \ˈlēn\ *vb* **1** : to bend from a vertical position : INCLINE **2** : to cast one's weight to one side for support **3** : to rely on for support **4** : to incline in opinion, taste, or desire — **lean** *n*

²**lean** *adj* **1** : lacking or deficient in flesh and esp. in fat ⟨~ meat⟩ **2** : lacking richness or productiveness ⟨~ profits⟩ **3** : low in fuel content — **lean·ness** *n*

leant \ˈlent\ *chiefly Brit past of* LEAN

lean–to \ˈlēn-ˌtü\ *n, pl* **lean–tos** \-ˌtüz\ : a wing or extension of a building having a roof of only one slope; *also* : a rough shed or shelter with a similar roof

¹**leap** \ˈlēp\ *vb* **leapt** \ˈlēpt, ˈlept\ *or* **leaped; leap·ing** : to spring free from a surface or over an obstacle : JUMP

²**leap** *n* : JUMP

leap·frog \ˈlēp-ˌfrȯg, -ˌfräg\ *n* : a game in which a player bends down and is vaulted over by another — **leapfrog** *vb*

leap year *n* : a year containing 366 days with February 29 as the extra day

learn \ˈlərn\ *vb* **learned** \ˈlərnd, ˈlərnt\; **learn·ing** **1** : to gain knowledge, understanding, or skill by study or experience; *also* : MEMORIZE ⟨~ the poem⟩ **2** : to find out : ASCERTAIN ⟨~ the truth⟩ — **learn·er** *n*

learn·ed \ˈlər-nəd\ *adj* : SCHOLARLY, ERUDITE — **learn·ed·ly** *adv* — **learn·ed·ness** *n*

learn·ing \ˈlər-niŋ\ *n* : KNOWLEDGE

learning disability *n* : any of various conditions (as dyslexia) that interfere with a person's ability to learn and so result in impaired functioning (as in language) — **learning disabled** *adj*

learnt \ˈlərnt\ *chiefly Brit past and past part of* LEARN

¹**lease** \ˈlēs\ *n* : a contract transferring real estate for a term of years or at will usu. for a specified rent

²**lease** *vb* **leased; leas·ing** [AF *lesser, lescher* to leave, hand over, lease, fr. L *laxare* to loosen, fr. *laxus* slack] **1** : to grant by lease **2** : to hold under a lease ♦ ***Synonyms*** LET, CHARTER, HIRE, RENT

lease·hold \ˈlēs-ˌhōld\ *n* **1** : a tenure by lease **2** : land held by lease — **lease·hold·er** *n*

leash \ˈlēsh\ *n* [ME *lees, leshe,* fr. AF **lesche, lesse* prob. fr. *lesser* to leave, let go] **1** : a line for leading or restraining an animal **2** : a state of restraint ⟨kept spending on a tight ~⟩ — **leash** *vb*

¹**least** \ˈlēst\ *adj* **1** : lowest in importance or position **2** : smallest in size or degree **3** : SLIGHTEST ⟨the ~ sign of trouble⟩

²**least** *n* : one that is least

³**least** *adv* : in the smallest or lowest degree

least common denominator *n* : the least common multiple of two or more denominators

least common multiple *n* : the smallest common multiple of two or more numbers

least·wise \ˈlēst-ˌwīz\ *adv* : at least

leath·er \ˈle-t͟hər\ *n* : animal skin dressed for use — **leath·ern** \-thərn\ *adj* — **leath·ery** *adj*

leath·er·back \-ˌbak\ *n* : the largest existing sea turtle with a flexible leathery carapace

leath·er·neck \-ˌnek\ *n* : MARINE
[1]**leave** \ˈlēv\ *vb* **left** \ˈleft\; **leav·ing** **1** : to allow or cause to remain behind **2** : to have as a remainder **3** : BEQUEATH **4** : to let stay without interference **5** : to go away : depart from **6** : GIVE UP, ABANDON ⟨*left* his wife for another woman⟩
[2]**leave** *n* **1** : PERMISSION; *also* : authorized absence from duty **2** : DEPARTURE
[3]**leave** *vb* **leaved; leav·ing** : LEAF
leaved \ˈlēvd\ *adj* : having leaves
[1]**leav·en** \ˈle-vən\ *n* **1** : a substance (as yeast) used to produce fermentation (as in dough) **2** : something that modifies or lightens
[2]**leaven** *vb* : to raise (dough) with a leaven; *also* : to permeate with a modifying or vivifying element ⟨lectures ~*ed* with humor⟩
leav·en·ing *n* : LEAVEN
leaves *pl of* LEAF
leave–tak·ing \ˈlēv-ˌtā-kiŋ\ *n* : DEPARTURE, FAREWELL
leav·ings \ˈlē-viŋz\ *n pl* : REMNANT, RESIDUE ⟨the ~ of a meal⟩
lech·ery \ˈle-chə-rē\ *n* : inordinate indulgence in sexual activity — **lech·er** \ˈle-chər\ *n* — **lech·er·ous** \ˈle-chə-rəs\ *adj* — **lech·er·ous·ly** *adv* — **lech·er·ous·ness** *n*
lec·i·thin \ˈle-sə-thən\ *n* : any of several waxy phosphorus-containing substances that are common in animals and plants, form colloidal solutions in water, and have emulsifying and wetting properties
lect *abbr* lecture; lecturer
lec·tern \ˈlek-tərn\ *n* : a stand to support a book for a standing reader
lec·tor \-tər\ *n* : one whose chief duty is to read the lessons in a church service
lec·ture \ˈlek-chər\ *n* **1** : a discourse given before an audience esp. for instruction **2** : REPRIMAND — **lec·ture** *vb* — **lec·tur·er** *n* — **lec·ture·ship** *n*
led *past and past part of* LEAD
LED \ˌel-(ˌ)ē-ˈdē\ *n* [*l*ight-*e*mitting *d*iode] : a semiconductor diode that emits light when a voltage is applied to it and is used esp. for electronic displays
le·der·ho·sen \ˈlā-dər-ˌhōz-ᵊn\ *n pl* : leather shorts often with suspenders worn esp. in Bavaria
ledge \ˈlej\ *n* [ME *legge* bar of a gate] **1** : a shelflike projection from a top or an edge **2** : REEF
led·ger \ˈle-jər\ *n* : a book containing accounts to which debits and credits are transferred in final form
lee \ˈlē\ *n* **1** : a protecting shelter **2** : the side (as of a ship) that is sheltered from the wind — **lee** *adj*
leech \ˈlēch\ *n* **1** : any of various bloodsucking segmented usu. freshwater worms that are related to the earthworms and have a sucker at each end **2** : a hanger-on who seeks gain
leek \ˈlēk\ *n* : an onionlike herb grown for its mildly pungent leaves and stalk
leer \ˈlir\ *n* : a suggestive, knowing, or malicious look — **leer** *vb*
leery \ˈlir-ē\ *adj* : SUSPICIOUS, WARY
lees \ˈlēz\ *n pl* : DREGS ⟨~ in the bottle⟩
[1]**lee·ward** \ˈlē-wərd, ˈlü-ərd\ *n* : the lee side
[2]**leeward** *adj* : situated away from the wind
lee·way \ˈlē-ˌwā\ *n* **1** : lateral movement of a ship when under way **2** : an allowable margin of freedom or variation
[1]**left** \ˈleft\ *adj* [ME, fr. OE, weak; fr. the left hand's being the weaker in most individuals] **1** : of, relating to, or being the side of the body in which the heart is mostly located; *also* : located nearer to this side than to the right **2** *often cap* : of, adhering to, or constituted by the political left — **left** *adv*
[2]**left** *n* **1** : the left hand; *also* : the side or part that is on or toward the left side **2** *often cap* : those professing political views marked by desire to reform the established order and usu. to give greater freedom to the common people — **left·ward** \-wərd\ *adv or adj*
[3]**left** *past and past part of* LEAVE
left–click \ˈleft-ˈklik\ *vb* : to press the leftmost button on a computer mouse or similar input device
left–hand *adj* **1** : situated on the left **2** : LEFT-HANDED
left–hand·ed \ˈleft-ˈhan-dəd\ *adj* **1** : using the left hand habitually or more easily than the right **2** : designed for or done with the left hand **3** : INSINCERE, BACKHANDED ⟨a ~ compliment⟩ **4** : COUNTERCLOCKWISE — **left–handed** *adv* — **left–hand·ed·ness** *n* — **left–hand·er** \-dər\ *n*
left·ism \ˈlef-ˌti-zəm\ *n* **1** : the principles and views of the left **2** : advocacy of the doctrines of the left — **left·ist** \-tist\ *n or adj*
left·over \ˈleft-ˌō-vər\ *n* : something that remains unused or unconsumed
lefty \ˈlef-tē\ *n, pl* **left·ies** **1** : a left-handed person **2** : an advocate of leftism
[1]**leg** \ˈleg\ *n* **1** : a limb of an animal used esp. for supporting the body and in walking; *also* : the part of the vertebrate leg between knee and foot **2** : something resembling or analogous to an animal leg ⟨table ~⟩ **3** : the part of an article of clothing that covers the leg **4** : a portion of a trip **5** *pl* : long-term appeal or interest ⟨a musical that has ~*s*⟩ — **leg·ged** \ˈle-gəd\ *adj* — **leg·less** *adj*
[2]**leg** *vb* **legged; leg·ging** : to use the legs in walking or esp. in running
[3]**leg** *abbr* **1** legal **2** legislative; legislature
leg·a·cy \ˈle-gə-sē\ *n, pl* **-cies** : INHERITANCE; *also* : something that has come from a predecessor or the past
le·gal \ˈlē-gəl\ *adj* **1** : of or relating to law or lawyers **2** : LAWFUL; *also* : STATUTORY **3** : enforced in courts of law — **le·gal·i·ty** \li-ˈga-lə-tē\ *n* — **le·gal·ize** \ˈlē-gə-ˌlīz\ *vb* — **le·gal·ly** *adv*
le·gal·ese \ˌlē-gə-ˈlēz\ *n* : the specialized language of the legal profession
le·gal·ism \ˈlē-gə-ˌli-zəm\ *n* **1** : strict, literal, or excessive conformity to the law or to a religious or moral code **2** : a legal term — **le·gal·is·tic** \ˌlē-gə-ˈlis-tik\ *adj*

leg·ate \ˈle-gət\ *n* : an official representative
leg·a·tee \ˌle-gə-ˈtē\ *n* : a person to whom a legacy is bequeathed
le·ga·tion \li-ˈgā-shən\ *n* **1** : a diplomatic mission headed by a minister **2** : the official residence and office of a minister in a foreign country
le·ga·to \li-ˈgä-tō\ *adv or adj* [It, lit., tied] : in a smooth and connected manner (as of music)
leg·end \ˈle-jənd\ *n* [ME *legende,* fr. AF & ML; AF *legende,* fr. ML *legenda,* fr. L *legere* to read] **1** : a story coming down from the past; *esp* : one popularly accepted as historical though not verifiable **2** : an inscription on an object; *also* : CAPTION **3** : an explanatory list of the symbols on a map or chart
leg·end·ary \ˈle-jən-ˌder-ē\ *adj* **1** : of, relating to, or characteristic of a legend **2** : FAMOUS ⟨~ actors⟩ — **leg·en·dari·ly** \-ˌder-ə-lē\ *adv*
leg·er·de·main \ˌle-jər-də-ˈmān\ *n* [ME, fr. MF *leger de main* light of hand] : SLEIGHT OF HAND
leg·ging *or* **leg·gin** \ˈle-gən, -giŋ\ *n* : a covering for the leg; *esp* : tightly fitting pants made of a stretchy material — usu. used in pl.
leg·gy \ˈle-gē\ *adj* **leg·gi·er; -est** **1** : having unusually long legs **2** : having long and attractive legs **3** : SPINDLY — used of a plant
leg·horn \ˈleg-ˌhȯrn, ˈle-gərn\ *n* **1** : a fine plaited straw; *also* : a hat made of this straw **2** : any of a Mediterranean breed of small hardy chickens
leg·i·ble \ˈle-jə-bəl\ *adj* : capable of being read : CLEAR — **leg·i·bil·i·ty** \ˌle-jə-ˈbi-lə-tē\ *n* — **leg·i·bly** \ˈle-jə-blē\ *adv*
[1]**le·gion** \ˈlē-jən\ *n* **1** : a unit of the Roman army comprising 3000 to 6000 soldiers **2** : MULTITUDE ⟨~*s* of fans⟩ **3** : an association of ex-servicemen — **le·gion·ary** \-jə-ˌner-ē\ *n* — **le·gion·naire** \ˌlē-jə-ˈnar\ *n*
[2]**legion** *adj* : MANY, NUMEROUS
Legionnaires' disease *also* **Legionnaire's disease** \-ˈnerz-\ *n* : a lobar pneumonia caused by a bacterium
legis *abbr* legislation; legislative; legislature
leg·is·late \ˈle-jəs-ˌlāt\ *vb* **-lat·ed; -lat·ing** : to make or enact laws; *also* : to bring about by legislation — **leg·is·la·tor** \-ˌlā-tər\ *n*
leg·is·la·tion \ˌle-jəs-ˈlā-shən\ *n* **1** : the action of legislating **2** : laws made by a legislative body
leg·is·la·tive \ˈle-jəs-ˌlā-tiv\ *adj* **1** : having the power of legislating **2** : of or relating to a legislature or legislation
leg·is·la·ture \ˈle-jəs-ˌlā-chər\ *n* : an organized body of persons having the authority to make laws
le·git \li-ˈjit\ *adj, slang* : LEGITIMATE
[1]**le·git·i·mate** \li-ˈji-tə-mət\ *adj* **1** : lawfully begotten **2** : GENUINE **3** : LAWFUL **4** : conforming to recognized principles or accepted rules or standards — **le·git·i·ma·cy** \-mə-sē\ *n* — **le·git·i·mate·ly** *adv*
[2]**le·git·i·mate** \-ˌmāt\ *vb* : to make legitimate
le·git·i·mise *Brit var of* LEGITIMIZE
le·git·i·mize \li-ˈji-tə-ˌmīz\ *vb* **-mized; -miz·ing** : LEGITIMATE
leg·man \ˈleg-ˌman\ *n* **1** : a reporter assigned usu. to gather information **2** : an assistant who gathers information and runs errands
le·gume \ˈle-ˌgyüm, li-ˈgyüm\ *n* [F] **1** : any of a large family of plants having fruits that are dry pods and split when ripe and including important food and forage plants (as beans and clover); *also* : the part (as seeds or pods) of a legume used as food **2** : the pod of a legume — **le·gu·mi·nous** \li-ˈgyü-mə-nəs\ *adj*
[1]**lei** \ˈlā, ˈlā-ˌē\ *n* : a wreath or necklace usu. of flowers
[2]**lei** \ˈlā\ *pl of* LEU
lei·sure \ˈlē-zhər, ˈle-, ˈlā-\ *n* **1** : time free from work or duties **2** : EASE; *also* : CONVENIENCE ⟨read it at your ~⟩ ♦ ***Synonyms*** RELAXATION, REST, REPOSE — **lei·sure·ly** *adj or adv*
leit·mo·tif *also* **leit·mo·tiv** \ˈlīt-mō-ˌtēf\ *n* [G *Leitmotiv,* fr. *leiten* to lead + *Motiv* motive] : a dominant recurring theme
lek \ˈlek\ *n, pl* **leks** *or* **le·ke** *or* **lekë** \ˈle-kə\ — see MONEY table
lem·ming \ˈle-miŋ\ *n* [Norwegian] : any of various short-tailed rodents found mostly in northern regions and noted for recurrent mass migrations
lem·on \ˈle-mən\ *n* **1** : an acid yellow usu. nearly oblong citrus fruit; *also* : a citrus tree that bears lemons **2** : something (as an automobile) unsatisfactory or defective — **lem·ony** *adj*
lem·on·ade \ˌle-mə-ˈnād\ *n* : a beverage of lemon juice, sugar, and water
lemon curd *n* : a custard made with lemon juice, butter, sugar, and eggs
lem·on·grass \ˈle-mən-ˌgras\ *n* : a tropical Asian grass grown for its lemon-scented foliage used as a seasoning
lem·pi·ra \lem-ˈpir-ə\ *n* — see MONEY table
le·mur \ˈlē-mər\ *n* : any of various arboreal primates largely of Madagascar that have large eyes, very soft woolly fur, and a long furry tail
Len·a·pe \ˈle-nə-pē, lə-ˈnä-pē\ *n, pl* **Lenape** *or* **Lenapes** : DELAWARE
lend \ˈlend\ *vb* **lent** \ˈlent\; **lend·ing** **1** : to give for temporary use on condition that the same or its equivalent be returned **2** : AFFORD, FURNISH **3** : ACCOMMODATE — **lend·er** *n*
lend–lease \-ˈlēs\ *n* : the transfer of goods and services to an ally to aid in a common cause with payment made by a return of the items or their use in the cause or by a similar transfer of other goods and services
length \ˈleŋth\ *n* **1** : the longer or longest dimension of an object; *also* : a measured distance **2** : duration or extent in time or space **3** : the length of something taken

as a unit of measure **4 :** a single piece of a series of pieces that may be joined together ⟨a ~ of pipe⟩ — **at length 1 :** in full **2 :** FINALLY

length·en \ˈleŋ-thən\ *vb* : to make or become longer ♦ ***Synonyms*** EXTEND, ELONGATE, PROLONG, PROTRACT

length·wise \ˈleŋth-ˌwīz\ *adv* : in the direction of the length — **lengthwise** *adj*

lengthy \ˈleŋ-thē\ *adj* **length·i·er; -est 1** : protracted excessively **2 :** EXTENDED, LONG ⟨a ~ journey⟩

le·nient \ˈlē-nē-ənt, -nyənt\ *adj* : of mild and tolerant disposition or effect ♦ ***Synonyms*** INDULGENT, FORBEARING, MERCIFUL, TOLERANT — **le·ni·en·cy** \ˈlē-nē-ən-sē, -nyən-sē\ *n* — **le·ni·ent·ly** *adv*

len·i·ty \ˈle-nə-tē\ *n* : LENIENCY

lens \ˈlenz\ *n* [L *lent-, lens* lentil; so called fr. the shape of a convex lens] **1 :** a curved piece of glass or plastic used singly or combined in an optical instrument for forming an image; *also* : a device for focusing radiation other than light **2 :** a transparent body in the eye that focuses light rays on receptors at the back of the eye

Lent \ˈlent\ *n* : a 40-day period of penitence and fasting observed from Ash Wednesday to Easter by many churches — **Lent·en** \ˈlen-tᵊn\ *adj*

len·til \ˈlen-tᵊl\ *n* : a Eurasian annual legume grown for its flat edible seeds and for fodder; *also* : its seed

Leo \ˈlē-ō\ *n* [L, lit., lion] **1 :** a zodiacal constellation between Cancer and Virgo usu. pictured as a lion **2 :** the 5th sign of the zodiac in astrology; *also* : one born under this sign

le·one \lē-ˈōn\ *n, pl* **leones** *or* **leone** — see MONEY table

le·o·nine \ˈlē-ə-ˌnīn\ *adj* : of, relating to, or resembling a lion

leop·ard \ˈle-pərd\ *n* : a large usu. tawny and black-spotted cat of southern Asia and Africa

le·o·tard \ˈlē-ə-ˌtärd\ *n* : a close-fitting garment worn esp. by dancers and for exercise

lep·er \ˈle-pər\ *n* **1 :** a person affected with leprosy **2 :** OUTCAST

lep·re·chaun \ˈle-prə-ˌkän\ *n* : a mischievous elf of Irish folklore

lep·ro·sy \ˈle-prə-sē\ *n* : a chronic bacterial disease marked esp. if not treated by slow-growing swellings with deformity and loss of sensation of affected parts — **lep·rous** \-prəs\ *adj*

lep·tin \ˈlep-tən\ *n* : a hormone that is produced by fat-containing cells and plays a role in body weight regulation

lep·ton \lep-ˈtän\ *n, pl* **lep·ta** \-ˈtä\ : a former monetary unit equal to $^{1}/_{100}$ drachma

les·bi·an \ˈlez-bē-ən\ *n* [fr. association with poetry written by Sappho of Lesbos to and about other women in the female community she led] : a gay woman — **lesbian** *adj* — **les·bi·an·ism** \-ə-ˌni-zəm\ *n*

lèse ma·jes·té *or* **lese maj·es·ty** \ˈlāz-ˈma-jə-stē, ˈlez-, ˈlēz-\ *n* [MF *lese majesté,* fr. L *laesa majestas,* lit., injured majesty] : an offense violating the dignity of a sovereign

le·sion \ˈlē-zhən\ *n* : an abnormal structural change in the body due to injury or disease; *esp* : one clearly marked off from healthy tissue around it

¹less \ˈles\ *adj, comparative of* ¹LITTLE **1** : FEWER ⟨~ than six⟩ **2 :** of lower rank, degree, or importance **3 :** SMALLER; *also* : more limited in quantity ⟨~ than a year⟩

²less *adv, comparative of* ²LITTLE : to a lesser extent or degree

³less *n, pl* **less 1 :** a smaller portion **2** : something of less importance

⁴less *prep* : diminished by : MINUS ⟨list price ~ the discount⟩

-less \ləs\ *adj suffix* **1 :** destitute of : not having ⟨child*less*⟩ **2 :** unable to be acted on or to act (in a specified way) ⟨daunt*less*⟩

les·see \le-ˈsē\ *n* : a tenant under a lease

less·en \ˈle-sᵊn\ *vb* : to make or become less ♦ ***Synonyms*** DECREASE, DIMINISH, DWINDLE, ABATE

less·er \ˈle-sər\ *adj, comparative of* ¹LITTLE : of less size, quality, or significance

les·son \ˈle-sᵊn\ *n* **1 :** a passage from sacred writings read in a service of worship **2 :** a reading or exercise to be studied by a pupil; *also* : something learned **3** : a period of instruction **4 :** an instructive example

les·sor \ˈle-ˌsȯr, le-ˈsȯr\ *n* : one who conveys property by a lease

lest \ˈlest\ *conj* : for fear that

¹let \ˈlet\ *n* [ME *lette,* fr. *letten* to delay, hinder, fr. OE *lettan*] **1 :** HINDRANCE, OBSTACLE **2 :** a shot or point in racket games that does not count

²let *vb* **let; let·ting** [ME *leten,* fr. OE *lǣtan*] **1 :** to cause to : MAKE ⟨~ it be known⟩ **2 :** RENT, LEASE; *also* : to assign esp. after bids **3 :** ALLOW, PERMIT ⟨~ me go⟩

-let *n suffix* **1 :** small one ⟨book*let*⟩ **2** : article worn on ⟨wrist*let*⟩

let·down \ˈlet-ˌdau̇n\ *n* **1 :** DISAPPOINTMENT **2 :** a slackening of effort

le·thal \ˈlē-thəl\ *adj* : DEADLY, FATAL ⟨~ weapons⟩ — **le·thal·ly** *adv*

leth·ar·gy \ˈle-thər-jē\ *n* **1 :** abnormal drowsiness **2 :** the quality or state of being lazy or indifferent ♦ ***Synonyms*** LANGUOR, LASSITUDE, TORPOR — **le·thar·gic** \li-ˈthär-jik\ *adj*

let on *vb* **1 :** REVEAL 1 ⟨knows a lot more than he *lets on*⟩ **2 :** PRETEND

¹let·ter \ˈle-tər\ *n* **1 :** a symbol that stands for a speech sound and constitutes a unit of an alphabet **2 :** a written or printed communication **3** *pl* : LITERATURE; *also* : LEARNING **4 :** the literal meaning ⟨the ~ of the law⟩ **5 :** a single piece of type

²letter *vb* : to mark with letters : INSCRIBE — **let·ter·er** *n*

letter bomb *n* : an explosive device concealed in an envelope and mailed to the intended victim

let·ter·boxed \ˈle-tər-ˌbäkst\ *adj* : being a

video recording formatted to display a frame size proportional to a standard theater screen

letter carrier *n* : a person who delivers mail

let·ter·head \ˈle-tər-ˌhed\ *n* : stationery with a printed or engraved heading; *also* : the heading itself

let·ter–per·fect \ˌle-tər-ˈpər-fikt\ *adj* : correct to the smallest detail

let·ter·press \ˈle-tər-ˌpres\ *n* : printing done directly by impressing the paper on an inked raised surface

letters of marque \-ˈmärk\ : a license granted to a private person by a government to fit out an armed ship to capture enemy shipping

letters patent *n pl* : a written grant from a government to a person in a form readily open for inspection by all

let·tuce \ˈle-təs\ *n* [ME *letuse,* fr. AF, prob. fr. pl. of *letue* lettuce plant, fr. L *lactuca,* fr. *lac* milk; fr. its milky juice] : a garden composite plant with crisp leaves used esp. in salads

let·up \ˈlet-ˌəp\ *n* : a lessening of effort

leu \ˈleu̇\ *n, pl* **lei** \ˈlā\ — see MONEY table

leu·kae·mia *chiefly Brit var of* LEUKEMIA

leu·ke·mia \lü-ˈkē-mē-ə\ *n* : a malignant disease characterized by an abnormal increase in the number of white blood cells in the blood-forming tissues — **leu·ke·mic** \-mik\ *adj or n*

leu·ko·cyte \ˈlü-kə-ˌsīt\ *n* : WHITE BLOOD CELL

lev \ˈlef\ *n, pl* **le·va** \ˈle-və\ — see MONEY table

Lev *or* **Levit** *abbr* Leviticus

[1]**le·vee** \ˈle-vē; lə-ˈvē, -ˈvā\ *n* [F *lever* act of arising] : a reception held by or for a person of distinction

[2]**lev·ee** \ˈle-vē\ *n* : an embankment to prevent or confine flooding; *also* : a river landing place

[1]**lev·el** \ˈle-vəl\ *n* **1** : a device for establishing a horizontal line or plane **2** : horizontal condition **3** : a horizontal position, line, or surface often taken as an index of altitude; *also* : a flat area of ground **4** : height, position, rank, or size in a scale

[2]**level** *vb* **-eled** *or* **-elled; -el·ing** *or* **-el·ling** **1** : to make flat or level; *also* : to come to a level **2** : AIM, DIRECT **3** : EQUALIZE **4** : RAZE — **lev·el·er** *n*

[3]**level** *adj* **1** : having a flat even surface **2** : HORIZONTAL **3** : of the same height or rank; *also* : UNIFORM **4** : steady and cool in judgment ⟨keep a ~ head when in danger⟩ — **lev·el·ly** *adv* — **lev·el·ness** *n*

lev·el·head·ed \ˌle-vəl-ˈhe-dəd\ *adj* : having or showing sound judgment : SENSIBLE ⟨a ~ decision⟩

le·ver \ˈle-vər, ˈlē-\ *n* **1** : a bar used for prying or dislodging something; *also* : a means for achieving one's purpose **2** : a rigid piece turning about an axis and used for transmitting and changing force and motion

le·ver·age \ˈle-vrij, ˈlē-, -və-rij\ *n* : the action or mechanical effect of a lever

le·vi·a·than \li-ˈvī-ə-thən\ *n* **1** : a large sea animal **2** : something large or formidable ⟨the ocean liner is a ~⟩

lev·i·tate \ˈle-və-ˌtāt\ *vb* **-tat·ed; -tat·ing** : to rise or cause to rise in the air in seeming defiance of gravitation — **lev·i·ta·tion** \ˌle-və-ˈtā-shən\ *n*

Le·vit·i·cus \li-ˈvi-tə-kəs\ *n* — see BIBLE table

lev·i·ty \ˈle-və-tē\ *n* : lack of seriousness ♦ ***Synonyms*** LIGHTNESS, FLIPPANCY, FRIVOLITY

levo·do·pa \ˌle-və-ˈdō-pə\ *n* : L-DOPA

[1]**levy** \ˈle-vē\ *n, pl* **lev·ies** **1** : the imposition or collection of an assessment; *also* : an amount levied **2** : the enlistment or conscription of men for military service; *also* : troops raised by levy

[2]**levy** *vb* **lev·ied; levy·ing** **1** : to impose or collect by legal authority ⟨~ taxes⟩ **2** : to enlist for military service **3** : WAGE ⟨~ war⟩ **4** : to seize property

lewd \ˈlüd\ *adj* [ME *lewed* vulgar, fr. OE *lǣwede* lay, ignorant] : sexually unchaste; *also* : OBSCENE, VULGAR — **lewd·ly** *adv* — **lewd·ness** *n*

lex·i·cog·ra·phy \ˌlek-sə-ˈkä-grə-fē\ *n* **1** : the editing or making of a dictionary **2** : the principles and practices of dictionary making — **lex·i·cog·ra·pher** \-fər\ *n* — **lex·i·co·graph·i·cal** \-kō-ˈgra-fi-kəl\ *or* **lex·i·co·graph·ic** \-fik\ *adj*

lex·i·con \ˈlek-sə-ˌkän\ *n, pl* **lex·i·ca** \-si-kə\ *or* **lexicons** **1** : DICTIONARY **2** : the vocabulary of a language, speaker, or subject

lg *abbr* **1** large **2** long

LGBT *abbr* lesbian, gay, bisexual, and transgender

LH *abbr* **1** left hand **2** lower half

li *abbr* link

Li *symbol* lithium

LI *abbr* Long Island

li·a·bil·i·ty \ˌlī-ə-ˈbi-lə-tē\ *n, pl* **-ties** **1** : the quality or state of being liable **2** *pl* : DEBTS **3** : DISADVANTAGE

li·a·ble \ˈlī-ə-bəl\ *adj* **1** : legally obligated : RESPONSIBLE **2** : LIKELY, APT ⟨~ to fall⟩ **3** : SUSCEPTIBLE ⟨~ to disease⟩

li·ai·son \ˈlē-ə-ˌzän, lē-ˈā-\ *n* [F] **1** : a close bond : INTERRELATIONSHIP **2** : an illicit sexual relationship **3** : communication for mutual understanding (as between parts of an armed force); *also* : one that carries on a liaison

li·ar \ˈlī(-ə)r\ *n* : a person who lies

[1]**lib** \ˈlib\ *n* : LIBERATION

[2]**lib** *abbr* **1** liberal **2** librarian; library

li·ba·tion \lī-ˈbā-shən\ *n* **1** : an act of pouring a liquid as a sacrifice (as to a god); *also* : the liquid poured **2** : DRINK

[1]**li·bel** \ˈlī-bəl\ *n* [ME, written declaration, fr. AF, fr. L *libellus,* dim. of *liber* book] **1** : a spoken or written statement or a representation that gives an unjustly unfavorable impression of a person or thing **2** : the action or crime of publishing a libel — **li·bel·ous** *or* **li·bel·lous** \-bə-ləs\ *adj*

[2]**libel** *vb* **-beled** *or* **-belled; -bel·ing** *or* **-bel·ling** : to make or publish a libel — **li·bel·er** *n* — **li·bel·ist** *n*

[1]**lib·er·al** \'li-brəl, -bə-rəl\ *adj* [ME, fr. AF, fr. L *liberalis* suitable for a freeman, generous, fr. *liber* free] **1** : of, relating to, or based on the liberal arts **2** : GENEROUS, BOUNTIFUL ⟨a ~ serving⟩ **3** : not literal **4** : not narrow in opinion or judgment : TOLERANT; *also* : not orthodox **5** : not conservative — **lib·er·al·i·ty** \ˌli-bə-'ra-lə-tē\ *n* — **lib·er·al·i·za·tion** \ˌli-brə-lə-'zā-shən, -bə-rə-\ *n* — **lib·er·al·ize** \'li-brə-ˌlīz, -bə-rə-\ *vb* — **lib·er·al·ly** *adv*

[2]**liberal** *n* : a person who holds liberal views

liberal arts *n pl* : the studies (as language, philosophy, history, literature, or abstract science) in a college or university intended to provide chiefly general knowledge and to develop the general intellectual capacities

lib·er·al·ism \'li-brə-ˌli-zəm, -bə-rə-\ *n* : liberal principles and theories

lib·er·ate \'li-bə-ˌrāt\ *vb* **-at·ed; -at·ing** **1** : to free from bondage or restraint; *also* : to raise to equal rights and status **2** : to free (as a gas) from combination — **lib·er·a·tion** \ˌli-bə-'rā-shən\ *n* — **lib·er·a·tor** \'li-bə-ˌrā-tər\ *n*

liberated *adj* : freed from or opposed to traditional social and sexual attitudes or roles ⟨a ~ marriage⟩

lib·er·tar·i·an \ˌli-bər-'ter-ē-ən\ *n* **1** : an advocate of the doctrine of free will **2** : one who upholds the principles of unrestricted liberty

lib·er·tine \'li-bər-ˌtēn\ *n* : a person who leads a dissolute life

lib·er·ty \'li-bər-tē\ *n, pl* **-ties** **1** : FREEDOM **2** : an action going beyond normal limits; *esp* : FAMILIARITY **3** : a short leave from naval duty

li·bid·i·nous \lə-'bi-də-nəs\ *adj* **1** : LASCIVIOUS **2** : LIBIDINAL

li·bi·do \lə-'bē-dō\ *n, pl* **-dos** [NL, fr. L, desire, lust] **1** : psychic energy derived from basic biological urges **2** : sexual drive — **li·bid·i·nal** \lə-'bi-də-nəl\ *adj*

Li·bra \'lē-brə\ *n* [L, lit., scales] **1** : a zodiacal constellation between Virgo and Scorpio usu. pictured as a balance scale **2** : the 7th sign of the zodiac in astrology; *also* : one born under this sign

li·brar·i·an \lī-'brer-ē-ən\ *n* : a specialist in the management of a library

li·brary \'lī-ˌbrer-ē\ *n, pl* **-brar·ies** **1** : a place in which books and related materials are kept for use but not for sale **2** : a collection of books

li·bret·to \lə-'bre-tō\ *n, pl* **-tos** *or* **-ti** \-tē\ [It, dim. of *libro* book, fr. L *liber*] : the text esp. of an opera — **li·bret·tist** \-tist\ *n*

lice *pl of* LOUSE

li·cense *or* **li·cence** \'lī-sᵊns\ *n* **1** : permission to act **2** : a permission granted by authority to engage in an activity **3** : a document, plate, or tag providing proof of a license **4** : freedom used irresponsibly — **license** *vb*

licensed practical nurse *n* : a specially trained person who is licensed (as by a state) to provide routine care for the sick

li·cens·ee \ˌlī-sᵊn-'sē\ *n* : a licensed person

licente *pl of* SENTE

li·cen·ti·ate \lī-'sen-chē-ət\ *n* : one licensed to practice a profession

li·cen·tious \lī-'sen-chəs\ *adj* : LEWD, LASCIVIOUS — **li·cen·tious·ly** *adv* — **li·cen·tious·ness** *n*

lichee *var of* LITCHI

li·chen \'lī-kən\ *n* : any of various complex plantlike organisms made up of an alga and a fungus growing as a unit on a solid surface — **li·chen·ous** *adj*

lic·it \'li-sət\ *adj* : LAWFUL

[1]**lick** \'lik\ *vb* **1** : to draw the tongue over; *also* : to flicker over like a tongue **2** : THRASH; *also* : DEFEAT

[2]**lick** *n* **1** : a stroke of the tongue **2** : a small amount **3** : a hasty careless effort **4** : BLOW **5** : a natural deposit of salt that animals lick

lick·e·ty–split \ˌli-kə-tē-'split\ *adv* : at great speed

lick·spit·tle \'lik-ˌspi-tᵊl\ *n* : a fawning subordinate : TOADY

lic·o·rice \'li-kə-rish, -rəs\ *n* [ME, fr. AF *licoris*, fr. LL *liquiritia*, alter. of L *glycyrrhiza*, fr. Gk *glykyrrhiza*, fr. *glykys* sweet + *rhiza* root] **1** : the dried root of a European leguminous plant; *also* : an extract from it used esp. as a flavoring and in medicine **2** : a candy flavored with licorice **3** : a plant yielding licorice

lid \'lid\ *n* **1** : a movable cover **2** : EYELID **3** : something that confines or suppresses — **lid·ded** \'li-dəd\ *adj*

li·do \'lē-dō\ *n, pl* **lidos** : a fashionable beach resort

[1]**lie** \'lī\ *vb* **lay** \'lā\; **lain** \'lān\; **ly·ing** \'lī-iŋ\ **1** : to be in, stay at rest in, or assume a horizontal position; *also* : to be in a helpless or defenseless state **2** : EXTEND ⟨our route *lay* to the west⟩ **3** : to occupy a certain relative position **4** : to have an effect esp. through mere presence

[2]**lie** *n* : the position in which something lies

[3]**lie** *vb* **lied; ly·ing** \'lī-iŋ\ : to tell a lie

[4]**lie** *n* : an untrue statement made with intent to deceive

lied \'lēt\ *n, pl* **lie·der** \'lē-dər\ [G] : a German song esp. of the 19th century

lie detector *n* : a polygraph for detecting physiological evidence of the tension that accompanies lying

lief \'lēv, 'lēf\ *adv* : GLADLY, WILLINGLY

[1]**liege** \'lēj\ *adj* : LOYAL, FAITHFUL

[2]**liege** *n* **1** : VASSAL **2** : a feudal superior

lien \'lēn, 'lē-ən\ *n* : a legal claim on the property of another for the satisfaction of a debt or duty

lieu \'lü\ *n, archaic* : PLACE, STEAD — **in lieu of** : in the place of

lieut *abbr* lieutenant

lieu·ten·ant \lü-'te-nənt\ *n* [ME, fr. AF *lieu tenant*, fr. *liu, lieu* place + *tenant* holding, fr. *tenir* to hold, fr. L *tenēre*] **1** : a representative of another in the performance of duty **2** : FIRST LIEUTENANT; *also* : SECOND LIEUTENANT **3** : a commissioned officer in the navy ranking next below a lieutenant commander — **lieu·ten·an·cy** \-nən-sē\ *n*

lieutenant colonel *n* : a commissioned officer (as in the army) ranking next below a colonel
lieutenant commander *n* : a commissioned officer in the navy ranking next below a commander
lieutenant general *n* : a commissioned officer (as in the army) ranking next below a general
lieutenant governor *n* : a deputy or subordinate governor
lieutenant junior grade *n, pl* **lieutenants junior grade** : a commissioned officer in the navy ranking next below a lieutenant
life \ˈlīf\ *n, pl* **lives** \ˈlīvz\ **1** : the quality that distinguishes a vital and functional being from a dead body or inanimate matter; *also* : a state of an organism characterized esp. by capacity for metabolism, growth, reaction to stimuli, and reproduction **2** : the physical and mental experiences of an individual **3** : BIOGRAPHY **4** : a specific phase or period ⟨adult ~⟩ **5** : the period from birth to death; *also* : a sentence of imprisonment for the remainder of a person's life **6** : a way of living **7** : PERSON ⟨a ~ was lost in the fire⟩ **8** : ANIMATION, SPIRIT ⟨danced with ~⟩ **9** : living beings ⟨forest ~⟩ **10** : animate activity ⟨signs of ~⟩ **11** : one providing interest and vigor ⟨~ of the party⟩ — **life·less** *adj* — **life·like** *adj*
life·blood \ˈlīf-ˌbləd\ *n* : a basic source of strength and vitality
life·boat \-ˌbōt\ *n* : a sturdy boat designed for use in saving lives at sea
life·guard \-ˌgärd\ *n* : a usu. expert swimmer employed to safeguard bathers
life·line \-ˌlīn\ *n* **1** : a line to which persons may cling for safety **2** : something considered vital for survival
life·long \-ˌlȯŋ\ *adj* : continuing through life
life preserver *n* : a buoyant device designed to save a person from drowning
lif·er \ˈlī-fər\ *n* **1** : a person sentenced to life imprisonment **2** : a person who makes a career in the armed forces
life raft *n* : a raft for use by people forced into the water
life·sav·ing \ˈlīf-ˌsā-viŋ\ *n* : the skill or practice of saving or protecting lives esp. of drowning persons — **life·sav·er** \-ˌsā-vər\ *n*
life science *n* : a branch of science (as biology, medicine, and sometimes anthropology or sociology) that deals with living organisms and life processes — usu. used in pl. — **life scientist** *n*
¹life·style \ˈlīf-stī(-ə)l\ *n* : a way of living
²lifestyle *adj* : associated with, reflecting, or promoting an enhanced or more desirable lifestyle
life·time \-ˌtīm\ *n* : the duration of an individual's existence
life·work \-ˈwərk\ *n* : the entire or principal work of one's lifetime; *also* : a work extending over a lifetime
life·world \-ˌwər(-ə)ld\ *n* : the total of an individual's physical surroundings and everyday experiences
LIFO *abbr* last in, first out
¹lift \ˈlift\ *vb* **1** : RAISE, ELEVATE; *also* : RISE, ASCEND **2** : to put an end to : STOP ⟨~ a ban⟩ **3** : to pay off ⟨~ a mortgage⟩ — **lift·er** *n*
²lift *n* **1** : LOAD **2** : the action or an instance of lifting **3** : HELP; *also* : a ride along one's way **4** : RISE, ADVANCE **5** *chiefly Brit* : ELEVATOR **6** : an elevation of the spirits **7** : the upward force that is developed by a moving airfoil and that opposes the pull of gravity
lift·off \-ˌȯf\ *n* : a vertical takeoff (as by a rocket)
lift truck *n* : a small truck for lifting and transporting loads
lig·a·ment \ˈli-gə-mənt\ *n* : a band of tough fibrous tissue that holds bones together or supports an organ in place
li·gate \ˈlī-ˌgāt\ *vb* **li·gat·ed; li·gat·ing** : to tie with a ligature — **li·ga·tion** \lī-ˈgā-shən\ *n*
lig·a·ture \ˈli-gə-ˌchu̇r, -chər\ *n* **1** : something that binds or ties; *also* : a thread used in surgery esp. for tying blood vessels **2** : a printed or written character consisting of two or more letters or characters (as æ) united
¹light \ˈlīt\ *n* **1** : something that makes vision possible : electromagnetic radiation visible to the human eye; *also* : the sensation aroused by stimulation of the visual sense organs **2** : DAYLIGHT **3** : a source of light (as a candle) **4** : ENLIGHTENMENT; *also* : TRUTH **5** : public knowledge ⟨facts brought to ~⟩ **6** : a particular aspect presented to view ⟨saw the matter in a different ~⟩ **7** : WINDOW **8** *pl* : STANDARDS ⟨according to his ~*s*⟩ **9** : CELEBRITY **10** : LIGHTHOUSE, BEACON; *also* : TRAFFIC LIGHT **11** : a flame for lighting something
²light *adj* **1** : having light : BRIGHT **2** : PALE 2 ⟨~ blue⟩ — **light·ness** *n*
³light *vb* **lit** \ˈlit\ *or* **light·ed; light·ing** **1** : to make or become light **2** : to cause to burn : BURN **3** : to conduct with a light **4** : ILLUMINATE
⁴light *adj* **1** : not heavy **2** : not serious ⟨~ reading⟩ **3** : SCANTY ⟨~ rain⟩ **4** : easily disturbed ⟨a ~ sleeper⟩ **5** : GENTLE ⟨a ~ blow⟩ **6** : easily endurable ⟨a ~ cold⟩; *also* : requiring little effort ⟨~ exercise⟩ **7** : SWIFT, NIMBLE **8** : FRIVOLOUS **9** : DIZZY **10** : made with lower calorie content or less of some ingredient than usual **11** : producing goods for direct consumption by the consumer ⟨~ industry⟩ — **light·ly** *adv* — **light·ness** *n*
⁵light *adv* **1** : LIGHTLY **2** : with little baggage ⟨travel ~⟩
⁶light *vb* **lit** \ˈlit\ *or* **light·ed; light·ing** **1** : SETTLE, ALIGHT **2** : to fall unexpectedly **3** : HAPPEN ⟨~*ed* on a solution⟩
light bulb *n* **1** : a lamp in which an electrically heated filament emits light **2** : FLUORESCENT LAMP
light–emitting diode *n* : LED
¹light·en \ˈlī-tᵊn\ *vb* **1** : ILLUMINATE, BRIGHTEN **2** : to give out flashes of lightning

[2]**lighten** *vb* **1** : to relieve of a burden **2** : GLADDEN **3** : to become lighter
lighten up *vb* : to take things less seriously ⟨*lighten up* and relax⟩
[1]**ligh·ter** \ˈlī-tər\ *n* : a barge used esp. in loading or unloading ships
[2]**light·er** \ˈlī-tər\ *n* : one that lights; *esp* : a device for lighting (as a fire or cigarette)
light·face \ˈlīt-ˌfās\ *n* : a type having light thin lines — **light·faced** \-ˌfāst\ *adj*
light–head·ed \ˈlīt-ˌhe-dəd\ *adj* **1** : feeling confused or dizzy **2** : lacking maturity or seriousness
light·heart·ed \-ˌhär-təd\ *adj* : free from worry — **light·heart·ed·ly** *adv* — **light·heart·ed·ness** *n*
light·house \-ˌhau̇s\ *n* : a structure with a powerful light for guiding sailors
light meter *n* : a usu. handheld device for indicating correct photographic exposure
[1]**light·ning** \ˈlīt-niŋ\ *n* : the flashing of light produced by a discharge of atmospheric electricity; *also* : the discharge itself
[2]**lightning** *adj* : extremely fast
lightning bug *n* : FIREFLY
lightning rod *n* : a grounded metallic rod set up on a structure to protect it from lightning
light out *vb* : to leave in a hurry
light·proof \ˈlīt-ˌprüf\ *adj* : impenetrable by light
lights \ˈlīts\ *n pl* : the lungs esp. of a slaughtered animal
light·ship \ˈlīt-ˌship\ *n* : a ship with a powerful light moored at a place dangerous to navigation
light show *n* : a kaleidoscopic display (as of colored lights)
light·some \ˈlīt-səm\ *adj* **1** : free from care **2** : NIMBLE
[1]**light·weight** \ˈlīt-ˌwāt\ *n* : one of less than average weight; *esp* : a boxer weighing not over 135 pounds
[2]**lightweight** *adj* **1** : INCONSEQUENTIAL **2** : of less than average weight
light–year \ˈlīt-ˌyir\ *n* **1** : an astronomical unit of distance equal to the distance that light travels in one year in a vacuum or about 5.88 trillion miles (9.46 trillion kilometers) **2** : an extremely large measure of comparison ⟨saw it ∼*s* ago⟩
lig·nin \ˈlig-nən\ *n* : a substance related to cellulose that occurs in the woody cell walls of plants and in the cementing material between them
lig·nite \ˈlig-ˌnīt\ *n* : brownish black soft coal
[1]**like** \ˈlīk\ *vb* **liked; lik·ing** **1** : ENJOY ⟨∼*s* baseball⟩ **2** : WANT ⟨would ∼ a drink⟩ **3** : CHOOSE ⟨does as she ∼*s*⟩ — **lik·able** *or* **like·able** \ˈlī-kə-bəl\ *adj*
[2]**like** *n* : PREFERENCE
[3]**like** *adj* : SIMILAR ♦ ***Synonyms*** ALIKE, ANALOGOUS, COMPARABLE, PARALLEL, UNIFORM
[4]**like** *prep* **1** : similar or similarly to ⟨seems ∼ a dream⟩ **2** : typical of **3** : comparable to **4** : as though there would be ⟨looks ∼ rain⟩ **5** : such as ⟨a subject ∼ physics⟩
[5]**like** *n* **1** : COUNTERPART **2** : one that is similar to another ⟨we may never see his ∼ again⟩ — **and the like** : ET CETERA
[6]**like** *conj* **1** : AS IF ⟨acted ∼ they were scared⟩ **2** : in the same way that ⟨do it ∼ mom said⟩
-like *adj comb form* : resembling or characteristic of ⟨lady*like*⟩ ⟨life*like*⟩
like·li·hood \ˈlī-klē-ˌhu̇d\ *n* : PROBABILITY
[1]**like·ly** \ˈlī-klē\ *adj* **like·li·er; -est** **1** : very probable **2** : BELIEVABLE **3** : PROMISING ⟨a ∼ place to fish⟩
[2]**likely** *adv* : in all probability
lik·en \ˈlī-kən\ *vb* : COMPARE
like·ness \ˈlīk-nəs\ *n* **1** : COPY, PORTRAIT **2** : SEMBLANCE **3** : RESEMBLANCE
like·wise \-ˌwīz\ *adv* **1** : in like manner **2** : in addition : ALSO
lik·ing \ˈlī-kiŋ\ *n* : favorable regard ⟨took a ∼ to the newcomer⟩; *also* : TASTE
li·lac \ˈlī-lək, -ˌlak, -ˌläk\ *n* [obs. F (now *lilas*), fr. Ar *līlak*, fr. Pers *nīlak* bluish, fr. *nīl* blue, fr. Skt *nīla* dark blue] **1** : a shrub related to the olive that produces large clusters of fragrant grayish pink, purple, or white flowers **2** : a moderate purple color
lil·an·ge·ni \ˌli-lən-ˈge-nē\ *n, pl* **em·a·lan·ge·ni** \ˌe-mə-lən-ˈge-nē\ — see MONEY table
lil·li·pu·tian \ˌli-lə-ˈpyü-shən\ *adj, often cap* **1** : SMALL, MINIATURE **2** : PETTY
lilt \ˈlilt\ *n* **1** : a cheerful lively song or tune **2** : a rhythmical swing or flow
lily \ˈli-lē\ *n, pl* **lil·ies** : any of a genus of tall bulbous herbs with leafy stems and usu. funnel-shaped flowers; *also* : any of various related plants
lily of the valley : a low perennial herb related to the lilies that produces a raceme of fragrant nodding bell-shaped white flowers
li·ma bean \ˈlī-mə-\ *n* : a bushy or tall-growing bean widely cultivated for its flat edible usu. pale green or whitish seeds; *also* : the seed
limb \ˈlim\ *n* **1** : one of the projecting paired appendages (as legs, arms, or wings) used by an animal esp. in moving or grasping **2** : a large branch of a tree : BOUGH — **limb·less** *adj*
[1]**lim·ber** \ˈlim-bər\ *adj* **1** : FLEXIBLE, SUPPLE **2** : LITHE, NIMBLE
[2]**limber** *vb* : to make or become limber
lim·bic \ˈlim-bik\ *adj* : of, relating to, or being a group of structures of the brain (**limbic system**) concerned esp. with emotion and motivation
[1]**lim·bo** \ˈlim-bō\ *n, pl* **limbos** [ME, fr. ML, abl. of *limbus* limbo, fr. L, border] **1** *often cap* : an abode of souls barred from heaven through no fault of their own **2** : a place or state of confinement, oblivion, or uncertainty ⟨a ∼ of forgotten things⟩
[2]**limbo** *n, pl* **limbos** : an acrobatic dance or contest that involves passing under a horizontal pole
Lim·burg·er \ˈlim-ˌbər-gər\ *n* : a pungent semisoft surface-ripened cheese

[1]**lime** \ˈlīm\ *n* : a caustic powdery white solid that consists of calcium and oxygen, is obtained from limestone or shells, and is used in making cement and in fertilizer — **lime** *vb* — **limy** \ˈlī-mē\ *adj*

[2]**lime** *n* : a small yellowish green citrus fruit with juicy acid pulp

lime·ade \ˌlīm-ˈād, ˈlī-ˌmād\ *n* : a beverage of lime juice, sugar, and water

lime·light \ˈlīm-ˌlīt\ *n* **1** : a device in which flame is directed against a cylinder of lime formerly used in the theater to cast a strong white light on the stage **2** : the center of public attention

lim·er·ick \ˈli-mə-rik\ *n* : a light or humorous poem of 5 lines

lime·stone \ˈlīm-ˌstōn\ *n* : a rock that is formed by accumulation of organic remains (as shells), is used in building, and yields lime when burned

[1]**lim·it** \ˈli-mət\ *n* **1** : something that restrains or confines; *also* : the utmost extent **2** : BOUNDARY; *also, pl* : BOUNDS **3** : a prescribed maximum or minimum **4** : a number whose value becomes arbitrarily close to that of a function as its independent variable approaches a given value — **lim·it·less** *adj* — **lim·it·less·ness** *n*

[2]**limit** *vb* **1** : to set limits to **2** : to reduce in quantity or extent — **lim·i·ta·tion** \ˌli-mə-ˈtā-shən\ *n*

lim·it·ed *adj* **1** : confined within limits **2** : offering faster service esp. by making fewer stops ⟨a ~ train⟩

limn \ˈlim\ *vb* **limned; limn·ing** \ˈli-miŋ, ˈlim-niŋ\ **1** : DRAW; *also* : PAINT **2** : DELINEATE **3** : DESCRIBE

limo \ˈli-(ˌ)mō\ *n, pl* **limos** : LIMOUSINE

li·mo·nite \ˈlī-mə-ˌnīt\ *n* : a ferric oxide that is a major ore of iron — **li·mo·nit·ic** \ˌlī-mə-ˈni-tik\ *adj*

lim·ou·sine \ˈli-mə-ˌzēn, ˌli-mə-ˈzēn\ *n* [F] **1** : a large luxurious often chauffeur-driven sedan **2** : a large vehicle for transporting passengers to and from an airport

[1]**limp** \ˈlimp\ *vb* : to walk lamely; *also* : to proceed with difficulty

[2]**limp** *n* : a limping movement or gait

[3]**limp** *adj* **1** : having no defined shape; *also* : not stiff or rigid **2** : lacking in strength or firmness ⟨went ~ from fatigue⟩ — **limp·ly** *adv* — **limp·ness** *n*

lim·pet \ˈlim-pət\ *n* : any of numerous gastropod sea mollusks with a conical shell that clings to rocks or timbers

lim·pid \ˈlim-pəd\ *adj* : CLEAR, TRANSPARENT ⟨~ water⟩

lin *abbr* **1** lineal **2** linear

lin·age \ˈlī-nij\ *n* : the number of lines of written or printed matter

linch·pin \ˈlinch-ˌpin\ *n* : a locking pin inserted crosswise (as through the end of an axle)

lin·den \ˈlin-dən\ *n* : any of a genus of trees with large heart-shaped leaves and clustered yellowish flowers; *also* : the light white wood of a linden

[1]**line** \ˈlīn\ *n* **1** : CORD, ROPE, WIRE; *also* : a length of material used in measuring and leveling **2** : pipes for conveying a fluid ⟨a gas ~⟩ **3** : a horizontal row of written or printed characters; *also* : VERSE **4** : NOTE **5** : the words making up a part in a drama — usu. used in pl. **6** : something distinct, long, and narrow; *also* : ROUTE **7** : a state of agreement **8** : a course of conduct, action, or thought; *also* : OCCUPATION **9** : LIMIT **10** : an arrangement of persons or objects of one kind in an orderly series ⟨waiting in ~⟩ **11** : a transportation system **12** : the football players who are stationed on the line of scrimmage **13** : a group of three players who play together as a unit in hockey **14** : a long narrow mark; *also* : EQUATOR **15** : a geometric element that is the path of a moving point **16** : CONTOUR **17** : a general plan ⟨thinking along these ~*s*⟩ **18** : an indication based on insight or investigation

[2]**line** *vb* **lined; lin·ing** **1** : to mark with a line **2** : to place or form a line along **3** : ALIGN ⟨~ up the sheets of paper⟩

[3]**line** *vb* **lined; lin·ing** : to cover the inner surface of ⟨~ the box with paper⟩

lin·eage \ˈli-nē-ij\ *n* : lineal descent from a common progenitor; *also* : FAMILY

lin·eal \ˈli-nē-əl\ *adj* **1** : LINEAR **2** : consisting of or being in a direct line of ancestry; *also* : HEREDITARY

lin·ea·ment \ˈli-nē-ə-mənt\ *n* : an outline, feature, or contour of a body and esp. of a face — usu. used in pl.

lin·ear \ˈli-nē-ər\ *adj* **1** : of, relating to, resembling, or having a graph that is a line and esp. a straight line : STRAIGHT **2** : composed of simply drawn lines with little attempt at pictorial representation ⟨~ script⟩ **3** : being long and uniformly narrow

line·back·er \ˈlīn-ˌba-kər\ *n* : a defensive football player who lines up just behind the line of scrimmage

line drive *n* : a batted baseball hit in a flatter path than a fly ball

line–item veto *n* : the power of a government executive to veto specific items in an appropriations bill

line·man \ˈlīn-mən\ *n* **1** : a person who sets up or repairs communication or power lines **2** : a player in the line in football

lin·en \ˈli-nən\ *n* **1** : cloth made of flax; *also* : thread or yarn spun from flax **2** : clothing or household articles made of linen cloth or similar fabric

line of scrimmage : an imaginary line in football parallel to the goal lines and tangent to the nose of the ball laid on the ground before a play

[1]**lin·er** \ˈlī-nər\ *n* : a ship or airplane of a regular transportation line

[2]**liner** *n* : one that lines or is used as a lining — **lin·er·less** *adj*

line score *n* : a score of a baseball game giving the runs, hits, and errors made by each team

lines·man \ˈlīnz-mən\ *n* **1** : LINEMAN 1 **2** : an official who assists a referee

line·up \ˈlī-ˌnəp\ *n* **1** : a list of players taking part in a game (as of baseball) **2**

: a line of persons arranged esp. for identification by police
ling \ˈliŋ\ *n* : any of various fishes related to the cod
-ling *n suffix* **1** : one associated with ⟨nest*ling*⟩ **2** : young, small, or minor one ⟨duck*ling*⟩
lin·ger \ˈliŋ-gər\ *vb* : TARRY; *also* : PROCRASTINATE — **lin·ger·er** *n*
lin·ge·rie \ˌlän-jə-ˈrā, ˌlaⁿ-zhə-, -ˈrē\ *n* [F, fr. MF, fr. *linge* linen, fr. L *lineus* made of linen, fr. *linum* flax, linen] : women's intimate apparel
lin·go \ˈliŋ-gō\ *n, pl* **lingoes** : a usu. strange or incomprehensible language
lin·gua fran·ca \ˌliŋ-gwə-ˈfraŋ-kə\ *n, pl* **lingua francas** *or* **lin·guae fran·cae** \-gwē-ˈfraŋ-ˌkē\ [It] **1** *often cap* : a common language consisting of Italian mixed with French, Spanish, Greek, and Arabic that was formerly spoken in Mediterranean ports **2** : a common or commercial tongue among speakers of different languages
lin·gual \ˈliŋ-gwəl\ *adj* : of, relating to, or produced by the tongue
lin·gui·ca \liŋ-ˈgwē-sə\ *n* : a spicy Portuguese sausage
lin·guist \ˈliŋ-gwist\ *n* **1** : a person skilled in languages **2** : a person who specializes in linguistics
lin·guis·tics \liŋ-ˈgwis-tiks\ *n* : the study of human speech including the units, nature, structure, and modification of language — **lin·guis·tic** \-tik\ *adj*
lin·i·ment \ˈli-nə-mənt\ *n* : a liquid preparation rubbed on the skin esp. to relieve pain
lin·ing \ˈlī-niŋ\ *n* : material used to line esp. an inner surface
link \ˈliŋk\ *n* **1** : a connecting structure; *esp* : a single ring of a chain **2** : BOND, TIE **3** : HYPERLINK — **link** *vb* — **link·er** *n*
link·age \ˈliŋ-kij\ *n* **1** : the manner or style of being united **2** : the quality or state of being linked **3** : a system of links
linking verb *n* : a word or expression (as a form of *be, become, feel,* or *seem*) that links a subject with its predicate
links \ˈliŋks\ *n pl* : a golf course
link·up \ˈliŋ-ˌkəp\ *n* **1** : MEETING **2** : something that serves as a linking device or factor
lin·net \ˈli-nət\ *n* : an Old World finch
li·no·leum \lə-ˈnō-lē-əm\ *n* [L *lin*um flax + *oleum* oil] : a floor covering with a canvas back and a surface of hardened linseed oil and a filler
lin·seed \ˈlin-ˌsēd\ *n* : the seeds of flax yielding a yellowish oil (**linseed oil**) used esp. in paints and linoleum
lin·sey–wool·sey \ˌlin-zē-ˈwu̇l-zē\ *n* : a coarse sturdy fabric of wool and linen or cotton
lint \ˈlint\ *n* **1** : linen made into a soft fleecy substance **2** : fine ravels and short fibers of yarn or fabric **3** : the fibers that surround cotton seeds and form the cotton staple
lin·tel \ˈlin-tᵊl\ *n* : a horizontal piece across the top of an opening (as of a door) that carries the weight of the structure above it
linz·er torte \ˈlin-sər-, -zər-\ *n, often cap L* : a baked buttery torte made with chopped almonds, sugar, and spices and filled with jam or preserves
li·on \ˈlī-ən\ *n, pl* **lions** : a large heavily built cat of Africa and southern Asia with a shaggy mane in the male
li·on·ess \ˈlī-ə-nəs\ *n* : a female lion
li·on·heart·ed \ˌlī-ən-ˈhär-təd\ *adj* : COURAGEOUS, BRAVE
li·on·ise *Brit var of* LIONIZE
li·on·ize \ˈlī-ə-ˌnīz\ *vb* **-ized; -iz·ing** : to treat as an object of great interest or importance — **li·on·i·za·tion** \lī-ə-nə-ˈzā-shən\ *n*
lion's den *n* : a place or state of extreme disadvantage, antagonism, or hostility
lip \ˈlip\ *n* **1** : either of the two fleshy folds that surround the mouth; *also* : the margin of the human lip **2** : a part or projection suggesting a lip **3** : the edge of a hollow vessel or cavity — **lipped** \ˈlipt\ *adj*
li·pa \ˈlē-ˌpä, -pə\ *n, pl* **lipa** — see *kuna* at MONEY table
lip·id \ˈli-pəd\ *n* : any of various substances (as fats and waxes) that with proteins and carbohydrates make up the principal structural parts of living cells
lip–lock \ˈlip-ˌläk\ *n* : a long amorous kiss
li·po·pro·tein \ˌlī-pō-ˈprō-ˌtēn, ˌli-\ *n* : a protein that is a complex of protein and lipid
li·po·suc·tion \ˈli-pə-ˌsək-shən, ˈlī-\ *n* : surgical removal of local fat deposits (as in the thighs) esp. for cosmetic purposes
lip·read·ing \ˈlip-ˌrē-diŋ\ *n* : the interpreting of a speaker's words by watching lip and facial movements without hearing the voice
lip service *n* : an avowal of allegiance that is not matched by action
lip·stick \ˈlip-ˌstik\ *n* : a waxy solid colored cosmetic in stick form for the lips — **lip·sticked** \-ˌstikt\ *adj*
liq *abbr* **1** liquid **2** liquor
liq·ue·fy *also* **liq·ui·fy** \ˈli-kwə-ˌfī\ *vb* **-fied; -fy·ing** : to make or become liquid — **liq·ue·fi·er** \-ˌfī(-ə)r\ *n*
li·queur \li-ˈkər\ *n* [F] : a distilled alcoholic liquor flavored with aromatic substances and usu. sweetened
¹liq·uid \ˈli-kwəd\ *adj* **1** : flowing freely like water **2** : neither solid nor gaseous **3** : shining and clear ⟨large ~ eyes⟩ **4** : smooth and musical in tone; *also* : smooth and unconstrained in movement **5** : consisting of or capable of ready conversion into cash ⟨~ assets⟩ — **li·quid·i·ty** \li-ˈkwi-də-tē\ *n*
²liquid *n* : a liquid substance
liq·ui·date \ˈli-kwə-ˌdāt\ *vb* **-dat·ed; -dat·ing** **1** : to settle the accounts and distribute the assets of (as a business) **2** : to pay off ⟨~ a debt⟩ **3** : to get rid of; *esp* : KILL — **liq·ui·da·tion** \ˌli-kwə-ˈdā-shən\ *n*
liquid crystal *n* : an organic liquid that

resembles a crystal in having ordered molecular arrays
liquid crystal display *n* : LCD
liquid measure *n* : a unit or series of units for measuring liquid capacity — see METRIC SYSTEM table, WEIGHT table
li·quor \ˈli-kər\ *n* [ME *licour*, fr. AF, fr. L *liquor*, fr. *liquēre* to be fluid] : a liquid substance; *esp* : a distilled alcoholic beverage
li·quo·rice *chiefly Brit var of* LICORICE
li·ra \ˈlir-ə, ˈlē-rə\ *n* **1** *pl* **li·re** \ˈlē-rā\ : the former basic monetary unit of Italy **2** : the basic monetary unit of Turkey — see MONEY table **3** *pl* **li·ri** \ˈlē-rē\ : the basic monetary unit of Malta until 2008
lisente *pl of* SENTE
lisle \ˈlī(-ə)l\ *n* : a smooth tightly twisted thread usu. made of long-staple cotton
lisp \ˈlisp\ *vb* : to pronounce \s\ and \z\ imperfectly esp. by turning them into \th\ and \th\; *also* : to speak childishly — **lisp** *n* — **lisp·er** *n*
lis·some *also* **lis·som** \ˈli-səm\ *adj* **1** : easily flexed **2** : LITHE 2 ⟨a ~ dancer⟩ **3** : NIMBLE — **lis·some·ly** *adv*
[1]**list** \ˈlist\ *vb, archaic* : PLEASE; *also* : WISH
[2]**list** *vb, archaic* : LISTEN
[3]**list** *n* : a leaning to one side : TILT
[4]**list** *vb* : TILT
[5]**list** *n* **1** : a simple series of words or numerals; *also* : an official roster **2** : CATALOG, CHECKLIST
[6]**list** *vb* : to make a list of; *also* : to include on a list — **list·ee** \li-ˈstē\ *n*
lis·ten \ˈli-sᵊn\ *vb* **1** : to pay attention in order to hear **2** : HEED — **lis·ten·er** *n*
lis·ten·er·ship \ˈli-sᵊn-ər-ˌship\ *n* : the audience for a radio program or recording
list·ing \ˈlis-tiŋ\ *n* **1** : an act or instance of making or including in a list **2** : something that is listed
list·less \ˈlist-ləs\ *adj* : SPIRITLESS, LANGUID ⟨a ~ performance⟩ — **list·less·ly** *adv* — **list·less·ness** *n*
list price *n* : the price of an item as published in a catalog, price list, or advertisement before being discounted
lists \ˈlists\ *n pl* : an arena for combat (as jousting)
[1]**lit** \ˈlit\ *past and past part of* LIGHT
[2]**lit** *abbr* **1** liter **2** literal; literally **3** literary **4** literature
lit·a·ny \ˈli-tə-nē\ *n, pl* **-nies** [ME *letanie*, fr. AF & LL; AF, fr. LL *litania*, fr. LGk *litaneia*, fr. Gk, entreaty, fr. *litanos* suppliant] **1** : a prayer consisting of a series of supplications and responses said alternately by a leader and a group **2** : a lengthy list or series ⟨a ~ of complaints⟩
li·tas \ˈlē-ˌtäs\ *n, pl* **li·tai** \-ˌtī\ *or* **li·tu** \-ˌtü\ : the basic monetary unit of Lithuania from 1923 to 1940 and from 1991 through 2014
litchi *var of* LYCHEE
lite \ˈlīt\ *adj* **1** : [4]LIGHT 10 ⟨~ beer⟩ **2** : lacking in substance or seriousness ⟨~ news⟩
li·ter \ˈlē-tər\ *n* — see METRIC SYSTEM table
lit·er·al \ˈli-tə-rəl\ *adj* **1** : adhering to fact or to the ordinary or usual meaning (as of a word) **2** : UNADORNED; *also* : PROSAIC **3** : VERBATIM
lit·er·al·ism \-rə-ˌli-zəm\ *n* **1** : adherence to the explicit substance (as of an idea) **2** : fidelity to observable fact — **lit·er·al·ist** \-list\ *n* — **lit·er·al·is·tic** \ˌli-tə-rə-ˈlis-tik\ *adj*
lit·er·al·ly \ˈli-tə-rə-lē, ˈli-trə-\ *adv* **1** : ACTUALLY ⟨was ~ soaked⟩ **2** : VIRTUALLY ⟨~ poured out new ideas⟩
lit·er·ary \ˈli-tə-ˌrer-ē\ *adj* **1** : of or relating to literature **2** : WELL-READ
lit·er·ate \ˈli-trət, -tə-rət\ *adj* **1** : EDUCATED; *also* : able to read and write **2** : LITERARY; *also* : POLISHED, LUCID — **lit·er·a·cy** \ˈli-trə-sē, -tə-rə-\ *n* — **literate** *n*
li·te·ra·ti \ˌli-tə-ˈrä-tē\ *n pl* **1** : the educated class **2** : persons interested in literature or the arts
lit·er·a·ture \ˈli-trə-ˌchu̇r, -tə-rə-, -chər\ *n* **1** : the production of written works having excellence of form or expression and dealing with ideas of permanent interest **2** : the written works produced in a particular language, country, or age
lithe \ˈlīth, ˈlīth\ *adj* **1** : SUPPLE **2** : characterized by effortless grace; *also* : athletically slim ⟨a ~ body⟩
lithe·some \ˈlīth-səm, ˈlīth-\ *adj* : LISSOME
lith·i·um \ˈli-thē-əm\ *n* : a light silver-white metallic chemical element
li·thog·ra·phy \li-ˈthä-grə-fē\ *n* : the process of printing from a plane surface (as a smooth stone or metal plate) on which the image to be printed is ink-receptive and the blank area ink-repellent — **lith·o·graph** \ˈli-thə-ˌgraf\ *vb* — **lithograph** *n* — **li·thog·ra·pher** \li-ˈthä-grə-fər, ˈli-thə-ˌgra-fər\ *n* — **lith·o·graph·ic** \ˌli-thə-ˈgra-fik\ *adj* — **lith·o·graph·i·cal·ly** \-fi-k(ə-)lē\ *adv*
li·thol·o·gy \li-ˈthä-lə-jē\ *n, pl* **-gies** : the study of rocks — **lith·o·log·ic** \ˌli-thə-ˈlä-jik\ *or* **lith·o·log·i·cal** \-ji-kəl\ *adj*
lith·o·sphere \ˈli-thə-ˌsfir\ *n* : the outer part of the solid earth
Lith·u·a·nian \ˌli-thə-ˈwā-nē-ən, -thyu̇-\ *n* **1** : a native or inhabitant of Lithuania **2** : the language of the Lithuanians — **Lithuanian** *adj*
lit·i·gant \ˈli-ti-gənt\ *n* : a party to a lawsuit — **litigant** *adj*
lit·i·gate \-ˌgāt\ *vb* **-gat·ed; -gat·ing** : to carry on a legal contest by judicial process; *also* : to contest at law — **lit·i·ga·tion** \ˌli-tə-ˈgā-shən\ *n*
li·ti·gious \lə-ˈti-jəs\ *adj* **1** : CONTENTIOUS **2** : prone to engage in lawsuits **3** : of or relating to litigation — **li·ti·gious·ly** *adv* — **li·ti·gious·ness** *n*
lit·mus \ˈlit-məs\ *n* : a coloring matter from lichens that turns red in acid solutions and blue in alkaline
litmus test *n* : a test in which a single factor (as an attitude) is decisive
Litt D *or* **Lit D** *abbr* [ML *litterarum doctor*] : doctor of letters; doctor of literature
[1]**lit·ter** \ˈli-tər\ *n* [ME, fr. AF *litere*, fr. *lit* bed,

fr. L *lectus*] **1** : a covered and curtained couch with shafts that is used to carry a single passenger; *also* : a device (as a stretcher) for carrying a sick or injured person **2** : material used as bedding for animals; *also* : material used to absorb the urine and feces of animals **3** : the offspring of an animal at one birth **4** : RUBBISH

²**litter** *vb* **1** : to give birth to young **2** : to strew or mark with scattered objects

lit·ter·bug \ˈli-tər-ˌbəg\ *n* : one who litters a public area

¹**lit·tle** \ˈli-tᵊl\ *adj* **lit·tler** \ˈli-tᵊl-ər\ *or* **less** \ˈles\ *or* **less·er** \ˈle-sər\; **lit·tlest** \ˈli-tᵊl-əst\ *or* **least** \ˈlēst\ **1** : not big; *also* : YOUNG **2** : not important **3** : PETTY 3 **4** : not much — **lit·tle·ness** *n*

²**little** *adv* **less** \ˈles\; **least** \ˈlēst\ **1** : SLIGHTLY; *also* : not at all **2** : INFREQUENTLY

³**little** *n* **1** : a small amount or quantity **2** : a short time or distance

Little Dipper *n* : the seven bright stars of Ursa Minor arranged in a form resembling a dipper

little finger *n* : PINKIE

little theater *n* : a small theater for low-cost dramatic productions designed for a limited audience

lit·to·ral \ˈli-tə-rəl; ˌli-tə-ˈral\ *adj* : of, relating to, or growing on or near a shore esp. of the sea — **littoral** *n*

lit·ur·gy \ˈli-tər-jē\ *n, pl* **-gies** : a rite or body of rites prescribed for public worship — **li·tur·gi·cal** \lə-ˈtər-ji-kəl\ *adj* — **li·tur·gi·cal·ly** \-k(ə-)lē\ *adv* — **lit·ur·gist** \ˈli-tər-jist\ *n*

liv·able *also* **live·able** \ˈli-və-bəl\ *adj* **1** : suitable for living in or with ⟨a ~ house⟩ ⟨~ wages⟩ **2** : ENDURABLE — **liv·a·bil·i·ty** \ˌli-və-ˈbi-lə-tē\ *n*

¹**live** \ˈliv\ *vb* **lived**; **liv·ing** **1** : to be or continue alive ⟨*lived* 80 years⟩ **2** : SUBSIST **3** : RESIDE ⟨~*s* next door⟩ **4** : to conduct one's life **5** : to remain in human memory or record ⟨his legacy ~*s*⟩

²**live** \ˈlīv\ *adj* **1** : having life ⟨~ worms⟩ **2** : ACTUAL ⟨a real ~ celebrity⟩ **3** : BURNING, GLOWING ⟨a ~ cigar⟩ **4** : connected to electric power ⟨a ~ wire⟩ **5** : UNEXPLODED ⟨a ~ bomb⟩ **6** : of continuing interest ⟨a ~ issue⟩ **7** : of or involving the actual presence of real people ⟨~ audience⟩; *also* : broadcast directly at the time of production **8** : being in play ⟨a ~ ball⟩

lived–in \ˈlivd-ˌin\ *adj* : of or suggesting long-term human habitation or use

live down *vb* : to live so as to wipe out the memory or effects of

live in *vb* : to live in one's place of employment — used of a servant — **live–in** \ˈliv-ˌin\ *adj*

live·li·hood \ˈlīv-lē-ˌhu̇d\ *n* : means of support or subsistence

live·long \ˈliv-ˌlȯŋ\ *adj* [ME *lef long,* fr. *lef* dear + *long* long] : WHOLE, ENTIRE ⟨the ~ day⟩

live·ly \ˈlīv-lē\ *adj* **live·li·er; -est** **1** : ANIMATED ⟨~ debate⟩ **2** : KEEN, VIVID ⟨~ interest⟩ **3** : showing activity or vigor ⟨a ~ manner⟩ **4** : quick to rebound ⟨a ~ ball⟩ **5** : full of life ♦ ***Synonyms*** VIVACIOUS, SPRIGHTLY, GAY, SPIRITED — **live·li·ness** *n* — **live·ly** *adv*

liv·en \ˈlī-vən\ *vb* : ENLIVEN

live oak *n* : any of several American evergreen oaks; *esp* : one of the southeastern U.S. that is often planted as a shade tree

¹**liv·er** \ˈli-vər\ *n* **1** : a large glandular organ of vertebrates that secretes bile and is a center of metabolic activity **2** : the liver of an animal (as a calf or chicken) eaten as food

²**liver** *n* : one that lives esp. in a specified way ⟨a fast ~⟩

liv·er·ish \ˈli-və-rish\ *adj* **1** : resembling liver esp. in color **2** : BILIOUS **3** : PEEVISH — **liv·er·ish·ness** *adj*

liv·er·mo·ri·um \ˌli-vər-ˈmȯr-ē-əm\ *n* : a short-lived artificially produced radioactive chemical element

liver spots *n pl* : AGE SPOTS

liv·er·wort \ˈli-vər-ˌwərt\ *n* : any of a class of flowerless plants resembling the related mosses

liv·er·wurst \-ˌwərst, -ˌwu̇rst\ *n* [part trans. of G *Leberwurst,* fr. *Leber* liver + *Wurst* sausage] : a sausage consisting chiefly of liver

liv·ery \ˈli-və-rē\ *n, pl* **-er·ies** **1** : a servant's uniform; *also* : distinctive dress **2** : the feeding, care, and stabling of horses for pay; *also* : an establishment (as a stable or business) keeping horses or vehicles for hire — **liv·er·ied** \-rēd\ *adj* — **liv·ery·man** \ˈli-və-rē-mən\ *n*

lives *pl of* LIFE

live·stock \ˈlīv-ˌstäk\ *n* : farm animals kept for use and profit

live·stream \ˈlī-strēm\ *vb* : to stream (a live event) over the Internet — **livestream** *n*

live wire *n* : an alert, active, or aggressive person — **live–wire** *adj*

liv·id \ˈli-vəd\ *adj* [F *livide,* fr. L *lividus,* fr. *livēre* to be blue] **1** : discolored by bruising **2** : ASHEN, PALLID **3** : REDDISH **4** : ENRAGED — **li·vid·ity** \li-ˈvi-də-tē\ *n*

¹**liv·ing** \ˈli-viŋ\ *adj* **1** : having life **2** : NATURAL **3** : full of life and vigor; *also* : VIVID ⟨in ~ color⟩

²**living** *n* **1** : the condition of being alive **2** : LIVELIHOOD **3** : manner of life

living room *n* : a room in a residence used for the common social activities of the occupants

living wage *n* : a wage sufficient to provide an acceptable standard of living

living will *n* : a document requesting that the signer not be kept alive by artificial means unless there is a reasonable expectation of recovery

livre \ˈlēvrᵊ\ *n* : the pound of Lebanon

liz·ard \ˈli-zərd\ *n* : any of a group of 4-legged reptiles with long tapering tails

Lk *abbr* Luke

ll *abbr* lines

lla·ma \ˈlä-mə\ *n* [Sp, fr. Quechua] : any of a genus of wild or domesticated So. American mammals related to the camels but smaller and without a hump

lla·no \ˈlä-nō\ *n, pl* **llanos** : an open grassy plain esp. of Latin America
LLD *abbr* [NL *legum doctor*] doctor of laws
LNG *abbr* liquefied natural gas
[1]**load** \ˈlōd\ *n* **1** : PACK; *also* : CARGO **2** : a mass of weight supported by something **3** : something that burdens the mind or spirits **4** : a large quantity — usu. used in pl. **5** : a standard, expected, or authorized burden
[2]**load** *vb* **1** : to put a load in or on; *also* : to receive a load **2** : to encumber with an obligation or something heavy or disheartening **3** : to increase the weight of by adding something **4** : to supply abundantly **5** : to put a charge in (as a firearm) **6** : to copy or transfer into a computer's memory esp. from an external source
load·ed *adj* **1** *slang* : HIGH 12 **2** : having a large amount of money **3** : equipped with an abundance of options ⟨a ~ car⟩
load·stone *var of* LODESTONE
[1]**loaf** \ˈlōf\ *n, pl* **loaves** \ˈlōvz\ : a shaped or molded mass esp. of bread
[2]**loaf** *vb* : to spend time in idleness : LOUNGE
loaf·er \ˈlō-fər\ *n* **1** : one that loafs : IDLER **2** : a low step-in shoe
loam \ˈlōm, ˈlüm\ *n* : SOIL; *esp* : a loose soil of mixed clay, sand, and silt — **loamy** *adj*
[1]**loan** \ˈlōn\ *n* **1** : money lent at interest; *also* : something lent for the borrower's temporary use **2** : the grant of temporary use
[2]**loan** *vb* : LEND
loan shark *n* : a person who lends money at excessive rates of interest — **loan·shark·ing** \ˈlōn-ˌshär-kiŋ\ *n*
loan·word \ˈlōn-ˌwərd\ *n* : a word taken from another language and at least partly naturalized
loath *also* **loth** \ˈlōth, ˈlōth\ *or* **loathe** \ˈlōth, ˈlōth\ *adj* : RELUCTANT
loathe \ˈlōth\ *vb* **loathed; loath·ing** : to dislike greatly ♦ ***Synonyms*** ABOMINATE, ABHOR, DETEST, HATE
loath·ing \ˈlō-thiŋ\ *n* : extreme disgust
loath·some \ˈlōth-səm, ˈlōth-\ *adj* : exciting loathing : REPULSIVE
lob \ˈläb\ *vb* **lobbed; lob·bing** **1** : to throw, hit, or propel something in a high arc **2** : to direct (as a question) so as to elicit a response — **lob** *n*
[1]**lob·by** \ˈlä-bē\ *n, pl* **lobbies** **1** : a corridor used esp. as a passageway or waiting room **2** : a group of persons engaged in lobbying
[2]**lobby** *vb* **lob·bied; lob·by·ing** : to try to influence public officials and esp. legislators — **lob·by·ist** *n*
lobe \ˈlōb\ *n* : a curved or rounded part esp. of a bodily organ — **lo·bar** \ˈlō-bər\ *adj* — **lobed** \ˈlōbd\ *adj*
lo·be·lia \lō-ˈbēl-yə\ *n* : any of a genus of plants often grown for their clusters of showy flowers
lo·bot·o·my \lō-ˈbä-tə-mē\ *n, pl* **-mies** : surgical severance of certain nerve fibers in the brain used esp. formerly to relieve some mental disorders
lob·ster \ˈläb-stər\ *n* [ME, fr. OE *loppestre*, fr. *loppe* spider] : any of a family of edible marine crustaceans with two large pincerlike claws and four other pairs of legs; *also* : SPINY LOBSTER
[1]**lo·cal** \ˈlō-kəl\ *adj* **1** : of, relating to, or occupying a particular place **2** : serving a particular limited district; *also* : making all stops ⟨a ~ train⟩ **3** : affecting a small part of the body ⟨a ~ infection⟩ — **lo·cal·ly** *adv*
[2]**local** *n* : one that is local
local area network *n* : a network of personal computers in a small area (as an office)
lo·cale \lō-ˈkal\ *n* : a place that is the setting for a particular event
lo·cal·ise *Brit var of* LOCALIZE
lo·cal·i·ty \lō-ˈka-lə-tē\ *n, pl* **-ties** : a particular spot, situation, or location
lo·cal·ize \ˈlō-kə-ˌlīz\ *vb* **-ized; -iz·ing** : to fix in or confine to a definite place or locality — **lo·cal·i·za·tion** \ˌlō-kə-lə-ˈzā-shən\ *n*
lo·cate \ˈlō-ˌkāt, lō-ˈkāt\ *vb* **lo·cat·ed; lo·cat·ing** **1** : STATION, SETTLE **2** : to determine the site of **3** : to find or fix the place of in a sequence
lo·ca·tion \lō-ˈkā-shən\ *n* **1** : SITUATION, PLACE **2** : the process of locating **3** : a place outside a studio where a motion picture is filmed
lo·ca·vore \ˈlō-kə-ˌvȯr\ *n* [*local* + *-vore* (as in *carnivore*)] : one who eats foods grown locally whenever possible
loc cit *abbr* [L *loco citato*] in the place cited
loch \ˈläk, ˈläk\ *n, Scot* : LAKE; *also* : a bay or arm of the sea esp. when nearly landlocked
[1]**lock** \ˈläk\ *n* : a tuft, strand, or ringlet of hair; *also* : a cohering bunch (as of wool or flax)
[2]**lock** *n* **1** : a fastening in which a bolt is operated **2** : the mechanism of a firearm by which the charge is exploded **3** : an enclosure (as in a canal) used in raising or lowering boats from level to level **4** : AIR LOCK **5** : a wrestling hold
[3]**lock** *vb* **1** : to fasten the lock of; *also* : to make fast with a lock **2** : to confine or exclude by means of a lock **3** : INTERLOCK **4** : to make or become motionless by the interlocking of parts
lock·down \ˈläk-ˌdau̇n\ *n* **1** : the confinement of prisoners to their cells as a security measure **2 a** : an emergency measure in which people are temporarily prevented from entering or leaving a restricted area during a threat of danger **b** : a temporary condition imposed by government authorities (as during the outbreak of an epidemic disease) in which people are required to stay in their homes and refrain from or limit activities outside the home (such as dining out)
lock·er \ˈlä-kər\ *n* **1** : a drawer, cupboard, or compartment for individual storage use **2** : an insulated compartment for storing frozen food

lock·et \ˈlä-kət\ *n* : a small usu. metal case for a memento worn suspended from a chain or necklace

lock·jaw \ˈläk-ˌjȯ\ *n* : a symptom of tetanus marked by spasms of the jaw muscles and inability to open the jaws; *also* : TETANUS

lock·nut \-ˌnət\ *n* **1** : a nut screwed tight on another to prevent it from slacking back **2** : a nut designed to lock itself when screwed tight

lock·out \-ˌau̇t\ *n* : the suspension of work by an employer during a labor dispute in order to make employees accept the terms being offered

lock·smith \-ˌsmith\ *n* : one who makes or repairs locks

lock·step \-ˌstep\ *n* : a mode of marching in step by a body of persons moving in a very close single file

lock·up \-ˌəp\ *n* : JAIL

lo·co \ˈlō-kō\ *adj* [Sp] *slang* : CRAZY, FRENZIED

lo·co·mo·tion \ˌlō-kə-ˈmō-shən\ *n* **1** : the act or power of moving from place to place **2** : TRAVEL

[1]**lo·co·mo·tive** \ˌlō-kə-ˈmō-tiv\ *adj* : of or relating to locomotion or a locomotive

[2]**locomotive** *n* : a self-propelled vehicle used to move railroad cars

lo·co·mo·tor \ˌlō-kə-ˈmō-tər\ *adj* : of or relating to locomotion or organs used in locomotion

lo·co·weed \ˈlō-kō-ˌwēd\ *n* : any of several leguminous plants of western No. America that are poisonous to livestock

lo·cus \ˈlō-kəs\ *n, pl* **lo·ci** \ˈlō-ˌsī\ [L] **1** : PLACE, LOCALITY **2** : the set of all points whose location is determined by stated conditions

lo·cust \ˈlō-kəst\ *n* **1** : a usu. destructive migratory grasshopper **2** : CICADA **3** : any of various leguminous trees; *also* : the wood of a locust

lo·cu·tion \lō-ˈkyü-shən\ *n* : a particular form of expression; *also* : PHRASEOLOGY

lode \ˈlōd\ *n* : an ore deposit

lode·stone \-ˌstōn\ *n* : an iron-containing rock with magnetic properties

[1]**lodge** \ˈläj\ *vb* **lodged; lodg·ing** **1** : to provide quarters for; *also* : to settle in a place **2** : CONTAIN **3** : to come to a rest and remain ⟨*lodged* in his throat⟩ **4** : to deposit for safekeeping **5** : to vest (as authority) in an agent **6** : FILE ⟨~ a complaint⟩

[2]**lodge** *n* **1** : a house set apart for residence in a special season or by an employee on an estate; *also* : INN **2** : a den or lair esp. of gregarious animals **3** : the meeting place of a branch of a fraternal organization; *also* : the members of such a branch

lodg·er \ˈlä-jər\ *n* : a person who occupies a rented room in another's house

lodg·ing \ˈlä-jiŋ\ *n* **1** : DWELLING **2** : a room or suite of rooms in another's house rented as a dwelling place — usu. used in pl.

lodg·ment *or* **lodge·ment** \ˈläj-mənt\ *n* **1** : a lodging place **2** : the act or manner of lodging **3** : DEPOSIT

loess \ˈles, ˈləs\ *n* : a usu. yellowish brown loamy deposit believed to be chiefly deposited by the wind

lo–fi \ˈlō-ˌfī\ *n* : audio production of rough or unpolished sound quality — **lo–fi** *adj*

[1]**loft** \ˈlȯft\ *n* [ME, fr. OE, air, sky, fr. ON *lopt*] **1** : ATTIC **2** : GALLERY ⟨organ ~⟩ **3** : an upper floor (as in a warehouse or barn) esp. when not partitioned **4** : the thickness of a fabric or insulated material (as of a sleeping bag)

[2]**loft** *vb* : to strike or throw a ball so that it rises high in the air

lofty \ˈlȯf-tē\ *adj* **loft·i·er; -est** **1** : NOBLE; *also* : SUPERIOR ⟨~ ideals⟩ **2** : extremely proud **3** : HIGH, TALL — **loft·i·ly** \ˈlȯf-tə-lē\ *adv* — **loft·i·ness** \-tē-nəs\ *n*

[1]**log** \ˈlȯg, ˈläg\ *n* **1** : a bulky piece of a cut or fallen tree **2** : an apparatus for measuring a ship's speed **3** : the daily record of a ship's progress; *also* : a regularly kept record of performance or events ⟨a pilot's ~⟩ ⟨a runner's ~⟩

[2]**log** *vb* **logged; log·ging** **1** : to cut (trees) for lumber; *also* : to clear (land) of trees in lumbering **2** : to enter in a log **3** : to sail a ship or fly an airplane for (an indicated distance or period of time) **4** : to have (an indicated record) to one's credit : ACHIEVE — **log·ger** \ˈlȯ-gər, ˈlä-\ *n*

[3]**log** *n* : LOGARITHM

lo·gan·ber·ry \ˈlō-gən-ˌber-ē\ *n* : a red-fruited upright-growing dewberry; *also* : its berry

log·a·rithm \ˈlȯ-gə-ˌri-t͟həm, ˈlä-\ *n* : the exponent that indicates the power to which a base is raised to produce a given number ⟨the ~ of 100 to base 10 is 2 since $10^2 = 100$⟩ — **log·a·rith·mic** \ˌlȯ-gə-ˈrit͟h-mik, ˌlä-\ *adj*

loge \ˈlōzh\ *n* **1** : a small compartment; *also* : a box in a theater **2** : a small partitioned area; *also* : the forward section of a theater mezzanine **3** : a raised level of seats in a stadium

log·ger·head \ˈlȯ-gər-ˌhed, ˈlä-\ *n* : a large sea turtle of subtropical and temperate waters — **at loggerheads** : in a state of quarrelsome disagreement

log·gia \ˈlō-jē-ə, ˈlȯ-jä\ *n, pl* **loggias** \ˈlō-jē-əz, ˈlȯ-jäz\ : a roofed open gallery

log·ic \ˈlä-jik\ *n* **1** : a science that deals with the rules and tests of sound thinking and proof by reasoning **2** : sound reasoning **3** : the arrangement of circuit elements for arithmetical computation in a computer — **log·i·cal** \-ji-kəl\ *adj* — **log·i·cal·ly** \-jik(ə-)lē\ *adv* — **lo·gi·cian** \lō-ˈji-shən\ *n*

log in *vb* : LOG ON

lo·gis·tics \lō-ˈjis-tiks\ *n sing or pl* : the procurement, maintenance, and transportation of matériel, facilities, and personnel — **lo·gis·tic** \-tik\ *or* **lo·gis·ti·cal** \-ti-kəl\ *adj*

log·jam \ˈlȯg-ˌjam, ˈläg-\ *n* **1** : a deadlocked jumble of logs in a watercourse **2** : DEADLOCK — **logjam** *vb*

logo \ˈlō-gō\ *n, pl* **log·os** \-gōz\ : an identifying symbol (as for advertising)

log off *vb* : to end the connection of a computer to a network or system
log on *vb* : to start the connection of a computer to a network or system
logo·type \ˈlȯ-gə-ˌtīp, ˈlä-\ *n* : LOGO
log out *vb* : LOG OFF
log·roll·ing \-ˌrō-liŋ\ *n* : the trading of votes by legislators to secure favorable action on projects of individual interest
lo·gy \ˈlō-gē\ *also* **log·gy** \ˈlȯ-gē, ˈlä-\ *adj* **lo·gi·er; -est** : deficient in vitality : SLUGGISH
loin \ˈlȯin\ *n* [ME *loyne,* fr. AF *loigne,* fr. VL **lumbea,* fr. L *lumbus*] **1** : the part of the body on each side of the spinal column and between the hip and the lower ribs; *also* : a cut of meat from this part of an animal **2** *pl* : the pubic region; *also* : the organs of reproduction
loin·cloth \-ˌklȯth\ *n* : a cloth worn about the loins often as the sole article of clothing in warm climates
loi·ter \ˈlȯi-tər\ *vb* **1** : LINGER **2** : to hang around idly ♦ ***Synonyms*** DAWDLE, DALLY, PROCRASTINATE, LAG, TARRY — **loi·ter·er** *n*
loll \ˈläl\ *vb* **1** : DROOP, DANGLE **2** : LOUNGE ⟨~*ing* by the pool⟩
lol·la·pa·loo·za \ˌlä-lə-pə-ˈlü-zə\ *n* : something extraordinarily impressive or outstanding
lol·li·pop *or* **lol·ly·pop** \ˈlä-li-ˌpäp\ *n* : a lump of hard candy on a stick
lol·ly·gag \ˈlä-lē-ˌgag\ *vb* **-gagged; -gag·ging** : DAWDLE
Lond *abbr* London
lone \ˈlōn\ *adj* **1** : SOLITARY ⟨a ~ sentinel⟩ **2** : SOLE, ONLY ⟨the ~ theater in town⟩ **3** : ISOLATED ⟨a ~ tree⟩
lone·ly \ˈlōn-lē\ *adj* **lone·li·er; -est** **1** : being without company **2** : UNFREQUENTED ⟨a ~ spot⟩ **3** : LONESOME — **lone·li·ness** *n*
lon·er \ˈlō-nər\ *n* : one that avoids others
lone·some \ˈlōn-səm\ *adj* **1** : sad from lack of companionship **2** : REMOTE; *also* : SOLITARY ⟨a ~ road⟩ — **lone·some·ly** *adv* — **lone·some·ness** *n*
¹**long** \ˈlȯŋ\ *adj* **lon·ger** \ˈlȯŋ-gər\; **lon·gest** \ˈlȯŋ-gəst\ **1** : extending for a considerable distance ⟨a ~ corridor⟩; *also* : TALL, ELONGATED ⟨~ legs⟩ **2** : having a specified length **3** : extending over a considerable time; *also* : TEDIOUS ⟨~ lectures⟩ **4** : containing many items in a series ⟨a ~ list⟩ **5** : being a syllable or speech sound of relatively great duration **6** : extending far into the future **7** : well furnished with something — used with *on* ⟨~ on talent⟩
²**long** *adv* : for or during a long time
³**long** *n* : a long period of time
⁴**long** *vb* **longed; long·ing** \ˈlȯŋ-iŋ\ : to feel a strong desire or wish ♦ ***Synonyms*** YEARN, HANKER, PINE, HUNGER, THIRST
⁵**long** *abbr* longitude
long·boat \ˈlȯŋ-ˌbōt\ *n* : a large boat usu. carried by a merchant sailing ship
long·bow \-ˌbō\ *n* : a wooden bow drawn by hand and used esp. by medieval English archers
long COVID *also* **long COVID–19** *or* **long–haul COVID** *or* **long–haul COVID–19** *n* : a condition that is marked by the presence of symptoms which persist for an extended period of time following a person's initial recovery from COVID-19 infection
lon·gev·i·ty \län-ˈje-və-tē\ *n* [LL *longaevitas,* fr. L *longaevus* long-lived, fr. *longus* long + *aevum* age] : a long duration of individual life; *also* : length of life
long·hair \ˈlȯŋ-ˌher\ *n* **1** : a lover of classical music **2** : HIPPIE **3** : a domestic cat having long outer fur — **long–haired** \-ˌherd\ *or* **long·hair** *adj*
long·hand \-ˌhand\ *n* : HANDWRITING
long haul *n* **1** : a long distance **2** : a long period of time — **long–haul** *adj*
long·horn \-ˌhȯrn\ *n* : any of the cattle with long horns formerly common in the southwestern U.S.
long hundredweight *n, Brit* — see WEIGHT table
long·ing \ˈlȯŋ-iŋ\ *n* : a strong desire esp. for something unattainable — **long·ing·ly** *adv*
lon·gi·tude \ˈlän-jə-ˌtüd, -ˌtyüd\ *n* : angular distance expressed usu. in degrees east or west from the prime meridian through Greenwich, England
lon·gi·tu·di·nal \ˌlän-jə-ˈtü-dᵊn-əl, -ˈtyüd-\ *adj* **1** : extending lengthwise **2** : of or relating to length — **lon·gi·tu·di·nal·ly** *adv*
long–range \ˈlȯŋ-ˈrānj\ *adj* **1** : relating to or fit for long distances **2** : involving a long period of time
long·shore·man \ˈlȯŋ-ˌshȯr-mən\ *n* : a laborer at a wharf who loads and unloads cargo
long–suf·fer·ing \-ˈsə-friŋ, -fə-riŋ\ *adj* : patiently enduring lasting offense or hardship
long–term \ˈlȯŋ-ˈtərm\ *adj* **1** : extending over or involving a long period of time **2** : constituting a financial obligation based on a term usu. of more than 10 years ⟨~ bonds⟩
long·time \ˈlȯŋ-ˈtīm\ *adj* : of long duration ⟨~ friends⟩
long ton *n* — see WEIGHT table
lon·gueur \lōⁿ-ˈgœr\ *n, pl* **longueurs** *same or* -ˈgœrz\ [F, lit., length] : a dull tedious portion (as of a book)
long–wind·ed \ˌlȯŋ-ˈwin-dəd\ *adj* : tediously long in speaking or writing
loo·fah \ˈlü-fə\ *n* : a sponge consisting of the fibrous skeleton of a gourd
¹**look** \ˈlu̇k\ *vb* **1** : to exercise the power of vision : SEE ⟨~ what I won⟩ **2** : EXPECT **3** : to have an appearance that befits ⟨~*s* the part⟩ **4** : SEEM ⟨~*s* thin⟩ **5** : to direct one's attention : HEED ⟨~ at the sign⟩ **6** : POINT, FACE ⟨~*s* east⟩ **7** : to show a tendency — **look after** : to take care of — **look at** **1** : CONSIDER ⟨*looking at* all possibilities⟩ **2** : CONFRONT, FACE ⟨*looking at* stiff fines⟩ — **look for** : EXPECT — **look forward** : to anticipate with pleasure ⟨*look forward* to summer⟩

[2]**look** *n* **1** : the action of looking : GLANCE **2** : EXPRESSION; *also* : physical appearance **3** : ASPECT
look down *vb* : to regard with contempt — used with *on* or *upon*
looking glass *n* : MIRROR
look·out \ˈlu̇k-ˌau̇t\ *n* **1** : a person assigned to watch (as on a ship) **2** : a careful watch **3** : VIEW **4** : a matter of concern
look up *vb* **1** : IMPROVE ⟨business is *looking up*⟩ **2** : to search for in or as if in a reference work **3** : to seek out esp. for a brief visit
[1]**loom** \ˈlüm\ *n* : a frame or machine for weaving together threads or yarns into cloth
[2]**loom** *vb* **1** : to come into sight in an unnaturally large, indistinct, or distorted form **2** : to appear in an impressively exaggerated form
loon \ˈlün\ *n* : any of several web-footed black-and-white fish-eating diving birds
loo·ny *or* **loo·ney** \ˈlü-nē\ *adj* **loo·ni·er; -est** : CRAZY, FOOLISH
loony bin *n, often offensive* : a psychiatric hospital
loop \ˈlüp\ *n* **1** : a fold or doubling of a line through which another line or hook can be passed; *also* : a loop-shaped figure or course ⟨a ~ in a river⟩ **2** : a circular airplane maneuver executed in the vertical plane **3** : a continuously repeated segment of film, music, or sound — **loop** *vb*
loop·er \ˈlü-pər\ *n* : any of numerous rather small hairless moth caterpillars that move with a looping motion
loop·hole \ˈlüp-ˌhōl\ *n* **1** : a small opening in a wall through which firearms may be discharged **2** : a means of escape; *esp* : an ambiguity or omission that allows one to evade the intent of a law or contract
loopy \ˈlü-pē\ *adj* **loop·i·er; -est** **1** : having loops **2** : CRAZY, BIZARRE — **loop·i·ly** \-pə-lē\ *adv* — **loop·i·ness** \-pē-nəs\ *n*
[1]**loose** \ˈlüs\ *adj* **loos·er; loos·est** **1** : not rigidly fastened **2** : free from restraint or obligation **3** : not dense or compact in structure **4** : not chaste : LEWD **5** : SLACK **6** : not precise or exact — **loose·ly** *adv* — **loose·ness** *n*
[2]**loose** *vb* **loosed; loos·ing** **1** : RELEASE **2** : UNTIE **3** : DETACH **4** : DISCHARGE **5** : RELAX, SLACKEN
[3]**loose** *adv* : LOOSELY
loos·en \ˈlü-sᵊn\ *vb* **1** : FREE **2** : to make or become loose **3** : to relax the severity of ⟨~ rules⟩
loot \ˈlüt\ *n* [Hindi & Urdu *lūṭ;* akin to Skt *luṇṭati* he plunders] : goods taken in war or by robbery : PLUNDER — **loot** *vb* — **loot·er** *n*
[1]**lop** \ˈläp\ *vb* **lopped; lop·ping** : to cut branches or twigs from : TRIM; *also* : to cut off
[2]**lop** *vb* **lopped; lop·ping** : to hang downward; *also* : to flop or sway loosely
lope \ˈlōp\ *n* : an easy bounding gait — **lope** *vb*
lop·sid·ed \ˈläp-ˈsī-dəd\ *adj* **1** : leaning to one side **2** : UNSYMMETRICAL — **lop·sid·ed·ly** *adv* — **lop·sid·ed·ness** *n*
lo·qua·cious \lō-ˈkwā-shəs\ *adj* : excessively talkative — **lo·quac·i·ty** \-ˈkwa-sə-tē\ *n*
[1]**lord** \ˈlȯrd\ *n* [ME *loverd, lord,* fr. OE *hlāford,* fr. *hlāf* loaf + *weard* keeper] **1** : one having power and authority over others; *esp* : a person from whom a feudal fee or estate is held **2** *cap* : GOD 1 **3** : a man of rank or high position; *esp* : a British nobleman **4** *pl, cap* : the upper house of the British parliament **5** : a person of great power in some field
[2]**lord** *vb* : to act like a lord; *esp* : to put on airs — usu. used with *it*
lord chancellor *n, pl* **lords chancellor** : a British officer of state who presides over the House of Lords, serves as head of the British judiciary, and is usu. a leading member of the cabinet
lord·ly \-lē\ *adj* **lord·li·er; -est** **1** : DIGNIFIED; *also* : NOBLE **2** : HAUGHTY
lord·ship \-ˌship\ *n* **1** : the rank or dignity of a lord — used as a title **2** : the authority or territory of a lord
Lord's Supper *n* : COMMUNION
lore \ˈlȯr\ *n* : KNOWLEDGE; *esp* : traditional knowledge or belief
lor·gnette \lȯrn-ˈyet\ *n* [F, fr. *lorgner* to take a sidelong look at, fr. MF, fr. *lorgne* squinting] : a pair of eyeglasses or opera glasses with a handle
lorn \ˈlȯrn\ *adj* : FORSAKEN, DESOLATE
lor·ry \ˈlȯr-ē\ *n, pl* **lorries** *chiefly Brit* : MOTORTRUCK
lose \ˈlüz\ *vb* **lost** \ˈlȯst\; **los·ing** \ˈlü-ziŋ\ **1** : DESTROY **2** : to miss from a customary place : MISLAY **3** : to suffer deprivation of **4** : to fail to use : WASTE ⟨no time to ~⟩ **5** : to fail to win or obtain ⟨~ the game⟩ **6** : to fail to keep or maintain ⟨~ his balance⟩ **7** : to wander from ⟨~ her way⟩ **8** : to get rid of ⟨should ~ the beard⟩ — **los·er** *n* — **lose it** **1** : to go crazy **2** : to fail to keep one's composure
loss \ˈlȯs\ *n* **1** : RUIN **2** : the harm resulting from losing **3** : something that is lost **4** *pl* : killed, wounded, or captured soldiers **5** : failure to win **6** : an amount by which the cost exceeds the selling price **7** : decrease in amount or degree
loss leader *n* : an article sold at a loss in order to draw customers
lost \ˈlȯst\ *adj* **1** : not used, won, or claimed **2** : no longer possessed or known **3** : ruined or destroyed physically or morally **4** : DENIED; *also* : HARDENED **5** : unable to find the way; *also* : HELPLESS **6** : ABSORBED, RAPT **7** : not appreciated or understood ⟨his jokes were ~ on me⟩ **8** : made obscure : OVERLOOKED ⟨~ in translation⟩ **9** : FUTILE ⟨a ~ cause⟩
lot \ˈlät\ *n* **1** : an object used in deciding something by chance; *also* : the use of lots to decide something **2** : SHARE, PORTION; *also* : FORTUNE, FATE **3** : a plot of land **4** : a group of individuals : SET **5** : a considerable quantity ⟨a ~ of trouble⟩

loth *var of* LOATH
lo·ti \ˈlō-tē\ *n, pl* **ma·lo·ti** \mə-ˈlō-tē\ — see MONEY table
lo·tion \ˈlō-shən\ *n* : a liquid preparation for cosmetic and external medicinal use
lot·tery \ˈlä-tə-rē\ *n, pl* **-ter·ies** **1** : a drawing of lots in which prizes are given to the winning names or numbers **2** : a matter determined by chance
lo·tus \ˈlō-təs\ *n* **1** : a fruit held in Greek legend to cause dreamy contentment and forgetfulness **2** : any of various water lilies represented esp. in ancient Egyptian and Hindu art **3** : any of several leguminous forage plants
loud \ˈlau̇d\ *adj* **1** : marked by intensity or volume of sound **2** : CLAMOROUS, NOISY **3** : obtrusive or offensive in color or pattern ⟨a ~ tie⟩ — **loud** *adv* — **loud·ly** *adv* — **loud·ness** *n*
loud·mouthed \-ˌmau̇tht, -ˌmau̇t͟hd\ *adj* : given to loud offensive talk
loud·speak·er \-ˌspē-kər\ *n* : a device that changes electrical signals into sound
¹lounge \ˈlau̇nj\ *vb* **lounged; loung·ing** : to act or move lazily or listlessly
²lounge *n* **1** : a room with comfortable furniture; *also* : a room (as in a theater) with lounging, smoking, and toilet facilities **2** : a long couch
lour, loury *var of* LOWER, LOWERY
louse \ˈlau̇s\ *n, pl* **lice** \ˈlīs\ **1** : any of various small wingless usu. flattened insects parasitic on warm-blooded animals **2** : a plant pest (as an aphid) **3** *pl* **lous·es** \ˈlau̇-səz\ : a contemptible person
lousy \ˈlau̇-zē\ *adj* **lous·i·er; -est** **1** : infested with lice **2** : POOR, INFERIOR **3** : somewhat ill **4** : amply supplied ⟨~ with money⟩ — **lous·i·ly** \-zə-lē\ *adv* — **lous·i·ness** \-zē-nəs\ *n*
lout \ˈlau̇t\ *n* : a stupid awkward fellow — **lout·ish** *adj* — **lout·ish·ly** *adv*
lou·ver *or* **lou·vre** \ˈlü-vər\ *n* **1** : an opening having parallel slanted slats to allow flow of air but to exclude rain or sun or to provide privacy; *also* : a slat in such an opening **2** : a device with movable slats for controlling the flow of air or light
¹love \ˈləv\ *n* **1** : strong affection **2** : warm attachment ⟨~ of the sea⟩ **3** : attraction based on sexual desire **4** : a beloved person **5** : unselfish loyal and benevolent concern for others **6** : a score of zero in tennis — **love·less** *adj*
²love *vb* **loved; lov·ing** **1** : CHERISH **2** : to feel a passion, devotion, or tenderness for **3** : CARESS **4** : to take pleasure in ⟨~*s* to play bridge⟩ — **lov·able** *also* **love·able** \ˈlə-və-bəl\ *adj* — **lov·er** *n*
love·bird \ˈləv-ˌbərd\ *n* **1** : any of various small usu. gray or green parrots that seem to show caring behavior for their mates **2** **lovebirds** *pl* : people who are lovers
love·lorn \-ˌlȯrn\ *adj* : deprived of love or of a lover
love·ly \ˈləv-lē\ *adj* **love·li·er; -est** : BEAUTIFUL — **love·li·ly** \ˈləv-lə-lē\ *adv* — **love·li·ness** *n* — **lovely** *adv*
love·mak·ing \-ˌmā-kiŋ\ *n* **1** : COURTSHIP **2** : sexual activity; *esp* : COPULATION
love·sick \-ˌsik\ *adj* **1** : YEARNING ⟨a ~ suitor⟩ **2** : expressing a lover's longing — **love·sick·ness** *n*
lov·ing \ˈlə-viŋ\ *adj* **1** : AFFECTIONATE **2** : PAINSTAKING — **lov·ing·ly** *adv*
¹low \ˈlō\ *vb* : MOO
²low *n* : MOO
³low *adj* **low·er** \ˈlō-ər\; **low·est** \ˈlō-əst\ **1** : not high or tall ⟨~ wall⟩; *also* : DÉCOLLETÉ **2** : situated or passing below the normal level or surface ⟨~ ground⟩; *also* : marking a nadir **3** : not loud ⟨~ voice⟩ **4** : being near the equator **5** : humble in status **6** : WEAK; *also* : DEPRESSED **7** : STRICKEN, PROSTRATE **8** : less than usual in number, amount, or value; *also* : of lesser degree than average **9** : falling short of a standard **10** : UNFAVORABLE — **low** *adv* — **low·ness** *n*
⁴low *n* **1** : something that is low **2** : a region of low barometric pressure **3** : the arrangement of gears in an automobile transmission that gives the slowest speed and greatest power
low·ball \ˈlō-ˌbȯl\ *vb* : to give a deceptively low price, cost estimate, or offer to
low beam *n* : a vehicle headlight beam with short-range focus
low blow *n* : an unprincipled attack
low·brow \ˈlō-ˌbrau̇\ *adj* : having little taste or intellectual interest ⟨~ humor⟩ — **lowbrow** *n*
low–density lipoprotein *n* : LDL
low·down \-ˌdau̇n\ *n* : pertinent and esp. guarded information
low–down \-ˌdau̇n\ *adj* **1** : MEAN, CONTEMPTIBLE **2** : deeply emotional
low–end \-ˌend\ *adj* : of, relating to, or being the lowest-priced merchandise in a manufacturer's line
¹low·er *also* **lour** \ˈlau̇(-ə)r\ *vb* **1** : FROWN **2** : to become dark, gloomy, and threatening — **lower** *also* **lour** *n*
²low·er \ˈlō-ər\ *adj* **1** : relatively low (as in rank) **2** : SOUTHERN ⟨the ~ states⟩ **3** : less advanced in the scale of evolutionary development ⟨~ animals⟩ **4** : situated beneath the earth's surface **5** : constituting the popular and more representative branch of a bicameral legislative body
³low·er \ˈlō-ər\ *vb* **1** : DROP; *also* : DIMINISH **2** : to let descend by its own weight; *also* : to reduce the height of **3** : to reduce in value, number, or amount **4** : DEGRADE; *also* : HUMBLE
low·er·case \ˌlō-ər-ˈkās\ *adj* : being a letter that belongs to or conforms to the series a, b, c, etc., rather than A, B, C, etc. — **lowercase** *n*
lower class *n* : a social class occupying a position below the middle class and having the lowest status in a society — **lower–class** \-ˈklas\ *adj*
low·er·most \ˈlō-ər-ˌmōst\ *adj* : LOWEST
low·ery *also* **loury** \ˈlau̇-(ə-)rē\ *adj* : GLOOMY, LOWERING ⟨a ~ sky⟩

lowest common denominator *n* **1** : LEAST COMMON DENOMINATOR **2** : something designed to appeal to a low-brow audience; *also* : such an audience
lowest common multiple *n* : LEAST COMMON MULTIPLE
low–key \ˈlō-ˈkē\ *also* **low–keyed** \-ˈkēd\ *adj* : of low intensity : RESTRAINED
low·land \ˈlō-lənd, -ˌland\ *n* : low and usu. level country
low–lev·el \ˈlō-ˈle-vəl\ *adj* **1** : being of low importance or rank **2** : being or relating to nuclear waste of low concentration
low·life \ˈlō-ˌlīf\ *n, pl* **low·lifes** \-ˌlīfs\ *also* **low·lives** \-ˌlīvz\ : a person of low social status or moral character
low·ly \ˈlō-lē\ *adj* **low·li·er; -est** **1** : HUMBLE, MEEK **2** : ranking low in some hierarchy — **low·li·ness** *n*
low–rise \ˈlō-ˈrīz\ *adj* **1** : having few stories and not equipped with elevators ⟨a ~ building⟩ **2** : of, relating to, or characterized by low-rise buildings
low–slung \ˈlō-ˌsləŋ\ *adj* : relatively low to the ground or floor ⟨a ~ building⟩ ⟨~ pants⟩
low–tech \ˈlō-ˈtek\ *adj* : technologically simple or unsophisticated
¹lox \ˈläks\ *n* : liquid oxygen
²lox *n, pl* **lox** *or* **lox·es** : salmon cured in brine and sometimes smoked
loy·al \ˈlȯi(-ə)l\ *adj* [MF, fr. OF *leial, leel,* fr. L *legalis* legal] **1** : faithful in allegiance to one's government **2** : faithful esp. to a cause or ideal : CONSTANT — **loy·al·ly** \ˈlȯi-ə-lē\ *adv* — **loy·al·ty** \ˈlȯi(-ə)l-tē\ *n*
loy·al·ist \ˈlȯi-ə-list\ *n* : one who is or remains loyal to a political party, government, or sovereign
loz·enge \ˈlä-zənj\ *n* **1** : a diamond-shaped figure **2** : a small flat often medicated candy
LP *abbr* low pressure
LPG *abbr* liquefied petroleum gas
LPGA *abbr* Ladies Professional Golf Association
LPN \ˌel-ˌpē-ˈen\ *n* : LICENSED PRACTICAL NURSE
Lr *symbol* Lawrencium
LSD \ˌel-(ˌ)es-ˈdē\ *n* [G *Lysergsäure-Diäthylamid* lysergic acid diethylamide] : an illicit and highly potent hallucinogenic drug derived from ergot or produced synthetically
lt *abbr* light
Lt *abbr* lieutenant
LT *abbr* long ton
LTC *or* **Lt Col** *abbr* lieutenant colonel
Lt Comdr *abbr* lieutenant commander
ltd *abbr* limited
LTG *or* **Lt Gen** *abbr* lieutenant general
LTJG *abbr* lieutenant, junior grade
ltr *abbr* letter
Lu *symbol* lutetium
lu·au \ˈlü-ˌau̇\ *n* : a Hawaiian feast
lub *abbr* lubricant; lubricating
lub·ber \ˈlə-bər\ *n* **1** : LOUT **2** : an unskilled seaman — **lub·ber·ly** *adj*
lube \ˈlüb\ *n* : LUBRICANT; *also* : an application of a lubricant
lu·bri·cant \ˈlü-bri-kənt\ *n* : a material capable of reducing friction when applied between moving parts
lu·bri·cate \ˈlü-brə-ˌkāt\ *vb* **-cat·ed; -cat·ing** : to apply a lubricant to — **lu·bri·ca·tion** \ˌlü-brə-ˈkā-shən\ *n* — **lu·bri·ca·tor** \ˈlü-brə-ˌkā-tər\ *n*
lu·bri·cious \lü-ˈbri-shəs\ *or* **lu·bri·cous** \ˈlü-bri-kəs\ *adj* **1** : SMOOTH, SLIPPERY **2** : LECHEROUS; *also* : SALACIOUS — **lu·bric·i·ty** \lü-ˈbri-sə-tē\ *n*
lu·cent \ˈlü-sᵊnt\ *adj* **1** : LUMINOUS **2** : CLEAR, LUCID — **lu·cent·ly** *adv*
lu·cerne \lü-ˈsərn\ *n, chiefly Brit* : ALFALFA
lu·cid \ˈlü-səd\ *adj* **1** : SHINING **2** : mentally sound **3** : easily understood ⟨a ~ explanation⟩ — **lu·cid·i·ty** \lü-ˈsi-də-tē\ *n* — **lu·cid·ly** *adv* — **lu·cid·ness** *n*
Lu·ci·fer \ˈlü-sə-fər\ *n* [ME, the morning star, a fallen rebel archangel, the Devil, fr. OE, fr. L, the morning star, fr. *lucifer* light-bearing] : DEVIL, SATAN
¹luck \ˈlək\ *n* **1** : CHANCE, FORTUNE **2** : good fortune — **luck·less** *adj*
²luck *vb* **1** : to prosper or succeed esp. through chance or good fortune — usu. used with *out* **2** : to come upon something desirable by chance — usu. used with *out, on, onto,* or *into*
luck·i·ly \ˈlə-kə-lē\ *adv* **1** : in a lucky manner **2** : FORTUNATELY 2
lucky \ˈlə-kē\ *adj* **luck·i·er; -est** **1** : favored by luck : FORTUNATE **2** : FORTUITOUS **3** : seeming to bring good luck ⟨a ~ penny⟩ — **luck·i·ness** *n*
lu·cra·tive \ˈlü-krə-tiv\ *adj* : PROFITABLE ⟨~ business deals⟩ — **lu·cra·tive·ly** *adv* — **lu·cra·tive·ness** *n*
lu·cre \ˈlü-kər\ *n* [ME, fr. AF, fr. L *lucrum*] : PROFIT; *also* : MONEY
lu·cu·bra·tion \ˌlü-kyə-ˈbrā-shən, -kə-\ *n* : laborious study : MEDITATION
Ludd·ite \ˈlə-ˌdīt\ *n* [perh. fr. Ned *Ludd,* 18th cent. Eng. workman who destroyed a knitting frame] : one who is opposed to technological change
lu·di·crous \ˈlü-də-krəs\ *adj* : LAUGHABLE, RIDICULOUS ⟨a ~ idea⟩ — **lu·di·crous·ly** *adv* — **lu·di·crous·ness** *n*
luff \ˈləf\ *vb* : to turn the head of a ship toward the wind
¹lug \ˈləg\ *vb* **lugged; lug·ging** **1** : DRAG, PULL **2** : to carry laboriously
²lug *n* **1** : a projecting piece (as for fastening, support, or traction) **2** : a nut securing a wheel on an automobile
lug·gage \ˈlə-gij\ *n* : containers (as suitcases) for carrying personal belongings : BAGGAGE
lu·gu·bri·ous \lu̇-ˈgü-brē-əs\ *adj* : mournful often to an exaggerated degree ⟨~ music⟩ — **lu·gu·bri·ous·ly** *adv* — **lu·gu·bri·ous·ness** *n*
Luke \ˈlük\ *n* — see BIBLE table
luke·warm \ˈlük-ˈwȯrm\ *adj* **1** : moderately warm : TEPID **2** : not enthusiastic ⟨~ praise⟩ — **luke·warm·ly** *adv*
¹lull \ˈləl\ *vb* **1** : SOOTHE, CALM **2** : to cause to relax vigilance

[2]**lull** *n* **1 :** a temporary calm (as during a storm) **2 :** a temporary drop in activity ⟨a ~ in sales⟩
lul·la·by \ˈlə-lə-ˌbī\ *n, pl* **-bies :** a song to lull children to sleep
lu·ma \ˌlü-ˈmä\ *n* — see *dram* at MONEY table
lum·ba·go \ˌləm-ˈbā-gō\ *n* **:** acute or chronic pain in the lower back
lum·bar \ˈləm-bər, -ˌbär\ *adj* **:** of, relating to, or constituting the loins or the vertebrae between the thoracic vertebrae and sacrum ⟨~ region⟩
[1]**lum·ber** \ˈləm-bər\ *vb* **:** to move heavily or clumsily ⟨an elephant ~*ed* along the road⟩
[2]**lumber** *n* **1 :** surplus or disused articles that are stored away **2 :** timber or logs esp. when dressed for use
[3]**lumber** *vb* **:** to cut logs; *also* **:** to saw logs into lumber — **lum·ber·man** \-mən\ *n*
lum·ber·jack \-ˌjak\ *n* **:** LOGGER
lum·ber·yard \-ˌyärd\ *n* **:** a place where lumber is kept for sale
lu·mi·nary \ˈlü-mə-ˌner-ē\ *n, pl* **-nar·ies 1 :** a very famous person **2 :** a source of light; *esp* **:** a celestial body
lu·mi·nes·cence \ˌlü-mə-ˈne-sᵊns\ *n* **:** the low-temperature emission of light (as by a chemical or physiological process); *also* **:** such light — **lu·mi·nes·cent** \-sᵊnt\ *adj*
lu·mi·nous \ˈlü-mə-nəs\ *adj* **1 :** emitting light; *also* **:** LIGHTED **2 :** CLEAR, INTELLIGIBLE **3 :** ILLUSTRIOUS — **lu·mi·nance** \-nəns\ *n* — **lu·mi·nos·i·ty** \ˌlü-mə-ˈnä-sə-tē\ *n* — **lu·mi·nous·ly** *adv*
lum·mox \ˈlə-məks\ *n* **:** a clumsy person
[1]**lump** \ˈləmp\ *n* **1 :** a piece or mass of indefinite size and shape **2 :** AGGREGATE, TOTALITY **3 :** a usu. abnormal swelling — **lump·ish** *adj* — **lumpy** *adj*
[2]**lump** *vb* **1 :** to heap together in a lump **2 :** to form into lumps
[3]**lump** *adj* **:** not divided into parts ⟨a ~ sum⟩
lump·ec·to·my \ˌləm-ˈpek-tə-mē\ *n, pl* **-mies :** excision of a breast tumor
lu·na·cy \ˈlü-nə-sē\ *n, pl* **-cies 1 :** INSANITY **2 :** extreme folly
lu·nar \ˈlü-nər\ *adj* **:** of or relating to the moon ⟨a ~ eclipse⟩
lu·na·tic \ˈlü-nə-ˌtik\ *adj* [ME *lunatik,* fr. AF & LL; AF *lunatik,* fr. LL *lunaticus,* fr. L *luna* moon; fr. the belief that lunacy fluctuated with the phases of the moon] **1 :** INSANE; *also* **:** used for insane persons **2 :** extremely foolish — **lunatic** *n*
[1]**lunch** \ˈlənch\ *n* **1 :** a light meal usu. eaten in the middle of the day **2 :** the food prepared for a lunch
[2]**lunch** *vb* **:** to eat lunch
lun·cheon \ˈlən-chən\ *n* **:** a usu. formal lunch
lun·cheon·ette \ˌlən-chə-ˈnet\ *n* **:** a small restaurant serving light lunches
lunch·room \ˈlənch-ˌrüm, -ˌrum\ *n* **1 :** LUNCHEONETTE **2 :** a room (as in a school) where lunches are sold and eaten or lunches brought from home may be eaten
lu·nette \lü-ˈnet\ *n* **:** something shaped like a crescent
lung \ˈləŋ\ *n* **1 :** one of the usu. paired baglike breathing organs in the chest of an air-breathing vertebrate **2 :** a mechanical device to promote breathing and make it easier — **lunged** \ˈləŋd\ *adj*
lunge \ˈlənj\ *n* **1 :** a sudden thrust or pass (as with a sword) **2 :** a sudden forward stride or leap — **lunge** *vb*
lu·pine \ˈlü-pən\ *n* **:** any of a genus of leguminous plants with long upright clusters of pealike flowers
lu·pus \ˈlü-pəs\ *n* [ML, fr. L, wolf] **:** any of several diseases characterized by skin lesions; *esp* **:** SYSTEMIC LUPUS ERYTHEMATOSUS
lurch \ˈlərch\ *n* **:** a sudden swaying or tipping movement — **lurch** *vb*
[1]**lure** \ˈlur\ *n* **1 :** ENTICEMENT; *also* **:** APPEAL ⟨the ~ of easy money⟩ **2 :** an artificial bait for catching fish
[2]**lure** *vb* **lured; lur·ing :** to draw on with a promise of pleasure or gain
lu·rid \ˈlur-əd\ *adj* **1 :** GRUESOME; *also* **:** SENSATIONAL **2 :** wan and ghostly pale in appearance **3 :** shining with the red glow of fire seen through smoke or cloud ♦ ***Synonyms*** GHASTLY, GRISLY, GRIM, HORRIBLE, MACABRE — **lu·rid·ly** *adv*
lurk \ˈlərk\ *vb* **1 :** to move furtively **:** SNEAK **2 :** to lie concealed
lus·cious \ˈlə-shəs\ *adj* **1 :** having a pleasingly sweet taste or smell **2 :** sensually appealing ⟨a ~ voice⟩ — **lus·cious·ly** *adv* — **lus·cious·ness** *n*
[1]**lush** \ˈləsh\ *adj* **:** having or covered with abundant growth ⟨~ pastures⟩
[2]**lush** *n* **:** a habitual heavy drinker
lust \ˈləst\ *n* **1 :** usu. intense or unbridled sexual desire **:** LASCIVIOUSNESS **2 :** an intense longing ⟨a ~ to succeed⟩ — **lust** *vb* — **lust·ful** *adj*
lus·ter *or* **lus·tre** \ˈləs-tər\ *n* **1 :** a shine or sheen esp. from reflected light **2 :** BRIGHTNESS, GLITTER **3 :** GLORY, SPLENDOR — **lus·ter·less** *adj* — **lus·trous** \-trəs\ *adj*
lus·tral \ˈləs-trəl\ *adj* **:** serving or intended to purify ⟨~ water⟩
lusty \ˈləs-tē\ *adj* **lust·i·er; -est :** full of vitality **:** ROBUST — **lust·i·ly** \ˈləs-tə-lē\ *adv* — **lust·i·ness** \-tē-nəs\ *n*
lute \ˈlüt\ *n* **:** a stringed musical instrument with a large pear-shaped body and a fretted fingerboard — **lu·te·nist** *or* **lu·ta·nist** \ˈlü-tə-nist\ *n*
lu·te·tium *also* **lu·te·cium** \lü-ˈtē-shē-əm, -shəm\ *n* **:** a metallic chemical element
Lu·ther·an \ˈlü-thə-rən\ *n* **:** a member of a Protestant denomination adhering to the doctrines of Martin Luther — **Lu·ther·an·ism** \-rə-ˌni-zəm\ *n*
lux·u·ri·ant \ˌləg-ˈzhur-ē-ənt, ˌlək-ˈshur-\ *adj* **1 :** yielding or growing abundantly **:** LUSH, PRODUCTIVE ⟨~ vegetation⟩ **2 :** abundantly rich and varied; *also* **:** FLORID ⟨a ~ fabric⟩ ♦ ***Synonyms*** EXUBERANT, LAVISH, OPULENT, PRODIGAL, PROFUSE, RIOTOUS — **lux·u·ri·ance** \-ē-əns\ *n* — **lux·u·ri·ant·ly** *adv*

lux·u·ri·ate \-ē-ˌāt\ *vb* **-at·ed; -at·ing** **1** : to grow profusely **2** : REVEL

lux·u·ry \ˈlək-shə-rē, ˈləg-zhə-\ *n, pl* **-ries** **1** : great ease and comfort **2** : something adding to pleasure or comfort but not absolutely necessary — **lux·u·ri·ous** \ˌləg-ˈzhu̇r-ē-əs, ˌlək-ˈshu̇r-\ *adj* — **lux·u·ri·ous·ly** *adv*

lv *abbr* leave

Lv *symbol* livermorium

lwei \lə-ˈwā\ *n, pl* **lwei** : a former monetary subunit of the kwanza

LWV *abbr* League of Women Voters

[1]**-ly** \lē\ *adj suffix* **1** : like in appearance, manner, or nature ⟨queen*ly*⟩ **2** : characterized by regular recurrence in (specified) units of time : every ⟨hour*ly*⟩ ⟨week*ly*⟩

[2]**-ly** *adv suffix* **1** : in a (specified) manner ⟨slow*ly*⟩ **2** : from a (specified) point of view ⟨grammatical*ly*⟩

ly·ce·um \lī-ˈsē-əm, ˈlī-sē-\ *n* **1** : a hall for public lectures **2** : an association providing public lectures, concerts, and entertainments

ly·chee *or* **li·tchi** \ˈlē-chē, ˈlī-\ *n* [Ch(Beijing) *lìzhī*] **1** : an oval fruit with a hard scaly outer covering, a small hard seed, and edible flesh **2** : an Asian tree bearing lychees

lye \ˈlī\ *n* : a corrosive alkaline substance used esp. in making soap

ly·ing \ˈlī-iŋ\ *adj* : UNTRUTHFUL, FALSE

ly·ing–in \ˌlī-iŋ-ˈin\ *n, pl* **lyings–in** *or* **ly·ing–ins** : the state during and consequent to childbirth : CONFINEMENT

Lyme disease \ˈlīm-\ *n* [*Lyme,* Connecticut, where it was first reported] : an acute inflammatory disease that is caused by a spirochete transmitted by ticks, is characterized usu. by chills and fever, and if left untreated may result in joint pain, arthritis, and cardiac and neurological disorders

lymph \ˈlimf\ *n* : a usu. clear fluid consisting chiefly of blood plasma and white blood cells, circulating in thin-walled tubes (**lymphatic vessels**), and bathing the body tissues — **lym·phat·ic** \lim-ˈfa-tik\ *adj*

lymph·ade·nop·a·thy \ˌlim-ˌfa-də-ˈnä-pə-thē\ *n, pl* **-thies** : abnormal enlargement of the lymph nodes

lymph node *n* : any of the rounded masses of lymphoid tissue surrounded by a capsule of connective tissue

lym·pho·cyte \ˈlim-fə-ˌsīt\ *n* : any of the white blood cells arising from lymphoid tissue that are typically found in lymph and blood and that include the cellular mediators (as a B cell or a T cell) of immunity — **lym·pho·cyt·ic** \ˌlim-fə-ˈsi-tik\ *adj*

lym·phoid \ˈlim-ˌfȯid\ *adj* **1** : of, relating to, or being tissue (as of the lymph nodes) containing lymphocytes **2** : of, relating to, or resembling lymph

lym·pho·ma \lim-ˈfō-mə\ *n, pl* **-mas** *also* **-ma·ta** \-mə-tə\ : a usu. malignant tumor of lymphoid tissue

lynch \ˈlinch\ *vb* : to put to death by mob action without legal sanction or due process of law — **lynch·er** *n*

lynx \ˈliŋks\ *n, pl* **lynx** *or* **lynx·es** : any of several wildcats with a short tail, long legs, and usu. tufted ears

lyre \ˈlī(-ə)r\ *n* : a stringed musical instrument of the harp class having a U-shaped frame and used by the ancient Greeks

[1]**lyr·ic** \ˈlir-ik\ *n* **1** : a lyric poem **2** *pl* : the words of a popular song — **lyr·i·cal** \-i-kəl\ *adj*

[2]**lyric** *adj* **1** : suitable for singing : MELODIC **2** : expressing direct and usu. intense personal emotion ⟨~ poetry⟩

ly·ser·gic acid di·eth·yl·am·ide \lə-ˈsər-jik . . . ˌdī-ˌe-thə-ˈla-ˌmīd, lī-, -ˈla-məd\ *n* : LSD

LZ *abbr* landing zone

M

[1]**m** \ˈem\ *n, pl* **m's** *or* **ms** \ˈemz\ *often cap* : the 13th letter of the English alphabet

[2]**m** *abbr, often cap* **1** Mach **2** male **3** married **4** masculine **5** medium **6** [L *meridies*] noon **7** meter **8** mile **9** [L *mille*] thousand **10** minute **11** month **12** moon

ma \ˈmä, ˈmȯ\ *n* : MOTHER

MA *abbr* **1** [ML *magister artium*] master of arts **2** Massachusetts **3** mental age

ma'am \ˈmam, *after "yes" often* əm\ *n* : MADAM

Mac *abbr* Machabees

Mac *or* **Macc** *abbr* Maccabees

ma·ca·bre \mə-ˈkäb; ˈkä-brə, -bər\ *adj* [F] **1** : having death as a subject **2** : GRUESOME **3** : HORRIBLE

mac·ad·am \mə-ˈka-dəm\ *n* [John L. *McAdam* †1836 Brit. engineer] : a roadway or pavement of small closely packed broken stone — **mac·ad·am·ize** \-də-ˌmīz\ *vb*

mac·a·da·mia nut \ˌma-kə-ˈdā-mē-ə-\ *n* : a hard-shelled richly flavored nut of any of several Australian trees

ma·caque \mə-ˈkak, -ˈkäk\ *n* : any of a genus of short-tailed chiefly Asian monkeys; *esp* : RHESUS MONKEY

mac·a·ro·ni \ˌma-kə-ˈrō-nē\ *n* **1** : pasta made chiefly of wheat flour and shaped in the form of slender tubes **2** *pl* **-nis** *or* **-nies** : FOP, DANDY

mac·a·roon \ˌma-kə-ˈrün\ *n* : a small cookie made chiefly of egg whites, sugar, and ground almonds or coconut

ma·caw \mə-ˈkȯ\ *n* : any of numerous parrots of Central and So. America

Mac·ca·bees \ˈma-kə-ˌbēz\ *n* — see BIBLE table

[1]**mace** \ˈmās\ *n* : a spice made from the fibrous coating of the nutmeg

[2]**mace** *n* **1** : a heavy often spiked club used as a weapon esp. in the Middle Ages **2** : an ornamental staff carried as a symbol of authority

mac·er·ate \ˈma-sə-ˌrāt\ *vb* **-at·ed; -at·ing** **1** : to cause to waste away **2** : to soften by steeping or soaking so as to separate the parts — **mac·er·a·tion** \ˌma-sə-ˈrā-shən\ *n*

Mac·Guf·fin *or* **Mc·Guf·fin** \mə-ˈgə-fən\ *n* : an object, event, or character whose main purpose is to advance the plot of a motion picture

mach *abbr* machine; machinery; machinist

Mach \ˈmäk\ *n* : a speed expressed by a Mach number

Mach·a·bees \ˈma-kə-ˌbēz\ *n* : MACCABEES

ma·chete \mə-ˈshe-tē\ *n* : a large heavy knife used for cutting sugarcane and underbrush and as a weapon

Ma·chi·a·vel·lian \ˌma-kē-ə-ˈve-lē-ən\ *adj* [Niccolò *Machiavelli,* †1527 Italian political philosopher] : characterized by cunning, duplicity, and bad faith — **Ma·chi·a·vel·lian·ism** *n*

mach·i·na·tion \ˌma-kə-ˈnā-shən, ˌma-shə-\ *n* : an act of planning esp. to do harm; *esp* : PLOT — **mach·i·nate** \ˈma-kə-ˌnāt, ˈma-shə-\ *vb*

[1]**ma·chine** \mə-ˈshēn\ *n* **1** : CONVEYANCE, VEHICLE; *esp* : AUTOMOBILE **2** : a combination of mechanical parts that transmit forces, motion, and energy one to another **3** : an instrument (as a lever) for transmitting or modifying force or motion **4** : an electrical, electronic, or mechanical device for performing a task 〈a sewing ~〉 **5** : a highly organized political group under the leadership of a boss or small clique

[2]**machine** *vb* **ma·chined; ma·chin·ing** : to shape or finish by machine-operated tools — **ma·chin·able** \-ˈshē-nə-bəl\ *adj*

machine gun *n* : an automatic gun capable of rapid continuous firing — **machine–gun** *vb* — **machine gunner** *n*

machine language *n* : the set of symbolic instruction codes used to represent operations and data in a machine (as a computer)

machine learning *n* : the process by which a computer is able to improve its own performance by incorporating new data into an existing statistical model

machine–readable *adj* : directly usable by a computer

ma·chin·ery \mə-ˈshē-nə-rē\ *n, pl* **-er·ies** **1** : MACHINES; *also* : the working parts of a machine **2** : the means by which something is done

ma·chin·ist \mə-ˈshē-nist\ *n* : a person who makes or works on machines

ma·chis·mo \mä-ˈchēz-(ˌ)mō, -ˈchiz-\ *n* : a strong or exaggerated pride in one's masculinity

Mach number \ˈmäk-\ *n* : a number representing the ratio of the speed of a body (as an aircraft) to the speed of sound in the surrounding atmosphere

ma·cho \ˈmä-chō\ *adj* [Sp, lit., male, fr. L *masculus*] : characterized by machismo

mack·er·el \ˈma-kə-rəl\ *n, pl* **mackerel** *or* **mackerels** : a No. Atlantic food fish greenish above and silvery below

mack·i·naw \ˈma-kə-ˌnȯ\ *n* : a short heavy plaid coat

mack·in·tosh *also* **mac·in·tosh** \ˈma-kən-ˌtäsh\ *n* **1** *chiefly Brit* : RAINCOAT **2** : a lightweight waterproof fabric

mac·ra·mé *also* **mac·ra·me** \ˈma-krə-ˌmā\ *n* [ultim. fr. Ar *miqrama* coverlet] : a coarse lace or fringe made by knotting threads or cords in a geometrical pattern

[1]**mac·ro** \ˈma-(ˌ)krō\ *adj* : very large; *also* : involving large quantities or being on a large scale 〈~ economic policies〉

[2]**macro** *n, pl* **macros** : a single computer instruction that stands for a sequence of operations

mac·ro·bi·ot·ic \ˌma-krō-bī-ˈä-tik, -bē-\ *adj* : relating to or being a very restricted diet (as one containing chiefly whole cereals or grains)

mac·ro·cosm \ˈma-krə-ˌkä-zəm\ *n* : the great world : UNIVERSE

ma·cron \ˈmā-ˌkrän, ˈma-\ *n* : a mark ¯ placed over a vowel (as in \māk\) to show that the vowel is long

mac·ro·scop·ic \ˌma-krə-ˈskä-pik\ *adj* : visible to the naked eye — **mac·ro·scop·i·cal·ly** \-pi-k(ə-)lē\ *adv*

mac·u·la \ˈma-kyə-lə\ *n, pl* **-lae** \-ˌlē, -ˌlī\ *also* **-las** : an anatomical spot distinguishable from surrounding tissues — **mac·u·lar** \-lər\ *adj*

mad \ˈmad\ *adj* **mad·der; mad·dest** **1** : disordered in mind : INSANE **2** : being rash and foolish **3** : FURIOUS, ENRAGED **4** : carried away by enthusiasm 〈~ about football〉 **5** : RABID **6** : marked by wild gaiety and merriment **7** : FRANTIC 〈a ~ rush〉 — **mad·ly** *adv* — **mad·ness** *n*

mad·am \ˈma-dəm\ *n* **1** *pl* **mes·dames** \mā-ˈdäm\ — used as a form of polite address to a woman **2** *pl* **madams** : the female head of a house of prostitution

ma·dame \mə-ˈdam, *before a surname also* ˈma-dəm\ *n, pl* **mes·dames** \mā-ˈdäm\ : MISTRESS — used as a title equivalent to *Mrs.* for a married woman not of English-speaking nationality

mad·cap \ˈmad-ˌkap\ *adj* : WILD, RECKLESS 〈a ~ scheme〉 — **madcap** *n*

mad cow disease *n* : a fatal encephalopathy of cattle that affects the nervous system causing the brain tissue to resemble a porous sponge

mad·den \ˈma-dᵊn\ *vb* : to make mad — **mad·den·ing·ly** *adv*

mad·der \ˈma-dər\ *n* : a Eurasian herb

with yellow flowers and fleshy red roots; *also* : its root or a dye prepared from it
made *past and past part of* MAKE
Ma·dei·ra \mə-ˈdir-ə\ *n* : an amber-colored dessert wine
ma·de·moi·selle \ˌma-də-mə-ˈzel, -mwə-, mam-ˈzel\ *n, pl* **ma·de·moi·selles** \-ˈzelz\ *or* **mes·de·moi·selles** \ˌmā-də-me-ˈzel, -mwə-\ : an unmarried girl or woman — used as a title for an unmarried woman not of English-speaking nationality
made–to–measure *adj* : CUSTOM-MADE
made–up \ˈmād-ˈəp\ *adj* **1** : fancifully conceived or falsely devised **2** : marked by the use of makeup
mad·house \ˈmad-ˌhau̇s\ *n, often offensive* **1** : an institution providing care to mentally ill individuals **2** : a place of great uproar
mad·man \ˈmad-ˌman, -mən\ *n* : a man who is or acts as if insane
Ma·don·na \mə-ˈdä-nə\ *n* : a representation (as a picture or statue) of the Virgin Mary
ma·dras \ˈma-drəs; ˌmə-ˈdras, -ˈdräs\ *n* [*Madras,* India] : a fine usu. cotton fabric with various designs (as plaid)
ma·dras·sa *or* **ma·dra·sa** \mə-ˈdra-sə, -ˈdrä-\ *n* : a Muslim school, college, or university that is often part of a mosque
mad·ri·gal \ˈma-dri-gəl\ *n* [It *madrigale*] **1** : a short lyrical poem in a strict poetic form **2** : an elaborate part-song esp. of the 16th and 17th centuries
mad·wom·an \ˈmad-ˌwu̇-mən\ *n* : a woman who is insane
mael·strom \ˈmāl-strəm\ *n* **1** : a violent whirlpool **2** : TUMULT
mae·stro \ˈmī-strō\ *n, pl* **maestros** *or* **mae·stri** \-ˌstrē\ [It] : a master in an art; *esp* : an eminent composer, conductor, or teacher of music
Ma·fia \ˈmä-fē-ə\ *n* [It] : a secret criminal society of Sicily or Italy; *also* : a similar organization elsewhere
ma·fi·o·so \ˌmä-fē-ˈō-(ˌ)sō\ *n, pl* **-si** \-(ˌ)sē\ : a member of the Mafia
[1]**mag** \ˈmag\ *n* : MAGAZINE
[2]**mag** *abbr* **1** magnetism **2** magneto **3** magnitude
mag·a·zine \ˈma-gə-ˌzēn\ *n* [MF, fr. Old Occitan, fr. Ar *makhāzin,* pl. of *makhzan* storehouse] **1** : a storehouse esp. for military supplies **2** : a place for keeping gunpowder in a fort or ship **3** : a publication usu. containing stories, articles, or poems and issued periodically **4** : a container in a gun for holding cartridges; *also* : a chamber (as on a camera) for film
ma·gen·ta \mə-ˈjen-tə\ *n* : a deep purplish red color
mag·got \ˈma-gət\ *n* : the legless wormlike larva of a dipteran fly — **mag·goty** *adj*
ma·gi \ˈmā-jī\ *n pl, often cap* : the three wise men from the East who paid homage to the infant Jesus
mag·ic \ˈma-jik\ *n* **1** : the use of means (as charms or spells) believed to have supernatural power over natural forces **2** : an extraordinary power or influence seemingly from a supernatural force **3** : SLEIGHT OF HAND — **magic** *adj* — **mag·i·cal** \-ji-kəl\ *adj* — **mag·i·cal·ly** \-ji-k(ə-)lē\ *adv*
ma·gi·cian \mə-ˈji-shən\ *n* : a person skilled in magic
mag·is·te·ri·al \ˌma-jə-ˈstir-ē-əl\ *adj* **1** : AUTHORITATIVE ⟨a ~ attitude⟩ **2** : of or relating to a magistrate or a magistrate's office or duties
ma·gis·tral \ˈma-jə-strəl\ *adj* : AUTHORITATIVE
mag·is·trate \ˈma-jə-ˌstrāt\ *n* : an official entrusted with administration of the laws — **mag·is·tra·cy** \-strə-sē\ *n*
mag·lev \ˈmag-lev\ *n* **1** : the use of magnetic fields to float an object above a solid surface **2** : a train using maglev technology
mag·ma \ˈmag-mə\ *n* : molten rock material within the earth — **mag·mat·ic** \mag-ˈma-tik\ *adj*
mag·nan·i·mous \mag-ˈna-nə-məs\ *adj* **1** : showing or suggesting a lofty and courageous spirit **2** : NOBLE, GENEROUS — **mag·na·nim·i·ty** \ˌmag-nə-ˈni-mə-tē\ *n* — **mag·nan·i·mous·ly** *adv* — **mag·nan·i·mous·ness** *n*
mag·nate \ˈmag-ˌnāt\ *n* : a person of rank, influence, or distinction
mag·ne·sia \mag-ˈnē-shə, -zhə\ *n* [NL, fr. *magnes carneus,* a white earth, lit., flesh magnet] : a light white oxide of magnesium used as a laxative
mag·ne·sium \mag-ˈnē-zē-əm, -zhəm\ *n* : a silver-white light malleable metallic chemical element
mag·net \ˈmag-nət\ *n* **1** : LODESTONE **2** : a body that is able to attract iron **3** : something that attracts
mag·net·ic \mag-ˈne-tik\ *adj* **1** : having an unusual ability to attract ⟨a ~ leader⟩ **2** : of or relating to a magnet or magnetism **3** : magnetized or capable of being magnetized — **mag·net·i·cal·ly** \-ti-k(ə-)lē\ *adv*
magnetic disk *n* : DISK 3
magnetic levitation *n* : MAGLEV 1
magnetic north *n* : the northerly direction in the earth's magnetic field indicated by the north-seeking pole of a compass needle
magnetic resonance imaging *n* : a noninvasive diagnostic technique that produces computerized images of internal body tissues based on electromagnetically induced activity of atoms within the body
magnetic tape *n* : a ribbon coated with a magnetic material on which information (as sound) may be stored
mag·ne·tise *Brit var of* MAGNETIZE
mag·ne·tism \ˈmag-nə-ˌti-zəm\ *n* **1** : the power (as of a magnet) to attract iron **2** : the science that deals with magnetic phenomena **3** : an ability to attract or charm
mag·ne·tite \ˈmag-nə-ˌtīt\ *n* : a black mineral that is an important iron ore
mag·ne·tize \ˈmag-nə-ˌtīz\ *vb* **-tized; -tiz-**

ing **1** : to induce magnetic properties in **2** : to attract like a magnet : CHARM — **mag·ne·tiz·able** *adj* — **mag·ne·ti·za·tion** \ˌmag-nə-tə-ˈzā-shən\ *n*

mag·ne·to \mag-ˈnē-tō\ *n, pl* **-tos** : a generator used to produce sparks in an internal combustion engine

mag·ne·tom·e·ter \ˌmag-nə-ˈtä-mə-tər\ *n* : an instrument for measuring the strength of a magnetic field

mag·ne·to·sphere \mag-ˈnē-tə-ˌsfir, -ˈne-\ *n* : a region around a celestial object (as the earth) in which charged particles are trapped by its magnetic field — **mag·ne·to·spher·ic** \-ˌnē-tə-ˈsfir-ik, -ˈsfer-\ *adj*

mag·ni·fi·ca·tion \ˌmag-nə-fə-ˈkā-shən\ *n* **1** : the act of magnifying **2** : the amount by which an optical lens or instrument magnifies

mag·nif·i·cent \mag-ˈni-fə-sənt\ *adj* **1** : characterized by grandeur or beauty : SPLENDID **2** : EXALTED, NOBLE ♦ ***Synonyms*** IMPOSING, STATELY, GRAND, MAJESTIC — **mag·nif·i·cence** \-səns\ *n* — **mag·nif·i·cent·ly** *adv*

mag·nif·i·co \mag-ˈni-fi-ˌkō\ *n, pl* **-coes** *or* **-cos** **1** : a nobleman of Venice **2** : a person of high position

mag·ni·fy \ˈmag-nə-ˌfī\ *vb* **-fied; -fy·ing** **1** : EXTOL, LAUD; *also* : to cause to be held in greater esteem **2** : INTENSIFY; *also* : EXAGGERATE **3** : to enlarge in fact or in appearance — **mag·ni·fi·er** \ˈmag-nə-ˌfī(-ə)r\ *n*

mag·nil·o·quent \mag-ˈni-lə-kwənt\ *adj* : characterized by an exalted and often bombastic style or manner — **mag·nil·o·quence** \-kwəns\ *n*

mag·ni·tude \ˈmag-nə-ˌtüd, -ˌtyüd\ *n* **1** : greatness of size or extent **2** : SIZE **3** : QUANTITY **4** : a number representing the brightness of a celestial body **5** : a number representing the intensity of an earthquake

mag·no·lia \mag-ˈnōl-yə\ *n* : any of a genus of usu. spring-flowering shrubs and trees with large often fragrant flowers

mag·num opus \ˈmag-nəm-ˈō-pəs\ *n* [L] : the greatest achievement of an artist or writer

mag·pie \ˈmag-ˌpī\ *n* : any of various long-tailed often black-and-white birds related to the jays

Mag·yar \ˈmag-ˌyär, ˈmäg-; ˈmä-ˌjär\ *n* : a member of the dominant people of Hungary — **Magyar** *adj*

ma·ha·ra·ja *or* **ma·ha·ra·jah** \ˌmä-hə-ˈrä-jə\ *n* : a Hindu prince ranking above a raja

ma·ha·ra·ni *or* **ma·ha·ra·nee** \-ˈrä-nē\ *n* **1** : the wife of a maharaja **2** : a Hindu princess ranking above a rani

ma·ha·ri·shi \ˌmä-hə-ˈrē-shē\ *n* : a Hindu teacher of mystical knowledge

ma·hat·ma \mə-ˈhät-mə, -ˈhat-\ *n* [Skt *mahātman,* fr. *mahātman* great-souled, fr. *mahat* great + *ātman* soul] : a person revered for high-mindedness, wisdom, and selflessness

Mahican *var of* MOHICAN

ma·hog·a·ny \mə-ˈhä-gə-nē\ *n, pl* **-nies** : the reddish wood of any of various chiefly tropical trees that is used in furniture; *also* : a tree yielding this wood

ma·hout \mə-ˈhau̇t\ *n* [Hindi & Urdu *mahāwat, mahāut*] : a keeper and driver of an elephant

maid \ˈmād\ *n* **1** : an unmarried girl or young woman **2** : MAIDSERVANT; *also* : a woman or girl employed to do domestic work

[1]**maid·en** \ˈmā-dᵊn\ *n* : MAID 1 — **maid·en·ly** *adj*

[2]**maiden** *adj* **1** : UNMARRIED; *also* : VIRGIN **2** : of, relating to, or befitting a maiden **3** : FIRST ⟨a ship's ~ voyage⟩

maid·en·hair fern \-ˌher-\ *n* : any of a genus of ferns with delicate feathery fronds

maid·en·head \ˈmā-dᵊn-ˌhed\ *n* **1** : VIRGINITY **2** : HYMEN

maid·en·hood \-ˌhu̇d\ *n* : the condition or time of being a maiden

maid–in–waiting *n, pl* **maids–in–waiting** : a young woman appointed to attend a queen or princess

maid of honor : a bride's principal unmarried wedding attendant

maid·ser·vant \ˈmād-ˌsər-vənt\ *n* : a girl or woman who is a servant

[1]**mail** \ˈmāl\ *n* [ME *male* bag, fr. AF, of Gmc origin] **1** : material sent or carried in the postal system **2** : a nation's postal system — often used in pl. **3** : EMAIL

[2]**mail** *vb* : to send by mail

[3]**mail** *n* [ME *maille* metal link, mail, fr. AF, fr. L *macula* spot, mesh] : armor made of metal links or plates

mail·box \ˈmāl-ˌbäks\ *n* **1** : a public box for the collection of mail **2** : a private box for the delivery of mail

mail·man \-ˌman\ *n* : a man who delivers mail

maim \ˈmām\ *vb* : to mutilate, disfigure, or wound seriously

[1]**main** \ˈmān\ *n* **1** : FORCE ⟨with might and ~⟩ **2** : MAINLAND; *also* : HIGH SEA **3** : the chief part **4** : a principal pipe, duct, or circuit of a utility system

[2]**main** *adj* **1** : CHIEF, PRINCIPAL ⟨the ~ idea⟩ **2** : fully exerted ⟨~ force⟩ **3** : expressing the chief predication in a complex sentence ⟨the ~ clause⟩ — **main·ly** *adv*

main·frame \ˈmān-ˌfrām\ *n* : a large fast computer

main·land \-ˌland, -lənd\ *n* : a continuous body of land constituting the chief part of a country or continent

main·line \-ˌlīn\ *vb, slang* : to inject a narcotic drug into a vein

main line *n* : a principal highway or railroad line

main·mast \ˈmān-ˌmast, -məst\ *n* : the principal mast on a sailing ship

main·sail \-ˌsāl, -səl\ *n* : the largest sail on the mainmast

main·spring \-ˌspriŋ\ *n* **1** : the chief spring in a mechanism (as of a watch) **2** : the chief motive, agent, or cause

main·stay \-ˌstā\ *n* **1** : a stay running from the head of the mainmast to the foot of the foremast **2** : a chief support

main·stream \-ˌstrēm\ *n* : a prevailing current or direction of activity or influence — **mainstream** *adj*

main·tain \mān-ˈtān\ *vb* [ME *mainteinen,* fr. AF *maintenir, maynteiner,* fr. ML *manutenēre,* fr. L *manu tenēre* to hold in the hand] **1** : to keep in an existing state (as of repair) **2** : to sustain against opposition or danger **3** : to continue in : CARRY ON **4** : to provide for : SUPPORT **5** : ASSERT ⟨~*ed* his innocence⟩ — **main·tain·abil·i·ty** \-ˌtā-nə-ˈbi-lə-tē\ *n* — **main·tain·able** \-ˈtā-nə-bəl\ *adj* — **main·te·nance** \ˈmān-tə-nəns\ *n*

main·top \ˈmān-ˌtäp\ *n* : a platform at the head of the mainmast of a square-rigged ship

mai·son·ette \ˌmā-zə-ˈnet\ *n* **1** : a small house **2** : an apartment often on two floors

mai tai \ˈmī-ˌtī\ *n* : a cocktail made with liquors and fruit juices

maî·tre d' *or* **mai·tre d'** \ˌmā-trə-ˈdē, ˌme-\ *n, pl* **maître d's** *or* **maitre d's** \-ˈdēz\ : MAÎTRE D'HÔTEL

maî·tre d'hô·tel \ˌmā-trə-dō-ˈtel, ˌme-\ *n, pl* **maîtres d'hôtel** *same*\ [F, lit., master of house] **1** : MAJORDOMO **2** : HEADWAITER

maize \ˈmāz\ *n* : CORN 2

Maj *abbr* major

maj·es·ty \ˈma-jə-stē\ *n, pl* **-ties** **1** : sovereign power, authority, or dignity; *also* : the person of a sovereign — used as a title **2** : GRANDEUR, SPLENDOR — **ma·jes·tic** \mə-ˈjes-tik\ *adj* — **ma·jes·ti·cal·ly** \-ti-k(ə-)lē\ *adv*

Maj Gen *abbr* Major General

ma·jol·i·ca \mə-ˈjä-li-kə\ *also* **ma·iol·i·ca** \-ˈyä-\ *n* : any of several faiences; *esp* : an Italian tin-glazed pottery

¹**ma·jor** \ˈmā-jər\ *adj* **1** : greater in number, extent, or importance ⟨a ~ poet⟩ **2** : notable or conspicuous in effect or scope ⟨a ~ improvement⟩ **3** : SERIOUS ⟨a ~ illness⟩ **4** : having half steps between the 3d and 4th and the 7th and 8th degrees ⟨~ scale⟩; *also* : based on a major scale ⟨~ key⟩ ⟨~ chord⟩

²**major** *n* **1** : a commissioned officer (as in the army) ranking next below a lieutenant colonel **2** : an academic subject chosen as a field of specialization; *also* : a student specializing in such a field ⟨a history ~⟩

³**major** *vb* : to pursue an academic major

ma·jor·do·mo \ˌmā-jər-ˈdō-mō\ *n, pl* **-mos** [Sp *mayordomo* or obs. It *maiordomo,* fr. ML *major domus,* lit., chief of the house] **1** : a head steward **2** : BUTLER

ma·jor·ette \ˌmā-jə-ˈret\ *n* : DRUM MAJORETTE

major general *n* : a commissioned officer (as in the army) ranking next below a lieutenant general

ma·jor·i·ty \mə-ˈjȯr-ə-tē\ *n, pl* **-ties** **1** : the age at which full civil rights are accorded; *also* : the status of one who has attained this age **2** : a number greater than half of a total; *also* : the excess of this greater number over the remainder **3** : the rank of a major

ma·jus·cule \ˈma-jəs-ˌkyül, mə-ˈjəs-\ *n* : a large letter (as a capital)

Ma·kah \ˈmä-kä\ *n, pl* **Makah** *or* **Makahs** : a member of an Indigenous people of the northwest coast of No. America; *also* : their language

¹**make** \ˈmāk\ *vb* **made** \ˈmād\; **mak·ing** **1** : to cause to exist, occur, or appear; *also* : DESTINE ⟨was *made* to be an actor⟩ **2** : FASHION ⟨~ a dress⟩; *also* : COMPOSE **3** : to formulate in the mind ⟨~ plans⟩ **4** : CONSTITUTE ⟨house *made* of stone⟩ **5** : to compute to be **6** : to set in order : PREPARE ⟨~ a bed⟩ **7** : to cause to be or become; *also* : APPOINT **8** : ENACT; *also* : EXECUTE ⟨~ a will⟩ **9** : CONCLUDE ⟨didn't know what to ~ of it⟩ **10** : CARRY OUT, PERFORM ⟨~ a gesture⟩ **11** : COMPEL **12** : to assure the success of ⟨will ~ us or break us⟩ **13** : to amount to in significance ⟨~*s* no difference⟩ **14** : to be capable of developing or being fashioned into **15** : REACH, ATTAIN; *also* : GAIN **16** : to start out : GO **17** : to have weight or effect ⟨courtesy ~*s* for safer driving⟩ ♦ ***Synonyms*** FORM, SHAPE, FABRICATE, MANUFACTURE — **mak·er** *n* — **make believe** : PRETEND — **make do** : to manage with the means at hand — **make fun of** : RIDICULE, MOCK — **make good** **1** : INDEMNIFY ⟨*make good* the loss⟩; *also* : to carry out successfully ⟨*make good* his promise⟩ **2** : SUCCEED — **make way** **1** : to give room for passing, entering, or occupying **2** : to make progress

²**make** *n* **1** : the manner or style of construction; *also* : BRAND 3 **2** : MAKEUP **3** : the action of manufacturing — **on the make** : in search of wealth, social status, or sexual adventure

¹**make–be·lieve** \ˈmāk-bə-ˌlēv\ *n* : a pretending that what is not real is real

²**make–believe** *adj* : IMAGINED, PRETENDED

make–do \-ˌdü\ *adj* : MAKESHIFT

make out *vb* **1** : to draw up in writing ⟨*make out* a list⟩ **2** : to find or grasp the meaning of ⟨can you *make* that *out*⟩ **3** : to represent as being **4** : to pretend to be true **5** : DISCERN ⟨*make out* a ship in the fog⟩ **6** : GET ALONG, FARE ⟨*make out* well in life⟩ **7** : to engage in amorous kissing and caressing

make over *vb* : REMAKE, REMODEL — **make·over** \ˈmā-ˌkō-vər\ *n*

make·shift \ˈmāk-ˌshift\ *n* : a temporary expedient — **makeshift** *adj*

make·up \ˈmā-ˌkəp\ *n* **1** : the way in which something is put together; *also* : physical, mental, and moral constitution **2** : cosmetics esp. for the face; *also* : materials (as wigs and cosmetics) used in making up

make up *vb* **1** : FORM, COMPOSE **2** : to compensate for a deficiency **3** : SETTLE ⟨*made up* my mind⟩ **4** : INVENT, IMPROVISE **5** : to become reconciled **6** : to put on makeup (as for a play)

make–work \ˈmāk-ˌwərk\ *n* : BUSYWORK

mak·ings \ˈmā-kiŋz\ *n pl* : the material from which something is made
Mal *abbr* Malachi
Mal·a·chi \ˈma-lə-ˌkī\ *n* — see BIBLE table
Mal·a·chi·as \ˌma-lə-ˈkī-əs\ *n* : MALACHI
mal·a·chite \ˈma-lə-ˌkīt\ *n* : a green mineral that is a carbonate of copper used for making ornamental objects
mal·adapt·ed \ˌma-lə-ˈdap-təd\ *adj* : poorly suited to a particular use, purpose, or situation
mal·ad·just·ed \ˌma-lə-ˈjəs-təd\ *adj* : poorly or inadequately adjusted (as to one's environment) — **mal·ad·just·ment** \-ˈjəst-mənt\ *n*
mal·adroit \ˌma-lə-ˈdrȯit\ *adj* : not adroit : INEPT ⟨the ~ handling of the crisis⟩
mal·a·dy \ˈma-lə-dē\ *n, pl* **-dies** : a disease or disorder of body or mind
mal·aise \mə-ˈlāz, ma-\ *n* [F] : a hazy feeling of not being well
mal·a·mute \ˈma-lə-ˌmyüt\ *n* : a dog often used to draw sleds esp. in northern No. America
mal·a·prop·ism \ˈma-lə-ˌprä-ˌpi-zəm\ *n* : a usu. humorous misuse of a word
mal·ap·ro·pos \ˌma-ˌla-prə-ˈpō, ma-ˈla-prə-ˌpō\ *adv* : in an inappropriate or inopportune way — **malapropos** *adj*
ma·lar·ia \mə-ˈler-ē-ə\ *n* [It, fr. *mala aria* bad air] : a disease marked by recurring chills and fever and caused by a protozoan parasite of the blood that is transmitted by anopheles mosquitoes — **ma·lar·i·al** \-əl\ *adj*
ma·lar·key \mə-ˈlär-kē\ *n* : insincere or foolish talk
mal·a·thi·on \ˌma-lə-ˈthī-ən, -ˌän\ *n* : an insecticide with a relatively low toxicity for mammals
Ma·lay \mə-ˈlā, ˈmā-ˌlā\ *n* **1** : a member of a people of the Malay Peninsula and Archipelago **2** : the language of the Malays — **Malay** *adj* — **Ma·lay·an** \mə-ˈlā-ən, ˈmā-ˌlā-\ *n or adj*
mal·con·tent \ˌmal-kən-ˈtent\ *adj* : marked by a dissatisfaction with the existing state of affairs : DISCONTENTED — **malcontent** *n*
mal de mer \ˌmal-də-ˈmer\ *n* [F] : SEASICKNESS
¹**male** \ˈmāl\ *n* : a male individual
²**male** *adj* **1** : of, relating to, or being the sex that produces germ cells which fertilize the eggs of a female; *also* : STAMINATE **2** : having a gender identity that is the opposite of female **3** : MASCULINE — **male·ness** *n*
male·dic·tion \ˌma-lə-ˈdik-shən\ *n* : CURSE, EXECRATION
male·fac·tor \ˈma-lə-ˌfak-tər\ *n* : EVILDOER; *esp* : one who commits an offense against the law — **mal·e·fac·tion** \ˌma-lə-ˈfak-shən\ *n*
ma·lef·ic \mə-ˈle-fik\ *adj* **1** : BALEFUL ⟨~ influences⟩ **2** : MALICIOUS
ma·lef·i·cent \-fə-sənt\ *adj* : working or productive of harm or evil
ma·lev·o·lent \mə-ˈle-və-lənt\ *adj* : having, showing, or arising from ill will, spite, or hatred ♦ ***Synonyms*** MALIGNANT, MALIGN, MALICIOUS, SPITEFUL — **ma·lev·o·lence** \-ləns\ *n*
mal·fea·sance \mal-ˈfē-zᵊns\ *n* : wrongful conduct esp. by a public official
mal·for·ma·tion \ˌmal-fȯr-ˈmā-shən\ *n* : irregular or faulty formation or structure; *also* : an instance of this — **malformed** \mal-ˈfȯrmd\ *adj*
mal·func·tion \mal-ˈfəŋk-shən\ *vb* : to fail to operate normally — **malfunction** *n*
mal·ice \ˈma-ləs\ *n* : desire to cause injury or distress to another — **ma·li·cious** \mə-ˈli-shəs\ *adj* — **ma·li·cious·ly** *adv*
¹**ma·lign** \mə-ˈlīn\ *adj* **1** : evil in nature, influence, or effect; *also* : MALIGNANT 2 **2** : moved by ill will
²**malign** *vb* : to speak evil of : DEFAME
ma·lig·nant \mə-ˈlig-nənt\ *adj* **1** : INJURIOUS, MALIGN **2** : tending to produce death or deterioration ⟨a ~ tumor⟩ — **ma·lig·nan·cy** \-nən-sē\ *n* — **ma·lig·nant·ly** *adv* — **ma·lig·ni·ty** \-nə-tē\ *n*
ma·lin·ger \mə-ˈliŋ-gər\ *vb* [F *malingre* sickly] : to pretend illness so as to avoid duty — **ma·lin·ger·er** *n*
mal·i·son \ˈma-lə-sən, -zən\ *n* : CURSE
mall \ˈmȯl, ˈmal\ *n* **1** : a shaded walk : PROMENADE **2** : an urban shopping area featuring a variety of shops surrounding a concourse **3** : a usu. large enclosed suburban shopping area containing various shops
mal·lard \ˈma-lərd\ *n, pl* **mallard** *or* **mallards** : a common wild duck that is the source of domestic ducks
mal·lea·ble \ˈma-lē-ə-bəl\ *adj* **1** : capable of being extended or shaped by beating with a hammer or by the pressure of rollers **2** : ADAPTABLE, PLIABLE ⟨~ young minds⟩ ♦ ***Synonyms*** PLASTIC, PLIANT, DUCTILE, SUPPLE — **mal·le·a·bil·i·ty** \ˌma-lē-ə-ˈbi-lə-tē\ *n*
mal·let \ˈma-lət\ *n* **1** : a tool with a large head for driving another tool or for striking a surface without marring it **2** : a long-handled hammerlike implement for striking a ball (as in croquet)
mal·le·us \ˈma-lē-əs\ *n, pl* **mal·lei** \-lē-ˌī, -lē-ˌē\ [NL, fr. L, hammer] : the outermost of the three small bones of the mammalian middle ear
mal·low \ˈma-lō\ *n* : any of a genus of herbs with lobed leaves, usu. showy flowers, and a disk-shaped fruit
malm·sey \ˈmälm-zē\ *n, often cap* : the sweetest variety of Madeira
mal·nour·ished \mal-ˈnər-isht\ *adj* : UNDERNOURISHED
mal·nu·tri·tion \ˌmal-nü-ˈtri-shən, -nyü-\ *n* : faulty and esp. inadequate nutrition
mal·oc·clu·sion \ˌma-lə-ˈklü-zhən\ *n* : faulty coming together of teeth in biting
mal·odor·ous \ma-ˈlō-də-rəs\ *adj* : ill-smelling — **mal·odor·ous·ly** *adv* — **mal·odor·ous·ness** *n*
maloti *pl of* LOTI
mal·prac·tice \mal-ˈprak-təs\ *n* : a dereliction of professional duty or a failure of professional skill that results in injury, loss, or damage

malt \ˈmȯlt\ *n* **1** : grain and esp. barley steeped in water until it has sprouted and used in brewing and distilling **2** : liquor made with malt — **malty** *adj*
malted milk \ˈmȯl-təd-\ *n* : a powder prepared from dried milk and an extract from malt; *also* : a beverage of this powder in milk or other liquid
Mal·thu·sian \mal-ˈthü-zhən, -ˈthyü-\ *adj* : of or relating to a theory that population unless checked (as by war) tends to increase faster than its means of subsistence — **Malthusian** *n* — **Mal·thu·sian·ism** \-zhə-ˌni-zəm\ *n*
malt·ose \ˈmȯl-ˌtōs\ *n* : a sugar formed esp. from starch by the action of enzymes
mal·treat \mal-ˈtrēt\ *vb* : to treat cruelly or roughly : ABUSE — **mal·treat·ment** *n*
mal·ware \ˈmal-ˌwer\ *n* : software designed to interfere with a computer's normal functioning
ma·ma *or* **mam·ma** \ˈmä-mə\ *n* : MOTHER
mam·bo \ˈmäm-bō\ *n, pl* **mambos** : a dance of Cuban origin related to the rumba — **mambo** *vb*
mam·mal \ˈma-məl\ *n* [NL *Mammalia,* fr. LL, neut. pl. of *mammalis* of the breast, fr. L *mamma* breast] : any of a class of warm-blooded vertebrates that includes humans and all other animals which nourish their young with milk and have the skin more or less covered with hair — **mam·ma·li·an** \mə-ˈmā-lē-ən, ma-\ *adj or n*
mam·ma·ry \ˈma-mə-rē\ *adj* : of, relating to, or being the glands (**mammary glands**) that in female mammals secrete milk
mam·mo·gram \ˈma-mə-ˌgram\ *n* : an X-ray photograph of the breasts
mam·mog·ra·phy \ma-ˈmä-grə-fē\ *n* : X-ray examination of the breasts (as for early detection of cancer)
mam·mon \ˈma-mən\ *n, often cap* : material wealth having a debasing influence
¹**mam·moth** \ˈma-məth\ *n* : any of a genus of large hairy extinct elephants
²**mammoth** *adj* : of very great size : GIGANTIC ♦ ***Synonyms*** COLOSSAL, ENORMOUS, IMMENSE, VAST, ELEPHANTINE
¹**man** \ˈman\ *n, pl* **men** \ˈmen\ **1** : a human being; *esp* : an adult male **2** : the human race : HUMANKIND **3** : one possessing in high degree the qualities considered distinctive of manhood **4** : an adult male servant or employee **5** : the individual who can fulfill one's requirements ⟨he's your ~⟩ **6** : one of the pieces with which various games (as chess) are played **7** : one of the players on a team **8** *often cap* : white society or people
²**man** *vb* **manned; man·ning** **1** : to supply with people ⟨~ a fleet⟩ **2** : FORTIFY, BRACE
³**man** *abbr* manual
Man *abbr* Manitoba
man–about–town *n, pl* **men–about–town** : a worldly and socially active man
man·a·cle \ˈma-ni-kəl\ *n* **1** : a shackle for the hand or wrist **2** : something used as a restraint
man·age \ˈma-nij\ *vb* **man·aged; man·ag·ing** **1** : HANDLE, CONTROL ⟨~*s* her skis well⟩; *also* : to direct or carry on business or affairs **2** : to make and keep compliant **3** : to treat with care : HUSBAND **4** : to achieve one's purpose : CONTRIVE — **man·age·abil·i·ty** \ˌma-ni-jə-ˈbi-lə-tē\ *n* — **man·age·able** \ˈma-ni-jə-bəl\ *adj* — **man·age·able·ness** *n* — **man·age·ably** \-blē\ *adv*
managed care *n* : a health-care system that controls costs by limiting doctor's fees and by restricting the patient's choice of doctors
man·age·ment \ˈma-nij-mənt\ *n* **1** : the act or art of managing : CONTROL **2** : judicious use of means to accomplish an end **3** : the group of those who manage or direct an enterprise
man·ag·er \ˈma-ni-jər\ *n* : one that manages — **man·a·ge·ri·al** \ˌma-nə-ˈjir-ē-əl\ *adj*
ma·ña·na \mən-ˈyä-nə\ *n* [Sp, lit., tomorrow] : an indefinite time in the future
ma·nat \mä-ˈnät\ *n, pl* **manat** *or* **manats** — see MONEY table
man–at–arms *n, pl* **men–at–arms** : SOLDIER; *esp* : one who is heavily armed and mounted
man·a·tee \ˈma-nə-ˌtē\ *n* : any of a genus of chiefly tropical plant-eating aquatic mammals having a broad rounded tail
man·ci·ple \ˈman-sə-pəl\ *n* : a steward or purveyor esp. for a college or monastery
man·da·mus \man-ˈdā-məs\ *n* [L, we enjoin] : a writ issued by a superior court commanding that an official act or duty be performed
man·da·rin \ˈman-də-rən\ *n* **1** : a public official of high rank under the Chinese Empire **2** *cap* : the chief dialect group of China **3** : a yellow to reddish orange loose-skinned citrus fruit; *also* : a tree that bears mandarins
man·date \ˈman-ˌdāt\ *n* **1** : an authoritative command **2** : an authorization to act given to a representative **3** : a commission granted by the League of Nations to a member nation for governing conquered territory; *also* : a territory so governed
man·da·to·ry \ˈman-də-ˌtȯr-ē\ *adj* **1** : containing or constituting a command : OBLIGATORY **2** : of or relating to a League of Nations mandate
man·di·ble \ˈman-də-bəl\ *n* **1** : JAW; *esp* : a lower jaw **2** : either segment of a bird's bill — **man·dib·u·lar** \man-ˈdi-byə-lər\ *adj*
man·do·lin \ˌman-də-ˈlin, ˈman-də-lən\ *n* : a stringed musical instrument with a pear-shaped body and a fretted neck
man·drake \ˈman-ˌdrāk\ *n* **1** : an Old World herb related to the nightshades or its large forked root formerly credited with magical properties **2** : MAYAPPLE
man·drel *also* **man·dril** \ˈman-drəl\ *n* **1** : an axle or spindle inserted into a hole in a piece of work to support it during

machining **2** : a metal bar used as a core around which material may be cast, shaped, or molded

man•drill \ˈman-drəl\ *n* : a large baboon of western central Africa

mane \ˈmān\ *n* : long heavy hair growing about the neck of some mammals (as horses) — **maned** \ˈmānd\ *adj*

man–eat•er \ˈman-ˌē-tər\ *n* : one (as a shark or cannibal) that has or is thought to have an appetite for human flesh — **man–eat•ing** *adj*

ma•nège \ma-ˈnezh, mə-\ *n* : the art of horsemanship or of training horses

ma•nes \ˈmä-ˌnās, ˈmā-ˌnēz\ *n pl, often cap* : the spirits of the dead and gods of the lower world in ancient Roman belief

ma•neu•ver \mə-ˈnü-vər, -ˈnyü-\ *n* [F *manœuvre,* fr. OF *maneuvre* work done by hand, fr. ML *manuopera,* fr. *manu operare* to work by hand] **1** : a military or naval movement; *also* : an armed forces training exercise — often used in pl. **2** : a procedure involving expert physical movement **3** : an evasive movement or shift of tactics; *also* : an action taken to gain a tactical end — **maneuver** *vb* — **ma•neu•ver•abil•i•ty** \-ˌnü-və-rə-ˈbi-lə-tē, -ˌnyü-\ *n* — **ma•neu•ver•able** \-ˈnü-və-rə-bəl, -ˈnyü-\ *adj*

man Friday *n* : an efficient and devoted aide or employee

man•ful \ˈman-fəl\ *adj* : having or showing courage and resolution ⟨a ~ struggle⟩ — **man•ful•ly** *adv*

man•ga \ˈmäŋ-gə\ *n* [Jp, comic, cartoon, fr. *man-* involuntary, aimless + *-ga* picture] : a Japanese comic book or graphic novel

man•ga•nese \ˈmaŋ-gə-ˌnēz, -ˌnēs\ *n* : a metallic chemical element resembling iron but not magnetic

mange \ˈmānj\ *n* : any of several contagious itchy skin diseases esp. of domestic animals — **mangy** \ˈmān-jē\ *adj*

man•ger \ˈmān-jər\ *n* : a trough or open box for livestock feed or fodder

[1]**man•gle** \ˈmaŋ-gəl\ *vb* **man•gled; man•gling** **1** : to cut, bruise, or hack with repeated blows **2** : to spoil or injure esp. through ineptitude — **man•gler** *n*

[2]**mangle** *n* : a machine with heated rollers for ironing laundry

man•go \ˈmaŋ-gō\ *n, pl* **mangoes** *also* **mangos** [Pg *manga,* prob. fr. Malayalam (Dravidian language of India) *māṅṅa*] : an edible juicy yellowish-red fruit borne by a tropical evergreen tree related to the sumacs; *also* : this tree

man•grove \ˈman-ˌgrōv\ *n* : any of a genus of tropical maritime trees that send out many prop roots and form dense thickets important in coastal land building

man•han•dle \ˈman-ˌhan-dᵊl\ *vb* : to handle roughly

man•hat•tan \man-ˈha-tᵊn\ *n, often cap* : a cocktail made of whiskey and vermouth

man•hole \ˈman-ˌhōl\ *n* : a hole through which a person may go esp. to gain access to an underground or enclosed structure

man•hood \-ˌhu̇d\ *n* **1** : the condition of being an adult male **2** : qualities associated with men : MANLINESS **3** : MEN ⟨the nation's ~⟩

man–hour \-ˈau̇(-ə)r\ *n* : a unit of one hour's work by one person

man•hunt \-ˌhənt\ *n* : an organized hunt for a person and esp. for one charged with a crime

ma•nia \ˈmā-nē-ə, -nyə\ *n* **1** : excitement manifested by mental and physical hyperactivity, disorganized behavior, and elevated mood **2** : excessive enthusiasm

ma•ni•ac \ˈmā-nē-ˌak\ *n* : LUNATIC, MADMAN

ma•ni•a•cal \mə-ˈnī-ə-kəl\ *also* **ma•ni•ac** \ˈmā-nē-ak\ *adj* **1** : affected with or suggestive of madness **2** : FRANTIC ⟨a ~ mob⟩

man•ic \ˈma-nik\ *adj* : affected with, relating to, characterized by, or resulting from mania — **manic** *n* — **man•i•cal•ly** \-ni-k(ə-)lē\ *adv*

manic depression *n* : BIPOLAR DISORDER

man•ic–de•pres•sive \ˌma-nik-di-ˈpre-siv\ *adj* : characterized by or affected with either mania or depression or alternating episodes of mania and depression — **manic–depressive** *n*

[1]**man•i•cure** \ˈma-nə-ˌkyu̇r\ *n* **1** : MANICURIST **2** : a treatment for the care of the hands and nails

[2]**manicure** *vb* **-cured; -cur•ing** **1** : to do manicure work on **2** : to trim closely and evenly

man•i•cur•ist \-ˌkyu̇r-ist\ *n* : a person who gives manicure treatments

[1]**man•i•fest** \ˈma-nə-ˌfest\ *adj* [ME, fr. AF or L; AF *manifeste,* fr. L *manifestus,* caught in the act, flagrant, obvious, perh. fr. *manus* hand + *-festus* (akin to L *infestus* hostile)] **1** : readily perceived by the senses and esp. by the sight **2** : easily understood : OBVIOUS — **man•i•fest•ly** *adv*

[2]**manifest** *vb* : to make evident or certain by showing or displaying ♦ ***Synonyms*** EVINCE, DEMONSTRATE, EXHIBIT

[3]**manifest** *n* : a list of passengers or an invoice of cargo for a ship or plane

man•i•fes•ta•tion \ˌma-nə-fə-ˈstā-shən\ *n* : DISPLAY, DEMONSTRATION

man•i•fes•to \ˌma-nə-ˈfes-tō\ *n, pl* **-tos** *or* **-toes** : a public declaration of intentions, motives, or views

[1]**man•i•fold** \ˈma-nə-ˌfōld\ *adj* **1** : marked by diversity or variety **2** : consisting of or operating many of one kind combined

[2]**manifold** *n* : a pipe fitting with several lateral outlets for connecting it with other pipes

[3]**manifold** *vb* **1** : MULTIPLY **2** : to make a number of copies of (as a letter)

man•i•kin *also* **man•ni•kin** \ˈma-ni-kən\ *n* **1** : MANNEQUIN **2** *dated, usu disparaging* : a little man : DWARF

Ma•nila hemp \mə-ˈni-lə-\ *n* : a tough fiber from a Philippine plant related to the banana that is used for cordage

manila paper *n, often cap M* : a tough brownish paper made orig. from Manila hemp

man·i·oc \ˈma-nē-ˌäk\ *n* : CASSAVA
ma·nip·u·late \mə-ˈni-pyə-ˌlāt\ *vb* **-lat·ed; -lat·ing** **1** : to treat or operate manually or mechanically esp. with skill **2** : to manage or use skillfully **3** : to influence esp. with intent to deceive — **ma·nip·u·la·tion** \mə-ni-pyə-ˈlā-shən\ *n* — **ma·nip·u·la·tive** \-ˈni-pyə-ˌlā-tiv\ *adj* — **ma·nip·u·la·tor** \-ˌlā-tər\ *n*
ma·nip·u·la·tives \mə-ˈni-pyə-ˌlā-tivz\ *n pl* : objects that a student is instructed to use in a way that teaches or reinforces a lesson
man·kind *n* **1** ˈman-ˈkīnd : the human race **2** -ˌkīnd : men as distinguished from women
[1]**man·ly** \ˈman-lē\ *adv* : in a manly manner
[2]**manly** *adj* **man·li·er; -est** : having qualities appropriate to or generally associated with a man : BOLD, RESOLUTE ⟨a ∼ competitor⟩ — **man·li·ness** *n*
man–made \ˈman-ˈmād\ *adj* : made by humans rather than nature ⟨∼ systems⟩; *esp* : SYNTHETIC ⟨∼ fibers⟩
man·na \ˈma-nə\ *n* **1** : food miraculously supplied to the Israelites in the wilderness **2** : something of value that comes unexpectedly : WINDFALL
manned \ˈmand\ *adj* : carrying or performed by a person ⟨∼ spaceflight⟩
man·ne·quin \ˈma-ni-kən\ *n* **1** : a form representing the human figure used esp. for displaying clothes **2** : a person employed to model clothing
man·ner \ˈma-nər\ *n* **1** : KIND, SORT ⟨what ∼ of man is he⟩ **2** : a way of acting or proceeding ⟨worked in a brisk ∼⟩; *also* : normal behavior ⟨spoke bluntly as was his ∼⟩ **3** : a method of artistic execution **4** *pl* : social conduct; *also* : BEARING **5** *pl* : BEHAVIOR ⟨taught the child good ∼*s*⟩
man·nered \ˈma-nərd\ *adj* **1** : having manners of a specified kind ⟨well-*mannered*⟩ **2** : having an artificial character ⟨a highly ∼ style⟩
man·ner·ism \ˈma-nə-ˌri-zəm\ *n* **1** : ARTIFICIALITY, PRECIOSITY **2** : a peculiarity of action, bearing, or treatment ♦ ***Synonyms*** POSE, AIR, AFFECTATION
man·ner·ly \ˈma-nər-lē\ *adj* : showing good manners : POLITE — **man·ner·li·ness** *n* — **mannerly** *adv*
man·nish \ˈma-nish\ *adj* **1** : resembling or suggesting a man rather than a woman **2** : generally associated with or characteristic of a man ⟨a ∼ voice⟩ — **man·nish·ly** *adv* — **man·nish·ness** *n*
ma·no a ma·no \ˌmä-nō-ä-ˈmä-nō\ *adv or adj* : in direct competition or conflict
ma·noeu·vre \mə-ˈnü-vər, -ˈnyü-\ *chiefly Brit var of* MANEUVER
man–of–war \ˌman-əv-ˈwȯr\ *n, pl* **men–of–war** \ˌmen-\ : WARSHIP
ma·nom·e·ter \mə-ˈnä-mə-tər\ *n* : an instrument for measuring the pressure of gases and vapors — **mano·met·ric** \ˌma-nə-ˈme-trik\ *adj*
man·or \ˈma-nər\ *n* **1** : the house or hall of an estate; *also* : a landed estate **2** : an English estate of a feudal lord — **ma·no·ri·al** \mə-ˈnȯr-ē-əl\ *adj* — **ma·no·ri·al·ism** \-ə-ˌli-zəm\ *n*
man power *n* **1** : power available from or supplied by the physical effort of human beings **2** *usu* **man·pow·er** : the total supply of persons available and fitted for service
man·qué \mäⁿ-ˈkā\ *adj* [F, fr. pp. of *manquer* to lack, fail] : short of or frustrated in the fulfillment of one's aspirations or talents ⟨a poet ∼⟩
man·sard \ˈman-ˌsärd, -sərd\ *n* : a roof having two slopes on all sides with the lower slope steeper than the upper one
manse \ˈmans\ *n* : the residence esp. of a Presbyterian minister
man·ser·vant \ˈman-ˌsər-vənt\ *n, pl* **men·ser·vants** \ˈmen-ˌsər-vənts\ : a male servant
man·sion \ˈman-chən\ *n* : a large imposing residence; *also* : a separate apartment in a large structure
man–size \ˈman-ˌsīz\ *or* **man–sized** \-ˌsīzd\ *adj* : suitable for or requiring a man ⟨a ∼ job⟩
man·slaugh·ter \-ˌslȯ-tər\ *n* : the unlawful killing of a human being without express or implied malice
man·ta \ˈman-tə\ *n* : a square piece of cloth or blanket used in southwestern U.S. and Latin America as a cloak or shawl
man·teau \man-ˈtō\ *n* : a loose cloak, coat, or robe
man·tel \ˈman-tᵊl\ *n* : a beam, stone, or arch serving as a lintel to support the masonry above a fireplace; *also* : a shelf above a fireplace
man·tel·piece \ˈman-tᵊl-ˌpēs\ *n* : the shelf of a mantel
man·til·la \man-ˈtē-yə, -ˈti-lə\ *n* : a light scarf worn over the head and shoulders esp. by Spanish and Latin-American women
man·tis \ˈman-təs\ *n, pl* **man·tis·es** *also* **man·tes** \-ˌtēz\ [NL, fr. Gk, lit., diviner, prophet] : any of a group of large usu. green insect-eating insects that hold their prey in forelimbs folded as if in prayer
man·tis·sa \man-ˈti-sə\ *n* : the part of a logarithm to the right of the decimal point
[1]**man·tle** \ˈman-tᵊl\ *n* **1** : a loose sleeveless garment worn over other clothes **2** : something that covers, enfolds, or envelops **3** : a lacy sheath that gives light by incandescence when placed over a flame **4** : the portion of the earth lying between the crust and the core **5** : MANTEL
[2]**mantle** *vb* **man·tled; man·tling** **1** : to cover with a mantle **2** : BLUSH
man·tra \ˈman-trə\ *n* : a mystical formula of invocation or incantation (as in Hinduism)
[1]**man·u·al** \ˈman-yə-wəl\ *adj* **1** : of, relating to, or involving the hands; *also* : worked by hand ⟨a ∼ pump⟩ **2** : requiring or using physical skill and energy ⟨∼ labor⟩ — **man·u·al·ly** *adv*
[2]**manual** *n* **1** : a small book; *esp* : HANDBOOK **2** : the prescribed movements in

the handling of a military item and esp. a weapon during a drill or ceremony ⟨the ~ of arms⟩ **3** : a keyboard esp. of an organ **4** : an automobile with a manual transmission

man·u·fac·to·ry \ˌman-yə-ˈfak-tə-rē\ *n* : FACTORY

[1]**man·u·fac·ture** \ˌman-yə-ˈfak-chər\ *n* [MF, fr. ML *manufactura,* L *manu factus* made by hand] **1** : something made from raw materials **2** : the process of making wares by hand or by machinery; *also* : a productive industry using machinery

[2]**manufacture** *vb* **-tured; -tur·ing** **1** : to make from raw materials by hand or by machinery; *also* : to engage in manufacture **2** : INVENT, FABRICATE; *also* : CREATE — **man·u·fac·tur·er** *n*

man·u·mit \ˌman-yə-ˈmit\ *vb* **-mit·ted; -mit·ting** : to free from slavery — **man·u·mis·sion** \-ˈmi-shən\ *n*

[1]**ma·nure** \mə-ˈnu̇r, -ˈnyu̇r\ *vb* **ma·nured; ma·nur·ing** : to fertilize land with manure

[2]**manure** *n* : FERTILIZER; *esp* : refuse from stables and barnyards — **ma·nu·ri·al** \-ˈnu̇r-ē-əl, -ˈnyu̇r-\ *adj*

man·u·script \ˈman-yə-ˌskript\ *n* [L *manu scriptus* written by hand] **1** : a written or typed composition or document; *also* : a document submitted for publication **2** : writing as opposed to print

Manx \ˈmaŋks\ *n pl* : the people of the Isle of Man — **Manx** *adj*

[1]**many** \ˈme-nē\ *adj* **more** \ˈmōr\; **most** \ˈmōst\ : consisting of or amounting to a large but indefinite number ⟨~ years ago⟩

[2]**many** *pron* : a large number ⟨~ are called⟩

[3]**many** *n* : a large but indefinite number ⟨a good ~ of them⟩

many·fold \ˌme-nē-ˈfōld\ *adv* : by many times

many–sid·ed \-ˈsī-dəd\ *adj* **1** : having many sides or aspects **2** : VERSATILE

Mao·ism \ˈmau̇-ˌi-zəm\ *n* : the theory and practice of Communism developed in China chiefly by Mao Zedong — **Mao·ist** \ˈmau̇-ist\ *n or adj*

Mao·ri \ˈmau̇(-ə)r-ē\ *n, pl* **Maori** *or* **Mao·ris** : a member of a Polynesian people native to New Zealand

[1]**map** \ˈmap\ *n* [ML *mappa,* fr. L, napkin, towel] **1** : a representation usu. on a flat surface of the whole or part of an area **2** : a representation of the celestial sphere or part of it

[2]**map** *vb* **mapped; map·ping** **1** : to make a map of **2** : to plan in detail ⟨~ out a program⟩ — **map·pa·ble** \ˈma-pə-bəl\ *adj* — **map·per** *n*

MAP *abbr* modified American plan

ma·ple \ˈmā-pəl\ *n* : any of a genus of trees or shrubs with 2-winged dry fruit and opposite leaves; *also* : the hard light-colored wood of a maple used esp. for floors and furniture

maple sugar *n* : sugar made by boiling maple syrup

maple syrup *n* : syrup made by concentrating the sap of maple trees and esp. the sugar maple

mar \ˈmär\ *vb* **marred; mar·ring** : to detract from the wholeness or perfection of : SPOIL ♦ ***Synonyms*** INJURE, HURT, HARM, DAMAGE, IMPAIR, BLEMISH

Mar *abbr* March

ma·ra·ca \mə-ˈrä-kə, -ˈra-\ *n* [Pg *maracá*] : a rattle usu. made from a gourd and used as a percussion instrument

mar·a·schi·no \ˌmer-ə-ˈskē-nō-, -ˈshē-\ *n, often cap* : a cherry preserved in a sweet liqueur made from the juice of a bitter wild cherry

mar·a·thon \ˈmer-ə-ˌthän\ *n* [*Marathon,* Greece, site of a victory of Greeks over Persians in 490 B.C. the news of which was carried to Athens by a long-distance runner] **1** : a long-distance race esp. on foot **2** : an endurance contest

mar·a·thon·er \ˈmer-ə-ˌthä-nər\ *n* : a person who takes part in a marathon — **mar·a·thon·ing** *n*

ma·raud \mə-ˈro̊d\ *vb* : to roam about and raid in search of plunder : PILLAGE — **ma·raud·er** *n*

mar·ble \ˈmär-bəl\ *n* **1** : a limestone that can be polished and used in fine building work **2** : something resembling marble (as in coldness) **3** : a small ball (as of glass) used in various games; *also, pl* : a children's game played with these small balls — **marble** *adj*

mar·bling \-bə-liŋ, -bliŋ\ *n* : an intermixture of fat through the lean of a cut of meat

mar·cel \mär-ˈsel\ *n* : a deep soft wave made in the hair by the use of a heated curling iron — **marcel** *vb*

[1]**march** \ˈmärch\ *n* : a border region : FRONTIER

[2]**march** *vb* **1** : to move along in or as if in military formation **2** : to walk in a direct purposeful manner; *also* : PROGRESS, ADVANCE **3** : TRAVERSE ⟨~*ed* 10 miles⟩ — **march·er** *n*

[3]**march** *n* **1** : the action of marching; *also* : the distance covered (as by a military unit) in a march **2** : a regular measured stride or rhythmic step used in marching **3** : forward movement **4** : a piece of music with marked rhythm suitable for marching to

March *n* [ME, fr. AF, fr. L *martius,* fr. *martius* of Mars, fr. *Mart-, Mars,* Roman god of war] : the 3d month of the year

mar·chio·ness \ˈmär-shə-nəs\ *n* **1** : the wife or widow of a marquess **2** : a woman holding the rank of a marquess in her own right

Mar·di Gras \ˈmär-dē-ˌgrä\ *n* [F, lit., fat Tuesday] : the Tuesday before Ash Wednesday often observed with parades and merrymaking

[1]**mare** \ˈmer\ *n* : an adult female of the horse or a related mammal

[2]**ma·re** \ˈmär-(ˌ)ā\ *n, pl* **ma·ria** \ˈmär-ē-ə\ : any of several large dark areas on the surface of the moon or Mars

mar·ga·rine \ˈmär-jə-rən\ *n* : a food product made usu. from vegetable oils churned with skimmed milk and used as a substitute for butter

mar·ga·ri·ta \ˌmär-gə-ˈrē-tə\ *n* : a cocktail consisting of tequila, lime or lemon juice, and an orange-flavored liqueur

mar·gin \ˈmär-jən\ *n* **1** : the part of a page outside the main body of printed or written matter **2** : EDGE ⟨continental ~⟩ **3** : a spare amount, measure, or degree allowed for use if needed ⟨a safety ~⟩ **4** : measure or degree of difference ⟨a one-vote ~⟩

mar·gin·al \-jə-nəl\ *adj* **1** : written or printed in the margin **2** : of, relating to, or situated at a margin or border **3** : close to the lower limit of quality or acceptability **4** : excluded from or existing outside the mainstream of society or a group — **mar·gin·al·ly** *adv*

mar·gi·na·lia \ˌmär-jə-ˈnā-lē-ə\ *n pl* : marginal notes or embellishments

mar·gin·al·ize \ˈmär-jə-nᵊl-ˌīz\ *vb* **-ized; -iz·ing** : to relegate to an unimportant position within a society or group

mar·grave \ˈmär-ˌgrāv\ *n* : the military governor esp. of a medieval German border province

ma·ri·a·chi \ˌmär-ē-ˈä-chē, ˌmer-\ *n* : a Mexican street band; *also* : a member of or the music of such a band

mari·gold \ˈmer-ə-ˌgōld\ *n* : any of a genus of tropical American herbs related to the daisies that are grown for their showy usu. yellow, orange, or maroon flower heads

mar·i·jua·na *also* **mar·i·hua·na** \ˌmer-ə-ˈwä-nə, -ˈhwä-\ *n* [MexSp *marihuana*] : the dried leaves and flowering tops of the female hemp plant smoked usu. illegally for their intoxicating effect; *also* : HEMP

ma·rim·ba \mə-ˈrim-bə\ *n* : a xylophone of southern Africa and Central America; *also* : a modern version of it

ma·ri·na \mə-ˈrē-nə\ *n* : a dock or basin providing secure moorings for pleasure boats

mar·i·nade \ˌmer-ə-ˈnād\ *n* : a savory usu. acidic sauce in which meat, fish, or a vegetable is soaked to enrich its flavor or to tenderize it

mar·i·na·ra \ˌmer-ə-ˈner-ə\ *adj* [It (*alla*) *marinara,* lit., in sailor style] : made with tomatoes, onions, garlic, and spices; *also* : served with marinara sauce

mar·i·nate \ˈmer-ə-ˌnāt\ *vb* **-nat·ed; -nat·ing** : to steep (as meat or fish) in a marinade

¹**ma·rine** \mə-ˈrēn\ *adj* **1** : of or relating to the sea or its navigation or commerce **2** : of or relating to marines

²**marine** *n* **1** : the mercantile and naval shipping of a country **2** : any of a class of soldiers serving on shipboard or with a naval force

mar·i·ner \ˈmer-ə-nər\ *n* : SAILOR

mar·i·o·nette \ˌmer-ē-ə-ˈnet\ *n* : a puppet moved by strings or by hand

mar·i·tal \ˈmer-ə-tᵊl\ *adj* : of or relating to marriage : CONJUGAL ♦ ***Synonyms*** MATRIMONIAL, CONNUBIAL, NUPTIAL

mar·i·time \ˈmer-ə-ˌtīm\ *adj* **1** : of, relating to, or bordering on the sea **2** : of or relating to navigation or commerce of the sea

mar·jo·ram \ˈmär-jə-rəm\ *n* : any of various fragrant mints often used as seasoning

¹**mark** \ˈmärk\ *n* **1** : something (as a line or fixed object) designed to record position; *also* : the starting line or position in a track event **2** : TARGET; *also* : GOAL, OBJECT **3** : an object of abuse or ridicule **4** : the question under discussion **5** : NORM ⟨not up to the ~⟩ **6** : a visible sign : INDICATION; *also* : CHARACTERISTIC **7** : a written or printed symbol **8** : GRADE 5 ⟨a ~ of B+⟩ **9** : IMPORTANCE, DISTINCTION **10** : a lasting impression ⟨made his ~ in the world⟩; *also* : a damaging impression left on a surface

²**mark** *vb* **1** : to set apart by a line or boundary **2** : to designate by a mark or make a mark on **3** : CHARACTERIZE ⟨the vehemence that ~*s* his speeches⟩; *also* : SIGNALIZE ⟨this year ~*s* our 50th anniversary⟩ **4** : to take notice of : OBSERVE ⟨~ my words⟩ — **mark·er** *n*

³**mark** *n* : DEUTSCHE MARK

Mark \ˈmärk\ *n* — see BIBLE table

mar·ka \ˈmär-kə\ *n, pl* **mar·a·ka** \ˈmär-ə-kə\ *or* **marka** *or* **mar·kas** — see MONEY table

mark·down \ˈmärk-ˌdau̇n\ *n* **1** : a lowering of price **2** : the amount by which an original price is reduced

mark down *vb* : to put a lower price on

marked \ˈmärkt\ *adj* : NOTICEABLE — **mark·ed·ly** \ˈmär-kəd-lē\ *adv*

¹**mar·ket** \ˈmär-kət\ *n* **1** : a meeting together of people for trade by purchase and sale; *also* : a public place where such a meeting is held **2** : the rate or price offered for a commodity or security **3** : the course of commercial activity by which the exchange of commodities is effected **4** : a geographical area of demand for commodities; *also* : extent of demand **5** : a retail establishment usu. of a specific kind

²**market** *vb* : to go to a market to buy or sell; *also* : SELL — **mar·ket·able** *adj*

mar·ket·place \ˈmär-kət-ˌplās\ *n* **1** : an open square in a town where markets are held **2** : the world of trade or economic activity

mark·ka \ˈmär-ˌkä\ *n, pl* **mark·kaa** \ˈmär-ˌkä\ *or* **markkas** \-ˌkäz\ : the basic monetary unit of Finland from 1860 to 2002

marks·man \ˈmärks-mən\ *n* : a person skillful at hitting a target — **marks·man·ship** *n*

mark·up \ˈmär-ˌkəp\ *n* **1** : a raising of price **2** : an amount added to the cost price of an article to determine the selling price

mark up *vb* : to put a higher price on

markup language *n* : a system for marking the components and layout of a computer document

marl \ˈmärl\ *n* : an earthy deposit rich in lime used esp. as fertilizer — **marly** \ˈmär-lē\ *adj*

mar·lin \ˈmär-lən\ *n* : any of several large oceanic sport fishes related to sailfishes

mar·line·spike *also* **mar·lin·spike** \ˈmär-lən-ˌspīk\ *n* : a pointed iron tool used to separate strands of rope or wire (as in splicing)

mar·ma·lade \ˈmär-mə-ˌlād\ *n* : a clear jelly holding in suspension pieces of fruit and fruit rind

mar·mo·re·al \mär-ˈmȯr-ē-əl\ *adj* : of, relating to, or suggestive of marble

mar·mo·set \ˈmär-mə-ˌset\ *n* : any of numerous small bushy-tailed monkeys of Central and So. America

mar·mot \ˈmär-mət\ *n* : any of a genus of stout short-legged burrowing No. American rodents

¹**ma·roon** \mə-ˈrün\ *vb* **1** : to put ashore (as on a desolate island) and leave to one's fate **2** : to leave in isolation and without hope of escape

²**maroon** *n* : a dark red color

¹**mar·quee** \mär-ˈkē\ *n* [modif. of F *marquise,* lit., marchioness] **1** : a large tent set up (as for an outdoor party) **2** : a usu. metal and glass canopy over an entrance (as of a theater) **3** : a sign over the entrance of a theater or arena advertising a performance

²**marquee** *adj* : having or being a great attraction : PREEMINENT ⟨~ athletes⟩

mar·quess \ˈmär-kwəs\ *or* **mar·quis** \ˈmär-kwəs, mär-ˈkē\ *n* **1** : a nobleman of hereditary rank in Europe and Japan **2** : a member of the British peerage ranking below a duke and above an earl

mar·que·try \ˈmär-kə-trē\ *n* : inlaid work of wood, shell, or ivory (as on a table or cabinet)

mar·quise \mär-ˈkēz\ *n, pl* **mar·quises** *same or* -ˈkē-zəz\ : MARCHIONESS

mar·riage \ˈmer-ij\ *n* **1** : the state of being united as spouses in a consensual and contractual relationship recognized by law **2** : a wedding ceremony and attendant festivities **3** : a close union ⟨a ~ of light and shadow⟩ — **mar·riage·able** *adj*

married name *n* : a surname acquired through marriage

mar·row \ˈmer-ō\ *n* : a soft vascular tissue that fills the cavities of most bones

mar·row·bone \ˈmer-ə-ˌbōn, ˈmer-ō-\ *n* : a bone (as a shinbone) rich in marrow

mar·ry \ˈmer-ē\ *vb* **mar·ried; mar·ry·ing 1** : to join in marriage **2** : to take as a spouse : WED **3** : to enter into a close union **4** : COMBINE, UNITE — **mar·ried** *adj or n*

Mars \ˈmärz\ *n* : the planet 4th from the sun and conspicuous for its red color

marsh \ˈmärsh\ *n* : a tract of soft wet land — **marshy** *adj*

¹**mar·shal** \ˈmär-shəl\ *n* [ME, fr. AF *mareschal,* of Gmc origin; akin to OHG *marahscalc* marshal, fr. *marah* horse + *scalc* servant] **1** : a high official in a medieval household; *also* : a person in charge of the ceremonial aspects of a gathering **2** : a general officer of the highest military rank **3** : an administrative officer (as of a U.S. judicial district) having duties similar to a sheriff's **4** : the administrative head of a city police or fire department

²**marshal** *vb* **mar·shaled** *or* **mar·shalled; mar·shal·ing** *or* **mar·shal·ling 1** : to arrange in order, rank, or position ⟨~ troops⟩ **2** : to bring together ⟨~ arguments⟩ **3** : to lead with ceremony : USHER

marsh gas *n* : METHANE

marsh·mal·low \ˈmärsh-ˌme-lō, -ˌma-\ *n* : a light spongy confection made from corn syrup, sugar, albumen, and gelatin

marsh marigold *n* : a swamp herb related to the buttercups that has bright yellow flowers

mar·su·pi·al \mär-ˈsü-pē-əl\ *n* : any of an order of primitive mammals (as opossums, kangaroos, or wombats) that bear very immature young which are nourished in a pouch on the abdomen of the female — **marsupial** *adj*

mart \ˈmärt\ *n* : MARKET

mar·ten \ˈmär-tᵊn\ *n, pl* **marten** *or* **martens** : a slender mammal that is larger than the related weasels and has soft gray or brown fur; *also* : this fur

mar·tial \ˈmär-shəl\ *adj* [L *martialis* of Mars, fr. *Mart-, Mars* Mars, Roman god of war] **1** : of, relating to, or suited for war or a warrior ⟨~ music⟩ **2** : of or relating to an army or military life **3** : WARLIKE

martial art *n* : any of several arts of combat (as karate and judo) practiced as sport

martial law *n* **1** : the law applied in occupied territory by the occupying military forces **2** : the established law of a country administered by military forces in an emergency when civilian law enforcement agencies are unable to maintain public order and safety

mar·tian \ˈmär-shən\ *adj, often cap* : of or relating to the planet Mars or its hypothetical inhabitants — **martian** *n, often cap*

mar·tin \ˈmär-tᵊn\ *n* : any of several swallows and esp. one of No. America with purplish blue plumage

mar·ti·net \ˌmär-tə-ˈnet\ *n* : a strict disciplinarian

mar·tin·gale \ˈmär-tᵊn-ˌgāl\ *n* : a strap connecting a horse's girth to the bit or reins so as to hold down its head

mar·ti·ni \mär-ˈtē-nē\ *n* : a cocktail made of gin or vodka and dry vermouth

¹**mar·tyr** \ˈmär-tər\ *n* [ME, fr. OE, fr. LL, fr. Gk *martyr-, martys* witness] **1** : a person who dies rather than renounce a religion; *also* : a person who makes a great sacrifice for the sake of principle **2** : a great or constant sufferer

²**martyr** *vb* **1** : to put to death for adhering to a belief **2** : TORTURE

mar·tyr·dom \ˈmär-tər-dəm\ *n* **1** : the suffering and death of a martyr **2** : TORTURE

¹**mar·vel** \ˈmär-vəl\ *n* **1** : one that causes wonder or astonishment **2** : intense surprise or interest

[2]**marvel** *vb* **mar·veled** *or* **mar·velled; mar·vel·ing** *or* **mar·vel·ling** : to feel surprise, wonder, or amazed curiosity ⟨~*ed* at the circus act⟩

mar·vel·ous *or* **mar·vel·lous** \ˈmär-və-ləs\ *adj* **1** : causing wonder **2** : of the highest kind or quality — **mar·vel·ous·ly** *adv* — **mar·vel·ous·ness** *n*

Marx·ism \ˈmärk-ˌsi-zəm\ *n* : the political, economic, and social principles and policies advocated by Karl Marx — **Marx·ist** \-sist\ *n or adj*

mar·zi·pan \ˈmärt-sə-ˌpän, -ˌpan; ˈmär-zə-ˌpan\ *n* [G, fr. It *marzapane*] : a confection of almond paste, sugar, and egg whites

masc *abbr* masculine

mas·cara \ma-ˈsker-ə\ *n* : a cosmetic esp. for darkening the eyelashes

mas·car·po·ne \ˌmas-kär-ˈpō-nā\ *n* : an Italian cream cheese

mas·cot \ˈmas-ˌkät, -kət\ *n* [F *mascotte,* fr. Occitan *mascoto,* fr. *masco* witch, fr. ML *masca*] : a person, animal, or object adopted usu. by a group to bring good luck

[1]**mas·cu·line** \ˈmas-kyə-lən\ *adj* **1** : MALE; *also* : MANLY **2** : of, relating to, or constituting the gender that includes most words or grammatical forms referring to males — **mas·cu·lin·i·ty** \ˌmas-kyə-ˈli-nə-tē\ *n*

[2]**masculine** *n* : a noun, pronoun, adjective, or inflectional form or class of the masculine gender; *also* : the masculine gender

[1]**mash** \ˈmash\ *n* **1** : a mixture of ground feeds for livestock **2** : crushed malt or grain steeped in hot water to make wort **3** : a soft pulpy mass

[2]**mash** *vb* **1** : to reduce to a soft pulpy state **2** : CRUSH, SMASH ⟨~ a finger⟩ — **mash·er** *n*

MASH *abbr* mobile army surgical hospital

mash–up \ˈmash-ˌəp\ *n* : something created by combining elements from two or more sources

[1]**mask** \ˈmask\ *n* **1** : a cover for the face usu. for disguise or protection **2** : MASQUE **3** : a figure of a head worn on the stage in antiquity **4** : a copy of a face made by means of a mold ⟨death ~⟩ **5** : something that conceals or disguises **6** : the face of an animal

[2]**mask** *vb* **1** : to conceal from view : DISGUISE **2** : to cover for protection **3** : to put on a mask

mask·er \ˈmas-kər\ *n* : a participant in a masquerade

mas·och·ism \ˈma-sə-ˌki-zəm, ˈma-zə-\ *n* **1** : a sexual perversion characterized by pleasure in being subjected to pain or humiliation **2** : pleasure in being abused or dominated — **mas·och·ist** \-kist\ *n* — **mas·och·is·tic** \ˌma-sə-ˈkis-tik, ˌma-zə-\ *adj*

ma·son \ˈmā-sᵊn\ *n* **1** : a skilled worker who builds with stone, brick, or concrete **2** *cap* : FREEMASON

Ma·son·ic \mə-ˈsä-nik\ *adj* : of or relating to Freemasons or Freemasonry

ma·son·ry \ˈmā-sᵊn-rē\ *n, pl* **-ries** **1** : something constructed of materials used by masons **2** : the art, trade, or work of a mason **3** *cap* : FREEMASONRY

masque \ˈmask\ *n* **1** : MASQUERADE **2** : a short allegorical dramatic performance (as of the 17th century)

[1]**mas·quer·ade** \ˌmas-kə-ˈrād\ *n* **1** : a social gathering of persons wearing masks; *also* : a costume for wear at such a gathering **2** : DISGUISE

[2]**masquerade** *vb* **-ad·ed; -ad·ing** **1** : to disguise oneself : POSE **2** : to take part in a masquerade — **mas·quer·ad·er** *n*

[1]**mass** \ˈmas\ *n* **1** *cap* : a sequence of prayers and ceremonies forming the eucharistic service of the Roman Catholic Church **2** *often cap* : a celebration of the Eucharist **3** : a musical setting for parts of the Mass

[2]**mass** *n* **1** : a quantity or aggregate of matter usu. of considerable size **2** : EXPANSE, BULK; *also* : MASSIVENESS **3** : the principal part **4** : AGGREGATE, WHOLE **5** : the quantity of matter that a body possesses as measured by its inertia **6** : a large quantity, amount, or number **7** : the great body of people — usu. used in pl. — **massy** *adj*

[3]**mass** *vb* : to form or collect into a mass

Mass *abbr* Massachusetts

mas·sa·cre \ˈma-si-kər\ *n* **1** : the killing of many persons under cruel or atrocious circumstances **2** : a wholesale slaughter — **massacre** *vb*

[1]**mas·sage** \mə-ˈsäzh, -ˈsäj\ *n* : manipulation of tissues (as by rubbing and kneading) for therapeutic purposes

[2]**massage** *vb* **mas·saged; mas·sag·ing** **1** : to subject to massage **2** : to treat flatteringly; *also* : MANIPULATE, DOCTOR ⟨~ data⟩

mas·seur \ma-ˈsər\ *n* : a man who practices massage

mas·seuse \-ˈsərz, -ˈsüz\ *n* : a woman who practices massage

mas·sif \ma-ˈsēf\ *n* : a principal mountain mass

mas·sive \ˈma-siv\ *adj* **1** : forming or consisting of a large mass **2** : large in structure, scope, or degree — **mas·sive·ly** *adv* — **mas·sive·ness** *n*

mass·less \ˈmas-ləs\ *adj* : having no mass ⟨~ particles⟩

mass medium *n, pl* **mass media** : a medium of communication (as the newspapers or television) that is designed to reach the mass of the people

mass–pro·duce \ˌmas-prə-ˈdüs, -ˈdyüs\ *vb* : to produce in quantity usu. by machinery — **mass production** *n*

[1]**mast** \ˈmast\ *n* **1** : a long pole or spar rising from the keel or deck of a ship and supporting the yards, booms, and rigging **2** : a slender vertical structure — **mast·ed** \ˈmas-təd\ *adj*

[2]**mast** *n* : nuts (as acorns) accumulated on the forest floor and often serving as food for animals (as hogs)

mas·tec·to·my \ma-ˈstek-tə-mē\ *n, pl* **-mies** : surgical removal of the breast

[1]**mas•ter** \ˈmas-tər\ *n* **1** : a male teacher; *also* : a person holding an academic degree higher than a bachelor's but lower than a doctor's **2** : one highly skilled (as in an art or profession) **3** : one having authority or control **4** : VICTOR, SUPERIOR **5** : the commander of a merchant ship **6** : a youth or boy too young to be called *mister* — used as a title **7** : an original from which copies are made

[2]**master** *vb* **1** : to become master of : OVERCOME **2** : to become skilled or proficient in **3** : to produce a master recording of (as a musical performance)

master chief petty officer *n* : a petty officer of the highest rank in the navy

mas•ter•ful \ˈmas-tər-fəl\ *adj* **1** : inclined and usu. competent to act as master **2** : having or reflecting the skill of a master ⟨~ verse⟩ — **mas•ter•ful•ly** *adv* — **mas•ter•ful•ness** *n*

master gunnery sergeant *n* : a noncommissioned officer in the marine corps ranking above a master sergeant

master key *n* : a key designed to open several different locks

mas•ter•ly \ˈmas-tər-lē\ *adj* **1** : indicating thorough knowledge or superior skill ⟨~ performance⟩ **2** : having the skill of a master ⟨a ~ writer⟩ — **mas•ter•ly** *adv*

mas•ter•mind \-ˌmīnd\ *n* : a person who directs or provides creative intelligence for a project — **mastermind** *vb*

master of ceremonies : a person who acts as host at a formal event or a program of entertainment

mas•ter•piece \ˈmas-tər-ˌpēs\ *n* : a work done with extraordinary skill

master plan *n* : an overall plan

mas•ter's \ˈmas-tərz\ *n* : a master's degree

master sergeant *n* **1** : a noncommissioned officer in the army ranking next below a sergeant major **2** : a noncommissioned officer in the air force ranking next below a senior master sergeant **3** : a noncommissioned officer in the marine corps ranking next below a master gunnery sergeant

mas•ter•stroke \ˈmas-tər-ˌstrōk\ *n* : a masterly performance or move

mas•ter•work \-ˌwərk\ *n* : MASTERPIECE

mas•tery \ˈmas-tə-rē\ *n* **1** : DOMINION; *also* : SUPERIORITY **2** : possession or display of great skill or knowledge

mast•head \ˈmast-ˌhed\ *n* **1** : the top of a mast **2** : the printed matter in a newspaper or periodical giving the title and details of ownership and rates of subscription or advertising

mas•tic \ˈmas-tik\ *n* : a pasty material used as a coating or cement

mas•ti•cate \ˈmas-tə-ˌkāt\ *vb* **-cat•ed; -cat•ing** : CHEW — **mas•ti•ca•tion** \ˌmas-tə-ˈkā-shən\ *n*

mas•tiff \ˈmas-təf\ *n* : any of a breed of large smooth-coated dogs used esp. as guard dogs

mast•odon \ˈmas-tə-ˌdän\ *n* [NL, fr. Gk *mastos* breast + *odōn, odous* tooth] : any of numerous huge extinct mammals related to the mammoths

mas•toid \ˈmas-ˌtȯid\ *n* : a bony prominence behind the ear — **mastoid** *adj*

mas•tur•ba•tion \ˌmas-tər-ˈbā-shən\ *n* : stimulation of the genital organs apart from sexual intercourse, usu. to orgasm, and esp. by use of one's own hand — **mas•tur•bate** \ˈmas-tər-ˌbāt\ *vb* — **mas•tur•ba•to•ry** \ˈmas-tər-bə-ˌtȯr-ē\ *adj*

[1]**mat** \ˈmat\ *n* **1** : a piece of coarse woven or plaited fabric **2** : something made up of many intertwined strands **3** : a large thick pad used as a surface for wrestling and gymnastics

[2]**mat** *vb* **mat•ted; mat•ting** **1** : to provide with a mat **2** : to form into a tangled mass ⟨dirt *matted* her hair⟩

[3]**mat** *vb* **mat•ted; mat•ting** **1** *also* **matte** *or* **matt** : to make (as a color) matte **2** : to provide (a picture) with a mat

[4]**mat** *var of* [2]MATTE

[5]**mat** *or* **matt** *or* **matte** *n* : a border going around a picture between picture and frame or serving as the frame

mat•a•dor \ˈma-tə-ˌdȯr\ *n* [Sp, fr. *matar* to kill] : a bullfighter whose role is to kill the bull in a bullfight

[1]**match** \ˈmach\ *n* **1** : a person or thing equal or similar to another; *also* : one able to cope with another : RIVAL **2** : a suitable pairing of persons or objects **3** : a contest or game between two or more individuals **4** : a marriage union; *also* : a prospective marriage partner — **match•less** *adj*

[2]**match** *vb* **1** : to meet as an antagonist; *also* : PIT ⟨~ wits⟩ **2** : to provide with a worthy competitor; *also* : to set in comparison with **3** : MARRY **4** : to combine suitably or congenially ⟨~*ed* the drapes with the rug⟩; *also* : ADAPT, SUIT **5** : to act in harmony ⟨his shoes and belt ~⟩ **6** : to provide with a counterpart

[3]**match** *n* : a short slender piece of flammable material (as wood) tipped with a combustible mixture that ignites through friction

matcha \ˈmä-chə, ˈma-\ *n* : a green powder made from ground green tea leaves that is used as a flavoring agent and esp. to make tea

match•book \ˈmach-ˌbu̇k\ *n* : a small folder containing rows of paper matches

match•lock \-ˌläk\ *n* : a musket with a slow-burning cord lowered over a hole in the breech to ignite the charge

match•mak•er \-ˌmā-kər\ *n* : one who arranges a match and esp. a marriage

match•wood \-ˌwu̇d\ *n* : small pieces of wood

[1]**mate** \ˈmāt\ *vb* **mat•ed; mat•ing** : CHECKMATE — **mate** *n*

[2]**mate** *n* **1** : ASSOCIATE, COMPANION; *also* : HELPER **2** : a deck officer on a merchant ship ranking below the captain **3** : one of a pair; *esp* : either member of a married couple or a breeding pair of animals

[3]**mate** *vb* **mat•ed; mat•ing** **1** : to join or fit

together **2** : to come or bring together as mates **3** : COPULATE

[1]**ma·te·ri·al** \mə-ˈtir-ē-əl\ *adj* **1** : PHYSICAL ⟨~ world⟩; *also* : BODILY ⟨~ needs⟩ **2** : of or relating to matter rather than form ⟨~ cause⟩; *also* : EMPIRICAL ⟨~ knowledge⟩ **3** : highly important : SIGNIFICANT **4** : of a physical or worldly nature ⟨~ progress⟩ — **ma·te·ri·al·ly** *adv*

[2]**material** *n* **1** : the elements or substance of which something is composed or made **2** : apparatus necessary for doing or making something

ma·te·ri·al·ise *Brit var of* MATERIALIZE

ma·te·ri·al·ism \mə-ˈtir-ē-ə-ˌli-zəm\ *n* **1** : a theory that everything can be explained as being or coming from matter **2** : a preoccupation with material rather than intellectual or spiritual things — **ma·te·ri·al·ist** \-list\ *n or adj* — **ma·te·ri·al·is·tic** \-ˌtir-ē-ə-ˈlis-tik\ *adj* — **ma·te·ri·al·is·ti·cal·ly** \-ti-k(ə-)lē\ *adv*

ma·te·ri·al·ize \mə-ˈtir-ē-ə-ˌlīz\ *vb* **-ized; -iz·ing** **1** : to give material form to; *also* : to assume bodily form **2** : to make an often unexpected appearance — **ma·te·ri·al·i·za·tion** \mə-ˌtir-ē-ə-lə-ˈzā-shən\ *n*

ma·té·ri·el *or* **ma·te·ri·el** \mə-ˌtir-ē-ˈel\ *n* [F *matériel*] : equipment, apparatus, and supplies used by an organization

ma·ter·nal \mə-ˈtər-nᵊl\ *adj* **1** : MOTHERLY **2** : related through or inherited or derived from a female parent ⟨his ~ grandparents⟩ — **ma·ter·nal·ly** *adv*

[1]**ma·ter·ni·ty** \mə-ˈtər-nə-tē\ *n, pl* **-ties** **1** : the quality or state of being a mother; *also* : MOTHERLINESS **2** : a hospital facility for the care of women before and during childbirth and for newborn babies

[2]**maternity** *adj* **1** : designed for wear during pregnancy ⟨a ~ dress⟩ **2** : effective for the period close to and including childbirth ⟨~ leave⟩

[1]**math** \ˈmath\ *n* : MATHEMATICS

[2]**math** *abbr* mathematical; mathematician

math·e·mat·ics \ˌma-thə-ˈma-tiks\ *n* : the science of numbers and their properties, operations, and relations and with shapes in space and their structure and measurement — **math·e·mat·i·cal** \-ˈma-ti-kəl\ *adj* — **math·e·mat·i·cal·ly** \-ti-k(ə-)lē\ *adv* — **math·e·ma·ti·cian** \ˌma-thə-mə-ˈti-shən\ *n*

mat·i·nee *or* **mat·i·née** \ˌma-tə-ˈnā\ *n* [F *matinée*, lit., morning, fr. OF, fr. *matin* morning, fr. L *matutinum*, fr. neut. of *matutinus* of the morning, fr. *Matuta*, goddess of morning] : a musical or dramatic performance in the daytime and esp. the afternoon

mat·ins \ˈma-tᵊnz\ *n pl, often cap* **1** : special prayers said between midnight and 4 a.m. **2** : a morning service of liturgical prayer in Anglican churches

ma·tri·arch \ˈmā-trē-ˌärk\ *n* : a woman who rules or dominates a family, group, or state — **ma·tri·ar·chal** \ˌmā-trē-ˈär-kəl\ *adj* — **ma·tri·ar·chy** \ˈmā-trē-ˌär-kē\ *n*

ma·tri·cide \ˈma-trə-ˌsīd, ˈmā-\ *n* : the murder of a mother by her child — **ma·tri·cid·al** \ˌma-trə-ˈsī-dᵊl, ˌmā-\ *adj*

ma·tric·u·late \mə-ˈtri-kyə-ˌlāt\ *vb* **-lat·ed; -lat·ing** : to enroll as a member of a body and esp. of a college or university — **ma·tric·u·la·tion** \-ˌtri-kyə-ˈlā-shən\ *n*

mat·ri·mo·ny \ˈma-trə-ˌmō-nē\ *n* [ME, fr. AF *matrimoignie*, fr. L *matrimonium*, fr. *mater* mother, matron] : MARRIAGE — **mat·ri·mo·nial** \ˌma-trə-ˈmō-nē-əl\ *adj* — **mat·ri·mo·nial·ly** *adv*

ma·trix \ˈmā-triks\ *n, pl* **ma·tri·ces** \ˈmā-trə-ˌsēz, ˈma-\ *or* **ma·trix·es** \ˈmā-trik-səz\ **1** : something within or from which something else originates, develops, or takes form **2** : a mold from which a relief surface (as a piece of type) is made

ma·tron \ˈmā-trən\ *n* **1** : a married woman usu. of dignified maturity or social distinction **2** : a woman supervisor (as in a school or police station) — **ma·tron·ly** *adj*

Matt *abbr* Matthew

[1]**matte** *or* **matt** *var of* [3]MAT

[2]**matte** *also* **matt** \ˈmat\ *adj* : not shiny : DULL

[1]**mat·ter** \ˈma-tər\ *n* **1** : a subject of interest or concern **2** *pl* : events or circumstances of a particular situation **3** : the subject of a discourse or writing **4** : TROUBLE, DIFFICULTY ⟨what's the ~⟩ **5** : the substance of which a physical object is composed **6** : PUS **7** : an indefinite amount or quantity ⟨a ~ of a few days⟩ **8** : something written or printed **9** : MAIL — **as a matter of fact** : ACTUALLY — **no matter** : without regard to ⟨will follow *no matter* where you go⟩ — **no matter what** : regardless of the consequences ⟨must win, *no matter what*⟩

[2]**matter** *vb* : to be of importance

mat·ter–of–fact \ˌma-tə-rəv-ˈfakt\ *adj* : adhering to fact; *also* : being plain, straightforward, or unemotional — **mat·ter–of–fact·ly** *adv* — **mat·ter–of–fact·ness** *n*

Mat·thew \ˈma-thyü\ *n* — see BIBLE table

mat·tins *often cap, chiefly Brit var of* MATINS

mat·tock \ˈma-tək\ *n* : a digging and grubbing tool with features of an adze and an ax or pick

mat·tress \ˈma-trəs\ *n* **1** : a fabric case filled with resilient material used as or for a bed **2** : an inflatable airtight sack for use as a mattress

mat·u·rate \ˈma-chə-ˌrāt\ *vb* **-rat·ed; -rat·ing** : MATURE

mat·u·ra·tion \ˌma-chə-ˈrā-shən\ *n* **1** : the process of becoming mature **2** : the emergence of personal and behavioral characteristics through growth processes — **mat·u·ra·tion·al** \-shə-nəl\ *adj*

[1]**ma·ture** \mə-ˈtür, -ˈtyür\ *adj* **ma·tur·er; -est** **1** : based on slow careful consideration **2** : having attained a final or desired state **3** : of or relating to a condition of full development **4** : suitable only for adults ⟨~ content⟩ **5** : due for payment — **ma·ture·ly** *adv*

[2]**mature** *vb* **ma·tured; ma·tur·ing** : to reach or bring to maturity or completion
ma·tu·ri·ty \mə-ˈtu̇r-ə-tē, -ˈtyu̇r-\ *n* **1** : the quality or state of being mature; *esp* : full development **2** : the date when a note becomes due for payment
ma·tu·ti·nal \ˌma-chu̇-ˈtī-nᵊl; mə-ˈtü-tə-ˈnəl, -ˈtyü-\ *adj* : of, relating to, or occurring in the morning : EARLY
mat·zo *or* **mat·zoh** \ˈmät-sə\ *n, pl* **mat·zoth** \-ˌsōt, -ˌsōth, -sōs\ *or* **mat·zos** *or* **mat·zohs** [Yiddish *matse,* fr. Heb *maṣṣāh*] : unleavened bread eaten esp. at the Passover
maud·lin \ˈmȯd-lən\ *adj* [alter. of Mary *Magdalene;* fr. her depiction as a weeping, penitent sinner] **1** : drunk enough to be silly **2** : weakly and effusively sentimental ⟨a ~ love story⟩
[1]**maul** \ˈmȯl\ *n* : a heavy hammer often with a wooden head used esp. for driving wedges
[2]**maul** *vb* **1** : BEAT, BRUISE; *also* : MANGLE **2** : to handle roughly
maun·der \ˈmȯn-dər\ *vb* **1** : to wander slowly and idly **2** : to speak indistinctly or disconnectedly
mau·so·le·um \ˌmȯ-sə-ˈlē-əm, ˌmȯ-zə-\ *n, pl* **-leums** *or* **-lea** \-ˈlē-ə\ [L, fr. Gk *mausōleion,* fr. *Mausōlos* Mausolus † *about* 353 B.C. ruler of Caria whose tomb was one of the seven wonders of the ancient world] : a large tomb; *esp* : a usu. stone building for entombment of the dead above ground
mauve \ˈmōv, ˈmȯv\ *n* : a moderate purple, violet, or lilac color
ma·ven *also* **ma·vin** \ˈmā-vən\ *n* [Yiddish *meyvn,* fr. Late Heb *mēbhīn*] : EXPERT
mav·er·ick \ˈma-vrik, -və-rik\ *n* [Samuel A. *Maverick* † 1870 Am. pioneer who did not brand his calves] **1** : an unbranded range animal **2** : NONCONFORMIST
maw \ˈmȯ\ *n* **1** : STOMACH; *also* : the crop of a bird **2** : the throat, gullet, or jaws esp. of a voracious animal
mawk·ish \ˈmȯ-kish\ *adj* : sickly sentimental ⟨~ poetry⟩ — **mawk·ish·ly** *adv* — **mawk·ish·ness** *n*
max *abbr* maximum
maxi \ˈmak-sē\ *n, pl* **max·is** : a long skirt, dress, or coat
maxi- *comb form* **1** : extra long ⟨*maxi*-kilt⟩ **2** : extra large ⟨*maxi*-problems⟩
max·il·la \mak-ˈsi-lə\ *n, pl* **max·il·lae** \-ˈsi-(ˌ)lē\ *or* **maxillas** : JAW 1; *esp* : an upper jaw — **max·il·lary** \ˈmak-sə-ˌler-ē\ *adj*
max·im \ˈmak-səm\ *n* : a proverbial saying
max·i·mal \ˈmak-sə-məl\ *adj* : MAXIMUM — **max·i·mal·ly** *adv*
max·i·mise *Brit var of* MAXIMIZE
max·i·mize \ˈmak-sə-ˌmīz\ *vb* **-mized; -miz·ing 1** : to increase to a maximum **2** : to make the most of **3** : to increase the size of a computer program's window to fill an entire screen — **max·i·mi·za·tion** \ˌmak-sə-mə-ˈzā-shən\ *n*
max·i·mum \ˈmak-sə-məm\ *n, pl* **-ma** \-mə\ *or* **-mums 1** : the greatest quantity, value, or degree **2** : an upper limit allowed by authority **3** : the largest of a set of numbers — **maximum** *adj*
max out *vb* **1** : to push to or reach a limit or an extreme **2** : to use up all available credit on (a credit card)
may \ˈmā\ *verbal auxiliary, past* **might** \ˈmīt\ *pres sing & pl* **may 1** : have permission or liberty to ⟨you ~ go now⟩ **2** : be in some degree likely to ⟨you ~ be right⟩ **3** — used as an auxiliary to express a wish, purpose, contingency, or concession ⟨~ the best man win⟩
May \ˈmā\ *n* [ME, fr. OF *mai,* fr. L *Maius,* fr. *Maia,* Roman goddess] : the 5th month of the year
Ma·ya \ˈmī-ə\ *n, pl* **Maya** *or* **Mayas** : a member of a group of Indigenous peoples of Yucatán, Guatemala, and adjacent areas — **Ma·yan** \ˈmī-ən\ *n or adj*
may·ap·ple \ˈmā-ˌa-pəl\ *n* : a No. American woodland herb related to the barberry that has a poisonous root, one or two large leaves, and an edible egg-shaped yellow fruit
may·be \ˈmā-bē, ˈme-\ *adv* : PERHAPS
May Day \ˈmā-ˌdā\ *n* : May 1 celebrated as a springtime festival and in some countries as Labor Day
may·flow·er \ˈmā-ˌflau̇(-ə)r\ *n* : any of several spring blooming herbs (as the trailing arbutus or an anemone)
may·fly \ˈmā-flī\ *n* : any of an order of insects with an aquatic nymph and a short-lived fragile adult having membranous wings
may·hem \ˈmā-ˌhem, ˈmā-əm\ *n* **1** : willful and permanent crippling, mutilation, or disfigurement of a person **2** : needless or willful damage
may·on·naise \ˈmā-ə-ˌnāz\ *n* [F] : a dressing made of egg yolks, vegetable oil, and vinegar or lemon juice
may·or \ˈmā-ər\ *n* : an official elected to act as chief executive or nominal head of a city or borough — **may·or·al** \-əl\ *adj* — **may·or·al·ty** \-əl-tē\ *n*
may·pole \ˈmā-ˌpōl\ *n, often cap* : a tall flower-wreathed pole forming a center for May Day sports and dances
maze \ˈmāz\ *n* : a confusing intricate network of passages — **mazy** *adj*
ma·zur·ka \mə-ˈzər-kə\ *n* : a Polish dance in moderate triple measure
MB *abbr* Manitoba
MBA *abbr* master of business administration
mc *abbr* megacycle
Mc *symbol* moscovium
[1]**MC** *n* : MASTER OF CEREMONIES
[2]**MC** *abbr* member of Congress
Mc- \mək; mə *before forms beginning with* k *or* g\ *prefix* : used to indicate a convenient, low-quality version of a specified thing ⟨*Mc*Book⟩
Mc·Coy \mə-ˈkȯi\ *n* : something that is neither imitation nor substitute ⟨the real ~⟩
McGuffin *var of* MACGUFFIN
MCPO *abbr* master chief petty officer
[1]**Md** *abbr* Maryland

[2]**Md** *symbol* mendelevium
MD *abbr* **1** [NL *medicinae doctor*] doctor of medicine **2** Maryland **3** muscular dystrophy
MDMA \ˌem-ˌdē-ˌem-ˈā\ *n* : ECSTASY 2
mdnt *abbr* midnight
mdse *abbr* merchandise
MDT *abbr* mountain daylight (saving) time
me \ˈmē\ *pron, objective case of* I
Me *abbr* Maine
ME *abbr* **1** Maine **2** mechanical engineer **3** medical examiner
[1]**mead** \ˈmēd\ *n* : an alcoholic beverage brewed from water and honey, malt, and yeast
[2]**mead** *n, archaic* : MEADOW
mead•ow \ˈme-dō\ *n* : land in or mainly in grass; *esp* : a tract of moist low-lying usu. level grassland — **mead•ow•land** \-ˌland\ *n* — **mead•owy** \ˈme-də-wē\ *adj*
mead•ow•lark \ˈme-dō-ˌlärk\ *n* : any of several American songbirds related to the orioles that are streaked brown above and in northernmost forms have a yellow breast marked with a black crescent
mead•ow•sweet \-ˌswēt\ *n* : a No. American native or naturalized spirea
mea•ger *or* **mea•gre** \ˈmē-gər\ *adj* **1** : THIN **2** : lacking richness, fertility, or strength; *also* : POOR ⟨a ~ income⟩ ♦ ***Synonyms*** SCANTY, SCANT, SPARE, SPARSE — **mea•ger•ly** *adv* — **mea•ger•ness** *n*
[1]**meal** \ˈmēl\ *n* **1** : an act or the time of eating a portion of food **2** : the portion of food eaten at a meal
[2]**meal** *n* **1** : usu. coarsely ground seeds of a cereal **2** : a product resembling seed meal — **mealy** *adj*
meal•time \ˈmēl-ˌtīm\ *n* : the usual time at which a meal is served
mealy•bug \ˈmē-lē-ˌbəg\ *n* : any of a family of scale insects with a white cottony or waxy covering that are destructive pests esp. of fruit trees
mealy•mouthed \ˈmē-lē-ˌmaůthd, -ˌmaůtht\ *adj* : not plain and straightforward : DEVIOUS ⟨a ~ politician⟩
[1]**mean** \ˈmēn\ *vb* **meant** \ˈment\; **mean•ing** **1** : to have in the mind as a purpose **2** : to serve to convey, show, or indicate : SIGNIFY ⟨red ~*s* stop⟩ **3** : to have importance to the degree of ⟨~*s* the world to me⟩ **4** : to direct to a particular individual ⟨a gift *meant* for me⟩
[2]**mean** *adj* **1** : HUMBLE **2** : lacking acumen : DULL **3** : SHABBY, CONTEMPTIBLE ⟨no ~ feat⟩ **4** : IGNOBLE, BASE ⟨a ~ trick⟩ **5** : STINGY **6** : pettily selfish or malicious **7** : VEXATIOUS ⟨a ~ dog⟩ **8** : EXCELLENT ⟨throws a ~ slider⟩ — **mean•ly** *adv* — **mean•ness** *n*
[3]**mean** *adj* **1** : occupying a middle position (as in space, order, or time) **2** : being a mean : AVERAGE ⟨a ~ value⟩
[4]**mean** *n* **1** : a middle point between extremes **2** *pl* : something helpful in achieving a desired end **3** *pl* : material resources affording a secure life **4** : ARITHMETIC MEAN
[1]**me•an•der** \mē-ˈan-dər\ *n* [L *maeander*, fr. Gk *maiandros*, fr. *Maiandros* (now *Menderes*), river in Asia Minor] **1** : a winding course **2** : a winding of a stream
[2]**meander** *vb* **1** : to follow a winding course **2** : to wander aimlessly or casually
mean•ing *n* **1** : the thing one intends to convey esp. by language; *also* : the thing that is thus conveyed **2** : AIM **3** : SIGNIFICANCE; *esp* : implication of a hidden significance **4** : CONNOTATION; *also* : DENOTATION — **mean•ing•ful** \-fəl\ *adj* — **mean•ing•ful•ly** *adv* — **mean•ing•less** *adj*
[1]**mean•time** \ˈmēn-ˌtīm\ *n* : the intervening time
[2]**meantime** *adv* : MEANWHILE
[1]**mean•while** \-ˌhwī(-ə)l\ *n* : MEANTIME
[2]**meanwhile** *adv* **1** : during the intervening time **2** : at the same time
meas *abbr* measure
mea•sles \ˈmē-zəlz\ *n sing or pl* : an acute virus disease marked by fever and an eruption of distinct circular red spots
mea•sly \ˈmēz-lē, -zə-lē\ *adj* **mea•sli•er; -est** : contemptibly small or insignificant
[1]**mea•sure** \ˈme-zhər, ˈmā-\ *n* **1** : an adequate or moderate portion; *also* : a suitable limit **2** : the dimensions, capacity, or amount of something ascertained by measuring; *also* : an instrument for measuring **3** : a unit of measurement; *also* : a system of such units **4** : the act or process of measuring **5** : rhythmic structure or movement **6** : the part of a musical staff between two bars **7** : CRITERION **8** : a means to an end **9** : a legislative bill — **mea•sure•less** *adj*
[2]**measure** *vb* **mea•sured; mea•sur•ing** **1** : to mark or fix in multiples of a specific unit ⟨~ off five centimeters⟩ **2** : to find out the size, extent, or amount of **3** : to bring into comparison or competition **4** : to serve as a means of measuring **5** : to have a specified measurement — **mea•sur•able** \ˈme-zhə-rə-bəl, ˈmā-\ *adj* — **mea•sur•ably** \-blē\ *adv* — **mea•sur•er** *n*
mea•sure•ment \ˈme-zhər-mənt, ˈmā-\ *n* **1** : the act or process of measuring **2** : a figure, extent, or amount obtained by measuring
measure up *vb* **1** : to have necessary or fitting qualifications **2** : to equal esp. in ability
meat \ˈmēt\ *n* **1** : FOOD; *esp* : solid food as distinguished from drink **2** : animal and esp. mammal flesh considered as food **3** : the edible part inside a covering (as a shell or rind) — **meaty** *adj*
meat•ball \-ˌbȯl\ *n* : a small ball of chopped or ground meat
meat loaf *n* : a dish of ground meat seasoned and baked in the form of a loaf
mec•ca \ˈme-kə\ *n, often cap* [*Mecca*, Saudi Arabia, a destination of pilgrims in the Islamic world] : a center of a specified activity or interest ⟨a shopping ~⟩
mech *abbr* mechanical; mechanics

[1]**me·chan·ic** \mi-ˈka-nik\ *adj* : of or relating to manual work or skill
[2]**mechanic** *n* **1** : a manual worker **2** : MACHINIST; *esp* : one who repairs cars
me·chan·i·cal \mi-ˈka-ni-kəl\ *adj* **1** : of or relating to machinery, to manual operations, or to mechanics **2** : done as if by a machine : AUTOMATIC ⟨a ~ response⟩ ♦ ***Synonyms*** INSTINCTIVE, IMPULSIVE, SPONTANEOUS — **me·chan·i·cal·ly** \-k(ə-)lē\ *adv*
mechanical drawing *n* : drawing done with the aid of instruments
me·chan·ics \mi-ˈka-niks\ *n sing or pl* **1** : a branch of physics that deals with energy and forces and their effect on bodies **2** : the practical application of mechanics (as to the operation of machines) **3** : mechanical or functional details ⟨the ~ of the brain⟩
mech·a·nism \ˈme-kə-ˌni-zəm\ *n* **1** : a piece of machinery; *also* : a process or technique for achieving a result **2** : mechanical operation or action **3** : the fundamental processes involved in or responsible for a natural phenomenon ⟨the visual ~⟩
mech·a·nis·tic \ˌme-kə-ˈnis-tik\ *adj* **1** : mechanically determined ⟨~ universe⟩ **2** : MECHANICAL — **mech·a·nis·ti·cal·ly** \-ti-k(ə-)lē\ *adv*
mech·a·nize \ˈme-kə-ˌnīz\ *vb* **-nized; -niz·ing** **1** : to make mechanical **2** : to equip with machinery esp. in order to replace human or animal labor **3** : to equip with armed and armored motor vehicles — **mech·a·ni·za·tion** \ˌme-kə-nə-ˈzā-shən\ *n* — **mech·a·niz·er** *n*
[1]**med** \ˈmed\ *adj* : MEDICAL ⟨~ school⟩
[2]**med** *n* : MEDICINE 1 — usu. used in pl.
[3]**med** *abbr* **1** medical; medicine **2** medieval **3** medium
MEd *abbr* master of education
med·al \ˈme-dᵊl\ *n* [MF *medaille,* fr. OIt *medaglia* coin worth half a denarius, medal, fr. VL **medalis* half, alter. of LL *medialis* middle, fr. L *medius*] **1** : a small usu. metal object bearing a religious emblem or picture **2** : a piece of metal issued to commemorate a person or event or to award excellence or achievement
med·al·ist *or* **med·al·list** \ˈme-dᵊl-ist\ *n* **1** : a designer or maker of medals **2** : a recipient of a medal as an award
me·dal·lion \mə-ˈdal-yən\ *n* **1** : a large medal **2** : a tablet or panel bearing a portrait or an ornament
med·dle \ˈme-dᵊl\ *vb* **med·dled; med·dling** : to interfere without right or propriety — **med·dler** \ˈme-dᵊl-ər\ *n*
med·dle·some \ˈme-dᵊl-səm\ *adj* : inclined to meddle ⟨a ~ neighbor⟩
med·e·vac *also* **med·i·vac** \ˈme-də-ˌvak\ *n* **1** : emergency evacuation of the sick or wounded **2** : a helicopter used for medevac
me·dia \ˈmē-dē-ə\ *n, pl* **me·di·as** **1** : MEDIUM 4 **2** *sing or pl in constr* : MASS MEDIA
me·di·al \ˈmē-dē-əl\ *adj* : occurring in or extending toward the middle
[1]**me·di·an** \ˈmē-dē-ən\ *n* **1** : a value in an ordered set of values below and above which there are an equal number of values **2** : MEDIAN STRIP
[2]**median** *adj* **1** : being in the middle or in an intermediate position **2** : relating to or constituting a statistical median
median strip *n* : a strip dividing a highway into lanes according to the direction of travel
me·di·ate \ˈmē-dē-ˌāt\ *vb* **-at·ed; -at·ing** **1** : to act as an intermediary; *esp* : to work with opposing sides in order to resolve (as a dispute) or bring about (as a settlement) **2** : to bring about, influence, or transmit (as a physical process or effect) by acting as an intermediate or controlling agent or mechanism ♦ ***Synonyms*** INTERCEDE, INTERVENE, INTERPOSE, INTERFERE — **me·di·a·tion** \ˌmē-dē-ˈā-shən\ *n* — **me·di·a·tor** \ˈmē-dē-ˌā-tər\ *n*
med·ic \ˈme-dik\ *n* : one engaged in medical work; *esp* : CORPSMAN
med·i·ca·ble \ˈme-di-kə-bəl\ *adj* : CURABLE
Med·ic·aid \ˈme-di-ˌkād\ *n* : a program of financial assistance for medical care designed for those unable to afford regular medical service and financed jointly by the state and federal governments
med·i·cal \ˈme-di-kəl\ *adj* : of or relating to the science or practice of medicine or the treatment of disease — **med·i·cal·ly** \-k(ə-)lē\ *adv*
medical examiner *n* : a public officer who performs autopsies on bodies to find the cause of death
me·di·ca·ment \mi-ˈdi-kə-mənt, ˈme-di-kə-\ *n* : a substance used in therapy
Medi·care \ˈme-di-ˌker\ *n* : a government program of financial assistance for medical care esp. for the aged
med·i·cate \ˈme-də-ˌkāt\ *vb* **-cat·ed; -cat·ing** : to treat with medicine
med·i·ca·tion \ˌme-də-ˈkā-shən\ *n* **1** : the act or process of medicating **2** : MEDICINE 1
me·dic·i·nal \mə-ˈdi-sᵊn-əl\ *adj* : tending or used to cure disease or relieve pain — **me·dic·i·nal·ly** *adv*
med·i·cine \ˈme-də-sən\ *n* **1** : a substance or preparation used in treating disease **2** : a science and art dealing with the prevention, alleviation, and cure of disease
medicine ball *n* : a heavy stuffed leather ball used for conditioning exercises
medicine man *n* : a person esp. among Indigenous Americans believed to possess supernatural powers that can heal illnesses and keep away evil spirits
med·i·co \ˈme-di-ˌkō\ *n, pl* **-cos** : a medical practitioner or student
me·di·e·val *also* **me·di·ae·val** \ˌmē-dē-ˈē-vəl, ˌme-, mē-ˈdē-vəl\ *adj* **1** : of, relating to, or characteristic of the Middle Ages **2** : having a quality (as cruelty) associated with the Middle Ages **3** : extremely outmoded or antiquated — **me·di·e·val·ism** \-və-ˌli-zəm\ *n* — **me·di·e·val·ist** \-list\ *n*
me·di·o·cre \ˌmē-dē-ˈō-kər\ *adj* [MF, fr.

L *mediocris,* fr. *medius* middle + *ocris* stony mountain] : of moderate or low quality : ORDINARY ⟨did a ~ job⟩ — **me·di·oc·ri·ty** \-ˈä-krə-tē\ *n*

med·i·tate \ˈme-də-ˌtāt\ *vb* **-tat·ed; -tat·ing** **1** : to muse over : CONTEMPLATE, PONDER **2** : to engage in deep mental exercise directed toward a heightened level of spiritual awareness **3** : INTEND, PLAN — **med·i·ta·tion** \ˌme-də-ˈtā-shən\ *n* — **med·i·ta·tive** \ˈme-də-ˌtā-tiv\ *adj* — **med·i·ta·tive·ly** *adv*

Med·i·ter·ra·nean \ˌme-də-tə-ˈrā-nē-ən, -ˈrā-nyən\ *adj* : of or relating to the Mediterranean Sea or to the lands or people around it

¹**me·di·um** \ˈmē-dē-əm\ *n, pl* **mediums** *or* **me·dia** \-dē-ə\ [L] **1** : something in a middle position; *also* : a middle position or degree **2** : a means of effecting or conveying something **3** : a surrounding or enveloping substance **4** : a channel or system of communication, information, or entertainment **5** : a mode of artistic expression **6** : an individual held to be a channel of communication between the earthly world and a world of spirits **7** : a condition or environment in which something may function or flourish

²**medium** *adj* : intermediate in amount, quality, position, or degree

me·di·um·is·tic \ˌmē-dē-ə-ˈmis-tik\ *adj* : of, relating to, or being a spiritualistic medium

medivac *var of* MEDEVAC

med·ley \ˈmed-lē\ *n, pl* **medleys** **1** : HODGEPODGE **2** : a musical composition made up esp. of a series of songs

me·dul·la \mə-ˈdə-lə\ *n, pl* **-las** *or* **-lae** \-(ˌ)lē, -ˌlī\ : an inner or deep anatomical part; *also* : the posterior part (**medulla ob·lon·ga·ta** \-ˌä-ˌblȯŋ-ˈgä-tə\) of the vertebrate brain that is continuous with the spinal cord

meed \ˈmēd\ *n* : a fitting return

meek \ˈmēk\ *adj* **1** : enduring injury with patience and without resentment **2** : deficient in spirit and courage **3** : MODERATE — **meek·ly** *adv* — **meek·ness** *n*

meer·schaum \ˈmir-shəm, -ˌshȯm\ *n* [G, fr. *Meer* sea + *Schaum* foam] : a tobacco pipe made of a light white clayey mineral

¹**meet** \ˈmēt\ *vb* **met** \ˈmet\; **meet·ing** **1** : to come upon : FIND **2** : JOIN, INTERSECT **3** : to appear to the perception of **4** : OPPOSE, FIGHT **5** : to join in conversation or discussion; *also* : ASSEMBLE **6** : to conform to ⟨~*s* requirements⟩ **7** : to pay fully **8** : to cope with **9** : to provide for **10** : to be introduced to

²**meet** *n* : an assembling esp. for a hunt or for competitive sports

³**meet** *adj* : SUITABLE, PROPER

meet·ing \ˈmē-tiŋ\ *n* **1** : an act of coming together : ASSEMBLY **2** : JUNCTION, INTERSECTION

meet·ing·house \-ˌhau̇s\ *n* : a building for public assembly and esp. for Protestant worship

meg \ˈmeg\ *n* : MEGABYTE

mega- *or* **meg-** *comb form* **1** : great : large ⟨*mega*hit⟩ **2** : million ⟨*mega*hertz⟩

mega·byte \ˈme-gə-ˌbīt\ *n* : 1024 kilobytes or 1,048,576 bytes; *also* : one million bytes

mega·cy·cle \-ˌsī-kəl\ *n* : MEGAHERTZ

mega·death \-ˌdeth\ *n* : one million deaths — used as a unit in reference to nuclear warfare

mega·hertz \ˈme-gə-ˌhərts, -ˌherts\ *n* : a unit of frequency equal to one million hertz

mega·lith \ˈme-gə-ˌlith\ *n* : a large stone used in prehistoric monuments — **mega·lith·ic** \ˌme-gə-ˈli-thik\ *adj*

meg·a·lo·ma·nia \ˌme-gə-lō-ˈmā-nē-ə, -nyə\ *n* : a mental disorder marked by feelings of personal omnipotence and grandeur — **meg·a·lo·ma·ni·ac** \-ˈmā-nē-ˌak\ *adj or n* — **meg·a·lo·ma·ni·a·cal** \-mə-ˈnī-ə-kəl\ *adj*

meg·a·lop·o·lis \ˌme-gə-ˈlä-pə-ləs\ *n* : a very large urban unit

mega·phone \ˈme-gə-ˌfōn\ *n* : a cone-shaped device used to intensify or direct the voice — **megaphone** *vb*

mega·pix·el \ˈme-gə-ˌpik-səl\ *n* : one million pixels

mega·plex \-ˌpleks\ *n* : a cineplex having usu. at least 16 movie theaters

mega·ton \-ˌtən\ *n* : an explosive force equivalent to that of one million tons of TNT

mega·vi·ta·min \-ˌvī-tə-mən\ *adj* : relating to or consisting of very large doses of vitamins — **mega·vi·ta·mins** *n pl*

meh \ˈme\ *interj* — used to express indifference or mild disappointment

mei·o·sis \mī-ˈō-səs\ *n* : a process of cell division in gamete-producing cells in which the number of chromosomes is reduced to one half — **mei·ot·ic** \mī-ˈä-tik\ *adj*

meit·ner·i·um \mīt-ˈnir-ē-əm, -ˈner-\ *n* : an artificially produced radioactive chemical element

mel·an·cho·lia \ˌme-lən-ˈkō-lē-ə\ *n* : a mental condition marked by extreme depression often with delusions

mel·an·chol·ic \ˌme-lən-ˈkä-lik\ *adj* **1** : DEPRESSED **2** : of or relating to melancholia

mel·an·choly \ˈme-lən-ˌkä-lē\ *n, pl* **-chol·ies** [ME *malencolie,* fr. AF, fr. LL *melancholia,* fr. Gk, fr. *melan-, melas* black + *cholē* bile; so called fr. the former belief that it was caused by an excess of black bile] : depression of spirits : DEJECTION — **melancholy** *adj*

Mel·a·ne·sian \ˌme-lə-ˈnē-zhən\ *n* : a member of the dominant native group of the Pacific island grouping of Melanesia — **Melanesian** *adj*

mé·lange \mā-ˈläⁿzh, -ˈlänj\ *n* : a mixture esp. of incongruous elements

mel·a·nin \ˈme-lə-nən\ *n* : any of various dark brown pigments of animal or plant structures (as skin or hair)

mel·a·nism \ˈme-lə-ˌni-zəm\ *n* : an increased amount of black or nearly black pigmentation

mel·a·no·ma \ˌme-lə-ˈnō-mə\ *n, pl* **-mas** *also* **-ma·ta** \-mə-tə\ : a usu. malignant tumor containing dark pigment

¹**meld** \ˈmeld\ *vb* : to show or announce for a score in a card game

²**meld** *n* : a card or combination of cards that is or can be melded

me·lee \ˈmā-ˌlā, mā-ˈlā\ *n* [F *mêlée*] : a confused struggle ♦ ***Synonyms*** FRACAS, ROW, BRAWL, DONNYBROOK

me·lio·rate \ˈmēl-yə-ˌrāt, ˈmē-lē-ə-\ *vb* **-rat·ed; -rat·ing** : AMELIORATE — **me·lio·ra·tion** \ˌmēl-yə-ˈrā-shən, ˌmē-lē-ə-\ *n* — **me·lio·ra·tive** \ˈmēl-yə-ˌrā-tiv, ˈmē-lē-ə-\ *adj*

mel·lif·lu·ous \me-ˈli-flə-wəs, mə-\ *adj* [ME *mellyfluous,* fr. LL *mellifluus,* fr. L *mel* honey + *fluere* to flow] : sweetly flowing ⟨a ~ voice⟩ — **mel·lif·lu·ous·ly** *adv* — **mel·lif·lu·ous·ness** *n*

¹**mel·low** \ˈme-lō\ *adj* **1** : soft and sweet because of ripeness; *also* : well aged and pleasingly mild ⟨~ wine⟩ **2** : made gentle by age or experience **3** : being rich and full but not garish or strident ⟨~ colors⟩ **4** : of soft loamy consistency ⟨~ soil⟩ — **mel·low·ness** *n*

²**mellow** *vb* : to make or become mellow — often used with *out*

me·lo·di·ous \mə-ˈlō-dē-əs\ *adj* : pleasing to the ear ⟨~ chimes⟩ — **me·lo·di·ous·ly** *adv* — **me·lo·di·ous·ness** *n*

melo·dra·ma \ˈme-lə-ˌdrä-mə, -ˌdra-\ *n* **1** : an extravagantly theatrical play in which action and plot predominate over characterization **2** : something having a sensational or theatrical quality — **melo·dra·mat·ic** \ˌme-lə-drə-ˈma-tik\ *adj* — **melo·dra·mat·i·cal·ly** \-ti-k(ə-)lē\ *adv* — **melo·dra·ma·tist** \ˌme-lə-ˈdra-mə-tist, -ˈdrä-\ *n*

mel·o·dy \ˈme-lə-dē\ *n, pl* **-dies** **1** : sweet or agreeable sound **2** : a particular succession of notes : TUNE, AIR — **me·lod·ic** \mə-ˈlä-dik\ *adj* — **me·lod·i·cal·ly** \-di-k(ə-)lē\ *adv*

mel·on \ˈme-lən\ *n* : any of various typically sweet fruits (as a muskmelon or watermelon) of the gourd family usu. eaten raw

¹**melt** \ˈmelt\ *vb* **1** : to change from a solid to a liquid state usu. by heat **2** : DISSOLVE, DISINTEGRATE; *also* : to disappear or cause to disperse or disappear ⟨her anger ~*ed* away⟩ **3** : to make or become tender or gentle

²**melt** *n* : a melted substance

melt·down \ˈmelt-ˌdau̇n\ *n* **1** : the melting of the core of a nuclear reactor **2** : a collapse of something (as one's self-control)

melting pot *n* : a place where a variety of peoples, cultures, or individuals assimilate into a cohesive whole

melt·wa·ter \-ˌwȯ-tər, -ˌwä-\ *n* : water derived from the melting of ice and snow

mem *abbr* **1** member **2** memoir **3** memorial

mem·ber \ˈmem-bər\ *n* **1** : a part (as an arm, leg, leaf, or branch) of an animal or plant **2** : one of the individuals composing a group **3** : a part of a whole ⟨~*s* of a set⟩

mem·ber·ship \-ˌship\ *n* **1** : the state or status of being a member **2** : the body of members

mem·brane \ˈmem-ˌbrān\ *n* : a thin pliable layer esp. of animal or plant origin — **mem·bra·nous** \-brə-nəs\ *adj*

me·men·to \mə-ˈmen-tō\ *n, pl* **-tos** *or* **-toes** [ME, fr. L, remember, imper. of *meminisse* to remember] : something that serves to warn or remind; *also* : SOUVENIR

memo \ˈme-mō\ *n, pl* **mem·os** : MEMORANDUM

mem·oir \ˈmem-ˌwär\ *n* **1** : MEMORANDUM **2** : AUTOBIOGRAPHY — usu. used in pl. **3** : an account of something noteworthy; *also, pl* : the record of the proceedings of a learned society

mem·o·ra·bil·ia \ˌme-mə-rə-ˈbi-lē-ə, -ˈbil-yə\ *n pl* [L] **1** : things worthy of remembrance **2** : things associated with a particular interest and that are usu. collected : MEMENTOS

mem·o·ra·ble \ˈme-mə-rə-bəl\ *adj* : worth remembering : NOTABLE ⟨a ~ quotation⟩ — **mem·o·ra·bil·i·ty** \ˌme-mə-rə-ˈbi-lə-tē\ *n* — **mem·o·ra·ble·ness** *n* — **mem·o·ra·bly** \-blē\ *adv*

mem·o·ran·dum \ˌme-mə-ˈran-dəm\ *n, pl* **-dums** *or* **-da** \-də\ **1** : an informal record; *also* : a written reminder **2** : an informal written note

¹**me·mo·ri·al** \mə-ˈmȯr-ē-əl\ *adj* : serving to preserve remembrance

²**memorial** *n* **1** : something designed to keep remembrance alive; *esp* : MONUMENT **2** : a statement of facts often accompanied with a petition — **me·mo·ri·al·ize** *vb*

Memorial Day *n* : the last Monday in May or formerly May 30 observed as a legal holiday in honor of those who died in war

mem·o·rise *Brit var of* MEMORIZE

mem·o·rize \ˈme-mə-ˌrīz\ *vb* **-rized; -riz·ing** : to learn by heart — **mem·o·ri·za·tion** \ˌme-mə-rə-ˈzā-shən\ *n* — **mem·o·riz·er** *n*

mem·o·ry \ˈme-mə-rē\ *n, pl* **-ries** **1** : the power or process of remembering **2** : the store of things remembered **3** : COMMEMORATION **4** : something remembered **5** : the time within which past events are remembered **6** : a device (as in a computer) in which information can be stored; *esp* : RAM **7** : capacity for storing information ⟨512 megabytes of ~⟩ ♦ ***Synonyms*** REMEMBRANCE, RECOLLECTION, REMINISCENCE

men *pl of* MAN

¹**men·ace** \ˈme-nəs\ *n* **1** : THREAT **2** : DANGER ⟨those dogs are a ~⟩; *also* : NUISANCE

²**menace** *vb* **men·aced; men·ac·ing** **1** : THREATEN **2** : ENDANGER — **men·ac·ing·ly** *adv*

mé·nage \mā-ˈnäzh\ *n* [F] : HOUSEHOLD

ménage à trois \-ä-ˈtrwä\ *n* : an arrangement in which three persons share sexual relations esp. while living together

me·nag·er·ie \mə-ˈna-jə-rē\ *n* : a collection of wild animals esp. for exhibition

[1]**mend** \ˈmend\ *vb* **1** : to improve in manners or morals **2** : to put into good shape : REPAIR **3** : to improve in or restore to health : HEAL — **mend·er** *n*

[2]**mend** *n* **1** : an act of mending **2** : a mended place

men·da·cious \men-ˈdā-shəs\ *adj* : given to deception or falsehood : UNTRUTHFUL ♦ ***Synonyms*** DISHONEST, DECEITFUL — **men·da·cious·ly** *adv* — **men·dac·i·ty** \-ˈda-sə-tē\ *n*

men·de·le·vi·um \ˌmen-də-ˈlē-vē-əm, -ˈlā-\ *n* : a radioactive metallic chemical element artificially produced

men·di·cant \ˈmen-di-kənt\ *n* **1** : BEGGAR **2** *often cap* : FRIAR — **men·di·can·cy** \-kən-sē\ *n* — **mendicant** *adj*

men·folk \ˈmen-ˌfōk\ *or* **men·folks** \-ˌfōks\ *n pl* **1** : men in general **2** : the men of a family or community

men·ha·den \men-ˈhā-dᵊn, mən-\ *n, pl* **-den** *also* **-dens** : a marine fish related to the herring that is abundant along the Atlantic coast of the U.S.

[1]**me·nial** \ˈmē-nē-əl, -nyəl\ *n* : a domestic servant

[2]**menial** *adj* **1** : of or relating to servants **2** : HUMBLE, SERVILE ⟨answered in ~ tones⟩ — **me·ni·al·ly** *adv*

men·in·gi·tis \ˌme-nən-ˈjī-təs\ *n, pl* **-git·i·des** \-ˈji-tə-ˌdēz\ : inflammation of the membranes enclosing the brain and spinal cord; *also* : a usu. bacterial disease marked by this

me·ninx \ˈmē-niŋks, ˈme-\ *n, pl* **me·nin·ges** \mə-ˈnin-(ˌ)jēz\ : any of the three membranes that envelop the brain and spinal cord — **men·in·ge·al** \ˌme-nən-ˈjē-əl\ *adj*

me·nis·cus \mə-ˈnis-kəs\ *n, pl* **me·nis·ci** \-ˈnis-ˌkī, -ˌkē\ *also* **me·nis·cus·es** **1** : CRESCENT **2** : the curved upper surface of a column of liquid

men·o·pause \ˈme-nə-ˌpȯz\ *n* : the period of life when menstruation stops naturally — **men·o·paus·al** \ˌme-nə-ˈpȯ-zəl\ *adj*

me·no·rah \mə-ˈnȯr-ə\ *n* [Heb *mĕnōrāh* candlestick] : a candelabrum that is used in Jewish worship

men·ses \ˈmen-ˌsēz\ *n sing or pl* : the menstrual flow

menstrual cycle *n* : the complete cycle of physiological changes from the beginning of one menstrual period to the beginning of the next

men·stru·a·tion \ˌmen-strə-ˈwā-shən, men-ˈstrā-\ *n* : a discharging of bloody matter at approximately monthly intervals from the uterus of breeding-age nonpregnant primate females; *also* : PERIOD 6 — **men·stru·al** \ˈmen-strə-wəl\ *adj* — **men·stru·ate** \ˈmen-strə-ˌwāt, -ˌstrāt\ *vb*

men·su·ra·ble \ˈmen-sə-rə-bəl, ˈ-chə-\ *adj* : MEASURABLE

men·su·ra·tion \ˌmen-sə-ˈrā-shən, ˌmen-chə-\ *n* : MEASUREMENT

-ment *n suffix* **1** : concrete result, object, or agent of a (specified) action ⟨embank*ment*⟩ ⟨entangle*ment*⟩ **2** : concrete means or instrument of a (specified) action ⟨entertain*ment*⟩ **3** : action : process ⟨encircle*ment*⟩ ⟨develop*ment*⟩ **4** : place of a (specified) action ⟨encamp*ment*⟩ **5** : state : condition ⟨amaze*ment*⟩

men·tal \ˈmen-tᵊl\ *adj* **1** : of or relating to the mind **2** : of, relating to, or affected with a disorder of the mind ⟨~ illness⟩ — **men·tal·ly** *adv*

mental age *n* : a measure of a child's mental development in terms of the number of years it takes an average child to reach the same level

mental deficiency *n* : INTELLECTUAL DISABILITY

men·tal·i·ty \men-ˈta-lə-tē\ *n, pl* **-ties** **1** : mental power or capacity **2** : mode or way of thought

mental retardation *n, sometimes offensive* : INTELLECTUAL DISABILITY — **mentally retarded** *adj*

men·tee \men-ˈtē\ *n* : PROTÉGÉ

men·thol \ˈmen-ˌthȯl, -ˌthōl\ *n* : an alcohol occurring esp. in mint oils that has the odor and cooling properties of peppermint — **men·tho·lat·ed** \-thə-ˌlā-təd\ *adj*

[1]**men·tion** \ˈmen-chən\ *n* **1** : a brief or casual reference **2** : a formal citation for outstanding achievement

[2]**mention** *vb* **1** : to refer to : CITE **2** : to cite for superior achievement — **not to mention** : not even yet counting or considering

men·tor \ˈmen-ˌtȯr, -tər\ *n* : a trusted counselor or guide; *also* : TUTOR, COACH — **mentor** *vb*

menu \ˈmen-yü, ˈmān-\ *n, pl* **menus** [F, fr. *menu* small, detailed, fr. OF, fr. L *minutus* minute (adj.)] **1** : a list of the dishes available (as in a restaurant) for a meal; *also* : the dishes served **2** : a list of offerings or options

me·ow \mē-ˈau̇\ *vb* : to make the characteristic cry of a cat — **meow** *n*

mer *abbr* meridian

mer·can·tile \ˈmər-kən-ˌtēl, -ˌtī(-ə)l\ *adj* : of or relating to merchants or trading

[1]**mer·ce·nary** \ˈmər-sə-ˌner-ē\ *n, pl* **-nar·ies** : a person who serves merely for wages; *esp* : a soldier hired into foreign service

[2]**mercenary** *adj* **1** : serving merely for pay or gain **2** : hired for service in a foreign army

mer·cer \ˈmər-sər\ *n, Brit* : a dealer in usu. expensive fabrics

mer·cer·ise *Brit var of* MERCERIZE

mer·cer·ize \ˈmər-sə-ˌrīz\ *vb* **-ized; -iz·ing** : to treat cotton yarn or cloth with alkali so that it looks silky or takes a better dye

[1]**mer·chan·dise** \ˈmər-chən-ˌdīz, -ˌdīs\ *n* : the commodities or goods that are bought and sold in business

[2]**mer·chan·dise** \-ˌdīz\ *vb* **-dised; -dis·ing** : to buy and sell in business : TRADE — **mer·chan·dis·er** *n*

mer·chant \ˈmər-chənt\ *n* **1** : a buyer and seller of commodities for profit **2** : STOREKEEPER

mer·chant·able \ˈmər-chən-tə-bəl\ *adj* : acceptable to buyers : MARKETABLE

mer·chant·man \ˈmər-chənt-mən\ *n* : a ship used in commerce

merchant marine *n* : the commercial ships of a nation

merchant ship *n* : MERCHANTMAN

mer·ci·ful·ly \ˈmər-si-fə-lē\ *adv* **1** : in a merciful manner **2** : FORTUNATELY 2 ⟨~ we didn't have to attend⟩

mer·cu·ri·al \ˌmər-ˈkyu̇r-ē-əl\ *adj* **1** : unpredictably changeable ⟨a ~ personality⟩ **2** : MERCURIC — **mer·cu·ri·al·ly** *adv* — **mer·cu·ri·al·ness** *n*

mer·cu·ric \ˌmər-ˈkyu̇r-ik\ *adj* : of, relating to, or containing mercury

mercuric chloride *n* : a poisonous compound of mercury and chlorine used as an antiseptic and fungicide

mer·cu·ry \ˈmər-kyə-rē\ *n, pl* **-ries** **1** : a heavy silver-white liquid metallic chemical element used esp. in scientific instruments **2** *cap* : the planet nearest the sun

mer·cy \ˈmər-sē\ *n, pl* **mercies** [ME, fr. AF *merci,* fr. ML *merced-, merces,* fr. L, price paid, wages, fr. *merc-, merx* merchandise] **1** : compassion shown to an offender; *also* : imprisonment rather than death for first-degree murder **2** : a blessing resulting from divine favor or compassion; *also* : a fortunate circumstance **3** : compassion shown to victims of misfortune — **mer·ci·ful** \-si-fəl\ *adj* — **mer·ci·less** \-si-ləs\ *adj* — **mer·ci·less·ly** *adv* — **mercy** *adj*

mercy killing *n* : EUTHANASIA

[1]**mere** \ˈmir\ *n* : LAKE, POOL

[2]**mere** *adj, superlative* **mer·est** **1** : not diluted : PURE **2** : being nothing more than ⟨a ~ child⟩ — **mere·ly** *adv*

mer·e·tri·cious \ˌmer-ə-ˈtri-shəs\ *adj* [L *meretricius,* fr. *meretrix* prostitute, fr. *merēre* to earn] : tawdrily attractive ⟨~ trinkets⟩; *also* : SPECIOUS — **mer·e·tri·cious·ly** *adv* — **mer·e·tri·cious·ness** *n*

mer·gan·ser \(ˌ)mər-ˈgan-sər\ *n* : any of various fish-eating wild ducks with a usu. crested head and a slender bill hooked at the end and serrated along the margins

merge \ˈmərj\ *vb* **merged; merg·ing** **1** : to blend gradually **2** : to combine, unite, or coalesce into one ♦ ***Synonyms*** MINGLE, AMALGAMATE, FUSE, INTERFUSE, INTERMINGLE

merg·er \ˈmər-jər\ *n* **1** : the act or process of merging **2** : absorption by a corporation of one or more others

me·rid·i·an \mə-ˈri-dē-ən\ *n* [ME, fr. AF *meridien,* fr. *meridien* of noon, fr. L *meridianus,* fr. *meridies* noon, south, irreg. fr. *medius* mid + *dies* day] **1** : the highest point : CULMINATION **2** : any of the imaginary circles on the earth's surface passing through the north and south poles **3** : any of the pathways along which the body's vital energy flows according to the theory behind acupuncture — **meridian** *adj*

me·ringue \mə-ˈraŋ\ *n* [F] : a baked dessert topping of stiffly beaten egg whites and powdered sugar

me·ri·no \mə-ˈrē-nō\ *n, pl* **-nos** [Sp] **1** : any of a breed of sheep noted for fine soft wool **2** : a fine soft fabric or yarn of wool or wool and cotton

[1]**mer·it** \ˈmer-ət\ *n* **1** : laudable or blameworthy traits or actions **2** : a praiseworthy quality; *also* : character or conduct deserving reward or honor **3** *pl* : the intrinsic nature of a legal case; *also* : legal significance

[2]**merit** *vb* : EARN, DESERVE

mer·i·toc·ra·cy \ˌmer-ə-ˈtä-krə-sē\ *n, pl* **-cies** : a system in which people are chosen and moved into positions of success, power, and influence based on their abilities and merit; *also* : leadership by the talented

mer·i·to·ri·ous \ˌmer-ə-ˈtȯr-ē-əs\ *adj* : deserving honor or esteem — **mer·i·to·ri·ous·ly** *adv* — **mer·i·to·ri·ous·ness** *n*

mer·lin \ˈmər-lən\ *n* : a small compact falcon of the northern hemisphere

mer·lot \mer-ˈlō, mər-\ *n* : a dry red wine made from a widely grown grape; *also* : the grape itself

mer·maid \ˈmər-ˌmād\ *n* : a legendary sea creature with a woman's upper body and a fish's tail

mer·man \-ˌman, -mən\ *n* : a legendary sea creature with a man's upper body and a fish's tail

mer·ri·ment \ˈmer-i-mənt\ *n* **1** : HILARITY **2** : FESTIVITY

mer·ry \ˈmer-ē\ *adj* **mer·ri·er; -est** **1** : full of gaiety or high spirits **2** : marked by festivity **3** : BRISK ⟨a ~pace⟩ ♦ ***Synonyms*** BLITHE, JOCUND, JOVIAL, JOLLY, MIRTHFUL — **mer·ri·ly** \ˈmer-ə-lē\ *adv*

merry–go–round \ˈmer-ē-gō-ˌrau̇nd\ *n* **1** : a circular revolving platform with benches and figures of animals on which people sit for a ride **2** : a busy round of activities

mer·ry·mak·ing \ˈmer-ē-ˌmā-kiŋ\ *n* **1** : jovial or festive activity **2** : a festive occasion — **mer·ry·mak·er** \-ˌmā-kər\ *n*

me·sa \ˈmā-sə\ *n* [Sp, lit., table, fr. L *mensa*] : a flat-topped hill with steep sides

mes·cal \me-ˈskal, mə-\ *n* **1** : PEYOTE 2 **2** : a usu. colorless liquor distilled from the leaves of an agave; *also* : this agave

mes·ca·line \ˈmes-kə-lən, -ˌlēn\ *n* : a hallucinatory alkaloid from the peyote cactus

mes·clun \ˈmes-klən\ *n* : a mixture of young tender greens; *also* : a salad made with mesclun

mesdames *pl of* MADAM *or of* MADAME *or of* MRS.

mesdemoiselles *pl of* MADEMOISELLE

[1]**mesh** \ˈmesh\ *n* **1** : one of the openings between the threads or cords of a net; *also* : one of the similar spaces in a network **2** : the fabric of a net **3** : NETWORK **4** : working contact (as of the teeth of gears) ⟨in ~⟩ — **meshed** \ˈmesht\ *adj*

[2]**mesh** *vb* **1** : to catch in or as if in a mesh **2** : to be in or come into mesh : ENGAGE **3** : to fit together properly

mesh·work \ˈmesh-ˌwərk\ *n* : NETWORK

me·si·al \ˈmē-zē-əl, -sē-\ *adj* : of, relating to, or being the surface of a tooth that is closest to the middle of the front of the jaw
mes·mer·ise *Brit var of* MESMERIZE
mes·mer·ize \ˈmez-mə-ˌrīz\ *vb* **-ized; -iz·ing** : HYPNOTIZE — **mes·mer·ic** \mez-ˈmer-ik\ *adj* — **mes·mer·ism** \ˈmez-mə-ˌri-zəm\ *n*
Me·so·lith·ic \ˌme-zə-ˈli-thik\ *adj* : of, relating to, or being a transitional period of the Stone Age between the Paleolithic and the Neolithic periods
me·so·sphere \ˈme-zə-ˌsfir\ *n* : a layer of the atmosphere between the stratosphere and the thermosphere
Me·so·zo·ic \ˌme-zə-ˈzō-ik, ˌmē-\ *adj* : of, relating to, or being the era of geologic history between the Paleozoic and the Cenozoic and extending from about 245 million years ago to about 65 million years ago — **Mesozoic** *n*
mes·quite \mə-ˈskēt, me-\ *n* : any of several spiny leguminous trees and shrubs chiefly of the southwestern U.S. with sugar-rich pods important as fodder; *also* : mesquite wood used esp. in grilling food
[1]**mess** \ˈmes\ *n* [ME *mes,* fr. AF, fr. LL *missus* course at a meal, fr. *missus,* pp. of *mittere* to put, fr. L, to send] **1** : a quantity of food; *also* : enough food of a specified kind for a dish or meal ⟨a ~ of beans⟩ **2** : a group of persons who regularly eat together; *also* : a meal eaten by such a group **3** : a place where meals are regularly served to a group **4** : a confused, dirty, or offensive state — **messy** *adj*
[2]**mess** *vb* **1** : to supply with meals; *also* : to take meals with a mess **2** : to make dirty or untidy; *also* : BUNGLE **3** : INTERFERE, MEDDLE ⟨don't ~ with me⟩ **4** : PUTTER, TRIFLE
mes·sage \ˈme-sij\ *n* : a communication sent by one person to another — **message** *vb*
message board *n* : BULLETIN BOARD 2
messeigneurs *pl of* MONSEIGNEUR
mes·sen·ger \ˈme-sᵊn-jər\ *n* : one who carries a message or does an errand
messenger RNA *n* : an RNA that carries the code for a particular protein from DNA in the nucleus to a ribosome in the cytoplasm and acts as a template for the formation of that protein
Mes·si·ah \mə-ˈsī-ə\ *n* **1** : the expected king and deliverer of the Jews **2** : Jesus **3** *not cap* : a professed or accepted leader of a cause — **mes·si·an·ic** \ˌme-sē-ˈa-nik\ *adj*
messieurs *pl of* MONSIEUR
mess·mate \ˈmes-ˌmāt\ *n* : a member of a group who eat regularly together
Messrs. \ˈme-sərz\ *pl of* MR.
mes·ti·zo \me-ˈstē-zō\ *n, pl* **-zos** [Sp] : a person of mixed blood
[1]**met** *past and past part of* MEET
[2]**met** *abbr* metropolitan
meta \ˈme-tə\ *adj* : cleverly self-referential
me·tab·o·lism \mə-ˈta-bə-ˌli-zəm\ *n* : the processes by which the substance of plants and animals incidental to life is built up and broken down; *also* : the processes by which a substance is handled in the living body ⟨the ~ of sugar⟩ — **met·a·bol·ic** \ˌme-tə-ˈbä-lik\ *adj* — **me·tab·o·lize** \mə-ˈta-bə-ˌlīz\ *vb*
me·tab·o·lite \-ˌlīt\ *n* **1** : a product of metabolism **2** : a substance essential to the metabolism of a particular organism or to a metabolic process
meta·car·pal \ˌme-tə-ˈkär-pəl\ *n* : any of usu. five more or less elongated bones of the part of the hand or forefoot between the wrist and the bones of the digits — **metacarpal** *adj*
meta·car·pus \-ˈkär-pəs\ *n* : the part of the hand or forefoot that contains the metacarpals
met·al \ˈme-tᵊl\ *n* **1** : any of various opaque, fusible, ductile, and typically lustrous substances that are good conductors of electricity and heat **2** : METTLE; *also* : the material out of which a person or thing is made — **me·tal·lic** \mə-ˈta-lik\ *adj*
met·al·lur·gy \ˈme-tᵊl-ˌər-jē\ *n* : the science and technology of metals — **met·al·lur·gi·cal** \ˌme-tᵊl-ˈər-ji-kəl\ *adj* — **met·al·lur·gist** \ˈme-tᵊl-ˌər-jist\ *n*
met·al·ware \ˈme-tᵊl-ˌwer\ *n* : metal utensils for household use
met·al·work \-ˌwərk\ *n* : work and esp. artistic work made of metal — **met·al·work·er** \-ˌwər-kər\ *n* — **met·al·work·ing** *n*
meta·mor·phism \ˌme-tə-ˈmȯr-ˌfi-zəm\ *n* : a change in the structure of rock; *esp* : a change to a more compact and more highly crystalline form produced by pressure, heat, and water — **meta·mor·phic** \-ˈmȯr-fik\ *adj*
meta·mor·pho·sis \ˌme-tə-ˈmȯr-fə-səs\ *n, pl* **-pho·ses** \-ˌsēz\ **1** : a change of physical form, structure, or substance esp. by supernatural means; *also* : a striking alteration (as in appearance or character) **2** : a fundamental change in form and often habits of an animal accompanying the transformation of a larva into an adult — **meta·mor·phose** \-ˌfōz, -ˌfōs\ *vb*
met·a·phor \ˈme-tə-ˌfȯr\ *n* : a figure of speech in which a word for one idea or thing is used in place of another to suggest a likeness between them (as in "the ship plows the sea") — **met·a·phor·ic** \ˌme-tə-ˈfȯr-ik\ *or* **met·a·phor·i·cal** \ˌme-tə-ˈfȯr-i-kəl\ *adj* — **met·a·phor·i·cal·ly** \-i-k(ə-)lē\ *adv*
meta·phys·ics \ˌme-tə-ˈfi-ziks\ *n* [ML *Metaphysica,* title of Aristotle's treatise on the subject, fr. Gk *(ta) meta (ta) physika,* lit., the (works) after the physical (works); fr. its position in his collected works] : the philosophical study of the ultimate causes and underlying nature of things — **meta·phys·i·cal** \-ˈfi-zi-kəl\ *adj* — **meta·phy·si·cian** \-fə-ˈzi-shən\ *n*
me·tas·ta·sis \mə-ˈtas-tə-səs\ *n, pl* **-ta·ses** \-ˌsēz\ : the spread of a health-

impairing agency (as cancer cells) from the initial or primary site of disease to another part of the body; *also* : a secondary growth of a malignant tumor — **me·tas·ta·size** \-tə-ˌsīz\ *vb* — **met·a·stat·ic** \ˌme-tə-ˈsta-tik\ *adj*

meta·tar·sal \ˌme-tə-ˈtär-səl\ *n* : any of the bones of the foot between the tarsus and the bones of the digits that in humans include five elongated bones — **metatarsal** *adj*

meta·tar·sus \-ˈtär-səs\ *n* : the part of the human foot or the hind foot in quadrupeds that contains the metatarsals

[1]**mete** \ˈmēt\ *vb* **met·ed; met·ing** **1** *archaic* : MEASURE **2** : ALLOT — usu. used with *out* ⟨~ out punishment⟩

[2]**mete** *n* : BOUNDARY ⟨~*s* and bounds⟩

me·te·or \ˈmē-tē-ər, -ˌȯr\ *n* **1** : a small particle of matter in the solar system directly observable only by its glow from frictional heating on falling into the earth's atmosphere **2** : the streak of light produced by a meteor

me·te·or·ic \ˌmē-tē-ˈȯr-ik\ *adj* **1** : of, relating to, or resembling a meteor **2** : transiently brilliant ⟨a ~ career⟩ — **me·te·or·i·cal·ly** \-i-k(ə-)lē\ *adv*

me·te·or·ite \ˈmē-tē-ə-ˌrīt\ *n* : a meteor that reaches the surface of the earth

me·te·or·oid \ˈmē-tē-ə-ˌrȯid\ *n* : a small particle of matter in the solar system

me·te·o·rol·o·gy \ˌmē-tē-ə-ˈrä-lə-jē\ *n* : a science that deals with the atmosphere and its phenomena and esp. with weather forecasting — **me·te·o·ro·log·ic** \ˌmē-tē-ˌȯr-ə-ˈlä-jik\ *or* **me·te·o·ro·log·i·cal** \-ˈlä-ji-kəl\ *adj* — **me·te·o·rol·o·gist** \ˌmē-tē-ə-ˈrä-lə-jist\ *n*

[1]**me·ter** \ˈmē-tər\ *n* : rhythm in verse or music

[2]**meter** *n* : the basic metric unit of length — see METRIC SYSTEM table

[3]**meter** *n* : a measuring and sometimes recording instrument

[4]**meter** *vb* **1** : to measure by means of a meter **2** : to print postal indicia on by means of a postage meter

meter–kilogram–second *adj* : of, relating to, or being a system of units based on the meter, the kilogram, and the second

meter maid *n* : a woman assigned to write tickets for parking violations

meth·a·done \ˈme-thə-ˌdōn\ *also* **meth·a·don** \-ˌdän\ *n* : a synthetic addictive narcotic drug used esp. as a substitute narcotic in the treatment of heroin addiction

meth·am·phet·amine \ˌme-tham-ˈfe-tə-ˌmēn, -thəm-, -mən\ *n* : a drug used medically in the form of its hydrochloride in the treatment of obesity and often illicitly as a stimulant

meth·ane \ˈme-ˌthān\ *n* : a colorless odorless flammable gas produced by decomposition of organic matter or from coal and used esp. as a fuel

meth·a·nol \ˈme-thə-ˌnȯl, -ˌnōl\ *n* : a volatile flammable poisonous liquid alcohol used esp. as a solvent and as an antifreeze

meth·aqua·lone \me-ˈtha-kwə-ˌlōn\ *n* : a sedative and hypnotic habit-forming drug that is not a barbiturate

meth·od \ˈme-thəd\ *n* [ME, prescribed treatment, fr. L *methodus,* fr. Gk *methodos,* fr. *meta* with + *hodos* way] **1** : a procedure or process for achieving an end **2** : orderly arrangement : PLAN ♦ ***Synonyms*** MODE, MANNER, WAY, FASHION, SYSTEM — **me·thod·i·cal** \mə-ˈthä-di-kəl\ *adj* — **me·thod·i·cal·ly** \-k(ə-)lē\ *adv* — **me·thod·i·cal·ness** *n*

meth·od·ise *Brit var of* METHODIZE

Meth·od·ist \ˈme-thə-dist\ *n* : a member of a Protestant denomination adhering to the doctrines of John Wesley — **Meth·od·ism** \-ˌdi-zəm\ *n*

meth·od·ize \ˈme-thə-ˌdīz\ *vb* **-ized; -iz·ing** : SYSTEMATIZE

meth·od·ol·o·gy \ˌme-thə-ˈdä-lə-jē\ *n, pl* **-gies** **1** : a body of methods and rules followed in a science or discipline **2** : the study of the principles or procedures of inquiry in a particular field

meth·yl \ˈme-thəl\ *n* : a chemical radical consisting of carbon and hydrogen

methyl alcohol *n* : METHANOL

meth·yl·mer·cury \ˌme-thəl-ˈmər-kyə-rē\ *n* : any of various toxic compounds of mercury that often occur as pollutants which accumulate in animals esp. at the top of a food chain

met·i·cal \ˈme-ti-kəl\ *n, pl* **met·i·cais** \-kī\ *also* **meticals** — see MONEY table

me·tic·u·lous \mə-ˈti-kyə-ləs\ *adj* [L *meticulosus* fearful, fr. *metus* fear] : extremely careful in attending to details — **me·tic·u·lous·ly** *adv* — **me·tic·u·lous·ness** *n*

mé·tier \ˈme-ˌtyā, me-ˈtyā\ *n* : an area of activity in which one is expert or successful

me·tre \ˈmē-tər\ *chiefly Brit var of* METER

met·ric \ˈme-trik\ *adj* **1** : of or relating to measurement; *esp* : of or relating to the metric system **2** : METRICAL 1

met·ri·cal \ˈme-tri-kəl\ *adj* **1** : of, relating to, or composed in meter **2** : METRIC 1 — **met·ri·cal·ly** \-k(ə-)lē\ *adv*

met·ri·ca·tion \ˌme-tri-ˈkā-shən\ *n* : the act or process of converting into or expressing in the metric system

met·ri·cize \ˈme-trə-ˌsīz\ *vb* **-cized; -ciz·ing** : to change into or express in the metric system

following full page **metric system** *n* : a decimal system of weights and measures based on the meter and on the kilogram

☞ the METRIC SYSTEM table is on page 459

metric ton *n* — see METRIC SYSTEM table

[1]**met·ro** \ˈme-trō\ *n, pl* **metros** : SUBWAY

[2]**metro** *adj* : of, relating to, or characteristic of a metropolis and sometimes including its suburbs

met·ro·nome \ˈme-trə-ˌnōm\ *n* : an instrument for marking exact time by a regularly repeated tick

me·trop·o·lis \mə-ˈträ-pə-ləs\ *n* [ME, fr. LL, fr. Gk *mētropolis,* fr. *mētēr* mother + *polis* city] : the chief or capital city of a country, state, or region — **met·ro·pol·i·tan** \ˌme-trə-ˈpä-lə-tən\ *adj*

METRIC SYSTEM

LENGTH

UNIT	SYMBOL	METRIC EQUIVALENT	U.S. EQUIVALENT
kilometer	km	1,000 meters	0.62 mile
hectometer	hm	100 meters	328.08 feet
dekameter	dam	10 meters	32.81 feet
meter	m		39.37 inches
decimeter	dm	0.1 meter	3.94 inches
centimeter	cm	0.01 meter	0.39 inch
millimeter	mm	0.001 meter	0.039 inch
micrometer	μm	0.000001 meter	0.000039 inch

AREA

UNIT	SYMBOL	METRIC EQUIVALENT	U.S. EQUIVALENT
square kilometer	sq km *or* km^2	1,000,000 square meters	0.39 square miles
hectare	ha	10,000 square meters	2.47 acres
are	a	100 square meters	119.60 square yards
square centimeter	sq cm *or* cm^2	0.0001 square meter	0.16 square inch

VOLUME

UNIT	SYMBOL	METRIC EQUIVALENT	U.S. EQUIVALENT
cubic meter	m^3		1.31 cubic yards
cubic decimeter	dm^3	0.001 cubic meter	61.02 cubic inches
cubic centimeter	cu cm *or* cm^3 *also* cc	0.000001 cubic meter	0.061 cubic inch

MASS AND WEIGHT

UNIT	SYMBOL	METRIC EQUIVALENT	U.S. EQUIVALENT
metric ton	t	1,000,000 grams	1.10 short tons
kilogram	kg	1,000 grams	2.20 pounds
hectogram	hg	100 grams	3.53 ounces
dekagram	dag	10 grams	0.35 ounce
gram	g		0.035 ounce
decigram	dg	0.1 gram	1.54 grains
centigram	cg	0.01 gram	0.15 grain
milligram	mg	0.001 gram	0.015 grain
microgram	μg *or* mcg	0.000001 gram	0.000015 grain

CAPACITY

UNIT	METRIC EQUIVALENT	U.S. EQUIVALENT UNITS		
		CUBIC	*DRY*	*LIQUID*
kiloliter (kl)	1,000 liters	1.31 cubic yards	28.38 bushels	264.17 gallons
hectoliter (hl)	100 liters	3.53 cubic feet	2.84 bushels	26.42 gallons
dekaliter (dal)	10 liters	0.35 cubic foot	1.14 pecks	2.64 gallons
liter (l)		61.02 cubic inches	0.91 quart	1.06 quarts
deciliter (dl)	0.1 liter	6.10 cubic inches	0.18 pint	0.21 pint
centiliter (cl)	0.01 liter	0.61 cubic inch		0.34 fluid ounce
milliliter (ml)	0.001 liter	0.061 cubic inch		0.27 fluid dram
microliter (μl)	0.000001 liter	0.000061 cubic inch		0.00027 fluid dram

For metric system equivalents of U.S. system units, see WEIGHTS AND MEASURES table.

met·tle \ˈme-tᵊl\ *n* **1** : SPIRIT, COURAGE **2** : quality of temperament

met·tle·some \ˈme-tᵊl-səm\ *adj* : full of mettle : COURAGEOUS ⟨a ~ opponent⟩

MeV *abbr* million electron volts

¹mew \ˈmyü\ *vb* : MEOW — **mew** *n*

²mew *vb* : CONFINE

mews \ˈmyüz\ *n sing or pl, chiefly Brit* : stables usu. with living quarters built around a court; *also* : a narrow street with dwellings converted from stables

Mex *abbr* Mexican; Mexico

mez·za·nine \ˈme-zə-ˌnēn, ˌme-zə-ˈ\ *n* **1** : a low-ceilinged story between two main stories of a building **2** : the lowest balcony in a theater; *also* : the first few rows of such a balcony

mez·zo for·te \ˌmet-(ˌ)sō-ˈfȯr-ˌtā, ˌmed-(ˌ)zō-, -tē\ *adj or adv* [It] : moderately loud — used as a direction in music

mez·zo pia·no \-pē-ˈä-(ˌ)nō\ *adj or adv* [It] : moderately soft — used as a direction in music

mez·zo–so·pra·no \-sə-ˈpra-nō, -ˈprä-\ *n* : a woman's voice having a range between that of the soprano and contralto; *also* : a singer having such a voice

MFA *abbr* master of fine arts

mfr *abbr* manufacture; manufacturer

mg *abbr* milligram

Mg *symbol* magnesium

MG *abbr* **1** machine gun **2** major general **3** military government

mgr *abbr* **1** manager **2** monseigneur **3** monsignor

mgt *or* **mgmt** *abbr* management

MGy Sgt *abbr* master gunnery sergeant

MHz *abbr* megahertz

mi *abbr* **1** mile; mileage **2** mill

MI *abbr* **1** Michigan **2** military intelligence

MIA \ˌem-(ˌ)ī-ˈā\ *n* [*m*issing *i*n *a*ction] : a member of the armed forces whose whereabouts following a combat mission are unknown

Mi·ami \mī-ˈa-mē, -mə\ *n, pl* **Mi·ami** *or* **Mi·am·is** : a member of an Indigenous people orig. of Wisconsin, Illinois, and Indiana

mi·as·ma \mī-ˈaz-mə, mē-\ *n, pl* **-mas** *also* **-ma·ta** \-mə-tə\ **1** : a vapor from a swamp formerly believed to cause disease **2** : a harmful influence or atmosphere ⟨a ~ of smog⟩ — **mi·as·mal** \-məl\ *adj* — **mi·as·mic** \-mik\ *adj*

mic \ˈmīk\ *n* : MICROPHONE

Mic *abbr* Micah

mi·ca \ˈmī-kə\ *n* [NL, fr. L, grain, crumb] : any of various mineral silicates readily separable into thin transparent sheets

Mi·cah \ˈmī-kə\ *n* — see BIBLE table

mice *pl of* MOUSE

Mich *abbr* Michigan

Mi·che·as \ˈmī-kē-əs, mī-ˈkē-əs\ *n* : MICAH

Micmac *var of* MI'KMAQ

micr- *or* **micro-** *comb form* **1** : small : minute ⟨*micro*capsule⟩ **2** : one millionth part of a specified unit ⟨*micro*second⟩

¹mi·cro \ˈmī-krō\ *adj* **1** : very small; *esp* : MICROSCOPIC **2** : involving minute quantities or variations

²micro *n, pl* **micros** : MICROCOMPUTER

mi·crobe \ˈmī-ˌkrōb\ *n* : MICROORGANISM; *esp* : one causing disease — **mi·cro·bi·al** \mī-ˈkrō-bē-əl\ *adj*

mi·cro·bi·ol·o·gy \ˌmī-krō-bī-ˈä-lə-jē\ *n* : a branch of biology dealing esp. with microscopic forms of life — **mi·cro·bi·o·log·i·cal** \-ˌbī-ə-ˈlä-ji-kəl\ *adj* — **mi·cro·bi·ol·o·gist** \-bī-ˈä-lə-jist\ *n*

mi·cro·brew·ery \ˈmī-krō-ˌbrü-ə-rē\ *n* : a small brewery making specialty beer in limited quantities

mi·cro·burst \-ˌbərst\ *n* : a violent short-lived localized downdraft that creates extreme wind shears at low altitudes

mi·cro·cap·sule \ˈmī-krō-ˌkap-səl, -sül\ *n* : a tiny capsule containing material (as a medicine) released when the capsule is broken, melted, or dissolved

mi·cro·chip \-ˌchip\ *n* : INTEGRATED CIRCUIT

mi·cro·cir·cuit \-ˌsər-kət\ *n* : a compact electronic circuit

mi·cro·com·put·er \-kəm-ˌpyü-tər\ *n* : a small computer that uses a microprocessor; *esp* : PERSONAL COMPUTER

mi·cro·cosm \ˈmī-krə-ˌkä-zəm\ *n* : an individual or community thought of as a miniature world or universe

mi·cro·elec·tron·ics \ˈmī-krō-i-ˌlek-ˈträ-niks\ *n* : a branch of electronics that deals with the miniaturization of electronic circuits and components — **mi·cro·elec·tron·ic** \-nik\ *adj*

mi·cro·en·cap·su·late \ˌmī-krō-in-ˈkap-sə-ˌlāt\ *vb* : to enclose (as a drug) in a microcapsule

mi·cro·fi·ber \ˈmī-krō-ˌfī-bər\ *n* : a fine usu. soft polyester fiber; *also* : fabric made from such fibers

mi·cro·fiche \ˈmī-krō-ˌfēsh, -ˌfish\ *n, pl* **-fiche** *or* **-fiches** *same or* -ˌfē-shəz, -ˌfi-\ : a sheet of microfilm containing rows of images of pages of printed matter

mi·cro·film \-ˌfilm\ *n* : a film bearing a photographic record (as of print) on a reduced scale — **microfilm** *vb*

mi·cro·graph \ˈmī-krə-ˌgraf\ *n* : a graphic reproduction of the image of an object formed by a microscope

mi·cro·man·age \ˌmī-krō-ˈma-nij\ *vb* : to manage esp. with excessive control or attention to details — **mi·cro·man·age·ment** \-mənt\ *n* — **mi·cro·man·ag·er** \-ni-jər\ *n*

mi·cro·me·te·or·ite \ˌmī-krō-ˈmē-tē-ə-ˌrīt\ *n* : a very small particle in interplanetary space

mi·crom·e·ter \mī-ˈkrä-mə-tər\ *n* : an instrument used with a telescope or microscope for measuring minute distances

mi·cro·min·ia·tur·i·za·tion \ˌmī-kro-ˌmi-nē-ə-ˌchu̇r-ə-ˈzā-shən, -ˌmi-ni-ˌchu̇r-, -chər-\ *n* : the process of producing things in a very small size and esp. in a size smaller than one considered miniature — **mi·cro·min·ia·tur·ized** \-ˈmi-nē-ə-chə-ˌrīzd, -ˈmi-ni-chə-\ *adj*

mi·cron \ˈmī-ˌkrän\ *n* : one millionth of a meter

mi·cro·or·gan·ism \ˌmī-krō-ˈȯr-gə-ˌni-zəm\ *n* : an organism (as a bacterium) too tiny to be seen by the unaided eye

mi·cro·phone \ˈmī-krə-ˌfōn\ *n* : an instrument for converting sound waves into variations of an electric current for transmitting or recording sound

mi·cro·pho·to·graph \ˌmī-krə-ˈfō-tə-ˌgraf\ *n* : PHOTOMICROGRAPH

mi·cro·pro·ces·sor \ˌmī-krō-ˈprä-ˌse-sər\ *n* : a computer processor contained on a microchip

mi·cro·scope \ˈmī-krə-ˌskōp\ *n* : an instrument for making magnified images of minute objects usu. using light — **mi·cros·co·py** \mī-ˈkräs-kə-pē\ *n*

mi·cro·scop·ic \ˌmī-krə-ˈskä-pik\ *also* **mi·cro·scop·i·cal** \-pi-kəl\ *adj* **1** : of, relating to, or involving the use of the microscope **2** : too tiny to be seen without the use of a microscope : very small — **mi·cro·scop·i·cal·ly** \-pi-k(ə-)lē\ *adv*

mi·cro·sec·ond \ˈmī-krō-ˌse-kənd\ *n* : one millionth of a second

mi·cro·sur·gery \ˌmī-krō-ˈsər-jə-rē\ *n* : minute dissection or manipulation (as by a laser beam) of living structures or tissue — **mi·cro·sur·gi·cal** \-ˈsər-ji-kəl\ *adj*

mi·cro·tech·nol·o·gy \-tek-ˈnä-lə-jē\ *n* : technology on a small or microscopic scale

¹mi·cro·wave \ˈmī-krə-ˌwāv\ *n* **1** : a radio wave between one millimeter and one meter in wavelength **2** : MICROWAVE OVEN

²microwave *vb* : to heat or cook in a microwave oven — **mi·cro·wav·able** *or* **mi·cro·wave·able** \ˌmī-krə-ˈwā-və-bəl\ *adj*

microwave oven *n* : an oven in which food is cooked by the absorption of microwave energy by water molecules in the food

¹mid \ˈmid\ *adj* : MIDDLE

²mid *abbr* middle

mid·air \ˈmid-ˈer\ *n* : a point or region in the air well above the ground

mid·day \ˈmid-ˌdā, -ˈdā\ *n* : NOON

mid·den \ˈmi-dᵊn\ *n* : a refuse heap

¹mid·dle \ˈmi-dᵊl\ *adj* **1** : equally distant from the extremes : MEDIAL, CENTRAL **2** : being at neither extreme : INTERMEDIATE **3** *cap* : constituting an intermediate period

²middle *n* **1** : a middle part, point, or position **2** : WAIST

middle age *n* : the period of life from about 45 to about 64 — **mid·dle–aged** \ˌmi-dᵊl-ˈājd\ *adj*

Middle Ages *n pl* : the period of European history from about A.D. 500 to about 1500

mid·dle·brow \ˈmi-dᵊl-ˌbrau̇\ *n* : a person who is moderately but not highly cultivated — **middlebrow** *adj*

middle class *n* : a social class holding a position between the upper class and the lower class — **middle–class** *adj*

middle ear *n* : a small membrane-lined cavity of the ear through which sound waves are transmitted by a chain of tiny bones

middle finger *n* : the midmost of the five digits of the hand

mid·dle·man \ˈmi-dᵊl-ˌman\ *n* : INTERMEDIARY; *esp* : one intermediate between the producer of goods and the retailer or consumer

middle–of–the–road *adj* : standing for or following a course of action midway between extremes; *esp* : being neither liberal nor conservative in politics — **mid·dle–of–the–road·er** \-ˈrō-dər\ *n* — **mid·dle–of–the–road·ism** \-ˈrō-ˌdi-zəm\ *n*

middle school *n* : a school usu. including grades 5 to 8 or 6 to 8

mid·dle·weight \ˈmi-dᵊl-ˌwāt\ *n* : one of average weight; *esp* : a boxer weighing not over 160 pounds

mid·dling \ˈmid-liŋ, -lən\ *adj* **1** : of middle, medium, or moderate size, degree, or quality **2** : MEDIOCRE

mid·dy \ˈmi-dē\ *n, pl* **middies** : MIDSHIPMAN

midge \ˈmij\ *n* : a very small fly : GNAT

midg·et \ˈmi-jət\ *n* **1** : something (as an animal) very small for its kind **2** *sometimes offensive* : a very small person

midi \ˈmi-dē\ *n* : a calf-length dress, coat, or skirt

MIDI \ˈmi-dē\ *n* [*m*usical *i*nstrument *d*igital *i*nterface] : a proctocol for the transmission of digitally encoded music

mid·land \ˈmid-lənd, -ˌland\ *n* : the interior or central region of a country

mid·life \ˈmid-ˈlīf\ *n* : MIDDLE AGE

midlife crisis *n* : a period of emotional turmoil in middle age characterized esp. by a strong desire for change

mid·most \-ˌmōst\ *adj* : being in or near the exact middle — **midmost** *adv*

mid·night \-ˌnīt\ *n* : 12 o'clock at night

mid–ocean ridge \ˈmid-ˈō-shən-\ *n* : an elevation on an ocean floor at the boundary of diverging tectonic plates

mid·point \ˈmid-ˌpȯint, -ˈpȯint\ *n* : a point at or near the center or middle

mid·riff \ˈmi-ˌdrif\ *n* [ME *midrif,* fr. OE *midhrif,* fr. *midde* mid + *hrif* belly] **1** : DIAPHRAGM 1 **2** : the mid-region of the human torso

mid·sec·tion \-ˌsek-shən\ *n* : a section midway between the extremes; *esp* : MIDRIFF 2

mid·ship·man \ˈmid-ˌship-mən, (ˌ)mid-ˈship-\ *n* : a student in a naval academy

mid·ships \-ˌships\ *adv* : AMIDSHIPS

midst \ˈmidst\ *n* **1** : the interior or central part or point **2** : a position of proximity to the members of a group ⟨in our ∼⟩ **3** : the condition of being surrounded or beset — **midst** *prep*

mid·stream \ˈmid-ˈstrēm, -ˌstrēm\ *n* : the middle of a stream

mid·sum·mer \-ˈsə-mər, -ˌsə-\ *n* **1** : the middle of summer **2** : the summer solstice

mid·town \ˈmid-ˌtau̇n, -ˈtau̇n\ *n* : a central section of a city; *esp* : one situated between sections called *downtown* and *uptown* — **midtown** *adj*

[1]**mid•way** \ˈmid-ˌwā, -ˈwā\ *adv* : in the middle of the way or distance

[2]**mid•way** \-ˌwā\ *n* : an avenue (as at a carnival) for concessions and amusements

mid•week \-ˌwēk\ *n* : the middle of the week — **mid•week•ly** \-ˌwē-klē, -ˈwē-\ *adj or adv*

mid•wife \ˈmid-ˌwīf\ *n* : a person who helps women in childbirth — **mid•wife•ry** \-ˌwi-fə-rē\ *n*

mid•win•ter \ˈmid-ˈwin-tər, -ˌwin-\ *n* **1** : the winter solstice **2** : the middle of winter

mid•year \-ˌyir\ *n* **1** : the middle of a year **2** : a midyear examination — **mid-year** *adj*

mien \ˈmēn\ *n* **1** : air or bearing esp. as expressive of mood or personality : DEMEANOR **2** : APPEARANCE, ASPECT ⟨dresses of formal ~⟩

miff \ˈmif\ *vb* : to put into an ill humor

[1]**might** \ˈmīt\ *verbal auxiliary, past of* MAY — used as an auxiliary to express permission or possibility in the past, a present condition contrary to fact, less probability or possibility than *may,* or as a polite alternative to *may, ought,* or *should*

[2]**might** *n* : the power, authority, or resources of an individual or a group

mighty \ˈmī-tē\ *adj* **might•i•er; -est** **1** : very strong : POWERFUL **2** : GREAT, NOTABLE — **might•i•ly** \ˈmī-tə-lē\ *adv* — **might•i•ness** \-tē-nəs\ *n* — **mighty** *adv*

mi•gnon•ette \ˌmin-yə-ˈnet\ *n* : an annual garden herb with spikes of tiny fragrant flowers

mi•graine \ˈmī-ˌgrān\ *n* [ME *mygreyn,* fr. MF *migraine,* fr. LL *hemicrania* pain in one side of the head, fr. Gk *hēmikrania,* fr. *hēmi-* half + *kranion* cranium] : a condition marked by recurrent severe headache and often nausea; *also* : an attack of migraine

mi•grant \ˈmī-grənt\ *n* : one that migrates; *esp* : a person who moves in order to find work (as picking crops) — **mi-grant** *adj*

mi•grate \ˈmī-ˌgrāt\ *vb* **mi•grat•ed; mi-grat•ing** **1** : to move from one country or place to another **2** : to pass usu. periodically from one region or climate to another for feeding or breeding — **mi-gra•tion** \mī-ˈgrā-shən\ *n* — **mi•gra•to•ry** \ˈmī-grə-ˌtȯr-ē\ *adj*

mi•ka•do \mə-ˈkä-dō\ *n, pl* **-dos** : an emperor of Japan

mike \ˈmīk\ *n* : MICROPHONE

Mi'k•maq *or* **Mic•mac** \ˈmik-ˌmak\ *n, pl* **Mi'kmaq** *or* **Mi'kmaqs** *or* **Micmac** *or* **Micmacs** : a member of a First Nations people of eastern Canada; *also* : their language

[1]**mil** \ˈmil\ *n* : a unit of length equal to $^1/_{1000}$ inch

[2]**mil** *abbr* military

milch \ˈmilk, ˈmilch\ *adj* : giving milk ⟨~ cow⟩

mild \ˈmī(-ə)ld\ *adj* **1** : gentle in nature or behavior **2** : moderate in action or effect **3** : TEMPERATE ⟨~ weather⟩ ♦ *Synonyms* EASY, COMPLAISANT, AMIABLE, LENIENT — **mild•ly** *adv* — **mild-ness** *n*

mil•dew \ˈmil-ˌdü, -ˌdyü\ *n* : a superficial usu. whitish growth produced on organic matter and on plants by a fungus; *also* : a fungus producing this growth — **mildew** *vb*

mile \ˈmī(-ə)l\ *n* [ME, fr. OE *mīl,* fr. L *milia* miles, fr. *milia passuum,* lit., thousands of paces] **1** — see WEIGHT table **2** : NAUTICAL MILE

mile•age \ˈmī-lij\ *n* **1** : an allowance for traveling expenses at a certain rate per mile **2** : distance in miles traveled (as in a day) **3** : the amount of service yielded (as by a tire) expressed in terms of miles of travel **4** : the average number of miles a motor vehicle will travel on a gallon of gasoline

mile•post \ˈmī(-ə)l-ˌpōst\ *n* : a post indicating the distance in miles from a given point

mile•stone \-ˌstōn\ *n* **1** : a stone serving as a milepost **2** : a significant point in development

mi•lieu \mēl-ˈyər, -ˈyü, -ˈyœ\ *n, pl* **mi-lieus** *or* **mi•lieux** *same or* -ˈyərz, -ˈyüz, -ˈyœz\ [F] : ENVIRONMENT, SETTING

mil•i•tant \ˈmi-lə-tənt\ *adj* **1** : engaged in warfare **2** : aggressively active esp. in a cause — **mil•i•tance** \-təns\ *n* — **mil•i-tan•cy** \-tən-sē\ *n* — **militant** *n* — **mil•i-tant•ly** *adv*

mil•i•ta•rise *Brit var of* MILITARIZE

mil•i•ta•rism \ˈmi-lə-tə-ˌri-zəm\ *n* **1** : predominance of the military class or its ideals **2** : a policy of aggressive military preparedness — **mil•i•ta•rist** \-rist\ *n* — **mil•i•ta•ris•tic** \ˌmi-lə-tə-ˈris-tik\ *adj*

mil•i•ta•rize \ˈmi-lə-tə-ˌrīz\ *vb* **-rized; -riz•ing** **1** : to equip with military forces and defenses ⟨~ a region⟩ **2** : to give a military character to

[1]**mil•i•tary** \ˈmi-lə-ˌter-ē\ *adj* **1** : of or relating to soldiers, arms, war, or the army **2** : performed by armed forces; *also* : supported by armed force ♦ *Synonyms* MARTIAL, WARLIKE — **mil•i•tar-i•ly** \ˌmi-lə-ˈter-ə-lē\ *adv*

[2]**military** *n, pl* **military** *also* **mil•i•tar•ies** **1** : the military, naval, and air forces of a nation **2** : military persons

military police *n* : a branch of an army that exercises guard and police functions

mil•i•tate \ˈmi-lə-ˌtāt\ *vb* **-tat•ed; -tat•ing** : to have weight or effect ⟨disagreements ~ against an alliance⟩

mi•li•tia \mə-ˈli-shə\ *n* **1** : a part of the organized armed forces of a country liable to call only in emergency **2** : a private group of armed individuals that operates as a paramilitary force — **mi•li•tia-man** \-mən\ *n*

[1]**milk** \ˈmilk\ *n* **1** : a nutritive usu. whitish fluid secreted by female mammals for feeding their young **2** : a milklike liquid (as a plant juice) — **milk•i•ness** \ˈmil-kē-nəs\ *n* — **milky** *adj*

[2]**milk** *vb* **1** : to draw off the milk of ⟨~ a

cow⟩ **2** : to draw something from as if by milking

milk•maid \'milk-ˌmād\ *n* : DAIRYMAID

milk•man \-ˌman, -mən\ *n* : a person who sells or delivers milk

milk of magnesia : a milk-white mixture of hydroxide of magnesium and water used as an antacid and laxative

milk shake *n* : a thoroughly blended drink made of milk, a flavoring syrup, and often ice cream

milk•sop \'milk-ˌsäp\ *n* : an unmanly man

milk•weed \-ˌwēd\ *n* : any of a genus of herbs with milky juice and clustered flowers

Milky Way *n* **1** : a broad irregular band of light that stretches across the sky and is caused by the light of a very great number of faint stars **2** : MILKY WAY GALAXY

Milky Way galaxy *n* : the galaxy of which the sun is a member and which includes the stars that create the light of the Milky Way

[1]**mill** \'mil\ *n* **1** : a building with machinery for grinding grain into flour **2** : a machine used in processing (as by grinding, stamping, cutting, or finishing) raw material **3** : FACTORY

[2]**mill** *vb* **1** : to process in a mill **2** : to move in a circle or in an eddying mass

[3]**mill** *n* : one tenth of a cent

mill•age \'mi-lij\ *n* : a rate (as of taxation) expressed in mills

[1]**mil•len•ni•al** \mə-'le-nē-əl\ *adj* : of or relating to a millennium

[2]**millennial** *n* : a person born in the 1980s or 1990s — usually used in pl.

mil•len•ni•um \mə-'le-nē-əm\ *n, pl* **-nia** \-nē-ə\ *or* **-niums** **1** : a period of 1000 years; *also* : a 1000th anniversary or its celebration **2** : the 1000 years mentioned in Revelation 20 when holiness is to prevail and Christ is to reign on earth **3** : a period of great happiness or human perfection

mill•er \'mi-lər\ *n* **1** : one that operates a mill and esp. a flour mill **2** : any of various moths having powdery wings

mil•let \'mi-lət\ *n* : any of several small-seeded cereal and forage grasses cultivated for grain or hay; *also* : the grain of a millet

milli- *comb form* : one thousandth part of

mil•li•am•pere \ˌmi-lē-'am-ˌpir\ *n* : one thousandth of an ampere

mil•liard \'mil-ˌyärd, 'mi-lē-ˌärd\ *n, Brit* : a thousand millions

mil•li•bar \'mi-lə-ˌbär\ *n* : a unit of atmospheric pressure

mil•li•gram \-ˌgram\ *n* — see METRIC SYSTEM table

mil•li•li•ter \-ˌlē-tər\ *n* — see METRIC SYSTEM table

mil•lime \mə-'lēm\ *n* — see *dinar* at MONEY table

mil•li•me•ter \'mi-lə-ˌmē-tər\ *n* — see METRIC SYSTEM table

mil•li•ner \'mi-lə-nər\ *n* [irreg. fr. *Milan*, Italy; fr. the importation of women's finery from Italy in the 16th century] : a person who designs, makes, trims, or sells women's hats

mil•li•nery \'mi-lə-ˌner-ē\ *n* **1** : women's apparel for the head **2** : the business or work of a milliner

mill•ing \'mi-liŋ\ *n* : a corrugated edge on a coin

mil•lion \'mil-yən\ *n, pl* **millions** *or* **million** : a thousand thousands — **million** *adj* — **mil•lionth** \-yənth\ *adj or n*

mil•lion•aire \ˌmil-yə-'ner, 'mil-yə-ˌner\ *n* : one whose wealth is estimated at a million or more (as of dollars or pounds)

mil•li•pede \'mi-lə-ˌpēd\ *n* : any of a class of arthropods related to the centipedes and having a long segmented body with a hard covering, two pairs of legs on most segments, and no poison fangs

mil•li•sec•ond \-ˌse-kənd\ *n* : one thousandth of a second

mil•li•volt \-ˌvōlt\ *n* : one thousandth of a volt

mill•pond \'mil-ˌpänd\ *n* : a pond made by damming a stream to produce a fall of water for operating a mill

mill•race \-ˌrās\ *n* : a canal in which water flows to and from a mill wheel

mill•stone \-ˌstōn\ *n* : either of two round flat stones used for grinding grain

mill•stream \-ˌstrēm\ *n* : a stream whose flow is used to run a mill; *also* : the stream in a millrace

mill wheel *n* : a waterwheel that drives a mill

mill•wright \'mil-ˌrīt\ *n* : a person who builds mills or sets up or maintains their machinery

milt \'milt\ *n* : the sperm-containing fluid of a male fish

mime \'mīm\ *n* **1** : MIMIC **2** : PANTOMIME — **mime** *vb*

mim•eo•graph \'mi-mē-ə-ˌgraf\ *n* : a machine for making many copies by means of a stencil through which ink is pressed — **mimeograph** *vb*

mi•me•sis \mə-'mē-səs, mī-\ *n* : IMITATION, MIMICRY

mi•met•ic \-'me-tik\ *adj* **1** : IMITATIVE **2** : relating to, characterized by, or exhibiting mimicry

[1]**mim•ic** \'mi-mik\ *n* : one that mimics

[2]**mimic** *vb* **mim•icked** \-mikt\; **mim•ick•ing** **1** : to imitate closely **2** : to ridicule by imitation **3** : to resemble by biological mimicry

mim•ic•ry \'mi-mi-krē\ *n, pl* **-ries** **1** : an instance of mimicking **2** : a superficial resemblance of one organism to another or to natural objects among which it lives that gives it an advantage (as protection from predation)

mi•mo•sa \mə-'mō-sə, mī-, -zə\ *n* : any of a genus of trees, shrubs, and herbs of the legume family that occur in warm regions and have ball-shaped heads of small white or pink flowers

min *abbr* **1** minim **2** minimum **3** mining **4** minister **5** minor **6** minute

min•a•ret \ˌmi-nə-'ret\ *n* [F, fr. Turk *minare*, fr. Ar *manāra* lighthouse] : a tall slender tower of a mosque from which a muezzin calls the faithful to prayer

mi•na•to•ry \'mi-nə-ˌtȯr-ē, 'mī-\ *adj* : THREATENING, MENACING

mince \ˈmins\ *vb* **minced; minc·ing** [ME, fr. AF *mincer,* fr. VL **minutiare,* fr. L *minutia* smallness, fr. *minutus* small, fr. pp. of *minuere* to lessen] **1** : to cut into very small pieces **2** : to restrain (words) within the bounds of decorum **3** : to walk in a prim affected manner

mince·meat \ˈmins-ˌmēt\ *n* : a finely chopped mixture esp. of raisins, apples, spices, and often meat used as a filling for a pie

¹mind \ˈmīnd\ *n* **1** : MEMORY **2** : the part of an individual that feels, perceives, thinks, wills, and esp. reasons **3** : INTENTION, DESIRE **4** : normal mental condition **5** : OPINION, VIEW ⟨changed her ~⟩ **6** : MOOD **7** : mental qualities of a person or group **8** : intellectual ability **9** : ATTENTION ⟨pay him no ~⟩

²mind *vb* **1** *chiefly dial* : REMEMBER **2** : to attend to closely **3** : HEED, OBEY **4** : to be concerned about; *also* : DISLIKE **5** : to be careful or cautious ⟨~ the broken stair⟩ **6** : to take charge of **7** : to regard with attention

mind–bend·ing \ˈmīnd-ˌben-diŋ\ *adj* : MIND-BLOWING — **mind–bend·ing·ly** *adv*

mind–blow·ing \-ˌblō-iŋ\ *adj* : PSYCHEDELIC 1; *also* : MIND-BOGGLING — **mind·blow·er** \-ˌblō-ər\ *n* — **mind–blow·ing·ly** *adv*

mind–bog·gling \-ˌbä-gə-liŋ\ *adj* : mentally or emotionally exciting or overwhelming ⟨~ special effects⟩

mind·ed \ˈmīn-dəd\ *adj* **1** : INCLINED, DISPOSED **2** : having a mind of a specified kind or concerned with a specific thing — usu. used in combination ⟨narrow-*minded*⟩ ⟨health-*minded*⟩

mind·ful \ˈmīnd-fəl\ *adj* : bearing in mind : AWARE ⟨~ of their needs⟩ — **mind·ful·ly** *adv* — **mind·ful·ness** *n*

mind·less \-ləs\ *adj* **1** : marked by a lack of mind or consciousness; *esp* : marked by no use of the intellect **2** : not mindful : HEEDLESS — **mind·less·ly** *adv* — **mind·less·ness** *n*

¹mine \ˈmīn\ *pron* : that which belongs to me

²mine *n* **1** : an excavation in the earth from which minerals are taken; *also* : an ore deposit **2** : an underground passage beneath an enemy position **3** : an explosive device for destroying enemy personnel, vehicles, or ships **4** : a rich source of supply

³mine *vb* **mined; min·ing** **1** : to dig a mine **2** : UNDERMINE **3** : to get ore from the earth **4** : to extract from a source **5** : to place military mines in **6** : to create or obtain more units of a cryptocurrency — **min·er** *n*

mine·field \ˈmīn-ˌfēld\ *n* **1** : an area set with mines **2** : something resembling a minefield esp. in having many dangers ⟨a political ~⟩

mine·lay·er \-ˌlā-ər\ *n* : a naval vessel for laying underwater mines

min·er·al \ˈmi-nə-rəl\ *n* **1** : a crystalline substance (as diamond or quartz) of inorganic origin **2** : a naturally occurring substance (as coal, salt, or water) obtained usu. from the ground — **mineral** *adj*

min·er·al·ise *Brit var of* MINERALIZE

min·er·al·ize \ˈmi-nə-rə-ˌlīz\ *vb* **-ized; -iz·ing** **1** : to impregnate or supply with minerals **2** : to change into mineral form — **min·er·al·i·za·tion** \-rə-lə-ˈzā-shən\ *n*

min·er·al·o·gy \ˌmi-nə-ˈrä-lə-jē, -ˈra-\ *n* : a science dealing with minerals — **min·er·al·og·i·cal** \ˌmi-nə-rə-ˈlä-ji-kəl\ *adj* — **min·er·al·o·gist** \ˌmi-nə-ˈrä-lə-jist, -ˈra-\ *n*

mineral oil *n* : an oil of mineral origin; *esp* : a refined petroleum oil used as a laxative

mineral water *n* : water infused with mineral salts or gases

min·e·stro·ne \ˌmi-nə-ˈstrō-nē, -ˈstrōn\ *n* [It, fr. *minestra,* fr. *minestrare* to serve, dish up, fr. L *ministrare,* fr. *minister* servant] : a rich thick vegetable soup

mine·sweep·er \ˈmīn-ˌswē-pər\ *n* : a warship for removing or neutralizing underwater mines

min·gle \ˈmiŋ-gəl\ *vb* **min·gled; min·gling** **1** : to bring or combine together : MIX ⟨*mingling* odors⟩ **2** : ASSOCIATE; *also* : to move about socially ⟨*mingled* with the guests⟩

ming tree \ˈmiŋ-\ *n* : a dwarfed usu. evergreen tree grown as bonsai; *also* : an artificial plant resembling this

mini \ˈmi-nē\ *n, pl* **min·is** : something small of its kind — **mini** *adj*

mini- *comb form* : smaller or briefer than usual, normal, or standard

min·ia·ture \ˈmi-nē-ə-ˌchu̇r, ˈmi-ni-ˌchu̇r, -chər\ *n* [It *miniatura* art of illuminating a manuscript, fr. ML, fr. L *miniare* to color with red lead, fr. *minium* red lead] **1** : a copy on a much reduced scale; *also* : something small of its kind **2** : a small painting — **miniature** *adj* — **min·ia·tur·ist** \-ˌchu̇r-ist, -chər-\ *n*

min·ia·tur·ize \ˈmi-nē-ə-ˌchə-ˌrīz, ˈmi-ni-\ *vb* **-ized; -iz·ing** : to design or construct in small size — **min·ia·tur·i·za·tion** \ˌmi-nē-ə-ˌchu̇r-ə-ˈzā-shən, ˌmi-ni-, -chər-\ *n*

mini·bar \ˈmi-nē-ˌbär\ *n* : a small refrigerator in a hotel room that is stocked with beverages and snacks

mini·bike \ˈmi-nē-ˌbīk\ *n* : a small one-passenger motorcycle

mini·bus \-ˌbəs\ *n* : a small bus or van

mini·com·put·er \-kəm-ˌpyü-tər\ *n* : a computer between a mainframe and a microcomputer in size and speed

mini·disc \ˈmi-nē-ˌdisk\ *n* : a miniature optical disk

min·im \ˈmi-nəm\ *n* — see WEIGHT table

min·i·mal \ˈmi-nə-məl\ *adj* **1** : relating to or being a minimum : LEAST **2** : of or relating to minimalism or minimal art — **min·i·mal·ly** *adv*

minimal art *n* : abstract art consisting primarily of simple geometric forms executed in an impersonal style — **minimal artist** *n*

min·i·mal·ism \ˈmi-nə-mə-ˌli-zəm\ *n*

: MINIMAL ART; *also* : a style (as in music or literature) marked by extreme spareness or simplicity — **min·i·mal·ist** \-list\ *n*

mini·mart \ˈmi-nē-ˌmärt\ *n* : CONVENIENCE STORE

min·i·mise *Brit var of* MINIMIZE

min·i·mize \ˈmi-nə-ˌmīz\ *vb* **-mized; -miz·ing 1** : to reduce or keep to a minimum **2** : to underestimate intentionally ⟨~ the defects⟩ **3** : to replace (a window) on a computer display with a small button or icon which will restore the window when selected ♦ ***Synonyms*** DEPRECIATE, DECRY, DISPARAGE

min·i·mum \ˈmi-nə-məm\ *n, pl* **-ma** \-mə\ *or* **-mums 1** : the least quantity assignable, admissible, or possible **2** : the least of a set of numbers **3** : the lowest degree or amount of variation (as of temperature) reached or recorded — **minimum** *adj*

min·ion \ˈmin-yən\ *n* [MF *mignon* darling] **1** : a servile dependent, follower, or underling **2** : one highly favored **3** : a subordinate official

min·is·cule \ˈmi-nəs-ˌkyül\ *var of* MINUSCULE

mini·se·ries \ˈmi-nē-ˌsir-ēz\ *n* : a television story presented in sequential episodes

mini·skirt \-ˌskərt\ *n* : a skirt with the hemline several inches above the knee

[1]**min·is·ter** \ˈmi-nə-stər\ *n* **1** : AGENT **2** : a member of the clergy esp. of a Protestant communion **3** : a high officer of state who heads a division of governmental activities **4** : a diplomatic representative to a foreign state — **min·is·te·ri·al** \ˌmi-nə-ˈstir-ē-əl\ *adj*

[2]**minister** *vb* **1** : to perform the functions of a minister of religion **2** : to give aid or service — **min·is·tra·tion** \ˌmi-nə-ˈstrā-shən\ *n*

[1]**min·is·trant** \ˈmi-nə-strənt\ *adj, archaic* : performing service as a minister

[2]**ministrant** *n* : one that ministers

min·is·try \ˈmi-nə-strē\ *n, pl* **-tries 1** : MINISTRATION **2** : the office, duties, or functions of a minister; *also* : the period of service or office **3** : CLERGY **4** : AGENCY **5** *often cap* : the body of ministers governing a nation or state; *also* : a government department headed by a minister

mini·tower \ˈmi-nē-ˌtau̇(-ə)r\ *n* : a computer tower of intermediate size

mini·van \ˈmi-nē-ˌvan\ *n* : a small van

mink \ˈmiŋk\ *n, pl* **mink** *or* **minks** : either of two slender flesh-eating mammals resembling the related weasels; *also* : the soft lustrous typically dark brown fur of a mink

min·ke whale \ˈmiŋ-kə-\ *n* : a small grayish baleen whale with a whitish underside

Minn *abbr* Minnesota

min·ne·sing·er \ˈmi-ni-ˌsiŋ-ər, -ˌziŋ-\ *n* [G, fr. Middle High German, fr. *minne* love + *singer* singer] : any of a class of German lyric poets and musicians of the 12th to the 14th centuries

min·now \ˈmi-nō\ *n, pl* **minnows** *also* **minnow** : any of numerous small freshwater fishes

[1]**mi·nor** \ˈmī-nər\ *adj* **1** : inferior in importance, size, or degree **2** : not having reached majority **3** : having the third, sixth, and sometimes the seventh degrees lowered by a half step ⟨~ scale⟩; *also* : based on a minor scale ⟨~ key⟩ **4** : not serious ⟨~ illness⟩

[2]**minor** *n* **1** : a person who has not attained majority **2** : a subject of academic study chosen as a secondary field of specialization

[3]**minor** *vb* : to pursue an academic minor ⟨~*ed* in philosophy⟩

mi·nor·i·ty \mə-ˈnȯr-ə-tē, mī-\ *n, pl* **-ties 1** : the period or state of being a minor **2** : the smaller in number of two groups; *esp* : a group having less than the number of votes necessary for control **3** : a part of a population differing from others (as in race); *also* : a member of a minority

mi·nox·i·dil \mə-ˈnäk-sə-ˌdil\ *n* : a drug used orally to treat hypertension and topically in solution to promote hair regrowth in some forms of baldness

min·ster \ˈmin-stər\ *n* : a large or important church

min·strel \ˈmin-strəl\ *n* **1** : a medieval singer of verses; *also* : MUSICIAN, POET **2** : a member of a type of performance troupe caricaturing Black performers in the U.S. in the early 19th century which promoted negative racial stereotypes

min·strel·sy \-sē\ *n* : the singing and playing of a minstrel; *also* : a body of minstrels

[1]**mint** \ˈmint\ *n* **1** : any of a large family of aromatic square-stemmed herbs and shrubs; *esp* : one (as spearmint) that is fragrant and is the source of a flavoring oil **2** : a mint-flavored piece of candy — **minty** *adj*

[2]**mint** *n* **1** : a place where coins are made **2** : a vast sum ⟨worth a ~⟩

[3]**mint** *vb* **1** : to make (as coins) out of metal **2** : CREATE; *also* : to give a certain status to ⟨newly ~*ed* lawyers⟩ — **mint·age** \-ij\ *n* — **mint·er** *n*

[4]**mint** *adj* : unmarred as if fresh from a mint ⟨in ~ condition⟩

min·u·end \ˈmin-yə-ˌwend\ *n* : a number from which another is to be subtracted

min·u·et \ˌmin-yə-ˈwet\ *n* : a slow graceful dance

[1]**mi·nus** \ˈmī-nəs\ *prep* **1** : diminished by : LESS ⟨seven ~ three equals four⟩ **2** : LACKING, WITHOUT ⟨~ his hat⟩

[2]**minus** *n* : a negative quantity or quality

[3]**minus** *adj* **1** : algebraically negative ⟨~ quantity⟩ **2** : having a negative quality

[1]**mi·nus·cule** \ˈmi-nəs-ˌkyül\ *n* : a lowercase letter

[2]**minuscule** *also* **min·is·cule** *adj* : very small

minus sign *n* : a sign − used in mathematics to indicate subtraction or a negative quantity

[1]**min·ute** \ˈmi-nət\ *n* **1** : the 60th part of

an hour or of a degree : 60 seconds **2** : a short space of time **3** *pl* : the official record of the proceedings of a meeting

²**mi·nute** \mī-ˈnüt, mə-, -ˈnyüt\ *adj* **mi·nut·er; -est 1** : very small **2** : of little importance : TRIFLING **3** : marked by close attention to details ♦ ***Synonyms*** DIMINUTIVE, TINY, MINIATURE, WEE — **mi·nute·ly** *adv* — **mi·nute·ness** *n*

min·ute·man \ˈmi-nət-ˌman\ *n* : a member of a group of armed men pledged to take the field at a minute's notice during and immediately before the American Revolution

mi·nu·tia \mə-ˈnü-shə, -ˈnyü-, -shē-ə\ *n, pl* **-ti·ae** \-shē-ˌē\ [L] : a minute or minor detail — usu. used in pl.

minx \ˈmiŋks\ *n* : a pert girl

Mio·cene \ˈmī-ə-ˌsēn\ *adj* : of, relating to, or being the epoch of the Tertiary between the Oligocene and the Pliocene — **Miocene** *n*

mir·a·cle \ˈmir-i-kəl\ *n* **1** : an extraordinary event manifesting divine intervention in human affairs **2** : an unusual event, thing, or accomplishment : WONDER, MARVEL — **mi·rac·u·lous** \mə-ˈra-kyə-ləs\ *adj* — **mi·rac·u·lous·ly** *adv*

miracle drug *n* : a usu. newly discovered drug that elicits a dramatic response in a patient's condition

mi·rage \mə-ˈräzh\ *n* **1** : an illusion that often appears as a pool of water or a mirror in which distant objects are seen inverted, is sometimes seen at sea, in the desert, or over a hot pavement, and results from atmospheric conditions **2** : something illusory and unattainable

¹**mire** \ˈmī(-ə)r\ *n* : heavy and often deep mud or slush — **miry** *adj*

²**mire** *vb* **mired; mir·ing** : to stick or sink in or as if in mire

mire·poix \mir-ˈpwä\ *n, pl* **mirepoix** : a mixture of diced vegetables and sometimes meats used in soups, stews, and sauces

¹**mir·ror** \ˈmir-ər\ *n* **1** : a polished or smooth surface (as of glass) that forms images by reflection **2** : a true representation

²**mirror** *vb* **1** : to reflect in or as if in a mirror **2** : RESEMBLE ⟨her mood ~*s* the gloomy weather⟩

mirth \ˈmərth\ *n* : gladness or gaiety accompanied with laughter ♦ ***Synonyms*** GLEE, JOLLITY, HILARITY, MERRIMENT — **mirth·ful** \-fəl\ *adj* — **mirth·ful·ly** *adv* — **mirth·ful·ness** *n* — **mirth·less** *adj*

MIRV \ˈmərv\ *n* [*m*ultiple *i*ndependently targeted *r*eentry *v*ehicle] : an ICBM with multiple warheads that have different targets — **MIRV** *vb*

mis·ad·ven·ture \ˌmi-səd-ˈven-chər\ *n* : MISFORTUNE, MISHAP

mis·aligned \ˌmi-sə-ˈlīnd\ *adj* : not properly aligned — **mis·align·ment** \-ˈlīn-mənt\ *n*

mis·al·li·ance \ˌmi-sə-ˈlī-əns\ *n* : an improper or unsuitable marriage

mis·al·lo·ca·tion \ˌmi-ˌsa-lə-ˈkā-shən\ *n* : faulty or improper allocation

mis·an·dry \ˈmi-ˌsan-drē\ *n* : a hatred of men — **mis·an·drist** \-drist\ *n or adj*

mis·an·thrope \ˈmi-sᵊn-ˌthrōp\ *n* : one who hates humankind — **mis·an·throp·ic** \ˌmi-sᵊn-ˈthrä-pik\ *adj* — **mis·an·throp·i·cal·ly** \-pi-k(ə-)lē\ *adv* — **mis·an·thro·py** \mi-ˈsan-thrə-pē\ *n*

mis·ap·ply \ˌmi-sə-ˈplī\ *vb* : to apply wrongly — **mis·ap·pli·ca·tion** \ˌmi-ˌsa-plə-ˈkā-shən\ *n*

mis·ap·pre·hend \ˌmi-ˌsa-pri-ˈhend\ *vb* : MISUNDERSTAND — **mis·ap·pre·hen·sion** \-ˈhen-chən\ *n*

mis·ap·pro·pri·ate \ˌmi-sə-ˈprō-prē-ˌāt\ *vb* : to appropriate wrongly (as by embezzlement) — **mis·ap·pro·pri·a·tion** \-ˌprō-prē-ˈā-shən\ *n*

mis·be·got·ten \-bi-ˈgä-tᵊn\ *adj* **1** *dated* : born to parents not married to each other **2** : badly planned

mis·be·have \ˌmis-bi-ˈhāv\ *vb* : to behave improperly — **mis·be·hav·er** *n* — **mis·be·hav·ior** \-ˈhā-vyər\ *n*

mis·be·liev·er \-bə-ˈlē-vər\ *n* : one who holds a false or unorthodox belief

mis·brand \mis-ˈbrand\ *vb* : to brand falsely or in a misleading manner

misc *abbr* miscellaneous

MIS–C \ˌem-ˌī-ˌes-ˈsē\ *abbr or n* : MULTISYSTEM INFLAMMATORY SYNDROME IN CHILDREN

mis·cal·cu·late \mis-ˈkal-kyə-ˌlāt\ *vb* : to calculate wrongly — **mis·cal·cu·la·tion** \ˌmis-ˌkal-kyə-ˈlā-shən\ *n*

mis·call \mis-ˈkȯl\ *vb* : MISNAME

mis·car·riage \-ˈker-ij\ *n* **1** : failure in the administration of justice **2** : spontaneous expulsion of a fetus before it is capable of independent life

mis·car·ry \-ˈker-ē\ *vb* **1** : to have a miscarriage of a fetus **2** : to go wrong; *also* : to be unsuccessful

mis·ce·ge·na·tion \mi-se-jə-ˈnā-shən, ˌmi-si-jə-ˈnā-\ *n* [L *miscēre* to mix + *genus* race] : marriage, cohabitation, or sexual intercourse between a white person and a member of another race

mis·cel·la·neous \ˌmi-sə-ˈlā-nē-əs\ *adj* **1** : consisting of diverse things or members **2** : having various traits; *also* : dealing with or interested in diverse subjects — **mis·cel·la·neous·ly** *adv* — **mis·cel·la·neous·ness** *n*

mis·cel·la·ny \ˈmi-sə-ˌlā-nē\ *n, pl* **-nies 1** : a collection of writings on various subjects **2** : HODGEPODGE

mis·chance \mis-ˈchans\ *n* : bad luck; *also* : MISHAP

mis·chief \ˈmis-chəf\ *n* [ME *meschief,* fr. AF, misfortune, hardship, fr. OF *mescheever* to come out badly, fr. *mes-* badly + *chief* head, end] **1** : injury caused by a particular agent **2** : a source of harm or irritation **3** : action that annoys; *also* : MISCHIEVOUSNESS

mis·chie·vous \ˈmis-chə-vəs\ *adj* **1** : HARMFUL, INJURIOUS **2** : causing annoyance or minor injury **3** : irresponsibly playful ⟨~ children⟩ — **mis·chie·vous·ly** *adv* — **mis·chie·vous·ness** *n*

mis·ci·ble \ˈmi-sə-bəl\ *adj* : capable of being mixed
mis·com·mu·ni·ca·tion \ˌmis-kə-ˌmyü-nə-ˈkā-shən\ *n* : failure to communicate clearly
mis·con·ceive \ˌmis-kən-ˈsēv\ *vb* : to interpret incorrectly — **mis·con·cep·tion** \-ˈsep-shən\ *n*
mis·con·duct \mis-ˈkän-(ˌ)dəkt\ *n* **1** : MISMANAGEMENT **2** : intentional wrongdoing **3** : improper behavior; *also* : a penalty in a sport for improper behavior
mis·con·strue \ˌmis-kən-ˈstrü\ *vb* : MISINTERPRET — **mis·con·struc·tion** \-ˈstrək-shən\ *n*
mis·count \mis-ˈkau̇nt\ *vb* : to count incorrectly : MISCALCULATE
mis·cre·ant \ˈmis-krē-ənt\ *n* : one who behaves criminally or viciously — **miscreant** *adj*
mis·cue \mis-ˈkyü\ *n* : MISTAKE, ERROR — **miscue** *vb*
mis·deed \mis-ˈdēd\ *n* : a wrong deed
mis·de·mean·or \ˌmis-di-ˈmē-nər\ *n* **1** : a crime less serious than a felony **2** : MISDEED
mis·di·rect \ˌmis-də-ˈrekt, -dī-\ *vb* : to give a wrong direction to — **mis·di·rec·tion** \-ˈrek-shən\ *n*
mis·do·ing \mis-ˈdü-iŋ\ *n* : WRONGDOING — **mis·do** \-ˈdü\ *vb* — **mis·do·er** \-ˈdü-ər\ *n*
mise–en–scène \ˌmē-ˌzäⁿ-ˈsen, -ˈsān\ *n, pl* **mise–en–scènes** *same or* -ˈsenz, -ˈsānz\ [F] **1** : the arrangement of the scenery, property, and actors on a stage **2** : SETTING; *also* : ENVIRONMENT
mi·ser \ˈmī-zər\ *n* [L *miser* miserable] : a person who hoards and is stingy with money — **mi·ser·li·ness** \-lē-nəs\ *n* — **mi·ser·ly** *adj*
mis·er·a·ble \ˈmi-zə-rə-bəl, ˈmiz-rə-\ *adj* **1** : wretchedly deficient; *also* : causing extreme discomfort **2** : being in a state of distress **3** : SHAMEFUL — **mis·er·a·ble·ness** *n* — **mis·er·a·bly** \-blē\ *adv*
mis·ery \ˈmi-zə-rē\ *n, pl* **-er·ies** **1** : suffering and want caused by poverty or affliction **2** : a cause of suffering or discomfort **3** : emotional distress
mis·fea·sance \mis-ˈfē-zᵊns\ *n* : the performance of a lawful action in an illegal or improper manner
mis·file \-ˈfī(-ə)l\ *vb* : to file in the wrong place
mis·fire \-ˈfī(-ə)r\ *vb* **1** : to fail to fire **2** : to miss an intended effect — **misfire** *n*
mis·fit \ˈmis-ˌfit, *sense 1 also* mis-ˈfit\ *n* **1** : something that fits badly **2** : a person who is poorly adjusted to a situation or environment
mis·for·tune \mis-ˈfȯr-chən\ *n* **1** : bad luck **2** : an unfortunate condition or event
mis·gen·der \-ˈjen-dər\ *vb* : to identify the gender of (a person) incorrectly
mis·giv·ing \-ˈgi-viŋ\ *n* : a feeling of doubt or suspicion esp. concerning a future event
mis·gov·ern \-ˈgə-vərn\ *vb* : to govern badly — **mis·gov·ern·ment** *n*
mis·guid·ance \mis-ˈgī-dᵊns\ *n* : faulty guidance — **mis·guide** \-ˈgīd\ *vb*
mis·guid·ed \-ˈgī-dəd\ *adj* : led or prompted by wrong or inappropriate motives or ideals — **mis·guid·ed·ly** *adv*
mis·han·dle \-ˈhan-dᵊl\ *vb* **1** : MALTREAT **2** : to manage wrongly
mis·hap \ˈmis-ˌhap\ *n* : an unfortunate accident
mish·mash \ˈmish-ˌmash, -ˌmäsh\ *n* : HODGEPODGE, JUMBLE
mis·in·form \ˌmi-sᵊn-ˈfȯrm\ *vb* : to give false or misleading information to — **mis·in·for·ma·tion** \ˌmi-ˌsin-fər-ˈmā-shən\ *n*
mis·in·ter·pret \ˌmi-sᵊn-ˈtər-prət\ *vb* : to understand or explain wrongly — **mis·in·ter·pre·ta·tion** \-ˌtər-prə-ˈtā- shən\ *n*
mis·judge \mis-ˈjəj\ *vb* **1** : to estimate wrongly **2** : to have an unjust opinion of — **mis·judg·ment** \mis-ˈjəj-mənt\ *n*
mis·la·bel \-ˈlā-bəl\ *vb* : to label incorrectly or falsely ⟨was ~*ed* a liar⟩
mis·lay \mis-ˈlā\ *vb* **-laid** \-ˈlād\; **-lay·ing** : MISPLACE, LOSE ⟨*mislaid* his keys⟩
mis·lead \mis-ˈlēd\ *vb* **-led** \-ˈled\; **-lead·ing** : to lead in a wrong direction or into a mistaken action or belief — **mis·lead·ing·ly** *adv*
mis·like \-ˈlīk\ *vb* : DISLIKE — **mis·like** *n*
mis·man·age \-ˈma-nij\ *vb* : to manage badly — **mis·man·age·ment** *n*
mis·match \-ˈmach\ *vb* : to match unsuitably or badly — **mis·match** \mis-ˈmach, ˈmis-ˌmach\ *n*
mis·name \-ˈnām\ *vb* : to name incorrectly : MISCALL
mis·no·mer \mis-ˈnō-mər\ *n* : a wrong or inappropriate name or designation
mi·so \ˈmē-sō\ *n* : a high-protein fermented food paste consisting chiefly of soybeans, salt, and usu. grain
mi·sog·y·ny \mə-ˈsä-jə-nē\ *n* [Gk *misogynia*, fr. *misein* to hate + *gynē* woman] : a hatred of women — **mi·sog·y·nist** \-nist\ *n or adj* — **mi·sog·y·nis·tic** \mə-ˌsä-jə-ˈnis-tik\ *adj*
mis·ori·ent \mi-ˈsȯr-ē-ˌent\ *vb* : to orient improperly or incorrectly — **mis·ori·en·ta·tion** \mi-ˌsȯr-ē-ən-ˈtā-shən\ *n*
mis·place \mis-ˈplās\ *vb* **1** : to put in a wrong or unremembered place **2** : to set on a wrong object ⟨~ trust⟩
mis·play \-ˈplā\ *n* : a wrong or unskillful play — **mis·play** \mis-ˈplā, ˈmis-ˌplā\ *vb*
mis·print \ˈmis-ˌprint\ *n* : a mistake in printed matter — **mis·print** \mis-ˈprint\ *vb*
mis·pro·nounce \ˌmis-prə-ˈnau̇ns\ *vb* : to pronounce incorrectly — **mis·pro·nun·ci·a·tion** \-prə-ˌnən-sē-ˈā-shən\ *n*
mis·quote \mis-ˈkwōt\ *vb* : to quote incorrectly — **mis·quo·ta·tion** \ˌmis-kwō-ˈtā-shən\ *n*
mis·read \-ˈrēd\ *vb* **-read** \-ˈred\; **-read·ing** \-ˈrē-diŋ\ : to read or interpret incorrectly ⟨~ her expression⟩
mis·rep·re·sent \ˌmis-ˌre-pri-ˈzent\ *vb* : to represent falsely or unfairly ⟨~ the facts⟩ — **mis·rep·re·sen·ta·tion** \-ˌzen-ˈtā-shən\ *n*

[1]**mis·rule** \mis-ˈrül\ *vb* : MISGOVERN

[2]**misrule** *n* **1** : MISGOVERNMENT **2** : DISORDER

[1]**miss** \ˈmis\ *vb* **1** : to fail to hit, reach, or contact **2** : to feel the absence of **3** : to fail to obtain **4** : AVOID ⟨just ~*ed* hitting the other car⟩ **5** : OMIT **6** : to fail to understand ⟨~ the point⟩ **7** : to fail to perform or attend; *also* : MISFIRE

[2]**miss** *n* **1** : a failure to hit or to attain a result **2** : MISFIRE

[3]**miss** *n* **1** *cap* — used as a title prefixed to the name of an unmarried woman or girl **2** : a young unmarried woman or girl

Miss *abbr* Mississippi

mis·sal \ˈmi-səl\ *n* : a book containing all that is said or sung at mass during the entire year

mis·send \mis-ˈsend\ *vb* : to send incorrectly (as to a wrong destination)

mis·shap·en \-ˈshā-pən\ *adj* : badly shaped : having an ugly shape

mis·sile \ˈmi-səl\ *n* [L, fr. neut. of *missilis* capable of being thrown, fr. *mittere* to let go, send] : an object (as a stone, bullet, or rocket) thrown or projected usu. so as to strike a target

miss·ing \ˈmi-siŋ\ *adj* : ABSENT; *also* : LOST ⟨~ in action⟩

mis·sion \ˈmi-shən\ *n* **1** : a group of missionaries; *also* : a place where missionaries work **2** : a group of envoys to a foreign country; *also* : a team of specialists or cultural leaders sent to a foreign country **3** : TASK, OBJECTIVE

[1]**mis·sion·ary** \ˈmi-shə-ˌner-ē\ *adj* : of, relating to, or engaged in missions

[2]**missionary** *n, pl* **-ar·ies** : a person commissioned by a church to spread its faith or carry on humanitarian work

mis·sion·er \ˈmi-shə-nər\ *n* : MISSIONARY

Mis·sis·sip·pi·an \ˌmi-sə-ˈsi-pē-ən\ *adj* **1** : of or relating to Mississippi, its people, or the Mississippi River **2** : of, relating to, or being the period of the Paleozoic era between the Devonian and the Pennsylvanian — **Mississippian** *n*

mis·sive \ˈmi-siv\ *n* : LETTER

mis·speak \mis-ˈspēk\ *vb* : to say imperfectly or incorrectly

mis·spell \-ˈspel\ *vb* : to spell incorrectly — **mis·spell·ing** *n*

mis·spend \-ˈspend\ *vb* **-spent** \-ˈspent\; **-spend·ing** : WASTE, SQUANDER ⟨my *misspent* youth⟩

mis·state \mis-ˈstāt\ *vb* : to state incorrectly — **mis·state·ment** *n*

mis·step \-ˈstep\ *n* **1** : a wrong step **2** : MISTAKE, BLUNDER

mist \ˈmist\ *n* **1** : water in the form of particles suspended or falling in the air **2** : something that obscures understanding — **mist** *vb*

mis·tak·able \mə-ˈstā-kə-bəl\ *adj* : capable of being misunderstood or mistaken

[1]**mis·take** \mi-ˈstāk\ *vb* **-took** \-ˈstu̇k\; **-tak·en** \-ˈstā-kən\; **-tak·ing** **1** : to blunder in the choice of **2** : MISINTERPRET **3** : to make a wrong judgment of the character or ability of **4** : to confuse with another — **mis·tak·en·ly** *adv* — **mis·tak·er** *n*

[2]**mistake** *n* **1** : a wrong judgment : MISUNDERSTANDING **2** : a wrong action or statement : ERROR

[1]**mis·ter** \ˈmis-tər\ *n* **1** *cap* — used sometimes instead of *Mr.* **2** : SIR — used without a name in addressing a man

[2]**mist·er** \ˈmis-tər\ *n* : a device for spraying mist

mis·tle·toe \ˈmi-səl-ˌtō\ *n* : a European parasitic green shrub that grows on trees and has yellowish flowers and waxy white berries

mis·tral \ˈmis-trəl, mi-ˈsträl\ *n* [F, fr. Occitan, fr. *mistral* masterful, fr. LL *magistralis* of a teacher, fr. L *magister* master] : a strong cold dry northerly wind of southern France

mis·treat \mis-ˈtrēt\ *vb* : to treat badly : ABUSE — **mis·treat·ment** *n*

mis·tress \ˈmis-trəs\ *n* **1** : a woman who has power, authority, or ownership ⟨~ of the house⟩ **2** : something personified as female that rules or dominates ⟨when Rome was ~ of the world⟩ **3** : a woman other than his wife with whom a married man has sexual relations; *also, archaic* : SWEETHEART **4** — used archaically as a title prefixed to the name of a married or unmarried woman

mis·tri·al \ˈmis-ˌtrī(-ə)l\ *n* : a trial that has no legal effect

[1]**mis·trust** \mis-ˈtrəst\ *n* : a lack of confidence : DISTRUST — **mis·trust·ful** \-fəl\ *adj* — **mis·trust·ful·ly** *adv* — **mis·trust·ful·ness** *n*

[2]**mistrust** *vb* : to have no trust or confidence in : SUSPECT

misty \ˈmis-tē\ *adj* **mist·i·er; -est** **1** : obscured by or as if by mist : INDISTINCT ⟨a ~ memory⟩ **2** : TEARFUL — **mist·i·ly** \-tə-lē\ *adv* — **mist·i·ness** \-tē-nəs\ *n*

mis·un·der·stand \ˌmi-ˌsən-dər-ˈstand\ *vb* **-stood** \-ˈstu̇d\; **-stand·ing** **1** : to fail to understand **2** : to interpret incorrectly

mis·un·der·stand·ing \-ˈstan-diŋ\ *n* **1** : MISINTERPRETATION **2** : DISAGREEMENT, QUARREL

mis·us·age \mis-ˈyü-sij\ *n* **1** : bad treatment : ABUSE **2** : wrong or improper use

mis·use \mis-ˈyüz\ *vb* **1** : to use incorrectly **2** : ABUSE, MISTREAT — **mis·use** \-ˈyüs\ *n*

[1]**mite** \ˈmīt\ *n* : any of numerous tiny arthropod animals related to the spiders that often live and feed on animals or plants

[2]**mite** *n* **1** : a small coin or sum of money **2** : a small amount : BIT

[1]**mi·ter** *or* **mi·tre** \ˈmī-tər\ *n* [ME *mitre,* fr. AF, fr. L *mitra* headband, turban, fr. Gk] **1** : a headdress worn by bishops and abbots **2** : MITER JOINT

[2]**miter** *or* **mitre** *vb* **mi·tered** *or* **mi·tred; mi·ter·ing** *or* **mi·tring** \ˈmī-tə-riŋ\ **1** : to match or fit together in a miter joint **2** : to bevel the ends of for making a miter joint

miter joint *n* : a usu. perpendicular joint made by fitting together two parts with the ends cut at an angle

mit·i·gate \ˈmi-tə-ˌgāt\ *vb* **-gat·ed; -gat·ing** **1** : to make less harsh or hostile **2** : to make less severe or painful — **mit·i·ga·tion** \ˌmi-tə-ˈgā-shən\ *n* — **mit·i·ga·tive** \ˈmi-tə-ˌgā-tiv\ *adj*

mi·to·chon·dri·on \ˌmī-tə-ˈkän-drē-ən\ *n, pl* **-dria** \-drē-ə\ : any of various round or long cellular organelles that produce energy for the cell — **mi·to·chon·dri·al** \-drē-əl\ *adj*

mi·to·sis \mī-ˈtō-səs\ *n, pl* **-to·ses** \-ˌsēz\ : a process that takes place in the nucleus of a dividing cell and results in the formation of two new nuclei each of which has the same number of chromosomes as the parent nucleus; *also* : cell division in which mitosis occurs — **mi·tot·ic** \-ˈtä-tik\ *adj*

mitt \ˈmit\ *n* **1** : a baseball catcher's or first baseman's glove **2** *slang* : HAND

mit·ten \ˈmi-tᵊn\ *n* : a covering for the hand having a separate section for the thumb only — **mit·tened** \-tᵊnd\ *adj*

¹**mix** \ˈmiks\ *vb* **1** : to combine into one mass **2** : ASSOCIATE **3** : to form by mingling components **4** : to produce (a recording) by electronically combining sounds from different sources **5** : HYBRIDIZE **6** : CONFUSE ⟨~*es* up the facts⟩ **7** : to become involved ♦ ***Synonyms*** BLEND, MERGE, COALESCE, AMALGAMATE, FUSE — **mix·able** *adj* — **mix it up** : to engage in a fight, contest, or dispute

²**mix** *n* : a product of mixing; *esp* : a commercially prepared mixture of food ingredients

mixed \ˈmikst\ *adj* **1** : combining features of more than one kind **2** : made up of or involving individuals or items of more than one kind **3** : including or accompanied by different or opposing elements ⟨a ~ blessing⟩ **4** : deriving from two or more races ⟨people of ~ race⟩ **5** : deriving from two or more breeds ⟨a stallion of ~ blood⟩

mixed number *n* : a number (as $5^2/_3$) composed of an integer and a fraction

mixed–race \ˈmikst-ˈrās\ *adj* : made up of two or more races ⟨~ families⟩; *esp* : having parents or ancestors of different races ⟨~ people⟩

mixed–up \ˈmikst-ˈəp\ *adj* : CONFUSED

mix·er \ˈmik-sər\ *n* **1** : one that mixes; *esp* : a machine or device for mixing **2** : an event (as a dance) that encourages meeting and socializing **3** : a nonalcoholic beverage used in a cocktail

mixt *abbr* mixture

mix·ture \ˈmiks-chər\ *n* **1** : the act or process of mixing; *also* : the state of being mixed **2** : a product of mixing

mix–up \ˈmiks-ˌəp\ *n* **1** : an instance of confusion **2** : CONFLICT, FIGHT

miz·zen *also* **miz·en** \ˈmi-zᵊn\ *n* **1** : a fore-and-aft sail set on the mizzenmast **2** : MIZZENMAST — **mizzen** *also* **mizen** *adj*

miz·zen·mast \-ˌmast, -məst\ *n* : the mast aft or next aft of the mainmast

mk *abbr* **1** mark **2** markka

Mk *abbr* Mark

mks *abbr* meter-kilogram-second

mkt *abbr* market

mktg *abbr* marketing

ml *abbr* milliliter

Mlle *abbr* [F] mademoiselle

Mlles *abbr* [F] mesdemoiselles

mm *abbr* millimeter

MM *abbr* [F] messieurs

Mme *abbr* [F] madame

Mmes *abbr* [F] mesdames

Mn *symbol* manganese

MN *abbr* Minnesota

mne·mon·ic \nə-ˈmä-nik\ *adj* : assisting or designed to assist memory; *also* : of or relating to memory

mo *abbr* month

¹**Mo** *abbr* **1** Missouri **2** Monday

²**Mo** *symbol* molybdenum

MO *abbr* **1** mail order **2** medical officer **3** Missouri **4** modus operandi **5** money order

moan \ˈmōn\ *n* : a low prolonged sound indicative of pain or grief — **moan** *vb*

moat \ˈmōt\ *n* : a deep wide usu. water-filled trench around a castle

¹**mob** \ˈmäb\ *n* [L *mobile vulgus* vacillating crowd] **1** : MASSES, RABBLE **2** : a disorderly crowd **3** : a criminal gang

²**mob** *vb* **mobbed; mob·bing** **1** : to crowd about and attack or annoy ⟨*mobbed* by fans⟩ **2** : to crowd into or around ⟨shoppers *mobbed* the stores⟩

¹**mo·bile** \ˈmō-bəl, -ˌbī(-ə)l, -ˌbēl\ *adj* **1** : capable of moving or being moved **2** : changeable in appearance, mood, or purpose; *also* : ADAPTABLE **3** : having the opportunity for or undergoing a shift in social status **4** : using vehicles for transportation ⟨~ warfare⟩ **5** : CELLULAR 2 — **mo·bil·i·ty** \mō-ˈbi-lə-tē\ *n*

²**mo·bile** \ˈmō-ˌbēl\ *n* : a construction or sculpture (as of wire and sheet metal) with parts that can be set in motion by air currents; *also* : a similar structure suspended so that it is moved by a current of air

mobile home *n* : a trailer used as a permanent dwelling

mobile phone *n* : CELL PHONE

mo·bi·lise *chiefly Brit var of* MOBILIZE

mo·bi·lize \ˈmō-bə-ˌlīz\ *vb* **-lized; -liz·ing** **1** : to put into movement or circulation **2** : to assemble and make ready for action ⟨~ army reserves⟩ — **mo·bi·li·za·tion** \ˌmō-bə-lə-ˈzā-shən\ *n* — **mo·bi·liz·er** \ˈmō-bə-ˌlī-zər\ *n*

mob·ster \ˈmäb-stər\ *n* : a member of a criminal gang

moc·ca·sin \ˈmä-kə-sən\ *n* **1** : a soft leather heelless shoe **2** : WATER MOCCASIN

mo·cha \ˈmō-kə\ *n* [*Mocha,* port in Yemen] **1** : choice coffee grown in Arabia **2** : a mixture of coffee and chocolate or cocoa **3** : a dark chocolate-brown color

¹**mock** \ˈmäk, ˈmȯk\ *vb* **1** : to treat with contempt or ridicule **2** : DELUDE **3** : DEFY **4** : to mimic in sport or derision — **mock·er** *n* — **mock·ery** \ˈmä-kə-rē, ˈmȯ-\ *n* — **mock·ing·ly** *adv*

²**mock** *adj* : SIMULATED ⟨a ~ trial⟩
mock–he·ro·ic \ˌmäk-hi-ˈrō-ik, ˌmȯk-\ *adj* : ridiculing or burlesquing heroic style, character, or action ⟨a ~ poem⟩
mock·ing·bird \ˈmä-kiŋ-ˌbərd, ˈmȯ-\ *n* : a grayish No. American songbird related to the catbirds and thrashers that mimics the calls of other birds
mock–up \ˈmä-ˌkəp, ˈmȯ-\ *n* **1** : a full-sized structural model built for study, testing, or display ⟨a ~ of a car⟩ **2** : a working sample (as of a magazine) for review
¹**mod** \ˈmäd\ *adj* **1** : of, relating to, or being the style of the 1960s British youth culture **2** : HIP, TRENDY
²**mod** *abbr* **1** moderate **2** modern **3** modification; modified
mode \ˈmōd\ *n* **1** : a particular form or variety of something; *also* : STYLE **2** : a manner of doing something **3** : the most frequent value of a set of data — **mod·al** \ˈmō-dᵊl\ *adj*
¹**mod·el** \ˈmä-dᵊl\ *n* **1** : structural design **2** : a miniature representation; *also* : a pattern of something to be made **3** : an example for imitation or emulation **4** : one who poses (as for an artist or to display clothes) **5** : TYPE, DESIGN ⟨a new car ~⟩
²**model** *vb* **mod·eled** *or* **mod·elled**; **mod·el·ing** *or* **mod·el·ling** **1** : SHAPE, FASHION, CONSTRUCT ⟨~*ed* in clay⟩ **2** : to work as a fashion model
³**model** *adj* **1** : serving as or worthy of being a pattern ⟨a ~ student⟩ **2** : being a miniature representation of something ⟨a ~ airplane⟩
mo·dem \ˈmō-dəm, -ˌdem\ *n* : a device that converts signals from one device (as a computer) to a form compatible with another (as a telephone)
¹**mod·er·ate** \ˈmä-də-rət\ *adj* **1** : avoiding extremes; *also* : TEMPERATE **2** : AVERAGE; *also* : MEDIOCRE **3** : limited in scope or effect **4** : not expensive — **moderate** *n* — **mod·er·ate·ly** *adv* — **mod·er·ate·ness** *n*
²**mod·er·ate** \ˈmä-də-ˌrāt\ *vb* **-at·ed**; **-at·ing** **1** : to lessen the intensity of : TEMPER **2** : to act as a moderator — **mod·er·a·tion** \ˌmä-də-ˈrā-shən\ *n*
mod·er·a·tor \ˈmä-də-ˌrā-tər\ *n* **1** : MEDIATOR **2** : one who presides over an assembly, meeting, or discussion
mod·ern \ˈmä-dərn\ *adj* [LL *modernus*, fr. L *modo* just now, fr. *modus* measure] : of, relating to, or characteristic of the present or the immediate past : CONTEMPORARY ⟨~ art⟩ — **modern** *n* — **mo·der·ni·ty** \mə-ˈdər-nə-tē\ *n* — **mod·ern·ly** *adv* — **mod·ern·ness** *n*
mod·ern·ise, mod·ern·i·sa·tion *Brit var of* MODERNIZE, MODERNIZATION
mod·ern·ism \ˈmä-dər-ˌni-zəm\ *n* : a practice, movement, or belief peculiar to modern times
mod·ern·ize \ˈmä-dər-ˌnīz\ *vb* **-ized**; **-iz·ing** : to make or become modern — **mod·ern·i·za·tion** \ˌmä-dər-nə-ˈzā-shən\ *n* — **mod·ern·iz·er** *n*
mod·est \ˈmä-dəst\ *adj* **1** : having a moderate estimate of oneself; *also* : DIFFIDENT **2** : observing the proprieties of dress and behavior **3** : limited in size, amount, or scope ⟨a ~ income⟩ — **mod·est·ly** *adv* — **mod·es·ty** \-də-stē\ *n*
mod·i·cum \ˈmä-di-kəm\ *n* : a small amount ⟨a ~ of privacy⟩
modif *abbr* modification
mod·i·fy \ˈmä-də-ˌfī\ *vb* **-fied**; **-fy·ing** **1** : MODERATE **2** : to limit the meaning of esp. in a grammatical construction **3** : CHANGE, ALTER — **mod·i·fi·ca·tion** \ˌmä-də-fə-ˈkā-shən\ *n* — **mod·i·fi·er** \ˈmä-də-ˌfī-ər\ *n*
mod·ish \ˈmō-dish\ *adj* : FASHIONABLE, STYLISH ⟨~ decor⟩ — **mod·ish·ly** *adv* — **mod·ish·ness** *n*
mo·diste \mō-ˈdēst\ *n* : a maker of fashionable dresses and hats
mod·u·lar \ˈmä-jə-lər\ *adj* : constructed with standardized units ⟨~ homes⟩
mod·u·lar·ized \ˈmä-jə-lə-ˌrīzd\ *adj* : containing or consisting of modules
mod·u·late \ˈmä-jə-ˌlāt\ *vb* **-lat·ed**; **-lat·ing** **1** : to tune to a key or pitch **2** : to keep in proper measure or proportion : TEMPER **3** : to vary the amplitude or frequency of a carrier wave for the transmission of information (as in radio or television) — **mod·u·la·tion** \ˌmä-jə-ˈlā-shən\ *n* — **mod·u·la·tor** \ˈmä-jə-ˌlā-tər\ *n* — **mod·u·la·to·ry** \-lə-ˌtȯr-ē\ *adj*
mod·ule \ˈmä-jül\ *n* **1** : any in a series of standardized units for use together **2** : an assembly of wired electronic parts for use with other such assemblies **3** : an independent unit that constitutes a part of the total structure of a space vehicle ⟨a propulsion ~⟩
mo·dus ope·ran·di \ˌmō-dəs-ˌä-pə-ˈran-dē, -ˌdī\ *n, pl* **mo·di operandi** \ˌmō-ˌdē-, ˌmō-ˌdī-\ [NL] : a method of procedure
¹**mo·gul** \ˈmō-gəl, mō-ˈgəl\ *n* [fr. *Mogul,* member of a Muslim dynasty ruling northern India] : an important person : MAGNATE ⟨a media ~⟩
²**mogul** \ˈmō-gəl\ *n* : a bump in a ski run
mo·hair \ˈmō-ˌher\ *n* [modif. of obs. It *mocaiarro,* fr. Ar *mukhayyar,* lit., choice] : a fabric or yarn made wholly or in part from the long silky hair of the Angora goat; *also* : this goat hair
Mo·ham·med·an *also* **Mu·ham·mad·an** \mō-ˈha-mə-dən, -ˈhä-, mü-\ *n* : MUSLIM
Mo·hawk \ˈmō-ˌhȯk\ *n, pl* **Mohawk** *or* **Mohawks** **1** : a member of an Indigenous people orig. of the Mohawk River valley, New York; *also* : the language of the Mohawk people **2** : a hairstyle with a narrow strip of upright hair down the center and the sides shaved
Mo·he·gan \mō-ˈhē-gən, mə-\ *or* **Mo·hi·can** \-ˈhē-kən\ *n, pl* **Mohegan** *or* **Mohegans** *or* **Mohican** *or* **Mohicans** : a member of an Indigenous people of southeastern Connecticut
mo·hel \ˈmō-(h)el, ˈmȯi(-ə)l\ *n, pl* **mohels** *also* **mo·hal·im** \ˌmō-hä-ˈlēm\ *also* **mo·hel·im** \-(h)e-ˈlēm\ : a person who performs Jewish circumcisions

Mo·hi·can \mō-ˈhē-kən, mə\ *or* **Ma·hi·can** \mə-\ *n, pl* **-can** *or* **-cans** : a member of an Indigenous people orig. of the upper Hudson River valley
moi·e·ty \ˈmȯi-ə-tē\ *n, pl* **-ties** : one of two equal or approximately equal parts
moil \ˈmȯi(-ə)l\ *vb* : to work hard : DRUDGE — **moil** *n* — **moil·er** *n*
moi·ré \mȯ-ˈrā, mwä-\ *or* **moire** *same or* ˈmȯir, ˈmwär\ *n* : a fabric (as silk) having a watered appearance
moist \ˈmȯist\ *adj* : slightly or moderately wet — **moist·ly** *adv* — **moist·ness** *n*
moist·en \ˈmȯi-sᵊn\ *vb* : to make or become moist — **moist·en·er** *n*
mois·ture \ˈmȯis-chər\ *n* : the small amount of liquid that causes dampness
mois·tur·ise *Brit var of* MOISTURIZE
mois·tur·ize \ˈmȯis-chə-ˌrīz\ *vb* **-ized; -iz·ing** : to add moisture to ⟨~ the skin⟩ — **mois·tur·iz·er** *n*
mo·ji·to \mō-ˈhē-tō\ *n, pl* **-tos** [AmerSp, dim. of *moje*, *mojo* citrus marinade, fr. Sp *mojar* to moisten] : a cocktail made of rum, sugar, mint, lime juice and soda water
mol *abbr* molecular; molecule
mo·lar \ˈmō-lər\ *n* [ME *molares,* pl., fr. L *molaris,* fr. *molaris* of a mill, fr. *mola* millstone] : any of the broad teeth adapted to grinding food and located in the back of the jaw — **molar** *adj*
mo·las·ses \mə-ˈla-səz\ *n* : the thick brown syrup that is separated from raw sugar in sugar manufacture
[1]**mold** \ˈmōld\ *n* : crumbly soil rich in organic matter
[2]**mold** *n* **1** : distinctive nature or character **2** : the frame on or around which something is constructed **3** : a cavity in which something is shaped; *also* : an object so shaped **4** : MOLDING
[3]**mold** *vb* **1** : to shape in or as if in a mold **2** : to ornament with molding — **mold·er** *n*
[4]**mold** *n* : a surface growth of fungus esp. on damp or decaying matter; *also* : a fungus that produces mold — **mold·i·ness** \ˈmōl-dē-nəs\ *n* — **moldy** *adj*
[5]**mold** *vb* : to become moldy
mold·board \ˈmōld-ˌbȯrd\ *n* : a curved iron plate attached above the plowshare to lift and turn the soil
mold·er \ˈmōl-dər\ *vb* : to crumble into small pieces
mold·ing \ˈmōl-diŋ\ *n* **1** : an act or process of shaping in a mold; *also* : an object so shaped **2** : a decorative surface, plane, or curved strip
[1]**mole** \ˈmōl\ *n* : a small often pigmented spot or protuberance on the skin
[2]**mole** *n* **1** : any of numerous small burrowing insect-eating mammals related to the shrews and hedgehogs **2** : a spy embedded within an organization
[3]**mole** *n* : a massive breakwater or jetty
molecular biology *n* : a branch of biology dealing with the ultimate physical and chemical organization of living matter and esp. with the molecular basis of inheritance and protein synthesis — **molecular biologist** *n*
molecular weight *n* : the mass of a molecule that is equal to the sum of the masses of all atoms contained in the molecule's formula
mol·e·cule \ˈmä-li-ˌkyül\ *n* : the smallest particle of matter that is the same chemically as the whole mass — **mo·lec·u·lar** \mə-ˈle-kyə-lər\ *adj*
mole·hill \ˈmōl-ˌhil\ *n* : a little ridge of earth thrown up by a mole
mole·skin \-ˌskin\ *n* **1** : the skin of the mole used as fur **2** : a heavy durable cotton fabric
mo·lest \mə-ˈlest\ *vb* **1** : ANNOY, DISTURB **2** : to make unwanted or improper sexual advances to; *esp* : to force physical and usu. sexual contact on — **mo·les·ta·tion** \ˌmō-ˌles-ˈtā-shən\ *n* — **mo·lest·er** *n*
moll \ˈmäl\ *n* : a gangster's girlfriend
mol·li·fy \ˈmä-lə-ˌfī\ *vb* **-fied; -fy·ing** **1** : to soothe in temper : APPEASE **2** : SOFTEN **3** : to reduce in intensity : ASSUAGE ⟨~ ill feelings⟩ — **mol·li·fi·ca·tion** \ˌmä-lə-fə-ˈkā-shən\ *n*
mol·lusk *or* **mol·lusc** \ˈmä-ləsk\ *n* : any of a large phylum of usu. shelled and aquatic invertebrate animals (as snails, clams, and squids) — **mol·lus·can** *also* **mol·lus·kan** \mə-ˈləs-kən\ *adj*
[1]**mol·ly·cod·dle** \ˈmä-lē-ˌkä-dᵊl\ *n* : a pampered man or boy
[2]**mollycoddle** *vb* **mol·ly·cod·dled; mol·ly·cod·dling** : PAMPER
Mo·lo·tov cocktail \ˈmä-lə-ˌtȯf-, ˈmȯ-\ *n* [Vyacheslav M. *Molotov* †1986 Soviet foreign minister] : a crude bomb made of a bottle filled usu. with gasoline and fitted with a wick (as a saturated rag) that is ignited just prior to hurling
[1]**molt** \ˈmōlt\ *vb* : to shed hair, feathers, outer skin, or horns periodically with the cast-off parts being replaced by new growth — **molt·er** *n*
[2]**molt** *n* : the act or process of molting
mol·ten \ˈmōl-tᵊn\ *adj* **1** : fused or liquefied by heat **2** : GLOWING
mo·ly \ˈmō-lē\ *n* : a mythical herb with black root, white flowers, and magic powers
mo·lyb·de·num \mə-ˈlib-də-nəm\ *n* : a metallic chemical element used in strengthening and hardening steel
mom \ˈmäm, ˈməm\ *n* : MOTHER
mom–and–pop *adj* : being a small owner-operated business
mo·ment \ˈmō-mənt\ *n* **1** : a minute portion of time : INSTANT **2** : a time of excellence ⟨he has his ~*s*⟩ **3** : IMPORTANCE ⟨an event of great ~⟩ ♦ ***Synonyms*** CONSEQUENCE, SIGNIFICANCE, WEIGHT, IMPORT
mo·men·tari·ly \ˌmō-mən-ˈter-ə-lē\ *adv* **1** : for a moment **2** *archaic* : INSTANTLY **3** : at any moment : SOON
mo·men·tary \ˈmō-mən-ˌter-ē\ *adj* **1** : continuing only a moment ⟨a ~ pause⟩; *also* : EPHEMERAL **2** : recurring at every

moment — **mo·men·tar·i·ness** \-ˌter-ē-nəs\ *n*
mo·men·tous \mō-ˈmen-təs\ *adj* : SIGNIFICANT ⟨a ~ decision⟩ — **mo·men·tous·ly** *adv* — **mo·men·tous·ness** *n*
mo·men·tum \mō-ˈmen-təm\ *n, pl* **mo·men·ta** \-ˈmen-tə\ *or* **momentums** : a property that a moving body has due to its mass and motion; *also* : IMPETUS
mom·my \ˈmä-mē, ˈmə-\ *n, pl* **mom·mies** : MOTHER
Mon *abbr* Monday
mon·arch \ˈmä-nərk, -ˌnärk\ *n* **1** : a person who reigns over a kingdom or an empire **2** : one holding preeminent position or power **3** : MONARCH BUTTERFLY — **mo·nar·chi·cal** \mə-ˈnär-ki-kəl\ *also* **mo·nar·chic** \-ˈnär-kik\ *adj*
monarch butterfly *n* : a large orange and black migratory American butterfly whose larva feeds on milkweed
mon·ar·chist \ˈmä-nər-kist\ *n* : a believer in monarchical government — **mon·ar·chism** \-ˌki-zəm\ *n*
mon·ar·chy \ˈmä-nər-kē\ *n, pl* **-chies** : a nation or state governed by a monarch
mon·as·tery \ˈmä-nə-ˌster-ē\ *n, pl* **-ter·ies** : a house for persons under religious vows (as monks)
mo·nas·tic \mə-ˈnas-tik\ *adj* : of or relating to monasteries or to monks or nuns — **monastic** *n* — **mo·nas·ti·cal·ly** \-ti-k(ə-)lē\ *adv* — **mo·nas·ti·cism** \-tə-ˌsi-zəm\ *n*
mon·au·ral \mä-ˈnȯr-əl\ *adj* : MONOPHONIC — **mon·au·ral·ly** *adv*
Mon·day \ˈmən-dē, -ˌdā\ *n* : the second day of the week
mon·e·tary \ˈmä-nə-ˌter-ē, ˈmə-\ *adj* : of or relating to money or to the mechanisms by which it is supplied and circulated in the economy
mon·ey \ˈmə-nē\ *n, pl* **moneys** *or* **mon·ies** \ˈmə-nēz\ **1** : something (as metal currency) accepted as a medium of exchange **2** : wealth reckoned in monetary terms **3** : the 1st, 2d, and 3d places in a horse or dog race
☞ the MONEY TABLE is on pages 472–473
mon·eyed \ˈmə-nēd\ *adj* **1** : having money : WEALTHY **2** : consisting in or derived from money
mon·ey·lend·er \ˈmə-nē-ˌlen-dər\ *n* : one (as a bank or pawnbroker) whose business is lending money
money market *n* : the trade in short-term negotiable financial instruments
money of account : a denominator of value or basis of exchange used in keeping accounts
money order *n* : an order purchased at a post office, bank, or telegraph office directing another office to pay a sum of money to a party named on it
mon·ger \ˈməŋ-gər, ˈmäŋ-\ *n* **1** : DEALER **2** : one who tries to stir up or spread something — usu. used in combination ⟨war*monger*⟩
mon·go \ˈmäŋ-(ˌ)gō\ *n, pl* **mongo** — see *tugrik* at MONEY table
Mon·gol \ˈmäŋ-gəl, ˈmän-ˌgōl\ *n* : a member of any of several traditionally pastoral peoples of Mongolia — **Mongol** *adj*
Mon·go·lian \män-ˈgōl-yən, mäŋ-, -ˈgō-lē-ən\ *n* **1** : a native or inhabitant of Mongolia **2** : a member of a group of people formerly considered to constitute a race of humans having Asian ancestry — **Mongolian** *adj*
Mon·gol·oid \ˈmäŋ-gə-ˌlȯid\ *adj* : of, constituting, or characteristic of a group of people formerly considered to constitute a race of humans having Asian ancestry — **Mongoloid** *n*
mon·goose \ˈmän-ˌgüs, ˈmäŋ-\ *n, pl* **mon·goos·es** *also* **mon·geese** \-ˌgēs\ : any of a group of small agile Old World mammals that are related to the civet cats and feed chiefly on small animals and fruits
mon·grel \ˈmäŋ-grəl, ˈməŋ-\ *n* : an offspring of parents of different breeds; *esp* : one of uncertain ancestry
mon·i·ker \ˈmä-ni-kər\ *n* : NAME, NICKNAME
mo·nism \ˈmō-ˌni-zəm, ˈmä-\ *n* : a view that reality is basically one unitary organic whole — **mo·nist** \ˈmō-nist, ˈmä-\ *n*
mo·ni·tion \mō-ˈni-shən, mə-\ *n* : WARNING, CAUTION
[1]**mon·i·tor** \ˈmä-nə-tər\ *n* **1** : a student appointed to assist a teacher **2** : one that monitors; *esp* : a video display screen (as for a computer)
[2]**monitor** *vb* : to watch, check, or observe for a special purpose
mon·i·to·ry \ˈmä-nə-ˌtȯr-ē\ *adj* : giving admonition : WARNING
[1]**monk** \ˈməŋk\ *n* [ME, fr. OE *munuc,* fr. LL *monachus,* fr. LGk *monachos,* fr. Gk, adj., single, fr. *monos* single, alone] : a man belonging to a religious order and living in a monastery — **monk·ish** *adj*
[2]**monk** *n* : MONKEY
[1]**mon·key** \ˈməŋ-kē\ *n, pl* **monkeys** : a nonhuman primate mammal; *esp* : one of the smaller, longer-tailed, and usu. more arboreal primates as contrasted with the apes
[2]**monkey** *vb* **mon·keyed; mon·key·ing** **1** : FOOL, TRIFLE — often used with *around* **2** : TAMPER — usu. used with *with* ⟨don't ~ around with the controls⟩
monkey bars *n pl* : a framework of bars on which children can play
mon·key·shine \ˈməŋ-kē-ˌshīn\ *n* : PRANK — usu. used in pl.
monkey wrench *n* : a wrench with one fixed and one adjustable jaw at right angles to a handle
monk·fish \ˈməŋk-ˌfish\ *n* : either of two marine bony fishes that have a large flattened head and are used for food
monks·hood \ˈməŋks-ˌhu̇d\ *n* : any of a genus of poisonous plants related to the buttercups; *esp* : a tall Eurasian herb with white or purplish flowers
[1]**mono** \ˈmä-nō\ *adj* : MONOPHONIC
[2]**mono** *n* : INFECTIOUS MONONUCLEOSIS
mono·chro·mat·ic \ˌmä-nə-krō-ˈma-tik\ *adj* **1** : having or consisting of one

color **2 :** consisting of radiation (as light) of a single wavelength

mono·chrome \ˈmä-nə-ˌkrōm\ *adj* **:** involving or producing visual images in a single color or in varying tones of a single color ⟨∼ television⟩

mon·o·cle \ˈmä-ni-kəl\ *n* **:** an eyeglass for one eye

mono·clo·nal \ˌmä-nə-ˈklō-nəl\ *adj* **:** produced by, being, or composed of cells derived from a single cell ⟨∼ antibodies⟩

mono·cot·y·le·don \ˌmä-nə-ˌkät-ᵊl-ˈē-dᵊn\ *n* **:** any of a class or subclass of chiefly herbaceous seed plants having an embryo with a single cotyledon and usu. parallel-veined leaves

mon·o·dy \ˈmä-nə-dē\ *n, pl* **-dies :** ELEGY, DIRGE — **mo·nod·ic** \mə-ˈnä-dik\ *or* **mo·nod·i·cal** \-di-kəl\ *adj* — **mon·o·dist** \ˈmä-nə-dist\ *n*

mo·nog·a·my \mə-ˈnä-gə-mē\ *n* **1 :** marriage with one person at a time **2 :** the practice of having a single mate at a time — **mo·nog·a·mist** \-mist\ *n* — **mo·nog·a·mous** \-məs\ *adj*

mono·gram \ˈmä-nə-ˌgram\ *n* **:** a sign of identity composed of the combined initials of a name — **monogram** *vb*

mono·graph \ˈmä-nə-ˌgraf\ *n* **:** a learned treatise on a small area of learning

mono·lin·gual \ˌmä-nə-ˈliŋ-gwəl\ *adj* **:** knowing or using only one language

mono·lith \ˈmä-nə-ˌlith\ *n* **1 :** a single great stone often in the form of a monument or column **2 :** something large and powerful that acts as a single unified force ⟨a bureaucratic ∼⟩ — **mono·lith·ic** \ˌmä-nə-ˈli-thik\ *adj*

mono·logue *also* **mono·log** \ˈmä-nə-ˌlȯg\ *n* **1 :** a dramatic soliloquy; *also* **:** a long speech monopolizing conversation **2 :** the routine of a stand-up comic — **mono·logu·ist** \-ˌlȯg-ist\ *or* **mo·no·lo·gist** \mə-ˈnä-lə-jist; ˈmä-nə-ˌlȯ-gist\ *n*

mono·ma·nia \ˌmä-nə-ˈmā-nē-ə, -nyə\ *n* **1 :** mental disorder limited in expression to one area of thought **2 :** excessive concentration on a single object or idea — **mono·ma·ni·ac** \-nē-ˌak\ *n or adj*

mono·mer \ˈmä-nə-mər\ *n* **:** a simple chemical compound that can be polymerized

mono·nu·cle·o·sis \ˌmä-nō-ˌnü-klē-ˈō-səs, -ˌnyü-\ *n* **:** INFECTIOUS MONONUCLEOSIS

mono·phon·ic \ˌmä-nə-ˈfä-nik\ *adj* **:** of or relating to sound recording or reproduction involving a single transmission path

mono·plane \ˈmä-nə-ˌplān\ *n* **:** an airplane with only one set of wings

mo·nop·o·ly \mə-ˈnä-pə-lē\ *n, pl* **-lies** [L *monopolium,* fr. Gk *monopōlion,* fr. *monos* alone, single + *pōlein* to sell] **1 :** exclusive ownership (as through command of supply) **2 :** a commodity controlled by one party **3 :** one that has a monopoly — **mo·nop·o·list** \-list\ *n* — **mo·nop·o·lis·tic** \mə-ˌnä-pə-ˈlis-tik\ *adj* — **mo·nop·o·li·za·tion** \-lə-ˈzā-shən\ *n* — **mo·nop·o·lize** \mə-ˈnä-pə-ˌlīz\ *vb*

mono·rail \ˈmä-nə-ˌrāl\ *n* **:** a single rail serving as a track for a vehicle; *also* **:** a vehicle traveling on such a track

mono·so·di·um glu·ta·mate \ˌmä-nə-ˌsō-dē-əm-ˈglü-tə-ˌmāt\ *n* **:** a crystalline salt used to enhance the flavor of food

mono·syl·la·ble \ˈmä-nə-ˌsi-lə-bəl\ *n* **:** a word of one syllable — **mono·syl·lab·ic** \ˌmä-nə-sə-ˈla-bik\ *adj* — **mono·syl·lab·i·cal·ly** \-bi-k(ə-)lē\ *adv*

mono·the·ism \ˈmä-nə-(ˌ)thē-ˌi-zəm\ *n* **:** a doctrine or belief that there is only one deity — **mono·the·ist** \-ˌthē-ist\ *n* — **mono·the·is·tic** \-thē-ˈis-tik\ *adj*

mono·tone \ˈmä-nə-ˌtōn\ *n* **:** a succession of syllables, words, or sentences in one unvaried key or pitch

mo·not·o·nous \mə-ˈnä-tə-nəs\ *adj* **1 :** uttered or sounded in one unvarying tone **2 :** tediously uniform — **mo·not·o·nous·ly** *adv* — **mo·not·o·nous·ness** *n*

mo·not·o·ny \mə-ˈnä-tə-nē\ *n* **:** tedious sameness or uniformity

mono·un·sat·u·rat·ed \ˌmä-nō-ˌən-ˈsa-chə-ˌrā-təd\ *adj* **:** containing one double or triple bond per molecule — used esp. of an oil, fat, or fatty acid

mon·ox·ide \mə-ˈnäk-ˌsīd\ *n* **:** an oxide containing one atom of oxygen in a molecule

mon·sei·gneur \ˌmōⁿ-ˌsān-ˈyər\ *n, pl* **mes·sei·gneurs** \ˌmā-ˌsān-ˈyər, -ˈyərz\ **:** a French dignitary — used as a title

mon·sieur \məs-ˈyər\ *n, pl* **mes·sieurs** *same or* -ˈyərz\ **:** a Frenchman of high rank or station — used as a title equivalent to *Mister*

mon·si·gnor \män-ˈsē-nyər\ *n, pl* **monsi·gnors** *or* **mon·si·gno·ri** \ˌmän-ˌsēn-ˈyȯr-ē\ [It *monsignore*] **:** a Roman Catholic prelate — used as a title

mon·soon \män-ˈsün\ *n* [obs. D *monssoen,* fr. Pg *monção,* fr. Ar *mawsim* time, season] **1 :** a periodic wind esp. in the Indian Ocean and southern Asia **2 :** the season of the southwest monsoon esp. in India **3 :** rainfall associated with the monsoon

¹**mon·ster** \ˈmän-stər\ *n* **1 :** an abnormally developed plant or animal **2 :** an animal of strange or terrifying shape; *also* **:** one unusually large of its kind **3 :** an extremely ugly, wicked, or cruel person — **mon·stros·i·ty** \män-ˈsträ-sə-tē\ *n* — **mon·strous** \ˈmän-strəs\ *adj* — **mon·strous·ly** *adv*

²**monster** *adj* **:** very large **:** ENORMOUS

mon·strance \ˈmän-strəns\ *n* **:** a vessel in which the consecrated Host is exposed for the adoration of the faithful

Mont *abbr* Montana

mon·tage \män-ˈtäzh\ *n* [F] **1 :** a composite photograph made by combining several separate pictures **2 :** an artistic composition made up of several different kinds of elements **3 :** a varied mixture **:** JUMBLE

month \ˈmənth\ *n, pl* **months** \ˈməns, ˈmənths\ **:** one of the 12 parts into which the year is divided — **month·ly** *adv or adj or n*

month·long \ˈmənth-ˈlȯŋ\ *adj* **:** lasting a month

mon·u·ment \ˈmän-yə-mənt\ *n* **1 :** a last-

MONEY — WORLD CURRENCIES

NAME	SUBDIVISION	COUNTRY
afghani	100 puls	Afghanistan
ariary	5 iraimbilanja	Madagascar
baht	100 satang	Thailand
balboa[1]	100 centesimos	Panama
birr	100 cents	Ethiopia
bolivar	100 centimos	Venezuela
boliviano	100 centavos	Bolivia
cedi	100 pesewas	Ghana
colón	100 centimos	Costa Rica
córdoba	100 centavos	Nicaragua
dalasi	100 bututs	Gambia
denar	100 deni[2]	Macedonia
dinar	100 centimes	Algeria
dinar	1000 fils	Bahrain
dinar	1000 fils	Iraq
dinar	1000 fils	Jordan
dinar	1000 fils	Kuwait
dinar	1000 dirhams	Libya
dinar	100 paras	Serbia
dinar	1000 millimes	Tunisia
dirham	100 centimes	Morocco
dirham	100 fils	United Arab Emirates
dobra	100 centimos	São Tomé and Príncipe
dollar[3]	100 cents	Antigua and Barbuda, Dominica, Grenada, St. Kitts-Nevis, St. Lucia, St. Vincent and the Grenadines
dollar	100 cents	Australia
dollar	100 cents	Bahamas
dollar	100 cents	Barbados
dollar	100 cents	Belize
dollar	100 cents	Bermuda
dollar	100 cents	Brunei
dollar	100 cents	Canada
dollar	100 cents	Fiji
dollar	100 cents	Guyana
dollar	100 cents	Hong Kong
dollar	100 cents	Jamaica
dollar	100 cents	Liberia
dollar	100 cents	Namibia
dollar	100 cents	New Zealand
dollar	100 cents	Singapore
dollar	100 cents	Solomon Islands
dollar	100 cents	Suriname
dollar	100 cents	Taiwan
dollar	100 cents	Trinidad and Tobago
dollar	100 cents	United States
dollar — see RINGGIT, below		
dong	100 xu	Vietnam
dram	100 luma	Armenia
escudo	100 centavos	Cape Verde
euro[4]	100 cents	Austria, Belgium, Cyprus, Estonia, Finland, France, Germany, Greece, Ireland, Italy, Latvia, Lithuania, Luxembourg, Malta, Netherlands, Portugal, Slovakia, Slovenia, Spain
forint	100 fillers[2]	Hungary
franc[5]	100 centimes	Cameroon, Central African Republic, Chad, Republic of the Congo, Equatorial Guinea[6], Gabon
franc[7]	100 centimes	Benin, Burkina Faso, Guinea-Bissau, Ivory Coast, Mali, Niger, Senegal, Togo
franc	100 centimes	Burundi
franc	100 centimes	Comoros
franc	100 centimes	Democratic Republic of the Congo
franc	100 centimes	Djibouti
franc	100 centimes[8]	Guinea
franc	100 centimes[8]	Rwanda
franc	100 centimes *or* rappen	Switzerland
gourde	100 centimes	Haiti
guarani	100 centimos[2]	Paraguay
hryvnia	100 kopiykas	Ukraine
kina	100 toea	Papua New Guinea
kip	100 at *or* att[2]	Laos
koruna	100 haleru	Czech Republic
krona	100 aurar[2] (*sing* eyrir)	Iceland
krona	100 ore[2]	Sweden
krone	100 øre	Denmark
krone	100 ore	Norway
kuna	100 lipa	Croatia
kwacha	100 tambala	Malawi
kwacha	100 ngwee	Zambia
kwanza	100 cêntimos	Angola
kyat	100 pyas	Myanmar
lari	100 tetri	Republic of Georgia
lek	100 qindarka[2] (*sing* qindar)	Albania
lempira	100 centavos	Honduras
leone	100 cents	Sierra Leone
leu	100 bani (*sing* ban)	Moldova
leu	100 bani (*sing* ban)	Romania
lev	100 stotinki	Bulgaria

See footnotes at end of table, p. 475.

MONEY — WORLD CURRENCIES

NAME	SUBDIVISION	COUNTRY
lilangeni (*pl* emalangeni)	100 cents	Eswatini
lira *or* pound	100 kuruş	Turkey
livre — see POUND, below		
loti (*pl* maloti)	100 lisente (*sing* sente)	Lesotho
manat	100 gopik	Azerbaijan
manat	100 tenesi (*sing* tenne)	Turkmenistan
marka	100 feninga (*sing* fening)	Bosnia and Herzegovina
metical	100 centavos	Mozambique
naira	100 kobo	Nigeria
nakfa	100 cents	Eritrea
ngultrum	100 chetrums	Bhutan
ouguiya	5 khoums	Mauritania
pa'anga	100 seniti	Tonga
pataca	100 avos	Macao
peso	100 centavos	Argentina
peso	100 centavos	Chile
peso	100 centavos	Colombia
peso	100 centavos	Cuba
peso	100 centavos	Dominican Republic
peso	100 centavos	Mexico
peso *or* piso	100 sentimos *or* centavos	Philippines
peso	100 centesimos	Uruguay
pound	100 piastres	Egypt
pound *or* livre	100 piastres	Lebanon
pound	100 piastres	South Sudan
pound	100 piastres	Sudan
pound	100 piastres	Syria
pound	100 pence (*sing* penny)	United Kingdom
pound — see LIRA, above		
pula	100 thebe	Botswana
quetzal	100 centavos	Guatemala
rand	100 cents	South Africa
real	100 centavos	Brazil
rial	100 dinars	Iran
rial	1000 baiza	Oman
rial *also* riyal	100 fils	Yemen
rial — see RIYAL, below		
riel	100 sen	Cambodia
ringgit *or* dollar	100 sen	Malaysia
riyal *also* rial	100 dirhams	Qatar
riyal *also* rial	100 halala	Saudi Arabia
riyal — see RIAL, above		
ruble *also* rouble	100 kapeek (*sing* kapeyka)	Belarus
ruble *also* rouble	100 kopecks	Russia
rufiyaa	100 laari	Maldives
rupee	100 paise	India
rupee	100 cents	Mauritius
rupee	100 paisa	Nepal
rupee	100 paisa	Pakistan
rupee	100 cents	Seychelles
rupee	100 cents	Sri Lanka
rupiah	100 sen	Indonesia
shekel *also* sheqel	100 agorot	Israel
shilling	100 cents	Kenya
shilling	100 cents	Somalia
shilling	100 cents	Tanzania
shilling	100 cents[2]	Uganda
sol	100 centimos	Peru
som	100 tyiyn	Kyrgyzstan
somoni	100 dirams	Tajikistan
sum *or* som	100 tiyin	Uzbekistan
taka	100 paisa *or* poisha	Bangladesh
tala	100 sene	Samoa
tenge	100 tiyns	Kazakhstan
tugrik	100 mongo	Mongolia
vatu		Vanuatu
won	100 chon	North Korea
won	100 jeon[2]	South Korea
yen	100 sen[8]	Japan
yuan	100 fen	China
zloty	100 groszy	Poland

[1]Used along with the U.S. dollar.
[2]No longer in circulation.
[3]Issued by the Eastern Caribbean Central Bank.
[4]Replaced the individual monetary units of participating European Union countries.
[5]Issued by the Bank of Central African States.
[6]The franc of Equatorial Guinea is also called the *franco*.
[7]Issued by the West African Economic and Monetary Union.
[8]A subdivision in name only.

ing reminder; *esp* : a structure erected in remembrance of a person or event 2 : NATIONAL MONUMENT

mon·u·men·tal \ˌmän-yə-ˈmen-tᵊl\ *adj* 1 : of or relating to a monument 2 : MASSIVE; *also* : OUTSTANDING ⟨a ~ achievement⟩ 3 : very great ⟨a ~ task⟩ — **mon·u·men·tal·ly** *adv*

moo \ˈmü\ *vb* : to make the natural throat noise of a cow — **moo** *n*

[1]**mood** \ˈmüd\ *n* 1 : a conscious state of mind or predominant emotion : FEELING 2 : a prevailing attitude : DISPOSITION 3 : a distinctive atmosphere

[2]**mood** *n* : distinction of form of a verb to express whether its action or state is conceived as fact or in some other manner (as wish)

moody \ˈmü-dē\ *adj* **mood·i·er; -est** 1 : GLOOMY 2 : subject to moods : TEMPERAMENTAL — **mood·i·ly** \-də-lē\ *adv* — **mood·i·ness** \-dē-nəs\ *n*

[1]**moon** \ˈmün\ *n* 1 : the earth's natural satellite 2 : SATELLITE 2

[2]**moon** *vb* : to engage in idle reverie

moon·beam \ˈmün-ˌbēm\ *n* : a ray of light from the moon

[1]**moon·light** \-ˌlīt\ *n* : the light of the moon — **moon·lit** \-ˌlit\ *adj*

[2]**moonlight** *vb* **moon·light·ed; moon·light·ing** : to hold a second job in addition to a regular one — **moon·light·er** *n*

moon·roof \-ˌrüf, -ˌru̇f\ *n* : a glass sunroof

moon·scape \-ˌskāp\ *n* : the surface of the moon as seen or as pictured

moon·shine \-ˌshīn\ *n* 1 : MOONLIGHT 2 : empty talk 3 : intoxicating liquor usu. illegally distilled

moon·stone \-ˌstōn\ *n* : a transparent or translucent feldspar of pearly luster used as a gem

moon·struck \-ˌstrək\ *adj* 1 : mentally unbalanced 2 : romantically sentimental 3 : lost in fantasy

[1]**moor** \ˈmu̇r\ *n* 1 *chiefly Brit* : an expanse of open rolling infertile land 2 : a boggy area; *esp* : one that is peaty and dominated by grasses and sedges

[2]**moor** *vb* : to make fast with or as if with cables, lines, or anchors

Moor \ˈmu̇r\ *n* : one of the Arab and Berber conquerors of Spain — **Moor·ish** *adj*

moor·ing \ˈmu̇r-iŋ\ *n* 1 : a place where or an object to which a craft can be made fast 2 : an established practice or stabilizing influence — usu. used in pl.

moor·land \-lənd, -ˌland\ *n* : land consisting of moors

moose \ˈmüs\ *n, pl* **moose** : a large heavy-antlered ruminant mammal related to the deer that has humped shoulders and long legs and inhabits northern forested areas

[1]**moot** \ˈmüt\ *vb* : to bring up for discussion; *also* : DEBATE

[2]**moot** *adj* 1 : open to question; *also* : DISPUTED ⟨a ~ assertion⟩ 2 : having no practical significance ⟨the issue is ~⟩

[1]**mop** \ˈmäp\ *n* : an implement made of absorbent material fastened to a handle and used esp. for cleaning floors

[2]**mop** *vb* **mopped; mop·ping** : to use a mop on : clean with a mop

mope \ˈmōp\ *vb* **moped; mop·ing** 1 : to become dull, dejected, or listless 2 : DAWDLE

mo·ped \ˈmō-ˌped\ *n* : a light low-powered motorbike that can be pedaled

mop·pet \ˈmä-pət\ *n* [obs. E *mop* fool, child] : CHILD

mo·raine \mə-ˈrān\ *n* : an accumulation of earth and stones left by a glacier

[1]**mor·al** \ˈmȯr-əl\ *adj* 1 : of or relating to principles of right and wrong 2 : conforming to a standard of right behavior; *also* : capable of right and wrong action 3 : probable but not proved ⟨a ~ certainty⟩ 4 : perceptual or psychological rather than tangible or practical in nature or effect ⟨a ~ victory⟩ ♦ ***Synonyms*** VIRTUOUS, RIGHTEOUS, NOBLE, ETHICAL, PRINCIPLED — **mor·al·ly** *adv*

[2]**moral** *n* 1 : the practical meaning (as of a story) 2 *pl* : moral practices or teachings ⟨protecting the public ~*s*⟩

mo·rale \mə-ˈral\ *n* 1 : MORALITY 2 : the mental and emotional attitudes of an individual to the tasks at hand; *also* : ESPRIT DE CORPS

mor·al·ise *Brit var of* MORALIZE

mor·al·ist \ˈmȯr-ə-list\ *n* 1 : one who leads a moral life 2 : a thinker or writer concerned with morals 3 : one concerned with regulating the morals of others — **mor·al·is·tic** \ˌmȯr-ə-ˈlis-tik\ *adj* — **mor·al·is·ti·cal·ly** \-ti-k(ə-)lē\ *adv*

mo·ral·i·ty \mə-ˈra-lə-tē\ *n, pl* **-ties** : moral conduct : VIRTUE

mor·al·ize \ˈmȯr-ə-ˌlīz\ *vb* **-ized; -iz·ing** : to make moral reflections — **mor·al·i·za·tion** \ˌmȯr-ə-lə-ˈzā-shən\ *n* — **mor·al·iz·er** \ˈmȯr-ə-ˌlī-zər\ *n*

mo·rass \mə-ˈras\ *n* [D *moeras,* fr. OF *maresc,* of Gmc origin; akin to OE *mersc* marsh] : SWAMP; *also* : something that entangles, impedes, or confuses

mor·a·to·ri·um \ˌmȯr-ə-ˈtȯr-ē-əm\ *n, pl* **-ri·ums** *or* **-ria** \-ē-ə\ [ultim. fr. L *mora* delay] : a suspension of activity

mo·ray eel \mə-ˈrā-, ˈmȯr-ˌā-\ *n* : any of numerous often brightly colored biting eels of warm seas

mor·bid \ˈmȯr-bəd\ *adj* 1 : of, relating to, or typical of disease; *also* : DISEASED, SICKLY 2 : characterized by gloomy or unwholesome ideas or feelings 3 : GRISLY, GRUESOME ⟨~ details⟩ — **mor·bid·i·ty** \mȯr-ˈbi-də-tē\ *n* — **mor·bid·ly** *adv* — **mor·bid·ness** *n*

mor·dant \ˈmȯr-dᵊnt\ *adj* 1 : biting or caustic in manner or style 2 : BURNING, PUNGENT — **mor·dant·ly** *adv*

[1]**more** \ˈmȯr\ *adj* 1 : GREATER ⟨something ~ than I expected⟩ 2 : ADDITIONAL ⟨wanted ~ coffee⟩

[2]**more** *adv* 1 : in addition 2 : to a greater or higher degree ⟨~ evenly matched⟩

[3]**more** *n* 1 : a greater quantity, number, or amount ⟨the ~ the merrier⟩ 2 : an additional amount ⟨costs a little ~⟩

[4]**more** *pron* : additional persons or things or a greater amount

mo•rel \mə-ˈrel\ *n* : any of several pitted edible fungi
more•over \mȯr-ˈō-vər\ *adv* : in addition : FURTHER
mo•res \ˈmȯr-ˌāz\ *n pl* [L, pl. of *mor-, mos* custom] **1** : the fixed morally binding customs of a group **2** : HABITS, MANNERS ⟨cultural ~⟩
Mor•gan \ˈmȯr-gən\ *n* : any of an American breed of lightly built horses
morgue \ˈmȯrg\ *n* : a place where the bodies of dead persons are kept until released for burial or autopsy
mor•i•bund \ˈmȯr-ə-(ˌ)bənd\ *adj* : being in a dying condition
Mor•mon \ˈmȯr-mən\ *n* : a member of the Church of Jesus Christ of Latter-day Saints — **Mor•mon•ism** \-mə-ˌni-zəm\ *n*
morn \ˈmȯrn\ *n* : MORNING
morn•ing \ˈmȯr-niŋ\ *n* **1** : the early part of the day; *esp* : the time from the sunrise to noon **2** : BEGINNING
morn•ing–after pill \ˌmȯr-niŋ-ˈaf-tər-\ *n* : a contraceptive drug taken up to usu. three days after sexual intercourse
morning glory *n* : any of various twining plants related to the sweet potato that have often showy bell-shaped or funnel-shaped flowers
morning sickness *n* : nausea and vomiting that typically occur in the morning esp. during early pregnancy
morning star *n* : a bright planet (as Venus) seen in the eastern sky before or at sunrise
mo•roc•co \mə-ˈrä-kō\ *n* : a fine leather made of goatskins tanned with sumac
mo•ron \ˈmȯr-ˌän\ *n* **1** : a very stupid person **2** *dated, now offensive* : a person affected with mild intellectual disability — **mo•ron•ic** \mə-ˈrä-nik\ *adj* — **mo•ron•i•cal•ly** \-ni-k(ə-)lē\ *adv*
mo•rose \mə-ˈrōs\ *adj* [L *morosus* hard to please, exacting, fr. *mor-, mos* custom, disposition] : having a sullen disposition; *also* : GLOOMY — **mo•rose•ly** *adv* — **mo•rose•ness** *n*
morph \ˈmȯrf\ *vb* : to change the form or character of : TRANSFORM
mor•pheme \ˈmȯr-ˌfēm\ *n* : a meaningful linguistic unit that contains no smaller meaningful parts — **mor•phe•mic** \mȯr-ˈfē-mik\ *adj*
mor•phia \ˈmȯr-fē-ə\ *n* : MORPHINE
mor•phine \ˈmȯr-ˌfēn\ *n* [F, fr. Gk *Morpheus,* Greek god of dreams] : an addictive drug obtained from opium and used to ease pain or induce sleep
mor•phol•o•gy \mȯr-ˈfä-lə-jē\ *n* **1** : a branch of biology dealing with the form and structure of organisms **2** : a study and description of word formation in a language — **mor•pho•log•i•cal** \ˌmȯr-fə-ˈlä-ji-kəl\ *adj* — **mor•phol•o•gist** \mȯr-ˈfä-lə-jist\ *n*
mor•ris \ˈmȯr-əs\ *n* : a vigorous English dance traditionally performed by men wearing costumes and bells
mor•row \ˈmär-ō\ *n* : the next day
Morse code \ˈmȯrs-\ *n* : either of two codes consisting of dots and dashes or long and short sounds used for transmitting messages
mor•sel \ˈmȯr-səl\ *n* [ME, fr. AF, dim. of *mors* bite, fr. L *morsus,* fr. *mordēre* to bite] **1** : a small piece or quantity ⟨chocolate ~*s*⟩ **2** : a tasty dish
mor•tal \ˈmȯr-tᵊl\ *adj* **1** : causing death : FATAL; *also* : leading to eternal punishment ⟨~ sin⟩ **2** : subject to death ⟨~ man⟩ **3** : implacably hostile ⟨~ foe⟩ **4** : very great : EXTREME ⟨~ fear⟩ **5** : HUMAN ⟨~ limitations⟩ — **mortal** *n* — **mor•tal•i•ty** \mȯr-ˈta-lə-tē\ *n* — **mor•tal•ly** \ˈmȯr-tᵊl-ē\ *adv*
[1]**mor•tar** \ˈmȯr-tər\ *n* **1** : a strong bowl in which substances are pounded or crushed with a pestle **2** : a short-barreled cannon used to fire shells at high angles
[2]**mortar** *n* : a building material (as a mixture of lime and cement with sand and water) that is spread between bricks or stones to bind them together as it hardens — **mortar** *vb*
mor•tar•board \ˈmȯr-tər-ˌbȯrd\ *n* **1** : a square board for holding mortar **2** : an academic cap with a flat square top
mort•gage \ˈmȯr-gij\ *n* [ME *morgage,* fr. AF *mortgage,* fr. *mort* dead + *gage* pledge] : a transfer of rights to a piece of property usu. as security for the payment of a loan or debt that becomes void when the debt is paid — **mortgage** *vb* — **mort•gag•ee** \ˌmȯr-gi-ˈjē\ *n* — **mort•gag•or** \ˌmȯr-gi-ˈjȯr\ *n*
mor•ti•cian \mȯr-ˈti-shən\ *n* [L *mort-, mors* death + E *-ician* (as in *physician*)] : UNDERTAKER
mor•ti•fy \ˈmȯr-tə-ˌfī\ *vb* **-fied; -fy•ing** **1** : to subdue (as the body) esp. by abstinence or self-inflicted pain **2** : HUMILIATE ⟨her behavior *mortified* her parents⟩ **3** : to become necrotic or gangrenous — **mor•ti•fi•ca•tion** \ˌmȯr-tə-fə-ˈkā-shən\ *n*
mor•tise *also* **mor•tice** \ˈmȯr-təs\ *n* : a hole cut in a piece of wood into which another piece fits to form a joint
mor•tu•ary \ˈmȯr-chə-ˌwer-ē\ *n, pl* **-ar•ies** : a place in which dead bodies are kept until burial
mos *abbr* months
mo•sa•ic \mō-ˈzā-ik\ *n* : a surface decoration made by inlaying small pieces (as of colored glass or stone) to form figures or patterns; *also* : a design made in mosaic — **mosaic** *adj*
mos•co•vi•um \mä-ˈskō-vē-əm\ *n* : a short-lived artificially produced radioactive chemical element
mo•sey \ˈmō-zē\ *vb* **mo•seyed; mo•sey•ing** : SAUNTER ⟨*moseyed* through the park⟩
mosh \ˈmäsh\ *vb* : to engage in rough uninhibited dancing near the stage at a rock concert
mosh pit *n* : an area in front of a stage where rough dancing takes place at a rock concert
Mos•lem \ˈmäz-ləm\ *var of* MUSLIM
mosque \ˈmäsk\ *n* : a building used for public worship by Muslims

mos·qui·to \mə-ˈskē-tō\ *n, pl* **-toes** *also* **-tos** : any of a family of dipteran flies the female of which sucks the blood of animals
mosquito net *n* : a net or screen for keeping out mosquitoes
moss \ˈmȯs\ *n* : any of a class of green plants that lack flowers but have small leafy stems and often grow in clumps — **mossy** *adj*
moss·back \ˈmȯs-ˌbak\ *n* : an extremely conservative person : FOGY
[1]**most** \ˈmōst\ *adj* **1** : GREATEST ⟨the ~ ability⟩ **2** : the majority of ⟨~ people⟩
[2]**most** *adv* **1** : to the greatest or highest degree ⟨~ beautiful⟩ **2** : to a very great degree ⟨a ~ careful driver⟩
[3]**most** *n* : the greatest amount ⟨the ~ I can do⟩
[4]**most** *pron* : the greatest number or part ⟨~ became discouraged⟩
-most *adj suffix* : most ⟨inner*most*⟩ : most toward ⟨end*most*⟩
most·ly \ˈmōst-lē\ *adv* : MAINLY
mot \ˈmō\ *n, pl* **mots** *same or* ˈmōz\ [F, word, saying, fr. LL *muttum* grunt] : a witty saying
mote \ˈmōt\ *n* : a small particle
mo·tel \mō-ˈtel\ *n* [blend of *motor* and *hotel*] : a hotel in which the rooms are accessible from the parking area
mo·tet \mō-ˈtet\ *n* : a choral work on a sacred text for several voices usu. without instrumental accompaniment
moth \ˈmȯth\ *n, pl* **moths** \ˈmȯt͟hz, ˈmȯths\ : any of various insects belonging to the same order as the butterflies but usu. night-flying and with a stouter body and smaller wings
moth·ball \ˈmȯth-ˌbȯl\ *n* **1** : a ball (as of naphthalene) used to keep moths out of clothing **2** *pl* : protective storage ⟨many ships were put in ~*s*⟩
[1]**moth·er** \ˈmə-t͟hər\ *n* **1** : a female parent **2** : the superior of a religious community of women **3** : SOURCE, ORIGIN ⟨necessity is the ~ of invention⟩ — **moth·er·hood** \-ˌhu̇d\ *n* — **moth·er·less** *adj* — **moth·er·li·ness** \-lē-nəs\ *n* — **moth·er·ly** *adj*
[2]**mother** *vb* **1** : to give birth to; *also* : PRODUCE **2** : to care for or protect like a mother
moth·er·board \ˈmə-t͟hər-ˌbȯrd\ *n* : the main circuit board esp. of a microcomputer
moth·er–in–law \ˈmə-t͟hər-ən-ˌlȯ\ *n, pl* **mothers–in–law** \ˈmə-t͟hərz-\ : the mother of one's spouse
moth·er·land \ˈmə-t͟hər-ˌland\ *n* **1** : the land of origin of something **2** : the native land of one's ancestors
moth·er–of–pearl \ˌmə-t͟hər-əv-ˈpərl\ *n* : the hard pearly matter forming the inner layer of a mollusk shell
mother ship *n* : a ship serving smaller craft
mo·tif \mō-ˈtēf\ *n* [F, motive, motif] : a dominant idea or central theme (as in a work of art)
mo·tile \ˈmō-tᵊl, ˈmō-ˌtī(-ə)l\ *adj* : capable of spontaneous movement ⟨~ cells⟩ — **mo·til·i·ty** \mō-ˈti-lə-tē\ *n*
[1]**mo·tion** \ˈmō-shən\ *n* **1** : an act, process, or instance of moving **2** : a proposal for action (as by a deliberative body) **3** *pl* : ACTIVITIES, MOVEMENTS — **mo·tion·less** *adj* — **mo·tion·less·ly** *adv* — **mo·tion·less·ness** *n*
[2]**motion** *vb* : to direct or signal by a movement
motion picture *n* : a series of pictures projected on a screen so rapidly that they produce a continuous picture in which persons and objects seem to move
motion sickness *n* : sickness induced by motion and characterized by nausea
mo·ti·vate \ˈmō-tə-ˌvāt\ *vb* **-vat·ed; -vat·ing** : to provide with a motive : IMPEL — **mo·ti·va·tion** \ˌmō-tə-ˈvā-shən\ *n* — **mo·ti·va·tion·al** \-shə-nəl\ *adj* — **mo·ti·va·tor** \ˈmō-tə-ˌvā-tər\ *n*
[1]**mo·tive** \ˈmō-tiv, *2 also* mō-ˈtēv\ *n* **1** : something (as a need or desire) that causes a person to act **2** : a recurrent theme in a musical composition **3** : MOTIF — **mo·tive·less** *adj*
[2]**mo·tive** \ˈmō-tiv\ *adj* **1** : moving to action **2** : of or relating to motion
mot·ley \ˈmät-lē\ *adj* **1** : variegated in color **2** : made up of diverse often incongruous elements ♦ ***Synonyms*** HETEROGENEOUS, MISCELLANEOUS, ASSORTED, MIXED, VARIED
[1]**mo·tor** \ˈmō-tər\ *n* [L, fr. *movēre* to move] **1** : one that imparts motion **2** : a machine that produces motion or power for doing work **3** : AUTOMOBILE
[2]**motor** *vb* : to travel or transport by automobile : DRIVE — **mo·tor·ist** *n*
mo·tor·bike \ˈmō-tər-ˌbīk\ *n* : a small lightweight motorcycle
mo·tor·boat \-ˌbōt\ *n* : a boat propelled by a motor
mo·tor·cade \-ˌkād\ *n* : a procession of motor vehicles
mo·tor·car \-ˌkär\ *n* : AUTOMOBILE
mo·tor·cy·cle \ˈmō-tər-ˌsī-kəl\ *n* : a 2-wheeled automotive vehicle — **motorcycle** *vb* — **mo·tor·cy·clist** \-k(ə-)list\ *n*
motor home *n* : a large motor vehicle equipped as living quarters
motor inn *n* : MOTEL
mo·tor·ise *Brit var of* MOTORIZE
mo·tor·ize \ˈmō-tə-ˌrīz\ *vb* **-ized; -iz·ing** **1** : to equip with a motor **2** : to equip with automobiles
mo·tor·man \ˈmō-tər-mən\ *n* : an operator of a motor-driven vehicle (as a streetcar or subway train)
motor scooter *n* : a low 2- or 3-wheeled automotive vehicle resembling a child's scooter but having a seat
mo·tor·truck \ˈmō-tər-ˌtrək\ *n* : an automotive truck
motor vehicle *n* : an automotive vehicle (as an automobile) not operated on rails
mot·tle \ˈmä-tᵊl\ *vb* **mot·tled; mot·tling** : to mark with spots of different color : BLOTCH
mot·to \ˈmä-tō\ *n, pl* **mottoes** *also* **mottos** [It, fr. LL *muttum* grunt, fr. L *muttire*

to mutter] **1** : a sentence, phrase, or word inscribed on something to indicate its character or use **2** : a short expression of a guiding rule of conduct

moue \ˈmü\ *n* : a little grimace

mould *chiefly Brit var of* MOLD

moult *chiefly Brit var of* MOLT

mound \ˈmau̇nd\ *n* **1** : an artificial bank or hill of earth or stones **2** : KNOLL **3** : HEAP, PILE ⟨a ~ of work⟩

[1]**mount** \ˈmau̇nt\ *n* : a high hill

[2]**mount** *vb* **1** : to increase in amount or extent; *also* : RISE, ASCEND **2** : to get up on something; *esp* : to seat oneself on (as a horse) for riding **3** : to put in position ⟨~ artillery⟩ **4** : to set on something that elevates **5** : to attach to a support **6** : to prepare esp. for examination or display — **mount·able** *adj* — **mount·er** *n*

[3]**mount** *n* **1** : FRAME, SUPPORT **2** : a means of conveyance; *esp* : SADDLE HORSE

moun·tain \ˈmau̇n-tᵊn\ *n* : a landmass higher than a hill — **moun·tain·ous** \-tə-nəs\ *adj* — **moun·tainy** \-tᵊn-ē\ *adj*

mountain ash *n* : any of various trees related to the roses that have pinnate leaves and red or orange-red fruits

mountain bike *n* : a bicycle with wide knobby tires, straight handlebars, and 18 or 21 gears that is designed to operate esp. over unpaved terrain

moun·tain·eer \ˌmau̇n-tə-ˈnir\ *n* **1** : a native or inhabitant of a mountainous region **2** : one who climbs mountains for sport

mountain goat *n* : a ruminant mammal of mountainous northwestern No. America that resembles a goat

mountain laurel *n* : a No. American evergreen shrub or small tree of the heath family with glossy leaves and clusters of rose-colored or white flowers

mountain lion *n* : COUGAR

moun·tain·side \ˈmau̇n-tᵊn-ˌsīd\ *n* : the side of a mountain

moun·tain·top \-ˌtäp\ *n* : the summit of a mountain

moun·te·bank \ˈmau̇n-ti-ˌbaŋk\ *n* [It *montimbanco,* fr. *montare* to mount + *in* in, on + *banco, banca* bench] : QUACK, CHARLATAN

Mount·ie \ˈmau̇n-tē\ *n* : a member of the Royal Canadian Mounted Police

mount·ing \ˈmau̇n-tiŋ\ *n* : something that serves as a frame or support

mourn \ˈmōrn\ *vb* : to feel or express grief or sorrow — **mourn·er** *n*

mourn·ful \-fəl\ *adj* : expressing, feeling, or causing sorrow ⟨a ~ song⟩ — **mourn·ful·ly** *adv* — **mourn·ful·ness** *n*

mourn·ing \ˈmōr-niŋ\ *n* **1** : an outward sign (as black clothes) of grief for a person's death **2** : a period of time during which signs of grief are shown

mouse \ˈmau̇s\ *n, pl* **mice** \ˈmīs\ **1** : any of numerous small rodents with pointed snout, long body, and slender tail **2** : a small manual device that controls cursor movement on a computer display

mouse pad *n* : a thin flat pad on which a computer mouse is used

mous·er \ˈmau̇-sər\ *n* : a cat proficient at catching mice

mouse·trap \ˈmau̇s-ˌtrap\ *n* **1** : a trap for catching mice **2** : a stratagem that lures one to defeat or destruction — **mouse-trap** *vb*

mousse \ˈmüs\ *n* [F, lit., froth, moss] **1** : a molded chilled dessert made with sweetened and flavored whipped cream or egg whites and gelatin **2** : a foamy preparation used in styling hair — **mousse** *vb*

moustache *var of* MUSTACHE

mousy *or* **mous·ey** \ˈmau̇-sē, -zē\ *adj* **mous·i·er; -est** **1** : QUIET, STEALTHY **2** : TIMID **3** : grayish brown — **mous·i·ness** \ˈmau̇-sē-nəs, -zē-\ *n*

[1]**mouth** \ˈmau̇th\ *n, pl* **mouths** \ˈmau̇t͟hz, ˈmau̇ths\ **1** : the opening through which an animal takes in food; *also* : the cavity that encloses the tongue, lips, and teeth in the typical vertebrate **2** : something resembling a mouth (as in affording entrance) — **mouthed** \ˈmau̇t͟hd, ˈmau̇tht\ *adj* — **mouth·ful** *n*

[2]**mouth** \ˈmau̇t͟h\ *vb* **1** : SPEAK; *also* : DECLAIM **2** : to repeat without comprehension or sincerity ⟨~*ed* platitudes⟩ **3** : to form soundlessly with the lips

mouth harp *n* : HARMONICA

mouth·part \ˈmau̇th-ˌpärt\ *n* : a structure or appendage near the mouth (as of an insect) esp. when adapted for eating

mouth·piece \-ˌpēs\ *n* **1** : a part (as of a musical instrument) that goes in the mouth or to which the mouth is applied **2** : SPOKESPERSON

mouth–to–mouth *adj* : of, relating to, or being a method of artificial respiration in which air from a rescuer's mouth is forced into a victim's lungs

mouth·wash \-ˌwȯsh, -ˌwäsh\ *n* : a usu. antiseptic liquid preparation for cleaning the mouth and teeth

mou·ton \ˈmü-ˌtän\ *n* : processed sheepskin that has been sheared or dyed to resemble beaver or seal

[1]**move** \ˈmüv\ *vb* **moved; mov·ing** **1** : to change or cause to change position or posture **2** : to go or cause to go from one point to another; *also* : DEPART **3** : to take or cause to take action **4** : to show marked activity **5** : to stir the emotions **6** : to make a formal request, application, or appeal **7** : to change one's residence **8** : EVACUATE 2 — **mov·able** *or* **move·able** \ˈmü-və-bəl\ *adj*

[2]**move** *n* **1** : an act of moving **2** : a calculated step taken to gain an objective **3** : a change of location **4** : an agile action esp. in sports

move·ment \ˈmüv-mənt\ *n* **1** : the act or process of moving : MOVE **2** : a series of organized activities working toward an objective **3** : the moving parts of a mechanism (as of a watch) **4** : RHYTHM **5** : a section of an extended musical composition **6** : BOWEL MOVEMENT; *also* : STOOL 4

mov·er \ˈmü-vər\ *n* : one that moves; *esp* : one that moves the belongings of others from one location to another

mov·ie \ˈmü-vē\ *n* **1** : MOTION PICTURE **2** *pl* : a showing of a motion picture **3** *pl* : the motion-picture industry

[1]**mow** \ˈmau̇\ *n* : the part of a barn where hay or straw is stored

[2]**mow** \ˈmō\ *vb* **mowed; mowed** *or* **mown** \ˈmōn\; **mow·ing** **1** : to cut (as grass) with a scythe or machine **2** : to cut the standing herbage of ⟨~ the lawn⟩ — **mow·er** *n*

mox·ie \ˈmäk-sē\ *n* **1** : ENERGY, PEP **2** : COURAGE, DETERMINATION

moz·za·rel·la \ˌmät-sə-ˈre-lə\ *n* [It] : a moist white unsalted unripened mild cheese of a smooth rubbery texture

[1]**MP** \ˈem-ˈpē\ *n* **1** : a member of the military police **2** : an elected member of a parliament

[2]**MP** *abbr* **1** melting point **2** metropolitan police

MPEG \ˈem-ˌpeg\ *n* : any of a group of computer file formats for the compression and storage of digital video and audio data; *also* : a computer file (as of a movie) in an MPEG format

mpg *abbr* miles per gallon

mph *abbr* miles per hour

MP3 \ˌem-(ˌ)pē-ˈthrē\ *n* : a computer file format for the compression and storage of digital audio data; *also* : a computer file (as of a song) in the MP3 format

Mr. \ˈmis-tər\ *n, pl* **Messrs.** \ˈme-sərz\ — used as a conventional title of courtesy before a man's surname or his title of office

MRI *n* : MAGNETIC RESONANCE IMAGING; *also* : the procedure in which magnetic resonance imaging is used

mRNA \ˈem-ˈär-ˈen-ˈā\ *n* MESSENGER RNA

Mr. Right *n* : a man who would make the perfect husband

Mrs. \ˈmi-səz, -səs, *esp Southern* ˈmi-zəz, -zəs\ *n, pl* **Mes·dames** \mā-ˈdäm, -ˈdam\ — used as a conventional title of courtesy before a married woman's surname

Ms. \ˈmiz\ *n, pl* **Mss.** *or* **Mses.** \ˈmi-zez\ — used as a conventional title of courtesy before a woman's surname

MS *abbr* **1** manuscript **2** master of science **3** military science **4** Mississippi **5** motor ship **6** multiple sclerosis

msec *abbr* millisecond

msg *abbr* message

MSG *abbr* **1** master sergeant **2** monosodium glutamate

msgr *abbr* **1** monseigneur **2** monsignor

MSgt *abbr* master sergeant

MSS *abbr* manuscripts

MST *abbr* mountain standard time

mt *abbr* mount; mountain

[1]**Mt** *abbr* Matthew

[2]**Mt** *symbol* meitnerium

MT *abbr* **1** metric ton **2** Montana **3** mountain time

mtg *abbr* **1** meeting **2** mortgage

mtge *abbr* mortgage

mu \ˈmyü, ˈmü\ *n* : the 12th letter of the Greek alphabet — Μ or μ

[1]**much** \ˈməch\ *adj* **more** \ˈmȯr\; **most** \ˈmōst\ : great in quantity, amount, extent, or degree ⟨~ money⟩

[2]**much** *adv* **more; most** **1** : to a great degree or extent ⟨~ happier⟩ **2** : ALMOST, NEARLY ⟨looks ~ as he did before⟩

[3]**much** *n* **1** : a great quantity, amount, extent, or degree **2** : something considerable or impressive

mu·ci·lage \ˈmyü-sə-lij\ *n* : a watery sticky solution (as of a gum) used esp. as an adhesive — **mu·ci·lag·i·nous** \ˌmyü-sə-ˈla-jə-nəs\ *adj*

muck \ˈmək\ *n* **1** : soft moist barnyard manure **2** : FILTH, DIRT **3** : a dark richly organic soil; *also* : MUD, MIRE — **mucky** *adj*

muck·rake \-ˌrāk\ *vb* : to expose publicly real or apparent misconduct of a prominent individual or business — **muck·rak·er** *n*

mu·cus \ˈmyü-kəs\ *n* : a slimy slippery protective secretion of membranes (**mucous membranes**) lining some body cavities — **mu·cous** \-kəs\ *adj*

mud \ˈməd\ *n* : soft wet earth : MIRE

mud·dle \ˈmə-dᵊl\ *vb* **mud·dled; mud·dling** **1** : to make muddy **2** : to confuse esp. with liquor **3** : to mix up or make a mess of ⟨*muddled* the household accounts⟩ **4** : to think or act in a confused way

mud·dle·head·ed \ˌmə-dᵊl-ˈhe-dəd\ *adj* **1** : mentally confused **2** : INEPT

[1]**mud·dy** \ˈmə-dē\ *adj* **mud·di·er; -est** **1** : full of or covered with mud **2** : suggestive of mud **3** : CLOUDY, OBSCURE — **mud·di·ness** *n*

[2]**muddy** *vb* **mud·died; mud·dy·ing** **1** : to soil or stain with or as if with mud **2** : to make cloudy or obscure **3** : CONFUSE

mud·flat \ˈməd-ˌflat\ *n* : a level tract alternately covered and left bare by the tide

mud·guard \ˈməd-ˌgärd\ *n* : a guard over or a flap behind a wheel of a vehicle to catch or deflect mud

mud·room \-ˌrüm, -ˌru̇m\ *n* : a room in a house for removing dirty or wet footwear and clothing

mud·sling·er \-ˌsliŋ-ər\ *n* : one who uses invective esp. against a political opponent — **mud·sling·ing** \-ˌsliŋ-iŋ\ *n*

Muen·ster \ˈmən-stər, ˈmün-, ˈmu̇n-\ *n* : a semisoft bland cheese

mu·ez·zin \mü-ˈe-zᵊn, myü-\ *n* : a Muslim crier who calls the hour of daily prayer

[1]**muff** \ˈməf\ *n* : a warm tubular covering for the hands

[2]**muff** *n* : a bungling performance; *esp* : a failure to hold a ball in attempting a catch — **muff** *vb*

muf·fin \ˈmə-fən\ *n* : a small soft cake baked in a cup-shaped container

muf·fle \ˈmə-fəl\ *vb* **muf·fled; muf·fling** **1** : to wrap up so as to conceal or protect **2** : to wrap or pad with something to dull the sound of **3** : to keep down : SUPPRESS ⟨*muffled* his feelings⟩

muf·fler \ˈmə-flər\ *n* **1** : a scarf worn around the neck **2** : a device (as on a car's exhaust) to deaden noise

muf·ti \ˈməf-tē\ *n* : civilian clothes

¹**mug** \ˈməg\ *n* : a usu. metal or earthenware cylindrical drinking cup

²**mug** *vb* **mugged; mug·ging** **1** : to pose or make faces esp. to attract attention or for a camera **2** : PHOTOGRAPH

³**mug** *vb* **mugged; mug·ging** : to assault usu. with intent to rob — **mug·ger** *n*

mug·gy \ˈmə-gē\ *adj* **mug·gi·er; -est** : being warm and humid — **mug·gi·ness** \-gē-nəs\ *n*

mug·wump \ˈməg-ˌwəmp\ *n* [obs. slang *mugwump* kingpin, fr. Massachusett (Algonquian language of New England) *mugquomp* war leader] : an independent in politics

Muhammadan *var of* MOHAMMEDAN

mu·ja·hid·een *or* **mu·ja·hed·in** \mü-ˌja-hi-ˈdēn, -ˌjä-\ *n pl* [Ar *mujāhidīn,* pl. of *mujāhid,* lit., person who wages jihad] : Islamic guerrilla fighters esp. in the Middle East

muk·luk \ˈmək-ˌlək\ *n* **1** : a boot of sealskin or reindeer skin typically worn by Indigenous peoples of usually arctic regions **2** : a boot with a soft leather sole worn over several pairs of socks

mu·lat·to \mu̇-ˈla-tō, myu̇-, -ˈlä-\ *n, pl* **-toes** *or* **-tos** [Sp *mulato,* fr. *mulo* mule, fr. L *mulus*] **1** *usually offensive* : the first-generation offspring of a Black person and a white person **2** *usually offensive* : a person of mixed white and Black ancestry

mul·ber·ry \ˈməl-ˌber-ē\ *n* : any of a genus of trees with edible berrylike fruit and leaves used as food for silkworms; *also* : the fruit

mulch \ˈməlch\ *n* : a protective covering (as of straw or leaves) spread on the ground esp. to reduce evaporation or control weeds — **mulch** *vb*

¹**mulct** \ˈməlkt\ *n* : FINE, PENALTY

²**mulct** *vb* **1** : FINE **2** : CHEAT, DEFRAUD

¹**mule** \ˈmyül\ *n* **1** : a hybrid offspring of a male donkey and a female horse **2** : a very stubborn person — **mul·ish** \ˈmyü-lish\ *adj* — **mul·ish·ly** *adv* — **mu·lish·ness** *n*

²**mule** *n* : a slipper whose upper does not extend around the heel of the foot

mule deer *n* : a long-eared deer of western No. America

mu·le·teer \ˌmyü-lə-ˈtir\ *n* : one who drives mules

¹**mull** \ˈməl\ *vb* : PONDER, MEDITATE

²**mull** *vb* : to heat, sweeten, and flavor (as wine) with spices

mul·lein \ˈmə-lən\ *n* : a tall herb related to the snapdragons that has coarse woolly leaves and flowers in spikes

mul·let \ˈmə-lət\ *n, pl* **mullet** *or* **mullets** : any of a family of largely gray chiefly marine bony fishes including valuable food fishes

mul·li·gan stew \ˈmə-li-gən-\ *n* : a stew made from whatever ingredients are available

mul·li·ga·taw·ny \ˌmə-li-gə-ˈtȯ-nē\ *n* : a soup usu. of chicken stock seasoned with curry

mul·lion \ˈməl-yən\ *n* : a vertical strip separating windowpanes

multi- *comb form* **1** : many : multiple ⟨*multi*unit⟩ **2** : many times over ⟨*multi*millionaire⟩

mul·ti·col·ored \ˌməl-ti-ˈkə-lərd\ *adj* : having many colors

mul·ti·cul·tur·al \ˌməl-tē-ˈkəl-chə-rəl, -ˌtī-\ *adj* : of, relating to, reflecting, or adapted to diverse cultures ⟨a ~ society⟩ — **mul·ti·cul·tur·al·ism** \-rə-ˌli-zəm\ *n* — **mul·ti·cul·tur·al·ist** \-rə-list\ *n or adj*

mul·ti·di·men·sion·al \-ti-də-ˈmen-chə-nəl, -ˌtī-, -dī-\ *adj* : of, relating to, or having many facets or dimensions ⟨a ~ problem⟩ ⟨~ space⟩

mul·ti·eth·nic \-ˈeth-nik\ *adj* : including, involving, or made up of people of various ethnic groups

mul·ti·fac·et·ed \-ˈfa-sə-təd\ *adj* : having many facets or aspects ⟨a ~ concept⟩

mul·ti·fam·i·ly \-ˈfam-lē, -ˈfa-mə-\ *adj* : designed for use by several families

mul·ti·far·i·ous \ˌməl-tə-ˈfer-ē-əs\ *adj* : having great variety : DIVERSE ⟨~ activities⟩ — **mul·ti·far·i·ous·ness** *n*

mul·ti·form \ˈməl-ti-ˌfȯrm\ *adj* : having many forms or appearances — **mul·ti·for·mi·ty** \ˌməl-ti-ˈfȯr-mə-tē\ *n*

mul·ti·lat·er·al \ˌməl-ti-ˈla-tə-rəl, -ˌtī-, -ˈla-trəl\ *adj* : having many sides or participants ⟨~ treaty⟩ — **mul·ti·lat·er·al·ism** \-ˈla-tə-rə-ˌli-zəm\ *n* — **mul·ti·lat·er·al·ly** *adv*

mul·ti·lay·ered \-ˈlā-ərd, -ˈlerd\ *or* **mul·ti·lay·er** \-ˈlā-ər, -ˈler\ *adj* : having or involving several distinct layers or levels

mul·ti·lev·el \-ˈle-vəl\ *adj* : having several levels

mul·ti·lin·gual \-ˈliŋ-gwəl\ *adj* : knowing or using several languages — **mul·ti·lin·gual·ism** \-gwə-ˌli-zəm\ *n*

¹**mul·ti·me·dia** \-ˈmē-dē-ə\ *adj* : using, involving, or encompassing several media ⟨a ~ advertising campaign⟩

²**multimedia** *n sing or pl* : the technique of using several media (as in art); *also* : something (as software) that uses or facilitates it

mul·ti·mil·lion·aire \ˌməl-ti-ˌmil-yə-ˈnar, -ˌtī-, -ˈmil-yə-ˌnar\ *n* : a person worth several million dollars

mul·ti·na·tion·al \-ˈna-shə-nəl\ *adj* **1** : of or relating to several nationalities **2** : relating to or involving several nations **3** : having divisions in several countries ⟨a ~ corporation⟩ — **multinational** *n*

mul·ti·pack \ˈməl-tē-ˌpak\ *n* : a package of several individually packed items sold as a unit

¹**mul·ti·ple** \ˈməl-tə-pəl\ *adj* **1** : more than one; *also* : MANY ⟨~ achievements⟩ **2** : VARIOUS

²**multiple** *n* : the product of a quantity by an integer ⟨35 is a ~ of 7⟩

multiple–choice *adj* : having several answers given from which the correct one is to be chosen ⟨a ~ question⟩

multiple personality disorder *n* : a neurosis in which the personality becomes separated into two or more parts each of which controls behavior part of the time

multiple sclerosis *n* : a disease marked

by patches of hardened tissue in the brain or spinal cord and associated esp. with partial or complete paralysis and muscular tremor

mul·ti·plex \ˈməl-tə-ˌpleks\ *n* : CINEPLEX

mul·ti·pli·cand \ˌməl-tə-pli-ˈkand\ *n* : the number that is to be multiplied by another

mul·ti·pli·ca·tion \ˌməl-tə-plə-ˈkā-shən\ *n* **1** : INCREASE **2** : a short method of finding the result of adding a figure the number of times indicated by another figure

multiplication sign *n* **1** : TIMES SIGN **2** : a centered dot indicating multiplication

mul·ti·plic·i·ty \ˌməl-tə-ˈpli-sə-tē\ *n, pl* **-ties** : a great number or variety

mul·ti·pli·er \ˈməl-tə-ˌplī(-ə)r\ *n* : one that multiplies; *esp* : a number by which another number is multiplied

mul·ti·ply \ˈməl-tə-ˌplī\ *vb* **-plied; -ply·ing** **1** : to increase in number (as by breeding) **2** : to find the product of by multiplication; *also* : to perform multiplication

mul·ti·pur·pose \ˌməl-ti-ˈpər-pəs, -ˌtī-\ *adj* : having or serving several purposes

mul·ti·ra·cial \-ˈrā-shəl\ *adj* **1** : composed of, involving, or representing various races **2** : having parents or ancestors of different races

mul·ti·sense \ˈməl-tē-ˌsens\ *adj* : having several meanings ⟨~ words⟩

mul·ti·sto·ry \ˌməl-ti-ˈstȯr-ē, -ˌtī-\ *adj* : having several stories ⟨~ buildings⟩

mul·ti·sys·tem inflammatory syndrome in children \ˈməl-tē-ˌsis-təm-, -ˌtī-\ *n* : an uncommon inflammatory condition that chiefly affects children and adolescents and usu. develops two to four weeks after infection with or exposure to the coronavirus causing COVID-19

mul·ti·task·ing \-ˌtas-kiŋ\ *n* **1** : the concurrent performance of several jobs by a computer **2** : the performance of multiple tasks at one time — **mul·ti·task** \-ˌtask\ *vb* — **mul·ti·task·er** \-ˌtas-kər\ *n*

mul·ti·tude \ˈməl-tə-ˌtüd, -ˌtyüd\ *n* : a great number — **mul·ti·tu·di·nous** \ˌməl-tə-ˈtü-dᵊn-əs, -ˈtyüd-\ *adj*

mul·ti·unit \ˌməl-ti-ˈyü-nət, -ˌtī-\ *adj* : having several units

mul·ti·vi·ta·min \-ˈvī-tə-mən\ *adj* : containing several vitamins and esp. all known to be essential to health — **multivitamin** *n*

[1]**mum** \ˈməm\ *adj* : SILENT

[2]**mum** *chiefly Brit var of* MOM

[3]**mum** *n* : CHRYSANTHEMUM

mum·ble \ˈməm-bəl\ *vb* **mum·bled; mum·bling** : to speak in a low indistinct manner — **mumble** *n* — **mum·bler** *n* — **mum·bly** *adj*

mum·ble·ty–peg \ˈməm-bəl-tē-ˌpeg\ *also* **mum·ble–the–peg** \ˈməm-bəl-t͟hə-\ *n* : a game in which the players try to flip a knife from various positions so that the blade will stick into the ground

mum·bo jum·bo \ˌməm-bō-ˈjəm-bō\ *n* **1** : a complicated ritual with elaborate trappings **2** : GIBBERISH, NONSENSE

mum·mer \ˈmə-mər\ *n* **1** : an actor esp. in a pantomime **2** : a person who goes merrymaking in disguise during festivals — **mum·mery** *n*

mum·my \ˈmə-mē\ *n, pl* **mummies** [ME *mummie* powdered parts of a mummified body used as a drug, fr. AF *mumie,* fr. ML *mumia,* fr. Ar *mūmiya* bitumen, mummy, fr. Pers *mūm* wax] : a body embalmed for burial in the manner of the ancient Egyptians — **mum·mi·fi·ca·tion** \ˌmə-mi-fə-ˈkā-shən\ *n* — **mum·mi·fy** \ˈmə-mi-ˌfī\ *vb*

mumps \ˈməmps\ *n sing or pl* [fr. pl. of obs. *mump* grimace] : a virus disease marked by fever and swelling esp. of the salivary glands

mun *or* **munic** *abbr* municipal

munch \ˈmənch\ *vb* : to eat with a chewing action; *also* : to snack on

munch·ies \ˈmən-chēz\ *n pl* **1** : hunger pangs **2** : light snack foods

mun·dane \ˌmən-ˈdān, ˈmən-ˌdān\ *adj* **1** : of or relating to the world **2** : concerned with the practical details of everyday life — **mun·dane·ly** *adv*

mung bean \ˈməŋ-\ *n* : an erect bushy bean widely grown in warm regions for its edible seeds and as the chief source of bean sprouts; *also* : its seed

mu·nic·i·pal \myu̇-ˈni-sə-pəl\ *adj* **1** : of, relating to, or characteristic of a municipality **2** : restricted to one locality — **mu·nic·i·pal·ly** *adv*

mu·nic·i·pal·i·ty \myu̇-ˌni-sə-ˈpa-lə-tē\ *n, pl* **-ties** : an urban political unit with corporate status and usu. powers of self-government

mu·nif·i·cent \myu̇-ˈni-fə-sənt\ *adj* : liberal in giving : GENEROUS — **mu·nif·i·cence** \-səns\ *n*

mu·ni·tion \myu̇-ˈni-shən\ *n* : ARMAMENT, AMMUNITION

[1]**mu·ral** \ˈmyu̇r-əl\ *adj* **1** : of or relating to a wall **2** : applied to and made part of a wall or ceiling surface

[2]**mural** *n* : a mural painting — **mu·ral·ist** *n*

[1]**mur·der** \ˈmər-dər\ *n* **1** : the crime of unlawfully killing a person esp. with malice aforethought **2** : something unusually difficult or dangerous

[2]**murder** *vb* **1** : to commit a murder; *also* : to kill brutally **2** : to put an end to **3** : to spoil by performing poorly ⟨~ a song⟩ — **mur·der·er** *n*

mur·der·ess \ˈmər-də-rəs\ *n* : a woman who murders

mur·der·ous \ˈmər-də-rəs\ *adj* **1** : having or appearing to have the purpose of murder ⟨~ impulses⟩ **2** : marked by or causing murder or bloodshed ⟨~ gunfire⟩ — **mur·der·ous·ly** *adv*

murk \ˈmərk\ *n* : DARKNESS, GLOOM — **murk·i·ly** \ˈmər-kə-lē\ *adv* — **murk·i·ness** \-kē-nəs\ *n* — **murky** *adj*

mur·mur \ˈmər-mər\ *n* **1** : a muttered complaint **2** : a low indistinct often continuous sound — **murmur** *vb* — **mur·mur·er** *n* — **mur·mur·ous** *adj*

mus *abbr* **1** museum **2** music; musical; musician

mus·ca·tel \ˌməs-kə-ˈtel\ *n* : a sweet fortified wine

[1]**mus·cle** \ˈmə-səl\ *n* [ME, fr. L *musculus,* fr. dim. of *mus* mouse] **1** : a body tissue consisting of long cells that contract when stimulated and produce motion; *also* : an organ consisting of this tissue and functioning in moving a body part **2** : STRENGTH, BRAWN — **mus·cled** \ˈmə-səld\ *adj* — **mus·cu·lar** \ˈməs-kyə-lər\ *adj* — **mus·cu·lar·i·ty** \ˌməs-kyə-ˈler-ə-tē\ *n*

[2]**muscle** *vb* **mus·cled; mus·cling** : to force one's way

mus·cle–bound \ˈmə-səl-ˌbau̇nd\ *adj* : having some of the muscles abnormally enlarged and lacking in elasticity (as from excessive exercise)

mus·cle·man \-ˌman\ *n* : a man with a muscular physique

muscular dystrophy *n* : any of a group of diseases characterized by progressive wasting of muscles

mus·cu·la·ture \ˈməs-kyə-lə-ˌchu̇r\ *n* : the muscles of the body or its parts

muscu·lo·skel·e·tal \ˌməs-kyə-lō-ˈske-lə-tᵊl\ *adj* : of, relating to, or involving both musculature and skeleton

[1]**muse** \ˈmyüz\ *vb* **mused; mus·ing** [ME, fr. AF *muser* to gape, idle, muse, fr. OF **mus* mouth of an animal, fr. ML *musus*] : to become absorbed in thought ⟨*mused* about what might have been⟩ — **mus·ing·ly** *adv*

[2]**muse** *n* [fr. *Muse* any of the nine sister goddesses of learning and the arts in Greek myth, fr. ME, fr. MF, fr. L *Musa,* fr. Gk *Mousa*] : a source of inspiration

mu·se·um \myu̇-ˈzē-əm\ *n* : an institution devoted to the procurement, care, and display of objects of lasting interest or value

[1]**mush** \ˈməsh\ *n* **1** : cornmeal boiled in water **2** : sentimental drivel

[2]**mush** *vb* : to travel esp. over snow with a sled drawn by dogs

[1]**mush·room** \ˈməsh-ˌrüm, -ˌru̇m\ *n* : the fleshy usu. caplike spore-bearing organ of various fungi esp. when edible; *also* : such a fungus

[2]**mushroom** *vb* **1** : to spread out : EXPAND **2** : to collect wild mushrooms **3** : to grow rapidly ⟨the population *~ed*⟩

mushy \ˈmə-shē\ *adj* **mush·i·er; -est** **1** : soft like mush **2** : excessively sentimental ⟨a ~ movie⟩

mu·sic \ˈmyü-zik\ *n* **1** : the science or art of combining tones into a composition having structure and continuity; *also* : vocal or instrumental sounds having rhythm, melody, or harmony **2** : an agreeable sound

[1]**mu·si·cal** \ˈmyü-zi-kəl\ *adj* **1** : of or relating to music or musicians **2** : having the pleasing tonal qualities of music **3** : fond of or gifted in music ⟨a ~ family⟩ — **mu·si·cal·ly** \-k(ə-)lē\ *adv*

[2]**musical** *n* : a film or theatrical production consisting of musical numbers and dialogue based on a unifying plot

mu·si·cale \ˌmyü-zi-ˈkal\ *n* : a usu. private social gathering featuring music

mu·si·cian \myu̇-ˈzi-shən\ *n* : a composer, conductor, or performer of music — **mu·si·cian·ly** *adj* — **mu·si·cian·ship** *n*

mu·si·col·o·gy \ˌmyü-zi-ˈkä-lə-jē\ *n* : the study of music as a field of knowledge or research — **mu·si·co·log·i·cal** \-kə-ˈlä-ji-kəl\ *adj* — **mu·si·col·o·gist** \-ˈkä-lə-jist\ *n*

musk \ˈməsk\ *n* : a substance obtained esp. from a small Asian deer (**musk deer**) and used as a perfume fixative — **musk·i·ness** \ˈməs-kē-nəs\ *n* — **musky** *adj*

mus·keg \ˈməs-ˌkeg\ *n* : BOG; *esp* : a mossy bog in northern No. America

mus·kel·lunge \ˈməs-kə-ˌlənj\ *n, pl* **muskellunge** : a large No. American pike that is a valuable sport fish

mus·ket \ˈməs-kət\ *n* [MF *mousquet,* fr. It *moschetto* small artillery piece, kind of small hawk, fr. dim. of *mosca* fly, fr. L *musca*] : a heavy large-caliber muzzle-loading shoulder firearm — **mus·ke·teer** \ˌməs-kə-ˈtir\ *n*

mus·ket·ry \ˈməs-kə-trē\ *n* **1** : MUSKETS **2** : MUSKETEERS **3** : musket fire

musk·mel·on \ˈməsk-ˌme-lən\ *n* : a small round to oval melon that has usu. a sweet edible green or orange flesh and a musky odor

musk ox *n* : a heavyset shaggy-coated wild ox of Greenland and the arctic tundra of northern No. America

musk·rat \ˈməs-ˌkrat\ *n, pl* **muskrat** *or* **muskrats** : a large No. American aquatic rodent with webbed feet and dark brown fur; *also* : its fur

Mus·lim \ˈməz-ləm\ *n* : an adherent of Islam — **Muslim** *adj*

mus·lin \ˈməz-lən\ *n* : a plain-woven sheer to coarse cotton fabric

[1]**muss** \ˈməs\ *n* : a state of disorder — **muss·i·ly** \ˈmə-sə-lē\ *adv* — **muss·i·ness** \-sē-nəs\ *n* — **mussy** *adj*

[2]**muss** *vb* : to make untidy : DISARRANGE

mus·sel \ˈmə-səl\ *n* **1** : a dark edible saltwater bivalve mollusk **2** : any of various freshwater bivalve mollusks of the central U.S. having shells with a pearly lining

[1]**must** \ˈməst\ *vb* — used as an auxiliary esp. to express a command, requirement, obligation, or necessity

[2]**must** *n* **1** : an imperative duty **2** : an indispensable item

mus·tache *also* **mous·tache** \ˈməs-ˌtash, (ˌ)məs-ˈtash\ *n* : the hair growing on the human upper lip — **mus·tached** *also* **mous·tached** \-ˌtasht, -ˈtasht\ *adj*

mus·tang \ˈməs-ˌtaŋ\ *n* [MexSp *mestengo,* fr. Sp, stray, fr. *mesteño* strayed, fr. *mesta* annual roundup of cattle that disposed of strays, fr. ML *(animalia) mixta* mixed animals] : a small hardy naturalized horse of the western plains of America; *also* : BRONC

mus·tard \ˈməs-tərd\ *n* **1** : a pungent yellow powder of the seeds of an herb related to the cabbage and used as a condiment or in medicine **2** : a plant that yields mustard; *also* : a closely related plant — **mus·tardy** *adj*

mustard gas *n* : a poison gas used in warfare that has violent irritating and blistering effects

[1]**mus·ter** \ˈməs-tər\ *n* **1** : an act of assembling (as for military inspection); *also* : critical examination **2** : an assembled group

[2]**muster** *vb* [ME *mustren* to show, muster, fr. AF *mustrer, monstrer,* fr. L *monstrare* to show, fr. *monstrum* evil omen, monster] **1** : CONVENE, ASSEMBLE ⟨~ an army⟩; *also* : to call the roll of **2** : ACCUMULATE **3** : to call forth : ROUSE ⟨~*ed* support⟩ **4** : to amount to : COMPRISE

muster out *vb* : to discharge from military service

musty \ˈməs-tē\ *adj* **mus·ti·er; -est** : MOLDY, STALE; *also* : tasting or smelling of damp or decay — **must·i·ly** \-tə-lē\ *adv* — **must·i·ness** \-tē-nəs\ *n*

mu·ta·ble \ˈmyü-tə-bəl\ *adj* **1** : prone to change : FICKLE **2** : capable of or liable to mutation : VARIABLE — **mu·ta·bil·i·ty** \ˌmyü-tə-ˈbi-lə-tē\ *n*

mu·tant \ˈmyü-t^{ə}nt\ *adj* : of, relating to, or produced by mutation — **mu·tant** *n*

mu·tate \ˈmyü-ˌtāt\ *vb* **mu·tat·ed; mu·tat·ing** : to undergo or cause to undergo mutation — **mu·ta·tive** \ˈmyü-ˌtā-tiv, -tə-tiv\ *adj*

mu·ta·tion \myü-ˈtā-shən\ *n* **1** : CHANGE **2** : an inherited physical or biochemical change in genetic material; *also* : the process of producing a mutation **3** : an individual, strain, or trait resulting from mutation — **mu·ta·tion·al** *adj*

[1]**mute** \ˈmyüt\ *adj* **mut·er; mut·est** **1** : unable to speak **2** : SILENT — **mute·ly** *adv* — **mute·ness** *n*

[2]**mute** *n* **1** *dated, offensive* : a person who cannot speak **2** : a device on a musical instrument that reduces, softens, or muffles the tone

[3]**mute** *vb* **mut·ed; mut·ing** : to muffle, reduce, or eliminate the sound of

mu·ti·late \ˈmyü-tə-ˌlāt\ *vb* **-lat·ed; -lat·ing** **1** : to cut up or alter radically so as to make imperfect **2** : MAIM, CRIPPLE — **mu·ti·la·tion** \ˌmyü-tə-ˈlā-shən\ *n* — **mu·ti·la·tor** \ˈmyü-tə-ˌlā-tər\ *n*

mu·ti·ny \ˈmyü-tə-nē\ *n, pl* **-nies** : willful refusal to obey constituted authority; *esp* : revolt against a superior officer — **mu·ti·neer** \ˌmyü-tə-ˈnir\ *n* — **mu·ti·nous** \ˈmyü-tə-nəs\ *adj* — **mu·ti·nous·ly** *adv* — **mutiny** *vb*

mutt \ˈmət\ *n* : MONGREL, CUR

mut·ter \ˈmə-tər\ *vb* **1** : to speak indistinctly or with a low voice and lips partly closed **2** : GRUMBLE — **mutter** *n*

mut·ton \ˈmə-t^{ə}n\ *n* [ME *motoun* mutton, sheep, fr. AF *mutun* ram, sheep, mutton] : the flesh of a mature sheep used for food — **mut·tony** *adj*

mut·ton·chops \ˈmə-t^{ə}n-ˌchäps\ *n pl* : whiskers on the side of the face that are narrow at the temple and broad and round by the lower jaws

mu·tu·al \ˈmyü-chə-wəl\ *adj* **1** : given and received in equal amount ⟨~ trust⟩ **2** : having the same feelings one for the other ⟨~ enemies⟩ **3** : COMMON, JOINT ⟨a ~ friend⟩ — **mu·tu·al·ly** *adv*

mutual fund *n* : an investment company that invests money of its shareholders in a usu. diversified group of securities of other corporations

muu·muu \ˈmü-ˌmü\ *n* : a loose dress of Hawaiian origin

[1]**muz·zle** \ˈmə-zəl\ *n* **1** : the nose and jaws of an animal; *also* : a covering for the muzzle to prevent biting or eating **2** : the mouth of a gun

[2]**muzzle** *vb* **muz·zled; muz·zling** **1** : to put a muzzle on **2** : to restrain from expression : GAG ⟨tried to ~ the press⟩

mV *abbr* millivolt

MV *abbr* motor vessel

MVP *abbr* most valuable player

MW *abbr* megawatt

my \ˈmī\ *adj* **1** : of or relating to me or myself **2** — used interjectionally esp. to express surprise

my·col·o·gy \mī-ˈkä-lə-jē\ *n* : a branch of biology dealing with fungi — **my·co·log·i·cal** \ˌmī-kə-ˈlä-ji-kəl\ *adj* — **my·col·o·gist** \mī-ˈkä-lə-jist\ *n*

my·elo·ma \ˌmī-ə-ˈlō-mə\ *n, pl* **-mas** *or* **-ma·ta** \-mə-tə\ : a primary tumor of the bone marrow

my·nah *or* **my·na** \ˈmī-nə\ *n* : any of several Asian starlings; *esp* : a dark brown slightly crested bird sometimes taught to mimic speech

my·o·pia \mī-ˈō-pē-ə\ *n* : a condition in which visual images come to a focus in front of the retina resulting esp. in defective vision of distant objects — **my·o·pic** \-ˈō-pik, -ˈä-\ *adj* — **my·o·pi·cal·ly** \-pi-k(ə-)lē\ *adv*

[1]**myr·i·ad** \ˈmir-ē-əd\ *n* [Gk *myriad-, myrias,* fr. *myrioi* countless, ten thousand] : an indefinitely large number

[2]**myriad** *adj* : consisting of a very great but indefinite number

myr·mi·don \ˈmər-mə-ˌdän\ *n* : a loyal follower; *esp* : one who executes orders without protest or pity

myrrh \ˈmər\ *n* : a fragrant aromatic plant gum used in perfumes and formerly for incense

myr·tle \ˈmər-t^{ə}l\ *n* : an evergreen shrub of southern Europe with shiny leaves, fragrant flowers, and black berries; *also* : PERIWINKLE

my·self \mī-ˈself, mə-\ *pron* : I, ME — used reflexively, for emphasis, or in absolute constructions ⟨I hurt ~⟩ ⟨I ~ did it⟩ ⟨~ busy, I sent him instead⟩

mys·tery \ˈmis-tə-rē\ *n, pl* **-ter·ies** **1** : a religious truth known by revelation alone **2** : something not understood or beyond understanding **3** : enigmatic quality or character **4** : a work of fiction dealing with the solution of a mysterious crime — **mys·te·ri·ous** \mis-ˈtir-ē-əs\ *adj* — **mys·te·ri·ous·ly** *adv* — **mys·te·ri·ous·ness** *n*

[1]**mys·tic** \ˈmis-tik\ *adj* **1** : of or relating to mystics or mysticism **2** : MYSTERIOUS; *also* : MYSTIFYING

[2]**mystic** *n* : a person who follows, advocates, or experiences mysticism

mys·ti·cal \ˈmis-ti-kəl\ *adj* **1** : SPIRITUAL, SYMBOLIC **2** : of or relating to an intimate knowledge of or direct communion with God (as through contemplation or visions)

mys·ti·cism \ˈmis-tə-ˌsi-zəm\ *n* : the belief that direct knowledge of God or ultimate reality is attainable through immediate intuition or insight

mys·ti·fy \ˈmis-tə-ˌfī\ *vb* **-fied; -fy·ing** **1** : to perplex the mind of **2** : to make mysterious — **mys·ti·fi·ca·tion** \ˌmis-tə-fə-ˈkā-shən\ *n*

mys·tique \mi-ˈstēk\ *n* [F] **1** : an air or attitude of mystery and reverence developing around something or someone **2** : the special esoteric skill essential in a calling or activity

myth \ˈmith\ *n* **1** : a usu. legendary narrative that presents part of the beliefs of a people or explains a practice or natural phenomenon **2** : an imaginary or unverifiable person or thing — **myth·i·cal** \ˈmi-thi-kəl\ *or* **myth·ic** \-thik\ *adj*

my·thol·o·gy \mi-ˈthä-lə-jē\ *n, pl* **-gies** : a body of myths and esp. of those dealing with the gods and heroes of a people — **myth·o·log·i·cal** \ˌmi-thə-ˈlä-ji-kəl\ *adj* — **my·thol·o·gist** \mi-ˈthä-lə-jist\ *n* — **my·thol·o·gize** \-ˌjīz\ *vb*

N

[1]**n** \ˈen\ *n, pl* **n's** *or* **ns** \ˈenz\ *often cap* **1** : the 14th letter of the English alphabet **2** : an unspecified quantity

[2]**n** *abbr, often cap* **1** net **2** neuter **3** noon **4** normal **5** north; northern **6** note **7** noun **8** number

N *symbol* nitrogen

-n — see -EN

Na *symbol* [NL *natrium*] sodium

NA *abbr* **1** no account **2** North America **3** not applicable **4** not available

NAACP \ˌen-ˌdə-bəl-ˌā-ˌsē-ˈpē, ˌen-ˌā-ˌā-ˌsē-\ *abbr* National Association for the Advancement of Colored People

nab \ˈnab\ *vb* **nabbed; nab·bing** : SEIZE; *esp* : ARREST

NAB *abbr* New American Bible

na·bob \ˈnā-ˌbäb\ *n* [Hindi *navāb* & Urdu *nawāb,* provincial governor (in the Mogul empire), fr. Ar *nuwwāb,* pl. of *nā'ib* governor] : a person of great wealth or prominence

na·celle \nə-ˈsel\ *n* : an enclosure (as for an engine) on an aircraft

na·cho \ˈnä-chō\ *n, pl* **nachos** [AmerSp] : a tortilla chip topped with melted cheese and often additional savory toppings

na·cre \ˈnā-kər\ *n* : MOTHER-OF-PEARL — **na·cre·ous** \ˈnā-krē-əs\ *adj*

na·dir \ˈnā-ˌdir, -dər\ *n* [ME, fr. MF, fr. Ar *naẓhīr* opposite] **1** : the point of the celestial sphere that is directly opposite the zenith and directly beneath the observer **2** : the lowest point

[1]**nag** \ˈnag\ *n* : HORSE; *esp* : an old or decrepit horse

[2]**nag** *vb* **nagged; nag·ging** **1** : to find fault incessantly : COMPLAIN **2** : to irritate by constant scolding or urging **3** : to be a continuing source of annoyance ⟨a *nagging* backache⟩

[3]**nag** *n* : one who nags habitually

Nah *abbr* Nahum

Na·huatl \ˈnä-ˌwä-tᵊl\ *n* : a group of languages that includes the speech of several peoples (as the Aztecs) of central and southern Mexico

Na·hum \ˈnā-həm, -əm\ *n* — see BIBLE table

NAIA *abbr* National Association of Intercollegiate Athletes

na·iad \ˈnā-əd, ˈnī-, -ˌad\ *n, pl* **naiads** *or* **na·ia·des** \-ə-ˌdēz\ **1** : one of the nymphs in ancient mythology living in lakes, rivers, springs, and fountains **2** : an aquatic young of some insects (as a dragonfly)

[1]**na·ïf** *or* **na·if** \nä-ˈēf\ *adj* : NAIVE

[2]**naïf** *or* **naif** *n* : a naive person

[1]**nail** \ˈnāl\ *n* **1** : a horny sheath protecting the end of each finger and toe in humans and related primates **2** : a slender pointed fastener with a head designed to be pounded in

[2]**nail** *vb* : to fasten with or as if with a nail — **nail·er** *n*

nail down *vb* : to settle or establish clearly and unmistakably ⟨*nailed down* the victory⟩

nain·sook \ˈnān-ˌsu̇k\ *n* : a soft lightweight muslin

nai·ra \ˈnī-rə\ *n* — see MONEY table

na·ive *or* **na·ïve** \nä-ˈēv\ *adj* **na·iv·er; -est** [F *naïve,* fem. of *naïf,* fr. OF, inborn, natural, fr. L *nativus* native] **1** : marked by unaffected simplicity : ARTLESS, INGENUOUS **2** : CREDULOUS ♦ ***Synonyms*** NATURAL, INNOCENT, SIMPLE, UNAFFECTED, UNSOPHISTICATED, UNSTUDIED — **na·ive·ly** *adv* — **na·ive·ness** *n*

na·ive·te *or* **na·ïve·té** *also* **na·ive·té** \ˌnä-ˌē-və-ˈtā, nä-ˈē-və-ˌtā\ *n* **1** : a naive remark or action **2** : the quality or state of being naive

na·ive·ty *also* **na·ïve·ty** \nä-ˈē-və-tē\ *n, pl* **-ties** : NAÏVETÉ

na·ked \ˈnā-kəd\ *adj* **1** : having no

clothes on : NUDE **2** : UNSHEATHED ⟨a ~ sword⟩ **3** : lacking a usual or natural covering (as of foliage or feathers) **4** : PLAIN, UNADORNED ⟨the ~ truth⟩ **5** : not aided by artificial means ⟨seen by the ~ eye⟩ — **na·ked·ly** *adv* — **na·ked·ness** *n*

nak·fa \ˈnäk-ˌfä\ *n, pl* **nakfa** — see MONEY table

nam·by–pam·by \ˌnam-bē-ˈpam-bē\ *adj* **1** : INSIPID **2** : WEAK, INDECISIVE ♦ ***Synonyms*** BLAND, FLAT, INANE, JEJUNE, VAPID, WISHY-WASHY

[1]**name** \ˈnām\ *n* **1** : a word or words by which a person or thing is known **2** : a disparaging epithet ⟨call him ~*s*⟩ **3** : REPUTATION; *esp* : distinguished reputation ⟨made a ~ for herself⟩ **4** : FAMILY, CLAN ⟨was a disgrace to their ~⟩ **5** : appearance as opposed to reality ⟨a friend in ~ only⟩

[2]**name** *vb* **named; nam·ing** **1** : to give a name to : CALL **2** : to mention or identify by name **3** : NOMINATE, APPOINT **4** : to decide on : CHOOSE ⟨*named* the wedding date⟩ **5** : to mention explicitly : SPECIFY ⟨~ a price⟩ — **name·able** *adj*

[3]**name** *adj* **1** : of, relating to, or bearing a name ⟨~ tag⟩ **2** : having an established reputation ⟨~ brands⟩

name day *n* : the church feast day of the saint after whom one is named

name·less \ˈnām-ləs\ *adj* **1** : having no name **2** : not marked with a name ⟨a ~ grave⟩ **3** : not known by name ⟨a ~ hero⟩ **4** : too distressing to be described ⟨~ fears⟩ — **name·less·ly** *adv*

name·ly \-lē\ *adv* : that is to say : AS ⟨the cat family, ~, lions, tigers, and similar animals⟩

name·plate \-ˌplāt\ *n* : a plate or plaque bearing a name (as of a resident)

name·sake \-ˌsāk\ *n* : one that has the same name as another; *esp* : one named after another

nan·keen \nan-ˈkēn\ *n* : a durable brownish yellow cotton fabric orig. woven by hand in China

nan·ny *also* **nan·nie** \ˈna-nē\ *n, pl* **-nies** : a child's nurse or caregiver

nan·ny goat \ˈna-nē-\ *n* : a female domestic goat

nano·me·ter \ˈna-nə-ˌmē-tər\ *n* : one billionth of a meter

nano·scale \-ˌskāl\ *adj* : having dimensions measured in nanometers

nano·sec·ond \-ˌse-kənd\ *n* : one billionth of a second

nano·tech \ˈna-nō-ˌtek\ *n* : NANOTECHNOLOGY

nano·tech·nol·o·gy \ˌna-nō-tek-ˈnä-lə-jē\ *n* : the manipulation of materials on an atomic or molecular scale esp. to build microscopic objects or devices

nano·tube \ˈna-nō-ˌtüb\ *n* : a microscope tube (as of carbon) whose diameter is measured in nanometers

[1]**nap** \ˈnap\ *vb* **napped; nap·ping** **1** : to sleep briefly esp. during the day : DOZE **2** : to be off guard ⟨was caught *napping*⟩

[2]**nap** *n* : a short sleep esp. during the day

[3]**nap** *n* : a soft downy fibrous surface (as on yarn and cloth) — **nap·less** *adj* — **napped** \ˈnapt\ *adj*

na·palm \ˈnā-ˌpälm, -ˌpäm\ *n* [*na*phthalene + *palm*itate, salt of a fatty acid] **1** : a thickener used in jelling gasoline (as for incendiary bombs) **2** : fuel jelled with napalm

nape \ˈnāp, ˈnap\ *n* : the back of the neck

na·pery \ˈnā-pə-rē\ *n* : household linen esp. for the table

naph·tha \ˈnaf-thə, ˈnap-\ *n* : any of various liquid hydrocarbon mixtures used chiefly as solvents

naph·tha·lene \-ˌlēn\ *n* : a crystalline substance used esp. in organic synthesis and as a moth repellent

nap·kin \ˈnap-kən\ *n* **1** : a piece of material (as cloth) used at table to wipe the lips or fingers and protect the clothes **2** : a small cloth or towel

na·po·leon \nə-ˈpōl-yən, -ˈpō-lē-ən\ *n* : an oblong pastry with a filling of cream, custard, or jelly

Na·po·le·on·ic \nə-ˌpō-lē-ˈä-nik\ *adj* : of, relating to, or characteristic of Napoleon I or his family

narc *also* **nark** \ˈnärk\ *n, slang* : a person (as a government agent) who investigates narcotics violations

nar·cis·sism \ˈnär-sə-ˌsi-zəm\ *n* [G *Narzissismus,* fr. *Narziss* Narcissus, beautiful youth of Greek mythology who fell in love with his own image] **1** : undue dwelling on one's own self or attainments **2** : love of or sexual desire for one's own body — **nar·cis·sist** \-sist\ *n or adj* — **nar·cis·sis·tic** \ˌnär-sə-ˈsis-tik\ *adj*

nar·cis·sus \när-ˈsi-səs\ *n, pl* **nar·cis·si** \-ˌsī, -ˌsē\ *or* **nar·cis·sus·es** *or* **narcissus** : DAFFODIL; *esp* : one with short-tubed flowers usu. borne separately

nar·co·lep·sy \ˈnär-kə-ˌlep-sē\ *n, pl* **-sies** : a condition characterized by brief attacks of deep sleep — **nar·co·lep·tic** \ˌnär-kə-ˈlep-tik\ *adj or n*

nar·co·sis \när-ˈkō-səs\ *n, pl* **-co·ses** \-ˌsēz\ : a state of stupor, unconsciousness, or arrested activity produced by the influence of chemicals (as narcotics)

nar·co–ter·ror·ism \ˈnär-kō-ˈter-ər-ˌi-zəm\ *n* : terrorism financed by profits from illegal drug trafficking

nar·cot·ic \när-ˈkä-tik\ *n* [ME *narkotik,* fr. MF *narcotique,* fr. *narcotique,* adj., fr. ML *narcoticus,* fr. Gk *narkōtikos,* fr. *narkoun* to benumb, fr. *narkē* numbness] **1** : a drug (as opium) that dulls the senses, relieves pain, and induces sleep **2** : an illegal drug (as marijuana or LSD) — **narcotic** *adj*

nar·co·tize \ˈnär-kə-ˌtīz\ *vb* **-tized; -tiz·ing** **1** : to treat with or subject to a narcotic; *also* : to put into a state of narcosis **2** : to soothe to unconsciousness or unawareness

nard \ˈnärd\ *n* : a fragrant ointment of the ancients

na·res \ˈner-(ˌ)ēz\ *n pl* [L] : the pair of openings of the nose

Nar·ra·gan·sett \ˌna-rə-ˈgan-sət\ *n, pl* **-sett** *or* **-setts** **1** : a member of an Algonquian-speaking Indigenous people of Rhode Island **2** : the Algonquian language of the Narragansett people

nar·rate \ˈner-ˌāt\ *vb* **nar·rat·ed; nar·rat·ing** : to recite the details of (as a story) : RELATE, TELL — **nar·ra·tion** \na-ˈrā-shən\ *n* — **nar·ra·tor** \ˈner-ˌā-tər\ *n*

nar·ra·tive \ˈner-ə-tiv\ *n* **1** : something that is narrated : STORY **2** : the art or practice of narrating

[1]**nar·row** \ˈner-ō\ *adj* **1** : of slender or less than standard width **2** : limited in size or scope : RESTRICTED **3** : not liberal in views : PREJUDICED **4** : interpreted or interpreting strictly **5** : CLOSE ⟨won by a ~ margin⟩; *also* : barely successful ⟨a ~ escape⟩ — **nar·row·ly** *adv* — **nar·row·ness** *n*

[2]**narrow** *vb* : to lessen in width or extent

[3]**narrow** *n* : a narrow passage : STRAIT — usu. used in pl.

nar·row–mind·ed \ˌner-ō-ˈmīn-dəd\ *adj* : not liberal or broad-minded ♦ ***Synonyms*** ILLIBERAL, BIGOTED, HIDEBOUND, INTOLERANT

nar·whal \ˈnär-ˌhwäl, ˈnär-wəl\ *n* : an arctic sea mammal about 20 feet (6 meters) long that is related to the dolphins and in the male has a long twisted ivory tusk

NAS *abbr* naval air station

NASA \ˈna-sə\ *abbr* National Aeronautics and Space Administration

[1]**na·sal** \ˈnā-zəl\ *n* **1** : a nasal part **2** : a nasal consonant or vowel

[2]**nasal** *adj* **1** : of or relating to the nose **2** : uttered through the nose — **na·sal·ly** *adv*

na·sal·ize \ˈnā-zə-ˌlīz\ *vb* **-ized; -iz·ing** : to make nasal or pronounce as a nasal sound

na·scent \ˈna-sᵊnt, ˈnā-\ *adj* : coming into existence : beginning to grow or develop — **na·scence** \-sᵊns\ *n*

nas·tur·tium \nə-ˈstər-shəm, na-\ *n* : either of two widely cultivated watery-stemmed herbs with showy spurred flowers and pungent edible seeds

nas·ty \ˈnas-tē\ *adj* **nas·ti·er; -est** **1** : FILTHY **2** : INDECENT, OBSCENE **3** : HARMFUL, DANGEROUS ⟨took a ~ fall⟩ **4** : DISAGREEABLE ⟨~ weather⟩ **5** : MEAN, ILL-NATURED ⟨a ~ temper⟩ **6** : DIFFICULT, VEXATIOUS ⟨a ~ problem⟩ **7** : UNFAIR, DIRTY ⟨a ~ trick⟩ — **nas·ti·ly** \ˈnas-tə-lē\ *adv* — **nas·ti·ness** \-tē-nəs\ *n*

nat *abbr* **1** national **2** native **3** natural

na·tal \ˈnā-tᵊl\ *adj* **1** : NATIVE **2** : of, relating to, or present at birth

na·ta·to·ri·um \ˌnā-tə-ˈtȯr-ē-əm, ˌna-\ *n* : a swimming pool esp. indoors

na·tion \ˈnā-shən\ *n* [ME *nacioun,* fr. AF *naciun* fr. L *nation-, natio* birth, race, nation, fr. *nasci* to be born] **1** : NATIONALITY 5; *also* : a politically organized nationality **2** : a community of people composed of one or more nationalities with its own territory and government **3** : the territory of a nation **4** : a tribe or federation of tribes (as of Indigenous peoples) — **na·tion·hood** *n*

[1]**na·tion·al** \ˈna-shə-nəl\ *adj* **1** : of or relating to a nation **2** : comprising or characteristic of a nationality **3** : FEDERAL 3 — **na·tion·al·ly** *adv*

[2]**national** *n* **1** : one who owes allegiance to a nation **2** : a competition that is national in scope — usu. used in pl.

national guard *n* **1** : a military force serving as a national constabulary and defense force **2** *cap N&G* : a militia force recruited by each state of the U.S., equipped by the federal government, and jointly maintained subject to the call of either — **national guardsman** *n, often cap*

na·tion·al·ise *chiefly Brit var of* NATIONALIZE

na·tion·al·ism \ˈna-shə-nə-ˌli-zəm\ *n* : devotion to national interests, unity, and independence

na·tion·al·ist \-list\ *n* **1** : an advocate of or believer in nationalism **2** : a member of a political party or group advocating national independence or strong national government — **nationalist** *adj* — **na·tion·al·is·tic** \ˌna-shə-nə-ˈlis-tik\ *adj*

na·tion·al·i·ty \ˌna-shə-ˈna-lə-tē\ *n, pl* **-ties** **1** : national character **2** : a legal relationship involving allegiance of an individual and protection on the part of the state **3** : membership in a particular nation **4** : political independence or existence as a separate nation **5** : a people having a common origin, tradition, and language and capable of forming a state **6** : an ethnic group within a larger unit (as a nation)

na·tion·al·ize \ˈna-shə-nə-ˌlīz\ *vb* **-ized; -iz·ing** **1** : to make national : make a nation of **2** : to remove from private ownership and place under government control — **na·tion·al·i·za·tion** \ˌna-shə-nə-lə-ˈzā-shən\ *n*

national monument *n* : a place of historic, scenic, or scientific interest set aside for preservation usu. by presidential proclamation

national park *n* : an area of special scenic, historical, or scientific importance set aside and maintained by a national government esp. for recreation or study

national seashore *n* : a recreational area adjacent to a seacoast and maintained by the federal government

na·tion·wide \ˌnā-shən-ˈwīd\ *adj* : extending throughout a nation

[1]**na·tive** \ˈnā-tiv\ *adj* **1** : INBORN, NATURAL ⟨~ talents⟩ **2** : born in a particular place or country **3** : belonging to a person because of the place or circumstances of birth ⟨her ~ language⟩ **4** : grown, produced, or originating in a particular place : INDIGENOUS **5** *cap* : of, relating to, or being a member of an Indigenous people of No. or So. America ♦ ***Synonyms*** ABORIGINAL, AUTOCHTHONOUS, ENDEMIC

[2]**native** *n* : one that is native; *esp* : a person who belongs to a particular place by birth

Native American *n* : a member of any of the Indigenous peoples of the western hemisphere; *esp* : an Indigenous person of No. America and esp. the U.S.

na·tiv·ism \ˈnā-ti-ˌvi-zəm\ *n* **1** : a policy of favoring native inhabitants over immigrants **2** : the revival or perpetuation of a native culture esp. in opposition to acculturation

na·tiv·i·ty \nə-ˈti-və-tē, nā-\ *n, pl* **-ties** **1** : the process or circumstances of being born : BIRTH **2** *cap* : the birth of Christ

natl *abbr* national

NATO \ˈnā-(ˌ)tō\ *abbr* North Atlantic Treaty Organization

nat·ty \ˈna-tē\ *adj* **nat·ti·er; -est** : trimly neat and tidy : SMART — **nat·ti·ly** \-tə-lē\ *adv* — **nat·ti·ness** \-tē-nəs\ *n*

[1]**nat·u·ral** \ˈna-chə-rəl\ *adj* **1** : determined by nature : INBORN, INNATE ⟨~ ability⟩ **2** : BORN ⟨a ~ fool⟩ **3** : begotten as distinguished from adopted ⟨their ~ son⟩ **4** : born to parents not married to each other **5** : HUMAN **6** : of or relating to nature **7** : not artificial **8** : being simple and sincere : not affected **9** : LIFELIKE **10** : being neither sharp nor flat ♦ ***Synonyms*** INGENUOUS, NAIVE, UNSOPHISTICATED, ARTLESS, GUILELESS — **nat·u·ral·ness** *n*

[2]**natural** *n* **1** : IDIOT **2** : a character ♮ placed on a line or space of the musical staff to nullify the effect of a preceding sharp or flat **3** : one obviously suitable for a purpose **4** : AFRO

natural-born *adj* **1** : born with the legal status of citizen or subject **2** : able to do something well immediately or from the first time

natural childbirth *n* : a system of managing childbirth in which the mother prepares to remain conscious and assist in delivery with little or no use of drugs

natural gas *n* : a combustible gaseous mixture of hydrocarbons coming from the earth's crust and used chiefly as a fuel and raw material

natural history *n* **1** : a treatise on some aspect of nature **2** : the study of natural objects esp. from an amateur or popular point of view

nat·u·ral·ise *Brit var of* NATURALIZE

nat·u·ral·ism \ˈna-chə-rə-ˌli-zəm\ *n* **1** : action or thought based only on natural desires and instincts **2** : a doctrine that denies a supernatural explanation of the origin or development of the universe and holds that scientific laws account for all of nature **3** : realism in art and literature — **nat·u·ral·is·tic** \ˌna-chə-rə-ˈlis-tik\ *adj*

nat·u·ral·ist \-list\ *n* **1** : one that advocates or practices naturalism **2** : a student of animals or plants esp. in the field

nat·u·ral·ize \-ˌlīz\ *vb* **-ized; -iz·ing** **1** : to confer the rights of a citizen on **2** : to become or cause to become established as if native ⟨~ new forage crops⟩ — **nat·u·ral·i·za·tion** \ˌna-chə-rə-lə-ˈzā-shən\ *n*

nat·u·ral·ly \ˈna-chə-rə-lē, ˈnach-rə-\ *adv* **1** : by nature : by natural character or ability **2** : as might be expected **3** : without artificial aid; *also* : without affectation **4** : REALISTICALLY

natural science *n* : a science (as physics, chemistry, or biology) that deals with matter, energy, and their interrelations and transformations or with objectively measurable phenomena — **natural scientist** *n*

natural selection *n* : the natural process that results in the survival of individuals or groups best adjusted to their environment

na·ture \ˈnā-chər\ *n* [ME, fr. MF, fr. L *natura,* fr. *natus,* pp. of *nasci* to be born] **1** : the inherent quality or basic constitution of a person or thing; *also* : DISPOSITION, TEMPERAMENT **2** : KIND, SORT ⟨letters of a personal ~⟩ **3** : the physical universe **4** : one's natural instincts or way of life ⟨quirks of human ~⟩; *also* : primitive state ⟨a return to ~⟩ **5** : natural scenery or environment

[1]**naught** *also* **nought** \ˈnȯt, ˈnät\ *pron* : NOTHING ⟨efforts came to ~⟩

[2]**naught** *also* **nought** *n* **1** : NOTHINGNESS, NONEXISTENCE **2** : the arithmetical symbol 0 : ZERO

naugh·ty \ˈnȯ-tē, ˈnä-\ *adj* **naugh·ti·er; -est** **1** : guilty of disobedience or misbehavior **2** : lacking in taste or propriety ⟨~ jokes⟩ — **naugh·ti·ly** \-tə-lē\ *adv* — **naugh·ti·ness** \-tē-nəs\ *n*

nau·sea \ˈnȯ-zē-ə, -sē-; ˈnȯ-zhə, -shə\ *n* [L, seasickness, nausea, fr. Gk *nautia, nausia,* fr. *nautēs* sailor] **1** : sickness of the stomach with a desire to vomit **2** : extreme disgust

nau·se·ate \ˈnȯ-zē-ˌāt, -sē-, -zhē-, -shē-\ *vb* **-at·ed; -at·ing** : to affect or become affected with nausea — **nau·se·at·ing·ly** *adv*

nau·seous \ˈnȯ-shəs, -zē-əs\ *adj* **1** : causing nausea or disgust **2** : affected with nausea or disgust

naut *abbr* nautical

nau·ti·cal \ˈnȯ-ti-kəl\ *adj* : of or relating to sailors, navigation, or ships ⟨~ terms⟩ — **nau·ti·cal·ly** \-k(ə-)lē\ *adv*

nautical mile *n* : a unit of distance equal to about 6080 feet (1852 meters)

nau·ti·lus \ˈnȯ-tə-ləs\ *n, pl* **-lus·es** *or* **-li** \ˌlī, -ˌlē\ : any of a genus of sea mollusks related to the octopuses but having a spiral chambered shell

nav *abbr* **1** naval **2** navigable; navigation

Na·va·jo *also* **Na·va·ho** \ˈna-və-ˌhō, ˈnä-\ *n, pl* **-jo** *or* **-jos** *also* **-ho** *or* **-hos** : a member of an Indigenous people of northern New Mexico, Arizona, and south Utah; *also* : their language

na·val \ˈnā-vəl\ *adj* : of, relating to, or possessing a navy ⟨a ~ power⟩

naval stores *n pl* : products (as pitch, turpentine, or rosin) obtained from resinous conifers (as pines)

nave \ˈnāv\ *n* [ML *navis,* fr. L, ship] : the central part of a church running lengthwise

na·vel \ˈnā-vəl\ *n* : a depression in the middle of the abdomen that marks the point of attachment of fetus and mother

navel–gaz·ing \ˈnā-vəl-ˈgā-ziŋ\ *n* : useless or excessive self-contemplation
navel orange *n* : a seedless orange having a pit at the blossom end where the fruit encloses a small secondary fruit
nav·i·ga·ble \ˈna-vi-gə-bəl\ *adj* **1** : capable of being navigated ⟨a ~ river⟩ **2** : capable of being steered — **nav·i·ga·bil·i·ty** \ˌna-vi-gə-ˈbi-lə-tē\ *n*
nav·i·gate \ˈna-və-ˌgāt\ *vb* **-gat·ed; -gat·ing** **1** : to sail on or through ⟨~ the Atlantic Ocean⟩ **2** : to steer or direct the course of a ship or aircraft **3** : MOVE; *esp* : WALK ⟨could hardly ~⟩ — **nav·i·ga·tion** \ˌna-və-ˈgā-shən\ *n* — **nav·i·ga·tor** \ˈna-və-ˌgā-tər\ *n*
na·vy \ˈnā-vē\ *n, pl* **navies** **1** : FLEET; *also* : the warships belonging to a nation **2** *often cap* : a nation's organization for naval warfare
navy yard *n* : a yard where naval vessels are built or repaired
[1]**nay** \ˈnā\ *adv* : NO
[2]**nay** *n* : a negative vote; *also* : a person casting such a vote
[3]**nay** *conj* : not merely this but also : not only so but ⟨he was happy, ~, ecstatic⟩
nay·say·er \ˈnā-ˌsā-ər\ *n* : one who denies, refuses, or opposes something
Na·zi \ˈnät-sē, ˈnat-\ *n* [G, fr. *Nationalsozialist,* lit., national socialist] : a member of a German fascist party controlling Germany from 1933 to 1945 under Adolf Hitler — **Nazi** *adj* — **Na·zism** \ˈnät-ˌsi-zəm, ˈnat-\ *also* **Na·zi·ism** \-sē-ˌi-zəm\ *n*
Nb *symbol* niobium
NB *abbr* **1** New Brunswick **2** nota bene
NBA *abbr* **1** National Basketball Association **2** National Boxing Association
NBC *abbr* National Broadcasting Company
NBS *abbr* National Bureau of Standards
NC *abbr* **1** no charge **2** North Carolina
NCAA *abbr* National Collegiate Athletic Association
NCO \ˌen-ˌsē-ˈō\ *n* : NONCOMMISSIONED OFFICER
nd *abbr* no date
Nd *symbol* neodymium
ND *abbr* North Dakota
N Dak *abbr* North Dakota
Ne *symbol* neon
NE *abbr* **1** Nebraska **2** New England **3** northeast
Ne·an·der·thal \nē-ˈan-dər-ˌthȯl, nā-ˈän-dər-ˌtäl\ *n* **1** *or* **Ne·an·der·tal** \-ˌtäl\ : an extinct Old World hominid that lived from about 30,000 to 200,000 years ago **2** : a person who resembles or suggests a caveman — **Neanderthal** *or* **Neandertal** *adj*
neap tide \ˈnēp-\ *n* : a tide of minimum range occurring at the first and third quarters of the moon
[1]**near** \ˈnir\ *adv* **1** : at, within, or to a short distance or time **2** : ALMOST ⟨was ~ dead⟩
[2]**near** *prep* : close to
[3]**near** *adj* **1** : closely related or associated; *also* : INTIMATE **2** : not far away; *also* : being the closer or left-hand member of a pair ⟨the ~ side of the lake⟩ **3** : barely avoided ⟨a ~ accident⟩ **4** : DIRECT, SHORT ⟨by the *~est* route⟩ **5** : STINGY **6** : not real but very like ⟨~ silk⟩ — **near·ly** *adv* — **near·ness** *n*
[4]**near** *vb* : APPROACH
near beer *n* : any of various malt liquors low in alcohol
near·by \nir-ˈbī, ˈnir-ˌbī\ *adv or adj* : close at hand
near·sight·ed \ˈnir-ˈsī-təd\ *adj* : able to see near things more clearly than distant ones : MYOPIC — **near·sight·ed·ly** *adv* — **near·sight·ed·ness** *n*
neat \ˈnēt\ *adj* [MF *net,* fr. L *nitidus* bright, neat, fr. *nitēre* to shine] **1** : being orderly and clean **2** : not mixed or diluted ⟨~ brandy⟩ **3** : marked by tasteful simplicity **4** : PRECISE, SYSTEMATIC **5** : SKILLFUL, ADROIT **6** : FINE, ADMIRABLE ♦ ***Synonyms*** SHIPSHAPE, TIDY, TRIG, TRIM — **neat** *adv* — **neat·ly** *adv* — **neat·ness** *n*
neath \ˈnēth\ *prep, dial* : BENEATH
neat·nik \ˈnēt-nik\ *n* : a person who is compulsively neat
neb \ˈneb\ *n* **1** : the beak of a bird or tortoise; *also* : NOSE, SNOUT **2** : NIB
Neb *or* **Nebr** *abbr* Nebraska
NEB *abbr* New English Bible
neb·u·la \ˈne-byə-lə\ *n, pl* **-lae** \-ˌlē, -ˌlī\ *also* **-las** [NL, fr. L, mist, cloud] **1** : any of numerous clouds of gas or dust in interstellar space **2** : GALAXY — **neb·u·lar** \-lər\ *adj*
neb·u·liz·er \ˈne-byə-ˌlī-zər\ *n* : ATOMIZER
neb·u·lous \ˈne-byə-ləs\ *adj* **1** : of or relating to a nebula **2** : HAZY, INDISTINCT
[1]**nec·es·sary** \ˈne-sə-ˌser-ē\ *adj* **1** : INEVITABLE, INESCAPABLE; *also* : CERTAIN **2** : PREDETERMINED **3** : COMPULSORY **4** : positively needed : INDISPENSABLE ⟨~ supplies⟩ ♦ ***Synonyms*** IMPERATIVE, NECESSITOUS, ESSENTIAL — **nec·es·sar·i·ly** \ˌne-sə-ˈser-ə-lē\ *adv*
[2]**necessary** *n, pl* **-sar·ies** : an indispensable item
ne·ces·si·tate \ni-ˈse-sə-ˌtāt\ *vb* **-tat·ed; -tat·ing** : to make necessary
ne·ces·si·tous \ni-ˈse-sə-təs\ *adj* **1** : NEEDY, IMPOVERISHED **2** : URGENT **3** : NECESSARY ⟨~ bargaining⟩
ne·ces·si·ty \ni-ˈse-sə-tē\ *n, pl* **-ties** **1** : conditions that cannot be changed **2** : WANT, POVERTY **3** : something that is necessary ⟨water is a ~⟩ **4** : very great need
[1]**neck** \ˈnek\ *n* **1** : the part of the body connecting the head and the trunk **2** : the part of a garment covering or near to the neck **3** : a relatively narrow part suggestive of a neck ⟨~ of a bottle⟩ ⟨~ of land⟩ **4** : a narrow margin esp. of victory ⟨won by a ~⟩ — **necked** \ˈnekt\ *adj*
[2]**neck** *vb* : to kiss and caress amorously
neck and neck *adv or adj* : very close (as in a race)
neck·er·chief \ˈne-kər-chəf, -ˌchēf\ *n, pl* **-chiefs** \-chəfs, -ˌchēfs\ *also* **-chieves**

\-ˌchēvz\ : a square of cloth worn folded about the neck like a scarf

neck·lace \ˈne-kləs\ *n* : an ornament worn around the neck

neck·line \ˈnek-ˌlīn\ *n* : the outline of the neck opening of a garment

neck·tie \-ˌtī\ *n* : a strip of cloth worn around the neck and tied in front

ne·crol·o·gy \nə-ˈkrä-lə-jē\ *n, pl* **-gies 1** : OBITUARY **2** : a list of the recently dead

nec·ro·man·cy \ˈne-krə-ˌman-sē\ *n* **1** : the art or practice of conjuring up the spirits of the dead for purposes of magically revealing the future **2** : MAGIC, SORCERY — **nec·ro·man·cer** \-sər\ *n*

ne·crop·o·lis \nə-ˈkrä-pə-ləs, ne-\ *n, pl* **-lis·es** *or* **-les** \-ˌlēz\ *or* **-leis** \-ˌlās\ *or* **-li** \-ˌlī, -ˌlē\ [LL, fr. Gk *nekropolis,* fr. *nekros* dead body + *polis* city] : CEMETERY; *esp* : a large elaborate cemetery of an ancient city

nec·rop·sy \ˈne-ˌkräp-sē\ *n, pl* **-sies** : AUTOPSY; *esp* : an autopsy performed on an animal

ne·cro·sis \nə-ˈkrō-səs, ne-\ *n, pl* **ne·cro·ses** \-ˌsēz\ : usu. local death of body tissue — **ne·crot·ic** \-ˈkrä-tik\ *adj*

nec·tar \ˈnek-tər\ *n* **1** : the drink of the Greek and Roman gods; *also* : any delicious drink **2** : a sweet plant secretion that is the raw material of honey

nec·tar·ine \ˌnek-tə-ˈrēn\ *n* : a smooth-skinned peach

née *or* **nee** \ˈnā\ *adj* [F, lit., born] — used to identify a woman by her maiden family name

[1]**need** \ˈnēd\ *n* **1** : OBLIGATION ⟨no ~ to hurry⟩ **2** : a lack of something requisite, desirable, or useful **3** : a condition requiring supply or relief ⟨when the ~ arises⟩ **4** : POVERTY ♦ ***Synonyms*** NECESSITY, EXIGENCY

[2]**need** *vb* **1** : to be in want **2** : to have cause or occasion for : REQUIRE ⟨he ~*s* advice⟩ **3** : to be under obligation or necessity ⟨we ~ to know the truth⟩

need·ful \ˈnēd-fəl\ *adj* : NECESSARY, REQUISITE ⟨bought only what was ~⟩

[1]**nee·dle** \ˈnē-dᵊl\ *n* **1** : a slender pointed usu. steel implement used in sewing **2** : a slender rod (as for knitting, controlling a small opening, or transmitting vibrations to or from a recording) ⟨a phonograph ~⟩ **3** : a slender hollow instrument by which material is introduced into or withdrawn from the body **4** : a slender indicator on a dial **5** : a needle-shaped leaf (as of a pine)

[2]**needle** *vb* **nee·dled; nee·dling** : PROD, GOAD; *esp* : to incite to action by repeated gibes ⟨*needled* him into a fight⟩

nee·dle–nose pliers \ˈnē-dᵊl-ˌnōz-\ *n pl* : pliers with long slender jaws for grasping small or thin objects

nee·dle·point \ˈnē-dᵊl-ˌpȯint\ *n* **1** : lace worked with a needle over a paper pattern **2** : embroidery done on canvas across counted threads — **needlepoint** *adj*

need·less \ˈnēd-ləs\ *adj* : UNNECESSARY ⟨~ waste⟩ — **need·less·ly** *adv* — **need·less·ness** *n*

nee·dle·wom·an \ˈnē-dᵊl-ˌwu̇-mən\ *n* : a woman who does needlework; *esp* : SEAMSTRESS

nee·dle·work \-ˌwərk\ *n* : work done with a needle; *esp* : work (as embroidery) other than plain sewing

needs \ˈnēdz\ *adv* : of necessity : NECESSARILY ⟨must ~ be recognized⟩

needy \ˈnē-dē\ *adj* **need·i·er; -est 1** : being in want : POVERTY-STRICKEN **2** : wanting affection or attention

ne'er \ˈner\ *adv* : NEVER

ne'er–do–well \ˈner-du̇-ˌwel\ *n* : an idle worthless person — **ne'er–do–well** *adj*

ne·far·i·ous \ni-ˈfer-ē-əs\ *adj* [L *nefarius,* fr. *nefas* crime, fr. *ne-* not + *fas* right, divine law] : very wicked : EVIL ♦ ***Synonyms*** BAD, IMMORAL, INIQUITOUS, SINFUL, VICIOUS — **ne·far·i·ous·ly** *adv*

neg *abbr* negative

ne·gate \ni-ˈgāt\ *vb* **ne·gat·ed; ne·gat·ing 1** : to deny the existence or truth of **2** : to cause to be ineffective or invalid : NULLIFY ⟨~ a contract⟩

ne·ga·tion \ni-ˈgā-shən\ *n* **1** : the action or operation of negating or making negative **2** : a negative doctrine or statement

[1]**neg·a·tive** \ˈne-gə-tiv\ *adj* **1** : marked by denial, prohibition, or refusal ⟨a ~ reply⟩ **2** : not positive or constructive; *esp* : not affirming the presence of what is sought or suspected to be present ⟨test results were ~⟩ **3** : less than zero ⟨a ~ number⟩ **4** : being, relating to, or charged with electricity of which the electron is the elementary unit **5** : having the light and dark parts opposite to what they were in the original photographic subject — **neg·a·tive·ly** *adv* — **neg·a·tive·ness** *n* — **neg·a·tiv·i·ty** \ˌne-gə-ˈti-və-tē\ *n*

[2]**negative** *n* **1** : a negative word or statement **2** : a negative vote or reply; *also* : REFUSAL **3** : something that is the opposite or negation of something else **4** : a negative number **5** : the side that votes or argues for the opposition (as in a debate) **6** : a negative photographic image on transparent material

[3]**negative** *vb* **-tived; -tiv·ing 1** : to refuse to accept or approve **2** : to vote against **3** : DISPROVE

negative income tax *n* : a system of federal subsidy payments to families with incomes below a stipulated level

neg·a·tiv·ism \ˈne-gə-ti-ˌvi-zəm\ *n* : an attitude of skepticism and denial of nearly everything affirmed by others

[1]**ne·glect** \ni-ˈglekt\ *vb* [L *neglectus,* pp. of *neglegere, neclegere,* fr. *nec-* not + *legere* to gather] **1** : DISREGARD **2** : to leave undone or unattended to esp. through carelessness ♦ ***Synonyms*** OMIT, IGNORE, OVERLOOK, SLIGHT, FORGET, MISS

[2]**neglect** *n* **1** : an act or instance of neglecting something **2** : the condition of being neglected — **ne·glect·ful** *adj*

neg·li·gee *also* **neg·li·gé** \ˌne-glə-ˈzhā\ *n* : a woman's long flowing dressing gown

neg·li·gent \ˈne-gli-jənt\ *adj* : marked by neglect ♦ ***Synonyms*** NEGLECTFUL, RE-

MISS, DELINQUENT, DERELICT — **neg·li·gence** \-jəns\ *n* — **neg·li·gent·ly** *adv*

neg·li·gi·ble \ˈne-gli-jə-bəl\ *adj* : so small as to be neglected or disregarded

ne·go·tiant \ni-ˈgō-shē-ənt\ *n* : NEGOTIATOR

ne·go·ti·ate \ni-ˈgō-shē-ˌāt\ *vb* **-at·ed; -at·ing** [L *negotiari* to carry on business, fr. *negotium* business, fr. *neg-* not + *otium* leisure] **1** : to confer with another so as to arrive at the settlement of some matter; *also* : to arrange for or bring about by such conferences ⟨~ a treaty⟩ **2** : to transfer to another by delivery or endorsement in return for equivalent value ⟨~ a check⟩ **3** : to get through, around, or over successfully ⟨~ a turn⟩ — **ne·go·tia·ble** \-shə-bəl, -shē-ə-\ *adj* — **ne·go·ti·a·tion** \ni-ˌgō-sē-ˈā-shən, -shē-\ *n* — **ne·go·ti·a·tor** \-ˈgō-shē-ˌā-tər\ *n*

ne·gri·tude \ˈne-grə-ˌtüd, -ˌtyüd, ˈnē-\ *n* : a consciousness of and pride in one's African heritage

Ne·gro \ˈnē-grō\ *n, pl* **Negroes** [Sp or Pg, fr. *negro* black] **1** *dated, often offensive* : a person of Black African ancestry **2** *dated, often offensive* : a member of a group of people formerly considered to constitute a race of humans having African ancestry and classified according to physical traits (such as dark skin pigmentation) — **Negro** *adj, dated, often offensive* — **ne·groid** \ˈnē-ˌgrȯid\ *n or adj, often cap, dated, often offensive*

Neh *abbr* Nehemiah

Ne·he·mi·ah \ˌnē-ə-ˈmī-ə\ *n* — see BIBLE table

neigh \ˈnā\ *n* : a loud prolonged cry of a horse — **neigh** *vb*

[1]**neigh·bor** \ˈnā-bər\ *n* **1** : one living or located near another **2** : FELLOW MAN

[2]**neighbor** *vb* : to be next to or near to : border on

neigh·bor·hood \ˈnā-bər-ˌhu̇d\ *n* **1** : NEARNESS **2** : a place or region near : VICINITY; *also* : a number or amount near ⟨costs in the ~ of $10⟩ **3** : the people living near one another **4** : a section lived in by neighbors and usu. having distinguishing characteristics

neigh·bor·ly \-lē\ *adj* : befitting congenial neighbors; *esp* : FRIENDLY ⟨a ~ welcome⟩ — **neigh·bor·li·ness** *n*

neigh·bour *chiefly Brit var of* NEIGHBOR

[1]**nei·ther** \ˈnē-t͟hər, ˈnī-\ *conj* **1** : not either ⟨~ good nor bad⟩ **2** : NOR ⟨~ did I⟩

[2]**neither** *pron* : neither one : not the one and not the other ⟨~ of the two⟩

[3]**neither** *adj* : not either ⟨~ hand⟩

nel·son \ˈnel-sən\ *n* : a wrestling hold in which one applies leverage against an opponent's arm, neck, and head

nem·a·tode \ˈne-mə-ˌtōd\ *n* : any of a phylum of elongated cylindrical worms parasitic in animals or plants or free-living in soil or water

nem·e·sis \ˈne-mə-səs\ *n, pl* **-e·ses** \-ˌsēz\ [L *Nemesis,* goddess of divine retribution, fr. Gk] **1** : one that inflicts retribution or vengeance **2** : a formidable and usu. victorious rival **3** : an act or effect of retribution; *also* : CURSE

neo·clas·sic \ˌnē-ō-ˈkla-sik\ *or* **neo·clas·si·cal** \-si-kəl\ *adj* : of or relating to a revival or adaptation of the classical style esp. in literature, art, or music

neo·co·lo·nial·ism \ˌnē-ō-kə-ˈlō-nē-ə-ˌli-zəm\ *n* : the economic and political policies by which a nation indirectly maintains or extends its influence over other areas or peoples — **neo·co·lo·nial** *adj* — **neo·co·lo·nial·ist** \-list\ *n or adj*

neo·con \ˈnē-ō-ˌkän\ *n* : NEOCONSERVATIVE

neo·con·ser·va·tive \-kən-ˈsər-və-tiv\ *n* : a former liberal espousing political conservatism — **neo·con·ser·va·tism** \-və-ˌti-zəm\ *n* — **neoconservative** *adj*

neo·dym·i·um \ˌnē-ō-ˈdi-mē-əm\ *n* : a silver-white to yellow metallic chemical element

neo–im·pres·sion·ism \ˌnē-ō-im-ˈpre-shə-ˌni-zəm\ *n, often cap N&I* : a late 19th century French art movement that attempted to make impressionism more precise and to use a pointillist painting technique

Neo·lith·ic \ˌnē-ə-ˈli-thik\ *adj* : of or relating to the latest period of the Stone Age characterized by polished stone implements

ne·ol·o·gism \nē-ˈä-lə-ˌji-zəm\ *n* : a new word or expression

ne·on \ˈnē-ˌän\ *n* [Gk, neut. of *neos* new] **1** : a gaseous colorless chemical element used in electric lamps and lasers **2** : a lamp in which a discharge through neon gives a reddish glow — **neon** *adj*

neo·na·tal \ˌnē-ō-ˈnā-tᵊl\ *adj* : of, relating to, or affecting the newborn ⟨a ~ infection⟩ — **neo·na·tal·ly** *adv*

ne·o·nate \ˈnē-ə-ˌnāt\ *n* : a newborn child

neo–pa·gan \ˌnē-ō-ˈpā-gən\ *n* : a person who practices a contemporary form of paganism — **neo–pagan** *adj*

neo·phyte \ˈnē-ə-ˌfīt\ *n* **1** : a new convert : PROSELYTE **2** : NOVICE **3** : BEGINNER
♦ ***Synonyms*** APPRENTICE, FRESHMAN, NEWCOMER, ROOKIE, TENDERFOOT, TYRO

neo·plasm \ˈnē-ə-ˌpla-zəm\ *n* : a new growth of tissue serving no useful purpose in the body : TUMOR — **neo·plas·tic** \ˌnē-ə-ˈplas-tik\ *adj*

neo·prene \ˈnē-ə-ˌprēn\ *n* : a synthetic rubber used esp. for special-purpose clothing (as wet suits)

neo·trop·i·cal \ˌnē-ō-ˈträ-pi-kəl\ *adj, often cap* : of or relating to a zoogeographic region of America that extends south from the central plateau of Mexico

ne·pen·the \nə-ˈpen-thē\ *n* **1** : a potion used by the ancients to dull pain and sorrow **2** : something capable of making one forget grief or suffering

neph·ew \ˈne-fyü, *chiefly Brit* -vyü\ *n* [ME *nevew,* fr. AF *neveu,* fr. LL *nepot-, nepos,* fr. L, grandson, descendant] : a son of one's brother, sister, brother-in-law, or sister-in-law

ne·phrit·ic \ni-ˈfri-tik\ *adj* **1** : RENAL **2** : of, relating to, or affected with nephritis

ne·phri·tis \ni-ˈfrī-təs\ *n, pl* **ne·phrit-**

i·des \-ˈfri-tə-ˌdēz\ : kidney inflammation

ne plus ul·tra \ˌnē-ˌpləs-ˈəl-trə\ *n* [NL, (go) no more beyond] : the highest point capable of being attained

nep·o·tism \ˈne-pə-ˌti-zəm\ *n* [F *népotisme,* fr. It *nepotismo,* fr. *nepote* nephew, fr. LL *nepot-, nepos*] : favoritism shown to a relative (as in the granting of jobs)

Nep·tune \ˈnep-ˌtün, -ˌtyün\ *n* : the planet 8th in order from the sun — **Nep·tu·ni·an** \nep-ˈtü-nē-ən, -ˈtyü-\ *adj*

nep·tu·ni·um \nep-ˈtü-nē-əm, -ˈtyü-\ *n* : a short-lived radioactive element

nerd \ˈnərd\ *n* **1** : a person devoted to intellectual or technical pursuits **2** : an unstylish or socially awkward person — **nerdy** *adj*

Ne·re·id \ˈnir-ē-əd\ *n* : a sea nymph in Greek mythology

[1]**nerve** \ˈnərv\ *n* **1** : SINEW, TENDON ⟨strain every ~⟩ **2** : any of the strands of nervous tissue that carry nerve impulses between the brain and spinal cord and every part of the body **3** : power of endurance or control : FORTITUDE; *also* : BOLDNESS, DARING **4** *pl* : NERVOUSNESS **5** : a vein of a leaf or insect wing — **nerved** \ˈnərvd\ *adj* — **nerve·less** *adj*

[2]**nerve** *vb* **nerved; nerv·ing** : to give strength or courage to

nerve cell *n* : NEURON; *also* : CELL BODY

nerve gas *n* : a chemical weapon damaging esp. to the nervous and respiratory systems

nerve impulse *n* : a physical and chemical change that moves along a process of a neuron after stimulation and carries a record of sensation or an instruction to act

nerve–rack·ing *or* **nerve–wrack·ing** \ˈnərv-ˌra-kiŋ\ *adj* : extremely trying on the nerves ⟨~ noise⟩

ner·vous \ˈnər-vəs\ *adj* **1** : FORCIBLE, SPIRITED **2** : of, relating to, or made up of neurons or nerves **3** : easily excited or annoyed : JUMPY ⟨a ~ horse⟩ **4** : TIMID, APPREHENSIVE ⟨a ~ smile⟩ **5** : UNEASY, UNSTEADY — **ner·vous·ly** *adv* — **ner·vous·ness** *n*

nervous breakdown *n* : an attack of mental or emotional disorder of sufficient severity to be incapacitating esp. when requiring hospitalization

nervous system *n* : a bodily system that in vertebrates is made up of the brain and spinal cord, nerves, ganglia, and parts of the sense organs and that receives and interprets stimuli and transmits nerve impulses

nervy \ˈnər-vē\ *adj* **nerv·i·er; -est** **1** : showing calm courage ⟨a ~ performer⟩ **2** : marked by impudence or presumption ⟨a ~ salesperson⟩ **3** : EXCITABLE, NERVOUS ♦ ***Synonyms*** BOLD, CHEEKY, FORWARD, FRESH, IMPUDENT, SAUCY

-ness \nəs\ *n suffix* : state : condition : quality : degree ⟨good*ness*⟩

[1]**nest** \ˈnest\ *n* **1** : the shelter prepared by a bird for its eggs and young **2** : a place where eggs (as of insects or fish) are laid and hatched **3** : a place of rest, retreat, or lodging **4** : DEN, HANGOUT ⟨a ~ of thieves⟩ **5** : the occupants of a nest **6** : a series of objects (as bowls or tables) fitting inside or under one another

[2]**nest** *vb* **1** : to build or occupy a nest **2** : to fit compactly together or within one another

nest egg *n* : a fund of money accumulated as a reserve

nes·tle \ˈne-səl\ *vb* **nes·tled; nes·tling** **1** : to settle snugly or comfortably **2** : to press closely and affectionately : CUDDLE **3** : to settle, shelter, or house as if in a nest

nest·ling \ˈnest-liŋ\ *n* : a bird too young to leave its nest

[1]**net** \ˈnet\ *n* **1** : a meshed fabric twisted, knotted, or woven together at regular intervals **2** : a device made all or partly of net and used esp. to catch birds, fish, or insects **3** : something made of net used esp. for protecting, confining, carrying, or dividing ⟨a tennis ~⟩ **4** : SNARE, TRAP **5** *often cap* : INTERNET

[2]**net** *vb* **net·ted; net·ting** **1** : to cover or enclose with or as if with a net **2** : to catch in or as if in a net

[3]**net** *adj* : free from all charges or deductions ⟨~ profit⟩ ⟨~ weight⟩

[4]**net** *vb* **net·ted; net·ting** : to gain or produce as profit : CLEAR, YIELD ⟨his business *netted* $50,000 a year⟩

[5]**net** *n* : a net amount, profit, weight, or price

Neth *abbr* Netherlands

neth·er \ˈne-t͟hər\ *adj* : situated down or below ⟨the ~ regions of the earth⟩

neth·er·most \-ˌmōst\ *adj* : LOWEST

neth·er·world \-ˌwərld\ *n* **1** : the world of the dead **2** : UNDERWORLD

net·i·quette \ˈne-ti-kət, -ˌket\ *n* : etiquette governing communication on the Internet

net·roots \ˈnet-ˌrüts, -ˌru̇ts\ *n pl* : the grass-roots political activists who communicate via the Internet

nett *Brit var of* NET

net·ting *n* **1** : NETWORK **2** : the act or process of making a net or network

[1]**net·tle** \ˈne-tᵊl\ *n* : any of a genus of coarse herbs with stinging hairs

[2]**nettle** *vb* **net·tled; net·tling** : PROVOKE, VEX, IRRITATE

net·tle·some \ˈne-tᵊl-səm\ *adj* : causing vexation : IRRITATING

net·work \ˈnet-ˌwərk\ *n* **1** : NET **2** : a system of elements (as lines or channels) that cross in the manner of the threads in a net **3** : a group or system of related or connected parts; *esp* : a chain of radio or television stations **4** : a system of computers that are connected (as by telephone wires)

net·work·ing \ˈnet-ˌwər-kiŋ\ *n* **1** : the exchange of information or services among individuals, groups, or institutions **2** : the cultivation of productive business relationships

neu·ral \ˈnu̇r-əl, ˈnyu̇r-\ *adj* : of, relating

to, or involving a nerve or the nervous system ⟨~ pathways⟩

neu·ral·gia \nu̇-ˈral-jə, nyu̇-\ *n* : acute pain that follows the course of a nerve — **neu·ral·gic** \-jik\ *adj*

neur·as·the·nia \ˌnu̇r-əs-ˈthē-nē-ə, ˌnyu̇r-\ *n* [NL, fr. Gk *neuron* nerve + *asthenia* weakness, fr. *asthenēs* weak, fr. *a-* not + *sthenos* strength] : a psychological disorder marked esp. by fatiguing easily, lack of motivation, feelings of inadequacy, and psychosomatic symptoms — **neur·as·then·ic** \-the-nik, -ˈthē-\ *adj or n*

neu·ri·tis \nu̇-ˈrī-təs, nyu̇-\ *n, pl* **-rit·i·des** \-ˈri-tə-ˌdēz\ *or* **-ri·tis·es** : inflammation of a nerve — **neu·rit·ic** \-ˈri-tik\ *adj or n*

neu·ro·bi·ol·o·gy \ˌnu̇r-ō-bī-ˈä-lə-jē\ *n* : a branch of biology that deals with the nervous system — **neu·ro·bi·o·log·i·cal** \-ˌbī-ə-ˈlä-ji-kəl\ *adj* — **neu·ro·bi·ol·o·gist** \-bī-ˈä-lə-jist\ *n*

neu·rol·o·gy \nu̇-ˈrä-lə-jē, nyu̇-\ *n* : the scientific study of the nervous system — **neu·ro·log·i·cal** \ˌnu̇r-ə-ˈlä-ji-kəl, ˌnyu̇r-\ *or* **neu·ro·log·ic** \-jik\ *adj* — **neu·ro·log·i·cal·ly** \-ji-k(ə-)lē\ *adv* — **neu·rol·o·gist** \nu̇-ˈrä-lə-jist, nyu̇-\ *n*

neu·ro·mus·cu·lar \ˌnu̇r-ō-ˈməs-kyə-lər, ˌnyu̇r-\ *adj* : of, relating to, or affecting nerves and muscles ⟨a ~ disease⟩

neu·ron \ˈnü-ˌrän, ˈnyü-\ *n* : a cell with specialized processes that is the fundamental functional unit of nervous tissue — **neu·ro·nal** \ˈnu̇r-ə-nᵊl, ˈnyu̇r-\ *adj*

neu·rone \-ˌrōn\ *chiefly Brit var of* NEURON

neu·ro·sci·ence \ˌnu̇r-ō-ˈsī-əns, ˌnyu̇r-\ *n* : a branch of the life sciences that deals with the anatomy, physiology, biochemistry, or molecular biology of nerves and nervous tissue and esp. with their relation to behavior and learning — **neu·ro·sci·en·tist** \-ən-tist\ *n*

neu·ro·sis \nu̇-ˈrō-səs, nyu̇-\ *n, pl* **-ro·ses** \-ˌsēz\ : a mental and emotional disorder that is less serious than a psychosis, is not characterized by disturbance of the use of language, and is accompanied by various bodily and mental disturbances (as visceral symptoms, anxieties, or phobias)

neu·ro·sur·gery \ˌnu̇r-ō-ˈsər-jə-rē, ˌnyu̇r-\ *n* : surgery of nervous structures (as nerves, the brain, or the spinal cord) — **neu·ro·sur·geon** \-ˈsər-jən\ *n*

[1]**neu·rot·ic** \nu̇-ˈrä-tik, nyu̇-\ *adj* : of, relating to, being, or affected with a neurosis — **neu·rot·i·cal·ly** \-ti-k(ə-)lē\ *adv*

[2]**neurotic** *n* : an emotionally unstable or neurotic person

neu·ro·trans·mit·ter \ˌnu̇r-ō-trans-ˈmi-tər, ˌnyu̇r-, -tranz-\ *n* : a substance (as acetylcholine) that transmits nerve impulses across a synapse

neut *abbr* neuter

[1]**neu·ter** \ˈnü-tər, ˈnyü-\ *adj* [ME *neutre,* fr. MF & L; MF *neutre,* fr. L *neuter,* lit., neither, fr. *ne-* not + *uter* which of two] **1** : of, relating to, or constituting the gender that includes most words or grammatical forms referring to things classed as neither masculine nor feminine **2** : lacking or having imperfectly developed sex organs

[2]**neuter** *n* **1** : a noun, pronoun, adjective, or inflectional form or class of the neuter gender; *also* : the neuter gender **2** : WORKER 2; *also* : a spayed or castrated animal

[3]**neuter** *vb* **1** : CASTRATE, SPAY **2** : to remove the force or effectiveness of

[1]**neu·tral** \ˈnü-trəl, ˈnyü-\ *n* **1** : one that is neutral **2** : a neutral color **3** : a position of disengagement (as of gears)

[2]**neutral** *adj* **1** : not favoring either side in a quarrel, contest, or war **2** : of or relating to a neutral state or power **3** : MIDDLING, INDIFFERENT **4** : having no hue : GRAY; *also* : not decided in color **5** : neither acid nor basic ⟨a ~ solution⟩ **6** : not electrically charged

neu·tral·ise *Brit var of* NEUTRALIZE

neu·tral·ism \ˈnü-trə-ˌli-zəm, ˈnyü-\ *n* : a policy or the advocacy of neutrality esp. in international affairs

neu·tral·i·ty \nü-ˈtra-lə-tē, nyü-\ *n* : the quality or state of being neutral; *esp* : refusal to take part in a war between other powers

neu·tral·ize \ˈnü-trə-ˌlīz, ˈnyü-\ *vb* **-ized; -iz·ing** : to make neutral; *esp* : COUNTERACT — **neu·tral·i·za·tion** \ˌnü-trə-lə-ˈzā-shən, ˌnyü-\ *n*

neu·tri·no \nü-ˈtrē-nō, nyü-\ *n, pl* **-nos** : an uncharged elementary particle held to be massless or very light

neu·tron \ˈnü-ˌträn, ˈnyü-\ *n* : an uncharged atomic particle that is nearly equal in mass to the proton

neutron bomb *n* : a nuclear bomb designed to produce lethal neutrons but less blast and fire damage than other nuclear bombs

neutron star *n* : a dense celestial object that results from the collapse of a large star

Nev *abbr* Nevada

nev·er \ˈne-vər\ *adv* **1** : not ever **2** : not in any degree, way, or condition

nev·er·more \ˌne-vər-ˈmōr\ *adv* : never again

nev·er–nev·er land \ˌne-vər-ˈne-vər-\ *n* : an ideal or imaginary place

nev·er·the·less \ˌne-vər-t͟hə-ˈles\ *adv* : in spite of that : HOWEVER

ne·vus \ˈnē-vəs\ *n, pl* **ne·vi** \-ˌvī\ : a usu. pigmented area on the skin : MOLE

[1]**new** \ˈnü, ˈnyü\ *adj* **1** : not old : RECENT, MODERN **2** : recently discovered, recognized, or learned about ⟨~ drugs⟩ **3** : UNFAMILIAR ⟨visit ~ places⟩ **4** : different from the former **5** : not accustomed ⟨~ to the work⟩ **6** : beginning as a repetition of a previous act or thing ⟨a ~ year⟩ **7** : REFRESHED, REGENERATED ⟨awoke a ~ person⟩ **8** : being in a position or place for the first time ⟨a ~ member⟩ **9** *cap* : having been in use after medieval times : MODERN ⟨*New* Latin⟩ ♦ ***Synonyms*** NOVEL, NEWFANGLED, FRESH — **new·ish** *adj* — **new·ness** *n*

[2]**new** *adv* : NEWLY ⟨*new*-mown hay⟩

[1]**new age** *adj, often cap N&A* **1** : of, relat-

ing to, or being New Age **2 :** CONTEMPORARY, MODERN

[2]**new age** *n* **1** *cap* : a group of late 20th century social attitudes adapted from a variety of ancient and modern beliefs relating to spirituality, right living, and health **2 :** a soft soothing form of instrumental music

new•bie \ˈnu̇-bē, ˈnyü-\ *n* : a newcomer esp. to cyberspace

new blood *n* : persons accepted into a group or organization and expected to provide fresh ideas and vitality

[1]**new•born** \-ˌbȯrn\ *adj* **1 :** recently born **2 :** born anew ⟨~ hope⟩

[2]**newborn** *n, pl* **newborn** *or* **newborns :** a newborn individual

new•com•er \-ˌkə-mər\ *n* **1 :** one recently arrived **2 :** BEGINNER

New Deal *n* : the legislative and administrative program of President F. D. Roosevelt to promote economic recovery and social reform during the 1930s — **New Dealer** *n*

new•el \ˈnü-əl, ˈnyü-\ *n* : a post about which the steps of a circular staircase wind; *also* : a post at the foot of a stairway or one at a landing

new•fan•gled \ˈnü-ˈfaŋ-gəld, ˈnyü-\ *adj* **1 :** attracted to novelty **2 :** of the newest style : NOVEL ⟨~ gadgets⟩

new–fash•ioned \-ˈfa-shənd\ *adj* **1 :** made in a new fashion or form ⟨~ automobiles⟩ **2 :** UP-TO-DATE

new•found \-ˈfau̇nd\ *adj* : newly found

New Left *n* : a radical political movement originating in the 1960s

new•ly \ˈnü-lē, ˈnyü-\ *adv* **1 :** LATELY, RECENTLY ⟨a ~ married couple⟩ **2 :** ANEW, AFRESH ⟨~ painted⟩

new•ly•wed \-ˌwed\ *n* : a person recently married

new moon *n* : the phase of the moon with its dark side toward the earth; *also* : the thin crescent moon seen for a few days after the new moon phase

news \ˈnüz, ˈnyüz\ *n* **1 :** a report of recent events : TIDINGS **2 :** material reported in a newspaper or news periodical or on a newscast

news•boy \ˈnüz-ˌbȯi, ˈnyüz-\ *n* : one who delivers or sells newspapers

news•cast \-ˌkast\ *n* : a radio or television broadcast of news — **news•cast•er** \-ˌkas-tər\ *n*

news•group \-ˌgrüp\ : an Internet bulletin devoted to a certain topic

news•let•ter \ˈnüz-ˌle-tər, ˈnyüz-\ *n* : a small newspaper containing news or information of interest chiefly to a special group

news•mag•a•zine \-ˌma-gə-ˌzēn\ *n* : a usu. weekly magazine devoted chiefly to summarizing and analyzing news

news•man \-mən, -ˌman\ *n* : a person who gathers, reports, or comments on the news : REPORTER

news•pa•per \-ˌpā-pər\ *n* : a paper that is published at regular intervals and contains news, articles of opinion, features, and advertising

news•pa•per•man \-ˌpā-pər-ˌman\ *n* : a person who owns or is employed by a newspaper

news•print \-ˌprint\ *n* : paper made chiefly from wood pulp and used mostly for newspapers

news•reel \-ˌrēl\ *n* : a short motion picture portraying current events

news•stand \-ˌstand\ *n* : a place where newspapers and periodicals are sold

news•week•ly \-ˌwēk-lē\ *n* : a weekly newspaper or newsmagazine

news•wire \-ˌwī(-ə)r\ *n* : WIRE SERVICE

news•wom•an \-ˌwu̇-mən\ *n* : a woman who is a reporter

news•wor•thy \-ˌwər-t͟hē\ *adj* : sufficiently interesting to the general public to warrant reporting

newsy \ˈnü-zē, ˈnyü-\ *adj* **news•i•er; -est :** filled with news; *esp* : TALKATIVE

newt \ˈnüt, ˈnyüt\ *n* [ME, alter. (from misdivision of *an ewte*) of *ewt, evete,* fr. OE *efete*] : any of various small chiefly aquatic salamanders

New Testament *n* : the second of the two chief divisions of the Christian Bible — see BIBLE table

new•ton \ˈnü-tᵊn, ˈnyü-\ *n* : the unit of force in the metric system equal to the force required to impart an acceleration of one meter per second per second to a mass of one kilogram

new wave *n, often cap N&W* : the latest and esp. the most outrageous style — **new–wave** *adj*

New World *n* : the western hemisphere ⟨colonized the *New World*⟩ — **new–world** *adj*

New Year *n* **1 :** NEW YEAR'S DAY; *also* : the first days of the year **2 :** ROSH HASHANAH

New Year's Day *n* : January 1 observed as a legal holiday

[1]**next** \ˈnekst\ *adj* : immediately preceding or following : NEAREST

[2]**next** *prep* : nearest or adjacent to

[3]**next** *adv* **1 :** in the time, place, or order nearest or immediately succeeding **2 :** on the first occasion to come

[4]**next** *n* : one that is next

nex•us \ˈnek-səs\ *n, pl* **nex•us•es** \-sə-səz\ *or* **nex•us** \-səs, -ˌsüs\ : CONNECTION, LINK

Nez Percé \ˈnez-ˈpərs\ *n* : a member of an Indigenous people originally of Idaho, Washington, and Oregon; *also* : the language of the Nez Percé

NF *abbr* Newfoundland

NFC *abbr* National Football Conference

NFL *abbr* National Football League

Nfld *abbr* Newfoundland

NFT \ˌen-ˌef-ˈtē\ *n* : NON-FUNGIBLE TOKEN

NG *abbr* **1** National Guard **2** no good

ngul•trum \eŋ-ˈgu̇l-trəm\ *n* — see MONEY table

ngwee \eŋ-ˈgwē\ *n, pl* **ngwee** — see *kwacha* at MONEY table

Nh *symbol* nihonium

NH *abbr* New Hampshire

NHL *abbr* National Hockey League

Ni *symbol* nickel
ni·a·cin \ˈnī-ə-sən\ *n* : an organic acid of the vitamin B complex found widely in plants and animals and used esp. against pellagra
nib \ˈnib\ *n* : POINT; *esp* : a pen point
[1]**nib·ble** \ˈni-bəl\ *vb* **nib·bled; nib·bling** : to bite gently or bit by bit
[2]**nibble** *n* : a small or cautious bite
ni·cad \ˈnī-ˌkad\ *n* : a rechargeable dry cell that has a nickel cathode and a cadmium anode
nice \ˈnīs\ *adj* **nic·er; nic·est** [ME, foolish, wanton, fr. AF, silly, simple, fr. L *nescius* ignorant, fr. *nescire* to not know] **1** : FASTIDIOUS, DISCRIMINATING **2** : marked by delicate discrimination or treatment ⟨a ~ distinction between those two words⟩ **3** : PLEASING, AGREEABLE ⟨had a ~ time⟩; *also* : well-executed ⟨a ~ shot⟩ **4** : WELL-BRED ⟨~ people⟩ **5** : VIRTUOUS, RESPECTABLE ♦ ***Synonyms*** CHOOSY, FINICKY, PARTICULAR, PERSNICKETY, PICKY — **nice·ly** *adv* — **nice·ness** *n*
nice–nel·ly \ˈnīs-ˈne-lē\ *adj, often cap 2d N* **1** : marked by euphemism **2** : PRUDISH ⟨his ~ sweetheart⟩ — **nice nelly** *n, often cap 2d N* — **nice–nel·ly·ism** \-ˌi-zəm\ *n, often cap 2d N*
nice·ty \ˈnī-sə-tē\ *n, pl* **-ties** **1** : a dainty, delicate, or elegant thing ⟨enjoy the *niceties* of life⟩ **2** : a fine point or distinction ⟨*niceties* of workmanship⟩ **3** : EXACTNESS, PRECISION, ACCURACY
niche \ˈnich\ *n* [F] **1** : a recess in a wall esp. for a statue **2** : a place, employment, or activity for which a person or thing is best fitted **3** : the living space or role of an organism in an ecological community esp. with regard to food consumption
[1]**nick** \ˈnik\ *n* **1** : a small notch, groove, or chip **2** : the final critical moment ⟨in the ~ of time⟩
[2]**nick** *vb* : NOTCH, CHIP
nick·el \ˈni-kəl\ *n* **1** : a hard silver-white metallic chemical element capable of a high polish and used in alloys **2** : the U.S. 5-cent piece made of copper and nickel; *also* : the Canadian 5-cent piece
nick·el·ode·on \ˌni-kə-ˈlō-dē-ən\ *n* **1** : an early movie theater to which admission cost five cents **2** : JUKEBOX
nick·er \ˈni-kər\ *vb* : NEIGH, WHINNY — **nicker** *n*
nick·name \ˈnik-ˌnām\ *n* [ME *nekename* additional name, alter. (from misdivision of *an ekename*) of *ekename,* fr. *eke* also + *name*] **1** : a usu. descriptive name given in addition to the one belonging to a person, place, or thing **2** : a familiar form of a proper name — **nickname** *vb*
nic·o·tine \ˈni-kə-ˌtēn\ *n* : a poisonous and addictive substance in tobacco that is used as an insecticide
nic·o·tin·ic acid \ˌni-kə-ˈtē-nik-, -ˈti-\ *n* : NIACIN
niece \ˈnēs\ *n* : a daughter of one's brother, sister, brother-in-law, or sister-in-law
nif·ty \ˈnif-tē\ *adj* **nif·ti·er; -est** : very good : very attractive
nig·gard \ˈni-gərd\ *n* : a stingy person : MISER — **nig·gard·li·ness** \-lē-nəs\ *n* — **nig·gard·ly** *adj or adv*
nig·gling \ˈni-gə-liŋ\ *adj* **1** : PETTY ⟨~ details⟩ **2** : bothersome in a petty way ♦ ***Synonyms*** INCONSEQUENTIAL, MEASLY, PICAYUNE, PIDDLING, TRIFLING, TRIVIAL
[1]**nigh** \ˈnī\ *adv* **1** : near in place, time, or relationship **2** : NEARLY, ALMOST
[2]**nigh** *adj* : CLOSE, NEAR
[3]**nigh** *prep* : NEAR
night \ˈnīt\ *n* **1** : the period between dusk and dawn **2** : the darkness of night **3** : a period of misery or unhappiness **4** : NIGHTFALL — **night** *adj*
night blindness *n* : reduced visual capacity in faint light (as at night)
night·cap \ˈnīt-ˌkap\ *n* **1** : a cloth cap worn with nightclothes **2** : a usu. alcoholic drink taken at bedtime
night·clothes \-ˌklōthz, -ˌklōz\ *n pl* : garments worn in bed
night·club \-ˌkləb\ *n* : a place open at night, usu. serving food and liquor, and having music for dancing or a show
night crawl·er \-ˌkrȯ-lər\ *n* : EARTHWORM; *esp* : a large earthworm found on the soil surface at night
night·dress \ˈnīt-ˌdres\ *n* : NIGHTGOWN
night·fall \-ˌfȯl\ *n* : the coming of night
night·gown \-ˌgau̇n\ *n* : a loose garment for wear in bed
night·hawk \-ˌhȯk\ *n* : any of a genus of American birds related to and resembling the whip-poor-will
night·in·gale \ˈnī-tᵊn-ˌgāl, ˈnī-tiŋ-\ *n* [ME, fr. OE *nihtegale,* fr. *niht* night + *galan* to sing] : any of several Old World thrushes noted for the sweet usu. nocturnal song of the male
night·life \ˈnīt-ˌlīf\ *n* : the activity of pleasure-seekers at night
night·ly \ˈnīt-lē\ *adj* **1** : happening, done, or produced by night or every night **2** : of or relating to the night or every night — **nightly** *adv*
night·mare \ˈnīt-ˌmer\ *n* **1** : a frightening dream **2** : a frightening or horrible experience — **nightmare** *adj* — **night·mar·ish** *adj*
night rider *n* : a member of a secret band who ride masked at night doing violence to punish or terrorize
night·shade \ˈnīt-ˌshād\ *n* : any of a large genus of herbs, shrubs, and trees that includes poisonous forms (as the belladonna), ornamentals (as the petunias), and important food plants (as the potato and eggplant)
night·shirt \-ˌshərt\ *n* : a nightgown resembling a shirt
night soil *n* : human feces used esp. for fertilizing the soil
night·stick \ˈnīt-ˌstik\ *n* : a police officer's club
night·time \-ˌtīm\ *n* : the time from dusk to dawn
night·walk·er \-ˌwȯ-kər\ *n* : a person who roves about at night esp. with criminal or immoral intent

ni·hil·ism \ˈnī-ə-ˌli-zəm, ˈnē-hə-\ *n* **1** : a viewpoint that traditional values and beliefs are unfounded and that existence is senseless and useless **2** : ANARCHISM — **ni·hil·ist** \-list\ *n or adj* — **ni·hil·is·tic** \ˌnī-ə-ˈlis-tik, ˌnē-hə-\ *adj*

ni·ho·ni·um \ni-ˈhō-nē-əm\ *n* : a short-lived artificially produced radioactive chemical element

nil \ˈnil\ *n* : ZERO, NOTHING

nim·ble \ˈnim-bəl\ *adj* **nim·bler; nim·blest** [ME *nimel,* fr. OE *numol* holding much, fr. *niman* to take] **1** : quick and light in motion : AGILE ⟨a ~ dancer⟩ **2** : quick in understanding and learning : CLEVER ⟨a ~ mind⟩ ♦ ***Synonyms*** ACTIVE, BRISK, SPRIGHTLY, SPRY, ZIPPY — **nim·ble·ness** *n* — **nim·bly** \-blē\ *adv*

nim·bus \ˈnim-bəs\ *n, pl* **nim·bi** \-ˌbī, -bē\ *or* **nim·bus·es** **1** : a figure (as a disk) in an art work suggesting radiant light about the head of a divinity, saint, or sovereign **2** : a rain cloud; *also* : THUNDERHEAD

NIMBY \ˈnim-bē\ *n* [*n*ot *i*n *m*y *b*ack*y*ard] : opposition to the placement of something undesirable (as a prison) in one's neighborhood

nim·rod \ˈnim-ˌräd\ *n* **1** : HUNTER **2** : IDIOT, JERK

nin·com·poop \ˈnin-kəm-ˌpüp\ *n, informal* : FOOL, SIMPLETON

nine \ˈnīn\ *n* **1** : one more than eight **2** : the 9th in a set or series **3** : something having nine units; *esp* : a baseball team — **nine** *adj or pron* — **ninth** \ˈnīnth\ *adj or adv or n* — **to the nines** **1** : to perfection **2** : in an elaborate manner ⟨dressed *to the nines*⟩

nine days' wonder *n* : something that creates a short-lived sensation

nine·pins \ˈnīn-ˌpinz\ *n* : a bowling game using nine pins arranged usu. in a diamond-shaped configuration

nine·teen \ˈnīn-ˈtēn\ *n* : one more than 18 — **nineteen** *adj or pron* — **nine·teenth** \-ˈtēnth\ *adj or n*

nine·ty \ˈnīn-tē\ *n, pl* **nineties** : nine times 10 — **nine·ti·eth** \-tē-əth\ *adj or n* — **ninety** *adj or pron*

nin·ja \ˈnin-jə, -(ˌ)jä\ *n, pl* **ninja** *or* **ninjas** [Jp] : a person trained in ancient Japanese martial arts and employed esp. for espionage and assassinations

nin·ny \ˈni-nē\ *n, pl* **ninnies** : FOOL

ni·o·bi·um \nī-ˈō-bē-əm\ *n* : a gray metallic chemical element used in alloys

[1]**nip** \ˈnip\ *vb* **nipped; nip·ping** **1** : to catch hold of and squeeze tightly between two surfaces, edges, or points **2** : [3]CLIP **3** : to destroy the growth, progress, or fulfillment of ⟨*nipped* in the bud⟩ **4** : to injure or make numb with cold : CHILL **5** : SNATCH, STEAL

[2]**nip** *n* **1** : a sharp stinging cold **2** : a biting or pungent flavor **3** : PINCH, BITE **4** : a small portion : BIT

[3]**nip** *n* : a small quantity of liquor : SIP

[4]**nip** *vb* **nipped; nip·ping** : to take liquor in nips : TIPPLE

nip and tuck *adj or adv* : so close that the lead shifts rapidly from one contestant to another

nip·per \ˈni-pər\ *n* **1** : one that nips **2** *pl* : PINCERS **3** : CHILD; *esp* : a small boy

nip·ple \ˈni-pəl\ *n* : the protuberance of a mammary gland through which milk is drawn off : TEAT; *also* : something resembling a nipple

nip·py \ˈni-pē\ *adj* **nip·pi·er; -est** **1** : PUNGENT, SHARP **2** : CHILLY

nir·va·na \nər-ˈvä-nə\ *n, often cap* [Skt *nirvāṇa,* lit., act of extinguishing, fr. *nis-* out + *vāti* it blows] **1** : the final state of bliss; *esp* : the supreme happiness that according to Buddhism comes through the extinction of desire and individual consciousness **2** : OBLIVION; *also* : PARADISE

ni·sei \nē-ˈsā, ˈnē-ˌsā\ *n, pl* **nisei** *often cap* : a son or daughter of immigrant Japanese parents who is born and educated in America

ni·si \ˈnī-ˌsī\ *adj* [L, unless, fr. *ne-* not + *si* if] : taking effect at a specified time unless previously modified or voided ⟨a divorce decree ~⟩

nit \ˈnit\ *n* **1** : the egg of a parasitic insect (as a louse); *also* : the young insect **2** : a minor shortcoming

nite *var of* NIGHT

ni·ter \ˈnī-tər\ *n* : POTASSIUM NITRATE

nit–pick·ing \ˈnit-ˌpi-kiŋ\ *n* : minute and usu. unjustified criticism — **nit·pick·er** *n*

[1]**ni·trate** \ˈnī-ˌtrāt, -trət\ *n* **1** : a salt or ester of nitric acid **2** : sodium nitrate or potassium nitrate used as a fertilizer

[2]**ni·trate** \-ˌtrāt\ *vb* **ni·trat·ed; ni·trat·ing** : to treat or combine with nitric acid or a nitrate — **ni·tra·tion** \nī-ˈtrā-shən\ *n*

ni·tre *chiefly Brit var of* NITER

ni·tric acid \ˈnī-trik-\ *n* : a corrosive liquid acid used esp. in making dyes, explosives, and fertilizers

ni·tri·fi·ca·tion \ˌnī-trə-fə-ˈkā-shən\ *n* : the oxidation (as by bacteria) of ammonium salts to nitrites and then to nitrates — **ni·tri·fy·ing** \ˈnī-trə-fī-iŋ\ *adj*

ni·trite \ˈnī-ˌtrīt\ *n* : a salt of nitrous acid

ni·tro \ˈnī-trō\ *n, pl* **nitros** : any of various nitrated products; *esp* : NITROGLYCERIN

ni·tro·gen \ˈnī-trə-jən\ *n* : a tasteless odorless gaseous chemical element constituting 78 percent of the atmosphere by volume — **ni·trog·e·nous** \nī-ˈträ-jə-nəs\ *adj*

nitrogen narcosis *n* : a state of euphoria and confusion caused by nitrogen forced into a diver's bloodstream from atmospheric air under pressure

ni·tro·glyc·er·in *or* **ni·tro·glyc·er·ine** \ˌnī-trə-ˈgli-sə-rən\ *n* : an oily explosive liquid used to make dynamite and in medicine to dilate blood vessels

ni·trous acid \ˈnī-trəs-\ *n* : an unstable nitrogen-containing acid known only in solution or in the form of its salts

nitrous oxide *n* : a colorless gas used esp. as an anesthetic in dentistry

nit·ty–grit·ty \ˈni-tē-ˌgri-tē, ˌni-tē-ˈgri-tē\ *n* : what is essential and basic : specific practical details

nit·wit \ˈnit-ˌwit\ *n* : a scatterbrained or stupid person

[1]nix \ˈniks\ *n* : NOTHING
[2]nix *vb* : VETO, REJECT
[3]nix *adv* : NO
NJ *abbr* New Jersey
NL *abbr* National League
NLRB *abbr* National Labor Relations Board
NM *abbr* **1** nautical mile **2** New Mexico
N Mex *abbr* New Mexico
NMI *abbr* no middle initial
NNE *abbr* north-northeast
NNW *abbr* north-northwest
[1]no \ˈnō\ *adv* **1** — used to express the negative of an alternative ⟨shall we continue or ~⟩ **2** : in no respect or degree ⟨he is ~ better than the others⟩ **3** : not so ⟨~, I'm not ready⟩ **4** — used with an adjective to imply a meaning opposite to the positive statement ⟨in ~ uncertain terms⟩ **5** — used to introduce a more emphatic or explicit statement ⟨has the right, ~, the duty to continue⟩ **6** — used as an interjection to express surprise or doubt ⟨~—you don't say⟩ **7** — used in combination with a verb to form a compound adjective ⟨*no*-bake pie⟩ **8** : in negation ⟨shook his head ~⟩
[2]no *adj* **1** : not any; *also* : hardly any **2** : not a ⟨she's ~ expert⟩
[3]no \ˈnō\ *n, pl* **noes** *or* **nos** \ˈnōz\ **1** : REFUSAL, DENIAL ⟨got a ~ in reply⟩ **2** : a negative vote or decision; *also, pl* : persons voting in the negative
[4]no *abbr* **1** north; northern **2** [L *numero*, abl. of *numerus*] number
[1]No *var of* NOH
[2]No *symbol* nobelium
No·bel·ist \nō-ˈbe-list\ *n* : a winner of a Nobel prize
no·bel·i·um \nō-ˈbe-lē-əm\ *n* : a radioactive metallic chemical element produced artificially
No·bel prize \nō-ˈbel-, ˈnō-ˌbel-\ *n* : any of various annual prizes (as in peace, literature, or medicine) established by the will of Alfred Nobel for the encouragement of persons who work for the interests of humanity
no·bil·i·ty \nō-ˈbi-lə-tē\ *n* **1** : the quality or state of being noble **2** : nobles considered as forming a class
[1]no·ble \ˈnō-bəl\ *adj* **no·bler; no·blest** [ME, fr. AF, fr. L *nobilis* well known, noble, fr. *noscere* to come to know] **1** : ILLUSTRIOUS; *also* : FAMOUS, NOTABLE **2** : of high birth, rank, or station : ARISTOCRATIC **3** : EXCELLENT **4** : STATELY, IMPOSING ⟨a ~ edifice⟩ **5** : of a superior nature ♦ ***Synonyms*** AUGUST, BARONIAL, GRAND, GRANDIOSE, MAGNIFICENT, MAJESTIC — **no·ble·ness** *n* — **no·bly** \-blē\ *adv*
[2]no·ble *n* : a person of noble rank or birth
no·ble·man \ˈnō-bəl-mən\ *n* : a member of the nobility : PEER
no·blesse oblige \nō-ˌbles-ə-ˈblēzh\ *n* [F, lit., nobility obligates] : the obligation of honorable, generous, and responsible behavior associated with high rank or birth
no·ble·wom·an \ˈnō-bəl-ˌwu̇-mən\ *n* : a woman of noble rank : PEERESS
[1]no·body \ˈnō-ˌbä-dē, -bə-\ *pron* : no person
[2]nobody *n, pl* **no·bod·ies** : a person of no influence or importance
no–brain·er \ˈnō-ˈbrā-nər\ *n* : something that requires a minimum of thought
noc·tur·nal \näk-ˈtər-nᵊl\ *adj* **1** : of, relating to, or occurring in the night **2** : active at night ⟨a ~ bird⟩
noc·turne \ˈnäk-ˌtərn\ *n* : a work of art dealing with night; *esp* : a dreamy pensive composition for the piano
noc·u·ous \ˈnä-kyə-wəs\ *adj* : HARMFUL — **noc·u·ous·ly** *adv*
nod \ˈnäd\ *vb* **nod·ded; nod·ding** **1** : to bend the head downward or forward (as in bowing, going to sleep, or giving assent) **2** : to move up and down ⟨tulips *nodding* in the breeze⟩ **3** : to show by a nod of the head ⟨~ agreement⟩ **4** : to make a slip or error in a moment of abstraction ⟨did many good things, but sometimes he *nodded*⟩ — **nod** *n*
nod·dle \ˈnä-dᵊl\ *n* : HEAD
nod·dy \ˈnä-dē\ *n, pl* **noddies** **1** : FOOL **2** : a stout-bodied tropical tern
node \ˈnōd\ *n* : a thickened, swollen, or differentiated area (as of tissue); *esp* : the part of a stem from which a leaf arises — **nod·al** \-ᵊl\ *adj*
nod·ule \ˈnä-jül\ *n* : a small lump or swelling — **nod·u·lar** \ˈnä-jə-lər\ *adj*
no·el \nō-ˈel\ *n* [F *noël* Christmas, carol, fr. OF *Nael* (*Deu*), *Noel* Christmas, fr. L *natalis* birthday] **1** : a Christmas carol **2** *cap* : the Christmas season
noes *pl of* NO
no–fault \ˈnō-ˈfȯlt\ *adj* **1** : of, relating to, or being a motor vehicle insurance plan under which someone involved in an accident is compensated usu. up to a stipulated limit for actual losses by that person's own insurance company regardless of who is responsible **2** : of, relating to, or being a divorce law under which neither party is held responsible for the breakup of the marriage
nog·gin \ˈnä-gən\ *n* **1** : a small mug or cup; *also* : a small quantity of drink **2** : a person's head
no–good \ˈnō-ˈgu̇d\ *adj* : having no worth, virtue, use, or chance of success — **no–good** \ˈnō-ˌgu̇d\ *n*
Noh *also* **No** \ˈnō\ *n, pl* **Noh** *also* **No** : classic Japanese dance-drama having a heroic theme, a chorus, and highly stylized action, costuming, and scenery
no–hit·ter \(ˌ)nō-ˈhi-tər\ *n* : a baseball game or part of a game in which a pitcher allows no base hits
no·how \ˈnō-ˌhau̇\ *adv* : in no manner
[1]noise \ˈnȯiz\ *n* [ME, fr. AF, disturbance, noise, fr. L *nausea* nausea] **1** : loud, confused, or senseless shouting or outcry **2** : SOUND; *esp* : one that lacks agreeable musical quality or is noticeably unpleasant **3** : unwanted electronic signal or disturbance — **noise·less** *adj* — **noise·less·ly** *adv*
[2]noise *vb* **noised; nois·ing** : to spread by rumor or report ⟨the story was *noised* abroad⟩

noise·mak·er \ˈnȯiz-ˌmā-kər\ *n* : one that makes noise; *esp* : a device used to make noise at parties

noise pollution *n* : annoying or harmful noise in an environment

noi·some \ˈnȯi-səm\ *adj* **1** : HARMFUL, UNWHOLESOME **2** : offensive to the senses (as smell) : DISGUSTING ⟨~ habits⟩ ♦ ***Synonyms*** INSALUBRIOUS, NOXIOUS, SICKLY, UNHEALTHFUL, UNHEALTHY

noisy \ˈnȯi-zē\ *adj* **nois·i·er; -est** **1** : making loud noises **2** : full of noises : LOUD — **nois·i·ly** \-zə-lē\ *adv* — **nois·i·ness** \-zē-nəs\ *n*

nol·le pro·se·qui \ˌnä-lē-ˈprä-sə-ˌkwī\ *n* [L, to be unwilling to pursue] : an entry on the record of a legal action that the prosecutor or plaintiff will proceed no further in an action or suit or in some aspect of it

no·lo con·ten·de·re \ˌnō-lō-kən-ˈten-də-rē\ *n* [L, I do not wish to contend] : a plea in a criminal prosecution that subjects the defendant to conviction but does not admit guilt or preclude denying the charges in another proceeding

nol–pros \ˈnäl-ˈpräs\ *vb* **nol–prossed; nol–pros·sing** : to discontinue by entering a nolle prosequi

nom *abbr* nominative

no·mad \ˈnō-ˌmad\ *n* **1** : a member of a people who have no fixed residence but move from place to place **2** : an individual who roams about aimlessly — **nomad** *adj* — **no·mad·ic** \nō-ˈma-dik\ *adj*

no–man's–land \ˈnō-ˌmanz-ˌland\ *n* **1** : an area of unowned, unclaimed, or uninhabited land **2** : an unoccupied area between opposing troops

nom de guerre \ˌnäm-di-ˈger\ *n, pl* **noms de guerre** *same or* ˌnämz-\ [F, lit., war name] : PSEUDONYM

nom de plume \-ˈplüm\ *n, pl* **noms de plume** *same or* ˌnämz-\ [F, pen name; prob. coined in E] : PEN NAME

no·men·cla·ture \ˈnō-mən-ˌklā-chər\ *n* **1** : NAME, DESIGNATION **2** : a system of terms used in a science or art

nom·i·nal \ˈnä-mə-nᵊl\ *adj* **1** : being something in name or form only ⟨~ head of a party⟩ **2** : TRIFLING ⟨a ~ price⟩ — **nom·i·nal·ly** *adv*

nom·i·nate \ˈnä-mə-ˌnāt\ *vb* **-nat·ed; -nat·ing** : to choose as a candidate for election, appointment, or honor ♦ ***Synonyms*** APPOINT, DESIGNATE, NAME, TAP — **nom·i·na·tion** \ˌnä-mə-ˈnā-shən\ *n*

nom·i·na·tive \ˈnä-mə-nə-tiv\ *adj* : of, relating to, or constituting a grammatical case marking typically the subject of a verb — **nominative** *n*

nom·i·nee \ˌnä-mə-ˈnē\ *n* : a person nominated for an office, duty, or position

non- \(ˈ)nän *or* ˌnän *before stressed syllables;* ˌnän *elsewhere*\ *prefix* **1** : not : reverse of : absence of **2** : having no importance

non·age \ˈnä-nij, ˈnō-\ *n* **1** : legal minority **2** : a period of youth **3** : IMMATURITY

no·na·ge·nar·i·an \ˌnō-nə-jə-ˈner-ē-ən, ˌnä-\ *n* : a person whose age is in the nineties

non·aligned \ˌnän-ə-ˈlīnd\ *adj* : not allied with other nations

no–name \ˈnō-ˌnām\ *adj* : not having a readily recognizable name ⟨~ brands⟩

non·bi·na·ry \ˌnän-ˈbī-nə-rē, -ˌner-ē\ *adj* **1** : not binary **2** : relating to or being a person who identifies with or expresses a gender identity that is neither entirely male nor entirely female

non·book \ˈnän-ˌbu̇k\ *n* : a book of little literary merit that is often a compilation (as of pictures or speeches)

¹nonce \ˈnäns\ *n* : the one, particular, or present occasion or purpose ⟨for the ~⟩

²nonce *adj* : occurring, used, or made only once or for a special occasion ⟨a ~ word⟩

non·cha·lant \ˌnän-shə-ˈlänt\ *adj* [F, fr. OF, fr. prp. of *nonchaloir* to disregard, fr. *non-* not + *chaloir* to concern, fr. L *calēre* to be warm] : giving an affect of unconcern or indifference ♦ ***Synonyms*** COLLECTED, COMPOSED, COOL, IMPERTURBABLE, UNFLAPPABLE, UNRUFFLED — **non·cha·lance** \-ˈläns\ *n* — **non·cha·lant·ly** *adv*

non·com \ˈnän-ˌkäm\ *n* : NONCOMMISSIONED OFFICER

non·com·ba·tant \ˌnän-kəm-ˈba-tᵊnt, nän-ˈkäm-bə-tənt\ *n* : a member (as a chaplain) of the armed forces whose duties do not include fighting; *also* : CIVILIAN — **noncombatant** *adj*

non·com·mis·sioned officer \ˌnän-kə-ˈmi-shənd-\ *n* : a subordinate officer in the armed forces appointed from enlisted personnel

non·com·mit·tal \ˌnän-kə-ˈmi-tᵊl\ *adj* : indicating neither consent nor dissent ⟨a ~ reply⟩

non com·pos men·tis \ˌnän-ˌkäm-pəs-ˈmen-təs\ *adj* : not of sound mind

non·con·duc·tor \ˌnän-kən-ˈdək-tər\ *n* : a substance that is a very poor conductor of heat, electricity, or sound

non·con·form·ist \-kən-ˈfȯr-mist\ *n* **1** *often cap* : a person who does not con-

---

nonabrasive
nonabsorbent
nonacademic
nonacceptance
nonaccredited
nonacid
nonactivated
nonadaptive
nonaddictive
nonadhesive
nonadjacent
nonadjustable
nonaggression
nonalcoholic
nonappearance
nonaromatic
nonathletic
nonattendance
nonbeliever
nonbelligerent
nonbiodegradable
nonbreakable
noncaloric
noncancerous
noncandidate
noncellular
noncitizen
nonclerical
noncoital
noncombat
noncombative
noncombustible
noncommercial
noncommunist
noncompeting
noncompetitive
noncompliance
noncomplying
nonconducting
nonconfidence
nonconflicting
nonconformance
nonconforming
nonconsensual

form to an established church and esp. the Church of England **2 :** a person who does not conform to a generally accepted pattern of thought or action ♦ ***Synonyms*** DISSENTER, DISSIDENT, HERETIC, SCHISMATIC, SEPARATIST — **non·con·for·mi·ty** \-ˈfȯr-mə-tē\ *n*

non·co·op·er·a·tion \ˌnän-kō-ˌä-pə-ˈrā-shən\ *n* **:** failure or refusal to cooperate; *esp* **:** refusal through civil disobedience of a people to cooperate with the government of a country

non·cred·it \(ˌ)nän-ˈkre-dət\ *adj* **:** not offering credit toward a degree

non·cus·to·di·al \ˌnän-kə-ˈstō-dē-əl\ *adj* **:** of or being a parent who does not have legal custody of a child

non·dairy \ˈnän-ˈder-ē\ *adj* **:** containing no milk or milk products ⟨~ margarine⟩

non·de·script \ˌnän-di-ˈskript\ *adj* **1 :** not belonging to any particular class or kind **2 :** lacking distinctive qualities ⟨a ~ building⟩

non·drink·er \-ˈdriŋ-kər\ *n* **:** a person who abstains from alcohol

[1]**none** \ˈnən\ *pron* **1 :** not any ⟨~ of them went⟩ **2 :** not one ⟨~ of the family⟩ **3 :** not any such thing or person ⟨half a loaf is better than ~⟩

[2]**none** *adj, archaic* **:** not any **:** NO

[3]**none** *adv* **:** by no means **:** not at all ⟨he got there ~ too soon⟩

non·en·ti·ty \ˌnän-ˈen-tə-tē\ *n* **1 :** something that does not exist or exists only in the imagination **2 :** one of no consequence or significance ♦ ***Synonyms*** NOBODY, NOTHING, WHIPPERSNAPPER

nones \ˈnōnz\ *n sing or pl* **:** the 7th day of March, May, July, or October or the 5th day of any other month in the ancient Roman calendar

non·es·sen·tial \ˌnän-i-ˈsen-shəl\ *adj* **1 :** not essential **2 :** being a substance synthesized by the body in sufficient quantity to satisfy dietary needs

none·such \ˈnən-ˌsəch\ *n* **:** one without an equal — **nonesuch** *adj*

none·the·less \ˌnən-thə-ˈles\ *adv* **:** NEVERTHELESS

non·event \ˈnän-i-ˌvent\ *n* **1 :** an event that fails to take place or to satisfy expectations **2 :** a highly promoted event of little intrinsic interest

non·fat \-ˈfat\ *adj* **:** lacking fat solids **:** having fat solids removed ⟨~ milk⟩

non-fungible token *n* **:** a unique digital identifier recorded in a blockchain that certifies authenticity and ownership (as of a specific digital asset and rights relating to it)

non·gono·coc·cal \ˌnän-ˌgä-nə-ˈkä-kəl\ *adj* **:** not caused by a gonococcus

non·he·ro \ˈnän-ˈhē-rō\ *n* **:** ANTIHERO

non–Hodg·kin's lymphoma \ˈnän-ˈhäj-kənz-\ *n* **:** any of numerous malignant lymphomas not classified as Hodgkin's disease

non·in·ter·ven·tion \ˌnän-ˌin-tər-ˈven-chən\ *n* **:** refusal or failure to intervene (as in the affairs of other countries)

non·is·sue \ˈnän-ˈi-shü\ *n* **:** an issue of little importance or concern

non·met·al \ˈnän-ˈme-tᵊl\ *n* **:** a chemical element (as carbon) that lacks the characteristics of a metal — **non·me·tal·lic** \ˌnän-mə-ˈta-lik\ *adj*

non·neg·a·tive \-ˈne-gə-tiv\ *adj* **:** not negative **:** being either positive or zero

non·nu·cle·ar \ˈnän-ˈnü-klē-ər\ *adj* **1 :** not nuclear **2 :** not having, using, or involving nuclear weapons

non·ob·jec·tive \ˌnän-əb-ˈjek-tiv\ *adj* **1 :** not objective **2 :** representing no natural or actual object, figure, or scene ⟨~ art⟩

[1]**non·pa·reil** \-pə-ˈrel\ *adj* **:** having no equal **:** PEERLESS ⟨a ~ performer⟩

[2]**nonpareil** *n* **1 :** an individual of unequaled excellence **:** PARAGON **2 :** a small flat disk of chocolate covered with white sugar pellets

---

nonconstructive
noncontagious
noncontinuous
noncorroding
noncorrosive
noncriminal
noncritical
noncrystalline
nondeductible
nondelivery
nondemocratic
nondenominational
nondepartmental
nondestructive
nondevelopment
nondiscrimination
nondiscriminatory
nondistinctive
nondurable
noneconomic
noneducational
nonelastic
nonelection
nonelective
nonelectric
nonelectrical
nonemotional
nonenforcement
nonethical
non-euclidean
nonexclusive
nonexempt
nonexistence
nonexistent
nonexplosive
nonfarm
nonfatal
nonfattening
nonfederated
nonferrous
nonfiction
nonfictional
nonfilamentous
nonfilterable
nonflammable
nonflowering
nonfood
nonfreezing
nonfulfillment
nonfunctional
nonglare
nongraded
nonhazardous
nonhereditary
nonhomogeneous
nonhomologous
nonhuman
nonidentical
nonimportation
nonindustrial
noninfectious
noninflammable
nonintellectual
nonintercourse
noninterference
nonintoxicant
nonintoxicating
noninvasive
nonionizing
nonirritating
nonlegal
nonlethal
nonlife
nonlinear
nonliterary
nonliterate
nonliving
nonlogical
nonmagnetic
nonmalignant
nonmaterial
nonmember
nonmembership
nonmigratory
nonmilitary
nonmoral
nonmotile
nonmoving
nonnegotiable
nonobservance
nonoccurrence
nonofficial
nonoily
nonorthodox
nonparallel
nonparasitic
nonparticipant
nonparticipating
nonpathogenic
nonpaying
nonpayment
nonperformance
nonperishable
nonphysical
nonpoisonous
nonpolar
nonpolitical
nonporous

non·par·ti·san \ˈnän-ˈpär-tə-zən\ *adj* : not partisan; *esp* : not influenced by political party spirit or interests

non·per·son \-ˈpər-sᵊn\ *n* **1** : UNPERSON **2** : a person having no social or legal status

non·plus \ˈnän-ˈpləs\ *vb* **-plussed** *also* **-plused** \-ˈpləst\; **-plus·sing** *also* **-plus·ing** : PUZZLE, PERPLEX

non·pre·scrip·tion \ˌnän-pri-ˈskrip-shən\ *adj* : available for sale legally without a doctor's prescription

non·prof·it \ˈnän-ˈprä-fət\ *adj* : not conducted or maintained for the purpose of making a profit ⟨a ~ organization⟩

non·pro·lif·er·a·tion \ˌnän-prə-ˌli-fə-ˈrā-shən\ *adj* : providing for the stoppage of proliferation (as of nuclear arms) ⟨a ~ treaty⟩

non·read·er \ˈnän-ˈrē-dər\ *n* : one who does not read or has difficulty reading

non·rep·re·sen·ta·tion·al \ˌnän-ˌre-pri-ˌzen-ˈtā-shə-nəl\ *adj* : NONOBJECTIVE 2

non·res·i·dent \ˈnän-ˈre-zə-dənt\ *adj* : not living in a particular place — **non·res·i·dence** \-dəns\ *n* — **nonresident** *n*

non·re·sis·tance \ˌnän-ri-ˈzis-təns\ *n* : the principles or practice of passive submission to authority even when unjust or oppressive

non·re·stric·tive \-ri-ˈstrik-tiv\ *adj* **1** : not serving or tending to restrict **2** : not limiting the reference of the word or phrase modified ⟨a ~ clause⟩

non·sched·uled \ˈnän-ˈske-jüld\ *adj* : licensed to carry passengers or freight by air without a regular schedule

non·sense \ˈnän-ˌsens, -səns\ *n* **1** : foolish or meaningless words or actions **2** : things of no importance or value — **non·sen·si·cal** \nän-ˈsen-si-kəl\ *adj* — **non·sen·si·cal·ly** \-k(ə-)lē\ *adv*

non se·qui·tur \nän-ˈse-kwə-tər\ *n* [L, it does not follow] : an inference that does not follow from the premises

non·skid \ˈnän-ˈskid\ *adj* : designed to prevent skidding ⟨a ~ surface⟩

non·slip \-ˈslip\ *adj* : designed to prevent slipping ⟨a ~ handle⟩

non·stan·dard \ˌnän-ˈstan-dərd\ *adj* **1** : not standard **2** : not conforming to the usage generally characteristic of educated native speakers of a language

non·start·er \ˈnän-ˈstär-tər\ *n* **1** : one that does not start **2** : one that is not productive or effective

non·stick \-ˈstik\ *adj* : allowing easy removal of cooked food particles

¹non·stop \-ˈstäp\ *adj* : done or made without a stop ⟨~ action⟩ — **nonstop** *adv*

²nonstop *n* : a nonstop airplane flight

non·sup·port \ˌnän-sə-ˈpȯrt\ *n* : failure to support; *esp* : failure on the part of one under obligation to provide maintenance

non·threat·en·ing \-ˈthret-niŋ, -ˈthre-tᵊn-iŋ\ *adj* : not likely to cause danger or anxiety ⟨a ~ illness⟩ ⟨a ~ idea⟩

non–U \ˈnän-ˈyü\ *adj* : not characteristic of the upper classes ⟨~ speech⟩

non·union \-ˈyü-nyən\ *adj* **1** : not belonging to a trade union ⟨~ carpenters⟩ **2** : not recognizing or favoring trade unions or their members ⟨~ employers⟩

non·us·er \-ˈyü-zər\ *n* : one who does not make use of something (as drugs)

non·vi·o·lence \ˈnän-ˈvī-ə-ləns\ *n* **1** : abstention from violence as a matter of principle **2** : avoidance of violence **3** : nonviolent political demonstrations — **non·vi·o·lent** \-lənt\ *adj*

non–white \ˌnän-ˈhwīt, -ˈwīt\ *n* : a person who is not white — **non–white** *adj*

non·wo·ven \ˈnän-ˈwō-vən\ *adj* : made of fibers held together by interlocking or bonding (as by chemical or thermal means) — **nonwoven** *n*

noo·dle \ˈnü-dᵊl\ *n* [G *Nudel*] : a food paste made usu. with egg and shaped typically in ribbon form

nook \ˈnu̇k\ *n* **1** : an interior angle or corner formed usu. by two walls ⟨a chimney ~⟩ **2** : a sheltered or hidden place ⟨searched every ~ and cranny⟩ **3** : a usu. recessed section of a larger room ⟨a breakfast ~⟩

noon \ˈnün\ *n* : the middle of the day : 12 o'clock in the daytime — **noon** *adj*

noon·day \ˈnün-ˌdā\ *n* : NOON, MIDDAY

no one *pron* : NOBODY

noon·tide \ˈnün-ˌtīd\ *n* : NOON

noon·time \-ˌtīm\ *n* : NOON

noose \ˈnüs\ *n* : a loop with a slipknot that binds closer the more it is drawn

nope \ˈnōp\ *adv, informal* : NO

---

nonpregnant
nonproductive
nonprofessional
nonprotein
nonradioactive
nonrandom
nonrated
nonreactive
nonreciprocal
nonrecognition
nonrecurrent
nonrecurring
nonrefillable
nonreligious
nonrenewable
nonresidential
nonrestricted
nonreturnable
nonreusable
nonreversible
nonrigid
nonruminant
nonsalable
nonscientific
nonscientist
nonseasonal
nonsectarian
nonsegregated
nonselective
non-self-governing
nonsexist
nonsexual
nonshrinkable
nonsinkable
nonsmoker
nonsmoking
nonsocial
nonspeaking
nonspecialist
nonspecific
nonsteroidal
nonstudent
nonsuccess
nonsurgical
nontaxable
nonteaching
nontechnical
nontemporal
nontenured
nontheistic
nonthreatening
nontoxic
nontraditional
nontransferable
nontypical
nonuniform
nonvascular
nonvenomous
nonverbal
nonveteran
nonviable
nonvisual
nonvocal
nonvolatile
nonvoter
nonvoting
nonworker
nonworking
nonzero

nor \ˈnȯr\ *conj* : and not ⟨not for you ~ for me⟩ — used esp. to introduce and negate the second member and each later member of a series of items preceded by *neither* ⟨neither here ~ there⟩

Nor·dic \ˈnȯr-dik\ *adj* **1** : of or relating to the Germanic peoples of northern Europe and esp. of Scandinavia **2** : of or relating to competitive ski events involving cross-country racing, ski jumping, or biathlon — **Nordic** *n*

nor·epi·neph·rine \ˌnȯr-ˌe-pə-ˈne-frən\ *n* : a nitrogen-containing neurotransmitter in parts of the sympathetic and central nervous systems

norm \ˈnȯrm\ *n* [L *norma,* lit., carpenter's square] **1** : an authoritative standard or model; *esp* : a set standard of development or achievement usu. derived from the average or median achievement of a large group **2** : a typical or widespread practice, procedure, or custom ♦ ***Synonyms*** AVERAGE, MEAN, MEDIAN, PAR

[1]**nor·mal** \ˈnȯr-məl\ *adj* **1** : REGULAR, STANDARD, NATURAL **2** : : sound in mind and body **3** : exhibiting healthy functioning — **nor·mal·cy** \-sē\ *n* — **nor·mal·i·ty** \nȯr-ˈma-lə-tē\ *n* — **nor·mal·ly** *adv*

[2]**normal** *n* **1** : one that is normal **2** : the usual condition, level, or quantity

nor·mal·ise *Brit var of* NORMALIZE

nor·mal·ize \ˈnȯr-mə-ˌlīz\ *vb* **-ized; -iz·ing** : to make or restore to normal ⟨*normalizing* relations⟩ — **nor·mal·i·za·tion** \ˌnȯr-mə-lə-ˈzā-shən\ *n*

Nor·man \ˈnȯr-mən\ *n* **1** : a native or inhabitant of Normandy **2** : one of the 10th century Scandinavian conquerors of Normandy **3** : one of the Norman-French conquerors of England in 1066 — **Norman** *adj*

nor·ma·tive \ˈnȯr-mə-tiv\ *adj* : of, relating to, or determining norms — **nor·ma·tive·ly** *adv* — **nor·ma·tive·ness** *n*

Norse \ˈnȯrs\ *n, pl* **Norse** **1** : NORWEGIAN; *also* : any of the western Scandinavian dialects or languages **2** *pl* : SCANDINAVIANS; *also* : NORWEGIANS

Norse·man \-mən\ *n* : any of the ancient Scandinavians

[1]**north** \ˈnȯrth\ *adv* : to, toward, or in the north

[2]**north** *adj* **1** : situated toward or at the north **2** : coming from the north

[3]**north** *n* **1** : the direction to the left of one facing east **2** : the compass point directly opposite to south **3** *cap* : regions or countries north of a specified or implied point — **north·er·ly** \ˈnȯr-thər-lē\ *adv or adj* — **north·ern** \-thərn\ *adj* — **North·ern·er** \-thər-nər\ *n* — **north·ern·most** \-thərn-ˌmōst\ *adj* — **north·ward** \ˈnȯrth-wərd\ *adv or adj* — **north·wards** \-wərdz\ *adv*

north·east \nȯrth-ˈēst\ *n* **1** : the general direction between north and east **2** : the compass point midway between north and east **3** *cap* : regions or countries northeast of a specified or implied point — **northeast** *adj or adv* — **north·east·er·ly** \-ˈthē-stər-lē\ *adv or adj* — **north·east·ern** \-stərn\ *adj*

north·east·er \-ˈēs-tər\ *n* **1** : a strong northeast wind **2** : a storm with northeast winds

north·er \ˈnȯr-thər\ *n* **1** : a strong north wind **2** : a storm with north winds

northern lights *n pl* : AURORA BOREALIS

north pole *n, often cap N&P* : the northernmost point of the earth

North Star *n* : the star toward which the northern end of the earth's axis points

north·west \nȯrth-ˈwest\ *n* **1** : the general direction between north and west **2** : the compass point midway between north and west **3** *cap* : regions or countries northwest of a specified or implied point — **northwest** *adj or adv* — **north·west·er·ly** \-ˈwe-stər-lē\ *adv or adj* — **north·west·ern** \-ˈwe-stərn\ *adj*

Norw *abbr* Norway; Norwegian

Nor·we·gian \nȯr-ˈwē-jən\ *n* **1** : a native or inhabitant of Norway **2** : the language of Norway — **Norwegian** *adj*

nos *abbr* numbers

[1]**nose** \ˈnōz\ *n* **1** : the part of the face or head containing the nostrils and covering the front of the nasal cavity **2** : the sense of smell **3** : something (as a point, edge, or projecting front part) that resembles a nose ⟨the ~ of a plane⟩ — **nosed** \ˈnōzd\ *adj* — **on the nose** : on target : ACCURATE — **under one's nose** : extremely near : in one's presence

[2]**nose** *vb* **nosed; nos·ing** **1** : to detect by or as if by smell : SCENT **2** : to push or move with the nose **3** : to touch or rub with the nose : NUZZLE **4** : PRY **5** : to move ahead slowly ⟨the ship *nosed* into her berth⟩

nose·bleed \ˈnōz-ˌblēd\ *n* : a bleeding from the nose

nose cone *n* : a protective cone constituting the forward end of an aerospace vehicle

nose·dive \ˈnōz-ˌdīv\ *n* **1** : a downward nose-first plunge (as of an airplane) **2** : a sudden extreme drop (as in prices)

nose·gay \ˈnōz-ˌgā\ *n* : a small bunch of flowers : POSY

nose out *vb* **1** : to discover often by prying **2** : to defeat by a narrow margin

nose·piece \-ˌpēs\ *n* **1** : a fitting at the lower end of a microscope tube to which the objectives are attached **2** : the bridge of a pair of eyeglasses

no–show \ˈnō-ˈshō\ *n* : a person who does not show up for an event as expected

nos·tal·gia \nä-ˈstal-jə\ *n* [NL, fr. Gk *nostos* return home + *algos* pain, grief] **1** : HOMESICKNESS **2** : a wistful yearning for something past or irrecoverable — **nos·tal·gic** \-jik\ *adj* — **nos·tal·gist** \-jist\ *n*

nos·tril \ˈnäs-trəl\ *n* [ME *nosethirl,* fr. OE *nosthyrl,* fr. *nosu* nose + *thyrel* hole] **1** : either of the nares usu. with the adjoining nasal wall and passage **2** : either fleshy lateral wall of the nose

nos·trum \ˈnäs-trəm\ *n* [L, neut. of *noster*

our, ours, fr. *nos* we] : a questionable medicine or remedy

nosy *or* **nos•ey** \ˈnō-zē\ *adj* **nos•i•er; -est** : INQUISITIVE, PRYING ⟨~ neighbors⟩

not \ˈnät\ *adv* **1** — used to make negative a group of words or a word ⟨the boys are ~ here⟩ **2** — used to stand for the negative of a preceding group of words ⟨sometimes easy and sometimes ~⟩

no•ta be•ne \ˌnō-tə-ˈbē-nē, -ˈbe-\ [L, mark well] — used to call attention to something important

no•ta•bil•i•ty \ˌnō-tə-ˈbi-lə-tē\ *n, pl* **-ties** **1** : the quality or state of being notable **2** : NOTABLE

[1]**no•ta•ble** \ˈnō-tə-bəl\ *adj* **1** : NOTEWORTHY, REMARKABLE ⟨a ~ achievement⟩ **2** : DISTINGUISHED, PROMINENT ⟨two ~ politicians made speeches⟩

[2]**notable** *n* : a person of note ♦ ***Synonyms*** BIGWIG, EMINENCE, NABOB, PERSONAGE, SOMEBODY, VIP

no•ta•bly \ˈnō-tə-blē\ *adv* **1** : in a notable manner **2** : ESPECIALLY, PARTICULARLY

no•tar•i•al \nō-ˈter-ē-əl\ *adj* : of, relating to, or done by a notary public

no•ta•rize \ˈnō-tə-ˌrīz\ *vb* **-rized; -riz•ing** : to acknowledge or make legally authentic as a notary public

no•ta•ry public \ˈnō-tə-rē-\ *n, pl* **notaries public** *or* **notary publics** : a public official who attests or certifies writings (as deeds) to make them legally authentic

no•ta•tion \nō-ˈtā-shən\ *n* **1** : ANNOTATION, NOTE **2** : the act, process, or method of representing data by marks, signs, figures, or characters; *also* : a system of symbols (as letters, numerals, or musical notes) used in such notation

[1]**notch** \ˈnäch\ *n* **1** : a V-shaped hollow in an edge or surface **2** : a narrow pass between two mountains

[2]**notch** *vb* **1** : to cut or make notches in **2** : to score or record by or as if by cutting a series of notches ⟨~*ed* 20 points for the team⟩

notch•back \ˈnäch-ˌbak\ *n* : an automobile with a trunk whose lid forms a distinct deck

[1]**note** \ˈnōt\ *vb* **not•ed; not•ing** **1** : to notice or observe with care ⟨*noted* her reaction⟩; *also* : to record or preserve in writing **2** : to make special mention of : REMARK

[2]**note** *n* **1** : a musical sound **2** : a cry, call, or sound esp. of a bird **3** : a special tone in a person's words or voice ⟨a ~ of fear⟩ **4** : a character in music used to indicate duration of a tone by its shape and pitch by its position on the staff **5** : a characteristic feature : MOOD, QUALITY ⟨a ~ of optimism⟩ **6** : MEMORANDUM **7** : a brief and informal record; *also* : a written or printed comment or explanation **8** : a written promise to pay a debt **9** : a piece of paper money **10** : a short informal letter **11** : a formal diplomatic or official communication **12** : DISTINCTION, REPUTATION ⟨an artist of ~⟩ **13** : OBSERVATION, NOTICE, HEED ⟨take ~ of the time⟩

note•book \ˈnōt-ˌbu̇k\ *n* **1** : a book for notes or memoranda **2** : a portable microcomputer smaller than a laptop computer

not•ed \ˈnō-təd\ *adj* : well known by reputation : EMINENT ⟨a ~ violinist⟩

note•wor•thy \ˈnōt-ˌwər-t͟hē\ *adj* : worthy of note : REMARKABLE

[1]**noth•ing** \ˈnə-thiŋ\ *pron* **1** : no thing ⟨leaves ~ to the imagination⟩ **2** : no part **3** : one of no interest, value, or importance ⟨she's ~ to me⟩ **4** : a light playful remark ⟨sweet ~*s*⟩

[2]**nothing** *adv* : not at all : in no degree

[3]**nothing** *n* **1** : something that does not exist **2** : ZERO **3** : a person or thing of little or no value or importance

[4]**nothing** *adj* : of no account : WORTHLESS

noth•ing•ness \ˈnə-thiŋ-nəs\ *n* **1** : the quality or state of being nothing **2** : NONEXISTENCE; *also* : utter insignificance **3** : something insignificant or valueless

[1]**no•tice** \ˈnō-təs\ *n* **1** : WARNING, ANNOUNCEMENT **2** : notification of the termination of an agreement or contract at a specified time **3** : ATTENTION, HEED ⟨bring the matter to my ~⟩ **4** : a written or printed announcement **5** : a short critical account or examination (as of a play) : REVIEW

[2]**notice** *vb* **no•ticed; no•tic•ing** **1** : to make mention of : remark on : NOTE **2** : to take notice of : OBSERVE, MARK

no•tice•able \ˈnō-tə-sə-bəl\ *adj* **1** : worthy of notice **2** : likely to be noticed ⟨a ~ scar⟩ — **no•tice•ably** \-blē\ *adv*

no•ti•fy \ˈnō-tə-ˌfī\ *vb* **-fied; -fy•ing** **1** : to give notice of : report the occurrence of **2** : to give notice to — **no•ti•fi•ca•tion** \ˌnō-tə-fə-ˈkā-shən\ *n*

no•tion \ˈnō-shən\ *n* **1** : IDEA, CONCEPTION ⟨have a ~ of what he means⟩ **2** : a belief held : OPINION, VIEW **3** : WHIM, FANCY ⟨a sudden ~ to go⟩ **4** *pl* : small useful articles (as pins, needles, or thread)

no•tion•al \ˈnō-shə-nəl\ *adj* **1** : existing in the mind only : IMAGINARY, UNREAL **2** : given to foolish or fanciful moods or ideas : WHIMSICAL

no•to•ri•ous \nō-ˈtȯr-ē-əs\ *adj* : generally known and talked of; *esp* : widely and unfavorably known — **no•to•ri•ety** \ˌnō-tə-ˈrī-ə-tē\ *n* — **no•to•ri•ous•ly** \nō-ˈtȯr-ē-əs-lē\ *adv*

[1]**not•with•stand•ing** \ˌnät-with-ˈstan-diŋ, -wit͟h-\ *prep* : in spite of

[2]**notwithstanding** *adv* : NEVERTHELESS

[3]**notwithstanding** *conj* : ALTHOUGH

nou•gat \ˈnü-gət\ *n* [F, fr. Occitan, fr. Old Occitan, *nogat,* fr. *noga* nut, ultim. fr. L *nuc-, nux*] : a confection of nuts or fruit pieces in a sugar paste

nought *var of* NAUGHT

noun \ˈnau̇n\ *n* : a word that is the name of a subject of discourse (as a person or place)

nour•ish \ˈnər-ish\ *vb* : to promote the growth or development of

nour·ish·ing *adj* : giving nourishment
nour·ish·ment \ˈnər-ish-mənt\ *n* **1** : FOOD, NUTRIENT **2** : the action or process of nourishing
nou·veau riche \ˌnü-ˌvō-ˈrēsh\ *n, pl* **nou·veaux riches** *same*\ [F] : a person newly rich : PARVENU
Nov *abbr* November
no·va \ˈnō-və\ *n, pl* **novas** *or* **no·vae** \-(ˌ)vē, -ˌvī\ [NL, fem. of L *novus* new] : a star that suddenly increases greatly in brightness and then within a few months or years grows dim again
¹nov·el \ˈnä-vəl\ *adj* **1** : having no precedent : NEW **2** : STRANGE, UNUSUAL
²novel *n* : a long invented prose narrative dealing with human experience through a connected sequence of events — **nov·el·ist** \-və-list\ *n*
nov·el·ette \ˌnä-və-ˈlet\ *n* : a brief novel or long short story
nov·el·ize \ˈnä-və-ˌlīz\ *vb* **-ized; -iz·ing** : to convert into the form of a novel — **nov·el·i·za·tion** \ˌnä-və-lə-ˈzā-shən\ *n*
no·vel·la \nō-ˈve-lə\ *n, pl* **novellas** *or* **no·vel·le** \-ˈve-lē\ : NOVELETTE
nov·el·ty \ˈnä-vəl-tē\ *n, pl* **-ties** **1** : something new or unusual **2** : NEWNESS **3** : a small manufactured article intended mainly for personal or household adornment — usu. used in pl.
No·vem·ber \nō-ˈvem-bər\ *n* [ME *Novembre,* fr. AF, fr. L *November* ninth month of the early Roman calendar, fr. *novem* nine] : the 11th month of the year
no·ve·na \nō-ˈvē-nə\ *n* : a Roman Catholic nine-day period of prayer
nov·ice \ˈnä-vəs\ *n* **1** : a new member of a religious order who is preparing to take the vows of religion **2** : one who is inexperienced or untrained
no·vi·tiate \nō-ˈvi-shət\ *n* **1** : the period or state of being a novice **2** : a house where novices are trained **3** : NOVICE
¹now \ˈnau̇\ *adv* **1** : at the present time or moment **2** : in the time immediately before the present **3** : IMMEDIATELY, FORTHWITH **4** — used with the sense of present time weakened or lost (as to express command, introduce an important point, or indicate a transition) ⟨~ hear this⟩ **5** : SOMETIMES ⟨~ one and ~ another⟩ **6** : under the present circumstances **7** : at the time referred to **8** : by this time
²now *conj* : in view of the fact ⟨~ that you're here, we'll start⟩
³now *n* : the present time or moment : PRESENT
⁴now *adj* **1** : of or relating to the present time ⟨the ~ president⟩ **2** : excitingly new ⟨~ clothes⟩; *also* : constantly aware of what is new ⟨~ people⟩
NOW *abbr* **1** National Organization for Women **2** negotiable order of withdrawal
now·a·days \ˈnau̇-ə-ˌdāz\ *adv* : at the present time
no·way \ˈnō-ˌwā\ *or* **no·ways** \-ˌwāz\ *adv* : NOWISE
no·where \-ˌhwer\ *adv* **1** : not anywhere **2** : not at all — usu. used with *near* ⟨~ near enough⟩ — **nowhere** *n*
no·wise \ˈnō-ˌwīz\ *adv* : in no way
nox·ious \ˈnäk-shəs\ *adj* : harmful esp. to health or morals
noz·zle \ˈnä-zəl\ *n* : a short tube constricted in the middle or at one end and used (as on a hose) to speed up or direct a flow of fluid
np *abbr* **1** no pagination **2** no place (of publication)
Np *symbol* neptunium
NP *abbr* notary public
NR *abbr* not rated
NRA *abbr* National Rifle Association
NS *abbr* **1** not specified **2** Nova Scotia
NSA *abbr* National Security Agency
NSC *abbr* National Security Council
NSF *abbr* **1** National Science Foundation **2** not sufficient funds
NSW *abbr* New South Wales
NT *abbr* **1** New Testament **2** Northern Territory **3** Northwest Territories
nth \ˈenth\ *adj* **1** : numbered with an unspecified or indefinitely large ordinal number ⟨for the ~ time⟩ **2** : EXTREME, UTMOST ⟨to the ~ degree⟩
NTP *abbr* normal temperature and pressure
nt wt *or* **n wt** *abbr* net weight
nu \ˈnü, ˈnyü\ *n* : the 13th letter of the Greek alphabet — Ν or ν
NU *abbr* name unknown
nu·ance \ˈnü-ˌäns, ˈnyü-, nü-ˈäns, nyü-\ *n* [F] : a shade of difference : a delicate variation (as in tone or meaning)
nub \ˈnəb\ *n* **1** : KNOB, LUMP **2** : GIST, POINT ⟨the ~ of the story⟩
nub·bin \ˈnə-bən\ *n* **1** : something (as an ear of corn) that is small for its kind, stunted, undeveloped, or imperfect **2** : a small projecting bit
nu·bile \ˈnü-ˌbī(-ə)l, ˈnyü-, -bəl\ *adj* **1** : of marriageable condition or age **2** : sexually attractive — used of a young woman
nu·cle·ar \ˈnü-klē-ər, ˈnyü-\ *adj* **1** : of, relating to, or constituting a nucleus **2** : of, relating to, or using the atomic nucleus or energy derived from it **3** : of, relating to, or being a weapon whose destructive power results from an uncontrolled nuclear reaction
nu·cle·ate \ˈnü-klē-ˌāt, ˈnyü-\ *vb* **-at·ed; -at·ing** : to form, act as, or have a nucleus — **nu·cle·ation** \ˌnü-klē-ˈā-shən, ˌnyü-\ *n*
nu·cle·ic acid \nu̇-ˈklē-ik-, nyu̇-, -ˈklā-\ *n* : any of various complex organic acids (as DNA or RNA) found esp. in cell nuclei
nu·cle·o·tide \ˈnü-klē-ə-ˌtīd, ˈnyü-\ *n* : any of several compounds that are the basic structural units of nucleic acids
nu·cle·us \ˈnü-klē-əs, ˈnyü-\ *n, pl* **nu·clei** \-klē-ˌī\ *also* **nu·cle·us·es** [NL, fr. L, kernel, dim. of *nuc-, nux* nut] **1** : a central mass or part about which matter gathers or is collected : CORE **2** : a cell part that is characteristic of all living things except viruses, bacteria, and certain algae, that

is necessary for heredity and for making proteins, that contains the chromosomes with their genes, and that is enclosed in a membrane **3** : a mass of gray matter or group of cell bodies of neurons in the central nervous system **4** : the central part of an atom that comprises nearly all of the atomic mass **5** : a basic or essential part

[1]**nude** \ˈnüd, ˈnyüd\ *adj* **nud·er; nud·est** **1** : BARE, NAKED, UNCLOTHED **2** : featuring or catering to naked people ⟨a ~ beach⟩ — **nu·di·ty** \ˈnü-də-tē, ˈnyü-\ *n*

[2]**nude** *n* **1** : a nude human figure esp. as depicted in art **2** : the condition of being nude ⟨in the ~⟩

nudge \ˈnəj\ *vb* **nudged; nudg·ing** : to touch or push gently (as with the elbow) usu. in order to seek attention — **nudge** *n*

nud·ism \ˈnü-ˌdi-zəm, ˈnyü-\ *n* : the practice of going nude esp. in mixed groups at specially secluded places — **nud·ist** \-dist\ *n*

nu·ga·to·ry \ˈnü-gə-ˌtȯr-ē\ *adj* **1** : INCONSEQUENTIAL, WORTHLESS ⟨his efforts were rendered ~⟩ **2** : having no force : INEFFECTUAL

nug·get \ˈnə-gət\ *n* **1** : a lump of precious metal (as gold) **2** : TIDBIT

nui·sance \ˈnü-sᵊns, ˈnyü-\ *n* : an annoying or troublesome person or thing

nuisance tax *n* : an excise tax collected in small amounts directly from the consumer

[1]**nuke** \ˈnük, ˈnyük\ *n* **1** : a nuclear weapon **2** : a nuclear power plant

[2]**nuke** *vb* **nuked; nuk·ing** **1** : to attack with nuclear weapons **2** : MICROWAVE

null \ˈnəl\ *adj* **1** : having no legal or binding force : INVALID, VOID **2** : amounting to nothing **3** : INSIGNIFICANT — **nul·li·ty** \ˈnə-lə-tē\ *n*

null and void *adj* : having no force, binding power, or validity

nul·li·fy \ˈnə-lə-ˌfī\ *vb* **-fied; -fy·ing** : to make null or valueless; *also* : ANNUL — **nul·li·fi·ca·tion** \ˌnə-lə-fə-ˈkā-shən\ *n*

num *abbr* numeral

Num *or* **Numb** *abbr* Numbers

numb \ˈnəm\ *adj* : lacking sensation or emotion : BENUMBED — **numb** *vb* — **numb·ly** *adv* — **numb·ness** *n*

[1]**num·ber** \ˈnəm-bər\ *n* **1** : the total of individuals or units taken together **2** : an indefinite total ⟨a small ~ of tickets remain unsold⟩ **3** : an ascertainable total ⟨the sands of the desert are without ~⟩ **4** : a distinction of word form to denote reference to one or more than one **5** : a unit belonging to a mathematical system and subject to its laws; *also, pl* : ARITHMETIC **6** : a symbol used to represent a mathematical number; *also* : such a number used to identify or designate ⟨a phone ~⟩ **7** : one in a series of musical or theatrical performances **8** : an act of transforming or impairing ⟨tripped and did a ~ on her knee⟩

[2]**number** *vb* **1** : COUNT, ENUMERATE **2** : to include with or be one of a group **3** : to restrict to a small or definite number **4** : to assign a number to **5** : to comprise in number : TOTAL

num·ber·less \-ləs\ *adj* : INNUMERABLE, COUNTLESS ⟨~ stars in the sky⟩

Numbers *n* — see BIBLE table

numb·ing \ˈnə-miŋ\ *adj* : tending to make numb ⟨a ~ lecture⟩ ⟨a ~ realization⟩

numbskull *var of* NUMSKULL

nu·mer·acy \ˈnü-mə-rə-sē, ˈnyü-\ *n* : the capacity for quantitative thought or expression

nu·mer·al \ˈnü-mə-rəl, ˈnyü-\ *n* : a conventional symbol representing a number — **numeral** *adj*

nu·mer·ate \ˈnü-mə-ˌrāt, ˈnyü-\ *vb* **-at·ed; -at·ing** : ENUMERATE

nu·mer·a·tor \-ˌrā-tər\ *n* : the part of a fraction above the line

nu·mer·ic \nu̇-ˈmer-ik, nyu̇-\ *adj* : NUMERICAL; *esp* : denoting a number or a system of numbers

nu·mer·i·cal \-ˈmer-i-kəl\ *adj* **1** : of or relating to numbers ⟨in ~ order⟩ **2** : expressed in or involving numbers — **nu·mer·i·cal·ly** \-k(ə-)lē\ *adv*

nu·mer·ol·o·gy \ˌnü-mə-ˈrä-lə-jē, ˌnyü-\ *n* : the study of the occult significance of numbers — **nu·mer·ol·o·gist** \-jist\ *n*

nu·mer·ous \ˈnü-mə-rəs, ˈnyü-\ *adj* : consisting of, including, or relating to a great number : MANY

nu·mis·mat·ics \ˌnü-məz-ˈma-tiks, ˌnyü-\ *n* : the study or collection of monetary objects — **nu·mis·mat·ic** \-tik\ *adj* — **nu·mis·ma·tist** \nü-ˈmiz-mə-tist, nyü-\ *n*

num·skull *also* **numb·skull** \ˈnəm-ˌskəl\ *n* : a stupid person : DUNCE

nun \ˈnən\ *n* : a woman belonging to a religious order; *esp* : one under solemn vows of poverty, chastity, and obedience

nun·cio \ˈnən-sē-ˌō, ˈnu̇n-\ *n, pl* **-ci·os** [It, fr. L *nuntius* messenger] : a permanent high-ranking papal representative to a civil government

nun·nery \ˈnə-nə-rē\ *n, pl* **-ner·ies** : a convent of nuns

[1]**nup·tial** \ˈnəp-shəl\ *adj* : of or relating to marriage or a wedding ⟨~ vows⟩

[2]**nuptial** *n* : MARRIAGE, WEDDING — usu. used in pl.

[1]**nurse** \ˈnərs\ *n* [ME *norice, nurse,* fr. AF *nurice,* fr. LL *nutricia,* fr. L, fem. of *nutricius* nourishing] **1** : a girl or woman employed to take care of children **2** : a person trained to care for sick people

[2]**nurse** *vb* **nursed; nurs·ing** **1** : SUCKLE **2** : to take charge of and watch over **3** : TEND ⟨~ an invalid⟩ **4** : to treat with special care ⟨~ a headache⟩ **5** : to hold in one's mind or consideration ⟨~ a grudge⟩ **6** : to act or serve as a nurse

nurse·maid \ˈnərs-ˌmād\ *n* : NURSE 1

nurse–prac·ti·tion·er \-prak-ˈti-shə-nər\ *n* : a registered nurse who is qualified to assume some of the duties formerly assumed only by a physician

nurs·ery \ˈnər-sə-rē\ *n, pl* **-er·ies** **1** : a room for children **2** : a place where children are temporarily cared for in their

parents' absence **3** : a place where young plants are grown usu. for transplanting
nurs·ery·man \-mən\ *n* : a person who keeps or works in a plant nursery
nursery school *n* : a school for children under kindergarten age
nursing home *n* : a private establishment providing care for persons (as the aged or the chronically ill) who are unable to care for themselves
nurs·ling \ˈnərs-liŋ\ *n* **1** : one that is solicitously cared for **2** : a nursing child
[1]**nur·ture** \ˈnər-chər\ *n* **1** : TRAINING, UPBRINGING; *also* : the influences that modify the expression of an individual's heredity **2** : FOOD, NOURISHMENT
[2]**nurture** *vb* **nur·tured; nur·tur·ing** **1** : to care for : FEED, NOURISH **2** : EDUCATE, TRAIN ⟨∼ students⟩ **3** : FOSTER ⟨∼ creativity⟩
nut \ˈnət\ *n* **1** : a dry fruit or seed with a hard shell and a firm inner kernel; *also* : its kernel **2** : a metal block with a hole through it that is fastened to a bolt or screw by means of a screw thread within the hole **3** : the ridge on the upper end of the fingerboard in a stringed musical instrument over which the strings pass **4** : a foolish, eccentric, or crazy person **5** : ENTHUSIAST
nut·crack·er \ˈnət-ˌkra-kər\ *n* : an instrument for cracking nuts
nut·hatch \-ˌhach\ *n* : any of various small tree-climbing chiefly insect-eating birds
nut·meg \-ˌmeg, -ˌmāg\ *n* [ME *notemuge,* ultim. fr. Old Occitan *noz muscada,* lit., musky nut] : a spice made by grinding the nutlike aromatic seed of a tropical tree; *also* : the seed or tree
nu·tria \ˈnü-trē-ə, ˈnyü-\ *n* [Sp] **1** : the durable usu. light brown fur of a nutria **2** : a large So. American aquatic rodent with webbed hind feet
[1]**nu·tri·ent** \ˈnü-trē-ənt, ˈnyü-\ *adj* : NOURISHING ⟨∼ deficiencies⟩
[2]**nutrient** *n* : a nutritive substance or ingredient ⟨fruits and vegetables are important ∼*s*⟩
nu·tri·ment \-trə-mənt\ *n* : NUTRIENT
nu·tri·tion \nu̇-ˈtri-shən, nyu̇-\ *n* : the act or process of nourishing; *esp* : the processes by which an individual takes in and utilizes food material — **nu·tri·tion·al** \-shə-nəl\ *adj* — **nu·tri·tion·al·ly** *adv* — **nu·tri·tion·ist** \-shə-nist\ *n* — **nu·tri·tive** \ˈnü-trə-tiv, ˈnyü-\ *adj*
nu·tri·tious \-shəs\ *adj* : NOURISHING — **nu·tri·tious·ly** *adv*
nuts \ˈnəts\ *adj, informal* **1** : ENTHUSIASTIC, KEEN **2** : CRAZY, DEMENTED
nut·shell \ˈnət-ˌshel\ *n* : the shell of a nut — **in a nutshell** : in a few words ⟨that's the story *in a nutshell*⟩
nut·ty \ˈnə-tē\ *adj* **nut·ti·er; -est** **1** : containing or suggesting nuts ⟨a ∼ flavor⟩ **2** : mentally unbalanced
nuz·zle \ˈnə-zəl\ *vb* **nuz·zled; nuz·zling** **1** : to root around, push, or touch with or as if with the nose **2** : NESTLE, SNUGGLE
NV *abbr* Nevada
NW *abbr* northwest
NWT *abbr* Northwest Territories
NY *abbr* New York
NYC *abbr* New York City
ny·lon \ˈnī-ˌlän\ *n* **1** : any of numerous strong tough elastic synthetic materials used esp. in textiles and plastics **2** *pl* : stockings made of nylon
nymph \ˈnimf\ *n* **1** : any of the lesser goddesses in ancient mythology represented as maidens living in the mountains, forests, meadows, and waters **2** : GIRL **3** : an immature insect resembling the adult but smaller, less differentiated, and usu. lacking developed wings
nym·pho·ma·nia \ˌnim-fə-ˈmā-nē-ə, -nyə\ *n* : excessive sexual desire by a female — **nym·pho·ma·ni·ac** \-nē-ˌak\ *n or adj*
NZ *abbr* New Zealand

O

[1]**o** \ˈō\ *n, pl* **o's** *or* **os** \ˈōz\ *often cap* **1** : the 15th letter of the English alphabet **2** : ZERO
[2]**o** *abbr, often cap* **1** ocean **2** Ohio **3** ohm
[1]**O** *var of* OH
[2]**O** *symbol* oxygen
o/a *abbr* on or about
oaf \ˈōf\ *n* : a stupid or awkward person — **oaf·ish** *adj*
oak \ˈōk\ *n, pl* **oaks** *or* **oak** : any of a genus of trees or shrubs related to the beech and chestnut and bearing a rounded thin-shelled nut surrounded at the base by a hardened cup; *also* : the usu. tough hard durable wood of an oak — **oak·en** \ˈō-kən\ *adj*
oa·kum \ˈō-kəm\ *n* [ME *okum,* fr. OE *ācumba* flax fiber, from *ā-* out + *-cumba* (akin to OE *camb* comb)] : loosely twisted hemp or jute fiber impregnated with tar and used esp. in caulking ships
oar \ˈȯr\ *n* : a long pole with a broad blade at one end used for propelling or steering a boat
oar·lock \ˈȯr-ˌläk\ *n* : a U-shaped device for holding an oar in place
oars·man \ˈȯrz-mən\ *n* : one who rows esp. in a racing crew
OAS *abbr* Organization of American States
oa·sis \ō-ˈā-səs\ *n, pl* **oa·ses** \-ˌsēz\ : a fertile or green area in an arid region

oat \ˈōt\ *n* : a cereal grass widely grown for its edible seed; *also* : this seed — **oat·en** \ˈō-tᵊn\ *adj*

oat·cake \ˈōt-ˌkāk\ *n* : a thin flat oatmeal cake

oath \ˈōth\ *n, pl* **oaths** \ˈōt͟hz, ˈōths\ **1** : a solemn appeal to God to witness to the truth of a statement or the sacredness of a promise **2** : an irreverent or careless use of a sacred name

oat·meal \ˈōt-ˌmēl\ *n* **1** : ground or rolled oats **2** : porridge made from ground or rolled oats

Ob *or* **Obad** *abbr* Obadiah

Oba·di·ah \ˌō-bə-ˈdī-ə\ *n* — see BIBLE table

ob·bli·ga·to \ˌä-blə-ˈgä-tō\ *n, pl* **-tos** *also* **-ti** \-ˈgä-tē\ [It] : an accompanying part usu. played by a solo instrument

ob·du·rate \ˈäb-də-rət, -dyə-\ *adj* : stubbornly resistant : UNYIELDING ⟨an ~ denial⟩ ♦ ***Synonyms*** INFLEXIBLE, ADAMANT, RIGID, UNCOMPROMISING — **ob·du·ra·cy** \-rə-sē\ *n*

obe·di·ent \ō-ˈbē-dē-ənt\ *adj* : submissive to the restraint or command of authority ♦ ***Synonyms*** DOCILE, TRACTABLE, AMENABLE, BIDDABLE — **obe·di·ence** \-əns\ *n* — **obe·di·ent·ly** *adv*

obei·sance \ō-ˈbē-səns, -ˈbā-\ *n* **1** : a bow made to show respect or submission **2** : DEFERENCE, HOMAGE ⟨makes ~ to her mentors⟩

obe·lisk \ˈä-bə-ˌlisk\ *n* [MF *obelisque,* fr. L *obeliscus,* fr. Gk *obeliskos,* fr. dim. of *obelos* spit, pointed pillar] : a 4-sided pillar that tapers toward the top and ends in a pyramid

obese \ō-ˈbēs\ *adj* [L *obesus,* fr. *ob-* against + *esus,* pp. of *edere* to eat] : having excessive body fat ♦ ***Synonyms*** CORPULENT, FLESHY, OVERWEIGHT, PORTLY, STOUT — **obe·si·ty** \-ˈbē-sə-tē\ *n*

obey \ō-ˈbā\ *vb* **obeyed; obey·ing** **1** : to follow the commands or guidance of : behave obediently **2** : to comply with ⟨~ orders⟩ ♦ ***Synonyms*** CONFORM, KEEP, MIND, OBSERVE

ob·fus·cate \ˈäb-fə-ˌskāt\ *vb* **-cat·ed; -cat·ing** **1** : to make dark or obscure **2** : to make difficult to understand — **ob·fus·ca·tion** \ˌäb-fəs-ˈkā-shən\ *n*

OB–GYN *abbr* obstetrician gynecologist; obstetrics gynecology

obi \ˈō-bē\ *n* [Jp] : a broad sash worn esp. with a Japanese kimono

obit \ō-ˈbit, ˈō-bət\ *n* : OBITUARY

obi·ter dic·tum \ˌō-bə-tər-ˈdik-təm\ *n, pl* **obiter dic·ta** \-tə\ [LL, lit., something said in passing] : an incidental remark or observation

obit·u·ary \ə-ˈbi-chə-ˌwer-ē\ *n, pl* **-ar·ies** : a notice of a person's death usu. with a short biographical account

obj *abbr* object; objective

¹**ob·ject** \ˈäb-jikt\ *n* **1** : something that may be seen or felt; *also* : something that may be perceived or examined mentally **2** : something that arouses an emotional response (as of affection or pity) **3** : AIM, PURPOSE ⟨the ~ is to raise money⟩ **4** : a word or word group denoting that which the action of the verb is directed on or toward; *also* : a noun or noun equivalent in a prepositional phrase

²**ob·ject** \əb-ˈjekt\ *vb* **1** : to offer in opposition **2** : to oppose something; *also* : DISAPPROVE ♦ ***Synonyms*** PROTEST, REMONSTRATE, EXPOSTULATE — **ob·jec·tor** \-ˈjek-tər\ *n*

object code *n* : a computer program after translation from source code

ob·jec·ti·fy \əb-ˈjek-tə-ˌfī\ *vb* **-fied; -fy·ing** : to make objective

ob·jec·tion \əb-ˈjek-shən\ *n* **1** : the act of objecting **2** : a reason for or a feeling of disapproval

ob·jec·tion·able \əb-ˈjek-shə-nə-bəl\ *adj* : UNDESIRABLE, OFFENSIVE — **ob·jec·tion·ably** \-blē\ *adv*

¹**ob·jec·tive** \əb-ˈjek-tiv\ *adj* **1** : of or relating to an object or end **2** : existing outside and independent of the mind **3** : of, relating to, or constituting a grammatical case marking typically the object of a verb or preposition **4** : treating or dealing with facts without distortion by personal feelings or prejudices — **ob·jec·tive·ly** *adv* — **ob·jec·tive·ness** *n* — **ob·jec·tiv·i·ty** \ˌäb-ˌjek-ˈti-və-tē\ *n*

²**objective** *n* **1** : the lens (as in a microscope) nearest the object and forming an image of it **2** : an aim, goal, or end of action

ob·jet d'art \ˌȯb-ˌzhā-ˈdär\ *n, pl* **ob·jets d'art** *same*\ [F] **1** : an article of artistic worth **2** : CURIO ♦ ***Synonyms*** KNICKKNACK, BAUBLE, BIBELOT, GEWGAW, NOVELTY, TRINKET

ob·jet trou·vé \ˈȯb-ˌzhā-trü-ˈvā\ *n, pl* **objets trouvés** *same*\ [F, lit., found object] : a found natural or discarded object (as a piece of driftwood or an old bathtub) held to have aesthetic value

ob·jur·ga·tion \ˌäb-jər-ˈgā-shən\ *n* : a harsh rebuke — **ob·jur·gate** \ˈäb-jər-ˌgāt\ *vb*

obl *abbr* **1** oblique **2** oblong

ob·late \ä-ˈblāt\ *adj* : flattened or depressed at the poles ⟨an ~ spheroid⟩

ob·la·tion \ə-ˈblā-shən\ *n* : a religious offering

ob·li·gate \ˈä-blə-ˌgāt\ *vb* **-gat·ed; -gat·ing** : to bind legally or morally

ob·li·ga·tion \ˌä-blə-ˈgā-shən\ *n* **1** : an act of obligating oneself to a course of action **2** : something (as a promise or a contract) that binds one to a course of action **3** : INDEBTEDNESS; *also* : LIABILITY **4** : DUTY — **oblig·a·to·ry** \ə-ˈbli-gə-ˌtȯr-ē\ *adj*

oblige \ə-ˈblīj\ *vb* **obliged; oblig·ing** [ME, fr. AF *obliger,* fr. L *obligare,* lit., to bind to, fr. *ob-* toward + *ligare* to bind] **1** : FORCE, COMPEL ⟨the soldiers were *obliged* to retreat⟩ **2** : to bind by a favor; *also* : to do a favor for or do something as a favor

oblig·ing *adj* : willing to do favors — **oblig·ing·ly** *adv*

oblique \ō-ˈblēk\ *adj* **1** : neither perpendicular nor parallel : SLANTING **2** : not straightforward : INDIRECT — **oblique·ly** *adv* — **oblique·ness** *n* — **obliq·ui·ty** \-ˈbli-kwə-tē\ *n*

oblique case *n* : a grammatical case other than the nominative or vocative

oblit·er·ate \ə-ˈbli-tə-ˌrāt\ *vb* **-at·ed; -at·ing** [L *oblitterare,* fr. *ob* in the way of + *littera* letter] **1** : to remove from recognition or memory **2** : to make undecipherable by wiping out or covering over **3** : CANCEL — **oblit·er·a·tion** \-ˌbli-tə-ˈrā-shən\ *n*

obliv·i·on \ə-ˈbli-vē-ən\ *n* **1** : the condition of being oblivious **2** : the condition or state of being forgotten

obliv·i·ous \ə-ˈbli-ve-əs\ *adj* **1** : lacking memory or mindful attention **2** : UNAWARE ⟨∼ of the risks⟩ — **obliv·i·ous·ly** *adv* — **obliv·i·ous·ness** *n*

ob·long \ˈä-ˌblȯŋ\ *adj* : deviating from a square, circular, or spherical form by elongation in one dimension — **oblong** *n*

ob·lo·quy \ˈä-blə-kwē\ *n, pl* **-quies** **1** : strongly condemnatory utterance or language **2** : bad repute : DISGRACE ♦ ***Synonyms*** DISHONOR, SHAME, INFAMY, DISREPUTE, IGNOMINY

ob·nox·ious \äb-ˈnäk-shəs\ *adj* : REPUGNANT, OFFENSIVE ⟨∼ behavior⟩ — **ob·nox·ious·ly** *adv* — **ob·nox·ious·ness** *n*

oboe \ˈō-bō\ *n* [It, fr. F *hautbois,* fr. *haut* high + *bois* wood] : a woodwind instrument with a slender conical tube and a double reed mouthpiece — **obo·ist** \ˈō-ˌbō-ist\ *n*

ob·scene \äb-ˈsēn\ *adj* **1** : REPULSIVE **2** : deeply offensive to morality or decency; *esp* : designed to incite to lust or depravity ♦ ***Synonyms*** GROSS, VULGAR, COARSE, CRUDE, INDECENT — **ob·scene·ly** *adv* — **ob·scen·i·ty** \-ˈse-nə-tē\ *n*

ob·scu·ran·tism \äb-ˈskyu̇r-ən-ˌti-zəm, ˌäb-skyu̇-ˈran-\ *n* **1** : opposition to the spread of knowledge **2** : deliberate vagueness or abstruseness — **ob·scu·ran·tist** \-tist\ *n or adj*

¹**ob·scure** \äb-ˈskyu̇r\ *adj* **1** : DIM, GLOOMY **2** : not readily understood : VAGUE **3** : REMOTE; *also* : HUMBLE ♦ ***Synonyms*** DARK, DUSKY, MURKY, TENEBROUS — **ob·scure·ly** *adv* — **ob·scu·ri·ty** \-ˈskyu̇r-ə-tē\ *n*

²**obscure** *vb* **ob·scured; ob·scur·ing** **1** : to make dark, dim, or indistinct **2** : to conceal or hide by or as if by covering

ob·se·qui·ous \əb-ˈsē-kwē-əs\ *adj* : humbly or excessively attentive (as to a person in authority) : FAWNING, SYCOPHANTIC ♦ ***Synonyms*** MENIAL, SERVILE, SLAVISH, SUBSERVIENT — **ob·se·qui·ous·ly** *adv* — **ob·se·qui·ous·ness** *n*

ob·se·quy \ˈäb-sə-kwē\ *n, pl* **-quies** : a funeral or burial rite — usu. used in pl.

ob·serv·able \əb-ˈzər-və-bəl\ *adj* **1** : NOTEWORTHY **2** : capable of being observed — **ob·serv·abil·ity** \-ˈbi-lə-tē\ *n*

ob·ser·vance \əb-ˈzər-vəns\ *n* **1** : a customary practice or ceremony **2** : an act or instance of following a custom, rule, or law **3** : OBSERVATION

ob·ser·vant \-vənt\ *adj* **1** : WATCHFUL ⟨∼ spectators⟩ **2** : KEEN, PERCEPTIVE **3** : MINDFUL ⟨∼ of the amenities⟩

¹**ob·ser·va·tion** \ˌäb-sər-ˈvā-shən, -zər-\ *n* **1** : an act or instance of observing **2** : the gathering of information (as for scientific studies) by noting facts or occurrences **3** : a conclusion drawn from observing; *also* : REMARK, STATEMENT **4** : the fact of being observed — **ob·ser·va·tion·al** \-shə-nəl\ *adj*

²**observation** *adj* : designed for use in viewing or in making observations

ob·ser·va·to·ry \əb-ˈzər-və-ˌtȯr-ē\ *n, pl* **-ries** : a place or institution equipped for observation of natural phenomena (as in astronomy)

ob·serve \əb-ˈzərv\ *vb* **ob·served; ob·serv·ing** **1** : to conform one's action or practice to **2** : CELEBRATE **3** : to make a scientific observation of **4** : to see or sense esp. through careful attention **5** : to come to realize esp. through consideration of noted facts **6** : REMARK — **ob·serv·er** *n*

ob·sess \əb-ˈses\ *vb* : to preoccupy intensely or abnormally

ob·ses·sion \äb-ˈse-shən\ *n* : a persistent disturbing preoccupation with an idea or feeling; *also* : an emotion or idea causing such a preoccupation — **ob·ses·sive** \-ˈse-siv\ *adj or n* — **ob·ses·sive·ly** *adv*

obsessive–compulsive *adj* : relating to, characterized by, or affected with recurring obsessions and compulsions esp. as symptoms of a neurotic state

ob·sid·i·an \əb-ˈsi-dē-ən\ *n* : a dark natural glass formed by the cooling of molten lava

ob·so·les·cent \ˌäb-sə-ˈle-sᵊnt\ *adj* : going out of use : becoming obsolete ⟨∼ computers⟩ — **ob·so·les·cence** \-sᵊns\ *n*

ob·so·lete \ˌäb-sə-ˈlēt, ˈäb-sə-ˌlēt\ *adj* : no longer in use; *also* : OLD-FASHIONED ⟨an ∼ technology⟩ ♦ ***Synonyms*** EXTINCT, OUTWORN, PASSÉ, SUPERSEDED

ob·sta·cle \ˈäb-sti-kəl\ *n* : something that stands in the way or opposes

ob·stet·rics \əb-ˈste-triks\ *n sing or pl* : a branch of medicine that deals with birth and with its antecedents and sequels — **ob·stet·ric** \-trik\ *or* **ob·stet·ri·cal** \-tri-kəl\ *adj* — **ob·ste·tri·cian** \ˌäb-stə-ˈtri-shən\ *n*

ob·sti·nate \ˈäb-stə-nət\ *adj* : fixed and unyielding (as in an opinion or course) despite reason or persuasion : STUBBORN ⟨∼ opposition⟩ — **ob·sti·na·cy** \-nə-sē\ *n* — **ob·sti·nate·ly** *adv*

ob·strep·er·ous \əb-ˈstre-pə-rəs\ *adj* **1** : uncontrollably noisy **2** : stubbornly resistant to control : UNRULY — **ob·strep·er·ous·ness** *n*

ob·struct \əb-ˈstrəkt\ *vb* **1** : to block by an obstacle **2** : to impede the passage, action, or operation of **3** : to cut off from sight — **ob·struc·tive** \-ˈstrək-tiv\ *adj* — **ob·struc·tor** \-tər\ *n*

ob·struc·tion \əb-ˈstrək-shən\ *n* **1** : an act of obstructing : the state of being obstructed **2** : something that obstructs : HINDRANCE

ob·struc·tion·ist \-shə-nist\ *n* : a person who hinders progress or business esp. in a legislative body — **ob·struc·tion·ism** \-shə-ˌni-zəm\ *n*

ob·tain \əb-ˈtān\ *vb* **1** : to gain or attain usu. by planning or effort **2** : to be generally recognized or established ♦ ***Synonyms*** PROCURE, SECURE, WIN, EARN, ACQUIRE — **ob·tain·able** *adj*

ob·trude \əb-ˈtrüd\ *vb* **ob·trud·ed; ob·trud·ing** **1** : to thrust out **2** : to thrust forward without warrant or request **3** : INTRUDE — **ob·tru·sion** \-ˈtrü-zhən\ *n* — **ob·tru·sive** \-ˈtrü-siv\ *adj* — **ob·tru·sive·ly** *adv* — **ob·tru·sive·ness** *n*

ob·tuse \äb-ˈtüs, -ˈtyüs\ *adj* **ob·tus·er; -est** **1** : exceeding 90 degrees but less than 180 degrees ⟨~ angle⟩ **2** : not pointed or acute : BLUNT **3** : not sharp or quick of wit ⟨is too ~ to take a hint⟩ — **ob·tuse·ly** *adv* — **ob·tuse·ness** *n*

obv *abbr* obverse

[1]**ob·verse** \äb-ˈvərs, ˈäb-ˌvərs\ *adj* **1** : facing the observer or opponent **2** : being a counterpart or complement — **ob·verse·ly** *adv*

[2]**ob·verse** \ˈäb-ˌvərs, äb-ˈvərs\ *n* **1** : the side (as of a coin) bearing the principal design and lettering **2** : a front or principal surface **3** : a counterpart having the opposite orientation or force

ob·vi·ate \ˈäb-vē-ˌāt\ *vb* **-at·ed; -at·ing** : to anticipate and prevent (as a situation) or make unnecessary (as an action) ♦ ***Synonyms*** PREVENT, AVERT, FORESTALL, FORFEND, PRECLUDE — **ob·vi·a·tion** \ˌäb-vē-ˈā-shən\ *n*

ob·vi·ous \ˈäb-vē-əs\ *adj* [L *obvius,* fr. *obviam* in the way, fr. *ob* in the way of + *viam,* accusative of *via* way] : easily found, seen, or understood : PLAIN ♦ ***Synonyms*** EVIDENT, MANIFEST, PATENT, CLEAR — **ob·vi·ous·ly** *adv* — **ob·vi·ous·ness** *n*

OC *abbr* officer candidate

oc·a·ri·na \ˌä-kə-ˈrē-nə\ *n* [It] : a wind instrument typically having an oval body with finger holes and a projecting mouthpiece

occas *abbr* occasionally

[1]**oc·ca·sion** \ə-ˈkā-zhən\ *n* **1** : a favorable opportunity **2** : a direct or indirect cause **3** : the time of an event **4** : EXIGENCY **5** *pl* : AFFAIRS, BUSINESS **6** : a special event : CELEBRATION

[2]**occasion** *vb* : BRING ABOUT, CAUSE

oc·ca·sion·al \ə-ˈkā-zhə-nəl\ *adj* **1** : happening or met with now and then ⟨~ visits⟩ **2** : used or designed for a special occasion ⟨~ verse⟩ ♦ ***Synonyms*** INFREQUENT, RARE, SPORADIC — **oc·ca·sion·al·ly** *adv*

oc·ci·den·tal \ˌäk-sə-ˈden-tᵊl\ *adj, often cap* [fr. *Occident* West, fr. ME, fr. AF, fr. L *occident-, occidens,* fr. prp. of *occidere* to fall, set (of the sun)] : WESTERN — **Occidental** *n*

Oc·ci·tan \ˈäk-sə-ˌtan\ *n* [F, fr. ML *occitanus,* fr. Old Occitan *oc* yes (contrasted with OF *oïl* yes)] : a Romance language spoken in southern France

oc·clude \ə-ˈklüd\ *vb* **oc·clud·ed; oc·clud·ing** **1** : OBSTRUCT ⟨an *occluded* artery⟩ **2** : to come together with opposing surfaces in contact — used of teeth — **oc·clu·sion** \-ˈklü-zhən\ *n* — **oc·clu·sive** \-ˈklü-siv\ *adj*

[1]**oc·cult** \ə-ˈkəlt\ *adj* **1** : not revealed : SECRET **2** : ABSTRUSE, MYSTERIOUS **3** : of or relating to supernatural agencies, their effects, or knowledge of them ⟨the ~ arts⟩ — **oc·cult·ism** \-ˈkəl-ˌti-zəm\ *n* — **oc·cult·ist** \-tist\ *n*

[2]**occult** *n* : occult matters — used with *the*

oc·cu·pan·cy \ˈä-kyə-pən-sē\ *n, pl* **-cies** **1** : the act of occupying : the state of being occupied **2** : an occupied building or part of a building

oc·cu·pant \-pənt\ *n* : one who occupies something; *esp* : RESIDENT

oc·cu·pa·tion \ˌä-kyə-ˈpā-shən\ *n* **1** : an activity in which one engages; *esp* : VOCATION **2** : the taking possession of property; *also* : the taking possession of an area by a foreign military force — **oc·cu·pa·tion·al** \-shə-nəl\ *adj* — **oc·cu·pa·tion·al·ly** *adv*

occupational therapy *n* : therapy that helps people with limitations in physical or mental functioning to learn to do the activities of daily life — **occupational therapist** *n*

oc·cu·py \ˈä-kyə-ˌpī\ *vb* **-pied; -py·ing** **1** : to engage the attention or energies of **2** : to fill up (an extent in space or time) **3** : to take or hold possession of **4** : to reside in as owner or tenant — **oc·cu·pi·er** *n*

oc·cur \ə-ˈkər\ *vb* **oc·curred; oc·cur·ring** [L *occurrere,* fr. *ob-* in the way + *currere* to run] **1** : to be found or met with : APPEAR **2** : HAPPEN ⟨the event will ~ at noon⟩ **3** : to come to mind

oc·cur·rence \ə-ˈkər-əns\ *n* **1** : something that takes place **2** : the action or process of occurring

ocean \ˈō-shən\ *n* **1** : the whole body of salt water that covers nearly three fourths of the surface of the earth **2** : any of the large bodies of water into which the great ocean is divided — **oce·an·ic** \ˌō-shē-ˈa-nik\ *adj*

ocean·ar·i·um \ˌō-shə-ˈnar-ē-əm\ *n, pl* **-iums** *or* **-ia** \-ē-ə\ : a large marine aquarium

ocean·front \ˈō-shən-ˌfrənt\ *n* : a shore area on the ocean

ocean·go·ing \-ˌgō-iŋ\ *adj* : of, relating to, or suitable for travel on the ocean

ocean·og·ra·phy \ˌō-shə-ˈnä-grə-fē\ *n* : a science dealing with the ocean and its phenomena — **ocean·og·ra·pher** \-fər\ *n* — **ocean·o·graph·ic** \-nə-ˈgra-fik\ *adj*

oce·lot \ˈä-sə-ˌlät, ˈō-\ *n* : a medium-sized American wildcat ranging southward from Texas to northern Argentina and having a tawny yellow or gray coat with black markings

ocher *or* **ochre** \ˈō-kər\ *n* : an earthy usu. red or yellow iron ore used as a pigment; *also* : the color esp. of yellow ocher
o'·clock \ə-ˈkläk\ *adv* : according to the clock
OCR *abbr* optical character reader; optical character recognition
OCS *abbr* officer candidate school
oct *abbr* octavo
Oct *abbr* October
oc·ta·gon \ˈäk-tə-ˌgän\ *n* : a polygon of eight angles and eight sides — **oc·tag·o·nal** \äk-ˈta-gə-nᵊl\ *adj*
oc·tane \ˈäk-ˌtān\ *n* : OCTANE NUMBER
octane number *n* : a number used to measure the antiknock properties of gasoline that increases as the likelihood of knocking decreases
oc·tave \ˈäk-tiv\ *n* **1** : a musical interval embracing eight degrees; *also* : a tone or note at this interval or the whole series of notes, tones, or keys within this interval **2** : a group of eight
oc·ta·vo \äk-ˈtā-vō, -ˈtä-\ *n, pl* **-vos** **1** : the size of a piece of paper cut eight from a sheet **2** : a book printed on octavo pages
oc·tet \äk-ˈtet\ *n* **1** : a musical composition for eight voices or eight instruments; *also* : the performers of such a composition **2** : a group or set of eight
Oc·to·ber \äk-ˈtō-bər\ *n* [ME *Octobre,* fr. OE *October,* fr. L, eighth month of the early Roman calendar, fr. *octo* eight] : the 10th month of the year
October surprise *n* : a significant revelation or event shortly before an esp. U.S. presidential election that may shift public opinion about a candidate
oc·to·ge·nar·i·an \ˌäk-tə-jə-ˈner-ē-ən\ *n* : a person whose age is in the eighties
oc·to·pus \ˈäk-tə-pəs\ *n, pl* **-pus·es** *or* **-pi** \-ˌpī\ : any of various sea mollusks with eight long muscular arms furnished with suckers
oc·to·syl·lab·ic \ˌäk-tə-sə-ˈla-bik\ *adj* : composed of verses having eight syllables — **octosyllabic** *n*
[1]**oc·u·lar** \ˈä-kyə-lər\ *adj* **1** : VISUAL **2** : of or relating to the eye or the eyesight
[2]**ocular** *n* : EYEPIECE
oc·u·list \ˈä-kyə-list\ *n* **1** : OPHTHALMOLOGIST **2** : OPTOMETRIST
[1]**OD** \ˌō-ˈdē\ *n* : an overdose of a drug and esp. a narcotic
[2]**OD** *vb* **OD'd** *or* **ODed; OD'ing; OD's** : to become ill or die from an OD
[3]**OD** *abbr* **1** doctor of optometry **2** [L *oculus dexter*] right eye **3** officer of the day **4** olive drab **5** overdraft **6** overdrawn
odd \ˈäd\ *adj* [ME *odde,* fr. ON *oddi* point of land, triangle, odd number] **1** : being only one of a pair or set ⟨an ~ shoe⟩ **2** : somewhat more than the number mentioned ⟨forty ~ years ago⟩ **3** : being an integer (as 1, 3, or 5) not divisible by two without leaving a remainder **4** : additional to what is usual ⟨~ jobs⟩ **5** : STRANGE ⟨an ~ way of behaving⟩ — **odd·ness** *n*
odd·ball \ˈäd-ˌbȯl\ *n* : one that is eccentric — **oddball** *adj*
odd·i·ty \ˈä-də-tē\ *n, pl* **-ties** **1** : one that is odd **2** : the quality or state of being odd
odd·ly \ˈäd-lē\ *adv* **1** : in an odd manner ⟨an ~ shaped roof⟩ **2** : as is odd
odd·ment \ˈäd-mənt\ *n* : something left over : REMNANT
odds \ˈädz\ *n pl* **1** : a difference by which one thing is favored over another **2** : DISAGREEMENT — usu. used with *at* **3** : the ratio between the amount to be paid for a winning bet and the amount of the bet ⟨the horse went off at ~ of 6–1⟩
odds and ends *n pl* : miscellaneous things or matters
odds–on \ˈädz-ˈȯn, -ˈän\ *adj* : having a better than even chance to win
ode \ˈōd\ *n* **1** : a lyric poem that expresses a noble feeling with dignity **2** : HOMAGE ⟨a film that's an ~ to LA⟩
odi·ous \ˈō-dē-əs\ *adj* : arousing or deserving hatred or repugnance — **odi·ous·ly** *adv* — **odi·ous·ness** *n*
odi·um \ˈō-dē-əm\ *n* **1** : merited loathing : HATRED **2** : DISGRACE ⟨the ~ of defeat⟩
odom·e·ter \ō-ˈdä-mə-tər\ *n* [F *odomètre,* fr. Gk *hodometron,* fr. *hodos* way, road + *metron* measure] : an instrument for measuring distance traveled (as by a vehicle)
odor \ˈō-dər\ *n* **1** : the quality of something that stimulates the sense of smell; *also* : a sensation resulting from such stimulation **2** : REPUTE, ESTIMATION — **odored** \ˈō-dərd\ *adj* — **odor·less** *adj* — **odor·ous** *adj*
odor·if·er·ous \ˌō-də-ˈri-fə-rəs\ *adj* : having or yielding an odor
odour *chiefly Brit var of* ODOR
od·ys·sey \ˈä-də-sē\ *n, pl* **-seys** [the *Odyssey,* epic poem attributed to Homer recounting the long wanderings of Odysseus] : a long wandering marked usu. by many changes of fortune
oe·cu·men·i·cal *esp Brit* ˌē-\ *chiefly Brit var of* ECUMENICAL
OED *abbr* Oxford English Dictionary
oe·de·ma *chiefly Brit var of* EDEMA
oe·di·pal \ˈe-də-pəl, ˈē-\ *adj, often cap* : of, relating to, or resulting from the Oedipus complex
Oe·di·pus complex \-pəs-\ *n* : the positive sexual feelings of a child toward the parent of the opposite sex and hostile or jealous feelings toward the parent of the same sex that may be a source of adult personality disorder when unresolved
o'er \ˈȯr\ *adv or prep* : OVER
OES *abbr* Order of the Eastern Star
oe·soph·a·gus *chiefly Brit var of* ESOPHAGUS
oeu·vre \ˈər-vrə, ˈœvrᵊ\ *n, pl* **oeuvres** *same*\ : a substantial body of work constituting the lifework of a writer, an artist, or a composer
of \ˈəv, ˈäv\ *prep* **1** : FROM ⟨a man ~ the West⟩ **2** : having as a significant background or character element ⟨a man ~ noble birth⟩ ⟨a woman ~ ability⟩ **3**

: owing to ⟨died ~ flu⟩ **4** : BY ⟨the plays ~ Shakespeare⟩ **5** : having as component parts or material, contents, or members ⟨a house ~ brick⟩ ⟨a glass ~ water⟩ ⟨a pack ~ fools⟩ **6** : belonging to or included by ⟨the front ~ the house⟩ ⟨a time ~ life⟩ ⟨one ~ you⟩ ⟨the best ~ its kind⟩ ⟨the son ~ a doctor⟩ **7** : ABOUT ⟨tales ~ the West⟩ **8** : connected with : OVER ⟨the queen ~ England⟩ **9** : that is : signified as ⟨the city ~ Rome⟩ **10** — used to indicate apposition of the words it joins ⟨that fool ~ a manager⟩ **11** : as concerns : FOR ⟨love ~ nature⟩ **12** — used to indicate the application of an adjective ⟨fond ~ candy⟩ **13** : BEFORE ⟨quarter ~ ten⟩

OF *abbr* outfield

[1]**off** \ˈȯf\ *adv* **1** : from a place or position ⟨drove ~ in a new car⟩; *also* : ASIDE ⟨turned ~ into a side road⟩ **2** : at a distance in time or space ⟨stood ~ a few yards⟩ ⟨several years ~⟩ **3** : so as to be unattached or removed ⟨the lid blew ~⟩ **4** : to a state of discontinuance, exhaustion, or completion ⟨shut the radio ~⟩ **5** : away from regular work ⟨took time ~ for lunch⟩

[2]**off** *prep* **1** : away from ⟨just ~ the highway⟩ ⟨take it ~ the table⟩ **2** : to seaward of ⟨two miles ~ the coast⟩ **3** : FROM ⟨borrowed a dollar ~ me⟩ **4** : at the expense of ⟨lives ~ his parents⟩ **5** : not now engaged in ⟨~ duty⟩ **6** : abstaining from ⟨~ liquor⟩ **7** : below the usual level of ⟨~ his game⟩

[3]**off** *adj* **1** : more removed or distant **2** : started on the way **3** : not operating **4** : not correct **5** : REMOTE, SLIGHT ⟨an ~ chance⟩ **6** : INFERIOR ⟨~ grade of oil⟩ **7** : provided for ⟨well ~⟩

[4]**off** *abbr* office; officer; official

of•fal \ˈȯ-fəl\ *n* [ME, fr. *of* off + *fall* fall] : the waste or by-product of a process; *esp* : the viscera and trimmings of a butchered animal removed in dressing

off and on *adv* : INTERMITTENTLY ⟨rained *off and on*⟩

[1]**off•beat** \ˈȯf-ˌbēt\ *n* : the unaccented part of a musical measure

[2]**offbeat** *adj* : ECCENTRIC, UNCONVENTIONAL ⟨an ~ style⟩

off–col•or \ˈȯf-ˈkə-lər\ *or* **off–col•ored** \-lərd\ *adj* **1** : not having the right or standard color **2** : of doubtful propriety : verging on indecency ⟨~ stories⟩

of•fend \ə-ˈfend\ *vb* **1** : SIN, TRANSGRESS **2** : to cause discomfort or pain : HURT **3** : to cause dislike or vexation : ANNOY ♦ ***Synonyms*** AFFRONT, INSULT, OUTRAGE — **of•fend•er** *n*

of•fense *or* **of•fence** \ə-ˈfens, *esp for 2 & 3* ˈä-ˌfens\ *n* **1** : something that outrages the senses **2** : ATTACK, ASSAULT **3** : the offensive team or members of a team playing offensive positions **4** : DISPLEASURE **5** : SIN, MISDEED **6** : an infraction of law : CRIME

[1]**of•fen•sive** \ə-ˈfen-siv, *esp for 1 & 2* ˈä-ˌfen-\ *adj* **1** : AGGRESSIVE **2** : of or relating to an attempt to score in a game; *also* : of or relating to a team in possession of the ball or puck **3** : OBNOXIOUS ⟨an ~ odor⟩ **4** : INSULTING ⟨~ remarks⟩ — **of•fen•sive•ly** *adv* — **of•fen•sive•ness** *n*

[2]**offensive** *n* : ATTACK

[1]**of•fer** \ˈȯ-fər\ *vb* **of•fered; of•fer•ing** **1** : SACRIFICE **2** : to present for acceptance : TENDER; *also* : to propose as payment **3** : PROPOSE, SUGGEST; *also* : to declare one's readiness **4** : to try or begin to exert ⟨~ resistance⟩ **5** : to place on sale — **of•fer•ing** *n*

[2]**offer** *n* **1** : PROPOSAL **2** : BID **3** : TRY

of•fer•to•ry \ˈȯ-fər-ˌtȯr-ē\ *n, pl* **-ries** : the presentation of offerings at a church service; *also* : the musical accompaniment during it

off–gas•sing \ˈȯf-ˌga-siŋ\ *n* : the emission of esp. noxious gases (as from a building material)

off•hand \ˈȯf-ˈhand\ *adv or adj* : without previous thought or preparation

off–hour \-ˌau̇(-ə)r\ *n* : a period of time other than a rush hour; *also* : a period of time other than business hours

of•fice \ˈȯ-fəs\ *n* **1** : a special duty or position; *esp* : a position of authority in government ⟨run for ~⟩ **2** : a prescribed form or service of worship; *also* : RITE **3** : an assigned or assumed duty or role **4** : a place where a business is transacted or a service is supplied

of•fice•hold•er \ˈȯ-fəs-ˌhōl-dər\ *n* : one holding a public office

of•fi•cer \ˈȯ-fə-sər\ *n* **1** : one charged with the enforcement of law **2** : one who holds an office of trust or authority **3** : a person who holds a position of authority or command in the armed forces; *esp* : COMMISSIONED OFFICER

[1]**of•fi•cial** \ə-ˈfi-shəl\ *n* : OFFICER 2

[2]**official** *adj* **1** : of or relating to an office or to officers **2** : AUTHORIZED, AUTHORITATIVE ⟨~ statement⟩ **3** : befitting or characteristic of a person in office — **of•fi•cial•ly** *adv*

of•fi•cial•dom \ə-ˈfi-shəl-dəm\ *n* : officials as a class

of•fi•cial•ism \ə-ˈfi-shə-ˌli-zəm\ *n* : lack of flexibility and initiative combined with excessive adherence to regulations

of•fi•ci•ant \ə-ˈfi-shē-ənt\ *n* : one (as a priest) who officiates at a religious rite

of•fi•ci•ate \ə-ˈfi-shē-ˌāt\ *vb* **-at•ed; -at•ing** **1** : to perform a ceremony, function, or duty **2** : to act in an official capacity

of•fi•cious \ə-ˈfi-shəs\ *adj* : volunteering one's services where they are neither asked for nor needed ⟨an ~ busybody⟩ — **of•fi•cious•ly** *adv* — **of•fi•cious•ness** *n*

off•ing \ˈȯ-fiŋ\ *n* : the near or foreseeable future

off–line \ˈȯf-ˈlīn\ *adj or adv* : not connected to or controlled directly by a computer

off of *prep* : OFF

off•print \ˈȯf-ˌprint\ *n* : a separately printed excerpt (as from a magazine)

off–road \-ˈrōd\ *adj* : of, relating to, or being a vehicle designed for use away

from public roads — **off–road·er** \-ˈrō-dər\ *n*
off–sea·son \-ˌsē-zᵊn\ *n* : a time of suspended or reduced activity
[1]**off·set** \-ˌset\ *n* **1** : a sharp bend (as in a pipe) by which one part is turned aside out of line **2** : a printing process in which an inked impression is first made on a rubber-blanketed cylinder and then transferred to the paper
[2]**off·set** *vb* **off·set; off·set·ting** **1** : to place over against : BALANCE **2** : to compensate for **3** : to form an offset in (∼ a wall)
off·shoot \ˈȯf-ˌshüt\ *n* **1** : a collateral or derived branch, descendant, or member **2** : a branch of a main stem (as of a plant)
[1]**off·shore** \ˈȯf-ˈshȯr\ *adv* **1** : at a distance from the shore **2** : outside the country : ABROAD
[2]**off·shore** \ˈȯf-ˌshȯr\ *adj* **1** : moving away from the shore **2** : situated off the shore but within waters under a country's control
off·side \-ˈsīd\ *adv or adj* : illegally in advance of the ball or puck
off·spring \-ˌspriŋ\ *n, pl* **offspring** *also* **offsprings** : PROGENY, YOUNG
off·stage \ˈȯf-ˈstāj, -ˌstāj\ *adv or adj* **1** : off or away from the stage **2** : out of the public view ⟨deals made ∼⟩
off–the–record *adj* : given or made in confidence and not for publication
off–the–shelf *adj* : available as a stock item : not specially designed or made
off–the–wall *adj* : highly unusual : BIZARRE ⟨an ∼ sense of humor⟩
off·track \ˈȯf-ˈtrak\ *adv or adj* : away from a racetrack
off–white \ˈȯf-ˈhwīt\ *n* : a yellowish or grayish white color
off year *n* **1** : a year in which no major election is held **2** : a year of diminished activity or production
oft \ˈȯft\ *adv* : OFTEN
of·ten \ˈȯ-fən\ *adv* : many times : FREQUENTLY
of·ten·times \-ˌtīmz\ *or* **oft·times** \ˈȯf-ˌtīmz, ˈȯft-\ *adv* : OFTEN
Og *symbol* oganesson
oga·nes·son \ˌō-gə-ˈne-ˌsän, ˌä-\ *n* : a short-lived artificially produced radioactive chemical element
ogle \ˈō-gəl\ *vb* **ogled; ogling** : to look at in a flirtatious way — **ogle** *n* — **ogler** *n*
ogre \ˈō-gər\ *n* **1** : a monster of fairy tales and folklore that eats people **2** : a dreaded person or object
ogress \ˈō-grəs\ *n* : a female ogre
oh *also* **O** \ˈō\ *interj* **1** — used to express an emotion or in response to physical stimuli **2** — used in direct address
OH *abbr* Ohio
ohm \ˈōm\ *n* : a unit of electrical resistance equal to the resistance of a circuit in which a potential difference of one volt produces a current of one ampere — **ohm·ic** \ˈō-mik\ *adj*
ohm·me·ter \ˈōm-ˌmē-tər\ *n* : an instrument for indicating resistance in ohms directly
[1]**oil** \ˈȯi(-ə)l\ *n* [ME *oile,* fr. AF, fr. L *oleum* olive oil, fr. Gk *elaion,* fr. *elaia* olive] **1** : any of numerous fatty or greasy liquid substances obtained from plants, animals, or minerals and used for fuel, food, medicines, and manufacturing **2** : PETROLEUM **3** : artists' colors made with oil; *also* : a painting in such colors — **oil·i·ness** \ˈȯi-lē-nəs\ *n* — **oily** \ˈȯi-lē\ *adj*
[2]**oil** *vb* : to put oil in or on — **oil·er** *n*
oil·cloth \ˈȯi(-ə)l-ˌklȯth\ *n* : cloth treated with oil or paint and used for table and shelf coverings
oil pan *n* : the lower section of a crankcase used as an oil reservoir
oil shale *n* : a rock (as shale) from which oil can be recovered
oil·skin \ˈȯi(-ə)l-ˌskin\ *n* **1** : an oiled waterproof cloth **2** : an oilskin raincoat **3** *pl* : an oilskin coat and pants
oink \ˈȯiŋk\ *n* : the natural noise of a hog — **oink** *vb*
oint·ment \ˈȯint-mənt\ *n* : a salve for use on the skin
OJ *abbr* orange juice
Ojib·wa *or* **Ojib·way** *or* **Ojibwe** \ō-ˈjib-ˌwā\ *n, pl* **Ojibwa** *or* **Ojibwas** *or* **Ojibway** *or* **Ojibways** *or* **Ojibwe** *or* **Ojibwes** **1** : a member of a First Nations people of the region around Lake Superior and westward **2** : the Algonquian language of the Ojibwa people
OJT *abbr* on-the-job training
[1]**OK** *or* **okay** \ō-ˈkā\ *adv or adj* : all right
[2]**OK** *or* **okay** *vb* **OK'd** *or* **okayed; OK'·ing** *or* **okay·ing** : APPROVE, AUTHORIZE — **OK** *or* **okay** *n*
[3]**OK** *abbr* Oklahoma
Okla *abbr* Oklahoma
okra \ˈō-krə\ *n* : a tall annual plant related to the mallows that has edible green pods; *also* : these pods
[1]**old** \ˈōld\ *adj* **1** : ANCIENT; *also* : of long standing **2** *cap* : belonging to an early period ⟨*Old* Irish⟩ **3** : having existed for a specified period of time **4** : of or relating to a past era **5** : advanced in years **6** : showing the effects of age or use **7** : no longer in use — **old·ish** \ˈōl-dish\ *adj*
[2]**old** *n* : old or earlier time ⟨days of ∼⟩
old·en \ˈōl-dən\ *adj* : of or relating to a bygone era
[1]**old–fash·ioned** \ˈōld-ˈfa-shənd\ *adj* **1** : OUT-OF-DATE, ANTIQUATED **2** : CONSERVATIVE
[2]**old–fashioned** *n* : a cocktail usu. made with whiskey, bitters, sugar, a twist of lemon peel, and water or soda water
old–growth \ˈōld-ˈgrōth\ *adj* : of, relating to, or being a forest with large old trees, numerous snags and woody debris, and a multilayered canopy
old guard *n, often cap O&G* : the conservative members of an organization
old hat *adj* **1** : OLD-FASHIONED ⟨equipment that is now *old hat*⟩ **2** : STALE, TRITE
old·ie \ˈōl-dē\ *n* : something old; *esp* : a popular song from the past
old–line \ˈōld-ˈlīn\ *adj* **1** : ORIGINAL, ES-

TABLISHED ⟨an ~ business⟩ **2** : adhering to old policies or practices
old maid *n* **1** : SPINSTER **2** : a prim fussy person — **old–maid·ish** \ˈōld-ˈmā-dish\ *adj*
old man *n* **1** : HUSBAND **2** : FATHER
old–school *adj* : adhering to traditional policies or practices ⟨an ~ politician⟩
old·ster \ˈōld-stər\ *n* : an old or elderly person
Old Testament *n* : the first of the two chief divisions of the Christian Bible — see BIBLE table
old–time \ˈōld-ˈtīm\ *adj* **1** : of, relating to, or characteristic of an earlier period **2** : of long standing
old–tim·er \-ˈtī-mər\ *n* : VETERAN; *also* : OLDSTER
old–world \-ˈwərld\ *adj* : characteristic of the Old World often in having old-fashioned charm ⟨an ~ hotel⟩
Old World *n* : the eastern hemisphere exclusive of Australia — used with *the*
ole·ag·i·nous \ˌō-lē-ˈa-jə-nəs\ *adj* : OILY
ole·an·der \ˈō-lē-ˌan-dər\ *n* : a poisonous evergreen shrub often grown for its fragrant white to red flowers
oleo \ˈō-lē-ˌō\ *n, pl* **ole·os** : MARGARINE
oleo·mar·ga·rine \ˌō-lē-ō-ˈmär-jə-rən\ *n* : MARGARINE
ol·fac·to·ry \äl-ˈfak-tə-rē, ōl-\ *adj* : of or relating to the sense of smell
oli·gar·chy \ˈä-lə-ˌgär-kē, ˈō-\ *n, pl* **-chies** **1** : a government in which power is in the hands of a few **2** : a state having an oligarchy; *also* : the group holding power in such a state — **oli·garch** \-ˌgärk\ *n* — **oli·gar·chic** \ˌä-lə-ˈgär-kik, ˌō-\ *or* **oli·gar·chi·cal** \-ki-kəl\ *adj*
Oli·go·cene \ˈä-li-gō-ˌsēn, ə-ˈli-gə-ˌsēn\ *adj* : of, relating to, or being the epoch of the Tertiary between the Eocene and the Miocene — **Oligocene** *n*
olio \ˈō-lē-ˌō\ *n, pl* **oli·os** : HODGEPODGE, MEDLEY
ol·ive \ˈä-liv\ *n* **1** : an Old World evergreen tree grown in warm regions for its fruit that is a food and the source of an edible oil (**olive oil**); *also* : the fruit **2** : a color resembling that of the unripe yellowish green fruit of the olive tree
olive drab *n* **1** : a grayish olive color **2** : an olive drab wool or cotton fabric; *also* : a uniform of this fabric
ol·iv·ine \ˈä-lə-ˌvēn\ *n* : a usu. greenish mineral that is a complex silicate of magnesium and iron
Olym·pi·an \ə-ˈlim-pē-ən\ *n* : a participant in the Olympic Games
Olym·pic Games \ə-ˈlim-pik-\ *n pl* : a modified revival of an ancient Greek festival consisting of international athletic contests that are held at separate winter and summer gatherings at four-year intervals
om \ˈōm\ *n* : a mantra consisting of the sound "om" used in contemplating ultimate reality
Oma·ha \ˈō-mə-ˌhä, -ˌhȯ\ *n, pl* **Omaha** *or* **Omahas** : a member of an Indigenous people of northeastern Nebraska; *also* : the language of the Omaha people
om·bre \ˈäm-ˌbrā\ *adj* : having colors or hues that shade into each other
om·buds·man \ˈäm-ˌbu̇dz-mən, äm-ˈbu̇dz-\ *n, pl* **-men** \-mən\ **1** : a government official appointed to investigate complaints made by individuals against abuses or capricious acts of public officials **2** : one that investigates reported complaints (as from students or consumers)
ome·ga \ō-ˈmā-gə\ *n* : the 24th and last letter of the Greek alphabet — Ω or ω
om·elet *or* **om·elette** \ˈäm-lət, ˈä-mə-\ *n* [F *omelette,* alter. of MF *amelette, alemette,* alter. of *alemelle* thin plate, ultim. fr. L *lamella,* dim. of *lamina*] : eggs beaten with milk or water, cooked without stirring until set, and folded over
omen \ˈō-mən\ *n* : an event or phenomenon believed to be a sign or warning of a future occurrence
om·i·cron \ˈä-mə-ˌkrän, ˈō-\ *n* : the 15th letter of the Greek alphabet — O or ο
om·i·nous \ˈä-mə-nəs\ *adj* : foretelling evil : THREATENING — **om·i·nous·ly** *adv* — **om·i·nous·ness** *n*
omis·si·ble \ō-ˈmi-sə-bəl\ *adj* : that may be omitted ⟨~ details⟩
omis·sion \ō-ˈmi-shən\ *n* **1** : something neglected or left undone **2** : the act of omitting : the state of being omitted
omit \ō-ˈmit\ *vb* **omit·ted; omit·ting** **1** : to leave out or leave unmentioned **2** : to leave undone: FAIL
[1]**om·ni·bus** \ˈäm-ni-(ˌ)bəs\ *n* : BUS
[2]**omnibus** *adj* : of, relating to, or providing for many things at once ⟨an ~ bill⟩
om·nip·o·tent \äm-ˈni-pə-tənt\ *adj* **1** *often cap* : ALMIGHTY 1 **2** : having unlimited authority or influence ⟨an ~ ruler⟩ — **om·nip·o·tence** \-təns\ *n* — **om·nip·o·tent·ly** *adv*
om·ni·pres·ent \ˌäm-ni-ˈpre-zᵊnt\ *adj* : present in all places at all times ⟨an ~ problem⟩ — **om·ni·pres·ence** \-zᵊns\ *n*
om·ni·scient \äm-ˈni-shənt\ *adj* : having infinite awareness, understanding, and insight — **om·ni·science** \-shəns\ *n* — **om·ni·scient·ly** *adv*
om·ni·um–gath·er·um \ˌäm-nē-əm-ˈga-t͟hə-rəm\ *n, pl* **omnium–gatherums** : a miscellaneous collection
om·niv·o·rous \äm-ˈni-və-rəs\ *adj* **1** : feeding on both animal and vegetable substances **2** : AVID ⟨an ~ reader⟩ — **om·ni·vore** \ˈäm-ni-ˌvȯr\ *n* — **om·niv·o·rous·ly** *adv*
[1]**on** \ˈȯn, ˈän\ *prep* **1** : in or to a position over and in contact with ⟨jumped ~ his horse⟩ **2** : touching the surface of ⟨shadows ~ the wall⟩ **3** : AT, TO ⟨~ the right were the mountains⟩ **4** : IN, ABOARD ⟨went ~ the train⟩ **5** : during or at the time of ⟨came ~ Monday⟩ ⟨every hour ~ the hour⟩ **6** : through the agency of ⟨was cut ~ a tin can⟩ **7** : in a state or process of ⟨~ fire⟩ ⟨~ the wane⟩ **8** : connected with as a member or participant ⟨~ a committee⟩ ⟨~ tour⟩ **9** — used to indicate a basis, source, or standard of computation ⟨has it ~ good authority⟩ ⟨10 cents ~ the dollar⟩ **10**

: with regard to ⟨a monopoly ~ wheat⟩ **11** : at or toward as an object ⟨crept up ~ her⟩ **12** : ABOUT, CONCERNING ⟨a book ~ minerals⟩

²**on** *adv* **1** : in or into a position of contact with or attachment to a surface **2** : FORWARD **3** : into operation

³**on** *adj* : being in operation or in progress

ON *abbr* Ontario

on–brand \ˈȯn-ˈbrand, ˈän-\ *adj* : typical of or consistent with a particular brand or public image or identity

¹**once** \ˈwəns\ *adv* [ME *ones,* fr. genitive of *on* one] **1** : one time only **2** : at any one time ⟨didn't ~ thank me⟩ **3** : FORMERLY ⟨was ~ young⟩ **4** : by one degree of relationship ⟨first cousin ~ removed⟩

²**once** *n* : one single time — **at once 1** : at the same time **2** : IMMEDIATELY

³**once** *adj* : FORMER ⟨a ~ successful actor⟩

⁴**once** *conj* : AS SOON AS ⟨~ we're finished, we can leave⟩

once–over \ˈwəns-ˌō-vər\ *n* : a swift examination or survey

on·co·gene \ˈäŋ-kō-ˌjēn\ *n* : a gene having the potential to cause a normal cell to become cancerous

on·col·o·gy \än-ˈkä-lə-jē\ *n* : the study of tumors — **on·co·log·i·cal** \ˌäŋ-kə-ˈlä-ji-kəl\ *also* **on·co·log·ic** \-jik\ *adj* — **on·col·o·gist** \än-ˈkä-lə-jist\ *n*

on·com·ing \ˈȯn-ˌkə-miŋ, ˈän-\ *adj* : APPROACHING ⟨~ traffic⟩

¹**one** \ˈwən\ *adj* **1** : being a single unit or thing ⟨~ person went⟩ **2** : being one in particular ⟨early ~ morning⟩ **3** : being the same in kind or quality ⟨both of ~ species⟩; *also* : UNITED **4** : being not specified or fixed ⟨~ day soon⟩

²**one** *n* **1** : the number denoting unity **2** : the 1st in a set or series **3** : a single person or thing — **one·ness** \ˈwən-nəs\ *n*

³**one** *pron* **1** : a certain indefinitely indicated person or thing ⟨saw ~ of his friends⟩ **2** : a person in general ⟨~ never knows⟩ **3** — used in place of a first-person pronoun

Onei·da \ō-ˈnī-də\ *n, pl* **Oneida** *or* **Oneidas** : a member of an Indigenous people orig. of New York; *also* : the language of the Oneida people

one–man band *n* **1** : a musician who plays several instruments during a solo performance **2** : a person who alone undertakes or is responsible for several tasks

oner·ous \ˈä-nə-rəs, ˈō-\ *adj* : imposing or constituting a burden : TROUBLESOME ⟨an ~ task⟩ ♦ ***Synonyms*** OPPRESSIVE, EXACTING, BURDENSOME, WEIGHTY

one·self \(ˌ)wən-ˈself\ *also* **one's self** *pron* : one's own self — usu. used reflexively or for emphasis

one–sid·ed \ˈwən-ˈsī-dəd\ *adj* **1** : having or occurring on one side only; *also* : having one side prominent or more developed **2** : PARTIAL ⟨a ~ interpretation⟩

one·time \-ˌtīm\ *adj* : FORMER ⟨a ~ actor⟩

one–to–one \ˌwən-tə-ˈwən\ *adj* : pairing each element of a set uniquely with an element of another set

one up *adj* : being in a position of advantage ⟨was *one up* on the others⟩

one–way *adj* : moving, allowing movement, or functioning in only one direction ⟨~ streets⟩

on·go·ing \ˈȯn-ˌgō-iŋ, ˈän-\ *adj* : continuously moving forward

on·ion \ˈən-yən\ *n* : the pungent edible bulb of a widely cultivated plant related to the lilies; *also* : this plant

on·ion·skin \-ˌskin\ *n* : a thin strong translucent paper of very light weight

on·line \ˈȯn-ˈlīn, ˈän-\ *adj or adv* : connected to, served by, or available through a computer network (as the Internet); *also* : done while online ⟨~ shopping⟩ — **online** *adv*

on·look·er \ˈȯn-ˌlu̇-kər, ˈän-\ *n* : SPECTATOR

¹**on·ly** \ˈōn-lē\ *adj* **1** : unquestionably the best **2** : SOLE ⟨the ~ one left⟩

²**only** *adv* **1** : MERELY, JUST ⟨~ $2⟩ **2** : SOLELY ⟨known ~ to me⟩ **3** : at the very least ⟨was ~ too true⟩ **4** : as a final result ⟨will ~ make you sick⟩

³**only** *conj* : except that

on·o·mato·poe·ia \ˌä-nə-ˌmä-tə-ˈpē-ə\ *n* [LL, fr. Gk *onomatopoiia,* fr. *onoma* name + *poiein* to make] **1** : formation of words in imitation of natural sounds (as *buzz* or *hiss*) **2** : the use of words whose sound suggests the sense — **on·o·mato·poe·ic** \-ˈpē-ik\ *or* **on·o·mato·po·et·ic** \-pō-ˈe-tik\ *adj* — **on·o·mato·poe·i·cal·ly** \-ˈpē-ə-k(ə-)lē\ *or* **on·o·mato·po·et·i·cal·ly** \-pō-ˈe-ti-k(ə-)lē\ *adv*

On·on·da·ga \ˌä-nən-ˈdȯ-gə, -ˈdā-, -ˈdä-\ *n, pl* **-ga** *or* **-gas** : a member of an Indigenous people of New York and Canada; *also* : the language of the Onondaga people

on·rush \ˈȯn-ˌrəsh, ˈän-\ *n* : a rushing onward — **on·rush·ing** *adj*

on–screen \ˈȯn-ˈskrēn, ˈän-\ *adv or adj* : on a computer or television screen

on·set \-ˌset\ *n* **1** : ATTACK **2** : BEGINNING ⟨the ~ of winter⟩

on·shore \-ˌshȯr\ *adj* **1** : moving toward the shore **2** : situated on or near the shore — **on·shore** \-ˈshȯr\ *adv*

on·slaught \ˈȯn-ˌslȯt, ˈän-\ *n* : a fierce attack; *also* : something resembling such an attack ⟨an ~ of questions⟩

Ont *abbr* Ontario

on·to \ˈȯn-tü, ˈän-\ *prep* : to a position or point on

onus \ˈō-nəs\ *n* **1** : BURDEN **2** : OBLIGATION **3** : BLAME

¹**on·ward** \ˈȯn-wərd, ˈän-\ *also* **on·wards** \-wərdz\ *adv* : FORWARD ⟨kept moving ~⟩

²**onward** *adj* : directed or moving onward : FORWARD

on·yx \ˈä-niks\ *n* [ME *oniche, onyx,* fr. AF & L; AF, fr. L *onyx,* fr. Gk, lit., claw, nail] : a translucent chalcedony in parallel layers of different colors

oo·dles \ˈü-dᵊlz\ *n pl* : a great quantity

oo·lite \ˈō-ə-ˌlīt\ *n* : a rock consisting of

small round grains cemented together — **oo·lit·ic** \ˌō-ə-ˈli-tik\ *adj*

[1]**ooze** \ˈüz\ *n* [ME *wose,* fr. OE *wāse* mire] **1** : a soft deposit (as of mud) on the bottom of a body of water **2** : soft wet ground : MUD — **oozy** \ˈü-zē\ *adj*

[2]**ooze** *vb* **oozed; ooz·ing** **1** : to flow or leak out slowly or imperceptibly **2** : EXUDE ⟨~ confidence⟩

[3]**ooze** *n* : something that oozes

op *abbr* **1** operation; operative; operator **2** opportunity **3** opus

OP *abbr* **1** observation post **2** out of print

opac·i·ty \ō-ˈpa-sə-tē\ *n, pl* **-ties** **1** : obscurity of meaning **2** : mental dullness **3** : the quality or state of being opaque **4** : an opaque spot in a normally transparent structure

opal \ˈō-pəl\ *n* : a mineral with iridescent colors that is used as a gem

opal·es·cent \ˌō-pə-ˈle-sᵊnt\ *adj* : IRIDESCENT — **opal·es·cence** \-sᵊns\ *n*

opaque \ō-ˈpāk\ *adj* **1** : blocking the passage of radiant energy and esp. light **2** : not easily understood; *also* : OBTUSE — **opaque·ly** *adv* — **opaque·ness** *n*

op art \ˈäp-\ *n* : OPTICAL ART — **op artist** *n*

op cit *abbr* [L *opere citato*] in the work cited

ope \ˈōp\ *vb* **oped; op·ing** *archaic* : OPEN

OPEC *abbr* Organization of Petroleum Exporting Countries

op–ed \ˈäp-ˈed\ *n, often cap O&E* : a page of special features usu. opposite the editorial page of a newspaper

[1]**open** \ˈō-pən\ *adj* **open·er; open·est** **1** : not shut or shut up ⟨an ~ door⟩ **2** : not secret or hidden; *also* : FRANK **3** : not enclosed or covered ⟨an ~ fire⟩; *also* : not protected **4** : free to be entered or used ⟨an ~ tournament⟩ **5** : easy to get through or see ⟨~ country⟩ **6** : spread out : EXTENDED **7** : not decided ⟨an ~ question⟩ **8** : readily accessible and cooperative; *also* : GENEROUS **9** : having openings, interruptions, or spaces ⟨an ~ mesh⟩; *also* : having components separated by a space in writing and printing ⟨the name *Spanish moss* is an ~ compound⟩ **10** : ready to operate ⟨stores are ~⟩ **11** : free from restraints or controls ⟨~ season⟩ — **open·ly** *adv* — **open·ness** *n*

[2]**open** \ˈō-pən\ *vb* **opened; open·ing** **1** : to change or move from a shut position; *also* : to make open by clearing away obstacles **2** : to make accessible **3** : to make openings in **4** : to make or become functional ⟨~ a store⟩ **5** : REVEAL; *also* : ENLIGHTEN **6** : BEGIN ⟨~ talks⟩ — **open·er** *n*

[3]**open** *n* **1** : OUTDOORS **2** : a contest or tournament open to all

open–air *adj* : OUTDOOR ⟨~ theaters⟩

open arms *n pl* : an eager or warm welcome

open–faced \-ˈfāst\ *also* **open–face** \-ˈfās\ *adj* : served without a covering layer of bread ⟨an ~ sandwich⟩

open·hand·ed \ˌō-pən-ˈhan-dəd\ *adj* : GENEROUS — **open·hand·ed·ly** *adv*

open–heart *adj* : of, relating to, or performed on a heart temporarily relieved of circulatory function and laid open for repair of defects or damage

open–hearth *adj* : of, relating to, or being a process of making steel in a furnace that reflects the heat from the roof onto the material

opening *n* **1** : an act or instance of making or becoming open **2** : BEGINNING **3** : something that is open **4** : OCCASION; *also* : an opportunity for employment

open mike *n* : an event in which amateurs may perform

open–mind·ed \ˌō-pən-ˈmīn-dəd\ *adj* : free from rigidly fixed preconceptions — **open–mind·ed·ness** *n*

open sentence *n* : a statement (as in mathematics) containing at least one blank or unknown so that when the blank is filled or a quantity substituted for the unknown the statement becomes a complete statement that is either true or false

open shop *n* : an establishment having members and nonmembers of a labor union on the payroll

open·work \ˈō-pən-ˌwərk\ *n* : work so made as to show openings through its substance ⟨a railing of wrought-iron ~⟩ — **open–worked** \-ˌwərkt\ *adj*

[1]**opera** *pl of* OPUS

[2]**op·era** \ˈä-prə, -pə-rə\ *n* : a drama set to music — **op·er·at·ic** \ˌä-pə-ˈra-tik\ *adj*

op·er·a·ble \ˈä-pə-rə-bəl\ *adj* **1** : fit, possible, or desirable to use **2** : likely to result in a favorable outcome upon surgical treatment

opera glasses *n pl* : small binoculars for use in a theater

op·er·ate \ˈä-pə-ˌrāt\ *vb* **-at·ed; -at·ing** **1** : to perform work : FUNCTION **2** : to produce an effect **3** : to put or keep in operation **4** : to perform or subject to an operation — **op·er·a·tor** \-ˌrā-tər\ *n*

operating system *n* : software that controls the operation of a computer

op·er·a·tion \ˌä-pə-ˈrā-shən\ *n* **1** : a doing or performing of a practical work **2** : an exertion of power or influence; *also* : method or manner of functioning **3** : a surgical procedure **4** : a process of deriving one mathematical expression from others according to a rule **5** : a military action or mission **6** : a usu. small business — **op·er·a·tion·al** \-shə-nəl\ *adj*

[1]**op·er·a·tive** \ˈä-pə-rə-tiv, -ˌrā-\ *adj* **1** : producing an appropriate effect; *also* : most significant or essential **2** : OPERATING ⟨an ~ force⟩ **3** : having to do with physical operations; *also* : WORKING ⟨an ~ craftsman⟩ **4** : based on or consisting of an operation ⟨~ dentistry⟩

[2]**operative** *n* **1** : OPERATOR; *esp* : a secret agent **2** : a person who works toward achieving the objectives of a larger interest

op·er·et·ta \ˌä-pə-ˈre-tə\ *n* [It, dim. of *opera* opera] : a light musical-dramatic work with a romantic plot, spoken dialogue, and dancing scenes

oph·thal·mic \äf-ˈthal-mik, äp-\ *adj* [Gk *ophthalmikos,* fr. *ophthalmos* eye] : of, relating to, or located near the eye

oph·thal·mol·o·gy \ˌäf-ˌthal-ˈmä-lə-jē, ˌäp-\ *n* : a branch of medicine dealing with the structure, functions, and diseases of the eye — **oph·thal·mol·o·gist** \-jist\ *n*

oph·thal·mo·scope \äf-ˈthal-mə-ˌskōp, äp-\ *n* : an instrument for use in viewing the interior of the eye and esp. the retina

opi·ate \ˈō-pē-ət, -pē-ˌāt\ *n* : a preparation or derivative of opium; *also* : a narcotic or a substance with similar activity — **opiate** *adj*

opine \ō-ˈpīn\ *vb* **opined; opin·ing** : to express an opinion : STATE

opin·ion \ə-ˈpin-yən\ *n* **1** : JUDGMENT **2** : a belief stronger than impression and less strong than positive knowledge **3** : a formal statement by an expert after careful study

opin·ion·at·ed \ə-ˈpin-yə-ˌnā-təd\ *adj* : obstinately adhering to personal opinions

opi·um \ˈō-pē-əm\ *n* [ME, fr. L, fr. Gk *opion,* fr. dim. of *opos* sap] : an addictive narcotic drug that is the dried latex of a Eurasian poppy

opos·sum \ə-ˈpä-səm\ *n, pl* **opossums** *also* **opossum** : an omnivorous tree-dwelling No. American marsupial that is active chiefly at night and has a pointed snout and a prehensile tail

opp *abbr* opposite

op·po·nent \ə-ˈpō-nənt\ *n* : one that opposes : ADVERSARY

op·por·tune \ˌä-pər-ˈtün, -ˈtyün\ *adj* [ME, fr. MF *opportun,* fr. L *opportunus,* fr. *ob-* toward + *portus* port, harbor] : SUITABLE ⟨an ~ moment⟩ — **op·por·tune·ly** *adv*

op·por·tun·ism \ˌä-pər-ˈtü-ˌni-zəm, -ˈtyü-\ *n* : a taking advantage of opportunities or circumstances esp. with little regard for principles or ultimate consequences — **op·por·tun·ist** \-nist\ *n* — **op·por·tu·nis·tic** \-tü-ˈnis-tik, -tyü-\ *adj*

op·por·tu·ni·ty \ˌä-pər-ˈtü-nə-tē, -ˈtyü-\ *n, pl* **-ties** **1** : a favorable combination of circumstances, time, and place **2** : a chance for advancement

op·pose \ə-ˈpōz\ *vb* **op·posed; op·pos·ing** **1** : to place opposite or against something (as to provide resistance or contrast) **2** : to strive against : RESIST — **op·po·si·tion** \ˌä-pə-ˈzi-shən\ *n*

¹**op·po·site** \ˈä-pə-zət\ *adj* **1** : set over against something that is at the other end or side **2** : OPPOSED, HOSTILE; *also* : CONTRARY **3** : contrarily turned or moving **4** : being the other of a matching or contrasting pair ⟨the ~ sex⟩ — **op·po·site·ly** *adv* — **op·po·site·ness** *n*

²**opposite** *n* : one that is opposed or contrary

³**opposite** *adv* : on or to an opposite side

⁴**opposite** *prep* : across from and usu. facing ⟨the house ~ ours⟩

op·press \ə-ˈpres\ *vb* **1** : to crush by abuse of power or authority ⟨~*ed* minorities⟩ **2** : to weigh down : BURDEN ♦ ***Synonyms*** AGGRIEVE, WRONG, PERSECUTE — **op·pres·sive** \-ˈpre-siv\ *adj* — **op·pres·sive·ly** *adv* — **op·pres·sor** \-ˈpre-sər\ *n*

op·pres·sion \ə-ˈpre-shən\ *n* **1** : unjust or cruel exercise of power or authority **2** : DEPRESSION

op·pro·bri·ous \ə-ˈprō-brē-əs\ *adj* : expressing or deserving opprobrium — **op·pro·bri·ous·ly** *adv*

op·pro·bri·um \-brē-əm\ *n* **1** : something that brings disgrace **2** : public disgrace or ill fame

¹**opt** \ˈäpt\ *vb* : to make a choice; *esp* : to decide in favor of something

²**opt** *abbr* **1** optical; optician; optics **2** option; optional

op·tic \ˈäp-tik\ *adj* : of or relating to vision or the eye

op·ti·cal \ˈäp-ti-kəl\ *adj* **1** : relating to optics **2** : OPTIC **3** : of, relating to, or using light

optical art *n* : nonobjective art characterized by the use of geometric patterns often for an illusory effect

optical disk *n* : a disk on which information has been recorded digitally and which is read using a laser

optical fiber *n* : a single fiber-optic strand

optical illusion *n* : a misleading image presented to the vision

op·ti·cian \äp-ˈti-shən\ *n* **1** : a maker of or dealer in optical items and instruments **2** : a person who makes or orders eyeglasses and contact lenses to prescription and sells them

op·tics \ˈäp-tiks\ *n* **1** : a science that deals with the nature and properties of light **2** : the aspects of an action, policy, or decision that relate to public perceptions

op·ti·mal \ˈäp-tə-məl\ *adj* : most desirable or satisfactory — **op·ti·mal·ly** *adv*

op·ti·mism \ˈäp-tə-ˌmi-zəm\ *n* [F *optimisme,* fr. L *optimum,* n., best, fr. neut. of *optimus* best] **1** : a doctrine that this world is the best possible world **2** : an inclination to anticipate the best possible outcome of actions or events — **op·ti·mist** \-mist\ *n* — **op·ti·mis·tic** \ˌäp-tə-ˈmis-tik\ *adj* — **op·ti·mis·ti·cal·ly** \-ti-k(ə-)lē\ *adv*

op·ti·mize \ˈäp-tə-ˌmīz\ *vb* **-mized; -miz·ing** : to make as perfect, effective, or functional as possible — **op·ti·mi·za·tion** \ˌäp-tə-mə-ˈzā-shən\ *n*

op·ti·mum \ˈäp-tə-məm\ *n, pl* **-ma** \-mə\ *also* **-mums** [L] : the amount or degree of something most favorable to an end; *also* : greatest degree attained under implied or specified conditions

op·tion \ˈäp-shən\ *n* **1** : the power or right to choose **2** : a right to buy or sell something at a specified price during a specified period **3** : something offered for choice — **op·tion·al** \-shə-nəl\ *adj*

op·tom·e·try \äp-ˈtä-mə-trē\ *n* : the health-care profession concerned esp. with examining the eyes for defects of vision and with prescribing corrective lenses or eye exercises — **op·to·met·ric** \ˌäp-tə-ˈme-trik\ *adj* — **op·tom·e·trist** \äp-ˈtä-mə-trist\ *n*

opt out *vb* : to choose not to participate

op·u·lence \ˈä-pyə-ləns\ *n* **1** : WEALTH **2** : ABUNDANCE

op·u·lent \ˈä-pyə-lənt\ *adj* **1** : WEALTHY **2** : richly abundant — **op·u·lent·ly** *adv*

opus \ˈō-pəs\ *n, pl* **opera** \ˈō-pə-rə, ˈä-\ *also* **opus·es** \ˈō-pə-səz\ : WORK; *esp* : a musical composition

or \ˈȯr\ *conj* — used as a function word to indicate an alternative ⟨sink ~ swim⟩

OR *abbr* **1** operating room **2** Oregon

-or *n suffix* : one that does a (specified) thing ⟨calculat*or*⟩

or·a·cle \ˈȯr-ə-kəl\ *n* **1** : one held to give divinely inspired answers or revelations **2** : an authoritative or wise utterance; *also* : a person of great authority or wisdom — **orac·u·lar** \ȯ-ˈra-kyə-lər\ *adj*

1**oral** \ˈȯr-əl\ *adj* **1** : SPOKEN ⟨an ~ report⟩ **2** : of, given through, or involving the mouth ⟨an ~ vaccine⟩ **3** : of, relating to, or characterized by the first stage of psychosexual development in psychoanalytic theory in which libidinal gratification is derived from intake (as of food), by sucking, and later by biting **4** : relating to or characterized by personality traits of passive dependency and aggressiveness — **oral·ly** *adv*

2**oral** *n* : an oral examination — usu. used in pl.

oral sex *n* : oral stimulation of the genitals : CUNNILINGUS, FELLATIO

orang \ə-ˈraŋ\ *n* : ORANGUTAN

or·ange \ˈär-inj, ˈȯr-\ *n* **1** : a juicy citrus fruit with reddish yellow rind; *also* : an evergreen tree with fragrant white flowers that bears this fruit **2** : a color between red and yellow — **or·ang·ey** *or* **or·angy** \ˈär-in-jē, ˈȯr-\ *adj*

or·ange·ade \ˌär-in-ˈjād, ˌȯr-\ *n* : a beverage of orange juice, sugar, and water

orange hawkweed *n* : a weedy herb related to the daisies with bright orange-red flower heads

or·ange·ry \ˈär-inj-rē, ˈȯr-\ *n, pl* **-ries** : a protected place (as a greenhouse) for raising oranges in cool climates

orang·utan \ə-ˈraŋ-ə-ˌtaŋ, -ˌtan\ *n* [Bazaar Malay (Malay-based pidgin), fr. Malay *orang* man + *hutan* forest] : a large reddish brown tree-living anthropoid ape of Borneo and Sumatra

orate \ȯ-ˈrāt\ *vb* **orat·ed; orat·ing** : to speak in a declamatory manner

ora·tion \ə-ˈrā-shən\ *n* : an elaborate discourse delivered in a formal and dignified manner

or·a·tor \ˈȯr-ə-tər\ *n* : one noted for skill and power as a public speaker

or·a·tor·i·cal \ˌȯr-ə-ˈtȯr-i-kəl\ *adj* : of, relating to, or characteristic of an orator or oratory — **or·a·tor·i·cal·ly** \-ˈtȯr-i-k(ə-)lē\ *adv*

or·a·to·rio \ˌȯr-ə-ˈtȯr-ē-ˌō\ *n, pl* **-rios** : a lengthy choral work usu. on a scriptural subject

1**or·a·to·ry** \ˈȯr-ə-ˌtȯr-ē\ *n, pl* **-ries** : a private or institutional chapel

2**oratory** *n* : the art of speaking eloquently and effectively in public ♦ ***Synonyms*** RHETORIC, ELOCUTION

orb \ˈȯrb\ *n* : a spherical body; *also* : EYE

1**or·bit** \ˈȯr-bət\ *n* [L *orbita,* lit., path, rut] **1** : a path described by one body in its revolution about another **2** : range or sphere of activity — **or·bit·al** \-bə-tᵊl\ *adj*

2**orbit** *vb* **1** : CIRCLE **2** : to send up and make revolve in an orbit ⟨~ a satellite⟩ — **or·bit·er** *n*

or·ca \ˈȯr-kə\ *n* : KILLER WHALE

orch *abbr* orchestra

or·chard \ˈȯr-chərd\ *n* [ME, fr. OE *ortgeard,* fr. *ort-* (fr. L *hortus* garden) + *geard* yard] : a place where fruit trees, sugar maples, or nut trees are grown; *also* : the trees of such a place — **or·chard·ist** \-chər-dist\ *n*

or·ches·tra \ˈȯr-kə-strə\ *n* **1** : the front section of seats on the main floor of a theater **2** : a group of instrumentalists organized to perform ensemble music — **or·ches·tral** \ȯr-ˈkes-trəl\ *adj* — **or·ches·tral·ly** *adv*

or·ches·trate \ˈȯr-kə-ˌstrāt\ *vb* **-trat·ed; -trat·ing** **1** : to compose or arrange for an orchestra **2** : to arrange so as to achieve a desired effect ⟨~ a campaign⟩ — **or·ches·tra·tion** \ˌȯr-kə-ˈstrā-shən\ *n*

or·chid \ˈȯr-kəd\ *n* : any of a large family of plants having often showy flowers with three petals of which the middle one is enlarged into a lip; *also* : a flower of an orchid

ord *abbr* **1** order **2** ordnance

or·dain \ȯr-ˈdān\ *vb* **1** : to admit to the ministry or priesthood by the ritual of a church **2** : DECREE, ENACT; *also* : DESTINE — **or·dain·ment** *n*

or·deal \ȯr-ˈdēl, ˈȯr-ˌdēl\ *n* : a severe trial or experience

1**or·der** \ˈȯr-dər\ *vb* **1** : ARRANGE, REGULATE **2** : COMMAND **3** : to place an order

2**order** *n* **1** : a group of people formally united; *also* : a badge or medal of such a group **2** : any of the several grades of the Christian ministry; *also, pl* : ORDINATION **3** : a rank, class, or special group of persons or things **4** : a category of biological classification ranking above the family and below the class **5** : ARRANGEMENT, SEQUENCE; *also* : the prevailing state of things **6** : a customary mode of procedure; *also* : the rule of law or proper authority **7** : a specific rule, regulation, or authoritative direction **8** : a style of building; *also* : an architectural column forming the unit of a style **9** : condition esp. with regard to repair **10** : a direction to pay money or to buy or sell goods; *also* : goods bought or sold — **in order** : APPROPRIATE, DESIRABLE ⟨apologies are *in order*⟩ — **in order to** : for the purpose of

1**or·der·ly** \ˈȯr-dər-lē\ *adj* **1** : arranged according to some order; *also* : NEAT, TIDY **2** : well behaved ⟨an ~ crowd⟩ ♦ ***Synonyms*** METHODICAL, SYSTEMATIC, REGULAR — **or·der·li·ness** *n*

[2]**orderly** *n, pl* **-lies** **1** : a soldier who attends a superior officer **2** : a hospital attendant who does general work

or·di·nal \'ȯr-də-nəl\ *adj* : indicating order or rank (as sixth) in a series

ordinal number *n* : a number (as first, second, or third) that designates the place of an item in an ordered sequence — compare CARDINAL NUMBER

or·di·nance \'ȯr-də-nəns\ *n* : an authoritative decree or law; *esp* : a municipal regulation

or·di·nary \'ȯr-də-ˌner-ē\ *adj* **1** : to be expected : USUAL **2** : of common quality, rank, or ability ⟨~ kids⟩; *also* : POOR, INFERIOR ⟨~ wine⟩ ♦ ***Synonyms*** CUSTOMARY, ROUTINE, NORMAL, EVERYDAY — **or·di·nar·i·ly** \ˌȯr-də-ner-ə-lē\ *adv* — **or·di·nar·i·ness** \'ȯr-də-ˌner-ē-nəs\ *n*

or·di·nate \'ȯr-də-nət, -ˌnāt\ *n* : the vertical coordinate of a point in a plane coordinate system obtained by measuring parallel to the y-axis

or·di·na·tion \ˌȯr-də-'nā-shən\ *n* : the act or ceremony by which a person is ordained

ord·nance \'ȯrd-nəns\ *n* **1** : military supplies **2** : CANNON, ARTILLERY

Or·do·vi·cian \ˌȯr-də-'vi-shən\ *adj* : of, relating to, or being the period of the Paleozoic era between the Cambrian and the Silurian — **Ordovician** *n*

or·dure \'ȯr-jər\ *n* : EXCREMENT

ore \'ȯr\ *n* : a naturally occurring mineral mined to obtain a substance that it contains

ore \'ər-ə\ *n, pl* **ore** — see *krona, krone* at MONEY table

Ore *or* **Oreg** *abbr* Oregon

oreg·a·no \ə-'re-gə-ˌnō\ *n* : a bushy perennial mint used as a seasoning and a source of oil

org *abbr* organization; organized

or·gan \'ȯr-gən\ *n* **1** : a musical instrument having sets of pipes sounded by compressed air and controlled by keyboards; *also* : an electronic keyboard instrument that approximates the sounds of the pipe organ **2** : a differentiated animal or plant structure (as a heart or a leaf) made up of cells and tissues and performing some bodily function **3** : a group that performs a specialized function ⟨the various ~*s* of government⟩ **4** : PERIODICAL ⟨the official ~ of the party⟩

or·gan·dy *also* **or·gan·die** \'ȯr-gən-dē\ *n, pl* **-dies** [F *organdi*] : a fine transparent muslin with a stiff finish

or·gan·elle \ˌȯr-gə-'nəl\ *n* : a specialized cell part that resembles an organ in having a special function

or·gan·ic \ȯr-'ga-nik\ *adj* **1** : of, relating to, or arising in a bodily organ **2** : of, relating to, or derived from living things **3** : of, relating to, or containing carbon compounds **4** : of or relating to a branch of chemistry dealing with carbon compounds **5** : involving, producing, or dealing in foods produced without the use of laboratory-made fertilizers, growth substances, antibiotics, or pesticides ⟨~ farming⟩ **6** : ORGANIZED ⟨an ~ whole⟩ — **or·gan·i·cal·ly** \-ni-k(ə-)lē\ *adv*

or·ga·ni·sa·tion, or·ga·nise *Brit var of* ORGANIZATION, ORGANIZE

or·gan·ism \'ȯr-gə-ˌni-zəm\ *n* : an individual living thing (as a person, animal, or plant) — **or·gan·is·mic** \ˌȯr-gə-'niz-mik\ *adj*

or·gan·ist \'ȯr-gə-nist\ *n* : a person who plays an organ

or·ga·ni·za·tion \ˌȯr-gə-nə-'zā-shən\ *n* **1** : the act or process of organizing or of being organized; *also* : the condition or manner of being organized **2** : ASSOCIATION, SOCIETY **3** : an administrative structure (as a business or a political party) — **or·ga·ni·za·tion·al** \-shə-nəl\ *adj*

or·ga·nize \'ȯr-gə-ˌnīz\ *vb* **-nized; -niz·ing** **1** : to develop an organic structure **2** : to form into a complete and functioning whole **3** : to set up an administrative structure for **4** : to arrange by systematic planning and united effort **5** : to join in a union; *also* : UNIONIZE ♦ ***Synonyms*** INSTITUTE, FOUND, ESTABLISH, CONSTITUTE — **or·ga·niz·er** *n*

or·gano·chlo·rine \ȯr-ˌga-nə-'klȯr-ˌēn\ *adj* : of, relating to, or being a chlorinated hydrocarbon pesticide (as DDT) — **organochlorine** *n*

or·gano·phos·phate \-'fäs-ˌfāt\ *n* : an organophosphorus pesticide — **organophosphate** *adj*

or·gano·phos·pho·rus \-'fäs-fə-rəs\ *also* **or·gano·phos·pho·rous** \-fäs-'fȯr-əs\ *adj* : of, relating to, or being a phosphorus-containing organic pesticide (as malathion)

or·gan·za \ȯr-'gan-zə\ *n* : a sheer dress fabric resembling organdy and usu. made of silk, rayon, or nylon

or·gasm \'ȯr-ˌga-zəm\ *n* : the climax of sexual excitement — **or·gas·mic** \ȯr-'gaz-mik\ *adj*

or·gi·as·tic \ˌȯr-jē-'as-tik\ *adj* : of, relating to, or marked by orgies

or·gu·lous \'ȯr-gyə-ləs, -gə-\ *adj* : PROUD

or·gy \'ȯr-jē\ *n, pl* **orgies** : a gathering marked by unrestrained indulgence (as in sexual activity, alcohol, or drugs)

ori·el \'ȯr-ē-əl\ *n* : a window built out from a wall and usu. supported by a bracket

ori·ent \'ȯr-ē-ˌent\ *vb* **1** : to set in a definite position esp. in relation to the points of the compass **2** : to acquaint with an existing situation or environment **3** : to direct toward the interests of a particular group

Orient *n* : EAST 3; *esp* : the countries of eastern Asia

ori·en·tal \ˌȯr-ē-'en-tᵊl\ *adj, often cap* [fr. *Orient* East, fr. ME, fr. AF, fr. L *orient-, oriens,* fr. prp. of *oriri* to rise] **1** : of or situated in the Orient **2** *sometimes offensive* : of, relating to, or coming from Asia and esp. eastern Asia ⟨~ food⟩

ori·en·tate \'ȯr-ē-ən-ˌtāt\ *vb* **-tat·ed; -tat·ing** **1** : ORIENT **2** : to face east

ori·en·ta·tion \ˌȯr-ē-ən-ˈtā-shən\ *n* **1** : the act or state of being oriented **2** : a person's sexual identity as bisexual, straight, gay, pansexual, etc.
or·i·fice \ˈȯr-ə-fəs\ *n* : OPENING, MOUTH
ori·flamme \ˈȯr-ə-ˌflam\ *n* : a brightly colored banner used as a standard or ensign in battle
orig *abbr* original; originally
ori·ga·mi \ˌȯr-ə-ˈgä-mē\ *n* : the Japanese art or process of paper folding
or·i·gin \ˈȯr-ə-jən\ *n* **1** : ANCESTRY **2** : rise, beginning, or derivation from a source; *also* : CAUSE **3** : the intersection of coordinate axes
¹**orig·i·nal** \ə-ˈri-jə-nəl\ *n* : something from which a copy, reproduction, or translation is made : PROTOTYPE
²**original** *adj* **1** : FIRST, INITIAL **2** : not copied from something else : FRESH **3** : INVENTIVE — **orig·i·nal·i·ty** \-ˌri-jə-ˈna-lə-tē\ *n* — **orig·i·nal·ly** \-ˈri-jə-nᵊl-ē\ *adv*
orig·i·nate \ə-ˈri-jə-ˌnāt\ *vb* **-nat·ed; -nat·ing** **1** : to give rise to : INITIATE **2** : to come into existence : BEGIN — **orig·i·na·tor** \-ˌnā-tər\ *n*
ori·ole \ˈȯr-ē-ˌōl\ *n* : any of various New World birds of which the males are usu. black and yellow or black and orange
or·i·son \ˈȯr-ə-sən\ *n* : PRAYER
or·mo·lu \ˈȯr-mə-ˌlü\ *n* : a golden or gilded brass used for decorative purposes
¹**or·na·ment** \ˈȯr-nə-mənt\ *n* : something that lends grace or beauty — **or·na·men·tal** \ˌȯr-nə-ˈmen-tᵊl\ *adj*
²**or·na·ment** \-ˌment\ *vb* : to provide with ornament : ADORN — **or·na·men·ta·tion** \ˌȯr-nə-mən-ˈtā-shən\ *n*
or·nate \ȯr-ˈnāt\ *adj* : elaborately decorated ⟨an ~ mantel⟩ — **or·nate·ly** *adv* — **or·nate·ness** *n*
or·nery \ˈȯr-nə-rē, ˈä-nə-\ *adj* : having an irritable disposition
or·ni·thol·o·gy \ˌȯr-nə-ˈthä-lə-jē\ *n, pl* **-gies** : a branch of zoology dealing with birds — **or·ni·tho·log·i·cal** \-thə-ˈlä-ji-kəl\ *adj* — **or·ni·thol·o·gist** \-ˈthä-lə-jist\ *n*
oro·tund \ˈȯr-ə-ˌtənd\ *adj* **1** : SONOROUS ⟨an ~ voice⟩ **2** : POMPOUS ⟨an ~ speech⟩ — **oro·tun·di·ty** \ȯr-ə-ˈtən-di-tē\ *n*
or·phan \ˈȯr-fən\ *n* : a child deprived by death of one or usu. both parents — **orphan** *vb*
or·phan·age \ˈȯr-fə-nij\ *n* : an institution for the care of orphans
or·tho·don·tia \ˌȯr-thə-ˈdän-chə, -chē-ə\ *n* : ORTHODONTICS
or·tho·don·tics \ˌȯr-thə-ˈdän-tiks\ *n* : a branch of dentistry concerned with the correction of faults in the arrangement and placing of the teeth — **or·tho·don·tic** \-tik\ *adj* — **or·tho·don·tist** \-ˈdän-tist\ *n*
or·tho·dox \ˈȯr-thə-ˌdäks\ *adj* [ME *orthodoxe*, fr. MF or LL; MF *orthodoxe*, fr. LL *orthodoxus*, fr. LGk *orthodoxos*, fr. Gk *orthos* right + *doxa* opinion] **1** : conforming to established doctrine esp. in religion **2** : CONVENTIONAL **3** *cap* : of or relating to a Christian church originating in the church of the Eastern Roman Empire — **or·tho·doxy** \-ˌdäk-sē\ *n*
or·thog·ra·phy \ȯr-ˈthä-grə-fē\ *n* : SPELLING — **or·tho·graph·ic** \ˌȯr-thə-ˈgra-fik\ *adj*
or·tho·pe·dics *also* **or·tho·pae·dics** \ˌȯr-thə-ˈpē-diks\ *n sing or pl* : a branch of medicine concerned with the correction or prevention of skeletal injuries or disorders — **or·tho·pe·dic** *also* **or·tho·pae·dic** \-dik\ *adj* — **or·tho·pe·dist** \-dist\ *n*
Or·well·ian \ȯr-ˈwe-lē-ən\ *adj* : of or relating to George Orwell or his writings; *esp* : relating to the dystopian reality depicted in the novel *1984*
-ory *adj suffix* **1** : of, relating to, or characterized by ⟨anticipat*ory*⟩ **2** : serving for, producing, or maintaining ⟨illus*ory*⟩
Os *symbol* osmium
OS *abbr* **1** [L *oculus sinister*] left eye **2** ordinary seaman **3** out of stock
Osage \ō-ˈsāj\ *n, pl* **Osag·es** *or* **Osage** : a member of an Indigenous people orig. of southwestern Missouri and adjacent parts of Kansas, Oklahoma, and Arkansas; *also* : the language of the Osage people
os·cil·late \ˈä-sə-ˌlāt\ *vb* **-lat·ed; -lat·ing** **1** : to swing backward and forward like a pendulum **2** : to move or travel back and forth between two points **3** : VARY, FLUCTUATE — **os·cil·la·tion** \ˌä-sə-ˈlā-shən\ *n* — **os·cil·la·tor** \ˈä-sə-ˌlā-tər\ *n* — **os·cil·la·to·ry** \ˈä-sə-lə-ˌtȯr-ē\ *adj*
os·cil·lo·scope \ä-ˈsi-lə-ˌskōp\ *n* : an instrument in which variations in current or voltage appear as a visible wave form on a fluorescent screen
os·cu·late \ˈäs-kyə-ˌlāt\ *vb* **-lat·ed; -lat·ing** : KISS — **os·cu·la·tion** \ˌäs-kyə-ˈlā-shən\ *n* — **os·cu·la·to·ry** \ˈäs-kyə-lə-ˌtōr-ē\ *adj*
Osee \ˈō-ˌzē, ō-ˈzā-ə\ *n* : HOSEA
OSHA \ˈō-shə\ *abbr* Occupational Safety and Health Administration
osier \ˈō-zhər\ *n* : any of various willows with pliable twigs used esp. in making baskets and furniture; *also* : a twig from an osier
os·mi·um \ˈäz-mē-əm\ *n* : a very heavy hard brittle metallic chemical element used esp. as a catalyst and in alloys
os·mo·sis \äz-ˈmō-səs, äs-\ *n* : movement of a solvent through a semipermeable membrane into a solution of higher concentration that tends to equalize the concentrations of the solutions on either side of the membrane — **os·mot·ic** \-ˈmä-tik\ *adj*
os·prey \ˈäs-prē, -ˌprā\ *n, pl* **ospreys** : a large dark brown and white fish-eating hawk
os·si·fy \ˈä-sə-ˌfī\ *vb* **-fied; -fy·ing** : to make or become hardened or set in one's ways ⟨an *ossified* regime⟩ — **os·si·fi·ca·tion** \ˌä-sə-fə-ˈkā-shən\ *n*
os·su·ary \ˈä-shə-ˌwer-ē, -syə-\ *n, pl* **-ar·ies** : a depository for the bones of the dead
os·ten·si·ble \ä-ˈsten-sə-bəl\ *adj* : shown

outwardly : PROFESSED, APPARENT — **os·ten·si·bly** \-blē\ *adv*

os·ten·ta·tion \ˌäs-tən-ˈtā-shən\ *n* : pretentious or excessive display — **os·ten·ta·tious** \-shəs\ *adj* — **os·ten·ta·tious·ly** *adv*

os·te·o·ar·thri·tis \ˌäs-tē-ō-är-ˈthrī-təs\ *n* : arthritis marked by degeneration of the cartilage and bone of joints

os·teo·path \ˈäs-tē-ə-ˌpath\ *n* : a practitioner of osteopathy

os·te·op·a·thy \ˌäs-tē-ˈä-pə-thē\ *n* : a system of treating diseases emphasizing manipulation (as of joints) but not excluding other agencies (as the use of medicine and surgery) — **os·teo·path·ic** \ˌäs-tē-ə-ˈpa-thik\ *adj*

os·teo·po·ro·sis \ˌäs-tē-ō-pə-ˈrō-səs\ *n, pl* **-ro·ses** \-ˌsēz\ : a condition affecting esp. older women and characterized by fragile and porous bones

os·tra·cise *Brit var of* OSTRACIZE

os·tra·cize \ˈäs-trə-ˌsīz\ *vb* **-cized; -ciz·ing** [Gk *ostrakizein* to banish by voting with potsherds, fr. *ostrakon* shell, potsherd] : to exclude from a group by common consent — **os·tra·cism** \-ˌsi-zəm\ *n*

os·trich \ˈäs-trich, ˈōs-\ *n* : a very large swift-footed flightless bird of Africa

Os·we·go tea \ä-ˈswē-gō-\ *n* : a No. American mint with showy scarlet flowers

OT *abbr* **1** occupational therapy **2** Old Testament **3** overtime

[1]**oth·er** \ˈə-thər\ *adj* **1** : being the one left; *also* : being the ones distinct from those first mentioned **2** : ALTERNATE ⟨every ~ day⟩ **3** : DIFFERENT **4** : ADDITIONAL **5** : recently past ⟨the ~ night⟩

[2]**other** *pron* **1** : remaining one or ones **2** : a different or additional one ⟨something or ~⟩

oth·er·wise \ˈə-thər-ˌwīz\ *adv* **1** : in a different way **2** : in different circumstances **3** : in other respects **4** : if not **5** : NOT — **otherwise** *adj*

oth·er·world \-ˌwərld\ *n* : a world beyond death or beyond present reality

oth·er·world·ly \ˌə-thər-ˈwərld-lē\ *adj* : not worldly : concerned with spiritual, intellectual, or imaginative matters

oti·ose \ˈō-shē-ˌōs, ˈō-tē-\ *adj* **1** : FUTILE **2** : IDLE **3** : USELESS ⟨~ details⟩

oto·lar·yn·gol·o·gy \ˌō-tō-ˌla-rən-ˈgä-lə-jē\ *n* : a medical specialty concerned esp. with the ear, nose, and throat — **oto·lar·yn·gol·o·gist** \-jist\ *n*

oto·rhi·no·lar·yn·gol·o·gy \ˌō-tō-ˌrī-nō-ˌla-rən-ˈgä-lə-jē\ *n* : OTOLARYNGOLOGY — **oto·rhi·no·lar·yn·gol·o·gist** \-jist\ *n*

OTS *abbr* officers' training school

Ot·ta·wa \ˈä-tə-wə, -ˌwä, -ˌwȯ\ *n, pl* **Ottawas** *or* **Ottawa** : a member of an Indigenous people of Michigan and southern Ontario

ot·ter \ˈä-tər\ *n, pl* **otters** *also* **otter** : any of various web-footed fish-eating mammals with dark brown fur that are related to the weasels; *also* : the fur

ot·to·man \ˈä-tə-mən\ *n* : an upholstered seat or couch usu. without a back; *also* : an overstuffed footstool

ou·bli·ette \ˌü-blē-ˈet\ *n* [F, fr. MF, fr. *oublier* to forget, ultim. fr. L *oblivisci*] : a dungeon with an opening at the top

ought \ˈȯt\ *verbal auxiliary* — used to express moral obligation, advisability, natural expectation, or logical consequence ⟨you ~ to apologize⟩

ou·gui·ya \ü-ˈgwē-ə, -ˈgē-\ *or* **ou·gi·ya** \-ˈgē-\ *n, pl* **ouguiya**; *or* **ougiya** — see MONEY table

ounce \ˈau̇ns\ *n* [ME, fr. AF *unce,* fr. L *uncia* twelfth part, ounce, fr. *unus* one] **1** : a unit of avoirdupois, troy, and apothecaries' weight — see WEIGHT table **2** : FLUID OUNCE

our \är, ˈau̇(-ə)r\ *adj* : of or relating to us or ourselves

ours \ˈau̇r(-ə)z, ˈärz\ *pron* : that which belongs to us

our·selves \är-ˈselvz, au̇(-ə)r-\ *pron* : our own selves — used reflexively, for emphasis, or in absolute constructions ⟨we pleased ~⟩ ⟨we'll do it ~⟩ ⟨we were tourists ~⟩

-ous *adj suffix* : full of : abounding in : having : possessing the qualities of ⟨clamor*ous*⟩ ⟨poison*ous*⟩

oust \ˈau̇st\ *vb* : to eject from or deprive of property or position : EXPEL ♦ ***Synonyms*** EVICT, DISMISS, BANISH, DEPORT

oust·er \ˈau̇s-tər\ *n* : EXPULSION

[1]**out** \ˈau̇t\ *adv* **1** : in a direction away from the inside or center **2** : beyond control **3** : to extinction, exhaustion, or completion **4** : in or into the open **5** : so as to retire a batter or base runner; *also* : so as to be retired

[2]**out** *vb* **1** : to become known ⟨the truth will ~⟩ **2** : to identify (someone) as being such secretly

[3]**out** *prep* **1** : out through ⟨looked ~ the window⟩ **2** : outward on or along ⟨drive ~ the river road⟩

[4]**out** *adj* **1** : situated outside or at a distance **2** : not in : ABSENT; *also* : not being in power **3** : removed from play as a batter or base runner **4** : not being in fashion : not up-to-date **5** : attempting a particular activity ⟨won his first time ~⟩

[5]**out** *n* **1** : one who is out of office **2** : the retiring of a batter or base runner

out·age \ˈau̇-tij\ *n* : a period or instance of interruption esp. of electricity

out–and–out *adj* : COMPLETE, THOROUGHGOING ⟨an ~ fraud⟩

out·bid \ˌau̇t-ˈbid\ *vb* : to make a higher bid than

[1]**out·board** \ˈau̇t-ˌbȯrd\ *adj* **1** : situated outboard **2** : having or using an outboard motor

[2]**outboard** *adv* **1** : outside a ship's hull : away from the long axis of a ship **2** : in a position closer to the wing tip of an airplane

outboard motor *n* : a small internal combustion engine with propeller attached for mounting at the stern of a small boat

out·bound \ˈau̇t-ˌbau̇nd\ *adj* : outward bound ⟨~ traffic⟩

out·break \-ˌbrāk\ *n* **1** : a sudden increase in activity, incidence, or numbers **2** : INSURRECTION, REVOLT

out·build·ing \-ˌbil-diŋ\ *n* : a building separate from but accessory to a main house
out·burst \-ˌbərst\ *n* : ERUPTION; *esp* : a violent expression of feeling
out·cast \-ˌkast\ *n* : one that is cast out by society
out·class \au̇t-ˈklas\ *vb* : SURPASS
out·come \ˈau̇t-ˌkəm\ *n* : a final consequence : RESULT
out·crop \-ˌkräp\ *n* : a coming out of bedrock to the surface of the ground; *also* : the part of a rock formation that thus appears — **outcrop** *vb*
out·cry \-ˌkrī\ *n* : a loud cry : CLAMOR
out·dat·ed \au̇t-ˈdā-təd\ *adj* : OUTMODED
out·dis·tance \-ˈdis-təns\ *vb* : to go far ahead of (as in a race) : OUTSTRIP
out·do \-ˈdü\ *vb* **-did** \-ˈdid\; **-done** \-ˈdən\; **-do·ing; -does** \-ˈdəz\ : to go beyond in action or performance
out·door \ˈau̇t-ˌdȯr, -ˈdȯr\ *also* **out·doors** \-ˌdȯrz, -ˈdȯrz\ *adj* **1** : of or relating to the outdoors **2** : performed outdoors **3** : not enclosed (as by a roof)
¹**out·doors** \au̇t-ˈdȯrz, -ˈdȯrz\ *adv* : in or into the open air
²**outdoors** *n* **1** : the open air **2** : the world away from human habitation — **outdoorsy** \ˌau̇t-ˈdȯr-zē\ *adj*
out·draw \au̇t-ˈdrȯ\ *vb* **-drew** \-ˈdrü\; **-drawn** \-ˈdrȯn\; **-draw·ing** **1** : to attract a larger audience than **2** : to draw a handgun more quickly than
out·er \ˈau̇-tər\ *adj* **1** : EXTERNAL **2** : situated farther out; *also* : being away from a center
outer ear *n* : the outer visible portion of the ear that collects and directs sound waves toward the eardrum
out·er·most \-ˌmōst\ *adj* : farthest out
outer space *n* : SPACE 5
out·er·wear \ˈau̇-tər-ˌwer\ *n* **1** : clothing for outdoor wear **2** : outer clothing as opposed to underwear
out·face \au̇t-ˈfās\ *vb* **1** : to cause to waver or submit **2** : DEFY
out·field \ˈau̇t-ˌfēld\ *n* : the part of a baseball field beyond the infield and within the foul lines; *also* : players in the outfield — **out·field·er** \-ˌfēl-dər\ *n*
out·fight \au̇t-ˈfīt\ *vb* : to surpass in fighting : DEFEAT
¹**out·fit** \ˈau̇t-ˌfit\ *n* **1** : the equipment or apparel for a special purpose or occasion **2** : GROUP ⟨an insurance ~⟩
²**outfit** *vb* **out·fit·ted; out·fit·ting** : EQUIP — **out·fit·ter** *n*
out·flank \au̇t-ˈflaŋk\ *vb* : to get around the flank of (an opposing force)
out·flow \ˈau̇t-ˌflō\ *n* **1** : a flowing out **2** : something that flows out
out·fox \au̇t-ˈfäks\ *vb* : OUTWIT
out·go \ˈau̇t-ˌgō\ *n, pl* **outgoes** : EXPENDITURES, OUTLAY
out·go·ing \-ˌgō-iŋ\ *adj* **1** : going out ⟨~ tide⟩ **2** : retiring from a place or position **3** : FRIENDLY
out·grow \au̇t-ˈgrō\ *vb* **-grew** \-ˈgrü\; **-grown** \-ˈgrōn\; **-grow·ing** **1** : to grow faster than **2** : to grow too large for
out·growth \ˈau̇t-ˌgrōth\ *n* : a product of growing out : OFFSHOOT; *also* : CONSEQUENCE, RESULT
out·guess \au̇t-ˈges\ *vb* : OUTWIT
out·gun \-ˈgən\ *vb* : to surpass in firepower
out·house \ˈau̇t-ˌhau̇s\ *n* : OUTBUILDING; *esp* : an outdoor toilet
out·ing \ˈau̇-tiŋ\ *n* : a brief stay or trip in the open ⟨a family ~⟩
out·land·ish \au̇t-ˈlan-dish\ *adj* **1** : of foreign appearance or manner; *also* : BIZARRE **2** : remote from civilization — **out·land·ish·ly** *adv*
out·last \-ˈlast\ *vb* : to last longer than
¹**out·law** \ˈau̇t-ˌlȯ\ *n* **1** : a person excluded from the protection of the law **2** : a lawless person
²**outlaw** *vb* **1** : to deprive of the protection of the law **2** : to make illegal — **out·law·ry** \ˈau̇t-ˌlȯr-ē\ *n*
out·lay \ˈau̇t-ˌlā\ *n* **1** : the act of spending **2** : EXPENDITURE
out·let \ˈau̇t-ˌlet, -lət\ *n* **1** : EXIT, VENT **2** : a means of release (as for an emotion) **3** : a medium for usu. public expression : a media organization **4** : a market for a commodity **5** : a receptacle for the plug of an electrical device
¹**out·line** \ˈau̇t-ˌlīn\ *n* **1** : a line marking the outer limits of an object or figure **2** : a drawing in which only contours are marked **3** : SUMMARY, SYNOPSIS ⟨an ~ of the novel⟩ **4** : PLAN
²**outline** *vb* **1** : to draw the outline of **2** : to indicate the chief features or parts of
out·live \au̇t-ˈliv\ *vb* : to live longer than
♦ ***Synonyms*** OUTLAST, SURVIVE
out·look \ˈau̇t-ˌlu̇k\ *n* **1** : a place offering a view; *also* : VIEW **2** : a position from which something is considered or evaluated **3** : the prospect for the future
out·ly·ing \-ˌlī-iŋ\ *adj* : distant from a center or main body
out·ma·neu·ver \ˌau̇t-mə-ˈnü-vər, -ˈnyü-\ *vb* : to defeat by more skillful maneuvering
out·mod·ed \au̇t-ˈmō-dəd\ *adj* **1** : no longer in style **2** : no longer acceptable or current ⟨~ technology⟩
out·num·ber \-ˈnəm-bər\ *vb* : to exceed in number
out of *prep* **1** : out from within or behind ⟨walk *out of* the room⟩ ⟨look *out of* the window⟩ **2** : from a state of ⟨wake up *out of* a deep sleep⟩ **3** : beyond the limits of ⟨*out of* sight⟩ **4** : BECAUSE OF ⟨asked *out of* curiosity⟩ **5** : FROM, WITH ⟨built it *out of* scrap⟩ **6** : in or into a state of loss or not having ⟨cheated him *out of* $5000⟩ ⟨we're *out of* matches⟩ **7** : from among ⟨one *out of* four⟩ — **out of it** : SQUARE, OLD-FASHIONED
out–of–bounds *adv or adj* : outside the prescribed boundaries or limits
out–of–date *adj* : no longer in fashion or in use : OUTMODED
out–of–door *or* **out–of–doors** *adj* : OUTDOOR
out–of–the–way *adj* **1** : UNUSUAL **2** : being off the beaten track

out·pa·tient \ˈau̇t-ˌpā-shənt\ *n* : a patient who visits a hospital or clinic for diagnosis or treatment without staying overnight
out·per·form \ˌau̇t-pər-ˈfȯrm\ *vb* : to perform better than
out·play \au̇t-ˈplā\ *vb* : to play more skillfully than
out·point \-ˈpȯint\ *vb* : to win more points than
out·post \ˈau̇t-ˌpōst\ *n* **1** : a security detachment dispatched by a main body of troops to protect it from enemy surprise; *also* : a military base established (as by treaty) in a foreign country **2** : an outlying or frontier settlement
out·pour·ing \-ˌpȯr-iŋ\ *n* : something that pours out or is poured out
out·pull \au̇t-ˈpu̇l\ *vb* : OUTDRAW 1
¹**out·put** \ˈau̇t-ˌpu̇t\ *n* **1** : the amount produced (as by a machine or factory) : PRODUCTION **2** : the information produced by a computer
²**output** *vb* **out·put·ted** *or* **output; out·put·ting** : to produce as output
¹**out·rage** \ˈau̇t-ˌrāj\ *n* [ME, fr. AF *utrage, outrage* insult, excess, fr. *utre, outre* beyond, fr. L *ultra*] **1** : a violent or shameful act **2** : INJURY, INSULT **3** : the anger or resentment aroused by injury or insult
²**outrage** *vb* **out·raged; out·rag·ing** **1** : RAPE **2** : to subject to violent injury or gross insult **3** : to arouse to extreme resentment
out·ra·geous \au̇t-ˈrā-jəs\ *adj* : extremely offensive, insulting, or shameful : SHOCKING — **out·ra·geous·ly** *adv*
out·rank \-ˈraŋk\ *vb* : to rank higher than
ou·tré \ü-ˈtrā\ *adj* [F] : violating convention or propriety : BIZARRE ⟨~ creations⟩
¹**out·reach** \au̇t-ˈrēch\ *vb* **1** : to surpass in reach **2** : to get the better of by trickery
²**out·reach** \ˈau̇t-ˌrēch\ *n* **1** : the act of reaching out **2** : the extent of reach **3** : the extending of services beyond usual limits
out·rid·er \-ˌrī-dər\ *n* : a mounted attendant
out·rig·ger \-ˌri-gər\ *n* **1** : a frame attached to the side of a boat to prevent capsizing **2** : a craft equipped with an outrigger
¹**out·right** \au̇t-ˈrīt\ *adv* **1** : COMPLETELY **2** : INSTANTANEOUSLY
²**out·right** \ˈau̇t-ˌrīt\ *adj* **1** : being exactly what is stated ⟨an ~ lie⟩ **2** : given or made without reservation or encumbrance ⟨an ~ sale⟩
out·ro \ˈau̇-trō\ *n* : a short, distinct closing section at the end of something (as a piece of music or a news report)
out·run \au̇t-ˈrən\ *vb* **-ran** \-ˈran\; **-run; -run·ning** : to run faster than; *also* : EXCEED
out·sell \-ˈsel\ *vb* **-sold** \-ˈsōld\; **-sell·ing** : to exceed in sales
out·set \ˈau̇t-ˌset\ *n* : BEGINNING, START
out·shine \au̇t-ˈshīn\ *vb* **-shone** \-ˈshōn\ *or* **-shined; -shin·ing** **1** : to shine brighter than **2** : SURPASS
¹**out·side** \au̇t-ˈsīd, ˈau̇t-ˌsīd\ *n* **1** : a place or region beyond an enclosure or boundary **2** : EXTERIOR **3** : the utmost limit or extent
²**outside** *adj* **1** : OUTER **2** : coming from without ⟨~ influences⟩ **3** : being apart from one's regular duties ⟨~ activities⟩ **4** : REMOTE ⟨an ~ chance⟩
³**outside** *adv* : on or to the outside
⁴**outside** *prep* **1** : on or to the outside of **2** : beyond the limits of **3** : EXCEPT
outside of *prep* **1** : OUTSIDE **2** : BESIDES
out·sid·er \au̇t-ˈsī-dər\ *n* : a person who does not belong to a group
out·size \ˈau̇t-ˌsīz\ *also* **out·sized** \-ˌsīzd\ *adj* : unusually large : extravagant in size or degree
out·skirts \-ˌskərts\ *n pl* : the outlying parts (as of a city) : BORDERS
out·smart \au̇t-ˈsmärt\ *vb* : OUTWIT
out·source \ˈau̇t-ˌsȯrs\ *vb* **-sourced; -sourcing** : to obtain (goods or services) from an outside supplier
out·spend \-ˈspend\ *vb* **1** : to exceed the limits of in spending ⟨~*s* his income⟩ **2** : to spend more than
out·spo·ken \au̇t-ˈspō-kən\ *adj* : direct and open in speech or expression — **out·spo·ken·ly** *adv* — **out·spo·ken·ness** *n*
out·spread \-ˈspred\ *vb* **-spread; -spread·ing** : to spread out
out·stand·ing \-ˈstan-diŋ\ *adj* **1** : PROJECTING **2** : UNPAID; *also* : UNRESOLVED ⟨~ warrants⟩ **3** : publicly issued and sold **4** : CONSPICUOUS; *also* : DISTINGUISHED — **out·stand·ing·ly** *adv*
out·stay \-ˈstā\ *vb* **1** : OVERSTAY **2** : to surpass in endurance
out·stretch \ˌau̇t-ˈstrech\ *vb* : to stretch out : EXTEND
out·strip \-ˈstrip\ *vb* **1** : to go faster than **2** : EXCEL, SURPASS
out·take \ˈau̇t-ˌtāk\ *n* : something taken out; *esp* : a take that is not used in an edited version of a film or videotape
out·vote \-ˈvōt\ *vb* : to defeat by a majority of votes
¹**out·ward** \ˈau̇t-wərd\ *adj* **1** : moving or directed toward the outside **2** : showing outwardly
²**outward** *or* **out·wards** \-wərdz\ *adv* : toward the outside
out·ward·ly \-wərd-lē\ *adv* : on the outside : EXTERNALLY
out·wear \au̇t-ˈwer\ *vb* **-wore** \-ˈwȯr\; **-worn** \-ˈwȯrn\; **-wear·ing** : to wear longer than : OUTLAST
out·weigh \-ˈwā\ *vb* : to exceed in weight, value, or importance
out·wit \-ˈwit\ *vb* : to get the better of by superior cleverness
¹**out·work** \-ˈwərk\ *vb* : to outdo in working
²**out·work** \ˈau̇t-ˌwərk\ *n* : a minor defensive position outside a fortified area
out·worn \au̇t-ˈwȯrn\ *adj* : OUTMODED
ou·zo \ˈü-(ˌ)zō\ *n* : a colorless anise-flavored unsweetened Greek liqueur
ova *pl of* OVUM
oval \ˈō-vəl\ *adj* [ML *ovalis,* fr. LL, of an egg, fr. L *ovum* egg] : egg-shaped; *also* : broadly elliptical — **oval** *n*

ova·ry \ˈō-və-rē\ *n, pl* **-ries** **1** : one of the usu. paired female reproductive organs producing eggs and in vertebrates sex hormones **2** : the part of a flower in which seeds are produced — **ovar·i·an** \ō-ˈver-ē-ən\ *adj*

ovate \ˈō-ˌvāt\ *adj* : egg-shaped

ova·tion \ō-ˈvā-shən\ *n* [L *ovation-, ovatio,* fr. *ovare* to exult] : an enthusiastic popular tribute

ov·en \ˈə-vən\ *n* : a chamber (as in a stove) for baking, heating, or drying

oven·bird \-ˌbərd\ *n* : a large olive-green American warbler that builds its dome-shaped nest on the ground

[1]**over** \ˈō-vər\ *adv* **1** : across a barrier or intervening space **2** : across the brim ⟨boil ~⟩ **3** : so as to bring the underside up **4** : out of a vertical position **5** : beyond some quantity, limit, or norm **6** : ABOVE **7** : at an end **8** : THROUGH ⟨read it ~⟩; *also* : THOROUGHLY ⟨still thinking it ~⟩ **9** : AGAIN ⟨do it ~⟩

[2]**over** *prep* **1** : above in position, authority, or scope ⟨towered ~ her⟩ ⟨obeyed those ~ him⟩ **2** : more than ⟨cost ~ $100⟩ **3** : ON, UPON ⟨a cape ~ her shoulders⟩ **4** : along the length of ⟨~ the road⟩ **5** : through the medium of : ON ⟨spoke ~ TV⟩ **6** : all through ⟨showed me ~ the house⟩ **7** : on or to the other side or beyond ⟨jump ~ a ditch⟩ **8** : DURING ⟨~ the past 25 years⟩ **9** : on account of ⟨trouble ~ money⟩

[3]**over** *adj* **1** : UPPER, HIGHER **2** : REMAINING **3** : ENDED ⟨those days are ~⟩

over- *prefix* **1** : so as to exceed or surpass **2** : excessive; excessively

over·act \ˌō-vər-ˈakt\ *vb* : to exaggerate in acting

[1]**over·age** \ˌō-vər-ˈāj\ *adj* **1** : too old to be useful **2** : older than is normal for one's position, function, or grade

[2]**over·age** \ˈō-və-rij\ *n* : SURPLUS

over·all \ˌō-vər-ˈȯl\ *adj* : including everything ⟨~ expenses⟩

over·alls \ˈō-vər-ˌȯlz\ *n pl* : pants of strong material usu. with a piece extending up to cover the chest

over·arm \-ˌärm\ *adj* : done with the arm raised above the shoulder

over·awe \ˌō-vər-ˈȯ\ *vb* : to restrain or subdue by awe

over·bal·ance \-ˈba-ləns\ *vb* **1** : OUTWEIGH **2** : to cause to lose balance

over·bear·ing \-ˈber-iŋ\ *adj* : ARROGANT, DOMINEERING

over·bite \ˈō-vər-ˌbīt\ *n* : the projection of the upper front teeth over the lower

over·blown \-ˈblōn\ *adj* **1** : PORTLY **2** : INFLATED, PRETENTIOUS

over·board \ˈō-vər-ˌbȯrd\ *adv* **1** : over the side of a ship into the water **2** : to extremes of enthusiasm

[1]**over·cast** \ˈō-vər-ˌkast\ *adj* : clouded over : GLOOMY

[2]**overcast** *n* : COVERING; *esp* : a covering of clouds

over·charge \ˌō-vər-ˈchärj\ *vb* **1** : to charge too much **2** : to fill or load too full — **over·charge** \ˈō-vər-ˌchärj\ *n*

over·coat \ˈō-vər-ˌkōt\ *n* : a warm coat worn over indoor clothing

over·come \ˌō-vər-ˈkəm\ *vb* **-came** \-ˈkām\; **-come; -com·ing** **1** : CONQUER **2** : to make helpless or exhausted

over·do \ˌō-vər-ˈdü\ *vb* **-did** \-ˈdid\; **-done** \-ˈdən\; **-do·ing; -does** \-ˈdəz\ **1** : to do too much; *also* : to tire oneself **2** : EXAGGERATE **3** : to cook too long

over·dose \ˈō-vər-ˌdōs\ *n* : too great a dose (as of medicine); *also* : a lethal or toxic amount (as of a drug) — **over·dose** \ˌō-vər-ˈdōs\ *vb*

over·draft \ˈō-vər-ˌdraft\ *n* : an overdrawing of a bank account; *also* : the sum overdrawn

over·draw \ˌō-vər-ˈdrȯ\ *vb* **-drew** \-ˈdrü\; **-drawn** \-ˈdrȯn\; **-draw·ing** **1** : to draw checks on a bank account for more than the balance **2** : EXAGGERATE

over·drive \ˈō-vər-ˌdrīv\ *n* : an automotive transmission gear that transmits to the driveshaft a speed greater than the engine speed

over·dub \ˌō-vər-ˈdəb\ *vb* : to transfer (recorded sound) onto an earlier recording for a combined effect — **over·dub** \ˈō-vər-ˌdəb\ *n*

over·due \-ˈdü, -ˈdyü\ *adj* **1** : unpaid when due ⟨an ~ bill⟩; *also* : not appearing or presented on time ⟨an ~ train⟩ **2** : more than ready

over·ex·pose \ˌō-vər-ik-ˈspōz\ *vb* : to expose (as film) for more time than is needed — **over·ex·po·sure** \-ˈspō-zhər\ *n*

[1]**over·flow** \-ˈflō\ *vb* **1** : INUNDATE; *also* : to pour forth in a flood **2** : to flow over the brim or top of

[2]**over·flow** \ˈō-vər-ˌflō\ *n* **1** : FLOOD; *also* : SURPLUS **2** : an outlet for surplus liquid

over·fly \ˌō-vər-ˈflī\ *vb* **-flew** \-ˈflü\; **-flown** \-ˈflōn\; **-fly·ing** : to fly over in an aircraft or spacecraft — **over·flight** \ˈō-vər-ˌflīt\ *n*

over·grow \ˌō-vər-ˈgrō\ *vb* **-grew** \-ˈgrü\; **-grown** \-ˈgrōn\; **-grow·ing** **1** : to grow over so as to cover **2** : OUTGROW **3** : to

---

overabundance
overabundant
overachiever
overactive
overaggressive
overambitious
overanxious
overbid
overbold
overbuild
overburden
overbuy
overcapacity
overcapitalize
overcareful
overcautious
overcompensation
overconfidence
overconfident
overconscientious
overcook
overcritical
overcrowd
overdecorated
overdependence
overdetermined
overdevelop
overdress
overeager
overeat
overeducated
overemphasis
overemphasize
overenthusiastic
overestimate
overexcite
overexcited
overexert
overexertion
overextend
overfatigued
overfeed
overfill
overgeneralization

grow excessively — **over•growth** \ˈō-vər-ˌgrōth\ *n*
over•hand \ˈō-vər-ˌhand\ *adj* : made with the hand brought down from above — **overhand** *adv* — **over•hand•ed** \-ˌhan-dəd\ *adv or adj*
¹**over•hang** \ˈō-vər-ˌhaŋ, ˌō-vər-ˈhaŋ\ *vb* **-hung** \-ˌhəŋ, -ˈhəŋ\; **-hang•ing** **1** : to project over : jut out **2** : to hang over threateningly
²**over•hang** \ˈō-vər-ˌhaŋ\ *n* : a part (as of a roof) that overhangs
over•haul \ˌō-vər-ˈhȯl\ *vb* **1** : to examine thoroughly and make necessary repairs and adjustments **2** : OVERTAKE
¹**over•head** \ˌō-vər-ˈhed\ *adv* : ALOFT
²**over•head** \ˈō-vər-ˌhed\ *adj* : operating or lying above ⟨~ storage bins⟩
³**over•head** \ˈō-vər-ˌhed\ *n* : business expenses not chargeable to a particular part of the work
over•hear \ˌō-vər-ˈhir\ *vb* **-heard** \-ˈhərd\; **-hear•ing** : to hear without the speaker's knowledge or intention
over•joyed \ˌō-vər-ˈjȯid\ *adj* : filled with great joy
over•kill \ˈō-vər-ˌkil\ *n* **1** : destructive capacity greatly exceeding that required for a target **2** : a large excess
over•land \ˈō-vər-ˌland, -lənd\ *adv or adj* : by, on, or across land
over•lap \ˌō-vər-ˈlap\ *vb* **1** : to lap over **2** : to have something in common — **over•lap** \ˈō-vər-ˌlap\ *n*
over•lay \ˌō-vər-ˈlā\ *vb* **-laid** \-ˈlād\; **-lay•ing** : to lay or spread over or across — **over•lay** \ˈō-vər-ˌlā\ *n*
over•leap \ˌō-vər-ˈlēp\ *vb* **-leaped** *or* **-leapt** \-ˈlēpt, -ˈlept\; **-leap•ing** **1** : to leap over or across **2** : to defeat (oneself) by going too far
over•lie \ˌō-vər-ˈlī\ *vb* **-lay** \-ˈlā\; **-lain** \-ˈlān\; **-ly•ing** : to lie over or upon
¹**over•look** \ˌō-vər-ˈlu̇k\ *vb* **1** : INSPECT **2** : to look down on from above **3** : to fail to see **4** : IGNORE ⟨~*ed* his faults⟩; *also* : EXCUSE **5** : SUPERINTEND
²**over•look** \ˈō-vər-ˌlu̇k\ *n* : a place from which to look upon a scene below
over•lord \-ˌlȯrd\ *n* : a lord who has supremacy over other lords
over•ly \ˈō-vər-lē\ *adv* : EXCESSIVELY
over•match \ˌō-vər-ˈmach\ *vb* : to be more than a match for : DEFEAT
over•much \-ˈməch\ *adj or adv* : too much
¹**over•night** \-ˈnīt\ *adv* **1** : on or during the night **2** : SUDDENLY ⟨became famous ~⟩
²**overnight** *adj* : of, lasting, or staying the night ⟨~ guests⟩
over•pass \ˈō-vər-ˌpas\ *n* **1** : a crossing (as of two highways) at different levels by means of a bridge **2** : the upper level of an overpass
over•play \ˌō-vər-ˈplā\ *vb* **1** : EXAGGERATE; *also* : OVEREMPHASIZE **2** : to rely too much on the strength of
over•pop•u•la•tion \ˌō-vər-ˌpä-pyə-ˈlā-shən\ *n* : the condition of having a population so dense as to cause a decline in population or in living conditions — **over•pop•u•la•ted** \-ˈpä-pyə-ˌlā-təd\ *adj*
over•pow•er \-ˈpau̇(-ə)r\ *vb* : to overcome by superior force
over•price \ˌō-vər-ˈprīs\ *vb* : to price too high
over•print \-ˈprint\ *vb* : to print over with something additional — **over•print** \ˈō-vər-ˌprint\ *n*
over•qual•i•fied \-ˈkwä-lə-ˌfīd\ *adj* : having more education, training, or experience than a job calls for
over•reach \ˌō-vər-ˈrēch\ *vb* : to defeat (oneself) by too great an effort
over•ride \-ˈrīd\ *vb* **-rode** \-ˈrōd\; **-rid•den** \-ˈri-dᵊn\; **-rid•ing** **1** : to ride over or across **2** : to prevail over; *also* : to set aside ⟨~ a veto⟩
over•rule \-ˈrül\ *vb* **1** : to prevail over **2** : to rule against **3** : to set aside
¹**over•run** \-ˈrən\ *vb* **-ran** \-ˈran\; **-run**; **-run•ning** **1** : to defeat and occupy the positions of **2** : OVERSPREAD; *also* : INFEST **3** : to go beyond **4** : to flow over
²**over•run** \ˈō-vər-ˌrən\ *n* **1** : an act or instance of overrunning; *esp* : an exceeding of estimated costs **2** : the amount by which something overruns
over•sea \ˌō-vər-ˈsē, ˈō-vər-ˌsē\ *adj or adv* : OVERSEAS
over•seas \ˌō-vər-ˈsēz, -ˌsēz\ *adv or adj* : beyond or across the sea : ABROAD
over•see \ˌō-vər-ˈsē\ *vb* **-saw** \-ˈsȯ\; **-seen** \-ˈsēn\; **-see•ing** **1** : OVERLOOK **2** : INSPECT; *also* : SUPERVISE ⟨~ the project⟩ — **over•seer** \ˈō-vər-ˌsir\ *n*
over•sell \ˌō-vər-ˈsel\ *vb* **-sold**; **-sel•ling** : to sell too much to or too much of
over•sexed \ˌō-vər-ˈsekst\ *adj* : exhibiting excessive sexual drive or interest
over•shad•ow \-ˈsha-dō\ *vb* **1** : to cast a shadow over **2** : to exceed in importance
over•shoe \ˈō-vər-ˌshü\ *n* : a protective outer shoe; *esp* : GALOSH
over•shoot \ˌō-vər-ˈshüt\ *vb* **-shot** \-ˈshät\; **-shoot•ing** **1** : to pass swiftly beyond **2** : to shoot over or beyond
over•sight \ˈō-vər-ˌsīt\ *n* **1** : SUPERVISION **2** : an inadvertent omission or error
over•size \ˌō-vər-ˈsīz\ *or* **over•sized** \-ˈsīzd\ *adj* : of more than ordinary size

---

overgeneralize
overgenerous
overgraze
overhasty
overheat
overhype
overindulge
overindulgence
overindulgent
overinflate
overlarge
overlearn
overload
overlong
overmodest
overnice
overoptimism
overoptimistic
overpay
overpraise
overproduce
overproduction
overprotect
overprotective
overrate
overreact
overreaction
overrefinement
overregulate
overreliance
overrepresented
overripe
oversensitive
oversensitiveness
oversimple
oversimplification

over·sleep \ˌō-vər-ˈslēp\ *vb* **-slept** \-ˈslept\; **-sleep·ing** : to sleep beyond the time for waking
over·spread \-ˈspred\ *vb* **-spread; -spread·ing** : to spread over or above
over·state \-ˈstāt\ *vb* : EXAGGERATE — **over·state·ment** *n*
over·stay \-ˈstā\ *vb* : to stay beyond the time or limits of ⟨~*ed* her welcome⟩
over·step \-ˈstep\ *vb* : EXCEED
over·sub·scribe \-səb-ˈskrīb\ *vb* : to subscribe for more of than is available, asked for, or offered for sale
overt \ō-ˈvərt, ˈō-ˌvərt\ *adj* [ME, fr. AF, fr. pp. of *ovrir* to open] : not secret ⟨~ hostility⟩ — **overt·ly** *adv*
over·take \ˌō-vər-ˈtāk\ *vb* **-took** \-ˈtu̇k\; **-tak·en** \-ˈtā-kən\; **-tak·ing** : to catch up with; *also* : to catch up with and pass by ⟨~ the lead runner⟩
over–the–counter *adj* : sold lawfully without a prescription ⟨~ drugs⟩
over–the–hill *adj* **1** : past one's prime **2** : advanced in age
over–the–top *adj* : extremely flamboyant or outrageous ⟨an ~ performance⟩
over·throw \ˌō-vər-ˈthrō\ *vb* **-threw** \-ˈthrü\; **-thrown** \-ˈthrōn\; **-throw·ing** **1** : UPSET **2** : to bring down : DEFEAT ⟨~ a government⟩ **3** : to throw over or past — **over·throw** \ˈō-vər-ˌthrō\ *n*
over·time \ˈō-vər-ˌtīm\ *n* : time beyond a set limit; *esp* : working time in excess of a standard day or week — **overtime** *adv*
over·tone \-ˌtōn\ *n* **1** : one of the higher tones in a complex musical tone **2** : IMPLICATION, SUGGESTION ⟨political ~*s*⟩
over·trick \ˈō-vər-ˌtrik\ *n* : a card trick won in excess of the number bid
over·ture \ˈō-vər-ˌchu̇r, -chər\ *n* [ME, lit., opening, fr. AF, fr. VL **opertura,* alter. of L *apertura*] **1** : an opening offer **2** : an orchestral introduction to a musical dramatic work
over·turn \ˌō-vər-ˈtərn\ *vb* **1** : to turn over : UPSET ⟨~ a vase⟩ **2** : INVALIDATE ⟨~ a court ruling⟩
over·view \ˈō-vər-ˌvyü\ *n* : a general survey : SUMMARY
over·ween·ing \ˌō-vər-ˈwē-niŋ\ *adj* **1** : ARROGANT ⟨~ pride⟩ **2** : IMMODERATE
over·weight \ˈō-vər-ˌwāt\ *n* **1** : weight above what is required or allowed **2** : bodily weight greater than normal — **overweight** *adj*
over·whelm \ˌō-vər-ˈhwelm\ *vb* **1** : OVERTHROW **2** : SUBMERGE **3** : to overcome completely
over·whelm·ing *adj* : EXTREME, GREAT ⟨~ joy⟩ — **over·whelm·ing·ly** *adv*
over·win·ter \-ˈwin-tər\ *vb* : to survive or pass the winter
over·work \-ˈwərk\ *vb* **1** : to work or cause to work too hard or long **2** : to use too much — **overwork** *n*
over·wrought \ˌō-vər-ˈrȯt\ *adj* **1** : extremely excited **2** : elaborated to excess
ovi·duct \ˈō-və-ˌdəkt\ *n* : a tube that serves for the passage of eggs from an ovary
ovip·a·rous \ō-ˈvi-pə-rəs\ *adj* : reproducing by eggs that hatch outside the parent's body
ovoid \ˈō-ˌvȯid\ *or* **ovoi·dal** \ō-ˈvȯi-dᵊl\ *adj* : egg-shaped : OVAL
ovu·la·tion \ˌäv-yə-ˈlā-shən, ˌōv-\ *n* : the discharge of a mature egg from the ovary — **ovu·late** \ˈäv-yə-ˌlāt, ˈōv-\ *vb*
ovule \ˈäv-yül, ˈōv-\ *n* : any of the bodies in a plant ovary that after fertilization become seeds
ovum \ˈō-vəm\ *n, pl* **ova** \-və\ : EGG 2
ow \ˈau̇\ *interj* — used esp. to express sudden pain
owe \ˈō\ *vb* **owed; ow·ing** **1** : to be under obligation to pay or render **2** : to be indebted to or for; *also* : to be in debt
owing to *prep* : BECAUSE OF
owl \ˈau̇(-ə)l\ *n* : any of an order of chiefly nocturnal birds of prey with a large head and eyes and strong talons — **owl·ish** *adj* — **owl·ish·ly** *adv*
owl·et \ˈau̇-lət\ *n* : a young or small owl
[1]**own** \ˈōn\ *adj* : belonging to oneself — used as an intensive after a possessive adjective ⟨her ~ car⟩
[2]**own** *vb* **1** : to have or hold as property **2** : to have power or control over **3** : ACKNOWLEDGE ⟨would not ~ up to his mistake⟩; *also* : CONFESS — **own·er** *n* — **own·er·ship** *n*
[3]**own** *pron* : one or ones belonging to oneself — **on one's own** : for or by oneself : left to one's own resources
ox \ˈäks\ *n, pl* **ox·en** \ˈäk-sən\ *also* **ox** : any of the large domestic bovine mammals kept for milk, draft, and meat; *esp* : an adult castrated male ox
ox·blood \ˈäks-ˌbləd\ *n* : a moderate reddish brown
ox·bow \-ˌbō\ *n* **1** : a U-shaped collar worn by a draft ox **2** : a U-shaped bend in a river — **oxbow** *adj*
ox·ford \ˈäks-fərd\ *n* : a low shoe laced or tied over the instep
ox·i·dant \ˈäk-sə-dənt\ *n* : OXIDIZING AGENT — **oxidant** *adj*
ox·i·da·tion \ˌäk-sə-ˈdā-shən\ *n* : the act or process of oxidizing; *also* : the condition of being oxidized — **ox·i·da·tive** \ˈäk-sə-ˌdā-tiv\ *adj*
ox·ide \ˈäk-ˌsīd\ *n* : a compound of oxygen with another element or group
ox·i·dize \ˈäk-sə-ˌdīz\ *vb* **-dized; -diz·ing** : to combine with oxygen ⟨iron rusts because it is *oxidized* by exposure to the air⟩ — **ox·i·diz·er** *n*
oxidizing agent *n* : a substance (as oxygen or nitric acid) that oxidizes by taking up electrons
ox·y·gen \ˈäk-si-jən\ *n* [F *oxygène,* fr. Gk

oversimplify
overspecialization
overspecialize
overspend
overstimulation
overstock
oversubtle
oversupply
overtax
overtired
overtrain
overuse
overvalue
overzealous

oxys acidic, lit., sharp + *-genēs* giving rise to; so called because it was once thought to be an essential element of all acids] : a colorless odorless gaseous chemical element that is found in the air, is essential to life, and is involved in combustion

ox·y·gen·ate \ˈäk-si-jə-ˌnāt\ *vb* **-at·ed; -at·ing** : to impregnate, combine, or supply with oxygen — **ox·y·gen·a·tion** \ˌäk-si-jə-ˈnā-shən\ *n*

oxygen mask *n* : a device worn over the nose and mouth through which oxygen is supplied

oxygen tent *n* : a canopy which can be placed over a bedridden person and within which a flow of oxygen can be maintained

ox·y·mo·ron \ˌäk-sē-ˈmȯr-ˌän\ *n* : a combination of contradictory words (as *cruel kindness*) — **ox·y·mo·ron·ic** \-mə-ˈrä-nik\ *adj*

oys·ter \ˈȯis-tər\ *n* : any of various marine mollusks with an irregular 2-valved shell that include commercially important edible shellfish and pearl producers — **oys·ter·ing** *n* — **oys·ter·man** \-mən\ *n*

oz *abbr* [obs. It *onza* (now *oncia*)] ounce; ounces

ozone \ˈō-ˌzōn\ *n* **1** : a bluish gaseous reactive form of oxygen that is formed naturally in the atmosphere and is used for disinfecting, deodorizing, and bleaching **2** : pure and refreshing air

ozone layer *n* : an atmospheric layer at heights of about 25 miles (40 kilometers) with high ozone content which blocks most solar ultraviolet radiation

P

¹p \ˈpē\ *n, pl* **p's** *or* **ps** \ˈpēz\ *often cap* : the 16th letter of the English alphabet

²p *abbr, often cap* **1** page **2** participle **3** past **4** pawn **5** pence; penny **6** per **7** petite **8** pint **9** pressure **10** purl

P *symbol* phosphorus

pa \ˈpä, ˈpȯ\ *n* : FATHER

¹Pa *abbr* **1** pascal **2** Pennsylvania

²Pa *symbol* protactinium

¹PA \(ˌ)pē-ˈā\ *n* : PHYSICIAN'S ASSISTANT

²PA *abbr* **1** Pennsylvania **2** per annum **3** power of attorney **4** press agent **5** private account **6** professional association **7** public address **8** purchasing agent

pa·'an·ga \pä-ˈäŋ-gə\ *n* — see MONEY table

pab·u·lum \ˈpa-byə-ləm\ *n* [L, food, fodder] : usu. soft digestible food

Pac *abbr* Pacific

PAC *abbr* political action committee

¹pace \ˈpās\ *n* **1** : rate of movement or progress (as in walking or working) **2** : a step in walking; *also* : a measure of length based on such a step **3** : GAIT; *esp* : a horse's gait in which the legs on the same side move together

²pace *vb* **paced; pac·ing** **1** : to go or cover at a pace or with slow steps **2** : to measure off by paces ⟨~ off a 15-yard penalty⟩ **3** : to set or regulate the pace of

³pace \ˈpā-sē; ˈpä-ˌkā, -ˌchā\ *prep* : contrary to the opinion of

pace·mak·er \ˈpās-ˌmā-kər\ *n* **1** : one that sets the pace for another **2** : a body part (as of the heart) that serves to establish and maintain a rhythmic activity **3** : an electrical device for stimulating or steadying the heartbeat

pac·er \ˈpā-sər\ *n* **1** : a horse that paces **2** : PACEMAKER

pachy·derm \ˈpa-ki-ˌdərm\ *n* [F *pachyderme,* fr. Gk *pachydermos* thick-skinned, fr. *pachys* thick + *derma* skin] : any of various thick-skinned hoofed mammals (as an elephant)

pach·ys·an·dra \ˌpa-ki-ˈsan-drə\ *n* : any of a genus of low perennial evergreen plants used as a ground cover

pa·cif·ic \pə-ˈsi-fik\ *adj* **1** : tending to lessen conflict **2** : CALM, PEACEFUL

Pacific Islander *n* : a native or a descendant of a native of Melanesia, Micronesia, or Polynesia in the Pacific Ocean

pac·i·fi·er \ˈpa-sə-ˌfī(-ə)r\ *n* : one that pacifies; *esp* : a device for a baby to chew or suck on

pac·i·fism \ˈpa-sə-ˌfi-zəm\ *n* : opposition to war or violence as a means of settling disputes — **pac·i·fist** \-fist\ *n or adj* — **pac·i·fis·tic** \ˌpa-sə-ˈfis-tik\ *adj*

pac·i·fy \ˈpa-sə-ˌfī\ *vb* **-fied; -fy·ing** **1** : to allay anger or agitation in : SOOTHE **2** : SETTLE; *also* : SUBDUE — **pac·i·fi·ca·tion** \ˌpa-sə-fə-ˈkā-shən\ *n*

¹pack \ˈpak\ *n* **1** : a compact bundle; *also* : a flexible container for carrying a bundle esp. on the back **2** : a large amount : HEAP **3** : a set of playing cards **4** : a group or band of people or animals **5** : wet absorbent material for application to the body

²pack *vb* **1** : to stow goods in for transportation **2** : to fill in or surround so as to prevent passage of air, steam, or water **3** : to put into a protective container **4** : to load with a pack ⟨~ a mule⟩ **5** : to crowd in **6** : to make into a pack **7** : to cause to go without ceremony ⟨~ them off to school⟩ **8** : WEAR, CARRY ⟨~ a gun⟩

³pack *vb* : to influence the composition of

so as to secure a desired result ⟨~ a jury⟩

¹**pack·age** \ˈpa-kij\ *n* **1** : BUNDLE, PARCEL **2** : a group of related things offered as a whole

²**package** *vb* **pack·aged; pack·ag·ing** : to make into or enclose in a package

package deal *n* : an offer containing several items all or none of which must be accepted

package store *n* : a store that sells alcoholic beverages in sealed containers for consumption off the premises

pack·er \ˈpa-kər\ *n* : one that packs; *esp* : a wholesale food dealer

pack·et \ˈpa-kət\ *n* **1** : a small bundle or package **2** : a passenger boat carrying mail and cargo on a regular schedule

pack·horse \ˈpak-ˌhȯrs\ *n* : a horse used to carry goods or supplies

pack·ing \ˈpa-kiŋ\ *n* : material used to pack something

pack·ing·house \-ˌhau̇s\ *n* : an establishment for processing and packing food and esp. meat and its by-products

pack rat *n* **1** : a bushy-tailed rodent of western No. America that hoards food and miscellaneous objects; *also* : any of several rodents of similar habit **2** : a person who collects or saves many esp. unneeded items

pack·sad·dle \ˈpak-ˌsa-dᵊl\ *n* : a saddle for supporting loads on the back of an animal

pack·thread \-ˌthred\ *n* : strong thread for tying

pact \ˈpakt\ *n* : AGREEMENT, TREATY

¹**pad** \ˈpad\ *n* **1** : a cushioning part or thing : CUSHION **2** : the cushioned underside of the foot or toes of some mammals **3** : the floating leaf of a water plant **4** : a writing tablet **5** : LAUNCHPAD **6** : living quarters; *also* : BED

²**pad** *vb* **pad·ded; pad·ding** **1** : to furnish with a pad or padding **2** : to expand with needless or fraudulent matter

pad·ding *n* : the material with which something is padded

¹**pad·dle** \ˈpa-dᵊl\ *vb* **pad·dled; pad·dling** : to move the hands and feet about in shallow water

²**paddle** *n* **1** : an implement with a flat blade used in propelling and steering a small craft (as a canoe) **2** : an implement used for stirring, mixing, or beating **3** : a broad board on the outer rim of a waterwheel or a paddle wheel

³**paddle** *vb* **pad·dled; pad·dling** **1** : to move on or through water by or as if by using a paddle **2** : to beat or stir with a paddle

paddle wheel *n* : a wheel with paddles around its outer edge used to move a boat

paddle wheeler *n* : a steam-driven vessel propelled by a paddle wheel

pad·dock \ˈpa-dək\ *n* **1** : a usu. enclosed area for pasturing or exercising animals; *esp* : one where racehorses are saddled and paraded before a race **2** : an area at a racecourse where racing cars are parked

pad·dy \ˈpa-dē\ *n, pl* **paddies** : wet land where rice is grown

paddy wagon *n* : an enclosed motortruck for carrying prisoners

pad·lock \ˈpad-ˌläk\ *n* : a removable lock with a curved piece that snaps into a catch — **padlock** *vb*

pa·dre \ˈpä-drā\ *n* [Sp or It or Pg, lit., father, fr. L *pater*] **1** : PRIEST **2** : a military chaplain

pad thai \ˈpäd-ˈtī\ *n, often cap T* : a Thai dish of rice noodles stir-fried with additional ingredients

pae·an \ˈpē-ən\ *n* : an exultant song of praise or thanksgiving

pae·di·at·ric, pae·di·a·tri·cian, pae·di·at·rics *chiefly Brit var of* PEDIATRIC, PEDIATRICIAN, PEDIATRICS

pa·el·la \pä-ˈe-lə; -ˈäl-yə, -ˈā-yə\ *n* : a saffron-flavored dish of rice, meat, seafood, and vegetables

pa·gan \ˈpā-gən\ *n* [ME, fr. LL *paganus,* fr. L, civilian, country dweller, fr. *pagus* country district] : an unconverted member of a people or nation who does not practice Christianity, Judaism, or Islam — **pagan** *adj* — **pa·gan·ism** \-gə-ˌni-zəm\ *n*

¹**page** \ˈpāj\ *n* : ATTENDANT; *esp* : one employed to deliver messages

²**page** *vb* **paged; pag·ing** **1** : to summon by repeatedly calling out the name of **2** : to send a message to via a pager

³**page** *n* **1** : a single leaf (as of a book); *also* : a single side of such a leaf **2** : the information at a single World Wide Web address

⁴**page** *vb* **paged; pag·ing** : to mark or number the pages of

pag·eant \ˈpa-jənt\ *n* [ME *pagyn, padgeant,* lit., scene of a play, fr. AF *pagine, pagent,* fr. ML *pagina,* perh. fr. L, page] : an elaborate spectacle, show, or procession esp. with tableaux or floats — **pag·eant·ry** \-jən-trē\ *n*

page·boy \ˈpāj-ˌbȯi\ *n* [¹*page*] : an often shoulder-length hairdo with the ends of the hair turned smoothly under

pag·er \ˈpā-jər\ *n* : one that pages; *esp* : a small radio receiver that alerts its user to incoming messages

pag·i·nate \ˈpa-jə-ˌnāt\ *vb* **-nat·ed; -nat·ing** : ⁴PAGE

pag·i·na·tion \ˌpa-jə-ˈnā-shən\ *n* **1** : the paging of written or printed matter **2** : the number and arrangement of pages (as of a book)

pa·go·da \pə-ˈgō-də\ *n* : a tower with roofs curving upward at the division of each of several stories

paid *past and past part of* PAY

pail \ˈpāl\ *n* : a usu. cylindrical vessel with a handle — **pail·ful** \-ˌfu̇l\ *n*

¹**pain** \ˈpān\ *n* **1** : PUNISHMENT, PENALTY **2** : suffering or distress of body or mind; *also* : a basic bodily sensation marked by discomfort (as throbbing or aching) **3** *pl* : great care **4** : one that irks or annoys — **pain·ful** \-fəl\ *adj* — **pain·ful·ly** *adv* — **pain·less** *adj* — **pain·less·ly** *adv*

[2]**pain** *vb* : to cause or experience pain
pain·kill·er \ˈpān-ˌki-lər\ *n* : something (as a drug) that relieves pain — **pain·kill·ing** *adj*
pains·tak·ing \-ˌstā-kiŋ\ *adj* : taking pains : showing care — **pains·taking** *n* — **pains·tak·ing·ly** *adv*
[1]**paint** \ˈpānt\ *vb* **1** : to apply color, pigment, or paint to **2** : to produce or portray in lines or colors on a surface; *also* : to practice the art of painting **3** : to decorate with colors **4** : to use cosmetics **5** : to describe vividly **6** : SWAB — **paint·er** *n*
[2]**paint** *n* **1** : something produced by painting **2** : MAKEUP **3** : a mixture of a pigment and a liquid that forms a thin adherent coating when spread on a surface; *also* : the dry pigment used in making this mixture **4** : an applied coating of paint
paint·ball \ˈpānt-ˌbȯl\ *n* : a game in which two teams try to capture each other's flag using guns that shoot paint-filled pellets
paint·brush \ˈpānt-ˌbrəsh\ *n* : a brush for applying paint
painted lady *n* : a migratory butterfly with wings mottled in brown, orange, black, and white
painting *n* **1** : a work (as a picture) produced by painting **2** : the art or occupation of painting
[1]**pair** \ˈper\ *n, pl* **pairs** *also* **pair** [ME *paire,* fr. AF, fr. L *paria* equal things, fr. neut. pl. of *par* equal] **1** : two things of a kind designed for use together **2** : something made up of two corresponding pieces ⟨a ~ of pants⟩ **3** : a set of two people or animals
[2]**pair** *vb* **1** : to arrange in pairs **2** : to form a pair : MATCH **3** : to become associated with another
pai·sa \pī-ˈsä\ *n* **1** *pl* **pai·se** \-ˈsā\ — see *rupee* at MONEY table **2** *pl* **paisa** — see *rupee, taka* at MONEY table
pais·ley \ˈpāz-lē\ *adj, often cap* : decorated with colorful curved abstract figures ⟨a ~ fabric⟩
Pai·ute \ˈpī-ˌüt, -ˌyüt\ *n* : a member of an Indigenous people orig. of the U.S. Great Basin; *also* : either of two languages of the Paiute people
pa·ja·mas \pə-ˈjä-məz, -ˈja-\ *n pl* : a loose suit for sleeping or lounging
pal \ˈpal\ *n* : a close friend
pal·ace \ˈpa-ləs\ *n* [ME *palais,* fr. AF, fr. L *palatium,* fr. *Palatium,* the Palatine Hill in Rome where the emperors' residences were built] **1** : the official residence of a chief of state **2** : MANSION
pal·a·din \ˈpa-lə-dən\ *n* **1** : a trusted military leader (as for a medieval prince) **2** : a leading champion of a cause
pa·laes·tra \pə-ˈles-trə\ *n, pl* **-trae** \-(ˌ)trē\ : a school in ancient Greece or Rome for sports (as wrestling)
pa·lan·quin \ˌpa-lən-ˈkēn\ *n* : an enclosed couch for one person borne on the shoulders of men by means of poles
pal·at·able \ˈpa-lə-tə-bəl\ *adj* : agreeable to the taste ♦ ***Synonyms*** APPETIZING, SAVORY, TASTY, TOOTHSOME
pal·a·tal \ˈpa-lə-tᵊl\ *adj* **1** : of or relating to the palate **2** : pronounced with some part of the tongue near or touching the hard palate ⟨the \y\ in *yeast* and the \sh\ in *she* are ~ sounds⟩
pal·a·tal·ize \ˈpa-lə-tə-ˌlīz\ *vb* **-ized; -iz·ing** : to pronounce as or change into a palatal sound — **pal·a·tal·i·za·tion** \ˌpa-lə-tə-lə-ˈzā-shən\ *n*
pal·ate \ˈpa-lət\ *n* **1** : the roof of the mouth separating the mouth from the nasal cavity **2** : TASTE
pa·la·tial \pə-ˈlā-shəl\ *adj* **1** : of, relating to, or being a palace **2** : MAGNIFICENT
pa·lat·i·nate \pə-ˈla-tə-nət\ *n* : the territory of a palatine
[1]**pal·a·tine** \ˈpa-lə-ˌtīn\ *adj* **1** : possessing royal privileges; *also* : of or relating to a palatine or a palatinate **2** : of or relating to a palace : PALATIAL
[2]**palatine** *n* **1** : a feudal lord having sovereign power within his domains **2** : a high officer of an imperial palace
pa·la·ver \pə-ˈla-vər, -ˈlä-\ *n* [Pg *palavra* word, speech, fr. LL *parabola* parable, speech] **1** : a long parley **2** : idle talk — **palaver** *vb*
[1]**pale** \ˈpāl\ *n* **1** : a stake or picket of a fence **2** : an enclosed place; *also* : a district or territory within certain bounds or under a particular jurisdiction **3** : LIMITS, BOUNDS ⟨conduct beyond the ~⟩
[2]**pale** *vb* **paled; pal·ing** : to enclose with or as if with pales : FENCE
[3]**pale** *adj* **pal·er; pal·est** **1** : deficient in color or intensity : WAN ⟨a ~ face⟩ **2** : lacking in brightness : DIM ⟨a ~ star⟩ **3** : not dark or intense in hue ⟨a ~ blue⟩ — **pale·ness** *n*
[4]**pale** *vb* **paled; pal·ing** : to make or become pale
pale ale *n* : a medium-colored very dry ale
pale·face \ˈpāl-ˌfās\ *n* *disparaging* : a white person
Pa·leo·cene \ˈpā-lē-ə-ˌsēn\ *adj* : of, relating to, or being the earliest epoch of the Tertiary — **Paleocene** *n*
pa·leo·con·ser·va·tive \ˌpā-lē-ō-kən-ˈsər-və-tiv\ *n* : a conservative espousing traditional principles and policies
pa·le·og·ra·phy \ˌpā-lē-ˈä-grə-fē\ *n* [NL *palaeographia,* fr. Gk *palaios* ancient + *graphein* to write] : the study of ancient writings and inscriptions — **pa·le·og·ra·pher** *n*
Pa·leo·lith·ic \ˌpā-lē-ə-ˈli-thik\ *adj* : of or relating to the earliest period of the Stone Age characterized by rough or chipped stone implements
pa·le·on·tol·o·gy \ˌpā-lē-ˌän-ˈtä-lə-jē\ *n* : a science dealing with the life of past geologic periods as known from fossil remains — **pa·le·on·to·log·i·cal** \-ˌän-tə-ˈlä-ji-kəl\ *adj* — **pa·le·on·tol·o·gist** \-ˌän-ˈtä-lə-jist, -ən-\ *n*
Pa·leo·zo·ic \ˌpā-lē-ə-ˈzō-ik\ *adj* : of, relating to, or being the era of geologic history extending from about 570 million years ago to about 245 million years ago — **Paleozoic** *n*

pal·ette \ˈpa-lət\ *n* : a thin often oval board that a painter holds and mixes colors on; *also* : the colors on a palette

pal·frey \ˈpȯl-frē\ *n, pl* **palfreys** *archaic* : a saddle horse that is not a warhorse; *esp* : one suitable for a woman

pa·limp·sest \ˈpa-ləmp-ˌsest\ *n* [L *palimpsestus,* fr. Gk *palimpsēstos* scraped again] : writing material (as a parchment) used after the erasure of earlier writing

pal·in·drome \ˈpa-lən-ˌdrōm\ *n* : a word, verse, or sentence (as "Able was I ere I saw Elba") or a number (as 1881) that reads the same backward or forward

pal·ing \ˈpā-liŋ\ *n* **1** : a fence of pales **2** : material for pales **3** : PALE, PICKET

pal·i·sade \ˌpa-lə-ˈsād\ *n* **1** : a high fence of stakes esp. for defense **2** : a line of steep cliffs

[1]**pall** \ˈpȯl\ *vb* **1** : to lose in interest or attraction **2** : SATIATE, CLOY

[2]**pall** *n* **1** : a heavy cloth draped over a coffin **2** : something that produces a gloomy atmosphere

pal·la·di·um \pə-ˈlā-dē-əm\ *n* : a silver-white metallic chemical element used esp. as a catalyst and in alloys

pall·bear·er \ˈpȯl-ˌber-ər\ *n* : a person who attends the coffin at a funeral

[1]**pal·let** \ˈpa-lət\ *n* : a small, hard, or makeshift bed

[2]**pallet** *n* : a portable platform for transporting and storing materials

pal·li·ate \ˈpa-lē-ˌāt\ *vb* **-at·ed; -at·ing 1** : to ease (as a disease) without curing **2** : to cover by excuses and apologies ⟨~ faults⟩ — **pal·li·a·tion** \ˌpa-lē-ˈā-shən\ *n* — **pal·li·a·tive** \ˈpa-lē-ˌā-tiv\ *adj or n*

pal·lid \ˈpa-ləd\ *adj* : PALE, WAN

pal·lor \ˈpa-lər\ *n* : PALENESS

[1]**palm** \ˈpäm, ˈpälm\ *n* [ME, fr. OE, fr. L *palma* palm of the hand, palm tree; fr. the resemblance of the tree's leaves to the outstretched hand] **1** : any of a family of mostly tropical trees, shrubs, or vines usu. with a tall unbranched stem topped by a crown of large leaves **2** : a symbol of victory; *also* : VICTORY

[2]**palm** *n* : the underpart of the hand between the fingers and the wrist

[3]**palm** *vb* **1** : to conceal in or with the hand ⟨~ a card⟩ **2** : to impose by fraud

pal·mate \ˈpal-ˌmāt, ˈpäl-\ *also* **pal·mat·ed** \-ˌmā-təd\ *adj* : resembling a hand with the fingers spread

pal·met·to \pal-ˈme-tō\ *n, pl* **-tos** *or* **-toes** : any of several usu. small palms with fan-shaped leaves

palm·ist·ry \ˈpä-mə-strē, ˈpäl-\ *n* : the practice of reading a person's character or future from the markings on the palms — **palm·ist** \ˈpä-mist, ˈpäl-\ *n*

Palm Sunday *n* : the Sunday preceding Easter and commemorating Christ's triumphal entry into Jerusalem

palm·top \ˈpäm-ˌtäp, ˈpälm-\ *n* : a portable computer small enough to hold in the hand

palmy \ˈpä-mē, ˈpäl-\ *adj* **palm·i·er; -est 1** : abounding in or bearing palms **2** : FLOURISHING, PROSPEROUS

pal·o·mi·no \ˌpa-lə-ˈmē-nō\ *n, pl* **-nos** [AmerSp, fr. Sp, like a dove, fr. L *palumbinus,* fr. *palumbes,* a species of dove] : a horse with a pale cream to golden coat and cream or white mane and tail

pal·pa·ble \ˈpal-pə-bəl\ *adj* **1** : capable of being touched or felt : TANGIBLE **2** : OBVIOUS, PLAIN ⟨the resentment was ~⟩ ♦ ***Synonyms*** PERCEPTIBLE, SENSIBLE, APPRECIABLE, TANGIBLE, DETECTABLE — **pal·pa·bly** \-blē\ *adv*

pal·pate \ˈpal-ˌpāt\ *vb* **pal·pat·ed; pal·pat·ing** : to examine by touch esp. medically — **pal·pa·tion** \pal-ˈpā-shən\ *n*

pal·pi·tate \ˈpal-pə-ˌtāt\ *vb* **-tat·ed; -tat·ing** : to beat rapidly and strongly : THROB — **pal·pi·ta·tion** \ˌpal-pə-ˈtā-shən\ *n*

pal·sy \ˈpȯl-zē\ *n, pl* **palsies 1** : PARALYSIS **2** : a condition marked by tremor — **pal·sied** \-zēd\ *adj*

pal·ter \ˈpȯl-tər\ *vb* **pal·tered; pal·ter·ing 1** : to act insincerely : EQUIVOCATE **2** : HAGGLE

pal·try \ˈpȯl-trē\ *adj* **pal·tri·er; -est 1** : TRASHY ⟨a ~ pamphlet⟩ **2** : MEAN, DESPICABLE ⟨a ~ trick⟩ **3** : TRIVIAL ⟨~ excuses⟩ **4** : MEAGER, MEASLY ⟨a ~ sum⟩

pam *abbr* pamphlet

pam·pas \ˈpam-pəz, ˈpäm-, -pəs\ *n pl* : wide grassy So. American plains

pam·per \ˈpam-pər\ *vb* : to treat with excessive attention : INDULGE ♦ ***Synonyms*** CODDLE, HUMOR, BABY, SPOIL

pam·phlet \ˈpam-flət\ *n* [ME *pamflet* unbound booklet, fr. *Pamphilus seu De Amore* Pamphilus or On Love, popular Latin love poem of the 12th cent.] : an unbound printed publication

pam·phle·teer \ˌpam-flə-ˈtir\ *n* : a writer of pamphlets attacking something or urging a cause

[1]**pan** \ˈpan\ *n* **1** : a usu. broad, shallow, and open container for domestic use; *also* : something resembling such a container **2** : a basin or depression in land **3** : HARDPAN

[2]**pan** *vb* **panned; pan·ning 1** : to wash earth or gravel in a pan in searching for gold **2** : to criticize severely

Pan *abbr* Panama

pan·a·cea \ˌpa-nə-ˈsē-ə\ *n* : a remedy for all ills or difficulties : CURE-ALL

pa·nache \pə-ˈnash, -ˈnäsh\ *n* [MF *pennache,* ultim. fr. LL *pinnaculum* small wing] **1** : an ornamental tuft (as of feathers) esp. on a helmet **2** : dash or flamboyance in style and action

pan·a·ma \ˈpa-nə-ˌmä, -ˌmȯ\ *n, often cap* : a handmade hat braided from strips of the leaves from a tropical American tree

pan·cake \ˈpan-ˌkāk\ *n* : a flat cake made of thin batter and fried on both sides

pan·chro·mat·ic \ˌpan-krō-ˈma-tik\ *adj* : sensitive to all colors of visible light ⟨~ film⟩

pan·cre·as \ˈpaŋ-krē-əs, ˈpan-\ *n* : a large compound gland of vertebrates that produces insulin and discharges enzymes into the intestine — **pan·cre·at·ic** \ˌpaŋ-krē-ˈa-tik, ˌpan-\ *adj*

pan·da \ˈpan-də\ *n* **1** : a long-tailed reddish brown Himalayan mammal related to and resembling the raccoon **2** : a large black-and-white mammal of China usu. classified with the bears

pan·dem·ic \pan-ˈde-mik\ *n* : a widespread outbreak of disease — **pandemic** *adj*

pan·de·mo·ni·um \ˌpan-də-ˈmō-nē-əm\ *n* : a wild uproar : TUMULT

[1]**pan·der** \ˈpan-dər\ *vb* : to act as a pander ⟨~*s* to the public's taste for violence⟩

[2]**pander** *n* **1** : a go-between in love intrigues; *also* : PIMP **2** : a person who caters to or exploits others' desires or weaknesses

P & I *abbr* principal and interest

P & L *abbr* profit and loss

Pan·do·ra's box \pan-ˈdȯr-əz-\ *n* : a prolific source of troubles

pan·dow·dy \pan-ˈdau̇-dē\ *n, pl* **-dies** : a deep-dish apple dessert spiced, sweetened, and covered with a crust

pane \ˈpān\ *n* : a sheet of glass (as in a door or window)

pan·e·gy·ric \ˌpa-nə-ˈjir-ik\ *n* : a eulogistic oration or writing ⟨a ~ on war heroes⟩ — **pan·e·gyr·ist** \-ˈjir-ist\ *n*

[1]**pan·el** \ˈpa-nᵊl\ *n* [ME, piece of cloth, jury list on a piece of parchment, fr. AF, fr. VL **pannellus,* dim. of L *pannus* cloth, rag] **1** : a list of persons appointed for special duty ⟨a jury ~⟩; *also* : a group of people taking part in a discussion or quiz program **2** : a section of something (as a wall or door) often sunk below the level of the frame; *also* : a flat piece of construction material **3** : a flat piece of wood on which a picture is painted **4** : a mount for controls or dials

[2]**panel** *vb* **-eled** *or* **-elled; -el·ing** *or* **-el·ling** : to decorate with panels

paneling *n* : decorative panels

pan·el·ist \ˈpa-nᵊl-ist\ *n* : a member of a discussion or quiz panel

panel truck *n* : a small motortruck with a fully enclosed body

pang \ˈpaŋ\ *n* : a sudden sharp spasm (as of pain) or attack (as of remorse)

pan·ga \ˈpäŋ-gə\ *n* : any of various small boats often used for fishing

[1]**pan·han·dle** \ˈpan-ˌhan-dᵊl\ *n* : a narrow projection of a larger territory (as a state) ⟨the Texas ~⟩

[2]**panhandle** *vb* **-dled; -dling** : to ask for money on the street — **pan·han·dler** *n*

[1]**pan·ic** \ˈpa-nik\ *n* : a sudden overpowering fright; *also* : extreme anxiety ⟨a ~ disorder⟩ ⟨~ attacks⟩ ♦ ***Synonyms*** TERROR, CONSTERNATION, DISMAY, ALARM, DREAD, FEAR — **pan·icky** \-ni-kē\ *adj*

[2]**panic** *vb* **pan·icked** \-nikt\; **pan·ick·ing** : to affect or be affected with panic

pan·i·cle \ˈpa-ni-kəl\ *n* : a branched flower cluster (as of a lilac) in which each branch from the main stem has one or more flowers

pa·ni·ni \pə-ˈnē-nē\ *also* **pa·ni·no** \pə-ˈnē-nō\ *n, pl* **panini** *or* **pa·ni·nis** : a usually grilled sandwich made with Italian bread

pan·jan·drum \pan-ˈjan-drəm\ *n, pl* **-drums** *also* **-dra** \-drə\ : a powerful personage or pretentious official

pan·nier *also* **pan·ier** \ˈpan-yər\ *n* : a large basket esp. for bearing on the back

pan·o·ply \ˈpa-nə-plē\ *n, pl* **-plies** **1** : a full suit of armor **2** : a protective covering **3** : an impressive array

pan·ora·ma \ˌpa-nə-ˈra-mə, -ˈrä-\ *n* **1** : a picture unrolled before one's eyes **2** : a complete view in every direction — **pan·oram·ic** \-ˈra-mik\ *adj*

pan out *vb* : TURN OUT; *esp* : SUCCEED

pan·sex·u·al \ˌpan-ˈsek-sh(ə-)wəl, -shəl\ *adj* : of, relating to, or characterized by sexual or romantic attraction that is not limited to people of a particular gender identity or sexual orientation; *also* : not solely gay or straight

pan·sy \ˈpan-zē\ *n, pl* **pansies** [ME *pancy, pensee,* fr. MF *pensée,* fr. *pensée* thought, fr. *penser* to think, fr. L *pensare* to ponder] : a low-growing garden herb related to the violet; *also* : its showy flower

[1]**pant** \ˈpant\ *vb* [ME, fr. AF *panteiser,* fr. VL **phantasiare* to have hallucinations, fr. Gk *phantasioun,* fr. *phantasia* appearance, imagination] **1** : to breathe in a labored manner **2** : YEARN **3** : THROB

[2]**pant** *n* : a panting breath or sound

[3]**pant** *n* **1** : an outer garment covering each leg separately and usu. extending from the waist to the ankle — usu. used in pl. **2** *pl* : PANTIE

pan·ta·loons \ˌpan-tə-ˈlünz\ *n pl* **1** : close-fitting pants of the 19th century usu. having straps passing under the instep **2** : loose-fitting usu. shorter than ankle-length trousers

pan·the·ism \ˈpan-thē-ˌi-zəm\ *n* : a doctrine that equates God with the forces and laws of the universe — **pan·the·ist** \-ist\ *n* — **pan·the·is·tic** \ˌpan-thē-ˈis-tik\ *adj*

pan·the·on \ˈpan-thē-ˌän, -ən\ *n* **1** : a temple dedicated to all the gods; *also* : the gods of a people **2** : a group of illustrious people ⟨a ~ of great writers⟩

pan·ther \ˈpan-thər\ *n, pl* **panthers** *also* **panther** **1** : LEOPARD; *esp* : a black one **2** : COUGAR **3** : JAGUAR

pant·ie *or* **panty** \ˈpan-tē\ *n, pl* **pant·ies** : a woman's or child's short underpants — usu. used in pl.

pan·to·mime \ˈpan-tə-ˌmīm\ *n* **1** : a play in which the actors use no words **2** : expression of something by bodily or facial movements only — **pantomime** *vb* — **pan·to·mim·ic** \ˌpan-tə-ˈmi-mik\ *adj*

pan·try \ˈpan-trē\ *n, pl* **pantries** : a storage room for food or dishes

pant·suit \ˈpant-ˌsüt\ *n* : a woman's outfit consisting usu. of a long jacket and pants of the same material

panty hose *n pl* : a one-piece undergarment for women consisting of hosiery combined with a pantie

panty·waist \ˈpan-tē-ˌwāst\ *n* : SISSY

pap \ˈpap\ *n* : soft food for infants or invalids

pa·pa \ˈpä-pə\ *n* : FATHER

pa·pa·cy \ˈpā-pə-sē\ *n, pl* **-cies** **1** : the office of pope **2** : a succession of popes **3** : the term of a pope's reign **4** *cap* : the system of government of the Roman Catholic Church

pa·pa·in \pə-ˈpā-ən, -ˈpī-ən\ *n* : an enzyme in papaya juice used esp. as a meat tenderizer and in medicine

pa·pal \ˈpā-pəl\ *adj* : of or relating to the pope or to the Roman Catholic Church

papaw *var of* PAWPAW

pa·pa·ya \pə-ˈpī-ə\ *n* : a tropical American tree with large yellow black-seeded edible fruit; *also* : its fruit

pa·per \ˈpā-pər\ *n* [ME *papir,* fr. AF, fr. L *papyrus* papyrus, paper, fr. Gk *papyros* papyrus] **1** : a pliable substance made usu. of vegetable matter and used to write or print on, to wrap things in, or to cover walls; *also* : a single sheet of this substance **2** : a printed or written document **3** : NEWSPAPER **4** : WALLPAPER 1 — **paper** *adj or vb* — **pa·pery** \ˈpā-pə-rē\ *adj*

pa·per·back \-ˌbak\ *n* : a paper-covered book

pa·per·board \-ˌbȯrd\ *n* : CARDBOARD

pa·per·hang·er \ˈpā-pər-ˌhaŋ-ər\ *n* : one that applies wallpaper — **pa·per·hang·ing** *n*

pa·per·weight \-ˌwāt\ *n* : an object used to hold down loose papers by its weight

pa·pier–mâ·ché \ˌpā-pər-mə-ˈshā, ˌpa-ˌpyā-mə-, -ma-\ *n* [F, lit., chewed paper] : a molding material of wastepaper and additives (as glue) — **papier–mâché** *adj*

pa·pil·la \pə-ˈpi-lə\ *n, pl* **-lae** \-(ˌ)lē, -ˌlī\ [L, nipple] : a small projecting bodily part (as one of the nubs on the surface of the tongue) that resembles a tiny nipple in form — **pap·il·lary** \ˈpa-pə-ˌler-ē, pə-ˈpi-lə-rē\ *adj*

papist *n, often cap, usu disparaging* : ROMAN CATHOLIC — **papist** *adj*

pa·poose \pa-ˈpüs, pə-\ *n* [Narragansett *papoòs*] *dated, offensive* : an Indigenous baby or young child of No. America

pa·pri·ka \pə-ˈprē-kə, pa-\ *n* [Hungarian] : a mild red spice made from the fruit of various cultivated sweet peppers

Pap smear \ˈpap-\ *n* : a method for the early detection of cancer esp. of the uterine cervix

Pap test *n* : PAP SMEAR

pap·ule \ˈpa-pyül\ *n* : a small solid usu. conical elevation of the skin — **pap·u·lar** \-pyə-lər\ *adj*

pa·py·rus \pə-ˈpī-rəs\ *n, pl* **-ri** \-(ˌ)rē, -ˌrī\ *or* **-rus·es** **1** : a tall grassy sedge of the Nile valley **2** : paper made from papyrus pith

[1]**par** \ˈpär\ *n* **1** : a stated value (as of a security) **2** : a common level : EQUALITY **3** : an accepted standard or normal condition **4** : the score standard set for each hole of a golf course — **par** *adj*

[2]**par** *abbr* **1** paragraph **2** parallel **3** parish

par·a·ble \ˈpa-rə-bəl\ *n* : a simple story told to illustrate a moral truth

pa·rab·o·la \pə-ˈra-bə-lə\ *n* : a plane curve formed by a point moving so that its distance from a fixed point is equal to its distance from a fixed line — **par·a·bol·ic** \ˌpar-ə-ˈbä-lik\ *adj*

para·chute \ˈpa-rə-ˌshüt\ *n* [F, fr. *para-* (as in *parasol*) + *chute* fall] : a device for slowing the descent of a person or object through the air that consists of a usu. hemispherical canopy beneath which the person or object is suspended — **parachute** *vb* — **para·chut·ist** \-ˈshü-tist\ *n*

parachute pants *n pl* : baggy casual pants of lightweight fabric

[1]**pa·rade** \pə-ˈrād\ *n* **1** : a pompous display : EXHIBITION **2** : MARCH, PROCESSION; *esp* : a ceremonial formation and march **3** : a place for strolling

[2]**parade** *vb* **pa·rad·ed; pa·rad·ing** **1** : to march in a parade **2** : PROMENADE **3** : SHOW OFF ⟨*paraded* her knowledge⟩ **4** : MASQUERADE

par·a·digm \ˈpa-rə-ˌdīm, -ˌdim\ *n* **1** : MODEL, PATTERN **2** : a systematic inflection of a verb or noun showing a complete conjugation or declension — **par·a·dig·mat·ic** \ˌpa-rə-dig-ˈma-tik\ *adj*

par·a·dise \ˈpa-rə-ˌdīs, -ˌdīz\ *n* [ME *paradis,* fr. AF, fr. LL *paradisus,* fr. Gk *paradeisos,* lit., enclosed park, of Iranian origin] **1** : HEAVEN **2** : a place or state of bliss

par·a·di·si·a·cal \ˌpa-rə-də-ˈsī-ə-kəl\ *or* **par·a·dis·i·ac** \-ˈdi-zē-ˌak, -sē-\ *adj* : of, relating to, or resembling paradise

par·a·dox \ˈpa-rə-ˌdäks\ *n* : a statement that seems contrary to common sense and yet is perhaps true — **par·a·dox·i·cal** \ˌpa-rə-ˈdäk-si-kəl\ *adj* — **par·a·dox·i·cal·ly** \-k(ə-)lē\ *adv*

par·af·fin \ˈpa-rə-fən\ *n* : a waxy substance used esp. for making candles and sealing foods

para·glid·ing \ˈpa-rə-ˌglī-diŋ\ *n* : the sport of soaring from a slope or cliff using a modified parachute

par·a·gon \ˈpa-rə-ˌgän, -gən\ *n* : a model of perfection : PATTERN ⟨a ~ of virtue⟩

[1]**para·graph** \ˈpa-rə-ˌgraf\ *n* : a subdivision of a written composition that deals with one point or gives the words of one speaker; *also* : a character (as ¶) marking the beginning of a paragraph

[2]**paragraph** *vb* : to divide into paragraphs

par·a·keet \ˈpa-rə-ˌkēt\ *n* : any of numerous usu. small slender parrots with a long graduated tail

para·le·gal \ˌpa-rə-ˈlē-gəl\ *adj* : of, relating to, or being a paraprofessional who assists a lawyer — **paralegal** *n*

Par·a·li·pom·e·non \ˌpa-rə-lə-ˈpä-mə-ˌnän\ *n* : CHRONICLES

par·al·lax \ˈpa-rə-ˌlaks\ *n* : the difference in apparent direction of an object as seen from two different points

[1]**par·al·lel** \ˈpa-rə-ˌlel\ *adj* [L *parallelus,* fr. Gk *parallēlos,* fr. *para* beside + *allēlōn* of one another, fr. *allos . . . allos* one . . . another, fr. *allos* other] **1** : lying or moving in the same direction but always the same distance apart **2** : similar in essential parts — **par·al·lel·ism** \-ˌle-ˌli-zəm\ *n*

[2]**parallel** *n* **1** : a parallel line, curve, or surface **2** : one of the imaginary circles on the earth's surface that parallel the equator and mark the latitude **3** : something essentially similar to another **4** : SIMILARITY, LIKENESS

[3]**parallel** *vb* **1** : COMPARE **2** : to correspond to **3** : to extend in a parallel direction with

par·al·lel·o·gram \ˌpa-rə-ˈle-lə-ˌgram\ *n* : a 4-sided geometric figure with opposite sides equal and parallel

par·a·lyse *Brit var of* PARALYZE

pa·ral·y·sis \pə-ˈra-lə-səs\ *n, pl* **-y·ses** \-ˌsēz\ : complete or partial loss of function esp. when involving the motion or sensation in a part of the body — **par·a·lyt·ic** \ˌpa-rə-ˈli-tik\ *adj or n*

par·a·lyze \ˈpa-rə-ˌlīz\ *vb* **-lyzed; -lyz·ing 1** : to affect with paralysis **2** : to make powerless or inactive ⟨*paralyzed* by fear⟩ — **par·a·lyz·ing·ly** *adv*

par·a·me·cium \ˌpa-rə-ˈmē-shəm, -shē-əm, -sē-əm\ *n, pl* **-cia** \-shə, -shē-ə, -sē-ə\ *also* **-ci·ums** : any of a genus of slipper-shaped protozoans that move by cilia

para·med·ic \ˌpa-rə-ˈme-dik\ *also* **para·med·i·cal** \-di-kəl\ *n* **1** : a person who assists a physician in a paramedical capacity **2** : a specially trained medical technician licensed to provide a wide range of emergency services before or during transportation to a hospital

para·med·i·cal \ˌpa-rə-ˈme-di-kəl\ *also* **para·med·ic** \-ˈme-dik\ *adj* : concerned with supplementing the work of trained medical professionals

pa·ram·e·ter \pə-ˈra-mə-tər\ *n* **1** : a quantity whose value characterizes a statistical population or a member of a system (as a family of curves) **2** : a physical property whose value determines the characteristics or behavior of a system **3** : a characteristic element : FACTOR

para·mil·i·tary \ˌpa-rə-ˈmi-lə-ˌter-ē\ *adj* : formed on a military pattern esp. as an auxiliary military force

par·a·mount \ˈpa-rə-ˌmau̇nt\ *adj* : superior to all others : SUPREME ♦ ***Synonyms*** PREPONDERANT, PREDOMINANT, DOMINANT, CHIEF, SOVEREIGN

par·amour \ˈpa-rə-ˌmu̇r\ *n* : an illicit lover

para·noia \ˌpa-rə-ˈnȯi-ə\ *n* : a psychosis marked by delusions and irrational suspicion usu. without hallucinations — **par·a·noid** \ˈpa-rə-ˌnȯid\ *adj or n*

para·nor·mal \ˌpa-rə-ˈnȯr-məl\ *adj* : not scientifically explainable : SUPERNATURAL ⟨~ phenomena⟩

par·a·pet \ˈpa-rə-pət, -ˌpet\ *n* **1** : a protecting rampart **2** : a low wall or railing (as at the edge of a bridge)

par·a·pher·na·lia \ˌpa-rə-fə-ˈnāl-yə, -fər-\ *n sing or pl* **1** : personal belongings **2** : EQUIPMENT, APPARATUS

para·phrase \ˈpa-rə-ˌfrāz\ *n* : a restatement of a text giving the meaning in different words — **paraphrase** *vb*

para·ple·gia \ˌpa-rə-ˈplē-jə, -jē-ə\ *n* : paralysis of the lower trunk and legs — **para·ple·gic** \-jik\ *adj or n*

para·pro·fes·sion·al \-prə-ˈfe-shə-nəl\ *n* : a trained aide who assists a professional — **paraprofessional** *adj*

para·psy·chol·o·gy \ˌpa-rə-sī-ˈkä-lə-jē\ *n* : a field of study concerned with investigating paranormal psychological phenomena (as extrasensory perception) — **para·psy·chol·o·gist** \-jist\ *n*

par·a·site \ˈpa-rə-ˌsīt\ *n* [MF, fr. L *parasitus,* fr. Gk *parasitos,* fr. *para-* beside + *sitos* grain, food] **1** : a plant or animal living in, with, or on another organism usu. to its harm **2** : one depending on another and not making adequate return — **par·a·sit·ic** \ˌpa-rə-ˈsi-tik\ *adj* — **par·a·sit·ism** \ˈpa-rə-sə-ˌti-zəm, -ˌsī-ˌti-\ *n* — **par·a·sit·ize** \-sə-ˌtīz\ *vb*

par·a·si·tol·o·gy \ˌpa-rə-sə-ˈtä-lə-jē\ *n* : a branch of biology dealing with parasites and parasitism esp. among animals — **par·a·si·tol·o·gist** \-jist\ *n*

para·sol \ˈpa-rə-ˌsȯl\ *n* [F, fr. It *parasole,* fr. *parare* to shield + *sole* sun, fr. L *sol*] : a lightweight umbrella used as a shield against the sun

para·sym·pa·thet·ic nervous system \ˌpa-rə-ˌsim-pə-ˈthe-tik-\ *n* : the part of the autonomic nervous system that tends to induce secretion, to increase the tone and contractility of smooth muscle, and to slow heart rate

para·thi·on \ˌpa-rə-ˈthī-ən, -ˌän\ *n* : an extremely toxic insecticide

para·thy·roid \-ˈthī-ˌrȯid\ *n* : PARATHYROID GLAND — **parathyroid** *adj*

parathyroid gland *n* : any of usu. four small endocrine glands adjacent to or embedded in the thyroid gland that produce a hormone (**parathyroid hormone**) concerned with calcium and phosphorus metabolism

para·tran·sit \ˌpa-rə-ˈtran-sət, -zət\ *n* : transportation service that provides individualized rules without fixed routes or timetables

para·troop·er \ˈpa-rə-ˌtrü-pər\ *n* : a member of the paratroops

para·troops \-ˌtrüps\ *n pl* : troops trained to parachute from an airplane

para·ty·phoid \ˌpa-rə-ˈtī-ˌfȯid\ *n* : a bacterial food poisoning resembling typhoid fever

par·boil \ˈpär-ˌbȯi(-ə)l\ *vb* : to boil briefly

[1]**par·cel** \ˈpär-səl\ *n* **1** : a tract or plot of land **2** : COLLECTION, LOT ⟨the story was a ~ of lies⟩ **3** : a wrapped bundle : PACKAGE

[2]**parcel** *vb* **-celed** *or* **-celled; -cel·ing** *or* **-cel·ling** . to divide into portions

parcel post *n* **1** : a mail service handling parcels **2** : packages handled by parcel post

parch \ˈpärch\ *vb* **1** : to toast under dry heat **2** : to shrivel with heat

parch·ment \ˈpärch-mənt\ *n* : the skin of an animal prepared for writing on; *also* : a writing on such material

pard \ˈpärd\ *n* : LEOPARD

[1]**par·don** \ˈpär-dᵊn\ *n* : excuse of an offense without penalty; *esp* : an official release from legal punishment

[2]**pardon** *vb* : to free from penalty : EXCUSE, FORGIVE ⟨~ a criminal⟩ ⟨~ a debt⟩ — **par·don·able** \'pär-dᵊn-ə-bəl\ *adj*

par·don·er \'pär-dᵊn-ər\ *n* **1** : a medieval preacher delegated to raise money for religious works by soliciting offerings and granting indulgences **2** : one that pardons

pare \'per\ *vb* **pared; par·ing** **1** : to trim off an outside part (as the skin or rind) of **2** : to reduce as if by paring ⟨~ expenses⟩ — **par·er** *n*

par·e·gor·ic \ˌper-ə-'gȯr-ik\ *n* : an alcoholic preparation of opium and camphor used esp. to relieve pain

par·ent \'per-ənt\ *n* **1** : one that begets or brings forth offspring : FATHER, MOTHER **2** : one who brings up and cares for another **3** : SOURCE, ORIGIN — **par·ent·age** \-ən-tij\ *n* — **pa·ren·tal** \pə-'ren-tᵊl\ *adj* — **par·ent·hood** *n*

pa·ren·the·sis \pə-'ren-thə-səs\ *n, pl* **-the·ses** \-ˌsēz\ **1** : a word, phrase, or sentence inserted in a passage to explain or modify the thought **2** : one of a pair of punctuation marks ( ) used esp. to enclose parenthetic matter — **par·en·thet·ic** \ˌper-ən-'the-tik\ *or* **par·en·thet·i·cal** \-ti-kəl\ *adj* — **par·en·thet·i·cal·ly** \-k(ə-)lē\ *adv*

pa·ren·the·size \pə-'ren-thə-ˌsīz\ *vb* **-sized; -siz·ing** : to make a parenthesis of

par·ent·ing \'per-ən-tiŋ\ *n* : the raising of a child by its parents

pa·re·sis \pə-'rē-səs, 'pa-rə-\ *n, pl* **pa·re·ses** \-ˌsēz\ : a usu. incomplete paralysis; *also* : insanity caused by syphilitic alteration of the brain that leads to dementia and paralysis

par ex·cel·lence \ˌpär-ˌek-sə-'läⁿs\ *adj* [F, lit., by excellence] : being the best of a kind : PREEMINENT

par·fait \pär-'fā\ *n* [F, lit., something perfect] : a cold dessert made of layers of fruit, syrup, ice cream, and whipped cream

pa·ri·ah \pə-'rī-ə\ *n* : OUTCAST

pa·ri·etal \pə-'rī-ə-tᵊl\ *adj* **1** : of, relating to, or forming the walls of an anatomical structure **2** : of or relating to college living or its regulation

pari–mu·tu·el \ˌper-i-'myü-chə-wəl\ *n* : a betting system in which winners share the total stakes minus a percentage for the management

paring *n* : a pared-off piece

pa·ri pas·su \'pa-ri-'pa-sü\ *adv or adj* [L, with equal step] : at an equal rate or pace

par·ish \'per-ish\ *n* **1** : a church district in the care of one pastor; *also* : the residents of such an area **2** : a local church community **3** : a civil division of the state of Louisiana : COUNTY

pa·rish·io·ner \pə-'ri-shə-nər\ *n* : a member or resident of a parish

par·i·ty \'per-ə-tē\ *n, pl* **-ties** : EQUALITY, EQUIVALENCE

[1]**park** \'pärk\ *n* **1** : a tract of ground kept as a game preserve or recreation area **2** : a place where vehicles (as automobiles) are parked **3** : an enclosed stadium used esp. for ball games

[2]**park** *vb* **1** : to leave a vehicle temporarily (as in a parking lot or garage) **2** : to set and leave temporarily

par·ka \'pär-kə\ *n* : a very warm jacket with a hood

Par·kin·son's disease \'pär-kən-sənz-\ *n* : a chronic progressive neurological disease chiefly of later life marked esp. by tremor and weakness of resting muscles and by a shuffling gait

Parkinson's Law *n* : an observation in office organization: work expands so as to fill the time available for its completion

par·kour \pär-'ku̇r, 'pär-ˌku̇r\ *n* [F, alter. of *parcours* course, route, fr. ML *percursus*, fr. L *percurrere* to run through] : the sport of traversing environmental obstacles by running, climbing, or leaping rapidly

park·way \'pärk-ˌwā\ *n* : a broad landscaped thoroughfare

par·lance \'pär-ləns\ *n* **1** : SPEECH **2** : manner of speaking ⟨military ~⟩

[1]**par·lay** \'pär-ˌlā, -lē\ *vb* : to increase or change into something of much greater value ⟨~*ed* a $1000 loan into a fortune⟩

[2]**parlay** *n* : a series of bets in which the original stake plus its winnings are risked on successive wagers

par·ley \'pär-lē\ *n, pl* **parleys** : a conference usu. over matters in dispute : DISCUSSION — **parley** *vb*

par·lia·ment \'pär-lə-mənt\ *n* [ME, fr. AF *parlement,* fr. *parler* to speak, fr. ML *parabolare,* fr. LL *parabola* speech, parable] **1** : a formal governmental conference **2** *cap* : an assembly that constitutes the supreme legislative body of a country (as the United Kingdom) — **par·lia·men·ta·ry** \ˌpär-lə-'men-tə-rē\ *adj*

par·lia·men·tar·i·an \ˌpär-lə-ˌmen-'ter-ē-ən\ *n* **1** *often cap* : an adherent of the parliament during the English Civil War **2** : an expert in parliamentary procedure

par·lor \'pär-lər\ *n* **1** : a room for conversation or the reception of guests **2** : a place of business ⟨beauty ~⟩

par·lour \'pär-lər\ *chiefly Brit var of* PARLOR

par·lous \'pär-ləs\ *adj* : full of danger or risk : PRECARIOUS — **par·lous·ly** *adv*

Par·me·san \'pär-mə-ˌzän, -ˌzhän, -ˌzan\ *n* : a hard dry cheese with a sharp flavor

par·mi·gia·na \ˌpär-mi-'jä-nə, ˌpär-mi-'zhän\ *or* **par·mi·gia·no** \-'jä-(ˌ)nō\ *adj* : made or covered with Parmesan cheese ⟨veal ~⟩

pa·ro·chi·al \pə-'rō-kē-əl\ *adj* **1** : of or relating to a church parish **2** : limited in scope : NARROW, PROVINCIAL — **pa·ro·chi·al·ism** \-ə-ˌli-zəm\ *n*

parochial school *n* : a school maintained by a religious body

par·o·dy \'per-ə-dē\ *n, pl* **-dies** [L *parodia,* fr. Gk *parōidia,* fr. *para-* beside + *aidein* to sing] : a humorous or satirical imitation — **parody** *vb*

pa·role \pə-ˈrōl\ *n* : a conditional release of a prisoner whose sentence has not expired — **parole** *vb* — **pa·rol·ee** \-ˌrō-ˈlē, -ˈrō-ˌlē\ *n*

par·ox·ysm \ˈpa-rək-ˌsi-zəm, pə-ˈräk-\ *n* : a sudden sharp attack (as of pain or coughing) : CONVULSION — **par·ox·ys·mal** \ˌpa-rək-ˈsiz-məl, pə-ˌräk-\ *adj*

par·quet \ˈpär-ˌkā, pär-ˈkā\ *n* [F] **1** : a flooring of parquetry **2** : the lower floor of a theater; *esp* : the forward part of the orchestra

par·que·try \ˈpär-kə-trē\ *n, pl* **-tries** : fine woodwork inlaid in patterns

par·ri·cide \ˈpa-rə-ˌsīd\ *n* **1** : one that murders a parent or a close relative **2** : the act of a parricide

par·rot \ˈper-ət\ *n* : any of numerous bright-colored tropical birds that have a stout hooked bill

parrot fever *n* : PSITTACOSIS

par·ry \ˈper-ē\ *vb* **par·ried; par·ry·ing** **1** : to ward off a weapon or blow **2** : to evade esp. by an adroit answer — **parry** *n*

parse \ˈpärs *also* ˈpärz\ *vb* **parsed; pars·ing** : to give a grammatical description of a word or a group of words

par·sec \ˈpär-ˌsek\ *n* : a unit of measure for interstellar space equal to 3.26 light-years

par·si·mo·ny \ˈpär-sə-ˌmō-nē\ *n* : extreme or excessive frugality — **par·si·mo·ni·ous** \ˌpär-sə-ˈmō-nē-əs\ *adj* — **par·si·mo·ni·ous·ly** *adv*

pars·ley \ˈpär-slē\ *n* : a garden plant related to the carrot that has finely divided leaves used as a seasoning or garnish; *also* : the leaves

pars·nip \ˈpär-snəp\ *n* : a garden plant related to the carrot that has a long edible usu. whitish root which is cooked as a vegetable; *also* : the root

par·son \ˈpär-sᵊn\ *n* [ME *persone,* fr. AF, fr. ML *persona,* lit., person, fr. L] : MINISTER 2, PASTOR

par·son·age \ˈpär-sə-nij\ *n* : a house provided by a church for its pastor

¹**part** \ˈpärt\ *n* **1** : a division or portion of a whole **2** : the melody or score for a particular voice or instrument **3** : a spare piece for a machine **4** : DUTY, FUNCTION **5** : one of the sides in a dispute **6** : ROLE; *also* : an actor's lines in a play **7** *pl* : TALENTS, ABILITY ⟨a man of many ~*s*⟩ **8** : the line where one's hair divides (as in combing)

²**part** *vb* **1** : to take leave of someone **2** : to divide or break into parts : SEPARATE **3** : to go away : DEPART; *also* : DIE **4** : to give up possession ⟨~*ed* with her jewels⟩ **5** : APPORTION, SHARE

³**part** *abbr* **1** participial; participle **2** particular

par·take \pär-ˈtāk\ *vb* **-took** \-ˈtu̇k\; **-tak·en** \-ˈtā-kən\; **-tak·ing** **1** : to have a share or part **2** : to take a portion (as of food) — **par·tak·er** *n*

par·terre \pär-ˈter\ *n* [F, fr. MF, fr. *par terre* on the ground] **1** : an ornamental garden with paths between the flower beds **2** : the part of a theater floor behind the orchestra

par·the·no·gen·e·sis \ˌpär-thə-nō-ˈje-nə-səs\ *n* [NL, fr. Gk *parthenos* virgin + L *genesis* genesis] : development of a new individual from an unfertilized usu. female sex cell — **par·the·no·ge·net·ic** \-jə-ˈne-tik\ *adj*

par·tial \ˈpär-shəl\ *adj* **1** : not total or general : affecting a part only **2** : favoring one party over the other : BIASED **3** : markedly fond — used with *to* — **par·tial·i·ty** \ˌpär-shē-ˈa-lə-tē\ *n* — **par·tial·ly** *adv*

par·tic·i·pate \pär-ˈti-sə-ˌpāt\ *vb* **-pat·ed; -pat·ing** **1** : to take part in something ⟨~ in a game⟩ **2** : SHARE — **par·tic·i·pant** \-pənt\ *adj or n* — **par·tic·i·pa·tion** \-ˌti-sə-ˈpā-shən\ *n* — **par·tic·i·pa·tor** \-ˈti-sə-ˌpā-tər\ *n* — **par·tic·i·pa·to·ry** \-ˈti-sə-pə-ˌtȯr-ē\ *adj*

par·ti·ci·ple \ˈpär-tə-ˌsi-pəl\ *n* : a word having the characteristics of both verb and adjective — **par·ti·cip·i·al** \ˌpär-tə-ˈsi-pē-əl\ *adj*

par·ti·cle \ˈpär-ti-kəl\ *n* **1** : a very small bit of matter **2** : a unit of speech (as an article, preposition, or conjunction) expressing some general aspect of meaning or some connective or limiting relation

par·ti·cle·board \-ˌbȯrd\ *n* : a board made of very small pieces of wood bonded together

par·ti–col·or \ˌpär-tē-ˈkə-lər\ *or* **par·ti–col·ored** \-lərd\ *adj* : showing different colors or tints; *esp* : having one main color broken by patches of one or more other colors

¹**par·tic·u·lar** \pər-ˈti-kyə-lər\ *adj* **1** : of or relating to a specific person or thing ⟨the laws of a ~ state⟩ **2** : DISTINCTIVE, SPECIAL ⟨the ~ point of his talk⟩ **3** : SEPARATE, INDIVIDUAL ⟨each ~ hair⟩ **4** : attentive to details : PRECISE **5** : hard to please : EXACTING ⟨is ~ about her clothes⟩ — **par·tic·u·lar·i·ty** \-ˌti-kyə-ˈlar-ə-tē\ *n* — **par·tic·u·lar·ly** *adv*

²**particular** *n* : an individual fact or detail

par·tic·u·lar·ise *Brit var of* PARTICULARIZE

par·tic·u·lar·ize \pər-ˈti-kyə-lə-ˌrīz\ *vb* **-ized; -iz·ing** **1** : to state in detail : SPECIFY **2** : to go into details

par·tic·u·late \pər-ˈti-kyə-lət, pär-, -ˌlāt\ *adj* : relating to or existing as minute separate particles — **particulate** *n*

¹**part·ing** *n* : a place or point of separation or divergence

²**parting** *adj* : given, taken, or done at parting ⟨a ~ kiss⟩

par·ti·san *also* **par·ti·zan** \ˈpär-tə-zən, -sən\ *n* **1** : one that takes the part of another : ADHERENT **2** : GUERRILLA — **partisan** *adj* — **par·ti·san·ship** *n*

par·tite \ˈpär-ˌtīt\ *adj* : divided into a usu. specified number of parts

par·ti·tion \pär-ˈti-shən\ *n* **1** : DIVISION **2** : something that divides or separates; *esp* : an interior dividing wall — **partition** *vb*

par·ti·tive \ˈpär-tə-tiv\ *adj* : of, relating to, or denoting a part

part·ly \ˈpärt-lē\ *adv* : in part : in some measure or degree

part·ner \ˈpärt-nər\ *n* **1** : ASSOCIATE, COLLEAGUE **2** : either of two persons who dance together **3** : one who plays on the same team with another **4** : SPOUSE **5** : one of two or more persons contractually associated as joint principals in a business — **part·ner·ship** *n*

part of speech : a class of words (as nouns or verbs) distinguished according to the kind of idea denoted and the function performed in a sentence

par·tridge \ˈpär-trij\ *n, pl* **partridge** *or* **par·tridg·es** : any of various stout-bodied Old World game birds

part–song \ˈpärt-ˌsȯŋ\ *n* : a song with two or more voice parts

part–time \-ˈtīm\ *adj or adv* : involving or working less than a full or regular schedule — **part–tim·er** \-ˌtī-mər\ *n*

par·tu·ri·tion \ˌpär-tə-ˈri-shən, ˌpär-chə-, ˌpär-tyu̇-\ *n* : CHILDBIRTH

part·way \ˈpärt-ˈwā\ *adv* : to some extent : PARTLY

par·ty \ˈpär-tē\ *n, pl* **parties** **1** : a person or group taking one side of a question; *esp* : a group of persons organized for the purpose of directing the policies of a government **2** : a person or group concerned in an action or affair : PARTICIPANT **3** : a group of persons detailed for a common task **4** : a social gathering

party animal *n* : a person known for frequent attendance at parties

par·ty·go·er \ˈpär-tē-ˌgō-ər\ *n* : a person who attends a party or who attends parties frequently

par·ve·nu \ˈpär-və-ˌnü, -ˌnyü\ *n* [F, fr. pp. of *parvenir* to arrive, fr. L *pervenire,* fr. *per* through + *venire* to come] : one who has recently or suddenly risen to wealth or power but has not yet secured the social position associated with it

pas \ˈpä\ *n, pl* **pas** *same or* ˈpäz\ : a dance step or combination of steps

pas·cal \pas-ˈkal\ *n* : a unit of pressure in the metric system equal to one newton per square meter

pas·chal \ˈpas-kəl\ *adj* : of, relating to, appropriate for, or used during Passover or Easter ceremonies

pa·sha \ˈpä-shə, ˈpa-; pə-ˈshä\ *n* : a man (as formerly a governor in Turkey) of high rank

pash·mi·na \ˌpəsh-ˈmē-nə\ *n* : a fine wool from the undercoat of domestic Himalayan goats; *also* : a shawl made from this wool

¹pass \ˈpas\ *vb* **1** : MOVE, PROCEED **2** : to go away; *also* : DIE **3** : to move past, beyond, or over **4** : to allow to elapse : SPEND **5** : to go or make way through **6** : to go or allow to go unchallenged **7** : to undergo transfer **8** : to render a legal judgment **9** : OCCUR **10** : to secure the approval of (as a legislature) **11** : to go or cause to go through an inspection, test, or course of study successfully **12** : to be regarded **13** : CIRCULATE ⟨~ a note⟩ **14** : VOID 2 **15** : to transfer the ball or puck to another player **16** : to decline to bid or bet on one's hand in a card game **17** : to give a base on balls to **18** : to let something go by without accepting ⟨~*ed* on his offer⟩ — **pass·er** *n*

²pass *n* : a gap in a mountain range

³pass *n* **1** : the act or an instance of passing **2** : REALIZATION, ACCOMPLISHMENT **3** : a state of affairs **4** : a written authorization to leave, enter, or move about freely **5** : a transfer of a ball or puck from one player to another **6** : BASE ON BALLS **7** : EFFORT, TRY **8** : a sexually inviting gesture or approach

⁴pass *abbr* **1** passenger **2** passive

pass·able \ˈpa-sə-bəl\ *adj* **1** : capable of being passed or traveled on **2** : just good enough : TOLERABLE ⟨did a ~ job⟩ — **pass·ably** \-blē\ *adv*

pas·sage \ˈpa-sij\ *n* **1** : a means (as a road or corridor) of passing **2** : the action or process of passing **3** : a voyage esp. by sea or air **4** : a right or permission to pass **5** : ENACTMENT **6** : a usu. brief portion or section (as of a book)

pas·sage·way \-ˌwā\ *n* : a way that allows passage

pass·book \ˈpas-ˌbu̇k\ *n* : BANKBOOK

pas·sé \pa-ˈsā\ *adj* **1** : past one's prime **2** : not up-to-date : OUTMODED

pas·sel \ˈpa-səl\ *n* : a large number ⟨a ~ of children⟩

pas·sen·ger \ˈpa-sᵊn-jər\ *n* : a traveler in a public or private conveyance

pass·er·by \ˈpa-sər-ˌbī\ *n, pl* **pass·ers·by** : one who passes by

pas·ser·ine \ˈpa-sə-ˌrīn\ *adj* : of or relating to the large order of birds comprising singing birds that perch

pas·sim \ˈpa-səm\ *adv* [L, fr. *passus* scattered, fr. pp. of *pandere* to spread] : here and there : THROUGHOUT

pass·ing *n* : the act of one that passes or causes to pass; *esp* : DEATH

pas·sion \ˈpa-shən\ *n* **1** *often cap* : the sufferings of Christ between the night of the Last Supper and his death **2** : strong feeling; *also, pl* : the emotions as distinguished from reason **3** : RAGE, ANGER **4** : LOVE; *also* : an object of affection or enthusiasm **5** : sexual desire — **pas·sion·ate** \ˈpa-shə-nət\ *adj* — **pas·sion·ate·ly** *adv* — **pas·sion·less** *adj*

pas·sion·flow·er \ˈpa-shən-ˌflau̇-(ə)r\ *n* [fr. the fancied resemblance of parts of the flower to the instruments of Christ's crucifixion] : any of a genus of chiefly tropical woody climbing vines or erect herbs with showy flowers and pulpy often edible berries (**passion fruit**)

pas·sive \ˈpa-siv\ *adj* **1** : not active : acted upon **2** : asserting that the grammatical subject is subjected to or affected by the action represented by the verb ⟨~ voice⟩ **3** : making use of the sun's heat usu. without the aid of mechanical devices **4** : SUBMISSIVE, PATIENT — **passive** *n* — **pas·sive·ly** *adv* — **pas·siv·i·ty** \pa-ˈsi-və-tē\ *n*

pas·sive–ma·trix \-ˈmā-triks\ *adj* : of, relating to, or being on LCD in which pixels are controlled in groups

pass·key \ˈpas-ˌkē\ *n* : a key for opening two or more locks

pass out *vb* : to lose consciousness

Pass·over \ˈpas-ˌō-vər\ *n* [fr. the exemption of the Israelites from the slaughter of the firstborn in Egypt (Exodus 12:23–27)] : a Jewish holiday celebrated in March or April in commemoration of the Hebrews' liberation from slavery in Egypt

pass·port \ˈpas-ˌpȯrt\ *n* : an official document issued by a country upon request to a citizen requesting protection during travel abroad

pass up *vb* : DECLINE, REJECT

pass·word \ˈpas-ˌwərd\ *n* **1** : a word or phrase that must be spoken by a person before being allowed to pass a guard **2** : a sequence of characters required for access to a computer system

1**past** \ˈpast\ *adj* **1** : AGO ⟨10 years ~⟩ **2** : just gone or elapsed ⟨the ~ month⟩ **3** : having existed or taken place in a period before the present : BYGONE **4** : of, relating to, or constituting a verb tense that expresses time gone by

2**past** *prep or adv* : BEYOND

3**past** *n* **1** : time gone by **2** : something that happened or was done in a former time **3** : the past tense; *also* : a verb form in it **4** : a secret past life

pas·ta \ˈpäs-tə\ *n* [It] **1** : a paste in processed form (as macaroni) or in the form of fresh dough (as ravioli) **2** : a dish of cooked pasta

1**paste** \ˈpāst\ *n* [ME, fr. AF, fr. LL *pasta* dough, paste] **1** : DOUGH **2** : a smooth food product made by evaporation or grinding ⟨tomato ~⟩ **3** : a shaped dough (as spaghetti or ravioli) **4** : a preparation (as of flour and water) for sticking things together **5** : a brilliant glass used for artificial gems

2**paste** *vb* **past·ed; past·ing** **1** : to cause to adhere by paste : STICK **2** : to put (something copied or cut from a computer document) into another place

paste·board \ˈpāst-ˌbȯrd\ *n* : CARDBOARD

1**pas·tel** \pas-ˈtel\ *n* **1** : a paste made of powdered pigment; *also* : a crayon of such paste **2** : a drawing in pastel **3** : a pale or light color

2**pastel** *adj* **1** : of or relating to a pastel **2** : pale in color

pas·tern \ˈpas-tərn\ *n* : the part of a horse's foot extending from the fetlock to the top of the hoof

pas·teur·i·za·tion \ˌpas-chə-rə-ˈzā-shən, ˌpas-tə-\ *n* : partial sterilization of a substance (as milk) by heat or radiation — **pas·teur·ize** \ˈpas-chə-ˌrīz, ˈpas-tə-\ *vb* — **pas·teur·iz·er** *n*

pas·tiche \pas-ˈtēsh\ *n* : a composition (as in literature or music) made up of selections from different works

pas·tille \pas-ˈtēl\ *n* : LOZENGE 2

pas·time \ˈpas-ˌtīm\ *n* : DIVERSION; *esp* : something that serves to make time pass agreeably

pas·tor \ˈpas-tər\ *n* [ME *pastour,* fr. AF, fr. L *pastor,* herdsman, fr. *pascere* to feed, pasture, nurture] : a minister or priest serving a local church or parish — **pas·tor·ate** \-tə-rət\ *n*

1**pas·to·ral** \ˈpas-tə-rəl\ *adj* **1** : of or relating to shepherds or to rural life **2** : of or relating to spiritual guidance esp. of a congregation **3** : of or relating to the pastor of a church

2**pastoral** *n* : a literary work dealing with shepherds or rural life

pas·to·rale \ˌpas-tə-ˈräl, -ˈral\ *n* [It] : a musical composition having a pastoral theme

past participle *n* : a participle that typically expresses completed action, that is one of the principal parts of the verb, and that is used in the formation of perfect tenses in the active voice and of all tenses in the passive voice

pas·tra·mi \pə-ˈsträ-mē\ *n* [Yiddish *pastrame*] : a highly seasoned smoked beef prepared esp. from shoulder cuts

pas·try \ˈpā-strē\ *n, pl* **pastries** : sweet baked goods made of dough or with a crust made of enriched dough

pas·tur·age \ˈpas-chə-rij\ *n* : PASTURE

1**pas·ture** \ˈpas-chər\ *n* **1** : plants (as grass) for the feeding esp. of grazing livestock **2** : land or a plot of land used for grazing

2**pasture** *vb* **pas·tured; pas·tur·ing** **1** : GRAZE **2** : to use as pasture

pasty \ˈpā-stē\ *adj* **past·i·er; -est** : resembling paste; *esp* : pallid and unhealthy in appearance

1**pat** \ˈpat\ *n* **1** : a light tap esp. with the hand or a flat instrument; *also* : the sound made by it **2** : something (as butter) shaped into a small flat usu. square individual portion

2**pat** *adv* : in a pat manner : PERFECTLY

3**pat** *vb* **pat·ted; pat·ting** **1** : to strike lightly with a flat instrument **2** : to flatten, smooth, or put into place or shape with a pat **3** : to tap gently or lovingly with the hand

4**pat** *adj* **1** : exactly suited to the occasion : APT **2** : memorized exactly **3** : UNYIELDING ⟨stood ~ on the issue⟩

PAT *abbr* point after touchdown

pa·ta·ca \pə-ˈtä-kə\ *n* — see MONEY table

1**patch** \ˈpach\ *n* **1** : a piece used to cover a torn or worn place; *also* : one worn on a garment as an ornament or insignia **2** : a small area distinct from that about it **3** : a shield worn over the socket of an injured or missing eye

2**patch** *vb* **1** : to mend or cover with a patch **2** : to make of fragments **3** : to repair usu. in hasty fashion

patch·ou·li \ˈpa-chə-lē, pə-ˈchü-lē\ *n* : a heavy perfume made from the fragrant essential oil of an Asian mint; *also* : the plant itself

patch test *n* : a test for allergic sensitivity made by applying to the unbroken skin small pads soaked with the allergen to be tested

patch·work \ˈpach-ˌwərk\ *n* : something made of pieces of different materials, shapes, or colors

patchy \ˈpa-chē\ *adj* **patch·i·er; -est** : marked by or consisting of patches; *also* : irregular in appearance or quality — **patch·i·ness** \-chē-nəs\ *n*

pate \ˈpāt\ *n* : HEAD; *esp* : the crown of the head

pâ·té *also* **pate** \pä-ˈtā\ *n* [F] **1** : a meat or fish pie or patty **2** : a spread of finely chopped or pureed seasoned meat

pa·tel·la \pə-ˈte-lə\ *n, pl* **-lae** \-ˈte-(ˌ)lē, -ˌlī\ *or* **-las** [L] : KNEECAP — **pa·tel·lar** \-ˈte-lər\ *adj*

pat·en \ˈpa-tᵊn\ *n* **1** : PLATE; *esp* : one of precious metal for the eucharistic bread **2** : a thin disk

¹pa·tent *1 & 4 are* ˈpa-tᵊnt, *Brit also* ˈpā-, *2 & 3 are* ˈpa-tᵊnt, ˈpā-\ *adj* **1** : open to public inspection — used chiefly in the phrase *letters patent* **2** : free from obstruction **3** : EVIDENT, OBVIOUS **4** : protected by a patent ♦ ***Synonyms*** MANIFEST, DISTINCT, APPARENT, PALPABLE, PLAIN, CLEAR — **pat·ent·ly** *adv*

²pat·ent \ˈpa-tᵊnt, *Brit also* ˈpā-\ *n* **1** : an official document conferring a right or privilege **2** : a document securing to an inventor for a term of years exclusive right to his or her invention **3** : something patented

³pat·ent *vb* : to secure by patent

pat·en·tee \ˌpa-tᵊn-ˈtē, *Brit also* ˌpā-\ *n* : one to whom a grant is made or a privilege secured by patent

pat·ent medicine \ˈpa-tᵊnt-\ *n* : a packaged nonprescription drug protected by a trademark; *also* : any proprietary drug

pa·ter·fa·mil·i·as \ˌpā-tər-fə-ˈmi-lē-əs\ *n, pl* **pa·tres·fa·mil·i·as** \ˌpā-ˌtrēz-\ [L] : the father of a family : the male head of a household

pa·ter·nal \pə-ˈtər-nᵊl\ *adj* **1** : FATHERLY **2** : related through or inherited or derived from a father — **pa·ter·nal·ly** *adv*

pa·ter·nal·ism \-nə-ˌli-zəm\ *n* : a system under which an authority treats those under its control paternally (as by regulating their conduct and supplying their needs)

¹pa·ter·ni·ty \pə-ˈtər-nə-tē\ *n* **1** : FATHERHOOD **2** : descent from a father

²paternity *adj* **1** : granted to a father ⟨~ leave⟩ **2** : of or relating to the determination of paternity ⟨a ~ suit⟩

¹path \ˈpath, ˈpäth\ *n, pl* **paths** \ˈpat͟hz, ˈpaths, ˈpät͟hz, ˈpäths\ **1** : a trodden way **2** : ROUTE, COURSE — **path·less** *adj*

²path *or* **pathol** *abbr* pathology

path·break·ing \ˈpath-ˌbrā-kiŋ\ *adj* : TRAILBLAZING

pa·thet·ic \pə-ˈthe-tik\ *adj* **1** : evoking tenderness, pity, or sorrow **2** : pitifully inadequate ⟨a ~ performance⟩ ♦ ***Synonyms*** PITIFUL, PITEOUS, PITIABLE, POOR — **pa·thet·i·cal·ly** \-ti-k(ə-)lē\ *adv*

path·find·er \ˈpath-ˌfīn-dər, ˈpäth-\ *n* : one that discovers a way; *esp* : one that explores untraveled regions to mark out a new route

patho·gen \ˈpa-thə-jən\ *n* : a specific agent (as a bacterium) causing disease — **patho·gen·ic** \ˌpa-thə-ˈje-nik\ *adj* — **patho·ge·nic·i·ty** \-jə-ˈni-sə-tē\ *n*

pa·thog·ra·phy \pə-ˈthä-grə-fē\ *n* : biography focusing on a person's flaws and misfortunes

pa·thol·o·gy \pə-ˈthä-lə-jē\ *n, pl* **-gies** **1** : the study of the essential nature of disease **2** : the abnormality of structure and function characteristic of a disease **3** : deviation giving rise to social ills — **path·o·log·i·cal** \ˌpa-thə-ˈlä-ji-kəl\ *adj* — **pa·thol·o·gist** \pə-ˈthä-lə-jist\ *n*

pa·thos \ˈpā-ˌthäs, -ˌthōs\ *n* : an element in experience or artistic representation evoking pity or compassion

path·way \ˈpath-ˌwā, ˈpäth-\ *n* : PATH

pa·tience \ˈpā-shəns\ *n* **1** : the capacity, habit, or fact of being patient **2** *chiefly Brit* : SOLITAIRE 2

¹pa·tient \ˈpā-shənt\ *adj* **1** : bearing pain or trials without complaint **2** : showing self-control : CALM **3** : STEADFAST, PERSEVERING — **pa·tient·ly** *adv*

²patient *n* : one under medical care

patient zero *n* : a person identified as the first to become infected with a disease in an outbreak

pa·ti·na \ˈpa-tə-nə, pə-ˈtē-\ *n, pl* **pa·ti·nas** \-nəz\ *or* **pa·ti·nae** \ˈpa-tə-ˌnē, -ˌnī\ **1** : a green film formed on copper and bronze by exposure to moist air **2** : a superficial covering or exterior

pa·tio \ˈpa-tē-ˌō, ˈpä-\ *n, pl* **pa·ti·os** **1** : COURTYARD **2** : an often paved area near a dwelling used esp. for outdoor dining

pa·tois \ˈpa-ˌtwä\ *n, pl* **pa·tois** \-ˌtwäz\ [F] **1** : a dialect other than the standard dialect; *esp* : uneducated or provincial speech **2** : JARGON 2

pa·tri·arch \ˈpā-trē-ˌärk\ *n* **1** : a man who is father or founder **2** : a venerable old man **3** : an ecclesiastical dignitary (as the bishop of an Eastern Orthodox see) — **pa·tri·ar·chal** \ˌpā-trē-ˈär-kəl\ *adj* — **pa·tri·arch·ate** \ˈpā-trē-ˌär-kət, -ˌkāt\ *n* — **pa·tri·ar·chy** \-ˌär-kē\ *n*

pa·tri·cian \pə-ˈtri-shən\ *n* : a person of high birth : ARISTOCRAT — **patrician** *adj*

pat·ri·cide \ˈpa-trə-ˌsīd\ *n* **1** : one who murders his or her own father **2** : the murder of one's own father

pat·ri·mo·ny \ˈpa-trə-ˌmō-nē\ *n* : something (as an estate) inherited or derived esp. from one's father : HERITAGE — **pat·ri·mo·ni·al** \ˌpa-trə-ˈmō-nē-əl\ *adj*

pa·tri·ot \ˈpā-trē-ət, -ˌät\ *n* [MF *patriote* compatriot, fr. LL *patriota,* fr. Gk *patriōtēs,* fr. *patria* lineage, fr. *patr-, patēr* father] : one who loves his or her country — **pa·tri·ot·ic** \ˌpā-trē-ˈä-tik\ *adj* — **pa·tri·ot·i·cal·ly** \-ti-k(ə-)lē\ *adv* — **pa·tri·o·tism** \ˈpā-trē-ə-ˌti-zəm\ *n*

pa·tris·tic \pə-ˈtris-tik\ *adj* : of or relating to the church fathers or their writings

¹pa·trol \pə-ˈtrōl\ *n* : the action of going the rounds (as of an area) for observation or the maintenance of security; *also* : a person or group performing such an action

[2]**patrol** *vb* **pa·trolled; pa·trol·ling** : to carry out a patrol

pa·trol·man \pə-ˈtrōl-mən\ *n* : a police officer assigned to a beat

patrol wagon *n* : PADDY WAGON

pa·tron \ˈpā-trən\ *n* [ME, fr. AF, fr. ML & L; ML *patronus* patron saint, patron of a benefice, pattern, fr. L, defender, fr. *patr-, pater* father] **1** : a person chosen or named as special protector **2** : a wealthy or influential supporter ⟨~ of poets⟩; *also* : BENEFACTOR **3** : a regular client or customer ⟨diner ~*s*⟩

pa·tron·age \ˈpa-trə-nij, ˈpā-\ *n* **1** : the support or influence of a patron **2** : the trade of customers **3** : control of appointment to government jobs

pa·tron·ess \ˈpā-trə-nəs\ *n* : a woman who is a patron

pa·tron·ise *Brit var of* PATRONIZE

pa·tron·ize \ˈpā-trə-ˌnīz, ˈpa-\ *vb* **-ized; -iz·ing** **1** : to be a customer of **2** : to treat condescendingly, haughtily, or coolly ⟨rich people who ~ the poor⟩

pat·ro·nym·ic \ˌpa-trə-ˈni-mik\ *n* : a name derived from the name of one's father or a paternal ancestor usu. by the addition of an affix

pa·troon \pə-ˈtrün\ *n* : the proprietor of a manorial estate esp. in New York under Dutch rule

pat·sy \ˈpat-sē\ *n, pl* **pat·sies** : a person who is easily duped or victimized

[1]**pat·ter** \ˈpa-tər\ *vb* : to talk glibly or mechanically ♦ ***Synonyms*** CHATTER, PRATE, CHAT, PRATTLE, BABBLE

[2]**patter** *n* **1** : a specialized lingo **2** : extremely rapid talk ⟨a comedian's ~⟩

[3]**patter** *vb* : to strike, pat, or tap rapidly

[4]**patter** *n* : a quick succession of taps or pats ⟨the ~ of rain⟩

[1]**pat·tern** \ˈpa-tərn\ *n* [ME *patron,* fr. AF, fr. ML *patronus,* fr. L, defender, fr. *patr-, pater* father] **1** : an ideal model **2** : something used as a model for making things ⟨a dressmaker's ~⟩ **3** : SAMPLE **4** : an artistic design **5** : CONFIGURATION **6** : a sample of a person's behaviors or characteristics ⟨a ~ of violence⟩

[2]**pattern** *vb* : to form according to a pattern

pat·ty *also* **pat·tie** \ˈpa-tē\ *n, pl* **patties** **1** : a little pie **2** : a small flat cake esp. of chopped food ⟨hamburger *patties*⟩

pau·ci·ty \ˈpȯ-sə-tē\ *n* : smallness of number or quantity

paunch \ˈpȯnch\ *n* : a usu. large belly : POTBELLY — **paunchy** *adj*

pau·per \ˈpȯ-pər\ *n* : a person without means of support except from charity — **pau·per·ism** \-pə-ˌri-zəm\ *n* — **pau·per·ize** \-pə-ˌrīz\ *vb*

[1]**pause** \ˈpȯz\ *n* **1** : a temporary stop; *also* : a period of inaction **2** : a brief suspension of the voice **3** : a sign ⌒ or ⌣ above or below a musical note or rest to show it is to be prolonged **4** : a reason for pausing **5** : a function of an electronic device that pauses a recording

[2]**pause** *vb* **paused; paus·ing** : to stop, rest, or linger for a time

pave \ˈpāv\ *vb* **paved; pav·ing** : to cover (as a road) with hard material in order to smooth or firm the surface

pave·ment \ˈpāv-mənt\ *n* **1** : a paved surface **2** : the material with which something is paved

pa·vil·ion \pə-ˈvil-yən\ *n* [ME *pavilloun, pavillioun,* fr. AF, fr. L *papilion-, papilio* butterfly] **1** : a large tent **2** : a usu. open structure (as in a park) used for entertainment or shelter

pav·ing \ˈpā-viŋ\ *n* : PAVEMENT

[1]**paw** \ˈpȯ\ *n* : the foot of a quadruped (as a dog or lion) having claws

[2]**paw** *vb* **1** : to touch or strike with a paw; *also* : to scrape with a hoof **2** : to feel or handle clumsily or rudely **3** : to flail about or grab for with the hands

pawl \ˈpȯl\ *n* : a pivoted tongue or sliding bolt designed to fall into notches on another machine part to permit motion in one direction only

[1]**pawn** \ˈpȯn\ *n* [ME *pown,* fr. AF *peoun, paun,* fr. ML *pedon-, pedo* foot soldier, fr. LL, one with broad feet, fr. L *ped-, pes* foot] **1** : a chess piece of the least value **2** : one used for the purposes of another

[2]**pawn** *n* **1** : something deposited as security for a loan; *also* : HOSTAGE **2** : the state of being pledged

[3]**pawn** *vb* : to deposit as a pledge

pawn·bro·ker \ˈpȯn-ˌbrō-kər\ *n* : one who lends money on goods pledged

Paw·nee \pȯ-ˈnē\ *n, pl* **Pawnee** *or* **Pawnees** : a member of an Indigenous people who lived in Nebraska and are now located in Oklahoma

pawn·shop \ˈpȯn-ˌshäp\ *n* : a pawnbroker's place of business

paw·paw *also* **pa·paw** **1** \pə-ˈpȯ\ : PAPAYA **2** \ˈpä-pȯ, ˈpȯ-\ : a No. American tree with green-skinned edible fruit; *also* : its fruit

[1]**pay** \ˈpā\ *vb* **paid** \ˈpād\ *also in sense 7* **payed; pay·ing** [ME, fr. AF *paier,* fr. L *pacare* to pacify, fr. *pac-, pax* peace] **1** : to make due return to for goods or services **2** : to discharge indebtedness for : SETTLE ⟨~ a bill⟩ **3** : to give in forfeit ⟨~ the penalty⟩ **4** : REQUITE **5** : to give, offer, or make freely or as fitting ⟨~ attention⟩ **6** : to be profitable to : RETURN **7** : to make slack and allow to run out ⟨~ out a rope⟩ — **pay·able** *adj* — **pay·ee** \pā-ˈē\ *n* — **pay·er** *n*

[2]**pay** *n* **1** : something paid; *esp* : WAGES **2** : the status of being paid by an employer : EMPLOY

[3]**pay** *adj* **1** : containing something valuable (as gold) ⟨~ dirt⟩ **2** : equipped to receive a fee for use ⟨~ telephone⟩ **3** : requiring payment

pay·back \ˈpā-ˌbak\ *n* **1** : a return on an investment equal to the original capital outlay **2** : something given in return, compensation, or retaliation

pay·check \ˈpā-ˌchek\ *n* **1** : a check in payment of wages or salary **2** : WAGES, SALARY

pay·load \-ˌlōd\ *n* : the load carried by a

vehicle in addition to what is necessary for its operation; *also* : the weight of such a load

pay·mas·ter \-ˌmas-tər\ *n* : one who distributes the payroll

pay·ment \ˈpā-mənt\ *n* **1** : the act of paying **2** : something paid

pay·off \-ˌȯf\ *n* **1** : PROFIT, REWARD; *also* : RETRIBUTION **2** : the climax of an incident or enterprise ⟨the ~ of a story⟩

pay–per–view *n* : a cable television service by which customers can order access to a single airing of a TV feature

pay·roll \-ˌrōl\ *n* : a list of persons entitled to receive pay; *also* : the money to pay those on such a list

payt *abbr* payment

pay up *vb* : to pay what is due; *also* : to pay in full

Pb *symbol* [L *plumbum*] lead

PBS *abbr* Public Broadcasting Service

PBX \ˌpē-(ˌ)bē-ˈeks\ *n* [*p*rivate *b*ranch e*x*change] : a private telephone switchboard

¹**PC** \ˌpē-ˈsē\ *n, pl* **PCs** *or* **PC's** [*p*ersonal *c*omputer] : MICROCOMPUTER

²**PC** *abbr* **1** Peace Corps **2** percent; percentage **3** politically correct **4** postcard **5** [L *post cibum*] after meals **6** professional corporation

PCB \ˌpē-ˌsē-ˈbē\ *n* : POLYCHLORINATED BIPHENYL

PCP \ˌpē-ˌsē-ˈpē\ *n* : PHENCYCLIDINE

pct *abbr* percent; percentage

pd *abbr* paid

Pd *symbol* palladium

PD *abbr* **1** per diem **2** police department **3** potential difference

PDA \ˌpē-ˌdē-ˈā\ *n* [*p*ersonal *d*igital *a*ssistant] : a small microprocessor device for storing and organizing personal information

PDQ \ˌpē-ˌdē-ˈkyü\ *adv, often not cap* [abbr. of *pretty damned quick*] : IMMEDIATELY

PDT *abbr* Pacific daylight (saving) time

PE *abbr* **1** physical education **2** printer's error **3** professional engineer

pea \ˈpē\ *n, pl* **peas** *also* **pease** \ˈpēz\ **1** : the round edible protein-rich seed borne in the pod of a widely grown leguminous vine; *also* : this vine **2** : any of various plants resembling or related to the pea

peace \ˈpēs\ *n* **1** : a state of calm and quiet; *esp* : public security under law **2** : freedom from disturbing thoughts or emotions **3** : a state of concord (as between persons or governments); *also* : an agreement to end hostilities — **peace·able** \ˈpē-sə-bəl\ *adj* — **peace·ably** \-blē\ *adv* — **peace·ful** *adj* — **peace·ful·ly** *adv*

peace·keep·ing \ˈpēs-ˌkē-piŋ\ *n* : the preserving of peace; *esp* : international enforcement and supervision of a truce — **peace·keep·er** *n*

peace·mak·er \-ˌmā-kər\ *n* : one who settles an argument or stops a fight

peace·time \-ˌtīm\ *n* : a time when a nation is not at war

peach \ˈpēch\ *n* [ME *peche*, fr. AF *pesche*, *peche*,, fr. LL *persica*, fr. L (*malum*) *Persicum*, lit., Persian fruit] : a sweet juicy fuzzy-skinned fruit of a small usu. pink-flowered tree related to the cherry and plums; *also* : this tree — **peachy** *adj*

pea·cock \ˈpē-ˌkäk\ *n* [ME *pecok*, fr. *pe-* (fr. OE *pēa* peafowl, fr. L *pavo* peacock) + *cok* cock] : the male peafowl that can spread its long tail feathers to make a colorful display

pea·fowl \-ˌfau̇(-ə)l\ *n* : either of two large domesticated Asian pheasants

pea·hen \-ˌhen\ *n* : the female peafowl

¹**peak** \ˈpēk\ *n* **1** : a pointed or projecting part **2** : the top of a hill or mountain; *also* : MOUNTAIN **3** : the front projecting part of a cap **4** : the narrow part of a ship's bow or stern **5** : the highest level or greatest degree — **peak** *adj*

²**peak** *vb* : to bring to or reach a maximum

peak·ed \ˈpē-kəd\ *adj* : THIN, SICKLY

¹**peal** \ˈpēl\ *n* **1** : the loud ringing of bells **2** : a set of tuned bells **3** : a loud sound or succession of sounds

²**peal** *vb* : to give out peals : RESOUND

pea·nut \ˈpē-(ˌ)nət\ *n* **1** : an annual herb related to the pea but having pods that ripen underground; *also* : this pod or one of the edible seeds it bears **2** *pl* : a very small amount **3** : a pellet of polystyrene foam

pear \ˈper\ *n* : the fleshy fruit of a tree related to the apple; *also* : this tree

pearl \ˈpərl\ *n* **1** : a small hard often lustrous body formed within the shell of some mollusks and used as a gem **2** : one that is choice or precious ⟨~*s* of wisdom⟩ **3** : a slightly bluish medium gray color — **pearly** \ˈpər-lē\ *adj*

peas·ant \ˈpe-zᵊnt\ *n* **1** : any of a class of small landowners or laborers tilling the soil **2** : a usu. uneducated person of low social status — **peas·ant·ry** \-zᵊn-trē\ *n*

pea·shoot·er \ˈpē-ˌshü-tər\ *n* : a toy blowgun for shooting peas

peat \ˈpēt\ *n* : a dark substance formed by partial decay of plants (as mosses) in water — **peaty** *adj*

peat moss *n* : SPHAGNUM

¹**peb·ble** \ˈpe-bəl\ *n* : a small usu. round stone — **peb·bly** \-b(ə-)lē\ *adj*

²**pebble** *vb* **peb·bled; peb·bling** : to produce a rough surface texture in ⟨~ leather⟩

pec \ˈpek\ *n* : PECTORAL MUSCLE

pe·can \pi-ˈkän, -ˈkan; ˈpē-ˌkan\ *n* : the smooth thin-shelled edible nut of a large American hickory; *also* : this tree

pec·ca·dil·lo \ˌpe-kə-ˈdi-lō\ *n, pl* **-loes** *or* **-los** : a slight offense

pec·ca·ry \ˈpe-kə-rē\ *n, pl* **-ries** : any of several American chiefly tropical mammals resembling but smaller than the related pigs

pec·ca·vi \pe-ˈkä-ˌvē\ *n* [L, I have sinned, fr. *peccare* to sin] : an acknowledgment of sin

¹**peck** \ˈpek\ *n* — see WEIGHT table

²**peck** *vb* **1** : to strike or pierce with or as if with the bill **2** : to make (as a hole) by pecking **3** : to pick up with or as if with the bill

³peck *n* **1** : an impression made by pecking **2** : a quick sharp stroke
pecking order *also* **peck order** *n* : a basic pattern of social organization within a flock of poultry in which each bird pecks another lower in the scale without being pecked in return and submits to pecking by one of higher rank; *also* : a social hierarchy
pec·tin \ˈpek-tən\ *n* : any of various water-soluble plant substances that cause fruit jellies to set — **pec·tic** \-tik\ *adj*
pec·to·ral \ˈpek-tə-rəl\ *adj* : of or relating to the breast or chest
pectoral muscle *n* : either of two muscles on each side of the body which connect the front walls of the chest with the bones of the upper arm and shoulder
pe·cu·liar \pi-ˈkyül-yər\ *adj* [ME *peculier,* fr. L *peculiaris* of private property, special, fr. *peculium* private property, fr. *pecus* cattle] **1** : belonging exclusively to one person or group **2** : CHARACTERISTIC, DISTINCTIVE **3** : UNUSUAL, ODD ⟨her ~ behavior⟩ ♦ *Synonyms* IDIOSYNCRATIC, ECCENTRIC, SINGULAR, STRANGE, WEIRD — **pe·cu·liar·i·ty** \-ˌkyül-ˈya-rə-tē, -ˌkyü-lē-ˈa-\ *n* — **pe·cu·liar·ly** *adv*
pe·cu·ni·ary \pi-ˈkyü-nē-ˌer-ē\ *adj* : of or relating to money : MONETARY
ped·a·gogue *also* **ped·a·gog** \ˈpe-də-ˌgäg\ *n* : TEACHER, SCHOOLMASTER
ped·a·go·gy \ˈpe-də-ˌgō-jē, -ˌgä-\ *n* : the art or profession of teaching; *esp* : EDUCATION 2 — **ped·a·gog·ic** \ˌpe-də-ˈgä-jik, -ˈgō-\ *or* **ped·a·gog·i·cal** \-ji-kəl\ *adj*
¹ped·al \ˈpe-dᵊl\ *n* : a lever worked by the foot
²pedal *adj* : of or relating to the foot
³pedal *vb* **ped·aled** *also* **ped·alled; ped·al·ing** *also* **ped·al·ling** **1** : to use or work a pedal (as of a piano or bicycle) **2** : to ride a bicycle
ped·ant \ˈpe-dᵊnt\ *n* **1** : a person who makes a show of knowledge **2** : a formal uninspired teacher ⟨his piano teacher was a ~⟩ — **pe·dan·tic** \pi-ˈdan-tik\ *adj* — **ped·ant·ry** \ˈpe-dᵊn-trē\ *n*
ped·dle \ˈpe-dᵊl\ *vb* **ped·dled; ped·dling** : to sell or offer for sale from place to place — **ped·dler** *also* **ped·lar** \ˈped-lər\ *n*
ped·er·ast \ˈpe-də-ˌrast\ *n* [Gk *paiderastēs,* lit., lover of boys] : a man who desires or engages in sexual activity with a boy — **ped·er·as·ty** \ˈpe-də-ˌras-tē\ *n*
ped·es·tal \ˈpe-dəs-tᵊl\ *n* **1** : the support or foot of something (as a column, statue, or vase) that is upright **2** : a position of high regard
¹pe·des·tri·an \pə-ˈdes-trē-ən\ *adj* **1** : ORDINARY **2** : going on foot
²pedestrian *n* : WALKER
pe·di·at·rics \ˌpē-dē-ˈa-triks\ *n* : a branch of medicine dealing with the development, care, and diseases of children — **pe·di·at·ric** \-trik\ *adj* — **pe·di·a·tri·cian** \ˌpē-dē-ə-ˈtri-shən\ *n*
pedi·cab \ˈpe-di-ˌkab\ *n* : a pedal-driven tricycle with seats for a driver and two passengers
ped·i·cure \ˈpe-di-ˌkyu̇r\ *n* : care of the feet, toes, and nails; *also* : a single treatment of these parts — **ped·i·cur·ist** \-ˌkyu̇r-ist\ *n*
ped·i·gree \ˈpe-də-ˌgrē\ *n* [ME *pedegru,* fr. AF *pé de grue,* lit., crane's foot; fr. the shape made by the lines of a genealogical chart] **1** : a record of a line of ancestors **2** : an ancestral line — **ped·i·greed** \-grēd\ *adj*
ped·i·ment \ˈpe-də-mənt\ *n* : a low triangular gablelike decoration (as over a door or window) on a building
pe·dom·e·ter \pi-ˈdä-mə-tər\ *n* : an instrument that measures the distance one walks
pe·do·phile \ˈpe-də-ˌfī(-ə)l, ˈpē-\ *n* : one affected with pedophilia
pe·do·phil·ia \ˌpe-də-ˈfi-lē-ə, ˌpē-\ *n* : sexual perversion in which children are the preferred sexual object
pe·dun·cle \ˈpē-ˌdəŋ-kəl\ *n* : a narrow supporting stalk
peek \ˈpēk\ *vb* **1** : to look furtively **2** : to peer from a place of concealment **3** : GLANCE — **peek** *n*
¹peel \ˈpēl\ *vb* [ME *pelen,* fr. AF *peler,* fr. L *pilare* to remove the hair from, fr. *pilus* hair] **1** : to strip the skin, bark, or rind from **2** : to strip off (as a coat); *also* : to come off **3** : to lose the skin, bark, or rind
²peel *n* : a skin or rind esp. of a fruit
peel·ing \ˈpē-liŋ\ *n* : a peeled-off piece or strip (as of skin or rind)
peen \ˈpēn\ *n* : the usu. hemispherical or wedge-shaped end of the head of a hammer opposite the face
¹peep \ˈpēp\ *vb* : to utter a feeble shrill sound or the slightest sound
²peep *n* : a feeble shrill sound
³peep *vb* **1** : to look slyly esp. through an aperture : PEEK **2** : to begin to emerge **3** : to look at : WATCH — **peep·er** *n*
⁴peep *n* **1** : a first faint appearance **2** : a brief or furtive look
peep·hole \ˈpēp-ˌhōl\ *n* : a hole to peep through
¹peer \ˈpir\ *n* **1** : one of equal standing with another : EQUAL **2** : NOBLE — **peer·age** \-ij\ *n*
²peer *vb* **1** : to look intently or curiously **2** : to come slightly into view
peer·ess \ˈpir-əs\ *n* : a woman who is a peer
peer·less \ˈpir-ləs\ *adj* : having no equal : MATCHLESS ⟨a ~ cellist⟩ ♦ *Synonyms* SUPREME, UNEQUALED, UNPARALLELED, INCOMPARABLE
¹peeve \ˈpēv\ *vb* **peeved; peev·ing** : to make resentful : ANNOY
²peeve *n* **1** : a feeling or mood of resentment **2** : a particular grievance
pee·vish \ˈpē-vish\ *adj* : querulous in temperament : FRETFUL ♦ *Synonyms* IRRITABLE, PETULANT, HUFFY — **pee·vish·ly** *adv* — **pee·vish·ness** *n*
pee·wee \ˈpē-(ˌ)wē\ *n* **1** : one that is diminutive or tiny **2** : a level of sports usu. for young children — **peewee** *adj*
¹peg \ˈpeg\ *n* **1** : a small pointed piece (as

of wood) used to pin down or fasten things or to fit into holes **2** : a projecting piece used as a support or boundary marker **3** : SUPPORT, PRETEXT **4** : STEP, DEGREE **5** : THROW

²peg *vb* **pegged; peg·ging** **1** : to put a peg into : fasten, pin down, or attach with or as if with pegs **2** : to work hard and steadily : PLUG **3** : HUSTLE **4** : to mark by pegs **5** : to hold (as prices) at a set level or rate **6** : IDENTIFY ⟨was *pegged* as an intellectual⟩ **7** : THROW

PEI *abbr* Prince Edward Island

pei·gnoir \pān-ˈwär, pen-\ *n* [F, lit., garment worn while combing the hair, fr. MF, fr. *peigner* to comb the hair, fr. L *pectinare,* fr. *pectin-, pecten* comb] : NEGLIGEE

¹pe·jo·ra·tive \pi-ˈjȯr-ə-tiv\ *n* : a pejorative word or phrase

²pejorative *adj* : having negative connotations : DISPARAGING — **pe·jo·ra·tive·ly** *adv*

peke \ˈpēk\ *n, often cap* : PEKINGESE

Pe·king·ese *or* **Pe·kin·ese** \ˌpē-kə-ˈnēz, -ˈnēs; -kiŋ-ˈēz, -ˈēs\ *n, pl* **Pekingese** *or* **Pekinese** : any of a breed of Chinese origin of small short-legged long-haired dogs

pe·koe \ˈpē-(ˌ)kō\ *n* : a black tea made from young tea leaves

pel·age \ˈpe-lij\ *n* : the hairy covering of a mammal

pe·lag·ic \pə-ˈla-jik\ *adj* : OCEANIC

pelf \ˈpelf\ *n* : MONEY, RICHES

pel·i·can \ˈpe-li-kən\ *n* : any of a genus of large web-footed birds having a pouched lower bill used to scoop in fish

pel·la·gra \pə-ˈla-grə, -ˈlā-\ *n* : a disease caused by a diet with too little niacin and protein and marked by a skin rash, disease of the digestive system, and mental disturbances

pel·let \ˈpe-lət\ *n* **1** : a little ball (as of medicine) **2** : BULLET — **pel·let·al** \-lə-təl\ *adj* — **pel·let·ize** \-ˌtīz\ *vb*

pell–mell \ˌpel-ˈmel\ *adv* **1** : in mingled confusion ⟨papers strewn ~ on the desk⟩ **2** : HEADLONG ⟨ran ~ for the door⟩

pel·lu·cid \pə-ˈlü-səd\ *adj* : extremely clear : LIMPID, TRANSPARENT ⟨a ~ stream⟩ ♦ ***Synonyms*** TRANSLUCENT, LUCID, LUCENT

pe·lo·ton \ˌpe-lə-ˈtän\ *n* : the main body of riders in a bicycle race

¹pelt \ˈpelt\ *n* : a skin esp. of a fur-bearing animal

²pelt *vb* : to strike with a succession of blows or missiles

pel·vis \ˈpel-vəs\ *n, pl* **pel·vis·es** \-və-səz\ *or* **pel·ves** \-ˌvēz\ : a basin-shaped part of the vertebrate skeleton consisting of the large bone of each hip and the nearby bones of the spine — **pel·vic** \-vik\ *adj*

pem·mi·can *also* **pem·i·can** \ˈpe-mi-kən\ *n* : dried meat pounded fine and mixed with melted fat

¹pen \ˈpen\ *vb* **penned; pen·ning** : to shut in or as if in a pen

²pen *n* **1** : a small enclosure for animals **2** : a small place of confinement or storage

³pen *n* **1** : an implement for writing or drawing with ink or a similar fluid **2** : a writing instrument regarded as a means of expression **3** : STYLUS 3

⁴pen *vb* **penned; pen·ning** : WRITE

⁵pen *n* : PENITENTIARY

⁶pen *abbr* peninsula

PEN *abbr* International Association of Poets, Playwrights, Editors, Essayists and Novelists

pe·nal \ˈpē-nᵊl\ *adj* : of or relating to punishment

pe·nal·ise *Brit var of* PENALIZE

pe·nal·ize \ˈpē-nə-ˌlīz, ˈpe-\ *vb* **-ized; -iz·ing** : to put a penalty on

pen·al·ty \ˈpe-nᵊl-tē\ *n, pl* **-ties** **1** : punishment for crime or offense **2** : something forfeited when a person fails to do something agreed to **3** : disadvantage, loss, or hardship (as to a competitor) due to some action

pen·ance \ˈpe-nəns\ *n* **1** : an act performed to show sorrow or repentance for sin **2** : a sacrament (as in the Roman Catholic Church) consisting of confession, absolution, and a penance directed by the confessor

pence \ˈpens\ *pl of* PENNY

pen·chant \ˈpen-chənt\ *n* [F, fr. prp. of *pencher* to incline, fr. VL **pendicare,* fr. L *pendere* to weigh] : a strong inclination : LIKING ⟨a ~ for taking risks⟩ ♦ ***Synonyms*** LEANING, PROPENSITY, PREDILECTION, PREDISPOSITION

¹pen·cil \ˈpen-səl\ *n* : a writing or drawing tool consisting of or containing a slender cylinder of a solid marking substance

²pencil *vb* **-ciled** *or* **-cilled; -cil·ing** *or* **-cil·ling** **1** : to draw or write with a pencil **2** : to plan or designate tentatively ⟨~*ed* in the appointment⟩

pen·dant *also* **pen·dent** \ˈpen-dənt\ *n* : a hanging ornament (as on a necklace)

pen·dent *or* **pen·dant** \ˈpen-dənt\ *adj* : SUSPENDED, OVERHANGING

¹pend·ing \ˈpen-diŋ\ *prep* **1** : DURING **2** : while awaiting ⟨~ approval⟩

²pending *adj* **1** : not yet decided ⟨a ~ application⟩ **2** : IMMINENT

pen·du·lous \ˈpen-jə-ləs, -də-\ *adj* : hanging loosely : DROOPING ⟨~ earrings⟩

pen·du·lum \-ləm\ *n* : a body that swings freely from a fixed point

pe·ne·plain *also* **pe·ne·plane** \ˈpē-ni-ˌplān\ *n* : a large almost flat land surface shaped by erosion

pen·e·trate \ˈpe-nə-ˌtrāt\ *vb* **-trat·ed; -trat·ing** **1** : to enter into : PIERCE **2** : PERMEATE **3** : to see into : UNDERSTAND **4** : to affect deeply — **pen·e·tra·ble** \-trə-bəl\ *adj* — **pen·e·tra·tion** \ˌpe-nə-ˈtrā-shən\ *n* — **pen·e·tra·tive** \ˈpe-nə-ˌtrā-tiv\ *adj*

penetrating *adj* **1** : having the power of entering, piercing, or pervading ⟨a ~ shriek⟩ ⟨a ~ odor⟩ **2** : ACUTE, DISCERNING ⟨a ~ look⟩

pen·guin \ˈpen-gwən, ˈpeŋ-\ *n* : any of

various erect short-legged flightless seabirds of the southern hemisphere
pen·i·cil·lin \ˌpe-nə-ˈsi-lən\ *n* : any of several antibiotics produced by molds or synthetically and used against various bacteria
pen·in·su·la \pə-ˈnin-sə-lə\ *n* [L *paeninsula,* fr. *paene* almost + *insula* island] : a long narrow portion of land extending out into the water — **pen·in·su·lar** \-lər\ *adj*
pe·nis \ˈpē-nəs\ *n, pl* **pe·nis·es** *also* **pe·nes** \-ˌnēz\ : a male organ of copulation that in the human male also functions as the channel by which urine leaves the body
[1]**pen·i·tent** \ˈpe-nə-tənt\ *adj* : feeling sorrow for sins or offenses : REPENTANT — **pen·i·tence** \-təns\ *n* — **pen·i·ten·tial** \ˌpe-nə-ˈten-chəl\ *adj*
[2]**penitent** *n* : a penitent person
[1]**pen·i·ten·tia·ry** \ˌpe-nə-ˈten-chə-rē\ *n, pl* **-ries** : a state or federal prison
[2]**penitentiary** *adj* : of, relating to, or incurring confinement in a penitentiary
pen·knife \ˈpen-ˌnīf\ *n* : a small pocketknife
pen·light *also* **pen·lite** \-ˌlīt\ *n* : a small flashlight resembling a fountain pen in size or shape
pen·man \ˈpen-mən\ *n* **1** : COPYIST **2** : one skilled in penmanship **3** : AUTHOR
pen·man·ship \-ˌship\ *n* : the art or practice of writing with the pen
Penn *or* **Penna** *abbr* Pennsylvania
pen name *n* : an author's pseudonym
pen·nant \ˈpe-nənt\ *n* **1** : a tapering flag used esp. for signaling **2** : a flag symbolic of championship
pen·ne \ˈpe-nā\ *n* : short diagonally cut tubular pasta
pen·ni \ˈpe-nē\ *n, pl* **pen·nia** \-nē-ə\ *or* **pen·nis** \-nēz\ : a former monetary unit equal to $\frac{1}{100}$ markka
pen·non \ˈpe-nən\ *n* **1** : a long narrow ribbonlike flag borne on a lance **2** : WING
Penn·syl·va·nian \ˌpen-səl-ˈvā-nyən\ *adj* **1** : of or relating to Pennsylvania or its people **2** : of, relating to, or being the period of the Paleozoic era between the Mississippian and the Permian — **Pennsylvanian** *n*
pen·ny \ˈpe-nē\ *n, pl* **pennies** \-nēz\ *or* **pence** \ˈpens\ **1** *pl usu pence* : a British monetary unit formerly equal to $\frac{1}{12}$ shilling but now equal to $\frac{1}{100}$ pound; *also* : a coin of this value — see *pound* at MONEY table **2** *pl pennies* : a cent of the U.S. or Canada **3** : a former monetary unit equal to $\frac{1}{100}$ Irish pound — **pen·ni·less** \ˈpe-ni-ləs\ *adj*
pen·ny–pinch·ing \ˈpe-nē-ˌpin-chiŋ\ *n* : PARSIMONY — **pen·ny–pinch·er** *n* — **penny–pinching** *adj*
pen·ny·weight \-ˌwāt\ *n* — see WEIGHT table
pen·ny–wise \-ˌwīz\ *adj* : wise or prudent only in small matters
pe·nol·o·gy \pi-ˈnä-lə-jē\ *n* : a branch of criminology dealing with prisons and the treatment of offenders
[1]**pen·sion** \ˈpen-chən\ *n* : a fixed sum paid regularly esp. to a person retired from service
[2]**pension** *vb* : to pay a pension to — **pen·sion·er** *n*
pen·sive \ˈpen-siv\ *adj* : musingly, dreamily, or sadly thoughtful ♦ ***Synonyms*** REFLECTIVE, SPECULATIVE, CONTEMPLATIVE, MEDITATIVE — **pen·sive·ly** *adv*
pen·stock \ˈpen-ˌstäk\ *n* **1** : a sluice or gate for regulating a flow **2** : a pipe for carrying water
pent \ˈpent\ *adj* : shut up : CONFINED
pen·ta·gon \ˈpen-tə-ˌgän\ *n* : a polygon of five angles and five sides — **pen·tag·o·nal** \pen-ˈta-gə-nᵊl\ *adj*
pen·tam·e·ter \pen-ˈta-mə-tər\ *n* : a line of verse containing five metrical feet
pen·tath·lon \pen-ˈtath-lən\ *n* : a composite athletic contest consisting of five events
Pen·te·cost \ˈpen-ti-ˌkȯst\ *n* : the 7th Sunday after Easter observed as a church festival commemorating the descent of the Holy Spirit on the apostles — **Pen·te·cos·tal** \ˌpen-ti-ˈkäs-tᵊl\ *adj*
Pentecostal *n* : a member of a Christian religious body that stresses expressive worship, evangelism, and spiritual gifts — **Pen·te·cos·tal·ism** \ˌpen-ti-ˈkäs-tə-ˌli-zəm\
pent·house \ˈpent-ˌhau̇s\ *n* [alter. of ME *pentis,* fr. AF *apentiz,* fr. *apent,* pp. of *apendre* to attach, hang against] **1** : a shed or sloping roof attached to a wall or building **2** : an apartment built on the top floor or roof of a building
pen·ul·ti·mate \pi-ˈnəl-tə-mət\ *adj* : next to the last ⟨~ syllable⟩
pen·um·bra \pə-ˈnəm-brə\ *n, pl* **-brae** \-(ˌ)brē\ *or* **-bras** **1** : the partial shadow surrounding a complete shadow (as in an eclipse) **2** : something that covers or obscures ⟨a ~ of secrecy⟩
pe·nu·ri·ous \pə-ˈnu̇r-ē-əs, -ˈnyu̇r-\ *adj* **1** : marked by penury **2** : MISERLY ♦ ***Synonyms*** STINGY, CLOSE, TIGHTFISTED, PARSIMONIOUS
pen·u·ry \ˈpe-nyə-rē\ *n* **1** : extreme poverty **2** : extreme frugality
pe·on \ˈpē-ˌän, -ən\ *n, pl* **peons** *or* **pe·o·nes** \pā-ˈō-nēz\ **1** : a member of the landless laboring class in Spanish America **2** : one bound to service for payment of a debt — **pe·on·age** \-ə-nij\ *n*
pe·o·ny \ˈpē-ə-nē\ *n, pl* **-nies** : any of a genus of chiefly Eurasian plants with large often double red, pink, or white flowers; *also* : the flower
[1]**peo·ple** \ˈpē-pəl\ *n, pl* **people** [ME *peple,* fr. AF *peple, peuple,* fr. L *populus*] **1** *pl* : human beings making up a group or linked by a common characteristic or interest **2** *pl* : human beings — often used in compounds instead of *persons* ⟨sales*people*⟩ or attributively ⟨~ skills⟩ **3** *pl* : the mass of persons in a community : POPULACE; *also* : ELECTORATE ⟨the ~'s choice⟩ **4** *pl* **peoples** : a body of persons

united by a common culture, sense of kinship, or political organization

²**people** *vb* **peo·pled; peo·pling** : to supply or fill with or as if with people

¹**pep** \ˈpep\ *n* : brisk energy or initiative — **pep·py** *adj*

²**pep** *vb* **pepped; pep·ping** : to put pep into : STIMULATE ⟨~ the team up⟩

¹**pep·per** \ˈpe-pər\ *n* **1** : either of two pungent condiments from the berry (**pep·per·corn** \-ˌkȯrn\) of an Indian climbing plant : BLACK PEPPER, WHITE PEPPER; *also* : this plant **2** : a plant related to the tomato and widely grown for its hot or mild sweet fruit; *also* : this fruit

²**pepper** *vb* **pep·pered; pep·per·ing** **1** : to shower with missiles or rapid blows **2** : to sprinkle or season with or as if with pepper **3** : to deliver something in rapid succession ⟨~*ed* him with questions⟩

pep·per·mint \-ˌmint, -mənt\ *n* : a pungent aromatic mint; *also* : candy flavored with its oil

pep·per·o·ni \ˌpe-pə-ˈrō-nē\ *n* : a highly seasoned beef and pork sausage

pepper spray *n* : a temporarily disabling aerosol that causes irritation and blinding of the eyes and inflammation of the nose, throat, and skin

pep·pery \ˈpe-pə-rē\ *adj* **1** : having the qualities of pepper : PUNGENT, HOT **2** : having a hot temper **3** : FIERY

pep·sin \ˈpep-sən\ *n* : an enzyme of the stomach that promotes digestion by breaking down proteins; *also* : a preparation of this used medicinally

pep·tic \ˈpep-tik\ *adj* [L *pepticus,* fr. Gk *peptikos,* fr. *peptos* cooked, *peptein* to cook, digest] **1** : relating to or promoting digestion **2** : caused by digestive juices ⟨a ~ ulcer⟩

pep·tide \ˈpep-ˌtīd\ *n* : any of various organic compounds composed of two or more amino acids bonded together

Pe·quot \ˈpē-ˌkwät\ *n* : a member of an Indigenous people of eastern Connecticut

¹**per** \ˈpər\ *prep* **1** : by means of **2** : to or for each **3** : ACCORDING TO

²**per** *adv* : for each : APIECE

³**per** *abbr* **1** period **2** person

¹**per·ad·ven·ture** \ˈpər-əd-ˌven-chər\ *adv, archaic* : PERHAPS

²**peradventure** *n* **1** : DOUBT **2** : CHANCE 4

per·am·bu·late \pə-ˈram-byə-ˌlāt\ *vb* **-lat·ed; -lat·ing** : to travel over esp. on foot — **per·am·bu·la·tion** \-ˌram-byə-ˈlā-shən\ *n*

per·am·bu·la·tor \pə-ˈram-byə-ˌlā-tər\ *n, chiefly Brit* : a baby carriage

per an·num \(ˌ)pər-ˈa-nəm\ *adv* [ML] : in or for each year : ANNUALLY

per·cale \(ˌ)pər-ˈkāl, ˈpər-ˌ; (ˌ)pər-ˈkal\ *n* : a fine woven cotton cloth

per cap·i·ta \(ˌ)pər-ˈka-pə-tə\ *adv or adj* [ML, by heads] : by or for each person

per·ceive \pər-ˈsēv\ *vb* **per·ceived; per·ceiv·ing** **1** : to attain awareness : REALIZE **2** : to become aware of through the senses — **per·ceiv·able** *adj*

¹**per·cent** \pər-ˈsent\ *adv* [*per* + L *centum* hundred] : in each hundred

²**percent** *n, pl* **percent** *or* **percents** **1** : one part in a hundred : HUNDREDTH **2** : PERCENTAGE

per·cent·age \pər-ˈsen-tij\ *n* **1** : a part of a whole expressed in hundredths **2** : the result obtained by multiplying a number by a percent **3** : ADVANTAGE, PROFIT **4** : PROBABILITY; *also* : favorable odds

percentage point *n* : one hundredth of a whole ⟨rates rose one *percentage point* from 6.5 to 7.5 percent⟩

per·cen·tile \pər-ˈsen-ˌtī(-ə)l\ *n* : a value on a scale of one hundred indicating the standing of a score or grade in terms of the percentage of scores or grades falling with or below it

per·cept \ˈpər-ˌsept\ *n* : an impression of an object obtained by use of the senses

per·cep·ti·ble \pər-ˈsep-tə-bəl\ *adj* : capable of being perceived ⟨a barely ~ light⟩ — **per·cep·ti·bly** \-blē\ *adv*

per·cep·tion \pər-ˈsep-shən\ *n* **1** : an act or result of perceiving **2** : awareness of one's environment through physical sensation **3** : ability to understand : INSIGHT, COMPREHENSION ♦ *Synonyms* PENETRATION, DISCERNMENT, DISCRIMINATION

per·cep·tive \pər-ˈsep-tiv\ *adj* : capable of or exhibiting keen perception : OBSERVANT — **per·cep·tive·ly** *adv*

per·cep·tu·al \pər-ˈsep-chə-wəl\ *adj* : of, relating to, or involving sensory stimulus as opposed to abstract concept ⟨~ stimulation⟩ — **per·cep·tu·al·ly** *adv*

¹**perch** \ˈpərch\ *n* **1** : a roost for a bird **2** : a high station or vantage point

²**perch** *vb* : ROOST

³**perch** *n, pl* **perch** *or* **perch·es** : either of two small freshwater bony fishes used for food; *also* : any of various fishes resembling or related to these

per·chance \pər-ˈchans\ *adv* : PERHAPS

per·cip·i·ent \pər-ˈsi-pē-ənt\ *adj* : capable of or characterized by perception — **per·cip·i·ence** \-əns\ *n*

per·co·late \ˈpər-kə-ˌlāt\ *vb* **-lat·ed; -lat·ing** **1** : to trickle or filter through a permeable substance **2** : to filter hot water through to extract the essence ⟨~ coffee⟩ — **per·co·la·tor** \-ˌlā-tər\ *n*

per con·tra \(ˌ)pər-ˈkän-trə\ *adv* [It, by the opposite side (of the ledger)] **1** : on the contrary **2** : by way of contrast

per·cus·sion \pər-ˈkə-shən\ *n* **1** : a sharp blow : IMPACT; *esp* : a blow upon a cap (**percussion cap**) designed to explode the charge in a firearm **2** : the beating or striking of a musical instrument; *also* : instruments sounded by striking, shaking, or scraping

per di·em \pər-ˈdē-əm, -ˈdī-\ *adv* [ML] : by the day — **per diem** *adj or n*

per·di·tion \pər-ˈdi-shən\ *n* **1** : eternal damnation **2** : HELL

per·du·ra·ble \(ˌ)pər-ˈdu̇r-ə-bəl, -ˈdyu̇r-\ *adj* : very durable — **per·du·ra·bil·i·ty** \-ˌdu̇r-ə-ˈbi-lə-tē, -ˌdyu̇r-\ *n*

père \ˈper\ *n* [F, fr. OF *paire, perre,* fr. L *pater*] : FATHER — used after a name to distinguish a father from a son

per·e·gri·na·tion \ˌper-ə-grə-ˈnā-shən\ *n* : a traveling about esp. on foot
per·e·grine falcon \ˈper-ə-grən, -ˌgrēn\ *n* : a swift nearly cosmopolitan falcon that often nests in cities and is often used in falconry
pe·remp·to·ry \pə-ˈremp-tə-rē\ *adj* **1** : barring a right of action or delay **2** : expressive of urgency or command : IMPERATIVE **3** : marked by arrogant self-assurance ♦ ***Synonyms*** IMPERIOUS, MASTERFUL, DOMINEERING, MAGISTERIAL — **pe·remp·to·ri·ly** \-tə-rə-lē\ *adv*
[1]**pe·ren·ni·al** \pə-ˈre-nē-əl\ *adj* **1** : present at all seasons of the year ⟨~ streams⟩ **2** : continuing to live from year to year ⟨~ plants⟩ **3** : recurring regularly : PERMANENT ⟨~ problems⟩ ♦ ***Synonyms*** LASTING, PERPETUAL, ENDURING, EVERLASTING — **pe·ren·ni·al·ly** *adv*
[2]**perennial** *n* : a perennial plant
perf *abbr* **1** perfect **2** perforated
[1]**per·fect** \ˈpər-fikt\ *adj* **1** : being without fault or defect **2** : EXACT, PRECISE **3** : COMPLETE **4** : relating to or being a verb tense that expresses an action or state completed at the time of speaking or at a time spoken of — **per·fect·ly** *adv* — **per·fect·ness** *n*
[2]**per·fect** \pər-ˈfekt\ *vb* : to make perfect
[3]**per·fect** \ˈpər-fikt\ *n* : the perfect tense; *also* : a verb form in it
per·fect·ible \pər-ˈfek-tə-bəl, ˈpər-fik-\ *adj* : capable of improvement or perfection — **per·fect·ibil·i·ty** \pər-ˌfek-tə-ˈbi-lə-tē, ˌpər-fik-\ *n*
per·fec·tion \pər-ˈfek-shən\ *n* **1** : the quality or state of being perfect **2** : the highest degree of excellence **3** : the act or process of perfecting
per·fec·tion·ist \-shə-nist\ *n* : a person who will not accept or be content with anything less than perfection
per·fec·to \pər-ˈfek-tō\ *n, pl* **-tos** : a cigar that is thick in the middle and tapers almost to a point at each end
per·fi·dy \ˈpər-fə-dē\ *n, pl* **-dies** [L *perfidia,* fr. *perfidus* faithless, fr. *per-* detrimental to + *fides* faith] : violation of faith or loyalty : TREACHERY — **per·fid·i·ous** \pər-ˈfi-dē-əs\ *adj* — **per·fid·i·ous·ly** *adv*
per·fo·rate \ˈpər-fə-ˌrāt\ *vb* **-rat·ed; -rat·ing** : to bore through : PIERCE; *esp* : to make a line of holes in to facilitate separation — **per·fo·ra·tion** \ˌpər-fə-ˈrā-shən\ *n*
per·force \pər-ˈfōrs\ *adv* : of necessity ⟨we attended ~⟩
per·form \pər-ˈfōrm\ *vb* **1** : FULFILL **2** : CARRY OUT, DO **3** : FUNCTION **4** : to do in a set manner **5** : to give a performance — **per·form·er** *n*
per·for·mance \pər-ˈfōr-ˌməns\ *n* **1** : the act or process of performing **2** : DEED, FEAT **3** : a public presentation
per·for·ma·tive \pər-ˈfōr-mə-tiv\ *adj* **1** : relating to or marked by public performance **2** : made or done for show ⟨a ~ gesture⟩
[1]**per·fume** \pər-ˈfyüm, ˈpər-ˌfyüm\ *n* **1** : a usu. pleasant odor : FRAGRANCE **2** : a preparation used for scenting
[2]**perfume** *vb* **per·fumed; per·fum·ing** : SCENT
per·fum·ery \ˌpər-ˈfyü-mə-rē\ *n, pl* **-er·ies** **1** : the art or process of making perfume **2** : PERFUMES **3** : an establishment where perfumes are made
per·func·to·ry \pər-ˈfəŋk-tə-rē\ *adj* : done merely as a duty — **per·func·to·ri·ly** *adv*
per·go·la \ˈpər-gə-lə\ *n* [It] : a structure consisting of posts supporting an open roof in the form of a trellis
perh *abbr* perhaps
per·haps \pər-ˈhaps\ *adv* : possibly but not certainly
per·i·gee \ˈper-ə-ˌjē\ *n* [MF, fr. NL *perigeum,* fr. Gk *perigeion,* fr. *peri* around, near + *gē* earth] : the point at which an orbiting object is nearest the body (as the earth) being orbited
peri·he·lion \ˌper-ə-ˈhēl-yən\ *n, pl* **-he·lia** \-ˈhēl-yə\ : the point in the path of a celestial body (as a planet) that is nearest to the sun
per·il \ˈper-əl\ *n* : DANGER; *also* : a source of danger : RISK — **per·il·ous** *adj* — **per·il·ous·ly** *adv*
pe·rim·e·ter \pə-ˈri-mə-tər\ *n* **1** : the boundary of a closed plane figure; *also* : its length **2** : a line bounding or protecting an area
peri·na·tal \ˌper-ə-ˈnā-tᵊl\ *adj* : occurring in, concerned with, or being in the period around the time of birth ⟨~ care⟩
[1]**pe·ri·od** \ˈpir-ē-əd\ *n* [ultim. fr. Gk *periodos* circuit, period of time, rhetorical period, fr. *peri* around + *hodos* way] **1** : SENTENCE; *also* : the full pause closing the utterance of a sentence **2** : END, STOP **3** : a punctuation mark . used esp. to mark the end of a declarative sentence or an abbreviation **4** : an extent of time; *esp* : one regarded as a stage or division in a process or development **5** : a portion of time in which a recurring phenomenon completes one cycle and is ready to begin again **6** : a single cyclic occurrence of menstruation
[2]**period** *adj* : of or relating to a particular historical period ⟨~ furniture⟩
pe·ri·od·ic \ˌpir-ē-ˈä-dik\ *adj* **1** : occurring at regular intervals of time **2** : happening repeatedly **3** : of or relating to a sentence that has no trailing elements following full grammatical statement of the essential idea
[1]**pe·ri·od·i·cal** \ˌpir-ē-ˈä-di-kəl\ *adj* **1** : PERIODIC **2** : published at regular intervals **3** : of or relating to a periodical — **pe·ri·od·i·cal·ly** \-k(ə-)lē\ *adv*
[2]**periodical** *n* : a periodical publication
periodic table *n* : an arrangement of chemical elements based on their atomic structure and on their properties
peri·odon·tal \ˌper-ē-ō-ˈdän-tᵊl\ *adj* **1** : surrounding a tooth **2** : of or affecting periodontal tissues or regions
per·i·pa·tet·ic \ˌper-ə-pə-ˈte-tik\ *adj* : performed or performing while moving about : ITINERANT ⟨~ salesmen⟩
pe·riph·er·al \pə-ˈri-fər-əl\ *n* : a device

PERIODIC TABLE

This is the common long form of the table. Roman numerals and letters heading the vertical columns indicate the groups. (There are differences of opinion regarding the letter designations, but those given here are probably the most generally used. Also, international standards favor numbering the groups 1–18 from left to right using Arabic numerals, but the designations shown below remain quite common.) The horizontal rows represent the periods, with two series removed from the two very long periods and represented below the main table. Atomic numbers are given above the symbols for the elements. Compare ELEMENT table.

IA[1]	IIA[2]	IIIB	IVB	VB	VIB	VIIB	VIII			IB	IIB	IIIA	IVA	VA	VIA	VIIA[3]	VIIIA[4]
1 H																1 H	2 He
3 Li	4 Be											5 B	6 C	7 N	8 O	9 F	10 Ne
11 Na	12 Mg											13 Al	14 Si	15 P	16 S	17 Cl	18 Ar
19 K	20 Ca	21 Sc	22 Ti	23 V	24 Cr	25 Mn	26 Fe	27 Co	28 Ni	29 Cu	30 Zn	31 Ga	32 Ge	33 As	34 Se	35 Br	36 Kr
37 Rb	38 Sr	39 Y	40 Zr	41 Nb	42 Mo	43 Tc	44 Ru	45 Rh	46 Pd	47 Ag	48 Cd	49 In	50 Sn	51 Sb	52 Te	53 I	54 Xe
55 Cs	56 Ba	57 *La	72 Hf	73 Ta	74 W	75 Re	76 Os	77 Ir	78 Pt	79 Au	80 Hg	81 Tl	82 Pb	83 Bi	84 Po	85 At	86 Rn
87 Fr	88 Ra	89 #Ac	104 Rf	105 Db	106 Sg	107 Bh	108 Hs	109 Mt	110 Ds	111 Rg	112 Cn	113 Nh	114 Fl	115 Mc	116 Lv	117 Ts	118 Og

* LANTHANIDE SERIES	58 Ce	59 Pr	60 Nd	61 Pm	62 Sm	63 Eu	64 Gd	65 Tb	66 Dy	67 Ho	68 Er	69 Tm	70 Yb	71 Lu
# ACTINIDE SERIES	90 Th	91 Pa	92 U	93 Np	94 Pu	95 Am	96 Cm	97 Bk	98 Cf	99 Es	100 Fm	101 Md	102 No	103 Lr

[1]Group IA (excluding hydrogen) comprises the alkali metals.

[2]Group IIA comprises the alkaline earth metals.

[3]Group VIIA (excluding hydrogen) comprises the halogens.

[4]Group VIIIA (also called group Zero) comprises the noble gases.

connected to a computer to provide communication or auxiliary functions

peripheral nervous system *n* : the part of the nervous system that is outside the central nervous system and comprises the spinal nerves, the cranial nerves except the one supplying the retina, and the autonomic nervous system

pe·riph·ery \pə-ˈri-fə-rē\ *n, pl* **-er·ies** **1** : the boundary of a rounded figure **2** : outward bounds : border area — **pe·riph·er·al** \-fə-rəl\ *adj*

pe·riph·ra·sis \pə-ˈri-frə-səs\ *n, pl* **-ra·ses** \-ˌsēz\ : CIRCUMLOCUTION

peri·scope \ˈper-ə-ˌskōp\ *n* : a tubular optical instrument enabling an observer to see an otherwise blocked field of view

per·ish \ˈper-ish\ *vb* : to become destroyed or ruined : cease to exist

per·ish·able \ˈper-i-shə-bəl\ *adj* : easily spoiled ⟨~ foods⟩ — **perishable** *n*

peri·stal·sis \ˌper-ə-ˈstȯl-səs, -ˈstal-\ *n, pl* **-stal·ses** : waves of contraction passing along the walls of a hollow muscular organ (as the intestine) and forcing its contents onward — **per·i·stal·tic** \-ˈstȯl-tik, -ˈstal-\ *adj*

peri·style \ˈper-ə-ˌstīl\ *n* : a row of columns surrounding a building or court

peri·to·ne·um \ˌper-ə-tə-ˈnē-əm\ *n, pl* **-ne·ums** *or* **-nea** : the smooth transparent serous membrane that lines the cavity of the abdomen — **peri·to·ne·al** \-ˈnē-əl\ *adj*

peri·to·ni·tis \ˌper-ə-tə-ˈnī-təs\ *n* : inflammation of the peritoneum

peri·wig \ˈper-i-ˌwig\ *n* : WIG

¹**per·i·win·kle** \ˈper-i-ˌwiŋ-kəl\ *n* : a usu. blue-flowered creeping plant cultivated as a ground cover

²**periwinkle** *n* : any of various small edible seashore snails

per·ju·ry \ˈpər-jə-rē\ *n* : the voluntary violation of an oath to tell the truth : lying under oath — **per·jure** \ˈpər-jər\ *vb* — **per·jur·er** *n*

¹**perk** \ˈpərk\ *vb* **1** : to thrust (as the head) up impudently or jauntily **2** : to regain vigor or spirit **3** : to make trim or brisk : FRESHEN — **perky** *adj*

²**perk** *vb* : PERCOLATE

³**perk** *n* : PERQUISITE — usu. used in pl.

per·lite \ˈpər-ˌlīt\ *n* : volcanic glass that when expanded by heat forms a lightweight material used esp. in concrete and plaster and for potting plants

¹**perm** \ˈpərm\ *n* : PERMANENT

²**perm** *vb* : to give (hair) a permanent

³**perm** *abbr* permanent

per·ma·frost \ˈpər-mə-ˌfrȯst\ *n* : a permanently frozen layer below the surface in frigid regions of a planet

¹**per·ma·nent** \ˈpər-mə-nənt\ *adj* **1** : existing or continuing a long while : LASTING, STABLE **2** : INDELIBLE — **per·ma·nence** \-nəns\ *n* — **per·ma·nen·cy** \-nən-sē\ *n* — **per·ma·nent·ly** *adv*

²**permanent** *n* : a long-lasting hair wave or straightening

permanent press *n* : the process of treating fabrics with chemicals (as resin) and heat for setting the shape and for aiding wrinkle resistance

per·me·able \ˈpər-mē-ə-bəl\ *adj* : having small openings that permit liquids or gases to seep through — **per·me·a·bil·i·ty** \ˌpər-mē-ə-ˈbi-lə-tē\ *n*

per·me·ate \ˈpər-mē-ˌāt\ *vb* **-at·ed; -at·ing** **1** : PERVADE **2** : to seep through the pores of : PENETRATE — **per·me·ation** \ˌpər-mē-ˈā-shən\ *n*

Perm·ian \ˈpər-mē-ən\ *adj* : of, relating to, or being the latest period of the Paleozoic era — **Permian** *n*

per·mis·si·ble \pər-ˈmi-sə-bəl\ *adj* : that may be permitted : ALLOWABLE

per·mis·sion \pər-ˈmi-shən\ *n* : formal consent : AUTHORIZATION

per·mis·sive \pər-ˈmi-siv\ *adj* : granting permission; *esp* : INDULGENT — **per·mis·sive·ly** *adv* — **per·mis·sive·ness** *n*

¹**per·mit** \pər-ˈmit\ *vb* **per·mit·ted; per·mit·ting** **1** : to consent to : ALLOW **2** : to make possible

²**per·mit** \ˈpər-ˌmit, pər-ˈmit\ *n* : a written permission : LICENSE ⟨a fishing ~⟩

per·mu·ta·tion \ˌpər-myu̇-ˈtā-shən\ *n* **1** : a major or fundamental change **2** : the act or process of changing the order of an ordered set of objects ♦ ***Synonyms*** INNOVATION, MUTATION, VICISSITUDE

per·ni·cious \pər-ˈni-shəs\ *adj* [ME, fr. AF, fr. L *perniciosus,* fr. *pernicies* destruction, fr. *per-* through + *nec-, nex* violent death] : very destructive or injurious ⟨a ~ influence⟩ — **per·ni·cious·ly** *adv*

per·ora·tion \ˈper-ə-ˌrā-shən, ˈpər-\ *n* : the concluding part of a speech

¹**per·ox·ide** \pə-ˈräk-ˌsīd\ *n* : an oxide containing a large proportion of oxygen; *esp* : HYDROGEN PEROXIDE

²**peroxide** *vb* **-id·ed; -id·ing** : to bleach with hydrogen peroxide

perp *abbr* **1** perpendicular **2** perpetrator

per·pen·dic·u·lar \ˌpər-pən-ˈdi-kyə-lər\ *adj* **1** : standing at right angles to the plane of the horizon **2** : forming a right angle with each other or with a given line or plane — **perpendicular** *n* — **per·pen·dic·u·lar·i·ty** \-ˌdi-kyə-ˈla-rə-tē\ *n* — **per·pen·dic·u·lar·ly** *adv*

per·pe·trate \ˈpər-pə-ˌtrāt\ *vb* **-trat·ed; -trat·ing** : to carry out (as a crime) : COMMIT — **per·pe·tra·tion** \ˌpər-pə-ˈtrā-shən\ *n* — **per·pe·tra·tor** \ˈpər-pə-ˌtrā-tər\ *n*

per·pet·u·al \pər-ˈpe-chə-wəl\ *adj* **1** : continuing forever : EVERLASTING **2** : occurring continually : CONSTANT ♦ ***Synonyms*** CEASELESS, UNCEASING, CONTINUAL, CONTINUOUS, INCESSANT, UNREMITTING — **per·pet·u·al·ly** *adv*

per·pet·u·ate \pər-ˈpe-chə-ˌwāt\ *vb* **-at·ed; -at·ing** : to make perpetual : cause to last indefinitely ⟨~ a belief⟩ — **per·pet·u·a·tion** \-ˌpe-chə-ˈwā-shən\ *n*

per·pe·tu·i·ty \ˌpər-pə-ˈtü-ə-tē, -ˈtyü-\ *n, pl* **-ties** **1** : ETERNITY 1 **2** : the quality or state of being perpetual

per·plex \pər-ˈpleks\ *vb* : to disturb mentally; *esp* : CONFUSE — **per·plex·i·ty** \-ˈplek-sə-tē\ *n*

per·plexed \-ˈplekst\ *adj* **1** : filled with uncertainty : PUZZLED ⟨a ~ look⟩ **2** : full of difficulty : COMPLICATED — **per·plexed·ly** \-ˈplek-səd-lē\ *adv*

per·qui·site \ˈpər-kwə-zət\ *n* : a privilege or profit beyond regular pay

pers *abbr* person; personal

[1]**per se** \(ˌ)pər-ˈsā\ *adv* [L] : by, of, or in itself : as such

[2]**per se** *adj* : being such inherently, clearly, or as a matter of law

per·se·cute \ˈpər-si-ˌkyüt\ *vb* **-cut·ed; -cut·ing** : to pursue in such a way as to injure or afflict : HARASS; *esp* : to cause to suffer because of belief — **per·se·cu·tion** \ˌpər-si-ˈkyü-shən\ *n* — **per·se·cu·tor** \ˈpər-si-ˌkyü-tər\ *n*

per·sev·er·ate \pər-ˈse-və-ˌrāt\ *vb* **1 a** : to recur or repeat continually **b** : to intently focus one's attention on a thought : FIXATE **2** : to have or display an involuntary repetitive behavior or thought — **per·sev·er·a·tion** \pər-ˌse-və-ˈrā-shən\ *n*

per·se·vere \ˌpər-sə-ˈvir\ *vb* **-vered; -ver·ing** : to persist (as in an undertaking) in spite of difficulties — **per·se·ver·ance** \-ˈvir-əns\ *n*

Per·sian \ˈpər-zhən\ *n* **1** : a native or inhabitant of ancient Persia **2** : a member of one of the peoples of modern Iran **3** : the language of the Persians

Persian cat *n* : any of a breed of stocky round-headed domestic cats that have a long silky coat

Persian lamb *n* : a pelt with very silky tightly curled fur that is obtained from newborn lambs which are older than those yielding broadtail

per·si·flage \ˈpər-si-ˌfläzh, ˈper-\ *n* [F, fr. *persifler* to banter, fr. *per-* thoroughly + *siffler* to whistle, hiss, boo, ultim. fr. L *sibilare*] : lightly jesting or mocking talk

per·sim·mon \pər-ˈsi-mən\ *n* : either of two trees related to the ebony; *also* : the edible usu. orange or red plumlike fruit of a persimmon

per·sist \pər-ˈsist, -ˈzist\ *vb* **1** : to go on resolutely or stubbornly in spite of difficulties **2** : to continue to exist — **per·sis·tence** \-ˈsis-təns, -ˈzis-\ *n* — **per·sis·ten·cy** \-tən-sē\ *n* — **per·sis·tent** \-tənt\ *adj* — **per·sis·tent·ly** *adv*

per·snick·e·ty \pər-ˈsni-kə-tē\ *adj* : fussy about small details

per·son \ˈpər-sən\ *n* [ME, fr. AF *persone*, fr. L *persona* actor's mask, character in a play, person, prob. fr. Etruscan *phersu* mask, fr. Gk *prosōpa*, pl. of *prosōpon* face, mask] **1** : a human being : INDIVIDUAL — used in combination esp. by those who prefer to avoid *man* in compounds applicable to both sexes ⟨chair*person*⟩ **2** : one of the three modes of being in the Godhead as understood by Trinitarians **3** : the body of a human being **4** : the individual personality of a human being : SELF **5** : reference of a segment of discourse to the speaker, to one spoken to, or to one spoken of esp. as indicated by certain pronouns

per·so·na \pər-ˈsō-nə\ *n, pl* **-nae** \-nē\ *or* **-nas** : the personality that a person projects in public

per·son·able \ˈpər-sə-nə-bəl\ *adj* : pleasant in person : ATTRACTIVE

per·son·age \ˈpər-sə-nij\ *n* : a person of rank, note, or distinction

[1]**per·son·al** \ˈpər-sə-nəl\ *adj* **1** : of, relating to, or affecting a person : PRIVATE ⟨~ correspondence⟩ **2** : done in person ⟨a ~ inquiry⟩ **3** : relating to the person or body ⟨~ injuries⟩ **4** : relating to an individual esp. in an offensive way ⟨resented such ~ remarks⟩ **5** : of or relating to temporary or movable property as distinguished from real estate **6** : denoting grammatical person **7** : intended for use by one person ⟨a ~ stereo⟩

[2]**personal** *n* **1** : a short newspaper paragraph relating to a person or group or to personal matters **2** : a short personal or private communication in the classified ads section of a newspaper

personal computer *n* : a computer with a microprocessor designed for an individual user to run esp. commercial software

personal digital assistant *n* : PDA

per·son·al·ise *Brit var of* PERSONALIZE

per·son·al·i·ty \ˌpər-sə-ˈna-lə-tē\ *n, pl* **-ties** **1** : an offensively personal remark ⟨indulges in *personalities*⟩ **2** : the collection of emotional and behavioral traits that characterize a person **3** : distinction of personal and social traits **4** : a well-known person ⟨a TV ~⟩ ♦ ***Synonyms*** INDIVIDUALITY, TEMPERAMENT, DISPOSITION, MAKEUP

per·son·al·ize \ˈpər-sə-nə-ˌlīz\ *vb* **-ized; -iz·ing** : to make personal or individual; *esp* : to mark as belonging to a particular person ⟨*personalized* stationery⟩

per·son·al·ly \-nə-lē\ *adv* **1** : in person **2** : as a person **3** : as far as oneself is concerned ⟨~, I don't want to go⟩

per·son·al·ty \ˈpər-sə-nəl-tē\ *n, pl* **-ties** : personal property

per·so·na non gra·ta \pər-ˈsō-nə-ˌnän-ˈgra-tə, -ˈgrä-\ *adj* [L] : being personally unacceptable or unwelcome

per·son·ate \ˈpər-sə-ˌnāt\ *vb* **-at·ed; -at·ing** : IMPERSONATE, REPRESENT

per·son·i·fy \pər-ˈsä-nə-ˌfī\ *vb* **-fied; -fy·ing** **1** : to think of or represent as a person **2** : to be the embodiment of : INCARNATE ⟨~ the law⟩ — **per·son·i·fi·ca·tion** \-ˌsä-nə-fə-ˈkā-shən\ *n*

per·son·nel \ˌpər-sə-ˈnel\ *n* : a body of persons employed

per·spec·tive \pər-ˈspek-tiv\ *n* **1** : the science of painting and drawing so that objects represented have apparent depth and distance **2** : the aspect in which a subject or its parts are mentally viewed; *esp* : a view of things (as objects or events) in their true relationship or relative importance

per·spi·ca·cious \ˌpər-spə-ˈkā-shəs\ *adj* : having or showing keen understanding or discernment ⟨a ~ observation⟩ — **per·spi·cac·i·ty** \-ˈka-sə-tē\ *n*

per·spic·u·ous \pər-ˈspi-kyə-wəs\ *adj*

: plain to the understanding ⟨a ~ argument⟩ — **per·spi·cu·i·ty** \ˌpər-spə-ˈkyü-ə-tē\ *n*

per·spire \pər-ˈspī(-ə)r\ *vb* **per·spired; per·spir·ing** : SWEAT — **per·spi·ra·tion** \ˌpər-spə-ˈrā-shən\ *n*

per·suade \pər-ˈswād\ *vb* **per·suad·ed; per·suad·ing** : to win over to a belief or course of action by argument or entreaty — **per·sua·sive** \-ˈswā-siv, -ziv\ *adj* — **per·sua·sive·ly** *adv* — **per·sua·sive·ness** *n*

per·sua·sion \pər-ˈswā-zhən\ *n* **1** : the act or process of persuading **2** : a system of religious beliefs; *also* : a group holding such beliefs

pert \ˈpərt\ *adj* [ME, evident, attractive, saucy, short for *apert* evident, fr. AF, fr. L *apertus* open, fr. pp. of *aperire* to open] **1** : saucily free and forward : IMPUDENT **2** : stylishly trim : JAUNTY **3** : LIVELY

per·tain \pər-ˈtān\ *vb* **1** : to belong to as a part, quality, or function ⟨duties ~*ing* to the office⟩ **2** : to have reference : RELATE ⟨books ~*ing* to birds⟩

per·ti·na·cious \ˌpər-tə-ˈnā-shəs\ *adj* **1** : holding resolutely to an opinion or purpose **2** : obstinately persistent ⟨a ~ bill collector⟩ ♦ ***Synonyms*** DOGGED, MULISH, HEADSTRONG, PERVERSE — **per·ti·nac·i·ty** \-ˈna-sə-tē\ *n*

per·ti·nent \ˈpər-tə-nənt\ *adj* : relating to the matter under consideration ♦ ***Synonyms*** RELEVANT, GERMANE, APPLICABLE, APROPOS — **per·ti·nence** \-əns\ *n*

per·turb \pər-ˈtərb\ *vb* : to disturb greatly esp. in mind : UPSET — **per·tur·ba·tion** \ˌpər-tər-ˈbā-shən\ *n*

per·tus·sis \pər-ˈtə-səs\ *n* : WHOOPING COUGH

pe·ruke \pə-ˈrük\ *n* : WIG

pe·ruse \pə-ˈrüz\ *vb* **pe·rused; pe·rus·ing** : READ; *esp* : to read over attentively or leisurely — **pe·rus·al** \-ˈrü-zəl\ *n*

perv \ˈpərv\ *n, slang* : PERVERT

per·vade \pər-ˈvād\ *vb* **per·vad·ed; per·vad·ing** : to spread through every part of : PERMEATE ⟨excitement *pervaded* the room⟩ — **per·va·sive** \-ˈvā-siv, -ziv\ *adj*

per·verse \pər-ˈvərs\ *adj* **1** : turned away from what is right or good : CORRUPT **2** : obstinate in opposing what is reasonable or accepted **3** : marked by perversion — **per·verse·ly** *adv* — **per·verse·ness** *n* — **per·ver·si·ty** \-ˈvər-sə-tē\ *n*

per·ver·sion \pər-ˈvər-zhən\ *n* **1** : the action of perverting : the condition of being perverted **2** : a perverted form of something; *esp* : aberrant sexual behavior

¹per·vert \pər-ˈvərt\ *vb* **1** : to lead astray : CORRUPT ⟨~ the young⟩ **2** : to divert to a wrong purpose : MISAPPLY ⟨~ evidence⟩ ♦ ***Synonyms*** DEPRAVE, DEBASE, DEBAUCH, DEMORALIZE — **per·ver·ter** *n*

²per·vert \ˈpər-ˌvərt\ *n* : one that is perverted; *esp* : one given to sexual perversion

pe·se·ta \pə-ˈsā-tə\ *n* : the former basic monetary unit of Spain

pe·se·wa \pə-ˈsā-wə\ *n* — see *cedi* at MONEY table

pes·ky \ˈpes-kē\ *adj* **pes·ki·er; -est** : causing annoyance : TROUBLESOME

pe·so \ˈpā-sō\ *n, pl* **pesos** — see MONEY table

pes·si·mism \ˈpe-sə-ˌmi-zəm\ *n* [F *pessimisme,* fr. L *pessimus* worst] : an inclination to take the least favorable view (as of events) or to expect the worst — **pes·si·mist** \-mist\ *n* — **pes·si·mis·tic** \ˌpe-sə-ˈmis-tik\ *adj*

pest \ˈpest\ *n* **1** : a destructive epidemic disease : PLAGUE **2** : a plant or animal detrimental to humans **3** : one that pesters : NUISANCE — **pesty** *adj*

pes·ter \ˈpes-tər\ *vb* : to harass with petty irritations : ANNOY

pes·ti·cide \ˈpes-tə-ˌsīd\ *n* : an agent used to destroy pests

pes·tif·er·ous \pes-ˈti-fə-rəs\ *adj* **1** : PESTILENT ⟨~ vermin⟩ **2** : ANNOYING

pes·ti·lence \ˈpes-tə-ləns\ *n* : a destructive infectious swiftly spreading disease; *esp* : BUBONIC PLAGUE

pes·ti·lent \-lənt\ *adj* **1** : dangerous to life : DEADLY **2** : PERNICIOUS, HARMFUL **3** : TROUBLESOME **4** : INFECTIOUS, CONTAGIOUS ⟨a ~ disease⟩

pes·ti·len·tial \ˌpes-tə-ˈlen-chəl\ *adj* **1** : causing or tending to cause pestilence : DEADLY **2** : morally harmful

pes·tle \ˈpes-əl, ˈpes-tᵊl\ *n* : an implement for grinding substances in a mortar — **pestle** *vb*

¹pet \ˈpet\ *n* **1** : FAVORITE, DARLING **2** : a domesticated animal kept for pleasure rather than utility

²pet *adj* **1** : kept or treated as a pet ⟨~ dog⟩ **2** : expressing fondness ⟨~ name⟩ **3** : particularly liked or favored

³pet *vb* **pet·ted; pet·ting** **1** : to stroke gently or lovingly **2** : to make a pet of : PAMPER **3** : to engage in amorous kissing and caressing

⁴pet *n* : a fit of peevishness, sulkiness, or anger — **pet·tish** *adj*

Pet *abbr* Peter

pet·al \ˈpe-tᵊl\ *n* : one of the modified leaves of a flower's corolla

pe·tard \pə-ˈtärd, -ˈtär\ *n* : a case containing an explosive to break down a door or gate or breach a wall

pe·ter \ˈpē-tər\ *vb* : to diminish gradually and come to an end ⟨his energy ~*ed* out⟩

Pe·ter \ˈpē-tər\ *n* — see BIBLE table

pet·i·ole \ˈpe-tē-ˌōl\ *n* : a slender stem that supports a leaf

pe·tite \pə-ˈtēt\ *adj* [F] : having a small trim figure — usu. used of a woman — **petite** *n*

pe·tit four \ˌpe-tē-ˈfȯr\ *n, pl* **petits fours** *or* **petit fours** \-ˈfȯrz\ [F, lit., small oven] : a small cake cut from pound or sponge cake and frosted

¹pe·ti·tion \pə-ˈti-shən\ *n* : an earnest request : ENTREATY; *esp* : a formal written request made to an authority

²petition *vb* : to make a request to or for — **pe·ti·tion·er** *n*

pe·trel \ˈpe-trəl\ *n* : any of numerous seabirds that fly far from land

pe·tri·chor \ˈpe-trə-ˌkȯr\ *n* : an earthy odor that is associated with rainfall esp. when following a warm dry period
pe·tri dish \ˈpē-trē-\ *n* **1** : a small shallow dish used esp. for growing bacteria **2** : something fostering development or innovation
pet·ri·fy \ˈpe-trə-ˌfī\ *vb* **-fied; -fy·ing** **1** : to convert (organic matter) into stone or stony material **2** : to make rigid or inactive (as from fear or awe) — **pet·ri·fac·tion** \ˌpe-trə-ˈfak-shən\ *n*
pet·ro·chem·i·cal \ˌpe-trō-ˈke-mi-kəl\ *n* : a chemical isolated or derived from petroleum or natural gas — **pet·ro·chem·is·try** \-ˈke-mə-strē\ *n*
pet·rol \ˈpe-trəl\ *n, chiefly Brit* : GASOLINE
pet·ro·la·tum \ˌpe-trə-ˈlā-təm\ *n* : PETROLEUM JELLY
pe·tro·leum \pə-ˈtrō-lē-əm\ *n* [ML, fr. Gk *petra* rock + L *oleum* oil] : an oily flammable liquid obtained from wells drilled in the ground and refined into gasoline, fuel oils, and other products
petroleum jelly *n* : a tasteless, odorless, and oily or greasy substance from petroleum that is used esp. in ointments and dressings
[1]**pet·ti·coat** \ˈpe-tē-ˌkōt\ *n* **1** : a skirt worn under a dress **2** : an outer skirt
[2]**petticoat** *adj* : of, relating to, or exercised by women : FEMALE
pet·ti·fog·ger \ˈpe-tē-ˌfȯ-gər, -ˌfä-\ *n* **1** : a lawyer whose methods are petty, underhanded, or disreputable **2** : one given to quibbling over trifles — **pet·ti·fog·ging** \-giŋ\ *adj or n*
pet·ty \ˈpe-tē\ *adj* **pet·ti·er; -est** [ME *pety* small, minor, alter. of *petit,* fr. AF, small] **1** : having secondary rank : MINOR ⟨~ prince⟩ **2** : of little importance : TRIFLING ⟨~ faults⟩ **3** : marked by narrowness or meanness — **pet·ti·ly** \ˈpe-tə-lē\ *adv* — **pet·ti·ness** \-tē-nəs\ *n*
petty officer *n* : a subordinate officer in the navy or coast guard appointed from among the enlisted personnel
petty officer first class *n* : a petty officer ranking below a chief petty officer
petty officer second class *n* : a petty officer ranking below a petty officer first class
petty officer third class *n* : a petty officer ranking below a petty officer second class
pet·u·lant \ˈpe-chə-lənt\ *adj* : marked by capricious ill humor ♦ ***Synonyms*** IRRITABLE, PEEVISH, FRETFUL, FRACTIOUS, QUERULOUS — **pet·u·lance** \-ləns\ *n* — **pet·u·lant·ly** *adv*
pe·tu·nia \pi-ˈtün-yə, -ˈtyün-\ *n* : any of a genus of tropical So. American herbs related to the potato and having bright funnel-shaped flowers
pew \ˈpyü\ *n* [ME *pewe,* fr. MF *puie* balustrade, fr. L *podia,* pl. of *podium* parapet, podium, fr. Gk *podion* base, dim. of *pod-, pous* foot] : any of the benches with backs fixed in rows in a church
pe·wee \ˈpē-(ˌ)wē\ *n* : any of various small American flycatchers
pew·ter \ˈpyü-tər\ *n* **1** : an alloy of tin used esp. for household utensils **2** : a bluish gray color — **pewter** *adj* — **pew·ter·er** *n*
pey·o·te \pā-ˈō-tē\ *also* **pey·otl** \-ˈō-tᵊl\ *n* **1** : a hallucinogenic drug derived from the peyote cactus and containing mescaline **2** : a small cactus of the southwestern U.S. and Mexico
pf *abbr* **1** pfennig **2** preferred
PFC *or* **Pfc** *abbr* private first class
pfd *abbr* preferred
pfen·nig \ˈfe-nig\ *n, pl* **pfennig** *also* **pfennigs** *or* **pfen·ni·ge** \ˈfe-ni-gə\ : a former monetary unit equal to $\frac{1}{100}$ deutsche mark
PFLAG *abbr* parents, families, and friends of lesbians and gays
pg *abbr* page
PG *abbr* postgraduate
PGA *abbr* Professional Golfers' Association
pH \(ˌ)pē-ˈāch\ *n* : a value used to express acidity and alkalinity; *also* : the condition represented by such a value
PH *abbr* **1** pinch hit **2** public health
pha·eton \ˈfā-ə-tᵊn\ *n* [F *phaéton,* fr. Gk *Phaethōn,* son of the sun god who persuaded his father to let him drive the chariot of the sun but who lost control of the horses with disastrous consequences] **1** : a light 4-wheeled horse-drawn vehicle **2** : an open automobile with two cross seats
phage \ˈfāj\ *n* : BACTERIOPHAGE
pha·lanx \ˈfā-ˌlaŋks\ *n, pl* **pha·lanx·es** *or* **pha·lan·ges** \fə-ˈlan-ˌjēz\ **1** : a group or body (as of troops) in compact formation **2** *pl phalanges* : one of the digital bones of the hand or foot of a vertebrate
phal·a·rope \ˈfa-lə-ˌrōp\ *n, pl* **-ropes** *also* **-rope** : any of a genus of small shorebirds related to sandpipers
phal·lic \ˈfa-lik\ *adj* **1** : of, relating to, or resembling a phallus **2** : relating to or being the stage of psychosexual development in psychoanalytic theory during which children become interested in their own sexual organs
phal·lus \ˈfa-ləs\ *n, pl* **phal·li** \ˈfa-ˌlī\ *or* **phal·lus·es** : PENIS; *also* : a symbolic representation of the penis
Phan·er·o·zo·ic \ˌfa-nə-rə-ˈzō-ik\ *adj* : of, relating to, or being an eon of geologic history comprising the Paleozoic, Mesozoic, and Cenozoic
phan·tasm \ˈfan-ˌta-zəm\ *n* : a product of the imagination : ILLUSION — **phan·tas·mal** \ˌfan-ˈtaz-məl\ *adj*
phan·tas·ma·go·ria \fan-ˌtaz-mə-ˈgȯr-ē-ə\ *n* : a constantly shifting complex succession of things seen or imagined; *also* : a scene that constantly changes or fluctuates
phantasy *var of* FANTASY
phan·tom \ˈfan-təm\ *n* **1** : something (as a specter) that is apparent to sense but has no substantial existence **2** : a mere show : SHADOW — **phantom** *adj*
pha·raoh \ˈfer-ō, ˈfā-rō\ *n, often cap* : a ruler of ancient Egypt

phar·i·sa·ical \ˌfa-rə-ˈsā-ə-kəl\ *adj* : hypocritically self-righteous

phar·i·see \ˈfa-rə-ˌsē\ *n* **1** *cap* : a member of an ancient Jewish sect noted for strict observance of rites and ceremonies of the traditional law **2** : a self-righteous or hypocritical person — **phar·i·sa·ic** \ˌfa-rə-ˈsā-ik\ *adj*

pharm *abbr* pharmaceutical; pharmacist; pharmacy

phar·ma·ceu·ti·cal \ˌfär-mə-ˈsü-ti-kəl\ *adj* : of, relating to, or engaged in pharmacy or the manufacture and sale of medicinal drugs — **pharmaceutical** *n*

phar·ma·col·o·gy \ˌfär-mə-ˈkä-lə-jē\ *n* **1** : the science of drugs esp. as related to medicinal uses **2** : the reactions and properties of one or more drugs — **phar·ma·co·log·i·cal** \-kə-ˈlä-ji-kəl\ *also* **phar·ma·co·log·ic** \-kə-ˈlä-jik\ *adj* — **phar·ma·col·o·gist** \-ˈkä-lə-jist\ *n*

phar·ma·co·poe·ia *also* **phar·ma·co·pe·ia** \-kə-ˈpē-ə\ *n* **1** : a book describing drugs and medicinal preparations **2** : a stock of drugs

phar·ma·cy \ˈfär-mə-sē\ *n, pl* **-cies** **1** : the art, practice, or profession of preparing and dispensing medical drugs **2** : DRUGSTORE — **phar·ma·cist** \-sist\ *n*

phar·ynx \ˈfa-riŋks\ *n, pl* **pha·ryn·ges** \fə-ˈrin-ˌjēz\ *also* **phar·ynx·es** : the muscular tubular passage extending from the back of the nasal cavity and mouth to the esophagus — **pha·ryn·ge·al** \fə-ˈrin-jəl, ˌfa-rən-ˈjē-əl\ *adj*

phase \ˈfāz\ *n* **1** : a particular appearance in a recurring series of changes ⟨~*s* of the moon⟩ **2** : a stage or interval in a process or cycle ⟨first ~ of an experiment⟩ **3** : an aspect or part under consideration — **pha·sic** \ˈfā-zik\ *adj*

phase down *vb* : to reduce the size or amount of by phases

phase in *vb* : to introduce in stages

phase·out \ˈfāz-ˌau̇t\ *n* : a gradual stopping of operations or production

phase out *vb* : to stop production or use of in stages ⟨*phase out* old equipment⟩

PhD *abbr* [L *philosophiae doctor*] doctor of philosophy

pheas·ant \ˈfe-zᵊnt\ *n, pl* **pheasant** *or* **pheasants** : any of numerous long-tailed brilliantly colored game birds related to the domestic chicken

phen·cy·cli·dine \ˌfen-ˈsī-klə-ˌdēn\ *n* : a drug used esp. as a veterinary anesthetic and sometimes illicitly as a hallucinogenic drug

phe·no·bar·bi·tal \ˌfē-nō-ˈbär-bə-ˌtȯl\ *n* : a crystalline drug used as a hypnotic and sedative

phe·nol \ˈfē-ˌnȯl\ *n* : a corrosive poisonous acidic compound present in coal and wood tars and used in solution as a disinfectant

phe·nom·e·non \fi-ˈnä-mə-ˌnän, -nən\ *n, pl* **-na** \-nə\ *or* **-nons** [LL *phaenomenon*, fr. Gk *phainomenon*, fr. neut. of *phainomenos*, prp. of *phainesthai* to appear] **1** *pl* *-na* : an observable fact or event **2** : an outward sign of the working of a law of nature **3** *pl* *-nons* : an extraordinary person or thing : PRODIGY — **phe·nom·e·nal** \-ˈnä-mə-nᵊl\ *adj* — **phe·nom·e·non·al·ly** *adv*

pher·o·mone \ˈfer-ə-ˌmōn\ *n* : a chemical substance that is usu. produced by an animal and serves to stimulate a behavioral response in other individuals of the same species — **pher·o·mon·al** \ˌfer-ə-ˈmō-nᵊl\ *adj*

phi \ˈfī\ *n* : the 21st letter of the Greek alphabet — Φ or ϕ

phi·al \ˈfī(-ə)l\ *n* : VIAL

Phil *abbr* Philippians

phi·lan·der \fə-ˈlan-dər\ *vb* : to have casual or illicit sexual relations with many women — **phi·lan·der·er** *n*

phi·lan·thro·py \fə-ˈlan-thrə-pē\ *n, pl* **-pies** **1** : goodwill toward all people; *esp* : effort to promote human welfare **2** : a charitable act or gift; *also* : an organization that distributes or is supported by donated funds — **phil·an·throp·ic** \ˌfi-lən-ˈthrä-pik\ *adj* — **phil·an·throp·i·cal·ly** \-pi-k(ə-)lē\ *adv* — **phi·lan·thro·pist** \fə-ˈlan-thrə-pist\ *n*

phi·lat·e·ly \fə-ˈla-tə-lē\ *n* : the collection and study of postage and imprinted stamps — **phil·a·tel·ic** \ˌfi-lə-ˈte-lik\ *adj* — **phi·lat·e·list** \fə-ˈla-tə-list\ *n*

Phi·le·mon \fə-ˈlē-mən, fī-\ *n* — see BIBLE table

Phi·lip·pi·ans \fə-ˈli-pē-ənz\ *n* — see BIBLE table

phi·lip·pic \fə-ˈli-pik\ *n* : TIRADE

phi·lis·tine \ˈfi-lə-ˌstēn; fə-ˈlis-tən\ *n, often cap* [*Philistine*, inhabitant of ancient Philistia (Palestine)] : a person who is smugly insensitive or indifferent to intellectual or artistic values — **philistine** *adj, often cap*

Phil·lips \ˈfi-ləps\ *adj* : of, relating to, or being a screw having a head with a cross slot or its corresponding screwdriver

philo·den·dron \ˌfi-lə-ˈden-drən\ *n, pl* **-drons** *also* **-dra** \-drə\ [NL, fr. Gk, neut. of *philodendros* loving trees, fr. *philos* dear, friendly + *dendron* tree] : any of various plants of the arum family grown for their showy foliage

phi·lol·o·gy \fə-ˈlä-lə-jē\ *n* **1** : the study of literature and relevant fields **2** : LINGUISTICS; *esp* : historical and comparative linguistics — **phil·o·log·i·cal** \ˌfi-lə-ˈlä-ji-kəl\ *adj* — **phi·lol·o·gist** \fə-ˈlä-lə-jist\ *n*

philos *abbr* philosopher; philosophy

phi·los·o·pher \fə-ˈlä-sə-fər\ *n* **1** : a reflective thinker : SCHOLAR **2** : a student of or specialist in philosophy **3** : a person whose philosophical perspective makes it possible to meet trouble calmly

phi·los·o·phise *Brit var of* PHILOSOPHIZE

phi·los·o·phize \fə-ˈlä-sə-ˌfīz\ *vb* **-phized; -phiz·ing** **1** : to reason like a philosopher : THEORIZE **2** : to expound a philosophy esp. superficially

phi·los·o·phy \fə-ˈlä-sə-fē\ *n, pl* **-phies** **1** : sciences and liberal arts exclusive of medicine, law, and theology ⟨doctor of

~> **2** : a critical study of fundamental beliefs and the grounds for them **3** : a system of philosophical concepts ⟨Aristotelian ~⟩ **4** : a basic theory concerning a particular subject or sphere of activity **5** : the sum of the ideas and convictions of an individual or group ⟨her ~ of life⟩ **6** : calmness of temper and judgment — **phil·o·soph·i·cal** \-fi-kəl\ *also* **phil·o·soph·ic** \ˌfi-lə-ˈsä-fik\ *adj* — **phil·o·soph·i·cal·ly** \-k(ə-)lē\ *adv*

phil·ter \ˈfil-tər\ *n* **1** : a magic potion **2** : a potion, drug, or charm held to arouse sexual passion

phil·tre *chiefly Brit var of* PHILTER

phish·ing \ˈfi-shiŋ\ *n* [alteration of *fishing*] : a scam by which an email user is fooled into revealing personal or confidential information which can be used illegally — **phish·er** \ˈfi-shər\ *n*

phle·bi·tis \fli-ˈbī-təs\ *n* : inflammation of a vein

phle·bot·o·my \fli-ˈbä-tə-mē\ *n, pl* **-mies** : the opening of a vein esp. for removing or releasing blood

phlegm \ˈflem\ *n* [ME *fleume,* fr. AF, fr. LL *phlegma,* fr. Gk, flame, inflammation, phlegm, fr. *phlegein* to burn] : thick mucus secreted in abnormal quantity esp. in the nose and throat

phleg·mat·ic \fleg-ˈma-tik\ *adj* : having or showing a slow and stolid temperament ⟨was ~ during the crisis⟩ ♦ ***Synonyms*** IMPASSIVE, APATHETIC, STOIC

phlo·em \ˈflō-ˌem\ *n* : a vascular plant tissue external to the xylem that carries dissolved food material and functions in support and storage

phlox \ˈfläks\ *n, pl* **phlox** *or* **phlox·es** : any of a genus of American herbs that have tall stalks with showy spreading terminal clusters of flowers

pho·bia \ˈfō-bē-ə\ *n* : an irrational persistent fear or dread — **pho·bic** \ˈfō-bik\ *adj*

phoe·be \ˈfē-(ˌ)bē\ *n* : a flycatcher of the eastern U.S. that has a slight crest and is grayish brown above and yellowish white below

phoe·nix \ˈfē-niks\ *n* : a legendary bird held to live for centuries and then to burn itself to death and rise fresh and young from its ashes

[1]**phone** \ˈfōn\ *n* **1** : TELEPHONE **2** : EARPHONE

[2]**phone** *vb* **phoned; phon·ing** : TELEPHONE

phone card *n* : a prepaid card used in paying for telephone calls

pho·neme \ˈfō-ˌnēm\ *n* : one of the elementary units of speech that distinguish one utterance from another — **pho·ne·mic** \fō-ˈnē-mik\ *adj*

pho·net·ics \fə-ˈne-tiks\ *n* : the study and systematic classification of the sounds made in spoken utterance — **pho·net·ic** \-tik\ *adj* — **pho·ne·ti·cian** \ˌfō-nə-ˈti-shən\ *n*

pho·nic \ˈfä-nik\ *adj* **1** : of, relating to, or producing sound **2** : of or relating to the sounds of speech or to phonics — **pho·ni·cal·ly** \-ni-k(ə-)lē\ *adv*

pho·nics \ˈfä-niks\ *n* : a method of teaching people to read and pronounce words by learning the phonetic value of letters, letter groups, and esp. syllables

pho·no·graph \ˈfō-nə-ˌgraf\ *n* : an instrument for reproducing sounds by means of the vibration of a needle following a spiral groove on a revolving disc

pho·nol·o·gy \fə-ˈnä-lə-jē\ *n* : a study and description of the sound changes in a language — **pho·no·log·i·cal** \ˌfō-nə-ˈlä-ji-kəl\ *adj* — **pho·nol·o·gist** \fə-ˈnä-lə-jist\ *n*

pho·ny *also* **pho·ney** \ˈfō-nē\ *adj* **pho·ni·er; -est** : not genuine or real : FAKE ⟨a ~ name⟩ — **phony** *n*

phos·phate \ˈfäs-ˌfāt\ *n* : a salt of a phosphoric acid — **phos·phat·ic** \fäs-ˈfa-tik\ *adj*

phos·phor \ˈfäs-fər\ *n* : a phosphorescent substance

phos·pho·res·cence \ˌfäs-fə-ˈre-sᵊns\ *n* **1** : luminescence caused by the absorption of radiations (as light or electrons) and continuing after these radiations stop **2** : an enduring luminescence without sensible heat — **phos·pho·res·cent** \-sᵊnt\ *adj* — **phos·pho·res·cent·ly** *adv*

phosphoric acid \ˌfäs-ˈfȯr-ik-, -ˈfär-\ *n* : any of several oxygen-containing acids of phosphorus

phos·pho·rus *also* **phos·pho·rous** \ˈfäs-fə-rəs\ *n* [NL, fr. Gk *phōsphoros* light-bearing, fr. *phōs* light + *pherein* to carry, bring] : a nonmetallic chemical element that has characteristics similar to nitrogen and occurs widely esp. as phosphates — **phos·pho·ric** \fäs-ˈfȯr-ik, -ˈfär-\ *adj* — **phos·pho·rous** \ˈfäs-fə-rəs; fäs-ˈfȯr-əs\ *adj*

phot- *or* **photo-** *comb form* **1** : light ⟨*photo*graphy⟩ **2** : photograph : photographic ⟨*photo*engraving⟩ **3** : photoelectric ⟨*photo*cell⟩

pho·to \ˈfō-tō\ *n, pl* **photos** : PHOTOGRAPH — **photo** *vb or adj*

pho·to·cell \ˈfō-tə-ˌsel\ *n* : PHOTOELECTRIC CELL

pho·to·chem·i·cal \ˌfō-tō-ˈke-mi-kəl\ *adj* : of, relating to, or resulting from the chemical action of radiant energy

pho·to·com·pose \-kəm-ˈpōz\ *vb* : to compose reading matter for reproduction by means of characters photographed on film — **pho·to·com·po·si·tion** \-ˌkäm-pə-ˈzi-shən\ *n*

pho·to·copy \ˈfō-tə-ˌkä-pē\ *n* : a photographic reproduction of graphic matter — **photocopy** *vb*

pho·to·elec·tric \ˌfō-tō-i-ˈlek-trik\ *adj* : relating to an electrical effect due to the interaction of light with matter — **pho·to·elec·tri·cal·ly** \-tri-k(ə-)lē\ *adv*

photoelectric cell *n* : a device whose electrical properties are modified by the action of light

pho·to·en·grave \ˌfō-tō-in-ˈgrāv\ *vb* : to make a photoengraving of

pho·to·en·grav·ing *n* : a process by which an etched printing plate is made from a photograph or drawing; *also* : a print made from such a plate

photo finish *n* : a race finish so close that a photograph of the finish is used to determine the winner

pho·tog \fə-ˈtäg\ *n* : PHOTOGRAPHER

pho·to·ge·nic \ˌfō-tə-ˈje-nik\ *adj* : eminently suitable esp. aesthetically for being photographed

pho·to·graph \ˈfō-tə-ˌgraf\ *n* : a picture taken by photography — **photograph** *vb* — **pho·tog·ra·pher** \fə-ˈtä-grə-fər\ *n*

pho·tog·ra·phy \fə-ˈtä-grə-fē\ *n* : the art or process of producing images on a sensitive surface (as film or a CCD chip) by the action of light — **pho·to·graph·ic** \ˌfō-tə-ˈgra-fik\ *adj* — **pho·to·graph·i·cal·ly** \-fi-k(ə-)lē\ *adv*

pho·to·gra·vure \ˌfō-tə-grə-ˈvyu̇r\ *n* : a process for making prints from an intaglio plate prepared by photographic methods

pho·to·li·thog·ra·phy \ˌfō-tō-li-ˈthä-grə-fē\ *n* : the process of photographically transferring a pattern to a surface for etching (as in making an integrated circuit)

pho·tom·e·ter \fō-ˈtä-mə-tər\ *n* : an instrument for measuring the intensity of light — **pho·to·met·ric** \ˌfō-tə-ˈme-trik\ *adj* — **pho·tom·e·try** \fō-ˈtä-mə-trē\ *n*

pho·to·mi·cro·graph \ˌfō-tə-ˈmī-krə-ˌgraf\ *n* : a photograph of a microscope image — **pho·to·mi·crog·ra·phy** \-mī-ˈkrä-grə-fē\ *n*

pho·ton \ˈfō-ˌtän\ *n* : a quantum of electromagnetic radiation

photo op *n* : a situation or event that lends itself to the taking of pictures which favor the individuals photographed

pho·to·play \ˈfō-tō-ˌplā\ *n* : MOTION PICTURE

pho·to·sen·si·tive \ˌfō-tə-ˈsen-sə-tiv\ *adj* : sensitive or sensitized to the action of radiant energy

pho·to·shop \ˈfō-(ˌ)tō-ˌshäp\ *vb, often cap* : to alter a digital image with image-editing software

pho·to·sphere \ˈfō-tə-ˌsfir\ *n* : the luminous surface of a star — **pho·to·spher·ic** \ˌfō-tə-ˈsfir-ik, -ˈsfer-\ *adj*

pho·to·syn·the·sis \ˌfō-tō-ˈsin-thə-səs\ *n* : the process by which chlorophyll-containing plants make carbohydrates from water and from carbon dioxide in the air in the presence of light — **pho·to·syn·the·size** \-ˌsīz\ *vb* — **pho·to·syn·thet·ic** \-sin-ˈthe-tik\ *adj*

phr *abbr* phrase

[1]**phrase** \ˈfrāz\ *n* **1** : a brief expression **2** : a group of two or more grammatically related words that form a sense unit expressing a thought

[2]**phrase** *vb* **phrased; phras·ing** : to express in words

phrase·ol·o·gy \ˌfrā-zē-ˈä-lə-jē\ *n, pl* **-gies** : a manner of phrasing : STYLE

phras·ing *n* : style of expression

phre·net·ic *archaic var of* FRENETIC

phren·ic \ˈfre-nik\ *adj* : of or relating to the diaphragm ⟨~ nerves⟩

phre·nol·o·gy \fri-ˈnä-lə-jē\ *n* : the study of the conformation of the skull based on the belief that it indicates mental faculties and character traits

phy·lac·tery \fə-ˈlak-tə-rē\ *n, pl* **-ter·ies** **1** : one of two small square leather boxes containing slips inscribed with scripture passages and traditionally worn on the left arm and forehead by Jewish men during morning weekday prayers **2** : AMULET

phy·lum \ˈfī-ləm\ *n, pl* **phy·la** \-lə\ [NL, fr. Gk *phylon* tribe, race] : a major category in biological classification esp. of animals that ranks above the class and below the kingdom; *also* : a group (as of people) apparently of common origin

phys *abbr* **1** physical **2** physics

[1]**phys·ic** \ˈfi-zik\ *n* **1** : the profession of medicine **2** : MEDICINE; *esp* : PURGATIVE

[2]**physic** *vb* **phys·icked; phys·ick·ing** : PURGE 2

[1]**phys·i·cal** \ˈfi-zi-kəl\ *adj* **1** : of or relating to nature or the laws of nature **2** : material as opposed to mental or spiritual **3** : of, relating to, or produced by the forces and operations of physics **4** : of or relating to the body — **phys·i·cal·ly** \-k(ə-)lē\ *adv*

[2]**physical** *n* : PHYSICAL EXAMINATION

physical education *n* : instruction in the development and care of the body ranging from simple calisthenics to training in hygiene, gymnastics, and the performance and management of athletic games

physical examination *n* : an examination of the bodily functions and condition of an individual

phys·i·cal·ize \ˈfi-zə-kə-ˌlīz\ *vb* **-ized; -iz·ing** : to give physical form or expression to

physical science *n* : any of the sciences (as physics and astronomy) that deal primarily with nonliving materials — **physical scientist** *n*

physical therapy *n* : the treatment of disease by physical and mechanical means (as massage, exercise, water, or heat) — **physical therapist** *n*

phy·si·cian \fə-ˈzi-shən\ *n* : a doctor of medicine

physician's assistant *n* : a person certified to provide basic medical care usu. under a licensed physician's supervision

phys·i·cist \ˈfi-zə-sist\ *n* : a scientist who specializes in physics

phys·ics \ˈfi-ziks\ *n* [L *physica,* pl., natural sciences, fr. Gk *physika,* fr. *physis* growth, nature, fr. *phyein* to bring forth] **1** : the science of matter and energy and their interactions **2** : the physical properties and composition of something

phys·i·og·no·my \ˌfi-zē-ˈäg-nə-mē\ *n, pl* **-mies** : facial appearance esp. as a reflection of inner character

phys·i·og·ra·phy \ˌfi-zē-ˈä-grə-fē\ *n* : geography dealing with physical features of the earth — **phys·io·graph·ic** \ˌfi-zē-ō-ˈgra-fik\ *adj*

phys·i·ol·o·gy \ˌfi-zē-ˈä-lə-jē\ *n* **1** : a branch of biology dealing with the functions and functioning of living matter and organisms **2** : functional processes in an organism or any of its parts — **phys·i·o·log·i·cal** \-zē-ə-ˈlä-ji-kəl\ *or* **phys·i·o·log·ic** \-jik\ *adj* — **phys·i·o·log·i·cal·ly** \-ji-k(ə-)lē\ *adv* — **phys·i·ol·o·gist** \-zē-ˈä-lə-jist\ *n*

phys·io·ther·a·py \ˌfi-zē-ō-ˈther-ə-pē\ *n* : PHYSICAL THERAPY — **phys·io·ther·a·pist** \-pist\ *n*

phy·sique \fə-ˈzēk\ *n* : the build of a person's body : bodily constitution

phy·to·chem·i·cal \ˌfī-tō-ˈke-mi-kəl\ *n* : a chemical compound occurring naturally in plants

phy·to·plank·ton \ˈfī-tō-ˌplaŋk-tən\ *n* : plant life of the plankton

pi \ˈpī\ *n, pl* **pis** \ˈpīz\ **1** : the 16th letter of the Greek alphabet — Π or *π* **2** : the symbol *π* denoting the ratio of the circumference of a circle to its diameter; *also* : the ratio itself equal to approximately 3.1416

PI *abbr* private investigator

pi·a·nis·si·mo \ˌpē-ə-ˈni-sə-ˌmō\ *adv or adj* : very softly — used as a direction in music

pi·a·nist \pē-ˈa-nist, ˈpē-ə-\ *n* : a person who plays the piano

[1]**pi·a·no** \pē-ˈä-nō\ *adv or adj* : SOFTLY — used as a direction in music

[2]**piano** \pē-ˈa-nō\ *n, pl* **pianos** [It, short for *pianoforte,* fr. *gravicembalo col piano e forte,* lit., harpsichord with soft and loud; fr. the fact that its tones could be varied in loudness] : a musical instrument having steel strings sounded by felt-covered hammers operated from a keyboard

pi·ano·forte \pē-ˌa-nō-ˈfȯr-ˌtā, -tē; pē-ˈa-nə-ˌfȯrt\ *n* : PIANO

pi·as·tre *also* **pi·as·ter** \pē-ˈas-tər\ *n* — see *pound* at MONEY table

pi·az·za \pē-ˈa-zə, *esp for 1* -ˈat-sə\ *n, pl* **piazzas** *or* **pi·az·ze** \-ˈat-(ˌ)sā, -ˈät-\ [It, fr. L *platea* broad street] **1** : an open square esp. in an Italian town **2** : a long hall with an arched roof **3** *dial* : VERANDA, PORCH

pi·broch \ˈpē-ˌbräk\ *n* : a set of variations for the bagpipe

pic \ˈpik\ *n, pl* **pics** *or* **pix** \ˈpiks\ **1** : PHOTOGRAPH **2** : MOTION PICTURE

pi·ca \ˈpī-kə\ *n* : a typewriter type with 10 characters to the inch

pi·ca·resque \ˌpi-kə-ˈresk, ˌpē-\ *adj* : of or relating to rogues ⟨~ fiction⟩

pic·a·yune \ˌpi-kē-ˈyün\ *adj* : of little value : TRIVIAL; *also* : PETTY

pic·ca·lil·li \ˌpi-kə-ˈli-lē\ *n* : a relish of chopped vegetables and spices

pic·co·lo \ˈpi-kə-ˌlō\ *n, pl* **-los** [It, short for *piccolo flauto* small flute] : a small shrill flute pitched an octave higher than the ordinary flute

pice \ˈpīs\ *n, pl* **pice** : PAISA

[1]**pick** \ˈpik\ *vb* **1** : to pierce or break up with a pointed instrument **2** : to remove bit by bit; *also* : to remove covering matter from **3** : to gather by plucking ⟨~ apples⟩ **4** : CULL, SELECT **5** : ROB ⟨~ a pocket⟩ **6** : PROVOKE ⟨~ a quarrel⟩ **7** : to dig into or pull lightly at **8** : to pluck with fingers or a pick ⟨~ a guitar⟩ **9** : to loosen or pull apart with a sharp point ⟨~ wool⟩ **10** : to unlock with a wire **11** : to eat sparingly ⟨~ at a salad⟩ — **pick·er** *n* — **pick on** : to single out for criticism, teasing, or bullying

[2]**pick** *n* **1** : the act or privilege of choosing **2** : the best or choicest one **3** : the part of a crop gathered at one time

[3]**pick** *n* **1** : a heavy wooden-handled tool pointed at one or both ends **2** : a pointed implement used for picking **3** : a small thin piece (as of plastic) used to pluck the strings of a stringed instrument

pick·a·back \ˈpi-gē-ˌbak, ˈpi-kə-\ *var of* PIGGYBACK

pick·ax \ˈpik-ˌaks\ *n* : [3]PICK 1

pick·er·el \ˈpi-kə-rəl\ *n, pl* **pickerel** *or* **pickerels** : either of two bony fishes related to the pikes; *also* : WALLEYE 2

pick·er·el·weed \-ˌwēd\ *n* : a No. American shallow-water herb that bears spikes of purplish blue flowers

[1]**pick·et** \ˈpi-kət\ *n* **1** : a pointed stake (as for a fence) **2** : a detached body of soldiers on outpost duty; *also* : SENTINEL **3** : a person posted by a labor union where workers are on strike; *also* : a person posted for a protest

[2]**picket** *vb* **1** : to guard with pickets **2** : TETHER ⟨~ a horse⟩ **3** : to post pickets at ⟨~ a factory⟩ **4** : to serve as a picket

pick·ings \ˈpi-kiŋz, -kənz\ *n pl* **1** : gleanable or eatable fragments : SCRAPS **2** : yield for effort expended : RETURN

pick·le \ˈpi-kəl\ *n* **1** : a brine or vinegar solution for preserving foods; *also* : a food (as a cucumber) preserved in a pickle **2** : a difficult situation : PLIGHT — **pickle** *vb*

pick·le·ball \-ˌbȯl\ *n* : a game resembling tennis played with paddles and a perforated plastic ball

pick·lock \ˈpik-ˌläk\ *n* **1** : BURGLAR, THIEF **2** : a tool for picking locks

pick·pock·et \ˈpik-ˌpä-kət\ *n* : one who steals from pockets

[1]**pick·up** \ˈpik-ˌəp\ *n* **1** : a hitchhiker who is given a ride **2** : a temporary chance acquaintance **3** : a picking up **4** : revival of business activity **5** : ACCELERATION **6** : the conversion of mechanical movements into electrical impulses in the reproduction of sound; *also* : a device for making such conversion **7** : a light truck having an enclosed cab and an open body with low sides and a tailgate **8** : a pickup game **9** : a player acquired from another team

[2]**pickup** *adj* : using or comprising local or available personnel ⟨a ~ game⟩

pick up *vb* **1** : to take hold of and lift **2** : IMPROVE **3** : to put in order

picky \ˈpi-kē\ *adj* **pick·i·er; -est** : FUSSY, FINICKY ⟨a ~ eater⟩

[1]**pic·nic** \ˈpik-ˌnik\ *n* : an outing with food usu. provided by members of the group and eaten in the open

[2]**picnic** *vb* **pic·nicked; pic·nick·ing** : to go on a picnic : eat in picnic fashion

pi·cot \ˈpē-ˌkō\ *n* : one of a series of small loops forming an edging on ribbon or lace

pic·to·ri·al \pik-ˈtȯr-ē-əl\ *adj* : of, relating to, or consisting of pictures

[1]**pic·ture** \ˈpik-chər\ *n* **1** : a representation made by painting, drawing, or photography **2** : a vivid description in words **3** : IMAGE, COPY ⟨was the ~ of his father⟩ **4** : a transitory visual image (as on a TV screen) **5** : MOTION PICTURE **6** : SITUATION ⟨a bleak economic ~⟩

[2]**picture** *vb* **pic·tured; pic·tur·ing** **1** : to paint or draw a picture of **2** : to describe vividly in words **3** : to form a mental image of

pic·tur·esque \ˌpik-chə-ˈresk\ *adj* **1** : resembling a picture ⟨a ~ landscape⟩ **2** : CHARMING, QUAINT ⟨a ~ character⟩ **3** : GRAPHIC 3, VIVID ⟨a ~ account⟩ — **pic·tur·esque·ness** *n*

picture tube *n* : a cathode-ray tube on which the picture appears in a television

pid·dle \ˈpi-dᵊl\ *vb* **pid·dled; pid·dling** : to act or work idly : DAWDLE

pid·dling \ˈpi-dᵊl-ən, -iŋ\ *adj* : TRIVIAL, PALTRY ⟨spent a ~ sum⟩

pid·dly \ˈpid-lē\ *adj* : TRIVIAL, PIDDLING

pid·gin \ˈpi-jən\ *n* [fr. *pidgin English,* fr. Chinese Pidgin English *pidgin* business] : a simplified speech used for communication between people with different languages

pie \ˈpī\ *n* : a dish consisting of a pastry crust and a filling (as of fruit or meat)

[1]**pie·bald** \ˈpī-ˌbȯld\ *adj* : of different colors; *esp* : blotched with white and black ⟨a ~ horse⟩

[2]**piebald** *n* : a piebald animal

[1]**piece** \ˈpēs\ *n* **1** : a part of a whole : FRAGMENT, PORTION **2** : one of a group, set, or mass ⟨~*s* of flatware⟩; *also* : a single item or instance ⟨a ~ of nonsense⟩ ⟨a ~ of news⟩ **3** : a movable object used in a board game **4** : a length, weight, or size in which something is made or sold **5** : a product (as an essay) of creative work **6** : FIREARM **7** : COIN

[2]**piece** *vb* **pieced; piec·ing** **1** : to repair or complete by adding pieces : PATCH **2** : to join into a whole

pièce de ré·sis·tance \pē-ˌes-də-rā-ˌzē-ˈstäⁿs\ *n, pl* **pièces de ré·sis·tance** *same*\ [F] **1** : the chief dish of a meal **2** : an outstanding item

piece·meal \ˈpēs-ˌmēl\ *adv or adj* : one piece at a time : GRADUALLY

piece·work \-ˌwərk\ *n* : work done and paid for by the piece — **piece·work·er** *n*

pie chart *n* : a circular chart that shows quantities or frequencies by parts of a circle shaped like pieces of pie

pied \ˈpīd\ *adj* : of two or more colors in blotches : VARIEGATED

pied–à–terre \pē-ˌā-də-ˈter\ *n, pl* **pieds–à–terre** *same*\ [F, lit., foot to the ground] : a temporary or second lodging

pier \ˈpir\ *n* **1** : a support for a bridge span **2** : a structure built out into the water for use as a landing place or a promenade or to protect or form a harbor **3** : an upright supporting part (as a pillar) of a building or structure

pierce \ˈpirs\ *vb* **pierced; pierc·ing** **1** : to enter or thrust into sharply or painfully : STAB **2** : to make a hole in or through : PERFORATE ⟨*pierced* ears⟩ **3** : to force or make a way into or through : PENETRATE **4** : to see through : DISCERN — **pierc·er** *n*

piercing *n* : a piece of jewelry attached to pierced flesh

pies *pl of* PI *or of* PIE

pi·ety \ˈpī-ə-tē\ *n, pl* **pi·et·ies** **1** : fidelity to natural obligations (as to parents) **2** : dutifulness in religion : DEVOUTNESS **3** : a pious act

pif·fle \ˈpi-fəl\ *n* : trifling talk or action

pig \ˈpig\ *n* **1** : SWINE; *esp* : a young domesticated swine **2** : PORK **3** : a dirty, gluttonous, or repulsive person **4** : a crude casting of metal (as iron)

pi·geon \ˈpi-jən\ *n* : any of numerous stout-bodied short-legged birds with smooth thick plumage

[1]**pi·geon·hole** \ˈpi-jən-ˌhōl\ *n* : a small open compartment (as in a desk) for keeping letters or documents

[2]**pigeonhole** *vb* **1** : to place in or as if in a pigeonhole : FILE **2** : to lay aside **3** : to assign to a usu. restrictive category

pi·geon–toed \-ˌtōd\ *adj* : having the toes and forefoot turned inward

pig·gish \ˈpi-gish\ *adj* **1** : GREEDY **2** : STUBBORN

pig·gy·back \ˈpi-gē-ˌbak\ *also* **pick·a·back** \ˈpi-gē-, ˈpi-kə-\ *adv or adj* **1** : up on the back and shoulders **2** : on a railroad flatcar

pig·head·ed \ˈpig-ˈhe-dəd\ *adj* : OBSTINATE, STUBBORN

pig latin *n, often cap L* : a jargon that is made by systematic alteration of English

pig·let \ˈpi-glət\ *n* : a small usu. young swine

pig·ment \ˈpig-mənt\ *n* **1** : coloring matter **2** : a powder mixed with a liquid to give color (as in paints) — **pig·ment·ed** \-mən-təd\ *adj*

pig·men·ta·tion \ˌpig-mən-ˈtā-shən\ *n* : coloration with or deposition of pigment; *esp* : an excessive deposition of bodily pigment

pigmy *var of* PYGMY

pig·nut \ˈpig-ˌnət\ *n* : the bitter nut of any of several hickory trees; *also* : any of these trees

pig·pen \-ˌpen\ *n* **1** : a pen for pigs **2** : a dirty place

pig·skin \-ˌskin\ *n* **1** : the skin of a swine or leather made of it **2** : FOOTBALL 2

pig·sty \-ˌstī\ *n* : PIGPEN

pig·tail \-ˌtāl\ *n* : lock of hair that is gathered and banded or braided together

PII *abbr* personally identifiable information

pi·ka \ˈpē-kə, ˈpī-\ *n* : any of various small short-eared mammals related to the rabbits and occurring in rocky uplands of Asia and western No. America

[1]**pike** \ˈpīk\ *n* : a sharp point or spike

[2]**pike** *n, pl* **pike** *or* **pikes** : a large slender

long-snouted freshwater bony fish valued for food; *also* : any of various related fishes

[3]**pike** *n* : a long wooden shaft with a pointed steel head formerly used as a foot soldier's weapon

[4]**pike** *n* : TURNPIKE

pik·er \ˈpī-kər\ *n* **1** : one who does things in a small way or on a small scale **2** : TIGHTWAD, CHEAPSKATE

pike·staff \ˈpīk-ˌstaf\ *n* : the staff of a foot soldier's pike

pi·laf *also* **pi·laff** \pi-ˈläf, ˈpē-ˌläf\ *or* **pi·lau** \pi-ˈlō, -ˈlȯ, ˈpē-lō, -lȯ\ *n* : a dish made of seasoned rice often with meat

pi·las·ter \pi-ˈlas-tər, ˈpī-ˌlas-tər\ *n* : an architectural support that looks like a rectangular column and projects slightly from a wall

pil·chard \ˈpil-chərd\ *n* : a small European marine fish related to the herrings and often packed as a sardine

[1]**pile** \ˈpī(-ə)l\ *n* : a long slender column (as of wood or steel) driven into the ground to support a vertical load

[2]**pile** *n* **1** : a quantity of things heaped together **2** : PYRE **3** : a great number or quantity : LOT ⟨~*s* of money⟩

[3]**pile** *vb* **piled; pil·ing** **1** : to lay in a pile : STACK **2** : to heap up : ACCUMULATE **3** : to press forward in a mass : CROWD

[4]**pile** *n* : a velvety surface of fine short hairs or threads (as on cloth) — **piled** \ˈpī(-ə)ld\ *adj* — **pile·less** *adj*

piles \ˈpī(-ə)lz\ *n pl* : HEMORRHOIDS

pil·fer \ˈpil-fər\ *vb* : to steal in small quantities ⟨~ pens from work⟩

pil·grim \ˈpil-grəm\ *n* [ME, fr. AF *pelerin, pilegrin,* fr. LL *pelegrinus,* alter. of L *peregrinus* foreigner, fr. *peregrinus* foreign, fr. *peregri* abroad, fr. *per* through + *ager* land] **1** : one who journeys in foreign lands : WAYFARER **2** : one who travels to a shrine or holy place as an act of devotion **3** *cap* : one of the English settlers founding Plymouth colony in 1620

pil·grim·age \-grə-mij\ *n* : a journey of a pilgrim esp. to a shrine or holy place

pil·ing \ˈpī-liŋ\ *n* : a structure of piles

pill \ˈpil\ *n* **1** : a small rounded mass usu. of medicine that is swallowed whole **2** : a disagreeable or tiresome person **3** *often cap* : an oral contraceptive — usu. used with *the*

pil·lage \ˈpi-lij\ *vb* **pil·laged; pil·lag·ing** : to take booty : LOOT, PLUNDER — **pillage** *n* — **pil·lag·er** *n*

pil·lar \ˈpi-lər\ *n* **1** : a strong upright support (as for a roof) **2** : a column or shaft standing alone esp. as a monument 3 : an integral or upstanding member or part **4** : a fundamental tenet ⟨the five ~*s* of Islam⟩ — **pil·lared** \-lərd\ *adj*

pill·box \ˈpil-ˌbäks\ *n* **1** : a shallow round box for pills **2** : a low concrete emplacement esp. for machine guns

pil·lion \ˈpil-yən\ *n* **1** : a pad or cushion placed behind a saddle for an extra rider **2** *chiefly Brit* : a motorcycle or bicycle saddle for a passenger

[1]**pil·lo·ry** \ˈpi-lə-rē\ *n, pl* **-ries** : a wooden frame for public punishment having holes in which the head and hands can be locked

[2]**pillory** *vb* **-ried; -ry·ing** **1** : to set in a pillory **2** : to expose to public scorn

[1]**pil·low** \ˈpi-lō\ *n* : a case filled with springy material (as feathers) and used to support the head of a resting person

[2]**pillow** *vb* : to rest or place on or as if on a pillow; *also* : to serve as a pillow for

pil·low·case \-ˌkās\ *n* : a removable covering for a pillow

[1]**pi·lot** \ˈpī-lət\ *n* **1** : HELMSMAN, STEERSMAN **2** : a person qualified and licensed to take ships into and out of a port **3** : GUIDE, LEADER **4** : one that flies an aircraft or spacecraft **5** : a television show filmed or taped as a sample of a proposed series — **pi·lot·less** *adj*

[2]**pilot** *vb* : CONDUCT, GUIDE; *esp* : to act as pilot of ⟨~ a ship⟩

[3]**pilot** *adj* : serving as a guiding or activating device or as a testing or trial unit ⟨a ~ light⟩ ⟨a ~ factory⟩

pi·lot·house \ˈpī-lət-ˌhau̇s\ *n* : a shelter on the upper deck of a ship for the steering gear and the helmsman

pilot whale *n* : either of two mostly black medium-sized whales

pil·sner *also* **pil·sen·er** \ˈpilz-nər, ˈpil-zə-\ *n* [G, lit., of Pilsen (Plzeň), city in the Czech Republic] **1** : a light beer with a strong flavor of hops **2** : a tall slender footed glass for beer

pi·men·to \pə-ˈmen-tō\ *n, pl* **pimentos** *or* **pimento** [Sp *pimienta* allspice, pepper, fr. LL *pigmenta,* pl. of *pigmentum* plant juice, fr. L, pigment] **1** : ALLSPICE **2** : PIMIENTO

pi·mien·to \pə-ˈmen-tō\ *n, pl* **-tos** : any of various mild red sweet pepper fruits used esp. to stuff olives and to make paprika

pimp \ˈpimp\ *n* : a criminal who lives off the earnings of and usu. exerts control over one or more prostitutes — **pimp** *vb*

pim·per·nel \ˈpim-pər-ˌnel, -nəl\ *n* : any of a genus of herbs related to the primroses

pim·ple \ˈpim-pəl\ *n* : a small inflamed swelling on the skin often containing pus — **pim·ply** \-p(ə-)lē\ *adj*

[1]**pin** \ˈpin\ *n* **1** : a piece of wood or metal used esp. for fastening things together or as a support by which one thing may be suspended from another; *esp* : a small pointed piece of wire with a head used for fastening clothes or attaching papers **2** : an ornament or emblem fastened to clothing with a pin **3** : one of the pieces constituting the target (as in bowling); *also* : the staff of the flag marking a hole on a golf course **4** : LEG

[2]**pin** *vb* **pinned; pin·ning** **1** : to fasten, join, or secure with a pin **2** : to hold fast or immobile **3** : ATTACH, HANG ⟨*pinned* their hopes on a miracle⟩ **4** : to assign the blame for ⟨~ a crime on someone⟩ **5** : to define clearly : ESTABLISH ⟨~ down an idea⟩

PIN *abbr* personal identification number

pi·ña co·la·da \ˌpēn-yə-kō-ˈlä-də, ˌpē-nə-\ *n* [Sp, lit., strained pineapple] : a tall

drink made of rum, cream of coconut, and pineapple juice mixed with ice
pin·afore \ˈpi-nə-ˌfōr\ *n* : a sleeveless dress or apron fastened at the back
pin·ball machine \ˈpin-ˌbȯl-\ *n* : an amusement device in which a ball is maneuvered along a slanted surface among a series of targets for points
pince–nez \paⁿs-ˈnā\ *n, pl* **pince–nez** *same or* -ˈnāz\ [F, fr. *pincer* to pinch + *nez* nose] : eyeglasses clipped to the nose by a spring
pin·cer \ˈpin-sər\ *n* **1** *pl* : a gripping instrument with two handles and two grasping jaws **2** : a claw (as of a lobster) resembling pincers
[1]**pinch** \ˈpinch\ *vb* [ME, fr. AF **pincher, pincer,* fr. VL **pinctiare,* **punctiare,* fr. L *punctum* puncture] **1** : to squeeze between the finger and thumb or between the jaws of an instrument **2** : to compress painfully **3** : CONTRACT, SHRIVEL **4** : to be miserly; *also* : to subject to strict economy **5** : to confine or limit narrowly **6** : STEAL **7** : ARREST
[2]**pinch** *n* **1** : a critical point : EMERGENCY **2** : painful effect **3** : an act of pinching **4** : a very small quantity **5** : ARREST
[3]**pinch** *adj* : SUBSTITUTE ⟨a ~ runner⟩
pinch–hit \ˌpinch-ˈhit\ *vb* **1** : to bat in the place of another player esp. when a hit is particularly needed **2** : to act or serve in place of another — **pinch hit** *n* — **pinch hitter** *n*
pin curl *n* : a curl made usu. by dampening a strand of hair, coiling it, and securing it by a hairpin or clip
pin·cush·ion \ˈpin-ˌku̇-shən\ *n* : a cushion for pins not in use
[1]**pine** \ˈpīn\ *n* : any of a genus of evergreen cone-bearing trees; *also* : the light durable resinous wood of a pine
[2]**pine** *vb* **pined; pin·ing** **1** : to lose vigor or health through distress **2** : to long for something intensely ⟨*pined* for home⟩
pi·ne·al \ˈpī-nē-əl, pī-ˈnē-əl\ *n* : PINEAL GLAND — **pineal** *adj*
pineal gland *n* : a small usu. conical appendage of the brain of all vertebrates with a cranium that functions primarily as an endocrine organ
pine·ap·ple \ˈpīn-ˌa-pəl\ *n* : a tropical plant bearing a large edible juicy fruit; *also* : its fruit
pin·feath·er \ˈpin-ˌfe-t͟hər\ *n* : a new feather just coming through the skin
ping \ˈpiŋ\ *n* **1** : a sharp sound like that of a bullet striking **2** : engine knock
pin·hole \ˈpin-ˌhōl\ *n* : a small hole made by, for, or as if by a pin
[1]**pin·ion** \ˈpin-yən\ *n* : the end section of a bird's wing; *also* : WING
[2]**pinion** *vb* : to restrain by binding the arms; *also* : SHACKLE
[3]**pinion** *n* : a gear with a small number of teeth designed to mesh with a larger wheel or rack
[1]**pink** \ˈpiŋk\ *n* **1** : any of a genus of plants with narrow leaves often grown for their showy flowers **2** : the highest degree : HEIGHT ⟨the ~ of condition⟩
[2]**pink** *n* : a light tint of red
[3]**pink** *adj* **1** : of the color pink **2** : holding socialistic views — **pink·ish** *adj*
[4]**pink** *vb* **1** : to perforate in an ornamental pattern **2** : PIERCE, STAB **3** : to cut a saw-toothed edge on
pink·eye \ˈpiŋk-ˌī\ *n* : an acute contagious eye inflammation
pin·kie *or* **pin·ky** \ˈpiŋ-kē\ *n, pl* **pinkies** : the smallest finger of the hand
pin·nace \ˈpi-nəs\ *n* **1** : a light sailing ship **2** : a ship's boat
pin·na·cle \ˈpi-ni-kəl\ *n* [ME *pinacle,* fr. AF, fr. LL *pinnaculum* small wing, gable, fr. L *pinna* wing, battlement] **1** : a turret ending in a small spire **2** : a lofty peak **3** : ACME
pin·nate \ˈpi-ˌnāt\ *adj* : resembling a feather esp. in having similar parts arranged on each side of an axis ⟨a ~ leaf⟩
pi·noch·le \ˈpē-ˌnə-kəl\ *n* : a card game played with a 48-card deck
pi·ñon *or* **pin·yon** \ˈpin-ˌyōn, -ˌyän\ *n, pl* **pi·ñons** *or* **pin·yons** *or* **pi·ño·nes** \pin-ˈyō-nēz\ [AmerSp *piñón*] : any of various small pines of western No. America with edible seeds; *also* : the edible seed of a piñon
pin·point \ˈpin-ˌpȯint\ *vb* : to locate, hit, or aim with great precision
pin·prick \-ˌprik\ *n* **1** : a small puncture made by or as if by a pin **2** : a petty irritation or annoyance
pins and needles *n pl* : a pricking tingling sensation in a limb growing numb or recovering from numbness — **on pins and needles** : in a nervous or jumpy state of anticipation
pin·stripe \ˈpin-ˌstrīp\ *n* : a narrow stripe on a fabric; *also* : a suit with such stripes — **pin–striped** \-ˌstrīpt\ *adj*
pint \ˈpīnt\ *n* — see WEIGHT table
pin·to \ˈpin-ˌtō\ *n, pl* **pintos** *also* **pintoes** : a spotted horse or pony
pinto bean *n* : a spotted seed produced by a kind of kidney bean and used for food
pin·up \ˈpin-ˌəp\ *adj* : suitable or designed for hanging on a wall; *also* : suited (as by beauty) to be the subject of a pinup photograph
pin·wheel \-ˌhwēl, -ˌwēl\ *n* **1** : a fireworks device in the form of a revolving wheel of colored fire **2** : a toy consisting of lightweight vanes that revolve at the end of a stick
pin·worm \-ˌwərm\ *n* : a nematode worm parasitic in the human intestine
pin·yin \ˈpin-ˈyin\ *n, often cap* : a system for writing Chinese ideograms by using Roman letters to represent the sounds
[1]**pi·o·neer** \ˌpī-ə-ˈnir\ *n* **1** : one that originates or helps open up a new line of thought or activity **2** : an early settler in a territory
[2]**pioneer** *vb* **1** : to act as a pioneer **2** : to open or prepare for others to follow ⟨~*ed* a new treatment⟩; *also* : SETTLE
pi·ous \ˈpī-əs\ *adj* **1** : marked by reverence for deity : DEVOUT **2** : excessively or affectedly religious **3** : SACRED, DE-

VOTIONAL **4** : showing loyal reverence for a person or thing : DUTIFUL **5** : marked by sham or hypocrisy ⟨~ hypocrites⟩ — **pi·ous·ly** *adv*

¹pip \ˈpip\ *n* : one of the dots used on dice and dominoes to indicate numerical value

²pip *n* : a small fruit seed (as of an apple)

¹pipe \ˈpīp\ *n* **1** : a tubular musical instrument played by forcing air through it **2** : BAGPIPE **3** : a tube designed to conduct something (as water, steam, or oil) **4** : a device for smoking having a tube with a bowl at one end and a mouthpiece at the other **5** : a means of transmission (as of computer data)

²pipe *vb* **piped; pip·ing** **1** : to play on a pipe **2** : to speak in a high or shrill voice **3** : to convey by or as if by pipes — **pip·er** *n*

pipe down *vb* : to stop talking or making noise

pipe dream *n* : an illusory or fantastic hope

pipe·line \ˈpīp-ˌlīn\ *n* **1** : a line of pipe with pumps, valves, and control devices for conveying fluids **2** : a channel for information **3** : PIPE 5

pi·pette *or* **pi·pet** \pī-ˈpet\ *n* : a device for measuring and transferring small volumes of liquid

pipe up *vb* : to speak loudly and distinctly; *also* : to express an opinion freely

pip·ing \ˈpī-piŋ\ *n* **1** : the music of pipes **2** : a narrow fold of material used to decorate edges or seams

piping hot *adj* : very hot

pip·pin \ˈpi-pən\ *n* : a crisp tart usu. yellowish apple

pip–squeak \ˈpip-ˌskwēk\ *n* : one that is small or insignificant

pi·quant \ˈpē-kənt\ *adj* **1** : pleasantly savory : PUNGENT ⟨a ~ sauce⟩ **2** : engagingly provocative; *also* : having a lively charm — **pi·quan·cy** \-kən-sē\ *n*

¹pique \ˈpēk\ *n* [F] : a passing feeling of wounded vanity : RESENTMENT

²pique *vb* **piqued; piqu·ing** **1** : IRRITATE 1 **2** : to arouse by a provocation or challenge : GOAD

pi·qué *or* **pi·que** \pi-ˈkā\ *n* : a durable ribbed clothing fabric

pi·quet \pi-ˈkā\ *n* : a 2-handed card game played with 32 cards

pi·ra·cy \ˈpī-rə-sē\ *n, pl* **-cies** **1** : robbery on the high seas; *also* : an act resembling such robbery **2** : the unauthorized use of another's production or invention

pi·ra·nha \pə-ˈrä-nə, -ˈrän-yə\ *n* [Pg, fr. Tupi (Indigenous language of Brazil) *pirãja,* fr. *pirá* fish + *ãja* tooth] : any of various usu. small So. American fishes with sharp teeth that include some known to attack humans and large animals

pi·rate \ˈpī-rət\ *n* [ME, fr. MF or L; MF, fr. L *pirata,* fr. Gk *peiratēs,* fr. *peiran* to attempt, test] : one who commits piracy — **pirate** *vb* — **pi·rat·i·cal** \pə-ˈra-ti-kəl, pī-\ *adj*

pir·ou·ette \ˌpir-ə-ˈwet\ *n* [F] : a rapid whirling about of the body; *esp* : a full turn on the toe or ball of one foot in ballet — **pirouette** *vb*

pis *pl of* PI

pis·ca·to·ri·al \ˌpis-kə-ˈtōr-ē-əl\ *adj* : of or relating to fishing

Pi·sces \ˈpī-sēz\ *n* [ME, fr. L, lit., fishes] **1** : a zodiacal constellation between Aquarius and Aries usu. pictured as a fish **2** : the 12th sign of the zodiac in astrology; *also* : one born under this sign

pis·mire \ˈpis-ˌmī(-ə)r\ *n* : ANT

pi·so \ˈpē-(ˌ)sō\ *n* : the peso of the Philippines

pis·ta·chio \pə-ˈsta-shē-ˌō, -ˈstä-\ *n, pl* **-chios** : the greenish edible seed of a small Asian tree related to the sumacs; *also* : the tree

pis·til \ˈpis-tᵊl\ *n* : the female reproductive organ in a flower — **pis·til·late** \ˈpis-tə-ˌlāt\ *adj*

pis·tol \ˈpis-tᵊl\ *n* : a handgun whose chamber is integral with the barrel

pis·tol–whip \-ˌhwip\ *vb* : to beat with a pistol

pis·ton \ˈpis-tən\ *n* : a sliding piece that receives and transmits motion and that usu. consists of a short cylinder inside a large cylinder

¹pit \ˈpit\ *n* **1** : a hole, shaft, or cavity in the ground **2** : an often sunken area designed for a particular use; *also* : an enclosed place (as for cockfights) **3** : HELL; *also, pl* : WORST ⟨it's the ~*s*⟩ **4** : a natural hollow or indentation in a surface **5** : a small indented mark or scar (as from disease or corrosion) **6** : an area beside a racecourse where cars are fueled and repaired during a race

²pit *vb* **pit·ted; pit·ting** **1** : to form pits in or become marred with pits **2** : to match for fighting

³pit *n* : the stony seed of some fruits (as the cherry, peach, and date)

⁴pit *vb* **pit·ted; pit·ting** : to remove the pit from

pi·ta \ˈpē-tə\ *n* [ModGk] : a thin flat bread

pit–a–pat \ˌpi-ti-ˈpat\ *n* : PITTER-PATTER — **pit–a–pat** *adv or adj*

pit bull *n* : a powerful compact short-haired dog developed for fighting

¹pitch \ˈpich\ *n* **1** : a dark sticky substance left over esp. from distilling tar or petroleum **2** : resin from various conifers — **pitchy** *adj*

²pitch *vb* **1** : to erect and fix firmly in place ⟨~ a tent⟩ **2** : THROW, FLING **3** : to deliver a baseball to a batter **4** : to toss (as coins) toward a mark **5** : to set at a particular level ⟨~ the voice low⟩ **6** : to fall headlong **7** : to have the front end (as of a ship) alternately plunge and rise **8** : to incline downward : SLOPE

³pitch *n* **1** : the action or a manner of pitching **2** : degree of slope ⟨~ of a roof⟩ **3** : the relative level of some quality or state ⟨a high ~ of excitement⟩ **4** : highness or lowness of sound; *also* : a standard frequency for tuning instruments **5** : a presentation delivered to sell or promote something **6** : the delivery of a baseball to a batter; *also* : the baseball delivered

pitch·blende \ˈpich-ˌblend\ *n* : a dark mineral that is the chief source of uranium

¹**pitch·er** \ˈpi-chər\ *n* : a container for liquids that usu. has a lip and a handle

²**pitcher** *n* : one that pitches esp. in a baseball game

pitcher plant *n* : any of various plants with leaves modified to resemble pitchers in which insects are trapped and digested

pitch·fork \ˈpich-ˌfȯrk\ *n* : a long-handled fork used esp. in pitching hay

pitch in *vb* **1** : to begin to work **2** : to contribute to a common effort

pitch·man \ˈpich-mən\ *n* : SALESMAN; *esp* : one who sells merchandise on the streets or from a concession

pitch–per·fect \ˈpich-ˈpər-fikt\ *adj* : having just the right tone or style ⟨a ~ translation⟩

pit·e·ous \ˈpi-tē-əs\ *adj* : arousing pity : PITIFUL — **pit·e·ous·ly** *adv*

pit·fall \ˈpit-ˌfȯl\ *n* **1** : TRAP, SNARE; *esp* : a covered pit used for capturing animals **2** : a hidden danger or difficulty

pith \ˈpith\ *n* **1** : loose spongy tissue esp. in the center of the stem of vascular plants **2** : the essential part : CORE

pithy \ˈpi-thē\ *adj* **pith·i·er; -est** **1** : consisting of or filled with pith **2** : having substance and point : CONCISE

piti·able \ˈpi-tē-ə-bəl\ *adj* : PITIFUL

piti·ful \ˈpi-ti-fəl\ *adj* **1** : arousing or deserving pity ⟨a ~ sight⟩ **2** : lamentably inadequate : MEAGER — **piti·ful·ly** *adv*

piti·less \ˈpi-ti-ləs\ *adj* : devoid of pity : HARSH, CRUEL — **pit·i·less·ly** *adv*

pi·ton \ˈpē-ˌtän\ *n* [F] : a spike, wedge, or peg that can be driven into a rock or ice surface as a support

pit·tance \ˈpi-tᵊns\ *n* : a small portion, amount, or allowance

pit·ted \ˈpi-təd\ *adj* : marked with pits

pit·ter–pat·ter \ˈpi-tər-ˌpa-tər, ˈpi-tē-\ *n* : a rapid succession of light taps or sounds ⟨the ~ of rain⟩ — **pitter–patter** \ˌpi-tər-ˈpa-tər, ˌpi-tē-\ *adv or adj* — **pitter–patter** *same as adv*\ *vb*

pi·tu·i·tary \pə-ˈtü-ə-ˌter-ē, -ˈtyü-\ *n, pl* **-itar·ies** : PITUITARY GLAND — **pituitary** *adj*

pituitary gland *n* : a small oval endocrine gland located at the base of the brain that produces various hormones that affect most basic bodily functions (as growth and reproduction)

pit viper *n* : any of various mostly New World venomous snakes with a sensory pit on each side of the head and hollow perforated fangs

¹**pity** \ˈpi-tē\ *n, pl* **pit·ies** [ME *pite,* fr. AF *pité,* fr. L *pietas* piety, pity, fr. *pius* pious] **1** : sympathetic sorrow : COMPASSION **2** : something to be regretted

²**pity** *vb* **pit·ied; pity·ing** : to feel pity for

¹**piv·ot** \ˈpi-vət\ *n* **1** : a fixed pin on which something turns **2 a** : a central member, part, or point **b** : an essential player or position **3** : the action of pivoting **4** : a usu. marked change — **pivot** *adj*

²**pivot** *vb* **1** : to turn on or as if on a pivot **2** : to adapt or improve by adjusting or modifying

piv·ot·al \ˈpi-və-tᵊl\ *adj* **1** : of or relating to a pivot **2** : vitally important : CRITICAL ⟨a ~ decision⟩

pix *pl of* PIC

pix·el \ˈpik-səl, -ˌsel\ *n* **1** : any of the small elements that together make up an image (as on a television screen) **2** : any of the detecting elements of a charge-coupled device used as an optical sensor

pix·ie *also* **pixy** \ˈpik-sē\ *n, pl* **pix·ies** : FAIRY; *esp* : a mischievous sprite

piz·za \ˈpēt-sə\ *n* [It] : an open pie made of rolled bread dough spread with a spiced mixture (as of tomatoes, cheese, and ground meat) and baked

piz·zazz *or* **pi·zazz** \pə-ˈzaz\ *n* **1** : GLAMOUR **2** : VITALITY

piz·ze·ria \ˌpēt-sə-ˈrē-ə\ *n* : an establishment where pizzas are made and sold

piz·zi·ca·to \ˌpit-si-ˈkä-tō\ *adv or adj* [It] : by means of plucking instead of bowing — used as a direction in music

pj's \ˈpē-ˌjāz\ *n pl* : PAJAMAS

pk *abbr* **1** park **2** peak **3** peck **4** pike

pkg *abbr* package

pkt *abbr* **1** packet **2** pocket

pkwy *abbr* parkway

pl *abbr* **1** place **2** plate **3** plural

¹**plac·ard** \ˈpla-kərd, -ˌkärd\ *n* : a notice posted in a public place : POSTER

²**plac·ard** \-ˌkärd, -kərd\ *vb* **1** : to cover with or as if with placards **2** : to announce by or as if by posting

pla·cate \ˈplā-ˌkāt, ˈpla-\ *vb* **pla·cat·ed; pla·cat·ing** : to soothe esp. by concessions : APPEASE — **pla·ca·ble** \ˈpla-kə-bəl, ˈplā-\ *adj*

¹**place** \ˈplās\ *n* [ME, fr. AF, open space, fr. L *platea* broad street, fr. Gk *plateia* (*hodos*), fr. fem. of *platys* broad, flat] **1** : SPACE, ROOM **2** : an indefinite region : AREA **3** : a building or locality used for a special purpose **4** : a center of population **5** : a particular part of a surface : SPOT **6** : relative position in a scale or sequence; *also* : position at the end of a competition ⟨last ~⟩ **7** : ACCOMMODATION; *esp* : SEAT **8** : the position of a figure within a numeral ⟨12 is a two ~ number⟩ **9** : JOB; *esp* : public office **10** : a public square **11** : 2d place at the finish (as of a horse race) — **in place of** : INSTEAD OF — **out of place** : not in the proper location : INAPPROPRIATE

²**place** *vb* **placed; plac·ing** **1** : to put in a particular place : SET **2** : to distribute in an orderly manner : ARRANGE **3** : IDENTIFY **4** : to give an order for ⟨~ a bet⟩ **5** : to earn a given spot in a competition; *esp* : to come in 2d

pla·ce·bo \plə-ˈsē-bō\ *n, pl* **-bos** [L, I shall please] : an inert medication used for its psychological effect or for purposes of comparison in an experiment

place·hold·er \ˈplās-ˌhōl-dər\ *n* : a symbol in a mathematical or logical expression that may be replaced by the name of any element of a set

place·kick \-ˌkik\ *n* : the kicking of a ball placed or held on the ground — **place-kick** *vb* — **place·kick·er** *n*

place·ment \ˈplās-mənt\ *n* : an act or instance of placing

place–name \-ˌnām\ *n* : the name of a geographical locality

pla·cen·ta \plə-ˈsen-tə\ *n, pl* **-tas** *or* **-tae** \-(ˌ)tē\ [NL, fr. L, flat cake] : the organ in most mammals by which the fetus is joined to the maternal uterus and is nourished — **pla·cen·tal** \-ˈsen-tᵊl\ *adj or n*

plac·er \ˈpla-sər\ *n* : a deposit of sand or gravel containing particles of valuable mineral (as gold)

plac·id \ˈpla-səd\ *adj* : UNDISTURBED, PEACEFUL ♦ ***Synonyms*** TRANQUIL, SERENE, CALM — **pla·cid·i·ty** \pla-ˈsi-də-tē\ *n* — **plac·id·ly** *adv*

plack·et \ˈpla-kət\ *n* : a slit in a garment

pla·gia·rise *Brit var of* PLAGIARIZE

pla·gia·rize \ˈplā-jə-ˌrīz\ *vb* **-rized; -riz·ing** : to present the ideas or words of another as one's own — **pla·gia·rism** \-ˌri-zəm\ *n* — **pla·gia·rist** \-rist\ *n*

[1]**plague** \ˈplāg\ *n* **1** : a disastrous evil or influx; *also* : NUISANCE **2** : PESTILENCE; *esp* : a destructive contagious bacterial disease (as bubonic plague)

[2]**plague** *vb* **plagued; plagu·ing** **1** : to afflict with or as if with disease or disaster **2** : TEASE, TORMENT ⟨*plagued* by guilt⟩

plaid \ˈplad\ *n* [ScGael *plaide*] **1** : a rectangular length of tartan worn esp. over the left shoulder as part of the Scottish national costume **2** : a twilled woolen fabric with a tartan pattern **3** : a pattern of unevenly spaced repeated stripes crossing at right angles — **plaid** *adj*

[1]**plain** \ˈplān\ *n* : an extensive area of level or rolling treeless country

[2]**plain** *adj* **1** : lacking ornament ⟨a ~ dress⟩ **2** : free of extraneous matter **3** : OPEN, UNOBSTRUCTED ⟨~ view⟩ **4** : EVIDENT, OBVIOUS **5** : easily understood : CLEAR **6** : CANDID, BLUNT **7** : SIMPLE, UNCOMPLICATED ⟨~ cooking⟩ **8** : lacking beauty or ugliness — **plain·ly** *adv* — **plain·ness** *n*

plain·clothes·man \ˈplān-ˈklōthz-mən, -ˈklōz-, -ˌman\ *n* : a police officer who wears civilian clothes instead of a uniform while on duty : DETECTIVE

plain·spo·ken \-ˈspō-kən\ *adj* : FRANK

plaint \ˈplānt\ *n* **1** : LAMENTATION, WAIL **2** : PROTEST, COMPLAINT

plain·tiff \ˈplān-təf\ *n* : the complaining party in a lawsuit

plain·tive \ˈplān-tiv\ *adj* : expressive of suffering or woe : MELANCHOLY ⟨a ~ sigh⟩ — **plain·tive·ly** *adv*

plait \ˈplāt, ˈplat\ *n* **1** : PLEAT **2** : a braid esp. of hair or straw — **plait** *vb*

[1]**plan** \ˈplan\ *n* **1** : a drawing or diagram showing the parts or details of something **2** : a method for accomplishing an objective; *also* : GOAL, AIM

[2]**plan** *vb* **planned; plan·ning** **1** : to form a plan of ⟨~ a new city⟩ **2** : INTEND ⟨*planned* to go⟩ — **plan·ner** *n*

[1]**plane** \ˈplān\ *vb* **planed; plan·ing** : to smooth or level off with or as if with a plane — **plan·er** *n*

[2]**plane** *n* : PLANE TREE

[3]**plane** *n* : a tool for smoothing or shaping a wood surface

[4]**plane** *n* **1** : a level or flat surface **2** : a level of existence, consciousness, or development **3** : AIRPLANE

[5]**plane** *adj* **1** : FLAT, LEVEL **2** : dealing with flat surfaces or figures ⟨~ geometry⟩

plane·load \ˈplān-ˌlōd\ *n* : a load that fills an airplane

bottom of this page **plan·et** \ˈpla-nət\ *n* [ME *planete,* fr. AF, fr. LL *planeta,* fr. Gk *planēt-, planēs,* lit., wanderer, fr. *planasthai* to wander] : any of the large bodies in the solar system that revolve around the sun — **plan·e·tary** \-nə-ˌter-ē\ *adj*

plan·e·tar·i·um \ˌpla-nə-ˈter-ē-əm\ *n, pl* **-i·ums** *or* **-ia** \-ē-ə\ : a building or room housing a device to project images of celestial bodies

plan·e·tes·i·mal \ˌpla-nə-ˈtes-ə-məl\ *n* : any of numerous small solid celestial bodies which may have existed during the formation of the solar system

plan·e·toid \ˈpla-nə-ˌtȯid\ *n* : a body resembling a planet; *esp* : ASTEROID

plane tree *n* : any of a genus of trees (as a sycamore) with large lobed leaves and globe-shaped fruit

plan·gent \ˈplan-jənt\ *adj* **1** : having a loud reverberating sound ⟨a ~ roar⟩ **2** : having an expressive esp. plaintive quality ⟨~ lyrics⟩ — **plan·gen·cy** \-jən-sē\ *n*

[1]**plank** \ˈplaŋk\ *n* **1** : a heavy thick board **2** : an article in the platform of a political party

[2]**plank** *vb* **1** : to cover with planks **2** : to set or lay down forcibly **3** : to cook and serve on a board

plank·ing \ˈplaŋ-kiŋ\ *n* : a quantity or covering of planks

plank·ton \ˈplaŋk-tən\ *n* [G, fr. Gk, neut. of *planktos* drifting] : the passively floating or weakly swimming animal and plant life of a body of water — **plank·ton·ic** \plaŋk-ˈtä-nik\ *adj*

[1]**plant** \ˈplant\ *vb* **1** : to set in the ground to grow **2** : ESTABLISH, SETTLE **3** : to stock or provide with something **4** : to place firmly or forcibly **5** : to hide or arrange with intent to deceive

[2]**plant** *n* **1** : any of a kingdom of living things that usu. have no locomotor ability or obvious sense organs and have cellulose cell walls and usu. capacity for indefinite growth **2** : the land, buildings, and machinery used in carrying on a trade or business

[1]**plan·tain** \ˈplan-tᵊn\ *n* [ME, fr. AF, fr. L *plantagin-, plantago,* fr. *planta* sole of the foot; fr. its broad leaves] : any of a genus of weedy herbs with spikes of tiny greenish flowers

[2]**plantain** *n* [Sp *plántano, plátano* plane tree, banana tree, fr. ML *plantanus* plane tree, alter. of L *platanus*] : a banana plant with starchy greenish fruit that is eaten cooked; *also* : its fruit

plan·tar \ˈplan-tər, -ˌtär\ *adj* : of or relating to the sole of the foot

plan·ta·tion \plan-ˈtā-shən\ *n* **1** : a large group of plants and esp. trees under cultivation **2** : an agricultural estate usu. worked by resident laborers

plant·er \ˈplan-tər\ *n* **1** : one that plants or sows; *esp* : an owner or operator of a plantation **2** : a container for plants

plant louse *n* : APHID

plaque \ˈplak\ *n* [F] **1** : an ornamental brooch **2** : a flat thin piece (as of metal) used for decoration; *also* : a commemorative tablet **3** : a bacteria-containing film on a tooth

plash \ˈplash\ *n* : SPLASH — **plash** *vb*

plas·ma \ˈplaz-mə\ *n* **1** : the fluid part of blood, lymph, or milk **2** : a gas composed of ionized particles **3** : a display (as a television screen) in which cells of plasma emit light upon receiving an electric current — **plas·mat·ic** \plaz-ˈma-tik\ *adj*

¹**plas·ter** \ˈplas-tər\ *n* **1** : a dressing consisting of a backing spread with an often medicated substance that clings to the skin ⟨adhesive ~⟩ **2** : a paste that hardens as it dries and is used for coating walls and ceilings

²**plaster** *vb* : to cover with or as if with plaster — **plas·ter·er** *n*

plas·ter·board \ˈplas-tər-ˌbȯrd\ *n* : DRYWALL

plaster of par·is \-ˈpa-rəs\ *often cap 2d P* : a white powder made from gypsum and used as a quick-setting paste with water for casts and molds

¹**plas·tic** \ˈplas-tik\ *adj* [L *plasticus* of molding, fr. Gk *plastikos,* fr. *plassein* to mold, form] **1** : capable of being molded ⟨~ clay⟩ **2** : characterized by or using modeling ⟨~ arts⟩ **3** : made or consisting of a plastic ♦ ***Synonyms*** PLIABLE, PLIANT, DUCTILE, MALLEABLE, ADAPTABLE — **plas·tic·i·ty** \plas-ˈti-sə-tē\ *n*

²**plastic** *n* : a plastic substance; *esp* : a synthetic or processed material that can be formed into rigid objects or into films or filaments

plastic surgery *n* : surgery to repair, restore, or improve lost, injured, defective, or misshapen body parts — **plastic surgeon** *n*

¹**plat** \ˈplat\ *n* **1** : a small plot of ground **2** : a plan of a piece of land with actual or proposed features (as lots)

²**plat** *vb* **plat·ted; plat·ting** : to make a plat of

¹**plate** \ˈplāt\ *n* **1** : a flat thin piece of material **2** : domestic hollowware made of or plated with gold, silver, or base metals **3** : DISH **4** : HOME PLATE **5** : the molded metal or plastic cast of a page of type to be printed from **6** : a sheet of glass or plastic coated with a chemical sensitive to light and used in photography **7** : the part of a denture that fits to the mouth; *also* : DENTURE **8** : something printed from an engraving **9** : a huge mobile segment of the earth's crust

²**plate** *vb* **plat·ed; plat·ing** **1** : to overlay with metal (as gold or silver) **2** : to make a printing plate of

pla·teau \pla-ˈtō\ *n, pl* **plateaus** *or* **pla·teaux** \-ˈtōz\ [F] : a large level area of high land

plate glass *n* : rolled, ground, and polished sheet glass

plate·let \ˈplāt-lət\ *n* : a minute flattened body; *esp* : a minute colorless disklike body of mammalian blood that assists in blood clotting

plat·en \ˈpla-tᵊn\ *n* **1** : a flat plate; *esp* : one that exerts or receives pressure (as in a printing press) **2** : the roller of a typewriter or printer

plate tectonics *n* **1** : a theory in geology that the lithosphere is divided into plates at the boundaries of which much of earth's seismic activity occurs **2** : the process and dynamics of tectonic plate movement — **plate–tectonic** *adj*

plat·form \ˈplat-ˌfȯrm\ *n* **1** : a raised flooring or stage for speakers, performers, or workers **2** : a declaration of the principles on which a group of persons (as a political party) stands **3** : a means or opportunity to communicate ideas or information to a group of people **4** : OPERATING SYSTEM

plat·ing \ˈplā-tiŋ\ *n* : a coating of metal plates or plate ⟨the ~ of a ship⟩

plat·i·num \ˈpla-tə-nəm\ *n* : a heavy grayish white metallic chemical element

plat·i·tude \ˈpla-tə-ˌtüd, -ˌtyüd\ *n* : a flat or trite remark — **plat·i·tu·di·nous** \-ˈtü-də-nəs, -ˈtyü-\ *adj*

pla·ton·ic love \plə-ˈtä-nik-, plā-\ *n, often cap P* : a close relationship between two persons without sexual desire

pla·toon \plə-ˈtün\ *n* [F *peloton* small detachment, lit., ball, fr. *pelote* little ball] **1** : a subdivision of a company-size military unit usu. consisting of two or more squads or sections **2** : a group of football players trained either for offense or for defense and sent into the game as a body

platoon sergeant *n* : a noncommissioned officer in the army ranking below a first sergeant

plat·ter \ˈpla-tər\ *n* **1** : a large serving plate **2** : a phonograph record

platy \ˈpla-tē\ *n, pl* **platy** *or* **plat·ys** *or* **plat·ies** : either of two small stocky usu. brilliantly colored bony fishes often kept in tropical aquariums

platy·pus \ˈpla-ti-pəs\ *n, pl* **platy·pus·es** *also* **platy·pi** \-ˌpī\ [NL, fr. Gk *platypous* flat-footed, fr. *platys* broad, flat + *pous* foot] : a small aquatic egg-laying marsupial mammal of Australia with webbed feet and a fleshy bill like a duck's

plau·dit \ˈplȯ-dət\ *n* : an act of applause

plau·si·ble \ˈplȯ-zə-bəl\ *adj* [L *plausibilis* worthy of applause, fr. *plausus,* pp. of *plaudere* to applaud] : seemingly worthy of belief — **plau·si·bil·i·ty** \ˌplȯ-zə-ˈbi-lə-tē\ *n* — **plau·si·bly** \ˈplȯ-zə-blē\ *adv*

¹**play** \ˈplā\ *n* **1** : brisk handling of something (as a weapon) **2** : the course of a game; *also* : a particular act or maneuver in a game **3** : recreational activity; *esp* : the spontaneous activity of children **4** : JEST ⟨said in ~⟩ **5** : the act or an in-

stance of punning **6** : GAMBLING **7** : OPERATION ⟨bring extra force into ~⟩ **8** : a brisk or light movement **9** : free motion (as of part of a machine) **10** : scope for action **11** : PUBLICITY **12** : an effort to arouse liking ⟨made a ~ for her⟩ **13** : a stage representation of a drama; *also* : a dramatic composition **14** : a function of an electronic device that causes a recording to play — **play·ful** \-fəl\ *adj* — **play·ful·ly** *adv* — **play·ful·ness** *n* — **in play** : in condition or position to be played

[2]**play** *vb* **1** : to engage in recreation : FROLIC **2** : to handle or behave lightly or absentmindedly **3** : to make a pun ⟨~ on words⟩ **4** : to take advantage ⟨~ on fears⟩ **5** : to move or operate in a brisk or irregular manner ⟨a flashlight ~*ed* over the wall⟩ **6** : to perform music ⟨~ on a violin⟩; *also* : to perform (music) on an instrument ⟨~ a waltz⟩ **7** : to perform music upon ⟨~ the piano⟩; *also* : to sound in performance ⟨the organ is ~*ing*⟩ **8** : to cause to emit sounds ⟨~ a radio⟩; *also* : to cause to reproduce recorded material ⟨~ a DVD⟩ **9** : to act in a dramatic medium; *also* : to act in the character of ⟨~ the hero⟩ **10** : GAMBLE **11** : to produce a specified impression in performance ⟨~*s* like a comedy⟩ **12** : to behave in a specified way ⟨~ safe⟩; *also* : COOPERATE ⟨~ along with him⟩ **13** : to deal with; *also* : EMPHASIZE ⟨~ up her good qualities⟩ **14** : to perform for amusement ⟨~ a trick⟩ **15** : WREAK **16** : to use as an esp. political strategy **17** : to contend with in a game; *also* : to fill (a certain position) on a team **18** : to make wagers on ⟨~ the races⟩ **19** : WIELD, PLY **20** : to keep in action — **play·er** *n*

play·act·ing \ˈplā-ˌak-tiŋ\ *n* **1** : performance in theatrical productions **2** : insincere or artificial behavior

play·back \-ˌbak\ *n* : an act of reproducing recorded sound or pictures — **play back** *vb*

play·bill \-ˌbil\ *n* : a poster advertising the performance of a play

play·book \-ˌbu̇k\ *n* **1** : a notebook containing diagrammed football plays **2** : a stock of usual tactics or methods

play·boy \-ˌbȯi\ *n* : a man whose chief interest is the pursuit of pleasure

play·date \-ˌdāt\ *n* : a usu. prearranged play session for small children

play·go·er \-ˌgō-ər\ *n* : a person who frequently attends plays

play·ground \-ˌgrau̇nd\ *n* : an area used for games and play esp. by children

play·house \-ˌhau̇s\ *n* **1** : THEATER **2** : a small house for children to play in

playing card *n* : any of a set of 24 to 78 cards marked to show its rank and suit and used to play a game of cards

play·let \ˈplā-lət\ *n* : a short play

play·mate \-ˌmāt\ *n* : a companion in play

play–off \-ˌȯf\ *n* : a contest or series of contests to break a tie or determine a championship

play out *vb* : DEVELOP, UNFOLD ⟨see how things *play out*⟩

play·pen \-ˌpen\ *n* : a portable enclosure in which a young child may play

play·scape \-ˌskāp\ *n* : a play area or structure for children

play·suit \-ˌsüt\ *n* : a sports and play outfit for women and children

play·thing \-ˌthiŋ\ *n* : TOY

play·wright \-ˌrīt\ *n* : a writer of plays

pla·za \ˈpla-zə, ˈplä-\ *n* [Sp, fr. L *platea* broad street] **1** : a public square in a city or town **2** : a shopping center

PLC *abbr, Brit* public limited company

plea \ˈplē\ *n* **1** : a defendant's answer in law to a charge or indictment **2** : something alleged as an excuse **3** : ENTREATY, APPEAL

plead \ˈplēd\ *vb* **plead·ed** *or* **pled** \ˈpled\; **plead·ing** **1** : to argue before a court or authority ⟨~ a case⟩ **2** : to answer to a charge or indictment ⟨~ guilty⟩ **3** : to argue for or against something ⟨~ for acquittal⟩ **4** : to appeal earnestly ⟨~*s* for help⟩ **5** : to offer as a plea (as in defense) ⟨~*ed* illness⟩ — **plead·er** *n*

pleas·ant \ˈple-zᵊnt\ *adj* **1** : giving pleasure : AGREEABLE ⟨a ~ experience⟩ **2** : marked by pleasing behavior or appearance ⟨a ~ person⟩ — **pleas·ant·ly** *adv* — **pleas·ant·ness** *n*

pleas·ant·ry \-zᵊn-trē\ *n, pl* **-ries** : a pleasant and casual act or speech

[1]**please** \ˈplēz\ *vb* **pleased; pleas·ing** **1** : to give pleasure or satisfaction to **2** : LIKE ⟨do as you ~⟩ **3** : to be the will or pleasure of ⟨may it ~ his Majesty⟩

[2]**please** *adv* — used as a function word to express politeness or emphasis in a request ⟨~ come in⟩

pleas·er \ˈplē-zər\ *n* : a person or thing that offers pleasure or satisfaction — often used in combination ⟨crowd-*pleaser*⟩

pleasing *adj* : giving pleasure ⟨a ~ fragrance⟩ — **pleas·ing·ly** *adv*

plea·sur·able \ˈple-zhə-rə-bəl\ *adj* : PLEASANT, GRATIFYING ⟨a ~ cruise⟩ — **plea·sur·ably** \-blē\ *adv*

plea·sure \ˈple-zhər\ *n* **1** : DESIRE, INCLINATION ⟨await your ~⟩ **2** : a state of gratification : ENJOYMENT **3** : a source of delight or joy ⟨a ~ to see you dance⟩

[1]**pleat** \ˈplēt\ *vb* **1** : FOLD; *esp* : to arrange in pleats **2** : BRAID

[2]**pleat** *n* : a fold (as in cloth) made by doubling material over on itself

plebe \ˈplēb\ *n* : a freshman at a military or naval academy

[1]**ple·be·ian** \pli-ˈbē-ən\ *n* **1** : a member of the Roman plebs **2** : one of the common people

[2]**plebeian** *adj* **1** : of or relating to plebeians **2** : COMMON, VULGAR ⟨~ tastes⟩

pleb·i·scite \ˈple-bə-ˌsīt, -sət\ *n* : a vote of the people (as of a country) on a proposal submitted to them

plebs \ˈplebz\ *n, pl* **ple·bes** \ˈplē-bēz\ **1** : the general populace **2** : the common people of ancient Rome

plec·trum \ˈplek-trəm\ *n, pl* **plec·tra** \-trə\ *or* **plec·trums** [L] : [3]PICK 3

[1]**pledge** \ˈplej\ *n* [ME *plegge* security, fr. AF *plege,* fr. LL *plebium,* fr. **plebere* to pledge, prob. of Gmc origin] **1** : something given as security for the performance of an act **2** : the state of being held as a security or guaranty **3** : TOAST 3 **4** : PROMISE, VOW

[2]**pledge** *vb* **pledged; pledg·ing** **1** : to deposit as a pledge **2** : TOAST **3** : to bind by a pledge : PLIGHT **4** : PROMISE

Pleis·to·cene \ˈplī-stə-ˌsēn\ *adj* : of, relating to, or being the earlier epoch of the Quaternary — **Pleistocene** *n*

ple·na·ry \ˈplē-nə-rē, ˈple-\ *adj* **1** : FULL ⟨~ power⟩ **2** : including all entitled to attend ⟨~ session⟩

pleni·po·ten·tia·ry \ˌple-nə-pə-ˈten-chə-rē, -ˈten-chē-ˌer-ē\ *n, pl* **-ries** : a diplomatic agent having full authority — **plenipotentiary** *adj*

plen·i·tude \ˈple-nə-ˌtüd, -ˌtyüd\ *n* **1** : COMPLETENESS **2** : ABUNDANCE

plen·te·ous \ˈplen-tē-əs\ *adj* **1** : FRUITFUL **2** : existing in plenty

plen·ti·ful \ˈplen-ti-fəl\ *adj* **1** : containing or yielding plenty ⟨a ~ harvest⟩ **2** : ABUNDANT — **plen·ti·ful·ly** *adv*

plen·ty \ˈplen-tē\ *n* : a more than adequate number or amount

ple·num \ˈple-nəm, ˈplē-\ *n, pl* **-nums** *or* **-na** \-nə\ : a general assembly of all members esp. of a legislative body

pleth·o·ra \ˈple-thə-rə\ *n* : an excessive quantity or fullness; *also* : PROFUSION

pleu·ri·sy \ˈplu̇r-ə-sē\ *n* : inflammation of the membrane that lines the chest and covers the lungs

plex·i·glass \ˈplek-si-ˌglas\ *n* [alter. of *Plexiglas,* a trademark] : a transparent acrylic plastic often used in place of glass

plex·us \ˈplek-səs\ *n, pl* **plex·us·es** \-sə-səz\ : an interlacing network esp. of blood vessels or nerves

pli·able \ˈplī-ə-bəl\ *adj* **1** : FLEXIBLE **2** : yielding easily to others ⟨a ~ child⟩ ♦ ***Synonyms*** PLASTIC, PLIANT, DUCTILE, MALLEABLE, ADAPTABLE — **pli·abil·i·ty** \ˌplī-ə-ˈbi-lə-tē\ *n*

pli·ant \ˈplī-ənt\ *adj* **1** : FLEXIBLE **2** : easily influenced : PLIABLE ⟨a ~ senator⟩ — **pli·an·cy** \-ən-sē\ *n*

pli·ers \ˈplī-ərz\ *n pl* : small pincers for bending or cutting wire or handling small objects

[1]**plight** \ˈplīt\ *vb* : to put or give in pledge : ENGAGE

[2]**plight** *n* : an unfortunate, difficult, or precarious situation

plinth \ˈplinth\ *n* : the lowest part of the base of an architectural column

Plio·cene \ˈplī-ə-ˌsēn\ *adj* : of, relating to, or being the latest epoch of the Tertiary — **Pliocene** *n*

PLO *abbr* Palestine Liberation Organization

plod \ˈpläd\ *vb* **plod·ded; plod·ding** **1** : to walk heavily or slowly : TRUDGE **2** : to work laboriously and monotonously : DRUDGE — **plod·der** *n* — **plod·ding·ly** *adv*

plonk *var of* PLUNK

plop \ˈpläp\ *vb* **plopped; plop·ping** **1** : to fall or move with a sound like that of something dropping into water **2** : to set, drop, or throw heavily or hastily ⟨*plopped* down on the couch⟩ ⟨~ down $20⟩ — **plop** *n*

[1]**plot** \ˈplät\ *n* **1** : a small area of ground **2** : a ground plan (as of an area) **3** : the main story (as of a book or movie) **4** : a secret scheme : INTRIGUE

[2]**plot** *vb* **plot·ted; plot·ting** **1** : to make a plot or plan of **2** : to mark on or as if on a chart **3** : to plan or contrive esp. secretly — **plot·ter** *n*

plo·ver \ˈplə-vər, ˈplō-\ *n, pl* **plover** *or* **plovers** [ME, fr. AF, fr. VL **pluviarius,* fr. L *pluvia* rain] : any of a family of shorebirds that differ from the sandpipers in having shorter stouter bills

[1]**plow** *or* **plough** \ˈplau̇\ *n* **1** : an implement used to cut, lift, turn over, and partly break up soil **2** : a device (as a snowplow) operating like a plow

[2]**plow** *or* **plough** *vb* **1** : to open, break up, or work with a plow **2** : to move through like a plow ⟨a ship ~*ing* the waves⟩ **3** : to proceed laboriously ⟨~*ed* through his work⟩ — **plow·able** *adj* — **plow·er** *n*

plow·boy \ˈplau̇-ˌbȯi\ *n* : a boy who leads the horse drawing a plow

plow·man \-mən, -ˌman\ *n* **1** : a man who guides a plow **2** : a farm laborer

plow·share \-ˌsher\ *n* : a part of a plow that cuts the earth

ploy \ˈplȯi\ *n* : a tactic intended to embarrass or frustrate an opponent

[1]**pluck** \ˈplək\ *vb* **1** : to pull off or out : PICK; *also* : to pull something from **2** : to play (an instrument) by pulling the strings **3** : TUG, TWITCH

[2]**pluck** *n* **1** : an act or instance of plucking **2** : SPIRIT, COURAGE

plucky \ˈplə-kē\ *adj* **pluck·i·er; -est** : COURAGEOUS, SPIRITED ⟨~ recruits⟩

[1]**plug** \ˈpləg\ *n* **1** : STOPPER; *also* : an obstructing mass **2** : a cake of tobacco **3** : a poor or worn-out horse **4** : SPARK PLUG **5** : a lure with several hooks used in fishing **6** : a device on the end of a cord for making an electrical connection **7** : a piece of favorable publicity

[2]**plug** *vb* **plugged; plug·ging** **1** : to stop, make tight, or secure by inserting a plug **2** : HIT, SHOOT **3** : to publicize insistently **4** : PLOD, DRUDGE

plug and play *n* : a computer feature enabling the operating system to automatically detect and configure peripherals — **plug–and–play** *adj*

plugged–in \ˈpləgd-ˈin\ *adj* : technologically or socially informed and connected

plug–in \ˈpləg-ˌin\ *n* : a small piece of software that supplements a larger program

plum \ˈpləm\ *n* [ME, fr. OE *plūme,* modif. of L *prunum* plum, fr. Gk *proumnon*] **1** : a smooth-skinned juicy fruit borne by trees related to the peach and cherry; *also* : a tree bearing plums **2** : a raisin when used in desserts (as puddings) **3** : something excellent; *esp* : something desirable given in return for a favor

plum·age \ˈplü-mij\ *n* : the feathers of a bird — **plum·aged** \-mijd\ *adj*
[1]**plumb** \ˈpləm\ *n* : a weight on the end of a line (**plumb line**) used esp. by builders to show vertical direction
[2]**plumb** *adv* **1** : VERTICALLY **2** : COMPLETELY ⟨~ tired out⟩ **3** : EXACTLY; *also* : IMMEDIATELY
[3]**plumb** *vb* : to sound, adjust, or test with a plumb ⟨~ the depth of a well⟩
[4]**plumb** *adj* **1** : VERTICAL **2** : COMPLETE
plumb·er \ˈplə-mər\ *n* : a worker who fits or repairs pipes and fixtures
plumb·ing \ˈplə-miŋ\ *n* : a system of pipes in a building for supplying and carrying off water
[1]**plume** \ˈplüm\ *n* : FEATHER; *esp* : a large, conspicuous, or showy feather — **plumed** \ˈplümd\ *adj* — **plumy** \ˈplü-mē\ *adj*
[2]**plume** *vb* **plumed; plum·ing** **1** : to provide or deck with feathers **2** : to indulge (oneself) in pride
[1]**plum·met** \ˈplə-mət\ *n* : PLUMB; *also* : PLUMB LINE
[2]**plummet** *vb* : to drop or plunge straight down
[1]**plump** \ˈpləmp\ *vb* **1** : to drop or fall suddenly or heavily **2** : to favor something strongly ⟨~*ing* for change⟩
[2]**plump** *n* : a sudden heavy fall or blow; *also* : the sound made by it
[3]**plump** *adv* **1** : straight down; *also* : straight ahead **2** : UNQUALIFIEDLY ⟨came out ~ for free trade⟩
[4]**plump** *adj* : having a full rounded usu. pleasing form ♦ ***Synonyms*** FLESHY, STOUT, ROLY-POLY, ROTUND — **plump·ness** *n*
[1]**plun·der** \ˈplən-dər\ *vb* : to take the goods of by force or wrongfully : PILLAGE — **plun·der·er** *n*
[2]**plunder** *n* : something taken by force or theft : LOOT
[1]**plunge** \ˈplənj\ *vb* **plunged; plung·ing** **1** : IMMERSE, SUBMERGE **2** : to enter or cause to enter a state or course of action suddenly or violently ⟨~ into war⟩ **3** : to cast oneself into or as if into water **4** : to gamble heavily and recklessly **5** : to descend suddenly
[2]**plunge** *n* : a sudden dive, leap, or rush
plung·er \ˈplən-jər\ *n* **1** : one that plunges **2** : a sliding piece driven by or against fluid pressure : PISTON **3** : a rubber cup on a handle pushed against an opening to free a waste outlet of an obstruction
plunk \ˈpləŋk\ *or* **plonk** \ˈpläŋk, ˈplȯŋk\ *vb* **1** : to make or cause to make a hollow metallic sound **2** : to drop heavily or suddenly — **plunk** *n*
plu·per·fect \(ˌ)plü-ˈpər-fikt\ *adj* [ME *pluperfyth,* modif. of LL *plusquamperfectus,* lit., more than perfect] : of, relating to, or constituting a verb tense that denotes an action or state as completed at or before a past time spoken of — **pluperfect** *n*
plu·ral \ˈplu̇r-əl\ *adj* [ME, fr. AF & L; AF *plurel,* fr. L *pluralis,* fr. *plur-, plus* more] : of, relating to, or constituting a word form used to denote more than one — **plural** *n*
plu·ral·i·ty \plu̇-ˈra-lə-tē\ *n, pl* **-ties** **1** : the state of being plural **2** : an excess of votes over those cast for an opposing candidate **3** : the greatest number of votes cast when not a majority
plu·ral·ize \ˈplu̇r-ə-ˌlīz\ *vb* **-ized; -iz·ing** : to make plural or express in the plural form — **plu·ral·i·za·tion** \ˌplu̇r-ə-lə-ˈzā-shən\ *n*
[1]**plus** \ˈpləs\ *adj* [L, more] **1** : mathematically positive **2** : having or being in addition to what is anticipated **3** : falling high in a specified range ⟨a grade of B ~⟩
[2]**plus** *n, pl* **plus·es** \ˈplə-səz\ *also* **plus·ses** **1** : a sign + (**plus sign**) used in mathematics to indicate addition or a positive quantity **2** : an added quantity; *also* : a positive quality **3** : SURPLUS
[3]**plus** *prep* **1** : increased by : with the addition of ⟨3 ~ 4⟩ **2** : BESIDES
[4]**plus** *conj* : AND ⟨soup ~ salad and bread⟩
[1]**plush** \ˈpləsh\ *n* : a fabric with a pile longer and less dense than velvet pile — **plushy** *adj*
[2]**plush** *adj* : notably luxurious ⟨a ~ suite⟩ — **plush·ly** *adv* — **plush·ness** *n*
plus/minus sign *n* : the sign ± used to indicate a quantity taking on both a positive value and its negative or to indicate a plus or minus quantity
plus or minus *adj* : indicating a quantity whose positive and negative values bracket a range of values ⟨*plus or minus* 3 inches⟩
plus–size \ˈpləs-ˈsīz\ *also* **plus–sized** \-ˈsīzd\ *adj* : extra large ⟨~ clothing⟩ ⟨~ shoppers⟩
Plu·to \ˈplü-tō\ *n* : a dwarf planet whose orbit crosses the orbit of Neptune — see PLANET table
plu·toc·ra·cy \plü-ˈtä-krə-sē\ *n, pl* **-cies** **1** : government by the wealthy **2** : a controlling class of the wealthy — **plu·to·crat** \ˈplü-tə-ˌkrat\ *n* — **plu·to·crat·ic** \ˌplü-tə-ˈkra-tik\ *adj*
plu·to·ni·um \plü-ˈtō-nē-əm\ *n* : a radioactive chemical element formed by the decay of neptunium
plu·vi·al \ˈplü-vē-əl\ *adj* **1** : of or relating to rain **2** : characterized by abundant rain
[1]**ply** \ˈplī\ *vb* **plied; ply·ing** **1** : to use, practice, or work diligently ⟨~ a trade⟩ **2** : to keep supplying something to ⟨*plied* them with liquor⟩ **3** : to go or travel regularly esp. by sea
[2]**ply** *n, pl* **plies** : one of the folds, thicknesses, or strands of which something (as plywood or yarn) is made
[3]**ply** *vb* **plied; ply·ing** : to twist together ⟨~ yarns⟩
ply·wood \ˈplī-ˌwu̇d\ *n* : material made of thin sheets of wood glued and pressed together
pm *abbr* premium
Pm *symbol* promethium
PM *abbr* **1** particulate matter **2** paymaster **3** postmaster **4** post meridiem — often not cap. and often punctuated **5**

postmortem **6** prime minister **7** provost marshal
pmk *abbr* postmark
PMS \ˌpē-ˌem-ˈes\ *n* : PREMENSTRUAL SYNDROME
pmt *abbr* payment
pneu·mat·ic \nu̇-ˈma-tik, nyu̇-\ *adj* **1** : of, relating to, or using air or wind **2** : moved by air pressure **3** : filled with compressed air ⟨~ tires⟩ — **pneu·mat·i·cal·ly** \-ti-k(ə-)lē\ *adv*
pneu·mo·coc·cus \ˌnü-mə-ˈkä-kəs, ˌnyü-\ *n, pl* **-coc·ci** \-ˈkäk-ˌsī, -ˌsē; -ˈkä-ˌkī, -ˌkē\ : a bacterium that causes pneumonia — **pneu·mo·coc·cal** \-ˈkä-kəl\ *adj*
pneu·mo·co·ni·o·sis \ˌnü-mō-ˌkō-nē-ˈō-səs, ˌnyü-\ *n* : a disease of the lungs caused by habitual inhalation of irritant mineral or metallic particles
pneu·mo·nia \nu̇-ˈmō-nyə, nyu̇-\ *n* : an inflammatory disease of the lungs
Po *symbol* polonium
PO *abbr* **1** petty officer **2** post office
[1]**poach** \ˈpōch\ *vb* [ME *pocchen,* fr. MF *pocher,* fr. OF *poché* poached, lit., bagged, fr. *poche* bag, pouch, of Gmc origin] : to cook (as an egg or fish) in simmering liquid
[2]**poach** *vb* : to hunt or fish unlawfully — **poach·er** *n*
POB *abbr* post office box
po·bla·no \pō-ˈblä-nō\ *n, pl* **-nos** : a heart-shaped usu. mild chili pepper esp. when fresh and dark green
po'·boy \ˈpō-ˌbȯi\ *also* **poor boy** *n* : SUBMARINE 2
POC *abbr* **1** : person of color **2** point of care **3** port of call **4** proof of concept
pock \ˈpäk\ *n* : a small swelling on the skin (as in smallpox); *also* : a spot suggesting this
[1]**pock·et** \ˈpä-kət\ *n* **1** : a small bag open at the top or side inserted in a garment **2** : supply of money : MEANS **3** : RECEPTACLE, CONTAINER **4** : a small isolated area or group ⟨~*s* of fog⟩ **5** : a small body of ore — **pock·et·ful** *n*
[2]**pocket** *vb* **1** : to put in or as if in a pocket **2** : STEAL ⟨~*ed* the profits⟩
[3]**pocket** *adj* **1** : small enough to fit in a pocket; *also* : SMALL, MINIATURE ⟨a ~ park⟩ **2** : carried in or paid from one's own pocket
[1]**pock·et·book** \-ˌbu̇k\ *n* **1** : PURSE; *also* : HANDBAG **2** : financial resources
[2]**pocketbook** *adj* : relating to money
pocket gopher *n* : GOPHER 2
pock·et·knife \ˈpä-kət-ˌnīf\ *n* : a knife with a folding blade to be carried in the pocket
pocket veto *n* : an indirect veto of a legislative bill by an executive through retention of the bill unsigned until after adjournment of the legislature
pock·mark \ˈpäk-ˌmärk\ *n* : a pit or scar caused by smallpox or acne; *also* : a small imperfection or depression — **pock·marked** \-ˌmärkt\ *adj*
po·co \ˈpō-kō, ˌpȯ-\ *adv* [It, little, fr. L *paucus*] : SOMEWHAT — used to qualify a direction in music ⟨~ allegro⟩
po·co a po·co \ˌpō-kō-ä-ˈpō-kō, ˌpȯ-kō-ä-ˈpȯ-\ *adv* : little by little : GRADUALLY — used as a direction in music
pod \ˈpäd\ *n* **1** : a dry fruit (as of a pea) that splits open when ripe **2** : an external streamlined compartment (as for a jet engine) on an airplane **3** : a compartment (as for personnel, a power unit, or an instrument) on a ship or craft **4** : BUBBLE 5
POD *abbr* pay on delivery
pod·cast \ˈpäd-ˌkast\ *n* [*iPod,* trademark for a portable media player + broad*cast*] : a program made available in digital format for download over the Internet — **podcast** *vb* — **pod·cast·er** *n*
po·di·a·try \pə-ˈdī-ə-trē, pō-\ *n* : the medical care and treatment of the human foot — **po·di·at·ric** \ˌpō-dē-ˈa-trik\ *adj* — **po·di·a·trist** \pə-ˈdī-ə-trist, pō-\ *n*
po·di·um \ˈpō-dē-əm\ *n, pl* **podiums** *or* **po·dia** \-dē-ə\ **1** : a dais esp. for an orchestral conductor **2** : LECTERN
POE *abbr* port of entry
po·em \ˈpō-əm\ *n* : a composition in verse
po·esy \ˈpō-ə-zē\ *n* : POETRY
po·et \ˈpō-ət\ *n* [ME, fr. AF *poete,* fr. L *poeta,* fr. Gk *poiētēs* maker, poet, fr. *poiein* to make] : a writer of poetry; *also* : a creative artist of great sensitivity
po·et·as·ter \ˈpō-ə-ˌtas-tər\ *n* : an inferior poet
po·et·ess \ˈpō-ə-təs\ *n* : a girl or woman who is a poet
poetic justice *n* : an outcome in which vice is punished and virtue rewarded usu. in a manner peculiarly or ironically appropriate
po·et·ry \ˈpō-ə-trē\ *n* **1** : metrical writing **2** : POEMS — **po·et·ic** \pō-ˈe-tik\ *or* **po·et·i·cal** \-ti-kəl\ *adj*
po·grom \ˈpō-grəm, pō-ˈgräm\ *n* [Yiddish, fr. Russ, lit., devastation] : an organized massacre of helpless people and esp. of Jews
poi \ˈpȯi\ *n, pl* **poi** *or* **pois** : a food prepared from the cooked corms of taro that are mashed with water to the consistency of a paste or thick liquid
poi·gnant \ˈpȯi-nyənt\ *adj* **1** : painfully affecting the feelings ⟨~ grief⟩ **2** : deeply moving ⟨~ scene⟩ — **poi·gnan·cy** \-nyən-sē\ *n*
poin·ci·ana \ˌpȯin-sē-ˈa-nə\ *n* : any of several ornamental tropical leguminous trees or shrubs with bright orange or red flowers
poin·set·tia \pȯin-ˈse-tē-ə\ *n* : a showy tropical American spurge with usu. scarlet bracts that suggest petals and surround small yellow flowers
[1]**point** \ˈpȯint\ *n* **1** : an individual detail; *also* : the most important essential **2** : PURPOSE ⟨no ~ in continuing⟩ **3** : a geometric element that has position but no size **4** : a particular place : LOCALITY **5** : a particular stage or degree **6** : a sharp end : TIP **7** : a projecting piece of land **8** : a punctuation mark; *esp* : PERIOD **9** : DECIMAL POINT **10** : one of the divisions of the compass **11** : a unit of counting (as in a game score) —

point·less *adj* — **pointy** \ˈpȯin-tē\ *adj* — **beside the point** : IRRELEVANT — **to the point** : RELEVANT, PERTINENT ⟨her remark was *to the point*⟩

[2]**point** *vb* **1** : to furnish with a point : SHARPEN **2** : PUNCTUATE **3** : to separate (a decimal fraction) from an integer by a decimal point — usu. used with *off* **4** : to indicate the position of esp. by extending a finger **5** : to direct attention to ⟨∼ out an error⟩ **6** : AIM, DIRECT **7** : to lie extended, aimed, or turned in a particular direction : FACE, LOOK

point–and–click *adj* : relating to or being a computer interface that allows the activation of a file by selection with a pointing device (as a mouse)

point–and–shoot *adj* : having or using preset or automatically adjusted controls ⟨a ∼ camera⟩

point–blank \ˈpȯint-ˈblaŋk\ *adj* **1** : so close to the target that a missile fired will travel in a straight line to the mark **2** : DIRECT, BLUNT ⟨a ∼ refusal⟩ — **point–blank** *adv*

point·ed \ˈpȯin-təd\ *adj* **1** : having a point **2** : being to the point : DIRECT **3** : aimed at a particular person or group; *also* : CONSPICUOUS, MARKED ⟨∼ indifference⟩ — **point·ed·ly** *adv*

point·er \ˈpȯin-tər\ *n* **1** : one that points out : INDICATOR **2** : a large short-haired hunting dog **3** : HINT, TIP ⟨gave me some ∼*s* on how to play⟩

poin·til·lism \ˈpwan-tē-ˌyi-zəm, ˈpȯin-tə-ˌli-zəm\ *n* [F *pointillisme,* fr. *pointiller* to stipple, fr. *point* spot, point] : the theory or practice in painting of applying small strokes or dots of color to a surface so that from a distance they blend together — **poin·til·list** \ˌpwan-tē-ˈyēst, ˈpȯin-tə-list\ *n or adj*

point man *n* : a principal spokesperson or advocate

point of no return : a critical point at which turning back or reversal is not possible

point of view : a position from which something is considered or evaluated

point person *n* : a principal spokesperson or advocate

point spread *n* : the number of points by which a favorite is expected to defeat an underdog

[1]**poise** \ˈpȯiz\ *vb* **poised; pois·ing** : BALANCE

[2]**poise** *n* **1** : BALANCE **2** : self-possessed calmness ⟨kept her ∼ even under attack⟩; *also* : a particular way of carrying oneself

poi·sha \ˈpȯi-shə\ *n, pl* **poisha** : the paisa of Bangladesh

[1]**poi·son** \ˈpȯi-zᵊn\ *n* [ME, fr. AF *poisun* drink, potion, poison, fr. L *potion-, potio* drink] : a substance that through its chemical action can injure or kill — **poi·son·ous** \-zᵊn-əs\ *adj*

[2]**poison** *vb* **1** : to injure or kill with poison **2** : to treat or taint with poison **3** : to affect destructively : CORRUPT ⟨∼*ed* her mind⟩ — **poi·son·er** *n*

poison hemlock *n* : a large branching poisonous herb with finely divided leaves and white flowers that is related to the carrot

poison ivy *n* **1** : a usu. climbing plant related to the sumacs that has leaves composed of three shiny leaflets and produces an irritating oil causing a usu. intensely itching skin rash; *also* : any of several related plants **2** : a skin rash caused by poison ivy

poison oak *n* : any of several shrubby plants closely related to poison ivy and having similar properties

poison sumac *n* : a No. American swamp shrub with pinnate leaves, greenish flowers, greenish white berries, and irritating properties

[1]**poke** \ˈpōk\ *n, chiefly Southern & Midland* : BAG, SACK

[2]**poke** *vb* **poked; pok·ing** **1** : PROD; *also* : to stir up by prodding **2** : to make a prodding or jabbing movement esp. repeatedly **3** : HIT, PUNCH **4** : to thrust forward obtrusively **5** : RUMMAGE ⟨*poking* around the attic⟩ **6** : MEDDLE, PRY **7** : DAWDLE ⟨*poking* along toward home⟩ — **poke fun at** : RIDICULE, MOCK

[3]**poke** *n* : a quick thrust; *also* : PUNCH

[1]**pok·er** \ˈpō-kər\ *n* : a metal rod for stirring a fire

[2]**po·ker** \ˈpō-kər\ *n* : any of several card games in which the player with the highest hand at the end of the betting wins

poker face *n* : a face that reveals no hint of a person's thoughts or feelings

poke·weed \ˈpōk-ˌwēd\ *n* : a coarse American perennial herb with clusters of white flowers and dark purple juicy berries

poky *or* **pok·ey** \ˈpō-kē\ *adj* **pok·i·er; -est** **1** : small and cramped **2** : SHABBY, DULL **3** : annoyingly slow

pol \ˈpäl\ *n* : POLITICIAN

po·lar \ˈpō-lər\ *adj* **1** : of or relating to a geographical pole **2** : of or relating to a pole (as of a magnet)

polar bear *n* : a large creamy-white bear that inhabits arctic regions

Po·lar·is \pə-ˈler-əs\ *n* : NORTH STAR

po·lar·ise *Brit var of* POLARIZE

po·lar·i·ty \pō-ˈler-ə-tē\ *n, pl* **-ties** : the condition of having poles and esp. magnetic or electrical poles

po·lar·i·za·tion \ˌpō-lə-rə-ˈzā-shən\ *n* **1** : the action of polarizing : the state of being polarized **2** : division into two sharply distinct opposites

po·lar·ize \ˈpō-lə-ˌrīz\ *vb* **-ized; -iz·ing** **1** : to cause (light waves) to vibrate in a definite way **2** : to give physical polarity to **3** : to break up into opposing groups

pol·der \ˈpōl-dər, ˈpäl-\ *n* [D] : a tract of low land reclaimed from the sea

[1]**pole** \ˈpōl\ *n* : a long slender piece of wood or metal ⟨telephone ∼⟩

[2]**pole** *vb* **poled; pol·ing** : to impel or push with a pole ⟨∼ a boat⟩

[3]**pole** *n* **1** : either end of an axis esp. of the earth **2** : either of the terminals of an electric device (as a battery or

generator) **3** : one of two or more regions in a magnetized body at which the magnetism is concentrated — **pole·ward** \ˈpōl-wərd\ *adj or adv*

¹**pole·ax** \ˈpōl-ˌaks\ *n* : a battle-ax with a short handle

²**poleax** *vb* : to attack or fell with or as if with a poleax

pole·cat \ˈpōl-ˌkat\ *n, pl* **polecats** *or* **polecat** **1** : a European carnivorous mammal of which the ferret is considered a domesticated variety **2** : SKUNK

po·lem·ic \pə-ˈle-mik\ *n* : the art or practice of disputation — usu. used in pl. — **po·lem·i·cal** \-mi-kəl\ *also* **po·lem·ic** \-mik\ *adj* — **po·lem·i·cist** \-sist\ *n*

pole·star \ˈpōl-ˌstär\ *n* **1** : NORTH STAR **2** : a directing principle : GUIDE

pole vault *n* : a field contest in which each contestant uses a pole to vault for height over a crossbar — **pole–vault** *vb* — **pole–vault·er** *n*

¹**po·lice** \pə-ˈlēs\ *vb* **po·liced; po·lic·ing** **1** : to control, regulate, or keep in order esp. by use of police ⟨~ a highway⟩ **2** : to make clean and put in order ⟨*policed* up the concert site⟩

²**police** *n, pl* **police** [F, government, fr. OF, fr. LL *politia,* fr. Gk *politeia,* fr. *politēs* citizen, fr. *polis* city, state] **1** : the department of government that keeps public order and safety and enforces the laws; *also* : the members of this department **2** : a private organization resembling a police force; *also* : its members **3** : military personnel detailed to clean and put in order

po·lice·man \-mən\ *n* : POLICE OFFICER

police officer *n* : a member of a police force

police state *n* : a state characterized by repressive, arbitrary, totalitarian rule by means of secret police

po·lice·wom·an \pə-ˈlēs-ˌwu̇-mən\ *n* : a woman who is a police officer

¹**pol·i·cy** \ˈpä-lə-sē\ *n, pl* **-cies** : a definite course or method of action selected to guide and determine present and future decisions

²**policy** *n, pl* **-cies** : a writing whereby a contract of insurance is made

pol·i·cy·hold·er \ˈpä-lə-sē-ˌhōl-dər\ *n* : one granted an insurance policy

po·lio \ˈpō-lē-ˌō\ *n* : POLIOMYELITIS — **polio** *adj*

po·lio·my·eli·tis \-ˌmī-ə-ˈlī-təs\ *n* : an acute virus disease marked by inflammation of the gray matter of the spinal cord leading usu. to paralysis

¹**pol·ish** \ˈpä-lish\ *vb* **1** : to make smooth and glossy usu. by rubbing **2** : to refine or improve in manners, condition, or style

²**polish** *n* **1** : a smooth glossy surface : LUSTER **2** : REFINEMENT, CULTURE **3** : the action or process of polishing **4** : a preparation used to produce a gloss

Pol·ish \ˈpō-lish\ *n* : the Slavic language of the Poles — **Polish** *adj*

polit *abbr* political; politician

po·lit·bu·ro \ˈpä-lət-ˌbyu̇r-ō, ˈpō-, pə-ˈlit-\ *n* [Russ *politbyuro*] : the principal policy-making committee of a Communist party

po·lite \pə-ˈlīt\ *adj* **po·lit·er; -est** **1** : REFINED, CULTIVATED ⟨~ society⟩ **2** : marked by correct social conduct : COURTEOUS; *also* : CONSIDERATE, TACTFUL — **po·lite·ly** *adv* — **po·lite·ness** *n*

po·li·tesse \ˌpä-li-ˈtes\ *n* [F] : formal politeness

pol·i·tic \ˈpä-lə-ˌtik\ *adj* **1** : wise in promoting a policy ⟨a ~ statesman⟩ **2** : shrewdly tactful ⟨a ~ move⟩

po·lit·i·cal \pə-ˈli-ti-kəl\ *adj* **1** : of or relating to government or politics **2** : involving or charged or concerned with acts against a government or a political system ⟨~ prisoners⟩ — **po·lit·i·cal·ly** \-k(ə-)lē\ *adv*

politically correct *adj* : conforming to a belief that language and practices which could offend sensibilities (as in matters of sex or race) should be eliminated — **political correctness** *n*

pol·i·ti·cian \ˌpä-lə-ˈti-shən\ *n* : a person actively engaged in government or politics

pol·i·tick \ˈpä-lə-ˌtik\ *vb* : to engage in political discussion or activity

po·lit·i·co \pə-ˈli-ti-ˌkō\ *n, pl* **-cos** *also* **-coes** : POLITICIAN

pol·i·tics \ˈpä-lə-ˌtiks\ *n sing or pl* **1** : the art or science of government, of guiding or influencing governmental policy, or of winning and holding control over a government **2** : political affairs or business; *esp* : competition between groups or individuals for power and leadership **3** : political opinions

pol·i·ty \ˈpä-lə-tē\ *n, pl* **-ties** : a politically organized unit; *also* : the form or constitution of such a unit

pol·ka \ˈpōl-kə, ˈpō-kə\ *n* [Czech, fr. *Polka* Polish woman, fem. of *Polák* Pole] : a lively couple dance of Bohemian origin; *also* : music for this dance — **polka** *vb*

pol·ka dot \ˈpō-kə-ˌdät\ *n* : a dot in a pattern of regularly distributed dots — **polka–dot** *or* **polka–dot·ted** \-ˌdä-təd\ *adj*

¹**poll** \ˈpōl\ *n* **1** : HEAD **2** : the casting and recording of votes; *also* : the total vote cast **3** : the place where votes are cast — usu. used in pl. **4** : a questioning of persons to obtain information or opinions to be analyzed

²**poll** *vb* **1** : to cut off or shorten a growth or part of : CLIP, SHEAR **2** : to receive and record the votes of **3** : to receive (as votes) in an election **4** : to question in a poll

pol·lack *or* **pol·lock** \ˈpä-lək\ *n, pl* **pollack** *or* **pollock** : an important No. Atlantic food fish that is related to the cods; *also* : a related food fish of the No. Pacific

pol·len \ˈpä-lən\ *n* [NL, fr. L, fine flour] : a mass of male spores of a seed plant usu. appearing as a yellow dust

pol·li·na·tion \ˌpä-lə-ˈnā-shən\ *n* : the carrying of pollen to the female part of a plant to fertilize the seed — **pol·li·nate** \ˈpä-lə-ˌnāt\ *vb* — **pol·li·na·tor** \-ˌnā-tər\ *n*

poll·ster \ˈpōl-stər\ *n* : one that conducts a poll or compiles data obtained by a poll
poll tax *n* : a tax of a fixed amount per person levied on adults and often linked to the right to vote
pol·lute \pə-ˈlüt\ *vb* **pol·lut·ed; pol·lut·ing** : to make impure; *esp* : to contaminate (an environment) esp. with man-made waste — **pol·lut·ant** \-ˈlü-tᵊnt\ *n* — **pol·lut·er** *n* — **pol·lu·tion** \-ˈlü-shən\ *n*
pol·ly·wog *or* **pol·li·wog** \ˈpä-lē-ˌwäg\ *n* : TADPOLE
po·lo \ˈpō-lō\ *n* [Balti (Tibetan language of northern Kashmir), ball] : a game played by two teams on horseback using long-handled mallets to drive a wooden ball
po·lo·ni·um \pə-ˈlō-nē-əm\ *n* : a radioactive metallic chemical element
pol·ter·geist \ˈpōl-tər-ˌgīst\ *n* [G, fr. *poltern* to knock + *Geist* spirit] : a noisy usu. mischievous ghost held to be responsible for unexplained noises
pol·troon \päl-ˈtrün\ *n* : COWARD
poly- *comb form* [Gk, fr. *polys* many] **1** : many : several ⟨*poly*syllabic⟩ **2** : polymeric ⟨*poly*ester⟩
poly·chlo·ri·nat·ed bi·phe·nyl \ˌpä-li-ˈklōr-ə-ˌnā-təd-ˌbī-ˈfen-ᵊl, -ˈfēn-\ *n* : any of several industrial compounds that are toxic environmental pollutants
poly·clin·ic \ˌpä-li-ˈkli-nik\ *n* : a clinic or hospital treating diseases of many sorts
poly·es·ter \ˈpä-lē-ˌes-tər\ *n* : a polymer composed of ester groups used esp. in making fibers or plastics; *also* : a product (as fabric) composed of polyester
poly·eth·yl·ene \ˌpä-lē-ˈe-thə-ˌlēn\ *n* : a lightweight plastic resistant to chemicals and moisture and used chiefly in packaging
po·lyg·a·my \pə-ˈli-gə-mē\ *n* : marriage in which a spouse of either sex may have more than one mate at the same time — **po·lyg·a·mist** \-mist\ *n* — **po·lyg·a·mous** \-məs\ *adj*
poly·glot \ˈpä-li-ˌglät\ *adj* **1** : speaking or writing several languages **2** : containing or made up of several languages — **polyglot** *n*
poly·gon \ˈpä-li-ˌgän\ *n* : a closed plane figure bounded by straight lines — **po·lyg·o·nal** \pə-ˈli-gə-nᵊl\ *adj*
poly·graph \ˈpä-li-ˌgraf\ *n* : an instrument (as a lie detector) for recording variations of several bodily functions (as blood pressure) simultaneously — **po·lyg·ra·pher** \pə-ˈli-grə-fər, ˈpä-li-ˌgra-fər\ *n*
poly·he·dron \ˌpä-li-ˈhē-drən\ *n* : a solid formed by plane faces that are polygons — **poly·he·dral** \-drəl\ *adj*
poly·math \ˈpä-li-ˌmath\ *n* : a person of encyclopedic learning
poly·mer \ˈpä-lə-mər\ *n* : a chemical compound formed by union of small molecules and usu. consisting of repeating structural units — **poly·mer·ic** \ˌpä-lə-ˈmer-ik\ *adj*
po·lym·er·i·za·tion \pə-ˌli-mə-rə-ˈzā-shən\ *n* : a chemical reaction in which two or more small molecules combine to form polymers — **po·lym·er·ize** \pə-ˈli-mə-ˌrīz\ *vb*
Poly·ne·sian \ˌpä-lə-ˈnē-zhən\ *n* **1** : a member of any of the Indigenous peoples of Polynesia **2** : a group of Austronesian languages spoken in Polynesia — **Polynesian** *adj*
poly·no·mi·al \ˌpä-lə-ˈnō-mē-əl\ *n* : an algebraic expression having one or more terms each of which consists of a constant multiplied by one or more variables raised to a nonnegative integral power — **polynomial** *adj*
pol·yp \ˈpä-ləp\ *n* **1** : an invertebrate animal (as a coral) that is a coelenterate having a hollow cylindrical body closed at one end **2** : a growth projecting from a mucous membrane (as of the colon or vocal cords)
po·lyph·o·ny \pə-ˈli-fə-nē\ *n* : music consisting of two or more melodically independent but harmonizing voice parts — **poly·phon·ic** \ˌpä-li-ˈfä-nik\ *adj*
poly·pro·pyl·ene \ˌpä-lē-ˈprō-pə-ˌlēn\ *n* : any of various polymer plastics or fibers
poly·sty·rene \ˌpä-li-ˈstī-ˌrēn\ *n* : a rigid transparent nonconducting thermoplastic used esp. in molded products and foams
poly·syl·lab·ic \-sə-ˈla-bik\ *adj* **1** : having more than three syllables **2** : characterized by polysyllabic words
poly·syl·la·ble \ˈpä-li-ˌsi-lə-bəl\ *n* : a polysyllabic word
poly·tech·nic \ˌpä-li-ˈtek-nik\ *adj* : of, relating to, or instructing in many technical arts or applied sciences
poly·the·ism \ˈpä-li-thē-ˌi-zəm\ *n* : belief in or worship of many gods — **poly·the·ist** \-ˌthē-ist\ *adj or n* — **poly·the·is·tic** \ˌpä-li-thē-ˈis-tik\ *adj*
poly·un·sat·u·rat·ed \ˌpä-lē-ˌən-ˈsa-chə-ˌrā-təd\ *adj* : having many double or triple bonds in a molecule — used esp. of an oil or fatty acid
poly·ure·thane \ˌpä-lē-ˈyůr-ə-ˌthān\ *n* : any of various polymers used esp. in foams and in resins (as for coatings)
poly·vi·nyl \ˌpä-li-ˈvī-nᵊl\ *adj* : of, relating to, or being a polymerized vinyl compound, resin, or plastic — often used in combination
pome·gran·ate \ˈpä-mə-ˌgra-nət\ *n* [ME *poumgrenet,* fr. AF *pome garnette,* lit., seedy fruit] : a many-seeded reddish fruit that has an edible crimson pulp and is borne by a tropical Asian tree; *also* : the tree
¹**pom·mel** \ˈpə-məl, ˈpä-\ *n* **1** : the knob on the hilt of a sword **2** : the knoblike bulge at the front and top of a saddlebow
²**pom·mel** \ˈpə-məl\ *vb* **-meled** *or* **-melled; -mel·ing** *or* **-mel·ling** : PUMMEL
pomp \ˈpämp\ *n* **1** : brilliant display : SPLENDOR **2** : OSTENTATION
pom·pa·dour \ˈpäm-pə-ˌdōr\ *n* : a style of dressing the hair high over the forehead
pom·pa·no \ˈpäm-pə-ˌnō, ˈpəm-\ *n, pl* **-no** *or* **-nos** : a narrow silvery fish of coastal waters of the western Atlantic

pom–pom \ˈpäm-ˌpäm\ *n* **1** : an ornamental ball or tuft used on a cap or costume **2** : a fluffy ball flourished by cheerleaders
pom·pon \ˈpäm-ˌpän\ *n* **1** : POM-POM **2** : a chrysanthemum or dahlia with small rounded flower heads
pomp·ous \ˈpäm-pəs\ *adj* **1** : suggestive of pomp; *esp* : OSTENTATIOUS **2** : pretentiously dignified ⟨~ politicians⟩ **3** : excessively elevated or ornate ♦ ***Synonyms*** ARROGANT, MAGISTERIAL, SELF-IMPORTANT — **pom·pos·i·ty** \päm-ˈpä-sə-tē\ *n* — **pomp·ous·ly** *adv*
pon·cho \ˈpän-chō\ *n, pl* **ponchos** [AmerSp, fr. Mapuche (Indigenous language of Chile)] **1** : a blanket with a slit in the middle for the head so that it can be worn as a garment **2** : a waterproof garment resembling a poncho
pond \ˈpänd\ *n* : a small body of water
pon·der \ˈpän-dər\ *vb* **pon·dered; pon·der·ing** **1** : to weigh in the mind **2** : to consider carefully
pon·der·o·sa pine \ˈpän-də-ˌrō-sə-, -zə-\ *n* : a tall pine of western No. America with long needles; *also* : its strong reddish wood
pon·der·ous \ˈpän-də-rəs\ *adj* **1** : of very great weight **2** : UNWIELDY, CLUMSY ⟨a ~ weapon⟩ **3** : oppressively dull ⟨a ~ speech⟩ ♦ ***Synonyms*** CUMBROUS, CUMBERSOME, WEIGHTY
pone \ˈpōn\ *n, Southern & Midland* : an oval-shaped cornmeal cake; *also* : corn bread in the form of pones
pon·iard \ˈpän-yərd\ *n* : DAGGER
pon·tiff \ˈpän-təf\ *n* : POPE — **pon·tif·i·cal** \pän-ˈti-fi-kəl\ *adj*
¹**pon·tif·i·cate** \pän-ˈti-fi-kət, -fə-ˌkāt\ *n* : the state, office, or term of office of a pontiff
²**pon·tif·i·cate** \pän-ˈti-fə-ˌkāt\ *vb* **-cat·ed; -cat·ing** : to deliver dogmatic opinions
pon·toon \pän-ˈtün\ *n* **1** : a flat-bottomed boat **2** : a boat or float used in building a floating temporary bridge **3** : a float of a seaplane
po·ny \ˈpō-nē\ *n, pl* **ponies** : a small horse
po·ny·tail \-ˌtāl\ *n* : a style of arranging hair to resemble the tail of a pony
pooch \ˈpüch\ *n* : DOG
poo·dle \ˈpü-dᵊl\ *n* [G *Pudel,* short for *Pudelhund,* fr. *pudeln* to splash + *Hund* dog] : any of a breed of active intelligent dogs with a dense curly solid-colored coat
pooh–pooh \ˈpü-ˈpü\ *also* **pooh** \ˈpü\ *vb* **1** : to express contempt or impatience **2** : DERIDE, SCORN ⟨~*ed* my idea⟩
¹**pool** \ˈpül\ *n* **1** : a small deep body of usu. fresh water **2** : a small body of standing liquid **3** : SWIMMING POOL
²**pool** *vb* : to form a pool
³**pool** *n* **1** : all the money bet on the result of a particular event **2** : any of several games of billiards played on a table having six pockets **3** : the amount contributed by the participants in a joint venture **4** : a combination between competing firms for mutual profit **5** : a readily available supply
⁴**pool** *vb* : to combine (as resources) in a common fund or effort
¹**poop** \ˈpüp\ *n* : an enclosed superstructure at the stern of a ship
²**poop** *n, slang* : INFORMATION
poop deck *n* : a partial deck above a ship's main afterdeck
poor \ˈpu̇r\ *adj* **1** : lacking material possessions ⟨~ people⟩ **2** : less than adequate : MEAGER ⟨a ~ crop⟩ **3** : arousing pity ⟨you ~ thing⟩ **4** : inferior in quality or value **5** : UNPRODUCTIVE, BARREN ⟨~ soil⟩ **6** : fairly unsatisfactory ⟨~ prospects⟩; *also* : UNFAVORABLE ⟨~ opinion⟩ — **poor·ly** *adv*
poor boy *var of* PO'BOY
poor·house \ˈpu̇r-ˌhau̇s\ *n* : a publicly supported home for needy or dependent persons
poor–mouth \-ˌmau̇t͟h, -ˌmau̇th\ *vb* : to plead poverty as a defense or excuse
¹**pop** \ˈpäp\ *vb* **popped; pop·ping** **1** : to go, come, enter, or issue forth suddenly or quickly ⟨~ into bed⟩ **2** : to put or thrust suddenly ⟨~ questions⟩ **3** : to burst or cause to burst with a sharp sound; *also* : to make a sharp sound **4** : to protrude from the sockets **5** : SHOOT **6** : to hit a pop-up
²**pop** *n* **1** : a sharp explosive sound **2** : SHOT **3** : SODA POP
³**pop** *n* : FATHER
⁴**pop** *adj* **1** : POPULAR ⟨~ music⟩ **2** : of or relating to pop music ⟨~ singer⟩ **3** : of or relating to the popular culture disseminated through the mass media ⟨~ psychology⟩ **4** : of, relating to, or imitating pop art ⟨~ painter⟩
⁵**pop** *n* : pop music or culture; *also* : POP ART
⁶**pop** *abbr* population
pop art *n, often cap P&A* : art in which commonplace objects (as comic strips or soup cans) are used as subject matter — **pop artist** *n*
¹**pop·corn** \ˈpäp-ˌkȯrn\ *n* : a corn whose kernels burst open into a white starchy mass when heated; *also* : the burst kernels
²**popcorn** *adj* : having widespread appeal but little artistic merit ⟨~ movies⟩
pope \ˈpōp\ *n, often cap* : the head of the Roman Catholic Church
pop–eyed \ˈpäp-ˌīd\ *adj* : having eyes that bulge (as from disease)
pop fly *n* : POP-UP 1
pop·gun \ˈpäp-ˌgən\ *n* : a toy gun for shooting pellets with compressed air
pop·in·jay \ˈpä-pən-ˌjā\ *n* [ME *papejay* parrot, fr. MF *papegai, papejai,* fr. Ar *babghā'*] : a strutting supercilious person
pop·lar \ˈpä-plər\ *n* **1** : any of a genus of slender quick-growing trees (as a cottonwood) related to the willows **2** : the wood of a poplar
pop·lin \ˈpä-plən\ *n* : a strong plain-woven fabric with crosswise ribs
pop·over \ˈpäp-ˌō-vər\ *n* : a hollow muffin made from a thin batter rich in egg

pop·per \ˈpä-pər\ *n* : a utensil for popping corn

pop·py \ˈpä-pē\ *n, pl* **poppies** : any of a genus of herbs with showy flowers including one that yields opium

pop·py·cock \-ˌkäk\ *n* : empty talk or writing : NONSENSE

pop·u·lace \ˈpä-pyə-ləs\ *n* **1** : the common people **2** : POPULATION

pop·u·lar \ˈpä-pyə-lər\ *adj* **1** : of or relating to the general public ⟨~ government⟩ **2** : suited to the tastes of the general public ⟨~ style⟩ **3** : INEXPENSIVE ⟨~ rates⟩ **4** : frequently encountered or widely accepted ⟨~ notion⟩ **5** : commonly liked or approved ⟨a ~ teacher⟩ — **pop·u·lar·i·ty** \ˌpä-pyə-ˈla-rə-tē\ *n* — **pop·u·lar·ize** \ˈpä-pyə-lə-ˌrīz\ *vb* — **pop·u·lar·ly** *adv*

pop·u·late \ˈpä-pyə-ˌlāt\ *vb* **-lat·ed; -lat·ing** **1** : to have a place in : INHABIT **2** : PEOPLE

pop·u·la·tion \ˌpä-pyə-ˈlā-shən\ *n* **1** : the people or number of people in an area **2** : the organisms inhabiting a particular locality **3** : a group of individuals or items from which samples are taken for statistical measurement

population explosion *n* : a pyramiding of numbers of a biological population; *esp* : the recent great increase in human numbers resulting from increased survival and exponential population growth

pop·u·list \ˈpä-pyə-list\ *n* : a believer in or advocate of the rights, wisdom, or virtues of the common people — **pop·u·lism** \-ˌli-zəm\ *n*

pop·u·lous \ˈpä-pyə-ləs\ *adj* **1** : densely populated; *also* : having a large population **2** : CROWDED — **pop·u·lous·ness** *n*

[1]**pop–up** \ˈpäp-ˌəp\ *n* **1** : a short high fly in baseball **2** : a pop-up window on a computer screen

[2]**pop–up** *adj* : of, relating to, or having a component or device that pops up **2** : appearing suddenly ⟨a ~ ad⟩ ⟨a ~ store⟩ ⟨~ windows⟩

por·ce·lain \ˈpȯr-sə-lən\ *n* : a fine-grained translucent ceramic ware

porch \ˈpȯrch\ *n* : a covered entrance usu. with a separate roof

por·cine \ˈpȯr-ˌsīn\ *adj* : of, relating to, or suggesting swine

por·ci·ni \pȯr-ˈchē-nē\ *n, pl* **porcini** [It] : a large edible brownish mushroom

por·ci·no \pȯr-ˈchē-nō\ *n, pl* **-ni** : PORCINI

por·cu·pine \ˈpȯr-kyə-ˌpīn\ *n* [ME *porke despyne,* fr. MF *porc espin,* fr. It *porcospino,* fr. L *porcus* pig + *spina* spine, prickle] : any of various mammals having stiff sharp spines mingled with their hair

[1]**pore** \ˈpȯr\ *vb* **pored; por·ing** **1** : to read studiously or attentively ⟨~ over a book⟩ **2** : PONDER, REFLECT

[2]**pore** *n* : a tiny hole or space (as in the skin or soil) — **pored** \ˈpȯrd\ *adj*

pork \ˈpȯrk\ *n* : the flesh of swine dressed for use as food

pork barrel *n* : government projects or appropriations yielding rich patronage benefits

pork·er \ˈpȯr-kər\ *n* : HOG; *esp* : a young pig suitable for use as fresh pork

por·nog·ra·phy \pȯr-ˈnä-grə-fē\ *n* : the depiction of erotic behavior intended to cause sexual excitement — **por·no·graph·ic** \ˌpȯr-nə-ˈgra-fik\ *adj*

po·rous \ˈpȯr-əs\ *adj* **1** : full of pores **2** : permeable to fluids : ABSORPTIVE — **po·ros·i·ty** \pə-ˈrä-sə-tē\ *n*

por·phy·ry \ˈpȯr-fə-rē\ *n, pl* **-ries** : a rock consisting of feldspar crystals embedded in a compact fine-grained base material — **por·phy·rit·ic** \ˌpȯr-fə-ˈri-tik\ *adj*

por·poise \ˈpȯr-pəs\ *n* [ME *porpoys,* fr. AF *porpeis,* fr. ML *porcopiscis,* fr. L *porcus* pig + *piscis* fish] : any of a family of small gregarious blunt-snouted whales with spadelike teeth; *also* : DOLPHIN 1

por·ridge \ˈpȯr-ij\ *n* : a soft food made by boiling meal of grains or legumes in milk or water

por·rin·ger \ˈpȯr-ən-jər\ *n* : a low one-handled metal bowl or cup

[1]**port** \ˈpȯrt\ *n* **1** : HARBOR **2** : a city with a harbor **3** : AIRPORT

[2]**port** *n* **1** : an inlet or outlet (as in an engine) for a fluid **2** : PORTHOLE **3** : JACK 7

[3]**port** *vb* : to turn or put a helm to the left

[4]**port** *n* : the left side of a ship or airplane looking forward — **port** *adj*

[5]**port** *n* : a sweet fortified wine

portabella *or* **portabello** *var of* PORTOBELLO

por·ta·bil·i·ty \ˌpȯr-tə-ˈbil-ə-tē\ *n, pl* **-ties** **1** : the quality or state of being portable **2** : the ability to transfer benefits from one pension fund to another when a worker changes jobs

por·ta·ble \ˈpȯr-tə-bəl\ *adj* : capable of being carried — **portable** *n*

[1]**por·tage** \ˈpȯr-tij, pȯr-ˈtäzh\ *n* [ME, fr. AF, fr. *porter* to carry] : the carrying of boats and goods overland between navigable bodies of water; *also* : a route for such carrying

[2]**portage** *vb* **por·taged; por·tag·ing** : to carry gear over a portage

por·tal \ˈpȯr-tᵊl\ *n* : DOOR, ENTRANCE; *esp* : a grand or imposing one

portal–to–portal *adj* : of or relating to the time spent by a worker in traveling from the entrance to an employer's property to the worker's actual job site (as in a mine)

port·cul·lis \pȯrt-ˈkə-ləs\ *n* : a grating at the gateway of a castle or fortress that can be let down to stop entrance

porte co·chere \ˌpȯrt-kō-ˈsher\ *n* [F *porte cochère,* lit., coach door] : a roofed structure extending from the entrance of a building over an adjacent driveway and sheltering those getting in or out of vehicles

por·tend \pȯr-ˈtend\ *vb* **1** : to give a sign or warning of beforehand **2** : INDICATE, SIGNIFY ♦ ***Synonyms*** AUGUR, PROGNOSTICATE, FORETELL, PREDICT, FORECAST, PROPHESY

por·tent \ˈpȯr-ˌtent\ *n* **1** : something that foreshadows a coming event : OMEN **2** : MARVEL, PRODIGY

por·ten·tous \pȯr-ˈten-təs\ *adj* **1** : of, relating to, or constituting a portent **2** : PRODIGIOUS **3** : self-consciously solemn : POMPOUS

¹por·ter \ˈpȯr-tər\ *n, chiefly Brit* : DOORKEEPER

²porter *n* **1** : a person who carries burdens; *esp* : one employed (as at a terminal) to carry baggage **2** : an attendant in a railroad car **3** : a dark heavy ale

por·ter·house \ˈpȯr-tər-ˌhau̇s\ *n* : a choice beefsteak with a large tenderloin

port·fo·lio \pȯrt-ˈfō-lē-ˌō\ *n, pl* **-li·os** **1** : a portable case for papers or drawings **2** : the office and functions of a minister of state **3** : the securities held by an investor

port·hole \ˈpȯrt-ˌhōl\ *n* : an opening (as a window) in the side of a ship or aircraft

por·ti·co \ˈpōr-ti-ˌkō\ *n, pl* **-coes** *or* **-cos** [It] : a row of columns supporting a roof around or at the entrance of a building

¹por·tion \ˈpōr-shən\ *n* **1** : one's part or share ⟨a ~ of food⟩ **2** : DOWRY **3** : an individual's lot **4** : a part of a whole

²portion *vb* **1** : to divide into portions **2** : to allot to as a portion

port·land cement \ˈpȯrt-lənd-\ *n* : a cement made by calcining and grinding a mixture of clay and limestone

port·ly \ˈpȯrt-lē\ *adj* **port·li·er; -est** : somewhat stout

port·man·teau \pȯrt-ˈman-ˌtō\ *n, pl* **-teaus** *or* **-teaux** \-ˌtōz\ [MF *portemanteau,* fr. *porter* to carry + *manteau* mantle, fr. L *mantellum*] : a large suitcase

por·to·bel·lo \pȯr-tə-ˈbe-lō\ *also* **por·ta·bel·la** \-lə\ *or* **por·ta·bel·lo** \-lō\ *n, pl* **-los** *also* **-las** : a large dark mature mushroom noted for its meaty texture

port of call : an intermediate port where ships customarily stop for supplies, repairs, or transshipment of cargo

port of entry **1** : a place where foreign goods may be cleared through a customhouse **2** : a place where an alien may enter a country

por·trait \ˈpȯr-trət, -ˌtrāt\ *n* : a picture (as a painting or photograph) of a person usu. showing the face — **por·trait·ist** \-trə-tist\ *n*

por·trai·ture \ˈpȯr-trə-ˌchu̇r\ *n* : the practice or art of making portraits

por·tray \pȯr-ˈtrā\ *vb* **1** : to make a picture of : DEPICT **2** : to describe in words **3** : to play the role of — **por·tray·al** *n*

Por·tu·guese \ˈpȯr-chə-ˌgēz, -ˌgēs; ˌpȯr-chə-ˈgēz, -ˈgēs\ *n, pl* **Portuguese** **1** : a native or inhabitant of Portugal **2** : the language of Portugal and Brazil — **Portuguese** *adj*

Portuguese man–of–war *n* : any of several large colonial marine invertebrate animals related to the jellyfishes and having a large sac by which the colony floats at the surface

por·tu·laca \ˌpȯr-chə-ˈla-kə\ *n* : any of a genus of succulent herbs cultivated for their showy flowers

pos *abbr* **1** position **2** positive

¹pose \ˈpōz\ *vb* **posed; pos·ing** **1** : to assume or cause to assume a posture usu. for artistic purposes **2** : to set forth : PROPOSE ⟨~ a question⟩ **3** : to affect an attitude or character

²pose *n* **1** : a sustained posture; *esp* : one assumed by a model **2** : an attitude assumed for effect : PRETENSE

¹pos·er \ˈpō-zər\ *n* : a puzzling question

²poser *n* : a person who poses

po·seur \pō-ˈzər\ *n* [F, lit., poser] : an affected or insincere person

posh \ˈpäsh\ *adj* : FASHIONABLE ⟨a ~ restaurant⟩

pos·it \ˈpä-zət\ *vb* : to assume the existence of : POSTULATE

po·si·tion \pə-ˈzi-shən\ *n* **1** : an arranging in order **2** : the stand taken on a question **3** : the point or area occupied by something : SITUATION **4** : a certain arrangement of bodily parts ⟨exercise in a sitting ~⟩ **5** : RANK, STATUS **6** : EMPLOYMENT, JOB — **position** *vb* — **po·si·tion·al** \-shə-nəl\ *adj*

¹pos·i·tive \ˈpä-zə-tiv\ *adj* **1** : expressed definitely ⟨her answer was a ~ *no*⟩ **2** : CONFIDENT, CERTAIN ⟨~ it was my book⟩ **3** : of, relating to, or constituting the degree of grammatical comparison that denotes no increase in quality, quantity, or relation **4** : not fictitious : REAL **5** : active and effective in function ⟨~ leadership⟩ **6** : having the light and shade as existing in the original subject ⟨a ~ photograph⟩ **7** : numerically greater than zero ⟨a ~ number⟩ **8** : being, relating to, or charged with electricity of which the proton is the elementary unit **9** : AFFIRMATIVE ⟨a ~ response⟩ **10** : FAVORABLE; *also* : marked by optimism ⟨a ~ attitude⟩ — **pos·i·tive·ly** *adv* — **pos·i·tive·ness** *n*

²positive *n* **1** : the positive degree or a positive form in a language **2** : a positive photograph

pos·i·tron \ˈpä-zə-ˌträn\ *n* : a positively charged particle having the same mass and magnitude of charge as the electron

po·so·le *or* **po·zo·le** \pō-ˈsō-lā\ *n* : a thick Mexican soup made with pork, hominy, garlic, and chili

poss *abbr* possessive

pos·se \ˈpä-sē\ *n* [ML *posse comitatus,* lit., power or authority of the county] **1** : a body of persons organized to assist a sheriff in an emergency **2** : a body of attendants or followers

pos·sess \pə-ˈzes\ *vb* **1** : to have as property : OWN **2** : to have as an attribute, knowledge, or skill **3** : to enter into and control firmly ⟨~*ed* by a devil⟩ — **pos·ses·sor** \-ˈze-sər\ *n*

pos·ses·sion \-ˈze-shən\ *n* **1** : control or occupancy of property **2** : OWNERSHIP **3** : something owned : PROPERTY **4** : domination by something (as an evil spirit, a passion, or an idea) **5** : SELF-CONTROL

pos·ses·sive \pə-ˈze-siv\ *adj* **1** : of, relating to, or constituting a grammatical case denoting ownership **2** : showing the desire to possess ⟨a ~ nature⟩ — **possessive** *n* — **pos·ses·sive·ness** *n*
pos·si·ble \ˈpä-sə-bəl\ *adj* **1** : being within the limits of ability, capacity, or realization **2** : being something that may or may not occur ⟨~ dangers⟩ **3** : able or fitted to become ⟨a ~ site for a bridge⟩ — **pos·si·bil·i·ty** \ˌpä-sə-ˈbi-lə-tē\ *n* — **pos·si·bly** \ˈpä-sə-blē\ *adv*
pos·sum \ˈpä-səm\ *n* : OPOSSUM
[1]**post** \ˈpōst\ *n* **1** : an upright piece of timber or metal serving esp. as a support : PILLAR **2** : a pole or stake set up as a mark or indicator
[2]**post** *vb* **1** : to affix to a usual place (as a wall) for public notices **2** : to publish or announce by or as if by a public notice ⟨~ grades⟩ **3** : to forbid (property) to trespassers by putting up a notice **4** : SCORE 4 ⟨~*ed* a 70 in the final round⟩ **5** : to publish in an online forum
[3]**post** *n* **1** *obs* : COURIER **2** *chiefly Brit* : [1]MAIL; *also* : POST OFFICE **3** : something that is published online
[4]**post** *vb* **1** : to ride or travel with haste : HURRY **2** : MAIL ⟨~ a letter⟩ **3** : to enter in a ledger **4** : INFORM ⟨kept him ~*ed* on new developments⟩
[5]**post** *n* **1** : the place at which a soldier is stationed; *esp* : a sentry's beat or station **2** : a station or task to which a person is assigned **3** : the place at which a body of troops is stationed : CAMP **4** : OFFICE, POSITION **5** : a trading settlement or station
[6]**post** *vb* **1** : to station in a given place **2** : to put up (as bond)
post·age \ˈpōs-tij\ *n* : the fee for postal service; *also* : stamps representing this fee
post·al \ˈpōs-tᵊl\ *adj* **1** : of or relating to the mails or the post office **2** : insanely or murderously violent ⟨he went ~⟩
postal card *n* : POSTCARD
postal service *n* : a government agency or department handling the transmission of mail
[1]**post·card** \ˈpōst-ˌkärd\ *n* : a card on which a message may be written for mailing without an envelope
[2]**postcard** *adj* : PICTURESQUE
post chaise *n* : a 4-wheeled closed carriage for two to four persons
post·con·sum·er \ˌpōst-kən-ˈsü-mər\ *adj* **1** : discarded by a consumer **2** : having been used and recycled for reuse in another product
post–COVID syndrome *also* **post–COVID–19 syndrome** *n* : LONG COVID
post·date \ˌpōst-ˈdāt\ *vb* : to date with a date later than that of execution ⟨~ a check⟩
post·doc·tor·al \-ˈdäk-tə-rəl\ *also* **post·doc·tor·ate** \-tə-rət\ *adj* : of, relating to, or engaged in advanced academic or professional work beyond a doctor's degree
post·er \ˈpō-stər\ *n* : a bill or placard for posting often in a public place
[1]**pos·te·ri·or** \pō-ˈstir-ē-ər, pä-\ *adj* **1** : later in time **2** : situated behind
[2]**pos·te·ri·or** \pä-ˈstir-ē-ər, pō-\ *n* : the hinder bodily parts; *esp* : BUTTOCKS
pos·ter·i·ty \pä-ˈster-ə-tē\ *n* **1** : the descendants from one ancestor **2** : all future generations
pos·tern \ˈpōs-tərn, ˈpäs-\ *n* **1** : a back door or gate **2** : a private or side entrance
post exchange *n* : a store at a military post that sells to military personnel and authorized civilians
post·grad \ˈpōst-ˌgrad\ *adj* : POSTGRADUATE
post·grad·u·ate \(ˌ)pōst-ˈgra-jə-wət\ *adj* : of or relating to studies beyond the bachelor's degree — **postgraduate** *n*
post·haste \ˈpōst-ˈhāst\ *adv* : with all possible speed
post·hole \-ˌhōl\ *n* : a hole for a post and esp. a fence post
post·hu·mous \ˈpäs-chə-məs\ *adj* [L *posthumus,* alter. of *postumus* last-born, posthumous, fr. superl. of *posterus* coming after] **1** : born after the death of the father **2** : published after the death of the author — **post·hu·mous·ly** *adv*
post·hyp·not·ic \ˌpōst-hip-ˈnä-tik\ *adj* : of, relating to, or characteristic of the period following a hypnotic trance
pos·til·ion *or* **pos·til·lion** \pō-ˈstil-yən\ *n* : a rider on the left-hand horse of a pair drawing a coach
Post·im·pres·sion·ism \ˌpōst-im-ˈpre-shəˌni-zəm\ *n* : a late 19th century French theory or practice of art that stresses variously volume, picture structure, or expressionism
post·lude \ˈpōst-ˌlüd\ *n* : an organ solo played at the end of a church service
post·man \-mən, -ˌman\ *n* : MAILMAN
post·mark \-ˌmärk\ *n* : an official postal marking on a piece of mail; *esp* : the mark canceling the postage stamp — **postmark** *vb*
post·mas·ter \-ˌmas-tər\ *n* : a person who has charge of a post office
postmaster general *n, pl* **postmasters general** : an official in charge of a national postal service
post·men·o·paus·al \ˌpōst-ˌme-nə-ˈpȯ-zəl\ *adj* **1** : having undergone menopause **2** : occurring or administered after menopause
post me·ri·di·em \ˌpōst-mə-ˈri-dē-əm\ *adj* [L] : being after noon
post·mis·tress \ˈpōst-ˌmis-trəs\ *n* : a woman who is a postmaster
post·mod·ern \ˌpōst-ˈmä-dərn\ *adj* : of, relating to, or being any of various movements in reaction to modernism
[1]**post·mor·tem** \ˌpōst-ˈmȯr-təm\ *adj* [L *post mortem* after death] **1** : done, occurring, or collected after death ⟨a ~ examination⟩ **2** : following the event
[2]**postmortem** *n* **1** : AUTOPSY **2** : an analysis or discussion of an event after it is over ⟨a ~ of the election⟩
post·na·sal drip \ˈpōst-ˌnā-zəl-\ *n* : flow of mucous secretion from the posterior

part of the nasal cavity onto the wall of the pharynx
post·na·tal \(ˌ)pōst-ˈnā-tᵊl\ *adj* : occurring or being after birth; *esp* : of or relating to a newborn infant
post office *n* **1** : POSTAL SERVICE **2** : a local branch of a post office department
post·op·er·a·tive \(ˌ)pōst-ˈä-prə-tiv, -pə-ˌrā-\ *adj* : following or having undergone a surgical operation ⟨~ care⟩
post·paid \ˈpōst-ˈpād\ *adj* : having the postage paid by the sender and not chargeable to the receiver
post·par·tum \(ˌ)pōst-ˈpär-təm\ *adj* [NL *post partum* after birth] : following parturition — **postpartum** *adv*
post·pone \pōst-ˈpōn\ *vb* **post·poned; post·pon·ing** : to put off to a later time — **post·pone·ment** *n*
post road *n* : a road over which mail is carried
post·script \ˈpōst-ˌskript\ *n* : a note added esp. to a completed letter
post time *n* : the designated time for the start of a horse race
post–traumatic *adj* : occurring after or as a result of trauma ⟨~ stress⟩
post–traumatic stress disorder *n* : a psychological reaction occurring after a highly stressful experience (as military combat) that is usu. characterized by depression, anxiety, flashbacks, and nightmares
pos·tu·lant \ˈpäs-chə-lənt\ *n* : a probationary candidate for membership in a religious order
¹**pos·tu·late** \ˈpäs-chə-ˌlāt\ *vb* **-lat·ed; -lat·ing** : to assume as true
²**pos·tu·late** \ˈpäs-chə-lət, -ˌlāt\ *n* : a proposition taken for granted as true esp. as a basis for a chain of reasoning
¹**pos·ture** \ˈpäs-chər\ *n* **1** : the position or bearing of the body or one of its parts **2** : STATE, CONDITION **3** : ATTITUDE ⟨a ~ of arrogance⟩
²**posture** *vb* **pos·tured; pos·tur·ing** : to strike a pose esp. for effect
post·war \ˈpōst-ˈwȯr\ *adj* : occurring or existing after a war
po·sy \ˈpō-zē\ *n, pl* **posies** **1** : a brief sentiment : MOTTO **2** : a bunch of flowers; *also* : FLOWER
¹**pot** \ˈpät\ *n* **1** : a rounded container used chiefly for domestic purposes **2** : the total of the bets at stake at one time **3** : RUIN ⟨go to ~⟩ — **pot·ful** *n*
²**pot** *vb* **pot·ted; pot·ting** **1** : to preserve or place in a pot **2** : SHOOT
³**pot** *n* : MARIJUANA
po·ta·ble \ˈpō-tə-bəl\ *adj* : suitable for drinking — **po·ta·bil·i·ty** \ˌpō-tə-ˈbi-lə-tē\ *n*
po·tage \pȯ-ˈtäzh\ *n* : a thick soup
pot·ash \ˈpät-ˌash\ *n* [sing. of *pot ashes*] : potassium or any of its various compounds esp. as used in agriculture
po·tas·si·um \pə-ˈta-sē-əm\ *n* : a silver-white soft metallic chemical element that occurs abundantly in nature
potassium bromide *n* : a crystalline salt used as a sedative and in photography
potassium carbonate *n* : a white salt used in making glass and soap
potassium nitrate *n* : a soluble salt used in making gunpowder, as a fertilizer, and in medicine
po·ta·tion \pō-ˈtā-shən\ *n* : a usu. alcoholic drink; *also* : the act of drinking
po·ta·to \pə-ˈtā-tō\ *n, pl* **-toes** : the edible starchy tuber of a plant related to the tomato; *also* : this plant
potato beetle *n* : COLORADO POTATO BEETLE
potato bug *n* : COLORADO POTATO BEETLE
potbellied pig *n* : any of an Asian breed of small pigs having a straight tail, potbelly, and black, white, or black and white coat
pot·bel·ly \ˈpät-ˌbe-lē\ *n* : a protruding abdomen — **pot·bel·lied** \-lēd\ *adj*
pot·boil·er \-ˌbȯi-lər\ *n* : a usu. inferior work of art or literature produced chiefly for profit
po·tent \ˈpō-tᵊnt\ *adj* **1** : having authority or influence : POWERFUL **2** : chemically or medicinally effective **3** : able to copulate — used esp. of the male ♦ ***Synonyms*** FORCEFUL, FORCIBLE, MIGHTY, PUISSANT — **po·ten·cy** \-tᵊn-sē\ *n*
po·ten·tate \ˈpō-tᵊn-ˌtāt\ *n* : one who wields controlling power : RULER
¹**po·ten·tial** \pə-ˈten-chəl\ *adj* : existing in possibility : capable of becoming actual ⟨a ~ champion⟩ ♦ ***Synonyms*** DORMANT, LATENT, QUIESCENT — **po·ten·ti·al·i·ty** \pə-ˌten-chē-ˈa-lə-tē\ *n* — **po·ten·tial·ly** \-ˈten-chə-lē\ *adv*
²**potential** *n* **1** : something that can develop or become actual ⟨a ~ for violence⟩ **2** : the work required to move a unit positive charge from infinity to a point in question; *also* : POTENTIAL DIFFERENCE
potential difference *n* : the difference in potential between two points that represents the work involved in the transfer of a unit quantity of electricity from one point to the other
potential energy *n* : the energy an object has because of its position or nature or the arrangement of its parts
po·ten·ti·ate \pə-ˈten-chē-ˌāt\ *vb* **-at·ed; -at·ing** : to make potent; *esp* : to augment the activity of (as a drug) synergistically — **po·ten·ti·a·tion** \-ˌten-chē-ˈā-shən\ *n*
pot·head \ˈpät-ˌhed\ *n* : a person who frequently smokes marijuana
poth·er \ˈpä-t͟hər\ *n* : a noisy disturbance; *also* : FUSS
pot·herb \ˈpät-ˌərb, -ˌhərb\ *n* : an herb whose leaves or stems are boiled for greens or used to season food
pot·hole \ˈpät-ˌhōl\ *n* : a large pit or hole (as in a road surface)
pot·hook \-ˌhu̇k\ *n* : an S-shaped hook for hanging pots and kettles over an open fire
po·tion \ˈpō-shən\ *n* : a mixture of liquids (as liquor or medicine)
pot·luck \ˈpät-ˈlək\ *n* : the regular meal

available to a guest for whom no special preparations have been made

pot·pie \-ˈpī\ *n* : pastry-covered meat and vegetables cooked in a deep dish

pot·pour·ri \ˌpō-pu̇-ˈrē\ *n* [F *pot pourri,* lit., rotten pot] **1** : a mixture of flowers, herbs, and spices used for scent **2** : a miscellaneous collection

pot·sherd \ˈpät-ˌshərd\ *n* : a pottery fragment

pot·shot \-ˌshät\ *n* **1** : a shot taken from ambush or at a random or easy target **2** : a critical remark made in a random or sporadic manner

pot sticker *n* : a crescent-shaped dumpling that is steamed and fried

pot·tage \ˈpä-tij\ *n* : a thick soup of vegetables and often meat

[1]**pot·ter** \ˈpä-tər\ *n* : one that makes pottery

[2]**potter** *vb* : PUTTER

pot·tery \ˈpä-tə-rē\ *n, pl* **-ter·ies** **1** : a place where earthen pots and dishes are made **2** : the art of the potter **3** : dishes, pots, and vases made from clay

pot·ty–mouthed \ˈpä-tē-ˌmau̇t͟hd, -ˌmau̇tht\ *adj* : given to the use of vulgar language

[1]**pouch** \ˈpau̇ch\ *n* [ME *pouche,* fr. AF, of Gmc origin; akin to OE *pocca* bag] **1** : a small bag (as for tobacco) carried on the person **2** : a bag for storing or transporting goods <mail ~> <diplomatic ~> **3** : an anatomical sac; *esp* : one for carrying the young on the abdomen of a female marsupial (as a kangaroo)

[2]**pouch** *vb* : to put or form into or as if into a pouch

poult \ˈpōlt\ *n* : a young fowl; *esp* : a young turkey

poul·ter·er \ˈpōl-tər-ər\ *n* : one that deals in poultry

poul·tice \ˈpōl-təs\ *n* : a soft usu. heated and medicated mass spread on cloth and applied to a sore or injury — **poultice** *vb*

poul·try \ˈpōl-trē\ *n* : domesticated birds kept for eggs or meat — **poul·try·man** \-mən\ *n*

pounce \ˈpau̇ns\ *vb* **pounced; pounc·ing** : to spring or swoop upon and seize something

[1]**pound** \ˈpau̇nd\ *n, pl* **pounds** *also* **pound** **1** : a unit of avoirdupois, troy, and apothecaries' weight — see WEIGHT table **2** — see MONEY table **3** : the former basic monetary unit of Ireland **4** : LIRA 3

[2]**pound** *n* : a public enclosure where stray animals are kept

[3]**pound** *vb* **1** : to crush to a powder or pulp by beating **2** : to strike or beat heavily or repeatedly **3** : DRILL 1 **4** : to move or move along heavily

pound·age \ˈpau̇n-dij\ *n* : POUNDS; *also* : weight in pounds

pound cake *n* : a rich cake made with a large proportion of eggs and shortening

pound–fool·ish \ˈpau̇nd-ˈfü-lish\ *adj* : imprudent in dealing with large sums or large matters

pour \ˈpȯr\ *vb* **1** : to flow or cause to flow in a stream or flood **2** : to rain hard **3** : to supply freely and copiously

pout \ˈpau̇t\ *vb* : to show displeasure by thrusting out the lips; *also* : to look sullen — **pout** *n*

pov·er·ty \ˈpä-vər-tē\ *n* [ME *poverte,* fr. AF *poverté,* fr. L *paupertat-, paupertas,* fr. *pauper* poor] **1** : lack of money or material possessions : WANT **2** : poor quality (as of soil)

poverty line *n* : a level of personal or family income below which one is classified as poor according to government standards

pov·er·ty–strick·en \ˈpä-vər-tē-ˌstri-kən\ *adj* : very poor : DESTITUTE

POW \ˌpē-(ˌ)ō-ˈdə-bəl-(ˌ)yü\ *n* : PRISONER OF WAR

[1]**pow·der** \ˈpau̇-dər\ *vb* **1** : to sprinkle or cover with or as if with powder **2** : to reduce to powder

[2]**powder** *n* [ME *poudre,* fr. AF *pudre, podre,* fr. L *pulver-, pulvis* dust] **1** : dry material made up of fine particles; *also* : a usu. medicinal or cosmetic preparation in this form **2** : a solid explosive (as gunpowder) — **pow·dery** *adj*

powder room *n* : a rest room for women

[1]**pow·er** \ˈpau̇(-ə)r\ *n* **1** : the ability to act or produce an effect **2** : a position of ascendancy over others : AUTHORITY **3** : one that has control or authority; *esp* : a sovereign state **4** : physical might; *also* : mental or moral vigor **5** : the number of times as indicated by an exponent that a number occurs as a factor in a product <5 to the third ~ is 125>; *also* : the product itself <8 is a ~ of 2> **6** : force or energy used to do work; *also* : the time rate at which work is done or energy transferred **7** : MAGNIFICATION 2 — **pow·er·ful** \-fəl\ *adj* — **pow·er·ful·ly** *adv* — **pow·er·less** *adj*

[2]**power** *vb* : to supply with power and esp. motive power

[3]**power** *adj* **1** : operated mechanically or electrically rather than manually **2** : of, relating to, or utilizing strength

pow·er·boat \-ˈbōt\ *n* : MOTORBOAT

pow·er·house \ˈpau̇(-ə)r-ˌhau̇s\ *n* **1** : POWER PLANT 1 **2** : one having great drive, energy, or ability

power plant *n* **1** : a building in which electric power is generated **2** : an engine and related parts supplying the motive power of a self-propelled vehicle

pow·wow \ˈpau̇-ˌwau̇\ *n* **1** : a ceremony (as for victory in war) of No. American Indigenous people **2** *offensive* : a meeting for discussion : CONFERENCE

pox \ˈpäks\ *n, pl* **pox** *or* **pox·es** : any of various diseases (as smallpox or syphilis) marked by a rash on the skin

pozole *var of* POSOLE

pp *abbr* **1** pages **2** pianissimo

PP *abbr* **1** parcel post **2** past participle **3** postpaid **4** prepaid

ppd *abbr* **1** postpaid **2** prepaid

PPE *abbr* personal protective equipment; personal protection equipment

PPO \ˌpē-ˌpē-ˈō\ *n, pl* **PPOs** [*p*referred

provider organization] : a health-care organization that gives economic incentives to enrolled individuals who use certain health-care providers

PPS *abbr* [L *post postscriptum*] an additional postscript

ppt *abbr* precipitate

PQ *abbr* Province of Quebec

pr *abbr* **1** pair **2** price

Pr *symbol* praseodymium

¹**PR** *or* **p.r.** \ˈpē-ˈär\ *n* : PUBLIC RELATIONS

²**PR** *abbr* **1** payroll **2** public relations **3** Puerto Rico

prac·ti·ca·ble \ˈprak-ti-kə-bəl\ *adj* : capable of being put into practice, done, or accomplished ⟨a ~ method⟩ — **prac·ti·ca·bil·i·ty** \ˌprak-ti-kə-ˈbi-lə-tē\ *n*

prac·ti·cal \ˈprak-ti-kəl\ *adj* **1** : of, relating to, or shown in practice ⟨~ questions⟩ **2** : VIRTUAL ⟨~ control⟩ **3** : capable of being put to use ⟨a ~ knowledge of French⟩ **4** : inclined to action as opposed to speculation ⟨a ~ person⟩ **5** : qualified by practice ⟨a good ~ mechanic⟩ — **prac·ti·cal·i·ty** \ˌprak-ti-ˈka-lə-tē\ *n* — **prac·ti·cal·ly** \-k(ə-)lē\ *adv*

practical joke *n* : a prank intended to trick or embarrass someone or cause physical discomfort

practical nurse *n* : a professional nurse without all of the qualifications of a registered nurse; *esp* : LICENSED PRACTICAL NURSE

¹**prac·tice** *also* **prac·tise** \ˈprak-təs\ *vb* **prac·ticed** *also* **prac·tised; prac·tic·ing** *also* **prac·tis·ing** **1** : CARRY OUT, APPLY ⟨~ what you preach⟩ **2** : to perform or work at repeatedly so as to become proficient ⟨~ tennis strokes⟩ **3** : to do or perform customarily ⟨~ politeness⟩ **4** : to be professionally engaged in ⟨~ law⟩

²**practice** *also* **practise** *n* **1** : actual performance or application **2** : customary action : HABIT **3** : systematic exercise for proficiency **4** : the exercise of a profession; *also* : a professional business

prac·ti·tion·er \prak-ˈti-shə-nər\ *n* : one who practices a profession

prae·tor \ˈprē-tər\ *n* : an ancient Roman magistrate ranking below a consul — **prae·to·ri·an** \prē-ˈtȯr-ē-ən\ *adj*

prag·mat·ic \prag-ˈma-tik\ *also* **prag·mat·i·cal** \-ti-kəl\ *adj* **1** : of or relating to practical affairs **2** : concerned with the practical consequences of actions or beliefs ⟨a ~ leader⟩ — **pragmatic** *n* — **prag·mat·i·cal·ly** \-ti-k(ə-)lē\ *adv*

prag·ma·tism \ˈprag-mə-ˌti-zəm\ *n* : a practical approach to problems and affairs

prai·rie \ˈprer-ē\ *n* [F, fr. OF *praierie*, fr. VL **prataria*, fr. L *pratum* meadow] : a broad tract of level or rolling grassland

prairie dog *n* : an American burrowing black-tailed rodent related to the squirrels and living in colonies

prairie schooner *n* : a covered wagon used by pioneers in cross-country travel

praise \ˈprāz\ *vb* **praised; prais·ing** **1** : to express approval of : COMMEND **2** : to glorify (a divinity or a saint) esp. in song — **praise** *n*

praise·wor·thy \-ˌwər-thē\ *adj* : LAUDABLE ⟨a ~ effort⟩

pra·line \ˈprä-ˌlēn, ˈprā-\ *n* [F] : a confection of nuts and sugar

pram \ˈpram\ *n, chiefly Brit* : PERAMBULATOR

prance \ˈprans\ *vb* **pranced; pranc·ing** **1** : to spring from the hind legs ⟨a *prancing* horse⟩ **2** : SWAGGER; *also* : CAPER — **prance** *n* — **pranc·er** *n*

prank \ˈpraŋk\ *n* : a playful or mildly mischievous act : TRICK

prank·ster \ˈpraŋk-stər\ *n* : a person who plays pranks

pra·seo·dym·i·um \ˌprā-zē-ō-ˈdi-mē-əm\ *n* : a yellowish white metallic chemical element

prate \ˈprāt\ *vb* **prat·ed; prat·ing** : to talk long and idly : chatter foolishly

prat·fall \ˈprat-ˌfȯl\ *n* **1** : a fall on the buttocks **2** : a humiliating blunder

¹**prat·tle** \ˈpra-tᵊl\ *vb* **prat·tled; prat·tling** : PRATE, BABBLE

²**prattle** *n* : trifling or childish talk

prawn \ˈprȯn\ *n* : any of various edible shrimplike crustaceans; *also* : SHRIMP 1

pray \ˈprā\ *vb* **1** : ENTREAT, IMPLORE **2** : to ask earnestly for something **3** : to address God or a god esp. with supplication

prayer \ˈprer\ *n* **1** : a supplication or expression addressed to God or a god; *also* : a set order of words used in praying **2** : an earnest request or wish **3** : the act or practice of praying to God or a god **4** : a religious service consisting chiefly of prayers — often used in pl. **5** : something prayed for **6** : a slight chance

prayer book *n* : a book containing prayers and often directions for worship

prayer·ful \ˈprer-fəl\ *adj* **1** : DEVOUT **2** : EARNEST — **prayer·ful·ly** *adv*

praying mantis *n* : MANTIS

PRC *abbr* People's Republic of China

preach \ˈprēch\ *vb* **1** : to deliver a sermon **2** : to set forth in a sermon **3** : to advocate earnestly ⟨~*ed* tolerance⟩ — **preach·er** *n* — **preach·ment** *n*

pre·ad·o·les·cence \ˈprē-ˌa-də-ˈle-sᵊns\ *n* : the period of human development just preceding adolescence — **pre·ad·o·les·cent** \-sᵊnt\ *adj or n*

pre·am·ble \ˈprē-ˌam-bəl\ *n* [ME, fr. MF *preambule*, fr. ML *preambulum*, fr. LL, neut. of *praeambulus* walking in front of, fr. L *prae* in front of + *ambulare* to walk] : an introductory part ⟨the ~ to a constitution⟩

pre·ap·prove \ˌprē-ə-ˈprüv\ *vb* : to approve in advance — **pre·ap·prov·al** \ˌprē-ə-ˈprü-vəl\ *n*

pre·ar·range \ˌprē-ə-ˈrānj\ *vb* : to arrange beforehand — **pre·ar·range·ment** *n*

pre·as·sign \ˌprē-ə-ˈsīn\ *vb* : to assign beforehand

pre·bake \ˌprē-ˈbāk\ *vb* : to bake in advance

Pre·cam·bri·an \ˈprē-ˈkam-brē-ən, -ˈkām-\ *adj* : of, relating to, or being the era that is earliest in geologic history and is characterized esp. by the appearance of single-celled organisms — **Precambrian** *n*

pre·can·cel \(,)prē-ˈkan-səl\ *vb* : to cancel (a postage stamp) in advance of use — **precancel** *n* — **pre·can·cel·la·tion** \ˌprē-ˌkan-sə-ˈlā-shən\ *n*

pre·can·cer·ous \(,)prē-ˈkan-sə-rəs\ *adj* : likely to become cancerous

pre·car·i·ous \pri-ˈker-ē-əs\ *adj* : dependent on uncertain conditions : dangerously insecure : UNSTABLE ⟨a ~ foothold⟩ ⟨~ prosperity⟩ ♦ ***Synonyms*** DELICATE, SENSITIVE, TICKLISH, TOUCHY, TRICKY — **pre·car·i·ous·ly** *adv* — **pre·car·i·ous·ness** *n*

pre·cau·tion \pri-ˈkȯ-shən\ *n* : a measure taken beforehand to prevent harm or secure good — **pre·cau·tion·ary** \-shə-ˌner-ē\ *adj*

pre·cede \pri-ˈsēd\ *vb* **pre·ced·ed; pre·ced·ing** : to be, go, or come ahead or in front of (as in rank or time)

pre·ce·dence \ˈpre-sə-dəns, pri-ˈsēd-ᵊns\ *n* **1** : the act or fact of preceding **2** : consideration based on order of importance : PRIORITY

¹**pre·ce·dent** \pri-ˈsē-dᵊnt, ˈpre-sə-dənt\ *adj* : prior in time, order, or significance

²**prec·e·dent** \ˈpre-sə-dənt\ *n* : something said or done that may serve to authorize or justify further words or acts of the same or a similar kind

pre·ced·ing \pri-ˈsē-diŋ\ *adj* : that precedes ♦ ***Synonyms*** ANTECEDENT, FOREGOING, PRIOR, FORMER, ANTERIOR

pre·cen·tor \pri-ˈsen-tər\ *n* : a leader of the singing of a choir or congregation

pre·cept \ˈprē-ˌsept\ *n* : a command or principle intended as a general rule of action or conduct

pre·cep·tor \pri-ˈsep-tər, ˈprē-ˌsep-\ *n* : TUTOR

pre·ces·sion \prē-ˈse-shən\ *n* : a slow gyration of the rotation axis of a spinning body (as the earth) — **pre·cess** \prē-ˈses\ *vb* — **pre·ces·sion·al** \-ˈsə-shə-nəl\ *adj*

pre·cinct \ˈprē-ˌsiŋkt\ *n* **1** : an administrative subdivision (as of a city) : DISTRICT ⟨police ~⟩ ⟨electoral ~⟩ **2** : an enclosure bounded by the limits of a building or place — often used in pl. **3** *pl* : ENVIRONS

pre·ci·os·i·ty \ˌpre-shē-ˈä-sə-tē\ *n, pl* **-ties** : fastidious refinement

pre·cious \ˈpre-shəs\ *adj* **1** : of great value ⟨~ jewels⟩ **2** : greatly cherished : DEAR ⟨~ memories⟩ **3** : AFFECTED ⟨~ language⟩

prec·i·pice \ˈpre-sə-pəs\ *n* : a steep cliff

pre·cip·i·tan·cy \pri-ˈsi-pə-tən-sē\ *n* : undue hastiness or suddenness

¹**pre·cip·i·tate** \pri-ˈsi-pə-ˌtāt\ *vb* **-tat·ed; -tat·ing** [L *praecipitare,* fr. *praecipit-, praeceps* headlong, fr. *prae* in front of + *caput* head] **1** : to throw violently **2** : to throw down **3** : to cause to happen quickly or abruptly ⟨~ a quarrel⟩ **4** : to cause to separate from solution or suspension **5** : to fall as rain, snow, or hail ♦ ***Synonyms*** SPEED, ACCELERATE, QUICKEN, HASTEN, HURRY

²**pre·cip·i·tate** \pri-ˈsi-pə-tət, -ˌtāt\ *n* : the solid matter that separates from a solution or suspension

³**pre·cip·i·tate** \pri-ˈsi-pə-tət\ *adj* **1** : showing extreme or unwise haste : RASH **2** : falling with steep descent; *also* : PRECIPITOUS — **pre·cip·i·tate·ly** *adv* — **pre·cip·i·tate·ness** *n*

pre·cip·i·ta·tion \pri-ˌsi-pə-ˈtā-shən\ *n* **1** : rash haste **2** : the process of precipitating or forming a precipitate **3** : water that falls to earth esp. as rain or snow; *also* : the quantity of this water

pre·cip·i·tous \pri-ˈsi-pə-təs\ *adj* **1** : PRECIPITATE **2** : having the character of a precipice : very steep ⟨a ~ slope⟩; *also* : containing precipices ⟨~ trails⟩ — **pre·cip·i·tous·ly** *adv*

pré·cis \prā-ˈsē\ *n, pl* **pré·cis** \-ˈsēz\ [F] : a concise summary of essentials

pre·cise \pri-ˈsīs\ *adj* **1** : exactly defined or stated : DEFINITE **2** : highly accurate : EXACT **3** : conforming strictly to a standard : SCRUPULOUS ⟨a ~ teacher⟩ — **pre·cise·ly** *adv* — **pre·cise·ness** *n*

pre·ci·sion \pri-ˈsi-zhən\ *n* : the quality or state of being precise

pre·clude \pri-ˈklüd\ *vb* **pre·clud·ed; pre·clud·ing** : to make impossible : BAR, PREVENT

pre·co·cious \pri-ˈkō-shəs\ *adj* [L *praecoc-, praecox,* lit., ripening early, fr. *prae-* ahead + *coquere* to cook] : early in development and esp. in mental development — **pre·co·cious·ly** *adv* — **pre·coc·i·ty** \pri-ˈkä-sə-tē\ *n*

pre·con·ceive \ˌprē-kən-ˈsēv\ *vb* : to form an opinion of beforehand — **pre·con·cep·tion** \-ˈsep-shən\ *n*

pre·con·di·tion \-ˈdi-shən\ *vb* : to put in proper or desired condition or frame of mind in advance

pre·cook \ˌprē-ˈku̇k\ *vb* : to cook partially or entirely before final cooking or reheating

pre·cur·sor \pri-ˈkər-sər\ *n* : one that precedes and indicates the approach of another : FORERUNNER

pred *abbr* predicate

pre·da·ceous *or* **pre·da·cious** \pri-ˈdā-shəs\ *adj* : living by preying on others : PREDATORY

pre·date \ˈprē-ˈdāt\ *vb* : ANTEDATE

pre·da·tion \pri-ˈdā-shən\ *n* **1** : the act of preying or plundering **2** : a mode of life in which food is primarily obtained by killing and consuming animals

pred·a·tor \ˈpre-də-tər\ *n* : an animal that lives by predation

pred·a·to·ry \ˈpre-də-ˌtȯr-ē\ *adj* **1** : of or relating to plunder ⟨~ warfare⟩ **2** : disposed to exploit others **3** : preying upon other animals

pre·dawn \(ˈ)prē-ˈdȯn\ *adj* : of or relating to the time just before dawn

pre·de·cease \ˌprē-di-ˈsēs\ *vb* **-ceased; -ceas·ing** : to die before another person

pre·de·ces·sor \ˈpre-də-ˌse-sər, ˈprē-\ *n* : a previous holder of a position to which another has succeeded

pre·des·ig·nate \(ˌ)prē-ˈde-zig-ˌnāt\ *vb* : to designate beforehand

pre·des·ti·na·tion \ˌprē-ˌdes-tə-ˈnā-shən\ *n* : the act of foreordaining to an earthly lot or eternal destiny by divine decree; *also* : the state of being so foreordained — **pre·des·ti·nate** \prē-ˈdes-tə-ˌnāt\ *vb*

pre·des·tine \prē-ˈdes-tən\ *vb* : to settle beforehand : FOREORDAIN

pre·de·ter·mine \ˌprē-di-ˈtər-mən\ *vb* : to determine beforehand

pre·dic·a·ment \pri-ˈdi-kə-mənt\ *n* : a difficult or trying situation ♦ ***Synonyms*** DILEMMA, PICKLE, QUAGMIRE, JAM

¹**pred·i·cate** \ˈpre-di-kət\ *n* : the part of a sentence or clause that expresses what is said of the subject

²**pred·i·cate** \ˈpre-də-ˌkāt\ *vb* **-cat·ed; -cat·ing** **1** : AFFIRM **2** : to assert to be a quality or attribute **3** : FOUND, BASE — usu. used with *on* — **pred·i·ca·tion** \ˌpre-də-ˈkā-shən\ *n*

pre·dict \pri-ˈdikt\ *vb* : to declare in advance — **pre·dict·abil·i·ty** \-ˌdik-tə-ˈbi-lə-tē\ *n* — **pre·dict·able** \-ˈdik-tə-bəl\ *adj* — **pre·dict·ably** \-blē\ *adv* — **pre·dic·tion** \-ˈdik-shən\ *n*

pre·di·gest \ˌprē-dī-ˈjest\ *vb* : to simplify for easy use; *also* : to subject to artificial or natural partial digestion

pre·di·lec·tion \ˌpre-də-ˈlek-shən, ˌprē-\ *n* : an established preference for something

pre·dis·pose \ˌprē-di-ˈspōz\ *vb* : to incline in advance : make susceptible ⟨was *predisposed* to infection⟩ — **pre·dis·po·si·tion** \ˌprē-ˌdis-pə-ˈzi-shən\ *n*

pre·dom·i·nant \pri-ˈdä-mə-nənt\ *adj* : greater in importance, strength, influence, or authority — **pre·dom·i·nance** \-nəns\ *n*

pre·dom·i·nant·ly \-nənt-lē\ *adv* : for the most part : MAINLY

pre·dom·i·nate \pri-ˈdä-mə-ˌnāt\ *vb* : to be superior esp. in power or numbers : PREVAIL

pre·dom·i·nate·ly \pri-ˈdä-mə-nət-lē\ *adv* : PREDOMINANTLY

pree·mie \ˈprē-mē\ *n* : a premature baby

pre·em·i·nent \prē-ˈe-mə-nənt\ *adj* : having highest rank : OUTSTANDING — **pre·em·i·nence** \-nəns\ *n* — **pre·em·i·nent·ly** *adv*

pre·empt \prē-ˈempt\ *vb* **1** : to settle upon (public land) with the right to purchase before others; *also* : to take by such right **2** : to seize upon before someone else can **3** : to take the place of ♦ ***Synonyms*** USURP, CONFISCATE, APPROPRIATE, EXPROPRIATE — **pre·emp·tion** \-ˈemp-shən\ *n*

pre·emp·tive \prē-ˈemp-tiv\ *adj* : marked by the seizing of the initiative : initiated by oneself ⟨~ attack⟩

preen \ˈprēn\ *vb* [ME *prenen,* alter. of *proynen, prunen,* fr. AF *puroindre, proindre,* fr. *pur-* thoroughly + *oindre* to anoint, rub, fr. L *unguere*] **1** : to groom with the bill — used of a bird **2** : to dress or smooth up : PRIMP **3** : to pride (oneself) for achievement

pre·ex·ist \ˌprē-ig-ˈzist\ *vb* : to exist before — **pre·ex·is·tence** \-ˈzis-təns\ *n* — **pre·ex·is·tent** \-tənt\ *adj*

pref *abbr* **1** preface **2** preference **3** preferred **4** prefix

¹**pre·fab** \(ˌ)prē-ˈfab, ˈprē-ˌfab\ *adj* : produced by prefabrication ⟨a ~ house⟩

²**prefab** *n* : a prefabricated structure

pre·fab·ri·cate \(ˌ)prē-ˈfa-brə-ˌkāt\ *vb* : to manufacture the parts of (a structure) beforehand for later assembly — **pre·fab·ri·ca·tion** \ˌprē-ˌfa-bri-ˈkā-shən\ *n*

¹**pref·ace** \ˈpre-fəs\ *n* : the introductory remarks of a speaker or writer — **pref·a·to·ry** \ˈpre-fə-ˌtȯr-ē\ *adj*

²**preface** *vb* **pref·aced; pref·ac·ing** : to introduce with a preface

pre·fect \ˈprē-ˌfekt\ *n* **1** : a high official; *esp* : a chief officer or magistrate **2** : a student monitor

pre·fec·ture \ˈprē-ˌfek-chər\ *n* : the office, term, or residence of a prefect

pre·fer \pri-ˈfər\ *vb* **pre·ferred; pre·fer·ring** **1** : PROMOTE **2** : to like better **3** : to bring (as a charge) against a person — **pref·er·a·ble** \ˈpre-fə-rə-bəl\ *adj* — **pref·er·a·bly** \-blē\ *adv*

pref·er·ence \ˈpre-frəns, -fə-rəns\ *n* **1** : a special liking for one thing over another **2** : CHOICE, SELECTION — **pref·er·en·tial** \ˌpre-fə-ˈren-chəl\ *adj*

pre·fer·ment \pri-ˈfər-mənt\ *n* : PROMOTION, ADVANCEMENT

preferred provider organization *n* : PPO

pre·fig·ure \prē-ˈfi-gyər\ *vb* **1** : FORESHADOW **2** : to imagine beforehand

¹**pre·fix** \ˈprē-ˌfiks, prē-ˈfiks\ *vb* : to place before ⟨~ a title to a name⟩

²**pre·fix** \ˈprē-ˌfiks\ *n* : an affix occurring at the beginning of a word

pre·flight \ˌprē-ˈflīt\ *adj* : preparing for or preliminary to flight

pre·form \(ˌ)prē-ˈfȯrm, ˈprē-ˌfȯrm\ *vb* : to form or shape beforehand

preg·na·ble \ˈpreg-nə-bəl\ *adj* : vulnerable to capture ⟨a ~ fort⟩

preg·nant \ˈpreg-nənt\ *adj* **1** : containing unborn offspring within the body **2** : rich in significance : MEANINGFUL — **preg·nan·cy** \-nən-sē\ *n*

pre·heat \ˌprē-ˈhēt\ *vb* : to heat beforehand; *esp* : to heat (an oven) to a designated temperature before using

pre·hen·sile \prē-ˈhen-səl, -ˌsī(-ə)l\ *adj* : adapted for grasping esp. by wrapping around ⟨a monkey with a ~ tail⟩

pre·his·tor·ic \ˌprē-his-ˈtȯr-ik\ *also* **pre·his·tor·i·cal** \-i-kəl\ *adj* : of, relating to, or existing in the period before written history began

pre·judge \(ˌ)prē-ˈjəj\ *vb* : to judge before full hearing or examination

¹**prej·u·dice** \ˈpre-jə-dəs\ *n* **1** : DAMAGE; *esp* : detriment to one's rights or claims **2** : an opinion made without adequate basis ⟨racial ~⟩ — **prej·u·di·cial** \ˌpre-jə-ˈdi-shəl\ *adj*

²**prejudice** *vb* **-diced; -dic·ing** **1** : to damage by a judgment or action esp. at law **2** : to cause to have prejudice

pre·kin·der·gar·ten \(ˈ)prē-ˈkin-dər-ˌgär-

tən\ *n* **1** : NURSERY SCHOOL **2** : a class or program preceding kindergarten
prel·ate \ˈpre-lət\ *n* : an ecclesiastic (as a bishop) of high rank — **prel·a·cy** \-lə-sē\ *n*
pre·launch \ˈprē-ˈlȯnch\ *adj* : preparing for or preliminary to launch
pre·lim \ˈprē-ˌlim, pri-ˈlim\ *n or adj* : PRELIMINARY
¹**pre·lim·i·nary** \pri-ˈli-mə-ˌner-ē\ *n, pl* **-nar·ies** : something that precedes or introduces the main business or event
²**preliminary** *adj* : preceding the main discourse or business
pre·lude \ˈprel-ˌyüd; ˈpre-ˌlüd, ˈprā-\ *n* **1** : an introductory performance or event **2** : a musical section or movement introducing the main theme; *also* : an organ solo played at the beginning of a church service
pre·mar·i·tal \(ˌ)prē-ˈmer-ə-tᵊl\ *adj* : existing or occurring before marriage
pre·ma·ture \ˌprē-mə-ˈtu̇r, -ˈtyu̇r, -ˈchu̇r\ *adj* : happening, coming, born, or done before the usual or proper time ⟨a ~ birth⟩ — **pre·ma·ture·ly** *adv*
¹**pre·med** \ˌprē-ˈmed\ *n* : a premedical student or course of study
²**premed** *adj* : PREMEDICAL
pre·med·i·cal \(ˌ)prē-ˈme-di-kəl\ *adj* : preceding and preparing for the professional study of medicine
pre·med·i·tate \pri-ˈme-də-ˌtāt\ *vb* : to consider and plan beforehand — **pre·med·i·ta·tion** \-ˌme-də-ˈtā-shən\ *n*
pre·men·o·paus·al \(ˌ)prē-ˌme-nə-ˈpȯ-zəl\ *adj* : of, relating to, or being in the period preceding menopause
pre·men·stru·al \(ˌ)prē-ˈmen-strə-wəl\ *adj* : of, relating to, or occurring in the period just before menstruation
premenstrual syndrome *n* : a varying group of symptoms manifested by some women prior to menstruation
premie *var of* PREEMIE
¹**pre·mier** \pri-ˈmir, -ˈmyir, ˈprē-mē-ər\ *adj* [ME *primer, primier,* fr. AF, first, chief, fr. L *primarius* of the first rank] : first in rank or importance : CHIEF; *also* : first in time : EARLIEST
²**premier** *n* : PRIME MINISTER — **pre·mier·ship** *n*
¹**pre·miere** \pri-ˈmyer, -ˈmir\ *n* : a first performance
²**premiere** *also* **pre·mier** *same as* ¹PREMIERE\ *vb* **pre·miered; pre·mier·ing** : to give or receive a first public performance
¹**prem·ise** \ˈpre-məs\ *n* **1** : a statement of fact or a supposition made or implied as a basis of argument **2** *pl* : a piece of land with the structures on it; *also* : the place of business of an enterprise
²**premise** *vb* **prem·ised; prem·is·ing** : to base on certain assumptions
pre·mi·um \ˈprē-mē-əm\ *n* [L *praemium* booty, profit, reward, fr. *prae* before + *emere* to take, buy] **1** : REWARD, PRIZE **2** : a sum over and above the stated value **3** : something paid over and above a fixed wage or price **4** : something given with a purchase **5** : the sum paid for a contract of insurance **6** : an unusually high value
pre·mix \ˌprē-ˈmiks\ *vb* : to mix before use
pre·mo·lar \(ˌ)prē-ˈmō-lər\ *adj* : situated in front of or preceding the molar teeth; *esp* : being or relating to those teeth of a mammal in front of the true molars and behind the canines — **premolar** *n*
pre·mo·ni·tion \ˌprē-mə-ˈni-shən, ˌpre-\ *n* **1** : previous warning **2** : PRESENTIMENT ⟨had a ~ of disaster⟩ — **pre·mon·i·to·ry** \pri-ˈmä-nə-ˌtȯr-ē\ *adj*
pre·na·tal \ˈprē-ˈnā-tᵊl\ *adj* : occurring, existing, or taking place before birth
pre·nup·tial \prē-ˈnəp-shəl\ *adj* : made or occurring before marriage
prenuptial agreement *n* : an agreement between a couple before marrying in which they give up future rights to each other's property in the event of divorce or death
pre·oc·cu·pa·tion \prē-ˌä-kyə-ˈpā-shən\ *n* : complete absorption of the mind or interests; *also* : something that causes such absorption
pre·oc·cu·pied \prē-ˈä-kyə-ˌpīd\ *adj* **1** : lost in thought; *also* : absorbed in some preoccupation **2** : already occupied ♦ ***Synonyms*** ABSTRACTED, ABSENT, ABSENTMINDED
pre·oc·cu·py \-ˌpī\ *vb* **1** : to occupy the attention of beforehand **2** : to take possession of before another
pre·op·er·a·tive \(ˌ)prē-ˈä-prə-tiv, -pə-ˌrā-\ *adj* : occurring before a surgical operation
pre·or·dain \ˌprē-ȯr-ˈdān\ *vb* : FOREORDAIN
pre–owned \(ˌ)prē-ˈōnd\ *adj* : SECONDHAND ⟨~ vehicles⟩
prep *abbr* **1** preparatory **2** preposition
pre·pack·age \(ˌ)prē-ˈpa-kij\ *vb* : to package (as food) before offering for sale to the customer
preparatory school *n* **1** : a usu. private school preparing students primarily for college **2** *Brit* : a private elementary school preparing students primarily for British public schools
pre·pare \pri-ˈper\ *vb* **pre·pared; pre·par·ing** **1** : to make or get ready ⟨~ dinner⟩ ⟨~ a student for college⟩ **2** : to get ready beforehand **3** : to put together : COMPOUND ⟨~ a prescription⟩ — **prep·a·ra·tion** \ˌpre-pə-ˈrā-shən\ *n* — **pre·pa·ra·to·ry** \pri-ˈper-ə-ˌtȯr-ē\ *adj*
pre·pared·ness \pri-ˈper-əd-nəs\ *n* : a state of adequate preparation
pre·pay \(ˌ)prē-ˈpā\ *vb* **-paid** \-ˈpād\; **-pay·ing** : to pay or pay the charge on in advance
pre·pon·der·ant \pri-ˈpän-də-rənt\ *adj* : having greater weight, force, influence, or frequency — **pre·pon·der·ance** \-rəns\ *n* — **pre·pon·der·ant·ly** *adv*
pre·pon·der·ate \pri-ˈpän-də-ˌrāt\ *vb* **-at·ed; -at·ing** [L *praeponderare,* fr. *prae-* ahead + *ponder-, pondus* weight] : to exceed in weight, force, influence, or frequency : PREDOMINATE
prep·o·si·tion \ˌpre-pə-ˈzi-shən\ *n* : a

word that combines with a noun or pronoun to form a phrase — **prep·o·si·tion·al** \-ˈzi-shə-nəl\ *adj*

pre·pos·sess \ˌprē-pə-ˈzes\ *vb* **1** : to cause to be preoccupied **2** : to influence beforehand esp. favorably

pre·pos·sess·ing *adj* : tending to create a favorable impression ⟨a ~ manner⟩

pre·pos·ses·sion \-ˈze-shən\ *n* **1** : PREJUDICE **2** : an exclusive concern with one idea or object

pre·pos·ter·ous \pri-ˈpäs-tə-rəs\ *adj* : contrary to nature or reason : ABSURD

prep·py *or* **prep·pie** \ˈpre-pē\ *n, pl* **prep·pies** **1** : a student at or a graduate of a preparatory school **2** : a person deemed to dress or behave like a preppy

pre·puce \ˈprē-ˌpyüs\ *n* : FORESKIN

pre·quel \ˈprē-kwəl\ *n* : a literary or dramatic work whose story precedes that of an earlier work

pre·re·cord·ed \(ˌ)prē-ri-ˈkȯr-dəd\ *adj* : recorded for later broadcast or play

pre·req·ui·site \prē-ˈre-kwə-zət\ *n* : something required beforehand or for the end in view — **prerequisite** *adj*

pre·rog·a·tive \pri-ˈrä-gə-tiv\ *n* : an exclusive or special right, power, or privilege ⟨presidential ~*s*⟩

pres *abbr* **1** present **2** president

¹**pres·age** \ˈpre-sij\ *n* [ME, fr. L *praesagium,* fr. *praesagus* having a foreboding, fr. *prae* before + *sagus* prophetic] **1** : something that foreshadows a future event : OMEN **2** : FOREBODING

²**pre·sage** \ˈpre-sij, pri-ˈsāj\ *vb* **pre·saged; pre·sag·ing** **1** : to give an omen or warning of : FORESHADOW **2** : FORETELL, PREDICT

pres·by·o·pia \ˌprez-bē-ˈō-pē-ə\ *n* : a visual condition in which loss of elasticity of the lens of the eye causes defective accommodation and inability to focus sharply for near vision — **pres·by·o·pic** \-ˈō-pik, -ˈä-\ *adj or n*

pres·by·ter \ˈprez-bə-tər\ *n* [LL, elder, priest, fr. Gk *presbyteros,* compar. of *presbys* elder, old man] **1** : PRIEST, MINISTER **2** : an elder in a Presbyterian church

¹**Pres·by·te·ri·an** \ˌprez-bə-ˈtir-ē-ən\ *n* : a member of a Presbyterian church

²**Presbyterian** *adj* **1** *often not cap* : characterized by a graded system of representative ecclesiastical bodies (as presbyteries) exercising legislative and judicial powers **2** : of or relating to a group of Protestant Christian bodies that are presbyterian in government — **Pres·by·te·ri·an·ism** \-ə-ˌni-zəm\ *n*

pres·by·tery \ˈprez-bə-ˌter-ē\ *n, pl* **-ter·ies** **1** : the part of a church reserved for the officiating clergy **2** : a ruling body in Presbyterian churches consisting of the ministers and representative elders of a district

¹**pre·school** \ˈprē-ˌskül\ *adj* : of or relating to the period in a child's life from infancy to the age of five or six — **pre·school·er** \-ˌskü-lər\ *n*

²**preschool** *n* : NURSERY SCHOOL

pre·science \ˈpre-shəns, ˈprē-\ *n* : foreknowledge of events; *also* : FORESIGHT — **pre·scient** \-shənt, -shē-ənt\ *adj*

pre·scribe \pri-ˈskrīb\ *vb* **pre·scribed; pre·scrib·ing** **1** : to lay down as a guide or rule of action **2** : to direct the use of (as a medicine) as a remedy

pre·scrip·tion \pri-ˈskrip-shən\ *n* **1** : the action of prescribing rules or directions **2** : a written direction for the preparation and use of a medicine; *also* : a medicine prescribed

pre·scrip·tive \pri-ˈskrip-tiv\ *adj* **1** : serving to prescribe ⟨~ rules⟩ **2** : acquired by, based on, or determined by prescription or by custom

pres·ence \ˈpre-zᵊns\ *n* **1** : the fact or condition of being present **2** : the space immediately around a person **3** : one that is present **4** : the bearing of a person; *esp* : stately bearing

¹**pres·ent** \ˈpre-zᵊnt\ *n* : something presented : GIFT

²**pre·sent** \pri-ˈzent\ *vb* **1** : to bring into the presence or acquaintance of : INTRODUCE **2** : to bring before the public ⟨~ a play⟩ **3** : to make a gift to **4** : to give formally **5** : to lay (as a charge) before a court for inquiry **6** : to aim or direct (as a weapon) so as to face in a particular direction — **pre·sent·able** *adj* — **pre·sen·ta·tion** \ˌprē-ˌzen-ˈtā-shən, ˌpre-zᵊn-\ *n* — **pre·sent·ment** \pri-ˈzent-mənt\ *n*

³**pres·ent** \ˈpre-zᵊnt\ *adj* **1** : now existing or in progress ⟨~ conditions⟩ **2** : being in view or at hand ⟨~ at the meeting⟩ **3** : under consideration ⟨the ~ problem⟩ **4** : of, relating to, or constituting a verb tense that expresses present time or the time of speaking

⁴**pres·ent** \ˈpre-zᵊnt\ *n* **1** *pl* : the present legal document **2** : the present tense; *also* : a verb form in it **3** : the present time

pres·ent–day \ˈpre-zᵊnt-ˈdā\ *adj* : now existing or occurring : CURRENT

pre·sen·ti·ment \pri-ˈzen-tə-mənt\ *n* : a feeling that something is about to happen : PREMONITION ⟨a ~ of danger⟩

pres·ent·ly \ˈpre-zᵊnt-lē\ *adv* **1** : SOON ⟨~ they arrived⟩ **2** : NOW ⟨~ busy⟩

present participle *n* : a participle that typically expresses present action and that in English is formed with the suffix *-ing* and is used in the formation of the progressive tenses

¹**pre·serve** \pri-ˈzərv\ *vb* **pre·served; pre·serv·ing** **1** : to keep safe : GUARD, PROTECT **2** : to keep from decaying; *esp* : to process food (as by canning or pickling) to prevent spoilage **3** : MAINTAIN ⟨~ silence⟩ — **pres·er·va·tion** \ˌpre-zər-ˈvā-shən\ *n* — **pre·ser·va·tive** \pri-ˈzər-və-tiv\ *adj or n* — **pre·serv·er** *n*

²**preserve** *n* **1** : preserved fruit — often used in pl. **2** : an area for the protection of natural resources (as animals)

pre·set \ˈprē-ˌset\ *vb* **-set; -set·ting** : to set beforehand — **preset** *n*

pre·shrink \prē-ˈshriŋk\ *vb* **-shrank** \-ˈshraŋk\; **-shrunk** \-ˈshrəŋk\ : to shrink (as a fabric) before making into a garment

pre·side \pri-ˈzīd\ *vb* **pre·sid·ed; pre·sid·ing** [L *praesidēre* to guard, preside over, fr. *prae* in front of + *sedēre* to sit] **1** : to exercise guidance or control **2** : to occupy the place of authority; *esp* : to act as chairman

pres·i·dent \ˈpre-zə-dənt\ *n* **1** : one chosen to preside ⟨~ of the assembly⟩ **2** : the chief officer of an organization (as a corporation or society) **3** : an elected official serving as both chief of state and chief political executive; *also* : a chief of state often with only minimal political powers — **pres·i·den·cy** \-dən-sē\ *n* — **pres·i·den·tial** \ˌpre-zə-ˈden-chəl\ *adj*

pre·si·dio \pri-ˈsē-dē-ˌō, -ˈsi-\ *n, pl* **-di·os** [Sp] : a military post or fortified settlement in an area currently or orig. under Spanish control

pre·sid·i·um \pri-ˈsi-dē-əm\ *n, pl* **-ia** \-dē-ə\ *or* **-iums** [Russ *prezidium,* fr. L *praesidium* garrison] : a permanent executive committee that acts for a larger body in a Communist country

¹**pre·soak** \(ˌ)prē-ˈsōk\ *vb* : to soak beforehand

²**pre·soak** \ˈprē-ˌsōk\ *n* **1** : an instance of presoaking **2** : a preparation used in presoaking clothes

pre·sort \(ˌ)prē-ˈsȯrt\ *vb* : to sort (mail) by zip code usu. before delivery to a post office

¹**press** \ˈpres\ *n* **1** : a crowded condition : THRONG **2** : a machine for exerting pressure **3** : CLOSET, CUPBOARD **4** : PRESSURE **5** : the properly creased condition of a freshly pressed garment **6** : PRINTING PRESS; *also* : the act or the process of printing **7** : a printing or publishing establishment **8** : the media (as newspapers and magazines) of public news and comment; *also* : persons (as reporters) employed in these media **9** : comment in newspapers and periodicals

²**press** *vb* **1** : to bear down upon : push steadily against **2** : ASSAIL, COMPEL **3** : to squeeze out the juice or contents of ⟨~ grapes⟩ **4** : to squeeze to a desired density, shape, or smoothness; *esp* : IRON **5** : to try hard to persuade : URGE **6** : to follow through : PROSECUTE **7** : CROWD ⟨reporters ~*ed* around the players⟩ **8** : to force one's way **9** : to require haste or speed in action — **press·er** *n*

press agent *n* : an agent employed to establish and maintain good public relations through publicity

press·ing *adj* : URGENT ⟨a ~ need⟩

press·man \ˈpres-mən, -ˌman\ *n* : the operator of a press and esp. a printing press

press·room \-rüm, -ˌrům\ *n* **1** : a room in a printing plant containing the printing presses **2** : a room for the use of reporters

¹**pres·sure** \ˈpre-shər\ *n* **1** : the burden of physical or mental distress **2** : the action of pressing; *esp* : the application of force to something by something else in direct contact with it **3** : the force exerted over a surface divided by its area **4** : the stress or urgency of matters demanding attention

²**pressure** *vb* **pres·sured; pres·sur·ing** : to apply pressure to

pressure group *n* : a group that seeks to influence governmental policy but not to elect candidates to office

pressure suit *n* : an inflatable suit for high-altitude flight or spaceflight to protect the body from low pressure

pres·sur·ise *Brit var of* PRESSURIZE

pres·sur·ize \ˈpre-shə-ˌrīz\ *vb* **-ized; -iz·ing** **1** : to maintain higher pressure within than without; *esp* : to maintain normal atmospheric pressure within (as an airplane cabin) during high-altitude flight or spaceflight **2** : to apply pressure to **3** : to design to withstand pressure — **pres·sur·i·za·tion** \ˌpre-shə-rə-ˈzā-shən\ *n*

pres·ti·dig·i·ta·tion \ˌpres-tə-ˌdi-jə-ˈtā-shən\ *n* : SLEIGHT OF HAND

pres·tige \pres-ˈtēzh, -ˈtēj\ *n* [F, fr. MF, conjuror's trick, illusion, fr. LL *praestigium,* fr. L *praestigiae,* pl., conjuror's tricks, fr. *praestringere* to graze, blunt, constrict, fr. *prae-* in front of + *stringere* to bind tight] : standing or estimation in the eyes of people : REPUTATION ♦ ***Synonyms*** INFLUENCE, AUTHORITY, WEIGHT, CACHET — **pres·ti·gious** \-ˈti-jəs, -ˈtē-\ *adj*

¹**pres·to** \ˈpres-tō\ *interj* [It, quick, quickly] — used to indicate the sudden appearance or occurrence of something

²**presto** *adv or adj* **1** : suddenly as if by magic : IMMEDIATELY **2** : at a rapid tempo — used as a direction in music

pre·stress \(ˌ)prē-ˈstres\ *vb* : to introduce internal stresses into (as a structural beam) to counteract later load stresses

pre·sum·ably \pri-ˈzü-mə-blē\ *adv* : by reasonable assumption

pre·sume \pri-ˈzüm\ *vb* **pre·sumed; pre·sum·ing** **1** : to take upon oneself without leave or warrant : DARE **2** : to take for granted : ASSUME **3** : to act or behave with undue boldness — **pre·sum·able** \-ˈzü-mə-bəl\ *adj*

pre·sump·tion \pri-ˈzəmp-shən\ *n* **1** : presumptuous attitude or conduct : AUDACITY **2** : an attitude or belief dictated by probability; *also* : the grounds lending probability to a belief — **pre·sump·tive** \-tiv\ *adj*

pre·sump·tu·ous \pri-ˈzəmp-chə-wəs\ *adj* : overstepping due bounds : taking liberties — **pre·sump·tu·ous·ly** *adv*

pre·sup·pose \ˌprē-sə-ˈpōz\ *vb* **1** : to suppose beforehand **2** : to require beforehand as a necessary condition — **pre·sup·po·si·tion** \(ˌ)prē-ˌsə-pə-ˈzi-shən\ *n*

pre·teen \ˈprē-ˈtēn\ *n* : a boy or girl not yet 13 years old — **preteen** *adj*

pre·tend \pri-ˈtend\ *vb* **1** : PROFESS ⟨doesn't ~ to be scientific⟩ **2** : FEIGN ⟨~ to be angry⟩ **3** : to lay claim ⟨~ to a throne⟩ — **pre·tend·er** *n*

pre·tense *or* **pre·tence** \ˈprē-ˌtens, pri-ˈtens\ *n* **1** : CLAIM; *esp* : one not supported by fact **2** : mere display : SHOW **3** : an attempt to attain a certain condition ⟨made a ~ at discipline⟩ **4** : false show : PRETEXT ⟨a ~ of objectivity⟩ — **pre·ten·sion** \pri-ˈten-chən\ *n*

pre·ten·tious \pri-ˈten-chəs\ *adj* **1** : making or possessing usu. unjustified claims (as to excellence) ⟨a ~ literary style⟩ **2** : making demands on one's ability or means : AMBITIOUS ⟨too ~ an undertaking⟩ — **pre·ten·tious·ly** *adv* — **pre·ten·tious·ness** *n*

pret·er·it *or* **pret·er·ite** \ˈpre-tə-rət\ *n* : a verb form expressing action in the past

pre·term \(ˌ)prē-ˈtərm, ˈprē-ˌ\ *adj* : of, relating to, being, or brought forth by premature birth ⟨a ~ infant⟩

pre·ter·nat·u·ral \ˌprē-tər-ˈna-chə-rəl\ *adj* **1** : exceeding what is natural ⟨his ~ stamina⟩ **2** : inexplicable by ordinary means — **pre·ter·nat·u·ral·ly** *adv*

pre·text \ˈprē-ˌtekst\ *n* : a purpose stated or assumed to cloak the real intention or state of affairs

pret·ti·fy \ˈpri-ti-ˌfī\ *vb* **-fied; -fy·ing** : to make pretty — **pret·ti·fi·ca·tion** \ˌpri-ti-fə-ˈkā-shən\ *n*

[1]**pret·ty** \ˈpri-tē\ *adj* **pret·ti·er; -est** [ME *praty, prety,* fr. OE *prættig* tricky, fr. *prætt* trick] **1** : pleasing by delicacy or grace : having conventionally accepted elements of beauty ⟨~ flowers⟩ **2** : MISERABLE, TERRIBLE ⟨a ~ state of affairs⟩ **3** : moderately large ⟨a ~ profit⟩ **4** : PLEASANT — usu. used in negative constructions ⟨the truth was not so ~⟩ ♦ ***Synonyms*** COMELY, FAIR, BEAUTIFUL, ATTRACTIVE, LOVELY — **pret·ti·ly** \-tə-lē\ *adv* — **pret·ti·ness** \-tē-nəs\ *n*

[2]**pretty** *adv* : in some degree : MODERATELY; *also* : QUITE, MAINLY

[3]**pretty** *vb* **pret·tied; pret·ty·ing** : to make pretty — usu. used with *up*

pretty boy *n, usu disparaging* : a man who is notably good-looking

pret·zel \ˈpret-səl\ *n* [G *Brezel,* ultim. fr. L *brachiatus* having branches like arms, fr. *brachium* arm] : a brittle or chewy glazed usu. salted slender bread often shaped like a loose knot

prev *abbr* previous; previously

pre·vail \pri-ˈvāl\ *vb* **1** : to win mastery : TRIUMPH **2** : to be or become effective : SUCCEED **3** : to urge successfully ⟨~*ed* upon her to sing⟩ **4** : to be frequent : PREDOMINATE — **pre·vail·ing·ly** *adv*

prev·a·lent \ˈpre-və-lənt\ *adj* : generally or widely existent : WIDESPREAD — **prev·a·lence** \-ləns\ *n*

pre·var·i·cate \pri-ˈver-ə-ˌkāt\ *vb* **-cat·ed; -cat·ing** [L *praevaricari* to act in collusion, lit., to straddle, fr. *prae* in front of + *varicare* to straddle, fr. *varus* bowlegged] : to deviate from the truth : EQUIVOCATE — **pre·var·i·ca·tion** \-ˌver-ə-ˈkā-shən\ *n* — **pre·var·i·ca·tor** \-ˈver-ə-ˌkā-tər\ *n*

pre·vent \pri-ˈvent\ *vb* **1** : to keep from happening or existing ⟨steps to ~ war⟩ **2** : to hold back : HINDER, STOP ⟨~ us from going⟩ — **pre·vent·able** *also* **pre·vent·ible** \-ˈven-tə-bəl\ *adj* — **pre·ven·ta·tive** \-ˈven-tə-tiv\ *adj or n* — **pre·ven·tion** \-ˈven-chən\ *n* — **pre·ven·tive** \-ˈven-tiv\ *adj or n*

pre·ver·bal \ˌprē-ˈvər-bəl\ *adj* : having not yet acquired the faculty of speech

[1]**pre·view** \ˈprē-ˌvyü\ *vb* : to see or discuss beforehand; *esp* : to view or show in advance of public presentation

[2]**preview** *n* **1** : FORETASTE **2** : an advance showing or viewing **3** *also* **pre·vue** \-ˌvyü\ : a showing of snatches from a motion picture advertised for future appearance

pre·vi·ous \ˈprē-vē-əs\ *adj* : going before : EARLIER, FORMER ♦ ***Synonyms*** FOREGOING, PRIOR, PRECEDING, ANTECEDENT — **pre·vi·ous·ly** *adv*

pre·vi·sion \prē-ˈvi-zhən\ *n* **1** : FORESIGHT, PRESCIENCE **2** : FORECAST, PREDICTION ⟨a ~ of success⟩

pre·war \ˈprē-ˈwȯr\ *adj* : occurring or existing before a war

[1]**prey** \ˈprā\ *n, pl* **prey** *also* **preys** **1** : an animal taken for food by a predator; *also* : VICTIM **2** : the act or habit of preying

[2]**prey** *vb* **1** : to raid for booty **2** : to seize and devour prey **3** : to have a harmful or wearing effect

prf *abbr* proof

[1]**price** \ˈprīs\ *n* **1** *archaic* : VALUE **2** : the amount of money paid or asked for the sale of a specified thing; *also* : the cost at which something is obtained

[2]**price** *vb* **priced; pric·ing** **1** : to set a price on **2** : to ask the price of **3** : to drive by raising prices ⟨*priced* themselves out of the market⟩

price–fix·ing \ˈprīs-ˌfik-siŋ\ *n* : the setting of prices artificially (as by producers or government)

price·less \-ləs\ *adj* : having a value beyond any price : INVALUABLE ♦ ***Synonyms*** PRECIOUS, COSTLY, EXPENSIVE

price support *n* : artificial maintenance of prices of a commodity at a level usu. fixed through government action

price war *n* : a period of commercial competition in which prices are repeatedly cut by the competitors

pric·ey *also* **pricy** \ˈprī-sē\ *adj* **pric·i·er; -est** : EXPENSIVE ⟨a ~ restaurant⟩

[1]**prick** \ˈprik\ *n* **1** : a mark or small wound made by a pointed instrument **2** : something sharp or pointed **3** : an instance of pricking; *also* : a sensation of being pricked

[2]**prick** *vb* **1** : to pierce slightly with a sharp point; *also* : to have or cause a pricking sensation **2** : to affect with anguish or remorse ⟨~*s* his conscience⟩ **3** : to outline with punctures ⟨~ out a pattern⟩ **4** : to stand or cause to stand erect ⟨the dog's ears ~*ed* up at the sound⟩ ♦ ***Synonyms*** PUNCH, PUNCTURE, PERFORATE, BORE, DRILL

prick·er \ˈpri-kər\ *n* : BRIAR; *also* : THORN

[1]**prick·le** \ˈpri-kəl\ *n* **1** : a small sharp process (as on a plant) **2** : a slight stinging pain — **prick·ly** \ˈpri-klē\ *adj*

[2]**prickle** *vb* **prick·led; prick·ling** **1** : to prick lightly **2** : TINGLE

prickly heat *n* : a red cutaneous eruption

with intense itching and tingling caused by inflammation around the ducts of the sweat glands

prickly pear *n* : any of numerous cacti with usu. yellow flowers and prickly flat or rounded joints; *also* : the sweet pulpy pear-shaped edible fruit of various prickly pears

[1]**pride** \ˈprīd\ *n* **1** : CONCEIT **2** : justifiable self-respect **3** : elation over an act or possession ⟨took ~ in her work⟩ **4** : haughty behavior : DISDAIN **5** : ostentatious display — **pride•ful** *adj*

[2]**pride** *vb* **prid•ed; prid•ing** : to indulge (as oneself) in pride

priest \ˈprēst\ *n* [ME *preist,* fr. OE *prēost,* ultim. fr. LL *presbyter* elder, priest, fr. Gk *presbyteros,* fr. compar. of *presbys* old man, elder] : a person having authority to perform the sacred rites of a religion; *esp* : a member of the Anglican, Eastern, or Roman Catholic clergy ranking below a bishop and above a deacon — **priest•hood** *n* — **priest•li•ness** *n* — **priest•ly** *adj*

priest•ess \ˈprēs-təs\ *n* : a woman authorized to perform the sacred rites of a religion

prig \ˈprig\ *n* : one who irritates by rigid or pointed observance of proprieties — **prig•gish** \ˈpri-gish\ *adj* — **prig•gish•ly** *adv*

[1]**prim** \ˈprim\ *adj* **prim•mer; prim•mest** : stiffly formal and precise — **prim•ly** *adv* — **prim•ness** *n*

[2]**prim** *abbr* **1** primary **2** primitive

pri•ma•cy \ˈprī-mə-sē\ *n* **1** : the state of being first (as in rank) **2** : the office, rank, or character of an ecclesiastical primate

pri•ma don•na \ˌpri-mə-ˈdä-nə\ *n, pl* **prima donnas** [It, lit., first lady] **1** : a principal female singer (as in an opera company) **2** : a vain undisciplined usu. uncooperative person

pri•ma fa•cie \ˈprī-mə-ˈfā-shə, -sē, -shē\ *adj or adv* [L, at first view] **1** : based on immediate impression : APPARENT **2** : SELF-EVIDENT

pri•mal \ˈprī-məl\ *adj* **1** : ORIGINAL, PRIMITIVE **2** : first in importance

pri•mar•i•ly \prī-ˈmer-ə-lē\ *adv* **1** : FUNDAMENTALLY **2** : ORIGINALLY

[1]**pri•ma•ry** \ˈprī-ˌmer-ē, -mə-rē\ *adj* **1** : first in order of time or development; *also* : PREPARATORY **2** : of first rank or importance; *also* : FUNDAMENTAL **3** : not derived from or dependent on something else ⟨~ sources⟩

[2]**primary** *n, pl* **-ries** : a preliminary election in which voters nominate or express a preference among candidates usu. of their own party

primary care *n* : health care provided by a medical professional with whom a patient has initial contact

primary color *n* : any of a set of colors from which all other colors may be derived

primary school *n* **1** : a school usu. including grades 1-3 and sometimes kindergarten **2** : ELEMENTARY SCHOOL

pri•mate \ˈprī-ˌmāt *or esp for 1* -mət\ *n* **1** *often cap* : the highest-ranking bishop of a province or nation **2** : any of an order of mammals including humans, apes, and monkeys

[1]**prime** \ˈprīm\ *n* **1** : the earliest stage of something; *esp* : SPRINGTIME **2** : the most active, thriving, or successful stage or period (as of one's life) **3** : the best individual; *also* : the best part of something **4** : any integer other than 0, +1, or −1 that is not divisible without remainder by any integer except +1, −1, and plus or minus itself; *esp* : any such integer that is positive

[2]**prime** *adj* **1** : standing first (as in time, rank, significance, or quality) ⟨~ requisite⟩ **2** : of, relating to, or being a number that is prime

[3]**prime** *vb* **primed; prim•ing** **1** : FILL, LOAD **2** : to lay a preparatory coating upon (as in painting) **3** : to put in working condition **4** : to instruct beforehand : COACH ⟨*primed* the witness⟩

prime meridian *n* : the meridian of 0° longitude which runs through Greenwich, England, and from which other longitudes are reckoned east and west

prime minister *n* **1** : the chief minister of a ruler or state **2** : the chief executive of a parliamentary government

[1]**prim•er** \ˈpri-mər\ *n* [ME, layperson's prayer book, fr. AF, fr. ML *primarium,* fr. LL, neut. of *primarius* primary] **1** : a small book for teaching children to read **2** : a small introductory book on a subject ⟨a ~ of modern art⟩ **3** : a short informative piece of writing

[2]**prim•er** \ˈprī-mər\ *n* **1** : one that primes **2** : a device for igniting an explosive **3** : material for priming a surface

prime rate *n* : an interest rate announced by a bank to be the lowest available to its most credit-worthy customers

prime time *n* **1** : the time period when the television or radio audience is largest; *also* : television shows aired in prime time **2** : the choicest or busiest time

pri•me•val \prī-ˈmē-vəl\ *adj* : of or relating to the earliest ages : PRIMITIVE

[1]**prim•i•tive** \ˈpri-mə-tiv\ *adj* **1** : ORIGINAL, PRIMARY **2** : of, relating to, or characteristic of an early stage of development or evolution **3** : ELEMENTAL, NATURAL **4** *sometimes offensive* : of, relating to, or produced by a people or culture that is nonindustrial and often nonliterate and tribal **5** : SELF-TAUGHT; *also* : produced by a self-taught artist — **prim•i•tive•ly** *adv* — **prim•i•tive•ness** *n* — **prim•i•tiv•i•ty** \ˌpri-mə-ˈti-və-tē\ *n*

[2]**primitive** *n* **1** : something primitive **2** : a primitive artist **3** : a member of a primitive people

prim•i•tiv•ism \ˈpri-mə-ti-ˌvi-zəm\ *n* **1** : primitive practices or procedures; *also* : a primitive quality or state **2** : belief in the superiority of a simple way of life close to nature **3** : the style of art of primitive peoples or primitive artists

pri•mo•gen•i•tor \ˌprī-mō-ˈje-nə-tər\ *n* : ANCESTOR, FOREFATHER

pri·mo·gen·i·ture \-ˈje-nə-ˌchu̇r\ *n* **1** : the state of being the firstborn of a family **2** : an exclusive right of inheritance belonging to the eldest son

pri·mor·di·al \prī-ˈmȯr-dē-əl\ *adj* : first created or developed : existing in its original state : PRIMEVAL

primp \ˈprimp\ *vb* : to dress in a careful or finicky manner

prim·rose \ˈprim-ˌrōz\ *n* : any of a genus of perennial herbs with large leaves arranged at the base of the stem and clusters of showy flowers

prin *abbr* **1** principal **2** principle

prince \ˈprins\ *n* [ME, fr. AF, fr. L *princeps* leader, initiator, fr. *primus* first + *capere* to take] **1** : MONARCH, KING **2** : a male member of a royal family; *esp* : a son of the monarch **3** : a person of high standing (as in a class) ⟨a ~ of poets⟩ — **prince·dom** \-dəm\ *n* — **prince·ly** *adj*

prince·ling \-liŋ\ *n* : a petty prince

prin·cess \ˈprin-səs, -ˌses\ *n* **1** : a female member of a royal family **2** : the consort of a prince

[1]**prin·ci·pal** \ˈprin-sə-pəl\ *adj* : most important — **prin·ci·pal·ly** *adv*

[2]**principal** *n* **1** : a leading person (as in a play) **2** : the chief officer of an educational institution **3** : the person from whom an agent's authority derives **4** : a capital sum earning interest or used as a fund

prin·ci·pal·i·ty \ˌprin-sə-ˈpa-lə-tē\ *n, pl* **-ties** : the position, territory, or jurisdiction of a prince

principal parts *n pl* : the inflected forms of a verb

prin·ci·ple \ˈprin-sə-pəl\ *n* **1** : a general or fundamental law, doctrine, or assumption **2** : a rule or code of conduct; *also* : devotion to such a code **3** : the laws or facts of nature underlying the working of an artificial device **4** : a primary source : ORIGIN; *also* : an underlying faculty or endowment **5** : the active part (as of a drug)

prin·ci·pled \-pəld\ *adj* : exhibiting, based on, or characterized by principle ⟨high-*principled*⟩

prink \ˈpriŋk\ *vb* : PRIMP

[1]**print** \ˈprint\ *n* [ME *prente,* fr. AF, fr. *preint, prient,* pp. of *priendre* to press, fr. L, *premere*] **1** : a mark made by pressure **2** : something stamped with an impression **3** : printed state or form **4** : printed matter **5** : a copy made by printing **6** : cloth with a pattern applied by printing

[2]**print** *vb* **1** : to stamp (as a mark) in or on something **2** : to produce impressions of (as from type) **3** : to write in letters like those of printer's type **4** : to make (a positive picture) from a photographic negative

print·able \ˈprin-tə-bəl\ *adj* **1** : capable of being printed or of being printed from **2** : worthy or fit to be published

print·er \ˈprin-tər\ *n* : one that prints; *esp* : a device that produces printout

print·ing *n* **1** : reproduction in printed form **2** : the art, practice, or business of a printer **3** : IMPRESSION 5

printing press *n* : a machine that produces printed copies

print·out \ˈprint-ˌau̇t\ *n* : a printed output produced by a computer — **print out** *vb*

[1]**pri·or** \ˈprī(-ə)r\ *n* **1** : the superior ranking next to the abbot or abbess of a religious house **2** : a previous instance of arrest or conviction for a crime

[2]**prior** *adj* **1** : earlier in time or order **2** : taking precedence logically or in importance — **pri·or·i·ty** \prī-ˈȯr-ə-tē\ *n*

pri·or·ess \ˈprī-ə-rəs\ *n* : a nun corresponding in rank to a prior

pri·or·i·tize \prī-ˈȯr-ə-ˌtīz, ˈprī-ə-rə-ˌtīz\ *vb* **-tized; -tiz·ing** : to list or rate in order of priority

prior to *prep* : in advance of : BEFORE

pri·o·ry \ˈprī-ə-rē\ *n, pl* **-ries** : a religious house under a prior or prioress

prise *chiefly Brit var of* [5]PRIZE

prism \ˈpri-zəm\ *n* [LL *prisma,* fr. Gk, lit., something sawed, fr. *priein* to saw] **1** : a solid whose sides are parallelograms and whose ends are parallel and alike in shape and size **2** : a usu. 3-sided transparent object that refracts light so that it breaks up into rainbow colors — **pris·mat·ic** \priz-ˈma-tik\ *adj*

pris·on \ˈpri-zᵊn\ *n* : a place or state of confinement esp. for criminals

pris·on·er \ˈpri-zᵊn-ər\ *n* : a person deprived of liberty; *esp* : one on trial or in prison

prisoner of war : a person captured in war

pris·sy \ˈpri-sē\ *adj* **pris·si·er; -est** : being overly prim and precise : PRIGGISH — **pris·si·ness** \-sē-nəs\ *n*

pris·tine \ˈpris-ˌtēn, pri-ˈstēn\ *adj* **1** : PRIMITIVE **2** : having the purity of its original state : UNSPOILED

prith·ee \ˈpri-t͟hē\ *interj, archaic* — used to express a wish or request

pri·va·cy \ˈprī-və-sē\ *n, pl* **-cies** **1** : the quality or state of being apart from others **2** : SECRECY

[1]**pri·vate** \ˈprī-vət\ *adj* **1** : belonging to or intended for a particular individual or group ⟨~ property⟩ **2** : restricted to the individual : PERSONAL ⟨~ opinion⟩ **3** : carried on by the individual independently ⟨~ study⟩ **4** : not holding public office ⟨a ~ citizen⟩ **5** : withdrawn from company or observation ⟨a ~ place⟩ **6** : not known publicly ⟨~ dealings⟩ — **pri·vate·ly** *adv*

[2]**private** *n* : an enlisted person of the lowest rank in the marine corps or of one of the two lowest ranks in the army — **in private** : not openly or in public

pri·va·teer \ˌprī-və-ˈtir\ *n* : an armed private ship licensed to attack enemy shipping; *also* : a sailor on such a ship

private first class *n* : an enlisted person ranking next below a corporal in the army and next below a lance corporal in the marine corps

pri·va·tion \prī-ˈvā-shən\ *n* **1** : DEPRIVATION 1 **2** : the state of being deprived; *esp* : lack of what is needed for existence

priv·et \ˈpri-vət\ *n* : a nearly evergreen

shrub related to the olive and widely used for hedges

[1]**priv·i·lege** \ˈpriv-lij, ˈpri-və-\ *n* [ME, fr. AF, fr. L *privilegium* law for or against a private person, fr. *privus* private + *leg-, lex* law] : a right or immunity granted as an advantage or favor esp. to some and not others

[2]**privilege** *vb* **-leged; -leg·ing** **1** : to grant a privilege to **2** : to accord a higher value to : FAVOR

privileged *adj* **1** : having or enjoying one or more privileges ⟨~ classes⟩ **2** : not subject to disclosure in a court of law ⟨a ~ communication⟩

[1]**privy** \ˈpri-vē\ *adj* **1** : PERSONAL, PRIVATE **2** : SECRET **3** : admitted as one sharing in a secret ⟨~ to the conspiracy⟩ — **priv·i·ly** \ˈpri-və-lē\ *adv*

[2]**privy** *n, pl* **priv·ies** : TOILET; *esp* : OUTHOUSE

[1]**prize** \ˈprīz\ *n* **1** : something offered or striven for in competition or in contests of chance **2** : something exceptionally desirable

[2]**prize** *adj* **1** : awarded or worthy of a prize ⟨a ~ essay⟩; *also* : awarded as a prize ⟨a ~ medal⟩ **2** : OUTSTANDING

[3]**prize** *vb* **prized; priz·ing** : to value highly : ESTEEM ⟨a *prized* possession⟩

[4]**prize** *n* : property (as a ship) lawfully captured in time of war

[5]**prize** *vb* **prized; priz·ing** : PRY

prize·fight \ˈprīz-ˌfīt\ *n* : a professional boxing match — **prize·fight·er** *n* — **prize·fight·ing** *n*

prize·win·ner \-ˌwi-nər\ *n* : a winner of a prize — **prize·win·ning** *adj*

[1]**pro** \ˈprō\ *n, pl* **pros** : a favorable argument, person, or position

[2]**pro** *adv* : in favor : FOR

[3]**pro** *n or adj* : PROFESSIONAL

PRO *abbr* public relations officer

pro·ac·tive \prō-ˈak-tiv\ *adj* : acting in anticipation of future problems or needs — **pro·ac·tive·ly** *adv*

pro–am \ˈprō-ˈam\ *adj* : involving professionals competing alongside or against amateurs ⟨a ~ tournament⟩ — **pro–am** *n*

prob *abbr* **1** probable; probably **2** problem

prob·a·bil·i·ty \ˌprä-bə-ˈbi-lə-tē\ *n, pl* **-ties** **1** : the quality or state of being probable **2** : something probable **3** : a measure of how often a particular event will occur if something (as tossing a coin) is done repeatedly which results in any of a number of possible events

prob·a·ble \ˈprä-bə-bəl\ *adj* **1** : apparently or presumably true ⟨a ~ hypothesis⟩ **2** : likely to be or become true or real ⟨a ~ result⟩ — **prob·a·bly** \-bə-blē\ *adv*

[1]**pro·bate** \ˈprō-ˌbāt\ *n* : the judicial determination of the validity of a will

[2]**pro·bate** *vb* **pro·bat·ed; pro·bat·ing** : to establish (a will) by probate as genuine and valid

pro·ba·tion \prō-ˈbā-shən\ *n* **1** : subjection of an individual to a period of testing and trial to ascertain fitness (as for a job) **2** : the action of giving a convicted offender freedom during good behavior under the supervision of a probation officer — **pro·ba·tion·ary** \-shə-ˌner-ē\ *adj*

pro·ba·tion·er \-shə-nər\ *n* **1** : a person (as a newly admitted student nurse) whose fitness is being tested during a trial period **2** : a convicted offender on probation

pro·ba·tive \ˈprō-bə-tiv\ *adj* **1** : serving to test or try **2** : serving to prove

[1]**probe** \ˈprōb\ *n* **1** : a slender instrument for examining a cavity (as a wound) **2** : an information-gathering device sent into outer space **3** : a penetrating investigation ♦ ***Synonyms*** INQUIRY, INQUEST, RESEARCH, INQUISITION

[2]**probe** *vb* **probed; prob·ing** **1** : to examine with a probe **2** : to investigate thoroughly

pro·bi·ty \ˈprō-bə-tē\ *n* : UPRIGHTNESS, HONESTY

prob·lem \ˈprä-bləm\ *n* **1** : a question raised for consideration or solution **2** : an intricate unsettled question **3** : a source of perplexity or vexation — **problem** *adj*

prob·lem·at·ic \ˌprä-blə-ˈma-tik\ *also* **prob·lem·at·i·cal** \-ti-kəl\ *adj* **1** : difficult to solve or decide : PUZZLING **2** : DUBIOUS, QUESTIONABLE

pro·bos·cis \prə-ˈbä-səs, -ˈbäs-kəs\ *n, pl* **-bos·cis·es** *also* **-bos·ci·des** \-ˈbä-sə-ˌdēz\ [L, fr. Gk *proboskis,* fr. *pro-* before + *boskein* to feed] : a long flexible snout (as the trunk of an elephant)

proc *abbr* proceedings

pro·caine \ˈprō-ˌkān\ *n* : a drug used esp. as a local anesthetic

pro·ce·dure \prə-ˈsē-jər\ *n* **1** : a particular way of doing something ⟨democratic ~⟩ **2** : a series of steps followed in a regular order ⟨a surgical ~⟩ — **pro·ce·dur·al** \-ˈsē-jə-rəl\ *adj*

pro·ceed \prō-ˈsēd\ *vb* **1** : to come forth : ISSUE **2** : to go on in an orderly way; *also* : CONTINUE **3** : to begin and carry on an action **4** : to take legal action **5** : to go forward : ADVANCE

pro·ceed·ing *n* **1** : PROCEDURE **2** *pl* : DOINGS **3** *pl* : legal action **4** : TRANSACTION **5** *pl* : an official record of things said or done

pro·ceeds \ˈprō-ˌsēdz\ *n pl* : the total amount or the profit arising from a business deal : RETURN

[1]**pro·cess** \ˈprä-ˌses, ˈprō-\ *n, pl* **pro·cess·es** \-ˌse-səz, -sə-səz, -sə-ˌsēz\ **1** : PROGRESS, ADVANCE **2** : something going on : PROCEEDING **3** : a natural phenomenon marked by gradual changes that lead toward a particular result ⟨the ~ of growth⟩ **4** : a series of actions or operations directed toward a particular result ⟨a manufacturing ~⟩ **5** : legal action **6** : a mandate issued by a court; *esp* : SUMMONS **7** : a projecting part of an organism or organic structure

[2]**process** *vb* : to subject to a special process

pro·ces·sion \prə-ˈse-shən\ *n* : a group of individuals moving along in an orderly often ceremonial way

pro·ces·sion·al \-ˈse-shə-nəl\ *n* **1** : music for a procession **2** : a ceremonial procession

pro·ces·sor \ˈprä-ˌse-sər, ˈprō-\ *n* **1** : one that processes **2** : CPU

pro–choice \(ˌ)prō-ˈchȯis\ *adj* : favoring the legalization of abortion

pro·claim \prō-ˈklām\ *vb* : to make known publicly : DECLARE

proc·la·ma·tion \ˌprä-klə-ˈmā-shən\ *n* : an official public announcement

pro·cliv·i·ty \prō-ˈkli-və-tē\ *n, pl* **-ties** : an inherent inclination esp. toward something objectionable

pro·con·sul \-ˈkän-səl\ *n* **1** : a governor or military commander of an ancient Roman province **2** : an administrator in a modern colony or occupied area — **pro·con·su·lar** \-sə-lər\ *adj*

pro·cras·ti·nate \prə-ˈkras-tə-ˌnāt, prō-\ *vb* **-nat·ed; -nat·ing** [L *procrastinare,* fr. *pro-* forward + *crastinus* of tomorrow, fr. *cras* tomorrow] : to put off usu. habitually doing something that should be done ♦ ***Synonyms*** DAWDLE, DELAY — **pro·cras·ti·na·tion** \-ˌkras-tə-ˈnā-shən\ *n* — **pro·cras·ti·na·tor** \-ˈkras-tə-ˌnā-tər\ *n*

pro·cre·ate \ˈprō-krē-ˌāt\ *vb* **-at·ed; -at·ing** : to beget or bring forth offspring ♦ ***Synonyms*** REPRODUCE, BREED, GENERATE, PROPAGATE — **pro·cre·ation** \ˌprō-krē-ˈā-shən\ *n* — **pro·cre·ative** \ˈprō-krē-ˌā-tiv\ *adj* — **pro·cre·ator** \-ˌā-tər\ *n*

pro·crus·te·an \prə-ˈkrəs-tē-ən\ *adj, often cap* [fr. *Procrustes,* villain of Greek mythology who made victims fit his bed by stretching them or cutting off their legs] : marked by arbitrary often ruthless disregard of individual differences or special circumstances

proc·tor \ˈpräk-tər\ *n* : one appointed to supervise students (as at an examination) — **proctor** *vb* — **proc·to·ri·al** \präk-ˈtȯr-ē-əl\ *adj*

proc·u·ra·tor \ˈprä-kyə-ˌrā-tər\ *n* : a Roman provincial administrator

pro·cure \prə-ˈkyu̇r\ *vb* **pro·cured; pro·cur·ing** **1** : to get possession of : OBTAIN **2** : to obtain (someone) to be employed for sexual intercourse **3** : ACHIEVE ♦ ***Synonyms*** SECURE, ACQUIRE, GAIN, WIN, EARN — **pro·cur·able** \-ˈkyu̇r-ə-bəl\ *adj* — **pro·cure·ment** *n* — **pro·cur·er** *n*

[1]**prod** \ˈpräd\ *vb* **prod·ded; prod·ding** **1** : to thrust a pointed instrument into : GOAD **2** : INCITE, STIR — **prod** *n*

[2]**prod** *abbr* product; production

prod·i·gal \ˈprä-di-gəl\ *adj* **1** : recklessly extravagant; *also* : LUXURIANT **2** : WASTEFUL, LAVISH ♦ ***Synonyms*** PROFUSE, LUSH, OPULENT — **prodigal** *n* — **prod·i·gal·i·ty** \ˌprä-də-ˈga-lə-tē\ *n*

pro·di·gious \prə-ˈdi-jəs\ *adj* **1** : exciting wonder **2** : extraordinary in size or degree : ENORMOUS ♦ ***Synonyms*** MONSTROUS, TREMENDOUS, STUPENDOUS, MONUMENTAL — **pro·di·gious·ly** *adv*

prod·i·gy \ˈprä-də-jē\ *n, pl* **-gies** **1** : something extraordinary : WONDER **2** : a highly talented child

[1]**pro·duce** \prə-ˈdüs, -ˈdyüs\ *vb* **pro·duced; pro·duc·ing** **1** : to present to view : EXHIBIT **2** : to give birth or rise to : YIELD **3** : EXTEND, PROLONG **4** : to give being or form to : BRING ABOUT, MAKE; *esp* : MANUFACTURE **5** : to sponsor or oversee the making of **6** : to cause to accrue ⟨~ a profit⟩ — **pro·duc·er** *n*

[2]**pro·duce** \ˈprä-(ˌ)düs, ˈprō- *also* -(ˌ)dyüs\ *n* : PRODUCT 2; *also* : agricultural products and esp. fresh fruits and vegetables

prod·uct \ˈprä-(ˌ)dəkt\ *n* **1** : the number resulting from multiplication **2** : something produced

pro·duc·tion \prə-ˈdək-shən\ *n* **1** : something produced : PRODUCT **2** : the act or process of producing — **pro·duc·tive** \-ˈdək-tiv\ *adj* — **pro·duc·tive·ness** *n* — **pro·duc·tiv·i·ty** \(ˌ)prō-ˌdək-ˈti-və-tē, ˌprä-(ˌ)dək-\ *n*

product placement *n* : the inclusion of a product in a television program or film as a means of advertising

pro·em \ˈprō-ˌem\ *n* **1** : preliminary comment : PREFACE **2** : PRELUDE

[1]**prof** \ˈpräf\ *n* : PROFESSOR

[2]**prof** *abbr* professional

[1]**pro·fane** \prō-ˈfān\ *vb* **pro·faned; pro·fan·ing** **1** : to treat (something sacred) with irreverence or contempt **2** : to debase by an unworthy use — **prof·a·na·tion** \ˌprä-fə-ˈnā-shən\ *n*

[2]**profane** *adj* [ME *prophane,* fr. MF, fr. L *profanus,* fr. *pro-* before + *fanum* temple] **1** : not concerned with religion : SECULAR **2** : not holy because unconsecrated, impure, or defiled **3** : serving to debase what is holy : IRREVERENT **4** : OBSCENE, VULGAR — **pro·fane·ly** *adv* — **pro·fane·ness** *n*

pro·fan·i·ty \prō-ˈfa-nə-tē\ *n, pl* **-ties** **1** : the quality or state of being profane **2** : the use of profane language **3** : profane language

pro·fess \prə-ˈfes\ *vb* **1** : to declare or admit openly : AFFIRM **2** : to declare in words only : PRETEND **3** : to confess one's faith in **4** : to practice or claim to be versed in (a calling or occupation) — **pro·fess·ed·ly** \-ˈfe-səd-lē\ *adv*

pro·fes·sion \prə-ˈfe-shən\ *n* **1** : an open declaration or avowal of a belief or opinion **2** : a calling requiring specialized knowledge and often long academic preparation **3** : the whole body of persons engaged in a calling

[1]**pro·fes·sion·al** \prə-ˈfe-shə-nəl\ *adj* **1** : of, relating to, or characteristic of a profession **2** : engaged in one of the professions **3** : participating for gain in an activity often engaged in by amateurs — **pro·fes·sion·al·ly** *adv*

[2]**professional** *n* : one that engages in an activity professionally

pro·fes·sion·al·ism \-nə-ˌli-zəm\ *n* **1** : the conduct, aims, or qualities that characterize or mark a profession or a professional person **2** : the following of a

profession (as athletics) for gain or livelihood
pro·fes·sion·al·ize \-nə-ˌlīz\ *vb* **-ized; -iz·ing** : to give a professional nature to
pro·fes·sor \prə-ˈfe-sər\ *n* : a teacher at a university or college; *esp* : a faculty member of the highest academic rank — **pro·fes·so·ri·al** \ˌprō-fə-ˈsȯr-ē-əl, ˌprä-\ *adj* — **pro·fes·sor·ship** *n*
prof·fer \ˈprä-fər\ *vb* **prof·fered; prof·fer·ing** : to present for acceptance : OFFER — **proffer** *n*
pro·fi·cient \prə-ˈfi-shənt\ *adj* : well advanced in an art, occupation, or branch of knowledge ♦ ***Synonyms*** ADEPT, SKILLFUL, EXPERT, MASTERFUL, MASTERLY — **pro·fi·cien·cy** \-shən-sē\ *n* — **proficient** *n* — **pro·fi·cient·ly** *adv*
¹**pro·file** \ˈprō-ˌfī(-ə)l\ *n* [It *profilo,* fr. *profilare* to draw in outline, fr. *pro-* forward (fr. L) + *filare* to spin, fr. LL, fr. L *filum* thread] **1** : a representation of something in outline; *esp* : a human head seen in side view **2** : a concise biographical sketch **3** : degree or level of public exposure ⟨keep a low ~⟩
²**profile** *vb* **pro·filed; pro·fil·ing** : to write or draw a profile of
profiling *n* : the act of suspecting or targeting a person solely on the basis of observed characteristics or behavior ⟨racial ~⟩
¹**prof·it** \ˈprä-fət\ *n* **1** : a valuable return : GAIN **2** : the excess of the selling price of goods over their cost — **prof·it·less** *adj*
²**profit** *vb* **1** : to be of use : BENEFIT **2** : to derive benefit : GAIN ⟨~*ed* from his mistakes⟩ — **prof·it·able** \ˈprä-fə-tə-bəl\ *adj* — **prof·it·ably** \-blē\ *adv*
prof·i·teer \ˌprä-fə-ˈtir\ *n* : one who makes what is considered an unreasonable profit — **profiteer** *vb*
prof·li·gate \ˈprä-fli-gət, -flə-ˌgāt\ *adj* **1** : completely given up to dissipation and licentiousness **2** : wildly extravagant — **prof·li·ga·cy** \-gə-sē\ *n* — **profligate** *n* — **prof·li·gate·ly** *adv*
pro for·ma \(ˌ)prō-ˈfȯr-mə\ *adj* : done or existing as a matter of form
pro·found \prə-ˈfau̇nd, prō-\ *adj* **1** : marked by intellectual depth or insight ⟨a ~ thought⟩ **2** : coming from or reaching to a depth ⟨a ~ sigh⟩ **3** : deeply felt : INTENSE ⟨~ sympathy⟩ — **pro·found·ly** *adv* — **pro·fun·di·ty** \-ˈfən-də-tē\ *n*
pro·fuse \prə-ˈfyüs, prō-\ *adj* : pouring forth liberally : ABUNDANT ⟨~ bleeding⟩ ♦ ***Synonyms*** LAVISH, PRODIGAL, LUXURIANT, EXUBERANT — **pro·fuse·ly** *adv* — **pro·fu·sion** \-ˈfyü-zhən\ *n*
prog *abbr* program
pro·gen·i·tor \prō-ˈje-nə-tər\ *n* **1** : a direct ancestor : FOREFATHER **2** : ORIGINATOR, PRECURSOR
prog·e·ny \ˈprä-jə-nē\ *n, pl* **-nies** : OFFSPRING, CHILDREN, DESCENDANTS
pro·ges·ter·one \prō-ˈjes-tə-ˌrōn\ *n* : a female hormone that causes the uterus to undergo changes so as to provide a suitable environment for a fertilized egg
prog·na·thous \ˈpräg-nə-thəs\ *adj* : having the lower jaw projecting beyond the upper part of the face
prog·no·sis \präg-ˈnō-səs\ *n, pl* **-no·ses** \-ˌsēz\ **1** : the prospect of recovery from disease **2** : FORECAST
¹**prog·nos·tic** \präg-ˈnäs-tik\ *n* **1** : PORTENT **2** : PROPHECY
²**prognostic** *adj* : of, relating to, or serving as ground for prognostication or a prognosis
prog·nos·ti·cate \präg-ˈnäs-tə-ˌkāt\ *vb* **-cat·ed; -cat·ing** : to foretell from signs or symptoms — **prog·nos·ti·ca·tion** \-ˌnäs-tə-ˈkā-shən\ *n* — **prog·nos·ti·ca·tor** \-ˈnäs-tə-ˌkā-tər\ *n*
¹**pro·gram** \ˈprō-ˌgram, -grəm\ *n* [F *programme* agenda, public notice, fr. Gk *programma,* fr. *prographein* to write in advance, fr. *pro-* before + *graphein* to write] **1** : a brief outline of the order to be pursued or the subjects included (as in a public entertainment); *also* : PERFORMANCE **2** : a plan of procedure esp. toward a goal **3** : coded instructions for a computer — **pro·gram·mat·ic** \ˌprō-grə-ˈma-tik\ *adj*
²**program** *also* **programme** *vb* **-grammed** *or* **-gramed; -gram·ming** *or* **-gram·ing** **1** : to arrange or furnish a program of or for **2** : to enter in a program **3** : to provide (as a computer) with a program — **pro·gram·ma·bil·i·ty** \(ˌ)prō-ˌgra-mə-ˈbi-lə-tē\ *n* — **pro·gram·ma·ble** \ˈprō-ˌgra-mə-bəl\ *adj* — **pro·gram·mer** *also* **pro·gram·er** \ˈprō-ˌgra-mər, -grə-\ *n*
programme *chiefly Brit var of* PROGRAM
programmed instruction *n* : instruction through information given in small steps with each requiring a correct response by the learner before going on to the next step
pro·gram·ming *also* **pro·gram·ing** *n* **1** : the planning, scheduling, or performing of a program **2** : the process of instructing or learning by means of an instruction program **3** : the process of preparing an instruction program
¹**prog·ress** \ˈprä-grəs, -ˌgres\ *n* **1** : a forward movement : ADVANCE **2** : a gradual betterment ⟨the ~ of science⟩
²**pro·gress** \prə-ˈgres\ *vb* **1** : to move forward : PROCEED **2** : to develop to a more advanced stage : IMPROVE
pro·gres·sion \prə-ˈgre-shən\ *n* **1** : an act of progressing : ADVANCE **2** : a continuous and connected series
¹**pro·gres·sive** \prə-ˈgre-siv\ *adj* **1** : of, relating to, or characterized by progress ⟨a ~ city⟩ **2** : moving forward or onward : ADVANCING **3** : increasing in extent or severity ⟨a ~ disease⟩ **4** *often cap* : of or relating to political Progressives **5** : of, relating to, or constituting a verb form that expresses action in progress at the time of speaking or a time spoken of — **pro·gres·sive·ly** *adv*
²**progressive** *n* **1** : one that is progressive **2** : a person believing in moderate political change and social improvement by government action; *esp, cap* : a member of a Progressive Party in the U.S.

pro·hib·it \prō-ˈhi-bət\ *vb* **1 :** to forbid by authority **2 :** to prevent from doing something

pro·hi·bi·tion \ˌprō-ə-ˈbi-shən\ *n* **1 :** the act of prohibiting **2 :** the forbidding by law of the sale or manufacture of alcoholic beverages — **pro·hi·bi·tion·ist** \-ˈbi-shə-nist\ *n* — **pro·hib·i·tive** \prō-ˈhi-bə-tiv\ *adj* — **pro·hib·i·tive·ly** *adv* — **pro·hib·i·to·ry** \-ˈhi-bə-ˌtȯr-ē\ *adj*

1proj·ect \ˈprä-ˌjekt, -jikt\ *n* **1 :** a specific plan or design **:** SCHEME **2 :** a planned undertaking ⟨a research ~⟩

2pro·ject \prə-ˈjekt\ *vb* **1 :** to devise in the mind **:** DESIGN **2 :** to throw forward **3 :** PROTRUDE **4 :** to cause (light or shadow) to fall into space or (an image) to fall on a surface ⟨~ a beam of light⟩ **5 :** to attribute (a thought, feeling, or personal characteristic) to a person, group, or object **6 :** to display outwardly — **pro·jec·tion** \-ˈjek-shən\ *n*

pro·jec·tile \prə-ˈjek-tᵊl, -ˈjek-tī(-ə)l\ *n* **1 :** a body hurled or projected by external force; *esp* **:** a missile for a firearm **2 :** a self-propelling weapon

pro·jec·tion·ist \prə-ˈjek-shə-nist\ *n* **:** one that operates a motion-picture projector or television equipment

pro·jec·tor \-ˈjek-tər\ *n* **:** one that projects; *esp* **:** a device for projecting pictures on a screen

pro·lapse \prō-ˈlaps, ˈprō-ˌ\ *n* **:** the falling down or slipping of a body part from its usual position

pro·le·gom·e·non \ˌprō-li-ˈgä-mə-ˌnän, -nən\ *n, pl* **-e·na** \-nə\ **:** prefatory remarks

pro·le·tar·i·an \ˌprō-lə-ˈter-ē-ən\ *n* [L *proletarius* belonging to the lowest class of citizens, fr. *proles* progeny, fr. *pro-* forth + *-oles* (akin to *alere* to nourish)] **:** a member of the proletariat — **proletarian** *adj*

pro·le·tar·i·at \-ē-ət\ *n* **:** the laboring class; *esp* **:** industrial workers who sell their labor to live

pro–life \(ˌ)prō-ˈlīf\ *n* **:** ANTIABORTION

pro·lif·er·ate \prə-ˈli-fə-ˌrāt\ *vb* **-at·ed; -at·ing :** to grow or increase by rapid production of new units (as cells, offspring, or nuclear weapons) — **pro·lif·er·a·tion** \-ˌli-fə-ˈrā-shən\ *n*

pro·lif·ic \prə-ˈli-fik\ *adj* **1 :** producing young or fruit abundantly **2 :** marked by abundant inventiveness or productivity ⟨a ~ writer⟩ — **pro·lif·i·cal·ly** \-fi-k(ə-)lē\ *adv*

pro·lix \prō-ˈliks, ˈprō-ˌliks\ *adj* **:** VERBOSE ♦ ***Synonyms*** WORDY, DIFFUSE, REDUNDANT — **pro·lix·i·ty** \prō-ˈlik-sə-tē\ *n*

pro·logue *also* **pro·log** \ˈprō-ˌlȯg, -ˌläg\ *n* **:** PREFACE ⟨~ of a play⟩

pro·long \prə-ˈlȯŋ\ *vb* **1 :** to lengthen in time **:** CONTINUE ⟨~ a meeting⟩ **2 :** to lengthen in extent or range ⟨~ an airport runway⟩ ♦ ***Synonyms*** PROTRACT, EXTEND, ELONGATE, STRETCH — **pro·lon·ga·tion** \ˌprō-ˌlȯŋ-ˈgā-shən\ *n*

prom \ˈpräm\ *n* **:** a formal dance given by a high school or college class

1prom·e·nade \ˌprä-mə-ˈnād, -ˈnäd\ *vb* **-nad·ed; -nad·ing 1 :** to take a promenade **2 :** to walk about in or on

2promenade *n* [F, fr. *promener* to take for a walk, fr. MF, alter. of OF *pourmener,* fr. *pour-* completely (fr. L *pro-*) + *mener* to lead, fr. LL *minare* to drive, fr. L *minari* to threaten] **1 :** a place for strolling **2 :** a leisurely walk for pleasure or display **3 :** an opening grand march at a formal ball

pro·me·thi·um \prə-ˈmē-thē-əm\ *n* **:** a metallic chemical element obtained from uranium or neodymium

prom·i·nence \ˈprä-mə-nəns\ *n* **1 :** something prominent **2 :** the quality, state, or fact of being prominent or conspicuous **3 :** a mass of cloudlike gas that arises from the sun's chromosphere

prom·i·nent \-nənt\ *adj* **1 :** jutting out **:** PROJECTING **2 :** readily noticeable **:** CONSPICUOUS **3 :** DISTINGUISHED, EMINENT ⟨a ~ lawyer⟩ ♦ ***Synonyms*** REMARKABLE, OUTSTANDING, STRIKING, SALIENT — **prom·i·nent·ly** *adv*

pro·mis·cu·ous \prə-ˈmis-kyə-wəs\ *adj* **1 :** consisting of various sorts and kinds **:** MIXED **2 :** not restricted to one class or person **3 :** having a number of sexual partners ♦ ***Synonyms*** MISCELLANEOUS, ASSORTED, HETEROGENEOUS, MOTLEY, VARIED — **pro·mis·cu·i·ty** \ˌprä-mis-ˈkyü-ə-tē, ˌprō-ˌmis-\ *n* — **pro·mis·cu·ous·ly** *adv* — **pro·mis·cu·ous·ness** *n*

1prom·ise \ˈprä-məs\ *n* **1 :** a pledge to do or not to do something specified **2 :** ground for expectation of success or improvement **3 :** something promised

2promise *vb* **prom·ised; prom·is·ing 1 :** to engage to do, bring about, or provide ⟨~ help⟩ **2 :** to suggest beforehand ⟨dark clouds ~ rain⟩ **3 :** to give ground for expectation ⟨it ~*s* to be fun⟩

promising *adj* **:** likely to succeed or yield good results ⟨a ~ new medicine⟩ — **prom·is·ing·ly** *adv*

prom·is·so·ry \ˈprä-mə-ˌsȯr-ē\ *adj* **:** containing a promise

prom·on·to·ry \ˈprä-mən-ˌtȯr-ē\ *n, pl* **-ries :** a point of land jutting into the sea **:** HEADLAND

pro·mote \prə-ˈmōt\ *vb* **pro·mot·ed; pro·mot·ing 1 :** to advance in station, rank, or honor **2 :** to contribute to the growth or prosperity of **:** FURTHER **3 :** LAUNCH — **pro·mo·tion** \-ˈmō-shən\ *n* — **pro·mo·tion·al** \-shə-nəl\ *adj*

pro·mot·er \-ˈmō-tər\ *n* **:** one that promotes; *esp* **:** one that assumes the financial responsibilities of a sports event

1prompt \ˈprämpt\ *vb* **1 :** INCITE **2 :** to assist (one acting or reciting) by suggesting the next words **3 :** INSPIRE, URGE — **prompt·er** *n*

2prompt *adj* **1 :** being ready and quick to act; *also* **:** PUNCTUAL **2 :** performed readily or immediately ⟨~ service⟩ — **prompt·ly** *adv* — **prompt·ness** *n*

prompt·book \-ˌbu̇k\ *n* **:** a copy of a play with directions for performance used by a theater prompter

promp·ti·tude \'prämp-tə-ˌtüd, -ˌtyüd\ *n* : the quality or habit of being prompt : PROMPTNESS
pro·mul·gate \'prä-məl-ˌgāt; prō-'məl-\ *vb* **-gat·ed; -gat·ing** : to make known or put into force by open declaration — **prom·ul·ga·tion** \ˌprä-məl-'gā-shən, ˌprō-(ˌ)məl-\ *n*
pron *abbr* **1** pronoun **2** pronounced **3** pronunciation
prone \'prōn\ *adj* **1** : having a tendency or inclination : DISPOSED **2** : lying face downward; *also* : lying flat or prostrate ♦ ***Synonyms*** SUBJECT, EXPOSED, OPEN, LIABLE, SUSCEPTIBLE — **prone·ness** *n*
prong \'prȯŋ\ *n* : one of the sharp points of a fork : TINE; *also* : a slender projecting part (as of an antler) — **pronged** \'prȯŋd\ *adj*
prong·horn \'prȯŋ-ˌhȯrn\ *n, pl* **prong·horn** *or* **pronghorns** : a swift horned ruminant mammal chiefly of grasslands of western No. America that resembles an antelope
pro·noun \'prō-ˌnau̇n\ *n* : a word used as a substitute for a noun
pro·nounce \prə-'nau̇ns\ *vb* **pro·nounced; pro·nounc·ing** **1** : to utter officially or as an opinion ⟨~ sentence⟩ **2** : to employ the organs of speech in order to produce ⟨~ a word⟩; *esp* : to say or speak correctly ⟨she can't ~ his name⟩ — **pro·nounce·able** *adj* — **pro·nun·ci·a·tion** \-ˌnən-sē-'ā-shən\ *n*
pro·nounced *adj* : strongly marked : DECIDED ⟨a ~ dislike⟩
pro·nounce·ment \prə-'nau̇ns-mənt\ *n* : a formal declaration of opinion; *also* : ANNOUNCEMENT
pron·to \'prän-ˌtō\ *adv* [Sp, fr. L *promptus* prompt] : QUICKLY
pro·nu·clear \'prō-'nü-klē-ər, -'nyü-\ *adj* : supporting the use of nuclear-powered electric generating stations
pro·nun·ci·a·men·to \prō-ˌnən-sē-ə-'men-tō\ *n, pl* **-tos** *or* **-toes** : PROCLAMATION, MANIFESTO
¹**proof** \'prüf\ *n* [ME *prof, prove,* alter. of *preve,* fr. AF *preove,* fr. LL *proba,* fr. L *probare* to test, prove, fr. *probus* good, honest] **1** : the evidence that compels acceptance by the mind of a truth or fact **2** : a process or operation that establishes validity or truth : TEST **3** : a trial impression (as from type) **4** : a trial print from a photographic negative **5** : alcoholic content (as of a beverage) indicated by a number that is twice the percent by volume of alcohol present ⟨whiskey of 90 ~ is 45% alcohol⟩
²**proof** *adj* **1** : successful in resisting or repelling ⟨~ against tampering⟩ ⟨water*proof*⟩ **2** : of standard strength or quality or alcoholic content
proof·read \-ˌrēd\ *vb* : to read and mark corrections in — **proof·read·er** *n*
¹**prop** \'präp\ *n* : something that props
²**prop** *vb* **propped; prop·ping** **1** : to support by placing something under or against **2** : SUSTAIN, STRENGTHEN
³**prop** *n* : PROPERTY 4
⁴**prop** *n* : PROPELLER
⁵**prop** *abbr* **1** property **2** proposition **3** proprietor
pro·pa·gan·da \ˌprä-pə-'gan-də, ˌprō-\ *n* [NL, fr. *Congregatio de propaganda fide* Congregation for propagating the faith, organization established by Pope Gregory XV] : the spreading of ideas or information to further or damage a cause; *also* : ideas or allegations spread for such a purpose — **pro·pa·gan·dist** \-dist\ *n or adj* — **pro·pa·gan·dis·tic** \-ˌgan-'dis-tik\ *adj*
pro·pa·gan·dize \-'gan-ˌdīz\ *vb* **-dized; -diz·ing** : to subject to or carry on propaganda
prop·a·gate \'prä-pə-ˌgāt\ *vb* **-gat·ed; -gat·ing** **1** : to reproduce or cause to reproduce biologically : MULTIPLY **2** : to cause to spread ⟨*propagating* the faith⟩ — **prop·a·ga·tion** \ˌprä-pə-'gā-shən\ *n*
pro·pane \'prō-ˌpān\ *n* : a heavy flammable gas found in petroleum and natural gas and used esp. as a fuel
pro·pel \prə-'pel\ *vb* **pro·pelled; pro·pel·ling** : to drive forward or onward ♦ ***Synonyms*** PUSH, SHOVE, THRUST
pro·pel·lant *also* **pro·pel·lent** \-'pe-lənt\ *n* : something (as a fuel) that propels — **propellant** *also* **propellent** *adj*
pro·pel·ler \prə-'pe-lər\ *n* : a device consisting of a hub fitted with blades that is used to propel a vehicle (as a motorboat or an airplane)
pro·pen·si·ty \prə-'pen-sə-tē\ *n, pl* **-ties** : an often intense natural inclination or preference
¹**prop·er** \'prä-pər\ *adj* **1** : referring to one individual only ⟨~ noun⟩ **2** : belonging characteristically to a species or individual : PECULIAR **3** : very satisfactory : EXCELLENT **4** : strictly limited to a specified thing ⟨the city ~⟩ **5** : CORRECT ⟨the ~ way to proceed⟩ **6** : strictly decorous : GENTEEL **7** : marked by suitability or rightness ⟨~ punishment⟩ ♦ ***Synonyms*** MEET, APPROPRIATE, FITTING, SEEMLY — **prop·er·ly** *adv*
²**proper** *n* : the parts of the Mass that vary according to the liturgical calendar
prop·er·tied \'prä-pər-tēd\ *adj* : owning property and esp. much property
prop·er·ty \'prä-pər-tē\ *n, pl* **-ties** **1** : a quality peculiar to an individual or thing **2** : something owned; *esp* : a piece of real estate **3** : OWNERSHIP **4** : an article or object used in a play or motion picture other than painted scenery and actor's costumes
proph·e·cy *also* **proph·e·sy** \'prä-fə-sē\ *n, pl* **-cies** *also* **-sies** **1** : an inspired utterance of a prophet **2** : PREDICTION
proph·e·sy \-ˌsī\ *vb* **-sied; -sy·ing** **1** : to speak or utter by divine inspiration **2** : PREDICT — **proph·e·si·er** *n*
proph·et \'prä-fət\ *n* [ME *prophete,* fr. AF, fr. L *propheta,* fr. Gk *prophētēs,* fr. *pro* for + *phanai* to speak] **1** : one who utters divinely inspired revelations **2** : one who foretells future events
proph·et·ess \'prä-fə-təs\ *n* : a woman who is a prophet

pro·phet·ic \prə-ˈfe-tik\ *or* **pro·phet·i·cal** \-ti-kəl\ *adj* : of, relating to, or characteristic of a prophet or prophecy — **pro·phet·i·cal·ly** \-ti-k(ə-)lē\ *adv*

Proph·ets \ˈprä-fəts\ *n pl* — see BIBLE table

[1]**pro·phy·lac·tic** \ˌprō-fə-ˈlak-tik, ˌprä-\ *adj* **1** : preventing or guarding from the spread or occurrence of disease or infection **2** : PREVENTIVE

[2]**prophylactic** *n* : something prophylactic; *esp* : a device (as a condom) for preventing venereal infection or conception

pro·phy·lax·is \-ˈlak-səs\ *n, pl* **-lax·es** \-ˈlak-ˌsēz\ : measures designed to preserve health and prevent the spread of disease

pro·pin·qui·ty \prə-ˈpiŋ-kwə-tē\ *n* **1** : KINSHIP **2** : nearness in place or time : PROXIMITY

pro·pi·ti·ate \prō-ˈpi-shē-ˌāt\ *vb* **-at·ed; -at·ing** : to gain or regain the favor of : APPEASE ⟨~ the angry gods⟩ — **pro·pi·ti·a·tion** \-ˌpi-shē-ˈā-shən\ *n* — **pro·pi·tia·to·ry** \-ˈpi-shē-ə-ˌtȯr-ē\ *adj*

pro·pi·tious \prə-ˈpi-shəs\ *adj* **1** : favorably disposed ⟨~ deities⟩ **2** : being of good omen ⟨~ circumstances⟩

prop·man \ˈpräp-ˌman\ *n* : one who is in charge of stage properties

pro·po·nent \prə-ˈpō-nənt\ *n* : one who argues in favor of something

[1]**pro·por·tion** \prə-ˈpȯr-shən\ *n* **1** : BALANCE, SYMMETRY **2** : SHARE, QUOTA **3** : the relation of one part to another or to the whole with respect to magnitude, quantity, or degree : RATIO **4** : SIZE, DEGREE — **in proportion** : PROPORTIONAL

[2]**proportion** *vb* **-tioned; -tion·ing** **1** : to adjust (a part or thing) in size relative to other parts or things **2** : to make the parts of harmonious

pro·por·tion·al \prə-ˈpȯr-shə-nəl\ *adj* : corresponding in size, degree, or intensity; *also* : having the same or a constant ratio — **pro·por·tion·al·ly** *adv*

pro·por·tion·ate \prə-ˈpȯr-shə-nət\ *adj* : PROPORTIONAL — **pro·por·tion·ate·ly** *adv*

pro·pose \prə-ˈpōz\ *vb* **pro·posed; pro·pos·ing** **1** : PLAN, INTEND ⟨~*s* to buy a house⟩ **2** : to make an offer of marriage **3** : to offer for consideration : SUGGEST ⟨~ a policy⟩ — **pro·pos·al** \-ˈpō-zəl\ *n* — **pro·pos·er** *n*

[1]**prop·o·si·tion** \ˌprä-pə-ˈzi-shən\ *n* **1** : something proposed for consideration : PROPOSAL **2** : a request for sexual intercourse **3** : a statement of something to be discussed, proved, or explained **4** : SITUATION, AFFAIR ⟨a tough ~⟩ — **prop·o·si·tion·al** \-ˈzi-shə-nəl\ *adj*

[2]**proposition** *vb* **-tioned; -tion·ing** : to make a proposal to; *esp* : to suggest sexual intercourse to

pro·pound \prə-ˈpau̇nd\ *vb* : to set forth for consideration ⟨~ a doctrine⟩

pro·pri·e·tary \prə-ˈprī-ə-ˌter-ē\ *adj* **1** : of, relating to, or characteristic of a proprietor ⟨~ rights⟩ **2** : made and sold by one with the sole right to do so ⟨~ medicines⟩ ⟨~ software⟩

pro·pri·e·tor \prə-ˈprī-ə-tər\ *n* : OWNER — **pro·pri·e·tor·ship** *n*

pro·pri·e·tress \-ˈprī-ə-trəs\ *n* : a woman who is a proprietor

pro·pri·e·ty \prə-ˈprī-ə-tē\ *n, pl* **-ties** **1** : the standard of what is socially acceptable in conduct or speech **2** *pl* : the customs of polite society

props \ˈpräps\ *n sing or pl* **1** *slang* : DUE 1 ⟨gave him his ~⟩ **2** *slang* : RESPECT 2 ⟨earned the ~ of his peers⟩ **3** *slang* : ACKNOWLEDGMENT ⟨deserves ~ for the effort⟩

pro·pul·sion \prə-ˈpəl-shən\ *n* **1** : the action or process of propelling **2** : something that propels — **pro·pul·sive** \-siv\ *adj*

pro ra·ta \(ˌ)prō-ˈrā-tə, -ˈrä-\ *adv* : in proportion to the share of each : PROPORTIONATELY

pro·rate \(ˌ)prō-ˈrāt\ *vb* **pro·rat·ed; pro·rat·ing** : to divide, distribute, or assess proportionately

pro·rogue \prə-ˈrōg\ *vb* **pro·rogued; pro·rogu·ing** : to suspend or end a session of (a legislative body) — **pro·ro·ga·tion** \ˌprō-rō-ˈgā-shən\ *n*

pros *pl of* PRO

pro·sa·ic \prō-ˈzā-ik\ *adj* : lacking imagination or excitement : DULL

pro·sce·ni·um \prō-ˈsē-nē-əm\ *n* **1** : the part of a stage in front of the curtain **2** : the wall containing the arch that frames the stage

pro·scribe \prō-ˈskrīb\ *vb* **pro·scribed; pro·scrib·ing** **1** : OUTLAW **2** : to condemn or forbid as harmful — **pro·scrip·tion** \-ˈskrip-shən\ *n*

prose \ˈprōz\ *n* [ME, fr. AF, fr. L *prosa,* fr. fem. of *prorsus, prosus,* straightforward, being in prose, alter. of *proversus,* pp. of *provertere* to turn forward] : the ordinary language people use in speaking or writing

pros·e·cute \ˈprä-si-ˌkyüt\ *vb* **-cut·ed; -cut·ing** **1** : to follow to the end ⟨~ an investigation⟩ **2** : to seek legal punishment of ⟨~ a forger⟩ — **pros·e·cu·tion** \ˌprä-si-ˈkyü-shən\ *n* — **pros·e·cu·tor** \ˈprä-si-ˌkyü-tər\ *n* — **pros·e·cu·to·ri·al** \ˌprä-si-kyü-ˈtȯr-ē-əl\ *adj*

[1]**pros·e·lyte** \ˈprä-sə-ˌlīt\ *n* : a new convert to a religion, belief, or party — **pros·e·ly·tism** \-ˌlī-ˌti-zəm\ *n*

[2]**proselyte** *vb* **-lyt·ed; -lyt·ing** : PROSELYTIZE

pros·e·ly·tise *Brit var of* PROSELYTIZE

pros·e·ly·tize \ˈprä-sə-lə-ˌtīz\ *vb* **-tized; -tiz·ing** **1** : to induce someone to convert to one's faith **2** : to recruit someone to join one's party, institution, or cause

pros·o·dy \ˈprä-sə-dē, -zə-\ *n, pl* **-dies** : the study of versification and esp. of metrical structure — **pro·sod·ic** \prə-ˈsä-dik\ *adj*

[1]**pros·pect** \ˈprä-ˌspekt\ *n* **1** : an extensive view; *also* : OUTLOOK **2** : the act of looking forward **3** : a mental vision of something to come **4** : something that is awaited or expected : POSSIBILITY **5** : a potential buyer or customer; *also* : a like-

ly candidate (as for a job) — **pro·spec·tive** \prə-ˈspek-tiv, ˈprä-ˌspek-\ *adj* — **pro·spec·tive·ly** *adv*

[2]**pros·pect** \ˈprä-ˌspekt\ *vb* : to explore esp. for mineral deposits — **pros·pec·tor** \-ˌspek-tər, prä-ˈspek-\ *n*

pro·spec·tus \prə-ˈspek-təs\ *n* : a preliminary statement that describes an enterprise and is distributed to prospective buyers or participants

pros·per \ˈpräs-pər\ *vb* **pros·pered; pros·per·ing** : SUCCEED; *esp* : to achieve economic success

pros·per·i·ty \präs-ˈper-ə-tē\ *n* : thriving condition : SUCCESS; *esp* : economic well-being

pros·per·ous \ˈpräs-pə-rəs\ *adj* **1** : FAVORABLE ⟨~ winds⟩ **2** : marked by success or economic well-being ⟨a ~ business⟩

pros·ta·glan·din \ˌpräs-tə-ˈglan-dən\ *n* : any of various oxygenated unsaturated fatty acids of animals that perform a variety of hormonelike actions

pros·tate \ˈpräs-ˌtāt\ *n* [NL *prostata,* fr. Gk *prostatēs,* fr. *proïstanai* to put in front] : PROSTATE GLAND — **pros·tat·ic** \prä-ˈsta-tik\ *adj*

prostate gland *n* : a glandular body about the base of the male urethra that produces a secretion which is a major part of the fluid ejaculated during an orgasm

pros·ta·ti·tis \ˌpräs-tə-ˈtī-təs\ *n* : inflammation of the prostate gland

pros·the·sis \präs-ˈthē-səs, ˈpräs-thə-\ *n, pl* **-the·ses** \-ˌsēz\ : an artificial replacement for a missing body part — **pros·thet·ic** \präs-ˈthe-tik\ *adj*

pros·thet·ics \-ˈthe-tiks\ *n pl* : the surgical or dental specialty concerned with the design, construction, and fitting of prostheses

[1]**pros·ti·tute** \ˈpräs-tə-ˌtüt, -ˌtyüt\ *vb* **-tut·ed; -tut·ing** **1** : to offer indiscriminately for sexual activity esp. for money **2** : to devote to corrupt or unworthy purposes — **pros·ti·tu·tion** \ˌpräs-tə-ˈtü-shən, -ˈtyü-\ *n*

[2]**prostitute** *n* : one who engages in sexual activities for money

[1]**pros·trate** \ˈprä-ˌstrāt\ *adj* **1** : stretched out with face on the ground in adoration or submission **2** : lying flat **3** : completely overcome ⟨~ with a cold⟩

[2]**prostrate** *vb* **pros·trat·ed; pros·trat·ing** **1** : to throw or put into a prostrate position **2** : to reduce to a weak or powerless condition — **pros·tra·tion** \prä-ˈstrā-shən\ *n*

prosy \ˈprō-zē\ *adj* **pros·i·er; -est** **1** : PROSAIC, ORDINARY **2** : TEDIOUS

Prot *abbr* Protestant

prot·ac·tin·i·um \ˌprō-ˌtak-ˈti-nē-əm\ *n* : a metallic radioactive chemical element of relatively short life

pro·tag·o·nist \prō-ˈta-gə-nist\ *n* **1** : the principal character in a drama or story **2** : a leader or supporter of a cause

pro·te·an \ˈprō-tē-ən\ *adj* : able to assume different shapes or roles

pro·tect \prə-ˈtekt\ *vb* : to shield from injury : GUARD

pro·tec·tion \prə-ˈtek-shən\ *n* **1** : the act of protecting : the state of being protected **2** : one that protects ⟨wear a helmet as a ~⟩ **3** : the supervision or support of one that is smaller and weaker **4** : the freeing of producers from foreign competition in their home market by high duties on foreign competitive goods — **pro·tec·tive** \-ˈtek-tiv\ *adj*

pro·tec·tion·ist \-shə-nist\ *n* : an advocate of government economic protection for domestic producers through restrictions on foreign competitors — **pro·tec·tion·ism** \-shə-ˌni-zəm\ *n*

pro·tec·tor \prə-ˈtek-tər\ *n* **1** : one that protects : GUARDIAN **2** : a device used to prevent injury : GUARD **3** : REGENT 1

pro·tec·tor·ate \-tə-rət\ *n* **1** : government by a protector **2** : the relationship of superior authority assumed by one state over a dependent one; *also* : the dependent political unit in such a relationship

pro·té·gé \ˈprō-tə-ˌzhā\ *n* [F] : one who is protected, trained, or guided by an influential person

pro·tein \ˈprō-ˌtēn\ *n* [F *protéine,* fr. LGk *prōteios* primary, fr. Gk *prōtos* first] : any of various complex nitrogen-containing substances that consist of chains of amino acids, are present in all living cells, and are an essential part of the human diet

pro tem \prō-ˈtem\ *adv* : PRO TEMPORE

pro tem·po·re \prō-ˈtem-pə-rē\ *adv* [L] : for the time being

Pro·te·ro·zo·ic \ˌprä-tə-rə-ˈzō-ik, ˌprō-\ *adj* : of, relating to, or being the eon of geologic history between the Archean and the Phanerozoic — **Proterozoic** *n*

[1]**pro·test** \ˈprō-ˌtest\ *n* **1** : the act of protesting; *esp* : an organized public demonstration of disapproval **2** : a complaint or objection against an idea, an act, or a course of action

[2]**pro·test** \prō-ˈtest\ *vb* **1** : to assert positively : make solemn declaration of ⟨~s his innocence⟩ **2** : to object strongly : make a protest against ⟨~ a ruling⟩ — **pro·tes·ta·tion** \ˌprä-təs-ˈtā-shən\ *n* — **pro·test·er** *or* **pro·tes·tor** \-tər\ *n*

Prot·es·tant \ˈprä-təs-tənt, *3 also* prə-ˈtes-\ *n* **1** : a member or adherent of one of the Christian churches deriving from the Reformation **2** : a Christian not of a Catholic or Orthodox church **3** *not cap* : one who makes a protest — **Prot·es·tant·ism** \ˈprä-təs-tən-ˌti-zəm\ *n*

pro·tha·la·mi·on \ˌprō-thə-ˈlā-mē-ən\ *or* **pro·tha·la·mi·um** \-mē-əm\ *n, pl* **-mia** \-mē-ə\ : a song in celebration of a marriage

pro·to·col \ˈprō-tə-ˌkȯl\ *n* [MF *prothocole,* fr. ML *protocollum,* fr. LGk *prōtokollon* first sheet of a papyrus roll bearing data of manufacture, fr. Gk *prōtos* first + *kollan* to glue together, fr. *kolla* glue] **1** : an original draft or record **2** : a preliminary memorandum of diplomatic negotiation **3** : a code of diplomatic or military etiquette **4** : a set of conventions for formatting data in an electronic communications system

pro·ton \ˈprō-ˌtän\ *n* [Gk *prōton,* neut. of *prōtos* first] : a positively charged atomic particle present in all atomic nuclei — **pro·ton·ic** \-ˈtä-nik\ *adj*

pro·to·plasm \ˈprō-tə-ˌpla-zəm\ *n* : the complex colloidal largely protein substance of living plant and animal cells — **pro·to·plas·mic** \ˌprō-tə-ˈplaz-mik\ *adj*

pro·to·type \ˈprō-tə-ˌtīp\ *n* : an original model : ARCHETYPE

pro·to·zo·an \ˌprō-tə-ˈzō-ən\ *n* : any of a phylum or subkingdom of unicellular lower invertebrate animals that include some pathogenic parasites of humans and domestic animals — **protozoan** *adj*

pro·tract \prō-ˈtrakt\ *vb* : to prolong in time or space ♦ ***Synonyms*** EXTEND, LENGTHEN, ELONGATE, STRETCH

pro·trac·tor \-ˈtrak-tər\ *n* : an instrument for drawing and measuring angles

pro·trude \prō-ˈtrüd\ *vb* **pro·trud·ed; pro·trud·ing** : to stick out or cause to stick out : jut out — **pro·tru·sion** \-ˈtrü-zhən\ *n*

pro·tu·ber·ance \prō-ˈtü-bə-rəns, -ˈtyü-\ *n* : something that protrudes

pro·tu·ber·ant \-rənt\ *adj* : extending beyond the surrounding surface in a bulge

proud \ˈpraủd\ *adj* **1** : having or showing excessive self-esteem : HAUGHTY **2** : highly pleased : EXULTANT **3** : having proper self-respect ⟨too ~ to beg⟩ **4** : GLORIOUS ⟨a ~ occasion⟩ **5** : SPIRITED ⟨a ~ steed⟩ ♦ ***Synonyms*** ARROGANT, INSOLENT, OVERBEARING, DISDAINFUL — **proud·ly** *adv*

prov *abbr* **1** province; provincial **2** provisional

Prov *abbr* Proverbs

prove \ˈprüv\ *vb* **proved; proved** *or* **prov·en** \ˈprü-vən\; **prov·ing** **1** : to test by experiment or by a standard **2** : to establish the truth of by argument or evidence **3** : to show to be correct, valid, or genuine **4** : to turn out esp. after trial or test ⟨the car *proved* to be a good choice⟩ — **prov·able** \ˈprü-və-bəl\ *adj*

prov·e·nance \ˈprä-və-nəns\ *n* : ORIGIN, SOURCE

Pro·ven·çal \ˌprō-ˌvän-ˈsäl, ˌprä-vən-\ *n* **1** : a native or inhabitant of Provence **2** : OCCITAN — **Provençal** *adj*

prov·en·der \ˈprä-vən-dər\ *n* **1** : dry food for domestic animals : FEED **2** : FOOD, VICTUALS

pro·ve·nience \prə-ˈvē-nyəns\ *n* : ORIGIN, SOURCE

prov·erb \ˈprä-ˌvərb\ *n* : a pithy popular saying : ADAGE

pro·ver·bi·al \prə-ˈvər-bē-əl\ *adj* **1** : of, relating to, or resembling a proverb **2** : commonly spoken of

Proverbs *n* — see BIBLE table

pro·vide \prə-ˈvīd\ *vb* **pro·vid·ed; pro·vid·ing** [ME, fr. L *providēre,* lit., to see ahead, fr. *pro-* forward + *vidēre* to see] **1** : to take measures beforehand ⟨~ against inflation⟩ **2** : to make a proviso or stipulation **3** : to supply what is needed ⟨~ for a family⟩ **4** : EQUIP **5** : to supply for use : YIELD — **pro·vid·er** *n*

pro·vid·ed *conj* : on condition that : IF

prov·i·dence \ˈprä-və-dəns\ *n* **1** *often cap* : divine guidance or care **2** *cap* : GOD 1 **3** : the quality or state of being provident

prov·i·dent \-dənt\ *adj* **1** : making provision for the future : PRUDENT **2** : FRUGAL — **prov·i·dent·ly** *adv*

prov·i·den·tial \ˌprä-və-ˈden-chəl\ *adj* **1** : of, relating to, or determined by Providence **2** : OPPORTUNE, LUCKY

providing *conj* : PROVIDED

prov·ince \ˈprä-vəns\ *n* **1** : an administrative district or division of a country **2** *pl* : all of a country except the metropolises **3** : proper business or scope : SPHERE ⟨the ~ of the jury⟩

pro·vin·cial \prə-ˈvin-chəl\ *adj* **1** : of or relating to a province **2** : limited in outlook : NARROW ⟨~ ideas⟩ — **pro·vin·cial·ism** \-chə-ˌli-zəm\ *n*

proving ground *n* : a place for scientific experimentation or testing

[1]**pro·vi·sion** \prə-ˈvi-zhən\ *n* **1** : the act or process of providing; *also* : a measure taken beforehand **2** : a stock of needed supplies; *esp* : a stock of food — usu. used in pl. **3** : PROVISO

[2]**provision** *vb* : to supply with provisions

pro·vi·sion·al \-ˈvi-zhə-nəl\ *adj* : provided for a temporary need : CONDITIONAL — **pro·vi·sion·al·ly** *adv*

pro·vi·so \prə-ˈvī-zō\ *n, pl* **-sos** *also* **-soes** [ME, fr. ML *proviso quod* provided that] : an article or clause that introduces a condition : STIPULATION

pro·vo·ca·teur \prō-ˌvä-kə-ˈtər\ *n* : one who provokes

prov·o·ca·tion \ˌprä-və-ˈkā-shən\ *n* **1** : the act of provoking **2** : something that provokes

pro·voc·a·tive \prə-ˈvä-kə-tiv\ *adj* : serving to provoke or excite

pro·voke \prə-ˈvōk\ *vb* **pro·voked; pro·vok·ing** **1** : to incite to anger : INCENSE **2** : to call forth : EVOKE ⟨a remark that *provoked* laughter⟩ **3** : to stir up on purpose ⟨~ an argument⟩ ♦ ***Synonyms*** IRRITATE, EXASPERATE, AGGRAVATE, INFLAME, RILE, PIQUE — **pro·vok·er** *n*

pro·vo·lo·ne \ˌprō-və-ˈlō-nē\ *n* : a usu. firm pliant often smoked Italian cheese

pro·vost \ˈprō-ˌvōst, ˈprä-vəst\ *n* : a high official : DIGNITARY; *esp* : a high-ranking university administrative officer

pro·vost mar·shal \ˈprō-ˌvō-ˈmär-shəl\ *n* : an officer who supervises the military police of a command

prow \ˈpraủ\ *n* : the bow of a ship

prow·ess \ˈpraủ-əs\ *n* **1** : military valor and skill **2** : extraordinary ability

prowl \ˈpraủ(-ə)l\ *vb* : to roam about stealthily — **prowl** *n* — **prowl·er** *n*

prox·i·mal \ˈpräk-sə-məl\ *adj* **1** : next to or nearest the point of attachment or origin; *esp* : located toward the center of the body **2** : of, relating to, or being the me-

sial and distal surfaces of a tooth — **prox·i·mal·ly** *adv*
prox·i·mate \ˈpräk-sə-mət\ *adj* **1** : DIRECT ⟨the ~ cause⟩ **2** : very near
prox·im·i·ty \präk-ˈsi-mə-tē\ *n* : NEARNESS ⟨lives in ~ to a bus stop⟩
prox·i·mo \ˈpräk-sə-ˌmō\ *adj* [L *proximo mense* in the next month] : of or occurring in the next month after the present
proxy \ˈpräk-sē\ *n, pl* **prox·ies** [ME *proxi, procucie,* alter. of *procuracie,* fr. AF, fr. ML *procuratia,* alter. of L *procuratio* appointment of another as an agent, fr. *procurare* to take care of] : the authority or power to act for another; *also* : a document giving such authorization — **proxy** *adj*
prude \ˈprüd\ *n* : a person who shows or affects extreme modesty — **prud·ery** \ˈprü-də-rē\ *n* — **prud·ish** *adj* — **prud·ish·ly** *adv*
pru·dent \ˈprü-dᵊnt\ *adj* **1** : shrewd in the management of practical affairs **2** : CAUTIOUS, DISCREET **3** : PROVIDENT, FRUGAL ♦ *Synonyms* JUDICIOUS, FORESIGHTED, SENSIBLE, SANE — **pru·dence** \-dᵊns\ *n* — **pru·den·tial** \prü-ˈden-chəl\ *adj* — **pru·dent·ly** *adv*
¹**prune** \ˈprün\ *n* : a dried plum
²**prune** *vb* **pruned; prun·ing** : to cut off unwanted parts (as of a tree)
pru·ri·ent \ˈprůr-ē-ənt\ *adj* : LASCIVIOUS; *also* : exciting to lasciviousness — **pru·ri·ence** \-ē-əns\ *n*
¹**pry** \ˈprī\ *vb* **pried; pry·ing** : to look closely or inquisitively; *esp* : SNOOP
²**pry** *vb* **pried; pry·ing** **1** : to raise, move, or pull apart with a pry or lever **2** : to detach or open with difficulty
³**pry** *n* : a tool for prying
Ps *or* **Psa** *abbr* Psalms
PS *abbr* **1** [L *postscriptum*] postscript **2** public school
PSA *abbr* public service announcement
psalm \ˈsäm, ˈsälm\ *n, often cap* [ME, fr. OE *psealm,* fr. LL *psalmus,* fr. Gk *psalmos,* lit., twanging of a harp, fr. *psallein* to pluck, play a stringed instrument] : a sacred song or poem; *esp* : one of the hymns collected in the Book of Psalms — **psalm·ist** *n*
Psalms *n* — see BIBLE table
Psal·ter \ˈsȯl-tər\ *n* : the Book of Psalms; *also* : a collection of the Psalms arranged for devotional use
pseud *abbr* pseudonym; pseudonymous
pseu·do \ˈsü-dō\ *adj* : SPURIOUS, SHAM
pseu·do·nym \ˈsü-də-ˌnim\ *n* : a fictitious name — **pseu·don·y·mous** \sü-ˈdä-nə-məs\ *adj*
pseu·do·sci·ence \ˌsü-dō-ˈsī-əns\ *n* : a system of theories, assumptions, and methods erroneously regarded as scientific — **pseu·do·sci·en·tif·ic** \-ˌsī-ən-ˈti-fik\ *adj*
PSG *abbr* platoon sergeant
¹**psi** \ˈsī, ˈpsī\ *n* : the 23d letter of the Greek alphabet — Ψ or ψ
²**psi** *abbr* pounds per square inch
psit·ta·co·sis \ˌsi-tə-ˈkō-səs\ *n* : an infectious disease of birds marked by diarrhea and wasting and transmissible to humans
pso·ri·a·sis \sə-ˈrī-ə-səs\ *n* : a chronic skin disease characterized by red patches covered with white scales
PST *abbr* Pacific standard time
¹**psych** *or* **psyche** \ˈsīk\ *vb* **psyched; psych·ing** **1** : OUTWIT, OUTGUESS; *also* : to analyze beforehand **2** : INTIMIDATE; *also* : to prepare oneself psychologically ⟨get *psyched* up for the game⟩
²**psych** *abbr* psychology
psy·che \ˈsī-kē\ *n* : SOUL, PERSONALITY; *also* : MIND
psy·che·del·ic \ˌsī-kə-ˈde-lik\ *adj* **1** : of, relating to, or causing abnormal psychic effects ⟨~ drugs⟩ **2** : relating to the taking of psychedelic drugs ⟨~ experience⟩ **3** : imitating, suggestive of, or reproducing the effects of psychedelic drugs ⟨~ art⟩ ⟨~ colors⟩ — **psychedelic** *n* — **psy·che·del·i·cal·ly** \-li-k(ə-)lē\ *adv*
psy·chi·a·try \sə-ˈkī-ə-trē, sī-\ *n* [prob. fr. F *psychiatrie,* fr. *psychiatre* psychiatrist, fr. Gk *psychē* breath, soul + *iatros* physician] : a branch of medicine dealing with mental, emotional, and behavioral disorders — **psy·chi·at·ric** \ˌsī-kē-ˈa-trik\ *adj* — **psy·chi·a·trist** \sə-ˈkī-ə-trist, sī-\ *n*
¹**psy·chic** \ˈsī-kik\ *also* **psy·chi·cal** \-ki-kəl\ *adj* **1** : of or relating to the psyche **2** : lying outside the sphere of physical science **3** : sensitive to nonphysical or supernatural forces — **psy·chi·cal·ly** \-k(ə-)lē\ *adv*
²**psychic** *n* : a person apparently sensitive to nonphysical forces; *also* : MEDIUM 6
psy·cho \ˈsī-kō\ *n, pl* **psychos** : a mentally disturbed person — **psycho** *adj*
psy·cho·ac·tive \ˌsī-kō-ˈak-tiv\ *adj* : affecting the mind or behavior
psy·cho·anal·y·sis \ˌsī-kō-ə-ˈna-lə-səs\ *n* : a method of dealing with psychic disorders by having the patient talk freely about personal experiences and esp. about early childhood and dreams — **psy·cho·an·a·lyst** \-ˈa-nə-list\ *n* — **psy·cho·an·a·lyt·ic** \-ˌa-nə-ˈli-tik\ *adj* — **psy·cho·an·a·lyze** \-ˈa-nə-ˌlīz\ *vb*
psy·cho·bab·ble \ˈsī-kō-ˌba-bəl\ *n* : psychological jargon esp. when used in a trite or simplistic manner
psy·cho·dra·ma \ˌsī-kə-ˈdrä-mə, -ˈdra-\ *n* **1** : an extemporized dramatization designed to afford catharsis for one or more of the participants from whose life the plot is taken **2** : a dramatic event or story with psychological overtones
psy·cho·gen·ic \-ˈje-nik\ *adj* : originating in the mind or in mental or emotional conflict
psy·cho·graph·ics \ˌsī-kə-ˈgra-fiks\ *n sing or pl* : market research or statistics classifying population groups according to psychological variables
psychol *abbr* psychologist; psychology
psy·chol·o·gy \sī-ˈkä-lə-jē\ *n, pl* **-gies** **1** : the science of mind and behavior **2** : the mental and behavioral characteristics of an individual or group — **psy·cho·log·i·cal** \ˌsī-kə-ˈlä-ji-kəl\ *adj* — **psy·cho·log·i·cal·ly** \-ji-k(ə-)lē\ *adv* — **psy·chol·o·gist** \sī-ˈkä-lə-jist\ *n*

psy·cho·path \ˈsī-kō-ˌpath\ *n* : a mentally ill or unstable person; *esp* : a person who engages in antisocial behavior and exhibits a pervasive disregard for the rights, feelings, and safety of others — **psy·cho·path·ic** \ˌsī-kə-ˈpa-thik\ *adj*

psy·cho·sex·u·al \ˌsī-kō-ˈsek-shə-wəl\ *adj* **1** : of or relating to the mental, emotional, and behavioral aspects of sexual development **2** : of or relating to the physiological psychology of sex

psy·cho·sis \sī-ˈkō-səs\ *n, pl* **-cho·ses** \-ˌsēz\ : a serious mental illness (as schizophrenia) marked by loss of or greatly lessened ability to test whether what one is thinking and feeling about the real world is really true

psy·cho·so·cial \ˌsī-kō-ˈsō-shəl\ *adj* **1** : involving both psychological and social aspects **2** : relating social conditions to mental health

psy·cho·so·mat·ic \ˌsī-kō-sə-ˈma-tik\ *adj* : of, relating to, involving, or concerned with bodily symptoms caused by mental or emotional disturbance

psy·cho·ther·a·py \ˌsī-kō-ˈther-ə-pē\ *n* : treatment of mental or emotional disorder or of related bodily ills by psychological means — **psy·cho·ther·a·pist** \-pist\ *n*

psy·chot·ic \sī-ˈkä-tik\ *adj* **1** : of or relating to psychosis ⟨~ behavior⟩ ⟨a ~ patient⟩ **2** *sometimes offensive* : exhibiting or suggestive of mental or emotional unsoundness or instability — not used technically — **psychotic** *n*

psy·cho·tro·pic \ˌsī-kə-ˈtrō-pik\ *adj* : acting on the mind ⟨~ drugs⟩

pt *abbr* **1** part **2** payment **3** pint **4** point **5** port

Pt *symbol* platinum

PT *abbr* **1** Pacific time **2** part-time **3** physical therapy **4** physical training

PTA *abbr* Parent-Teacher Association

ptar·mi·gan \ˈtär-mi-gən\ *n, pl* **-gan** *or* **-gans** : any of various grouses of northern regions with completely feathered feet

PT boat \(ˌ)pē-ˈtē-\ *n* [*p*atrol *t*orpedo] : a small fast patrol craft usu. armed with torpedos

pte *abbr, Brit* private

ptg *abbr* printing

PTO *abbr* **1** paid time off **2** Parent-Teacher Organization **3** please turn over

pto·maine \ˈtō-ˌmān\ *n* : any of various chemical substances formed by bacteria in decaying matter (as meat) and including a few poisonous ones

PTSD *abbr* post-traumatic stress disorder

Pu *symbol* plutonium

[1]**pub** \ˈpəb\ *n* **1** *chiefly Brit* : PUBLIC HOUSE 2 **2** : TAVERN

[2]**pub** *abbr* **1** public **2** publication **3** published; publisher; publishing

pu·ber·ty \ˈpyü-bər-tē\ *n* : the condition of being or period of becoming first capable of reproducing sexually — **pu·ber·tal** \-bər-tᵊl\ *adj*

pu·bes \ˈpyü-bēz\ *n, pl* **pubes** [NL, fr. L, manhood, body hair, pubic region] **1** : the hair that appears upon the lower middle region of the abdomen at puberty **2** : the pubic region

pu·bes·cence \pyü-ˈbe-sᵊns\ *n* **1** : the quality or state of being pubescent **2** : a pubescent covering or surface

pu·bes·cent \-sᵊnt\ *adj* **1** : arriving at or having reached puberty **2** : covered with fine soft short hairs

pu·bic \ˈpyü-bik\ *adj* : of, relating to, or situated near the pubes or the pubis

pu·bis \ˈpyü-bəs\ *n, pl* **pu·bes** \-bēz\ : the ventral and anterior of the three principal bones composing either half of the pelvis

publ *abbr* **1** publication **2** published; publisher

[1]**pub·lic** \ˈpə-blik\ *adj* **1** : exposed to general view ⟨the story became ~⟩ **2** : of, relating to, or affecting the people as a whole ⟨~ opinion⟩ **3** : CIVIC, GOVERNMENTAL ⟨~ expenditures⟩ **4** : of, relating to, or serving the community ⟨~ officials⟩ **5** : not private : SOCIAL ⟨~ morality⟩ **6** : open to all ⟨~ library⟩ **7** : well known : PROMINENT ⟨~ figures⟩ **8** : supported by public funds and private contributions rather than by income from commercials — **pub·lic·ly** *adv*

[2]**public** *n* **1** : the people as a whole : POPULACE **2** : a group of people having common interests ⟨the movie-going ~⟩

pub·li·can \ˈpə-bli-kən\ *n* **1** : a Jewish tax collector for the ancient Romans **2** *chiefly Brit* : the licensee of a pub

pub·li·ca·tion \ˌpə-blə-ˈkā-shən\ *n* **1** : the act or process of publishing **2** : a published work

public house *n* **1** : INN **2** *chiefly Brit* : a licensed saloon or bar

pub·li·cise *Brit var of* PUBLICIZE

pub·li·cist \ˈpə-blə-sist\ *n* : one that publicizes; *esp* : PRESS AGENT

pub·lic·i·ty \(ˌ)pə-ˈbli-sə-tē\ *n* **1** : information with news value issued to gain public attention or support **2** : public attention or acclaim

pub·li·cize \ˈpə-blə-ˌsīz\ *vb* **-cized; -cizing** : to bring to public attention : ADVERTISE ⟨*publicizing* his book⟩

pub·lic–key \ˈpə-blik-ˈkē\ *n* : the publicly shared element of a code usable only to encode messages

public relations *n sing or pl* : the business of fostering public goodwill toward a person, firm, or institution; *also* : the degree of goodwill and understanding achieved

public school *n* **1** : an endowed secondary boarding school in Great Britain offering a classical curriculum and preparation for the universities or public service **2** : a free tax-supported school controlled by a local governmental authority

public–spirited *adj* : motivated by devotion to the general or national welfare

public works *n pl* : works (as schools or highways) constructed with public funds for public use

pub·lish \ˈpə-blish\ *vb* **1** : to make generally known : announce publicly **2** : to produce or release literature, information, musical scores or sometimes recordings, or art for sale to the public — **pub·lish·er** *n*

[1]**puck** \ˈpək\ *n* : a mischievous sprite — **puck·ish** *adj* — **puck·ish·ly** *adv*

[2]**puck** *n* : a disk used in ice hockey

[1]**puck·er** \ˈpə-kər\ *vb* : to contract into folds or wrinkles

[2]**pucker** *n* : FOLD, WRINKLE

pud·ding \ˈpu̇-diŋ\ *n* : a soft, spongy, or thick creamy dessert

pud·dle \ˈpə-dᵊl\ *n* : a very small pool of usu. dirty or muddy water

pu·den·dum \pyu̇-ˈden-dəm\ *n, pl* **-da** \-də\ [NL, fr. L *pudēre* to be ashamed] : the human external genital organs esp. of a woman

pudgy \ˈpə-jē\ *adj* **pudg·i·er; -est** : being short and plump : CHUBBY

pueb·lo \ˈpwe-blō, pü-ˈe-\ *n, pl* **-los** [Sp, village, lit., people, fr. L *populus*] **1** : a village of Indigenous people of Arizona or New Mexico that consists of flat-roofed stone or adobe houses joined in groups sometimes several stories high **2** *cap* : a member of a group of Indigenous peoples of the southwestern U.S.

pu·er·ile \ˈpyu̇-ə-rəl\ *adj* : CHILDISH, SILLY ⟨~ remarks⟩ — **pu·er·il·i·ty** \ˌpyü-ə-ˈri-lə-tē\ *n*

pu·er·per·al \pyü-ˈər-pə-rəl\ *adj* : of, relating to, or occurring during childbirth or the period immediately following ⟨~ infection⟩ ⟨~ depression⟩

puerperal fever *n* : an abnormal condition that results from infection of the placental site following childbirth or abortion

[1]**puff** \ˈpəf\ *vb* **1** : to blow in short gusts **2** : PANT **3** : to emit small whiffs or clouds **4** : BLUSTER, BRAG **5** : INFLATE, SWELL **6** : to make proud or conceited **7** : to praise extravagantly

[2]**puff** *n* **1** : a short discharge (as of air or smoke); *also* : a slight explosive sound accompanying it **2** : a light fluffy pastry **3** : a slight swelling **4** : a fluffy mass; *also* : a small pad for applying cosmetic powder **5** : a laudatory notice or review — **puffy** *adj*

[3]**puff** *adj* : of, relating to, or designed for promotion or flattery ⟨~ articles on the new TV series⟩

puff·ball \ˈpəf-ˌbȯl\ *n* : any of various globe-shaped and often edible fungi

puf·fin \ˈpə-fən\ *n* : any of several seabirds having a short neck and a deep grooved parti-colored bill

[1]**pug** \ˈpəg\ *n* **1** : any of a breed of small stocky short-haired dogs with a wrinkled face **2** : a close coil of hair

[2]**pug** *n* : [1]BOXER

pu·gi·lism \ˈpyü-jə-ˌli-zəm\ *n* : BOXING — **pu·gi·list** \-list\ *n* — **pu·gi·lis·tic** \ˌpyü-jə-ˈlis-tik\ *adj*

pug·na·cious \ˌpəg-ˈnā-shəs\ *adj* : having a quarrelsome or combative nature

◆ ***Synonyms*** BELLIGERENT, BELLICOSE, CONTENTIOUS, TRUCULENT — **pug·nac·i·ty** \-ˈna-sə-tē\ *n*

puis·sance \ˈpwi-səns, ˈpyü-ə-\ *n* : POWER, STRENGTH ⟨the ~ of the king⟩ — **puis·sant** \-sənt\ *adj*

puke \ˈpyük\ *vb* **puked; puk·ing** : VOMIT — **puke** *n*

puk·ka \ˈpə-kə\ *adj* [Hindi *pakkā* cooked, ripe, solid, fr. Skt *pakva*] : GENUINE, AUTHENTIC; *also* : FIRST-CLASS, COMPLETE

pul \ˈpül\ *n, pl* **puls** \ˈpülz\ *or* **pul** — see *afghani* at MONEY table

pu·la \ˈpü-lə, ˈpyü-\ *n, pl* **pula** — see MONEY table

pul·chri·tude \ˈpəl-krə-ˌtüd, -ˌtyüd\ *n* : BEAUTY — **pul·chri·tu·di·nous** \ˌpəl-krə-ˈtü-dᵊn-əs, -ˈtyü-\ *adj*

[1]**pull** \ˈpu̇l\ *vb* **1** : to exert force so as to draw (something) toward the force; *also* : MOVE ⟨~ out of a driveway⟩ **2** : PLUCK; *also* : EXTRACT ⟨~ a tooth⟩ **3** : STRETCH, STRAIN ⟨~ a tendon⟩ **4** : to draw apart : TEAR **5** : to make (as a proof) by printing **6** : REMOVE ⟨~*ed* the pitcher in the third inning⟩ **7** : DRAW ⟨~ a gun⟩ **8** : to carry out esp. with daring ⟨~ a robbery⟩ **9** : PERPETRATE, COMMIT **10** : ATTRACT **11** : to express strong sympathy — **pull·er** *n*

[2]**pull** *n* **1** : the act or an instance of pulling **2** : the effort expended in moving **3** : ADVANTAGE ⟨had the ~ of a respected family name⟩; *esp* : special influence **4** : a device for pulling something or for operating by pulling **5** : a force that attracts or compels **6** : an injury from abnormal straining or stretching ⟨a muscle ~⟩

pull·back \ˈpu̇l-ˌbak\ *n* : an orderly withdrawal of troops

pull–down *adj* : appearing below a selected item (as a menu title) on a computer display ⟨a ~ menu⟩

pul·let \ˈpu̇-lət\ *n* : a young hen esp. of the domestic chicken when less than a year old

pul·ley \ˈpu̇-lē\ *n, pl* **pulleys** : a wheel used to transmit power by means of a belt, rope, or chain; *esp* : one with a grooved rim that forms part of a tackle for hoisting or for changing the direction of a force

Pull·man \ˈpu̇l-mən\ *n* : a railroad passenger car with comfortable furnishings esp. for night travel

pull off *vb* : to accomplish successfully

pull·out \ˈpu̇l-ˌau̇t\ *n* : PULLBACK

pull·over \ˈpu̇l-ˌō-vər\ *adj* : put on by being pulled over the head ⟨~ sweater⟩ — **pull·over** *n*

pull–up \ˈpu̇l-ˌəp\ *n* : CHIN-UP

pull up *vb* : to bring or come to an often abrupt halt : STOP

pul·mo·nary \ˈpu̇l-mə-ˌner-ē, ˈpəl-\ *adj* : of, relating to, or carried on by the lungs ⟨the ~ circulation⟩

pulp \ˈpəlp\ *n* **1** : the soft juicy or fleshy part of a fruit or vegetable **2** : a soft moist mass **3** : the soft sensitive tissue that fills the central cavity of a tooth **4** : a material (as from wood) used in making paper **5** : a magazine using cheap paper and often dealing with sensational material — **pulpy** *adj*

pul·pit \ˈpu̇l-ˌpit\ *n* : a raised platform or high reading desk used in preaching or conducting a worship service

pulp·wood \ˈpəlp-ˌwu̇d\ *n* : wood used in making pulp for paper

pul·sar \ˈpəl-ˌsär\ *n* : a celestial source of pulsating electromagnetic radiation (as radio waves)

pul·sate \ˈpəl-ˌsāt\ *vb* **pul·sat·ed; pul·sat·ing** : to expand and contract rhythmically : BEAT ⟨an artery ~*s*⟩ — **pul·sa·tion** \ˌpəl-ˈsā-shən\ *n*

pulse \ˈpəls\ *n* **1** : the regular throbbing in the arteries caused by the contractions of the heart **2** : rhythmical beating, vibrating, or sounding **3** : a brief change in electrical current or voltage — **pulse** *vb*

pul·ver·ise *Brit var of* PULVERIZE

pul·ver·ize \ˈpəl-və-ˌrīz\ *vb* **-ized; -iz·ing** **1** : to reduce (as by crushing or grinding) or be reduced to very small particles **2** : DEMOLISH

pu·ma \ˈpü-mə, ˈpyü-\ *n, pl* **pumas** *also* **puma** [Sp, fr. Quechua] : COUGAR

pum·ice \ˈpə-məs\ *n* : a light porous volcanic glass used esp. for smoothing and polishing

pum·mel \ˈpə-məl\ *vb* **-meled** *also* **-melled; -mel·ing** *also* **-mel·ling** : POUND, BEAT ⟨~*ed* the intruder⟩

¹pump \ˈpəmp\ *n* : a device for raising, transferring, or compressing fluids esp. by suction or pressure

²pump *vb* **1** : to raise (as water) with a pump **2** : to draw fluid from with a pump; *also* : to fill by means of a pump ⟨~ up a tire⟩ **3** : to force or propel in the manner of a pump — **pump·er** *n*

³pump *n* : a low shoe that grips the foot chiefly at the toe and heel

pumped \ˈpəmpt\ *adj* : filled with energetic excitement and enthusiasm

pum·per·nick·el \ˈpəm-pər-ˌni-kəl\ *n* : a dark rye bread

pump·kin \ˈpəmp-kən, ˈpəŋ-kən\ *n* : the large usu. orange fruit of a vine of the gourd family that is widely used as food; *also* : this vine

pun \ˈpən\ *n* : the humorous use of a word in a way that suggests two or more interpretations — **pun** *vb*

¹punch \ˈpənch\ *n* : a tool for piercing, stamping, cutting, or forming

²punch *vb* **1** : PROD, POKE; *also* : DRIVE, HERD ⟨~*ing* cattle⟩ **2** : to strike with the fist **3** : to emboss, perforate, or make with a punch **4** : to operate, produce, or enter (as data) by or as if by punching — **punch·er** *n*

³punch *n* **1** : a quick blow with or as if with the fist **2** : effective energy or forcefulness

⁴punch *n* [perh. fr. Hindi *pā̃c* five, fr. Skt *pañca;* fr. the number of ingredients] : a drink usu. composed of wine or alcoholic liquor and nonalcoholic beverages; *also* : a drink composed of nonalcoholic beverages

punch card *n* : a card with holes punched in particular positions to represent data

punch–drunk \ˈpənch-ˌdrəŋk\ *adj* **1** : suffering from brain injury resulting from repeated head blows received in boxing **2** : DAZED, CONFUSED

pun·cheon \ˈpən-chən\ *n* : a large cask

punch line *n* : the sentence or phrase in a joke that makes the point

punch list *n* : a list of tasks to be completed at the end of a project

punchy \ˈpən-chē\ *adj* **punch·i·er; -est** **1** : having punch : FORCEFUL **2** : DAZED, CONFUSED ⟨a ~ boxer⟩ **3** : VIVID, VIBRANT ⟨~ graphics⟩

punc·til·io \ˌpəŋk-ˈti-lē-ˌō\ *n, pl* **-i·os** **1** : a nice detail of conduct in a ceremony or in observance of a code **2** : careful observance of forms (as in social conduct)

punc·til·i·ous \ˌpəŋk-ˈti-lē-əs\ *adj* : marked by precise accordance with codes or conventions ♦ ***Synonyms*** METICULOUS, SCRUPULOUS, CAREFUL, PUNCTUAL

punc·tu·al \ˈpəŋk-chə-wəl\ *adj* : being on time : PROMPT — **punc·tu·al·i·ty** \ˌpəŋk-chə-ˈwa-lə-tē\ *n* — **punc·tu·al·ly** *adv*

punc·tu·ate \ˈpəŋk-chə-ˌwāt\ *vb* **-at·ed; -at·ing** **1** : to mark or divide (written matter) with punctuation marks **2** : to break into at intervals **3** : EMPHASIZE

punc·tu·a·tion \ˌpəŋk-chə-ˈwā-shən\ *n* : the act, practice, or system of inserting standardized marks in written matter to clarify the meaning and separate structural units

¹punc·ture \ˈpəŋk-chər\ *n* **1** : an act of puncturing **2** : a small hole or wound made by puncturing

²puncture *vb* **punc·tured; punc·tur·ing** **1** : to make a hole in : PIERCE **2** : to make useless as if by a puncture

pun·dit \ˈpən-dət\ *n* [Hindi *paṇḍit,* fr. Skt *paṇḍita,* fr. *paṇḍita* learned] **1** : a learned person : TEACHER **2** : AUTHORITY, CRITIC

pun·dit·oc·ra·cy \ˌpən-dət-ˈä-krə-sē\ *n, pl* **-cies** : a group of powerful and influential political commentators

pun·gent \ˈpən-jənt\ *adj* **1** : having a sharp incisive quality : CAUSTIC ⟨a ~ editorial⟩ **2** : causing a sharp, intense, or irritating sensation (as of taste or smell); *esp* : ACRID ⟨a ~ odor⟩ — **pun·gen·cy** \-jən-sē\ *n* — **pun·gent·ly** *adv*

pun·ish \ˈpə-nish\ *vb* **1** : to impose a penalty on for a fault or crime ⟨~ an offender⟩ **2** : to inflict a penalty for ⟨~ treason with death⟩ **3** : to inflict injury on : HURT ♦ ***Synonyms*** CHASTISE, CASTIGATE, CHASTEN, DISCIPLINE, CORRECT — **pun·ish·able** *adj*

pun·ish·ment *n* **1** : retributive suffering, pain, or loss : PENALTY **2** : rough treatment

pu·ni·tive \ˈpyü-nə-tiv\ *adj* : inflicting, involving, or aiming at punishment

¹punk \ˈpəŋk\ *n* **1** : a young inexperienced person **2** : a petty hoodlum

²punk *adj* : very poor : INFERIOR

³punk *n* : dry crumbly wood useful for tinder; *also* : a substance made from fungi for use as tinder

pun·ster \ˈpən-stər\ *n* : one who is given to punning

[1]**punt** \ˈpənt\ *n* : a long narrow flat-bottomed boat with square ends

[2]**punt** *vb* : to propel (as a punt) with a pole

[3]**punt** *vb* : to kick a football or soccer ball dropped from the hands before it touches the ground

[4]**punt** *n* : the act or an instance of punting a ball

pu·ny \ˈpyü-nē\ *adj* **pu·ni·er; -est** [AF *puisné* younger, weakly, lit., born afterward, fr. *puis* afterward (fr. L *post*) + *né* born, fr. L *natus*] : slight in power, size, or importance : WEAK ⟨a ~ body⟩ ⟨~ sales⟩

pup \ˈpəp\ *n* : a young dog; *also* : one of the young of some other animals

pu·pa \ˈpyü-pə\ *n, pl* **pu·pae** \-(ˌ)pē\ *or* **pupas** [NL, fr. L *pupa* doll] : a form of some insects (as a bee, moth, or beetle) between the larva and the adult that usu. has a protective covering (as a cocoon) — **pu·pal** \-pəl\ *adj*

[1]**pu·pil** \ˈpyü-pəl\ *n* **1** : a child or young person in school or in the charge of a tutor **2** : DISCIPLE

[2]**pupil** *n* : the dark central opening of the iris of the eye

pup·pet \ˈpə-pət\ *n* [ME *popet* youth, doll, fr. MF *poupette,* ultim. fr. L *pupa* doll] **1** : a small figure of a person or animal moved by hand or by strings or wires **2** : DOLL **3** : one whose acts are controlled by an outside force or influence

pup·pe·teer \ˌpə-pə-ˈtir\ *n* : one who manipulates puppets

pup·py \ˈpə-pē\ *n, pl* **puppies** : a young domestic dog

pu·pu \ˈpü-ˌpü\ *n* : an Asian dish consisting of a variety of foods

pur·blind \ˈpər-ˌblīnd\ *adj* **1** : partly blind **2** : lacking in insight : OBTUSE

[1]**pur·chase** \ˈpər-chəs\ *vb* **pur·chased; pur·chas·ing** : to obtain by paying money or its equivalent : BUY — **pur·chas·able** \-chə-sə-bəl\ *adj* — **pur·chas·er** *n*

[2]**purchase** *n* **1** : an act or instance of purchasing **2** : something purchased **3** : a secure hold or grasp; *also* : advantageous leverage

pur·dah \ˈpər-də\ *n* : seclusion of women from public observation among Muslims and some Hindus esp. in India; *also* : a state of seclusion

pure \ˈpyu̇r\ *adj* **pur·er; pur·est** **1** : unmixed with any other matter : free from taint ⟨~ gold⟩ ⟨~ water⟩ **2** : SHEER, ABSOLUTE ⟨~ nonsense⟩ **3** : ABSTRACT, THEORETICAL ⟨~ mathematics⟩ **4** : free from what vitiates, weakens, or pollutes ⟨speaks a ~ French⟩ **5** : free from moral fault : INNOCENT **6** : CHASTE, CONTINENT — **pure·ly** *adv*

pure–blood·ed \-ˌblə-dəd\ *or* **pure–blood** \-ˌbləd\ *adj* : FULL-BLOODED — **pure-blood** *n*

pure·bred \-ˈbred\ *adj* : bred from members of a recognized breed, strain, or kind without crossbreeding over many generations — **pure·bred** \-ˌbred\ *n*

[1]**pu·ree** \pyu̇-ˈrā, -ˈrē\ *n* [F *purée,* fr. MF, fr. fem. of *puré,* pp. of *purer* to purify, strain, fr. L *purare* to purify] : a paste or thick liquid suspension usu. made from finely ground cooked food; *also* : a thick soup made of pureed vegetables

[2]**puree** *vb* **pu·reed; pu·ree·ing** : to make a puree of

pur·ga·tion \ˌpər-ˈgā-shən\ *n* : the act or result of purging

[1]**pur·ga·tive** \ˈpər-gə-tiv\ *adj* : purging or tending to purge

[2]**purgative** *n* : a strong laxative : CATHARTIC

pur·ga·to·ry \ˈpər-gə-ˌtȯr-ē\ *n, pl* **-ries** **1** : an intermediate state after death for expiatory purification **2** : a place or state of temporary punishment — **pur·ga·tor·i·al** \ˌpər-gə-ˈtȯr-ē-əl\ *adj*

[1]**purge** \ˈpərj\ *vb* **purged; purg·ing** **1** : to cleanse or purify esp. from sin **2** : to have or cause strong and usu. repeated emptying of the bowels **3** : to get rid of ⟨the leaders had been *purged*⟩

[2]**purge** *n* **1** : something that purges; *esp* : PURGATIVE **2** : an act or result of purging; *esp* : a ridding of persons regarded as treacherous or disloyal

pu·ri·fy \ˈpyu̇r-ə-ˌfī\ *vb* **-fied; -fy·ing** : to make or become pure ⟨~ water⟩ ⟨~ the mind⟩ — **pu·ri·fi·ca·tion** \ˌpyu̇r-ə-fə-ˈkā-shən\ *n* — **pu·ri·fi·ca·to·ry** \pyu̇-ˈri-fi-kə-ˌtȯr-ē\ *adj* — **pu·ri·fi·er** *n*

Pu·rim \ˈpu̇r-(ˌ)im\ *n* : a Jewish holiday celebrated in February or March in commemoration of the deliverance of the Jews from the massacre plotted by Haman

pu·rine \ˈpyu̇r-ˌēn\ *n* : any of a group of bases including several (as adenine or guanine) that are constituents of DNA or RNA

pur·ism \ˈpyu̇r-ˌi-zəm\ *n* : rigid adherence to or insistence on purity or nicety esp. in use of words — **pur·ist** \-ist\ *n* — **pu·ris·tic** \pyu̇-ˈris-tik\ *adj*

pu·ri·tan \ˈpyu̇r-ə-tən\ *n* **1** *cap* : a member of a 16th and 17th century Protestant group in England and New England opposing the ceremonies and government of the Church of England **2** : one who practices or preaches a stricter or professedly purer moral code than that which prevails — **pu·ri·tan·i·cal** \ˌpyu̇r-ə-ˈta-ni-kəl\ *adj* — **pu·ri·tan·i·cal·ly** *adv*

pu·ri·ty \ˈpyu̇r-ə-tē\ *n* : the quality or state of being pure

[1]**purl** \ˈpərl\ *n* : a stitch in knitting

[2]**purl** *vb* : to knit in purl stitch

[3]**purl** *n* : a gentle murmur or movement (as of purling water)

[4]**purl** *vb* **1** : EDDY, SWIRL **2** : to make a soft murmuring sound

pur·lieu \ˈpər-lü, ˈpərl-yü\ *n* **1** : an outlying district : SUBURB **2** *pl* : ENVIRONS

pur·loin \(ˌ)pər-ˈlȯin, ˈpər-ˌlȯin\ *vb* : STEAL, FILCH

[1]**pur·ple** \ˈpər-pəl\ *adj* **pur·pler; pur·plest** **1** : of the color purple **2** : highly rhetorical ⟨a ~ passage⟩ **3** : PROFANE **4** : having roughly equal levels of support

for Democratic and Republican candidates or policies — **pur·plish** *adj*

[2]**purple** *n* **1** : a bluish red color **2** : a purple robe emblematic esp. of regal rank or authority

[1]**pur·port** \ˈpər-ˌpȯrt\ *n* [ME, fr. AF, content, tenor, fr. *purporter* to carry, mean, purport, fr. *pur-* thoroughly + *porter* to carry] : meaning conveyed or implied; *also* : GIST ⟨the ~ of her letter⟩

[2]**pur·port** \(ˌ)pər-ˈpȯrt\ *vb* : to convey or profess outwardly as the meaning or intention : CLAIM ⟨~*s* to be objective⟩ — **pur·port·ed·ly** \-ˈpȯr-təd-lē\ *adv*

[1]**pur·pose** \ˈpər-pəs\ *n* **1** : an object or result aimed at : INTENTION **2** : RESOLUTION, DETERMINATION — **pur·pose·ful** \-fəl\ *adj* — **pur·pose·ful·ly** *adv* — **purpose·less** *adj* — **pur·pose·ly** *adv*

[2]**purpose** *vb* **pur·posed; pur·pos·ing** : to propose as an aim to oneself

purr \ˈpər\ *n* : a low murmur typical of a contented cat — **purr** *vb*

[1]**purse** \ˈpərs\ *n* **1** : a receptacle (as a pouch) to carry money and often other small objects in **2** : RESOURCES **3** : a sum of money offered as a prize or present

[2]**purse** *vb* **pursed; purs·ing** : PUCKER

purs·er \ˈpər-sər\ *n* : an official on a ship who keeps accounts and attends to the comfort of passengers

purs·lane \ˈpər-slən, -ˌslān\ *n* : a fleshy-leaved weedy trailing plant with tiny yellow flowers that is sometimes used in salads

pur·su·ance \pər-ˈsü-əns\ *n* : the act of carrying out or into effect

pur·su·ant to \-ˈsü-ənt-\ *prep* : in carrying out : ACCORDING TO

pur·sue \pər-ˈsü\ *vb* **pur·sued; pur·su·ing** **1** : to follow in order to overtake or overcome : CHASE **2** : to seek to accomplish ⟨~ a goal⟩ **3** : to proceed along ⟨~ a course⟩ **4** : to engage in ⟨~ a career⟩ — **pur·su·er** *n*

pur·suit \pər-ˈsüt\ *n* **1** : the act of pursuing **2** : OCCUPATION, BUSINESS

pu·ru·lent \ˈpyu̇r-ə-lənt, -yə-\ *adj* : containing or accompanied by pus ⟨a ~ discharge⟩ — **pu·ru·lence** \-ləns\ *n*

pur·vey \(ˌ)pər-ˈvā\ *vb* **pur·veyed; pur·vey·ing** : to supply (as provisions) usu. as a business — **pur·vey·ance** \-əns\ *n* — **pur·vey·or** \-ər\ *n*

pur·view \ˈpər-ˌvyü\ *n* **1** : the range or limit esp. of authority, responsibility, or intention **2** : range of vision, understanding, or cognizance

pus \ˈpəs\ *n* : thick yellowish white fluid matter (as in a boil) formed at a place of inflammation and infection (as an abscess) and containing germs, white blood cells, and tissue debris

[1]**push** \ˈpu̇sh\ *vb* [ME *possen, pusshen,* prob. fr. OF *pousser* to exert pressure, fr. L *pulsare,* fr. *pellere* to drive, strike] **1** : to press against with force in order to drive or impel **2** : to thrust forward, downward, or outward **3** : to urge on : press forward **4** : to cause to increase ⟨~ prices to record levels⟩ **5** : to urge or press the advancement, adoption, or practice of; *esp* : to make aggressive efforts to sell **6** : to engage in the illicit sale of narcotics

[2]**push** *n* **1** : a vigorous effort : DRIVE ⟨a ~ for higher wages⟩ **2** : an act of pushing **3** : vigorous enterprise : ENERGY

push–button *adj* **1** : operated or done by means of push buttons **2** : using or dependent on complex and more or less automatic mechanisms ⟨~ warfare⟩

push button *n* : a small button or knob that when pushed operates something esp. by closing an electric circuit

push·cart \ˈpu̇sh-ˌkärt\ *n* : a cart or barrow pushed by hand

push·er \ˈpu̇-shər\ *n* : one that pushes; *esp* : one that pushes illegal drugs

push·over \-ˌō-vər\ *n* **1** : something easily accomplished **2** : an opponent easy to defeat **3** : SUCKER ⟨she's nobody's ~⟩

push–up \-ˌəp\ *n* : a conditioning exercise performed in a prone position by raising and lowering the body with the straightening and bending of the arms while keeping the back straight and supporting the body on the hands and toes

pushy \ˈpu̇-shē\ *adj* **push·i·er; -est** : aggressive often to an objectionable degree

pu·sil·lan·i·mous \ˌpyü-sə-ˈla-nə-məs\ *adj* [LL *pusillanimis,* fr. L *pusillus* very small (dim. of *pusus* boy) + *animus* spirit] : contemptibly timid : COWARDLY — **pu·sil·la·nim·i·ty** \ˌpyü-sə-lə-ˈni-mə-tē\ *n*

[1]**puss** \ˈpu̇s\ *n* : CAT

[2]**puss** *n, slang* : FACE

[1]**pussy** \ˈpu̇-sē\ *n, pl* **puss·ies** : CAT

[2]**pus·sy** \ˈpə-sē\ *adj* **pus·si·er; -est** : full of or resembling pus

pussy·cat \ˈpu̇-sē-ˌkat\ *n* : CAT

pussy·foot \-ˌfu̇t\ *vb* **1** : to tread or move warily or stealthily **2** : to refrain from committing oneself

pussy willow \ˈpu̇-sē-\ *n* : a willow having large silky catkins

pus·tule \ˈpəs-chül\ *n* : a pus-filled pimple

put \ˈpu̇t\ *vb* **put; put·ting** **1** : to bring into a specified position : PLACE ⟨~ the book on the table⟩ **2** : SEND, THRUST **3** : to throw with an upward pushing motion ⟨~ the shot⟩ **4** : to bring into a specified state ⟨~ the plan into effect⟩ **5** : SUBJECT ⟨~ traitors to death⟩ **6** : IMPOSE **7** : to set before one for decision ⟨~ the question⟩ **8** : EXPRESS, STATE ⟨~ my feelings into words⟩ **9** : TRANSLATE, ADAPT **10** : APPLY, ASSIGN ⟨~ them to work⟩ **11** : ESTIMATE ⟨~ the number at 20⟩ **12** : ATTACH, ATTRIBUTE ⟨~ a high value on it⟩ **13** : to take a specified course ⟨the ship ~ out to sea⟩

pu·ta·tive \ˈpyü-tə-tiv\ *adj* **1** : commonly accepted ⟨~ expert⟩ **2** : assumed to exist or to have existed

put–down \ˈpu̇t-ˌdau̇n\ *n* : a belittling remark

put in *vb* **1** : to come in with : INTERPOSE ⟨*put in* a good word for me⟩ **2** : to spend time at some occupation or job ⟨*put in* eight hours at the office⟩

put off *vb* : POSTPONE, DELAY ⟨*put off* my visit⟩

[1]**put–on** \ˈpu̇t-ˌȯn, -ˌän\ *adj* : PRETENDED, ASSUMED ⟨a ~ accent⟩

[2]**put–on** *n* **1** : a deliberate act of misleading someone **2** : PARODY, SPOOF

put·out \ˈpu̇t-ˌau̇t\ *n* : the retiring of a base runner or batter in baseball

put out *vb* **1** : EXTINGUISH **2** : ANNOY; *also* : INCONVENIENCE **3** : to cause to be out (as in baseball)

pu·tre·fy \ˈpyü-trə-ˌfī\ *vb* **-fied; -fy·ing** : to make or become putrid : ROT ⟨*putrefied* meat⟩ — **pu·tre·fac·tion** \ˌpyü-trə-ˈfak-shən\ *n* — **pu·tre·fac·tive** \-tiv\ *adj*

pu·tres·cent \pyü-ˈtre-sᵊnt\ *adj* : becoming putrid : ROTTING ⟨~ carcasses⟩ — **pu·tres·cence** \-sᵊns\ *n*

pu·trid \ˈpyü-trəd\ *adj* **1** : ROTTEN, DECAYED ⟨~ meat⟩ **2** : VILE, CORRUPT — **pu·trid·i·ty** \pyü-ˈtri-də-tē\ *n*

putsch \ˈpu̇ch\ *n* [G] : a secretly plotted and suddenly executed attempt to overthrow a government

putt \ˈpət\ *n* : a golf stroke made on the green to cause the ball to roll into the hole — **putt** *vb*

put·ta·nes·ca \ˌpü-tä-ˈnes-kä\ *adj* : served with or being a pungent tomato sauce

[1]**put·ter** \ˈpu̇-tər\ *n* : one that puts

[2]**putt·er** \ˈpə-tər\ *n* **1** : a golf club used in putting **2** : one that putts

[3]**put·ter** \ˈpə-tər\ *vb* **1** : to move or act aimlessly or idly **2** : TINKER

put·ty \ˈpə-tē\ *n, pl* **putties** [F *potée* potter's glaze, lit., potful, fr. OF, fr. *pot* pot] **1** : a doughlike cement used esp. to fasten glass in sashes **2** : one who is easily manipulated — **putty** *vb*

put up *vb* **1** : SHEATHE **2** : to prepare so as to preserve for later use **3** : to offer for public sale ⟨*put* the house *up* for auction⟩ **4** : ACCOMMODATE, LODGE ⟨*put* us *up* for the night⟩ **5** : BUILD **6** : to engage in ⟨*put up* a struggle⟩ **7** : CONTRIBUTE, PAY — **put up with** : TOLERATE 2

[1]**puz·zle** \ˈpə-zəl\ *vb* **puz·zled; puz·zling** **1** : to bewilder mentally : PERPLEX **2** : to solve with difficulty or ingenuity ⟨~ out a riddle⟩ **3** : to be in a quandary ⟨~ over what to do⟩ **4** : to attempt a solution of a puzzle ⟨~ over a person's words⟩ ♦ ***Synonyms*** MYSTIFY, BEWILDER, NONPLUS, CONFOUND — **puz·zle·ment** *n* — **puz·zler** *n*

[2]**puzzle** *n* **1** : something that puzzles **2** : a question, problem, or contrivance designed for testing ingenuity

PVC *abbr* polyvinyl chloride

pvt *abbr* private

PW *abbr* prisoner of war

pwt *abbr* pennyweight

PX *abbr* post exchange

pya \pē-ˈä\ *n* — see *kyat* at MONEY table

pyg·my *also* **pig·my** \ˈpig-mē\ *n, pl* **pygmies** *also* **pigmies** [ME *pigmei,* fr. L *pygmaeus* of a pygmy, dwarfish, fr. Gk *pygmaios,* fr. *pygmē* fist, measure of length] **1** *cap* : any of a small people of equatorial Africa **2** : an unusually small person; *also* : an insignificant or unimpressive person — **pygmy** *adj*

py·ja·mas \pə-ˈjä-məz\ *chiefly Brit var of* PAJAMAS

py·lon \ˈpī-ˌlän, -lən\ *n* **1** : a usu. massive gateway; *esp* : an Egyptian one flanked by flat-topped pyramids **2** : a tower that supports wires over a long span **3** : a post or tower marking the course in an airplane race

py·or·rhea \ˌpī-ə-ˈrē-ə\ *n* : an inflammation with pus of the sockets of the teeth

[1]**pyr·a·mid** \ˈpir-ə-ˌmid\ *n* **1** : a massive structure with a square base and four triangular faces meeting at a point **2** : a geometrical solid having a polygon for its base and three or more triangles for its sides that meet at a point to form the top — **py·ra·mi·dal** \pə-ˈra-mə-dᵊl, ˌpir-ə-ˈmid-\ *adj*

[2]**pyramid** *vb* **1** : to build up in the form of a pyramid : heap up **2** : to increase rapidly on a broadening base

pyramid scheme *n* : a usu. illegal operation in which participants pay to join and profit from payments made by subsequent participants

pyre \ˈpī(-ə)r\ *n* : a combustible heap for burning a dead body as a funeral rite

py·re·thrum \pī-ˈrē-thrəm\ *n* : an insecticide made from the dried heads of any of several Old World chrysanthemums

py·rim·i·dine \pī-ˈri-mə-ˌdēn\ *n* : any of a group of bases including several (as cytosine, thymine, or uracil) that are constituents of DNA or RNA

py·rite \ˈpī-ˌrīt\ *n* : a mineral containing sulfur and iron that is brass-yellow in color

py·rol·y·sis \pī-ˈrä-lə-səs\ *n* : chemical change caused by the action of heat

py·ro·ma·nia \ˌpī-rō-ˈmā-nē-ə\ *n* : an irresistible impulse to start fires — **py·ro·ma·ni·ac** \-nē-ˌak\ *n*

py·ro·tech·nics \ˌpī-rə-ˈtek-niks\ *n pl* **1** : a display of fireworks **2** : a spectacular display (as of extreme virtuosity) ⟨musical ~⟩ — **py·ro·tech·nic** \-nik\ *also* **py·ro·tech·ni·cal** \-ni-kəl\ *adj*

Pyr·rhic \ˈpir-ik\ *adj* : achieved at excessive cost ⟨a ~ victory⟩; *also* : costly to the point of outweighing expected benefits

Py·thag·o·re·an theorem \pī-ˌtha-gə-ˈrē-ən-\ *n* : a theorem in geometry: the square of the length of the hypotenuse of a right triangle equals the sum of the squares of the lengths of the other two sides

py·thon \ˈpī-ˌthän, -thən\ *n* [L, monstrous serpent killed by the god Apollo, fr. Gk *Pythōn*] : a large snake (as a boa) that squeezes and suffocates its prey; *esp* : any of the large Old World snakes that include the largest snakes living at the present time

pyx \ˈpiks\ *n* : a small case used to carry the Eucharist to the sick

Q

[1]**q** \ˈkyü\ *n, pl* **q's** *or* **qs** \ˈkyüz\ *often cap* : the 17th letter of the English alphabet

[2]**q** *abbr, often cap* **1** quart **2** quarto **3** queen **4** query **5** question

QB *abbr* quarterback

QED *abbr* [L *quod erat demonstrandum*] which was to be demonstrated

qin·dar \k(y)in-ˈdär\ *n, pl* **qin·dar·ka** \-ˈdär-kə\ — see *lek* at MONEY table

qi·vi·ut \ˈkē-vē-ˌüt\ *n* [Inuit] : the wool of the undercoat of the musk ox

Qld *abbr* Queensland

QM *abbr* quartermaster

QMC *abbr* quartermaster corps

QMG *abbr* quartermaster general

qq v *abbr* [L *quae vide*] which (*pl*) see

qr *abbr* quarter

Q rating *n* [*q*uotient] : a scale measuring popularity based on dividing an assessment of familiarity or recognition by an assessment of favorable opinion; *also* : position on such a scale

qt *abbr* **1** quantity **2** quart

q.t. \ˌkyü-ˈtē\ *n, often cap Q&T* : QUIET — usu. used in the phrase *on the q.t.*

qto *abbr* quarto

qty *abbr* quantity

qu *or* **ques** *abbr* question

[1]**quack** \ˈkwak\ *vb* : to make the characteristic cry of a duck

[2]**quack** *n* : a sound made by quacking

[3]**quack** *n* **1** : CHARLATAN **2** : a pretender to medical skill ♦ ***Synonyms*** FAKER, IMPOSTOR, MOUNTEBANK — **quack** *adj* — **quack·ery** \ˈkwa-kə-rē\ *n* — **quack·ish** *adj*

[1]**quad** \ˈkwäd\ *n* : QUADRANGLE

[2]**quad** *n* **1** : QUADRUPLET **2** : a ski lift that accommodates four people

[3]**quad** *abbr* quadrant

quad·ran·gle \ˈkwä-ˌdraŋ-gəl\ *n* **1** : QUADRILATERAL **2** : a 4-sided courtyard or enclosure — **quad·ran·gu·lar** \kwä-ˈdraŋ-gyə-lər\ *adj*

quad·rant \ˈkwä-drənt\ *n* **1** : one quarter of a circle : an arc of 90° **2** : any of the four quarters into which something is divided by two lines intersecting each other at right angles

qua·drat·ic \kwä-ˈdra-tik\ *adj* : having or being a term in which the variable (as *x*) is squared but containing no term in which the variable is raised to a higher power than a square ⟨a ∼ equation⟩ — **quadratic** *n*

qua·dren·ni·al \kwä-ˈdre-nē-əl\ *adj* **1** : consisting of or lasting for four years **2** : occurring every four years

qua·dren·ni·um \-nē-əm\ *n, pl* **-ni·ums** *or* **-nia** \-nē-ə\ : a period of four years

quad·ri·ceps \ˈkwä-drə-ˌseps\ *n* : a muscle of the front of the thigh that is divided into four parts

[1]**quad·ri·lat·er·al** \ˌkwä-drə-ˈla-tə-rəl\ *n* : a polygon of four sides

[2]**quadrilateral** *adj* : having four sides

qua·drille \kwä-ˈdril, kə-\ *n* : a square dance made up of five or six figures in various rhythms

quad·ri·par·tite \ˌkwä-drə-ˈpär-ˌtīt\ *adj* **1** : consisting of four parts **2** : shared by four parties or persons

quad·ri·ple·gia \ˌkwä-drə-ˈplē-jə, -jē-ə\ *n* : paralysis of both arms and both legs — **quad·ri·ple·gic** \-jik\ *adj or n*

qua·driv·i·um \kwä-ˈdri-vē-əm\ *n* : the four liberal arts of arithmetic, music, geometry, and astronomy in a medieval university

quad·ru·ped \ˈkwä-drə-ˌped\ *n* : an animal having four feet — **qua·dru·pe·dal** \kwä-ˈdrü-pə-dᵊl, ˌkwä-drə-ˈpe-\ *adj*

[1]**qua·dru·ple** \kwä-ˈdrü-pəl, -ˈdrə-; ˈkwä-drə-\ *vb* **qua·dru·pled; qua·dru·pling** : to make or become four times as great or as many

[2]**quadruple** *adj* : FOURFOLD

qua·dru·plet \kwä-ˈdrə-plət, -ˈdrü-; ˈkwä-drə-\ *n* **1** : a combination of four of a kind **2** : one of four offspring born at one birth

[1]**qua·dru·pli·cate** \kwä-ˈdrü-pli-kət\ *adj* **1** : repeated four times **2** : FOURTH

[2]**qua·dru·pli·cate** \-plə-ˌkāt\ *vb* **-cat·ed; -cat·ing** **1** : QUADRUPLE **2** : to prepare in quadruplicate — **qua·dru·pli·ca·tion** \-ˌdrü-plə-ˈkā-shən\ *n*

[3]**qua·dru·pli·cate** \-ˈdrü-pli-kət\ *n* **1** : four copies all alike ⟨typed in ∼⟩ **2** : one of four like things

quaff \ˈkwäf, ˈkwaf\ *vb* : to drink deeply or repeatedly — **quaff** *n*

quag·ga mussel \ˈkwa-gə-, ˈkwä-\ *n* : a freshwater Eurasian mollusk introduced into U.S. waterways where it colonizes and clogs water intake pipes

quag·mire \ˈkwag-ˌmī(-ə)r, ˈkwäg-\ *n* **1** : soft miry land that yields under the foot **2** : PREDICAMENT

qua·hog \ˈkō-ˌhȯg, ˈkwȯ-, ˈkwō-, -ˌhäg\ *n* [modif. of Narragansett *poquaûhock*] : a round thick-shelled edible clam of the U.S.

quai \ˈkā\ *n* : QUAY

[1]**quail** \ˈkwāl\ *n, pl* **quail** *or* **quails** [ME *quaile,* fr. AF, fr. ML *quaccula,* of imitative origin] : any of numerous small short-winged plump game birds (as a bobwhite) related to the domestic chicken

[2]**quail** *vb* [ME, to grow feeble, fr. MD *quelen*] : to lose heart : COWER ⟨∼*ed* at the daunting task⟩ ♦ ***Synonyms*** RECOIL, SHRINK, FLINCH, WINCE, BLANCH

quaint \ˈkwānt\ *adj* : unusual or different in character or appearance; *esp* : pleasingly old-fashioned or unfamiliar ♦ ***Synonyms*** ODD, CURIOUS, STRANGE — **quaint·ly** *adv* — **quaint·ness** *n*

[1]**quake** \ˈkwāk\ *vb* **quaked; quak·ing** **1**

: to shake usu. from shock or instability 2 : to tremble usu. from cold or fear

[2]**quake** *n* : a shaking or trembling; *esp* : EARTHQUAKE

Quak•er \ˈkwā-kər\ *n* : FRIEND 5

qual *abbr* quality

qual•i•fi•ca•tion \ˌkwä-lə-fə-ˈkā-shən\ *n* 1 : LIMITATION, MODIFICATION ⟨her statement stands without ~⟩ 2 : a special skill that fits a person for some work or position 3 : REQUIREMENT

qual•i•fied \ˈkwä-lə-ˌfīd\ *adj* 1 : fitted for a given purpose or job 2 : limited in some way ⟨~ approval⟩

qual•i•fi•er \ˈkwä-lə-ˌfī(-ə)r\ *n* 1 : one that satisfies requirements 2 : a word or word group that limits the meaning of another word or word group

qual•i•fy \ˈkwä-lə-ˌfī\ *vb* **-fied; -fy•ing** 1 : to reduce from a general to a particular form : MODIFY 2 : to make less harsh 3 : to limit the meaning of (as a noun) 4 : to fit by skill or training for some purpose 5 : to give or have a legal right to do something 6 : to demonstrate the necessary ability ⟨~ for the finals⟩ ♦ ***Synonyms*** MODERATE, TEMPER

qual•i•ta•tive \ˈkwä-lə-ˌtā-tiv\ *adj* : of, relating to, or involving quality — **qual•i•ta•tive•ly** *adv*

[1]**qual•i•ty** \ˈkwä-lə-tē\ *n, pl* **-ties** 1 : peculiar and essential character : NATURE 2 : degree of excellence 3 : high social status 4 : a distinguishing attribute

[2]**quality** *adj* : being of high quality

qualm \ˈkwäm, ˈkwälm\ *n* 1 : a sudden attack (as of nausea) 2 : a sudden feeling of doubt, fear, or uneasiness esp. in not following one's conscience or better judgment

qualm•ish \ˈkwä-mish, ˈkwäl-\ *adj* 1 : feeling qualms : NAUSEATED 2 : overly scrupulous : SQUEAMISH 3 : of, relating to, or producing qualms

quan•da•ry \ˈkwän-drē\ *n, pl* **-ries** : a state of perplexity or doubt

quan•ti•fy \ˈkwän-tə-ˌfī\ *vb* **-fied; -fy•ing** : to determine, express, or measure the quantity of — **quan•ti•fi•able** \ˌkwän-tə-ˈfī-ə-bəl\ *adj*

quan•ti•ta•tive \ˈkwän-tə-ˌtā-tiv\ *adj* : of, relating to, or involving quantity — **quan•ti•ta•tive•ly** *adv*

quan•ti•ty \ˈkwän-tə-tē\ *n, pl* **-ties** 1 : AMOUNT, NUMBER 2 : a considerable amount ⟨buys food in ~⟩

quan•tize \ˈkwän-ˌtīz\ *vb* **quan•tized; quan•tiz•ing** : to subdivide (as energy) into small units

[1]**quan•tum** \ˈkwän-təm\ *n, pl* **quan•ta** \-tə\ [L, neut. of *quantus* how much] 1 : QUANTITY, AMOUNT 2 : an elemental unit of energy

[2]**quantum** *adj* 1 : LARGE, SIGNIFICANT 2 : relating to or employing the principles of quantum mechanics

quantum mechanics *n sing or pl* : a theory of matter based on the concept of possession of wave properties by elementary particles — **quantum mechanical** *adj* — **quantum mechanically** *adv*

quantum theory *n* 1 : a theory in physics based on the idea that radiant energy (as light) is composed of small separate packets of energy 2 : QUANTUM MECHANICS

quar *abbr* quarterly

quar•an•tine \ˈkwȯr-ən-ˌtēn\ *n* [modif. of It *quarantena,* lit., period of forty days, fr. *quaranta* forty, fr. L *quadraginta*] 1 : a period during which a ship suspected of carrying contagious disease is forbidden contact with the shore 2 : a restraint on the movements of persons or goods to prevent the spread of pests or disease 3 : a place or period of quarantine 4 : a state of enforced isolation — **quarantine** *vb*

quark \ˈkwȯrk, ˈkwärk\ *n* : a hypothetical elementary particle that carries a fractional charge and is held to be a constituent of heavier particles (as protons and neutrons)

[1]**quar•rel** \ˈkwȯr-əl\ *n* 1 : a ground of dispute 2 : a verbal clash : CONFLICT — **quar•rel•some** \-səm\ *adj*

[2]**quarrel** *vb* **-reled** *or* **-relled; -rel•ing** *or* **-rel•ling** 1 : to find fault 2 : to dispute angrily : WRANGLE

[1]**quar•ry** \ˈkwȯr-ē\ *n, pl* **quarries** [ME *querre* entrails of game given to the hounds, fr. AF *cureie, quereie,* fr. *quir, cuir* skin, hide (on which the entrails were placed), fr. L *corium*] 1 : game hunted with hawks 2 : PREY

[2]**quarry** *n, pl* **quarries** [ME *quarey,* alter. of *quarrere,* fr. AF, fr. VL **quadraria,* fr. LL *quadrus* hewn (lit., squared) stone, fr. L *quadrum* square] : an open excavation usu. for obtaining building stone or limestone — **quarry** *vb*

quart \ˈkwȯrt\ *n* — see WEIGHT table

[1]**quar•ter** \ˈkwȯr-tər\ *n* 1 : one of four equal parts 2 : a fourth of a dollar; *also* : a coin of this value 3 : a district of a city 4 *pl* : LODGINGS ⟨moved into new ~*s*⟩ 5 : MERCY, CLEMENCY ⟨gave no ~⟩ 6 : a fourth part of the moon's period

[2]**quarter** *vb* 1 : to divide into four equal parts 2 : to provide with shelter

[1]**quar•ter•back** \-ˌbak\ *n* : a football player who calls the signals and directs the offensive play for the team

[2]**quarterback** *vb* 1 : to direct the offensive play of a football team 2 : LEAD, BOSS

quar•ter•deck \-ˌdek\ *n* : the stern area of a ship's upper deck

quarter horse *n* : any of a breed of compact muscular saddle horses characterized by great endurance and by high speed for short distances

[1]**quar•ter•ly** \ˈkwȯr-tər-lē\ *adv* : at 3-month intervals

[2]**quarterly** *adj* : occurring, issued, or payable at 3-month intervals

[3]**quarterly** *n, pl* **-lies** : a periodical published four times a year

quar•ter•mas•ter \-ˌmas-tər\ *n* 1 : a petty officer who attends to a ship's helm, binnacle, and signals 2 : an army officer who provides clothing and subsistence for troops

quar·ter·staff \-ˌstaf\ *n, pl* **-staves** \-ˌstavz, -ˌstāvz\ : a long stout staff formerly used as a weapon

quar·tet *also* **quar·tette** \kwȯr-ˈtet\ *n* **1** : a musical composition for four instruments or voices **2** : a group of four and esp. of four musicians

quar·to \ˈkwȯr-tō\ *n, pl* **quartos** **1** : the size of a piece of paper cut four from a sheet **2** : a book printed on quarto pages

quartz \ˈkwȯrts\ *n* : a common often transparent crystalline mineral that is a form of silica

quartz·ite \ˈkwȯrt-ˌsīt\ *n* : a compact granular rock composed of quartz and derived from sandstone

qua·sar \ˈkwā-ˌzär, -ˌsär\ *n* : any of a class of extremely distant starlike celestial objects

[1]**quash** \ˈkwäsh, ˈkwȯsh\ *vb* : to suppress or extinguish summarily and completely : QUELL

[2]**quash** *vb* : to nullify by judicial action

qua·si \ˈkwā-ˌzī, -ˌsī; ˈkwä-zē, -sē\ *adj* : being in some sense or degree ⟨a ~ corporation⟩

quasi- *comb form* [L, as if, as it were, approximately, fr. *quam* as + *si* if] : in some sense or degree ⟨*quasi*-historical⟩

qua·si–gov·ern·men·tal \-gə-vərn-ˈment°l\ *adj* : supported by the government but managed privately

Qua·ter·na·ry \ˈkwä-tər-ˌner-ē, kwə-ˈtər-nə-rē\ *adj* : of, relating to, or being the geologic period from the end of the Tertiary to the present — **Quaternary** *n*

qua·train \ˈkwä-ˌtrān\ *n* : a unit of four lines of verse

qua·tre·foil \ˈka-tər-ˌfȯi(-ə)l, ˈka-trə-\ *n* : a stylized figure often of a flower with four petals

qua·ver \ˈkwā-vər\ *vb* **1** : TREMBLE, SHAKE ⟨~*ed* with nervousness⟩ **2** : TRILL **3** : to speak in tremulous tones ♦ ***Synonyms*** SHUDDER, QUAKE, TWITTER, QUIVER, SHIVER — **quaver** *n*

quay \ˈkē, ˈkwā, ˈkā\ *n* : WHARF

Que *abbr* Quebec

quean \ˈkwēn\ *n* : PROSTITUTE

quea·sy \ˈkwē-zē\ *adj* **quea·si·er; -est** : NAUSEATED — **quea·si·ly** \-zə-lē\ *adv* — **quea·si·ness** \-zē-nəs\ *n*

Que·chua \ˈke-chə-wə, ˈkech-wə\ *n* **1** : a member of an Indigenous people of central Peru **2** : a group of peoples forming the dominant element of the Inca Empire **3** : a family of languages spoken in Peru and adjacent countries of the So. American Andes — **Quechuan** *adj or n*

queen \ˈkwēn\ *n* [ME *quene,* fr. OE *cwēn* woman, wife, queen] **1** : the wife or widow of a king **2** : a female monarch **3** : a woman notable in rank, power, or attractiveness **4** : the most powerful piece in the game of chess **5** : a playing card bearing the figure of a queen **6** : a fertile female of a social insect (as a bee or termite) — **queen·ly** *adj*

Queen Anne's lace \-ˈanz-\ *n* : a widely naturalized Eurasian herb from which the cultivated carrot originated

queen consort *n, pl* **queens consort** : the wife of a reigning king

queen mother *n* : a dowager queen who is mother of the reigning sovereign

queen–size *adj* : having dimensions of approximately 60 inches by 80 inches ⟨a ~ bed⟩; *also* : of a size that fits a queen-size bed

[1]**queer** \ˈkwir\ *adj* **1 a** : differing from what is usual or normal : ODD, STRANGE **b** : ECCENTRIC, UNCONVENTIONAL **2** *sometimes disparaging + offensive* **a** : GAY 5 **b** : of, relating to, or characterized by sexual or romantic attraction not limited to people of a particular gender identity or sexual orientation **c** : of, relating to, or being a person who is not heterosexual and/or who is not cisgender **d** : NONBINARY 2 **e** : TRANSGENDER — **queer·ly** *adv* — **queer·ness** *n*

[2]**queer** *n, sometimes disparaging + offensive* : a person who is queer

[3]**queer** *vb* : to spoil the effect of : DISRUPT ⟨~*ed* our plans⟩

queer theory *n* : an approach to literary and cultural study that rejects traditional categories of gender and sexuality

quell \ˈkwel\ *vb* **1** : to put an end to by force ⟨~ a riot⟩ **2** : CALM, PACIFY

quench \ˈkwench\ *vb* **1** : PUT OUT, EXTINGUISH **2** : SUBDUE **3** : SLAKE, SATISFY ⟨~*ed* his thirst⟩ — **quench·able** *adj* — **quench·er** *n* — **quench·less** *adj*

quer·u·lous \ˈkwer-ə-ləs, -yə-\ *adj* **1** : constantly complaining **2** : FRETFUL, WHINING ⟨a ~ voice⟩ ♦ ***Synonyms*** PETULANT, PETTISH, IRRITABLE, PEEVISH, HUFFY — **quer·u·lous·ly** *adv* — **quer·u·lous·ness** *n*

que·ry \ˈkwir-ē, ˈkwer-\ *n, pl* **queries** : QUESTION — **query** *vb*

que·sa·dil·la \ˌkā-sə-ˈdē-ə\ *n* : a tortilla filled with a savory mixture, folded, and usu. fried

quest \ˈkwest\ *n* : SEARCH ⟨in ~ of game⟩ — **quest** *vb*

[1]**ques·tion** \ˈkwes-chən\ *n* **1** : an interrogative expression **2** : a subject for debate; *also* : a proposition to be voted on **3** : INQUIRY **4** : DISPUTE ⟨true beyond ~⟩

[2]**question** *vb* **1** : to ask questions **2** : DOUBT, DISPUTE ⟨~*ed* the verdict⟩ **3** : to subject to analysis : EXAMINE ♦ ***Synonyms*** INTERROGATE, QUIZ, QUERY — **ques·tion·er** *n*

ques·tion·able \ˈkwes-chə-nə-bəl\ *adj* **1** : not certain or exact : DOUBTFUL **2** : not believed to be true, sound, or moral ♦ ***Synonyms*** DUBIOUS, PROBLEMATICAL, MOOT, DEBATABLE — **ques·tion·ably** \-blē\ *adv*

question mark *n* : a punctuation mark ? used esp. at the end of a sentence to indicate a direct question

ques·tion·naire \ˌkwes-chə-ˈner\ *n* : a set of questions for obtaining information

quet·zal \ket-ˈsäl, -ˈsal\ *n, pl* **quetzals** *or* **quet·za·les** \-ˈsä-lās, -ˈsa-\ **1** : a Central American bird with brilliant plumage **2** *pl quetzales* — see MONEY table

[1]**queue** \ˈkyü\ *n* [F, lit., tail, fr. OF *cue, coe,* fr. L *cauda, coda*] **1** : a braid of hair usu. worn hanging at the back of the head **2** : a waiting line (as of persons)

[2]**queue** *vb* **queued; queu·ing** *or* **queue·ing** : to line up in a queue

quib·ble \ˈkwi-bəl\ *n* **1** : an evasion of or shifting from the point at issue **2** : a minor objection or criticism — **quibble** *vb* — **quib·bler** *n*

[1]**quick** \ˈkwik\ *adj* **1** : LIVING **2** : RAPID, SPEEDY ⟨∼ steps⟩ **3** : prompt to understand, think, or perceive : ALERT **4** : easily aroused ⟨a ∼ temper⟩ **5** : turning or bending sharply ⟨a ∼ turn in the road⟩ ♦ *Synonyms* FLEET, FAST, HASTY, EXPEDITIOUS — **quick** *adv* — **quick·ly** *adv* — **quick·ness** *n*

[2]**quick** *n* **1** : a sensitive area of living flesh **2** : a vital part : HEART

quick bread *n* : a bread made with a leavening agent that permits immediate baking of the dough or batter

quick·en \ˈkwi-kən\ *vb* **1** : to come to life : REVIVE **2** : AROUSE, STIMULATE ⟨curiosity ∼*ed* my interest⟩ **3** : to increase in speed : HASTEN **4** : to show vitality (as by growing or moving) ♦ *Synonyms* ANIMATE, ENLIVEN, LIVEN, VIVIFY

quick–freeze \ˈkwik-ˈfrēz\ *vb* **-froze** \-ˈfrōz\; **-fro·zen** \-ˈfrō-zᵊn\; **-freez·ing** : to freeze (food) for preservation so rapidly that the natural juices and flavor are not lost

quick·ie \ˈkwi-kē\ *n* : something hurriedly done or made

quick·lime \ˈkwik-ˌlīm\ *n* : [1]LIME

quick·sand \-ˌsand\ *n* : a deep mass of loose sand mixed with water

quick·sil·ver \-ˌsil-vər\ *n* : MERCURY 1

quick·step \-ˌstep\ *n* : a spirited march tune or dance

quick–wit·ted \ˈkwik-ˈwi-təd\ *adj* : mentally alert ♦ *Synonyms* CLEVER, BRIGHT, SMART, INTELLIGENT

quid \ˈkwid\ *n* : a lump of something chewable ⟨a ∼ of tobacco⟩

quid pro quo \ˌkwid-ˌprō-ˈkwō\ *n* [NL, something for something] : something given or received for something else

qui·es·cent \kwī-ˈe-sᵊnt\ *adj* : being at rest : QUIET ⟨a ∼ state⟩ ♦ *Synonyms* LATENT, DORMANT, POTENTIAL — **qui·es·cence** \-sᵊns\ *n*

[1]**qui·et** \ˈkwī-ət\ *n* : REPOSE

[2]**quiet** *adj* **1** : marked by little motion or activity : CALM **2** : GENTLE, MILD ⟨a ∼ disposition⟩ **3** : enjoyed in peace and relaxation ⟨a ∼ cup of tea⟩ **4** : free from noise or uproar **5** : not showy : MODEST ⟨∼ clothes⟩ **6** : SECLUDED ⟨a ∼ nook⟩ — **quiet** *adv* — **qui·et·ly** *adv* — **qui·et·ness** *n*

[3]**quiet** *vb* **1** : CALM, PACIFY **2** : to become quiet — usu. used with *down*

qui·etude \ˈkwī-ə-ˌtüd, -ˌtyüd\ *n* : QUIETNESS, REPOSE

qui·etus \kwī-ˈē-təs\ *n* [ME *quietus est,* fr. ML, he is quit, formula of discharge from obligation] **1** : final settlement (as of a debt) **2** : DEATH

quill \ˈkwil\ *n* **1** : a large stiff feather; *also* : the hollow tubular part of a feather **2** : one of the hollow sharp spines of a hedgehog or porcupine **3** : a pen made from a feather

[1]**quilt** \ˈkwilt\ *n* : a padded bed coverlet

[2]**quilt** *vb* **1** : to fill, pad, or line like a quilt **2** : to stitch or sew in layers with padding in between **3** : to make quilts

quince \ˈkwins\ *n* : a hard yellow applelike fruit; *also* : a tree related to the roses that bears this fruit

quin·ce·a·ñe·ra *or* **quin·ce·a·ne·ra** \ˌkēn-sā-än-ˈyer-ə\ *n* : a celebration of a girl's fifteenth birthday in Latin American cultures

qui·nine \ˈkwī-ˌnīn\ *n* : a bitter white drug obtained from cinchona bark and used esp. in treating malaria

qui·noa \ˈkēn-ˌwä, kē-ˈnō-ə\ *n* [Sp, fr. Quechua *kinua*] : the starchy seeds of an annual herb related to spinach which are used as food and ground into flour; *also* : this herb

quint \ˈkwint\ *n* : QUINTUPLET

quin·tal \ˈkwin-tᵊl, ˈkan-\ *n* : HUNDREDWEIGHT

quin·tes·sence \kwin-ˈte-sᵊns\ *n* **1** : the purest essence of something **2** : the most typical example ⟨the ∼ of self-control⟩ — **quin·tes·sen·tial** \ˌkwin-tə-ˈsen-chəl\ *adj* — **quin·tes·sen·tial·ly** *adv*

quin·tet \kwin-ˈtet\ *n* **1** : a musical composition for five instruments or voices **2** : a group of five and esp. of five musicians

[1]**quin·tu·ple** \kwin-ˈtü-pəl, -ˈtyü-, -ˈtə-\ *adj* **1** : having five units or members **2** : being five times as great or as many — **quintuple** *n*

[2]**quintuple** *vb* **quin·tu·pled; quin·tu·pling** : to make or become five times as great or as many

quin·tu·plet \kwin-ˈtə-plət, -ˈtü-, -ˈtyü-\ *n* **1** : a group of five of a kind **2** : one of five offspring born at one birth

[1]**quin·tu·pli·cate** \kwin-ˈtü-pli-kət, -ˈtyü-\ *adj* **1** : repeated five times **2** : FIFTH

[2]**quintuplicate** *n* **1** : one of five like things **2** : five copies all alike ⟨typed in ∼⟩

[3]**quin·tu·pli·cate** \-plə-ˌkāt\ *vb* **-cat·ed; -cat·ing 1** : QUINTUPLE **2** : to provide in quintuplicate

[1]**quip** \ˈkwip\ *n* : a clever remark : GIBE

[2]**quip** *vb* **quipped; quip·ping 1** : to make quips : GIBE **2** : to jest or gibe at

quire \ˈkwī(-ə)r\ *n* : a set of 24 or sometimes 25 sheets of paper of the same size and quality

quirk \ˈkwərk\ *n* : a peculiarity of action or behavior — **quirky** *adj*

quirt \ˈkwərt\ *n* : a riding whip with a short handle and a rawhide lash

quis·ling \ˈkwiz-liŋ\ *n* [Vidkun *Quisling* †1945 Norwegian politician who collaborated with the Nazis] : one who helps the invaders of one's own country

quit \ˈkwit\ *vb* **quit** *also* **quit·ted; quit·ting 1** : CONDUCT, BEHAVE ⟨∼ themselves well⟩ **2** : to depart from : LEAVE;

also : to bring to an end **3** : to give up for good ⟨~ smoking⟩ ⟨~ my job⟩ ♦ ***Synonyms*** ACQUIT, COMPORT, DEPORT, DEMEAN — **quit·ter** *n*

quite \ˈkwīt\ *adv* **1** : COMPLETELY, WHOLLY ⟨not ~ finished⟩ **2** : to an extreme : POSITIVELY **3** : to a considerable extent : RATHER ⟨~ rich⟩

quits \ˈkwits\ *adj* : even or equal with another

quit·tance \ˈkwi-tᵊns\ *n* : REQUITAL

[1]**quiv·er** \ˈkwi-vər\ *n* : a case for carrying arrows

[2]**quiver** *vb* **quiv·ered; quiv·er·ing** : to shake with a slight trembling motion ⟨~*ed* with rage⟩ ♦ ***Synonyms*** SHIVER, SHUDDER, QUAVER, QUAKE, TREMBLE — **quiv·er·ing·ly** *adv*

[3]**quiver** *n* : the act or action of quivering : TREMOR

qui vive \kē-ˈvēv\ *n* [F *qui-vive,* fr. *qui vive?* long live who?, challenge of a French sentry] : ALERT ⟨on the *qui vive* for prowlers⟩

quix·ot·ic \kwik-ˈsä-tik\ *adj* [fr. Don *Quixote,* hero of the novel *Don Quixote de la Mancha* by Cervantes] : foolishly impractical esp. in the pursuit of ideals — **quix·ot·i·cal·ly** \-ti-kə-lē\ *adv*

[1]**quiz** \ˈkwiz\ *n, pl* **quiz·zes** **1** : an eccentric person **2** : PRACTICAL JOKE **3** : a short oral or written test

[2]**quiz** *vb* **quizzed; quiz·zing** **1** : MOCK **2** : to look at inquisitively **3** : to question closely ♦ ***Synonyms*** ASK, INTERROGATE, QUERY

quiz·zi·cal \ˈkwi-zi-kəl\ *adj* **1** : comically quaint **2** : mildly teasing or mocking **3** : expressive of puzzlement, curiosity, or disbelief ⟨gave me a ~ look⟩

quoit \ˈkwāt, ˈkwȯit, ˈkȯit\ *n* **1** : a flattened ring of iron or circle of rope used in a throwing game **2** *pl* : a game in which quoits are thrown at an upright pin in an attempt to ring the pin

quon·dam \ˈkwän-dəm, -ˌdam\ *adj* [L, at one time, formerly, fr. *quom, cum* when] : FORMER ⟨a ~ friend⟩

quo·rum \ˈkwȯr-əm\ *n* : the number of members required to be present for business to be legally transacted

quot *abbr* quotation

quo·ta \ˈkwō-tə\ *n* : a proportional part esp. when assigned : SHARE

quot·able \ˈkwō-tə-bəl\ *adj* : fit for or worth quoting ⟨a ~ comment⟩ — **quot·abil·i·ty** \-ˈbi-lə-tē\ *n*

quo·ta·tion \kwō-ˈtā-shən\ *n* **1** : the act or process of quoting **2** : the price currently bid or offered for something **3** : something that is quoted

quotation mark *n* : one of a pair of punctuation marks " " or ' ' used esp. to indicate the beginning and end of a quotation in which exact phraseology is directly cited

quote \ˈkwōt\ *vb* **quot·ed; quot·ing** [ML *quotare* to mark the number of, number references, fr. L *quotus* of what number or quantity, fr. *quot* how many, (as) many as] **1** : to speak or write a passage from another usu. with acknowledgment; *also* : to repeat a passage in substantiation or illustration **2** : to state the market price of a commodity, stock, or bond **3** : to inform a hearer or reader that matter following is quoted — **quote** *n*

quoth \ˈkwōth\ *vb past* [ME, past of *quethen* to say, fr. OE *cwethan*] *archaic* : SAID — usu. used in the 1st and 3d persons with the subject following

quo·tid·i·an \kwō-ˈti-dē-ən\ *adj* **1** : DAILY **2** : COMMONPLACE, ORDINARY ⟨~ concerns⟩

quo·tient \ˈkwō-shənt\ *n* : the number obtained by dividing one number by another

Quran *also* **Qur'an** *var of* KORAN

qv *abbr* [L *quod vide*] which see

qy *abbr* query

R

[1]**r** \ˈär\ *n, pl* **r's** *or* **rs** \ˈärz\ *often cap* : the 18th letter of the English alphabet

[2]**r** *abbr, often cap* **1** rabbi **2** radius **3** rare **4** Republican **5** rerun **6** resistance **7** right **8** river **9** roentgen **10** rook **11** run

Ra *symbol* radium

RA *abbr* **1** regular army **2** research assistant **3** : resident advisor; resident assistant **4** : Royal Academy

[1]**rab·bet** \ˈra-bət\ *n* : a groove in the edge or face of a surface (as a board) esp. to receive another piece

[2]**rabbet** *vb* : to cut a rabbet in; *also* : to join by means of a rabbet

rab·bi \ˈra-ˌbī\ *n* [ME, fr. OE, fr. LL, fr. Gk *rhabbi,* fr. Heb *rabbī* my master, fr. *rabh* master + *-ī* my] **1** : MASTER, TEACHER — used by Jews as a term of address **2** : a Jew trained and ordained for professional religious leadership — **rab·bin·ic** \rə-ˈbi-nik\ *or* **rab·bin·i·cal** \-ni-kəl\ *adj*

rab·bin·ate \ˈra-bə-nət, -ˌnāt\ *n* **1** : the office of a rabbi **2** : the whole body of rabbis

rab·bit \ˈra-bət\ *n, pl* **rabbit** *or* **rabbits** : any of various long-eared short-tailed burrowing mammals distinguished from the related hares by being blind, furless, and helpless at birth; *also* : the pelt of a rabbit

rabbit ears *n pl* : an indoor V-shaped television antenna

rabble \ˈra-bəl\ *n* **1** : MOB 2 **2** : the lowest class of people

rab•ble–rous•er \ˈra-bəl-ˌrau̇-zər\ *n* : one that stirs up (as to hatred or violence) the masses of the people

ra•bid \ˈra-bəd\ *adj* **1** : VIOLENT, FURIOUS **2** : being fanatical or extreme ⟨~ supporters⟩ **3** : affected with rabies — **ra•bid•ly** *adv*

ra•bies \ˈrā-bēz\ *n, pl* **rabies** [NL, fr. L, madness] : an acute deadly virus disease of the nervous system transmitted by the bite of an affected animal

rac•coon \ra-ˈkün\ *n, pl* **raccoon** *or* **raccoons** : a gray No. American chiefly tree-dwelling mammal with a black mask, a bushy ringed tail, and nocturnal habits; *also* : its pelt

[1]**race** \ˈrās\ *n* **1** : a strong current of running water; *also* : its channel **2** : an onward course (as of time or life) **3** : a contest of speed **4** : a contest for a desired end (as election to office)

[2]**race** *vb* **raced; rac•ing** **1** : to run in a race **2** : to run swiftly : RUSH **3** : to engage in a race with **4** : to drive or ride at high speed — **rac•er** *n*

[3]**race** *n* **1** *dated* : a group of people sharing a common cultural, geographical, linguistic, or religious origin or background **2** : a group of individuals within a biological species able to breed together **3** : any one of the groups that humans are often divided into based on physical traits regarded as common among people of shared ancestry; *also* : categorization into such groups **4** : a group of living things considered as a category ⟨the human ~⟩ — **ra•cial** \ˈrā-shəl\ *adj* — **ra•cial•ly** *adv*

race•course \ˈrās-ˌkȯrs\ *n* : a course for racing

race•horse \-ˌhȯrs\ *n* : a horse bred or kept for racing

ra•ceme \rā-ˈsēm\ *n* [L *racemus* bunch of grapes] : a flower cluster with flowers borne along a stem and blooming from the base toward the tip — **rac•e•mose** \ˈra-sə-ˌmōs\ *adj*

race•track \ˈrās-ˌtrak\ *n* : a usu. oval course on which races are run

race•way \-ˌwā\ *n* **1** : a channel for a current of water **2** : RACECOURSE

ra•cial•ism \ˈrā-shə-ˌli-zəm\ *n* : a belief that race determines human traits and capacities; *also* : RACISM — **ra•cial•ist** \-list\ *n* — **ra•cial•is•tic** \ˌrā-shə-ˈlis-tik\ *adj*

ra•cial•ize \ˈrā-shə-ˌlīz\ *vb* **-ized; -iz•ing** : to give a racial character to — **ra•cial•iza•tion** \ˌrā-shə-lə-ˈzā-shən\ *n*

racing form *n* : a paper giving data about racehorses for use by bettors

rac•ism \ˈrā-ˌsi-zəm\ *n* **1** : a belief that race is a fundamental determinant of human traits and capacities and that racial differences produce an inherent superiority of a particular race; *also* : racial discrimination or prejudice **2 a** : the systemic oppression of a racial group to the advantage of another; *specif* : WHITE SUPREMACY **b** : a political or social system founded on racism and designed to execute its principles — **rac•ist** \-sist\ *n*

[1]**rack** \ˈrak\ *n* **1** : an instrument of torture on which a body is stretched **2** : a framework on or in which something may be placed (as for display or storage) **3** : a bar with teeth on one side to mesh with a pinion or worm gear

[2]**rack** *vb* **1** : to torture on or as if on a rack **2** : to stretch or strain by force **3** : TORMENT **4** : to place on or in a rack

[1]**rack•et** *or* **rac•quet** \ˈra-kət\ *n* [MF *raquette,* ultim. fr. ML *rasceta* wrist, carpus, fr. Ar *rusgh* wrist] : a light bat made of netting stretched in an oval open frame having a handle and used for striking a ball or shuttlecock

[2]**racket** *n* **1** : confused noise : DIN **2** : a fraudulent or dishonest scheme or activity ⟨a criminal ~⟩

[3]**racket** *vb* : to make a racket

rack•e•teer \ˌra-kə-ˈtir\ *n* : a person who obtains money by an illegal enterprise usu. involving intimidation — **rack•e•teer•ing** *n*

rack up *vb* : ACHIEVE, GAIN ⟨*racked up* their 10th victory⟩

ra•con•teur \ˌra-ˌkän-ˈtər\ *n* : one good at telling anecdotes

rac•quet•ball \ˈra-kət-ˌbȯl\ *n* : a game similar to handball played on a 4-walled court with a short-handled racket

racy \ˈrā-sē\ *adj* **rac•i•er; -est** **1** : full of zest **2** : PUNGENT, SPICY **3** : RISQUÉ, SUGGESTIVE ⟨~ jokes⟩ — **rac•i•ly** \ˈrā-sə-lē\ *adv* — **rac•i•ness** \-sē-nəs\ *n*

rad *abbr* **1** radical **2** radio **3** radius

ra•dar \ˈrā-ˌdär\ *n* [*ra*dio *d*etecting *a*nd *r*anging] : a device that emits radio waves for detecting and locating an object by the reflection of the radio waves and that may use this reflection to determine the object's direction and speed

radar gun *n* : a handheld device that uses radar to measure the speed of a moving object

ra•dar•scope \ˈrā-ˌdär-ˌskōp\ *n* : a visual display for a radar receiver

[1]**ra•di•al** \ˈrā-dē-əl\ *adj* : arranged or having parts arranged like rays around a common center — **ra•di•al•ly** *adv*

[2]**radial** *n* : a pneumatic tire with cords laid perpendicular to the center line

radial engine *n* : an internal combustion engine with cylinders arranged radially like the spokes of a wheel

ra•di•an \ˈrā-dē-ən\ *n* : a unit of measure for angles that is equal to approximately 57.3 degrees

ra•di•ant \ˈrā-dē-ənt\ *adj* **1** : SHINING, GLOWING **2** : beaming with happiness ⟨a ~ smile⟩ **3** : transmitted by radiation ♦ ***Synonyms*** BRILLIANT, BRIGHT, LUMINOUS, LUSTROUS — **ra•di•ance** \-əns\ *n* — **ra•di•ant•ly** *adv*

radiant energy *n* : energy traveling as electromagnetic waves

ra·di·ate \ˈrā-dē-ˌāt\ *vb* **-at·ed; -at·ing** **1** : to send out rays : SHINE, GLOW **2** : to issue in or as if in rays ⟨light ~*s*⟩ **3** : to spread around as from a center

ra·di·a·tion \ˌrā-dē-ˈā-shən\ *n* **1** : the action or process of radiating **2** : the process of emitting radiant energy in the form of waves or particles; *also* : something (as an X-ray beam) that is radiated

radiation sickness *n* : sickness that results from exposure to radiation and is commonly marked by fatigue, nausea, vomiting, loss of teeth and hair, and in more severe cases by damage to blood-forming tissue

radiation therapy *n* : RADIOTHERAPY

ra·di·a·tor \ˈrā-dē-ˌā-tər\ *n* : any of various devices (as a set of pipes or tubes) for transferring heat from a fluid within to an area or object outside

[1]**rad·i·cal** \ˈra-di-kəl\ *adj* [ME, fr. LL *radicalis,* fr. L *radic-, radix* root] **1** : FUNDAMENTAL, EXTREME, THOROUGHGOING **2** : of or relating to radicals in politics — **rad·i·cal·ism** \-kə-ˌli-zəm\ *n* — **rad·i·cal·ly** *adv*

[2]**radical** *n* **1** : a person who favors rapid and sweeping changes in laws and methods of government **2** : FREE RADICAL; *also* : a group of atoms considered as a unit in certain reactions or as a subunit of a larger molecule **3** : a mathematical expression indicating a root by means of a radical sign; *also* : RADICAL SIGN

rad·i·cal·ise *Brit var of* RADICALIZE

rad·i·cal·ize \-kə-ˌlīz\ *vb* **-ized; -iz·ing** : to make radical esp. in politics — **rad·i·cal·i·za·tion** \ˌra-di-kə-lə-ˈzā-shən\ *n*

radical sign *n* : the sign √ placed before a mathematical expression to indicate that its root is to be taken

ra·dic·chio \ra-ˈdi-kē-ō\ *n, pl* **–chios** : a chicory with reddish variegated leaves

radii *pl of* RADIUS

[1]**ra·dio** \ˈrā-dē-ˌō\ *n, pl* **ra·di·os** **1** : the wireless transmission or reception of signals using electromagnetic waves **2** : a radio receiving set **3** : the radio broadcasting industry — **radio** *adj*

[2]**radio** *vb* : to communicate or send a message to by radio

ra·dio·ac·tiv·i·ty \ˌrā-dē-ō-ˌak-ˈti-və-tē\ *n* : the property that some elements or isotopes have of spontaneously emitting energetic particles by the disintegration of their atomic nuclei — **ra·dio·ac·tive** \-ˈak-tiv\ *adj*

radio astronomy *n* : astronomy dealing with radio waves received from outside the earth's atmosphere

ra·dio·car·bon \ˌrā-dē-ō-ˈkär-bən\ *n* : CARBON 14

radio frequency *n* : an electromagnetic wave frequency intermediate between audio frequencies and infrared frequencies used esp. for communication and radar signals

ra·dio·gram \ˈrā-dē-ō-ˌgram\ *n* : a message transmitted by radio

ra·dio·graph \-ˌgraf\ *n* : a photograph made by some form of radiation other than light; *esp* : an X-ray photograph — **radiograph** *vb* — **ra·di·og·ra·pher** \ˌrā-dē-ˈä-grə-fər\ *n* — **ra·dio·graph·ic** \ˌrā-dē-ō-ˈgra-fik\ *adj* — **ra·dio·graph·i·cal·ly** \-fi-k(ə-)lē\ *adv* — **ra·di·og·ra·phy** \ˌrā-dē-ˈä-grə-fē\ *n*

ra·dio·iso·tope \ˌrā-dē-ō-ˈī-sə-ˌtōp\ *n* : a radioactive isotope

ra·di·ol·o·gy \ˌrā-dē-ˈä-lə-jē\ *n* : the use of radiant energy (as X-rays and radium radiations) in medicine — **ra·di·ol·o·gist** \-jist\ *n*

ra·dio·man \ˈrā-dē-ō-ˌman\ *n* : a radio operator or technician

ra·di·om·e·ter \ˌrā-dē-ˈä-mə-tər\ *n* : an instrument for measuring the intensity of radiant energy — **ra·dio·met·ric** \ˌrā-dē-ō-ˈme-trik\ *adj* — **ra·di·om·e·try** \-mə-trē\ *n*

ra·dio·phone \ˈrā-dē-ə-ˌfōn\ *n* : RADIOTELEPHONE

ra·dio·sonde \ˈrā-dē-ō-ˌsänd\ *n* : a small radio transmitter carried aloft (as by balloon) and used to transmit meteorological data

ra·dio·tele·phone \ˌrā-dē-ō-ˈte-lə-ˌfōn\ *n* : a telephone that uses radio waves wholly or partly instead of connecting wires — **ra·dio·te·le·pho·ny** \-tə-ˈle-fə-nē, -ˈte-lə-ˌfō-nē\ *n*

radio telescope *n* : a radio receiver-antenna combination used for observation in radio astronomy

ra·dio·ther·a·py \ˌrā-dē-ō-ˈther-ə-pē\ *n* : the treatment of disease by means of radiation (as X-rays) — **ra·dio·ther·a·pist** \-pist\ *n*

rad·ish \ˈra-dish\ *n* [ME, alter. of OE *rædic,* fr. L *radic-, radix* root, radish] : a pungent fleshy root usu. eaten raw; *also* : a plant related to the mustards that produces this root

ra·di·um \ˈrā-dē-əm\ *n* [NL, fr. L *radius* ray] : a very radioactive metallic chemical element that is used in the treatment of cancer

ra·di·us \ˈrā-dē-əs\ *n, pl* **ra·dii** \-ē-ˌī\ *also* **ra·di·us·es** **1** : a straight line extending from the center of a circle or a sphere to the circumference or surface; *also* : the length of a radius **2** : the bone on the thumb side of the human forearm **3** : a circular area defined by the length of its radius ♦ ***Synonyms*** RANGE, REACH, SCOPE, COMPASS

RADM *abbr* rear admiral

ra·don \ˈrā-ˌdän\ *n* : a heavy radioactive gaseous chemical element

RAF *abbr* Royal Air Force

raf·fia \ˈra-fē-ə\ *n* : fiber used esp. for making baskets and hats that is obtained from the stalks of the leaves of a tropical African palm **(raffia palm)**

raff·ish \ˈra-fish\ *adj* : jaunty or sporty esp. in a flashy or vulgar manner — **raff·ish·ly** *adv* — **raff·ish·ness** *n*

[1]**raf·fle** \ˈra-fəl\ *vb* **raf·fled; raf·fling** : to dispose of by a raffle

[2]**raffle** *n* : a lottery in which the prize is won by one of a number of persons buying chances

[1]**raft** \'raft\ *n* **1** : a number of logs or timbers fastened together to form a float **2** : a flat structure for support or transportation on water; *also* : an inflatable watercraft with a flat bottom

[2]**raft** *vb* **1** : to travel or transport by raft **2** : to make into a raft

[3]**raft** *n* : a large amount or number

raf·ter \'raf-tər\ *n* : any of the parallel beams that support a roof

[1]**rag** \'rag\ *n* **1** : a waste piece of cloth **2** : a sleazy newspaper

[2]**rag** *n* : a composition in ragtime

ra·ga \'rä-gə\ *n* **1** : a traditional melodic pattern or mode in Indian music **2** : an improvisation based on a raga

rag·a·muf·fin \'ra-gə-ˌmə-fən\ *n* [ME *Ragamuffyn,* name for a ragged, oafish person] : a ragged dirty person; *esp* : a poorly clothed often dirty child

[1]**rage** \'rāj\ *n* **1** : violent and uncontrolled anger **2** : VOGUE, FASHION

[2]**rage** *vb* **raged; rag·ing** **1** : to be furiously angry : RAVE **2** : to continue out of control ⟨the fire *raged*⟩

rag·ged \'ra-gəd\ *adj* **1** : TORN, TATTERED ⟨a ~ dress⟩; *also* : wearing tattered clothes **2** : done in an uneven way — **rag·ged·ly** *adv* — **rag·ged·ness** *n*

rag·lan \'ra-glən\ *n* : an overcoat with sleeves (**raglan sleeves**) sewn in with seams slanting from neck to underarm

ra·gout \ra-'gü\ *n* [F *ragoût,* fr. *ragoûter* to revive the taste, fr. MF *ragouster,* fr. *re-* + *a-* to (fr. L *ad-*) + *goust* taste, fr. L *gustus*] : a highly seasoned meat stew with vegetables

rag·pick·er \'rag-ˌpi-kər\ *n* : one who collects rags and refuse for a living

rag·time \-ˌtīm\ *n* : music in which there is more or less continuous syncopation in the melody

rag·top \'rag-ˌtäp\ *n* : CONVERTIBLE

rag·weed \-ˌwēd\ *n* : any of several chiefly No. American weedy composite herbs with allergenic pollen

[1]**raid** \'rād\ *n* : a sudden usu. surprise attack or invasion : FORAY

[2]**raid** *vb* : to make a raid on — **raid·er** *n*

[1]**rail** \'rāl\ *n* [ME *raile,* fr. AF *raille, reille* bar, rule, fr. L *regula* straightedge, rule, fr. *regere* to keep straight, direct] **1** : a bar extending from one support to another as a guard or barrier **2** : a bar of steel forming a track for wheeled vehicles **3** : RAILROAD

[2]**rail** *vb* : to provide with a railing

[3]**rail** *n, pl* **rail** *or* **rails** : any of numerous small wading birds often hunted as game

[4]**rail** *vb* [ME, fr. MF *railler* to mock, prob. fr. OF *reillier* to growl, mutter, fr. VL **ragulare* to bray, fr. LL *ragere* to neigh] : to criticize angrily : SCOLD, REVILE — **rail·er** *n*

rail·ing \'rā-liŋ\ *n* : a barrier of rails

rail·lery \'rā-lə-rē\ *n, pl* **-ler·ies** : good-natured ridicule : BANTER

[1]**rail·road** \'rāl-ˌrōd\ *n* : a permanent road with rails fixed to ties providing a track for cars; *also* : such a road and its assets constituting a property

[2]**railroad** *vb* **1** : to put through (as a law) too hastily **2** : to convict hastily or with insufficient or improper evidence **3** : to send by rail **4** : to work on a railroad — **rail·road·er** *n* — **rail·road·ing** *n*

rail·way \-ˌwā\ *n* : RAILROAD

rai·ment \'rā-mənt\ *n* : CLOTHING

[1]**rain** \'rān\ *n* **1** : water falling in drops from the clouds **2** : a shower of objects ⟨a ~ of bullets⟩ — **rainy** *adj*

[2]**rain** *vb* **1** : to send down rain **2** : to fall as or like rain **3** : to pour down

[1]**rain·bow** \-ˌbō\ *n* : an arc or circle of colors formed by the refraction and reflection of the sun's rays in rain, spray, or mist

[2]**rainbow** *adj* **1** : having many colors **2** : of, relating to, or made up of people of different races or cultural backgrounds

rainbow trout *n* : a large stout-bodied fish of western No. America closely related to the salmons of the Pacific and usu. having red or pink stripes with black dots along its sides

rain check *n* **1** : a ticket stub good for a later performance when the scheduled one is rained out **2** : an assurance of a deferred extension of an offer

rain·coat \'rān-ˌkōt\ *n* : a waterproof or water-repellent coat

rain date *n* : an alternative date for an event postponed due to rain

rain·drop \-ˌdräp\ *n* : a drop of rain

rain·fall \-ˌfȯl\ *n* **1** : amount of precipitation measured by depth **2** : a fall of rain

rain forest *n* : a tropical woodland having an annual rainfall of at least 100 inches (254 centimeters) and marked by lofty broad-leaved evergreen trees forming a continuous canopy

rain·mak·ing \'rān-ˌmā-kiŋ\ *n* : the action or process of producing or attempting to produce rain by artificial means — **rain·mak·er** *n*

rain out *vb* : to interrupt or prevent by rain

rain·storm \'rān-ˌstȯrm\ *n* : a storm of or with rain

rain·wa·ter \-ˌwȯ-tər, -ˌwä-\ *n* : water fallen as rain

[1]**raise** \'rāz\ *vb* **raised; rais·ing** **1** : to cause or help to rise : LIFT ⟨~ a window⟩ **2** : AWAKEN, AROUSE ⟨enough to ~ the dead⟩ **3** : BUILD, ERECT ⟨~ a monument⟩ **4** : PROMOTE ⟨was *raised* to captain⟩ **5** : END ⟨~ a siege⟩ **6** : COLLECT ⟨~ money⟩ **7** : BREED, GROW ⟨~ cattle⟩ ⟨~ corn⟩; *also* : BRING UP ⟨~ a family⟩ **8** : PROVOKE ⟨~ a laugh⟩ **9** : to bring to notice ⟨~ an objection⟩ **10** : INCREASE ⟨~ prices⟩; *also* : to bet more than **11** : to make light and spongy ⟨~ dough⟩ **12** : to multiply a quantity by itself a specified number of times ⟨~ 2 to the third power⟩ **13** : to cause to form ⟨~ a blister⟩ ♦ ***Synonyms*** LIFT, HOIST, BOOST, ELEVATE — **rais·er** *n* — **raise the bar** : to set a higher standard

[2]**raise** *n* : an increase in amount (as of a bid or bet); *also* : an increase in pay

rai·sin \'rā-zᵊn\ *n* [ME, fr. AF, grape, raisin, fr. L *racemus* cluster of grapes or berries] : a grape dried for food

rai·son d'être \ˌrā-ˌzōⁿ-ˈdetrᵊ\ *n, pl* **raisons d'être** \-ˌzōⁿz-\ : reason or justification for existence

ra·ja *or* **ra·jah** \ˈrä-jə\ *n* [Hindi *rājā,* fr. Skt *rājan* king] : an Indian or Malay prince or chief

¹**rake** \ˈrāk\ *n* : a long-handled garden tool having a crossbar with prongs

²**rake** *vb* **raked; rak·ing** **1** : to gather, loosen, or smooth with or as if with a rake **2** : to sweep the length of (as a trench or ship) with gunfire

³**rake** *n* : inclination from either perpendicular or horizontal : SLANT

⁴**rake** *n* : a dissolute person : LIBERTINE

rake–off \ˈrāk-ˌȯf\ *n* : a percentage or cut taken

¹**rak·ish** \ˈrā-kish\ *adj* : DISSOLUTE — **rak·ish·ly** *adv* — **rak·ish·ness** *n*

²**rakish** *adj* **1** : having a trim appearance indicative of speed ⟨a ~ sloop⟩ **2** : JAUNTY, SPORTY ⟨~ clothes⟩ — **rak·ish·ly** *adv* — **rak·ish·ness** *n*

¹**ral·ly** \ˈra-lē\ *vb* **ral·lied; ral·ly·ing** **1** : to bring together for a common purpose; *also* : to bring back to order ⟨a leader ~*ing* his forces⟩ **2** : to arouse to activity or from depression or weakness **3** : to make a comeback ♦ ***Synonyms*** STIR, ROUSE, AWAKEN, WAKEN, KINDLE

²**rally** *n, pl* **rallies** **1** : an act of rallying **2** : a mass meeting to arouse enthusiasm **3** : a competitive automobile event run over public roads

³**rally** *vb* **ral·lied; ral·ly·ing** : BANTER

rallying cry *n* : WAR CRY 2

¹**ram** \ˈram\ *n* **1** : a male sheep **2** : BATTERING RAM

²**ram** *vb* **rammed; ram·ming** **1** : to force or drive in or through **2** : CRAM, CROWD **3** : to strike against violently

RAM \ˈram\ *n* : a computer memory that provides the main internal storage for programs and data

Ram·a·dan \ˈrä-mə-ˌdän, ˌrä-mə-ˈdän\ *n* : the ninth month of the Islamic year observed as sacred with daily fasting from dawn to sunset

¹**ram·ble** \ˈram-bəl\ *vb* **ram·bled; ram·bling** : to go about aimlessly : ROAM, WANDER

²**ramble** *n* : a leisurely excursion; *esp* : an aimless walk

ram·bler \ˈram-blər\ *n* **1** : a person who rambles **2** : any of various climbing roses with large clusters of small often double flowers

ram·bunc·tious \ram-ˈbəŋk-shəs\ *adj* : UNRULY

ra·mie \ˈrā-mē, ˈra-\ *n* : a strong lustrous bast fiber from an Asian nettle

ram·i·fi·ca·tion \ˌra-mə-fə-ˈkā-shən\ *n* **1** : the act or process of branching **2** : CONSEQUENCE, OUTGROWTH

ram·i·fy \ˈra-mə-ˌfī\ *vb* **-fied; -fy·ing** : to branch out

¹**ramp** \ˈramp\ *n* : a sloping passage or roadway connecting different levels

²**ramp** *vb* : to speed up, expand, or increase esp. quickly or at a constant rate — used with *up* ⟨~ up production⟩

¹**ram·page** \ˈram-ˌpāj, (ˌ)ram-ˈpāj\ *vb* **ram·paged; ram·pag·ing** : to rush about wildly ⟨*rampaging* soccer fans⟩

²**ram·page** \ˈram-ˌpāj\ *n* : a course of violent or riotous action or behavior — **ram·pa·geous** \ram-ˈpā-jəs\ *adj*

ram·pant \ˈram-pənt\ *adj* : unchecked in growth or spread : RIFE ⟨fear was ~ in the town⟩ — **ram·pan·cy** \-pən-sē\ *n* — **ram·pant·ly** *adv*

ram·part \ˈram-ˌpärt\ *n* **1** : a protective barrier **2** : a broad embankment raised as a fortification

¹**ram·rod** \ˈram-ˌräd\ *n* **1** : a rod used to ram a charge into a muzzle-loading gun **2** : a cleaning rod for small arms **3** : BOSS, OVERSEER

²**ramrod** *adj* : marked by rigidity or severity ⟨his ~ posture⟩

³**ramrod** *vb* : to direct, supervise, and control ⟨*ramrodded* the project forward⟩

ram·shack·le \ˈram-ˌsha-kəl\ *adj* : RICKETY, TUMBLEDOWN

ran *past of* RUN

¹**ranch** \ˈranch\ *n* [MexSp *rancho* small ranch, fr. Sp, camp, hut & Sp dial., small farm, fr. Old Spanish *ranchear* (*se*) to take up quarters, fr. MF (*se*) *ranger* to take up a position, fr. *ranger* to set in a row] **1** : an establishment for the raising and grazing of livestock (as cattle, sheep, or horses) **2** : a large farm devoted to a specialty **3** : RANCH HOUSE 2

²**ranch** *vb* : to live or work on a ranch — **ranch·er** *n*

ranch house *n* **1** : the main house on a ranch **2** : a one-story house typically with a low-pitched roof

ran·cho \ˈran-chō, ˈrän-\ *n, pl* **ranchos** : RANCH 1

ran·cid \ˈran-səd\ *adj* **1** : having a rank smell or taste **2** : OFFENSIVE 3 — **ran·cid·i·ty** \ran-ˈsi-də-tē\ *n*

ran·cor \ˈraŋ-kər\ *n* : bitter deep-seated ill will ♦ ***Synonyms*** ANTAGONISM, ANIMOSITY, ANTIPATHY, ENMITY, HOSTILITY — **ran·cor·ous** *adj*

ran·cour *Brit var of* RANCOR

rand \ˈrand, ˈränd, ˈränt\ *n, pl* **rand** — see MONEY table

R & B *abbr* rhythm and blues

R & D *abbr* research and development

ran·dom \ˈran-dəm\ *adj* : CHANCE, HAPHAZARD — **ran·dom·ly** *adv* — **ran·dom·ness** *n*

random–access *adj* : allowing access to stored data in any order the user desires

random–access memory *n* : RAM

ran·dom·ize \ˈran-də-ˌmīz\ *vb* **-ized; -iz·ing** : to select, assign, or arrange in a random way — **ran·dom·i·za·tion** \ˌran-də-mə-ˈzā-shən\ *n*

R & R *abbr* rest and recreation; rest and recuperation

rang *past of* RING

¹**range** \ˈrānj\ *n* **1** : a series of things in a row **2** : a cooking stove having an oven and a flat top with burners **3** : open land where animals (as livestock) may roam

and graze **4** : the region throughout which an organism occurs **5** : the act of ranging about **6** : the distance a weapon will shoot or is to be shot **7** : a place where shooting is practiced **8** : the space or extent included, covered, or used : SCOPE **9** : a variation within limits ♦ ***Synonyms*** REACH, COMPASS, RADIUS, CIRCLE

[2]**range** *vb* **ranged; rang·ing** [ME, fr. AF *renger,* fr. *renc, reng* line, place, row, of Gmc origin] **1** : to set in a row or in proper order **2** : to set in place among others of the same kind **3** : to roam over or through : EXPLORE **4** : to roam at large or freely **5** : to correspond in direction or line **6** : to vary within limits **7** : to find the range of an object by instrument (as radar)

rang·er \ˈrān-jər\ *n* **1** : FOREST RANGER **2** : a member of a body of troops who range over a region **3** : an expert in close-range fighting and raiding tactics

rangy \ˈrān-jē\ *adj* **rang·i·er; -est** : being long-limbed and slender ⟨a ~ teenager⟩ — **rang·i·ness** \ˈrān-jē-nəs\ *n*

ra·ni *or* **ra·nee** \rä-ˈnē, ˈrä-ˌnē\ *n* : a Hindu queen : a raja's wife

[1]**rank** \ˈraŋk\ *adj* **1** : strong and vigorous and usu. coarse in growth **2** : unpleasantly strong-smelling — **rank·ly** *adv* — **rank·ness** *n*

[2]**rank** *n* **1** : ROW **2** : a line of soldiers ranged side by side **3** *pl* : the body of enlisted personnel ⟨rose from the ~*s*⟩ **4** : position in a group **5** : superior position **6** : a grade of official standing (as in an army) **7** : an orderly arrangement **8** : CLASS, DIVISION — usu. used in pl.

[3]**rank** *vb* **1** : to arrange in lines or in regular formation **2** : RATE **3** : to rate above (as in official standing) **4** : to take or have a relative position

rank and file *n* : the general membership of a body as contrasted with its leaders

rank·ing \ˈraŋ-kiŋ\ *adj* **1** : having a high position : of the highest rank **2** : being next to the chairman in seniority

ran·kle \ˈraŋ-kəl\ *vb* **ran·kled; ran·kling** [ME *ranclen* to fester, fr. AF *rancler,* fr. OF *draoncler, raoncler,* fr. *draoncle, raoncle* festering sore, fr. ML *dracunculus,* fr. L, dim. of *draco* serpent] : to cause anger, irritation, or bitterness

ran·sack \ˈran-ˌsak\ *vb* : to search thoroughly; *esp* : to search through and rob

[1]**ran·som** \ˈran-səm\ *n* [ME *ransoun,* fr. OF *rançun,* fr. L *redemption-, redemptio* act of buying back, fr. *redimere* to buy back, redeem] **1** : something paid or demanded for the freedom of a captive **2** : the act of ransoming

[2]**ransom** *vb* : to free from captivity or punishment by paying a price — **ran·som·er** *n*

ran·som·ware \ˈran(t)-səm-ˌwer\ *n* : malware that requires the victim to pay a ransom to access encrypted files

rant \ˈrant\ *vb* **1** : to talk loudly and wildly **2** : to scold violently — **rant·er** *n* — **rant·ing·ly** *adv*

[1]**rap** \ˈrap\ *n* **1** : a sharp blow **2** : a sharp rebuke **3** : a negative often undeserved reputation ⟨a bum ~⟩ **4** : responsibility for or consequences of an action ⟨take the ~⟩

[2]**rap** *vb* **rapped; rap·ping** **1** : to strike sharply : KNOCK **2** : to utter sharply **3** : to criticize sharply

[3]**rap** *vb* **rapped; rap·ping** **1** : to talk freely and frankly **2** : to perform rap music — **rap·per** *n*

[4]**rap** *n* **1** : TALK, CONVERSATION **2** : a rhythmic chanting of usu. rhymed couplets to a musical accompaniment; *also* : a piece so performed

ra·pa·cious \rə-ˈpā-shəs\ *adj* **1** : excessively greedy or covetous **2** : living on prey **3** : RAVENOUS 2 ⟨a ~ appetite⟩ — **ra·pa·cious·ly** *adv* — **ra·pa·cious·ness** *n* — **ra·pac·i·ty** \-ˈpa-sə-tē\ *n*

[1]**rape** \ˈrāp\ *n* : an Old World herb related to the mustards that is grown as a forage crop and for its seeds (**rapeseed** \-ˌsēd\)

[2]**rape** *vb* **raped; rap·ing** : to commit rape on — **rap·er** *n* — **rap·ist** \ˈrā-pist\ *n*

[3]**rape** *n* **1** : a carrying away by force **2** : unlawful sexual activity and usu. sexual intercourse carried out forcibly or under threat of injury

[1]**rap·id** \ˈra-pəd\ *adj* [L *rapidus* strong-flowing, rapid, fr. *rapere* to seize, carry away] : very fast : SWIFT ♦ ***Synonyms*** FLEET, QUICK, SPEEDY — **ra·pid·i·ty** \rə-ˈpi-də-tē\ *n* — **rap·id·ly** *adv*

[2]**rapid** *n* : a place in a stream where the current flows very fast usu. over obstructions — usu. used in pl.

rapid eye movement *n* : rapid conjugate movement of the eyes associated with REM sleep

rapid transit *n* : fast passenger transportation (as by subway) in cities

[1]**ra·pi·er** \ˈrā-pē-ər\ *n* : a straight 2-edged sword with a narrow pointed blade

[2]**rapier** *adj* : extremely sharp or keen ⟨~ wit⟩

rap·ine \ˈra-pən, -pīn\ *n* : PILLAGE, PLUNDER

rap·pel \rə-ˈpel, ra-\ *vb* **-pelled; -pel·ling** : to descend by sliding down a rope

rap·pen \ˈrä-pən\ *n, pl* **rappen** : the centime of Switzerland

rap·port \ra-ˈpȯr\ *n* : RELATION; *esp* : relation characterized by harmony

rap·proche·ment \ˌra-ˌprōsh-ˈmäⁿ, ra-ˈprōsh-ˌmäⁿ\ *n* : the establishment of or a state of having cordial relations

rap·scal·lion \rap-ˈskal-yən\ *n* : RASCAL, SCAMP

rapt \ˈrapt\ *adj* **1** : carried away with emotion **2** : ABSORBED, ENGROSSED — **rapt·ly** \ˈrapt-lē\ *adv* — **rapt·ness** *n*

rap·tor \ˈrap-tər, -ˌtȯr\ *n* **1** : BIRD OF PREY **2** : a usu. small-to-medium-sized predatory dinosaur

rap·ture \ˈrap-chər\ *n* : spiritual or emotional ecstasy — **rap·tur·ous** \-chə-rəs\ *adj* — **rap·tur·ous·ly** *adv*

rapture of the deep : NITROGEN NARCOSIS

ra·ra avis \ˌrer-ə-ˈā-vəs, ˌrär-ə-ˈä-wəs\ *n, pl* **ra·ra avis·es** \-ˈā-və-səz\ *or* **ra·rae**

aves \ˌrär-ˌī-ˈä-ˌwās\ [L, rare bird] : a rare person or thing : RARITY

¹**rare** \ˈrer\ *adj* **rar·er; rar·est** 1 : not thick or dense : THIN ⟨~ air⟩ 2 : unusually fine : EXCELLENT, SPLENDID 3 : seldom met with — **rare·ly** *adv* — **rare·ness** *n* — **rar·i·ty** \ˈrar-ə-tē\ *n*

²**rare** *adj* **rar·er; rar·est** : cooked so that the inside is still red ⟨~ beef⟩

rare·bit \ˈrer-bət\ *n* : WELSH RABBIT

rar·efac·tion \ˌrer-ə-ˈfak-shən\ *n* 1 : the action or process of rarefying 2 : the state of being rarefied

rar·e·fy *also* **rar·i·fy** \ˈrer-ə-ˌfī\ *vb* **-fied; -fy·ing** : to make or become rare, thin, or less dense

rar·ing \ˈrer-ən, -iŋ\ *adj* : full of enthusiasm or eagerness ⟨~ to go⟩

ras·cal \ˈras-kəl\ *n* 1 : a mean or dishonest person 2 : a mischievous person — **ras·cal·i·ty** \ra-ˈska-lə-tē\ *n* — **ras·cal·ly** \ˈras-kə-lē\ *adj*

¹**rash** \ˈrash\ *adj* : having or showing little regard for consequences : too hasty in decision, action, or speech : RECKLESS ♦ ***Synonyms*** DARING, FOOLHARDY, ADVENTUROUS, VENTURESOME — **rash·ly** *adv* — **rash·ness** *n*

²**rash** *n* : an eruption on the body

rash·er \ˈra-shər\ *n* : a thin slice of bacon or ham broiled or fried; *also* : a portion consisting of several such slices

¹**rasp** \ˈrasp\ *vb* 1 : to rub with or as if with a rough file 2 : to grate harshly on (as one's nerves) 3 : to speak in a grating tone ⟨"Don't touch me," she ~*ed*⟩

²**rasp** *n* : a coarse file with cutting points instead of ridges

rasp·ber·ry \ˈraz-ˌber-ē, -bə-rē\ *n* 1 : any of various edible usu. black or red berries produced by some brambles; *also* : such a bramble 2 : a sound of contempt made by protruding the tongue through the lips and expelling air forcibly

¹**rat** \ˈrat\ *n* 1 : any of numerous rodents larger than the related mice 2 : a contemptible person; *esp* : one that betrays friends or associates

²**rat** *vb* **rat·ted; rat·ting** 1 : to betray or inform on one's associates 2 : to hunt or catch rats

rat cheese *n* : CHEDDAR

ratch·et \ˈra-chət\ *n* : a device that consists of a bar or wheel having slanted teeth into which a pawl drops so as to allow motion in only one direction

¹**rate** \ˈrāt\ *vb* **rat·ed; rat·ing** : to scold violently

²**rate** *n* 1 : quantity, amount, or degree measured by some standard 2 : an amount (as of payment) measured by its relation to some other amount (as of time) 3 : a charge, payment, or price fixed according to a ratio, scale, or standard ⟨tax ~⟩ 4 : RANK, CLASS

³**rate** *vb* **rat·ed; rat·ing** 1 : ESTIMATE 2 : CONSIDER, REGARD ⟨*rated* as a good pianist⟩ 3 : to settle the relative rank or class of 4 : to be classed : RANK 5 : to have a right to : DESERVE 6 : to be of consequence — **rat·er** *n*

rath·er \ˈra-t͟hər, ˈrä-, ˈrə-\ *adv* [ME, fr. OE *hrathor,* compar. of *hrathe* quickly] 1 : more properly 2 : PREFERABLY ⟨I'd ~ not go⟩ 3 : more correctly speaking 4 : to the contrary : INSTEAD 5 : SOMEWHAT ⟨~ warm⟩

rather than *prep* : INSTEAD OF

rat·i·fy \ˈra-tə-ˌfī\ *vb* **-fied; -fy·ing** : to approve and accept formally — **rat·i·fi·ca·tion** \ˌra-tə-fə-ˈkā-shən\ *n*

rat·ing \ˈrā-tiŋ\ *n* 1 : a classification according to grade : RANK 2 *chiefly Brit* : an enlisted person in the navy 3 : an estimate of the credit standing and business responsibility of a person or firm

ra·tio \ˈrā-shō, -shē-ō\ *n, pl* **ra·tios** 1 : the indicated quotient of two numbers or mathematical expressions 2 : the relationship in number, quantity, or degree between two or more things

ra·ti·o·ci·na·tion \ˌra-tē-ˌō-sə-ˈnā-shən, -ˌä-\ *n* : exact thinking : REASONING — **ra·ti·o·ci·nate** \-ˈō-sə-ˌnāt, -ˈä-\ *vb* — **ra·ti·o·ci·na·tive** \-ˈō-sə-ˌnā-tiv, -ˈä-\ *adj* — **ra·ti·o·ci·na·tor** \-ˈō-sə-ˌnā-tər, -ˈä-sə-\ *n*

¹**ra·tion** \ˈra-shən, ˈrā-\ *n* 1 : a food allowance for one day 2 : FOOD, PROVISIONS, DIET — usu. used in pl. 3 : SHARE, ALLOTMENT

²**ration** *vb* 1 : to supply with or allot as rations 2 : to use or allot sparingly ♦ ***Synonyms*** APPORTION, PORTION, PRORATE, PARCEL

¹**ra·tio·nal** \ˈra-shə-nəl\ *adj* 1 : having reason or understanding 2 : of or relating to reason 3 : relating to, consisting of, or being one or more rational numbers — **ra·tio·nal·ly** *adv*

²**rational** *n* : RATIONAL NUMBER

ra·tio·nale \ˌra-shə-ˈnal\ *n* 1 : an explanation of principles controlling belief or practice 2 : an underlying reason

ra·tio·nal·ise *Brit var of* RATIONALIZE

ra·tio·nal·ism \ˈra-shə-nə-ˌli-zəm\ *n* : the practice of guiding one's actions and opinions solely by what seems reasonable — **ra·tio·nal·ist** \-list\ *n* — **rationalist** *or* **ra·tio·nal·is·tic** \ˌra-shə-nə-ˈlis-tik\ *adj* — **ra·tio·nal·is·ti·cal·ly** \-ti-k(ə-)lē\ *adv*

ra·tio·nal·i·ty \ˌra-shə-ˈna-lə-tē\ *n, pl* **-ties** : the quality or state of being rational

ra·tio·nal·ize \ˈra-shə-nə-ˌlīz\ *vb* **-ized; -iz·ing** 1 : to make (something irrational) appear rational or reasonable 2 : to provide a natural explanation of (as a myth) 3 : to justify (as one's behavior or weaknesses) esp. to oneself 4 : to find plausible but untrue reasons for conduct — **ra·tio·nal·i·za·tion** \ˌra-shə-nə-lə-ˈzā-shən\ *n*

rational number *n* : a number that can be expressed as an integer or the quotient of an integer divided by a nonzero integer

rat race *n* : strenuous, tiresome, and usu. competitive activity or rush

rat·tan \ra-ˈtan, rə-\ *n* : a cane or switch made from one of the long stems of an Asian climbing palm; *also* : this palm

rat·ter \ˈra-tər\ *n* : a rat-catching dog or cat

[1]**rat·tle** \ˈra-tᵊl\ *vb* **rat·tled; rat·tling 1 :** to make or cause to make a series of clattering sounds **2 :** to move with a clattering sound **3 :** to say or do in a brisk lively fashion ⟨~ off the answers⟩ **4 :** CONFUSE, UPSET ⟨~ a witness⟩

[2]**rattle** *n* **1 :** a toy that produces a rattle when shaken **2 :** a series of clattering and knocking sounds **3 :** a rattling organ at the end of a rattlesnake's tail

rat·tler \ˈrat-lər\ *n* **:** RATTLESNAKE

rat·tle·snake \ˈra-tᵊl-ˌsnāk\ *n* **:** any of various American pit vipers with a rattle at the end of the tail

rat·tle·trap \ˈra-tᵊl-ˌtrap\ *n* **:** something (as an old car) rickety and full of rattles

rat·tling \ˈrat-liŋ\ *adj* **1 :** LIVELY, BRISK ⟨a ~ pace⟩ **2 :** FIRST-RATE, SPLENDID

rat·trap \ˈrat-ˌtrap\ *n* **1 :** a trap for rats **2 :** a dilapidated building

rat·ty \ˈra-tē\ *adj* **rat·ti·er; -est 1 :** infested with rats **2 :** of, relating to, or suggestive of rats **3 :** SHABBY ⟨a ~ old coat⟩

rau·cous \ˈrò-kəs\ *adj* **1 :** HARSH, HOARSE, STRIDENT ⟨~ voices⟩ **2 :** boisterously disorderly — **rau·cous·ly** *adv* — **rau·cous·ness** *n*

raun·chy \ˈròn-chē, ˈrän-\ *adj* **raun·chi·er; -est 1 :** SLOVENLY, DIRTY **2 :** OBSCENE, SMUTTY ⟨~ jokes⟩ — **raun·chi·ness** \-chē-nəs\ *n*

[1]**rav·age** \ˈra-vij\ *n* [F] **:** an act or result of ravaging **:** DEVASTATION

[2]**ravage** *vb* **rav·aged; rav·ag·ing :** to lay waste **:** DEVASTATE — **rav·ag·er** *n*

[1]**rave** \ˈrāv\ *vb* **raved; rav·ing 1 :** to talk wildly in or as if in delirium **:** STORM, RAGE **2 :** to talk with extreme enthusiasm ⟨*raved* about the show⟩ — **rav·er** *n*

[2]**rave** *n* **1 :** an act or instance of raving **2 :** an extravagantly favorable criticism

[1]**rav·el** \ˈra-vəl\ *vb* **-eled** *or* **-elled; -el·ing** *or* **-el·ling 1 :** UNRAVEL, UNTWIST **2 :** TANGLE, CONFUSE

[2]**ravel** *n* **1 :** something tangled **2 :** something raveled out; *esp* **:** a loose thread

[1]**ra·ven** \ˈrā-vən\ *n* **:** a large black bird related to the crow

[2]**raven** *adj* **:** black and glossy like a raven's feathers

[3]**rav·en** \ˈra-vən\ *vb* **1 :** to devour greedily **2 :** DESPOIL, PLUNDER **3 :** PREY

rav·en·ous \ˈra-və-nəs\ *adj* **1 :** RAPACIOUS, VORACIOUS ⟨~ wolves⟩ **2 :** eager for food **:** very hungry — **rav·en·ous·ly** *adv* — **rav·en·ous·ness** *n*

ra·vine \rə-ˈvēn\ *n* **:** a small narrow steep-sided valley larger than a gully

rav·i·o·li \ˌra-vē-ˈō-lē\ *n, pl* **ravioli** *also* **raviolis** [It, fr. It dial., pl. of *raviolo,* lit., little turnip, dim. of *rava* turnip, fr. L *rapa*] **:** small cases of dough with a savory filling (as of meat or cheese)

rav·ish \ˈra-vish\ *vb* **1 :** to seize and take away by violence **2 :** to overcome with emotion and esp. with joy or delight ⟨~*ed* by her beauty⟩ **3 :** RAPE — **rav·ish·er** *n* — **rav·ish·ment** *n*

[1]**raw** \ˈrò\ *adj* **raw·er** \ˈrò-ər\; **raw·est** \ˈrò-əst\ **1 :** not cooked **2 :** changed little from the original form **:** not processed ⟨~ materials⟩ **3 :** having the surface abraded or irritated ⟨a ~ sore⟩ **4 :** not trained or experienced ⟨~ recruits⟩ **5 :** VULGAR, COARSE ⟨~ language⟩ **6 :** disagreeably cold and damp ⟨a ~ day⟩ **7 :** UNFAIR ⟨~ deal⟩ — **raw·ness** *n*

[2]**raw** *n* **:** a raw place or state — **in the raw :** NAKED

raw·boned \ˈrò-ˌbōnd\ *adj* **:** LEAN, GAUNT; *also* **:** having a heavy frame that seems to have little flesh

raw·hide \ˈrò-ˌhīd\ *n* **:** the untanned skin of cattle; *also* **:** a whip made of this

[1]**ray** \ˈrā\ *n* **:** any of an order of large flat cartilaginous fishes that have the eyes on the upper surface and the hind end of the body slender and taillike

[2]**ray** *n* [ME, fr. AF *rai,* fr. L *radius* rod, ray] **1 :** any of the lines of light that appear to radiate from a bright object **2 :** a thin beam of radiant energy (as light) **3 :** light from a beam **4 :** a thin line like a beam of light **5 :** an animal or plant structure resembling a ray **6 :** a tiny bit ⟨a ~ of hope⟩

ray·on \ˈrā-ˌän\ *n* **:** a fiber made from cellulose; *also* **:** a yarn, thread, or fabric made from such fibers

raze \ˈrāz\ *vb* **razed; raz·ing 1 :** to scrape, cut, or shave off **2 :** to destroy to the ground **:** DEMOLISH

ra·zor \ˈrā-zər\ *n* **:** a sharp cutting instrument used to shave off hair

ra·zor–backed \ˈrā-zər-ˌbakt\ *or* **ra·zor·back** \-ˌbak\ *adj* **:** having a sharp narrow back ⟨a ~ horse⟩

razor clam *n* **:** any of a family of marine bivalve mollusks having a long narrow curved thin shell

razor wire *n* **:** coiled wire fitted with sharp edges and used as an obstacle or barrier

[1]**razz** \ˈraz\ *n* **:** RASPBERRY 2

[2]**razz** *vb* **:** RIDICULE, TEASE

Rb *symbol* rubidium

RBC *abbr* red blood cells

RBI \ˌär-(ˌ)bē-ˈī, ˈri-bē\ *n, pl* **RBIs** *or* **RBI** [*r*un *b*atted *i*n] **:** a run in baseball that is driven in by a batter

RC *abbr* **1** Red Cross **2** Roman Catholic

RCAF *abbr* Royal Canadian Air Force

RCMP *abbr* Royal Canadian Mounted Police

RCN *abbr* Royal Canadian Navy

rct *abbr* recruit

rd *abbr* **1** road **2** rod **3** round

RD *abbr* rural delivery

RDA *abbr* recommended daily allowance; recommended dietary allowance

re \ˈrā, ˈrē\ *prep* **:** with regard to

Re *symbol* rhenium

re- \rē, ˌrē, ˈrē\ *prefix* **1 :** again **:** for a second time **2 :** anew **:** in a new or different form **3 :** back **:** backward

[1]**reach** \ˈrēch\ *vb* **1 :** to stretch out **2 :** to touch or attempt to touch or seize **3 :** to extend to **4 :** to communicate with **5 :** to

arrive at ♦ ***Synonyms*** GAIN, REALIZE, ACHIEVE, ATTAIN — **reach·able** *adj* — **reach·er** *n*

²reach *n* **1** : an unbroken stretch of a river **2** : the act of reaching **3** : a reachable distance; *also* : ability to reach **4** : a range of knowledge or comprehension

re·act \rē-ˈakt\ *vb* **1** : to exert a return or counteracting influence **2** : to have or show a reaction **3** : to act in opposition to a force or influence **4** : to move or tend in a reverse direction **5** : to undergo chemical reaction

re·ac·tant \rē-ˈak-tənt\ *n* : a chemically reacting substance

re·ac·tion \rē-ˈak-shən\ *n* **1** : the act or process of reacting **2** : a counter tendency; *esp* : a tendency toward a former esp. outmoded political or social order or policy **3** : bodily, mental, or emotional response to a stimulus **4** : chemical change **5** : a process involving change in atomic nuclei

re·ac·tion·ary \rē-ˈak-shə-ˌner-ē\ *adj* : relating to, marked by, or favoring esp. political reaction — **reactionary** *n*

re·ac·tive \rē-ˈak-tiv\ *adj* : reacting or tending to react ⟨a ∼ chemical⟩

re·ac·tor \rē-ˈak-tər\ *n* **1** : one that reacts **2** : a device for the controlled release of nuclear energy

¹read \ˈrēd\ *vb* **read** \ˈred\; **read·ing** [ME *reden* to advise, interpret, read, fr. OE *rǣdan*] **1** : to understand language by interpreting written symbols for speech sounds **2** : to utter aloud written or printed words **3** : to learn by observing ⟨∼ nature's signs⟩ **4** : to study by a course of reading ⟨∼*s* law⟩ **5** : to discover the meaning of ⟨∼ the clues⟩ **6** : to recognize or interpret as if by reading **7** : to attribute (a meaning) to something ⟨∼ guilt in his manner⟩ **8** : INDICATE ⟨thermometer ∼*s* 10°⟩ **9** : to consist in phrasing or meaning ⟨the two versions ∼ differently⟩ — **read·abil·i·ty** \ˌrē-də-ˈbi-lə-tē\ *n* — **read·able** \ˈrē-də-bəl\ *adj* — **read·ably** \-blē\ *adv* — **read·er** *n*

²read \ˈred\ *adj* : informed by reading ⟨widely ∼⟩

read·er·ship \ˈrē-dər-ˌship\ *n* : the mass or a particular group of readers

read·ing *n* **1** : something read or for reading **2** : a particular version **3** : data indicated by an instrument ⟨thermometer ∼⟩ **4** : a particular interpretation (as of a law) **5** : a particular performance (as of a musical work) **6** : an indication of a certain state of affairs

read–only memory *n* : ROM

read·out \ˈrēd-ˌau̇t\ *n* **1** : the process of removing information from an automatic device (as a computer) and displaying it in an understandable form; *also* : the information removed from such a device **2** : an electronic device that presents information in visual form

read out *vb* **1** : to read aloud **2** : to expel from an organization

¹ready \ˈre-dē\ *adj* **read·i·er; -est** **1** : prepared for use or action **2** : likely to do something indicated; *also* : willingly disposed : INCLINED **3** : spontaneously prompt ⟨her ∼ wit⟩ **4** : immediately available ⟨∼ cash⟩ — **read·i·ly** \ˈre-də-lē\ *adv* — **read·i·ness** \-dē-nəs\ *n* — **at the ready** : ready for immediate use

²ready *vb* **read·ied; ready·ing** : to make ready : PREPARE

ready–made \ˌre-dē-ˈmād\ *adj* : already made up for general sale : not specially made — **ready–made** *n*

ready room *n* : a room in which pilots are briefed and await orders

re·agent \rē-ˈā-jənt\ *n* : a substance that takes part in or brings about a particular chemical reaction

¹re·al \ˈrēl\ *adj* [ME, real, relating to things (in law), fr. AF, fr. ML & LL; ML *realis* relating to things (in law), fr. LL, real, fr. L *res* thing, fact] **1** : of or relating to fixed or immovable things (as land) ⟨∼ property⟩ **2** : not artificial : GENUINE; *also* : not imaginary — **re·al·ness** *n* — **for real** **1** : in earnest **2** : GENUINE ⟨the threat was *for real*⟩

²real *adv* : VERY ⟨had a ∼ good time⟩

³re·al \rā-ˈäl\ *n* — see MONEY table

real estate *n* : property in buildings and land

re·al·ism \ˈrē-ə-ˌli-zəm\ *n* **1** : the disposition to face facts and to deal with them practically **2** : true and faithful portrayal of nature and of people in art or literature — **re·al·ist** \-list\ *adj or n* — **re·al·is·tic** \ˌrē-ə-ˈlis-tik\ *adj* — **re·al·is·ti·cal·ly** \-ti-k(ə-)lē\ *adv*

re·al·i·ty \rē-ˈa-lə-tē\ *n, pl* **-ties** **1** : the quality or state of being real **2** : something real **3** : the totality of real things and events

re·al·ize \ˈrē-ə-ˌlīz\ *vb* **-ized; -iz·ing** **1** : to make actual : ACCOMPLISH **2** : to convert into money ⟨∼ assets⟩ **3** : OBTAIN, GAIN ⟨∼ a profit⟩ **4** : to be aware of : UNDERSTAND — **re·al·iz·able** *adj* — **re·al·i·za·tion** \ˌrē-ə-lə-ˈzā-shən\ *n*

re·al·ly \ˈrē-lē, ˈri-\ *adv* : in truth : in fact : ACTUALLY

realm \ˈrelm\ *n* **1** : KINGDOM **2** : SPHERE, DOMAIN ⟨within the ∼ of possibility⟩

real number *n* : a number that has no imaginary part ⟨the set of all *real*

readdress	**reallocate**	**reappearance**	**rearm**
readjust	**reallocation**	**reapplication**	**rearmament**
readjustment	**reanalysis**	**reapply**	**rearouse**
readmission	**reanalyze**	**reappoint**	**rearrange**
readmit	**reanimate**	**reappointment**	**rearrangement**
reaffirm	**reanimation**	**reapportion**	**rearrest**
reaffirmation	**reannex**	**reapportionment**	**reascend**
realign	**reannexation**	**reappraisal**	
realignment	**reappear**	**reappraise**	

numbers comprises the rationals and the irrationals〉

re•al•po•li•tik \rā-ˈäl-ˌpō-li-ˌtēk\ *n, often cap* [G] : politics based on practical and material factors rather than on theoretical or ethical objectives

real time *n* : the actual time during which something takes place — **real–time** *adj*

re•al•ty \ˈrēl-tē\ *n* : REAL ESTATE

[1]**ream** \ˈrēm\ *n* [ME *reme,* fr. AF, ultim. fr. Ar *rizma,* lit., bundle] : a quantity of paper that is variously 480, 500, or 516 sheets

[2]**ream** *vb* : to enlarge, shape, or clear with a reamer

ream•er \ˈrē-mər\ *n* : a tool with cutting edges that is used to enlarge or shape a hole

reap \ˈrēp\ *vb* **1** : to cut or clear with a scythe, sickle, or machine **2** : to gather by or as if by cutting : HARVEST 〈∼ a reward〉 — **reap•er** *n*

[1]**rear** \ˈrir\ *vb* **1** : to erect by building **2** : to set or raise upright **3** : to breed and raise for use or market 〈∼ livestock〉 **4** : BRING UP, FOSTER **5** : to lift or rise up; *esp* : to rise on the hind legs

[2]**rear** *n* **1** : the unit (as of an army) or area farthest from the enemy **2** : BACK; *also* : the position at the back of something

[3]**rear** *adj* : being at the back

rear admiral *n* : a commissioned officer in the navy or coast guard ranking next below a vice admiral

[1]**rear•ward** \ˈrir-wərd\ *adj* **1** : being at or toward the rear **2** : directed toward the rear 〈a ∼ glance〉

[2]**rear•ward** *also* **rear•wards** \-wərdz\ *adv* : at or toward the rear 〈looking ∼〉

reas *abbr* reasonable

[1]**rea•son** \ˈrē-zᵊn\ *n* [ME *resoun,* fr. AF *raisun,* fr. L *ration-, ratio* reason, computation] **1** : a statement offered in explanation or justification **2** : GROUND, CAUSE **3** : the power to think : INTELLECT **4** : a sane or sound mind **5** : due exercise of the faculty of logical thought

[2]**reason** *vb* **1** : to talk with another to cause a change of mind **2** : to use the faculty of reason : THINK **3** : to discover or formulate by the use of reason — **rea•son•er** *n* — **rea•son•ing** *n*

rea•son•able \ˈrē-zᵊn-ə-bəl\ *adj* **1** : being within the bounds of reason : not extreme **2** : INEXPENSIVE **3** : able to reason : RATIONAL — **rea•son•able•ness** *n* — **rea•son•ably** \-blē\ *adv*

re•as•sure \ˌrē-ə-ˈshu̇r\ *vb* **1** : to assure again **2** : to restore confidence to : free from fear — **re•as•sur•ance** \-ˈshu̇r-əns\ *n* — **re•as•sur•ing•ly** *adv*

[1]**re•bate** \ˈrē-ˌbāt\ *vb* **re•bat•ed; re•bat•ing** : to make or give a rebate

[2]**rebate** *n* : a return of part of a payment ♦ ***Synonyms*** DEDUCTION, ABATEMENT, DISCOUNT

[1]**reb•el** \ˈre-bəl\ *adj* [ME, fr. AF, fr. L *rebellis,* fr. *re-* + *bellum* war] : of or relating to rebels

[2]**rebel** *n* : one that rebels against authority

[3]**re•bel** \ri-ˈbel\ *vb* **re•belled; re•bel•ling** **1** : to resist the authority of one's government **2** : to act in or show disobedience **3** : to feel or exhibit anger or revulsion

re•bel•lion \ri-ˈbel-yən\ *n* : resistance to authority; *esp* : defiance against a government through uprising or revolt

re•bel•lious \-yəs\ *adj* **1** : given to or engaged in rebellion **2** : inclined to resist authority — **re•bel•lious•ly** *adv* — **re•bel•lious•ness** *n*

re•birth \ˌrē-ˈbərth\ *n* **1** : a new or second birth **2** : RENAISSANCE, REVIVAL

re•born \-ˈbȯrn\ *adj* : born again : REGENERATED, REVIVED

[1]**re•bound** \ˌrē-ˈbau̇nd, ˈrē-ˌbau̇nd\ *vb* **1** : to spring back on or as if on striking another body **2** : to recover from a setback or frustration 〈∼*ed* quickly from the loss〉

[2]**re•bound** \ˈrē-ˌbau̇nd\ *n* **1** : the action of rebounding **2** : a rebounding ball **3** : a reaction to setback or frustration

re•buff \ri-ˈbəf\ *vb* : to reject or criticize sharply : SNUB — **rebuff** *n*

re•build \(ˌ)rē-ˈbild\ *vb* **-built** \-ˈbilt\; **-build•ing** **1** : REPAIR, RECONSTRUCT; *also* : REMODEL **2** : to build again

[1]**re•buke** \ri-ˈbyük\ *vb* **re•buked; re•buk•ing** : to reprimand sharply : REPROVE

[2]**rebuke** *n* : a sharp reprimand

re•bus \ˈrē-bəs\ *n* [L, by things, abl. pl. of *res* thing] : a representation of syllables or words by means of pictures; *also* : a riddle composed of such pictures

re•but \ri-ˈbət\ *vb* **re•but•ted; re•but•ting** : to refute esp. formally (as in debate) by evidence and arguments ♦ ***Synonyms*** DISPROVE, CONTROVERT, CONFUTE — **re•but•ter** *n*

re•but•tal \ri-ˈbə-tᵊl\ *n* : the act of rebutting

rec *abbr* **1** receipt **2** record; recording **3** recreation

re•cal•ci•trant \ri-ˈkal-sə-trənt\ *adj* [LL *recalcitrant-, recalcitrans,* prp. of *recalcitrare* to be stubbornly disobedient, fr. L, to kick back, fr. *re-* back, again + *calcitrare* to kick, fr. *calc-, calx* heel] **1** : stubbornly resisting authority 〈a ∼ prisoner〉 **2** : resistant to handling or treatment ♦ ***Synonyms*** REFRACTORY, HEADSTRONG, WILLFUL, UNRULY, UNGOVERNABLE — **re•cal•ci•trance** \-trəns\ *n*

[1]**re•call** \ri-ˈkȯl\ *vb* **1** : REVOKE, CANCEL **2** : to call back **3** : REMEMBER, RECOLLECT 〈∼*ed* their last meeting〉

[2]**re•call** \ri-ˈkȯl, ˈrē-ˌkȯl\ *n* **1** : a summons

---

reassemble
reassembly
reassert
reassess
reassessment
reassign
reassignment
reassume
reattach
reattachment
reattain
reattempt
reauthorization
reauthorize
reawaken
rebaptism
rebaptize
rebid
rebind
reboil
rebroadcast
reburial
rebury
recalculate
recalculation

to return **2** : the procedure of removing an official by popular vote **3** : remembrance of things learned or experienced **4** : the act of revoking **5** : a call by a manufacturer for the return of a product that may be defective or contaminated

re·cant \ri-ˈkant\ *vb* : to take back (something one has said) publicly : make an open confession of error — **re·can·ta·tion** \ˌrē-ˌkan-ˈtā-shən\ *n*

¹**re·cap** \ˈrē-ˌkap, rē-ˈkap\ *vb* **re·capped; re·cap·ping** : RECAPITULATE — **re·cap** \ˈrē-ˌkap\ *n*

²**recap** *vb* **re·capped; re·cap·ping** : RETREAD — **re·cap** \ˈrē-ˌkap\ *n*

re·ca·pit·u·late \ˌrē-kə-ˈpi-chə-ˌlāt\ *vb* **-lat·ed; -lat·ing** : to restate briefly : SUMMARIZE ⟨~ recent news stories⟩ — **re·ca·pit·u·la·tion** \-ˌpi-chə-ˈlā-shən\ *n*

re·cap·ture \(ˌ)rē-ˈkap-chər\ *vb* **1** : to capture again **2** : to experience again ⟨~ happy times⟩

re·cast \(ˌ)rē-ˈkast\ *vb* **1** : to cast again **2** : REVISE, REMODEL ⟨~ a sentence⟩

recd *abbr* received

re·cede \ri-ˈsēd\ *vb* **re·ced·ed; re·ced·ing** **1** : to move back or away ⟨a *receding* hairline⟩ **2** : to slant backward **3** : DIMINISH, CONTRACT ⟨a *receding* deficit⟩

¹**re·ceipt** \ri-ˈsēt\ *n* **1** : RECIPE **2** : the act of receiving **3** : something received — usu. used in pl. **4** : a written acknowledgment of something received

²**receipt** *vb* **1** : to give a receipt for **2** : to mark as paid

re·ceiv·able \ri-ˈsē-və-bəl\ *adj* **1** : capable of being received; *esp* : acceptable as legal ⟨~ certificates⟩ **2** : subject to call for payment ⟨notes ~⟩

re·ceive \ri-ˈsēv\ *vb* **re·ceived; re·ceiv·ing** **1** : to take in or accept (as something sent or paid) : come into possession of : GET **2** : CONTAIN, HOLD **3** : to permit to enter : GREET, WELCOME **4** : to be at home to visitors **5** : to accept as true or authoritative **6** : to be the subject of : UNDERGO, EXPERIENCE ⟨~ a shock⟩ **7** : to change incoming radio waves into sounds or pictures ⟨~ a broadcast⟩

re·ceiv·er \ri-ˈsē-vər\ *n* **1** : one that receives **2** : a person legally appointed to receive and have charge of property or money involved in a lawsuit **3** : a device for converting electromagnetic waves or signals into audio or visual form

re·ceiv·er·ship \-ˌship\ *n* **1** : the office or function of a receiver **2** : the condition of being in the hands of a receiver

re·cen·cy \ˈrē-sᵊn-sē\ *n* : RECENTNESS

re·cent \ˈrē-sᵊnt\ *adj* **1** : of the present time or time just past ⟨~ history⟩ **2** : having lately come into existence : NEW, FRESH ⟨~ buds⟩ **3** *cap* : HOLOCENE — **re·cent·ly** *adv* — **re·cent·ness** *n*

re·cep·ta·cle \ri-ˈsep-ti-kəl\ *n* **1** : something used to receive and hold something else : CONTAINER **2** : the enlarged end of a flower stalk upon which the parts of the flower grow **3** : an electrical fitting containing the live parts of a circuit

re·cep·tion \ri-ˈsep-shən\ *n* **1** : the act of receiving **2** : a social gathering at which guests are formally welcomed

re·cep·tion·ist \ri-ˈsep-shə-nist\ *n* : a person employed to greet callers

re·cep·tive \ri-ˈsep-tiv\ *adj* : able or inclined to receive; *esp* : open and responsive to ideas, impressions, or suggestions ⟨a ~ audience⟩ — **re·cep·tive·ly** *adv* — **re·cep·tive·ness** *n* — **re·cep·tiv·i·ty** \ˌrē-ˌsep-ˈti-və-tē\ *n*

re·cep·tor \ri-ˈsep-tər\ *n* **1** : one that receives stimuli : SENSE ORGAN **2** : a chemical group or molecule in the outer cell membrane or in the cell interior that has an affinity for a specific chemical group, molecule, or virus

¹**re·cess** \ˈrē-ˌses, ri-ˈses\ *n* **1** : a secret or secluded place **2** : an indentation in a line or surface (as an alcove in a room) **3** : a suspension of business or procedure for rest or relaxation

²**recess** *vb* **1** : to put into a recess **2** : to make a recess in **3** : to interrupt for a recess **4** : to take a recess

re·ces·sion \ri-ˈse-shən\ *n* **1** : the act of receding : WITHDRAWAL **2** : a departing procession (as at the end of a church service) **3** : a period of reduced economic activity

re·ces·sion·al \ri-ˈse-shə-nəl\ *n* **1** : a hymn or musical piece at the conclusion of a service or program **2** : RECESSION 2

¹**re·ces·sive** \ri-ˈse-siv\ *adj* **1** : tending to recede **2** : producing or being a bodily characteristic that is masked or not expressed when a contrasting dominant gene or trait is present ⟨~ genes⟩ ⟨~ traits⟩

²**recessive** *n* : a recessive characteristic or gene; *also* : an individual that has one or more recessive characteristics

re·cher·ché \rə-ˌsher-ˈshā, -ˈsher-ˌshā\ *adj* [F] **1** : CHOICE, RARE **2** : excessively refined ⟨~ poetry⟩

re·cid·i·vism \ri-ˈsi-də-ˌvi-zəm\ *n* : a tendency to relapse into a previous condition; *esp* : relapse into criminal behavior — **re·cid·i·vist** \-vist\ *n*

rec·i·pe \ˈre-sə-(ˌ)pē\ *n* [L, take, imperative of *recipere* to take, receive, fr. *re-* back + *capere* to take] **1** : a set of instructions for making something from various ingredients **2** : a method of procedure : FORMULA

re·cip·i·ent \ri-ˈsi-pē-ənt\ *n* : one that receives

¹**re·cip·ro·cal** \ri-ˈsi-prə-kəl\ *adj* **1** : inversely related **2** : MUTUAL, SHARED **3** : serving to reciprocate **4** : mutually corresponding — **re·cip·ro·cal·ly** *adv*

²**reciprocal** *n* **1** : something in a reciprocal relationship to another **2** : one of a pair of numbers (as ⅔ and ³⁄₂) whose product is one

rechannel
recharge
rechargeable
recharter
recheck
rechristen
reclassification
reclassify

re·cip·ro·cate \-ˌkāt\ *vb* **-cat·ed; -cat·ing** **1** : to move backward and forward alternately **2** : to give and take mutually **3** : to make a return for something done or given — **re·cip·ro·ca·tion** \-ˌsi-prə-ˈkā-shən\ *n*

rec·i·proc·i·ty \ˌre-sə-ˈprä-sə-tē\ *n, pl* **-ties** **1** : the quality or state of being reciprocal **2** : mutual exchange of privileges (as trade advantages between countries)

re·cit·al \ri-ˈsī-tᵊl\ *n* **1** : an act or instance of reciting : ACCOUNT **2** : a public reading or recitation ⟨a poetry ~⟩ **3** : a concert given by a musician, dancer, or dance troupe **4** : a public exhibition of skill given by music or dance pupils — **re·cit·al·ist** \-tᵊl-ist\ *n*

rec·i·ta·tion \ˌre-sə-ˈtā-shən\ *n* **1** : RECITING, RECITAL **2** : delivery before an audience usu. of something memorized ⟨~ of a poem⟩ **3** : a classroom exercise in which pupils answer questions on a lesson they have studied

re·cite \ri-ˈsīt\ *vb* **re·cit·ed; re·cit·ing** **1** : to repeat verbatim (as something memorized) **2** : to recount in some detail : RELATE **3** : to reply to a teacher's questions on a lesson — **re·cit·er** *n*

reck·less \ˈre-kləs\ *adj* : lacking caution ⟨a ~ driver⟩ ♦ ***Synonyms*** HASTY, BRASH, HOTHEADED, THOUGHTLESS — **reck·less·ly** *adv* — **reck·less·ness** *n*

reck·on \ˈre-kən\ *vb* **1** : COUNT, CALCULATE, COMPUTE **2** : CONSIDER, REGARD ⟨was ~*ed* as the leader⟩ **3** *chiefly dial* : THINK, SUPPOSE, GUESS

reck·on·ing *n* **1** : an act or instance of reckoning **2** : a settling of accounts ⟨day of ~⟩

re·claim \ri-ˈklām\ *vb* **1** : to recall from wrong conduct : REFORM **2** : to change from an undesirable to a desired condition ⟨~ marshy land⟩ **3** : to obtain from a waste product or by-product ⟨~*ed* plastic⟩ **4** : to demand or obtain the return of — **re·claim·able** *adj* — **rec·la·ma·tion** \ˌre-klə-ˈmā-shən\ *n*

re·cline \ri-ˈklīn\ *vb* **re·clined; re·clin·ing** **1** : to lean or incline backward **2** : to lie down : REST

re·clin·er \ri-ˈklī-nər\ *n* : a chair with an adjustable back and footrest

re·cluse \ˈre-ˌklüs, ri-ˈklüs\ *n* : a person who leads a secluded or solitary life : HERMIT — **re·clu·sive** \ri-ˈklü-siv\ *adj*

rec·og·nise *chiefly Brit var of* RECOGNIZE

rec·og·ni·tion \ˌre-kəg-ˈni-shən\ *n* **1** : the act of recognizing : the state of being recognized : ACKNOWLEDGMENT ⟨in ~ of their achievements⟩ **2** : special notice or attention

re·cog·ni·zance \ri-ˈkäg-nə-zəns\ *n* : a promise recorded before a court or magistrate to do something (as to appear in court or to keep the peace) usu. under penalty of a money forfeiture

rec·og·nize \ˈre-kəg-ˌnīz\ *vb* **-nized; -niz·ing** **1** : to acknowledge (as a speaker in a meeting) as one entitled to be heard at the time **2** : to acknowledge the existence or the independence of (a country or government) **3** : to take notice of **4** : to acknowledge with appreciation **5** : to acknowledge acquaintance with **6** : to identify as previously known **7** : to perceive clearly : REALIZE — **rec·og·niz·able** \ˈre-kəg-ˌnī-zə-bəl\ *adj* — **rec·og·niz·ably** \-blē\ *adv*

¹**re·coil** \ri-ˈkȯi(-ə)l\ *vb* [ME *reculen, recoilen,* fr. AF *reculer, recuiler,* fr. *re-* back + *cul* backside, fr. L *culus*] **1** : to draw back : RETREAT **2** : to spring back to or as if to a starting point ♦ ***Synonyms*** SHRINK, FLINCH, WINCE, QUAIL, BLENCH

²**re·coil** \ˈrē-ˌkȯi(-ə)l, ri-ˈkȯil\ *n* : the action of recoiling (as by a gun or spring)

rec·ol·lect \ˌre-kə-ˈlekt\ *vb* : to recall to mind : REMEMBER ♦ ***Synonyms*** RECALL, REMIND, REMINISCE, BETHINK

rec·ol·lec·tion \ˌre-kə-ˈlek-shən\ *n* **1** : the act or power of recollecting **2** : something recollected

re·com·bi·nant \(ˌ)rē-ˈkäm-bə-nənt\ *adj* **1** : relating to genetic recombination **2** : containing or produced by recombinant DNA ⟨~ vaccines⟩

recombinant DNA *n* : genetically engineered DNA prepared in vitro by joining together DNA usu. from more than one species of organism

re·com·bi·na·tion \ˌrē-ˌkäm-bə-ˈnā-shən\ *n* : the formation of new combinations of genes

rec·om·mend \ˌre-kə-ˈmend\ *vb* **1** : to present as deserving of acceptance or trial **2** : to give in charge : COMMIT **3** : to make acceptable **4** : ADVISE, COUNSEL — **rec·om·mend·able** \-ˈmen-də-bəl\ *adj*

rec·om·men·da·tion \ˌre-kə-mən-ˈdā-shən\ *n* **1** : the act of recommending **2** : something recommended **3** : something that recommends

¹**rec·om·pense** \ˈre-kəm-ˌpens\ *vb* **-pensed; -pens·ing** **1** : to give compensation to : pay for ⟨were *recompensed* for their losses⟩ **2** : to return in kind : REQUITE ♦ ***Synonyms*** REIMBURSE, INDEMNIFY, REPAY, COMPENSATE

²**recompense** *n* : COMPENSATION

rec·on·cile \ˈre-kən-ˌsī(-ə)l\ *vb* **-ciled; -cil·ing** **1** : to cause to be friendly or harmonious again **2** : ADJUST, SETTLE ⟨~ differences⟩ **3** : to bring to submission or

---

recoin
recolonization
recolonize
recolor
recombine
recommence
recommission
recommit
recompile
recompose
recomputation
recompute
reconceive
reconcentrate
reconception
recondensation
recondense
reconfirm
reconfirmation
reconnect
reconquer
reconquest
reconsecrate
reconsecration
recontact
recontaminate
recontamination
reconvene
reconvert
recook
recopy

acceptance ♦ ***Synonyms*** CONFORM, ACCOMMODATE, HARMONIZE, COORDINATE — **rec•on•cil•able** *adj* — **rec•on•cile•ment** *n* — **rec•on•cil•er** *n*

rec•on•cil•i•a•tion \ˌre-kən-ˌsi-lē-ˈā-shən\ *n* **1** : the action of reconciling **2** : the Roman Catholic sacrament of penance

re•con•dite \ˈre-kən-ˌdīt\ *adj* **1** : hard to understand : ABSTRUSE ⟨~ terminology⟩ **2** : little known : OBSCURE

re•con•di•tion \ˌrē-kən-ˈdi-shən\ *vb* **1** : to restore to good condition (as by replacing parts) **2** : to condition anew

re•con•nais•sance \ri-ˈkä-nə-zəns, -səns\ *n* [F, lit., recognition] : a preliminary survey of an area; *esp* : an exploratory military survey of enemy territory

re•con•noi•ter *or* **re•con•noi•tre** \ˌrē-kə-ˈnȯi-tər, ˌre-\ *vb* **-noi•tered** *or* **-noi•tred; -noi•ter•ing** *or* **-noi•tring** : to make a reconnaissance of : engage in reconnaissance ⟨~*ed* to locate enemy positions⟩

re•con•sid•er \ˌrē-kən-ˈsi-dər\ *vb* : to consider again with a view to changing or reversing ⟨~*ed* his decision⟩ — **re•con•sid•er•a•tion** \-ˌsi-də-ˈrā-shən\ *n*

re•con•sti•tute \ˌrē-ˈkän-stə-ˌtüt, -ˌtyüt\ *vb* : to restore to a former condition by adding water ⟨~ powdered milk⟩

re•con•struct \ˌrē-kən-ˈstrəkt\ *vb* **1** : to construct again : REBUILD **2** : to subject (a body part) to surgery to re-form its structure or correct a defect **3** : to re-create or reimagine (something from the past) esp. by using information from research

re•con•struc•tion \ˌrē-kən-ˈstrək-shən\ *n* **1** : the action of reconstructing : the state of being reconstructed **2** *often cap* : the reorganization and reestablishment of the seceded states in the Union after the American Civil War **3** : something reconstructed

[1]**re•cord** \ri-ˈkȯrd\ *vb* [ME, lit., to recall, fr. AF *recorder,* fr. L *recordari,* fr. *re-* back, again + *cord-, cors* heart] **1** : to set down in writing ⟨~*ed* her observations⟩ **2** : to register permanently **3** : INDICATE, READ **4** : to give evidence of **5** : to cause (as sound or visual images) to be registered (as on a disc or a magnetic tape) in a form that permits reproduction

[2]**rec•ord** \ˈre-kərd\ *n* **1** : the act of being recorded **2** : a written account of proceedings **3** : known facts about a person; *also* : a collection of items of information (as in a database) treated as a unit **4** : an attested top performance **5** : something on which sound or visual images have been recorded

[3]**re•cord** \ri-ˈkȯrd\ *n* : a function of an electronic device that causes it to record

re•cord•er \ri-ˈkȯr-dər\ *n* **1** : a judge in some city courts **2** : one who records transactions officially **3** : a recording device **4** : a wind instrument with a whistle mouthpiece and eight fingerholes

re•cord•ing *n* : RECORD 5

re•cord•ist \ri-ˈkȯr-dist\ *n* : one who records sound esp. on film

[1]**re•count** \ri-ˈkau̇nt\ *vb* : to relate in detail : TELL ♦ ***Synonyms*** RECITE, REHEARSE, NARRATE, DESCRIBE, STATE, REPORT

[2]**re•count** \ˈrē-ˌkau̇nt, (ˌ)rē-ˈkau̇nt\ *vb* : to count again

[3]**re•count** \ˈrē-ˌkau̇nt, (ˌ)rē-ˈkau̇nt\ *n* : a second or fresh count

re•coup \ri-ˈküp\ *vb* : to get an equivalent or compensation for : make up for something lost ⟨~*ed* their costs⟩

re•course \ˈrē-ˌkȯrs, ri-ˈkȯrs\ *n* **1** : a turning to someone or something for assistance or protection **2** : a source of aid : RESORT

re•cov•er \ri-ˈkə-vər\ *vb* **1** : to get back again : REGAIN, RETRIEVE **2** : to regain normal health, poise, or status **3** : to make up for : RECOUP ⟨~*ed* all his losses⟩ **4** : RECLAIM ⟨~ land from the sea⟩ **5** : to obtain a legal judgment in one's favor — **re•cov•er•able** *adj*

re–cov•er \ˌrē-ˈkə-vər\ *vb* : to cover again

recovering *adj* : being in the process of overcoming a shortcoming or problem ⟨a ~ alcoholic⟩

re•cov•ery \ri-ˈkə-və-rē\ *n* **1** : an act or instance of recovering; *esp* : an economic upturn **2** : the process of combating a disorder or problem

[1]**rec•re•ant** \ˈre-krē-ənt\ *adj* [ME, fr. AF, fr. prp. of (*se*) *recreire* to give up, yield, fr. ML (*se*) *recredere* to resign oneself (to a judgment), fr. L *re-* back + *credere* to believe] **1** : COWARDLY **2** : UNFAITHFUL

[2]**recreant** *n* **1** : COWARD **2** : DESERTER

rec•re•ate \ˈre-krē-ˌāt\ *vb* **-at•ed; -at•ing 1** : to give new life or freshness to **2** : to take recreation ⟨*recreated* at the beach⟩ — **rec•re•ative** \-ˌā-tiv\ *adj*

re–cre•ate \ˌrē-krē-ˈāt\ *vb* : to create again ⟨*re-created* the battle scene⟩ — **re–cre•ation** \-ˈā-shən\ *n* — **re–cre•ative** \-ˈā-tiv\ *adj*

rec•re•ation \ˌre-krē-ˈā-shən\ *n* : a refreshing of strength or spirits after work; *also* : a means of refreshment ♦ ***Synonyms*** DIVERSION, ENTERTAINMENT, AMUSEMENT — **rec•re•ation•al** \-shə-nəl\ *adj*

recreational vehicle *n* : a vehicle designed for recreational use (as camping)

re•crim•i•na•tion \ri-ˌkri-mə-ˈnā-shən\ *n* : a retaliatory accusation — **re•crim•i•nate** \-ˈkri-mə-nāt\ *vb* — **re•crim•i•na•tory** \-ˈkri-mə-nə-ˌtȯr-ē\ *adj*

re•cru•des•cence \ˌrē-krü-ˈde-sᵊns\ *n* : a renewal or breaking out again esp. of something unhealthful or dangerous

[1]**re•cruit** \ri-ˈkrüt\ *vb* **1** : to form or strengthen with new members ⟨~ an army⟩ **2** : to enlist as a member of an armed service **3** : to secure the services of **4** : to seek to enroll **5** : to restore or increase in health or vigor ⟨resting to ~ his strength⟩ — **re•cruit•er** *n* — **re•cruit•ment** *n*

[2]**recruit** *n* [F *recrute, recrue* fresh growth, new levy of soldiers, fr. MF, fr. *recroistre* to grow up again, fr. L *recrescere*] : a new-

comer to an activity or field; *esp* : a newly enlisted member of the armed forces

rec·tal \'rek-tᵊl\ *adj* : of or relating to the rectum — **rec·tal·ly** *adv*

rect·an·gle \'rek-ˌtaŋ-gəl\ *n* : a 4-sided figure with four right angles; *esp* : one with adjacent sides of unequal length — **rect·an·gu·lar** \rek-'taŋ-gyə-lər\ *adj*

rec·ti·fi·er \'rek-tə-ˌfī(-ə)r\ *n* : one that rectifies; *esp* : a device for converting alternating current into direct current

rec·ti·fy \'rek-tə-ˌfī\ *vb* **-fied; -fy·ing** : to make or set right : CORRECT ♦ ***Synonyms*** EMEND, AMEND, MEND, RIGHT — **rec·ti·fi·ca·tion** \ˌrek-tə-fə-'kā-shən\ *n*

rec·ti·lin·ear \ˌrek-tə-'li-nē-ər\ *adj* **1** : moving in a straight line ⟨~ motion⟩ **2** : characterized by straight lines

rec·ti·tude \'rek-tə-ˌtüd, -ˌtyüd\ *n* **1** : moral integrity **2** : correctness of procedure ♦ ***Synonyms*** VIRTUE, GOODNESS, MORALITY, PROBITY

rec·to \'rek-tō\ *n, pl* **rectos** : a right-hand page

rec·tor \'rek-tər\ *n* **1** : a priest or minister in charge of a parish **2** : the head of a university or school — **rec·to·ri·al** \rek-'tȯr-ē-əl\ *adj*

rec·to·ry \'rek-tə-rē\ *n, pl* **-ries** : the residence of a rector or a parish priest

rec·tum \'rek-təm\ *n, pl* **rectums** *or* **rec·ta** \-tə\ [ME, fr. ML, fr. *rectum intestinum,* lit., straight intestine] : the last part of the intestine joining the colon and anus

re·cum·bent \ri-'kəm-bənt\ *adj* : lying down : RECLINING

re·cu·per·ate \ri-'kü-pə-ˌrāt-, -'kyü-\ *vb* **-at·ed; -at·ing** : to get back (as health or strength) : RECOVER — **re·cu·per·a·tion** \-ˌkü-pə-'rā-shən, -ˌkyü-\ *n* — **re·cu·per·a·tive** \-'kü-pə-ˌrā-tiv, -'kyü-\ *adj*

re·cur \ri-'kər\ *vb* **re·curred; re·cur·ring 1** : to go or come back in thought or discussion **2** : to occur or appear again esp. after an interval : occur time after time ⟨*recurring* headaches⟩ — **re·cur·rence** \-'kər-əns\ *n* — **re·cur·rent** \-ənt\ *adj*

re·cy·cle \rē-'sī-kəl\ *vb* **1** : to pass again through a cycle of changes or treatment **2** : to process (as liquid body waste, glass, or cans) in order to regain materials for human use — **re·cy·cla·bil·i·ty** \-ˌsī-klə-'bil-ə-tē\ *n* — **re·cy·cla·ble** \-k(ə)lə-bəl\ *adj* — **recycle** *n*

¹**red** \'red\ *adj* **red·der; red·dest 1** : of the color red **2** : endorsing radical social or political change esp. by force **3** *often cap* : of or relating to the former U.S.S.R. or its allies **4** : tending to support Republican candidates or policies ⟨~ states⟩ — **red·ly** *adv* — **red·ness** *n*

²**red** *n* **1** : the color of blood or of the ruby **2** : a revolutionary in politics **3** *cap* : COMMUNIST **4** : the condition of showing a loss ⟨in the ~⟩

re·dact \ri-'dakt\ *vb* **1** : to put in writing : FRAME ⟨~*ed* the proclamation⟩ **2** : EDIT — **re·dac·tor** \-'dak-tər\ *n*

re·dac·tion \-'dak-shən\ *n* **1** : an act or instance of redacting **2** : EDITION

red alga *n* : any of a group of reddish usu. marine algae

red blood cell *n* : any of the hemoglobin-containing cells that carry oxygen from the lungs to the tissues and are responsible for the red color of vertebrate blood

red·breast \'red-ˌbrest\ *n* : ROBIN

red–carpet *adj* : marked by ceremonial courtesy ⟨was given the ~ treatment⟩

red cedar *n* : an American juniper with scalelike leaves and fragrant close-grained red wood; *also* : its wood

red clover *n* : a European clover that has globe-shaped heads of reddish flowers and is widely cultivated for hay and forage

red·coat \'red-ˌkōt\ *n* : a British soldier esp. during the Revolutionary War

red·den \'re-dᵊn\ *vb* : to make or become red or reddish : FLUSH, BLUSH

red·dish \'re-dish\ *adj* : tinged with red — **red·dish·ness** *n*

red dwarf *n* : a star with lower temperature and less mass than the sun

re·deem \ri-'dēm\ *vb* [ME *redemen,* fr. AF *redemer,* modif. of L *redimere,* fr. *re-, red-* back, again + *emere* to take, buy] **1** : to recover (property) by discharging an obligation **2** : to ransom, free, or rescue by paying a price **3** : to free from the consequences of sin **4** : to remove the obligation of by payment ⟨the government ~*s* savings bonds⟩; *also* : to convert into something of value **5** : to make good (a promise) by performing : FULFILL **6** : to atone for — **re·deem·able** *adj* — **re·deem·er** *n*

re·demp·tion \ri-'demp-shən\ *n* : the act of redeeming : the state of being redeemed — **re·demp·tive** \-tiv\ *adj* — **re·demp·to·ry** \-tə-rē\ *adj*

re·de·ploy \ˌrē-di-'plȯi\ *vb* **1** : to transfer from one area or activity to another **2** : to relocate personnel or equipment — **re·de·ploy·ment** *n*

red–eye \'red-ˌī\ *n* **1** : cheap whiskey **2** : a late night or overnight flight

red·fish \'red-ˌfish\ *n* : any of various reddish marine fishes of the Atlantic including some used for food

red flag *n* : a warning signal or sign

red fox *n* : a fox with orange-red to reddish brown fur

red giant *n* : a very large star with a relatively low surface temperature

---

redecorate
redecoration
rededicate
rededication
redefine
redefinition
redeposit
redesign
redetermination
redetermine
redevelop
redevelopment
redirect
rediscount
rediscover
rediscovery
redissolve
redistill
redistillation
redraft
redraw

red–hand·ed \ˈred-ˈhan-dəd\ *adv or adj* : in the act of committing a misdeed

red·head \-ˌhed\ *n* : a person having red hair — **red·head·ed** \-ˌhe-dəd\ *adj*

red herring *n* : a diversion intended to distract attention from the real issue

red–hot \ˈred-ˈhät\ *adj* **1** : extremely hot; *esp* : glowing with heat **2** : EXCITED, FURIOUS **3** : very new ⟨~ news⟩

re·dial \ˈrē-ˌdī(-ə)l\ *n* : a telephone function that automatically repeats the dialing of the last number called — **redial** *vb*

re·dis·trib·ute \ˌrē-də-ˈstri-byüt\ *vb* **1** : to alter the distribution of **2** : to spread to other areas — **re·dis·tri·bu·tion** \(ˌ)rē-ˌdis-trə-ˈbyü-shən\ *n*

re·dis·trict \ˌrē-ˈdis-(ˌ)trikt\ *vb* : to organize into new territorial and esp. political divisions

red–let·ter \ˈred-ˌle-tər\ *adj* : of special significance : MEMORABLE ⟨a ~ day⟩

red–light *adj* : having many houses of prostitution ⟨a ~ district⟩

re·do \(ˌ)rē-ˈdü\ *vb* : to do over or again; *esp* : REDECORATE

red oak *n* : any of various No. American oaks with leaves usu. having spiny-tipped lobes and acorns that take two years to mature; *also* : the wood of a red oak

red·o·lent \ˈre-də-lənt\ *adj* **1** : FRAGRANT, AROMATIC **2** : having a specified fragrance ⟨a room ~ of cooked cabbage⟩ **3** : REMINISCENT, SUGGESTIVE ⟨a tavern ~ of colonial times⟩ — **red·o·lence** \-ləns\ *n* — **red·o·lent·ly** *adv*

re·dou·ble \(ˌ)rē-ˈdə-bəl\ *vb* : to make twice as great in size or amount; *also* : INTENSIFY

re·doubt \ri-ˈdau̇t\ *n* [F *redoute,* fr. It *ridotto,* fr. ML *reductus* secret place, fr. L, withdrawn, fr. *reducere* to lead back, fr. *re-* back + *ducere* to lead] : a small usu. temporary fortification

re·doubt·able \ri-ˈdau̇-tə-bəl\ *adj* [ME *redoutable,* fr. AF, fr. *reduter* to dread, fr. *re-* back, again + *duter* to doubt] : arousing dread or fear : FORMIDABLE

re·dound \ri-ˈdau̇nd\ *vb* **1** : to have an effect ⟨the change may ~ to her benefit⟩ **2** : to become added or transferred : ACCRUE

red pepper *n* **1** : CAYENNE PEPPER **2** : a mature red hot pepper or sweet pepper

[1]**re·dress** \ri-ˈdres\ *vb* **1** : to set right : REMEDY ⟨~ injustice⟩ **2** : COMPENSATE **3** : to remove the cause of (a grievance) **4** : AVENGE

[2]**re·dress** *n* **1** : relief from distress **2** : means or possibility of seeking a remedy **3** : compensation for loss or injury **4** : an act or instance of redressing

red·shift \ˈred-ˈshift\ *n* : displacement of the spectrum of a heavenly body toward longer wavelengths; *also* : a measure of this displacement

red snapper *n* : any of various reddish fishes including several food fishes

red spider *n* : SPIDER MITE

red squirrel *n* : a common No. American squirrel with the upper parts chiefly red

red–tailed hawk \ˈred-ˌtāld-\ *n* : a rodent-eating No. American hawk with a rather short typically reddish tail

red tape *n* [fr. the red tape formerly used to bind legal documents in England] : official routine or procedure marked by excessive complexity which results in delay or inaction

red tide *n* : seawater discolored by the presence of large numbers of dinoflagellates which produce a toxin that renders infected shellfish poisonous

re·duce \ri-ˈdüs, -ˈdyüs\ *vb* **re·duced; re·duc·ing** **1** : LESSEN **2** : to bring to a specified state or condition ⟨*reduced* them to tears⟩ **3** : to put in a lower rank or grade **4** : CONQUER ⟨~ a fort⟩ **5** : to bring into a certain order or classification **6** : to correct (as a fracture) by restoration of displaced parts **7** : to lessen one's weight ♦ ***Synonyms*** DECREASE, DIMINISH, ABATE, DWINDLE, RECEDE — **re·duc·er** *n* — **re·duc·ible** \-ˈdü-sə-bəl, -ˈdyü-\ *adj*

re·duc·tion \ri-ˈdək-shən\ *n* **1** : the act of reducing : the state of being reduced **2** : something made by reducing **3** : the amount taken off in reducing something

re·dun·dan·cy \ri-ˈdən-dən-sē\ *n, pl* **-cies** **1** : the quality or state of being redundant : SUPERFLUITY **2** : something redundant or in excess **3** : the use of surplus words

re·dun·dant \-dənt\ *adj* **1** : exceeding what is needed or normal : SUPERFLUOUS; *esp* : using more words than necessary **2** : marked by repetition — **re·dun·dant·ly** *adv*

red–winged blackbird \ˈred-ˌwiŋd-\ *n* : a No. American blackbird of which the adult male is black with a patch of bright scarlet on the wings

red·wood \ˈred-ˌwu̇d\ *n* : a tall coniferous timber tree esp. of coastal California; *also* : its durable wood

reed \ˈrēd\ *n* **1** : any of various tall slender grasses of wet areas; *also* : a stem or growth of reed **2** : a musical instrument made from the hollow stem of a reed **3** : an elastic tongue of cane, wood, or metal by which tones are produced in organ pipes and certain other wind instruments — **reedy** *adj*

re·ed·u·cate \(ˌ)rē-ˈe-jə-ˌkāt\ *vb* : to train again; *esp* : to rehabilitate through education — **re·ed·u·ca·tion** *n*

[1]**reef** \ˈrēf\ *n* **1** : a part of a sail taken in or let out in regulating the sail's size **2** : reduction in sail area by reefing

[2]**reef** *vb* : to reduce the area of a sail by rolling or folding part of it

[3]**reef** *n* : a ridge of rocks, sand or coral at or near the surface of the water

reef·er \ˈrē-fər\ *n* : a marijuana cigarette

[1]**reek** \ˈrēk\ *n* : a strong or disagreeable fume or odor

---

reecho
reedit
reelect
reelection
reemerge
reemergence
reemphasis
reemphasize

[2]**reek** *vb* **1 :** to give off or become permeated with a strong or offensive odor **2 :** to give a strong impression of some constituent quality ⟨an excuse that ~*ed* of falsehood⟩ — **reek·er** *n* — **reeky** \ˈrē-kē\ *adj*
[1]**reel** \ˈrēl\ *n* **:** a revolvable device on which something flexible (as film or tape) is wound; *also* **:** a quantity of something wound on such a device
[2]**reel** *vb* **1 :** to wind on or as if on a reel **2 :** to pull or draw (as a fish) by reeling a line — **reel·able** *adj* — **reel·er** *n*
[3]**reel** *vb* **1 :** WHIRL; *also* **:** to be giddy **2 :** to waver or fall back (as from a blow) **3 :** to walk or move unsteadily
[4]**reel** *n* **:** a reeling motion
[5]**reel** *n* **:** a lively Scottish dance or its music
reel off *vb* **1 :** to tell or recite rapidly and easily ⟨*reeled off* the right answers⟩ **2 :** to achieve usu. consecutively ⟨*reeled off* six straight wins⟩
re·en·try \rē-ˈen-trē\ *n* **1 :** a second or new entry **2 :** the action of reentering the earth's atmosphere from space
reeve \ˈrēv\ *vb* **rove** \ˈrōv\ *or* **reeved; reev·ing :** to pass (as a rope) through a hole in a block or cleat
[1]**ref** \ˈref\ *n* **:** REFEREE 2
[2]**ref** *abbr* **1** reference **2** referred **3** reformed **4** refunding
re·fec·tion \ri-ˈfek-shən\ *n* **1 :** refreshment esp. after hunger or fatigue **2 :** food and drink together **:** REPAST
re·fec·to·ry \ri-ˈfek-tə-rē\ *n, pl* **-ries :** a dining hall (as in a monastery or college)
re·fer \ri-ˈfər\ *vb* **re·ferred; re·fer·ring** [ME *referren,* fr. AF *referer, referir,* fr. L *referre* to bring back, report, refer, fr. *re-* back + *ferre* to carry] **1 :** to assign to a certain source, cause, or relationship **2 :** to direct or send to some person or place (as for information or help) **3 :** to submit to someone else for consideration or action **4 :** to have recourse (as for information or aid) **5 :** to have connection **:** RELATE **6 :** to direct attention **:** speak of **:** MENTION, ALLUDE ♦ ***Synonyms*** RECUR, REPAIR, RESORT, APPLY, GO, TURN — **re·fer·able** \ˈre-fə-rə-bəl, ri-ˈfər-ə-\ *adj*
[1]**ref·er·ee** \ˌre-fə-ˈrē\ *n* **1 :** a person to whom an issue esp. in law is referred for investigation or settlement **2 :** an umpire in certain games
[2]**referee** *vb* **-eed; -ee·ing :** to act as referee
ref·er·ence \ˈre-frəns, -fə-rəns\ *n* **1 :** the act of referring **2 :** RELATION, RESPECT **3 :** ALLUSION, MENTION **4 :** something that refers a reader to another passage or book **5 :** consultation esp. for obtaining information ⟨books for ~⟩ **6 :** a person of whom inquiries as to character or ability can be made **7 :** a written recommendation of a person for employment
ref·er·en·dum \ˌre-fə-ˈren-dəm\ *n, pl* **-da** \-də\ *or* **-dums :** the submitting of legislative measures to the voters for approval or rejection; *also* **:** a vote on a measure so submitted
ref·er·ent \ˈre-frənt, -fə-rənt\ *n* **:** one that refers or is referred to; *esp* **:** the thing a word stands for — **referent** *adj*
re·fer·ral \ri-ˈfər-əl\ *n* **1 :** the act or an instance of referring **2 :** one that is referred
[1]**re·fill** \ˌrē-ˈfil\ *vb* **:** to fill again **:** REPLENISH — **re·fill·able** *adj*
[2]**re·fill** \ˈrē-ˌfil\ *n* **:** a new or fresh supply of something
re·fi·nance \ˌrē-fə-ˈnans, (ˌ)rē-ˈfī-nans\ *vb* **:** to renew or reorganize the financing of
re·fine \ri-ˈfīn\ *vb* **re·fined; re·fin·ing 1 :** to free from impurities or waste matter **2 :** IMPROVE, PERFECT **3 :** to free or become free of what is coarse or uncouth **4 :** to make improvements by introducing subtle changes — **re·fin·er** *n*
re·fined \ri-ˈfīnd\ *adj* **1 :** freed from impurities **2 :** CULTURED, CULTIVATED **3 :** PRECISE, EXACT
re·fine·ment \ri-ˈfīn-mənt\ *n* **1 :** the action of refining **2 :** the quality or state of being refined **3 :** a refined feature or method; *also* **:** something intended to improve or perfect
re·fin·ery \ri-ˈfī-nə-rē\ *n, pl* **-er·ies :** a building and equipment for refining metals, oil, or sugar
re·flect \ri-ˈflekt\ *vb* [ME, fr. L *reflectere* to bend back, fr. *re-* back + *flectere* to bend] **1 :** to bend or cast back (as light, heat, or sound) **2 :** to give back a likeness or image of as a mirror does **3 :** to bring as a result ⟨~*ed* credit on him⟩ **4 :** to make apparent **:** SHOW ⟨figures that ~ economic growth⟩ **5 :** to cast reproach or blame ⟨their bad conduct ~*ed* on their training⟩ **6 :** PONDER, MEDITATE — **re·flec·tion** \-ˈflek-shən\ *n* — **re·flec·tive** \-tiv\ *adj* — **re·flec·tiv·ity** \(ˌ)rē-ˌflek-ˈti-və-tē\ *n*
re·flec·tor \ri-ˈflek-tər\ *n* **:** one that reflects; *esp* **:** a polished surface for reflecting radiation (as light)
[1]**re·flex** \ˈrē-ˌfleks\ *n* **1 :** an automatic and usu. inborn response to a stimulus not involving higher mental centers **2** *pl* **:** the power of acting or responding with enough speed ⟨an athlete with great ~*es*⟩
[2]**reflex** *adj* **1 :** bent or directed back **2 :** of, relating to, or produced by a reflex ⟨a ~ action⟩ — **re·flex·ly** *adv*
[1]**re·flex·ive** \ri-ˈflek-siv\ *adj* **:** of or relating to an action directed back upon the doer or the grammatical subject ⟨a ~ verb⟩

---

reemploy
reemployment
reenact
reenactment
reenergize
reenlist
reenlistment
reenter
reequip
reestablish
reestablishment
reevaluate
reevaluation
reexamination
reexamine
reexport
refashion
refight
refigure
refinish
refit

⟨the ~ pronoun *himself*⟩ — **re·flex·ive·ly** *adv* — **re·flex·ive·ness** *n*

[2]reflexive *n* : a reflexive verb or pronoun

re·flex·ol·o·gy \ˌrē-ˌflek-ˈsä-lə-jē\ *n* : massage in which pressure is applied to specific points on the hands or feet

re·flux \ˈrē-ˌfləks\ *n* : a flowing back

re·fo·cus \(ˌ)rē-ˈfō-kəs\ *vb* **1** : to focus again **2** : to change the emphasis or direction of ⟨~*ed* her life⟩

re·for·es·ta·tion \ˌrē-ˌfȯr-ə-ˈstā-shən\ *n* : the action of renewing forest cover by planting seeds or young trees — **re·for·est** \rē-ˈfȯr-əst\ *vb*

[1]re·form \ri-ˈfȯrm\ *vb* **1** : to make better or improve by removal of faults **2** : to correct or improve one's own character or habits ♦ ***Synonyms*** CORRECT, RECTIFY, EMEND, REMEDY, REDRESS, REVISE — **re·form·able** *adj* — **re·for·ma·tive** \-ˈfȯr-mə-tiv\ *adj*

[2]reform *n* : improvement or correction of what is corrupt or defective

re–form \ˌrē-ˈfȯrm\ *vb* : to form again

ref·or·ma·tion \ˌre-fər-ˈmā-shən\ *n* **1** : the act of reforming : the state of being reformed **2** *cap* : a 16th century religious movement marked by the establishment of the Protestant churches

[1]re·for·ma·to·ry \ri-ˈfȯr-mə-ˌtȯr-ē\ *adj* : aiming at or tending toward reformation : REFORMATIVE

[2]reformatory *n, pl* **-ries** : a penal institution for reforming esp. young or first offenders

re·form·er \ri-ˈfȯr-mər\ *n* **1** : one that works for or urges reform **2** *cap* : a leader of the Protestant Reformation

refr *abbr* refraction

re·fract \ri-ˈfrakt\ *vb* [L *refractus,* pp. of *refringere* to break open, break up, fr. *re-* back + *frangere* to break] : to subject to refraction

re·frac·tion \ri-ˈfrak-shən\ *n* : the bending of a ray (as of light) when it passes obliquely from one medium into another in which its speed is different — **re·frac·tive** \-tiv\ *adj*

refractive index *n* : the ratio of the speed of radiation in one medium to that in another medium

re·frac·to·ry \ri-ˈfrak-tə-rē\ *adj* **1** : OBSTINATE, STUBBORN, UNMANAGEABLE **2** : capable of enduring high temperature ⟨~ bricks⟩ ♦ ***Synonyms*** RECALCITRANT, INTRACTABLE, UNGOVERNABLE, UNRULY, HEADSTRONG, WILLFUL — **re·frac·to·ri·ness** \ri-ˈfrak-tə-rē-nəs\ *n* — **refractory** *n*

[1]re·frain \ri-ˈfrān\ *vb* : to hold oneself back : FORBEAR ⟨~ from interfering⟩ — **re·frain·ment** *n*

[2]refrain *n* : a phrase or verse recurring regularly in a poem or song

re·fresh \ri-ˈfresh\ *vb* **1** : to make or become fresh or fresher **2** : to revive by or as if by renewal of supplies ⟨~ one's memory⟩ **3** : to freshen up **4** : to supply or take refreshment **5** : to update or renew esp. by sending a new signal ⟨~ the Web page⟩ ♦ ***Synonyms*** RESTORE, REJUVENATE, RENOVATE, REFURBISH — **re·fresh·er** *n* — **re·fresh·ing·ly** *adv*

re·fresh·ment \-mənt\ *n* **1** : the act of refreshing : the state of being refreshed **2** : something that refreshes **3** *pl* : a light meal; *also* : assorted light foods

re·fried beans \ˈrē-ˌfrīd-\ *n pl* : beans cooked with seasonings, fried, then mashed and fried again

refrig *abbr* refrigerating; refrigeration

re·frig·er·ate \ri-ˈfri-jə-ˌrāt\ *vb* **-at·ed; -at·ing** : to make cool; *esp* : to chill or freeze (food) for preservation — **re·frig·er·ant** \-jə-rənt\ *adj or n* — **re·frig·er·a·tion** \-ˌfri-jə-ˈrā-shən\ *n* — **re·frig·er·a·tor** \-ˈfri-jə-ˌrā-tər\ *n*

ref·uge \ˈre-ˌfyüj\ *n* **1** : shelter or protection from danger or distress **2** : a place that provides protection

ref·u·gee \ˌre-fyu̇-ˈjē\ *n* : one who flees for safety esp. to a foreign country

re·ful·gence \ri-ˈfu̇l-jəns, -ˈfəl-\ *n* : a radiant or resplendent quality or state — **re·ful·gent** \-jənt\ *adj*

[1]re·fund \ri-ˈfənd, ˈrē-ˌfənd\ *vb* : to give or put back (money) : REPAY — **re·fund·able** *adj*

[2]re·fund \ˈrē-ˌfənd\ *n* **1** : the act of refunding **2** : a sum refunded

re·fur·bish \ri-ˈfər-bish\ *vb* : to brighten or freshen up : RENOVATE

[1]re·fuse \ri-ˈfyüz\ *vb* **re·fused; re·fus·ing** **1** : to decline to accept : REJECT **2** : to decline to do, give, or grant : DENY — **re·fus·al** \-ˈfyü-zəl\ *n*

[2]ref·use \ˈre-ˌfyüs, -ˌfyüz\ *n* : rejected or worthless matter : RUBBISH, TRASH

re·fute \ri-ˈfyüt\ *vb* **re·fut·ed; re·fut·ing** [L *refutare* to check, suppress, refute] : to prove to be false by argument or evidence — **ref·u·ta·tion** \ˌre-fyu̇-ˈtā-shən\ *n* — **re·fut·er** *n*

[1]reg \ˈreg\ *n* : REGULATION

[2]reg *abbr* **1** region **2** register; registered; registration **3** regular

re·gal \ˈrē-gəl\ *adj* **1** : of, relating to, or befitting a king : ROYAL **2** : STATELY, SPLENDID — **re·gal·ly** *adv*

re·gale \ri-ˈgāl\ *vb* **re·galed; re·gal·ing** **1** : to entertain richly or agreeably **2** : to give pleasure or amusement to ⟨*regaled* us with stories⟩ ♦ ***Synonyms*** GRATIFY, DELIGHT, PLEASE, REJOICE, GLADDEN

re·ga·lia \ri-ˈgāl-yə\ *n pl* **1** : the emblems, symbols, or paraphernalia of royalty (as the crown and scepter) **2** : the insignia of an office or order **3** : special costume : FINERY

[1]re·gard \ri-ˈgärd\ *n* **1** : CONSIDERATION, HEED; *also* : CARE, CONCERN **2** : GAZE, GLANCE, LOOK **3** : RESPECT, ESTEEM ⟨held in high ~⟩ **4** *pl* : friendly greetings implying respect and esteem **5** : an as-

---

refix	reforge	refortify	refuel
refloat	reformulate	refound	refurnish
refold	reformulation	refreeze	regain

pect to be considered : PARTICULAR — **re·gard·ful** *adj* — **re·gard·less** *adj*

²regard *vb* **1** : to think of : CONSIDER **2** : to pay attention to **3** : to show respect for ⟨~*s* his elders⟩ **4** : to hold in high esteem **5** : to look at : gaze upon ⟨~*ed* the landscape⟩ **6** *archaic* : to relate to

re·gard·ing *prep* : CONCERNING

regardless of \ri-ˈgärd-ləs-\ *prep* : in spite of

re·gat·ta \ri-ˈgä-tə, -ˈga-\ *n* : a boat race or a series of boat races

re·gen·cy \ˈrē-jən-sē\ *n, pl* **-cies** **1** : the office or government of a regent or body of regents **2** : a body of regents **3** : the period during which a regent governs

re·gen·er·a·cy \ri-ˈje-nə-rə-sē\ *n* : the state of being regenerated

¹re·gen·er·ate \ri-ˈje-nə-rət\ *adj* **1** : formed or created again **2** : spiritually reborn or converted

²re·gen·er·ate \ri-ˈje-nə-ˌrāt\ *vb* **1** : to subject to spiritual renewal **2** : to reform completely **3** : to replace (a body part) by a new growth of tissue **4** : to give new life to : REVIVE — **re·gen·er·a·tion** \-ˌje-nə-ˈrā-shən\ *n* — **re·gen·er·a·tive** \-ˈje-nə-ˌrā-tiv\ *adj* — **re·gen·er·a·tor** \-ˌrā-tər\ *n*

re·gent \ˈrē-jənt\ *n* **1** : a person who rules during the childhood, absence, or incapacity of the sovereign **2** : a member of a governing board (as of a state university) — **regent** *adj*

reg·gae \ˈre-ˌgā\ *n* : popular music of Jamaican origin that combines native styles with elements of rock and soul music

reg·i·cide \ˈre-jə-ˌsīd\ *n* **1** : one who murders a king **2** : murder of a king

re·gift \(ˌ)rē-ˈgift\ *vb* : to give a previously received gift to someone else

re·gime *also* **ré·gime** \rā-ˈzhēm, ri-\ *n* **1** : REGIMEN **2** : a form or system of government **3** : a government in power; *also* : a period of rule

reg·i·men \ˈre-jə-mən\ *n* [ME, fr. ML, position of authority, direction, set of rules, fr. L, steering, control, fr. *regere* to direct] **1** : a systematic course of treatment or training **2** : GOVERNMENT

¹reg·i·ment \ˈre-jə-mənt\ *n* : a military unit consisting usu. of a number of battalions — **reg·i·men·tal** \ˌre-jə-ˈment-təl\ *adj*

²reg·i·ment \ˈre-jə-ˌment\ *vb* : to organize rigidly esp. for regulation or central control; *also* : to subject to order or uniformity — **reg·i·men·ta·tion** \ˌre-jə-mən-ˈtā-shən\ *n*

reg·i·men·tals \ˌre-jə-ˈmen-təlz\ *n pl* **1** : a regimental uniform **2** : military dress

re·gion \ˈrē-jən\ *n* [ME, fr. AF *regiun,* fr. L *region-, regio,* line, direction, area, fr. *regere* to rule] : an often indefinitely defined part or area

re·gion·al \ˈrē-jə-nəl\ *adj* **1** : affecting a particular region : LOCALIZED **2** : of, relating to, characteristic of, or serving a region — **re·gion·al·ly** *adv*

¹reg·is·ter \ˈre-jə-stər\ *n* **1** : a record of items or details; *also* : a book or system for keeping such a record **2** : the range of a voice or instrument **3** : a device to regulate ventilation or heating **4** : an automatic device recording a number or quantity **5** : CASH REGISTER

²register *vb* **-tered; -ter·ing** **1** : to enter in a register (as in a list of guests) **2** : to record automatically **3** : to secure special care for (mail matter) by paying additional postage **4** : to convey an impression of : EXPRESS **5** : to make or adjust so as to correspond exactly

registered nurse *n* : a graduate trained nurse who has been licensed to practice by a state authority after passing qualifying examinations

reg·is·trant \ˈre-jə-strənt\ *n* : one that registers or is registered

reg·is·trar \-ˌsträr\ *n* : an official recorder or keeper of records (as at an educational institution)

reg·is·tra·tion \ˌre-jə-ˈstrā-shən\ *n* **1** : the act of registering **2** : an entry in a register **3** : the number of persons registered : ENROLLMENT **4** : a document certifying an act of registering

reg·is·try \ˈre-jə-strē\ *n, pl* **-tries** **1** : ENROLLMENT, REGISTRATION **2** : a place of registration **3** : an official record book or an entry in one

reg·nant \ˈreg-nənt\ *adj* **1** : REIGNING **2** : DOMINANT **3** : of common or widespread occurrence

¹re·gress \ˈrē-ˌgres\ *n* **1** : an act or the privilege of going or coming back **2** : RETROGRESSION

²re·gress \ri-ˈgres\ *vb* : to go or cause to go back or to a lower level — **re·gres·sive** *adj* — **re·gres·sor** \-ˈgre-sər\ *n*

re·gres·sion \ri-ˈgre-shən\ *n* : the act or an instance of regressing; *esp* : reversion to an earlier mental or behavioral level

¹re·gret \ri-ˈgret\ *vb* **re·gret·ted; re·gret·ting** **1** : to mourn the loss or death of **2** : to be very sorry for **3** : to experience regret — **re·gret·ta·ble** \-ˈgre-tə-bəl\ *adj* — **re·gret·ter** *n*

²regret *n* **1** : sorrow caused by something beyond one's power to remedy **2** : an expression of sorrow **3** *pl* : a note politely declining an invitation — **re·gret·ful** \-fəl\ *adj* — **re·gret·ful·ly** *adv*

re·gret·ta·bly \-ˈgre-tə-blē\ *adv* **1** : to a regrettable extent **2** : it is to be regretted

re·group \(ˌ)rē-ˈgrüp\ *vb* : to form into a new grouping

regt *abbr* regiment

¹reg·u·lar \ˈre-gyə-lər\ *adj* [ME *reguler,* fr. AF, fr. LL *regularis* regular, fr. L, of a bar, fr. *regula* rule, straightedge, fr. *regere* to keep straight, direct] **1** : belonging to a religious order **2** : made, built, or arranged according to a rule, standard, or type; *also* : even or symmetrical in form or structure **3** : ORDERLY, METHODICAL ⟨~ habits⟩; *also* : not varying : STEADY

---

regather **regive** **regrade** **regrind**
regild

⟨a ~ pace⟩ **4** : made, selected, or conducted according to rule or custom **5** : properly qualified ⟨not a ~ lawyer⟩ **6** : conforming to the normal or usual manner or inflection **7** : of, relating to, or constituting the permanent standing military force of a state — **reg·u·lar·i·ty** \ˌre-gyə-ˈla-rə-tē\ *n* — **reg·u·lar·ize** \ˈre-gyə-lə-ˌrīz\ *vb* — **reg·u·lar·ly** *adv*

²**regular** *n* **1** : one that is regular (as in attendance) **2** : a member of the regular clergy **3** : a soldier in a regular army **4** : a player on an athletic team who is usu. in the starting lineup

reg·u·late \ˈre-gyə-ˌlāt\ *vb* **-lat·ed; -lat·ing** **1** : to govern or direct according to rule : CONTROL **2** : to bring under the control of law or authority **3** : to put in good order **4** : to fix or adjust the time, amount, degree, or rate of — **reg·u·la·tive** \-ˌlā-tiv\ *adj* — **reg·u·la·tor** \-ˌlā-tər\ *n* — **reg·u·la·to·ry** \-lə-ˌtȯr-ē\ *adj*

reg·u·la·tion \ˌre-gyə-ˈlā-shən\ *n* **1** : the act of regulating : the state of being regulated **2** : a rule dealing with details of procedure **3** : an order issued by an executive authority of a government and having the force of law

re·gur·gi·tate \rē-ˈgər-jə-ˌtāt\ *vb* **-tat·ed; -tat·ing** [ML *regurgitare,* fr. L *re-* re- + LL *gurgitare* to engulf, fr. L *gurgit-, gurges* whirlpool] : to throw or be thrown back, up, or out ⟨~ food⟩ — **re·gur·gi·ta·tion** \-ˌgər-jə-ˈtā-shən\ *n*

re·hab \ˈrē-ˌhab\ *n* **1** : REHABILITATION **2** : a rehabilitated building — **rehab** *vb*

re·ha·bil·i·tate \ˌrē-hə-ˈbi-lə-ˌtāt, ˌrē-ə-\ *vb* **-tat·ed; -tat·ing** **1** : to restore to a former capacity, rank, or right : REINSTATE **2** : to restore to good condition or health — **re·ha·bil·i·ta·tion** \-ˌbi-lə-ˈtā-shən\ *n* — **re·ha·bil·i·ta·tive** \-ˌtā-tiv\ *adj*

re·hash \ˌrē-ˈhash\ *vb* : to present again in another form without real change or improvement — **rehash** *n*

re·hear·ing \ˌrē-ˈhir-iŋ\ *n* : a second or new hearing by the same tribunal

re·hears·al \ri-ˈhər-səl\ *n* **1** : something told again : RECITAL **2** : a private performance or practice session preparatory to a public appearance

re·hearse \ri-ˈhərs\ *vb* **re·hearsed; re·hears·ing** **1** : to say again : REPEAT **2** : to recount in order : ENUMERATE; *also* : RELATE 1 **3** : to give a rehearsal of **4** : to train by rehearsal **5** : to engage in a rehearsal — **re·hears·er** *n*

¹**reign** \ˈrān\ *n* **1** : the authority or rule of a sovereign **2** : the time during which a sovereign rules

²**reign** *vb* **1** : to rule as a sovereign **2** : to be predominant or prevalent

re·im·burse \ˌrē-əm-ˈbərs\ *vb* **-bursed; -burs·ing** [*re-* re- + obs. E *imburse* to put in the pocket, pay, fr. ML *imbursare* to put into a purse, fr. L *in-* in + ML *bursa* purse, fr. LL, hide of an ox, fr. Gk *byrsa*] : to pay back : make restitution : REPAY ⟨was *reimbursed* for her travel expenses⟩ ♦ ***Synonyms*** INDEMNIFY, RECOMPENSE, REQUITE, COMPENSATE — **re·im·burs·able** *adj* — **re·im·burse·ment** *n*

¹**rein** \ˈrān\ *n* **1** : a strap fastened to a bit by which a rider or driver controls an animal **2** : a restraining influence : CHECK **3** : controlling or guiding power **4** : complete freedom — usu. used in the phrase *give rein to*

²**rein** *vb* : to check or direct by reins

re·in·car·na·tion \ˌrē-(ˌ)in-(ˌ)kär-ˈnā-shən\ *n* : rebirth of the soul in a new body — **re·in·car·nate** \ˌrē-in-ˈkär-ˌnāt\ *vb*

rein·deer \ˈrān-ˌdir\ *n* [ME *reindere,* fr. ON *hreinn* reindeer + ME *deer* animal, deer] : CARIBOU — used esp. for one of the Old World

reindeer moss *n* : a gray, erect, tufted, and much-branched edible lichen of northern regions that is an important food of reindeer

re·in·fec·tion \ˌrē-in-ˈfek-shən\ *n* : infection following another infection of the same type

re·in·force \ˌrē-ən-ˈfȯrs\ *vb* **1** : to strengthen with additional forces ⟨~ our troops⟩ **2** : to strengthen with new force, aid, material, or support — **re·in·force·ment** *n* — **re·in·forc·er** *n*

re·in·scribe \ˌrē-ən-ˈskrīb\ *vb* : to reestablish or rename in a new and esp. stronger form or context

re·in·state \ˌrē-in-ˈstāt\ *vb* **-stat·ed; -stat·ing** : to restore to a former position, condition, or capacity — **re·in·state·ment** *n*

re·in·vent \ˌrē-in-ˈvent\ *vb* **1** : to make as if for the first time something already invented ⟨~ the wheel⟩ **2** : to remake completely

re·it·er·ate \rē-ˈi-tə-ˌrāt\ *vb* **-at·ed; -at·ing** : to state or do over again or repeatedly — **re·it·er·a·tion** \-ˌi-tə-ˈrā-shən\ *n*

¹**re·ject** \ri-ˈjekt\ *vb* **1** : to refuse to accept, consider, use, or submit to **2** : to refuse to hear, receive, or admit : REPEL **3** : to rebuff or withhold love from **4** : to throw out esp. as useless or unsatisfactory **5** : to subject (a transplanted tissue) to an attack by immune system components of the recipient organism — **re·jec·tion** \-ˈjek-shən\ *n*

²**re·ject** \ˈrē-ˌjekt\ *n* : a rejected person or thing

re·joice \ri-ˈjȯis\ *vb* **re·joiced; re·joic·ing** **1** : to give joy to : GLADDEN **2** : to feel joy or great delight — **re·joic·er** *n*

re·join \(ˌ)rē-ˈjȯin *for 1,* ri- *for 2*\ *vb* **1** : to join again **2** : to say in answer (as to a plaintiff's plea in court) : REPLY

re·join·der \ri-ˈjȯin-dər\ *n* : REPLY; *esp* : an answer to a reply

re·ju·ve·nate \ri-ˈjü-və-ˌnāt\ *vb* **-nat·ed;**

regrow	rehear	reimagine	reincorporate
regrowth	reheat	reimpose	reinsert
rehandle	rehouse	reimposition	reinsertion

-nat·ing : to make young or youthful again : give new vigor to ♦ ***Synonyms*** RENEW, REFRESH, RENOVATE, RESTORE — **re·ju·ve·na·tion** \-ˌjü-və-ˈnā-shən\ *n*

rel *abbr* **1** relating; relative **2** religion; religious

¹re·lapse \ri-ˈlaps, ˈrē-ˌlaps\ *n* [ME, fr. ML *relapsus,* fr. L *relabi* to slide back] **1** : the act or process of backsliding or worsening **2** : a recurrence of illness after a period of improvement

²re·lapse \ri-ˈlaps\ *vb* **re·lapsed; re·laps·ing** : to slip or fall back into a former worse state (as of illness)

re·late \ri-ˈlāt\ *vb* **re·lat·ed; re·lat·ing** **1** : to give an account of : TELL, NARRATE **2** : to show or establish logical or causal connection between **3** : to have relationship or connection **4** : to have or establish relationship ⟨the way a child ∼*s* to a teacher⟩ **5** : to respond favorably ⟨can't ∼ to that kind of music⟩ — **re·lat·able** *adj* — **re·lat·er** *or* **re·la·tor** \-ˈlā-tər\ *n*

re·lat·ed *adj* **1** : connected by some understood relationship **2** : connected through membership in the same family — **re·lat·ed·ness** *n*

re·la·tion \ri-ˈlā-shən\ *n* **1** : NARRATION, ACCOUNT **2** : CONNECTION, RELATIONSHIP **3** : connection by blood or marriage : KINSHIP; *also* : RELATIVE **4** : REFERENCE, RESPECT ⟨in ∼ to⟩ **5** : the state of being mutually interested or involved (as in social or commercial matters) **6** *pl* : DEALINGS, AFFAIRS ⟨foreign ∼*s*⟩ **7** *pl* : SEXUAL INTERCOURSE — **re·la·tion·al** \-shə-nəl\ *adj*

re·la·tion·ship \-ˌship\ *n* : the state of being related or interrelated

¹rel·a·tive \ˈre-lə-tiv\ *n* **1** : a word referring grammatically to an antecedent **2** : a thing having a relation to or a dependence upon another thing **3** : a person connected with another by blood or marriage

²relative *adj* **1** : introducing a subordinate clause qualifying an expressed or implied antecedent ⟨∼ pronoun⟩; *also* : introduced by such a connective ⟨∼ clause⟩ **2** : PERTINENT, RELEVANT ⟨matters ∼ to world peace⟩ **3** : not absolute or independent : COMPARATIVE **4** : expressed as the ratio of the specified quantity to the total magnitude or to the mean of all quantities involved ♦ ***Synonyms*** DEPENDENT, CONTINGENT, CONDITIONAL — **rel·a·tive·ly** *adv* — **rel·a·tive·ness** *n*

relative humidity *n* : the ratio of the amount of water vapor actually present in the air to the greatest amount possible at the same temperature

rel·a·tiv·is·tic \ˌre-lə-ti-ˈvis-tik\ *adj* **1** : of, relating to, or characterized by relativity **2** : moving at a velocity that is a significant fraction of the speed of light so that effects predicted by the theory of relativity become evident ⟨a ∼ electron⟩ — **rel·a·tiv·is·ti·cal·ly** \-ti-k(ə-)lē\ *adv*

rel·a·tiv·i·ty \ˌre-lə-ˈti-və-tē\ *n, pl* **-ties** **1** : the quality or state of being relative **2** : a theory in physics that considers mass and energy to be equivalent and that predicts changes in mass, dimension, and time which are related to speed but are noticeable esp. at speeds approaching that of light; *also* : an extension of the theory to include gravitation and related acceleration phenomena

re·lax \ri-ˈlaks\ *vb* **1** : to make or become less firm, tense, or rigid **2** : to make less severe or strict **3** : to seek rest or recreation — **re·lax·er** *n*

¹re·lax·ant \ri-ˈlak-sənt\ *adj* : of, relating to, or producing relaxation

²relaxant *n* : a relaxing agent; *esp* : a drug that induces muscular relaxation

re·lax·ation \ˌrē-ˌlak-ˈsā-shən\ *n* **1** : the act of relaxing or state of being relaxed : a lessening of tension **2** : DIVERSION, RECREATION

¹re·lay \ˈrē-ˌlā\ *n* [ME, set of fresh hounds, fr. *relayen* to release fresh hounds, take a fresh horse, fr. MF *relaier,* fr. *re-* again + *laier* to let go, leave] **1** : a fresh supply (as of horses) arranged beforehand to relieve others **2** : a race between teams in which each team member covers a specified part of a course **3** : an electromagnetic device in which the opening or closing of one circuit activates another device (as a switch in another circuit) **4** : the act of passing along by stages

²re·lay \ˈrē-ˌlā, ri-ˈlā\ *vb* **re·layed; re·lay·ing** **1** : to place in or provide with relays **2** : to pass along by relays **3** : to control or operate by a relay

³re·lay \(ˌ)rē-ˈlā\ *vb* **-laid** \-ˈlād\; **-lay·ing** : to lay again

¹re·lease \ri-ˈlēs\ *vb* **re·leased; re·leas·ing** **1** : to set free from confinement or restraint; *also* : DISMISS ⟨*released* from her job⟩ **2** : to relieve from something that oppresses, confines, or burdens **3** : RELINQUISH ⟨∼ a claim⟩ **4** : to permit publication, performance, exhibition, or sale of; *also* : to make available to the public ♦ ***Synonyms*** EMANCIPATE, DISCHARGE, FREE, LIBERATE

²release *n* **1** : relief or deliverance from sorrow, suffering, or trouble **2** : discharge from an obligation or responsibility **3** : an act of setting free : the state of being freed **4** : a document effecting a legal release **5** : a releasing for performance or publication; *also* : the matter released (as to the press) **6** : a device for holding or releasing a mechanism as required

rel·e·gate \ˈre-lə-ˌgāt\ *vb* **-gat·ed; -gat·ing** **1** : to send into exile : BANISH **2** : to

---

reintegrate	reintroduction	reinvigorate	rekindle
reinterpret	reinvention	reinvigoration	reknit
reinterpretation	reinvest	reissue	relaunch
reintroduce	reinvestment	rejudge	relearn

remove or dismiss to some less prominent position **3** : to assign to a particular class or sphere **4** : to submit to someone or something for appropriate action : DELEGATE ♦ ***Synonyms*** COMMIT, ENTRUST, CONSIGN, COMMEND — **rel·e·ga·tion** \ˌre-lə-ˈgā-shən\ *n*

re·lent \ri-ˈlent\ *vb* **1** : to become less stern, severe, or harsh **2** : SLACKEN

re·lent·less \-ləs\ *adj* : showing or promising no abatement of severity, intensity, or pace ⟨~ pressure⟩ — **re·lent·less·ly** *adv* — **re·lent·less·ness** *n*

rel·e·vance \ˈre-lə-vəns\ *n* : relation to the matter at hand; *also* : practical and esp. social applicability

rel·e·van·cy \-vən-sē\ *n* : RELEVANCE

rel·e·vant \ˈre-lə-vənt\ *adj* : bearing on the matter at hand : PERTINENT ♦ ***Synonyms*** GERMANE, MATERIAL, APPLICABLE, APROPOS — **rel·e·vant·ly** *adv*

re·li·able \ri-ˈlī-ə-bəl\ *adj* : fit to be trusted or relied on : DEPENDABLE, TRUSTWORTHY — **re·li·abil·i·ty** \-ˌlī-ə-ˈbi-lə-tē\ *n* — **re·li·able·ness** *n* — **re·li·ably** \-ˈlī-ə-blē\ *adv*

re·li·ance \ri-ˈlī-əns\ *n* **1** : the act of relying **2** : the state of being reliant **3** : one relied on

re·li·ant \ri-ˈlī-ənt\ *adj* : having reliance on someone or something : DEPENDENT

rel·ic \ˈre-lik\ *n* **1** : an object venerated because of its association with a saint or martyr **2** : SOUVENIR, MEMENTO **3** *pl* : REMAINS, RUINS **4** : a remaining trace : VESTIGE

rel·ict \ˈre-likt\ *n* : WIDOW

re·lief \ri-ˈlēf\ *n* **1** : removal or lightening of something oppressive, painful, or distressing **2** : WELFARE 2 **3** : military assistance to an endangered post or force **4** : release from a post or from performance of a duty; *also* : one that takes the place of another on duty **5** : legal remedy or redress **6** : projection of figures or ornaments from the background (as in sculpture) **7** : the state of being distinguished by contrast **8** : the elevations of a land surface

relief pitcher *n* : a baseball pitcher who takes over for another during a game

re·lieve \ri-ˈlēv\ *vb* **re·lieved; re·liev·ing** **1** : to free partly or wholly from a burden or from distress **2** : to bring about the removal or alleviation of : MITIGATE **3** : to release from a post or duty; *also* : to take the place of **4** : to break the monotony of **5** : to discharge the bladder or bowels of (oneself) ♦ ***Synonyms*** ALLEVIATE, LIGHTEN, ASSUAGE, ALLAY — **re·liev·er** *n*

relig *abbr* religion

re·li·gion \ri-ˈli-jən\ *n* **1** : the service and worship of God or the supernatural **2** : devotion to a religious faith **3** : a personal set or institutionalized system of religious beliefs, attitudes, and practices **4** : a cause, principle, or belief held to with faith and ardor — **re·li·gion·ist** *n*

¹re·li·gious \ri-ˈli-jəs\ *adj* **1** : relating or devoted to an acknowledged ultimate reality or deity **2** : of or relating to religious beliefs or observances **3** : scrupulously and conscientiously faithful **4** : FERVENT, ZEALOUS ⟨~ about football⟩ — **re·li·gious·ly** *adv*

²religious *n, pl* **religious** : a member of a religious order under monastic vows

re·lin·quish \ri-ˈliŋ-kwish, -ˈlin-\ *vb* **1** : to withdraw or retreat from : ABANDON, QUIT **2** : GIVE UP ⟨~ a title⟩ **3** : to let go of : RELEASE ♦ ***Synonyms*** YIELD, LEAVE, RESIGN, SURRENDER, CEDE, WAIVE — **re·lin·quish·ment** *n*

rel·i·quary \ˈre-lə-ˌkwer-ē\ *n, pl* **-quar·ies** : a container for religious relics

¹rel·ish \ˈre-lish\ *n* [ME *reles* taste, fr. OF, something left behind, release, fr. *relessier* to relax, release, fr. L *relaxare*] **1** : characteristic flavor : SAVOR **2** : keen enjoyment or delight in something : GUSTO **3** : APPETITE, INCLINATION ⟨has no ~ for sports⟩ **4** : a highly seasoned sauce (as of pickles) eaten with other food to add flavor

²relish *vb* **1** : to add relish to **2** : to take pleasure in : ENJOY **3** : to eat with pleasure — **rel·ish·able** *adj*

re·live \(ˌ)rē-ˈliv\ *vb* : to live again or over again; *esp* : to experience again in the imagination

re·lo·cate \(ˌ)rē-ˈlō-ˌkāt, ˌrē-lō-ˈkāt\ *vb* **1** : to locate again **2** : to move to a new location — **re·lo·ca·tion** \ˌrē-lō-ˈkā-shən\ *n*

re·luc·tant \ri-ˈlək-tənt\ *adj* : feeling or showing aversion, hesitation, or unwillingness ⟨~ to get involved⟩ ♦ ***Synonyms*** DISINCLINED, INDISPOSED, HESITANT, LOATH, AVERSE — **re·luc·tance** \-təns\ *n* — **re·luc·tant·ly** *adv*

re·ly \ri-ˈlī\ *vb* **re·lied; re·ly·ing** [ME *relien* to rally, fr. AF *relier* to retie, gather, rally, fr. L *religare* to tie out of the way, fr. *re-* back + *ligare* to tie] : to place faith or confidence : DEPEND

REM \ˈrem\ *n* : RAPID EYE MOVEMENT

re·main \ri-ˈmān\ *vb* **1** : to be left after others have been removed, subtracted, or destroyed **2** : to be something yet to be shown, done, or treated ⟨it ~*s* to be seen⟩ **3** : to stay after others have gone **4** : to continue unchanged

re·main·der \ri-ˈmān-dər\ *n* **1** : that which is left over : a remaining group, part, or trace **2** : the number left after a subtraction **3** : the number that is left over from the dividend after division and that is less than the divisor **4** : a book sold at a reduced price by the publisher after sales have slowed ♦ ***Synonyms*** LEAVINGS, REST, BALANCE, REMNANT, RESIDUE

re·mains \-ˈmānz\ *n pl* **1** : a remaining part or trace ⟨the ~ of a meal⟩ **2** : a dead body

¹re·make \(ˌ)rē-ˈmāk\ *vb* **-made** \-ˈmād\; **-mak·ing** : to make anew or in a different form

relight reline reload remanufacture

²**re·make** \ˈrē-ˌmāk\ *n* : one that is remade; *esp* : a new version of a motion picture
re·mand \ri-ˈmand\ *vb* : to order back; *esp* : to return to custody pending trial or for further detention
¹**re·mark** \ri-ˈmärk\ *n* **1** : the act of remarking : OBSERVATION, NOTICE **2** : a passing observation or comment
²**remark** *vb* **1** : to take notice of : OBSERVE **2** : to express as an observation or comment : SAY
re·mark·able \ri-ˈmär-kə-bəl\ *adj* : worthy of being or likely to be noticed : UNUSUAL, EXTRAORDINARY, NOTEWORTHY — **re·mark·able·ness** *n*
re·mark·ably \ri-ˈmär-kə-blē\ *adv* **1** : in a remarkable manner **2** : as is remarkable ⟨~, no one was hurt⟩
re·me·di·a·ble \ri-ˈmē-dē-ə-bəl\ *adj* : capable of being remedied
re·me·di·al \ri-ˈmē-dē-əl\ *adj* : intended to remedy or improve ⟨a class in ~ math⟩
¹**rem·e·dy** \ˈre-mə-dē\ *n, pl* **-dies** [ME *remedie,* fr. AF, fr. L *remedium,* fr. *re-* back, again + *mederi* to heal] **1** : a medicine or treatment that cures or relieves a disease or condition **2** : something that corrects or counteracts an evil or compensates for a loss
²**remedy** *vb* **-died; -dy·ing** : to provide or serve as a remedy for
re·mem·ber \ri-ˈmem-bər\ *vb* **-bered; -ber·ing** **1** : to bring to mind or think of again : RECOLLECT **2** : to keep from forgetting : keep in mind **3** : to convey greetings from **4** : COMMEMORATE
re·mem·brance \-brəns\ *n* **1** : an act of remembering : RECOLLECTION **2** : the ability to remember : MEMORY **3** : the period over which one's memory extends **4** : a memory of a person, thing, or event **5** : something that serves to bring to mind : REMINDER **6** : a greeting or gift recalling or expressing friendship or affection
re·mind \ri-ˈmīnd\ *vb* : to put in mind of something : cause to remember — **re·mind·er** *n*
rem·i·nisce \ˌre-mə-ˈnis\ *vb* **-nisced; -nisc·ing** : to indulge in reminiscence
rem·i·nis·cence \-ˈni-sᵊns\ *n* **1** : a recalling or telling of a past experience **2** : an account of a memorable experience
rem·i·nis·cent \-sᵊnt\ *adj* **1** : of or relating to reminiscence **2** : marked by or given to reminiscence **3** : serving to remind : SUGGESTIVE — **rem·i·nis·cent·ly** *adv*
re·miss \ri-ˈmis\ *adj* **1** : negligent or careless in the performance of work or duty **2** : showing neglect or inattention ♦ ***Synonyms*** LAX, NEGLECTFUL, DELINQUENT, DERELICT — **re·miss·ness** *n*
re·mis·sion \ri-ˈmi-shən\ *n* **1** : the act or process of remitting **2** : a state or period during which something is remitted
re·mit \ri-ˈmit\ *vb* **re·mit·ted; re·mit·ting** **1** : FORGIVE, PARDON ⟨~ sins⟩ **2** : to give or gain relief from (as pain) **3** : to refer for consideration, report, or decision **4** : to refrain from exacting or enforcing (as a penalty) **5** : to send (money) in payment of a bill
re·mit·tal \ri-ˈmi-tᵊl\ *n* : REMISSION
re·mit·tance \ri-ˈmi-tᵊns\ *n* **1** : a sum of money remitted **2** : transmittal of money (as to a distant place)
rem·nant \ˈrem-nənt\ *n* **1** : a usu. small part or trace remaining **2** : an unsold or unused end of a fabric that is sold by the yard
re·mod·el \ˌrē-ˈmä-dᵊl\ *vb* : to alter the structure of : MAKE OVER
re·mon·strance \ri-ˈmän-strəns\ *n* : an act or instance of remonstrating
re·mon·strant \-strənt\ *adj* : vigorously objecting or opposing — **remonstrant** *n* — **re·mon·strant·ly** *adv*
re·mon·strate \ri-ˈmän-ˌstrāt\ *vb* **-strat·ed; -strat·ing** : to plead in opposition to something : speak in protest or reproof ♦ ***Synonyms*** EXPOSTULATE, OBJECT, PROTEST — **re·mon·stra·tion** \ri-ˌmän-ˈstrā-shən, ˌre-mən-\ *n* — **re·mon·stra·tor** \ri-ˈmän-ˌstrā-tər\ *n*
rem·o·ra \ˈre-mə-rə\ *n* : any of a family of marine bony fishes with sucking organs on the head by which they cling esp. to other fishes
re·morse \ri-ˈmȯrs\ *n* [ME, fr. AF *remors,* fr. ML *remorsus,* fr. LL, act of biting again, fr. L *remordēre* to bite again, fr. *re-* again + *mordēre* to bite] : a gnawing distress arising from a sense of guilt for past wrongs ♦ ***Synonyms*** PENITENCE, REPENTANCE, CONTRITION — **re·morse·ful** *adj*
re·morse·less \-ləs\ *adj* **1** : MERCILESS **2** : PERSISTENT, RELENTLESS
¹**re·mote** \ri-ˈmōt\ *adj* **re·mot·er; -est** **1** : far off in place or time : not near **2** : not closely related : DISTANT **3** : located out of the way : SECLUDED **4** : acting, acted on, or controlled indirectly or from a distance **5** : small in degree : SLIGHT ⟨a ~ chance⟩ **6** : distant in manner ⟨became ~ in her old age⟩ — **re·mote·ly** *adv* — **re·mote·ness** *n*
²**remote** *n* **1** : a radio or television program or a portion of a program originating outside the studio **2** : REMOTE CONTROL 2
remote control *n* **1** : control (as by radio signal) of operation from a point at some distance removed **2** : a device or mechanism for controlling something from a distance
¹**re·mount** \(ˌ)rē-ˈmau̇nt\ *vb* **1** : to mount again **2** : to furnish remounts to
²**re·mount** \ˈrē-ˌmau̇nt\ *n* : a fresh horse to replace one no longer available
¹**re·move** \ri-ˈmüv\ *vb* **re·moved; re·mov·ing** **1** : to move from one place to another : TRANSFER **2** : to move by lifting or taking off or away **3** : DISMISS,

remap	remarry	remelt	remold
remarriage	rematch	remigration	

DISCHARGE **4** : to get rid of : ELIMINATE ⟨~ a fire hazard⟩ **5** : to change one's residence or location **6** : to go away : DEPART **7** : to be capable of being removed — **re·mov·able** *adj* — **re·mov·al** \-ˈmü-vəl\ *n* — **re·mov·er** *n*

²**remove** *n* **1** : a transfer from one location to another : MOVE **2** : a degree or stage of separation

REM sleep *n* : a state of sleep that recurs cyclically several times during normal sleep and is associated with rapid eye movements and dreaming

re·mu·ner·ate \ri-ˈmyü-nə-ˌrāt\ *vb* **-at·ed; -at·ing** : to pay an equivalent for or to : RECOMPENSE ⟨my services were *remunerated*⟩ — **re·mu·ner·a·tor** \-ˌrā-tər\ *n*

re·mu·ner·a·tion \ri-ˌmyü-nə-ˈrā-shən\ *n* : COMPENSATION, PAYMENT

re·mu·ner·a·tive \ri-ˈmyü-nə-rə-tiv, -ˌrā-\ *adj* : serving to remunerate : GAINFUL

re·nais·sance \ˌre-nə-ˈsäns, -ˈzäns\ *n* **1** *cap* : the cultural revival and beginnings of modern science in Europe in the 14th–17th centuries; *also* : the period of the Renaissance **2** *often cap* : a movement or period of vigorous artistic and intellectual activity **3** : REBIRTH, REVIVAL

re·nal \ˈrē-nᵊl\ *adj* : of, relating to, or located in or near the kidneys

re·na·scence \ri-ˈna-sᵊns, -ˈnā-\ *n, often cap* : RENAISSANCE

rend \ˈrend\ *vb* **rent** \ˈrent\; **rend·ing** **1** : to remove by violence : WREST **2** : to tear forcibly apart : SPLIT

ren·der \ˈren-dər\ *vb* **1** : to extract (as lard) by heating **2** : to give to another; *also* : YIELD **3** : to give in return **4** : to do (a service) for another ⟨~ aid⟩ **5** : to cause to be or become : MAKE **6** : to reproduce or represent by artistic or verbal means **7** : TRANSLATE ⟨~ into English⟩

¹**ren·dez·vous** \ˈrän-di-ˌvü, -dā-\ *n, pl* **ren·dez·vous** \-ˌvüz\ [MF, fr. *rendez vous* present yourselves] **1** : a place appointed for a meeting; *also* : a meeting at an appointed place **2** : a place of popular resort **3** : the process of bringing two spacecraft together

²**rendezvous** *vb* **-voused** \-ˌvüd\; **-vous·ing** \-ˌvü-iŋ\; **-vouses** \-ˌvüz\ : to come or bring together at a rendezvous

ren·di·tion \ren-ˈdi-shən\ *n* : an act or a result of rendering ⟨first ~ of the work into English⟩

ren·e·gade \ˈre-ni-ˌgād\ *n* [Sp *renegado,* fr. ML *renegatus,* fr. pp. of *renegare* to deny, fr. L *re-* re- + *negare* to deny] : a deserter from one faith, cause, principle, or party for another

re·nege \ri-ˈneg\ *vb* **re·neged; re·neg·ing** **1** : to go back on a promise or commitment **2** : to fail to follow suit when able in a card game in violation of the rules — **re·neg·er** *n*

re·new \ri-ˈnü, -ˈnyü\ *vb* **1** : to make or become new, fresh, or strong again **2** : to restore to existence : RECREATE, REVIVE **3** : to make or do again : REPEAT ⟨~ a complaint⟩ **4** : to begin again : RESUME ⟨~*ed* his efforts⟩ **5** : REPLACE ⟨~ the lining of a coat⟩ **6** : to grant or obtain an extension of or on ⟨~ a lease⟩ ⟨~ a subscription⟩ — **re·new·er** *n*

re·new·able \ri-ˈnü-ə-bəl, -ˈnyü-\ *adj* **1** : capable of being renewed **2** : capable of being replaced by natural ecological cycles or sound management procedures ⟨~ resources⟩

re·new·al \ri-ˈnü-əl, -ˈnyü-\ *n* **1** : the act of renewing : the state of being renewed **2** : something renewed

ren·net \ˈre-nət\ *n* **1** : the contents of the stomach of an unweaned animal (as a calf) or the lining membrane of the stomach used for curdling milk **2** : rennin or a substitute used to curdle milk

ren·nin \ˈre-nən\ *n* : a stomach enzyme that coagulates casein and is used commercially to curdle milk in the making of cheese

re·nounce \ri-ˈnau̇ns\ *vb* **re·nounced; re·nounc·ing** **1** : to give up, refuse, or resign usu. by formal declaration **2** : to refuse further to follow, obey, or recognize : REPUDIATE — **re·nounce·ment** *n*

ren·o·vate \ˈre-nə-ˌvāt\ *vb* **-vat·ed; -vat·ing** **1** : to make like new again : put in good condition : REPAIR ⟨*renovated* the kitchen⟩ **2** : to restore to vigor or activity — **ren·o·va·tion** \ˌre-nə-ˈvā-shən\ *n* — **ren·o·va·tor** \ˈre-nə-ˌvā-tər\ *n*

re·nown \ri-ˈnau̇n\ *n* : a state of being widely acclaimed and honored : FAME, CELEBRITY ⟨writers of ~⟩ ♦ ***Synonyms*** HONOR, GLORY, REPUTATION, REPUTE — **re·nowned** \-ˈnau̇nd\ *adj*

¹**rent** \ˈrent\ *n* **1** : money or the amount of money paid or due at intervals for the use of another's property **2** : property rented or for rent

²**rent** *vb* **1** : to give possession and use of in return for rent **2** : to take and hold under an agreement to pay rent **3** : to be for rent ⟨~*s* for $100 a month⟩ — **rent·er** *n*

³**rent** *n* **1** : a tear made by or as if by rending **2** : a split in a party or organized group : SCHISM

¹**rent·al** \ˈren-tᵊl\ *n* **1** : an amount paid or collected as rent **2** : something that is rented **3** : an act of renting

²**rental** *adj* : of or relating to rent

re·nun·ci·a·tion \ri-ˌnən-sē-ˈā-shən\ *n* : the act of renouncing : REPUDIATION

¹**rep** \ˈrep\ *n* : REPRESENTATIVE ⟨sales ~*s*⟩

²**rep** *abbr* **1** repair **2** repeat **3** report; reporter **4** republic

Rep *abbr* Republican

re·pack·age \(ˌ)rē-ˈpa-kij\ *vb* : to package again or anew; *esp* : to put into a more attractive form

¹**re·pair** \ri-ˈper\ *vb* [ME, fr. AF *repairer* to go back, return, fr. LL *repatriare* to go home again, fr. L *re-* back + *patria* native

---

rename **renegotiation** **renomination** **renumber**
renegotiate **renominate**

country] : to make one's way : GO ⟨~*ed* to the drawing room⟩

[2]**repair** *vb* [ME, fr. AF *reparer*, fr. L *reparare*, fr. *re-* back + *parare* to prepare] **1** : to restore to good condition : FIX **2** : to restore to a healthy state **3** : REMEDY ⟨~ a wrong⟩ — **re·pair·er** *n* — **re·pair·man** \-ˌman\ *n*

[3]**repair** *n* **1** : a result of repairing **2** : an act of repairing **3** : condition with respect to need of repairing ⟨in bad ~⟩

rep·a·ra·tion \ˌre-pə-ˈrā-shən\ *n* **1** : the act of making amends for a wrong **2** : amends made for a wrong; *esp* : money paid by a defeated nation in compensation for damages caused during hostilities — usu. used in pl. ♦ ***Synonyms*** REDRESS, RESTITUTION, INDEMNITY

re·par·a·tive \ri-ˈpa-rə-tiv\ *adj* **1** : of, relating to, or effecting repairs **2** : serving to make amends

rep·ar·tee \ˌre-pər-ˈtē\ *n* **1** : a witty reply **2** : a succession of clever replies; *also* : skill in making such replies

re·past \ri-ˈpast, ˈrē-ˌpast\ *n* : a supply of food and drink served as a meal

re·pa·tri·ate \rē-ˈpā-trē-ˌāt\ *vb* **-at·ed; -at·ing** : to send or bring back to the country of origin or citizenship ⟨~ prisoners of war⟩ — **re·pa·tri·ate** \-trē-ət, -trē-ˌāt\ *n* — **re·pa·tri·a·tion** \-ˌpā-trē-ˈā-shən\ *n*

re·pay \rē-ˈpā\ *vb* **-paid** \-ˈpād\; **-pay·ing** **1** : to pay back : REFUND **2** : to give or do in return or requital **3** : to make a return payment to : RECOMPENSE, REQUITE ♦ ***Synonyms*** REMUNERATE, COMPENSATE, REIMBURSE, INDEMNIFY — **re·pay·able** *adj* — **re·pay·ment** *n*

re·peal \ri-ˈpēl\ *vb* [ME *repelen*, fr. AF *repeler*, lit., to call back, fr. *re-* back + *apeler* to appeal, call] : to annul by authoritative and esp. legislative action ⟨~ a law⟩ — **repeal** *n* — **re·peal·er** *n*

[1]**re·peat** \ri-ˈpēt\ *vb* **1** : to say again **2** : to do again **3** : to say over from memory — **re·peat·able** *adj* — **re·peat·er** *n*

[2]**re·peat** \ri-ˈpēt, ˈrē-ˌpēt\ *n* **1** : the act of repeating **2** : something repeated or to be repeated (as a television show)

[3]**re·peat** \ri-ˈpēt\ *adj* : of, relating to, or being one that repeats an offense, achievement, or action

re·peat·ed \ri-ˈpē-təd\ *adj* : done or recurring again and again : FREQUENT ⟨~ requests⟩ — **re·peat·ed·ly** *adv*

re·pel \ri-ˈpel\ *vb* **re·pelled; re·pel·ling** **1** : to drive away : REPULSE **2** : to fight against : RESIST **3** : to turn away : REJECT **4** : to cause aversion in : DISGUST

[1]**re·pel·lent** *also* **re·pel·lant** \ri-ˈpe-lənt\ *adj* **1** : tending to drive away ⟨a mosquito-*repellent* spray⟩ **2** : causing disgust

[2]**repellent** *also* **repellant** *n* : something that repels; *esp* : a substance that repels insects

re·pent \ri-ˈpent\ *vb* **1** : to turn from sin and resolve to reform one's life **2** : to feel sorry for (something done) : REGRET ⟨~*ed* his decision⟩ — **re·pen·tance** \ri-ˈpen-tᵊns\ *n* — **re·pen·tant** \-tᵊnt\ *adj*

re·per·cus·sion \ˌrē-pər-ˈkə-shən, ˌre-\ *n* **1** : REVERBERATION **2** : a reciprocal action or effect **3** : a widespread, indirect, or unforeseen effect of something done or said

rep·er·toire \ˈre-pər-ˌtwär\ *n* [F] **1** : a list of plays, operas, pieces, or parts which a company or performer is prepared to present **2** : a list of the skills or devices possessed by a person or needed in a person's occupation

rep·er·to·ry \ˈre-pər-ˌtȯr-ē\ *n, pl* **-ries** **1** : REPOSITORY **2** : REPERTOIRE **3** : a company that presents its repertoire in the course of one season at one theater

rep·e·ti·tion \ˌre-pə-ˈti-shən\ *n* **1** : the act or an instance of repeating **2** : the fact of being repeated

rep·e·ti·tious \-ˈti-shəs\ *adj* : REPETITIVE — **rep·e·ti·tious·ly** *adv* — **rep·e·ti·tious·ness** *n*

re·pet·i·tive \ri-ˈpe-ti-tiv\ *adj* : marked by repetition; *esp* : tediously repeating ⟨~ work⟩ — **re·pet·i·tive·ly** *adv* — **re·pet·i·tive·ness** *n*

re·pine \ri-ˈpīn\ *vb* **re·pined; re·pin·ing** **1** : to feel or express discontent or dejection **2** : to long for something

repl *abbr* replace; replacement

re·place \ri-ˈplās\ *vb* **1** : to restore to a former place or position **2** : to take the place of : SUPPLANT **3** : to put something new in the place of — **re·place·able** *adj* — **re·plac·er** *n*

re·place·ment \ri-ˈplās-mənt\ *n* **1** : the act of replacing : the state of being replaced **2** : one that replaces another esp. in a job or function

[1]**re·play** \(ˌ)rē-ˈplā\ *vb* : to play again or over

[2]**re·play** \ˈrē-ˌplā\ *n* **1** : an act or instance of replaying **2** : the playing of a tape (as a videotape)

re·plen·ish \ri-ˈple-nish\ *vb* : to fill or build up again : stock or supply anew — **re·plen·ish·ment** *n*

re·plete \ri-ˈplēt\ *adj* **1** : fully provided ⟨a kit ~ with instructions⟩ **2** : FULL; *esp* : full of food — **re·plete·ness** *n* — **re·ple·tion** \ri-ˈplē-shən\ *n*

rep·li·ca \ˈre-pli-kə\ *n* [It, repetition, fr. *replicare* to repeat, fr. LL, fr. L, to fold back, fr. *re-* back + *plicare* to fold] **1** : an exact reproduction (as of a painting) executed by the original artist **2** : a copy exact in all details : DUPLICATE

[1]**rep·li·cate** \ˈre-plə-ˌkāt\ *vb* **-cat·ed; -cat·ing** : DUPLICATE, REPEAT

[2]**rep·li·cate** \-pli-kət\ *n* : one of several identical experiments or procedures

rep·li·ca·tion \ˌre-plə-ˈkā-shən\ *n* **1** : ANSWER, REPLY **2** : precise copying or re-

---

reoccupy	**reorganization**	**repack**	**rephotograph**
reoccur	**reorganize**	**repaint**	**rephrase**
reopen	**reorient**	**repass**	**replant**
reorder	**reorientation**	**repeople**	**repopulate**

production; *also* : an act or process of this ⟨~ of DNA⟩

[1]**re·ply** \ri-ˈplī\ *vb* **re·plied; re·ply·ing** : to say or do in answer : RESPOND

[2]**reply** *n, pl* **replies** : ANSWER, RESPONSE

repo \ˈrē-ˌpō\ *adj* : of, relating to, or being in the business of repossessing property (as a car)

[1]**re·port** \ri-ˈpȯrt\ *n* [ME, fr. AF, fr. *reporter* to bring back, report, fr. L *reportare,* fr. *re-* back + *portare* to carry] **1** : common talk : RUMOR **2** : FAME, REPUTATION ⟨a person of good ~⟩ **3** : a usu. detailed account or statement **4** : an explosive noise

[2]**report** *vb* **1** : to give an account of : RELATE, TELL **2** : to serve as carrier of (a message) **3** : to prepare or present (as an account of an event) for a newspaper or a broadcast **4** : to make a charge of misconduct against **5** : to present oneself (as for work) **6** : to make known to the authorities ⟨~ a fire⟩ **7** : to return or present (as a matter referred to a committee) with conclusions and recommendations **8** : to work as a subordinate ⟨~*s* to the vice president⟩ — **re·port·able** *adj*

re·port·age \ri-ˈpȯr-tij, *esp for 2* ˌre-pər-ˈtäzh, ˌre-ˌpȯr-ˈ\ *n* [F] **1** : the act or process of reporting news **2** : writing intended to give an account of observed or documented events

report card *n* : a periodic report on a student's grades

re·port·ed·ly \ri-ˈpȯr-təd-lē\ *adv* : according to report ⟨is ~ about to be fired⟩

re·port·er \ri-ˈpȯr-tər\ *n* : one that reports; *esp* : a person who gathers and reports news for a news medium — **re·por·to·ri·al** \ˌre-pər-ˈtȯr-ē-əl\ *adj*

[1]**re·pose** \ri-ˈpōz\ *vb* **re·posed; re·pos·ing** **1** : to lay at rest **2** : to lie at rest **3** : to lie dead **4** : to take a rest **5** : to rest for support : LIE

[2]**repose** *n* **1** : a state of resting (as after exertion); *esp* : SLEEP **2** : eternal or heavenly rest **3** : CALM, PEACE ⟨the ~ of the bayous⟩ **4** : cessation or absence of activity, movement, or animation **5** : POISE, COMPOSURE — **re·pose·ful** *adj*

[3]**repose** *vb* **re·posed; re·pos·ing** **1** : to place (as trust) in someone or something **2** : to place for control, management, or use

re·pos·i·to·ry \ri-ˈpä-zə-ˌtȯr-ē\ *n, pl* **-ries** **1** : a place where something is deposited or stored **2** : a person to whom something is entrusted

re·pos·sess \ˌrē-pə-ˈzes\ *vb* **1** : to regain possession of **2** : to take possession of in default of the payment of installments due — **re·pos·ses·sion** \-ˈze-shən\ *n*

re·post \(ˌ)rē-ˈpōst\ *vb* : to post again ⟨~ a message⟩

rep·re·hend \ˌre-pri-ˈhend\ *vb* : to express disapproval of : CENSURE ♦ ***Synonyms*** CRITICIZE, CONDEMN, DENOUNCE, BLAME, PAN — **rep·re·hen·sion** \-ˈhen-chən\ *n*

rep·re·hen·si·ble \-ˈhen-sə-bəl\ *adj* : deserving blame or censure : CULPABLE — **rep·re·hen·si·bly** \-blē\ *adv*

rep·re·sent \ˌre-pri-ˈzent\ *vb* **1** : to present a picture or a likeness of : PORTRAY, DEPICT **2** : to serve as a sign or symbol of **3** : to act the role of **4** : to stand in the place of : act or speak for; *also* : to manage the legal and business affairs of **5** : to be a member or example of : TYPIFY **6** : to serve as an elected representative of **7** : to describe as having a specified quality or character **8** : to state with the purpose of affecting judgment or action

rep·re·sen·ta·tion \ˌre-pri-ˌzen-ˈtā-shən\ *n* **1** : the act of representing **2** : one (as a picture or image) that represents something else **3** : the state of being represented in a legislative body; *also* : the body of persons representing a constituency **4** : a usu. formal statement made to effect a change

[1]**rep·re·sen·ta·tive** \ˌre-pri-ˈzen-tə-tiv\ *adj* **1** : serving to represent **2** : standing or acting for another **3** : founded on the principle of representation : carried on by elected representatives ⟨~ government⟩ — **rep·re·sen·ta·tive·ly** *adv* — **rep·re·sen·ta·tive·ness** *n*

[2]**representative** *n* **1** : one that represents another; *esp* : one representing a district in a legislative body usu. as a member of a lower house **2** : a typical example of a group, class, or quality

re·press \ri-ˈpres\ *vb* **1** : CURB, SUBDUE **2** : RESTRAIN, SUPPRESS **3** : to exclude from consciousness ⟨~ a painful memory⟩ — **re·pres·sion** \-ˈpre-shən\ *n* — **re·pres·sive** \-ˈpre-siv\ *adj*

[1]**re·prieve** \ri-ˈprēv\ *vb* **re·prieved; re·priev·ing** **1** : to delay the punishment or execution of **2** : to give temporary relief to

[2]**reprieve** *n* **1** : the act of reprieving : the state of being reprieved **2** : a formal temporary suspension of a sentence esp. of death **3** : a temporary respite

[1]**rep·ri·mand** \ˈre-prə-ˌmand\ *n* : a severe or formal reproof

[2]**reprimand** *vb* : to reprove severely or formally ⟨~*ed* the sergeant⟩

[1]**re·print** \(ˌ)rē-ˈprint\ *vb* : to print again

[2]**re·print** \ˈrē-ˌprint\ *n* : a reproduction of printed matter

re·pri·sal \ri-ˈprī-zəl\ *n* : an act in retaliation for something done by another

re·prise \ri-ˈprēz\ *n* : a recurrence, renewal, or resumption of an action; *also* : a musical repetition

[1]**re·proach** \ri-ˈprōch\ *n* **1** : an expression of disapproval **2** : DISGRACE, DISCREDIT **3** : the act of reproaching : REBUKE **4** : a cause or occasion of blame or disgrace — **re·proach·ful** \-fəl\ *adj* — **re·proach·ful·ly** *adv* — **re·proach·ful·ness** *n*

[2]**reproach** *vb* **1** : CENSURE, REBUKE **2** : to cast discredit on ♦ ***Synonyms*** CHIDE, ADMONISH, REPROVE, REPRIMAND — **re·proach·able** *adj*

rep·ro·bate \ˈre-prə-ˌbāt\ *n* **1** : a person

foreordained to damnation **2** : a thoroughly bad person : SCOUNDREL — **rep·robate** *adj*

rep·ro·ba·tion \ˌre-prə-ˈbā-shən\ *n* : strong disapproval : CONDEMNATION

re·pro·duce \ˌrē-prə-ˈdüs, -ˈdyüs\ *vb* **1** : to produce again or anew **2** : to produce offspring — **re·pro·duc·ible** \-ˈdü-sə-bəl, -ˈdyü-\ *adj* — **re·pro·duc·tion** \-ˈdək-shən\ *n* — **re·pro·duc·tive** \-ˈdək-tiv\ *adj*

re·proof \ri-ˈprüf\ *n* : blame or censure for a fault

re·prove \ri-ˈprüv\ *vb* **re·proved; re·prov·ing** **1** : to administer a rebuke to **2** : to express disapproval of ♦ ***Synonyms*** REPRIMAND, ADMONISH, REPROACH, CHIDE — **re·prov·er** *n*

rept *abbr* report

rep·tile \ˈrep-tī(-ə)l, -tᵊl\ *n* [ME *reptil,* fr. MF or LL; MF *reptile,* fr. LL *reptile,* fr. L *repere* to crawl] : any of a large class of air-breathing scaly vertebrates including snakes, lizards, alligators, turtles, and extinct related forms (as dinosaurs) — **rep·til·i·an** \rep-ˈti-lē-ən\ *adj or n*

re·pub·lic \ri-ˈpə-blik\ *n* [F *république,* fr. MF *republique,* fr. L *respublica,* fr. *res* thing, wealth + *publica,* fem. of *publicus* public] **1** : a government having a chief of state who is not a monarch and is usu. a president; *also* : a nation or other political unit having such a government **2** : a government in which supreme power is held by the citizens entitled to vote and is exercised by elected officers and representatives governing according to law; *also* : a nation or other political unit having such a form of government **3** : a constituent political and territorial unit of the former nations of Czechoslovakia, the U.S.S.R., or Yugoslavia

¹**re·pub·li·can** \-bli-kən\ *n* **1** : one that favors or supports a republican form of government **2** *cap* : a member of a republican party and esp. of the Republican party of the U.S.

²**republican** *adj* **1** : of, relating to, or resembling a republic **2** : favoring or supporting a republic **3** *cap* : of, relating to, or constituting one of the two major political parties in the U.S. evolving in the mid-19th century — **re·pub·li·can·ism** *n, often cap*

re·pu·di·ate \ri-ˈpyü-dē-ˌāt\ *vb* **-at·ed; -at·ing** [L *repudiare* to cast off, divorce, fr. *repudium* rejection of a prospective spouse, divorce] **1** : to cast off : DISOWN **2** : to refuse to have anything to do with : refuse to acknowledge, accept, or pay ⟨~ a charge⟩ ⟨~ a debt⟩ ♦ ***Synonyms*** SPURN, REJECT, DECLINE — **re·pu·di·a·tion** \-ˌpyü-dē-ˈā-shən\ *n* — **re·pu·di·a·tor** \-ˈpyü-dē-ˌā-tər\ *n*

re·pug·nance \ri-ˈpəg-nəns\ *n* **1** : the quality or fact of being contradictory or inconsistent **2** : strong dislike, distaste, or antagonism

re·pug·nant \-nənt\ *adj* **1** : marked by repugnance **2** : contrary to a person's tastes or principles : exciting distaste or aversion ♦ ***Synonyms*** REPELLENT, ABHORRENT, DISTASTEFUL, OBNOXIOUS, REVOLTING, LOATHSOME — **re·pug·nant·ly** *adv*

¹**re·pulse** \ri-ˈpəls\ *vb* **re·pulsed; re·puls·ing** **1** : to drive or beat back : REPEL **2** : to repel by discourtesy or denial : REBUFF **3** : to cause a feeling of repulsion in : DISGUST ⟨*repulsed* by the violence⟩

²**repulse** *n* **1** : REBUFF, REJECTION **2** : the action of repelling an attacker : the fact of being repelled

re·pul·sion \ri-ˈpəl-shən\ *n* **1** : the action of repulsing : the state of being repulsed **2** : the force with which bodies, particles, or like forces repel one another **3** : a feeling of aversion

re·pul·sive \-siv\ *adj* **1** : serving or tending to repel or reject **2** : arousing aversion or disgust ♦ ***Synonyms*** REPUGNANT, REVOLTING, LOATHSOME, NOISOME — **re·pul·sive·ly** *adv* — **re·pul·sive·ness** *n*

re·pur·pose \(ˌ)rē-ˈpər-pəs\ *vb* : to give a new purpose or use to

rep·u·ta·ble \ˈre-pyə-tə-bəl\ *adj* : having a good reputation : ESTIMABLE ⟨a ~ lawyer⟩ — **rep·u·ta·bly** \-blē\ *adv*

rep·u·ta·tion \ˌre-pyü-ˈtā-shən\ *n* **1** : overall quality or character as seen or judged by people in general **2** : place in public esteem or regard

¹**re·pute** \ri-ˈpyüt\ *vb* **re·put·ed; re·put·ing** : BELIEVE, CONSIDER ⟨*reputed* to be a millionaire⟩

²**repute** *n* **1** : REPUTATION ⟨knew her by ~⟩ **2** : the state of being favorably known or spoken of

re·put·ed \ri-ˈpyü-təd\ *adj* **1** : REPUTABLE **2** : according to reputation : SUPPOSED — **re·put·ed·ly** *adv*

req *abbr* **1** request **2** require; required **3** requisition

¹**re·quest** \ri-ˈkwest\ *n* **1** : an act or instance of asking for something **2** : a thing asked for **3** : the condition of being asked for ⟨available on ~⟩

²**request** *vb* **1** : to make a request to or of **2** : to ask for — **re·quest·er** *or* **re·quest·or** *n*

re·qui·em \ˈre-kwē-əm, ˈrā-\ *n* [ME, fr. L (first word of the requiem mass), accusative of *requies* rest, fr. *quies* quiet, rest] **1** : a mass for a dead person; *also* : a musical setting for this **2** : a musical service or hymn in honor of the dead

re·quire \ri-ˈkwī(-ə)r\ *vb* **re·quired; re·quir·ing** **1** : to demand as necessary or essential **2** : COMMAND, ORDER ⟨the law ~*s* that everyone pay the tax⟩

re·quire·ment \-mənt\ *n* **1** : something (as a condition or quality) required ⟨entrance ~*s*⟩ **2** : NECESSITY ⟨production was sufficient to satisfy military ~*s*⟩

req·ui·site \ˈre-kwə-zət\ *adj* : REQUIRED, NECESSARY — **requisite** *n*

req·ui·si·tion \ˌre-kwə-ˈzi-shən\ *n* **1**

: formal application or demand (as for supplies) **2** : the state of being in demand or use — **requisition** *vb*

re·quite \ri-ˈkwīt\ *vb* **re·quit·ed; re·quit·ing** **1** : to make return for : REPAY **2** : to make retaliation for : AVENGE **3** : to make return to — **re·quit·al** \-ˈkwī-tᵊl\ *n*

rere·dos \ˈrer-ə-ˌdäs\ *n* : a usu. ornamental wood or stone screen or partition wall behind an altar

re·run \ˈrē-ˌrən, (ˌ)rē-ˈrən\ *n* : the act or an instance of running again or anew; *esp* : a showing of a motion picture or television program after its first run — **re·run** \(ˌ)rē-ˈrən\ *vb*

res *abbr* **1** research **2** reservation; reserve **3** reservoir **4** residence; resident **5** resolution

re·sale \ˈrē-ˌsāl, (ˌ)rē-ˈsāl\ *n* : the act of selling again usu. to a new party — **re·sal·able** \(ˌ)rē-ˈsā-lə-bəl\ *adj*

re·scind \ri-ˈsind\ *vb* : REPEAL, CANCEL, ANNUL — **re·scis·sion** \-ˈsi-zhən\ *n*

re·script \ˈrē-ˌskript\ *n* : an official or authoritative order or decree

res·cue \ˈres-kyü\ *vb* **res·cued; res·cu·ing** [ME *rescouen, rescuen,* fr. AF *rescure,* fr. *re-* back, again + *escure* to shake off, fr. L *excutere*] : to free from danger, harm, or confinement — **rescue** *n* — **res·cu·er** *n*

re·search \ri-ˈsərch, ˈrē-ˌsərch\ *n* **1** : careful or diligent search **2** : studious inquiry or examination aimed at the discovery and interpretation of new knowledge **3** : the collecting of information about a particular subject — **research** *vb* — **re·search·er** *n*

re·sec·tion \ri-ˈsek-shən\ *n* : the surgical removal of part of an organ or structure

re·sem·blance \ri-ˈzem-bləns\ *n* : the quality or state of resembling

re·sem·ble \ri-ˈzem-bəl\ *vb* **-bled; -bling** : to be like or similar to

re·sent \ri-ˈzent\ *vb* : to feel or exhibit annoyance or indignation at ⟨*~ed* his interference⟩ — **re·sent·ful** \-fəl\ *adj* — **re·sent·ful·ly** *adv* — **re·sent·ment** *n*

re·ser·pine \ri-ˈsər-ˌpēn, -pən\ *n* : a drug used in treating high blood pressure and nervous tension

res·er·va·tion \ˌre-zər-ˈvā-shən\ *n* **1** : an act of reserving **2** : something (as a room in a hotel) arranged for in advance **3** : something reserved; *esp* : a tract of public land set aside for special use **4** : a limiting condition

¹re·serve \ri-ˈzərv\ *vb* **re·served; re·serv·ing** **1** : to store for future or special use **2** : to hold back for oneself **3** : to set aside or arrange to have set aside or held for special use

²reserve *n* **1** : something reserved : STOCK, STORE **2** : a military force withheld from action for later use — usu. used in pl. **3** : the military forces of a country not part of the regular services; *also* : RESERVIST **4** : a tract set apart : RESERVATION **5** : an act of reserving **6** : restraint or caution in one's words or bearing **7** : money or its equivalent kept in hand or set apart to meet liabilities

re·served \ri-ˈzərvd\ *adj* **1** : restrained in words and actions **2** : set aside for future or special use — **re·serv·ed·ly** \-ˈzər-vəd-lē\ *adv* — **re·serv·ed·ness** \-vəd-nəs\ *n*

re·serv·ist \ri-ˈzər-vist\ *n* : a member of a military reserve

res·er·voir \ˈre-zə-ˌvwär, -zər-, -ˌvwȯr\ *n* [F] : a place where something is kept in store; *esp* : an artificial lake where water is collected and kept for use

re·shuf·fle \rē-ˈshə-fəl\ *vb* **1** : to shuffle again **2** : to reorganize usu. by redistribution of existing elements ⟨*reshuffled* our schedule⟩ — **reshuffle** *n*

re·side \ri-ˈzīd\ *vb* **re·sid·ed; re·sid·ing** **1** : to make one's home : DWELL **2** : to be present as a quality or vested as a right

res·i·dence \ˈre-zə-dəns\ *n* **1** : the act or fact of residing in a place as a dweller or in discharge of a duty or an obligation **2** : the place where one actually lives **3** : a building used as a home : DWELLING **4** : the period of living in a place

res·i·den·cy \ˈre-zə-dən-sē\ *n, pl* **-cies** **1** : the residence of or the territory under a diplomatic resident **2** : a period of advanced training in a medical specialty

¹res·i·dent \-dənt\ *adj* **1** : RESIDING **2** : being in residence **3** : not migratory

²resident *n* **1** : one who resides in a place **2** : a diplomatic representative with governing powers (as in a protectorate) **3** : a physician serving a residency

res·i·den·tial \ˌre-zə-ˈden-chəl\ *adj* **1** : used as a residence or by residents **2** : occupied by or restricted to residences — **res·i·den·tial·ly** *adv*

¹re·sid·u·al \ri-ˈzi-jə-wəl\ *n* **1** : a residual product or substance **2** : a payment (as to an actor or writer) for each rerun after an initial showing (as of a taped TV show)

²residual *adj* : being a residue or remainder

re·sid·u·ary \ri-ˈzi-jə-ˌwer-ē\ *adj* : of, relating to, or constituting a residue esp. of an estate

res·i·due \ˈre-zə-ˌdü, -ˌdyü\ *n* : a part remaining after another part has been taken away : REMAINDER

re·sid·u·um \ri-ˈzi-jə-wəm\ *n, pl* **re·sid·ua** \-jə-wə\ [L] **1** : something remaining or residual after certain deductions are made **2** : a residual product

re·sign \ri-ˈzīn\ *vb* [ME, fr. AF *resigner,* fr. L *resignare,* lit., to unseal, cancel, fr. *signare* to sign, seal] **1** : to give up deliberately (as one's position) esp. by a formal act **2** : to give (oneself) over (as to grief or despair) without resistance — **re·sign·ed·ly** \-ˈzī-nəd-lē\ *adv*

---

reradiate	**rerecord**	**rescore**	**reseed**
reread	**reroute**	**rescreen**	**resell**
rereading	**reschedule**	**reseal**	**reset**

re–sign \(ˌ)rē-ˈsīn\ *vb* : to sign again
res·ig·na·tion \ˌre-zig-ˈnā-shən\ *n* **1** : an act or instance of resigning; *also* : a formal notification of such an act **2** : the quality or state of being resigned
re·sil·ience \ri-ˈzil-yəns\ *n* **1** : the ability of a body to regain its original size and shape after being compressed, bent, or stretched **2** : an ability to recover from or adjust easily to change or misfortune
re·sil·ien·cy \-yən-sē\ *n* : RESILIENCE
re·sil·ient \-yənt\ *adj* : marked by resilience ⟨~ players⟩
res·in \ˈre-zᵊn\ *n* : any of various substances obtained from the gum or sap of some trees and used esp. in varnishes, plastics, and medicine; *also* : a comparable synthetic product — **res·in·ous** *adj*
1**re·sist** \ri-ˈzist\ *vb* **1** : to fight against : OPPOSE ⟨~ aggression⟩ **2** : to withstand the force or effect of ⟨~*ed* temptation⟩ ⟨~ disease⟩ ♦ ***Synonyms*** COMBAT, REPEL — **re·sist·ible** \-ˈzis-tə-bəl\ *adj* — **re·sist·less** *adj*
2**resist** *n* : something (as a coating) that resists or prevents a particular action
re·sis·tance \ri-ˈzis-təns\ *n* **1** : the act or an instance of resisting : OPPOSITION **2** : the power or capacity to resist; *esp* : the inherent ability of an organism to resist harmful influences (as disease or infection) **3** : the opposition offered by a body to the passage through it of a steady electric current
re·sis·tant \-tənt\ *adj* : giving, capable of, or exhibiting resistance
re·sis·tor \ri-ˈzis-tər\ *n* : a device used to provide resistance to the flow of an electric current in a circuit
res·o·lute \ˈre-zə-ˌlüt\ *adj* : firmly determined in purpose : RESOLVED ⟨a ~ leader⟩ ♦ ***Synonyms*** STEADFAST, STAUNCH, FAITHFUL, TRUE, LOYAL — **res·o·lute·ly** *adv* — **res·o·lute·ness** *n*
res·o·lu·tion \ˌre-zə-ˈlü-shən\ *n* **1** : the act or process of resolving **2** : the action of solving; *also* : SOLUTION **3** : the quality of being resolute : FIRMNESS, DETERMINATION **4** : a formal statement expressing the opinion, will, or intent of a body of persons **5** : a measure of the sharpness of an image or of the fineness with which a device can produce or record such an image
1**re·solve** \ri-ˈzälv\ *vb* **re·solved; re·solv·ing** **1** : to break up into constituent parts : ANALYZE **2** : to distinguish between or make visible adjacent parts of **3** : to find an answer to : SOLVE ⟨~ a dispute⟩ **4** : DETERMINE, DECIDE **5** : to make or pass a formal resolution — **re·solv·able** *adj*
2**resolve** *n* **1** : fixity of purpose **2** : something resolved
res·o·nance \ˈre-zə-nəns\ *n* **1** : the quality or state of being resonant **2** : a reinforcement of sound in a vibrating body caused by waves from another body vibrating at nearly the same rate
res·o·nant \-nənt\ *adj* **1** : continuing to sound : RESOUNDING **2** : relating to or exhibiting resonance **3** : intensified and enriched by or as if by resonance — **res·o·nant·ly** *adv*
res·o·nate \-ˌnāt\ *vb* **-nat·ed; -nat·ing** **1** : to produce or exhibit resonance **2** : REVERBERATE, RESOUND **3** : to relate harmoniously ⟨~ with voters⟩
res·o·na·tor \-ˌnā-tər\ *n* : something that resounds or exhibits resonance
re·sorp·tion \rē-ˈsȯrp-shən, -ˈzȯrp-\ *n* : the action or process of breaking down and assimilating something (as a tooth or an embryo)
1**re·sort** \ri-ˈzȯrt\ *n* [ME, return, source of aid, fr. AF, fr. *resortir* to rebound, resort, fr. *sortir* to go out, leave] **1** : one looked to for help : REFUGE **2** : RECOURSE **3** : frequent or general visiting ⟨place of ~⟩ **4** : a frequently visited place : HAUNT **5** : a place providing recreation esp. to vacationers
2**resort** *vb* **1** : to go often or habitually **2** : to have recourse ⟨~*ed* to violence⟩
re·sound \ri-ˈzau̇nd\ *vb* **1** : to become filled with sound : REVERBERATE, RING **2** : to sound loudly
re·sound·ing *adj* **1** : RESONATING, RESONANT **2** : impressively sonorous ⟨~ name⟩ **3** : EMPHATIC, UNEQUIVOCAL ⟨a ~ success⟩ — **re·sound·ing·ly** *adv*
re·source \ˈrē-ˌsȯrs, ri-ˈsȯrs\ *n* [F *ressource,* fr. OF *ressourse* relief, resource, fr. *resourdre* to relieve, lit., to rise again, fr. L *resurgere,* fr. *re-* again + *surgere* to rise] **1** : a source of supply or support — usu. used in pl. **2** : a natural feature or phenomenon that enhances the quality of human life **3** *pl* : available funds **4** : a possibility of relief or recovery **5** : a means of spending leisure time **6** : ability to meet and handle situations — **re·source·ful** \ri-ˈsȯrs-fəl\ *adj* — **re·source·ful·ness** *n*
1**re·spect** \ri-ˈspekt\ *n* **1** : relation to something usu. specified : REGARD ⟨in ~ to⟩ **2** : high or special regard : ESTEEM **3** *pl* : an expression of respect or deference **4** : DETAIL, PARTICULAR — **re·spect·ful** \-fəl\ *adj* — **re·spect·ful·ly** *adv* — **re·spect·ful·ness** *n*
2**respect** *vb* **1** : to consider deserving of high regard : ESTEEM **2** : to refrain from interfering with ⟨~ another's privacy⟩ **3** : to have reference to : CONCERN — **re·spect·er** *n*
re·spect·able \ri-ˈspek-tə-bəl\ *adj* **1** : worthy of respect : ESTIMABLE **2** : decent or correct in conduct : PROPER **3** : fair in size, quantity, or quality ⟨a ~ score⟩ : MODERATE, TOLERABLE **4** : fit to be seen : PRESENTABLE — **re·spect·a·bil·i·ty** \-ˌspek-tə-ˈbi-lə-tē\ *n* — **re·spect·ably** \-ˈspek-tə-blē\ *adv*
re·spect·ing *prep* : with regard to
re·spec·tive \-tiv\ *adj* : PARTICULAR, SEPARATE ⟨returned to their ~ homes⟩

---

resettle
resettlement
resew
reshow
resocialization
resow

re·spec·tive·ly \-lē\ *adv* **1** : as relating to each **2** : each in the order given
res·pi·ra·tion \ˌres-pə-ˈrā-shən\ *n* **1** : an act or the process of breathing **2** : the physical and chemical processes (as breathing and oxidation) by which a living thing obtains oxygen and eliminates waste gases (as carbon dioxide) — **re·spi·ra·to·ry** \ˈres-pə-rə-ˌtȯr-ē, ri-ˈspī-rə-\ *adj* — **re·spire** \ri-ˈspī(-ə)r\ *vb*
res·pi·ra·tor \ˈres-pə-ˌrā-tər\ *n* **1** : a device covering the mouth and nose esp. to prevent inhaling harmful substances **2** : a device for artificial respiration
re·spite \ˈres-pət\ *n* [ME *respit,* fr. AF, fr. ML *respectus,* fr. L, act of looking back] **1** : a temporary delay **2** : an interval of rest or relief
re·splen·dent \ri-ˈsplen-dənt\ *adj* : shining brilliantly : gloriously bright : SPLENDID ⟨~ uniforms⟩ — **re·splen·dence** \-dəns\ *n* — **re·splen·dent·ly** *adv*
re·spond \ri-ˈspänd\ *vb* **1** : ANSWER, REPLY **2** : REACT ⟨~*ed* to a call for help⟩ **3** : to show favorable reaction ⟨~ to medication⟩ — **re·spond·er** *n*
re·spon·dent \ri-ˈspän-dənt\ *n* : one who responds; *esp* : one who answers in various legal proceedings — **respondent** *adj*
re·sponse \ri-ˈspäns\ *n* **1** : an act of responding **2** : something constituting a reply or a reaction
re·spon·si·bil·i·ty \ri-ˌspän-sə-ˈbi-lə-tē\ *n, pl* **-ties** **1** : the quality or state of being responsible **2** : something for which one is responsible
re·spon·si·ble \ri-ˈspän-sə-bəl\ *adj* **1** : liable to be called upon to answer for one's acts or decisions : ANSWERABLE **2** : able to fulfill one's obligations : RELIABLE, TRUSTWORTHY **3** : able to choose for oneself between right and wrong **4** : involving accountability or important duties ⟨~ position⟩ — **re·spon·si·ble·ness** *n* — **re·spon·si·bly** \-blē\ *adv*
re·spon·sive \-siv\ *adj* **1** : RESPONDING **2** : quick to respond : SENSITIVE **3** : using responses ⟨~ readings⟩ — **re·spon·sive·ly** *adv* — **re·spon·sive·ness** *n*
[1]**rest** \ˈrest\ *n* **1** : REPOSE, SLEEP **2** : freedom from work or activity **3** : a state of motionlessness or inactivity **4** : a place of shelter or lodging **5** : a silence in music equivalent in duration to a note of the same value; *also* : a character indicating this **6** : something used as a support — **rest·ful** \-fəl\ *adj* — **rest·ful·ly** *adv*
[2]**rest** *vb* **1** : to get rest by lying down; *esp* : SLEEP **2** : to cease from action or motion **3** : to give rest to : set at rest **4** : to sit or lie fixed or supported **5** : to place on or against a support **6** : to remain based or founded **7** : to cause to be firmly fixed : GROUND **8** : to remain for action : DEPEND
[3]**rest** *n* : something left over
res·tau·rant \ˈres-trənt, -tə-ˌränt\ *n* [F, fr. prp. of *restaurer* to restore, fr. L *restaurare*] : a public eating place
res·tau·ra·teur \ˌres-tə-rə-ˈtər\ *also* **res·tau·ran·teur** \-ˌrän-\ *n* : the operator or proprietor of a restaurant
rest home *n* : an establishment that gives care for the aged or convalescent
res·ti·tu·tion \ˌres-tə-ˈtü-shən, -ˈtyü-\ *n* : the act of restoring : the state of being restored; *esp* : restoration of something to its rightful owner ♦ ***Synonyms*** AMENDS, REDRESS, REPARATION, INDEMNITY, COMPENSATION
res·tive \ˈres-tiv\ *adj* [ME *restyf,* fr. AF *restif,* fr. *rester* to stop, resist, remain, fr. L *restare,* fr. *re-* back + *stare* to stand] **1** : BALKY **2** : UNEASY, FIDGETY ♦ ***Synonyms*** RESTLESS, IMPATIENT, NERVOUS — **res·tive·ly** *adv* — **res·tive·ness** *n*
rest·less \ˈrest-ləs\ *adj* **1** : lacking or denying rest ⟨a ~ night⟩ **2** : never resting or settled : always moving ⟨the ~ sea⟩ **3** : marked by or showing unrest esp. of mind ⟨~ pacing back and forth⟩ ♦ ***Synonyms*** RESTIVE, IMPATIENT, NERVOUS, FIDGETY — **rest·less·ly** *adv* — **rest·less·ness** *n*
re·stor·able \ri-ˈstȯr-ə-bəl\ *adj* : fit for restoring or reclaiming
res·to·ra·tion \ˌres-tə-ˈrā-shən\ *n* **1** : an act of restoring : the state of being restored **2** : something (as a building) that has been restored
re·stor·ative \ri-ˈstȯr-ə-tiv\ *n* : something that restores esp. to consciousness or health — **restorative** *adj*
re·store \ri-ˈstȯr\ *vb* **re·stored; re·stor·ing** **1** : to give back : RETURN **2** : to put back into use or service **3** : to put or bring back into a former or original state **4** : to put again in possession of something — **re·stor·er** *n*
re·strain \ri-ˈstrān\ *vb* **1** : to prevent from doing something **2** : to limit, restrict, or keep under control : CURB **3** : to place under restraint or arrest — **re·strain·able** *adj* — **re·strain·er** *n*
re·strained \ri-ˈstrānd\ *adj* : marked by restraint : DISCIPLINED — **re·strain·ed·ly** \-ˈstrā-nəd-lē\ *adv*
restraining order *n* : a legal order directing one person to stay away from another
re·straint \ri-ˈstrānt\ *n* **1** : an act of restraining : the state of being restrained **2** : a restraining force, agency, or device **3** : deprivation or limitation of liberty : CONFINEMENT **4** : control over one's feelings : RESERVE
re·strict \ri-ˈstrikt\ *vb* **1** : to confine within bounds : LIMIT **2** : to place under restriction as to use — **re·stric·tive** *adj* — **re·stric·tive·ly** *adv*
re·stric·tion \ri-ˈstrik-shən\ *n* **1** : something (as a law or rule) that restricts **2** : an act of restricting : the state of being restricted

---

respell
restaff
restart
restate
restatement
restock
restrengthen
restructure
restudy
restuff
restyle

rest room *n* : a room or suite of rooms that includes sinks and toilets

[1]**re·sult** \ri-ˈzəlt\ *vb* [ME, fr. ML *resultare,* fr. L, to rebound, fr. *re-* re- + *saltare* to leap] : to come about as an effect or consequence ⟨an injury ~*ing* from a fall⟩ — **re·sul·tant** \-ˈzəl-tᵊnt\ *adj or n*

[2]**result** *n* **1** : something that results : EFFECT, CONSEQUENCE **2** : beneficial or discernible effect **3** : something obtained by calculation or investigation

re·sume \ri-ˈzüm\ *vb* **re·sumed; re·sum·ing** **1** : to take or assume again **2** : to return to or begin again after interruption **3** : to take back to oneself — **re·sump·tion** \-ˈzəmp-shən\ *n*

ré·su·mé *or* **re·su·me** *or* **re·su·mé** \ˈre-zə-ˌmā, ˌre-zə-ˈmā\ *n* [F *résumé*] **1** : SUMMARY; *esp* : a short account of one's career and qualifications usu. prepared by a job applicant **2** : a set of accomplishments ⟨a musical ~⟩

re·sur·gence \ri-ˈsər-jəns\ *n* : a rising again into life, activity, or prominence — **re·sur·gent** \-jənt\ *adj*

res·ur·rect \ˌre-zə-ˈrekt\ *vb* **1** : to raise from the dead **2** : to bring to attention or use again

res·ur·rec·tion \ˌre-zə-ˈrek-shən\ *n* **1** *cap* : the rising of Christ from the dead **2** *often cap* : the rising to life of all human dead before the final judgment **3** : REVIVAL ⟨the ~ of her career⟩

re·sus·ci·tate \ri-ˈsə-sə-ˌtāt\ *vb* **-tat·ed; -tat·ing** : to revive from apparent death or unconsciousness; *also* : REVITALIZE — **re·sus·ci·ta·tion** \ri-ˌsə-sə-ˈtā-shən, ˌrē-\ *n* — **re·sus·ci·ta·tor** \ri-ˈsə-sə-ˌtā-tər\ *n*

ret *abbr* retired

[1]**re·tail** \ˈrē-ˌtāl, *esp for 2 also* ri-ˈtāl\ *vb* **1** : to sell in small quantities directly to the ultimate consumer **2** : to tell in detail or to one person after another — **re·tail·er** *n*

[2]**re·tail** \ˈrē-ˌtāl\ *n* : the sale of goods in small amounts to ultimate consumers — **retail** *adj or adv*

re·tain \ri-ˈtān\ *vb* **1** : to hold in possession or use **2** : to engage (as a lawyer) by paying a fee in advance **3** : to keep in a fixed place or position ♦ ***Synonyms*** DETAIN, WITHHOLD, RESERVE

[1]**re·tain·er** \ri-ˈtā-nər\ *n* **1** : one that retains **2** : a servant in a wealthy household; *also* : EMPLOYEE **3** : a device that holds something (as teeth) in place

[2]**retainer** *n* : a fee paid to secure services (as of a lawyer)

[1]**re·take** \(ˌ)rē-ˈtāk\ *vb* **-took** \-ˈtu̇k\; **-tak·en** \-ˈtā-kən\; **-tak·ing** **1** : to take or seize again **2** : to photograph again

[2]**re·take** \ˈrē-ˌtāk\ *n* : a second photographing of a motion-picture scene

re·tal·i·ate \ri-ˈta-lē-ˌāt\ *vb* **-at·ed; -at·ing** : to return like for like; *esp* : to get revenge — **re·tal·i·a·tion** \-ˌta-lē-ˈā-shən\ *n* — **re·tal·ia·to·ry** \-ˈtal-yə-ˌtȯr-ē\ *adj*

re·tard \ri-ˈtärd\ *vb* : to hold back : delay the progress of ♦ ***Synonyms*** SLOW, SLACKEN, DETAIN — **re·tar·da·tion** \ˌrē-ˌtär-ˈdā-shən, ri-\ *n* — **re·tard·er** *n*

re·tar·dant \ri-ˈtär-dᵊnt\ *adj* : serving or tending to retard — **retardant** *n*

re·tard·ed *adj, dated, offensive* : affected by intellectual disability

retch \ˈrech\ *vb* : to try to vomit; *also* : VOMIT

re·ten·tion \ri-ˈten-chən\ *n* **1** : the act of retaining : the state of being retained **2** : the power of retaining esp. in the mind : RETENTIVENESS

re·ten·tive \-ˈten-tiv\ *adj* : having the power of retaining; *esp* : retaining knowledge easily — **re·ten·tive·ness** *n*

re·think \(ˌ)rē-ˈthiŋk\ *vb* **-thought** \-ˈthȯt\; **-think·ing** : to think about again : RECONSIDER

ret·i·cent \ˈre-tə-sənt\ *adj* **1** : tending not to talk or give out information **2** : RELUCTANT ♦ ***Synonyms*** RESERVED, TACITURN, CLOSEMOUTHED — **ret·i·cence** \-səns\ *n* — **ret·i·cent·ly** *adv*

ret·i·na \ˈre-tə-nə\ *n, pl* **retinas** *or* **ret·i·nae** \-ˌnē\ : the sensory membrane lining the eye that receives the image formed by the lens — **ret·i·nal** \ˈre-tə-nəl\ *adj*

ret·i·nue \ˈre-tə-ˌnü, -ˌnyü\ *n* : the body of attendants or followers of a distinguished person

re·tire \ri-ˈtī(-ə)r\ *vb* **re·tired; re·tir·ing** **1** : RETREAT **2** : to withdraw esp. for privacy **3** : to withdraw from one's occupation or position : conclude one's career **4** : to withdraw from use or service **5** : to go to bed **6** : to cause to be out in baseball — **re·tire·ment** *n*

re·tired \ri-ˈtī(-ə)rd\ *adj* **1** : SECLUDED, QUIET **2** : withdrawn from active duty or from one's career

re·tir·ee \ri-ˌtī-ˈrē\ *n* : a person who has retired from a career

re·tir·ing *adj* : SHY, RESERVED

re·tool \(ˌ)rē-ˈtül\ *vb* **1** : to reequip with tools **2** : to modify with usu. minor improvements ⟨~*ed* the team for next year⟩

[1]**re·tort** \ri-ˈtȯrt\ *vb* [L *retortus,* pp. of *retorquēre,* lit., to twist back, hurl back, fr. *re-* back + *torquēre* to twist] **1** : to say in reply : answer back usu. sharply **2** : to answer (an argument) by a counter argument **3** : RETALIATE

[2]**retort** *n* : a quick, witty, or cutting reply

[3]**re·tort** \ri-ˈtȯrt, ˈrē-ˌtȯrt\ *n* [MF *retorte,* fr. ML *retorta,* fr. L, fem. of *retortus,* pp. of *retorquēre* to twist back; fr. its shape] : a vessel in which substances are distilled or broken up by heat

re·touch \(ˌ)rē-ˈtəch\ *vb* : TOUCH UP; *esp* : to change (as a photographic negative) in order to produce a more desirable appearance

re·trace \(ˌ)rē-ˈtrās\ *vb* : to go over again

---

resubmit
resubscribe
resummon
resupply
resurface
resurvey
resynthesis
resynthesize
retarget
retaste
retell
retest

or in a reverse direction ⟨*retraced* his steps⟩

re·tract \ri-ˈtrakt\ *vb* **1** : to draw back or in **2** : to withdraw (as a charge or promise) : DISAVOW — **re·tract·able** *adj* — **re·trac·tion** \-ˈtrak-shən\ *n*

re·trac·tile \ri-ˈtrak-t^{ə}l, -ˈtrak-ˌtī(-ə)l\ *adj* : capable of being drawn back or in ⟨~ claws⟩

[1]**re·tread** \(ˌ)rē-ˈtred\ *vb* **re·tread·ed; re·tread·ing** : to put a new tread on (a worn tire)

[2]**re·tread** \ˈrē-ˌtred\ *n* **1** : a retreaded tire **2** : one pressed into service again; *also* : REMAKE

[1]**re·treat** \ri-ˈtrēt\ *n* **1** : an act of withdrawing esp. from something dangerous, difficult, or disagreeable **2** : a military signal for withdrawal; *also* : a military flag-lowering ceremony **3** : a place of privacy or safety : REFUGE **4** : a group withdrawal for prayer, meditation, or study

[2]**retreat** *vb* **1** : to make a retreat : WITHDRAW **2** : to slope backward

re·trench \ri-ˈtrench\ *vb* [obs. F *retrencher* (now *retrancher*), fr. MF *retrenchier,* fr. *re-* + *trenchier* to cut] **1** : to cut down or pare away : REDUCE, CURTAIL **2** : to cut down expenses : ECONOMIZE ⟨the company had to ~⟩ — **re·trench·ment** *n*

ret·ri·bu·tion \ˌre-trə-ˈbyü-shən\ *n* : something administered or exacted in recompense; *esp* : PUNISHMENT ♦ ***Synonyms*** REPRISAL, VENGEANCE, REVENGE, RETALIATION — **re·trib·u·tive** \ri-ˈtri-byə-tiv\ *adj* — **re·trib·u·to·ry** \-byə-ˌtȯr-ē\ *adj*

re·trieve \ri-ˈtrēv\ *vb* **re·trieved; re·triev·ing** **1** : to search about for and bring in (killed or wounded game) **2** : RECOVER, RESTORE — **re·triev·able** *adj* — **re·triev·al** \-ˈtrē-vəl\ *n*

re·triev·er \ri-ˈtrē-vər\ *n* : one that retrieves; *esp* : a dog of any of several breeds used esp. for retrieving game

ret·ro \ˈre-trō\ *adj* : relating to or being the styles and fashions of the past ⟨~ clothing⟩

ret·ro·ac·tive \ˌre-trō-ˈak-tiv\ *adj* : made effective as of a date prior to enactment ⟨a ~ pay raise⟩ — **ret·ro·ac·tive·ly** *adv*

ret·ro·fit \ˈre-trō-ˌfit, ˌre-trō-ˈfit\ *vb* **1** : to furnish (as an aircraft) with newly available equipment **2** : to adapt to a new purpose or need : MODIFY — **ret·ro·fit** \ˈre-trō-ˌfit\ *n*

[1]**ret·ro·grade** \ˈre-trə-ˌgrād\ *adj* **1** : moving or tending backward **2** : tending toward or resulting in a worse condition

[2]**retrograde** *vb* **1** : RETREAT **2** : DETERIORATE, DEGENERATE

ret·ro·gres·sion \ˌre-trə-ˈgre-shən\ *n* : return to a former and less complex level of development or organization — **ret·ro·gress** \ˌre-trə-ˈgres\ *vb* — **ret·ro·gres·sive** \ˌre-trə-ˈgre-siv\ *adj*

ret·ro–rock·et \ˈre-trō-ˌrä-kət\ *n* : an auxiliary rocket engine (as on a spacecraft) used to slow forward motion

ret·ro·spect \ˈre-trə-ˌspekt\ *n* : a review of past events — **ret·ro·spec·tion** \ˌre-trə-ˈspek-shən\ *n*

ret·ro·spec·tive \ˌre-trə-ˈspek-tiv\ *n* **1** : a comprehensive examination of an artist's work over many years **2** : REVIEW 4 ⟨a war ~⟩ — **retrospective** *adj* — **ret·ro·spec·tive·ly** *adv*

ret·ro·vi·rus \ˈre-trō-ˌvī-rəs\ *n* : any of a group of RNA-containing viruses (as HIV) that make DNA using RNA instead of the reverse — **re·tro·vi·ral** \-rəl\ *adj*

[1]**re·turn** \ri-ˈtərn\ *vb* **1** : to go or come back **2** : to pass, give, or send back to an earlier possessor **3** : to put back to or in a former place or state **4** : REPLY, ANSWER **5** : to report esp. officially **6** : to elect to office **7** : to bring in (as profit) : YIELD **8** : to give or perform in return ⟨~ a favor⟩ — **re·turn·er** *n*

[2]**return** *n* **1** : an act of coming or going back to or from a former place or state **2** : RECURRENCE **3** : a report of the results of balloting **4** : a formal statement of taxable income **5** : the profit from labor, investment, or business : YIELD **6** : the act of returning something **7** : something that returns or is returned; *also* : a means for conveying something (as water) back to its starting point **8** : something given in repayment or reciprocation; *also* : ANSWER, RETORT **9** : an answering play — **return** *adj*

[1]**re·turn·able** \ri-ˈtər-nə-bəl\ *adj* : capable of being returned (as for reuse); *also* : permitted to be returned

[2]**returnable** *n* : a returnable beverage container

re·turn·ee \ri-ˌtər-ˈnē\ *n* : one who returns

re·tweet \(ˌ)rē-ˈtwēt\ *vb* : to repost to the Twitter online message service ⟨fans ~*ed* her tweet⟩

re·union \rē-ˈyün-yən\ *n* **1** : an act of reuniting : the state of being reunited **2** : a meeting of persons after separation

[1]**rev** \ˈrev\ *n* : a revolution of a motor

[2]**rev** *vb* **revved; rev·ving** **1** : to increase the revolutions per minute of (a motor) **2** : STIMULATE, EXCITE

[3]**rev** *abbr* **1** revenue **2** reverse **3** review; reviewed **4** revised; revision **5** revolution

Rev *abbr* **1** Revelation **2** Reverend

re·vamp \(ˌ)rē-ˈvamp\ *vb* : RECONSTRUCT, REVISE; *also* : RENOVATE

re·vanche \rə-ˈvä^{n}sh\ *n* [F] : REVENGE; *esp* : a usu. political policy designed to recover lost territory or status

re·veal \ri-ˈvēl\ *vb* **1** : to make known **2** : to show plainly : open up to view

rev·eil·le \ˈre-və-lē\ *n* [modif. of F *réveillez,* imper. pl. of *réveiller* to awaken, fr. MF *eveiller* to awaken, fr. VL **exvigilare,* fr. L *vigilare* to keep watch, stay awake] : a military signal sounded at about sunrise

retrain **retransmission** **retransmit** **retrial**

[1]**rev·el** \ˈre-vəl\ *vb* **-eled** *or* **-elled; -el·ing** *or* **-el·ling** **1** : to take part in a revel **2** : to take great pleasure or satisfaction ⟨~*ed* in the quiet⟩ — **rev·el·er** *or* **rev·el·ler** *n* — **rev·el·ry** \-vəl-rē\ *n*

[2]**revel** *n* : a usu. wild party or celebration

rev·e·la·tion \ˌre-və-ˈlā-shən\ *n* **1** : an act of revealing **2** : something revealed; *esp* : an enlightening or astonishing disclosure

Revelation *n* — see BIBLE table

[1]**re·venge** \ri-ˈvenj\ *vb* **re·venged; re·veng·ing** : to inflict harm or injury in return for (a wrong) : AVENGE — **re·veng·er** *n*

[2]**revenge** *n* **1** : a desire for revenge **2** : an act or instance of retaliation to get even **3** : an opportunity for getting satisfaction ♦ ***Synonyms*** VENGEANCE, RETRIBUTION, REPRISAL — **re·venge·ful** *adj*

rev·e·nue \ˈre-və-ˌnü, -ˌnyü\ *n* [ME, return, revenue, fr. AF, fr. *revenir* to return, fr. L *revenire,* fr. *re-* back + *venire* to come] **1** : investment income **2** : money collected by a government (as through taxes)

re·verb \ri-ˈvərb, ˈrē-ˌvərb\ *n* : an electronically produced echo effect in recorded music; *also* : a device for producing reverb

re·ver·ber·ate \ri-ˈvər-bə-ˌrāt\ *vb* **-at·ed; -at·ing** **1** : REFLECT ⟨~ light or heat⟩ **2** : to resound in or as if in a series of echoes — **re·ver·ber·a·tion** \-ˌvər-bə-ˈrā-shən\ *n*

re·vere \ri-ˈvir\ *vb* **re·vered; re·ver·ing** : to show honor and devotion to : VENERATE ⟨a teacher *revered* by students⟩ ♦ ***Synonyms*** REVERENCE, WORSHIP, ADORE

[1]**rev·er·ence** \ˈre-vrəns, -və-rəns\ *n* **1** : honor or respect felt or shown **2** : a gesture (as a bow or curtsy) of respect

[2]**reverence** *vb* **-enced; -enc·ing** : to regard or treat with reverence

[1]**rev·er·end** \ˈre-vrənd, -və-rənd\ *adj* **1** : worthy of reverence : REVERED **2** : being a member of the clergy — used as a title

[2]**reverend** *n* : a member of the clergy

rev·er·ent \ˈre-vrənt, -və-rənt\ *adj* : expressing reverence — **rev·er·ent·ly** *adv*

rev·er·en·tial \ˌre-və-ˈren-chəl\ *adj* : REVERENT

rev·er·ie *also* **rev·ery** \ˈre-və-rē\ *n, pl* **-er·ies** [F *rêverie,* fr. MF, delirium, fr. *resver, rever* to wander, be delirious] **1** : DAYDREAM **2** : the state of being lost in thought

re·ver·sal \ri-ˈvər-səl\ *n* : an act or process of reversing

[1]**re·verse** \ri-ˈvərs\ *adj* **1** : opposite to a previous or normal condition ⟨in ~ order⟩ **2** : acting or working in a manner opposite the usual **3** : bringing about reverse movement ⟨~ gear⟩ — **re·verse·ly** *adv*

[2]**reverse** *vb* **re·versed; re·vers·ing** **1** : to turn upside down or completely about in position or direction **2** : to set aside or change (as a legal decision) **3** : to change to the contrary ⟨~ a policy⟩ **4** : to go or cause to go in the opposite direction **5** : to put (as a car) in reverse — **re·vers·ible** \-ˈvər-sə-bəl\ *adj*

[3]**reverse** *n* **1** : something contrary to something else : OPPOSITE **2** : an act or instance of reversing; *esp* : a change for the worse **3** : the back side of something (as a coin or card) **4** : a gear that reverses something

reverse engineer *vb* : to disassemble or analyze in detail in order to discover concepts involved in manufacture — **reverse engineering** *n*

re·ver·sion \ri-ˈvər-zhən\ *n* **1** : the right of succession or future possession (as to a title or property) **2** : return toward some former or ancestral condition; *also* : a product of this — **re·ver·sion·ary** \-zhə-ˌner-ē\ *adj*

re·vert \ri-ˈvərt\ *vb* **1** : to come or go back ⟨~*ed* to my old habits⟩ **2** : to return to a proprietor or his or her heirs **3** : to return to an ancestral type

[1]**re·view** \ri-ˈvyü\ *n* **1** : an act of revising **2** : a formal military inspection **3** : a general survey **4** : INSPECTION, EXAMINATION; *esp* : REEXAMINATION **5** : a critical evaluation (as of a book) **6** : a magazine devoted to reviews and essays **7** : a renewed study of previously studied material **8** : REVUE

[2]**re·view** \ri-ˈvyü, *1 also* ˈrē-\ *vb* **1** : to examine or study again; *esp* : to reexamine judicially **2** : to hold a review of ⟨~ troops⟩ **3** : to write a critical examination of ⟨~ a novel⟩ **4** : to look back over ⟨~*ed* her accomplishments⟩ **5** : to study material again

re·view·er \ri-ˈvyü-ər\ *n* : one that reviews; *esp* : a writer of critical reviews

re·vile \ri-ˈvī(-ə)l\ *vb* **re·viled; re·vil·ing** : to abuse verbally : rail at ♦ ***Synonyms*** VITUPERATE, BERATE, RATE, UPBRAID, SCOLD — **re·vile·ment** *n* — **re·vil·er** *n*

re·vise \ri-ˈvīz\ *vb* **re·vised; re·vis·ing** **1** : to look over something written in order to correct or improve ⟨~ an essay⟩ **2** : to make a new version of ⟨~ an almanac⟩ — **re·vis·able** *adj* — **re·vise** *n* — **re·vis·er** *or* **re·vi·sor** \-ˈvī-zər\ *n* — **re·vi·sion** \-ˈvi-zhən\ *n*

re·vi·tal·ise *Brit var of* REVITALIZE

re·vi·tal·ize \ˌrē-ˈvīt-tə-ˌlīz\ *vb* **-ized; -iz·ing** : to give new life or vigor to ⟨~ the shopping district⟩ — **re·vi·tal·i·za·tion** \(ˌ)rē-ˌvī-tə-lə-ˈzā-shən\ *n*

re·viv·al \ri-ˈvī-vəl\ *n* **1** : an act of reviving : the state of being revived **2** : a new publication or presentation (as of a book or play) **3** : an evangelistic meeting or series of meetings

re·vive \ri-ˈvīv\ *vb* **re·vived; re·viv·ing** **1**

---

reunification	**reusable**	**revaluate**	**revalue**
reunify	**reuse**	**revaluation**	**revisit**
reunite			

: to bring back to life, consciousness, or activity : make or become fresh or strong again **2** : to bring back into use ⟨*revived* an old tradition⟩ — **re·viv·er** *n*

re·viv·i·fy \rē-ˈvi-və-ˌfī\ *vb* : REVIVE — **re·viv·i·fi·ca·tion** \-ˌvi-və-fə-ˈkā-shən\ *n*

re·vo·ca·ble \ˈre-və-kə-bəl *also* ri-ˈvō-kə-bəl\ *adj* : capable of being revoked

re·vo·ca·tion \ˌre-və-ˈkā-shən\ *n* : an act or instance of revoking

re·voke \ri-ˈvōk\ *vb* **re·voked; re·vok·ing** **1** : to annul by recalling or taking back : REPEAL, RESCIND ⟨~ a license⟩ **2** : RENEGE 2 — **re·vok·er** *n*

¹re·volt \ri-ˈvōlt\ *vb* [MF *revolter,* fr. It *rivoltare* to overthrow, fr. VL **revolvitare,* fr. L *revolvere* to revolve, roll back] **1** : to throw off allegiance to a ruler or government : REBEL **2** : to experience disgust or shock **3** : to turn or cause to turn away with disgust or abhorrence ⟨violence ~*ed* her⟩ — **re·volt·er** *n*

²revolt *n* : REBELLION, INSURRECTION

re·volt·ing *adj* : extremely offensive ⟨a ~ odor⟩ — **re·volt·ing·ly** *adv*

rev·o·lu·tion \ˌre-və-ˈlü-shən\ *n* **1** : the action by a heavenly body of going round in an orbit **2** : ROTATION **3** : a sudden, radical, or complete change; *esp* : the overthrow or renunciation of one ruler or government and substitution of another by the governed

¹rev·o·lu·tion·ary \-shə-ˌner-ē\ *adj* **1** : of or relating to revolution **2** : tending to or promoting revolution **3** : constituting or bringing about a major change

²revolutionary *n, pl* **-ar·ies** : one who takes part in a revolution or who advocates revolutionary doctrines

rev·o·lu·tion·ise *Brit var of* REVOLUTIONIZE

rev·o·lu·tion·ist \ˌre-və-ˈlü-shə-nist\ *n* : REVOLUTIONARY — **revolutionist** *adj*

rev·o·lu·tion·ize \-ˌnīz\ *vb* **-ized; -iz·ing** : to change fundamentally or completely ⟨~ an industry⟩ — **rev·o·lu·tion·iz·er** *n*

re·volve \ri-ˈvälv\ *vb* **re·volved; re·volv·ing** **1** : to turn over in the mind : reflect upon : PONDER **2** : to move in an orbit; *also* : ROTATE **3** : to have a specified focus ⟨the debate *revolved* around taxes⟩ — **re·volv·able** *adj*

re·volv·er \ri-ˈväl-vər\ *n* : a pistol with a revolving cylinder of several chambers

re·vue \ri-ˈvyü\ *n* : a theatrical production consisting typically of brief often satirical sketches and songs

re·vul·sion \ri-ˈvəl-shən\ *n* **1** : a strong sudden reaction or change of feeling **2** : a feeling of complete distaste or repugnance

revved *past and past part of* REV

revving *pres part of* REV

¹re·ward \ri-ˈwȯrd\ *vb* **1** : to give a reward to or for **2** : RECOMPENSE

²reward *n* **1** : something given in return for good or evil done or received or for some service or attainment **2** : a stimulus that is administered to an organism after a response and that increases the probability of occurrence of the response

♦ *Synonyms* PREMIUM, PRIZE, AWARD

re·warm \(ˌ)rē-ˈwȯrm\ *vb* : to make warm again ⟨~ food⟩ ⟨~*ed* herself by the fire⟩

¹re·wind \(ˌ)rē-ˈwīnd\ *vb* **-wound; -wind·ing** **1** : to wind again **2** : to reverse the winding of (as film)

²re·wind \ˈrē-ˌwīnd\ *n* **1** : something that rewinds **2** : an act of rewinding **3** : a function of an electronic device that reverses a recording to a previous portion

re·work \(ˌ)rē-ˈwərk\ *vb* **1** : REVISE **2** : to reprocess for further use

¹re·write \(ˌ)rē-ˈrīt\ *vb* **-wrote; -writ·ten; -writ·ing** : to make a revision of : REVISE

²re·write \ˈrē-ˌrīt\ *n* : an instance or a piece of rewriting

RF *abbr* radio frequency

RFD *abbr* rural free delivery

Rg *abbr* roentgenium

Rh *symbol* rhodium

RH *abbr* right hand

rhap·so·dy \ˈrap-sə-dē\ *n, pl* **-dies** [L *rhapsodia* portion of an epic poem adapted for recitation, fr. Gk *rhapsōidia* recitation of selections from epic poetry, ultim. fr. *rhaptein* to sew, stitch together + *aidein* to sing] **1** : an expression of extravagant praise or ecstasy **2** : a musical composition of irregular form — **rhap·sod·ic** \rap-ˈsä-dik\ *adj* — **rhap·sod·i·cal·ly** \-di-k(ə-)lē\ *adv* — **rhap·so·dize** \ˈrap-sə-ˌdīz\ *vb*

rhea \ˈrē-ə\ *n* : either of two large flightless 3-toed So. American birds that resemble but are smaller than the African ostrich

rhe·ni·um \ˈrē-nē-əm\ *n* : a rare heavy metallic chemical element

rheo·stat \ˈrē-ə-ˌstat\ *n* : a resistor for regulating an electric current by means of variable resistances — **rheo·stat·ic** \ˌrē-ə-ˈsta-tik\ *adj*

rhe·sus monkey \ˈrē-səs-\ *n* : a pale brown Asian monkey often used in medical research

rhet·o·ric \ˈre-tə-rik\ *n* [ME *rethorik,* fr. AF *rethorique,* fr. L *rhetorica,* fr. Gk *rhētorikē,* lit., art of oratory, fr. *rhētōr* public speaker, fr. *eirein* to speak] : the art of speaking or writing effectively — **rhet·o·ri·cian** \ˌre-tə-ˈri-shən\ *n*

rhe·tor·i·cal \ri-ˈtȯr-i-kəl\ *adj* **1** : of or relating to rhetoric **2** : asked merely for effect with no answer expected ⟨a ~ question⟩

rheum \ˈrüm\ *n* : a watery discharge from the mucous membranes esp. of the eyes or nose — **rheumy** *adj*

rheu·mat·ic fever \rü-ˈma-tik-\ *n* : an acute disease chiefly of children and young adults that is characterized by fever, by inflammation and pain in and around the joints, and by inflammation of the membranes surrounding the heart and the heart valves

rewarm	rewatch	rewed	rewire
rewash	reweave	reweigh	rezone

rheu·ma·tism \'rü-mə-ˌti-zəm, 'ru̇-\ *n* **1** : any of various conditions marked by stiffness, pain, or swelling in muscles or joints **2** : RHEUMATOID ARTHRITIS — **rheu·mat·ic** \ru̇-'ma-tik\ *adj*
rheu·ma·toid arthritis \-ˌtȯid-\ *n* : a usu. chronic progressive autoimmune disease characterized by inflammation and swelling of joint structures
rheu·ma·tol·o·gy \ˌrü-mə-'tä-lə-jē, ˌru̇-\ *n* : a medical science dealing with rheumatic diseases — **rheu·ma·tol·o·gist** \-jist\ *n*
Rh factor \ˌär-'āch-\ *n* [*rh*esus monkey (in which it was first detected)] : any of one or more inherited substances in red blood cells that may cause dangerous reactions in some infants or in transfusions
rhine·stone \'rīn-ˌstōn\ *n* : a colorless imitation stone of high luster made of glass, paste, or gem quartz
rhi·no \'rī-nō\ *n, pl* **rhinos** *also* **rhino** : RHINOCEROS
rhi·noc·er·os \rī-'nä-sə-rəs\ *n, pl* **-noc·er·os·es** *also* **-noc·er·os** *or* **-noc·eri** \-'nä-sə-ˌrī\ [ME *rinoceros,* fr. AF, fr. L *rhinoceros,* fr. Gk *rhinokerōs,* fr. *rhin-, rhis* nose + *keras* horn] : any of a family of large thick-skinned mammals of Africa and Asia with one or two upright horns of keratin on the snout and three toes on each foot
rhi·zome \'rī-ˌzōm\ *n* : a fleshy, rootlike, and usu. horizontal underground plant stem that forms shoots above and roots below — **rhi·zom·a·tous** \rī-'zä-mə-təs\ *adj*
Rh–neg·a·tive \ˌär-ˌāch-'ne-gə-tiv\ *adj* : lacking Rh factors in the red blood cells
rho \'rō\ *n* : the 17th letter of the Greek alphabet — P or ρ
rho·di·um \'rō-dē-əm\ *n* : a rare hard ductile metallic chemical element
rho·do·den·dron \ˌrō-də-'den-drən\ *n* : any of a genus of shrubs or trees of the heath family with clusters of large bright flowers
rhom·boid \'räm-ˌbȯid\ *n* : a parallelogram with unequal adjacent sides and angles that are not right angles — **rhomboid** *or* **rhom·boi·dal** \räm-'bȯi-dᵊl\ *adj*
rhom·bus \'räm-bəs\ *n, pl* **rhom·bus·es** *or* **rhom·bi** \-ˌbī\ : a parallelogram having all four sides equal
Rh–pos·i·tive \ˌär-ˌāch-'pä-zə-tiv\ *adj* : containing one or more Rh factors in the red blood cells
rhu·barb \'rü-ˌbärb\ *n* [ME *rubarbe,* fr. AF *reubarbe,* fr. ML *reubarbarum,* alter. of *rha barbarum,* lit., barbarian rhubarb] : a garden plant related to the buckwheat having leaves with thick juicy edible pink and red stems
¹**rhyme** *also* **rime** \'rīm\ *n* **1** : a composition in verse that rhymes; *also* : POETRY **2** : correspondence in terminal sounds (as of two lines of verse)
²**rhyme** *also* **rime** *vb* **rhymed** *also* **rimed; rhym·ing** *also* **rim·ing** **1** : to make rhymes; *also* : to write poetry **2** : to have rhymes : be in rhyme
rhythm \'ri-t͟həm\ *n* **1** : regular rise and fall in the flow of sound in speech **2** : a movement or activity in which some action or element recurs regularly — **rhyth·mic** \'rit͟h-mik\ *or* **rhyth·mi·cal** \-mi-kəl\ *adj* — **rhyth·mi·cal·ly** \-k(ə-)lē\ *adv*
rhythm and blues *n* : popular music based on blues and African American folk music
rhythm method *n* : birth control by refraining from sexual intercourse during the time when ovulation is most likely to occur
RI *abbr* Rhode Island
ri·al \rē-'ȯl, -'äl\ *n* — see MONEY table
¹**rib** \'rib\ *n* **1** : any of the series of curved bones of the chest of most vertebrates that are joined to the backbone in pairs and help to support the body wall and protect the organs inside **2** : something resembling a rib in shape or function **3** : an elongated ridge (as in fabric)
²**rib** *vb* **ribbed; rib·bing** **1** : to furnish or strengthen with ribs **2** : to knit so as to form ridges
³**rib** *vb* **ribbed; rib·bing** : to poke fun at : TEASE — **rib·ber** *n*
rib·ald \'ri-bəld\ *adj* : coarse or indecent esp. in language ⟨~ jokes⟩ — **rib·ald·ry** \-bəl-drē\ *n*
rib·and \'ri-bənd\ *n* : RIBBON
rib·bon \'ri-bən\ *n* **1** : a narrow fabric typically of silk or velvet used for trimming and for badges **2** : a strip of inked cloth (as in a typewriter) **3** : TATTER, SHRED ⟨torn to ~*s*⟩
ri·bo·fla·vin \ˌrī-bə-'flā-vən, 'rī-bə-ˌflā-vən\ *n* : a growth-promoting vitamin of the vitamin B complex occurring esp. in milk and liver
ri·bo·nu·cle·ic acid \ˌrī-bō-nu̇-ˌklē-ik-, -nyu̇-, -ˌklā-\ *n* : RNA
ri·bose \'rī-ˌbōs\ *n* : a sugar with five carbon atoms and five oxygen atoms in each molecule that is part of RNA
ri·bo·some \'rī-bə-ˌsōm\ *n* : any of the RNA-rich cytoplasmic granules in a cell that are sites of protein synthesis — **ri·bo·som·al** \ˌrī-bə-'sō-məl\ *adj*
¹**rice** \'rīs\ *n* : the starchy seeds of an annual grass that are cooked and used for food; *also* : this widely cultivated grass of warm wet areas
²**rice** *vb* **riced; ric·ing** : to finely chop or process (a food) so that it resembles rice
rich \'rich\ *adj* **1** : possessing or controlling great wealth : WEALTHY **2** : COSTLY, VALUABLE **3** : deep and pleasing in color or tone **4** : ABUNDANT **5** : containing much sugar, fat, or seasoning; *also* : high in combustible content **6** : FRUITFUL, FERTILE — **rich·ly** *adv* — **rich·ness** *n*
rich·es \'ri-chəz\ *n pl* [ME, sing. or pl., fr. *richesse* wealth, fr. AF *richesce,* fr. *riche* rich] : things that make one rich : WEALTH
Rich·ter scale \'rik-tər-\ *n* : a scale for expressing the magnitude of a seismic disturbance (as an earthquake) in terms of the energy dissipated in it
rick \'rik\ *n* : a large stack (as of hay) in the open air

rick•ets \ˈri-kəts\ *n* : a childhood deficiency disease marked esp. by soft deformed bones and caused by lack of vitamin D

rick•ett•sia \ri-ˈket-sē-ə\ *n, pl* **-si•as** *or* **-si•ae** \-sē-ˌē\ : any of a group of usu. rod-shaped bacteria that cause various diseases (as typhus)

rick•ety \ˈri-kə-tē\ *adj* **1** : affected with rickets **2** : SHAKY; *also* : in unsound physical condition ⟨~ stairs⟩

rick•shaw *also* **rick•sha** \ˈrik-ˌshȯ\ *n* : a small covered 2-wheeled carriage pulled by one person and used orig. in Japan

[1]**ric•o•chet** \ˈri-kə-ˌshā, *Brit also* -ˌshet\ *n* [F] : a bouncing off at an angle (as of a bullet off a wall); *also* : an object that ricochets

[2]**ricochet** *vb* **-cheted** \-ˌshād\ *also* **-chet•ted** \-ˌshe-təd\; **-chet•ing** \-ˌshā-iŋ\ *or* **-chet•ting** \-ˌshe-tiŋ\ : to bounce or skip with or as if with a glancing rebound

ri•cot•ta \ri-ˈkä-tə, -ˈkȯ-\ *n* : a white unripened whey cheese of Italy that resembles cottage cheese

rid \ˈrid\ *vb* **rid** *also* **rid•ded; rid•ding** : to make free : CLEAR, RELIEVE ⟨~ the house of mice⟩ — **rid•dance** \ˈri-dᵊns\ *n*

rid•den \ˈri-dᵊn\ *adj* **1** : harassed, oppressed, or obsessed by ⟨debt-*ridden*⟩ **2** : excessively full of or supplied with ⟨slum-*ridden*⟩

[1]**rid•dle** \ˈri-dᵊl\ *n* : a puzzling question to be solved or answered by guessing

[2]**riddle** *vb* **rid•dled; rid•dling** **1** : EXPLAIN, SOLVE **2** : to speak in riddles

[3]**riddle** *n* : a coarse sieve

[4]**riddle** *vb* **rid•dled; rid•dling** **1** : to sift with a riddle **2** : to pierce with many holes **3** : PERMEATE

[1]**ride** \ˈrīd\ *vb* **rode** \ˈrōd\; **rid•den** \ˈri-dᵊn\; **rid•ing** **1** : to go on an animal's back or in a conveyance (as a boat, car, or airplane); *also* : to sit on and control so as to be carried along ⟨~ a bicycle⟩ **2** : to float or move on water ⟨~ at anchor⟩; *also* : to move like a floating object **3** : to bear along : CARRY ⟨*rode* her on their shoulders⟩ **4** : to travel over a surface ⟨the car ~*s* well⟩ **5** : to proceed over on horseback **6** : to torment by nagging or teasing

[2]**ride** *n* **1** : an act of riding; *esp* : a trip on horseback or by vehicle **2** : a way (as a road or path) suitable for riding **3** : a mechanical device (as a merry-go-round) for riding on **4** : a means of transportation

rid•er \ˈrī-dər\ *n* **1** : one that rides **2** : an addition to a document often attached on a separate piece of paper **3** : a clause dealing with an unrelated matter attached to a legislative bill during passage — **rid•er•less** *adj*

[1]**ridge** \ˈrij\ *n* [ME *rigge,* fr. OE *hrycg*] **1** : an elevated body part or structure **2** : a range of hills **3** : a raised line or strip **4** : the line made where two sloping surfaces (as of a roof) meet — **ridgy** *adj*

[2]**ridge** *vb* **ridged; ridg•ing** **1** : to form into a ridge **2** : to extend in ridges

[1]**rid•i•cule** \ˈri-də-ˌkyül\ *n* : the act of ridiculing : DERISION, MOCKERY

[2]**ridicule** *vb* **-culed; -cul•ing** : to laugh at or make fun of mockingly or contemptuously ⟨was *ridiculed* by his peers⟩ ♦ ***Synonyms*** DERIDE, TAUNT, TWIT, MOCK

ri•dic•u•lous \rə-ˈdi-kyə-ləs\ *adj* : arousing or deserving ridicule : ABSURD, PREPOSTEROUS ♦ ***Synonyms*** LAUGHABLE, LUDICROUS, FARCICAL, RISIBLE — **ri•dic•u•lous•ly** *adv* — **ri•dic•u•lous•ness** *n*

rid•ley \ˈrid-lē\ *n* : either of two relatively small sea turtles

ri•el \rē-ˈel\ *n* — see MONEY table

Ries•ling \ˈrēz-liŋ, ˈrēs-\ *n* : a sweet to very dry white wine made from a single variety of grape orig. grown in Germany

RIF *abbr* reduction in force

rife \ˈrīf\ *adj* : WIDESPREAD, PREVALENT, ABOUNDING — **rife** *adv* — **rife•ly** *adv*

[1]**riff** \ˈrif\ *n* **1** : a repeated phrase in jazz typically supporting a solo improvisation; *also* : a piece based on such a phrase **2** : a usu. witty or improvised remark or outpouring **3** : a distinct variation : TAKE — **riff** *vb*

riff•raff \ˈrif-ˌraf\ *n* [ME *riffe raffe,* fr. *rif and raf* every single one, fr. AF *rif et raf* altogether] **1** : RABBLE ⟨did not associate with the ~⟩ **2** : REFUSE, RUBBISH

[1]**ri•fle** \ˈrī-fəl\ *vb* **ri•fled; ri•fling** : to ransack esp. with the intent to steal — **ri•fler** *n*

[2]**rifle** *vb* **ri•fled; ri•fling** : to cut spiral grooves into the bore of ⟨*rifled* pipe⟩ — **rifling** *n*

[3]**rifle** *n* **1** : a shoulder weapon with a rifled bore **2** *pl* : soldiers armed with rifles — **ri•fle•man** \-fəl-mən\ *n*

rift \ˈrift\ *n* **1** : CLEFT, FISSURE **2** : FAULT 6 **3** : ESTRANGEMENT, SEPARATION ⟨a ~ between spouses⟩ — **rift** *vb*

[1]**rig** \ˈrig\ *vb* **rigged; rig•ging** **1** : to fit out (as a ship) with rigging **2** : CLOTHE, DRESS **3** : EQUIP **4** : to set up esp. as a makeshift ⟨~ up a shelter⟩

[2]**rig** *n* **1** : the distinctive shape, number, and arrangement of sails and masts of a ship **2** : a carriage with its horse **3** : CLOTHING, DRESS **4** : EQUIPMENT

[3]**rig** *vb* **rigged; rig•ging** **1** : to manipulate or control esp. by deceptive or dishonest means **2** : to fix in advance for a desired result — **rig•ger** *n*

rig•ging \ˈri-giŋ, -gən\ *n* **1** : the ropes and chains that hold and move masts, sails, and spars of a ship **2** : a network (as in theater scenery) used for support and manipulation

[1]**right** \ˈrīt\ *adj* **1** : RIGHTEOUS, UPRIGHT **2** : JUST, PROPER **3** : conforming to truth or fact : CORRECT **4** : APPROPRIATE, SUITABLE **5** : STRAIGHT ⟨a ~ line⟩ **6** : GENUINE, REAL **7** : of, relating to, or being the side of the body which is away from the side on which the heart is mostly located **8** : located nearer to the right hand; *esp* : being on the right when facing in the same direction as the observer **9** : made to be placed or worn outward ⟨~ side of a rug⟩ **10** : NORMAL, SOUND ⟨not in her ~ mind⟩

♦ *Synonyms* CORRECT, ACCURATE, EXACT, PRECISE, NICE — **right·ness** *n*

²right *n* **1** : qualities that constitute what is correct, just, proper, or honorable **2** : something (as a power or privilege) to which one has a just or lawful claim **3** : just action or decision : the cause of justice **4** : the side or part that is on or toward the right side **5** *cap* : political conservatives **6** *often cap* : a conservative position — **right·ward** \-wərd\ *adj or adv*

³right *adv* **1** : according to what is right ⟨live ~⟩ **2** : EXACTLY, PRECISELY ⟨~ here and now⟩ **3** : DIRECTLY ⟨went ~ home⟩ **4** : according to fact or truth ⟨guess ~⟩ **5** : all the way : COMPLETELY ⟨~ to the end⟩ **6** : IMMEDIATELY ⟨~ after lunch⟩ **7** : QUITE, VERY ⟨~ nice weather⟩ **8** : on or to the right ⟨looked ~ and left⟩

⁴right *vb* **1** : to relieve from wrong **2** : to adjust or restore to a proper state or position **3** : to bring or restore to an upright position **4** : to become upright — **right·er** *n*

right angle *n* : an angle whose measure is 90° : an angle whose sides are perpendicular to each other — **right–an·gled** \ˈrīt-ˈaŋ-gəld\ *or* **right–an·gle** \-gəl\ *adj*

right circular cone *n* : CONE 2

right–click \ˈrīt-ˈklik\ *vb* : to press the rightmost button on a computer mouse or similar input device

righ·teous \ˈrī-chəs\ *adj* : acting or being in accordance with what is just, honorable, and free from guilt or wrong : UPRIGHT ♦ *Synonyms* VIRTUOUS, NOBLE, MORAL, ETHICAL — **righ·teous·ly** *adv* — **righ·teous·ness** *n*

right·ful \ˈrīt-fəl\ *adj* **1** : JUST; *also* : FITTING **2** : having or held by a legally just claim — **right·ful·ly** *adv* — **right·ful·ness** *n*

right–hand \ˈrīt-ˌhand\ *adj* **1** : situated on the right **2** : RIGHT-HANDED **3** : chiefly relied on ⟨his ~ man⟩

right–hand·ed \-ˈhan-dəd\ *adj* **1** : using the right hand habitually or better than the left **2** : designed for or done with the right hand **3** : CLOCKWISE ⟨a ~ twist⟩ — **right–handed** *adv* — **right–hand·ed·ly** *adv* — **right–hand·ed·ness** *n*

right·ly \ˈrīt-lē\ *adv* **1** : FAIRLY, JUSTLY **2** : PROPERLY **3** : CORRECTLY, EXACTLY

right–of–way *n, pl* **rights–of–way** **1** : a legal right of passage over another person's ground **2** : the area over which a right-of-way exists **3** : the land on which a public road is built **4** : the land occupied by a railroad **5** : the land used by a public utility **6** : the right of traffic to take precedence over other traffic

right on *interj* — used to express agreement or give encouragement

right–to–life *adj* : ANTIABORTION — **right–to–lifer** *n*

right triangle *n* : a triangle having one right angle

right whale *n* : any of a family of large baleen whales having a very large head on a stocky body

rig·id \ˈri-jəd\ *adj* **1** : lacking flexibility **2** : strictly observed ♦ *Synonyms* SEVERE, STERN, RIGOROUS, STRINGENT — **ri·gid·i·ty** \rə-ˈji-də-tē\ *n* — **rig·id·ly** *adv*

rig·ma·role \ˈri-gə-mə-ˌrōl\ *n* [alter. of obs. *ragman roll* long list, catalog] **1** : confused or senseless talk **2** : a complex and ritualistic procedure

rig·or \ˈri-gər\ *n* **1** : the quality of being inflexible or unyielding : STRICTNESS **2** : HARSHNESS, SEVERITY **3** : a tremor caused by a chill **4** : strict precision : EXACTNESS ⟨scientific ~⟩ — **rig·or·ous** *adj* — **rig·or·ous·ly** *adv*

rig·or mor·tis \ˌri-gər-ˈmȯr-təs\ *n* [NL, stiffness of death] : temporary rigidity of muscles occurring after death

rig·our *chiefly Brit var of* RIGOR

rile \ˈrī(-ə)l\ *vb* **riled; ril·ing** **1** : to make angry **2** : ROIL 1

rill \ˈril\ *n* : a very small brook

¹rim \ˈrim\ *n* **1** : the outer part of a wheel **2** : an outer edge esp. of something curved : BORDER, MARGIN

²rim *vb* **rimmed; rim·ming** **1** : to serve as a rim for : BORDER **2** : to run around the rim of

¹rime \ˈrīm\ *n* : FROST 2 — **rimy** \ˈrī-mē\ *adj*

²rime *var of* RHYME

rind \ˈrīnd\ *n* : a usu. hard or tough outer layer ⟨lemon ~⟩

¹ring \ˈriŋ\ *n* **1** : a circular band worn as an ornament or token or used for holding or fastening ⟨wedding ~⟩ ⟨key ~⟩ **2** : something circular in shape ⟨smoke ~⟩ **3** : a place for contest or display ⟨boxing ~⟩; *also* : PRIZEFIGHTING **4** : ANNUAL RING **5** : a group of people who work together for selfish or dishonest purposes ⟨a ~ of smugglers⟩ — **ringed** *adj* — **ring·like** \ˈriŋ-ˌlīk\ *adj*

²ring *vb* **ringed; ring·ing** \ˈriŋ-iŋ\ **1** : ENCIRCLE **2** : to throw a ring over (a mark) in a game (as quoits) **3** : to move in a ring or spirally

³ring *vb* **rang** \ˈraŋ\; **rung** \ˈrəŋ\; **ring·ing** \ˈriŋ-iŋ\ **1** : to sound resonantly when struck; *also* : to feel as if filled with such sound **2** : to cause to make a clear metallic sound by striking **3** : to announce or call by or as if by striking a bell ⟨~ an alarm⟩ **4** : to repeat loudly and persistently **5** : to summon esp. by a bell ⟨~ for the butler⟩ — **ring a bell** : to arouse a response ⟨that name *rings a bell*⟩

⁴ring *n* **1** : a set of bells **2** : the clear resonant sound of vibrating metal **3** : resonant tone : SONORITY **4** : a sound or character expressive of a particular quality **5** : an act or instance of ringing; *esp* : a telephone call

¹ring·er \ˈriŋ-ər\ *n* **1** : one that sounds by ringing **2** : one that enters a competition under false representations **3** : one that closely resembles another

²ringer *n* : one that encircles or puts a ring around

ring finger *n* : the third finger of the left hand counting the index finger as the first

ring·git \ˈriŋ-git\ *n* — see MONEY table
ring·lead·er \ˈriŋ-ˌlē-dər\ *n* : a leader esp. of a group of troublemakers
ring·let \-lət\ *n* : a long curl
ring·mas·ter \-ˌmas-tər\ *n* : one in charge of performances in a circus ring
ring·tone \ˈriŋ-ˌtōn\ *n* : the sound made by a cell phone to signal an incoming call
ring up *vb* **1** : to total and record esp. by means of a cash register **2** : ACHIEVE ⟨*rang up* many triumphs⟩
ring·worm \ˈriŋ-ˌwərm\ *n* : any of several contagious skin diseases caused by fungi and marked by ring-shaped discolored patches
rink \ˈriŋk\ *n* : a level extent of ice marked off for skating or various games; *also* : a similar surface (as of wood) marked off or enclosed for a sport or game ⟨roller-skating ~⟩
[1]**rinse** \ˈrins\ *vb* **rinsed; rins·ing** [ME *rincen,* AF *rincer,* alter. of OF *recincier,* fr. VL **recentiare,* fr. L *recent-, recens* fresh, recent] **1** : to wash lightly or in water only **2** : to cleanse (as of soap) with clear water **3** : to treat (hair) with a rinse — **rins·er** *n*
[2]**rinse** *n* **1** : an act of rinsing **2** : a liquid used for rinsing **3** : a solution that temporarily tints hair
ri·ot \ˈrī-ət\ *n* **1** *archaic* : disorderly behavior **2** : disturbance of the public peace; *esp* : a violent public disorder **3** : random or disorderly profusion ⟨a ~ of color⟩ **4** : one that is wildly amusing ⟨the comedy is a ~⟩ — **riot** *vb* — **ri·ot·er** *n* — **ri·ot·ous** *adj*
[1]**rip** \ˈrip\ *vb* **ripped; rip·ping** **1** : to cut or tear open **2** : to saw or split (wood) with the grain **3** : CRITICIZE, DISPARAGE ⟨*ripped* into the team⟩ — **rip·per** *n*
[2]**rip** *n* : a rent made by ripping
RIP *abbr* [L *requiescat in pace*] may he rest in peace, may she rest in peace; [L *requiescant in pace*] may they rest in peace
ri·par·i·an \rə-ˈper-ē-ən\ *adj* : of or relating to the bank of a stream, river, or lake ⟨~ trees⟩
rip cord *n* : a cord that is pulled to release a parachute out of its container
ripe \ˈrīp\ *adj* **rip·er; rip·est** **1** : fully grown and developed : MATURE ⟨~ fruit⟩ **2** : fully prepared : READY ⟨~ for action⟩ — **ripe·ly** *adv* — **ripe·ness** *n*
rip·en \ˈrī-pən\ *vb* **rip·ened; rip·en·ing** **1** : to grow or make ripe **2** : to bring to completeness or perfection; *also* : to age or cure (cheese) to develop characteristic flavor, odor, body, texture, and color
rip–off \ˈrip-ˌȯf\ *n* **1** : an act of stealing : THEFT **2** : a cheap imitation — **rip off** *vb*
ri·poste \ri-ˈpōst\ *n* [F, modif. of It *risposta,* lit., answer] **1** : a fencer's return thrust after a parry **2** : a retaliatory maneuver or response; *esp* : a quick retort — **riposte** *vb*
ripped \ˈript\ *adj* : having high muscle definition ⟨a ~ body⟩
rip·ple \ˈri-pəl\ *vb* **rip·pled; rip·pling** **1** : to become lightly ruffled on the surface **2** : to make a sound like that of rippling water — **ripple** *n*
rip·saw \ˈrip-ˌsȯ\ *n* : a coarse-toothed saw used to cut wood in the direction of the grain
rip·stop \-ˌstäp\ *adj* : being a fabric woven in such a way that small tears do not spread ⟨~ nylon⟩ — **ripstop** *n*
[1]**rise** \ˈrīz\ *vb* **rose** \ˈrōz\; **ris·en** \ˈriz-ᵊn\; **ris·ing** **1** : to get up from sitting, kneeling, or lying **2** : to get up from sleep or from one's bed **3** : to return from death **4** : to take up arms **5** : to end a session : ADJOURN **6** : to appear above the horizon **7** : to move upward : ASCEND **8** : to extend above other objects **9** : to attain a higher level or rank **10** : to increase in quantity, intensity, or pitch **11** : to come into being : HAPPEN, BEGIN, ORIGINATE
[2]**rise** *n* **1** : a spot higher than surrounding ground **2** : an upward slope **3** : an act of rising : a state of being risen **4** : BEGINNING, ORIGIN **5** : the elevation of one point above another **6** : an increase in amount, number, or volume **7** : an angry reaction ⟨tried to get a ~ out of me⟩
ris·er \ˈrī-zər\ *n* **1** : one that rises **2** : the upright part between stair treads
ris·i·bil·i·ty \ˌri-zə-ˈbi-lə-tē\ *n, pl* **-ties** : the ability or inclination to laugh — often used in pl.
ris·i·ble \ˈri-zə-bəl\ *adj* **1** : able or inclined to laugh **2** : arousing laughter; *esp* : amusingly ridiculous
[1]**risk** \ˈrisk\ *n* **1** : exposure to possible loss or injury : DANGER, PERIL ⟨health ~*s*⟩ **2** : the chance that an investment will lose value — **risk·i·ness** \ˈris-kē-nəs\ *n* — **risky** *adj*
[2]**risk** *vb* **1** : to expose to danger ⟨~*ed* his life⟩ **2** : to incur the danger of
ri·sot·to \ri-ˈsȯ-tō, -ˈzȯ-\ *n, pl* **-tos** : rice cooked usu. in meat or seafood stock and seasoned
ris·qué \ris-ˈkā\ *adj* [F] : verging on impropriety or indecency ⟨~ jokes⟩
ri·tard \ri-ˈtärd\ *adv or adj* : with a gradual slackening in tempo — used as a direction in music
rite \ˈrīt\ *n* **1** : a set form for conducting a ceremony **2** : the liturgy of a church **3** : a ceremonial act or action
rit·u·al \ˈri-chə-wəl\ *n* **1** : the established form esp. for a religious ceremony **2** : a system of rites **3** : a ceremonial act or action **4** : an act or series of acts regularly repeated in a precise manner — **ritual** *adj* — **rit·u·al·ism** \-wə-ˌli-zəm\ *n* — **rit·u·al·is·tic** \ˌri-chə-wə-ˈlis-tik\ *adj* — **rit·u·al·is·ti·cal·ly** \-ti-k(ə-)lē\ *adv* — **rit·u·al·ly** *adv*
ritzy \ˈrit-sē\ *adj* **ritz·i·er; -est** : showily elegant : POSH
riv *abbr* river
[1]**ri·val** \ˈrī-vəl\ *n* [MF or L; MF, fr. L *rivalis* one using the same stream as another, rival in love, fr. *rivalis* of a stream, fr. *rivus* stream] **1** : one of two or more trying to get what only one can have **2** : one

striving for competitive advantage **3** : one that equals another esp. in desired qualities : MATCH, PEER

[2]**rival** *adj* : COMPETING

[3]**rival** *vb* **-valed** *or* **-valled; -val·ing** *or* **-val·ling 1** : to be in competition with **2** : to try to equal or excel **3** : to have qualities that approach or equal another's

ri·val·ry \ˈrī-vəl-rē\ *n, pl* **-ries** : COMPETITION

rive \ˈrīv\ *vb* **rived** \ˈrīvd\; **riv·en** \ˈri-vən\ *also* **rived; riv·ing 1** : SPLIT, REND **2** : SHATTER ⟨nations *riven* by war⟩

riv·er \ˈri-vər\ *n* **1** : a natural stream larger than a brook **2** : a large stream or flow

riv·er·bank \-ˌbaŋk\ *n* : the bank of a river

riv·er·bed \-ˌbed\ *n* : the channel occupied by a river

riv·er·boat \-ˌbōt\ *n* : a boat for use on a river

riv·er·front \-ˌfrənt\ *n* : the land or area along a river

riv·er·side \-ˌsīd\ *n* : the side or bank of a river

[1]**riv·et** \ˈri-vət\ *n* : a metal bolt with a head at one end used to join parts by being put through holes in them and then being flattened on the plain end to make another head

[2]**rivet** *vb* : to fasten with or as if with a rivet — **riv·et·er** *n*

riv·u·let \ˈri-vyə-lət, -və-\ *n* : a small stream

ri·yal *also* **ri·al** \rē-ˈäl, -ˈal\ *n* — see MONEY table

rm *abbr* room

Rn *symbol* radon

[1]**RN** \ˌär-ˈen\ *n* : REGISTERED NURSE

[2]**RN** *abbr* Royal Navy

RNA \ˌär-(ˌ)en-ˈā\ *n* : any of various nucleic acids (as messenger RNA) that are found esp. in the cytoplasm of cells, have ribose as the 5-carbon sugar, and are associated with the control of cellular chemical activities

rnd *abbr* round

[1]**roach** \ˈrōch\ *n, pl* **roach** *also* **roach·es** : any of various bony fishes related to the carp; *also* : any of several sunfishes

[2]**roach** *n* **1** : COCKROACH **2** : the butt of a marijuana cigarette

road \ˈrōd\ *n* [ME *rode,* fr. OE *rād* ride, journey] **1** : ROADSTEAD — often used in pl. **2** : an open way for vehicles, persons, and animals : HIGHWAY **3** : a way to a conclusion or end ⟨the ~ to success⟩ **4** : a series of scheduled visits (as games or performances) in several locations or the travel necessary to make these visits ⟨the team is on the ~⟩

road·bed \ˈrōd-ˌbed\ *n* **1** : the foundation of a road or railroad **2** : the part of the surface of a road on which vehicles travel

road·block \-ˌbläk\ *n* **1** : a barricade on the road ⟨a police ~⟩ **2** : an obstruction to progress

road·ie \ˈrō-dē\ *n* : a person who works for traveling entertainers

road·kill \ˈrōd-ˌkil\ *n* **1** : the remains of an animal that has been killed on a road by a motor vehicle **2** : one that falls victim to intense competition ⟨political ~⟩

road·run·ner \-ˌrə-nər\ *n* : a largely terrestrial bird of the southwestern U.S. and Mexico that is a speedy runner

road·side \ˈrōd-ˌsīd\ *n* : the strip of land along a road — **roadside** *adj*

road·stead \-ˌsted\ *n* : an anchorage for ships usu. less sheltered than a harbor

road·ster \ˈrōd-stər\ *n* **1** : a driving horse **2** : an open automobile that seats two often with a storage compartment or rumble seat in the rear

road·way \-ˌwā\ *n* : ROAD; *esp* : ROADBED

road·work \-ˌwərk\ *n* **1** : work done in constructing or repairing roads **2** : conditioning for an athletic contest (as a boxing match) consisting mainly of long runs

roam \ˈrōm\ *vb* **1** : WANDER, ROVE **2** : to range or wander over or about **3** : to use a cell phone outside one's local calling area

[1]**roan** \ˈrōn\ *adj* : of dark color (as black, red, or brown) sprinkled with white

[2]**roan** *n* : an animal (as a horse) with a roan coat; *also* : its color

[1]**roar** \ˈrȯr\ *vb* **1** : to utter a full loud prolonged sound **2** : to make a loud confused sound (as of wind or waves) — **roar·er** *n*

[2]**roar** *n* : a sound of roaring

[1]**roast** \ˈrōst\ *vb* **1** : to cook by exposure to dry heat or an open flame **2** : to criticize severely or kiddingly

[2]**roast** *n* **1** : a piece of meat suitable for roasting **2** : an outing at which food is roasted ⟨corn ~⟩ **3** : severe criticism or kidding

[3]**roast** *adj* : ROASTED

roast·er \ˈrō-stər\ *n* **1** : one that roasts **2** : a device for roasting **3** : something (as a young chicken) fit for roasting

rob \ˈräb\ *vb* **robbed; rob·bing 1** : to steal from **2** : to deprive of something due or expected **3** : to commit robbery — **rob·ber** *n*

robber fly *n* : any of a family of predaceous flies resembling bumblebees

rob·bery \ˈrä-bə-rē\ *n, pl* **-ber·ies** : the act or practice of robbing; *esp* : theft of something from a person by use of violence or threat

[1]**robe** \ˈrōb\ *n* **1** : a long flowing outer garment; *esp* : one used for ceremonial occasions **2** : a wrap or covering for the lower body (as for sitting outdoors)

[2]**robe** *vb* **robed; rob·ing 1** : to clothe with or as if with a robe **2** : DRESS

rob·in \ˈrä-bən\ *n* **1** : a small chiefly European thrush with a somewhat orange face and breast **2** : a large No. American thrush with a grayish back, a streaked throat, and a chiefly dull reddish breast

ro·bo·call \ˈrō-bō-ˌkȯl\ *n* : a telephone call from an automated source that delivers a message to a large number of people — **ro·bo·call·er** *n*

ro·bot \ˈrō-ˌbät, -bət\ *n* [Czech, fr. *robota* compulsory labor] **1** : a machine that looks and acts like a human being **2** : an efficient but insensitive person **3 :** a device that automatically performs esp. repetitive tasks **4 :** something guided by automatic controls — **ro•bot•ic** \rō-ˈbä-tik\ *adj*

ro•bot•ics \rō-ˈbä-tiks\ *n* **:** technology dealing with the design, construction, and operation of robots

ro•bust \rō-ˈbəst, ˈrō-(ˌ)bəst\ *adj* [L *robustus* oaken, strong, fr. *robur* oak, strength] **1 :** strong and vigorously healthy **2 :** capable of performing without failure under a wide range of conditions ⟨~ software⟩ — **ro•bust•ly** *adv* — **ro•bust•ness** *n*

ROC *abbr* Republic of China (Taiwan)

[1]**rock** \ˈräk\ *vb* **1 :** to move back and forth in or as if in a cradle **2 :** to sway or cause to sway back and forth **3 :** to arouse to excitement (as with rock music) ⟨~*ed* the crowd⟩ **4** *slang* **:** to be extremely enjoyable or effective ⟨this car ~*s*⟩

[2]**rock** *n* **1 :** a rocking movement **2 :** popular music usu. played on electric instruments and characterized by a strong beat and much repetition

[3]**rock** *n* **1 :** a mass of stony material; *also* **:** broken pieces of stone **2 :** solid mineral deposits **3 :** something like a rock in firmness **4 :** GEM; *esp* **:** DIAMOND — **rock** *adj* — **rock•like** *adj* — **rocky** *adj* — **on the rocks 1 :** in a state of ruin ⟨a marriage *on the rocks*⟩ **2 :** on ice cubes ⟨bourbon *on the rocks*⟩

rock and roll *n* **:** [2]ROCK 2

rock•bound \ˈräk-ˌbau̇nd\ *adj* **:** fringed or covered with rocks

rock•er \ˈrä-kər\ *n* **1 :** one of the curved pieces on which something (as a chair or cradle) rocks **2 :** a chair that rocks on rockers **3 :** a device that works with a rocking motion **4 :** a rock performer, song, or enthusiast

[1]**rock•et** \ˈrä-kət\ *n* [It *rocchetta*, lit., small distaff] **1 :** a firework that is propelled through the air by the discharge of gases produced by a burning substance **2 :** a jet engine that operates on the same principle as a firework rocket but carries the oxygen needed for burning its fuel **3 :** a rocket-propelled bomb or missile

[2]**rocket** *vb* **1 :** to convey by means of a rocket **2 :** to rise abruptly and rapidly

rock•et•ry \ˈrä-kə-trē\ *n* **:** the study or use of rockets

rocket ship *n* **:** a rocket-propelled spacecraft

rock•fall \ˈräk-ˌfȯl\ *n* **:** a mass of falling or fallen rocks

rock•fish \-ˌfish\ *n* **:** any of various bony fishes that live among rocks or on rocky bottoms

rock salt *n* **:** common salt in rocklike masses or large crystals

Rocky Mountain sheep *n* **:** BIGHORN

ro•co•co \rə-ˈkō-kō\ *adj* [F, irreg. fr. *rocaille* style of ornament, lit., stone debris] **:** of or relating to an artistic style esp. of the 18th century marked by fanciful curved forms and elaborate ornamentation — **rococo** *n*

rod \ˈräd\ *n* **1 :** a straight slender stick **2 :** a stick or bundle of twigs used in punishing a person; *also* **:** PUNISHMENT **3 :** a staff borne to show rank **4** — see WEIGHT table **5 :** any of the rod-shaped receptor cells of the retina that are sensitive to faint light **6** *slang* **:** HANDGUN

rode *past of* RIDE

ro•dent \ˈrō-dᵊnt\ *n* [ultim. fr. L *rodent-, rodens*, prp. of *rodere* to gnaw] **:** any of an order of relatively small mammals (as mice, squirrels, and beavers) with sharp front teeth used for gnawing

ro•deo \ˈrō-dē-ˌō, rə-ˈdā-ō\ *n, pl* **ro•de•os** [Sp, fr. *rodear* to surround, fr. *rueda* wheel, fr. L *rota*] **1 :** ROUNDUP 1 **2 :** a public performance featuring cowboy skills (as riding and roping)

[1]**roe** \ˈrō\ *n, pl* **roe** *or* **roes :** DOE

[2]**roe** *n* **:** the eggs of a fish esp. while bound together in a mass

roe•buck \ˈrō-ˌbək\ *n, pl* **roebuck** *or* **roebucks :** a male roe deer

roe deer *n* **:** either of two small nimble European or Asian deers

roent•gen \ˈrent-gən, ˈrənt-, -jən\ *n* **:** the international unit of measurement for X-rays and gamma rays

roent•gen•i•um \rent-ˈge-nē-əm, rənt-, -ˈje-\ *n* **:** a short-lived radioactive chemical element

rog•er \ˈrä-jər\ *interj* — used esp. in radio and signaling to indicate that a message has been received and understood

[1]**rogue** \ˈrōg\ *n* **1 :** a dishonest person **:** SCOUNDREL **2 :** a mischievous person **:** SCAMP — **rogu•ery** \ˈrō-gə-rē\ *n* — **rogu•ish** *adj* — **rogu•ish•ly** *adv* — **rogu•ish•ness** *n*

[2]**rogue** *adj* **1 :** CORRUPT, DISHONEST ⟨~ cops⟩ **2 :** of or being a nation whose leaders defy international law or norms — **go rogue :** to begin to behave in an unexpected or uncontrolled way

roil \ˈrȯi(-ə)l, *for 2 also* ˈrī(-ə)l\ *vb* **1 :** to make cloudy or muddy by stirring up **2 :** RILE 1 — **roily** \ˈrȯi-lē\ *adj*

rois•ter \ˈrȯi-stər\ *vb* **rois•tered; rois•ter•ing :** to engage in noisy revelry **:** CAROUSE — **rois•ter•er** *n* — **rois•ter•ous** \-stə-rəs\ *adj*

ROK *abbr* Republic of Korea (South Korea)

role *also* **rôle** \ˈrōl\ *n* **1 :** an assigned or assumed character; *also* **:** a part played (as by an actor) **2 :** FUNCTION

role model *n* **:** a person whose behavior in a particular role is imitated by others

[1]**roll** \ˈrōl\ *n* [ME *rolle* scroll, fr. AF, fr. ML *rolla*, alter. of *rotula*, fr. L, dim. of *rota* wheel] **1 :** a document containing an official record **2 :** an official list of names **3 :** bread baked in a small rounded mass **4 :** something that rolls **:** ROLLER

[2]**roll** *vb* **1 a :** to move by causing to revolve or turn over and over ⟨~ dice⟩ **b :** to cause to move in a circular manner ⟨~*ed* her eyes⟩ **2 :** to press with a roller ⟨~ dough⟩ **3 :** to move on wheels **4 :** to sound with a full reverberating tone **5**

: to make a continuous beating sound (as on a drum) **6** : to utter with a trill **7** : to move onward as if by completing a revolution ⟨years ~*ed* by⟩ **8** : to flow or seem to flow in a continuous stream or with a rising and falling motion ⟨the river ~*ed* on⟩ **9** : to swing or sway from side to side **10** : to shape or become shaped in rounded form ⟨~ up the paper⟩ **11** : to move by or as if by turning a crank ⟨~ down the window⟩

[3]**roll** *n* **1** : a sound produced by rapid strokes on a drum **2** : a heavy reverberating sound **3** : a rolling movement or action **4** : a swaying movement (as of a ship) **5** : a somersault made in contact with the ground

roll•back \ˈrōl-ˌbak\ *n* : the act or an instance of rolling back

roll back *vb* **1** : to reduce (as a commodity price) on a national scale **2** : to cause to withdraw : push back

roll bar *n* : an overhead metal bar on an automobile designed to protect riders in case the automobile overturns

roll call *n* : the act or an instance of calling off a list of names (as of soldiers); *also* : a time for a roll call

roll•er \ˈrō-lər\ *n* **1** : a revolving cylinder used for moving, pressing, shaping, applying, or smoothing something **2** : a rod on which something is rolled up **3** : a long heavy ocean wave

roll•er coast•er \ˈrō-lər-ˌkō-stər\ *n* : an amusement ride consisting of an elevated railway having sharp curves and steep slopes

roller skate *n* : a skate with wheels instead of a runner — **roller–skate** *vb* — **roller skater** *n*

rol•lick \ˈrä-lik\ *vb* : ROMP, FROLIC

rol•lick•ing *adj* : full of fun and good spirits ⟨a ~ good time⟩

roly–poly \ˌrō-lē-ˈpō-lē\ *adj* : ROTUND

Rom *abbr* **1** Roman **2** Romance **3** Romania; Romanian **4** Romans

ROM \ˈräm\ *n* : a computer memory that contains special-purpose information (as a program) which cannot be altered

ro•maine \rō-ˈmān\ *n* [F, lit., Roman] : a garden lettuce with a tall loose head of long crisp leaves

[1]**Ro•man** \ˈrō-mən\ *n* **1** : a native or resident of Rome **2** *not cap* : roman letters or type

[2]**Roman** *adj* **1** : of or relating to Rome or the Romans and esp. the ancient Romans **2** *not cap* : relating to type in which the letters are upright **3** : of or relating to the Roman Catholic Church

Roman candle *n* : a cylindrical firework that discharges balls of fire

Roman Catholic *n* : a member of a Christian church led by the pope and having a liturgy centered in the Mass — **Roman Catholic** *adj* — **Roman Catholicism** *n*

[1]**ro•mance** \rō-ˈmans, ˈrō-ˌmans\ *n* [ME *romauns,* fr. AF *romanz* French, something written in French, tale in verse, fr. ML *Romanice* in a vernacular language, ultim. fr. L *Romanus* Roman] **1** : a medieval tale of knightly adventure **2** : a prose narrative dealing with heroic or mysterious events set in a remote time or place **3** : a love story **4** : a romantic attachment or episode between lovers — **ro•manc•er** *n*

[2]**romance** *vb* **ro•manced; ro•manc•ing** **1** : to exaggerate or invent detail or incident **2** : to have romantic fancies **3** : to carry on a romantic episode with

Ro•mance \rō-ˈmans, ˈrō-ˌmans\ *adj* : of or relating to any of several languages developed from Latin

Romani *or* **Romany** *n, pl* **-ni** *or* **-nis** *or* **nies** : a member of a traditionally traveling people coming orig. from India and living chiefly in Europe and in smaller numbers throughout the world; *also* : the language of the Romani

Ro•ma•nian \rü-ˈmā-nē-ən, rō-, -nyən\ *also* **Ru•ma•nian** \rü-\ *n* **1** : a native or inhabitant of Romania **2** : the language of the Romanians

Roman numeral *n* : a numeral in a system of notation that is based on the ancient Roman system

Ro•ma•no \rō-ˈmä-nō\ *n* : a hard Italian cheese that is sharper than Parmesan

Ro•mans \ˈrō-mənz\ *n* — see BIBLE table

[1]**ro•man•tic** \rō-ˈman-tik\ *adj* **1** : IMAGINARY **2** : VISIONARY **3** : having an imaginative or emotional appeal **4** : of, relating to, or having the characteristics of romanticism — **ro•man•ti•cal•ly** \-ti-k(ə-)lē\ *adv*

[2]**romantic** *n* : a romantic person; *esp* : a romantic writer, composer, or artist

ro•man•ti•cism \rō-ˈman-tə-ˌsi-zəm\ *n, often cap* : a literary movement (as in early 19th century England) marked esp. by emphasis on the imagination and the emotions and by the use of autobiographical material — **ro•man•ti•cist** \-sist\ *n, often cap*

ro•man•ti•cize \-ˈman-tə-ˌsīz\ *vb* **-cized; -ciz•ing** **1** : to make romantic **2** : to have romantic ideas

Romany *var of* ROMANI

romp \ˈrämp\ *vb* **1** : to play actively and noisily **2** : to win a contest easily — **romp** *n*

romp•er \ˈräm-pər\ *n* **1** : one that romps **2** : a jumpsuit usu. for infants — usu. used in pl.

rood \ˈrüd\ *n* : CROSS, CRUCIFIX

[1]**roof** \ˈrüf, ˈru̇f\ *n, pl* **roofs** \ˈrüfs, ˈru̇fs; ˈrüvz, ˈru̇vz\ **1** : the upper covering part of a building **2** : something suggesting a roof of a building — **roofed** \ˈrüft, ˈru̇ft\ *adj* — **roof•ing** *n* — **roof•less** *adj* — **through the roof** : to an extremely high level ⟨prices went *through the roof*⟩

[2]**roof** *vb* : to cover with a roof

roof•top \-ˌtäp\ *n* : a roof esp. of a house

[1]**rook** \ˈru̇k\ *n* : a crow that nests and roosts in usu. treetop colonies

[2]**rook** *vb* : CHEAT, SWINDLE

[3]**rook** *n* : a chess piece that can move parallel to the sides of the board across any number of unoccupied squares

rook•ery \ˈru̇-kə-rē\ *n, pl* **-er•ies** : a

breeding ground or haunt of gregarious birds or mammals; *also* : a colony of such birds or mammals

rook·ie \ˈru̇-kē\ *n* : BEGINNER, RECRUIT; *esp* : a first-year player in a professional sport

[1]**room** \ˈrüm, ˈru̇m\ *n* **1** : an extent of space occupied by or sufficient or available for something **2** : a partitioned part of a building : CHAMBER; *also* : the people in a room **3** : OPPORTUNITY, CHANCE ⟨~ to develop his talents⟩ — **room·ful** *n* — **roomy** *adj*

[2]**room** *vb* : to occupy or share lodgings : LODGE — **room·er** *n*

room·ette \rü-ˈmet, ru̇-\ *n* : a small private room on a railroad sleeping car

room·ie \ˈrü-mē, ˈru̇-\ *n* : ROOMMATE

room·mate \ˈrüm-ˌmāt, ˈru̇m-\ *n* : one of two or more persons sharing the same room or dwelling

[1]**roost** \ˈrüst\ *n* : a support on which or a place where birds perch

[2]**roost** *vb* : to settle on or as if on a roost

roost·er \ˈrüs-tər, ˈru̇s-\ *n* : an adult male domestic chicken : COCK

[1]**root** \ˈrüt, ˈru̇t\ *n* **1** : the leafless usu. underground part of a seed plant that functions in absorption, aeration, and storage or as a means of anchorage; *also* : an underground plant part esp. when fleshy and edible **2** : something (as the basal part of a tooth or hair) resembling a root **3** : SOURCE, ORIGIN; *esp* : ANCESTRY — usu. used in pl. **4** : the essential core : HEART ⟨get to the ~ of the matter⟩ **5** : a number that when taken as a factor an indicated number of times gives a specified number **6** : the lower part — **root·less** *adj* — **root·like** *adj*

[2]**root** *vb* **1** : to form roots **2** : to fix or become fixed by or as if by roots : ESTABLISH **3** : UPROOT

[3]**root** *vb* **1** : to turn up or dig with the snout ⟨pigs ~*ing*⟩ **2** : to poke or dig around (as in search of something)

[4]**root** \ˈrüt\ *vb* **1** : to applaud or encourage noisily : CHEER **2** : to wish success or lend support to — **root·er** *n*

root beer *n* : a sweetened carbonated beverage flavored with extracts of roots and herbs

root canal *n* : a dental operation to save a tooth by removing the pulp in the root of the tooth and filling the cavity with a protective substance

root·let \ˈrüt-lət, ˈru̇t-\ *n* : a small root

root·stock \-ˌstäk\ *n* : an underground part of a plant that resembles a rhizome

[1]**rope** \ˈrōp\ *n* **1** : a large strong cord made of strands of fiber **2** : a hangman's noose **3** : a thick string (as of pearls) made by twisting or braiding

[2]**rope** *vb* **roped; rop·ing 1** : to bind, tie, or fasten together with a rope **2** : to separate or divide by means of a rope **3** : LASSO

Ror·schach test \ˈrȯr-ˌshäk-\ *n* : a psychological test in which a subject interprets ink-blot designs in terms that reveal intellectual and emotional factors

ro·sa·ry \ˈrō-zə-rē\ *n, pl* **-ries 1** *often cap* : a Roman Catholic devotion consisting of meditation on sacred mysteries during recitation of Hail Marys **2** : a string of beads used in praying

[1]**rose** *past of* RISE

[2]**rose** \ˈrōz\ *n* **1** : any of a genus of usu. prickly often climbing shrubs with divided leaves and bright often fragrant flowers; *also* : one of these flowers **2** : something resembling a rose in form **3** : a moderate purplish red color — **rose** *adj*

ro·sé \rō-ˈzā\ *n* [F] : a light pink wine

ro·se·ate \ˈrō-zē-ət, -zē-ˌāt\ *adj* **1** : resembling a rose esp. in color **2** : OPTIMISTIC ⟨a ~ view of the future⟩

rose·bud \ˈrōz-ˌbəd\ *n* : the flower of a rose when it is at most partly open

rose·bush \-ˌbu̇sh\ *n* : a shrubby rose

rose·mary \ˈrōz-ˌmer-ē\ *n, pl* **-mar·ies** [ME *rosmarine,* fr. AF *rosmarin,* fr. L *rosmarinus,* fr. *ros* dew + *marinus* of the sea, fr. *mare* sea] : a fragrant shrubby Mediterranean mint; *also* : its leaves used as a seasoning

ro·sette \rō-ˈzet\ *n* [F] **1** : a usu. small badge or ornament of ribbon gathered in the shape of a rose **2** : a circular ornament filled with representations of leaves

rose wa·ter \ˈrōz-ˌwȯ-tər, -ˌwä-\ *n* : a watery solution of the fragrant constituents of the rose used as a perfume

rose·wood \-ˌwu̇d\ *n* : any of various tropical trees with dark red wood streaked with black; *also* : this wood

Rosh Ha·sha·nah \ˌräsh-hə-ˈshä-nə, ˌrōsh-, -ˈshō-\ *n* [Heb *rōsh hashshānāh,* lit., beginning of the year] : the Jewish New Year observed as a religious holiday in September or October

ros·in \ˈrä-zᵊn\ *n* : a brittle resin obtained esp. from pine trees and used esp. in varnishes and on violin bows

ros·ter \ˈräs-tər\ *n* **1** : a list of personnel; *also* : the persons listed on a roster **2** : an itemized list

ros·trum \ˈräs-trəm\ *n, pl* **rostrums** *or* **ros·tra** \-trə\ [L *Rostra,* pl., a platform for speakers in the Roman Forum decorated with the beaks of captured ships, fr. pl. of *rostrum* beak, ship's beak, fr. *rodere* to gnaw] : a stage or platform for public speaking

rosy \ˈrō-zē\ *adj* **ros·i·er; -est 1** : of the color rose **2** : HOPEFUL, PROMISING ⟨a ~ outlook⟩ — **ros·i·ly** \ˈrō-zə-lē\ *adv* — **ros·i·ness** \-zē-nəs\ *n*

[1]**rot** \ˈrät\ *vb* **rot·ted; rot·ting** : to undergo decomposition : DECAY

[2]**rot** *n* **1** : DECAY **2** : any of various diseases of plants or animals in which tissue breaks down **3** : NONSENSE

[1]**ro·ta·ry** \ˈrō-tə-rē\ *adj* **1** : turning on an axis like a wheel **2** : having a rotating part ⟨a ~ telephone⟩

[2]**rotary** *n, pl* **-ries 1** : a rotary machine **2** : a one-way circular road junction

ro·tate \ˈrō-ˌtāt\ *vb* **ro·tat·ed; ro·tat·ing 1** : to turn or cause to turn about an axis or a center : REVOLVE **2** : to alternate in a series ♦ ***Synonyms***

TURN, CIRCLE, SPIN, WHIRL, TWIRL — **ro·ta·tion** \rō-ˈtā-shən\ *n* — **ro·ta·tor** \ˈrō-ˌtā-tər\ *n* — **ro·ta·to·ry** \ˈrō-tə-ˌtȯr-ē\ *adj*

ROTC *abbr* Reserve Officers' Training Corps

rote \ˈrōt\ *n* **1** : repetition from memory often without attention to meaning ⟨learn by ~⟩ **2** : mechanical or unthinking routine or repetition — **rote** *adj*

ro·ti·ni \rō-ˈtē-nē\ *n* : short, corkscrew-shaped pasta

ro·tis·ser·ie \rō-ˈti-sə-rē\ *n* [F] **1** : a restaurant specializing in broiled and barbecued meats **2** : an appliance fitted with a spit on which food is rotated before or over a source of heat

ro·tor \ˈrō-tər\ *n* **1** : a part that rotates; *esp* : the rotating part of an electrical machine **2** : a system of rotating horizontal blades for supporting a helicopter

ro·to·till·er \ˈrō-tō-ˌti-lər\ *n* : an engine-powered machine with rotating blades used to lift and turn over soil

rot·ten \ˈrä-tᵊn\ *adj* **1** : having rotted **2** : CORRUPT **3** : extremely unpleasant or inferior — **rot·ten·ness** *n*

rot·ten·stone \ˈrä-tᵊn-ˌstōn\ *n* : a decomposed siliceous limestone used for polishing

rott·wei·ler \ˈrät-ˌwī-lər\ *n, often cap* : any of a breed of tall powerful black-and-tan short-haired dogs

ro·tund \rō-ˈtənd\ *adj* : rounded out ♦ ***Synonyms*** PLUMP, CHUBBY, PORTLY, STOUT — **ro·tun·di·ty** \-ˈtən-də-tē\ *n*

ro·tun·da \rō-ˈtən-də\ *n* **1** : a round building; *esp* : one covered by a dome **2** : a large round room

rouble *var of* RUBLE

roué \rü-ˈā\ *n* [F, lit., broken on the wheel, fr. pp. of *rouer* to break on the wheel, fr. ML *rotare,* fr. L, to rotate; fr. the feeling that such a person deserves this punishment] : a man devoted to a life of sensual pleasure : RAKE

rouge \ˈrüzh, ˈrüj\ *n* [F, lit., red] : a cosmetic used to give a red color to cheeks and lips — **rouge** *vb*

¹rough \ˈrəf\ *adj* **rough·er; rough·est** **1** : uneven in surface : not smooth **2** : SHAGGY **3** : not calm : TURBULENT, TEMPESTUOUS **4** : marked by harshness or violence **5** : DIFFICULT, TRYING **6** : coarse or rugged in character or appearance **7** : marked by lack of refinement **8** : CRUDE, UNFINISHED **9** : done or made hastily or tentatively ⟨a ~ estimate⟩ — **rough·ly** *adv* — **rough·ness** *n*

²rough *n* **1** : uneven ground covered with high grass esp. along a golf fairway **2** : a crude, unfinished, or preliminary state; *also* : something in such a state **3** : ROWDY, TOUGH

³rough *vb* **1** : ROUGHEN **2** : MANHANDLE **3** : to make or shape roughly esp. in a preliminary way — **rough·er** *n*

rough·age \ˈrə-fij\ *n* : FIBER 2; *also* : food containing much indigestible material acting as fiber

rough–and–ready \ˌrə-fən-ˈre-dē\ *adj* : rude or unpolished in nature, method, or manner but effective in action or use ⟨a ~ solution⟩

rough–and–tum·ble \-ˈtəm-bəl\ *n* : rough unrestrained fighting or struggling — **rough–and–tumble** *adj*

rough·en \ˈrə-fən\ *vb* **rough·ened; rough·en·ing** : to make or become rough

rough–hewn \ˈrəf-ˈhyün\ *adj* **1** : being rough and unfinished ⟨~ beams⟩ **2** : lacking smooth manners or social grace — **rough–hew** \-ˈhyü\ *vb*

rough·house \ˈrəf-ˌhau̇s\ *vb* **rough·housed; rough·hous·ing** : to participate in rough noisy behavior — **rough·house** *n*

rough·neck \ˈrəf-ˌnek\ *n* **1** : ROWDY, TOUGH **2** : a worker on a crew drilling oil wells

rough·shod \ˈrəf-ˌshäd\ *adv* : in a roughly forceful manner ⟨rode ~ over the opposition⟩

rou·lette \rü-ˈlet\ *n* [F, lit., small wheel] **1** : a gambling game in which a whirling wheel is used **2** : a wheel or disk with teeth around the outside

¹round \ˈrau̇nd\ *adj* **1** : having every part of the surface or circumference the same distance from the center **2** : CYLINDRICAL **3** : COMPLETE, FULL **4** : approximately correct; *esp* : exact only to a specific decimal or place ⟨~ numbers⟩ **5** : liberal or ample in size or amount **6** : BLUNT, OUTSPOKEN **7** : moving in or forming a circle **8** : having curves rather than angles — **round·ish** *adj* — **round·ness** *n*

²round *prep or adv* : AROUND

³round *n* **1** : something round (as a circle, globe, or ring) **2** : a curved or rounded part (as a rung of a ladder) **3** : an indirect path or course; *also* : a regularly covered route (as of a security guard) **4** : a series or cycle of recurring actions or events **5** : one shot fired by a soldier or a gun; *also* : ammunition for one shot **6** : a period of time or a unit of play in a game or contest **7** : a cut of meat (as beef) esp. between the rump and the lower leg — **in the round** **1** : FREESTANDING **2** : with a center stage surrounded by an audience ⟨theater *in the round*⟩

⁴round *vb* **1** : to make or become round **2** : to go or pass around or part way around **3** : COMPLETE, FINISH **4** : to become plump or shapely **5** : to express as a round number — often used with *off* **6** : to follow a winding course : BEND

¹round·about \ˈrau̇n-də-ˌbau̇t\ *adj* : INDIRECT, CIRCUITOUS ⟨a ~ explanation⟩

²roundabout *n* **1** *Brit* : MERRY-GO-ROUND **2** : ROTARY 2

roun·de·lay \ˈrau̇n-də-ˌlā\ *n* **1** : a simple song with a refrain **2** : a poem with a recurring refrain

round·house \ˈrau̇nd-ˌhau̇s\ *n* **1** : a circular building for housing and repairing locomotives **2** : a blow with the hand made with a wide swing — **roundhouse** *adj*

round·ly \ˈrau̇nd-lē\ *adv* **1** : in a complete manner; *also* : WIDELY **2** : in a blunt way **3** : with vigor
round–rob·in \ˈrau̇nd-ˌrä-bən\ *n* : a tournament in which each contestant meets every other contestant in turn
round–shoul·dered \-ˌshōl-dərd\ *adj* : having the shoulders stooping or rounded
round–trip *n* : a trip to a place and back
round·up \ˈrau̇nd-ˌəp\ *n* **1** : the gathering together of cattle on the range by riding around them and driving them in; *also* : the ranch hands and horses engaged in a roundup **2** : a gathering in of scattered persons or things **3** : SUMMARY ⟨news ~⟩ — **round up** *vb*
round·worm \-ˌwərm\ *n* : NEMATODE
rouse \ˈrau̇z\ *vb* **roused; rous·ing** **1** : to excite to activity : stir up **2** : to wake from sleep — **rous·er** *n*
roust·about \ˈrau̇s-tə-ˌbau̇t\ *n* **1** : one who does heavy unskilled labor (as on a dock or in an oil field) **2** : a laborer at a circus **3** : a person with no established home or occupation
[1]**rout** \ˈrau̇t\ *n* **1** : MOB 1, 2 **2** : DISTURBANCE **3** : a fashionable gathering
[2]**rout** *vb* **1** : RUMMAGE **2** : to gouge out **3** : to expel by force ⟨~*ed* out of their homes⟩
[3]**rout** *n* **1** : a state of wild confusion or disorderly retreat **2** : a disastrous defeat
[4]**rout** *vb* **1** : to put to flight **2** : to defeat decisively
[1]**route** \ˈrüt, ˈrau̇t\ *n* [ME, fr. AF *rute*, fr. VL **rupta (via)*, lit., broken way] **1** : a traveled way **2** : CHANNEL **3** : a line of travel
[2]**route** *vb* **rout·ed; rout·ing** : to send by a selected route : DIRECT
[1]**rout·er** \ˈrau̇-tər\ *n* : a machine with a revolving spindle and cutter for shaping a surface (as of wood)
[2]**rout·er** \ˈrü-tər, ˈrau̇-\ *n* : a device that sends data from one place to another within a computer network or between computer networks
rou·tine \rü-ˈtēn\ *n* [F, fr. MF, fr. *route* traveled way] **1** : a regular course of procedure **2** : an often repeated speech or formula **3** : a part fully worked out ⟨a comedy ~⟩ **4** : a set of computer instructions that will perform a certain task — **routine** *adj* — **rou·tine·ly** *adv* — **rou·tin·ize** \-ˈtē-ˌnīz\ *vb*
[1]**rove** \ˈrōv\ *vb* **roved; rov·ing** : to wander over or through — **rov·er** *n*
[2]**rove** *past and past part of* REEVE
[1]**row** \ˈrō\ *vb* **1** : to propel a boat with oars **2** : to transport in a rowboat **3** : to pull an oar in a crew — **row·er** \ˈrō-ər\ *n*
[2]**row** *n* : an act or instance of rowing
[3]**row** *n* **1** : a number of objects in an orderly sequence **2** : WAY, STREET
[4]**row** \ˈrau̇\ *n* : a noisy quarrel
[5]**row** \ˈrau̇\ *vb* : to engage in a row
row·boat \ˈrō-ˌbōt\ *n* : a small boat designed to be rowed
row·dy \ˈrau̇-dē\ *adj* **row·di·er; -est** : coarse or boisterous in behavior : ROUGH ⟨a ~ crowd⟩ — **row·di·ness** \ˈrau̇-dē-nəs\ *n* — **rowdy** *n* — **row·dy·ish** *adj* — **row·dy·ism** *n*
row·el \ˈrau̇(-ə)l\ *n* : a small pointed wheel on a rider's spur — **rowel** *vb*
[1]**roy·al** \ˈrȯi(-ə)l\ *adj* [ME *roial*, fr. AF *real*, *roial*, fr. L *regalis*, fr. *reg-*, *rex* king] **1** : of or relating to a sovereign : REGAL **2** : fit for a king or queen ⟨a ~ welcome⟩ — **roy·al·ly** *adv*
[2]**royal** *n* : a person of royal blood
royal flush *n* : a straight flush having an ace as the highest card
roy·al·ist \ˈrȯi-ə-list\ *n* : an adherent of a king or of monarchical government
roy·al·ty \ˈrȯi-əl-tē\ *n, pl* **-ties** **1** : the state of being royal **2** : royal persons **3** : a share of a product or profit (as of a mine or oil well) claimed by the owner for allowing another person to use the property **4** : a payment made to an author or composer for each copy of a work sold or to an inventor for each article sold under a patent
RP *abbr* **1** relief pitcher **2** Republic of the Philippines
rpm *abbr* revolutions per minute
rps *abbr* revolutions per second
rpt *abbr* **1** repeat **2** report
RPV \ˌär-ˌpē-ˈvē\ *n* : an uncrewed aircraft flown by remote control and used esp. for reconnaissance
RR *abbr* **1** railroad **2** rural route
RS *abbr* **1** recording secretary **2** revised statutes **3** Royal Society
RSV *abbr* Revised Standard Version
RSVP *abbr* [F *répondez s'il vous plaît*] please reply
rt *abbr* **1** right **2** route
RT *abbr* round-trip
rte *abbr* route
Ru *symbol* ruthenium
[1]**rub** \ˈrəb\ *vb* **rubbed; rub·bing** **1** : to use pressure and friction on a body or object **2** : to fret or chafe with friction **3** : to scour, polish, erase, or smear by pressure and friction
[2]**rub** *n* **1** : DIFFICULTY, OBSTRUCTION **2** : something grating to the feelings
[1]**rub·ber** \ˈrə-bər\ *n* **1** : one that rubs **2** : ERASER **3** : a flexible waterproof elastic substance made from the milky juice of various tropical plants or made synthetically; *also* : something made of this material **4** : CONDOM — **rubber** *adj* — **rub·ber·ize** \ˈrə-bə-ˌrīz\ *vb* — **rub·bery** *adj*
[2]**rubber** *n* **1** : a contest that consists of an odd number of games and is won by the side that takes a majority **2** : an extra game played to decide a tie
[1]**rub·ber·neck** \-ˌnek\ *n* **1** : an idly or overly inquisitive person **2** : a person on a guided tour
[2]**rubberneck** *vb* : to look about, stare, or listen with excessive curiosity ⟨~*ing* drivers⟩ — **rub·ber·neck·er** *n*
rub·bish \ˈrə-bish\ *n* **1** : useless waste or rejected matter : TRASH **2** : something worthless or nonsensical
rub·ble \ˈrə-bəl\ *n* : broken fragments esp. of a destroyed building

ru·bel·la \rü-ˈbe-lə\ *n* : GERMAN MEASLES
ru·bi·cund \ˈrü-bi-(ˌ)kənd\ *adj* : RED, RUDDY ⟨a ~ face⟩
ru·bid·i·um \rü-ˈbi-dē-əm\ *n* : a soft silvery metallic chemical element
ru·ble *also* **rou·ble** \ˈrü-bəl\ *n* — see MONEY table
ru·bric \ˈrü-brik\ *n* [ME *rubrike* red ocher, heading in red letters of part of a book, fr. AF, fr. L *rubrica,* fr. *ruber* red] **1** : HEADING, TITLE; *also* : CLASS, CATEGORY **2** : a rule esp. for the conduct of a religious service
ru·by \ˈrü-bē\ *n, pl* **rubies** : a clear red precious stone — **ruby** *adj*
ru·by–throat·ed hummingbird \ˈrü-bē-ˌthrō-təd-\ *n* : a bright green and whitish hummingbird of eastern No. America with a red throat in the male
ruck·us \ˈrə-kəs\ *n* : ROW, DISTURBANCE
rud·der \ˈrə-dər\ *n* : a movable flat piece attached at the rear of a ship or aircraft for steering
rud·dy \ˈrə-dē\ *adj* **rud·di·er; -est** : REDDISH; *esp* : of a healthy reddish complexion — **rud·di·ness** \ˈrə-dē-nəs\ *n*
rude \ˈrüd\ *adj* **rud·er; rud·est** **1** : roughly made : CRUDE **2** : UNDEVELOPED, PRIMITIVE **3** : IMPOLITE **4** : UNSKILLED — **rude·ly** *adv* — **rude·ness** *n*
ru·di·ment \ˈrü-də-mənt\ *n* **1** : an elementary principle or basic skill — usu. used in pl. ⟨the ~*s* of mathematics⟩ **2** : something not fully developed — usu. used in pl. ⟨the ~*s* of a plan⟩ — **ru·di·men·ta·ry** \ˌrü-də-ˈmen-tə-rē\ *adj*
[1]**rue** \ˈrü\ *n* : REGRET, SORROW — **rue·ful** \-fəl\ *adj* — **rue·ful·ly** *adv* — **rue·ful·ness** *n*
[2]**rue** *vb* **rued; ru·ing** : to feel regret, remorse, or penitence for ⟨~*s* his decision now⟩
[3]**rue** *n* : a European strong-scented woody herb with bitter-tasting leaves
ruff \ˈrəf\ *n* **1** : a large round pleated collar worn about 1600 **2** : a fringe of long hair or feathers around the neck of an animal — **ruffed** \ˈrəft\ *adj*
ruf·fi·an \ˈrə-fē-ən\ *n* : a brutal person — **ruf·fi·an·ly** *adj*
[1]**ruf·fle** \ˈrə-fəl\ *vb* **ruf·fled; ruf·fling** **1** : to roughen the surface of **2** : IRRITATE, VEX **3** : to erect (as hair or feathers) in or like a ruff **4** : to flip through (as pages) **5** : to draw into or provide with plaits or folds
[2]**ruffle** *n* **1** : a strip of fabric gathered or pleated on one edge **2** : RUFF 2 **3** : RIPPLE — **ruf·fly** \ˈrə-fə-lē, -flē\ *adj*
ru·fi·yaa \ˈrü-fē-ˌyä\ *n, pl* **rufiyaa** — see MONEY table
RU–486 \ˈär-ˌyü-ˌfȯr-ˌā-tē-ˈsiks\ *n* : a drug taken orally to induce abortion esp. early in pregnancy
rug \ˈrəg\ *n* **1** : a covering for the legs, lap, and feet **2** : a piece of heavy fabric usu. with a nap or pile used as a floor covering
rug·by \ˈrəg-bē\ *n, often cap* [*Rugby* School, Rugby, England, where it was first played] : a football game in which play is continuous and interference and forward passing are not permitted
rug·ged \ˈrə-gəd\ *adj* **1** : having a rough uneven surface **2** : TURBULENT, STORMY **3** : HARSH, STERN **4** : ROBUST, STURDY — **rug·ged·ize** \ˈrə-gə-ˌdīz\ *vb* — **rug·ged·ly** *adv* — **rug·ged·ness** *n*
[1]**ru·in** \ˈrü-ən\ *n* **1** : complete collapse or destruction **2** : the remains of something destroyed — usu. used in pl. **3** : a cause of destruction **4** : the action of destroying
[2]**ruin** *vb* **1** : DESTROY **2** : to damage beyond repair **3** : BANKRUPT
ru·in·ation \ˌrü-ə-ˈnā-shən\ *n* : RUIN, DESTRUCTION
ru·in·ous \ˈrü-ə-nəs\ *adj* **1** : RUINED, DILAPIDATED **2** : causing ruin ⟨~ conflicts⟩ — **ru·in·ous·ly** *adv*
[1]**rule** \ˈrül\ *n* [ME *reule,* fr. AF, fr. L *regula* straightedge, rule, fr. *regere* to keep straight, direct] **1** : a guide or principle for governing action : REGULATION **2** : the usual way of doing something **3** : the exercise of authority or control : GOVERNMENT **4** : RULER 2
[2]**rule** *vb* **ruled; rul·ing** **1** : CONTROL; *also* : GOVERN **2** : to be supreme or outstanding in **3** : to give or state as a considered decision **4** : to mark on paper with or as if with a ruler **5** *slang* : to be extremely cool or popular
rul·er \ˈrü-lər\ *n* **1** : SOVEREIGN **2** : a straight strip of material (as wood or metal) marked off in units and used for measuring or as a straightedge
rum \ˈrəm\ *n* **1** : an alcoholic liquor made from sugarcane products (as molasses) **2** : alcoholic liquor
Ru·ma·nian *var of* ROMANIAN
rum·ba \ˈrəm-bə, ˈrüm-\ *n* : a dance of Cuban origin marked by strong rhythmic movements
[1]**rum·ble** \ˈrəm-bəl\ *vb* **rum·bled; rum·bling** : to make a low heavy rolling sound; *also* : to move along with such a sound — **rum·bler** *n*
[2]**rumble** *n* **1** : a low heavy rolling sound **2** : a street fight esp. among gangs
rumble seat *n* : a folding seat in the back of an automobile that is not covered by the top
rum·bling \ˈrəm-bliŋ\ *n* **1** : RUMBLE **2** : widespread talk or complaints — usu. used in pl.
ru·men \ˈrü-mən\ *n, pl* **ru·mi·na** \-mə-nə\ *or* **rumens** : the large first compartment of the stomach of a ruminant (as a cow)
[1]**ru·mi·nant** \ˈrü-mə-nənt\ *n* : a ruminant mammal
[2]**ruminant** *adj* **1** : chewing the cud; *also* : of or relating to a group of hoofed mammals (as cattle, deer, and camels) that chew the cud and have a complex 3- or 4-chambered stomach **2** : MEDITATIVE
ru·mi·nate \ˈrü-mə-ˌnāt\ *vb* **-nat·ed; -nat·ing** [L *ruminari* to chew the cud, muse upon, fr. *rumin-, rumen* first stomach chamber of a ruminant] **1** : MEDITATE, MUSE **2** : to chew the cud — **ru·mi·na·tion** \ˌrü-mə-ˈnā-shən\ *n*

[1]**rum·mage** \ˈrə-mij\ *vb* **rum·maged; rum·mag·ing** : to search thoroughly ⟨*rummaged* the room for his key⟩ — **rum·mag·er** *n*

[2]**rummage** *n* **1** : a miscellaneous collection **2** : an act of rummaging

rum·my \ˈrə-mē\ *n* : any of several card games for two or more players

ru·mor \ˈrü-mər\ *n* **1** : common talk **2** : a statement or report current but not authenticated — **rumor** *vb*

ru·mour *chiefly Brit var of* RUMOR

rump \ˈrəmp\ *n* **1** : the rear part of an animal; *also* : a cut of meat (as beef) behind the upper sirloin **2** : a small or inferior remnant (as of a group)

rum·ple \ˈrəm-pəl\ *vb* **rum·pled; rum·pling** : TOUSLE, MUSS, WRINKLE — **rumple** *n* — **rum·ply** \ˈrəm-pə-lē\ *adj*

rum·pus \ˈrəm-pəs\ *n* : DISTURBANCE, RUCKUS

rumpus room *n* : a room usu. in the basement of a home that is used for games, parties, and recreation

[1]**run** \ˈrən\ *vb* **ran** \ˈran\; **run; run·ning** **1** : to go faster than a walk **2** : to take to flight : FLEE **3** : to go without restraint ⟨let chickens ~ loose⟩ **4** : to go rapidly or hurriedly : HASTEN, RUSH **5** : to make a quick or casual trip or visit **6** : to contend in a race; *esp* : to enter an election ⟨~ for mayor⟩ **7** : to put forward as a candidate for office **8** : to move on or as if on wheels : pass or slide freely **9** : to go back and forth : PLY **10** : to move in large numbers esp. to a spawning ground ⟨shad are *running*⟩ **11** : FUNCTION, OPERATE ⟨~*s* on gasoline⟩ ⟨software that ~*s* on her computer⟩ **12** : to continue in force ⟨two years to ~⟩ **13** : to flow rapidly or under pressure : MELT, FUSE, DISSOLVE; *also* : DISCHARGE 7 ⟨my nose is *running*⟩ **14** : to tend to produce or to recur ⟨family ~*s* to blonds⟩ ⟨stubbornness ~*s* in the family⟩ **15** : to take a certain direction **16** : to be worded or written **17** : to be current ⟨rumors *running* wild⟩ **18** : to cause to produce a flow ⟨*ran* the faucet⟩ **19** : TRACE ⟨~ down a rumor⟩ **20** : to perform or bring about by running **21** : to cause to pass ⟨~ a wire from the antenna⟩ **22** : to cause to collide **23** : SMUGGLE **24** : MANAGE, CONDUCT, OPERATE ⟨~ a business⟩ **25** : INCUR ⟨~ a risk⟩ **26** : to permit to accumulate before settling ⟨~ up a bill⟩ **27** : PRINT, PUBLISH ⟨~ a news story⟩

[2]**run** *n* **1** : an act or the action of running **2** : a migration of fish; *also* : the migrating fish **3** : a score in baseball **4** : BROOK, CREEK **5** : a continuous series esp. of similar things **6** : persistent heavy demands from depositors, creditors, or customers **7** : the quantity of work turned out in a continuous operation; *also* : a period of operation (as of a machine or plant) **8** : the usual or normal kind ⟨the ordinary ~ of students⟩ **9** : the distance covered in continuous travel or sailing **10** : a regular course or trip **11** : freedom of movement in a place or area ⟨has the ~ of the house⟩ **12** : an enclosure for animals **13** : an inclined course (as for skiing) **14** : a lengthwise ravel (as in a stocking) — **run·less** *adj*

run·about \ˈrə-nə-ˌbau̇t\ *n* : a light wagon, automobile, or motorboat

run·around \ˈrə-nə-ˌrau̇nd\ *n* : evasive or delaying action esp. in response to a request

[1]**run·away** \ˈrə-nə-ˌwā\ *n* **1** : one that runs away : FUGITIVE **2** : the act of running away out of control; *also* : something (as a horse) that is running out of control

[2]**runaway** *adj* **1** : FUGITIVE **2** : won by a long lead; *also* : extremely successful **3** : subject to uncontrolled changes ⟨~ inflation⟩ **4** : operating out of control ⟨a ~ locomotive⟩

run·down \ˈrən-ˌdau̇n\ *n* : an item-by-item report or review : SUMMARY

run–down \ˈrən-ˈdau̇n\ *adj* **1** : EXHAUSTED, WORN-OUT ⟨that ~ feeling⟩ **2** : being in poor repair ⟨a ~ farm⟩

run down *vb* **1** : to collide with and knock down **2** : to chase until exhausted or captured **3** : to find by search **4** : DISPARAGE **5** : to cease to operate for lack of motive power **6** : to decline in physical condition

rune \ˈrün\ *n* **1** : any of the characters of any of several alphabets formerly used by the Germanic peoples **2** : MYSTERY, MAGIC **3** : a poem esp. in Finnish or Old Norse — **ru·nic** \ˈrü-nik\ *adj*

[1]**rung** *past part of* RING

[2]**rung** \ˈrəŋ\ *n* **1** : a rounded crosspiece between the legs of a chair **2** : one of the crosspieces of a ladder

run–in \ˈrən-ˌin\ *n* **1** : ALTERCATION, QUARREL **2** : something run in

run in *vb* **1** : to insert as additional matter **2** : to arrest esp. for a minor offense **3** : to pay a casual visit

run·nel \ˈrə-nᵊl\ *n* : BROOK, STREAMLET

run·ner \ˈrə-nər\ *n* **1** : one that runs **2** : BASE RUNNER **3** : BALLCARRIER **4** : a thin piece or part on which something (as a sled or an ice skate) slides **5** : the support of a drawer or a sliding door **6** : a horizontal branch from the base of a plant that produces new plants **7** : a plant producing runners **8** : a long narrow carpet **9** : a narrow decorative cloth cover for a table or dresser top

run·ner–up \ˈrə-nər-ˌəp\ *n, pl* **runners–up** *also* **runner–ups** : the competitor in a contest who finishes second

[1]**run·ning** *adj* **1** : FLOWING **2** : FLUID, RUNNY **3** : CONTINUOUS, INCESSANT **4** : measured in a straight line ⟨cost per ~ foot⟩ **5** : of or relating to an act of running **6** : made or trained for running ⟨~ horse⟩ ⟨~ shoes⟩

[2]**running** *adv* : in succession

running light *n* : any of the lights carried by a vehicle (as a ship) at night

run·ny \ˈrə-nē\ *adj* : having a tendency to run ⟨a ~ dough⟩ ⟨a ~ nose⟩

run·off \ˈrən-ˌȯf\ *n* : a final contest (as an election) to decide a previous indecisive contest

run–of–the–mill *adj* : not outstanding : AVERAGE ⟨a ~ performance⟩
run on *vb* **1** : to talk at length **2** : to continue (matter in type) without a break or a new paragraph **3** : to place or add (as an entry in a dictionary) at the end of a paragraphed item — **run–on** \ˈrən-ˌȯn, -ˌän\ *n*
run out *vb* : to use up or exhaust a supply ⟨*ran out* of gas⟩
runt \ˈrənt\ *n* **1** : an animal unusually small of its kind **2** *usu disparaging* : a person of small stature — **runty** *adj*
run•way \ˈrən-ˌwā\ *n* **1** : a beaten path made by animals; *also* : a passage for animals **2** : a paved strip of ground for the landing and takeoff of aircraft **3** : a narrow platform from a stage into an auditorium **4** : a support (as a track) on which something runs
ru•pee \rü-ˈpē, ˈrü-ˌpē\ *n* — see MONEY table
ru•pi•ah \rü-ˈpē-ə\ *n, pl* **rupiah** *or* **rupiahs** — see MONEY table
[1]**rup•ture** \ˈrəp-chər\ *n* : a breaking or tearing apart; *also* : HERNIA
[2]**rupture** *vb* **rup•tured; rup•tur•ing** : to cause or undergo rupture
ru•ral \ˈru̇r-əl\ *adj* : of or relating to the country, country people, or agriculture
ruse \ˈrüs, ˈrüz\ *n* : a wily subterfuge : TRICK, ARTIFICE
[1]**rush** \ˈrəsh\ *n* : any of various often tufted and hollow-stemmed grasslike marsh plants — **rushy** *adj*
[2]**rush** *vb* [ME *russhen,* fr. AF *reuser, ruser, russher* to drive back, repulse, fr. L *recusare* to oppose] **1** : to move forward or act with too great haste or eagerness or without preparation **2** : to perform in a short time or at high speed **3** : ATTACK, CHARGE **4** : to advance a football by running — **rush•er** *n*
[3]**rush** *n* **1** : a violent forward motion **2** : unusual demand or activity **3** : a crowding of people to one place **4** : a running play in football **5** : a sudden feeling of pleasure
[4]**rush** *adj* : requiring or marked by special speed or urgency ⟨~ orders⟩
rush hour *n* : a time when the amount of traffic or business is at a peak
rusk \ˈrəsk\ *n* : a sweet or plain bread baked, sliced, and baked again until dry and crisp
rus•set \ˈrə-sət\ *n* **1** : a coarse reddish brown cloth **2** : a reddish brown **3** : a baking potato — **russet** *adj*
Rus•sian \ˈrə-shən\ *n* **1** : a native or inhabitant of Russia **2** : a Slavic language of the Russian people — **Russian** *adj*
rust \ˈrəst\ *n* **1** : a reddish coating formed on iron when it is exposed to esp. moist air **2** : any of numerous plant diseases characterized by usu. reddish spots; *also* : a fungus causing rust **3** : a strong reddish brown — **rust** *vb* — **rusty** *adj*
[1]**rus•tic** \ˈrəs-tik\ *adj* : of, relating to, or suitable for the country or country people ⟨a ~ inn⟩ — **rus•ti•cal•ly** \-ti-k(ə-)lē\ *adv* — **rus•tic•i•ty** \ˌrəs-ˈti-sə-tē\ *n*
[2]**rustic** *n* : a rustic person
rus•ti•cate \ˈrəs-ti-ˌkāt\ *vb* **-cat•ed; -cat•ing** : to go into or reside in the country — **rus•ti•ca•tion** \ˌrəs-ti-ˈkā-shən\ *n*
[1]**rus•tle** \ˈrə-səl\ *vb* **rus•tled; rus•tling** **1** : to make or cause a rustle **2** : to cause to rustle ⟨~ a newspaper⟩ **3** : to act or move with energy or speed; *also* : to procure in this way **4** : to forage food **5** : to steal cattle from the range — **rus•tler** *n*
[2]**rustle** *n* : a quick series of small sounds ⟨~ of leaves⟩
[1]**rut** \ˈrət\ *n* : state or period of sexual excitement esp. in male deer — **rut** *vb*
[2]**rut** *n* **1** : a track worn by wheels or by habitual passage of something **2** : a usual or fixed routine
ru•ta•ba•ga \ˌrü-tə-ˈbā-gə, ˌru̇-\ *n* : a turnip with a large yellowish root
Ruth \ˈrüth\ *n* — see BIBLE table
ru•the•ni•um \rü-ˈthē-nē-əm\ *n* : a rare hard metallic chemical element
ruth•er•ford•ium \ˌrə-thər-ˈfȯr-dē-əm\ *n* : an artifically produced radioactive chemical element
ruth•less \ˈrüth-ləs\ *adj* [fr. *ruth* compassion, pity, fr. ME *ruthe,* fr. *ruen* to rue, fr. OE *hrēowan*] : having no pity : MERCILESS, CRUEL ⟨a ~ tyrant⟩ — **ruth•less•ly** *adv* — **ruth•less•ness** *n*
[1]**RV** \ˌär-ˈvē\ *n* : RECREATIONAL VEHICLE
[2]**RV** *abbr* Revised Version
R–value \ˈär-ˌval-yü\ *n* : a measure of resistance to the flow of heat through a substance (as insulation)
RW *abbr* **1** right worshipful **2** right worthy
rwy *or* **ry** *abbr* railway
Rx \ˌär-ˈeks\ *n* : PRESCRIPTION 2
-ry *n suffix* : -ERY ⟨bigot*ry*⟩
rye \ˈrī\ *n* **1** : a hardy annual grass grown for grain or as a cover crop; *also* : its seed **2** : a whiskey distilled from a rye mash

S

¹s \ˈes\ *n, pl* **s's** *or* **ss** \ˈe-səz\ *often cap* : the 19th letter of the English alphabet

²s *abbr, often cap* **1** saint **2** second **3** senate **4** series **5** shilling **6** singular **7** small **8** son **9** south; southern

¹-s \s *after sounds* f, k, k̲, p, t, th; əz *after sounds* ch, j, s, sh, z, zh; z *after other sounds*\ *n pl suffix* — used to form the plural of most nouns that do not end in *s, z, sh,* or *ch* or *y* following a consonant ⟨head*s*⟩ ⟨book*s*⟩ ⟨boy*s*⟩ ⟨belief*s*⟩, to form the plural of proper nouns that end in *y* following a consonant ⟨Mary*s*⟩, and with or without a preceding apostrophe to form the plural of abbreviations, numbers, letters, and symbols used as nouns ⟨MC*s*⟩ ⟨4*s*⟩ ⟨#*s*⟩ ⟨B'*s*⟩

²-s *adv suffix* — used to form adverbs denoting usual or repeated action or state ⟨works night*s*⟩

³-s *vb suffix* — used to form the third person singular present of most verbs that do not end in *s, z, sh,* or *ch* or *y* following a consonant ⟨fall*s*⟩ ⟨take*s*⟩ ⟨play*s*⟩

S *symbol* sulfur

SA *abbr* **1** Salvation Army **2** seaman apprentice **3** sex appeal **4** [L *sine anno* without year] without date **5** South Africa **6** South America **7** subject to approval

Saami *var of* SAMI

Sab·bath \ˈsa-bəth\ *n* [ME *sabat,* fr. AF & OE, fr. L *sabbatum,* fr. Gk *sabbaton,* fr. Heb *shabbāth,* lit., rest] **1** : the 7th day of the week observed as a day of worship by Jews and some Christians **2** : Sunday observed among Christians as a day of worship

sab·bat·i·cal \sə-ˈba-ti-kəl\ *n* : a leave often with pay granted (as to a college professor) usu. every 7th year for rest, travel, or research

sa·ber *or* **sa·bre** \ˈsā-bər\ *n* [F *sabre*] : a cavalry sword with a curved blade and thick back

saber saw *n* : a portable electric saw with a pointed reciprocating blade; *esp* : JIGSAW

sa·ble \ˈsā-bəl\ *n, pl* **sables** **1** : the color black **2** *pl* : mourning garments **3** : a dark brown mammal chiefly of northern Asia related to the weasels; *also* : its fur or pelt

¹sab·o·tage \ˈsa-bə-ˌtäzh\ *n* [F] **1** : deliberate destruction of an employer's property or hindering of production by workers **2** : destructive or hampering action by enemy agents or sympathizers in time of war

²sabotage *vb* **-taged; -tag·ing** : to practice sabotage on : WRECK

sab·o·teur \ˌsa-bə-ˈtər\ *n* : a person who practices sabotage

sac \ˈsak\ *n* : a pouch in an animal or plant often containing a fluid

SAC *abbr* Strategic Air Command

sac·cha·rin \ˈsa-kə-rən\ *n* : a white crystalline compound used as an artificial calorie-free sweetener

sac·cha·rine \ˈsa-kə-rən\ *adj* : nauseatingly sweet ⟨~ poetry⟩

sac·er·do·tal \ˌsa-sər-ˈdō-tᵊl, -kər-\ *adj* : PRIESTLY

sac·er·do·tal·ism \-tə-ˌli-zəm\ *n* : a religious belief emphasizing the powers of priests as essential mediators between God and humankind

sa·chem \ˈsā-chəm\ *n* [Narragansett *sâchim*] : a No. American Indigenous chief

sa·chet \sa-ˈshā\ *n* [MF, fr. OF, dim. of *sac* bag] : a small bag filled with perfumed powder for scenting clothes

¹sack \ˈsak\ *n* **1** : a usu. rectangular-shaped bag (as of paper or burlap) **2** : a loose jacket or short coat

²sack *vb* : DISMISS, FIRE

³sack *n* [modif. of MF *sec* dry, fr. L *siccus*] : a white wine popular in England in the 16th and 17th centuries

⁴sack *vb* : to plunder a captured town

sack·cloth \-ˌklȯth\ *n* : a rough garment worn as a sign of penitence

sac·ra·ment \ˈsa-krə-mənt\ *n* **1** : a formal religious act or rite; *esp* : one (as baptism or the Eucharist) held to have been instituted by Christ **2** : the elements of the Eucharist — **sac·ra·men·tal** \ˌsa-krə-ˈmen-tᵊl\ *adj*

sa·cred \ˈsā-krəd\ *adj* **1** : set apart for the service or worship of deity **2** : devoted exclusively to one service or use **3** : worthy of veneration or reverence **4** : of or relating to religion : RELIGIOUS ♦ ***Synonyms*** BLESSED, DIVINE, HALLOWED, HOLY, SANCTIFIED — **sa·cred·ly** *adv* — **sa·cred·ness** *n*

sacred cow *n* : one that is often unreasonably immune from criticism

¹sac·ri·fice \ˈsa-krə-ˌfīs\ *n* **1** : the offering of something precious to deity **2** : something offered in sacrifice **3** : LOSS, DEPRIVATION **4** : a bunt allowing a base runner to advance while the batter is put out; *also* : a fly ball allowing a runner to score after the catch — **sac·ri·fi·cial** \ˌsa-krə-ˈfi-shəl\ *adj* — **sac·ri·fi·cial·ly** *adv*

²sac·ri·fice *vb* **-ficed; -fic·ing** **1** : to offer up or kill as a sacrifice **2** : to accept the loss or destruction of for an end, cause, or ideal **3** : to make a sacrifice in baseball

sac·ri·lege \ˈsa-krə-lij\ *n* [ME, fr. AF, fr. L *sacrilegium,* fr. *sacrilegus* one who robs sacred property fr. *sacr-, sacer* sacred + *legere* to gather, steal] **1** : violation of something consecrated to God **2** : gross irreverence toward a hallowed person, place, or thing — **sac·ri·le·gious** \ˌsa-krə-ˈli-jəs, -ˈlē-\ *adj* — **sac·ri·le·gious·ly** *adv*

sac·ris·tan \ˈsa-krə-stən\ *n* **1 :** a church officer in charge of the sacristy **2 :** SEXTON
sac·ris·ty \ˈsa-krə-stē\ *n, pl* **-ties :** VESTRY
sac·ro·il·i·ac \ˌsa-krō-ˈi-lē-ˌak\ *n* **:** the joint between the upper part of the hipbone and the sacrum
sac·ro·sanct \ˈsa-krō-ˌsaŋkt\ *adj* **:** SACRED, INVIOLABLE
sa·crum \ˈsa-krəm, ˈsā-\ *n, pl* **sa·cra** \ˈsa-krə, ˈsā-\ **:** the part of the vertebral column that is directly connected with or forms a part of the pelvis and in humans consists of five fused vertebrae
sad \ˈsad\ *adj* **sad·der; sad·dest** **1 :** GRIEVING, MOURNFUL, DOWNCAST **2 :** causing sorrow **3 :** DULL, SOMBER — **sad·ly** *adv* — **sad·ness** *n*
sad·den \ˈsa-dᵊn\ *vb* **:** to make sad
[1]**sad·dle** \ˈsa-dᵊl\ *n* **:** a usu. padded leather-covered seat (as for a rider on horseback)
[2]**saddle** *vb* **sad·dled; sad·dling** **1 :** to put a saddle on **2 :** OPPRESS, BURDEN
sad·dle·bow \ˈsa-dᵊl-ˌbō\ *n* **:** the arch in the front of a saddle
saddle horse *n* **:** a horse suited for or trained for riding
Sad·du·cee \ˈsa-jə-ˌsē, ˈsa-dyə-\ *n* **:** a member of an ancient Jewish sect consisting of a ruling class of priests and rejecting certain doctrines — **Sad·du·ce·an** \ˌsa-jə-ˈsē-ən, ˌsa-dyə-\ *adj*
sa·dism \ˈsā-ˌdi-zəm, ˈsa-\ *n* **:** a sexual perversion in which gratification is obtained by inflicting physical or mental pain on others — **sa·dist** \ˈsā-dist, ˈsa-\ *n* — **sa·dis·tic** \sə-ˈdis-tik\ *adj* — **sa·dis·ti·cal·ly** \-ti-k(ə-)lē\ *adv*
sa·do·mas·och·ism \ˌsā-(ˌ)dō-ˈma-sə-ˌki-zəm, ˌsa-, -ˈma-zə-\ *n* **:** the derivation of pleasure from the infliction of physical or mental pain either on others or on oneself — **sa·do·mas·och·is·tic** \-ˌma-sə-ˈkis-tik, -ˌma-zə-\ *adj*
SAE *abbr* **1** self-addressed envelope **2** Society of Automotive Engineers **3** stamped addressed envelope
sa·fa·ri \sə-ˈfär-ē\ *n* [Swahili, trip, fr. Ar *safarī* of a trip] **1 :** a hunting expedition esp. in eastern Africa **2 :** JOURNEY, TRIP
[1]**safe** \ˈsāf\ *adj* **saf·er; saf·est** **1 :** free from harm or risk **2 :** affording safety; *also* **:** secure from danger or loss **3 :** RELIABLE — **safe·ly** *adv*
[2]**safe** *n* **:** a container for keeping articles (as valuables) safe
safe–con·duct \-ˈkän-(ˌ)dəkt\ *n* **:** a pass permitting a person to go through enemy lines
[1]**safe·guard** \-ˌgärd\ *n* **:** a measure or device for preventing accident
[2]**safeguard** *vb* **:** to provide a safeguard for **:** PROTECT ⟨~ your valuables⟩
safe·keep·ing \ˈsāf-ˈkē-piŋ\ *n* **:** a keeping or being kept in safety
safer sex *n* **:** SAFE SEX
safe sex *n* **:** sexual activity and esp. sexual intercourse in which various measures (as the use of latex condoms) are taken to avoid disease (as AIDS) transmitted by sexual contact
safe·ty \ˈsāf-tē\ *n, pl* **safeties** **1 :** freedom from danger **:** SECURITY **2 :** a protective device **3 :** a football play in which the ball is downed by the offensive team behind its own goal line **4 :** a defensive football back in the deepest position — **safety** *adj*
safety glass *n* **:** shatter-resistant material formed of two sheets of glass with a sheet of clear plastic between them
safety match *n* **:** a match that ignites only when struck on a special surface
saf·flow·er \ˈsa-ˌflau̇(-ə)r\ *n* **:** a widely grown Old World herb related to the daisies that has large orange or red flower heads yielding a dyestuff and seeds rich in edible oil
saf·fron \ˈsa-frən\ *n* **:** a deep orange powder from the flower of a crocus used to color and flavor foods
sag \ˈsag\ *vb* **sagged; sag·ging** **1 :** to droop or settle from or as if from pressure ⟨a *sagging* mattress⟩ **2 :** to lose firmness or vigor — **sag** *n*
sa·ga \ˈsä-gə\ *n* [ON] **:** a narrative of heroic deeds; *esp* **:** one recorded in Iceland in the 12th and 13th centuries
sa·ga·cious \sə-ˈgā-shəs\ *adj* **:** of keen mind **:** SHREWD ⟨a ~ counselor⟩ — **sa·gac·i·ty** \-ˈga-sə-tē\ *n*
sag·a·more \ˈsa-gə-ˌmȯr\ *n* **:** a subordinate No. American Indigenous chief
[1]**sage** \ˈsāj\ *adj* [ME, fr. AF, fr. VL **sapius,* fr. L *sapere* to taste, have good taste, be wise] **:** WISE, PRUDENT — **sage·ly** *adv*
[2]**sage** *n* **:** one who is distinguished for wisdom
[3]**sage** *n* [ME, fr. AF *sage, salge,* fr. L *salvia,* fr. *salvus* healthy; fr. its use as a medicinal herb] **1 :** a perennial mint with aromatic leaves used in flavoring; *also* **:** its leaves **2 :** SAGEBRUSH **3 :** a light grayish green
sage·brush \ˈsāj-ˌbrəsh\ *n* **:** any of several low shrubby No. American composite plants; *esp* **:** one of the western U.S. with a sagelike odor
Sag·it·tar·i·us \ˌsa-jə-ˈter-ē-əs\ *n* [L, lit., archer] **1 :** a zodiacal constellation between Scorpio and Capricorn usu. pictured as a centaur archer **2 :** the 9th sign of the zodiac in astrology; *also* **:** one born under this sign
sa·go \ˈsā-gō\ *n, pl* **sagos :** a dry granulated starch esp. from the pith of various tropical palms **(sago palm)**
sa·gua·ro \sə-ˈwär-ə, -ˈgwär-, -ō\ *n, pl* **-ros** [MexSp] **:** a tall columnar usu. sparsely-branched cactus of dry areas of the southwestern U.S. and Mexico that may attain a height of up to 50 feet (16 meters)
said *past and past part of* SAY
[1]**sail** \ˈsāl\ *n* **1 :** a piece of fabric by means of which the wind is used to propel a ship **2 :** a sailing ship **3 :** something resembling a sail **4 :** a trip on a sailboat
[2]**sail** *vb* **1 :** to travel on a sailing ship **2 :** to pass over in a ship **3 :** to manage or direct the course of a ship **4 :** to move with ease, grace, or nonchalance

sail·board \ˈsāl-ˌbȯrd\ *n* : a modified surfboard having a mast and sailed by a standing person
sail·boat \-ˌbōt\ *n* : a boat propelled primarily by sail
sail·cloth \-ˌklȯth\ *n* : a heavy canvas used for sails, tents, or upholstery
sail·fish \-ˌfish\ *n* : any of a genus of large marine bony fishes with a large dorsal fin that are related to marlins
sail·ing *n* : the sport of handling or riding in a sailboat
sail·or \ˈsā-lər\ *n* : one that sails; *esp* : a member of a ship's crew
sail·plane \ˈsāl-ˌplān\ *n* : a glider designed to rise in an upward air current
saint \ˈsānt, *before a name* (ˌ)sānt *or* sənt\ *n* **1** : one officially recognized as preeminent for holiness **2** : one of the spirits of the departed in heaven **3** : a holy or godly person — **saint·ed** \-ˈsān-təd\ *adj* — **saint·hood** \-ˌhu̇d\ *n*
Saint Ber·nard \-bər-ˈnärd\ *n* : any of a Swiss alpine breed of tall powerful working dogs used esp. formerly in aiding lost travelers
Saint–John's–wort \ˈsānt-ˈjänz-ˌwərt, -ˌwȯrt\ *n* **1** : any of a genus of herbs and shrubs with showy yellow flowers **2** : the dried aerial parts of a Saint-John's-wort used esp. in herbal remedies
saint·ly \ˈsānt-lē\ *adj* : relating to, resembling, or befitting a saint ⟨~ zeal⟩ — **saint·li·ness** \-lē-nəs\ *n*
Saint Val·en·tine's Day \-ˈva-lən-ˌtīnz-\ *n* : VALENTINE'S DAY
¹**sake** \ˈsāk\ *n* **1** : END, PURPOSE **2** : personal or social welfare, safety, or well-being
²**sa·ke** *or* **sa·ki** \ˈsä-kē\ *n* : a Japanese alcoholic beverage of fermented rice
sa·laam \sə-ˈläm\ *n* [Ar *salām,* lit., peace] **1** : a salutation or ceremonial greeting in the East **2** : an obeisance performed by bowing very low and placing the right palm on the forehead — **salaam** *vb*
sa·la·cious \sə-ˈlā-shəs\ *adj* **1** : arousing sexual desire or imagination **2** : LUSTFUL — **sa·la·cious·ly** *adv* — **sa·la·cious·ness** *n*
sal·ad \ˈsa-ləd\ *n* : a cold dish (as of lettuce, vegetables, fish, eggs, or fruit) served with dressing
sal·a·man·der \ˈsa-lə-ˌman-dər\ *n* : any of numerous amphibians that look like lizards but have scaleless usu. smooth moist skin
sa·la·mi \sə-ˈlä-mē\ *n* [It] : a highly seasoned sausage of pork and beef
sal·a·ry \ˈsa-lə-rē\ *n, pl* **-ries** [ME *salarie,* fr. AF, fr. L *salarium* pension, salary, fr. neut. of *salarius* of salt, fr. *sal* salt] : payment made at regular intervals for services
sale \ˈsāl\ *n* **1** : transfer of ownership of property from one person to another in return for money **2** : ready market : DEMAND **3** : AUCTION **4** : a selling of goods at bargain prices — **sal·able** *or* **sale·able** \ˈsā-lə-bəl\ *adj*
sales·girl \ˈsālz-ˌgərl\ *n* : SALESWOMAN
sales·man \-mən\ *n* : one who sells in a given territory, in a store, or by telephone — **sales·man·ship** *n*
sales·per·son \-ˌpər-sən\ *n* : a salesman or saleswoman
sales·wom·an \-ˌwu̇-mən\ *n* : a woman who sells in a given territory, in a store, or by telephone
sal·i·cyl·ic acid \ˌsa-lə-ˈsi-lik-\ *n* : a crystalline organic acid used in making aspirin and other medicinal preparations
¹**sa·lient** \ˈsāl-yənt, ˈsā-lē-ənt\ *adj* : jutting forward beyond a line; *also* : PROMINENT ⟨a ~ feature⟩ ♦ ***Synonyms*** CONSPICUOUS, STRIKING, NOTICEABLE
²**salient** *n* : a projecting part in a line of defense
¹**sa·line** \ˈsā-ˌlēn, -ˌlīn\ *adj* : consisting of or containing salt : SALTY — **sa·lin·i·ty** \sā-ˈli-nə-tē, sə-\ *n*
²**saline** *n* **1** : a metallic salt esp. with a purgative action **2** : a saline solution
sa·li·va \sə-ˈlī-və\ *n* : a liquid secreted into the mouth that helps digestion — **sal·i·vary** \ˈsa-lə-ˌver-ē\ *adj*
sal·i·vate \ˈsa-lə-ˌvāt\ *vb* **-vat·ed; -vat·ing** : to produce saliva esp. in excess — **sal·i·va·tion** \ˌsa-lə-ˈvā-shən\ *n*
sal·low \ˈsa-lō\ *adj* : of a yellowish sickly color ⟨a ~ face⟩
sal·ly \ˈsa-lē\ *n, pl* **sallies** **1** : a rushing attack on besiegers by troops of a besieged place **2** : a witty remark or retort **3** : a brief excursion — **sally** *vb*
salm·on \ˈsa-mən\ *n, pl* **salmon** *also* **salmons** **1** : any of several bony fishes with pinkish flesh that are used for food and are related to the trouts **2** : a strong yellowish pink color
sal·mo·nel·la \ˌsal-mə-ˈne-lə\ *n, pl* **-nel·lae** \-ˈne-(ˌ)lē, -ˌlī\ *or* **-nellas** *or* **-nella** : any of a genus of rod-shaped bacteria that cause various illnesses (as food poisoning)
sa·lon \sə-ˈlän, ˈsa-ˌlän, sa-ˈlōⁿ\ *n* [F] : an elegant drawing room; *also* : a fashionable shop ⟨beauty ~⟩
sa·loon \sə-ˈlün\ *n* **1** : a large public cabin on a ship **2** : a place where liquors are sold and drunk : BARROOM **3** *Brit* : SEDAN 2
sal·sa \ˈsȯl-sə, ˈsäl-\ *n* : a spicy sauce of tomatoes, onions, and hot peppers
¹**salt** \ˈsȯlt\ *n* **1** : a white crystalline substance that consists of sodium and chlorine and is used in seasoning foods **2** : a saltlike cathartic substance (as Epsom salts) **3** : a compound formed usu. by action of an acid on metal **4** : SAILOR — **salt·i·ness** \ˈsȯl-tē-nəs\ *n* — **salty** \ˈsȯl-tē\ *adj*
²**salt** *vb* : to preserve, season, or feed with salt
³**salt** *adj* : preserved or treated with salt ⟨~ pork⟩; *also* : SALTY
SALT *abbr* Strategic Arms Limitation Talks
salt away *vb* : to lay away safely : SAVE
salt·box \ˈsȯlt-ˌbäks\ *n* : a frame dwelling with two stories in front and one behind and a long sloping roof

salt·cel·lar \-ˌse-lər\ *n* : a small container for holding salt at the table
sal·tine \sȯl-ˈtēn\ *n* : a thin crisp cracker sprinkled with salt
salt lick *n* : LICK 5
salt·pe·ter \ˈsȯlt-ˈpē-tər\ *n* [ME *salt petre,* alter. of *salpetre,* fr. ML *sal petrae,* lit., salt of the rock] **1** : POTASSIUM NITRATE **2** : SODIUM NITRATE
salt·wa·ter \-ˌwȯ-tər, -ˌwä-\ *adj* : of, relating to, or living in salt water
sa·lu·bri·ous \sə-ˈlü-brē-əs\ *adj* : favorable to health ⟨a ~ climate⟩
sal·u·tary \ˈsal-yə-ˌter-ē\ *adj* : health-giving; *also* : BENEFICIAL ⟨~ effects⟩
sal·u·ta·tion \ˌsal-yə-ˈtā-shən\ *n* : an expression of greeting, goodwill, or courtesy usu. by word or gesture
sa·lu·ta·to·ri·an \sə-ˌlü-tə-ˈtȯr-ē-ən\ *n* : the student having the 2d highest rank in a graduating class who delivers the salutatory address
sa·lu·ta·to·ry \sə-ˈlü-tə-ˌtȯr-ē\ *adj* : relating to or being the welcoming oration delivered at an academic commencement
[1]**sa·lute** \sə-ˈlüt\ *vb* **sa·lut·ed; sa·lut·ing** **1** : GREET **2** : to honor by special ceremonies **3** : to show respect to (a superior officer) by a formal position of hand, rifle, or sword
[2]**salute** *n* **1** : GREETING **2** : the formal position assumed in saluting a superior
[1]**sal·vage** \ˈsal-vij\ *n* **1** : money paid for saving a ship, its cargo, or passengers when the ship is wrecked or in danger **2** : the saving of a ship **3** : the saving of possessions in danger of being lost **4** : things saved from loss or destruction (as by a wreck or fire)
[2]**salvage** *vb* **sal·vaged; sal·vag·ing** : to rescue from destruction
sal·va·tion \sal-ˈvā-shən\ *n* **1** : the saving of a person from sin or its consequences esp. in the life after death **2** : the saving from danger, difficulty, or evil **3** : something that saves
[1]**salve** \ˈsav, ˈsäv\ *n* **1** : a medicinal substance applied to the skin **2** : a soothing influence
[2]**salve** *vb* **salved; salv·ing** : EASE, SOOTHE
sal·ver \ˈsal-vər\ *n* [F *salve,* fr. Sp *salva* sampling of food to detect poison, tray, fr. *salvar* to save, sample food to detect poison, fr. LL *salvare* to save, fr. L *salvus* safe] : a small serving tray
sal·vo \ˈsal-vō\ *n, pl* **salvos** *or* **salvoes** : a simultaneous discharge of guns
Sam *or* **Saml** *abbr* Samuel
SAM \ˈsam, ˌes-ˌā-ˈem\ *n* [*s*urface-to-*a*ir *m*issile] : a guided missile for use against aircraft by ground units
Sa·mar·i·tan \sə-ˈmer-ə-tən\ *n* **1** : a native or inhabitant of Samaria **2** : a person who is generous in helping those in distress
sa·mar·i·um \sə-ˈmer-ē-əm\ *n* : a silvery-white lustrous rare metallic chemical element
[1]**same** \ˈsām\ *adj* **1** : being the one referred to : not different **2** : SIMILAR — **same·ness** *n*
[2]**same** *pron* : the same one or ones
[3]**same** *adv* : in the same manner
same–sex \ˈsām-ˈseks\ *adj* : of, relating to, or involving members of the same sex
Sa·mi *also* **Saa·mi** \ˈsä-mē\ *n, pl* **Sami** *or* **Samis** *also* **Saami** *or* **Saamis** : a member of a people of northern Scandinavia, Finland, and the Kola Peninsula of Russia
Sa·mo·an \sə-ˈmō-ən\ *n* : a native or inhabitant of Samoa — **Samoan** *adj*
sa·mo·sa \sə-ˈmō-sə\ *n* : a small triangular pastry filled with spiced meat or vegetables and fried
sam·o·var \ˈsa-mə-ˌvär\ *n* [Russ, fr. *samo-* self + *varit'* to boil] : an urn with a spigot at the base used esp. in Russia to boil water for tea
sam·pan \ˈsam-ˌpan\ *n* : a flat-bottomed skiff of eastern Asia usu. propelled by two short oars
[1]**sam·ple** \ˈsam-pəl\ *n* : a representative piece, item, or set of individuals that shows the quality or nature of the whole from which it was taken : EXAMPLE, SPECIMEN
[2]**sample** *vb* **sam·pled; sam·pling** : to judge the quality of by a sample
sam·pler \ˈsam-plər\ *n* **1** : a piece of needlework; *esp* : one testing skill in embroidering **2** : a collection of various examples of something ⟨a chocolate ~⟩
Sam·u·el \ˈsam-yə-wəl\ *n* — see BIBLE table
sam·u·rai \ˈsa-mə-ˌrī, ˈsam-yə-\ *n, pl* **samurai** : a military retainer of a Japanese feudal lord who adhered to strict principles of honor and duty
san·a·to·ri·um \ˌsa-nə-ˈtȯr-ē-əm\ *n, pl* **-ri·ums** *or* **-ria** \-ē-ə\ **1** : a health resort **2** : an establishment for the care esp. of convalescents or the chronically ill
sanc·ti·fy \ˈsaŋk-tə-ˌfī\ *vb* **-fied; -fy·ing** **1** : to make holy : CONSECRATE **2** : to free from sin — **sanc·ti·fi·ca·tion** \ˌsaŋk-tə-fə-ˈkā-shən\ *n*
sanc·ti·mo·nious \ˌsaŋk-tə-ˈmō-nē-əs\ *adj* : hypocritically pious ⟨~ politicians⟩ — **sanc·ti·mo·nious·ly** *adv*
[1]**sanc·tion** \ˈsaŋk-shən\ *n* **1** : authoritative approval **2** : a measure (as a threat or fine) designed to enforce a law or standard ⟨economic ~*s*⟩
[2]**sanction** *vb* : to give approval to : RATIFY ♦ ***Synonyms*** ENDORSE, ACCREDIT, CERTIFY, APPROVE
sanc·ti·ty \ˈsaŋk-tə-tē\ *n, pl* **-ties** **1** : GODLINESS **2** : SACREDNESS
sanc·tu·ary \ˈsaŋk-chə-ˌwer-ē\ *n, pl* **-ar·ies** **1** : a consecrated place (as the part of a church in which the altar is placed) **2** : a place of refuge ⟨bird ~⟩
sanc·tum \ˈsaŋk-təm\ *n, pl* **sanctums** *also* **sanc·ta** \-tə\ : a private office or study : DEN ⟨an editor's ~⟩
[1]**sand** \ˈsand\ *n* : loose particles of hard broken rock — **sandy** *adj*
[2]**sand** *vb* **1** : to cover or fill with sand **2** : to scour, smooth, or polish with an abrasive (as sandpaper) — **sand·er** *n*
san·dal \ˈsan-dᵊl\ *n* : a shoe consisting of

a sole strapped to the foot; *also* : a low or open slipper or rubber overshoe

san·dal·wood \-ˌwu̇d\ *n* : the fragrant yellowish heartwood of a parasitic tree of southern Asia that is much used in ornamental carving and cabinetwork; *also* : the tree

sand·bag \ˈsand-ˌbag\ *n* : a bag filled with sand and used in fortifications, as ballast, or as a weapon

sand·bank \-ˌbaŋk\ *n* : a deposit of sand (as in a bar or shoal)

sand·bar \-ˌbär\ *n* : a ridge of sand formed in water by tides or currents

sand·blast \-ˌblast\ *vb* : to treat with a stream of sand blown by compressed air — **sand·blast·er** *n*

sand dollar *n* : any of numerous flat circular sea urchins living chiefly on sandy bottoms in shallow water

S & H *abbr* shipping and handling

sand·hog \ˈsand-ˌho̊g, -ˌhäg\ *n* : a laborer who builds underwater tunnels

sand·lot \-ˌlät\ *n* : a vacant lot esp. when used for the unorganized sports of children — **sand·lot** *adj* — **sand·lot·ter** *n*

sand·man \-ˌman\ *n* : the genie of folklore who makes children sleepy

sand·pa·per \-ˌpā-pər\ *n* : paper with abrasive (as sand) glued on one side used in smoothing and polishing surfaces — **sandpaper** *vb*

sand·pip·er \-ˌpī-pər\ *n* : any of various shorebirds with a soft-tipped bill longer than that of the related plovers

sand·stone \-ˌstōn\ *n* : rock made of sand united by a natural cement

sand·storm \-ˌsto̊rm\ *n* : a windstorm that drives clouds of sand

sand trap *n* : a hazard on a golf course consisting of a hollow containing sand

¹**sand·wich** \ˈsand-(ˌ)wich\ *n* [after John Montagu, 4th Earl of *Sandwich* †1792 Eng. diplomat] **1** : two or more slices of bread with a layer (as of meat or cheese) spread between them **2** : something resembling a sandwich

²**sandwich** *vb* : to squeeze or crowd in

sane \ˈsān\ *adj* **san·er; san·est** : mentally sound and healthy; *also* : SENSIBLE, RATIONAL — **sane·ly** *adv*

sang *past of* SING

sang·froid \ˈsäⁿ-ˈfrwä\ *n* [F *sang-froid,* lit., cold blood] : self-possession or an imperturbable state esp. under strain

san·gui·nary \ˈsaŋ-gwə-ˌner-ē\ *adj* : BLOODY ⟨∼ battle⟩

san·guine \ˈsaŋ-gwən\ *adj* **1** : RUDDY **2** : CHEERFUL, HOPEFUL ⟨a ∼ disposition⟩

sanit *abbr* sanitary; sanitation

san·i·tar·i·an \ˌsa-nə-ˈter-ē-ən\ *n* : a specialist in sanitation and public health

san·i·tar·i·um \ˌsa-nə-ˈter-ē-əm\ *n, pl* **-i·ums** *or* **-ia** \-ē-ə\ : SANATORIUM

san·i·tary \ˈsa-nə-ˌter-ē\ *adj* **1** : of or relating to health : HYGIENIC **2** : free from filth or infective matter

sanitary napkin *n* : a disposable absorbent pad used to absorb uterine flow (as during menstruation)

san·i·ta·tion \ˌsa-nə-ˈtā-shən\ *n* : the act or process of making sanitary; *also* : protection of health by maintenance of sanitary conditions

san·i·tize \ˈsa-nə-ˌtīz\ *vb* **-tized; -tiz·ing** **1** : to make sanitary **2** : to make more acceptable by removing unpleasant features — **san·i·tiz·er** *n*

san·i·ty \ˈsa-nə-tē\ *n* : soundness of mind

sank *past of* SINK

sans \ˈsanz\ *prep* : WITHOUT

San·skrit \ˈsan-ˌskrit\ *n* : an ancient language that is the classical language of India and of Hinduism — **Sanskrit** *adj*

San·ta Ana \ˌsan-tə-ˈa-nə\ *n* [*Santa Ana* Mountains in southern California] : a hot dry wind from the north, northeast, or east in southern California

san·tims \ˈsän-ˌtims\ *n, pl* **san·ti·mi** \-ti-mē\ : a monetary unit equal to $\frac{1}{100}$ lats formerly used in Latvia

¹**sap** \ˈsap\ *n* **1** : a vital fluid; *esp* : a watery fluid that circulates through a vascular plant **2** : a foolish gullible person — **sap·less** *adj*

²**sap** *vb* **sapped; sap·ping** **1** : UNDERMINE **2** : to weaken gradually

sa·pi·ent \ˈsā-pē-ənt, ˈsa-\ *adj* : WISE, DISCERNING — **sa·pi·ence** \-əns\ *n*

sa·pi·o·sex·u·al \ˌsā-pē-ō-ˈsek-shə-wəl, ˌsa-\ *adj* : of, relating to, or characterized by sexual or romantic attraction to highly intelligent people — **sapiosexual** *n*

sap·ling \ˈsa-pliŋ\ *n* : a young tree

sap·phire \ˈsa-ˌfī(-ə)r\ *n* : a hard transparent usu. rich blue gem

sap·py \ˈsa-pē\ *adj* **sap·pi·er; -est** **1** : full of sap **2** : overly sentimental ⟨a ∼ movie⟩ **3** : SILLY, FOOLISH

sap·ro·phyte \ˈsa-prə-ˌfīt\ *n* : a living thing and esp. a plant living on dead or decaying organic matter — **sap·ro·phyt·ic** \ˌsa-prə-ˈfi-tik\ *adj*

sap·suck·er \ˈsap-ˌsə-kər\ *n* : any of a genus of No. American woodpeckers

sap·wood \-ˌwu̇d\ *n* : the younger active and usu. lighter and softer outer layer of wood (as of a tree trunk)

sar·casm \ˈsär-ˌka-zəm\ *n* **1** : a cutting or contemptuous remark **2** : ironic criticism or reproach — **sar·cas·tic** \sär-ˈkas-tik\ *adj* — **sar·cas·ti·cal·ly** \-ti-k(ə-)lē\ *adv*

sar·co·ma \sär-ˈkō-mə\ *n, pl* **-mas** *also* **-ma·ta** \-mə-tə\ : a malignant tumor esp. of connective tissue, bone, cartilage, or striated muscle

sar·coph·a·gus \sär-ˈkä-fə-gəs\ *n, pl* **-gi** \-ˌgī, -ˌjī\ *also* **-gus·es** [L *sarcophagus* (*lapis*) limestone used for coffins, fr. Gk (*lithos*) *sarkophagos,* lit., flesh-eating stone, fr. *sark-, sarx* flesh + *phagein* to eat] : a large stone coffin

sar·dine \sär-ˈdēn\ *n, pl* **sardines** *also* **sardine** : a young or small fish preserved for use as food

sar·don·ic \sär-ˈdä-nik\ *adj* : disdainfully or skeptically humorous : derisively mocking ♦ ***Synonyms*** IRONIC, SATIRIC, SARCASTIC — **sar·don·i·cal·ly** \-ni-k(ə-)lē\ *adv*

sa·ri *also* **sa·ree** \ˈsär-ē\ *n* [Hindi *sāṛī*] : a

garment worn by women in southern Asia that consists of a long cloth draped around the body and head or shoulder

sa·rin \ˈsär-ən, zä-ˈrēn\ *n* : an extremely toxic chemical weapon used as a lethal nerve gas

sa·rong \sə-ˈrȯŋ, -ˈräŋ\ *n* : a loose garment wrapped around the body and worn by men and women of the Malay Archipelago and the Pacific islands

SARS \ˈsärz\ *n* [*s*evere *a*cute *r*espiratory *s*yndrome] : a severe respiratory illness that is caused by a coronavirus, is transmitted esp. by contact with infectious material (as respiratory droplets or body fluids), and is characterized by fever, headache, body aches, a dry cough, shortness of breath, and usu. pneumonia

sar·sa·pa·ril·la \ˌsas-pə-ˈri-lə, ˌsärs-\ *n* **1** : the dried roots of a tropical American smilax used esp. for flavoring; *also* : the plant **2** : a sweetened carbonated beverage flavored with sassafras and an oil from a birch

sar·to·ri·al \sär-ˈtȯr-ē-əl\ *adj* : of or relating to a tailor or tailored clothes — **sar·to·ri·al·ly** *adv*

SASE *abbr* self-addressed stamped envelope

[1]**sash** \ˈsash\ *n* : a broad band worn around the waist or over the shoulder

[2]**sash** *n, pl* **sash** *also* **sash·es** : a frame for panes of glass in a door or window; *also* : the movable part of a window

sa·shay \sa-ˈshā\ *vb* **1** : WALK, GLIDE, GO **2** : to strut or move about in an ostentatious manner **3** : to proceed in a diagonal or sideways manner

Sask *abbr* Saskatchewan

Sas·quatch \ˈsas-ˌkwach, -ˌkwäch\ *n* [Halkomelem (Indigenous language of British Columbia) *sésq̓əc*] : a large hairy humanlike creature reported to exist in the northwestern U.S. and western Canada

sas·sa·fras \ˈsa-sə-ˌfras\ *n* [Sp *sasafrás*] : an aromatic No. American tree related to the laurel; *also* : its carcinogenic dried root bark

sassy \ˈsa-sē\ *adj* **sass·i·er; -est** : SAUCY

[1]**sat** *past and past part of* SIT

[2]**sat** *abbr* **1** satellite **2** saturated

Sat *abbr* Saturday

Sa·tan \ˈsā-tᵊn\ *n* : DEVIL

sa·tang \sə-ˈtäŋ\ *n, pl* **satang** *or* **satangs** — see *baht* at MONEY table

sa·tan·ic \sə-ˈta-nik, sā-\ *adj* **1** : of or characteristic of Satan **2** : extremely malicious or wicked — **sa·tan·i·cal·ly** \-ni-k(ə-)lē\ *adv*

satch·el \ˈsa-chəl\ *n* : SUITCASE

sate \ˈsāt\ *vb* **sat·ed; sat·ing** : to satisfy to the full; *also* : SURFEIT, GLUT

sa·teen \sa-ˈtēn, sə-\ *n* : a cotton cloth finished to resemble satin

sat·el·lite \ˈsa-tə-ˌlīt\ *n* [MF, fr. L *satelles* attendant] **1** : an obsequious follower of a distinguished person : TOADY **2** : a celestial body that orbits a larger body **3** : a manufactured object that orbits a celestial body

satellite dish *n* : a microwave dish for receiving usu. television transmissions from an orbiting satellite

sa·ti·ate \ˈsā-shē-ˌāt\ *vb* **-at·ed; -at·ing** : to satisfy fully or to excess

sa·ti·ety \sə-ˈtī-ə-tē\ *n* : fullness to the point of excess

sat·in \ˈsa-tᵊn\ *n* : a fabric (as of silk) with a glossy surface — **sat·iny** *adj*

sat·in·wood \ˈsa-tᵊn-ˌwu̇d\ *n* : a hard yellowish brown wood of satiny luster; *also* : a tree yielding this wood

sat·ire \ˈsa-ˌtī(-ə)r\ *n* : biting wit, irony, or sarcasm used to expose vice or folly; *also* : a literary work having these qualities — **sa·tir·ic** \sə-ˈtir-ik\ *or* **sa·tir·i·cal** \-i-kəl\ *adj* — **sa·tir·i·cal·ly** *adv* — **sat·i·rist** \ˈsa-tə-rist\ *n* — **sat·i·rize** \-tə-ˌrīz\ *vb*

sat·is·fac·tion \ˌsa-təs-ˈfak-shən\ *n* **1** : payment through penance of punishment incurred by sin **2** : CONTENTMENT, GRATIFICATION **3** : reparation for an insult **4** : settlement of a claim

sat·is·fac·to·ry \-ˈfak-tə-rē\ *adj* : giving satisfaction : ADEQUATE — **sat·is·fac·to·ri·ly** \-ˈfak-tə-rə-lē\ *adv*

sat·is·fy \ˈsa-təs-ˌfī\ *vb* **-fied; -fy·ing** **1** : to answer or discharge (a claim) in full **2** : to make happy : GRATIFY **3** : to pay what is due to **4** : CONVINCE **5** : to meet the requirements of — **sat·is·fy·ing·ly** *adv*

sa·trap \ˈsā-ˌtrap, ˈsa-\ *n* [ME, fr. L *satrapes,* fr. Gk *satrapēs,* fr. Old Pers *khshathrapāvan,* lit., protector of the dominion] : a petty prince : a subordinate ruler

sat·u·rate \ˈsa-chə-ˌrāt\ *vb* **-rat·ed; -rat·ing** **1** : to soak thoroughly **2** : to treat or charge with something to the point where no more can be absorbed, dissolved, or retained — **sat·u·ra·ble** \ˈsa-chə-rə-bəl\ *adj* — **sat·u·ra·tion** \ˌsa-chə-ˈrā-shən\ *n*

saturated *adj* **1** : full of moisture **2** : having no double or triple bonds between carbon atoms ⟨~ fats⟩

Sat·ur·day \ˈsa-tər-dē, -ˌdā\ *n* : the 7th day of the week

Saturday night special *n* : a cheap easily concealed handgun

Sat·urn \ˈsa-tərn\ *n* : the planet 6th in order from the sun

sat·ur·nine \ˈsa-tər-ˌnīn\ *adj* : SULLEN, SARDONIC

sa·tyr \ˈsā-tər\ *n* **1** *often cap* : a woodland deity in Greek mythology having certain characteristics of a horse or goat **2** : a lecherous man

[1]**sauce** \ˈsȯs, *3 usu* ˈsas\ *n* **1** : a fluid dressing or topping for food **2** : stewed fruit **3** : IMPUDENCE

[2]**sauce** \ˈsȯs, *2 usu* ˈsas\ *vb* **sauced; sauc·ing** **1** : to put sauce on; *also* : to add zest to **2** : to be impudent to

sauce·pan \ˈsȯs-ˌpan\ *n* : a small deep cooking pan with a handle

sau·cer \ˈsȯ-sər\ *n* : a rounded shallow dish for use under a cup

saucy \ˈsa-sē, ˈsȯ-\ *adj* **sauc·i·er; -est** : IMPUDENT, PERT — **sauc·i·ly** \-sə-lē\ *adv* — **sauc·i·ness** \-sē-nəs\ *n*

Sau·di \ˈsau̇-dē, ˈsȯ-; sä-ˈü-dē\ *n* : SAUDI ARABIAN — **Saudi** *adj*

Saudi Arabian *n* : a native or inhabitant of Saudi Arabia — **Saudi Arabian** *adj*

sau·er·kraut \ˈsau̇(-ə)r-ˌkrau̇t\ *n* [G, fr. *sauer* sour + *Kraut* greens] : finely cut cabbage fermented in brine

Sauk \ˈsȯk\ *or* **Sac** \ˈsak, ˈsȯk\ *n, pl* **Sauk** *or* **Sauks** *or* **Sac** *or* **Sacs** : a member of an Algonquian-speaking Indigenous people formerly living in what is now Wisconsin

sau·na \ˈsȯ-nə, ˈsau̇-nə\ *n* **1** : a Finnish steam bath in which the steam is provided by water thrown on hot stones **2** : a dry heat bath; *also* : a room or cabinet used for such a bath

saun·ter \ˈsȯn-tər, ˈsän-\ *vb* : STROLL

sau·ro·pod \ˈsȯr-ə-ˌpäd\ *n* : any of a suborder of plant-eating dinosaurs (as a brontosaurus) with a long neck and tail and a small head — **sauropod** *adj*

sau·sage \ˈsȯ-sij\ *n* [ME *sausige,* fr. AF *sauseche,* fr. LL *salsicia,* fr. L *salsus* salted] : minced and highly seasoned meat (as pork) usu. enclosed in a tubular casing

S Aust *abbr* South Australia

sau·té \sȯ-ˈtā, sō-\ *vb* **sau·téed** *or* **sau·téd; sau·té·ing** [F] : to fry lightly in a little fat — **sauté** *n*

sau·terne \sō-ˈtərn, sȯ-\ *n, often cap* : a usu. semisweet American white wine

[1]**sav·age** \ˈsa-vij\ *adj* [ME, fr. AF *salvage, savage,* fr. LL *salvaticus,* alter. of L *silvaticus* of the woods, wild, fr. *silva* forest] **1** : WILD, UNTAMED **2** *dated, offensive* : UNCIVILIZED, BARBAROUS **3** : CRUEL, FIERCE — **sav·age·ly** *adv* — **sav·age·ness** *n* — **sav·age·ry** \-rē\ *n*

[2]**savage** *n* **1** *dated, offensive* : a member of a primitive human society **2** : a rude, unmannerly, or brutal person

sa·van·na *or* **sa·van·nah** \sə-ˈva-nə\ *n* [Sp *zavana*] : grassland containing scattered trees

sa·vant \sa-ˈvänt, sə-, ˈsa-vənt\ *n* : a learned person : SCHOLAR

[1]**save** \ˈsāv\ *vb* **saved; sav·ing** **1** : to redeem from sin **2** : to rescue from danger **3** : to preserve or guard from destruction or loss; *also* : to store (data) in a computer or on a storage device **4** : to put aside as a store or reserve — **sav·er** *n*

[2]**save** *n* : a play that prevents an opponent from scoring or winning

[3]**save** *prep* : EXCEPT

[4]**save** *conj* : BUT

savings and loan association *n* : a cooperative association that holds savings of members in the form of dividend-bearing shares and that invests chiefly in mortgage loans

savings bank *n* : a bank that holds funds of individual depositors in interest-bearing accounts and makes long-term investments (as mortgage loans)

savings bond *n* : a registered U.S. bond issued in denominations of $50 to $10,000

sav·ior *or* **sav·iour** \ˈsāv-yər\ *n* **1** : one who saves **2** *cap* : Jesus Christ

sa·voir faire \ˌsav-ˌwär-ˈfer\ *n* [F *savoir faire,* lit., knowing how to do] : sureness in social behavior

[1]**sa·vor** *also* **sa·vour** \ˈsā-vər\ *n* **1** : the taste and odor of something **2** : a special flavor or quality — **sa·vory** *adj*

[2]**savor** *also* **savour** *vb* **1** : to have a specified taste, smell, or quality **2** : to taste with pleasure ⟨~*ed* every morsel⟩

sa·vo·ry \ˈsā-və-rē\ *n, pl* **-ries** : either of two aromatic mints used in cooking

[1]**sav·vy** \ˈsa-vē\ *vb* **sav·vied; sav·vy·ing** : UNDERSTAND, COMPREHEND

[2]**savvy** *n* : practical know-how ⟨political ~⟩ — **savvy** *adj*

[1]**saw** *past of* SEE

[2]**saw** \ˈsȯ\ *n* : a cutting tool with a blade having a line of teeth along its edge

[3]**saw** *vb* **sawed** \ˈsȯd\; **sawed** *or* **sawn** \ˈsȯn\; **saw·ing** : to cut or shape with or as if with a saw

[4]**saw** *n* : a common saying : MAXIM

saw·dust \ˈsȯ-(ˌ)dəst\ *n* : fine particles made by a saw in cutting

saw·fly \-ˌflī\ *n* : any of numerous insects belonging to the same order as bees and wasps and including many whose larvae are plant-feeding pests

saw·horse \-ˌhȯrs\ *n* : a rack on which wood is rested while being sawed by hand

saw·mill \-ˌmil\ *n* : a mill for sawing logs

saw palmetto *n* **1** : any of several shrubby palms with spiny-toothed petioles **2** : the fruit of a saw palmetto used esp. in herbal remedies

saw·yer \ˈsȯ-yər\ *n* : a person who saws timber

sax \ˈsaks\ *n* : SAXOPHONE

sax·i·frage \ˈsak-sə-frij, -ˌfrāj\ *n* [ME, fr. AF, fr. LL *saxifraga,* fr. L, fem. of *saxifragus,* breaking rocks] : any of a genus of plants with showy flowers and usu. with leaves growing in tufts close to the ground

sax·o·phone \ˈsak-sə-ˌfōn\ *n* : a musical instrument having a conical metal tube with a reed mouthpiece and finger keys — **sax·o·phon·ist** \-ˌfō-nist\ *n*

[1]**say** \ˈsā\ *vb* **said** \ˈsed\; **say·ing; says** \ˈsez\ **1** : to express in words ⟨~ what you mean⟩ **2** : to state as opinion or belief **3** : PRONOUNCE; *also* : RECITE, REPEAT ⟨~ your prayers⟩ **4** : INDICATE ⟨the clock ~*s* noon⟩

[2]**say** *n, pl* **says** \ˈsāz\ **1** : an expression of opinion **2** : power of decision

say·ing *n* : a commonly repeated statement

say–so \ˈsā-(ˌ)sō\ *n* : an esp. authoritative assertion or decision; *also* : the right to decide ⟨he has the ~ on this matter⟩

sb *abbr* substantive

Sb *symbol* [L *stibium*] antimony

SB *abbr* [NL *scientiae baccalaureus*] bachelor of science

SBA *abbr* Small Business Administration

sc *abbr* **1** scene **2** science

Sc *symbol* scandium

SC *abbr* **1** South Carolina **2** supreme court

[1]**scab** \ˈskab\ *n* **1** : scabies of domestic animals **2** : a crust of hardened blood

forming over a wound **3** : a worker who replaces a striker or works under conditions not authorized by a union **4** : any of various bacterial or fungus plant diseases marked by crusted spots on stems or leaves — **scab·by** *adj*

[2]**scab** *vb* **scabbed; scab·bing** **1** : to become covered with a scab **2** : to work as a scab

scab·bard \ˈska-bərd\ *n* : a sheath for the blade of a weapon (as a sword)

sca·bies \ˈskā-bēz\ *n* [L] : contagious itch or mange caused by mites living as parasites under the skin

sca·brous \ˈska-brəs, ˈskā-\ *adj* **1** : DIFFICULT, KNOTTY **2** : rough to the touch : SCALY, SCURFY ⟨a ~ leaf⟩ **3** : dealing with suggestive, indecent, or scandalous themes ⟨~ lyrics⟩; *also* : SQUALID

scad \ˈskad\ *n* : a large number or quantity — usu. used in pl.

scaf·fold \ˈska-fəld, -ˌfōld\ *n* **1** : a raised platform for workers to sit or stand on **2** : a platform on which a criminal is executed (as by hanging)

scaf·fold·ing *n* : a system of scaffolds; *also* : materials for scaffolds

scal·a·wag *or* **scal·ly·wag** \ˈska-li-ˌwag\ *n* : RASCAL

[1]**scald** \ˈskȯld\ *vb* **1** : to burn with or as if with hot liquid or steam **2** : to heat to just below the boiling point

[2]**scald** *n* : a burn caused by scalding

[1]**scale** \ˈskāl\ *n* **1** : either pan of a balance **2** : BALANCE — usu. used in pl. **3** : a weighing instrument

[2]**scale** *vb* **scaled; scal·ing** : WEIGH

[3]**scale** *n* **1** : one of the small thin plates that cover the body esp. of a fish or reptile **2** : a thin plate or flake **3** : a thin coating, layer, or incrustation **4** : SCALE INSECT — **scaled** \ˈskāld\ *adj* — **scale·less** \ˈskāl-ləs\ *adj* — **scaly** *adj*

[4]**scale** *vb* **scaled; scal·ing** : to strip of scales

[5]**scale** *n* [ME, fr. LL *scala* ladder, staircase, fr. L *scalae,* pl., stairs, rungs, ladder] **1** : something divided into regular spaces as a help in drawing or measuring **2** : a graduated series **3** : the size of a sample (as a model) in proportion to the size of the actual thing **4** : a standard of estimation or judgment **5** : a series of musical tones going up or down in pitch according to a specified scheme

[6]**scale** *vb* **scaled; scal·ing** **1** : to climb by or as if by a ladder **2** : to arrange in a graded series

scale insect *n* : any of numerous small insects with wingless scale-covered females that are related to aphids and feed on and are often pests of plants

scale·pan \ˈskāl-ˌpan\ *n* : [1]SCALE 1

scal·lion \ˈskal-yən\ *n* [ultim. fr. L *ascalonia* (*caepa*) onion of Ascalon (seaport in Palestine)] : an onion without an enlarged bulb; *also* : GREEN ONION

[1]**scal·lop** \ˈskä-ləp, ˈska-\ *n* **1** : any of numerous marine bivalve mollusks with radially ridged shells; *also* : a large edible muscle of this mollusk **2** : one of a continuous series of rounded projections forming an edge

[2]**scallop** *vb* **1** : to bake in a casserole ⟨~*ed* potatoes⟩ **2** : to shape, cut, or finish in scallops ⟨~*ed* edges⟩

[1]**scalp** \ˈskalp\ *n* : the part of the skin and flesh of the head usu. covered with hair

[2]**scalp** *vb* **1** : to remove the scalp from **2** : to resell at greatly increased prices ⟨~ tickets⟩ — **scalp·er** *n*

scal·pel \ˈskal-pəl\ *n* : a small straight knife with a thin blade used esp. in surgery

scam \ˈskam\ *n* : a fraudulent or deceptive act or operation — **scam** *vb*

scamp \ˈskamp\ *n* : RASCAL

scam·per \ˈskam-pər\ *vb* : to run nimbly and playfully — **scamper** *n*

scam·pi \ˈskam-pē\ *n, pl* **scampi** [It] : a usu. large shrimp; *also* : large shrimp prepared with a garlic-flavored sauce

[1]**scan** \ˈskan\ *vb* **scanned; scan·ning** **1** : to read (verses) so as to show metrical structure **2** : to examine closely **3** : to input or examine systematically in order to obtain data esp. for display or storage **4** : to make a scan of (as the human body) — **scan·ner** *n*

[2]**scan** *n* **1** : the act or process of scanning **2** : a picture of the distribution of radioactive material in something; *also* : an image of a bodily part produced (as by computer) by combining radiographic data obtained from several angles or sections

Scand *abbr* Scandinavia

scan·dal \ˈskan-dᵊl\ *n* [ME, fr. LL *scandalum* stumbling block, offense, fr. Gk *skandalon*] **1** : DISGRACE, DISHONOR **2** : malicious gossip : SLANDER — **scan·dal·ize** *vb* — **scan·dal·ous** *adj* — **scan·dal·ous·ly** *adv*

scan·dal·mon·ger \-ˌməŋ-gər, -ˌmäŋ-\ *n* : a person who circulates scandal

Scan·di·na·vian \ˌskan-də-ˈnā-vē-ən\ *n* : a native or inhabitant of Scandinavia — **Scandinavian** *adj*

scan·di·um \ˈskan-dē-əm\ *n* : a silvery-white metallic chemical element

scan·ner \ˈska-nər\ *n* **1** : a radio receiver that sequentially scans a range of frequencies for a signal **2** : a device that scans an image or document esp. for use or storage on a computer

[1]**scant** \ˈskant\ *adj* **1** : barely sufficient ⟨food is in ~ supply⟩ **2** : having scarcely enough ♦ ***Synonyms*** SCANTY, SKIMPY, MEAGER, SPARSE, EXIGUOUS

[2]**scant** *vb* **1** : SKIMP **2** : STINT

scant·ling \ˈskant-liŋ\ *n* : a small piece of lumber (as an upright in a house)

scanty \ˈskan-tē\ *adj* **scant·i·er; -est** : barely sufficient : SCANT ⟨wore ~ outfits⟩ — **scant·i·ly** \ˈskan-tə-lē\ *adv* — **scant·i·ness** \-tē-nəs\ *n*

scape·goat \ˈskāp-ˌgōt\ *n* : one that bears the blame for others

scape·grace \-ˌgrās\ *n* [*scape* (escape)] : an incorrigible rascal

scap·u·la \ˈska-pyə-lə\ *n, pl* **-lae** \-ˌlē\ *or* **-las** [L] : SHOULDER BLADE

scap•u•lar \-lər\ *n* : a pair of small cloth squares worn on the breast and back under the clothing esp. for religious purposes

scar \ˈskär\ *n* : a mark left after injured tissue has healed — **scar** *vb*

scar•ab \ˈska-rəb\ *n* [MF *scarabee,* fr. L *scarabaeus*] : any of a family of large stout beetles; *also* : an ornament (as a gem) representing such a beetle

scarce \ˈskers\ *adj* **scarc•er; scarc•est** **1** : deficient in quantity or number : not plentiful **2** : intentionally absent ⟨made himself ~ at inspection time⟩ — **scar•ci•ty** \ˈsker-sə-tē\ *n*

scarce•ly \-lē\ *adv* **1** : BARELY ⟨can ~ see them⟩ **2** : almost not **3** : very probably not

[1]**scare** \ˈsker\ *vb* **scared; scar•ing** : FRIGHTEN, STARTLE

[2]**scare** *n* : FRIGHT — **scary** *adj*

scare•crow \ˈsker-ˌkrō\ *n* : a crude figure set up to scare birds away from crops

[1]**scarf** \ˈskärf\ *n, pl* **scarves** \ˈskärvz\ *or* **scarfs** **1** : a broad band (as of cloth) worn about the shoulders, around the neck, over the head, or about the waist **2** : a long narrow cloth cover for a table or dresser top

[2]**scarf** *vb* [alter. of earlier *scoff* eat greedily] : to eat greedily ⟨~*ed* down his lunch⟩

scar•i•fy \ˈsker-ə-ˌfī\ *vb* **-fied; -fy•ing** **1** : to make scratches or small cuts in ⟨~ skin for vaccination⟩ ⟨~ seeds to help them germinate⟩ **2** : to lacerate the feelings of **3** : to break up and loosen the surface of (as a road) — **scar•i•fi•ca•tion** \ˌskar-ə-fə-ˈkā-shən\ *n*

scar•let \ˈskär-lət\ *n* : a bright red color — **scarlet** *adj*

scarlet fever *n* : an acute contagious disease marked by fever, sore throat, and red rash and caused by certain streptococci

scarp \ˈskärp\ *n* : a line of cliffs produced by faulting or erosion

scath•ing \ˈskā-thiŋ\ *adj* : bitterly severe ⟨a ~ condemnation⟩

scat•o•log•i•cal \ˌska-tə-ˈlä-ji-kəl\ *adj* : concerned with obscene matters

scat•ter \ˈska-tər\ *vb* **1** : to distribute or strew about irregularly **2** : DISPERSE

scat•ter•brain \ˈska-tər-ˌbrān\ *n* : a silly careless person — **scat•ter•brained** \-ˌbrānd\ *adj*

scav•enge \ˈska-vənj\ *vb* **scav•enged; scav•eng•ing** : to work or function as a scavenger

scav•en•ger \ˈska-vən-jər\ *n* [alter. of earlier *scavager,* fr. AF *scawageour* collector of scavage (duty imposed on nonresident street merchants), fr. *skawage* scavage, fr. MF dial. (Flanders) *escauver* to inspect, fr. MD *scouwen*] : a person or animal that collects, eats, or disposes of refuse or waste

sce•nar•io \sə-ˈner-ē-ˌō\ *n, pl* **-i•os** : the plot or outline of a dramatic work; *also* : an account of a possible action

scene \ˈsēn\ *n* [MF, stage, fr. L *scena, scaena* stage, scene, prob. fr. Etruscan, fr. Gk *skēnē* temporary shelter, tent, building forming the background for a dramatic performance, stage] **1** : a division of one act of a play **2** : a single situation or sequence in a play or motion picture **3** : a stage setting **4** : VIEW, PROSPECT **5** : the place of an occurrence or action **6** : a display of strong feeling and esp. anger **7** : a sphere of activity ⟨the fashion ~⟩ — **sce•nic** \ˈsē-nik\ *adj*

scen•ery \ˈsē-nə-rē\ *n, pl* **-er•ies** **1** : the painted scenes or hangings and accessories used on a theater stage **2** : a picturesque view or landscape

[1]**scent** \ˈsent\ *n* **1** : ODOR, SMELL **2** : sense of smell **3** : course of pursuit : TRACK **4** : PERFUME 2 — **scent•ed** \ˈsen-təd\ *adj* — **scent•less** *adj*

[2]**scent** *vb* **1** : SMELL **2** : to imbue or fill with odor

scep•ter \ˈsep-tər\ *n* : a staff borne by a sovereign as an emblem of authority

sceptic *var of* SKEPTIC

scep•tre *Brit var of* SCEPTER

sch *abbr* school

[1]**sched•ule** \ˈske-jül, *esp Brit* ˈshe-dyül\ *n* **1** : a list of items or details **2** : TIMETABLE

[2]**schedule** *vb* **sched•uled; sched•ul•ing** **1** : to appoint, assign, or designate for a fixed time **2** : to make a schedule of; *also* : to enter on a schedule

sche•ma \ˈskē-mə\ *n, pl* **sche•ma•ta** \-mə-tə\ *also* **schemas** : a diagrammatic presentation or plan : OUTLINE

sche•mat•ic \ski-ˈma-tik\ *adj* : of or relating to a scheme or diagram : DIAGRAMMATIC — **schematic** *n* — **sche•mat•i•cal•ly** \-ti-k(ə-)lē\ *adv*

[1]**scheme** \ˈskēm\ *n* **1** : a plan for doing something; *esp* : a crafty plot **2** : a systematic design ⟨a color ~⟩

[2]**scheme** *vb* **schemed; schem•ing** : to form a plot : INTRIGUE — **schem•er** *n*

schil•ling \ˈshi-liŋ\ *n* : a former basic monetary unit of Austria

schism \ˈsi-zəm, ˈski-\ *n* **1** : DIVISION, SPLIT; *also* : DISCORD, DISSENSION **2** : a formal division in or separation from a religious body

schis•mat•ic \siz-ˈma-tik, ski-\ *n* : one who creates or takes part in schism — **schismatic** *adj*

schist \ˈshist\ *n* : a metamorphic crystalline rock

schizo•phre•nia \ˌskit-sə-ˈfrē-nē-ə\ *n* [NL, fr. Gk *schizein* to split + *phrēn* diaphragm, mind] : a psychotic mental illness that is characterized by a distorted view of the real world, by a greatly reduced ability to carry out one's daily tasks, and by abnormal ways of thinking, feeling, perceiving, and behaving — **schiz•oid** \ˈskit-ˌsȯid\ *adj or n* — **schizo•phren•ic** \ˌskit-sə-ˈfre-nik\ *adj or n*

schle•miel *also* **shle•miel** \shlə-ˈmēl\ *n* : an unlucky bungler : CHUMP

schlep *or* **schlepp** \ˈshlep\ *vb* [Yiddish *shlepn*] **1** : DRAG, HAUL **2** : to move slowly or awkwardly

schlock \ˈshläk\ *or* **schlocky** \ˈshlä-kē\ *adj* : of low quality or value — **schlock** *n*
schlub *also* **shlub** \ˈshləb\ *n* [Yiddish *zhlob, zhlub* yokel, boor] *slang* : a stupid, ineffectual, or unattractive person
schmaltz *also* **schmalz** \ˈshmȯlts, ˈshmälts\ *n* [Yiddish *shmalts,* lit., rendered fat] : sentimental or florid music or art — **schmaltzy** *adj*
schmooze *or* **shmooze** \ˈshmüz\ *vb* : to chat informally esp. to gain favor — **schmooze** *n*
schnapps \ˈshnaps\ *n, pl* **schnapps** : a liquor (as gin) of high alcoholic content
schnau·zer \ˈshnau̇-zər, ˈshnau̇t-sər\ *n* [G, fr. *Schnauze* snout] : a dog of any of three breeds that are characterized by a wiry coat, long head, pointed ears, heavy eyebrows, and long hair on the muzzle
schol·ar \ˈskä-lər\ *n* **1** : STUDENT, PUPIL **2** : a learned person — **schol·ar·ly** *adj*
schol·ar·ship \-ˌship\ *n* **1** : the qualities or learning of a scholar **2** : money awarded to a student to help pay for further education
scho·las·tic \skə-ˈlas-tik\ *adj* : of or relating to schools, scholars, or scholarship
¹school \ˈskül\ *n* **1** : an institution for teaching and learning; *also* : the pupils in attendance **2** : a body of persons of like opinions or beliefs ⟨the radical ~⟩
²school *vb* : TEACH, TRAIN, DRILL
³school *n* : a large number of one kind of water animal swimming and feeding together ⟨a ~ of fish⟩
school·boy \-ˌbȯi\ *n* : a boy attending school
school·fel·low \-ˌfe-lō\ *n* : SCHOOLMATE
school·girl \-ˌgərl\ *n* : a girl attending school
school·house \-ˌhau̇s\ *n* : a building used as a school
school·marm \-ˌmärm\ *or* **school·ma'am** \-ˌmäm, -ˌmam\ *n* **1** : a woman who is a schoolteacher **2** : a person who exhibits characteristics popularly attributed to schoolteachers
school·mas·ter \-ˌmas-tər\ *n* : a man who is a schoolteacher
school·mate \-ˌmāt\ *n* : a school companion
school·mis·tress \-ˌmis-trəs\ *n* : a woman who is a schoolteacher
school·room \-ˌrüm, -ˌru̇m\ *n* : CLASSROOM
school·teach·er \-ˌtē-chər\ *n* : one who teaches in a school
schoo·ner \ˈskü-nər\ *n* : a fore-and-aft rigged sailing ship
schtick *var of* SHTICK
schuss \ˈshu̇s, ˈshüs\ *vb* [G *Schuss,* n., lit., shot] : to ski down a slope at high speed — **schuss** *n*
sci *abbr* science; scientific
sci·at·i·ca \sī-ˈa-ti-kə\ *n* : pain in the region of the hips or along the course of the nerve at the back of the thigh
sci·ence \ˈsī-əns\ *n* [ME, fr. AF, fr. L *scientia,* fr. *scient-, sciens* having knowledge, fr. prp. of *scire* to know] **1** : an area of knowledge that is an object of study; *esp* : NATURAL SCIENCE **2** : knowledge covering general truths or the operation of general laws especially as obtained and tested through the scientific method — **sci·en·tif·ic** \ˌsī-ən-ˈti-fik\ *adj* — **sci·en·tif·i·cal·ly** \-fi-k(ə-)lē\ *adv* — **sci·en·tist** \ˈsī-ən-tist\ *n*
science fiction *n* : fiction dealing principally with the impact of actual or imagined science on society or individuals
scientific method *n* : the rules and methods for the pursuit of knowledge involving the finding and stating of a problem, the collection of facts through observation and experiment, and the making and testing of ideas that need to be proven right or wrong
scim·i·tar \ˈsi-mə-tər\ *n* : a curved sword used chiefly by Arabs and Turks
scin·til·la \sin-ˈti-lə\ *n* : BIT, TRACE
scin·til·late \ˈsin-tə-ˌlāt\ *vb* **-lat·ed; -lat·ing** : SPARKLE, GLEAM — **scin·til·la·tion** \ˌsin-tə-ˈlā-shən\ *n*
sci·on \ˈsī-ən\ *n* **1** : a shoot of a plant joined to a stock in grafting **2** : DESCENDANT ⟨a ~ of a powerful family⟩
scis·sors \ˈsi-zərz\ *n pl* : a cutting instrument like shears but usu. smaller
scissors kick *n* : a swimming kick in which the legs move like scissors
sclero·der·ma \ˌskler-ə-ˈdər-mə\ *n* : a chronic disease characterized by the usu. progressive hardening and thickening of the skin
scle·ro·sis \sklə-ˈrō-səs\ *n* : abnormal hardening of tissue (as of an artery); *also* : a disease characterized by this — **scle·rot·ic** \-ˈrä-tik\ *adj*
scoff \ˈskäf\ *vb* : MOCK, JEER ⟨~*ed* at his proposal⟩ — **scoff·er** *n*
scoff·law \-ˌlȯ\ *n* : a contemptuous law violator
¹scold \ˈskōld\ *n* : a person who scolds
²scold *vb* : to censure severely or angrily
sconce \ˈskäns\ *n* : a candlestick or an electric light fixture fastened to a wall
scone \ˈskōn, ˈskän\ *n* : a biscuit (as of oatmeal) baked on a griddle
¹scoop \ˈsküp\ *n* **1** : a large shovel; *also* : a utensil with a shovellike or rounded end **2** : the amount contained by a scoop **3** : an act of scooping **4** : information of immediate interest
²scoop *vb* **1** : to take out or up or empty with or as if with a scoop **2** : to make hollow **3** : to report a news item in advance of ⟨~*ed* the other newspapers⟩
scoot \ˈsküt\ *vb* : to move swiftly
scoot·er \ˈskü-tər\ *n* **1** : a vehicle ridden while standing that consists of a narrow board mounted between two wheels tandem with an upright steering handle attached to the front wheel and that is moved by pushing with one foot or by an electric motor **2** : MOTOR SCOOTER **3** : a vehicle ridden while seated that usu. has three or four wheels and is propelled by an electric motor
¹scope \ˈskōp\ *n* [It *scopo* purpose, goal, fr. Gk *skopos*] **1** : space or opportunity

for action or thought **2** : extent covered : RANGE ⟨is beyond the ~ of this essay⟩

²**scope** *n* : an instrument (as a microscope or telescope) for viewing

scorch \ˈskȯrch\ *vb* : to burn the surface of; *also* : to dry or shrivel with heat

¹**score** \ˈskȯr\ *n, pl* **scores 1** *or pl* **score** : TWENTY **2** : CUT, SCRATCH, SLASH **3** : a record of points made (as in a game) **4** : DEBT **5** : REASON, GROUND **6** : the music of a composition or arrangement with different parts indicated **7** : success in obtaining something esp. illegally

²**score** *vb* **scored; scor·ing 1** : RECORD **2** : to keep score in a game **3** : to mark with lines, grooves, scratches, or notches **4** : to gain or tally in or as if in a game ⟨*scored* a point⟩ **5** : to assign a grade or score to ⟨~ the tests⟩ **6** : to compose a score for **7** : SUCCEED **8** : ACQUIRE ⟨*scored* tickets to the game⟩ — **score·less** *adj* — **scor·er** *n*

¹**scorn** \ˈskȯrn\ *n* : an emotion involving both anger and disgust : CONTEMPT — **scorn·ful** \-fəl\ *adj* — **scorn·ful·ly** *adv*

²**scorn** *vb* : to hold in contempt : DISDAIN ⟨were ~*ed* as fanatics⟩ — **scorn·er** *n*

Scor·pio \ˈskȯr-pē-ˌō\ *n* [L, lit., scorpion] **1** : a zodiacal constellation between Libra and Sagittarius usu. pictured as a scorpion **2** : the 8th sign of the zodiac in astrology; *also* : one born under this sign

scor·pi·on \ˈskȯr-pē-ən\ *n* : any of an order of arthropods related to the spiders that have a poisonous stinger at the tip of a long jointed tail

¹**Scot** \ˈskät\ *n* : a native or inhabitant of Scotland

²**Scot** *abbr* Scotland; Scottish

Scotch \ˈskäch\ *n* **1** : SCOTS **2 Scotch** *pl* : the people of Scotland **3** : a whiskey distilled in Scotland esp. from malted barley — **Scotch** *adj* — **Scotch·man** \-mən\ *n* — **Scotch·wom·an** \-ˌwu̇-mən\ *n*

Scotch bonnet *n* : a small roundish very hot chili pepper esp. of the Caribbean

Scotch pine *n* : a pine that is naturalized in the U.S. from northern Europe and Asia and is a valuable timber tree

Scotch terrier *n* : SCOTTISH TERRIER

scot–free \ˈskät-ˈfrē\ *adj* : free from obligation, harm, or penalty

Scots \ˈskäts\ *n* : the English language of Scotland

Scots·man \ˈskäts-mən\ *n* : SCOT

Scots·wom·an \-ˌwu̇-mən\ *n* : a woman who is a Scot

Scot·tie \ˈskä-tē\ *n* : SCOTTISH TERRIER

Scot·tish \ˈskä-tish\ *adj* : of, relating to, or characteristic of Scotland, Scots, or the Scots

Scottish terrier *n* : any of an old Scottish breed of terrier with short legs, a long head with small erect ears, a broad deep chest, and a thick rough coat

scoun·drel \ˈskau̇n-drəl\ *n* : a disreputable person : VILLAIN

¹**scour** \ˈskau̇(-ə)r\ *vb* **1** : to rub (as with a gritty substance) in order to clean **2** : to cleanse by or as if by rubbing

²**scour** *vb* **1** : to move rapidly through : RUSH **2** : to examine thoroughly

¹**scourge** \ˈskərj\ *n* **1** : LASH, WHIP **2** : PUNISHMENT; *also* : a cause of affliction

²**scourge** *vb* **scourged; scourg·ing 1** : LASH, FLOG **2** : to punish severely

¹**scout** \ˈskau̇t\ *vb* [ME, fr. AF *escuter* to listen, fr. L *auscultare*] **1** : to look around : RECONNOITER **2** : to inspect or observe to get information

²**scout** *n* **1** : a person sent out to get information; *also* : a soldier, airplane, or ship sent out to reconnoiter **2** : BOY SCOUT **3** : GIRL SCOUT — **scout·mas·ter** \-ˌmas-tər\ *n*

³**scout** *vb* : SCORN, SCOFF

scow \ˈskau̇\ *n* : a large flat-bottomed boat with square ends

scowl \ˈskau̇(-ə)l\ *vb* : to make a frowning expression of displeasure — **scowl** *n*

SCPO *abbr* senior chief petty officer

scrab·ble \ˈskra-bəl\ *vb* **scrab·bled; scrab·bling 1** : SCRAPE, SCRATCH **2** : CLAMBER, SCRAMBLE ⟨*scrabbled* on the slippery rocks⟩ **3** : to work hard and long **4** : SCRIBBLE — **scrabble** *n* — **scrab·bler** *n*

scrag·gly \ˈskra-glē\ *adj* : IRREGULAR; *also* : RAGGED, UNKEMPT ⟨a ~ beard⟩

scram \ˈskram\ *vb* **scrammed; scram·ming** : to go away at once

scram·ble \ˈskram-bəl\ *vb* **scram·bled; scram·bling 1** : to clamber clumsily around **2** : to struggle for or as if for possession of something **3** : to spread irregularly **4** : to mix together **5** : to cook (eggs) by stirring during frying — **scramble** *n*

¹**scrap** \ˈskrap\ *n* **1** : FRAGMENT, PIECE **2** : discarded material : REFUSE

²**scrap** *vb* **scrapped; scrap·ping 1** : to make into scrap ⟨~ a battleship⟩ **2** : to get rid of as useless ⟨*scrapped* the plans⟩

³**scrap** *n* : FIGHT

⁴**scrap** *vb* **scrapped; scrap·ping** : FIGHT, QUARREL — **scrap·per** *n*

scrap·book \ˈskrap-ˌbu̇k\ *n* : a blank book in which mementos are kept

¹**scrape** \ˈskrāp\ *vb* **scraped; scrap·ing 1** : to remove by drawing a knife over; *also* : to clean or smooth by rubbing off the covering **2** : to damage or injure the surface of by contact with something rough **3** : to draw across a surface with a grating sound **4** : to get together (money) by strict economy **5** : to get along with difficulty ⟨barely *scraping* by on her income⟩ — **scrap·er** *n*

²**scrape** *n* **1** : the act or the effect of scraping **2** : a bow accompanied by a drawing back of the foot **3** : an unpleasant predicament

scra·pie \ˈskrā-pē\ *n* : a usu. fatal degenerative disease of the brain esp. of sheep that is related to mad cow disease

¹**scrap·py** \ˈskra-pē\ *adj* **scrap·pi·er; -est** : DISCONNECTED, FRAGMENTARY

²**scrappy** *adj* **scrap·pi·er; -est 1** : QUARRELSOME **2** : having an aggressive and determined spirit ⟨a ~ competitor⟩

¹**scratch** \ˈskrach\ *vb* **1** : to scrape, dig, or rub with or as if with claws or nails ⟨a dog ~*ing* at the door⟩ ⟨~*ed* my arm⟩ **2**

: SCRAPE 3 ⟨~*ed* his nails across the blackboard⟩ **3** : SCRAPE 4 **4** : to cancel or erase by or as if by drawing a line through **5** : to withdraw from a contest — **scratchy** *adj* — **scratch one's head** : to become confused or perplexed

²**scratch** *n* **1** : a mark or injury made by or as if by scratching; *also* : a sound so made **2** : the starting line in a race — **from scratch** : with no steps completed or ingredients prepared ahead of time ⟨built from ~⟩

³**scratch** *adj* **1** : made or done by chance ⟨a ~ hit⟩ **2** : made as or used for a trial attempt ⟨~ paper⟩

scratch card *n* : a card with a small area covered by an opaque coating which may be scraped away to reveal hidden information

scrawl \ˈskrȯl\ *vb* : to write hastily and carelessly — **scrawl** *n*

scraw·ny \ˈskrȯ-nē\ *adj* **scraw·ni·er; -est** : very thin : SKINNY

¹**scream** \ˈskrēm\ *vb* : to cry out loudly and shrilly

²**scream** *n* : a loud shrill cry

scream·ing \ˈskrē-miŋ\ *adj* : so striking as to attract notice as if by screaming ⟨~ headlines⟩

screech \ˈskrēch\ *vb* : SHRIEK — **screech** *n* — **screechy** \ˈskrē-chē\ *adj*

screech·ing \ˈskrē-chiŋ\ *adj* : ABRUPT ⟨came to a ~ halt⟩

¹**screen** \ˈskrēn\ *n* **1** : a device or partition used to hide, restrain, protect, or decorate ⟨a window ~⟩; *also* : something that shelters, protects, or conceals **2** : a sieve or perforated material for separating finer from coarser parts (as of sand) **3** : a surface on which an image is made to appear (as in television); *also* : the information displayed on a computer screen at one time **4** : the motion-picture industry

²**screen** *vb* **1** : to shield with or as if with a screen **2** : to separate with a screen; *also* : to select or categorize methodically ⟨~ contestants⟩ **3** : to present (as a motion picture) on the screen

screen·ing \ˈskrē-niŋ\ *n* **1** : metal or plastic mesh (as for window screens) **2** : a showing of a motion picture

screen saver *n* : a computer program that displays something (as images) on the screen of a computer that is on but not in use

screen time *n* **1** : the amount of time someone or something appears on-screen in a movie or television show **2** : time spent watching television, playing a video game, or using an electronic device

¹**screw** \ˈskrü\ *n* [ME, fr. MF *escroe* female screw, nut, fr. ML *scrofa,* fr. L, sow] **1** : a machine consisting of a solid cylinder with a spiral groove around it and a corresponding hollow cylinder into which it fits **2** : a naillike metal piece with a spiral groove and a head with a slot that is inserted into material by rotating and is used to fasten pieces of solid material together **3** : PROPELLER

²**screw** *vb* **1** : to fasten or close by means of a screw **2** : to operate or adjust by means of a screw **3** : to move or cause to move spirally; *also* : to close or set in position by such an action

screw·ball \ˈskrü-ˌbȯl\ *n* **1** : a baseball pitch breaking in a direction opposite to a curve **2** : a whimsical, eccentric, or crazy person

screw·driv·er \-ˌdrī-vər\ *n* **1** : a tool for turning screws **2** : a drink made of vodka and orange juice

screw·worm \ˈskrü-ˌwərm\ *n* : an American blowfly of warm regions whose larva matures in wounds or sores of mammals and may cause disease or death; *esp* : its larva

screwy \ˈskrü-ē\ *adj* **screw·i·er; -est** **1** : crazily absurd, eccentric, or unusual ⟨a ~ idea⟩ **2** *informal* : CRAZY, INSANE

scrib·ble \ˈskri-bəl\ *vb* **scrib·bled; scrib·bling** : to write hastily or carelessly — **scribble** *n* — **scrib·bler** *n*

scribe \ˈskrīb\ *n* **1** : a scholar of Jewish law in New Testament times **2** : a person whose business is the copying of writing **3** : JOURNALIST

scrim \ˈskrim\ *n* : a light loosely woven cotton or linen cloth

scrim·mage \ˈskri-mij\ *n* : the play between two football teams beginning with the snap of the ball; *also* : practice play between two teams — **scrimmage** *vb*

scrimp \ˈskrimp\ *vb* : to economize greatly ⟨~ and save⟩

scrim·shaw \ˈskrim-ˌshȯ\ *n* : carved or engraved articles made orig. by American whalers usu. from baleen or whale ivory — **scrimshaw** *vb*

scrip \ˈskrip\ *n* **1** : a certificate showing its holder is entitled to something (as stock or land) **2** : paper money issued for temporary use in an emergency

¹**script** \ˈskript\ *n* **1** : written matter (as lines for a play or broadcast) **2** : HANDWRITING **3** : a sequence of instructions or commands for a computer to execute

²**script** *abbr* scripture

scrip·ture \ˈskrip-chər\ *n* **1** *cap* : the books of the Bible — often used in pl. **2** : the sacred writings of a religion — **scrip·tur·al** \ˈskrip-chə-rəl\ *adj* — **scrip·tur·al·ly** *adv*

scriv·en·er \ˈskri-və-nər\ *n* : SCRIBE, COPYIST, WRITER

scrod \ˈskräd\ *n* [prob. fr. Brit. dial. (Cornwall) *scrawed,* pp. of *scraw, scrawl* to split, salt, and dry (young fish)] : a young fish (as a cod or haddock); *esp* : one split and boned for cooking

scrof·u·la \ˈskrȯ-fyə-lə\ *n* : tuberculosis of lymph nodes esp. in the neck

¹**scroll** \ˈskrōl\ *n* : a roll of paper or parchment for writing a document; *also* : a spiral or coiled ornamental form suggesting a loosely or partly rolled scroll

²**scroll** *vb* : to move or cause to move text or graphics up, down, or across a display screen

scroll saw *n* **1** : FRETSAW **2** : a machine saw with a narrow vertically reciprocating blade for cutting curved lines or openwork

scro·tum \ˈskrō-təm\ *n, pl* **scro·ta** \-tə\ *or* **scrotums** [L] : a pouch that in most male mammals contains the testes

scrounge \ˈskraůnj\ *vb* **scrounged; scroung·ing** : to collect by or as if by foraging

1**scrub** \ˈskrəb\ *n* **1** : a thick growth of stunted trees or shrubs; *also* : an area of land covered with scrub **2** : an inferior domestic animal **3** : a person of insignificant size or standing **4** : a player not on the first team — **scrub** *adj* — **scrub·by** *adj*

2**scrub** *vb* **scrubbed; scrub·bing** **1** : to clean or wash by rubbing ⟨~ clothes⟩ ⟨~ out a spot⟩ **2** : CANCEL

3**scrub** *n* **1** : an act or instance of scrubbing **2** *pl* : loose-fitting clothing worn by hospital staff ⟨surgical ~*s*⟩

scrub·ber \ˈskrə-bər\ *n* : one that scrubs; *esp* : an apparatus for removing impurities esp. from gases

scruff \ˈskrəf\ *n* : the back of the neck : NAPE

scruffy \ˈskrə-fē\ *adj* **scruff·i·er; -est** : UNKEMPT, SLOVENLY ⟨a ~ tramp⟩

scrump·tious \ˈskrəmp-shəs\ *adj* : DELIGHTFUL, EXCELLENT; *esp* : DELICIOUS ⟨a ~ cake⟩ — **scrump·tious·ly** *adv*

scrunch·ie *or* **scrunchy** \ˈskrən-chē, ˈskrůn-\ *n* : a fabric-covered elastic for the hair

1**scru·ple** \ˈskrü-pəl\ *n* [ME *scrupil, scriple,* fr. AF *scruble,* fr. L *scrupulus,* dim. of *scrupus* source of uneasiness, lit., sharp stone] **1** : a point of conscience or honor **2** : hesitation due to ethical considerations

2**scruple** *vb* **scru·pled; scru·pling** : to be reluctant on grounds of conscience : HESITATE

scru·pu·lous \ˈskrü-pyə-ləs\ *adj* **1** : having moral integrity **2** : PAINSTAKING ⟨was ~ about her work⟩ — **scru·pu·lous·ly** *adv* — **scru·pu·lous·ness** *n*

scru·ti·nise *Brit var of* SCRUTINIZE

scru·ti·nize \ˈskrü-tə-ˌnīz\ *vb* **-nized; -niz·ing** : to examine closely

scru·ti·ny \ˈskrü-tə-nē\ *n, pl* **-nies** [L *scrutinium,* fr. *scrutari* to search, examine, prob. fr. *scruta* trash] : a careful looking over ♦ ***Synonyms*** INSPECTION, EXAMINATION, ANALYSIS

scu·ba \ˈskü-bə\ *n* [*s*elf-*c*ontained *u*nderwater *b*reathing *a*pparatus] : an apparatus for breathing while swimming underwater

scuba diver *n* : one who swims underwater with the aid of scuba gear

1**scud** \ˈskəd\ *vb* **scud·ded; scud·ding** : to move speedily

2**scud** *n* : light clouds driven by the wind

1**scuff** \ˈskəf\ *vb* **1** : to scrape the feet while walking : SHUFFLE **2** : to scratch or become scratched or worn away

2**scuff** *n* **1** : a mark or injury caused by scuffing **2** : a flat-soled slipper without heel strap

scuf·fle \ˈskə-fəl\ *vb* **scuf·fled; scuf·fling** **1** : to struggle confusedly at close quarters ⟨*scuffled* with the police⟩ **2** : to shuffle one's feet — **scuffle** *n*

1**scull** \ˈskəl\ *n* **1** : an oar for use in sculling; *also* : one of a pair of short oars for a single oarsman **2** : a racing shell propelled by one or two persons using sculls

2**scull** *vb* : to propel (a boat) by an oar over the stern

scul·lery \ˈskə-lə-rē\ *n, pl* **-ler·ies** [ME *squilerie, sculerie* department of household in charge of dishes, fr. AF *esquilerie,* fr. *escuele* bowl, fr. L *scutella* drinking bowl] : a small room near the kitchen used for cleaning dishes, cooking utensils, and vegetables

scul·lion \ˈskəl-yən\ *n* : a kitchen helper

sculpt \ˈskəlpt\ *vb* : CARVE, SCULPTURE

sculp·tor \ˈskəlp-tər\ *n* : a person who produces works of sculpture

1**sculp·ture** \ˈskəlp-chər\ *n* : the act, process, or art of carving or molding material (as stone, wood, or plastic); *also* : work produced this way — **sculp·tur·al** \ˈskəlp-chə-rəl\ *adj*

2**sculpture** *vb* **sculp·tured; sculp·tur·ing** : to form or alter as or as if a work of sculpture ⟨*sculptured* hedges⟩

scum \ˈskəm\ *n* **1** : a slimy or filmy covering on the surface of a liquid **2** : waste matter **3** : RABBLE

scup·per \ˈskə-pər\ *n* [ME *skopper-,* perh. fr. AF **escopoir,* fr. *escopir* to spit out] : an opening in the side of a ship through which water on deck is drained overboard

scurf \ˈskərf\ *n* : thin dry scales of skin (as dandruff); *also* : a scaly deposit or covering — **scurfy** \ˈskər-fē\ *adj*

scur·ri·lous \ˈskər-ə-ləs\ *adj* : coarsely jesting : OBSCENE, VULGAR

scur·ry \ˈskər-ē\ *vb* **scur·ried; scur·ry·ing** : SCAMPER ⟨*scurried* for cover⟩

1**scur·vy** \ˈskər-vē\ *n* : a disease caused by a lack of vitamin C and characterized by spongy gums, loosened teeth, and bleeding under the skin

2**scurvy** *adj* : MEAN, CONTEMPTIBLE — **scur·vi·ly** \ˈskər-və-lē\ *adv*

scutch·eon \ˈskə-chən\ *n* : ESCUTCHEON

1**scut·tle** \ˈskə-tᵊl\ *n* : a pail for carrying coal

2**scuttle** *n* : a small opening with a lid esp. in the deck, side, or bottom of a ship

3**scuttle** *vb* **scut·tled; scut·tling** : to cut a hole in the deck, side, or bottom of (a ship) in order to sink

4**scuttle** *vb* **scut·tled; scut·tling** : SCURRY, SCAMPER

scut·tle·butt \ˈskə-tᵊl-ˌbət\ *n* : GOSSIP

scythe \ˈsīth\ *n* : an implement for mowing (as grass or grain) by hand — **scythe** *vb*

SD *abbr* **1** South Dakota **2** special delivery

S Dak *abbr* South Dakota

SDI *abbr* Strategic Defense Initiative

Se *symbol* selenium

SE *abbr* southeast

sea \ˈsē\ *n* **1** : a large body of salt water **2** : OCEAN **3** : rough water; *also* : a large wave **4** : something likened to the sea esp. in vastness ⟨a ~ of wheat⟩ — **sea** *adj* — **at sea** : LOST, BEWILDERED

sea anemone *n* : any of numerous coelenterate polyps whose form, bright and varied colors, and cluster of tentacles superficially resemble a flower

sea·bird \ˈsē-ˌbərd\ *n* : a bird (as a gull) frequenting the open ocean

sea·board \-ˌbȯrd\ *n* : SEACOAST; *also* : the land bordering a coast

sea·borg·i·um \sē-ˈbȯr-gē-əm\ *n* : a short-lived radioactive chemical element produced artificially

sea·coast \-ˌkōst\ *n* : the shore of the sea

sea·far·er \-ˌfer-ər\ *n* : SEAMAN 1

sea·far·ing \-ˌfer-iŋ\ *n* : the use of the sea for travel or transportation — **seafaring** *adj*

sea·food \-ˌfüd\ *n* : edible marine fish and shellfish

sea·go·ing \-ˌgō-iŋ\ *adj* : OCEANGOING

sea·gull \ˈsē-ˌgəl\ : GULL

sea horse *n* : any of a genus of small marine fishes with the head and forepart of the body sharply flexed like the head and neck of a horse

[1]seal \ˈsēl\ *n, pl* **seals** *also* **seal** [ME *sele,* fr. OE *seolh*] **1** : any of numerous large carnivorous sea mammals occurring chiefly in cold regions and having limbs adapted for swimming **2** : the pelt of a seal

[2]seal *vb* : to hunt seals

[3]seal *n* [ME *sele, seel,* fr. AF *seal, sel,* fr. L *sigillum,* fr. dim. of *signum* sign, seal] **1** : GUARANTEE, PLEDGE **2** : a device having a raised design that can be stamped on clay or wax; *also* : the impression made by stamping with such a device **3** : something that seals or closes up ⟨safety ~⟩

[4]seal *vb* **1** : to affix a seal to; *also* : AUTHENTICATE **2** : to fasten with or as if with a seal to prevent tampering **3** : to close or make secure against access, leakage, or passage **4** : to determine irrevocably ⟨~*ed* his fate⟩

sea–lane \ˈsē-ˌlān\ *n* : an established sea route

seal·ant \ˈsē-lənt\ *n* : a sealing agent

seal·er \ˈsē-lər\ *n* : a coat applied to prevent subsequent coats of paint or varnish from sinking in

sea level *n* : the level of the surface of the sea esp. at its mean midway between mean high and low water

sea·lift \ˈsē-ˌlift\ *n* : transport of military personnel and equipment by ship

sea lion *n* : any of several large Pacific seals with small external ears

seal·skin \ˈsēl-ˌskin\ *n* **1** : [1]SEAL 2 **2** : a garment of sealskin

[1]seam \ˈsēm\ *n* **1** : the line of junction of two edges and esp. of edges of fabric sewn together **2** : a layer of mineral matter **3** : WRINKLE

[2]seam *vb* **1** : to join by or as if by sewing **2** : WRINKLE, FURROW

sea·man \ˈsē-mən\ *n* **1** : one who assists in the handling of ships : MARINER **2** : an enlisted person in the navy ranking next below a petty officer third class

seaman apprentice *n* : an enlisted person in the navy ranking next below a seaman

seaman recruit *n* : an enlisted person of the lowest rank in the navy

sea·man·ship \ˈsē-mən-ˌship\ *n* : the art or skill of handling a ship

seam·less \ˈsēm-ləs\ *adj* : having no flaws or interruptions ⟨a ~ transition⟩ — **seam·less·ly** *adv*

sea·mount \ˈsē-ˌmau̇nt\ *n* : an underwater mountain

seam·stress \ˈsēm-strəs\ *n* : a woman whose occupation is sewing

seamy \ˈsē-mē\ *adj* **seam·i·er; -est** **1** : UNPLEASANT **2** : DEGRADED, SORDID ⟨the ~ part of town⟩

sé·ance \ˈsā-ˌäns\ *n* [F] : a meeting to receive communications from spirits

sea·plane \ˈsē-ˌplān\ *n* : an airplane that can take off from and land on water

sea·port \-ˌpȯrt\ *n* : a port for oceangoing ships

sear \ˈsir\ *vb* **1** : WITHER **2** : to cook, burn, or scorch esp. on the surface; *also* : BRAND — **sear** *n*

[1]search \ˈsərch\ *vb* [ME *cerchen,* fr. AF *cercher* to travel about, investigate, search, fr. LL *circare* to go about, fr. L *circum* round about] **1** : to look through in trying to find something **2** : SEEK **3** : PROBE — **search·er** *n*

[2]search *n* : the act of searching

search engine *n* : computer software or a website used to search data (as text or other websites) for specified information

search·light \-ˌlīt\ *n* : an apparatus for projecting a powerful beam of light; *also* : the light projected

sear·ing \ˈsir-iŋ\ *adj* : very sharp, harsh or intense ⟨~ pain⟩ ⟨a ~ review⟩

sea scallop *n* : a large scallop of the Atlantic coast of No. America that is harvested for food

sea·scape \ˈsē-ˌskāp\ *n* **1** : a view of the sea **2** : a picture representing a scene at or of the sea

sea·shell \ˈsē-ˌshel\ *n* : the shell of a marine animal and esp. a mollusk

sea·shore \-ˌshȯr\ *n* : the shore of a sea

sea·sick \-ˌsik\ *adj* : nauseated by or as if by the motion of a ship — **sea·sick·ness** *n*

sea·side \ˈsē-ˌsīd\ *n* : SEASHORE

[1]sea·son \ˈsē-zən\ *n* [ME *sesoun,* fr. AF *seison* natural season, appropriate time, fr. L *sation-, satio* action of sowing, fr. *serere* to sow] **1** : one of the divisions of the year (as spring or summer) **2** : a period of the year associated with a particular activity, event, or holiday ⟨the Easter ~⟩ ⟨hunting ~⟩ — **sea·son·al** \-zə-nəl\ *adj* — **sea·son·al·ly** *adv*

[2]season *vb* **1** : to make pleasant to the taste by use of salt, pepper, or spices **2** : to make (as by aging or drying) suitable for use **3** : to accustom or habituate to something (as hardship) ♦ ***Synonyms*** HARDEN, INURE, ACCLIMATE, TOUGHEN — **sea·son·er** *n*

sea·son·able \ˈsē-zə-nə-bəl\ *adj* : occurring at a good or proper time ⟨~ weather⟩

♦ *Synonyms* TIMELY, PROPITIOUS, OPPORTUNE — **sea·son·ably** \-blē\ *adv*

seasonal affective disorder *n* : depression that recurs as the days grow shorter during the fall and winter

sea·son·ing *n* : something that seasons : CONDIMENT

1**seat** \ˈsēt\ *n* **1** : a chair, bench, or stool for sitting on **2** : a place which serves as a capital or center

2**seat** *vb* **1** : to place in or on a seat **2** : to provide seats for

seat belt *n* : straps designed to hold a person in a seat

SEATO \ˈsē-ˌtō\ *abbr* Southeast Asia Treaty Organization

seat–of–the–pants *adj* : employing or based on personal experience, judgment, and effort rather than technological aids ⟨~ navigation⟩

sea turtle *n* : any of two families of marine turtles that have the feet modified into paddles

sea urchin *n* : any of numerous spiny marine echinoderms having thin brittle globular shells

sea·wall \ˈsē-ˌwȯl\ *n* : an embankment to protect the shore from erosion

1**sea·ward** \ˈsē-wərd\ *n* : the direction or side away from land and toward the open sea

2**seaward** *also* **sea·wards** \-wərdz\ *adv* : toward the sea

3**seaward** *adj* **1** : directed or situated toward the sea **2** : coming from the sea

sea·wa·ter \ˈsē-ˌwȯ-tər, -ˌwä-\ *n* : water in or from the sea

sea·way \-ˌwā\ *n* : an inland waterway that admits ocean shipping

sea·weed \-ˌwēd\ *n* : a marine alga (as a kelp); *also* : a mass of marine algae

sea·wor·thy \-ˌwər-t͟hē\ *adj* : fit for a sea voyage ⟨a ~ ship⟩

se·ba·ceous \si-ˈbā-shəs\ *adj* : of, relating to, or secreting fatty material

sec *abbr* **1** second; secondary **2** secretary **3** section **4** [L *secundum*] according to

SEC *abbr* Securities and Exchange Commission

se·cede \si-ˈsēd\ *vb* **se·ced·ed; se·ced·ing** : to withdraw from an organized body and esp. from a political body

se·ces·sion \si-ˈse-shən\ *n* : the act of seceding — **se·ces·sion·ist** *n*

se·clude \si-ˈklüd\ *vb* **se·clud·ed; se·clud·ing** : to keep or shut away from others ⟨*secluded* herself in her room⟩

se·clu·sion \si-ˈklü-zhən\ *n* : the act of secluding : the state of being secluded — **se·clu·sive** \-siv\ *adj*

1**sec·ond** \ˈse-kənd\ *adj* [ME, fr. AF *secund*, fr. L *secundus* second, following, favorable, fr. *sequi* to follow] **1** : being number two in a countable series **2** : next after the first **3** : ALTERNATE ⟨every ~ year⟩ — **second** *or* **sec·ond·ly** *adv*

2**second** *n* **1** : one that is second **2** : one who assists another (as in a duel) **3** : an inferior or flawed article **4** : the second forward gear in a motor vehicle

3**second** *n* [ME *secounde*, fr. ML *secunda*, fr. L, fem. of *secundus* second; fr. its being the second division of a unit into 60 parts, as a minute is the first] **1** : the 60th part of a minute of time or angular measure **2** : an instant of time

4**second** *vb* **1** : to encourage or give support to **2** : to act as a second to **3** : to support (a motion) by adding one's voice to that of a proposer

1**sec·ond·ary** \ˈse-kən-ˌder-ē\ *adj* **1** : second in rank, value, or occurrence : LESSER **2** : belonging to a second or later stage of development **3** : coming after the primary or elementary ⟨~ schools⟩

♦ *Synonyms* SUBORDINATE, COLLATERAL, DEPENDENT

2**secondary** *n, pl* **-ar·ies** : the defensive backfield of a football team

secondary sex characteristic *n* : a physical characteristic that appears in members of one sex at puberty or in seasonal breeders at breeding season and is not directly concerned with reproduction

second fiddle *n* : one that plays a supporting or subservient role

second gentleman *n, often cap S&G* : the husband or male partner of a vice president or of a second in command of a country or jurisdiction

sec·ond–guess \ˌse-kənd-ˈges\ *vb* **1** : to think out other strategies or explanations for after the event **2** : to seek to anticipate or predict ⟨~ the stock market⟩

sec·ond·hand \-ˈhand\ *adj* **1** : not original **2** : not new : USED ⟨~ clothes⟩ **3** : dealing in used goods

second lady *n, often cap S&L* : the wife or female partner of a vice president or of a second in command of a country or jurisdiction

secondhand smoke *n* : tobacco smoke that is exhaled by smokers or is given off by burning tobacco and is inhaled by persons nearby

second lieutenant *n* : a commissioned officer (as in the army) ranking next below a first lieutenant

sec·ond–rate \ˌse-kənd-ˈrāt\ *adj* : INFERIOR ⟨~ hotels⟩

sec·ond–string \ˈse-kənd-ˈstriŋ\ *adj* : being a substitute (as on a team)

se·cre·cy \ˈsē-krə-sē\ *n, pl* **-cies** **1** : the habit or practice of being secretive **2** : the condition of being hidden or concealed

1**se·cret** \ˈsē-krət\ *adj* **1** : HIDDEN, CONCEALED ⟨a ~ staircase⟩ **2** : COVERT, STEALTHY; *also* : engaged in detecting or spying ⟨a ~ agent⟩ **3** : kept from general knowledge — **se·cret·ly** *adv*

2**secret** *n* **1** : MYSTERY **2** : something kept from the knowledge of others

sec·re·tar·i·at \ˌse-krə-ˈter-ē-ət\ *n* **1** : the office of a secretary **2** : the secretarial staff in an office **3** : the administrative department of a governmental organization ⟨the UN ~⟩

sec·re·tary \ˈse-krə-ˌter-ē\ *n, pl* **-tar·ies** **1** : a person employed to handle records, correspondence, and routine work for another person **2 :** an officer of a corporation or business who is in charge of correspondence and records **3 :** an official at the head of a department of government **4 :** a writing desk — **sec·re·tari·al** \ˌse-krə-ˈter-ē-əl\ *adj* — **sec·re·tary·ship** \ˈse-krə-ˌter-ē-ˌship\ *n*

[1]**se·crete** \si-ˈkrēt\ *vb* **se·cret·ed; se·cret·ing :** to form and give off (a secretion)

[2]**se·crete** \si-ˈkrēt, ˈsē-krət\ *vb* **se·cret·ed; se·cret·ing :** HIDE, CONCEAL

se·cre·tion \si-ˈkrē-shən\ *n* **1 :** the process of secreting something **2 :** a product of glandular activity; *esp* **:** one (as a hormone) useful in the organism **3 :** the act of hiding something — **se·cre·to·ry** \ˈsē-krə-ˌtȯr-ē\ *adj*

se·cre·tive \ˈsē-krə-tiv, si-ˈkrē-\ *adj* **:** tending to keep secrets or to act secretly ⟨~ about his work⟩ — **se·cre·tive·ly** *adv* — **se·cre·tive·ness** *n*

[1]**sect** \ˈsekt\ *n* **1 :** a dissenting religious body **2 :** a religious denomination **3 :** a group adhering to a distinctive doctrine or to a leader

[2]**sect** *abbr* section; sectional

[1]**sec·tar·i·an** \sek-ˈter-ē-ən\ *adj* **1 :** of or relating to a sect or sectarian **2 :** limited in character or scope — **sec·tar·i·an·ism** *n*

[2]**sectarian** *n* **1 :** an adherent of a sect **2 :** a narrow or bigoted person

[1]**sec·tion** \ˈsek-shən\ *n* **1 :** a part cut off or separated **2 :** a distinct part **3 :** the appearance that a thing has or would have if cut straight through

[2]**section** *vb* **1 :** to separate or become separated into sections ⟨~ an orange⟩ **2 :** to represent in sections

sec·tion·al \ˈsek-shə-nəl\ *adj* **1 :** of, relating to, or characteristic of a section **2 :** local or regional rather than general in character **3 :** divided into sections — **sec·tion·al·ism** *n*

sec·tor \ˈsek-tər\ *n* **1 :** a part of a circle between two radii **2 :** an area assigned to a military leader to defend **3 :** a subdivision of society

sec·u·lar \ˈse-kyə-lər\ *adj* **1 :** not sacred or ecclesiastical **2 :** not bound by monastic vows ⟨a ~ priest⟩

sec·u·lar·ise *Brit var of* SECULARIZE

sec·u·lar·ism \ˈse-kyə-lə-ˌri-zəm\ *n* **:** indifference to or exclusion of religion — **sec·u·lar·ist** \-rist\ *n* — **secularist** *also* **sec·u·lar·is·tic** \ˌse-kyə-lə-ˈris-tik\ *adj*

sec·u·lar·ize \ˈse-kyə-lə-ˌrīz\ *vb* **-ized; -iz·ing 1 :** to make secular **2 :** to transfer from ecclesiastical to civil or lay use, possession, or control — **sec·u·lar·i·za·tion** \ˌse-kyə-lə-rə-ˈzā-shən\ *n*

[1]**se·cure** \si-ˈkyu̇r\ *adj* **se·cur·er; -est** [L *securus* safe, secure, fr. *se* without + *cura* care] **1 :** easy in mind **:** free from fear **2 :** free from danger or risk of loss **:** SAFE **3 :** CERTAIN, SURE — **se·cure·ly** *adv*

[2]**secure** *vb* **se·cured; se·cur·ing 1 :** to make safe **:** GUARD **2 :** to assure payment of by giving a pledge or collateral **3 :** to fasten safely ⟨~ a door⟩ **4 :** GET, ACQUIRE ⟨~ permission⟩

se·cu·ri·ty \si-ˈkyu̇r-ə-tē\ *n, pl* **-ties 1 :** SAFETY **2 :** freedom from worry **3 :** something given as pledge of payment ⟨a ~ deposit⟩ **4** *pl* **:** bond or stock certificates **5 :** PROTECTION

secy *abbr* secretary

se·dan \si-ˈdan\ *n* **1 :** a covered chair borne on poles by two people **2 :** an automobile seating four or more people and usu. having a permanent top

[1]**se·date** \si-ˈdāt\ *adj* **:** quiet and dignified in behavior ♦ ***Synonyms*** STAID, SOBER, SERIOUS, SOLEMN — **se·date·ly** *adv*

[2]**sedate** *vb* **se·dat·ed; se·dat·ing :** to dose with sedatives — **se·da·tion** \si-ˈdā-shən\ *n*

[1]**sed·a·tive** \ˈse-də-tiv\ *adj* **:** serving or tending to relieve tension

[2]**sedative** *n* **:** a sedative drug

sed·en·tary \ˈse-dᵊn-ˌter-ē\ *adj* **:** characterized by or requiring much sitting

sedge \ˈsej\ *n* **:** any of a family of plants esp. of marshy areas that differ from the related grasses esp. in having solid stems — **sedgy** \ˈse-jē\ *adj*

sed·i·ment \ˈse-də-mənt\ *n* **1 :** the material that settles to the bottom of a liquid **2 :** material (as stones and sand) deposited by water, wind, or a glacier — **sed·i·men·ta·ry** \ˌse-də-ˈmen-tə-rē\ *adj* — **sed·i·men·ta·tion** \-mən-ˈtā-shən, -ˌmen-\ *n*

se·di·tion \si-ˈdi-shən\ *n* **:** the causing of discontent, insurrection, or resistance against a government — **se·di·tious** \-shəs\ *adj*

se·duce \si-ˈdüs, -ˈdyüs\ *vb* **se·duced; se·duc·ing 1 :** to persuade to disobedience or disloyalty **2 :** to lead astray **3 :** to entice to sexual intercourse ♦ ***Synonyms*** TEMPT, ENTICE, INVEIGLE, LURE — **se·duc·er** *n* — **se·duc·tion** \-ˈdək-shən\ *n* — **se·duc·tive** \-tiv\ *adj*

sed·u·lous \ˈse-jə-ləs\ *adj* [L *sedulus,* fr. *sedulo* sincerely, diligently, fr. *se* without + *dolus* guile] **:** DILIGENT

[1]**see** \ˈsē\ *vb* **saw** \ˈsȯ\; **seen** \ˈsēn\; **see·ing 1 :** to perceive by the eye; *also* **:** to have the power of sight **2 :** EXPERIENCE **3 :** UNDERSTAND **4 :** to make sure ⟨~ that order is kept⟩ **5 :** to meet with **6 :** to keep company with esp. in dating **7 :** ACCOMPANY, ESCORT ⟨~ the guests to the door⟩ ♦ ***Synonyms*** BEHOLD, DESCRY, ESPY, VIEW, OBSERVE, NOTE, DISCERN — **see red :** to become very angry — **see the light :** to realize an obscured truth

[2]**see** *n* **:** the authority or jurisdiction of a bishop

[1]**seed** \ˈsēd\ *n, pl* **seed** *or* **seeds 1 :** the grains of plants used for sowing **2 :** a ripened ovule of a flowering plant that may develop into a new plant; *also* **:** a plant structure (as a spore or small dry fruit) capable of producing a new plant **3 :** DESCENDANTS **4 :** SOURCE, ORIGIN **5 :** a competitor seeded in a tournament — **seed·less** *adj* — **go to seed** *or* **run to seed 1 :** to develop seed **2 :** DECAY, DETERIORATE

[2]**seed** *vb* **1** : SOW, PLANT ⟨~ land with grass⟩ **2** : to bear or shed seeds **3** : to remove seeds from **4** : to rank or schedule (contestants) in a tournament — **seed·er** *n*
seed·bed \-ˌbed\ *n* : soil or a bed of soil prepared for planting seed
seed·ling \ˈsēd-liŋ\ *n* **1** : a young plant grown from seed **2** : a young tree before it becomes a sapling
seed·time \ˈsēd-ˌtīm\ *n* : the season for sowing
seedy \ˈsē-dē\ *adj* **seed·i·er; -est** **1** : containing or full of seeds **2** : SHABBY
seek \ˈsēk\ *vb* **sought** \ˈsȯt\; **seek·ing** **1** : to search for **2** : to try to reach or obtain **3** : ATTEMPT — **seek·er** *n*
seem \ˈsēm\ *vb* **1** : to appear to the observation or understanding **2** : to give the impression of being : APPEAR
seem·ing *adj* : outwardly apparent ⟨~ indifference⟩ — **seem·ing·ly** *adv*
seem·ly \ˈsēm-lē\ *adj* **seem·li·er; -est** **1** : conventionally proper **2** : FIT
seep \ˈsēp\ *vb* : to flow or pass slowly through fine pores or cracks — **seep·age** \ˈsē-pij\ *n*
seer \ˈsir\ *n* : a person who foresees or predicts events : PROPHET
seer·suck·er \ˈsir-ˌsə-kər\ *n* [Hindi *śīrśakar,* fr. Pers *shīr-o-shakar,* lit., milk and sugar] : a light fabric of linen, cotton, or rayon usu. striped and slightly puckered
see·saw \ˈsē-ˌsȯ\ *n* **1** : a contest in which each side assumes then relinquishes the lead **2** : a children's sport of riding up and down on the ends of a plank supported in the middle; *also* : the plank so used — **seesaw** *vb*
seethe \ˈsēth\ *vb* **seethed; seeth·ing** [archaic *seethe* boil] : to become violently agitated ⟨~ with jealousy⟩
seg·ment \ˈseg-mənt\ *n* **1** : a part cut off from a geometrical figure (as a circle) by one or more points, lines, or planes **2** : a division of a thing : SECTION — **seg·men·tal** \seg-ˈmen-tᵊl\ *adj* — **seg·men·ta·tion** \ˌseg-mən-ˈtā-shən\ *n* — **seg·ment·ed** \ˈseg-ˌmen-təd\ *adj*
seg·re·gate \ˈse-gri-ˌgāt\ *vb* **-gat·ed; -gat·ing** [L *segregare,* fr. *se-* apart + *greg-, grex* herd, flock] : to cut off from others; *esp* : to separate esp. by races or ethnic groups — **seg·re·ga·tion** \ˌse-gri-ˈgā-shən\ *n*
seg·re·ga·tion·ist \ˌse-gri-ˈgā-shə-nist\ *n* : one who believes in or practices the segregation of races
[1]**se·gue** \ˈse-(ˌ)gwā, ˈsā-\ *vb* **se·gued; se·gue·ing** **1** : to proceed without pause from one musical number to another **2** : to make a transition without interruption from one activity, topic, scene, or part to another
[2]**segue** *n* : the act or an instance of segueing
sei·gneur \sān-ˈyər\ *n, often cap* [MF, fr. ML *senior,* fr. L, adj., elder] : a feudal lord
[1]**seine** \ˈsān\ *n* : a large weighted fishing net
[2]**seine** *vb* **seined; sein·ing** : to fish or catch with a seine — **sein·er** *n*
seis·mic \ˈsīz-mik, ˈsīs-\ *adj* : of, relating to, resembling, or caused by an earthquake — **seis·mi·cal·ly** \-mi-k(ə-)lē\ *adv* — **seis·mic·i·ty** \sīz-ˈmi-sə-tē, sīs-\ *n*
seis·mo·gram \ˈsīz-mə-ˌgram, ˈsīs-\ *n* : the record of an earth tremor made by a seismograph
seis·mo·graph \-ˌgraf\ *n* : an apparatus to measure and record seismic vibrations — **seis·mo·graph·ic** \ˌsīz-mə-ˈgra-fik, ˌsīs-\ *adj* — **seis·mog·ra·phy** \sīz-ˈmä-grə-fē, sīs-\ *n*
seis·mol·o·gy \sīz-ˈmä-lə-jē, sīs-\ *n* : a science that deals with earthquakes — **seis·mo·log·i·cal** \ˌsīz-mə-ˈlä-ji-kəl, ˌsīs-\ *adj* — **seis·mol·o·gist** \sīz-ˈmä-lə-jist, sīs-\ *n*
seis·mom·e·ter \sīz-ˈmä-mə-tər, sīs-\ *n* : a seismograph measuring the actual movement of the ground
seize \ˈsēz\ *vb* **seized; seiz·ing** **1** : to lay hold of or take possession of by force **2** : ARREST **3** : UNDERSTAND **4** : to attack or overwhelm physically : AFFLICT ⟨*seized* by panic⟩ ♦ ***Synonyms*** TAKE, GRASP, CLUTCH, SNATCH, GRAB
sei·zure \ˈsē-zhər\ *n* **1** : the act of seizing : the state of being seized **2** : a sudden attack (as of disease)
sel *abbr* select; selected; selection
sel·dom \ˈsel-dəm\ *adv* : not often : RARELY
[1]**se·lect** \sə-ˈlekt\ *adj* **1** : CHOSEN, PICKED; *also* : CHOICE **2** : judicious or restrictive in choice : DISCRIMINATING
[2]**select** *vb* : to choose from a number or group : pick out
se·lec·tion \sə-ˈlek-shən\ *n* **1** : the act or process of selecting **2** : something selected : CHOICE **3** : a natural or artificial process that tends to favor the survival and reproduction of individuals with certain traits but not those with others
se·lec·tive \sə-ˈlek-tiv\ *adj* : of or relating to selection : selecting or tending to select ⟨~ shoppers⟩
selective service *n* : a system for calling men up for military service : DRAFT
se·lect·man \si-ˈlekt-ˌman, -mən\ *n* : one of a board of officials elected in towns of most New England states to administer town affairs
se·le·ni·um \sə-ˈlē-nē-əm\ *n* : a photosensitive chemical element
self \ˈself\ *n, pl* **selves** \ˈselvz\ **1** : the essential person distinct from all other persons in identity **2** : a particular side of a person's character **3** : personal interest : SELFISHNESS
self- *comb form* **1** : oneself : itself **2** : of oneself or itself **3** : by oneself or itself;

---

self–abasement
self–absorbed
self–absorption
self–acceptance
self–accusation
self–acting
self–addressed
self–adjusting
self–administer
self–advancement
self–aggrandizement

also : automatic **4** : to, for, or toward oneself

self–cen·tered \'self-'sen-tərd\ *adj* : concerned only with one's own self — **self–cen·tered·ness** *n*

self–com·posed \,self-kəm-'pōzd\ *adj* : having control over one's emotions

self–con·scious \'self-'kän-chəs\ *adj* : uncomfortably conscious of oneself as an object of observation by others — **self–con·scious·ly** *adv* — **self–con·scious·ness** *n*

self–con·tained \,self-kən-'tānd\ *adj* **1** : complete in itself **2** : showing self-control; *also* : reserved in manner

self–de·fense \'self-di-'fens\ *n* **1** : a plea of justification for the use of force or for homicide **2** : the act of defending oneself, one's property, or a close relative

self–ef·fac·ing \-ə-'fā-siŋ\ *adj* : RETIRING, SHY ⟨is quiet and ~⟩

self–ev·i·dent \,self-'e-və-dənt\ *adj* : evident without proof or reasoning

self–fer·til·i·za·tion \,self-,fər-tə-lə-'zā-shən\ *n* : fertilization of a plant or animal by its own pollen or sperm

self–ful·fill·ing \,self-fül-'fi-liŋ\ *adj* : becoming real or true by virtue of having been predicted or expected ⟨a ~ prophecy⟩

self–help \'self-'help\ *n* : the process of bettering oneself or coping with one's problems without the aid of others — **self–help** *adj*

self·ie \'sel-fē\ *n* : a digital image of oneself taken by oneself ⟨post a ~⟩

self·ish \'sel-fish\ *adj* : concerned with one's own welfare excessively or without regard for others — **self·ish·ly** *adv* — **self·ish·ness** *n*

self·less \'self-ləs\ *adj* : UNSELFISH ⟨~ dedication⟩ — **self·less·ness** *n*

self–made \'self-'mād\ *adj* : having achieved success or prominence by one's own efforts ⟨a ~ millionaire⟩

self–pol·li·na·tion \,self-,pä-lə-'nā-shən\ *n* : pollination of a flower by its own pollen or sometimes by pollen from another flower on the same plant

self–reg·u·lat·ing \'self-'re-gyə-,lā-tiŋ\ *adj* : AUTOMATIC

self–righ·teous \-'rī-chəs\ *adj* : strongly convinced of one's own righteousness — **self–righ·teous·ly** *adv*

self·same \'self-,sām\ *adj* : precisely the same : IDENTICAL

self–seal·ing \'self-'sē-liŋ\ *adj* : capable of sealing itself (as after puncture)

self–seek·ing \'self-'sē-kiŋ\ *adj* : seeking only to further one's own interests — **self–seeking** *n*

self–start·er \-'stär-tər\ *n* : a person who has initiative

self–will \'self-'wil\ *n* : OBSTINACY

sell \'sel\ *vb* **sold** \'sōld\; **sell·ing** **1** : to transfer (property) in return for money or something else of value **2** : to deal in as a business **3** : to be sold ⟨cars are ~*ing* well⟩ — **sell·er** *n*

sell out *vb* **1** : to dispose of entirely by sale; *esp* : to sell one's business **2** : BETRAY — **sell·out** \'sel-,au̇t\ *n*

selt·zer \'selt-sər\ *n* [modif. of G *Selterser (Wasser)* water of Selters, fr. Nieder *Selters,* Germany] : artificially carbonated water

sel·vage *or* **sel·vedge** \'sel-vij\ *n* : the edge of a woven fabric so formed as to prevent raveling

selves *pl of* SELF

---

self–aggrandizing
self–analysis
self–anointed
self–appointed
self–appraisal
self–asserting
self–assertion
self–assertive
self–assurance
self–assured
self–awareness
self–betrayal
self–care
self–cleaning
self–closing
self–complacent
self–conceit
self–concern
self–condemned
self–confessed
self–confidence
self–confident
self–congratulation
self–congratulatory
self–constituted
self–contempt
self–contradiction
self–contradictory
self–control
self–correcting
self–created
self–criticism
self–cultivation
self–deceit
self–deception
self–defeating
self–definition
self–delusion
self–denial
self–denying
self–deprecating
self–deprecation
self–depreciation
self–described
self–despair
self–destruct
self–destruction
self–destructive
self–determination
self–directed
self–discipline
self–distrust
self–doubt
self–educated
self–employed
self–employment
self–enhancement
self–esteem
self–examination
self–explaining
self–explanatory
self–expression
self–forgetful
self–giving
self–governing
self–government
self–hate
self–hypnosis
self–identity
self–image
self–importance
self–important
self–imposed
self–improvement
self–incrimination
self–induced
self–indulgence
self–indulgent
self–inflicted
self–instruction
self–interest
self–isolate
self–knowledge
self–limiting
self–love
self–lubricating
self–luminous
self–operating
self–perception
self–perpetuating
self–pity
self–portrait
self–possessed
self–possession
self–preservation
self–proclaimed
self–professed
self–promotion
self–propelled
self–propelling
self–protection
self–quarantine
self–realization
self–referential
self–regard
self–reliance
self–reliant
self–renewing
self–reproach
self–respect
self–respecting
self–restraint
self–revelation
self–rule
self–sacrifice
self–sacrificing
self–satisfaction
self–satisfied
self–service
self–serving
self–starting
self–styled
self–sufficiency
self–sufficient
self–supporting
self–sustaining
self–taught
self–torment
self–winding
self–worth

sem *abbr* **1** semicolon **2** seminar **3** seminary

se·man·tic \si-ˈman-tik\ *also* **se·man·ti·cal** \-ti-kəl\ *adj* : of or relating to meaning in language ⟨~ change⟩

se·man·tics \si-ˈman-tiks\ *n sing or pl* : the study of meanings in language

sema·phore \ˈse-mə-ˌfȯr\ *n* **1** : a visual signaling apparatus with movable arms **2** : signaling by hand-held flags

sem·blance \ˈsem-bləns\ *n* **1** : outward appearance **2** : IMAGE, LIKENESS

se·men \ˈsē-mən\ *n* [NL, fr. L, seed] : a sticky whitish fluid of the male reproductive tract that contains the sperm

se·mes·ter \sə-ˈmes-tər\ *n* [G, fr. L *semestris* half-yearly, fr. *sex* six + *mensis* month] **1** : half a year **2** : one of the two terms into which many colleges divide the school year

semi \ˈse-ˌmī\ *n, pl* **sem·is** : SEMITRAILER

semi- \ˈse-mi, -ˌmī\ *prefix* **1** : precisely half of **2** : half in quantity or value; *also* : half of or occurring halfway through a specified period **3** : partly : incompletely **4** : partial : incomplete **5** : having some of the characteristics of

semi·au·to·mat·ic \ˌse-mē-ˌȯ-tə-ˈma-tik\ *adj, of a firearm* : able to fire repeatedly but requiring release and another press of the trigger for each successive shot

semi·co·lon \ˈse-mi-ˌkō-lən\ *n* : a punctuation mark ; used esp. to separate major sentence elements

semi·con·duc·tor \ˌse-mi-kən-ˈdək-tər\ *n* : a substance whose electrical conductivity is between that of a conductor and an insulator — **semi·con·duct·ing** *adj*

[1]**semi·fi·nal** \ˌse-mi-ˈfī-nᵊl\ *adj* : being next to the last in an elimination tournament

[2]**semi·fi·nal** \ˈse-mi-ˌfī-nᵊl\ *n* : a semifinal round or match — **semi·fi·nal·ist** \-ist\ *n*

sem·i·nal \ˈse-mə-nᵊl\ *adj* **1** : of, relating to, or consisting of seed or semen **2** : containing or contributing the seeds of later development : CREATIVE, ORIGINAL — **sem·i·nal·ly** *adv*

sem·i·nar \ˈse-mə-ˌnär\ *n* **1** : a course of study pursued by a group of advanced students doing original research under a professor **2** : CONFERENCE

sem·i·nary \ˈse-mə-ˌner-ē\ *n, pl* **-nar·ies** [ME, seedbed, nursery, fr. L *seminarium*, fr. *semen* seed] : an educational institution; *esp* : one that gives theological training — **sem·i·nar·i·an** \ˌse-mə-ˈner-ē-ən\ *n*

Sem·i·nole \ˈse-mə-ˌnōl\ *n, pl* **Semi·noles** *or* **Seminole** : a member of an Indigenous people of Florida and Oklahoma

semi·per·me·able \ˌse-mi-ˈpər-mē-ə-bəl\ *adj* : partially but not freely or wholly permeable; *esp* : permeable to some usu. small molecules but not to other usu. larger particles — **semi·per·me·abil·i·ty** \-ˌpər-mē-ə-ˈbi-lə-tē\ *n*

Sem·ite \ˈse-ˌmīt\ *n* : a member of any of a group of peoples (as the Hebrews or Arabs) of southwestern Asia — **Se·mit·ic** \sə-ˈmi-tik\ *adj*

semi·trail·er \ˈse-mi-ˌtrā-lər, -ˌmī-\ *n* : a freight trailer that when attached is supported at its forward end by the truck tractor; *also* : a semitrailer with attached tractor

sem·o·li·na \ˌse-mə-ˈlē-nə\ *n* : the purified hard grains produced from the milling of wheat and used esp. for pasta

[1]**sen** \ˈsen\ *n, pl* **sen** — see *yen* at MONEY table

[2]**sen** *n, pl* **sen** — see *ringgit, rupiah* at MONEY table

[3]**sen** *n, pl* **sen** — see *riel* at MONEY table

[4]**sen** *abbr* **1** senate; senator **2** senior

sen·ate \ˈse-nət\ *n* : the second of two chambers of a legislature

sen·a·tor \ˈse-nə-tər\ *n* : a member of a senate — **sen·a·to·ri·al** \ˌse-nə-ˈtȯr-ē-əl\ *adj*

send \ˈsend\ *vb* **sent** \ˈsent\; **send·ing** **1** : to cause to go **2** : EMIT **3** : to propel or drive esp. with force **4** : to put or bring into a certain condition ⟨*sent* them into a rage⟩ **5** : to convey or transmit by an agent — **send·er** *n*

send–off \ˈsend-ˌȯf\ *n* : a demonstration of goodwill and enthusiasm at the start of a new venture (as a trip)

send–up \ˈsend-ˌəp\ *n* : PARODY

se·ne \ˈsā-(ˌ)nā\ *n, pl* **sene** — see *tala* at MONEY table

Sen·e·ca \ˈse-ni-kə\ *n, pl* **Seneca** *or* **Sen·ecas** : a member of an Indigenous people of western New York; *also* : the language of the Seneca people

Sen·e·ga·lese \ˌse-ni-gə-ˈlēz, -ˈlēs\ *n, pl* **Senegalese** : a native or inhabitant of Senegal — **Senegalese** *adj*

se·nes·cence \si-ˈne-sᵊns\ *n* : the state of being old; *also* : the process of becoming old — **se·nes·cent** \-ᵊnt\ *adj*

se·nile \ˈsē-ˌnī(-ə)l, ˈse-\ *adj* : OLD, AGED; *esp* : exhibiting a loss of cognitive abilities associated with old age — **se·nil·i·ty** \si-ˈni-lə-tē\ *n*

[1]**se·nior** \ˈsē-nyər\ *n* **1** : a person older or of higher rank than another **2** : a member of the graduating class of a high school or college

[2]**senior** *adj* [ME, fr. L, older, elder, compar. of *senex* old] **1** : ELDER **2** : more advanced in dignity or rank **3** : belonging to the final year of a school or college course

senior airman *n* : an enlisted person in

---

semiannual
semiarid
semicentennial
semicircle
semicircular
semicivilized
semiclassical
semiconscious
semidarkness
semidivine
semiformal
semigloss
semi–independent
semiliquid
semiliterate
semimonthly
semiofficial
semipermanent
semipolitical
semiprecious
semiprivate
semiprofessional
semireligious
semiretired
semiskilled
semisoft
semisolid
semisweet
semitransparent
semiweekly
semiyearly

the air force ranking next below a staff sergeant

senior chief petty officer *n* : a petty officer in the navy or coast guard ranking next below a master chief petty officer

senior citizen *n* : an elderly person; *esp* : one who has retired

senior high school *n* : a school usu. including grades 10 to 12

se·nior·i·ty \sēn-ˈyȯr-ə-tē\ *n* **1** : the quality or state of being senior **2** : a privileged status owing to length of continuous service

senior master sergeant *n* : a noncommissioned officer in the air force ranking next below a chief master sergeant

sen·i·ti \ˈse-nə-tē\ *n, pl* **seniti** — see *pa'anga* at MONEY table

sen·na \ˈse-nə\ *n* **1** : CASSIA 2; *esp* : one used medicinally **2** : the dried leaflets or pods of a cassia used as a purgative

sen·sa·tion \sen-ˈsā-shən\ *n* **1** : awareness (as of noise or heat) or a mental process (as seeing or hearing) due to stimulation of a sense organ; *also* : an indefinite bodily feeling **2** : a condition of excitement; *also* : the thing that causes this condition

sen·sa·tion·al \-shə-nəl\ *adj* **1** : of or relating to sensation or the senses **2** : arousing an intense and usu. superficial interest or emotional reaction — **sen·sa·tion·al·ly** *adv*

sen·sa·tion·al·ise *Brit var of* SENSATIONALIZE

sen·sa·tion·al·ism \-nə-ˌli-zəm\ *n* : the use or effect of sensational subject matter or treatment — **sen·sa·tion·al·ist** \-nə-list\ *adj or n* — **sen·sa·tion·al·is·tic** \-ˌsā-shə-nə-ˈlis-tik\ *adj*

sen·sa·tion·al·ize \-nə-ˌlīz\ *vb* **-ized; -iz·ing** : to present in a sensational manner

[1]**sense** \ˈsens\ *n* **1** : semantic content : MEANING **2** : the faculty of perceiving by means of sense organs; *also* : a bodily function or mechanism (as sight, hearing, or smell) involving the action and effect of a stimulus on a sense organ **3** : SENSATION, AWARENESS **4** : INTELLIGENCE, JUDGMENT **5** : OPINION ⟨the ~ of the meeting⟩ — **sense·less** *adj* — **sense·less·ly** *adv* — **sense·less·ness** *n*

[2]**sense** *vb* **sensed; sens·ing** **1** : to be or become aware of ⟨~ danger⟩; *also* : to perceive by the senses **2** : to detect (as radiation) automatically

sense organ *n* : a bodily structure (as an eye or ear) that receives stimuli (as heat or light) which excite neurons to send information to the brain

sen·si·bil·i·ty \ˌsen-sə-ˈbi-lə-tē\ *n, pl* **-ties** : delicacy of feeling : SENSITIVITY

sen·si·ble \ˈsen-sə-bəl\ *adj* **1** : capable of being perceived by the senses or the mind; *also* : capable of receiving sense impressions **2** : AWARE, CONSCIOUS **3** : REASONABLE, RATIONAL ⟨a ~ decision⟩ — **sen·si·bly** \-blē\ *adv*

sen·si·tive \ˈsen-sə-tiv\ *adj* **1** : subject to excitation by or responsive to stimuli **2** : having power of feeling **3** : of such a nature as to be easily affected **4** : TOUCHY ⟨a ~ issue⟩ — **sen·si·tive·ly** *adv* — **sen·si·tive·ness** *n* — **sen·si·tiv·i·ty** \ˌsen-sə-ˈti-və-tē\ *n*

sensitive plant *n* : any of several mimosas with leaves that fold or droop when touched

sen·si·tize \ˈsen-sə-ˌtīz\ *vb* **-tized; -tiz·ing** : to make or become sensitive or hypersensitive — **sen·si·ti·za·tion** \ˌsen-sə-tə-ˈzā-shən\ *n*

sen·sor \ˈsen-ˌsȯr, -sər\ *n* : a device that responds to a physical stimulus

sen·so·ry \ˈsen-sə-rē\ *adj* **1** : of or relating to sensation or the senses ⟨~ perception⟩ **2** : AFFERENT

sen·su·al \ˈsen-shə-wəl\ *adj* **1** : relating to gratification of the senses **2** : devoted to the pleasures of the senses — **sen·su·al·ist** *n* — **sen·su·al·i·ty** \ˌsen-shə-ˈwa-lə-tē\ *n* — **sen·su·al·ly** *adv*

sen·su·ous \ˈsen-shə-wəs\ *adj* **1** : relating to the senses or to things that can be perceived by the senses **2** : VOLUPTUOUS ⟨~ lips⟩ — **sen·su·ous·ly** *adv* — **sen·su·ous·ness** *n*

[1]**sent** *past and past part of* SEND

[2]**sent** \ˈsent\ *n, pl* **sen·ti** \ˈsen-tē\ : a monetary unit equal to $\frac{1}{100}$ kroon formerly used in Estonia

sen·te \ˈsen-tē\ *n, pl* **li·cen·te** *or* **li·sen·te** \li-ˈsen-tē\ — see *loti* at MONEY table

[1]**sen·tence** \ˈsen-t^{ə}ns, -t^{ə}nz\ *n* [ME, fr. AF, fr. L *sententia,* lit., feeling, opinion, fr. *sentire* to feel] **1** : the punishment set by a court **2** : a grammatically self-contained speech unit that expresses an assertion, a question, a command, a wish, or an exclamation

[2]**sentence** *vb* **sen·tenced; sen·tenc·ing** : to impose a sentence on

sen·ten·tious \sen-ˈten-chəs\ *adj* : using wise sayings or proverbs; *also* : using pompous language — **sen·ten·tious·ly** *adv* — **sen·ten·tious·ness** *n*

sen·tient \ˈsen-chənt, -chē-ənt\ *adj* : capable of feeling : having perception

sen·ti·ment \ˈsen-tə-mənt\ *n* **1** : FEELING; *also* : thought and judgment influenced by feeling : emotional attitude **2** : OPINION, NOTION

sen·ti·men·tal \ˌsen-tə-ˈmen-t^{ə}l\ *adj* **1** : influenced by tender feelings **2** : affecting the emotions ♦ ***Synonyms*** BATHETIC, MAUDLIN, MAWKISH, MUSHY — **sen·ti·men·tal·ism** *n* — **sen·ti·men·tal·ist** *n* — **sen·ti·men·tal·i·ty** \-ˌmen-ˈta-lə-tē, -mən-\ *n* — **sen·ti·men·tal·ly** *adv*

sen·ti·men·tal·ise *Brit var of* SENTIMENTALIZE

sen·ti·men·tal·ize \-ˈmen-tə-ˌlīz\ *vb* **-ized; -iz·ing** **1** : to indulge in sentiment **2** : to look upon or imbue with sentiment ⟨~*s* the past⟩ — **sen·ti·men·tal·i·za·tion** \-ˌmen-tə-lə-ˈzā-shən\ *n*

sen·ti·mo \sen-ˈtē-(ˌ)mō\ *n, pl* **-mos** — see *peso* at MONEY table

sen·ti·nel \ˈsen-t^{ə}n-əl\ *n* [MF *sentinelle,* fr. It *sentinella,* fr. *sentina* vigilance, fr. *sentire* to perceive, fr. L] : SENTRY

sen·try \ˈsen-trē\ *n, pl* **sentries** : a guard at a point of passage
SEO *abbr* search engine optimization
sep *abbr* separate; separated
Sep *abbr* September
SEP *abbr* simplified employee pension
se·pal \ˈsē-pəl, ˈse-\ *n* : one of the modified leaves comprising a flower calyx
sep·a·ra·ble \ˈse-pə-rə-bəl\ *adj* : capable of being separated — **sep·a·ra·bil·i·ty** \ˌse-pə-rə-ˈbi-lə-tē\
[1]**sep·a·rate** \ˈse-pə-ˌrāt\ *vb* **-rat·ed; -rat·ing** **1** : to set or keep apart : DISCONNECT, SEVER **2** : to keep apart by something intervening **3** : to cease to be together : PART ⟨the couple decided to ~⟩
[2]**sep·a·rate** \ˈse-prət, -pə-rət\ *adj* **1** : not connected **2** : divided from each other **3** : SINGLE, PARTICULAR ⟨the ~ pieces of the puzzle⟩ — **sep·a·rate·ly** *adv*
[3]**sep·a·rate** \ˈse-prət, -pə-rət\ *n* : an article of dress designed to be worn interchangeably with others to form various combinations
sep·a·ra·tion \ˌse-pə-ˈrā-shən\ *n* **1** : the act or process of separating : the state of being separated **2** : a point, line, means, or area of division **3** : a formal separating of a married couple by agreement but without divorce
sep·a·rat·ist \ˈse-prə-tist, ˈse-pə-ˌrā-\ *n* : an advocate of separation (as from a political body) — **sep·a·rat·ism** \ˈse-prə-ˌti-zəm\ *n*
sep·a·ra·tive \ˈse-pə-ˌrā-tiv, ˈse-prə-tiv\ *adj* : tending toward, causing, or expressing separation ⟨~ influences⟩
sep·a·ra·tor \ˈse-pə-ˌrā-tər\ *n* : one that separates; *esp* : a device for separating cream from milk
se·pia \ˈsē-pē-ə\ *n* : a brownish gray to dark brown color
sep·sis \ˈsep-səs\ *n, pl* **sep·ses** \ˈsep-ˌsēz\ : a toxic condition due to spread of bacteria or their toxic products in the body
Sept *abbr* September
Sep·tem·ber \sep-ˈtem-bər\ *n* [ME *Septembre,* fr. AF & OE, both fr. L *September* (seventh month), fr. *septem* seven] : the 9th month of the year
sep·tic \ˈsep-tik\ *adj* **1** : PUTREFACTIVE **2** : relating to or involving sepsis **3** : of, relating to, or used for sewage treatment and disposal
sep·ti·ce·mia \ˌsep-tə-ˈsē-mē-ə\ *n* : BLOOD POISONING
septic tank *n* : a tank in which sewage is disintegrated by bacteria
sep·tu·a·ge·nar·i·an \sep-ˌtü-ə-jə-ˈner-ē-ən, -ˌtyü-\ *n* : a person whose age is in the seventies — **septuagenarian** *adj*
Sep·tu·a·gint \sep-ˈtü-ə-jənt, -ˈtyü-\ *n* : a Greek version of the Old Testament prepared in the 3d and 2d centuries B.C. by Jewish scholars
sep·tum \ˈsep-təm\ *n, pl* **sep·ta** \-tə\ : a dividing wall or membrane esp. between bodily spaces or masses of soft tissue
se·pul·chral \sə-ˈpəl-krəl\ *adj* **1** : relating to burial or the grave **2** : GLOOMY
[1]**sep·ul·chre** *or* **sep·ul·cher** \ˈse-pəl-kər\ *n* : a burial vault : TOMB
[2]**sepulchre** *or* **sepulcher** *vb* **-chred** *or* **-chered; -chring** *or* **-cher·ing** : BURY, ENTOMB
sep·ul·ture \ˈse-pəl-ˌchu̇r\ *n* **1** : BURIAL **2** : SEPULCHRE
se·quel \ˈsē-kwəl\ *n* **1** : logical consequence **2** : a literary or cinematic work continuing a story begun in a preceding one
[1]**se·quence** \ˈsē-kwəns\ *n* **1** : SERIES **2** : chronological order of events **3** : RESULT, SEQUEL ♦ ***Synonyms*** SUCCESSION, CHAIN, PROGRESSION, TRAIN — **se·quen·tial** \si-ˈkwen-chəl\ *adj* — **se·quen·tial·ly** *adv*
[2]**sequence** *vb* **se·quenced; se·quenc·ing** **1** : to arrange in a sequence **2** : to determine the sequence of chemical constituents in ⟨~ DNA⟩
se·quent \ˈsē-kwənt\ *adj* **1** : SUCCEEDING, CONSECUTIVE **2** : RESULTANT
se·ques·ter \si-ˈkwes-tər\ *vb* : to set apart : SEGREGATE ⟨~ a jury⟩
se·ques·trate \ˈsē-kwəs-ˌtrāt, si-ˈkwes-\ *vb* **-trat·ed; -trat·ing** : SEQUESTER — **se·ques·tra·tion** \ˌsē-kwəs-ˈtrā-shən, ˌse-\ *n*
se·quin \ˈsē-kwən\ *n* **1** : an old gold coin of Turkey and Italy **2** : a small metal or plastic plate used for ornamentation esp. on clothing — **se·quined** *or* **se·quinned** \-kwənd\ *adj*
se·quoia \si-ˈkwȯi-ə\ *n* : either of two huge California coniferous trees
ser *abbr* **1** serial **2** series **3** service
sera *pl of* SERUM
se·ra·glio \sə-ˈral-yō\ *n, pl* **-glios** [It *serraglio*] : HAREM
se·ra·pe \sə-ˈrä-pē\ *n* : a colorful woolen shawl worn over the shoulders esp. by Mexican men
ser·aph \ˈser-əf\ *n, pl* **ser·a·phim** \-ə-ˌfim, -ˌfēm\ *or* **seraphs** : one of the 6-winged angels standing in the presence of God
ser·a·phim \ˈser-ə-ˌfim, -ˌfēm\ *n pl* **1** : the highest order of angels **2** *sing, pl* **seraphim** : SERAPH — **se·raph·ic** \sə-ˈra-fik\ *adj*
Serb \ˈsərb\ *n* **1** : a native or inhabitant of Serbia **2** : SERBIAN 2 — **Serb** *adj*
Ser·bi·an \ˈsər-bē-ən\ *n* **1** : SERB **2** : a south Slavic language spoken by the Serbian people — **Serbian** *adj*
Ser·bo–Cro·a·tian \ˌsər-(ˌ)bō-krō-ˈā-shən\ *n* : the Serbian and Croatian languages together with the Slavic speech of Bosnia, Herzegovina, and Montenegro taken as a single language with regional variants
sere \ˈsir\ *adj* : DRY, WITHERED
[1]**ser·e·nade** \ˌser-ə-ˈnād\ *n* [F, fr. It *serenata,* fr. *sereno* clear, calm (of weather) fr. L *serenus*] : music sung or played as a compliment esp. outdoors at night for a woman being courted
[2]**serenade** *vb* **-nad·ed; -nad·ing** : to entertain with or perform a serenade
ser·en·dip·i·ty \ˌser-ən-ˈdi-pə-tē\ *n* [fr. its

possession by the heroes of the Persian fairy tale *The Three Princes of Serendip*] : the gift of finding valuable or agreeable things not sought for — **ser·en·dip·i·tous** \-təs\ *adj* — **ser·en·dip·i·tous·ly** *adv*

se·rene \sə-ˈrēn\ *adj* **1** : CLEAR ⟨~ skies⟩ **2** : QUIET, CALM ♦ ***Synonyms*** TRANQUIL, PEACEFUL, PLACID — **se·rene·ly** *adv* — **se·ren·i·ty** \sə-ˈre-nə-tē\ *n*

serf \ˈsərf\ *n* : a member of a servile class bound to the land and subject to the will of the landowner — **serf·dom** \-dəm\ *n*

serge \ˈsərj\ *n* : a twilled woolen cloth

ser·geant \ˈsär-jənt\ *n* [ME, servant, attendant, sergeant, fr. AF *sergant, serjant,* fr. L *servient-, serviens,* prp. of *servire* to serve] **1** : a noncommissioned officer (as in the army) ranking next below a staff sergeant **2** : an officer in a police force

sergeant at arms : an officer of an organization who preserves order and executes commands

sergeant first class *n* : a noncommissioned officer in the army ranking next below a master sergeant

sergeant major *n, pl* **sergeants major** *or* **sergeant majors** **1** : a noncommissioned officer in the army or marine corps serving as chief administrative assistant in a headquarters **2** : a noncommissioned officer in the marine corps ranking above a first sergeant

[1]**se·ri·al** \ˈsir-ē-əl\ *adj* **1** : appearing in parts that follow regularly ⟨a ~ story⟩ **2** : performing a series of similar acts over a period of time ⟨a ~ killer⟩; *also* : occurring in such a series — **se·ri·al·ly** *adv*

[2]**serial** *n* : a serial story or other writing — **se·ri·al·ist** \-ə-list\ *n*

se·ries \ˈsir-ēz\ *n, pl* **series** : a number of things or events arranged in order and connected by being alike in some way ♦ ***Synonyms*** SUCCESSION, PROGRESSION, SEQUENCE, CHAIN, TRAIN, STRING

seri·graph \ˈser-ə-ˌgraf\ *n* : an original silk-screen print — **se·rig·ra·pher** \sə-ˈri-grə-fər\ *n* — **se·rig·ra·phy** \-fē\ *n*

se·ri·ous \ˈsir-ē-əs\ *adj* **1** : thoughtful or subdued in appearance or manner : SOBER **2** : requiring much thought or work **3** : EARNEST, DEVOTED **4** : DANGEROUS, HARMFUL ⟨a ~ illness⟩ **5** : excessive or impressive in quantity or degree ⟨making ~ money⟩ ♦ ***Synonyms*** GRAVE, SEDATE, STAID — **se·ri·ous·ly** *adv* — **se·ri·ous·ness** *n*

ser·mon \ˈsər-mən\ *n* [ME, fr. AF *sermun,* fr. ML *sermon, sermo,* fr. L, speech, conversation, fr. *serere* to link together] **1** : a religious discourse esp. as part of a worship service **2** : a lecture on conduct or duty

ser·mon·ize \ˈsər-mə-ˌnīz\ *vb* **-ized; -iz·ing** **1** : to compose or deliver a sermon **2** : to preach to or on at length

se·rol·o·gy \sə-ˈrä-lə-jē\ *n* : a science dealing with serums and esp. their reactions and properties — **se·ro·log·i·cal** \ˌsir-ə-ˈlä-ji-kəl\ *or* **se·ro·log·ic** \-jik\ *adj* — **se·ro·log·i·cal·ly** \-ji-k(ə-)lē\ *adv*

se·ro·to·nin \ˌsir-ə-ˈtō-nən, ˌser-\ *n* : a neurotransmitter that is a powerful vasoconstrictor

se·rous \ˈsir-əs\ *adj* : of, relating to, resembling, or producing serum; *esp* : of thin watery constitution

ser·pent \ˈsər-pənt\ *n* : SNAKE

[1]**ser·pen·tine** \ˈsər-pən-ˌtēn, -ˌtīn\ *adj* **1** : SLY, CRAFTY **2** : WINDING, TURNING

[2]**ser·pen·tine** \-ˌtēn\ *n* : a dull-green mineral having a mottled appearance

ser·rate \ˈser-ˌāt\ *adj* : having a saw-toothed edge ⟨a ~ leaf⟩

ser·ried \ˈser-ēd\ *adj* : crowded together

se·rum \ˈsir-əm\ *n, pl* **serums** *or* **se·ra** \-ə\ [L, whey, wheylike fluid] **1** : the clear yellowish antibody-containing fluid that can be separated from blood when it clots; *also* : a preparation of animal serum containing specific antibodies and used to prevent or cure disease **2** : a usu. lightweight cosmetic preparation esp. for use on the face

serv *abbr* service

ser·vant \ˈsər-vənt\ *n* : one that serves others; *esp* : a person employed for domestic or personal work

[1]**serve** \ˈsərv\ *vb* **served; serv·ing** **1** : to work as a servant **2** : to render obedience and worship to (God) **3** : to comply with the commands or demands of **4** : to work through or perform a term of service (as in the army) **5** : PUT IN ⟨*served* five years in jail⟩ **6** : to be of use ⟨pine boughs *served* for a bed⟩ **7** : BENEFIT **8** : to prove adequate or satisfactory for ⟨a pie that ~*s* eight people⟩ **9** : to make ready and pass out ⟨~ drinks⟩ **10** : to furnish or supply with something **11** : to wait on ⟨~ a customer⟩ **12** : to treat or act toward in a specified way ⟨*served* as her maid⟩ **13** : to put the ball in play (as in tennis)

[2]**serve** *n* : the act of serving a ball (as in tennis)

ser·ver \ˈsər-vər\ *n* **1** : one that serves **2** : a computer in a network that is used to provide services (as access to files) to other computers in the network

[1]**ser·vice** \ˈsər-vəs\ *n* **1** : the occupation of a servant **2** : HELP, BENEFIT **3** : a meeting for worship; *also* : a form followed in worship or in a ceremony ⟨burial ~⟩ **4** : the act, fact, or means of serving **5** : performance of official or professional duties **6** : SERVE **7** : a set of dishes or silverware **8** : a branch of public employment; *also* : the persons in it ⟨civil ~⟩ **9** : military or naval duty

[2]**service** *vb* **ser·viced; ser·vic·ing** : to do maintenance or repair work on or for

ser·vice·able \ˈsər-və-sə-bəl\ *adj* : prepared for service : USEFUL, USABLE

ser·vice·man \ˈsər-vəs-ˌman, -mən\ *n* **1** : a man who is a member of the armed forces **2** : a man employed to repair or maintain equipment

service mark *n* : a mark or device used to identify a service (as transportation or insurance) offered to customers

service member *n* : a member of the armed forces

service station *n* : GAS STATION
ser·vice·wom·an \ˈsər-vəs-ˌwu̇-mən\ *n* : a woman who is a member of the armed forces
ser·vile \ˈsər-vəl, -ˌvī(-ə)l\ *adj* **1** : of or befitting a menial position **2** : lacking spirit or independence : SUBMISSIVE — **ser·vile·ly** *adv* — **ser·vil·i·ty** \ˌsər-ˈvi-lə-tē\ *n*
serv·ing \ˈsər-viŋ\ *n* : HELPING
ser·vi·tor \ˈsər-və-tər\ *n* : a male servant
ser·vi·tude \ˈsər-və-ˌtüd, -ˌtyüd\ *n* : SLAVERY, BONDAGE
ser·vo \ˈsər-vō\ *n, pl* **servos** **1** : SERVOMOTOR **2** : SERVOMECHANISM
ser·vo·mech·a·nism \ˈsər-vō-ˌme-kə-ˌni-zəm\ *n* : a device for automatically correcting the performance of a mechanism
ser·vo·mo·tor \-ˌmō-tər\ *n* : a mechanism that supplements a primary control
ses·a·me \ˈse-sə-mē\ *n* : a widely cultivated annual herb of warm regions; *also* : its seeds that yield an edible oil (**sesame oil**) and are used in flavoring
ses·qui·cen·ten·ni·al \ˌses-kwi-sen-ˈte-nē-əl\ *n* [L *sesqui-* one and a half, half again] : a 150th anniversary or its celebration — **sesquicentennial** *adj*
ses·qui·pe·da·lian \ˌses-kwə-pə-ˈdāl-yən\ *adj* **1** : having many syllables : LONG **2** : using long words
ses·sile \ˈse-sī(-ə)l, -səl\ *adj* : permanently attached and not free to move about
ses·sion \ˈse-shən\ *n* **1** : a meeting or series of meetings of a body (as a court or legislature) for the transaction of business **2** : a meeting or period devoted to a particular activity
[1]**set** \ˈset\ *vb* **set; set·ting** **1** : to cause to sit **2** : PLACE **3** : ARRANGE, ADJUST **4** : to cause to be or do **5** : SETTLE, DECREE **6** : to fix in a frame **7** : to fix at a certain amount **8** : WAGER, STAKE **9** : to make or become fast or rigid **10** : to adapt (as words) to something (as music) **11** : to become fixed or firm or solid **12** : to be suitable : FIT **13** : BROOD **14** : to have a certain direction **15** : to pass below the horizon **16** : to defeat in bridge — **set about** : to begin to do — **set forth** : to begin a trip — **set off** **1** : to start out on a course or a trip **2** : to cause to explode — **set out** : to begin a trip or undertaking — **set sail** : to begin a voyage — **set upon** : to attack usu. with violence
[2]**set** *n* **1** : a setting or a being set **2** : DIRECTION, COURSE; *also* : TENDENCY **3** : FORM, BUILD **4** : the fit of something (as a coat) **5** : an artificial setting for the scene of a play or motion picture **6** : a group of tennis games in which one side wins at least six **7** : a group of persons or things of the same kind or having a common characteristic usu. classed together **8** : a collection of things and esp. of mathematical elements (as numbers or points) **9** : an electronic apparatus ⟨a television ~⟩
[3]**set** *adj* **1** : DELIBERATE, INTENT **2** : fixed by authority or custom ⟨a ~ price⟩ **3** : RIGID ⟨a ~ frown⟩ ⟨~ in their ways⟩ **4** : PERSISTENT **5 a** : READY, PREPARED **b** : needing or wanting nothing further
set·back \ˈset-ˌbak\ *n* : a temporary defeat : REVERSE
set back *vb* **1** : HINDER, DELAY; *also* : REVERSE **2** : COST
set piece **1** : a composition (as in literature or music) executed in fixed or ideal form often with brilliant effect **2** : a scene, depiction, speech, or event obviously designed to have an imposing effect **3** : a precisely planned and conducted military operation **4** : a carefully planned sequence of movements performed by members of a sports team
set·screw \ˈset-ˌskrü\ *n* : a screw screwed through one part tightly upon or into another part to prevent relative movement
set·tee \se-ˈtē\ *n* : a bench or sofa with a back and arms
set·ter \ˈse-tər\ *n* : a large long-coated hunting dog
set·ting \ˈse-tiŋ\ *n* **1** : the frame in which a gem is set **2** : the time, place, and circumstances in which something occurs or develops; *also* : SCENERY **3** : music written for a text (as of a poem) **4** : the eggs that a fowl sits on for hatching at one time
set·tle \ˈse-tᵊl\ *vb* **set·tled; set·tling** [ME *settlen* to seat, bring to rest, come to rest, fr. OE *setlan*, fr. *setl* seat] **1** : to place so as to stay **2** : to establish in residence; *also* : COLONIZE **3** : to make compact **4** : QUIET, CALM **5** : to establish or secure permanently **6** : to direct one's efforts **7** : to fix by agreement **8** : to give legally **9** : ADJUST, ARRANGE **10** : DECIDE, DETERMINE **11** : to make a final disposition of ⟨~ an account⟩ **12** : to come to rest **13** : to reach an agreement on **14** : to sink gradually to a lower level **15** : to become clear by depositing sediment — **set·tler** *n*
set·tle·ment \ˈse-tᵊl-mənt\ *n* **1** : the act or process of settling **2** : BESTOWAL ⟨a marriage ~⟩ **3** : payment or adjustment of an account **4** : COLONY **5** : a small village **6** : an institution providing various community services esp. to large city populations **7** : adjustment of doubts and differences
set–to \ˈset-ˌtü\ *n, pl* **set–tos** : FIGHT
set·up \ˈset-ˌəp\ *n* **1** : the manner or act of arranging **2** : glass, ice, and nonalcoholic beverage for mixing served to patrons who supply their own liquor **3** : something (as a plot) that has been constructed or contrived; *also* : FRAME-UP
set up *vb* **1** : to place in position; *also* : ASSEMBLE **2** : CAUSE **3** : FOUND, ESTABLISH ⟨*set up* a school⟩ **4** : FRAME 5
sev·en \ˈse-vən\ *n* **1** : one more than six **2** : the 7th in a set or series **3** : something having seven units — **seven** *adj or pron* — **sev·enth** \-vənth\ *adj or adv or n*
sev·en·teen \ˌse-vən-ˈtēn\ *n* : one more than 16 — **seventeen** *adj or pron* — **sev·en·teenth** \-ˈtēnth\ *adj or n*

seventeen–year locust *n* : a cicada of the U.S. that lives most of its life as a wingless underground nymph and emerges from the ground after seventeen years in the North and after thirteen years in the South to spend only a few weeks as a winged adult
sev•en•ty \ˈse-vən-tē\ *n, pl* **-ties** : seven times 10 — **sev•en•ti•eth** \-tē-əth\ *adj or n* — **seventy** *adj or pron*
sev•er \ˈse-vər\ *vb* **sev•ered; sev•er•ing** : DIVIDE; *esp* : to separate by or as if by cutting ⟨~*ed* ties with his brother⟩ — **sev•er•ance** \ˈsev-rəns, ˈse-və-\ *n*
sev•er•al \ˈsev-rəl, ˈse-və-\ *adj* [ME, fr. AF, fr. ML *separalis,* fr. L *separ* separate, fr. *separare* to separate] **1** : INDIVIDUAL, DISTINCT ⟨federal union of the ~ states⟩ **2** : consisting of an indefinite number but yet not very many ⟨ate ~ cookies⟩ — **sev•er•al•ly** *adv*
severance pay *n* : extra pay given an employee on termination of employment
se•vere \sə-ˈvir\ *adj* **se•ver•er; -est 1** : marked by strictness or sternness : AUSTERE **2** : strict in discipline **3** : causing distress and esp. physical discomfort or pain ⟨~ weather⟩ ⟨a ~ wound⟩ **4** : hard to endure ⟨~ trials⟩ **5** : SERIOUS ⟨~ depression⟩ ♦ ***Synonyms*** STERN, ASCETIC, ASTRINGENT — **se•vere•ly** *adv* — **se•ver•i•ty** \-ˈver-ə-tē\ *n*
sew \ˈsō\ *vb* **sewed; sewn** \ˈsōn\ *or* **sewed; sew•ing 1** : to unite or fasten by stitches **2** : to engage in sewing
sew•age \ˈsü-ij\ *n* : waste materials carried off by sewers
[1]**sew•er** \ˈsō-ər\ *n* : one that sews
[2]**sew•er** \ˈsü-ər\ *n* : an artificial pipe or channel to carry off waste matter
sew•er•age \ˈsü-ə-rij\ *n* **1** : a system of sewers **2** : SEWAGE
sew•ing *n* **1** : the activity of one who sews **2** : material that has been or is to be sewed
sex \ˈseks\ *n* **1** : either of the two major forms that occur in many living things and are designated male or female according to their role in reproduction; *also* : the qualities by which these sexes are differentiated and which directly or indirectly function in reproduction involving two parents **2** : sexual activity or behavior; *also* : SEXUAL INTERCOURSE — **sexed** \ˈsekst\ *adj* — **sex•less** *adj*
sex•a•ge•nar•i•an \ˌsek-sə-jə-ˈner-ē-ən\ *n* : a person whose age is in the sixties — **sexagenarian** *adj*
sex appeal *n* : the quality of being sexually attractive
sex cell *n* : an egg cell or sperm cell
sex chromosome *n* : one of usu. a pair of chromosomes that are usu. similar in one sex but different in the other sex and are concerned with the inheritance of sex
sex hormone *n* : a steroid hormone (as estrogen or testosterone) that is produced esp. by the gonads or adrenal cortex and chiefly affects the growth or function of the reproductive organs
sex•ism \ˈsek-ˌsi-zəm\ *n* : prejudice or discrimination based on sex; *esp* : discrimination against women — **sex•ist** \ˈsek-sist\ *adj or n*
sex•ol•o•gy \sek-ˈsä-lə-jē\ *n* : the study of sex or of the interactions of the sexes — **sex•ol•o•gist** \-jist\ *n*
sex•pot \ˈseks-ˌpät\ *n* : a conspicuously sexy woman
sex symbol *n* : a usu. renowned person (as an entertainer) noted and admired for conspicuous attractiveness
sex•tant \ˈsek-stənt\ *n* [NL *sextant-, sextans* sixth part of a circle, fr. L, sixth part, fr. *sextus* sixth] : a navigational instrument for determining latitude
sex•tet \sek-ˈstet\ *n* **1** : a musical composition for six voices or instruments; *also* : the performers of such a composition **2** : a group or set of six
sex•ting \ˈsek-stiŋ\ *n* : the sending of sexually explicit messages or images by cell phone
sex•ton \ˈsek-stən\ *n* : one who takes care of church property
sex•u•al \ˈsek-shə-wəl\ *adj* : of, relating to, or involving sex or the sexes ⟨a ~ spore⟩ ⟨~ relations⟩ — **sex•u•al•i•ty** \ˌsek-shə-ˈwa-lə-tē\ *n* — **sex•u•al•ly** \ˈsek-shə-wə-lē\ *adv*
sexual intercourse *n* **1** : intercourse between a male and a female in which the penis is inserted into the vagina **2** : intercourse between individuals involving genital contact other than insertion of the penis into the vagina
sexually transmitted disease *n* : a disease (as syphilis, gonorrhea, AIDS, or the genital form of herpes simplex) that is caused by a microorganism or virus usu. or often transmitted by direct sexual contact
sexual relations *n pl* : SEXUAL INTERCOURSE
sexy \ˈsek-sē\ *adj* **sex•i•er; -est** : sexually suggestive or stimulating : EROTIC — **sex•i•ly** \-sə-lē\ *adv* — **sex•i•ness** \-sē-nəs\ *n*
SF *abbr* **1** sacrifice fly **2** science fiction **3** square feet
SFC *abbr* sergeant first class
[1]**SG** *abbr* **1** sergeant **2** solicitor general **3** surgeon general
[2]**SG** *symbol* seaborgium
sgd *abbr* signed
Sgt *abbr* sergeant
Sgt Maj *abbr* sergeant major
sh *abbr* share
shab•by \ˈsha-bē\ *adj* **shab•bi•er; -est 1** : dressed in worn clothes **2** : threadbare and faded from wear **3** : DESPICABLE, MEAN; *also* : UNFAIR ⟨~ treatment⟩ — **shab•bi•ly** \ˈsha-bə-lē\ *adv* — **shab•bi•ness** \-bē-nəs\ *n*
shack \ˈshak\ *n* : HUT, SHANTY
[1]**shack•le** \ˈsha-kəl\ *n* **1** : something (as a manacle or fetter) that confines the legs or arms **2** : a check on free action made as if by fetters **3** : a device for making something fast or secure
[2]**shackle** *vb* **shack•led; shack•ling** : to bind or fasten with shackles

shad \ˈshad\ *n, pl* **shad** : any of several sea fishes related to the herrings that swim up rivers to spawn and include some important food fishes

[1]**shade** \ˈshād\ *n* **1** : partial obscurity **2** : space sheltered from the light esp. of the sun **3** : PHANTOM **4** : something that shelters from or intercepts light or heat; *also, pl* : SUNGLASSES **5** : a dark color or a variety of a color **6** : a small difference

[2]**shade** *vb* **shad•ed; shad•ing** **1** : to shelter from light and heat **2** : DARKEN, OBSCURE **3** : to mark with degrees of light or color **4** : to show slight differences esp. in color or meaning

shad•ing *n* : the color and lines representing darkness or shadow in a drawing or painting

[1]**shad•ow** \ˈsha-dō\ *n* **1** : partial darkness in a space from which light rays are cut off **2** : SHELTER **3** : shade cast upon a surface by something intercepting rays from a light ⟨the ~ of a tree⟩ **4** : PHANTOM **5** : a shaded portion of a picture **6** : a small portion or degree : TRACE ⟨a ~ of doubt⟩ **7** : a source of gloom or unhappiness — **shad•owy** *adj*

[2]**shadow** *vb* **1** : to cast a shadow on **2** : to represent faintly or vaguely **3** : to follow and watch closely : TRAIL

shad•ow•box \ˈsha-dō-ˌbäks\ *vb* : to box with an imaginary opponent esp. for training

shady \ˈshā-dē\ *adj* **shad•i•er; -est** **1** : affording shade **2** : of questionable honesty or reputation ⟨a ~ politician⟩

[1]**shaft** \ˈshaft\ *n, pl* **shafts** **1** : the long handle of a spear or lance **2** : SPEAR, LANCE **3** *or pl* **shaves** \ˈshavz\ : POLE; *esp* : one of two poles between which a horse is hitched to pull a vehicle **4** : something (as a column) long and slender **5** : a bar to support a rotating piece or to transmit power by rotation **6** : an inclined opening in the ground (as for finding or mining ore) **7** : a vertical opening (as for an elevator) through the floors of a building **8** : harsh or unfair treatment — usu. used with *the*

[2]**shaft** *vb* **1** : to fit with a shaft **2** : to treat unfairly or harshly

shag \ˈshag\ *n* : a shaggy tangled mass or covering (as of wool) : long coarse or matted fiber, nap, or pile

shag•gy \ˈsha-gē\ *adj* **shag•gi•er; -est** **1** : rough with or as if with long hair or wool **2** : tangled or rough in surface

shah \ˈshä, ˈshȯ\ *n, often cap* : a sovereign of Iran

Shak *abbr* Shakespeare

[1]**shake** \ˈshāk\ *vb* **shook** \ˈshu̇k\; **shak•en** \ˈshā-kən\; **shak•ing** **1** : to move or cause to move jerkily or irregularly **2** : BRANDISH, WAVE ⟨*shaking* his fist⟩ **3** : to disturb emotionally ⟨*shaken* by her death⟩ **4** : WEAKEN ⟨*shook* his faith⟩ **5** : to bring or come into a certain position, condition, or arrangement by or as if by moving jerkily **6** : to clasp (hands) in greeting or as a sign of goodwill or agreement ♦ ***Synonyms*** TREMBLE, QUAKE, QUAVER, SHIVER, QUIVER — **shak•able** *or* **shake•able** \ˈshā-kə-bəl\ *adj*

[2]**shake** *n* **1** : the act or a result of shaking **2** : DEAL, TREATMENT ⟨a fair ~⟩

shake•down \ˈshāk-ˌdau̇n\ *n* **1** : an improvised bed **2** : EXTORTION ⟨was a victim of a ~⟩ **3** : a process or period of adjustment **4** : a test (as of a new ship or airplane) under operating conditions

shake down *vb* **1** : to take up temporary quarters **2** : to occupy a makeshift bed **3** : to become accustomed esp. to new surroundings or duties **4** : to settle down **5** : to give a shakedown test to **6** : to obtain money from in a deceitful or illegal manner **7** : to bring about a reduction of

shak•er \ˈshā-kər\ *n* **1** : one that shakes ⟨pepper ~⟩ **2** *cap* : a member of a religious sect founded in England in 1747

Shake•spear•ean *or* **Shake•spear•ian** \shāk-ˈspir-ē-ən\ *adj* : of, relating to, or having the characteristics of Shakespeare or his writings

shake–up \ˈshāk-ˌəp\ *n* : an extensive often drastic reorganization

shaky \ˈshā-kē\ *adj* **shak•i•er; -est** : UNSOUND, WEAK — **shak•i•ly** \ˈshā-kə-lē\ *adv* — **shak•i•ness** \-kē-nəs\ *n*

shale \ˈshāl\ *n* : a finely layered rock formed from clay, mud, or silt

shall \shəl, ˈshal\ *vb, past* **should** \shəd, ˈshu̇d\ *pres sing & pl* **shall** — used as an auxiliary to express a command, what seems inevitable or likely in the future, simple futurity, or determination

shal•lop \ˈsha-ləp\ *n* : a light open boat

shal•lot \shə-ˈlät, ˈsha-lət\ *n* [modif. of F *échalote*] **1** : a small clustered bulb that is used in seasoning and is produced by a perennial herb belonging to a subspecies of the onion; *also* : this herb **2** : GREEN ONION

[1]**shal•low** \ˈsha-lō\ *adj* **1** : not deep **2** : not intellectually profound

[2]**shallow** *n* : a shallow place in a body of water — usu. used in pl.

[1]**sham** \ˈsham\ *n* **1** : an ornamental covering for a pillow **2** : COUNTERFEIT, IMITATION **3** : a person who shams

[2]**sham** *vb* **shammed; sham•ming** : FEIGN, PRETEND — **sham•mer** *n*

[3]**sham** *adj* : not genuine : FALSE, FEIGNED

sha•man \ˈshä-mən, ˈshā-\ *n* [ultim. fr. Evenki (a language of Siberia) *šamān*] : a priest or priestess who uses magic to cure the sick, to divine the hidden, and to control events

sham•ble \ˈsham-bəl\ *vb* **sham•bled; sham•bling** : to shuffle along — **shamble** *n*

sham•bles \ˈsham-bəlz\ *n* **1** : a scene of great slaughter **2** : a scene or state of great destruction or disorder; *also* : MESS

[1]**shame** \ˈshām\ *n* **1** : a painful sense of having done something wrong, improper, or immodest **2** : DISGRACE, DISHONOR **3** : a cause of feeling shame **4** : something to be regretted ⟨it's a ~ you'll miss the party⟩ — **shame•ful** \-fəl\ *adj* — **shame•ful•ly** *adv* — **shame•less** *adj* — **shame•less•ly** *adv*

[2]**shame** *vb* **shamed; sham·ing** **1** : DISGRACE **2** : to make ashamed

shame·faced \ˈshām-ˌfāst\ *adj* : ASHAMED, ABASHED — **shame·faced·ly** \-ˌfā-səd-lē, -ˌfāst-lē\ *adv*

[1]**sham·poo** \sham-ˈpü\ *vb* [Hindi *cā̃po,* imper. of *cā̃pnā* to press, shampoo] : to wash (as the hair) with soap and water or with a special preparation; *also* : to clean (as a rug) similarly

[2]**shampoo** *n, pl* **shampoos** **1** : the act or an instance of shampooing **2** : a preparation for use in shampooing

sham·rock \ˈsham-ˌräk\ *n* [Ir *seamróg,* dim. of *seamar* clover] : a plant of folk legend with leaves composed of three leaflets that is associated with St. Patrick and Ireland

shang·hai \shaŋ-ˈhī\ *vb* **shang·haied; shang·hai·ing** [*Shanghai,* China] : to force aboard a ship for service as a sailor; *also* : to trick or force into an undesirable position

Shan·gri–la \ˌshaŋ-gri-ˈlä\ *n* [*Shangri-La,* imaginary land depicted in the novel *Lost Horizon* (1933) by James Hilton] : a remote idyllic hideaway

shank \ˈshaŋk\ *n* **1** : the part of the leg between the knee and the human ankle or a corresponding part of a quadruped **2** : a cut of meat from the leg **3** : the narrow part of the sole of a shoe beneath the instep **4** : the part of a tool or instrument (as a key or anchor) connecting the functioning part with a part by which it is held or moved

shan·tung \ˌshan-ˈtəŋ\ *n* : a fabric in plain weave having a slightly irregular surface

shan·ty \ˈshan-tē\ *n, pl* **shanties** [prob. fr. CanF *chantier* lumber camp, hut, fr. F, builder's yard, ways, support for barrels, fr. OF, support, fr. L *cantherius* rafter, trellis] : a small roughly built shelter or dwelling

[1]**shape** \ˈshāp\ *vb* **shaped; shap·ing** **1** : to form esp. in a particular shape **2** : DESIGN **3** : ADAPT, ADJUST **4** : REGULATE ♦ ***Synonyms*** MAKE, FASHION, FABRICATE, MANUFACTURE, FRAME, MOLD

[2]**shape** *n* **1** : APPEARANCE ⟨the ~ of an apple⟩ **2** : surface configuration : FORM **3** : bodily contour apart from the head and face : FIGURE **4** : PHANTOM **5** : CONDITION ⟨was in fine ~⟩ — **shaped** *adj*

shape·less \ˈshā-pləs\ *adj* **1** : having no definite shape **2** : not shapely — **shape·less·ly** *adv* — **shape·less·ness** *n*

shape·ly \ˈshā-plē\ *adj* **shape·li·er; -est** : having a pleasing shape ⟨a ~ model⟩ — **shape·li·ness** *n*

shape–shift·er \ˈshāp-ˌshif-tər\ *n* : one that seems able to change form or identity at will

shard \ˈshärd\ *also* **sherd** \ˈshərd\ *n* : a broken piece : FRAGMENT

[1]**share** \ˈsher\ *n* : PLOWSHARE

[2]**share** *n* **1** : a portion belonging to one person or group **2** : any of the equal interests into which the capital stock of a corporation is divided

[3]**share** *vb* **shared; shar·ing** **1** : APPORTION **2** : to use or enjoy with others **3** : PARTICIPATE **4** : to post (something) on a social media platform — **shar·er** *n*

share·crop·per \-ˌkrä-pər\ *n* : a farmer who works another's land in return for a share of the crop — **share·crop** *vb*

share·hold·er \-ˌhōl-dər\ *n* : STOCKHOLDER

share·ware \ˈsher-ˌwer\ *n* : software available for usu. limited trial use at little or no cost but that can be upgraded for a fee

[1]**shark** \ˈshärk\ *n* : any of various active, usu. predatory, and mostly large marine cartilaginous fishes

[2]**shark** *n* : a greedy crafty person

shark·skin \-ˌskin\ *n* **1** : the hide of a shark or leather made from it **2** : a fabric woven from strands of many fine threads and having a sleek appearance and silky feel

[1]**sharp** \ˈshärp\ *adj* **1** : having a thin cutting edge or fine point : not dull or blunt **2** : COLD, NIPPING ⟨a ~ wind⟩ **3** : keen in intellect, perception, or attention **4** : BRISK, ENERGETIC **5** : IRRITABLE ⟨a ~ temper⟩ **6** : causing intense distress ⟨a ~ pain⟩ **7** : HARSH, CUTTING ⟨a ~ rebuke⟩ **8** : affecting the senses as if cutting or piercing ⟨a ~ sound⟩ ⟨a ~ smell⟩ **9** : not smooth or rounded ⟨~ features⟩ **10** : involving an abrupt or extreme change ⟨a ~ turn⟩ **11** : CLEAR, DISTINCT ⟨mountains in ~ relief⟩; *also* : easy to perceive ⟨a ~ contrast⟩ **12** : higher than the true pitch; *also* : raised by a half step **13** : STYLISH ⟨a ~ dresser⟩ ♦ ***Synonyms*** KEEN, ACUTE, QUICK-WITTED, PENETRATIVE — **sharp·ly** *adv* — **sharp·ness** *n*

[2]**sharp** *adv* **1** : in a sharp manner **2** : EXACTLY, PRECISELY ⟨left at 8 ~⟩

[3]**sharp** *n* **1** : a sharp edge or point **2** : a character # which indicates that a specified note is to be raised by a half step; *also* : the resulting note **3** : SHARPER

[4]**sharp** *vb* : to raise in pitch by a half step

shar–pei \ˌshä-ˈpā, ˌshär-\ *n, pl* **shar–peis** *often cap S&P* [Chin (Guangdong dial.) *sà* sand + *péi* fur] : any of a Chinese breed of dogs that have loose wrinkled skin esp. when young

sharp·en \ˈshär-pən\ *vb* : to make or become sharp — **sharp·en·er** *n*

sharp·er \ˈshär-pər\ *n* : SWINDLER; *esp* : a cheating gambler

sharp·ie *or* **sharpy** \ˈshär-pē\ *n, pl* **sharp·ies** **1** : SHARPER **2** : a person who is exceptionally keen or alert

sharp·shoot·er \ˈshärp-ˌshü-tər\ *n* : a proficient marksman — **sharp·shoot·ing** *n*

shat·ter \ˈsha-tər\ *vb* : to dash or burst into fragments — **shat·ter·proof** \ˈsha-tər-ˌprüf\ *adj*

[1]**shave** \ˈshāv\ *vb* **shaved; shaved** *or* **shav·en** \ˈshā-vən\; **shav·ing** **1** : to slice

in thin pieces **2** : to make bare or smooth by cutting the hair from **3** : to cut or pare off by the sliding movement of a razor **4** : to skim along or near the surface of

²**shave** *n* **1** : any of various tools for cutting thin slices **2** : an act or process of shaving

shav·er \ˈshā-vər\ *n* **1** : an electric razor **2** : BOY, YOUNGSTER

shaves *pl of* SHAFT

shaving *n* **1** : the act of one that shaves **2** : something shaved off

shawl \ˈshȯl\ *n* : a square or oblong piece of fabric used esp. by women as a loose covering for the head or shoulders

Shaw·nee \shȯ-ˈnē, shä-\ *n, pl* **Shawnee** *or* **Shawnees** : a member of an Indigenous people orig. of the central Ohio valley; *also* : their language

shd *abbr* should

she \ˈshē\ *pron* : that female one ⟨who is ~⟩; *also* : that one regarded as feminine ⟨~'s a fine ship⟩

sheaf \ˈshēf\ *n, pl* **sheaves** \ˈshēvz\ **1** : a bundle of stalks and ears of grain **2** : a group of things bound together

¹**shear** \ˈshir\ *vb* **sheared; sheared** *or* **shorn** \ˈshōrn\; **shear·ing** **1** : to cut the hair or wool from : CLIP, TRIM **2** : to deprive by or as if by cutting ⟨*shorn* of power⟩ **3** : to cut or break sharply

²**shear** *n* **1** : any of various cutting tools that consist of two blades fastened together so that the edges slide one by the other — usu. used in pl. **2** *chiefly Brit* : the act, an instance, or the result of shearing **3** : an action or stress caused by applied forces that causes two parts of a body to slide on each other

shear·wa·ter \ˈshir-ˌwȯ-tər, -ˌwä-\ *n* : any of several seabirds related to the petrels that often skim along waves in flight

sheath \ˈshēth\ *n, pl* **sheaths** \ˈshēt͟hz, ˈshēths\ **1** : a case for a blade (as of a knife); *also* : an anatomical covering suggesting such a case **2** : a close-fitting dress usu. worn without a belt

sheathe \ˈshēt͟h\ *also* **sheath** \ˈshēth\ *vb* **sheathed; sheath·ing** **1** : to put into a sheath **2** : to cover with something that guards or protects

sheath·ing \ˈshē-t͟hiŋ, -thiŋ\ *n* : material used to sheathe something; *esp* : the first covering of boards or of waterproof material on the outside wall of a frame house or on a timber roof

sheave \ˈshiv, ˈshēv\ *n* : a grooved wheel or pulley (as on a pulley block)

she·bang \shi-ˈbaŋ\ *n* : everything involved in what is under consideration ⟨sold the whole ~⟩

¹**shed** \ˈshed\ *vb* **shed; shed·ding** **1** : to cause to flow from a cut or wound ⟨~ blood⟩ **2** : to pour down in drops ⟨~ tears⟩ **3** : to give out (as light) : DIFFUSE **4** : to throw off (as a natural covering) : DISCARD ⟨~ skin⟩

²**shed** *n* : a slight structure built for shelter or storage

sheen \ˈshēn\ *n* : a subdued luster

sheep \ˈshēp\ *n, pl* **sheep** **1** : any of various cud-chewing mammals that are stockier than the related goats and lack a beard in the male; *esp* : one raised for meat or for its wool or skin **2** : a timid or defenseless person **3** : SHEEPSKIN

sheep·dog \ˈshēp-ˌdȯg\ *n* : a dog used to tend, drive, or guard sheep

sheep·fold \ˈshēp-ˌfōld\ *n* : a pen or shelter for sheep

sheep·herd·er \-ˌhər-dər\ *n* : a worker in charge of sheep esp. on open range — **sheep·herd·ing** *n*

sheep·ish \ˈshē-pish\ *adj* : BASHFUL, TIMID; *esp* : embarrassed by consciousness of a fault — **sheep·ish·ly** *adv*

sheep·skin \ˈshēp-ˌskin\ *n* **1** : the hide of a sheep or leather prepared from it; *also* : PARCHMENT **2** : DIPLOMA

¹**sheer** \ˈshir\ *vb* : to turn from a course

²**sheer** *adj* **1** : very thin or transparent **2** : UNQUALIFIED ⟨~ folly⟩ **3** : very steep ♦ ***Synonyms*** PURE, SIMPLE, ABSOLUTE, UNADULTERATED, UNMITIGATED — **sheer** *adv*

¹**sheet** \ˈshēt\ *n* **1** : a broad piece of cloth (as for a bed); *also* : SAIL 1 **2** : a single piece of paper **3** : a broad flat surface ⟨a ~ of ice⟩ **4** : something broad and long and relatively thin

²**sheet** *n* : a rope used to trim a sail

sheet cake *n* : a large, one-layer, usu. frosted cake

sheet·ing \ˈshē-tiŋ\ *n* : material in the form of sheets or suitable for forming into sheets

sheikh *or* **sheik** \ˈshēk, ˈshāk\ *n* : an Arab chief — **sheikh·dom** *or* **sheik·dom** \-dəm\ *n*

shek·el *or* **sheq·el** \ˈshe-kəl\ *n* — see MONEY table

shelf \ˈshelf\ *n, pl* **shelves** \ˈshelvz\ **1** : a thin flat usu. long and narrow structure fastened horizontally (as on a wall) above the floor to hold things **2** : something (as a sandbar) that suggests a shelf

shelf life *n* : the period of storage time during which a material will remain useful

¹**shell** \ˈshel\ *n* **1** : a hard or tough often thin outer covering of an animal (as a beetle, turtle, or mollusk) or of an egg or a seed or fruit (as a nut); *also* : something that resembles a shell ⟨a pastry ~⟩ **2** : a light narrow racing boat propelled by oarsmen **3** : a case holding an explosive and designed to be fired from a cannon; *also* : a case holding the charge of powder and shot or bullet for small arms **4** : a plain usu. sleeveless blouse or sweater — **shelled** \ˈsheld\ *adj* — **shelly** \ˈshe-lē\ *adj*

²**shell** *vb* **1** : to remove from a shell or husk **2** : BOMBARD — **shell·er** *n*

¹**shel·lac** \shə-ˈlak\ *n* **1** : a purified lac **2** : lac dissolved in alcohol and used as a wood filler or finish

²**shellac** *vb* **shel·lacked; shel·lack·ing** **1** : to coat or treat with shellac **2** : to defeat decisively ⟨*shellacked* their opponents⟩

shellacking *n* : a sound drubbing

shell bean *n* : a bean grown esp. for its edible seeds; *also* : its edible seed
shell•fish \-ˌfish\ *n* : an invertebrate water animal (as an oyster or lobster) with a shell
shell out *vb* : PAY
shell shock *n* : COMBAT FATIGUE — **shell–shocked** \ˈshel-ˌshäkt\ *adj*
¹**shel•ter** \ˈshel-tər\ *n* : something that gives protection : REFUGE
²**shelter** *vb* **shel•tered; shel•ter•ing** : to give protection or refuge to
shelve \ˈshelv\ *vb* **shelved; shelv•ing** **1** : to slope gradually **2** : to store on shelves **3** : to dismiss from service or use **4** : to put aside : DEFER ⟨∼ a proposal⟩
shelv•ing \ˈshel-viŋ\ *n* : material for shelves; *also* : SHELVES
she•nan•i•gan \shə-ˈna-ni-gən\ *n* **1** : an underhand trick **2** : questionable conduct — usu. used in pl. **3** : high-spirited or mischievous activity — usu. used in pl.
¹**shep•herd** \ˈshe-pərd\ *n* **1** : one who tends sheep **2** : GERMAN SHEPHERD
²**shepherd** *vb* : to tend as or in the manner of a shepherd
shep•herd•ess \ˈshe-pər-dəs\ *n* : a woman who tends sheep
shepherd's pie *n* : a meat pie with a mashed potato crust
sheqel *n, pl* **sheqalim** *var of* SHEKEL
sher•bet \ˈshər-bət\ *n* [Turk *şerbet,* fr. Pers *sharbat,* fr. Ar *sharba* drink] **1** : a drink of sweetened diluted fruit juice **2** *also* **sher•bert** \-bərt\ : a frozen dessert of fruit juices, sugar, milk or water, and egg whites or gelatin
sherd *var of* SHARD
sher•iff \ˈsher-əf\ *n* [ME *shirreve,* fr. OE *scīrgerēfa,* lit., shire reeve (local official)] : a county officer charged with the execution of the law and the preservation of order
sher•ry \ˈsher-ē\ *n, pl* **sherries** [alter. of earlier *sherris* (taken as pl.), fr. *Xeres* (now *Jerez*), Spain] : a fortified wine with a nutty flavor
Shet•land pony \ˈshet-lənd-\ *n* : any of a breed of small stocky hardy ponies
shew \ˈshō\ *Brit var of* SHOW
Shia \ˈshē-(ˌ)ä\ *n* **1** : one of the two main branches of Islam **2** : a Muslim who is a member of this branch
shi•at•su *also* **shi•at•zu** \shē-ˈät-sü\ *n* : a form of acupressure originating in Japan
shib•bo•leth \ˈshi-bə-ləth\ *n* [Heb *shibbōleth* stream; fr. the use of this word as a test to distinguish the men of Gilead from members of the tribe of Ephraim (Judges 12:5, 6)] **1** : CATCHPHRASE **2** : language that is a criterion for distinguishing members of a group
¹**shield** \ˈshēld\ *n* **1** : a broad piece of defensive armor carried on the arm **2** : something that protects or hides **3** : a police officer's badge
²**shield** *vb* : to protect or hide with a shield ♦ ***Synonyms*** PROTECT, GUARD, SAFEGUARD
shier *comparative of* SHY
shiest *superlative of* SHY
¹**shift** \ˈshift\ *vb* **1** : EXCHANGE, REPLACE **2** : to change place, position, or direction : MOVE; *also* : to change gears **3** : GET BY, MANAGE
²**shift** *n* **1** : SCHEME, TRICK **2** : a woman's slip or loose-fitting dress **3** : a change in direction, emphasis, or attitude **4** : a group working together alternating with other groups **5** : TRANSFER **6** : GEARSHIFT
shift•less \ˈshift-ləs\ *adj* : LAZY, INEFFICIENT — **shift•less•ness** *n*
shifty \ˈshif-tē\ *adj* **shift•i•er; -est** **1** : TRICKY; *also* : ELUSIVE **2** : indicative of a tricky nature ⟨∼ eyes⟩
shih tzu \ˈshēd-ˈzü, ˈshēt-ˈsü\ *n, pl* **shih tzus** *also* **shih tzu** *often cap S&T* [Chin (Beijing) *shīzi (gǒu),* fr. *shīzi* lion + *gǒu* dog] : any of a breed of small short-legged dogs of Chinese origin that have a short muzzle and a long dense coat
shii•ta•ke \shē-ˈtä-kē\ *n* [Jp] : a dark Asian mushroom widely cultivated for its edible cap
Shi•ite \ˈshēˌīt\ *n* : a Muslim of the Shia branch of Islam
shill \ˈshil\ *n* : one who acts as a decoy (as for a pitchman) — **shill** *vb*
shil•le•lagh *also* **shil•la•lah** \shə-ˈlā-lē\ *n* [*Shillelagh,* town in Ireland] : CUDGEL, CLUB
shil•ling \ˈshi-liŋ\ *n* — see MONEY table
shilly–shally \ˈshi-lē-ˌsha-lē\ *vb* **shilly–shall•ied; shilly–shally•ing** **1** : to show hesitation or lack of decisiveness **2** : to waste time
shim \ˈshim\ *n* : a thin often tapered piece of wood, metal, or stone used (as in leveling) to fill in space
shim•mer \ˈshi-mər\ *vb* : to shine waveringly or tremulously : GLIMMER ⟨∼*ing* light⟩ ♦ ***Synonyms*** FLASH, GLEAM, GLINT, SPARKLE, GLITTER — **shimmer** *n* — **shim•mery** *adj*
shim•my \ˈshi-mē\ *n, pl* **shimmies** : an abnormal vibration esp. in the front wheels of a motor vehicle — **shimmy** *vb*
¹**shin** \ˈshin\ *n* : the front part of the leg below the knee
²**shin** *vb* **shinned; shin•ning** : to climb (as a pole) by gripping alternately with arms or hands and legs
shin•bone \ˈshin-ˌbōn\ *n* : TIBIA
¹**shine** \ˈshīn\ *vb* **shone** \ˈshōn\ *or* **shined; shin•ing** **1** : to give or cause to give light **2** : GLEAM, GLITTER **3** : to be eminent, conspicuous, or distinguished ⟨gave her a chance to ∼⟩ **4** : POLISH ⟨∼ your shoes⟩
²**shine** *n* **1** : BRIGHTNESS, RADIANCE **2** : LUSTER, BRILLIANCE **3** : fair weather : SUNSHINE ⟨rain or ∼⟩ **4** : LIKING, FANCY ⟨took a ∼ to them⟩ **5** : a polish given to shoes
shin•er \ˈshī-nər\ *n* **1** : a silvery fish; *esp* : any of numerous small freshwater American fishes related to the carp **2** : BLACK EYE
¹**shin•gle** \ˈshiŋ-gəl\ *n* **1** : a small thin

piece of building material used in overlapping rows for covering a roof or outside wall **2** : a small sign

[2]**shingle** *vb* **shin·gled; shin·gling** : to cover with shingles

[3]**shingle** *n* : a beach strewn with gravel; *also* : coarse gravel (as on a beach)

shin·gles \ˈshiŋ-gəlz\ *n* : an acute inflammation of the spinal and cranial nerves caused by reactivation of the chicken pox virus and associated with eruptions and pain along the course of the affected nerves

shin·ny \ˈshi-nē\ *vb* **shin·nied; shin·ny·ing** : SHIN

shin splints *n sing or pl* : a condition marked by pain and sometimes tenderness and swelling in the shin caused by repeated small injuries to muscles and associated tissue esp. from running

Shin·to \ˈshin-ˌtō\ *n* : the indigenous religion of Japan consisting esp. in reverence of the spirits of natural forces and imperial ancestors — **Shin·to·ism** *n* — **Shin·to·ist** *n or adj*

shiny \ˈshī-nē\ *adj* **shin·i·er; -est** : BRIGHT, RADIANT; *also* : POLISHED

[1]**ship** \ˈship\ *n* **1** : a large oceangoing boat **2** : a ship's officers and crew **3** : AIRSHIP, AIRCRAFT, SPACECRAFT

[2]**ship** *vb* **shipped; ship·ping** **1** : to put or receive on board a ship for transportation **2** : to have transported by a carrier **3** : to take or draw into a boat ⟨~ oars⟩ ⟨~ water⟩ **4** : to engage to serve on a ship — **ship·per** *n*

-ship \ˌship\ *n suffix* **1** : state : condition : quality ⟨friend*ship*⟩ **2** : office : dignity : profession ⟨lord*ship*⟩ ⟨clerk*ship*⟩ **3** : art : skill ⟨horseman*ship*⟩ **4** : something showing, exhibiting, or embodying a quality or state ⟨town*ship*⟩ **5** : one entitled to a (specified) rank, title, or appellation ⟨his Lord*ship*⟩ **6** : the body of persons engaged in a specified activity ⟨reader*ship*⟩

ship·board \ˈship-ˌbȯrd\ *n* : SHIP

ship·build·er \-ˌbil-dər\ *n* : one who designs or builds ships

ship·fit·ter \-ˌfi-tər\ *n* **1** : one who constructs ships **2** : a naval enlisted person who works as a plumber

ship·mate \-ˌmāt\ *n* : a fellow sailor

ship·ment \-mənt\ *n* : the process of shipping; *also* : the goods shipped

shipping *n* **1** : SHIPS; *esp* : ships in one port or belonging to one country **2** : transportation of goods

ship·shape \ˈship-ˌshāp\ *adj* : TRIM, TIDY

ship·worm \-ˌwərm\ *n* : any of various wormlike marine clams that have a shell used for burrowing in wood and damage wooden ships and wharves

[1]**ship·wreck** \-ˌrek\ *n* **1** : a wrecked ship **2** : destruction or loss of a ship **3** : total loss or failure : RUIN

[2]**shipwreck** *vb* : to cause or meet disaster at sea through destruction or foundering

ship·wright \ˈship-ˌrīt\ *n* : a carpenter skilled in ship construction and repair

ship·yard \-ˌyärd\ *n* : a place where ships are built or repaired

shire \ˈshī(-ə)r, *in place-name compounds* ˌshir, shər\ *n* : a county in Great Britain

shirk \ˈshərk\ *vb* : to avoid performing (duty or work) — **shirk·er** *n*

shirr \ˈshər\ *vb* **1** : to make shirring in **2** : to bake (eggs removed from the shell) until set

shirr·ing \ˈshər-iŋ\ *n* : a decorative gathering in cloth made by drawing up parallel lines of stitches

shirt \ˈshərt\ *n* **1** : a loose cloth garment usu. having a collar, sleeves, a front opening, and a tail long enough to be tucked inside pants or a skirt **2** : UNDERSHIRT — **shirt·less** *adj*

shirt·ing \ˈshər-tiŋ\ *n* : cloth suitable for making shirts

shish ke·bab \ˈshish-kə-ˌbäb\ *n* [Turk *şiş kebabı*, fr. *şiş* spit + *kebap* roast meat] : kebab cooked on skewers

shiv \ˈshiv\ *n, slang* : KNIFE

shi·va *also* **shi·vah** \ˈshi-və, ˈshē-\ *n* : a traditional seven-day period of mourning the death of a family member observed in Jewish homes

[1]**shiv·er** \ˈshi-vər\ *vb* : TREMBLE, QUIVER
♦ ***Synonyms*** SHUDDER, QUAVER, SHAKE, QUAKE

[2]**shiver** *n* : an instance of shivering — **shiv·ery** *adj*

shlemiel *var of* SCHLEMIEL

shlub *var of* SCHLUB

shmooze *var of* SCHMOOZE

Sho·ah \ˈshō-ə, -ˌä\ *n* : HOLOCAUST 2

[1]**shoal** \ˈshōl\ *n* **1** : SHALLOW **2** : a sandbank or bar creating a shallow

[2]**shoal** *n* : a large group (as of fish)

shoat \ˈshōt\ *n* : a weaned young pig

[1]**shock** \ˈshäk\ *n* : a pile of sheaves of grain or cornstalks set up in a field

[2]**shock** *n* [MF *choc*, fr. *choquer* to strike against] **1** : a sharp impact or violent shake or jar **2** : a sudden violent mental or emotional disturbance **3** : a state of bodily collapse that is often marked by a drop in blood pressure and volume and that is caused esp. by crushing wounds, blood loss, or burns **4** : the effect of a charge of electricity passing through the body **5** : SHOCK ABSORBER — **shock·proof** \-ˌprüf\ *adj*

[3]**shock** *vb* **1** : to strike with surprise, horror, or disgust **2** : to subject to the action of an electrical discharge

[4]**shock** *n* : a thick bushy mass (as of hair)

shock absorber *n* : any of several devices for absorbing the energy of sudden shocks in machinery

shock·er \ˈshä-kər\ *n* : one that shocks; *esp* : a sensational work of fiction or drama

shock·ing \ˈshä-kiŋ\ *adj* : extremely startling and offensive — **shock·ing·ly** *adv*

shock therapy *n* : the treatment of mental disorder by induction of coma or convulsions by drugs or electricity

shock wave *n* : a wave formed by the sudden violent compression of the medium through which it travels

[1]**shod·dy** \ˈshä-dē\ *n* **1** : wool reclaimed from old rags; *also* : a fabric made from it **2** : inferior or imitation material

[2]**shoddy** *adj* **shod·di·er; -est** **1** : made of shoddy **2** : poorly done or made ⟨~ workmanship⟩ — **shod·di·ly** \ˈshä-də-lē\ *adv* — **shod·di·ness** \-dē-nəs\ *n*

[1]**shoe** \ˈshü\ *n* **1** : a covering for the human foot **2** : HORSESHOE **3** : the part of a brake that presses on the wheel

[2]**shoe** *vb* **shod** \ˈshäd\ *also* **shoed** \ˈshüd\; **shoe·ing** : to put a shoe or shoes on

shoebox \ˈshü-ˌbäks\ *n* **1** : a box that shoes are sold in **2** : a very small space ⟨a ~ apartment⟩

shoe·horn \-ˌhȯrn\ *n* : a curved implement (as of horn or plastic) used in putting on a shoe

shoe·lace \ˈshü-ˌlās\ *n* : a lace or string for fastening a shoe

shoe·mak·er \-ˌmā-kər\ *n* : one who makes or repairs shoes

shoe·string \-ˌstriŋ\ *n* **1** : SHOELACE **2** : a small sum of money

sho·gun \ˈshō-gən\ *n* [Jp *shōgun* general] : any of a line of military governors ruling Japan until the revolution of 1867–68 — **sho·gun·ate** \ˈshō-gə-nət, -ˌnāt\ *n*

shone *past and past part of* SHINE

shook *past of* SHAKE

shook–up \(ˌ)shu̇k-ˈəp\ *adj* : nervously upset : AGITATED

[1]**shoot** \ˈshüt\ *vb* **shot** \ˈshät\; **shoot·ing** **1** : to drive (as an arrow or bullet) forward quickly or forcibly **2** : to hit, kill, or wound with a missile **3** : to cause a missile to be driven forth or forth from ⟨~ a gun⟩ **4** : to send forth (as a ray of light) **5** : to thrust forward or out **6** : to pass rapidly along ⟨~ the rapids⟩ **7** : PHOTOGRAPH, FILM **8** : to move swiftly : DART **9** : to grow by or as if by sending out shoots; *also* : MATURE, DEVELOP — **shoot·er** *n*

[2]**shoot** *n* **1** : a plant stem with its leaves and branches esp. when not yet mature **2** : an act of shooting **3** : a shooting match

shooting *n* **1** : the act of one that shoots a gun **2** : an instance of gun violence ⟨a school ~⟩ **3** : the act of photographing or filming

shooting iron *n* : FIREARM

shooting star *n* : METEOR 2

shoot up *vb* : to inject a narcotic into a vein

[1]**shop** \ˈshäp\ *n* [ME *shoppe,* fr. OE *sceoppa* booth] **1** : a place where things are made or worked on : FACTORY, MILL **2** : a retail store ⟨dress ~⟩

[2]**shop** *vb* **shopped; shop·ping** : to visit stores for purchasing or examining goods — **shop·per** *n*

shop·keep·er \ˈshäp-ˌkē-pər\ *n* : a retail merchant

shop·lift \-ˌlift\ *vb* : to steal goods on display from a store — **shop·lift·er** *n*

shopping cart *n* **1** : a cart used for holding merchandise when shopping in a store **2** : a temporary record of items selected for purchase from a website

shop·talk \-tȯk\ *n* : talk about one's business or special interests

shop·worn \-ˌwȯrn\ *adj* : soiled or frayed from much handling in a store

[1]**shore** \ˈshȯr\ *n* : land along the edge of a body of water — **shore·less** *adj*

[2]**shore** *vb* **shored; shor·ing** : to give support to : BRACE

[3]**shore** *n* : [1]PROP

shore·bird \-ˌbərd\ *n* : any of a suborder of birds (as the plovers and sandpipers) found mostly along the seashore

shore patrol *n* : a branch of a navy that exercises guard and police functions

shor·ing \ˈshȯr-iŋ\ *n* : a group of things that shore something up

shorn *past part of* SHEAR

[1]**short** \ˈshȯrt\ *adj* **1** : not long or tall **2** : not great in distance **3** : brief in time **4** : not coming up to standard or to an expected amount **5** : CURT, ABRUPT ⟨was ~ with the busybody⟩ **6** : insufficiently supplied ⟨~ of cash⟩ **7** : made with shortening : FLAKY **8** : consisting of or relating to a sale of securities or commodities that the seller does not possess or has not contracted for at the time of the sale ⟨~ sale⟩ — **short·ness** *n*

[2]**short** *adv* **1** : ABRUPTLY, CURTLY **2** : at some point before a goal aimed at

[3]**short** *n* **1** : something shorter than normal or standard **2** *pl* : drawers or pants of less than knee length **3** : SHORT CIRCUIT

[4]**short** *vb* **1** : SHORT-CIRCUIT **2** : SHORTCHANGE, CHEAT **3** : to sell (a security) in expectation of a fall in prices

short·age \ˈshȯr-tij\ *n* : LACK, DEFICIT

short·cake \ˈshȯrt-ˌkāk\ *n* : a dessert consisting of short biscuit spread with sweetened fruit

short·change \-ˈchānj\ *vb* : to cheat esp. by giving less than the correct amount of change

short circuit *n* : a connection made between points in an electric circuit where current is not intended to flow — **short–circuit** *vb*

short·com·ing \ˈshȯrt-ˌkə-miŋ\ *n* : FAULT 1, FLAW

short·cut \-ˌkət\ *n* **1** : a route more direct than that usu. taken **2** : a quicker way of doing something

short·en \ˈshȯr-tᵊn\ *vb* : to make or become short ♦ ***Synonyms*** CURTAIL, ABBREVIATE, ABRIDGE, RETRENCH

short·en·ing \ˈshȯr-tᵊn-iŋ\ *n* : a substance (as lard or butter) that makes pastry tender and flaky

short·hand \ˈshȯrt-ˌhand\ *n* : a method of writing rapidly by using symbols and abbreviations for letters, words, or phrases : STENOGRAPHY

short·hand·ed \ˌshȯrt-ˈhan-dəd\ *adj* : short of the needed number of people

short·horn \ˈshȯrt-ˌhȯrn\ *n, often cap* : any of a breed of red, roan, or white cattle of English origin

short hundredweight *n* — see WEIGHT table

short–lived \ˈshȯrt-ˌlivd, -ˈlīvd\ *adj* : of short life or duration

short·ly \ˈshȯrt-lē\ *adv* **1** : in a few words **2** : in a short time : SOON

short–or·der \ˈshȯrt-ˌȯr-dər\ *adj* : preparing or serving food that can be quickly cooked ⟨a ~ cook⟩

short shrift *n* **1** : a brief respite from death **2** : little consideration

short·sight·ed \'shȯrt-ˌsī-təd\ *adj* **1** : lacking foresight **2** : NEARSIGHTED — **short·sight·ed·ness** *n*

short·stop \-ˌstäp\ *n* : a baseball player defending the area between second and third base

short story *n* : a short work of fiction usu. dealing with a few characters and a single event

short–tem·pered \ˌshȯrt-'tem-pərd\ *adj* : having a quick temper

short–term \'shȯrt-ˌtərm\ *adj* **1** : occurring over or involving a relatively short period of time **2** : of or relating to a financial transaction based on a term usu. of less than a year

short ton *n* — see WEIGHT table

short·wave \'shȯrt-ˌwāv\ *n* : a radio wave with a wavelength between 10 and 100 meters

Sho·sho·ne *or* **Sho·sho·ni** \shə-'shō-nē\ *n, pl* **Shoshones** *or* **Shoshoni** : a member of an Indigenous people orig. ranging through California, Idaho, Nevada, Utah, and Wyoming; *also* : their language

[1]**shot** \'shät\ *n* **1** : an act of shooting **2** : a stroke or throw in some games **3** : something that is shot : MISSILE, PROJECTILE; *esp* : small pellets forming a charge for a shotgun **4** : a metal sphere that is thrown for distance in the shot put **5** : RANGE, REACH **6** : MARKSMAN **7** : a single photographic exposure **8** : a single sequence of a motion picture or a television program made by one camera **9** : an injection (as of medicine) into the body **10** : a small serving of undiluted liquor or other beverage

[2]**shot** *past and past part of* SHOOT

shot·gun \'shät-ˌgən\ *n* : a gun with a smooth bore used to fire shot at short range

shot put *n* : a field event in which a shot is heaved for distance

should \'shu̇d, shəd\ *past of* SHALL — used as an auxiliary to express condition, obligation or propriety, probability, or futurity from a point of view in the past

[1]**shoul·der** \'shōl-dər\ *n* **1** : the part of the body of a person or animal where the arm or foreleg joins the body **2** : either edge of a roadway **3** : a rounded or sloping part (as of a bottle) where the neck joins the body

[2]**shoulder** *vb* **1** : to push or thrust with the shoulder **2** : to bear on the shoulder **3** : to take the responsibility of

shoulder belt *n* : an automobile safety belt worn across the torso and over the shoulder

shoulder blade *n* : a flat triangular bone at the back of each shoulder

shout \'shau̇t\ *vb* : to utter a sudden loud cry — **shout** *n*

shout–out \-ˌau̇t\ *n* : a public expression of greeting, praise, or acknowledgment directed toward a person or group often as part of a performance, broadcast, or recording

shove \'shəv\ *vb* **shoved; shov·ing** : to push along, aside, or away — **shove** *n*

[1]**shov·el** \'shə-vəl\ *n* **1** : a broad long-handled scoop used to lift and throw material **2** : the amount a shovel will hold — **shov·el·ful** \'shə-vəl-ˌfu̇l\ *n*

[2]**shovel** *vb* **-eled** *or* **-elled; -el·ing** *or* **-el·ling** **1** : to take up and throw with a shovel **2** : to dig or clean out with a shovel

[1]**show** \'shō\ *vb* **showed** \'shōd\; **shown** \'shōn\ *or* **showed; show·ing** **1** : to cause or permit to be seen : EXHIBIT ⟨~ anger⟩ **2** : CONFER, BESTOW ⟨~ mercy⟩ **3** : REVEAL, DISCLOSE ⟨~*ed* courage in battle⟩ **4** : INSTRUCT ⟨~ me how⟩ **5** : PROVE ⟨~*s* he was guilty⟩ **6** : APPEAR **7** : to be noticeable **8** : to be third in a horse race

[2]**show** *n* **1** : a demonstrative display **2** : outward appearance ⟨a ~ of courage⟩ **3** : SPECTACLE **4** : a theatrical presentation **5** : a regularly distributed program (as on radio, television, or the Internet) **6** : third place in a horse race

[1]**show·case** \'shō-ˌkās\ *n* : a cabinet for displaying items (as in a store)

[2]**showcase** *vb* **show·cased; show·cas·ing** : EXHIBIT

show·down \'shō-ˌdau̇n\ *n* : a decisive confrontation or contest; *esp* : the showing of poker hands to determine the winner of a pot

[1]**show·er** \'shau̇(-ə)r\ *n* **1** : a brief fall of rain **2** : a party given by friends who bring gifts **3** : a bath in which water is showered on the person; *also* : a facility for such a bath — **show·ery** *adj*

[2]**shower** *vb* **1** : to rain or fall in a shower **2** : to bathe in a shower

show·man \'shō-mən\ *n* : a notably spectacular, dramatic, or effective performer — **show·man·ship** *n*

show–off \'shō-ˌȯf\ *n* : one that seeks attention by conspicuous behavior

show off *vb* **1** : to display proudly **2** : to act as a show-off

show·piece \'shō-ˌpēs\ *n* : an outstanding example used for exhibition

show·place \-ˌplās\ *n* : an estate or building that is a showpiece

show up *vb* : ARRIVE

showy \'shō-ē\ *adj* **show·i·er; -est** : superficially impressive or striking ⟨a ~ orchid⟩ — **show·i·ly** \'shō-ə-lē\ *adv* — **show·i·ness** \-ē-nəs\ *n*

shpt *abbr* shipment

shrap·nel \'shrap-nəl\ *n, pl* **shrapnel** [Henry *Shrapnel* †1842 Eng. artillery officer] : bomb, mine, or shell fragments

[1]**shred** \'shred\ *n* : a narrow strip cut or torn off : a small fragment

[2]**shred** *vb* **shred·ded; shred·ding** : to cut or tear into shreds

shrew \'shrü\ *n* **1** : any of a family of very small mammals with short velvety fur that are related to the moles **2** : a scolding woman

shrewd \ˈshrüd\ *adj* : CLEVER, ASTUTE — **shrewd·ly** *adv* — **shrewd·ness** *n*

shrew·ish \ˈshrü-ish\ *adj* : having an irritable disposition : ILL-TEMPERED — **shrew·ish·ly** *adv* — **shrew·ish·ness** *n*

shriek \ˈshrēk\ *n* : a shrill cry : SCREAM, YELL — **shriek** *vb*

shrift \ˈshrift\ *n, archaic* : the act of shriving : CONFESSION

shrike \ˈshrīk\ *n* : any of numerous usu. largely grayish or brownish birds that often impale their usu. insect prey upon thorns before devouring it

¹shrill \ˈshril\ *vb* : to make a high-pitched piercing sound

²shrill *adj* : high-pitched : PIERCING ⟨~ whistle⟩ — **shril·ly** *adv*

shrimp \ˈshrimp\ *n, pl* **shrimps** *or* **shrimp** **1** : any of various small marine crustaceans related to the lobsters **2** *usu disparaging* : a small or puny person

shrine \ˈshrīn\ *n* [ME, receptacle for the relics of a saint, fr. OE *scrīn*, fr. L *scrinium* case, chest] **1** : the tomb of a saint; *also* : a place where devotion is paid to a saint or deity **2** : a place or object hallowed by its associations

¹shrink \ˈshriŋk\ *vb* **shrank** \ˈshraŋk\ *or* **shrunk** \ˈshrəŋk\; **shrunk** *or* **shrunk·en** \ˈshrəŋ-kən\; **shrink·ing** **1** : to draw back or away **2** : to become smaller or more compact **3** : to lessen in value ♦ ***Synonyms*** CONTRACT, CONSTRICT, COMPRESS, CONDENSE — **shrink·able** *adj*

²shrink *n* : a clinical psychiatrist or psychologist

shrink·age \ˈshriŋ-kij\ *n* **1** : the act of shrinking **2** : the amount lost by shrinkage

shrive \ˈshrīv\ *vb* **shrived** *or* **shrove** \ˈshrōv\; **shriv·en** \ˈshri-vən\ *or* **shrived** [ME, fr. OE *scrīfan* to prescribe, allot, shrive, fr. L *scribere* to write] : to administer the sacrament of reconciliation to

shriv·el \ˈshri-vəl\ *vb* **-eled** *or* **-elled; -el·ing** *or* **-el·ling** : to shrink and draw into wrinkles : DWINDLE

¹shroud \ˈshrau̇d\ *n* **1** : something that covers or screens **2** : a cloth placed over a dead body **3** : any of the ropes leading from the masthead of a ship to the side to support the mast

²shroud *vb* : to veil or screen from view

shrub \ˈshrəb\ *n* : a low usu. several-stemmed woody plant — **shrub·by** *adj*

shrub·bery \ˈshrə-bə-rē\ *n, pl* **-ber·ies** : a planting or growth of shrubs

shrug \ˈshrəg\ *vb* **shrugged; shrug·ging** : to hunch (the shoulders) up to express aloofness, indifference, or uncertainty — **shrug** *n*

shrug off *vb* **1** : to brush aside : MINIMIZE ⟨she *shrugged* off their concerns⟩ **2** : to shake off **3** : to remove (a garment) by wriggling out

shtick *also* **schtick** *or* **shtik** \ˈshtik\ *n* [Yiddish *shtik* pranks, lit., piece] **1** : a usu. comic or repetitive performance or routine **2** : one's special trait, interest, or activity

¹shuck \ˈshək\ *n* : SHELL, HUSK

²shuck *vb* : to strip of shucks

shud·der \ˈshə-dər\ *vb* : TREMBLE, QUAKE — **shudder** *n*

shuf·fle \ˈshə-fəl\ *vb* **shuf·fled; shuf·fling** **1** : to mix in a disorderly mass **2** : to rearrange the order of (cards in a pack) by mixing two parts of the pack together **3** : to shift from place to place **4** : to move with a sliding or dragging gait **5** : to dance in a slow lagging manner — **shuffle** *n*

shuf·fle·board \ˈshə-fəl-ˌbȯrd\ *n* : a game in which players use long-handled cues to shove disks into scoring areas marked on a smooth surface

shun \ˈshən\ *vb* **shunned; shun·ning** : to avoid deliberately or habitually ♦ ***Synonyms*** EVADE, ELUDE, ESCAPE, DUCK

¹shunt \ˈshənt\ *vb* [ME, to turn away] **1 a** : to turn off to one side **b** : to switch (a train) from one track to another **2** : to provide with or divert by means of an electrical shunt **3** : to divert (blood or other bodily fluid) from one part of the body to another by surgical shunt **4** : SHUTTLE

²shunt *n* **1** : a method or device for turning or thrusting aside **2** : a conductor joining two points in an electrical circuit forming an alternate path through which a portion of the current may pass

shut \ˈshət\ *vb* **shut; shut·ting** **1** : CLOSE **2** : to forbid entrance into **3** : to lock up **4** : to fold together ⟨~ a penknife⟩ **5** : to cease or suspend activity ⟨~ down an assembly line⟩

shut·down \-ˌdau̇n\ *n* : a temporary cessation of activity (as in a factory)

shut–in \ˈshət-ˌin\ *n* : a person confined to home, a room, or bed because of illness or incapacity

shut·out \ˈshət-ˌau̇t\ *n* : a game or contest in which one side fails to score

shut out *vb* **1** : EXCLUDE **2** : to prevent (an opponent) from scoring in a game or contest

shut·ter \ˈshə-tər\ *n* **1** : a movable cover for a door or window : BLIND **2** : the part of a camera that opens and closes to allow light to enter

shut·ter·bug \ˈshə-tər-ˌbəg\ *n* : a photography enthusiast

¹shut·tle \ˈshə-tᵊl\ *n* **1** : an instrument used in weaving for passing the horizontal threads between the vertical threads **2** : a vehicle traveling back and forth over a short route ⟨a ~ bus⟩ **3** : SPACE SHUTTLE

²shuttle *vb* **shut·tled; shut·tling** : to move back and forth frequently

shut·tle·cock \ˈshə-tᵊl-ˌkäk\ *n* : a light conical object (as of cork or plastic) used in badminton

shut up *vb* : to cease or cause to cease talking

¹shy \ˈshī\ *adj* **shi·er** *or* **shy·er** \ˈshī-ər\; **shi·est** *or* **shy·est** \ˈshī-əst\ **1** : easily frightened : TIMID **2** : WARY **3** : BASHFUL **4** : DEFICIENT, LACKING ⟨a nickel

∼ of a quarter⟩ — **shy·ly** *adv* — **shy·ness** *n*

[2]**shy** *vb* **shied; shy·ing** **1** : to show a dislike : RECOIL **2** : to start suddenly aside through fright ⟨the horse *shied*⟩

shy·ster \ˈshīs-tər\ *n* : an unscrupulous lawyer or politician

Si *symbol* silicon

SI *abbr* [F *Système International d'Unités*] International System of Units

Si·a·mese \ˌsī-ə-ˈmēz, -ˈmēs\ *n, pl* **Siamese** : THAI — **Siamese** *adj*

Siamese cat *n* : any of a breed of slender blue-eyed short-haired domestic cats of Asian origin

Siamese twin *n* [fr. Chang †1874 and Eng †1874 twins born in Siam with bodies united] : one of a pair of twins with bodies joined together at birth

Siberian husky *n* : any of a breed of thick-coated compact dogs orig. developed in Siberia to pull sleds

[1]**sib·i·lant** \ˈsi-bə-lənt\ *adj* : having, containing, or producing the sound of or a sound resembling that of the *s* or the *sh* in *sash* — **sib·i·lant·ly** *adv*

[2]**sibilant** *n* : a sibilant speech sound (as English \s\, \z\, \sh\, \zh\, \ch (=tsh)\, or \j (=dzh)\)

sib·ling \ˈsi-bliŋ\ *n* : a brother or sister considered irrespective of sex; *also* : one of two or more offspring having one common parent

sib·yl \ˈsi-bəl\ *n, often cap* : PROPHETESS — **sib·yl·line** \-bə-ˌlīn, -ˌlēn\ *adj*

sic \ˈsik, ˈsēk\ *adv* : intentionally so written — used after a printed word or passage to indicate that it exactly reproduces an original ⟨said he seed [∼] it all⟩

sick \ˈsik\ *adj* **1** : not in good health : ILL; *also* : of, relating to, or intended for use in sickness ⟨∼ pay⟩ **2** : NAUSEATED **3** : DISGUSTED **4** : PINING **5** : mentally or emotionally unsound **6** : MACABRE, SADISTIC ⟨∼ jokes⟩ — **sick·ly** *adj*

sick·bed \ˈsik-ˌbed\ *n* : a bed on which one lies sick

sick·en \ˈsi-kən\ *vb* : to make or become sick — **sick·en·ing·ly** *adv*

sick·le \ˈsi-kəl\ *n* : a cutting tool consisting of a curved metal blade with a short handle

sickle–cell anemia *n* : an inherited anemia in which red blood cells tend to become crescent-shaped and clog small blood vessels and which occurs esp. in individuals of African, Mediterranean, or southwest Asian ancestry

sick·ness \ˈsik-nəs\ *n* **1** : ill health; *also* : a specific disease **2** : NAUSEA

side \ˈsīd\ *n* **1** : the right or left part of the trunk of a body **2** : a place away from a central point or line **3** : a border of an object; *esp* : one of the longer borders as contrasted with an end **4** : an outer surface of an object **5** : a position regarded as opposite to another **6** : a body of contestants — **side** *adj* — **on the side** : in addition to the main portion

side·arm \-ˌärm\ *adj* : made with a sideways sweep of the arm ⟨a ∼ pitch⟩ — **sidearm** *adv*

side arm *n* : a weapon worn at the side or in the belt

side·bar \ˈsīd-ˌbär\ *n* : a short news story accompanying a major story and presenting related information

side·board \-ˌbȯrd\ *n* : a piece of dining-room furniture for holding articles of table service

side·burns \-ˌbərnz\ *n pl* : whiskers on the side of the face in front of the ears

side by side *adv* **1** : beside one another **2** : in the same place, time, or circumstance — **side–by–side** *adj*

side·car \-ˌkär\ *n* : a one-wheeled passenger car attached to the side of a motorcycle

side effect *n* : a secondary and usu. adverse effect (as of a drug)

side·kick \ˈsīd-ˌkik\ *n* : PAL, PARTNER

side·line \ˈsīd-ˌlīn\ *n* **1** : an activity pursued in addition to one's regular occupation **2** : the space immediately outside the lines of an athletic field or court **3** : a sphere of little or no participation — usu. used in pl.

[1]**side·long** \ˈsīd-ˌlȯŋ\ *adv* : in the direction of or along the side : OBLIQUELY

[2]**sidelong** *adj* : directed to one side ⟨a ∼ look⟩

side·man \ˈsīd-ˌman\ *n* : a member of a jazz or swing orchestra

side·piece \-ˌpēs\ *n* : a piece forming or contained in the side of something

si·de·re·al \sī-ˈdir-ē-əl, sə-\ *adj* [L *sidereus*, fr. *sider-, sidus* star, constellation] **1** : of or relating to the stars **2** : measured by the apparent motion of the stars

side·sad·dle \ˈsīd-ˌsa-dᵊl\ *n* : a saddle for women in which the rider sits with both legs on the same side of the horse — **sidesaddle** *adv*

side·show \ˈsīd-ˌshō\ *n* **1** : a minor show offered in addition to a main exhibition (as of a circus) **2** : an incidental diversion

side·step \-ˌstep\ *vb* **1** : to step aside **2** : AVOID, EVADE ⟨*sidestepped* the question⟩

side·stroke \-ˌstrōk\ *n* : a swimming stroke which is executed on the side and in which the arms are swept backward and downward and the legs do a scissors kick

side·swipe \-ˌswīp\ *vb* : to strike with a glancing blow along the side — **sideswipe** *n*

[1]**side·track** \-ˌtrak\ *n* : SIDING 1

[2]**sidetrack** *vb* **1** : to switch from a main railroad line to a siding **2** : to turn aside from a purpose

side·walk \ˈsīd-ˌwȯk\ *n* : a paved walk at the side of a road or street

side·wall \-ˌwȯl\ *n* **1** : a wall forming the side of something **2** : the side of an automobile tire

side·ways \-ˌwāz\ *adv or adj* **1** : from the side **2** : with one side to the front **3** : to, toward, or at one side

side·wind·er \-ˌwīn-dər\ *n* : a small pale-colored desert rattlesnake of the southwestern U.S.

sid·ing \'sī-diŋ\ *n* **1** : a short railroad track connected with the main track **2** : material (as boards) covering the outside of frame buildings

si·dle \'sī-dᵊl\ *vb* **si·dled; si·dling** : to move sideways or with one side foremost

SIDS *abbr* sudden infant death syndrome

siege \'sēj\ *n* **1** : the placing of an army around or before a fortified place to force its surrender **2** : a persistent attack (as of illness)

sie·mens \'sē-mənz, 'zē-\ *n* : a unit of conductance equivalent to one ampere per volt

si·er·ra \sē-'er-ə\ *n* [Sp, lit., saw, fr. L *serra*] : a range of mountains esp. with jagged peaks

si·es·ta \sē-'es-tə\ *n* [Sp, fr. L *sexta (hora)* noon, lit., sixth hour] : a midday rest or nap

sieve \'siv\ *n* : a utensil with meshes or holes to separate finer particles from coarser or solids from liquids

sift \'sift\ *vb* **1** : to pass through a sieve **2** : to separate with or as if with a sieve **3** : to examine carefully **4** : to scatter by or as if by passing through a sieve — **sift·er** *n*

sig *abbr* signature

SIG *abbr* special interest group

sigh \'sī\ *vb* **1** : to let out a deep audible breath (as in weariness or sorrow) **2** : GRIEVE, YEARN — **sigh** *n*

¹sight \'sīt\ *n* **1** : something seen or worth seeing **2** : the process or power of seeing; *esp* : the sense of which the eye is the receptor and by which qualities of appearance (as position, shape, and color) are perceived **3** : INSPECTION **4** : a device (as a small bead on a gun barrel) that aids the eye in aiming **5** : VIEW, GLIMPSE **6** : the range of vision — **sight·less** *adj*

²sight *vb* **1** : to get sight of **2** : to aim by means of a sight

sight·ed \'sī-təd\ *adj* : having sight

sight·ly \-lē\ *adj* : pleasing to the sight

sight·see·ing \'sīt-ˌsē-iŋ\ *adj* : engaged in or used for seeing sights of interest — **sight·seer** \-ˌsē-ər\ *n*

sig·ma \'sig-mə\ *n* : the 18th letter of the Greek alphabet — Σ or σ or ς

¹sign \'sīn\ *n* **1** : a gesture expressing a command, wish, or thought **2** : SYMBOL **3** : a notice publicly displayed for advertising purposes or for giving direction or warning **4** : OMEN, PORTENT **5** : TRACE, VESTIGE ⟨left without a ~⟩

²sign *vb* **1** : to mark with a sign **2** : to represent by a sign **3** : to make a sign or signal **4** : to write one's name on in token of assent or obligation **5** : to assign legally **6** : to use sign language — **sign·er** *n*

¹sig·nal \'sig-nəl\ *n* **1** : a sign agreed on as the start of some joint action **2** : a sign giving warning or notice of something **3** : the message, sound, or image transmitted in electronic communication (as radio)

²signal *vb* **-naled** *or* **-nalled; -nal·ing** *or* **-nal·ling** **1** : to notify by a signal **2** : to communicate by signals

³signal *adj* : DISTINGUISHED ⟨a ~ honor⟩ — **sig·nal·ly** *adv*

sig·nal·ize \'sig-nə-ˌlīz\ *vb* **-ized; -iz·ing** : to point out or make conspicuous — **sig·nal·i·za·tion** \ˌsig-nə-lə-'zā-shən\ *n*

sig·nal·man \'sig-nəl-mən, -ˌman\ *n* : a person who signals or works with signals

sig·na·to·ry \'sig-nə-ˌtȯr-ē\ *n, pl* **-ries** : a person or government that signs jointly with others — **signatory** *adj*

sig·na·ture \'sig-nə-ˌchu̇r\ *n* **1** : the name of a person written by himself or herself **2** : the sign placed after the clef to indicate the key or the meter of a piece of music

sign·board \'sīn-ˌbȯrd\ *n* : a board bearing a sign or notice

sig·net \'sig-nət\ *n* : a small intaglio seal (as in a ring)

sig·nif·i·cance \sig-'ni-fi-kəns\ *n* **1** : something signified : MEANING **2** : SUGGESTIVENESS **3** : CONSEQUENCE, IMPORTANCE ⟨the ~ of the treaty⟩

sig·nif·i·cant \-kənt\ *adj* **1** : having meaning; *esp* : having a hidden or special meaning **2** : having or likely to have considerable influence or effect : IMPORTANT — **sig·nif·i·cant·ly** *adv*

sig·ni·fy \'sig-nə-ˌfī\ *vb* **-fied; -fy·ing** **1** : to show by a sign **2** : MEAN, IMPORT **3** : to have significance — **sig·ni·fi·ca·tion** \ˌsig-nə-fə-'kā-shən\ *n*

sign in *vb* : to make a record of arrival (as by signing a register)

sign language *n* : a formal system of hand gestures used for communication esp. by deaf people

sign off *vb* : to announce the end (as of a program or broadcast)

sign of the cross : a gesture of the hand forming a cross (as to invoke divine blessing)

sign on *vb* **1** : ENLIST **2** : to announce the start of broadcasting for the day

sign out *vb* : to make a record of departure (as by signing a register)

sign·post \'sīn-ˌpōst\ *n* **1** : a post bearing a sign **2** : GUIDE, BEACON **3** : SIGN, INDICATION

sign up *vb* : to sign one's name in order to obtain, do, or join something

Sikh \'sēk\ *n* : an adherent of a religion of India marked by rejection of caste — **Sikh·ism** *n*

si·lage \'sī-lij\ *n* : fodder fermented (as in a silo) to produce a rich moist animal feed

¹si·lence \'sī-ləns\ *n* **1** : the state of being silent **2** : STILLNESS **3** : SECRECY

²silence *vb* **si·lenced; si·lenc·ing** **1** : to reduce to silence : STILL **2** : to cause to cease hostile firing or criticism

si·lenc·er \'sī-lən-sər\ *n* : a device for muffling the noise of a gunshot

si·lent \'sī-lənt\ *adj* **1** : not speaking : MUTE; *also* : TACITURN **2** : STILL, QUIET **3** : performed or borne without utterance ⟨a ~ prayer⟩ ♦ ***Synonyms*** RETI-

CENT, RESERVED, CLOSEMOUTHED, CLOSE — **si·lent·ly** *adv*

[1]**sil·hou·ette** \ˌsi-lə-ˈwet\ *n* [F] **1 :** a representation of the outlines of an object filled in with black or some other uniform color **2 :** OUTLINE ⟨~ of a ship⟩

[2]**silhouette** *vb* **-ett·ed; -ett·ing :** to represent by a silhouette; *also* **:** to show against a light background

sil·i·ca \ˈsi-li-kə\ *n* **:** a mineral that consists of silicon and oxygen

sil·i·cate \ˈsi-lə-ˌkāt, ˈsi-li-kət\ *n* **:** a chemical salt that consists of a metal combined with silicon and oxygen

si·li·ceous *also* **si·li·cious** \sə-ˈli-shəs\ *adj* **:** of, relating to, or containing silica or a silicate

sil·i·con \ˈsi-li-kən, ˈsi-lə-ˌkän\ *n* **:** a nonmetallic chemical element that occurs in combination as the most abundant element next to oxygen in the earth's crust and is used esp. in alloys and semiconductors

sil·i·cone \ˈsi-lə-ˌkōn\ *n* **:** an organic silicon compound used esp. for lubricants and varnishes

sil·i·co·sis \ˌsi-lə-ˈkō-səs\ *n* **:** a lung disease caused by prolonged inhaling of silica dusts

silk \ˈsilk\ *n* **1 :** a fine strong lustrous protein fiber produced by insect larvae usu. for their cocoons; *esp* **:** one from moth larvae (**silk·worms** \-ˌwərmz\) used for cloth **2 :** thread or cloth made from silk — **silk·en** \ˈsil-kən\ *adj* — **silky** *adj*

silk screen *n* **:** a stencil process in which coloring matter is forced through the meshes of a prepared silk or organdy screen; *also* **:** a print made by this process — **silk–screen** *vb*

sill \ˈsil\ *n* **:** a heavy crosspiece (as of wood or stone) that forms the bottom member of a window frame or a doorway; *also* **:** a horizontal supporting piece at the base of a structure

sil·ly \ˈsi-lē\ *adj* **sil·li·er; -est** [ME *sely, silly* happy, innocent, pitiable, feeble, fr. OE *sǣlig,* fr. *sǣl* happiness] **:** FOOLISH, ABSURD, STUPID — **sil·li·ness** *n*

si·lo \ˈsī-lō\ *n, pl* **silos** [Sp] **1 :** a trench, pit, or esp. a tall cylinder for making and storing silage **2 :** an underground structure for housing a guided missile

[1]**silt** \ˈsilt\ *n* **1 :** fine earth; *esp* **:** particles of such soil floating in rivers, ponds, or lakes **2 :** a deposit (as by a river) of silt — **silty** *adj*

[2]**silt** *vb* **:** to obstruct or cover with silt — **silt·ation** \sil-ˈtā-shən\ *n*

Si·lu·ri·an \sī-ˈlu̇r-ē-ən\ *adj* **:** of, relating to, or being the period of the Paleozoic era between the Ordovician and the Devonian marked by the appearance of the first land plants — **Silurian** *n*

[1]**sil·ver** \ˈsil-vər\ *n* **1 :** a white ductile metallic chemical element that takes a high polish and is a better conductor of heat and electricity than any other substance **2 :** coin made of silver **3 :** FLATWARE **4 :** a grayish white color — **sil·very** *adj*

[2]**silver** *adj* **1 :** relating to, made of, or coated with silver **2 :** SILVERY

[3]**silver** *vb* **sil·vered; sil·ver·ing :** to coat with or as if with silver — **sil·ver·er** *n*

silver bromide *n* **:** a light-sensitive compound used esp. in photography

sil·ver·fish \ˈsil-vər-ˌfish\ *n* **:** any of various small wingless insects found in houses and sometimes injurious esp. to sized paper and starched clothes

silver iodide *n* **:** a light-sensitive compound used in photography, rainmaking, and medicine

silver maple *n* **:** a No. American maple with deeply cut leaves that are green above and silvery white below

silver nitrate *n* **:** a soluble compound used in photography and as an antiseptic

sil·ver·ware \ˈsil-vər-ˌwer\ *n* **:** FLATWARE

sim *abbr* simulation; simulator

sim·i·an \ˈsi-mē-ən\ *n* **:** MONKEY, APE — **simian** *adj*

simian immunodeficiency virus *n* **:** SIV

sim·i·lar \ˈsi-mə-lər\ *adj* **:** marked by correspondence or resemblance ♦ ***Synonyms*** ALIKE, AKIN, COMPARABLE, PARALLEL — **sim·i·lar·i·ty** \ˌsi-mə-ˈler-ə-tē\ *n* — **sim·i·lar·ly** *adv*

sim·i·le \ˈsi-mə-(ˌ)lē\ *n* [ME, fr. L, likeness, comparison, fr. neut. of *similis* like, similar] **:** a figure of speech in which two dissimilar things are compared by the use of *like* or *as* (as in "cheeks like roses")

si·mil·i·tude \sə-ˈmi-lə-ˌtüd, -ˌtyüd\ *n* **:** LIKENESS, RESEMBLANCE

sim·mer \ˈsi-mər\ *vb* **sim·mered; sim·mer·ing 1 :** to stew at or just below the boiling point **2 :** to be on the point of bursting out with violence or emotional disturbance — **simmer** *n*

simmer down *vb* **:** to become calm or peaceful

si·mo·nize \ˈsī-mə-ˌnīz\ *vb* **-nized; -niz·ing :** to polish with or as if with wax

si·mo·ny \ˈsī-mə-nē, ˈsi-\ *n* [ME *symonie,* fr. AF *simonie,* fr. LL *simonia,* fr. *Simon* Magus sorcerer of Samaria in Acts 8:9–24] **:** the buying or selling of a church office

sim·pa·ti·co \sim-ˈpä-ti-ˌkō, -ˈpa-\ *adj* **:** CONGENIAL, LIKABLE

sim·per \ˈsim-pər\ *vb* **:** to smile in a silly manner — **simper** *n*

sim·ple \ˈsim-pəl\ *adj* **sim·pler** \-pə-lər\; **sim·plest** \-pə-ləst\ [ME, fr. AF, plain, uncomplicated, artless, fr. L *simplus, simplex,* lit., single; L *simplus* fr. *sim-* one + *-plus* multiplied by; L *simplex* fr. *sim-* + *-plex* -fold] **1 :** free from dishonesty or vanity **:** INNOCENT **2 :** free from ostentation **3 :** of humble origin or modest position **4 :** STUPID **5 :** not complex **:** PLAIN ⟨a ~ melody⟩ ⟨~ directions⟩ **6 :** lacking education, experience, or intelligence **7 :** developing from a single ovary ⟨a ~ fruit⟩ ♦ ***Synonyms*** EASY, FACILE, LIGHT, EFFORTLESS — **sim·ple·ness** *n* — **sim·ply** *adv*

simple interest *n* **:** interest paid or computed on the original principal only of a loan or on the amount of an account

sim·ple·ton \ˈsim-pəl-tən\ *n* **:** FOOL

sim·plic·i·ty \sim-ˈpli-sə-tē\ *n, pl* **-ties 1**

: lack of complication : CLEARNESS ⟨the ~ of his reasoning⟩ **2** : CANDOR, ARTLESSNESS **3** : plainness in manners or way of life **4** : SILLINESS, FOLLY

sim·pli·fy \ˈsim-plə-ˌfī\ *vb* **-fied; -fy·ing** : to make less complex — **sim·pli·fi·ca·tion** \ˌsim-plə-fə-ˈkā-shən\ *n*

sim·plis·tic \sim-ˈplis-tik\ *adj* : excessively simple : tending to overlook complexities ⟨a ~ solution⟩

sim·u·late \ˈsim-yə-ˌlāt\ *vb* **-lat·ed; -lat·ing** : to give or create the effect or appearance of : IMITATE; *also* : to make a simulation of — **sim·u·la·tor** \ˈsim-yə-ˌlā-tər\ *n*

sim·u·la·tion \ˌsim-yə-ˈlā-shən\ *n* **1** : the act or process of simulating **2** : an object that is not genuine **3** : the imitation by one system or process of the way in which another system or process works

si·mul·ta·ne·ous \ˌsī-məl-ˈtā-nē-əs, ˌsi-\ *adj* : occurring or operating at the same time — **si·mul·ta·ne·ous·ly** *adv* — **si·mul·ta·ne·ous·ness** *n*

¹sin \ˈsin\ *n* **1** : an offense esp. against God **2** : FAULT **3** : a weakened state of human nature in which the self is estranged from God — **sin·less** *adj*

²sin *vb* **sinned; sin·ning** : to commit a sin — **sin·ner** *n*

³sin *abbr* sine

¹since \ˈsins\ *adv* **1** : from a past time until now **2** : backward in time : AGO **3** : after a time in the past

²since *conj* **1** : from the time when **2** : seeing that : BECAUSE

³since *prep* **1** : in the period after ⟨changes made ~ the war⟩ **2** : continuously from ⟨has been here ~ 1980⟩

sin·cere \sin-ˈsir\ *adj* **sin·cer·er; sin·cer·est** **1** : free from hypocrisy : HONEST **2** : GENUINE, REAL — **sin·cere·ly** *adv* — **sin·cer·i·ty** \-ˈser-ə-tē\ *n*

sine \ˈsīn\ *n* [ML *sinus,* fr. L, curve] : the trigonometric function that is the ratio between the side opposite an acute angle in a right triangle and the hypotenuse

si·ne·cure \ˈsī-ni-ˌkyu̇r, ˈsi-\ *n* : a paying job that requires little or no work

si·ne die \ˌsī-ni-ˈdī-ˌē, ˌsi-nā-ˈdē-ˌā\ *adv* [L, without day] : INDEFINITELY ⟨the meeting adjourned *sine die*⟩

si·ne qua non \ˌsi-ni-ˌkwä-ˈnän, -ˈnōn\ *n, pl* **sine qua nons** *also* **sine qui·bus non** \-ˌkwi-(ˌ)bu̇s-\ [LL, without which not] : something indispensable or essential

sin·ew \ˈsin-yü\ *n* **1** : TENDON **2** : physical strength — **sin·ewy** *adj*

sin·ful \ˈsin-fəl\ *adj* : marked by or full of sin : WICKED — **sin·ful·ly** *adv* — **sin·ful·ness** *n*

¹sing \ˈsiŋ\ *vb* **sang** \ˈsaŋ\ *or* **sung** \ˈsəŋ\; **sung; sing·ing** **1** : to produce musical tones with the voice; *also* : to utter with musical tones **2** : to make a prolonged shrill sound ⟨locusts ~*ing*⟩ **3** : to produce harmonious sustained sounds ⟨birds ~*ing*⟩ **4** : CHANT, INTONE **5** : to write poetry; *also* : to celebrate in song or verse **6** : to give information or evidence — **sing·er** *n*

²sing *abbr* singular

singe \ˈsinj\ *vb* **singed; singe·ing** : to scorch lightly the outside of; *esp* : to remove the hair or down from usu. by passing over a flame

¹sin·gle \ˈsiŋ-gəl\ *adj* **1** : UNMARRIED **2** : being alone : being the only one **3** : having only one feature or part **4** : made for one person ♦ ***Synonyms*** SOLE, UNIQUE, LONE, SOLITARY, SEPARATE, PARTICULAR — **sin·gle·ness** *n* — **sin·gly** *adv*

²single *n* **1** : a separate person or thing; *also* : an unmarried person **2** : a hit in baseball that enables the batter to reach first base **3** *pl* : a tennis match with one player on each side

³single *vb* **sin·gled; sin·gling** **1** : to select (one) from a group **2** : to hit a single

single bond *n* : a chemical bond in which one pair of electrons is shared by two atoms in a molecule

single–lens reflex *n* : a camera having a single lens that forms an image which is reflected to the viewfinder or recorded on film

sin·gle–mind·ed \ˌsiŋ-gəl-ˈmīn-dəd\ *adj* : having one driving purpose or resolve ⟨~ determination⟩ — **sin·gle–mind·ed·ly** *adv* — **sin·gle–mind·ed·ness** *n*

sing·song \ˈsiŋ-ˌsȯŋ\ *n* **1** : verse with marked and regular rhythm and rhyme **2** : a voice delivery marked by monotonous rhythm — **sing·songy** \-ˌsȯŋ-ē\ *adj*

sin·gu·lar \ˈsiŋ-gyə-lər\ *adj* **1** : of, relating to, or constituting a word form denoting one person, thing, or instance **2** : OUTSTANDING, EXCEPTIONAL **3** : of unusual quality **4** : ODD, PECULIAR — **singular** *n* — **sin·gu·lar·i·ty** \ˌsiŋ-gyə-ˈler-ə-tē\ *n* — **sin·gu·lar·ly** *adv*

sin·is·ter \ˈsi-nəs-tər\ *adj* [ME *sinistre,* fr. AF *senestre* on the left, fr. L *sinister* on the left side, inauspicious] **1** : singularly evil or productive of evil **2** : accompanied by or leading to disaster ♦ ***Synonyms*** BALEFUL, MALIGN, MALEFIC, MALEFICENT — **sin·is·ter·ly** *adv*

¹sink \ˈsiŋk\ *vb* **sank** \ˈsaŋk\ *or* **sunk** \ˈsəŋk\; **sunk; sink·ing** **1** : SUBMERGE **2** : to descend lower and lower **3** : to grow less in volume or height **4** : to slope downward **5** : to penetrate downward **6** : to fail in health or strength **7** : LAPSE, DEGENERATE **8** : to cause (a ship) to descend to the bottom **9** : to make (a hole or shaft) by digging, boring, or cutting **10** : INVEST — **sink·able** *adj*

²sink *n* **1** : DRAIN, SEWER **2** : a basin connected with a drain **3** : an extensive depression in the land surface

sink·er \ˈsiŋ-kər\ *n* : a weight for sinking a fishing line or net

sink·hole \ˈsiŋk-ˌhōl\ *n* : a hollow place in which drainage collects

si·nol·o·gy \sī-ˈnä-lə-jē\ *n, often cap* : the study of the Chinese and esp. their language, history, and culture — **si·no·log·i·cal** \ˌsī-nə-ˈlä-ji-kəl\ *adj, often cap* — **si·nol·o·gist** \sī-ˈnä-lə-jist\ *n, often cap*

sin tax *n* : a tax on substances or activities considered sinful or harmful

sin·u·ous \'sin-yə-wəs\ *adj* : bending in and out : WINDING — **sin·u·os·i·ty** \ˌsin-yə-'wä-sə-tē\ *n* — **sin·u·ous·ly** *adv*

si·nus \'sī-nəs\ *n* [ME, fr. ML, fr. L, curve, hollow] **1** : any of several cavities of the skull usu. connecting with the nostrils **2** : a space forming a channel (as for the passage of blood)

si·nus·itis \ˌsī-nə-'sī-təs\ *n* : inflammation of a sinus of the skull

Sioux \'sü\ *n, pl* **Sioux** *same or* 'süz\ [AmerF, short for *Nadouessioux,* fr. Ojibwa *na·towe·ssiw-,* prob. fr. Algonquian **a·towe·-* speak another language] : DAKOTA

sip \'sip\ *vb* **sipped; sip·ping** : to drink in small quantities — **sip** *n*

¹**si·phon** *also* **sy·phon** \'sī-fən\ *n* **1** : a bent tube through which a liquid can be transferred by means of air pressure up and over the edge of one container and into another container placed at a lower level **2** *usu* **sy·phon** : a bottle that ejects soda water through a tube when a valve is opened

²**siphon** *also* **syphon** *vb* **si·phoned** *also* **sy·phoned; si·phon·ing** *also* **sy·phon·ing** : to draw off by means of a siphon

sip·py cup \'si-pē-\ *n* : a cup having a lid with a perforated spout for a young child

sir \'sər\ *n* [ME *sir, sire,* fr. AF, lord, feudal superior, fr. VL **seior,* alter. of L *senior,* compar. of *senex* old, old man] **1** : a man of rank or position — used as a title before the given name of a knight or baronet **2** — used as a usu. respectful form of address

Si·rach \'sī-rak, sə-'räk\ *n* — see BIBLE table

¹**sire** \'sī(-ə)r\ *n* **1** : FATHER; *also, archaic* : FOREFATHER **2** *archaic* : LORD — used as a form of address and a title **3** : the male parent of an animal (as a horse or dog)

²**sire** *vb* **sired; sir·ing** : BEGET

si·ren \'sī-rən\ *n* **1** : a seductive or alluring woman **2** : an electrically operated device for producing a loud shrill warning signal — **siren** *adj*

sir·loin \'sər-ˌlȯin\ *n* [alter. of earlier *surloin,* modif. of MF *surlonge,* fr. *sur* over (fr. L *super*) + *longe* loin] : a cut of beef taken from the part in front of the round

sirup *var of* SYRUP

si·sal \'sī-səl, -zəl\ *n* : a strong cordage fiber from an agave; *also* : this agave

sis·sy \'si-sē\ *n, pl* **sissies** *disparaging* : an effeminate boy or man; *also* : a timid or cowardly person

sis·ter \'sis-tər\ *n* **1** : a female having one or both parents in common with another individual **2** : a member of a religious order of women : NUN **3** *chiefly Brit* : NURSE **4 a** : a girl or woman regarded as a comrade **b** : a girl or woman who shares with another a common national or racial origin — **sis·ter·ly** *adj*

sis·ter·hood \-ˌhu̇d\ *n* **1** : the state of being a sister **2** : a community or society of sisters **3** : the solidarity of women based on shared conditions

sis·ter–in–law \'sis-tə-rən-ˌlȯ\ *n, pl* **sisters–in–law** : the sister of one's spouse; *also* : the wife of one's sibling or of one's spouse's sibling

sit \'sit\ *vb* **sat** \'sat\; **sit·ting** **1** : to rest upon the buttocks or haunches **2** : ROOST, PERCH **3** : to occupy a seat **4** : to hold a session **5** : to cover eggs for hatching : BROOD **6** : to pose for a portrait **7** : to remain quiet or inactive **8** : FIT **9** : to cause (oneself) to be seated **10** : to place in position **11** : to keep one's seat on ⟨~ a horse⟩ **12** : BABYSIT — **sit·ter** *n*

si·tar \si-'tär\ *n* [Hindi & Urdu *sitār*] : an Indian lute with a long neck and a varying number of strings

sit·com \'sit-ˌkäm\ *n* : SITUATION COMEDY

site \'sīt\ *n* **1** : LOCATION **2** : WEBSITE

sit–in \'sit-ˌin\ *n* : an act of sitting in the seats or on the floor of an establishment as a means of organized protest

sit·u·at·ed \'si-chə-ˌwā-təd\ *adj* : LOCATED, PLACED

sit·u·a·tion \ˌsi-chə-'wā-shən\ *n* **1** : LOCATION, SITE **2** : JOB **3** : CONDITION, CIRCUMSTANCES — **sit·u·a·tion·al** \-shə-nəl\ *adj*

situation comedy *n* : a radio or television comedy series that involves a continuing cast of characters in a succession of episodes

sit–up \'sit-ˌəp\ *n* : an exercise performed from a supine position by raising the torso to a sitting position and returning to the original position without lifting the feet

SIV \ˌes-ˌī-'vē\ *n* [*s*imian *i*mmunodeficiency *v*irus] : a retrovirus related to HIV that causes a disease in monkeys similar to AIDS

six \'siks\ *n* **1** : one more than five **2** : the 6th in a set or series **3** : something having six units — **six** *adj or pron* — **sixth** \'siksth\ *adj or adv or n*

six–gun \'siks-ˌgən\ *n* : a 6-chambered revolver

six–pack \-ˌpak\ *n* : six bottles or cans (as of beer) packaged and purchased together; *also* : the contents of a six-pack

six·pence \-pəns, *US also* -ˌpens\ *n* : the sum of six pence; *also* : an English silver coin of this value

six–shoot·er \'siks-ˌshü-tər\ *n* : SIX-GUN

six·teen \ˌsiks-'tēn\ *n* : one more than 15 — **sixteen** *adj or pron* — **six·teenth** \-'tēnth\ *adj or n*

six·ty \'siks-tē\ *n, pl* **sixties** : six times 10 — **six·ti·eth** \'siks-tē-əth\ *adj or n* — **sixty** *adj or pron*

siz·able *or* **size·able** \'sī-zə-bəl\ *adj* : quite large — **siz·ably** \-blē\ *adv*

¹**size** \'sīz\ *n* [ME *sise* assize, judgment, quantity, fr. AF, short for *assise* assize] : physical extent or bulk : DIMENSIONS; *also* : considerable proportions — **sized** \'sīzd\ *adj*

²**size** *vb* **sized; siz·ing** **1** : to grade or

classify according to size **2 :** to form a judgment of ⟨~ up the situation⟩
[3]size *n* **:** a gluey material used for filling the pores in paper, plaster, or textiles — **siz·ing** *n*
[4]size *vb* **sized; siz·ing :** to cover, stiffen, or glaze with size
siz·zle \ˈsi-zəl\ *vb* **siz·zled; siz·zling :** to fry or shrivel up with a hissing sound — **sizzle** *n*
SJ *abbr* Society of Jesus
SK *abbr* Saskatchewan
ska \ˈskä\ *n* **:** popular music of Jamaican origin combining traditional Caribbean rhythms and jazz
[1]skate \ˈskāt\ *n, pl* **skates** *also* **skate :** any of a family of rays with thick broad winglike fins
[2]skate *n* **1 :** a metal frame and runner attached to a shoe and used for gliding over ice **2 :** ROLLER SKATE; *esp* **:** IN-LINE SKATE — **skate** *vb* — **skat·er** *n*
skate·board \ˈskāt-ˌbȯrd\ *n* **:** a short board mounted on small wheels — **skateboard** *vb* — **skate·board·er** *n*
skeet \ˈskēt\ *n* **:** trapshooting in which clay targets are thrown in such a way that their angle of flight simulates that of a flushed game bird
skein \ˈskān\ *n* **:** a loosely twisted quantity of yarn or thread wound on a reel
skel·e·ton \ˈske-lə-t[ə]n\ *n* **1 :** a usu. bony supporting framework of an animal body **2 :** a bare minimum **3 :** FRAMEWORK — **skel·e·tal** \-lə-t[ə]l\ *adj*
skep·tic \ˈskep-tik\ *n* **1 :** one who believes in skepticism **2 :** a person disposed to skepticism esp. regarding religion — **skep·ti·cal** \-ti-kəl\ *adj* — **skep·ti·cal·ly** \-k(ə-)lē\ *adv*
skep·ti·cism \ˈskep-tə-ˌsi-zəm\ *n* **1 :** a doubting state of mind **2 :** a doctrine that certainty of knowledge cannot be attained **3 :** doubt concerning religion
sketch \ˈskech\ *n* [D *schets,* fr. It *schizzo,* lit., splash] **1 :** a rough drawing or outline **2 :** a short or light literary composition (as a story or essay); *also* **:** a short comedy piece — **sketch** *vb* — **sketchy** *adj*
[1]skew \ˈskyü\ *vb* **:** TWIST, SWERVE
[2]skew *n* **:** SLANT
skew·er \ˈskyü-ər\ *n* **:** a long pin for holding small pieces of meat and vegetables for broiling — **skewer** *vb*
[1]ski \ˈskē\ *n, pl* **skis** [Norw, fr. ON *skīth* stick of wood, ski] **:** one of a pair of long strips (as of wood, metal or plastic) curving upward in front that are used for gliding over snow or water
[2]ski *vb* **skied** \ˈskēd\; **ski·ing :** to glide on skis — **ski·able** \ˈskē-ə-bəl\ *adj* — **ski·er** *n*
[1]skid \ˈskid\ *n* **1 :** a plank for supporting something above the ground **2 :** a device placed under a wheel to prevent turning **3 :** a timber or rail over or on which something is slid or rolled **4 :** the act of skidding **5 :** a runner on the landing gear of an aircraft **6 :** [2]PALLET
[2]skid *vb* **skid·ded; skid·ding 1 :** to slide without rotating ⟨a *skidding* wheel⟩ **2 :** to slide sideways on the road ⟨the car *skidded* on ice⟩ **3 :** SLIDE, SLIP
skid row *n* **:** a district of cheap saloons frequented by vagrants and alcoholics
skiff \ˈskif\ *n* **:** a small boat
ski jump *n* **:** a jump made by a person wearing skis; *also* **:** a course or track prepared for such jumping — **ski jump** *vb* — **ski jumper** *n*
skil·ful *chiefly Brit var of* SKILLFUL
ski lift *n* **:** a mechanical device (as a chairlift) for carrying skiers up a long slope
skill \ˈskil\ *n* **1 :** ability to use one's knowledge effectively in doing something **2 :** developed or acquired ability
♦ ***Synonyms*** ART, CRAFT, CUNNING, DEXTERITY, EXPERTISE, KNOW-HOW — **skilled** \ˈskild\ *adj*
skil·let \ˈski-lət\ *n* **:** a frying pan
skill·ful \ˈskil-fəl\ *adj* **1 :** having or displaying skill **:** EXPERT **2 :** accomplished with skill — **skill·ful·ly** *adv* — **skill·ful·ness** *n*
[1]skim \ˈskim\ *vb* **skimmed; skim·ming 1 :** to take off from the top of a liquid; *also* **:** to remove (scum or cream) from ⟨~ milk⟩ **2 :** to read rapidly and superficially **3 :** to pass swiftly over — **skim·mer** *n*
[2]skim *adj* **:** having the cream removed
skimp \ˈskimp\ *vb* **:** to give insufficient attention, effort, or funds; *also* **:** to save by skimping
skimpy \ˈskim-pē\ *adj* **skimp·i·er; -est :** deficient in supply or execution — **skimp·i·ly** \-pə-lē\ *adv*
[1]skin \ˈskin\ *n* **1 :** the outer limiting layer of an animal body; *also* **:** the usu. thin tough tissue of which this is made **2 :** an outer or surface layer (as a rind or peel) — **skin·less** *adj* — **skinned** *adj*
[2]skin *vb* **skinned; skin·ning :** to free from skin **:** remove the skin of ⟨~ a rabbit⟩
[3]skin *adj* **:** devoted to showing nudes ⟨~ magazines⟩
skin diving *n* **:** the sport of swimming under water with a face mask and flippers and esp. without a portable breathing device — **skin–dive** *vb* — **skin diver** *n*
skin·flint \ˈskin-ˌflint\ *n* **:** a very stingy person
skin graft *n* **:** a piece of skin surgically removed from one area to replace skin in another area — **skin grafting** *n*
skin·head \ˈskin-ˌhed\ *n* **1 :** a person whose hair is cut very short **2 :** a usu. white male belonging to a youth gang whose members have close-shaven hair and often believe in white supremacy
[1]skin·ny \ˈski-nē\ *adj* **skin·ni·er; -est 1 :** resembling skin **2 :** very thin
[2]skinny *n* **:** inside information
skin·ny–dip \ˈski-nē-ˌdip\ *vb* **:** to swim in the nude — **skin·ny–dip·per** \-ˌdi-pər\ *n*
skin·tight \ˈskin-ˈtīt\ *adj* **:** closely fitted to the figure ⟨~ pants⟩
[1]skip \ˈskip\ *vb* **skipped; skip·ping 1 :** to move with leaps and bounds **2 :** to leap lightly over **3 :** to pass from point to point (as in reading) disregarding what is in between **4 :** to pass over without notice or mention

[2]**skip** *n* : a light bouncing step; *also* : a gait of alternate hops and steps

skip·jack \ˈskip-ˌjak\ *n* : a small sailboat with vertical sides and a bottom similar to a flat V

skip·per \ˈski-pər\ *n* [ME, fr. MD *schipper,* fr. *schip* ship] : the master of a ship; *also* : the manager of a baseball team — **skipper** *vb*

skir·mish \ˈskər-mish\ *n* : a minor engagement in war; *also* : a minor dispute or contest — **skirmish** *vb*

[1]**skirt** \ˈskərt\ *n* : a free-hanging garment or part of a garment extending from the waist down

[2]**skirt** *vb* **1** : to pass around the outer edge of **2** : BORDER **3** : EVADE ⟨~ the issue⟩

skit \ˈskit\ *n* : a brief dramatic sketch

ski tow *n* : SKI LIFT

skit·ter \ˈski-tər\ *vb* : to glide or skip lightly or quickly : skim along a surface

skit·tish \ˈski-tish\ *adj* **1** : CAPRICIOUS **2** : easily frightened ⟨a ~ horse⟩; *also* : WARY ⟨~ investors⟩

ski·wear \ˈskē-ˌwer\ *n* : clothing suitable for wear while skiing

skosh \ˈskōsh\ *n* [Jp *sukoshi*] : a small amount : BIT ⟨has a ~ more room⟩

skul·dug·gery *or* **skull·dug·gery** \ˌskəl-ˈdə-gə-rē\ *n, pl* **-ger·ries** : underhanded or unscrupulous behavior

skulk \ˈskəlk\ *vb* : to move furtively : SNEAK, LURK — **skulk·er** *n*

skull \ˈskəl\ *n* : the skeleton of the head of a vertebrate that protects the brain and supports the jaws

skull and crossbones *n, pl* **skulls and crossbones** : a depiction of a human skull over crossbones usu. indicating a danger

skull·cap \ˈskəl-ˌkap\ *n* : a close-fitting brimless cap

[1]**skunk** \ˈskəŋk\ *n, pl* **skunks** *also* **skunk** **1** : any of various black-and-white New World mammals related to the weasels that can forcibly eject an ill-smelling fluid when startled **2** : a contemptible person

[2]**skunk** *vb* : to defeat decisively; *esp* : to prevent entirely from scoring in a game

skunk cabbage *n* : either of two No. American perennial herbs related to the arums that occur in shaded wet to swampy areas and have a fetid odor suggestive of a skunk

sky \ˈskī\ *n, pl* **skies** [ME, sky, cloud, fr. ON *ský* cloud] **1** : the upper air **2** : HEAVEN — **sky·ey** \ˈskī-ē\ *adj*

sky·cap \-ˌkap\ *n* : a person employed to carry luggage at an airport

sky·div·ing \-ˌdī-viŋ\ *n* : the sport of jumping from an airplane and executing various body maneuvers before opening a parachute — **skydiver** *n*

sky·jack \-ˌjak\ *vb* : to commandeer an airplane in flight by threat of violence — **sky·jack·er** *n* — **sky·jack·ing** *n*

[1]**sky·lark** \-ˌlärk\ *n* : a European lark noted for singing during flight

[2]**skylark** *vb* : FROLIC, SPORT

sky·light \ˈskī-ˌlīt\ *n* : a window in a roof or ceiling — **sky·light·ed** \-ˌlī-təd\ *adj*

sky·line \-ˌlīn\ *n* **1** : HORIZON **2** : an outline (as of buildings) against the sky

[1]**sky·rock·et** \-ˌrä-kət\ *n* : ROCKET 1

[2]**skyrocket** *vb* : ROCKET 2

sky·scrap·er \-ˌskrā-pər\ *n* : a very tall building

sky·surf·ing \-ˌsər-fiŋ\ *n* : skydiving with a short modified surfboard attached to the feet — **sky·surf·er** \-fər\ *n*

sky·walk \-ˌwȯk\ *n* : an aerial walkway connecting two buildings

sky·ward \-wərd\ *adv* : toward the sky

sky·writ·ing \-ˌrī-tiŋ\ *n* : writing in the sky formed by smoke emitted from an airplane — **sky·writ·er** *n*

sl *abbr* **1** slightly **2** slip **3** slow

slab \ˈslab\ *n* : a thick flat piece or slice

[1]**slack** \ˈslak\ *adj* **1** : CARELESS, NEGLIGENT **2** : SLUGGISH, LISTLESS **3** : not taut : LOOSE **4** : not busy or active ⟨a ~ season⟩ ♦ ***Synonyms*** LAX, REMISS, NEGLECTFUL, DELINQUENT, DERELICT — **slack·ly** *adv* — **slack·ness** *n*

[2]**slack** *vb* **1** : to make or become slack : LOOSEN, RELAX **2** : SLAKE 2

[3]**slack** *n* **1** : cessation of movement or flow : LETUP **2** : a part that hangs loose without strain ⟨~ of a rope⟩ **3** : pants esp. for casual wear — usu. used in pl.

slack·en \ˈsla-kən\ *vb* : to make or become slack

slack·er \ˈsla-kər\ *n* **1** : one that shirks work or evades military duty **2** : a young person perceived to be disaffected, apathetic, cynical, or lacking ambition

slag \ˈslag\ *n* : the waste left after the melting of ores and the separation of metal from them

slain *past part of* SLAY

slake \ˈslāk, *for 2 also* ˈslak\ *vb* **slaked; slak·ing** **1** : to relieve or satisfy with or as if with refreshing drink ⟨~ thirst⟩ **2** : to cause (lime) to crumble by mixture with water

sla·lom \ˈslä-ləm\ *n* [Norw *slalåm,* lit., sloping track] : skiing in a zigzag course between obstacles

[1]**slam** \ˈslam\ *n* : the winning of every trick or of all tricks but one in bridge

[2]**slam** *n* **1** : a heavy jarring impact : BANG **2** : harsh criticism **3** : a poetry competition

[3]**slam** *vb* **slammed; slam·ming** **1** : to shut violently and noisily **2** : to throw or strike with a loud impact **3** : to criticize harshly ⟨was *slammed* in the press⟩

slam·mer \ˈsla-mər\ *n* : JAIL, PRISON

[1]**slan·der** \ˈslan-dər\ *vb* : to utter slander against : DEFAME — **slan·der·er** *n*

[2]**slander** *n* [ME *sclaundre, slaundre,* fr. AF *esclandre,* alter. of *escandle,* fr. LL *scandalum* stumbling block, offense] : a false report maliciously uttered and tending to injure the reputation of a person — **slan·der·ous** *adj*

slang \ˈslaŋ\ *n* : an informal nonstandard vocabulary composed typically of invented words, arbitrarily changed words, and extravagant figures of speech — **slangy** *adj*

[1]**slant** \ˈslant\ *n* **1** : a sloping direction,

line, or plane **2 :** a particular or personal viewpoint ⟨has a liberal ~⟩ — **slant** *adj* — **slant·wise** \-ˌwīz\ *adv or adj*

²**slant** *vb* **1 :** SLOPE **2 :** to interpret or present in accordance with a special viewpoint or bias ⟨~*ed* the story for their benefit⟩ ♦ ***Synonyms*** INCLINE, LEAN, LIST, TILT, HEEL — **slant·ing·ly** *adv*

slap \ˈslap\ *vb* **slapped; slap·ping 1 :** to strike sharply with the open hand **2 :** REBUFF, INSULT — **slap** *n*

slap·stick \-ˌstik\ *n* **:** comedy stressing horseplay

¹**slash** \ˈslash\ *vb* **1 :** to cut with sweeping strokes **2 :** to cut slits in (a garment) **3 :** to reduce sharply ⟨~*ed* prices⟩ — **slash·er** \ˈsla-shər\ *n*

²**slash** *n* **1 :** GASH **2 :** an ornamental slit in a garment **3 :** a mark / used to denote "or" (as in *and/or*), "and or" (as in *straggler/deserter*), or "per" (as in *feet/second*)

slat \ˈslat\ *n* **:** a thin narrow flat strip

¹**slate** \ˈslāt\ *n* **1 :** a dense fine-grained rock that splits into thin layers **2 :** a roofing tile or a writing tablet made from this rock **3 :** a written or unwritten record ⟨start with a clean ~⟩ **4 :** a list of candidates for election

²**slate** *vb* **slat·ed; slat·ing 1 :** to cover with slate **2 :** to designate for action or appointment ⟨is *slated* to open soon⟩

slath·er \ˈsla-t͟hər\ *vb* **:** to spread with or on thickly or lavishly

slat·tern \ˈsla-tərn\ *n* **:** a slovenly woman — **slat·tern·ly** *adj*

¹**slaugh·ter** \ˈslȯ-tər\ *n* **1 :** the butchering of livestock for market **2 :** great destruction of lives esp. in battle

²**slaughter** *vb* **1 :** to kill (animals) for food **:** BUTCHER **2 :** to kill in large numbers or in a bloody way **:** MASSACRE

slaugh·ter·house \-ˌhau̇s\ *n* **:** an establishment where animals are butchered

Slav \ˈsläv, ˈslav\ *n* **:** a person speaking a Slavic language

¹**slave** \ˈslāv\ *n* [ME *sclave,* fr. AF or ML; AF *esclave,* fr. ML *sclavus,* fr. *Sclavus* Slav; fr. the enslavement of Slavs in central Europe in the Middle Ages] **1 :** a person held in forced servitude **2 :** a person who is completely subservient to a dominating influence **3 :** a device (as the printer of a computer) that is directly responsive to another — **slave** *adj*

²**slave** *vb* **slaved; slav·ing :** to work very hard for long hours or under difficult conditions **:** DRUDGE

¹**sla·ver** \ˈsla-vər, ˈslā-\ *n* **:** SLOBBER — **slaver** *vb*

²**slav·er** \ˈslā-vər\ *n* **:** a ship or a person engaged in the trafficking of enslaved people

slav·ery \ˈslāv-rē, ˈslā-və-\ *n* **1 :** wearisome drudgery **2 :** the state of a person who is held in forced servitude **3 :** the practice of owning enslaved people ♦ ***Synonyms*** SERVITUDE, BONDAGE, ENSLAVEMENT

¹**Slav·ic** \ˈsla-vik, ˈslä-\ *n* **:** a branch of the Indo-European language family including various languages (as Russian or Polish) of eastern Europe

²**Slavic** *adj* **:** of or relating to the Slavs or their languages

slav·ish \ˈslā-vish\ *adj* **1 :** SERVILE **2 :** obeying or imitating with no freedom of judgment or choice — **slav·ish·ly** *adv*

slaw \ˈslȯ\ *n* **:** COLESLAW

slay \ˈslā\ *vb* **slew** \ˈslü\; **slain** \ˈslān\; **slay·ing :** KILL — **slay·er** *n*

SLBM *abbr* submarine-launched ballistic missile

sleaze \ˈslēz\ *n* **:** a sleazy quality, appearance, or behavior

slea·zy \ˈslē-zē\ *adj* **slea·zi·er; -est 1 :** FLIMSY, SHODDY **2 :** marked by low character or quality ⟨a ~ lawyer⟩

¹**sled** \ˈsled\ *n* **:** a vehicle usu. on runners adapted esp. for sliding on snow

²**sled** *vb* **sled·ded, sled·ding :** to ride or carry on a sled

¹**sledge** \ˈslej\ *n* **:** SLEDGEHAMMER

²**sledge** *n* **:** a strong heavy sled

sledge·ham·mer \ˈslej-ˌha-mər\ *n* **:** a large heavy hammer wielded with both hands — **sledgehammer** *adj or vb*

¹**sleek** \ˈslēk\ *vb* **1 :** to make smooth or glossy **2 :** to gloss over

²**sleek** *adj* **1 :** having a smooth well-groomed look **2 :** trim and graceful in design ⟨a ~ car⟩

¹**sleep** \ˈslēp\ *n* **1 :** the natural periodic suspension of consciousness during which bodily powers are restored **2 :** a state (as death or coma) suggesting sleep — **sleep·less** *adj* — **sleep·less·ness** *n*

²**sleep** *vb* **slept** \ˈslept\; **sleep·ing 1 :** to rest or be in a state of sleep; *also* **:** to spend in sleep **2 :** to have sexual intercourse — usu. used with *with* **3 :** to provide sleeping space for

sleep·er \ˈslē-pər\ *n* **1 :** one that sleeps **2 :** a horizontal beam to support something on or near ground level **3 :** SLEEPING CAR **4 :** someone or something unpromising or unnoticed that suddenly attains prominence or value

sleeping bag *n* **:** a warmly lined bag for sleeping esp. outdoors

sleeping car *n* **:** a railroad car with berths for sleeping

sleeping pill *n* **:** a drug in tablet or capsule form taken to induce sleep

sleeping sickness *n* **:** a serious disease of tropical Africa that is marked by fever, lethargy, confusion, and sleep disturbances and is caused by protozoans transmitted by the tsetse fly

sleep·over \ˈslēp-ˌō-vər\ *n* **:** an overnight stay (as at another's home)

sleep·walk·er \ˈslēp-ˌwȯ-kər\ *n* **:** one that walks while or as if while asleep — **sleep·walk** \-ˌwȯk\ *vb*

sleepy \ˈslē-pē\ *adj* **sleep·i·er; -est 1 :** ready for sleep **2 :** quietly inactive — **sleep·i·ly** \ˈslē-pə-lē\ *adv* — **sleep·i·ness** \-pē-nəs\ *n*

sleet \ˈslēt\ *n* **:** frozen or partly frozen rain — **sleet** *vb* — **sleety** *adj*

sleeve \ˈslēv\ *n* **1 :** a part of a garment covering an arm **2 :** a tubular part designed to fit over another part — **sleeved** *adj* — **sleeve·less** *adj*

[1]**sleigh** \'slā\ *n* : an open usu. horse-drawn vehicle on runners for use on snow or ice
[2]**sleigh** *vb* : to drive or travel in a sleigh
sleight \'slīt\ *n* **1** : TRICK **2** : DEXTERITY
sleight of hand : a trick requiring skillful manual manipulation
slen·der \'slen-dər\ *adj* **1** : SLIM, THIN **2** : WEAK, SLIGHT **3** : MEAGER, INADEQUATE ⟨~ opportunities⟩
slen·der·ize \-də-ˌrīz\ *vb* **-ized; -iz·ing** : to make slender
sleuth \'slüth\ *n* [short for *sleuthhound* bloodhound, fr. ME (Sc) *sleuth hund,* fr. ME *sleuth, sloith, sloth* track of an animal or person, fr. ON *slōth*] : DETECTIVE
[1]**slew** \'slü\ *past of* SLAY
[2]**slew** *vb* : TURN, VEER, SKID
[1]**slice** \'slīs\ *vb* **sliced; slic·ing** **1** : to cut a slice from; *also* : to cut into slices **2** : to hit (a ball) so that a slice results
[2]**slice** *n* **1** : a thin flat piece cut from something **2** : a flight of a ball (as in golf) that curves in the direction of the dominant hand of the player hitting it
[1]**slick** \'slik\ *vb* : to make smooth or sleek
[2]**slick** *adj* **1** : very smooth : SLIPPERY **2** : CLEVER, SMART ⟨a ~ salesperson⟩
[3]**slick** *n* **1** : a smooth patch of water covered with a film of oil **2** : a popular magazine printed on coated paper
slick·er \'sli-kər\ *n* **1** : a long loose raincoat **2** : a sly tricky person **3** : a city dweller esp. of stylish appearance or sophisticated mannerisms
[1]**slide** \'slīd\ *vb* **slid** \'slid\; **slid·ing** \'slī-diŋ\ **1** : to move smoothly along a surface **2** : to fall or dive towards a base in baseball **3** : to fall by a loss of support **4** : to pass unobtrusively **5** : to move or pass smoothly; *also* : to pass unnoticed ⟨let it ~ by⟩ **6** : to become worse gradually
[2]**slide** *n* **1** : an act or instance of sliding **2** : something (as a cover or fastener) that operates by sliding **3** : a fall of a mass of earth or snow down a hillside **4** : a surface on which something slides **5** : a flat piece of glass or plastic on which a specimen is mounted for examination under a microscope **6 a** : a small transparent photograph that can be projected on a screen **b** : an electronic image presented as part of a series
slid·er \'slī-dər\ *n* **1** : one that slides **2** : a baseball pitch that looks like a fastball but curves slightly **3** : a small hamburger
slide rule *n* : a manual device for calculation consisting of a ruler and a movable middle piece graduated with logarithmic scales
slier *comparative of* SLY
sliest *superlative of* SLY
[1]**slight** \'slīt\ *adj* **1** : SLENDER; *also* : FRAIL **2** : UNIMPORTANT ⟨a ~ movie⟩ **3** : small of its kind or in amount ⟨a ~ odor⟩ — **slight·ly** *adv*
[2]**slight** *vb* **1** : to treat as unimportant **2** : to ignore discourteously ⟨~*ed* the mayor⟩ **3** : to perform or attend to carelessly
[3]**slight** *n* : a humiliating discourtesy
[1]**slim** \'slim\ *adj* **slim·mer; slim·mest** [D, bad, inferior, fr. MD, *slimp* crooked, bad] **1** : SLENDER, SLIGHT, THIN **2** : SMALL, SLIGHT ⟨a ~ chance⟩
[2]**slim** *vb* **slimmed; slim·ming** : to make or become slender
slime \'slīm\ *n* **1** : sticky mud **2** : a slippery substance (as on the skin of a slug or catfish) — **slimy** *adj*
[1]**sling** \'sliŋ\ *vb* **slung** \'sləŋ\; **sling·ing** **1** : to throw forcibly : FLING **2** : to hurl with or as if with a sling
[2]**sling** *n* **1** : a short strap with strings attached for hurling stones or shot **2** : something (as a rope or chain) used to hoist, lower, support, or carry; *esp* : a bandage hanging from the neck to support an arm or hand
sling·shot \'sliŋ-ˌshät\ *n* : a forked stick with elastic bands for shooting small stones or shot
slink \'sliŋk\ *vb* **slunk** \'sləŋk\ *also* **slinked** \'sliŋkt\; **slink·ing** **1** : to move stealthily or furtively **2** : to move sinuously — **slinky** *adj*
[1]**slip** \'slip\ *vb* **slipped; slip·ping** **1** : to escape quietly or secretly **2** : to slide along or cause to slide along smoothly **3** : to make a mistake **4** : to pass unnoticed or undone **5** : to fall off from a standard or level
[2]**slip** *n* **1** : a ramp for repairing ships **2** : a ship's berth between two piers **3** : secret or hurried departure, escape, or evasion **4** : BLUNDER **5** : a sudden mishap **6** : a thin one-piece garment worn under a dress or skirt **7** : PILLOWCASE
[3]**slip** *n* **1** : a shoot or twig from a plant for planting or grafting **2** : a long narrow strip; *esp* : one of paper used for a record
[4]**slip** *vb* **slipped; slip·ping** : to take slips from (a plant)
slip·knot \'slip-ˌnät\ *n* : a knot that slips along the rope around which it is made
slipped disk *n* : a protrusion of one of the disks of cartilage between vertebrae with pressure on spinal nerves resulting esp. in low back pain
slip·per \'sli-pər\ *n* : a light low shoe that may be easily slipped on and off
slip·pery \'sli-pə-rē\ *adj* **slip·per·i·er; -est** **1** : icy, wet, smooth, or greasy enough to cause one to fall or lose one's hold **2** : not to be trusted : TRICKY ⟨a ~ salesman⟩ — **slip·per·i·ness** *n*
slip·shod \'slip-'shäd\ *adj* : SLOVENLY, CARELESS ⟨~ work⟩
slip·stream \'slip-ˌstrēm\ *n* : a stream (as of air) driven aft by a propeller
slip·up \'slip-ˌəp\ *n* **1** : MISTAKE **2** : ACCIDENT
[1]**slit** \'slit\ *vb* **slit; slit·ting** **1** : SLASH **2** : to cut off or away
[2]**slit** *n* : a long narrow cut or opening
slith·er \'sli-thər\ *vb* : to slip or glide along like a snake — **slith·ery** *adj*
sliv·er \'sli-vər\ *n* : SPLINTER
slob \'släb\ *n* : a slovenly or boorish person
slob·ber \'slä-bər\ *vb* **slob·bered; slob·ber·ing** : to dribble saliva — **slob·ber** *n*

sloe \ˈslō\ *n* : the fruit of the blackthorn

slog \ˈsläg\ *vb* **slogged; slog·ging 1** : to hit hard : BEAT **2** : to work hard and steadily

slo·gan \ˈslō-gən\ *n* [alter. of earlier *slogorn,* fr. ScGael *sluagh-ghairm,* fr. *sluagh* army, host + *gairm* cry] : a word or phrase expressing the spirit or aim of a party, group, or cause

slo–mo \ˈslō-ˌmō\ *n* : SLOW MOTION — **slo–mo** *adj*

sloop \ˈslüp\ *n* [D *sloep*] : a single-masted sailboat with a jib and a fore-and-aft mainsail

[1]**slop** \ˈsläp\ *n* **1** : thin tasteless drink or liquid food — usu. used in pl. **2** : food waste for animal feed : SWILL **3** : excreted body waste — usu. used in pl.

[2]**slop** *vb* **slopped; slop·ping 1** : SPILL **2** : to feed with slop ⟨~ hogs⟩

[1]**slope** \ˈslōp\ *vb* **sloped; slop·ing** : SLANT, INCLINE

[2]**slope** *n* **1** : upward or downward slant or degree of slant **2** : ground that forms an incline **3** : the part of a landmass draining into a particular ocean

slop·py \ˈslä-pē\ *adj* **slop·pi·er; -est 1** : MUDDY, SLUSHY **2** : SLOVENLY, MESSY

sloppy joe \-ˈjō\ *n* : ground beef cooked in a thick spicy sauce and usu. served on a bun

slosh \ˈsläsh\ *vb* **1** : to flounder through or splash about in or with water, mud, or slush **2** : to move with a splashing motion

slot \ˈslät\ *n* **1** : a long narrow opening or groove **2** : a position in a sequence

slot car *n* : an electric toy racing car that runs on a grooved track

sloth \ˈsloth\ *n, pl* **sloths** \ˈsloths, ˈslo<u>th</u>z\ **1** : LAZINESS, INDOLENCE **2** : any of several slow-moving plant-eating arboreal mammals of So. and Central America — **sloth·ful** *adj*

slot machine *n* **1** : a machine whose operation is begun by dropping a coin into a slot **2** : a coin-operated gambling machine that pays off according to the matching of symbols on wheels spun by a handle

[1]**slouch** \ˈslauch\ *n* **1** : a lazy or incompetent person **2** : a loose or drooping gait or posture

[2]**slouch** *vb* : to walk, stand, or sit with a slouch : SLUMP

[1]**slough** \ˈslü, *2 usu* ˈslau\ *n* **1** : a wet and marshy or muddy place (as a swamp) **2** : a discouraged state of mind

[2]**slough** \ˈsləf\ *also* **sluff** *n* : something that has been or may be shed or cast off

[3]**slough** \ˈsləf\ *also* **sluff** *vb* : to cast off

Slo·vak \ˈslō-ˌväk, -ˌvak\ *n* **1** : a member of a Slavic people of Slovakia **2** : the language of the Slovaks — **Slovak** *adj* — **Slo·va·ki·an** \slō-ˈvä-kē-ən, -ˈva-\ *adj or n*

slov·en \ˈslə-vən\ *n* [ME *sloveyn* slut, rascal, perh. fr. MD *slof* negligent] : an untidy person

Slo·vene \ˈslō-ˌvēn\ *n* **1** : a member of a Slavic people living largely in Slovenia **2** : the language of the Slovenes — **Slovene** *adj* — **Slo·ve·nian** \slō-ˈvē-nē-ən\ *adj or n*

slov·en·ly \ˈslə-vən-lē\ *adj* **1** : untidy in dress or person **2** : lazily or carelessly done : SLIPSHOD ⟨~ thinking⟩

[1]**slow** \ˈslō\ *adj* **1** : SLUGGISH; *also* : dull in mind : STUPID **2** : moving, flowing, or proceeding at less than the usual speed **3** : taking more than the usual time **4** : registering behind the correct time **5** : not lively : BORING ♦ ***Synonyms*** DILATORY, LAGGARD, DELIBERATE, LEISURELY — **slow** *adv* — **slow·ly** *adv* — **slow·ness** *n*

[2]**slow** *vb* **1** : to make slow : hold back **2** : to go slower

slow motion *n* : motion-picture action photographed so as to appear much slower than normal — **slow–motion** *adj*

SLR *abbr* single-lens reflex

sludge \ˈsləj\ *n* : a slushy mass : OOZE; *esp* : solid matter produced by sewage treatment processes

slue *var of* [2]SLEW

[1]**slug** \ˈsləg\ *n* **1** : a small mass of metal; *esp* : BULLET **2** : a metal disk for use (as in a slot machine) in place of a coin **3** : any of numerous wormlike mollusks related to the snails **4** : a quantity of liquor drunk

[2]**slug** *vb* **slugged; slug·ging** : to strike forcibly and heavily — **slug·ger** *n*

slug·gard \ˈslə-gərd\ *n* : a lazy person

slug·gish \ˈslə-gish\ *adj* **1** : SLOTHFUL, LAZY **2** : slow in movement, flow, or growth ⟨a ~ economy⟩ **3** : STAGNANT, DULL — **slug·gish·ly** *adv* — **slug·gish·ness** *n*

[1]**sluice** \ˈslüs\ *n* [ME *sluse, scluse,* fr. AF *escluse,* fr. LL *exclusa,* fr. L, fem. of *exclusus,* pp. of *excludere* to shut out, exclude] **1** : an artificial passage for water with a gate for controlling the flow; *also* : the gate so used **2** : a channel that carries off surplus water **3** : an inclined trough or flume for washing ore or floating logs

[2]**sluice** *vb* **sluiced; sluic·ing 1** : to draw off through a sluice **2** : to wash with running water : FLUSH

[1]**slum** \ˈsləm\ *n* : a thickly populated area marked by poverty and dirty or deteriorated houses — **slum·my** \ˈslə-mē\ *adj*

[2]**slum** *vb* **slummed; slum·ming** : to visit slums esp. out of curiosity; *also* : to go somewhere or do something that might be considered beneath one's station

[1]**slum·ber** \ˈsləm-bər\ *vb* **slum·bered; slum·ber·ing 1** : DOZE; *also* : SLEEP **2** : to be in a sluggish or torpid state

[2]**slumber** *n* : SLEEP

slum·ber·ous \ˈsləm-bə-rəs\ *or* **slum·brous** \-brəs\ *adj* **1** : SLUMBERING, SLEEPY **2** : PEACEFUL, INACTIVE

slum·lord \ˈsləm-ˌlord\ *n* : a landlord who receives unusually large profits from substandard properties

slump \ˈsləmp\ *vb* **1** : to sink down suddenly : COLLAPSE **2** : SLOUCH **3** : to decline sharply — **slump** *n*

slung *past and past part of* SLING
slunk *past and past part of* SLINK
[1]**slur** \ˈslər\ *n* **:** a slighting remark **:** ASPERSION — **slur** *vb*
[2]**slur** *vb* **slurred; slur·ring 1 :** to slide or slip over without due mention or emphasis **2 :** to perform two or more successive notes of different pitch in a smooth or connected way
[3]**slur** *n* **:** a curved line connecting notes to be slurred; *also* **:** a group of slurred notes
slurp \ˈslərp\ *vb* **:** to eat or drink noisily — **slurp** *n*
slur·ry \ˈslər-ē\ *n, pl* **slur·ries :** a watery mixture of insoluble matter
slush \ˈsləsh\ *n* **1 :** partly melted or watery snow **2 :** soft mud — **slushy** *adj*
slush fund *n* **:** an unregulated fund often for illicit purposes
slut \ˈslət\ *n* **1** *dated* **a** *chiefly Brit, disparaging* **:** a slovenly woman **b :** MINX **2** *disparaging + offensive* **:** a promiscuous person — **slut·tish** *adj*
sly \ˈslī\ *adj* **sly·er** *also* **sli·er** \ˈslī-ər\; **sly·est** *also* **sli·est** \ˈslī-əst\ **1 :** CRAFTY, CUNNING **2 :** SECRETIVE, FURTIVE **3 :** ROGUISH ♦ ***Synonyms*** TRICKY, WILY, ARTFUL, FOXY, GUILEFUL — **sly·ly** *also* **sli·ly** *adv* — **sly·ness** *n*
sm *abbr* small
Sm *symbol* samarium
SM *abbr* **1** master of science **2** sergeant major **3** service mark **4** stage manager
SMA *abbr* sergeant major of the army
[1]**smack** \ˈsmak\ *n* **:** characteristic flavor; *also* **:** a slight trace
[2]**smack** *vb* **1 :** to have a taste **2 :** to have a trace or suggestion ⟨∼*s* of treason⟩
[3]**smack** *vb* **1 :** to move (the lips) so as to make a sharp noise **2 :** to kiss or slap with a loud noise
[4]**smack** *n* **1 :** a sharp noise made by the lips **2 :** a loud kiss or slap
[5]**smack** *adv* **:** squarely and sharply
[6]**smack** *n* **:** a sailing ship used in fishing
[7]**smack** *n, slang* **:** HEROIN
smack·down \ˈsmak-ˌdau̇n\ *n* **1 :** the act of knocking down an opponent **2 :** a wrestling match **3 :** a decisive defeat **4 :** a competition between rivals
SMaj *abbr* sergeant major
[1]**small** \ˈsmȯl\ *adj* **1 :** little in size or amount **2 :** operating on a limited scale **3 :** little or close to zero (as in number or value) **4 :** made up of little things **5 :** TRIFLING, UNIMPORTANT **6 :** MEAN, PETTY ♦ ***Synonyms*** DIMINUTIVE, PETITE, WEE, TINY, MINUTE — **small·ish** *adj* — **small·ness** *n*
[2]**small** *n* **:** a small part or product ⟨the ∼ of the back⟩
small ball *n* **1 a :** a strategy in baseball that involves batters attempting to advance base runners into scoring position **b :** a strategy in basketball based on speed and agility of players as opposed to height and physical power **2 :** a strategy for progressing towards a goal by proceeding in small steps or by addressing small matters
small·pox \ˈsmȯl-ˌpäks\ *n* **:** a contagious virus disease of humans formerly common but now eradicated
small talk *n* **:** light or casual conversation
small–time \ˈsmȯl-ˈtīm\ *adj* **:** insignificant in performance and standing **:** MINOR — **small–tim·er** *n*
smarmy \ˈsmär-mē\ *adj* **smarm·i·er; -est :** marked by a smug, ingratiating, or false earnestness ⟨∼ politeness⟩
[1]**smart** \ˈsmärt\ *adj* **1 :** causing a sharp stinging ⟨a ∼ blow⟩ **2 :** mentally quick **:** BRIGHT **3 a :** WITTY, CLEVER **b :** RUDE, DISRESPECTFUL **4 :** STYLISH **5 :** being a guided missile **6 :** containing a microprocessor for limited computing capability ⟨∼ terminal⟩ ♦ ***Synonyms*** KNOWING, QUICK-WITTED, INTELLIGENT, BRAINY, SHARP — **smart·ly** *adv* — **smart·ness** *n*
[2]**smart** *vb* **1 :** to cause or feel a stinging pain **2 :** to feel or endure distress — **smart** *n*
smart al·eck \ˈsmärt-ˌa-lik\ *n* **:** a person given to obnoxious cleverness
smart card *n* **:** a small plastic card that has a built-in microprocessor to store and handle data
smart·en \ˈsmär-tᵊn\ *vb* **:** to make smart or smarter — usu. used with *up*
smart·phone \ˈsmärt-ˌfōn\ *n* **:** a cell phone that includes additional software functions (as email or an Internet browser)
[1]**smash** \ˈsmash\ *n* **1 :** a smashing blow **2 :** a hard, overhand stroke in tennis **3 :** the act or sound of smashing **4 :** collision of vehicles **:** CRASH **5 :** COLLAPSE, RUIN; *esp* **:** BANKRUPTCY **6 :** a striking success **:** HIT — **smash** *adj*
[2]**smash** *vb* **1 :** to break or be broken into pieces **2 :** to move forward with force and shattering effect **3 :** to destroy utterly **:** WRECK
smat·ter·ing \ˈsma-tə-riŋ\ *n* **1 :** superficial knowledge **2 :** a small scattered number or amount
[1]**smear** \ˈsmir\ *n* **1 :** a spot left by an oily or sticky substance **2 :** material smeared on a surface (as of a microscope slide)
[2]**smear** *vb* **1 :** to overspread esp. with something oily or sticky **2 :** SMUDGE, SOIL **3 :** to injure by slander or insults
[1]**smell** \ˈsmel\ *vb* **smelled** \ˈsmeld\ *or* **smelt** \ˈsmelt\; **smell·ing 1 :** to perceive the odor of by sense organs of the nose; *also* **:** to detect or seek with or as if with these organs **2 :** to have or give off an odor
[2]**smell** *n* **1 :** ODOR, SCENT **2 :** the process or power of perceiving odor; *also* **:** the sense by which one perceives odor **3 :** an act of smelling — **smelly** *adj*
smelling salts *n pl* **:** an aromatic preparation used as a stimulant and restorative (as to relieve faintness)
[1]**smelt** \ˈsmelt\ *n, pl* **smelts** *or* **smelt :** any of a family of small food fishes of coastal or fresh waters that are related to the trouts and salmons
[2]**smelt** *vb* **:** to melt or fuse (ore) in order to separate the metal; *also* **:** REFINE
smelt·er \ˈsmel-tər\ *n* **1 :** one that smelts **2 :** an establishment for smelting

smid·gen *also* **smid·geon** *or* **smid·gin** \ˈsmi-jən\ *n* : a small amount : BIT

smi·lax \ˈsmī-ˌlaks\ *n* **1** : any of various mostly climbing and prickly plants related to the lilies **2** : an ornamental plant related to the asparagus

¹smile \ˈsmī(-ə)l\ *vb* **smiled; smil·ing 1** : to look with a smile **2** : to be favorable **3** : to express by a smile

²smile *n* : a change of facial expression to express amusement, pleasure, or affection — **smile·less** \ˈsmī(-ə)l-ləs\ *adj*

smil·ey \ˈsmī-lē\ *adj* : exhibiting a smile : frequently smiling

smiley face *n* : a line drawing that symbolizes a smiling face

smirch \ˈsmərch\ *vb* **1** : to make dirty or stained **2** : to bring disgrace on — **smirch** *n*

smirk \ˈsmərk\ *vb* : to smile in an affected or smug manner : SIMPER — **smirk** *n*

smite \ˈsmīt\ *vb* **smote** \ˈsmōt\; **smit·ten** \ˈsmi-tᵊn\ *or* **smote; smit·ing** \ˈsmī-tiŋ\ **1** : to strike heavily; *also* : to kill by striking **2** : to affect as if by a heavy blow

smith \ˈsmith\ *n* : a worker in metals; *esp* : BLACKSMITH

smith·er·eens \ˌsmi-thə-ˈrēnz\ *n pl* [perh. fr. Ir *smidiríní*] : FRAGMENTS, BITS

smithy \ˈsmi-thē\ *n, pl* **smith·ies 1** : a smith's workshop **2** : BLACKSMITH

¹smock \ˈsmäk\ *n* : a loose garment worn over other clothes as a protection

²smock *vb* : to gather (cloth) in regularly spaced tucks — **smock·ing** *n*

smog \ˈsmäg, ˈsmȯg\ *n* [blend of *smoke* and *fog*] : a thick haze caused by the action of sunlight on air polluted by smoke and automobile exhaust fumes — **smog·gy** *adj*

¹smoke \ˈsmōk\ *n* **1** : the gas from burning material (as coal, wood, or tobacco) in which are suspended particles of soot **2** : a mass or column of smoke **3** : something (as a cigarette) to smoke; *also* : the act of smoking — **smoke·less** *adj* — **smoky** *adj*

²smoke *vb* **smoked; smok·ing 1** : to emit smoke **2** : to inhale and exhale the fumes of burning tobacco; *also* : to use in smoking ⟨~ a pipe⟩ **3** : to stupefy or drive away by smoke **4** : to discolor with smoke **5** : to cure (as meat) with smoke — **smok·er** *n*

smoke detector *n* : an alarm that sounds automatically when it detects smoke

smoke jumper *n* : a forest firefighter who parachutes to locations otherwise difficult to reach

smoke screen *n* **1** : a screen of smoke to hinder enemy observation **2** : something designed to obscure, confuse, or mislead

smoke·stack \ˈsmōk-ˌstak\ *n* : a pipe or funnel through which smoke and gases are discharged

smol·der *or* **smoul·der** \ˈsmōl-dər\ *vb* **smol·dered** *or* **smoul·dered; smol·der·ing** *or* **smoul·der·ing 1** : to burn and smoke without flame **2** : to burn inwardly — **smolder** *n*

smooch \ˈsmüch\ *vb* : KISS, PET — **smooch** *n*

¹smooth \ˈsmüth\ *adj* **1** : not rough or uneven **2** : not jarring or jolting **3** : BLAND, MILD **4** : fluent in speech and agreeable in manner — **smooth·ly** *adv* — **smooth·ness** *n*

²smooth *vb* **1** : to make smooth **2** : to free from trouble or difficulty

smooth muscle *n* : muscle with no cross striations that is typical of visceral organs (as the stomach and bladder) and is not under voluntary control

smoothy *or* **smooth·ie** \ˈsmü-thē\ *n, pl* **smooth·ies 1** : an artfully suave person **2** *smoothie* : a creamy beverage of fruit blended with juice, milk, or yogurt

s'more \ˈsmȯr\ *n* : a dessert of marshmallow and pieces of chocolate sandwiched between graham crackers

smor·gas·bord \ˈsmȯr-gəs-ˌbȯrd\ *n* [Sw *smörgåsbord*, fr. *smörgås* open sandwich + *bord* table] : a luncheon or supper buffet consisting of many foods

smote *past and past part of* SMITE

¹smoth·er \ˈsmə-thər\ *n* **1** : thick stifling smoke **2** : a dense cloud (as of fog or dust) **3** : a confused multitude of things

²smother *vb* **smoth·ered; smoth·er·ing 1** : to be overcome by or die from lack of air **2** : to kill by depriving of air **3** : SUPPRESS **4** : to cover thickly

SMSgt *abbr* senior master sergeant

¹smudge \ˈsməj\ *vb* **smudged; smudg·ing** : to soil or blur by rubbing or smearing ⟨his face was *smudged* with grease⟩

²smudge *n* : a dirty or blurred spot — **smudgy** *adj*

smug \ˈsməg\ *adj* **smug·ger; smug·gest** : conscious of one's virtue and importance : SELF-SATISFIED — **smug·ly** *adv* — **smug·ness** *n*

smug·gle \ˈsmə-gəl\ *vb* **smug·gled; smug·gling 1** : to import or export secretly, illegally, or without paying the duties required by law **2** : to convey secretly — **smug·gler** \ˈsmə-glər\ *n*

smut \ˈsmət\ *n* **1** : something (as soot) that smudges; *also* : SMUDGE, SPOT **2** : any of various destructive diseases of plants caused by fungi; *also* : a fungus causing smut **3** : indecent language or matter — **smut·ty** *adj*

Sn *symbol* [LL *stannum*] tin

SN *abbr* seaman

snack \ˈsnak\ *n* : a light meal : BITE — **snack** *vb*

snaf·fle \ˈsna-fəl\ *n* : a simple jointed bit for a horse's bridle

¹snag \ˈsnag\ *n* **1** : a stump or piece of a tree esp. when under water **2** : an unexpected difficulty ♦ ***Synonyms*** OBSTACLE, OBSTRUCTION, IMPEDIMENT, BAR

²snag *vb* **snagged; snag·ging 1** : to become caught on or as if on a snag **2** : to seize quickly : SNATCH

snail \ˈsnāl\ *n* : any of numerous small gastropod mollusks with a spiral shell into which they can withdraw

snail mail *n* **1** : mail delivered by a postal system **2** : MAIL 2

snake \ˈsnāk\ *n* **1** : any of numerous long-bodied limbless reptiles **2** : a treacherous person **3** : something that resembles a snake — **snake·like** \-ˌlīk\ *adj* — **snaky** *adj*

snake·bite \-ˌbīt\ *n* : the bite of a snake and esp. a venomous snake

¹**snap** \ˈsnap\ *vb* **snapped; snap·ping** **1** : to grasp or slash at something with the teeth **2** : to get or buy quickly **3** : to utter sharp or angry words **4** : to break suddenly with a sharp sound **5** : to give a sharp cracking noise **6** : to throw with a quick motion **7** : FLASH ⟨her eyes *snapped*⟩ **8** : to put a football into play — **snap·per** *n* — **snap·pish** *adj*

²**snap** *n* **1** : the act or sound of snapping **2** : something very easy to do : CINCH **3** : a short period of cold weather **4** : a catch or fastening that closes with a click **5** : a thin brittle cookie **6** : ENERGY, VIM; *also* : smartness of movement **7** : the putting of the ball into play in football

snap bean *n* : a bean grown primarily for its long pods that are cooked as a vegetable when young and tender

snap·drag·on \ˈsnap-ˌdra-gən\ *n* : any of a genus of herbs with long spikes of showy flowers

snapping turtle *n* : either of two large American turtles with powerful jaws and a strong musky odor

snap·py \ˈsna-pē\ *adj* **1** : quickly made or done **2** : marked by vigor **3** : STYLISH ⟨a ~ dresser⟩

snap·shot \ˈsnap-ˌshät\ *n* : a photograph taken usu. with an inexpensive hand-held camera

snare \ˈsner\ *n* : a trap often consisting of a noose for catching birds or mammals — **snare** *vb*

¹**snarl** \ˈsnärl\ *vb* : to cause to become knotted and intertwined

²**snarl** *n* : TANGLE — **snarly** \ˈsnär-lē\ *adj*

³**snarl** *vb* : to growl angrily or threateningly

⁴**snarl** *n* : an angry ill-tempered growl

¹**snatch** \ˈsnach\ *vb* **1** : to try to grasp something suddenly **2** : to seize or take away suddenly ♦ ***Synonyms*** CLUTCH, SEIZE, GRAB, NAB

²**snatch** *n* **1** : a short period **2** : an act of snatching **3** : something brief or fragmentary ⟨~*es* of song⟩

¹**sneak** \ˈsnēk\ *vb* **sneaked** \ˈsnēkt\ *or* **snuck** \ˈsnək\; **sneak·ing** : to move, act, or take in a furtive manner ⟨~*ed* past the guard⟩ — **sneak·ing·ly** *adv*

²**sneak** *n* **1** : one who acts in a furtive or shifty manner **2** : a stealthy or furtive move or escape — **sneak·i·ly** \ˈsnē-kə-lē\ *adv* — **sneaky** *adj*

sneak·er \ˈsnē-kər\ *n* : a sports shoe with a pliable rubber sole

sneer \ˈsnir\ *vb* : to show scorn or contempt by curling the lip or by a jeering tone — **sneer** *n*

sneeze \ˈsnēz\ *vb* **sneezed; sneez·ing** [ME *snesen,* alter. of *fnesen,* fr. OE *fnēosan*] : to force the breath out suddenly and violently as a reflex act — **sneeze** *n*

SNF *abbr* skilled nursing facility

snick·er \ˈsni-kər\ *n* : a partly suppressed laugh — **snicker** *vb*

snide \ˈsnīd\ *adj* **1** : MEAN, LOW ⟨a ~ trick⟩ **2** : slyly disparaging ⟨a ~ remark⟩ — **snide·ly** *adv* — **snide·ness** *n*

sniff \ˈsnif\ *vb* **1** : to draw air audibly up the nose esp. for smelling **2** : to show disdain or scorn **3** : to detect by or as if by smelling — **sniff** *n*

snif·fle \ˈsni-fəl\ *n* **1** *pl* : a head cold marked by nasal discharge **2** : SNUFFLE — **sniffle** *vb*

¹**snip** \ˈsnip\ *n* **1** : a fragment snipped off **2** : a simple stroke of the scissors or shears

²**snip** *vb* **snipped; snip·ping** : to cut off by bits : CLIP; *also* : to remove by cutting off ⟨~ a flower⟩

¹**snipe** \ˈsnīp\ *n, pl* **snipes** *or* **snipe** : any of several long-billed game birds esp. of marshy areas that belong to the same family as the sandpipers

²**snipe** *vb* **sniped; snip·ing** : to shoot at an exposed enemy from a concealed position — **snip·er** *n*

snip·py \ˈsni-pē\ *adj* **snip·pi·er; -est** : CURT, SNAPPISH ⟨~ comments⟩ — **snip·pi·ly** \ˈsni-pə-lē\ *adv*

snips \ˈsnips\ *n pl* : hand shears used esp. for cutting sheet metal ⟨tin ~⟩

snitch \ˈsnich\ *vb* **1** : INFORM, TATTLE **2** : PILFER, SNATCH — **snitch** *n*

sniv·el \ˈsni-vəl\ *vb* **-eled** *or* **-elled; -el·ing** *or* **-el·ling** **1** : to have a running nose; *also* : SNUFFLE **2** : to whine in a snuffling manner — **snivel** *n*

snob \ˈsnäb\ *n* : one who seeks association with persons of higher social position and looks down on those considered inferior — **snob·bish** *adj* — **snob·bish·ly** *adv* — **snob·bish·ness** *n* — **snob·by** \ˈsnä-bē\ *adj*

snob·bery \ˈsnä-bə-rē\ *n, pl* **-ber·ies** : snobbish conduct

¹**snoop** \ˈsnüp\ *vb* [D *snoepen* to buy or eat on the sly] : to pry in a furtive or meddlesome way

²**snoop** *n* : a prying meddlesome person

snoopy \ˈsnü-pē\ *adj* **snoop·i·er; -est** : given to snooping

snooty \ˈsnü-tē\ *adj* **snoot·i·er; -est** : DISDAINFUL, SNOBBISH ⟨~ rich people⟩ — **snoot·i·ly** \ˈsnü-tə-lē\ *adv*

snooze \ˈsnüz\ *vb* **snoozed; snooz·ing** : to take a nap : DOZE — **snooze** *n*

snore \ˈsnȯr\ *vb* **snored; snor·ing** : to breathe with a rough hoarse noise while sleeping — **snore** *n*

snor·kel \ˈsnȯr-kəl\ *n* [G *Schnorchel*] : a tube projecting above the water used by swimmers for breathing with the face under water — **snorkel** *vb*

snort \ˈsnȯrt\ *vb* **1** : to force air violently and noisily through the nose ⟨his horse ~*ed*⟩ **2** : to inhale (a drug) through the nostrils — **snort** *n*

snot \ˈsnät\ *n* **1** *often vulgar* : nasal mucus **2** : a snotty person

snot·ty \ˈsnä-tē\ *adj* **snot·ti·er; -est** **1** : soiled with snot **2** : rude and arrogant ⟨a ~ remark⟩ ⟨a ~ person⟩

snout \ˈsnau̇t\ *n* **1** : a long projecting muzzle (as of a pig) **2** : a usu. large or grotesque nose

[1]**snow** \ˈsnō\ *n* **1** : crystals of ice formed from water vapor in the air **2** : a descent or shower of snow crystals

[2]**snow** *vb* **1** : to fall or cause to fall in or as snow **2** : to cover or shut in with or as if with snow

[1]**snow·ball** \ˈsnō-ˌbȯl\ *n* : a round mass of snow pressed into shape in the hand for throwing

[2]**snowball** *vb* **1** : to throw snowballs at **2** : to increase or expand at a rapidly accelerating rate

snow·bank \-ˌbaŋk\ *n* : a mound or slope of snow

snow·belt \-ˌbelt\ *n, often cap* : a region that receives an appreciable amount of annual snowfall

snow·blow·er \-ˌblō-ər\ *n* : a machine in which a rotating spiral blade picks up and propels snow aside

snow·board \-ˌbȯrd\ *n* : a board like a wide ski ridden in a surfing position downhill over snow

snow·drift \-ˌdrift\ *n* : a bank of drifted snow

snow·drop \-ˌdräp\ *n* : a plant with narrow leaves and a nodding white flower that blooms early in the spring

snow·fall \-ˌfȯl\ *n* : a fall of snow

snow fence *n* : a fence across the path of prevailing winds to protect something (as a road) from drifting snow

snow·field \ˈsnō-ˌfēld\ *n* : a mass of perennial snow at the head of a glacier

snow·flake \-ˌflāk\ *n* **1** : a flake or crystal of snow **2** *usu disparaging* **a** : someone regarded or treated as unique or special **b** : someone who is overly sensitive

snow·mo·bile \ˈsnō-mō-ˌbēl\ *n* : any of various automotive vehicles for travel on snow — **snow·mo·bil·er** \-ˌbē-lər\ *n* — **snow·mo·bil·ing** \-liŋ\ *n*

snow pea *n* : a cultivated pea with flat edible pods

snow·plow \ˈsnō-ˌplau̇\ *n* **1** : a device for clearing away snow **2** : a skiing maneuver in which the heels of both skis are slid outward for slowing down or stopping

[1]**snow·shoe** \-ˌshü\ *n* : a lightweight platform for the foot designed to enable a person to walk on soft snow without sinking

[2]**snowshoe** *vb* **snow·shoed; snow·shoe·ing** : to travel on snowshoes

snow·storm \-ˌstȯrm\ *n* : a storm of falling snow

snow thrower *n* : SNOWBLOWER

snowy \ˈsnō-ē\ *adj* **snow·i·er; -est** **1** : marked by snow **2** : white as snow

snowy egret *n* : a white American egret with a slender black bill

snub \ˈsnəb\ *vb* **snubbed; snub·bing** : to treat with disdain : SLIGHT — **snub** *n*

snub–nosed \ˈsnəb-ˌnōzd\ *adj* : having a nose slightly turned up at the end

snuck *past and past part of* SNEAK

[1]**snuff** \ˈsnəf\ *vb* **1** : to pinch off the charred end of (a candle) **2** : to put out (a candle) — **snuff·er** *n*

[2]**snuff** *vb* **1** : to draw forcibly into or through the nose **2** : SMELL

[3]**snuff** *n* : SNIFF

[4]**snuff** *n* : pulverized tobacco

snuf·fle \ˈsnə-fəl\ *vb* **snuf·fled; snuf·fling** **1** : to snuff or sniff audibly and repeatedly **2** : to breathe with a sniffing sound — **snuf·fle** *n*

snug \ˈsnəg\ *adj* **snug·ger; snug·gest** **1** : fitting closely and comfortably **2** : CONCEALED ⟨a ~ position⟩ — **snug·ly** *adv* — **snug·ness** *n*

snug·gle \ˈsnə-gəl\ *vb* **snug·gled; snug·gling** : to curl up or draw close comfortably : NESTLE

[1]**so** \ˈsō\ *adv* **1** : in the manner indicated **2** : in the same way ⟨he's hungry and ~ am I⟩ **3** : THUS **4** : FINALLY **5** : to an indicated or great extent ⟨I'm ~ bored⟩ **6** : THEREFORE

[2]**so** *conj* : for that reason ⟨he wanted it, ~ he took it⟩

[3]**so** *pron* **1** : the same ⟨became chairman and remained ~⟩ **2** : approximately that ⟨a dozen or ~⟩

[4]**so** *abbr* south; southern

SO *abbr* strikeout

[1]**soak** \ˈsōk\ *vb* **1** : to remain in a liquid **2** : WET, SATURATE **3** : to draw in by or as if by absorption ⟨~ up the sunshine⟩ ♦ ***Synonyms*** DRENCH, STEEP, IMPREGNATE

[2]**soak** *n* **1** : the act of soaking **2** : the liquid in which something is soaked **3** : DRUNKARD

soap \ˈsōp\ *n* : a cleansing substance made usu. by action of alkali on fat — **soap** *vb* — **soapy** *adj*

soap·box \ˈsōp-ˌbäks\ *n* : an improvised platform used for delivering informal speeches

soap opera *n* [fr. its sponsorship by soap manufacturers] : a radio or television daytime serial drama

soap·stone \ˈsōp-ˌstōn\ *n* : a soft talc-containing stone with a soapy feel

soar \ˈsȯr\ *vb* : to fly upward or at a height on or as if on wings

sob \ˈsäb\ *vb* **sobbed; sob·bing** : to weep with convulsive heavings of the chest or contractions of the throat — **sob** *n*

so·ba \ˈsō-bə\ *n* [Jp] : a Japanese noodle made from buckwheat flour

so·ber \ˈsō-bər\ *adj* **so·ber·er** \-bər-ər\; **so·ber·est** \-bə-rəst\ **1** : temperate in the use of liquor **2** : not drunk **3** : serious or grave in mood or disposition **4** : having a quiet tone or color ♦ ***Synonyms*** SOLEMN, EARNEST, STAID, SEDATE — **so·ber·ly** *adv* — **so·ber·ness** *n*

so·bri·ety \sō-ˈbrī-ə-tē\ *n* : the quality or state of being sober

so·bri·quet \ˈsō-bri-ˌkā, -ˌket\ *n* [F] : NICKNAME

soc *abbr* **1** social; society **2** sociology

so·ca \ˈsō-kə, -kä\ *n* : soul music blended with calypso

so–called \ˈsō-ˈkȯld\ *adj* : commonly but often inaccurately so termed

soc·cer \ˈsä-kər\ *n* [by shortening & alter. fr. *association football*] : a game played on a field by two teams with a round inflated ball that is kicked or hit with any body part other than the hands or arms

¹**so·cia·ble** \ˈsō-shə-bəl\ *adj* **1** : liking companionship : FRIENDLY **2** : characterized by pleasant social relations ♦ ***Synonyms*** GRACIOUS, CORDIAL, AFFABLE, GENIAL — **so·cia·bil·i·ty** \ˌsō-shə-ˈbi-lə-tē\ *n* — **so·cia·bly** \ˈsō-shə-blē\ *adv*

²**sociable** *n* : SOCIAL

¹**so·cial** \ˈsō-shəl\ *adj* **1** : marked by pleasant companionship with one's friends **2** : naturally living and breeding in organized communities ⟨~ insects⟩ **3** : of or relating to human society ⟨~ institutions⟩ **4** : of, relating to, or based on rank in a particular society ⟨~ circles⟩; *also* : of or relating to fashionable society — **so·cial·ly** *adv*

²**social** *n* : a social gathering

so·cial·ise *Brit var of* SOCIALIZE

so·cial·ism \ˈsō-shə-ˌli-zəm\ *n* : any of various social systems based on shared or government ownership and administration of the means of production and distribution of goods — **so·cial·ist** \ˈsō-shə-list\ *n or adj* — **so·cial·is·tic** \ˌsō-shə-ˈlis-tik\ *adj*

so·cial·ite \ˈsō-shə-ˌlīt\ *n* : a person prominent in fashionable society

so·cial·ize \ˈsō-shə-ˌlīz\ *vb* **-ized; -iz·ing 1** : to regulate according to the theory and practice of socialism **2** : to adapt to social needs or uses **3** : to participate actively in a social gathering — **so·cial·i·za·tion** \ˌso-shə-lə-ˈzā-shən\ *n*

social media *n pl* : forms of electronic communication (as websites) for sharing content (such as messages, photos, or videos) with other users

social networking *n* : the creation and maintenance of personal and business relationships especially online

social science *n* : a science (as economics or political science) dealing with a particular aspect of human society — **social scientist** *n*

social work *n* : services, activities, or methods providing social services esp. to the economically or socially disadvantaged — **social worker** *n*

so·ci·e·ty \sə-ˈsī-ə-tē\ *n, pl* **-ties** [MF *societé*, fr. L *societat-, societas,* fr. *socius* companion] **1** : COMPANY ⟨in the ~ of others⟩ **2** : an association of persons for some purpose ⟨a literary ~⟩ **3** : a part of a community bound together by common interests and values; *esp* : the group or set of fashionable people ⟨high ~⟩ **4** : people in general ⟨the benefit of ~⟩ — **so·ci·e·tal** \-tᵊl\ *adj*

so·cio·eco·nom·ic \ˌsō-sē-ō-ˌe-kə-ˈnä-mik, ˌsō-shē-, -ˌē-kə-\ *adj* : of, relating to, or involving both social and economic factors

sociol *abbr* sociologist; sociology

so·ci·ol·o·gy \ˌsō-sē-ˈä-lə-jē, ˌsō-shē-\ *n* : the science of society, social institutions, and social relationships — **so·cio·log·i·cal** \ˌsō-sē-ə-ˈlä-ji-kəl, ˌsō-shē-\ *adj* — **so·ci·ol·o·gist** \-ˈä-lə-jist\ *n*

so·cio·path \ˈsō-sē-ə-ˌpath, ˈsō-sh(ē-)ə-\ *n* : a person exhibiting antisocial behavior : PSYCHOPATH — **so·cio·path·ic** \ˌsō-sē-ə-ˈpa-thik, ˌsō-sh(ē-)ə-\ *adj*

¹**sock** \ˈsäk\ *n, pl* **socks** *or* **sox** \ˈsäks\ : a stocking with a short leg

²**sock** *vb* : to hit, strike, or apply forcefully

³**sock** *n* : a vigorous blow : PUNCH

sock·et \ˈsä-kət\ *n* : an opening or hollow that forms a holder for something

socket wrench *n* : a wrench usu. in the form of a bar and removable socket made to fit a bolt or nut

sock·eye salmon \ˈsäk-ˌī-\ *n* : a commercially important Pacific salmon

¹**sod** \ˈsäd\ *n* : TURF 1

²**sod** *vb* **sod·ded; sod·ding** : to cover with sod

so·da \ˈsō-də\ *n* **1** : SODIUM CARBONATE **2** : SODIUM BICARBONATE **3** : SODIUM **4** : SODA WATER **5** : SODA POP **6** : a sweet drink of soda water, flavoring, and often ice cream

soda pop *n* : a carbonated, sweetened, and flavored soft drink

soda water *n* : a beverage of water charged with carbon dioxide

sod·den \ˈsä-dᵊn\ *adj* **1** : lacking spirit : DULLED **2** : SOAKED, DRENCHED **3** : heavy or doughy from being improperly cooked ⟨~ biscuits⟩

so·di·um \ˈsō-dē-əm\ *n* : a soft waxy silver white metallic chemical element occurring in nature in combined form (as in salt)

sodium bicarbonate *n* : a white weakly alkaline salt used esp. in baking powders, fire extinguishers, and medicine

sodium carbonate *n* : a carbonate of sodium used esp. in washing and bleaching textiles

sodium chloride *n* : SALT 1

sodium fluoride *n* : a salt used chiefly in tiny amounts (as in fluoridation) to prevent tooth decay

sodium hydroxide *n* : a white brittle caustic substance used in making soap and rayon and in bleaching

sodium nitrate *n* : a crystalline salt used as a fertilizer and in curing meat

sodium thiosulfate *n* : a hygroscopic crystalline salt used as a photographic fixing agent

sod·omy \ˈsä-də-mē\ *n* : anal or oral sexual intercourse with a member of the same or opposite sex; *also* : sexual intercourse with an animal — **sod·om·ize** \ˈsä-də-ˌmīz\ *vb*

so·ev·er \sō-ˈe-vər\ *adv* **1** : in any degree or manner ⟨how bad ~⟩ **2** : at all : of any kind ⟨any help ~⟩

so·fa \ˈsō-fə\ *n* [earlier, raised carpeted floor, fr. It *sofà,* fr. Turk *sofa,* fr. Ar *ṣuffa* carpet, divan] : a couch usu. with upholstered back and arms

soft \ˈsȯft\ *adj* **1** : not hard or rough : NONVIOLENT **2** : RESTFUL, GENTLE, SOOTHING **3** : emotionally susceptible **4**

: not prepared to endure hardship **5** : not containing certain salts that prevent lathering ⟨~ water⟩ **6** : occurring at such a speed as to avoid destructive impact ⟨~ landing of a spacecraft on the moon⟩ **7** : BIODEGRADABLE ⟨a ~ pesticide⟩ **8** : not alcoholic ⟨~ drinks⟩ **9** : less detrimental than a hard narcotic ⟨~ drugs⟩ — **soft·ly** *adv* — **soft·ness** *n*

soft·ball \ˈsȯft-ˌbȯl\ *n* : a game similar to baseball played with a ball larger and softer than a baseball; *also* : the ball used in this game

soft·bound \-ˌbau̇nd\ *adj* : not bound in hard covers ⟨~ books⟩

soft coal *n* : BITUMINOUS COAL

soft·en \ˈsȯ-fən\ *vb* : to make or become soft — **soft·en·er** *n*

soft palate *n* : the fold at the back of the hard palate that partially separates the mouth from the pharynx

soft·ware \ˈsȯft-ˌwer\ *n* : the entire set of programs, procedures, and related documentation associated with a system; *esp* : computer programs

soft·wood \-ˌwu̇d\ *n* **1** : the wood of a coniferous tree as compared to that of a broad-leaved deciduous tree **2** : a tree yielding softwood — **softwood** *adj*

sog·gy \ˈsä-gē\ *adj* **sog·gi·er; -est** : heavy with water or moisture — **sog·gi·ly** \ˈsä-gə-lē\ *adv* — **sog·gi·ness** \-gē-nəs\ *n*

soi·gné *or* **soi·gnée** \swän-ˈyā\ *adj* : elegantly maintained; *esp* : WELL-GROOMED

[1]**soil** \ˈsȯi(-ə)l\ *vb* **1** : CORRUPT, POLLUTE **2** : to make or become dirty **3** : STAIN, DISGRACE ⟨~*ed* his reputation⟩

[2]**soil** *n* **1** : STAIN, DEFILEMENT **2** : EXCREMENT, WASTE

[3]**soil** *n* **1** : firm land : EARTH **2** : the upper layer of earth in which plants grow **3** : COUNTRY, REGION

soi·ree *or* **soi·rée** \swä-ˈrā\ *n* [F *soirée* evening period, evening party, fr. MF, fr. *soir* evening, fr. L *sero* at a late hour] : an evening party

so·journ \ˈsō-ˌjərn, sō-ˈjərn\ *vb* : to dwell in a place temporarily — **so·journ** *n* — **so·journ·er** *n*

[1]**sol** \ˈsäl, ˈsȯl\ *n* — see MONEY table

[2]**sol** *n* : a fluid colloidal system

[3]**sol** *abbr* **1** solicitor **2** soluble **3** solution

Sol \ˈsäl\ *n* : SUN

[1]**sol·ace** \ˈsä-ləs\ *n* : COMFORT

[2]**solace** *vb* **so·laced; so·lac·ing** : to give solace to : CONSOLE

so·lar \ˈsō-lər\ *adj* **1** : of, derived from, or relating to the sun **2** : measured by the earth's course in relation to the sun ⟨the ~ year⟩ **3** : operated by or using the sun's light or heat ⟨~ energy⟩

solar cell *n* : a photoelectric cell used as a power source

solar collector *n* : a device for the absorption of solar radiation for the heating of water or buildings or the production of electricity

solar flare *n* : a sudden temporary outburst of energy from a small area of the sun's surface

so·lar·i·um \sō-ˈler-ē-əm\ *n, pl* **-ia** \-ē-ə\ *also* **-i·ums** : a room exposed to the sun; *esp* : a room (as in a hospital) for exposure of the body to sunshine

solar mass *n* : a unit of mass equal to the mass of the sun or about 2×10^{30} kilograms

solar plexus *n* : the general area of the stomach below the sternum

solar system *n* : the sun together with the group of celestial bodies that revolve around it

solar wind *n* : plasma continuously ejected from the sun's surface

sold *past and past part of* SELL

sol·der \ˈsä-dər, ˈsȯ-\ *n* : a metallic alloy used when melted to mend or join metallic surfaces — **solder** *vb*

soldering iron *n* : a metal device for applying heat in soldering

[1]**sol·dier** \ˈsōl-jər\ *n* [ME *soudeour,* fr. AF, mercenary, fr. *soudee* shilling's worth, wage, fr. *sou, soud* shilling, fr. LL *solidus* a Roman coin, fr. L, solid] : a person in military service; *esp* : an enlisted man or woman — **sol·dier·ly** *adj or adv*

[2]**soldier** *vb* **sol·diered; sol·dier·ing** **1** : to serve as a soldier **2** : to pretend to work while actually doing nothing

soldier of fortune : ADVENTURER 2

sol·diery \ˈsōl-jə-rē\ *n* : a body of soldiers

[1]**sole** \ˈsōl\ *n* : any of various flatfishes including some used for food

[2]**sole** *n* **1** : the undersurface of the foot **2** : the bottom of a shoe

[3]**sole** *vb* **soled; sol·ing** : to furnish (a shoe) with a sole

[4]**sole** *adj* : SINGLE, ONLY ⟨the ~ survivor⟩ — **sole·ly** \ˈsōl-lē\ *adv*

so·le·cism \ˈsä-lə-ˌsi-zəm, ˈsō-\ *n* **1** : a mistake in grammar **2** : a breach of etiquette

sol·emn \ˈsä-ləm\ *adj* **1** : marked by or observed with full religious ceremony ⟨a ~ oath⟩ **2** : FORMAL, CEREMONIOUS **3** : highly serious : GRAVE ⟨a ~ gathering⟩ **4** : SOMBER, GLOOMY ⟨a ~ city⟩ — **so·lem·ni·ty** \sə-ˈlem-nə-tē\ *n* — **sol·emn·ly** \ˈsä-ləm-lē\ *adv*

sol·em·nize \ˈsä-ləm-ˌnīz\ *vb* **-nized; -niz·ing** **1** : to observe or honor with solemnity **2** : to celebrate (a marriage) with religious rites — **sol·em·ni·za·tion** \ˌsä-ləm-nə-ˈzā-shən\ *n*

so·le·noid \ˈsō-lə-ˌnȯid, ˈsä-\ *n* : a coil of wire usu. in cylindrical form that when carrying a current acts like a magnet

so·lic·it \sə-ˈli-sət\ *vb* **1** : ENTREAT, BEG **2** : to approach with a request or plea **3** : TEMPT, LURE **4** : to try to obtain by request ⟨~ donations⟩ — **so·lic·i·ta·tion** \-ˌli-sə-ˈtā-shən\ *n*

so·lic·i·tor \sə-ˈli-sə-tər\ *n* **1** : one that solicits **2** : LAWYER; *esp* : a legal official of a city or state

so·lic·i·tous \sə-ˈli-sə-təs\ *adj* **1** : WORRIED, CONCERNED **2** : EAGER, WILLING ♦ ***Synonyms*** AVID, IMPATIENT, KEEN, ANXIOUS — **so·lic·i·tous·ly** *adv*

so·lic·i·tude \sə-ˈli-sə-ˌtüd, -ˌtyüd\ *n* : CONCERN, ANXIETY

[1]**sol·id** \ˈsä-ləd\ *adj* **1 :** not hollow; *also* **:** written as one word without a hyphen ⟨a ~ compound⟩ **2 :** having, involving, or dealing with three dimensions or with solids ⟨~ geometry⟩ **3 :** not loose or spongy **:** COMPACT ⟨a ~ mass of rock⟩; *also* **:** neither gaseous nor liquid **:** HARD, RIGID ⟨~ ice⟩ **4 :** of good substantial quality or kind ⟨~ comfort⟩ **5 :** thoroughly dependable **:** RELIABLE ⟨a ~ citizen⟩; *also* **:** serious in purpose or character ⟨~ reading⟩ **6 :** UNANIMOUS, UNITED ⟨~ for pay increases⟩ **7 :** of one substance or character — **solid** *adv* — **so·lid·i·ty** \sə-ˈli-də-tē\ *n* — **sol·id·ly** *adv* — **sol·id·ness** *n*

[2]**solid** *n* **1 :** a geometrical figure (as a cube or sphere) having three dimensions **2 :** a solid substance

sol·i·dar·i·ty \ˌsä-lə-ˈder-ə-tē\ *n* **:** unity based on shared interests, objectives, or standards

so·lid·i·fy \sə-ˈli-də-ˌfī\ *vb* **-fied; -fy·ing** **:** to make or become solid — **so·lid·i·fi·ca·tion** \-ˌli-də-fə-ˈkā-shən\ *n*

solid–state *adj* **1 :** relating to the structure and properties of solid material **2 :** using semiconductor devices rather than vacuum tubes

so·lil·o·quize \sə-ˈli-lə-ˌkwīz\ *vb* **-quized; -quiz·ing** **:** to talk to oneself **:** utter a soliloquy

so·lil·o·quy \sə-ˈli-lə-kwē\ *n, pl* **-quies** [LL *soliloquium,* fr. L *solus* alone + *loqui* to speak] **1 :** the act of talking to oneself **2 :** a dramatic monologue that represents unspoken reflections by a character

sol·i·taire \ˈsä-lə-ˌter\ *n* **1 :** a single gem (as a diamond) set alone **2 :** a card game for one person

sol·i·tary \ˈsä-lə-ˌter-ē\ *adj* **1 :** being or living apart from others **2 :** LONELY, SECLUDED **3 :** SOLE, ONLY ⟨a ~ example⟩

sol·i·tude \ˈsä-lə-ˌtüd, -ˌtyüd\ *n* **1 :** the state of being alone **:** SECLUSION ⟨worked in ~⟩ **2 :** a lonely place

soln *abbr* solution

[1]**so·lo** \ˈsō-lō\ *n, pl* **solos** [It, fr. *solo* alone, fr. L *solus*] **1 :** a piece of music for a single voice or instrument with or without accompaniment **2 :** an action in which there is only one performer — **solo** *adj or vb* — **so·lo·ist** *n*

[2]**solo** *adv* **:** without a companion **:** ALONE

so·lon \ˈsō-lən\ *n* **1 :** a wise and skillful lawgiver **2 :** a member of a legislative body

sol·stice \ˈsäl-stəs, ˈsōl-\ *n* [ME, fr. L *solstitium,* fr. *sol* sun + *-stit-, -stes* standing] **:** the time of the year when the sun is farthest north of the equator (**summer solstice**) about June 22 or farthest south (**winter solstice**) about Dec. 22 — **sol·sti·tial** \säl-ˈsti-shəl, sōl-\ *adj*

sol·u·ble \ˈsäl-yə-bəl\ *adj* **1 :** capable of being dissolved in or as if in a liquid **2 :** capable of being solved or explained — **sol·u·bil·i·ty** \ˌsäl-yə-ˈbi-lə-tē\ *n*

sol·ute \ˈsäl-ˌyüt\ *n* **:** a dissolved substance

so·lu·tion \sə-ˈlü-shən\ *n* **1 :** an action or process of solving a problem; *also* **:** an answer to a problem **2 :** an act or the process by which one substance is homogeneously mixed with another usu. liquid substance; *also* **:** a mixture thus formed

solve \ˈsälv\ *vb* **solved; solv·ing** **:** to find the answer to or a solution for — **solv·able** *adj*

sol·ven·cy \ˈsäl-vən-sē\ *n* **:** the condition of being solvent

[1]**sol·vent** \-vənt\ *adj* **1 :** able or sufficient to pay all legal debts **2 :** dissolving or able to dissolve

[2]**solvent** *n* **:** a usu. liquid substance capable of dissolving or dispersing one or more other substances

som \ˈsōm\ *n, pl* **som** **1** — see MONEY table **2 :** the sum of Uzbekistan

so·mat·ic \sō-ˈma-tik\ *adj* **:** of, relating to, or affecting the body in contrast to the mind or the sex cells and their precursors

som·ber *or* **som·bre** \ˈsäm-bər\ *adj* **1 :** DARK, GLOOMY **2 :** GRAVE, MELANCHOLY ⟨a ~ mood⟩ — **som·ber·ly** *adv*

som·bre·ro \səm-ˈbrer-ō\ *n, pl* **-ros** [Sp, fr. *sombra* shade] **:** a broad-brimmed felt hat worn esp. in the Southwest and in Mexico

[1]**some** \ˈsəm\ *adj* **1 :** one unspecified ⟨~ man called⟩ **2 :** an unspecified or indefinite number of ⟨~ berries are ripe⟩ **3 :** at least a few or a little ⟨~ years ago⟩

[2]**some** *pron* **:** a certain number or amount ⟨~ of the berries are ripe⟩ ⟨~ of it is missing⟩

[1]**-some** \səm\ *adj suffix* **:** characterized by a (specified) thing, quality, state, or action ⟨awe*some*⟩ ⟨burden*some*⟩

[2]**-some** *n suffix* **:** a group of (so many) members and esp. persons ⟨four*some*⟩

[1]**some·body** \ˈsəm-ˌbä-dē, -bə-\ *pron* **:** some person

[2]**somebody** *n* **:** a person of importance

some·day \ˈsəm-ˌdā\ *adv* **:** at some future time

some·how \-ˌhau̇\ *adv* **:** by some means

some·one \-(ˌ)wən\ *pron* **:** some person

som·er·sault *also* **sum·mer·sault** \ˈsə-mər-ˌsȯlt\ *n* [MF *sombresaut* leap, ultim. fr. L *super* over + *saltus* leap, fr. *salire* to jump] **:** a leap or roll in which a person turns heels over head — **somersault** *vb*

som·er·set \-ˌset\ *n or vb* **:** SOMERSAULT

some·thing \ˈsəm-thiŋ\ *pron* **:** some undetermined or unspecified thing

some·time \-ˌtīm\ *adv* **1 :** at a future time **2 :** at an unknown or unnamed time

some·times \-ˌtīmz\ *adv* **:** OCCASIONALLY

[1]**some·what** \-ˌhwät, -ˌhwət\ *pron* **:** SOMETHING

[2]**somewhat** *adv* **:** in some degree

some·where \-ˌhwer\ *adv* **:** in, at, or to an unknown or unnamed place

som·nam·bu·lism \säm-ˈnam-byə-ˌli-zəm\ *n* **:** performance of motor acts (as walking) during sleep; *also* **:** an abnormal condition of sleep characterized by this — **som·nam·bu·list** \-list\ *n*

som·no·lent \ˈsäm-nə-lənt\ *adj* **:** SLEEPY, DROWSY — **som·no·lence** \-ləns\ *n*

so·mo·ni \ˌsō-mō-ˈnē\ *n, pl* **somoni** — see MONEY table

son \ˈsən\ *n* **1** : a male offspring or descendant **2** *cap* : Jesus Christ **3** : a person deriving from a particular source (as a country, race, or school)

so·nar \ˈsō-ˌnär\ *n* [*so*und *na*vigation *r*anging] : a method or device for detecting and locating submerged objects (as submarines) by sound waves

so·na·ta \sə-ˈnä-tə\ *n* [It] : an instrumental composition with three or four movements differing in rhythm and mood but related in key

son·a·ti·na \ˌsä-nə-ˈtē-nə\ *n* [It, dim. of *sonata*] : a short usu. simplified sonata

song \ˈsȯŋ\ *n* **1** : vocal music; *also* : a short composition of words and music **2** : poetic composition **3** : a distinctive or characteristic sound (as of a bird) **4** : a small amount ⟨sold for a ~⟩

song·bird \ˈsȯŋ-ˌbərd\ *n* : a bird that utters a series of musical tones

Song of Sol·o·mon \-ˈsä-lə-mən\ — see BIBLE table

Song of Songs — see BIBLE table

song·ster \ˈsȯŋ-stər\ *n* : one that sings

song·stress \-strəs\ *n* : a girl or woman who is a singer

son·ic \ˈsä-nik\ *adj* : of or relating to sound waves or the speed of sound

sonic boom *n* : an explosive sound produced by an aircraft traveling at supersonic speed

son–in–law \ˈsən-ən-ˌlȯ\ *n, pl* **sons–in–law** : the husband of one's daughter or son

son·net \ˈsä-nət\ *n* : a poem of 14 lines usu. in iambic pentameter with a definite rhyme scheme

son of a gun *n, pl* **sons of guns** : an offensive or disagreeable person

so·no·rous \sə-ˈnȯr-əs, ˈsä-nə-rəs\ *adj* **1** : giving out sound when struck **2** : loud, deep, or rich in sound : RESONANT ⟨a ~ voice⟩ **3** : high-sounding : IMPRESSIVE — **so·nor·i·ty** \sə-ˈnȯr-ə-tē\ *n*

soon \ˈsün\ *adv* **1** : before long **2** : PROMPTLY, QUICKLY **3** *archaic* : EARLY **4** : WILLINGLY, READILY

soot \ˈsu̇t, ˈsət, ˈsüt\ *n* : a fine black powder consisting chiefly of carbon that is formed when something burns and that colors smoke — **sooty** *adj*

sooth \ˈsüth\ *n, archaic* : TRUTH

soothe \ˈsüth\ *vb* **soothed; sooth·ing 1** : to please by flattery or attention **2** : RELIEVE, ALLEVIATE ⟨~ a burn⟩ **3** : to calm down : COMFORT ⟨~ a child⟩ — **sooth·er** *n* — **sooth·ing·ly** *adv*

sooth·say·er \ˈsüth-ˌsā-ər\ *n* : one who foretells events — **sooth·say·ing** *n*

¹sop \ˈsäp\ *n* : a conciliatory bribe, gift, or concession

²sop *vb* **sopped; sop·ping 1** : to steep or dip in or as if in a liquid **2** : to wet thoroughly : SOAK; *also* : to mop up (a liquid)

SOP *abbr* standard operating procedure; standing operating procedure

soph *abbr* sophomore

soph·ism \ˈsä-ˌfi-zəm\ *n* **1** : an argument correct in form but embodying a subtle fallacy **2** : SOPHISTRY

soph·ist \ˈsä-fist\ *n* : PHILOSOPHER; *esp* : a captious or fallacious reasoner

so·phis·tic \sä-ˈfis-tik, sə-\ *or* **so·phis·ti·cal** \-ti-kəl\ *adj* : of or characteristic of sophists or sophistry ♦ ***Synonyms*** FALLACIOUS, ILLOGICAL, UNREASONABLE, SPECIOUS

so·phis·ti·cat·ed \sə-ˈfis-tə-ˌkā-təd\ *adj* **1** : COMPLEX ⟨~ instruments⟩ **2** : made worldly-wise by wide experience **3** : intellectually appealing ⟨a ~ novel⟩ — **so·phis·ti·ca·tion** \-ˌfis-tə-ˈkā-shən\ *n*

soph·ist·ry \ˈsä-fə-strē\ *n* : subtly deceptive reasoning or argument

soph·o·more \ˈsäf-ˌmȯr, ˈsä-fə-\ *n* : a student in the second year of high school or college

soph·o·mor·ic \ˌsäf-ˈmȯr-ik, ˌsä-fə-\ *adj* **1** : being overconfident of knowledge but poorly informed and immature ⟨~ reasoning⟩ **2** : of, relating to, or characteristic of a sophomore ⟨~ humor⟩

So·pho·ni·as \ˌsä-fə-ˈnī-əs, ˌsō-\ *n* : ZEPHANIAH

sop·o·rif·ic \ˌsä-pə-ˈri-fik\ *adj* **1** : causing sleep or drowsiness **2** : LETHARGIC

so·pra·no \sə-ˈpra-nō, -ˈprä-\ *n, pl* **-nos** [It, fr. *sopra* above, fr. L *supra*] **1** : the highest singing voice; *also* : a singer with this voice **2** : the highest part in a 4-part chorus — **soprano** *adj*

sor·bet \sȯr-ˈbā\ *n* : a usu. fruit-flavored ice served for dessert or between courses as a palate refresher

sor·cery \ˈsȯr-sə-rē\ *n* [ME *sorcerie,* fr. AF, fr. *sorcer* sorcerer, fr. ML *sortiarius,* fr. L *sort-, sors* chance, lot] : the use of magic : WITCHCRAFT — **sor·cer·er** \-rər\ *n* — **sor·cer·ess** \-rəs\ *n*

sor·did \ˈsȯr-dəd\ *adj* **1** : marked by baseness or grossness : VILE **2** : DIRTY, SQUALID ⟨~ living conditions⟩ — **sor·did·ly** *adv* — **sor·did·ness** *n*

¹sore \ˈsȯr\ *adj* **sor·er; sor·est 1** : causing pain or distress ⟨a ~ bruise⟩ **2** : painfully sensitive ⟨~ muscles⟩ **3** : SEVERE, INTENSE **4** : IRRITATED, ANGRY — **sore·ly** *adv* — **sore·ness** *n*

²sore *n* **1** : a sore spot on the body; *esp* : one (as an ulcer) with the tissues broken and usu. infected **2** : a source of pain or vexation

sore·head \ˈsȯr-ˌhed\ *n* : a person easily angered or discontented

sore throat *n* : painful throat due to inflammation of the fauces and pharynx

sor·ghum \ˈsȯr-gəm\ *n* : a tall variable Old World tropical grass grown widely for its edible seed, for forage, or for its sweet juice which yields a syrup

so·ror·i·ty \sə-ˈrȯr-ə-tē\ *n, pl* **-ties** [ML *sororitas* sisterhood, fr. L *soror* sister] : a club or organization usu. of female students for social purposes

¹sor·rel \ˈsȯr-əl\ *n* : a brownish orange to light brown color; *also* : a sorrel-colored animal (as a horse)

²sorrel *n* : any of various herbs having a sour juice

sor·row \ˈsär-ō\ *n* **1** : deep distress, sadness, or regret; *also* : resultant unhappy or unpleasant state **2** : a cause of grief or sadness **3** : a display of grief or sadness — **sorrow** *vb* — **sor·row·ful** \-fəl\ *adj* — **sor·row·ful·ly** \-f(ə-)lē\ *adv*

sor·ry \ˈsär-ē\ *adj* **sor·ri·er; -est** **1** : feeling sorrow, regret, or penitence ⟨~ for yelling at her⟩ **2** : MOURNFUL, SAD **3** : causing sorrow, pity, or scorn : PITIFUL ⟨a ~ lot of ragamuffins⟩

[1]**sort** \ˈsȯrt\ *n* **1** : a group of persons or things that have similar characteristics : CLASS **2** : QUALITY, NATURE **3** : an instance of sorting — **all sorts of** : many different — **out of sorts** **1** : somewhat ill **2** : GROUCHY, IRRITABLE

[2]**sort** *vb* **1** : to put in a certain place according to kind, class, or nature **2** : to be in accord : AGREE **3** : SEARCH ⟨~ through this mess⟩ — **sort·er** *n*

sor·tie \ˈsȯr-tē, sȯr-ˈtē\ *n* **1** : a sudden issuing of troops from a defensive position against the enemy **2** : one mission or attack by one airplane

sort of *adv* : to a moderate degree

SOS \ˌes-(ˌ)ō-ˈes\ *n* : a call or request for help or rescue

so–so \ˈsō-ˈsō\ *adv or adj* : PASSABLY

sot \ˈsät\ *n* : a habitual drunkard — **sot·tish** *adj* — **sot·tish·ly** *adv*

souf·flé \sü-ˈflā\ *n* [F, fr. *soufflé,* pp. of *souffler* to blow, puff up, fr. OF *sufler,* fr. L *sufflare,* fr. *sub-* up + *flare* to blow] : a spongy dish made light in baking by stiffly beaten egg whites

sough \ˈsau̇, ˈsəft\ *vb* : to make a moaning or sighing sound — **sough** *n*

sought *past and past part of* SEEK

[1]**soul** \ˈsōl\ *n* **1** : the immaterial essence of an individual life **2** : the spiritual principle embodied in human beings or the universe **3** : an active or essential part **4** : the moral and emotional nature of human beings **5** : spiritual or moral force **6** : PERSON ⟨a kindly ~⟩ **7** : a strong, positive feeling (as of intense sensitivity and emotional fervor) conveyed esp. by African American performers **8** : music that is closely related to rhythm and blues and characterized by intensity of feeling — **souled** \ˈsōld\ *adj* — **soul·less** \ˈsōl-ləs\ *adj*

[2]**soul** *adj* **1** : of, relating to, or characteristic of African Americans or their culture ⟨~ food⟩ **2** : designed for or controlled by African Americans ⟨~ radio stations⟩

soul brother *n* : an African American man or boy

soul·ful \ˈsōl-fəl\ *adj* : full of or expressing deep feeling ⟨a ~ ballad⟩ — **soul·ful·ly** *adv*

[1]**sound** \ˈsau̇nd\ *adj* **1** : not diseased or sickly **2** : free from flaw or defect ⟨a ~ structure⟩ **3** : FIRM, STRONG **4** : free from error or fallacy : RIGHT ⟨~ logic⟩ **5** : LEGAL, VALID **6** : THOROUGH **7** : UNDISTURBED ⟨~ sleep⟩ **8** : showing good judgment ⟨~ reasoning⟩ — **sound·ly** *adv* — **sound·ness** *n*

[2]**sound** *n* **1** : the sensation of hearing; *also* : mechanical energy transmitted by longitudinal pressure waves (**sound waves**) (as in air) that is the stimulus to hearing **2** : something heard : NOISE, TONE; *also* : hearing distance : EARSHOT **3** : a musical style ⟨the band's ~⟩ — **sound·less** *adj* — **sound·less·ly** *adv*

[3]**sound** *vb* **1** : to make or cause to make a sound **2** : to order or proclaim by a sound ⟨~ the alarm⟩ **3** : to convey a certain impression : SEEM ⟨that ~*s* like fun⟩ **4** : to examine the condition of by causing to give out sounds — **sound·able** \ˈsau̇n-də-bəl\ *adj*

[4]**sound** *n* : a long passage of water wider than a strait often connecting two larger bodies of water

[5]**sound** *vb* **1** : to measure the depth of (water) esp. by a weighted line dropped from the surface : FATHOM **2** : PROBE **3** : to dive down suddenly ⟨the hooked fish ~*ed*⟩ — **sound·ing** *n*

sound·bar \-ˌbär\ *n* : a bar-shaped audio device that transmits sound (as from a television) by way of internal speakers

sound bite *n* : a brief recorded statement broadcast esp. on a news program — **sound–bite** *adj*

sound card *n* : a circuit board in a computer system designed to produce or reproduce sound

sound·er \ˈsau̇n-dər\ *n* : one that sounds; *esp* : a device for making soundings

sound·proof \ˈsau̇n(d)-ˌprüf\ *vb* : to insulate so as to obstruct the passage of sound — **soundproof** *adj*

sound·stage \ˈsau̇nd-ˌstāj\ *n* : the part of a motion-picture studio in which a production is filmed

sound·track \ˈsau̇n(d)-ˌtrak\ *n* : music recorded to accompany a film or videotape

soup \ˈsüp\ *n* **1** : a liquid food with stock as its base and often containing pieces of solid food **2** : something having the consistency of soup **3** : an unfortunate predicament ⟨in the ~⟩

soup·çon \süp-ˈsōⁿ\ *n* [F, lit., suspicion] : a little bit : [1]TRACE 2 ⟨a ~ of garlic⟩

soup up *vb* : to increase the power of — **souped–up** \ˈsüpt-ˈəp\ *adj*

soupy \ˈsü-pē\ *adj* **soup·i·er; -est** **1** : having the consistency of soup **2** : densely foggy or cloudy

[1]**sour** \ˈsau̇(-ə)r\ *adj* **1** : having an acid or tart taste ⟨~ pickles⟩ **2** : SPOILED, PUTRID ⟨a ~ odor⟩ **3** : UNPLEASANT, DISAGREEABLE ⟨a ~ mood⟩ — **sour·ish** *adj* — **sour·ly** *adv* — **sour·ness** *n*

[2]**sour** *vb* : to become or make sour

source \ˈsȯrs\ *n* **1** : ORIGIN, BEGINNING **2** : a supplier of information **3** : the beginning of a stream of water

source code *n* : a computer program in its original programming language and before translation (as by a compiler)

sous–chef \ˈsü-ˌshef\ *n* : the top assistant chef in a professional kitchen

[1]**souse** \ˈsau̇s\ *vb* **soused; sous·ing** **1** : PICKLE **2** : to plunge into a liquid **3** : DRENCH **4** : to make drunk

[2]**souse** *n* **1** : something (as pigs' feet)

steeped in pickle **2** : a soaking in liquid **3** : DRUNKARD

[1]**south** \ˈsau̇th\ *adv* : to or toward the south; *also* : into a state of decline

[2]**south** *adj* **1** : situated toward or at the south **2** : coming from the south

[3]**south** *n* **1** : the direction to the right of one facing east **2** : the compass point directly opposite to north **3** *cap* : regions or countries south of a specified or implied point; *esp* : the southeastern part of the U.S. — **south·er·ly** \ˈsə-t͟hər-lē\ *adj or adv* — **south·ern** \ˈsə-t͟hərn\ *adj* — **South·ern·er** *n* — **south·ern·most** \-ˌmōst\ *adj* — **south·ward** \ˈsau̇th-wərd\ *adv or adj* — **south·wards** \-wərdz\ *adv*

south·east \sau̇-ˈthēst, *naut* sau̇-ˈēst\ *n* **1** : the general direction between south and east **2** : the compass point midway between south and east **3** *cap* : regions or countries southeast of a specified or implied point — **southeast** *adj or adv* — **south·east·er·ly** *adv or adj* — **south·east·ern** \-ˈēs-tərn\ *adj*

south·paw \ˈsau̇th-ˌpȯ\ *n* : a left-handed person; *esp* : a left-handed baseball pitcher — **southpaw** *adj*

south pole *n, often cap S&P* : the southernmost point of the earth

south·west \sau̇th-ˈwest, *naut* sau̇-ˈwest\ *n* **1** : the general direction between south and west **2** : the compass point midway between south and west **3** *cap* : regions or countries southwest of a specified or implied point — **southwest** *adj or adv* — **south·west·er·ly** *adv or adj* — **south·west·ern** \-ˈwes-tərn\ *adj*

sou·ve·nir \ˌsü-və-ˈnir\ *n* [F] : something serving as a reminder

sou'·west·er \sau̇-ˈwes-tər\ *n* : a long waterproof coat worn at sea in stormy weather; *also* : a waterproof hat

[1]**sov·er·eign** \ˈsä-vrən, -və-rən\ *n* **1** : one possessing the supreme power and authority in a state **2** : a gold coin of the United Kingdom

[2]**sovereign** *adj* **1** : EXCELLENT, FINE **2** : supreme in power or authority **3** : CHIEF, HIGHEST **4** : having independent authority ♦ ***Synonyms*** DOMINANT, PREDOMINANT, PARAMOUNT, PREPONDERANT

sov·er·eign·ty \-tē\ *n, pl* **-ties** **1** : supremacy in rule or power **2** : power to govern without external control **3** : the supreme political power in a state

so·vi·et \ˈsō-vē-ˌet, ˈsä-, -ət\ *n* **1** : an elected governmental council in a Communist country **2** *pl, cap* : the people and esp. the leaders of the U.S.S.R. — **soviet** *adj, often cap* — **so·vi·et·ize** *vb, often cap*

[1]**sow** \ˈsau̇\ *n* : an adult female swine

[2]**sow** \ˈsō\ *vb* **sowed; sown** \ˈsōn\ *or* **sowed; sow·ing** **1** : to plant seed for growing esp. by scattering **2** : to strew with seed **3** : to scatter abroad — **sow·er** \ˈsō-ər\ *n*

sow bug \ˈsau̇-\ *n* : WOOD LOUSE

sox *pl of* SOCK

soy \ˈsȯi\ *n* : a sauce made from soybeans fermented in brine

soy·bean \ˈsȯi-ˌbēn\ *n* : an Asian legume widely grown for forage and for its edible seeds that yield a valuable oil (**soybean oil**); *also* : its seed

sp *abbr* **1** special **2** species **3** specimen **4** spelling **5** spirit

Sp *abbr* Spain

SP *abbr* **1** shore patrol; shore patrolman **2** shore police **3** specialist

spa \ˈspä\ *n* [*Spa,* watering place in Belgium] **1** : a mineral spring; *also* : a resort with mineral springs **2** : a health and fitness facility **3** : a hot tub with a whirlpool device

[1]**space** \ˈspās\ *n* **1** : a period of time **2** : some small measurable distance, area, or volume **3** : the limitless area in which all things exist and move **4** : an empty place **5** : the region beyond the earth's atmosphere **6** : a definite place (as a seat on a train or ship) **7** : the distance from others that a person needs for comfort

[2]**space** *vb* **spaced; spac·ing** **1** : to place at intervals **2** : to fail to remember — **spac·er** *n*

space–age \ˈspās-ˌāj\ *adj* : of or relating to the age of space exploration

space·craft \-ˌkraft\ *n* : a vehicle for travel beyond the earth's atmosphere

space·flight \-ˌflīt\ *n* : flight beyond the earth's atmosphere

space heater *n* : a usu. portable device for heating a relatively small area

space·man \ˈspās-ˌman, -mən\ *n* : one who travels outside the earth's atmosphere

space out *vb* : to become distracted or inattentive

space·ship \-ˌship\ *n* : a vehicle used for space travel

space shuttle *n* : a reusable spacecraft designed to transport people and cargo between earth and space

space station *n* : a large artificial satellite serving as a base (as for scientific observation)

space suit *n* : a suit equipped to make life in space possible for its wearer

space walk *n* : a period of activity outside a spacecraft by an astronaut in space — **space·walk** \ˈspās-ˌwȯk\ *vb* — **space·walk·er** *n*

spa·cious \ˈspā-shəs\ *adj* : very large in extent : ROOMY ♦ ***Synonyms*** COMMODIOUS, CAPACIOUS, AMPLE — **spa·cious·ly** *adv* — **spa·cious·ness** *n*

[1]**spade** \ˈspād\ *n* : a shovel with a blade for digging — **spade·ful** *n*

[2]**spade** *vb* **spad·ed; spad·ing** : to dig with a spade — **spad·er** *n*

[3]**spade** *n* : any of a suit of playing cards marked with a black figure resembling an inverted heart with a short stem at the bottom

spa·dix \ˈspā-diks\ *n, pl* **spa·di·ces** \ˈspā-də-ˌsēz\ : a floral spike with a fleshy or succulent axis usu. enclosed in a spathe

spa·ghet·ti \spə-ˈge-tē\ *n* [It, fr. pl. of *spaghetto,* dim. of *spago* cord, string] : pasta made in thin solid strings

spam \ˈspam\ *n* : unsolicited usu. commercial email sent to a large number of addresses — **spam** *vb*

[1]span \ˈspan\ *n* **1** : an English unit of length equal to nine inches (about 23 centimeters) **2** : a limited portion of time **3** : the spread (as of an arch) from one support to another

[2]span *vb* **spanned; span·ning** **1** : MEASURE **2** : to extend across

[3]span *n* : a pair of animals (as mules) driven together

Span *abbr* Spanish

span·dex \ˈspan-ˌdeks\ *n* : any of various elastic synthetic textile fibers

span·gle \ˈspaŋ-gəl\ *n* : a small disk of shining metal or plastic used esp. on a dress for ornament — **spangle** *vb*

Span·glish \ˈspaŋ-glish\ *n* : Spanish with many English words included; *also* : a combination of Spanish and English

Span·iard \ˈspan-yərd\ *n* : a native or inhabitant of Spain

span·iel \ˈspan-yəl\ *n* [ME *spaynel, spaniell,* fr. AF *espainnel,* alter. of *espaignol,* Spaniard] : a dog of any of several breeds of mostly small and short-legged dogs usu. with long wavy hair and large drooping ears

Span·ish \ˈspa-nish\ *n* **1** : the chief language of Spain and of the countries colonized by the Spanish **2 Spanish** *pl* : the people of Spain — **Spanish** *adj*

Spanish American *n* : a resident of the U.S. whose native language is Spanish and whose culture is of Spanish origin; *also* : a native or inhabitant of one of the countries of America in which Spanish is the national language — **Spanish–American** *adj*

Spanish fly *n* : a toxic preparation of dried green European beetles that causes the skin to blister and is thought to be an aphrodisiac

Spanish moss *n* : a plant related to the pineapple that grows in pendent tufts of grayish green filaments on trees from the southern U.S. to Argentina

Spanish onion *n* : a large mild-flavored onion

spank \ˈspaŋk\ *vb* : to hit on the buttocks with the open hand — **spank** *n*

spank·ing \ˈspaŋ-kiŋ\ *adj* : BRISK, LIVELY ⟨~ breeze⟩ — **spanking** *adv*

[1]spar \ˈspär\ *n* : a rounded wood or metal piece (as a mast, yard, boom, or gaff) for supporting sail rigging

[2]spar *vb* **sparred; spar·ring** : to box for practice without serious hitting; *also* : SKIRMISH, WRANGLE

[1]spare \ˈsper\ *vb* **spared; spar·ing** **1** : to refrain from punishing or injuring : show mercy to **2** : to exempt from something **3** : to get along without ⟨can you ~ ten dollars?⟩ **4** : to use frugally or rarely

[2]spare *adj* **spar·er; spar·est** **1** : held in reserve **2** : SUPERFLUOUS **3** : not liberal or profuse **4** : LEAN, THIN **5** : SCANTY ♦ ***Synonyms*** MEAGER, SPARSE, SKIMPY, EXIGUOUS, SCANT — **spare·ness** *n*

[3]spare *n* **1** : a duplicate kept in reserve; *esp* : a spare tire **2** : the knocking down of all the bowling pins with the first two balls

sparing *adj* : SAVING, FRUGAL ♦ ***Synonyms*** THRIFTY, ECONOMICAL, PROVIDENT — **spar·ing·ly** *adv*

[1]spark \ˈspärk\ *n* **1** : a small particle of a burning substance or a hot glowing particle struck from a mass (as by steel on flint) **2** : a short bright flash of electricity between two points **3** : SPARKLE **4** : a particle capable of being kindled or developed : GERM

[2]spark *vb* **1** : to emit or produce sparks **2** : to stir to activity : INCITE

[3]spark *vb* : WOO, COURT

[1]spar·kle \ˈspär-kəl\ *vb* **spar·kled; spar·kling** **1** : FLASH, GLEAM **2** : to perform brilliantly **3** : EFFERVESCE ⟨*sparkling* wine⟩ — **spar·kler** *n*

[2]sparkle *n* **1** : GLEAM **2** : ANIMATION

spark plug *n* : a device that produces a spark to ignite the fuel mixture in an engine cylinder

spar·row \ˈspa-rō\ *n* : any of several small dull-colored singing birds

sparse \ˈspärs\ *adj* **spars·er; spars·est** : thinly scattered : SCANTY ⟨~ vegetation⟩ ♦ ***Synonyms*** MEAGER, SPARE, SKIMPY, EXIGUOUS, SCANT — **sparse·ly** *adv* — **sparse·ness** *n*

[1]Spar·tan \ˈspär-tᵊn\ *n* **1** : a native or inhabitant of ancient Sparta **2** : a person of great courage and self-discipline

[2]Spartan *adj* **1** : of or relating to Sparta or Spartans **2** *often not cap* : marked by simplicity, frugality, or avoidance of luxury and comfort ⟨a ~ room⟩

spasm \ˈspa-zəm\ *n* **1** : an involuntary and abnormal muscular contraction **2** : a sudden, violent, and temporary effort, emotion, or sensation — **spas·mod·ic** \spaz-ˈmä-dik\ *adj* — **spas·mod·i·cal·ly** \-di-k(ə-)lē\ *adv*

spas·tic \ˈspas-tik\ *adj* : of, relating to, marked by, or affected with muscular spasm ⟨~ paralysis⟩ — **spastic** *n*

[1]spat \ˈspat\ *past and past part of* SPIT

[2]spat *n, pl* **spat** *or* **spats** : a young bivalve mollusk (as an oyster)

[3]spat *n* : a gaiter covering instep and ankle

[4]spat *n* : a brief petty quarrel : DISPUTE

[5]spat *vb* **spat·ted; spat·ting** : to quarrel briefly

spate \ˈspāt\ *n* : a sudden outburst

spathe \ˈspāth\ *n* : a sheathing bract or pair of bracts enclosing an inflorescence (as of the calla lily) and esp. a spadix on the same axis

spa·tial \ˈspā-shəl\ *adj* : of or relating to space or to the facility to perceive objects in space — **spa·tial·ly** *adv*

spat·ter \ˈspa-tər\ *vb* **1** : to splash with drops of liquid ⟨clothes ~*ed* with paint⟩ **2** : to sprinkle around — **spatter** *n*

spat·u·la \ˈspa-chə-lə\ *n* : a flexible knifelike implement for scooping, spreading, or mixing soft substances

spav·in \ˈspa-vən\ *n* : a bony enlargement of the hock of a horse — **spav·ined** \-vənd\ *adj*

[1]**spawn** \'spȯn\ *vb* [ME, fr. AF *espandre* to spread out, shed, scatter, spawn, fr. L *expandere,* fr. *ex-* out + *pandere* to spread] **1 :** to produce eggs or offspring esp. in large numbers **2 :** GENERATE ⟨~*ed* much protest⟩ — **spawn·er** *n*

[2]**spawn** *n* **1 :** the eggs of water animals (as fishes or oysters) that lay many small eggs **2 :** offspring esp. when produced in great numbers

spay \'spā\ *vb* **spayed; spay·ing :** to remove the ovaries of (a female animal)

SPCA *abbr* Society for the Prevention of Cruelty to Animals

SPCC *abbr* Society for the Prevention of Cruelty to Children

speak \'spēk\ *vb* **spoke** \'spōk\; **spo·ken** \'spō-kən\; **speak·ing** **1 :** to utter words **2 :** to express orally **3 :** to mention in speech or writing **4 :** to address an audience **5 :** to use or be able to use (a language) in talking — **to speak of :** worthy of mention ⟨no progress *to speak of*⟩

speak·easy \'spēk-ˌē-zē\ *n, pl* **-eas·ies :** an illicit drinking place

speak·er \'spē-kər\ *n* **1 :** one that speaks **2 :** the presiding officer of a deliberative assembly **3 :** LOUDSPEAKER

[1]**spear** \'spir\ *n* **1 :** a long-shafted weapon with a sharp point for thrusting or throwing **2 :** a sharp-pointed instrument with barbs used in spearing fish — **spear·man** \-mən\ *n*

[2]**spear** *vb* **:** to strike or pierce with or as if with a spear — **spear·er** *n*

[3]**spear** *n* **:** a usu. young blade, shoot, or sprout (as of asparagus)

spear·head \-ˌhed\ *n* **:** a leading force, element, or influence — **spearhead** *vb*

spear·mint \-ˌmint\ *n* **:** a common highly aromatic garden mint

[1]**spec** *abbr* **1** special; specialist **2** specifically

[2]**spec** \'spek\ *n* **:** SPECIFICATION 2 — usu. used in pl.

spe·cial \'spe-shəl\ *adj* **1 :** UNCOMMON, NOTEWORTHY **2 :** particularly favored **3 :** INDIVIDUAL, UNIQUE **4 :** EXTRA, ADDITIONAL **5 :** confined to or designed for a definite field of action, purpose, or occasion ⟨a ~ assignment⟩ — **special** *n*

special delivery *n* **:** delivery of mail by messenger for an extra fee

special effects *n pl* **:** visual or sound effects introduced into a motion picture, video recording, or taped television production

Special Forces *n pl* **:** a branch of the army composed of soldiers specially trained in guerrilla warfare

spe·cial·ise *Brit var of* SPECIALIZE

spe·cial·ist \'spe-shə-list\ *n* **1 :** a person who specializes in a particular branch of learning or activity **2 :** a rank in the U.S. Army corresponding to that of corporal

spe·cial·ize \'spe-shə-ˌlīz\ *vb* **-ized; -iz·ing :** to concentrate one's efforts in a special activity or field; *also* **:** to change in an adaptive manner — **spe·cial·i·za·tion** \ˌspe-shə-lə-'zā-shən\ *n*

spe·cial·ly \'spe-shə-lē\ *adv* **1 :** in a special manner **2 :** for a special purpose **:** in particular

spe·cial·ty \'spe-shəl-tē\ *n, pl* **-ties** **1 :** a particular quality or detail **2 :** a product of a special kind or of special excellence **3 :** a skill or discipline in which one specializes ⟨the doctor's ~ is dermatology⟩

spe·cie \'spē-shē, -sē\ *n* **:** money in coin

spe·cies \'spē-shēz, -sēz\ *n, pl* **spe·cies** [ME, fr. L, appearance, kind, species, fr. *specere* to look] **1 :** SORT, KIND **2 :** a category of biological classification ranking just below the genus or subgenus and comprising closely related organisms potentially able to breed with one another

spe·cies·ism \'spē-shēz-ˌi-zəm, -sēz-\ *n* **:** discrimination against animals; *also* **:** the assumption of human superiority on which such discrimination is based

specif *abbr* specific; specifically

[1]**spe·cif·ic** \spi-'si-fik\ *adj* **1 :** having a unique effect or influence or reacting in only one way or with only one thing ⟨~ antibodies⟩ ⟨~ enzymes⟩ **2 :** DEFINITE, EXACT ⟨a ~ agreement⟩ **3 :** of, relating to, or constituting a species — **spe·cif·i·cal·ly** \-fi-k(ə-)lē\ *adv* — **spec·i·fic·i·ty** \ˌspe-sə-'fi-sə-tē\ *n*

[2]**specific** *n* **:** something specific **:** DETAIL, PARTICULAR — usu. used in pl.

spec·i·fi·ca·tion \ˌspe-sə-fə-'kā-shən\ *n* **1 :** the act or process of specifying **2 :** a description of work to be done and materials to be used (as in building) — usu. used in pl.

specific gravity *n* **:** the ratio of the density of a substance to the density of some substance (as water) taken as a standard when both densities are obtained by weighing in air

spec·i·fy \'spe-sə-ˌfī\ *vb* **-fied; -fy·ing :** to mention or name explicitly

spec·i·men \'spe-sə-mən\ *n* **:** an item or part typical of a group or whole

spe·cious \'spē-shəs\ *adj* **:** seeming to be genuine, correct, or beautiful but not really so ⟨~ reasoning⟩

speck \'spek\ *n* **1 :** a small spot or blemish **2 :** a small particle — **speck** *vb*

speck·le \'spe-kəl\ *n* **:** a little speck — **speckle** *vb*

specs \'speks\ *n pl, chiefly Brit* **:** GLASSES

spec·ta·cle \'spek-ti-kəl\ *n* **1 :** an unusual or impressive public display **2** *pl* **:** GLASSES — **spec·ta·cled** \-kəld\ *adj*

spec·tac·u·lar \spek-'ta-kyə-lər\ *adj* **:** exciting to see **:** SENSATIONAL

spec·ta·tor \'spek-ˌtā-tər\ *n* **:** a person who looks on (as at a sports event) ♦ ***Synonyms*** OBSERVER, WITNESS, BYSTANDER, ONLOOKER, EYEWITNESS

spec·ter *or* **spec·tre** \'spek-tər\ *n* **:** a visible disembodied spirit **:** GHOST

spec·tral \'spek-trəl\ *adj* **1 :** of, relating to, or resembling a specter **2 :** of, relating to, or made by a spectrum

spec·tro·gram \'spek-trə-ˌgram\ *n* **:** a photograph, image, or diagram of a spectrum

spec·tro·graph \-ˌgraf\ *n* : an instrument for dispersing radiation into a spectrum and recording or mapping the spectrum — **spec·tro·graph·ic** \ˌspek-trə-ˈgra-fik\ *adj* — **spec·tro·graph·i·cal·ly** \-fi-k(ə-)lē\ *adv*

spec·trom·e·ter \spek-ˈträ-mə-tər\ *n* : an instrument for measuring spectra — **spec·tro·met·ric** \ˌspek-trə-ˈme-trik\ *adj* — **spec·trom·e·try** \spek-ˈträ-mə-trē\ *n*

spec·tro·scope \ˈspek-trə-ˌskōp\ *n* : an instrument that produces spectra esp. of visible electromagnetic radiation — **spec·tro·scop·ic** \ˌspek-trə-ˈskä-pik\ *adj* — **spec·tro·scop·i·cal·ly** \-pi-k(ə-)lē\ *adv* — **spec·tros·co·pist** \spek-ˈträs-kə-pist\ *n* — **spec·tros·co·py** \-pē\ *n*

spec·trum \ˈspek-trəm\ *n, pl* **spec·tra** \-trə\ *or* **spectrums** [NL, fr. L, appearance, fr. *specere* to look] **1** : a series of colors formed when a beam of white light is dispersed (as by a prism) so that its parts are arranged in the order of their wavelengths **2** : a series of radiations arranged in regular order **3** : a continuous sequence or range ⟨a wide ~ of opinions⟩

spec·u·late \ˈspe-kyə-ˌlāt\ *vb* **-lat·ed; -lat·ing** [L *speculari* to spy out, examine, fr. *specula* lookout post, fr. *specere* to look, look at] **1** : to think or wonder about a subject **2** : to take a business risk in hope of gain ♦ *Synonyms* REASON, THINK, DELIBERATE, COGITATE — **spec·u·la·tion** \ˌspe-kyə-ˈlā-shən\ *n* — **spec·u·la·tive** \ˈspe-kyə-ˌlā-tiv\ *adj* — **spec·u·la·tive·ly** *adv* — **spec·u·la·tor** \-ˌlā-tər\ *n*

speech \ˈspēch\ *n* **1** : the act of speaking **2** : TALK, CONVERSATION **3** : a public talk or lecture **4** : LANGUAGE, DIALECT **5** : an individual manner of speaking **6** : the power of speaking — **speech·less** *adj*

[1]**speed** \ˈspēd\ *n* **1** *archaic* : SUCCESS **2** : SWIFTNESS, RAPIDITY **3** : rate of motion or performance **4** : a transmission gear (as of a bicycle) **5** : METHAMPHETAMINE; *also* : a related drug ♦ *Synonyms* HASTE, HURRY, DISPATCH, CELERITY — **speed·i·ly** \ˈspē-də-lē\ *adv* — **speedy** *adj*

[2]**speed** *vb* **sped** \ˈsped\ *or* **speed·ed; speed·ing** **1** *archaic* : PROSPER; *also* : GET ALONG, FARE **2** : to go fast; *esp* : to go at an excessive or illegal speed **3** : to cause to go faster — **speed·er** *n*

speed·boat \-ˌbōt\ *n* : a fast motorboat

speed bump *n* : a low raised ridge across a roadway (as in a parking lot) to limit vehicle speed

speed of light : a fundamental physical constant that is the speed of electromagnetic radiation propagation in a vacuum and has the value of 299,792,458 meters per second

speed·om·e·ter \spi-ˈdä-mə-tər\ *n* : an instrument for indicating speed

speed·up \ˈspēd-ˌəp\ *n* : ACCELERATION

speed·way \-ˌwā\ *n* : a racecourse for motor vehicles

speed·well \ˈspēd-ˌwel\ *n* : VERONICA

[1]**spell** \ˈspel\ *vb* **spelled** \ˈspeld, ˈspelt\; **spell·ing** [ME, to signify, read by spelling out, fr. AF *espeleir,* of Gmc origin] **1** : to name, write, or print in order the letters of a word **2** : MEAN ⟨another drought may ~ famine⟩

[2]**spell** *n* [ME, talk, tale, fr. OE] **1** : a magic formula : INCANTATION **2** : a compelling influence ⟨under the ~ of a guru⟩

[3]**spell** *n* **1** : one's turn at work or duty **2** : a stretch of a specified kind of weather **3** : a period of bodily or mental distress or disorder : ATTACK ⟨a dizzy ~⟩

[4]**spell** *vb* **spelled** \ˈspeld\; **spell·ing** : to take the place of for a time in work or duty : RELIEVE

spell·bind·er \-ˌbīn-dər\ *n* : a speaker of compelling eloquence; *also* : one that compels attention

spell·bound \-ˌbau̇nd\ *adj* : held by or as if by a spell : FASCINATED

spell·check·er \ˈspel-ˌche-kər\ *n* : a computer program that identifies possible misspellings in a block of text — **spell–check** \-ˌchek\ *vb*

spell·er \ˈspe-lər\ *n* **1** : one who spells words **2** : a book with exercises for teaching spelling

spelt \ˈspelt\ *chiefly Brit past and past part of* [1]SPELL

spe·lunk·er \spi-ˈləŋ-kər, ˈspē-ˌləŋ-kər\ *n* [L *spelunca* cave, fr. Gk *spēlynx*] : one who makes a hobby of exploring caves — **spe·lunk·ing** *n*

spend \ˈspend\ *vb* **spent** \ˈspent\; **spend·ing** **1** : to pay out : EXPEND **2** : WEAR OUT, EXHAUST; *also* : to consume wastefully **3** : to cause or permit to elapse : PASS — **spend·er** *n*

spend·thrift \ˈspend-ˌthrift\ *n* : one who spends wastefully or recklessly

spent \ˈspent\ *adj* : drained of energy

sperm \ˈspərm\ *n, pl* **sperm** *or* **sperms** **1** : SEMEN **2** : a male gamete

sper·ma·to·zo·on \(ˌ)spər-ˌma-tə-ˈzō-ˌän, -ˈzō-ən\ *n, pl* **-zoa** \-ˈzō-ə\ : a motile male gamete of an animal usu. with a rounded or elongated head and a long posterior flagellum

sperm cell *n* : SPERM 2

sper·mi·cide \ˈspər-mə-ˌsīd\ *n* : a preparation or substance used to kill sperm — **sper·mi·cid·al** \ˌspər-mə-ˈsī-dəl\ *adj*

sperm whale *n* : a large whale with a massive square-shaped head containing a fluid-filled cavity

spew \ˈspyü\ *vb* : VOMIT

SPF *abbr* sun protection factor

sp gr *abbr* specific gravity

sphag·num \ˈsfag-nəm\ *n* : any of a genus of atypical mosses that grow in wet acid areas where their remains become compacted with other plant debris to form peat; *also* : a mass of these mosses

sphere \ˈsfir\ *n* [ME *spere* globe, celestial sphere, fr. AF *espere,* fr. L *sphaera,* fr. Gk *sphaira,* lit., ball] **1** : a globe-shaped body : BALL **2** : a celestial body **3** : a solid figure so shaped that every point on its surface is an equal distance from the center **4** : range of action or influence —

spher·i·cal \ˈsfir-i-kəl, ˈsfer-\ *adj* — **spher·i·cal·ly** \-i-k(ə-)lē\ *adv*

spher·oid \ˈsfir-ˌȯid, ˈsfer-\ *n* : a figure similar to a sphere but not perfectly round — **sphe·roi·dal** \sfir-ˈȯi-dəl\ *adj*

sphinc·ter \ˈsfiŋk-tər\ *n* : a muscular ring that closes a bodily opening

sphinx \ˈsfiŋks\ *n, pl* **sphinx·es** *or* **sphin·ges** \ˈsfin-ˌjēz\ **1** : a winged monster in Greek mythology having a woman's head and a lion's body and noted for killing anyone unable to answer its riddle **2** : an enigmatic or mysterious person **3** : an ancient Egyptian image having the body of a lion and the head of a man, ram, or hawk

spice \ˈspīs\ *n* **1** : any of various aromatic plant products (as pepper or nutmeg) used to season or flavor foods **2** : something that adds interest and relish — **spice** *vb* — **spicy** *adj*

spick–and–span *or* **spic–and–span** \ˌspik-ənd-ˈspan\ *adj* : quite new; *also* : spotlessly clean

spic·ule \ˈspi-kyül\ *n* : a slender pointed body esp. of calcium or silica

spi·der \ˈspī-dər\ *n* **1** : any of an order of arachnids that have a 2-part body, eight legs, and two or more pairs of abdominal organs for spinning threads of silk used esp. in making webs for catching prey **2** : a cast-iron frying pan — **spi·dery** *adj*

spider mite *n* : any of various small web-spinning mites that feed on and are pests of plants

spider plant *n* : a houseplant of the asparagus family having long green leaves usu. striped with white and producing tufts of small plants on long hanging stems

spi·der·web \ˈspī-dər-ˌweb\ *n* : the web spun by a spider

spiel \ˈspēl\ *vb* : to talk in a fast, smooth, and usu. colorful manner — **spiel** *n*

spig·ot \ˈspi-gət, -kət\ *n* : FAUCET

¹**spike** \ˈspīk\ *n* **1** : a very large nail **2** : any of various pointed projections (as on the sole of a shoe to prevent slipping) — **spiky** *adj*

²**spike** *vb* **spiked; spik·ing** **1** : to fasten with spikes **2** : to put an end to : QUASH ⟨~ a rumor⟩ **3** : to pierce with or impale on a spike **4** : to add alcoholic liquor to (a drink)

³**spike** *n* **1** : an ear of grain **2** : a long cluster of usu. stemless flowers

¹**spill** \ˈspil\ *vb* **spilled** \ˈspild, ˈspilt\ *also* **spilt** \ˈspilt\; **spill·ing** **1** : to cause or allow to fall, flow, or run out esp. unintentionally **2** : to cause (blood) to be lost by wounding **3** : to run out or over with resulting loss or waste **4** : to let out : DIVULGE — **spill·able** *adj*

²**spill** *n* **1** : an act of spilling; *also* : a fall from a horse or vehicle or an erect position **2** : something spilled

spill·way \-ˌwā\ *n* : a passage for surplus water to run over or around an obstruction (as a dam)

¹**spin** \ˈspin\ *vb* **spun** \ˈspən\; **spin·ning** **1** : to draw out (fiber) and twist into thread; *also* : to form (thread) by such means **2** : to form thread by extruding a sticky quickly hardening fluid; *also* : to construct from such thread ⟨spiders ~ their webs⟩ **3** : to produce slowly and by degrees ⟨~ a story⟩ **4** : TWIRL **5** : WHIRL, REEL ⟨my head is *spinning*⟩ **6** : to move rapidly along **7** : to present (as information) with a particular spin — **spin·ner** *n*

²**spin** *n* **1** : a rapid rotating motion **2** : an excursion in a wheeled vehicle **3** : a particular point of view, emphasis, or interpretation

spi·na bi·fi·da \ˌspī-nə-ˈbi-fə-də\ *n* : a birth defect in which the spinal column has a fissure

spin·ach \ˈspi-nich\ *n* : a dark green herb grown for its edible leaves

spi·nal \ˈspī-nᵊl\ *adj* : of or relating to the backbone or spinal cord — **spi·nal·ly** *adv*

spinal column *n* : BACKBONE 1

spinal cord *n* : the thick cord of nervous tissue that extends from the brain along the back in the cavity of the backbone and carries nerve impulses to and from the brain

spinal nerve *n* : any of the paired nerves which arise from the spinal cord and pass to various parts of the body and of which there are normally 31 pairs in human beings

spin control *n* : the act or practice of attempting to manipulate the way an event is interpreted

spin·dle \ˈspin-dᵊl\ *n* **1** : a round tapering stick or rod by which fibers are twisted in spinning **2** : a turned part of a piece of furniture ⟨the ~*s* of a chair⟩ **3** : a slender pin or rod which turns or on which something else turns

spin·dling \ˈspind-liŋ\ *adj* : SPINDLY

spin·dly \ˈspind-lē\ *adj* : being long or tall and thin and usu. weak

spin·drift \ˈspin-ˌdrift\ *n* : spray blown from waves

spine \ˈspīn\ *n* **1** : BACKBONE **2** : a stiff sharp process esp. on a plant or animal **3** : the part of a book where the pages are attached — **spiny** *adj*

spi·nel \spə-ˈnel\ *n* : a hard crystalline mineral of variable color used as a gem

spine·less \ˈspīn-ləs\ *adj* **1** : having no spines, thorns, or prickles **2** : lacking a backbone **3** : lacking courage or determination ⟨a ~ politician⟩

spin·et \ˈspi-nət\ *n* **1** : an early harpsichord having a single keyboard and only one string for each note **2** : a small upright piano

spin·na·ker \ˈspi-ni-kər\ *n* : a large triangular sail set on a long light pole

spinning jen·ny \-ˈje-nē\ *n* : an early multiple-spindle machine for spinning wool or cotton

spinning wheel *n* : a small machine for spinning thread or yarn in which a large wheel drives a single spindle

spin–off \ˈspin-ˌȯf\ *n* **1** : a usu. useful by-product **2** : something (as a TV show) derived from an earlier work — **spin off** *vb*

spin·ster \ˈspin-stər\ *n* : an unmarried woman past the common age for marrying — **spin·ster·hood** \-ˌhu̇d\ *n*

spiny lobster *n* : any of several edible crustaceans differing from the related lobsters in lacking the large front claws and in having a spiny carapace

¹**spi·ral** \ˈspī-rəl\ *adj* : winding or coiling around a center or axis and usu. getting closer to or farther away from it — **spi·ral·ly** *adv*

²**spiral** *n* **1** : something that has a spiral form; *also* : a single turn in a spiral object **2** : a continuously spreading and accelerating increase or decrease

³**spiral** *vb* **-raled** *or* **-ralled**; **-ral·ing** *or* **-ral·ling** **1** : to move and esp. to rise or fall in a spiral course **2** : to form into a spiral

spi·rant \ˈspī-rənt\ *n* : a consonant (as \f\, \s\, \sh\) uttered with decided friction of the breath against some part of the oral passage — **spirant** *adj*

spire \ˈspī(-ə)r\ *n* **1** : a slender tapering stalk (as of grass) **2** : a pointed tip (as of an antler) **3** : STEEPLE — **spiry** *adj*

spi·rea *or* **spi·raea** \spī-ˈrē-ə\ *n* : any of a genus of shrubs related to the roses with dense clusters of small usu. white or pink flowers

¹**spir·it** \ˈspir-ət\ *n* [ME, fr. AF or L; AF, fr. L *spiritus,* lit., breath, fr. *spirare* to blow, breathe] **1** : a life-giving force; *also* : the animating principle : SOUL **2** *cap* : HOLY SPIRIT **3** : SPECTER, GHOST **4** : PERSON ⟨a bold ~⟩ **5** : DISPOSITION, MOOD ⟨in good ~*s*⟩ **6** : VIVACITY, ARDOR **7** : essential or real meaning : INTENT **8** : distilled alcoholic liquor **9** : LOYALTY ⟨school ~⟩ — **spir·it·less** *adj*

²**spirit** *vb* : to carry off secretly or mysteriously

spir·it·ed \ˈspir-ə-təd\ *adj* : full of energy, animation, or courage

¹**spir·i·tu·al** \ˈspir-i-chəl, -chə-wəl\ *adj* **1** : of, relating to, consisting of, or affecting the spirit : INCORPOREAL ⟨~ needs⟩ **2** : of or relating to sacred matters **3** : ecclesiastical rather than lay or temporal — **spir·i·tu·al·i·ty** \ˌspir-i-chə-ˈwa-lə-tē\ *n* — **spir·i·tu·al·ize** \ˈspir-i-chə-ˌlīz, -chə-wə-\ *vb* — **spir·i·tu·al·ly** *adv*

²**spiritual** *n* : a religious song originating among Black people of the southern U.S.

spir·i·tu·al·ism \ˈspir-i-chə-ˌli-zəm, -chə-wə-\ *n* : a belief that spirits of the dead communicate with the living usu. through a medium — **spir·i·tu·al·ist** \-list\ *n, often cap* — **spir·i·tu·al·is·tic** \ˌspir-i-chə-ˈlis-tik, -chə-wə-\ *adj*

spir·i·tu·ous \ˈspir-i-chəs, -chə-wəs; ˈspir-ə-təs\ *adj* : containing alcohol

spi·ro·chete *also* **spi·ro·chaete** \ˈspī-rə-ˌkēt\ *n* : any of an order of spirally undulating bacteria including those causing syphilis and Lyme disease

spirt *var of* SPURT

¹**spit** \ˈspit\ *n* **1** : a thin pointed rod for holding meat over a fire **2** : a point of land that runs out into the water

²**spit** *vb* **spit·ted; spit·ting** : to pierce with or as if with a spit

³**spit** *vb* **spit** *or* **spat** \ˈspat\; **spit·ting** **1** : to eject (saliva) from the mouth **2** : to express by or as if by spitting **3** : to rain or snow lightly

⁴**spit** *n* **1** : SALIVA **2** : perfect likeness ⟨~ and image of his father⟩

spit·ball \ˈspit-ˌbȯl\ *n* **1** : paper chewed and rolled into a ball to be thrown as a missile **2** : a baseball pitch delivered after the ball has been moistened with saliva or sweat

¹**spite** \ˈspīt\ *n* : ill will with a wish to annoy, anger, or frustrate : petty malice ♦ ***Synonyms*** MALIGNITY, SPLEEN, GRUDGE, MALEVOLENCE — **spite·ful** \-fəl\ *adj* — **spite·ful·ly** *adv* — **spite·ful·ness** *n* — **in spite of** : in defiance or contempt of : NOTWITHSTANDING

²**spite** *vb* **spit·ed; spit·ing** : to treat maliciously : ANNOY, OFFEND

spit·tle \ˈspi-tᵊl\ *n* : SALIVA

spit·tle·bug \-ˌbəg\ *n* : any of a family of leaping insects with froth-secreting larvae that are related to aphids

spit·toon \spi-ˈtün\ *n* : a receptacle for spit

splash \ˈsplash\ *vb* **1** : to dash a liquid about **2** : to scatter a liquid on : SPATTER **3** : to fall or strike with a splashing noise ♦ ***Synonyms*** SPRINKLE, BESPATTER, DOUSE, SPLATTER — **splash** *n*

splash·down \ˈsplash-ˌdau̇n\ *n* : the landing of a crewed spacecraft in the ocean — **splash down** *vb*

splashy \ˈspla-shē\ *adj* **splash·i·er; -est** : conspicuously showy : OSTENTATIOUS

¹**splat·ter** \ˈspla-tər\ *vb* : SPATTER — **splatter** *n*

²**splatter** *adj* : extremely gory or violent ⟨a ~ movie⟩

¹**splay** \ˈsplā\ *vb* : to spread outward or apart ⟨~*ed* out her fingers⟩ — **splay** *n*

²**splay** *adj* **1** : spread out : turned outward **2** : AWKWARD, CLUMSY

spleen \ˈsplēn\ *n* **1** : a vascular organ located near the stomach in most vertebrates that is concerned esp. with the filtration and storage of blood, destruction of red blood cells, and production of lymphocytes **2** : SPITE, MALICE ♦ ***Synonyms*** MALIGNITY, GRUDGE, MALEVOLENCE, ILL WILL, SPITEFULNESS

splen·did \ˈsplen-dəd\ *adj* [L *splendidus,* fr. *splendēre* to shine] **1** : SHINING, BRILLIANT **2** : SHOWY, GORGEOUS **3** : ILLUSTRIOUS **4** : EXCELLENT ⟨a ~ opportunity⟩ ♦ ***Synonyms*** RESPLENDENT, GLORIOUS, SUBLIME, SUPERB — **splen·did·ly** *adv*

splen·dor \ˈsplen-dər\ *n* **1** : BRILLIANCE ⟨the ~ of the sun⟩ **2** : POMP, MAGNIFICENCE

splen·dour \ˈsplen-dər\ *chiefly Brit var of* SPLENDOR

sple·net·ic \spli-ˈne-tik\ *adj* : marked by bad temper or spite

splen·ic \ˈsple-nik\ *adj* : of, relating to, or located in the spleen

splice \ˈsplīs\ *vb* **spliced; splic·ing** **1** : to unite (as two ropes) by weaving the strands together **2** : to unite (as two lengths of film) by connecting the ends together — **splice** *n*

splint \ˈsplint\ *n* **1** : a thin strip of wood interwoven with others to make something (as a basket) **2** : material or a device used to protect and keep in place an injured body part (as a broken arm)

[1]**splin·ter** \ˈsplin-tər\ *n* : a thin piece of something split off lengthwise : SLIVER

[2]**splinter** *vb* : to split into splinters

split \ˈsplit\ *vb* **split; split·ting** **1** : to divide lengthwise or along a grain or seam **2** : to burst or break in pieces **3** : to divide into parts or sections **4** : LEAVE ⟨~ the party⟩ ♦ ***Synonyms*** REND, CLEAVE, RIP, TEAR — **split** *n*

split–lev·el \ˈsplit-ˈle-vəl\ *n* : a house divided so that the floor in one part is about halfway between two floors in the other

split personality *n* : SCHIZOPHRENIA; *also* : MULTIPLE PERSONALITY DISORDER

split–second \ˈsplit-ˈse-kənd\ *adj* **1** : occurring in a very brief time **2** : extremely precise ⟨~ timing⟩

split·ting *adj* : causing a piercing sensation ⟨a ~ headache⟩

splotch \ˈspläch\ *n* : BLOTCH

splurge \ˈsplərj\ *vb* **splurged; splurg·ing** : to spend more than usual esp. on oneself — **splurge** *n*

splut·ter \ˈsplə-tər\ *n* : SPUTTER — **splutter** *vb*

[1]**spoil** \ˈspȯi(-ə)l\ *n* : PLUNDER ⟨~*s* of war⟩

[2]**spoil** *vb* **spoiled** \ˈspȯi(-ə)ld, ˈspȯi(-ə)lt\ *or* **spoilt** \ˈspȯi(-ə)lt\; **spoil·ing** **1** : ROB, PILLAGE **2** : to damage seriously : RUIN **3** : to impair the quality or effect of **4** : to damage the disposition of by pampering; *also* : INDULGE, CODDLE **5** : DECAY, ROT **6** : to have an eager desire ⟨~*ing* for a fight⟩ ♦ ***Synonyms*** INJURE, HARM, HURT, MAR — **spoil·age** \ˈspȯi-lij\ *n*

spoil·er \ˈspȯi-lər\ *n* **1** : one that spoils **2** : a device (as on an airplane or automobile) used to disrupt airflow and decrease lift **3** : information about a movie or TV plot that can spoil a viewer's sense of surprise or suspense

spoil·sport \ˈspȯi(-ə)l-ˌspȯrt\ *n* : one who spoils the fun of others

[1]**spoke** \ˈspōk\ *past & archaic past part of* SPEAK

[2]**spoke** *n* : any of the rods extending from the hub of a wheel to the rim

spo·ken \ˈspō-kən\ *past part of* SPEAK

spokes·man \ˈspōks-mən\ *n* SPOKESPERSON

spokes·mod·el \-ˌmä-dᵊl\ *n* : a model who is a spokesperson

spokes·per·son \-ˌpər-sən\ *n* : a person who speaks as the representative of another or others

spokes·wom·an \-ˌwu̇-mən\ *n* : a woman who speaks as the representative of another or others

spo·li·a·tion \ˌspō-lē-ˈā-shən\ *n* : the act of plundering : the state of being plundered

[1]**sponge** \ˈspənj\ *n* **1** : an elastic porous water-absorbing mass of fibers that forms the skeleton of various primitive sea animals; *also* : any of a phylum of chiefly marine sea animals that are the source of natural sponges **2** : a spongelike or porous mass or material — **spongy** \ˈspən-jē\ *adj*

[2]**sponge** *vb* **sponged; spong·ing** **1** : to bathe or wipe with a sponge **2** : to live at another's expense **3** : to gather sponges — **spong·er** *n*

sponge cake *n* : a light cake made without shortening

sponge rubber *n* : a cellular rubber resembling natural sponge

spon·sor \ˈspän-sər\ *n* [LL, fr. L, guarantor, surety, fr. *spondēre* to promise] **1** : one who takes the responsibility for some other person or thing : SURETY **2** : GODPARENT **3** : a business firm that pays the cost of a radio or television program usu. in return for advertising time during its course — **sponsor** *vb* — **spon·sor·ship** *n*

spon·ta·ne·ous \spän-ˈtā-nē-əs\ *adj* [LL *spontaneus,* fr. L *sponte* of one's free will, voluntarily] **1** : done or produced freely or naturally **2** : acting or taking place without external force or cause ♦ ***Synonyms*** IMPULSIVE, INSTINCTIVE, AUTOMATIC, UNPREMEDITATED — **spon·ta·ne·ity** \ˌspän-tə-ˈnē-ə-tē, -ˈnā-\ *n* — **spon·ta·ne·ous·ly** *adv*

spontaneous combustion *n* : a bursting into flame of material through heat produced within itself by chemical action (as oxidation)

spoof \ˈspüf\ *vb* **1** : DECEIVE, HOAX **2** : to make good-natured fun of ⟨the movie ~*s* horror films⟩ — **spoof** *n*

[1]**spook** \ˈspük\ *n* **1** : GHOST, APPARITION **2** : SPY 2 — **spooky** *adj*

[2]**spook** *vb* : FRIGHTEN

[1]**spool** \ˈspül\ *n* : a cylinder on which flexible material (as thread) is wound

[2]**spool** *vb* **1** : to wind on a spool **2** : to regulate data flow by means of a spooler

spool·er \ˈspü-lər\ *n* : a computer program or routine for regulating data flow

spoon \ˈspün\ *n* [ME, fr. OE *spōn* splinter, chip] **1** : an eating or cooking implement consisting of a small shallow bowl with a handle **2** : a metal piece used on a fishing line as a lure — **spoon** *vb* — **spoon·ful** *n*

spoon·bill \ˈspün-ˌbil\ *n* : any of several wading birds related to the ibises that have a bill with a broad flat tip

spoon–feed \-ˌfēd\ *vb* **-fed** \-ˌfed\; **-feed·ing** : to feed by means of a spoon

spoor \ˈspu̇r, ˈspȯr\ *n, pl* **spoor** *or* **spoors** : a track, a trail, a scent, or droppings esp. of a wild animal

spo·rad·ic \spə-ˈra-dik\ *adj* : occurring now and then ⟨~ outbreaks of disease⟩ ♦ ***Synonyms*** OCCASIONAL, RARE, SCARCE, INFREQUENT, UNCOMMON — **spo·rad·i·cal·ly** \-di-k(ə-)lē\ *adv*

spore \ˈspȯr\ *n* : a primitive usu. one-celled often environmentally resistant dormant or reproductive body produced by plants, fungi, and some microorganisms

spork \ˈspȯrk\ *n* : an eating utensil that combines the bowl of a spoon with the tines of a fork

¹**sport** \ˈspȯrt\ *vb* [ME, to divert, amuse, short for *disporten,* fr. AF *desporter,* to carry away, comfort, entertain, fr. *des-* (fr. L *dis-* apart) + *porter* to carry, fr. L *portare*] **1** : to amuse oneself : FROLIC **2** : SHOW OFF 1 ⟨~*ing* new shoes⟩ — **sport·ive** *adj*

²**sport** *n* **1** : a source of diversion : PASTIME **2** : physical activity engaged in for pleasure **3** : JEST **4** : MOCKERY ⟨make ~ of his efforts⟩ **5** : BUTT, LAUGHINGSTOCK **6** : one who accepts results cheerfully whether favorable or not **7** : an individual exhibiting marked deviation from its normal type esp. as a result of mutation ♦ ***Synonyms*** PLAY, FROLIC, FUN, RECREATION — **sporty** *adj*

³**sport** *or* **sports** *adj* : of, relating to, or suitable for sport or casual wear ⟨~ coats⟩

sport fish *n* : a fish noted for the sport it affords anglers

sports·cast \ˈspȯrts-ˌkast\ *n* : a broadcast dealing with sports events — **sports·cast·er** \-ˌkas-tər\ *n*

sports·man \ˈspȯrts-mən\ *n* **1** : a person who engages in sports (as in hunting or fishing) **2** : one who plays fairly and wins or loses gracefully — **sports·man·like** \-ˌlīk\ *adj* — **sports·man·ship** *n*

sports medicine *n* : a field of medicine dealing with the prevention and treatment of sports-related injuries

sports·wom·an \-ˌwu̇-mən\ *n* : a woman who engages in sports

sports·writ·er \-ˌrī-tər\ *n* : one who writes about sports esp. for a newspaper — **sports·writ·ing** *n*

sport utility vehicle *n* : SUV

¹**spot** \ˈspät\ *n* **1** : STAIN, BLEMISH **2** : a small part different (as in color) from the main part **3** : LOCATION, SITE — **spot·less** *adj* — **spot·less·ly** *adv* — **on the spot** **1** : at the place of action **2** : in difficulty or danger

²**spot** *vb* **spot·ted; spot·ting** **1** : to mark or disfigure with spots **2** : to pick out : RECOGNIZE, IDENTIFY

³**spot** *adj* **1** : being, done, or originating on the spot ⟨a ~ broadcast⟩ **2** : paid upon delivery **3** : made at random or at a few key points ⟨a ~ check⟩

spot–check \ˈspät-ˌchek\ *vb* : to make a spot check of

spot·light \-ˌlīt\ *n* **1** : a circle of brilliant light projected upon a particular area, person, or object (as on a stage); *also* : the device that produces this light **2** : public notice — **spotlight** *vb*

spot–on \ˈspät-ˈän\ *adj* : exactly correct ⟨a ~ forecast⟩

spotted owl *n* : a rare large dark brown dark-eyed owl of humid old growth forests and thickly wooded canyons from British Columbia to southern California and central Mexico

spot·ter \ˈspä-tər\ *n* **1** : one that keeps watch : OBSERVER **2** : one that removes spots

spot·ty \ˈspä-tē\ *adj* **spot·ti·er; -est** : uneven in quality; *also* : sparsely distributed ⟨~ attendance⟩

spou·sal \ˈspau̇-zəl, -səl\ *n* : MARRIAGE 2, WEDDING — usu. used in pl.

spouse \ˈspau̇s\ *n* : one's husband or wife — **spou·sal** \ˈspau̇-zəl, -səl\ *adj*

¹**spout** \ˈspau̇t\ *vb* **1** : to eject or issue forth forcibly and freely ⟨wells ~*ing* oil⟩ **2** : to speak pompously

²**spout** *n* **1** : a pipe or hole through which liquid spouts **2** : a jet of liquid; *esp* : WATERSPOUT 2

spp *abbr* species (*pl*)

¹**sprain** \ˈsprān\ *n* : a sudden or severe twisting of a joint with stretching or tearing of ligaments; *also* : a sprained condition

²**sprain** *vb* : to subject to sprain

sprat \ˈsprat\ *n* : a small European fish related to the herring; *also* : SARDINE

sprawl \ˈsprȯl\ *vb* **1** : to lie or sit with limbs spread out awkwardly **2** : to spread out irregularly — **sprawl** *n*

¹**spray** \ˈsprā\ *n* : a usu. flowering branch; *also* : a decorative arrangement of flowers and foliage

²**spray** *n* **1** : liquid flying in small drops like water blown from a wave **2** : a jet of fine vapor (as from an atomizer) **3** : an instrument (as an atomizer) for scattering fine liquid

³**spray** *vb* **1** : to discharge spray on or into **2** : to scatter or let fall in a spray — **spray·er** *n*

spray can *n* : a pressurized container from which aerosols are sprayed

spray gun *n* : a device for spraying liquids (as paint or insecticide)

¹**spread** \ˈspred\ *vb* **spread; spread·ing** **1** : to scatter over a surface **2** : to flatten out : open out **3** : to distribute over a period of time or among many persons **4** : to cover something with ⟨~ rugs on the floor⟩ **5** : to prepare for a meal ⟨~ a table⟩ **6** : to pass on from person to person **7** : to stretch, force, or push apart ⟨a bird ~*ing* its wings⟩ — **spread·er** *n*

²**spread** *n* **1** : the act or process of spreading **2** : EXPANSE, EXTENT **3** : a prominent display in a periodical **4** : a food to be spread on bread or crackers **5** : a cloth cover for a bed **6** : distance between two points : GAP

spread·sheet \ˈspred-ˌshēt\ *n* : an accounting program for a computer

spree \ˈsprē\ *n* : an unrestrained outburst ⟨buying ~⟩; *also* : a drinking bout

sprig \ˈsprig\ *n* : a small shoot or twig

spright·ly \ˈsprīt-lē\ *adj* **spright·li·er; -est** : LIVELY, SPIRITED ⟨a ~ musical⟩ ♦ ***Synonyms*** ANIMATED, VIVACIOUS, ENERGETIC — **spright·li·ness** *n*

¹**spring** \ˈspriŋ\ *vb* **sprang** \ˈspraŋ\ *or* **sprung** \ˈsprəŋ\; **sprung; spring·ing** **1** : to move suddenly upward or forward **2** : to grow quickly ⟨weeds *sprang* up overnight⟩ **3** : to come from by birth or de-

scent 4 : to move quickly by elastic force 5 : WARP 6 : to develop (a leak) through the seams 7 : to cause to close suddenly ⟨~ a trap⟩ 8 : to make known suddenly ⟨~ a surprise⟩ 9 : to make lame : STRAIN ⟨*sprang* a leg muscle⟩

²**spring** *n* 1 : a source of supply; *esp* : an issuing of water from the ground 2 : SOURCE, ORIGIN; *also* : MOTIVE 3 : the season between winter and summer 4 : an elastic body or device that recovers its original shape when it is released after being distorted 5 : the act or an instance of leaping up or forward 6 : RESILIENCE — **springy** *adj*

spring·board \ˈspriŋ-ˌbȯrd\ *n* : a springy board used in jumping or vaulting or for diving

spring fever *n* : a lazy or restless feeling often associated with the onset of spring

spring tide *n* : a tide of greater-than-average range that occurs at each new moon and full moon

spring·time \ˈspriŋ-ˌtīm\ *n* : the season of spring

¹**sprin·kle** \ˈspriŋ-kəl\ *vb* **sprin·kled; sprin·kling** : to scatter in small drops or particles — **sprin·kler** *n*

²**sprinkle** *n* : a light rainfall

sprin·kling *n* : SMATTERING

¹**sprint** \ˈsprint\ *vb* : to run at top speed esp. for a short distance — **sprint·er** *n*

²**sprint** *n* 1 : a short run at top speed 2 : a short distance race

sprite \ˈsprīt\ *n* 1 : GHOST, SPIRIT 2 : ELF, FAIRY

spritz \ˈsprits, ˈshprits\ *vb* : SPRAY ⟨~ the plants⟩ — **spritz** *n*

sprock·et \ˈsprä-kət\ *n* : a toothed wheel whose teeth engage the links of a chain

¹**sprout** \ˈsprau̇t\ *vb* : to send out new growth ⟨~*ing* seeds⟩

²**sprout** *n* : a usu. young and growing plant shoot (as from a seed)

¹**spruce** \ˈsprüs\ *vb* **spruced; spruc·ing** : to make or become spruce

²**spruce** *adj* **spruc·er; spruc·est** : neat and smart in appearance ♦ *Synonyms* STYLISH, FASHIONABLE, MODISH, DAPPER, NATTY

³**spruce** *n, pl* **spruc·es** *also* **spruce** : any of a genus of evergreen pyramid-shaped trees related to the pines and having soft light wood; *also* : the wood of a spruce

sprung *past and past part of* SPRING

spry \ˈsprī\ *adj* **spri·er** *or* **spry·er** \ˈsprī-ər\; **spri·est** *or* **spry·est** \ˈsprī-əst\ : NIMBLE, ACTIVE ⟨a ~ 75-year-old⟩ ♦ *Synonyms* AGILE, BRISK, LIVELY, SPRIGHTLY

spud \ˈspəd\ *n* 1 : a sharp narrow spade 2 : POTATO

spume \ˈspyüm\ *n* : frothy matter on liquids : FOAM — **spumy** \ˈspyü-mē\ *adj*

spu·mo·ni *also* **spu·mo·ne** \spu̇-ˈmō-nē\ *n* [It *spumone,* fr. *spuma* foam] : ice cream in layers of different colors, flavors, and textures often with candied fruits and nuts

spun *past and past part of* SPIN

spun glass *n* : FIBERGLASS

spunk \ˈspəŋk\ *n* [fr. *spunk* tinder, fr. ScGael *spong* sponge, tinder, fr. Middle Irish *spongc,* fr. L *spongia* sponge] : PLUCK, COURAGE — **spunky** *adj*

¹**spur** \ˈspər\ *n* 1 : a pointed device fastened to a rider's boot and used to urge on a horse 2 : something that urges to action 3 : a stiff sharp spine (as on the leg of a cock); *also* : a hollow projecting appendage of a flower (as a columbine) 4 : a ridge extending sideways from a mountain 5 : a branch of railroad track extending from the main line ♦ *Synonyms* GOAD, MOTIVE, IMPULSE, INCENTIVE, INDUCEMENT — **spurred** \ˈspərd\ *adj* — **on the spur of the moment** : on hasty impulse

²**spur** *vb* **spurred; spur·ring** 1 : to urge a horse on with spurs 2 : INCITE

spurge \ˈspərj\ *n* : any of a family of herbs and woody plants with a bitter milky juice

spu·ri·ous \ˈspyu̇r-ē-əs\ *adj* [LL *spurius* false, fr. L, *spurius,* n., son of an unknown father] : not genuine : FALSE

spurn \ˈspərn\ *vb* 1 : to kick away or trample on 2 : to reject with disdain

¹**spurt** \ˈspərt\ *vb* : to gush out : SPOUT

²**spurt** *n* : a sudden gushing or spouting

³**spurt** *n* 1 : a sudden brief burst of effort, speed, or development 2 : a sharp increase of activity ⟨~ in sales⟩

⁴**spurt** *vb* : to make a spurt

sput·ter \ˈspə-tər\ *vb* 1 : to spit small scattered particles : SPLUTTER 2 : to utter words hastily or explosively in excitement or confusion 3 : to make small popping sounds — **sputter** *n*

spu·tum \ˈspyü-təm\ *n, pl* **spu·ta** \-tə\ [L] : material (as phlegm) that is spit out or coughed up esp. during illness

¹**spy** \ˈspī\ *vb* **spied; spy·ing** 1 : to watch or search for information secretly : act as a spy 2 : to get a momentary or quick glimpse of : SEE

²**spy** *n, pl* **spies** 1 : one who secretly watches others 2 : a secret agent who tries to get information for one country in the territory of an enemy

spy·glass \ˈspī-ˌglas\ *n* : a small telescope

sq *abbr* 1 squadron 2 square

squab \ˈskwäb\ *n, pl* **squabs** *or* **squab** : a young bird and esp. a pigeon

squab·ble \ˈskwä-bəl\ *n* : a noisy altercation : WRANGLE ♦ *Synonyms* QUARREL, SPAT, ROW, TIFF — **squabble** *vb*

squad \ˈskwäd\ *n* 1 : a small organized group of military personnel 2 : a small group engaged in a common effort

squad car *n* : a police car connected by two-way radio with headquarters

squad·ron \ˈskwä-drən\ *n* : any of several units of military organization

squal·id \ˈskwä-ləd\ *adj* 1 : filthy or degraded through neglect or poverty 2 : SORDID, DEBASED ⟨a ~ political ploy⟩ ♦ *Synonyms* NASTY, FOUL, DIRTY, GRUBBY

squall \ˈskwȯl\ *n* : a sudden violent gust of wind often with rain or snow — **squally** *adj*

squa·lor \ˈskwä-lər\ *n* : the quality or state of being squalid

squa·mous cell \ˈskwā-məs-\ *n* : a scale-like cell of the outer layers of the skin from which a type of carcinoma arises

squan·der \ˈskwän-dər\ *vb* : to spend wastefully or foolishly

[1]**square** \ˈskwer\ *n* **1** : an instrument used to lay out or test right angles **2** : a rectangle with all four sides equal **3** : something square **4** : the product of a number multiplied by itself **5** : an area bounded by four streets **6** : an open area in a city where streets meet **7** : a highly conventional person

[2]**square** *adj* **squar·er; squar·est** **1** : having four equal sides and four right angles **2** : forming a right angle ⟨cut a ~ corner⟩ **3** : multiplied by itself : SQUARED ⟨x^2 is the symbol for *x* ~⟩ **4** : being a unit of square measure equal to a square each side of which measures one unit ⟨a ~ foot⟩ **5** : being of a specified length in each of two dimensions ⟨an area 10 feet ~⟩ **6** : exactly adjusted **7** : JUST, FAIR ⟨a ~ deal⟩ **8** : leaving no balance ⟨make accounts ~⟩ **9** : SUBSTANTIAL ⟨a ~ meal⟩ **10** : highly conservative or conventional — **square·ly** *adv*

[3]**square** *vb* **squared; squar·ing** **1** : to form with four equal sides and right angles or with flat surfaces ⟨~ a timber⟩ **2** : to multiply (a number) by itself **3** : CONFORM, AGREE **4** : BALANCE, SETTLE ⟨~ an account⟩

square dance *n* : a dance for four couples arranged to form a square

square measure *n* : a unit or system of units for measuring area — see METRIC SYSTEM table, WEIGHT table

square–rigged \ˈskwer-ˈrigd\ *adj* : having the chief sails extended on yards that are fastened to the masts horizontally and at their center

square–rig·ger \-ˌri-gər\ *n* : a square-rigged craft

square root *n* : either of the two numbers whose squares are equal to a given number ⟨the *square root* of 9 is +3 or −3⟩

[1]**squash** \ˈskwäsh, ˈskwȯsh\ *vb* **1** : to beat or press into a pulp or flat mass **2** : QUASH, SUPPRESS ⟨~ a revolt⟩

[2]**squash** *n* **1** : the impact of something soft and heavy; *also* : the sound of such impact **2** : a crushed mass **3** : a game played on a 4-wall court with a racket and rubber ball

[3]**squash** *n, pl* **squash·es** *or* **squash** : any of various fruits of plants of the gourd family that are used esp. as vegetables; *also* : a plant and esp. a vine bearing squashes

squash racquets *n* : SQUASH 3

[1]**squat** \ˈskwät\ *vb* **squat·ted; squat·ting** [ME *squatten* to crush, crouch in hiding, fr. MF (dial. of Picardy) *esquatir, escuater,* fr. OF *es-* ex- + *quatir* to hide, fr. VL **coactire* to squeeze, alter. of L *coactare* to compel, fr. *cogere* to compel] **1** : to sit down upon the hams or heels **2** : to settle on land without right or title; *also* : to settle on public land with a view to acquiring title — **squat·ter** *n*

[2]**squat** *adj* **squat·ter; squat·test** : low to the ground; *also* : short and thick in stature ♦ ***Synonyms*** THICKSET, STOCKY, HEAVYSET, STUBBY

[3]**squat** *n* : the act or posture of squatting

squawk \ˈskwȯk\ *n* : a harsh loud cry; *also* : a noisy protest — **squawk** *vb*

squeak \ˈskwēk\ *vb* **1** : to utter or speak in a weak shrill tone **2** : to make a thin high-pitched sound ⟨the door ~*s*⟩ — **squeak** *n* — **squeaky** *adj*

[1]**squeal** \ˈskwēl\ *vb* **1** : to make a shrill sound or cry **2** : to betray a secret or turn informer **3** : COMPLAIN, PROTEST

[2]**squeal** *n* : a shrill sharp cry or noise

squea·mish \ˈskwē-mish\ *adj* **1** : easily nauseated; *also* : NAUSEATED **2** : easily disgusted ♦ ***Synonyms*** FUSSY, NICE, DAINTY, FASTIDIOUS, PERSNICKETY — **squea·mish·ness** *n*

squee·gee \ˈskwē-ˌjē\ *n* : a blade set crosswise on a handle and used for spreading or wiping liquid on, across, or off a surface — **squeegee** *vb*

[1]**squeeze** \ˈskwēz\ *vb* **squeezed; squeez·ing** **1** : to exert pressure on the opposite sides or parts of **2** : to obtain by pressure ⟨~ juice from a lemon⟩ **3** : to force or move into a small space ⟨we all *squeezed* into the room⟩ — **squeez·er** *n*

[2]**squeeze** *n* **1** : an act of squeezing **2** : a quantity squeezed out

squeeze bottle *n* : a flexible plastic bottle that dispenses its contents when it is squeezed

squelch \ˈskwelch\ *vb* **1** : to suppress completely : CRUSH ⟨~ resistance⟩ **2** : to move in soft mud — **squelch** *n*

squib \ˈskwib\ *n* : a brief witty writing or speech

squid \ˈskwid\ *n, pl* **squid** *or* **squids** : any of an order of long-bodied sea mollusks having eight short arms and two longer tentacles and usu. a slender internal shell

squint \ˈskwint\ *vb* **1** : to look or aim obliquely **2** : to look or peer with the eyes partly closed ⟨~*ing* into the sun⟩ **3** : to be cross-eyed — **squint** *n or adj*

[1]**squire** \ˈskwī(-ə)r\ *n* [ME *squier,* fr. AF *esquier,* fr. LL *scutarius,* fr. L *scutum* shield] **1** : an armor-bearer of a knight **2** : a man gallantly devoted to a lady **3** : a member of the British gentry ranking below a knight and above a gentleman; *also* : a prominent landowner **4** : a local magistrate

[2]**squire** *vb* **squired; squir·ing** : to attend as a squire or escort

squirm \ˈskwərm\ *vb* : to twist about like a worm : WRIGGLE

[1]**squir·rel** \ˈskwər-əl\ *n, pl* **squirrels** *also* **squirrel** [ME *squirel,* fr. AF *escurel, esquirel,* fr. VL **scuriolus,* dim. of **scurius,* alter. of L *sciurus,* fr. Gk *skiouros,* prob. fr. *skia* shadow + *oura* tail] : any of various rodents usu. with a long bushy tail and strong hind legs; *also* : the fur of a squirrel

²squirrel *vb* **-reled** *or* **-relled; -rel·ing** *or* **-rel·ling** : to store up for future use

¹squirt \ˈskwərt\ *vb* : to eject liquid in a thin spurt

²squirt *n* **1** : an instrument (as a syringe) for squirting **2** : a small forcible jet of liquid

¹Sr *abbr* **1** senior **2** sister

²Sr *symbol* strontium

SR *abbr* seaman recruit

¹SRO \ˌes-(ˌ)är-ˈō\ *n* [*s*ingle-*r*oom *o*ccupancy] : a house or apartment building in which low-income tenants live in single rooms

²SRO *abbr* standing room only

SRP *abbr* suggested retail price

SS *abbr* **1** saints **2** Social Security **3** steamship **4** sworn statement

SSA *abbr* Social Security Administration

SSE *abbr* south-southeast

SSG *or* **SSgt** *abbr* staff sergeant

SSI *abbr* supplemental security income

SSM *abbr* staff sergeant major

SSN *abbr* Social Security Number

ssp *abbr* subspecies

SSR *abbr* Soviet Socialist Republic

SSS *abbr* Selective Service System

SST \ˌes-(ˌ)es-ˈtē\ *n* [*s*uper*s*onic *t*ransport] : a supersonic passenger airplane

SSW *abbr* south-southwest

st *abbr* **1** stanza **2** state **3** stitch **4** stone **5** street

St *abbr* saint

ST *abbr* **1** short ton **2** standard time

-st — see -EST

sta *abbr* station; stationary

¹stab \ˈstab\ *n* **1** : a wound produced by a pointed weapon **2** : a quick thrust **3** : a brief attempt

²stab *vb* **stabbed; stab·bing** : to pierce or wound with or as if with a pointed weapon; *also* : THRUST, DRIVE

sta·bile \ˈstā-ˌbēl\ *n* : an abstract sculpture or construction similar to a mobile but made to be stationary

sta·bi·lize \ˈstā-bə-ˌlīz\ *vb* **-lized; -liz·ing** **1** : to make stable **2** : to hold steady ⟨~ prices⟩ — **sta·bi·li·za·tion** \ˌstā-bə-lə-ˈzā-shən\ *n* — **sta·bi·liz·er** \ˈstā-bə-ˌlī-zər\ *n*

¹sta·ble \ˈstā-bəl\ *n* : a building in which domestic animals are sheltered and fed — **sta·ble·man** \-mən, -ˌman\ *n*

²stable *vb* **sta·bled; sta·bling** : to put or keep in a stable

³stable *adj* **sta·bler; sta·blest** **1** : firmly established; *also* : mentally and emotionally healthy **2** : steady in purpose : CONSTANT **3** : DURABLE, ENDURING ⟨~ civilizations⟩ **4** : resistant to chemical or physical change ♦ ***Synonyms*** LASTING, PERMANENT, PERPETUAL, PERDURABLE — **sta·bil·i·ty** \stə-ˈbi-lə-tē\ *n*

stac·ca·to \stə-ˈkä-tō\ *adj or adv* [It] : cut short so as not to sound connected ⟨~ notes⟩

¹stack \ˈstak\ *n* **1** : a large pile (as of hay or grain) **2** : an orderly pile (as of poker chips) **3** : a large quantity **4** : a vertical pipe : SMOKESTACK **5** : a rack with shelves for storing books ⟨library ~*s*⟩

²stack *vb* **1** : to pile up **2** : to arrange (cards) secretly for cheating

stack up *vb* : MEASURE UP ⟨how do they *stack up* against the competition?⟩

sta·di·um \ˈstā-dē-əm\ *n, pl* **-dia** \-dē-ə\ *or* **-di·ums** : a structure with tiers of seats for spectators built around a field for sports events

¹staff \ˈstaf\ *n, pl* **staffs** \ˈstafs, ˈstavz\ *or* **staves** \ˈstavz, ˈstāvz\ **1** : a pole, stick, rod, or bar used for supporting, for measuring, or as a symbol of authority; *also* : CLUB, CUDGEL **2** : something that sustains ⟨bread is the ~ of life⟩ **3** : the five horizontal lines on which music is written **4** : a body of assistants to an executive **5** : a group of officers holding no command but having duties concerned with planning and managing

²staff *vb* : to supply with a staff or with workers ⟨~ a hotel⟩

staff·er \ˈsta-fər\ *n* : a member of a staff (as of a newspaper)

staff sergeant *n* : a noncommissioned officer ranking in the army next below a sergeant first class, in the air force next below a technical sergeant, and in the marine corps next below a gunnery sergeant

¹stag \ˈstag\ *n, pl* **stags** *or* **stag** : an adult male of various large deer

²stag *adj* : restricted to or intended for men ⟨a ~ party⟩ ⟨~ movies⟩

³stag *adv* : unaccompanied by a date

¹stage \ˈstāj\ *n* [ME, fr. AF *estage* abode, story of a building, stage, fr. VL **staticum*, fr. L *stare* to stand] **1** : a raised platform on which an orator may speak or a play may be presented **2** : the acting profession : THEATER **3** : the scene of a notable action or event **4** : a station or resting place on a traveled road **5** : STAGECOACH **6** : a degree of advance in an undertaking, process, or development **7** : a propulsion unit in a rocket — **stagy** \ˈstā-jē\ *adj*

²stage *vb* **staged; stag·ing** : to produce or perform on or as if on a stage ⟨~ a play⟩ — **stage·able** *adj*

stage·coach \ˈstāj-ˌkōch\ *n* : a horse-drawn coach that runs regularly between stations

stage manager *n* : one who supervises the physical aspects of a stage production

stag·fla·tion \ˌstag-ˈflā-shən\ *n* : inflation with stagnant economic activity and high unemployment

¹stag·ger \ˈsta-gər\ *vb* **1** : to reel from side to side : TOTTER **2** : to begin to doubt : WAVER **3** : to cause to reel or waver **4** : to arrange in overlapping or alternating positions or times ⟨~ working hours⟩ **5** : ASTONISH ⟨their indifference ~*s* me⟩ — **stag·ger·ing·ly** *adv*

²stagger *n* **1** *sing or pl* : an abnormal condition of domestic animals associated with damage to the central nervous system and marked by lack of coordination and a reeling unsteady gait **2** : a reeling or unsteady gait or stance

stag·ing \ˈstā-jiŋ\ *n* **1** : SCAFFOLDING **2**

: the assembling of troops and matériel in transit in a particular place
staging post *n* : STOPOVER 2
stag·nant \'stag-nənt\ *adj* **1** : not flowing : MOTIONLESS ⟨~ water in a pond⟩ **2** : DULL, INACTIVE ⟨~ business⟩
stag·nate \'stag-ˌnāt\ *vb* **stag·nat·ed; stag·nat·ing** : to be or become stagnant — **stag·na·tion** \stag-'nā-shən\ *n*
staid \'stād\ *adj* : SOBER, SEDATE ♦ ***Synonyms*** GRAVE, SERIOUS, EARNEST
[1]**stain** \'stān\ *vb* **1** : DISCOLOR, SOIL **2** : TAINT, CORRUPT **3** : DISGRACE **4** : to color (as wood, paper, or cloth) by processes affecting the material itself
[2]**stain** *n* **1** : a small soiled or discolored area **2** : a taint of guilt : STIGMA **3** : a preparation (as a dye or pigment) used in staining — **stain·less** *adj*
stainless steel *n* : steel alloyed with chromium that is highly resistant to stain, rust, and corrosion
stair \'ster\ *n* **1** : a series of steps or flights of steps for passing from one level to another — often used in pl. **2** : one step of a stairway
stair·case \-ˌkās\ *n* : a flight of steps with their supporting framework, casing, and balusters
stair·way \-ˌwā\ *n* : one or more flights of stairs with connecting landings
stair·well \-ˌwel\ *n* : a vertical shaft in which stairs are located
[1]**stake** \'stāk\ *n* **1** : a pointed piece of material (as of wood) driven into the ground as a marker or a support **2** : a post to which a person is bound for death by burning; *also* : execution by burning at the stake **3** : something that is staked for gain or loss **4** : the prize in a contest
[2]**stake** *vb* **staked; stak·ing** **1** : to mark the limits of by or as if by stakes **2** : to tie to a stake **3** : to support or secure with stakes **4** : BET, WAGER
stake·out \'stāk-ˌau̇t\ *n* : a surveillance by police (as of a suspected criminal)
sta·lac·tite \stə-'lak-ˌtīt\ *n* [NL *stalactites,* fr. Gk *stalaktos* dripping, fr. *stalassein* to let drip] : an icicle-shaped deposit hanging from the roof or sides of a cavern
sta·lag·mite \stə-'lag-ˌmīt\ *n* [NL *stalagmites,* fr. Gk *stalagma* drop or *stalagmos* dripping, fr. *stalassein* to let drip] : a deposit resembling an inverted stalactite rising from the floor of a cavern
stale \'stāl\ *adj* **stal·er; stal·est** **1** : having lost good taste and quality from age ⟨~ bread⟩ **2** : used or heard so often as to be dull ⟨~ news⟩ **3** : not as strong or effective as before ⟨~ from lack of practice⟩ — **stale·ness** *n*
stale·mate \'stāl-ˌmāt\ *n* : a drawn contest : DEADLOCK — **stalemate** *vb*
[1]**stalk** \'stȯk\ *n* : a plant stem; *also* : any slender usu. upright supporting or connecting part — **stalked** \'stȯkt\ *adj*
[2]**stalk** *vb* **1** : to pursue (game) stealthily **2** : to walk stiffly or haughtily **3** : to follow (a person) obsessively — **stalk·er** *n*
[1]**stall** \'stȯl\ *n* **1** : a compartment in a stable or barn for one animal **2** : a booth or counter where articles may be displayed for sale **3** : a seat in a church choir; *also* : a church pew **4** *chiefly Brit* : a front orchestra seat in a theater
[2]**stall** *vb* : to bring or come to a standstill unintentionally ⟨~ an engine⟩
[3]**stall** *n* : the condition of an airfoil or aircraft in which lift is lost and the airfoil or aircraft tends to drop
[4]**stall** *n* [alter. of *stale* lure] : a ruse to deceive or delay
[5]**stall** *vb* : to hold off, divert, or delay by evasion or deception
stal·lion \'stal-yən\ *n* : a male horse
stal·wart \'stȯl-wərt\ *adj* : STOUT, STRONG; *also* : BRAVE, VALIANT
sta·men \'stā-mən\ *n* : an organ of a flower that produces pollen
stam·i·na \'sta-mə-nə\ *n* [L, pl. of *stamen* warp, thread of life spun by the Fates] : VIGOR, ENDURANCE ⟨had the ~ to win⟩
sta·mi·nate \'stā-mə-nət, 'sta-mə-, -ˌnāt\ *adj* **1** : having or producing stamens **2** : having stamens but no pistils
stam·mer \'sta-mər\ *vb* : to hesitate or stumble in speaking — **stammer** *n* — **stam·mer·er** *n*
[1]**stamp** \'stamp; *for 2 also* 'stämp *or* 'stȯmp\ *vb* **1** : to pound or crush with a heavy instrument **2** : to strike or beat with the bottom of the foot **3** : IMPRESS, IMPRINT ⟨~ "paid" on the bill⟩ **4** : to cut out or indent with a stamp or die **5** : to attach a postage stamp to
[2]**stamp** *n* **1** : a device or instrument for stamping **2** : the mark made by stamping; *also* : a distinctive mark or quality **3** : the act of stamping **4** : a stamped or printed paper affixed to show that a charge has been paid ⟨postage ~⟩
[1]**stam·pede** \stam-'pēd\ *n* : a wild headlong rush or flight esp. of frightened animals
[2]**stampede** *vb* **stam·ped·ed; stam·ped·ing** **1** : to flee or cause to flee in panic **2** : to act or cause to act together suddenly and heedlessly
stance \'stans\ *n* : a way of standing
[1]**stanch** \'stȯnch, 'stänch, 'stanch\ *or* **staunch** \'stȯnch, 'stänch\ *vb* : to check the flowing of (as blood); *also* : to cease flowing or bleeding
[2]**stanch** *var of* [2]STAUNCH
stan·chion \'stan-chən\ *n* : an upright bar, post, or support
[1]**stand** \'stand\ *vb* **stood** \'stu̇d\; **stand·ing** **1** : to take or be at rest in an upright or firm position **2** : to assume a specified position **3** : to remain stationary or unchanged **4** : to be steadfast **5** : to act in resistance ⟨~ against a foe⟩ **6** : to maintain a relative position or rank **7** : to gather slowly and remain ⟨tears *stood* in her eyes⟩ **8** : to set upright **9** : ENDURE, TOLERATE ⟨I won't ~ for that⟩ **10** : to submit to ⟨~ trial⟩ — **stand pat** : to oppose or resist change
[2]**stand** *n* **1** : an act of standing, staying, or resisting **2** : a stop made to give a performance **3** : POSITION, VIEWPOINT **4** : a

place taken by a witness to testify in court **5** *pl* : tiered seats for spectators **6** : a raised platform (as for speakers) **7** : a structure for a small retail business **8** : a structure for supporting or holding something upright ⟨music ~⟩ **9** : a group of plants growing in a continuous area

stand–alone \'stan-də-ˌlōn\ *adj* : SELF-CONTAINED; *esp* : capable of operation independent of a computer system

[1]**stan·dard** \'stan-dərd\ *n* **1** : a figure adopted as an emblem by a people **2** : the personal flag of a ruler; *also* : FLAG **3** : something set up as a rule for measuring or as a model to be followed **4** : an upright support ⟨lamp ~⟩

[2]**standard** *adj* **1** : used as or meeting a standard established by law or custom **2** : regularly and widely used ⟨a ~ practice⟩ **3** : well established by usage in speech or writing

stan·dard–bear·er \-ˌber-ər\ *n* : the leader of a cause

standard deviation *n* : a measure of dispersion in a set of data

stan·dard·ise *Brit var of* STANDARDIZE

stan·dard–is·sue \'stan-dərd-'i-shü\ *adj* : STANDARD, TYPICAL ⟨a ~ blue suit⟩

stan·dard·ize \'stan-dər-ˌdīz\ *vb* **-ized; -iz·ing** : to make standard or uniform — **stan·dard·i·za·tion** \ˌstan-dər-də-'zā-shən\ *n*

standard of living : the necessities, comforts, and luxuries that a person or group is accustomed to

standard time *n* : the time established by law or by general usage over a region or country

[1]**stand·by** \'stand-ˌbī\ *n, pl* **stand·bys** \-ˌbīz\ **1** : one that can be relied on **2** : a substitute in reserve — **on standby** : ready or available for immediate action or use

[2]**standby** *adj* **1** : ready for use **2** : relating to airline travel in which the passenger must wait for an available unreserved seat — **standby** *adv*

stand–in \'stan-ˌdin\ *n* **1** : someone employed to occupy an actor's place while lights and camera are readied **2** : SUBSTITUTE

[1]**stand·ing** \'stan-diŋ\ *adj* **1** : ERECT ⟨~ timber⟩ **2** : not flowing : STAGNANT **3** : remaining at the same level or amount for an indefinite period ⟨~ offer⟩ **4** : PERMANENT ⟨a ~ army⟩ **5** : done from a standing position ⟨a ~ jump⟩

[2]**standing** *n* **1** : length of service; *also* : relative position in society or in a profession : RANK **2** : DURATION ⟨a custom of long ~⟩

stand·off \'stan-ˌdȯf\ *n* : TIE, DRAW

stand·off·ish \stan-'dȯ-fish\ *adj* : somewhat cold and reserved

stand·out \'stan-ˌdau̇t\ *n* : something conspicuously excellent

stand·pipe \'stand-ˌpīp\ *n* : a high vertical pipe or reservoir for water used to produce a uniform pressure

stand·point \-ˌpȯint\ *n* : OUTLOOK

stand·still \-ˌstil\ *n* : a state of rest

stand–up \'stan-ˌdəp\ *adj* : done or performing in a standing position ⟨a ~ comic⟩ ⟨~ comedy⟩

stank *past of* STINK

stan·za \'stan-zə\ *n* [It] : a group of lines forming a division of a poem

sta·pes \'stā-ˌpēz\ *n, pl* **stapes** *or* **sta·pe·des** \'stā-pə-ˌdēz\ : the innermost bone of the middle ear of mammals

staph \'staf\ *n* : STAPHYLOCOCCUS

staph·y·lo·coc·cus \ˌsta-fə-lō-'kä-kəs\ *n, pl* **-coc·ci** \-'kä-ˌkī, -'käk-ˌsī\ : any of a genus of spherical bacteria including some pathogens of skin and mucous membranes — **staph·y·lo·coc·cal** \-'kä-kəl\ *adj*

[1]**sta·ple** \'stā-pəl\ *n* : a U-shaped piece of metal or wire with sharp points to be driven into a surface or through thin layers (as paper) for attaching or holding together — **staple** *vb* — **sta·pler** *n*

[2]**staple** *n* **1** : a chief commodity or product **2** : a chief part of something ⟨a ~ of their diet⟩ **3** : unmanufactured or raw material **4** : a textile fiber suitable for spinning into yarn

[3]**staple** *adj* **1** : regularly produced in large quantities **2** : PRINCIPAL, MAIN ⟨the ~ crop⟩

[1]**star** \'stär\ *n* **1** : a celestial body that appears as a fixed point of light; *esp* : such a body that is gaseous, self-luminous, and of great mass **2** : a planet or configuration of planets that is held in astrology to influence one's fortune — usu. used in pl. **3** *obs* : DESTINY **4** : a conventional figure representing a star; *esp* : ASTERISK **5** : an actor or actress playing the leading role **6** : a brilliant performer — **star·dom** \'stär-dəm\ *n* — **star·less** *adj* — **star·like** *adj* — **star·ry** *adj*

[2]**star** *vb* **starred; star·ring** **1** : to adorn with stars **2** : to mark with an asterisk **3** : to play the leading role

star anise *n* : the small brown star-shaped fruit of an Asian tree used as a spice esp. in Chinese cooking

star·board \'stär-bərd\ *n* [ME *sterbord,* fr. OE *stēorbord,* fr. *stēor-* steering oar + *bord* ship's side] : the right side of a ship or airplane looking forward — **starboard** *adj*

star·burst \'stär-bərst\ *n* : a pattern that resembles diverging rays of light

[1]**starch** \'stärch\ *vb* : to stiffen with or as if with starch

[2]**starch** *n* : a complex carbohydrate that is stored in plants, is an important foodstuff, and is used in adhesives and sizes, in laundering, and in pharmacy — **starchy** *adj*

stare \'ster\ *vb* **stared; star·ing** : to look fixedly with wide-open eyes ⟨*stared* in disbelief⟩ — **stare** *n* — **star·er** *n*

star·fish \'stär-ˌfish\ *n* : any of a class of echinoderms that have usu. five arms arranged around a central disk and feed largely on mollusks

star fruit *n* : CARAMBOLA 1

[1]**stark** \'stärk\ *adj* **1** : rigid as if in death;

also : STRICT **2** *archaic* : STRONG, ROBUST **3** : SHEER, UTTER ⟨~ nonsense⟩ **4** : BARREN, DESOLATE ⟨~ landscape⟩; *also* : UNADORNED ⟨~ realism⟩ **5** : sharply delineated — **stark·ly** *adv*

[2]**stark** *adv* : WHOLLY, ABSOLUTELY ⟨~ naked⟩

star·light \ˈstär-ˌlīt\ *n* : the light given by the stars

star·ling \ˈstär-liŋ\ *n* : a dark brown or in summer glossy greenish black European bird that is naturalized nearly worldwide and often considered a pest

[1]**start** \ˈstärt\ *vb* **1** : to give an involuntary twitch or jerk (as from surprise) **2** : BEGIN, COMMENCE **3** : to set going ⟨~ an engine⟩ **4** : to enter or cause to enter a game or contest; *also* : to be in the starting lineup — **start·er** *n*

[2]**start** *n* **1** : a sudden involuntary motion : LEAP **2** : a spasmodic and brief effort or action **3** : BEGINNING; *also* : the place of beginning

start·er \ˈstär-tər\ *adj* : being an item acquired with the expectation that a more elaborate one will be acquired in the future ⟨a ~ home⟩

star·tle \ˈstär-t^{ə}l\ *vb* **star·tled; star·tling** : to frighten or surprise suddenly : cause to start ⟨the noise *startled* the dog⟩

star·tling *adj* : causing sudden fear, surprise, or anxiety — **star·tling·ly** *adv*

starve \ˈstärv\ *vb* **starved; starv·ing** [ME *sterven* to die, fr. OE *steorfan*] **1** : to die or cause to die from hunger **2** : to suffer extreme hunger or deprivation ⟨*starving* for affection⟩ **3** : to subdue by famine — **star·va·tion** \stär-ˈvā-shən\ *n*

starve·ling \ˈstärv-liŋ\ *n* : one that is thin from lack of nourishment

stash \ˈstash\ *vb* : to store in a secret place for future use — **stash** *n*

sta·sis \ˈstā-səs, ˈsta-\ *n, pl* **sta·ses** \ˈstā-ˌsēz, ˈsta-\ **1** : a stoppage or slowing of the normal flow of a bodily fluid (as blood) **2** : a state of static balance : STAGNATION

[1]**stat** \ˈstat\ *adv* [L *statim*] : without delay : IMMEDIATELY

[2]**stat** *abbr* statute

[1]**state** \ˈstāt\ *n* [ME *stat,* fr. AF & L; AF *estat,* fr. L *status,* fr. *stare* to stand] **1** : mode or condition of being ⟨the four ~*s* of matter⟩ **2** : condition of mind **3** : social position **4** : a body of people occupying a territory and organized under one government; *also* : the government of such a body of people **5** : one of the constituent units of a nation having a federal government — **state·hood** \-ˌhu̇d\ *n*

[2]**state** *vb* **stat·ed; stat·ing** **1** : to set by regulation or authority **2** : to express in words

state·craft \ˈstāt-ˌkraft\ *n* : the art of conducting state affairs

state·house \-ˌhau̇s\ *n* : the building in which a state legislature meets

state·ly \ˈstāt-lē\ *adj* **state·li·er; -est** **1** : having lofty dignity : HAUGHTY **2** : IMPRESSIVE, MAJESTIC ⟨~ homes⟩ ♦ ***Synonyms*** MAGNIFICENT, IMPOSING, AUGUST — **state·li·ness** *n*

state·ment \ˈstāt-mənt\ *n* **1** : the act or result of presenting in words **2** : a summary of a financial account

state·room \ˈstāt-ˌrüm, -ˌru̇m\ *n* : a private room on a ship or railroad car

state·side \ˈstāt-ˌsīd\ *adj* : of or relating to the U.S. as regarded from outside its continental limits — **stateside** *adv*

states·man \ˈstāts-mən\ *n* : a person engaged in fixing the policies and conducting the affairs of a government; *esp* : one wise and skilled in such matters — **states·man·like** *adj* — **states·man·ship** *n*

[1]**stat·ic** \ˈsta-tik\ *adj* **1** : acting by mere weight without motion ⟨~ pressure⟩ **2** : relating to bodies at rest or forces in equilibrium **3** : showing little change **4** : not moving : not active **5** : of or relating to stationary charges of electricity **6** : of, relating to, or caused by radio static

[2]**static** *n* : noise produced in a radio or television receiver by atmospheric or other electrical disturbances

stat·in \ˈsta-t^{ə}n\ *n* : any of a group of drugs that inhibit the synthesis of cholesterol

[1]**sta·tion** \ˈstā-shən\ *n* **1** : the place where a person or thing stands or is assigned to remain **2** : a regular stopping place on a transportation route : DEPOT **3** : a place where a fleet is assigned for duty **4** : a stock farm or ranch esp. in Australia or New Zealand **5** : social standing **6** : a complete assemblage of radio or television equipment for sending or receiving

[2]**station** *vb* : to assign to a station

sta·tion·ary \ˈstā-shə-ˌner-ē\ *adj* **1** : fixed in a station, course, or mode **2** : unchanging in condition ⟨a ~ population⟩

stationary front *n* : the boundary between two air masses neither of which is advancing

station break *n* : a pause in a radio or television broadcast to announce the identity of the network or station

sta·tio·ner \ˈstā-shə-nər\ *n* : one that sells stationery

sta·tio·nery \ˈstā-shə-ˌner-ē\ *n* : materials (as paper, pens, or ink) for writing; *esp* : letter paper with envelopes

station wagon *n* : an automobile having a long interior, one or more folding or removable rear seats, and usu. a door at the rear

sta·tis·tic \stə-ˈtis-tik\ *n* **1** : a single term or datum in a collection of statistics **2** : a quantity (as the mean) that is computed from a sample

sta·tis·tics \-tiks\ *n sing or pl* [G *Statistik* study of political facts and figures, fr. NL *statisticus* of politics, fr. L *status* state] : a branch of mathematics dealing with the collection, analysis, and interpretation of masses of numerical data; *also* : a collection of such numerical data — **sta·tis·ti·cal** \-ti-kəl\ *adj* — **sta·tis·ti·cal·ly** \-ti-k(ə-)lē\ *adv* — **stat·is·ti·cian** \ˌsta-tə-ˈsti-shən\ *n*

stat·u·ary \ˈsta-chə-ˌwer-ē\ *n, pl* **-ar·ies** **1** : the art of making statues **2** : STATUES

stat·ue \ˈsta-chü\ *n* : a likeness (as of a person or animal) sculptured, modeled, or cast in a solid substance

stat·u·esque \ˌsta-chə-ˈwesk\ *adj* : tall and shapely

stat·u·ette \ˌsta-chə-ˈwet\ *n* : a small statue

stat·ure \ˈsta-chər\ *n* **1** : natural height (as of a person) **2** : quality or status gained (as by achievement)

sta·tus \ˈstā-təs, ˈsta-\ *n* **1** : the condition of a person in the eyes of others or of the law **2** : state or condition with respect to circumstances

sta·tus quo \-ˈkwō\ *n* [L, state in which] : the existing state of affairs

stat·ute \ˈsta-chüt\ *n* : a law enacted by a legislative body

stat·u·to·ry \ˈsta-chə-ˌtȯr-ē\ *adj* : imposed by statute : LAWFUL

statutory rape *n* : sexual intercourse with a person who is below the statutory age of consent

[1]**staunch** *var of* [1]STANCH

[2]**staunch** \ˈstȯnch, ˈstänch\ *adj* **1** : WATERTIGHT ⟨a ~ ship⟩ **2** : FIRM, STRONG; *also* : STEADFAST, LOYAL ⟨a ~ supporter⟩ ♦ ***Synonyms*** RESOLUTE, CONSTANT, TRUE, FAITHFUL — **staunch·ly** *adv*

[1]**stave** \ˈstāv\ *n* **1** : CUDGEL, STAFF **2** : any of several narrow strips of wood placed edge to edge to make something (as a barrel) **3** : STANZA

[2]**stave** *vb* **staved** *or* **stove** \ˈstōv\; **stav·ing** **1** : to break in the staves of; *also* : to break a hole in **2** : to drive or thrust away ⟨~ off hunger⟩

staves *pl of* STAFF

[1]**stay** \ˈstā\ *n* **1** : a strong rope or wire used to support a mast **2** : [1]GUY

[2]**stay** *vb* **stayed** \ˈstād\ *also* **staid** \ˈstād\; **stay·ing** **1** : PAUSE, WAIT **2** : REMAIN **3** : to stand firm **4** : LIVE, DWELL **5** : DELAY, POSTPONE **6** : to last out (as a race) **7** : STOP, CHECK **8** : to satisfy (as hunger) for a time ♦ ***Synonyms*** REMAIN, ABIDE, LINGER, TARRY

[3]**stay** *n* **1** : STOP, HALT **2** : a residence or sojourn in a place

[4]**stay** *n* **1** : PROP, SUPPORT **2** : CORSET — usu. used in pl.

[5]**stay** *vb* : to hold up : PROP

staying power *n* : STAMINA

stbd *abbr* starboard

std *abbr* standard

STD \ˌes-(ˌ)tē-ˈdē\ *n* : SEXUALLY TRANSMITTED DISEASE

Ste *abbr* [F *sainte*] saint (female)

stead \ˈsted\ *n* **1** : ADVANTAGE ⟨stood him in good ~⟩ **2** : the place or function ordinarily occupied or carried out by another ⟨acted in her brother's ~⟩

stead·fast \ˈsted-ˌfast\ *adj* **1** : firmly fixed in place **2** : not subject to change **3** : firm in belief, determination, or adherence : LOYAL ♦ ***Synonyms*** RESOLUTE, TRUE, FAITHFUL, STAUNCH — **stead·fast·ly** *adv* — **stead·fast·ness** *n*

[1]**steady** \ˈste-dē\ *adj* **steadi·er; -est** **1** : direct or sure in movement; *also* : CALM **2** : FIRM, FIXED ⟨held the pole ~⟩ **3** : STABLE ⟨~ prices⟩ **4** : not easily disturbed **5** : RELIABLE ⟨~ friends⟩ **6** : temperate in character or demeanor ♦ ***Synonyms*** UNIFORM, EVEN — **steadi·ly** \-də-lē\ *adv* — **steadi·ness** \-dē-nəs\ *n* — **steady** *adv*

[2]**steady** *vb* **stead·ied; steady·ing** : to make or become steady

steak \ˈstāk\ *n* : a slice of meat and esp. beef; *also* : a slice of a large fish

[1]**steal** \ˈstēl\ *vb* **stole** \ˈstōl\; **sto·len** \ˈstō-lən\; **steal·ing** **1** : to take and carry away without right or permission **2** : to come or go secretly or gradually **3** : to get for oneself slyly or by skill and daring ⟨~ the ball in basketball⟩ **4** : to gain or attempt to gain a base in baseball by running without the aid of a hit or an error ♦ ***Synonyms*** PILFER, FILCH, SWIPE

[2]**steal** *n* **1** : an act of stealing **2** : BARGAIN

[1]**stealth** \ˈstelth\ *n* **1** : secret or unobtrusive procedure **2** : an aircraft design intended to produce a weak radar return

[2]**stealth** *adj* : STEALTHY ⟨a ~ campaign⟩

stealthy \ˈstel-thē\ *adj* **stealth·i·er; -est** : done by stealth : FURTIVE, SLY ⟨a ~ burglar⟩ ♦ ***Synonyms*** SECRET, COVERT, CLANDESTINE, SURREPTITIOUS, UNDERHANDED — **stealth·i·ly** \ˈstel-thə-lē\ *adv*

[1]**steam** \ˈstēm\ *n* **1** : the vapor into which water is changed when heated to the boiling point **2** : water vapor when compressed so that it supplies heat and power **3** : POWER, FORCE, ENERGY — **steamy** *adj*

[2]**steam** *vb* **1** : to pass off as vapor **2** : to emit vapor **3** : to move by or as if by the agency of steam — **steam·er** *n*

steam·boat \ˈstēm-ˌbōt\ *n* : a boat driven by steam

steam engine *n* : a reciprocating engine having a piston driven by steam

steam·fit·ter \ˈstēm-ˌfi-tər\ *n* : a worker who puts in or repairs equipment (as steam pipes) for heating, ventilating, or refrigerating systems

steam·punk \ˈstēm-ˌpəŋk\ *n* : science fiction involving historical or imagined steam-powered technology

steam·roll·er \-ˌrō-lər\ *n* : a machine for compacting roads or pavements — **steam·roll·er** *also* **steam·roll** \-ˌrōl\ *vb*

steam·ship \-ˌship\ *n* : a ship driven by steam

steed \ˈstēd\ *n* : HORSE

[1]**steel** \ˈstēl\ *n* **1** : iron treated with intense heat and mixed with carbon to make it hard and tough **2** : an article made of steel **3** : a quality (as hardness of mind) that suggests steel — **steel** *adj* — **steely** *adj*

[2]**steel** *vb* : to fill with courage or determination ⟨~*ed* himself for her rage⟩

steel wool *n* : long fine steel shavings used esp. for cleaning and polishing

[1]**steep** \ˈstēp\ *adj* **1** : having a very sharp slope : PRECIPITOUS **2** : too high ⟨~ prices⟩ — **steep·ly** *adv* — **steep·ness** *n*

[2]**steep** *n* : a steep slope

³steep *vb* **1 :** to soak in a liquid; *esp* **:** to extract the essence of by soaking ⟨~ tea⟩ **2 :** SATURATE ⟨~*ed* in learning⟩
stee·ple \ˈstē-pəl\ *n* **:** a tall tapering structure built on top of a church tower; *also* **:** a church tower
stee·ple·chase \-ˌchās\ *n* [fr. the use of church steeples as landmarks to guide the riders] **:** a horse race across country; *also* **:** a race over a course obstructed by hurdles
¹steer \ˈstir\ *n* **:** a male bovine animal castrated before sexual maturity and usu. raised for beef
²steer *vb* **1 :** to direct the course of (as by a rudder or wheel) **2 :** GUIDE, CONTROL **3 :** to pursue a course of action **4 :** to be subject to guidance or direction — **steers·man** \ˈstirz-mən\ *n*
steer·age \ˈstir-ij\ *n* **1 :** DIRECTION, GUIDANCE **2 :** a section in a passenger ship for passengers paying the lowest fares
stego·sau·rus \ˌste-gə-ˈsȯr-əs\ *n* **:** any of a genus of plant-eating armored dinosaurs with a series of bony plates along the backbone
stein \ˈstīn\ *n* **:** an earthenware mug
stel·lar \ˈste-lər\ *adj* **:** of or relating to stars **:** resembling a star
¹stem \ˈstem\ *n* **1 :** the main stalk of a plant; *also* **:** a plant part that supports another part (as a leaf or fruit) **2 :** the bow of a ship **3 :** a line of ancestry **:** STOCK **4 :** that part of an inflected word which remains unchanged throughout a given inflection **5 :** something resembling the stem of a plant — **stem·less** *adj* — **stemmed** \ˈstemd\ *adj*
²stem *vb* **stemmed; stem·ming :** to have a specified source **:** DERIVE
³stem *vb* **stemmed; stem·ming :** to make headway against ⟨~ the tide⟩
⁴stem *vb* **stemmed; stem·ming :** to stop or check by or as if by damming
STEM *abbr* science, technology, engineering, and math
stem cell *n* **:** an undifferentiated cell that may give rise to many different types of cells
stench \ˈstench\ *n* **:** STINK
sten·cil \ˈsten-səl\ *n* [prob. ultim. fr. ME *stanseld* brightly ornamented, fr. AF *estencelé* spangled, pp. of *estenceler* to sparkle, fr. *estencele* spark, fr. VL **stincilla,* alter. of L *scintilla*] **:** an impervious material (as metal or paper) perforated with lettering or a design through which a substance (as ink or paint) is applied to a surface to be printed — **stencil** *vb*
ste·nog·ra·phy \stə-ˈnä-grə-fē\ *n* **:** the art or process of writing in shorthand — **ste·nog·ra·pher** \-fər\ *n* — **steno·graph·ic** \ˌste-nə-ˈgra-fik\ *adj*
ste·no·sis \stə-ˈnō-səs\ *n, pl* **-no·ses** \-ˌsēz\ **:** a narrowing of a bodily passage or orifice
stent \ˈstent\ *n* **:** a short narrow tube inserted into an anatomical vessel esp. to keep a passage open
sten·to·ri·an \sten-ˈtȯr-ē-ən\ *adj* **:** extremely loud ⟨~ tones⟩
¹step \ˈstep\ *n* **1 :** a rest for the foot in ascending or descending **:** STAIR **2 :** an advance made by raising one foot and putting it down elsewhere **3 :** manner of walking **4 :** a small space or distance **5 :** a degree, rank, or plane in a series **6 :** a sequential measure leading to a result
²step *vb* **stepped; step·ping 1 :** to advance or recede by steps **2 :** to go on foot **:** WALK **3 :** to move along briskly **4 :** to press down with the foot **5 :** to measure by steps **6 :** to construct or arrange in or as if in steps
step aerobics *n sing or pl* **:** aerobics that involves repeatedly stepping on and off a raised platform
step aside *vb* **:** STEP DOWN 1
step·broth·er \ˈstep-ˌbrə-t͟hər\ *n* **:** the son of one's stepparent by a former marriage
step·child \-ˌchī(-ə)ld\ *n* **:** a child of one's husband or wife by a former marriage
step·daugh·ter \-ˌdȯ-tər\ *n* **:** a daughter of one's wife or husband by a former marriage
step down *vb* **1 :** to give up a position **:** RETIRE, RESIGN **2 :** to lower (a voltage) by means of a transformer
step·fa·ther \-ˌfä-t͟hər\ *n* **:** the husband of one's parent when distinct from one's natural or legal father
step·lad·der \ˈstep-ˌla-dər\ *n* **:** a light portable set of steps in a hinged frame
step·moth·er \-ˌmə-t͟hər\ *n* **:** the wife of one's parent when distinct from one's natural or legal mother
step·par·ent \-ˌper-ənt\ *n* **:** a person who is a stepfather or stepmother
steppe \ˈstep\ *n* [Russ *step'*] **:** dry level grass-covered treeless land in regions of wide temperature range esp. in southeastern Europe and Asia
step·sis·ter \ˈstep-ˌsis-tər\ *n* **:** the daughter of one's stepparent by a former marriage
step·son \-ˌsən\ *n* **:** a son of one's wife or husband by a former marriage
step up *vb* **1 :** to increase (a voltage) by means of a transformer **2 :** INCREASE, ACCELERATE **3 :** to come forward — **step–up** \ˈstep-ˌəp\ *n*
ster *abbr* sterling
ste·reo \ˈster-ē-ˌō, ˈstir-\ *n, pl* **ste·re·os 1 :** stereophonic reproduction **2 :** a stereophonic sound system — **stereo** *adj*
ste·reo·phon·ic \ˌster-ē-ə-ˈfä-nik, ˌstir-\ *adj* **:** of or relating to sound reproduction designed to create the effect of listening to the original — **ste·reo·phon·i·cal·ly** \-ˈfä-ni-k(ə-)lē\ *adv*
ster·e·o·scope \ˈster-ē-ə-ˌskōp, ˈstir-\ *n* [Gk *stereos* solid + *-skopion* means for viewing] **:** an optical instrument that blends two slightly different pictures of the same subject to give the effect of depth
ste·reo·scop·ic \ˌster-ē-ə-ˈskä-pik, ˌstir-\ *adj* **1 :** of or relating to the stereoscope **2 :** characterized by the seeing of objects in three dimensions ⟨~ vision⟩ — **ste·reo·scop·i·cal·ly** \-ˈskä-pi-k(ə-)lē\ *adv* — **ste·re·os·co·py** \ˌster-ē-ˈäs-kə-pē, ˌstir-\ *n*
ste·reo·type \ˈster-ē-ə-ˌtīp, ˈstir-\ *n* **1 :** a

metal printing plate cast from a mold made from set type **2 :** something agreeing with a pattern; *esp* **:** an idea that many people have about a thing or a group and that may often be untrue or only partly true — **stereotype** *vb* — **ste·reo·typ·i·cal** \ˌster-ē-ə-ˈti-pi-kəl\ *adj* — **ste·reo·typ·i·cal·ly** \-pi-k(ə-)lē\ *adv*

ste·reo·typed \-ˌtīpt\ *adj* **:** lacking originality or individuality ♦ ***Synonyms*** TRITE, CLICHÉD, COMMONPLACE, HACKNEYED, STALE, THREADBARE

ster·ile \ˈster-əl\ *adj* **1 :** unable to bear fruit, crops, or offspring **2 :** free from living things and esp. germs — **ste·ril·i·ty** \stə-ˈri-lə-tē\ *n*

ster·il·ize \ˈster-ə-ˌlīz\ *vb* **-ized; -iz·ing :** to make sterile; *esp* **:** to free from germs — **ster·il·i·za·tion** \ˌster-ə-lə-ˈzā-shən\ *n* — **ster·il·iz·er** \ˈster-ə-ˌlī-zər\ *n*

[1]**ster·ling** \ˈstər-liŋ\ *n* **1 :** British money **2 :** sterling silver

[2]**sterling** *adj* **1 :** of, relating to, or calculated in terms of British sterling **2 :** having a fixed standard of purity represented by an alloy of 925 parts of silver with 75 parts of copper **3 :** made of sterling silver **4 :** EXCELLENT ⟨a ~ reputation⟩

[1]**stern** \ˈstərn\ *adj* **1 :** SEVERE, AUSTERE ⟨~ taskmasters⟩ **2 :** STOUT, STURDY ⟨~ resolve⟩ — **stern·ly** *adv* — **stern·ness** *n*

[2]**stern** *n* **:** the rear end of a boat

ster·num \ˈstər-nəm\ *n, pl* **sternums** *or* **ster·na** \-nə\ **:** a long flat bone or cartilage at the center front of the chest connecting the ribs of the two sides

ste·roid \ˈstir-ˌȯid, ˈster-\ *n* **:** any of various compounds including numerous hormones (as anabolic steroids) and sugar derivatives — **steroid** *or* **ste·roi·dal** \stə-ˈrȯi-dᵊl\ *adj*

stetho·scope \ˈste-thə-ˌskōp\ *n* **:** an instrument used to detect and listen to sounds produced in the body

ste·ve·dore \ˈstē-və-ˌdȯr\ *n* [Sp *estibador,* fr. *estibar* to pack, fr. L *stipare* to press together] **:** one who works at loading and unloading ships

ste·via \ˈstē-vē-ə\ *n* [NL, plant from which it is derived, fr. Petrus *Stevus* †1555 Sp. botanist] **:** a plant-derived powder used as a noncaloric sweetener

[1]**stew** \ˈstü, ˈstyü\ *n* **1 :** a dish of stewed meat and vegetables served in gravy **2 :** a state of agitation, worry, or resentment

[2]**stew** *vb* **1 :** to boil slowly **:** SIMMER **2 :** to be in a state of agitation, worry, or resentment ⟨~*ed* about her predicament⟩

stew·ard \ˈstü-ərd, ˈstyü-\ *n* [ME, fr. OE *stīweard,* fr. *stī, stig* hall, sty + *weard* ward] **1 :** one employed on a large estate to manage domestic concerns **2 :** one who supervises the provision and distribution of food (as on a ship); *also* **:** an employee on a ship or airplane who serves passengers **3 :** one actively concerned with the direction of the affairs of an organization — **stew·ard·ship** *n*

stew·ard·ess \ˈstü-ər-dəs, ˈstyü-\ *n* **:** a woman who is a steward esp. on an airplane

stg *abbr* sterling

[1]**stick** \ˈstik\ *n* **1 :** a cut or broken branch or twig; *also* **:** a long slender piece of wood **2 :** ROD, STAFF **3 :** something resembling a stick **4 :** a dull uninteresting person **5** *pl* **:** remote usu. rural areas

[2]**stick** *vb* **stuck** \ˈstək\; **stick·ing 1 :** STAB, PRICK **2 :** IMPALE **3 :** ATTACH, FASTEN **4 :** to thrust or project in some direction or manner **5 :** to be unable to proceed or move freely **6 :** to hold fast by or as if by gluing **:** ADHERE **7 :** to hold to something firmly or closely **:** CLING **8 :** to become jammed or blocked ⟨the door ~*s*⟩

stick·er \ˈsti-kər\ *n* **:** one that sticks (as a bur) or causes sticking (as glue); *esp* **:** an adhesive label

sticker shock *n* **:** astonishment and dismay on being informed of a product's unexpectedly high price

stick insect *n* **:** any of various usu. wingless insects with a long round body resembling a stick

stick·ler \ˈsti-klər, -kə-lər\ *n* **:** one who insists on exactness or completeness

stick shift *n* **:** a manually operated automobile gearshift usu. mounted on the floor

stick–to–it·ive·ness \stik-ˈtü-ə-tiv-nəs\ *n* **:** dogged perseverance **:** TENACITY

stick up *vb* **:** to rob at gunpoint — **stick·up** \ˈstik-ˌəp\ *n*

sticky \ˈsti-kē\ *adj* **stick·i·er; -est 1 :** ADHESIVE **2 :** VISCOUS, GLUEY **3 :** tending to stick ⟨~ valve⟩ **4 :** DIFFICULT ⟨a ~ problem⟩

[1]**stiff** \ˈstif\ *adj* **1 :** not pliant **:** RIGID **2 :** not limber ⟨~ joints⟩; *also* **:** TENSE, TAUT **3 :** not flowing or working easily ⟨~ paste⟩ **4 :** not natural and easy **:** FORMAL **5 :** STRONG, FORCEFUL ⟨~ breeze⟩ **6 :** HARSH, SEVERE ⟨a ~ penalty⟩ ♦ ***Synonyms*** INFLEXIBLE, INELASTIC — **stiff·ly** *adv* — **stiff·ness** *n*

[2]**stiff** *vb* **:** to refuse to pay or tip

stiff–arm \ˈstif-ˌärm\ *vb* **:** to treat with disdain or neglect ⟨~*ed* her advice⟩

stiff·en \ˈsti-fən\ *vb* **:** to make or become stiff — **stiff·en·er** *n*

stiff–necked \ˈstif-ˈnekt\ *adj* **:** STUBBORN, HAUGHTY ⟨too ~ to ask for help⟩

sti·fle \ˈstī-fəl\ *vb* **sti·fled; sti·fling 1 :** to kill by depriving of or die from lack of oxygen or air **:** SMOTHER **2 :** to keep in check by effort **:** SUPPRESS ⟨~ a sneeze⟩ — **sti·fling·ly** *adv*

stig·ma \ˈstig-mə\ *n, pl* **stig·ma·ta** \stig-ˈmä-tə, ˈstig-mə-tə\ *or* **stigmas** [L] **1 :** a mark of disgrace or discredit **2** *stigmata pl* **:** bodily marks resembling the wounds of the crucified Jesus **3 :** the upper part of the pistil of a flower that receives the pollen in fertilization — **stig·mat·ic** \stig-ˈma-tik\ *adj*

stig·ma·tize \ˈstig-mə-ˌtīz\ *vb* **-tized; -tiz·ing 1 :** to mark with a stigma **2 :** to characterize as disgraceful ⟨was *stigmatized* by the scandal⟩

stile \ˈstī(-ə)l\ *n* **:** steps used for crossing a fence or wall

sti·let·to \stə-ˈle-tō\ *n, pl* **-tos** *or* **-toes** [It, dim. of *stilo* stylus, dagger] : a slender dagger

[1]**still** \ˈstil\ *adj* **1** : MOTIONLESS **2** : making no sound : SILENT — **still·ness** *n*

[2]**still** *vb* : to make or become still

[3]**still** *adv* **1** : without motion ⟨sit ~⟩ **2** : up to and during this or that time **3** : in spite of that : NEVERTHELESS **4** : EVEN ⟨ran ~ faster⟩ **5** : YET ⟨has ~ to be recognized⟩

[4]**still** *n* **1** : STILLNESS, SILENCE **2** : a static photograph esp. from a motion picture

[5]**still** *n* **1** : DISTILLERY **2** : apparatus used in distillation

still·birth \ˈstil-ˌbərth\ *n* : the birth of a dead fetus

still·born \-ˈbȯrn\ *adj* : born dead

still life *n, pl* **still lifes** : a picture of inanimate objects

stilt \ˈstilt\ *n* : one of a pair of poles for walking with each having a step or loop for the foot to elevate the wearer above the ground; *also* : a polelike support of a structure above ground or water level

stilt·ed \ˈstil-təd\ *adj* : not easy and natural ⟨~ language⟩

Stil·ton \ˈstil-tᵊn\ *n* : a blue cheese of English origin

stim·u·lant \ˈsti-myə-lənt\ *n* **1** : an agent (as a drug) that temporarily increases the activity of an organism or any of its parts **2** : STIMULUS **3** : an alcoholic beverage — **stimulant** *adj*

stim·u·late \-ˌlāt\ *vb* **-lat·ed; -lat·ing** : to make active or more active : ANIMATE, AROUSE ⟨~ interest⟩ ♦ ***Synonyms*** EXCITE, PROVOKE, MOTIVATE, QUICKEN — **stim·u·la·tion** \ˌsti-myə-ˈlā-shən\ *n* — **stim·u·la·tive** \ˈsti-myə-ˌlā-tiv\ *adj* — **stim·u·la·tor** \-ˌlā-tər\ *n* — **stim·u·la·to·ry** \-lə-ˌtȯr-ē\ *adj*

stim·u·lus \ˈsti-myə-ləs\ *n, pl* **-li** \-ˌlī\ [L] **1** : something that moves to activity **2** : an agent that directly influences the activity of a living organism or one of its parts

[1]**sting** \ˈstiŋ\ *vb* **stung** \ˈstəŋ\; **sting·ing** **1** : to prick painfully esp. with a sharp or poisonous process **2** : to cause to suffer acutely — **sting·er** *n*

[2]**sting** *n* **1** : an act of stinging; *also* : a resultant wound, sore, or pain **2** : a pointed often venom-bearing organ (as of a bee) : STINGER **3** : an elaborate confidence game; *esp* : one worked by undercover police to trap criminals

sting·ray \ˈstiŋ-ˌrā\ *n* : any of numerous rays with sharp stinging spines on a whiplike tail

stin·gy \ˈstin-jē\ *adj* **stin·gi·er; -est** : not generous : giving or spending as little as possible — **stin·gi·ness** *n*

stink \ˈstiŋk\ *vb* **stank** \ˈstaŋk\ *or* **stunk** \ˈstəŋk\; **stunk; stink·ing** : to give forth a strong and offensive smell; *also* : to be extremely bad in quality or repute — **stink** *n* — **stink·er** *n*

stink·bug \ˈstiŋk-ˌbəg\ *n* : any of various true bugs that emit a disagreeable odor

[1]**stint** \ˈstint\ *vb* **1** : to be sparing or frugal **2** : to cut short in amount

[2]**stint** *n* **1** : an assigned amount of work **2** : RESTRAINT, LIMITATION **3** : a period of time spent at a particular activity

sti·pend \ˈstī-ˌpend, -pənd\ *n* [ME, alter. of *stipendy*, fr. L *stipendium*, fr. *stips* gift + *pendere* to weigh, pay] : a fixed sum of money paid periodically for services or to defray expenses

stip·ple \ˈsti-pəl\ *vb* **stip·pled; stip·pling** **1** : to engrave by means of dots and light strokes **2** : to apply (as paint or ink) with small short touches — **stipple** *n*

stip·u·late \ˈsti-pyə-ˌlāt\ *vb* **-lat·ed; -lat·ing** : to make an agreement; *esp* : to make a special demand for something as a condition in an agreement — **stip·u·la·tion** \ˌsti-pyə-ˈlā-shən\ *n*

[1]**stir** \ˈstər\ *vb* **stirred; stir·ring** **1** : to move slightly **2** : AROUSE, EXCITE **3** : to mix, dissolve, or make by continued circular movement ⟨~ eggs into cake batter⟩ **4** : to move to activity (as by pushing, beating, or prodding)

[2]**stir** *n* **1** : a state of agitation or activity **2** : an act of stirring

stir–fry \ˈstər-ˌfrī\ *vb* : to fry quickly over high heat while stirring continuously — **stir–fry** *n*

[1]**stir·ring** \ˈstər-iŋ\ *adj* **1** : ACTIVE, BUSTLING **2** : ROUSING, INSPIRING ⟨a ~ speech⟩

[2]**stirring** *n* : a beginning of activity ⟨the first ~*s* of revolution⟩

stir·rup \ˈstər-əp\ *n* [ME *stirop*, fr. OE *stigrāp*, lit., mounting rope] **1** : a light frame hung from a saddle to support the rider's foot **2** : STAPES

[1]**stitch** \ˈstich\ *n* **1** : a sudden sharp pain esp. in the side **2** : one of the series of loops formed by or over a needle in sewing

[2]**stitch** *vb* **1** : to fasten or join with stitches **2** : to make (as a design) with stitches **3** : SEW

stk *abbr* stock

stoat \ˈstōt\ *n, pl* **stoats** *also* **stoat** : the common Old and New World ermine esp. in its brown summer coat

[1]**stock** \ˈstäk\ *n* **1** *archaic* : a block of wood **2** : a stupid person **3** : a wooden part of a thing serving as its support, frame, or handle **4** *pl* : a device for publicly punishing offenders consisting of a wooden frame with holes in which the feet and hands can be locked **5** : the original from which others derive; *also* : a group having a common origin : FAMILY **6** : LIVESTOCK **7** : a supply of goods **8** : the ownership element in a corporation divided to give the owners an interest and usu. voting power **9** : a company of actors playing at a particular theater and presenting a series of plays **10** : liquid in which meat, fish, or vegetables have been simmered that is used as a basis for soup, gravy, or sauce

[2]**stock** *vb* : to provide with stock

[3]**stock** *adj* : kept regularly for sale or use; *also* : commonly used : STANDARD

stock·ade \stä-ˈkād\ *n* [Sp *estacada*, fr. *estaca* stake, pale, of Gmc origin] : an enclosure (as of posts and stakes) for defense or confinement

stock·bro·ker \-ˌbrō-kər\ *n* : one who executes orders to buy and sell securities

stock car *n* : a racing car that is similar to a regular car

stock exchange *n* : a place where the buying and selling of securities is conducted

stock·hold·er \ˈstäk-ˌhōl-dər\ *n* : one who owns corporate stock

stock·i·nette *or* **stock·i·net** \ˌstä-kə-ˈnet\ *n* : an elastic knitted fabric used esp. for infants' wear and bandages

stock·ing \ˈstä-kiŋ\ *n* : a close-fitting knitted covering for the foot and leg

stock market *n* **1** : STOCK EXCHANGE **2** : a market for stocks

stock·pile \ˈstäk-ˌpī(-ə)l\ *n* : a reserve supply esp. of something essential — **stockpile** *vb*

stocky \ˈstä-kē\ *adj* **stock·i·er; -est** : being short and relatively thick : STURDY ♦ ***Synonyms*** THICKSET, SQUAT, HEAVYSET, STUBBY

stock·yard \ˈstäk-ˌyärd\ *n* : a yard for stock; *esp* : one for livestock about to be slaughtered or shipped

stodgy \ˈstä-jē\ *adj* **stodg·i·er; -est 1** : thick in texture : HEAVY ⟨∼ bread⟩ **2** : not interesting : DULL ⟨a ∼ accountant⟩ **3** : extremely old-fashioned

¹sto·ic \ˈstō-ik\ *n* [ME, fr. L *stoicus,* fr. Gk *stōïkos,* lit., of the portico, fr. *Stoa* (*Poikilē*) the Painted Portico, portico at Athens where the philosopher Zeno taught] : one who suffers without complaining

²stoic *or* **sto·i·cal** \-i-kəl\ *adj* : not affected by passion or feeling; *esp* : showing indifference to pain ♦ ***Synonyms*** IMPASSIVE, PHLEGMATIC, APATHETIC, STOLID — **sto·ical·ly** \-i-k(ə-)lē\ *adv* — **sto·icism** \ˈstō-ə-ˌsi-zəm\ *n*

stoke \ˈstōk\ *vb* **stoked; stok·ing 1** : to stir up a fire **2** : to tend and supply fuel to a furnace — **stok·er** *n*

STOL *abbr* short takeoff and landing

¹stole *past of* STEAL

²stole \ˈstōl\ *n* **1** : a long narrow band worn round the neck by some members of the clergy **2** : a long wide scarf or similar covering worn by women

stolen *past part of* STEAL

stol·id \ˈstä-ləd\ *adj* : not easily aroused or excited : showing little or no emotion ⟨a ∼ face⟩ ♦ ***Synonyms*** PHLEGMATIC, APATHETIC, IMPASSIVE, STOIC — **sto·lid·i·ty** \stä-ˈli-də-tē\ *n* — **stol·id·ly** *adv*

sto·lon \ˈstō-lən, -ˌlän\ *n* : RUNNER 6

¹stom·ach \ˈstə-mək\ *n* **1** : a saclike digestive organ of a vertebrate into which food goes from the mouth by way of the throat and which opens below into the intestine **2** : a cavity in an invertebrate animal that is analogous to a stomach **3** : ABDOMEN **4** : desire for food caused by hunger : APPETITE **5** : INCLINATION, DESIRE ⟨had no ∼ for an argument⟩

²stomach *vb* : to bear without open resentment : put up with

stom·ach·ache \-ˌāk\ *n* : pain in or in the region of the stomach

stom·ach·er \ˈstə-mi-kər, -chər\ *n* : the front of a bodice often appearing between the laces of an outer garment (as in 16th century costume)

stomp \ˈstämp, ˈstómp\ *vb* : STAMP — **stomp** *n*

¹stone \ˈstōn\ *n* **1** : hardened earth or mineral matter : ROCK **2** : a small piece of rock **3** : a precious stone : GEM **4** : CALCULUS 3 **5** : a hard stony seed (as of a date) or one (as of a plum) with a stony covering **6** *pl usu* **stone** : a British unit of weight equal to 14 pounds — **stony** *also* **ston·ey** \ˈstō-nē\ *adj*

²stone *vb* **stoned; ston·ing 1** : to pelt or kill with stones **2** : to remove the stones of (a fruit)

Stone Age *n* : the first known period of prehistoric human culture characterized by the use of stone tools

stoned \ˈstōnd\ *adj* **1** : DRUNK **2** : being under the influence of a drug

stone·wall \ˈstōn-ˌwól\ *vb* : to refuse to comply or cooperate with

stone·washed \ˈstōn-ˌwósht, -ˌwäsht\ *adj* : having been washed with stones during manufacture to create a softer fabric ⟨∼ jeans⟩

stood *past and past part of* STAND

stooge \ˈstüj\ *n* **1** : a person who plays a subordinate or compliant role to a principal **2** : STRAIGHT MAN

stool \ˈstül\ *n* **1** : a seat usu. without back or arms **2** : FOOTSTOOL **3** : a seat used while urinating or defecating **4** : a discharge of fecal matter

stool pigeon *n* : DECOY, INFORMER

¹stoop \ˈstüp\ *vb* **1** : to bend forward and downward **2** : CONDESCEND **3** : to lower oneself morally ⟨∼ to lying⟩

²stoop *n* **1** : an act of bending forward **2** : a bent position of head and shoulders

³stoop *n* [D *stoep*] : a porch, platform, or entrance stairway at a house door

¹stop \ˈstäp\ *vb* **stopped; stop·ping 1** : to close (an opening) by filling or covering closely **2** : BLOCK, HALT **3** : to cease to go on **4** : to bring activity or operation to an end **5** : STAY, TARRY ♦ ***Synonyms*** QUIT, DISCONTINUE, DESIST, CEASE

²stop *n* **1** : END, CESSATION **2** : a set of organ pipes of one tone quality; *also* : a control knob for such a set **3** : OBSTRUCTION **4** : PLUG, STOPPER **5** : an act of stopping : CHECK **6** : a delay in a journey : STAY **7** : a place for stopping **8** *chiefly Brit* : any of several punctuation marks **9** : a function of an electronic device that stops a recording

stop–ac·tion \ˈstäp-ˈak-shən\ *n* : STOP-MOTION

stop·gap \ˈstäp-ˌgap\ *n* : something that serves as a temporary expedient

stop·light \-ˌlīt\ *n* : TRAFFIC LIGHT

stop–mo·tion \ˈstäp-ˈmō-shən\ *n* : a filming technique in which successive positions of objects are photographed to produce the appearance of movement

stop·over \ˈstäp-ˌō-vər\ *n* **1** : a stop at an intermediate point in one's journey **2** : a stopping place on a journey

stop·page \ˈstä-pij\ *n* : the act of stopping : the state of being stopped
stop·per \ˈstä-pər\ *n* : something (as a cork) for sealing an opening
stop·watch \ˈstäp-ˌwäch\ *n* : a watch that can be started or stopped at will for exact timing
stor·age \ˈstȯr-ij\ *n* **1** : space for storing; *also* : cost of storing **2** : MEMORY 6 **3** : the act of storing; *esp* : the safekeeping of goods (as in a warehouse)
storage battery *n* : a group of connected rechargeable electrochemical cells used to provide electric current
1store \ˈstȯr\ *vb* **stored; stor·ing** **1** : to place or leave in a safe location for preservation or future use **2** : to provide esp. for a future need ⟨~ information⟩
2store *n* **1** : something accumulated and kept for future use **2** : a large or ample quantity **3** : STOREHOUSE **4** : a retail business establishment
store·house \-ˌhau̇s\ *n* : a building for storing goods or supplies; *also* : an abundant source or supply
store·keep·er \-ˌkē-pər\ *n* : one who operates a retail store
store·room \-ˌrüm, -ˌru̇m\ *n* : a room for storing goods or supplies
sto·ried \ˈstȯr-ēd\ *adj* : celebrated in story or history ⟨a ~ career⟩
stork \ˈstȯrk\ *n* : any of various large stout-billed Old World wading birds related to the herons and ibises
1storm \ˈstȯrm\ *n* **1** : a heavy fall of rain, snow, or hail with high wind **2** : a violent outbreak or disturbance **3** : a mass attack on a defended position — **storm·i·ly** \ˈstȯr-mə-lē\ *adv* — **storm·i·ness** \-mē-nəs\ *n* — **stormy** *adj*
2storm *vb* **1** : to blow with violence; *also* : to rain, snow, or hail heavily **2** : to make a mass attack against **3** : to be violently angry : RAGE **4** : to rush along furiously ⟨*~ed* out of the room⟩
1sto·ry \ˈstȯr-ē\ *n, pl* **stories** **1** : NARRATIVE, ACCOUNT **2** : REPORT, STATEMENT **3** : ANECDOTE **4** : SHORT STORY **5** : LIE, FALSEHOOD **6** : a news article or broadcast ♦ ***Synonyms*** UNTRUTH, TALE, CANARD
2story *also* **sto·rey** \ˈstȯr-ē\ *n, pl* **stories** *also* **storeys** : a floor of a building or the space between two adjacent floor levels
sto·ry·tell·er \-ˌte-lər\ *n* : a teller of stories
sto·tin \stō-ˈtēn\ *n, pl* **sto·ti·nov** \stō-ˈtē-ˌnȯv\ : a monetary unit equal to $\frac{1}{100}$ tolar formerly used in Slovenia
sto·tin·ka \stō-ˈtiŋ-kə\ *n, pl* **-tin·ki** \-kē\ — see *lev* at MONEY table
1stout \ˈstau̇t\ *adj* **1** : BRAVE **2** : FIRM ⟨a ~ refusal⟩ **3** : STURDY **4** : STAUNCH, ENDURING ⟨~ loyalty⟩ **5** : SOLID **6** : FORCEFUL, VIOLENT ⟨a ~ attack⟩ ⟨a ~ wind⟩ **7** : BULKY, THICKSET ♦ ***Synonyms*** FLESHY, FAT, PORTLY, CORPULENT, OBESE, PLUMP — **stout·ly** *adv* — **stout·ness** *n*
2stout *n* : a dark heavy ale
1stove \ˈstōv\ *n* : an apparatus that burns fuel or uses electricity to provide heat (as for cooking or heating)
2stove *past and past part of* STAVE
stow \ˈstō\ *vb* **1** : HIDE, STORE ⟨~ baggage⟩ **2** : to pack in a compact mass
stow·away \ˈstō-ə-ˌwā\ *n* : one who hides on a vehicle to ride free
STP *abbr* standard temperature and pressure
strad·dle \ˈstra-dᵊl\ *vb* **strad·dled; strad·dling** **1** : to stand, sit, or walk with legs spread apart **2** : to favor or seem to favor two apparently opposite sides — **straddle** *n*
strafe \ˈstrāf\ *vb* **strafed; straf·ing** [G *Gott strafe England* may God punish England, propaganda slogan during World War I] : to fire upon with machine guns from a low-flying airplane
strag·gle \ˈstra-gəl\ *vb* **strag·gled; strag·gling** **1** : to wander from the direct course : ROVE, STRAY **2** : to become separated from others of the same kind — **strag·gler** *n* — **strag·gly** \ˈstra-g(ə-)lē\ *adj*
1straight \ˈstrāt\ *adj* **1** : free from curves, bends, angles, or irregularities **2** : not wandering from the main point or proper course ⟨~ thinking⟩ **3** : HONEST ⟨a ~ answer⟩ **4** : having the elements in correct order **5** : UNMIXED, UNDILUTED ⟨~ whiskey⟩ **6** : CONVENTIONAL, SQUARE **7** : of, relating to, or characterized by sexual or romantic attraction between people of the opposite sex : HETEROSEXUAL; *also* : of, relating to, or involving sexual activity between individuals of the opposite sex
2straight *adv* : in a straight manner
3straight *n* **1** : a straight line, course, or arrangement **2** : the part of a racetrack between the last turn and the finish **3** : a sequence of five cards in a poker hand
straight–arm \ˈstrāt-ˌärm\ *n* : an act of warding off a person with the arm fully extended — **straight–arm** *vb*
straight·away \ˈstrā-tə-ˌwā\ *n* : a straight stretch (as at a racetrack)
straight·edge \ˈstrāt-ˌej\ *n* : a piece of material with a straight edge for testing straight lines and surfaces or for cutting along or drawing straight lines
straight·en \ˈstrā-tᵊn\ *vb* : to make or become straight
straight flush *n* : a poker hand containing five cards of the same suit in sequence
straight·for·ward \strāt-ˈfȯr-wərd\ *adj* **1** : FRANK, CANDID, HONEST ⟨a ~ account⟩ **2** : proceeding in a straight course or manner
straight man *n* : an entertainer who feeds lines to a comedian who replies with usu. humorous quips
straight shooter *n* : a thoroughly upright straightforward person
straight·way \ˈstrāt-ˈwā, -ˌwā\ *adv* : IMMEDIATELY ⟨get ~ to work⟩
1strain \ˈstrān\ *n* [ME *streen* progeny, lineage, fr. OE *strēon* gain, acquisition] **1** : LINEAGE, ANCESTRY **2** : a group (as of

people or plants) of presumed common ancestry **3** : an inherited or inherent character or quality ⟨a ~ of madness in the family⟩ **4** : STREAK, TRACE ⟨a ~ of fanaticism⟩ **5** : MELODY **6** : the general style or tone

²**strain** *vb* [ME, fr. AF *estreindre,* fr. L *stringere* to bind or draw tight, press together] **1** : to draw taut **2** : to exert to the utmost **3** : to strive violently **4** : to injure by improper or excessive use **5** : to filter or remove by filtering **6** : to stretch beyond a proper limit — **strain·er** *n*

³**strain** *n* **1** : excessive tension or exertion (as of body or mind) **2** : bodily injury from excessive tension, effort, or use; *esp* : one in which muscles or ligaments are unduly stretched usu. from a wrench or twist **3** : deformation of a material body under the action of applied forces

¹**strait** \ˈstrāt\ *adj* [ME, fr. AF *estreit,* fr. L *strictus* strait, strict, fr. pp. of *stringere*] **1** *archaic* : STRICT **2** *archaic* : NARROW **3** *archaic* : CONSTRICTED **4** : DIFFICULT, STRAITENED

²**strait** *n* **1** : a narrow channel connecting two bodies of water **2** *pl* : DISTRESS

strait·en \ˈstrā-tᵊn\ *vb* **1** : to hem in : CONFINE **2** : to subject to distress or difficulty ⟨~*ed* by misfortune⟩

strait·jack·et *also* **straight·jack·et** \ˈstrāt-ˌja-kət\ *n* : a cover or garment of strong material (as canvas) used to bind the body and esp. the arms closely in restraining a violent prisoner or patient — **straitjacket** *vb*

strait·laced *or* **straight·laced** \-ˈlāst\ *adj* : strict in manners, morals, or opinion

¹**strand** \ˈstrand\ *n* : SHORE, BEACH

²**strand** *vb* **1** : to run, drift, or drive upon the shore ⟨a ~*ed* ship⟩ **2** : to place or leave in a helpless position

³**strand** *n* **1** : one of the fibers twisted or plaited together into a cord, rope, or cable; *also* : a cord, rope, or cable made up of such fibers **2** : a twisted or plaited ropelike mass ⟨a ~ of pearls⟩ — **strand·ed** \ˈstran-dəd\ *adj*

¹**strange** \ˈstrānj\ *adj* **strang·er; strang·est** [ME, fr. AF *estrange,* fr. L *extraneus,* lit., external, fr. *extra* outside] **1** : of external origin, kind, or character **2** : NEW, UNFAMILIAR ⟨moved to a ~ neighborhood⟩ **3** *dated* : DISTANT 6 **4** : UNACCUSTOMED, INEXPERIENCED ⟨she was ~ to his ways⟩ ♦ ***Synonyms*** SINGULAR, PECULIAR, ECCENTRIC, ERRATIC, ODD, QUAINT, CURIOUS — **strange·ly** *adv* — **strange·ness** *n*

²**strange** *n* : a quark with a charge of −⅓ and a measured energy of approximately 150 million electron volts

strang·er \ˈstrān-jər\ *n* **1** : FOREIGNER **2** : INTRUDER **3** : a person with whom one is unacquainted

stran·gle \ˈstraŋ-gəl\ *vb* **stran·gled; stran·gling** **1** : to choke to death : THROTTLE **2** : STIFLE, SUPPRESS ⟨repression ~*s* free speech⟩ — **stran·gler** *n*

strangler fig *n* : any of several figs that begin life atop a host tree and then send down roots that surround it

stran·gu·late \ˈstraŋ-gyə-ˌlāt\ *vb* **-lat·ed; -lat·ing** **1** : STRANGLE, CONSTRICT **2** : to become so constricted as to stop circulation

stran·gu·la·tion \ˌstraŋ-gyə-ˈlā-shən\ *n* : the act or process of strangling or strangulating; *also* : the state of being strangled or strangulated

¹**strap** \ˈstrap\ *n* : a narrow strip of flexible material used esp. for fastening, holding together, or wrapping

²**strap** *vb* **strapped; strap·ping** **1** : to secure with a strap **2** : BIND, CONSTRICT **3** : to flog with a strap **4** : STROP

strap·less \-ləs\ *adj* : having no straps; *esp* : having no shoulder straps

¹**strapping** *adj* : LARGE, STRONG, HUSKY

²**strapping** *n* : material for a strap

strat·a·gem \ˈstra-tə-jəm, -ˌjem\ *n* **1** : a trick to deceive or outwit the enemy; *also* : a deceptive scheme **2** : skill in deception

strat·e·gy \ˈstra-tə-jē\ *n, pl* **-gies** [Gk *stratēgia* generalship, fr. *stratēgos* general, fr. *stratos* camp, army + *agein* to lead] **1** : the science and art of military command aimed at meeting the enemy under conditions advantageous to one's own force **2** : a careful plan or method esp. for achieving an end — **stra·te·gic** \strə-ˈtē-jik\ *adj* — **strat·e·gist** \ˈstra-tə-jist\ *n*

strat·i·fy \ˈstra-tə-ˌfī\ *vb* **-fied; -fy·ing** : to form or arrange in layers — **strat·i·fi·ca·tion** \ˌstra-tə-fə-ˈkā-shən\ *n*

stra·tig·ra·phy \strə-ˈti-grə-fē\ *n* : geology that deals with rock strata — **strati·graph·ic** \ˌstra-tə-ˈgra-fik\ *adj*

strato·sphere \ˈstra-tə-ˌsfir\ *n* : the part of the earth's atmosphere between about 7 miles (11 kilometers) and 31 miles (50 kilometers) above the earth — **strato·spher·ic** \ˌstra-tə-ˈsfir-ik, -ˈsfer-\ *adj*

stra·tum \ˈstrā-təm, ˈstra-\ *n, pl* **stra·ta** \ˈstrā-tə, ˈstra-\ [NL, fr. L, spread, bed, fr. neut. of *stratus,* pp. of *sternere* to spread out] **1** : a bed, layer, or sheetlike mass (as of one kind of rock lying between layers of other kinds of rock) **2** : a level of culture; *also* : a group of people representing one stage in cultural development

¹**straw** \ˈstrȯ\ *n* **1** : stalks of grain after threshing; *also* : a single coarse dry stem (as of a grass) **2** : a thing of small worth : TRIFLE **3** : a tube (as of paper or plastic) for sucking up a beverage

²**straw** *adj* **1** : made of straw **2** : having no real force or validity ⟨a ~ vote⟩

straw·ber·ry \ˈstrȯ-ˌber-ē, -bə-rē\ *n* : an edible juicy usu. red pulpy fruit of any of several low herbs with white flowers and long slender runners; *also* : one of these herbs

straw boss *n* : a foreman of a small group of workers

straw·flow·er \ˈstrȯ-ˌflau̇(-ə)r\ *n* : any of several plants whose flowers can be dried with little loss of form or color

¹**stray** \ˈstrā\ *n* **1** : a domestic animal wandering at large or lost **2** : WAIF

[2]**stray** *vb* **1** : to wander or roam without purpose **2** : DEVIATE ⟨~*ed* from the topic⟩
[3]**stray** *adj* **1** : having strayed : separated from the group or the main body **2** : occurring at random ⟨~ remarks⟩
[1]**streak** \ˈstrēk\ *n* **1** : a line or mark of a different color or texture from its background **2** : a narrow band of light; *also* : a lightning bolt **3** : a slight admixture : TRACE **4** : a brief run (as of luck); *also* : an unbroken series ⟨a winning ~⟩
[2]**streak** *vb* **1** : to form streaks in or on **2** : to move very swiftly
[1]**stream** \ˈstrēm\ *n* **1** : a body of water (as a river) flowing on the earth; *also* : any body of flowing fluid (as water or gas) **2** : a continuous procession ⟨a ~ of traffic⟩
[2]**stream** *vb* **1** : to flow in or as if in a stream **2** : to pour out streams of liquid **3** : to trail out in length **4** : to move forward in a steady stream **5** : to transfer (digital data, such as audio or video material) in a continuous stream esp. for immediate processing or playback
stream·bed \ˈstrēm-ˌbed\ *n* : the channel occupied by a stream
stream·er \ˈstrē-mər\ *n* **1** : a long narrow ribbonlike flag **2** : a long ribbon on a dress or hat **3** : a newspaper headline that runs across the entire sheet **4** *pl* : AURORA
stream·ing \ˈstrē-miŋ\ *adj* : relating to or being the transfer of data (as music or videos) in a continuous stream esp. for immediate processing or playback
stream·let \ˈstrēm-lət\ *n* : a small stream
stream·lined \-ˌlīnd\ *adj* **1** : made with contours to reduce resistance to motion through water or air **2** : SIMPLIFIED **3** : MODERNIZED — **stream·line** *vb*
street \ˈstrēt\ *n* [ME *strete,* fr. OE *strǣt,* fr. LL *strata* paved road, fr. L, fem. of *stratus,* pp. of *sternere* to spread out] **1** : a thoroughfare esp. in a city, town, or village **2** : the occupants of the houses on a street ⟨the whole ~ likes the idea⟩
street·car \-ˌkär\ *n* : a passenger vehicle running on rails on city streets
street fighter *n* : a tough belligerent person
street hockey *n* : a game resembling ice hockey played on a hard surface with hockey sticks and a small ball
street railway *n* : a company operating streetcars or buses
street·walk·er \ˈstrēt-ˌwȯ-kər\ *n* : PROSTITUTE
strength \ˈstreŋth\ *n* **1** : the quality of being strong : ability to do or endure : POWER **2** : TOUGHNESS, SOLIDITY **3** : power to resist attack **4** : INTENSITY **5** : force as measured in numbers ⟨the ~ of an army⟩
strength·en \ˈstreŋ-thən\ *vb* : to make or become stronger — **strength·en·er** *n*
stren·u·ous \ˈstren-yə-wəs\ *adj* **1** : VIGOROUS, ENERGETIC **2** : requiring energy or stamina — **stren·u·ous·ly** *adv*
strep \ˈstrep\ *n* : STREPTOCOCCUS
strep throat *n* : an inflammatory sore throat caused by streptococci and marked by fever, prostration, and toxemia
strep·to·coc·cus \ˌstrep-tə-ˈkä-kəs\ *n, pl* **-coc·ci** \-ˈkä-ˌkī, -ˈkäk-ˌsī, -ˈkä-ˌkē, -ˈkäk-ˌsē\ : any of various spherical bacteria that usu. grow in chains and include some causing serious diseases — **strep·to·coc·cal** \-kəl\ *adj*
strep·to·my·cin \-ˈmī-sᵊn\ *n* : an antibiotic produced by soil bacteria and used esp. in treating tuberculosis
[1]**stress** \ˈstres\ *n* **1** : PRESSURE, STRAIN; *esp* : a force that tends to distort a body **2** : a factor that induces bodily or mental tension; *also* : a state induced by such a stress **3** : EMPHASIS **4** : relative prominence of sound **5** : ACCENT; *also* : any syllable carrying the accent — **stress·ful** \ˈstres-fəl\ *adj*
[2]**stress** *vb* **1** : to put pressure or strain on **2** : to put emphasis on : ACCENT
[1]**stretch** \ˈstrech\ *vb* **1** : to spread or reach out : EXTEND ⟨~*ed* out her arm⟩ **2** : to draw out in length or breadth : EXPAND **3** : to make tense : STRAIN **4** : EXAGGERATE ⟨~*ed* the truth⟩ **5** : to become extended without breaking ⟨rubber ~*es* easily⟩ — **stretchy** \ˈstre-chē\ *adj*
[2]**stretch** *n* **1** : an act of extending or drawing out beyond ordinary or normal limits **2** : a continuous extent in length, area, or time **3** : the extent to which something may be stretched **4** : either of the straight sides of a racecourse
[3]**stretch** *adj* : easily stretched ⟨~ pants⟩
[1]**stretch·er** \ˈstre-chər\ *n* **1** : one that stretches **2** : a device for carrying a sick, injured, or dead person
[2]**stretcher** *vb* : to carry or transport on a stretcher
stretch marks *n pl* : striae on the skin (as of the abdomen) due to excessive stretching and rupture of elastic fibers (as from pregnancy)
strew \ˈstrü\ *vb* **strewed; strewed** *or* **strewn** \ˈstrün\; **strew·ing** **1** : to spread by scattering **2** : to cover by or as if by scattering something over or on ⟨a floor *strewn* with toys⟩ **3** : DISSEMINATE
stria \ˈstrī-ə\ *n, pl* **stri·ae** \ˈstrī-ˌē\ **1** : STRIATION 3 **2** : a stripe or line (as in the skin)
stri·at·ed muscle \ˈstrī-ˌā-təd-\ *n* : muscle tissue made up of long thin cells with many nuclei and alternate light and dark stripes that includes esp. the muscle of the heart and muscle that moves the vertebrate skeleton and is mostly under voluntary control
stri·a·tion \strī-ˈā-shən\ *n* **1** : the state of being marked with stripes or lines **2** : arrangement of striations or striae **3** : a minute groove, scratch, or channel esp. when one of a parallel series
strick·en \ˈstri-kən\ *adj* **1** : afflicted by or as if by disease, misfortune, or sorrow **2** : WOUNDED ⟨was ~ by an arrow⟩
strict \ˈstrikt\ *adj* **1** : allowing no evasion or escape : RIGOROUS ⟨~ discipline⟩ **2**

: ACCURATE, PRECISE ⟨the ~ sense of the word⟩ ♦ ***Synonyms*** STRINGENT, RIGID — **strict·ly** *adv* — **strict·ness** *n*

stric·ture \ˈstrik-chər\ *n* **1** : an abnormal narrowing of a bodily passage; *also* : the narrowed part **2** : hostile criticism : a critical remark

¹**stride** \ˈstrīd\ *vb* **strode** \ˈstrōd\; **strid·den** \ˈstri-dᵊn\; **strid·ing** : to walk or run with long regular steps — **strid·er** *n*

²**stride** *n* **1** : a long step **2** : a stage of progress **3** : manner of striding : GAIT

stri·dent \ˈstrī-dᵊnt\ *adj* : harsh sounding : GRATING, SHRILL ⟨a ~ voice⟩

strife \ˈstrīf\ *n* : CONFLICT, FIGHT, STRUGGLE ♦ ***Synonyms*** DISCORD, CONTENTION, DISSENSION

¹**strike** \ˈstrīk\ *vb* **struck** \ˈstrək\; **struck** *also* **strick·en** \ˈstri-kən\; **strik·ing** **1** : to take a course : GO ⟨*struck* off through the brush⟩ **2** : to touch or hit sharply; *also* : to deliver a blow **3** : to produce by or as if by a blow ⟨*struck* terror in the foe⟩ **4** : to lower (as a flag or sail) **5** : to collide with; *also* : to injure or destroy by collision **6** : DELETE, CANCEL **7** : to produce by impressing ⟨*struck* a medal⟩; *also* : COIN ⟨~ a new cent⟩ **8** : to cause to sound ⟨~ a bell⟩ **9** : to afflict suddenly : lay low ⟨*stricken* with a high fever⟩ **10** : to appear to; *also* : to appear to as remarkable : IMPRESS **11** : to reach by reckoning ⟨~ an average⟩ **12** : to stop work in order to obtain a change in conditions of employment **13** : to cause (a match) to ignite by rubbing **14** : to come upon ⟨~ gold⟩ **15** : TAKE ON, ASSUME ⟨~ a pose⟩ — **strik·er** *n*

²**strike** *n* **1** : an act or instance of striking **2** : a sudden discovery of rich ore or oil deposits **3** : a pitched baseball that is swung at but not hit **4** : the knocking down of all the bowling pins with the 1st ball **5** : a military attack

strike·break·er \-ˌbrā-kər\ *n* : a person hired to replace a striking worker

strike·out \-ˌau̇t\ *n* : an out in baseball as a result of a batter's being charged with three strikes

strike out *vb* **1** : to enter upon a course of action **2** : to start out vigorously **3** : to make an out in baseball by a strikeout

strike–slip \ˈstrīk-ˌslip\ *n* : a fault about which movement is predominantly horizontal

strike up *vb* **1** : to begin or cause to begin to sing or play ⟨*strike up* the band⟩ **2** : BEGIN ⟨~ a conversation⟩

strike zone *n* : the area over home plate through which a pitched baseball must pass to be called a strike

striking *adj* : attracting attention : very noticeable ♦ ***Synonyms*** ARRESTING, SALIENT, CONSPICUOUS, OUTSTANDING, REMARKABLE, PROMINENT — **strik·ing·ly** *adv*

¹**string** \ˈstriŋ\ *n* **1** : a line usu. composed of twisted threads **2** : a series of things arranged as if strung on a cord **3** : a plant fiber (as a leaf vein) **4** *pl* : the stringed instruments of an orchestra ♦ ***Synonyms*** SUCCESSION, PROGRESSION, SEQUENCE, CHAIN, TRAIN

²**string** *vb* **strung** \ˈstrəŋ\; **string·ing** **1** : to provide with strings ⟨~ a racket⟩ **2** : to make tense **3** : to thread on or as if on a string ⟨~ pearls⟩ **4** : to hang, tie, or fasten by a string **5** : to take the strings out of ⟨~ beans⟩ **6** : to extend like a string

string bean *n* : a bean of one of the older varieties of kidney bean that have stringy fibers on the lines of separation of the pods; *also* : SNAP BEAN

string bikini *n* : a scanty bikini

string cheese *n* : cheese that can be pulled apart in narrow strips

stringed \ˈstriŋd\ *adj* **1** : having strings ⟨~ instruments⟩ **2** : produced by strings

strin·gen·cy \ˈstrin-jən-sē\ *n* **1** : STRICTNESS, SEVERITY **2** : SCARCITY ⟨~ of money⟩ — **strin·gent** \-jənt\ *adj*

string·er \ˈstriŋ-ər\ *n* **1** : a long horizontal member in a framed structure or a bridge **2** : a news correspondent paid by the amount of copy

stringy \ˈstriŋ-ē\ *adj* **string·i·er; -est** **1** : resembling string esp. in tough, fibrous, or disordered quality ⟨~ meat⟩ ⟨~ hair⟩ **2** : lean and sinewy in build

¹**strip** \ˈstrip\ *vb* **stripped** \ˈstript\ *also* **stript; strip·ping** **1** : to take the covering or clothing from **2** : to take off one's clothes **3** : to pull or tear off **4** : to make bare or clear (as by cutting or grazing) **5** : PLUNDER, PILLAGE ♦ ***Synonyms*** DIVEST, DENUDE, DEPRIVE, DISMANTLE — **strip·per** *n*

²**strip** *n* **1** : a long narrow flat piece **2** : AIRSTRIP

¹**stripe** \ˈstrīp\ *vb* **striped** \ˈstrīpt\; **strip·ing** : to make stripes on

²**stripe** *n* **1** : a line or long narrow division having a different color from the background **2** : a strip of braid (as on a sleeve) indicating military rank or length of service **3** : TYPE, CHARACTER — **striped** \ˈstrīpt, ˈstrī-pəd\ *adj*

striped bass *n* : a large black-striped marine bony fish that occurs along the Atlantic and Pacific coasts of the U.S. and is an excellent food and sport fish

strip·ling \ˈstri-pliŋ\ *n* : YOUTH, LAD

strip mall *n* : a long building or group of buildings housing several retail stores or service establishments

strip mine *n* : a mine that is worked from the earth's surface by the stripping of the topsoil — **strip–mine** *vb*

strip·tease \ˈstrip-ˌtēz\ *n* : an act or dance in which a performer removes clothing piece by piece — **strip·teas·er** *n*

strive \ˈstrīv\ *vb* **strove** \ˈstrōv\ *also* **strived** \ˈstrīvd\; **striv·en** \ˈstri-vən\ *or* **strived; striv·ing** **1** : to make effort : labor hard **2** : to struggle in opposition : CONTEND ♦ ***Synonyms*** ENDEAVOR, ATTEMPT, TRY, ASSAY

strobe \ˈstrōb\ *n* **1** : STROBOSCOPE **2** : a device for high-speed intermittent illumination (as in photography)

stro·bo·scope \ˈstrō-bə-ˌskōp\ *n* : an instrument for studying rapid motion by means of a rapidly flashing light
strode *past of* STRIDE
[1]**stroke** \ˈstrōk\ *vb* **stroked; strok·ing** **1** : to rub gently **2** : to flatter in a manner designed to persuade
[2]**stroke** *n* **1** : the act of striking : BLOW, KNOCK **2** : a sudden action or process producing an impact ⟨~ of lightning⟩; *also* : an unexpected result **3** : sudden weakening or loss of consciousness or the power to move or feel caused by rupture or obstruction (as by a clot) of a blood vessel of the brain **4** : one of a series of movements against air or water to get through or over it ⟨the ~ of a bird's wing⟩ **5** : a rower who sets the pace for a crew **6** : a vigorous effort **7** : the sound of striking (as of a clock) **8** : a single movement with or as if with a tool or implement (as a pen)
stroll \ˈstrōl\ *vb* : to walk in a leisurely or idle manner — **stroll** *n* — **stroll·er** *n*
strong \ˈstrȯŋ\ *adj* **stron·ger** \ˈstrȯŋ-gər\; **stron·gest** \ˈstrȯŋ-gəst\ **1** : POWERFUL, VIGOROUS **2** : HEALTHY, ROBUST **3** : of a specified number ⟨an army 10 thousand ~⟩ **4** : not mild or weak **5** : VIOLENT ⟨~ wind⟩ **6** : ZEALOUS ⟨a ~ supporter⟩ **7** : not easily broken **8** : FIRM, SOLID ⟨~ beliefs⟩ ♦ ***Synonyms*** STOUT, STURDY, STALWART, TOUGH — **strong·ly** *adv*
strong–arm \ˈstrȯŋ-ˈärm\ *adj* : having or using undue force ⟨~ operatives⟩
strong force *n* : the physical force responsible for binding together nucleons in the atomic nucleus
strong·hold \-ˌhōld\ *n* : a fortified place : FORTRESS
strong·man \-ˌman\ *n* : one who leads or controls by force of will and character or by military strength
stron·tium \ˈsträn-chē-əm, ˈsträn-tē-əm\ *n* : a soft malleable metallic chemical element
[1]**strop** \ˈsträp\ *n* : STRAP; *esp* : one for sharpening a razor
[2]**strop** *vb* **stropped; strop·ping** : to sharpen a razor on a strop
stro·phe \ˈstrō-fē\ *n* [Gk *strophē*, lit., act of turning] : a division of a poem — **stroph·ic** \ˈsträ-fik\ *adj*
strove *past of* STRIVE
struck *past and past part of* STRIKE
[1]**struc·ture** \ˈstrək-chər\ *n* [ME, fr. L *structura*, fr. *structus*, pp. of *struere* to heap up, build] **1** : the action of building : CONSTRUCTION **2** : something built (as a house or a dam); *also* : something made up of interdependent parts in a definite pattern of organization **3** : arrangement or relationship of elements (as particles, parts, or organs) in a substance, body, or system — **struc·tur·al** *adj*
[2]**structure** *vb* **struc·tured; struc·tur·ing** : to make into a structure
stru·del \ˈstrü-dᵊl, ˈshtrü-\ *n* [G, lit., whirlpool] : a pastry made of a thin sheet of dough rolled up with filling and baked ⟨apple ~⟩
[1]**strug·gle** \ˈstrə-gəl\ *vb* **strug·gled; strug·gling** **1** : to make strenuous efforts against opposition : STRIVE **2** : to proceed with difficulty or with great effort ♦ ***Synonyms*** ENDEAVOR, ATTEMPT, TRY, ASSAY
[2]**struggle** *n* **1** : CONTEST, STRIFE **2** : a violent effort or exertion
strum \ˈstrəm\ *vb* **strummed; strumming** : to play on a stringed instrument by brushing the strings with the fingers ⟨~ a guitar⟩
strum·pet \ˈstrəm-pət\ *n*, *dated, usu disparaging* : PROSTITUTE
strung \ˈstrəŋ\ *past and past part of* STRING
[1]**strut** \ˈstrət\ *vb* **strut·ted; strut·ting** : to walk with an affectedly proud gait
[2]**strut** *n* **1** : a bar or rod for resisting lengthwise pressure **2** : a haughty or pompous gait
strych·nine \ˈstrik-ˌnīn, -nən, -ˌnēn\ *n* : a bitter poisonous plant alkaloid used as a poison (as for rats) and medicinally as a stimulant of the central nervous system
[1]**stub** \ˈstəb\ *n* **1** : STUMP 2 **2** : a short blunt end **3** : a small part of each leaf (as of a checkbook) kept as a memorandum of the items on the detached part
[2]**stub** *vb* **stubbed; stub·bing** : to strike (as one's toe) against something
stub·ble \ˈstə-bəl\ *n* **1** : the cut stem ends of herbs and esp. grasses left in the soil after harvest **2** : a rough surface or growth resembling stubble ⟨his face covered with ~⟩ — **stub·bly** \-b(ə-)lē\ *adj*
stub·born \ˈstə-bərn\ *adj* **1** : FIRM, DETERMINED **2** : done or continued in a willful, unreasonable, or persistent manner **3** : not easily controlled or remedied ⟨a ~ cold⟩ — **stub·born·ly** *adv* — **stub·born·ness** *n*
stub·by \ˈstə-bē\ *adj* : short, blunt, and thick like a stub ⟨~ fingers⟩
stuc·co \ˈstə-kō\ *n, pl* **stuccos** *or* **stuccoes** [It] : plaster for coating exterior walls — **stuc·coed** \ˈstə-kōd\ *adj*
stuck *past and past part of* STICK
stuck–up \ˈstək-ˈəp\ *adj* : CONCEITED
[1]**stud** \ˈstəd\ *n* : a male animal and esp. a horse (**stud·horse** \-ˌhȯrs\) kept for breeding
[2]**stud** *n* **1** : one of the smaller uprights in a building to which the wall materials are fastened **2** : a removable device like a button used as a fastener or ornament ⟨shirt ~*s*⟩ **3** : a projecting nail, pin, or rod
[3]**stud** *vb* **stud·ded; stud·ding** **1** : to supply with or adorn with studs **2** : DOT ⟨the sky was *studded* with stars⟩
[4]**stud** *abbr* student
stud·book \ˈstəd-ˌbu̇k\ *n* : an official record of the pedigree of purebred animals (as horses or dogs)
studding *n* : the studs in a building or wall
stu·dent \ˈstü-dᵊnt, ˈstyü-\ *n* : SCHOLAR, PUPIL; *esp* : one who attends a school
stud·ied \ˈstə-dēd\ *adj* : INTENTIONAL ⟨a ~ insult⟩ ♦ ***Synonyms*** DELIBERATE,

CONSIDERED, PREMEDITATED, DESIGNED

stu·dio \'stü-dē-,ō, 'styü-\ *n, pl* **-dios** **1** : a place where an artist works; *also* : a place for the study of an art **2** : a place where motion pictures are made **3** : a place equipped for the transmission of radio or television programs

stu·di·ous \'stü-dē-əs, 'styü-\ *adj* : devoted to study — **stu·di·ous·ly** *adv*

[1]**study** \'stə-dē\ *n, pl* **stud·ies** **1** : the use of the mind to gain knowledge **2** : the act or process of learning about something **3** : careful examination **4** : INTENT, PURPOSE **5** : a branch of learning **6** : a room esp. for reading and writing

[2]**study** *vb* **stud·ied; study·ing** **1** : to engage in study or the study of **2** : to consider attentively or in detail ♦ ***Synonyms*** CONSIDER, CONTEMPLATE, WEIGH

[1]**stuff** \'stəf\ *n* [ME, fr. AF *estuffes* goods, fr. *estuffer* to fill in (with rubble), furnish, equip, of Gmc origin] **1** : personal property **2** : raw material **3** : a finished textile fabric; *esp* : a worsted fabric **4** : writing, talk, or ideas of little or transitory worth **5** : an unspecified material substance or aggregate of matter **6** : fundamental material **7** : special knowledge or capability

[2]**stuff** *vb* **1** : to fill by packing things in : CRAM **2** : to eat greedily : GORGE **3** : to prepare (as meat) by filling with a stuffing **4** : to fill (as a cushion) with a soft material **5** : to stop up : PLUG

stuffed shirt \'stəft-\ *n* : a smug, conceited, and usu. pompous and inflexibly conservative person

stuff·ing *n* : material used to fill tightly; *esp* : a mixture of bread crumbs and spices used to stuff food

stuffy \'stə-fē\ *adj* **stuff·i·er; -est** **1** : STODGY **2** : lacking fresh air : CLOSE; *also* : blocked up ⟨a ~ nose⟩

stul·ti·fy \'stəl-tə-,fī\ *vb* **-fied; -fy·ing** **1** : to cause to appear foolish or stupid **2** : to impair, invalidate, or make ineffective **3** : to have a dulling effect on — **stul·ti·fi·ca·tion** \,stəl-tə-fə-'kā-shən\ *n*

stum·ble \'stəm-bəl\ *vb* **stum·bled; stum·bling** **1** : to blunder morally **2** : to trip in walking or running **3** : to walk unsteadily; *also* : to speak or act in a blundering or clumsy manner **4** : to happen by chance — **stumble** *n*

stumbling block *n* : an obstacle to belief, understanding, or progress

[1]**stump** \'stəmp\ *n* **1** : the base of a bodily part (as a leg or tooth) left after the rest is removed **2** : the part of a plant and esp. a tree remaining with the root after the trunk is cut off **3** : a place or occasion for political public speaking — **stumpy** *adj*

[2]**stump** *vb* **1** : BAFFLE, PERPLEX **2** : to clear (land) of stumps **3** : to tour (a region) making political speeches **4** : to walk clumsily and heavily

stun \'stən\ *vb* **stunned; stun·ning** **1** : to make senseless or dizzy by or as if by a blow **2** : BEWILDER, STUPEFY ⟨*stunned* by the news⟩

stung *past and past part of* STING

stunk *past and past part of* STINK

stun·ning *adj* **1** : causing astonishment or disbelief **2** : strikingly beautiful — **stun·ning·ly** *adv*

[1]**stunt** \'stənt\ *vb* : to hinder the normal growth or progress of

[2]**stunt** *n* : an unusual or spectacular feat

stu·pe·fy \'stü-pə-,fī, 'styü-\ *vb* **-fied; -fy·ing** **1** : to make stupid, groggy, or insensible **2** : ASTONISH — **stu·pe·fac·tion** \,stü-pə-'fak-shən, ,styü-\ *n*

stu·pen·dous \stu̇-'pen-dəs, styu̇-\ *adj* : causing astonishment esp. because of great size or height ♦ ***Synonyms*** TREMENDOUS, PRODIGIOUS, MONUMENTAL, MONSTROUS — **stu·pen·dous·ly** *adv*

stu·pid \'stü-pəd, 'styü-\ *adj* [MF *stupide,* fr. L *stupidus,* fr. *stupēre* to be numb, be astonished] **1** : very dull in mind **2** : showing or resulting from dullness of mind — **stu·pid·i·ty** \stu̇-'pi-də-tē, styu̇-\ *n* — **stu·pid·ly** *adv*

stu·por \'stü-pər, 'styü-\ *n* **1** : a condition of greatly dulled or completely suspended sense or feeling **2** : a state of extreme apathy or torpor often following stress or shock — **stu·por·ous** *adj*

stur·dy \'stər-dē\ *adj* **stur·di·er; -est** [ME, brave, stubborn, fr. AF *esturdi* stunned, fr. pp. of *esturdir* to stun, fr. VL **exturdire*, fr. L *ex-* + VL **turdus* simpleton, fr. L *turdus* thrush] **1** : STRONG, ROBUST **2** : RESOLUTE, UNYIELDING ♦ ***Synonyms*** STOUT, STALWART, TOUGH, TENACIOUS — **stur·di·ly** \-də-lē\ *adv* — **stur·di·ness** \-dē-nəs\ *n*

stur·geon \'stər-jən\ *n* : any of a family of large bony fishes including some whose roe are made into caviar

stut·ter \'stə-tər\ *vb* : to speak with involuntary disruption or blocking of sounds — **stutter** *n* — **stut·ter·er** *n*

stutter step *n* : a move made by a runner (as in football) done to fake a defender out of position

[1]**sty** \'stī\ *n, pl* **sties** : PIGPEN

[2]**sty** *or* **stye** *n, pl* **sties** *or* **styes** : an inflamed swelling of a skin gland on the edge of an eyelid

[1]**style** \'stī(-ə)l\ *n* **1** : mode of address : TITLE **2** : a way of speaking or writing; *esp* : one characteristic of an individual, period, school, or nation ⟨ornate ~⟩ **3** : manner or method of acting, making, or performing; *also* : a distinctive or characteristic manner **4** : a slender pointed instrument or process; *esp* : STYLUS **5** : a fashionable manner or mode **6** : overall excellence, skill, or grace in performance, manner, or appearance **7** : the custom followed in spelling, capitalization, punctuation, and typography — **sty·lis·tic** \stī-'lis-tik\ *adj*

[2]**style** *vb* **styled; styl·ing** **1** : NAME, DESIGNATE **2** : to make or design in accord with a prevailing mode ⟨~ hair⟩

styling *n* : the way in which something is styled

styl·ise *Brit var of* STYLIZE

styl·ish \ˈstī-lish\ *adj* : conforming to current fashion ♦ ***Synonyms*** MODISH, SMART, CHIC — **styl·ish·ly** *adv* — **stylish·ness** *n*

styl·ist \ˈstī-list\ *n* **1** : one (as a writer) noted for a distinctive style **2** : a developer or designer of styles

styl·ize \ˈstī-ˌlīz, ˈstī-ə-\ *vb* **styl·ized; styliz·ing** : to conform to a style; *esp* : to represent or design according to a pattern or style rather than according to nature or tradition ⟨*stylized* flower prints⟩ — **styli·za·tion** \ˌstī-lə-ˈzā-shən\ *n*

sty·lus \ˈstī-ləs\ *n, pl* **sty·li** \ˈstī-ˌlī\ *also* **sty·lus·es** \ˈstī-lə-səz\ [L *stylus, stilus* spike, stylus] **1** : a pointed implement used by the ancients for writing on wax **2** : a phonograph needle **3** : a pen-shaped pointing device for entering data into a computer

sty·mie \ˈstī-mē\ *vb* **sty·mied; sty·mie·ing** : BLOCK, FRUSTRATE ⟨managed to ~ the opposition⟩

styp·tic \ˈstip-tik\ *adj* : tending to check bleeding — **styptic** *n*

suave \ˈswäv\ *adj* [F, fr. MF, pleasant, sweet, fr. L *suavis*] : persuasively pleasing : smoothly agreeable ♦ ***Synonyms*** URBANE, SMOOTH, BLAND — **suave·ly** *adv* — **sua·vi·ty** \ˈswä-və-tē\ *n*

[1]**sub** \ˈsəb\ *n* : SUBSTITUTE — **sub** *vb*

[2]**sub** *n* : SUBMARINE

[3]**sub** *abbr* **1** subtract **2** suburb

sub- \ˈsəb\ *prefix* **1** : under : beneath **2** : subordinate : secondary **3** : subordinate portion of : subdivision of **4** : with repetition of a process described in a simple verb so as to form, stress, or deal with subordinate parts or relations **5** : somewhat **6** : falling nearly in the category of : bordering on

sub·al·pine \ˌsəb-ˈal-ˌpīn\ *adj* **1** : of or relating to the region about the foot and lower slopes of the Alps **2** : of, relating to, or inhabiting high upland slopes esp. just below the timberline

sub·al·tern \sə-ˈbȯl-tərn\ *n* : SUBORDINATE; *esp* : a junior officer (as in the British army)

sub·as·sem·bly \ˌsəb-ə-ˈsem-blē\ *n* : an assembled unit to be incorporated with other units in a finished product

sub·atom·ic \ˌsəb-ə-ˈtä-mik\ *adj* : of or relating to the inside of the atom or to particles smaller than atoms

sub·clin·i·cal \ˌsəb-ˈkli-nə-kəl\ *adj* : not detectable by the usual clinical tests ⟨a ~ infection⟩

sub·com·pact \ˈsəb-ˈkäm-ˌpakt\ *n* : an automobile smaller than a compact

[1]**sub·con·scious** \ˌsəb-ˈkän-chəs, ˈsəb-\ *adj* : existing in the mind without entering conscious awareness — **sub·con·scious·ly** *adv* — **sub·con·scious·ness** *n*

[2]**subconscious** *n* : mental activities just below the threshold of consciousness

sub·con·ti·nent \ˌsəb-ˈkän-tə-nənt\ *n* : a major subdivision of a continent — **sub·con·ti·nen·tal** \ˌsəb-ˌkän-tə-ˈnen-tᵊl\ *adj*

sub·di·vide \ˌsəb-də-ˈvīd, ˈsəb-də-ˌvīd\ *vb* : to divide the parts of into more parts; *esp* : to divide (a tract of land) into building lots — **sub·di·vi·sion** \-ˈvi-zhən, -ˌvi-\ *n*

sub·duc·tion \səb-ˈdək-shən\ *n* : the descent of the edge of one crustal plate beneath the edge of an adjacent plate

sub·due \səb-ˈdü, -ˈdyü\ *vb* **sub·dued; sub·du·ing** **1** : to bring into subjection : VANQUISH **2** : to bring under control : CURB **3** : to reduce the intensity of

subj *abbr* **1** subject **2** subjunctive

[1]**sub·ject** \ˈsəb-jikt\ *n* [ME *suget, subget,* fr. AF, fr. L *subjectus* one under authority & *subjectum* subject of a proposition, fr. *subicere* to subject, lit., to throw under, fr. *sub-* under + *jacere* to throw] **1** : a person under the authority of another **2** : a person subject to a sovereign **3** : an individual that is studied or experimented on **4** : the person or thing discussed or treated : TOPIC, THEME **5** : a word or word group denoting that of which something is predicated

[2]**subject** *adj* **1** : being under the power or rule of another **2** : LIABLE, EXPOSED ⟨~ to floods⟩ **3** : dependent on some act or condition ⟨appointment ~ to senate approval⟩ ♦ ***Synonyms*** SUBORDINATE, SECONDARY, TRIBUTARY, COLLATERAL, DEPENDENT

[3]**sub·ject** \səb-ˈjekt\ *vb* **1** : to bring under control : CONQUER **2** : to make liable **3** : to cause to undergo or endure — **sub·jec·tion** \-ˈjek-shən\ *n*

sub·jec·tive \(ˌ)səb-ˈjek-tiv\ *adj* **1** : of, relating to, or constituting a subject **2** : of, relating to, or arising within one's self or mind in contrast to what is outside : PERSONAL ⟨~ judgments⟩ ⟨a ~ sensation⟩ — **sub·jec·tive·ly** *adv* — **sub·jec·tiv·i·ty** \-ˌjek-ˈti-və-tē\ *n*

subject matter *n* : matter presented for consideration, discussion, or study

sub·join \(ˌ)səb-ˈjȯin\ *vb* : APPEND ⟨~*ed* a statement of expenses to her report⟩

sub ju·di·ce \(ˌ)su̇b-ˈyü-di-ˌkā, ˈsəb-ˈjü-də-(ˌ)sē\ *adv* [L] : before a judge or court : not yet legally decided

sub·ju·gate \ˈsəb-ji-ˌgāt\ *vb* **-gat·ed; -gat·ing** : CONQUER, SUBDUE ♦ ***Synonyms*** REDUCE, OVERCOME, OVERTHROW, VANQUISH, DEFEAT, BEAT — **sub·ju·ga·tion** \ˌsəb-ji-ˈgā-shən\ *n*

---

subacute
subagency
subagent
subaqueous
subarctic
subarea
subatmospheric
subaverage
subbasement
subcategory
subcellular
subchapter
subclass
subclassify
subcommittee
subcontract
subcontractor
subculture
subcutaneous
subdiscipline
subentry
subfamily
subfield
subfreezing
subgenre
subgenus
subgroup
subhead

sub·junc·tive \səb-ˈjəŋk-tiv\ *adj* : of, relating to, or constituting a verb form that represents an act or state as contingent or possible or viewed emotionally (as with desire) ⟨the ~ mood⟩ — **subjunctive** *n*

sub·lease \ˈsəb-ˈlēs, -ˌlēs\ *n* : a lease by a lessee of part or all of leased premises to another person with the original lessee retaining some right under the original lease — **sublease** *vb*

¹**sub·let** \ˈsəb-ˈlet\ *vb* **-let; -let·ting** : to let all or a part of (a leased property) to another; *also* : to rent (a property) from a lessee

²**sublet** \-ˌlet\ *n* : property and esp. housing obtained by or available through a sublease

sub·li·mate \ˈsə-blə-ˌmāt\ *vb* **-mat·ed; -mat·ing** 1 : SUBLIME 2 : to direct the expression of (as a desire or impulse) from a primitive to a more socially and culturally acceptable form — **sub·li·ma·tion** \ˌsə-blə-ˈmā-shən\ *n*

¹**sub·lime** \sə-ˈblīm\ *vb* **sub·limed; sub·lim·ing** : to pass or cause to pass directly from the solid to the vapor state

²**sublime** *adj* 1 : EXALTED, NOBLE 2 : having awe-inspiring beauty or grandeur ♦ ***Synonyms*** GLORIOUS, SPLENDID, SUPERB, RESPLENDENT, GORGEOUS — **sub·lime·ly** *adv* — **sub·lim·i·ty** \-ˈbli-mə-tē\ *n*

sub·lim·i·nal \(ˌ)səb-ˈli-mə-nᵊl, ˈsəb-\ *adj* [*sub-* + L *limin-, limen* threshold] 1 : inadequate to produce a sensation or mental awareness ⟨~ stimuli⟩ 2 : existing or functioning below the threshold of consciousness ⟨the ~ mind⟩ ⟨~ advertising⟩

sub·ma·chine gun \ˌsəb-mə-ˈshēn-ˌgən\ *n* : an automatic firearm fired from the shoulder or hip

¹**sub·ma·rine** \ˈsəb-mə-ˌrēn, ˌsəb-mə-ˈrēn\ *adj* : UNDERWATER; *esp* : UNDERSEA

²**submarine** *n* 1 : a naval vessel designed to operate underwater 2 : a large sandwich made from a long split roll with any of a variety of fillings

sub·merge \səb-ˈmərj\ *vb* **sub·merged; sub·merg·ing** 1 : to put or plunge under the surface of water 2 : INUNDATE — **sub·mer·gence** \-ˈmər-jəns\ *n*

sub·merse \səb-ˈmərs\ *vb* **sub·mersed; sub·mers·ing** : SUBMERGE — **sub·mer·sion** \-ˈmər-zhən\ *n*

¹**sub·mers·ible** \səb-ˈmər-sə-bəl\ *adj* : capable of being submerged

²**submersible** *n* : something that is submersible; *esp* : a small underwater craft used for deep-sea research

sub·mi·cro·sco·pic \ˌsəb-ˌmī-krə-ˈskä-pik\ *adj* : too small to be seen in an ordinary light microscope

sub·min·ia·ture \ˌsəb-ˈmi-nē-ə-ˌchu̇r, ˈsəb-, -ˈmi-ni-ˌchu̇r, -chər\ *adj* : very small

sub·mit \səb-ˈmit\ *vb* **sub·mit·ted; sub·mit·ting** 1 : to commit to the discretion or decision of another or of others 2 : YIELD, SURRENDER 3 : to put forward as an opinion — **sub·mis·sion** \-ˈmi-shən\ *n* — **sub·mis·sive** \-ˈmi-siv\ *adj*

sub·nor·mal \ˌsəb-ˈnȯr-məl\ *adj* : falling below what is normal; *also* : having less of something and esp. intelligence than is normal — **sub·nor·mal·i·ty** \ˌsəb-nȯr-ˈma-lə-tē\ *n*

sub·or·bit·al \ˌsəb-ˈȯr-bə-tᵊl, ˈsəb-\ *adj* : being or involving less than one orbit

¹**sub·or·di·nate** \sə-ˈbȯr-də-nət\ *adj* 1 : of lower class or rank ⟨a ~ officer⟩ 2 : INFERIOR 3 : submissive to authority 4 : subordinated to other elements in a sentence : DEPENDENT ⟨~ clause⟩ ♦ ***Synonyms*** SECONDARY, SUBJECT, TRIBUTARY, COLLATERAL

²**subordinate** *n* : one that is subordinate

³**sub·or·di·nate** \sə-ˈbȯr-də-ˌnāt\ *vb* **-nat·ed; -nat·ing** 1 : SUBDUE 2 : to place in a lower rank or class — **sub·or·di·na·tion** \-ˌbȯr-də-ˈnā-shən\ *n*

sub·orn \sə-ˈbȯrn\ *vb* 1 : to induce secretly to do an unlawful thing 2 : to induce to commit perjury — **sub·or·na·tion** \ˌsə-ˌbȯr-ˈnā-shən\ *n*

¹**sub·poe·na** \sə-ˈpē-nə\ *n* [ME *suppena,* fr. L *sub poena* under penalty] : a writ commanding the person named in it to attend court under penalty for failure to do so

²**subpoena** *vb* **-naed; -na·ing** : to summon with a subpoena

sub–Sa·ha·ran \ˌsəb-sə-ˈher-ən\ *adj* : of, relating to, or being the part of Africa south of the Sahara

sub·scribe \səb-ˈskrīb\ *vb* **sub·scribed; sub·scrib·ing** 1 : to sign one's name to a document 2 : to give consent by or as if by signing one's name 3 : to promise to contribute by signing one's name with the amount promised 4 : to place an order by signing 5 : to receive a periodical or service regularly on order 6 : FAVOR, APPROVE ⟨~ to the theory⟩ ♦ ***Synonyms*** AGREE, ACQUIESCE, ASSENT, ACCEDE — **sub·scrib·er** *n*

sub·script \ˈsəb-ˌskript\ *n* : a symbol (as a letter or number) immediately below or below and to the right or left of another written character — **subscript** *adj*

sub·scrip·tion \səb-ˈskrip-shən\ *n* 1 : the act of subscribing : SIGNATURE 2 : a purchase by signed order

sub·se·quent \ˈsəb-si-kwənt, -sə-ˌkwent\ *adj* : following after : SUCCEEDING ⟨~ events⟩ — **sub·se·quent·ly** *adv*

sub·ser·vi·ence \səb-ˈsər-vē-əns\ *n* 1 : a subordinate place or condition 2 : SERVILITY — **sub·ser·vi·en·cy** \-ən-sē\ *n* — **sub·ser·vi·ent** \-ənt\ *adj*

sub·set \ˈsəb-ˌset\ *n* : a set each of whose elements is an element of an inclusive set

---

subheading
subhuman
subkingdom
sublethal
subliterate
subminimal
subminimum
suboptimal
suborder
subparagraph
subparallel
subphylum
subplot
subpopulation
subproblem
subprofessional
subprogram
subregion
subroutine
subsection

sub·side \səb-ˈsīd\ *vb* **sub·sid·ed; sub·sid·ing** [L *subsidere,* fr. *sub-* under + *sidere* to sit down, sink] **1 :** to settle to the bottom of a liquid **2 :** to tend downward : DESCEND **3 :** SINK, SUBMERGE ⟨*subsided* into a chair⟩ **4 :** to become quiet and tranquil ♦ ***Synonyms*** ABATE, WANE, MODERATE, SLACKEN — **sub·sid·ence** \səb-ˈsī-dᵊns, ˈsəb-sə-dəns\ *n*

¹**sub·sid·iary** \səb-ˈsi-dē-ˌer-ē\ *adj* **1 :** furnishing aid or support **2 :** of secondary importance **3 :** of or relating to a subsidy ♦ ***Synonyms*** AUXILIARY, CONTRIBUTORY, SUBSERVIENT, ACCESSORY

²**subsidiary** *n, pl* **-iar·ies :** one that is subsidiary; *esp* **:** a company controlled by another

sub·si·dise *Brit var of* SUBSIDIZE

sub·si·dize \ˈsəb-sə-ˌdīz\ *vb* **-dized; -diz·ing :** to aid or furnish with a subsidy

sub·si·dy \ˈsəb-sə-dē\ *n, pl* **-dies** [ME, *subsidie,* fr. AF, fr. L *subsidium* reserve troops, support, assistance, fr. *sub-* near + *sedēre* to sit] **:** a gift of public money to a private person or company or to another government

sub·sist \səb-ˈsist\ *vb* **1 :** EXIST, PERSIST **2 :** to have the means (as food and clothing) of maintaining life; *esp* **:** to nourish oneself

sub·sis·tence \səb-ˈsis-təns\ *n* **1 :** EXISTENCE **2 :** means of subsisting **:** the minimum (as of food and clothing) necessary to support life

sub·son·ic \ˌsəb-ˈsä-nik, ˈsəb-\ *adj* **:** being or relating to a speed less than that of sound; *also* **:** moving at such a speed

sub·species \ˈsəb-ˌspē-shēz, -sēz\ *n* **:** a subdivision of a species; *esp* **:** a category in biological classification ranking just below a species that designates a geographic population genetically distinct from other such populations and potentially able to breed with them where its range overlaps theirs

sub·stance \ˈsəb-stəns\ *n* **1 :** essential nature **:** ESSENCE ⟨divine ~⟩; *also* **:** the fundamental or essential part or quality ⟨the ~ of the speech⟩ **2 :** physical material from which something is made or which has discrete existence; *also* **:** matter of particular or definite chemical constitution **3 :** something (as drugs or alcohol) deemed harmful and usu. subject to legal restriction ⟨~ abuse⟩ **4 :** material possessions **:** PROPERTY, WEALTH

sub·stan·dard \ˌsəb-ˈstan-dərd\ *adj* **:** falling short of a standard or norm

sub·stan·tial \səb-ˈstan-chəl\ *adj* **1 :** existing as or in substance **:** MATERIAL; *also* **:** not illusory **:** REAL **2 :** IMPORTANT, ESSENTIAL ⟨a ~ difference in the stories⟩ **3 :** NOURISHING, SATISFYING ⟨~ meal⟩ **4 :** having means **:** WELL-TO-DO **5 :** CONSIDERABLE ⟨~ profit⟩ **6 :** STRONG, FIRM — **sub·stan·tial·ly** *adv*

sub·stan·ti·ate \səb-ˈstan-chē-ˌāt\ *vb* **-at·ed; -at·ing 1 :** to give substance or body to **2 :** VERIFY, PROVE ⟨~ a charge⟩ — **sub·stan·ti·a·tion** \-ˌstan-chē-ˈā-shən\ *n*

¹**sub·stan·tive** \ˈsəb-stən-tiv\ *n* **:** NOUN; *also* **:** a word or phrase used as a noun

²**substantive** *adj* **:** having substance **:** REAL ⟨~ changes⟩

¹**sub·sti·tute** \ˈsəb-stə-ˌtüt, -ˌtyüt\ *n* **:** a person or thing replacing another — **substitute** *adj*

²**substitute** *vb* **-tut·ed; -tut·ing 1 :** to put or use in the place of another **2 :** to serve as a substitute — **sub·sti·tu·tion** \ˌsəb-stə-ˈtü-shən, -ˈtyü-\ *n*

sub·strate \ˈsəb-ˌstrāt\ *n* **1 :** the base on which a plant or animal lives **2 :** a substance acted upon (as by an enzyme)

sub·stra·tum \ˈsəb-ˌstrā-təm, -ˌstra-\ *n, pl* **-stra·ta** \-tə\ **:** the layer or structure (as subsoil) lying underneath

sub·struc·ture \ˈsəb-ˌstrək-chər\ *n* **:** FOUNDATION, GROUNDWORK

sub·sume \səb-ˈsüm\ *vb* **sub·sumed; sub·sum·ing :** to include or place within something larger or more comprehensive

sub·sur·face \ˈsəb-ˌsər-fəs\ *n* **:** earth material near the surface of the ground — **subsurface** *adj*

sub·ter·fuge \ˈsəb-tər-ˌfyüj\ *n* **:** a trick or device used in order to conceal, escape, or evade ♦ ***Synonyms*** FRAUD, DECEPTION, TRICKERY

sub·ter·ra·nean \ˌsəb-tə-ˈrā-nē-ən\ *adj* **1 :** lying or being underground **2 :** SECRET, HIDDEN ⟨a ~ network of criminals⟩

sub·tile \ˈsə-tᵊl\ *adj* **sub·til·er** \ˈsə-tᵊl-ər\; **sub·til·est** \ˈsə-tᵊl-əst\ **:** SUBTLE ⟨a ~ aroma⟩

sub·ti·tle \ˈsəb-ˌtī-tᵊl\ *n* **1 :** a secondary or explanatory title (as of a book) **2 :** printed matter projected on a motion-picture screen during or between the scenes

sub·tle \ˈsə-tᵊl\ *adj* **sub·tler** \ˈsə-tᵊl-ər\; **sub·tlest** \ˈsə-tᵊl-əst\ **1 :** hardly noticeable ⟨~ differences⟩ **2 :** SHREWD, PERCEPTIVE ⟨a ~ mind⟩ **3 :** CLEVER, SLY ⟨a ~ rogue⟩ — **sub·tle·ty** \-tē\ *n* — **sub·tly** \ˈsə-tᵊl-ē\ *adv*

sub·tract \səb-ˈtrakt\ *vb* **:** to take away (as one part or number) from another; *also* **:** to perform the operation of deducting one number from another — **sub·trac·tion** \-ˈtrak-shən\ *n*

sub·tra·hend \ˈsəb-trə-ˌhend\ *n* **:** a number that is to be subtracted from another

sub·trop·i·cal \ˌsəb-ˈträ-pi-kəl, ˈsəb-\ *also* **sub·trop·ic** \-pik\ *adj* **:** of, relating to, or being regions bordering on the tropical zone ⟨a ~ environment⟩ — **sub·trop·ics** \-piks\ *n pl*

sub·urb \ˈsə-ˌbərb\ *n* **1 :** an outlying part of a city; *also* **:** a small community adjacent to a city **2** *pl* **:** a residential area adjacent to a city — **sub·ur·ban** \sə-ˈbər-

---

subsense
subsoil
substage
substation
subsystem
subteen
subthreshold
subtopic
subtotal
subtreasury
subtype
subunit

bən\ *adj or n* — **sub·ur·ban·ite** \sə-ˈbər-bə-ˌnīt\ *n*

sub·ur·bia \sə-ˈbər-bē-ə\ *n* **1** : SUBURBS **2** : suburban people or customs

sub·ven·tion \səb-ˈven-chən\ *n* : SUBSIDY, ENDOWMENT

sub·vert \səb-ˈvərt\ *vb* **1** : OVERTHROW, RUIN **2** : CORRUPT ⟨~ the rule of law⟩ — **sub·ver·sion** \-ˈvər-zhən\ *n* — **sub·ver·sive** \-ˈvər-siv\ *adj*

sub·way \ˈsəb-ˌwā\ *n* : an underground way; *esp* : an underground electric railway

sub·woof·er \ˈsəb-ˈwu̇-fər\ *n* : a loudspeaker responsive only to the lowest acoustic frequencies

suc·ceed \sək-ˈsēd\ *vb* **1** : to follow next in order or next after another; *esp* : to inherit sovereignty, rank, title, or property **2** : to attain a desired object or end : be successful

suc·cess \sək-ˈses\ *n* **1** : favorable or desired outcome **2** : the gaining of wealth and fame **3** : one that succeeds — **suc·cess·ful** \-fəl\ *adj* — **suc·cess·ful·ly** *adv*

suc·ces·sion \sək-ˈse-shən\ *n* **1** : the order, act, or right of succeeding to a property, title, or throne **2** : the act or process of following in order **3** : a series of persons or things that follow one after another ♦ ***Synonyms*** PROGRESSION, SEQUENCE, CHAIN, TRAIN, STRING

suc·ces·sive \sək-ˈse-siv\ *adj* : following in order : CONSECUTIVE ⟨three ~ days⟩ — **suc·ces·sive·ly** *adv*

suc·ces·sor \sək-ˈse-sər\ *n* : one that succeeds (as to a throne, title, estate, or office)

suc·cinct \(ˌ)sək-ˈsiŋkt, sə-ˈsiŋkt\ *adj* : BRIEF, CONCISE ⟨a ~ description⟩ ♦ ***Synonyms*** TERSE, LACONIC, SUMMARY, CURT, SHORT — **suc·cinct·ly** *adv* — **suc·cinct·ness** *n*

suc·cor \ˈsə-kər\ *n* [ME *socour, sucurs* (taken as pl.), fr. AF *sucur, sucors,* fr. ML *succursus,* fr. L *succurrere* to run to the rescue, bring aid] : AID, HELP, RELIEF — **succor** *vb*

suc·co·tash \ˈsə-kə-ˌtash\ *n* [Narragansett *msíckquatash* boiled corn kernels] : beans and corn kernels cooked together

suc·cour *chiefly Brit var of* SUCCOR

[1]**suc·cu·lent** \ˈsə-kyə-lənt\ *adj* : full of juice : JUICY; *also* : having fleshy tissues that conserve moisture ⟨~ plants⟩ — **suc·cu·lence** \-ləns\ *n*

[2]**succulent** *n* : a succulent plant (as a cactus or an aloe)

suc·cumb \sə-ˈkəm\ *vb* **1** : to yield to superior strength or force or overpowering appeal or desire **2** : DIE ♦ ***Synonyms*** SUBMIT, CAPITULATE, RELENT, DEFER

[1]**such** \ˈsəch, ˈsich\ *adj* **1** : of this or that kind **2** : having a quality just specified or to be specified

[2]**such** *pron* **1** : such a one or ones ⟨he's a star, and acted as ~⟩ **2** : that or those similar or related thereto ⟨boards and nails and ~⟩

[3]**such** *adv* : to that degree : so

such·like \ˈsəch-ˌlīk\ *adj* : SIMILAR

[1]**suck** \ˈsək\ *vb* **1** : to draw in liquid and esp. mother's milk with the mouth **2** : to draw liquid from by action of the mouth ⟨~ an orange⟩ **3** : to take in or up or remove by or as if by suction **4** *slang* : to be objectionable

[2]**suck** *n* **1** : a sucking movement or force **2** : the act of sucking

suck·er \ˈsə-kər\ *n* **1** : one that sucks **2** : a part of an animal's body used for sucking or for clinging **3** : any of numerous freshwater fishes with thick soft lips for sucking in food **4** : a shoot from the roots or lower part of a plant **5** : a person easily deceived **6** — used as a generalized term of reference ⟨see if you can get that ~ working again⟩

suck·le \ˈsə-kəl\ *vb* **suck·led; suck·ling** : to give or draw milk from the breast or udder; *also* : NURTURE

suck·ling \ˈsə-kliŋ\ *n* : a young unweaned mammal

suck–up \ˈsək-ˌəp\ *n* : a person who seeks to gain favor by flattery ⟨a ~ to the teacher⟩

su·cre \ˈsü-(ˌ)krā\ *n* : the basic monetary unit of Ecuador until 2000

su·crose \ˈsü-ˌkrōs, -ˌkrōz\ *n* : a sweet sugar obtained commercially esp. from sugarcane or sugar beets

suc·tion \ˈsək-shən\ *n* **1** : the act of sucking **2** : the act or process of drawing something (as liquid or dust) into a space (as in a vacuum cleaner or a pump) by partially exhausting the air in the space — **suc·tion·al** \-shə-nəl\ *adj*

suction cup *n* : a cup-shaped device in which a partial vacuum is produced when applied to a surface

sud·den \ˈsə-dᵊn\ *adj* [ME *sodain,* fr. AF *sudain,* fr. L *subitaneus,* fr. *subitus* sudden, fr. pp. of *subire* to come up] **1** : happening or coming unexpectedly ⟨~ shower⟩; *also* : changing angle or character all at once ⟨~ turn⟩ ⟨~ descent⟩ **2** : HASTY, RASH ⟨~ decision⟩ **3** : made or brought about in a short time : PROMPT ⟨~ cure⟩ ♦ ***Synonyms*** PRECIPITATE, HEADLONG, IMPETUOUS — **sud·den·ly** *adv* — **sud·den·ness** *n*

sudden infant death syndrome *n* : death due to unknown causes of an apparently healthy infant usu. before one year of age and esp. during sleep

su·do·ku \sü-ˈdō-kü\ *n* [Jp *sūdoku*, short for *sūji wa dokushin ni kagiru* "the numerals must remain single"] : a puzzle in which several numbers are to be filled into a 9x9 grid of squares so that every row, every column, and every 3x3 box contains the numbers 1 through 9

suds \ˈsədz\ *n pl* : soapy water esp. when frothy — **sudsy** \ˈsəd-zē\ *adj*

sue \ˈsü\ *vb* **sued; su·ing** [ME *sewen, siuen* to follow, strive for, petition, fr. AF *sivre, siure,* fr. VL **sequere,* fr. L *sequi* to follow] **1** : PETITION, SOLICIT ⟨*sued* for peace⟩ **2** : to seek justice or right by bringing legal action ⟨*sued* the company⟩

suede *also* **suède** \ˈswād\ *n* [F *gants de Suède* Swedish gloves] **1** : leather with a napped surface **2** : a fabric with a suedelike nap

su•et \ˈsü-ət\ *n* : the hard fat from beef and mutton that yields tallow

suff *abbr* **1** sufficient **2** suffix

suf•fer \ˈsə-fər\ *vb* **suf•fered; suf•fer•ing** **1** : to feel or endure pain **2** : EXPERIENCE, UNDERGO ⟨~ a defeat⟩ **3** : to bear loss, damage, or injury **4** : ALLOW, PERMIT ♦ ***Synonyms*** ENDURE, ABIDE, TOLERATE, STAND, BROOK, STOMACH — **suf•fer•able** \ˈsə-fə-rə-bəl\ *adj* — **suf•fer•er** *n*

suf•fer•ance \ˈsə-frəns, -fə-rəns\ *n* **1** : consent or approval implied by lack of interference or resistance **2** : ENDURANCE, PATIENCE

suf•fer•ing \ˈsə-friŋ, -fə-riŋ\ *n* : PAIN, MISERY, HARDSHIP ⟨human ~⟩

suf•fice \sə-ˈfīs\ *vb* **suf•ficed; suf•fic•ing** **1** : to satisfy a need : be sufficient **2** : to be capable or competent

suf•fi•cien•cy \sə-ˈfi-shən-sē\ *n* **1** : a sufficient quantity to meet one's needs **2** : ADEQUACY

suf•fi•cient \sə-ˈfi-shənt\ *adj* : adequate to accomplish a purpose or meet a need — **suf•fi•cient•ly** *adv*

1**suf•fix** \ˈsə-ˌfiks\ *n* : an affix occurring at the end of a word

2**suf•fix** \ˈsə-fiks, (ˌ)sə-ˈfiks\ *vb* : to attach as a suffix — **suf•fix•ation** \ˌsə-ˌfik-ˈsā-shən\ *n*

suf•fo•cate \ˈsə-fə-ˌkāt\ *vb* **-cat•ed; -cat•ing** : STIFLE, SMOTHER, CHOKE — **suf•fo•cat•ing•ly** *adv* — **suf•fo•ca•tion** \ˌsə-fə-ˈkā-shən\ *n*

suf•fra•gan \ˈsə-fri-gən\ *n* : an assistant bishop; *esp* : one not having the right of succession — **suffragan** *adj*

suf•frage \ˈsə-frij\ *n* [L *suffragium*] **1** : VOTE **2** : the right to vote : FRANCHISE

suf•frag•ette \ˌsə-fri-ˈjet\ *n* : a woman who advocates suffrage for women

suf•frag•ist \ˈsəf-ri-jist\ *n* : one who advocates extension of suffrage esp. to women

suf•fuse \sə-ˈfyüz\ *vb* **suf•fused; suf•fus•ing** : to spread over or through in the manner of a fluid or light ♦ ***Synonyms*** INFUSE, IMBUE, INGRAIN, STEEP — **suf•fu•sion** \-ˈfyü-zhən\ *n*

1**sug•ar** \ˈshu̇-gər\ *n* **1** : a sweet substance that is colorless or white when pure and is chiefly sucrose from sugarcane or sugar beets **2** : a water-soluble compound (as glucose) similar to sucrose — **sug•ary** *adj*

2**sugar** *vb* **sug•ared; sug•ar•ing** **1** : to mix, cover, or sprinkle with sugar **2** : SWEETEN ⟨~ advice with flattery⟩ **3** : to form sugar ⟨a syrup that ~*s*⟩ **4** : GRANULATE

sugar beet *n* : a large beet with a white root from which sugar is made

sug•ar•cane \ˈshu̇-gər-ˌkān\ *n* : a tall grass widely grown in warm regions for the sugar in its stalks

sugar daddy *n* **1** : a well-to-do usu. older man who supports or spends lavishly on a mistress, girlfriend, or boyfriend **2** : a generous benefactor of a cause

sugar maple *n* : a maple with a sweet sap; *esp* : one of eastern No. America with sap that is the chief source of maple syrup and maple sugar

sugar pea *n* : SNOW PEA

sug•ar•plum \ˈshu̇-gər-ˌpləm\ *n* : a small ball of candy

sug•gest \səg-ˈjest, sə-\ *vb* **1** : to put (as a thought, plan, or desire) into a person's mind **2** : to remind or evoke by association of ideas ♦ ***Synonyms*** IMPLY, HINT, INTIMATE, INSINUATE, CONNOTE

sug•gest•ible \səg-ˈjes-tə-bəl, sə-\ *adj* : easily influenced by suggestion

sug•ges•tion \-ˈjes-chən\ *n* **1** : an act or instance of suggesting; *also* : something suggested **2** : a slight indication

sug•ges•tive \-ˈjes-tiv\ *adj* : tending to suggest something; *esp* : suggesting something improper or indecent — **sug•ges•tive•ly** *adv* — **sug•ges•tive•ness** *n*

1**sui•cide** \ˈsü-ə-ˌsīd\ *n* **1** : the act of killing oneself purposely **2** : one that commits or attempts suicide — **sui•cid•al** \ˌsü-ə-ˈsī-dᵊl\ *adj*

2**suicide** *adj* : being or performing a deliberate act resulting in the voluntary death of the person who does it ⟨a ~ mission⟩ ⟨a ~ bomber⟩

sui ge•ner•is \ˌsü-ˌī-ˈje-nə-rəs; ˌsü-ē-\ *adj* [L, of its own kind] : being in a class by itself : UNIQUE

1**suit** \ˈsüt\ *n* **1** : an action in court to recover a right or claim **2** : an act of suing or entreating; *esp* : COURTSHIP **3** : a number of things used together ⟨~ of clothes⟩ **4** : all the playing cards in a pack bearing the same symbol

2**suit** *vb* **1** : to be appropriate or fitting **2** : to be becoming to **3** : to meet the needs or desires of : PLEASE

suit•able \ˈsü-tə-bəl\ *adj* : FITTING, PROPER, APPROPRIATE ⟨~ dress⟩ ♦ ***Synonyms*** FIT, MEET, APT, HAPPY — **suit•abil•i•ty** \ˌsü-tə-ˈbi-lə-tē\ *n* — **suit•able•ness** \ˈsü-tə-bəl-nəs\ *n* — **suit•ably** \-tə-blē\ *adv*

suit•case \ˈsüt-ˌkās\ *n* : a portable case designed to hold a traveler's clothing and personal articles

suite \ˈswēt, *for 4 also* ˈsüt\ *n* **1** : RETINUE **2** : a group of rooms occupied as a unit **3** : a modern instrumental composition in several movements of different character; *also* : a long orchestral concert arrangement in suite form of material drawn from a longer work **4** : a set of matched furniture for a room

suit•ing \ˈsü-tiŋ\ *n* : fabric for suits of clothes

suit•or \ˈsü-tər\ *n* **1** : one who sues or petitions **2** : one who courts a woman or seeks to marry her

su•ki•ya•ki \skē-ˈyä-kē, ˌsu̇-kē-ˈyä-\ *n* : thin slices of meat, tofu, and vegetables cooked in soy sauce and sugar

sul•fa drug \ˈsəl-fə-\ *n* : any of various

synthetic organic bacteria-inhibiting drugs
sul·fate \ˈsəl-ˌfāt\ *n* : a salt or ester of sulfuric acid
sul·fide \ˈsəl-ˈfīd\ *n* : a compound of sulfur
sul·fur *also* **sul·phur** \ˈsəl-fər\ *n* : a nonmetallic chemical element used esp. in the chemical and paper industries and in vulcanizing rubber
sulfur di·ox·ide \-dī-ˈäk-sīd\ *n* : a heavy pungent toxic gas that is used esp. in bleaching, as a preservative, and as a refrigerant, and is a major air pollutant
sul·fu·ric \ˌsəl-ˈfyu̇r-ik\ *adj* : of, relating to, or containing sulfur
sulfuric acid *or* **sul·phu·ric acid** \ˌsəl-ˈfyu̇r-ik-\ *n* : a heavy corrosive oily strong acid
sul·fu·rous *also* **sul·phu·rous** \ˈsəl-fə-rəs, -fyə-, *also esp for 1* ˌsəl-ˈfyu̇r-əs\ *adj* **1** : of, relating to, or containing sulfur **2** : of or relating to brimstone or the fire of hell : INFERNAL **3** : FIERY, INFLAMED ⟨~ sermons⟩
¹**sulk** \ˈsəlk\ *vb* : to be or become moodily silent or irritable
²**sulk** *n* : a sulky mood or spell
¹**sulky** \ˈsəl-kē\ *adj* **sulk·i·er; -est** : inclined to sulk : MOROSE, MOODY ⟨a ~ mood⟩ ♦ ***Synonyms*** SURLY, GLUM, SULLEN, GLOOMY — **sulk·i·ly** \ˈsəl-kə-lē\ *adv* — **sulk·i·ness** \-kē-nəs\ *n*
²**sulky** *n, pl* **sulkies** : a light 2-wheeled horse-drawn vehicle with a seat for the driver and usu. no body
sul·len \ˈsə-lən\ *adj* **1** : gloomily silent : MOROSE **2** : DISMAL, GLOOMY ⟨a ~ sky⟩ ♦ ***Synonyms*** GLUM, SURLY, DOUR, SATURNINE — **sul·len·ly** *adv* — **sul·len·ness** *n*
sul·ly \ˈsə-lē\ *vb* **sul·lied; sul·ly·ing** : SOIL, SMIRCH, DEFILE ⟨~ his name⟩
sul·tan \ˈsəl-tᵊn\ *n* : a sovereign esp. of a Muslim state — **sul·tan·ate** \-ˌāt\ *n*
sul·ta·na \ˌsəl-ˈta-nə\ *n* **1** : a female member of a sultan's family **2** : a pale seedless grape; *also* : a raisin of this grape
sul·try \ˈsəl-trē\ *adj* **sul·tri·er; -est** [obs. E *sulter* to swelter, alter. of E *swelter*] : very hot and moist : SWELTERING; *also* : exciting sexual desire ⟨a ~ look⟩
¹**sum** \ˈsəm\ *n* [ME *summe*, fr. AF *sume, somme*, fr. L *summa*, fr. fem. of *summus* highest] **1** : a quantity of money **2** : the whole amount **3** : GIST ⟨the ~ of an argument⟩ **4** : the result obtained by adding numbers **5** : a problem in arithmetic
²**sum** *vb* **summed; sum·ming** : to find the sum of by adding or counting
³**sum** *n* : — see MONEY table
su·mac *also* **su·mach** \ˈsü-ˌmak, ˈshü-\ *n* : any of a genus of trees, shrubs, and woody vines having spikes or loose clusters of red or whitish berries
sum·ma·rise *Brit var of* SUMMARIZE
sum·ma·rize \ˈsə-mə-ˌrīz\ *vb* **-rized; -riz·ing** : to tell in a summary
¹**sum·ma·ry** \ˈsə-mə-rē\ *adj* **1** : covering the main points briefly : CONCISE **2** : done without delay or formality ⟨~ punishment⟩ ♦ ***Synonyms*** TERSE, SUCCINCT, LACONIC — **sum·mar·i·ly** \(ˌ)sə-ˈmer-ə-lē, ˈsə-mə-rə-lē\ *adv*
²**summary** *n, pl* **-ries** : a concise statement of the main points
sum·ma·tion \(ˌ)sə-ˈmā-shən\ *n* : a summing up; *esp* : a speech in court summing up the arguments in a case
sum·mer \ˈsə-mər\ *n* : the season of the year in a region in which the sun shines most directly : the warmest period of the year — **sum·mery** *adj*
sum·mer·house \ˈsə-mər-ˌhau̇s\ *n* : a covered structure in a garden or park to provide a shady retreat
summersault *var of* SOMERSAULT
summer squash *n* : any of various squashes (as zucchini) used as a vegetable while immature
sum·mit \ˈsə-mət\ *n* **1** : the highest point **2** : a conference of highest-level officials ⟨an economic ~⟩
sum·mon \ˈsə-mən\ *vb* [ME *somnen, somonen*, fr. AF *somondre*, fr. VL **summonere*, alter. of L *summonēre* to remind secretly] **1** : to call to a meeting : CONVOKE **2** : to send for; *also* : to order to appear in court **3** : to evoke esp. by an act of the will ⟨~ up courage⟩ — **sum·mon·er** *n*
sum·mons \ˈsə-mənz\ *n, pl* **sum·mons·es** **1** : an authoritative call to appear at a designated place or to attend to a duty **2** : a warning or citation to appear in court at a specified time to answer charges
sump·tu·ous \ˈsəmp-shə-wəs, -chə-\ *adj* : LAVISH, LUXURIOUS ⟨a ~ banquet⟩ ⟨a ~ residence⟩
sum up *vb* : SUMMARIZE
¹**sun** \ˈsən\ *n* **1** : the shining celestial body around which the earth and other planets revolve and from which they receive light and heat **2** : a celestial body like the sun **3** : SUNSHINE — **sun·less** *adj* — **sun·ny** *adj*
²**sun** *vb* **sunned; sun·ning** **1** : to expose to or as if to the rays of the sun **2** : to sun oneself
Sun *abbr* Sunday
sun·bath \ˈsən-ˌbath, -ˌbäth\ *n* : an exposure to sunlight or a sunlamp — **sun·bathe** \-ˌbāt͟h\ *vb*
sun·beam \-ˌbēm\ *n* : a ray of sunlight
sun·block \ˈsən-ˌbläk\ *n* : a preparation used on the skin to prevent sunburn (as by blocking ultraviolet radiation)
sun·bon·net \-ˌbä-nət\ *n* : a bonnet with a wide brim to shield the face and neck from the sun
¹**sun·burn** \-ˌbərn\ *vb* **-burned** \-ˌbərnd\ *or* **-burnt** \-ˌbərnt\; **-burn·ing** : to cause or become affected with sunburn
²**sunburn** *n* : a skin inflammation caused by overexposure to ultraviolet radiation esp. from sunshine
sun·dae \ˈsən-(ˌ)dā, -dē\ *n* : ice cream served with topping
Sun·day \ˈsən-ˌdā, -dē\ *n* : the 1st day of the week : the Christian Sabbath
sun·der \ˈsən-dər\ *vb* : to force apart ⟨a family ~*ed* by scandal⟩ ♦ ***Synonyms*** SEVER, PART, DISJOIN, DISUNITE

sun·di·al \ˈsən-ˌdī(-ə)l\ *n* : a device for showing the time of day from the shadow cast on a plate by an object with a straight edge
sun·down \-ˌdau̇n\ *n* : SUNSET 2
sun·dries \ˈsən-drēz\ *n pl* : various small articles or items
sun·dry \ˈsən-drē\ *adj* : SEVERAL, DIVERS, VARIOUS ⟨for ~ reasons⟩
sun·fish \ˈsən-ˌfish\ *n* **1** : a large marine fish with a deep flattened body **2** : any of numerous often brightly colored No. American freshwater fishes related to the perches and usu. having the body flattened from side to side
sun·flow·er \-ˌflau̇(-ə)r\ *n* : any of a genus of tall New World plants related to the daisies and often grown for the oil-rich seeds of their yellow-petaled dark-centered flower heads
sung *past and past part of* SING
sun·glasses \ˈsən-ˌgla-səz\ *n pl* : glasses to protect the eyes from the sun
sunk *past and past part of* SINK
sunk·en \ˈsəŋ-kən\ *adj* **1** : SUBMERGED ⟨~ ships⟩ **2** : fallen in : HOLLOW ⟨~ cheeks⟩ **3** : lying in a depression ⟨~ garden⟩; *also* : constructed below the general floor level ⟨a ~ living room⟩
sun·lamp \ˈsən-ˌlamp\ *n* : an electric lamp designed to emit radiation of wavelengths from ultraviolet to infrared
sun·light \-ˌlīt\ *n* : SUNSHINE
sun·lit \-ˌlit\ *adj* : lighted by or as if by the sun
Sun·ni \ˈsu̇-nē\ *n* **1** : one of the two main branches of Islam **2** : a Muslim who is a member of this branch
sun protection factor *n* : a number that is the factor by which the time required for unprotected skin to become sunburned is increased when a sunscreen is used
sun·rise \-ˌrīz\ *n* **1** : the apparent rising of the sun above the horizon **2** : the time at which the sun rises
sun·roof \-ˌrüf, -ˌru̇f\ *n* : a panel in an automobile roof that can be opened
sun·screen \-ˌskrēn\ *n* : a preparation on the skin to prevent sunburn (as by absorbing ultraviolet radiation)
sun·set \-ˌset\ *n* **1** : the apparent descent of the sun below the horizon **2** : the time at which the sun sets
sun·shade \ˈsən-ˌshād\ *n* : something (as a parasol or awning) used as a protection from the sun's rays
sun·shine \-ˌshīn\ *n* : the direct light of the sun — **sun·shiny** *adj*
sun·spot \-ˌspät\ *n* : any of the dark spots that appear at times on the sun's surface
sun·stroke \-ˌstrōk\ *n* : heatstroke caused by direct exposure to the sun
sun·tan \-ˌtan\ *n* : a browning of the skin from exposure to the sun's rays
sun·up \-ˌəp\ *n* : SUNRISE 2
¹sup \ˈsəp\ *vb* **supped; sup·ping** : to take or drink in swallows or gulps
²sup *n* : a mouthful esp. of liquor or broth; *also* : a small quantity of liquid
³sup *vb* **supped; sup·ping** **1** : to eat the evening meal **2** : to make one's supper ⟨*supped* on roast beef⟩
⁴sup *abbr* **1** superior **2** supplement; supplementary **3** supply **4** supra
¹su·per \ˈsü-pər\ *adj* **1** : very fine : EXCELLENT **2** : EXTREME, EXCESSIVE ⟨~ secrecy⟩
²super *n* : SUPERINTENDENT
super- \ˌsü-pər\ *prefix* **1** : over and above : higher in quantity, quality, or degree than : more than **2** : in addition : extra **3** : exceeding a norm **4** : in excessive degree or intensity **5** : surpassing all or most others of its kind **6** : situated above, on, or at the top of **7** : next above or higher **8** : more inclusive than **9** : superior in status or position
su·per·abun·dant \ˌsü-pər-ə-ˈbən-dənt\ *adj* : more than ample — **su·per·abun·dance** \-dəns\ *n*
su·per·an·nu·ate \ˌsü-pər-ˈan-yə-ˌwāt\ *vb* **-at·ed; -at·ing** **1** : to make out-of-date **2** : to retire and pension because of age or infirmity — **su·per·an·nu·at·ed** *adj*
su·perb \su̇-ˈpərb\ *adj* [L *superbus* excellent, proud, fr. *super* above] : marked to the highest degree by excellence, brilliance, or competence ♦ ***Synonyms*** RESPLENDENT, GLORIOUS, GORGEOUS, SUBLIME — **su·perb·ly** *adv*
su·per·charg·er \ˈsü-pər-ˌchär-jər\ *n* : a device for increasing the amount of air supplied to an internal combustion engine
su·per·cil·ious \ˌsü-pər-ˈsi-lē-əs\ *adj* [L *superciliosus*, fr. *supercilium* eyebrow, haughtiness] : haughtily contemptuous ♦ ***Synonyms*** DISDAINFUL, OVERBEARING, ARROGANT, LORDLY, SUPERIOR
su·per·com·pu·ter \ˈsü-pər-kəm-ˌpyü-tər\ *n* : a large very fast mainframe
su·per·con·duc·tiv·i·ty \ˌsü-pər-ˌkän-ˌdək-ˈti-və-tē\ *n* : a complete disappearance of electrical resistance in a substance esp. at very low temperatures — **su·per·con·duc·tive** \-kən-ˈdək-tiv\ *adj* — **su·per·con·duc·tor** \-ˈdək-tər\ *n*
su·per·con·ti·nent \ˈsü-pər-ˌkän-tə-nənt\ *n* : a former large continent from which other continents are held to have broken off and drifted away
su·per·ego \ˌsü-pər-ˈē-gō\ *n* : the one of the three divisions of the psyche in psychoanalytic theory that functions to reward and punish through a system of moral attitudes, conscience, and a sense of guilt
su·per·fi·cial \ˌsü-pər-ˈfi-shəl\ *adj* **1** : of or relating to the surface or appearance only **2** : not thorough : SHALLOW ⟨a ~ analysis⟩ — **su·per·fi·ci·al·i·ty** \-ˌfi-shē-ˈa-lə-tē\ *n* — **su·per·fi·cial·ly** *adv*
su·per·flu·ous \su̇-ˈpər-flə-wəs\ *adj* : exceeding what is sufficient or necessary : SURPLUS ⟨~ details⟩ ♦ ***Synonyms***

---

superabsorbent
superachiever
superagency
superblock
superbomb
supercity
superclean
superexpensive
superfast
superfine

EXTRA, SPARE, SUPERNUMERARY — **su·per·flu·i·ty** \ˌsü-pər-ˈflü-ə-tē\ *n*

su·per·high·way \ˌsü-pər-ˈhī-ˌwā\ *n* : a broad highway designed for high-speed traffic

su·per·im·pose \-im-ˈpōz\ *vb* : to lay (one thing) over or above something else

su·per·in·tend \ˌsü-pə-rin-ˈtend\ *vb* : to have or exercise the charge and oversight of : DIRECT ⟨~*ed* the school system⟩ — **su·per·in·ten·dence** \-ˈten-dəns\ *n* — **su·per·in·ten·den·cy** \-dən-sē\ *n* — **su·per·in·ten·dent** \-dənt\ *n*

¹**su·pe·ri·or** \su̇-ˈpir-ē-ər\ *adj* **1** : situated higher up, over, or near the top; *also* : higher in rank or numbers **2** : of greater value or importance **3** : courageously indifferent (as to pain or misfortune) **4** : better than most others of its kind **5** : ARROGANT, HAUGHTY — **su·pe·ri·or·i·ty** \-ˌpir-ē-ˈȯr-ə-tē\ *n*

²**superior** *n* **1** : one who is above another in rank, office, or station; *esp* : the head of a religious house or order **2** : one higher in quality or merit

¹**su·per·la·tive** \su̇-ˈpər-lə-tiv\ *adj* **1** : of, relating to, or constituting the degree of grammatical comparison that denotes an extreme or unsurpassed level or extent **2** : surpassing others : SUPREME ♦ ***Synonyms*** PEERLESS, INCOMPARABLE, SUPERB — **su·per·la·tive·ly** *adv*

²**superlative** *n* **1** : the superlative degree or a superlative form in a language **2** : the utmost degree : ACME

su·per·mar·ket \ˈsü-pər-ˌmär-kət\ *n* : a self-service retail market selling foods and household merchandise

su·per·mod·el \ˈsü-pər-ˌmä-dᵊl\ *n* : a famous and successful fashion model

su·per·mom \ˈsü-pər-ˌmäm\ *n* : an exemplary mother; *also* : a woman who performs the traditional duties of housekeeping and raising children while also having a full-time job

su·per·nal \su̇-ˈpər-nəl\ *adj* **1** : being or coming from on high **2** : of heavenly or spiritual character

su·per·nat·u·ral \ˌsü-pər-ˈna-chə-rəl\ *adj* : of or relating to phenomena beyond or outside of nature; *esp* : relating to or attributed to a divinity, ghost, or devil — **su·per·nat·u·ral·ly** *adv*

su·per·no·va \ˌsü-pər-ˈnō-və\ *n* : the explosion of a very large star

¹**su·per·nu·mer·ary** \-ˈnü-mə-ˌrer-ē, -ˈnyü-\ *adj* : exceeding the usual or required number : EXTRA ♦ ***Synonyms*** SURPLUS, SUPERFLUOUS, SPARE

²**supernumerary** *n, pl* **-ar·ies** : an extra person or thing; *esp* : an actor hired for a nonspeaking part

su·per·pose \ˌsü-pər-ˈpōz\ *vb* **-posed; -pos·ing** : SUPERIMPOSE — **su·per·po·si·tion** \-pə-ˈzi-shən\ *n*

su·per·pow·er \ˈsü-pər-ˌpau̇(-ə)r\ *n* **1** : excessive or superior power **2** : one of a few politically and militarily dominant nations

su·per·sat·u·rat·ed \-ˈsa-chə-ˌrā-təd\ *adj* : containing an amount of a substance greater than that required for saturation

su·per·script \ˈsü-pər-ˌskript\ *n* : a symbol (as a numeral or letter) written immediately above or above and to one side of another character

su·per·sede \ˌsü-pər-ˈsēd\ *vb* **-sed·ed; -sed·ing** [ME (Sc) *superceden* to defer, fr. MF *superceder,* fr. L *supersedēre* to be superior to, refrain from, fr. *super-* above + *sedēre* to sit] : to take the place of : REPLACE ⟨this edition ~*s* the previous one⟩

su·per·son·ic \-ˈsä-nik\ *adj* **1** : ULTRASONIC **2** : being or relating to speeds from one to five times the speed of sound; *also* : capable of moving at such a speed ⟨a ~ airplane⟩

su·per·sti·tion \ˌsü-pər-ˈsti-shən\ *n* **1** : beliefs or practices resulting from ignorance, fear of the unknown, or trust in magic or chance **2** : an unreasoning fear of nature, the unknown, or God resulting from superstition — **su·per·sti·tious** \-shəs\ *adj*

su·per·struc·ture \ˈsü-pər-ˌstrək-chər\ *n* : something built on a base or as a vertical extension

su·per·ti·tle \ˈsü-pər-ˌtī-tᵊl\ *n* : a translation of foreign-language dialogue displayed above a screen or performance

su·per·vene \ˌsü-pər-ˈvēn\ *vb* **-vened; -ven·ing** : to occur as something additional or unexpected

su·per·vise \ˈsü-pər-ˌvīz\ *vb* **-vised; -vis·ing** : OVERSEE, SUPERINTEND — **su·per·vi·sion** \ˌsü-pər-ˈvi-zhən\ *n* — **su·per·vi·sor** \ˈsü-pər-ˌvī-zər\ *n* — **su·per·vi·so·ry** \ˌsü-pər-ˈvī-zə-rē\ *adj*

su·pine \su̇-ˈpīn\ *adj* **1** : lying on the back or with the face upward **2** : LETHARGIC, SLUGGISH; *also* : ABJECT ⟨a ~ legislature⟩ ♦ ***Synonyms*** INACTIVE, INERT, PASSIVE, IDLE

supp *or* **suppl** *abbr* supplement; supplementary

sup·per \ˈsə-pər\ *n* : the evening meal esp. when dinner is taken at midday — **sup·per·time** \-ˌtīm\ *n*

sup·plant \sə-ˈplant\ *vb* **1** : to take the place of (another) esp. by force or trickery **2** : REPLACE

sup·ple \ˈsə-pəl\ *adj* **sup·pler; sup·plest** **1** : COMPLIANT, ADAPTABLE **2** : capable of bending without breaking or

---

superheat
superheavy
superhero
superhuman
superhumanly
superindividual
superliner
superman
supernormal
superpatriot
superpatriotic
superpatriotism
superpremium
superrich
supersalesman
supersecret
supersize
supersized
supersmart
supersophisticated
superspy
superstar
superstate
superstore
superstratum
superstrength
superstrong
supersubtle
supersystem
supertanker
superthin
superwoman

creasing : LIMBER ♦ *Synonyms* RESILIENT, ELASTIC, FLEXIBLE

¹**sup·ple·ment** \ˈsə-plə-mənt\ *n* **1** : something that supplies a want or makes an addition **2** : DIETARY SUPPLEMENT **3** : a continuation (as of a book) containing corrections or additional material — **sup·ple·men·tal** \ˌsə-plə-ˈmen-tᵊl\ *adj* — **sup·ple·men·ta·ry** \-ˈmen-tə-rē\ *adj*

²**sup·ple·ment** \ˈsə-plə-ˌment\ *vb* : to fill up the deficiencies of : add to — **sup·ple·men·ta·tion** \ˌsə-plə-ˌmen-ˈtā-shən, -mən-\ *n*

sup·pli·ant \ˈsə-plē-ənt\ *n* : one who supplicates : PETITIONER, PLEADER

sup·pli·cant \ˈsə-pli-kənt\ *n* : SUPPLIANT

sup·pli·cate \ˈsə-plə-ˌkāt\ *vb* **-cat·ed; -cat·ing** **1** : to make a humble entreaty; *esp* : to pray to God **2** : to ask earnestly and humbly : BESEECH ♦ *Synonyms* IMPLORE, BEG, ENTREAT, PLEAD — **sup·pli·ca·tion** \ˌsə-plə-ˈkā-shən\ *n*

¹**sup·ply** \sə-ˈplī\ *vb* **sup·plied; sup·ply·ing** [ME *supplien,* to complete, compensate for, fr. MF *soupplier* fr. L *supplēre* to fill up, supplement, supply, fr. *sub-* under, up to + *plēre* to fill] **1** : to add as a supplement **2** : to satisfy the needs of **3** : FURNISH, PROVIDE — **sup·pli·er** *n*

²**supply** *n, pl* **supplies** **1** : the quantity or amount (as of a commodity) needed or available; *also* : PROVISIONS, STORES — usu. used in pl. **2** : the act or process of filling a want or need : PROVISION **3** : the quantities of goods or services offered for sale at a particular time or at one price

sup·ply–side \sə-ˈplī-ˌsīd\ *adj* : of, relating to, or being an economic theory that recommends the reduction of tax rates to expand economic activity

¹**sup·port** \sə-ˈpȯrt\ *vb* **1** : BEAR, TOLERATE **2** : to take sides with : BACK, ASSIST **3** : to provide with food, clothing, and shelter **4** : to hold up or serve as a foundation for ♦ *Synonyms* UPHOLD, ADVOCATE, CHAMPION — **sup·port·able** *adj* — **sup·port·er** *n* — **sup·port·ive** \-ˈpȯr-tiv\ *adj*

²**support** *n* **1** : the act of supporting : the state of being supported **2** : one that supports : PROP, BASE **3** : help given in the form of money, information, or services

support group *n* : a group of people with common experiences and concerns who provide emotional and moral support for one another

sup·pose \sə-ˈpōz\ *vb* **sup·posed; sup·pos·ing** **1** : to assume to be true (as for the sake of argument) **2** : EXPECT ⟨I am *supposed* to go⟩ **3** : to think probable ⟨I ∼ so⟩ — **sup·pos·al** *n*

sup·posed \sə-ˈpōzd, -ˈpō-zəd\ *adj* : BELIEVED; *also* : mistakenly believed ⟨a ∼ cure⟩ — **sup·pos·ed·ly** \-ˈpō-zəd-lē, -ˈpōzd-lē\ *adv*

sup·pos·ing *conj* : if by way of hypothesis : on the assumption that ⟨∼ I did agree with you⟩

sup·po·si·tion \ˌsə-pə-ˈzi-shən\ *n* **1** : something that is supposed : HYPOTHESIS **2** : the act of supposing

sup·pos·i·to·ry \sə-ˈpä-zə-ˌtȯr-ē\ *n, pl* **-ries** [ME *suppositorie,* fr. AF, fr. ML *suppositorium,* fr. LL, neut. of *suppositorius* placed beneath] : a small easily melted mass of usu. medicated material for insertion (as into the rectum)

sup·press \sə-ˈpres\ *vb* **1** : to put down by authority or force : SUBDUE ⟨∼ a revolt⟩ **2** : to keep from being known; *also* : to stop the publication or circulation of **3** : to hold back : REPRESS ⟨∼ anger⟩ ⟨∼ a cough⟩ — **sup·press·ible** \-ˈpre-sə-bəl\ *adj* — **sup·pres·sion** \-ˈpre-shən\ *n* — **sup·pres·sor** \-ˈpre-sər\ *n*

sup·pres·sant \sə-ˈpre-sᵊnt\ *n* : an agent (as a drug) suppressing rather than eliminating something ⟨a cough ∼⟩

sup·pu·rate \ˈsə-pyə-ˌrāt\ *vb* **-rat·ed; -rat·ing** : to form or give off pus — **sup·pu·ra·tion** \ˌsə-pyə-ˈrā-shən\ *n*

su·pra \ˈsü-prə, -ˌprä\ *adv* : earlier in this writing : ABOVE

su·pra·na·tion·al \ˌsü-prə-ˈna-shə-nəl, -ˌprä-\ *adj* : going beyond national boundaries, authority, or interests ⟨∼ organizations⟩

su·prem·a·cist \sů-ˈpre-mə-sist\ *n* **1** : an advocate of group supremacy **2** : WHITE SUPREMACIST

su·prem·a·cy \sů-ˈpre-mə-sē\ *n, pl* **-cies** : supreme rank, power, or authority

su·preme \sů-ˈprēm\ *adj* [L *supremus,* superl. of *superus* upper, fr. *super* over, above] **1** : highest in rank or authority **2** : highest in degree or quality ⟨∼ among poets⟩ **3** : ULTIMATE ⟨the ∼ sacrifice⟩ ♦ *Synonyms* SUPERLATIVE, SURPASSING, PEERLESS, INCOMPARABLE — **su·preme·ly** *adv* — **su·preme·ness** *n*

Supreme Being *n* : GOD 1

supt *abbr* superintendent

sur·cease \ˈsər-ˌsēs\ *n* : CESSATION, RESPITE ⟨a ∼ from pain⟩

¹**sur·charge** \ˈsər-ˌchärj\ *vb* **1** : to fill to excess : OVERLOAD **2** : to apply a surcharge to (postage stamps)

²**surcharge** *n* **1** : an extra fee or cost **2** : an excessive load or burden **3** : something officially printed on a postage stamp esp. to change its value

sur·cin·gle \ˈsər-ˌsiŋ-gəl\ *n* : a band put around a horse's body to make something (as a saddle) fast

¹**sure** \ˈshůr\ *adj* **sur·er; sur·est** [ME, *seur, sure,*fr. AF *seur,* fr. L *securus* secure] **1** : firmly established **2** : TRUSTWORTHY, RELIABLE ⟨a ∼ friend⟩ **3** : CONFIDENT ⟨I'm ∼ I'm right⟩ **4** : not to be disputed : UNDOUBTED **5** : bound to happen **6** : careful to remember or attend to something ⟨be ∼ to lock the door⟩ ♦ *Synonyms* CERTAIN, COCKSURE, POSITIVE — **sure·ness** *n*

²**sure** *adv* : SURELY

sure·fire \ˈshůr-ˈfī(-ə)r\ *adj* : certain to get results : DEPENDABLE

sure·ly \ˈshůr-lē\ *adv* **1** : in a sure manner **2** : without doubt **3** : INDEED, REALLY ⟨∼, you don't believe that⟩

sure·ty \ˈshůr-ə-tē\ *n, pl* **-ties** **1** : SURENESS, CERTAINTY **2** : something that makes sure : GUARANTEE **3** : one who is a guarantor for another person

[1]**surf** \ˈsərf\ *n* : waves that break upon the shore; *also* : the sound or foam of breaking waves

[2]**surf** *vb* **1** : to ride the surf (as on a surfboard) **2** : to scan the offerings of (as television or the Internet) for something of interest — **surf·er** *n* — **surf·ing** *n*

[1]**sur·face** \ˈsər-fəs\ *n* **1** : the outside of an object or body **2** : outward aspect or appearance — **surface** *adj*

[2]**surface** *vb* **sur·faced; sur·fac·ing** **1** : to give a surface to : make smooth **2** : to rise to the surface

surf·board \ˈsərf-ˌbȯrd\ *n* : a buoyant board used in surfing

[1]**sur·feit** \ˈsər-fət\ *n* **1** : EXCESS, SUPERABUNDANCE **2** : excessive indulgence (as in food or drink) **3** : disgust caused by excess

[2]**surfeit** *vb* : to feed, supply, or indulge to the point of surfeit : CLOY

surg *abbr* surgeon; surgery; surgical

[1]**surge** \ˈsərj\ *vb* **surged; surg·ing** **1** : to rise and fall actively : TOSS **2** : to move in waves **3** : to rise suddenly to an excessive or abnormal value

[2]**surge** *n* **1** : a sweeping onward like a wave of the sea ⟨a ~ of emotion⟩ **2** : a large billow **3** : a transient sudden increase of current or voltage in an electrical circuit

sur·geon \ˈsər-jən\ *n* : a physician who specializes in surgery

sur·gery \ˈsər-jə-rē\ *n, pl* **-ger·ies** [ME *surgerie,* fr. AF *cirurgerie, surgerie,* fr. L *chirurgia,* fr. Gk *cheirourgia,* fr. *cheirourgos* surgeon, fr. *cheirourgos* doing by hand, fr. *cheir* hand + *ergon* work] **1** : a branch of medicine concerned with the correction of physical defects, the repair of injuries, and the treatment of disease esp. by operations **2** : a room or area where surgery is performed **3** : the work done by a surgeon

sur·gi·cal \ˈsər-ji-kəl\ *adj* : of, relating to, or associated with surgeons or surgery — **sur·gi·cal·ly** \-k(ə-)lē\ *adv*

sur·ly \ˈsər-lē\ *adj* **sur·li·er; -est** [alter. of ME *serreli* lordly, imperious, prob. fr. *sire, ser* sire] : having a rude unfriendly disposition ⟨a ~ customer⟩ ♦ ***Synonyms*** MOROSE, GLUM, SULLEN, SULKY, GLOOMY — **sur·li·ness** \-lē-nəs\ *n*

sur·mise \sər-ˈmīz\ *vb* **sur·mised; sur·mis·ing** : to form a notion of from scanty evidence ♦ ***Synonyms*** CONJECTURE, PRESUME, SUPPOSE — **surmise** *n*

sur·mount \sər-ˈmau̇nt\ *vb* **1** : to prevail over : OVERCOME ⟨~ a problem⟩ **2** : to get to or lie at the top of

sur·name \ˈsər-ˌnām\ *n* **1** : NICKNAME **2** : the name borne in common by members of a family

sur·pass \sər-ˈpas\ *vb* **1** : to be superior to in quality, degree, or performance : EXCEL **2** : to go beyond the reach or powers of ♦ ***Synonyms*** TRANSCEND, OUTDO, OUTSTRIP, EXCEED — **sur·pass·ing·ly** *adv*

sur·plice \ˈsər-pləs\ *n* : a loose white outer vestment usu. of knee length

sur·plus \ˈsər-(ˌ)pləs\ *n* **1** : quantity left over : EXCESS **2** : the excess of assets over liabilities ♦ ***Synonyms*** SUPERFLUITY, OVERABUNDANCE, SURFEIT

[1]**sur·prise** \sər-ˈprīz\ *n* **1** : an attack made without warning **2** : a taking unawares **3** : something that surprises **4** : AMAZEMENT, ASTONISHMENT

[2]**surprise** *vb* **sur·prised; sur·pris·ing** **1** : to come upon and attack unexpectedly **2** : to take unawares **3** : AMAZE ⟨his conduct *surprised* me⟩ **4** : to cause astonishment or surprise ⟨her success didn't ~⟩ ♦ ***Synonyms*** ASTONISH, ASTOUND, DUMBFOUND — **sur·pris·ing** *adj*

sur·pris·ing·ly \-ˈprī-ziŋ-lē\ *adv* **1** : in a surprising manner or degree **2** : it is surprising that ⟨~, voter turnout was high⟩

sur·re·al \sə-ˈrē-əl, -ˈrēl\ *adj* **1** : having the intense irrational reality of a dream **2** : of or relating to surrealism ⟨~ art⟩ — **sur·re·al·ly** *adv*

sur·re·al·ism \sə-ˈrē-ə-ˌli-zəm\ *n* : art, literature, or theater characterized by fantastic or incongruous imagery or effects produced by unnatural juxtapositions and combinations — **sur·re·al·ist** \-list\ *n or adj* — **sur·re·al·is·tic** \sə-ˌrē-ə-ˈlis-tik\ *adj* — **sur·re·al·is·ti·cal·ly** \-ti-k(ə-)lē\ *adv*

[1]**sur·ren·der** \sə-ˈren-dər\ *vb* **1** : to yield to the power of another : give up under compulsion **2** : RELINQUISH

[2]**surrender** *n* : the act of giving up or yielding oneself or the possession of something to another

sur·rep·ti·tious \ˌsər-əp-ˈti-shəs\ *adj* : done, made, or acquired by stealth : CLANDESTINE ⟨a ~ relationship⟩ ♦ ***Synonyms*** UNDERHAND, COVERT, FURTIVE — **sur·rep·ti·tious·ly** *adv*

sur·rey \ˈsər-ē\ *n, pl* **surreys** : a 2-seated horse-drawn carriage

sur·ro·ga·cy \ˈsər-ə-gə-sē\ *n* : SURROGATE MOTHERHOOD

sur·ro·gate \ˈsər-ə-ˌgāt, -gət\ *n* **1** : DEPUTY, SUBSTITUTE **2** : a law officer in some states with authority in the probate of wills, the settlement of estates, and the appointment of guardians **3** : SURROGATE MOTHER

surrogate mother *n* : a woman who becomes pregnant (as by surgical implantation of a fertilized egg) in order to carry the fetus for another woman — **surrogate motherhood** *n*

sur·round \sə-ˈrau̇nd\ *vb* **1** : to enclose on all sides : ENCIRCLE **2** : to enclose so as to cut off retreat or escape

sur·round·ings \sə-ˈrau̇n-diŋz\ *n pl* : conditions by which one is surrounded

surround sound *n* : sound reproduction that uses three or more transmission channels

sur·tax \ˈsər-ˌtaks\ *n* : an additional tax over and above a normal tax

sur·tout \(ˌ)sər-ˈtü\ *n* [F, fr. *sur* over + *tout* all] : a man's long close-fitting overcoat

surv *abbr* survey; surveying; surveyor
sur·veil·lance \sər-ˈvā-ləns\ *n* [F] : close watch; *also* : SUPERVISION
[1]**sur·vey** \sər-ˈvā\ *vb* **sur·veyed; sur·vey·ing** [ME, fr. AF *surveer* to look over, fr. *sur-* over + *veer* to see, fr. L *vidēre*] **1** : to look over and examine closely **2** : to find and represent the contours, measurements, and position of a part of the earth's surface (as a tract of land) **3** : to view or study something as a whole ♦ ***Synonyms*** SCRUTINIZE, EXAMINE, INSPECT, STUDY — **sur·vey·or** \-ər\ *n*
[2]**sur·vey** \ˈsər-ˌvā\ *n, pl* **surveys** : the act or an instance of surveying; *also* : something that is surveyed
sur·viv·al·ism \sər-ˈvī-və-ˌli-zəm\ *n* : an attitude, policy, or practice based on the primacy of survival as a value — **sur·viv·al·ist** \-və-list\ *n or adj*
sur·vive \sər-ˈvīv\ *vb* **sur·vived; sur·viv·ing** **1** : to remain alive or existent **2** : OUTLIVE, OUTLAST — **sur·viv·al** *n* — **sur·vi·vor** \-ˈvī-vər\ *n*
sus·cep·ti·ble \sə-ˈsep-tə-bəl\ *adj* **1** : of such a nature as to permit ⟨words ~ of being misunderstood⟩ **2** : having little resistance to a stimulus or agency ⟨~ to colds⟩ **3** : IMPRESSIONABLE, RESPONSIVE ⟨a ~ mind⟩ ♦ ***Synonyms*** SENSITIVE, SUBJECT, EXPOSED, PRONE, LIABLE, OPEN — **sus·cep·ti·bil·i·ty** \-ˌsep-tə-ˈbi-lə-tē\ *n*
su·shi \ˈsü-shē\ *n* [Jp] : cold rice formed into various shapes and garnished esp. with bits of raw fish or seafood
[1]**sus·pect** \ˈsəs-ˌpekt, sə-ˈspekt\ *adj* : regarded with suspicion; *also* : QUESTIONABLE ⟨his claim is ~⟩
[2]**sus·pect** \ˈsəs-ˌpekt\ *n* : one who is suspected (as of a crime)
[3]**sus·pect** \sə-ˈspekt\ *vb* **1** : to have doubts of : MISTRUST **2** : to imagine to be guilty without proof **3** : SURMISE
sus·pend \sə-ˈspend\ *vb* **1** : to bar temporarily from a privilege, office, or function **2** : to stop temporarily : make inactive for a time **3** : to withhold (judgment) for a time **4** : HANG; *esp* : to hang so as to be free except at one point **5** : to put or hold in suspension **6** : to keep from falling or sinking by some invisible support
sus·pend·er \sə-ˈspen-dər\ *n* : one of two supporting straps which pass over the shoulders and to which the pants are fastened
sus·pense \sə-ˈspens\ *n* **1** : SUSPENSION **2** : mental uncertainty : ANXIETY **3** : excitement as to an outcome — **sus·pense·ful** *adj*
sus·pen·sion \sə-ˈspen-chən\ *n* **1** : the act of suspending : the state or period of being suspended **2** : the state of a substance when its particles are mixed with but undissolved in a fluid or solid; *also* : a substance in this state **3** : something suspended **4** : the system of devices supporting the upper part of a vehicle on the axles
sus·pi·cion \sə-ˈspi-shən\ *n* **1** : the act or an instance of suspecting something wrong without proof **2** : TRACE, SOUPÇON ⟨a ~ of garlic⟩ ♦ ***Synonyms*** MISTRUST, UNCERTAINTY, DOUBT, SKEPTICISM
sus·pi·cious \sə-ˈspi-shəs\ *adj* **1** : open to or arousing suspicion **2** : inclined to suspect **3** : showing suspicion ⟨is ~ of strangers⟩ — **sus·pi·cious·ly** *adv*
sus·tain \sə-ˈstān\ *vb* **1** : to provide with nourishment **2** : to keep going : PROLONG ⟨~*ed* effort⟩ **3** : to hold up : PROP **4** : to hold up under : ENDURE **5** : SUFFER ⟨~ a broken arm⟩ **6** : to support as true, legal, or valid ⟨the objection was ~*ed*⟩ **7** : PROVE, CORROBORATE — **sus·tain·able** \səs-ˈtā-nə-bəl\ *adj*
sus·te·nance \ˈsəs-tə-nəns\ *n* **1** : FOOD, NOURISHMENT **2** : a supplying with the necessities of life **3** : something that sustains or supports
su·ture \ˈsü-chər\ *n* **1** : material or a stitch for sewing a wound together **2** : a seam or line along which two things or parts are joined by or as if by sewing
SUV \ˌes-ˌyü-ˈvē\ *n* [*s*port *u*tility *v*ehicle] : a vehicle similar to a station wagon but built on a light-truck chassis
su·zer·ain \ˈsü-zə-rən, -ˌrān\ *n* [F] **1** : a feudal lord **2** : a nation that has political control over the foreign relations of another nation — **su·zer·ain·ty** \-tē\ *n*
svc *or* **svce** *abbr* service
svelte \ˈsfelt\ *adj* **svelt·er; svelt·est** [F, fr. It *svelto,* fr. pp. of *svellere* to pluck out, modif. of L *evellere,* fr. *e-* out + *vellere* to pluck] : SLENDER, LITHE ⟨a ~ figure⟩
svgs *abbr* savings
SW *abbr* **1** shortwave **2** southwest
[1]**swab** \ˈswäb\ *n* **1** : MOP **2** : a wad of absorbent material esp. for applying medicine or for cleaning; *also* : a sample taken with a swab **3** : SAILOR
[2]**swab** *vb* **swabbed; swab·bing** : to use a swab on : MOP
swad·dle \ˈswä-dᵊl\ *vb* **swad·dled; swad·dling** **1** : to bind (an infant) in bands of cloth **2** : to wrap up : SWATHE
swaddling clothes *n pl* : bands of cloth wrapped around an infant
swag \ˈswag\ *n* **1 a** : FESTOON **b** : a hanging cluster (as of evergreen branches) **2 a** : stolen goods : LOOT **b** : valuable articles or goods **c** : promotional goods or items
swag·ger \ˈswa-gər\ *vb* **1** : to walk with a conceited swing or strut **2** : BOAST, BRAG — **swagger** *n*
Swa·hi·li \swä-ˈhē-lē\ *n* : a language that is a trade and governmental language over much of eastern Africa and the Congo region
swain \ˈswān\ *n* [ME *swein* boy, servant, fr. ON *sveinn*] **1** : RUSTIC; *esp* : SHEPHERD **2** : ADMIRER, SUITOR
SWAK *abbr* sealed with a kiss
[1]**swal·low** \ˈswä-lō\ *n* : any of numerous small long-winged migratory birds that often have a deeply forked tail
[2]**swallow** *vb* **1** : to take into the stomach through the throat **2** : to envelop or take

in as if by swallowing **3 :** to accept or believe without question, protest, or anger

[3]**swallow** *n* **1 :** an act of swallowing **2 :** an amount that can be swallowed at one time

swal·low·tail \ˈswä-lō-ˌtāl\ *n* **1 :** a deeply forked and tapering tail like that of a swallow **2 :** TAILCOAT **3 :** any of various large butterflies with the border of each hind wing usu. drawn out into a process resembling a tail — **swal·low–tailed** \-ˌtāld\ *adj*

swam *past of* SWIM

swa·mi \ˈswä-mē\ *n* [Hindi *svāmī,* fr. Skt *svāmin* owner, lord] **:** a Hindu ascetic or religious teacher

[1]**swamp** \ˈswämp\ *n* **:** a spongy wetland — **swamp** *adj* — **swampy** *adj*

[2]**swamp** *vb* **1 :** to fill or become filled with or as if with water **2 :** OVERWHELM 3

swamp·land \-ˌland\ *n* **:** SWAMP

swan \ˈswän\ *n, pl* **swans** *also* **swan :** any of various heavy-bodied long-necked mostly pure white swimming birds related to the geese

[1]**swank** \ˈswaŋk\ *or* **swanky** \ˈswaŋ-kē\ *adj* **swank·er** *or* **swank·i·er; -est :** showily smart and dashing; *also* **:** fashionably elegant ⟨a ~ hotel⟩

[2]**swank** *n* **1 :** PRETENTIOUSNESS **2 :** ELEGANCE

swans·down \ˈswänz-ˌdau̇n\ *n* **1 :** the very soft down of a swan used esp. for trimming **2 :** a soft thick cotton flannel

swan song *n* **:** a farewell appearance, act, or pronouncement

swap \ˈswäp\ *vb* **swapped; swap·ping :** TRADE, EXCHANGE — **swap** *n*

sward \ˈswȯrd\ *n* **:** the grassy surface of land

[1]**swarm** \ˈswȯrm\ *n* **1 :** a great number of honeybees leaving together from a hive with a queen to start a new colony; *also* **:** a hive of bees **2 :** a large crowd

[2]**swarm** *vb* **1 :** to form in a swarm and depart from a hive **2 :** to throng together **:** gather in great numbers

swart \ˈswȯrt\ *adj* **:** SWARTHY

swar·thy \ˈswȯr-t͟hē, -thē\ *adj* **swar·thi·er; -est :** dark in color or complexion **:** dark-skinned

swash \ˈswäsh\ *vb* **:** to move about with a splashing sound — **swash** *n*

swash·buck·ler \-ˌbə-klər\ *n* **:** a swaggering or daring soldier or adventurer — **swash·buck·ling** *adj*

swas·ti·ka \ˈswäs-ti-kə\ *n* [Skt *svastika,* fr. *svasti* well-being, fr. *su-* well + *as-* to be] **:** a symbol or ornament in the form of a cross with the ends of the arms bent at right angles

swat \ˈswät\ *vb* **swat·ted; swat·ting :** to hit sharply ⟨~ a fly⟩ ⟨~ a ball⟩ — **swat** *n* — **swat·ter** *n*

SWAT *abbr* Special Weapons and Tactics

swatch \ˈswäch\ *n* **:** a sample piece (as of fabric) or a collection of samples

swath \ˈswäth, ˈswȯth\ *or* **swathe** \ˈswät͟h, ˈswȯt͟h, ˈswāt͟h\ *n* [ME, fr. OE *swæth* footstep, trace] **1 :** a row of cut grass or grain **2 :** the sweep of a scythe or mowing machine or the path cut in mowing

swathe \ˈswät͟h, ˈswȯt͟h, ˈswāt͟h\ *vt* **swathed; swath·ing :** to bind or wrap with or as if with a bandage

[1]**sway** \ˈswā\ *n* **1 :** a gentle swinging from side to side **2 :** controlling influence or power **:** DOMINION

[2]**sway** *vb* **1 :** to swing gently from side to side **2 :** RULE, GOVERN **3 :** to cause to swing from side to side **4 :** BEND, SWERVE; *also* **:** INFLUENCE ⟨tried to ~ the jury⟩ ♦ ***Synonyms*** OSCILLATE, FLUCTUATE, VIBRATE, WAVER

sway·backed \ˈswā-ˌbakt\ *also* **sway·back** \-ˌbak\ *adj* **:** having an abnormally sagging back ⟨a ~ mare⟩ — **swayback** *n*

swear \ˈswer\ *vb* **swore** \ˈswȯr\; **sworn** \ˈswȯrn\; **swear·ing 1 :** to make a solemn statement or promise under oath **2 :** to assert or promise emphatically or earnestly **3 :** to administer an oath to **4 :** to bind by or as if by an oath **5 :** to use profane or obscene language — **swear·er** *n*

swear in *vb* **:** to induct into office by administration of an oath

sweat \ˈswet\ *vb* **sweat** *or* **sweat·ed; sweat·ing 1 :** to excrete salty moisture from glands of the skin **:** PERSPIRE **2 :** to form drops of moisture on the surface **3 :** to work so that one sweats **:** TOIL **4 :** to cause to sweat **5 :** to draw out or get rid of by or as if by sweating **6 :** to make a person overwork — **sweat** *n* — **sweaty** *adj*

sweat·er \ˈswe-tər\ *n* **1 :** one that sweats **2 :** a knitted or crocheted jacket or pullover

sweat·shirt \ˈswet-ˌshərt\ *n* **:** a loose collarless pullover or jacket usu. of heavy cotton jersey

sweat·shop \ˈswet-ˌshäp\ *n* **:** a shop or factory in which workers are employed for long hours at low wages and under unhealthy conditions

Swed *abbr* Sweden

swede \ˈswēd\ *n* **1** *cap* **:** a native or inhabitant of Sweden **2** *chiefly Brit* **:** RUTABAGA

Swed·ish \ˈswē-dish\ *n* **1 :** the language of Sweden **2 Swedish** *pl* **:** the people of Sweden — **Swedish** *adj*

[1]**sweep** \ˈswēp\ *vb* **swept** \ˈswept\; **sweep·ing 1 :** to remove or clean by or as if by brushing **2 :** to destroy completely; *also* **:** to remove or take with a single swift movement **3 :** to remove from sight or consideration **4 :** to move over with speed and force ⟨the tide *swept* over the shore⟩ **5 :** to win an overwhelming victory in; *also* **:** to win all the games or contests of **6 :** to move or extend in a wide curve — **sweep·er** *n*

[2]**sweep** *n* **1 :** something (as a long oar) that operates with a sweeping motion **2 :** a clearing off or away **3 :** a winning of all the contests or prizes in a competition **4 :** a sweeping movement **5 :** CURVE, BEND **6 :** RANGE, SCOPE

sweeping *adj* : EXTENSIVE ⟨~ reforms⟩; *also* : indiscriminately inclusive ⟨~ generalities⟩
sweep·ings \ˈswē-piŋz\ *n pl* : things collected by sweeping
sweep–sec·ond hand \ˈswēp-ˌse-kənd-\ *n* : a hand marking seconds on a timepiece
sweep·stakes \ˈswēp-ˌstāks\ *also* **sweep·stake** \-ˌstāk\ *n, pl* **sweep·stakes 1** : a race or contest in which the entire prize may go to the winner **2** : any of various lotteries
¹**sweet** \ˈswēt\ *adj* **1** : being or causing the one of the basic taste sensations that is caused esp. by sugars; *also* : pleasing to the taste **2** : AGREEABLE ⟨how ~ it is⟩ **3** : pleasing to a sense other than taste ⟨a ~ smell⟩ ⟨~ music⟩ **4** : not stale or spoiled : WHOLESOME ⟨~ milk⟩ **5** : not salted ⟨~ butter⟩ — **sweet·ish** *adj* — **sweet·ly** *adv* — **sweet·ness** *n*
²**sweet** *n* **1** : something sweet : CANDY **2** : DARLING
sweet·bread \ˈswēt-ˌbred\ *n* : the pancreas or thymus of an animal (as a calf or lamb) used for food
sweet·bri·ar *or* **sweet·bri·er** \-ˌbrī-ər\ *n* : a thorny Old World rose with fragrant white to deep pink flowers
sweet clover *n* : any of a genus of erect legumes widely grown for soil improvement or hay
sweet corn *n* : corn of a variety having soft kernels containing a high percentage of sugar
sweet·en \ˈswē-tᵊn\ *vb* **sweet·ened; sweet·en·ing** : to make sweet — **sweet·en·er** *n* — **sweet·en·ing** *n*
sweet·heart \ˈswēt-ˌhärt\ *n* : one who is loved
sweet·meat \-ˌmēt\ *n* : CANDY 1
sweet pea *n* : a garden plant of the legume family with climbing stems and fragrant flowers of many colors; *also* : its flower
sweet pepper *n* : any of various large mild thick-walled fruits of a pepper; *also* : a plant bearing sweet peppers
sweet potato *n* : a tropical vine related to the morning glory; *also* : its large sweet edible root
sweet–talk \ˈswēt-ˌtȯk\ *vb* : FLATTER, COAX — **sweet talk** *n*
sweet tooth *n* : a craving or fondness for sweet food
sweet wil·liam \ˌswēt-ˈwil-yəm\ *n, often cap W* : a widely cultivated Old World pink with small white to deep red or purple flowers often showily spotted, banded, or mottled
¹**swell** \ˈswel\ *vb* **swelled; swelled** *or* **swol·len** \ˈswō-lən\; **swell·ing 1** : to grow big or make bigger **2** : to expand or distend abnormally or excessively ⟨a *swollen* joint⟩; *also* : BULGE **3** : to fill or be filled with emotion (as pride) ♦ ***Synonyms*** EXPAND, AMPLIFY, DISTEND, INFLATE, DILATE — **swell·ing** *n*
²**swell** *n* **1** : a long crestless wave or series of waves in the open sea **2** : the condition of being protuberant **3** : a person dressed in the height of fashion; *also* : a person of high social position
³**swell** *adj* **1** : STYLISH; *also* : socially prominent **2** : EXCELLENT ⟨a ~ party⟩
swelled head *n* : an exaggerated opinion of oneself : SELF-CONCEIT
swel·ter \ˈswel-tər\ *vb* [ME *sweltren,* fr. *swelten* to die, be overcome by heat, fr. OE *sweltan* to die] **1** : to be faint or oppressed with the heat **2** : to become exceedingly hot — **swel·ter·ing** \-tə-riŋ\ *adj*
swept *past and past part of* SWEEP
swerve \ˈswərv\ *vb* **swerved; swerv·ing** : to move abruptly aside from a straight line or course — **swerve** *n*
¹**swift** \ˈswift\ *adj* **1** : moving or capable of moving with great speed **2** : occurring suddenly **3** : READY, ALERT ⟨~ for vengeance⟩ — **swift·ly** *adv* — **swift·ness** *n*
²**swift** *n* : any of numerous small insect-eating birds with long narrow wings
swig \ˈswig\ *vb* **swigged; swig·ging** : to drink in long drafts — **swig** *n*
¹**swill** \ˈswil\ *vb* **1** : to swallow greedily : GUZZLE **2** : to feed (as hogs) on swill
²**swill** *n* **1** : food for animals composed of edible refuse mixed with liquid **2** : GARBAGE
¹**swim** \ˈswim\ *vb* **swam** \ˈswam\; **swum** \ˈswəm\; **swim·ming 1** : to propel oneself along in water by natural means (as by hands and legs, by tail, or by fins) **2** : to glide smoothly along **3** : FLOAT **4** : to be covered with or as if with a liquid **5** : to be dizzy ⟨his head *swam*⟩ **6** : to cross or go over by swimming ⟨*swam* the river⟩ — **swim·mer** *n*
²**swim** *n* **1** : an act of swimming **2** : the main current of activity ⟨in the ~⟩
swim·ming *n* : the action, art, or sport of swimming and diving
swimming pool *n* : a tank (as of concrete or plastic) designed for swimming
swim·suit \ˈswim-ˌsüt\ *n* : a suit for swimming or bathing
swim·wear \ˈswim-ˌwer\ *n* : clothing for wear while swimming or bathing
swin·dle \ˈswin-dᵊl\ *vb* **swin·dled; swin·dling** [fr. *swindler,* fr. G *Schwindler* giddy person, fr. *schwindeln* to be dizzy] : CHEAT, DEFRAUD — **swindle** *n* — **swin·dler** *n*
swine \ˈswīn\ *n, pl* **swine 1** : any of a family of stout short-legged hoofed mammals with bristly skin and a long flexible snout; *esp* : one widely raised as a meat animal **2** : a contemptible person — **swin·ish** *adj*
¹**swing** \ˈswiŋ\ *vb* **swung** \ˈswəŋ\; **swing·ing 1** : to move or cause to move rapidly in an arc **2** : to sway or cause to sway back and forth **3** : to hang so as to move freely back and forth or in a curve **4** : to be executed by hanging **5** : to move or turn on a hinge or pivot **6** : to manage or handle successfully **7** : to march or walk with free swaying movements **8** : to have a steady pulsing rhythm; *also* : to play swing music **9** : to

be lively and up-to-date; *also* : to engage freely in sex ♦ ***Synonyms*** WIELD, MANIPULATE, PLY, MANEUVER — **swing·er** *n* — **swing·ing** *adj*

[2]**swing** *n* **1** : the act of swinging **2** : a swinging blow, movement, or rhythm **3** : the distance through which something swings : FLUCTUATION **4** : progression of an activity or process ⟨in full ~⟩ **5** : a seat suspended by a rope or chain for swinging back and forth for pleasure **6** : jazz music played esp. by a large band and marked by a steady lively rhythm, simple harmony, and a basic melody often submerged in improvisation

[3]**swing** *adj* **1** : of or relating to musical swing **2** : that may swing decisively either way (as on an issue) ⟨~ voters⟩

[1]**swipe** \ˈswīp\ *n* : a strong sweeping blow

[2]**swipe** *vb* **swiped; swip·ing** **1** : to strike or wipe with a sweeping motion **2** : PILFER, SNATCH **3** : to slide (a card having a magnetic code) through a reading device

swirl \ˈswərl\ *vb* : to move or cause to move with a whirling motion — **swirl** *n* — **swirly** \ˈswər-lē\ *adj*

swish \ˈswish\ *n* **1** : a prolonged hissing sound **2** : a light sweeping or brushing sound — **swish** *vb*

Swiss \ˈswis\ *n* **1** *pl* **Swiss** : a native or inhabitant of Switzerland **2** : a hard cheese with large holes — **Swiss** *adj*

Swiss chard *n* : a beet having large leaves and succulent stalks often cooked as a vegetable

[1]**switch** \ˈswich\ *n* **1** : a slender flexible whip, rod, or twig **2** : a blow with a switch **3** : a shift from one thing to another; *also* : change from the usual **4** : a device for adjusting the rails of a track so that a locomotive or train may be turned from one track to another; *also* : a railroad siding **5** : a device for making, breaking, or changing the connections in an electrical circuit **6** : a heavy strand of hair often used in addition to a person's own hair for some coiffures

[2]**switch** *vb* **1** : to punish or urge on with a switch **2** : WHISK ⟨a cow *~ing* her tail⟩ **3** : to shift or turn by operating a switch **4** : CHANGE, EXCHANGE

switch·back \ˈswich-ˌbak\ *n* : a zigzag road, trail, or section of railroad tracks for climbing a steep hill

switch·blade \-ˌblād\ *n* : a pocket-knife with a spring-operated blade

switch·board \-ˌbōrd\ *n* : a panel for controlling the operation of a number of electric circuits; *esp* : one used to make and break telephone connections

switch–hit·ter \-ˈhi-tər\ *n* : a baseball player who bats either right-handed or left-handed — **switch–hit** \-ˈhit\ *vb*

switch·man \ˈswich-mən\ *n* : one who attends a railroad switch

Switz *abbr* Switzerland

[1]**swiv·el** \ˈswi-vəl\ *n* : a device joining two parts so that one or both can turn freely

[2]**swivel** *vb* **-eled** *or* **-elled; -el·ing** *or* **-el·ling** : to swing or turn on or as if on a swivel

swiv·et \ˈswi-vət\ *n* : an agitated state

swiz·zle stick \ˈswi-zəl-\ *n* : a stick used to stir mixed drinks

swollen *past part of* SWELL

swoon \ˈswün\ *vb* : FAINT — **swoon** *n*

swoop \ˈswüp\ *vb* : to move with a sweep ⟨the eagle *~ed* down on its prey⟩ — **swoop** *n*

swoopy \ˈswü-pē\ *adj* : having lines that extend in a wide curve ⟨a ~ silhouette⟩

swop *chiefly Brit var of* SWAP

sword \ˈsȯrd\ *n* **1** : a weapon with a long blade for cutting or thrusting **2** : the use of force

sword·fish \-ˌfish\ *n* : a very large ocean fish used for food that has the upper jaw prolonged into a long swordlike beak

sword·play \-ˌplā\ *n* : the art or skill of wielding a sword

swords·man \ˈsȯrdz-mən\ *n* : one skilled in swordplay; *esp* : FENCER

sword·tail \ˈsȯrd-ˌtāl\ *n* : a small brightly marked Central American fish often kept in aquariums

swore *past of* SWEAR

sworn *past part of* SWEAR

swum *past part of* SWIM

swung *past and past part of* SWING

syb·a·rite \ˈsi-bə-ˌrīt\ *n* : a lover of luxury : VOLUPTUARY — **syb·a·rit·ic** \ˌsi-bə-ˈri-tik\ *adj*

syc·a·more \ˈsi-kə-ˌmȯr\ *n* : a large spreading tree chiefly of the eastern and central U.S. that has light brown flaky bark and small round fruits hanging on long stalks

sy·co·phant \ˈsi-kə-fənt\ *n* : a servile flatterer — **sy·co·phan·cy** \ˈsi-kə-fən-sē\ *n* — **sy·co·phan·tic** \ˌsi-kə-ˈfan-tik\ *adj*

syl *or* **syll** *abbr* syllable

syl·lab·i·ca·tion \sə-ˌla-bə-ˈkā-shən\ *n* : the division of words into syllables

syl·lab·i·fy \sə-ˈla-bə-ˌfī\ *vb* **-fied; -fy·ing** : to form or divide into syllables — **syl·lab·i·fi·ca·tion** \-ˌla-bə-fə-ˈkā-shən\ *n*

syl·la·ble \ˈsi-lə-bəl\ *n* [ME, fr. AF *sillabe, silable,* fr. L *syllaba,* fr. Gk *syllabē,* fr. *syllambanein* to gather together, fr. *syn-* with + *lambanein* to take] : a unit of spoken language consisting of an uninterrupted utterance and forming either a whole word (as *cat*) or a commonly recognized division of a word (as *syl* in *syl-la-ble*); *also* : one or more letters representing such a unit — **syl·lab·ic** \sə-ˈla-bik\ *adj*

syl·la·bus \ˈsi-lə-bəs\ *n, pl* **-bi** \-ˌbī\ *or* **-bus·es** : a summary containing the heads or main topics of a speech, book, or course of study

syl·lo·gism \ˈsi-lə-ˌji-zəm\ *n* : a logical scheme of a formal argument consisting of a major and a minor premise and a conclusion which must logically be true if the premises are true — **syl·lo·gis·tic** \ˌsi-lə-ˈjis-tik\ *adj*

sylph \ˈsilf\ *n* **1** : an imaginary being inhabiting the air **2** : a slender graceful woman or girl

syl·van \ˈsil-vən\ *adj* **1** : living or located in a wooded area; *also* : of, relating to, or characteristic of forest **2 :** abounding in woods or trees

sym *abbr* **1** symbol **2** symmetrical

sym·bi·o·sis \ˌsim-ˌbī-ˈō-səs, -bē-\ *n, pl* **-o·ses** \-ˌsēz\ **:** the living together in close association of two dissimilar organisms esp. when mutually beneficial — **sym·bi·ot·ic** \-ˈä-tik\ *adj*

sym·bol \ˈsim-bəl\ *n* **1 :** something that stands for something else; *esp* **:** something concrete that represents or suggests another thing that cannot in itself be pictured ⟨the lion is a ∼ of bravery⟩ **2 :** a letter, character, or sign used in writing or printing to represent operations, quantities, elements, sounds, or other ideas — **sym·bol·ic** \sim-ˈbä-lik\ *also* **sym·bol·i·cal** \-li-kəl\ *adj* — **sym·bol·i·cal·ly** \-k(ə-)lē\ *adv*

sym·bol·ise *Brit var of* SYMBOLIZE

sym·bol·ism \ˈsim-bə-ˌli-zəm\ *n* **:** representation of abstract or intangible things by means of symbols

sym·bol·ize \ˈsim-bə-ˌlīz\ *vb* **-ized; -iz·ing** **1 :** to serve as a symbol of **2 :** to represent by symbols — **sym·bol·i·za·tion** \ˌsim-bə-lə-ˈzā-shən\ *n*

sym·me·try \ˈsi-mə-trē\ *n, pl* **-tries** **1 :** an arrangement marked by regularity and balanced proportions **2 :** correspondence in size, shape, and position of parts that are on opposite sides of a dividing line or center — **sym·met·ri·cal** \sə-ˈme-tri-kəl\ *or* **sym·met·ric** \sə-ˈme-trik\ *adj* — **sym·met·ri·cal·ly** \-k(ə-)lē\ *adv*

sympathetic nervous system *n* **:** the part of the autonomic nervous system that is concerned esp. with the body's response to stress and that tends to decrease the tone and contractility of smooth muscle and increase blood pressure and the activity of the heart

sym·pa·thise *chiefly Brit var of* SYMPATHIZE

sym·pa·thize \ˈsim-pə-ˌthīz\ *vb* **-thized; -thiz·ing :** to feel or show sympathy — **sym·pa·thiz·er** *n*

sym·pa·thy \ˈsim-pə-thē\ *n, pl* **-thies** **1 :** a relationship between persons or things wherein whatever affects one similarly affects the other **2 :** harmony of interests and aims **3 :** FAVOR, SUPPORT **4 :** the capacity for entering into and sharing the feelings or interests of another; *also* **:** COMPASSION, PITY **5 :** an expression of sorrow for another's loss, grief, or misfortune — **sym·pa·thet·ic** \ˌsim-pə-ˈthe-tik\ *adj* — **sym·pa·thet·i·cal·ly** \-ti-k(ə-)lē\ *adv*

sym·pho·ny \ˈsim-fə-nē\ *n, pl* **-nies** **1 :** harmony of sounds **2 :** a large and complex composition for a full orchestra **3 :** a large orchestra of a kind that plays symphonies — **sym·phon·ic** \sim-ˈfä-nik\ *adj*

sym·po·sium \sim-ˈpō-zē-əm\ *n, pl* **-sia** \-zē-ə\ *or* **-siums :** a conference at which a particular topic is discussed by various speakers; *also* **:** a collection of opinions about a subject

symp·tom \ˈsimp-təm\ *n* [LL *symptoma,* fr. Gk *symptōma* happening, attribute, symptom, fr. *sympiptein* to happen, fr. *syn-* with + *piptein* to fall] **1 :** something that indicates the presence of disease or abnormality; *esp* **:** something (as a headache) that can be sensed only by the individual affected **2 :** SIGN, INDICATION ⟨∼*s* of inner turmoil⟩ — **symp·tom·at·ic** \ˌsimp-tə-ˈma-tik\ *adj*

syn *abbr* synonym; synonymous; synonymy

syn·a·gogue *also* **syn·a·gog** \ˈsi-nə-ˌgäg\ *n* [ME *synagoge,* fr. AF, fr. LL *synagoga,* fr. Gk *synagōgē* assembly, synagogue, fr. *synagein* to bring together] **1 :** a Jewish congregation **2 :** the house of worship of a Jewish congregation

syn·apse \ˈsi-ˌnaps, sə-ˈnaps\ *n* **:** the point at which a nervous impulse passes from one neuron to another — **syn·ap·tic** \sə-ˈnap-tik\ *adj*

[1]**sync** *also* **synch** \ˈsiŋk\ *vb* **synced** *also* **synched** \ˈsiŋkt\; **sync·ing** *also* **synch·ing** \ˈsiŋ-kiŋ\ **:** SYNCHRONIZE

[2]**sync** *also* **synch** *n* **:** SYNCHRONIZATION, SYNCHRONISM — **sync** *adj*

syn·chro·ni·sa·tion, syn·chro·nise *Brit var of* SYNCHRONIZATION, SYNCHRONIZE

syn·chro·nize \ˈsiŋ-krə-ˌnīz, ˈsin-\ *vb* **-nized; -niz·ing** **1 :** to occur or cause to occur at the same instant **2 :** to represent, arrange, or tabulate according to dates or time **3 :** to cause to agree in time **4 :** to make synchronous in operation — **syn·chro·nism** \-ˌni-zəm\ *n* — **syn·chro·ni·za·tion** \ˌsiŋ-krə-nə-ˈzā-shən, ˌsin-\ *n* — **syn·chro·niz·er** *n*

syn·chro·nous \ˈsiŋ-krə-nəs, ˈsin-\ *adj* **1 :** happening at the same time **:** CONCURRENT **2 :** working, moving, or occurring together at the same rate and at the proper time

syn·co·pa·tion \ˌsiŋ-kə-ˈpā-shən, ˌsin-\ *n* **:** a shifting of the regular musical accent **:** occurrence of accented notes on the weak beat — **syn·co·pate** \ˈsiŋ-kə-ˌpāt, ˈsin-\ *vb*

syn·co·pe \ˈsiŋ-kə-(ˌ)pē, ˈsin-\ *n* **:** the loss of one or more sounds or letters in the interior of a word (as in *fo'c'sle* for *forecastle*)

[1]**syn·di·cate** \ˈsin-di-kət\ *n* **1 :** a group of persons who combine to carry out a financial or industrial undertaking **2 :** a loose association of racketeers **3 :** a business concern that sells materials for publication in many newspapers and periodicals at the same time

[2]**syn·di·cate** \-də-ˌkāt\ *vb* **-cat·ed; -cat·ing** **1 :** to combine into or manage as a syndicate **2 :** to publish through a syndicate — **syn·di·ca·tion** \ˌsin-də-ˈkā-shən\ *n*

syn·drome \ˈsin-ˌdrōm\ *n* **:** a group of signs and symptoms that occur together and characterize a particular abnormality or condition

syn·er·gism \ˈsin-ər-ˌji-zəm\ *n* **:** interaction of discrete agencies (as industrial firms), agents (as drugs), or conditions such that the total effect is greater than the sum of the individual effects — **syn·er·gist** \-jist\ *n* — **syn·er·gis·tic** \ˌsi-nər-ˈjis-tik\ *adj* — **syn·er·gis·ti·cal·ly** \-ti-k(ə-)lē\ *adv*

syn·er·gy \ˈsi-nər-jē\ *n, pl* **-gies** : SYNERGISM

syn·fuel \ˈsin-ˌfyül\ *n* [*syn*thetic] : a fuel derived esp. from a fossil fuel

syn·od \ˈsi-nəd\ *n* : COUNCIL, ASSEMBLY; *esp* : a religious governing body — **syn·od·al** \-nə-dᵊl, -ˌnä-dᵊl\ *adj* — **syn·od·ic** \sə-ˈnä-dik\ *or* **syn·od·i·cal** \-di-kəl\ *adj*

syn·o·nym \ˈsi-nə-ˌnim\ *n* : one of two or more words in the same language which have the same or very nearly the same meaning — **syn·on·y·mous** \sə-ˈnä-nə-məs\ *adj* — **syn·on·y·mous·ly** *adv* — **syn·on·y·my** \-mē\ *n*

syn·op·sis \sə-ˈnäp-səs\ *n, pl* **-op·ses** \-ˌsēz\ : a condensed statement or outline (as of a treatise) : ABSTRACT

syn·op·tic \sə-ˈnäp-tik\ *also* **syn·op·ti·cal** \-ti-kəl\ *adj* : characterized by or affording a comprehensive view

syn·tax \ˈsin-ˌtaks\ *n* : the way in which words are put together to form phrases, clauses, or sentences — **syn·tac·tic** \sin-ˈtak-tik\ *or* **syn·tac·ti·cal** \-ti-kəl\ *adj*

syn·the·sis \ˈsin-thə-səs\ *n, pl* **-the·ses** \-ˌsēz\ : the combination of parts or elements into a whole; *esp* : the production of a substance by union of chemically simpler substances — **syn·the·size** \-ˌsīz\ *vb* — **syn·the·siz·er** *n*

syn·thet·ic \sin-ˈthe-tik\ *adj* : produced artificially esp. by chemical means; *also* : not genuine — **synthetic** *n* — **syn·thet·i·cal·ly** \-ti-k(ə-)lē\ *adv*

syph·i·lis \ˈsi-fə-ləs\ *n* [NL, fr. *Syphilus,* hero of the poem *Syphilis sive Morbus Gallicus* (*Syphilis or the French disease*) (1530) by Girolamo Fracastoro †1553 Italian physician] : an infectious usu. venereal disease caused by a spirochete — **syph·i·lit·ic** \ˌsi-fə-ˈli-tik\ *adj or n*

syphon *var of* SIPHON

Sy·rah \sē-ˈrä\ *n* : a red wine

¹sy·ringe \sə-ˈrinj\ *n* : a device used esp. for injecting liquids into or withdrawing them from the body

²syringe *vb* **sy·ringed; sy·ring·ing** : to flush or cleanse with or as if with a syringe

syr·up *also* **sir·up** \ˈsər-əp, ˈsir-əp\ *n* **1** : a thick sticky solution of sugar and water often flavored or medicated **2** : the concentrated juice of a fruit or plant — **syr·upy** *adj*

syst *abbr* system

sys·tem \ˈsis-təm\ *n* **1** : a group of units so combined as to form a whole and to operate in unison **2** : the body as a functioning whole; *also* : a group of bodily organs (as the nervous system) that together carry on some vital function **3** : a definite scheme or method of procedure or classification **4** : regular method or order — **sys·tem·at·ic** \ˌsis-tə-ˈma-tik\ — **sys·tem·at·i·cal·ly** \-ti-k(ə-)lē\ *adv*

sys·tem·a·tise *Brit var of* SYSTEMATIZE

sys·tem·a·tize \ˈsis-tə-mə-ˌtīz\ *vb* **-tized; -tiz·ing** : to make into a system : arrange methodically

¹sys·tem·ic \sis-ˈte-mik\ *adj* **1** : of, relating to, or affecting the whole body ⟨~ disease⟩ **2** : of, relating to, or being a pesticide that when absorbed into the sap or bloodstream makes the entire plant or animal toxic to a pest (as an insect or fungus)

²systemic *n* : a systemic pesticide

systemic lupus er·y·the·ma·to·sus \ˌer-ə-ˌthē-mə-ˈtō-səs\ *n* : a systemic disease esp. of women characterized by fever, skin rash, and arthritis, often by anemia, by small hemorrhages of the skin and mucous membranes, and in serious cases by involvement of internal organs

sys·tem·ize \ˈsis-tə-ˌmīz\ *vb* **-ized; -iz·ing** : SYSTEMATIZE

systems analyst *n* : a person who studies a procedure or business to determine its goals or purposes and to discover the best ways to accomplish them — **systems analysis** *n*

sys·to·le \ˈsis-tə-(ˌ)lē\ *n* : a rhythmically recurrent contraction of the heart — **sys·tol·ic** \sis-ˈtä-lik\ *adj* N

T

¹t \ˈtē\ *n, pl* **t's** *or* **ts** \ˈtēz\ *often cap* : the 20th letter of the English alphabet

²t *abbr, often cap* **1** tablespoon **2** teaspoon **3** temperature **4** ton **5** transitive **6** troy **7** true

T *abbr* **1** toddler **2** T-shirt

Ta *symbol* tantalum

TA *abbr* teaching assistant

¹tab \ˈtab\ *n* **1** : a short projecting flap, loop, or tag; *also* : a small insert or addition **2** : close surveillance : WATCH ⟨keep ~*s* on him⟩ **3** : BILL, CHECK **4** : a key on a keyboard esp. for putting data in columns

²tab *vb* **tabbed; tab·bing** : DESIGNATE

tab·by \ˈta-bē\ *n, pl* **tabbies** : a usu. striped or mottled domestic cat; *also* : a female domestic cat

tab·er·na·cle \ˈta-bər-ˌna-kəl\ *n* [ME, fr. AF, fr. LL *tabernaculum,* fr. L, tent, fr. *taberna* hut] **1** *often cap* : a tent sanctuary used by the Israelites during the Exodus

2 : a receptacle for the consecrated elements of the Eucharist 3 : a house of worship

[1]ta·ble \ˈtā-bəl\ *n* 1 : TABLET 1 2 : a piece of furniture consisting of a smooth flat top fixed on legs 3 : a supply of food : BOARD, FARE 4 : a group of people assembled at or as if at a table 5 : an orderly arrangement of data usu. in rows and columns 6 : a short list ⟨~ of contents⟩ — **ta·ble·top** \-ˌtäp\ *n*

[2]table *vb* **ta·bled; ta·bling** 1 *Brit* : to place on the agenda 2 : to remove (a parliamentary motion) from consideration indefinitely

tab·leau \ˈta-ˌblō\ *n, pl* **tab·leaux** \-ˌblōz\ *also* **tableaus** [F] : a scene or event usu. presented on a stage by silent and motionless costumed participants

ta·ble·cloth \ˈtā-bəl-ˌklȯth\ *n* : a covering spread over a dining table before the table is set

ta·ble·land \ˈtā-bəl-ˌland\ *n* : PLATEAU

ta·ble·spoon \-ˌspün\ *n* 1 : a large spoon used esp. for serving 2 : a unit of measure equal to ½ fluid ounce (15 milliliters)

ta·ble·spoon·ful \-ˌfu̇l\ *n, pl* **-spoonfuls** \-ˌfu̇lz\ *also* **-spoons·ful** \-ˌspünz-fu̇l\ : TABLESPOON 2

tab·let \ˈta-blət\ *n* 1 : a flat slab suited for or bearing an inscription 2 : a collection of sheets of paper glued together at one edge 3 : a compressed or molded block of material; *esp* : a usu. disk-shaped medicated mass 4 : GRAPHICS TABLET 5 *or* **tablet computer** : a mobile computing device that has a flat rectangular form, is usually controlled by means of a touch screen, and is typically used for accessing the Internet, watching videos, and reading e-books

table tennis *n* : a game resembling tennis played on a tabletop with wooden paddles and a small hollow plastic ball

ta·ble·ware \ˈtā-bəl-ˌwer\ *n* : utensils (as of china or silver) for table use

[1]tab·loid \ˈta-ˌblȯid\ *adj* : condensed into small scope

[2]tabloid *n* : a newspaper marked by small pages, condensation of the news, and usu. many photographs

[1]ta·boo *also* **ta·bu** \tə-ˈbü, ta-\ *adj* [Tongan (a Polynesian language) *tabu*] : prohibited by a taboo

[2]taboo *also* **tabu** *n, pl* **taboos** *also* **tabus** 1 : a prohibition against touching, saying, or doing something for fear of immediate harm from a supernatural force 2 : a prohibition imposed by social custom

ta·bor *also* **ta·bour** \ˈtā-bər\ *n* : a small drum used to accompany a pipe or fife played by the same person

tab·u·lar \ˈta-byə-lər\ *adj* 1 : having a flat surface 2 : arranged in a table; *esp* : set up in rows and columns 3 : computed by means of a table

tab·u·late \-ˌlāt\ *vb* **-lat·ed; -lat·ing** : to put into tabular form — **tab·u·la·tion** \ˌta-byə-ˈlā-shən\ *n* — **tab·u·la·tor** \ˈta-byə-ˌlā-tər\ *n*

TAC \ˈtak\ *abbr* Tactical Air Command

tach \ˈtak\ *n* : TACHOMETER

ta·chom·e·ter \ta-ˈkä-mə-tər, tə-\ *n* [ultim. fr. Gk *tachos* speed] : a device to indicate speed of rotation

tachy·car·dia \ˌta-ki-ˈkär-dē-ə\ *n* : relatively rapid heart action

tachy·on \ˈta-kē-ˌän\ *n* : a hypothetical particle held to travel faster than light

tac·it \ˈta-sət\ *adj* [F or L; F *tacite,* fr. L *tacitus* silent, fr. *tacēre* to be silent] 1 : expressed without words or speech 2 : implied or indicated but not actually expressed ⟨~ consent⟩ — **tac·it·ly** *adv* — **tac·it·ness** *n*

tac·i·turn \ˈta-sə-ˌtərn\ *adj* : disinclined to talk ♦ ***Synonyms*** UNCOMMUNICATIVE, RESERVED, RETICENT, CLOSEMOUTHED — **tac·i·tur·ni·ty** \ˌta-sə-ˈtər-nə-tē\ *n*

[1]tack \ˈtak\ *vb* 1 : to fasten with tacks; *also* : to add on 2 : to change the direction of (a sailing ship) from one tack to another 3 : to follow a zigzag course

[2]tack *n* 1 : a small sharp nail with a broad flat head 2 : the direction toward the wind that a ship is sailing ⟨starboard ~⟩; *also* : the run of a ship on one tack 3 : a change of course from one tack to another 4 : a zigzag course 5 : a course of action

[3]tack *n* : gear for harnessing a horse

[1]tack·le \ˈta-kəl, *naut often* ˈtā-\ *n* 1 : GEAR, APPARATUS, EQUIPMENT 2 : the rigging of a ship 3 : an arrangement of ropes and pulleys for hoisting or pulling heavy objects 4 : the act or an instance of tackling; *also* : a football lineman playing between guard and end

[2]tackle *vb* **tack·led; tack·ling** 1 : to attach and secure with or as if with tackle 2 : to seize, grapple with, or throw down with the intention of subduing or stopping 3 : to set about dealing with ⟨~ a problem⟩ — **tack·ler** *n*

[1]tacky \ˈta-kē\ *adj* **tack·i·er; -est** : sticky to the touch

[2]tacky *adj* **tack·i·er; -est** 1 : SHABBY, SEEDY 2 : marked by lack of style or good taste; *also* : cheaply showy ⟨a ~ publicity stunt⟩ ⟨a ~ outfit⟩

ta·co \ˈtä-kō\ *n, pl* **tacos** \-kōz\ [MexSp] : a usu. fried tortilla rolled up with or folded over a filling

tact \ˈtakt\ *n* [F, sense of touch, fr. L *tactus,* fr. *tangere* to touch] : a keen sense of what to do or say to keep good relations with others ⟨a diplomat with ~⟩ — **tact·ful** \-fəl\ *adj* — **tact·ful·ly** *adv* — **tact·less** *adj* — **tact·less·ly** *adv*

tac·tic \ˈtak-tik\ *n* : a planned action for accomplishing an end

tac·tics \ˈtak-tiks\ *n sing or pl* 1 : the science of maneuvering forces in combat 2 : the skill of using available means to accomplish an end — **tac·ti·cal** \-ti-kəl\ *adj* — **tac·ti·cian** \tak-ˈti-shən\ *n*

tac·tile \ˈtak-tᵊl, ˈtak-ˌtī(-ə)l\ *adj* : of, relating to, or perceptible through the sense of touch

tad·pole \ˈtad-ˌpōl\ *n* [ME *taddepol,* fr.

tode toad + *polle* head] : an aquatic larva of a frog or toad that has a tail and gills

tae kwon do \ˈtī-ˈkwän-ˈdō\ *n* : a Korean martial art of self-defense

taf·fe·ta \ˈta-fə-tə\ *n* : a crisp lustrous fabric (as of silk or rayon)

taff·rail \ˈtaf-ˌrāl, -rəl\ *n* : the rail around a ship's stern

taf·fy \ˈta-fē\ *n, pl* **taffies** : a candy usu. of molasses or brown sugar stretched until porous and light-colored

[1]**tag** \ˈtag\ *n* **1** : a metal or plastic binding on an end of a shoelace **2** : a piece of hanging or attached material **3** : a hackneyed quotation or saying **4** : a descriptive or identifying epithet

[2]**tag** *vb* **tagged; tag·ging 1** : to provide or mark with or as if with a tag; *esp* : IDENTIFY **2** : to attach as an addition **3** : to follow closely and persistently ⟨~*s* along everywhere we go⟩ **4** : to hold responsible for something

[3]**tag** *n* : a game in which one player chases others and tries to touch one of them

[4]**tag** *vb* **tagged; tag·ging 1** : to touch in or as if in a game of tag **2** : SELECT

TAG *abbr* the adjutant general

tag sale *n* : GARAGE SALE

Ta·hi·tian \tə-ˈhē-shən\ *n* **1** : a native or inhabitant of Tahiti **2** : the Polynesian language of the Tahitians — **Tahitian** *adj*

tai·ga \ˈtī-gə\ *n* [Russ *taĭga*] : a moist coniferous subarctic forest extending south from the tundra

[1]**tail** \ˈtāl\ *n* **1** : the rear end or a process extending from the rear end of an animal **2** : something resembling an animal's tail **3** *pl* : full evening dress for men **4** : the back, last, lower, or inferior part of something; *esp* : the reverse of a coin — usu. used in pl. ⟨~*s*, I win⟩ **5** : one who follows or keeps watch on someone — **tailed** \ˈtāld\ *adj* — **tail·less** \ˈtāl-ləs\ *adj*

[2]**tail** *vb* : FOLLOW; *esp* : to follow for the purpose of surveillance

tail·coat \-ˈkōt\ *n* : a coat with tails; *esp* : a man's full-dress coat with two long tapering skirts at the back

[1]**tail·gate** \-ˌgāt\ *n* : a board or gate at the back end of a vehicle that can be let down (as for loading)

[2]**tailgate** *vb* **tail·gat·ed; tail·gat·ing 1** : to drive dangerously close behind another vehicle **2** : to hold a tailgate picnic

[3]**tailgate** *adj* : relating to or being a picnic set up on a tailgate ⟨a ~ party⟩

tail·light \-ˌlīt\ *n* : a usu. red warning light mounted at the rear of a vehicle

[1]**tai·lor** \ˈtā-lər\ *n* [ME *taillour,* fr. AF *taillur,* fr. *tailler* to cut, fr. LL *taliare,* fr. L *talea* twig, cutting] : a person whose occupation is making or altering garments

[2]**tailor** *vb* **1** : to make or fashion as the work of a tailor **2** : to make or adapt to suit a special purpose

tail·pipe \ˈtāl-ˌpīp\ *n* : an outlet by which engine exhaust gases are expelled from a vehicle (as an automobile)

tail·spin \ˈtāl-ˌspin\ *n* : a rapid descent or downward spiral

tail·wind \ˈtāl-ˌwind\ *n* : a wind blowing in the same general direction as a course of movement (as of an aircraft)

[1]**taint** \ˈtānt\ *vb* **1** : CORRUPT, CONTAMINATE **2** : to affect or become affected with something bad (as putrefaction)

[2]**taint** *n* : a contaminating mark or influence

ta·ka \ˈtä-kə\ *n* — see MONEY table

[1]**take** \ˈtāk\ *vb* **took** \ˈtu̇k\; **tak·en** \ˈtā-kən\; **tak·ing** [ME, fr. OE *tacan,* fr. ON *taka*] **1** : to get into one's hands or possession : GRASP, SEIZE **2** : CAPTURE; *also* : DEFEAT **3** : to obtain or secure for use **4** : to catch or attack through the effect of a sudden force or influence ⟨*taken* ill⟩ **5** : CAPTIVATE, DELIGHT **6** : to bring into a relation ⟨~ a wife⟩ **7** : REMOVE, SUBTRACT ⟨~ three from eight⟩ **8** : to pick out : CHOOSE **9** : ASSUME, UNDERTAKE **10** : RECEIVE, ACCEPT **11** : to use for transportation ⟨~ a bus⟩ **12** : to become impregnated with : ABSORB ⟨~*s* a dye⟩ **13** : to receive into one's body (as by swallowing) ⟨~ a pill⟩ **14** : ENDURE, UNDERGO ⟨~ a cut in pay⟩ **15** : to lead, carry, or cause to go along to another place **16** : NEED, REQUIRE ⟨~*s* a size nine shoe⟩ **17** : to obtain as the result of a special procedure ⟨~ a snapshot⟩ **18** : to undertake and do, make, or perform ⟨~ a walk⟩ **19** : to take effect : ACT, OPERATE ♦ ***Synonyms*** GRAB, CLUTCH, SNATCH, SEIZE, NAB, GRAPPLE — **tak·er** *n* — **take advantage of 1** : to profit by **2** : EXPLOIT — **take after** : RESEMBLE — **take care** : to be careful — **take care of** : to attend to — **take effect** : to become operative — **take exception** : OBJECT — **take for** : to suppose to be; *esp* : to mistake for — **take place** : HAPPEN — **take to 1** : to go to **2** : to apply or devote oneself to **3** : to conceive a liking for

[2]**take** *n* **1** : the number or quantity taken; *also* : PROCEEDS, RECEIPTS **2** : an act or the action of taking **3** : a television or movie scene filmed or taped at one time; *also* : a sound recording made at one time **4** : a distinct or personal point of view

take·off \ˈtāk-ˌȯf\ *n* **1** : IMITATION; *esp* : PARODY ⟨did a ~ of the president⟩ **2** : an act or instance of taking off

take off *vb* **1** : REMOVE **2** : DEDUCT **3** : to set out : go away **4** : to begin flight

take on *vb* **1** : to begin to perform or deal with; *also* : to contend with as an opponent **2** : ENGAGE, HIRE **3** : to assume or acquire as or as if one's own **4** : to make an unusual show of one's feelings esp. of grief or anger

take over *vb* : to assume control or possession of or responsibility for — **takeover** \ˈtāk-ˌō-vər\ *n*

take up *vb* **1** : PICK UP **2** : to begin to occupy (land) **3** : to absorb or incorporate into itself **4** : to begin to engage in ⟨*took up* jogging⟩ **5** : to make tighter or shorter ⟨*take up* the slack⟩

tak·ings \ˈtā-kiŋz\ *n pl, chiefly Brit* : receipts esp. of money

ta·la \ˈtä-lə\ *n, pl* **tala** *or* **talas** — see MONEY table

talc \ˈtalk\ *n* : a soft mineral with a soapy feel used esp. in making a soothing powder (**tal·cum powder** \ˈtal-kəm-\) for the skin

tale \ˈtāl\ *n* **1** : a relation of a series of events **2** : a report of a confidential matter **3** : idle talk; *esp* : harmful gossip **4** : a usu. imaginative narrative **5** : FALSEHOOD **6** : COUNT, TALLY

tal·ent \ˈta-lənt\ *n* **1** : an ancient unit of weight and value **2** : the natural endowments of a person **3** : a special often creative or artistic aptitude **4** : mental power : ABILITY **5** : a person of talent ♦ ***Synonyms*** GENIUS, GIFT, FACULTY, APTITUDE, KNACK — **tal·ent·ed** *adj*

ta·ler \ˈtä-lər\ *n* : any of numerous silver coins issued by German states from the 15th to the 19th centuries

tal·is·man \ˈta-ləs-mən, -ləz-\ *n, pl* **-mans** [F *talisman* or Sp *talismán* or It *talismano,* fr. Ar *ṭilsam,* fr. MGk *telesma,* fr. Gk, consecration, fr. *telein* to initiate into the mysteries, complete, fr. *telos* end] : an object thought to act as a charm

[1]**talk** \ˈtȯk\ *vb* **1** : to express in speech : utter words : SPEAK **2** : DISCUSS ⟨~ business⟩ **3** : to influence or cause by talking ⟨~*ed* him into going⟩ **4** : to use (a language) for communicating **5** : CONVERSE **6** : to reveal confidential information; *also* : GOSSIP **7** : to give a talk : LECTURE — **talk·er** *n* — **talk back** : to answer impertinently

[2]**talk** *n* **1** : the act of talking **2** : a way of speaking **3** : a formal discussion **4** : REPORT, RUMOR **5** : the topic of comment or gossip ⟨the ~ of the town⟩ **6** : an informal address or lecture

talk·ative \ˈtȯ-kə-tiv\ *adj* : given to talking ♦ ***Synonyms*** LOQUACIOUS, CHATTY, GABBY, GARRULOUS — **talk·ative·ly** *adv* — **talk·ative·ness** *n*

talk·ing–to \ˈtȯ-kiŋ-ˌtü\ *n* : REPRIMAND, REPROOF

talk radio *n* : radio programming consisting of call-in shows

tall \ˈtȯl\ *adj* **1** : high in stature; *also* : of a specified height ⟨six feet ~⟩ **2** : LARGE, FORMIDABLE ⟨a ~ order⟩ **3** : UNBELIEVABLE, IMPROBABLE ⟨a ~ story⟩ — **tall·ness** *n*

tal·low \ˈta-lō\ *n* : a hard white fat rendered usu. from cattle or sheep tissues and used esp. in candles

[1]**tal·ly** \ˈta-lē\ *n, pl* **tallies** **1** : a device for visibly recording or accounting esp. business transactions **2** : a recorded account **3** : a corresponding part; *also* : CORRESPONDENCE

[2]**tally** *vb* **tal·lied; tal·ly·ing** **1** : to mark on or as if on a tally **2** : to make a count of : RECKON; *also* : SCORE **3** : CORRESPOND, MATCH ♦ ***Synonyms*** SQUARE, ACCORD, HARMONIZE, CONFORM, JIBE

tal·ly·ho \ˌta-lē-ˈhō\ *n, pl* **-hos** : a call of a huntsman at sight of the fox

Tal·mud \ˈtäl-ˌmu̇d, ˈtal-məd\ *n* [Late Heb *talmūdh,* lit., instruction] : the authoritative body of Jewish tradition — **Tal·mu·dic** \tal-ˈmü-dik, -ˈmyü-, -ˈmə-; täl-ˈmu̇-\ *adj* — **Tal·mud·ist** \ˈtäl-ˌmu̇-dist, ˈtal-mə-\ *n*

tal·on \ˈta-lən\ *n* : the claw of an animal and esp. of a bird of prey

ta·lus \ˈtā-ləs, ˈta-\ *n* : rock debris at the base of a cliff

tam \ˈtam\ *n* : TAM-O'-SHANTER

ta·ma·le \tə-ˈmä-lē\ *n* [MexSp *tamales,* pl. of *tamal* tamale, fr. Nahuatl *tamalli* steamed cornmeal dough] : ground meat seasoned with chili, rolled in cornmeal dough, wrapped in corn husks, and steamed

tam·a·rack \ˈta-mə-ˌrak\ *n* : a larch of northern No. America; *also* : its hard resinous wood

tam·a·rin \ˈta-mə-rən\ *n* : any of several small So. American monkeys related to the marmosets

tam·a·rind \ˈta-mə-rənd, -ˌrind\ *n* [Sp & Pg *tamarindo,* fr. Ar *tamr hindī,* lit., Indian date] : a tropical tree of the legume family with hard yellowish wood and feathery leaves; *also* : its acid fruit

tam·ba·la \täm-ˈbä-lə\ *n, pl* **-la** *or* **-las** — see *kwacha* at MONEY table

tam·bou·rine \ˌtam-bə-ˈrēn\ *n* : a small shallow drum with loose disks at the sides played by shaking or striking with the hand

[1]**tame** \ˈtām\ *adj* **tam·er; tam·est** **1** : reduced from a state of native wildness esp. so as to be useful to humans : DOMESTICATED **2** : made docile : SUBDUED **3** : lacking spirit or interest : INSIPID ♦ ***Synonyms*** SUBMISSIVE, DOMESTIC, DOMESTICATED — **tame·ly** *adv* — **tame·ness** *n*

[2]**tame** *vb* **tamed; tam·ing** **1** : to make or become tame; *also* : to subject (land) to cultivation **2** : HUMBLE, SUBDUE — **tam·able** *or* **tame·able** \ˈtā-mə-bəl\ *adj* — **tame·less** *adj* — **tam·er** *n*

tam–o'–shan·ter \ˈta-mə-ˌshan-tər\ *n* [fr. poem *Tam o' Shanter* (1790) by Robert Burns †1796 Scot. poet] : a Scottish woolen cap with a wide flat circular crown and usu. a pom-pom in the center

ta·mox·i·fen \tə-ˈmäk-sə-ˌfen\ *n* : a drug used esp. to treat breast cancer

tamp \ˈtamp\ *vb* : to drive down or in by a series of light blows

tam·per \ˈtam-pər\ *vb* **1** : to carry on underhand negotiations (as by bribery) ⟨~ with a witness⟩ **2** : to interfere so as to weaken or change for the worse ⟨~ with a document⟩ **3** : to try foolish or dangerous experiments

tam·pon \ˈtam-ˌpän\ *n* [F, lit., plug] : a plug (as of cotton) introduced into a body cavity usu. to absorb secretions (as from menstruation) or to arrest bleeding

[1]**tan** \ˈtan\ *vb* **tanned; tan·ning** **1** : to change (hide) into leather esp. by soaking in a liquid containing tannin **2** : to make or become brown (as by exposure to the sun) **3** : WHIP, THRASH

[2]**tan** *n* **1** : a brown skin color induced by sun or weather **2** : a light yellowish brown color

[3]**tan** *abbr* tangent

tan·a·ger \'ta-ni-jər\ *n* : any of numerous American birds that are often brightly colored

tan·bark \'tan-ˌbärk\ *n* : bark (as of oak or sumac) that is rich in tannin and used in tanning

[1]**tan·dem** \'tan-dəm\ *n* [L, at last, at length (taken to mean "lengthwise"), fr. *tam* so] **1** : a 2-seated carriage with horses hitched tandem; *also* : its team **2** : a bicycle for two persons sitting one behind the other — **in tandem** : in a tandem arrangement

[2]**tandem** *adv* : one behind another

[3]**tandem** *adj* **1** : consisting of things arranged one behind the other **2** : working in conjunction with each other

tang \'taŋ\ *n* **1** : a part in a tool that connects the blade with the handle **2** : a sharp distinctive flavor; *also* : a pungent odor — **tangy** *adj*

[1]**tan·gent** \'tan-jənt\ *adj* [L *tangent-, tangens,* prp. of *tangere* to touch] : TOUCHING; *esp* : touching a circle or sphere at only one point

[2]**tangent** *n* **1** : the trigonometric function that is the ratio between the side opposite and the side adjacent to an acute angle in a right triangle **2** : a tangent line, curve, or surface **3** : an abrupt change of course

tan·gen·tial \tan-'jen-chəl\ *adj* **1** : TANGENT **2** : touching lightly : INCIDENTAL ⟨~ involvement⟩ — **tan·gen·tial·ly** *adv*

tan·ger·ine \'tan-jə-ˌrēn, ˌtan-jə-'rēn\ *n* : a deep orange loose-skinned citrus fruit; *also* : a tree that bears tangerines

[1]**tan·gi·ble** \'tan-jə-bəl\ *adj* **1** : perceptible esp. by the sense of touch : PALPABLE **2** : substantially real : MATERIAL ⟨~ rewards⟩ **3** : capable of being appraised ⟨~ assets⟩ ♦ ***Synonyms*** APPRECIABLE, PERCEPTIBLE, SENSIBLE, DISCERNIBLE — **tan·gi·bil·i·ty** \ˌtan-jə-'bi-lə-tē\ *n*

[2]**tangible** *n* : something tangible; *esp* : a tangible asset

[1]**tan·gle** \'taŋ-gəl\ *vb* **tan·gled; tan·gling** **1** : to involve so as to hamper or embarrass; *also* : ENTRAP **2** : to unite or knit together in intricate confusion : ENTANGLE

[2]**tangle** *n* **1** : a matted twisted mass **2** : a confusedly complicated state : MUDDLE

tan·go \'taŋ-gō\ *n, pl* **tangos** : a dance of Latin-American origin — **tango** *vb*

tank \'taŋk\ *n* **1** : a large artificial receptacle for liquids **2** : a heavily armed and armored combat vehicle that moves on tracks — **tank·ful** *n*

tan·kard \'taŋ-kərd\ *n* : a tall one-handled drinking vessel

tank·er \'taŋ-kər\ *n* : a vehicle equipped for transporting a liquid

tank top *n* : a sleeveless collarless pullover shirt with shoulder straps

tank town *n* : a small town

tan·ner \'ta-nər\ *n* : one that tans hides

tan·nery \'ta-nə-rē\ *n, pl* **-ner·ies** : a place where tanning is carried on

tan·nic acid \'ta-nik-\ *n* : TANNIN

tan·nin \'ta-nən\ *n* : any of various plant substances used esp. in tanning and dyeing, in inks, and as astringents

tan·sy \'tan-zē\ *n, pl* **tansies** : a common weedy herb related to the daisies with an aromatic odor and bitter-tasting finely divided leaves

tan·ta·lise *Brit var of* TANTALIZE

tan·ta·lize \'tan-tə-ˌlīz\ *vb* **-lized; -liz·ing** [fr. *Tantalus,* king of Greek myth punished in Hades by having to stand up to his chin in water that receded as he bent to drink] : to tease or torment by presenting something desirable but keeping it out of reach — **tan·ta·liz·er** *n* — **tan·ta·liz·ing·ly** *adv*

tan·ta·lum \'tan-tə-ləm\ *n* : a gray-white ductile metallic chemical element

tan·ta·mount \'tan-tə-ˌmau̇nt\ *adj* : equivalent in value or meaning ⟨a relationship ~ to marriage⟩

tan·trum \'tan-trəm\ *n* : a fit of bad temper

Tao·ism \'tau̇-ˌi-zəm, 'dau̇-\ *n* : a Chinese mystical philosophy; *also* : a religion developed from Taoist philosophy and Buddhism — **Tao·ist** \-ist\ *adj or n*

[1]**tap** \'tap\ *n* **1** : FAUCET, COCK **2** : liquor drawn through a tap **3** : the removing of fluid from a container or cavity by tapping **4** : a tool for forming an internal screw thread **5** : a point in an electric circuit where a connection may be made

[2]**tap** *vb* **tapped; tap·ping** **1** : to release or cause to flow by piercing or by drawing a plug from a container or cavity **2** : to pierce so as to let out or draw off a fluid **3** : to draw from ⟨~ resources⟩ **4** : to cut in on (as a telephone signal) to get information **5** : to form an internal screw thread in by means of a tap **6** : to connect (as a gas or water main) with a local supply — **tap·per** *n*

[3]**tap** *vb* **tapped; tap·ping** **1** : to rap lightly **2** : to bring about by repeated light blows **3** : SELECT; *esp* : to elect to membership

[4]**tap** *n* **1** : a light blow or stroke; *also* : its sound **2** : a small metal plate for the sole or heel of a shoe

ta·pa \'tä-pə, 'ta-\ *n* [Sp, lit., cover, lid] : an hors d'oeuvre served with drinks esp. in Spanish bars — usu. used in pl.

[1]**tape** \'tāp\ *n* **1** : a narrow flexible band or strip (as of woven fabric) **2** : MAGNETIC TAPE; *also* : CASSETTE

[2]**tape** *vb* **taped; tap·ing** **1** : to fasten or support with tape **2** : to record on magnetic tape

tape deck *n* : a device used to play back cassette tapes that usu. has to be connected to an audio system

tape measure *n* : a tape marked off in units (as inches) for measuring

[1]**ta·per** \'tā-pər\ *n* **1** : a slender wax candle; *also* : a long waxed wick **2** : a gradual lessening of thickness or width in a long object

[2]**taper** *vb* **ta·pered; ta·per·ing** **1** : to make or become gradually smaller toward one end **2** : to diminish gradually

tape–re·cord \ˌtāp-ri-'kȯrd\ *vb* : to make

a recording of on magnetic tape — **tape recorder** *n* — **tape recording** *n*

tap·es·try \ˈta-pə-strē\ *n, pl* **-tries** : a heavy reversible textile that has designs or pictures woven into it and is used esp. as a wall hanging

tape·worm \ˈtāp-ˌwərm\ *n* : any of a class of long flat segmented worms parasitic esp. in vertebrate intestines

tap·i·o·ca \ˌta-pē-ˈō-kə\ *n* : a usu. granular preparation of cassava starch used esp. in puddings; *also* : a dish (as pudding) that contains tapioca

ta·pir \ˈtā-pər\ *n, pl* **tapirs** *also* **tapir** [Pg *tapir, tapira,* fr. Tupi (Indigenous language of Brazil) *tapiʔira*] : any of a genus of large herbivorous hoofed mammals of tropical America and southeastern Asia

tap·pet \ˈta-pət\ *n* : a lever or projection moved by some other piece (as a cam) or intended to move something else

tap·room \ˈtap-ˌrüm, -ˌru̇m\ *n* : BARROOM

tap·root \-ˌrüt, -ˌru̇t\ *n* : a large main root growing straight down and giving off small side roots

taps \ˈtaps\ *n sing or pl* : the last bugle call at night blown as a signal that lights are to be put out; *also* : a similar call blown at military funerals and memorial services

tap·ster \ˈtap-stər\ *n* : BARTENDER

¹**tar** \ˈtär\ *n* **1** : a thick dark sticky liquid distilled from organic material (as wood or coal) **2** : SAILOR, SEAMAN

²**tar** *vb* **tarred; tar·ring** : to cover or smear with or as if with tar

tar·an·tel·la \ˌta-rən-ˈte-lə\ *n* : a lively folk dance of southern Italy in 6/8 time

ta·ran·tu·la \tə-ˈran-chə-lə, -tə-lə\ *n, pl* **tarantulas** *also* **ta·ran·tu·lae** \-ˈran-chə-ˌlē, -tə-ˌlē\ : any of a family of large hairy American spiders with a sharp bite that is not very poisonous to human beings

tar·dy \ˈtär-dē\ *adj* **tar·di·er; -est** **1** : moving slowly : SLUGGISH **2** : LATE ♦ ***Synonyms*** BEHINDHAND, OVERDUE, BELATED — **tar·di·ly** \-də-lē\ *adv* — **tar·di·ness** \-dē-nəs\ *n*

¹**tare** \ˈter\ *n* : a weed of grain fields

²**tare** *n* : a deduction from the gross weight of a substance and its container made in allowance for the weight of the container — **tare** *vb*

¹**tar·get** \ˈtär-gət\ *n* [ME, fr. MF *targette,* dim. of *targe* light shield, of Gmc origin] **1** : a mark to shoot at **2** : an object of ridicule or criticism **3** : a goal to be achieved

²**target** *vb* : to make a target of

tar·iff \ˈta-rəf\ *n* [It *tariffa,* fr. Ar *taʿrīf* notification] **1** : a schedule of duties imposed by a government esp. on imported goods; *also* : a duty or rate of duty imposed in such a schedule **2** : a schedule of rates or charges

tar·mac \ˈtär-ˌmak\ *n* : a surface paved with crushed stone covered with tar

tarn \ˈtärn\ *n* : a small mountain lake

tar·nish \ˈtär-nish\ *vb* : to make or become dull or discolored — **tarnish** *n*

ta·ro \ˈtär-ō, ˈter-\ *n, pl* **taros** : a large-leaved tropical plant related to the arums that is grown for its edible starchy corms; *also* : its corms

tar·ot \ˈter-ō, ˈta-rō\ *n* : one of a set of usu. 78 playing cards used esp. for fortune-telling

tar·pau·lin \tär-ˈpȯ-lən, ˈtär-pə-\ *n* : a piece of material (as durable plastic) used for protecting exposed objects

tar·pon \ˈtär-pən\ *n, pl* **tarpon** *or* **tarpons** : a large silvery bony fish often caught for sport in the warm coastal waters of the Atlantic esp. off Florida

tar·ra·gon \ˈter-ə-gän\ [MF *targon,* ultim. fr. Ar *ṭarkhūn*] : a small widely cultivated perennial wormwood with aromatic leaves used as a seasoning; *also* : its leaves

¹**tar·ry** \ˈta-rē\ *vb* **tar·ried; tar·ry·ing** **1** : to be tardy : DELAY; *esp* : to be slow in leaving **2** : to stay in or at a place : SOJOURN ♦ ***Synonyms*** REMAIN, WAIT, LINGER, ABIDE

²**tar·ry** \ˈtär-ē\ *adj* : of, resembling, or smeared with tar

tar sand *n* : sand or sandstone that is naturally soaked with the heavy sticky portions of petroleum

tar·sus \ˈtär-səs\ *n, pl* **tar·si** \-ˌsī\ [NL] : the part of a vertebrate foot between the metatarsus and the leg; *also* : the small bones that support this part — **tar·sal** \-səl\ *adj or n*

¹**tart** \ˈtärt\ *adj* **1** : agreeably sharp to the taste : PUNGENT **2** : BITING, CAUSTIC ⟨~ comments⟩ — **tart·ly** *adv* — **tart·ness** *n*

²**tart** *n* **1** : a small pie or pastry shell containing jelly, custard, or fruit **2** : PROSTITUTE

tar·tan \ˈtärt-ᵊn\ *n* : a plaid textile design of Scottish origin usu. distinctively patterned to designate a particular clan

tar·tar \ˈtär-tər\ *n* **1** : a substance in the juice of grapes deposited (as in wine casks) as a reddish crust or sediment **2** : a crust on the teeth formed from plaque hardened by calcium salts

tar·tar sauce *or* **tar·tare sauce** \ˈtär-tər-\ *n* : mayonnaise with chopped pickles, olives, or capers

¹**task** \ˈtask\ *n* [ME *taske,* fr. MF dial. *tasque,* fr. ML *tasca* tax or service imposed by a feudal superior, fr. *taxare* to tax] : a piece of assigned work ♦ ***Synonyms*** JOB, DUTY, CHORE, STINT, ASSIGNMENT

²**task** *vb* : to oppress with great labor

task bar *n* : a strip of icons usually at the bottom of a computer screen showing programs that may be used by selecting their icons

task force *n* : a temporary grouping to accomplish a particular objective

task·mas·ter \ˈtask-ˌmas-tər\ *n* : one that imposes a task or burdens another with labor

¹**tas·sel** \ˈta-səl, ˈtä-\ *n* **1** : a hanging ornament made of a bunch of cords of even length fastened at one end **2** : something suggesting a tassel; *esp* : a male flower cluster of corn

²**tassel** *vb* **-seled** *or* **-selled; -sel·ing** *or*

-sel·ling : to adorn with or put forth tassels

¹taste \ˈtāst\ *vb* **tast·ed; tast·ing** **1** : EXPERIENCE, UNDERGO **2** : to try or determine the flavor of by taking a bit into the mouth **3** : to eat or drink esp. in small quantities : SAMPLE **4** : to have a specific flavor ⟨the milk ~*s* sour⟩

²taste *n* **1** : a small amount tasted **2** : BIT; *esp* : a sample of experience **3** : the special sense that perceives and identifies sweet, sour, bitter, or salty qualities and is mediated by taste buds on the tongue **4** : a quality perceptible to the sense of taste; *also* : the sensation obtained from a substance in the mouth : FLAVOR **5** : individual preference **6** : critical judgment, discernment, or appreciation; *also* : aesthetic quality ♦ ***Synonyms*** TANG, RELISH, FLAVOR, SAVOR — **taste·ful** \-fəl\ *adj* — **taste·ful·ly** *adv* — **taste·less** *adj* — **taste·less·ly** *adv* — **tast·er** *n*

taste bud *n* : a sense organ mediating the sensation of taste

tasting *n* : an occasion for sampling a selection of foods or drinks ⟨a wine ~⟩

tasty \ˈtā-stē\ *adj* **tast·i·er; -est** : pleasing to the taste : SAVORY ⟨a very ~ meal⟩ ♦ ***Synonyms*** PALATABLE, APPETIZING, TOOTHSOME, FLAVORSOME — **tast·i·ness** \ˈtā-stē-nəs\ *n*

tat \ˈtat\ *vb* **tat·ted; tat·ting** : to work at or make by tatting

¹tat·ter \ˈta-tər\ *vb* : to make or become ragged

²tatter *n* **1** : a part torn and left hanging **2** *pl* : tattered clothing

tat·ter·sall \ˈta-tər-ˌsȯl, -səl\ *n* : a pattern of colored lines forming squares on solid background; *also* : a fabric in a tattersall pattern

tat·ting \ˈta-tiŋ\ *n* : a delicate handmade lace formed usu. by looping and knotting with a single thread and a small shuttle; *also* : the act or process of making such lace

tat·tle \ˈta-tᵊl\ *vb* **tat·tled; tat·tling** **1** : CHATTER, PRATE **2** : to tell secrets; *also* : to inform against another — **tat·tler** *n*

tat·tle·tale \ˈta-tᵊl-ˌtāl\ *n* : one that tattles : INFORMER

¹tat·too \ta-ˈtü\ *n, pl* **tattoos** [alter. of earlier *taptoo,* fr. D *taptoe,* fr. the phrase *tap toe!* taps shut!] **1** : a call sounded before taps as notice to go to quarters **2** : a rapid rhythmic rapping

²tattoo *vb* : to mark (the skin) with tattoos

³tattoo *n, pl* **tattoos** [Tahitian *tatau*] : an indelible figure fixed upon the body esp. by insertion of pigment under the skin

tau \ˈtau̇, ˈtȯ\ *n* : the 19th letter of the Greek alphabet — Τ or τ

taught *past and past part of* TEACH

¹taunt \ˈtȯnt\ *n* : a sarcastic challenge or insult

²taunt *vb* : to reproach or challenge in a mocking manner : jeer at ⟨the boys ~*ed* each other⟩ ♦ ***Synonyms*** MOCK, DERIDE, RIDICULE, TWIT — **taunt·er** *n*

taupe \ˈtōp\ *n* : a brownish gray

Tau·rus \ˈtȯr-əs\ *n* [L, lit., bull] **1** : a zodiacal constellation between Aries and Gemini usu. pictured as a bull **2** : the 2d sign of the zodiac in astrology; *also* : one born under this sign

taut \ˈtȯt\ *adj* **1** : tightly drawn : not slack **2** : extremely nervous : TENSE **3** : TRIM, TIDY ⟨a ~ ship⟩ — **taut·ly** *adv* — **taut·ness** *n*

tau·tol·o·gy \tȯ-ˈtä-lə-jē\ *n, pl* **-gies** : needless repetition of an idea, statement, or word; *also* : an instance of such repetition — **tau·to·log·i·cal** \ˌtȯ-tə-ˈlä-ji-kəl\ *adj* — **tau·to·log·i·cal·ly** \-ji-k(ə-)lē\ *adv* — **tau·tol·o·gous** \tȯ-ˈtä-lə-gəs\ *adj* — **tau·tol·o·gous·ly** *adv*

tav·ern \ˈta-vərn\ *n* [ME *taverne,* fr. AF, fr. L *taberna* hut, shop] **1** : an establishment where alcoholic liquors are sold to be drunk on the premises **2** : INN

taw \ˈtȯ\ *n* **1** : a marble used as a shooter **2** : the line from which players shoot at marbles

taw·dry \ˈtȯ-drē\ *adj* **taw·dri·er; -est** [*tawdry lace* a tie of lace for the neck, fr. *St. Audrey* (St. Etheldreda) †679 queen of Northumbria] **1** : cheap and gaudy in appearance and quality ⟨~ decorations⟩ **2** : morally sordid, base, or distasteful ♦ ***Synonyms*** GARISH, FLASHY, CHINTZY, MERETRICIOUS — **taw·dri·ly** *adv*

taw·ny \ˈtȯ-nē\ *adj* **taw·ni·er; -est** : of a brownish orange color

¹tax \ˈtaks\ *vb* **1** : to levy a tax on **2** : CHARGE, ACCUSE **3** : to put under pressure — **tax·able** \ˈtak-sə-bəl\ *adj* — **tax·a·tion** \tak-ˈsā-shən\ *n*

²tax *n* **1** : a charge usu. of money imposed by authority on persons or property for public purposes **2** : a heavy demand : STRAIN

¹taxi \ˈtak-sē\ *n, pl* **tax·is** \-sēz\ *also* **tax·ies** : TAXICAB; *also* : a similarly operated boat or aircraft

²taxi *vb* **tax·ied; taxi·ing** *or* **taxy·ing; tax·is** *or* **tax·ies** **1** : to move along the ground or on the water under an aircraft's own power when starting or after a landing **2** : to go by taxicab

taxi·cab \ˈtak-sē-ˌkab\ *n* : an automobile that carries passengers for a fare usu. based on the distance traveled

taxi·der·my \ˈtak-sə-ˌdər-mē\ *n* : the skill or occupation of preparing, stuffing, and mounting skins of animals — **taxi·der·mist** \-mist\ *n*

tax·on \ˈtak-ˌsän\ *n, pl* **taxa** \-sə\; *also* **taxons** : a taxonomic group or entity

tax·on·o·my \tak-ˈsä-nə-mē\ *n* : classification esp. of animals or plants according to natural relationships — **tax·o·nom·ic** \ˌtak-sə-ˈnä-mik\ *adj* — **tax·on·o·mist** \tak-ˈsä-nə-mist\ *n*

tax·pay·er \ˈtaks-ˌpā-ər\ *n* : one who pays or is liable for a tax — **tax·pay·ing** *adj*

Tay–Sachs disease \ˈtā-ˈsaks-\ *n* : a hereditary disorder caused by the absence of an enzyme needed to break down fatty material, marked by buildup of lipids in nervous tissue, and causing death in childhood

tb *abbr* tablespoon; tablespoonful
Tb *symbol* terbium
TB \ˌtē-ˈbē\ *n* : TUBERCULOSIS
TBA *abbr, often not cap* to be announced
T–bar \ˈtē-ˌbär\ *n* : a ski lift with a series of T-shaped bars
TBI *abbr* traumatic brain injury
tbs *or* **tbsp** *abbr* tablespoon; tablespoonful
Tc *symbol* technetium
TC *abbr* teachers college
T cell *n* : any of several lymphocytes (as a helper T cell) specialized esp. for activity in and control of immunity and the immune response
TCP/IP \ˌtē-(ˌ)sē-ˈpē-ˌī-ˈpē\ *n* [*t*ransmission *c*ontrol *p*rotocol/*I*nternet *p*rotocol] : a set of communications protocols used over networks and esp. the Internet
TD *abbr* **1** touchdown **2** Treasury Department
TDD *abbr* telecommunications device for the deaf
TDY *abbr* temporary duty
Te *symbol* tellurium
tea \ˈtē\ *n* [Chin (dialect of Fujian province) *dé*] **1** : the cured leaves and leaf buds of a shrub grown chiefly in China, Japan, India, and Sri Lanka; *also* : this shrub **2** : a drink made by steeping tea in boiling water **3** : refreshments usu. including tea served in late afternoon; *also* : a reception at which tea is served
teach \ˈtēch\ *vb* **taught** \ˈtȯt\; **teach·ing** **1** : to cause to know something : act as a teacher **2** : to show how ⟨~ a child to swim⟩ **3** : to make to know the disagreeable consequences of an action **4** : to guide the studies of **5** : to impart the knowledge of ⟨~ algebra⟩ — **teach·able** *adj* — **teach·er** *n*
teach·ing *n* **1** : the act, practice, or profession of a teacher **2** : something taught; *esp* : DOCTRINE
tea·cup \ˈtē-ˌkəp\ *n* : a small cup used with a saucer for hot beverages
teak \ˈtēk\ *n* : the hard durable yellowish brown wood of a tall tropical Asian timber tree related to the vervains; *also* : this tree
tea·ket·tle \ˈtē-ˌke-tᵊl\ *n* : a covered kettle with a handle and spout for boiling water
teal \ˈtēl\ *n, pl* **teal** *or* **teals** **1** : any of various small short-necked wild ducks **2** : a dark greenish blue color
¹**team** \ˈtēm\ *n* [ME *teme,* fr. OE *tēam* offspring, lineage, group of draft animals] **1** : two or more draft animals harnessed to the same vehicle or implement **2** : a number of persons associated in work or activity; *esp* : a group on one side in a match
²**team** *adj* : of or performed by a team; *also* : marked by devotion to teamwork ⟨a ~ player⟩
³**team** *vb* **1** : to haul with or drive a team **2** : to form a team : join forces
team·mate \-ˌmāt\ *n* : a fellow member of a team
team·ster \ˈtēm-stər\ *n* : one who drives a team or truck
team·work \-ˌwərk\ *n* : the work or activity of a number of persons acting in close association as members of a unit
tea·pot \ˈtē-ˌpät\ *n* : a vessel with a spout for brewing and serving tea
¹**tear** \ˈtir\ *n* : a drop of the salty liquid that moistens the eye and inner side of the eyelids; *also, pl* : an act of weeping or grieving — **tear·ful** \-fəl\ *adj* — **tear·ful·ly** *adv* — **teary** \ˈtir-ē\ *adj*
²**tear** \ˈtir\ *vb* : to fill with or shed tears
³**tear** \ˈter\ *vb* **tore** \ˈtȯr\; **torn** \ˈtȯrn\; **tear·ing** **1** : to separate parts of or pull apart by force : REND **2** : LACERATE **3** : to disrupt by the pull of contrary forces **4** : to remove by force : WRENCH ⟨~ down a house⟩ **5** : to move or act with violence, haste, or force ♦ ***Synonyms*** RIP, SPLIT, CLEAVE, REND
⁴**tear** \ˈter\ *n* **1** : the act of tearing **2** : a hole or flaw made by tearing : RENT
tear gas \ˈtir-\ *n* : a substance that on dispersion in the atmosphere blinds the eyes with tears — **tear–gas** *vb*
tear·jerk·er \ˈtir-ˌjər-kər\ *n* : an extravagantly pathetic story, song, play, movie, or broadcast
¹**tease** \ˈtēz\ *vb* **teased; teas·ing** **1** : to disentangle and lay parallel by combing or carding ⟨~ wool⟩ **2** : to scratch the surface of (cloth) so as to raise a nap **3** : to annoy persistently esp. in fun by goading, coaxing, or tantalizing ⟨stop *teasing* the dog⟩ **4** : to comb (hair) by taking a strand and pushing the short hairs toward the scalp with the comb ♦ ***Synonyms*** HARASS, WORRY, PESTER, ANNOY
²**tease** *n* **1** : the act of teasing or state of being teased **2** : one that teases
tea·sel \ˈtē-zəl\ *n* : a prickly herb or its flower head covered with stiff hooked bracts and used to raise the nap on cloth; *also* : an artificial device used for this purpose
tea·spoon \ˈtē-ˌspün\ *n* **1** : a small spoon suitable for stirring beverages **2** : a unit of measure equal to ⅙ fluid ounce (5 milliliters)
tea·spoon·ful \-ˌfu̇l\ *n, pl* **-spoonfuls** *also* **-spoons·ful** \-ˌspünz-ˌfu̇l\ : TEASPOON 2
teat \ˈtit, ˈtēt\ *n* : the protuberance through which milk is drawn from an udder or breast
tech *abbr* **1** technical; technically; technician **2** technological; technology
tech·ne·tium \tek-ˈnē-shē-əm\ *n* : a radioactive metallic chemical element
tech·nic \ˈtek-nik, tek-ˈnēk\ *n* : TECHNIQUE 1
tech·ni·cal \ˈtek-ni-kəl\ *adj* [Gk *technikos* of art, skillful, fr. *technē* art, craft, skill] **1** : having special knowledge esp. of a mechanical or scientific subject ⟨~ experts⟩ **2** : of or relating to a particular and esp. a practical or scientific subject ⟨~ training⟩ **3** : according to a strict interpretation of the rules **4** : of or relating to technique — **tech·ni·cal·ly** \-k(ə-)lē\ *adv*

tech·ni·cal·i·ty \ˌtek-nə-ˈka-lə-tē\ *n, pl* **-ties** **1** : a detail meaningful only to a specialist **2** : the quality or state of being technical

technical sergeant *n* : a noncommissioned officer in the air force ranking next below a master sergeant

tech·ni·cian \tek-ˈni-shən\ *n* : a person who has acquired the technique of a specialized skill or subject

tech·nique \tek-ˈnēk\ *n* [F] **1** : the manner in which technical details are treated or basic physical movements are used **2** : technical methods

tech·no \ˈtek-nō\ *n* : dance music featuring a fast beat and electronically created sounds usu. without vocals

tech·noc·ra·cy \tek-ˈnä-krə-sē\ *n* : management of society by technical experts — **tech·no·crat** \ˈtek-nə-ˌkrat\ *n* — **tech·no·crat·ic** \ˌtek-nə-ˈkra-tik\ *adj*

tech·nol·o·gy \tek-ˈnä-lə-jē\ *n, pl* **-gies** : ENGINEERING; *also* : a manner of accomplishing a task using technical methods or knowledge — **tech·no·log·i·cal** \ˌtek-nə-ˈlä-ji-kəl\ *adj*

tec·ton·ics \tek-ˈtä-niks\ *n sing or pl* **1** : geological structural features **2** : geology dealing esp. with the faulting and folding of a planet or moon — **tec·ton·ic** \-nik\ *adj*

ted·dy bear \ˈte-dē-ˌber\ *n* [*Teddy* Roosevelt; fr. a cartoon depicting the president sparing the life of a bear cub while hunting] : a stuffed toy bear

te·dious \ˈtē-dē-əs\ *adj* : tiresome because of length or dullness ⟨a ~ speech⟩ ♦ ***Synonyms*** BORING, TIRING, IRKSOME — **te·dious·ly** *adv* — **te·dious·ness** *n*

te·di·um \ˈtē-dē-əm\ *n* : TEDIOUSNESS; *also* : BOREDOM

¹tee \ˈtē\ *n* **1** : a small mound or peg on which a golf ball is placed to be hit at the beginning of play on a hole; *also* : the area from which the ball is hit to begin play **2** : an adjustable post on which a ball is placed for batting

²tee *vb* **teed; tee·ing** : to place (a ball) on a tee

teem \ˈtēm\ *vb* : to become filled to overflowing : ABOUND ♦ ***Synonyms*** SWARM, CRAWL, FLOW

teen \ˈtēn\ *n* : a teenage person : TEENAGER — **teen** *adj*

teen·age \ˈtē-ˌnāj\ *or* **teen·aged** \-ˌnājd\ *adj* : of, being, or relating to people in their teens — **teen·ag·er** \-ˌnā-jər\ *n*

teens \ˈtēnz\ *n pl* : the numbers 13 to 19 inclusive; *esp* : the years 13 to 19 in a person's life

tee·ny \ˈtē-nē\ *adj* **tee·ni·er; -est** : TINY

teepee *var of* TEPEE

tee shirt *var of* T-SHIRT

tee·ter \ˈtē-tər\ *vb* **1** : to move unsteadily **2** : SEESAW — **teeter** *n*

teeth *pl of* TOOTH

teethe \ˈtēth\ *vb* **teethed; teeth·ing** : to experience the rising of one's teeth through the gums : to grow teeth

teething *n* : growth of the first set of teeth through the gums with its accompanying phenomena

tee·to·tal·er *or* **tee·to·tal·ler** \ˈtē-ˈtō-tᵊl-ər\ *n* : a person who practices complete abstinence from alcoholic drinks — **tee·to·tal** \ˈtē-ˈtō-tᵊl, -ˌtō-\ *adj* — **tee·to·tal·ism** \-tᵊl-ˌi-zəm\ *n*

TEFL *abbr* teaching English as a foreign language

Te·ja·no \tā-ˈhä-(ˌ)nō\ *n, pl* **-nos** [Mex Sp, fr. *Tejas* Texas] : a Texan of Hispanic descent

tek·tite \ˈtek-ˌtīt\ *n* : a glassy body of probably meteoric origin

tel *abbr* **1** telegram **2** telegraph **3** telephone

tele·cast \ˈte-li-ˌkast\ *vb* **-cast** *also* **-cast·ed; -cast·ing** : to broadcast by television — **telecast** *n* — **tele·cast·er** *n*

tel·e·com \ˈte-li-ˌkäm\ *n* : TELECOMMUNICATION; *also* : the telecommunications industry

tele·com·mu·ni·ca·tion \ˌte-li-kə-ˌmyü-nə-ˈkā-shən\ *n* : communication at a distance (as by telephone or radio)

tele·com·mute \ˈte-li-kə-ˌmyüt\ *vb* : to work at home by the use of an electronic linkup with a central office

tele·con·fer·ence \ˈte-li-ˌkän-fə-rəns\ *n* : a conference among people remote from one another held using telecommunications — **tele·con·fer·enc·ing** *n*

teleg *abbr* telegraphy

tele·ge·nic \ˌte-lə-ˈje-nik, -ˈjē-\ *adj* : very attractive to television viewers

tele·gram \ˈte-lə-ˌgram\ *n* : a message sent by telegraph

¹tele·graph \-ˌgraf\ *n* : an electric apparatus or system for sending messages by a code over wires — **tele·graph·ic** \ˌte-lə-ˈgra-fik\ *adj*

²telegraph *vb* : to send or communicate by or as if by telegraph — **te·leg·ra·pher** \tə-ˈle-grə-fər\ *n*

te·leg·ra·phy \tə-ˈle-grə-fē\ *n* : the use or operation of a telegraph apparatus or system

tele·health \ˌte-lə-ˈhelth\ *n* : TELEMEDICINE

tele·mar·ket·ing \ˌte-lə-ˈmär-kə-tiŋ\ *n* : the marketing of goods or services by telephone — **tele·mar·ket·er** \-tər\ *n*

tele·med·i·cine \ˌte-lə-ˈme-də-sən\ *n* : medical care provided remotely to a patient in a separate location using two-way voice and visual communication (as by computer or cell phone)

te·lem·e·try \tə-ˈle-mə-trē\ *n* : the transmission esp. by radio of measurements made by automatic instruments to a distant station — **tele·me·ter** \ˈte-lə-ˌmē-tər\ *n*

tel·e·no·vela \ˌte-lə-nō-ˈve-lə\ *n* : a soap opera televised in or from many Latin-American countries

te·lep·a·thy \tə-ˈle-pə-thē\ *n* : apparent communication from one mind to another by extrasensory means — **tele·path·ic** \ˌte-lə-ˈpa-thik\ *adj* — **tele·path·i·cal·ly** \-thi-k(ə-)lē\ *adv*

¹tele·phone \ˈte-lə-ˌfōn\ *n* : an instrument for sending and receiving sounds over long distances by electricity

²telephone *vb* **-phoned; -phon·ing** **1** : to

send or communicate by telephone **2** : to speak to (a person) by telephone — **tele·phon·er** *n*

te·le·pho·ny \tə-ˈle-fə-nē, ˈte-lə-ˌfō-\ *n* : use or operation of an apparatus for transmission of sounds as electrical signals between distant points — **tel·e·phon·ic** \ˌte-lə-ˈfä-nik\ *adj*

tele·pho·to \ˌte-lə-ˈfō-tō\ *adj* : being a camera lens giving a large image of a distant object — **tele·pho·tog·ra·phy** \-fə-ˈtä-grə-fē\ *n*

tele·play \ˈte-li-ˌplā\ *n* : a story prepared for television production

tele·pres·ence \ˌte-lə-ˈpre-zᵊns\ *n* : technology that enables a person to perform actions in a distant or virtual location as if physically present in that location; *also* : the practice or experience of using such technology

tele·print·er \ˈte-lə-ˌprin-tər\ *n* : TELETYPEWRITER

tele·prompt·er \ˈte-lə-ˌprämp-tər\ *n* : a device for displaying prepared text to a speaker or performer

¹tele·scope \ˈte-lə-ˌskōp\ *n* **1** : a cylindrical instrument equipped with lenses or mirrors for viewing distant objects **2** : RADIO TELESCOPE

²telescope *vb* **-scoped; -scop·ing 1** : to slide or pass or cause to slide or pass one within another like the sections of a collapsible hand telescope **2** : COMPRESS, CONDENSE

tele·scop·ic \ˌte-lə-ˈskä-pik\ *adj* **1** : of or relating to a telescope **2** : seen only by a telescope **3** : able to discern objects at a distance **4** : having parts that telescope — **tele·scop·i·cal·ly** \-pi-k(ə-)lē\ *adv*

tele·text \ˈte-lə-ˌtekst\ *n* : a system for broadcasting text over a television signal and displaying it on a decoder-equipped television

tele·thon \ˈte-lə-ˌthän\ *n* : a long television program usu. to solicit funds for a charity

tele·type·writ·er \ˌte-lə-ˈtīp-ˌrī-tər\ *n* : a printing device resembling a typewriter used to send and receive signals over telephone lines

tele·vise \ˈte-lə-ˌvīz\ *vb* **-vised; -vis·ing** : to broadcast by television

tele·vi·sion \ˈte-lə-ˌvi-zhən\ *n* [F *télévision,* fr. Gk *tēle* far, at a distance + F *vision* vision] : a system for transmitting images and sound by converting them into electrical or radio waves which are converted back into images and sound by a receiver; *also* : a television receiving set

tell \ˈtel\ *vb* **told** \ˈtōld\; **tell·ing 1** : COUNT, ENUMERATE **2** : to relate in detail : NARRATE ⟨*told* us what happened⟩ **3** : SAY, UTTER **4** : to make known : REVEAL **5** : to report to : INFORM ⟨*told* me her name⟩ **6** : ORDER, DIRECT **7** : to find out by observing ⟨can ~ the difference⟩ **8** : to have a marked effect **9** : to serve as evidence ♦ ***Synonyms*** DISCLOSE, DISCOVER, BETRAY

tell·er \ˈte-lər\ *n* **1** : one that relates : NARRATOR **2** : one that counts **3** : a bank employee handling money received or paid out

tell·ing \ˈte-liŋ\ *adj* : producing a marked effect : EFFECTIVE ⟨~ evidence⟩ ♦ ***Synonyms*** COGENT, CONVINCING, SOUND

tell off *vb* : REPRIMAND, SCOLD

tell·tale \ˈtel-ˌtāl\ *n* **1** : INFORMER, TATTLETALE **2** : something that serves to disclose : INDICATION — **telltale** *adj*

tel·lu·ri·um \tə-ˈlu̇r-ē-əm\ *n* : a chemical element used esp. in alloys

tem·blor \ˈtem-blər\ *n* [Sp, lit., trembling] : EARTHQUAKE

te·mer·i·ty \tə-ˈmer-ə-tē\ *n, pl* **-ties** : rash or presumptuous daring : BOLDNESS ♦ ***Synonyms*** AUDACITY, EFFRONTERY, GALL, NERVE, CHEEK

¹temp \ˈtemp\ *n* **1** : TEMPERATURE **2** : a temporary worker

²temp *abbr* temporary

¹tem·per \ˈtem-pər\ *vb* **1** : to dilute or soften by the addition of something else ⟨~ justice with mercy⟩ **2** : to bring (as steel) to a desired hardness by reheating and cooling **3** : to toughen (glass) by gradual heating and cooling **4** : TOUGHEN **5** : TUNE

²temper *n* **1** : characteristic tone : TENDENCY **2** : the hardness or toughness of a substance ⟨the ~ of a knife blade⟩ **3** : a characteristic frame of mind : DISPOSITION **4** : calmness of mind : COMPOSURE **5** : state of feeling or frame of mind at a particular time **6** : heat of mind or emotion ♦ ***Synonyms*** TEMPERAMENT, CHARACTER, PERSONALITY, MAKEUP — **tem·pered** \ˈtem-pərd\ *adj*

tem·pera \ˈtem-pə-rə\ *n* [It] : a painting process using an albuminous or colloidal medium as a vehicle; *also* : a painting done in tempera

tem·per·a·ment \ˈtem-prə-mənt, -pər-mənt\ *n* **1** : characteristic or habitual inclination or mode of emotional response : DISPOSITION **2** : excessive sensitiveness or irritability ♦ ***Synonyms*** CHARACTER, PERSONALITY, NATURE, MAKEUP — **tem·per·a·men·tal** \ˌtem-prə-ˈmen-tᵊl, -pər-ˈment-\ *adj*

tem·per·ance \ˈtem-prəns, -pə-rəns\ *n* : habitual moderation in the indulgence of the appetites or passions; *esp* : moderation in or abstinence from the use of alcoholic beverages

tem·per·ate \ˈtem-prət, -pə-rət\ *adj* **1** : not extreme or excessive : MILD **2** : moderate in indulgence of appetite or desire **3** : moderate in the use of alcoholic beverages **4** : having a moderate climate ♦ ***Synonyms*** SOBER, CONTINENT, ABSTEMIOUS

temperate zone *n, often cap T&Z* : the region between the Tropic of Cancer and the arctic circle or between the Tropic of Capricorn and the antarctic circle

tem·per·a·ture \ˈtem-pər-ˌchu̇r, -prə-ˌchu̇r, -chər\ *n* **1** : degree of hotness or coldness of something (as air, water, or the body) as shown by a thermometer **2** : FEVER 1

tem·pest \ˈtem-pəst\ *n* [ME *tempeste,* fr.

AF, ultim. fr. L *tempestas* season, weather, storm, fr. *tempus* time] : a violent storm

tempest in a teapot : a great commotion over an unimportant matter

tem·pes·tu·ous \tem-ˈpes-chə-wəs\ *adj* : of, involving, or resembling a tempest : STORMY — **tem·pes·tu·ous·ly** *adv* — **tem·pes·tu·ous·ness** *n*

tem·plate \ˈtem-plət\ *n* : a gauge, mold, or pattern used as a guide to the form or structure of something being made

¹tem·ple \ˈtem-pəl\ *n* **1** : a building reserved for religious practice **2** : a place devoted to a special or exalted purpose

²temple *n* : the flattened space on each side of the forehead esp. of humans

tem·po \ˈtem-pō\ *n, pl* **tem·pi** \-(ˌ)pē\ *or* **tempos** [It, lit., time] **1** : the rate of speed of a musical piece or passage **2** : rate of motion or activity : PACE

¹tem·po·ral \ˈtem-pə-rəl\ *adj* **1** : of, relating to, or limited by time ⟨~ and spatial bounds⟩ **2** : of or relating to earthly life or secular concerns ⟨~ power⟩

²temporal *adj* : of or relating to the temples or the sides of the skull

¹tem·po·rary \ˈtem-pə-ˌrer-ē\ *adj* : lasting for a time only : TRANSITORY ♦ ***Synonyms*** TRANSIENT, EPHEMERAL, MOMENTARY, IMPERMANENT — **tem·po·rar·i·ly** \ˌtem-pə-ˈrer-ə-lē\ *adv*

²temporary *n, pl* **-rar·ies** : one serving for a limited time

tem·po·rise *Brit var of* TEMPORIZE

tem·po·rize \ˈtem-pə-ˌrīz\ *vb* **-rized; -riz·ing 1** : to adapt one's actions to the time or the dominant opinion : COMPROMISE **2** : to draw out matters so as to gain time — **tem·po·riz·er** *n*

tempt \ˈtempt\ *vb* **1** : to entice to do wrong by promise of pleasure or gain **2** : PROVOKE ⟨~ fate⟩ **3** : to risk the dangers of **4** : to induce to do something : INCITE ♦ ***Synonyms*** INVEIGLE, DECOY, SEDUCE, LURE — **tempt·er** *n* — **tempt·ing·ly** *adv*

temp·ta·tion \temp-ˈtā-shən\ *n* **1** : the act of tempting : the state of being tempted **2** : something that tempts

tempt·ress \ˈtemp-trəs\ *n* : a woman who tempts

ten \ˈten\ *n* **1** : one more than nine **2** : the 10th in a set or series **3** : something having 10 units — **ten** *adj or pron* — **tenth** \ˈtenth\ *adj or adv or n*

ten·a·ble \ˈte-nə-bəl\ *adj* : capable of being held, maintained, or defended

te·na·cious \tə-ˈnā-shəs\ *adj* **1** : not easily pulled apart : COHESIVE ⟨a ~ metal⟩ **2** : holding fast ⟨~ of his rights⟩ **3** : RETENTIVE ⟨a ~ memory⟩ — **te·na·cious·ly** *adv* — **te·nac·i·ty** \tə-ˈna-sə-tē\ *n*

ten·an·cy \ˈte-nən-sē\ *n, pl* **-cies** : the temporary possession or occupancy of something (as a house) that belongs to another; *also* : the period of a tenant's occupancy

ten·ant \ˈte-nənt\ *n* **1** : one who rents or leases (as a house) from a landlord **2** : DWELLER, OCCUPANT — **tenant** *vb*

tenant farmer *n* : a farmer who works land owned by another and pays rent either in cash or in shares of produce

Ten Commandments *n pl* : the commandments of God given to Moses on Mount Sinai

¹tend \ˈtend\ *vb* **1** : to apply oneself ⟨~ to your affairs⟩ **2** : to take care of ⟨~ a plant⟩ **3** : to manage the operations of

²tend *vb* **1** : to move or develop one's course in a particular direction **2** : to show an inclination or tendency

ten·den·cy \ˈten-dən-sē\ *n, pl* **-cies 1** : DRIFT, TREND **2** : a proneness to or readiness for a particular kind of thought or action : PROPENSITY ⟨a ~ to overreact⟩ ♦ ***Synonyms*** BENT, LEANING, DISPOSITION, INCLINATION

ten·den·tious \ten-ˈden-chəs\ *adj* : marked by a tendency in favor of a particular point of view : BIASED ⟨~ remarks⟩ — **ten·den·tious·ly** *adv* — **ten·den·tious·ness** *n*

¹ten·der \ˈten-dər\ *adj* [ME, fr. AF *tendre*, fr. L *tener*] **1** : having a soft texture : easily broken, chewed, or cut **2** : physically weak : DELICATE; *also* : IMMATURE **3** : expressing or responsive to love or sympathy : LOVING, COMPASSIONATE ⟨a ~ smile⟩ **4** : SENSITIVE, TOUCHY ⟨a ~ ego⟩ ♦ ***Synonyms*** SYMPATHETIC, WARM, WARMHEARTED — **ten·der·ly** *adv* — **ten·der·ness** *n*

²tender *n* [AF *tendre*, fr. *tendre*, v., to stretch, hold out, offer, fr. L *tendere* to stretch, direct] **1** : an offer or proposal made for acceptance; *esp* : an offer of a bid for a contract **2** : something (as money) that may be offered in payment

³tender *vb* : to present for acceptance

⁴tend·er \ˈten-dər\ *n* **1** : one that tends or takes care **2** : a boat carrying passengers and freight to a larger ship **3** : a car attached to a steam locomotive for carrying fuel and water

⁵tender *n* [prob. short for *tenderloin*] : a strip of meat (as chicken) often breaded

ten·der·foot \ˈten-dər-ˌfu̇t\ *n, pl* **-feet** \-ˌfēt\ *also* **-foots** \-ˌfu̇ts\ **1** : one not hardened to frontier or rough outdoor life **2** : an inexperienced beginner

ten·der·heart·ed \ˌten-dər-ˈhär-təd\ *adj* : easily moved to love, pity, or sorrow

ten·der·ize \ˈten-də-ˌrīz\ *vb* **-ized; -iz·ing** : to make (meat) tender — **ten·der·iz·er** \ˈten-də-ˌrī-zər\ *n*

ten·der·loin \ˈten-dər-ˌlȯin\ *n* **1** : a tender strip of beef or pork from near the backbone **2** : a district of a city largely devoted to vice

ten·di·ni·tis *or* **ten·don·itis** \ˌten-də-ˈnī-təs\ *n* : inflammation of a tendon

ten·don \ˈten-dən\ *n* : a tough cord of dense white fibrous tissue uniting a muscle with another part (as a bone) — **ten·di·nous** \-də-nəs\ *adj*

ten·dril \ˈten-drəl\ *n* : a slender coiling organ by which some climbing plants attach themselves to a support

ten·e·brous \ˈte-nə-brəs\ *adj* : shut off from the light : GLOOMY, OBSCURE

ten·e·ment \ˈte-nə-mənt\ *n* **1** : a house used as a dwelling **2** : a building divided into apartments for rent; *esp* : one meeting only minimum standards of safety and comfort **3** : APARTMENT, FLAT

te·net \ˈte-nət\ *n* [L, he holds, fr. *tenēre* to hold] : one of the principles or doctrines held in common by members of a group (as a church or profession) ♦ ***Synonyms*** DOCTRINE, DOGMA, BELIEF

ten·fold \ˈten-ˌfōld, -ˈfōld\ *adj* : being 10 times as great or as many — **ten·fold** \-ˈfōld\ *adv*

ten–gallon hat *n* : a wide-brimmed hat with a large soft crown

tenge \ˈteŋ-ˌgā\ *n, pl* **tenge** — see MONEY table

Tenn *abbr* Tennessee

ten·ne \ˈteŋ-ā\ *n, pl* **ten·e·si** \ˈteŋ-ə-sē\ *or* **tenne** *or* **ten·ne·si** \ˈteŋ-ə-sē\ — see *manat* at MONEY table

ten·nes·sine \ˈte-nə-ˌsēn\ *n* : a short-lived artificially produced radioactive element

ten·nis \ˈte-nəs\ *n* : a game played with a ball and racket on a court divided by a net

ten·on \ˈte-nən\ *n* : a projecting part in a piece of material (as wood) for insertion into a mortise to make a joint

ten·or \ˈte-nər\ *n* **1** : the general drift of something spoken or written ⟨his speech had an angry ~⟩ **2** : the highest natural adult male voice; *also* : a singer having this voice **3** : a continuing in a course, movement, or activity ⟨the ~ of my life⟩

tenpenny nail *n* : a nail three inches (about 7.6 centimeters) long

ten·pin \ˈten-ˌpin\ *n* : a bottle-shaped bowling pin set in groups of 10 and bowled at in a game (**tenpins**)

¹**tense** \ˈtens\ *n* [ME *tens* time, tense, fr. AF, fr. L *tempus*] : distinction of form of a verb to indicate the time of the action or state

²**tense** *adj* **tens·er; tens·est** [L *tensus,* fr. pp. of *tendere* to stretch] **1** : stretched tight : TAUT **2** : feeling or showing nervous tension ⟨a ~ smile⟩ ♦ ***Synonyms*** STIFF, RIGID, INFLEXIBLE — **tense·ly** *adv* — **tense·ness** *n* — **ten·si·ty** \ˈten-sə-tē\ *n*

³**tense** *vb* **tensed; tens·ing** : to make or become tense

ten·sile \ˈten-səl, -ˌsī(-ə)l\ *adj* : of or relating to tension ⟨~ strength⟩

ten·sion \ˈten-chən\ *n* **1** : the act of straining or stretching; *also* : the condition of being strained or stretched **2** : a state of mental unrest often with signs of bodily stress **3** : a state of latent hostility or opposition

ten–speed \ˈten-ˌspēd\ *n* : a bicycle with a derailleur having 10 possible combinations of gears

¹**tent** \ˈtent\ *n* **1** : a collapsible shelter of material stretched and supported by poles **2** : a canopy placed over the head and shoulders to retain vapors or oxygen given for medical reasons

²**tent** *vb* **1** : to lodge in tents **2** : to cover with or as if with a tent

ten·ta·cle \ˈten-ti-kəl\ *n* : any of various long flexible projections about the head or mouth (as of an insect, mollusk, or fish) — **ten·ta·cled** \-kəld\ *adj* — **ten·tac·u·lar** \ten-ˈta-kyə-lər\ *adj*

ten·ta·tive \ˈten-tə-tiv\ *adj* **1** : not fully worked out or developed ⟨~ plans⟩ **2** : HESITANT, UNCERTAIN ⟨a ~ smile⟩ — **ten·ta·tive·ly** *adv* — **ten·ta·tive·ness** *n*

ten·u·ous \ˈten-yə-wəs\ *adj* **1** : not dense : RARE ⟨a ~ fluid⟩ **2** : not thick : SLENDER ⟨a ~ rope⟩ **3** : having little substance : FLIMSY, WEAK ⟨~ influences⟩ **4** : lacking stability : SHAKY ⟨~ reasoning⟩ — **te·nu·i·ty** \te-ˈnü-ə-tē, tə-, -ˈnyü-\ *n* — **ten·u·ous·ly** *adv* — **ten·u·ous·ness** *n*

ten·ure \ˈten-yər\ *n* : the act, right, manner, or period of holding something (as a landed property, an office, or a position)

ten·ured \ˈten-yərd\ *adj* : having tenure ⟨~ faculty members⟩

te·o·sin·te \ˌtā-ō-ˈsin-tē\ *n* : a tall annual grass of Mexico that is closely related to and usu. considered ancestral to corn

te·pee *or* **tee·pee** \ˈtē-(ˌ)pē\ *n* [Dakota *tʰípi,* fr. *tʰi-* to dwell] : a conical tent usu. consisting of skins and used esp. by Indigenous people of the Great Plains

tep·id \ˈte-pəd\ *adj* **1** : moderately warm : LUKEWARM **2** : HALFHEARTED

te·qui·la \tə-ˈkē-lə, tā-\ *n* : a Mexican liquor distilled from an agave's sap

ter *abbr* **1** terrace **2** territory

tera·byte \ˈter-ə-ˌbīt\ *n* [*tera-* trillion (10^{12}), fr. Gk *terat-, teras* monster] : 1024 gigabytes; *also* : one trillion bytes

ter·bi·um \ˈtər-bē-əm\ *n* : a metallic chemical element

ter·cen·te·na·ry \ˌtər-ˌsen-ˈte-nə-rē, tər-ˈsen-tə-ˌner-ē\ *n, pl* **-ries** : a 300th anniversary or its celebration — **tercentenary** *adj*

ter·cen·ten·ni·al \ˌtər-ˌsen-ˈte-nē-əl\ *adj or n* : TERCENTENARY

te·re·do \tə-ˈrē-dō, -ˈrā-\ *n, pl* **-dos** [L] : SHIPWORM

ter·i·ya·ki \ˌter-ē-ˈyä-kē\ *n* [Jp] : a Japanese dish of meat or fish soaked in a soy marinade and cooked

¹**term** \ˈtərm\ *n* **1** : END, TERMINATION **2** : DURATION; *esp* : a period of time fixed esp. by law or custom **3** : a mathematical expression connected with another by a plus or minus sign; *also* : an element (as a numerator) of a fraction or proportion **4** : a word or expression that has a precise meaning in some uses or is limited to a particular subject or field **5** *pl* : PROVISIONS, CONDITIONS ⟨~*s* of a contract⟩ **6** *pl* : mutual relationship ⟨on good ~*s*⟩ **7** : AGREEMENT, CONCORD **8** : a state of acceptance ⟨come to ~*s* with his grief⟩

²**term** *vb* : to apply a term to : CALL

ter·ma·gant \ˈtər-mə-gənt\ *n* : an overbearing or nagging woman : SHREW

¹**ter·mi·nal** \ˈtər-mə-nᵊl\ *adj* **1** : of, relating to, or forming an end, limit, or terminus **2** : FATAL 2 ⟨~ cancer⟩; *also* : being in or relating to the final stages of a fatal disease ⟨a ~ patient⟩ ♦ ***Synonyms*** FINAL, CONCLUDING, LAST, LATEST — **ter·mi·nal·ly** *adv*

²terminal *n* **1** : EXTREMITY, END **2** : a device at the end of a wire or on electrical equipment for making a connection **3** : either end of a transportation line (as a railroad) with its offices and freight and passenger stations; *also* : a freight or passenger station **4** : a device (as in a computer system) for data entry and display

ter·mi·nate \ˈtər-mə-ˌnāt\ *vb* **-nat·ed; -nat·ing** : to bring or come to an end ♦ ***Synonyms*** CONCLUDE, FINISH, COMPLETE — **ter·mi·na·ble** \-nə-bəl\ *adj* — **ter·mi·na·tion** \ˌtər-mə-ˈnā-shən\ *n* — **ter·mi·na·tor** \ˈtər-mə-ˌnā-tər\ *n*

ter·mi·nol·o·gy \ˌtər-mə-ˈnä-lə-jē\ *n, pl* **-gies** : the technical or special terms used in a business, art, science, or special subject

ter·mi·nus \ˈtər-mə-nəs\ *n, pl* **-ni** \-ˌnī\ *or* **-nus·es** [L] **1** : final goal : END **2** : either end of a transportation line or travel route; *also* : the station or city at such a place

ter·mite \ˈtər-ˌmīt\ *n* : any of numerous pale soft-bodied social insects that feed on wood

tern \ˈtərn\ *n* : any of various chiefly marine birds with narrow wings and often a forked tail

ter·na·ry \ˈtər-nə-rē\ *adj* **1** : of, relating to, or proceeding by threes **2** : having three elements or parts

terr *abbr* territory

¹ter·race \ˈter-əs\ *n* **1** : a flat roof or open platform **2** : a level area next to a building **3** : an embankment with level top **4** : a bank or ridge on a slope to conserve moisture and soil **5** : a row of houses on raised land; *also* : a street with such a row of houses **6** : a strip of park in the middle of a street

²terrace *vb* **ter·raced; ter·rac·ing** : to form into a terrace or supply with terraces

ter·ra–cot·ta \ˌter-ə-ˈkä-tə\ *n* [It *terra cotta,* lit., baked earth] : a reddish brown earthenware

terra fir·ma \-ˈfər-mə\ *n* [NL] : solid ground

ter·rain \tə-ˈrān\ *n* : the surface features of an area of land ⟨a rough ~⟩

ter·ra in·cog·ni·ta \ˈter-ə-ˌin-ˌkäg-ˈnē-tə\ *n, pl* **ter·rae in·cog·ni·tae** \ˈter-ˌī-ˌin-ˌkäg-ˈnē-tī\ [L] : an unexplored area or field of knowledge

ter·ra·pin \ˈter-ə-pən\ *n* : any of various turtles of fresh or brackish water

ter·rar·i·um \tə-ˈrer-ē-əm\ *n, pl* **-ia** \-ē-ə\ *or* **-i·ums** : a usu. transparent enclosure for keeping or raising plants or small animals indoors

ter·res·tri·al \tə-ˈres-trē-əl\ *adj* **1** : of or relating to the earth or its inhabitants **2** : living or growing on land ⟨~ plants⟩ ♦ ***Synonyms*** MUNDANE, EARTHLY, WORLDLY

ter·ri·ble \ˈter-ə-bəl\ *adj* **1** : exciting terror : FEARFUL, DREADFUL ⟨~ weapons⟩ **2** : hard to bear : DISTRESSING ⟨a ~ situation⟩ **3** : extreme in degree : INTENSE ⟨~ heat⟩ **4** : of very poor quality : AWFUL ⟨a ~ play⟩ ♦ ***Synonyms*** FRIGHTFUL, HORRIBLE, SHOCKING, APPALLING — **ter·ri·bly** \-blē\ *adv*

ter·ri·er \ˈter-ē-ər\ *n* [ME *terryer, terrer,* fr. AF (*chen*) *terrer,* lit., earth dog, fr. *terre* earth, fr. L *terra*] : any of various usu. small energetic dogs orig. used by hunters to drive small game animals from their holes

ter·rif·ic \tə-ˈri-fik\ *adj* **1** : exciting terror ⟨a ~ explosion⟩ **2** : EXTRAORDINARY, ASTOUNDING ⟨~ speed⟩ **3** : MAGNIFICENT ⟨makes ~ chili⟩

ter·ri·fy \ˈter-ə-ˌfī\ *vb* **-fied; -fy·ing** : to fill with terror : FRIGHTEN ♦ ***Synonyms*** SCARE, TERRORIZE, STARTLE, ALARM — **ter·ri·fy·ing·ly** *adv*

ter·ri·to·ri·al·i·ty \ˌter-ə-ˌtȯr-ē-ˈa-lə-tē\ *n* : persistent attachment to a specific territory ⟨~ in bears⟩

ter·ri·to·ry \ˈter-ə-ˌtȯr-ē\ *n, pl* **-ries** **1** : a geographic area belonging to or under the jurisdiction of a governmental authority **2** : a part of the U.S. not included within any state but organized with a separate legislature **3** : REGION, DISTRICT; *also* : a region in which one feels at home **4** : a field of knowledge or interest **5** : an assigned area **6** : an area occupied and defended by one or a group of animals — **ter·ri·to·ri·al** \ˌter-ə-ˈtȯr-ē-əl\ *adj* — **go with the territory** *or* **come with the territory** : to accompany a situation naturally

ter·ror \ˈter-ər\ *n* **1** : a state of intense fear : FRIGHT **2** : one that inspires fear **3** : violent or destructive acts committed to intimidate a people or government ♦ ***Synonyms*** PANIC, CONSTERNATION, DREAD, ALARM, DISMAY, HORROR, TREPIDATION

ter·ror·ism \ˈter-ər-ˌi-zəm\ *n* : the systematic use of terror esp. as a means of coercion — **ter·ror·ist** \-ist\ *adj or n*

ter·ror·ize \ˈter-ər-ˌīz\ *vb* **-ized; -iz·ing** **1** : to fill with terror : SCARE **2** : to coerce by threat or violence ♦ ***Synonyms*** TERRIFY, FRIGHTEN, ALARM, STARTLE

ter·ry \ˈter-ē\ *n, pl* **terries** : an absorbent fabric with a loose pile of uncut loops

terse \ˈtərs\ *adj* **ters·er; ters·est** [L *tersus* clean, neat, fr. pp. of *tergēre* to wipe off] : effectively brief : CONCISE — **terse·ly** *adv* — **terse·ness** *n*

ter·tia·ry \ˈtər-shē-ˌer-ē\ *adj* **1** : of third rank, importance, or value **2** *cap* : of, relating to, or being the earlier period of the Cenozoic era **3** : occurring in or being the third stage ⟨~ medical care⟩

Tertiary *n* : the Tertiary period

TESL *abbr* teaching English as a second language

TESOL *abbr* Teachers of English to Speakers of Other Languages

¹test \ˈtest\ *n* [ME, vessel in which metals were assayed, potsherd, fr. AF, pot, fr. L *testum* earthen vessel] **1** : a critical examination or evaluation : TRIAL **2** : a means or result of testing

²test *vb* **1** : to put to test : TRY, EXAMINE **2** : to undergo or score on tests

[3]**test** *adj* : relating to or used in testing ⟨a ~ group⟩

tes·ta·ment \ˈtes-tə-mənt\ *n* **1** *cap* : either of two main divisions of the Bible **2** : EVIDENCE, WITNESS **3** : CREED **4** : the legal instructions for the disposition of one's property after death : WILL — **tes·ta·men·ta·ry** \ˌtes-tə-ˈmen-tə-rē\ *adj*

tes·tate \ˈtes-ˌtāt, -tət\ *adj* : having left a valid will

tes·ta·tor \ˈtes-ˌtā-tər, tes-ˈtā-\ *n* : a person who dies leaving a valid will

tes·ta·trix \tes-ˈtā-triks\ *n* : a woman who is a testator

[1]**tes·ter** \ˈtēs-tər, ˈtes-\ *n* : a canopy over a bed, pulpit, or altar

[2]**test·er** \ˈtes-tər\ *n* : one that tests

tes·ti·cle \ˈtes-ti-kəl\ *n* : TESTIS; *esp* : one of a mammal usu. with its enclosing structures — **tes·tic·u·lar** *adj*

tes·ti·fy \ˈtes-tə-ˌfī\ *vb* **-fied; -fy·ing** **1** : to make a statement based on personal knowledge or belief : bear witness **2** : to serve as evidence or proof

tes·ti·mo·ni·al \ˌtes-tə-ˈmō-nē-əl\ *n* **1** : a statement testifying to benefits received; *also* : a character reference **2** : an expression of appreciation : TRIBUTE — **testimonial** *adj*

tes·ti·mo·ny \ˈtes-tə-ˌmō-nē\ *n, pl* **-nies** **1** : evidence based on observation or knowledge **2** : an outward sign : SYMBOL **3** : a solemn declaration made by a witness under oath esp. in a court ♦ ***Synonyms*** EVIDENCE, CONFIRMATION, PROOF, TESTAMENT

tes·tis \ˈtes-təs\ *n, pl* **tes·tes** \ˈtes-ˌtēz\ [L, witness, testis] : a typically paired male reproductive gland that produces sperm and testosterone and that in most mammals is contained within the scrotum at sexual maturity

tes·tos·ter·one \te-ˈstäs-tə-ˌrōn\ *n* : a male sex hormone causing development of the male reproductive system and secondary sex characteristics

test–tube *adj* **1** : IN VITRO ⟨~ experiments⟩ **2** : produced by in vitro fertilization ⟨~ babies⟩

test tube *n* : a glass tube closed at one end and used esp. in chemistry and biology

tes·ty \ˈtes-tē\ *adj* **tes·ti·er; -est** [ME *testif,* fr. AF, headstrong, fr. *teste* head, fr. LL *testa* skull, fr. L, shell] : easily annoyed; *also* : marked by ill humor

tet·a·nus \ˈte-tə-nəs\ *n* : an infectious disease caused by bacterial poisons and marked by muscle stiffness and spasms esp. of the jaws — **tet·a·nal** \-əl\ *adj*

tetchy \ˈte-chē\ *adj* **tetchi·er; -est** : irritably or peevishly sensitive

[1]**tête–à–tête** \ˈtāt-ə-ˌtāt\ *n* [F, lit., head to head] : a private conversation between two persons

[2]**tête–à–tête** \ˌtāt-ə-ˈtāt\ *adv* : in private

[3]**tête–à–tête** \ˈtāt-ə-ˌtāt\ *adj* : being face-to-face : PRIVATE

[1]**teth·er** \ˈte-t͟hər\ *n* **1** : something (as a rope) by which an animal is fastened **2** : the limit of one's strength or resources

[2]**tether** *vb* : to fasten or restrain by or as if by a tether

tet·ra·eth·yl lead \ˌte-trə-ˈe-thəl-\ *n* : a heavy oily poisonous liquid used esp. formerly as an antiknock agent in gasoline

tet·ra·he·dron \-ˈhē-drən\ *n, pl* **-drons** *or* **-dra** \-drə\ : a polyhedron that has four faces — **tet·ra·he·dral** \-drəl\ *adj*

tet·ra·hy·dro·can·nab·i·nol \-ˌhī-drə-kə-ˈna-bə-ˌnȯl, -ˌnōl\ *n* : THC

te·tram·e·ter \te-ˈtra-mə-tər\ *n* : a line of verse consisting of four metrical feet

tet·ri \ˈte-trē\ *n, pl* **tetri** — see *lari* at MONEY table

Teu·ton·ic \tü-ˈtä-nik, tyü-\ *adj* : GERMANIC

Tex *abbr* Texas

Tex–Mex \ˈteks-ˈmeks\ *adj* : characteristic of Mexican-American culture and esp. that of southern Texas

[1]**text** \ˈtekst\ *n* **1** : the actual words of an author's work **2** : the main body of printed or written matter on a page **3** : a scriptural passage chosen as the subject esp. of a sermon **4** : THEME, TOPIC **5** : matter handled with a computer that is chiefly in the form of words **6** : TEXTBOOK **7** : TEXT MESSAGE — **tex·tu·al** \ˈteks-chə-wəl\ *adj*

[2]**text** *vb* : to communicate by text messaging — **texting** *n*

text·book \ˈtekst-ˌbu̇k\ *n* : a book used in the study of a subject

tex·tile \ˈtek-ˌstī(-ə)l, ˈteks-tᵊl\ *n* : CLOTH; *esp* : a woven or knit cloth

text message *n* : a short message sent electronically usu. from one cell phone to another

text messaging *n* : the sending of short text messages electronically esp. from one cell phone to another

tex·ture \ˈteks-chər\ *n* **1** : the visual or tactile surface characteristics and appearance of something ⟨a coarse ~⟩ **2** : essential part **3** : basic scheme or structure : FABRIC **4** : overall structure — **tex·tur·al** \-chə-rəl\ *adj*

TGIF *abbr* thank God it's Friday

[1]**Th** *abbr* Thursday

[2]**Th** *symbol* thorium

[1]**-th** — see [1]-ETH

[2]**-th** *or* **-eth** *adj suffix* — used in forming ordinal numbers ⟨hundred*th*⟩

[3]**-th** *n suffix* **1** : act or process **2** : state or condition ⟨dear*th*⟩

Thai \ˈtī\ *n, pl* **Thai** *or* **Thais** **1** : a native or inhabitant of Thailand **2** : the official language of Thailand — **Thai** *adj*

thal·a·mus \ˈtha-lə-məs\ *n, pl* **-mi** \-ˌmī\ [NL] : a subdivision of the brain that serves as a relay station to and from the cerebral cortex and functions in arousal and the integration of sensory information — **tha·lam·ic** \thə-ˈla-mik\ *adj*

thal·as·se·mia \ˌtha-lə-ˈsē-mē-ə\ *n* : any of a group of inherited disorders of hemoglobin synthesis

tha·las·so·ther·a·py \thə-ˌla-sō-ˈther-ə-pē\ *n* [Gk *thalassa* sea] : the use of seawater or sea products (as seaweed) for the benefit of health or beauty

thal·li·um \ˈtha-lē-əm\ *n* : a poisonous metallic chemical element

¹than \ˈthən, ˈthan\ *conj* **1** — used after a comparative adjective or adverb to introduce the second part of a comparison expressing inequality ⟨older ~ I am⟩ **2** — used after *other* or a word of similar meaning to express a difference of kind, manner, or identity ⟨adults other ~ parents⟩

²than *prep* : in comparison with ⟨older ~ me⟩

thane \ˈthān\ *n* **1** : a free retainer of an Anglo-Saxon lord **2** : a Scottish feudal lord

thank \ˈthaŋk\ *vb* : to express gratitude to ⟨~*ed* them for the present⟩

thank·ful \ˈthaŋk-fəl\ *adj* **1** : conscious of benefit received **2** : expressive of thanks **3** : GLAD — **thank·ful·ness** *n*

thank·ful·ly \-fə-lē\ *adv* **1** : in a thankful manner **2** : as makes one thankful

thank·less \ˈthaŋ-kləs\ *adj* **1** : UNAPPRECIATED **2** : UNGRATEFUL

thanks \ˈthaŋks\ *n pl* : an expression of gratitude

thanks·giv·ing \thaŋks-ˈgi-viŋ\ *n* **1** : the act of giving thanks **2** : a prayer expressing gratitude **3** *cap* : the 4th Thursday in November observed as a legal holiday for giving thanks for divine goodness

¹that \ˈthat, thət\ *pron, pl* **those** \ˈthōz\ **1** : the one indicated, mentioned, or understood ⟨~ is my house⟩ **2** : the one farther away or first mentioned ⟨this is an elm, ~'s a maple⟩ **3** : what has been indicated or mentioned ⟨after ~, we left⟩ **4** : the one or ones : IT, THEY ⟨*those* who wish to leave may do so⟩

²that \thət, ˈthat\ *conj* **1** : the following, namely ⟨he said ~ he would⟩; *also* : which is, namely ⟨there's a chance ~ it may fail⟩ **2** : to this end or purpose ⟨shouted ~ all might hear⟩ **3** : as to result in the following, namely ⟨so heavy ~ it can't be moved⟩ **4** : for this reason, namely : BECAUSE ⟨we're glad ~ you came⟩

³that *adj, pl* **those** **1** : being the one mentioned, indicated, or understood ⟨~ boy⟩ ⟨*those* people⟩ **2** : being the one farther away or less immediately under discussion ⟨this chair or ~ one⟩

⁴that \thət, ˈthat\ *pron* **1** : WHO, WHOM, WHICH ⟨the woman ~ saw you⟩ ⟨the woman ~ you saw⟩ ⟨the money ~ was spent⟩ **2** : in, on, or at which ⟨the way ~ he drives⟩ ⟨the day ~ it rained⟩

⁵that \ˈthat\ *adv* : to such an extent or degree ⟨I like it, but not ~ much⟩

¹thatch \ˈthach\ *vb* : to cover with or as if with thatch — **thatch·er** *n*

²thatch *n* **1** : plant material (as straw) for use as roofing **2** : a mat of grass clippings accumulated next to the soil on a lawn **3** : a covering of or as if of thatch

thaw \ˈthȯ\ *vb* **1** : to melt or cause to melt **2** : to become so warm as to melt ice or snow **3** : to abandon aloofness or hostility — **thaw** *n*

THC \ˌtē-(ˌ)āch-ˈsē\ *n* [*t*etra*h*ydro*c*annabinol] : a physiologically active chemical from hemp plant resin that is the chief intoxicant in marijuana

¹the \thə, *before vowel sounds usu* thē\ *definite article* **1** : that in particular **2** — used before adjectives functioning as nouns ⟨a word to ~ wise⟩

²the *adv* **1** : to what extent ⟨~ sooner, the better⟩ **2** : to that extent ⟨the sooner, ~ better⟩

theat *abbr* theater; theatrical

the·ater *or* **the·atre** \ˈthē-ə-tər\ *n* [ME *theatre,* fr. MF, fr. L *theatrum,* fr. Gk *theatron,* fr. *theasthai* to view, fr. *thea* act of seeing] **1** : a building or area for dramatic performances; *also* : a building or area for showing motion pictures **2** : a place of enactment of significant events ⟨~ of war⟩ **3** : a place (as a lecture room) resembling a theater **4** : dramatic literature or performance

theater–in–the–round *n* : a theater with the stage in the center of the auditorium

the·at·ri·cal \thē-ˈa-tri-kəl\ *also* **the·at·ric** \-trik\ *adj* **1** : of or relating to the theater **2** : marked by artificiality of emotion : HISTRIONIC ⟨a ~ gesture⟩ **3** : marked by extravagant display : SHOWY

the·at·ri·cals \-kəlz\ *n pl* : the performance of plays

the·at·rics \thē-ˈa-triks\ *n pl* **1** : THEATRICALS **2** : staged or contrived effects

the·be \ˈthā-bā\ *n, pl* **thebe** — see *pula* at MONEY table

thee \ˈthē\ *pron, archaic objective case of* THOU

theft \ˈtheft\ *n* : the act of stealing

thegn \ˈthān\ *n* : THANE 1

their \thər, ˈther\ *adj* : of or relating to them or themselves

theirs \ˈtherz\ *pron* : their one : their ones

the·ism \ˈthē-ˌi-zəm\ *n* : belief in the existence of a god or gods — **the·ist** \-ist\ *n or adj* — **the·is·tic** \thē-ˈis-tik\ *adj*

them \thəm, ˈthem\ *pron, objective case of* THEY

theme \ˈthēm\ *n* **1** : a subject or topic of discourse or of artistic representation **2** : a written exercise : COMPOSITION **3** : a melodic subject of a musical composition or movement — **the·mat·ic** \thi-ˈma-tik\ *adj*

them·selves \thəm-ˈselvz, them-\ *pron pl* : THEY, THEM — used reflexively, for emphasis, or in absolute constructions ⟨they govern ~⟩ ⟨they ~ came⟩ ⟨~ busy, they sent me⟩

¹then \ˈthen\ *adv* **1** : at that time **2** : soon after that : NEXT **3** : in addition : BESIDES **4** : in that case **5** : CONSEQUENTLY

²then *n* : that time ⟨since ~⟩

³then *adj* : existing or acting at that time ⟨the ~ attorney general⟩

thence \ˈthens, ˈthens\ *adv* **1** : from that place **2** *archaic* : THENCEFORTH **3** : from that fact : THEREFROM

thence·forth \-ˌfȯrth\ *adv* : from that time forward : THEREAFTER

thence·for·ward \thens-ˈfȯr-wərd, thens-\ *also* **thence·for·wards** \-wərdz\ *adv* : onward from that place or time

the·oc·ra·cy \thē-ˈä-krə-sē\ *n, pl* **-cies** **1** : government by officials regarded as divinely inspired **2** : a state governed by a theocracy — **the·o·crat·ic** \ˌthē-ə-ˈkra-tik\ *adj*

theol *abbr* theological; theology

the·ol·o·gy \thē-ˈä-lə-jē\ *n, pl* **-gies** **1** : the study of religious faith, practice, and experience; *esp* : the study of God and of God's relation to the world **2** : a theory or system of theology — **the·o·lo·gian** \ˌthē-ə-ˈlō-jən\ *n* — **the·o·log·i·cal** \-ˈlä-ji-kəl\ *adj*

the·o·rem \ˈthē-ə-rəm, ˈthir-əm\ *n* **1** : a statement esp. in mathematics that has been or is to be proved **2** : an idea accepted or proposed as a demonstrable truth : PROPOSITION

the·o·ret·i·cal \ˌthē-ə-ˈre-ti-kəl\ *also* **the·o·ret·ic** \-tik\ *adj* **1** : relating to or having the character of theory **2** : existing only in theory : HYPOTHETICAL — **the·o·ret·i·cal·ly** \-ti-k(ə-)lē\ *adv*

the·o·rise *Brit var of* THEORIZE

the·o·rize \ˈthē-ə-ˌrīz\ *vb* **-rized; -riz·ing** : to form a theory : SPECULATE — **the·o·rist** \-rist\ *n*

the·o·ry \ˈthē-ə-rē, ˈthir-ē\ *n, pl* **-ries** **1** : abstract thought **2** : the general principles of a subject **3** : a plausible or scientifically acceptable general principle offered to explain observed facts **4** : HYPOTHESIS, CONJECTURE

theory of games : GAME THEORY

the·os·o·phy \thē-ˈä-sə-fē\ *n* : belief about God and the world held to be based on mystical insight — **theo·soph·i·cal** \ˌthē-ə-ˈsä-fi-kəl\ *adj* — **the·os·o·phist** \thē-ˈä-sə-fist\ *n*

ther·a·peu·tic \ˌther-ə-ˈpyü-tik\ *adj* [Gk *therapeutikos,* fr. *therapeuein* to attend, treat, fr. *theraps* attendant] : of, relating to, or dealing with healing and esp. with remedies for diseases — **ther·a·peu·ti·cal·ly** \-ti-k(ə-)lē\ *adv*

ther·a·peu·tics \ˌther-ə-ˈpyü-tiks\ *n* : a branch of medical or dental science dealing with the use of remedies

ther·a·py \ˈther-ə-pē\ *n, pl* **-pies** : treatment of bodily, mental, or behavioral disorders — **ther·a·pist** \-pist\ *n*

¹there \ˈther\ *adv* **1** : in or at that place — often used interjectionally **2** : to or into that place ⟨went ~ after work⟩ **3** : in that matter or respect

²there \ˈther, thər\ *pron* — used as a function word to introduce a sentence or clause ⟨~'s a pen here⟩

³there \ˈther\ *n* **1** : that place ⟨get away from ~⟩ **2** : that point ⟨you take it from ~⟩

there·abouts \ˌthr-ə-ˈbau̇ts, ˈther-ə-ˌbau̇ts\ *or* **there·about** \-ˈbau̇t, -ˌbau̇t\ *adv* **1** : near that place or time **2** : near that number, degree, or quantity

there·af·ter \ther-ˈaf-tər\ *adv* : after that : AFTERWARD

there·at \-ˈat\ *adv* **1** : at that place **2** : at that occurrence : on that account

there·by \ther-ˈbī, ˈther-ˌbī\ *adv* **1** : by that : by that means **2** : connected with or with reference to that

there·for \ther-ˈfȯr\ *adv* : for or in return for that ⟨wanted a refund ~⟩

there·fore \ˈther-ˌfōr\ *adv* : for that reason : CONSEQUENTLY

there·from \ther-ˈfrəm\ *adv* : from that or it

there·in \ther-ˈin\ *adv* **1** : in or into that place, time, or thing **2** : in that respect

there·of \-ˈəv, -ˈäv\ *adv* **1** : of that or it **2** : from that : THEREFROM

there·on \-ˈȯn, -ˈän\ *adv* **1** : on that **2** *archaic* : THEREUPON 3

there·to \ther-ˈtü\ *adv* : to that

there·un·to \ther-ˈən-(ˌ)tü, ˌther-ən-ˈtü\ *adv, archaic* : THERETO

there·upon \ˈther-ə-ˌpȯn, -ˌpän; ˌther-ə-ˈpȯn, -ˈpän\ *adv* **1** : on that matter **2** : THEREFORE **3** : immediately after that : at once

there·with \ther-ˈwith, -with\ *adv* **1** : with that **2** : THEREUPON, FORTHWITH

there·with·al \ˈther-wi-ˌthȯl, -ˌthȯl\ *adv* **1** *archaic* : BESIDES **2** : THEREWITH

therm *abbr* thermometer

ther·mal \ˈthər-məl\ *adj* **1** : of, relating to, or caused by heat **2** : designed to prevent the loss of body heat ⟨~ underwear⟩ — **ther·mal·ly** *adv*

thermal pollution *n* : the discharge of heated liquid (as waste water from a factory) into natural waters at a temperature harmful to the environment

therm·is·tor \ˈthər-ˌmis-tər\ *n* : an electrical resistor whose resistance varies sharply with temperature

ther·mo·cline \ˈthər-mə-ˌklīn\ *n* : the region in a thermally stratified body of water that separates warmer surface water from cold deep water

ther·mo·cou·ple \ˈthər-mə-ˌkə-pəl\ *n* : a device for measuring temperature by measuring the temperature-dependent potential difference created at the junction of two dissimilar metals

ther·mo·dy·nam·ics \ˌthər-mə-dī-ˈna-miks\ *n* : physics that deals with the mechanical action or relations of heat — **ther·mo·dy·nam·ic** \-mik\ *adj* — **ther·mo·dy·nam·i·cal·ly** \-mi-k(ə-)lē\ *adv*

ther·mom·e·ter \thər-ˈmä-mə-tər\ *n* [F *thermomètre,* fr. Gk *thermē* heat + *metron* measure] : an instrument for determining temperature — **ther·mo·met·ric** \ˌthər-mə-ˈme-trik\ *adj* — **ther·mo·met·ri·cal·ly** \-tri-k(ə-)lē\ *adv*

ther·mo·nu·cle·ar \ˌthər-mō-ˈnü-klē-ər, -ˈnyü-\ *adj* **1** : of or relating to changes in the nucleus of atoms of low atomic weight (as hydrogen) that require a very high temperature (as in the hydrogen bomb) **2** : utilizing or relating to a thermonuclear bomb ⟨~ war⟩

ther·mo·plas·tic \ˌthər-mə-ˈplas-tik\ *adj* : capable of softening when heated and of hardening again when cooled ⟨~ resins⟩ — **thermoplastic** *n*

ther·mos \ˈthər-məs\ *n* : a cylindrical container with a vacuum between an inner and an outer wall used to keep liquids hot or cold

ther·mo·sphere \ˈthər-mə-ˌsfir\ *n* : the

part of the earth's atmosphere that lies above the mesosphere and that is characterized by steadily increasing temperature with height

ther·mo·stat \ˈthər-mə-ˌstat\ *n* : a device that automatically controls temperature — **ther·mo·stat·ic** \ˌthər-mə-ˈsta-tik\ *adj* — **ther·mo·stat·i·cal·ly** \-ti-k(ə-)lē\ *adv*

the·sau·rus \thi-ˈsȯr-əs\ *n, pl* **-sau·ri** \-ˈsȯr-ˌī\ *or* **-sau·rus·es** \-ˈsȯr-ə-səz\ [NL, fr. L, treasure, collection, fr. Gk *thēsauros*] : a book of words and their synonyms — **the·sau·ral** \-ˈsȯr-əl\ *adj*

these *pl of* THIS

the·sis \ˈthē-səs\ *n, pl* **the·ses** \ˈthē-ˌsēz\ **1** : a proposition that a person advances and offers to maintain by argument **2** : an essay embodying results of original research; *esp* : one written for an academic degree

[1]**thes·pi·an** \ˈthes-pē-ən\ *adj, often cap* [fr. *Thespis,* 6th cent. B.C. Greek poet and reputed originator of tragedy] : relating to the drama : DRAMATIC

[2]**thespian** *n* : ACTOR

Thess *abbr* Thessalonians

Thes·sa·lo·nians \ˌthe-sə-ˈlō-nyənz, -nē-ənz\ *n* — see BIBLE table

the·ta \ˈthā-tə\ *n* : the 8th letter of the Greek alphabet — Θ or θ

thew \ˈthü, ˈthyü\ *n* : MUSCLE, SINEW — usu. used in pl.

they \ˈthā\ *pron* **1** : those ones : those people, animals, or things **2** : unspecified persons : PEOPLE **3** : that one — used for a single person whose gender is nonbinary, unknown, or intentionally not revealed

thi·a·mine \ˈthī-ə-mən, -ˌmēn\ *also* **thi·a·min** \-mən\ *n* : a vitamin of the vitamin B complex essential to normal metabolism and nerve function

[1]**thick** \ˈthik\ *adj* **1** : having relatively great depth or extent from one surface to its opposite ⟨a ~ plank⟩; *also* : heavily built : THICKSET **2** : densely massed : CROWDED; *also* : FREQUENT, NUMEROUS **3** : dense or viscous in consistency ⟨~ syrup⟩ **4** : marked by haze, fog, or mist ⟨~ weather⟩ **5** : measuring in thickness ⟨one meter ~⟩ **6** : imperfectly articulated : INDISTINCT ⟨~ speech⟩ **7** : STUPID, OBTUSE **8** : associated on close terms : INTIMATE **9** : EXCESSIVE ♦ ***Synonyms*** COMPACT, CLOSE, TIGHT — **thick·ly** *adv*

[2]**thick** *n* **1** : the most crowded or active part **2** : the part of greatest thickness

thick and thin *n* : every difficulty and obstacle ⟨was loyal through *thick and thin*⟩

thick·en \ˈthi-kən\ *vb* : to make or become thick — **thick·en·er** *n*

thick·et \ˈthi-kət\ *n* : a dense growth of bushes or small trees

thick·ness \-nəs\ *n* **1** : the smallest of three dimensions ⟨length, width, and ~⟩ **2** : the quality or state of being thick **3** : LAYER, SHEET ⟨a single ~ of canvas⟩

thick·set \ˈthik-ˈset\ *adj* **1** : closely placed or planted **2** : having a thick body : BURLY

thick–skinned \-ˈskind\ *adj* **1** : having a thick skin **2** : not easily bothered by criticism or insult ⟨a ~ politician⟩

thief \ˈthēf\ *n, pl* **thieves** \ˈthēvz\ : one that steals esp. secretly

thieve \ˈthēv\ *vb* **thieved; thiev·ing** : STEAL, ROB ♦ ***Synonyms*** FILCH, PILFER, PURLOIN, SWIPE

thiev·ery \ˈthē-və-rē\ *n, pl* **-er·ies** : the act of stealing : THEFT

thigh \ˈthī\ *n* : the part of the vertebrate hind or lower limb between the knee and the hip

thigh·bone \ˈthī-ˌbōn\ *n* : FEMUR

thim·ble \ˈthim-bəl\ *n* : a cap or guard worn on the finger to push the needle in sewing — **thim·ble·ful** *n*

[1]**thin** \ˈthin\ *adj* **thin·ner; thin·nest** **1** : having little extent from one surface through to its opposite : not thick : SLENDER **2** : not closely set or placed : SPARSE ⟨~ hair⟩ **3** : not dense or not dense enough : more fluid or rarefied than normal ⟨~ air⟩ ⟨~ syrup⟩ **4** : lacking substance, fullness, or strength ⟨~ broth⟩ **5** : FLIMSY ⟨a ~ excuse⟩ — **thin·ly** *adv* — **thin·ness** *n*

[2]**thin** *vb* **thinned; thin·ning** : to make or become thin

thine \ˈthīn\ *pron, archaic* : that which belongs to thee

thing \ˈthiŋ\ *n* **1** : a matter of concern : AFFAIR ⟨~*s* to do⟩ **2** *pl* : state of affairs ⟨~*s* are improving⟩ **3** : EVENT, CIRCUMSTANCE ⟨the crime was a terrible ~⟩ **4** : DEED, ACT ⟨expected great ~*s* of him⟩ **5** : a distinct entity : OBJECT **6** : an inanimate object distinguished from a living being **7** *pl* : POSSESSIONS, EFFECTS **8** : an article of clothing **9** : DETAIL, POINT **10** : IDEA, NOTION ⟨says the first ~ he thinks of⟩ **11** : something one likes to do : SPECIALTY ⟨doing her ~⟩

think \ˈthiŋk\ *vb* **thought** \ˈthȯt\; **think·ing** **1** : to form or have in the mind **2** : to have as an opinion : BELIEVE **3** : to reflect on : PONDER **4** : to call to mind : REMEMBER **5** : REASON **6** : to form a mental picture of : IMAGINE **7** : to devise by thinking ⟨*thought* up a plan to escape⟩ ♦ ***Synonyms*** CONCEIVE, FANCY, REALIZE, ENVISAGE — **think·er** *n*

think tank *n* : an institute, corporation, or group organized for interdisciplinary research

thin·ner \ˈthi-nər\ *n* : a volatile liquid (as turpentine) used to thin paint

thin–skinned \ˈthin-ˈskind\ *adj* **1** : having a thin skin or rind **2** : extremely sensitive to criticism or insult

[1]**third** \ˈthərd\ *adj* : next after the second — **third** *or* **third·ly** *adv*

[2]**third** *n* **1** : one of three equal parts of something **2** : one that is number three in a countable series **3** : the 3d forward gear in an automotive vehicle

third degree *n* : the subjection of a prisoner to mental or physical torture to force a confession

third dimension *n* **1** : thickness, depth,

or apparent thickness or depth that confers solidity on an object **2** : a quality that confers reality — **third–dimensional** *adj*

third world *n, often cap T&W sometimes offensive* : the aggregate of the underdeveloped nations of the world

[1]**thirst** \ˈthərst\ *n* **1** : a feeling of dryness in the mouth and throat associated with a desire to drink; *also* : a bodily condition producing this **2** : an ardent desire : CRAVING ⟨a ~ for knowledge⟩ — **thirsty** *adj*

[2]**thirst** *vb* **1** : to need drink : suffer thirst **2** : to have a strong desire : CRAVE

thir·teen \ˌthər-ˈtēn\ *n* : one more than 12 — **thirteen** *adj or pron* — **thir·teenth** \-ˈtēnth\ *adj or n*

thir·ty \ˈthər-tē\ *n, pl* **thirties** : three times 10 — **thir·ti·eth** \-tē-əth\ *adj or n* — **thirty** *adj or pron*

[1]**this** \ˈthis\ *pron, pl* **these** \ˈthēz\ **1** : the one close or closest in time or space ⟨~ is your book⟩ **2** : what is in the present or under immediate observation or discussion ⟨~ is a mess⟩; *also* : what is happening or being done now ⟨after ~ we'll leave⟩

[2]**this** *adj, pl* **these** **1** : being the one near, present, just mentioned, or more immediately under observation ⟨~ book⟩ **2** : constituting the immediate past or future ⟨friends all *these* years⟩

[3]**this** *adv* : to such an extent or degree ⟨didn't expect to wait ~ long⟩

this·tle \ˈthi-səl\ *n* : any of various tall prickly composite plants with often showy heads of tightly packed tubular flowers

this·tle·down \-ˌdau̇n\ *n* : the down from the ripe flower head of a thistle

[1]**thith·er** \ˈthi-thər\ *adv* : to that place

[2]**thither** *adj* : being on the farther side

thith·er·ward \-wərd\ *adv* : toward that place : THITHER

thong \ˈthȯŋ\ *n* **1** : a strip esp. of leather or hide **2** : a sandal held on the foot by a thong between the toes **3** : a narrow strip of swimwear or underwear that passes between the buttocks

tho·rax \ˈthȯr-ˌaks\ *n, pl* **tho·rax·es** *or* **tho·ra·ces** \ˈthȯr-ə-ˌsēz\ **1** : the part of the body of a mammal between the neck and the abdomen; *also* : its cavity containing the heart and lungs **2** : the middle of the three main divisions of the body of an insect — **tho·rac·ic** \thə-ˈra-sik\ *adj*

tho·ri·um \ˈthȯr-ē-əm\ *n* : a radioactive metallic chemical element

thorn \ˈthȯrn\ *n* **1** : a woody plant bearing sharp processes **2** : a sharp rigid plant process that is usu. a modified leafless branch **3** : something that causes distress — **thorny** *adj*

thor·ough \ˈthər-ō\ *adj* **1** : COMPLETE, EXHAUSTIVE ⟨a ~ search⟩ **2** : very careful : PAINSTAKING ⟨a ~ scholar⟩ **3** : having full mastery — **thor·ough·ly** *adv* — **thor·ough·ness** *n*

[1]**thor·ough·bred** \ˈthər-ə-ˌbred\ *adj* **1** : bred from the best blood through a long line : PUREBRED **2** *cap* : of or relating to the Thoroughbred breed of horses **3** : marked by high-spirited grace

[2]**thoroughbred** *n* **1** *cap* : any of an English breed of light speedy horses kept chiefly for racing **2** : one (as a pedigreed animal) of excellent quality

thor·ough·fare \-ˌfer\ *n* : a public road or street

thor·ough·go·ing \ˌthər-ə-ˈgō-iŋ\ *adj* : marked by thoroughness or zeal

those *pl of* THAT

[1]**thou** \ˈthau̇\ *pron, archaic* : the person addressed

[2]**thou** \ˈthau̇\ *n, pl* **thou** : a thousand of something (as dollars)

[1]**though** \ˈthō\ *conj* **1** : despite the fact that ⟨~ the odds are hopeless, they fight on⟩ **2** : granting that ⟨~ it may look bad, still, all is not lost⟩

[2]**though** *adv* : HOWEVER, NEVERTHELESS ⟨not for long, ~⟩

[1]**thought** \ˈthȯt\ *past and past part of* THINK

[2]**thought** *n* **1** : the process of thinking **2** : serious consideration : REGARD **3** : reasoning power **4** : the power to imagine : CONCEPTION **5** : IDEA, NOTION **6** : OPINION, BELIEF ⟨spoke his ~*s* freely⟩

thought·ful \ˈthȯt-fəl\ *adj* **1** : absorbed in thought **2** : marked by careful thinking ⟨a ~ essay⟩ **3** : considerate of others ⟨a ~ host⟩ — **thought·ful·ly** *adv* — **thought·ful·ness** *n*

thought·less \-ləs\ *adj* **1** : insufficiently alert : CARELESS ⟨a ~ worker⟩ **2** : RECKLESS ⟨a ~ act⟩ **3** : lacking concern for others : INCONSIDERATE ⟨~ remarks⟩ — **thought·less·ly** *adv* — **thought·less·ness** *n*

thou·sand \ˈthau̇z-ᵊnd\ *n, pl* **thousands** *or* **thousand** : 10 times 100 — **thousand** *adj* — **thou·sandth** \-ᵊnth\ *adj or n*

thousands place *n* : the place four to the left of the decimal point in an Arabic number

thrall \ˈthrȯl\ *n* **1** : an enslaved person who performs the duties of a servant : BONDMAN **2** : a state of servitude — **thrall·dom** *or* **thral·dom** \ˈthrȯl-dəm\ *n*

[1]**thrash** \ˈthrash\ *vb* **1** : THRESH 1 **2** : BEAT, WHIP; *also* : DEFEAT **3** : to move about violently **4** : to go over again and again ⟨~ over the matter⟩; *also* : to hammer out ⟨~ out a plan⟩

[2]**thrash** *n* : rock music that is extremely fast and loud

[1]**thrash·er** \ˈthra-shər\ *n* : one that thrashes or threshes

[2]**thrasher** *n* : any of various long-tailed American songbirds related to the mockingbird

[1]**thread** \ˈthred\ *n* **1** : a thin continuous strand of spun and twisted textile fibers **2** : something resembling a textile thread **3** : the ridge or groove that winds around a screw **4** : a line of reasoning or train of thought **5** : a continuing element **6** : a tenuous or feeble support

[2]**thread** *vb* **1** : to pass a thread through the eye of (a needle) **2** : to pass (as film)

through something **3** : to make one's way through or between **4** : to put together on a thread ⟨~ beads⟩ **5** : to form a screw thread on or in

thread·bare \-ˌber\ *adj* **1** : having the nap worn off so that the thread shows : SHABBY **2** : TRITE ⟨~ excuses⟩

thready \ˈthre-dē\ *adj* **1** : consisting of or bearing fibers of filaments ⟨a ~ bark⟩ **2** : lacking in fullness, body, or vigor ⟨a ~ voice⟩

threat \ˈthret\ *n* **1** : an expression of intent to do harm **2** : one that threatens

threat·en \ˈthre-tᵊn\ *vb* **1** : to utter threats against **2** : to give signs or warning of : PORTEND **3** : to hang over as a threat : MENACE **4** : to cause to feel insecure or anxious — **threat·en·ing·ly** *adv*

threat·ened \-tᵊnd\ *adj* : having an uncertain chance of continued survival; *esp* : likely to become an endangered species

three \ˈthrē\ *n* **1** : one more than two **2** : the 3d in a set or series **3** : something having three units — **three** *adj or pron*

3D \ˈthrē-ˈdē\ *n* : a three-dimensional form or picture — **3D** *adj*

three–dimensional *adj* **1** : relating to or having three dimensions **2** : giving the illusion of varying distances ⟨a ~ picture⟩

3D printer *n* : a device used to manufacture objects by depositing material in successive layers according to a prescribed pattern or model

three·fold \ˈthrē-ˌfōld, -ˈfōld\ *adj* **1** : having three parts : TRIPLE **2** : being three times as great or as many — **three·fold** \-ˈfōld\ *adv*

three·pence \ˈthre-pəns, ˈthri-, ˈthrə-, *US also* ˈthrē-pens\ *n* **1** *pl* **threepence** *or* **three·penc·es** : a coin worth three pennies **2** : the sum of three British pennies

three·score \ˈthrē-ˈskȯr\ *adj* : being three times twenty : SIXTY

three·some \ˈthrē-səm\ *n* : a group of three persons or things

thren·o·dy \ˈthre-nə-dē\ *n, pl* **-dies** : a song of lamentation : ELEGY

thresh \ˈthresh, ˈthrash\ *vb* **1** : to separate (as grain from straw) mechanically **2** : THRASH — **thresh·er** *n*

thresh·old \ˈthresh-ˌhōld\ *n* **1** : the sill of a door **2** : a point or place of beginning or entering : OUTSET **3** : a point at which a physiological or psychological effect begins to be produced ⟨pain ~*s*⟩

threw *past of* THROW

thrice \ˈthrīs\ *adv* **1** : three times **2** : in a threefold manner or degree

thrift \ˈthrift\ *n* [ME, fr. ON, prosperity, fr. *thrīfask* to thrive] : careful management esp. of money : FRUGALITY — **thrift·i·ly** \ˈthrif-tə-lē\ *adv* — **thrift·less** *adj* — **thrifty** *adj*

thrill \ˈthril\ *vb* [ME *thirlen, thrillen* to pierce, fr. OE *thyrlian,* fr. *thyrel* hole, fr. *thurh* through] **1** : to have or cause to have a sudden sharp feeling of excitement ⟨was *thrilled* by the news⟩; *also* : TINGLE, SHIVER **2** : TREMBLE, VIBRATE — **thrill** *n* — **thrill·er** *n* — **thrill·ing·ly** *adv*

thrips \ˈthrips\ *n, pl* **thrips** : any of an order of minute sucking insects including many plant-feeding pests

thrive \ˈthrīv\ *vb* **thrived** *or* **throve** \ˈthrōv\; **thrived** *also* **thriv·en** \ˈthri-vən\; **thriv·ing** **1** : to grow luxuriantly : FLOURISH **2** : to gain in wealth or possessions : PROSPER ⟨her business ~*s*⟩

throat \ˈthrōt\ *n* : the part of the neck in front of the spinal column; *also* : the passage through it to the stomach and lungs — **throat·ed** *adj*

throaty \ˈthrō-tē\ *adj* **throat·i·er; -est** **1** : uttered or produced from low in the throat ⟨a ~ voice⟩ **2** : heavy, thick, or deep as if from the throat ⟨~ notes of a horn⟩ — **throat·i·ly** \-tə-lē\ *adv* — **throat·i·ness** \-tē-nəs\ *n*

1**throb** \ˈthräb\ *vb* **throbbed; throb·bing** : to pulsate or pound esp. with abnormal force or rapidity : BEAT, VIBRATE

2**throb** *n* : BEAT, PULSE

throe \ˈthrō\ *n* **1** : PANG, SPASM ⟨death ~*s*⟩ **2** *pl* : a hard or painful struggle

throm·bo·lyt·ic \ˌthräm-bə-ˈli-tik\ *adj* : destroying or breaking up a thrombus — **thrombolytic** *n*

throm·bo·sis \thräm-ˈbō-səs\ *n, pl* **-bo·ses** \-ˌsēz\ : the formation or presence of a clot in a blood vessel — **throm·bot·ic** \-ˈbä-tik\ *adj*

throm·bus \ˈthräm-bəs\ *n, pl* **throm·bi** \-ˌbī\ [NL, fr. Gk *thrombos* lump, clot] : a clot of blood formed within a blood vessel and remaining attached to its place of origin

throne \ˈthrōn\ *n* **1** : the chair of state of a sovereign or high dignitary **2** : royal power : SOVEREIGNTY

1**throng** \ˈthrȯŋ\ *n* **1** : MULTITUDE **2** : a crowding together of many persons

2**throng** *vb* **thronged; throng·ing** : CROWD

1**throt·tle** \ˈthrä-tᵊl\ *vb* **throt·tled; throt·tling** [ME *throtlen,* fr. *throte* throat] **1** : CHOKE, STRANGLE **2** : SUPPRESS ⟨policies that ~ creativity⟩ **3** : to reduce the speed of (an engine) by closing the throttle — **throt·tler** *n*

2**throttle** *n* : a valve regulating the flow of steam or fuel to an engine; *also* : the lever controlling this valve

1**through** \ˈthrü\ *prep* **1** : into at one side and out at the other side of ⟨go ~ the door⟩ **2** : by way of ⟨entered ~ a skylight⟩ **3** : in the midst of ⟨a path ~ the trees⟩ **4** : by means of ⟨succeeded ~ hard work⟩ **5** : over the whole of ⟨rumors swept ~ the office⟩ **6** : during the whole of ⟨~ the night⟩ **7** : to and including ⟨Monday ~ Friday⟩

2**through** *adv* **1** : from one end or side to the other **2** : from beginning to end : to completion ⟨see it ~⟩ **3** : to the core : THOROUGHLY ⟨he was wet ~⟩ **4** : into the open : OUT ⟨break ~⟩

3**through** *adj* **1** : permitting free passage ⟨a ~ street⟩ **2** : going from point of origin to destination without change or transfer ⟨a ~ train⟩ **3** : coming from or going to points outside a local area ⟨~ traffic⟩ **4** : FINISHED ⟨~ with the job⟩

¹through·out \thrü-ˈau̇t\ *adv* **1** : EVERYWHERE **2** : from beginning to end
²throughout *prep* **1** : in or to every part of **2** : during the whole period of
through·put \ˈthrü-ˌpu̇t\ *n* : OUTPUT, PRODUCTION ⟨the ~ of a computer⟩
throve *past of* THRIVE
¹throw \ˈthrō\ *vb* **threw** \ˈthrü\; **thrown** \ˈthrōn\; **throw·ing** [ME, to cause to twist, throw, fr. OE *thrāwan* to cause to twist] **1** : to propel through the air esp. with a forward motion of the hand and arm ⟨~ a ball⟩ **2** : to cause to fall or fall off **3** : to put suddenly in a certain position or condition ⟨~ into panic⟩ **4** : to put on or take off hastily ⟨~ on a coat⟩ **5** : to lose intentionally ⟨~ a game⟩ **6** : to move (a lever) so as to connect or disconnect parts of something (as a clutch) **7** : to put (an automobile) into a different gear **8** : to act as host for ⟨~ a party⟩ ♦ ***Synonyms*** TOSS, FLING, PITCH, SLING — **throw·er** *n*
²throw *n* **1** : an act of throwing, hurling, or flinging; *also* : CAST **2** : the distance a missile may be thrown **3** : a light coverlet **4** : a woman's scarf or light wrap
¹throw·away \ˈthrō-ə-ˌwā\ *n* : something that is or is designed to be thrown away esp. after one use
²throwaway *adj* : overly wasteful ⟨a ~ society⟩
throw·back \-ˌbak\ *n* : reversion to an earlier type or phase; *also* : an instance or product of this
throw up *vb* **1** : to build hurriedly **2** : VOMIT
thrum \ˈthrəm\ *vb* **thrummed; thrum·ming** : to play or pluck a stringed instrument idly : STRUM
thrush \ˈthrəsh\ *n* : any of numerous small or medium-sized songbirds that are mostly of a plain color often with spotted underparts
¹thrust \ˈthrəst\ *vb* **thrust; thrust·ing** **1** : to push or drive with force : SHOVE **2** : STAB, PIERCE **3** : INTERJECT **4** : to press the acceptance of upon someone
²thrust *n* **1** : a lunge with a pointed weapon **2** : ATTACK **3** : the pressure of one part of a construction against another (as of an arch against an abutment) **4** : the force produced by a propeller or jet or rocket engine that drives a vehicle (as an aircraft) forward **5** : a violent push : SHOVE **6** : prominent or essential element ⟨the ~ of the argument⟩
thrust·er *also* **thrust·or** \ˈthrəs-tər\ *n* : one that thrusts; *esp* : a rocket engine
thru·way \ˈthrü-ˌwā\ *n* : EXPRESSWAY
¹thud \ˈthəd\ *n* **1** : ⁴BLOW **2** : a dull sound
²thud *vb* **thud·ded; thud·ding** : to move or strike so as to make a thud
thug \ˈthəg\ *n* [Hindi & Urdu *ṭhag,* lit., thief] : a violent or brutal criminal or bully — **thug·gish** *adj*
thu·li·um \ˈthü-lē-əm, ˈthyü-\ *n* : a rare metallic chemical element
¹thumb \ˈthəm\ *n* **1** : the short thick first digit of the human hand or a corresponding digit of a lower animal **2** : the part of a glove or mitten that covers the thumb
²thumb *vb* **1** : to leaf through (pages) with the thumb **2** : to wear or soil with the thumb by frequent handling **3** : to request or obtain (a ride) in a passing automobile by signaling with the thumb
thumb drive *n* : FLASH DRIVE
¹thumb·nail \ˈthəm-ˌnāl\ *n* : the nail of the thumb
²thumbnail *adj* : BRIEF, CONCISE ⟨a ~ description⟩ ⟨a ~ picture⟩
thumb·print \-ˌprint\ *n* : an impression made by the thumb
thumb·screw \-ˌskrü\ *n* **1** : a device of torture for squeezing the thumb **2** : a screw with a head that may be turned by the thumb and index finger
thumb·tack \-ˌtak\ *n* : a tack with a broad flat head for pressing with one's thumb into a board or wall
¹thump \ˈthəmp\ *vb* **1** : to strike with or as if with something thick or heavy so as to cause a dull sound **2** : POUND
²thump *n* : a blow with or as if with something blunt or heavy; *also* : the sound made by such a blow
¹thun·der \ˈthən-dər\ *n* **1** : the sound following a flash of lightning; *also* : a noise like such a sound **2** : a loud utterance or threat
²thunder *vb* **1** : to produce thunder **2** : ROAR, SHOUT ⟨jets ~*ed* overhead⟩
thun·der·bolt \-ˌbōlt\ *n* : a flash of lightning with its accompanying thunder
thun·der·clap \-ˌklap\ *n* : a crash of thunder
thun·der·cloud \-ˌklau̇d\ *n* : a cloud charged with electricity and producing lightning and thunder
thun·der·head \-ˌhed\ *n* : a large cumulus or cumulonimbus cloud often appearing before a thunderstorm
thun·der·ous \ˈthən-də-rəs\ *adj* : producing thunder; *also* : making a noise like thunder — **thun·der·ous·ly** *adv*
thun·der·show·er \ˈthən-dər-ˌshau̇(-ə)r\ *n* : a shower accompanied by thunder and lightning
thun·der·storm \-ˌsto̊rm\ *n* : a storm accompanied by thunder and lightning
thun·der·struck \-ˌstrək\ *adj* : stunned as if struck by a thunderbolt
Thurs *or* **Thu** *abbr* Thursday
Thurs·day \ˈthərz-ˌdā, -dē\ *n* [ME, fr. OE *thursdæg,* fr. ON *thōrsdagr,* lit., day of Thor (Norse god)] : the 5th day of the week
thus \ˈt͟həs\ *adv* **1** : in this or that manner **2** : to this degree or extent : SO **3** : because of this or that : HENCE
¹thwack \ˈthwak\ *vb* : to strike with or as if with something flat or heavy
²thwack *n* : a heavy blow : WHACK
¹thwart \ˈthwo̊rt\ *vb* **1** : FOIL, BAFFLE **2** : BLOCK, DEFEAT ⟨~*ed* the attack⟩ ♦ ***Synonyms*** BALK, OUTWIT, FRUSTRATE
²thwart \ˈthwo̊rt, *naut often* ˈtho̊rt\ *adv* : ATHWART
³thwart *adj* : situated or placed across something else
⁴thwart *n* : a seat extending across a boat

thy \'thī\ *adj, archaic* : of, relating to, or done by or to thee or thyself

thyme \'tīm, 'thīm\ *n* [ME, fr. AF *time,* fr. L *thymum,* fr. Gk *thymon,* prob. fr. *thyein* to make a burnt offering, sacrifice] : a garden mint with small aromatic leaves used esp. in seasoning; *also* : its leaves so used

thy·mine \'thī-ˌmēn\ *n* : a pyrimidine base that is one of the four bases coding genetic information in the molecular chain of DNA

thy·mus \'thī-məs\ *n, pl* **thy·mus·es** : a glandular organ of the neck region that is composed largely of lymphoid tissue, functions esp. in the development of the immune system, and tends to atrophy in the adult

thy·ris·tor \thī-'ris-tər\ *n* : a semiconductor device that acts as a switch, rectifier, or voltage regulator

thy·roid \'thī-ˌrȯid\ *n* [NL *thyroides,* fr. Gk *thyreoeidēs* shield-shaped, thyroid, fr. *thyreos* shield shaped like a door, fr. *thyra* door] : a large 2-lobed endocrine gland that lies at the base of the neck and produces several iodine-containing hormones that affect growth, development, and metabolism — **thyroid** *also* **thy·roi·dal** \thī-'rȯi-dᵊl\ *adj*

thy·rox·ine *or* **thy·rox·in** \thī-'räk-ˌsēn, -sən\ *n* : an iodine-containing hormone that is produced by the thyroid gland, increases metabolic rate, and is used to treat thyroid disorders

thy·self \thī-'self\ *pron, archaic* : YOURSELF

Ti *symbol* titanium

ti·ara \tē-'er-ə, -'är-\ *n* **1** : a 3-tiered crown worn by the pope **2** : a decorative headband or semicircle for formal wear by women

Ti·bet·an \tə-'be-tᵊn\ *n* **1** : the language of the Tibetan people **2** : a native or inhabitant of Tibet — **Tibetan** *adj*

tib·ia \'ti-bē-ə\ *n, pl* **-i·ae** \-bē-ˌē\ *also* **-i·as** [L] : the inner of the two bones of the vertebrate hind or lower limb between the knee and the ankle

tic \'tik\ *n* : a local and habitual twitching of muscles esp. of the face

¹tick \'tik\ *n* : any of a large group of small bloodsucking arachnids

²tick *n* : the fabric case of a mattress or pillow; *also* : a mattress consisting of a tick and its filling

³tick *n* **1** : a light rhythmic audible tap or beat **2** : a small mark used to draw attention to or check something

⁴tick *vb* **1** : to make the sound of a tick or series of ticks **2** : to mark, count, or announce by or as if by ticking beats **3** : to mark or check with a tick **4** : to function as an operating mechanism : RUN

⁵tick *n, chiefly Brit* : CREDIT; *also* : a credit account

tick·er \'ti-kər\ *n* **1** : something (as a watch) that ticks **2** : a telegraph instrument that prints information (as stock prices) on paper tape **3** *slang* : HEART

ticker tape *n* : the paper ribbon on which a telegraphic ticker prints

¹tick·et \'ti-kət\ *n* [MF *etiquet, estiquette* notice attached to something, fr. MF dial. *estiquier* to attach, fr. MD *steken* to stick] **1** : CERTIFICATE, LICENSE, PERMIT; *esp* : a certificate or token showing that a fare or admission fee has been paid **2** : TAG, LABEL **3** : SLATE 4 **4** : a summons issued to a traffic offender

²ticket *vb* **1** : to attach a ticket to **2** : to furnish or serve with a ticket

tick·ing \'ti-kiŋ\ *n* : a strong fabric used in upholstering and as a mattress covering

tick·le \'ti-kəl\ *vb* **tick·led; tick·ling** **1** : to excite or stir up agreeably : PLEASE, AMUSE **2** : to have a tingling sensation **3** : to touch (as a body part) lightly so as to cause uneasiness, laughter, or spasmodic movements ⟨*tickled* her under the chin⟩ — **tickle** *n* — **tick·ler** *n*

tick·lish \-kə-lish\ *adj* **1** : OVERSENSITIVE, TOUCHY **2** : UNSTABLE ⟨a ~ foothold⟩ **3** : requiring delicate handling ⟨~ subject⟩ **4** : sensitive to tickling — **tick·lish·ly** *adv* — **tick·lish·ness** *n*

tidal wave *n* **1** : an unusually high sea wave that sometimes follows an earthquake **2** : an unusual rise of water alongshore due to strong winds

tid·bit \'tid-ˌbit\ *n* : a choice morsel

¹tide \'tīd\ *n* [ME, time, fr. OE *tīd*] **1** : the alternate rising and falling of the surface of the ocean **2** : something that fluctuates like the tides of the sea ⟨the ~ of public opinion⟩ — **tid·al** \'tī-dᵊl\ *adj*

²tide *vb* **tid·ed; tid·ing** : to carry through or help along as if by the tide ⟨a loan to ~ us over⟩

tide·land \'tīd-ˌland, -lənd\ *n* **1** : land overflowed during flood tide **2** : land under the ocean within a nation's territorial waters — often used in pl.

tide·wa·ter \-ˌwȯ-tər, -ˌwä-\ *n* **1** : water overflowing land at flood tide **2** : low-lying coastal land

tid·ings \'tī-diŋz\ *n pl* : NEWS, MESSAGE

¹ti·dy \'tī-dē\ *adj* **ti·di·er; -est** **1** : well ordered and cared for : NEAT **2** : LARGE, SUBSTANTIAL ⟨a ~ sum⟩ — **ti·di·ness** \'tī-dē-nəs\ *n*

²tidy *vb* **ti·died; ti·dy·ing** **1** : to put in order **2** : to make things tidy

³tidy *n, pl* **tidies** : a decorated covering used to protect the back or arms of a chair from wear or soil

¹tie \'tī\ *n* **1** : a line, ribbon, or cord used for fastening, uniting, or closing **2** : a structural element (as a beam or rod) holding two pieces together **3** : one of the cross supports to which railroad rails are fastened **4** : a connecting link : BOND ⟨family ~*s*⟩ **5** : an equality in number (as of votes or scores); *also* : an undecided or deadlocked contest **6** : NECKTIE

²tie *vb* **tied; ty·ing** *or* **tie·ing** **1** : to fasten, attach, or close by means of a tie **2** : to bring together firmly : UNITE **3** : to form a knot or bow in ⟨~ a scarf⟩ **4** : to restrain from freedom of action : CONSTRAIN **5** : to make or have an equal score with

tie·back \'tī-ˌbak\ *n* : a decorative strip

for draping a curtain to the side of a window

tie–dye·ing \ˈtī-ˌdī-iŋ\ *n* : a method of producing patterns in textiles by tying parts of the fabric so that they will not absorb the dye — **tie–dyed** \-ˌdīd\ *adj*

tie–in \ˈtī-ˌin\ *n* : CONNECTION

tier \ˈtir\ *n* : ROW, LAYER; *esp* : one of two or more rows arranged one above another — **tiered** \ˈtird\ *adj*

tie–rod \ˈtī-ˌräd\ *n* : a rod used as a connecting member or brace

tie–up \-ˌəp\ *n* **1** : a slowing or stopping of traffic or business **2** : CONNECTION

tiff \ˈtif\ *n* : a petty quarrel — **tiff** *vb*

Tif·fa·ny \ˈti-fə-nē\ *adj* : made of pieces of stained glass ⟨a ~ lamp⟩

ti·ger \ˈtī-gər\ *n* : a very large tawny black-striped Asian cat — **ti·ger·ish** *adj*

[1]**tight** \ˈtīt\ *adj* **1** : so close in structure as to prevent passage of a liquid or gas **2** : strongly fixed or held : SECURE **3** : TAUT **4** : fitting usu. too closely ⟨~ shoes⟩ **5** : set close together : COMPACT ⟨a ~ formation⟩ **6** : DIFFICULT, TRYING ⟨get in a ~ spot⟩ **7** : STINGY, MISERLY **8** : evenly contested : CLOSE **9** : INTOXICATED **10** : low in supply : hard to get ⟨money is ~⟩ — **tight·ly** *adv* — **tight·ness** *n*

[2]**tight** *adv* **1** : TIGHTLY, FIRMLY **2** : SOUNDLY ⟨sleep ~⟩

tight·en \ˈtī-tᵊn\ *vb* : to make or become tight

tight·fist·ed \ˈtīt-ˈfis-təd\ *adj* : STINGY

tight·rope \-ˌrōp\ *n* : a taut rope or wire for acrobats to perform on

tights \ˈtīts\ *n pl* : skintight garments covering the body esp. below the waist; *also, Brit* : PANTY HOSE

tight·wad \ˈtīt-ˌwäd\ *n* : a stingy person

ti·gress \ˈtī-grəs\ *n* : a female tiger

ti·la·pia \tə-ˈlä-pē-ə, -ˈlā-\ *n, pl* **tilapia** *also* **ti·la·pi·as** : any of numerous chiefly African freshwater fishes widely raised for food

til·de \ˈtil-də\ *n* [Sp, fr. ML *titulus* tittle] : a mark ˜ placed esp. over the letter *n* (as in Spanish *señor* sir) to denote the sound \n^{y}\ or over vowels (as in Portuguese *irmã* sister) to indicate nasal quality

[1]**tile** \ˈtī(-ə)l\ *n* **1** : a flat or curved piece of fired clay, stone, or concrete used for roofs, floors, or walls; *also* : a pipe of earthenware or concrete used for a drain **2** : a thin piece (as of linoleum) used for covering walls or floors — **til·ing** \ˈtī-liŋ\ *n*

[2]**tile** *vb* **tiled; til·ing** : to cover with tiles — **til·er** *n*

[1]**till** \ˈtil\ *prep or conj* : UNTIL

[2]**till** *vb* : to work by plowing, sowing, and raising crops : CULTIVATE — **till·able** *adj*

[3]**till** *n* : DRAWER; *esp* : a money drawer in a store or bank

till·age \ˈti-lij\ *n* **1** : the work of tilling land **2** : cultivated land

[1]**til·ler** \ˈti-lər\ *n* [OE *telgor, telgra* twig, shoot] : a sprout or stalk esp. from the base or lower part of a plant

[2]**till·er** \ˈti-lər\ *n* : one that tills

[3]**til·ler** \ˈti-lər\ *n* [ME *tiler* stock of a crossbow, tiller, fr. AF *teiler* stock of a crossbow] : a lever used for turning a boat's rudder from side to side

[1]**tilt** \ˈtilt\ *n* **1** : a contest in which two combatants charging usu. with lances try to unhorse each other : JOUST; *also* : a tournament of tilts **2** : a verbal contest : DISPUTE **3** : a sloping surface : SLANT

[2]**tilt** *vb* **1** : to move or shift so as to incline : TIP **2** : to engage in or as if in combat with lances : JOUST, ATTACK

tilth \ˈtilth\ *n* **1** : TILLAGE 2 **2** : the state of a soil esp. in relation to the suitability of its particle size and structure for growing crops

Tim *abbr* Timothy

tim·ber \ˈtim-bər\ *n* [ME, fr. OE, building, wood] **1** : growing trees or their wood — often used interjectionally to warn of a falling tree **2** : wood for use in making something **3** : a usu. large squared or dressed piece of wood

tim·bered \ˈtim-bərd\ *adj* : having walls framed by exposed timbers

tim·ber·land \ˈtim-bər-ˌland\ *n* : wooded land

tim·ber·line \ˈtim-bər-ˌlīn\ *n* : the upper limit of tree growth in mountains or high latitudes

timber rattlesnake *n* : a widely distributed rattlesnake of the eastern U.S.

timber wolf *n* : GRAY WOLF

tim·bre *also* **tim·ber** \ˈtam-bər, ˈtim-\ *n* [F, fr. MF, bell struck by a hammer, fr. OF, drum, fr. MGk *tymbanon* kettledrum, fr. Gk *tympanon*] : the distinctive quality given to a sound by its overtones

tim·brel \ˈtim-brəl\ *n* : a small hand drum or tambourine

[1]**time** \ˈtīm\ *n* **1** : a period during which an action, process, or condition exists or continues ⟨gone a long ~⟩ **2** : LEISURE ⟨found ~ to read⟩ **3** : a point or period when something occurs : OCCASION ⟨the last ~ we met⟩ **4** : a set or customary moment or hour for something to occur ⟨arrived on ~⟩ **5** : AGE, ERA **6** : state of affairs : CONDITIONS ⟨hard ~*s*⟩ **7** : a rate of speed : TEMPO **8** : a moment, hour, day, or year as indicated by a clock or calendar ⟨what ~ is it⟩ **9** : a system of reckoning time ⟨solar ~⟩ **10** : one of a series of recurring instances; *also, pl* : added or accumulated quantities or examples ⟨five ~*s* greater⟩ **11** : a person's experience during a particular period ⟨had a good ~⟩ **12** : the hours or days of one's work; *also* : an hourly pay rate ⟨straight ~⟩ **13** : TIME-OUT 1

[2]**time** *vb* **timed; tim·ing** **1** : to arrange or set the time of : SCHEDULE ⟨~*s* his calls conveniently⟩ **2** : to set the tempo or duration of ⟨~ a performance⟩ **3** : to cause to keep time with **4** : to determine or record the time, duration, or rate of ⟨~ a sprinter⟩ — **tim·er** *n*

time bomb *n* **1** : a bomb so made as to explode at a predetermined time **2** : something with a potentially dangerous delayed reaction

time clock *n* : a clock that records the time workers arrive and depart
time frame *n* : a period of time esp. with respect to some action or project
time–hon·ored \ˈtīm-ˌä-nərd\ *adj* : honored because of age or long usage
time·keep·er \-ˌkē-pər\ *n* **1** : a clerk who keeps records of the time worked by employees **2** : one appointed to mark and announce the time in an athletic game or contest
time·less \-ləs\ *adj* **1** : ETERNAL **2** : not limited or affected by time ⟨~ works of art⟩ — **time·less·ly** *adv* — **time·less·ness** *n*
time·ly \-lē\ *adj* **time·li·er; -est** **1** : coming early or at the right time ⟨a ~ decision⟩ ⟨~ payment⟩ **2** : appropriate to the time ⟨a ~ book⟩ — **time·li·ness** *n*
time–out \ˈtīm-ˈau̇t\ *n* **1** : a brief suspension of activity esp. in an athletic game **2** : a quiet period used esp. as a disciplinary measure for a child
time·piece \-ˌpēs\ *n* : a device (as a clock) to show the passage of time
times \ˈtīmz\ *prep* : multiplied by ⟨2 ~ 2 is 4⟩
time–shar·ing \ˈtīm-ˌsher-iŋ\ *n* **1** : simultaneous use of a computer by many users **2** *or* **time–share** \-ˌsher\ : joint ownership or rental of a vacation lodging by several persons with each taking turns using the place
times sign *n* : the symbol × used to indicate multiplication
time·ta·ble \ˈtīm-ˌtā-bəl\ *n* **1** : a table of the departure and arrival times (as of trains) **2** : a schedule showing a planned order or sequence
time warp *n* : an anomaly, discontinuity, or suspension held to occur in the progress of time
time·worn \-ˌwȯrn\ *adj* **1** : worn by time **2** : HACKNEYED, STALE ⟨a ~ joke⟩
tim·id \ˈti-məd\ *adj* : lacking in courage or self-confidence : FEARFUL — **ti·mid·i·ty** \tə-ˈmi-də-tē\ *n* — **tim·id·ly** *adv*
tim·o·rous \ˈti-mə-rəs\ *adj* : of a timid disposition : AFRAID ⟨a ~ kitten⟩ — **tim·o·rous·ly** *adv* — **tim·o·rous·ness** *n*
tim·o·thy \ˈti-mə-thē\ *n* : a perennial grass with long cylindrical spikes widely grown for hay in the U.S.
Tim·o·thy \ˈti-mə-thē\ *n* — see BIBLE table
tim·pa·ni \ˈtim-pə-nē\ *n sing or pl* [It] : a set of kettledrums played by one performer in an orchestra — **tim·pa·nist** \-nist\ *n*
[1]**tin** \ˈtin\ *n* **1** : a soft white crystalline metallic chemical element malleable at ordinary temperatures that is used esp. in solders and alloys **2** : a container (as a can) made of metal (as tinplate)
[2]**tin** *vb* **tinned; tin·ning** **1** : to cover or plate with tin **2** : to pack in tins
TIN *abbr* taxpayer identification number
tinct \ˈtiŋkt\ *n* : TINCTURE, TINGE
[1]**tinc·ture** \ˈtiŋk-chər\ *n* **1** *archaic* : a substance that colors **2** : a slight admixture : TRACE **3** : an alcoholic solution of a medicinal substance ♦ *Synonyms* TOUCH, SUGGESTION, SUSPICION, TINGE
[2]**tincture** *vb* **tinc·tured; tinc·tur·ing** **1** : COLOR, TINGE **2** : AFFECT
tin·der \ˈtin-dər\ *n* **1** : a very flammable substance used as kindling **2** : something serving to incite or inflame
tin·der·box \ˈtin-dər-ˌbäks\ *n* **1** : a metal box for holding tinder and usu. flint and steel for striking a spark **2** : a highly flammable object or place
tine \ˈtīn\ *n* : a slender pointed part (as of a fork or an antler) : PRONG
tin·foil \ˈtin-ˌfȯi(-ə)l\ *n* : a thin metal sheeting usu. of aluminum or tin-lead alloy
[1]**tinge** \ˈtinj\ *vb* **tinged; tinge·ing** *or* **ting·ing** **1** : to color slightly : TINT **2** : to affect or modify esp. with a slight odor or taste
[2]**tinge** *n* : a slight coloring, flavor, or quality : TRACE ⟨a ~ of color⟩ ⟨a ~ of regret⟩ ♦ *Synonyms* TOUCH, SUGGESTION, SUSPICION, TINCTURE, SOUPÇON
tin·gle \ˈtiŋ-gəl\ *vb* **tin·gled; tin·gling** **1** : to feel a prickling or thrilling sensation **2** : TINKLE — **tingle** *n*
[1]**tin·ker** \ˈtiŋ-kər\ *n* **1** : a usu. itinerant mender of household utensils **2** : an unskillful mender : BUNGLER
[2]**tinker** *vb* : to repair or adjust something in an unskillful or experimental manner — **tin·ker·er** *n*
[1]**tin·kle** \ˈtiŋ-kəl\ *vb* **tin·kled; tin·kling** : to make or cause to make a tinkle
[2]**tinkle** *n* : a series of short high ringing or clinking sounds
tin·ni·tus \ˈtī-nə-təs, tə-ˈnī-təs\ *n* : a sensation of noise (as ringing or roaring) in the ears
tin·ny \ˈti-nē\ *adj* **tin·ni·er; -est** **1** : abounding in or yielding tin **2** : resembling tin; *also* : LIGHT, CHEAP **3** : thin in tone ⟨a ~ voice⟩ — **tin·ni·ly** \-nə-lē\ *adv* — **tin·ni·ness** \-nē-nəs\ *n*
tin·plate \ˈtin-ˈplāt\ *n* : thin sheet iron or steel coated with tin — **tin–plate** *vb*
tin·sel \ˈtin-səl\ *n* [ME *tyneseyle* cloth interwoven with metallic thread, prob. fr. AF *tencelé*, pp. of *tenceler, estenceler* to sparkle] **1** : threads, strips, or sheets of metal, paper, or plastic used to produce a glittering appearance **2** : something superficially attractive but of little worth
tin·smith \ˈtin-ˌsmith\ *n* : one that works with sheet metal (as tinplate)
[1]**tint** \ˈtint\ *n* **1** : a slight or pale coloration : HUE **2** : any of various shades of a color
[2]**tint** *vb* : to impart a tint to : COLOR
tin·tin·nab·u·la·tion \ˌtin-tə-ˌna-byə-ˈlā-shən\ *n* **1** : the ringing of bells **2** : a tinkling or jingling sound as if of bells
tin·ware \ˈtin-ˌwer\ *n* : articles and esp. utensils made of tinplate
ti·ny \ˈtī-nē\ *adj* **ti·ni·er; -est** : very small : MINUTE ♦ *Synonyms* MINIATURE, DIMINUTIVE, WEE, LILLIPUTIAN
[1]**tip** \ˈtip\ *vb* **tipped; tip·ping** **1** : OVERTURN, UPSET **2** : LEAN, SLANT; *also* : to raise and tilt forward ⟨*tipped* his hat⟩
[2]**tip** *n* : the act or an instance of tipping

³tip *vb* **tipped; tip·ping 1** : to furnish with a tip **2** : to cover or adorn the tip of

⁴tip *n* **1** : the usu. pointed end of something **2** : a small piece or part serving as an end, cap, or point

⁵tip *n* : a light touch or blow

⁶tip *vb* **tipped; tip·ping** : to strike lightly : TAP

⁷tip *n* : a piece of advice or expert or confidential information : HINT

⁸tip *vb* **tipped; tip·ping** : to impart a piece of information about or to

⁹tip *vb* **tipped; tip·ping** : to give a gratuity to — **tip·per** *n*

¹⁰tip *n* : a gift or small sum given for a service performed or anticipated

tip–off \ˈtip-ˌȯf\ *n* : WARNING, TIP

tip·pet \ˈti-pət\ *n* : a long scarf or shoulder cape

tipping point *n* : the critical point in a situation or process beyond which a significant effect takes place

tip·ple \ˈti-pəl\ *vb* **tip·pled; tip·pling** : to drink intoxicating liquor esp. habitually or excessively — **tipple** *n* — **tip·pler** *n*

tip·ster \ˈtip-stər\ *n* : a person who gives or sells tips esp. for gambling

tip·sy \ˈtip-sē\ *adj* **tip·si·er; -est** : unsteady or foolish from the effects of alcohol — **tip·si·ly** \-sə-lē\ *adv* — **tip·si·ness** \-sē-nəs\ *n*

¹tip·toe \ˈtip-ˌtō\ *n* : the position of being balanced on the balls of the feet and toes with the heels raised; *also* : the ends of the toes

²tiptoe *adv or adj* : on or as if on tiptoe

³tiptoe *vb* **tip·toed; tip·toe·ing** : to walk or proceed on or as if on tiptoe ⟨~ around the issue⟩

¹tip–top \ˈtip-ˈtäp\ *n* : the highest point

²tip–top *adj* : EXCELLENT, FIRST-RATE

ti·rade \ˈtī-ˌrād\ *n* [F, shot, tirade, fr. MF, fr. It *tirata,* fr. *tirare* to draw, shoot] : a prolonged speech of abuse or condemnation

tir·a·mi·su \ˌtir-ə-ˈmē-sü, -mē-ˈsü\ *n* [It *tiramisù*] : a dessert made with ladyfingers, mascarpone, and espresso

¹tire \ˈtī(-ə)r\ *vb* **tired; tir·ing 1** : to make or become weary : FATIGUE **2** : to wear out the patience of : BORE

²tire *n* **1** : a metal hoop that forms the tread of a wheel **2** : a rubber cushion usu. containing compressed air that encircles a wheel (as of a bike)

tired *adj* **1** : WEARY, FATIGUED **2** : HACKNEYED — **tired·ness** *n*

tire·less \ˈtī(-ə)r-ləs\ *adj* : not tiring : UNTIRING, INDEFATIGABLE ⟨~ workers⟩ — **tire·less·ly** *adv* — **tire·less·ness** *n*

tire·some \-səm\ *adj* : tending to bore : WEARISOME, TEDIOUS ⟨~ lectures⟩ — **tire·some·ly** *adv* — **tire·some·ness** *n*

ti·ro *chiefly Brit var of* TYRO

tis·sue \ˈti-shü\ *n* [ME *tysshewe, tyssew,* a rich fabric, fr. AF, fr. *tistre* to weave, fr. L *texere*] **1** : a fine lightweight often sheer fabric **2** : NETWORK, WEB ⟨a ~ of lies⟩ **3** : a soft absorbent paper **4** : a mass or layer of cells forming a basic structural material of an animal or plant

¹tit \ˈtit\ *n* : TEAT

²tit *n* : any of various small plump Old World songbirds related to the titmice

Tit *abbr* Titus

ti·tan \ˈtī-tᵊn\ *n* **1** *cap* : one of a family of giants overthrown by the gods in Greek mythology **2** : one gigantic in size or power ⟨a media ~⟩

ti·tan·ic \tī-ˈta-nik\ *adj* : enormous in size, force, or power ♦ ***Synonyms*** IMMENSE, GIGANTIC, GIANT, COLOSSAL, MAMMOTH

ti·ta·ni·um \tī-ˈtā-nē-əm\ *n* : a gray light strong metallic chemical element used esp. in alloys

titbit *var of* TIDBIT

tithe \ˈtīth\ *n* [ME, fr. OE *teogotha* tenth] : a 10th part paid or given esp. for the support of a church — **tithe** *vb* — **tith·er** *n*

tit·il·late \ˈti-tᵊl-ˌāt\ *vb* **-lat·ed; -lat·ing 1** : to excite pleasurably **2** : TICKLE 3 — **tit·il·la·tion** \ˌti-tᵊl-ˈā-shən\ *n*

ti·tle \ˈtī-tᵊl\ *n* **1** : CLAIM, RIGHT; *esp* : a legal right to the ownership of property **2** : the distinguishing name of a written, filmed, or musical production or a work of art **3** : an appellation of honor, rank, or office **4** : CHAMPIONSHIP ♦ ***Synonyms*** DESIGNATION, DENOMINATION, APPELLATION

ti·tled \ˈtī-tᵊld\ *adj* : having a title esp. of nobility

title page *n* : a page of a book bearing the title and usu. the names of the author and publisher

tit·mouse \ˈtit-ˌmau̇s\ *n, pl* **tit·mice** \-ˌmīs\ : any of several small long-tailed No. American songbirds related to the chickadees

ti·tra·tion \tī-ˈtrā-shən\ *n* : a process of finding the concentration of a solution (as of an acid) by adding small portions of a second solution of known concentration (as of a base) to a fixed amount of the first until an expected change (as in color) occurs

tit·ter \ˈti-tər\ *vb* : to laugh in an affected or in a nervous or half-suppressed manner : GIGGLE — **titter** *n*

tit·tle \ˈti-tᵊl\ *n* : a tiny part

tit·tle–tat·tle \ˈti-tᵊl-ˌta-tᵊl\ *n* : idle talk : GOSSIP — **tittle–tattle** *vb*

tit·u·lar \ˈti-chə-lər\ *adj* **1** : existing in title only : NOMINAL ⟨~ ruler⟩ **2** : of, relating to, or bearing a title ⟨~ role⟩

Ti·tus \ˈtī-təs\ *n* — see BIBLE table

ti·yin \ˈtē-ēn\ *n, pl* **tiyin** *or* **tiyins** — see *sum* at MONEY table

ti·yn \ˈtē-in\ *n* — see *tenge* at MONEY table

tiz·zy \ˈti-zē\ *n, pl* **tizzies** : a highly excited and distracted state of mind

tk *abbr* **1** tank **2** truck

TKO \ˌtē-ˌkā-ˈō\ *n* [*t*echnical *k*nock*o*ut] : the termination of a boxing match when a boxer is declared unable to continue the fight

tkt *abbr* ticket

Tl *symbol* thallium

TLC *abbr* tender loving care

T lymphocyte *n* : T CELL

Tm *symbol* thulium
TM *abbr* trademark
T–man \ˈtē-ˌman\ *n* : a special agent of the U.S. Treasury Department
TMI *abbr* too much information
tn *abbr* **1** ton **2** town
TN *abbr* Tennessee
tng *abbr* training
tnpk *abbr* turnpike
TNT \ˌtē-(ˌ)en-ˈtē\ *n* : a flammable toxic compound used as a high explosive and in chemical synthesis
[1]**to** \tə, ˈtü\ *prep* **1** : in the direction of and reaching ⟨drove ~ town⟩ **2** : in the direction of : TOWARD **3** : ON, AGAINST ⟨apply salve ~ a burn⟩ **4** : as far as ⟨can pay up ~ a dollar⟩ **5** : so as to become or bring about ⟨beaten ~ death⟩ ⟨broken ~ pieces⟩ **6** : BEFORE ⟨it's five minutes ~ six⟩ **7** : UNTIL ⟨from May ~ December⟩ **8** : fitting or being a part of : FOR ⟨key ~ the lock⟩ **9** : with the accompaniment of ⟨sing ~ the music⟩ **10** : in relation or comparison with ⟨similar ~ that one⟩ ⟨won 10 ~ 6⟩ **11** : in accordance with ⟨add salt ~ taste⟩ **12** : within the range of ⟨~ my knowledge⟩ **13** : contained, occurring, or included in ⟨two pints ~ a quart⟩ **14** : as regards ⟨agreeable ~ everyone⟩ **15** : affecting as the receiver or beneficiary ⟨whispered ~ her⟩ ⟨gave it ~ me⟩ **16** : for no one except ⟨a room ~ myself⟩ **17** : into the action of ⟨we got ~ talking⟩ **18** — used for marking the following verb as an infinitive ⟨wants ~ go⟩ and often used by itself at the end of a clause in place of an infinitive suggested by the preceding context ⟨goes to town whenever he wants ~⟩ ⟨can leave if you'd like ~⟩
[2]**to** \ˈtü\ *adv* **1** : in a direction toward ⟨run ~ and fro⟩ **2** : into contact esp. with the frame of a door ⟨the door slammed ~⟩ **3** : to the matter in hand ⟨fell ~ and ate heartily⟩ **4** : to a state of consciousness or awareness ⟨he came ~ hours later⟩
TO *abbr* turn over
toad \ˈtōd\ *n* : any of numerous tailless leaping amphibians differing typically from the related frogs in having a shorter stockier build, rough dry warty skin, and less aquatic habits
toad·stool \-ˌstül\ *n* : MUSHROOM; *esp* : one that is poisonous or inedible
toady \ˈtō-dē\ *n, pl* **toad·ies** : a person who flatters in the hope of gaining favors : SYCOPHANT — **toady** *vb*
to–and–fro \ˌtü-ən-ˈfrō\ *adj* : forward and backward — **to–and–fro** *n*
[1]**toast** \ˈtōst\ *vb* **1** : to warm thoroughly **2** : to make (as bread) crisp, hot, and brown by heat **3** : to become toasted
[2]**toast** *n* **1** : sliced toasted bread **2** : someone or something in whose honor persons drink **3** : an act of drinking in honor of a toast
[3]**toast** *vb* : to propose or drink to as a toast
toast·er \ˈtō-stər\ *n* : an electrical appliance for toasting
toaster oven *n* : a portable electrical appliance that bakes, broils, and toasts
toast·mas·ter \ˈtōst-ˌmas-tər\ *n* : a person who presides at a banquet and introduces the after-dinner speakers
toast·mis·tress \-ˌmis-trəs\ *n* : a woman who acts as toastmaster
toasty \ˈtō-stē\ *adj* **toast·i·er; -est** : pleasantly warm
Tob *abbr* Tobit
to·bac·co \tə-ˈba-kō\ *n, pl* **-cos** [Sp *tabaco*] **1** : a tall broad-leaved herb related to the potato; *also* : its leaves prepared for smoking or chewing or as snuff **2** : manufactured tobacco products; *also* : smoking as a practice
to·bac·co·nist \tə-ˈba-kə-nist\ *n* : a dealer in tobacco
To·bi·as \tō-ˈbī-əs\ *n* : TOBIT
To·bit \ˈtō-bət\ *n* — see BIBLE table
[1]**to·bog·gan** \tə-ˈbä-gən\ *n* : a long flat-bottomed light sled made of thin boards curved up at one end
[2]**toboggan** *vb* **1** : to coast on or as if on a toboggan **2** : to decline suddenly (as in value) — **to·bog·gan·er** *n*
toc·sin \ˈtäk-sən\ *n* **1** : an alarm bell **2** : a warning signal
[1]**to·day** \tə-ˈdā\ *adv* **1** : on or for this day **2** : at the present time
[2]**today** *n* : the present day, time, or age
tod·dle \ˈtäd-ᵊl\ *vb* **tod·dled; tod·dling** : to walk with short tottering steps in the manner of a young child — **toddle** *n* — **tod·dler** *n*
tod·dy \ˈtä-dē\ *n, pl* **toddies** [Hindi & Urdu *tāṛī* juice of a palm, fr. *tāṛ* a palm, fr. Skt *tāla*] : a drink made of liquor, sugar, spices, and hot water
to–do \tə-ˈdü\ *n, pl* **to–dos** \-ˈdüz\ : BUSTLE, STIR, FUSS
[1]**toe** \ˈtō\ *n* **1** : one of the jointed parts of the front end of the vertebrate foot **2** : the front part of a foot or hoof
[2]**toe** *vb* **toed; toe·ing** : to touch, reach, or drive with the toes
toea \ˈtȯi-ə\ *n* — see *kina* at MONEY table
toe·hold \ˈtō-ˌhōld\ *n* **1** : a place of support for the toes **2** : a slight footing
toe·nail \ˈtō-ˌnāl\ *n* : a nail of a toe
tof·fee *or* **tof·fy** \ˈtȯ-fē, ˈtä-\ *n, pl* **toffees** *or* **toffies** : candy of brittle but tender texture made by boiling sugar and butter together
to·fu \ˈtō-(ˌ)fü\ *n* [Jp *tōfu*] : a soft white food product made from soybeans
tog \ˈtäg, ˈtȯg\ *vb* **togged; tog·ging** : to put togs on : DRESS
to·ga \ˈtō-gə\ *n* : the loose outer garment worn in public by citizens of ancient Rome — **to·gaed** \-gəd\ *adj*
[1]**to·geth·er** \tə-ˈge-t͟hər\ *adv* **1** : in or into one place or group **2** : in or into contact or association ⟨mix ~⟩ **3** : at one time : SIMULTANEOUSLY ⟨talk and work ~⟩ **4** : in succession ⟨for days ~⟩ **5** : in or into harmony or coherence ⟨get ~ on a plan⟩ **6** : as a group : JOINTLY — **to·geth·er·ness** *n*
[2]**together** *adj* : composed in mind or manner

together with *prep* : in addition to : in association with
tog·gery \ˈtä-gə-rē, ˈtȯ-\ *n* : CLOTHING
tog·gle \ˈtä-gəl\ *vb* : to switch between two options esp. of an electronic device
toggle switch *n* : an electric switch operated by pushing a projecting lever through a small arc
togs \ˈtägz, ˈtȯgz\ *n pl* : CLOTHING; *esp* : clothes for a specified use ⟨riding ~⟩
[1]**toil** \ˈtȯi(-ə)l\ *n* **1** : laborious effort **2** : long fatiguing labor : DRUDGERY — **toil·ful** \-fəl\ *adj* — **toil·some** *adj*
[2]**toil** *vb* [ME, to argue, struggle, fr. AF *toiller* to make dirty, fight, wrangle, fr. L *tudiculare* to crush, grind, fr. *tudicula* machine for crushing olives, dim. of *tudes* hammer] **1** : to work hard and long **2** : to proceed with great effort : PLOD — **toil·er** *n*
[3]**toil** *n* [ME *toile* cloth, net, fr. OF *teile,* fr. L *tela* cloth on a loom] : NET, TRAP — usu. used in pl. ⟨caught in the ~*s* of the law⟩
toi·let \ˈtȯi-lət\ *n* **1** : the act or process of dressing and grooming oneself **2** : BATHROOM **3** : a fixture for use in urinating and defecating; *esp* : one consisting essentially of a water-flushed bowl and seat — **toilet** *vb*
toilet paper *n* : an absorbent paper for drying or cleaning oneself after defecation and urination
toi·let·ry \ˈtȯi-lə-trē\ *n, pl* **-ries** : an article or preparation used in cleaning or grooming oneself — usu. used in pl.
toi·lette \twä-ˈlet\ *n* **1** : TOILET 1 **2** : formal attire; *also* : a particular costume
toilet training *n* : the process of training a child to control bladder and bowel movements and to use the toilet — **toilet train** *vb*
toil·worn \ˈtȯi(-ə)l-ˌwōrn\ *adj* : showing the effects of toil
To·kay \tō-ˈkā\ *n* : naturally sweet wine from Hungary
toke \ˈtōk\ *n, slang* : a puff on a marijuana cigarette or pipe
[1]**to·ken** \ˈtō-kən\ *n* **1** : an outward sign **2** : SYMBOL, EMBLEM **3** : SOUVENIR, KEEPSAKE **4** : a small part representing the whole **5** : a piece resembling a coin issued as money or for use by a particular group on specified terms
[2]**token** *adj* **1** : done or given as a token esp. in partial fulfillment of an obligation **2** : representing only a symbolic effort : MINIMAL, PERFUNCTORY
to·ken·ism \ˈtō-kə-ˌni-zəm\ *n* : the policy or practice of making only a symbolic effort (as to desegregate)
tolar \ˈtō-lär\ *n, pl* **to·lar·ja** \ˈtō-lär-ˌyä\ *or* **to·lar·jev** \ˈtō-lär-ˌyev\ *or* **tolars** : the basic monetary unit of Slovenia from 1992 to 2007
told *past and past part of* TELL
tole \ˈtōl\ *n* : sheet metal and esp. tinplate for use in domestic and ornamental wares
tol·er·a·ble \ˈtä-lə-rə-bəl\ *adj* **1** : capable of being borne or endured **2** : moderately good — **tol·er·a·bly** \-blē\ *adv*
tol·er·ance \ˈtä-lə-rəns\ *n* **1** : the act or practice of tolerating; *esp* : sympathy or indulgence for beliefs or practices differing from one's own **2** : the allowable deviation from a standard (as of size) **3** : the body's capacity to become less responsive over time to something (as a drug used repeatedly) — **tol·er·ant** *adj* — **tol·er·ant·ly** *adv*
tol·er·ate \ˈtä-lə-ˌrāt\ *vb* **-at·ed; -at·ing** **1** : to exhibit physiological tolerance for (as a drug) **2** : to allow to be or to be done without hindrance ♦ ***Synonyms*** ABIDE, BEAR, SUFFER, STAND, BROOK — **tol·er·a·tion** \ˌtä-lə-ˈrā-shən\ *n*
[1]**toll** \ˈtōl\ *n* **1** : a tax paid for a privilege (as for passing over a bridge) **2** : a charge for a service (as for a long-distance telephone call) **3** : the cost in life, health, loss, or suffering
[2]**toll** *vb* **1** : to cause the slow regular sounding of (a bell) esp. by pulling a rope **2** : to give signal of : SOUND **3** : to sound with slow measured strokes **4** : to announce by tolling
[3]**toll** *n* : the sound of a tolling bell
toll·booth \ˈtōl-ˌbüth\ *n* : a booth where tolls are paid
toll·gate \-ˌgāt\ *n* : a point where vehicles stop to pay a toll
toll·house \-ˌhau̇s\ *n* : a house or booth where tolls are paid
tol·u·ene \ˈtäl-yə-ˌwēn\ *n* : a liquid hydrocarbon used esp. as a solvent
tom \ˈtäm\ *n* : the male of various animals (as a cat or turkey)
[1]**tom·a·hawk** \ˈtä-mə-ˌhȯk\ *n* : a light ax used as a missile and as a hand weapon esp. by Indigenous people of No. America
[2]**tomahawk** *vb* : to strike or kill with a tomahawk
to·ma·til·lo \ˌtō-mə-ˈtē-(ˌ)yō\ *n, pl* **-los** : a small round usu. pale green edible fruit of a Mexican herb related to the tomato; *also* : this herb
to·ma·to \tə-ˈmā-tō, -ˈmä-\ *n, pl* **-toes** [alter. of earlier *tomate,* fr. Sp, fr. Nahuatl *tomatl*] : a usu. large, rounded, and red or yellow pulpy edible berry of a widely grown tropical herb related to the potato; *also* : this herb
tomb \ˈtüm\ *n* **1** : a place of burial : GRAVE **2** : a house, chamber, or vault for the dead — **tomb** *vb*
tom·boy \ˈtäm-ˌbȯi\ *n* : a girl who behaves in a manner usu. considered boyish — **tom·boy·ish** *adj*
tomb·stone \ˈtüm-ˌstōn\ *n* : a stone marking a grave
tom·cat \ˈtäm-ˌkat\ *n* : a male domestic cat
Tom Col·lins \ˈtäm-ˈkä-lənz\ *n* : a tall iced drink with a base of gin
tome \ˈtōm\ *n* : BOOK; *esp* : a large or weighty one
tom·fool·ery \täm-ˈfü-lə-rē\ *n* : playful or foolish behavior
tom·my gun \ˈtä-mē-ˌgən\ *n* : SUBMACHINE GUN — **tommy–gun** *vb*
to·mog·ra·phy \tō-ˈmä-grə-fē\ *n* : a meth-

od of producing a three-dimensional image of the internal structures of a solid object (as the human body or the earth) — **to·mo·graph·ic** \ˌtō-mə-ˈgra-fik\ *adj*

to·mor·row \tə-ˈmär-ō\ *adv* : on or for the day after today — **tomorrow** *n*

tom–tom \ˈtäm-ˌtäm\ *n* : a small-headed drum beaten with the hands

ton \ˈtən\ *n, pl* **tons** *also* **ton** **1** — see WEIGHT table **2** : a unit equal to the volume of a long ton weight of seawater used in reckoning the displacement of ships and equal to 35 cubic feet

to·nal·i·ty \tō-ˈna-lə-tē\ *n, pl* **-ties** : tonal quality

[1]**tone** \ˈtōn\ *n* [ME, fr. L *tonus* tension, tone, fr. Gk *tonos,* lit., act of stretching; fr. the dependence of the pitch of a musical string on its tension] **1** : vocal or musical sound; *esp* : sound quality **2** : a sound of definite pitch **3** : WHOLE STEP **4** : accent or inflection expressive of an emotion **5** : the pitch of a word often used to express differences of meaning **6** : style or manner of expression **7** : color quality; *also* : SHADE, TINT **8** : the effect in painting of light and shade together with color **9** : healthy and vigorous condition of a living body or bodily part; *also* : the state of partial contraction characteristic of normal muscle **10** : general character, quality, or trend ♦ ***Synonyms*** ATMOSPHERE, FEELING, MOOD, VEIN — **ton·al** \ˈtō-nᵊl\ *adj*

[2]**tone** *vb* **toned; ton·ing** **1** : to give a particular intonation or inflection to **2** : to impart tone to **3** : SOFTEN, MELLOW ⟨~ down your language⟩ **4** : to harmonize in color : BLEND

tone·arm *n* : the movable part of a record player that carries the pickup and the needle

toney *var of* TONY

tong \ˈtäŋ, ˈtȯŋ\ *n* : a Chinese secret society in the U.S.

tongs \ˈtäŋz, ˈtȯŋz\ *n pl* : a grasping device consisting of two pieces joined at one end by a pivot or hinged like scissors — **tong** *vb*

[1]**tongue** \ˈtəŋ\ *n* **1** : a fleshy movable process of the floor of the mouth used in tasting and in taking and swallowing food and in humans as a speech organ **2** : the flesh of a tongue (as of the ox) used as food **3** : the power of communication **4** : LANGUAGE 1 **5** : manner or quality of utterance; *also* : intended meaning **6** : ecstatic usu. unintelligible utterance accompanying religious excitation — usu. used in pl. **7** : something resembling an animal's tongue esp. in being elongated and fastened at one end only — **tongued** \ˈtəŋd\ *adj* — **tongue·less** *adj*

[2]**tongue** *vb* **tongued; tongu·ing** **1** : to touch or lick with the tongue **2** : to articulate notes on a wind instrument

tongue–in–cheek *adj* : characterized by insincerity, irony, or whimsical exaggeration — **tongue in cheek** *adv*

tongue–lash \ˈtəŋ-ˌlash\ *vb* : CHIDE, REPROVE — **tongue–lash·ing** \-iŋ\ *n*

tongue–tied \-ˌtīd\ *adj* : unable or disinclined to speak clearly or freely (as from shyness or a tongue impairment)

tongue twister *n* : an utterance that is difficult to articulate because of a succession of similar consonants

[1]**ton·ic** \ˈtä-nik\ *adj* **1** : of, relating to, or producing a healthy physical or mental condition : INVIGORATING **2** : relating to or based on the 1st tone of a scale — **to·nic·i·ty** \tō-ˈni-sə-tē\ *n*

[2]**tonic** *n* **1** : the 1st degree of a musical scale **2** : something that invigorates, restores, or refreshes

tonic water *n* : a carbonated beverage flavored with a bit of quinine, lemon, and lime

[1]**to·night** \tə-ˈnīt\ *adv* : on this present night or the coming night

[2]**tonight** *n* : the present or the coming night

ton·nage \ˈtə-nij\ *n* **1** : a duty on ships based on tons carried **2** : ships in terms of the number of tons registered or carried **3** : total weight in tons shipped, carried, or mined

ton·sil \ˈtän-səl\ *n* : either of a pair of oval masses of lymphoid tissue that lie one on each side of the throat at the back of the mouth

ton·sil·lec·to·my \ˌtän-sə-ˈlek-tə-mē\ *n, pl* **-mies** : the surgical removal of the tonsils

ton·sil·li·tis \-ˈlī-təs\ *n* : inflammation of the tonsils

ton·so·ri·al \tän-ˈsȯr-ē-əl\ *adj* : of or relating to a barber or a barber's work

ton·sure \ˈtän-chər\ *n* [ME, fr. AF, ML *tonsura,* fr. L, act of shearing, fr. *tonsus,* pp. of *tondēre* to shear] **1** : the rite of admission to the clerical state by the clipping or shaving of the head **2** : the shaven crown or patch worn by clerics (as monks) — **tonsure** *vb*

tony *also* **ton·ey** \ˈtō-nē\ *adj* **ton·i·er; -est** : marked by an aristocratic manner or style

too \ˈtü\ *adv* **1** : in addition : ALSO **2** : EXCESSIVELY ⟨the music is ~ loud⟩ **3** : to such a degree as to be regrettable **4** : VERY ⟨didn't seem ~ interested⟩

took *past of* TAKE

[1]**tool** \ˈtül\ *n* **1** : a hand instrument that aids in accomplishing a task **2** : the cutting or shaping part in a machine; *also* : a machine for shaping metal in any way **3** : something used in doing a job ⟨a scholar's books are his ~*s*⟩; *also* : a means to an end **4** : a person used by another : DUPE **5** *pl* : natural ability

[2]**tool** *vb* **1** : to shape, form, or finish with a tool; *esp* : to letter or decorate (as a book cover) by means of hand tools **2** : to equip a plant or industry with machines and tools for production **3** : DRIVE, RIDE ⟨~*ing* along at 60 miles per hour⟩

tool bar *n* : a strip of icons on a computer display providing quick access to the pictured functions

[1]**toot** \ˈtüt\ *vb* **1** : to sound or cause to sound in short blasts **2** : to blow an instrument (as a horn) — **toot·er** *n*

²**toot** *n* : a short blast (as on a horn)
tooth \'tüth\ *n, pl* **teeth** \'tēth\ **1** : one of the hard bony structures borne esp. on the jaws of vertebrates and used for seizing and chewing food and as weapons; *also* : a hard sharp structure esp. around the mouth of an invertebrate **2** : something resembling an animal's tooth **3** : any of the projections on the edge of a wheel that fits into corresponding projections on another wheel **4** *pl* : effective means of enforcement — **toothed** \'tütht\ *adj* — **tooth·less** *adj*
tooth·ache \'tüth-ˌāk\ *n* : pain in or about a tooth
tooth·brush \-ˌbrəsh\ *n* : a brush for cleaning the teeth
tooth·paste \-ˌpāst\ *n* : a paste for cleaning the teeth
tooth·pick \-ˌpik\ *n* : a pointed instrument for removing food particles caught between the teeth
tooth powder *n* : a powder for cleaning the teeth
tooth·some \'tüth-səm\ *adj* **1** : AGREEABLE, ATTRACTIVE **2** : pleasing to the taste : DELICIOUS ♦ *Synonyms* PALATABLE, APPETIZING, SAVORY, TASTY
toothy \'tü-thē\ *adj* **tooth·i·er; -est** : having or showing prominent teeth
¹**top** \'täp\ *n* **1** : the highest part, point, or level of something **2** : the part of a plant with edible roots lying above the ground ⟨beet ~*s*⟩ **3** : the upper end, edge, or surface ⟨the ~ of a page⟩ **4** : an upper piece, lid, or covering **5** : the highest degree, pitch, or rank **6** : a quark with a charge of +⅔ and a measured energy of approximately 175 billion electron volts
²**top** *vb* **topped; top·ping** **1** : to remove or trim the top of : PRUNE ⟨~ a tree⟩ **2** : to cover with a top or on the top : CROWN, CAP **3** : to be superior to : EXCEL, SURPASS **4** : to go over the top of **5** : to strike (a ball) above the center **6** : to make an end or conclusion ⟨~ off a meal with coffee⟩
³**top** *adj* **1** : of, relating to, or being at the top : HIGHEST ⟨is ~ in her class⟩ **2** : CHIEF
⁴**top** *n* : a toy that has a tapering point on which it is made to spin
to·paz \'tō-ˌpaz\ *n* : a hard silicate of aluminum; *esp* : a yellow transparent topaz used as a gem
top·coat \'täp-ˌkōt\ *n* **1** : a lightweight overcoat **2** : a protective coating (as of paint)
top dollar *n* : the highest amount being paid for a commodity or service
top–dress \-ˌdres\ *vb* : to apply material to (as land) without working it in; *esp* : to scatter fertilizer over
top·dress·ing \-ˌdre-siŋ\ *n* : a material used to top-dress soil
top–end \'täp-'end\ *adj* : TOPFLIGHT
top·flight \'täp-'flīt\ *adj* : of, relating to, or being the highest level of excellence or rank ⟨a ~ staff⟩ — **top flight** *n*
top hat *n* : a tall-crowned hat usu. of beaver or silk
top–heavy \'täp-ˌhe-vē\ *adj* : having the top part too heavy for the lower part
to·pi·ary \'tō-pē-ˌer-ē\ *n, pl* **-ar·ies** : the art of training and trimming trees or shrubs with decorative shapes — **topiary** *adj*
top·ic \'tä-pik\ *n* **1** : a heading in an outlined argument **2** : the subject of a discourse or a section of it : THEME
top·i·cal \-pi-kəl\ *adj* **1** : of, relating to, or arranged by topics ⟨a ~ outline⟩ **2** : relating to current or local events **3** : designed to be applied to or to work on a part (as of the body) — **top·i·cal·ly** \-k(ə-)lē\ *adv*
top·knot \'täp-ˌnät\ *n* **1** : an ornament (as a knot of ribbons) forming a headdress **2** : a crest of feathers or tuft of hair on the top of the head **3** : hair gathered high on the head usu. in a knot
top·less \-ləs\ *adj* **1** : wearing no clothing on the upper body **2** : featuring topless waitresses or entertainers
top·mast \'täp-ˌmast, -məst\ *n* : the 2d mast above a ship's deck
top·most \'täp-ˌmōst\ *adj* : highest of all : UPPERMOST
top–notch \-'näch\ *adj* : of the highest quality : FIRST-RATE
top–of–the–line *adj* : being or belonging to the highest or most expensive class
to·pog·ra·phy \tə-'pä-grə-fē\ *n* **1** : the art of showing in detail on a map or chart the physical features of a place or region **2** : the outline of the form of a place showing its relief and the position of features (as rivers, roads, or cities) — **to·pog·ra·pher** \-fər\ *n* — **top·o·graph·ic** \ˌtä-pə-'gra-fik\ *or* **top·o·graph·i·cal** \-fi-kəl\ *adj*
topping *n* : a food served on top of another to make it look or taste better
top·ple \'tä-pəl\ *vb* **top·pled; top·pling** **1** : to fall from or as if from being top-heavy **2** : to push over : OVERTURN; *also* : OVERTHROW ⟨*toppled* the dictator⟩
¹**tops** \'täps\ *adj* : topmost in quality or importance ⟨~ in his field⟩
²**tops** *adv* : at the very most
top·sail \'täp-ˌsāl, -səl\ *also* **top·s'l** \-səl\ *n* : the sail next above the lowest sail on a mast in a square-rigged ship
top secret *adj* : demanding complete secrecy among those concerned
top·side \'täp-'sīd\ *adv or adj* **1** : to or on the top or surface **2** : on deck
top·sides \-'sīdz\ *n pl* : the top portion of the outer surface of a ship on each side above the waterline
top·soil \'täp-ˌsȯi(-ə)l\ *n* : surface soil usu. including the organic layer in which plants have most of their roots
top·sy–tur·vy \ˌtäp-sē-'tər-vē\ *adv* **1** : in utter confusion **2** : UPSIDE DOWN — **topsy–turvy** *adj*
toque \'tōk\ *n* : a woman's small hat without a brim
tor \'tȯr\ *n* : a high craggy hill
To·rah \'tȯr-ə\ *n* **1** : a scroll of the first five books of the Old Testament used in a synagogue; *also* : these five books **2** : the

body of divine knowledge and law found in the Jewish scriptures and tradition

[1]**torch** \ˈtȯrch\ *n* **1** : a flaming light made of something that burns brightly and usu. carried in the hand **2** : something that resembles a torch in giving light, heat, or guidance **3** : a portable burner for producing a hot flame **4** *chiefly Brit* : FLASHLIGHT

[2]**torch** *vb* : to set fire to

torch·bear·er \ˈtȯrch-ˌber-ər\ *n* **1** : a person who carries a torch **2** : one in the forefront (as of a political campaign)

torch·light \-ˌlīt\ *n* : light given by torches

torch song *n* : a popular sentimental song of unrequited love

tore *past of* TEAR

to·re·ador \ˈtȯr-ē-ə-ˌdȯr\ *n* : BULLFIGHTER

to·re·ro \tə-ˈrer-ō\ *n, pl* **-ros** [Sp] : BULLFIGHTER

[1]**tor·ment** \ˈtȯr-ˌment\ *n* **1** : extreme pain or anguish of body or mind **2** : a source of vexation or pain

[2]**tor·ment** \tȯr-ˈment\ *vb* **1** : to cause severe suffering of body or mind to **2** : DISTORT, TWIST ♦ ***Synonyms*** RACK, AFFLICT, TRY, TORTURE — **tor·men·tor** \-ˈmen-tər\ *n*

torn *past part of* TEAR

tor·na·do \tȯr-ˈnā-dō\ *n, pl* **-does** *or* **-dos** [modif of Sp *tronada* thunderstorm, fr. *tronar* to thunder, fr. L *tonare*] : a violent destructive whirling wind accompanied by a funnel-shaped cloud that moves over a narrow path

[1]**tor·pe·do** \tȯr-ˈpē-dō\ *n, pl* **-does** : a thin cylindrical self-propelled underwater weapon

[2]**torpedo** *vb* **tor·pe·doed; tor·pe·do·ing** : to hit or destroy with or as if with a torpedo

torpedo boat *n* : a small very fast boat for firing torpedoes

tor·pid \ˈtȯr-pəd\ *adj* **1** : having lost motion or the power of exertion : DORMANT **2** : SLUGGISH **3** : lacking vigor — **tor·pid·i·ty** \tȯr-ˈpi-də-tē\ *n*

tor·por \ˈtȯr-pər\ *n* **1** : DULLNESS, APATHY **2** : extreme sluggishness : STAGNATION ♦ ***Synonyms*** STUPOR, LETHARGY, LANGUOR, LASSITUDE

[1]**torque** \ˈtȯrk\ *n* : a force that produces or tends to produce rotation or torsion

[2]**torque** *vb* **torqued; torqu·ing** : to impart torque to : cause to twist (as about an axis)

tor·rent \ˈtȯr-ənt\ *n* [F, fr. L *torrent-, torrens,* fr. *torrent-, torrens* burning, seething, rushing, fr. prp. of *torrēre* to parch, burn] **1** : a tumultuous outburst **2** : a rushing stream (as of water)

tor·ren·tial \tȯ-ˈren-chəl\ *adj* : relating to or resembling a torrent ⟨~ rains⟩

tor·rid \ˈtȯr-əd\ *adj* **1** : parched with heat esp. of the sun : HOT **2** : ARDENT

torrid zone *n* : the region of the earth between the Tropic of Cancer and the Tropic of Capricorn

tor·sion \ˈtȯr-shən\ *n* **1** : a wrenching by which one part of a body is under pressure to turn about a longitudinal axis while the other part is held fast or is under pressure to turn in the opposite direction **2** : a twisting of a bodily organ or part on its own axis — **tor·sion·al** \ˈtȯr-shə-nəl\ *adj* — **tor·sion·al·ly** *adv*

tor·so \ˈtȯr-sō\ *n, pl* **torsos** *or* **tor·si** \ˈtȯr-ˌsē\ [It, lit., stalk] : the trunk of the human body

tort \ˈtȯrt\ *n* : a wrongful act which does not involve a breach of contract and for which the injured party can recover damages in a civil action

tor·ti·lla \tȯr-ˈtē-ə\ *n* : a round thin cake of unleavened cornmeal or wheat flour bread

tor·toise \ˈtȯr-təs\ *n* : TURTLE; *esp* : any of a family of land turtles

tor·toise·shell \-ˌshel\ *n* : the mottled horny substance of the shell of some turtles used in inlaying and in making various ornamental articles — **tortoiseshell** *adj*

tor·to·ni \tȯr-ˈtō-nē\ *n* : rich ice cream often made with minced almonds and chopped cherries and flavored with rum

tor·tu·ous \ˈtȯr-chə-wəs\ *adj* **1** : marked by twists or turns : WINDING ⟨a ~ path⟩ **2** : DEVIOUS, TRICKY

[1]**tor·ture** \ˈtȯr-chər\ *n* **1** : anguish of body or mind **2** : the infliction of severe pain esp. to punish or coerce — **tor·tur·ous** \ˈtȯrch-rəs, ˈtȯr-chə-\ *adj*

[2]**torture** *vb* **tor·tured; tor·tur·ing** **1** : to cause intense suffering to : TORMENT **2** : to punish or coerce by inflicting severe pain **3** : TWIST, DISTORT ♦ ***Synonyms*** RACK, HARROW, AFFLICT, TRY — **tor·tur·er** *n*

To·ry \ˈtȯr-ē\ *n, pl* **Tories** **1** : a member of a chiefly 18th century British party upholding the established church and the traditional political structure **2** : an American supporter of the British during the American Revolution **3** *often not cap* : an extreme conservative — **Tory** *adj*

[1]**toss** \ˈtȯs, ˈtäs\ *vb* **1** : to fling to and fro or up and down **2** : to throw with a quick light motion; *also* : BANDY **3** : to fling or lift with a sudden motion ⟨~*ed* her head angrily⟩ **4** : to move restlessly or turbulently ⟨~*es* on the waves⟩ **5** : to twist and turn repeatedly **6** : FLOUNCE **7** : to accomplish readily ⟨~ off an article⟩ **8** : to decide an issue by flipping a coin

[2]**toss** *n* : an act or instance of tossing; *esp* : TOSS-UP 1

toss–up \-ˌəp\ *n* **1** : a deciding by flipping a coin **2** : an even chance **3** : something that offers no clear basis for choice

[1]**tot** \ˈtät\ *n* **1** : a small child **2** : a small drink of alcoholic liquor : SHOT

[2]**tot** *vb* **tot·ted; tot·ting** : to add up

[3]**tot** *abbr* total

[1]**to·tal** \ˈtō-tᵊl\ *adj* **1** : making up a whole : ENTIRE ⟨~ amount⟩ **2** : COMPLETE, UTTER ⟨a ~ failure⟩ ⟨a ~ stranger⟩ **3** : involving a complete and unified effort esp. to achieve a desired effect — **to·tal·ly** *adv*

[2]**total** *n* **1** : SUM 4 **2** : the entire amount

♦ ***Synonyms*** AGGREGATE, WHOLE, GROSS, TOTALITY

³**total** *vb* **to·taled** *or* **to·talled; to·tal·ing** *or* **to·tal·ling** **1** : to add up : COMPUTE **2** : to amount to : NUMBER **3** : to make a total wreck of (a car)

to·tal·i·tar·i·an \tō-ˌta-lə-ˈter-ē-ən\ *adj* : of, relating to, or advocating a political regime based on subordination of the individual to the state and strict control of all aspects of life esp. by coercive measures — **totalitarian** *n* — **to·tal·i·tar·i·an·ism** \-ē-ə-ˌni-zəm\ *n*

to·tal·i·ty \tō-ˈta-lə-tē\ *n, pl* **-ties** **1** : an aggregate amount : SUM, WHOLE **2** : ENTIRETY, WHOLENESS

to·tal·iza·tor *or* **to·tal·isa·tor** \ˈtō-tᵊl-ə-ˌzā-tər\ *n* : a machine for registering and indicating the number of bets and the odds on a horse or dog race

¹**tote** \ˈtōt\ *vb* **tot·ed; tot·ing** : CARRY

²**tote** *vb* **tot·ed; tot·ing** : ADD, TOTAL — usu. used with *up*

to·tem \ˈtō-təm\ *n* [Ojibwa *oto·te·man* his totem] : an object (as an animal or plant) serving as the emblem of a family or clan and often as a reminder of its ancestry; *also* : something usu. carved or painted to represent such an object

totem pole *n* : a pole that is carved and painted with a series of totems and is erected by Indigenous people of the northwest coast of No. America

tot·ter \ˈtä-tər\ *vb* **1** : to tremble or rock as if about to fall : SWAY **2** : to move unsteadily : STAGGER

tou·can \ˈtü-ˌkan\ *n* [F, fr. Pg *tucano,* fr. Tupi (Indigenous language of Brazil) *tukána*] : any of a family of chiefly fruit-eating birds of tropical America with brilliant coloring and a very large bill

¹**touch** \ˈtəch\ *vb* **1** : to bring a bodily part (as the hand) into contact with so as to feel **2** : to be or cause to be in contact **3** : to strike or push lightly esp. with the hand or foot **4** : DISTURB, HARM **5** : to make use of ⟨never ~*es* alcohol⟩ **6** : to induce to give or lend **7** : to get to : REACH **8** : to refer to in passing : MENTION **9** : to affect the interest of : CONCERN **10** : to leave a mark on; *also* : BLEMISH **11** : to move to sympathetic feeling **12** : to come close : VERGE **13** : to have a bearing : RELATE **14** : to make a usu. brief or incidental stop in port ♦ ***Synonyms*** AFFECT, INFLUENCE, IMPRESS, STRIKE, SWAY

²**touch** *n* **1** : a light stroke or tap **2** : the act or fact of touching or being touched **3** : the sense by which pressure or traction on the skin or mucous membrane is perceived; *also* : a particular sensation conveyed by this sense **4** : mental or moral sensitiveness : TACT **5** : a small quantity : HINT ⟨a ~ of spring in the air⟩ **6** : a manner of striking or touching esp. the keys of a keyboard instrument **7** : an improving detail ⟨add a few ~*es* to the painting⟩ **8** : distinctive manner or skill ⟨the ~ of a master⟩ **9** : the state of being in contact ⟨keep in ~⟩ ♦ ***Synonyms*** SUGGESTION, SUSPICION, TINCTURE, TINGE

touch·down \ˈtəch-ˌdau̇n\ *n* : the act of scoring six points in American football by being lawfully in possession of the ball on, above, or behind an opponent's goal line

tou·ché \tü-ˈshā\ *interj* [F] — used to acknowledge a hit in fencing or the success of an argument, an accusation, or a witty point

touch football *n* : football in which touching is substituted for tackling

touch·ing \ˈtə-chiŋ\ *adj* : capable of stirring emotions ♦ ***Synonyms*** MOVING, IMPRESSIVE, POIGNANT, AFFECTING

touch off *vb* **1** : to describe with precision **2** : to start by or as if by touching with fire ⟨*touched off* a riot⟩

touch screen *n* : a display screen (as for a computer) on which the user selects options by touching the screen

touch·stone \ˈtəch-ˌstōn\ *n* **1** : a test or criterion of genuineness or quality **2** : a fundamental or typical part or feature ♦ ***Synonyms*** STANDARD, GAUGE, BENCHMARK, YARDSTICK

touch–tone \ˈtəch-ˈtōn\ *adj* : of, relating to, or being a telephone having push buttons that produce tones corresponding to numbers

touch up *vb* : to improve or perfect by small additional strokes or alterations ⟨*touch up* a photo⟩ — **touch–up** \ˈtəch-ˌəp\ *n*

touchy \ˈtə-chē\ *adj* **touch·i·er; -est** **1** : easily offended : PEEVISH **2** : calling for tact in treatment ⟨a ~ subject⟩ ♦ ***Synonyms*** IRASCIBLE, CRANKY, CROSS, TETCHY, TESTY

¹**tough** \ˈtəf\ *adj* **1** : strong or firm in texture but flexible and not brittle **2** : not easily chewed **3** : characterized by severity and determination ⟨a ~ policy⟩ **4** : capable of enduring strain or hardship : ROBUST **5** : hard to influence : STUBBORN **6** : difficult to accomplish, resolve, or cope with ⟨a ~ problem⟩ **7** : ROWDYISH ♦ ***Synonyms*** TENACIOUS, STOUT, STURDY, STALWART — **tough·ly** *adv* — **tough·ness** *n*

²**tough** *n* : a tough person : ROWDY

tough·en \ˈtə-fən\ *vb* **tough·ened; tough·en·ing** : to make or become tough ⟨training camp ~*ed* him up⟩

tou·pee \tü-ˈpā\ *n* [F *toupet* forelock] : a small wig for a bald spot

¹**tour** \ˈtu̇r, *1 is also* ˈtau̇(-ə)r\ *n* **1** : one's turn : SHIFT **2** : a journey in which one returns to the starting point

²**tour** *vb* : to make a tour

tour de force \ˌtu̇r-də-ˈfȯrs\ *n, pl* **tours de force** *same*\ [F] : a feat or display of strength, skill, or ingenuity

Tou·rette's syndrome \tu̇-ˈrets-\ *n* : a familial neurological disorder marked by recurrent involuntary tics and vocal sounds

tour·ism \ˈtu̇r-ˌi-zəm\ *n* **1** : the practice of traveling for recreation **2** : promotion of touring **3** : accommodation of tourists — **tour·ist** \-ist\ *n*

tourist class *n* : economy accommodations (as on a ship)

tour•ma•line \'tu̇r-mə-lən, -ˌlēn\ *n* : a mineral that when transparent is valued as a gem

tour•na•ment \'tu̇r-nə-mənt, 'tər-\ *n* **1** : a medieval sport in which mounted armored knights contended with blunted lances or swords **2** : a championship series of games or athletic contests

tour•ney \-nē\ *n, pl* **tourneys** : TOURNAMENT

tour•ni•quet \'tu̇r-ni-kət, 'tər-\ *n* : a device (as a tight bandage) to check bleeding or blood flow

tou•sle \'tau̇-zəl\ *vb* **tou•sled; tou•sling** : to disorder by rough handling : DISHEVEL, MUSS ⟨*tousled* his hair⟩

tout \'tau̇t, *2 is also* 'tüt\ *vb* **1** : to give a tip or solicit bets on a racehorse **2** : to praise or publicize loudly — **tout** *n*

[1]**tow** \'tō\ *vb* : to draw or pull along behind

[2]**tow** *n* **1** : an act of towing or condition of being towed **2** : something (as a barge) that is towed

[3]**tow** *n* : short or broken fiber (as of flax or hemp) used esp. for yarn, twine, or stuffing

to•ward \'tȯrd, 'tō-ərd, tə-'wȯrd\ *or* **to•wards** \'tȯrdz, 'tō-ərdz, tə-'wȯrdz\ *prep* **1** : in the direction of ⟨heading ~ the river⟩ **2** : along a course leading to ⟨efforts ~ reconciliation⟩ **3** : in regard to ⟨tolerance ~ minorities⟩ **4** : so as to face ⟨turn the chair ~ the window⟩ **5** : close upon ⟨it was getting along ~ sundown⟩ **6** : for part payment of ⟨here's $100 ~ your tuition⟩

tow•boat \'tō-ˌbōt\ *n* : TUGBOAT

tow•el \'tau̇(-ə)l\ *n* : an absorbent cloth or paper for wiping or drying

tow•el•ing *or* **tow•el•ling** *n* : a cotton or linen fabric for making towels

[1]**tow•er** \'tau̇(-ə)r\ *n* **1** : a tall structure either isolated or built upon a larger structure ⟨an observation ~⟩ **2** : a towering citadel **3** : a personal computer case that stands in an upright position — **tow•ered** *adj*

[2]**tower** *vb* : to reach or rise to a great height

tow•er•ing \'tau̇(-ə)r-iŋ\ *adj* **1** : LOFTY ⟨~ pines⟩ **2** : reaching high intensity ⟨a ~ rage⟩ **3** : EXCESSIVE ⟨~ ambition⟩

tow•head \'tō-ˌhed\ *n* : a person having whitish blond hair — **tow•head•ed** \-ˌhedəd\ *adj*

to•whee \'tō-ˌhē, 'tō-(ˌ)ē, tō-'hē\ *n* : a common finch of eastern No. America having the male black, white, and reddish; *also* : any of several closely related finches

to wit *adv* : NAMELY

town \'tau̇n\ *n* **1** : a compactly settled area usu. larger than a village but smaller than a city **2** : CITY **3** : the inhabitants of a town **4** : a New England territorial and political unit usu. containing both rural and urban areas; *also* : a New England community in which matters of local government are decided by a general assembly (**town meeting**) of qualified voters

town•home \-ˌhōm\ *n* : TOWN HOUSE 2

town house *n* **1** : the city residence of a person having a country home **2** : a single-family house of two or sometimes three stories connected to another house by a common wall

town•ie *or* **towny** \'tau̇-nē\ *n, pl* **townies** : a permanent resident of a town as distinguished from a member of another group

towns•folk \'tau̇nz-ˌfōk\ *n pl* : TOWNSPEOPLE

town•ship \'tau̇n-ˌship\ *n* **1** : TOWN 4 **2** : a unit of local government in some states **3** : an unorganized subdivision of a county **4** : a division of territory in surveys of U.S. public land containing 36 square miles **5** : an area in the Republic of South Africa that was segregated under apartheid for occupation by persons of non-European descent

towns•man \'tau̇nz-mən\ *n* **1** : a native or resident of a town or city **2** : a fellow citizen of a town

towns•peo•ple \-ˌpē-pəl\ *n pl* **1** : the inhabitants of a town or city **2** : town-bred persons

towns•wom•an \-ˌwu̇-mən\ *n* **1** : a woman who is a native or resident of a town or city **2** : a woman who is a fellow citizen of a town

tow•path \'tō-ˌpath, -ˌpäth\ *n* : a path (as along a canal) traveled esp. by draft animals towing boats

tow truck *n* : a truck equipped for towing vehicles

tox•emia \täk-'sē-mē-ə\ *n* : a bodily disorder associated with the presence of toxic substances in the blood

tox•ic \'täk-sik\ *adj* [LL *toxicus,* fr. L *toxicum* poison, fr. Gk *toxikon* arrow poison, fr. neut. of *toxikos* of a bow, fr. *toxon* bow, arrow] : of, relating to, or caused by poison or a toxin : POISONOUS — **tox•ic•i•ty** \täk-'si-sə-tē\ *n*

tox•i•col•o•gy \ˌtäk-si-'kä-lə-jē\ *n* : a science that deals with poisons and esp. with problems of their use and control — **tox•i•co•log•i•cal** \-kə-'lä-ji-kəl\ *also* **tox•i•co•log•ic** \-kə-'lä-jik\ *adj* — **tox•i•col•o•gist** \-'kä-lə-jist\ *n*

toxic shock syndrome *n* : an acute disease associated with the presence of a bacterium that is characterized by fever, diarrhea, nausea, diffuse erythema, and shock and occurs esp. in menstruating females using tampons

tox•in \'täk-sən\ *n* : a poisonous substance produced by metabolic activities of a living organism that is usu. unstable, very toxic when introduced into the tissues, and usu. capable of inducing antibodies

[1]**toy** \'tȯi\ *n* **1** : something trifling **2** : a small ornament : BAUBLE **3** : something for a child to play with

[2]**toy** *vb* **1** : to deal with something lightly : TRIFLE **2** : FLIRT **3** : to amuse oneself as if with a plaything

[3]**toy** *adj* **1** : DIMINUTIVE ⟨a ~ dog⟩ **2** : designed for use as a toy

tp *abbr* **1** title page **2** township
tpk *or* **tpke** *abbr* turnpike
tr *abbr* **1** translated; translation; translator **2** transpose **3** troop
[1]**trace** \ˈtrās\ *n* **1** : a mark (as a footprint or track) left by something that has passed **2** : a minute or barely detectable amount ⟨disappeared without a ~⟩
[2]**trace** *vb* **traced; trac•ing** **1** : to mark out : SKETCH **2** : to form (as letters) carefully **3** : to copy (a drawing) by marking lines on transparent paper laid over the drawing to be copied **4** : to follow the trail of : track down **5** : to study out and follow the development of ⟨~*ed* his family's history⟩ — **trace•able** *adj*
[3]**trace** *n* : either of two lines of a harness for fastening a draft animal to a vehicle
trac•er \ˈtrā-sər\ *n* **1** : one that traces **2** : ammunition containing a chemical to mark the flight of projectiles by a trail of smoke or light
trac•ery \ˈtrā-sə-rē\ *n, pl* **-er•ies** : ornamental work having a design with branching or interlacing lines
tra•chea \ˈtrā-kē-ə\ *n, pl* **-che•ae** \-kē-ˌē\ *also* **-che•as** *or* **-chea** : the main tube by which air passes from the larynx to the lungs of vertebrates — **tra•che•al** \-kē-əl\ *adj*
tra•che•ot•o•my \ˌtrā-kē-ˈä-tə-mē\ *n, pl* **-mies** : the surgical operation of cutting into the trachea esp. through the skin
tracing *n* **1** : the act of one that traces **2** : something that is traced **3** : a graphic record made by an instrument for measuring vibrations or pulsations
[1]**track** \ˈtrak\ *n* **1** : a mark left in passing **2** : PATH, ROUTE, TRAIL **3** : a course laid out for racing; *also* : track-and-field sports **4** : one of a series of paths along which material (as music) is recorded (as on a CD or magnetic tape) **5** : the course along which something moves; *esp* : a way made by two parallel lines of metal rails **6** : awareness of a fact or progression ⟨lost ~ of time⟩ **7** : either of two endless metal belts on which a vehicle (as a bulldozer) travels
[2]**track** *vb* **1** : to follow the tracks or traces of : TRAIL **2** : to observe the moving path of (as a missile) **3** : to make tracks on **4** : to carry (as mud) on the feet and deposit — **track•er** *n*
track•age \ˈtra-kij\ *n* : lines of railway track
track–and–field *adj* : of or relating to athletic contests held on a running track or on the adjacent field
[1]**tract** \ˈtrakt\ *n* **1** : an area without precise boundaries ⟨huge ~*s* of land⟩ **2** : a defined area of land **3** : a system of body parts or organs that act together to perform some function ⟨the digestive ~⟩
[2]**tract** *n* : a pamphlet of political or religious propaganda
trac•ta•ble \ˈtrak-tə-bəl\ *adj* : easily controlled : DOCILE ♦ ***Synonyms*** AMENABLE, OBEDIENT, BIDDABLE
tract house *n* : any of many similar houses built on a tract of land
trac•tion \ˈtrak-shən\ *n* **1** : the act of drawing : the state of being drawn **2** : the drawing of a vehicle by motive power; *also* : the particular form of motive power used **3** : the adhesive friction of a body on a surface on which it moves **4** : a pulling force applied to a skeletal structure (as a broken bone) by means of a special device; *also* : a state of tension created by such a pulling force ⟨a leg in ~⟩ — **trac•tion•al** \-shə-nəl\ *adj* — **trac•tive** \ˈtrak-tiv\ *adj*
trac•tor \ˈtrak-tər\ *n* **1** : an automotive vehicle used esp. for drawing farm equipment **2** : a truck for hauling a trailer
[1]**trade** \ˈtrād\ *n* **1** : one's regular business or work : OCCUPATION **2** : an occupation requiring manual or mechanical skill **3** : the persons engaged in a business or industry **4** : the business of buying and selling or bartering commodities **5** : an act of trading : TRANSACTION
[2]**trade** *vb* **trad•ed; trad•ing** **1** : to give in exchange for another commodity : BARTER **2** : to engage in the exchange, purchase, or sale of goods **3** : to deal regularly as a customer — **trade on** : EXPLOIT ⟨*trades on* his family name⟩
trade–in \ˈtrād-ˌin\ *n* : an item of merchandise traded in
trade in *vb* : to turn in as part payment for a purchase
[1]**trade•mark** \ˈtrād-ˌmärk\ *n* : a device (as a word or mark) that points distinctly to the origin or ownership of merchandise to which it is applied and that is legally reserved for the exclusive use of the owner; *also* : something that identifies a person or thing
[2]**trademark** *vb* : to secure the trademark rights for ⟨that name is ~*ed*⟩
trade name *n* : a name that is given by a manufacturer or merchant to a product to distinguish it as made or sold by that manufacturer or merchant and that may be used and protected as a trademark
trad•er \ˈtrā-dər\ *n* **1** : a person whose business is buying or selling **2** : a ship engaged in trade
trades•man \ˈtrādz-mən\ *n* **1** : one who runs a retail store : SHOPKEEPER **2** : CRAFTSMAN
trades•peo•ple \-ˌpē-pəl\ *n pl* : people engaged in trade
trade union *n* : LABOR UNION
trade wind *n* : a wind blowing almost constantly in one direction
trading stamp *n* : a printed stamp given as a premium to a retail customer that when accumulated may be redeemed for merchandise
tra•di•tion \trə-ˈdi-shən\ *n* **1** : an inherited, established, or customary pattern of thought or action **2** : the handing down of beliefs and customs by word of mouth or by example without written instruction; *also* : a belief or custom thus handed down — **tra•di•tion•al** \-ˌdi-shə-nəl\ *adj* — **tra•di•tion•al•ly** *adv*
tra•duce \trə-ˈdüs, -ˈdyüs\ *vb* **tra•duced; tra•duc•ing** : to lower the reputation of

: DEFAME, SLANDER ⟨he was *traduced* in the past⟩ ♦ ***Synonyms*** MALIGN, LIBEL, CALUMNIATE — **tra·duc·er** *n*

¹traf·fic \'tra-fik\ *n* **1** : the business of bartering or buying and selling **2** : communication or dealings between individuals or groups **3** : the movement (as of vehicles) along a route; *also* : the vehicles, people, ships, or planes moving along a route **4** : the passengers or cargo carried by a transportation system

²traffic *vb* **traf·ficked; traf·fick·ing** **1** : to carry on business dealings **2** : to engage in commerce : DEAL, TRADE ⟨*trafficked* in illegal drugs⟩ — **traf·fick·er** *n*

traffic circle *n* : ROTARY 2

traffic light *n* : a visual signal (as a system of lights) for controlling traffic

tra·ge·di·an \trə-'jē-dē-ən\ *n* **1** : a writer of tragedies **2** : an actor who plays tragic roles

tra·ge·di·enne \trə-ˌjē-dē-'en\ *n* [F] : an actress who plays tragic roles

trag·e·dy \'tra-jə-dē\ *n, pl* **-dies** [ME *tragedie,* fr. MF, fr. L *tragoedia,* fr. Gk *tragōidia,* fr. *tragos* goat + *aeidein* to sing] **1** : a serious drama with a sorrowful or disastrous conclusion **2** : a disastrous event : CALAMITY; *also* : MISFORTUNE **3** : tragic quality or element ⟨the ∼ of life⟩

trag·ic \'tra-jik\ *also* **trag·i·cal** \-ji-kəl\ *adj* **1** : of, relating to, or expressive of tragedy **2** : appropriate to tragedy **3** : LAMENTABLE, UNFORTUNATE ⟨a ∼ mistake⟩ — **trag·i·cal·ly** \-ji-k(ə-)lē\ *adv*

¹trail \'trāl\ *vb* **1** : to hang down so as to drag along or sweep the ground **2** : to draw or drag along behind **3** : to extend over a surface in a straggling manner **4** : to lag behind **5** : to follow the track of : PURSUE **6** : DWINDLE ⟨her voice ∼*ed* off⟩

²trail *n* **1** : something that trails or is trailed ⟨a ∼ of smoke⟩ **2** : a trace or mark left by something that has passed or been drawn along : SCENT, TRACK ⟨a ∼ of blood⟩ **3** : a beaten path; *also* : a marked path through woods

trail bike *n* : a small motorcycle for off-road use

trail·blaz·er \-ˌblā-zər\ *n* : PATHFINDER, PIONEER — **trail·blaz·ing** *adj or n*

trail·er \'trā-lər\ *n* **1** : one that trails; *esp* : a creeping plant (as an ivy) **2** : a vehicle that is hauled by another (as a tractor) **3** : a vehicle equipped to serve wherever parked as a dwelling or place of business **4** : PREVIEW 3

trailer park *n* : a site equipped to accommodate mobile homes

trailing arbutus *n* : a creeping spring-flowering plant of the heath family with fragrant pink or white flowers

¹train \'trān\ *n* [ME, fr. AF, fr. *trainer* to draw, drag] **1** : a part of a gown that trails behind the wearer **2** : RETINUE **3** : a moving file of persons, vehicles, or animals **4** : a connected series ⟨a ∼ of thought⟩ **5** : AFTERMATH **6** : a connected line of railroad cars usu. hauled by a locomotive ♦ ***Synonyms*** SUCCESSION, SEQUENCE, PROCESSION, CHAIN

²train *vb* [ME, to trail, drag, train, fr. AF *trainer*] **1** : to cause to grow as desired ⟨∼ a vine on a trellis⟩ **2** : to form by instruction, discipline, or drill **3** : to make or become prepared (as by exercise) for a test of skill **4** : to aim or point at an object ⟨∼ guns on a fort⟩ ♦ ***Synonyms*** DISCIPLINE, SCHOOL, EDUCATE, INSTRUCT — **train·er** *n*

train·ee \trā-'nē\ *n* : one who is being trained esp. for a job

train·ing \'trā-niŋ\ *n* **1** : the act, process, or method of one who trains **2** : the skill, knowledge, or experience gained by one who trains

train·man \-mən\ *n* : a member of a train crew

traipse \'trāps\ *vb* **traipsed; traips·ing** : TRAMP, WALK ⟨∼ the countryside⟩

trait \'trāt\ *n* **1** : a distinguishing quality (as of personality) 2 : an inherited characteristic

trai·tor \'trā-tər\ *n* [ME *traytour,* fr. AF *traitre,* fr. L *traditor,* fr. *tradere* to hand over, deliver, betray, fr. *trans-* across + *dare* to give] **1** : one who betrays another's trust or is false to an obligation **2** : one who commits treason — **trai·tor·ous** *adj*

tra·jec·to·ry \trə-'jek-tə-rē\ *n, pl* **-ries** : the curve that a body (as a planet in its orbit) describes in space

tram \'tram\ *n* **1** : a boxlike car running on rails (as in a mine) **2** *chiefly Brit* : STREETCAR **3** : an overhead cable car

¹tram·mel \'tra-məl\ *n* [ME *tramayle,* a kind of net, fr. OF *tramail,* fr. LL *tremaculum,* fr. L *tres* three + *macula* mesh, spot] : something impeding activity, progress, or freedom — usu. used in pl.

²trammel *vb* **-meled** *or* **-melled; -mel·ing** *or* **-mel·ling** **1** : to catch and hold in or as if in a net **2** : HAMPER ♦ ***Synonyms*** CLOG, FETTER, SHACKLE, HOBBLE

¹tramp \'tramp, *1 & 3 are also* 'trämp, 'trȯmp\ *vb* **1** : to walk, tread, or step heavily **2** : to walk about or through; *also* : HIKE ⟨∼*ed* through the woods⟩ **3** : to tread on forcibly and repeatedly

²tramp \'tramp, *5 is also* 'trämp, 'trȯmp\ *n* **1** : VAGRANT **2** : a foot traveler **3** : an immoral woman; *esp* : PROSTITUTE **4** : a walking trip : HIKE **5** : the succession of sounds made by the beating of feet on a road **6** : a ship that does not follow a regular course but takes cargo to any port — **trampy** \'tram-pē\ *adj*

tram·ple \'tram-pəl\ *vb* **tram·pled; tram·pling** **1** : to tread heavily so as to bruise, crush, or injure **2** : to inflict injury or destruction **3** : to press down or crush by or as if by treading — **trample** *n* — **tram·pler** *n*

tram·po·line \ˌtram-pə-'lēn, 'tram-pə-ˌlēn\ *n* [It *trampolino* springboard] : a resilient sheet or web (as of nylon) supported by springs in a metal frame and used as a springboard in tumbling — **tram·po·lin·ist** \-'lē-nist, -ˌlē-\ *n*

trance \ˈtrans\ *n* [ME, fr. AF *transe,* death, coma, rapture, fr. *transir* to depart, die, fr. L *transire* to cross, pass by, fr. *trans-* across + *ire* to go] **1 :** STUPOR, DAZE **2 :** a sleeplike state of altered consciousness (as of deep hypnosis) **3 :** a state of very deep absorption — **trance·like** \-ˌlīk\ *adj*

tran·quil \ˈtraŋ-kwəl, ˈtran-\ *adj* **:** free from agitation or disturbance **:** QUIET ♦ ***Synonyms*** SERENE, PLACID, PEACEFUL — **tran·quil·i·ty** *also* **tran·quil·li·ty** \tran-ˈkwi-lə-tē, traŋ-\ *n* — **tran·quil·ly** *adv*

tran·quil·ize *also* **tran·quil·lize** \ˈtraŋ-kwə-ˌlīz, ˈtran-\ *vb* **-ized** *also* **-lized; -iz·ing** *also* **-liz·ing :** to make or become tranquil; *esp* **:** to relieve of mental tension and anxiety by means of drugs

tran·quil·iz·er *also* **tran·quil·liz·er** \-ˌlī-zər\ *n* **:** a drug used to relieve mental disturbance (as tension and anxiety)

¹trans \ˈtranz\ *adj* **:** TRANSGENDER, TRANSSEXUAL

²trans *abbr* **1** transaction **2** transitive **3** translated; translation; translator **4** transmission **5** transportation **6** transverse

trans·act \tran-ˈzakt, -ˈsakt\ *vb* **:** CARRY OUT, PERFORM; *also* **:** CONDUCT

trans·ac·tion \-ˈzak-shən, -ˈsak-\ *n* **1 :** something transacted; *esp* **:** a business deal **2 :** an act or process of transacting **3** *pl* **:** the records of the proceedings of a society or organization — **trans·ac·tion·al** \-shnəl, -shə-nᵊl\ *adj*

trans·at·lan·tic \ˌtrans-ət-ˈlan-tik, ˌtranz-\ *adj* **:** crossing or extending across or situated beyond the Atlantic Ocean ⟨a ~ flight⟩

trans·ax·le \trans-ˈak-səl\ *n* **:** a unit combining the transmission and differential gear of a front-wheel-drive automobile

trans·ceiv·er \tran-ˈsē-vər\ *n* **:** a radio transmitter-receiver that uses many of the same components for both transmission and reception

tran·scend \tran-ˈsend\ *vb* **1 :** to rise above the limits of ⟨music that ~*s* cultural boundaries⟩ **2 :** SURPASS ♦ ***Synonyms*** EXCEED, OUTDO, OUTSHINE, OUTSTRIP

tran·scen·dent \-ˈsen-dənt\ *adj* **1 :** exceeding usual limits **:** SURPASSING **2 :** transcending material existence ♦ ***Synonyms*** SUPERLATIVE, SUPREME, PEERLESS, INCOMPARABLE

tran·scen·den·tal \ˌtran-ˌsen-ˈden-tᵊl, -sən-\ *adj* **1 :** TRANSCENDENT 2 **2 :** of, relating to, or characteristic of transcendentalism; *also* **:** ABSTRUSE

tran·scen·den·tal·ism \-tə-ˌli-zəm\ *n* **:** a philosophy holding that ultimate reality is unknowable or asserting the primacy of the spiritual over the material and empirical — **tran·scen·den·tal·ist** \-tə-list\ *adj or n*

trans·con·ti·nen·tal \ˌtrans-ˌkän-tə-ˈnen-tᵊl\ *adj* **:** extending or going across a continent ⟨a ~ railroad⟩

tran·scribe \tran-ˈskrīb\ *vb* **tran·scribed; tran·scrib·ing 1 :** to write a copy of **2 :** to make a copy of (dictated or recorded matter) in longhand or on a typewriter **3 :** to represent (speech sounds) by means of phonetic symbols; *also* **:** to make a musical transcription of

tran·script \ˈtran-ˌskript\ *n* **1 :** a written, printed, or typed copy **2 :** an official copy esp. of a student's educational record

tran·scrip·tion \tran-ˈskrip-shən\ *n* **1 :** an act or process of transcribing **2 :** COPY, TRANSCRIPT **3 :** an arrangement of a musical composition for some instrument or voice other than the original **4 :** the process of constructing a messenger RNA molecule using a DNA molecule as a template

tran·scrip·tion·ist \-shə-nist\ *n* **:** one that transcribes; *esp* **:** a typist who transcribes medical reports

trans·der·mal \trans-ˈdər-məl, ˈtranz-\ *adj* **:** relating to, being, or supplying a medication in a form for absorption through the skin ⟨~ nicotine patch⟩

trans·duc·er \trans-ˈdü-sər, tranz-, -ˈdyü-\ *n* **:** a device that is actuated by power from one system and supplies power usu. in another form to a second system

tran·sept \ˈtran-ˌsept\ *n* **:** the part of a cruciform church that crosses at right angles to the greatest length; *also* **:** either of the projecting ends

trans fat \ˈtran(t)s-, ˈtranz-\ *n* **:** a fat containing unsaturated fatty acids (**trans–fatty acids**) that have been linked to an increase in blood cholesterol

¹trans·fer \trans-ˈfər, ˈtrans-ˌfər\ *vb* **trans·ferred; trans·fer·ring 1 :** to pass or cause to pass from one person, place, or situation to another **:** MOVE, TRANSMIT **2 :** to make over the possession of **:** CONVEY **3 :** to print or copy from one surface to another by contact **4 :** to change from one vehicle or transportation line to another — **trans·fer·able** \trans-ˈfər-ə-bəl\ *adj* — **trans·fer·al** \-əl\ *n*

²trans·fer \ˈtrans-ˌfər\ *n* **1 :** conveyance of right, title, or interest in property from one person to another **2 :** an act or process of transferring **3 :** one that transfers or is transferred **4 :** a ticket entitling a passenger to continue a trip on another route

trans·fer·ence \trans-ˈfər-əns\ *n* **:** an act, process, or instance of transferring

trans·fig·ure \trans-ˈfi-gyər\ *vb* **-ured; -ur·ing 1 :** to change the form or appearance of **2 :** EXALT, GLORIFY — **trans·fig·u·ra·tion** \ˌtrans-ˌfi-gyə-ˈrā-shən, -gə-\ *n*

trans·fix \trans-ˈfiks\ *vb* **1 :** to pierce through with or as if with a pointed weapon **2 :** to hold motionless by or as if by piercing ⟨stood ~*ed* by her gaze⟩

trans·form \trans-ˈfȯrm\ *vb* **:** to change in structure, appearance, or character ♦ ***Synonyms*** TRANSMUTE, TRANSFIGURE, TRANSMOGRIFY — **trans·for·ma·tion** \ˌtrans-fər-ˈmā-shən\ *n* — **trans·for·ma·tive** \trans-ˈfȯr-mə-tiv\ *adj*

trans·form·er \trans-ˈfȯr-mər\ *n* : one that transforms; *esp* : a device for converting variations of current in one circuit into variations of voltage and current in another circuit
trans·fuse \trans-ˈfyüz\ *vb* **trans·fused; trans·fus·ing** **1** : to cause to pass from one to another **2** : to diffuse into or through **3** : to transfer (as blood) into a vein or an artery of a person or animal — **trans·fu·sion** \-ˈfyü-zhən\ *n*
trans·gen·der \tranz-ˈjen-dər\ *adj* : of, relating to, or being a person whose gender identity differs from the sex the person had or was identified as having at birth
trans·gen·dered \-dərd\ *adj, now sometimes offensive* : TRANSGENDER
trans·gen·ic \tran(t)s-ˈje-nik\ *adj* : being or used to produce an organism or cell with genes introduced from another species of organism ⟨~ crops⟩
trans·gress \trans-ˈgres, tranz-\ *vb* [ME, fr. MF *transgresser,* fr. L *transgressus,* pp. of *transgredi* to step beyond or across, fr. *trans-* across + *gradi* to step] **1** : to go beyond the limits set by ⟨~ the divine law⟩ **2** : to go beyond : EXCEED **3** : SIN — **trans·gres·sion** \-ˈgre-shən\ *n* — **trans·gres·sor** \-ˈgre-sər\ *n*
[1]**tran·sient** \ˈtran-shənt; -sē-ənt, -shē-, -zē-\ *adj* **1** : not lasting long : SHORT-LIVED ⟨~ optimism⟩ **2** : passing through a place with only a brief stay ⟨~ visitors⟩ ♦ ***Synonyms*** TRANSITORY, PASSING, MOMENTARY, FLEETING — **tran·sient·ly** *adv*
[2]**transient** *n* : one that is transient; *esp* : a transient guest
tran·sis·tor \tran-ˈzis-tər, -ˈsis-\ *n* [*transfer* + *resistor;* fr. its transferring an electrical signal across a resistor] **1** : a small electronic semiconductor device used in electronic equipment **2** : a radio having transistors
tran·sis·tor·ized \-tə-ˌrīzd\ *adj* : having or using transistors
tran·sit \ˈtran-sət, -zət\ *n* **1** : a passing through, across, or over : PASSAGE **2** : conveyance of persons or things from one place to another **3** : usu. local transportation esp. of people by public conveyance **4** : a surveyor's instrument for measuring angles
tran·si·tion \tran-ˈsi-shən, -ˈzi-\ *n* : passage from one state, condition, place, stage, or subject to another : CHANGE — **transition** *vb* — **tran·si·tion·al** \-ˈsi-shə-nəl, ˈzi-\ *adj*
tran·si·tive \ˈtran-sə-tiv, -zə-\ *adj* **1** : having or containing an object required to complete the meaning ⟨a ~ verb⟩ **2** : TRANSITIONAL — **tran·si·tive·ly** *adv* — **tran·si·tive·ness** *n* — **tran·si·tiv·i·ty** \ˌtran-sə-ˈti-və-tē, -zə-\ *n*
tran·si·to·ry \ˈtran-sə-ˌtȯr-ē, -zə-\ *adj* : of brief duration : SHORT-LIVED, TEMPORARY ♦ ***Synonyms*** TRANSIENT, PASSING, MOMENTARY, FLEETING
transl *abbr* translated; translation
trans·late \trans-ˈlāt, tranz-\ *vb* **trans·lat·ed; trans·lat·ing** **1** : to change from one place, state, or form to another **2** : to convey to heaven without death **3** : to turn into one's own or another language — **trans·lat·able** *adj* — **trans·la·tor** \-ˈlā-tər\ *n*
trans·la·tion \tran(t)s-ˈlā-shən, tranz-\ *n* **1** : an act, process, or instance of translating **2** : the process of forming a protein molecule from information in messenger RNA — **trans·la·tion·al** \-shnəl, -shə-nᵊl\ *adj*
trans·lit·er·ate \trans-ˈli-tə-ˌrāt, tranz-\ *vb* **-at·ed; -at·ing** : to represent or spell in the characters of another alphabet — **trans·lit·er·a·tion** \ˌtrans-ˌli-tə-ˈrā-shən, ˌtranz-\ *n*
trans·lu·cent \trans-ˈlü-sᵊnt, tranz-\ *adj* : not transparent but clear enough to allow light to pass through — **trans·lu·cence** \-sᵊns\ *n* — **trans·lu·cen·cy** \-sᵊn-sē\ *n* — **trans·lu·cent·ly** *adv*
trans·mi·grate \-ˈmī-ˌgrāt\ *vb* : to pass at death from one body or being to another — **trans·mi·gra·tion** \ˌtrans-mī-ˈgrā-shən, ˌtranz-\ *n* — **trans·mi·gra·to·ry** \trans-ˈmī-grə-ˌtȯr-ē\ *adj*
trans·mis·sion \-ˈmi-shən\ *n* **1** : an act or process of transmitting **2** : the passage of radio waves between transmitting stations and receiving stations **3** : the gears by which power is transmitted from the engine of an automobile to the axle that propels the vehicle **4** : something transmitted
trans·mit \-ˈmit\ *vb* **trans·mit·ted; trans·mit·ting** **1** : to transfer from one person or place to another : FORWARD **2** : to pass on by or as if by inheritance **3** : to cause or allow to spread abroad or to another ⟨~ a disease⟩ **4** : to cause (as light, electricity, or force) to pass through space or a medium **5** : to send out (radio or television signals) ♦ ***Synonyms*** CONVEY, COMMUNICATE, IMPART — **trans·mis·si·ble** \-ˈmi-sə-bəl\ *adj* — **trans·mit·ta·ble** \-ˈmi-tə-bəl\ *adj* — **trans·mit·tal** \-ˈmit-ᵊl\ *n*
trans·mit·ter \-ˈmi-tər\ *n* : one that transmits; *esp* : an apparatus for transmitting telegraph, radio, or television signals
trans·mog·ri·fy \trans-ˈmä-grə-ˌfī, tranz-\ *vb* **-fied; -fy·ing** : to change or alter often with grotesque or humorous effect — **trans·mog·ri·fi·ca·tion** \-ˌmä-grə-fə-ˈkā-shən\ *n*
trans·mute \-ˈmyüt\ *vb* **trans·mut·ed; trans·mut·ing** : to change or alter in form, appearance, or nature ♦ ***Synonyms*** TRANSFORM, CONVERT, TRANSFIGURE, METAMORPHOSE — **trans·mu·ta·tion** \ˌtrans-myu̇-ˈtā-shən, ˌtranz-\ *n*
trans·na·tion·al \-ˈna-shə-nəl\ *adj* : extending beyond national boundaries
trans·oce·an·ic \ˌtrans-ˌō-shē-ˈa-nik, ˌtranz-\ *adj* **1** : lying or dwelling beyond the ocean **2** : crossing or extending across the ocean
tran·som \ˈtran-səm\ *n* **1** : a piece (as a crossbar in the frame of a window or door) that lies crosswise in a structure **2**

: a window above an opening (as a door) built on and often hinged to a horizontal crossbar

tran·son·ic *also* **trans–son·ic** \trans-ˈsä-nik\ *adj* : being or relating to speeds near that of sound in air or about 741 miles (1185 kilometers) per hour

trans·pa·cif·ic \ˌtrans-pə-ˈsi-fik\ *adj* : crossing, extending across, or situated beyond the Pacific Ocean

trans·par·ent \trans-ˈper-ənt\ *adj* **1** : clear enough to be seen through **2** : SHEER, DIAPHANOUS ⟨a ~ fabric⟩ **3** : readily understood : CLEAR; *also* : easily detected ⟨a ~ lie⟩ ♦ ***Synonyms*** LUCID, TRANSLUCENT, LUCENT — **trans·par·en·cy** \-ən-sē\ *n* — **trans·par·ent·ly** *adv*

trans·pho·bia \trans-ˈfō-bē-ə\ *n* : irrational fear of, aversion to, or discrimination against transgender people — **trans·pho·bic** \-bik\ *adj*

tran·spire \trans-ˈpi(-ə)r\ *vb* **trans·pired; trans·pir·ing** [MF *transpirer,* fr. ML *transpirare,* fr. L *trans-* across + *spirare* to breathe] **1** : to pass or give off (as water vapor) through pores or a membrane **2** : to become known **3** : to take place : HAPPEN — **tran·spi·ra·tion** \ˌtrans-pə-ˈrā-shən\ *n*

¹**trans·plant** \trans-ˈplant\ *vb* **1** : to dig up and plant elsewhere **2** : to remove from one place and settle or introduce elsewhere : TRANSPORT **3** : to transfer (an organ or tissue) from one part or individual to another — **trans·plan·ta·tion** \ˌtrans-ˌplan-ˈtā-shən\ *n*

²**trans·plant** \ˈtrans-ˌplant\ *n* **1** : a person or thing transplanted **2** : the act or process of transplanting

trans·po·lar \trans-ˈpō-lər\ *adj* : going or extending across either of the polar regions

transponder \tran-ˈspän-dər\ *n* [*trans*mitter + re*sponder*] : a radio or radar set that upon receiving a certain signal emits a radio signal and that is used to locate and identify objects and in satellites to relay communications signals

¹**trans·port** \trans-ˈpȯrt\ *vb* **1** : to convey from one place to another : CARRY **2** : to carry away by strong emotion : ENRAPTURE **3** : to send to a penal colony overseas ♦ ***Synonyms*** BEAR, FERRY — **trans·por·ta·tion** \ˌtrans-pər-ˈtā-shən\ *n* — **trans·port·er** *n*

²**trans·port** \ˈtrans-ˌpȯrt\ *n* **1** : an act of transporting **2** : strong or intensely pleasurable emotion ⟨~*s* of joy⟩ **3** : a ship used in transporting troops or supplies; *also* : a vehicle (as a truck or plane) used to transport persons or goods

trans·pose \trans-ˈpōz\ *vb* **trans·posed; trans·pos·ing 1** : to change the position or sequence of ⟨~ the letters in a word⟩ **2** : to write or perform (a musical composition) in a different key — **trans·po·si·tion** \ˌtrans-pə-ˈzi-shən\ *n*

trans·sex·u·al \(ˌ)tran(t)s-ˈsek-sh(ə-)wəl, -shəl\ *adj* : of, relating to, or being a person whose gender identity is opposite the sex the person had or was identified as having at birth

trans·ship \tran-ˈship, trans-\ *vb* : to transfer for further transportation from one ship or conveyance to another — **trans·ship·ment** *n*

tran·sub·stan·ti·a·tion \ˌtran-səb-ˌstan-chē-ˈā-shən\ *n* : the change in the eucharistic elements from the substance of bread and wine to the substance of the body of Christ with only the appearances of bread and wine remaining

trans·verse \trans-ˈvərs, tranz-\ *adj* : lying across : set crosswise — **transverse** \ˈtrans-ˌvərs, ˈtranz-\ *n* — **trans·verse·ly** *adv*

trans·ves·tite \trans-ˈves-ˌtīt, tranz-\ *n* : a person and esp. a male who adopts the dress and often the behavior of the opposite sex — **transvestite** *adj* — **trans·ves·tism** \-ˌti-zəm\ *n*

¹**trap** \ˈtrap\ *n* **1** : a device for catching animals **2** : something by which one is caught unawares; *also* : a situation from which escape is difficult or impossible **3** : a machine for throwing clay pigeons into the air; *also* : SAND TRAP **4** : a light one-horse carriage on springs **5** : a device to allow some one thing to pass through while keeping other things out ⟨a ~ in a drainpipe⟩ **6** *pl* : a group of percussion instruments (as in a dance orchestra)

²**trap** *vb* **trapped; trap·ping 1** : to catch in or as if in a trap; *also* : CONFINE **2** : to provide or set (a place) with traps **3** : to set traps for animals esp. as a business ♦ ***Synonyms*** SNARE, ENTRAP, ENSNARE, BAG, LURE, DECOY — **trap·per** *n*

trap·door \ˈtrap-ˈdȯr\ *n* : a lifting or sliding door covering an opening in a floor or roof

tra·peze \tra-ˈpēz\ *n* : a gymnastic apparatus consisting of a horizontal bar suspended by two parallel ropes

trap·e·zoid \ˈtra-pə-ˌzȯid\ *n* [NL *trapezoïdes,* fr. Gk *trapezoeidēs* trapezoidal, fr. *trapeza* table, fr. *tra-* four + *peza* foot] : a 4-sided polygon with exactly two sides parallel — **trap·e·zoi·dal** \ˌtra-pə-ˈzȯi-dᵊl\ *adj*

trap·pings \ˈtra-piŋz\ *n pl* **1** : CAPARISON 1 **2** : outward decoration or dress; *also* : outward sign ⟨~ of success⟩

traps \ˈtraps\ *n pl* : personal belongings : LUGGAGE

trap·shoot·ing \ˈtrap-ˌshü-tiŋ\ *n* : shooting at clay pigeons sprung from a trap into the air away from the shooter

¹**trash** \ˈtrash\ *n* **1** : something of little worth : RUBBISH **2** : empty or disparaging talk **3** : a worthless person; *also* : such persons as a group : RIFFRAFF — **trashy** *adj*

²**trash** *vb* **1** : to dispose of : DISCARD ⟨~*ed* the plans⟩ **2** : VANDALIZE, DESTROY **3** : ATTACK **4** : SPOIL, RUIN **5** : to criticize or disparage harshly

trau·ma \ˈtrau̇-mə, ˈtrȯ-\ *n, pl* **traumas** *also* **trau·ma·ta** \-mə-tə\ [Gk, wound] : a bodily or mental injury usu. caused by an external agent; *also* : a cause of trauma — **trau·mat·ic** \trə-ˈma-tik, trȯ-, trau̇-\ *adj*

traumatic brain injury *n* : a brain injury caused by external forces (as a blow to the head)

trau·ma·tize \-ˌtīz\ *vb* **-tized; -tiz·ing** : to inflict trauma upon

[1]**tra·vail** \trə-ˈvāl, ˈtra-ˌvāl\ *n* **1** : painful work or exertion : TOIL **2** : AGONY, TORMENT **3** : CHILDBIRTH, LABOR

[2]**travail** *vb* : to labor hard : TOIL

[1]**trav·el** \ˈtra-vəl\ *vb* **-eled** *or* **-elled; -el·ing** *or* **-el·ling** [ME *travailen* to torment, labor, journey, fr. AF *travailler* strive, fr. VL **trepaliare* to torture, fr. LL *trepalium* instrument of torture] **1** : to go on or as if on a trip or tour : JOURNEY **2** : to move as if by traveling ⟨news ~*s* fast⟩ **3** : ASSOCIATE **4** : to go from place to place as a sales representative **5** : to move from point to point ⟨light waves ~ very fast⟩ **6** : to journey over or through ⟨~*ing* the highways⟩ **7** : to take excessive steps while holding a basketball — **trav·el·er** *or* **trav·el·ler** *n*

[2]**travel** *n* **1** : the act of traveling : PASSAGE **2** : JOURNEY, TRIP — often used in pl. **3** : the number traveling : TRAFFIC **4** : the motion of a piece of machinery and esp. when to and fro

traveler's check *n* : a check paid for in advance that is signed when bought and signed again when cashed

traveling bag *n* : SUITCASE

trav·el·ogue *or* **trav·el·og** \ˈtra-və-ˌlȯg, -ˌläg\ *n* : a usu. illustrated lecture on travel

[1]**tra·verse** \ˈtra-vərs\ *n* : something that crosses or lies across

[2]**tra·verse** \trə-ˈvərs, tra-ˈvərs *or* ˈtra-vərs\ *vb* **tra·versed; tra·vers·ing** **1** : to go or travel across or over **2** : to move or pass along or through **3** : to extend over **4** : SWIVEL

[3]**tra·verse** \ˈtra-ˌvərs\ *adj* : TRANSVERSE

trav·er·tine \ˈtra-vər-ˌtēn, -tən\ *n* : a crystalline mineral formed by deposition from spring waters

[1]**trav·es·ty** \ˈtra-və-stē\ *vb* **-tied; -ty·ing** : to make a travesty of

[2]**travesty** *n, pl* **-ties** [obs. E *travesty* disguised, parodied, fr. F *travesti,* pp. of *travestir* to disguise, fr. It *travestire,* fr. *tra-* across (fr. L *trans-*) + *vestire* to dress] : an imitation that makes crude fun of something; *also* : an inferior imitation

[1]**trawl** \ˈtrȯl\ *vb* : to fish or catch with a trawl — **trawl·er** *n*

[2]**trawl** *n* **1** : a large conical net dragged along the sea bottom in fishing **2** : a long heavy fishing line equipped with many hooks in series

tray \ˈtrā\ *n* : an open receptacle with flat bottom and low rim for holding, carrying, or exhibiting articles

treach·er·ous \ˈtre-chə-rəs\ *adj* **1** : characterized by treachery **2** : UNTRUSTWORTHY, UNRELIABLE ⟨a ~ coworker⟩ **3** : providing insecure footing or support ⟨a ~ slope⟩ ♦ ***Synonyms*** TRAITOROUS, FAITHLESS, FALSE, DISLOYAL — **treach·er·ous·ly** *adv*

treach·ery \ˈtre-chə-rē\ *n, pl* **-er·ies** : violation of allegiance or trust

trea·cle \ˈtrē-kəl\ *n* [ME *triacle* a medicinal compound, fr. AF, fr. L *theriaca,* fr. Gk *thēriakē* antidote against a poisonous bite, fr. *thērion* wild animal] *chiefly Brit* : MOLASSES — **trea·cly** \-k(ə-)lē\ *adj*

[1]**tread** \ˈtred\ *vb* **trod** \ˈträd\; **trod·den** \ˈträ-dᵊn\ *or* **trod; tread·ing** **1** : to step or walk on or over **2** : to move on foot : WALK; *also* : DANCE **3** : to beat or press with the feet — **tread water** : to stay afloat and upright in water by sustaining a walking motion

[2]**tread** *n* **1** : a mark made by or as if by treading **2** : the manner or sound of stepping **3** : the part of a wheel that makes contact with a road **4** : the horizontal part of a step

trea·dle \ˈtre-dᵊl\ *n* : a lever device pressed by the foot to drive a machine — **treadle** *vb*

tread·mill \ˈtred-ˌmil\ *n* **1** : a mill worked by persons who tread on steps around the edge of a wheel or by animals that walk on an endless belt **2** : a device with an endless belt on which a person walks or runs in place **3** : a wearisome routine

treas *abbr* treasurer; treasury

trea·son \ˈtrē-zᵊn\ *n* : the offense of attempting to overthrow the government of one's country or of assisting its enemies in war — **trea·son·able** \-zᵊn-ə-bəl\ *adj* — **trea·son·ous** \-zᵊn-əs\ *adj*

[1]**trea·sure** \ˈtre-zhər, ˈtrā-\ *n* [ME *tresor,* fr. AF, fr. L *thesaurus,* fr. Gk *thēsauros*] **1** : wealth stored up or held in reserve **2** : something of great value

[2]**treasure** *vb* **trea·sured; trea·sur·ing** **1** : HOARD **2** : to keep as precious : CHERISH ♦ ***Synonyms*** PRIZE, VALUE, APPRECIATE, ESTEEM

trea·sur·er \ˈtre-zhə-rər, ˈtrā-\ *n* : an officer of a club, business, or government who has charge of money taken in and paid out

treasure trove \-ˌtrōv\ *n* **1** : treasure of unknown ownership found buried or hidden **2** : a valuable discovery

trea·sury \ˈtre-zhə-rē, ˈtrā-\ *n, pl* **-sur·ies** **1** : a place in which stores of wealth are kept **2** : the place where collected funds are stored and paid out **3** *cap* : a governmental department in charge of finances

[1]**treat** \ˈtrēt\ *vb* **1** : NEGOTIATE **2** : to deal with esp. in writing; *also* : HANDLE **3** : to pay for the food or entertainment of **4** : to behave or act toward ⟨~ them well⟩ **5** : to regard in a specified manner ⟨~ as inferiors⟩ **6** : to give medical or surgical care to **7** : to subject to some action ⟨~ soil with lime⟩

[2]**treat** *n* **1** : an entertainment given free to those invited; *also* : food, drink, or entertainment provided at another's expense **2** : a source of joy or amusement

trea·tise \ˈtrē-təs\ *n* : a systematic written exposition or argument

treat·ment \ˈtrēt-mənt\ *n* : the act or manner or an instance of treating someone or something; *also* : a substance or method used in treating

trea·ty \ˈtrē-tē\ *n, pl* **treaties** : an agreement made by negotiation or diplomacy esp. between two or more states or governments

[1]**tre·ble** \ˈtre-bəl\ *n* **1** : the highest of the four voice parts in vocal music : SOPRANO **2** : a high-pitched or shrill voice or sound **3** : the upper half of the musical pitch range

[2]**treble** *adj* **1** : triple in number or amount **2** : relating to or having the range of a musical treble **3** : high-pitched : SHRILL — **tre·bly** *adv*

[3]**treble** *vb* **tre·bled; tre·bling** : to make or become three times the size, amount, or number

[1]**tree** \ˈtrē\ *n* **1** : a woody perennial plant usu. with a single main stem and a head of branches and leaves at the top **2** : a piece of wood adapted to a particular use ⟨a shoe ~⟩ **3** : something resembling a tree ⟨a genealogical ~⟩ — **tree·less** *adj*

[2]**tree** *vb* **treed; tree·ing** : to drive to or up a tree ⟨~ a raccoon⟩

tree farm *n* : an area of forest land managed to ensure continuous commercial production

tree frog *n* : any of numerous small usu. tree-dwelling amphibians with adhesive disks on the toes

tree line *n* : TIMBERLINE

tree of heaven : a Chinese ailanthus widely grown as an ornamental tree

tree surgery *n* : operative treatment of diseased trees esp. for control of decay — **tree surgeon** *n*

tre·foil \ˈtrē-ˌfȯi(-ə)l, ˈtre-\ *n* **1** : an herb (as a clover) with leaves that have three leaflets **2** : a decorative design with three leaflike parts

[1]**trek** \ˈtrek\ *vb* **trekked; trek·king** **1** *chiefly South Africa* : to travel or migrate by ox wagon **2** : to make one's way arduously

[2]**trek** *n* **1** *chiefly South Africa* : a migration esp. of settlers by ox wagon **2** : a slow or difficult journey

[1]**trel·lis** \ˈtre-ləs\ *n* [ME *trelis,* fr. AF *treleis,* fr. OF *treille* arbor, fr. L *trichila* summerhouse] : a frame of latticework used esp. to support climbing plants

[2]**trellis** *vb* : to provide with a trellis; *esp* : to train (as a vine) on a trellis

trem·a·tode \ˈtre-mə-ˌtōd\ *n* : any of a class of parasitic worms

[1]**trem·ble** \ˈtrem-bəl\ *vb* **trem·bled; trem·bling** **1** : to shake involuntarily (as with fear or cold) : SHIVER **2** : to move, sound, pass, or come to pass as if shaken or tremulous **3** : to be affected with fear or doubt

[2]**tremble** *n* : a spell of shaking or quivering

tre·men·dous \tri-ˈmen-dəs\ *adj* **1** : causing dread, awe, or terror : TERRIFYING **2** : unusually large, powerful, great, or excellent ⟨~ strength⟩ ♦ ***Synonyms*** STUPENDOUS, MONUMENTAL, MONSTROUS — **tre·men·dous·ly** *adv*

trem·o·lo \ˈtre-mə-ˌlō\ *n, pl* **-los** [It] : a rapid fluttering of a tone or alternating tones

trem·or \ˈtre-mər\ *n* **1** : a trembling or shaking esp. from weakness, emotional stress, or disease **2** : a quivering motion of the earth (as during an earthquake)

trem·u·lous \ˈtrem-yə-ləs\ *adj* **1** : marked by trembling or tremors : QUIVERING ⟨~ hands⟩ **2** : TIMOROUS, TIMID — **trem·u·lous·ly** *adv*

[1]**trench** \ˈtrench\ *n* [ME *trenche* track cut through a wood, fr. AF, act of cutting, fr. *trencher* to cut, prob. fr. VL **trinicare* to cut in three, fr. L *trini* three each] **1** : a long narrow cut in the ground : DITCH; *esp* : a ditch protected by banks of earth and used to shelter soldiers **2** *pl* : a place or situation likened to warfare conducted from trenches **3** : a long narrow steep-sided depression in the ocean floor

[2]**trench** *vb* **1** : to cut or dig trenches in **2** : to protect (troops) with trenches **3** : to come close : VERGE

tren·chant \ˈtren-chənt\ *adj* **1** : vigorously effective; *also* : CAUSTIC ⟨~ comments⟩ **2** : sharply perceptive : KEEN ⟨a ~ wit⟩ **3** : CLEAR-CUT, DISTINCT

tren·cher \ˈtren-chər\ *n* : a wooden platter for serving food

tren·cher·man \ˈtren-chər-mən\ *n* : a hearty eater

trench foot *n* : a painful foot disorder resembling frostbite and resulting from exposure to cold and wet

trench mouth *n* : a progressive painful bacterial infection of the mouth and adjacent parts marked by ulceration, bleeding gums, and foul breath

[1]**trend** \ˈtrend\ *vb* **1** : to have or take a general direction : TEND **2** : to show a tendency : INCLINE

[2]**trend** *n* **1** : a general direction taken (as by a stream or mountain range) **2** : a prevailing tendency : DRIFT **3** : a current style or preference : VOGUE

trendy \ˈtren-dē\ *adj* **trend·i·er; -est** : very fashionable; *also* : marked by superficial or faddish appeal or taste

trep·i·da·tion \ˌtre-pə-ˈdā-shən\ *n* : nervous agitation : APPREHENSION ♦ ***Synonyms*** HORROR, TERROR, PANIC, CONSTERNATION, DREAD, FRIGHT, DISMAY

[1]**tres·pass** \ˈtres-pəs, -ˌpas\ *n* **1** : SIN, OFFENSE **2** : unlawful entry on someone else's land ♦ ***Synonyms*** TRANSGRESSION, VIOLATION, INFRACTION, INFRINGEMENT

[2]**trespass** *vb* **1** : to commit an offense : ERR, SIN **2** : INTRUDE, ENCROACH; *esp* : to enter unlawfully upon the land of another — **tres·pass·er** *n*

tress \ˈtres\ *n* : a long lock of hair — usu. used in pl.

tres·tle *also* **tres·sel** \ˈtre-səl\ *n* **1** : a supporting framework consisting usu. of a horizontal piece with spreading legs at each end **2** : a braced framework of timbers, piles, or steel for carrying a road or railroad over a depression

T. rex \ˈtē-ˈreks\ *n* : TYRANNOSAUR

trey \ˈtrā\ *n, pl* **treys** : a card or the side of a die with three spots

tri·ad \ˈtrī-ˌad, -əd\ *n* : a union or group of

three usu. closely related persons or things

tri·age \trē-ˈäzh, ˈtrē-ˌäzh\ *n* [F, sorting] : the sorting of and allocation of treatment to patients and esp. battle or disaster victims according to a system of priorities designed to maximize the number of survivors

tri·al \ˈtrī-əl\ *n* **1** : the action or process of trying or putting to the proof : TEST **2** : the hearing and judgment of a matter in issue before a competent tribunal **3** : a source of vexation or annoyance **4** : an experiment to test quality, value, or usefulness **5** : EFFORT, ATTEMPT ♦ ***Synonyms*** CROSS, ORDEAL, TRIBULATION, AFFLICTION — **trial** *adj*

tri·an·gle \ˈtrī-ˌaŋ-gəl\ *n* **1** : a polygon that has three sides **2** : something shaped like a triangle — **tri·an·gu·lar** \trī-ˈaŋ-gyə-lər\ *adj* — **tri·an·gu·lar·ly** *adv*

tri·an·gu·la·tion \(ˌ)trī-ˌaŋ-gyə-ˈlā-shən\ *n* : a method using trigonometry to find the location of a point using bearings from two fixed points a known distance apart — **tri·an·gu·late** \trī-ˈaŋ-gyə-ˌlāt\ *vb*

Tri·as·sic \trī-ˈa-sik\ *adj* : of, relating to, or being the earliest period of the Mesozoic era marked by the first appearance of the dinosaurs — **Triassic** *n*

tri·ath·lon \trī-ˈath-lən, -ˌlän\ *n* : an athletic contest consisting of three phases (as swimming, bicycling, and running)

trib *abbr* tributary

tribe \ˈtrīb\ *n* **1** : a social group comprising numerous families, clans, or generations **2** : a group of persons having a common character, occupation, or interest **3** : a group of related plants or animals ⟨the cat ~⟩ — **trib·al** \ˈtrī-bəl\ *adj*

tribes·man \ˈtrībz-mən\ *n* : a member of a tribe

trib·u·la·tion \ˌtri-byə-ˈlā-shən\ *n* [ME *tribulacion,* fr. AF, fr. L *tribulatio,* fr. *tribulare* to press, oppress, fr. *tribulum* drag used in threshing] : distress or suffering resulting from oppression or persecution; *also* : a trying experience ♦ ***Synonyms*** TRIAL, AFFLICTION, CROSS, ORDEAL

tri·bu·nal \trī-ˈbyü-nᵊl, tri-\ *n* **1** : the seat of a judge **2** : a court of justice **3** : something that decides or determines ⟨the ~ of public opinion⟩

tri·bune \ˈtri-ˌbyün, tri-ˈbyün\ *n* **1** : an official in ancient Rome with the function of protecting the interests of plebeian citizens from the patricians **2** : a defender of the people

[1]**trib·u·tary** \ˈtri-byə-ˌter-ē\ *adj* **1** : paying tribute : SUBJECT **2** : flowing into a larger stream or a lake ♦ ***Synonyms*** SUBORDINATE, SECONDARY, DEPENDENT

[2]**tributary** *n, pl* **-tar·ies** **1** : a ruler or state that pays tribute **2** : a tributary stream

trib·ute \ˈtri-(ˌ)byüt, -byət\ *n* **1** : a payment by one ruler or nation to another as an act of submission or price of protection **2** : a usu. excessive tax, rental, or levy exacted by a sovereign or superior **3** : a gift or service showing respect, gratitude, or affection; *also* : PRAISE ♦ ***Synonyms*** EULOGY, CITATION, ENCOMIUM, PANEGYRIC

trice \ˈtrīs\ *n* : INSTANT, MOMENT

tri·ceps \ˈtrī-ˌseps\ *n, pl* **triceps** : a large muscle along the back of the upper arm that is attached at its upper end by three main parts and acts to extend the forearm at the elbow joint

tri·cer·a·tops \(ˌ)trī-ˈser-ə-ˌtäps\ *n, pl* **-tops** *also* **-tops·es** [NL, fr. Gk *tri-* three + *kerat-, keras* horn + *ōps* face] : any of a genus of large plant-eating Cretaceous dinosaurs with three horns, a bony crest on the neck, and hoofed toes

tri·chi·na \tri-ˈkī-nə\ *n, pl* **-nae** \-(ˌ)nē\ *also* **-nas** : a small slender nematode worm that in the larval state is parasitic in the striated muscles of flesh-eating mammals (as humans)

trich·i·no·sis \ˌtri-kə-ˈnō-səs\ *n* : infestation with or disease caused by trichinae and marked esp. by muscular pain, fever, and swelling

[1]**trick** \ˈtrik\ *n* **1** : a crafty procedure meant to deceive **2** : a mischievous action : PRANK **3** : a childish action **4** : a deceptive or ingenious feat designed to puzzle or amuse **5** : PECULIARITY, MANNERISM **6** : a quick or artful way of getting a result : KNACK ⟨~*s* of the trade⟩ **7** : the cards played in one round of a card game **8** : a tour of duty : SHIFT ♦ ***Synonyms*** RUSE, MANEUVER, ARTIFICE, WILE, FEINT

[2]**trick** *vb* **1** : to deceive by cunning or artifice : CHEAT **2** : to dress ornately

trick·ery \ˈtri-kə-rē\ *n* : deception by tricks and strategems

trick·le \ˈtri-kəl\ *vb* **trick·led; trick·ling** **1** : to run or fall in drops **2** : to flow in a thin gentle stream — **trickle** *n*

trick·ster \ˈtrik-stər\ *n* : one who tricks or cheats

tricky \ˈtri-kē\ *adj* **trick·i·er; -est** **1** : inclined to trickery **2** : requiring skill or caution ⟨a ~ situation to handle⟩ **3** : UNRELIABLE ⟨a ~ lock⟩

tri·col·or \ˈtrī-ˌkə-lər\ *n* : a flag of three colors ⟨the French ~⟩

tri·cy·cle \ˈtrī-(ˌ)si-kəl\ *n* : a 3-wheeled vehicle usu. propelled by pedals

tri·dent \ˈtrī-dᵊnt\ *n* [L *trident-, tridens,* fr. *tri-* three + *dent-, dens* tooth] : a 3-pronged spear

tried \ˈtrīd\ *adj* **1** : found trustworthy through testing **2** : subjected to trials

tri·en·ni·al \trī-ˈe-nē-əl\ *adj* **1** : occurring or being done every three years **2** : lasting for three years — **triennial** *n*

[1]**tri·fle** \ˈtrī-fəl\ *n* **1** : something of little value or importance **2** : a dessert of cake soaked with liqueur and served with toppings (as fruit or cream)

[2]**trifle** *vb* **tri·fled; tri·fling** **1** : to talk in a jesting or mocking manner **2** : to treat someone or something as unimportant **3** : DALLY, FLIRT **4** : to handle idly : TOY — **tri·fler** *n*

tri·fling \ˈtrī-fliŋ\ *adj* **1** : FRIVOLOUS **2** : TRIVIAL, INSIGNIFICANT ⟨~ details⟩

♦ ***Synonyms*** PETTY, PALTRY, MEASLY, INCONSEQUENTIAL

tri·fo·cals \trī-ˈfō-kəlz\ *n pl* : eyeglasses with lenses having one part for close focus, one for intermediate focus, and one for distant focus

tri·fo·li·ate \trī-ˈfō-lē-ət\ *adj* : having three leaves or leaflets

¹trig \ˈtrig\ *adj* : stylishly trim : SMART

²trig *n* : TRIGONOMETRY

¹trig·ger \ˈtri-gər\ *n* [alter. of earlier *tricker*, fr. D *trekker*, fr. MD *trecker* one that pulls, fr. *trecken* to pull] : a movable lever that activates a device when it is squeezed; *esp* : the part of a firearm lock moved by the finger to fire a gun — **trigger** *adj* — **trig·gered** *adj*

²trigger *vb* **1** : to fire by pulling a trigger **2** : to initiate, actuate, or set off as if by a trigger ⟨remarks that ~*ed* a fight⟩

tri·glyc·er·ide \trī-ˈgli-sə-ˌrīd\ *n* : any of a group of lipids that are formed from glycerol and fatty acids and are widespread in animal tissue

trig·o·nom·e·try \ˌtri-gə-ˈnä-mə-trē\ *n* : the branch of mathematics dealing with the properties of triangles and esp. with finding unknown angles or sides given the size or length of some angles or sides — **trig·o·no·met·ric** \-nə-ˈme-trik\ *also* **trig·o·no·met·ri·cal** \-tri-kəl\ *adj*

trike \ˈtrīk\ *n* : TRICYCLE

¹trill \ˈtril\ *n* **1** : the alternation of two musical tones a scale degree apart **2** : WARBLE **3** : the rapid vibration of one speech organ against another (as of the tip of the tongue against the teeth)

²trill *vb* : to utter as or with a trill

tril·lion \ˈtril-yən\ *n* **1** : a thousand billions **2** : an indeterminately large number — **trillion** *adj* — **tril·lionth** \-yənth\ *adj or n*

tril·li·um \ˈtri-lē-əm\ *n* : any of a genus of spring-blooming herbs that are related to the lilies and have an erect stem bearing a whorl of three leaves and a solitary flower

tril·o·gy \ˈtri-lə-jē\ *n, pl* **-gies** : a series of three dramas or literary or musical compositions that are closely related and develop one theme

¹trim \ˈtrim\ *vb* **trimmed; trim·ming** [OE *trymian, trymman* to strengthen, arrange, fr. *trum* strong, firm] **1** : to put ornaments on : ADORN **2** : to defeat esp. resoundingly **3** : to make trim, neat, regular, or less bulky by or as if by cutting ⟨~ a beard⟩ ⟨~ a budget⟩ **4** : to cause (a boat) to assume a desired position in the water by arrangement of the load; *also* : to adjust (as a submarine or airplane) esp. for horizontal motion **5** : to adjust (a sail) to a desired position **6** : to change one's views for safety or expediency — **trim·ly** *adv* — **trim·mer** *n* — **trim·ness** *n*

²trim *adj* **trim·mer; trim·mest** : showing neatness, good order, or compactness ⟨a ~ figure⟩ ♦ ***Synonyms*** TIDY, TRIG, SMART, SPRUCE, SHIPSHAPE

³trim *n* **1** : good condition : FITNESS **2** : material used for ornament or trimming; *esp* : the woodwork in the finish of a house esp. around doors and windows **3** : the position of a ship or boat esp. with reference to the horizontal; *also* : the relation between the plane of a sail and the direction of a ship **4** : the position of an airplane at which it will continue in level flight with no adjustments to the controls **5** : something that is trimmed off

tri·ma·ran \ˈtrī-mə-ˌran, ˌtrī-mə-ˈran\ *n* : a sailboat with three hulls

tri·mes·ter \trī-ˈmes-tər, ˈtrī-ˌmes-tər\ *n* **1** : a period of three or about three months (as in pregnancy) **2** : one of three terms into which an academic year is sometimes divided

trim·e·ter \ˈtri-mə-tər\ *n* : a line of verse consisting of three metrical feet

trim·ming \ˈtri-miŋ\ *n* **1** : DEFEAT **2** : the action of one that trims **3** : something that trims, ornaments, or completes

tri·month·ly \trī-ˈmənth-lē\ *adj* : occurring every three months

trine \ˈtrīn\ *adj* : THREEFOLD, TRIPLE

Trin·i·da·di·an \ˌtri-nə-ˈdā-dē-ən, -ˈda-\ *n* : a native or inhabitant of the island of Trinidad — **Trinidadian** *adj*

Trin·i·tar·i·an \ˌtri-nə-ˈter-ē-ən\ *n* : a believer in the doctrine of the Trinity — **Trin·i·tar·i·an·ism** \-ē-ə-ˌni-zəm\ *n*

Trin·i·ty \ˈtri-nə-tē\ *n* **1** : the unity of Father, Son, and Holy Spirit as three persons in one Godhead **2** *not cap* : TRIAD

trin·ket \ˈtriŋ-kət\ *n* **1** : a small ornament (as a jewel or ring) **2** : TRIFLE 1

trio \ˈtrē-ō\ *n, pl* **tri·os** **1** : a musical composition for three voices or three instruments **2** : the performers of a trio **3** : a group or set of three

¹trip \ˈtrip\ *vb* **tripped; trip·ping** **1** : to move with light quick steps **2** : to catch the foot against something so as to stumble or cause to stumble **3** : to make a mistake : SLIP; *also* : to detect in a misstep : EXPOSE **4** : to release (as a spring or switch) by moving a catch; *also* : ACTIVATE ⟨~ an alarm⟩ **5** : to get high on a usu. hallucinatory drug

²trip *n* **1** : JOURNEY, VOYAGE **2** : a quick light step **3** : a false step : STUMBLE; *also* : ERROR **4** : the action of tripping mechanically; *also* : a device for tripping **5** : an intense experience; *esp* : one triggered by a hallucinatory drug **6** : absorption in an attitude or state of mind ⟨an ego ~⟩

tri·par·tite \trī-ˈpär-ˌtīt\ *adj* **1** : divided into three parts **2** : having three corresponding parts or copies **3** : made between three parties ⟨a ~ treaty⟩

tripe \ˈtrīp\ *n* **1** : stomach tissue esp. of a ruminant (as an ox) used as food **2** : something poor, worthless, or offensive : TRASH

¹tri·ple \ˈtri-pəl\ *vb* **tri·pled; tri·pling** **1** : to make or become three times as great or as many **2** : to hit a triple

²triple *n* **1** : a triple quantity **2** : a group of three **3** : a hit in baseball that lets the batter reach third base

[3]**triple** *adj* **1** : being three times as great or as many **2** : having three units or members **3** : repeated three times

triple bond *n* : a chemical bond in which three pairs of electrons are shared by two atoms in a molecule

triple point *n* : the condition of temperature and pressure under which the gaseous, liquid, and solid forms of a substance can exist in equilibrium

trip•let \ˈtri-plət\ *n* **1** : a unit of three lines of verse **2** : a group of three of a kind **3** : one of three offspring born at one birth

tri•plex \ˈtri-ˌpleks, ˈtrī-\ *adj* : THREEFOLD, TRIPLE

[1]**trip•li•cate** \ˈtri-pli-kət\ *adj* : made in three identical copies

[2]**trip•li•cate** \-plə-ˌkāt\ *vb* **-cat•ed; -cat•ing 1** : TRIPLE **2** : to provide three copies of ⟨~ a document⟩

[3]**trip•li•cate** \-pli-kət\ *n* : three copies all alike — used with *in* ⟨typed in ~⟩

tri•ply \ˈtri-plē, ˈtri-pə-lē\ *adv* : in a triple degree, amount, or manner

tri•pod \ˈtrī-ˌpäd\ *n* : something (as a cauldron, stool, or camera stand) that rests on three legs — **tripod** *or* **tri•po•dal** \ˈtri-pə-dᵊl, ˈtrī-ˌpä-\ *adj*

trip•tych \ˈtrip-tik\ *n* : a picture or carving in three panels side by side

tri•reme \ˈtrī-ˌrēm\ *n* : an ancient galley having three banks of oars

tri•sect \ˈtrī-ˌsekt, trī-ˈsekt\ *vb* : to divide into three usu. equal parts — **tri•sec•tion** \ˈtrī-ˌsek-shən\ *n*

trite \ˈtrīt\ *adj* **trit•er; trit•est** [L *tritus,* fr. pp. of *terere* to rub, wear away] : used so commonly that the novelty is worn off : STALE ♦ ***Synonyms*** HACKNEYED, STEREOTYPED, COMMONPLACE, CLICHÉD

tri•ti•um \ˈtri-tē-əm, ˈtri-shē-\ *n* : a radioactive form of hydrogen with one proton and two neutrons in its nucleus and three times the mass of ordinary hydrogen

tri•ton \ˈtrī-tᵊn\ *n* : any of various large marine gastropod mollusks with a heavy elongated conical shell; *also* : the shell of a triton

trit•u•rate \ˈtri-chə-ˌrāt\ *vb* **-rat•ed; -rat•ing** : to rub or grind to a fine powder

[1]**tri•umph** \ˈtrī-əmf\ *n* **1** : the joy or exultation of victory or success **2** : VICTORY, CONQUEST — **tri•um•phal** \trī-ˈəm-fəl\ *adj*

[2]**triumph** *vb* **1** : to obtain victory : PREVAIL **2** : to celebrate victory or success exultantly — **tri•um•phant** \trī-ˈəm-fənt\ *adj* — **tri•um•phant•ly** *adv*

tri•um•vir \trī-ˈəm-vər\ *n, pl* **-virs** *also* **-vi•ri** \-və-ˌrī\ : a member of a triumvirate

tri•um•vi•rate \-və-rət\ *n* : a ruling body of three persons

tri•une \ˈtrī-ˌün, -ˌyün\ *adj* : being three in one ⟨the ~ God⟩

triv•et \ˈtri-vət\ *n* **1** : a 3-legged stand : TRIPOD **2** : a usu. metal stand with short feet for use under a hot dish

triv•ia \ˈtri-vē-ə\ *n sing or pl* : unimportant matters : obscure facts or details ⟨movie ~⟩

triv•i•al \ˈtri-vē-əl\ *adj* [L *trivialis* found everywhere, commonplace, fr. *trivium* crossroads, fr. *tri-* three + *via* way] : of little importance — **triv•i•al•i•ty** \ˌtri-vē-ˈa-lə-tē\ *n*

triv•i•um \ˈtri-vē-əm\ *n, pl* **triv•ia** \-vē-ə\ : the three liberal arts of grammar, rhetoric, and logic in a medieval university

tri•week•ly \trī-ˈwē-klē\ *adj* **1** : occurring or appearing three times a week **2** : occurring or appearing every three weeks — **triweekly** *adv*

tro•che \ˈtrō-kē\ *n* : LOZENGE 2

tro•chee \ˈtrō-(ˌ)kē\ *n* : a metrical foot of one accented syllable followed by one unaccented syllable — **tro•cha•ic** \trō-ˈkā-ik\ *adj*

trod *past and past part of* TREAD

trodden *past part of* TREAD

troi•ka \ˈtrȯi-kə\ *n* [Russ *troĭka,* fr. *troe* three] : a group of three; *esp* : an administrative or ruling body of three

[1]**troll** \ˈtrōl\ *vb* **1** : to sing the parts of (a song) in succession **2** : to fish by trailing a lure or baited hook from a moving boat **3** : to sing or play jovially **4** : to deliberately antagonize (others) esp. online

[2]**troll** *n* **1** : a lure used in trolling; *also* : the line with its lure **2** : a person who trolls others esp. online

[3]**troll** *n* : a dwarf or giant in Scandinavian folklore inhabiting caves or hills

trol•ley *also* **trol•ly** \ˈträ-lē\ *n, pl* **trolleys** *also* **trollies 1** : a device (as a grooved wheel on the end of a pole) to carry current from a wire to an electrically driven vehicle **2** : a streetcar powered electrically by overhead wires **3** : a wheeled carriage running on an overhead rail or track

trol•ley•bus \ˈträ-lē-ˌbəs\ *n* : a bus powered electrically by overhead wires

trolley car *n* : TROLLEY 2

trol•lop \ˈträ-ləp\ *n* : a disreputable woman; *esp* : one who engages in sex promiscuously

trom•bone \träm-ˈbōn, ˈträm-ˌbōn\ *n* [It, fr. *tromba* trumpet] : a brass wind instrument that consists of a long metal tube with two turns and a flaring end and that usu. has a movable slide to vary the pitch — **trom•bon•ist** \-ˈbō-nist, -ˌbō-\ *n*

tromp \ˈträmp, ˈtrȯmp\ *vb* **1** : TRAMP, MARCH **2** : to stamp with the foot **3** : to defeat decisively

trompe l'oeil \(ˌ)trȯmp-ˈlə-ē, trōⁿp-ˈlœi\ *n* [F *trompe-l'oeil,* lit., deceives the eye] : a style of painting in which objects are depicted with photographic detail

[1]**troop** \ˈtrüp\ *n* **1** : a cavalry unit corresponding to an infantry company **2** *pl* : armed forces : SOLDIERS **3** : a collection of people, animals, or things **4** : a unit of Girl Scouts or Boy Scouts under an adult leader

[2]**troop** *vb* : to move or gather in crowds

troop•er \ˈtrü-pər\ *n* **1** : an enlisted cavalryman; *also* : a cavalry horse **2** : a mounted or a state police officer

troop•ship \ˈtrüp-ˌship\ *n* : a ship or aircraft for carrying troops

trope \ˈtrōp\ *n* : a word or expression used in a figurative sense

tro·phic \ˈtrō-fik\ *adj* : of or relating to nutrition

tro·phy \ˈtrō-fē\ *n, pl* **trophies** : something gained or given in conquest or victory esp. when preserved or mounted as a memorial

trop·ic \ˈträ-pik\ *n* [ME *tropik,* fr. L *tropicus* of the solstice, fr. Gk *tropikos,* fr. *tropē* turn] **1** : either of the two parallels of latitude approximately 23½ degrees north (**Tropic of Can·cer**) or south (**Tropic of Cap·ri·corn**) of the equator where the sun is directly overhead when it reaches its most northerly or southerly point in the sky **2** *pl, often cap* : the region lying between the tropics — **trop·i·cal** \-pi-kəl\ *or* **tropic** *adj*

tro·pism \ˈtrō-ˌpi-zəm\ *n* : an automatic movement by an organism in response to a source of stimulation; *also* : a reflex reaction involving this

tro·po·sphere \ˈtrō-pə-ˌsfir, ˈträ-\ *n* : the part of the atmosphere between the earth's surface and the stratosphere in which most weather changes occur — **tro·po·spher·ic** \ˌtrō-pə-ˈsfir-ik, ˌträ-, -ˈsfer-\ *adj*

1**trot** \ˈträt\ *n* **1** : a moderately fast gait of a 4-footed animal (as a horse) in which the legs move in diagonal pairs **2** : a human jogging gait between a walk and a run

2**trot** *vb* **trot·ted; trot·ting** **1** : to ride, drive, or go at a trot **2** : to proceed briskly : HURRY — **trot·ter** *n*

troth \ˈträth, ˈtröth, ˈtrōth\ *n* **1** : pledged faithfulness **2** : one's pledged word; *also* : BETROTHAL

trou·ba·dour \ˈtrü-bə-ˌdȯr\ *n* [F, fr. Old Occitan *trobador,* fr. *trobar* to compose] : any of a class of poet-musicians flourishing esp. in southern France and northern Italy during the 11th, 12th, and 13th centuries

1**trou·ble** \ˈtrə-bəl\ *vb* **trou·bled; trou·bling** **1** : to agitate mentally or spiritually : DISTURB, WORRY **2** : to produce physical disorder in : AFFLICT **3** : to put to inconvenience **4** : RUFFLE ⟨~ the waters⟩ **5** : to make an effort ♦ ***Synonyms*** DISTRESS, AIL, UPSET — **trou·ble·some** *adj* — **trou·ble·some·ly** *adv* — **trou·blous** \-bə-ləs\ *adj*

2**trouble** *n* **1** : the quality or state of being troubled esp. mentally **2** : an instance of distress or annoyance **3** : DISEASE, AILMENT ⟨heart ~⟩ **4** : EXERTION, PAINS ⟨took the ~ to phone⟩ **5** : a cause of disturbance or distress

trou·ble·mak·er \-ˌmā-kər\ *n* : a person who causes trouble

trou·ble·shoot·er \-ˌshü-tər\ *n* **1** : a worker employed to locate trouble and make repairs in equipment **2** : an expert in resolving disputes or problems — **trou·ble·shoot** *vb*

trough \ˈtrȯf, ˈtrȯth\ *n, pl* **troughs** \ˈtrȯfs, ˈtrȯvz; ˈtrȯths, ˈtrȯt͟hz\ **1** : a long shallow open boxlike container esp. for water or feed for livestock **2** : a gutter along the eaves of a house **3** : a long channel or depression (as between waves or hills) **4** : an elongated area of low barometric pressure

trounce \ˈtrau̇ns\ *vb* **trounced; trounc·ing** **1** : to thrash or punish severely **2** : to defeat decisively

troupe \ˈtrüp\ *n* : COMPANY; *esp* : a group of performers on the stage — **troup·er** *n*

trou·sers \ˈtrau̇-zərz\ *n pl* [alter. of earlier *trouse,* fr. ScGael *triubhas*] : PANTS — **trouser** *adj*

trous·seau \ˈtrü-sō, trü-ˈsō\ *n, pl* **trous·seaux** \-sōz, -ˈsōz\ *or* **trous·seaus** [F] : the personal outfit of a bride

trout \ˈtrau̇t\ *n, pl* **trout** *also* **trouts** [ME, fr. OE *trūht,* fr. LL *tructa,* a fish with sharp teeth, fr. Gk *trōktēs,* lit., gnawer] : any of various mostly freshwater food and game fishes usu. smaller than the related salmons

trow \ˈtrō\ *vb, archaic* : THINK, SUPPOSE

trow·el \ˈtrau̇(-ə)l\ *n* **1** : a hand tool used for spreading, shaping, or smoothing loose or plastic material (as mortar or plaster) **2** : a scoop-shaped tool used in gardening — **trowel** *vb*

troy \ˈtrȯi\ *adj* : expressed in troy weight ⟨~ ounce⟩

troy weight *n* : a system of weights based on a pound of 12 ounces and an ounce of 480 grains (31 grams) — see WEIGHT table

tru·ant \ˈtrü-ənt\ *n* [ME, vagabond, idler, fr. AF, of Celtic origin] : a student who stays out of school without permission — **tru·an·cy** \-ən-sē\ *n* — **truant** *adj*

truce \ˈtrüs\ *n* **1** : ARMISTICE **2** : a respite esp. from something unpleasant

1**truck** \ˈtrək\ *vb* **1** : EXCHANGE, BARTER **2** : to have dealings : TRAFFIC

2**truck** *n* **1** : BARTER **2** : DEALINGS **3** : small goods or merchandise; *esp* : vegetables grown for market

3**truck** *n* **1** : a wheeled vehicle (as a strong heavy automobile) designed for carrying heavy articles or hauling a trailer **2** : a swiveling frame with springs and one or more pairs of wheels used to carry and guide one end of a locomotive or railroad car

4**truck** *vb* **1** : to transport on a truck ⟨~s vegetables⟩ **2** : to be employed in driving a truck — **truck·er** *n*

truck farm *n* : a farm growing vegetables for market — **truck farmer** *n*

truck·le \ˈtrə-kəl\ *vb* **truck·led; truck·ling** : to act in a subservient manner : SUBMIT ♦ ***Synonyms*** FAWN, TOADY, CRINGE, COWER

truc·u·lent \ˈtrə-kyə-lənt\ *adj* **1** : feeling or showing ferocity : SAVAGE **2** : aggressively self-assertive : BELLIGERENT — **truc·u·lence** \-ləns\ *n* — **truc·u·len·cy** \-lən-sē\ *n* — **truc·u·lent·ly** *adv*

trudge \ˈtrəj\ *vb* **trudged; trudg·ing** : to walk or march steadily and usu. laboriously ⟨*trudged* through the snow⟩

1**true** \ˈtrü\ *adj* **tru·er; tru·est** **1** : STEADFAST, LOYAL **2** : agreeing with facts or reality ⟨a ~ description⟩ **3** : CONSISTENT ⟨~ to expectations⟩ **4** : properly so called ⟨~ love⟩ **5** : RIGHTFUL ⟨~ and lawful king⟩ **6** : conformable to a standard or pattern; *also* : placed or formed accurately ♦ ***Synonyms*** CONSTANT, STAUNCH, RESOLUTE, STEADFAST

²true *adv* **1** : TRUTHFULLY **2** : ACCURATELY ⟨the bullet flew straight and ~⟩; *also* : without variation from type ⟨breed ~⟩

³true *n* **1** : TRUTH, REALITY — usu. used with *the* **2** : the state of being accurate (as in alignment) ⟨out of ~⟩

⁴true *vb* **trued; true·ing** *also* **tru·ing** : to bring or restore to a desired precision

true–blue *adj* : marked by unswerving loyalty ⟨a ~ patriot⟩

true bug *n* : BUG 2

true·heart·ed \ˈtrü-ˈhär-təd\ *adj* : FAITHFUL, LOYAL ⟨a ~ soldier⟩

truf·fle \ˈtrə-fəl, ˈtrü-\ *n* **1** : the dark or light edible spore-bearing organ of any of several European fungi that grow underground; *also* : one of these fungi **2** : a candy made of chocolate, butter, and sugar shaped into balls and coated with cocoa

tru·ism \ˈtrü-ˌi-zəm\ *n* : an undoubted or self-evident truth ♦ ***Synonyms*** COMMONPLACE, PLATITUDE, CLICHÉ

tru·ly \ˈtrü-lē\ *adv* **1** : in all sincerity ⟨is ~ sorry⟩ **2** : in agreement with fact ⟨report it ~⟩ **3** : ACCURATELY **4** : in a proper or suitable manner

¹trump \ˈtrəmp\ *n* : TRUMPET

²trump *n* : a card of a designated suit any of whose cards will win over a card that is not of this suit; *also* : the suit itself — often used in pl.

³trump *vb* : to take with a trump

trumped–up \ˈtrəmpt-ˈəp\ *adj* : fraudulently concocted : SPURIOUS ⟨~ charges⟩

trum·pery \ˈtrəm-pə-rē\ *n* **1** : NONSENSE **2** : trivial articles : JUNK

¹trum·pet \ˈtrəm-pət\ *n* **1** : a wind instrument consisting of a long curved metal tube flaring at one end and with a cup-shaped mouthpiece at the other **2** : something that resembles a trumpet or its tonal quality **3** : a funnel-shaped instrument for collecting, directing, or intensifying sound

²trumpet *vb* **1** : to blow a trumpet **2** : to proclaim on or as if on a trumpet ⟨~ the news⟩ — **trum·pet·er** *n*

¹trun·cate \ˈtrəŋ-ˌkāt, ˈtrən-\ *adj* : having the end square or blunt

²truncate *vb* **trun·cat·ed; trun·cat·ing** : to shorten by or as if by cutting : LOP — **trun·ca·tion** \ˌtrəŋ-ˈkā-shən\ *n*

trun·cheon \ˈtrən-chən\ *n* : a police officer's billy club

trun·dle \ˈtrən-dᵊl\ *vb* **trun·dled; trun·dling** : to roll along : WHEEL

trundle bed *n* : a low bed that can be stored under a higher bed

trunk \ˈtrəŋk\ *n* **1** : the main stem of a tree **2** : the body of a person or animal apart from the head and limbs **3** : the main or central part of something **4** : a box or chest used to hold usu. clothes or personal effects (as of a traveler); *also* : the enclosed luggage space in the rear of an automobile **5** : the long muscular nose of an elephant **6** *pl* : men's shorts worn chiefly for sports ⟨swimming ~*s*⟩ **7** : a usu. major channel or passage

trunk line *n* : a transportation system handling long-distance through traffic

¹truss \ˈtrəs\ *vb* **1** : to secure tightly : BIND **2** : to arrange for cooking by binding close the wings or legs of (a fowl) **3** : to support, strengthen, or stiffen by or as if by a truss

²truss *n* **1** : a collection of structural parts (as beams) forming a rigid framework (as in bridge or building construction) **2** : a device worn to reduce a hernia by pressure

¹trust \ˈtrəst\ *n* **1** : assured reliance on the character, strength, or truth of someone or something **2** : a basis of reliance, faith, or hope **3** : confident hope **4** : financial credit **5** : a property interest held by one person for the benefit of another **6** : a combination of firms formed by a legal agreement; *esp* : one that reduces competition **7** : something entrusted to one to be cared for in the interest of another **8** : CARE, CUSTODY ♦ ***Synonyms*** CONFIDENCE, DEPENDENCE, FAITH, RELIANCE

²trust *vb* **1** : to place confidence : DEPEND **2** : to be confident : HOPE **3** : ENTRUST **4** : to permit to stay or go or to do something without fear or misgiving **5** : to rely on or on the truth of : BELIEVE **6** : to extend credit to

trust·ee \ˌtrəs-ˈtē\ *n* **1** : a person to whom property is legally committed in trust **2** : a country charged with the supervision of a trust territory

trust·ee·ship \ˌtrəs-ˈtē-ˌship\ *n* **1** : the office or function of a trustee **2** : supervisory control by one or more nations over a trust territory

trust·ful \ˈtrəst-fəl\ *adj* : full of trust : CONFIDING — **trust·ful·ly** *adv* — **trust·ful·ness** *n*

trust territory *n* : a non-self-governing territory placed under a supervisory authority by the Trusteeship Council of the United Nations

trust·wor·thy \-ˌwər-t͟hē\ *adj* : worthy of confidence : DEPENDABLE ⟨a ~ assistant⟩ ♦ ***Synonyms*** TRUSTY, TRIED, RELIABLE — **trust·wor·thi·ness** *n*

¹trusty \ˈtrəs-tē\ *adj* **trust·i·er; -est** : TRUSTWORTHY, DEPENDABLE ⟨a ~ friend⟩

²trusty \ˈtrəs-tē, ˌtrəs-ˈtē\ *n, pl* **trust·ies** : a trusted person; *esp* : a convict considered trustworthy and allowed special privileges

truth \ˈtrüth\ *n, pl* **truths** \ˈtrü t͟hz, ˈtrüths\ **1** : TRUTHFULNESS, HONESTY **2** : the real state of things : FACT **3** : the body of real events or facts : ACTUALITY **4** : a true or accepted statement or proposition ⟨the ~*s* of science⟩ **5** : agreement with fact or reality : CORRECTNESS ♦ ***Synonyms*** VERACITY, VERITY

truth·ful \ˈtrüth-fəl\ *adj* : telling or disposed to tell the truth — **truth·ful·ly** *adv* — **truth·ful·ness** *n*

truth serum *n* : a drug held to induce a subject under questioning to talk freely

[1]**try** \ˈtrī\ *vb* **tried; try·ing** [ME *trien,* fr. AF *trier* to select, sort, examine, prob. fr. LL *tritare* to grind] **1 :** to examine or investigate judicially **2 :** to conduct the trial of **3 :** to put to test or trial **4 :** to subject to strain, affliction, or annoyance **5 :** to extract or clarify (as lard) by melting **6 :** to make an effort to do something **:** ATTEMPT, ENDEAVOR ♦ ***Synonyms*** ESSAY, ASSAY, STRIVE, STRUGGLE

[2]**try** *n, pl* **tries :** an experimental trial

try·ing *adj* **:** severely straining the powers of endurance

try on *vb* **:** to put on (a garment) to test the fit and looks

try out *vb* **:** to participate in competition esp. for a position on an athletic team or a part in a play — **try·out** \ˈtrī-ˌau̇t\ *n*

tryp·to·phan \ˈtrip-tə-ˌfan\ *n* **:** a crystalline essential amino acid that is widely distributed in proteins

tryst \ˈtrist\ *n* **1 :** an agreement (as between lovers) to meet **2 :** an appointed meeting or meeting place — **tryst** *vb* — **tryst·er** *n*

Ts *symbol* tennessine

TSA *abbr* Transportation Security Administration

tsar, tsarist *var of* CZAR, CZARIST

tsarina *var of* CZARINA

tset·se fly \ˈtset-sē-, ˈtsēt-, ˈtet-, ˈtēt-, ˈset-, ˈsēt-\ *n* **:** any of several sub-Saharan African dipteran flies including the vector of sleeping sickness

TSgt *abbr* technical sergeant

T–shirt \ˈtē-ˌshərt\ *n* **:** a collarless short-sleeved or sleeveless cotton undershirt; *also* **:** an outer shirt of similar design — **T–shirt·ed** \-ˌshər-təd\ *adj*

tsk *a click; often read as* ˈtisk\ *interj* — used to express disapproval

tsp *abbr* teaspoon; teaspoonful

T square *n* **:** a ruler with a crosspiece at one end for making parallel lines

tsu·na·mi \su̇-ˈnä-mē, tsu̇-\ *n* [Jp] **:** a tidal wave caused esp. by an underwater earthquake or volcanic eruption

TT *abbr* Trust Territories

TTY *abbr* teletypewriter

Tu *abbr* Tuesday

tub \ˈtəb\ *n* **1 :** a wide low bucketlike vessel **2 :** BATHTUB; *also* **:** BATH **3 :** the amount that a tub will hold

tu·ba \ˈtü-bə, ˈtyü-\ *n* **:** a large low-pitched brass wind instrument

tub·al \ˈtü-bəl, ˈtyü-\ *adj* **:** of, relating to, or involving a tube and esp. a fallopian tube ⟨~ infection⟩

tube \ˈtüb, ˈtyüb\ *n* **1 :** any of various usu. cylindrical structures or devices; *esp* **:** one to convey fluids **2 :** a slender hollow anatomical part (as a fallopian tube) functioning as a channel in a plant or animal body **:** DUCT **3 :** a soft round container from which a paste is squeezed **4 :** a tunnel for vehicular or rail travel **5** *Brit* **:** SUBWAY **6 :** INNER TUBE **7 :** ELECTRON TUBE **8 :** TELEVISION — **tubed** \ˈtübd, ˈtyübd\ *adj* — **tube·less** *adj* — **tube·like** \ˈtüb-ˌlīk, ˈtyüb-\ *adj*

tu·ber \ˈtü-bər, ˈtyü-\ *n* **:** a short fleshy usu. underground stem (as of a potato plant) bearing minute scalelike leaves each with a bud at its base

tu·ber·cle \ˈtü-bər-kəl, ˈtyü-\ *n* **1 :** a small knobby prominence or outgrowth esp. on an animal or plant **2 :** a small abnormal lump in an organ or on the skin; *esp* **:** one caused by tuberculosis

tubercle bacillus *n* **:** a bacterium that is the cause of tuberculosis

tu·ber·cu·lar \tu̇-ˈbər-kyə-lər, tyu̇-\ *adj* **1 :** TUBERCULOUS **2 :** of, resembling, or being a tubercle

tu·ber·cu·lin \tu̇-ˈbər-kyə-lən, tyu̇-\ *n* **:** a sterile liquid extracted from the tubercle bacillus and used in the diagnosis of tuberculosis esp. in children and cattle

tu·ber·cu·lo·sis \tu̇-ˌbər-kyə-ˈlō-səs, tyu̇-\ *n, pl* **-lo·ses** \-ˌsēz\ **:** a communicable bacterial disease that affects esp. the lungs and is typically marked by fever, cough, difficulty in breathing, and formation of tubercles — **tu·ber·cu·lous** \-ˈbər-kyə-ləs\ *adj*

tube·rose \ˈtüb-ˌrōz, ˈtyüb-\ *n* **:** a bulbous herb related to the agaves and often grown for its spike of fragrant waxy-white flowers

tu·ber·ous \ˈtü-bə-rəs, ˈtyü-\ *adj* **:** of, resembling, or being a tuber

tub·ing \ˈtü-biŋ, ˈtyü-\ *n* **1 :** material in the form of a tube; *also* **:** a length of tube **2 :** a series or system of tubes

tu·bu·lar \ˈtü-byə-lər, ˈtyü-\ *adj* **:** having the form of or consisting of a tube; *also* **:** made with tubes

tu·bule \ˈtü-byül, ˈtyü-\ *n* **:** a small tube

[1]**tuck** \ˈtək\ *vb* **1 :** to pull up into a fold ⟨~*ed* up her skirt⟩ **2 :** to make tucks in **3 :** to put into a snug often concealing place ⟨~ a book under the arm⟩ **4 :** to secure in place by pushing the edges under ⟨~ in a blanket⟩ **5 :** to cover by tucking in bedclothes

[2]**tuck** *n* **1 :** a fold stitched into cloth to shorten, decorate, or control fullness **2 :** a cosmetic surgical operation for the removal of excess skin or fat ⟨a tummy ~⟩

tuck·er \ˈtə-kər\ *vb* **tuck·ered; tuck·er·ing :** EXHAUST, FATIGUE ⟨was ~*ed* out after a long day's work⟩

Tues *or* **Tue** *abbr* Tuesday

Tues·day \ˈtüz-dē, ˈtyüz-, -dā\ *n* **:** the 3d day of the week

tu·fa \ˈtü-fə, ˈtyü-\ *n* **:** a porous rock (as travertine) formed as a deposit from springs or streams

tuff \ˈtəf\ *n* **:** a rock composed of volcanic detritus

[1]**tuft** \ˈtəft\ *n* **1 :** a small cluster of long flexible outgrowths (as hairs); *also* **:** a bunch of soft fluffy threads cut off short and used as ornament **2 :** CLUMP, CLUSTER — **tuft·ed** *adj*

[2]**tuft** *vb* **1 :** to provide or adorn with a tuft **2 :** to make (as a mattress) firm by stitching at intervals and sewing on tufts — **tuft·er** *n*

[1]**tug** \ˈtəg\ *vb* **tugged; tug·ging 1 :** to pull hard **2 :** to struggle in opposition **:** CON-

TEND **3** : to move by pulling hard : HAUL **4** : to tow with a tugboat

[2]**tug** *n* **1** : a harness trace **2** : an act of tugging : PULL **3** : a straining effort **4** : a struggle between opposing people or forces **5** : TUGBOAT

tug·boat \-ˌbōt\ *n* : a strongly built boat used for towing or pushing

tug–of–war \ˌtəg-əv-ˈwȯr\ *n, pl* **tugs–of–war** **1** : a struggle for supremacy **2** : an athletic contest in which two teams pull against each other at opposite ends of a rope

tu·grik *or* **tu·ghrik** \ˈtü-grik\ *n* — see MONEY table

tu·ition \tu̇-ˈi-shən, tyu̇-\ *n* : money paid for instruction ⟨college ~⟩

tu·la·re·mia \ˌtü-lə-ˈrē-mē-ə, ˌtyü-\ *n* : an infectious bacterial disease esp. of wild rabbits, rodents, humans, and some domestic animals that in humans is marked by symptoms (as fever) similar to those of influenza

tu·lip \ˈtü-ləp, ˈtyü-\ *n* [NL *tulipa,* fr. Turk *tülbent* turban] : any of a genus of Eurasian bulbous herbs related to the lilies and grown for their large showy erect cup-shaped flowers; *also* : a flower or bulb of a tulip

tulip tree *n* : a tall No. American timber tree that is related to the magnolias and has greenish tulip-shaped flowers and soft white wood

tulle \ˈtül\ *n* : a sheer often stiffened silk, rayon, or nylon net ⟨a veil of ~⟩

[1]**tum·ble** \ˈtəm-bəl\ *vb* **tum·bled; tum·bling** [ME, fr. *tumben* to dance, fr. OE *tumbian*] **1** : to fall or cause to fall suddenly and helplessly **2** : to fall into ruin **3** : to perform gymnastic feats of rolling and turning **4** : to roll over and over : TOSS **5** : to issue forth hurriedly and confusedly **6** : to come to understand **7** : to throw together in a confused mass

[2]**tumble** *n* **1** : a disorderly state **2** : an act or instance of tumbling

tum·ble·down \ˈtəm-bəl-ˈdau̇n\ *adj* : DILAPIDATED, RAMSHACKLE ⟨a ~ shack⟩

tum·bler \ˈtəm-blər\ *n* **1** : one that tumbles; *esp* : ACROBAT **2** : a drinking glass without foot or stem **3** : a movable obstruction in a lock that must be adjusted to a particular position (as by a key) before the bolt can be thrown

tum·ble·weed \ˈtəm-bəl-ˌwēd\ *n* : a plant that breaks away from its roots in autumn and is driven about by the wind

tum·brel *or* **tum·bril** \ˈtəm-brəl\ *n* **1** : CART **2** : a vehicle carrying condemned persons (as during the French Revolution) to a place of execution

tu·mid \ˈtü-məd, ˈtyü-\ *adj* **1** : SWOLLEN, DISTENDED **2** : BOMBASTIC, TURGID

tum·my \ˈtə-mē\ *n, pl* **tummies** : BELLY, ABDOMEN, STOMACH

tu·mor \ˈtü-mər, ˈtyü-\ *n* : an abnormal and functionless new growth of tissue that arises from uncontrolled cellular proliferation — **tu·mor·ous** *adj*

tu·mour *chiefly Brit var of* TUMOR

tu·mult \ˈtü-ˌməlt, ˈtyü-\ *n* **1** : UPROAR **2** : violent agitation of mind or feelings

tu·mul·tu·ous \tu̇-ˈməl-chə-wəs, tyu̇-, -chəs\ *adj* **1** : marked by tumult ⟨~ applause⟩ **2** : tending to incite a tumult **3** : marked by violent upheaval ⟨~ war years⟩

tun \ˈtən\ *n* : a large cask

tu·na \ˈtü-nə, ˈtyü-\ *n, pl* **tuna** *or* **tunas** : any of several mostly large marine fishes related to the mackerels and caught for food and sport; *also* : the flesh of a tuna

tun·able \ˈtü-nə-bəl, ˈtyü-\ *adj* : capable of being tuned — **tun·abil·i·ty** \ˌtü-nə-ˈbi-lə-tē, ˌtyü-\ *n*

tun·dra \ˈtən-drə\ *n* [Russ] : a treeless plain of arctic and subarctic regions

[1]**tune** \ˈtün, ˈtyün\ *n* **1** : a succession of pleasing musical tones : MELODY **2** : correct musical pitch **3** : harmonious relationship : AGREEMENT ⟨in ~ with the times⟩ **4** : general attitude ⟨changed his ~⟩ **5** : AMOUNT, EXTENT ⟨in debt to the ~ of millions⟩

[2]**tune** *vb* **tuned; tun·ing** **1** : to adjust in musical pitch **2** : to bring or come into harmony : ATTUNE **3** : to put in good working order **4** : to adjust a radio or television receiver so as to receive a broadcast **5** : to adjust the frequency of the output of (a device) to a chosen frequency — **tun·er** *n*

tune·ful \-fəl\ *adj* : MELODIOUS, MUSICAL ⟨a ~ ballad⟩ — **tune·ful·ly** *adv* — **tune·ful·ness** *n*

tune·less \-ləs\ *adj* **1** : UNMELODIOUS **2** : not producing music — **tune·less·ly** *adv*

tune–up \ˈtün-ˌəp, ˈtyün-\ *n* : an adjustment to ensure efficient functioning

tung·sten \ˈtəŋ-stən\ *n* [Sw, fr. *tung* heavy + *sten* stone] : a gray-white hard heavy ductile metallic chemical element used esp. in carbide materials, electrical components, and alloys

tu·nic \ˈtü-nik, ˈtyü-\ *n* **1** : a usu. knee-length belted garment worn by ancient Greeks and Romans **2** : a hip-length or longer blouse or jacket

tuning fork *n* : a 2-pronged metal implement that gives a fixed tone when struck and is useful for tuning musical instruments

[1]**tun·nel** \ˈtə-nᵊl\ *n* : an enclosed passage (as a tube or conduit); *esp* : one underground (as in a mine)

[2]**tunnel** *vb* **-neled** *or* **-nelled; -nel·ing** *or* **-nel·ling** : to make a tunnel through or under — **tun·nel·er** \ˈtən-lər, ˈtə-nᵊl-ər\ *n*

tun·ny \ˈtə-nē\ *n, pl* **tunnies** *also* **tunny** : TUNA

tuque \ˈtük, ˈtyük\ *n* [CanF] : a warm knitted cone-shaped cap

tur·ban \ˈtər-bən\ *n* **1** : a headdress worn esp. by Muslims and made of a cap around which is wound a long cloth **2** : a headdress resembling a turban; *esp* : a woman's close-fitting hat without a brim

tur·bid \ˈtər-bəd\ *adj* [L *turbidus* confused, turbid, fr. *turba* confusion, crowd] **1** : cloudy or discolored by suspended particles ⟨a ~ stream⟩ **2** : CONFUSED, MUDDLED — **tur·bid·i·ty** \ˌtər-ˈbi-də-tē\ *n*

tur·bine \ˈtər-bən, -ˌbīn\ *n* [F, fr. L *turbin-, turbo* top, whirlwind, whirl] : an engine whose central driveshaft is fitted with curved vanes spun by the pressure of water, steam, or gas

tur·bo·fan \ˈtər-bō-ˌfan\ *n* : a jet engine having a fan driven by a turbine for supplying air for combustion

tur·bo·jet \-ˌjet\ *n* : an airplane powered by a jet engine (**turbojet engine**) having a turbine-driven air compressor supplying compressed air to the combustion chamber

tur·bo·prop \-ˌpräp\ *n* : an airplane powered by a jet engine (**turboprop engine**) having a turbine-driven propeller

tur·bot \ˈtər-bət\ *n, pl* **turbot** *also* **turbots** : a European flatfish that is a popular food fish; *also* : any of several similar flatfishes

tur·bu·lence \ˈtər-byə-ləns\ *n* : the quality or state of being turbulent

tur·bu·lent \-lənt\ *adj* **1** : causing violence or disturbance **2** : marked by agitation or tumult : TEMPESTUOUS ⟨a ~ marriage⟩ — **tur·bu·lent·ly** *adv*

tu·reen \tə-ˈrēn, tyu̇-\ *n* [F *terrine,* fr. MF, fr. fem. of *terrin* of earth] : a deep bowl from which foods (as soup) are served at the table

[1]**turf** \ˈtərf\ *n, pl* **turfs** \ˈtərfs\ *also* **turves** \ˈtərvz\ **1** : the upper layer of soil bound by grass and roots into a close mat; *also* : a piece of this **2** : an artificial substitute for turf (as on a playing field) **3** : a piece of peat dried for fuel **4** : a track or course for horse racing; *also* : horse racing as a sport or business

[2]**turf** *vb* : to cover with turf

tur·gid \ˈtər-jəd\ *adj* **1** : being in a swollen state **2** : excessively embellished in style or language : BOMBASTIC ⟨~ writing⟩ — **tur·gid·i·ty** \ˌtər-ˈji-də-tē\ *n*

tur·key \ˈtər-kē\ *n, pl* **turkeys** [*Turkey,* country in western Asia and southeastern Europe; fr. confusion with the guinea fowl, supposed to be imported from Turkish territory] : a large No. American bird related to the domestic chicken and widely raised for food

turkey buzzard *n* : TURKEY VULTURE

turkey vulture *n* : an American vulture with a red head and whitish bill

Turk·ish \ˈtər-kish\ *n* : the language of Turkey — **Turkish** *adj*

tur·mer·ic \ˈtər-mə-rik\ *n* : a spice or dyestuff obtained from the large aromatic deep-yellow rhizome of an Indian perennial herb related to the ginger; *also* : this herb

tur·moil \ˈtər-ˌmȯi(-ə)l\ *n* : an extremely confused or agitated condition

[1]**turn** \ˈtərn\ *vb* **1** : to move or cause to move around an axis or center : ROTATE, REVOLVE ⟨~ a wheel⟩ **2** : to effect a desired end by turning something ⟨~ the oven on⟩ **3** : WRENCH ⟨~ an ankle⟩ **4** : to change or cause to change position by moving through an arc of a circle ⟨~*ed* her chair to the fire⟩ **5** : to cause to move around a center so as to show another side of ⟨~ a page⟩ **6** : to revolve mentally : PONDER **7** : to become dizzy : REEL **8** : to reverse the sides or surfaces of ⟨~ a pancake⟩ **9** : UPSET, DISORDER ⟨things were ~*ed* topsy-turvy⟩ **10** : to set in another esp. contrary direction **11** : to change one's course or direction **12** : to go around ⟨~ a corner⟩ **13** : BECOME ⟨my hair ~*ed* gray⟩ ⟨~*ed* twenty-one⟩ **14** : to direct toward or away from something; *also* : DEVOTE, APPLY **15** : to have recourse **16** : to become or make hostile **17** : to cause to become of a specified nature or appearance ⟨~*s* the leaves yellow⟩ **18** : to make or become spoiled : SOUR **19** : to pass from one state to another ⟨water ~*s* to ice⟩ **20** : CONVERT, TRANSFORM **21** : TRANSLATE, PARAPHRASE **22** : to give a rounded form to; *esp* : to shape by means of a lathe **23** : to gain by passing in trade ⟨~ a quick profit⟩ — **turn·able** \ˈtər-nə-bəl\ *adj* — **turn color 1** : BLUSH **2** : to become pale — **turn loose** : to set free

[2]**turn** *n* **1** : a turning about a center or axis : REVOLUTION, ROTATION **2** : the action or an act of giving or taking a different direction ⟨make a left ~⟩ **3** : a change of course or tendency ⟨a ~ for the better⟩ **4** : a place at which something turns : BEND, CURVE **5** : a short walk or trip round about ⟨take a ~ around the block⟩ **6** : an act affecting another ⟨did him a good ~⟩ **7** : a place, time, or opportunity accorded in a scheduled order ⟨waited his ~ in line⟩ **8** : a period of duty : SHIFT **9** : a short act esp. in a variety show **10** : a special purpose or requirement ⟨the job serves his ~⟩ **11** : a skillful fashioning ⟨neat ~ of phrase⟩ **12** : a single round (as of rope passed around an object) **13** : natural or special aptitude **14** : a usu. sudden and brief disorder of body or spirits; *esp* : a spell of nervous shock or faintness

turn·about \ˈtərn-ə-ˌbau̇t\ *n* **1** : a reversal of direction, trend, or policy **2** : RETALIATION

turn·buck·le \ˈtərn-ˌbə-kəl\ *n* : a link with a screw thread at one or both ends for tightening a rod or stay

turn·coat \-ˌkōt\ *n* : one who switches to an opposing side or party : TRAITOR

turn down *vb* : to decline to accept : REJECT — **turn·down** \ˈtərn-ˌdau̇n\ *n*

turn·er \ˈtər-nər\ *n* **1** : one that turns or is used for turning **2** : one that forms articles with a lathe

turn·ery \ˈtər-nə-rē\ *n, pl* **-er·ies** : the work, products, or shop of a turner

turn in *vb* **1** : to deliver up **2** : to inform on **3** : to acquit oneself of ⟨*turn in* a good job⟩ **4** : to go to bed

turn·ing \ˈtər-niŋ\ *n* **1** : the act or course of one that turns **2** : a place of a change of direction

tur·nip \ˈtər-nəp\ *n* **1** : a garden herb related to the cabbage with a thick edible usu. white root **2** : RUTABAGA **3** : the root of a turnip

turn·key \ˈtərn-ˌkē\ *n, pl* **turnkeys** : one who has charge of a prison's keys

turn·off \ˈtərn-ˌȯf\ *n* : a place for turning off esp. from an expressway

turn off *vb* **1** : to deviate from a straight course or a main road **2** : to stop the functioning or flow of **3** : to cause to lose interest; *also* : to evoke a negative feeling in ⟨violence on TV *turns* her *off*⟩

turn on *vb* **1** : to cause to flow, function, or operate **2** : to get high or cause to get high as a result of using a drug (as marijuana) **3** : EXCITE, STIMULATE

turn•out \ˈtərn-ˌau̇t\ *n* **1** : an act of turning out **2** : the number of people who participate or attend an event **3** : a widened place in a highway for vehicles to pass or park **4** : manner of dress **5** : net yield : OUTPUT

turn out *vb* **1** : EXPEL, EVICT **2** : PRODUCE **3** : to cause to stop functioning by turning a switch **4** : to come forth and assemble **5** : to get out of bed **6** : to prove to be in the end

[1]**turn•over** \ˈtərn-ˌō-vər\ *n* **1** : UPSET **2** : SHIFT, REVERSAL **3** : a filled pastry made by turning half of the crust over the other half **4** : the volume of business done **5** : movement (as of goods or people) into, through, and out of a place **6** : the number of persons hired within a period to replace those leaving or dropped **7** : an instance of a team's losing possession of the ball esp. through error

[2]**turnover** *adj* : capable of being turned over

turn over *vb* : TRANSFER ⟨*turn* the job *over* to her⟩

turn•pike \ˈtərn-ˌpīk\ *n* [ME *turnepike* revolving frame bearing spikes and serving as a barrier, fr. *turnen* to turn + *pike*] **1** : TOLLGATE; *also* : an expressway on which tolls are charged **2** : a main road

turn•stile \-ˌstī(-ə)l\ *n* : a post with arms pivoted on the top set in a passageway so that persons can pass through only on foot one by one

turn•ta•ble \-ˌtā-bəl\ *n* : a circular platform that revolves (as for turning a locomotive or a phonograph record)

turn to *vb* : to apply oneself to work

turn up *vb* **1** : to come to light or bring to light : DISCOVER, APPEAR **2** : to raise or increase by or as if by turning a control **3** : to arrive at an appointed time or place **4** : to happen unexpectedly

tur•pen•tine \ˈtər-pən-ˌtīn\ *n* **1** : a mixture of oil and resin obtained from various cone-bearing trees (as pines) **2** : an oil distilled from turpentine or pine wood and used as a solvent and paint thinner

tur•pi•tude \ˈtər-pə-ˌtüd, -ˌtyüd\ *n* : inherent baseness : DEPRAVITY

tur•quoise *also* **tur•quois** \ˈtər-ˌkȯiz, -ˌkwȯiz\ *n* [ME *turkeys,* fr. AF *turkeise,* fr. fem. of *turkeis* Turkish, fr. *Turc* Turk] **1** : a blue, bluish green, or greenish gray mineral that is valued as a gem **2** : a light greenish blue color

tur•ret \ˈtər-ət\ *n* **1** : a little ornamental tower often at a corner of a building **2** : a low usu. revolving structure (as on a tank or warship) in which one or more guns are mounted — **tur•ret•ed** \ˈtər-ə-təd\ *adj*

[1]**tur•tle** \ˈtər-tᵊl\ *n, archaic* : TURTLEDOVE

[2]**turtle** *n, pl* **turtles** *also* **turtle** : any of an order of horny-beaked land, freshwater, or sea reptiles with the trunk enclosed in a bony shell

tur•tle•dove \ˈtər-tᵊl-ˌdəv\ *n* : any of several small pigeons noted for plaintive cooing

tur•tle•neck \-ˌnek\ *n* : a high close-fitting turnover collar (as on a sweater); *also* : a sweater or shirt with a turtleneck — **tur•tle•necked** \-ˌnekt\ *adj*

turves *pl of* TURF

Tus•ca•ro•ra \ˌtəs-kə-ˈrȯr-ə\ *n, pl* **Tuscarora** *or* **Tuscaroras** : a member of an Indigenous people orig. of No. Carolina and later of New York and Ontario; *also* : the language of the Tuscarora people

tusk \ˈtəsk\ *n* : a long enlarged protruding tooth (as of an elephant, walrus, or boar) used esp. to dig up food or as a weapon — **tusked** \ˈtəskt\ *adj*

tusk•er \ˈtəs-kər\ *n* : an animal with tusks; *esp* : a male elephant with two normally developed tusks

[1]**tus•sle** \ˈtə-səl\ *n* **1** : a physical struggle : SCUFFLE **2** : an intense argument, controversy, or struggle

[2]**tussle** *vb* **tus•sled; tus•sling** : to struggle roughly ⟨players *tussled* for the ball⟩

tus•sock \ˈtə-sək\ *n* : a dense tuft esp. of grass or sedge; *also* : a hummock in a marsh or bog bound together by roots — **tus•socky** *adj*

tu•te•lage \ˈtü-tᵊl-ij, ˈtyü-\ *n* **1** : an act of guarding or protecting **2** : the state of being under a guardian or tutor **3** : instruction esp. of an individual

tu•te•lary \ˈtü-tə-ˌler-ē, ˈtyü-\ *adj* : acting as a guardian ⟨~ deity⟩

[1]**tu•tor** \ˈtü-tər, ˈtyü-\ *n* **1** : a person charged with the instruction and guidance of another **2** : a private teacher

[2]**tutor** *vb* **1** : to have the guardianship of **2** : to teach or guide individually : COACH ⟨~*ed* her in Latin⟩ **3** : to receive instruction esp. privately

tu•to•ri•al \tü-ˈtȯr-ē-əl, tyü-\ *n* : a class conducted by a tutor for one student or a small number of students

tut•ti \ˈtü-tē, ˈtu̇-, -ˌtē\ *adj or adv* [It, pl. of *tutto* all] : with all voices and instruments playing together — used as a direction in music

tut•ti–frut•ti \ˌtü-ti-ˈfrü-tē, ˌtu̇-\ *n* [It, lit., all fruits] : a confection or ice cream containing chopped usu. candied fruits

tu•tu \ˈtü-(ˌ)tü\ *n* [F] : a short projecting skirt worn by a ballerina

tux•e•do \ˌtək-ˈsē-dō\ *n, pl* **-dos** *or* **-does** [*Tuxedo* Park, N.Y.] **1** : a usu. black or blackish blue jacket **2** : a semiformal evening suit for men

TV \ˈtē-ˈvē\ *n* : TELEVISION

TVA *abbr* Tennessee Valley Authority

TV dinner *n* : a frozen packaged dinner that needs only heating before serving

twad•dle \ˈtwä-dᵊl\ *n* : silly idle talk : DRIVEL — **twaddle** *vb*

twain \ˈtwān\ *n* **1** : TWO **2** : PAIR

[1]**twang** \ˈtwaŋ\ *n* **1** : a harsh quick ringing sound like that of a plucked bowstring **2**

: nasal speech or resonance **3** : the characteristic speech of a region

[2]**twang** *vb* **twanged; twang·ing** **1** : to sound or cause to sound with a twang **2** : to speak with a nasal twang

tweak \'twēk\ *vb* **1** : to pinch and pull with a sudden jerk and twitch **2** : to make small adjustments to — **tweak** *n*

tweed \'twēd\ *n* **1** : a rough woolen fabric made usu. in twill weaves **2** *pl* : tweed clothing; *esp* : a tweed suit

tweedy \'twē-dē\ *adj* **tweed·i·er; -est** **1** : of or resembling tweed **2** : given to wearing tweeds **3** : suggestive of the outdoors in taste or habits **4** : ACADEMIC, SCHOLARLY

[1]**tween** \'twēn\ *prep* : BETWEEN

[2]**tween** *n* : PRETEEN

[1]**tweet** \'twēt\ *n* **1** : a chirping note **2** : a short message posted on the Twitter online service

[2]**tweet** *vb* **1** : to make a chirping sound **2** : to post a tweet

tweet·er \'twē-tər\ *n* : a small loudspeaker that reproduces sounds of high pitch

twee·zers \'twē-zərz\ *n pl* [obs. E *tweeze,* n., case for small implements, short for obs. E *etweese,* fr. pl. of obs. E *etwee,* fr. F *étui*] : a small pincerlike implement usu. held between the thumb and index finger and used for grasping something

twelve \'twelv\ *n* **1** : one more than 11 **2** : the 12th in a set or series **3** : something having 12 units — **twelfth** \'twelfth\ *adj or n* — **twelve** *adj or pron*

twelve·month \-ˌmənth\ *n* : YEAR

12–step \'twelv-ˌstep\ *adj* : of, relating to, or being a program designed esp. to help someone overcome a problem (as an addiction) by following 12 tenets

twen·ty \'twen-tē\ *n, pl* **twenties** : two times 10 — **twen·ti·eth** \-tē-əth\ *adj or n* — **twenty** *adj or pron*

twenty–twenty *or* **20/20** \ˌtwen-tē-'twen-tē\ *adj* : characterized by a visual capacity for seeing detail that is normal for the human eye ⟨~ vision⟩

twice \'twīs\ *adv* **1** : on two occasions **2** : two times ⟨~ two is four⟩

[1]**twid·dle** \'twi-dᵊl\ *vb* **twid·dled; twid·dling** **1** : to be busy with trifles; *also* : to play idly with something **2** : to rotate lightly or idly

[2]**twiddle** *n* : TURN, TWIST

twig \'twig\ *n* : a small branch — **twig·gy** *adj*

twi·light \'twī-ˌlīt\ *n* **1** : the light from the sky between full night and sunrise or between sunset and full night **2** : a state of imperfect clarity **3** : a period of decline

twilight zone *n* **1** : an area just beyond ordinary legal or ethical limits **2** : TWILIGHT 2 **3** : a world of fantasy or unreality

twill \'twil\ *n* [ME *twyll,* fr. OE *twilic* having a double thread, part trans. of L *bilic-, bilix,* fr. *bi-* two + *licium* thread] **1** : a fabric with a twill weave **2** : a textile weave that gives an appearance of diagonal lines

twilled \'twild\ *adj* : made with a twill weave

[1]**twin** \'twin\ *n* **1** : either of two offspring produced at a birth **2** : one of two persons or things closely related to or resembling each other

[2]**twin** *vb* **twinned; twin·ning** **1** : to be coupled with another **2** : to bring forth twins

[3]**twin** *adj* **1** : born with one other or as a pair at one birth ⟨~ brother⟩ ⟨~ girls⟩ **2** : made up of two similar or related members or parts **3** : being one of a pair ⟨~ city⟩

[1]**twine** \'twīn\ *n* **1** : a strong thread of two or three strands twisted together **2** : an act of entwining or interlacing — **twiny** *adj*

[2]**twine** *vb* **twined; twin·ing** **1** : to twist together; *also* : to form by twisting **2** : INTERLACE, WEAVE **3** : to coil about a support **4** : to stretch or move in a sinuous manner — **twin·er** *n*

[1]**twinge** \'twinj\ *vb* **twinged; twing·ing** *or* **twinge·ing** : to affect with or feel a sharp sudden pain

[2]**twinge** *n* : a sudden sharp stab (as of pain or distress)

[1]**twin·kle** \'twiŋ-kəl\ *vb* **twin·kled; twin·kling** **1** : to shine or cause to shine with a flickering or sparkling light **2** : to appear bright with merriment **3** : to flutter or flit rapidly — **twin·kler** *n*

[2]**twinkle** *n* **1** : a wink of the eyelids; *also* : the duration of a wink **2** : an intermittent radiance **3** : a rapid flashing motion — **twin·kly** \'twiŋ-klē\ *adj*

twin·kling \'twiŋ-kliŋ\ *n* : the time required for a wink : INSTANT

[1]**twirl** \'twərl\ *vb* : to turn or cause to turn rapidly ⟨~ a baton⟩ ♦ ***Synonyms*** REVOLVE, ROTATE, CIRCLE, SPIN, SWIRL, PIROUETTE — **twirl·er** *n*

[2]**twirl** *n* **1** : an act of twirling **2** : COIL, WHORL — **twirly** \'twər-lē\ *adj*

[1]**twist** \'twist\ *vb* **1** : to unite by winding one thread or strand round another **2** : WREATHE, TWINE **3** : to turn so as to hurt : SPRAIN ⟨~*ed* my ankle⟩ **4** : to twirl into spiral shape **5** : to subject (as a shaft) to torsion **6** : to turn from the true form or meaning **7** : to pull off or break by torsion **8** : to follow a winding course **9** : to turn around

[2]**twist** *n* **1** : something formed by twisting or winding **2** : an act of twisting : the state of being twisted **3** : a spiral turn or curve; *also* : SPIN **4** : a turning aside **5** : ECCENTRICITY **6** : a distortion of meaning **7** : an unexpected turn or development **8** : DEVICE, TRICK **9** : a variant approach or method

twist·er \'twis-tər\ *n* **1** : one that twists; *esp* : a ball with a forward and spinning motion **2** : TORNADO; *also* : WATERSPOUT 2

[1]**twit** \'twit\ *n* : a silly or foolish person

[2]**twit** *vb* **twit·ted; twit·ting** : to ridicule as a fault; *also* : TAUNT ♦ ***Synonyms*** DERIDE, MOCK, RAZZ

[1]**twitch** \'twich\ *vb* **1** : to move or pull with a sudden motion : JERK **2** : to move jerkily : QUIVER **3** : to have a twitch

[2]**twitch** *n* **1** : an act or movement of twitching **2** : a brief spasmodic contraction of muscle fibers

¹twit·ter \ˈtwi-tər\ *vb* **1** : to make a succession of chirping noises **2** : to talk in a chattering fashion **3** : to tremble with agitation : FLUTTER

²twitter *n* **1** : a slight agitation of the nerves **2** : a small tremulous intermittent noise (as made by a swallow) **3** : a light chattering

twixt \ˈtwikst\ *prep* : BETWEEN ⟨~ the two extremes⟩

two \ˈtü\ *n, pl* **twos** **1** : one more than one **2** : the second in a set or series **3** : something having two units — **two** *adj or pron*

two cents *n* **1** *or* **two cents' worth** : an opinion offered on a topic under discussion **2** : a sum or object of very small value

2D \ˈtü-ˈdē\ *n* : a two-dimensional form — **2D** *adj*

two–faced \ˈtü-ˈfāst\ *adj* **1** : DOUBLE-DEALING, FALSE **2** : having two faces

two·fold \ˈtü-ˌfōld, -ˈfōld\ *adj* **1** : having two units or members **2** : being twice as much or as many — **twofold** \-ˈfōld\ *adv*

2,4–D \ˌtü-ˌfȯr-ˈdē\ *n* : an irritant compound used esp. as a weed killer

2,4,5–T \-ˌfīv-ˈtē\ *n* : an irritant compound used esp. as an herbicide and defoliant

two·pence \ˈtə-pəns, *US also* ˈtü-ˌpens\ *n* : the sum of two pence

two·pen·ny \ˈtə-pə-nē, *US also* ˈtü-ˌpe-nē\ *adj* : of the value of or costing twopence

two–ply \ˈtü-ˈplī\ *adj* **1** : woven as a double cloth **2** : consisting of two strands or thicknesses ⟨~ toilet paper⟩

two·some \ˈtü-səm\ *n* **1** : a group of two persons or things : COUPLE **2** : a golf match between two players

two–step \ˈtü-ˌstep\ *n* : a ballroom dance performed with a sliding step in march or polka time; *also* : a piece of music for this dance — **two–step** *vb*

two–time \ˈtü-ˌtīm\ *vb* : to betray (a spouse or lover) by secret lovemaking with another — **two–tim·er** *n*

two–way *adj* : involving two elements or allowing movement or use in two directions or manners

2WD *abbr* two-wheel drive

twp *abbr* township

TWX *abbr* teletypewriter exchange

TX *abbr* Texas

ty·coon \tī-ˈkün\ *n* [Jp *taikun* feudal lord] **1** : a top leader (as in politics) **2** : a powerful businessman or industrialist

tying *pres part of* TIE

ty·iyn \tē-ˈen\ *n, pl* **tiyin** — see *som* at MONEY table

tyke \ˈtīk\ *n* : a small child

tym·pan·ic membrane \tim-ˈpa-nik-\ *n* : EARDRUM

tym·pa·num \ˈtim-pə-nəm\ *n, pl* **-na** \-nə\ *also* **-nums** : EARDRUM; *also* : MIDDLE EAR — **tym·pan·ic** \tim-ˈpa-nik\ *adj*

¹type \ˈtīp\ *n* [ME, fr. LL *typus,* fr. L & Gk; L *typus* image, fr. Gk *typos* blow, impression, model, fr. *typtein* to strike, beat] **1** : a person, thing, or event that foreshadows another to come : TOKEN, SYMBOL **2** : MODEL, EXAMPLE **3** : a distinctive stamp, mark, or sign : EMBLEM **4** : rectangular blocks usu. of metal each having a face so shaped as to produce a character when printed **5** : the letters or characters printed from or as if from type **6** : general character or form common to a number of individuals and setting them off as a distinguishable class ⟨horses of draft ~⟩ **7** : a class, kind, or group set apart by common characteristics ⟨a seedless ~ of orange⟩; *also* : something distinguishable as a variety ⟨reactions of this ~⟩ ♦ ***Synonyms*** SORT, NATURE, CHARACTER, DESCRIPTION

²type *vb* **typed; typ·ing** **1** : to represent beforehand as a type **2** : to produce a copy of; *also* : REPRESENT, TYPIFY **3** : to write with a typewriter or computer keyboard **4** : to identify as belonging to a type **5** : TYPECAST

type A *adj* : relating to, having, or being a personality marked esp. by impatience and aggressiveness

type·cast \-ˌkast\ *vb* **-cast; -cast·ing** **1** : to cast (an actor) in a part calling for characteristics possessed by the actor **2** : to cast repeatedly in the same type of role

type·face \-ˌfās\ *n* : all type of a single design

type 1 diabetes \ˈtīp-ˈwən-\ *n* : a form of diabetes mellitus usu. developing before adulthood and marked by severe insulin deficiency

type·script \ˈtīp-ˌskript\ *n* : typewritten matter

type·set \-ˌset\ *vb* **-set; -set·ting** : to set in type : COMPOSE — **type·set·ter** *n*

type 2 diabetes \-ˈtü-\ *n* : a form of diabetes mellitus developing esp. in adults and usu. in obese individuals and marked by excess sugar in the blood

type·write \-ˌrīt\ *vb* **-wrote** \-ˌrōt\; **-writ·ten** \-ˌri-tᵊn\ : TYPE 3

type·writ·er \-ˌrī-tər\ *n* **1** : a machine for writing in characters similar to those produced by printers' type by means of types striking a ribbon to transfer ink or carbon impressions onto paper **2** : TYPIST

type·writ·ing \-ˌrī-tiŋ\ *n* : the use of a typewriter ⟨teach ~⟩; *also* : writing produced with a typewriter

¹ty·phoid \ˈtī-ˌfȯid, tī-ˈfȯid\ *adj* : of, relating to, or being a communicable bacterial disease (**typhoid fever**) marked by fever, diarrhea, prostration, and intestinal inflammation

²typhoid *n* : TYPHOID FEVER

ty·phoon \tī-ˈfün\ *n* : a hurricane occurring esp. in the region of the Philippines or the China sea

ty·phus \ˈtī-fəs\ *n* : a severe infectious disease transmitted esp. by body lice, caused by a rickettsia, and marked by high fever, stupor and delirium, intense headache, and a dark red rash

typ·i·cal \ˈti-pi-kəl\ *adj* **1** : being or having the nature of a type **2** : exhibiting the essential characteristics of a group **3** : conforming to a type — **typ·i·cal·i·ty** \ˌti-pə-ˈka-lə-tē\ *n* — **typ·i·cal·ness** *n*

typ·i·cal·ly \-pi-k(ə-)lē\ *adv* **1** : in a typical manner **2** : in typical circumstances

typ·i·fy \ˈti-pə-ˌfī\ *vb* **-fied; -fy·ing** **1 :** to represent by an image, form, model, or resemblance **2 :** to embody the essential or common characteristics of
typ·ist \ˈtī-pist\ *n* **:** a person who types esp. as a job
ty·po \ˈtī-pō\ *n, pl* **typos :** an error (as of spelling) in typed or typeset material
ty·pog·ra·pher \tī-ˈpä-grə-fər\ *n* **:** one who designs or arranges printing
ty·pog·ra·phy \tī-ˈpä-grə-fē\ *n* **:** the art of printing with type; *also* **:** the style, arrangement, or appearance of printed matter — **ty·po·graph·ic** \ˌtī-pə-ˈgra-fik\ *or* **ty·po·graph·i·cal** \-fi-kəl\ *adj* — **ty·po·graph·i·cal·ly** *adv*
ty·ran·ni·cal \tə-ˈra-ni-kəl, tī-\ *also* **ty·ran·nic** \-nik\ *adj* **:** of or relating to a tyrant **:** DESPOTIC ♦ ***Synonyms*** ARBITRARY, ABSOLUTE, AUTOCRATIC — **ty·ran·ni·cal·ly** \-ni-k(ə-)lē\ *adv*
tyr·an·nise *Brit var of* TYRANNIZE
tyr·an·nize \ˈtir-ə-ˌnīz\ *vb* **-nized; -niz·ing :** to act as a tyrant **:** rule with unjust severity — **tyr·an·niz·er** *n*
ty·ran·no·saur \tə-ˈra-nə-ˌsȯr\ *n* **:** a massive American flesh-eating dinosaur of the Cretaceous that had small forelegs and walked on its hind legs
ty·ran·no·sau·rus \tə-ˌra-nə-ˈsȯr-əs\ *n* **:** TYRANNOSAUR
tyr·an·nous \ˈtir-ə-nəs\ *adj* **:** unjustly severe — **tyr·an·nous·ly** *adv*
tyr·an·ny \ˈtir-ə-nē\ *n, pl* **-nies** **1 :** oppressive power **2 :** the rule or authority of a tyrant **:** government in which absolute power is vested in a single ruler **3 :** a tyrannical act
ty·rant \ˈtī-rənt\ *n* **1 :** an absolute ruler **:** DESPOT **2 :** a ruler who governs oppressively or brutally **3 :** one who uses authority or power harshly
tyre *chiefly Brit var of* ²TIRE
ty·ro \ˈtī-rō\ *n, pl* **tyros** [ML, fr. L *tiro* young soldier, tyro] **:** a beginner in learning **:** NOVICE
tzar, tzarist *var of* CZAR, CZARIST

U

¹u \ˈyü\ *n, pl* **u's** *or* **us** \ˈyüz\ *often cap* **:** the 21st letter of the English alphabet
²u *abbr, often cap* unit
¹U \ˈyü\ *adj* **:** characteristic of the upper classes
²U *abbr* **1** [abbr. of *Union of Orthodox Hebrew Congregations* kosher certification] — often enclosed in a circle **2** university **3** unsatisfactory
³U *symbol* uranium
UAE *abbr* United Arab Emirates
UAR *abbr* United Arab Republic
UAW *abbr* United Automobile Workers
ubiq·ui·tous \yü-ˈbi-kwə-təs\ *adj* **:** existing or being everywhere at the same time **:** OMNIPRESENT — **ubiq·ui·tous·ly** *adv* — **ubiq·ui·ty** \-kwə-tē\ *n*
U–boat \ˈyü-ˌbōt\ *n* [trans. of G *U-boot,* short for *Unterseeboot,* lit., undersea boat] **:** a German submarine
UC *abbr* uppercase
ud·der \ˈə-dər\ *n* **:** an organ (as of a cow) consisting of two or more milk glands enclosed in a large hanging sac and each provided with a nipple
UFO \ˌyü-(ˌ)ef-ˈō\ *n, pl* **UFO's** *or* **UFOs** \-ˈōz\ **:** an unidentified flying object; *esp* **:** FLYING SAUCER
ug·ly \ˈə-glē\ *adj* **ug·li·er; -est** [ME, fr. ON *uggligr,* fr. *uggr* fear] **1 :** FRIGHTFUL, DIRE **2 :** offensive to the sight **:** HIDEOUS **3 :** offensive or unpleasant to any sense **4 :** morally objectionable **:** REPULSIVE **5 :** likely to cause inconvenience or discomfort **6 :** SURLY, QUARRELSOME ⟨an ~ disposition⟩ — **ug·li·ness** \-glē-nəs\ *n*
UHF *abbr* ultrahigh frequency
UK *abbr* United Kingdom
ukase \yü-ˈkās, -ˈkāz\ *n* [F & Russ; F, fr. Russ *ukaz,* fr. *ukazat'* to show, order] **:** an edict esp. of a Russian emperor or government
Ukrai·ni·an \yü-ˈkrā-nē-ən\ *n* **1 :** a native or inhabitant of Ukraine **2 :** a Slavic language of the Ukrainian people — **Ukrainian** *adj*
uku·le·le *also* **uke·le·le** \ˌyü-kə-ˈlā-lē\ *n* [Hawaiian *ʻukulele,* fr. *ʻuku* flea + *lele* jumping] **:** a small usu. 4-stringed guitar popularized in Hawaii
ul·cer \ˈəl-sər\ *n* **1 :** an open eroded sore of skin or mucous membrane often discharging pus **2 :** something that festers and corrupts like an open sore — **ul·cer·ous** *adj*
ul·cer·ate \ˈəl-sə-ˌrāt\ *vb* **-at·ed; -at·ing** **:** to become affected with an ulcer — **ul·cer·a·tive** \ˈəl-sə-ˌrā-tiv\ *adj*
ul·cer·a·tion \ˌəl-sə-ˈrā-shən\ *n* **1 :** the process of forming or state of having an ulcer **2 :** ULCER 1
ul·na \ˈəl-nə\ *n* **:** the bone on the little-finger side of the human forearm; *also* **:** a corresponding bone of the forelimb of vertebrates above fishes
ul·ster \ˈəl-stər\ *n* **:** a long loose overcoat
ult *abbr* **1** ultimate **2** ultimo
ul·te·ri·or \ˌəl-ˈtir-ē-ər\ *adj* **1 :** lying farther away **:** more remote **2 :** situated beyond or on the farther side **3 :** going beyond what is openly said or shown **:** HIDDEN ⟨~ motives⟩

[1]**ul·ti·mate** \ˈəl-tə-mət\ *adj* **1** : most remote in space or time : FARTHEST **2** : last in a progression : FINAL **3** : the best or most extreme of its kind **4** : arrived at as the last resort **5** : FUNDAMENTAL, ABSOLUTE, SUPREME ⟨~ reality⟩ **6** : incapable of further analysis or division : ELEMENTAL **7** : MAXIMUM ♦ ***Synonyms*** CONCLUDING, EVENTUAL, LATEST, TERMINAL — **ul·ti·mate·ly** *adv*

[2]**ultimate** *n* : something ultimate

ul·ti·ma·tum \ˌəl-tə-ˈmā-təm, -ˈmä-\ *n, pl* **-tums** *or* **-ta** \-tə\ : a final condition or demand whose rejection will bring about a resort to forceful action

ul·ti·mo \ˈəl-tə-ˌmō\ *adj* [L *ultimo mense* in the last month] : of or occurring in the month preceding the present

[1]**ul·tra** \ˈəl-trə\ *adj* : going beyond others or beyond due limits : EXTREME

[2]**ultra** *n* : EXTREMIST

ul·tra·con·ser·va·tive \-kən-ˈsər-və-tiv\ *adj* : extremely conservative

ul·tra·high frequency \-ˈhī-\ *n* : a radio frequency between 300 and 3000 megahertz

[1]**ul·tra·light** \ˈəl-trə-ˌlīt\ *adj* : extremely light esp. in weight

[2]**ultralight** *n* : a very light recreational aircraft typically carrying only one person

ul·tra·ma·rine \ˌəl-trə-mə-ˈrēn\ *n* **1** : a deep blue pigment **2** : a very bright deep blue color

ul·tra·mi·cro·scop·ic \-ˌmī-krə-ˈskä-pik\ *adj* : too small to be seen with an ordinary microscope

ul·tra·mod·ern \-ˈmä-dərn\ *adj* : extremely or excessively modern in idea, style, or tendency

ul·tra·pure \-ˈpyu̇r\ *adj* : of the utmost purity

ul·tra·short \-ˈshȯrt\ *adj* **1** : having a wavelength below 10 meters **2** : very short in duration

ul·tra·son·ic \ˌəl-trə-ˈsä-nik\ *adj* : having a frequency too high to be heard by the human ear — **ul·tra·son·i·cal·ly** \-ni-k(ə-)lē\ *adv*

ul·tra·son·ics \-ˈsä-niks\ *n sing or pl* **1** : ultrasonic vibrations **2** : the science of ultrasonic phenomena

ul·tra·sound \-ˌsau̇nd\ *n* **1** : ultrasonic vibrations **2** : the diagnostic or therapeutic use of ultrasound and esp. a technique involving the formation of a two-dimensional image of internal body structures **3** : a diagnostic examination using ultrasound

ul·tra·vi·o·let \-ˈvī-ə-lət\ *adj* : having a wavelength shorter than those of visible light and longer than those of X-rays ⟨~ radiation⟩; *also* : producing or employing ultraviolet radiation — **ultraviolet** *n*

ul·tra vi·res \ˈəl-trə-ˈvī-rēz\ *adv or adj* [NL, lit., beyond power] : beyond the scope of legal power or authority

ul·u·late \ˈəl-yə-ˌlāt\ *vb* **-lat·ed; -lat·ing** : HOWL, WAIL

uma·mi \ü-ˈmä-mē\ *n* [Jp, flavor] : a meaty or savory taste sensation produced by several amino acids and nucleotides

um·bel \ˈəm-bəl\ *n* : a flat-topped or rounded flower cluster in which the individual flower stalks all arise near one point on the main stem

um·ber \ˈəm-bər\ *n* : a brown earthy substance valued as a pigment either in its raw state or burnt — **umber** *adj*

umbilical cord *n* : a cord containing blood vessels that connects the navel of a fetus with the placenta of its mother

um·bi·li·cus \ˌəm-ˈbi-li-kəs, ˌəm-bə-ˈlī-\ *n, pl* **um·bi·li·ci** \ˌəm-ˈbi-lə-ˌkī; ˌəm-bə-ˈlī-ˌkī, -ˌsī\ *or* **um·bi·li·cus·es** : NAVEL — **um·bil·i·cal** \ˌəm-ˈbi-li-kəl\ *adj*

um·bra \ˈəm-brə\ *n, pl* **umbras** *or* **um·brae** \-(ˌ)brē, -ˌbrī\ **1** : SHADE, SHADOW **2** : the conical part of the shadow of a celestial body from which the sun's light is completely blocked

um·brage \ˈəm-brij\ *n* **1** : SHADE; *also* : FOLIAGE **2** : RESENTMENT, OFFENSE ⟨take ~ at a remark⟩

um·brel·la \ˌəm-ˈbre-lə\ *n* **1** : a collapsible shade for protection against weather consisting of fabric stretched over hinged ribs radiating from a center pole **2** : something that provides protection **3** : something that covers a range of elements

umi·ak \ˈü-mē-ˌak\ *n* : an open Inuit boat made of a wooden frame covered with skins

ump \ˈəmp\ *n* : UMPIRE

um·pire \ˈəm-ˌpī(-ə)r\ *n* [ME *oumpere,* alter. of *noumpere* (the phrase *a noumpere* being understood as *an oumpere*), fr. AF *nounpier* single, odd, fr. *non* not + *per* equal, fr. L *par*] **1** : one having authority to decide finally a controversy or question between parties **2** : an official in a sport who rules on plays — **umpire** *vb*

ump·teen \ˈəmp-ˌtēn\ *adj* : very many : indefinitely numerous — **ump·teenth** \-ˌtēnth\ *adj*

UN *abbr* United Nations

un- \ˌən, ˈən\ *prefix* **1** : not : IN-, NON- **2** : opposite of : contrary to

un·able \ˌən-ˈā-bəl\ *adj* **1** : not able **2** : UNQUALIFIED, INCOMPETENT

un·abridged \ˌən-ə-ˈbrijd\ *adj* **1** : not abridged ⟨an ~ edition of Shakespeare⟩ **2** : complete of its class : not based on one larger ⟨an ~ dictionary⟩

un·ac·com·pa·nied \ˌən-ə-ˈkəm-pə-nēd\ *adj* : not accompanied; *esp* : being without instrumental accompaniment

un·ac·count·able \ˌən-ə-ˈkau̇n-tə-bəl\ *adj* **1** : not to be accounted for : INEXPLICABLE **2** : not responsible — **un·ac·count·ably** \-blē\ *adv*

---

unabashed
unabated
unabsorbed
unabsorbent
unacademic
unaccented
unacceptable
unacclimatized
unaccommodating

un·ac·count·ed \-ˈkau̇n-təd\ *adj* : not accounted ⟨the loss was ~ for⟩
un·ac·cus·tomed \ˌən-ə-ˈkəs-təmd\ *adj* **1** : not customary : not usual or common **2** : not accustomed or habituated ⟨~ to noise⟩
un·adul·ter·at·ed \ˌən-ə-ˈdəl-tə-ˌrā-təd\ *adj* : PURE, UNMIXED ⟨~ meat⟩ ♦ ***Synonyms*** ABSOLUTE, SHEER, SIMPLE, UNALLOYED, UNDILUTED, UNMITIGATED
un·af·fect·ed \ˌən-ə-ˈfek-təd\ *adj* **1** : not influenced or changed mentally, physically, or chemically **2** : free from affectation : NATURAL, GENUINE — **un·af·fect·ed·ly** *adv*
un·alien·able \-ˈāl-yə-nə-bəl, -ˈā-lē-ə-\ *adj* : INALIENABLE
un·aligned \ˌən-ə-ˈlīnd\ *adj* : not associated with any one of competing international blocs ⟨~ nations⟩
un·al·loyed \ˌən-ə-ˈlȯid\ *adj* : UNMIXED, UNQUALIFIED, PURE ⟨~ happiness⟩
un·al·ter·able \ˌən-ˈȯl-tə-rə-bəl\ *adj* : not capable of being altered or changed ⟨an ~ rule⟩ — **un·al·ter·ably** \-blē\ *adv*
un–Amer·i·can \ˌən-ə-ˈmer-ə-kən\ *adj* : not characteristic of or consistent with American customs or principles
unan·i·mous \yu̇-ˈna-nə-məs\ *adj* [L *unanimus,* fr. *unus* one + *animus* mind] **1** : being of one mind : AGREEING **2** : formed with or indicating the agreement of all — **una·nim·i·ty** \yü-nə-ˈni-mə-tē\ *n* — **unan·i·mous·ly** *adv*
un·arm \ˌən-ˈärm\ *vb* : DISARM
un·armed \-ˈärmd\ *adj* : not armed or armored ⟨~ civilians⟩
un·as·sail·able \ˌən-ə-ˈsā-lə-bəl\ *adj* : not liable to doubt, attack, or question ⟨an ~ argument⟩
un·as·sum·ing \ˌən-ə-ˈsü-miŋ\ *adj* : MODEST ⟨an ~ librarian⟩ ⟨an ~ manner⟩ ⟨an ~ neighborhood⟩ ♦ ***Synonyms*** HUMBLE, LOWLY, MEEK
un·at·tached \ˌən-ə-ˈtacht\ *adj* **1** : not married or engaged **2** : not joined or united
un·avail·ing \ˌən-ə-ˈvā-liŋ\ *adj* : being of no avail — **un·avail·ing·ly** *adv*
un·avoid·able \ˌən-ə-ˈvȯi-də-bəl\ *adj* : not avoidable : INEVITABLE ⟨an ~ fact⟩ ♦ ***Synonyms*** CERTAIN, INELUCTABLE, INESCAPABLE, NECESSARY — **un·avoid·ably** \-blē\ *adv*
¹un·aware \ˌən-ə-ˈwer\ *adv* : UNAWARES
²unaware *adj* : not aware : IGNORANT ⟨~ of the danger⟩ — **un·aware·ness** *n*
un·awares \-ˈwerz\ *adv* **1** : without knowing : UNINTENTIONALLY **2** : without warning : by surprise ⟨taken ~⟩
un·bal·anced \ˌən-ˈba-lənst\ *adj* **1** : not in a state of balance **2** : mentally disordered **3** : not adjusted so as to make credits equal to debits
un·bar \-ˈbär\ *vb* : UNBOLT, OPEN
un·bear·able \ˌən-ˈber-ə-bəl\ *adj* : greater than can be borne ⟨~ pain⟩ ♦ ***Synonyms*** INSUFFERABLE, INSUPPORTABLE, INTOLERABLE, UNENDURABLE, UNSUPPORTABLE — **un·bear·ably** \-blē\ *adv*
un·beat·able \-ˈbē-tə-bəl\ *adj* : not capable of being defeated ♦ ***Synonyms*** INDOMITABLE, INVINCIBLE, INVULNERABLE, UNCONQUERABLE
un·beat·en \-ˈbē-tᵊn\ *adj* **1** : not pounded, beaten, or whipped **2** : UNTRODDEN **3** : UNDEFEATED
un·be·com·ing \ˌən-bi-ˈkə-miŋ\ *adj* : not becoming : UNSUITABLE, IMPROPER ⟨conduct ~ an officer⟩ ♦ ***Synonyms*** INDECORUS, INDECENT, INDELICATE, UNSEEMLY — **un·be·com·ing·ly** *adv*
un·be·knownst \ˌən-bi-ˈnōnst\ *also* **un·be·known** \-ˈnōn\ *adj* : happening or existing without one's knowledge
un·be·lief \ˌən-bə-ˈlēf\ *n* : the withholding or absence of belief : DOUBT — **un·be·liev·ing** \-ˈlē-viŋ\ *adj*
un·be·liev·able \-ˈlē-və-bəl\ *adj* : too improbable for belief; *also* : of such a superlative degree as to be hard to believe ⟨an ~ catch for a touchdown⟩ ♦ ***Synonyms*** INCONCEIVABLE, UNIMAGINABLE, UNTHINKABLE — **un·be·liev·ably** \-blē\ *adv*
un·be·liev·er \-ˈlē-vər\ *n* **1** : INFIDEL **2** : DOUBTER
un·bend \-ˈbend\ *vb* **-bent** \-ˈbent\; **-bend·ing** **1** : to free from being bent : make or become straight **2** : UNTIE **3** : to make or become less stiff or more affable : RELAX
un·bend·ing *adj* : formal and distant in manner : INFLEXIBLE
un·bi·ased \ˌən-ˈbī-əst\ *adj* : free from bias; *esp* : UNPREJUDICED ⟨an ~ opinion⟩ ♦ ***Synonyms*** DISINTERESTED, DISPASSIONATE, IMPARTIAL, NONDISCRIMINATORY, NONPARTISAN, OBJECTIVE, UNCOLORED
un·bid·den \-ˈbi-dᵊn\ *also* **un·bid** \-ˈbid\ *adj* : not bidden : UNASKED
un·bind \-ˈbīnd\ *vb* **-bound** \-ˈbau̇nd\; **-bind·ing** **1** : to remove bindings from : UNTIE **2** : RELEASE

---

unaccredited
unacknowledged
unacquainted
unadapted
unadjusted
unadorned
unadventurous
unadvertised
unaesthetic
unaffiliated
unafraid
unaggressive
unaided
unalike
unaltered
unambiguous
unambiguously
unambitious
unanchored
unannounced
unanswerable
unanswered
unanticipated
unapologetic
unapparent
unappealing
unappeased
unappetizing
unappreciated
unappreciative
unapproachable
unappropriated
unapproved
unarguable
unarguably
unarmored
unartistic
unashamed
unasked
unassertive
unassisted
unathletic
unattainable
unattended
unattested
unattractive
unauthentic
unauthorized
unavailable
unavowed
unawakened
unbaked
unbaptized
unbeloved

un·blessed *also* **un·blest** \ˌən-ˈblest\ *adj* **1** : not blessed **2** : EVIL

un·block \-ˈbläk\ *vb* : to free from being blocked

un·blush·ing \-ˈblə-shiŋ\ *adj* **1** : not blushing **2** : SHAMELESS ⟨~ greed⟩ — **un·blush·ing·ly** *adv*

un·bod·ied \-ˈbä-dēd\ *adj* **1** : having no body; *also* : DISEMBODIED **2** : FORMLESS

un·bolt \ˌən-ˈbōlt\ *vb* : to open or unfasten by withdrawing a bolt

un·bolt·ed \-ˈbōl-təd\ *adj* : not fastened by bolts

un·born \-ˈbȯrn\ *adj* : not yet born

un·bos·om \-ˈbu̇-zəm, -ˈbü-\ *vb* **1** : DISCLOSE, REVEAL **2** : to disclose the thoughts or feelings of oneself

un·bound·ed \-ˈbau̇n-dəd\ *adj* : having no bounds or limits ⟨~ enthusiasm⟩ ♦ ***Synonyms*** BOUNDLESS, ENDLESS, IMMEASURABLE, LIMITLESS, MEASURELESS, UNLIMITED

un·bowed \ˌən-ˈbau̇d\ *adj* **1** : not bowed down **2** : UNSUBDUED ⟨~ by failure⟩

un·bri·dled \-ˈbrī-d^{ə}ld\ *adj* **1** : UNRESTRAINED ⟨~ enthusiasm⟩ **2** : not confined by a bridle

un·bro·ken \-ˈbrō-kən\ *adj* **1** : not damaged **2** : not subdued or tamed **3** : not interrupted : CONTINUOUS

un·buck·le \-ˈbə-kəl\ *vb* : to loose the buckle of : UNFASTEN ⟨~ a belt⟩

un·bur·den \-ˈbər-d^{ə}n\ *vb* **1** : to free or relieve from a burden **2** : to relieve oneself of (as cares or worries)

un·but·ton \-ˈbə-t^{ə}n\ *vb* : to unfasten the buttons of ⟨~ your coat⟩

un·called–for \ˌən-ˈkȯld-ˌfȯr\ *adj* : not called for, needed, or wanted

un·can·ny \-ˈka-nē\ *adj* **1** : GHOSTLY, MYSTERIOUS, EERIE **2** : suggesting superhuman or supernatural powers ♦ ***Synonyms*** SPOOKY, UNEARTHLY, WEIRD — **un·can·ni·ly** \-ˈka-nə-lē\ *adv*

un·ceas·ing \-ˈsē-siŋ\ *adj* : never ceasing ♦ ***Synonyms*** CEASELESS, CONTINUOUS, ENDLESS, INTERMINABLE, UNENDING, UNREMITTING — **un·ceas·ing·ly** *adv*

un·cer·e·mo·ni·ous \ˌən-ˌser-ə-ˈmō-nē-əs\ *adj* : acting without or lacking ordinary courtesy : ABRUPT ⟨his ~ dismissal⟩ — **un·cer·e·mo·ni·ous·ly** *adv*

un·cer·tain \ˌən-ˈsər-t^{ə}n\ *adj* **1** : not determined or fixed ⟨an ~ quantity⟩ **2** : subject to chance or change : not dependable ⟨~ weather⟩ **3** : not definitely known **4** : not sure ⟨~ of the truth⟩ — **un·cer·tain·ly** *adv*

un·cer·tain·ty \-t^{ə}n-tē\ *n* **1** : lack of certainty : DOUBT **2** : something that is uncertain ♦ ***Synonyms*** CONCERN, DOUBT, DUBIETY, INCERTITUDE, SKEPTICISM, SUSPICION

un·chain \ˌən-ˈchān\ *vb* : to free by or as if by removing a chain

un·charged \ˌən-ˈchärjd\ *adj* : having no electrical charge

un·char·i·ta·ble \-ˈcha-rə-tə-bəl\ *adj* : not charitable; *esp* : severe in judging others — **un·char·i·ta·ble·ness** *n* — **un·char·i·ta·bly** \-blē\ *adv*

un·chart·ed \-ˈchär-təd\ *adj* **1** : not recorded on a map, chart, or plan **2** : UNKNOWN ⟨discussion moving into ~ territory⟩

un·chris·tian \-ˈkris-chən\ *adj* **1** : not of the Christian faith **2** : contrary to the Christian spirit

un·churched \-ˈchərcht\ *adj* : not belonging to or connected with a church

un·cial \ˈən-shəl, -chəl; ˈən-sē-əl\ *adj* : relating to or written in a form of script with rounded letters used esp. in early Greek and Latin manuscripts — **uncial** *n*

un·cir·cu·lat·ed \ˌən-ˈsər-kyə-ˌlā-təd\ *adj* : issued for use as money but kept out of circulation

un·cir·cum·cised \ˌən-ˈsər-kəm-ˌsīzd\ *adj* **1** : not circumcised **2** : spiritually impure

un·civ·il \ˌən-ˈsi-vəl\ *adj* **1** : not civilized : BARBAROUS **2** : DISCOURTEOUS, ILL-MANNERED, IMPOLITE ⟨~ remarks⟩

un·civ·i·lized \-ˈsi-və-ˌlīzd\ *adj* **1** : not civilized : BARBAROUS **2** : remote from civilization : WILD

un·clasp \-ˈklasp\ *vb* : to open by or as if by loosing the clasp

un·cle \ˈəŋ-kəl\ *n* [ME, fr. AF, fr. L *avunculus* mother's brother] **1** : the brother of one's father or mother **2** : the husband of one's aunt or uncle

un·clean \ˌən-ˈklēn\ *adj* **1** : morally or spiritually impure **2** : prohibited by ritual law for use or contact **3** : DIRTY, SOILED — **un·clean·li·ness** \-lē-nəs\ *n* — **un·clean·ly** *adj* — **un·clean·ness** *n*

un·clench \-ˈklench\ *vb* : to open from a clenched position : RELAX

Uncle Tom \-ˈtäm\ *n* [fr. *Uncle Tom,* enslaved character in Harriet Beecher Stowe's novel *Uncle Tom's Cabin* (1851-52)] *disparaging* : a Black person who is eager to win the approval of white people

un·cloak \ˌən-ˈklōk\ *vb* **1** : to remove a cloak or cover from **2** : UNMASK, REVEAL ⟨~ an impostor⟩

un·clog \-ˈkläg\ *vb* : to remove an obstruction from

---

unbleached
unblemished
unblinking
unbound
unbranched
unbranded
unbreakable
unbridgeable
unbruised
unbrushed
unbudging
unburied
unburned
uncanceled
uncanonical
uncap
uncapitalized
uncared–for
uncataloged
uncaught
uncensored
uncensured
unchallenged
unchangeable
unchanged
unchanging
unchaperoned
uncharacteristic
unchaste
unchastely
unchasteness
unchastity
unchecked
unchivalrous
unchristened
unclad
unclaimed
unclassified
uncleaned
unclear
uncleared

un·close \-ˈklōz\ *vb* : OPEN — **un·closed** \-ˈklōzd\ *adj*

un·clothe \-ˈklōth\ *vb* : to strip of clothes or a covering — **un·clothed** \-ˈklōthd\ *adj*

un·coil \ˌən-ˈkȯi(-ə)l\ *vb* : to release or become released from a coiled state

un·com·fort·able \ˌən-ˈkəmf-tə-bəl, -ˈkəm-fər-tə-\ *adj* **1** : causing discomfort **2** : feeling discomfort — **un·com·fort·ably** \-blē\ *adv*

un·com·mit·ted \ˌən-kə-ˈmi-təd\ *adj* : not committed; *esp* : not pledged to a particular belief, allegiance, or program ⟨~ voters⟩

un·com·mon \ˌən-ˈkä-mən\ *adj* **1** : not ordinarily encountered : UNUSUAL, RARE **2** : REMARKABLE, EXCEPTIONAL ⟨a soldier of ~ courage⟩ ♦ ***Synonyms*** EXTRAORDINARY, PHENOMENAL, SINGULAR, UNIQUE — **un·com·mon·ly** *adv*

un·com·mu·ni·ca·tive \ˌən-kə-ˈmyü-nə-ˌkā-tiv, -ni-kə-\ *adj* : not inclined to talk or impart information : RESERVED ♦ ***Synonyms*** CLOSEMOUTHED, RETICENT, SILENT, TACITURN

un·com·pro·mis·ing \ˌən-ˈkäm-prə-ˌmī-ziŋ\ *adj* : not making or accepting a compromise : UNYIELDING ♦ ***Synonyms*** ADAMANT, INFLEXIBLE, OBDURATE, RIGID, UNBENDING

un·con·cern \ˌən-kən-ˈsərn\ *n* **1** : lack of care or interest : INDIFFERENCE **2** : freedom from excessive concern

un·con·cerned \-ˈsərnd\ *adj* **1** : not having any part or interest **2** : not anxious or upset : free of worry ♦ ***Synonyms*** ALOOF, DETACHED, INCURIOUS, REMOTE, UNCURIOUS, UNINTERESTED — **un·con·cern·ed·ly** \-ˈsər-nəd-lē\ *adv*

un·con·di·tion·al \ˌən-kən-ˈdi-shə-nəl\ *adj* : not limited in any way ⟨~ surrender⟩ — **un·con·di·tion·al·ly** *adv*

un·con·di·tioned \-ˈdi-shənd\ *adj* **1** : not subject to conditions **2** : not acquired or learned : NATURAL ⟨~ responses⟩ **3** : producing an unconditioned response ⟨~ stimuli⟩

un·con·quer·able \ˌən-ˈkäŋ-kə-rə-bəl\ *adj* : incapable of being conquered or overcome : INDOMITABLE

un·con·scio·na·ble \-ˈkän-shə-nə-bəl\ *adj* **1** : not guided or controlled by conscience **2** : not in accordance with what is right or just ⟨~ sales practices⟩ ♦ ***Synonyms*** UNREASONABLE, UNDUE, UNJUSTIFIABLE, UNWARRANTABLE, UNWARRANTED — **un·con·scio·na·bly** \-blē\ *adv*

[1]**un·con·scious** \ˌən-ˈkän-chəs, -shəs\ *adj* **1** : not knowing or perceiving : not aware **2** : not done consciously or on purpose **3** : having lost consciousness **4** : of or relating to the unconscious — **un·con·scious·ly** *adv* — **un·con·scious·ness** *n*

[2]**unconscious** *n* : the part of one's mental life of which one is not ordinarily aware but which is often a powerful force in influencing behavior

un·con·sti·tu·tion·al \ˌən-ˌkän-stə-ˈtü-shə-nəl, -ˈtyü-\ *adj* : not according to or consistent with the constitution of a state or society — **un·con·sti·tu·tion·al·i·ty** \-tü-shə-ˈna-lə-tē, -ˈtyü-\ *n* — **un·con·sti·tu·tion·al·ly** \-ˈtü-shə-nə-lē, -ˈtyü-\ *adv*

un·con·trol·la·ble \ˌən-kən-ˈtrō-lə-bəl\ *adj* : incapable of being controlled : UNGOVERNABLE — **un·con·trol·la·bly** \-blē\ *adv*

un·con·ven·tion·al \-ˈven-chə-nəl\ *adj* : not conventional : being out of the ordinary — **un·con·ven·tion·al·i·ty** \-ˌven-chə-ˈna-lə-tē\ *n* — **un·con·ven·tion·al·ly** \-ˈven-chə-nə-lē\ *adv*

un·cork \ˌən-ˈkȯrk\ *vb* **1** : to draw a cork from **2** : to release from a sealed or pent-up state; *also* : to let go

un·count·ed \-ˈkaùn-təd\ *adj* **1** : not counted **2** : INNUMERABLE

un·cou·ple \-ˈkə-pəl\ *vb* : DISCONNECT ⟨~ railroad cars⟩

un·couth \-ˈküth\ *adj* [ME, unfamiliar, fr. OE *uncūth,* fr. *un-* + *cūth* known] **1** : strange, awkward, and clumsy in shape or appearance **2** : vulgar in conduct or speech : RUDE ♦ ***Synonyms*** DISCOURTEOUS, ILL-MANNERED, IMPOLITE, UNGRACIOUS, UNMANNERED, UNMANNERLY

un·cov·er \-ˈkə-vər\ *vb* **1** : to make known : DISCLOSE, REVEAL **2** : to expose to view by removing some covering **3** : to take the cover from **4** : to remove the hat from; *also* : to take off the hat as a token of respect — **un·cov·ered** *adj*

un·crewed \-ˌkrüd\ *adj* : having no crew

un·crit·i·cal \ˌən-ˈkri-ti-kəl\ *adj* **1** : not critical : lacking in discrimination **2** : showing lack or improper use of critical standards or procedures — **un·crit·i·cal·ly** \-k(ə-)lē\ *adv*

un·cross \-ˈkrȯs\ *vb* : to change from a crossed position ⟨~*ed* his legs⟩

unc·tion \ˈəŋk-shən\ *n* **1** : the act of anointing as a rite of consecration or healing **2** : exaggerated or insincere earnestness of language or manner

---

unclouded
uncluttered
uncoated
uncollected
uncolored
uncombed
uncombined
uncomely
uncomic
uncommercial
uncompensated
uncomplaining
uncompleted
uncomplicated
uncomplimentary
uncompounded
uncomprehending
unconcealed
unconfined
unconfirmed
unconformable
uncongenial
unconnected
unconquered
unconsecrated
unconsidered
unconsolidated
unconstrained
unconsumed
unconsummated
uncontaminated
uncontested
uncontrolled
uncontroversial
unconverted
unconvincing
uncooked
uncooperative
uncoordinated
uncorrected
uncorroborated
uncountable
uncreative
uncredited
uncropped
uncrowded
uncrowned
uncrystallized

unc·tu·ous \ˈəŋk-chə-wəs\ *adj* [ME, fr. MF or ML; MF *unctueus,* fr. ML *unctuosus,* fr. L *unctus* act of anointing, fr. *unguere* to anoint] **1 :** FATTY, OILY **2 :** insincerely smooth in speech and manner ⟨an ~ politician⟩ — **unc·tu·ous·ly** *adv*

un·curl \ˌən-ˈkərl\ *vb* : to make or become straightened out from a curled or coiled position

un·cut \ˌən-ˈkət\ *adj* **1 :** not cut down or into **2 :** not shaped by cutting ⟨an ~ diamond⟩ **3 :** not having the folds of the leaves slit ⟨an ~ book⟩ **4 :** not abridged or curtailed ⟨the ~ version of the film⟩ **5 :** not diluted ⟨~ heroin⟩

un·daunt·ed \-ˈdȯn-təd\ *adj* : not daunted : not discouraged or dismayed ♦ ***Synonyms*** BOLD, BRAVE, DAUNTLESS, FEARLESS, INTREPID, VALIANT — **un·daunt·ed·ly** *adv*

un·de·ceive \ˌən-di-ˈsēv\ *vb* : to free from deception, illusion, or error

un·de·mon·stra·tive \ˌən-di-ˈmän-strə-tiv\ *adj* : restrained in expression of feeling : RESERVED

un·de·ni·able \ˌən-di-ˈnī-ə-bəl\ *adj* **1** : plainly true : INCONTESTABLE **2 :** unquestionably excellent or genuine ♦ ***Synonyms*** INCONTROVERTIBLE, INDISPUTABLE, INDUBITABLE, UNQUESTIONABLE — **un·de·ni·ably** \-blē\ *adv*

[1]**un·der** \ˈən-dər\ *adv* **1 :** in or into a position below or beneath something **2 :** below some quantity, level, or limit ⟨$10 or ~⟩ **3 :** in or into a condition of subjection, subordination, or unconsciousness ⟨the ether put him ~⟩

[2]**un·der** \ˌən-dər, ˈən-\ *prep* **1 :** lower than and overhung, surmounted, or sheltered by ⟨~ a tree⟩ **2 :** subject to the authority or guidance of ⟨served ~ him⟩ ⟨was ~ contract⟩ **3 :** subject to the action or effect of ⟨~ the influence of alcohol⟩ **4** : within the division or grouping of ⟨items ~ this heading⟩ **5 :** less or lower than (as in size, amount, or rank) ⟨earns ~ $5000⟩

[3]**under** \ˈən-dər\ *adj* **1 :** lying below, beneath, or on the ventral side **2 :** facing or protruding downward **3 :** SUBORDINATE **4 :** lower than usual, proper, or desired in amount, quality, or degree

un·der·achiev·er \ˌən-dər-ə-ˈchē-vər\ *n* : one (as a student) who performs below an expected level of proficiency

un·der·act \-ˈakt\ *vb* : to perform feebly or with restraint

un·der·ac·tive \-ˈak-tiv\ *adj* : characterized by abnormally low activity ⟨an ~ thyroid gland⟩ — **un·der·ac·tiv·i·ty** \-ˌak-ˈti-və-tē\ *n*

un·der·age \-ˈāj\ *adj* : of less than mature or legal age

un·der·arm \-ˈärm\ *adj* **1 :** UNDERHAND **2** ⟨an ~ throw⟩ **2 :** placed under or on the underside of the arms ⟨~ seams⟩ — **underarm** *adv or n*

un·der·bel·ly \ˈən-dər-ˌbe-lē\ *n* **1 :** a vulnerable area **2 :** the underside of a body or mass

un·der·bid \ˌən-dər-ˈbid\ *vb* **-bid; -bidding 1 :** to bid less than another **2 :** to bid too low

un·der·bite \ˌən-dər-ˈbīt\ *n* : the projection of the lower front teeth over the upper

un·der·body \-ˌbä-dē\ *n* : the lower parts of the body of a vehicle

un·der·bred \ˌən-dər-ˈbred\ *adj* : marked by lack of good breeding

un·der·brush \ˈən-dər-ˌbrəsh\ *n* : shrubs, bushes, or small trees growing beneath large trees

un·der·car·riage \-ˌka-rij\ *n* **1 :** a supporting framework or underside (as of an automobile) **2 :** the landing gear of an airplane

un·der·charge \ˌən-dər-ˈchärj\ *vb* : to charge (as a person) too little — **undercharge** \ˈən-dər-ˌchärj\ *n*

un·der·class \ˈən-dər-ˌklas\ *n* : LOWER CLASS

un·der·class·man \ˌən-dər-ˈklas-mən\ *n* : a member of the freshman or sophomore class

un·der·clothes \ˈən-dər-ˌklōthz\ *n pl* : UNDERWEAR

un·der·cloth·ing \-ˌklō-thiŋ\ *n* : UNDERWEAR

un·der·coat \-ˌkōt\ *n* **1 :** a coat worn under another **2 :** a growth of short hair or fur partly concealed by the longer and usu. coarser hairs of a mammal **3 :** a coat of paint under another

un·der·coat·ing \-ˌkō-tiŋ\ *n* : a special waterproof coating applied to the underside of a vehicle

un·der·cov·er \ˌən-dər-ˈkə-vər\ *adj* : acting or executed in secret; *esp* : employed or engaged in secret investigation ⟨an ~ agent⟩

un·der·croft \ˈən-dər-ˌkrȯft\ *n* [ME, fr. *under* + *crofte* crypt, fr. MD, fr. ML *crupta,* fr. L *crypta*] : a vaulted chamber under a church

un·der·cur·rent \-ˌkər-ənt\ *n* **1 :** a current below the surface **2 :** a hidden tendency of feeling or opinion ⟨an ~ of dread⟩

un·der·cut \ˌən-dər-ˈkət\ *vb* **-cut; -cutting 1 :** to cut away the underpart of **2** : to offer to sell or to work at a lower rate than **3 :** to strike (the ball) obliquely downward so as to give a backward spin or elevation to the shot — **un·der·cut** \ˈən-dər-ˌkət\ *n*

un·der·de·vel·oped \ˌən-dər-di-ˈve-ləpt\ *adj* **1 :** not normally or adequately developed ⟨~ muscles⟩ **2 :** having a relatively

---

uncultivated
uncultured
uncured
uncurious
uncurtained
uncustomary
undamaged
undamped
undated
undecided
undecipherable
undeclared
undecorated
undefeated
undefended
undefiled
undefinable
undefined
undemanding
undemocratic
undenominational
undependable

low level of economic development ⟨the ~ nations⟩

un·der·dog \ˈən-dər-ˌdȯg\ *n* : the loser or predicted loser in a struggle

un·der·done \ˌən-dər-ˈdən\ *adj* : not thoroughly done or cooked : RARE

un·der·draw·ers \ˈən-dər-ˌdrȯrz, -ˌdrȯ-ərz\ *n pl* : UNDERPANTS

un·der·draw·ing \ˈən-dər-ˌdrȯ-iŋ\ *n* : a preliminary sketch made prior to painting

un·der·em·pha·size \ˌən-dər-ˈem-fə-sīz\ *vb* : to emphasize inadequately — **un·der·em·pha·sis** \-səs\ *n*

un·der·em·ployed \-im-ˈplȯid\ *adj* : having less than full-time or adequate employment

un·der·es·ti·mate \-ˈes-tə-ˌmāt\ *vb* : to set too low a value on

un·der·ex·pose \-ik-ˈspōz\ *vb* : to expose (a photographic plate or film) for less time than is needed — **un·der·ex·po·sure** \-ˈspō-zhər\ *n*

un·der·feed \ˌən-dər-ˈfēd\ *vb* **-fed** \-ˈfed\; **-feed·ing** : to feed with too little food

un·der·foot \-ˈfu̇t\ *adv* **1** : under the feet ⟨flowers trampled ~⟩ **2** : close about one's feet : in the way

un·der·fur \ˈən-dər-ˌfər\ *n* : an undercoat of fur esp. when thick and soft

un·der·gar·ment \-ˌgär-mənt\ *n* : a garment to be worn under another

un·der·gird \ˌən-dər-ˈgərd\ *vb* : to brace up : STRENGTHEN

un·der·go \ˌən-dər-ˈgō\ *vb* **-went** \-ˈwent\; **-gone** \-ˈgȯn, -ˈgän\; **-go·ing** **1** : to submit to : ENDURE **2** : to go through : EXPERIENCE ⟨~ a change⟩

un·der·grad \ˈən-dər-ˌgrad\ *n* : UNDERGRADUATE

un·der·grad·u·ate \ˌən-dər-ˈgra-jə-wət, -jə-ˌwāt\ *n* : a student at a university or college who has not received a first degree

¹un·der·ground \ˌən-dər-ˈgrau̇nd\ *adv* **1** : beneath the surface of the earth **2** : in or into hiding or secret operation

²un·der·ground \ˈən-dər-ˌgrau̇nd\ *n* **1** : a space under the surface of the ground; *esp* : SUBWAY **2** : a secret political movement or group; *esp* : an organized body working in secret to overthrow a government or an occupying power **3** : an avant-garde group or movement that operates outside the establishment

³underground \ˈən-dər-ˌgrau̇nd\ *adj* **1** : being, growing, operating, or located below the surface of the ground ⟨~ stems⟩ **2** : conducted by secret means **3** : produced or published by the underground ⟨~ publications⟩; *also* : of or relating to the avant-garde underground

un·der·growth \ˈən-dər-ˌgrōth\ *n* : low growth (as of herbs and shrubs) on the floor of a forest

¹un·der·hand \ˈən-dər-ˌhand\ *adv* **1** : in an underhanded or secret manner **2** : with an underhand motion

²underhand *adj* **1** : UNDERHANDED **2** : made with the hand kept below the level of the shoulder ⟨an ~ pitch⟩

¹un·der·hand·ed \ˌən-dər-ˈhan-dəd\ *adv* : UNDERHAND

²underhanded *adj* : marked by secrecy and deception ⟨~ tactics⟩ — **un·der·hand·ed·ly** *adv* — **un·der·hand·ed·ness** *n*

un·der·lie \-ˈlī\ *vb* **-lay** \-ˈlā\; **-lain** \-ˈlān\; **-ly·ing** \-ˈlī-iŋ\ **1** : to lie or be situated under **2** : to be at the basis of : form the foundation of : SUPPORT

un·der·line \ˈən-dər-ˌlīn\ *vb* **1** : to draw a line under **2** : EMPHASIZE, STRESS — **underline** *n*

un·der·ling \ˈən-dər-liŋ\ *n* : SUBORDINATE, INFERIOR

un·der·lip \ˌən-dər-ˈlip\ *n* : the lower lip

un·der·ly·ing \ˌən-dər-ˈlī-iŋ\ *adj* **1** : lying under or below **2** : FUNDAMENTAL, BASIC ⟨~ principles⟩

un·der·mine \-ˈmīn\ *vb* **1** : to excavate beneath **2** : to weaken or wear away secretly or gradually ⟨~ authority⟩

un·der·most \ˈən-dər-ˌmōst\ *adj* : lowest in relative position — **undermost** *adv*

¹un·der·neath \ˌən-dər-ˈnēth\ *prep* **1** : directly under **2** : under subjection to

²underneath *adv* **1** : below a surface or object : BENEATH **2** : on the lower side

un·der·nour·ished \ˌən-dər-ˈnər-isht\ *adj* : supplied with insufficient nourishment — **un·der·nour·ish·ment** \-ˈnər-ish-mənt\ *n*

un·der·pants \ˈən-dər-ˌpants\ *n pl* : a usu. short undergarment for the lower trunk : DRAWERS

un·der·part \-ˌpärt\ *n* : a part lying on the lower side (as of a bird or mammal)

un·der·pass \-ˌpas\ *n* : a crossing of a highway and another way (as a road) at different levels; *also* : the lower level

un·der·pay \ˌən-dər-ˈpā\ *vb* : to pay less than what is normal or required

un·der·pin·ning \ˈən-dər-ˌpi-niŋ\ *n* : the material and construction (as a foundation) used for support of a structure — **un·der·pin** \ˌən-dər-ˈpin\ *vb*

un·der·play \ˌən-dər-ˈplā\ *vb* : to treat or handle with restraint; *esp* : to play a role with subdued force

un·der·pop·u·lat·ed \ˌən-dər-ˈpä-pyə-ˌlā-təd\ *adj* : having a lower than normal or desirable density of population

un·der·priv·i·leged \-ˈpriv-lijd, -ˈpri-və-lijd\ *adj* : having fewer esp. economic and social privileges than others

un·der·pro·duc·tion \ˌən-dər-prə-ˈdək-shən\ *n* : the production of less than enough to satisfy the demand or of less than the usual supply

un·der·rate \-ˈrāt\ *vb* : to rate or value too low

un·der·rep·re·sent·ed \-ˌre-pri-ˈzen-təd\ *adj* : inadequately represented

un·der·score \ˈən-dər-ˌskȯr\ *vb* **1** : to draw a line under : UNDERLINE **2** : EMPHASIZE — **underscore** *n*

¹un·der·sea \ˌən-dər-ˈsē\ *adj* : being, carried on, or used beneath the surface of the sea

²undersea *or* **un·der·seas** \-ˈsēz\ *adv* : beneath the surface of the sea

un·der·sec·re·tary \ˌən-dər-ˈse-krə-ˌter-ē\ *n* : a secretary immediately subordinate to a principal secretary ⟨~ of state⟩

un·der·sell \-ˈsel\ *vb* **-sold** \-ˈsōld\; **-sell·ing** **1** : to sell articles cheaper than **2** : UNDERRATE

un·der·sexed \-ˈsekst\ *adj* : deficient in sexual desire

un·der·shirt \ˈən-dər-ˌshərt\ *n* : a collarless undergarment with or without sleeves

un·der·shoot \ˌən-dər-ˈshüt\ *vb* **-shot** \-ˈshät\; **-shoot·ing** **1** : to shoot short of or below (a target) **2** : to fall short of (a runway) in landing an airplane

un·der·shorts \ˈən-dər-ˌshȯrts\ *n pl* : underpants for men or boys

un·der·shot \ˈən-dər-ˌshät\ *adj* **1** : moved by water passing beneath ⟨an ~ waterwheel⟩ **2** : having the lower front teeth projecting beyond the upper when the mouth is closed

un·der·side \ˈən-dər-ˌsīd, ˌən-dər-ˈsīd\ *n* : the side or surface lying underneath

un·der·signed \ˈən-dər-ˌsīnd\ *n, pl* **undersigned** : one whose name is signed at the end of a document

un·der·sized \ˌən-dər-ˈsīzd\ *also* **un·der·size** \-ˈsīz\ *adj* : of a size less than is common, proper, or normal

un·der·skirt \ˈən-dər-ˌskərt\ *n* : a skirt worn under an outer skirt; *esp* : PETTICOAT

un·der·staffed \ˌən-dər-ˈstaft\ *adj* : inadequately staffed

un·der·stand \ˌən-dər-ˈstand\ *vb* **-stood** \-ˈstu̇d\; **-stand·ing** **1** : to grasp the meaning of : COMPREHEND **2** : to have thorough or technical acquaintance with or expertness in ⟨~ finance⟩ **3** : to have reason to believe ⟨I ~ you are leaving tomorrow⟩ **4** : INTERPRET ⟨we ~ this to be a refusal⟩ **5** : to have a sympathetic attitude **6** : to accept as settled ⟨it is *understood* that he will pay the expenses⟩ — **un·der·stand·able** \-ˈstan-də-bəl\ *adj*

un·der·stand·ably \-blē\ *adv* : as can be easily understood

[1]**un·der·stand·ing** \ˌən-dər-ˈstan-diŋ\ *n* **1** : knowledge and ability to judge : INTELLIGENCE ⟨a person of ~⟩ **2** : agreement of opinion or feeling **3** : a mutual agreement informally or tacitly entered into

[2]**understanding** *adj* : endowed with understanding : TOLERANT, SYMPATHETIC

un·der·state \ˌən-dər-ˈstāt\ *vb* **1** : to represent as less than is the case **2** : to state with restraint esp. for effect — **un·der·state·ment** *n*

un·der·stood \ˌən-dər-ˈstu̇d\ *adj* **1** : agreed upon **2** : IMPLICIT

un·der·sto·ry \ˈən-dər-ˌstȯr-ē\ *n* : the vegetative layer between the top layer of a forest and the ground cover

un·der·study \ˈən-dər-ˌstə-dē\ *n* : one who is prepared to act another's part or take over another's duties — **understudy** \ˈən-dər-ˌstə-dē, ˌən-dər-ˈstə-dē\ *vb*

un·der·sur·face \ˈən-dər-ˌsər-fəs\ *n* : UNDERSIDE

un·der·take \ˌən-dər-ˈtāk\ *vb* **-took** \-ˈtu̇k\; **-tak·en** \-ˈtā-kən\; **-tak·ing** **1** : to take upon oneself : set about ⟨~ a task⟩ **2** : to put oneself under obligation **3** : GUARANTEE, PROMISE

un·der·tak·er \ˈən-dər-ˌtā-kər\ *n* : one whose business is to prepare the dead for burial and to arrange and manage funerals

un·der·tak·ing \ˈən-dər-ˌtā-kiŋ, ˌən-dər-ˈtā-kiŋ; *2 is* ˈən-dər-ˌtā-kiŋ *only*\ *n* **1** : the act of one who undertakes or engages in any project **2** : the business of an undertaker **3** : something undertaken **4** : PROMISE, GUARANTEE

under–the–counter *adj* : UNLAWFUL, ILLICIT ⟨~ sale of drugs⟩

un·der·tone \ˈən-dər-ˌtōn\ *n* **1** : a low or subdued tone or utterance **2** : a subdued color (as seen through and modifying another color)

un·der·tow \-ˌtō\ *n* : the current beneath the surface that flows seaward when waves are breaking upon the shore

un·der·val·ue \ˌən-dər-ˈval-yü\ *vb* **1** : to value or estimate below the real worth **2** : to esteem lightly

un·der·wa·ter \ˌən-dər-ˈwȯ-tər, -ˈwä-\ *adj* : lying, growing, worn, or operating below the surface of the water ⟨an ~ camera⟩ — **un·der·wa·ter** *adv*

under way \-ˈwā\ *adv* **1** : into motion from a standstill **2** : in progress

un·der·wear \ˈən-dər-ˌwer\ *n* : clothing or a garment worn next to the skin and under other clothing

un·der·weight \ˌən-dər-ˈwāt\ *adj* : weighing below what is normal, average, or necessary — **underweight** *n*

un·der·wire \ˈən-dər-ˌwī(-ə)r\ *n* : a wire running through the bottom of a brassiere to aid in support

un·der·world \ˈən-dər-ˌwərld\ *n* **1** : the place of departed souls : HADES **2** : the side of the world opposite to one **3** : the world of organized crime

un·der·write \ˈən-dər-ˌrīt, ˌən-dər-ˈrīt\ *vb* **-wrote** \-ˌrōt, -ˈrōt\; **-writ·ten** \-ˌri-tᵊn, -ˈri-tᵊn\; **-writ·ing** **1** : to write under or at the end of something else **2** : to set one's name to an insurance policy and thereby become answerable for a designated loss or damage **3** : to subscribe to : agree to **4** : to guarantee financial support of — **un·der·writ·er** *n*

un·de·sign·ing \ˌən-di-ˈzī-niŋ\ *adj* : having no artful, ulterior, or fraudulent purpose : SINCERE

un·de·sir·able \-ˈzī-rə-bəl\ *adj* : not desirable — **undesirable** *n*

un·de·vi·at·ing \ˌən-ˈdē-vē-ˌā-tiŋ\ *adj* : keeping a true course

un·dies \ˈən-dēz\ *n pl* : UNDERWEAR; *esp* : women's underwear

undeserved
undeserving
undesired
undetected
undetermined
undeterred
undeveloped
undifferentiated
undigested
undignified
undiluted
undiminished
undimmed
undiplomatic
undirected
undisciplined
undisclosed
undiscovered
undiscriminating
undisguised
undismayed
undisputed
undissolved
undistinguished
undistributed
undisturbed
undivided

un·do \ˌən-ˈdü\ *vb* **-did** \-ˈdid\; **-done** \-ˈdən\; **-do·ing** **1** : to make or become unfastened or loosened : OPEN **2** : to make null or as if not done : REVERSE **3** : to bring to ruin; *also* : UPSET
un·doc·u·ment·ed \ən-ˈdä-kyə-ˌmen-təd\ *adj* **1** : not supported by documentary evidence **2** : lacking documents required for legal immigration
un·do·ing *n* : a cause of ruin
un·doubt·ed \-ˈdau̇-təd\ *adj* : not doubted or called into question : CERTAIN — **un·doubt·ed·ly** *adv*
[1]**un·dress** \ˌən-ˈdres\ *vb* : to remove the clothes or covering of : STRIP, DISROBE
[2]**undress** *n* **1** : informal dress; *esp* : a loose robe or dressing gown **2** : ordinary dress **3** : NUDITY
un·due \-ˈdü, -ˈdyü\ *adj* **1** : not due **2** : exceeding or violating propriety or fitness : EXCESSIVE ⟨~ force⟩
un·du·lant \ˈən-jə-lənt, ˈən-də-, -dyə-\ *adj* : rising and falling in waves ⟨~ hills⟩
undulant fever *n* : a human disease caused by bacteria from infected domestic animals or their products and marked by intermittent fever, chills, headache, weakness, and weight loss
un·du·late \-ˌlāt\ *vb* **-lat·ed; -lat·ing** [LL *undula* small wave, fr. L *unda* wave] **1** : to have a wavelike motion or appearance **2** : to rise and fall in pitch or volume ⟨*undulating* music⟩
un·du·la·tion \ˌən-jə-ˈlā-shən, ˌən-də-, -dyə-\ *n* **1** : wavy or wavelike motion **2** : pulsation of sound **3** : a wavy appearance or outline — **un·du·la·to·ry** \ˈən-jə-lə-ˌtōr-ē, ˈən-də-, -dyə-\ *adj*
un·du·ly \ˌən-ˈdü-lē, ˈən-, -ˈdyü-\ *adv* : in an undue manner : EXCESSIVELY
un·dy·ing \-ˈdī-iŋ\ *adj* : not dying : IMMORTAL, PERPETUAL
un·earned \-ˈərnd\ *adj* : not earned by labor, service, or skill ⟨~ income⟩
un·earth \ˌən-ˈərth\ *vb* **1** : to dig up out of or as if out of the earth ⟨~ buried treasure⟩ **2** : to bring to light : DISCOVER ⟨~ a secret⟩
un·earth·ly \-lē\ *adj* **1** : not of or belonging to the earth **2** : SUPERNATURAL, WEIRD; *also* : ABSURD
un·easy \ˌən-ˈē-zē\ *adj* **1** : AWKWARD, EMBARRASSED ⟨~ among strangers⟩ **2** : disturbed by pain or worry; *also* : RESTLESS **3** : UNSTABLE ⟨an ~ truce⟩ — **un·eas·i·ly** \-ˈē-zə-lē\ *adv* — **un·eas·i·ness** \-ˈē-zē-nəs\ *n*
un·em·ployed \ˌən-im-ˈplȯid\ *adj* : not being used; *also* : having no job
un·em·ploy·ment \-ˈplȯi-mənt\ *n* **1** : lack of employment **2** : money paid at regular intervals (as by a government agency) to an unemployed person
un·end·ing \ˌən-ˈen-diŋ\ *adj* : having no ending : ENDLESS
un·equal \ˌən-ˈē-kwəl\ *adj* **1** : not alike (as in size, amount, number, or value) **2** : not uniform : VARIABLE **3** : badly balanced or matched **4** : INADEQUATE, INSUFFICIENT ⟨~ to the task⟩ — **un·equal·ly** *adv*
un·equaled *or* **un·equalled** \-kwəld\ *adj* : not equaled : UNPARALLELED ⟨an artist of ~ talent⟩
un·equiv·o·cal \ˌən-i-ˈkwi-və-kəl\ *adj* : leaving no doubt : CLEAR — **un·equiv·o·cal·ly** *adv*
un·err·ing \ˌən-ˈer-iŋ, ˌən-ˈər-\ *adj* : making no errors : CERTAIN, UNFAILING ⟨~ accuracy⟩ — **un·err·ing·ly** *adv*
UNES·CO \yu̇-ˈnes-kō\ *abbr* United Nations Educational, Scientific, and Cultural Organization
un·even \ˌən-ˈē-vən\ *adj* **1** : ODD 3 **2** : not even : not level or smooth : RUGGED, RAGGED **3** : IRREGULAR; *also* : varying in quality — **un·even·ly** *adv* — **un·even·ness** *n*
un·event·ful \ˌən-i-ˈvent-fəl\ *adj* : lacking interesting or noteworthy incidents — **un·event·ful·ly** *adv*
un·evolved \ˌən-i-ˈvälvd\ *adj* **1** : not fully developed ⟨an ~ wine⟩ **2** : lacking cultural refinement
un·ex·am·pled \ˌən-ig-ˈzam-pəld\ *adj* : UNPRECEDENTED, UNPARALLELED ⟨fought with ~ passion⟩
un·ex·cep·tion·able \ˌən-ik-ˈsep-shə-nə-bəl\ *adj* : not open to exception or objection : beyond reproach
un·ex·pect·ed \ˌən-ik-ˈspek-təd\ *adj* : not expected : UNFORESEEN — **un·ex·pect·ed·ly** *adv*
un·fail·ing \ˌən-ˈfā-liŋ\ *adj* **1** : not failing, flagging, or waning : CONSTANT **2** : INEXHAUSTIBLE ⟨a subject of ~ interest⟩ **3** : INFALLIBLE, SURE ⟨an ~ test⟩ — **un·fail·ing·ly** *adv*
un·fair \-ˈfer\ *adj* **1** : marked by injustice, partiality, or deception : UNJUST **2** : not equitable in business dealings — **un·fair·ly** *adv* — **un·fair·ness** *n*
un·faith·ful \ˌən-ˈfāth-fəl\ *adj* **1** : not observant of vows, allegiance, or duty : DISLOYAL **2** : INACCURATE, UNTRUST-

undogmatic
undomesticated
undone
undoubled
undramatic
undraped
undreamed
undressed
undrinkable
undulled
undutiful
undyed
uneager
uneatable
uneaten
uneconomic
uneconomical
unedifying
unedited
uneducated
unembarrassed
unemotional
unemphatic
unenclosed
unencumbered
unendurable
unenforceable
unenforced
unenlightened
unenterprising
unenthusiastic
unenviable
unequipped
unessential
unethical
unexamined
unexcelled
unexceptional
unexcited
unexciting
unexpired
unexplained
unexploded
unexplored
unexposed
unexpressed
unexpurgated
unfading
unfaltering

WORTHY ⟨an ~ copy of a document⟩ — **un·faith·ful·ly** *adv* — **un·faith·ful·ness** *n*

un·fa·mil·iar \ˌən-fə-ˈmil-yər\ *adj* **1** : not well-known : STRANGE **2** : not well acquainted ⟨~ with the subject⟩ — **un·fa·mil·iar·i·ty** \-ˌmi-lē-ˈer-ə-tē, -ˈyer-\ *n*

un·fas·ten \ˌən-ˈfa-sᵊn\ *vb* : to make or become loose : UNDO, DETACH

un·feel·ing \-ˈfē-liŋ\ *adj* **1** : lacking feeling : INSENSATE **2** : HARDHEARTED, CRUEL — **un·feel·ing·ly** *adv*

un·feigned \-ˈfānd\ *adj* : not feigned : not hypocritical : GENUINE

un·fet·ter \-ˈfe-tər\ *vb* **1** : to free from fetters **2** : LIBERATE

un·fil·ial \ˌən-ˈfi-lē-əl, -ˈfil-yəl\ *adj* : not observing the obligations of a child to a parent : UNDUTIFUL

un·fin·ished \ˌən-ˈfi-nisht\ *adj* **1** : not brought to an end **2** : being in a rough or unpolished state

1**un·fit** \-ˈfit\ *adj* : not fit or suitable; *esp* : physically or mentally unsound ⟨~ for army service⟩ — **un·fit·ness** *n*

2**unfit** *vb* : to make unfit : DISQUALIFY

un·fix \-ˈfiks\ *vb* **1** : to loosen from a fastening : DETACH **2** : UNSETTLE

un·flap·pa·ble \-ˈfla-pə-bəl\ *adj* : not easily upset or panicked — **un·flap·pa·bly** *adv*

un·fledged \ˌən-ˈflejd\ *adj* : not feathered or ready for flight; *also* : IMMATURE, CALLOW

un·flinch·ing \-ˈflin-chiŋ\ *adj* : not flinching or shrinking : STEADFAST — **un·flinch·ing·ly** *adv*

un·fold \-ˈfōld\ *vb* **1** : to open the folds of : open up **2** : to lay open to view : DISCLOSE **3** : BLOSSOM, DEVELOP

un·for·get·ta·ble \ˌən-fər-ˈge-tə-bəl\ *adj* : incapable of being forgotten ⟨an ~ event⟩ — **un·for·get·ta·bly** \-blē\ *adv*

un·formed \-ˈfȯrmd\ *adj* : not regularly formed or ordered : UNDEVELOPED

un·for·tu·nate \-ˈfȯr-chə-nət\ *adj* **1** : not fortunate : UNLUCKY **2** : attended with misfortune **3** : UNSUITABLE ⟨an ~ choice of words⟩ — **unfortunate** *n*

un·for·tu·nate·ly \-nət-lē\ *adv* **1** : in an unfortunate manner **2** : it is unfortunate

un·found·ed \ˌən-ˈfau̇n-dəd\ *adj* : lacking a sound basis : GROUNDLESS

un·freeze \-ˈfrēz\ *vb* **-froze** \-ˈfrōz\; **-frozen** \-ˈfrō-zᵊn\; **-freez·ing** **1** : to cause to thaw **2** : to remove from a freeze ⟨~ prices⟩

un·fre·quent·ed \ˌən-frē-ˈkwen-təd; ˌən-ˈfrē-kwən-\ *adj* : seldom visited or traveled over

un·friend·ly \ˌən-ˈfrend-lē\ *adj* **1** : not friendly or kind : HOSTILE **2** : UNFAVORABLE ⟨~ to new business⟩ — **un·friend·li·ness** \-lē-nəs\ *n*

un·frock \-ˈfräk\ *vb* : DEFROCK

un·fruit·ful \-ˈfrüt-fəl\ *adj* **1** : not producing fruit or offspring : BARREN **2** : yielding no valuable result : UNPROFITABLE — **un·fruit·ful·ness** *n*

un·furl \-ˈfərl\ *vb* : to loose from a furled state : UNFOLD

un·gain·ly \-ˈgān-lē\ *adj* [*un-* + obs. *gainly* proper, becoming, fr. *gain* direct, handy, fr. ME *geyn,* fr. OE *gēn,* fr. ON *gegn* against] : CLUMSY, AWKWARD — **un·gain·li·ness** \-lē-nəs\ *n*

un·gen·er·ous \ˌən-ˈje-nə-rəs\ *adj* : not generous or liberal : STINGY

un·glued \ˌən-ˈglüd\ *adj* : UPSET, DISORDERED ⟨became ~ when she was refused⟩

un·god·ly \ˌən-ˈgäd-lē, -ˈgȯd-\ *adj* **1** : IMPIOUS, IRRELIGIOUS **2** : SINFUL, WICKED **3** : OUTRAGEOUS ⟨an ~ hour⟩ — **un·god·li·ness** \-lē-nəs\ *n*

un·gov·ern·able \-ˈgə-vər-nə-bəl\ *adj* : not capable of being governed, guided, or restrained : UNRULY

un·gra·cious \-ˈgrā-shəs\ *adj* **1** : not courteous : RUDE **2** : not pleasing : DISAGREEABLE ⟨an ~ task⟩

un·grate·ful \ˌən-ˈgrāt-fəl\ *adj* **1** : not thankful for favors **2** : DISAGREEABLE; *also* : THANKLESS — **un·grate·ful·ly** *adv* — **un·grate·ful·ness** *n*

un·guard·ed \-ˈgär-dəd\ *adj* **1** : UNPROTECTED **2** : DIRECT, INCAUTIOUS ⟨~ remarks⟩

un·guent \ˈəŋ-gwənt, ˈən-\ *n* : a soothing or healing salve : OINTMENT

1**un·gu·late** \ˈəŋ-gyə-lət, ˈən-, -ˌlāt\ *adj* [LL *ungulatus,* fr. L *ungula* hoof, fr. *unguis* nail, hoof] : having hoofs

2**ungulate** *n* : a hoofed mammal (as a cow, horse, or rhinoceros)

un·hal·lowed \ˌən-ˈha-lōd\ *adj* **1** : not consecrated : UNHOLY **2** : IMPIOUS, PROFANE **3** : contrary to accepted standards : IMMORAL

un·hand \ˌən-ˈhand\ *vb* : to remove the hand from : let go

un·hand·some \-ˈhan-səm\ *adj* **1** : not beautiful or handsome : HOMELY **2** : UNBECOMING **3** : DISCOURTEOUS, RUDE

un·handy \-ˈhan-dē\ *adj* : INCONVENIENT; *also* : AWKWARD

un·hap·py \-ˈha-pē\ *adj* **1** : UNLUCKY,

---

unfashionable
unfashionably
unfathomable
unfavorable
unfavorably
unfeasible
unfeminine
unfenced
unfermented
unfertilized
unfilled
unfiltered
unfitted
unflagging
unflattering
unflavored
unfocused
unfolded
unforced
unforeseeable
unforeseen
unforgivable
unforgiving
unformulated
unfortified
unframed
unfree
unfulfilled
unfunded
unfunny
unfurnished
unfussy
ungentle
ungentlemanly
ungerminated
unglamorous
unglazed
ungoverned
ungraceful
ungracefully
ungraded
ungrammatical
unground
ungrudging
unguided
unhackneyed
unhampered

UNFORTUNATE ⟨an ~ coincidence⟩ **2** : SAD, MISERABLE **3** : INAPPROPRIATE ⟨an ~ choice⟩ — **un·hap·pi·ly** \-ˈha-pə-lē\ *adv* — **un·hap·pi·ness** \-pē-nəs\ *n*
un·har·ness \-ˈhär-nəs\ *vb* : to remove the harness from (as a horse)
un·healthy \-ˈhel-thē\ *adj* **1** : not conducive to health : UNWHOLESOME ⟨~ foods⟩ **2** : SICKLY, DISEASED
un·heard \-ˈhərd\ *adj* **1** : not heard **2** : not granted a hearing
unheard–of *adj* : previously unknown; *esp* : UNPRECEDENTED ⟨~ speeds⟩
un·hinge \ˌən-ˈhinj\ *vb* **1** : to make unstable esp. mentally ⟨~*ed* by grief⟩ **2** : to take from the hinges
un·hitch \-ˈhich\ *vb* : UNFASTEN, LOOSE
un·ho·ly \-ˈhō-lē\ *adj* **1** : not holy : PROFANE, WICKED **2** : very unpleasant ⟨an ~ mess⟩ — **un·ho·li·ness** \-lē-nəs\ *n*
un·hook \-ˈhu̇k\ *vb* : to loose from a hook
un·horse \-ˈho̊rs\ *vb* : to dislodge from or as if from a horse
uni·cam·er·al \ˌyü-ni-ˈka-mə-rəl\ *adj* : having a single legislative house or chamber
UNI·CEF \ˈyü-nə-ˌsef\ *abbr* [*U*nited *N*ations *I*nternational *C*hildren's *E*mergency *F*und, its former name] United Nations Children's Fund
uni·cel·lu·lar \ˌyü-ni-ˈsel-yə-lər\ *adj* : having or consisting of a single cell
uni·corn \ˈyü-nə-ˌko̊rn\ *n* [ME *unicorne,* fr. AF, fr. LL *unicornis,* fr. L, having one horn, fr. *unus* one + *cornu* horn] : a mythical animal with one horn in the middle of the forehead
uni·cy·cle \ˈyü-ni-ˌsī-kəl\ *n* : a vehicle that has a single wheel and is usu. propelled by pedals
uni·di·rec·tion·al \ˌyü-ni-də-ˈrek-shə-nəl, -dī-\ *adj* : having, moving in, or responsive in a single direction
uni·fi·ca·tion \ˌyü-nə-fə-ˈkā-shən\ *n* : the act, process, or result of unifying : the state of being unified
[1]**uni·form** \ˈyü-nə-ˌfo̊rm\ *adj* **1** : not varying ⟨~ procedures⟩ **2** : of the same form with others — **uni·form·ly** *adv*
[2]**uniform** *vb* : to clothe with a uniform
[3]**uniform** *n* : distinctive dress worn by members of a particular group (as an army or a police force)
uni·for·mi·ty \ˌyü-nə-ˈfo̊r-mə-tē\ *n, pl* **-ties** : the state of being uniform
uni·fy \ˈyü-nə-ˌfī\ *vb* **-fied; -fy·ing** : to make into a coherent whole : UNITE
uni·lat·er·al \ˌyü-nə-ˈla-tə-rəl\ *adj* : of, having, affecting, or done by one side only — **uni·lat·er·al·ly** *adv*
un·im·peach·able \ˌən-im-ˈpē-chə-bəl\ *adj* : not liable to accusation : IRREPROACHABLE ⟨an ~ reputation⟩
un·in·hib·it·ed \ˌən-in-ˈhi-bə-təd\ *adj* : free from inhibition; *also* : boisterously informal — **un·in·hib·it·ed·ly** *adv*
un·in·stall \ˌən-in-ˈsto̊l\ *vb* : to remove (software) from a computer system
un·in·tel·li·gent \-ˈte-lə-jənt\ *adj* : lacking intelligence
un·in·tel·li·gi·ble \-jə-bəl\ *adj* : not intelligible : OBSCURE ⟨an ~ voice mail⟩ — **un·in·tel·li·gi·bly** \-blē\ *adv*
un·in·ter·est·ed \ˌən-ˈin-trəs-təd, -tə-rəs-, -tə-ˌres-\ *adj* : not interested : not having the mind or feelings engaged or aroused
un·in·ter·rupt·ed \ˌən-ˌin-tə-ˈrəp-təd\ *adj* : not interrupted : CONTINUOUS
union \ˈyün-yən\ *n* **1** : an act or instance of uniting two or more things into one : the state of being so united : COMBINATION, JUNCTION **2** : a uniting in marriage **3** : something formed by a combining of parts or members; *esp* : a confederation of independent individuals (as nations or persons) for some common purpose **4** : an organization of workers (as a labor union or a trade union) formed to advance its members' interests esp. in respect to wages and working conditions **5** : a device emblematic of union used on or as a national flag; *also* : the upper inner corner of a flag **6** : a device for connecting parts (as of a machine); *esp* : a coupling for pipes
union·ise *Brit var of* UNIONIZE
union·ism \ˈyün-yə-ˌni-zəm\ *n* **1** : the principle or policy of forming or adhering to a union; *esp, cap* : adherence to the policy of a firm federal union before or during the U.S. Civil War **2** : the principles or system of trade unions — **union·ist** *n*
union·ize \ˈyün-yə-ˌnīz\ *vb* **-ized; -iz·ing** : to form into or cause to join a labor union — **union·i·za·tion** \ˌyün-yə-nə-ˈzā-shən\ *n*
union jack *n* **1** : a flag consisting of the part of a national flag that signifies union **2** *cap U&J* : the national flag of the United Kingdom
unique \yu̇-ˈnēk\ *adj* **1** : being the only one of its kind : SINGLE, SOLE ⟨each

---

unhardened
unharmed
unharvested
unhatched
unhealed
unhealthful
unheated
unheeded
unhelpful
unheralded
unheroic
unhesitating
unhindered
unhistorical
unhonored
unhoused
unhurried
unhurt
unhygienic
unidentifiable
unidentified
unidiomatic
unimaginable
unimaginative
unimpaired
unimpassioned
unimpeded
unimportant
unimposing
unimpressed
unimpressive
unimproved
unincorporated
uninfected
uninfluenced
uninformative
uninformed
uninhabitable
uninhabited
uninitiated
uninjured
uninspired
uninstructed
uninstructive
uninsured
unintelligent
unintelligible
unintelligibly
unintended
unintentional
unintentionally
uninteresting
uninterrupted
uninvited
uninviting

snowflake is ~⟩ **2** : very unusual : NOTABLE — **unique·ly** *adv* — **unique·ness** *n*

uni·sex \ˈyü-nə-ˌseks\ *adj* : not distinguishable as male or female; *also* : suitable or designed for both males and females ⟨~ clothing⟩ — **unisex** *n*

uni·sex·u·al \ˌyü-nə-ˈsek-shə-wəl\ *adj* **1** : having only male or only female sex organs **2** : UNISEX

uni·son \ˈyü-nə-sən, -zən\ *n* [ME *unisoun,* fr. MF *unisson,* fr. ML *unisonus* having the same sound, fr. L *unus* one + *sonus* sound] **1** : sameness or identity in musical pitch **2** : the condition of being tuned or sounded at the same pitch or in octaves ⟨sing in ~⟩ **3** : harmonious agreement or union : ACCORD

unit \ˈyü-nət\ *n* **1** : the smallest whole number greater than zero : ONE **2** : a definite amount or quantity used as a standard of measurement **3** : a single thing, person, or group that is a constituent of a whole; *also* : a part of a military establishment that has a prescribed organization — **unit** *adj*

Uni·tar·i·an \ˌyü-nə-ˈter-ē-ən\ *n* : a member of a religious denomination stressing individual freedom of belief — **Uni·tar·i·an·ism** *n*

uni·tary \ˈyü-nə-ˌter-ē\ *adj* **1** : of or relating to a unit **2** : not divided — **uni·tar·i·ly** \ˌyü-nə-ˈter-ə-lē\ *adv*

unite \yu̇-ˈnīt\ *vb* **unit·ed; unit·ing** **1** : to put or join together so as to make one : COMBINE, COALESCE **2** : to join by a legal or moral bond; *also* : to join in interest or fellowship **3** : AMALGAMATE, CONSOLIDATE **4** : to act in concert

unit·ed \yu̇-ˈnī-təd\ *adj* **1** : made one : COMBINED **2** : relating to or produced by joint action **3** : being in agreement : HARMONIOUS

unit·ize \ˈyü-nə-ˌtīz\ *vb* **-ized; -iz·ing** **1** : to form or convert into a unit **2** : to divide into units

uni·ty \ˈyü-nə-tē\ *n, pl* **-ties** **1** : the quality or state of being or being made one : ONENESS **2** : a definite quantity or combination of quantities taken as one or for which 1 is made to stand in calculation **3** : CONCORD, ACCORD, HARMONY **4** : continuity without change ⟨~ of purpose⟩ **5** : reference of all the parts of a literary or artistic composition to a single main idea **6** : totality of related parts ♦ ***Synonyms*** SOLIDARITY, UNION, INTEGRITY

univ *abbr* **1** universal **2** university

uni·valve \ˈyü-ni-ˌvalv\ *n* : a mollusk having a shell with only one piece; *esp* : GASTROPOD — **univalve** *adj*

uni·ver·sal \ˌyü-nə-ˈvər-səl\ *adj* **1** : including, covering, or affecting the whole without limit or exception : available or applying to everyone ⟨~ privileges⟩ ⟨a ~ rule⟩ **2** : present or occurring everywhere **3** : used or for use among all ⟨a ~ language⟩ **4** : adaptable for various purposes ⟨a ~ remote control⟩ — **uni·ver·sal·ly** *adv*

uni·ver·sal·i·ty \-vər-ˈsa-lə-tē\ *n* : the quality or state of being universal

uni·ver·sal·ize \-ˈvər-sə-ˌlīz\ *vb* **-ized; -iz·ing** : to make universal : GENERALIZE ⟨would ~ equal rights⟩ — **uni·ver·sal·i·za·tion** \-ˌvər-sə-lə-ˈzā-shən\ *n*

universal joint *n* : a shaft coupling for transmitting rotation from one shaft to another not in a straight line with it

Universal Product Code *n* : a combination of a barcode and numbers by which a scanner can identify a product and usu. assign a price

uni·verse \ˈyü-nə-ˌvərs\ *n* [ME, fr. L *universum,* fr. neut. of *universus* entire, whole, fr. *unus* one + *versus* turned toward, fr. pp. of *vertere* to turn] : the whole body of things observed or assumed : COSMOS

uni·ver·si·ty \ˌyü-nə-ˈvər-sə-tē\ *n, pl* **-ties** : an institution of higher learning authorized to confer degrees in various special fields (as theology, law, and medicine) as well as in the arts and sciences generally

un·just \ˌən-ˈjəst\ *adj* : characterized by injustice — **un·just·ly** *adv*

un·kempt \-ˈkempt\ *adj* **1** : lacking order or neatness; *also* : ROUGH, UNPOLISHED **2** : not combed : DISHEVELED

un·kind \-ˈkīnd\ *adj* : not kind or sympathetic ⟨an ~ remark⟩ — **un·kind·ly** *adv* — **un·kind·ness** *n*

un·kind·ly \-ˈkīnd-lē\ *adj* : UNKIND — **un·kind·li·ness** *n*

un·know·ing \ˌən-ˈnō-iŋ\ *adj* : not knowing — **un·know·ing·ly** *adv*

un·known \-ˈnōn\ *adj* : not known or not well-known — **unknown** *n*

un·lace \ˌən-ˈlās\ *vb* : to loose by undoing a lace

un·lade \-ˈlād\ *vb* **-lad·ed; -laded** *or* **-lad·en** \-ˈlā-dᵊn\; **-lad·ing** : to take the load or cargo from : UNLOAD

un·latch \-ˈlach\ *vb* **1** : to open or loose by lifting the latch **2** : to become loosed or opened

un·law·ful \ˌən-ˈlȯ-fəl\ *adj* **1** : not lawful : ILLEGAL **2** : not morally right or conventional — **un·law·ful·ly** *adv*

un·lead·ed \-ˈle-dəd\ *adj* : not treated or mixed with lead or lead compounds

un·learn \-ˈlərn\ *vb* : to put out of one's knowledge or memory; *also* : to discard the habit of

un·learned \-ˈlər-nəd *for 1;* -ˈlərnd *for 2*\ *adj* **1** : UNEDUCATED, ILLITERATE **2** : not gained by study or training

un·leash \-ˈlēsh\ *vb* : to free from or as if from a leash : let loose

un·less \ən-ˈles, ˈən-ˌles\ *conj* : except on condition that ⟨won't go ~ you do⟩

un·let·tered \ˌən-ˈle-tərd\ *adj* : not educated : ILLITERATE

[1]**un·like** \-ˈlīk\ *adj* **1** : not like : DISSIMI-

---

unjointed
unjustifiable
unjustified
unkept
unknowable
unknowledgeable
unlabeled
unladylike
unlamented
unleavened
unlicensed
unlighted
unlikable

LAR, DIFFERENT **2** : UNEQUAL — **un·like·ness** *n*

[2]**unlike** *prep* **1** : different from ⟨she's quite ~ her sister⟩ **2** : unusual for ⟨it's ~ you to be late⟩ **3** : differently from ⟨behaves ~ his brother⟩

un·like·li·hood \ˌən-ˈlī-klē-ˌhu̇d\ *n* : IMPROBABILITY

un·like·ly \-ˈlī-klē\ *adj* **1** : not likely : IMPROBABLE **2** : likely to fail

un·lim·ber \ˌən-ˈlim-bər\ *vb* : to get ready for action

un·list·ed \ˌən-ˈlis-təd\ *adj* **1** : not appearing on a list; *esp* : not appearing in a telephone book **2** : not listed on a stock exchange

un·load \-ˈlōd\ *vb* **1** : to take away or off : REMOVE ⟨~ cargo from a hold⟩; *also* : to get rid of **2** : to take a load from ⟨~ the ship⟩; *also* : to relieve or set free : UNBURDEN ⟨~ one's mind of worries⟩ **3** : to draw the charge from ⟨~*ed* the gun⟩ **4** : to sell in volume

un·lock \-ˈläk\ *vb* **1** : to open or unfasten through release of a lock **2** : RELEASE ⟨~ a flood of emotions⟩ **3** : DISCLOSE, REVEAL ⟨~ nature's secrets⟩

un·looked–for \-ˈlu̇kt-ˌfȯr\ *adj* : UNEXPECTED

un·loose \ˌən-ˈlüs\ *vb* : to relax the strain of : set free; *also* : UNTIE

un·loos·en \-ˈlü-sᵊn\ *vb* : UNLOOSE

un·love·ly \-ˈləv-lē\ *adj* : having no charm or appeal : not amiable

un·luck·i·ly \-ˈlə-kə-lē\ *adv* : UNFORTUNATELY

un·lucky \-ˈlə-kē\ *adj* **1** : UNFORTUNATE, ILL-FATED **2** : likely to bring misfortune : INAUSPICIOUS **3** : REGRETTABLE

un·man \ˌən-ˈman\ *vb* **1** : to deprive of manly courage **2** : CASTRATE

un·man·ly \-ˈman-lē\ *adj* : not manly : COWARDLY; *also* : EFFEMINATE

un·man·ner·ly \-ˈma-nər-lē\ *adj* : RUDE, IMPOLITE — **unmannerly** *adv*

un·mask \ˌən-ˈmask\ *vb* **1** : to strip of a mask or a disguise : EXPOSE **2** : to remove one's mask

un·mean·ing \-ˈmē-niŋ\ *adj* : having no meaning : SENSELESS

un·me·di·at·ed \ˌən-ˈmē-dē-ˌā-təd\ *adj* : not mediated : not communicated or transformed by an intervening agency

un·meet \-ˈmēt\ *adj* : not meet or fit : UNSUITABLE, IMPROPER

un·men·tion·able \-ˈmen-chə-nə-bəl\ *adj* : not fit or proper to be talked about

un·mer·ci·ful \-ˈmər-si-fəl\ *adj* : not merciful : CRUEL, MERCILESS — **un·mer·ci·ful·ly** *adv*

un·mind·ful \-ˈmīnd-fəl\ *adj* : not mindful : CARELESS, UNAWARE

un·mis·tak·able \ˌən-mə-ˈstā-kə-bəl\ *adj* : not capable of being mistaken or misunderstood : CLEAR, OBVIOUS — **un·mis·tak·ably** \-blē\ *adv*

un·mit·i·gat·ed \ˌən-ˈmi-tə-ˌgā-təd\ *adj* **1** : not softened or lessened **2** : ABSOLUTE, DOWNRIGHT ⟨an ~ liar⟩

un·moor \-ˈmu̇r\ *vb* : to loose from or as if from moorings

un·mor·al \-ˈmȯr-əl\ *adj* : having no moral perception or quality : AMORAL — **un·mo·ral·i·ty** \ˌən-mə-ˈra-lə-tē\ *n*

un·mute \-ˌmyüt\ *vb* **-mu·ted; -mu·ting** : to stop muting (something)

un·muz·zle \-ˈmə-zəl\ *vb* : to remove a muzzle from

un·nat·u·ral \ˌən-ˈna-chə-rəl\ *adj* : contrary to or acting contrary to nature or natural instincts; *also* : ABNORMAL — **un·nat·u·ral·ly** *adv* — **un·nat·u·ral·ness** *n*

un·nec·es·sar·i·ly \ˌən-ˌne-sə-ˈser-ə-lē\ *adv* **1** : not by necessity **2** : to an unnecessary degree ⟨~ harsh⟩

un·nerve \ˌən-ˈnərv\ *vb* : to deprive of courage, strength, or steadiness ⟨fear *unnerved* them⟩; *also* : UPSET

un·num·bered \ˌən-ˈnəm-bərd\ *adj* : not numbered or counted : INNUMERABLE

un·ob·tru·sive \ˌən-əb-ˈtrü-siv\ *adj* : not obtrusive or forward : not bold : INCONSPICUOUS — **un·ob·tru·sive·ly** *adv*

un·oc·cu·pied \ˌən-ˈä-kyə-ˌpīd\ *adj* **1** : not busy : UNEMPLOYED **2** : not occupied : EMPTY, VACANT

un·or·ga·nized \-ˈȯr-gə-ˌnīzd\ *adj* **1** : not formed or brought into an integrated or ordered whole **2** : not organized into unions ⟨~ labor⟩

un·pack \ˌən-ˈpak\ *vb* **1** : to separate and remove things packed **2** : to open and remove the contents of

un·par·al·leled \ˌən-ˈpa-rə-ˌleld\ *adj* : having no parallel; *esp* : having no equal or match ⟨an ~ achievement⟩

un·par·lia·men·ta·ry \ˌən-ˌpär-lə-ˈmen-tə-rē\ *adj* : contrary to parliamentary practice

---

unlimited
unlined
unlit
unliterary
unlivable
unlovable
unloved
unloving
unmade
unmalicious
unmanageable
unmanned
unmapped
unmarked
unmarketable
unmarred
unmarried
unmasculine
unmatched
unmeant
unmeasurable
unmeasured
unmelodious
unmentioned
unmerited
unmilitary
unmilled
unmixed
unmodified
unmolested
unmotivated
unmounted
unmovable
unmoved
unmusical
unnameable
unnamed
unnecessary
unneeded
unnewsworthy
unnoticeable
unnoticed
unobjectionable
unobservant
unobserved
unobstructed
unobtainable
unofficial
unofficially
unopened
unopposed
unoriginal
unorthodox
unorthodoxy
unostentatious
unowned
unpaged
unpaid
unpainted
unpaired
unpalatable
unpardonable
unpasteurized
unpatriotic
unpaved

un·peg \ˌən-ˈpeg\ *vb* **1** : to remove a peg from **2** : to unfasten by or as if by removing a peg
un·per·son \ˈən-ˈpər-sᵊn, -ˌpər-\ *n* : a person who usu. for political or ideological reasons is removed from recognition or consideration
un·pile \ˌən-ˈpī(-ə)l\ *vb* : to take or disentangle from a pile
un·pin \-ˈpin\ *vb* : to remove a pin from : UNFASTEN
un·pleas·ant \-ˈple-zᵊnt\ *adj* : not pleasant : DISAGREEABLE — **un·pleas·ant·ly** *adv* — **un·pleas·ant·ness** *n*
un·plug \ˌən-ˈpləg\ *vb* **1** : UNCLOG **2** : to remove (a plug) from a receptacle; *also* : to disconnect from an electric circuit by removing a plug **3** : to temporarily stop using electronic devices; *also* : to temporarily withdraw from everyday responsibilities ⟨~ while on vacation⟩
un·plumbed \-ˈpləmd\ *adj* **1** : not tested or measured with a plumb line **2** : not thoroughly explored
un·pop·u·lar \ˌən-ˈpä-pyə-lər\ *adj* : not popular : looked upon or received unfavorably — **un·pop·u·lar·i·ty** \ˌən-ˌpä-pyə-ˈla-rə-tē\ *n*
un·prec·e·dent·ed \ˌən-ˈpre-sə-ˌden-təd\ *adj* : having no precedent : NOVEL
un·pre·ten·tious \ˌən-pri-ˈten-chəs\ *adj* : not pretentious : MODEST
un·prin·ci·pled \ˌən-ˈprin-sə-pəld\ *adj* : lacking sound or honorable principles : UNSCRUPULOUS ⟨an ~ criminal⟩
un·print·able \-ˈprin-tə-bəl\ *adj* : unfit or too offensive to be printed
un·prof·it·able \ˌən-ˈprä-fə-tə-bəl\ *adj* : not profitable : USELESS, VAIN
un·pro·tect·ed \ˌən-prə-ˈtek-təd\ *adj* **1** : lacking protection **2** : performed without measures to prevent pregnancy or sexually transmitted disease ⟨~ sex⟩
un·qual·i·fied \ˌən-ˈkwä-lə-ˌfīd\ *adj* **1** : not having requisite qualifications **2** : not modified or restricted by reservations : COMPLETE — **un·qual·i·fied·ly** \-ˌfī-əd-lē\ *adv*
un·ques·tion·able \-ˈkwes-chə-nə-bəl\ *adj* : not questionable : INDISPUTABLE — **un·ques·tion·ably** \-blē\ *adv*
un·ques·tion·ing \-chə-niŋ\ *adj* : not questioning : accepting without examination or hesitation ⟨~ obedience⟩ — **un·ques·tion·ing·ly** *adv*
un·qui·et \-ˈkwī-ət\ *adj* **1** : not quiet : AGITATED, DISTURBED **2** : physically, emotionally, or mentally restless : UNEASY
un·quote \ˈən-ˌkwōt\ *n* — used orally to indicate the end of a direct quotation
un·rav·el \ˌən-ˈra-vəl\ *vb* **1** : to separate the threads of **2** : SOLVE ⟨~ a mystery⟩ **3** : to become unraveled
un·read \-ˈred\ *adj* **1** : not read; *also* : left unexamined **2** : lacking the benefits or the experience of reading
un·re·al \-ˈrēl\ *adj* : lacking in reality, substance, or genuineness — **un·re·al·i·ty** \ˌən-rē-ˈa-lə-tē\ *n*
un·rea·son·able \-ˈrē-zᵊn-ə-bəl\ *adj* **1** : not governed by or acting according to reason; *also* : not conformable to reason : ABSURD **2** : exceeding the bounds of reason or moderation — **un·rea·son·able·ness** *n* — **un·rea·son·ably** *adv*
un·rea·soned \-ˈrē-zᵊnd\ *adj* : not based on reason or reasoning ⟨~ fears⟩
un·rea·son·ing \-ˈrē-zᵊn-iŋ\ *adj* : not using or showing the use of reason as a guide or control
un·re·con·struct·ed \ˌən-ˌrē-kən-ˈstrək-təd\ *adj* : not reconciled to some political, economic, or social change; *esp* : holding stubbornly to a particular belief, view, place, or style
un·reel \ˌən-ˈrēl\ *vb* **1** : to unwind from or as if from a reel **2** : to perform successfully
un·re·gen·er·ate \ˌən-ri-ˈje-nə-rət\ *adj* : not regenerated or reformed
un·re·lent·ing \-ˈlen-tiŋ\ *adj* **1** : not yielding in determination : STERN ⟨~ leader⟩ **2** : not letting up or weakening in vigor or pace : CONSTANT — **un·re·lent·ing·ly** *adv*
un·re·mit·ting \-ˈmi-tiŋ\ *adj* : CONSTANT, INCESSANT — **un·re·mit·ting·ly** *adv*
un·re·quit·ed \ˌən-ri-ˈkwī-təd\ *adj* : not requited : not reciprocated or returned in kind ⟨~ love⟩
un·re·served \-ˈzərvd\ *adj* **1** : not limited

unpeeled
unperceived
unperceptive
unperformed
unpersuaded
unpersuasive
unperturbed
unplanned
unplanted
unpleasing
unplowed
unpoetic
unpolished
unpolitical
unpolluted
unposed
unpractical
unpredictability
unpredictable
unprejudiced
unpremeditated
unprepared
unpreparedness
unprepossessing
unpressed
unpretending
unpretty
unprivileged
unprocessed
unproductive
unprofessed
unprofessional
unprogrammed
unprogressive
unpromising
unprompted
unpronounceable
unpropitious
unproven
unprovided
unprovoked
unpublished
unpunished
unquenchable
unquestioned
unraised
unrated
unratified
unreachable
unreadable
unready
unrealistic
unrealized
unrecognizable
unrecognized
unrecorded
unrecoverable
unredeemable
unrefined
unreflecting
unreflective
unregistered
unregulated
unrehearsed
unrelated
unreliable
unrelieved
unremarkable
unremembered
unremovable
unrepentant
unreported
unrepresentative
unrepresented
unrepressed
unresistant
unresisting
unresolved
unresponsive
unresponsiveness

or partial ⟨~ enthusiasm⟩ **2** : not cautious or reticent : FRANK, OPEN **3** : not set aside for special use — **un·re·serv·ed·ly** \-ˈzər-vəd-lē\ *adv*

un·rest \ˌən-ˈrest\ *n* : a disturbed or uneasy state : TURMOIL

un·re·strained \ˌən-ri-ˈstrānd\ *adj* **1** : IMMODERATE, UNCONTROLLED ⟨~ anger⟩ **2** : SPONTANEOUS

un·re·straint \-ri-ˈstrānt\ *n* : lack of restraint

un·rid·dle \ˌən-ˈri-dᵊl\ *vb* : to find the explanation of : SOLVE

un·righ·teous \-ˈrī-chəs\ *adj* **1** : SINFUL, WICKED **2** : UNJUST — **un·righ·teous·ness** *n*

un·ripe \-ˈrīp\ *adj* : not ripe : IMMATURE

un·ri·valed *or* **un·ri·valled** \ˌən-ˈrī-vəld\ *adj* : having no rival : SUPREME

un·robe \-ˈrōb\ *vb* : DISROBE, UNDRESS

un·roll \-ˈrōl\ *vb* **1** : to unwind a roll of : open out **2** : DISPLAY, DISCLOSE **3** : to become unrolled or spread out

un·roof \-ˈrüf, -ˈru̇f\ *vb* : to strip off the roof or covering of

un·ruf·fled \ˌən-ˈrə-fəld\ *adj* **1** : not agitated or upset **2** : not ruffled : SMOOTH ⟨~ water⟩

un·ruly \-ˈrü-lē\ *adj* [ME *unreuly*, fr. *un-* + *reuly* disciplined, fr. *reule* rule, fr. AF, fr. L *regula* straightedge, rule, fr. *regere* to direct] : not submissive to rule or restraint : TURBULENT ⟨~ passions⟩ — **un·rul·i·ness** \-ˈrü-lē-nəs\ *n*

un·sad·dle \ˌən-ˈsa-dᵊl\ *vb* **1** : to remove the saddle from a horse **2** : UNHORSE

un·sat·u·rat·ed \-ˈsa-chə-ˌrā-təd\ *adj* **1** : capable of absorbing or dissolving more of something **2** : containing double or triple bonds between carbon atoms ⟨~ fat⟩ — **un·sat·u·rate** \-rət\ *n*

un·saved \ˌən-ˈsāvd\ *adj* : not saved; *esp* : not rescued from eternal punishment

un·sa·vory \-ˈsā-və-rē\ *adj* **1** : TASTELESS **2** : unpleasant to taste or smell **3** : morally offensive ⟨~ characters⟩

un·say \-ˈsā\ *vb* **-said** \-ˈsed\; **-say·ing** : to take back (something said) : RETRACT, WITHDRAW

un·scathed \-ˈskāt͟hd\ *adj* : wholly unharmed : not injured

un·schooled \-ˈsküld\ *adj* : not schooled : UNTAUGHT, UNTRAINED

un·sci·en·tif·ic \ˌən-ˌsī-ən-ˈti-fik\ *adj* : not scientific : not in accord with the principles and methods of science

un·scram·ble \ˌən-ˈskram-bəl\ *vb* **1** : RESOLVE, CLARIFY **2** : to restore (as a radio message) to intelligible form

un·screw \-ˈskrü\ *vb* **1** : to draw the screws from **2** : to loosen by turning

un·scru·pu·lous \-ˈskrü-pyə-ləs\ *adj* : not scrupulous : UNPRINCIPLED — **un·scru·pu·lous·ly** *adv* — **un·scru·pu·lous·ness** *n*

un·seal \-ˈsēl\ *vb* : to break or remove the seal of : OPEN

un·search·able \-ˈsər-chə-bəl\ *adj* : not capable of being searched or explored ⟨~ forests⟩

un·sea·son·able \-ˈsē-zᵊn-ə-bəl\ *adj* : not seasonable : happening or coming at the wrong time : UNTIMELY — **un·sea·son·ably** \-blē\ *adv*

un·seat \-ˈsēt\ *vb* **1** : to throw from one's seat esp. on horseback **2** : to remove from political office

un·seem·ly \-ˈsēm-lē\ *adj* : not according with established standards of good form or taste ⟨~ behavior⟩; *also* : not suitable — **un·seem·li·ness** *n*

un·seen \ˌən-ˈsēn\ *adj* : not seen : INVISIBLE ⟨~ dangers⟩

un·seg·re·gat·ed \-ˈse-gri-ˌgā-təd\ *adj* : not segregated; *esp* : free from racial segregation

un·self·ish \-ˈsel-fish\ *adj* : not selfish : GENEROUS — **un·self·ish·ly** *adv* — **un·self·ish·ness** *n*

un·set·tle \ˌən-ˈse-tᵊl\ *vb* : to move or loosen from a settled position : DISPLACE, DISTURB

un·set·tled \-ˈse-tᵊld\ *adj* **1** : not settled : not fixed (as in position or character) **2** : not calm : DISTURBED **3** : not decided in mind : UNRESOLVED **4** : not paid ⟨~ accounts⟩ **5** : not occupied by settlers

un·shack·le \-ˈsha-kəl\ *vb* : to free from shackles

un·shaped \-ˈshāpt\ *adj* : not shaped; *esp* : not being in finished, final, or perfect form ⟨~ ideas⟩ ⟨~ timber⟩

un·sheathe \ˌən-ˈshēt͟h\ *vb* : to draw from or as if from a sheath

un·ship \-ˈship\ *vb* **1** : to remove from a ship **2** : to remove or become removed from position ⟨~ an oar⟩

un·shod \ˌən-ˈshäd\ *adj* : not wearing or provided with shoes

un·sight·ly \ˌən-ˈsīt-lē\ *adj* : unpleasant to the sight : UGLY ⟨an ~ mess⟩

un·skilled \-ˈskild\ *adj* **1** : not skilled; *esp* : not skilled in a specified branch of work **2** : not requiring skill

un·skill·ful \-ˈskil-fəl\ *adj* : lacking in skill or proficiency — **un·skill·ful·ly** *adv*

un·sling \-ˈsliŋ\ *vb* **-slung** \-ˈsləŋ\; **-sling·ing** : to remove from being slung

---

unrestful
unrestricted
unreturnable
unrewarding
unrhymed
unrhythmic
unripened
unromantic
unromantically
unsafe
unsaid
unsalable
unsalted
unsanctioned
unsanitary
unsatisfactory
unsatisfied
unscented
unscheduled
unscholarly
unsealed
unseasoned
unseaworthy
unsegmented
unself–conscious
unself–consciously
unsensational
unsentimental
unserious
unserviceable
unsexual
unshaded
unshakable
unshaken
unshapely
unshaven
unshorn
unsifted
unsigned
unsinkable
unsmiling
unsociable
unsoiled
unsold
unsoldierly
unsolicited
unsolvable
unsolved

un·snap \-ˈsnap\ *vb* : to loosen or free by or as if by undoing a snap
un·snarl \-ˈsnärl\ *vb* : to remove snarls from : UNTANGLE
un·so·phis·ti·cat·ed \ˌən-sə-ˈfis-tə-ˌkā-təd\ *adj* **1** : not worldly-wise : lacking sophistication **2** : SIMPLE ⟨~ designs⟩
un·sought \ˌən-ˈsȯt\ *adj* : not sought : not searched for or asked for : not obtained by effort ⟨~ honors⟩
un·sound \-ˈsau̇nd\ *adj* **1** : not healthy or whole; *also* : not mentally normal ⟨of ~ mind⟩ **2** : not valid **3** : not firmly made or fixed ⟨structurally ~⟩ — **un·sound·ly** *adv* — **un·sound·ness** *n*
un·spar·ing \-ˈsper-iŋ\ *adj* **1** : HARD, RUTHLESS ⟨~ criticism⟩ **2** : not frugal : LIBERAL, PROFUSE ⟨~ generosity⟩
un·speak·able \-ˈspē-kə-bəl\ *adj* **1** : impossible to express in words **2** : extremely bad ⟨~ offenses⟩ — **un·speak·ably** \-blē\ *adv*
un·spool \ˌən-ˈspül\ *vb* **1** : to unwind from a spool **2** : to present artfully ⟨~ a new film⟩
un·spot·ted \-ˈspä-təd\ *adj* : not spotted or stained; *esp* : free from moral stain
un·sprung \-ˈsprəŋ\ *adj* : not sprung; *esp* : not equipped with springs
un·sta·ble \-ˈstā-bəl\ *adj* **1** : not stable **2** : FICKLE, VACILLATING; *also* : lacking effective emotional control **3** : readily changing (as by decomposing) in chemical or physical composition or in biological activity ⟨an ~ atomic nucleus⟩
un·steady \ˌən-ˈste-dē\ *adj* : not steady : UNSTABLE — **un·stead·i·ly** \-ˈste-də-lē\ *adv* — **un·stead·i·ness** \-ˈste-dē-nəs\ *n*
un·stint·ing \-ˈstin-tiŋ\ *adj* **1** : not restricting or holding back **2** : giving or being given freely or generously ⟨~ praise⟩
un·stop \-ˈstäp\ *vb* **1** : UNCLOG **2** : to remove a stopper from
un·stop·pa·ble \ˌən-ˈstä-pə-bəl\ *adj* : incapable of being stopped
un·strap \-ˈstrap\ *vb* : to remove or loose a strap from
un·stressed \ˌən-ˈstrest\ *adj* : not stressed; *esp* : not bearing a stress or accent ⟨~ syllables⟩
un·strung \-ˈstrəŋ\ *adj* **1** : having the strings loose or detached **2** : made weak, disordered, or unstable
un·stud·ied \-ˈstə-dēd\ *adj* **1** : not acquired by study **2** : NATURAL, UNFORCED ⟨moved with ~ grace⟩
un·sub·stan·tial \ˌən-səb-ˈstan-chəl\ *adj* : INSUBSTANTIAL
un·sung \ˌən-ˈsəŋ\ *adj* **1** : not sung **2** : not celebrated in song or verse ⟨~ heroes⟩
un·swerv·ing \ˌən-ˈswər-viŋ\ *adj* **1** : not swerving or turning aside **2** : STEADY
un·tan·gle \-ˈtaŋ-gəl\ *vb* **1** : DISENTANGLE **2** : to straighten out : RESOLVE ⟨~ a problem⟩
un·taught \-ˈtȯt\ *adj* **1** : not instructed or taught : IGNORANT **2** : NATURAL, SPONTANEOUS ⟨~ kindness⟩
un·think·able \-ˈthiŋ-kə-bəl\ *adj* : not to be thought of or considered as possible ⟨~ cruelty⟩
un·think·ing \ˌən-ˈthiŋ-kiŋ\ *adj* : not thinking; *esp* : THOUGHTLESS, HEEDLESS ⟨~ remarks⟩ — **un·think·ing·ly** *adv*
un·thought \ˌən-ˈthȯt\ *adj* : not anticipated : UNEXPECTED — often used with *of* ⟨*unthought*-of development⟩
un·tie \-ˈtī\ *vb* **-tied; -ty·ing** *or* **-tie·ing** **1** : to free from something that ties, fastens, or restrains : UNBIND **2** : DISENTANGLE, RESOLVE **3** : to become loosened or unbound
[1]**un·til** \ˌən-ˈtil\ *prep* : up to the time of ⟨worked ~ 5 o'clock⟩
[2]**until** *conj* **1** : up to the time that ⟨wait ~ he calls⟩ **2** : to the point or degree that ⟨ran ~ she was breathless⟩
[1]**un·time·ly** \ˌən-ˈtīm-lē\ *adv* : at an inopportune time : UNSEASONABLY; *also* : PREMATURELY
[2]**untimely** *adj* : PREMATURE ⟨~ death⟩; *also* : INOPPORTUNE, UNSEASONABLE
un·tir·ing \ˌən-ˈtī-riŋ\ *adj* : not becoming tired : INDEFATIGABLE ⟨an ~ worker⟩ — **un·tir·ing·ly** *adv*
un·to \ˈən-ˌtü\ *prep* : TO
un·told \ˌən-ˈtōld\ *adj* **1** : too great or numerous to count **2** : not told : not revealed
[1]**un·touch·able** \ˌən-ˈtə-chə-bəl\ *adj* : forbidden to the touch
[2]**untouchable** *n* : a member of the lowest social class in India having in traditional Hindu belief the quality of defiling by contact a member of a higher caste
un·touched \ˌən-ˈtəcht\ *adj* **1** : not subjected to touching **2** : not described or dealt with **3** : not tasted **4** : being in a primeval state or condition **5** : UNAFFECTED ⟨~ by scandals⟩

---

unsorted
unspecified
unspectacular
unspent
unspiritual
unspoiled
unspoken
unsportsmanlike
unstained
unstated
unsterile
unstructured
unstylish
unsubdued
unsubstantiated
unsubtle
unsuccessful
unsuccessfully
unsuitable
unsuited
unsullied
unsupervised
unsupportable
unsupported
unsure
unsurpassed
unsurprising
unsurprisingly
unsuspected
unsuspecting
unsuspicious
unsweetened
unsymmetrical
unsympathetic
unsystematic
untactful
untainted
untalented
untamed
untanned
untapped
untarnished
untaxed
unteachable
untenable
untenanted
untended
untested
unthrifty
untidy
untilled
untitled
untraceable
untraditional
untrained
untrammeled
untranslatable
untranslated
untraveled
untraversed
untreated

un·tow·ard \,ən-'tȯrd, -'tō-ərd; ,ən-tə-'wȯrd\ *adj* **1** : difficult to manage : STUBBORN, WILLFUL ⟨an ~ child⟩ **2** : INCONVENIENT, TROUBLESOME ⟨an ~ encounter⟩

un·tried \,ən-'trīd\ *adj* : not tested or proved by experience or trial; *also* : not tried in court

un·true \-'trü\ *adj* **1** : not faithful : DISLOYAL **2** : not according with a standard of correctness **3** : FALSE

un·truth \,ən-'trüth, 'ən-,trüth\ *n* **1** : lack of truthfulness **2** : FALSEHOOD

un·tune \-'tün, -'tyün\ *vb* **1** : to put out of tune **2** : DISARRANGE, DISCOMPOSE

un·tu·tored \-'tü-tərd, -'tyü-\ *adj* : UNTAUGHT, UNLEARNED, IGNORANT

un·twine \-'twīn\ *vb* : UNWIND, DISENTANGLE

un·twist \,ən-'twist\ *vb* **1** : to separate the twisted parts of : UNTWINE **2** : to become untwined

un·used \-'yüst, -'yüzd *for 1;* -'yüzd *for 2*\ *adj* **1** : UNACCUSTOMED ⟨~ to such treatment⟩ **2** : not used

un·usu·al \-'yü-zhə-wəl\ *adj* : not usual : UNCOMMON, RARE — **un·usu·al·ly** *adv*

un·ut·ter·able \,ən-'ə-tə-rə-bəl\ *adj* : being beyond the powers of description : INEXPRESSIBLE ⟨~ shame⟩ — **un·ut·ter·ably** \-blē\ *adv*

un·var·nished \-'vär-nisht\ *adj* **1** : not varnished **2** : not embellished : PLAIN ⟨the ~ truth⟩

un·veil \,ən-'vāl\ *vb* **1** : to remove a veil or covering from : DISCLOSE **2** : to remove a veil : reveal oneself

un·voiced \-'vȯist\ *adj* **1** : not verbally expressed : UNSPOKEN **2** : VOICELESS 2

un·war·rant·able \-'wȯr-ən-tə-bəl\ *adj* : not justifiable : INEXCUSABLE — **un·war·rant·ably** \-blē\ *adv*

un·weave \-'wēv\ *vb* **-wove** \-'wōv\; **-wo·ven** \-'wō-vən\; **-weav·ing** : DISENTANGLE, RAVEL

un·well \,ən-'wel\ *adj* : SICK, AILING

un·whole·some \-'hōl-səm\ *adj* **1** : harmful to physical, mental, or moral well-being ⟨~ food⟩ **2** : CORRUPT, UNSOUND ⟨~ deals⟩; *also* : offensive to the senses : LOATHSOME ⟨an ~ stench⟩

un·wieldy \-'wēl-dē\ *adj* : not easily managed, handled, or used (as because of bulk, weight, or complexity) : AWKWARD ⟨an ~ tool⟩

un·wind \-'wīnd\ *vb* **-wound** \-'waůnd\; **-wind·ing** **1** : to undo something that is wound : loose from coils **2** : to become unwound : be capable of being unwound **3** : RELAX ⟨~ after work⟩

un·wise \,ən-'wīz\ *adj* : not wise : FOOLISH — **un·wise·ly** *adv*

un·wit·ting \-'wi-tiŋ\ *adj* **1** : not knowing : UNAWARE **2** : not intended : INADVERTENT ⟨~ mistake⟩ — **un·wit·ting·ly** *adv*

un·wont·ed \-'wȯn-təd, -'wōn-\ *adj* **1** : RARE, UNUSUAL **2** : not accustomed by experience — **un·wont·ed·ly** *adv*

un·world·ly \-'wərld-lē\ *adj* **1** : not of this world; *esp* : SPIRITUAL **2** : NAIVE **3** : not swayed by worldly considerations — **un·world·li·ness** \-lē-nəs\ *n*

un·wor·thy \,ən-'wər-thē\ *adj* **1** : DISHONORABLE, BASE **2** : not meritorious : not worthy : UNDESERVING **3** : not deserved : UNMERITED ⟨~ treatment⟩ — **un·wor·thi·ly** \-thə-lē\ *adv* — **un·wor·thi·ness** \-thē-nəs\ *n*

un·wrap \-'rap\ *vb* : to remove the wrapping from : DISCLOSE

un·writ·ten \-'ri-tᵊn\ *adj* **1** : not in writing : ORAL, TRADITIONAL ⟨an ~ law⟩ **2** : containing no writing : BLANK

un·yield·ing \,ən-'yēl-diŋ\ *adj* **1** : characterized by lack of softness or flexibility **2** : characterized by firmness or obduracy ⟨~ opposition⟩

un·yoke \-'yōk\ *vb* : to remove a yoke from; *also* : SEPARATE, DISCONNECT

un·zip \-'zip\ *vb* : to zip open : open by means of a zipper

¹up \'əp\ *adv* **1** : in or to a higher position or level; *esp* : away from the center of the earth **2** : from beneath a surface (as ground or water) **3** : from below the horizon **4** : in or into an upright position; *esp* : out of bed **5** : with greater intensity ⟨speak ~⟩ **6** : to or at a greater rate or amount ⟨prices went ~⟩ **7** : in or into a better or more advanced state or a state of greater intensity or activity ⟨stir ~ a fire⟩ **8** : into existence, evidence, or knowledge ⟨the missing book turned ~⟩ **9** : into consideration ⟨brought the matter ~⟩ **10** : to or at bat **11** : into possession or custody ⟨gave himself ~⟩ **12** : ENTIRELY, COMPLETELY ⟨eat it ~⟩ **13** — used for emphasis ⟨clean ~ a room⟩ **14** : ASIDE, BY ⟨lay ~ supplies⟩ **15** : so as to arrive or approach ⟨ran ~ the path⟩ **16** : in a direction opposite to down **17** : in or into parts ⟨tear ~ paper⟩ **18** : to a stop ⟨pull ~ at the curb⟩ **19** : for each side ⟨the score was 15 ~⟩

²up *adj* **1** : risen above the horizon ⟨the sun is ~⟩ **2** : being out of bed ⟨~ by 6 o'clock⟩ **3** : relatively high ⟨prices are ~⟩ **4** : RAISED, LIFTED ⟨windows are ~⟩ **5** : BUILT, CONSTRUCTED ⟨the house is ~⟩ **6** : grown above a surface ⟨the corn is ~⟩ **7** : moving, inclining, or directed upward **8** : marked by agitation,

---

untrimmed
untrod
untrodden
untroubled
untrustworthy
untruthful
untypical
unusable
unvaried
unvarying
unventilated
unverifiable
unverified
unversed
unvisited
unwanted
unwarranted
unwary
unwashed
unwavering
unweaned
unwearable
unwearied
unweathered
unwed
unwelcome
unwilling
unwillingly
unwillingness
unwomanly
unworkable
unworn
unworried
unwounded
unwoven

excitement, or activity **9** : READY; *esp* : highly prepared **10** : going on : taking place ⟨find out what is ~⟩ **11** : EXPIRED, ENDED ⟨the time is ~⟩ **12** : extensively aware or informed ⟨~ on the news⟩ **13** : being ahead or in advance of an opponent ⟨one hole ~ in a match⟩ **14** : presented for or being under consideration ⟨~ for promotion⟩ **15** : charged before a court ⟨~ for robbery⟩

³**up** *prep* **1** : to, toward, or at a higher point of ⟨~ a ladder⟩ **2** : to or toward the source of ⟨~ the river⟩ **3** : to or toward the northern part of ⟨~ the coast⟩ **4** : to or toward the interior of ⟨traveling ~ the country⟩ **5** : ALONG ⟨walk ~ the street⟩

⁴**up** *n* **1** : an upward course or slope **2** : a period or state of prosperity or success ⟨he had his ~*s* and downs⟩ **3** : a quark with a charge of +⅔ that is one of the constituents of the proton and neutron

⁵**up** *vb* **upped** \ˈəpt\ *or in 2* **up; upped; up·ping; ups** *or in 2* **up** **1** : to rise from a lying or sitting position **2** : to act abruptly or surprisingly ⟨she *upped* and left home⟩ **3** : to move or cause to move upward ⟨*upped* the prices⟩

Upa·ni·shad \ü-ˈpän-i-ˌshäd\ *n* : one of a set of Vedic philosophical treatises

¹**up·beat** \ˈəp-ˌbēt\ *n* : an unaccented beat in a musical measure; *esp* : the last beat of the measure

²**upbeat** *adj* : OPTIMISTIC, CHEERFUL

up·braid \ˌəp-ˈbrād\ *vb* : to criticize, reproach, or scold severely

up·bring·ing \ˈəp-ˌbriŋ-iŋ\ *n* : the process of bringing up and training

UPC *abbr* Universal Product Code

up·chuck \ˈəp-ˌchək\ *vb* : VOMIT

up·com·ing \ˈəp-ˌkə-miŋ\ *adj* : FORTHCOMING, APPROACHING ⟨the ~ election⟩

up–coun·try \ˈəp-ˌkən-trē\ *adj* : of or relating to the interior of a country or a region — **up–country** \ˈəp-ˈkən-\ *adv*

up·date \ˌəp-ˈdāt\ *vb* : to bring up to date — **update** \ˈəp-ˌdāt\ *n*

up·draft \ˈəp-ˌdraft, -ˌdräft\ *n* : an upward movement of gas (as air)

up·end \ˌəp-ˈend\ *vb* : to set, stand, or rise on end; *also* : OVERTURN

up–front \ˈəp-ˌfrənt, ˌəp-ˈfrənt\ *adj* **1** : HONEST, CANDID ⟨an ~ answer⟩ **2** : ADVANCE ⟨~ payment⟩

up front *adv* : in advance ⟨paid *up front*⟩

¹**up·grade** \ˈəp-ˌgrād\ *n* **1** : an upward grade or slope **2** : INCREASE, RISE

²**up·grade** \ˈəp-ˌgrād, ˌəp-ˈgrād\ *vb* **1** : to raise to a higher grade or position; *esp* : to advance to a job requiring a higher level of skill **2** : to improve or replace (as software or a device) for increased usefulness

up·growth \ˈəp-ˌgrōth\ *n* : the process of growing upward : DEVELOPMENT; *also* : a product or result of this

up·heav·al \ˌəp-ˈhē-vəl\ *n* **1** : the action or an instance of uplifting esp. of part of the earth's crust **2** : a violent agitation or change

¹**up·hill** \ˈəp-ˈhil\ *adv* : upward on a hill or incline; *also* : against difficulties

²**up·hill** \-ˌhil\ *adj* **1** : situated on elevated ground **2** : ASCENDING **3** : DIFFICULT, LABORIOUS ⟨an ~ struggle⟩

up·hold \ˌəp-ˈhōld\ *vb* **-held** \-ˈheld\; **-hold·ing** **1** : to give support to ⟨~ the law⟩ **2** : to support against an opponent **3** : to keep elevated — **up·hold·er** *n*

up·hol·ster \ˌəp-ˈhōl-stər\ *vb* : to furnish with or as if with upholstery — **up·hol·ster·er** *n*

up·hol·stery \-stə-rē\ *n, pl* **-ster·ies** [ME *upholdester* upholsterer, fr. *upholden* to uphold, fr. *up* + *holden* to hold] : materials (as fabrics, padding, and springs) used to make a soft covering esp. for a seat

UPI *abbr* United Press International

up·keep \ˈəp-ˌkēp\ *n* : the act or cost of keeping up or maintaining; *also* : the state of being maintained

up·land \ˈəp-lənd, -ˌland\ *n* : high land esp. at some distance from the sea — **upland** *adj*

¹**up·lift** \ˌəp-ˈlift\ *vb* **1** : to lift or raise up : ELEVATE **2** : to improve the condition of esp. morally, socially, or intellectually

²**up·lift** \ˈəp-ˌlift\ *n* **1** : a lifting up; *esp* : an upheaval of the earth's surface **2** : moral or social improvement ⟨spiritual ~⟩; *also* : a movement to make such improvement

up·load \(ˌ)əp-ˈlōd, ˈəp-ˌlōd\ *vb* : to transfer (information) from a computer to a remote computer or other device

up·mar·ket \ˌəp-ˈmär-kət\ *adj* : appealing to wealthy consumers

up·most \ˈəp-ˌmōst\ *adj* : UPPERMOST

up·on \ə-ˈpȯn, -ˈpän\ *prep* : ON

¹**up·per** \ˈə-pər\ *adj* **1** : higher in physical position, rank, or order ⟨~ management⟩ **2** : constituting the smaller and more restricted branch of a bicameral legislature **3** *cap* : being a later part or formation of a specific geological period **4** : being toward the interior ⟨the ~ Amazon⟩ **5** : NORTHERN ⟨~ Minnesota⟩

²**upper** *n* : one that is upper; *esp* : the parts of a shoe or boot above the sole

up·per·case \ˌə-pər-ˈkās\ *adj* : CAPITAL 1 — **uppercase** *n*

upper class *n* : a social class occupying a position above the middle class and having the highest status in a society — **upper–class** *adj*

up·per·class·man \ˌə-pər-ˈklas-mən\ *n* : a junior or senior in a college or high school

upper crust *n* : the highest social class or group; *esp* : the highest circle of the upper class

up·per·cut \ˈə-pər-ˌkət\ *n* : a short swinging punch delivered (as in boxing) in an upward direction usu. with a bent arm

upper hand *n* : MASTERY, ADVANTAGE

up·per·most \ˈə-pər-ˌmōst\ *adv* : in or into the highest or most prominent position — **uppermost** *adj*

up·pish \ˈə-pish\ *adj* : UPPITY

up·pi·ty \ˈə-pə-tē\ *adj* : ARROGANT, PRESUMPTUOUS ⟨~ technicians⟩

up·raise \ˌəp-ˈrāz\ *vb* : to lift up : ELEVATE

¹**up·right** \ˈəp-ˌrīt\ *adj* **1** : PERPENDICULAR, VERTICAL **2** : erect in carriage or posture **3** : morally correct : JUST ⟨an ~ citizen⟩ — **upright** *adv* — **up·right·ly** *adv* — **up·right·ness** *n*

²**upright** *n* **1** : the state of being upright : a vertical position **2** : something that stands upright

upright piano *n* : a piano whose strings run vertically

up·ris·ing \ˈəp-ˌrī-ziŋ\ *n* : INSURRECTION, REVOLT, REBELLION

up·riv·er \ˈəp-ˈri-vər\ *adv or adj* : toward or at a point nearer the source of a river

up·roar \ˈəp-ˌrȯr\ *n* [D *oproer,* fr. MD, fr. *op* up + *roer* motion] : a state of commotion, excitement, or violent disturbance

up·roar·i·ous \ˌəp-ˈrȯr-ē-əs\ *adj* **1** : marked by uproar **2** : extremely funny — **up·roar·i·ous·ly** *adv*

up·root \ˌəp-ˈrüt, -ˈru̇t\ *vb* **1** : to remove by or as if by pulling up by the roots **2** : DISPLACE 1 ⟨families were *~ed*⟩

up·scale \ˌəp-ˌskāl\ *adj* : relating to, being, or appealing to wealthy consumers ⟨~ restaurants⟩ — **upscale** *vb*

up·sell \ˌəp-ˌsel\ *vb* **-sold** \-ˌsōld\; **-selling** : to try to convince (a customer) to purchase something additional or at a higher cost

¹**up·set** \ˌəp-ˈset\ *vb* **-set; -set·ting** **1** : to force or be forced out of the usual upright, level, or proper position **2** : to disturb emotionally : WORRY; *also* : to make somewhat ill **3** : UNSETTLE, DISARRANGE **4** : to defeat unexpectedly

²**up·set** \ˈəp-ˌset\ *n* **1** : an upsetting or being upset; *esp* : a minor illness **2** : a derangement of plans or ideas **3** : an unexpected defeat

³**up·set** \(ˌ)əp-ˈset\ *adj* : emotionally disturbed or agitated ⟨~ about the divorce⟩

up·shot \ˈəp-ˌshät\ *n* : the final result

¹**up·side** \ˈəp-ˌsīd\ *n* **1** : the upper side **2** : a positive aspect **3** : PROMISE ⟨rookies with much ~⟩

²**up·side** \ˌəp-ˈsīd\ *prep* : up on or against the side of ⟨knocked him ~ the head⟩

up·side down \ˌəp-ˌsīd-ˈdau̇n\ *adv* **1** : with the upper and the lower parts reversed in position **2** : in or into confusion or disorder — **upside–down** *adj*

up·si·lon \ˈüp-sə-ˌlän, ˈyüp-, ˈəp-\ *n* : the 20th letter of the Greek alphabet — Υ or υ

¹**up·stage** \ˈəp-ˈstāj\ *adv or adj* : toward or at the rear of a theatrical stage

²**up·stage** \ˌəp-ˈstāj\ *vb* : to draw attention away from (as an actor)

¹**up·stairs** \ˌəp-ˈsterz\ *adv* **1** : up the stairs : to or on a higher floor **2** : to or at a higher position

²**up·stairs** \ˈəp-ˈsterz\ *adj* : situated above the stairs esp. on an upper floor ⟨~ bedroom⟩

³**up·stairs** \ˈəp-ˈsterz, ˈəp-ˌsterz\ *n sing or pl* : the part of a building above the ground floor

up·stand·ing \ˌəp-ˈstan-diŋ, ˈəp-\ *adj* **1** : ERECT **2** : STRAIGHTFORWARD, HONEST ⟨~ citizens⟩

¹**up·start** \ˌəp-ˈstärt\ *vb* : to jump up suddenly

²**up·start** \ˈəp-ˌstärt\ *n* : one that has risen suddenly; *esp* : one that claims more personal importance than is warranted — **up·start** \-ˈstärt\ *adj*

up·state \ˈəp-ˈstāt\ *adj* : of, relating to, or characteristic of a part of a state away from a large city and esp. to the north — **upstate** *adv* — **upstate** *n*

up·stream \ˈəp-ˈstrēm\ *adv* : at or toward the source of a stream — **upstream** *adj*

up·stroke \ˈəp-ˌstrōk\ *n* : an upward stroke (as of a pen)

up·surge \-ˌsərj\ *n* : a rapid or sudden rise ⟨an ~ in interest⟩

up·swept \ˈəp-ˌswept\ *adj* : swept upward ⟨~ hairdo⟩

up·swing \ˈəp-ˌswiŋ\ *n* : an upward swing; *esp* : a marked increase or rise (as in activity)

up·take \ˈəp-ˌtāk\ *n* **1** : UNDERSTANDING, COMPREHENSION ⟨quick on the ~⟩ **2** : an act or instance of absorbing and incorporating esp. into a living organism, tissue, or cell

up·thrust \ˈəp-ˌthrəst\ *n* : an upward thrust (as of the earth's crust) — **upthrust** *vb*

up·tick \-ˈtik\ *n* : an increase, rise, or upward trend

up·tight \ˈəp-ˈtīt\ *adj* **1** : TENSE, NERVOUS, UNEASY; *also* : ANGRY, INDIGNANT **2** : rigidly conventional

up–to–date *adj* **1** : extending up to the present time **2** : abreast of the times : MODERN — **up–to–date·ness** *n*

up·town \ˈəp-ˌtau̇n\ *n* : the upper part of a town or city; *esp* : the residential district — **up·town** \ˈəp-ˈtau̇n\ *adj or adv*

¹**up·turn** \ˈəp-ˌtərn, ˌəp-ˈtərn\ *vb* **1** : to turn (as earth) up or over **2** : to turn or direct upward

²**up·turn** \ˈəp-ˌtərn\ *n* : an upward turn esp. toward better conditions or higher prices

¹**up·ward** \ˈəp-wərd\ *or* **up·wards** \-wərdz\ *adv* **1** : in a direction from lower to higher **2** : toward a higher or better condition **3** : toward a greater amount or higher number, degree, or rate

²**upward** *adj* : directed or moving toward or situated in a higher place or level : ASCENDING — **up·ward·ly** *adv*

upwards of *also* **upward of** *adv* : more than : in excess of ⟨they cost *upwards of* $25 each⟩

up·well \ˌəp-ˈwel\ *vb* : to move or flow upward

up·well·ing \-ˈwe-liŋ\ *n* : a rising or an appearance of rising to the surface and flowing outward; *esp* : the movement of deep cold usu. nutrient-rich ocean water to the surface

up·wind \ˈəp-ˈwind\ *adv or adj* : in the direction from which the wind is blowing

ura·cil \ˈyu̇r-ə-ˌsil\ *n* : a pyrimidine base that is one of the four bases coding genetic information in the molecular chain of RNA

ura·ni·um \yu̇-ˈrā-nē-əm\ *n* : a silvery heavy radioactive metallic chemical element used as a source of atomic energy

Ura·nus \ˈyu̇r-ə-nəs, yu̇-ˈrā-\ *n* [LL, the sky personified as a god, fr. Gk *Ouranos,* fr. *ouranos* sky, heaven] : the planet 7th in order from the sun

ur·ban \ˈər-bən\ *adj* : of, relating to, characteristic of, or constituting a city

ur·bane \ˌər-ˈbān\ *adj* [L *urbanus* urban, urbane, fr. *urbs* city] : very polite and polished in manner : SUAVE

ur·ban·ite \ˈər-bə-ˌnīt\ *n* : a person who lives in a city

ur·ban·i·ty \ˌər-ˈba-nə-tē\ *n, pl* **-ties** : the quality or state of being urbane

ur·ban·ize \ˈər-bə-ˌnīz\ *vb* **-ized; -iz·ing** : to cause to take on urban characteristics — **ur·ban·i·za·tion** \ˌər-bə-nə-ˈzā-shən\ *n*

ur·chin \ˈər-chən\ *n* [ME, hedgehog, fr. AF *heriçun, hirechoun,* ultim. fr. L *ericius*] : a pert or mischievous youngster

Ur·du \ˈu̇r-dü, ˈər-\ *n* [Hindi & Urdu *urdū,* fr. Pers *zabān-e-urdū-e-muallā* language of the Exalted Camp (the imperial bazaar in Delhi)] : an Indo-Aryan language that is the official language of Pakistan and that is widely used by Muslims in urban areas of India

urea \yu̇-ˈrē-ə\ *n* : a soluble nitrogenous compound that is the chief solid constituent of mammalian urine

ure·mia \yu̇-ˈrē-mē-ə\ *n* : accumulation in the blood of materials normally passed off in the urine resulting in a poisoned condition — **ure·mic** \-mik\ *adj*

ure·ter \ˈyu̇r-ə-tər\ *n* : a duct that carries the urine from a kidney to the bladder

ure·thra \yu̇-ˈrē-thrə\ *n, pl* **-thras** *or* **-thrae** \-(ˌ)thrē\ : the canal that in most mammals carries off the urine from the bladder and in the male also serves to carry semen from the body — **ure·thral** \-thrəl\ *adj*

ure·thri·tis \ˌyu̇r-i-ˈthrī-təs\ *n* : inflammation of the urethra

[1]**urge** \ˈərj\ *vb* **urged; urg·ing** **1** : to present, advocate, or demand earnestly **2** : to try to persuade or sway ⟨~ a guest to stay⟩ **3** : to serve as a motive or reason for **4** : to impress or impel to some course or activity ⟨the dog *urged* the sheep onward⟩

[2]**urge** *n* **1** : the act or process of urging **2** : a force or impulse that urges or drives

ur·gent \ˈər-jənt\ *adj* **1** : calling for immediate attention : PRESSING **2** : urging insistently — **ur·gen·cy** \-jən-sē\ *n* — **ur·gent·ly** *adv*

uric \ˈyu̇r-ik\ *adj* : of, relating to, or found in urine

uric acid *n* : a nearly insoluble acid that is the chief nitrogenous excretory product of birds but is present in only small amounts in mammalian urine

uri·nal \ˈyu̇r-ə-nᵊl\ *n* **1** : a receptacle for urine **2** : a place for urinating

uri·nal·y·sis \ˌyu̇r-ə-ˈna-lə-səs\ *n* : chemical analysis of urine

uri·nary \ˈyu̇r-ə-ˌner-ē\ *adj* **1** : relating to, occurring in, or being organs for the formation and discharge of urine **2** : of, relating to, or for urine

urinary bladder *n* : a membranous sac in many vertebrates that serves for the temporary retention of urine and discharges by the urethra

uri·nate \ˈyu̇r-ə-ˌnāt\ *vb* **-nat·ed; -nat·ing** : to release or give off urine — **uri·na·tion** \ˌyu̇r-ə-ˈnā-shən\ *n*

urine \ˈyu̇r-ən\ *n* : a waste material from the kidneys that is usu. a yellowish watery liquid in mammals but is semisolid in birds and reptiles

URL \ˌyü-(ˌ)är-ˈel, ˈər(-ə)l\ *n* [*u*niform (or *u*niversal) *r*esource *l*ocator] : a series of usu. alphanumeric characters that specifies the storage location of a resource on the Internet

urn \ˈərn\ *n* **1** : a vessel that typically has the form of a vase on a pedestal and often is used to hold the ashes of the dead **2** : a closed vessel usu. with a spout for serving a hot beverage

uro·gen·i·tal \ˌyu̇r-ō-ˈje-nə-tᵊl\ *adj* : of, relating to, or being the excretory and reproductive organs or functions

urol·o·gy \yu̇-ˈrä-lə-jē\ *n* : a branch of medical science dealing with the urinary or urogenital tract and its disorders — **uro·log·i·cal** \ˌyu̇r-ə-ˈlä-ji-kəl\ *also* **uro·log·ic** \-jik\ *adj* — **urol·o·gist** \yu̇-ˈrä-lə-jist\ *n*

Ur·sa Ma·jor \ˌər-sə-ˈmā-jər\ *n* [L, lit., greater bear] : the northern constellation that contains the stars which form the Big Dipper

Ursa Mi·nor \-ˈmī-nər\ *n* [L, lit., lesser bear] : the constellation including the north pole of the heavens and the stars that form the Little Dipper with the North Star at the tip of the handle

ur·sine \ˈər-ˌsīn\ *adj* : of, relating to, or resembling a bear

ur·ti·car·ia \ˌər-tə-ˈker-ē-ə\ *n* [NL, fr. L *urtica* nettle] : HIVES

us \ˈəs\ *pron, objective case of* WE

US *abbr* United States

USA *abbr* **1** United States Army **2** United States of America

us·able *also* **use·able** \ˈyü-zə-bəl\ *adj* : suitable or fit for use — **us·abil·i·ty** \ˌyü-zə-ˈbi-lə-tē\ *n*

USAF *abbr* United States Air Force

us·age \ˈyü-sij, -zij\ *n* **1** : habitual or customary practice or procedure **2** : the way in which words and phrases are actually used **3** : the action or mode of using **4** : manner of treating

USB \ˌyü-(ˌ)es-ˈbē\ *n* [*u*niversal *s*erial *b*us] : a standardized computer interface for attaching peripherals

USCG *abbr* United States Coast Guard

USDA *abbr* United States Department of Agriculture

[1]**use** \ˈyüs\ *n* **1** : the act or practice of using or employing something : EMPLOYMENT, APPLICATION **2** : the fact or state of being used **3** : the way of using **4** : USAGE, CUSTOM **5** : the privilege or benefit

of using something **6** : the ability or power to use something (as a limb) **7** : the legal enjoyment of property that consists in its employment, occupation, or exercise; *also* : the benefit or profit esp. from property held in trust **8** : USEFULNESS, UTILITY; *also* : the end served : OBJECT, FUNCTION **9** : something useful or beneficial ⟨it's no ~ arguing⟩ **10** : the occasion or need to employ ⟨he had no more ~ for it⟩ **11** : ESTEEM, LIKING ⟨had no ~ for modern art⟩

²**use** \ˈyüz\ *vb* **used** \ˈyüzd; "*used to*" *usu* ˈyüs-tə\; **us·ing** **1** : to put into action or service : EMPLOY **2** : to consume or take (as drugs) regularly **3** : UTILIZE ⟨~ tact⟩; *also* : MANIPULATE ⟨*used* his friends to get ahead⟩ **4** : to expend or consume by putting to use **5** : to behave toward : TREAT ⟨*used* the horse cruelly⟩ **6** : to benefit from ⟨house could ~ a coat of paint⟩ **7** — used in the past with *to* to indicate a former practice, fact, or state ⟨we *used* to work harder⟩ — **us·er** *n*

used \ˈyüzd\ *adj* **1** : having been used by another : SECONDHAND ⟨~ cars⟩ **2** : ACCUSTOMED, HABITUATED ⟨~ to the heat⟩

use·ful \ˈyüs-fəl\ *adj* : capable of being put to use : ADVANTAGEOUS; *esp* : serviceable for a beneficial end — **use·ful·ly** *adv* — **use·ful·ness** *n*

use·less \-ləs\ *adj* : having or being of no use : WORTHLESS, INEFFECTUAL — **use·less·ly** *adv* — **use·less·ness** *n*

us·er·name \ˈyü-zər-ˌnām\ *n* : a sequence of characters that identifies a user when logging onto a computer or website — called also user ID

USES *abbr* United States Employment Service

use up *vb* : to consume completely

¹**ush·er** \ˈə-shər\ *n* [ME *ussher,* fr. AF *ussier, usscher,* fr. VL **ustiarius* doorkeeper, fr. L *ostium, ustium* door, mouth of a river] **1** : an officer who walks before a person of rank **2** : one who escorts people to their seats (as in a church or theater)

²**usher** *vb* **1** : to conduct to a place **2** : to precede as an usher, forerunner, or harbinger **3** : INAUGURATE, INTRODUCE ⟨~ in a new era⟩

ush·er·ette \ˌə-shə-ˈret\ *n* : a girl or woman who is an usher (as in a theater)

USIA *abbr* United States Information Agency

USMC *abbr* United States Marine Corps

USN *abbr* United States Navy

USO *abbr* United Service Organizations

USP *abbr* United States Pharmacopeia

USPS *abbr* United States Postal Service

USS *abbr* United States ship

USSR *abbr* Union of Soviet Socialist Republics

usu *abbr* usual; usually

usu·al \ˈyü-zhə-wəl\ *adj* **1** : accordant with usage, custom, or habit : NORMAL **2** : commonly or ordinarily used **3** : ORDINARY ♦ ***Synonyms*** CUSTOMARY, HABITUAL, ACCUSTOMED, ROUTINE — **usu·al·ly** \ˈyü-zhə-wə-lē, ˈyü-zhə-lē\ *adv*

usu·fruct \ˈyü-zə-ˌfrəkt\ *n* [L *ususfructus,* fr. *usus et fructus* use and enjoyment] : the legal right to use and enjoy the benefits and profits of something belonging to another

usu·rer \ˈyü-zhər-ər\ *n* : one that lends money esp. at an exorbitant rate

usu·ri·ous \yu̇-ˈzhu̇r-ē-əs\ *adj* : practicing, involving, or constituting usury ⟨a ~ rate of interest⟩

usurp \yu̇-ˈsərp, -ˈzərp\ *vb* [ME, fr. AF *usorper,* fr. L *usurpare,* to take possession of without legal claim, fr. *usu* (abl. of *usus* use) + *rapere* to seize] : to seize and hold by force or without right ⟨~ a throne⟩ — **usur·pa·tion** \ˌyü-sər-ˈpā-shən, -zər-\ *n* — **usurp·er** \yu̇-ˈsər-pər, -ˈzər-\ *n*

usu·ry \ˈyü-zhə-rē\ *n, pl* **-ries** **1** : the lending of money with an interest charge for its use **2** : an excessive rate or amount of interest charged; *esp* : interest above an established legal rate

UT *abbr* Utah

Ute \ˈyüt\ *n, pl* **Ute** *or* **Utes** : a member of an Indigenous people orig. ranging through Utah, Colorado, Arizona, and New Mexico; *also* : their language

uten·sil \yu̇-ˈten-səl\ *n* [ME, vessels for domestic use, fr. MF *utensile,* fr. L *utensilia,* fr. neut. pl. of *utensilis* useful, fr. *uti* to use] **1** : an instrument or vessel used in a household and esp. a kitchen **2** : a useful tool

uter·us \ˈyü-tə-rəs\ *n, pl* **uter·us·es** *or* **uteri** \ˈyü-tə-ˌrī\ : the muscular organ of a female mammal in which the young develop before birth — **uter·ine** \-ˌrīn, -rən\ *adj*

utile \ˈyüt-ᵊl, ˈyü-ˌtī(-ə)l\ *adj* : USEFUL

uti·lise *Brit var of* UTILIZE

¹**util·i·tar·i·an** \yu̇-ˌti-lə-ˈter-ē-ən\ *n* : a person who believes in utilitarianism

²**utilitarian** *adj* **1** : of or relating to utilitarianism **2** : of or relating to utility : aiming at usefulness rather than beauty; *also* : serving a useful purpose

util·i·tar·i·an·ism \yu̇-ˌti-lə-ˈter-ē-ə-ˌni-zəm\ *n* : a theory that the greatest good for the greatest number should be the main consideration in making a choice of actions

¹**util·i·ty** \yü-ˈti-lə-tē\ *n, pl* **-ties** **1** : USEFULNESS **2** : something useful or designed for use **3** : a business organization performing a public service and subject to special governmental regulation **4** : a public service or a commodity (as electricity or water) provided by a public utility; *also* : equipment to provide such or a similar service

²**utility** *adj* **1** : capable of serving esp. as a substitute in various uses or positions ⟨a ~ outfielder⟩ ⟨a ~ cord⟩ **2** : being of a usable but poor quality ⟨~ beef⟩

utility knife *n* : a knife designed for general use; *esp* : one with a retractable blade

uti·lize \ˈyü-tə-ˌlīz\ *vb* **-lized; -liz·ing** : to make use of : turn to profitable account or use — **uti·li·za·tion** \ˌyü-tə-lə-ˈzā-shən\ *n*

ut·most \ˈət-ˌmōst\ *adj* **1** : situated at the farthest or most distant point : EXTREME **2** : of the greatest or highest degree, quantity, number, or amount — **utmost** *n*

uto·pia \yu̇-ˈtō-pē-ə\ *n* [*Utopia,* imaginary island described in Sir Thomas More's *Utopia,* fr. Gk *ou* not, no + *topos* place] **1** *often cap* : a place of ideal perfection esp. in laws, government, and social conditions **2** : an impractical scheme for social improvement

¹uto·pi·an \-pē-ən\ *adj, often cap* **1** : of, relating to, or resembling a utopia **2** : proposing ideal social and political schemes that are impractical **3** : VISIONARY

²utopian *n* **1** : a believer in the perfectibility of human society **2** : one who proposes or advocates utopian schemes

¹ut·ter \ˈə-tər\ *adj* [ME, remote, fr. OE *ūtera* outer, compar. adj. fr. *ūt* out, adv.] : ABSOLUTE, TOTAL 〈~ ruin〉 — **ut·ter·ly** *adv*

²utter *vb* [ME *uttren,* fr. *utter* outside, adv., fr. OE *ūtor,* compar. of *ūt* out] **1** : to send forth as a sound : express in usu. spoken words : PRONOUNCE, SPEAK **2** : to put (as currency) into circulation — **ut·ter·er** *n*

ut·ter·ance \ˈə-tə-rəns\ *n* **1** : something uttered; *esp* : an oral or written statement **2** : the action of uttering with the voice : SPEECH **3** : power, style, or manner of speaking

ut·ter·most \ˈə-tər-ˌmōst\ *adj* : EXTREME, UTMOST 〈the ~ parts of the earth〉 — **uttermost** *n*

U–turn \ˈyü-ˌtərn\ *n* : a turn resembling the letter U; *esp* : a 180-degree turn made by a vehicle in a road

UV *abbr* ultraviolet

uvu·la \ˈyü-vyə-lə\ *n, pl* **-las** *or* **-lae** \-ˌlē, -ˌlī\ : the fleshy lobe hanging at the back of the roof of the mouth — **uvu·lar** \-lər\ *adj*

UW *abbr* underwriter

UX *abbr* user experience

ux·o·ri·ous \ˌək-ˈsȯr-ē-əs, ˌəg-ˈzȯr-\ *adj* : excessively devoted or submissive to a wife

V

¹v \ˈvē\ *n, pl* **v's** *or* **vs** \ˈvēz\ *often cap* : the 22d letter of the English alphabet

²v *abbr, often cap* **1** vector **2** velocity **3** verb **4** verse **5** versus **6** very **7** victory **8** vide **9** voice **10** voltage **11** volume **12** vowel

V *symbol* **1** vanadium **2** volt

Va *abbr* Virginia

VA *abbr* **1** Veterans Administration **2** vice admiral **3** Virginia

va·can·cy \ˈvā-kən-sē\ *n, pl* **-cies** **1** : a vacating esp. of an office, position, or piece of property **2** : a vacant office, position, or tenancy; *also* : the period during which it stands vacant **3** : empty space : VOID **4** : the state of being vacant

va·cant \ˈvā-kənt\ *adj* **1** : not occupied 〈~ seat〉 〈~ room〉 **2** : EMPTY 〈~ space〉 **3** : free from business or care 〈a few ~ hours〉 **4** : devoid of thought, reflection, or expression 〈a ~ smile〉 — **va·cant·ly** *adv*

va·cate \ˈvā-ˌkāt\ *vb* **va·cat·ed; va·cat·ing** **1** : to make void : ANNUL **2** : to make vacant (as an office or house); *also* : to give up the occupancy of

¹va·ca·tion \vā-ˈkā-shən, və-\ *n* : a period of rest from work : HOLIDAY

²vacation *vb* : to take or spend a vacation — **va·ca·tion·er** *n*

va·ca·tion·ist \-shə-nist\ *n* : a person taking a vacation

va·ca·tion·land \-shən-ˌland\ *n* : an area with recreational attractions and facilities for vacationists

va·cay \ˈvā-ˌkā\ *n, slang* VACATION

vac·ci·nate \ˈvak-sə-ˌnāt\ *vb* **-nat·ed; -nat·ing** : to administer a vaccine to usu. by injection

vac·ci·na·tion \ˌvak-sə-ˈnā-shən\ *n* **1** : the act of vaccinating **2** : the scar left by vaccinating

vac·cine \vak-ˈsēn, ˈvak-ˌsēn\ *n* [F *vaccin,* fr. *vaccine* cowpox, fr. NL *vaccina* (in *variolae vaccinae* cowpox), fr. L, fem. of *vaccinus* of or from cows, fr. *vacca* cow] : a preparation that is administered (as by injection) to stimulate the body's immune response against a specific infectious agent or disease

vac·cin·ia \vak-ˈsi-nē-ə\ *n* : COWPOX

vac·il·late \ˈva-sə-ˌlāt\ *vb* **-lat·ed; -lat·ing** **1** : SWAY, TOTTER; *also* : FLUCTUATE **2** : to incline first to one course or opinion and then to another : WAVER — **vac·il·la·tion** \ˌva-sə-ˈlā-shən\ *n*

va·cu·ity \va-ˈkyü-ə-tē\ *n, pl* **-ities** **1** : an empty space **2** : the state, fact, or quality of being vacuous **3** : something that is vacuous

vac·u·ole \ˈva-kyə-ˌwōl\ *n* : a usu. fluid-filled cavity esp. in the cytoplasm of an individual cell — **vac·u·o·lar** \ˌva-kyə-ˈwō-lər, -ˌlär\ *adj*

vac·u·ous \ˈva-kyə-wəs\ *adj* **1** : EMPTY, VACANT, BLANK **2** : DULL, STUPID, INANE 〈~ movies〉 — **vac·u·ous·ly** *adv* — **vac·u·ous·ness** *n*

¹vac·u·um \ˈva-(ˌ)kyüm, -kyəm\ *n, pl* **vac-**

uums *or* **vac·ua** \-kyə-wə\ [L, fr. neut. of *vacuus* empty] **1 :** a space entirely empty of matter **2 :** a space from which most of the air has been removed (as by a pump) **3 :** VOID, GAP **4 :** VACUUM CLEANER — **vacuum** *adj*

²**vacuum** *vb* **:** to use a vacuum device (as a vacuum cleaner) on ⟨~ the den⟩

vacuum bottle *n* **:** THERMOS

vacuum cleaner *n* **:** a household appliance for cleaning (as floors or rugs) by suction

vacuum–packed *adj* **:** having much of the air removed before being hermetically sealed ⟨~ fish⟩

vacuum tube *n* **:** an electron tube from which most of the air has been removed

va·de me·cum \ˌvā-dē-ˈmē-kəm, ˌvä-dē-ˈmā-\ *n, pl* **vade mecums** [L, go with me] **:** something (as a handbook or manual) regularly carried about

VADM *abbr* vice admiral

¹**vag·a·bond** \ˈva-gə-ˌbänd\ *adj* **1 :** WANDERING, HOMELESS **2 :** of, characteristic of, or leading the life of a vagrant or tramp **3 :** leading an unsettled or irresponsible life

²**vagabond** *n* **:** one leading a vagabond life; *esp* **:** VAGRANT, TRAMP

va·ga·ry \ˈvā-gə-rē, və-ˈger-ē\ *n, pl* **-ries** **:** an odd or eccentric idea or action **:** WHIM, CAPRICE ⟨the *vagaries* of life⟩

va·gi·na \və-ˈjī-nə\ *n, pl* **-nae** \-(ˌ)nē\ *or* **-nas** [L, lit., sheath] **:** a canal that leads from the uterus to the external opening of the female sex organs — **vag·i·nal** \ˈva-jə-nᵊl\ *adj* — **vag·i·nal·ly** \-nᵊl-ē\ *adv*

vag·i·ni·tis \ˌva-jə-ˈnī-təs\ *n* **:** inflammation of the vagina

va·gran·cy \ˈvā-grən-sē\ *n, pl* **-cies** **1 :** the quality or state of being vagrant; *also* **:** a vagrant act or notion **2 :** the offense of being a vagrant

¹**va·grant** \ˈvā-grənt\ *n* **:** a person who has no job and wanders from place to place

²**vagrant** *adj* **1 :** of, relating to, or characteristic of a vagrant **2 :** following no fixed course **:** RANDOM, CAPRICIOUS ⟨~ thoughts⟩ — **va·grant·ly** *adv*

vague \ˈvāg\ *adj* **vagu·er; vagu·est** [MF, fr. L *vagus,* lit., wandering] **1 :** not clear, definite, or distinct ⟨a ~ plan⟩ ⟨~ silhouettes⟩ **2 :** not clearly felt or analyzed ⟨a ~ unrest⟩ ♦ ***Synonyms*** OBSCURE, DARK, ENIGMATIC, AMBIGUOUS, EQUIVOCAL — **vague·ly** *adv* — **vague·ness** *n*

vain \ˈvān\ *adj* [ME, fr. AF, empty, futile, fr. L *vanus*] **1 :** of no real value **:** IDLE, WORTHLESS **2 :** FUTILE, UNSUCCESSFUL **3 :** proud of one's looks or abilities ♦ ***Synonyms*** CONCEITED, NARCISSISTIC, VAINGLORIOUS — **vain·ly** *adv* — **in vain** **1 :** without success ⟨her efforts were *in vain*⟩ **2 :** in a blasphemous manner ⟨took the Lord's name *in vain*⟩

vain·glo·ri·ous \ˌvān-ˈglȯr-ē-əs\ *adj* **:** marked by vainglory **:** BOASTFUL

vain·glo·ry \ˈvān-ˌglȯr-ē\ *n* **1 :** excessive or ostentatious pride esp. in one's own achievements **2 :** vain display **:** VANITY

val *abbr* value; valued

va·lance \ˈva-ləns, ˈvā-\ *n* **1 :** drapery hanging from an edge (as of an altar, table, or bed) **2 :** a drapery or a decorative frame across the top of a window

vale \ˈvāl\ *n* **:** VALLEY, DALE

vale·dic·tion \ˌva-lə-ˈdik-shən\ *n* [L *valedicere* to say farewell, fr. *vale* farewell + *dicere* to say] **:** an act or utterance of leave-taking **:** FAREWELL

vale·dic·to·ri·an \-ˌdik-ˈtȯr-ē-ən\ *n* **:** the student usu. of the highest rank in a graduating class who delivers the valedictory address at commencement

vale·dic·to·ry \-ˈdik-tə-rē\ *adj* **:** bidding farewell **:** delivered as a valediction ⟨a ~ address⟩ — **valedictory** *n*

va·lence \ˈvā-ləns\ *n* [LL *valentia* power, capacity, fr. L *valēre* to be strong] **:** the combining power of an atom as shown by the number of its electrons that are lost, gained, or shared in the formation of chemical bonds

Va·len·ci·ennes \və-ˌlen-sē-ˈen, ˌva-lən-sē-, -ˈenz\ *n* **:** a fine handmade lace

val·en·tine \ˈva-lən-ˌtīn\ *n* **:** a sweetheart chosen or complimented on Valentine's Day; *also* **:** a gift or greeting given on this day

Valentine's Day *also* **Valentine Day** *n* **:** February 14 observed in honor of St. Valentine and as a time for exchanging valentines

¹**va·let** \ˈva-lət, -(ˌ)lā; va-ˈlā\ *n* **1 :** a male servant who takes care of a man's clothes and performs personal services **2 :** an attendant in a hotel or restaurant who performs personal services (as parking cars) for customers

²**valet** *vb* **:** to serve as a valet

val·e·tu·di·nar·i·an \ˌva-lə-ˌtü-də-ˈner-ē-ən, -ˌtyü-\ *n* **:** a person of a weak or sickly constitution; *esp* **:** one whose chief concern is his or her ill health — **val·e·tu·di·nar·i·an·ism** \-ē-ə-ˌni-zəm\ *n*

val·iant \ˈval-yənt\ *adj* **:** having or showing valor **:** BRAVE, HEROIC ♦ ***Synonyms*** VALOROUS, DOUGHTY, COURAGEOUS, BOLD, AUDACIOUS, DAUNTLESS, UNDAUNTED, INTREPID — **val·iant·ly** *adv*

val·id \ˈva-ləd\ *adj* **1 :** having legal force ⟨a ~ contract⟩ **2 :** founded on truth or fact **:** capable of being justified or defended **:** SOUND ⟨a ~ argument⟩ ⟨~ reasons⟩ — **va·lid·i·ty** \və-ˈli-də-tē\ *n* — **val·id·ly** *adv*

val·i·date \ˈva-lə-ˌdāt\ *vb* **-dat·ed; -dat·ing** **1 :** to make legally valid **2 :** to confirm the validity of **3 :** VERIFY — **val·i·da·tion** \ˌva-lə-ˈdā-shən\ *n*

va·lise \və-ˈlēs\ *n* [F] **:** SUITCASE

val·ley \ˈva-lē\ *n, pl* **valleys** **:** a long depression between ranges of hills or mountains

val·or \ˈva-lər\ *n* [ME *valour* worth, worthiness, bravery, fr. AF, fr. ML *valor,* fr. L *valēre* to be strong] **:** personal bravery ♦ ***Synonyms*** HEROISM, PROWESS, GALLANTRY — **val·or·ous** \ˈva-lə-rəs\ *adj*

val·o·ri·za·tion \ˌva-lə-rə-ˈzā-shən\ *n* **:** the support of commodity prices by any of various forms of government subsidy — **val·o·rize** \ˈva-lə-ˌrīz\ *vb*

val·our *chiefly Brit var of* VALOR

¹valu·able \ˈval-yə-bəl, -yə-wə-bəl\ *adj* **1** : having money value **2** : having great money value **3** : of great use or service ♦ ***Synonyms*** INVALUABLE, PRICELESS, COSTLY, EXPENSIVE, DEAR, PRECIOUS

²valuable *n* : a usu. personal possession of considerable value ⟨put ~*s* in a safe⟩

val·u·ate \ˈval-yə-ˌwāt\ *vb* **-at·ed; -at·ing** : to place a value on : APPRAISE — **val·u·a·tor** \-ˌwā-tər\ *n*

val·u·a·tion \ˌval-yə-ˈwā-shən\ *n* **1** : the act or process of valuing; *esp* : appraisal of property **2** : the estimated or determined market value of a thing

¹val·ue \ˈval-yü\ *n* **1** : a fair return or equivalent in money, goods, or services for something exchanged **2** : the monetary worth of a thing; *also* : relative worth, utility, or importance ⟨nothing of ~ to say⟩ **3** : an assigned or computed numerical quantity ⟨the ~ of *x* in an equation⟩ **4** : relative lightness or darkness of a color : LUMINOSITY **5** : the relative length of a tone or note **6** : something (as a principle or ideal) intrinsically valuable or desirable ⟨human rather than material ~*s*⟩ — **val·ue·less** *adj*

²value *vb* **val·ued; valu·ing** **1** : to estimate the monetary worth of : APPRAISE **2** : to rate in usefulness, importance, or general worth **3** : to consider or rate highly : PRIZE, ESTEEM ⟨*valued* your opinions⟩ — **val·u·er** *n*

val·ue–add·ed tax *n* : an incremental excise tax that is levied on the value added at each stage of the processing of a raw material or the production and distribution of a commodity

valve \ˈvalv\ *n* **1** : a structure (as in a vein) that temporarily closes a passage or that permits movement in one direction only **2** : a device by which the flow of a fluid material may be regulated by a movable part; *also* : the movable part of such a device **3** : a device in a brass wind instrument for quickly varying the tube length in order to change the fundamental tone by some definite interval **4** : one of the separate usu. hinged pieces of which the shell of some animals and esp. bivalve mollusks consists **5** : one of the pieces into which a ripe seed capsule or pod separates — **valved** \ˈvalvd\ *adj* — **valve·less** *adj*

val·vu·lar \ˈval-vyə-lər\ *adj* : of, relating to, or affecting a valve esp. of the heart ⟨~ heart disease⟩

va·moose \və-ˈmüs, va-\ *vb* **va·moosed; va·moos·ing** [Sp *vamos* let us go] : to leave or go away quickly

¹vamp *n* **1** : the part of a boot or shoe upper covering esp. the front part of the foot **2** : a short introductory musical passage often repeated

²vamp \ˈvamp\ *vb* **1** : to provide with a new vamp **2** : to patch up with a new part **3** : INVENT, IMPROVISE ⟨~ up an excuse⟩

³vamp *n* : a woman who uses her charm or wiles to seduce and exploit men

⁴vamp *vb* : to practice seductive wiles on : to act like a vamp

vam·pire \ˈvam-ˌpī(-ə)r\ *n* [F, fr. G *Vampir*, fr. Serbian *vampir*] **1** : a reanimated corpse of folklore that bites and sucks the blood of the living **2** : a person who preys on other people; *esp* : a woman who exploits and ruins her lover **3** : VAMPIRE BAT

vampire bat *n* : any of various bats of Central and South America that feed on the blood of animals; *also* : any of several other bats that do not feed on blood but are sometimes reputed to do so

¹van \ˈvan\ *n* : VANGUARD

²van *n* : a usu. enclosed wagon or motortruck for moving goods or animals; *also* : a versatile enclosed box-like motor vehicle

va·na·di·um \və-ˈnā-dē-əm\ *n* : a soft grayish ductile metallic chemical element used esp. to form alloys

Van Al·len belt \van-ˈa-lən-\ *n* : a belt of intense radiation in the magnetosphere composed of charged particles trapped by earth's magnetic field

van·co·my·cin \ˌvaŋ-kə-ˈmī-sᵊn\ *n* : an antibiotic used esp. against staphylococci

van·dal \ˈvan-dᵊl\ *n* **1** *cap* : a member of a Germanic people who sacked Rome in A.D. 455 **2** : a person who willfully mars or destroys property

van·dal·ise *Brit var of* VANDALIZE

van·dal·ism \ˈvan-də-ˌli-zəm\ *n* : willful or malicious destruction or defacement of public or private property

van·dal·ize \-ˌlīz\ *vb* **-ized; -iz·ing** : to subject to vandalism : DAMAGE

Van·dyke \van-ˈdīk\ *n* : a trim pointed beard

vane \ˈvān\ *n* [ME, fr. OE *fana* banner] **1** : a movable device attached to a high object for showing wind direction **2** : a thin flat or curved object that is rotated about an axis by a flow of fluid or that rotates to cause a fluid to flow or that redirects a flow of fluid ⟨the ~*s* of a windmill⟩ **3** : a feather fastened near the back end of an arrow for stability in flight

van·guard \ˈvan-ˌgärd\ *n* **1** : the troops moving at the front of an army **2** : the forefront of an action or movement

va·nil·la \və-ˈni-lə\ *n* [NL, genus name, fr. Sp *vainilla* vanilla (plant and fruit), dim. of *vaina* sheath, fr. L *vagina*] : a flavoring extract made synthetically or obtained from the long beanlike pods (**vanilla beans**) of a tropical American climbing orchid; *also* : this orchid

van·ish \ˈva-nish\ *vb* : to pass from sight or existence : disappear completely — **van·ish·er** *n*

van·i·ty \ˈva-nə-tē\ *n, pl* **-ties** **1** : something that is vain, empty, or useless **2** : the quality or fact of being useless or futile : FUTILITY **3** : undue pride in oneself or one's appearance : CONCEIT **4** : a small case for cosmetics : COMPACT

vanity plate *n* : an automobile license

plate bearing distinctive letters or numbers designated by the owner
van·quish \ˈvaŋ-kwish, ˈvan-\ *vb* **1** : to overcome in battle or in a contest **2** : to gain mastery over (as an emotion)
van·tage \ˈvan-tij\ *n* **1** : superiority in a contest **2** : a position giving a strategic advantage or a commanding perspective
va·pid \ˈva-pəd, ˈvā-\ *adj* : lacking spirit, liveliness, or zest : FLAT, INSIPID ⟨~ gossip⟩ — **va·pid·i·ty** \va-ˈpi-də-tē\ *n* — **vap·id·ly** *adv* — **vap·id·ness** *n*
va·por \ˈvā-pər\ *n* **1** : fine separated particles (as fog or smoke) floating in the air and clouding it **2** : a substance in the gaseous state; *esp* : one that is liquid under ordinary conditions **3** : something insubstantial or fleeting **4** *pl* : a depressed or hysterical nervous condition
va·por·ing \ˈvā-pə-riŋ\ *n* : an idle, boastful, or high-flown expression or speech — usu. used in pl. ⟨political ~*s*⟩
va·por·ise *Brit var of* VAPORIZE
va·por·ize \ˈvā-pə-ˌrīz\ *vb* **-ized; -iz·ing** **1** : to convert into vapor **2** : to destroy as if by converting to vapor ⟨*vaporized* enemy tanks⟩ — **va·por·i·za·tion** \ˌvā-pə-rə-ˈzā-shən\ *n*
va·por·iz·er \-ˌrī-zər\ *n* : a device that vaporizes something (as a medicated liquid)
vapor lock *n* : an interruption of flow of a fluid (as fuel in an engine) caused by the formation of vapor in the feeding system
va·por·ous \ˈvā-pə-rəs\ *adj* **1** : full of vapors : FOGGY, MISTY **2** : UNSUBSTANTIAL, VAGUE ⟨~ speculations⟩ — **va·por·ous·ly** *adv* — **va·por·ous·ness** *n*
va·pour *chiefly Brit var of* VAPOR
va·que·ro \vä-ˈker-ō\ *n, pl* **-ros** [Sp, fr. *vaca* cow, fr. L *vacca*] : a ranch hand : COWBOY
var *abbr* **1** variable **2** variant; variation **3** variety **4** various
¹**var·i·able** \ˈver-ē-ə-bəl\ *adj* **1** : able or apt to vary : CHANGEABLE **2** : FICKLE **3** : not true to type : ABERRANT ⟨a ~ wheat⟩ — **var·i·abil·i·ty** \ˌver-ē-ə-ˈbi-lə-tē, ˌvar-\ *n* — **var·i·ably** \-blē\ *adv*
²**variable** *n* **1** : a quantity that may take on any of a set of values; *also* : a mathematical symbol representing a variable **2** : something that is variable
var·i·ance \ˈver-ē-əns\ *n* **1** : variation or a degree of variation : DEVIATION **2** : DISAGREEMENT, DISPUTE **3** : a license to do something contrary to the usual rule ⟨a zoning ~⟩ **4** : the square of the standard deviation ♦ ***Synonyms*** DISCORD, CONTENTION, DISSENSION, STRIFE, CONFLICT
¹**var·i·ant** \ˈver-ē-ənt\ *adj* **1** : differing from others of its kind or class **2** : varying usu. slightly from the standard or type
²**variant** *n* **1** : one that exhibits variation from a type or norm **2** : one of two or more different spellings or pronunciations of a word
var·i·a·tion \ˌver-ē-ˈā-shən\ *n* **1** : the act, process, or an instance of varying : a change in form, position, or condition : MODIFICATION, ALTERATION **2** : extent of change or difference **3** : divergence in the characteristics of an organism from those typical or usual for its group; *also* : one exhibiting such variation **4** : repetition of a musical theme with modifications in rhythm, tune, harmony, or key
vari·col·ored \ˈver-i-ˌkə-lərd\ *adj* : having various colors : VARIEGATED
var·i·cose \ˈva-rə-ˌkōs\ *adj* : abnormally swollen and dilated ⟨~ veins⟩ — **var·i·cos·i·ty** \ˌva-rə-ˈkä-sə-tē\ *n*
var·ied \ˈver-ēd\ *adj* **1** : having many forms or types : DIVERSE ⟨~ interests⟩ **2** : VARIEGATED — **var·ied·ly** *adv*
var·ie·gat·ed \ˈver-ē-ə-ˌgā-təd\ *adj* **1** : having patches, stripes, or marks of different colors ⟨~ flowers⟩ **2** : VARIED 1 — **var·ie·gate** \-ˌgāt\ *vb* — **var·ie·ga·tion** \ˌver-ē-ə-ˈgā-shən\ *n*
¹**va·ri·etal** \və-ˈrī-ə-tᵊl\ *adj* : of or relating to a variety; *esp* : of, relating to, or producing a varietal
²**varietal** *n* : a wine bearing the name of the principal grape from which it is made
va·ri·ety \və-ˈrī-ə-tē\ *n, pl* **-et·ies** **1** : the state of being varied or various : DIVERSITY **2** : a collection of different things : ASSORTMENT **3** : something varying from others of the same general kind **4** : any of various groups of plants or animals within a species distinguished by characteristics insufficient to separate species : SUBSPECIES **5** : entertainment such as is given in a stage presentation comprising a series of performances (as songs, dances, or acrobatic acts)
var·i·o·rum \ˌver-ē-ˈōr-əm\ *n* : an edition or text of a work containing notes by various persons or variant readings of the text
var·i·ous \ˈver-ē-əs\ *adj* **1** : VARICOLORED **2** : of differing kinds : MULTIFARIOUS **3** : UNLIKE ⟨animals as ~ as the jaguar and the sloth⟩ **4** : having a number of different aspects **5** : NUMEROUS, MANY **6** : INDIVIDUAL, SEPARATE ♦ ***Synonyms*** DIVERGENT, DISPARATE, DIFFERENT, DISSIMILAR, DIVERSE, UNALIKE — **var·i·ous·ly** *adv*
var·let \ˈvär-lət\ *n* **1** : ATTENDANT **2** : SCOUNDREL, KNAVE
var·mint \ˈvär-mənt\ *n* [alter. of *vermin*] **1** : an animal considered a pest; *esp* : one classed as vermin and unprotected by game law **2** : a contemptible person : RASCAL
¹**var·nish** \ˈvär-nish\ *n* **1** : a liquid preparation that is applied to a surface and dries into a hard glossy coating; *also* : the glaze of this coating **2** : something suggesting varnish by its gloss **3** : outside show : deceptive or superficial appearance
²**varnish** *vb* **1** : to cover with varnish **2** : to cover or conceal with something that gives a fair appearance : GLOSS
var·si·ty \ˈvär-sə-tē\ *n, pl* **-ties** [by shortening & alter. fr. *university*] **1** *Brit* : UNIVERSITY **2** : the principal team representing a college, school, or club

vary \ˈver-ē\ *vb* **var·ied; vary·ing** **1** : ALTER, CHANGE **2** : to make or be of different kinds : introduce or have variety : DIVERSIFY, DIFFER **3** : DEVIATE, SWERVE **4** : to change in bodily structure or function away from what is usual for members of a group

vas·cu·lar \ˈvas-kyə-lər\ *adj* [NL *vascularis,* fr. L *vasculum* small vessel, dim. of *vas* vase, vessel] : of or relating to a channel or system of channels for the conveyance of a body fluid (as blood or sap); *also* : supplied with or containing such vessels and esp. blood vessels ⟨the ~ system⟩

vascular plant *n* : a plant having a specialized system for carrying fluids that includes xylem and phloem

vas def·er·ens \ˈvas-ˈde-fə-rənz\ *n, pl* **va·sa def·er·en·tia** \ˈvā-zə-ˌde-fə-ˈren-shē-ə\ : a sperm-carrying duct of the testis

vase \ˈvās, ˈvāz\ *n* : a usu. round vessel of greater depth than width used chiefly for ornament or for flowers

va·sec·to·my \və-ˈsek-tə-mē, vā-ˈzek-\ *n, pl* **-mies** : surgical excision of all or part of the vas deferens usu. to induce sterility

va·so·con·stric·tion \ˌvā-zō-kən-ˈstrik-shən\ *n* : narrowing of the interior diameter of blood vessels

va·so·con·stric·tor \-tər\ *n* : an agent (as a nerve fiber or a drug) that initiates or induces vasoconstriction

vas·sal \ˈva-səl\ *n* **1** : a person under the protection of a feudal lord to whom he owes homage and loyalty : a feudal tenant **2** : one occupying a dependent or subordinate position — **vassal** *adj*

vas·sal·age \-sə-lij\ *n* **1** : the state of being a vassal **2** : the homage and loyalty due from a vassal **3** : SERVITUDE, SUBJECTION

¹**vast** \ˈvast\ *adj* : very great in size, amount, degree, intensity, or esp. extent ⟨~ plains⟩ ⟨~ knowledge⟩ ♦ ***Synonyms*** ENORMOUS, HUGE, GIGANTIC, COLOSSAL, MAMMOTH — **vast·ly** *adv* — **vast·ness** *n*

²**vast** *n* : a great expanse : IMMENSITY

vasty \ˈvas-tē\ *adj* : VAST, IMMENSE

vat \ˈvat\ *n* : a large vessel (as a tub or barrel) esp. for holding liquids in manufacturing processes

VAT *abbr* value-added tax

vat·ic \ˈva-tik\ *adj* : PROPHETIC, ORACULAR ⟨~ pronouncements⟩

Vat·i·can \ˈva-ti-kən\ *n* **1** : the papal headquarters in Rome **2** : the papal government

va·tu \ˈvä-ˌtü\ *n, pl* **vatu** — see MONEY table

vaude·ville \ˈvȯd-vəl, ˈväd-, ˈvōd-, -ˌvil\ *n* [F, fr. MF, satirical song, alter. of *vaudevire,* fr. *vau-de-Vire* valley of Vire, town in northwest France where such songs were composed] : a stage entertainment consisting of unrelated acts (as of acrobats, comedians, dancers, or singers)

¹**vault** \ˈvȯlt\ *n* **1** : an arched masonry structure usu. forming a ceiling or roof; *also* : something (as the sky) resembling a vault **2** : a room or space covered by a vault esp. when underground **3** : a room or compartment for the safekeeping of valuables **4** : a burial chamber; *also* : a usu. metal or concrete case in which a casket is enclosed at burial — **vaulty** *adj*

²**vault** *vb* : to form or cover with a vault

³**vault** *vb* : to leap vigorously esp. by aid of the hands or a pole — **vault·er** *n*

⁴**vault** *n* : an act of vaulting : LEAP

vault·ed \ˈvȯl-təd\ *adj* **1** : built in the form of a vault : ARCHED **2** : covered with a vault

vault·ing \-tiŋ\ *adj* : reaching for the heights ⟨~ ambition⟩

vaunt \ˈvȯnt\ *vb* [ME, fr. AF *vanter,* fr. LL *vanitare,* ultim. fr. L *vanus* vain] : to boast of ⟨~*s* his successes⟩ — **vaunt** *n*

vaunt·ed \ˈvȯn-təd\ *adj* : much praised or boasted of

vb *abbr* verb; verbal

V–chip \ˈvē-ˌchip\ *n* : a computer chip in a television set used to block based on content the viewing of certain programs

VCR \ˌvē-(ˌ)sē-ˈär\ *n* [*v*ideo*c*assette *r*ecorder] : a device that records and plays back videotapes

VD *abbr* venereal disease

VDT *abbr* video display terminal

veal \ˈvēl\ *n* : the flesh of a young calf

vec·tor \ˈvek-tər\ *n* **1** : a quantity that has magnitude and direction **2** : an organism (as a fly or tick) that transmits a pathogen

Ve·da \ˈvā-də\ *n* [Skt, lit., knowledge] : any of a class of Hindu sacred writings — **Ve·dic** \ˈvā-dik\ *adj*

Ve·dan·ta \vā-ˈdän-tə, və-, -ˈdan-\ *n* : an orthodox Hindu philosophy based on the Upanishads

vee·jay \ˈvē-ˌjā\ *n* : an announcer of a program featuring music videos

veep \ˈvēp\ *n* : VICE PRESIDENT

veer \ˈvir\ *vb* : to shift from one direction or course to another ♦ ***Synonyms*** TURN, AVERT, DEFLECT, DIVERT — **veer** *n*

veg·an \ˈvē-gən, ˈvā-; ˈve-jən, -ˌjan\ *n* : a strict vegetarian who consumes no animal food or dairy products — **veg·an·ism** \ˈvē-gə-ˌni-zəm, ˈvā-, ˈve-\ *n*

¹**veg·e·ta·ble** \ˈvej-tə-bəl, ˈve-jə-\ *adj* [ME, fr. ML *vegetabilis* vegetative, fr. *vegetare* to grow, fr. L, to animate, fr. *vegetus* lively, fr. *vegēre* to enliven] **1** : of, relating to, or growing like plants ⟨the ~ kingdom⟩ **2** : made from, obtained from, or containing plants or plant products ⟨~ oils⟩ **3** : suggesting that of a plant (as in inertness) ⟨a ~ existence⟩

²**vegetable** *n* **1** : PLANT 1 **2** : a usu. herbaceous plant grown for an edible part that is usu. eaten as part of a meal; *also* : such an edible part

veg·e·tal \ˈve-jə-tᵊl\ *adj* **1** : VEGETABLE **2** : VEGETATIVE

veg·e·tar·i·an \ˌve-jə-ˈter-ē-ən\ *n* : one that believes in or practices living on a diet of vegetables, fruits, grains, nuts, and sometimes animal products (as milk and cheese) — **vegetarian** *adj* — **veg·e·tar·i·an·ism** \-ē-ə-ˌni-zəm\ *n*

veg·e·tate \ˈve-jə-ˌtāt\ *vb* **-tat·ed; -tat·ing** : to live or grow in the manner of a plant; *esp* : to lead a dull inert life

veg·e·ta·tion \ˌve-jə-ˈtā-shən\ *n* **1** : the act or process of vegetating; *also* : inert existence **2** : plant life or cover (as of an area) — **veg·e·ta·tion·al** \-shə-nəl\ *adj*

veg·e·ta·tive \ˈve-jə-ˌtā-tiv\ *adj* **1** : of or relating to nutrition and growth esp. as contrasted with reproduction **2** : of, relating to, or composed of vegetation ⟨~ cover⟩ **3** : VEGETABLE 3

veg out \ˈvej-\ *vb* **vegged out; vegging out** [short for *vegetate*] : to spend time idly or passively

ve·he·ment \ˈvē-ə-mənt\ *adj* **1** : marked by great force or energy **2** : marked by strong feeling or expression : PASSIONATE, FERVID ⟨~ opposition⟩ — **ve·he·mence** \-məns\ *n* — **ve·he·ment·ly** *adv*

ve·hi·cle \ˈvē-ə-kəl, ˈvē-ˌhi-\ *n* **1** : a medium by which a thing is applied or administered ⟨linseed oil is a ~ for pigments⟩ **2** : a medium through or by means of which something is conveyed or expressed **3** : a means of transporting persons or goods ♦ ***Synonyms*** INSTRUMENT, AGENT, AGENCY, ORGAN, CHANNEL — **ve·hic·u·lar** \vē-ˈhi-kyə-lər\ *adj*

[1]**veil** \ˈvāl\ *n* **1** : a piece of often sheer or diaphanous material used to screen or curtain something or to cover the head or face **2** : the life of a nun ⟨take the ~⟩ **3** : something that hides or obscures like a veil ⟨a ~ of secrecy⟩

[2]**veil** *vb* : to cover with or as if with a veil : wear a veil

[1]**vein** \ˈvān\ *n* **1** : a fissure in rock filled with mineral matter; *also* : a bed of useful mineral matter **2** : any of the tubular branching vessels that carry blood from the capillaries toward the heart **3** : any of the bundles of vascular vessels forming the framework of a leaf **4** : any of the thickened ribs that stiffen the wings of an insect **5** : something (as a wavy variegation in marble) suggesting veins **6** : a distinctive style of expression **7** : a distinctive element or quality : STRAIN **8** : MOOD, HUMOR — **veined** \ˈvānd\ *adj*

[2]**vein** *vb* : to pattern with or as if with veins — **vein·ing** *n*

vel *abbr* velocity

ve·lar \ˈvē-lər\ *adj* : of or relating to a velum and esp. that of the soft palate

veld *or* **veldt** \ˈvelt, ˈfelt\ *n* [Afrikaans *veld,* fr. D, field] : an open grassland esp. in southern Africa usu. with scattered shrubs or trees

vel·lum \ˈve-ləm\ *n* [ME *velym,* fr. AF *velim, veeslin,* fr. **veelin,* adj., of a calf, fr. *veel* calf] **1** : a fine-grained lambskin, kidskin, or calfskin prepared for writing on or for binding books **2** : a strong cream-colored paper — **vellum** *adj*

ve·loc·i·pede \və-ˈlä-sə-ˌpēd\ *n* : an early bicycle

ve·loc·i·rapt·or \və-ˈlä-sə-ˌrap-tər\ *n* : any of a genus of agile flesh-eating bipedal dinosaurs of the Cretaceous having a sickle-shaped claw on each foot

ve·loc·i·ty \və-ˈlä-sə-tē\ *n, pl* **-ties** : quickness of motion : SPEED ⟨the ~ of light⟩

ve·lour *or* **ve·lours** \və-ˈlu̇r\ *n, pl* **velours** \-ˈlu̇rz\ : any of various textile fabrics with pile like that of velvet

ve·lum \ˈvē-ləm\ *n, pl* **ve·la** \-lə\ : a membranous body part (as the soft palate) resembling a veil

vel·vet \ˈvel-vət\ *n* [ME *veluet, velvet,* fr. AF, fr. *velu* shaggy, ultim. fr. L *villus* shaggy hair] **1** : a fabric having a short soft dense warp pile **2** : something resembling or suggesting velvet (as in softness or luster) **3** : the soft skin covering the growing antlers of deer — **velvet** *adj* — **velvety** *adj*

vel·ve·teen \ˌvel-və-ˈtēn\ *n* **1** : a fabric woven usu. of cotton in imitation of velvet **2** *pl* : clothes made of velveteen

Ven *abbr* venerable

ve·nal \ˈvē-nᵊl\ *adj* : capable of being bought or bribed : MERCENARY, CORRUPT ⟨~ legislators⟩ — **ve·nal·i·ty** \vi-ˈna-lə-tē\ *n* — **ve·nal·ly** \ˈvē-nᵊl-ē\ *adv*

ve·na·tion \ve-ˈnā-shən, vē-\ *n* : an arrangement or system of veins ⟨the ~ of the hand⟩ ⟨leaf ~⟩

vend \ˈvend\ *vb* : SELL; *esp* : to sell as a hawker or peddler — **vend·ible** *adj*

vend·ee \ven-ˈdē\ *n* : one to whom a thing is sold : BUYER

ven·det·ta \ven-ˈde-tə\ *n* : a feud marked by acts of revenge

vending machine *n* : a coin-operated machine for selling merchandise

ven·dor \ˈven-dər, *for 1 also* ven-ˈdȯr\ *n* **1** : one that vends : SELLER **2** : VENDING MACHINE

[1]**ve·neer** \və-ˈnir\ *n* [G *Furnier,* fr. *furnieren* to veneer, fr. F *fournir* to furnish] **1** : a thin usu. superficial layer of material ⟨brick ~⟩; *esp* : a thin layer of fine wood glued over a cheaper wood **2** : superficial display : GLOSS

[2]**veneer** *vb* : to overlay with a veneer

ven·er·a·ble \ˈve-nə-rə-bəl\ *adj* **1** : deserving to be venerated — often used as a religious title **2** : made sacred by association

ven·er·ate \ˈve-nə-ˌrāt\ *vb* **-at·ed; -at·ing** : to regard with reverential respect ♦ ***Synonyms*** ADORE, REVERE, REVERENCE, WORSHIP — **ven·er·a·tion** \ˌve-nə-ˈrā-shən\ *n*

ve·ne·re·al \və-ˈnir-ē-əl\ *adj* : of or relating to sexual intercourse or to diseases transmitted by it ⟨a ~ infection⟩

venereal disease *n* : a contagious disease (as gonorrhea or syphilis) usu. acquired by having sexual intercourse with someone who already has it

ve·ne·tian blind \və-ˈnē-shən-\ *n* : a blind having thin horizontal parallel slats that can be adjusted to admit a desired amount of light

ven·geance \ˈven-jəns\ *n* : punishment inflicted in retaliation for an injury or offense : REVENGE

venge·ful \ˈvenj-fəl\ *adj* : filled with a desire for revenge : VINDICTIVE ⟨a ~ former employee⟩ — **venge·ful·ly** *adv*

ve·nial \ˈvē-nē-əl\ *adj* : capable of being forgiven : EXCUSABLE ⟨~ sin⟩

ve·ni·re \və-ˈnī-rē\ *n* : a panel from which a jury is drawn

ve·ni·re fa·ci·as \-ˈfā-shē-əs\ *n* [ME, fr. ML, you should cause to come] : a writ summoning persons to appear in court to serve as jurors

ve·ni·re·man \və-ˈnī-rē-mən, -ˈnir-ē-\ *n* : a member of a venire

ven·i·son \ˈven-ə-sən, -zən\ *n, pl* **venisons** *also* **venison** [ME, fr. AF *veneisun* game, venison, fr. L *venatio,* fr. *venari* to hunt, pursue] : the edible flesh of a deer

ven·om \ˈve-nəm\ *n* [ME *venim,* fr. AF, ultim. fr. L *venenum* magic charm, drug, poison] **1** : poisonous material secreted by some animals (as snakes, spiders, or bees) and transmitted usu. by biting or stinging **2** : ILL WILL, MALEVOLENCE

ven·om·ous \ˈve-nə-məs\ *adj* **1** : full of venom : POISONOUS **2** : SPITEFUL, MALEVOLENT ⟨~ comments⟩ **3** : secreting and using venom ⟨~ snakes⟩ — **ven·om·ous·ly** *adv*

ve·nous \ˈvē-nəs\ *adj* **1** : of, relating to, or full of veins **2** : being purplish red oxygen-deficient blood rich in carbon dioxide that is present in most veins

[1]**vent** \ˈvent\ *vb* **1** : to provide with a vent **2** : to serve as a vent for **3** : EXPEL, DISCHARGE **4** : to relieve oneself by vigorous or emotional expression

[2]**vent** *n* **1** : an opportunity or way of escape or passage : OUTLET **2** : an opening for the escape of a gas or liquid or for the relief of pressure

[3]**vent** *n* : a slit in a garment esp. in the lower part of a seam (as of a jacket or skirt)

ven·ti·late \ˈven-tə-ˌlāt\ *vb* **-lat·ed; -lat·ing** **1** : to discuss freely and openly ⟨~ a question⟩ **2** : to give vent to ⟨~ one's grievances⟩ **3** : to cause fresh air to circulate through (as a room or mine) so as to replace foul air **4** : to provide with artificial respiration esp. using a ventilator **5** : to provide with a vent or outlet ♦ ***Synonyms*** EXPRESS, VENT, AIR, UTTER, VOICE, BROACH

ven·ti·la·tion \ˌven-tə-ˈlā-shən\ *n* **1** : the act or process of ventilating **2** : circulation of air (as in a room) **3** : a system or means of providing fresh air

ven·ti·la·tor \-lā-tər\ *n* **1** : a device for introducing fresh air **2** : a device for maintaining artificial respiration

ven·tral \ˈven-trəl\ *adj* **1** : of or relating to the belly : ABDOMINAL **2** : of, relating to, or located on or near the surface of the body that in humans is the front but in most other animals is the lower surface — **ven·tral·ly** *adv*

ven·tri·cle \ˈven-tri-kəl\ *n* **1** : a chamber of the heart that receives blood from the atrium of the same side and pumps it into the arteries **2** : any of the communicating cavities of the brain that are continuous with the central canal of the spinal cord — **ven·tric·u·lar** \ven-ˈtri-kyə-lər\ *adj*

ven·tril·o·quism \ven-ˈtri-lə-ˌkwi-zəm\ *n* [LL *ventriloquus* ventriloquist, fr. L *venter* belly + *loqui* to speak; fr. the belief that the voice is produced from the ventriloquist's stomach] : the production of the voice in such a manner that the sound appears to come from a source other than the speaker — **ven·tril·o·quist** \-kwist\ *n*

ven·tril·o·quy \-kwē\ *n* : VENTRILOQUISM

[1]**ven·ture** \ˈven-chər\ *vb* **ven·tured; ven·tur·ing** **1** : to expose to hazard : RISK **2** : to undertake the risks of : BRAVE **3** : to offer at the risk of rebuff, rejection, or censure ⟨~ an opinion⟩ **4** : to proceed despite danger : DARE

[2]**venture** *n* **1** : an undertaking involving chance or risk; *esp* : a speculative business enterprise **2** : something risked in a speculative venture : STAKE

ven·ture·some \ˈven-chər-səm\ *adj* **1** : involving risk : DANGEROUS, HAZARDOUS **2** : inclined to venture : BOLD, DARING ♦ ***Synonyms*** ADVENTUROUS, VENTUROUS, RASH, RECKLESS, FOOLHARDY — **ven·ture·some·ly** *adv* — **ven·ture·some·ness** *n*

ven·tur·ous \ˈven-chə-rəs\ *adj* : VENTURESOME — **ven·tur·ous·ly** *adv* — **ven·tur·ous·ness** *n*

ven·ue \ˈven-yü\ *n* [AF, alter. of *vinné, visné,* lit., neighborhood, neighbors, ultim. fr. L *vicinitas* vicinity] **1** : the place from which the jury is taken and where the trial is held **2** : the place in which the alleged events from which a legal action arises took place **3** : a place where events are held ⟨music ~*s*⟩

Ve·nus \ˈvē-nəs\ *n* : the planet 2d in order from the sun

Venus fly·trap *or* **Ve·nus's–fly·trap** \ˈvē-nə-səz-ˈflī-ˌtrap\ *n* : an insect-eating plant of the Carolina coast that has the leaf tip modified into an insect trap

Ve·nu·sian \vi-ˈnü-zhən, -ˈnyü-\ *adj* : of or relating to the planet Venus

ve·ra·cious \və-ˈrā-shəs\ *adj* **1** : TRUTHFUL, HONEST **2** : TRUE, ACCURATE ⟨~ details⟩ — **ve·ra·cious·ly** *adv*

ve·rac·i·ty \və-ˈra-sə-tē\ *n, pl* **-ties** **1** : devotion to truth : TRUTHFULNESS **2** : conformity with fact : ACCURACY **3** : something true

ve·ran·da *or* **ve·ran·dah** \və-ˈran-də\ *n* : a long open usu. roofed porch

verb \ˈvərb\ *n* : a word that is the grammatical center of a predicate and expresses an act, occurrence, or mode of being

[1]**ver·bal** \ˈvər-bəl\ *adj* **1** : of, relating to, or consisting of words; *esp* : having to do with words rather than with the ideas to be conveyed **2** : expressed in usu. spoken words : not written : ORAL ⟨a ~ contract⟩ **3** : of, relating to, or formed from a verb ⟨a ~ adjective⟩ **4** : LITERAL, VERBATIM — **ver·bal·ly** *adv*

[2]**verbal** *n* : a word that combines characteristics of a verb with those of a noun or adjective

verbal auxiliary *n* : an auxiliary verb
ver·bal·ize \ˈvər-bə-ˌlīz\ *vb* **-ized; -iz·ing** **1** : to speak or write in wordy or empty fashion **2** : to express something in words : describe verbally ⟨*verbalized* her feelings⟩ **3** : to convert into a verb — **ver·bal·i·za·tion** \ˌvər-bə-lə-ˈzā-shən\ *n*
verbal noun *n* : a noun derived directly from a verb or verb stem and in some uses having the sense and constructions of a verb
ver·ba·tim \(ˌ)vər-ˈbā-təm\ *adv or adj* : in the same words : word for word
ver·be·na \(ˌ)vər-ˈbē-nə\ *n* : VERVAIN; *esp* : any of several garden vervains of hybrid origin with showy spikes of bright often fragrant flowers
ver·biage \ˈvər-bē-ij, -bij\ *n* **1** : superfluity of words usu. of little or obscure content **2** : DICTION, WORDING
ver·bose \(ˌ)vər-ˈbōs\ *adj* : using more words than are needed : WORDY ♦ ***Synonyms*** PROLIX, DIFFUSE, REDUNDANT, WINDY — **ver·bos·i·ty** \-ˈbä-sə-tē\ *n*
ver·bo·ten \vər-ˈbō-tᵊn, fər-\ *adj* [G] : forbidden usu. by dictate
ver·dant \ˈvər-dᵊnt\ *adj* : green with growing plants — **ver·dant·ly** *adv*
ver·dict \ˈvər-(ˌ)dikt\ *n* [ME *verdit, verdict,* fr. AF *veirdit,* fr. *veir* true (fr. L *verus*) + *dit* saying, dictum, fr. L *dictum,* fr. *dicere* to say] **1** : the finding or decision of a jury **2** : DECISION, JUDGMENT
ver·di·gris \ˈvər-də-ˌgrēs, -ˌgris\ *n* : a green or bluish deposit that forms on copper, brass, or bronze surfaces
ver·dure \ˈvər-jər\ *n* : the greenness of growing vegetation; *also* : such vegetation
[1]**verge** \ˈvərj\ *n* [ME, rod, measuring rod, margin, fr. AF, rod, area of jurisdiction, fr. L *virga* twig, rod, line] **1** : a staff carried as an emblem of authority or office **2** : something that borders or bounds : EDGE, MARGIN **3** : BRINK, THRESHOLD ⟨on the ~ of collapse⟩
[2]**verge** *vb* **verged; verg·ing** **1** : to be contiguous **2** : to be on the verge
[3]**verge** *vb* **verged; verg·ing** **1** : to move or extend in some direction or toward some condition : INCLINE **2** : to be in transition or change
verg·er \ˈvər-jər\ *n* **1** *chiefly Brit* : an attendant who carries a verge (as before a bishop) **2** : SEXTON
ve·rid·i·cal \və-ˈri-di-kəl\ *adj* **1** : TRUTHFUL **2** : not illusory : GENUINE
ver·i·fy \ˈver-ə-ˌfī\ *vb* **-fied; -fy·ing** **1** : to confirm in law by oath **2** : to establish the truth, accuracy, or reality of ⟨~ the claim⟩ ♦ ***Synonyms*** AUTHENTICATE, CORROBORATE, SUBSTANTIATE, VALIDATE — **ver·i·fi·able** *adj* — **ver·i·fi·ca·tion** \ˌver-ə-fə-ˈkā-shən\ *n*
ver·i·ly \ˈver-ə-lē\ *adv* **1** : in very truth : CERTAINLY **2** : TRULY, CONFIDENTLY
veri·si·mil·i·tude \ˌver-ə-sə-ˈmi-lə-ˌtüd, -ˌtyüd\ *n* : the quality or state of appearing to be true or real
ver·i·ta·ble \ˈver-ə-tə-bəl\ *adj* : ACTUAL, GENUINE, TRUE — **ver·i·ta·bly** *adv*
ver·i·ty \ˈver-ə-tē\ *n, pl* **-ties** **1** : the quality or state of being true or real : TRUTH, REALITY **2** : something (as a statement) that is true **3** : HONESTY, VERACITY
ver·meil *n* [MF] **1** \ˈvər-məl, -ˌmāl\ : VERMILION **2** \ver-ˈmā\ : gilded silver
ver·mi·cel·li \ˌvər-mə-ˈche-lē, -ˈse-\ *n* [It, fr. pl. of *vermicello,* dim. of *verme* worm] : a pasta made in thinner strings than spaghetti
ver·mic·u·lite \vər-ˈmi-kyə-ˌlīt\ *n* : any of various lightweight water-absorbent minerals derived from mica
ver·mi·form appendix \ˈvər-mə-ˌform-\ *n* : APPENDIX 2
ver·mil·ion *also* **ver·mil·lion** \vər-ˈmil-yən\ *n* : a bright reddish orange color; *also* : any of various red pigments
ver·min \ˈvər-mən\ *n, pl* **vermin** **1** : small common harmful or objectionable animals (as lice or mice) that are difficult to get rid of **2** : birds and mammals that prey on game — **ver·min·ous** *adj*
ver·mouth \vər-ˈmüth\ *n* [F *vermout,* fr. G *Wermut* wormwood] : a dry or sweet wine flavored with herbs and often used in mixed drinks
[1]**ver·nac·u·lar** \vər-ˈna-kyə-lər\ *adj* [L *vernaculus* native, fr. *verna* slave born in the master's house, native] **1** : of, relating to, or being a language or dialect native to a region or country rather than a literary, cultured, or foreign language **2** : of, relating to, or being the normal spoken form of a language **3** : applied to a plant or animal in common speech as distinguished from biological nomenclature ⟨~ names⟩
[2]**vernacular** *n* **1** : a vernacular language **2** : the mode of expression of a group or class **3** : a vernacular name of a plant or animal
ver·nal \ˈvər-nᵊl\ *adj* : of, relating to, or occurring in the spring ⟨~ equinox⟩
ver·ni·er \ˈvər-nē-ər\ *n* : a short scale made to slide along the divisions of a graduated instrument to indicate parts of divisions
ve·ron·i·ca \və-ˈrä-ni-kə\ *n* : any of a genus of herbs related to the snapdragons that have small usu. bluish flowers
ver·sa·tile \ˈvər-sə-tᵊl\ *adj* : turning with ease from one thing or position to another; *esp* : having many aptitudes — **ver·sa·til·i·ty** \ˌvər-sə-ˈti-lə-tē\ *n*
[1]**verse** \ˈvərs\ *n* **1** : a line of poetry; *also* : STANZA **2** : metrical writing distinguished from poetry esp. by its lower level of intensity **3** : POETRY **4** : POEM **5** : one of the short divisions of a chapter in the Bible
[2]**verse** *vb* **versed; vers·ing** : to familiarize by experience, study, or practice ⟨well *versed* in the theater⟩
ver·si·cle \ˈvər-si-kəl\ *n* : a verse or sentence said or sung by a leader in public worship and followed by a response from the people
ver·si·fi·ca·tion \ˌvər-sə-fə-ˈkā-shən\ *n* **1** : the making of verses **2** : metrical structure
ver·si·fy \ˈvər-sə-ˌfī\ *vb* **-fied; -fy·ing** **1**

: to write verse **2** : to turn into verse — **ver·si·fi·er** \-ˌfī-ər\ *n*

ver·sion \ˈvər-zhən\ *n* **1** : TRANSLATION; *esp* : a translation of the Bible **2** : an account or description from a particular point of view esp. as contrasted with another **3** : a form or variant of a type or original

vers li·bre \ˌver-ˈlēbrᵊ\ *n, pl* **vers li·bres** *same*\ [F] : FREE VERSE

ver·so \ˈvər-sō\ *n, pl* **versos** : a left-hand page

ver·sus \ˈvər-səs\ *prep* **1** : AGAINST 1 ⟨the champion ~ the challenger⟩ **2** : in contrast or as an alternative to ⟨free trade ~ protection⟩

vert *abbr* vertical

ver·te·bra \ˈvər-tə-brə\ *n, pl* **-brae** \-ˌbrā, -(ˌ)brē\ *or* **-bras** [L] : one of the segments of bone or cartilage making up the backbone

ver·te·bral \(ˌ)vər-ˈtē-brəl, ˈvər-tə-\ *adj* : of, relating to, or made up of vertebrae : SPINAL

vertebral column *n* : BACKBONE 1

¹**ver·te·brate** \ˈvər-tə-brət, -ˌbrāt\ *adj* **1** : having a backbone **2** : of or relating to the vertebrates

²**vertebrate** *n* : any of a large group of animals (as mammals, birds, reptiles, amphibians, or fishes) that have a backbone or in some primitive forms (as a lamprey) a flexible rod of cells and that have a tubular nervous system arranged along the back and divided into a brain and spinal cord

ver·tex \ˈvər-ˌteks\ *n, pl* **ver·ti·ces** \ˈvər-tə-ˌsēz\ *also* **ver·tex·es** [ME, top of the head, fr. L *vertex, vortex* whirl, whirlpool, top of the head, summit, fr. *vertere* to turn] **1** : the point opposite to and farthest from the base of a geometrical figure **2** : the point where the sides of an angle or three or more edges of a polyhedron (as a cube) meet **3** : the highest point : TOP, SUMMIT

ver·ti·cal \ˈvər-ti-kəl\ *adj* **1** : of, relating to, or located at the vertex : directly overhead **2** : rising perpendicularly from a level surface : UPRIGHT — **vertical** *n* — **ver·ti·cal·i·ty** \ˌvər-tə-ˈka-lə-tē\ *n* — **ver·ti·cal·ly** \-k(ə-)lē\ *adv*

ver·tig·i·nous \(ˌ)vər-ˈti-jə-nəs\ *adj* : marked by, affected with, or tending to cause dizziness

ver·ti·go \ˈvər-ti-ˌgō\ *n, pl* **-goes** *or* **-gos** : DIZZINESS, GIDDINESS

vertu *var of* VIRTU

ver·vain \ˈvər-ˌvān\ *n* : any of a genus of chiefly American herbs or low woody plants with often showy heads or spikes of tubular flowers

verve \ˈvərv\ *n* : liveliness of imagination; *also* : VIVACITY

¹**very** \ˈver-ē\ *adj* **veri·er; -est** [ME *verray, verry,* fr. AF *verai,* ultim. fr. L *verax* truthful, fr. *verus* true] **1** : EXACT, PRECISE ⟨the ~ heart of the city⟩ **2** : exactly suitable ⟨the ~ tool for the job⟩ **3** : ABSOLUTE, UTTER ⟨the *veriest* nonsense⟩ **4** — used as an intensive esp. to emphasize identity ⟨before my ~ eyes⟩ **5** : MERE, BARE ⟨the ~ idea scared him⟩ **6** : SELFSAME, IDENTICAL ⟨the ~ man I saw⟩

²**very** *adv* **1** : in actual fact : TRULY **2** : to a high degree : EXTREMELY

very high frequency *n* : a radio frequency of between 30 and 300 megahertz

ves·i·cant \ˈve-si-kənt\ *n* : an agent that causes blistering — **vesicant** *adj*

ves·i·cle \ˈve-si-kəl\ *n* : a membranous and usu. fluid-filled cavity in a plant or animal; *also* : BLISTER — **ve·sic·u·lar** \və-ˈsi-kyə-lər\ *adj*

¹**ves·per** \ˈves-pər\ *n* **1** *cap, archaic* : EVENING STAR **2** : a vesper bell **3** *archaic* : EVENING, EVENTIDE

²**vesper** *adj* : of or relating to vespers or the evening ⟨a ~ service⟩

ves·pers \-pərz\ *n pl, often cap* : a late afternoon or evening worship service

ves·sel \ˈve-səl\ *n* **1** : a container (as a barrel, bottle, bowl, or cup) for holding something **2** : a person held to be the recipient of a quality (as grace) **3** : a craft bigger than a rowboat **4** : a tube in which a body fluid (as blood or sap) is contained and circulated

¹**vest** \ˈvest\ *vb* **1** : to place or give into the possession or discretion of some person or authority **2** : to grant or endow with a particular authority, right, or property **3** : to become legally vested **4** : to clothe with or as if with a garment; *esp* : to garb in ecclesiastical vestments

²**vest** *n* **1** : a sleeveless garment for the upper body usu. worn over a shirt **2** *chiefly Brit* : a man's sleeveless undershirt **3** : a front piece of a dress resembling the front of a vest

¹**ves·tal** \ˈves-tᵊl\ *adj* : CHASTE

²**vestal** *n* : VESTAL VIRGIN

vestal virgin *n* **1** : a virgin consecrated to the Roman goddess Vesta and to the service of watching the sacred fire perpetually kept burning on her altar **2** : a chaste woman

vest·ed \ˈves-təd\ *adj* : fully and unconditionally guaranteed as a legal right, benefit, or privilege

vested interest *n* : an interest (as in an existing political, economic, or social arrangement) to which the holder has a strong commitment; *also* : one (as a corporation) having a vested interest

ves·ti·bule \ˈves-tə-ˌbyül\ *n* **1** : a passage or room between the outer door and the interior of a building **2** : any of various bodily cavities forming or suggesting an entrance to some other cavity or space — **ves·tib·u·lar** \ve-ˈsti-byə-lər\ *adj*

ves·tige \ˈves-tij\ *n* [F, fr. L *vestigium* footprint, track, vestige] : a trace or visible sign left by something lost or vanished; *also* : a minute remaining amount — **ves·ti·gial** \ve-ˈsti-jē-əl, -jəl\ *adj* — **ves·ti·gial·ly** *adv*

vest·ing \ˈves-tiŋ\ *n* : the conveying to an employee of inalienable rights to share in a pension fund; *also* : the right so conveyed

vest·ment \ˈvest-mənt\ *n* **1** : an outer garment; *esp* : a ceremonial or official robe **2** *pl* : CLOTHING, GARB **3** : a garment or insignia worn by a cleric when officiating or assisting at a religious service
vest–pocket *adj* : very small ⟨a ~ park⟩
ves·try \ˈves-trē\ *n, pl* **vestries** **1** : a room in a church for vestments, altar linens, and sacred vessels **2** : a room used for church meetings and classes **3** : a body administering the temporal affairs of an Episcopal parish
ves·try·man \-mən\ *n* : a member of a vestry
ves·ture \ˈves-chər\ *n* **1** : a covering garment **2** : CLOTHING, APPAREL
[1]**vet** \ˈvet\ *n* : VETERINARIAN
[2]**vet** *adj or n* : VETERAN
[3]**vet** *vb* : to evaluate for appraisal or acceptance ⟨~ a manuscript⟩
vetch \ˈvech\ *n* : any of a genus of twining leguminous herbs including some grown for fodder and green manure
vet·er·an \ˈve-trən, -tə-rən\ *n* [L *veteranus,* fr. *veteranus* old, of long experience, fr. *veter-, vetus* old] **1** : an old soldier of long service **2** : a former member of the armed forces **3** : a person of long experience usu. in an occupation or skill — **veteran** *adj*
Veterans Day *n* : November 11 observed as a legal holiday in commemoration of the end of hostilities in 1918 and 1945
vet·er·i·nar·i·an \ˌve-trə-ˈner-ē-ən, ˌve-tə-rə-\ *n* : one qualified and authorized to practice veterinary medicine
[1]**vet·er·i·nary** \ˈve-trə-ˌner-ē, ˈve-tə-rə-\ *adj* : of, relating to, or being the medical care of animals and esp. domestic animals
[2]**veterinary** *n, pl* **-nar·ies** : VETERINARIAN
[1]**ve·to** \ˈvē-tō\ *n, pl* **vetoes** [L, I forbid] **1** : an authoritative prohibition **2** : a power of one part of a government to forbid the carrying out of projects attempted by another part; *esp* : a power vested in a chief executive to prevent the carrying out of measures adopted by a legislature **3** : the exercise of the power of veto
[2]**veto** *vb* **1** : FORBID, PROHIBIT **2** : to refuse assent to (a legislative bill) so as to prevent enactment or cause reconsideration — **ve·to·er** *n*
vex \ˈveks\ *vb* **vexed** *also* **vext; vex·ing** **1** : to bring trouble, distress, or agitation to ⟨a ~*ing* problem⟩ **2** : to annoy continually with little irritations
vex·a·tion \vek-ˈsā-shən\ *n* **1** : the act of vexing **2** : the quality or state of being vexed : IRRITATION **3** : a cause of trouble or annoyance
vex·a·tious \-shəs\ *adj* **1** : causing vexation : ANNOYING **2** : full of distress or annoyance : TROUBLED — **vex·a·tious·ly** *adv* — **vex·a·tious·ness** *n*
vexed \ˈvekst\ *adj* : fully debated or discussed ⟨a ~ question⟩
VF *abbr* **1** video frequency **2** visual field
VFD *abbr* volunteer fire department
VFW *abbr* Veterans of Foreign Wars
VG *abbr* **1** very good **2** vicar-general
VHF *abbr* very high frequency
VI *abbr* Virgin Islands
via \ˈvī-ə, ˈvē-ə\ *prep* **1** : by way of **2** : by means of
vi·a·ble \ˈvī-ə-bəl\ *adj* **1** : capable of living; *esp* : sufficiently developed as to be capable of surviving outside the mother's womb ⟨a ~ fetus⟩ **2** : capable of growing and developing ⟨~ seeds⟩ **3** : capable of being put into practice : WORKABLE **4** : having a reasonable chance of succeeding ⟨a ~ candidate⟩ — **vi·a·bil·i·ty** \ˌvī-ə-ˈbi-lə-tē\ *n* — **vi·a·bly** \ˈvī-ə-blē\ *adv*
via·duct \ˈvī-ə-ˌdəkt\ *n* : a long elevated roadway usu. consisting of a series of short spans supported on arches, piers, or columns
vi·al \ˈvī-əl\ *n* : a small vessel for liquids
vi·and \ˈvī-ənd\ *n* : an article of food
vi·at·i·cum \vī-ˈa-ti-kəm, vē-\ *n, pl* **-cums** *or* **-ca** \-kə\ **1** : the Christian Eucharist given to a person in danger of death **2** : an allowance esp. in money for traveling needs and expenses
vibes \ˈvībz\ *n pl* **1** : VIBRAPHONE **2** : VIBRATIONS
vi·brant \ˈvī-brənt\ *adj* **1** : VIBRATING, PULSATING **2** : pulsating with vigor or activity ⟨a ~ personality⟩ **3** : readily set in vibration : RESPONSIVE **4** : sounding from vibration **5** : BRIGHT ⟨~ colors⟩ — **vi·bran·cy** \-brən-sē\ *n*
vi·bra·phone \ˈvī-brə-ˌfōn\ *n* : a percussion instrument like the xylophone but with metal bars and motor-driven resonators
vi·brate \ˈvī-ˌbrāt\ *vb* **vi·brat·ed; vi·brat·ing** **1** : OSCILLATE **2** : to set in vibration **3** : to be in vibration **4** : WAVER, FLUCTUATE **5** : to respond sympathetically : THRILL
vi·bra·tion \vī-ˈbrā-shən\ *n* **1** : a rapid to-and-fro motion of the particles of an elastic body or medium (as a stretched cord) that produces sound **2** : an act of vibrating : a state of being vibrated : OSCILLATION **3** : a trembling motion **4** : VACILLATION **5** : a feeling or impression that someone or something gives off — usu. used in pl. ⟨good ~*s*⟩ — **vi·bra·tion·al** \-shə-nəl\ *adj*
vi·bra·to \vi-ˈbrä-tō\ *n, pl* **-tos** [It] : a slightly tremulous effect imparted to vocal or instrumental music
vi·bra·tor \ˈvī-ˌbrā-tər\ *n* : one that vibrates or causes vibration; *esp* : a vibrating electrical device used in massage or for sexual stimulation
vi·bra·to·ry \ˈvī-brə-ˌtȯr-ē\ *adj* : consisting of, capable of, or causing vibration
vi·bur·num \vī-ˈbər-nəm\ *n* : any of a genus of widely distributed shrubs or small trees related to the honeysuckle and bearing small usu. white flowers in broad clusters
vic *abbr* vicinity
Vic *abbr* Victoria
vic·ar \ˈvi-kər\ *n* **1** : an administrative deputy **2** : a minister in charge of a

church who serves under the authority of another minister — **vi·car·i·ate** \vī-ˈker-ē-ət\ *n*
vic·ar·age \ˈvi-kə-rij\ *n* : a vicar's home
vicar–general *n, pl* **vicars–general** : an administrative deputy (as of a Roman Catholic or Anglican bishop)
vi·car·i·ous \vī-ˈker-ē-əs\ *adj* [L *vicarius,* fr. *vicis* change, alternation, stead] **1** : acting for another **2** : done or suffered by one person on behalf of another or others ⟨a ~ sacrifice⟩ **3** : sharing in someone else's experience through the use of the imagination or sympathetic feelings ⟨~ thrills⟩ — **vi·car·i·ous·ly** *adv* — **vi·car·i·ous·ness** *n*
¹**vice** \ˈvīs\ *n* **1** : DEPRAVITY, WICKEDNESS **2** : a moral fault or failing **3** : a habitual usu. trivial fault **4** : an undesirable behavior pattern in a domestic animal
²**vice** *chiefly Brit var of* VISE
³**vi·ce** \ˈvī-sē\ *prep* : in the place of; *also* : rather than
vice admiral *n* : a commissioned officer in the navy or coast guard ranking above a rear admiral
vice·ge·rent \ˈvīs-ˈjir-ənt\ *n* : an administrative deputy of a king or magistrate — **vice·ge·ren·cy** \-ən-sē\ *n*
vi·cen·ni·al \vī-ˈse-nē-əl\ *adj* : occurring once every 20 years
vice presidency *n* : the office of vice president
vice president *n* **1** : an officer ranking next to a president and usu. empowered to act for the president during an absence or disability **2** : any of several of a president's deputies
vice·re·gal \ˈvīs-ˈrē-gəl\ *adj* : of or relating to a viceroy
vice·roy \ˈvīs-ˌrȯi\ *n* : the governor of a country or province who rules as representative of the sovereign — **vice·roy·al·ty** \-əl-tē\ *n*
vice ver·sa \ˌvī-si-ˈvər-sə, ˈvīs-ˈvər-\ *adv* : with the order reversed
vi·chys·soise \ˌvi-shē-ˈswäz, ˌvē-\ *n* [F] : a soup made esp. from leeks or onions and potatoes, cream, and chicken stock and usu. served cold
vic·i·nage \ˈvi-sə-nij\ *n* : a neighboring or surrounding district : VICINITY
vi·cin·i·ty \və-ˈsi-nə-tē\ *n, pl* **-ties** [MF *vicinité,* fr. L *vicinitas,* fr. *vicinus* neighboring, fr. *vicus* row of houses, village] **1** : NEARNESS, PROXIMITY **2** : a surrounding area : NEIGHBORHOOD
vi·cious \ˈvi-shəs\ *adj* **1** : having the quality of vice : WICKED, DEPRAVED **2** : DEFECTIVE, FAULTY; *also* : INVALID **3** : IMPURE, FOUL **4** : having a savage disposition; *also* : marked by violence or ferocity ⟨a ~ attack⟩ **5** : MALICIOUS, SPITEFUL ⟨~ gossip⟩ **6** : worsened by internal causes that augment each other ⟨~ wage-price spiral⟩ — **vi·cious·ly** *adv* — **vi·cious·ness** *n*
vi·cis·si·tude \və-ˈsi-sə-ˌtüd, vī-, -ˌtyüd\ *n* : an irregular, unexpected, or surprising change ⟨the ~*s* of business⟩
vic·tim \ˈvik-təm\ *n* **1** : a living being offered as a sacrifice in a religious rite **2** : an individual injured or killed (as by disease or accident) **3** : a person cheated, fooled, or injured ⟨a ~ of fraud⟩
vic·tim·ise *Brit var of* VICTIMIZE
vic·tim·ize \ˈvik-tə-ˌmīz\ *vb* **-ized; -iz·ing** : to make a victim of — **vic·tim·i·za·tion** \ˌvik-tə-mə-ˈzā-shən\ *n* — **vic·tim·iz·er** \ˈvik-tə-ˌmī-zər\ *n*
vic·tim·less \ˈvik-təm-ləs\ *adj* : having no victim ⟨considered gambling to be a ~ crime⟩
vic·tor \ˈvik-tər\ *n* : WINNER, CONQUEROR
vic·to·ria \vik-ˈtȯr-ē-ə\ *n* : a low 4-wheeled carriage with a folding top and a raised driver's seat in front
¹**Vic·to·ri·an** \vik-ˈtȯr-ē-ən\ *adj* **1** : of or relating to the reign of Queen Victoria of England or the art, letters, or tastes of her time **2** : typical of the standards, attitudes, or conduct of the age of Victoria esp. when considered prudish or narrow
²**Victorian** *n* **1** : a person and esp. an author of the Victorian period **2** : a typically large ornate house built during Queen Victoria's reign
vic·to·ri·ous \vik-ˈtȯr-ē-əs\ *adj* **1** : having won a victory **2** : of, relating to, or characteristic of victory ⟨~ exuberance⟩ — **vic·to·ri·ous·ly** *adv*
vic·to·ry \ˈvik-tə-rē\ *n, pl* **-ries** **1** : the overcoming of an enemy or an antagonist **2** : achievement of mastery or success in a struggle or endeavor
¹**vict·ual** \ˈvi-tᵊl\ *n* [ME *vitaille, victuayle,* fr. AF, fr. LL *victualia,* pl., provisions, food, fr. neut. pl. of *victualis* of nourishment, fr. L *victus* nourishment, way of living, fr. *vivere* to live] **1** : food fit for humans **2** *pl* : food supplies
²**victual** *vb* **-ualed** *or* **-ualled; -ual·ing** *or* **-ual·ling** **1** : to supply with food **2** : to store up provisions
vict·ual·ler *or* **vict·ual·er** \ˈvi-tᵊl-ər\ *n* : one that supplies provisions (as to an army or a ship)
vi·cu·ña *or* **vi·cu·na** \vi-ˈkün-yə, vī-; vī-ˈkü-nə, -ˈkyü-\ *n* **1** : a So. American wild mammal related to the llama and alpaca; *also* : its wool **2** : a soft fabric woven from the wool of the vicuña; *also* : a sheep's wool imitation of this
vi·de \ˈvī-dē, ˈvē-ˌdā\ *vb imper* [L] : SEE — used to direct a reader to another item
vi·de·li·cet \və-ˈde-lə-ˌset, vī-; vi-ˈdā-li-ˌket\ *adv* [ME, fr. L, fr. *vidēre* to see + *licet* it is permitted] : that is to say : NAMELY
¹**vid·eo** \ˈvi-dē-ˌō\ *n* **1** : TELEVISION **2** : VIDEOTAPE; *also* : a recording similar to a videotape but stored in digital form **3** : a videotaped performance ⟨music ~*s*⟩
²**video** *adj* **1** : relating to or used in transmission or reception of the television image **2** : relating to or being images on a television screen or computer display ⟨a ~ terminal⟩
video camera *n* : a camera that records visual images and usu. sound; *esp* : CAMCORDER

vid·eo·cas·sette \ˌvi-dē-ō-kə-ˈset\ *n* **1 :** a case containing videotape for use with a VCR **2 :** a recording (as of a movie) on a videocassette
videocassette recorder *n* **:** VCR
vid·eo·con·fer·enc·ing \ˌvi-dē-ō-ˈkän-f(ə-)rən-siŋ\ *n* **:** the holding of a conference among people at remote locations by means of transmitted audio and video signals
vid·eo·disc *or* **vid·eo·disk** \ˈvi-dē-ō-ˌdisk\ *n* **1 :** OPTICAL DISK **2 :** a recording (as of a movie) on a videodisc
video game *n* **:** an electronic game played on a video screen
vid·e·o·gen·ic \ˌvi-dē-ō-ˈje-nik\ *adj* **:** TELEGENIC
vid·eo·phone \ˈvid-ē-ə-ˌfōn\ *n* **:** a telephone for transmitting both audio and video signals
[1]**vid·eo·tape** \ˈvid-ē-ō-ˌtāp\ *n* **:** a recording of visual images and sound made on magnetic tape; *also* **:** the magnetic tape used for such a recording
[2]**videotape** *vb* **:** to make a videotape of
videotape recorder *n* **:** a device for recording and playing back videotapes
vie \ˈvī\ *vb* **vied; vy·ing** \ˈvī-iŋ\ **:** to compete for superiority **:** CONTEND — **vi·er** \ˈvī-ər\ *n*
Viet·cong \vē-ˈet-ˈkäŋ, ˌvē-ət-, -ˈkȯŋ\ *n, pl* **Vietcong :** a guerrilla member of the Vietnamese communist movement
[1]**view** \ˈvyü\ *n* **1 :** the act of seeing or examining **:** INSPECTION; *also* **:** SURVEY **2 :** a way of looking at or regarding something **3 :** ESTIMATE, JUDGMENT ⟨stated his ~*s*⟩ **4 :** a sight (as of a landscape) regarded for its pictorial quality **5 :** extent or range of vision ⟨within ~⟩ **6 :** OBJECT, PURPOSE ⟨done with a ~ to promotion⟩ **7 :** a picture of a scene
[2]**view** *vb* **1 :** to look at attentively **:** EXAMINE **2 :** SEE, WATCH ⟨~ a film⟩ **3 :** to examine mentally **:** CONSIDER ⟨~ a problem⟩ — **view·able** *adj* — **view·er** *n*
view·er·ship \ˈvyü-ər-ˌship\ *n* **:** a television audience esp. with respect to size or makeup
view·find·er \ˈvyü-ˌfīn-dər\ *n* **:** a device on a camera for showing the view to be included in the picture
view·point \-ˌpȯint\ *n* **:** POINT OF VIEW, OUTLOOK
vi·ges·i·mal \vī-ˈje-sə-məl\ *adj* **:** based on the number 20
vig·il \ˈvi-jəl\ *n* **1 :** a religious observance formerly held on the night before a religious feast **2 :** the day before a religious feast observed as a day of spiritual preparation **3 :** evening or nocturnal devotions or prayers — usu. used in pl. **4 :** an act or a time of keeping awake when sleep is customary; *esp* **:** WATCH 1
vigilance committee *n* **:** a committee of vigilantes
vig·i·lant \ˈvi-jə-lənt\ *adj* **:** alertly watchful esp. to avoid danger — **vig·i·lance** \-ləns\ *n* — **vig·i·lant·ly** *adv*
vig·i·lan·te \ˌvi-jə-ˈlan-tē\ *n* **:** a member of a volunteer committee organized to suppress and punish crime summarily (as when the processes of law are viewed as inadequate); *also* **:** a self-appointed doer of justice — **vig·i·lan·tism** \-ˈlan-ˌti-zəm\ *n*
[1]**vi·gnette** \vin-ˈyet\ *n* [F, fr. MF *vignete,* fr. dim. of *vigne* vine] **1 :** a small decorative design **2 :** a picture (as an engraving or a photograph) that shades off gradually into the surrounding ground **3 :** a short descriptive literary sketch
[2]**vignette** *vb* **vi·gnett·ed; vi·gnett·ing 1 :** to finish (as a photograph) like a vignette **2 :** to describe briefly
vig·or \ˈvi-gər\ *n* **1 :** active strength or energy of body or mind **2 :** INTENSITY, FORCE ⟨the ~ of their quarrel⟩
vig·or·ous \ˈvi-gə-rəs\ *adj* **1 :** having vigor **:** ROBUST **2 :** done with force and energy ⟨a ~ debate⟩ — **vig·or·ous·ly** *adv* — **vig·or·ous·ness** *n*
vig·our *chiefly Brit var of* VIGOR
Vi·king \ˈvī-kiŋ\ *n* [ON *vīkingr*] **:** any of the pirate Norsemen who raided or invaded the coasts of Europe in the 8th to 10th centuries
vile \ˈvī(-ə)l\ *adj* **vil·er; vil·est 1 :** morally despicable **2 :** physically repulsive **:** FOUL **3 :** of little worth **4 :** DEGRADING, IGNOMINIOUS **5 :** utterly bad or contemptible ⟨~ weather⟩ — **vile·ly** \ˈvī(-ə)l-lē\ *adv* — **vile·ness** *n*
vil·i·fy \ˈvi-lə-ˌfī\ *vb* **-fied; -fy·ing :** to blacken the character of with abusive language **:** DEFAME ♦ ***Synonyms*** MALIGN, CALUMNIATE, SLANDER, LIBEL, TRADUCE — **vil·i·fi·ca·tion** \ˌvi-lə-fə-ˈkā-shən\ *n* — **vil·i·fi·er** \ˈvi-lə-ˌfī-ər\ *n*
vil·la \ˈvi-lə\ *n* **1 :** a country estate **2 :** the rural or suburban residence of a wealthy person
vil·lage \ˈvi-lij\ *n* [ME, fr. AF *vilage,* fr. *vile* manorial estate, farmstead, fr. L *villa*] **1 :** a settlement usu. larger than a hamlet and smaller than a town **2 :** an incorporated minor municipality **3 :** the people of a village
vil·lag·er \ˈvi-li-jər\ *n* **:** an inhabitant of a village
vil·lain \ˈvi-lən\ *n* **1 :** VILLEIN **2 :** an evil person **:** SCOUNDREL
vil·lain·ess \-lə-nəs\ *n* **:** a woman who is a villain
vil·lain·ous \-lə-nəs\ *adj* **1 :** befitting a villain **:** WICKED, EVIL **2 :** highly objectionable **:** DETESTABLE ♦ ***Synonyms*** VICIOUS, INIQUITOUS, NEFARIOUS, INFAMOUS, CORRUPT, DEGENERATE — **vil·lain·ous·ly** *adv* — **vil·lain·ous·ness** *n*
vil·lainy \-lə-nē\ *n, pl* **-lain·ies 1 :** villainous conduct; *also* **:** a villainous act **2 :** villainous character or nature
vil·lein \ˈvi-lən, -ˌlān\ *n* **1 :** a free villager of Anglo-Saxon times **2 :** an unfree peasant enslaved to a feudal lord
vil·lous \ˈvi-ləs\ *adj* **:** covered with fine hairs or villi
vil·lus \ˈvi-ləs\ *n, pl* **vil·li** \-ˌlī, -(ˌ)lē\ **:** a slender usu. vascular process; *esp* **:** one of the tiny projections of the mucous membrane of the small intestine that function in the absorption of food

vim \ˈvim\ *n* : robust energy and enthusiasm : VITALITY

VIN *abbr* vehicle identification number

vin·ai·grette \ˌvi-ni-ˈgret\ *n* [F] : a sauce made typically of oil, vinegar, and seasonings

vin·ci·ble \ˈvin-sə-bəl\ *adj* : capable of being overcome or subdued

vin·di·cate \ˈvin-də-ˌkāt\ *vb* **-cat·ed; -cat·ing** **1** : AVENGE **2** : EXONERATE, ABSOLVE **3** : CONFIRM, SUBSTANTIATE **4** : to provide defense for : JUSTIFY **5** : to maintain a right to : ASSERT — **vin·di·ca·tor** \-ˌkā-tər\ *n*

vin·di·ca·tion \ˌvin-də-ˈkā-shən\ *n* : the act of vindicating or the state of being vindicated; *esp* : justification against denial or censure : DEFENSE

vin·dic·tive \vin-ˈdik-tiv\ *adj* **1** : disposed to revenge **2** : intended for or involving revenge ⟨~ punishment⟩ **3** : VICIOUS, SPITEFUL — **vin·dic·tive·ly** *adv* — **vin·dic·tive·ness** *n*

vine \ˈvīn\ *n* [ME, fr. AF *vigne,* fr. L *vinea* vine, vineyard, fr. fem. of *vineus* of wine, fr. *vinum* wine] **1** : GRAPE 2 **2** : a plant whose stem requires support and which climbs (as by tendrils) or trails along the ground; *also* : the stem of such a plant

vin·e·gar \ˈvi-ni-gər\ *n* [ME *vinegre,* fr. AF *vin egre,* lit., sour wine] : a sour liquid obtained by fermentation (as of cider, wine, or malt) and used to flavor or preserve foods

vin·e·gary \-gə-rē\ *adj* **1** : resembling vinegar : SOUR **2** : disagreeable in manner or disposition : CRABBED

vine·yard \ˈvin-yərd\ *n* **1** : a field of grapevines esp. to produce grapes for wine production **2** : a sphere of activity : field of endeavor

vi·nous \ˈvī-nəs\ *adj* **1** : of, relating to, or made with wine ⟨~ medications⟩ **2** : showing the effects of the use of wine ⟨~ bloodshot eyes⟩

¹**vin·tage** \ˈvin-tij\ *n* **1** : a season's yield of grapes or wine **2** : WINE; *esp* : a usu. superior wine which comes from a single year **3** : the act or period of gathering grapes or making wine **4** : a period of origin ⟨clothes of 1890 ~⟩

²**vintage** *adj* **1** : of, relating to, or produced in a particular vintage **2** : of old, recognized, and enduring interest, importance, or quality : CLASSIC ⟨~ cars⟩ **3** : of the best and most characteristic — used with a proper noun

vint·ner \ˈvint-nər\ *n* : a dealer in wines

vi·nyl \ˈvī-nᵊl\ *n* **1** : a chemical derived from ethylene by the removal of one hydrogen atom **2** : a polymer of a vinyl compound or a product (as a textile fiber) made from one

vinyl chloride *n* : a flammable gaseous carcinogenic compound used esp. to make vinyl resins

vi·ol \ˈvī-əl\ *n* : a bowed stringed instrument chiefly of the 16th and 17th centuries having a fretted neck and usu. six strings

¹**vi·o·la** \vī-ˈō-lə, ˈvī-ə-lə\ *n* : VIOLET 1; *esp* : any of various hybrid garden plants with white, yellow, purple, or variously colored flowers that resemble but are smaller than those of the related pansies

²**vi·o·la** \vē-ˈō-lə\ *n* : an instrument of the violin family slightly larger and tuned lower than a violin — **vi·o·list** \-list\ *n*

vi·o·la·ble \ˈvī-ə-lə-bəl\ *adj* : capable of being violated ⟨~ boundaries⟩

vi·o·late \ˈvī-ə-ˌlāt\ *vb* **-lat·ed; -lat·ing** **1** : BREAK, DISREGARD ⟨~ a law⟩ ⟨~ a frontier⟩ **2** : RAPE **3** : PROFANE, DESECRATE **4** : INTERRUPT, DISTURB ⟨*violated* his privacy⟩ — **vi·o·la·tor** \-ˌlā-tər\ *n*

vi·o·la·tion \ˌvī-ə-ˈlā-shən\ *n* : an act or instance of violating : the state of being violated ◆ ***Synonyms*** BREACH, INFRACTION, TRESPASS, INFRINGEMENT, TRANSGRESSION

vi·o·lence \ˈvī-ləns, ˈvī-ə-\ *n* **1** : exertion of physical force so as to injure or abuse **2** : injury by or as if by infringement or profanation **3** : intense or furious often destructive action or force **4** : vehement feeling or expression : INTENSITY **5** : jarring quality : DISCORDANCE ◆ ***Synonyms*** COMPULSION, COERCION, DURESS, CONSTRAINT

vi·o·lent \-lənt\ *adj* **1** : marked by extreme force or sudden intense activity **2** : caused by or showing strong feeling ⟨~ words⟩ **3** : EXTREME, INTENSE ⟨~ pain⟩ ⟨~ colors⟩ **4** : emotionally agitated to the point of loss of self-control **5** : caused by force : not natural ⟨~ death⟩ — **vi·o·lent·ly** *adv*

vi·o·let \ˈvī-ə-lət\ *n* **1** : any of a genus of herbs or small shrubs usu. with heart-shaped leaves and both aerial and underground flowers; *esp* : one with small usu. solid-colored flowers **2** : a reddish blue color

vi·o·lin \ˌvī-ə-ˈlin\ *n* : a bowed stringed instrument with four strings that has a shallow body, a fingerboard without frets, and a curved bridge — **vi·o·lin·ist** \-ˈli-nist\ *n*

vi·o·lon·cel·lo \ˌvī-ə-lən-ˈche-lō\ *n* [It] : CELLO — **vi·o·lon·cel·list** \-list\ *n*

VIP \ˌvē-ˌī-ˈpē\ *n, pl* **VIPs** \-ˈpēz\ [*very important person*] : a person of great influence or prestige; *esp* : a high official with special privileges

vi·per \ˈvī-pər\ *n* **1** : a common stout-bodied Eurasian venomous snake having a bite only rarely fatal to humans; *also* : any snake (as a pit viper) of the same family as the viper **2** : any venomous or reputedly venomous snake **3** : a vicious or treacherous person — **vi·per·ine** \-pə-ˌrīn\ *adj*

vi·ra·go \və-ˈrä-gō, -ˈrā-\ *n, pl* **-goes** *or* **-gos** [ME, fr. L, strong or heroic woman, fr. *vir* man] **1** : a loud overbearing woman **2** : a woman of great strength and courage

vi·ral \ˈvī-rəl\ *adj* **1** : of, relating to, or caused by a virus ⟨a ~ infection⟩ **2** : quickly and widely spread or popularized esp. by means of social media ⟨a ~ video⟩ — **vi·ral·ly** *adv*

vir·eo \ˈvir-ē-ˌō\ *n, pl* **-e·os** [L, a small bird, fr. *virēre* to be green] : any of various small insect-eating American songbirds mostly olive green and grayish in color

[1]**vir·gin** \ˈvər-jən\ *n* **1** : an unmarried woman devoted to religion **2** : an unmarried girl or woman **3** *cap* : the mother of Jesus **4** : a person who has not had sexual intercourse

[2]**virgin** *adj* **1** : free from stain : PURE, SPOTLESS **2** : CHASTE **3** : befitting a virgin : MODEST **4** : FRESH, UNSPOILED; *esp* : not altered by human activity ⟨~ forest⟩ **5** : INITIAL, FIRST

[1]**vir·gin·al** \ˈvər-jə-nᵊl\ *adj* : of, relating to, or characteristic of a virgin or virginity ⟨~ innocence⟩ — **vir·gin·al·ly** *adv*

[2]**virginal** *n* : a small rectangular spinet without legs popular in the 16th and 17th centuries

Vir·gin·ia creeper \vər-ˈjin-yə-\ *n* : a No. American vine related to the grapes that has leaves with five leaflets and bluish-black berries

Virginia reel *n* : an American country-dance

vir·gin·i·ty \vər-ˈji-nə-tē\ *n, pl* **-ties** **1** : the quality or state of being virgin; *esp* : MAIDENHOOD **2** : the unmarried life : CELIBACY

Vir·go \ˈvər-ˌgō\ *n* [L, lit., virgin] **1** : a zodiacal constellation between Leo and Libra usu. pictured as a young woman **2** : the 6th sign of the zodiac in astrology; *also* : one born under this sign

vir·gule \ˈvər-gyül\ *n* : [2]SLASH 3

vir·i·des·cent \ˌvir-ə-ˈde-sᵊnt\ *adj* : slightly green : GREENISH

vir·ile \ˈvir-əl\ *adj* **1** : having the nature, properties, or qualities of a man **2** : MASCULINE, MALE **3** : MASTERFUL, FORCEFUL — **vi·ril·i·ty** \və-ˈri-lə-tē\ *n*

vi·ri·on \ˈvī-rē-ˌän, ˈvir-ē-\ *n* : a complete virus particle consisting of an RNA or DNA core with a protein coat

vi·rol·o·gy \vī-ˈrä-lə-jē\ *n* : a branch of science that deals with viruses and viral diseases — **vi·rol·o·gist** \-jist\ *n*

vir·tu \ˌvər-ˈtü, ˌvir-\ *or* **ver·tu** \ˌvər-, ˌver-\ *n* [It *virtù,* lit., virtue] **1** : a love of or taste for objects of art **2** : objects of art (as curios and antiques)

vir·tu·al \ˈvər-chə-wəl\ *adj* **1** : being in essence or in effect though not formally recognized or admitted ⟨a ~ dictator⟩ **2** : being on or simulated on a computer or computer network ⟨~ shopping⟩

vir·tu·al·ly \ˈvər-chə-wə-lē\ *adv* **1** : almost entirely : NEARLY **2** : for all practical purposes ⟨~ unknown⟩

virtual private network *n* : a private computer network that functions over a public network (as the Internet) and usu. uses data encryption to provide secure access to something (as an internal business server)

virtual reality *n* : an artificial environment that is experienced through sensory stimuli (as sights and sounds) provided by an interactive computer program; *also* : the technology used to create or access a virtual reality

vir·tue \ˈvər-chü\ *n* [ME *vertu,* fr. AF, fr. L *virtus* strength, manliness, virtue, fr. *vir* man] **1** : conformity to a standard of right : MORALITY **2** : a particular moral excellence **3** : manly strength or courage : VALOR **4** : a commendable quality : MERIT **5** : active power to accomplish a given effect : POTENCY, EFFICACY **6** : chastity esp. in a woman

vir·tu·os·i·ty \ˌvər-chə-ˈwä-sə-tē\ *n, pl* **-ties** : great technical skill in the practice of a fine art

vir·tu·o·so \ˌvər-chə-ˈwō-sō, -zō\ *n, pl* **-sos** *or* **-si** \-sē, -zē\ [It] **1** : one skilled in or having a taste for the fine arts **2** : one who excels in the technique of an art; *esp* : a highly skilled musical performer ♦ ***Synonyms*** EXPERT, ADEPT, ARTIST, DOYEN, MASTER — **vir·tu·o·sic** \-ˈwä-sik, -ˈwō-, -zik\ *adj* — **vir·tu·o·sic·al·ly** \-si-k(ə-)lē-, -zi-\ *adv* — **virtuoso** *adj*

vir·tu·ous \ˈvər-chə-wəs\ *adj* **1** : having or showing virtue and esp. moral virtue **2** : CHASTE — **vir·tu·ous·ly** *adv*

vir·u·lent \ˈvir-ə-lənt, ˈvir-yə-\ *adj* **1** : highly infectious ⟨a ~ germ⟩; *also* : marked by a rapid, severe, and often deadly course ⟨a ~ disease⟩ **2** : extremely poisonous or venomous : NOXIOUS **3** : full of malice : MALIGNANT — **vir·u·lence** \-ləns\ *n* — **vir·u·lent·ly** *adv*

vi·rus \ˈvī-rəs\ *n, pl* **vi·rus·es** [L, venom, poisonous emanation] **1** : any of a large group of submicroscopic infectious agents that have an outside coat of protein around a core of RNA or DNA, that can grow and multiply only in living cells, and that cause important diseases in human beings, lower animals, and plants; *also* : a disease caused by a virus **2** : something (as a corrupting influence) that poisons the mind or spirit **3** : a computer program that is usu. hidden within another program and that reproduces itself and inserts the copies into other programs and usu. performs a malicious action (as destroying data)

vis *abbr* **1** visibility **2** visual

[1]**vi·sa** \ˈvē-zə, -sə\ *n* [F] **1** : an endorsement by the proper authorities on a passport to show that it has been examined and the bearer may proceed **2** : a signature by a superior official signifying approval of a document

[2]**visa** *vb* **vi·saed** \-zəd, -səd\; **vi·sa·ing** \-zə-iŋ, -sə-\ : to give a visa to (a passport)

vis·age \ˈvi-zij\ *n* : the face or countenance of a person or sometimes an animal; *also* : LOOK, APPEARANCE

[1]**vis-à-vis** \ˌvēz-ə-ˈvē, ˌvēs-\ *prep* [F, lit., face-to-face] **1** : face-to-face with : OPPOSITE **2** : in relation to **3** : as compared with

[2]**vis-à-vis** *n, pl* **vis-à-vis** *same or* -ˈvēz\ **1** : one that is face-to-face with another **2** : ESCORT **3** : COUNTERPART **4** : TÊTE-À-TÊTE

[3]**vis-à-vis** *adv* : in company : TOGETHER

viscera *pl of* VISCUS

vis·cer·al \ˈvi-sə-rəl\ *adj* **1** : felt in or as if in the viscera **2** : not intellectual : INSTINCTIVE **3** : of or relating to the viscera — **vis·cer·al·ly** *adv*

vis·cid \ˈvi-səd\ *adj* : VISCOUS — **vis·cid·i·ty** \vi-ˈsi-də-tē\ *n*

vis·cos·i·ty \vis-ˈkä-sə-tē\ *n, pl* **-ties** : the quality of being viscous; *esp* : the property of resistance to flow in a fluid

vis·count \ˈvī-ˌkau̇nt\ *n* : a member of the British peerage ranking below an earl and above a baron

vis·count·ess \-ˌkau̇n-təs\ *n* **1** : the wife or widow of a viscount **2** : a woman who holds the rank of viscount in her own right

vis·cous \ˈvis-kəs\ *adj* [ME *viscouse,* fr. AF *viscos,* fr. LL *viscosus* full of birdlime, viscous, fr. L *viscum* mistletoe, birdlime] **1** : having the sticky consistency of glue **2** : having or characterized by viscosity

vis·cus \ˈvis-kəs\ *n, pl* **vis·cera** \ˈvi-sə-rə\ : an internal organ of the body; *esp* : one (as the heart or liver) located in the cavity of the trunk

vise \ˈvīs\ *n* [ME *vys, vice* screw, fr. AF *vyz,* fr. L *vitis* vine] : a tool with two jaws for holding work that typically close by a screw or lever

vis·i·bil·i·ty \ˌvi-zə-ˈbi-lə-tē\ *n, pl* **-ties** **1** : the quality, condition, or degree of being visible **2** : the degree of clearness of the atmosphere

vis·i·ble \ˈvi-zə-bəl\ *adj* : capable of being seen ⟨~ stars⟩; *also* : MANIFEST, APPARENT ⟨has no ~ means of support⟩ — **vis·i·bly** \-blē\ *adv*

[1]**vi·sion** \ˈvi-zhən\ *n* **1** : something seen otherwise than by ordinary sight (as in a dream or trance) **2** : a vivid picture created by the imagination ⟨~*s* of fame and fortune⟩ **3** : the act or power of imagination **4** : unusual wisdom in foreseeing what is going to happen **5** : the act or power of seeing : SIGHT **6** : something seen; *esp* : a lovely sight

[2]**vision** *vb* : IMAGINE, ENVISION

[1]**vi·sion·ary** \ˈvi-zhə-ˌner-ē\ *adj* **1** : of the nature of a vision : ILLUSORY, UNREAL **2** : not practical : UTOPIAN **3** : seeing or likely to see visions : given to dreaming or imagining ♦ ***Synonyms*** IMAGINARY, FANTASTIC, CHIMERICAL, QUIXOTIC

[2]**visionary** *n, pl* **-ar·ies** **1** : one whose ideas or projects are impractical : DREAMER **2** : one who sees visions

[1]**vis·it** \ˈvi-zət\ *vb* **1** : to go to see in order to comfort or help **2** : to call on either as an act of courtesy or friendship **3** : to dwell with for a time as a guest **4** : to come to or upon as a reward, affliction, or punishment **5** : INFLICT ⟨~*ed* his wrath upon them⟩ **6** : to make a visit or regular or frequent visits **7** : CHAT, CONVERSE ⟨enjoys ~*ing* with the neighbors⟩ — **vis·it·able** *adj*

[2]**visit** *n* **1** : a short stay : CALL **2** : a brief residence as a guest **3** : a journey to and stay at a place **4** : a formal or professional call (as by a doctor)

vis·i·tant \ˈvi-zə-tənt\ *n* : VISITOR

vis·i·ta·tion \ˌvi-zə-ˈtā-shən\ *n* **1** : VISIT; *esp* : an official visit **2** : a special dispensation of divine favor or wrath; *also* : a severe trial

visiting nurse *n* : a nurse employed to visit sick persons or perform public health services in a community

vis·i·tor \ˈvi-zə-tər\ *n* : one that visits

vi·sor \ˈvī-zər\ *n* **1** : the front piece of a helmet; *esp* : a movable upper piece **2** : VIZARD **3** : a projecting part (as on a cap) to shade the eyes — **vi·sored** \-zərd\ *adj*

vis·ta \ˈvis-tə\ *n* **1** : a distant view through or along an avenue or opening **2** : an extensive mental view over a series of years or events

VISTA *abbr* Volunteers in Service to America

[1]**vi·su·al** \ˈvi-zhə-wəl\ *adj* **1** : of, relating to, or used in vision ⟨~ organs⟩ **2** : perceived by vision ⟨a ~ impression⟩ **3** : VISIBLE ⟨~ objects⟩ **4** : done by sight only ⟨~ navigation⟩ **5** : of or relating to instruction by means of sight ⟨~ aids⟩ — **vi·su·al·ly** *adv*

[2]**visual** *n* : something (as a graphic) that appeals to the sight and is used for illustration, demonstration, or promotion — usu. used in pl.

vi·su·al·ize \ˈvi-zhə-wə-ˌlīz\ *vb* **-ized; -iz·ing** : to make visible; *esp* : to form a mental image of — **vi·su·al·i·za·tion** \ˌvi-zhə-wə-lə-ˈzā-shən\ *n* — **vi·su·al·iz·er** *n*

vi·ta \ˈvē-tə, ˈvī-\ *n, pl* **vi·tae** \ˈvē-ˌtī, ˈvī-tē\ [L, lit., life] : a brief autobiographical sketch

vi·tal \ˈvī-tᵊl\ *adj* **1** : concerned with or necessary to the maintenance of life ⟨~ organs⟩ **2** : full of life and vigor : ANIMATED **3** : of, relating to, or characteristic of life or living beings **4** : FATAL, MORTAL ⟨~ wound⟩ **5** : FUNDAMENTAL, INDISPENSABLE — **vi·tal·ly** *adv*

vi·tal·i·ty \vī-ˈta-lə-tē\ *n, pl* **-ties** **1** : the property distinguishing the living from the nonliving **2** : mental and physical vigor **3** : enduring quality **4** : ANIMATION, LIVELINESS ⟨the ~ of youth⟩

vi·tal·ize \ˈvī-tə-ˌlīz\ *vb* **-ized; -iz·ing** : to impart life or vigor to : ANIMATE — **vi·tal·i·za·tion** \ˌvī-tə-lə-ˈzā-shən\ *n*

vi·tals \ˈvī-tᵊlz\ *n pl* **1** : vital organs (as the heart and brain) **2** : essential parts **3** : VITAL STATISTICS **4** : VITAL SIGNS

vital signs *n pl* : the pulse rate, respiratory rate, body temperature, and blood pressure of a person

vital statistics *n pl* : statistics dealing with births, deaths, marriages, health, and disease

vi·ta·min \ˈvī-tə-mən\ *n* : any of various organic substances that are essential in tiny amounts to the nutrition of most animals and some plants and are mostly obtained from foods

vitamin A *n* : any of several vitamins (as from egg yolk or fish-liver oils) required esp. for good vision

vitamin B *n* **1** : VITAMIN B COMPLEX **2** *or* **vitamin B_1** : THIAMINE

vitamin B complex *n* : a group of vitamins that are found widely in foods and are essential for normal function of certain enzymes and for growth

vitamin B_6 \-ˈbē-ˈsiks\ *n* : any of several compounds that are considered essential to vertebrate nutrition

vitamin B_{12} \-ˈbē-ˈtwelv\ *n* : a complex cobalt-containing compound that occurs esp. in liver and is essential to normal blood formation, neural function, and growth; *also* : any of several compounds of similar action

vitamin C *n* : a vitamin found esp. in fruits and vegetables that is needed by the body to prevent scurvy

vitamin D *n* : any or all of several vitamins that are needed for normal bone and tooth structure and are found esp. in fish-liver oils, egg yolk, and milk or are produced by the body in response to ultraviolet light

vitamin E *n* : any of various oily fat-soluble liquid vitamins whose absence in the body is associated with such ailments as infertility, the breakdown of muscles, and vascular problems and which are found esp. in leaves and in seed germ oils

vitamin K *n* : any of several vitamins needed for blood to clot properly

vi·ti·ate \ˈvi-shē-ˌāt\ *vb* **-at·ed; -at·ing** **1** : CONTAMINATE, POLLUTE; *also* : DEBASE, PERVERT **2** : to make legally ineffective : INVALIDATE ⟨~ a contract⟩ — **vi·ti·a·tion** \ˌvi-shē-ˈā-shən\ *n* — **vi·ti·a·tor** \ˈvi-shē-ˌā-tər\ *n*

vi·ti·cul·ture \ˈvi-tə-ˌkəl-chər\ *n* : the growing of grapes — **vi·ti·cul·tur·al** \ˌvi-tə-ˈkəl-chə-rəl\ *adj* — **vi·ti·cul·tur·ist** \-rist\ *n*

vit·re·ous \ˈvi-trē-əs\ *adj* **1** : of, relating to, or resembling glass : GLASSY ⟨~ rocks⟩ **2** : of, relating to, or being the clear colorless transparent jelly (**vitreous humor**) behind the lens in the eyeball

vit·ri·ol \ˈvi-trē-əl\ *n* : something resembling acid in being caustic, corrosive, or biting — **vit·ri·ol·ic** \ˌvi-trē-ˈä-lik\ *adj*

vit·tles \ˈvi-tᵊlz\ *n pl* : VICTUALS

vi·tu·per·ate \vī-ˈtü-pə-ˌrāt, və-, -ˈtyü-\ *vb* **-at·ed; -at·ing** : to abuse in words : SCOLD ♦ ***Synonyms*** REVILE, BERATE, RATE, UPBRAID, RAIL, LASH — **vi·tu·per·a·tive** \-ˈtü-pə-rə-tiv, -ˈtyü-, -ˌrā-\ *adj* — **vi·tu·per·a·tive·ly** *adv*

vi·tu·per·a·tion \(ˌ)vī-tü-pə-ˈrā-shən, və-, -tyü-\ *n* : lengthy harsh criticism or abuse

vi·va \ˈvē-və\ *interj* [It & Sp, long live] — used to express goodwill or approval

vi·va·ce \vē-ˈvä-chā\ *adv or adj* [It] : in a brisk spirited manner — used as a direction in music

vi·va·cious \və-ˈvā-shəs, vī-\ *adj* : lively in temper, conduct, or spirit : SPRIGHTLY ⟨a ~ personality⟩ — **vi·va·cious·ly** *adv* — **vi·va·cious·ness** *n*

vi·vac·i·ty \-ˈva-sə-tē\ *n* : the quality or state of being vivacious

vi·va vo·ce \ˌvī-və-ˈvō-sē, ˌvē-və-ˈvō-ˌchā\ *adj* [ML, with the living voice] : expressed or conducted by word of mouth : ORAL — **viva voce** *adv*

viv·id \ˈvi-vəd\ *adj* **1** : BRILLIANT, INTENSE ⟨a ~ red⟩ **2** : having the appearance of vigorous life **3** : producing a strong impression on the senses; *esp* : producing distinct mental pictures ⟨a ~ description⟩ — **viv·id·ly** *adv* — **viv·id·ness** *n*

viv·i·fy \ˈvi-və-ˌfī\ *vb* **-fied; -fy·ing** **1** : to put life into : ANIMATE ⟨details that ~ a story⟩ **2** : to make vivid — **viv·i·fi·ca·tion** \ˌvi-və-fə-ˈkā-shən\ *n* — **viv·i·fi·er** *n*

vi·vip·a·rous \vī-ˈvi-pə-rəs, və-\ *adj* : producing living young from within the body rather than from eggs — **vi·vi·par·i·ty** \ˌvī-və-ˈpa-rə-tē, ˌvi-\ *n*

viv·i·sec·tion \ˌvi-və-ˈsek-shən, ˈvi-və-ˌsek-\ *n* : the cutting of or operation on a living animal; *also* : animal experimentation esp. if causing distress to the subject

vix·en \ˈvik-sən\ *n* **1** : an ill-tempered scolding woman **2** : a female fox

viz *abbr* videlicet

viz·ard \ˈvi-zərd\ *n* : a mask for disguise or protection

vi·zier \və-ˈzir\ *n* : a high executive officer of many Muslim countries

VJ *abbr* veejay

vlog \ˈvlȯg, ˈvläg\ *n* [*v*ideo + b*log*] : a blog that contains video material — **vlog** *vb* — **vlog·ger** *n*

VOA *abbr* Voice of America

voc *abbr* **1** vocational **2** vocative

vocab *abbr* vocabulary

vo·ca·ble \ˈvō-kə-bəl\ *n* : TERM, NAME; *esp* : a word as such without regard to its meaning

vo·cab·u·lary \vō-ˈka-byə-ˌler-ē\ *n, pl* **-lar·ies** **1** : a list or collection of words usu. alphabetically arranged and defined or explained : LEXICON **2** : a stock of words in a language used by a class or individual or in relation to a subject

vocabulary entry *n* : a word (as the noun *book*), hyphened or open compound (as the verb *cross-refer* or the noun *boric acid*), word element (as the affix *-an*), abbreviation (as *agt*), verbalized symbol (as *Na*), or term (as *master of ceremonies*) entered alphabetically in a dictionary for the purpose of definition or identification or expressly included as an inflected form (as the noun *mice* or the verb *saw*) or as a derived form (as the noun *godlessness* or the adverb *globally*) or related phrase (as *in spite of*) run on at its base word and usu. set in a type (as boldface) readily distinguishable from that of the lightface running text which defines, explains, or identifies the entry

¹**vo·cal** \ˈvō-kəl\ *adj* **1** : uttered by the voice : ORAL **2** : relating to, composed or arranged for, or sung by the human voice ⟨~ music⟩ **3** : given to expressing oneself freely or insistently : OUTSPOKEN ⟨a ~ critic⟩ **4** : of or relating to the voice

²**vocal** *n* **1** : a vocal sound **2** : a vocal composition or its performance

vocal cords *n pl* : either of two pairs of elastic folds of mucous membrane that project into the cavity of the larynx and function in the production of vocal sounds

vo·cal·ic \vō-ˈka-lik\ *adj* : of, relating to, or functioning as a vowel

vo·cal·ise *Brit var of* VOCALIZE

vo·cal·ist \ˈvō-kə-list\ *n* : SINGER

vo·cal·ize \-ˌlīz\ *vb* **-ized; -iz·ing** **1** : to give vocal expression to : UTTER; *esp* : SING **2** : to make voiced rather than voiceless — **vo·cal·iz·er** *n*

vo·ca·tion \vō-ˈkā-shən\ *n* **1** : a summons or strong inclination to a particular state or course of action ⟨religious ~⟩ **2** : regular employment : OCCUPATION, PROFESSION — **vo·ca·tion·al** \-shə-nəl\ *adj*

vo·ca·tion·al·ism \-shə-nə-ˌli-zəm\ *n* : emphasis on vocational training in education

voc·a·tive \ˈvä-kə-tiv\ *adj* : of, relating to, or constituting a grammatical case marking the one addressed — **vocative** *n*

vo·cif·er·ate \vō-ˈsi-fə-ˌrāt\ *vb* **-at·ed; -at·ing** [L *vociferari,* fr. *voc-, vox* voice + *ferre* to bear] : to cry out loudly : CLAMOR, SHOUT — **vo·cif·er·a·tion** \-ˌsi-fə-ˈrā-shən\ *n*

vo·cif·er·ous \vō-ˈsi-fə-rəs\ *adj* : making or given to loud outcry — **vo·cif·er·ous·ly** *adv* — **vo·cif·er·ous·ness** *n*

vod·ka \ˈväd-kə\ *n* [Russ, fr. *voda* water] : a colorless liquor distilled from a mash (as of rye or wheat)

vogue \ˈvōg\ *n* [MF, action of rowing, course, fashion, fr. *voguer* to sail, fr. OF, fr. OIt *vogare* to row] **1** : popular acceptance or favor : POPULARITY **2** : a period of popularity **3** : one that is in fashion at a particular time ♦ ***Synonyms*** MODE, FAD, RAGE, CRAZE, TREND, FASHION

vogu·ish \ˈvō-gish\ *adj* **1** : FASHIONABLE, SMART **2** : suddenly or temporarily popular ⟨~ expressions⟩

[1]**voice** \ˈvȯis\ *n* **1** : sound produced through the mouth by vertebrates and esp. by human beings (as in speaking or singing) **2** : musical sound produced by the vocal cords : the power to produce such sound; *also* : one of the melodic parts in a vocal or instrumental composition **3** : the vocal organs as a means of tone production ⟨train the ~⟩ **4** : sound produced by vibration of the vocal cords as heard in vowels and some consonants **5** : the power of speaking **6** : a sound suggesting a voice ⟨the ~ of the sea⟩ **7** : an instrument or medium of expression **8** : a choice, opinion, or wish openly expressed; *also* : right of expression **9** : distinction of form of a verb to indicate the relation of the subject to the action expressed by the verb

[2]**voice** *vb* **voiced; voic·ing** : to give voice or expression to : UTTER ⟨~ a complaint⟩ ♦ ***Synonyms*** EXPRESS, VENT, AIR, VENTILATE

voice box *n* : LARYNX

voiced \ˈvȯist\ *adj* **1** : having a voice ⟨soft-*voiced*⟩ **2** : uttered with voice ⟨a ~ consonant⟩ — **voiced·ness** \ˈvȯist-nəs, ˈvȯi-səd-nəs\ *n*

voice·less \ˈvȯis-ləs\ *adj* **1** : having no voice **2** : not pronounced with voice — **voice·less·ly** *adv* — **voice·less·ness** *n*

voice mail *n* : an electronic communication system in which spoken messages are recorded for later playback to the intended recipient; *also* : such a message

voice–over *n* : the voice in a film or television program of a person who is heard but not seen or not seen talking

voice·print \ˈvȯis-ˌprint\ *n* : an individually distinctive pattern of voice characteristics that is spectrographically produced

[1]**void** \ˈvȯid\ *adj* **1** : UNOCCUPIED, VACANT ⟨a ~ bishopric⟩ **2** : containing nothing : EMPTY **3** : LACKING, DEVOID ⟨proposals ~ of sense⟩ **4** : VAIN, USELESS **5** : of no legal force or effect : NULL

[2]**void** *n* **1** : empty space : EMPTINESS, VACUUM **2** : a feeling of want or hollowness

[3]**void** *vb* **1** : to make or leave empty; *also* : VACATE, LEAVE **2** : DISCHARGE, EMIT ⟨~ urine⟩ **3** : to render void : ANNUL, NULLIFY ⟨~ a contract⟩ — **void·able** *adj* — **void·er** *n*

voi·là \vwä-ˈlä\ *interj* [F] — used to call attention or to express satisfaction or approval

voile \ˈvȯi(-ə)l\ *n* : a sheer fabric used esp. for women's clothing and curtains

vol *abbr* **1** volume **2** volunteer

vol·a·tile \ˈvä-lə-tᵊl\ *adj* **1** : readily becoming a vapor at a relatively low temperature ⟨a ~ liquid⟩ **2** : tending to erupt into violence **3** : likely to change suddenly — **vol·a·til·i·ty** \ˌvä-lə-ˈti-lə-tē\ *n* — **vol·a·til·ize** \ˈvä-lə-tə-ˌlīz\ *vb*

vol·ca·nic \väl-ˈka-nik\ *adj* **1** : of, relating to, or produced by a volcano **2** : explosively violent ⟨~ emotions⟩

vol·ca·nism \ˈväl-kə-ˌni-zəm\ *n* : volcanic action or activity

vol·ca·no \väl-ˈkā-nō\ *n, pl* **-noes** *or* **-nos** [It or Sp; It *vulcano,* fr. Sp *vulcán,* ultim. fr. L *Volcanus,* Roman god of fire and metalworking] : an opening in the crust of the earth, a planet, or a moon from which molten rock and steam issue; *also* : a hill or mountain composed of the ejected material

vol·ca·nol·o·gy \ˌväl-kə-ˈnä-lə-jē\ *n* : a branch of geology that deals with volcanic phenomena — **vol·ca·nol·o·gist** \-kə-ˈnä-lə-jist\ *n*

vole \ˈvōl\ *n* : any of various small rodents that are closely related to the lemmings and muskrats

vo·li·tion \vō-ˈli-shən\ *n* **1** : the act or the power of making a choice or decision : WILL **2** : a choice or decision made — **vo·li·tion·al** \-ˈli-shə-nəl\ *adj*

[1]**vol·ley** \ˈvä-lē\ *n, pl* **volleys** **1** : a flight of missiles (as arrows) **2** : simultaneous discharge of a number of missile weapons **3** : an act of volleying **4** : a burst of many things at once ⟨a ~ of angry letters⟩

[2]**volley** *vb* **vol·leyed; vol·ley·ing** **1** : to discharge or become discharged in or as if in a volley **2** : to hit an object of play (as a ball) in the air before it touches the ground

vol·ley·ball \-ˌbȯl\ *n* : a game played by volleying an inflated ball over a net; *also* : the ball used in this game

volt \ˈvōlt\ *n* : the meter-kilogram-second unit of electrical potential difference and electromotive force equal to the difference in potential between two points in a wire carrying a constant current of one ampere when the power dissipated between the points is equal to one watt

volt·age \ˈvōl-tij\ *n* : potential difference measured in volts

vol·ta·ic \väl-ˈtā-ik, vōl-\ *adj* : of, relating to, or producing direct electric current by chemical action

volte–face \ˌvȯlt-ˈfäs, ˌvȯl-tə-\ *n* : a reversal in policy : ABOUT-FACE

volt·me·ter \ˈvōlt-ˌmē-tər\ *n* : an instrument for measuring in volts the difference in potential between different points of an electrical circuit

vol·u·ble \ˈväl-yə-bəl\ *adj* : fluent and smooth in speech : GLIB ♦ ***Synonyms*** GARRULOUS, LOQUACIOUS, TALKATIVE — **vol·u·bil·i·ty** \ˌväl-yə-ˈbi-lə-tē\ *n* — **vol·u·bly** \ˈväl-yə-blē\ *adv*

vol·ume \ˈväl-yəm, -(ˌ)yüm\ *n* [ME, fr. AF, fr. L *volumen* roll, scroll, fr. *volvere* to roll] **1** : a series of printed sheets bound typically in book form; *also* : an arbitrary number of issues of a periodical **2** : space occupied as measured by cubic units ⟨the ~ of a cylinder⟩ **3** : sufficient matter to fill a book ⟨her glance spoke ~*s*⟩ **4** : AMOUNT ⟨increasing ~ of business⟩ **5** : the degree of loudness of a sound ♦ ***Synonyms*** BODY, BULK, MASS

vo·lu·mi·nous \və-ˈlü-mə-nəs\ *adj* : having or marked by great volume or bulk : LARGE — **vo·lu·mi·nous·ly** *adv* — **vo·lu·mi·nous·ness** *n*

[1]**vol·un·tary** \ˈvä-lən-ˌter-ē\ *adj* **1** : done, made, or given freely and without compulsion ⟨a ~ sacrifice⟩ **2** : done on purpose : INTENTIONAL ⟨~ manslaughter⟩ **3** : of, relating to, or regulated by the will ⟨~ behavior⟩ **4** : having power of free choice **5** : provided or supported by voluntary action ⟨a ~ organization⟩ ♦ ***Synonyms*** DELIBERATE, WILLFUL, WILLING, WITTING — **vol·un·tar·i·ly** \ˌvä-lən-ˈter-ə-lē\ *adv*

[2]**voluntary** *n, pl* **-tar·ies** : an organ solo played in a religious service

voluntary muscle *n* : muscle (as most striated muscle) under voluntary control

[1]**vol·un·teer** \ˌvä-lən-ˈtir\ *n* **1** : a person who voluntarily undertakes a service or duty **2** : a plant growing spontaneously esp. from seeds lost from a previous crop

[2]**volunteer** *vb* **1** : to offer or give voluntarily **2** : to offer oneself as a volunteer

vo·lup·tu·ary \və-ˈləp-chə-ˌwer-ē\ *n, pl* **-ar·ies** : a person whose chief interest in life is the indulgence of sensual appetites

vo·lup·tu·ous \-chə-wəs\ *adj* **1** : giving sensual gratification **2** : given to or spent in enjoyment of luxury or pleasure ♦ ***Synonyms*** LUXURIOUS, EPICUREAN, SENSUOUS — **vo·lup·tu·ous·ly** *adv* — **vo·lup·tu·ous·ness** *n*

vo·lute \və-ˈlüt\ *n* : a spiral or scroll-shaped decoration

[1]**vom·it** \ˈvä-mət\ *n* : an act or instance of throwing up the contents of the stomach through the mouth; *also* : the matter thrown up

[2]**vomit** *vb* **1** : to throw up the contents of the stomach through the mouth **2** : to belch forth : GUSH

voo·doo \ˈvü-dü\ *n, pl* **voodoos** **1** : a religion that is derived from African polytheism and is practiced chiefly in Haiti **2** : a person who deals in spells and necromancy **3** : a charm used in voodoo; *also* : [2]SPELL 1 — **voodoo** *adj*

voo·doo·ism \-ˌi-zəm\ *n* **1** : VOODOO 1 **2** : the practice of witchcraft

vo·ra·cious \vȯ-ˈrā-shəs, və-\ *adj* **1** : having a huge appetite : RAVENOUS **2** : very eager ⟨a ~ reader⟩ ♦ ***Synonyms*** GLUTTONOUS, RAVENING, RAPACIOUS — **vo·ra·cious·ly** *adv* — **vo·ra·cious·ness** *n* — **vo·rac·i·ty** \-ˈra-sə-tē\ *n*

vor·tex \ˈvȯr-ˌteks\ *n, pl* **vor·ti·ces** \ˈvȯr-tə-ˌsēz\ *also* **vor·tex·es** \ˈvȯr-ˌtek-səz\ : WHIRLPOOL; *also* : something resembling a whirlpool

vo·ta·ry \ˈvō-tə-rē\ *n, pl* **-ries** **1** : ENTHUSIAST, DEVOTEE; *also* : a devoted adherent or admirer **2** : a devout or zealous worshiper

[1]**vote** \ˈvōt\ *n* [ME (Sc), fr. L *votum* vow, wish, fr. *vovēre* to vow] **1** : a choice or opinion of a person or body of persons expressed usu. by a ballot, spoken word, or raised hand; *also* : the ballot, word, or gesture used to express a choice or opinion **2** : the decision reached by voting **3** : the right of suffrage **4** : a group of voters with some common characteristics ⟨the big city ~⟩ — **vote·less** *adj*

[2]**vote** *vb* **vot·ed; vot·ing** **1** : to cast a vote **2** : to elect, decide, pass, defeat, grant, or make legal by a vote **3** : to declare by general agreement **4** : to offer as a suggestion : PROPOSE **5** : to cause to vote esp. in a given way — **vot·er** *n*

vo·tive \ˈvō-tiv\ *adj* : consisting of or expressing a vow, wish, or desire

votive candle *n* : a short thick candle used esp. as a prayer offering or for decoration

vou *abbr* voucher

vouch \ˈvau̇ch\ *vb* **1** : PROVE, SUBSTANTIATE **2** : to verify by examining documentary evidence **3** : to give a guarantee **4** : to supply supporting evidence or testimony; *also* : to give personal assurance

vouch·er \ˈvau̇-chər\ *n* **1** : an act of vouching **2** : one that vouches for another **3** : a documentary record of a business transaction **4** : a written affidavit or authorization **5** : a form indicating a credit against future purchases or expenditures

vouch·safe \vau̇ch-ˈsāf\ *vb* **vouch·safed; vouch·saf·ing** : to grant or give as or as if a privilege or a special favor

[1]**vow** \ˈvau̇\ *n* : a solemn promise or statement; *esp* : one by which a person is bound to an act, service, or condition ⟨marriage ~*s*⟩

[2]**vow** *vb* **1** : to make a vow or as a vow **2** : to bind or commit by a vow — **vow·er** *n*

vow·el \ˈvau̇(-ə)l\ *n* **1** : a speech sound produced without obstruction or friction in the mouth **2** : a letter representing such a sound

vox po·pu·li \ˈväks-ˈpä-pyə-ˌlī\ *n* [L, voice of the people] : popular sentiment

[1]**voy·age** \ˈvȯi-ij\ *n* [ME, *viage, veyage,* fr. AF *veiage,* fr. LL *viaticum,* fr. L, traveling money, fr. neut. of *viaticus* of a journey, fr. *via* way] : a journey esp. by water from one place or country to another

[2]**voyage** *vb* **voy·aged; voy·ag·ing** : to take or make a voyage — **voy·ag·er** *n*

voya·geur \ˌvȯi-ə-ˈzhər, ˌvwä-yä-\ *n* [CanF] : a person employed by a fur company to transport goods to and from remote stations esp. in the Canadian Northwest

voy·eur \vwä-ˈyər, vȯi-ˈər\ *n* **1** : one who obtains sexual pleasure from viewing esp. covertly the nudity or sexual activity of others **2** : an observer of the sordid — **voy·eur·ism** \-ˌi-zəm\ *n* — **voy·eur·is·tic** \ˌvwä-(ˌ)yər-ˈis-tik, ˌvȯi-ər-\ *adj*

VP *abbr* **1** verb phrase **2** vice president

VPN *n* VIRTUAL PRIVATE NETWORK

vs *abbr* **1** verse **2** versus

vss *abbr* **1** verses **2** versions

V/STOL *abbr* vertical or short takeoff and landing

Vt *or* **VT** *abbr* Vermont

VTOL *abbr* vertical takeoff and landing

VTR *abbr* videotape recorder

vul·ca·nize \ˈvəl-kə-ˌnīz\ *vb* **-nized; -niz·ing** : to treat rubber or rubberlike material chemically to give useful properties (as elasticity and strength)

Vulg *abbr* Vulgate

vul·gar \ˈvəl-gər\ *adj* [ME, fr. L *vulgaris* of the mob, vulgar, fr. *vulgus* mob, common people] **1** : VERNACULAR ⟨the ~ tongue⟩ **2** : of or relating to the common people : GENERAL, COMMON **3** : lacking cultivation or refinement : BOORISH; *also* : offensive to good taste or refined feelings ⟨~ language⟩ ♦ ***Synonyms*** GROSS, OBSCENE, RIBALD, DIRTY, INDECENT, PROFANE — **vul·gar·ly** *adv*

vul·gar·i·an \ˌvəl-ˈger-ē-ən\ *n* : a vulgar person

vul·gar·ism \ˈvəl-gə-ˌri-zəm\ *n* **1** : VULGARITY **2** : a word or expression originated or used chiefly by illiterate persons **3** : a coarse expression : OBSCENITY

vul·gar·i·ty \ˌvəl-ˈga-rə-tē\ *n, pl* **-ties 1** : something vulgar **2** : the quality or state of being vulgar

vul·gar·ize \ˈvəl-gə-ˌrīz\ *vb* **-ized; -iz·ing** : to make vulgar — **vul·gar·i·za·tion** \ˌvəl-gə-rə-ˈzā-shən\ *n* — **vul·gar·iz·er** \ˈvəl-gə-ˌrī-zər\ *n*

Vul·gate \ˈvəl-ˌgāt\ *n* [ML *vulgata,* fr. LL *vulgata editio* edition in general circulation] : a Latin version of the Bible used by the Roman Catholic Church

vul·ner·a·ble \ˈvəl-nə-rə-bəl\ *adj* **1** : capable of being wounded : susceptible to wounds **2** : open to attack **3** : liable to increased penalties in contract bridge — **vul·ner·a·bil·i·ty** \ˌvəl-nə-rə-ˈbi-lə-tē\ *n* — **vul·ner·a·bly** \ˈvəl-nə-rə-blē\ *adv*

vul·pine \ˈvəl-ˌpīn\ *adj* : of, relating to, or resembling a fox esp. in cunning ⟨~ charms⟩

vul·ture \ˈvəl-chər\ *n* **1** : any of various large birds (as a turkey vulture) related to the hawks, eagles, and falcons but having weaker claws and the head usu. naked and living chiefly on carrion **2** : a rapacious person

vul·va \ˈvəl-və\ *n, pl* **vul·vae** \-ˌvē\ [ME, fr. ML, fr. L *volva, vulva* womb, female genitals] : the external parts of the female genital organs — **vul·val** \ˈvəl-vəl\ *or* **vul·var** \-vər, -ˌvär\ *adj*

vv *abbr* **1** verses **2** vice versa

VX \ˈvē-ˈeks\ *n* : an extremely toxic chemical weapon

vying *pres part of* VIE

W

[1]**w** \ˈdə-bəl-(ˌ)yü\ *n, pl* **w's** *or* **ws** *often cap* : the 23d letter of the English alphabet

[2]**w** *abbr, often cap* **1** water **2** watt **3** week **4** weight **5** west; western **6** wide; width **7** wife **8** with

W *symbol* [G *Wolfram*] tungsten

WA *abbr* **1** Washington **2** Western Australia

wacky \ˈwa-kē\ *adj* **wack·i·er; -est** : ECCENTRIC, CRAZY

[1]**wad** \ˈwäd\ *n* **1** : a little mass, bundle, or tuft ⟨~*s* of clay⟩ **2** : a soft mass of usu. light fibrous material **3** : a pliable plug (as of felt) used to retain a powder charge (as in a cartridge) **4** : a considerable amount (as of money) **5** : a roll of paper money

[2]**wad** *vb* **wad·ded; wad·ding 1** : to push a wad into ⟨~ a gun⟩ **2** : to form into a wad **3** : to hold in by a wad ⟨~ a bullet in a gun⟩ **4** : to stuff or line with a wad : PAD

wad·ding \ˈwä-diŋ\ *n* **1** : WADS; *also* : material for making wads **2** : a soft mass or sheet of short loose fibers used for stuffing or padding

wad·dle \ˈwä-dᵊl\ *vb* **wad·dled; wad·dling** : to walk with short steps swaying from side to side like a duck — **waddle** *n*

wade \ˈwād\ *vb* **wad·ed; wad·ing** **1** : to step in or through a medium (as water) more resistant than air **2** : to move or go with difficulty or labor and often with determination ⟨~ through a dull book⟩ — **wad·able** *or* **wade·able** \ˈwā-də-bəl\ *adj* — **wade** *n*

wad·er \ˈwā-dər\ *n* **1** : one that wades **2** : SHOREBIRD; *also* : WADING BIRD **3** *pl* : a waterproof garment consisting of pants with attached boots for wading

wa·di \ˈwä-dē\ *n* [Ar *wādī*] : a streambed of southwest Asia and northern Africa that is dry except in the rainy season

wading bird *n* : any of an order of long-legged birds (as sandpipers, cranes, or herons) that wade in water in search of food

wa·fer \ˈwā-fər\ *n* **1** : a thin crisp cake or cracker **2** : a thin round piece of unleavened bread used in the Eucharist **3** : something (as a piece of candy) that resembles a wafer

1**waf·fle** \ˈwä-fəl\ *n* : a soft but crisped cake of batter cooked in a special hinged metal utensil (**waffle iron**)

2**waffle** *vb* **waf·fled; waf·fling** \-f(ə)liŋ\ : to speak or write in a vague or evasive manner ⟨*waffled* on important issues⟩

1**waft** \ˈwäft, ˈwaft\ *vb* : to cause to move or go lightly by or as if by the impulse of wind or waves

2**waft** *n* **1** : a slight breeze : PUFF **2** : the act of waving

1**wag** \ˈwag\ *vb* **wagged; wag·ging** **1** : to sway or swing shortly from side to side or to-and-fro ⟨the dog *wagged* his tail⟩ **2** : to move in chatter or gossip ⟨scandal caused tongues to ~⟩

2**wag** *n* : an act of wagging : a wagging movement

3**wag** *n* : WIT, JOKER

1**wage** \ˈwāj\ *n* **1** : payment for labor or services usu. according to contract **2** *pl* : RECOMPENSE, REWARD

2**wage** *vb* **waged; wag·ing** **1** : to engage in : CARRY ON ⟨~ a war⟩ **2** : to be in process of being waged

1**wa·ger** \ˈwā-jər\ *n* **1** : BET, STAKE **2** : something on which bets are laid : GAMBLE

2**wager** *vb* : BET — **wa·ger·er** *n*

wag·gish \ˈwa-gish\ *adj* **1** : resembling or characteristic of a wag : MISCHIEVOUS **2** : SPORTIVE, HUMOROUS

wag·gle \ˈwa-gəl\ *vb* **wag·gled; wag·gling** : to move backward and forward or from side to side : WAG — **waggle** *n*

wag·gon *chiefly Brit var of* WAGON

wag·on \ˈwa-gən\ *n* **1** : a 4-wheeled vehicle; *esp* : one drawn by animals and used for freight or merchandise **2** : PADDY WAGON **3** : a child's 4-wheeled cart **4** : STATION WAGON

wag·on·er \ˈwa-gə-nər\ *n* : the driver of a wagon

wag·on·ette \ˌwa-gə-ˈnet\ *n* : a light wagon with two facing seats along the sides behind a cross seat in front

wa·gon–lit \vä-gōⁿ-ˈlē\ *n, pl* **wagons–lits** *or* **wagon–lits** *same or* -ˈlēz\ [F, fr. *wagon* railroad car + *lit* bed] : a railroad sleeping car

wagon train *n* : a column of wagons traveling overland

wag·tail \ˈwag-ˌtāl\ *n* : any of various slender-bodied mostly Old World birds with a long tail that jerks up and down

wa·hi·ne \wä-ˈhē-nē, -ˌnā\ *n* **1** : a Polynesian woman **2** : a female surfer

wa·hoo \ˈwä-ˌhü\ *n, pl* **wahoos** : a large vigorous food and sport fish related to the mackerel and found in warm seas

waif \ˈwāf\ *n* **1** : something found without an owner and esp. by chance **2** : a stray person or animal; *esp* : a homeless child

wail \ˈwāl\ *vb* **1** : LAMENT, WEEP **2** : to make a sound suggestive of a mournful cry **3** : COMPLAIN — **wail** *n*

wail·ful \-fəl\ *adj* : SORROWFUL, MOURNFUL ♦ ***Synonyms*** MELANCHOLY, DOLEFUL, LUGUBRIOUS, LAMENTABLE, PLAINTIVE, WOEFUL — **wail·ful·ly** *adv*

wain \ˈwān\ *n* : a usu. large heavy farm wagon

wain·scot \ˈwān-skət, -ˌskōt, -ˌskät\ *n* **1** : a usu. paneled wooden lining of an interior wall of a room **2** : the lower part of an interior wall when finished differently from the rest — **wainscot** *vb*

wain·scot·ing *or* **wain·scot·ting** \-ˌskō-tiŋ, -ˌskä-, -skə-\ *n* : material for a wainscot; *also* : WAINSCOT

waist \ˈwāst\ *n* **1** : the narrowed part of the body between the chest and hips **2** : a part resembling the human waist esp. in narrowness or central position ⟨the ~ of a ship⟩ **3** : a garment or part of a garment (as a blouse or bodice) for the upper part of the body

waist·band \-ˌband\ *n* : a band (as on pants or a skirt) that fits around the waist

waist·coat \ˈwes-kət, ˈwāst-ˌkōt\ *n, chiefly Brit* : VEST 1

waist·line \ˈwāst-ˌlīn\ *n* **1** : a line around the waist at its narrowest part; *also* : the length of this **2** : the line at which the bodice and skirt of a dress meet

1**wait** \ˈwāt\ *vb* **1** : to remain inactive in readiness or expectation : AWAIT ⟨~ for orders⟩ **2** : to delay serving (a meal) **3** : to act as attendant or servant ⟨~ on customers⟩ **4** : to serve food and drinks to the people sitting at ⟨~ tables⟩ **5** : to be ready ⟨a letter ~*ing* for you⟩

2**wait** *n* **1** : a position of concealment usu. with intent to attack or surprise ⟨lie in ~⟩ **2** : an act or period of waiting

wait·er \ˈwā-tər\ *n* **1** : one that waits on another; *esp* : a person who waits tables **2** : TRAY

waiting game *n* : a strategy in which one or more participants withhold action in the hope of an opportunity for more effective action later

waiting room *n* : a room (as at a doctor's office) for the use of persons who are waiting

wait·per·son \ˈwāt-ˌpər-sən\ *n* : a waiter or waitress

wait·ress \ˈwā-trəs\ *n* : a woman who waits tables

waive \ˈwāv\ *vb* **waived; waiv·ing** [ME *weiven* to decline, reject, give up, fr. AF *waiver, gaiver,* fr. *waif* lost, stray] **1** : to give up claim to ⟨*waived* his right to a trial⟩ **2** : POSTPONE

waiv·er \ˈwā-vər\ *n* : the act of waiving right, claim, or privilege; *also* : a document containing a declaration of such an act

[1]**wake** \ˈwāk\ *vb* **woke** \ˈwōk\ *also* **waked** \ˈwākt\; **wo·ken** \ˈwō-kən\ *also* **waked** *or* **woke; wak·ing** **1** : to be or remain awake; *esp* : to keep watch (as over a corpse) **2** : AWAKE, AWAKEN ⟨the baby *woke* up early⟩

[2]**wake** *n* **1** : the state of being awake **2** : a watch held over the body of a dead person prior to burial

[3]**wake** *n* : the track left by a ship in the water; *also* : a track left behind

wake·board \ˈwāk-ˌbȯrd\ *n* : a short board with foot bindings on which a rider is towed by a motorboat across its wake — **wake·board·er** *n* — **wake·board·ing** *n*

wake·ful \ˈwāk-fəl\ *adj* : not sleeping or able to sleep : SLEEPLESS, ALERT — **wake·ful·ness** *n*

wak·en \ˈwā-kən\ *vb* : WAKE

wake–rob·in \ˈwāk-ˌrä-bən\ *n* : TRILLIUM

wak·ing \ˈwā-kiŋ\ *adj* : passed in a conscious or alert state ⟨every ∼ hour⟩

wale \ˈwāl\ *n* : a ridge esp. on cloth; *also* : the texture esp. of a fabric

[1]**walk** \ˈwȯk\ *vb* **1** : to move or cause to move on foot usu. at a natural unhurried gait ⟨∼ to town⟩ ⟨∼ a horse⟩ **2** : to pass over, through, or along by walking ⟨∼ the streets⟩ **3** : to perform or accomplish by walking ⟨∼ guard⟩ **4** : to follow a course of action or way of life ⟨∼ humbly in the sight of God⟩ **5** : WALK OUT **6** : to receive a base on balls; *also* : to give a base on balls to — **walk·er** *n*

[2]**walk** *n* **1** : a going on foot ⟨go for a ∼⟩ **2** : a place, path, or course for walking **3** : distance to be walked ⟨a quarter-mile ∼ from here⟩ **4** : manner of living : CONDUCT, BEHAVIOR **5** : social or economic status ⟨various ∼*s* of life⟩ **6** : manner of walking : GAIT; *esp* : a slow 4-beat gait of a horse **7** : BASE ON BALLS

walk·away \ˈwȯ-kə-ˌwā\ *n* : an easily won contest

walk·ie–talk·ie \ˌwȯ-kē-ˈtȯ-kē\ *n* : a small portable radio transmitting and receiving set

[1]**walk–in** \ˈwȯk-ˌin\ *adj* : large enough to be walked into ⟨a ∼ refrigerator⟩

[2]**walk–in** *n* **1** : an easy election victory **2** : one that walks in

walking papers *n pl* : DISMISSAL, DISCHARGE

walking stick *n* **1** : a stick used in walking **2** : STICK INSECT; *esp* : one of the U.S. and Canada

walk–on \ˈwȯk-ˌȯn, -ˌän\ *n* : a small part in a dramatic production

walk·out \-ˌau̇t\ *n* **1** : a labor strike **2** : the action of leaving a meeting or organization as an expression of disapproval

walk out *vb* **1** : to leave suddenly often as an expression of disapproval **2** : to go on strike

walk·over \-ˌō-vər\ *n* : a one-sided contest : an easy victory

walk–up \ˈwȯk-ˌəp\ *n* : a building or apartment house without an elevator — **walk–up** *adj*

walk·way \-ˌwā\ *n* : a passage for walking

[1]**wall** \ˈwȯl\ *n* [ME, fr. OE *weall,* fr. L *vallum* rampart, fr. *vallus* stake, palisade] **1** : a structure (as of stone or brick) intended for defense or security or for enclosing something **2** : one of the upright enclosing parts of a building or room **3** : the inside surface of a cavity or container ⟨the ∼ of a boiler⟩ **4** : something like a wall in appearance, function, or effect ⟨a tariff ∼⟩ — **walled** \ˈwȯld\ *adj*

[2]**wall** *vb* **1** : to provide, separate, or surround with or as if with a wall ⟨∼ in a garden⟩ **2** : to close (an opening) with or as if with a wall ⟨∼ up a door⟩

wal·la·by \ˈwä-lə-bē\ *n, pl* **wallabies** *also* **wallaby** : any of various small or medium-sized kangaroos

wall·board \ˈwȯl-ˌbȯrd\ *n* : a structural material (as of wood pulp or plaster) made in large sheets and used for sheathing interior walls and ceilings

wal·let \ˈwä-lət\ *n* **1** : a bag or sack for carrying things on a journey **2** : a pocketbook with compartments (as for personal papers and usu. unfolded money) : BILLFOLD

wall·eye \ˈwȯl-ˌī\ *n* **1** : an eye with a whitish iris or an opaque white cornea **2** : a large vigorous No. American food and sport fish related to the perches — **wall-eyed** \-ˌlīd\ *adj*

wall·flow·er \ˈwȯl-ˌflau̇(-ə)r\ *n* **1** : any of several Old World herbs related to the mustards; *esp* : one with showy fragrant flowers **2** : a person who usu. from shyness or unpopularity remains alone (as at a dance)

Wal·loon \wä-ˈlün\ *n* : a member of a people of southern and southeastern Belgium and adjacent parts of France — **Walloon** *adj*

[1]**wal·lop** \ˈwä-ləp\ *vb* **1** : to beat soundly : TROUNCE **2** : to hit hard : SOCK ♦ ***Synonyms*** BATTER, BEAT, LAMBASTE, POUND, PUMMEL, THRASH

[2]**wallop** *n* **1** : a powerful blow or impact **2** : the ability to hit hard **3** : emotional, sensory, or psychological force : IMPACT ⟨a story with a ∼⟩

wal·lop·ing \ˈwä-lə-piŋ\ *adj* **1** : LARGE, WHOPPING ⟨a ∼ storm⟩ **2** : exceptionally fine or impressive ⟨a ∼ fun party⟩

[1]**wal·low** \ˈwä-lō\ *vb* **1** : to roll oneself about sluggishly in or as if in deep mud ⟨hogs ∼*ing* in the mire⟩ **2** : to indulge oneself excessively ⟨∼ in luxury⟩ **3** : to become or remain helpless ⟨∼ in ignorance⟩ ♦ ***Synonyms*** BASK, INDULGE, LUXURIATE, REVEL, WELTER

[2]**wallow** *n* : a muddy or dust-filled area where animals wallow

wall·pa·per \ˈwȯl-ˌpā-pər\ *n* **1** : decorative paper for the walls of a room **2** : the background image or set of images displayed on a computer screen — **wallpaper** *vb*

wall–to–wall *adj* **1** : covering the entire floor ⟨*wall-to-wall* carpeting⟩ **2** : covering or filling one entire space or time ⟨crowds of *wall-to-wall* people⟩

wal·nut \ˈwȯl-(ˌ)nət\ *n* [ME *walnot,* fr. OE *wealhhnutu,* lit., foreign nut, fr. *Wealh* Welshman, foreigner + *hnutu* nut] **1** : a nut with a furrowed usu. rough shell and an adherent husk from any of a genus of trees related to the hickories; *esp* : the large edible nut of a Eurasian tree **2** : a tree that bears walnuts **3** : the usu. reddish to dark brown wood of a walnut used esp. in cabinetwork and veneers

wal·rus \ˈwȯl-rəs, ˈwäl-\ *n, pl* **walrus** *or* **wal·rus·es** : a large mammal of arctic waters that is related to the seals and has long ivory tusks

¹**waltz** \ˈwȯlts\ *n* [G *Walzer,* fr. *walzen* to turn from one side to another, roll] **1** : a gliding dance done to music having three beats to the measure **2** : music for or suitable for waltzing

²**waltz** *vb* **1** : to dance a waltz **2** : to move or advance easily, successfully, or conspicuously ⟨he ~*ed* off with the championship⟩ — **waltz·er** *n*

wam·ble \ˈwäm-bəl\ *vb* **wam·bled; wam·bling** : to progress unsteadily or with a lurching shambling gait

Wam·pa·no·ag \ˌwäm-pə-ˈnō-(ˌ)ag; ˌwȯm-\ *n, pl* **Wampanoag** *or* **Wampanoags** [Narragansett, lit., easterners] : a member of an Indigenous people of parts of Rhode Island and Massachusetts

wam·pum \ˈwäm-pəm\ *n* [short for *wampumpeag,* fr. Massachuset (an Algonquian language) *wampompeag,* fr. *wampan* white + *api* string + *-ag,* pl. suffix] **1** : beads made of shells strung in strands, belts, or sashes and used by No. American Indigenous people as money and ornaments **2** *slang* : MONEY

wan \ˈwän\ *adj* **wan·ner; wan·nest** **1** : SICKLY, PALLID; *also* : FEEBLE **2** : DIM, FAINT **3** : LANGUID ⟨a ~ smile⟩ ♦ ***Synonyms*** ASHEN, BLANCHED, DOUGHY, LIVID, PALE, WAXEN — **wan·ly** *adv* — **wan·ness** *n*

wand \ˈwänd\ *n* **1** : a slender staff carried in a procession **2** : the staff of a fairy, diviner, or magician

wan·der \ˈwän-dər\ *vb* **1** : to move about aimlessly or without a fixed course or goal : RAMBLE **2** : to go astray in conduct or thought; *esp* : to become delirious ♦ ***Synonyms*** GAD, GALLIVANT, MEANDER, RANGE, ROAM, ROVE — **wan·der·er** *n*

wandering Jew *n* : either of two trailing or creeping plants cultivated for their showy and often white-striped foliage

wan·der·lust \ˈwän-dər-ˌləst\ *n* : strong longing for or impulse toward wandering

¹**wane** \ˈwān\ *vb* **waned; wan·ing** **1** : to grow gradually smaller or less ⟨the full moon ~*s* to new⟩ ⟨his strength *waned*⟩ **2** : to lose power, prosperity, or influence **3** : to draw near an end ⟨summer is *waning*⟩ ♦ ***Synonyms*** ABATE, EBB, MODERATE, RELENT, SLACKEN, SUBSIDE

²**wane** *n* : a waning (as in size or power); *also* : a period in which something is waning

wan·gle \ˈwaŋ-gəl\ *vb* **wan·gled; wan·gling** **1** : to obtain by sly or devious means; *also* : to use trickery or questionable means to achieve an end **2** : MANIPULATE; *also* : FINAGLE

wan·na–be *also* **wan·na·bee** \ˈwä-nə-ˌbē\ *n* : a person who wants or aspires to be someone or something else or who tries to look or act like someone else

¹**want** \ˈwȯnt, ˈwänt\ *vb* **1** : to fail to possess : LACK ⟨they ~ the necessities of life⟩ **2** : to feel or suffer the need of **3** : NEED, REQUIRE ⟨the house ~*s* painting⟩ **4** : to desire earnestly : WISH

²**want** *n* **1** : a lack of a required or usual amount : SHORTAGE **2** : dire need : DESTITUTION **3** : something wanted : DESIRE **4** : personal defect : FAULT

¹**want·ing** \ˈwȯn-tiŋ, ˈwän-\ *adj* **1** : not present or in evidence : ABSENT **2** : falling below standards or expectations **3** : lacking in ability or capacity : DEFICIENT ⟨~ in common sense⟩

²**wanting** *prep* **1** : LESS, MINUS ⟨a month ~ two days⟩ **2** : WITHOUT ⟨a book ~ a cover⟩

¹**wan·ton** \ˈwȯn-tᵊn, ˈwän-\ *adj* [ME, undisciplined, fr. *wan-* deficient, wrong + *towen,* pp. of *teen* to draw, train, discipline] **1** : UNCHASTE, LEWD, LUSTFUL; *also* : SENSUAL **2** : having no regard for justice or for other persons' feelings, rights, or safety : MERCILESS, INHUMANE ⟨~ cruelty⟩ **3** : having no just cause ⟨a ~ attack⟩ — **wan·ton·ly** *adv* — **wan·ton·ness** *n*

²**wanton** *n* : a wanton individual; *esp* : a lewd or immoral person

³**wanton** *vb* **1** : to be wanton : act wantonly **2** : to pass or waste wantonly

wa·pi·ti \ˈwä-pə-tē\ *n, pl* **wapiti** *or* **wapitis** : ELK 2

¹**war** \ˈwȯr\ *n* **1** : a state or period of usu. open and declared armed fighting between states or nations **2** : the art or science of warfare **3** : a state of hostility, conflict, or antagonism **4** : a struggle between opposing forces or for a particular end ⟨~ against disease⟩ — **war·less** \-ləs\ *adj*

²**war** *vb* **warred; war·ring** : to engage in warfare : be in conflict

³**war** *abbr* warrant

¹**war·ble** \ˈwȯr-bəl\ *n* **1** : a melodious succession of low pleasing sounds **2** : a musical trill

²**warble** *vb* **war·bled; war·bling** **1** : to sing or utter in a trilling manner or with variations **2** : to express by or as if by warbling

³**warble** *n* : a swelling under the skin esp. of the back of cattle, horses, and wild

mammals caused by the maggot of a fly (**warble fly**); *also* : its maggot

war·bler \ˈwȯr-blər\ *n* **1** : SONGSTER **2** : any of various small slender-billed chiefly Old World songbirds related to the thrushes and noted for their singing **3** : any of numerous small bright-colored insect-eating American birds with a usu. weak and unmusical song

war·bon·net \ˈwȯr-ˌbä-nət\ *n* : a feathered ceremonial headdress worn mainly by Indigenous People of the Great Plains

war crime *n* : a crime (as genocide) committed during or in connection with war

war cry *n* **1** : a cry used by fighters in war **2** : a slogan used esp. to rally people to a cause

[1]**ward** \ˈwȯrd\ *n* **1** : a guarding or being under guard or guardianship; *esp* : CUSTODY **2** : a body of guards **3** : a division of a prison **4** : a division in a hospital **5** : a division of a city for electoral or administrative purposes **6** : a person (as a child) under the protection of a guardian or a law court **7** : a person or body of persons under the protection or tutelage of a government **8** : a means of defense : PROTECTION

[2]**ward** *vb* : to turn aside : DEFLECT — usu. used with *off* ⟨~ off a blow⟩

[1]**-ward** *also* **-wards** *adj suffix* **1** : that moves, tends, faces, or is directed toward ⟨wind*ward*⟩ **2** : that occurs or is situated in the direction of ⟨sea*ward*⟩

[2]**-ward** *or* **-wards** *adv suffix* **1** : in a (specified) direction ⟨up*wards*⟩ ⟨after*ward*⟩ **2** : toward a (specified) point, position, or area ⟨sky*ward*⟩

war dance *n* : a dance performed by members of tribal societies before going to war or in celebration of victory

war·den \ˈwȯr-dᵊn\ *n* **1** : GUARDIAN, KEEPER **2** : the governor of a town, district, or fortress **3** : an official charged with special supervisory or enforcement duties ⟨game ~⟩ ⟨air raid ~⟩ **4** : an official in charge of the operation of a prison **5** : one of two ranking lay officers of an Episcopal parish **6** : any of various British college officials

ward·er \ˈwȯr-dər\ *n* : WATCHMAN, WARDEN

ward heel·er \-ˌhē-lər\ *n* : a local worker for a political boss

ward·robe \ˈwȯr-ˌdrōb\ *n* [ME *warderobe,* fr. AF **warderobe, garderobe,* fr. *warder, garder* to guard + *robe* robe] **1** *chiefly Brit* : a room or closet where clothes are kept **2** : CLOTHESPRESS; *esp* : a tall freestanding cabinet with a rod for hanging clothes **3** : a collection of wearing apparel ⟨his summer ~⟩

ward·room \-ˌdrüm, -ˌdrům\ *n* : the dining area for officers aboard a warship

ward·ship \ˈwȯrd-ˌship\ *n* **1** : GUARDIANSHIP **2** : the state of being under care of a guardian

ware \ˈwer\ *n* **1** : manufactured articles or products of art or craft : GOODS ⟨glass*ware*⟩ **2** : an article of merchandise ⟨a peddler hawking his ~*s*⟩ **3** : items (as dishes) of fired clay : POTTERY

ware·house \-ˌhau̇s\ *n* : a place for the storage of merchandise or commodities : STOREHOUSE — **warehouse** *vb* — **ware·house·man** \-mən\ *n* — **ware·hous·er** \-ˌhau̇-zər, -sər\ *n*

ware·room \ˈwer-ˌrüm, -ˌrům\ *n* : a room in which goods are exhibited for sale

war·fare \ˈwȯr-ˌfer\ *n* **1** : military operations between enemies : WAR; *also* : an activity undertaken by one country to weaken or destroy another ⟨economic ~⟩ **2** : STRUGGLE, CONFLICT

war·fa·rin \ˈwȯr-fə-rən\ *n* : an anticoagulant compound used as a rodent poison and in medicine

war·head \ˈwȯr-ˌhed\ *n* : the section of a missile containing the charge

war·horse \-ˌhȯrs\ *n* **1** : a horse for use in war **2** : a veteran soldier or public person (as a politician) **3** : a musical composition that is often performed

war·like \-ˌlīk\ *adj* **1** : fond of war ⟨~ peoples⟩ **2** : of, relating to, or useful in war : MILITARY, MARTIAL ⟨~ supplies⟩ **3** : befitting or characteristic of war or of soldiers ⟨~ attitudes⟩

war·lock \-ˌläk\ *n* [ME *warloghe,* fr. OE *wǣrloga* one that breaks faith, the Devil, fr. *wǣr* faith, troth + *-loga* (fr. *lēogan* to lie)] : SORCERER, WIZARD

war·lord \-ˌlȯrd\ *n* **1** : a high military leader **2** : a military commander exercising local civil power by force ⟨former Chinese ~*s*⟩

[1]**warm** \ˈwȯrm\ *adj* **1** : having or giving out heat to a moderate or adequate degree ⟨~ milk⟩ ⟨a ~ stove⟩ **2** : serving to retain heat ⟨~ clothes⟩ **3** : feeling or inducing sensations of heat ⟨~ from exercise⟩ ⟨a ~ climb⟩ **4** : showing or marked by strong feeling : ARDENT ⟨~ support⟩ **5** : marked by tense excitement or hot anger ⟨a ~ campaign⟩ **6** : giving a pleasant impression of warmth, cheerfulness, or friendliness ⟨~ colors⟩ ⟨a ~ tone of voice⟩ **7** : marked by or tending toward injury, distress, or pain ⟨made things ~ for the enemy⟩ **8** : newly made : FRESH ⟨a ~ scent⟩ **9** : near to a goal ⟨getting ~ in a search⟩ — **warm·ly** *adv*

[2]**warm** *vb* **1** : to make or become warm **2** : to give a feeling of warmth or vitality to **3** : to experience feelings of affection or pleasure ⟨she ~*ed* to her guest⟩ **4** : to reheat for eating ⟨~*ed* over the roast⟩ **5** : to make ready for operation or performance by preliminary exercise or operation ⟨~ up the motor⟩ **6** : to become increasingly ardent, interested, or competent ⟨the speaker ~*ed* to his topic⟩ — **warm·er** *n*

warm–blood·ed \-ˈblə-dəd\ *adj* : able to maintain a relatively high and constant body temperature relatively independent of that of the surroundings

warmed–over \ˈwȯrmd-ˈō-vər\ *adj* **1** : REHEATED ⟨~ cabbage⟩ **2** : not fresh or new ⟨~ ideas⟩

warm front *n* : an advancing edge of a warm air mass

warm·heart·ed \ˈwȯrm-ˈhär-təd\ *adj*

: marked by warmth of feeling : CORDIAL — **warm·heart·ed·ness** *n*

warming pan *n* : a long-handled covered pan filled with live coals and formerly used to warm a bed

war·mon·ger \ˈwȯr-ˌməŋ-gər, -ˌmäŋ-\ *n* : one who urges or attempts to stir up war — **war·mon·ger·ing** \-g(ə-)riŋ\ *n*

warmth \ˈwȯrmth\ *n* **1** : the quality or state of being warm **2** : ZEAL, ARDOR, FERVOR

warm up *vb* : to engage in exercise or practice esp. before entering a game or contest — **warm–up** \ˈwȯrm-ˌəp\ *n*

warn \ˈwȯrn\ *vb* **1** : to put on guard : CAUTION; *also* : ADMONISH, COUNSEL **2** : to notify esp. in advance : INFORM **3** : to order to go or keep away

[1]**warn·ing** \ˈwȯr-niŋ\ *n* **1** : the act of warning : the state of being warned **2** : something that warns or serves to warn ⟨a tornado ~⟩

[2]**warning** *adj* : serving as an alarm, signal, summons, or admonition ⟨a ~ bell⟩ — **warn·ing·ly** *adv*

[1]**warp** \ˈwȯrp\ *n* **1** : the lengthwise threads on a loom or in a woven fabric **2** : a twist out of a true plane or straight line ⟨a ~ in a board⟩

[2]**warp** *vb* [ME, fr. OE *weorpan* to throw] **1** : to turn or twist out of shape; *also* : to become so twisted **2** : to lead astray : PERVERT; *also* : FALSIFY, DISTORT

war paint *n* : paint put on the face and body by American Indigenous communities as a sign of going to war

war·path \ˈwȯr-ˌpath, -ˌpäth\ *n* : the course taken by a party of Indigenous warriors going on a hostile expedition — **on the warpath** : ready to fight or argue

war·plane \-ˌplān\ *n* : a military airplane; *esp* : one armed for combat

warp speed *n* : the highest possible speed

[1]**war·rant** \ˈwȯr-ənt, ˈwär-\ *n* **1** : AUTHORIZATION; *also* : JUSTIFICATION, GROUND **2** : evidence (as a document) of authorization; *esp* : a legal writ authorizing an officer to take action (as in making an arrest, seizure, or search) **3** : a certificate of appointment issued to an officer of lower rank than a commissioned officer

[2]**warrant** *vb* **1** : to guarantee security or immunity to : SECURE **2** : to declare or maintain positively ⟨I ~ this is so⟩ **3** : to assure (a person) of the truth of what is said **4** : to guarantee to be as it appears or as it is represented ⟨~ goods as of the first quality⟩ **5** : SANCTION, AUTHORIZE **6** : to give proof of : ATTEST; *also* : GUARANTEE **7** : JUSTIFY ⟨his need ~*s* the expenditure⟩

warrant officer *n* **1** : an officer in the armed forces ranking next below a commissioned officer **2** : a commissioned officer ranking below an ensign in the navy or coast guard and below a second lieutenant in the marine corps

war·ran·ty \ˈwȯr-ən-tē, ˈwär-\ *n, pl* **-ties** : an expressed or implied statement that some situation or thing is as it appears to be or is represented to be; *esp* : a usu. written guarantee of the integrity of a product and of the maker's responsibility for the repair or replacement of defective parts

war·ren \ˈwȯr-ən, ˈwär-\ *n* **1** : an area where rabbits breed; *also* : a structure where rabbits are bred or kept **2** : a crowded tenement or district

war·rior \ˈwȯr-yər; ˈwȯr-ē-ər, ˈwär-\ *n* : a person engaged or experienced in warfare

war·ship \ˈwȯr-ˌship\ *n* : a naval vessel

wart \ˈwȯrt\ *n* **1** : a small usu. horny projecting growth on the skin; *esp* : one caused by a virus **2** : a protuberance resembling a wart (as on a plant) — **warty** *adj*

wart·hog \ˈwȯrt-ˌhȯg, -ˌhäg\ *n* : a wild African hog that has large tusks and in the male two pairs of rough warty protuberances below the eyes

war·time \ˈwȯr-ˌtīm\ *n* : a period during which a war is in progress

wary \ˈwer-ē\ *adj* **war·i·er; -est** : very cautious; *esp* : careful in guarding against danger or deception — **war·i·ly** \ˈwer-ə-lē\ *adv* — **war·i·ness** \ˈwer-ē-nəs\ *n*

was *past 1st & 3d sing of* BE

wa·sa·bi \ˈwä-sə-bē; wä-ˈsä-\ *n* [Jp] : a condiment prepared from the ground greenish root of an Asian herb and similar in flavor and use to horseradish; *also* : the herb or its root

[1]**wash** \ˈwȯsh, ˈwäsh\ *vb* **1** : to clean with water and usu. soap or detergent ⟨~ clothes⟩ ⟨~ your hands⟩ **2** : to wet thoroughly : DRENCH **3** : to flow along the border of ⟨waves ~ the shore⟩ **4** : to pour or flow in a stream or current **5** : to move or remove by or as if by the action of water **6** : to cover or daub lightly with a liquid (as whitewash) **7** : to run water over (as gravel or ore) in order to separate valuable matter from refuse ⟨~ sand for gold⟩ **8** : to undergo laundering ⟨a dress that doesn't ~ well⟩ **9** : to stand a test ⟨that story will not ~⟩ **10** : to be worn away by water

[2]**wash** *n* **1** : the act or process or an instance of washing or being washed **2** : articles to be washed or being washed **3** : a thin coat of paint (as watercolor) **4** : the flow or action of a mass of water (as a wave) **5** : worthless esp. liquid waste : REFUSE, SWILL **6** : erosion by waves (as of the sea) **7** : a disturbance in a fluid (as water or the air) caused by the passage of a wing or propeller **8** *West* : the dry bed of a stream

[3]**wash** *adj* : WASHABLE

Wash *abbr* Washington

wash·able \ˈwȯ-shə-bəl, ˈwä-\ *adj* : capable of being washed without damage — **wash·abil·i·ty** \ˌwȯ-shə-ˈbi-lə-tē, ˌwä-\ *n*

wash–and–wear *adj* : of, relating to, or being a fabric or garment that needs little or no ironing after washing

wash·ba·sin \ˈwȯsh-ˌbā-sᵊn, ˈwäsh-\ *n* : WASHBOWL

wash·board \-ˌbȯrd\ *n* : a grooved board to scrub clothes on

wash·bowl \-ˌbōl\ *n* : a large bowl for water for washing hands and face

wash·cloth \-ˌklȯth\ *n* : a cloth used for washing one's face and body

washed–out \ˈwȯsht-ˈau̇t, ˈwäsht-\ *adj* **1** : faded in color **2** : EXHAUSTED ⟨felt ~ after working all night⟩

washed–up \-ˈəp\ *adj* : no longer successful, popular, skillful, or needed

wash·er \ˈwȯ-shər, ˈwä-\ *n* **1** : a ring or perforated plate used around a bolt or screw to ensure tightness or relieve friction **2** : one that washes; *esp* : a machine for washing

wash·er·wom·an \-ˌwu̇-mən\ *n* : a woman whose occupation is washing clothes

wash·ing \ˈwȯ-shiŋ, ˈwä-\ *n* **1** : material obtained by washing **2** : articles washed or to be washed

washing soda *n* : SODIUM CARBONATE

Wash·ing·ton's Birthday \ˈwȯ-shiŋ-tənz-, ˈwä-\ *n* : the 3d Monday in February observed as a legal holiday

wash·out \ˈwȯsh-ˌau̇t, ˈwäsh-\ *n* **1** : the washing away of earth (as from a road); *also* : a place where earth is washed away **2** : a complete failure

wash·room \-ˌrüm, -ˌru̇m\ *n* : BATHROOM

wash·stand \-ˌstand\ *n* **1** : a stand holding articles needed for washing face and hands **2** : LAVATORY 1

wash·tub \-ˌtəb\ *n* : a tub for washing or soaking clothes

wash·wom·an \ˈwȯsh-ˌwu̇-mən, ˈwäsh-\ *n* : WASHERWOMAN

washy \ˈwȯ-shē, ˈwä-\ *adj* **wash·i·er; -est 1** : WEAK, WATERY **2** : PALLID ⟨a ~ yellow⟩ **3** : lacking in vigor, individuality, or definiteness

wasp \ˈwäsp, ˈwȯsp\ *n* : any of numerous social or solitary winged insects related to the bees and ants with biting mouthparts and in females and workers an often formidable sting

WASP *or* **Wasp** *n* [*w*hite *A*nglo-*S*axon *P*rotestant] *sometimes disparaging* : an American of northern European and esp. British ancestry and of Protestant background

wasp·ish \ˈwäs-pish, ˈwȯs-\ *adj* **1** : SNAPPISH, IRRITABLE ⟨a ~ temper⟩ **2** : resembling a wasp in form; *esp* : slightly built ♦ ***Synonyms*** FRACTIOUS, FRETFUL, HUFFY, PEEVISH, PETULANT, QUERULOUS

wasp waist *n* : a very slender waist

[1]**was·sail** \ˈwä-səl, wä-ˈsāl\ *n* [ME *wæs hæil, washayl,* fr. ON *ves heill* be well] **1** : an early English toast to someone's health **2** : a hot drink made with wine, beer, or cider, spices, sugar, and usu. baked apples and traditionally served at Christmas **3** : riotous drinking : REVELRY

[2]**wassail** *vb* **1** : CAROUSE **2** : to drink to the health of — **was·sail·er** *n*

Was·ser·mann test \ˈwä-sər-mən-, ˈvä-\ *n* : a blood test for the detection of syphilis

wast·age \ˈwā-stij\ *n* : WASTE 3

[1]**waste** \ˈwāst\ *n* **1** : a sparsely settled or barren region : DESERT; *also* : uncultivated land **2** : the act or an instance of wasting : the state of being wasted **3** : gradual loss or decrease by use, wear, or decay **4** : material left over, rejected, or thrown away; *also* : an unwanted by-product of a manufacturing or chemical process **5** : refuse (as garbage) that accumulates about habitations **6** : material (as feces) produced but not used by a living organism — **waste·ful** \-fəl\ *adj* — **waste·ful·ly** *adv* — **waste·ful·ness** *n*

[2]**waste** *vb* **wast·ed; wast·ing 1** : DEVASTATE **2** : to wear away or diminish gradually : CONSUME **3** : to spend or use carelessly or uselessly : SQUANDER **4** : to lose or cause to lose weight, strength, or energy ⟨*wasting* away from fever⟩ **5** : to become diminished in bulk or substance : DWINDLE ♦ ***Synonyms*** DEPREDATE, DESOLATE, DESPOIL, RAVAGE, SPOIL, STRIP — **wast·er** *n*

[3]**waste** *adj* **1** : being wild and uninhabited : BARREN, DESOLATE; *also* : UNCULTIVATED **2** : being in a ruined condition **3** : discarded as worthless after being used ⟨~ water⟩ **4** : excreted from or stored in inert form in a living organism as a by-product of vital activity ⟨~ matter from birds⟩

waste·bas·ket \ˈwāst-ˌbas-kət\ *n* : a receptacle for refuse

waste·land \-ˌland, -lənd\ *n* : land that is barren or unfit for cultivation

waste·pa·per \-ˈpā-pər\ *n* : paper thrown away as used, not needed, or not fit for use

wast·rel \ˈwā-strəl\ *n* : a person who wastes resources : SPENDTHRIFT

[1]**watch** \ˈwäch, ˈwȯch\ *vb* **1** : to be or stay awake intentionally : keep vigil ⟨~*ed* by the patient's bedside⟩ ⟨~ and pray⟩ **2** : to be on the lookout for danger : be on one's guard **3** : to keep guard ⟨~ outside the door⟩ **4** : OBSERVE ⟨~ a game⟩ **5** : to keep in view so as to prevent harm or warn of danger ⟨~ a brush fire carefully⟩ **6** : to keep oneself informed about ⟨~ his progress⟩ **7** : to lie in wait for esp. so as to take advantage of ⟨~*ed* her opportunity⟩ — **watch·er** *n*

[2]**watch** *n* **1** : the act of keeping awake to guard, protect, or attend; *also* : a state of alert and continuous attention **2** : a public weather alert ⟨a winter storm ~⟩ **3** : close observation **4** : LOOKOUT, WATCHMAN, GUARD **5** : a period during which a part of a ship's crew is on duty; *also* : the part of a crew on duty during a watch **6** : a portable timepiece carried on the person

watch·band \ˈwäch-ˌband, ˈwȯch-\ *n* : the bracelet or strap of a wristwatch

watch·dog \-ˌdȯg\ *n* **1** : a dog kept to guard property **2** : one that guards or protects

watch·ful \-fəl\ *adj* : steadily attentive and alert esp. to danger : VIGILANT — **watch·ful·ly** *adv* — **watch·ful·ness** *n*

watch·mak·er \-ˌmā-kər\ *n* : a person who makes or repairs watches — **watch·mak·ing** \-ˌmā-kiŋ\ *n*

watch·man \-mən\ *n* : a person assigned to watch : GUARD
watch night *n* : a devotional service lasting until after midnight esp. on New Year's Eve
watch·tow·er \ˈwäch-ˌtau̇(-ə)r, ˈwȯch-\ *n* : a tower for a lookout
watch·word \-ˌwərd\ *n* **1** : a secret word used as a signal or sign of recognition **2** : a word or motto used as a slogan or rallying cry
[1]**wa·ter** \ˈwȯ-tər, ˈwä-\ *n* **1** : the liquid that descends as rain and forms rivers, lakes, and seas **2** : a natural mineral water — usu. used in pl. **3** *pl* : the water occupying or flowing in a particular bed; *also* : a band of seawater bordering on and under the control of a country **4** : any of various liquids containing or resembling water; *esp* : a watery fluid (as tears, urine, or sap) formed or circulating in a living organism **5** : a specified degree of thoroughness or completeness ⟨a scoundrel of the first ~⟩
[2]**water** *vb* **1** : to supply with or get or take water ⟨~ horses⟩ ⟨the ship ~*ed* at each port⟩ **2** : to treat (as cloth) so as to give a lustrous appearance in wavy lines **3** : to dilute by or as if by adding water to **4** : to form or secrete water or watery matter ⟨her eyes ~*ed*⟩ ⟨my mouth ~*ed*⟩
wa·ter·bed \ˈwȯ-tər-ˌbed, ˈwä-\ *n* : a bed whose mattress is a watertight bag filled with water
wa·ter·borne \-ˌbȯrn\ *adj* : supported, carried, or transmitted by water
water buffalo *n* : a common oxlike often domesticated Asian bovine
water chestnut *n* : a whitish crunchy vegetable used esp. in Chinese cooking that is the peeled tuber of a widely cultivated Asian sedge; *also* : the tuber or the sedge itself
water closet *n* : a compartment or room with a toilet bowl : BATHROOM; *also* : a toilet bowl along with its accessories
wa·ter·col·or \ˈwȯ-tər-ˌkə-lər, ˈwä-\ *n* **1** : a paint whose liquid part is water **2** : the art of painting with watercolors **3** : a picture made with watercolors
wa·ter·course \-ˌkȯrs\ *n* : a stream of water; *also* : the bed of a stream
wa·ter·craft \-ˌkraft\ *n* : a craft for water transport : SHIP, BOAT
wa·ter·cress \-ˌkres\ *n* : an aquatic perennial Eurasian cress that is naturalized in the U.S. and has edible leaves used esp. in salads
wa·ter·fall \-ˌfȯl\ *n* : a very steep descent of the water of a stream
wa·ter·fowl \ˈwȯ-tər-ˌfau̇(-ə)l, ˈwä-\ *n, pl* **-fowl** *also* **-fowls** : a bird that frequents water; *esp* : a swimming bird (as a duck) hunted as game
wa·ter·front \-ˌfrənt\ *n* : land or a section of a town fronting or abutting on a body of water
water gap *n* : a pass in a mountain ridge through which a stream runs
water glass *n* : a drinking glass
water hyacinth *n* : a showy floating aquatic plant of tropical America that often clogs waterways (as in the southern U.S.)
watering hole *n* : a place (as a bar) where people gather socially
watering place *n* : a resort that features mineral springs or bathing
water lily *n* : any of various aquatic plants with floating roundish leaves and showy solitary flowers
wa·ter·line \ˈwȯ-tər-ˌlīn, ˈwä-\ *n* : a line that marks the level of the surface of water on something (as a ship or the shore)
wa·ter·logged \-ˌlȯgd, -ˌlägd\ *adj* : so filled or soaked with water as to be heavy or unmanageable ⟨a ~ boat⟩
wa·ter·loo \ˌwȯ-tər-ˈlü, ˌwä-\ *n, pl* **-loos** [*Waterloo,* Belgium, scene of Napoleon's defeat in 1815] : a decisive or final defeat or setback
[1]**wa·ter·mark** \ˈwȯ-tər-ˌmärk, ˈwä-\ *n* **1** : a mark indicating height to which water has risen **2** : a marking in paper visible when the paper is held up to the light
[2]**watermark** *vb* : to mark (paper) with a watermark
wa·ter·mel·on \-ˌme-lən\ *n* : a large roundish or oblong fruit with sweet juicy usu. red pulp; *also* : a widely grown African vine related to the squashes that produces watermelons
water moccasin *n* : a venomous pit viper chiefly of the southeastern U.S. that is related to the copperhead
water ou·zel \-ˈü-zəl\ *n* : DIPPER 1
water park *n* : an amusement park with a pool and wetted slides
water pill *n* : DIURETIC
water pipe *n* : a pipe for smoking that has a long flexible tube whereby the smoke is cooled by passing through water
water pistol *n* : a toy pistol for squirting a jet of liquid
water polo *n* : a team game played in a swimming pool with a ball resembling a soccer ball
wa·ter·pow·er \ˈwȯ-tər-ˌpau̇(-ə)r, ˈwä-\ *n* : the power of moving water used to run machinery
[1]**wa·ter·proof** \ˈwȯ-tər-ˌprüf, ˈwä-\ *adj* : not letting water through; *esp* : covered or treated with a material to prevent permeation by water — **wa·ter·proof·ing** *n*
[2]**waterproof** *n* **1** : a waterproof fabric **2** *chiefly Brit* : RAINCOAT
[3]**waterproof** *vb* : to make waterproof
wa·ter–re·pel·lent \ˌwȯ-tər-ri-ˈpe-lənt, ˌwä-\ *adj* : treated with a finish that is resistant to water penetration
wa·ter–re·sis·tant \-ri-ˈzis-tənt\ *adj* : WATER-REPELLENT
wa·ter·shed \ˈwȯ-tər-ˌshed, ˈwä-\ *n* **1** : a dividing ridge between two drainage areas **2** : the region or area drained by a particular body of water
wa·ter·side \-ˌsīd\ *n* : the land bordering a body of water
water ski *n* : a ski used on water when the wearer is towed — **wa·ter–ski** *vb* — **wa·ter–ski·er** \-ˌskē-ər\ *n*
water snake *n* : any of various snakes

found in or near freshwater and feeding largely on aquatic animals

wa·ter·spout \ˈwȯ-tər-ˌspau̇t, ˈwä-\ *n* **1** : a pipe for carrying water from a roof **2** : a funnel-shaped cloud extending from a cloud down to a spray torn up by whirling winds from an ocean or lake

water strider *n* : any of various long-legged bugs that move about swiftly on the surface of water

water table *n* : the upper limit of the portion of the ground wholly saturated with water

wa·ter·tight \ˌwȯ-tər-ˈtīt, ˌwä-\ *adj* **1** : constructed so as to keep water out **2** : allowing no possibility for doubt or uncertainty ⟨a ~ case against the accused⟩

wa·ter·way \ˈwȯ-tər-ˌwā, ˈwä-\ *n* : a navigable body of water

wa·ter·wheel \-ˌhwēl, -ˌwēl\ *n* : a wheel made to turn by water flowing against it

water wings *n pl* : an air-filled device to give support to a person's body esp. when learning to swim

wa·ter·works \ˈwȯ-tər-ˌwərks, ˈwä-\ *n pl* : a system for supplying water (as to a city)

wa·tery \ˈwȯ-tə-rē, ˈwä-\ *adj* **1** : containing, full of, or giving out water ⟨~ clouds⟩ **2** : being like water : THIN, WEAK ⟨~ lemonade⟩; *also* : being soft and soggy ⟨~ turnips⟩

WATS \ˈwäts\ *abbr* Wide-Area Telecommunications Service

watt \ˈwät\ *n* [James *Watt* †1819 Scottish engineer and inventor] : the metric unit of power equal to the work done at the rate of one joule per second or to the power produced by a current of one ampere across a potential difference of one volt

watt·age \ˈwä-tij\ *n* : amount of power expressed in watts

wat·tle \ˈwä-tᵊl\ *n* **1** : a framework of rods with flexible branches or reeds interlaced used esp. formerly in building; *also* : material for this framework **2** : a naked fleshy process hanging usu. from the head or neck (as of a bird) — **wat·tled** \-tᵊld\ *adj*

W Aust *abbr* Western Australia

[1]**wave** \ˈwāv\ *vb* **waved; wav·ing** **1** : FLUTTER ⟨flags *waving* in the breeze⟩ **2** : to motion with the hands or with something held in them in signal or salute **3** : to become moved or brandished to-and-fro; *also* : BRANDISH, FLOURISH ⟨~ a sword⟩ **4** : to move before the wind with a wavelike motion ⟨fields of *waving* grain⟩ **5** : to curve up and down like a wave : UNDULATE

[2]**wave** *n* **1** : a moving ridge or swell on the surface of water **2** : a wavelike formation or shape ⟨a ~ in the hair⟩ **3** : the action or process of making wavy or curly **4** : a waving motion; *esp* : a signal made by waving something **5** : FLOW, GUSH ⟨a ~ of anger swept over her⟩ **6** : a peak of activity ⟨a ~ of selling⟩ **7** : a disturbance that transfers energy progressively from point to point in a medium ⟨light travels in ~*s*⟩ ⟨a sound ~⟩ **8** : a period of hot or cold weather — **wave·like** *adj*

wave·length \ˈwāv-ˌleŋth\ *n* **1** : the distance in the line of advance of a wave from any one point (as a crest) to the next corresponding point **2** : a line of thought that reveals a common understanding

wave·let \-lət\ *n* : a little wave : RIPPLE

wa·ver \ˈwā-vər\ *vb* **1** : to fluctuate in opinion, allegiance, or direction **2** : REEL, TOTTER; *also* : QUIVER, FLICKER ⟨~*ing* flames⟩ **3** : FALTER **4** : to give an unsteady sound : QUAVER ♦ ***Synonyms*** FALTER, HESITATE, SHILLY-SHALLY, VACILLATE — **waver** *n* — **wa·ver·er** *n* — **wa·ver·ing·ly** *adv*

wavy \ˈwā-vē\ *adj* **wav·i·er; -est** : having waves : moving in waves

[1]**wax** \ˈwaks\ *n* **1** : a yellowish plastic substance secreted by bees for constructing the honeycomb **2** : any of various substances like beeswax

[2]**wax** *vb* : to treat or rub with wax — **wax·er** *n*

[3]**wax** *vb* **1** : to increase in size, numbers, strength, volume, or duration **2** : to increase in apparent size ⟨the moon ~*es* toward the full⟩ **3** : to take on a quality or state : BECOME ⟨~*ed* indignant⟩

wax bean *n* : a kidney bean with pods that turn creamy yellow to bright yellow when mature enough to use as snap beans

wax·en \ˈwak-sən\ *adj* **1** : made of or covered with wax **2** : resembling wax (as in color or consistency)

wax museum *n* : a place where wax effigies are exhibited

wax myrtle *n* : any of a genus of shrubs or trees with aromatic leaves; *esp* : an evergreen shrub or small tree of the eastern U.S. that produces small hard berries with a thick coating of bluish-white wax used for candles

wax·wing \ˈwaks-ˌwiŋ\ *n* : any of a genus of chiefly brown to gray singing birds with a showy crest and red waxy material on the tips of some wing feathers

wax·work \-ˌwərk\ *n* **1** : an effigy usu. of a person in wax **2** *pl* : an exhibition of wax figures

waxy \ˈwak-sē\ *adj* **wax·i·er; -est** **1** : made of or full of wax **2** : WAXEN 2

way \ˈwā\ *n* **1** : a thoroughfare for travel or passage : ROAD, PATH, STREET **2** : ROUTE ⟨knew the ~ home⟩ **3** : a course of action ⟨chose the easy ~⟩; *also* : opportunity, capability, or fact of doing as one pleases ⟨always had your own ~⟩ **4** : a possible course : POSSIBILITY ⟨no two ~*s* about it⟩ **5** : METHOD, MODE ⟨this ~ of thinking⟩ ⟨a new ~ of painting⟩ **6** : FEATURE, RESPECT ⟨a good worker in many ~*s*⟩ **7** : the usual or characteristic state of affairs ⟨as is the ~ with old people⟩; *also* : individual characteristic or peculiarity ⟨used to her ~*s*⟩ **8** : DISTANCE ⟨a short ~ from here⟩ ⟨a long ~ from success⟩ **9** : progress along a course ⟨working my ~ through college⟩ **10** : something having direction : LOCALITY ⟨out our ~⟩ **11** : STATE, CONDITION ⟨the ~ things are⟩ **12** *pl* : an inclined structure upon which a ship is built or is supported in launching **13** : CATEGORY, KIND ⟨get what you need in the ~ of supplies⟩ **14** : motion or speed of a boat through the water — **by the way** : by way of interjection or digression — **by way of 1** : for the purpose of ⟨*by way of* illustration⟩ **2** : by the route through : VIA — **out of the way 1** : WRONG, IMPROPER **2** : SECLUDED, REMOTE

way·bill \ˈwā-ˌbil\ *n* : a paper that accompanies a freight shipment and gives details of goods, route, and charges

way·far·er \ˈwā-ˌfer-ər\ *n* : a traveler esp. on foot — **way·far·ing** \-ˌfer-iŋ\ *adj*

way·lay \ˈwā-ˌlā\ *vb* **-laid** \-ˌlād\; **-lay·ing 1** : to lie in wait for or attack from ambush **2** : to temporarily stop the movement or progress of

way–out \ˈwā-ˈau̇t\ *adj* : FAR-OUT

-ways *adv suffix* : in (such) a way, course, direction, or manner ⟨side*ways*⟩

ways and means *n pl* : methods and resources esp. for raising revenues needed by a state; *also* : a legislative committee concerned with this function

way·side \ˈwā-ˌsīd\ *n* : the side of or land adjacent to a road or path

way station *n* : an intermediate station on a line of travel (as a railroad)

way·ward \ˈwā-wərd\ *adj* [ME, short for *awayward* turned away, fr. *away*, adv. + *-ward* directed toward] **1** : following one's own capricious or wanton inclinations ⟨~ children⟩ **2** : UNPREDICTABLE, IRREGULAR ⟨a ~ act⟩

WBC *abbr* white blood cells

WC *abbr* **1** water closet **2** without charge

WCTU *abbr* Women's Christian Temperance Union

we \ˈwē\ *pron* **1** — used of a group that includes the speaker or writer **2** — used for the singular *I* by a monarch, editor, or writer

weak \ˈwēk\ *adj* **1** : lacking strength or vigor : FEEBLE **2** : not able to sustain or resist much weight, pressure, or strain **3** : deficient in vigor of mind or character; *also* : resulting from or indicative of such deficiency ⟨a ~ policy⟩ ⟨a ~ will⟩ **4** : not supported by truth or logic ⟨a ~ argument⟩ **5** : lacking skill or proficiency; *also* : indicative of a lack of skill or aptitude **6** : lacking vigor of expression or effect **7** : of less than usual strength ⟨~ tea⟩ **8** : not having or exerting authority ⟨~ government⟩; *also* : INEFFECTIVE, IMPOTENT ⟨~ measures to control crime⟩ **9** : of, relating to, or constituting a verb or verb conjugation that forms the past tense and past participle by adding *-ed* or *-d* or *-t* — **weak·ly** *adv*

weak·en \ˈwē-kən\ *vb* : to make or become weak ⟨bodies ~*ed* by hunger⟩ ♦ ***Synonyms*** ENFEEBLE, DEBILITATE, UNDERMINE, SAP, CRIPPLE, DISABLE

weak·fish \ˈwēk-ˌfish\ *n* [obs. D *weekvis*, fr. D *week* soft + *vis* fish] : a common marine fish of the Atlantic coast of the U.S. caught for food and sport; *also* : any of several related food fishes

weak force *n* : the physical force responsible for particle decay processes in radioactivity

weak–kneed \ˈwēk-ˈnēd\ *adj* : lacking willpower or resolution ⟨~ appeasers⟩

weak·ling \ˈwē-kliŋ\ *n* : a person who is physically, mentally, or morally weak

weak·ly \ˈwē-klē\ *adj* : FEEBLE, WEAK

weak·ness \ˈwēk-nəs\ *n* **1** : the quality or state of being weak; *also* : an instance or period of being weak ⟨in a moment of ~ he agreed to go⟩ **2** : FAULT, DEFECT **3** : an object of special desire or fondness ⟨chocolate is her ~⟩

[1]**weal** \ˈwēl\ *n* : WELL-BEING, PROSPERITY

[2]**weal** *n* : WELT

weald \ˈwēld\ *n* [The *Weald*, wooded district in England, fr. ME *Weeld*, fr. OE *weald* forest] **1** : FOREST **2** : WOLD

wealth \ˈwelth\ *n* [ME *welthe* welfare, prosperity, fr. *wele* weal] **1** : abundance of possessions or resources : AFFLUENCE, RICHES **2** : abundant supply : PROFUSION ⟨a ~ of detail⟩ **3** : all property that has a money or an exchange value; *also* : all objects or resources that have economic value ♦ ***Synonyms*** FORTUNE, PROPERTY, SUBSTANCE, WORTH

wealthy \ˈwel-thē\ *adj* **wealth·i·er**; **-est** : having wealth : RICH

wean \ˈwēn\ *vb* **1** : to accustom (a young mammal) to take food by means other than nursing **2** : to free from a source of dependence; *also* : to free from a usu. unwholesome habit or interest

weap·on \ˈwe-pən\ *n* **1** : something (as a gun, knife, or club) used to injure, defeat, or destroy **2** : a means of contending against another ⟨a ~ against cancer⟩ — **weap·on·less** \-ləs\ *adj*

weap·on·ry \-rē\ *n* : WEAPONS

[1]**wear** \ˈwear\ *vb* **wore** \ˈwȯr\; **worn** \ˈwȯrn\; **wear·ing 1** : to use as an article of clothing or adornment ⟨~ a coat⟩ ⟨~*s* earrings⟩; *also* : to carry on the person ⟨~ a gun⟩ **2** : EXHIBIT, PRESENT ⟨~ a smile⟩ **3** : to impair, diminish, or decay by use or by scraping or rubbing ⟨clothes *worn* to shreds⟩; *also* : to produce gradually by friction, rubbing, or wasting away ⟨~ a hole in the rug⟩ **4** : to exhaust or lessen the strength of : WEARY, FATIGUE ⟨*worn* by care and toil⟩ **5** : to endure use : last under use or the passage of time ⟨this cloth ~*s* well⟩ **6** : to diminish or fail with the passage of time ⟨the day ~*s* on⟩ ⟨the effect of the drug *wore* off⟩ **7** : to grow or become by attrition, use, or age ⟨the coin was *worn* thin⟩ — **wear·able** \ˈwer-ə-bəl\ *adj* — **wear·er** *n*

[2]**wear** *n* **1** : the act of wearing : the state of being worn ⟨clothes for everyday ~⟩ **2** : clothing usu. of a particular kind or for a special occasion or use ⟨children's ~⟩ **3** : wearing or lasting quality ⟨the coat still has lots of ~ in it⟩ **4** : the result

of wearing or use : impairment due to use ⟨the suit shows ~⟩
wear and tear *n* : the loss, injury, or stress to which something is subjected in the course of use; *esp* : normal depreciation
wear down *vb* : to weary and overcome by persistent resistance or pressure
wea·ri·some \ˈwir-ē-səm\ *adj* : causing weariness : TIRESOME — **wea·ri·some·ly** *adv* — **wea·ri·some·ness** *n*
wear out *vb* **1** : TIRE **2** : to make or become useless by wear
¹**wea·ry** \ˈwir-ē\ *adj* **wea·ri·er; -est** **1** : worn out in strength, energy, or freshness **2** : expressing or characteristic of weariness ⟨a ~ sigh⟩ **3** : having one's patience, tolerance, or pleasure exhausted ⟨~ of war⟩ — **wea·ri·ly** \ˈwir-ə-lē\ *adv* — **wea·ri·ness** \-ē-nəs\ *n*
²**weary** *vb* **wea·ried; wea·ry·ing** : to become or make weary : TIRE
¹**wea·sel** \ˈwē-zəl\ *n, pl* **weasels** : any of various small slender flesh-eating mammals related to the minks — **wea·sel·ly** *also* **wea·sely** \ˈwēz-lē, ˈwē-zə-lē\ *adj*
²**weasel** *vb* **wea·seled; wea·sel·ing** **1** : to use weasel words : EQUIVOCATE **2** : to escape from or evade a situation or obligation — often used with *out*
weasel word *n* [fr. the weasel's reputed habit of sucking the contents out of an egg while leaving the shell intact] : a word used to avoid a direct or forthright statement or position
¹**weath·er** \ˈwe-t͟hər\ *n* **1** : the state of the atmosphere with respect to heat or cold, wetness or dryness, calm or storm, clearness or cloudiness **2** : a particular and esp. a disagreeable atmospheric state : RAIN, STORM
²**weather** *vb* **1** : to expose to or endure the action of weather; *also* : to alter (as in color or texture) by such exposure **2** : to bear up against successfully ⟨~ a storm⟩ ⟨~ troubles⟩
³**weather** *adj* : WINDWARD
weath·er–beat·en \ˈwe-t͟hər-ˌbē-tᵊn\ *adj* : worn or damaged by exposure to the weather; *also* : toughened or tanned by the weather ⟨~ face⟩
weath·er·cock \-ˌkäk\ *n* : a weather vane shaped like a rooster
weath·er·ing \ˈwe-t͟hə-riŋ\ *n* : the action of the weather in altering the color, texture, composition, or form of exposed objects; *also* : alteration thus effected
weath·er·ize \ˈwe-t͟hə-ˌrīz\ *vb* **-ized; -iz·ing** : to make (as a house) better protected against winter weather (as by adding insulation)
weath·er·man \-ˌman\ *n* : one who reports and forecasts the weather : METEOROLOGIST
weath·er·per·son \-ˌpər-sən\ *n* : a person who reports and forecasts the weather : METEOROLOGIST
weath·er·proof \ˈwe-t͟hər-ˌprüf\ *adj* : able to withstand exposure to weather — **weatherproof** *vb*
weath·er·strip·ping \ˈwe-t͟hər-ˌstri-piŋ\ *n* : material used to seal a door or window at the edges — **weath·er–strip** *vb* — **weather strip** *n*
weather vane *n* : VANE 1
weath·er·worn \ˈwe-t͟hər-ˌwōrn\ *adj* : worn by exposure to the weather
¹**weave** \ˈwēv\ *vb* **wove** \ˈwōv\ *or* **weaved; wo·ven** \ˈwō-vən\ *or* **weaved; weav·ing** **1** : to form by interlacing strands of material; *esp* : to make on a loom by interlacing warp and filling threads ⟨~ cloth⟩ **2** : to interlace (as threads) into a fabric and esp. cloth **3** : SPIN 2 **4** : to make as if by weaving together parts **5** : to insert as a part : work in **6** : to move in a winding or zigzag course esp. to avoid obstacles ⟨we *wove* our way through the crowd⟩ — **weav·er** *n*
²**weave** *n* : something woven; *also* : a pattern or method of weaving ⟨a loose ~⟩
¹**web** \ˈweb\ *n* **1** : a fabric on a loom or coming from a loom **2** : COBWEB; *also* : SNARE, ENTANGLEMENT ⟨caught in a ~ of deceit⟩ **3** : an animal or plant membrane; *esp* : one uniting the toes (as in many birds) **4** : NETWORK ⟨a ~ of highways⟩ **5** : the series of barbs on each side of the shaft of a feather **6** : WORLD WIDE WEB — **webbed** \ˈwebd\ *adj*
²**web** *vb* **webbed; web·bing** **1** : to make a web **2** : to cover or provide with webs or a network **3** : ENTANGLE, ENSNARE
web·bing \ˈwe-biŋ\ *n* : a strong closely woven tape designed for bearing weight and used esp. for straps, harness, or upholstery
web·cam \ˈweb-ˌkam\ *n* : a camera used in transmitting live images over the World Wide Web
web·cast \ˈweb-ˌkast\ *n* : a transmission of sound and images via the World Wide Web — **webcast** *vb*
web–foot·ed \ˈweb-ˈfu̇-təd\ *adj* : having webbed feet
web·log \ˈweb-ˌlȯg, -ˌläg\ *n* : BLOG
web·mas·ter \ˈweb-ˌmas-tər\ *n, often cap* : a person responsible for the creation or maintenance of a website
web page *n* : ³PAGE 2
web·site *or* **Web site** \ˈweb-ˌsīt\ *n* : a group of World Wide Web pages made available online (as by an individual or business)
wed \ˈwed\ *vb* **wed·ded** *also* **wed; wed·ding** **1** : to take, give, enter into, or join in marriage : MARRY **2** : to unite firmly
Wed *abbr* Wednesday
wed·ding \ˈwe-diŋ\ *n* **1** : a marriage ceremony usu. with accompanying festivities : NUPTIALS **2** : a joining in close association **3** : a wedding anniversary or its celebration
¹**wedge** \ˈwej\ *n* **1** : a piece of wood or metal that tapers to a thin edge and is used to split logs or rocks or to raise heavy weights **2** : something (as an action or policy) that serves to open up a way for a breach, change, or intrusion **3** : a wedge-shaped object or part ⟨a ~ of pie⟩
²**wedge** *vb* **wedged; wedg·ing** **1** : to hold

firm by or as if by driving in a wedge **2** : to force (something) into a narrow space

wed·lock \ˈwed-ˌläk\ *n* [ME *wedlok,* fr. OE *wedlāc* marriage bond, fr. *wedd* pledge + *-lāc,* suffix denoting activity] : the state of being married : MARRIAGE, MATRIMONY

Wednes·day \ˈwenz-(ˌ)dā, -dē\ *n* [ME, fr. OE *wōdensdæg,* lit., day of Woden (supreme god of the pagan Anglo-Saxons)] : the 4th day of the week

wee \ˈwē\ *adj* [ME (Sc) *we,* fr. *we,* n., little bit, fr. OE *wǣge* weight] **1** : very small : TINY **2** : very early ⟨~ hours of the morning⟩

¹weed \ˈwēd\ *n* **1** : a plant that tends to grow thickly where it is not wanted and to choke out more desirable plants **2** : MARIJUANA

²weed *vb* **1** : to clear of or remove weeds or something harmful, inferior, or superfluous ⟨~ a garden⟩ **2** : to get rid of ⟨~ out the troublemakers⟩ — **weed·er** *n*

³weed *n* : mourning clothes — usu. used in pl. ⟨widow's ~*s*⟩

weedy \ˈwē-dē\ *adj* **1** : full of weeds **2** : resembling a weed esp. in vigor of growth or spread **3** : noticeably lean and scrawny : LANKY

week \ˈwēk\ *n* **1** : seven successive days; *esp* : a calendar period of seven days beginning with Sunday and ending with Saturday **2** : the working or school days of the calendar week

week·day \ˈwēk-ˌdā\ *n* : a day of the week except Sunday or sometimes except Saturday and Sunday

¹week·end \-ˌend\ *n* : the period between the close of one working or business or school week and the beginning of the next

²weekend *vb* : to spend the weekend

¹week·ly \ˈwē-klē\ *adj* **1** : occurring, appearing, or done every week **2** : computed in terms of one week ⟨~ rental rates⟩ — **weekly** *adv*

²weekly *n, pl* **weeklies** : a weekly publication

ween \ˈwēn\ *vb, archaic* : SUPPOSE 3

wee·ny \ˈwē-nē\ *also* **ween·sy** \ˈwēn-sē\ *adj* : exceptionally small

weep \ˈwēp\ *vb* **wept** \ˈwept\; **weep·ing** **1** : to express emotion and esp. sorrow by shedding tears : BEWAIL, CRY **2** : to give off fluid slowly : OOZE — **weep·er** *n*

weeping *adj* **1** : TEARFUL ⟨~ gratitude⟩ **2** : having slender drooping branches

weeping willow *n* : a willow with slender drooping branches

weepy \ˈwē-pē\ *adj* : inclined to weep

wee·vil \ˈwē-vəl\ *n* : any of a large group of beetles having a long head usu. curved into a snout and including many whose larvae are destructive plant-feeding pests — **wee·vily** *or* **wee·vil·ly** \ˈwē-və-lē\ *adj*

weft \ˈweft\ *n* **1** : a filling thread or yarn in weaving **2** : WEB, FABRIC; *also* : something woven

¹weigh \ˈwā\ *vb* [ME *weyen,* fr. OE *wegan* to move, carry, weigh] **1** : to find the heaviness of **2** : to have weight or a specified weight **3** : to consider carefully : PONDER **4** : to merit consideration as important : COUNT ⟨evidence ~*ing* against him⟩ **5** : to raise before sailing ⟨~ anchor⟩ **6** : to press down with or as if with a heavy weight

²weigh *n* [alter. of *way*] : WAY — used in the phrase *under weigh*

¹weight \ˈwāt\ *n* **1** : the amount that something weighs; *also* : the standard amount that something should weigh **2** : a quantity or object weighing a usu. specified amount **3** : a unit (as a pound or kilogram) of weight or mass; *also* : a system of such units **4** : a heavy object for holding or pressing something down; *also* : a heavy object for throwing or lifting in an athletic contest **5** : a mental or emotional burden **6** : IMPORTANCE; *also* : INFLUENCE ⟨threw his ~ around⟩ **7** : overpowering force **8** : relative thickness (as of a textile) ⟨summer-*weight* clothes⟩ ♦ ***Synonyms*** SIGNIFICANCE, MOMENT, CONSEQUENCE, IMPORT, AUTHORITY, PRESTIGE, CREDIT

²weight *vb* **1** : to oppress with a burden ⟨~*ed* down with cares⟩ **2** : to load with or as if with a weight

weight·less \ˈwāt-ləs\ *adj* : having little weight : lacking apparent gravitational pull ⟨a ~ environment⟩ — **weight·less·ly** *adv* — **weight·less·ness** *n*

weighty \ˈwā-tē\ *adj* **weight·i·er; -est** **1** : of much importance or consequence : MOMENTOUS, SERIOUS ⟨~ problems⟩ **2** : SOLEMN ⟨a ~ manner⟩ **3** : HEAVY **4** : POWERFUL, TELLING ⟨~ arguments⟩

weiner *var of* WIENER

weir \ˈwer, ˈwir\ *n* **1** : a fence set in a waterway for catching fish **2** : a dam in a stream to raise the water level or divert its flow

weird \ˈwird\ *adj* [ME *wird, werd* fate, destiny, fr. OE *wyrd*] **1** : MAGICAL **2** : ODD, UNUSUAL ⟨~ noises⟩ ♦ ***Synonyms*** EERIE, UNCANNY, SPOOKY — **weird·ly** *adv* — **weird·ness** *n*

weirdo \ˈwir-(ˌ)dō\ *n, pl* **weird·os** : a person who is extraordinarily strange or eccentric

Welch *var of* WELSH

¹wel·come \ˈwel-kəm\ *vb* **wel·comed; wel·com·ing** **1** : to greet cordially or courteously **2** : to accept, meet, or face with pleasure ⟨he ~*s* criticism⟩

²welcome *adj* **1** : received gladly into one's presence ⟨a ~ visitor⟩ **2** : giving pleasure : PLEASING ⟨~ news⟩ **3** : willingly permitted or admitted ⟨all are ~ to use the books⟩ **4** — used in the phrase "You're welcome" as a reply to an expression of thanks

³welcome *n* **1** : a cordial greeting or reception **2** : the state of being welcome ⟨overstayed their ~⟩

¹weld \ˈweld\ *vb* **1** : to unite (metal or plastic parts) either by heating and allow-

U.S. WEIGHTS AND MEASURES

LENGTH

UNIT	SYMBOL	U.S. EQUIVALENT	METRIC EQUIVALENT
mile	mi	5280 feet, 1760 yards	1.609 kilometers
rod	rd	5.50 yards, 16.5 feet	5.029 meters
yard	yd	3 feet, 36 inches	0.9144 meter
foot	ft *or* ′	12 inches, 0.333 yard	30.48 centimeters
inch	in *or* ″	0.083 foot, 0.028 yard	2.54 centimeters

AREA

UNIT	SYMBOL	U.S. EQUIVALENT	METRIC EQUIVALENT
square mile	sq mi *or* mi^2	640 acres	2.590 square kilometers
acre	ac	4840 square yards, 43,560 square feet	4047 square meters
square rod	sq rd *or* rd^2	30.25 square yards	25.293 square meters
square yard	sq yd *or* yd^2	9 square feet	0.836 square meter
square foot	sq ft *or* ft^2	144 square inches	0.093 square meter
square inch	sq in *or* in^2	0.0069 square foot	6.452 square centimeter

VOLUME

UNIT	SYMBOL	U.S. EQUIVALENT	METRIC EQUIVALENT
cubic yard	cu yd *or* yd^3	27 cubic feet	0.765 cubic meter
cubic foot	cu ft *or* ft^3	1728 cubic inches	0.028 cubic meter
cubic inch	cu in *or* in^3	0.00058 cubic foot	16.387 cubic centimeters

WEIGHT—AVOIRDUPOIS

UNIT	SYMBOL	U.S. EQUIVALENT	METRIC EQUIVALENT
ton			
short ton		2000 pounds	0.907 metric ton
long ton		2240 pounds	1.016 metric tons
hundredweight	cwt		
short hundredweight		100 pounds	45.359 kilograms
long hundredweight		112 pounds	50.802 kilograms
pound	lb *also* #	16 ounces	0.454 kilogram
ounce	oz	16 drams, 437.5 grains	28.350 grams
dram	dr	27.344 grains	1.772 grams
grain	gr	0.037 dram	0.0648 gram

CAPACITY

UNIT	SYMBOL	U.S. EQUIVALENT	METRIC EQUIVALENT
		LIQUID MEASURE	
gallon	gal	4 quarts	3.785 liters
quart	qt	2 pints	0.946 liter
pint	pt	4 gills	473.176 milliliters
gill	gi	4 fluid ounces	118.294 milliliters
fluid ounce	fl oz *or* f℥	8 fluid drams	29.573 milliliters
fluid dram	fl dr *or* fʒ	60 minims	3.697 milliliters
minim	min *or* ♏	1/60 fluid dram	0.061610 milliliter
		DRY MEASURE	
bushel	bu	4 pecks	35.239 liters
peck	pk	8 quarts	8.810 liters
quart	qt	2 pints	1.101 liters
pint	pt	½ quart	0.551 liter

ing the parts to flow together or by hammering or pressing together **2** : to unite closely or intimately ⟨~*ed* together in friendship⟩ — **weld·er** *n*

²**weld** *n* **1** : a welded joint **2** : union by welding

wel·fare \ˈwel-ˌfer\ *n* **1** : the state of doing well esp. in respect to happiness, well-being, or prosperity **2** : aid in the form of money or necessities for those in need; *also* : the agency through which the aid is given

welfare state *n* : a nation or state that assumes primary responsibility for the individual and social welfare of its citizens

wel·kin \ˈwel-kən\ *n* : SKY; *also* : AIR

¹**well** \ˈwel\ *n* **1** : a spring with its pool : FOUNTAIN; *also* : a source of supply ⟨a ~ of information⟩ **2** : a hole sunk in the earth to obtain a natural deposit (as of water, oil, or gas) **3** : an open space (as for a staircase) extending vertically through floors of a structure **4** : something suggesting a well

²**well** *vb* : to rise up and flow out

³**well** *adv* **bet·ter** \ˈbe-tər\; **best** \ˈbest\ **1** : in a good or proper manner : RIGHTLY; *also* : EXCELLENTLY, SKILLFULLY **2** : SATISFACTORILY, FORTUNATELY ⟨the party turned out ~⟩ **3** : ABUNDANTLY ⟨eat ~⟩ **4** : with reason or courtesy : PROPERLY ⟨I cannot ~ refuse⟩ **5** : COMPLETELY, FULLY, QUITE ⟨~ worth the price⟩ ⟨*well*-hidden⟩ **6** : INTIMATELY, CLOSELY ⟨I know him ~⟩ **7** : CONSIDERABLY, FAR ⟨~ over a million⟩ ⟨~ ahead⟩ **8** : without trouble or difficulty ⟨we could ~ have gone⟩ **9** : EXACTLY, DEFINITELY ⟨remember it ~⟩

⁴**well** *adj* **1** : PROSPEROUS; *also* : being in satisfactory condition or circumstances **2** : SATISFACTORY, PLEASING ⟨all is ~⟩ **3** : ADVISABLE, DESIRABLE ⟨it is not ~ to anger him⟩ **4** : free or recovered from ill health : HEALTHY **5** : FORTUNATE ⟨it is ~ that this has happened⟩

well–ad·just·ed \ˌwel-ə-ˈjəs-təd\ *adj* : WELL-BALANCED 2

well–ad·vised \-əd-ˈvīzd\ *adj* **1** : PRUDENT ⟨~ restraint⟩ **2** : resulting from, based on, or showing careful deliberation or wise counsel ⟨~ plans⟩

well–ap·point·ed \-ə-ˈpȯin-təd\ *adj* : properly fitted out ⟨a ~ house⟩

well–ba·lanced \ˈwel-ˈba-lənst\ *adj* **1** : nicely or evenly balanced or arranged ⟨a ~ meal⟩ **2** : emotionally or psychologically untroubled

well–be·ing \-ˈbē-iŋ\ *n* : the state of being happy, healthy, or prosperous

well·born \-ˈbȯrn\ *adj* : born of noble or wealthy lineage

well–bred \-ˈbred\ *adj* : having or indicating good breeding : REFINED

well–de·fined \-di-ˈfīnd\ *adj* : having clearly distinguishable limits or boundaries

well–dis·posed \-di-ˈspōzd\ *adj* : disposed to be friendly, favorable, or sympathetic ⟨~ to the idea⟩

well–done \ˈwel-ˈdən\ *adj* **1** : rightly or properly performed **2** : cooked thoroughly

well–en·dowed \ˈwel-in-ˈdau̇d\ *adj* **1** : having plenty of money or property **2** : having large breasts **3** : having a large penis

well–fa·vored \-ˈfā-vərd\ *adj* : GOOD-LOOKING, HANDSOME ⟨a ~ face⟩

well–fixed \-ˈfikst\ *adj* : WELL-HEELED

well–found·ed \-ˈfau̇n-dəd\ *adj* : based on good reasons

well–groomed \-ˈgrümd, -ˈgru̇md\ *adj* : neatly dressed or cared for

well–ground·ed \-ˈgrau̇n-dəd\ *adj* **1** : having a firm foundation **2** : WELL-FOUNDED

well·head \-ˌhed\ *n* **1** : the source of a spring or a stream **2** : principal source **3** : the top of or a structure built over a well

well–heeled \-ˈhēld\ *adj* : financially well-off

well–known \-ˈnōn\ *adj* : fully or widely known

well–mean·ing \-ˈmē-niŋ\ *adj* : having or based on good intentions

well·ness \-nəs\ *n* : good health esp. as an actively sought goal ⟨~ clinics⟩ ⟨lifestyles that promote ~⟩

well–nigh \-ˈnī\ *adv* : ALMOST, NEARLY ⟨~ impossible⟩

well–off \-ˈȯf\ *adj* : being in good condition or circumstances; *esp* : WELL-TO-DO

well–or·dered \-ˈȯr-dərd\ *adj* : having an orderly procedure or arrangement

well–placed \-ˈplāst\ *adj* : appropriately or advantageously directed or positioned

well–read \-ˈred\ *adj* : well informed through reading

well–round·ed \-ˈrau̇n-dəd\ *adj* **1** : broadly trained, educated, and experienced **2** : COMPREHENSIVE ⟨a ~ program of activities⟩

well–spo·ken \ˈwel-ˈspō-kən\ *adj* **1** : speaking well and esp. courteously **2** : spoken with propriety ⟨~ words⟩

well·spring \-ˌspriŋ\ *n* : a source of continuous supply ⟨a ~ of information⟩

well–timed \-ˈtīmd\ *adj* : TIMELY ⟨a ~ announcement⟩

well–to–do \ˌwel-tə-ˈdü\ *adj* : having more than adequate financial resources : PROSPEROUS

well–turned \ˈwel-ˈtərnd\ *adj* **1** : pleasingly shaped ⟨a ~ ankle⟩ **2** : pleasingly expressed ⟨a ~ phrase⟩

well–wish·er \ˈwel-ˌwi-shər\ *n* : an admiring supporter or fan — **well–wish·ing** *adj or n*

welsh \ˈwelsh, ˈwelch\ *vb* **1** *sometimes offensive* : to avoid payment **2** *sometimes offensive* : to break one's word ⟨~*ed* on his promises⟩

Welsh \ˈwelsh\ *also* **Welch** \ˈwelch\ *n* [ME *walisch, welisch,* adj., Welsh, fr. OE *wælisc* foreign, British, Welsh, fr. *Wealh* foreigner, Briton, Welshman] **1 Welsh** *pl* : the people of Wales **2** : the Celtic language of Wales — **Welsh** *adj* — **Welshman** \-mən\ *n*

Welsh cor·gi \-ˈkȯr-gē\ *n* [W *corgi,* fr. *cor* dwarf + *ci* dog] : a short-legged long-backed dog with foxy head of either of two breeds of Welsh origin

Welsh rabbit *n* : melted often seasoned cheese served over toast or crackers

Welsh rare·bit \-ˈrer-bət\ *n* : WELSH RABBIT

¹**welt** \ˈwelt\ *n* **1** : the narrow strip of leather between a shoe upper and sole to which other parts are stitched **2** : a doubled edge, strip, insert, or seam for ornament or reinforcement **3** : a ridge or lump raised on the skin usu. by a blow; *also* : a heavy blow

²**welt** *vb* **1** : to furnish (as a shoe) with a welt **2** : to hit hard

¹**wel·ter** \ˈwel-tər\ *vb* **1** : WRITHE, TOSS; *also* : WALLOW **2** : to rise and fall or toss about in or with waves **3** : to become deeply sunk, soaked, or involved **4** : to be in turmoil

²**welter** *n* **1** : TURMOIL **2** : a chaotic mass or jumble ⟨a ~ of data⟩

wel·ter·weight \ˈwel-tər-ˌwāt\ *n* : a boxer weighing more than 135 but not over 147 pounds

wen \ˈwen\ *n* : an abnormal growth or a cyst protruding from a surface esp. of the skin

wench \ˈwench\ *n* [ME *wenche,* short for *wenchel* child, fr. OE *wencel*] **1** : a young woman **2** : a female servant

wend \ˈwend\ *vb* : to direct one's course : proceed on (one's way)

went *past of* GO

wept *past and past part of* WEEP

were *past 2d sing, past pl, or past subjunctive of* BE

were·wolf \ˈwer-ˌwu̇lf, ˈwir-, ˈwər-\ *n, pl* **were·wolves** \-ˌwu̇lvz\ [ME, fr. OE *werwulf,* fr. *wer* man + *wulf* wolf] : a person who in stories is transformed into a wolf or is capable of assuming a wolf's form

wes·kit \ˈwes-kət\ *n* : VEST 1

¹**west** \ˈwest\ *adv* : to or toward the west

²**west** *adj* **1** : situated toward or at the west **2** : coming from the west

³**west** *n* **1** : the general direction of sunset **2** : the compass point directly opposite to east **3** *cap* : regions or countries west of a specified or implied point **4** *cap* : Europe and the Americas — **west·er·ly** \ˈwes-tər-lē\ *adv or adj* — **west·ward** *adv or adj* — **west·wards** *adv*

¹**west·ern** \ˈwes-tərn\ *adj* **1** : lying toward or coming from the west **2** *cap* : of, relating to, or characteristic of a region conventionally designated West **3** *cap* : of or relating to the Roman Catholic or Protestant segment of Christianity — **West·ern·er** *n* — **west·ern·most** \-ˌmōst\ *adj*

²**western** *n, often cap* : a novel, story, film, or radio or television show about life in the western U.S. during the latter half of the 19th century

west·ern·ize \ˈwes-tər-ˌnīz\ *vb* **-ized; -iz·ing** : to give western characteristics to ⟨wanted to ~ the country⟩ — **west·ern·i·zation** \ˌwes-tər-nə-ˈzā-shən\ *n*

West Nile virus \-ˈnī(-ə)l-\ *n* [*West Nile* province of Uganda] : a virus that is transmitted to humans by mosquitoes and causes an illness marked by fever, headache, muscle ache, and sometimes encephalitis or meningitis; *also* : this illness

¹**wet** \ˈwet\ *adj* **wet·ter; wet·test** **1** : consisting of or covered or soaked with liquid (as water) **2** : RAINY ⟨~ days⟩ **3** : not dry ⟨~ paint⟩ **4** : permitting or advocating the manufacture and sale of alcoholic beverages ⟨a ~ town⟩ ⟨a ~ candidate⟩ ♦ ***Synonyms*** DAMP, DANK, MOIST, HUMID — **wet·ly** *adv* — **wet·ness** *n*

²**wet** *n* **1** : WATER; *also* : WETNESS, MOISTURE **2** : rainy weather : RAIN **3** : an advocate of a wet liquor policy

³**wet** *vb* **wet** *or* **wet·ted; wet·ting** : to make or become wet — **wet·ter** *n*

wet blanket *n* : one that quenches or dampens enthusiasm or pleasure

weth·er \ˈwe-t͟hər\ *n* : a castrated male sheep or goat

wet·land \ˈwet-ˌland, -lənd\ *n* : land or areas (as swamps) containing much soil moisture — usu. used in pl.

wet market *n* : a market that sells perishable items and sometimes live animals

wet nurse *n* : a woman who cares for and suckles children not her own

wet suit *n* : a rubber suit for swimmers that acts to retain body heat by keeping a layer of water against the body as insulation

WFH *abbr* work from home; working from home

wh *abbr* **1** which **2** white

¹**whack** \ˈhwak\ *vb* **1** : to strike with a smart or resounding blow **2** : to cut with or as if with a whack

²**whack** *n* **1** : a smart or resounding blow; *also* : the sound of such a blow **2** : PORTION, SHARE ⟨must each pay our ~⟩ **3** : CONDITION, STATE ⟨my neck is out of ~⟩ **4** : an opportunity or attempt to do something : CHANCE **5** : a single action or occasion ⟨made three pies at a ~⟩

¹**whale** \ˈhwāl\ *n, pl* **whales** **1** *or pl* **whale** : CETACEAN; *esp* : one (as a sperm whale or killer whale) of large size **2** : a person or thing impressive in size or quality ⟨a ~ of a story⟩

²**whale** *vb* **whaled; whal·ing** : to fish or hunt for whales

³**whale** *vb* **whaled; whal·ing** **1** : THRASH **2** : to strike or hit vigorously

whale·boat \-ˌbōt\ *n* : a long narrow rowboat originally used by whalers

whale·bone \-ˌbōn\ *n* : BALEEN

whal·er \ˈhwā-lər\ *n* **1** : a person or ship that hunts whales **2** : WHALEBOAT

whale shark *n* : a shark of warm waters that is the largest known fish

wham·my \ˈhwa-mē\ *n, pl* **wham·mies** : JINX, HEX ⟨put the ~ on him⟩

wharf \ˈhwȯrf\ *n, pl* **wharves** \ˈhwȯrvz\ *also* **wharfs** : a structure alongside which ships lie to load and unload

¹**what** \ˈhwät, ˈhwət\ *pron* **1** — used to inquire about the identity or nature of

a being, an object, or some matter or situation ⟨~'s that⟩ ⟨~ happened⟩ **2** : that which ⟨I know ~ you want⟩ **3** : WHATEVER 1 ⟨take ~ you want⟩

²**what** *adv* **1** : in what respect : HOW ⟨~ does he care⟩ **2** — used with *with* to introduce a prepositional phrase that expresses cause ⟨kept busy ~ with school and work⟩

³**what** *adj* **1** — used to inquire about the identity or nature of a person, object, or matter ⟨~ books do you read⟩ **2** : how remarkable or surprising ⟨~ an idea⟩ **3** : WHATEVER

¹**what·ev·er** \hwät-ˈe-vər, hwət-\ *pron* **1** : anything or everything that ⟨does ~ he wants to⟩ **2** : no matter what ⟨~ you do, don't cheat⟩ **3** : WHAT 1 — used as an intensive ⟨~ do you mean⟩

²**whatever** *adj* : of any kind at all ⟨no food ~⟩

³**whatever** *adv* : in any case : whatever the case may be — often used to suggest the unimportance of an issue or choice ⟨see a movie, watch TV,—~⟩

¹**what·not** \ˈhwät-ˌnät, ˈhwət-\ *pron* : any of various other things that might also be mentioned ⟨needles, pins, and ~⟩

²**whatnot** *n* : a light open set of shelves for small ornaments

what·so·ev·er \ˌhwät-sō-ˈe-vər, ˌhwət-\ *pron or adj* : WHATEVER

wheal \ˈhwēl\ *n* : a rapidly formed flat slightly raised itching or burning patch on the skin; *also* : WELT

wheat \ˈhwēt\ *n* : a cereal grain that yields a fine white flour used chiefly in breads, baked goods, and pastas; *also* : any of several widely grown grasses yielding wheat — **wheat·en** *adj*

wheat germ *n* : the vitamin-rich wheat embryo separated in milling

whee·dle \ˈhwē-dᵊl\ *vb* **whee·dled; whee·dling** **1** : to entice by flattery **2** : to gain or get by wheedling

¹**wheel** \ˈhwēl\ *n* **1** : a disk or circular frame that turns on a central axis **2** : a device whose main part is a wheel **3** : something resembling a wheel in shape or motion **4** : a curving or circular movement **5** : machinery that imparts motion : moving power ⟨the ~*s* of government⟩ **6** : a person of importance **7** *pl, slang* : AUTOMOBILE — **wheeled** \ˈhwēld\ *adj* — **wheel·less** *adj*

²**wheel** *vb* **1** : ROTATE, REVOLVE **2** : to change direction as if turning on a pivot **3** : to convey or move on wheels or in a vehicle

wheel·bar·row \-ˌber-ō\ *n* : a vehicle with handles and usu. one wheel for carrying small loads

wheel·base \-ˌbās\ *n* : the distance in inches between the front and rear axles of an automotive vehicle

wheel·chair \-ˌcher\ *n* : a chair mounted on wheels esp. for the use of disabled persons

wheel·er \ˈhwē-lər\ *n* **1** : one that wheels **2** : WHEELHORSE **3** : something that has wheels — used in combination ⟨a side-*wheeler*⟩

wheel·er–deal·er \ˌhwē-lər-ˈdē-lər\ *n* : a shrewd operator esp. in business or politics

wheel·horse \ˈhwēl-ˌhȯrs\ *n* **1** : a horse in a position nearest the front wheels of a wagon **2** : a steady and effective worker esp. in a political body

wheel·house \-ˌhau̇s\ *n* **1** : PILOTHOUSE **2** : a place of control or leadership (as in an organization) **3** : an area that matches a person's skills or expertise

wheel–thrown \ˈhwēl-ˌthrōn\ *adj* : made on a potter's wheel

wheel·wright \-ˌrīt\ *n* : a maker and repairer of wheels and wheeled vehicles

¹**wheeze** \ˈhwēz\ *vb* **wheezed; wheez·ing** : to breathe with difficulty usu. with a whistling sound

²**wheeze** *n* **1** : a sound of wheezing ⟨the ~ of an engine⟩ **2** : an often repeated and well-known joke **3** : a trite saying

wheezy \ˈhwē-zē\ *adj* **wheez·i·er; -est** **1** : inclined to wheeze **2** : having a wheezing sound — **wheez·i·ly** \-zə-lē\ *adv* — **wheez·i·ness** \-zē-nəs\ *n*

whelk \ˈhwelk\ *n* : a large sea snail; *esp* : one much used as food in Europe

whelm \ˈhwelm\ *vb* : to overcome or engulf completely : OVERWHELM

¹**whelp** \ˈhwelp\ *n* : any of the young of various carnivorous mammals (as a dog)

²**whelp** *vb* : to give birth to (whelps); *also* : bring forth young

¹**when** \ˈhwen\ *adv* **1** : at what time ⟨~ will you return⟩ **2** : at or during which time ⟨a time ~ things were better⟩

²**when** *conj* **1** : at or during the time that ⟨leave ~ I do⟩ **2** : every time that ⟨they all clapped ~ he sang⟩ **3** : in the event that : IF ⟨disqualified ~ you cheat⟩ **4** : ALTHOUGH ⟨quit politics ~ he might have had a great career in it⟩

³**when** *pron* : what or which time ⟨since ~ have you been the boss⟩

⁴**when** *n* : the time of a happening

whence \ˈhwens\ *adv or conj* : from what place, source, or cause

when·ev·er \hwe-ˈne-vər, hwə-\ *conj or adv* : at whatever time

when·so·ev·er \ˈhwen-sō-ˌe-vər\ *conj* : at any or every time that

¹**where** \ˈhwer\ *adv* **1** : at, in, or to what place ⟨~ is it⟩ ⟨~ will we go⟩ **2** : at, in, or to what situation, position, direction, circumstances, or respect ⟨~ does this road lead⟩

²**where** *conj* **1** : at, in, or to what place ⟨knows ~ the house is⟩ **2** : at, in, or to what situation, position, direction, circumstances, or respect ⟨shows ~ the road leads⟩ **3** : WHEREVER ⟨goes ~ she likes⟩ **4** : at, in, or to which place ⟨the town ~ we live⟩ **5** : at, in, or to the place at, in, or to which ⟨stay ~ you are⟩ **6** : in a case, situation, or respect in which ⟨outstanding ~ endurance is called for⟩

³**where** *n* : PLACE, LOCATION ⟨the ~ and how of the accident⟩

¹**where·abouts** \-ə-ˌbau̇ts\ *also* **where·about** \-ˌbau̇t\ *adv* : about where : near what place ⟨~ does he live⟩

²whereabouts *n sing or pl* : the place where a person or thing is ⟨his present ~ are unknown⟩

where·as \hwer-ˈaz\ *conj* **1** : while on the contrary; *also* : ALTHOUGH **2** : in view of the fact that : SINCE

where·at \-ˈat\ *conj* **1** : at or toward which **2** : in consequence of which : WHEREUPON

where·by \-ˈbī\ *conj* : by, through, or in accordance with which ⟨the means ~ we achieved our goals⟩

¹where·fore \ˈhwer-ˌfȯr\ *adv* **1** : for what reason or purpose : WHY **2** : THEREFORE

²wherefore *n* : an answer or statement giving an explanation : REASON

¹where·in \hwer-ˈin\ *adv* : in what : in what respect ⟨~ was I wrong⟩

²wherein *conj* **1** : in which : WHERE ⟨the city ~ we live⟩ **2** : during which **3** : in what way : HOW ⟨showed me ~ I was wrong⟩

where·of \-ˈəv, -ˈäv\ *conj* **1** : of what ⟨knows ~ he speaks⟩ **2** : of which or whom ⟨books ~ the best are lost⟩

where·on \-ˈȯn, -ˈän\ *conj* : on which ⟨the base ~ it rests⟩

where·so·ev·er \ˈhwer-sō-ˌe-vər\ *conj* : WHEREVER

where·to \ˈhwer-ˌtü\ *conj* : to which

where·up·on \ˈhwer-ə-ˌpȯn, -ˌpän\ *conj* **1** : on which **2** : closely following and in consequence of which

¹wher·ev·er \hwer-ˈe-vər\ *adv* : where in the world ⟨~ did he get that tie⟩

²wherever *conj* **1** : at, in, or to whatever place ⟨thrives ~ he goes⟩ **2** : in any circumstance in which

where·with \ˈhwer-ˌwith, -ˌwith\ *conj* : with or by means of which ⟨lack the tools ~ to repair the damage⟩

where·with·al \ˈhwer-wi-ˌthȯl, -ˌthȯl\ *n* : MEANS, RESOURCES; *esp* : MONEY

wher·ry \ˈhwer-ē\ *n, pl* **wherries** : a long light rowboat sharp at both ends

whet \ˈhwet\ *vb* **whet·ted; whet·ting** **1** : to sharpen by rubbing on or with something abrasive (as a whetstone) **2** : to make keen : STIMULATE ⟨~ the appetite⟩

wheth·er \ˈhwe-thər\ *conj* **1** : if it is or was true that ⟨ask ~ he is going⟩ **2** : if it is or was better ⟨uncertain ~ to go or stay⟩ **3** : whichever is or was the case, namely that ⟨~ we succeed or fail, we must try⟩ **4** : EITHER ⟨turned out well ~ by accident or design⟩

whet·stone \ˈhwet-ˌstōn\ *n* : a stone for sharpening blades

whey \ˈhwā\ *n* : the watery part of milk that separates after the milk sours and thickens

¹which \ˈhwich\ *adj* **1** : being what one or ones out of a group ⟨~ shirt should I wear⟩ **2** : WHICHEVER

²which *pron* **1** : which one or ones ⟨~ is yours⟩ ⟨~ are his⟩ ⟨it's in May or June, I'm not sure ~⟩ **2** : WHICHEVER ⟨we have all kinds; take ~ you like⟩ **3** — used to introduce a relative clause and to serve as a substitute therein for the noun modified by the clause ⟨the money ~ is coming to me⟩

¹which·ev·er \hwich-ˈe-vər\ *adj* : no matter which ⟨~ way you go⟩

²whichever *pron* : whatever one or ones

which·so·ev·er \ˌhwich-sō-ˈe-vər\ *pron or adj, archaic* : WHICHEVER

whick·er \ˈhwi-kər\ *vb* : NEIGH, WHINNY — **whicker** *n*

¹whiff \ˈhwif\ *n* **1** : a quick puff or slight gust (as of air) **2** : an inhalation of odor, gas, or smoke **3** : a slight trace ⟨a ~ of scandal⟩ **4** : STRIKEOUT

²whiff *vb* **1** : to expel, puff out, or blow away in or as if in whiffs **2** : to inhale an odor **3** : STRIKE OUT 3

Whig \ˈhwig\ *n* [short for *Whiggamore,* member of a Scottish group that marched to Edinburgh in 1648 to oppose the court party] **1** : a member or supporter of a British political group of the late 17th through early 19th centuries seeking to limit royal authority and increase parliamentary power **2** : an American favoring independence from Great Britain during the American Revolution **3** : a member or supporter of an American political party formed about 1834 to oppose the Democrats

¹while \ˈhwī(-ə)l\ *n* **1** : a period of time ⟨stay a ~⟩ **2** : the time and effort used : TROUBLE ⟨worth your ~⟩

²while *conj* **1** : during the time that ⟨she called ~ you were out⟩ **2** : AS LONG AS ⟨~ there's life there's hope⟩ **3** : ALTHOUGH ⟨~ he's respected, he's not liked⟩

³while *vb* **whiled; whil·ing** : to cause to pass esp. pleasantly ⟨~ away an hour⟩

¹whi·lom \ˈhwī-ləm\ *adv* [ME, lit., at times, fr. OE *hwīlum,* dative pl. of *hwīl* time, while] *archaic* : FORMERLY

²whilom *adj* : FORMER ⟨his ~ friends⟩

whilst \ˈhwīlst\ *conj, chiefly Brit* : WHILE

whim \ˈhwim\ *n* : a sudden wish, desire, or change of mind

whim·per \ˈhwim-pər\ *vb* : to make a low whining plaintive or broken sound — **whimper** *n*

whim·si·cal \ˈhwim-zi-kəl\ *adj* **1** : full of whims : CAPRICIOUS **2** : resulting from or characterized by whim or caprice : ERRATIC ⟨~ notions⟩ — **whim·si·cal·i·ty** \ˌhwim-zə-ˈka-lə-tē\ *n* — **whim·si·cal·ly** \ˈhwim-zi-k(ə-)lē\ *adv*

whim·sy *also* **whim·sey** \ˈhwim-zē\ *n, pl* **whimsies** *also* **whimseys** **1** : WHIM, CAPRICE **2** : a fanciful or fantastic device, object, or creation esp. in writing or art ⟨decorative ~⟩

whine \ˈhwīn\ *vb* **whined; whin·ing** [ME, fr. OE *hwīnan* to whiz] **1** : to utter a usu. high-pitched plaintive or distressed cry; *also* : to make a sound similar to such a cry **2** : to complain with or as if with a whine — **whine** *n* — **whin·er** *n* — **whiny** *also* **whin·ey** \ˈhwī-nē\ *adj*

¹whin·ny \ˈhwi-nē\ *vb* **whin·nied; whin·ny·ing** : to neigh usu. in a low or gentle manner

²whinny *n, pl* **whinnies** : NEIGH

[1]**whip** \ˈhwip\ *vb* **whipped; whip·ping** **1** : to move, snatch, or jerk quickly or forcefully ⟨~ out a gun⟩ **2** : to strike with a slender lithe implement (as a lash) esp. as a punishment; *also* : SPANK **3** : to drive or urge on by or as if by using a whip **4** : to bind or wrap (as a rope or rod) with cord in order to protect and strengthen; *also* : to wind or wrap around something **5** : DEFEAT **6** : to stir up : INCITE ⟨~ up enthusiasm⟩ **7** : to produce in a hurry ⟨~ up a meal⟩ **8** : to beat (as eggs or cream) into a froth **9** : to proceed nimbly or briskly; *also* : to flap about forcefully ⟨flags *whipping* in the wind⟩ — **whip·per** *n* — **whip into shape** : to bring forcefully to a desired state or condition

[2]**whip** *n* **1** : a flexible instrument used for whipping **2** : a stroke or cut with or as if with a whip **3** : a dessert made by whipping a portion of the ingredients ⟨prune ~⟩ **4** : a person who handles a whip **5** : a member of a legislative body appointed by a party to enforce party discipline **6** : a whipping or thrashing motion

whip·cord \-ˌkȯrd\ *n* **1** : a thin tough braided cord **2** : a strong cloth with fine diagonal cords or ribs

whip hand *n* : positive control : ADVANTAGE

whip·lash \ˈhwip-ˌlash\ *n* **1** : the lash of a whip **2** : injury resulting from a sudden sharp movement of the neck and head (as of a person in a vehicle that is struck from the rear)

whip·per·snap·per \ˈhwi-pər-ˌsna-pər\ *n* : a small, insignificant, or presumptuous person

whip·pet \ˈhwi-pət\ *n* : any of a breed of small swift slender dogs that are used for racing

whipping boy *n* : SCAPEGOAT

whip–poor–will \ˈhwi-pər-ˌwil\ *n* : an American insect-eating bird with dull variegated plumage whose call at nightfall and just before dawn is suggestive of its name

whip·saw \ˈhwip-ˌsȯ\ *vb* : to beset with two or more adverse conditions or situations at once

[1]**whir** *also* **whirr** \ˈhwər\ *vb* **whirred; whir·ring** : to move, fly, or revolve with a whir

[2]**whir** *also* **whirr** *n* : a continuous fluttering or vibratory sound made by something in rapid motion

[1]**whirl** \ˈhwərl\ *vb* **1** : to move or drive in a circle or curve esp. with force or speed **2** : to turn or cause to turn rapidly in circles **3** : to turn abruptly : WHEEL **4** : to move or go quickly **5** : to become dizzy or giddy : REEL

[2]**whirl** *n* **1** : a rapid rotating or circling movement; *also* : something whirling **2** : COMMOTION, BUSTLE ⟨the social ~⟩ **3** : a state of mental confusion **4** : TRY ⟨gave it a ~⟩

whirl·i·gig \ˈhwər-li-ˌgig\ *n* [ME *whirlegigg,* fr. *whirlen* to whirl + *gigg* top] **1** : a child's toy having a whirling motion **2** : something that continuously whirls or changes

whirl·pool \ˈhwərl-ˌpül\ *n* : water moving rapidly in a circle so as to produce a depression in the center into which floating objects may be drawn

whirl·wind \-ˌwind\ *n* **1** : a small whirling windstorm **2** : a confused rush **3** : a violent or destructive force

whirly·bird \ˈhwər-lē-ˌbərd\ *n* : HELICOPTER

[1]**whish** \ˈhwish\ *vb* : to move with a whish or swishing sound

[2]**whish** *n* : a rushing sound : SWISH

[1]**whisk** \ˈhwisk\ *n* **1** : a quick light sweeping or brushing motion **2** : a usu. wire kitchen implement for beating food by hand **3** : WHISK BROOM

[2]**whisk** *vb* **1** : to move nimbly and quickly **2** : to move or convey briskly ⟨~*ed* the children off to bed⟩ **3** : to beat or whip lightly ⟨~ eggs⟩ **4** : to brush or wipe off lightly ⟨~ a coat⟩

whisk broom *n* : a small broom with a short handle used esp. as a clothes brush

whis·ker \ˈhwis-kər\ *n* **1** : one hair of the beard **2** *pl* : the part of the beard that grows on the sides of the face or on the chin **3** : one of the long bristles or hairs growing near the mouth of an animal (as a cat or mouse) — **whis·kered** \-kərd\ *adj*

whis·key *or* **whis·ky** \ˈhwis-kē\ *n, pl* **whiskeys** *or* **whiskies** [Ir *uisce beatha* & ScGael *uisge beatha,* lit., water of life] : a liquor distilled from fermented wort (as that obtained from rye, corn, or barley mash)

[1]**whis·per** \ˈhwis-pər\ *vb* **1** : to speak very low or under the breath; *also* : to tell or utter by whispering ⟨~ a secret⟩ **2** : to make a low rustling sound — **whis·per·er** \-pər-ər\ *n*

[2]**whisper** *n* **1** : something communicated by or as if by whispering : HINT, RUMOR **2** : an act or instance of whispering

whist \ˈhwist\ *n* : a card game played by four players in two partnerships with a deck of 52 cards

[1]**whis·tle** \ˈhwi-səl\ *n* **1** : a device by which a shrill sound is produced ⟨steam ~⟩ ⟨tin ~⟩ **2** : a shrill clear sound made by forcing breath out or air in through the puckered lips **3** : the sound or signal produced by a whistle or as if by whistling **4** : the shrill clear note of an animal (as a bird)

[2]**whistle** *vb* **whis·tled; whis·tling** **1** : to utter a shrill clear sound by blowing or drawing air through the puckered lips **2** : to utter a shrill note or call resembling a whistle **3** : to make a shrill clear sound esp. by rapid movements ⟨the wind *whistled*⟩ **4** : to blow or sound a whistle **5** : to signal or call by a whistle **6** : to produce, utter, or express by whistling ⟨~ a tune⟩ — **whis·tler** *n*

whis·tle·blow·er \ˈhwi-səl-ˌblō-ər\ *n* : INFORMER

whis·tle–stop \-ˌstäp\ *n* : a brief personal appearance by a political candidate orig. on the rear platform of a touring train

whit \ˈhwit\ *n* [prob. alter. of ME *wiht,*

wight creature, thing, fr. OE *wiht*] : the smallest part or particle : BIT

[1]**white** \'hwīt\ *adj* **whit·er; whit·est** **1** : free from color **2** : of the color of new snow or milk; *esp* : of the color white **3** : light or pallid in color ⟨lips ~ with fear⟩ **4** : SILVERY; *also* : made of silver **5** : of, relating to, or being a member of a group or race characterized by light skin pigmentation **6** : free from spot or blemish : PURE, INNOCENT **7** : BLANK 2 ⟨~ space in printed matter⟩ **8** : not intended to cause harm ⟨a ~ lie⟩ **9** : wearing white ⟨~ friars⟩ **10** : marked by snow ⟨~ Christmas⟩ **11** : consisting of a wide range of frequencies ⟨~ light⟩ — **white·ness** \-nəs\ *n* — **whit·ish** \'hwī-tish\ *adj*

[2]**white** *n* **1** : the color of maximal lightness that characterizes objects which both reflect and transmit light : the opposite of black **2** : a white or light-colored part or thing ⟨the ~ of an egg⟩; *also, pl* : white garments **3** : the light-colored pieces in a 2-player board game; *also* : the person by whom these are played **4** : one that is or approaches the color white **5** : a person having light skin pigmentation

white ant *n* : TERMITE

white blood cell *n* : any of the colorless blood cells (as lymphocytes) that do not contain hemoglobin but do have a nucleus

white–bread \'hwīt-'bred\ *adj* : being, typical of, or having qualities (as blandness) associated with the white middle class ⟨~ values⟩

white·cap \'hwīt-ˌkap\ *n* : a wave crest breaking into white foam

white chocolate *n* : a whitish confection chiefly of cocoa butter, milk, and sugar

white–col·lar \'hwīt-'kä-lər\ *adj* : of, relating to, or constituting the class of salaried workers whose duties do not require the wearing of work clothes or protective clothing ⟨~ jobs⟩

white dwarf *n* : a small very dense whitish star of low luminosity

white elephant *n* **1** : an Indian elephant of a pale color that is sometimes venerated in India, Sri Lanka, Thailand, and Myanmar **2** : something requiring much care and expense and giving little profit or enjoyment

white feather *n* [fr. the superstition that a white feather in the plumage of a gamecock is a mark of a poor fighter] : a mark or symbol of cowardice

white·fish \'hwīt-ˌfish\ *n* : any of various freshwater food fishes related to the salmons and trouts

white flag *n* : a flag of pure white used to signify truce or surrender

white flight *n* : the departure of white people from places (as neighborhoods or schools) increasingly or predominantly populated by minorities

white gold *n* : a pale alloy of gold resembling platinum in appearance

white goods *n pl* : white fabrics or articles (as sheets or towels) typically made of cotton or linen

White·hall \'hwīt-ˌhȯl\ *n* : the British government

white hat *n* **1** : an admirable and honorable person **2** : a mark or symbol of goodness

white·head \-ˌhed\ *n* : a small whitish lump in the skin due to retention of secretion in an oil gland duct

white heat *n* : a temperature higher than red heat at which a body becomes brightly incandescent

white–hot *adj* **1** : being at or radiating white heat **2** : FERVID ⟨~ enthusiasm⟩

White House \-ˌhau̇s\ *n* **1** : a residence of the president of the U.S. **2** : the executive department of the U.S. government

white lead *n* : a heavy white poisonous carbonate of lead used esp. formerly as a pigment in exterior paints

white matter *n* : whitish nerve tissue esp. of the brain and spinal cord that consists largely of neuron processes enclosed in a fatty material and that typically lies under the cortical gray matter

whit·en \'hwī-tᵊn\ *vb* : to make or become white ♦ ***Synonyms*** BLANCH, BLEACH — **whit·en·er** *n*

white oak *n* : any of various oaks with acorns that take one year to mature; *also* : its hard durable wood

white pepper *n* : a spice that consists of the berry of a pepper plant ground after removal of its black husk

white pine *n* : a tall-growing pine of eastern No. America with needles in clusters of five; *also* : its wood

white privilege *n* : the set of social and economic advantages that white people have by virtue of their race in a culture characterized by racial inequality

white sale *n* : a sale on white goods

white shark *n* : GREAT WHITE SHARK

white slave *n, dated* : a woman or girl held unwillingly for purposes of prostitution — **white slavery** *n*

white supremacist *n* : a person who believes that the white race is inherently superior to other races

white supremacy *n* **1** : the belief that the white race is inherently superior to other races **2** : the social, economic, and political systems that enable white people to maintain power over people of other races

white·tail \'hwīt-ˌtāl\ *n* : WHITE-TAILED DEER

white–tailed deer *n* : a No. American deer with a rather long tail white on the underside and the males of which have forward-arching antlers

white–tie \-tī\ *adj* : characterized by or requiring formal evening clothes consisting of usu. white tie and tailcoat for men and a formal gown for women

white·wall \'hwīt-ˌwȯl\ *n* : an automobile tire having a white band on the sidewall

[1]**white·wash** \-ˌwȯsh, -ˌwäsh\ *vb* **1** : to whiten with whitewash **2** : to clear of a charge of wrongdoing by offering excuses, hiding facts, or conducting a perfunctory investigation **3** : SHUT OUT 2 **4** : to

alter in a way that favors, features, or caters to white people ⟨a ~ed remake of the movie⟩

[2]**whitewash** *n* **1** : a liquid mixture (as of lime and water) for whitening a surface **2** : a clearing of wrongdoing by whitewashing

white water *n* : frothy water (as in breakers, rapids, or falls)

white•wood \-ˌwu̇d\ *n* : any of various trees and esp. a tulip tree having light-colored wood; *also* : such wood

[1]**whith•er** \ˈhwi-t͟hər\ *adv* **1** : to what place **2** : to what situation, position, degree, or end ⟨~ will this drive him⟩

[2]**whither** *conj* **1** : to the place at, in, or to which; *also* : to which place **2** : to whatever place

whith•er•so•ev•er \ˌhwi-t͟hər-sō-ˈe-vər\ *conj* : to whatever place

[1]**whit•ing** \ˈhwī-tiŋ\ *n, pl* **whiting** *also* **whit•ings** : any of several usu. light or silvery food fishes (as a hake) found mostly near seacoasts

[2]**whiting** *n* : calcium carbonate in powdered form used esp. as a pigment and in putty

whit•low \ˈhwit-ˌlō\ *n* : a deep inflammation of a finger or toe with pus formation

Whit•sun•day \ˈhwit-ˈsən-dē, -sən-ˌdā\ *n* [ME *Whitsonday,* fr. OE *hwīta sunnandæg,* lit., white Sunday; prob. fr. the custom of wearing white robes by those newly baptized at this season] : PENTECOST

whit•tle \ˈhwi-tᵊl\ *vb* **whit•tled; whit•tling** **1** : to pare or cut off chips from the surface of (wood) with a knife; *also* : to cut or shape by such paring **2** : to reduce as if by paring down ⟨~ down expenses⟩

[1]**whiz** *or* **whizz** \ˈhwiz\ *vb* **whizzed; whiz•zing** : to hum, whir, or hiss like a speeding object (as an arrow or ball) passing through air

[2]**whiz** *or* **whizz** *n, pl* **whiz•zes** : a hissing, buzzing, or whizzing sound

[3]**whiz** *n, pl* **whiz•zes** : WIZARD 2

who \ˈhü\ *pron* **1** : what or which person or persons ⟨~ did it⟩ ⟨~ is he⟩ ⟨~ are they⟩ **2** : the person or persons that ⟨knows ~ did it⟩ **3** — used to introduce a relative clause and to serve as a substitute therein for the substantive modified by the clause ⟨the person ~ lives there is rich⟩

WHO *abbr* World Health Organization

whoa \ˈwō, ˈhwō, ˈhō\ *vb imper* **1** — a command to an animal to stand still **2** : cease or slow a course of action or a line of thought

who•dun•it *also* **who•dun•nit** \hü-ˈdə-nət\ *n* : a detective or mystery story

who•ev•er \hü-ˈe-vər\ *pron* : whatever person : no matter who

[1]**whole** \ˈhōl\ *adj* [ME *hool* healthy, unhurt, entire, fr. OE *hāl*] **1** : being in healthy or sound condition : free from defect or damage **2** : having all its proper parts or elements ⟨~ milk⟩ **3** : constituting the total sum of : ENTIRE ⟨owns the ~ island⟩ **4** : each or all of the ⟨the ~ family⟩ **5** : not scattered or divided : CONCENTRATED ⟨gave me his ~ attention⟩ **6** : seemingly complete or total ⟨the ~ idea is to help, not hinder⟩ ♦ ***Synonyms*** PERFECT, INTACT, SOUND — **whole•ness** *n*

[2]**whole** *n* **1** : a complete amount or sum **2** : something whole or entire — **on the whole** **1** : in view of all the circumstances or conditions **2** : in general

[3]**whole** *adv* : COMPLETELY, WHOLLY, ENTIRELY ⟨a ~ new term⟩

whole food *n* : a food eaten in its natural state with little or no artificial additives

whole•heart•ed \ˈhōl-ˈhär-təd\ *adj* : undivided in purpose, enthusiasm, will, or commitment

whole hog *adv* : to the fullest extent : COMPLETELY ⟨accepted the proposals *whole hog*⟩

whole note *n* : a musical note equal to one measure of four beats

whole number *n* : any of the set of nonnegative integers; *also* : INTEGER

[1]**whole•sale** \ˈhōl-ˌsāl\ *n* : the sale of goods in quantity usu. for resale by a retail merchant

[2]**wholesale** *adj* **1** : performed on a large scale without discrimination ⟨~ slaughter⟩ **2** : of, relating to, or engaged in wholesaling — **wholesale** *adv*

[3]**wholesale** *vb* **whole•saled; whole•sal•ing** : to sell at wholesale — **whole•sal•er** *n*

whole•some \ˈhōl-səm\ *adj* **1** : promoting mental, spiritual, or bodily health or well-being ⟨a ~ environment⟩ **2** : sound in body, mind, or morals : HEALTHY **3** : PRUDENT ⟨~ respect for the law⟩ — **whole•some•ness** *n*

whole step *n* : a musical interval comprising two half steps (as C–D or F♯–G♯)

whole wheat *adj* : made of ground entire wheat kernels

whol•ly \ˈhōl-lē\ *adv* **1** : COMPLETELY, TOTALLY **2** : SOLELY, EXCLUSIVELY

whom \ˈhüm\ *pron, objective case of* WHO

whom•ev•er \hü-ˈme-vər\ *pron, objective case of* WHOEVER

whom•so•ev•er \ˌhüm-sō-ˈe-vər\ *pron, objective case of* WHOSOEVER

[1]**whoop** \ˈhwüp, ˈhwu̇p, ˈhüp, ˈhu̇p\ *vb* **1** : to shout or call loudly and vigorously **2** : to make the characteristic whoop of whooping cough **3** : to go or pass with a loud noise **4** : to utter or express with a whoop; *also* : to urge, drive, or cheer with a whoop

[2]**whoop** *n* **1** : a whooping sound or utterance : SHOUT, HOOT **2** : a crowing intake of breath after a fit of coughing in whooping cough

[1]**whoop•ee** \ˈhwu̇-(ˌ)pē, ˈhwü-\ *interj* — used to express exuberance

[2]**whoopee** *n* **1** : boisterous fun **2** : sexual play — usu. used with *make*

whooping cough *n* : an infectious bacterial disease esp. of children marked by convulsive coughing fits often followed by a shrill gasping intake of breath

whooping crane *n* : a large white nearly

extinct No. American crane noted for its loud whooping call

whoop·la \ˈhwüp-ˌlä, ˈhwu̇p-\ *n* **1** : HOOPLA **2** : boisterous merrymaking

whop·per \ˈhwä-pər\ *n* : something unusually large or extreme of its kind; *esp* : a monstrous lie

whop·ping \ˈhwä-piŋ\ *adj* : extremely large ⟨a ~ increase⟩

whore \ˈhȯr\ *n* : PROSTITUTE

whorl \ˈhwȯrl, ˈhwərl\ *n* **1** : a group of parts (as leaves or petals) encircling an axis and esp. a plant stem **2** : something that whirls or coils around a center : COIL, SPIRAL **3** : one of the turns of a snail shell

whorled \ˈhwȯrld, ˈhwərld\ *adj* : having or arranged in whorls

¹**whose** \ˈhüz\ *adj* : of or relating to whom or which esp. as possessor or possessors, agent or agents, or object or objects of an action ⟨asked ~ bag it was⟩

²**whose** *pron* : whose one or ones ⟨~ is this car⟩ ⟨~ are those books⟩

who·so \ˈhü-ˌsō\ *pron* : WHOEVER

who·so·ev·er \ˌhü-sō-ˈe-vər\ *pron* : WHOEVER

whs *or* **whse** *abbr* warehouse

whsle *abbr* wholesale

¹**why** \ˈhwī\ *adv* : for what reason, cause, or purpose ⟨~ did you do it?⟩

²**why** *conj* **1** : the cause, reason, or purpose for which ⟨that is ~ you did it⟩ **2** : for which : on account of which ⟨knows the reason ~ you did it⟩

³**why** *n, pl* **whys** : REASON, CAUSE ⟨the ~*s* of racial prejudice⟩

⁴**why** \ˈwī, ˈhwī\ *interj* — used to express surprise, hesitation, approval, disapproval, or impatience ⟨~, here's what I was looking for⟩

WI *abbr* **1** West Indies **2** Wisconsin

WIA *abbr* wounded in action

Wic·ca \ˈwi-kə\ *n* [prob. fr. OE *wicca* wizard] : a religion that affirms the existence of supernatural power (as magic) and of deities who inhere in nature and that ritually observes seasonal and life cycles

wick \ˈwik\ *n* : a loosely bound bundle of soft fibers that draws up oil, tallow, or wax to be burned in a candle, oil lamp, or stove

wick·ed \ˈwi-kəd\ *adj* **1** : morally bad : EVIL, SINFUL **2** : FIERCE, VICIOUS **3** : ROGUISH ⟨a ~ glance⟩ **4** : REPUGNANT, VILE ⟨a ~ odor⟩ **5** : HARMFUL, DANGEROUS ⟨a ~ attack⟩ **6** : impressively excellent ⟨throws a ~ fastball⟩ — **wick·ed·ly** *adv* — **wick·ed·ness** *n*

wick·er \ˈwi-kər\ *n* **1** : a small pliant branch (as an osier or a withe) **2** : WICKERWORK — **wicker** *adj*

wick·er·work \-ˌwərk\ *n* : work made of osiers, twigs, or rods : BASKETRY

wick·et \ˈwi-kət\ *n* **1** : a small gate or door; *esp* : one forming a part of or placed near a larger one **2** : a window-like opening usu. with a grille or grate (as at a ticket office) **3** : a set of three upright rods topped by two crosspieces bowled at in cricket **4** : an arch or hoop in croquet

wick·i·up \ˈwi-kē-ˌəp\ *n* : a hut used by nomadic Indigenous Americans of the western and southwestern U.S. with a usu. oval base and a rough frame covered with reed mats, grass, or brushwood

wid *abbr* widow; widower

¹**wide** \ˈwīd\ *adj* **wid·er; wid·est** **1** : covering a vast area **2** : measured across or at right angles to the length **3** : not narrow : BROAD; *also* : ROOMY **4** : opened to full width ⟨eyes ~ with wonder⟩ **5** : not limited : EXTENSIVE ⟨~ experience⟩ **6** : far from the goal, mark, or truth ⟨was ~ of the truth⟩ — **wide·ly** *adv*

²**wide** *adv* **wid·er; wid·est** **1** : over a great distance or extent : WIDELY ⟨searched far and ~⟩ **2** : over a specified distance, area, or extent **3** : so as to leave a wide space between ⟨~ apart⟩ **4** : so as to clear by a considerable distance ⟨ran ~ around left end⟩ **5** : COMPLETELY, FULLY ⟨opened her eyes ~⟩

wide area network *n* : a computer network (as the Internet) over a large area (as a country or the globe) for sharing resources or exchanging data

wide–awake \ˌwīd-ə-ˈwāk\ *adj* : fully awake; *also* : KNOWING, ALERT

wide–body \ˈwīd-ˌbä-dē\ *n* : a large jet aircraft having a wide cabin

wide–eyed \ˈwīd-ˈīd\ *adj* **1** : having the eyes wide open esp. with wonder or astonishment **2** : NAIVE ⟨~ innocence⟩

wide·mouthed \-ˈmau̇thd, -ˈmau̇tht\ *adj* **1** : having one's mouth opened wide (as in awe) **2** : having a wide mouth ⟨~ jars⟩

wid·en \ˈwī-dᵊn\ *vb* : to increase in width, scope, or extent

wide·spread \ˈwīd-ˈspred\ *adj* **1** : widely scattered or prevalent **2** : widely extended or spread out ⟨~ wings⟩

widgeon *var of* WIGEON

¹**wid·ow** \ˈwi-dō\ *n* : a woman who has lost her spouse or partner by death and has not married again — **wid·ow·hood** *n*

²**widow** *vb* : to cause to become a widow or widower

wid·ow·er \ˈwi-də-wər\ *n* : a man who has lost his spouse or partner by death and has not married again

width \ˈwidth\ *n* **1** : a distance from side to side : the measurement taken at right angles to the length : BREADTH **2** : largeness of extent or scope; *also* : FULLNESS **3** : a measured and cut piece of material ⟨a ~ of calico⟩

wield \ˈwēld\ *vb* **1** : to use or handle esp. effectively ⟨~ a broom⟩ **2** : to exert authority by means of : EMPLOY ⟨~ influence⟩ — **wield·er** *n*

wie·ner *also* **wei·ner** \ˈwē-nər\ *n* [short for *wienerwurst,* fr. G, lit., Vienna sausage] : FRANKFURTER

wife \ˈwīf\ *n, pl* **wives** \ˈwīvz\ **1** *dial* : WOMAN **2** : a woman acting in a specified capacity — used in combination ⟨fish*wife*⟩ **3** : a female partner in a marriage — **wife·hood** *n* — **wife·less** *adj* — **wife·ly** *adj*

wig \ˈwig\ *n* [short for *periwig,* modif. of

MF *perruque,* fr. It *parrucca, perrucca* hair, wig] : a manufactured covering of natural or synthetic hair for the head; *also* : TOUPEE

wi·geon *or* **wid·geon** \ˈwi-jən\ *n, pl* **wi·geon** *or* **wigeons** *or* **widgeon** *or* **wid·geons** : any of several medium-sized freshwater ducks

wig·gle \ˈwi-gəl\ *vb* **wig·gled; wig·gling** 1 : to move to and fro with quick jerky or shaking movements : JIGGLE ⟨*wiggled* his toes⟩ 2 : WRIGGLE — **wiggle** *n*

wig·gler \ˈwi-glər, -gə-lər\ *n* 1 : a larva or pupa of a mosquito 2 : one that wiggles

wig·gly \ˈwi-glē, -gə-lē\ *adj* 1 : tending to wiggle ⟨a ~ worm⟩ 2 : WAVY ⟨~ lines⟩

wight \ˈwīt\ *n* : a living being : CREATURE

wig·let \ˈwi-glət\ *n* : a small wig used esp. to enhance a hairstyle

[1]**wig·wag** \ˈwig-ˌwag\ *vb* 1 : to signal by or as if by a flag or light waved according to a code 2 : to make or cause to make a signal (as with the hand or arm)

[2]**wigwag** *n* : the art or practice of wigwagging

wig·wam \ˈwig-ˌwäm\ *n* : a hut used by Indigenous peoples of the eastern U.S. having typically an arched framework of poles overlaid with bark, rush mats, or hides

[1]**wild** \ˈwī(-ə)ld\ *adj* 1 : living in a state of nature and not ordinarily tamed ⟨~ ducks⟩ 2 : growing or produced without human aid or care ⟨~ honey⟩ ⟨~ plants⟩ 3 : WASTE, DESOLATE ⟨~ country⟩ 4 : UNCONTROLLED, UNRESTRAINED, UNRULY ⟨~ passions⟩ ⟨a ~ young stallion⟩ 5 : TURBULENT, STORMY ⟨a ~ night⟩ 6 : EXTRAVAGANT, FANTASTIC, CRAZY ⟨~ ideas⟩ 7 : indicative of strong passion, desire, or emotion ⟨a ~ stare⟩ 8 : UNCIVILIZED, BARBAROUS 9 : deviating from the natural or expected course : ERRATIC ⟨a ~ throw⟩ 10 : able to represent any playing card designated by the holder ⟨deuces ~⟩ — **wild·ly** *adv* — **wild·ness** *n*

[2]**wild** *adv* 1 : WILDLY 2 : without regulation or control ⟨running ~⟩

[3]**wild** *n* 1 : WILDERNESS 2 : a natural or undomesticated state or existence

wild boar *n* : an Old World wild hog from which most domestic swine have been derived

wild card *n* 1 : an unknown or unpredictable factor 2 : one picked to fill a leftover play-off or tournament position 3 *usu* **wild·card** : a symbol (as ? or *) used in a keyword search to represent the presence of unspecified characters

wild carrot *n* : QUEEN ANNE'S LACE

[1]**wild·cat** \ˈwī(-ə)ld-ˌkat\ *n, pl* **wildcats** 1 : any of various small or medium-sized cats (as a lynx or ocelot) 2 : a quick-tempered hard-fighting person

[2]**wildcat** *adj* 1 : not sound or safe ⟨~ schemes⟩ 2 : initiated by a group of workers without formal union approval ⟨~ strike⟩

[3]**wildcat** *vb* **wild·cat·ted; wild·cat·ting** : to drill an oil or gas well in a region not known to be productive

wil·de·beest \ˈwil-də-ˌbēst\ *n, pl* **wildebeests** *also* **wildebeest** [Afrikaans *wildebees,* fr. *wilde* wild + *bees* ox] : either of two large African antelopes with an oxlike head and horns and a horselike mane and tail

wil·der·ness \ˈwil-dər-nəs\ *n* [ME, fr. *wildern* wild, fr. OE *wilddēoren* of wild beasts] : an uncultivated and uninhabited region

wild·fire \ˈwī(-ə)ld-ˌfī(-ə)r\ *n* : an uncontrollable fire — **like wildfire** : very rapidly

wild·flow·er \-ˌflau̇(-ə)r\ *n* : the flower of a wild or uncultivated plant or the plant bearing it

wild·fowl \-ˌfau̇(-ə)l\ *n* : a bird and esp. a waterfowl hunted as game

wild–goose chase *n* : the pursuit of something unattainable

wild·life \ˈwī(-ə)ld-ˌlīf\ *n* : nonhuman living things and esp. wild animals living in their natural environment

wild oat *n* 1 : any of several Old World wild grasses 2 *pl* : offenses and indiscretions attributed to youthful exuberance — usu. used in the phrase *sow one's wild oats*

wild rice *n* : a No. American aquatic grass; *also* : its edible seed

wild type *n* : a gene or trait that is typical of a natural population of organisms in contrast to that of mutant forms; *also* : an organism with such a gene or trait

wild·wood \ˈwī(-ə)ld-ˌwu̇d\ *n* : a wood unaltered or unfrequented by humans

[1]**wile** \ˈwī(-ə)l\ *n* 1 : a trick or stratagem intended to ensnare or deceive; *also* : a playful trick 2 : TRICKERY, GUILE

[2]**wile** *vb* **wiled; wil·ing** : LURE, ENTICE

[1]**will** \ˈwil\ *vb, past* **would** \ˈwu̇d\ *pres sing & pl* **will** 1 : WISH, DESIRE ⟨call it what you ~⟩ 2 — used as an auxiliary verb to express (1) desire, willingness, or in negative constructions refusal ⟨~ you have another⟩ ⟨he *won't* do it⟩, (2) customary or habitual action ⟨~ get angry over nothing⟩, (3) simple futurity ⟨tomorrow we ~ go shopping⟩, (4) capability or sufficiency ⟨the back seat ~ hold three⟩, (5) determination or willfulness ⟨I ~ go despite them⟩, (6) probability ⟨that ~ be the mailman⟩, (7) inevitability ⟨accidents ~ happen⟩, or (8) a command ⟨you ~ do as I say⟩

[2]**will** *n* 1 : wish or desire often combined with determination ⟨the ~ to win⟩ 2 : something desired; *esp* : a choice or determination of one having authority or power 3 : the act, process, or experience of willing : VOLITION 4 : the mental powers manifested as wishing, choosing, desiring, or intending 5 : a disposition to act according to principles or ends 6 : power of controlling one's own actions or emotions ⟨a leader of iron ~⟩ 7 : a legal document in which a person declares to whom his or her possessions are to go after death

[3]**will** *vb* 1 : to dispose of by or as if by a will : BEQUEATH 2 : to determine by an

act of choice; *also* : DECREE, ORDAIN **3** : INTEND, PURPOSE; *also* : CHOOSE

will·ful *or* **wil·ful** \ˈwil-fəl\ *adj* **1** : governed by will without regard to reason : OBSTINATE **2** : INTENTIONAL ⟨~ murder⟩ — **will·ful·ly** *adv*

wil·lies \ˈwi-lēz\ *n pl* : a fit of nervousness : JITTERS — used with *the*

will·ing \ˈwi-liŋ\ *adj* **1** : inclined or favorably disposed in mind : READY ⟨~ to go⟩ **2** : prompt to act or respond ⟨~ workers⟩ **3** : done, borne, or accepted voluntarily or without reluctance **4** : of or relating to the will : VOLITIONAL — **will·ing·ly** *adv* — **will·ing·ness** *n*

wil·li·waw \ˈwi-lē-ˌwȯ\ *n* : a sudden violent gust of cold land air common along mountainous coasts of high latitudes

will–o'–the–wisp \ˌwil-ə-t͟hə-ˈwisp\ *n* **1** : a light that appears at night over marshy grounds **2** : a misleading or elusive goal or hope

wil·low \ˈwi-lō\ *n* **1** : any of a genus of quick-growing shrubs and trees with tough pliable shoots **2** : an object made of willow wood

wil·low·ware \-ˌwer\ *n* : dinnerware that is usu. blue and white and that is decorated with a story-telling design featuring a large willow tree by a little bridge

wil·lowy \ˈwi-lə-wē\ *adj* : PLIANT; *also* : gracefully tall and slender

will·pow·er \ˈwil-ˌpau̇-(ə)r\ *n* : energetic determination : RESOLUTENESS

wil·ly–nil·ly \ˌwi-lē-ˈni-lē\ *adv or adj* [alter. of *will I nill I* or *will ye nill ye* or *will he nill he*; *nill* fr. archaic *nill* to be unwilling, fr. ME *nilen*, fr. OE *nyllan*, fr. *ne* not + *wyllan* to wish] : without regard for one's choice : by compulsion ⟨they rushed us along ~⟩

[1]**wilt** \ˈwilt\ *vb* **1** : to lose or cause to lose freshness and become limp esp. from lack of water : DROOP ⟨the roses were ~*ing*⟩ **2** : to grow weak or faint : LANGUISH

[2]**wilt** *n* : any of various plant disorders marked by wilting and often shriveling

wily \ˈwī-lē\ *adj* **wil·i·er; -est** : full of guile : TRICKY — **wil·i·ness** \-lē-nəs\ *n*

wimp \ˈwimp\ *n* : a weak, cowardly, or ineffectual person — **wimpy** \ˈwim-pē\ *adj*

[1]**wim·ple** \ˈwim-pəl\ *n* : a cloth covering worn over the head and around the neck and chin by women esp. in the late medieval period and by some nuns

[2]**wimple** *vb* **wim·pled; wim·pling** **1** : to cover with or as if with a wimple **2** : to ripple or cause to ripple

[1]**win** \ˈwin\ *vb* **won** \ˈwən\; **win·ning** [ME *winnen*, fr. OE *winnan* to struggle] **1** : to get possession of esp. by effort : GAIN; *also* : to obtain by work : EARN **2** : to gain in or as if in battle or contest; *also* : to be the victor in ⟨*won* the war⟩ **3** : to solicit and gain the favor of; *esp* : to induce to accept oneself in marriage

[2]**win** *n* : VICTORY; *esp* : 1st place at the finish (as of a horse race)

wince \ˈwins\ *vb* **winced; winc·ing** : to shrink back involuntarily (as from pain) : FLINCH — **wince** *n*

winch \ˈwinch\ *n* : a machine that has a drum on which is wound a rope or cable for hauling or hoisting — **winch** *vb*

[1]**wind** \ˈwind\ *n* **1** : a movement of the air **2** : a prevailing force or influence : TENDENCY, TREND **3** : BREATH ⟨he had the ~ knocked out of him⟩ **4** : gas produced in the stomach or intestines **5** : something insubstantial; *esp* : idle words **6** : air carrying a scent (as of game) **7** : INTIMATION ⟨they got ~ of our plans⟩ **8** *pl* : WIND INSTRUMENTS; *also* : players of wind instruments

[2]**wind** *vb* **1** : to get a scent of ⟨the dogs ~*ed* the game⟩ **2** : to cause to be out of breath ⟨he was ~*ed* from the climb⟩ **3** : to allow (as a horse) to rest so as to recover breath

[3]**wind** \ˈwīnd, ˈwind\ *vb* **wind·ed** \ˈwīn-dəd, ˈwin-\ *or* **wound** \ˈwau̇nd\; **wind·ing** : to sound by blowing ⟨~ a horn⟩

[4]**wind** \ˈwīnd\ *vb* **wound** \ˈwau̇nd\ *also* **wind·ed; wind·ing** **1** : ENTANGLE, INVOLVE **2** : to introduce stealthily : INSINUATE **3** : to encircle or cover with something pliable : WRAP, COIL, TWINE ⟨~ a bobbin⟩ **4** : to hoist or haul by a rope or chain and a winch **5** : to tighten the spring of; *also* : CRANK **6** : to raise to a high level (as of excitement) **7** : to cause to move in a curving line or path **8** : to have a curving course or shape ⟨a river ~*ing* through the valley⟩ **9** : to move or lie so as to encircle

[5]**wind** \ˈwīnd\ *n* : COIL, TURN

wind·age \ˈwin-dij\ *n* : the influence of the wind in deflecting the course of a projectile through the air; *also* : the amount of such deflection

wind·bag \ˈwind-ˌbag\ *n* : an overly talkative person

wind·blown \-ˌblōn\ *adj* : blown by the wind; *also* : having the appearance of being blown by the wind ⟨~ hair⟩

wind·break \-ˌbrāk\ *n* : a growth of trees or shrubs serving to break the force of the wind; *also* : a shelter from the wind

wind·burned \-ˌbərnd\ *adj* : irritated and inflamed by exposure to the wind — **wind·burn** \-ˌbərn\ *n*

wind·chill \-ˌchil\ *n* : a still-air temperature that would have the same cooling effect on exposed human skin as a given combination of temperature and wind speed

windchill factor *n* : WINDCHILL

wind down *vb* **1** : to draw toward an end **2** : RELAX, UNWIND

wind·er \ˈwīn-dər\ *n* : one that winds

wind·fall \ˈwind-ˌfȯl\ *n* **1** : something (as a tree or fruit) blown down by the wind **2** : an unexpected or sudden gift, gain, or advantage ⟨won a ~ from the lottery⟩

wind·flow·er \-ˌflau̇-(ə)r\ *n* : ANEMONE

[1]**wind·ing** \ˈwīn-diŋ\ *n* : material (as wire) wound or coiled about an object

[2]**winding** *adj* **1** : having a pronounced curve or spiral ⟨~ stairs⟩ **2** : having a course that winds ⟨a ~ road⟩

wind·ing–sheet \-ˌshēt\ *n* : SHROUD

wind instrument *n* : a musical instrument (as a flute or horn) sounded by wind and esp. by the breath

wind·jam·mer \ˈwind-ˌja-mər\ *n* : a sailing ship; *also* : one of its crew

wind·lass \ˈwind-ləs\ *n* [ME *wyndlas,* alter. of *wyndase,* fr. OF *guindas, windas,* fr. ON *vindāss,* fr. *vinda* to wind + *āss* pole] : a winch used esp. on ships for hoisting or hauling

wind·mill \ˈwind-ˌmil\ *n* : a mill or machine worked by the wind turning sails or vanes that radiate from a central shaft

win·dow \ˈwin-dō\ *n* [ME *windowe,* fr. ON *vindauga,* fr. *vindr* wind + *auga* eye] **1** : an opening in the wall of a building to let in light and air; *also* : the framework with fittings that closes such an opening **2** : WINDOWPANE **3** : an opening resembling or suggesting that of a window in a building **4** : an interval of time during which certain conditions or an opportunity exists **5** : a rectangular box appearing on a computer screen on which information (as files or program output) is displayed — **win·dow·less** *adj*

window box *n* : a box for growing plants in or by a window

window dressing *n* **1** : display of merchandise in a store window **2** : a showing made to create a deceptively favorable impression

win·dow·pane \ˈwin-dō-ˌpān\ *n* : a pane in a window

win·dow–shop \-ˌshäp\ *vb* : to look at the displays in store windows without going inside the stores to make purchases — **win·dow–shop·per** *n*

win·dow·sill \-ˌsil\ *n* : the horizontal member at the bottom of a window

wind·pipe \ˈwind-ˌpīp\ *n* : TRACHEA

wind·proof \-ˈprüf\ *adj* : impervious to wind ⟨a ~ jacket⟩

wind·row \ˈwind-ˌrō\ *n* **1** : hay raked up into a row to dry **2** : a row of something (as dry leaves) swept up by or as if by the wind

wind shear *n* : a radical shift in wind speed and direction that occurs over a very short distance

wind·shield \ˈwind-ˌshēld\ *n* : a transparent screen (as of glass) in front of the occupants of a vehicle

wind sock *n* : an open-ended truncated cloth cone mounted in an elevated position to indicate wind direction

wind·storm \-ˌstȯrm\ *n* : a storm with high wind and little or no rain

wind·surf·ing \-ˌsər-fiŋ\ *n* : the sport or activity of riding a sailboard — **wind·surf** \-ˌsərf\ *vb* — **wind·surf·er** *n*

wind·swept \ˈwind-ˌswept\ *adj* : swept by or as if by wind ⟨~ plains⟩

wind tunnel *n* : an enclosed passage through which air is blown to investigate air flow around an object

wind·up \ˈwīn-ˌdəp\ *n* **1** : CONCLUSION, FINISH **2** : a series of regular and distinctive motions made by a pitcher preliminary to delivering a pitch

wind up *vb* **1** : to bring or come to a conclusion : END ⟨*wind up* the meeting⟩ **2** : to put in order for the purpose of bringing to an end **3** : to arrive in a place, situation, or condition at the end or as a result of a course of action ⟨*wound up* as paupers⟩ **4** : to make a pitching windup

¹wind·ward \ˈwin-dwərd\ *n* : the side or direction from which the wind is blowing

²windward *adj* : being in or facing the direction from which the wind is blowing

windy \ˈwin-dē\ *adj* **wind·i·er; -est** **1** : having wind : exposed to winds ⟨a ~ day⟩ ⟨a ~ prairie⟩ **2** : STORMY **3** : FLATULENT **4** : indulging in or characterized by useless talk : VERBOSE

¹wine \ˈwīn\ *n* [ME *win,* fr. OE *wīn,* ultim. fr. L *vinum*] **1** : fermented grape juice used as a beverage **2** : the usu. fermented juice of a plant product (as fruit) used as a beverage ⟨rice ~⟩

²wine *vb* **wined; win·ing** : to treat to or drink wine

wine cellar *n* : a room for storing wines; *also* : a stock of wines

wine·grow·er \-ˌgrō-ər\ *n* : one that cultivates a vineyard and makes wine

wine·press \-ˌpres\ *n* : a vat in which juice is pressed from grapes

win·ery \ˈwī-nə-rē, ˈwīn-rē\ *n, pl* **-eries** : a wine-making establishment

¹wing \ˈwiŋ\ *n* **1** : one of the movable feathered or membranous paired appendages by means of which a bird, bat, or insect flies **2** : something suggesting a wing; *esp* : an airfoil that develops the lift which supports an aircraft in flight **3** : a plant or animal appendage or part likened to a wing **4** : a turned-back or extended edge on an article of clothing **5** : a means of flight or rapid progress **6** : the act or manner of flying : FLIGHT **7** *pl* : the area at the side of the stage out of sight **8** : one of the positions or players on either side of a center position or line **9** : either of two opposing groups within an organization : FACTION **10** : a unit in military aviation consisting of two or more squadrons — **wing·less** *adj* — **wing·like** \-ˌlīk\ *adj* — **on the wing** : in flight : FLYING — **under one's wing** : in one's charge or care

²wing *vb* **1** : to fit with wings; *also* : to enable to fly easily **2** : to pass through in flight : FLY ⟨~ the air⟩ ⟨swallows *~ing* southward⟩ **3** : to let fly : DISPATCH **4** : to wound in the wing ⟨~ a bird⟩; *also* : to wound without killing **5** : to perform without preparation : IMPROVISE ⟨~ it⟩

wing·ding \ˈwiŋ-ˌdiŋ\ *n* : a wild, lively, or lavish party

winged \ˈwiŋd, ˈwiŋ-əd, *in compounds* ˈwiŋd\ *adj* **1** : having wings esp. of a specified character **2** : soaring with or as if with wings : ELEVATED **3** : SWIFT, RAPID

wing nut *n* : a nut with winglike extensions that can be gripped with the thumb and finger

wing·span \ˈwiŋ-ˌspan\ *n* : the distance between the tips of a pair of wings

wing·spread \-ˌspred\ *n* : the spread of the wings; *esp* : the distance between the tips of the fully extended wings of a winged animal

[1]**wink** \ˈwiŋk\ *vb* **1** : to close and open one eye quickly as a signal or hint **2** : to close and open the eyes quickly : BLINK **3** : to avoid seeing or noticing something ⟨~ at a traffic violation⟩ **4** : TWINKLE, FLICKER — **wink·er** \ˈwiŋ-kər\ *n*

[2]**wink** *n* **1** : a brief period of sleep : NAP **2** : an act of winking; *esp* : a hint or sign given by winking **3** : INSTANT ⟨dries in a ~⟩

win·ner \ˈwi-nər\ *n* : one that wins

[1]**win·ning** \ˈwi-niŋ\ *n* **1** : VICTORY **2** : something won; *esp* : money won at gambling ⟨large ~*s*⟩

[2]**winning** *adj* **1** : successful esp. in competition **2** : ATTRACTIVE, CHARMING

win·now \ˈwi-nō\ *vb* **1** : to remove (as chaff) by a current of air; *also* : to free (as grain) from waste in this manner **2** : to sort or separate as if by winnowing

wino \ˈwī-nō\ *n, pl* **win·os** : one who is addicted to drinking wine

win·some \ˈwin-səm\ *adj* [ME *winsum,* fr. OE *wynsum,* fr. *wynn* joy] **1** : generally pleasing and engaging ⟨a ~ smile⟩ **2** : CHEERFUL, GAY — **win·some·ly** *adv* — **win·some·ness** *n*

[1]**win·ter** \ˈwin-tər\ *n* : the season of the year in any region in which the noonday sun shines most obliquely : the coldest period of the year

[2]**winter** *vb* **1** : to pass the winter ⟨~*ed* in Florida⟩ **2** : to feed or find food during the winter ⟨~*ed* on hay⟩

[3]**winter** *adj* : sown in autumn for harvesting in the following spring or summer ⟨~ wheat⟩

win·ter·green \ˈwin-tər-ˌgrēn\ *n* **1** : a low evergreen plant of the heath family with white bell-shaped flowers and spicy red berries **2** : an aromatic oil or its flavor from the wintergreen

win·ter·ize \ˈwin-tə-ˌrīz\ *vb* **-ized; -iz·ing** : to make ready for winter

win·ter–kill \ˈwin-tər-ˌkil\ *vb* : to kill or die by exposure to winter weather

winter squash *n* : any of various hard-shelled squashes that keep well in storage

win·ter·tide \-ˌtīd\ *n* : WINTER

win·ter·time \-ˌtīm\ *n* : WINTER

win·try \ˈwin-trē\ *also* **win·tery** \ˈwin-tə-rē\ *adj* **win·tri·er; -est** **1** : of, relating to, or characteristic of winter ⟨~ weather⟩ **2** : CHILLING, CHEERLESS ⟨a ~ welcome⟩

[1]**wipe** \ˈwīp\ *vb* **wiped; wip·ing** **1** : to clean or dry by rubbing ⟨~ dishes⟩ **2** : to remove by or as if by rubbing ⟨~ away tears⟩ **3** : to erase completely : OBLITERATE **4** : to pass or draw over a surface ⟨*wiped* his hand across his face⟩ — **wip·er** *n*

[2]**wipe** *n* **1** : an act or instance of wiping; *also* : BLOW, STRIKE, SWIPE **2** : something used for wiping ⟨disposable ~*s*⟩

wipe out *vb* : to destroy completely

[1]**wire** \ˈwī(-ə)r\ *n* **1** : metal in the form of a thread or slender rod; *also* : a thread or rod of metal **2** : hidden or secret influences controlling the action of a person or organization — usu. used in pl. ⟨pull ~*s*⟩ **3** : a line of wire for conducting electric current **4** : a telegraph or telephone wire or system **5** : TELEGRAM, CABLEGRAM **6** : the finish line of a race

[2]**wire** *vb* **wired; wir·ing** **1** : to provide or equip with wire ⟨~ a house⟩ **2** : to bind, string, or mount with wire **3** : to send or send word to by telegraph

wired *adj* **1** : furnished with wires **2** : connected to the Internet **3** : feverishly excited ⟨~ fans⟩

wire·hair \ˈwī(-ə)r-ˌher\ *n* : a wirehaired dog or cat

wire·haired \-ˈherd\ *adj* : having a stiff wiry outer coat of hair

[1]**wire·less** \-ləs\ *adj* **1** : having no wire or wires **2** : RADIO **3** : of or relating to data communications using radio waves

[2]**wireless** *n* **1** : telecommunication involving signals transmitted by radio waves; *also* : the technology used in radio telecommunication **2** *chiefly Brit* : RADIO **3** : access to a wireless Internet network ⟨a cafe with ~⟩

wire service *n* : a news agency that sends out syndicated news copy to subscribers by wire or satellite

wire·tap \-ˌtap\ *n* : the act or an instance of tapping a telephone or telegraph wire to get information; *also* : an electrical connection used for such tapping — **wiretap** *vb* — **wire·tap·per** \-ˌta-pər\ *n*

wire·worm \-ˌwərm\ *n* : any of various slender hard-coated beetle larvae esp. destructive to plant roots

wir·ing \ˈwī(-ə)r-iŋ\ *n* : a system of wires

wiry \ˈwī(-ə)r-ē\ *adj* **wir·i·er** \ˈwī-rē-ər\; **-est** **1** : made of or resembling wire **2** : slender yet strong and sinewy ⟨~ arms⟩ — **wir·i·ness** \ˈwī-rē-nəs\ *n*

Wis *or* **Wisc** *abbr* Wisconsin

Wisd *abbr* Wisdom

wis·dom \ˈwiz-dəm\ *n* [ME, fr. OE *wīsdom,* fr. *wīs* wise] **1** : accumulated philosophic or scientific learning : KNOWLEDGE; *also* : INSIGHT **2** : good sense : JUDGMENT **3** : a wise attitude or course of action

Wisdom *n* — see BIBLE table

Wisdom of Sol·o·mon \-ˈsä-lə-mən\ — see BIBLE table

wisdom tooth *n* : the last tooth of the full set on each side of the upper and lower jaws of humans

[1]**wise** \ˈwīz\ *n* : WAY, MANNER, FASHION ⟨in no ~⟩ ⟨in this ~⟩

[2]**wise** *adj* **wis·er; wis·est** **1** : having wisdom : SAGE **2** : having or showing good sense or good judgment **3** : aware of what is going on : KNOWING ⟨got ~ to his secrets⟩; *also* : CRAFTY, SHREWD **4** : possessing inside information **5** : saying things that are or being rude or insulting ⟨a ~ retort⟩ — **wise·ly** *adv*

-wise \-ˌwīz\ *adv comb form* : in the manner or direction of ⟨slant*wise*⟩

wise·acre \ˈwīz-ˌā-kər\ *n* [MD *wijssegger* soothsayer] : SMART ALECK

[1]**wise·crack** \ˈwīz-ˌkrak\ *n* : a clever, smart, or flippant remark
[2]**wisecrack** *vb* : to make a wisecrack
wise guy *n* : SMART ALECK
[1]**wish** \ˈwish\ *vb* **1** : to have a desire : long for ⟨~ you were here⟩ ⟨~ for a puppy⟩ **2** : to form or express a wish concerning ⟨~*ed* him a happy birthday⟩ **3** : BID ⟨he ~*ed* me good morning⟩ **4** : to request by expressing a desire ⟨I ~ you to go now⟩
[2]**wish** *n* **1** : an act or instance of wishing or desire : WANT; *also* : GOAL **2** : an expressed will or desire
wish·bone \-ˌbōn\ *n* : a forked bone in front of the breastbone in most birds
wish·ful \ˈwish-fəl\ *adj* **1** : expressive of a wish; *also* : having a wish **2** : according with wishes rather than fact ⟨~ thinking⟩
wishy–washy \ˈwi-shē-ˌwȯ-shē, -ˌwä-\ *adj* : WEAK, INSIPID; *also* : morally feeble
wisp \ˈwisp\ *n* **1** : a small handful (as of hay or straw) **2** : a thin strand, strip, or fragment ⟨a ~ of hair⟩; *also* : a thready streak ⟨a ~ of smoke⟩ **3** : something frail, slight, or fleeting ⟨a ~ of a smile⟩ — **wispy** *adj*
wis·te·ria \wis-ˈtir-ē-ə\ *also* **wis·tar·ia** \-ˈtir-ē-ə *also* -ˈter-\ *n* : any of a genus of chiefly Asian mostly woody vines related to the peas and widely grown for their long showy clusters of blue, white, purple, or rose flowers
wist·ful \ˈwist-fəl\ *adj* : feeling or showing a timid desire ⟨~ memories⟩ — **wist·ful·ly** *adv* — **wist·ful·ness** *n*
wit \ˈwit\ *n* **1** : reasoning power : INTELLIGENCE **2** : mental soundness : SANITY — usu. used in pl. **3** : RESOURCEFULNESS, INGENUITY; *esp* : quickness and cleverness in handling words and ideas **4** : a talent for making clever remarks; *also* : a person noted for making witty remarks — **wit·ted** \ˈwi-təd\ *adj* — **at one's wit's end** : at a loss for a means of solving a problem
[1]**witch** \ˈwich\ *n* **1** : a person believed to have magic power; *esp* : SORCERESS **2** : an ugly old woman : HAG **3** : a charming or alluring girl or woman **4** : an adherent of Wicca
[2]**witch** *vb* : BEWITCH
witch·craft \ˈwich-ˌkraft\ *n* **1** : the power or practices of a witch : SORCERY **2** : WICCA
witch doctor *n* : a person in a primitive society who uses magic to treat sickness and to fight off evil spirits
witch·ery \ˈwi-chə-rē\ *n, pl* **-er·ies** **1** : SORCERY **2** : FASCINATION, CHARM
witch·grass \ˈwich-ˌgras\ *n* : any of several grasses that are weeds in cultivated areas
witch ha·zel \ˈwich-ˌhā-zəl\ *n* **1** : a shrub of eastern No. America bearing small yellow flowers in the fall **2** : a soothing alcoholic lotion made from witch hazel bark
witch–hunt \ˈwich-ˌhənt\ *n* **1** : a searching out and persecution of persons accused of witchcraft **2** : the searching out and deliberate harassment esp. of political opponents
witch·ing \ˈwi-chiŋ\ *adj* : of, relating to, or suitable for sorcery or supernatural occurrences
with \ˈwit͟h, ˈwith\ *prep* **1** : AGAINST ⟨a fight ~ his brother⟩ **2** : FROM ⟨parting ~ friends⟩ **3** : in mutual relation to ⟨talk ~ a friend⟩ **4** : in the company of ⟨went there ~ her⟩ **5** : AS REGARDS, TOWARD ⟨is patient ~ children⟩ **6** : compared to ⟨on equal terms ~ another⟩ **7** : in support of ⟨I'm ~ you all the way⟩ **8** : in the presence of : CONTAINING ⟨tea ~ sugar⟩ **9** : in the opinion of : as judged by ⟨their arguments had weight ~ her⟩ **10** : BECAUSE OF, THROUGH ⟨pale ~ anger⟩; *also* : by means of ⟨hit him ~ a club⟩ **11** : in a manner indicating ⟨work ~ a will⟩ **12** : GIVEN, GRANTED ⟨~ your permission I'll leave⟩ **13** : HAVING ⟨came ~ good news⟩ ⟨stood there ~ his mouth open⟩ **14** : characterized by ⟨boys ~ good morals⟩ **15** : at the time of : right after ⟨~ that we left⟩ **16** : DESPITE ⟨~ all her cleverness, she failed⟩ **17** : in the direction of ⟨swim ~ the tide⟩
with·al \wi-ˈt͟hȯl, -ˈthȯl\ *adv* **1** : together with this : BESIDES **2** : on the other hand : NEVERTHELESS
with·draw \wit͟h-ˈdrȯ, with-\ *vb* **-drew** \-ˈdrü\; **-drawn** \-ˈdrȯn\; **-draw·ing** \-ˈdrȯ-iŋ\ **1** : to take back or away : REMOVE **2** : to call back (as from consideration); *also* : RETRACT **3** : to go away : RETREAT, LEAVE **4** : to terminate one's participation in or use of something
with·draw·al \-ˈdrȯ-əl\ *n* **1** : an act or instance of withdrawing **2** : the discontinuance of the use or administration of a drug and esp. an addicting drug; *also* : the period following such discontinuance marked by often painful physiological and psychological symptoms **3** : a pathological retreat from the real world (as in some schizophrenic states)
with·drawn \wit͟h-ˈdrȯn\ *adj* **1** : ISOLATED, SECLUDED **2** : socially detached and unresponsive ⟨became depressed and ~⟩
withe \ˈwith\ *n* : a slender flexible twig or branch
with·er \ˈwi-t͟hər\ *vb* **1** : to shrivel from or as if from loss of bodily moisture and esp. sap **2** : to lose or cause to lose vitality, force, or freshness ⟨their enthusiasm ~*ed*⟩ **3** : to cause to feel shriveled ⟨~*ed* him with a glance⟩
with·ers \ˈwi-t͟hərz\ *n pl* : the ridge between the shoulder bones of a horse; *also* : the corresponding part in other 4-footed animals
with·hold \with-ˈhōld, wit͟h-\ *vb* **-held** \-ˈheld\; **-hold·ing** **1** : to hold back : RESTRAIN; *also* : RETAIN **2** : to refrain from granting, giving, or allowing ⟨~ permission⟩ ⟨~ names⟩
withholding tax *n* : a tax on income withheld at the source
[1]**with·in** \wi-ˈt͟hin, -ˈthin-\ *adv* **1** : in or into the interior : INSIDE **2** : inside oneself : INWARDLY

[2]**within** *prep* **1** : inside the limits or influence of ⟨~ call⟩ **2** : in the limits or compass of ⟨~ a mile⟩ **3** : in or to the inner part of ⟨~ the room⟩

with–it \ˈwi-t͟hət, -thət\ *adj* : socially or culturally up-to-date

[1]**with·out** \wi-ˈt͟hau̇t, -ˈthau̇t\ *prep* **1** : OUTSIDE **2** : LACKING ⟨~ hope⟩; *also* : not accompanied by or showing ⟨spoke ~ thinking⟩

[2]**without** *adv* **1** : on the outside : EXTERNALLY **2** : with something lacking or absent ⟨has learned to do ~⟩

with·stand \with-ˈstand, wit͟h-\ *vb* **-stood** \-ˈstu̇d\; **-stand·ing** : to stand against : RESIST; *esp* : to oppose (as an attack) successfully

wit·less \ˈwit-ləs\ *adj* : lacking wit or understanding : FOOLISH — **wit·less·ly** *adv* — **wit·less·ness** *n*

[1]**wit·ness** \ˈwit-nəs\ *n* [ME *witnesse,* fr. OE *witnes* knowledge, testimony, witness, fr. *wit* mind, intelligence] **1** : TESTIMONY ⟨bear ~ to the fact⟩ **2** : one that gives evidence; *esp* : one who testifies in a cause or before a court **3** : one present at a transaction so as to be able to testify that it has taken place **4** : one who has personal knowledge or experience of something **5** : something serving as evidence or proof : SIGN

[2]**witness** *vb* **1** : to bear witness : TESTIFY **2** : to act as legal witness of **3** : to furnish proof of : BETOKEN **4** : to be a witness of **5** : to be the scene of ⟨this region has ~*ed* many wars⟩

wit·ti·cism \ˈwi-tə-ˌsi-zəm\ *n* : a witty saying or phrase

wit·ting \ˈwi-tiŋ\ *adj* : done knowingly : INTENTIONAL — **wit·ting·ly** *adv*

wit·ty \ˈwi-tē\ *adj* **wit·ti·er; -est** : marked by or full of wit : AMUSING ⟨a ~ writer⟩ ⟨a ~ remark⟩ ♦ ***Synonyms*** HUMOROUS, FACETIOUS, JOCULAR, JOCOSE — **wit·ti·ly** \-tə-lē\ *adv* — **wit·ti·ness** \-tē-nəs\ *n*

wive \ˈwīv\ *vb* **wived; wiv·ing** : to take a wife

wives *pl of* WIFE

wiz \ˈwiz\ *n* : a person who is very good at something ⟨a math ~⟩

wiz·ard \ˈwi-zərd\ *n* [ME *wysard* wise man, fr. *wys* wise] **1** : MAGICIAN, SORCERER **2** : a very clever or skillful person ⟨a ~ at chess⟩

wiz·ard·ry \ˈwi-zər-drē\ *n, pl* **-ries** **1** : magic skill : SORCERY **2** : great skill or cleverness in an activity

wiz·en \ˈwi-zᵊn, ˈwē-\ *vb* : to become or cause to become dry, shrunken, or wrinkled ⟨a face ~*ed* by age⟩

wk *abbr* **1** week **2** work

WL *abbr* wavelength

wmk *abbr* watermark

WNW *abbr* west-northwest

WO *abbr* warrant officer

w/o *abbr* without

woad \ˈwōd\ *n* : a European herb related to the mustards; *also* : a blue dyestuff made from its leaves

wob·ble \ˈwä-bəl\ *vb* **wob·bled; wob·bling** **1** : to move or cause to move with an irregular rocking or side-to-side motion **2** : TREMBLE, QUAVER **3** : WAVER, VACILLATE — **wobble** *n* — **wob·bly** \-bə-lē\ *adj*

WOC *abbr* woman of color; women of color

woe \ˈwō\ *n* **1** : deep suffering from misfortune, affliction, or grief **2** : TROUBLE, MISFORTUNE ⟨economic ~*s*⟩

woe·be·gone \ˈwō-bi-ˌgȯn\ *adj* : exhibiting woe, sorrow, or misery ⟨~ faces⟩; *also* : being in a sorry condition

woe·ful *also* **wo·ful** \ˈwō-fəl\ *adj* **1** : full of woe : AFFLICTED **2** : involving, bringing, or relating to woe ⟨~ stories⟩ **3** : DEPLORABLE ⟨~ test scores⟩ — **woe·ful·ly** *adv*

wok \ˈwäk\ *n* [Chin (Guangzhou & Hong Kong dial.) *wohk*] : a bowl-shaped cooking utensil used esp. in stir-frying

[1]**woke** *past and past part of* WAKE

[2]**woke** \ˈwōk\ *adj* **wok·er; wok·est** *slang* : aware of and actively attentive to important facts and issues (especially issues of racial and social justice)

woken *past part of* WAKE

wold \ˈwōld\ *n* : an upland plain or stretch of rolling land without woods

[1]**wolf** \ˈwu̇lf\ *n, pl* **wolves** \ˈwu̇lvz\ **1** : any of several large erect-eared bushy-tailed doglike predatory mammals that live and hunt in packs; *esp* : GRAY WOLF **2** : a fierce or destructive person — **wolf·ish** *adj* — **wolf in sheep's clothing** : one who hides a hostile intention with a friendly manner

[2]**wolf** *vb* : to eat greedily : DEVOUR

wolf·hound \-ˌhau̇nd\ *n* : any of several large dogs orig. used in hunting wolves

wol·fram \ˈwu̇l-frəm\ *n* : TUNGSTEN

wol·ver·ine \ˌwu̇l-və-ˈrēn\ *n, pl* **wolverines** *also* **wolverine** : a dark shaggy-coated flesh-eating mammal of northern forests and associated tundra that is related to the weasels

wom·an \ˈwu̇-mən\ *n, pl* **wom·en** \ˈwi-mən\ [ME, fr. OE *wīfman,* fr. *wīf* woman, wife + *man* human being, man] **1** : an adult female person **2** : WOMANKIND **3** : feminine nature : WOMANLINESS **4** : a female servant or attendant

wom·an·hood \ˈwu̇-mən-ˌhu̇d\ *n* **1** : the state of being a woman : the distinguishing qualities of a woman or of womankind **2** : WOMEN, WOMANKIND

wom·an·ish \ˈwu̇-mə-nish\ *adj* **1** : associated with or characteristic of women rather than men **2** : suggestive of a weak character : EFFEMINATE ⟨a ~ voice⟩

wom·an·ize \ˈwu̇-mə-ˌnīz\ *vb* : to pursue casual sexual relationships with numerous women — **wom·an·iz·er** *n*

wom·an·kind \ˈwu̇-mən-ˌkīnd\ *n* : female human beings : women esp. as distinguished from men

wom·an·like \-ˌlīk\ *adj* : WOMANLY

wom·an·ly \-lē\ *adj* : having qualities characteristic of a woman — **wom·an·li·ness** \-lē-nəs\ *n*

woman suffrage *n* : possession and exercise of suffrage by women

womb \ˈwüm\ *n* **1** : UTERUS **2** : a place where something is generated

wom•bat \ˈwäm-ˌbat\ *n* : any of several stocky burrowing Australian marsupials that resemble small bears

wom•en•folk \ˈwi-mən-ˌfōk\ *also* **wom•en•folks** \-ˌfōks\ *n pl* : WOMEN

[1]**won** \ˈwən\ *past and past part of* WIN

[2]**won** \ˈwȯn\ *n, pl* **won** — see MONEY table

[1]**won•der** \ˈwən-dər\ *n* **1** : a cause of astonishment or surprise : MARVEL; *also* : MIRACLE **2** : the quality of exciting wonder ⟨the charm and ~ of the scene⟩ **3** : a feeling (as of awed astonishment or uncertainty) aroused by something extraordinary or affecting

[2]**wonder** *vb* **1** : to feel surprise or amazement **2** : to feel curiosity or doubt ⟨~ about the future⟩

wonder drug *n* : MIRACLE DRUG

won•der•ful \ˈwən-dər-fəl\ *adj* **1** : exciting wonder : MARVELOUS, ASTONISHING **2** : unusually good : ADMIRABLE ⟨did a ~ job⟩ — **won•der•ful•ly** \-f(ə-)lē\ *adv* — **won•der•ful•ness** *n*

won•der•land \-ˌland, -lənd\ *n* **1** : an imaginary place of delicate beauty or magical charm **2** : a place that excites admiration or wonder ⟨a scenic ~⟩

won•der•ment \-mənt\ *n* **1** : ASTONISHMENT, SURPRISE **2** : a cause of or occasion for wonder **3** : curiosity about something

won•drous \ˈwən-drəs\ *adj* : WONDERFUL, MARVELOUS ⟨a ~ feat⟩ — **won•drous•ly** *adv* — **won•drous•ness** *n*

wonk \ˈwäŋk, ˈwȯŋk\ *n* : one who works in a specialized usu. intellectual field ⟨computer ~*s*⟩

[1]**wont** \ˈwȯnt, ˈwōnt\ *adj* [ME *woned, wont,* fr. pp. of *wonen* to dwell, be used to, fr. OE *wunian*] **1** : ACCUSTOMED, USED ⟨as we are ~ to do⟩ **2** : INCLINED, APT

[2]**wont** *n* : CUSTOM, USAGE, HABIT ⟨according to her ~⟩

won't \ˈwōnt\ : will not

wont•ed \ˈwȯn-təd, ˈwōn-\ *adj* : ACCUSTOMED, CUSTOMARY ⟨his ~ courtesy⟩

woo \ˈwü\ *vb* **1** : to try to gain the love of : COURT **2** : SOLICIT, ENTREAT **3** : to try to gain or bring about ⟨~ public favor⟩ — **woo•er** *n*

[1]**wood** \ˈwu̇d\ *n* **1** : a dense growth of trees usu. larger than a grove and smaller than a forest — often used in pl. **2** : a hard fibrous substance that is basically xylem and forms the bulk of trees and shrubs beneath the bark; *also* : this material fit or prepared for some use (as burning or building) **3** : something made of wood

[2]**wood** *adj* **1** : WOODEN **2** : suitable for holding, cutting, or working with wood **3** *or* **woods** \ˈwu̇dz\ : living or growing in woods

[3]**wood** *vb* **1** : to supply or load with wood esp. for fuel **2** : to cover with a growth of trees

wood alcohol *n* : METHANOL

wood•bine \ˈwu̇d-ˌbīn\ *n* : any of several honeysuckles; *also* : VIRGINIA CREEPER

wood•block \-ˌbläk\ *n* : WOODCUT

wood•chop•per \-ˌchä-pər\ *n* : one engaged esp. in chopping down trees

wood•chuck \-ˌchək\ *n* : a thickset grizzled marmot of Alaska, Canada, and the northeastern U.S.

wood•cock \ˈwu̇d-ˌkäk\ *n, pl* **wood•cocks** : a brown eastern No. American game bird with a short neck and long bill that is related to the snipe; *also* : a related and similar Old World bird

wood•craft \-ˌkraft\ *n* **1** : skill and practice in matters relating to the woods and esp. in how to take care of oneself in them **2** : skill in shaping or constructing articles from wood

wood•cut \-ˌkət\ *n* **1** : a relief printing surface engraved on a block of wood **2** : a print from a woodcut

wood•cut•ter \-ˌkə-tər\ *n* : a person who cuts wood

wood duck *n* : a showy crested American duck of which the male has iridescent multicolored plumage

wood•ed \ˈwu̇-dəd\ *adj* : covered with woods or trees ⟨~ slopes⟩

wood•en \ˈwu̇-dᵊn\ *adj* **1** : made of wood **2** : lacking flexibility : awkwardly stiff ⟨~ acting⟩ — **wood•en•ly** *adv* — **wood•en•ness** *n*

wood•en•ware \ˈwu̇-dᵊn-ˌwer\ *n* : articles made of wood for domestic use

wood•land \ˈwu̇d-lənd, -ˌland\ *n* : land covered with trees : FOREST — **wood•land** *adj*

wood•lot \ˈwu̇d-ˌlät\ *n* : a restricted area of woodland usu. privately kept to meet fuel and timber needs

wood louse *n* : any of various small flat crustaceans that live esp. in ground litter and under stones and bark

wood•man \ˈwu̇d-mən\ *n* : WOODSMAN

wood nymph *n* : a nymph living in the woods

wood•peck•er \ˈwu̇d-ˌpe-kər\ *n* : any of numerous usu. brightly marked climbing birds with stiff spiny tail feathers and a chisellike bill used to drill into trees for insects

wood•pile \-ˌpī(-ə)l\ *n* : a pile of wood and esp. firewood

wood rat *n* : PACK RAT

wood•shed \-ˌshed\ *n* : a shed for storing wood and esp. firewood

woods•man \ˈwu̇dz-mən\ *n* : a person who frequents or works in the woods; *esp* : one skilled in woodcraft

woodsy \ˈwu̇d-zē\ *adj* **woods•i•er; -est** : relating to or suggestive of woods ⟨a ~ odor⟩

wood•wind \ˈwu̇d-ˌwind\ *n* : one of a group of wind instruments including flutes, clarinets, oboes, bassoons, and sometimes saxophones

wood•work \-ˌwərk\ *n* : work made of wood; *esp* : interior fittings (as moldings or stairways) of wood

woody \ˈwu̇-dē\ *adj* **wood•i•er; -est** **1** : abounding or overgrown with woods ⟨a ~ trail⟩ **2** : of or containing wood or wood fibers ⟨~ plants⟩ **3** : characteristic or suggestive of wood ⟨a ~ flavor⟩ — **wood·i·ness** \ˈwu̇-dē-nəs\ *n*

woof \ˈwu̇f\ *n* [alter. of ME *oof,* fr. OE *ōwef,* fr. *ō-* (fr. *on* on) + *wefan* to weave] **1** : WEFT 1 **2** : a woven fabric; *also* : its texture

woof·er \ˈwu̇-fər\ *n* : a loudspeaker that reproduces sounds of low pitch

wool \ˈwu̇l\ *n* **1** : the soft wavy or curly hair of some mammals and esp. the domestic sheep; *also* : something (as a textile or garment) made of wool **2** : material that resembles a mass of wool — **wooled** \ˈwu̇ld\ *adj*

¹**wool·en** *or* **wool·len** \ˈwu̇-lən\ *adj* **1** : made of wool **2** : of or relating to the manufacture or sale of woolen products ⟨~ mills⟩

²**woolen** *or* **woollen** *n* **1** : a fabric made of wool **2** : garments of woolen fabric — usu. used in pl.

wool·gath·er·ing \-ˌga-t͟hə-riŋ\ *n* : idle daydreaming

¹**wool·ly** *also* **wooly** \ˈwu̇-lē\ *adj* **wool·li·er; -est** **1** : of, relating to, or bearing wool **2** : consisting of or resembling wool **3** : mentally confused ⟨~ thinking⟩ **4** : marked by a lack of order or restraint ⟨the wild and ~ West⟩

²**wool·ly** *also* **wool·ie** *or* **wooly** \ˈwu̇-lē\ *n, pl* **wool·lies** : a garment made from wool; *esp* : underclothing of knitted wool — usu. used in pl.

woolly adel·gid \-ə-ˈdel-jəd\ *n* : either of two aphids accidentally introduced into No. America where they are serious pests of firs and hemlocks

woolly bear *n* : any of numerous very hairy moth caterpillars

woolly mammoth *n* : a heavy-coated mammoth formerly inhabiting colder parts of the northern hemisphere

woo·zy \ˈwü-zē\ *adj* **woo·zi·er; -est** **1** : BEFUDDLED **2** : somewhat dizzy, nauseated, or weak ⟨~ from fatigue⟩ **3** : somewhat indistinct or unfocused : FUZZY — **woo·zi·ness** \ˈwü-zē-nəs\ *n*

¹**word** \ˈwərd\ *n* **1** : something that is said; *esp* : a brief remark **2** : a speech sound or series of speech sounds that communicates a meaning; *also* : a graphic representation of such a sound or series of sounds **3** : ORDER, COMMAND **4** *often cap* : the 2d person of the Trinity; *also* : GOSPEL **5** : NEWS, INFORMATION **6** : PROMISE **7** *pl* : QUARREL, DISPUTE **8** : a verbal signal : PASSWORD — **word·less** *adj*

²**word** *vb* : to express in words : PHRASE

word·age \ˈwər-dij\ *n* **1** : WORDS **2** : number of words **3** : WORDING

word·book \ˈwərd-ˌbu̇k\ *n* : VOCABULARY, DICTIONARY

word·ing \ˈwər-diŋ\ *n* : verbal expression : PHRASEOLOGY

word of mouth : oral communication

word·play \ˈwərd-ˌplā\ *n* : playful use of words

word processing *n* : the production of typewritten documents with automated and usu. computerized text-editing equipment — **word process** *vb*

word processor *n* : a keyboard-operated terminal for use in word processing; *also* : software to perform word processing

wordy \ˈwər-dē\ *adj* **word·i·er; -est** : using or having too many words ⟨~ sentences⟩ ♦ ***Synonyms*** PROLIX, DIFFUSE, REDUNDANT — **word·i·ness** \-dē-nəs\ *n*

wore *past of* WEAR

¹**work** \ˈwərk\ *n* **1** : TOIL, LABOR; *also* : EMPLOYMENT ⟨out of ~⟩ **2** : TASK, JOB ⟨have ~ to do⟩ **3** : the energy used when a force is applied over a given distance **4** : DEED, ACHIEVEMENT **5** : a fortified structure **6** *pl* : engineering structures **7** *pl* : a place where industrial labor is done : PLANT, FACTORY **8** *pl* : the moving parts of a mechanism **9** : something produced by mental effort or physical labor; *esp* : an artistic production (as a book or needlework) **10** : WORKMANSHIP ⟨careless ~⟩ **11** : material in the process of manufacture **12** *pl* : everything possessed, available, or belonging ⟨the whole ~*s* went overboard⟩; *also* : drastic treatment ⟨gave him the ~*s*⟩ ♦ ***Synonyms*** OCCUPATION, EMPLOYMENT, BUSINESS, PURSUIT, CALLING — **in the works** : in process of preparation

²**work** *adj* **1** : used for work ⟨~ vehicles⟩ **2** : suitable or styled for wear while working ⟨~ clothes⟩ **3** : involving or engaged in work ⟨~ hours⟩ ⟨a ~ crew⟩

³**work** *vb* **worked** \ˈwərkt\ *or* **wrought** \ˈrȯt\; **work·ing** **1** : to bring to pass : EFFECT **2** : to fashion or create a useful or desired product through labor or exertion **3** : to prepare for use (as by kneading) **4** : to bring into a desired form by a manufacturing process ⟨~ cold steel⟩ **5** : to set or keep in operation : OPERATE ⟨a pump ~*ed* by hand⟩ **6** : to solve by reasoning or calculation ⟨~ out a problem⟩ **7** : to cause to toil or labor ⟨~*ed* the team hard⟩; *also* : to make use of ⟨~ a mine⟩ **8** : to pay for with labor or service ⟨~ off a debt⟩ **9** : to bring or get into some position or condition by stages ⟨the stream ~*ed* itself clear⟩ ⟨the knot ~*ed* loose⟩ **10** : CONTRIVE, ARRANGE ⟨~ it so you can leave early⟩ **11** : to practice trickery or cajolery on ⟨~*ed* the management for a free ticket⟩ **12** : EXCITE, PROVOKE ⟨~*ed* himself into a rage⟩ **13** : to exert oneself physically or mentally; *esp* : to perform work regularly for wages **14** : to function according to plan or design **15** : to produce a desired effect : SUCCEED ⟨the plan ~*ed*⟩ **16** : to make way slowly and with difficulty ⟨he ~*ed* forward through the crowd⟩ **17** : to permit of being worked ⟨this wood ~*s* easily⟩ **18** : to be in restless motion; *also* : FERMENT 1 — **work on** **1** : AFFECT **2** : to try to influence or persuade — **work upon** : to have effect upon : operate on : INFLUENCE

work·able \ˈwər-kə-bəl\ *adj* **1** : capable of being worked ⟨~ clay⟩ **2** : PRACTICABLE, FEASIBLE — **work·able·ness** *n*

work·a·day \ˈwər-kə-ˌdā\ *adj* **1** : relating to or suited for working days **2** : PROSAIC, ORDINARY ⟨~ chores⟩

work·a·hol·ic \ˌwər-kə-ˈhȯ-lik, -ˈhä-\ *n* : a compulsive worker
work·bench \-ˌbench\ *n* : a bench on which work esp. of mechanics, machinists, and carpenters is performed
work·book \-ˌbu̇k\ *n* **1** : a worker's manual **2** : a student's book of problems to be answered directly on the pages
work·day \ˈwərk-ˌdā\ *n* **1** : a day on which work is done as distinguished from a day off **2** : the period of time in a day when work is performed
work·er \ˈwər-kər\ *n* **1** : one that works; *esp* : a person who works for wages **2** : any of the sexually undeveloped individuals of a colony of social insects (as bees, ants, or termites) that perform the work of the community
workers' compensation *n* : a system of insurance that reimburses an employer for damages paid to an employee who was injured while working
work ethic *n* : belief in work as a moral good
work farm *n* : a farm on which persons guilty of minor law violations are confined
work·horse \ˈwərk-ˌhȯrs\ *n* **1** : a horse used for hard work **2** : a person who does most of the work of a group task **3** : something that is useful, durable, or dependable
work·house \-ˌhau̇s\ *n* **1** *Brit* : POORHOUSE **2** : a house of correction for persons guilty of minor law violations
[1]**work·ing** \ˈwər-kiŋ\ *n* **1** : manner of functioning — usu. used in pl. **2** *pl* : an excavation made in mining or tunneling
[2]**working** *adj* **1** : engaged in work ⟨a ~ journalist⟩ **2** : adequate to allow work to be done ⟨a ~ majority⟩ ⟨a ~ knowledge of French⟩ **3** : adopted or assumed to help further work or activity ⟨a ~ draft⟩ **4** : spent at work ⟨~ life⟩
work·ing·man \ˈwər-kiŋ-ˌman\ *n* : WORKER 1
work·man \ˈwərk-mən\ *n* **1** : WORKER 1 **2** : ARTISAN, CRAFTSMAN
work·man·like \-ˌlīk\ *adj* : worthy of a good workman : SKILLFUL
work·man·ship \-ˌship\ *n* : the art or skill of a workman : CRAFTSMANSHIP; *also* : the quality of a piece of work ⟨a vase of exquisite ~⟩
work·out \ˈwərk-ˌau̇t\ *n* **1** : a practice or exercise to test or improve one's fitness, ability, or performance **2** : a test or trial to determine ability or capacity or suitability
work out *vb* **1** : to bring about esp. by resolving difficulties **2** : DEVELOP, ELABORATE **3** : to prove effective, practicable, or suitable ⟨our plan didn't *work out*⟩ **4** : to amount to a total or calculated figure — used with *at* **5** : to engage in a workout
work·place \ˈwərk-ˌplās\ *n* : a place (as an office) where work is done
work·room \ˈwərk-ˌrüm, -ˌru̇m\ *n* : a room used for work
work·shop \-ˌshäp\ *n* **1** : a shop where manufacturing or handicrafts are carried on **2** : a seminar emphasizing exchange of ideas and practical methods
work·sta·tion \-ˌstā-shən\ *n* : an area with equipment for the performance of a specialized task; *also* : a personal computer usu. connected to a computer network
world \ˈwərld\ *n* [ME, fr. OE *woruld* human existence, this world, age, fr. a prehistoric compound whose first constituent is represented by OE *wer* man and whose second constituent is akin to OE *eald* old] **1** : the earth with its inhabitants and all things upon it **2** : people in general : HUMANKIND **3** : human affairs ⟨withdraw from the ~⟩ **4** : CREATION 3 **5** : a state of existence : scene of life and action ⟨the ~ of the future⟩ **6** : a distinctive class of persons or their sphere of interest ⟨the musical ~⟩ **7** : a part or section of the earth or its inhabitants by itself **8** : a great number or quantity ⟨a ~ of troubles⟩ **9** : a celestial body
world–beat·er \-ˌbē-tər\ *n* : one that excels all others of its kind : CHAMPION
world–class *adj* : of the highest caliber in the world ⟨a ~ athlete⟩
world·ling \-liŋ\ *n* : a person absorbed in the concerns of the present world
world·ly \-lē\ *adj* **1** : of, relating to, or devoted to this world and its pursuits rather than to religion or spiritual affairs ⟨~ pleasures⟩ **2** : WORLDLY-WISE, SOPHISTICATED — **world·li·ness** \-lē-nəs\ *n*
world·ly–wise \-ˌwīz\ *adj* : possessing a practical and often shrewd understanding of human affairs
world·wide \ˈwərld-ˈwīd\ *adj* : extended throughout the entire world ⟨attracted ~ attention⟩ — **worldwide** *adv*
World Wide Web *n* : a part of the Internet usu. accessed through a browser and containing files connected by hyperlinks
[1]**worm** \ˈwərm\ *n* **1** : any of various small long usu. naked and soft-bodied round or flat invertebrate animals (as an earthworm, nematode, tapeworm, or maggot) **2** : a human being who is an object of contempt, loathing, or pity : WRETCH **3** : something that inwardly torments or devours **4** *pl* : infestation with or disease caused by parasitic worms **5** : a spiral or wormlike thing (as the thread of a screw) — **worm·like** \-ˌlīk\ *adj* — **wormy** *adj*
[2]**worm** *vb* **1** : to move or cause to move or proceed slowly and deviously **2** : to insinuate or introduce (oneself) by devious or subtle means **3** : to obtain or extract by artful or insidious pleading, asking, or persuading ⟨~*ed* the truth out of him⟩ **4** : to treat (an animal) with a drug to destroy or expel parasitic worms
worm–eat·en \ˈwərm-ˌē-tᵊn\ *adj* : eaten or burrowed by worms
worm gear *n* : a mechanical linkage consisting of a short rotating screw whose threads mesh with the teeth of a gear wheel
worm·hole \ˈwərm-ˌhōl\ *n* : a hole or passage burrowed by a worm

worm·wood \-ˌwu̇d\ *n* **1** : any of a genus of aromatic woody plants (as a sagebrush); *esp* : one of Europe used in absinthe **2** : something bitter or grievous : BITTERNESS

worn *past part of* WEAR

worn–out \ˈwōrn-ˈau̇t\ *adj* : exhausted or used up by or as if by wear

wor·ri·some \ˈwər-ē-səm\ *adj* **1** : causing distress or worry ⟨~ news⟩ **2** : inclined to worry or fret ⟨a ~ mother⟩

¹wor·ry \ˈwər-ē\ *vb* **wor·ried; wor·ry·ing** **1** : to shake and mangle with the teeth ⟨a terrier *~ing* a rat⟩ **2** : to make anxious or upset ⟨her poor health *worries* me⟩ **3** : to feel or express great care or anxiety : FRET ⟨*~ing* about his health⟩ — **wor·ri·er** *n*

²worry *n, pl* **worries** **1** : ANXIETY **2** : a cause of anxiety : TROUBLE

wor·ry·wart \ˈwər-ē-ˌwȯrt\ *n* : one who is inclined to worry unduly

¹worse \ˈwərs\ *adj, comparative of* BAD *or of* ILL **1** : bad or evil in a greater degree : less good **2** : more unfavorable, unpleasant, or painful; *also* : SICKER

²worse *n* **1** : one that is worse **2** : a greater degree of ill or badness ⟨a turn for the ~⟩

³worse *adv, comparative of* BAD *or of* ILL : in a worse manner : to a worse extent or degree ⟨you drive ~ than he does⟩

wors·en \ˈwər-sᵊn\ *vb* : to make or become worse ⟨the rash *~ed*⟩

¹wor·ship \ˈwər-shəp\ *n* [ME *worshipe* worthiness, respect, reverence paid to a divine being, fr. OE *weorthscipe* worthiness, respect, fr. *weorth* worthy, worth + *-scipe* -ship, suffix denoting quality or condition] **1** *chiefly Brit* : a person of importance — used as a title for officials **2** : reverence toward a divine being or supernatural power; *also* : the expression of such reverence **3** : extravagant respect or admiration or devotion ⟨~ of the dollar⟩

²worship *vb* **-shipped** *also* **-shiped; -shipp·ing** *also* **-ship·ing** **1** : to honor or reverence as a divine being or supernatural power **2** : IDOLIZE ⟨*~s* his brother⟩ **3** : to perform or take part in worship — **wor·ship·er** *or* **wor·ship·per** *n*

wor·ship·ful \ˈwər-shəp-fəl\ *adj* **1** *archaic* : NOTABLE, DISTINGUISHED **2** *chiefly Brit* — used as a title for various persons or groups of rank or distinction **3** : VENERATING, WORSHIPING ⟨~ fans⟩

¹worst \ˈwərst\ *adj, superlative of* BAD *or of* ILL **1** : most bad, evil, ill, or corrupt ⟨the ~ criminals⟩ **2** : most unfavorable, unpleasant, or painful ⟨the ~ scenario⟩; *also* : most unsuitable, faulty, or unattractive **3** : least skillful or efficient ⟨her ~ students⟩

²worst *adv, superlative of* ILL *or of* BAD *or* BADLY **1** : to the extreme degree of badness or inferiority ⟨the ~ dressed person⟩ : in the worst manner **2** : MOST ⟨those who need help ~⟩

³worst *n* : one that is worst

⁴worst *vb* : DEFEAT

wor·sted \ˈwu̇s-təd, ˈwər-stəd\ *n* [ME, fr. *Worsted* (now *Worstead*), England] : a smooth compact yarn from long wool fibers; *also* : a fabric made from such yarn

wort \ˈwərt, ˈwȯrt\ *n* : a sweet liquid drained from mash and fermented to form beer and whiskey

¹worth \ˈwərth\ *n* **1** : monetary value; *also* : the equivalent of a specified amount or figure ⟨$5 ~ of gas⟩ **2** : the value of something measured by its qualities **3** : MERIT, EXCELLENCE

²worth *prep* **1** : equal in value to; *also* : having possessions or income equal to **2** : deserving of ⟨well ~ the effort⟩

worth·less \ˈwərth-ləs\ *adj* **1** : lacking worth : VALUELESS; *also* : USELESS **2** : LOW, DESPICABLE ⟨a ~ coward⟩ — **worth·less·ness** *n*

worth·while \ˈwərth-ˈhwī(-ə)l\ *adj* : being worth the time or effort spent

¹wor·thy \ˈwər-t͟hē\ *adj* **wor·thi·er; -est** **1** : having worth or value : ESTIMABLE ⟨a ~ cause⟩ **2** : HONORABLE, MERITORIOUS ⟨my ~ opponent⟩ **3** : having sufficient worth ⟨~ of the honor⟩ — **wor·thi·ly** \ˈwər-t͟hə-lē\ *adv* — **wor·thi·ness** \-t͟hē-nəs\ *n*

²worthy *n, pl* **worthies** : a worthy person

would \ˈwu̇d\ *past of* WILL **1** *archaic* : wish for : WANT **2** : strongly desire : WISH ⟨I ~ I were young again⟩ **3** — used as an auxiliary to express (1) preference ⟨~ rather run than fight⟩, (2) wish, desire, or intent ⟨those who ~ forbid gambling⟩, (3) habitual action ⟨we ~ meet often for lunch⟩, (4) a contingency or possibility ⟨if he were coming, he ~ be here by now⟩, (5) probability ⟨~ have won if he hadn't tripped⟩, or (6) a request ⟨~ you help us⟩ **4** : COULD **5** : SHOULD

would–be \ˈwu̇d-ˈbē\ *adj, disparaging* : desiring or pretending to be ⟨a ~ artist⟩

¹wound \ˈwünd\ *n* **1** : an injury involving cutting or breaking of bodily tissue (as by violence, accident, or surgery) **2** : an injury or hurt to feelings or reputation

²wound *vb* : to inflict a wound to or in

³wound \ˈwau̇nd\ *past and past part of* WIND

wove *past of* WEAVE

woven *past part of* WEAVE

¹wow \ˈwau̇\ *n* : a striking success : HIT

²wow *vb* : to arouse enthusiastic approval ⟨*~ed* the critics⟩

WP *abbr* word processing; word processor

WPM *abbr* words per minute

wpn *abbr* weapon

wrack \ˈrak\ *n* [ME, fr. OE *wræc* misery, punishment, something driven by the sea] : violent or total destruction

wraith \ˈrāth\ *n, pl* **wraiths** \ˈrāths, ˈrāt͟hz\ **1** : GHOST, SPECTER **2** : an insubstantial appearance : SHADOW

¹wran·gle \ˈraŋ-gəl\ *vb* **wran·gled; wran·gling** **1** : to quarrel angrily or peevishly : BICKER **2** : ARGUE ⟨they *wrangled* about money⟩ **3** : to obtain by persistent arguing **4** : to herd and care for (livestock) on the range — **wran·gler** *n*

[2]**wrangle** *n* : an angry, noisy, or prolonged dispute; *also* : CONTROVERSY

[1]**wrap** \ˈrap\ *vb* **wrapped; wrap·ping** **1** : to cover esp. by winding or folding **2** : to envelop and secure for transportation or storage **3** : to enclose wholly : ENFOLD **4** : to coil, fold, draw, or twine about something **5** : SURROUND, ENVELOP ⟨*wrapped* in mystery⟩ **6** : INVOLVE, ENGROSS ⟨*wrapped* up in a hobby⟩ **7** : to complete filming or recording

[2]**wrap** *n* **1** : WRAPPER, WRAPPING **2** : an article of clothing that may be wrapped around a person **3** *pl* : SECRECY ⟨kept under ∼*s*⟩ **4** : completion of filming or recording **5** : a thin piece of bread that is rolled around a filling

wrap·around \ˈra-pə-ˌraủnd\ *n* : a garment (as a dress) adjusted to the figure by wrapping around

wrap·per \ˈra-pər\ *n* **1** : that in which something is wrapped **2** : one that wraps **3** : an article of clothing worn wrapped around the body

wrap·ping \ˈra-piŋ\ *n* : something used to wrap an object : WRAPPER

wrap–up \ˈrap-ˌəp\ *n* : SUMMARY

wrap up *vb* **1** : SUMMARIZE, SUM UP **2** : to bring to a usu. successful conclusion

wrasse \ˈras\ *n* : any of a large family of usu. brightly colored marine fishes including many food fishes

wrath \ˈrath\ *n* **1** : violent anger : RAGE **2** : divine punishment ♦ ***Synonyms*** INDIGNATION, IRE, FURY, ANGER

wrath·ful \-fəl\ *adj* **1** : filled with wrath : very angry **2** : showing, marked by, or arising from anger ⟨a ∼ assault⟩ — **wrath·ful·ly** *adv* — **wrath·ful·ness** *n*

wreak \ˈrēk\ *vb* [ME *wreken,* fr. OE *wrecan* to drive, punish, avenge] **1** : to exact as a punishment : INFLICT ⟨∼ vengeance on an enemy⟩ **2** : to give free scope or rein to ⟨∼*ed* his wrath⟩ **3** : BRING ABOUT, CAUSE ⟨∼ havoc⟩

wreath \ˈrēth\ *n, pl* **wreaths** \ˈrēt͟hz, ˈrēths\ : a circular band of flowers or leaves usu. for decoration; *also* : something having a circular or coiling form ⟨a ∼ of smoke⟩

wreathe \ˈrēt͟h\ *vb* **wreathed; wreath·ing** **1** : to shape or take on the shape of a wreath **2** : to crown, decorate, or cover with or as if with a wreath ⟨a face *wreathed* in smiles⟩

[1]**wreck** \ˈrek\ *n* **1** : something (as goods) cast up on the land by the sea after a shipwreck **2** : SHIPWRECK **3** : a destructive crash ⟨a car ∼⟩ **4** : the action of breaking up or destroying something **5** : broken remains (as of a vehicle after a crash) **6** : something disabled or in a state of ruin; *also* : an individual broken in health, strength, or spirits ⟨he's a nervous ∼⟩

[2]**wreck** *vb* **1** : SHIPWRECK **2** : to ruin or damage by breaking up ⟨∼*ed* his marriage⟩ : involve in disaster or ruin

wreck·age \ˈre-kij\ *n* **1** : the act of wrecking : the state of being wrecked : RUIN **2** : the remains of a wreck

wreck·er \ˈre-kər\ *n* **1** : one that searches for or works upon the wrecks of ships **2** : TOW TRUCK **3** : one that wrecks; *esp* : one whose work is the demolition of buildings

wren \ˈren\ *n* : any of a family of small mostly brown singing birds with short wings and often a tail that points upward

[1]**wrench** \ˈrench\ *vb* **1** : to move with a violent twist **2** : to pull, strain, or tighten with violent twisting or force **3** : to injure or disable by a violent twisting or straining ⟨∼*ed* her back⟩ **4** : to snatch forcibly : WREST

[2]**wrench** *n* **1** : a forcible twisting; *also* : an injury (as to one's ankle) by twisting **2** : a tool for holding, twisting, or turning (as nuts or bolts)

[1]**wrest** \ˈrest\ *vb* **1** : to pull or move by a forcible twisting movement **2** : to gain with difficulty by or as if by force or violence ⟨∼ control of the government from the dictator⟩

[2]**wrest** *n* : a forcible twist : WRENCH

[1]**wres·tle** \ˈre-səl, ˈra-\ *vb* **wres·tled; wres·tling** **1** : to grapple with and try to throw down an opponent **2** : to compete against in wrestling **3** : to struggle for control (as of something difficult) ⟨∼ with a problem⟩ — **wres·tler** \ˈres-lər, ˈras-\ *n*

[2]**wrestle** *n* : the action or an instance of wrestling : STRUGGLE

wres·tling \ˈres-liŋ\ *n* : the sport in which two opponents wrestle each other

wretch \ˈrech\ *n* [ME *wrecche,* fr. OE *wrecca* outcast, exile] **1** : a miserable unhappy person **2** : a base, despicable, or vile person

wretch·ed \ˈre-chəd\ *adj* **1** : deeply afflicted, dejected, or distressed : MISERABLE **2** : WOEFUL, GRIEVOUS ⟨a ∼ accident⟩ **3** : DESPICABLE ⟨a ∼ trick⟩ **4** : poor in quality or ability : INFERIOR ⟨∼ workmanship⟩ — **wretch·ed·ly** *adv* — **wretch·ed·ness** *n*

wrig·gle \ˈri-gəl\ *vb* **wrig·gled; wrig·gling** **1** : to twist or move to and fro like a worm : SQUIRM ⟨*wriggled* in his chair⟩ ⟨∼ your toes⟩; *also* : to move along by twisting and turning ⟨a snake *wriggled* along the path⟩ **2** : to extricate oneself as if by wriggling ⟨∼ out of difficulty⟩ — **wriggle** *n*

wrig·gler *n* **1** : one that wriggles **2** : WIGGLER 1

wring \ˈriŋ\ *vb* **wrung** \ˈrəŋ\; **wring·ing** \ˈriŋ-iŋ\ **1** : to squeeze or twist esp. so as to make dry or to extract moisture or liquid ⟨∼ wet clothes⟩ **2** : to get by or as if by twisting or pressing ⟨∼ the truth out of him⟩ **3** : to twist so as to strain or sprain : CONTORT ⟨∼ his neck⟩ **4** : to twist together as a sign of anguish ⟨*wrung* her hands⟩ **5** : to affect painfully as if by wringing : TORMENT ⟨her plight *wrung* my heart⟩

wring·er \ˈriŋ-ər\ *n* : one that wrings; *esp* : a device for squeezing out liquid or moisture ⟨clothes ∼⟩

[1]**wrin·kle** \ˈriŋ-kəl\ *n* **1** : a crease or small fold on a smooth surface (as in the skin or in cloth) **2** : a clever or new method, trick, or idea — **wrin·kly** \-k(ə-)lē\ *adj*

[2]**wrinkle** *vb* **wrin·kled; wrin·kling** : to develop or cause to develop wrinkles

wrist \ˈrist\ *n* : the joint or region between the hand and the arm; *also* : a corresponding part in a lower animal

wrist·band \-ˌband\ *n* : a band or the part of a sleeve encircling the wrist

wrist·let \-lət\ *n* : WRISTBAND; *esp* : a close-fitting knitted band attached to the top of a glove or the end of a sleeve

wrist·watch \-ˌwäch\ *n* : a small watch attached to a bracelet or strap to fasten about the wrist

writ \ˈrit\ *n* **1** : something written **2** : a written legal order signed by a court officer

writ·able \ˈrī-tə-bəl\ *adj* : being an electronic storage medium on which it is possible to introduce new data ⟨a ~ DVD⟩

write \ˈrīt\ *vb* **wrote** \ˈrōt\; **writ·ten** \ˈri-tᵊn\ *also* **writ** \ˈrit\; **writ·ing** \ˈrī-tiŋ\ [ME, fr. OE *wrītan* to scratch, draw, inscribe] **1** : to form characters, letters, or words on a surface ⟨learn to read and ~⟩ **2** : to form the letters or the words of ⟨~ your name⟩ ⟨~ a check⟩ **3** : to put down on paper : express in writing **4** : to make up and set down for others to read ⟨~ a book⟩ ⟨~ music⟩ **5** : to write a letter to **6** : to communicate by letter : CORRESPOND

write–in \ˈrīt-ˌin\ *n* : a vote cast by writing in the name of a candidate; *also* : a candidate whose name is written in

write in *vb* : to insert (a name not listed on a ballot) in an appropriate space; *also* : to cast (a vote) in this manner

write off *vb* : to eliminate (an asset) from a bookkeeping record : enter as a loss or expense

writ·er \ˈrī-tər\ *n* : one that writes esp. as a business or occupation : AUTHOR

writer's cramp *n* : a painful spasmodic contraction of muscles of the hand or fingers brought on by excessive writing

write–up \ˈrīt-ˌəp\ *n* : a written account (as in a newspaper); *esp* : a flattering article

writhe \ˈrīth\ *vb* **writhed; writh·ing** **1** : to twist and turn this way and that ⟨~ in pain⟩ **2** : to suffer with shame or confusion

writing *n* **1** : the act of one that writes; *also* : HANDWRITING **2** : something that is written or printed **3** : a style or form of composition **4** : the occupation of a writer

Writings \ˈrī-tiŋz\ *n pl* : the third part of the Jewish scriptures

wrnt *abbr* warrant

[1]**wrong** \ˈrȯŋ\ *n* **1** : an injurious, unfair, or unjust act **2** : a violation of the legal rights of another person **3** : something that is wrong : wrong principles, practices, or conduct ⟨know right from ~⟩ **4** : the state, position, or fact of being wrong ⟨was in the ~⟩

[2]**wrong** *adj* **wrong·er** \ˈrȯŋ-ər\; **wrong·est** \ˈrȯŋ-əst\ **1** : SINFUL, IMMORAL **2** : not right according to a standard or code : IMPROPER **3** : INCORRECT ⟨a ~ solution⟩ **4** : UNSATISFACTORY **5** : UNSUITABLE, INAPPROPRIATE **6** : constituting a surface that is considered the back, bottom, inside, or reverse of something ⟨iron only on the ~ side of the fabric⟩ ♦ ***Synonyms*** FALSE, ERRONEOUS, INCORRECT, INACCURATE, UNTRUE — **wrong·ly** *adv*

[3]**wrong** *adv* **1** : INCORRECTLY **2** : in a wrong direction, manner, or relation

[4]**wrong** *vb* **wronged; wrong·ing** \ˈrȯŋ-iŋ\ **1** : to do wrong to : INJURE, HARM **2** : to treat unjustly : DISHONOR, MALIGN ♦ ***Synonyms*** OPPRESS, PERSECUTE, AGGRIEVE

wrong·do·er \ˈrȯŋ-ˌdü-ər\ *n* : a person who does wrong and esp. moral wrong — **wrong·do·ing** \-ˌdü-iŋ\ *n*

wrong·ful \ˈrȯŋ-fəl\ *adj* **1** : WRONG, UNJUST **2** : UNLAWFUL ⟨~ conduct⟩ — **wrong·ful·ly** *adv* — **wrong·ful·ness** *n*

wrong·head·ed \-ˈhe-dəd\ *adj* : stubborn in clinging to wrong opinion or principles — **wrong·head·ed·ly** *adv* — **wrong·head·ed·ness** *n*

wrote *past of* WRITE

wroth \ˈrȯth, ˈrōth\ *adj* : filled with wrath : ANGRY

wrought \ˈrȯt\ *adj* [ME, fr. pp. of *worken* to work] **1** : FASHIONED, FORMED ⟨carefully ~ essays⟩ **2** : ORNAMENTED **3** : beaten into shape by tools : HAMMERED ⟨~ metals⟩ **4** : deeply stirred : EXCITED ⟨gets easily ~ up⟩

wrung *past and past part of* WRING

wry \ˈrī\ *adj* **wry·er** \ˈrī-ər\; **wry·est** \ˈrī-əst\ **1** : having a bent or twisted shape ⟨a ~ smile⟩; *also* : turned abnormally to one side : CONTORTED ⟨a ~ neck⟩ **2** : cleverly and often ironically humorous — **wry·ly** *adv* — **wry·ness** *n*

wry·neck \ˈrī-ˌnek\ *n* **1** : either of two Old World woodpeckers that differ from typical woodpeckers in having a peculiar manner of twisting the head and neck **2** : an abnormal twisting of the neck and head to one side caused by muscle spasms

WSW *abbr* west-southwest

wt *abbr* weight

wurst \ˈwərst, ˈwu̇rst\ *n* : SAUSAGE

wu·shu \ˈwü-ˈshü\ *n* [Chin (Beijing) *wǔshù*, fr. *wǔ* martial + *shù* art] : Chinese martial arts

wuss \ˈwu̇s\ *n* : WIMP — **wussy** \ˈwu̇-sē\ *adj*

WV *or* **W Va** *abbr* West Virginia

WW *abbr* World War

w/w *abbr* wall-to-wall

WY *or* **Wyo** *abbr* Wyoming

WYS·I·WYG \ˈwi-zē-ˌwig\ *adj* [*w*hat *y*ou *s*ee *i*s *w*hat *y*ou *g*et] : of, relating to, or being a computer display that shows a document exactly as it will appear when printed out

X

[1]**x** \ˈeks\ *n, pl* **x's** *or* **xs** \ˈek-səz\ *often cap* **1 :** the 24th letter of the English alphabet **2 :** an unknown quantity
[2]**x** *vb* **x-ed** *also* **x'd** *or* **xed** \ˈekst\; **x-ing** *or* **x'ing** \ˈek-siŋ\ **:** to cancel or obliterate with a series of *x*'s — usu. used with *out*
[3]**x** *abbr* **1** ex **2** experimental **3** extra
[4]**x** *symbol* **1** times ⟨3 *x* 2 is 6⟩ **2** by ⟨a 3 *x* 5 index card⟩ **3** *often cap* power of magnification
Xan•a•du \ˈza-nə-ˌdü, -ˌdyü\ *n* [fr. *Xanadu,* locality in *Kubla Khan* (1798), poem by Eng. poet Samuel Taylor Coleridge †1834] **:** an idyllic, exotic, or luxurious place
Xan•thip•pe \zan-ˈthi-pē, -ˈti-\ *or* **Xan•tip•pe** \-ˈti-pē\ *n* [Gk *Xanthippē,* shrewish wife of Socrates] **:** an ill-tempered woman
x–ax•is \ˈeks-ˌak-səs\ *n* **:** the axis of a graph or of a system of coordinates in a plane parallel to which abscissas are measured
XC *abbr* cross-country
X chromosome *n* **:** a sex chromosome that usu. occurs paired in each female cell and single in each male cell in organisms (as humans) in which the male normally has two unlike sex chromosomes
Xe *symbol* xenon
xe•non \ˈzē-ˌnän, ˈze-\ *n* [Gk, neut. of *xenos* strange] **:** a heavy gaseous chemical element occurring in minute quantities in air
xe•no•pho•bia \ˌze-nə-ˈfō-bē-ə, ˌzē-\ *n* **:** fear and hatred of strangers or foreigners or of what is strange or foreign — **xe•no•phobe** \ˈze-nə-ˌfōb, ˈzē-\ *n* — **xe•no•pho•bic** \ˌze-nə-ˈfō-bik, ˌzē-\ *adj*
xe•ric \ˈzir-ik, ˈzer-\ *adj* **:** characterized by or requiring only a small amount of moisture ⟨a ~ habitat⟩
xeri•scape \ˈzir-ə-ˌskāp, ˈzer-\ *n, often cap* **:** a landscaping method utilizing water-conserving techniques
xe•rog•ra•phy \zə-ˈrä-grə-fē\ *n* **:** a process for copying printed matter by the action of light on an electrically charged surface in which the latent image is developed with a powder — **xe•ro•graph•ic** \ˌzir-ə-ˈgra-fik\ *adj*
xe•ro•phyte \ˈzir-ə-ˌfīt\ *n* **:** a plant adapted for growth with a limited water supply — **xe•ro•phyt•ic** \ˌzir-ə-ˈfi-tik\ *adj*
xi \ˈzī, ˈksī\ *n* **:** the 14th letter of the Greek alphabet — Ξ or ξ
XL *abbr* **1** extra large **2** extra long
Xmas \ˈkris-məs *also* ˈeks-məs\ *n* [*X* (symbol for *Christ,* fr. the Gk letter chi (X), initial of *Christos* Christ) + *-mas* (in *Christmas*)] **:** CHRISTMAS
XML \ˌeks-(ˌ)em-ˈel\ *n* **:** a markup language that indicates the structural type of data
XO *abbr* executive officer
x–ra•di•a•tion \ˌeks-ˌrā-dē-ˈā-shən\ *n, often cap* **1 :** exposure to X-rays **2 :** radiation consisting of X-rays
x–ray \ˈeks-ˌrā\ *vb, often cap* **:** to examine, treat, or photograph with X-rays
X–ray \ˈeks-ˌrā\ *n* **1 :** a radiation with an extremely short wavelength of less than 100 angstroms that is able to penetrate through various thicknesses of solids and to act on photographic film **2 :** a photograph taken with X-rays — **X–ray** *adj*
XS *abbr* extra small
xu \ˈsü\ *n, pl* **xu** — see *dong* at MONEY table
xy•lem \ˈzī-ləm, -ˌlem\ *n* **:** a woody tissue of vascular plants that transports water and dissolved materials upward, functions in support and storage, and lies central to the phloem
xy•lo•phone \ˈzī-lə-ˌfōn\ *n* [Gk *xylon* wood + *phōnē* voice, sound] **:** a musical instrument consisting of a series of wooden bars graduated in length to produce the musical scale, supported on belts of straw or felt, and sounded by striking with two small wooden hammers — **xy•lo•phon•ist** \-ˌfō-nist\ *n*

Y

[1]**y** \ˈwī\ *n, pl* **y's** *or* **ys** \ˈwīz\ *often cap* **:** the 25th letter of the English alphabet
[2]**y** *abbr* **1** yard **2** year
[1]**Y** \ˈwī\ *n* **:** YMCA, YWCA
[2]**Y** *symbol* yttrium
[1]**-y** *also* **-ey** \ē\ *adj suffix* **1 :** characterized by **:** full of ⟨dirt*y*⟩ ⟨clay*ey*⟩ **2 :** having the character of **:** composed of ⟨ic*y*⟩ **3 :** like **:** like that of ⟨home*y*⟩ ⟨wintr*y*⟩ ⟨stag*y*⟩ **4 :** tending or inclined to ⟨sleep*y*⟩ ⟨chatt*y*⟩ **5 :** giving occasion for (specified) action ⟨tear*y*⟩ **6 :** performing (specified) action ⟨curl*y*⟩
[2]**-y** \ē\ *n suffix, pl* **-ies** **1 :** state **:** condition **:** quality ⟨beggar*y*⟩ **2 :** activity, place of business, or goods dealt with ⟨laundr*y*⟩ **3 :** whole body or group ⟨soldier*y*⟩
[3]**-y** *n suffix, pl* **-ies** **:** instance of a (specified) action ⟨entreat*y*⟩ ⟨inquir*y*⟩

YA *abbr* young adult

[1]**yacht** \ˈyät\ *n* [obs. D *jaght,* fr. Middle Low German *jacht,* short for *jachtschip,* lit., hunting ship] : a usu. large recreational watercraft

[2]**yacht** *vb* : to race or cruise in a yacht

yacht•ing \ˈyä-tiŋ\ *n* : the sport of racing or cruising in a yacht

yachts•man \ˈyäts-mən\ *n* : a person who owns or sails a yacht

ya•hoo \ˈyā-hü, ˈyä-\ *n, pl* **yahoos** [fr. *Yahoo,* one of a race of brutes having the form of humans in Jonathan Swift's *Gulliver's Travels*] : a boorish, crass, or stupid person

Yah•weh \ˈyä-ˌwā\ *also* **Yah•veh** \-ˌvā\ *n* : GOD 1 — used esp. by the Hebrews

[1]**yak** \ˈyak\ *n, pl* **yaks** *also* **yak** : a large long-haired wild or domesticated ox of Tibet and adjacent Asian uplands

[2]**yak** *also* **yack** \ˈyak\ *n* : persistent or voluble talk — **yak** *also* **yack** *vb*

yam \ˈyam\ *n* **1** : the edible starchy root of various twining plants used as a staple food in tropical areas; *also* : a plant that produces yams **2** : a usu. deep orange sweet potato

yam•mer \ˈya-mər\ *vb* [ME *yameren,* alter. of *yomeren* to murmur, be sad, fr. OE *gēomrian*] **1** : WHIMPER **2** : CHATTER — **yammer** *n*

[1]**yank** \ˈyaŋk\ *vb* : to pull with a quick vigorous movement

[2]**yank** *n* : a strong sudden pull : JERK

Yank \ˈyaŋk\ *n* : YANKEE

Yan•kee \ˈyaŋ-kē\ *n* **1** : a native or inhabitant of New England; *also* : a native or inhabitant of the northern U.S. **2** : a native or inhabitant of the U.S.

yan•qui \ˈyäŋ-kē\ *n, often cap* [Sp] : a citizen of the U.S. as distinguished from a Latin American

[1]**yap** \ˈyap\ *vb* **yapped; yap•ping 1** : BARK, YELP **2** : GAB

[2]**yap** *n* **1** : a quick sharp bark **2** : CHATTER

[1]**yard** \ˈyärd\ *n* [ME, fr. OE *geard* enclosure, yard] **1** : a small enclosed area open to the sky and adjacent to a building **2** : the grounds of a building **3** : the grounds surrounding a house usu. covered with grass **4** : an enclosure for livestock **5** : an area set aside for a particular business or activity **6** : a system of railroad tracks for storing cars and making up trains

[2]**yard** *n* [ME *yarde,* fr. OE *gierd* twig, measure, yard] **1** — see WEIGHT table **2** : a long spar tapered toward the ends that supports and spreads the head of a sail — **the whole nine yards** : all of a set of circumstances, conditions, or details

yard•age \ˈyär-dij\ *n* : an aggregate number of yards; *also* : the length, extent, or volume of something as measured in yards

yard•arm \ˈyärd-ˌärm\ *n* : either end of the yard of a square-rigged ship

yard•man \-mən, -ˌman\ *n* : a person employed in or about a yard

yard•mas•ter \-ˌmas-tər\ *n* : the person in charge of a railroad yard

yard•stick \-ˌstik\ *n* **1** : a graduated measuring stick three feet long **2** : a standard for making a critical judgment : CRITERION ♦ ***Synonyms*** GAUGE, TOUCHSTONE, BENCHMARK, MEASURE

yar•mul•ke \ˈyä-mə-kə, ˈyär-, -məl-\ *n* [Yiddish *yarmlke*] : a skullcap worn esp. by Jewish males in the synagogue and the home

yarn \ˈyärn\ *n* **1** : a continuous often plied strand composed of fibers or filaments and used in weaving and knitting to form cloth **2** : STORY; *esp* : a tall tale

yar•row \ˈya-rō\ *n* : a strong-scented herb related to the daisies that has white or pink flowers in flat clusters

yaw \ˈyȯ\ *vb* : to deviate erratically from a course ⟨the ship ~*ed* in the heavy seas⟩ — **yaw** *n*

yawl \ˈyȯl\ *n* : a 2-masted sailboat with the shorter mast aft of the rudder

[1]**yawn** \ˈyȯn\ *vb* : to open wide; *esp* : to open the mouth wide and take a deep breath usu. as an involuntary reaction to fatigue or boredom — **yawn•er** *n*

[2]**yawn** *n* : the act of yawning

yawp *or* **yaup** \ˈyȯp\ *vb* **1** : to make a raucous noise : SQUAWK **2** : CLAMOR, COMPLAIN — **yawp•er** *n*

yaws \ˈyȯz\ *n pl* : a contagious tropical disease caused by a spirochete closely resembling the causative agent of syphilis and marked by skin lesions

y–ax•is \ˈwī-ˌak-səs\ *n* : the axis of a graph or of a system of coordinates in a plane parallel to which the ordinates are measured

Yb *symbol* ytterbium

YB *abbr* yearbook

Y chromosome *n* : a sex chromosome that is characteristic of male cells in organisms (as humans) in which the male typically has two unlike sex chromosomes

yd *abbr* yard

[1]**ye** \ˈyē\ *pron* : YOU 1

[2]**ye** \yē, yə, *originally same as* the\ *definite article, archaic* : THE — used by early printers to represent the manuscript word *þe* (*the*)

[1]**yea** \ˈyā\ *adv* **1** : YES — used in oral voting **2** : INDEED, TRULY

[2]**yea** *n* : an affirmative vote; *also* : a person casting such a vote

yeah \ˈyeə, ˈyaə\ *adv* : YES

year \ˈyir\ *n* **1** : the period of about 365¼ solar days required for one revolution of the earth around the sun; *also* : the time in which a planet completes a revolution about the sun **2** : a cycle of 365 or 366 days beginning with January 1; *also* : a calendar year specified usu. by a number **3** *pl* : a time of special significance ⟨their glory ~*s*⟩ **4** *pl* : AGE ⟨advanced in ~*s*⟩ **5** : a period of time other than a calendar year ⟨the school ~⟩

year•book \-ˌbu̇k\ *n* **1** : a book published annually esp. as a report **2** : a school publication recording the history and activities of a graduating class

year•ling \ˈyir-liŋ, ˈyər-lən\ *n* **1** : one that

is a year old **2** : a racehorse between January of the year after the year in which it was born and the next January

year·long \ˈyir-ˈlȯŋ\ *adj* : lasting through a year

[1]**year·ly** \ˈyir-lē\ *adj* : ANNUAL

[2]**yearly** *adv* : every year

yearn \ˈyərn\ *vb* **1** : to feel a longing or craving ⟨~*ing* for freedom⟩ **2** : to feel tenderness or compassion ♦ ***Synonyms*** LONG, PINE, HANKER, HUNGER, THIRST

yearn·ing *n* : a tender or urgent longing

year–round \ˈyir-ˈraủnd\ *adj* : effective, employed, or operating for the full year : not seasonal ⟨a ~ resort⟩

yeast \ˈyēst\ *n* **1** : a surface froth or a sediment in sugary liquids (as fruit juices) that consists largely of cells of a tiny fungus and is used in making alcoholic liquors and as a leaven in baking **2** : a commercial product containing yeast fungi in a moist or dry medium **3** : a minute one-celled fungus present and functionally active in yeast that reproduces by budding; *also* : any of several similar fungi **4** *archaic* : the foam of waves : SPUME **5** : something that causes ferment or activity

yeast infection *n* : infection of the vagina with an excess growth of a normally present fungus that resembles a yeast

yeasty \ˈyē-stē\ *adj* **yeast·i·er; -est** **1** : of, relating to, or resembling yeast **2** : UNSETTLED **3** : full of vitality ⟨~ youths⟩; *also* : FRIVOLOUS

[1]**yell** \ˈyel\ *vb* : to utter a loud cry or scream : SHOUT — **yell·er** *n*

[2]**yell** *n* **1** : SHOUT **2** : a cheer used esp. to encourage an athletic team (as at a college)

[1]**yel·low** \ˈye-lō\ *adj* **1** : of the color yellow **2** *sometimes offensive* : having a light olive or light brown complexion **3** : SENSATIONAL ⟨~ journalism⟩ **4** : COWARDLY ⟨was too ~ to fight⟩ — **yel·low·ish** \ˈye-lə-wish\ *adj*

[2]**yellow** *n* **1** : a color between green and orange in the spectrum : the color of ripe lemons or sunflowers **2** : something yellow; *esp* : the yolk of an egg **3** *pl* : any of several plant diseases marked by stunted growth and yellowing of foliage

[3]**yellow** *vb* : to make or turn yellow

yellow birch *n* : a No. American birch with thin lustrous gray or yellow bark; *also* : its strong hard wood

yellow fever *n* : an acute infectious viral disease marked by prostration, jaundice, fever, and often hemorrhage and transmitted by a mosquito

yellow jack *n* : YELLOW FEVER

yellow jacket *n* : any of various small social wasps having the body barred with bright yellow

yel·low·tail \ˈye-lō-ˌtāl\ *n* : any of various fishes with a yellow or yellowish tail including several valuable food fishes

yelp \ˈyelp\ *vb* [ME, to boast, cry out, fr. OE *gielpan* to boast, exult] : to utter a sharp quick shrill cry — **yelp** *n*

Ye·me·ni \ˈye-mə-nē\ *n* : YEMENITE — **Yemeni** *adj*

Ye·men·ite \ˈye-mə-ˌnīt\ *n* : a native or inhabitant of Yemen — **Yemenite** *adj*

[1]**yen** \ˈyen\ *n, pl* **yen** — see MONEY table

[2]**yen** *n* [obs. E argot *yen-yen* craving for opium, fr. Chin (Guangdong dial.) *yīn-yáhn*, fr. *yīn* opium + *yáhn* craving] : a strong desire : LONGING ⟨a ~ to travel⟩

yeo·man \ˈyō-mən\ *n* **1** : an attendant or officer in a royal or noble household **2** : a naval petty officer who performs clerical duties **3** : a person who owns and cultivates a small farm; *esp* : one of a class of English freeholders below the gentry — **yeo·man·ly** \-lē\ *adj*

yeo·man·ry \-rē\ *n* : the body of yeomen and esp. of small landed proprietors

yep \ˈyep\ *adv* : YES

-yer — see -ER

[1]**yes** \ˈyes\ *adv* — used as a function word esp. to express assent or agreement or to introduce a more emphatic or explicit phrase

[2]**yes** *n* : an affirmative reply

ye·shi·va *also* **ye·shi·vah** \yə-ˈshē-və\ *n, pl* **yeshivas** *or* **ye·shi·voth** \-ˌshē-ˈvōt, -ˈvōth\ : a Jewish school esp. for religious instruction

yes–man \ˈyes-ˌman\ *n* : a person who endorses uncritically every opinion or proposal of a superior

[1]**yes·ter·day** \ˈyes-tər-dē, -ˌdā\ *adv* **1** : on the day preceding today **2** : only a short time ago

[2]**yesterday** *n* **1** : the day last past **2** : time not long past

yes·ter·year \ˈyes-tər-ˌyir\ *n* **1** : last year **2** : the recent past

[1]**yet** \ˈyet\ *adv* **1** : in addition : BESIDES; *also* : EVEN 6 **2** : up to now; *also* : STILL **3** : so soon as now ⟨not time to go ~⟩ **4** : EVENTUALLY **5** : NEVERTHELESS, HOWEVER

[2]**yet** *conj* : but nevertheless : BUT

ye·ti \ˈye-tē, ˈyā-\ *n* : ABOMINABLE SNOWMAN

yew \ˈyü\ *n* **1** : any of a genus of evergreen trees and shrubs with dark stiff poisonous needles and fleshy fruits **2** : the wood of a yew; *esp* : that of an Old World yew

Yid·dish \ˈyi-dish\ *n* [Yiddish *yidish*, short for *yidish daytsh*, lit., Jewish German] : a language derived from medieval German and spoken by Jews esp. of eastern European origin — **Yiddish** *adj*

[1]**yield** \ˈyēld\ *vb* **1** : to give as fitting, owed, or required **2** : GIVE UP; *esp* : to give up possession of on claim or demand **3** : to bear as a natural product **4** : PRODUCE, SUPPLY **5** : to bring in : RETURN **6** : to give way (as to force or influence) **7** : to give place ♦ ***Synonyms*** RELINQUISH, CEDE, WAIVE, SURRENDER

[2]**yield** *n* : something yielded; *esp* : the amount or quantity produced or returned

yield·ing \ˈyēl-diŋ\ *adj* **1** : not rigid or stiff : FLEXIBLE **2** : SUBMISSIVE, COMPLIANT

yikes \ˈyīks\ *interj* — used to express fear or astonishment

yip \'yip\ *vb* **yipped; yip·ping** : YAP
YK *abbr* Yukon; Yukon Territory
YMCA \ˌwī-ˌem-(ˌ)sē-'ā\ *n* : Young Men's Christian Association
YMHA \ˌwī-ˌem-ˌāch-'ā\ *n* : Young Men's Hebrew Association
yo \'yō\ *interj* — used to call attention, indicate attentiveness, or express affirmation
YOB *abbr* year of birth
yo·del \'yō-dᵊl\ *vb* **yo·deled** *or* **yo·delled; yo·del·ing** *or* **yo·del·ling** : to sing by suddenly changing from chest voice to falsetto and back; *also* : to shout or call in this manner — **yodel** *n* — **yo·del·er** *n*
yo·ga \'yō-gə\ *n* [Skt, lit., yoking, fr. *yunakti* he yokes] **1** *cap* : a Hindu theistic philosophy teaching the suppression of all activity of body, mind, and will in order that the self may realize its distinction from them and attain liberation **2** : a system of exercises for attaining bodily or mental control and well-being — **yo·gic** \-gik\ *adj, often cap*
yo·gi \'yō-gē\ *also* **yo·gin** \-gən, -ˌgin\ *n* **1** : a person who practices yoga **2** *cap* : an adherent of Yoga philosophy
yo·gurt *also* **yo·ghurt** \'yō-gərt\ *n* [Turk *yoğurt*] : a soured slightly acid often flavored semisolid food made of milk and milk solids to which cultures of bacteria have been added
¹**yoke** \'yōk\ *n, pl* **yokes** **1** : a wooden bar or frame by which two draft animals (as oxen) are coupled at the heads or necks for working together; *also* : a frame fitted to a person's shoulders to carry a load in two equal portions **2** : a clamp that embraces two parts to hold or unite them in position **3** *pl usu* **yoke** : two animals yoked together **4** : SERVITUDE, BONDAGE **5** : TIE, LINK ⟨the ~ of matrimony⟩ **6** : a fitted or shaped piece esp. at the shoulder of a garment ◆ ***Synonyms*** COUPLE, PAIR, BRACE
²**yoke** *vb* **yoked; yok·ing** **1** : to put a yoke on : couple with a yoke **2** : to attach a draft animal to ⟨~ a plow⟩ **3** : JOIN; *esp* : MARRY
yo·kel \'yō-kəl\ *n* : a naive or gullible country person
yolk \'yōk\ *n* **1** : the yellow rounded inner mass of the egg of a bird or reptile **2** : the stored food material of an egg that supplies nutrients (as proteins and cholesterol) to the developing embryo — **yolked** \'yōkt\ *adj*
Yom Kip·pur \ˌyōm-ki-'pu̇r, ˌyäm-, -'kipər\ *n* [Heb *yōm kippūr,* lit., day of atonement] : a Jewish holiday observed in September or October with fasting and prayer as a day of atonement
¹**yon** \'yän\ *adj* : YONDER
²**yon** *adv* **1** : YONDER **2** : THITHER ⟨ran hither and ~⟩
¹**yon·der** \'yän-dər\ *adv* : at or to that place
²**yonder** *adj* **1** : more distant ⟨the ~ side of the river⟩ **2** : being at a distance within view ⟨~ hills⟩
yore \'yȯr\ *n* [ME, fr. *yore,* adv., long ago, fr. OE *geāra,* fr. *gēar* year] : time long past ⟨in days of ~⟩
York·ie \'yȯr-kē\ *n* : YORKSHIRE TERRIER
York·shire terrier \'yȯrk-ˌshir-, -shər-\ *n* : any of a breed of compact toy terriers with long straight silky hair
you \'yü\ *pron* **1** : the person or persons addressed ⟨~ are a nice person⟩ ⟨~ are nice people⟩ **2** : ONE 2 ⟨~ turn this knob to open it⟩
¹**young** \'yəŋ\ *adj* **youn·ger** \'yəŋ-gər\; **youn·gest** \'yəŋ-gəst\ **1** : being in the first or an early stage of life, growth, or development **2** : having little experience **3** : recently come into being **4** : YOUTHFUL **5** *cap* : belonging to or representing a new or revived usu. political group or movement — **young·ish** \'yəŋ-ish\ *adj*
²**young** *n, pl* **young** : young persons; *also* : young animals
young adult *adj* : of, relating to, or being a category of fiction that is primarily intended for adolescent readers
young·ling \'yəŋ-liŋ\ *n* : one that is young — **youngling** *adj*
young·ster \-stər\ *n* **1** : a young person **2** : CHILD
your \'yu̇r, 'yȯr, yər\ *adj* : of or relating to you or yourself
yours \'yu̇rz, 'yȯrz\ *pron* : one or the ones belonging to you
your·self \yər-'self\ *pron, pl* **yourselves** \-'selvz\ : YOU — used reflexively, for emphasis, or in absolute constructions ⟨you'll hurt ~⟩ ⟨do it ~⟩
youth \'yüth\ *n, pl* **youths** \'yüt͟hz, 'yüths\ **1** : the period of life between childhood and maturity **2** : a young man; *also* : young persons **3** : YOUTHFULNESS
youth·ful \'yüth-fəl\ *adj* **1** : of, relating to, or appropriate to youth **2** : being young and not yet mature **3** : FRESH, VIGOROUS ⟨~ fervor⟩ — **youth·ful·ly** *adv* — **youth·ful·ness** *n*
youth hostel *n* : HOSTEL 2
You·Tu·ber \'yü-'tü-bər\ *n* : a person who creates and uploads videos on the YouTube online video sharing service
yowl \'yau̇(-ə)l\ *vb* : to utter a loud long mournful cry : WAIL — **yowl** *n*
yo–yo \'yō-(ˌ)yō\ *n, pl* **yo–yos** [prob. fr. Ilocano (a Philippine language) *yóyo*] : a thick grooved double disk with a string attached to its center that is made to fall and rise to the hand by unwinding and rewinding on the string — **yo–yo** *vb*
yr *abbr* **1** year **2** your
yrbk *abbr* yearbook
YT *abbr* Yukon Territory
yt·ter·bi·um \i-'tər-bē-əm\ *n* : a rare metallic chemical element
yt·tri·um \'i-trē-əm\ *n* : a rare metallic chemical element
yu·an \'yü-ən, yü-'än\ *n, pl* **yuan** — see MONEY table
yuc·ca \'yə-kə\ *n* : any of a genus of plants related to the agaves that grow esp. in warm dry regions and bear large clusters of white cup-shaped flowers atop a long stiff stalk

yuck *also* **yuk** \ˈyək\ *interj* — used to express rejection or disgust

yule \ˈyül\ *n, often cap* : CHRISTMAS

Yule log *n* : a large log formerly put on the hearth on Christmas Eve as the foundation of the fire

yule·tide \ˈyül-ˌtīd\ *n, often cap* : CHRISTMASTIDE

yum·my \ˈyə-mē\ *adj* **yum·mi·er; -est** : DELICIOUS

yup \ˈyəp\ *adv* : YES

yup·pie \ˈyə-pē\ *n* [prob. fr. *y*oung *u*rban *p*rofessional + *-ie* (as in hipp*ie*)] : a young college-educated adult employed in a well-paying profession and living and working in or near a large city — **yup·pie·dom** \-dəm\ *n*

yurt \ˈyu̇rt\ *n* : a light round tent of skins or felt stretched over a lattice framework used by pastoral peoples of inner Asia

YWCA \ˌwī-ˌdə-bəl-yü-(ˌ)sē-ˈā\ *n* : Young Women's Christian Association

YWHA \-ˌāch-ˈā\ *n* : Young Women's Hebrew Association

Z

[1]**z** \ˈzē\ *n, pl* **z's** *or* **zs** \ˈzēz\ *often cap* : the 26th letter of the English alphabet

[2]**z** *abbr* **1** zero **2** zone

Z *symbol* atomic number

Zach *abbr* Zacharias

Zach·a·ri·as \ˌza-kə-ˈrī-əs\ *n* : ZECHARIAH

[1]**za·ny** \ˈzā-nē\ *n, pl* **zanies** [It *zanni,* a traditional masked clown, fr. It dial. *Zanni,* nickname for It *Giovanni* John] **1** : CLOWN, BUFFOON **2** : a silly or foolish person

[2]**zany** *adj* **za·ni·er; -est** **1** *archaic* : characteristic of a zany **2** : very eccentric or absurd ⟨a ~ movie⟩ — **za·ni·ly** \ˈzā-nə-lē\ *adv* — **za·ni·ness** \ˈzā-nē-nəs\ *n*

zap \ˈzap\ *vb* **zapped; zap·ping** **1** : DESTROY, KILL **2** : to heat or cook in a microwave oven ⟨*zapped* the soup⟩

zeal \ˈzēl\ *n* : eager and ardent interest in the pursuit of something : FERVOR ♦ ***Synonyms*** ENTHUSIASM, PASSION, ARDOR

zeal·ot \ˈze-lət\ *n* : a zealous person; *esp* : a fanatical partisan ⟨a religious ~⟩ ♦ ***Synonyms*** ENTHUSIAST, BIGOT

zeal·ous \ˈze-ləs\ *adj* : filled with, characterized by, or due to zeal — **zeal·ous·ly** *adv* — **zeal·ous·ness** *n*

ze·bra \ˈzē-brə\ *n, pl* **zebras** *also* **zebra** : any of several African mammals related to the horse but conspicuously striped with black or dark brown and white or buff

zebra mussel *n* : a freshwater Eurasian mollusk introduced into U.S. waterways where it colonizes and clogs water intake pipes

ze·bu \ˈzē-bü, -byü\ *n* : any of various breeds of domestic oxen developed in India that have a large fleshy hump over the shoulders, a dewlap, drooping ears, and marked resistance to heat and to insect attack

Zech *abbr* Zechariah

Zech·a·ri·ah \ˌze-kə-ˈrī-ə\ *n* — see BIBLE table

zed \ˈzed\ *n, chiefly Brit* : the letter *z*

zeit·geist \ˈtsīt-ˌgīst, ˈzīt-\ *n* [G, fr. *Zeit* time + *Geist* spirit] : the general intellectual, moral, and cultural state of an era

Zen \ˈzen\ *n* : a Japanese Buddhist sect that teaches self-discipline, meditation, and attainment of enlightenment through direct intuitive insight

ze·na·na \zə-ˈnä-nə\ *n* : HAREM

ze·nith \ˈzē-nəth\ *n* **1** : the point in the heavens directly overhead **2** : the highest point : ACME ⟨the ~ of her career⟩ ♦ ***Synonyms*** CULMINATION, PINNACLE, APEX

ze·o·lite \ˈzē-ə-ˌlīt\ *n* : any of various feldsparlike silicates used esp. as water softeners

Zeph *abbr* Zephaniah

Zeph·a·ni·ah \ˌze-fə-ˈnī-ə\ *n* — see BIBLE table

zeph·yr \ˈze-fər\ *n* : a breeze from the west; *also* : a gentle breeze

zep·pe·lin \ˈze-plən, -pə-lən\ *n* [Count Ferdinand von *Zeppelin* †1917 German airship manufacturer] : a cylindrical rigid blimplike airship

[1]**ze·ro** \ˈzē-rō, ˈzir-ō\ *n, pl* **zeros** *also* **zeroes** [ultim. fr. Ar *ṣifr*] **1** : the numerical symbol 0 **2** : the number represented by the symbol 0 **3** : the point at which the graduated degrees or measurements on a scale (as of a thermometer) begin **4** : the lowest point

[2]**zero** *adj* **1** : of, relating to, or being a zero **2** : having no magnitude or quantity **3** : ABSENT, LACKING; *esp* : having no modified inflectional form

[3]**zero** *vb* : to adjust the sights of a firearm to hit the point aimed at — usu. used with *in*

zero hour *n* : the time at which an event (as a military operation) is scheduled to begin

zest \ˈzest\ *n* **1** : a quality of enhancing enjoyment : PIQUANCY **2** : keen enjoyment : GUSTO ⟨a ~ for life⟩ — **zest·ful** \-fəl\ *adj* — **zest·ful·ly** *adv* — **zest·ful·ness** *n* — **zesty** \ˈzes-tē\ *adj*

ze·ta \ˈzā-tə, ˈzē-\ *n* : the 6th letter of the Greek alphabet — Z or ζ

zi·do·vu·dine \zi-ˈdō-vyü-ˌdēn\ *n* : AZT

[1]**zig·zag** \ˈzig-ˌzag\ *n* : one of a series of short sharp turns, angles, or alterations in a course; *also* : something marked by such a series

[2]**zigzag** *adv* : in or by a zigzag path

[3]**zigzag** *adj* : having short sharp turns or angles

[4]**zigzag** *vb* **zig·zagged; zig·zag·ging** : to form into or proceed along a zigzag

zil·lion \ˈzil-yən\ *n* : a large indeterminate number

zinc \ˈziŋk\ *n* : a bluish-white metallic chemical element that is commonly found in minerals and is used esp. in alloys and as a protective coating for iron and steel

zinc oxide *n* : a white solid used esp. as a pigment, in compounding rubber, and in ointments and sunblocks

zine \ˈzēn\ *n* : a noncommercial publication usu. devoted to specialized subject matter

zin·fan·del \ˈzin-fən-ˌdel\ *n, often cap* : a dry red table wine made chiefly in California

zing \ˈziŋ\ *n* **1** : a shrill humming noise **2** : VITALITY 4 — **zing** *vb*

zing·er \ˈziŋ-ər\ *n* : a pointed witty remark or retort

zin·nia \ˈzi-nē-ə, ˈzēn-yə\ *n* : any of a genus of tropical American herbs or low shrubs related to the daisies and widely grown for their showy long-lasting flowers

Zi·on \ˈzī-ən\ *n* **1** : the Jewish people **2** : the Jewish homeland as a symbol of Judaism or of Jewish national aspiration **3** : HEAVEN **4** : UTOPIA

Zi·on·ism \ˈzī-ə-ˌni-zəm\ *n* : an international movement orig. for the establishment of a Jewish national or religious community in Palestine and later for the support of modern Israel — **Zi·on·ist** \-nist\ *adj or n*

[1]**zip** \ˈzip\ *vb* **zipped; zip·ping** : to move, act, or function with speed or vigor

[2]**zip** *n* **1** : a sudden sharp hissing sound **2** : ENERGY, VIM ⟨the performance lacked ~⟩

[3]**zip** *n* : NOTHING, ZERO ⟨the score was 27 to ~⟩

[4]**zip** *vb* **zipped; zip·ping** : to close or open with a zipper

zip code *n, often cap Z&I&P* [zone *i*mprovement *p*lan] : a number that identifies each postal delivery area in the U.S.

zip line *n* : a cable suspended usu. over an incline to which a rider is harnessed

zip·per \ˈzi-pər\ *n* : a fastener consisting of two rows of metal or plastic teeth on strips of tape and a sliding piece that closes an opening by drawing the teeth together

zip·py \ˈzi-pē\ *adj* **zip·pi·er; -est 1** : very speedy ⟨a ~ car⟩ **2** : strikingly appealing ⟨~ clothes⟩

zir·con \ˈzər-ˌkän\ *n* : a zirconium-containing mineral transparent varieties of which are used as gems

zir·co·ni·um \ˌzər-ˈkō-nē-əm\ *n* : a gray corrosion-resistant metallic chemical element used esp. in alloys and ceramics

zit \ˈzit\ *n* : PIMPLE

zith·er \ˈzi-t͟hər, -thər\ *n* : a musical instrument having 30 to 40 strings played with plectrum and fingers

zi·ti \ˈzē-tē\ *n, pl* **ziti** [It] : medium-size tubular pasta

zlo·ty \ˈzlȯ-tē\ *n, pl* **zlo·tys** \-tēz\ *or* **zloty** — see MONEY table

Zn *symbol* zinc

zo·di·ac \ˈzō-dē-ˌak\ *n* [ME, fr. AF, fr. L *zodiacus,* fr. Gk *zōidiakos,* fr. *zōidion* carved figure, sign of the zodiac, fr. dim. of *zōion* living being, figure] **1** : an imaginary belt in the heavens that encompasses the paths of most of the planets and that is divided into 12 constellations or signs **2** : a figure representing the signs of the zodiac and their symbols — **zo·di·a·cal** \zō-ˈdī-ə-kəl\ *adj*

zom·bie *also* **zom·bi** \ˈzäm-bē\ *n* : a person who is believed to have died and been brought back to life without speech or free will

zon·al \ˈzō-nᵊl\ *adj* : of, relating to, or having the form of a zone — **zon·al·ly** *adv*

[1]**zone** \ˈzōn\ *n* [ME, fr. AF, fr. L *zona* belt, zone, fr. Gk *zōnē*] **1** : any of five great divisions of the earth's surface made according to latitude and temperature including the torrid zone, two temperate zones, and two frigid zones **2** : something that forms an encircling band ⟨a ~ of tissue⟩ **3** : a region or area set off as distinct from surrounding parts ⟨business ~⟩ ⟨postal ~⟩

[2]**zone** *vb* **zoned; zon·ing 1** : ENCIRCLE **2** : to arrange in or mark off into zones; *esp* : to divide (as a city) into sections reserved for different purposes

zonked \ˈzäŋkt\ *adj* : being or acting as if under the influence of alcohol or a drug : HIGH

zoo \ˈzü\ *n, pl* **zoos** : a park where wild animals are kept for exhibition

zoo·ge·og·ra·phy \ˌzō-ə-jē-ˈä-grə-fē\ *n* : a branch of biogeography concerned with the geographical distribution of animals — **zoo·ge·og·ra·pher** \-fər\ *n* — **zoo·geo·graph·ic** \-ˌjē-ə-ˈgra-fik\ *also* **zoo·geo·graph·i·cal** \-fi-kəl\ *adj*

zoo·keep·er \ˈzü-ˌkē-pər\ *n* : a person who cares for animals in a zoo

zool *abbr* zoological; zoology

zoological garden *n* : ZOO

zo·ol·o·gy \zō-ˈä-lə-jē\ *n* : a branch of biology that deals with the classification and the properties and vital phenomena of animals — **zo·o·log·i·cal** \ˌzō-ə-ˈlä-ji-kəl\ *adj* — **zo·ol·o·gist** \zō-ˈä-lə-jist\ *n*

zoom \ˈzüm\ *vb* **1** : to move with a loud hum or buzz **2** : to gain altitude quickly **3** : to focus a camera or microscope using a special lens that permits the apparent distance of the object to be varied — **zoom** *n*

zoom lens *n* : a camera lens in which the image size can be varied continuously while the image remains in focus

zoo·mor·phic \ˌzō-ə-ˈmȯr-fik\ *adj* **1**

: having the form of an animal **2** : of, relating to, or being the representation of a deity in the form or with the attributes of an animal
zoo·plank·ton \ˌzō-ə-ˈplaŋk-tən, -ˌtän\ *n* : plankton composed of animals
zoo·spore \ˈzō-ə-ˌspȯr\ *n* : a motile spore
zoot suit \ˈzüt-\ *n* : a flashy suit of extreme cut typically consisting of a thigh-length jacket with wide padded shoulders and pants that are wide at the top and narrow at the bottom — **zoot·suit·er** \-ˌsü-tər\ *n*
Zo·ro·as·tri·an·ism \ˌzȯr-ə-ˈwas-trē-ə-ˌni-zəm\ *n* : a religion founded by the Persian prophet Zoroaster — **Zo·ro·as·tri·an** \-trē-ən\ *adj or n*
zounds \ˈzau̇ndz\ *interj* [euphemism for *God's wounds*] — used as a mild oath
zoy·sia \ˈzȯi-shə, -zhə, -sē-ə, -zē-ə\ *n* : any of a genus of creeping perennial grasses having fine wiry leaves and including some used as lawn grasses
ZPG *abbr* zero population growth
Zr *symbol* zirconium
zuc·chet·to \zü-ˈke-tō, tsü-\ *n, pl* **-tos** [It] : a small round skullcap worn by Roman Catholic ecclesiastics
zuc·chi·ni \zu̇-ˈkē-nē\ *n, pl* **-ni** *or* **-nis** [It] : a smooth cylindrical usu. dark green summer squash; *also* : a plant that bears zucchini
Zu·lu \ˈzü-ˌlü\ *n, pl* **Zulu** *or* **Zulus** : a member of a Bantu-speaking people of South Africa; *also* : the Bantu language of the Zulus
Zu·ni \ˈzü-nē\ *or* **Zu·ñi** \-nyē\ *n, pl* **Zuni** *or* **Zunis** *or* **Zuñi** *or* **Zuñis** : a member of an Indigenous people of western New Mexico; *also* : the language of the Zuni people
zwie·back \ˈswē-ˌbak, ˈswī-, ˈzwē-, ˈzwī-, -ˌbäk\ *n* [G, lit., twice baked, fr. *zwie-* twice + *backen* to bake] : a usu. sweetened bread that is baked and then sliced and toasted until dry and crisp
Zwing·li·an \ˈzwiŋ-glē-ən, ˈswiŋ-, -lē-; ˈtsfiŋ-lē-\ *adj* : of or relating to the Swiss religious reformer Ulrich Zwingli or his teachings — **Zwinglian** *n*
zy·de·co \ˈzī-də-ˌkō\ *n* : popular music of southern Louisiana that combines tunes of French origin with elements of Caribbean music and the blues
zy·gote \ˈzī-ˌgōt\ *n* : a cell formed by the union of two sexual cells; *also* : the developing individual produced from such a cell — **zy·got·ic** \zī-ˈgä-tik\ *adj*

Foreign Words & Phrases

Geographical Names

FOREIGN WORDS & PHRASES

These words and phrases occur frequently enough in English context to be included in a general English dictionary, but they merit a special section because they have not become a part of the English vocabulary.

---

ab·eunt stu·dia in mo·res \ˈä-be-ˌu̇nt-ˈstü-dē-ˌä-ˌin-ˈmō-ˌrās\ [L] : practices zealously pursued pass into habits

à bien·tôt \ä-bya^{n}-tō\ [F] : so long

ab in·cu·na·bu·lis \ˌäb-ˌiŋ-ku̇-ˈnä-bu̇-ˌlēs\ [L] : from the cradle : from infancy

à bon chat, bon rat \ä-bō^{n}-ˈshä bō^{n}-ˈrä\ [F] : to a good cat, a good rat : retaliation in kind

à bouche ou·verte \ä-bü-shü-vert\ [F] : with open mouth : eagerly : uncritically

ab ovo us·que ad ma·la \äb-ˈō-vō-ˌu̇s-kwe-ˌäd-ˈmä-lä\ [L] : from egg to apples : from soup to nuts : from beginning to end

à bras ou·verts \ä-brä-zü-ver\ [F] : with open arms : cordially

ab·sit in·vi·dia \ˈäb-ˌsit-in-ˈwi-dē-ˌä\ [L] : let there be no envy or ill will

ab uno dis·ce om·nes \äb-ˈü-nō-ˌdis-ke-ˈȯm-ˌnās\ [L] : from one learn to know all

ab ur·be con·di·ta \äb-ˈu̇r-be-ˈkȯn-di-ˌtä\ [L] : from the founding of the city (Rome, founded 753 B.C.) — used by the Romans in reckoning dates

ab·usus non tol·lit usum \ˈä-ˌbü-su̇s-ˌnōn-ˌtȯ-lit-ˈü-su̇m\ [L] : abuse does not take away use, i.e., is not an argument against proper use

à compte \ä-ˈkō^{n}t\ [F] : on account

à coup sûr \ä-kü-sɶr\ [F] : with sure stroke : surely

acte gra·tuit \äk-tə-grä-tw^{y}ē\ [F] : gratuitous impulsive act

ad ar·bi·tri·um \ˌad-är-ˈbi-trē-u̇m\ [L] : at will : arbitrarily

ad as·tra per as·pe·ra \ad-ˈas-trə-ˌpər-ˈas-pə-rə\ [L] : to the stars by hard ways — motto of Kansas

ad ex·tre·mum \ˌäd-ek-ˈstrā-ˌmu̇m, ˌad-ik-ˈstrē-məm\ [L] : to the extreme : at last

ad ma·jo·rem Dei glo·ri·am \äd-mä-ˈyȯr-ˌem-ˈde-ˌē-ˈglȯr-ē-ˌäm\ [L] : to the greater glory of God — motto of the Society of Jesus

ad pa·tres \äd-ˈpä-ˌtrās\ [L] : (gathered) to his fathers : deceased

ad re·fe·ren·dum \ˌäd-ˌre-fe-ˈren-du̇m\ [L] : for reference : for further consideration by one having the authority to make a final decision

à droite \ä-drwät\ [F] : to or on the right hand

ad utrum·que pa·ra·tus \ˌäd-u̇-ˈtru̇m-kwe-pä-ˈrä-tu̇s\ [L] : prepared for either (event)

ad vi·vum \äd-ˈwē-ˌwu̇m\ [L] : to the life

ae·gri som·nia \ˌī-grē-ˈsȯm-nē-ˌä\ [L] : a sick man's dreams

ae·quam ser·va·re men·tem \ˈī-ˌkwäm-ser-ˌwä-rā-ˈmen-ˌtem\ [L] : to preserve a calm mind

ae·quo ani·mo \ˌī-ˌkwō-ˈä-ni-ˌmō\ [L] : with even mind : calmly

à gauche \ä-gōsh\ [F] : to or on the left hand

age quod agis \ˈä-ge-ˌkwȯd-ˈä-ˌgis\ [L] : do what you are doing : to the business at hand

à grands frais \ä-grä^{n}-fre\ [F] : at great expense

à huis clos \ä-w^{y}ē-klō\ [F] : with closed doors : behind closed doors

aide–toi, le ciel t'ai·dera \ed-twä lə-ˈsyel-te-drä\ [F] : help yourself (and) heaven will help you

aî·né \e-nā\ [F] : elder : senior (masc.)

aî·née \e-nā\ [F] : elder : senior (fem.)

à l'aban·don \ä-lä-bä^{n}-dō^{n}\ [F] : carelessly : in disorder

à la belle étoile \ä-lä-bel-ā-twäl\ [F] : under the beautiful star : in the open air at night

à la bonne heure \ä-lä-bȯ-nœr\ [F] : at a good time : well and good : all right

à la fran·çaise \ä-lä-frä^{n}-sez\ [F] : in the French manner

à l'amé·ri·caine \ä-lä-mā-rē-ken\ [F] : in the American manner : of the American kind

à l'an·glaise \ä-lä^{n}-glez\ [F] : in the English manner

à la page \ä-lä-päzh\ [F] : at the page : up-to-the-minute

à la russe \ä-lä-rɶs\ [F] : in the Russian manner

alea jac·ta est \ˈä-lē-ˌä-ˌyäk-tä-ˈest\ [L] : the die is cast

à l'im·pro·viste \ä-la^{n}-prȯ-vēst\ [F] : unexpectedly

alis vo·lat pro·pri·is \ˈä-ˌlēs-ˈwȯ-ˌlät-ˈprō-prē-ˌēs\ [L] : she flies with her own wings — motto of Oregon

al–ki \ˈal-ˌkī, -kē\ [Chinook Jargon] : by and by — motto of Washington

alo·ha oe \ä-ˌlō-hä-ˈȯi, -ˈō-ē\ [Hawaiian] : love to you : greetings : farewell

al·ter idem \ˌȯl-tər-ˈī-ˌdem, ˌäl-ter-ˈē-\ [L] : second self

à mer·veille \ä-mer-vā\ [F] : marvelously : wonderfully

ami·cus hu·ma·ni ge·ne·ris \ä-ˈmē-ku̇s-hü-ˌmä-nē-ˈge-ne-ris\ [L] : friend of the human race

ami·cus us·que ad aras \-ˌu̇s-kwe-ˌäd-ˈär-ˌäs\ [L] : a friend as far as to the altars, i.e., except in what is contrary to one's religion; *also* : a friend to the last extremity

ami de cour \ä-ˌmē-də-ˈku̇r\ [F] : court friend : insincere friend

amor pa·tri·ae \ˈä-ˌmȯr-ˈpä-trē-ˌī\ [L] : love of one's country

amor vin·cit om·nia \ˈä-ˌmȯr-ˌwiŋ-kit-ˈȯm-nē-ä\ [L] : love conquers all things

an·guis in her·ba \ˌäŋ-gwis-in-ˈher-ˌbä\ [L] : snake in the grass

ani·mal bi·pes im·plu·me \ˈä-ni-ˌmäl-ˌbi-ˌpās-im-ˈplü-me\ [L] : two-legged animal without feathers (i.e., the human race)

ani·mis opi·bus·que pa·ra·ti \ˈä-ni-ˌmēs-ˌȯ-pi-ˈbu̇s-kwe-pä-ˈrä-tē\ [L] : prepared in mind and resources — one of the mottoes of South Carolina

an·no ae·ta·tis su·ae \ˈä-nō-ī-ˌtä-tis-ˈsü-ˌī\ [L] : in the (specified) year of his (or her) age

an·no mun·di \ˌä-nō-ˈmu̇n-dē\ [L] : in the year of the world — used in reckoning dates from the supposed period of the creation of the world, esp. as fixed by James Ussher at 4004 B.C. or by the Jews at 3761 B.C.

an·no ur·bis con·di·tae \ˌä-nō-ˌu̇r-bis-ˈkȯn-di-ˌtī\ [L] : in the year of the founded city : in the year that the city was founded (Rome, founded 753 B.C.)

an·nu·it coep·tis \ˌä-nü-ˌit-ˈkȯip-ˌtēs\ [L] : He (God) has approved our beginnings — motto on the reverse of the Great Seal of the United States

à peu près \ä-pœ-pre\ [F] : nearly : approximately

à pied \ä-pyā\ [F] : on foot

à point \ä-pwa^n\ [F] : at the right time

après moi le dé·luge \ä-pre-mwä-lə-dā-lu̇ezh\ *or* **après nous le déluge** \ä-pre-nü-\ [F] : after me the deluge — attributed to Louis XV

à pro·pos de rien \-rya^n\ [F] : apropos of nothing

aqua et ig·ni in·ter·dic·tus \ˌä-kwä-et-ˈig-nē-ˌin-ter-ˈdik-tu̇s\ [L] : forbidden to be furnished with water and fire : outlawed

Ar·ca·des am·bo \ˈär-kä-ˌdes-ˈäm-bō\ [L] : both Arcadians : two persons of like occupations or tastes; *also* : two rascals

ar·rec·tis au·ri·bus \ä-ˈrek-ˌtēs-ˈau̇-ri-ˌbu̇s\ [L] : with ears pricked up : attentively

ar·ri·ve·der·ci \ˌär-ē-vā-ˈder-chē\ [It] : till we meet again : farewell

ars lon·ga, vi·ta bre·vis \ärs-ˈlȯŋ-ˌgä ˌwē-ˌtä-ˈbre-wis\ [L] : art is long, life is short : human life span limits all that might be accomplished

as–sa·laam alai·kum \əs-sə-ˈläm-ə-ˈlī-ku̇m\ [Ar *as-salāmu ʿalaykum*] : peace to you — used as a traditional greeting among Muslims

a ter·go \ä-ˈter-(ˌ)gō\ [L] : from behind

à tort et à tra·vers \ä-tȯr-ā-ä-trä-ver\ [F] : wrong and crosswise : at random : without rhyme or reason

au bout de son la·tin \ō-büd-sō^n-lä-ta^n, -bü-də-\ [F] : at the end of one's Latin : at the end of one's mental resources

au con·traire \ō-kō^n-trer\ [F] : on the contrary

au·de·mus ju·ra nos·tra de·fen·de·re \au̇-ˈdā-mu̇s-ˌyu̇r-ä-ˈnȯ-strä-dā-ˈfen-de-rā\ [L] : we dare defend our rights — motto of Alabama

au·den·tes for·tu·na ju·vat \au̇-ˈden-ˌtās-fȯr-ˌtü-nä-ˈyü-ˌwät\ [L] : fortune favors the bold

au·di al·te·ram par·tem \ˈau̇-ˌdē-ˌäl-te-ˌräm-ˈpär-ˌtem\ [L] : hear the other side

au fait \ō-fet, -fe\ [F] : to the point : fully competent : fully informed : socially correct

au fond \ō-fō^n\ [F] : at bottom : fundamentally

au grand sé·rieux \ō-grä^n-sā-ryœ\ [F] : in all seriousness

au mieux \ō-myœ\ [F] : on the best terms : on intimate terms

au pays des aveugles les borgnes sont rois \ō-pā-ē-dā-zä-vœgl^ə-lā-bȯrn^y-ə-sō^n-rwä\ [F] : in the country of the blind the one-eyed men are kings

au·rea me·di·o·cri·tas \ˈau̇-rē-ä-ˌme-dē-ˈȯ-kri-ˌtäs\ [L] : the golden mean

au reste \ō-rest\ [F] : for the rest : besides

au sé·rieux \ō-sā-ryœ\ [F] : seriously

aus·si·tôt dit, aus·si·tôt fait \ō-sē-tō-dē ō-sē-tō-fe\ [F] : no sooner said than done

aut Cae·sar aut ni·hil \au̇t-ˈkī-sär-ˌau̇t-ˈni-ˌhil\ [L] : either a Caesar or nothing

au·tres temps, au·tres mœurs \ō-trə-tä^n ō-trə-mœrs\ [F] : other times, other customs

aut vin·ce·re aut mo·ri \au̇t-ˈwiŋ-ke-rā-ˌau̇t-ˈmȯ-ˌrē\ [L] : either to conquer or to die

aux armes \ō-zärm\ [F] : to arms

avant la lettre \ä-vä^n-lä-letr^ə\ [F] : before the letter : before a (specified) name or entity existed

ave at·que va·le \ˈä-ˌwā-ˌät-kwe-ˈwä-ˌlā\ [L] : hail and farewell

à vo·tre san·té \ä-vȯt-sä^n-tā, -vȯ-trə-\ [F] : to your health — used as a toast

ax·is mun·di \ˈak-səs-ˈmu̇n-dē\ [L] : turning point of the world : line through the earth's center around which the universe revolves

bel·la fi·gu·ra \ˈbel-lə-fē-ˈgü-rä\ [It] : fine appearance or impression

bel·lum om·ni·um con·tra om·nes \ˈbe-lu̇m-ˈōm-nē-u̇m-ˌkȯn-trä-ˈōm-ˌnās\ [L] : war of all against all

bien en·ten·du \bya^{n}-nä^{n}-tä^{n}-dæ\ [F] : well understood : of course

bien–pen·sant \bya^{n}-pä^{n}-sä^{n}\ [F] : right-minded : one who holds orthodox views

bis dat qui ci·to dat \ˈbis-ˌdät-kwē-ˈki-tō-ˌdät\ [L] : he gives twice who gives promptly

bon ap·pé·tit \bȯ-nä-pā-tē\ [F] : good appetite : enjoy your meal

bon gré, mal gré \ˈbō^{n}-ˌgrā ˈmäl-ˌgrā\ [F] : whether with good grace or bad : willy-nilly

bon·jour \bō^{n}-zhür\ [F] : good day : good morning

bonne foi \bȯn-fwä\ [F] : good faith

bon·soir \bō^{n}-swär\ [F] : good evening

bru·tum ful·men \ˌbrü-tu̇m-ˈfu̇l-men\ [L] : insensible thunderbolt : a futile threat or display of force

ca·dit quae·stio \ˌkä-dit-ˈkwī-stē-ˌō\ [L] : the question drops : the argument collapses

carte d'iden·ti·té \kärt-dē-dä^{n}-tē-tā\ [F] : identity card

cau·sa si·ne qua non \ˈkau̇-ˌsä-ˌsi-nā-kwä-ˈnōn\ [L] : an indispensable cause or condition

ça va sans dire \sä-vä-sä^{n}-dir\ [F] : it goes without saying

ca·ve ca·nem \ˌkä-wā-ˈkä-ˌnem\ [L] : beware the dog

ce·dant ar·ma to·gae \ˈkā-ˌdänt-ˌär-mə-ˈtō-ˌgī\ [L] : let arms yield to the toga : let military power give way to civil power — motto of Wyoming

ce n'est que le pre·mier pas qui coûte \snek-lə-prə-myā-pä-kē-küt\ [F] : it is only the first step that costs

c'est–à–dire \se-tä-dir\ [F] : that is to say : namely

c'est au·tre chose \se-tōt-shōz, -tō-trə-\ [F] : that's a different thing

c'est la guerre \se-lä-ger\ [F] : that's war : it cannot be helped

c'est la vie \se-lä-vē\ [F] : that's life : that's how things happen

c'est plus qu'un crime, c'est une faute \se-plæ-kœ^{n}-krēm se-tæn-fōt\ [F] : it is worse than a crime, it is a blunder

ce·te·ra de·sunt \ˌkā-te-ˌrä-ˈdā-ˌsu̇nt\ [L] : the rest is missing

cha·cun à son goût \shä-kœ^{n}-nä-sō^{n}-gü\ [F] : everyone to his taste

châ·teau en Es·pagne \shä-tō-ä^{n}-nes-pän^{y}\ [F] : castle in Spain : a visionary project

cher·chez la femme \sher-shā-lä-fäm\ [F] : look for the woman

che sa·rà, sa·rà \ˌkā-sä-ˌrä sä-ˈrä\ [It] : what will be, will be

che·val de ba·taille \shə-väl-də-bä-tä^{y}\ [F] : warhorse : argument constantly relied on : favorite subject

co·gi·to, er·go sum \ˈkō-gi-ˌtō ˌer-gō-ˈsu̇m\ [L] : I think, therefore I exist

co·mé·die hu·maine \kȯ-mā-dē-æ-men\ [F] : human comedy : the whole variety of human life

comme ci, comme ça \kȯm-sē kȯm-sä\ [F] : so-so

com·pa·gnon de voy·age \kō^{n}-pä-n^{y}ō^{n}-də-vwä-yäzh\ [F] : traveling companion

compte ren·du \kō^{n}t-rä^{n}-dæ\ [F] : report (as of proceedings in an investigation)

con·cor·dia dis·cors \kȯn-ˈkȯr-dē-ä-ˈdis-ˌkȯrs\ [L] : discordant harmony

con·fes·sio fi·dei \kȯn-ˈfe-sē-ō-ˈfi-dē-ˌē\ [L] : confession of faith

cor·rup·tio op·ti·mi pes·si·ma \kȯ-ˈru̇p-tē-ˌō-ˈäp-ti-ˌmē-ˈpe-si-ˌmä\ [L] : the corruption of the best is the worst of all

coup de maî·tre \küd-metr^{ə}, kü-də-\ [F] : masterstroke

coup d'es·sai \kü-dā-se\ [F] : experiment : trial

coûte que coûte \küt-kə-küt\ [F] : cost what it may

cre·do quia ab·sur·dum est \ˌkrā-dō-ˈkwē-ä-äp-ˌsu̇r-du̇m-ˈest\ [L] : I believe it because it is absurd

cres·cit eun·do \ˌkres-kit-ˈeu̇n-dō\ [L] : it grows as it goes — motto of New Mexico

crise de nerfs *or* **crise des nerfs** \krēz-də-ner\ [F] : crisis of nerves : nervous collapse : hysterical fit

cuj·us re·gio, ej·us re·li·gio \ˌkü-yu̇s-ˈre-gē-ˌō ˌe-yu̇s-re-ˈli-gē-ˌō\ [L] : whose region, his or her religion : subjects are to accept the religion of their ruler

cum gra·no sa·lis \ku̇m-ˌgrä-nō-ˈsä-lis\ [L] : with a grain of salt

cus·tos mo·rum \ˌku̇s-tōs-ˈmȯr-u̇m\ [L] : guardian of manners or morals : censor

d'ac·cord \dä-kȯr\ [F] : in accord : agreed

dame d'hon·neur \däm-dȯ-nœr\ [F] : lady-in-waiting

dam·nant quod non in·tel·li·gunt \ˈdäm-ˌnänt-ˌkwȯd-ˌnōn-in-ˈte-li-ˌgu̇nt\ [L] : they condemn what they do not understand

de bonne grâce \də-bȯn-gräs\ [F] : with good grace : willingly

de gus·ti·bus non est dis·pu·tan·dum \dā-ˈgu̇s-tə-ˌbu̇s-ˌnōn-ˌest-ˌdis-pu̇-ˈtän-ˌdu̇m\ [L] : there is no disputing about tastes

Dei gra·tia \ˌde-ˌē-ˈgrä-tē-ˌä\ [L] : by the grace of God

de in·te·gro \dā-ˈin-te-ˌgrō\ [L] : anew : afresh

de·len·da est Car·tha·go \dā-ˈlen-dä-ˌest-kär-ˈtä-gō\ [L] : Carthage must be destroyed

de mal en pis \də-mä-lä^{n}-pē\ [F] : from bad to worse

de mi·ni·mis non cu·rat lex \dā-ˈmi-ni-ˌmēs-ˌnōn-ˌkü-ˌrät-ˈleks\ [L] : the law takes no account of trifles

de mor·tu·is nil ni·si bo·num \dā-ˈmȯr-

tù-ˌēs-ˌnēl-ˌni-sē-ˈbò-ˌnùm\ [L] : of the dead (say) nothing but good
de nos jours \də-nō-zhür\ [F] : of our time : contemporary — used postpositively esp. after a proper name
Deo fa·ven·te \ˌdā-ō-fä-ˈven-tā\ [L] : with God's favor
Deo gra·ti·as \ˌdā-ō-ˈgrä-tē-ˌäs\ [L] : thanks (be) to God
de pro·fun·dis \ˌdā-prō-ˈfùn-dēs\ [L] : out of the depths
de·si·pe·re in lo·co \dā-ˈsi-pe-rā-in-ˈlò-kō\ [L] : to indulge in trifling at the proper time
de te fa·bu·la nar·ra·tur \ˌdā-ˌtā-ˈfä-bù-lä-nä-ˈrä-ˌtùr\ [L] : the story applies to you
De·us ab·scon·di·tus \ˌdā-ùs-ˌäp-ˈskòn-di-ˌtùs\ [L] : hidden God : God unknowable by the human mind
De·us vult \ˌdā-ùs-ˈwùlt\ [L] : God wills it — rallying cry of the First Crusade
di·es fau·stus \ˌdē-ˌās-ˈfaù-stùs\ [L] : lucky day
dies in·fau·stus \-ˈin-ˌfaù-stùs\ [L] : unlucky day
dies irae \-ˈē-ˌrī, -ˌrā\ [L] : day of wrath — used of the Judgment Day
Dieu et mon droit \dyœ-ā-mòⁿ-drwä\ [F] : God and my right — motto on the British royal arms
Dieu vous garde \dyœ-vü-gärd\ [F] : God keep you
di·ri·go \ˈdē-ri-ˌgō\ [L] : I direct — motto of Maine
dis ali·ter vi·sum \ˌdēs-ˌä-li-ˌter-ˈwē-ˌsùm\ [L] : the Gods decreed otherwise
di·tat De·us \ˌdē-ˌtät-ˈdā-ˌùs\ [L] : God enriches — motto of Arizona
di·vi·de et im·pe·ra \ˈdē-wi-ˌde-ˌet-ˈim-pe-ˌrä\ [L] : divide and rule
do·cen·do dis·ci·mus \dò-ˌken-dō-ˈdis-ki-ˌmùs\ [L] : we learn by teaching
Do·mi·ne, di·ri·ge nos \ˈdò-mi-ˌne ˈdē-ri-ˌge-ˈnōs\ [L] : Lord, direct us — motto of the City of London
Do·mi·nus vo·bis·cum \ˌdò-mi-ˌnùs-wō-ˈbēs-ˌkùm\ [L] : the Lord be with you
dul·ce et de·co·rum est pro pa·tria mori \ˌdùl-ˌke-et-de-ˈkòr-ùm-ˌest-prō-ˌpä-trē-ˌä-ˈmò-ˌrē\ [L] : it is sweet and seemly to die for one's country
dum spi·ro, spe·ro \dùm-ˈspē-rō ˈspā-rō\ [L] : while I breathe, I hope — one of the mottoes of South Carolina
dum vi·vi·mus vi·va·mus \dùm-ˈwē-wē-ˌmùs-wē-ˈwä-mùs\ [L] : while we live, let us live
d'un cer·tain âge \dœⁿ-ser-te-näzh\ [F] : of a certain age : no longer young
dux fe·mi·na fac·ti \ˌdùks-ˌfā-mi-nä-ˈfäk-ˌtē\ [L] : a woman was leader of the exploit
ec·ce sig·num \ˌe-ke-ˈsig-ˌnùm\ [L] : behold the sign : look at the proof
e con·tra·rio \ˌā-kòn-ˈträr-ē-ˌō\ [L] : on the contrary
écra·sez l'in·fâme \ā-krä-zā-laⁿ-fäm\ [F] : crush the infamous thing
eheu fu·ga·ces la·bun·tur an·ni \ˌā-ˌheù-fù-ˈgä-ˌkās-lä-ˈbùn-ˌtùr-ˈä-ˌnē\ [L] : alas! the fleeting years glide on
ein' fes·te Burg ist un·ser Gott \īn-ˌfes-tə-ˈbùrk-ist-ˌùn-zər-ˈgòt\ [G] : a mighty fortress is our God
em·bar·ras de choix \äⁿ-bä-rä-də-shwä\ *or* **embarras du choix** \-dœ-shwä\ [F] : embarrassing variety of choice
em·bar·ras de ri·chesses *or* **embarras de ri·chesse** \äⁿ-bä-räd-rē-shes, -rä-də-\ [F] : embarrassing surplus of riches : confusing abundance
en ami \äⁿ-nä-mē\ [F] : as a friend
en ef·fet \äⁿ-nā-fe\ [F] : in fact : indeed
en fa·mille \äⁿ-fä-mē\ [F] : in or with one's family : at home : informally
en·fant ché·ri \äⁿ-fäⁿ-shā-rē\ [F] : loved or pampered child : one that is highly favored
en·fant gâ·té \äⁿ-fäⁿ-gä-tā\ [F] : spoiled child
en·fants per·dus \äⁿ-fäⁿ-per-dœ\ [F] : lost children : soldiers sent to a dangerous post
en·fin \äⁿ-faⁿ\ [F] : in conclusion : in a word
en gar·çon \äⁿ-gär-sōⁿ\ [F] : as or like a bachelor
en garde \äⁿ-gärd\ [F] : on guard
en plein air \äⁿ-ple-ner\ [F] : in the open air
en plein jour \äⁿ-plaⁿ-zhür\ [F] : in broad day
en règle \äⁿ-reglᵊ\ [F] : in order : in due form
en re·tard \äⁿr-(ə-)tär\ [F] : behind time : late
en re·traite \äⁿr-(ə-)tret\ [F] : in retreat : in retirement
en re·vanche \äⁿr-(ə-)väⁿsh\ [F] : in return : in compensation
en·se pe·tit pla·ci·dam sub li·ber·ta·te qui·e·tem \ˌen-se-ˌpe-tit-ˈplä-ki-ˌdäm-sùb-ˌlē-ber-ˌtä-te-kwē-ˈā-ˌtem\ [L] : with the sword she seeks calm repose under liberty : by the sword we seek peace, but peace only under liberty — motto of Massachusetts
eo ip·so \ā-ō-ˈip-(ˌ)sō\ [L] : by that itself : by that fact alone
épa·ter le bour·geois \ā-pä-tā-lə-bür-zhwä\ *or* **épater les bour·geois** \-lā-bür-\ [F] : to shock the middle classes
e plu·ri·bus unum \ˌē-ˌplùr-ə-bəs-ˈ(y)ü-nəm, ˌā-ˌplùr-i-bùs-ˈü-nùm\ [L] : one out of many — used on the Great Seal of the U.S. and on several U.S. coins
ep·pur si muo·ve \āp-ˌpür-sē-ˈmwò-vā\ [It] : and yet it does move — attributed to Galileo after recanting his assertion of the earth's motion

Erin go bragh \ˌer-ən-gə-ˈbrȯ, -gō-ˈbrä\ [Ir *go brách* or *go bráth*, lit., till doomsday] : Ireland forever

er·ra·re hu·ma·num est \e-ˈrär-ā-hü-ˌmä-nu̇m-ˈest\ [L] : to err is human

es·prit de l'es·ca·lier \es-prēd-les-kä-lyā\ *or* **es·prit d'es·ca·lier** \-prē-des-\ [F] : wit of the staircase : repartee thought of only too late

es·se quam vi·de·ri \ˈe-sā-ˌkwäm-wi-ˈdā-rē\ [L] : to be rather than to seem — motto of North Carolina

est mo·dus in re·bus \est-ˈmȯ-ˌdu̇s-in-ˈrā-ˌbu̇s\ [L] : there is a proper measure in things, i.e., the golden mean should always be observed

es·to per·pe·tua \ˈes-ˌtō-per-ˈpe-tu̇-ˌä\ [L] : may she endure forever — motto of Idaho

et hoc ge·nus om·ne \et-ˌhōk-ˌge-nu̇s-ˈȯm-ne\ *or* **et id genus omne** \et-ˌid-\ [L] : and everything of this kind

et sic de si·mi·li·bus \et-ˌsēk-dā-si-ˈmi-li-ˌbu̇s\ [L] : and so of like things

et tu Bru·te \et-ˈtü-ˈbrü-te\ [L] : thou too, Brutus — exclamation attributed to Julius Caesar on seeing his friend Brutus among his assassins

eu·re·ka \yu̇-ˈrē-kä\ [Gk] : I have found it — motto of California

Ewig–Weib·li·che \ˌā-vik-ˈvīp-li-kə\ [G] : eternal feminine

ex·al·té \eg-zäl-tā\ [F] : emotionally excited or elated : fanatic

ex ani·mo \eks-ˈä-ni-ˌmō\ [L] : from the heart : sincerely

ex·cel·si·or \ik-ˈsel-sē-ər, eks-ˈkel-sē-ˌȯr\ [L] : still higher — motto of New York

ex·cep·tio pro·bat re·gu·lam de re·bus non ex·cep·tis \eks-ˈkep-tē-ˌō-ˌprō-bät-ˈrā-gu̇-ˌläm-dā-ˈrā-ˌbu̇s-ˌnōn-eks-ˈkep-ˌtēs\ [L] : an exception establishes the rule as to things not excepted

ex·cep·tis ex·ci·pi·en·dis \eks-ˈkep-ˌtēs-eks-ˌki-pē-ˈen-ˌdēs\ [L] : with the proper or necessary exceptions

ex·i·tus ac·ta pro·bat \ˈek-si-ˌtu̇s-ˌäk-tä-ˈprȯ-ˌbät\ [L] : the outcome justifies the deed

ex li·bris \eks-ˈlē-bris\ [L] : from the books of — used on bookplates

ex me·ro mo·tu \ˌeks-ˌmer-ō-ˈmō-tü\ [L] : out of mere impulse : of one's own accord

ex ne·ces·si·ta·te rei \ˌeks-ne-ˌke-si-ˈtä-te-ˈrā(-ˌē)\ [L] : from the necessity of the case

ex ni·hi·lo ni·hil fit \eks-ˈni-hi-ˌlō-ˌni-ˌhil-ˈfit\ [L] : from nothing nothing is produced

ex pe·de Her·cu·lem \eks-ˌpe-de-ˈher-ku̇-ˌlem\ [L] : from the foot (we may judge of the size of) Hercules : from a part we may judge of the whole

ex·per·to cre·de \eks-ˌper-tō-ˈkrā-de\ *or* **experto cre·di·te** \-ˈkrā-di-ˌte\ [L] : believe one who has had experience

ex un·gue le·o·nem \eks-ˈu̇ŋ-gwe-le-ˈō-ˌnem\ [L] : from the claw (we may judge of) the lion : from a part we may judge of the whole

ex vi ter·mi·ni \eks-ˌwē-ˈter-mə-ˌnē\ [L] : from the force of the term

fa·ci·le prin·ceps \ˌfä-ki-le-ˈpriŋ-ˌkeps\ [L] : easily first

fa·ci·lis de·scen·sus Aver·no \ˈfä-ki-ˌlis-dā-ˌskān-ˌsu̇s-ä-ˈwer-nō\ *or* **facilis descensus Aver·ni** \-(ˌ)nē\ [L] : the descent to Avernus is easy : the road to evil is easy

fa·çon de par·ler \fä-sōⁿ-də-pär-lā\ [F] : manner of speaking : figurative or conventional expression

fas est et ab ho·ste do·ce·ri \fäs-ˈest-et-äb-ˈhȯ-ste-dȯ-ˈkā-(ˌ)rē\ [L] : it is right to learn even from an enemy

Fa·ta vi·am in·ve·ni·ent \ˌfä-tä-ˈwē-ˌäm-in-ˈwe-nē-ˌent\ [L] : the Fates will find a way

fat·ti mas·chii, pa·ro·le fe·mi·ne \ˌfät-tē-ˈmäs-ˌkē pä-ˌrȯ-lā-ˈfā-mē-ˌnā\ [It] : deeds are males, words are females : deeds are more effective than words — motto of Maryland, where it is generally interpreted as meaning "manly deeds, womanly words"

faux bon·homme \fō-bȯ-nȯm\ [F] : pretended good fellow

faux–naïf \fœ-nä-ēf\ [F] : spuriously or affectedly childlike : artfully simple

fe·lix cul·pa \ˈfā-liks-ˈku̇l-pä\ [L] : fortunate fault — used esp. of original sin in relation to the consequent coming of Christ

femme de cham·bre \fäm-də-shäⁿbrᵊ\ [F] : chambermaid : lady's maid

fe·sti·na len·te \fe-ˌstē-nä-ˈlen-ˌtā\ [L] : make haste slowly

feux d'ar·ti·fice \fœ-där-tē-fēs\ [F] : fireworks : display of wit

fi·at ju·sti·tia, ru·at cae·lum \ˌfē-ˌät-yu̇s-ˈti-tē-ä ˌrü-ˌät-ˈkī-ˌlu̇m\ [L] : let justice be done though the heavens fall

fi·at lux \ˌfē-ˌät-ˈlu̇ks\ [L] : let there be light

Fi·dei De·fen·sor \ˌfi-de-ˌē-dā-ˈfān-ˌsȯr\ [L] : Defender of the Faith — a title of the sovereigns of England

fille de cham·bre \fē-də-shäⁿbrᵊ\ [F] : lady's maid

fille d'hon·neur \fē-dȯ-nœr\ [F] : maid of honor

fi·nem re·spi·ce \ˌfē-ˌnem-ˈrā-spi-ˌke\ [L] : consider the end

fi·nis co·ro·nat opus \ˌfē-nis-kȯ-ˌrō-ˌnät-ˈō-ˌpu̇s\ [L] : the end crowns the work

flo·re·at \ˈflō-re-ˌät\ [L] : may (he, she, or it) flourish — usu. followed by a name

fluc·tu·at nec mer·gi·tur \ˈflu̇k-tü-ˌät-ˌnek-ˈmer-gi-ˌtu̇r\ [L] : it is tossed by the waves but does not sink — motto of Paris

fo·lie de gran·deur *or* **fo·lie des gran-**

deurs \fȯ-lē-də-grä^{n}-dœr\ [F] : delusion of greatness : megalomania

force de frappe \fȯrs-də-fräp\ [F] : a force equipped to deal a retaliatory blow

fors·an et haec olim me·mi·nis·se ju·va·bit \ˌfȯr-ˌsän-ˌet-ˈhīk-ˌō-lim-ˌme-mi-ˈni-se-yü-ˈwä-bit\ [L] : perhaps this too will be a pleasure to look back on one day

for·tes for·tu·na ju·vat \ˈfȯr-ˌtās-fȯr-ˌtü-nä-ˈyü-ˌwät\ [L] : fortune favors the brave

fron·ti nul·la fi·des \ˈfrȯn-ˌtē-ˌnü-lä-ˈfi-ˌdās\ [L] : no reliance can be placed on appearance

fu·it Ili·um \ˈfü-it-ˈi-lē-ům\ [L] : Troy has been (i.e., is no more)

fu·ror lo·quen·di \ˌfür-ˌȯr-lō-ˈkwen-(ˌ)dē\ [L] : rage for speaking

furor po·e·ti·cus \-pō-ˈā-ti-kůs\ [L] : poetic frenzy

furor scri·ben·di \-skrē-ˈben-(ˌ)dē\ [L] : rage for writing

Gal·li·ce \ˈgä-li-ˌke\ [L] : in French : after the French manner

gar·çon d'hon·neur \gär-sō^{n}-dȯ-nœr\ [F] : bridegroom's attendant

garde du corps \gärd-dæ-kȯr\ [F] : bodyguard

gar·dez la foi \gär-dā-lä-fwä\ [F] : keep faith

gau·de·a·mus igi·tur \ˌgaů-dē-ˈä-mùs-ˈi-gi-ˌtůr\ [L] : let us then be merry

gens d'é·glise \zhä^{n}-dā-glēz\ [F] : church people : clergy

gens de guerre \zhä^{n}-də-ger\ [F] : military people : soldiery

gens du monde \zhä^{n}-dæ-mō^{n}d\ [F] : people of the world : fashionable people

gno·thi se·au·ton \ˈgnō-thē-ˌse-aů-ˈtȯn\ [Gk] : know thyself

goût de ter·roir \gü-də-te-rwär\ [F] : taste of the earth

grand monde \grä^{n}-mō^{n}d\ [F] : great world : high society

gros·so mo·do \ˈgrȯs-(ˌ)sō-ˈmō-(ˌ)dō\ [It] : roughly

guerre à ou·trance \ger-ä-ü-trä^{n}s\ [F] : war to the uttermost

gu·ten Tag \ˌgü-tən-ˈtäk\ [G] : good day

has·ta la vis·ta \ˌäs-tə-lä-ˈvēs-tə\ [Sp] : good-bye

haute vul·ga·ri·sa·tion \ōt-vœl-gä-rē-zä-syō^{n}\ [F] : high popularization : effective presentation of a difficult subject to a general audience

hic et nunc \ˈhēk-et-ˈnůŋk\ [L] : here and now

hic et ubi·que \ˌhēk-et-ů-ˈbē-kwe\ [L] : here and everywhere

hic ja·cet \hik-ˈjā-sət, hēk-ˈyä-ket\ [L] : here lies — used preceding a name on a tombstone

hinc il·lae la·cri·mae \ˌhiŋk-ˌi-ˌlī-ˈlä-kri-ˌmī\ [L] : hence those tears

hoc age \hōk-ˈä-ge\ [L] : do this : apply yourself to what you are about

homme d'af·faires \ȯm-dä-fer\ [F] : man of business : business agent

homme d'es·prit \ȯm-des-prē\ [F] : man of wit

homme moyen sen·suel \ȯm-mwä-ya^{n}-sä^{n}-sw^{y}el\ [F] : the average nonintellectual man

ho·mo sum: hu·ma·ni nil a me ali·e·num pu·to \ˈhō-mō-ˌsům hü-ˌmä-nē-ˈnēl-ä-ˌmā-ˌä-lē-ˈā-nům-ˈpů-tō\ [L] : I am a human being: I regard nothing of human concern as foreign to my interests

ho·ni soit qui mal y pense \ȯ-nē-swä-kē-mäl-ē-pä^{n}s\ [F] : shamed be he who thinks evil of it — motto of the Order of the Garter

hu·ma·num est er·ra·re \hü-ˌmä-nům-ˌest-e-ˈrär-ā\ [L] : to err is human

ich dien \ik-ˈdēn\ [G] : I serve — motto of the Prince of Wales

ici on parle fran·çais \ē-sē-ō^{n}-pärl-frä^{n}-se\ [F] : French is spoken here

idées re·çues \ē-dār-(ə-)sue\ [F] : received ideas : conventional opinions

id est \id-ˈest\ [L] : that is

ig·no·ran·tia ju·ris ne·mi·nem ex·cu·sat \ˌig-nō-ˌrän-tē-ä-ˈyůr-is-ˈnā-mi-ˌnem-eks-ˈkü-ˌsät\ [L] : ignorance of the law excuses no one

ig·no·tum per ig·no·ti·us \ig-ˈnō-tům-ˌper-ig-ˈnō-tē-ˌůs\ [L] : (explaining) the unknown by means of the more unknown

il faut cul·ti·ver no·tre jar·din \ēl-fō-kœl-tē-vā-nȯt-zhär-da^{n}, -nȯ-trə-zhär-\ [F] : we must cultivate our garden : we must tend to our own affairs

in ae·ter·num \ˌin-ī-ˈter-ˌnům\ [L] : forever

in du·bio \in-ˈdů-bē-ˌō\ [L] : in doubt : undetermined

in fu·tu·ro \ˌin-fů-ˈtůr-ō\ [L] : in the future

in hoc sig·no vin·ces \in-hōk-ˈsig-nō-ˈwiŋ-ˌkās\ [L] : by this sign (the Cross) you will conquer

in li·mi·ne \in-ˈlē-mi-ˌne\ [L] : on the threshold : at the beginning

in om·nia pa·ra·tus \in-ˈȯm-nē-ä-pä-ˈrä-ˌtůs\ [L] : ready for all things

in par·ti·bus in·fi·de·li·um \in-ˈpär-ti-ˌbůs-ˌin-fi-ˈdā-lē-ˌům\ [L] : in the regions of the infidels — used of a titular bishop having no diocesan jurisdiction, usu. in non-Christian countries

in prae·sen·ti \ˌin-prī-ˈsen-ˌtē\ [L] : at the present time

in sae·cu·la sae·cu·lo·rum \in-ˈsī-ků-ˌlä-ˌsī-ků-ˈlȯr-ům, -ˈsā-ků-ˌlä-ˌsā-\ [L] : for ages of ages : forever and ever

in·shal·lah \ˌin-shä-ˈlä\ [Ar *in shā' Allāh*] : if Allah wills : God willing

in·te·ger vi·tae sce·le·ris·que pu·rus \ˌin-te-ˌger-ˈwē-ˌtī-ˌske-le-ˈris-kwe-ˈpü-rüs\ [L] : upright of life and free from wickedness

in·ter nos \ˌin-ter-ˈnōs\ [L] : between ourselves
in·tra mu·ros \ˌin-trä-ˈmü-ˌrōs\ [L] : within the walls
in utrum·que pa·ra·tus \ˌin-ü-ˈtrum-kwe-pä-ˈrä-ˌtus\ [L] : prepared for either (event)
in·ve·nit \in-ˈwā-nit\ [L] : he or she devised it
in vi·no ve·ri·tas \in-wē-nō-ˈwā-ri-ˌtäs\ [L] : there is truth in wine
ip·sis·si·ma ver·ba \ip-ˈsi-si-ˌmä-ˈwer-ˌbä\ [L] : the very words
ira fu·ror bre·vis est \ˌē-rä-ˈfu̇r-ˌȯr-ˈbre-wis-ˌest\ [L] : anger is a brief madness
j'ac·cuse \zhä-kuez\ [F] : I accuse : bitter denunciation
jac·ta alea est \ˈyäk-ˌtä-ˌä-lē-ˌä-ˈest\ [L] : the die is cast
j'adoube \zhä-düb\ [F] : I adjust — used in chess when touching a piece without intending to move it
ja·nu·is clau·sis \ˌyä-nu̇-ˌēs-ˈklau̇-ˌsēs\ [L] : behind closed doors
je main·tien·drai \zhə-maⁿ-tyaⁿ-drā\ [F] : I will maintain — motto of the Netherlands
jeu de mots \zhœd-mō, zhœ-də-\ [F] : play on words : pun
Jo·an·nes est no·men eius \yō-ˈä-näs-est-ˌnō-men-ˈā-yu̇s\ [L] : John is his name — motto of Puerto Rico
jour·nal in·time \zhür-näl-aⁿ-tēm\ [F] : intimate journal : private diary
jus di·vi·num \ˌyüs-di-ˈwē-ˌnu̇m\ [L] : divine law
jus·ti·tia om·ni·bus \yu̇s-ˌti-tē-ˌä-ˈȯm-ni-ˌbu̇s\ [L] : justice for all — motto of the District of Columbia
j'y suis, j'y reste \zhē-swʸē zhē-rest\ [F] : here I am, here I remain
Kin·der, Kir·che, Küche \ˈkin-dər ˈkir-k̲ə ˈkue-k̲ə\ [G] : children, church, kitchen
la belle dame sans mer·ci \lä-bel-däm-säⁿ-mer-sē\ [F] : the beautiful lady without mercy
la·bo·ra·re est ora·re \ˈlä-bō-ˌrär-ā-ˌest-ˈō-ˌrär-ā\ [L] : to work is to pray
la·bor om·nia vin·cit \ˈlä-ˌbȯr-ˌȯm-nē-ˌä-ˈwiŋ-kit\ [L] : labor conquers all things — motto of Oklahoma
la·cri·mae re·rum \ˌlä-kri-ˌmī-ˈrā-ˌru̇m\ [L] : tears for things : pity for misfortune; *also* : tears in things : tragedy of life
lais·sez–al·ler *or* **lais·ser–al·ler** \le-sā-ä-lā\ [F] : letting go : lack of restraint
lap·sus ca·la·mi \ˌläp-su̇s-ˈkä-lä-ˌmē\ [L] : slip of the pen
lap·sus lin·guae \ˌ-ˈliŋ-ˌgwī\ [L] : slip of the tongue
la reine le veut \lä-ren-lə-vœ\ [F] : the queen wills it
la·scia·te ogni spe·ran·za, voi ch'en·tra·te \läsh-ˈshä-tā-ˌō-nʸē-spā-ˈrän-tsä ˌvō-ē-kān-ˈträ-tā\ [It] : abandon all hope, ye who enter
lau·da·tor tem·po·ris ac·ti \lau̇-ˈdä-ˌtȯr-ˌtem-pȯ-ris-ˈäk-ˌtē\ [L] : one who praises past times
laus Deo \lau̇s-ˈdā-ō\ [L] : praise (be) to God
Le·bens·welt \ˈlā-bəns-ˌvelt\ [G] : life world : world of lived experience
le cœur a ses rai·sons que la rai·son ne con·naît point \lə-kœr-ä-sā-re-zōⁿk-lä-re-zōⁿn-kȯ-ne-pwaⁿ\ [F] : the heart has its reasons that reason knows nothing of
le roi est mort, vive le roi \lə-rwä-e-mȯr vēv-lə-rwä\ [F] : the king is dead, long live the king
le roi le veut \lə-rwä-lə-vœ\ [F] : the king wills it
le style, c'est l'homme \lə-stēl se-lȯm\ [F] : the style is the man
l'état, c'est moi \lā-tä se-mwä\ [F] : the state, it is I
l'étoile du nord \lā-twäl-due-nȯr\ [F] : the star of the north — motto of Minnesota
Lie·der·kranz \ˈlē-dər-ˌkränts\ [G] : wreath of songs : German singing society
lit·tera scrip·ta ma·net \ˌli-te-ˌrä-ˌskrip-tä-ˈmä-net\ [L] : the written letter abides
lo·cus in quo \ˌlō-ku̇s-in-ˈkwō\ [L] : place in which
l'union fait la force \lue-nyōⁿ-fe-lä-fȯrs\ [F] : union makes strength — motto of Belgium
lu·sus na·tu·rae \ˌlü-su̇s-nä-ˈtu̇r-ē, -ˈtu̇r-ˌī\ [L] : freak of nature
ma foi \mä-fwä\ [F] : my faith! : indeed
mag·na est ve·ri·tas et prae·va·le·bit \ˌmäg-nä-ˌest-ˈwā-ri-ˌtäs-et-ˌprī-wä-ˈlā-bit\ [L] : truth is mighty and will prevail
ma·ha·lo \ˈmä-hä-lō\ [Hawaiian] : thank you
ma·lade ima·gi·naire \mä-läd-ē-mä-zhē-ner\ [F] : imaginary invalid : hypochondriac
mal de siècle \mäl-də-syeklᵊ\ [F] : illness from worldly concerns : world-weariness
ma·lis avi·bus \ˌmä-ˌlēs-ˈä-wi-ˌbu̇s\ [L] : under evil auspices
man spricht Deutsch \män-shprik̲t-ˈdȯich\ [G] : German spoken
ma·riage de con·ve·nance \mä-ryäzh-də-kōⁿv-näⁿs\ [F] : marriage of convenience
ma·ri com·plai·sant \mä-rē-kōⁿ-ple-zäⁿ\ [F] : complaisant husband : cuckold who accepts his wife's infidelity
mau·vaise honte \mȯ-vez-ōⁿt\ [F] : bad shame : bashfulness
mau·vais quart d'heure \mȯ-ve-kär-dœr\ [F] : bad quarter hour : an uncomfortable though brief experience
me·dio tu·tis·si·mus ibis \ˈme-dē-ˌō-tü-ˌti-si-mu̇s-ˈē-bis\ [L] : you will go most safely by the middle course
me ju·di·ce \mā-ˈyü-di-ke\ [L] : I being judge : in my judgment

mens sa·na in cor·po·re sa·no \māns-ˈsä-nä-in-ˌkȯr-pȯ-re-ˈsä-nō\ [L] : a sound mind in a sound body
me·um et tu·um \ˌmē-əm-ˌet-ˈtü-əm, ˌme-u̇m-ˌet-ˈtü-u̇m\ [L] : mine and thine : distinction of private property
mi·ra·bi·le vi·su \mi-ˌrä-bi-lā-ˈwē-sü\ [L] : wonderful to behold
mi·ra·bi·lia \ˌmir-ə-ˈbi-lē-ˌä\ [L] : wonders : miracles
mœurs \mœr(s)\ [F] : mores : attitudes, customs, and manners of a society
mo·le ru·it sua \ˈmō-le-ˈru̇-it-ˌsu̇-ä\ [L] : it collapses from its own bigness
monde \mōⁿd\ [F] : world : fashionable world : society
mon·ta·ni sem·per li·be·ri \mȯn-ˈtä-nē-ˌsem-per-ˈlē-be-ˌrē\ [L] : mountaineers are always free — motto of West Virginia
mo·nu·men·tum ae·re per·en·ni·us \ˌmȯ-nu̇-ˈmen-tu̇m-ˌī-re-pe-ˈre-nē-u̇s\ [L] : a monument more lasting than bronze — used of an immortal work of art or literature
mo·re suo \ˌmȯr-ā-ˈsü-ō\ [L] : in his (or her) own manner
mo·ri·tu·ri te sa·lu·ta·mus \ˌmȯr-i-ˈtu̇r-ē-ˌtā-ˌsä-lu̇-ˈtä-mu̇s\ *or* **morituri te sa·lu·tant** \-ˈsä-lu̇-ˌtänt\ [L] : we (or those) who are about to die salute thee
mul·tum in par·vo \ˌmu̇l-tu̇m-in-ˈpär-vō, -ˈpär-wō\ [L] : much in little
mu·ta·to no·mi·ne de te fa·bu·la nar·ra·tur \mü-ˌtä-tō-ˈnō-mi-ne-ˌdā-ˌtā-ˈfä-bu̇-lä-nä-ˈrä-ˌtu̇r\ [L] : with the name changed the story applies to you
my·ster·i·um tre·men·dum \mi-ˈster-ē-ˌu̇m-tre-ˈmen-du̇m\ [L] : overwhelming mystery
na·tu·ram ex·pel·las fur·ca, ta·men us·que re·cur·ret \nä-ˈtü-ˌräm-ek-ˌspe-läs-ˈfu̇r-ˌkä ˌtä-men-ˈu̇s-kwe-re-ˈku̇r-et\ [L] : you may drive nature out with a pitchfork, but she will keep coming back
na·tu·ra non fa·cit sal·tum \nä-ˈtü-rä-ˌnōn-ˌfä-kit-ˈsäl-ˌtu̇m\ [L] : nature makes no leap
ne ce·de ma·lis \nā-ˌkā-de-ˈmä-ˌlēs\ [L] : yield not to misfortunes
ne·mo me im·pu·ne la·ces·sit \ˈnā-mō-ˈmā-im-ˌpü-nā-lä-ˈke-sit\ [L] : no one attacks me with impunity — motto of Scotland and of the Order of the Thistle
ne quid ni·mis \ˌnā-ˌkwid-ˈni-mis\ [L] : not anything in excess
n'est–ce pas? \nes-pä\ [F] : isn't it so?
nicht wahr? \nikt-ˈvär\ [G] : not true? : isn't it so?
nil ad·mi·ra·ri \ˈnēl-ˌäd-mi-ˈrär-ē\ [L] : to be excited by nothing : equanimity
nil de·spe·ran·dum \ˈnēl-ˌdā-spā-ˈrän-du̇m\ [L] : never despair
nil si·ne nu·mi·ne \ˈnēl-ˌsi-nā-ˈnü-mi-ne\ [L] : nothing without the divine will — motto of Colorado
n'im·porte \naⁿ-pȯrt\ [F] : it's no matter
no·lens vo·lens \ˌnō-ˌlenz-ˈvō-ˌlenz\ [L] : unwilling (or) willing : willy-nilly
non om·nia pos·su·mus om·nes \nōn-ˈȯm-nē-ä-ˌpȯ-su̇-mu̇s-ˈȯm-ˌnās\ [L] : we can't all (do) all things
non sans droict \nōⁿ-säⁿ-drwä\ [OF] : not without right — motto on Shakespeare's coat of arms
non sum qua·lis eram \ˌnōn-ˌsu̇m-ˌkwä-lis-ˈer-ˌäm\ [L] : I am not what I used to be
nos·ce te ip·sum \ˌnȯs-ke-ˌtā-ˈip-ˌsu̇m\ [L] : know thyself
nos·tal·gie de la boue \nȯs-täl-zhēd-lä-bü, -zhē-də-\ [F] : yearning for the mud : attraction to what is unworthy, crude, or degrading
nous avons chan·gé tout ce·la \nü-zä-vōⁿ-shäⁿ-zhā-tü-sə-lä\ [F] : we have changed all that
nous ver·rons ce que nous ver·rons \nü-ve-rōⁿs-kə-nü-ve-rōⁿ, -rōⁿ-sə-kə-\ [F] : we shall see what we shall see
no·vus ho·mo \ˌnȯ-wu̇s-ˈhȯ-mō\ [L] : new man : man newly ennobled : upstart
novus or·do se·clo·rum \-ˈȯr-ˌdō-sā-ˈklȯr-u̇m\ [L] : a new cycle of the ages — motto on the reverse of the Great Seal of the United States
nu·gae \ˈnü-ˌgī\ [L] : trifles
nuit blanche \nwʸē-bläⁿsh\ [F] : white night : a sleepless night
nyet \ˈnyet\ [Russ] : no
ob·iit \ˈȯ-bē-ˌit\ [L] : he or she died
ob·scu·rum per ob·scu·ri·us \ȯb-ˈskyu̇r-u̇m-ˌper-ȯb-ˈskyu̇r-ē-u̇s\ [L] : (explaining) the obscure by means of the more obscure
ode·rint dum me·tu·ant \ˈō-de-ˌrint-ˌdu̇m-me-tu̇-ˌänt\ [L] : let them hate, so long as they fear
odi et amo \ˈō-ˌdē-et-ˈä-(ˌ)mō\ [L] : I hate and I love
omer·tà \ȯ-ˈmer-tä\ [It] : conspiracy of silence
om·ne ig·no·tum pro mag·ni·fi·co \ˌȯm-ne-ig-ˈnō-ˌtu̇m-prō-mäg-ˈni-fi-ˌkō\ [L] : everything unknown (is taken) as grand : the unknown tends to be exaggerated in importance or difficulty
om·nia mu·tan·tur, nos et mu·ta·mur in il·lis \ˌȯm-nē-ä-mü-ˈtän-ˌtu̇r ˌnōs-ˌet-mü-ˌtä-mu̇r-in-ˈi-ˌlēs\ [L] : all things are changing, and we are changing with them
om·nia vin·cit amor \ˈȯm-nē-ä-ˈwiŋ-kit-ˈä-ˌmȯr\ [L] : love conquers all
onus pro·ban·di \ˌō-nu̇s-prō-ˈban-ˌdī, -dē\ [L] : burden of proof
ora pro no·bis \ˌō-rä-prō-ˈnō-ˌbēs\ [L] : pray for us
ore ro·tun·do \ˌōr-ē-rō-ˈtən-dō\ [L] : with round mouth : eloquently
oro y pla·ta \ˌōr-ō-ē-ˈplä-tə\ [Sp] : gold and silver — motto of Montana

o tem·po·ra! o mo·res! \ō-ˈtem-pȯ-rä ō-ˈmō-ˌrās\ [L] : oh the times! oh the manners!
oti·um cum dig·ni·ta·te \ˈō-tē-ˌu̇m-ku̇m-ˌdig-ni-ˈtä-te\ [L] : leisure with dignity
où sont les neiges d'an·tan? \ü-sōⁿ-lā-nezh-däⁿ-täⁿ\ [F] : where are the snows of yesteryear?
outre–mer \ütrᵊ-mer\ [F] : overseas : distant lands
pal·li·da Mors \ˌpa-li-dä-ˈmȯrz\ [L] : pale Death
pa·nem et cir·cen·ses \ˈpä-ˌnem-et-kir-ˈkān-ˌsās\ [L] : bread and circuses : provision of the means of life and recreation by government to appease discontent
pan·ta rhei \ˌpän-ˌtä-ˈrā\ [Gk] : all things are in flux
par avance \pär-ä-väⁿs\ [F] : in advance : by anticipation
par avion \pär-ä-vyōⁿ\ [F] : by airplane — used on airmail
par ex·em·ple \pär-āg-zäⁿplᵊ\ [F] : for example
pars pro to·to \ˈpärs-(ˌ)prō-ˈtō-(ˌ)tō\ [L] : part (taken) for the whole
par·tu·ri·unt mon·tes, nas·ce·tur ri·di·cu·lus mus \pär-ˈtu̇r-ē-ˌu̇nt-ˈmȯn-ˌtās näs-ˈkā-ˌtu̇r-ri-ˌdi-ku̇-lu̇s-ˈmüs\ [L] : the mountains are in labor, and a ridiculous mouse will be brought forth
pa·ter pa·tri·ae \ˈpä-ˌter-ˈpä-trē-ˌī\ [L] : father of his country
pau·cis ver·bis \ˌpau̇-ˌkēs-ˈwer-ˌbēs\ [L] : in a few words
pax vo·bis·cum \ˌpäks-vō-ˈbēs-ˌku̇m\ [L] : peace (be) with you
peine forte et dure \pen-fȯr-tā-dœr\ [F] : strong and hard punishment : torture
per an·gus·ta ad au·gus·ta \per-ˈän-ˌgu̇s-tä-äd-ˈau̇-ˌgu̇s-tä\ [L] : through difficulties to honors
per·fide Al·bion \per-fēd-äl-byōⁿ\ [F] : perfidious Albion (England)
peu à peu \pœ-ä-pœ\ [F] : little by little
peu de chose \pœd-shōz, pœ-də-\ [F] : a trifle
pinx·it \ˈpiŋk-sit\ [L] : he or she painted it
place aux dames \pläs-ō-däm\ [F] : (make) room for the ladies
ple·no ju·re \ˌplā-nō-ˈyu̇r-e\ [L] : with full right
plus ça change, plus c'est la même chose \plue-sä-shäⁿzh plue-se-lä-mem-shōz\ [F] : the more that changes, the more it's the same thing — often shortened to *plus ça change*
plus roy·a·liste que le roi \plue-rwä-yä-lēst-kəl-rwä\ [F] : more royalist than the king
po·cas pa·la·bras \ˌpō-käs-pä-ˈlä-vräs\ [Sp] : few words
po·eta nas·ci·tur, non fit \pȯ-ˌā-tä-ˈnäs-ki-ˌtu̇r nōn-ˈfit\ [L] : a poet is born, not made
po·ète mau·dit \pȯ-et-mō-dē\ [F] : accursed poet : a writer dogged by misfortune and lack of recognition
pol·li·ce ver·so \ˌpȯ-li-ke-ˈwer-sō\ [L] : with thumb turned : with a gesture or expression of condemnation
post hoc, er·go prop·ter hoc \ˈpōst-ˌhōk ˌer-gō-ˈprȯp-ter-ˌhōk\ [L] : after this, therefore on account of it (a fallacy of argument)
post ob·itum \pōst-ˈō-bi-ˌtu̇m\ [L] : after death
pour en·cou·ra·ger les autres \pür-äⁿ-kü-rä-zhā-lā-zōtrᵊ\ [F] : in order to encourage the others — said ironically of an action (as an execution) carried out in order to compel others to obey
pri·mum non no·ce·re \ˌprē-mu̇m-ˌnōn-nȯ-ˈkā-rā\ [L] : the first thing (is) to do no harm
pro bo·no pu·bli·co \prō-ˌbō-nō-ˈpü-bli-ˌkō\ [L] : for the public good
pro hac vi·ce \prō-ˌhäk-ˈwi-ke\ [L] : for this occasion
pro pa·tria \prō-ˈpä-trē-ˌä\ [L] : for one's country
pro re·ge, le·ge, et gre·ge \prō-ˈrā-ˌge ˈlā-ˌge et-ˈgre-ˌge\ [L] : for the king, the law, and the people
pro re na·ta \ˌprō-ˌrā-ˈnä-tä\ [L] : for an occasion that has arisen : as needed — used in medical prescriptions
quand même \käⁿ-mem\ [F] : even so : all the same
quan·tum mu·ta·tus ab il·lo \ˌkwän-tu̇m-mü-ˈtä-tu̇s-äb-ˈi-lō\ [L] : how changed from what he once was
quan·tum suf·fi·cit \ˌkwän-təm-ˈsə-fə-ˌkit\ [L] : as much as suffices : a sufficient quantity — used chiefly in medical prescriptions
¿quién sa·be? \kyān-ˈsä-vā\ [Sp] : who knows?
qui fa·cit per ali·um fa·cit per se \kwē-ˌfä-kit-ˌper-ˈä-lē-ˌu̇m-ˌfä-kit-ˌper-ˈsā\ [L] : he who does (something) through another does it through himself
quis cus·to·di·et ip·sos cus·to·des? \ˌkwis-ku̇s-ˈtō-dē-ˌet-ˌip-ˌsōs-ku̇s-ˈtō-ˌdās\ [L] : who will keep the keepers themselves?
qui s'ex·cuse s'ac·cuse \kē-ˈsek-ˌskuez-ˈsä-ˌkuez\ [F] : he who excuses himself accuses himself
quis se·pa·ra·bit? \ˌkwis-ˌsā-pə-ˈrä-bit\ [L] : who shall separate (us)? — motto of the Order of St. Patrick
qui trans·tu·lit sus·ti·net \kwē-ˈträns-tu̇-ˌlit-ˈsu̇s-ti-ˌnet\ [L] : He who transplanted sustains (us) — motto of Connecticut
qui va là? \kē-vä-lä\ [F] : who goes there?
quo·ad hoc \ˌkwō-ˌäd-ˈhōk\ [L] : as far as this : to this extent
quod erat de·mon·stran·dum \ˌkwȯd-ˈer-ˌät-ˌde-mən-ˈstran-dəm, -ˌdā-ˌmȯn-ˈsträn-ˌdu̇m\ [L] : which was to be proved

quod erat fa·ci·en·dum \-ˌfä-kē-ˈen-ˌdu̇m\ [L] : which was to be done

quod sem·per, quod ubi·que, quod ab om·ni·bus \kwȯd-ˈsem-ˌper kwȯd-ˈü-bi-ˌkwā ˌkwȯd-äb-ˈȯm-ni-ˌbu̇s, -ˌkwȯd-ü-ˈbē-(ˌ)kwā-\ [L] : what (has been held) always, everywhere, by everybody

quod vi·de \kwȯd-ˈwi-ˌde\ [L] : which see

quo·rum pars mag·na fui \ˈkwȯr-u̇m-ˌpärs-ˌmäg-nä-ˈfu̇-ē\ [L] : in which I played a great part

quos de·us vult per·de·re pri·us de·men·tat \kwōs-ˈdā-u̇s-ˌwu̇lt-ˈper-de-ˌrā-ˌpri-u̇s-dā-ˈmen-ˌtät\ [L] : those whom a god wishes to destroy he first drives mad

quot ho·mi·nes, tot sen·ten·ti·ae \kwȯt-ˈhȯ-mi-ˌnās ˌtȯt-sen-ˈten-tē-ˌī\ [L] : there are as many opinions as there are men

quo va·dis? \kwō-ˈwä-dis, -ˈvä-dəs\ [L] : whither are you going?

rai·son d'état \re-zōⁿ-dā-tä\ [F] : reason of state

reg·nat po·pu·lus \ˌreg-ˌnät-ˈpȯ-pu̇-ˌlu̇s\ [L] : the people rule — motto of Arkansas

re in·fec·ta \ˌrā-in-ˈfek-ˌtä\ [L] : the business being unfinished : without accomplishing one's purpose

re·li·gio lo·ci \re-ˈli-gē-ˌō-ˈlȯ-ˌkē\ [L] : religious sanctity of a place

rem acu te·ti·gis·ti \rem-ˈä-ˌkü-ˌte-ti-ˈgis-tē\ [L] : you have touched the point with a needle : you have hit the nail on the head

ré·pon·dez s'il vous plaît \rā-pōⁿ-dā-sēl-vü-ple\ [F] : reply, if you please

re·qui·es·cat in pa·ce \ˌre-kwē-ˈes-ˌkät-in-ˈpä-ˌke, ˌrā-kwē-ˈes-ˌkät-in-ˈpä-ˌchā\ [L] : may he or she rest in peace — used on tombstones

re·spi·ce fi·nem \ˌrā-spi-ˌke-ˈfē-ˌnem\ [L] : look to the end : consider the outcome

re·sur·gam \re-ˈsu̇r-ˌgäm\ [L] : I shall rise again

re·te·nue \rət-nœ\ [F] : self-restraint : reserve

re·ve·nons à nos mou·tons \rəv-nōⁿ-ä-nō-mü-tōⁿ\ [F] : let us return to our sheep : let us get back to the subject

ruse de guerre \rœz-də-ger\ [F] : war stratagem

rus in ur·be \ˌrüs-in-ˈu̇r-ˌbe\ [L] : country in the city

sae·va in·dig·na·tio \ˌsī-wä-ˌin-dig-ˈnä-tē-ō\ [L] : fierce indignation

salle à man·ger \säl-ä-mäⁿ-zhā\ [F] : dining room

sa·lus po·pu·li su·pre·ma lex es·to \ˌsä-ˌlüs-ˈpȯ-pu̇-ˌlē-sü-ˌprā-mä-ˌleks-ˈes-tō\ [L] : let the welfare of the people be the supreme law — motto of Missouri

sanc·ta sim·pli·ci·tas \ˌsäŋk-tä-sim-ˈpli-ki-ˌtäs\ [L] : holy simplicity — often used ironically in reference to another's naïveté

sans doute \säⁿ-düt\ [F] : without doubt

sans gêne \säⁿ-zhen\ [F] : without embarrassment or constraint

sans peur et sans re·proche \säⁿ-pœr-ā-säⁿ-rə-ˈprȯsh\ [F] : without fear and without reproach

sans sou·ci \säⁿ-sü-sē\ [F] : without worry

sa·yo·na·ra \ˌsī-ə-ˈnär-ə, ˌsä-yə-\ [Jp] : good-bye

sculp·sit \ˈskəlp-sət, ˈsku̇lp-sit\ [L] : he or she carved it

scu·to bo·nae vo·lun·ta·tis tu·ae co·ro·nas·ti nos \ˈskü-ˌtō-ˈbȯ-ˌnī-ˌvȯ-lu̇n-ˌtä-tis-ˈtu̇-ˌī-ˈkȯr-ō-ˌnäs-tē-ˈnōs\ [L] : Thou hast crowned us with the shield of Thy good will — a motto on the Great Seal of Maryland

se·cun·dum ar·tem \se-ˌku̇n-du̇m-ˈär-ˌtem\ [L] : according to the art : according to the accepted practice of a profession or trade

secundum na·tu·ram \-nä-ˈtü-ˌräm\ [L] : according to nature : naturally

se de·fen·den·do \ˈsā-ˌdā-ˌfen-ˈden-dō\ [L] : in self-defense

se ha·bla es·pa·ñol \sā-ˌäv-lä-ˌäs-pä-ˈnʸȯl\ [Sp] : Spanish spoken

sem·per ea·dem \ˌsem-ˌper-ˈe-ä-ˌdem\ [L] : always the same (fem.) — motto of Queen Elizabeth I

sem·per fi·de·lis \ˌsem-pər-fə-ˈdā-ləs\ [L] : always faithful — motto of the U.S. Marine Corps

sem·per idem \ˌsem-ˌper-ˈē-ˌdem\ [L] : always the same (masc.)

sem·per pa·ra·tus \ˌsem-pər-pə-ˈrä-təs\ [L] : always prepared — motto of the U.S. Coast Guard

se non è ve·ro, è ben tro·va·to \sā-ˌnōn-e-ˈvā-rō e-ˌben-trō-ˈvä-tō\ [It] : even if it is not true, it is well conceived

sha·lom alei·chem \ˌshȯ-ləm-ə-ˈlā-kəm, ˌshō-, -k̲əm\ [Heb *shālōm ʿalēkhem*] : peace to you — used as a traditional Jewish greeting

sic itur ad as·tra \sēk-ˈi-ˌtu̇r-ˌäd-ˈäs-trə\ [L] : thus one goes to the stars : such is the way to immortality

sic sem·per ty·ran·nis \ˌsik-ˌsem-pər-tə-ˈra-nəs\ [L] : thus ever to tyrants — motto of Virginia

sic trans·it glo·ria mun·di \sēk-ˈträn-sit-ˌglȯr-ē-ä-ˈmu̇n-dē\ [L] : so passes away the glory of the world

si jeu·nesse sa·vait, si vieil·lesse pou·vait! \sē-ˈzhœ-nes-ˈsä-ve sē-ˈvye-yes-ˈpü-ve\ [F] : if youth only knew, if age only could!

si·lent le·ges in·ter ar·ma \ˌsi-ˌlent-ˈlā-ˌgās-ˌin-ter-ˈär-mä\ [L] : the laws are silent in the midst of arms (i.e., in time of war)

s'il vous plaît \sēl-vü-ple\ [F] : if you please

si·mi·lia si·mi·li·bus cu·ran·tur \si-ˈmi-lē-ä-si-ˈmi-li-bu̇s-kü-ˈrän-ˌtu̇r\ [L] : like is cured by like

si·mi·lis si·mi·li gau·det \ˈsi-mi-lis-ˈsi-mi-lē-ˈgau̇-ˌdet\ [L] : like takes pleasure in like

si mo·nu·men·tum re·qui·ris, cir·cum·spi·ce \ˌsē-ˌmo̊-nu̇-ˌmen-tu̇m-re-ˈkwē-ris kir-ˈku̇m-spi-ke\ [L] : if you seek his monument, look around — epitaph of Sir Christopher Wren in St. Paul's, London, of which he was architect

sim·pliste \sa^{n}-plēst\ [F] : simplistic : overly simple or naïve

si quae·ris pen·in·su·lam amoe·nam, cir·cum·spi·ce \sē-ˈkwī-ris-pā-ˈnin-sə-ˌläm-ä-ˈmo̊i-ˌnäm kir-ˈku̇m-spi-ke\ [L] : if you seek a beautiful peninsula, look around — motto of Michigan

sis·te vi·a·tor \ˌsis-te-wē-ˈä-ˌto̊r\ [L] : stop, traveler — used on Roman roadside tombs

si vis pa·cem, pa·ra bel·lum \sē-ˈwēs-ˈpä-ˌkem ˈpä-rä-ˈbe-ˌlu̇m\ [L] : if you wish peace, prepare for war

sol·vi·tur am·bu·lan·do \ˈso̊l-wi-ˌtu̇r-ˌäm-bu̇-ˈlän-dō\ [L] : it is solved by walking : the problem is solved by a practical experiment

spo·lia opi·ma \ˌspo̊-lē-ä-ō-ˈpē-mä\ [L] : rich spoils : the arms taken by the victorious from the vanquished general

sta·tus quo an·te bel·lum \ˈstä-tu̇s-kwō-ˌän-te-ˈbe-lu̇m\ [L] : the state existing before the war

sua·vi·ter in mo·do, for·ti·ter in re \ˈswä-wi-ˌter-in-ˈmo̊-dō ˈfo̊r-ti-ˌter-in-ˈrā\ [L] : gently in manner, strongly in deed

sub ver·bo \su̇b-ˈwer-bō, ˌsəb-ˈvər-bō\ *or* **sub vo·ce** \su̇b-ˈwō-ke, ˌsəb-ˈvō-sē\ [L] : under the word — introducing a cross-reference in a dictionary or index

sunt la·cri·mae re·rum \su̇nt-ˌlä-kri-ˌmī-ˈrā-ru̇m\ [L] : there are tears for things : tears attend trials

suo ju·re \ˌsu̇-ō-ˈyu̇r-e\ [L] : in his or her own right

suo lo·co \-ˈlo̊-kō\ [L] : in its proper place

suo Mar·te \-ˈmär-te\ [L] : by one's own exertions

su·um cui·que \ˌsu̇-u̇m-ˈkwi-kwe\ [L] : to each his own

tant mieux \tä^{n}-myœ\ [F] : so much the better

tant pis \-pē\ [F] : so much the worse : too bad

tem·po·ra mu·tan·tur, nos et mu·ta·mur in il·lis \ˌtem-po̊-rä-mü-ˈtän-ˌtu̇r ˌnōs-ˌet-mü-ˌtä-mu̇r-in-ˈi-ˌlēs\ [L] : the times are changing, and we are changing with them

tem·pus edax re·rum \ˈtem-pu̇s-ˌe-ˌdäks-ˈrā-ru̇m\ [L] : time, that devours all things

tem·pus fu·git \ˌtem-pəs-ˈfyü-jət, ˌtem-pu̇s-ˈfü-git\ [L] : time flies

ti·meo Da·na·os et do·na fe·ren·tes \ˌti-mē-ˌō-ˈdä-nä-ˌōs-ˌet-ˌdō-nä-fe-ˈren-ˌtās\ [L] : I fear the Greeks even when they bring gifts

to·ti·dem ver·bis \ˌto̊-ti-ˌdem-ˈwer-ˌbēs\ [L] : in so many words

to·tis vi·ri·bus \ˌtō-ˌtēs-ˈwē-ri-ˌbu̇s\ [L] : with all one's might

to·to cae·lo \ˌtō-tō-ˈkī-lō\ *or* **toto coe·lo** \-ˈko̊i-lō\ [L] : by the whole extent of the heavens : diametrically

tou·jours per·drix \tü-zhür-per-drē\ [F] : always partridge : too much of a good thing

tour d'ho·ri·zon \tür-do̊-rē-zō^{n}\ [F] : circuit of the horizon : general survey

tous frais faits \tü-fre-fe\ [F] : all expenses defrayed

tout à fait \tü-tä-fe\ [F] : altogether : quite

tout au con·traire \tü-tō-kō^{n}-trer\ [F] : quite the contrary

tout à vous \tü-tä-vü\ [F] : wholly yours : at your service

tout bien ou rien \tü-ˈbya^{n}-nü-ˈrya^{n}\ [F] : everything well (done) or nothing (attempted)

tout com·pren·dre c'est tout par·don·ner \ˈtü-kō^{n}-prä^{n}-drə-se-ˈtü-pär-do̊-nā\ [F] : to understand all is to forgive all

tout court \tü-kür\ [F] : quite short : and nothing else : simply : just; *also* : brusquely

tout de même \tüt-mem\ [F] : all the same : nevertheless

tout de suite \tüt-sw^{y}ēt\ [F] : immediately; *also* : all at once : consecutively

tout en·sem·ble \tü-tä^{n}-sä^{n}bl^{ə}\ [F] : all together : general effect

tout est per·du fors l'hon·neur \tü-te-per-dœ-fo̊r-lo̊-nœr\ *or* **tout est perdu hors l'honneur** \-dœ-o̊r-\ [F] : all is lost save honor

tout le monde \tü-lə-mō^{n}d\ [F] : all the world : everybody

tra·hi·son des clercs \trä-ē-zo̊^{n}-dā-klerk\ [F] : treason of the intellectuals

tranche de vie \trä^{n}sh-də-ˈvē\ [F] : slice of life

trist·esse \trē-stes\ [F] : melancholy

tu·e·bor \tu̇-ˈā-ˌbo̊r\ [L] : I will defend — a motto on the Great Seal of Michigan

ua mau ke ea o ka ai·na i ka po·no \ˌü-ä-ˈmä-ü-kā-ˈā-ä-ō-kä-ˈä-ē-nä-ˌē-kä-ˈpō-nō\ [Hawaiian] : the life of the land is perpetuated in righteousness — motto of Hawaii

über al·les \ˌœ-ber-ˈä-les\ [G] : above everything else

Über·mensch \ˈœ-bər-ˌmench\ [G] : superman

ul·ti·ma ra·tio re·gum \ˈu̇l-ti-mä-ˌrä-tē-ō-ˈrā-gu̇m\ [L] : the final argument of kings, i.e., war

und so wei·ter \u̇nt-zō-ˈvī-tər\ [G] : and so on

uno ani·mo \ˌü-nō-ˈä-ni-ˌmō\ [L] : with one mind : unanimously

ur·bi et or·bi \ˌu̇r-bē-ˌet-ˈȯr-bē\ [L] : to the city (Rome) and the world : to everyone
uti·le dul·ci \ˌü-ti-le-ˈdu̇l-ˌkē\ [L] : the useful with the agreeable
ut in·fra \u̇t-ˈin-frä\ [L] : as below
ut su·pra \u̇t-ˈsü-prä\ [L] : as above
va·de re·tro me, Sa·ta·na \ˌwä-de-ˈrā-trō-ˌmā ˈsä-tä-ˌnä\ [L] : get thee behind me, Satan
vae vic·tis \wī-ˈwik-ˌtēs\ [L] : woe to the vanquished
va·ri·um et mu·ta·bi·le sem·per fe·mi·na \ˌwär-ē-u̇m-ˌet-ˌmü-ˈtä-bi-le-ˌsem-ˌper-ˈfā-mi-nä\ [L] : woman is ever a fickle and changeable thing
ve·di Na·po·li e poi mo·ri \ˌvā-dē-ˈnä-pō-lē-ā-ˌpȯ-ē-ˈmȯ-rē\ [It] : see Naples and then die
ve·ni, vi·di, vi·ci \ˌwā-nē ˌwē-dē ˈwē-kē, ˌvā-nē ˌvē-dē ˈvē-chē\ [L] : I came, I saw, I conquered
ven·tre à terre \väⁿ-trä-ter\ [F] : belly to the ground : at very great speed
ver·ba·tim ac lit·te·ra·tim \wer-ˈbä-tim-ˌäk-ˌli-te-ˈrä-tim\ [L] : word for word and letter for letter
ver·bum sat sa·pi·en·ti est \ˌwer-bu̇m-ˈsät-ˌsä-pē-ˈen-tē-ˌest\ [L] : a word to the wise is sufficient
via cru·cis \wē-ä-ˈkrü-sis\ [L] : Way of the Cross : path of suffering
vieux jeu \vyœ-zhœ\ [F] : old game : old hat
vin·cit om·nia ve·ri·tas \ˌwiŋ-kit-ˈȯm-nē-ä-ˈwā-ri-ˌtäs\ [L] : truth conquers all things
vin·cu·lum ma·tri·mo·nii \ˌwiŋ-ku̇-lu̇m-ˌmä-tri-ˈmō-nē-ˌē\ [L] : bond of marriage
vin du pays \vaⁿ-dᵫ-pā-ē\ *or* **vin de pays** \vaⁿ-də-\ [F] : wine of the locality
vir·gi·ni·bus pu·e·ris·que \wir-ˈgi-ni-bu̇s-ˌpu̇-e-ˈrēs-kwe\ [L] : for girls and boys
vir·go in·tac·ta \ˈvir-ˌgō-in-ˈtäk-tä\ [L] : untouched virgin
vir·tu·te et ar·mis \wir-ˈtü-te-ˌet-ˈär-mēs\ [L] : by valor and arms — motto of Mississippi
vis me·di·ca·trix na·tu·rae \ˈwēs-ˌme-di-ˈkä-triks-nä-ˈtü-ˌrī\ [L] : the healing power of nature
vive la dif·fé·rence \vēv-lä-dē-fā-räⁿs\ [F] : long live the difference (between the sexes)
vive la reine \vēv-lä-ren\ [F] : long live the queen
vive le roi \vēv-lə-rwä\ [F] : long live the king
vogue la ga·lère \vȯg-lä-gä-ler\ [F] : let the galley be kept rowing : keep on, whatever may happen
voi·là tout \vwä-lä-tü\ [F] : that's all
vox et prae·te·rea ni·hil \ˈwōks-et-prī-ˈter-e-ä-ˈni-ˌhil\ [L] : voice and nothing more
vox po·pu·li vox Dei \wōks-ˈpȯ-pu̇-ˌlē-ˌwōks-ˈdā-ē\ [L] : the voice of the people is the voice of God
Wan·der·jahr \ˈvän-dər-ˌyär\ [G] : year of wandering
wie geht's? \vē-ˈgāts\ [G] : how goes it? : how is it going? — used as a greeting
wun·der·bar \ˈvu̇n-dər-ˌbär\ [G] : wonderful

GEOGRAPHICAL NAMES

This section gives basic information about the world's countries, regions, cities, and major physical features. For many of these entries, derived nouns and adjectives are also listed (as **Iceland** . . . **Icelander** . . . *n*). Other derived words not shown here have been separately entered in the main A-Z section, because of the presence of additional senses (as **Chinese**).

Abbreviations used here are listed in the front section Abbreviations in This Work. The capital letters N, E, S, and W, used singly or in combination and without a period, indicate direction. For example, "N India" means "northern India." Where direction is a part of the name, the word is spelled out.

The symbol ✻ denotes a capital. Sizes are given in conventional U.S. units, with metric equivalents following.

Ab·er·deen \ˌa-bər-ˈdēn\ city NE Scotland — **Ab·er·do·ni·an** \ˌa-bər-ˈdō-nē-ən\ *adj or n*

Ab·i·djan \ˌä-bē-ˈjän, ˌa-bi-\ city, seat of government of Côte d'Ivoire

Ab·i·lene \ˈa-bə-ˌlēn\ city NW *cen* Texas

Abu Dha·bi \ˌä-bü-ˈdä-bē, -ˈthä-\ city, ✻ of United Arab Emirates

Abu·ja \ä-ˈbü-jä\ city *cen* Nigeria; its ✻

Ab·ys·sin·ia \ˌa-bə-ˈsi-nē-ə, -nyə\ — see ETHIOPIA — **Ab·ys·sin·i·an** \-nē-ən, -nyən\ *adj or n*

Aca·dia \ə-ˈkā-dē-ə\ *or French* **Aca·die** \ä-kä-ˈdē\ NOVA SCOTIA — an early name — **Aca·di·an** \-ē-ən\ *adj or n*

Aca·pul·co \ˌä-kä-ˈpül-(ˌ)kō, ˌa-\ city & port S Mexico on the Pacific

Ac·cra \ˈä-krə, ˈa-; ə-ˈkrä\ city & port, ✻ of Ghana

Acon·ca·gua \ˌä-kōn-ˈkä-gwä\ mountain 22,834 ft. (6960 m.) W Argentina; highest in the Andes & in Western Hemisphere

Ad·dis Aba·ba \ˈä-dis-ˈä-bä-ˌbä, ˌa-dəs-ˈa-bə-bə\ city, ✻ of Ethiopia

Ad·e·laide \ˈa-də-ˌlād\ city S Australia, ✻ of South Australia

Aden \ˈä-dᵊn, ˈā-\ city & port S Yemen

Aden, Gulf of arm of Indian Ocean between Yemen (Arabia) & Somalia (Africa)

Ad·i·ron·dack \ˌa-də-ˈrän-ˌdak\ mountains NE New York; highest Mount Marcy 5344 ft. (1629 m.)

Admiralty \ˈad-m(ə-)rəl-tē\ **1** island SE Alaska **2** islands W Pacific N of New Guinea; part of Papua New Guinea

Adri·at·ic Sea \ˌā-drē-ˈa-tik, ˌa-\ arm of Mediterranean between Italy & Balkan Peninsula

Ae·ge·an Sea \i-ˈjē-ən\ arm of Mediterranean between Asia Minor & Greece

Af·ghan·i·stan \af-ˈga-nə-ˌstan, -ˈgä-nə-ˌstän\ country W Asia E of Iran; ✻, Kabul

Af·ri·ca \ˈa-fri-kə\ continent S of the Mediterranean

Agana — see HAGÅTÑA

Agra \ˈä-grə, ˈə-\ city N India SSE of Delhi

Aguas·ca·lien·tes \ˌä-gwäs-ˌkäl-ˈyen-ˌtās\ city *cen* Mexico NE of Guadalajara

Agul·has, Cape \ə-ˈgə-ləs\ cape Republic of South Africa; most southerly point of Africa, at 34° 52′ S latitude

Ahag·gar \ə-ˈhä-gər, ˌä-hə-ˈgär\ mountains S Algeria in W *cen* Sahara

Ah·mad·abad \ˈä-mə-də-ˌbäd, -ˌbad\ city W India N of Mumbai

Ak·ron \ˈa-krən\ city NE Ohio

Al·a·bama \ˌa-lə-ˈba-mə\ state SE U.S.; ✻, Montgomery — **Al·a·bam·i·an** \-ˈba-mē-ən\ *or* **Al·a·bam·an** \-ˈba-mən\ *adj or n*

Alas·ka \ə-ˈlas-kə\ **1** peninsula SW Alaska SW of Cook Inlet **2** state of U.S. in NW North America; ✻, Juneau **3** mountain range S Alaska extending from Alaska Peninsula to Yukon boundary — **Alas·kan** \-kən\ *adj or n*

Alaska, Gulf of inlet of Pacific off S Alaska between Alaska Peninsula on W & Alexander Archipelago on E

Al·ba·nia \al-ˈbā-nē-ə, -nyə\ country S Europe in Balkan Peninsula on Adriatic; ✻, Tirane

Al·ba·ny \ˈȯl-bə-nē\ city, ✻ of New York

Albemarle Sound \ˈal-bə-ˌmärl\ inlet of the Atlantic in NE North Carolina

Albert, Lake \ˈal-bərt\ lake E Africa between Uganda & Democratic Republic of the Congo in course of the Nile

Al·ber·ta \al-ˈbər-tə\ province W Canada; ✻, Edmonton — **Al·ber·tan** \-ˈbər-tᵊn\ *adj or n*

Al·bu·quer·que \ˈal-bə-ˌkər-kē\ city *cen* New Mexico

Al·ca·traz \ˈal-kə-ˌtraz\ island California in San Francisco Bay

Al·da·bra \äl-ˈdä-brə\ island NW Indian Ocean N of Madagascar; belongs to Seychelles
Al·der·ney \ˈȯl-dər-nē\ — see CHANNEL
Alep·po \ə-ˈle-(ˌ)pō\ city N Syria
Aleu·tian \ə-ˈlü-shən\ islands SW Alaska extending 1700 mi. (2735 km.) W from Alaska Peninsula
Al·ex·an·der \ˌal-ig-ˈzan-dər, ˌel-\ archipelago SE Alaska
Al·ex·an·dria \ˌa-lig-ˈzan-drē-ə, ˌe-\ **1** city N Virginia S of District of Columbia **2** city N Egypt on the Mediterranean — **Al·ex·an·dri·an** \-drē-ən\ *adj or n*
Al·ge·ria \al-ˈjir-ē-ə\ country NW Africa on Mediterranean; ✽, Algiers — **Al·ge·ri·an** \-ē-ən\ *adj or n*
Al·giers \al-ˈjirz\ city, ✽ of Algeria — **Al·ge·rine** \ˌal-jə-ˈrēn\ *adj or n*
Al·lah·a·bad \ˈä-lä-hä-ˌbäd, ˈa-lə-hə-ˌbad\ city N India on the Ganges
Al·le·ghe·ny \ˌa-lə-ˈgā-nē\ **1** river 325 mi. (523 km.) long W Pennsylvania & SW New York **2** mountains of Appalachian system E U.S. in Pennsylvania, Maryland, Virginia, & West Virginia
Al·len·town \ˈa-lən-ˌtau̇n\ city E Pennsylvania
Al·maty \əl-ˈmä-tē\ *or* **Al·ma–Ata** \əl-ˈmä-ə-ˈtä; ˌal-mə-ˈä-tə, -ə-ˈtä\ city, former ✽ of Kazakhstan
Alps \ˈalps\ mountain system *cen* Europe — see MONT BLANC
Al·tai *or* **Al·tay** \ˌal-ˈtī\ mountain system *cen* Asia between Mongolia & W China & between Kazakhstan & Russia
Ama·ga·sa·ki \ˌä-mä-gä-ˈsä-kē\ city Japan in W *cen* Honshu
Am·a·ril·lo \ˌa-mə-ˈri-(ˌ)lō, -lə\ city NW Texas
Am·a·zon \ˈa-mə-ˌzän, -zən\ river 3900 mi. (6436 km.) long N South America flowing from Peruvian Andes into Atlantic in N Brazil
Amer·i·ca \ə-ˈmer-ə-kə, -ˈme-rə-\ **1** either continent (**North America** or **South America**) of Western Hemisphere **2** *or* **the Amer·i·cas** \-kəz\ lands of Western Hemisphere including North, Central, & South America & West Indies **3** UNITED STATES OF AMERICA — **American** *adj or n*
American Falls — see NIAGARA FALLS
American Samoa *or* **Eastern Samoa** islands SW *cen* Pacific; U.S. territory; ✽, Pago Pago (on Tutuila Island)
Am·man \ä-ˈmän, a-, -ˈman\ city, ✽ of Jordan
Am·ster·dam \ˈam(p)-stər-ˌdam, ˈäm(p)-stər-ˌdäm\ city, official ✽ of the Netherlands
Amur \ä-ˈmu̇r\ river 1780 mi. (2784 km.) long E Asia flowing into the Pacific & forming part of boundary between China & Russia
An·a·heim \ˈa-nə-ˌhīm\ city SW California E of Long Beach
An·a·to·lia \ˌa-nə-ˈtō-lē-ə, -ˈtōl-yə\ — see ASIA MINOR — **An·a·to·li·an** \-ˈtō-lē-ən, -ˈtōl-yən\ *adj or n*
An·chor·age \ˈaŋ-k(ə-)rij\ city S *cen* Alaska
An·da·man \ˈan-də-mən, -ˌman\ **1** islands India in Bay of Bengal S of Myanmar & N of Nicobar Islands **2** sea, arm of Bay of Bengal S of Myanmar — **An·da·man·ese** \ˌan-də-mə-ˈnēz, -ˈnēs\ *adj or n*
An·des \ˈan-(ˌ)dēz\ mountain system W South America extending from Panama to Tierra del Fuego — see ACONCAGUA — **An·de·an** \ˈan-(ˌ)dē-ən, an-ˈ\ *adj* — **An·dine** \ˈan-ˌdēn, -ˌdīn\ *adj*
An·dor·ra \an-ˈdȯr-ə, -ˈdär-ə\ country SW Europe in E Pyrenees between France & Spain; ✽, Andorra la Vella — **An·dor·ran** \-ən\ *adj or n*
Andorra la Vel·la \lä-ˈvel-yä\ town, ✽ of Andorra
An·dros \ˈan-drəs\ island, largest of Bahamas
An·gel Falls \ˈān-jəl\ waterfall 3212 ft. (979 m.) SE Venezuela; world's highest waterfall
Ang·kor \ˈaŋ-ˌkȯr\ ruins of ancient city NW Cambodia
An·gle·sey \ˈaŋ-gəl-sē\ island NW Wales
An·go·la \aŋ-ˈgō-lə, an-\ country SW Africa S of mouth of Congo River; ✽, Luanda — **An·go·lan** \-lən\ *adj or n*
An·i·ak·chak Crater \ˌa-nē-ˈak-ˌchak\ volcanic crater SW Alaska on Alaska Peninsula; 6 mi. (10 km.) in diameter
An·ka·ra \ˈaŋ-kə-rə, ˈäŋ-\ city, ✽ of Turkey in N *cen* Anatolia
An·nap·o·lis \ə-ˈna-pə-lis\ city, ✽ of Maryland
Ann Ar·bor \(ˌ)an-ˈär-bər\ city SE Michigan
An·shan \ˈän-ˈshän\ city NE China
An·ta·nan·a·ri·vo \ˌän-tä-ˌnä-nä-ˈrē-(ˌ)vō\ city, ✽ of Madagascar
Ant·arc·ti·ca \ˌant-ˈärk-ti-kə, -ˈär-ti-\ body of land around the South Pole; plateau covered by great ice cap
An·ti·gua \an-ˈtē-gə, -gwə\ island West Indies in the Leewards; with Barbuda forms independent **Antigua and Barbuda**; ✽, Saint John's
An·til·les \an-ˈti-lēz\ the West Indies except for the Bahamas — see GREATER ANTILLES, LESSER ANTILLES — **An·til·le·an** \-lē-ən\ *adj*
An·trim \ˈan-trəm\ district E Northern Ireland
Ant·werp \ˈant-ˌwərp, ˈan-ˌtwərp\ city N Belgium
Aomen — see MACAO
Aoraki — see COOK, MOUNT
Ap·en·nines \ˈa-pə-ˌnīnz\ mountain chain Italy extending length of the peninsula; highest peak Monte Corno (NE of

Rome) 9560 ft. (2897 m.) — **Ap·en·nine** \ˈa-pə-ˌnīn\ *adj*

Apia \ä-ˈpē-ä\ town, ✱ of Samoa

Apo, Mount \ˈä-(ˌ)pō\ volcano Philippines in SE Mindanao 9692 ft. (2954 m.); highest peak in the Philippines

Ap·pa·la·chia \ˌa-pə-ˈlā-chə, -ˈla-chə, -ˈlā-shə\ region E U.S. including Appalachian Mountains from S *cen* New York to *cen* Alabama

Ap·pa·la·chian Mountains \ˌa-pə-ˈlā-ch(ē-)ən, -sh(ē-)ən\ mountain system E North America extending from S Quebec to *cen* Alabama — see MITCHELL, MOUNT

Aqa·ba, Gulf of \ˈä-kä-bə\ arm of Red Sea E of Sinai Peninsula

Aquid·neck \ə-ˈkwid-ˌnek\ *or* **Rhode** island SE Rhode Island in Narragansett Bay

Ara·bia \ə-ˈrā-bē-ə\ peninsula of SW Asia including Saudi Arabia, Yemen, Oman, & Persian Gulf States

Ara·bi·an Sea \ə-ˈrā-bē-ən\ NW section of Indian Ocean between Arabia & India

Ara·fu·ra \ˌä-rä-ˈfü-rä\ sea between N Australia & W New Guinea

Ar·al Sea \ˈa-rəl\ *formerly* **Lake Aral** formerly large lake W Asia which has shrunk into sections some of which are now entirely in Kazakhstan and others between Kazakhstan & Uzbekistan

Ar·a·rat \ˈa-rə-ˌrat\ mountain 16,946 ft. (5165 m.) E Turkey near border of Iran

Arc·tic \ˈärk-tik, ˈär-tik\ **1** ocean N of Arctic Circle **2** Arctic regions **3** archipelago N Canada in Nunavut & Northwest Territories

Ar·da·bil *or* **Ar·de·bil** \ˌär-də-ˈbēl\ city NW Iran

Ards \ˈärdz\ district E Northern Ireland

Are·ci·bo \ˌä-rā-ˈsē-(ˌ)bō\ city & port N Puerto Rico

Ar·gen·ti·na \ˌär-jən-ˈtē-nə\ country S South America between the Andes & the Atlantic; ✱, Buenos Aires — **Ar·gen·tine** \ˈär-jən-ˌtīn, -ˌtēn\ *adj or n* — **Ar·gen·tin·ean** *or* **Ar·gen·tin·i·an** \ˌär-jən-ˈti-nē-ən\ *adj or n*

Ar·gos \ˈär-ˌgȯs, -gəs\ ancient Greek city–state S Greece

Ar·i·zo·na \ˌa-rə-ˈzō-nə\ state SW U.S.; ✱, Phoenix — **Ar·i·zo·nan** \-nən\ *or* **Ar·i·zo·nian** \-nē-ən, -nyən\ *adj or n*

Ar·kan·sas \ˈär-kən-ˌsȯ\ **1** river 1450 mi. (2334 km.) long SW *cen* U.S. flowing SE into the Mississippi **2** state S *cen* U.S.; ✱, Little Rock — **Ar·kan·san** \är-ˈkan-zən\ *adj or n*

Ar·ling·ton \ˈär-liŋ-tən\ city N Texas

Ar·magh \är-ˈmä, ˈär-ˌ\ **1** district S Northern Ireland

Ar·me·nia \är-ˈmē-nē-ə, -nyə\ **1** region W Asia in mountainous area SE of Black Sea & SW of Caspian Sea divided among Iran, Turkey, & Armenia (country) **2** country W Asia; ✱, Yerevan

Arn·hem Land \ˈär-nəm\ region N Australia on N coast of Northern Territory

Ar·no \ˈär-(ˌ)nō\ river 150 mi. (241 km.) long *cen* Italy flowing through Florence

Aru·ba \ə-ˈrü-bə\ Dutch island in Caribbean Sea off coast of NW Venezuela

Ar·vada \är-ˈva-də\ city N *cen* Colorado NW of Denver

Ash·ga·bat \ˈäsh-gə-ˌbät\ *or* **Ashkh·a·bad** \ˈash-kə-ˌbad, -ˌbäd\ city, ✱ of Turkmenistan

Asia \ˈā-zhə, -shə\ continent of Eastern Hemisphere N of the Equator — see EURASIA

Asia Mi·nor \-ˈmī-nər\ *or* **An·a·to·lia** \ˌa-nə-ˈtō-lē-ə, -ˈtōl-yə\ peninsula in modern Turkey between Black Sea on N & the Mediterranean on S

As·ma·ra \az-ˈmä-rə, -ˈma-rə\ city, ✱ of Eritrea

As·syr·ia \ə-ˈsir-ē-ə\ ancient empire W Asia extending along the middle Tigris & over foothills to the E — **As·syr·i·an** \-ən\ *adj or n*

Astana — see NUR-SULTAN

Asun·ción \ä-sün-ˈsyōn\ city, ✱ of Paraguay

As·wân \a-ˈswän, ä-\ city S Egypt on the Nile near site of **Aswân High Dam**

Ata·ca·ma \ˌä-tä-ˈkä-mä\ desert N Chile

Atchaf·a·laya \(ə-)ˌcha-fə-ˈlī-ə\ river 225 mi. (362 km.) long S Louisiana flowing S into Gulf of Mexico

Ath·a·bas·ca \ˌa-thə-ˈbas-kə, ˌä-\ river 765 mi. (1231 km.) long NE Alberta flowing into **Lake Athabasca** on Alberta–Saskatchewan border

Ath·ens \ˈa-thənz\ **1** city NE Georgia **2** city, ✱ of Greece — **Athe·nian** \ə-ˈthē-nē-ən, -nyən\ *adj or n*

At·lan·ta \ət-ˈlan-tə, at-\ city, ✱ of Georgia

At·lan·tic \ət-ˈlan-tik, at-\ ocean separating North America & South America from Europe & Africa; often divided into **North Atlantic** and **South Atlantic** — **Atlantic** *adj*

At·las \ˈat-ləs\ mountains NW Africa extending from SW Morocco to N Tunisia

At·ti·ca \ˈa-ti-kə\ ancient state E Greece; chief city Athens — **At·tic** \ˈat-ik\ *adj*

Auck·land \ˈȯ-klənd\ city N New Zealand on NW North Island

Au·gus·ta \ȯ-ˈgəs-tə, ə-\ **1** city E Georgia **2** city, ✱ of Maine

Au·ro·ra \ə-ˈrȯr-ə, ȯ-\ **1** city NE *cen* Colorado **2** city NE Illinois

Auschwitz — see OSWIECIM

Aus·tin \ˈȯs-tən, ˈäs-\ city, ✱ of Texas

Aus·tral·asia \ˌȯs-trə-ˈlā-zhə, ˌäs-, -ˈlā-shə\ Australia, Tasmania, New Zealand, & Melanesia — **Aus·tral·asian** \-zhən, -shən\ *adj or n*

Aus·tra·lia \ȯ-ˈstrāl-yə, ä-, ə-\ **1** continent of Eastern Hemisphere SE of Asia **2** country including continent of

Australia & island of Tasmania; ✻, Canberra — **Aus·tra·lian** \-yən\ *adj or n*

Australian Alps mountain range SE Australia in E Victoria & SE New South Wales; part of Great Dividing Range

Australian Capital Territory district SE Australia including two areas, one containing Canberra (✻ of Australia) & the other on Jervis Bay (inlet of the South Pacific); surrounded by New South Wales

Aus·tria \ˈȯs-trē-ə, ˈäs-\ country *cen* Europe; ✻, Vienna — **Aus·tri·an** \-ən\ *adj or n*

Aus·tria–Hun·ga·ry \-ˈhəŋ-gə-rē\ country 1867–1918 *cen* Europe including Bohemia, Moravia, Transylvania, Galicia, and what are now Austria, Hungary, Slovenia, Croatia, & part of NE Italy — **Aus·tro–Hun·gar·i·an** \ˈȯs-(ˌ)trō-ˌhəŋ-ˈger-ē-ən, ˈäs-\ *adj or n*

Aus·tro·ne·sia \ˌȯs-trə-ˈnē-zhə, ˌäs-, -ˈnē-shə\ **1** islands of the South Pacific **2** area extending from Madagascar through Malay Peninsula & Malay Archipelago to Hawaii & Easter Island — **Aus·tro·ne·sian** \-zhən, -shən\ *adj or n*

Avon \ˈā-vən, ˈa-\ river 96 mi. (154 km.) long *cen* England flowing WSW into the Severn

Ayers Rock — see ULURU

Ayles·bury \ˈālz-b(ə-)rē\ town SE *cen* England

Ayr \ˈer\ *or* **Ayr·shire** \-ˌshir, -shər\ former county SW Scotland

Azer·bai·jan \ˌa-zər-ˌbī-ˈjän, ˌä-\ country W Asia & SE Europe bordering on Caspian Sea; ✻, Baku — **Azer·bai·ja·ni** \ˌa-zər-ˌbī-ˈjä-nē, ˌä-\ *adj or n*

Azores \ˈā-ˌzȯrz, ə-ˈ\ islands Portugal in North Atlantic lying 800 mi. (1287 km.) W of Portuguese coast — **Azor·e·an** \ā-ˈzȯr-ē-ən, ə-\ *adj or n*

Bab·y·lon \ˈba-bə-lən, -ˌlän\ ancient city, ✻ of Babylonia; site 55 mi. (89 km.) S of Baghdad near the Euphrates — **Bab·y·lo·nian** \ˌba-bə-ˈlō-nyən, -nē-ən\ *adj or n*

Bab·y·lo·nia \ˌba-bə-ˈlō-nyə, -nē-ə\ ancient country W Asia in valley of lower Euphrates and Tigris rivers

Bac·tria \ˈbak-trē-ə\ ancient country W Asia in present NE Afghanistan — **Bac·tri·an** \ˈbak-trē-ən\ *adj or n*

Bad·lands barren region SW South Dakota & NW Nebraska

Baf·fin \ˈba-fən\ **1** bay of the Atlantic between W Greenland & E Baffin Island **2** island NE Canada in Arctic Archipelago N of Hudson Strait

Bagh·dad \ˈbag-ˌdad, ˌbäg-ˈdäd\ city, ✻ of Iraq on the Tigris

Ba·guio \ˌbä-gē-ˈō\ city, former summer ✻ of the Philippines in NW *cen* Luzon

Ba·ha·mas \bə-ˈhä-məz\ islands in N Atlantic SE of Florida; ✻, Nassau — **Ba·ha·mi·an** \bə-ˈhā-mē-ən, -ˈhä-\ *or* **Ba·ha·man** \-ˈhā-mən, -ˈhäm-ən\ *adj or n*

Bahia — see SALVADOR

Bah·rain \bä-ˈrān\ islands in Persian Gulf off coast of Arabia; country; ✻, Manama — **Bah·raini** \-ˈrā-nē\ *adj or n*

Bai·kal, Lake *or* **Lake Bay·kal** \bī-ˈkäl, -ˈkal\ lake Russia, in mountains N of Mongolia

Ba·ja California \ˈbä-(ˌ)hä\ peninsula NW Mexico W of Gulf of California

Ba·kers·field \ˈbā-kərz-ˌfēld\ city S California

Ba·ku \bä-ˈkü\ city, ✻ of Azerbaijan on W coast of Caspian Sea

Bal·a·ton \ˈba-lə-ˌtän, ˈbȯ-lȯ-ˌtōn\ lake W Hungary

Bal·boa Heights \(ˌ)bal-ˈbō-ə\ town Panama; formerly the center of administration for Canal Zone

Bal·e·ar·ic Islands \ˌba-lē-ˈa-rik\ islands E Spain in the W Mediterranean

Ba·li \ˈbä-lē, ˈba-\ island Indonesia off E end of Java — **Ba·li·nese** \ˌbäl-i-nēz, ˌbal-, -ˈnēs\ *adj or n*

Bal·kans \ˈbȯl-kənz\ **1** *or* **Balkan Mountains** mountains N Bulgaria extending from Serbia border to Black Sea; highest 7793 ft. (2375 m.) **2** *or* **Balkan Peninsula** peninsula SE Europe between Adriatic & Ionian seas on the W & Aegean & Black seas on the E **3** *or* **Balkan States** countries occupying the Balkan Peninsula: Slovenia, Croatia, Bosnia and Herzegovina, North Macedonia, Kosovo, Serbia, Montenegro, Romania, Bulgaria, Albania, Greece, Turkey (in Europe)

Bal·ly·me·na \ˌba-lē-ˈmē-nə\ district NE *cen* Northern Ireland

Bal·ly·mon·ey \ˌba-lē-ˈmə-nē\ district N *cen* Northern Ireland

Bal·tic Sea \ˈbȯl-tik\ arm of the Atlantic N Europe E of Scandinavian Peninsula

Bal·ti·more \ˈbȯl-tə-ˌmȯr, -mər\ city N *cen* Maryland

Ba·ma·ko \ˈbä-mä-ˌkō\ city, ✻ of Mali on the Niger

Ban·bridge \ban-ˈbrij\ district SE *cen* Northern Ireland

Ban·dar Se·ri Be·ga·wan \ˌbən-dər-ˌser-ē-bə-ˈgä-wän\ town, ✻ of Brunei

Ban·dung \ˈbän-ˌdu̇ŋ\ city Indonesia in W Java SE of Jakarta

Ban·ga·lore \ˈbaŋ-gə-ˌlȯr\ *or now officially* **Ben·ga·lu·ru** \ˈbeŋ-gə-ˌlü-rü\ city S India W of Chennai

Banghazi — see BENGHAZI

Bang·kok \ˈbaŋ-ˌkäk, baŋ-ˈ\ city, ✻ of Thailand

Ban·gla·desh \ˌbäŋ-glə-ˈdesh, ˌbaŋ-, ˌbəŋ-, -ˈdāsh\ country S Asia E of India; ✻, Dhaka — see EAST PAKISTAN — **Ban·gla·deshi** \-ˈde-shē, -ˈdā-\ *adj or n*

Ban·gor \ˈbaŋ-ˌgȯr, ˈban-ˌgȯr\ town E Northern Ireland

Ban·gui \bäŋ-ˈgē\ city, * of Central African Republic

Ban·jul \ˈbän-ˌjül\ *formerly* **Bath·urst** \ˈbath-(ˌ)ərst\ city & port, * of Gambia

Bao·tou *or* **Pao–t'ou** \ˈbau̇-ˈtō\ city N China

Bar·ba·dos \bär-ˈbā-(ˌ)dōs, -dəs, -(ˌ)dōz\ island West Indies in Lesser Antilles E of Windward Islands; country, *, Bridgetown — **Bar·ba·di·an** \-ˈbā-dē-ən\ *adj or n*

Bar·bu·da \bär-ˈbü-də\ island West Indies; part of independent Antigua and Barbuda

Bar·ce·lo·na \ˌbär-sə-ˈlō-nə\ city NE Spain on the Mediterranean; chief city of Catalonia

Bar·king and Dag·en·ham \ˈbär-kiŋ-ən(d)-ˈda-gə-nəm\ borough of E Greater London, England

Bar·na·ul \ˌbär-nə-ˈül\ city S Russia

Bar·net \ˈbär-nət\ borough of N Greater London, England

Bar·ran·qui·lla \ˌbär-än-ˈkē-yä\ city N Colombia

Barren Grounds treeless plains N Canada W of Hudson Bay

Bar·row, Point \ˈba-(ˌ)rō\ most northerly point of Alaska & of U.S. at about 71°25′ N latitude

Ba·si·lan \bä-ˈsē-ˌlän\ island S Philippines SW of Mindanao

Bas·il·don \ˈba-zəl-dən\ town SE England

Bass \ˈbas\ strait separating Tasmania & continent of Australia

Basse·terre \bas-ˈter, bäs-\ seaport Saint Kitts, * of Saint Kitts and Nevis

Basutoland — see LESOTHO

Bathurst — see BANJUL

Bat·on Rouge \ˌba-tᵊn-ˈrüzh\ city, * of Louisiana

Ba·var·ia \bə-ˈver-ē-ə\ *or German* **Bay·ern** \ˈbī-ərn\ state SE Germany bordering on Czech Republic & Austria — **Ba·var·i·an** \bə-ˈver-ē-ən, -ˈvar-\ *adj or n*

Ba·ya·mon \ˌbī-ä-ˈmōn\ city NE *cen* Puerto Rico

Beau·fort \ˈbō-fərt\ sea consisting of part of Arctic Ocean NE of Alaska & NW of Canada

Beau·mont \ˈbō-ˌmänt, bō-ˈ\ city SE Texas

Bech·u·a·na·land \ˌbech-ˈwä-nə-ˌland, ˌbe-chə-\ **1** region S Africa N of Orange River **2** — see BOTSWANA

Bed·ford·shire \ˈbed-fərd-ˌshir, -shər\ *or* **Bedford** county SE England

Bedloe's — see LIBERTY

Bei·jing \ˈbā-ˈjiŋ\ *or* **Pe·king** \ˈpē-ˈkiŋ, ˈpā-\ city, * of China

Bei·rut \bā-ˈrüt\ city, * of Lebanon

Be·la·rus \ˌbē-lə-ˈrüs, ˌbye-lə-\ country *cen* Europe; *, Minsk — **Be·la·ru·si·an** \-ˈrü-sē-ən, -ˈrə-shən\ *or* **Be·la·rus·sian** \-ˈrə-shən\ *adj or n*

Belau — see PALAU

Be·lém \be-ˈlem\ city N Brazil

Bel·fast \ˈbel-ˌfast, bel-ˈ\ city, * of Northern Ireland

Bel·gium \ˈbel-jəm\ *or French* **Bel·gique** \bel-ˈzhēk\ *or Flemish* **Bel·gië** \ˈbel-kē-ə\ country W Europe; *, Brussels — **Bel·gian** \ˈbel-jən\ *adj or n*

Bel·grade \ˈbel-ˌgrād, -ˌgräd, -ˌgrad, bel-ˈ\ *or* **Beo·grad** \bā-ˈō-ˌgräd\ city, * of Serbia on the Danube

Be·lize \bə-ˈlēz\ *formerly* **British Honduras** country Central America on the Caribbean; *, Belmopan — **Be·liz·ean** *adj or n*

Belize City seaport E Belize

Belle·vue \ˈbel-ˌvyü\ city W Washington E of Seattle

Bel·mo·pan \ˌbel-mō-ˈpän\ city, * of Belize

Be·lo Ho·ri·zon·te \ˈbā-lō-ˌȯr-ē-ˈzōn-tē\ city E Brazil N of Rio de Janeiro

Be·lo·rus·sia \ˌbe-lō-ˈrə-shə, ˌbye-lō-\ *or* **Bye·lo·rus·sia** \bē-ˌe-lō-, ˌbye-lō-\ former republic of U.S.S.R.; became independent Belarus in 1991 — **Belo·rus·sian** \ˌbe-lō-ˈrə-shən, ˌbye-\ *adj or n*

Ben·gal \ben-ˈgȯl, beŋ-, -ˈgäl\ region S Asia including delta of Ganges & Brahmaputra rivers; divided between Bangladesh & India — **Ben·gal·ese** \ˌbeŋ-gə-ˈlēz, ˌben-, -ˈlēs\ *adj or n*

Bengal, Bay of arm of Indian Ocean between India & Myanmar

Ben·gha·zi *or* **Ban·gha·zi** \ben-ˈgä-zē\ city NE Libya; former * of Libya

Be·nin \bə-ˈnēn, -ˈnin; ˈbe-nin\ *formerly* **Da·ho·mey** \də-ˈhō-mē\ country W Africa on Gulf of Guinea; *, Porto-Novo — **Ben·i·nese** \bə-ˌni-ˈnēz, -ˌnē-, -ˈnēs; ˌbe-ni-ˈnēz, -ˈnēs\ *adj or n*

Ben Nev·is \ben-ˈne-vəs\ mountain 4406 ft. (1343 m.) W Scotland in the Grampians; highest in Great Britain

Beograd — see BELGRADE

Ber·gen \ˈbər-gən, ˈber-\ city & port SW Norway

Be·ring \ˈbir-iŋ, ˈber-\ **1** sea, arm of the North Pacific between Alaska & NE Siberia **2** strait at narrowest point 53 mi. (85 km.) wide between North America (Alaska) and Asia (Russia)

Berke·ley \ˈbər-klē\ city W California on San Francisco Bay N of Oakland

Berk·shire \ˈbərk-ˌshir, -shər\ hills W Massachusetts; highest point Mount Greylock 3491 ft. (1064 m.)

Ber·lin \(ˌ)bər-ˈlin, *G* ber-ˈlēn\ city, * of Germany; divided 1945–90 into **East Berlin** (* of East Germany) & **West Berlin** (city of West Germany lying within East Germany) — **Ber·lin·er** \(ˌ)bər-ˈli-nər\ *n*

Ber·mu·da \(ˌ)bər-ˈmyü-də\ islands W Atlantic ESE of Cape Hatteras; a British colony; ✻, Hamilton — **Ber·mu·dan** \-dᵊn\ *or* **Ber·mu·di·an** \-dē-ən\ *adj or n*

Bern \ˈbərn, ˈbern\ city, ✻ of Switzerland — **Ber·nese** \(ˌ)bər-ˈnēz, -ˈnēs\ *adj or n*

Bes·sa·ra·bia \ˌbe-sə-ˈrā-bē-ə\ region SE Europe now chiefly in Moldova — **Bes·sa·ra·bi·an** \-bē-ən\ *adj or n*

Beth·le·hem \ˈbeth-li-ˌhem, -lē-həm, -lē-əm\ town of ancient Palestine in Judaea; the present-day town is SW of Jerusalem in the West Bank

Bev·er·ly Hills \ˈbe-vər-lē\ city SW California within Los Angeles

Bex·ley \ˈbek-slē\ borough of E Greater London, England

Bho·pal \bō-ˈpäl\ city N *cen* India

Bhu·tan \bü-ˈtän, -ˈtan\ country S Asia in the Himalayas on NE border of India; ✻, Thimphu — **Bhu·ta·nese** \ˌbü-tə-ˈnēz, -ˈnēs\ *adj or n*

Bi·ki·ni \bi-ˈkē-nē\ atoll W Pacific in Marshall Islands

Bil·lings \ˈbi-liŋz\ city S *cen* Montana; largest in state

Bi·loxi \bə-ˈlək-sē, -ˈläk-\ city & port SE Mississippi on Gulf of Mexico

Bi·o·ko \bē-ˈō-(ˌ)kō\ *formerly* **Fer·nan·do Póo** \fer-ˈnän-(ˌ)dō-ˈpō\ island portion of Equatorial Guinea in Gulf of Guinea

Bir·ken·head \ˈbər-kən-ˌhed, ˌbər-kən-ˈ\ borough NW England on the Mersey opposite Liverpool

Bir·ming·ham \ˈbər-miŋ-ˌham\ **1** city N *cen* Alabama

Bis·cay, Bay of \ˈbis-ˌkā, -kē\ inlet of the Atlantic between W coast of France & N coast of Spain

Bish·kek \bish-ˈkek\ *formerly 1926–91* **Frun·ze** \ˈfrün-zi\ city, ✻ of Kyrgyzstan

Bis·marck \ˈbiz-ˌmärk\ **1** city, ✻ of North Dakota **2** archipelago W Pacific N of E end of New Guinea

Bis·sau \bi-ˈsau̇\ city, ✻ of Guinea-Bissau

Bi·thyn·ia \bə-ˈthi-nē-ə\ ancient country NW Asia Minor bordering on Sea of Marmara and Black Sea — **Bi·thyn·i·an** \-nē-ən\ *adj or n*

Bit·ter·root \ˈbi-tə(r)-ˌrüt, -ˌru̇t\ range of the Rockies along Idaho–Montana boundary

Black·burn \ˈblak-(ˌ)bərn\ town NW England

Black Forest forested mountain region Germany along E bank of the upper Rhine

Black Hills mountains W South Dakota & NE Wyoming

Black·pool \ˈblak-ˌpül\ town NW England on Irish Sea

Black Sea sea between Europe & Asia connected with Aegean Sea through the Bosporus, Sea of Marmara, & Dardanelles

Blanc, Mont — see MONT BLANC

Blan·tyre \ˈblan-ˌtī(-ə)r\ city S Malawi

Bloem·fon·tein \ˈblüm-fən-ˌtān, -ˌfān-\ city Republic of South Africa, judicial ✻ of the country

Blue Ridge E range of the Appalachians E U.S. extending from S Pennsylvania to N Georgia

Bodh Gaya \ˈbȯd-ˈgī-ä\ village NE India; one of the holiest sites of Buddhism

Boe·o·tia \bē-ˈō-sh(ē-)ə\ ancient state E *cen* Greece NW of Attica; chief ancient city, Thebes — **Boe·o·tian** \bē-ˈō-shən\ *adj or n*

Bo·go·tá \ˌbō-gō-ˈtä, -ˈtȯ, ˈbō-gə-ˌ\ city, ✻ of Colombia

Bo Hai *or* **Po Hai** \ˈbō-ˈhī\ *or* **Gulf of Chih·li** \ˈchē-ˈlē, ˈjir-\ arm of Yellow Sea NE China

Bo·he·mia \bō-ˈhē-mē-ə\ region W Czech Republic; chief city, Prague

Bo·hol \bō-ˈhȯl\ island S *cen* Philippines

Boi·se \ˈbȯi-sē, -zē\ city, ✻ of Idaho

Bo·liv·ia \bə-ˈli-vē-ə\ country W *cen* South America; administrative ✻, La Paz; constitutional ✻, Sucre — **Bo·liv·i·an** \-vē-ən\ *adj or n*

Bo·lo·gna \bō-ˈlō-nyä\ city N Italy

Bol·ton \ˈbōl-tᵊn\ town NW England

Bom·bay \bäm-ˈbā\ *or now officially* **Mum·bai** \ˈməm-ˌbī\ city & port W India

Bonn \ˈbän, ˈbȯn\ city Germany on the Rhine SSE of Cologne, formerly (1949–99) ✻ of West Germany

Boo·thia \ˈbü-thē-ə\ peninsula N Canada W of Baffin Island; its N tip is most northerly point in mainland North America

Bor·ders \ˈbȯr-dərz\ former administrative region SE Scotland

Bor·neo \ˈbȯr-nē-ˌō\ island Malay Archipelago SW of the Philippines; divided between Brunei, Indonesia, and Malaysia

Bos·nia \ˈbäz-nē-ə, ˈbȯz-\ region S Europe; with Herzegovina forms independent **Bosnia and Her·ze·go·vi·na** \ˌhert-sə-gō-ˈvē-nə, ˌhərt-, -ˈgō-və-nə\ ; ✻, Sarajevo — **Bos·ni·an** \-nē-ən\ *adj or n*

Bos·po·rus \ˈbäs-p(ə-)rəs\ strait 18 mi. (29 km.) long between Turkey in Europe & Turkey in Asia connecting Sea of Marmara & Black Sea

Bos·ton \ˈbȯs-tən\ city, ✻ of Massachusetts — **Bos·to·nian** \bȯ-ˈstō-nē-ən, -nyən\ *adj or n*

Bot·a·ny Bay \ˈbä-tə-nē\ inlet of South Pacific SE Australia in New South Wales S of Sydney

Both·nia, Gulf of \ˈbäth-nē-ə\ arm of Baltic Sea between Sweden & Finland

Bo·tswa·na \bät-ˈswä-nə\ *formerly* **Bech·u·a·na·land** \ˌbech-ˈwä-nə-land\ country S Africa; ✻, Gaborone

Boul·der \ˈbōl-dər\ city N *cen* Colorado

Boulder Dam — see HOOVER DAM

Bourne·mouth \ˈbȯrn-məth, ˈbu̇rn-\ town S England on English Channel

Brad·ford \ˈbrad-fərd\ city N England

Brah·ma·pu·tra \ˌbrä-mə-ˈpü-trə\ river about 1800 mi. (2900 km.) long S Asia flowing from the Himalayas in Tibet to Ganges Delta

Bra·sí·lia \brə-ˈzil-yə\ city, * of Brazil

Bra·ti·sla·va \ˌbra-tə-ˈslä-və, ˌbrä-\ city on the Danube; * of Slovakia

Bra·zil \brə-ˈzil\ country E & *cen* South America; *, Brasília — **Bra·zil·ian** \brə-ˈzil-yən\ *adj or n*

Braz·za·ville \ˈbra-zə-ˌvil, ˈbrä-zə-ˌvēl\ city, * of Republic of the Congo on W bank of lower Congo River

Bre·men \ˈbre-mən, ˈbrā-\ city & port NW Germany

Bren·ner \ˈbre-nər\ pass 4495 ft. (1370 m.) high in the Alps between Austria & Italy

Brent \ˈbrent\ borough of W Greater London, England

Bret·on, Cape \kāp-ˈbre-tᵊn, kə-ˈbre-, -ˈbri-\ cape Canada; most easterly point of Cape Breton Island & of Nova Scotia

Bridge·port \ˈbrij-ˌpȯrt\ city SW Connecticut on Long Island Sound

Bridge·town \ˈbrij-ˌtau̇n\ city, * of Barbados

Brigh·ton \ˈbrī-tᵊn\ town S England on English Channel

Bris·bane \ˈbriz-bən, -ˌbān\ city & port E Australia, * of Queensland

Bris·tol \ˈbris-tᵊl\ **1** city & port SW England **2** channel between S Wales & SW England

Brit·ain \ˈbri-tᵊn\ **1** the island of Great Britain **2** UNITED KINGDOM

British Columbia province W Canada on Pacific coast; *, Victoria

British Commonwealth — see COMMONWEALTH, THE

British Empire former empire consisting of Great Britain & the British dominions & dependencies

British Guiana — see GUYANA

British Honduras — see BELIZE

British India the part of India formerly under direct British administration

British Indian Ocean Territory British colony in Indian Ocean consisting of Chagos Archipelago

British Isles island group W Europe consisting of Great Britain, Ireland, & nearby islands

British Virgin Islands E islands of Virgin Islands; a British possession

British West Indies islands of the West Indies including Jamaica, Trinidad and Tobago, & the Bahama & Cayman islands, Windward Islands, Leeward Islands, & British Virgin Islands

Brit·ta·ny \ˈbri-tə-nē\ region NW France SW of Normandy

Brom·ley \ˈbräm-lē\ borough of SE Greater London, England

Bronx \ˈbräŋks\ *or* **The Bronx** borough of New York City NE of Manhattan

Brook·lyn \ˈbru̇k-lən\ borough of New York City at SW end of Long Island

Brooks Range \ˈbru̇ks\ mountains N Alaska

Browns·ville \ˈbrau̇nz-ˌvil, -vəl\ city S Texas on the Rio Grande

Bru·nei \bru̇-ˈnī, ˈbrü-ˌnī\ country NE Borneo; *, Bandar Seri Begawan — **Bru·nei·an** \bru̇-ˈnī-ən\ *adj or n*

Brus·sels \ˈbrə-səlz\ city, * of Belgium

Bu·cha·rest \ˈbü-kə-ˌrest, ˈbyü-\ city, * of Romania

Buck·ing·ham·shire \ˈbə-kiŋ-əm-ˌshir\ *or* **Buckingham** county SE *cen* England

Bu·da·pest \ˈbü-də-ˌpest\ city, * of Hungary

Bue·nos Ai·res \ˌbwā-nəs-ˈa-rēz, *Sp* ˌbwā-nōs-ˈī-rās\ city, * of Argentina

Buf·fa·lo \ˈbə-fə-ˌlō\ city W New York on Lake Erie

Bu·jum·bu·ra \ˌbü-jəm-ˈbu̇r-ə\ city, former * of Burundi

Bu·ko·vi·na \ˌbü-kō-ˈvē-nə\ region E *cen* Europe in foothills of E Carpathians

Bul·gar·ia \ˌbəl-ˈger-ē-ə, bu̇l-\ country SE Europe on Black Sea; *, Sofia — **Bul·gar·i·an** \ˌbəl-ˈger-ē-ən, bu̇l-\ *adj or n*

Bull Run \ˈbu̇l-ˈrən\ stream NE Virginia

Bun·ker Hill \ˈbəŋ-kər\ height in Boston, Massachusetts

Bur·bank \ˈbər-ˌbaŋk\ city SW California

Bur·gun·dy \ˈbər-gən-dē\ region E France — **Bur·gun·di·an** \(ˌ)bər-ˈgən-dē-ən\ *adj or n*

Bur·ki·na Fa·so \bu̇r-ˈkē-nə-ˈfä-sō, bər-\ *formerly* **Upper Vol·ta** \ˈvōl-tə, ˈvȯl-\ country W Africa N of Côte d'Ivoire, Ghana, & Togo; *, Ouagadougou

Bur·ling·ton \ˈbər-liŋ-tən\ city NW Vermont; largest in state

Bur·ma \ˈbər-mə\ — see MYANMAR — **Bur·mese** \ˌbər-ˈmēz, -ˈmēs\ *adj or n*

Bu·run·di \bu̇-ˈrün-dē, -ˈru̇n-\ country E *cen* Africa; *, Gitega — **Bu·run·di·an** \-dē-ən\ *adj or n*

Bu·san \ˈbü-ˌsän\ *or* **Pu·san** \ˈpü-sän, ˈbü-\ city SE South Korea

Bute \ˈbyüt\ island SW Scotland in Firth of Clyde

Butte \ˈbyüt\ city SW Montana

Byelorussia — see BELORUSSIA

By·zan·tine Empire \ˈbi-zᵊn-ˌtēn, ˈbī-, -ˌtīn; bə-ˈzan-ˌtēn, -tīn, bī-\ empire of SE & S Europe and W Asia from 4th to 15th century

By·zan·ti·um \bə-ˈzan-sh(ē-)əm, -ˈzant-ē-əm\ ancient city on site of modern Istanbul

Cabo Verde — see CAPE VERDE

Caer·nar·von \kär-ˈnär-vən, kə(r)-\ town & seaport NW Wales

Ca·guas \ˈkä-ˌgwäs\ town E *cen* Puerto Rico

Cai·ro \ˈkī-(ˌ)rō\ city, ✻ of Egypt — **Cai·rene** \kī-ˈrēn\ *adj or n*

Ca·la·bria \kə-ˈlā-brē-ə, -ˈlä-\ district of ancient Italy consisting of area forming heel of Italian Peninsula — **Ca·la·bri·an** \kə-ˈlā-brē-ən, -ˈlä-\ *adj or n*

Cal·cut·ta \kal-ˈkə-tə\ *or* **Kol·ka·ta** \kōl-ˈkä-tä\ city E India on Hugli River — **Cal·cut·tan** \-ˈkə-tᵊn\ *adj or n*

Cal·e·do·nia \ˌka-lə-ˈdō-nyə, -nē-ə\ — see SCOTLAND — **Cal·e·do·nian** \-nyən, -nē-ən\ *adj or n*

Cal·ga·ry \ˈkal-gə-rē\ city SW Alberta, Canada

Ca·li \ˈkä-lē\ city W Colombia

Cal·i·for·nia \ˌka-lə-ˈfȯr-nyə\ state SW U.S.; ✻, Sacramento — **Cal·i·for·nian** \-nyən\ *adj or n*

California, Gulf of arm of the Pacific NW Mexico

Cal·va·ry \ˈkal-v(ə-)rē\ place outside ancient Jerusalem where Jesus was crucified

Cambay, Gulf of — see KHAMBHAT (Gulf of)

Cam·bo·dia \kam-ˈbō-dē-ə\ *or* **Kam·pu·chea** \ˌkam-pu̇-ˈchē-ə\ country SE Asia in S Indochina; ✻, Phnom Penh — **Cam·bo·di·an** \kam-ˈbō-dē-ən\ *adj or n*

Cam·bria \ˈkam-brē-ə\ WALES — an old name

Cam·bridge \ˈkām-brij\ **1** city E Massachusetts W of Boston **2** city E England

Cam·bridge·shire \ˈkām-brij-ˌshir, -shər\ *or* **Cambridge** county E England

Cam·den \ˈkam-dən\ borough of N Greater London, England

Cam·er·oon *or French* **Cam·er·oun** \ˌka-mə-ˈrün\ country W Africa; ✻, Yaoundé — **Cam·er·oo·nian** \-ˈrü-nē-ən, -rü-nyən\ *adj or n*

Ca·mi·guin \ˌkä-mē-ˈgēn\ island Philippines, off N coast of Mindanao

Ca·naan \ˈkā-nən\ the part of ancient Palestine between Jordan River & Mediterranean Sea; sometimes used to refer to all of ancient Palestine — **Ca·naan·ite** \ˈkā-nə-ˌnīt\ *adj or n*

Can·a·da \ˈka-nə-də\ country N North America; ✻, Ottawa — **Ca·na·di·an** \kə-ˈnā-dē-ən\ *adj or n*

Canadian Falls — see NIAGARA FALLS

Canadian Shield *or* **Lau·ren·tian Plateau** \lȯ-ˈren(t)-shən\ plateau region E Canada & NE U.S. extending from Mackenzie River basin E to Davis Strait & S to S Quebec, S *cen* Ontario, NE Minnesota, N Wisconsin, NW Michigan, and NE New York including the Adirondacks

Canal Zone *or* **Panama Canal Zone** strip of territory Panama leased to U.S. (until 1979) for Panama Canal

Ca·nary \kə-ˈner-ē\ islands Spain in the Atlantic off NW coast of Africa

Ca·nav·er·al, Cape \kə-ˈnav-rəl, -ˈna-və-\ *or 1963–73* **Cape Ken·ne·dy** \-ˈken-ə-dē\ cape E Florida in the Atlantic on **Canaveral Peninsula** E of Indian River

Can·ber·ra \ˈkan-b(ə-)rə, -ˌber-ə\ city, ✻ of Australia in Australian Capital Territory

Cannes \ˈkan, ˈkän\ port SE France

Can·ter·bury \ˈkan-tə(r)-ˌber-ē, -b(ə-)rē\ city SE England

Canton — see GUANGZHOU

Cape Bret·on Island \kāp-ˈbre-tᵊn, kə-ˈbre-, -ˈbri-\ island NE Nova Scotia

Cape Coral city SW Florida

Cape Horn — see HORN, CAPE

Cape of Good Hope — see GOOD HOPE, CAPE OF

Cape Province *or* **Cape of Good Hope** *or before 1910* **Cape Colony** former province S Republic of South Africa

Cape Town \ˈkāp-ˌtau̇n\ city, legislative ✻ of Republic of South Africa and formerly ✻ of Cape Province

Cape Verde \ˈvərd\ *or* **Ca·bo Ver·de** \ˌkä-bü-ˈver-də\ islands in the North Atlantic off W Africa; country; ✻, Praia — **Cape Verd·ean** \ˈvər-dē-ən\ *adj or n*

Cape York Peninsula \ˈyȯrk\ peninsula NE Australia in N Queensland

Ca·pri \ka-ˈprē, kə-; ˈkä-(ˌ)prē, ˈka-\ island Italy S of Bay of Naples

Ca·ra·cas \kä-ˈrä-käs\ city, ✻ of Venezuela

Car·diff \ˈkär-dif\ city, ✻ of Wales

Ca·rib·be·an Sea \ˌka-rə-ˈbē-ən, kə-ˈri-bē-\ arm of the Atlantic; on N & E are the West Indies, on S is South America, & on W is Central America — **Caribbean** *adj*

Car·lisle \kär-ˈlī(-ə)l, kər-, ˈkär-ˌ\ city NW England

Carls·bad Caverns \ˈkär(-ə)lz-ˌbad\ series of caves SE New Mexico

Car·mar·then \kär-ˈmär-t͟hən, kə(r)-\ port S Wales

Car·o·li·na \ˌka-rə-ˈlī-nə\ English colony on E coast of North America founded 1663 & divided 1729 into North Carolina & South Carolina (the **Carolinas**) — **Car·o·lin·i·an** \ˌka-rə-ˈli-nē-ən, -nyən\ *adj or n*

Ca·ro·li·na \ˌkä-rō-ˈlē-nä\ city NE Puerto Rico

Car·o·line \ˈka-rə-ˌlīn, -lən\ islands W Pacific E of S Philippines; comprising Palau & the Federated States of Micronesia

Car·pa·thi·an \kär-ˈpā-thē-ən\ mountains E *cen* Europe between Slovakia & Poland & in N & *cen* Romania; highest Gerlachovsky 8711 ft. (2655 m.)

Car·pen·tar·ia, Gulf of \ˌkär-pən-ˈter-ē-ə\ inlet of Arafura Sea N of Australia

Car·rick·fer·gus \ˌka-rik-ˈfər-gəs\ district E Northern Ireland

Car·roll·ton \ˈka-rəl-tən\ city N Texas

Car·son City \ˈkär-sᵊn\ city, ✻ of Nevada

Car·thage \ˈkär-thij\ ancient city N Africa NE of modern Tunis; ✻ of an empire that once included much of NW Africa, E Spain, & Sicily — **Car·tha·gin·ian** \ˌkär-thə-ˈji-nyən, -nē-ən\ *adj or n*

Ca·sa·blan·ca \ˌka-sə-ˈblaŋ-kə, ˌkä-sə-ˈbläŋ-, -zə-\ city W Morocco on the Atlantic

Cas·cade Range \(ˌ)kas-ˈkād\ mountains NW U.S. in Washington, Oregon, & N California — see RAINIER, MOUNT

Cas·per \ˈkas-pər\ city *cen* Wyoming

Cas·pi·an Sea \ˈkas-pē-ən\ salt lake between Europe and Asia about 90 ft. (27 m.) below sea level

Cas·tile \ka-ˈstēl\ *or in full* **Cas·ti·lla** \kä-ˈstēl-yä, -ˈstē-yä\ region & ancient kingdom *cen* & N Spain

Cast·le·reagh \ˈka-səl-(ˌ)rā\ district E Northern Ireland

Cas·tries \ˈkas-ˌtrēz, -ˌtrēs\ seaport, ✻ of Saint Lucia

Cat·a·lo·nia \ˌka-tə-ˈlō-nyə, -nē-ə\ region NE Spain bordering on France & the Mediterranean; chief city, Barcelona — **Cat·a·lo·nian** \-ˈō-nyən, -nē-ən\ *adj or n*

Ca·thay \ka-ˈthā\ an old name for China

Cats·kill \ˈkat-ˌskil\ mountains in Appalachian system SE New York W of the Hudson

Cau·ca·sus \ˈkȯ-kə-səs\ mountain system SE Europe between Black & Caspian seas in Russia, Georgia, Azerbaijan, & Armenia

Cay·enne \kī-ˈen, kā-\ city, ✻ of French Guiana

Cay·man \(ˌ)kā-ˈman, *attributively* ˈkā-mən\ islands West Indies NW of Jamaica; a British colony

Ce·bu \sā-ˈbü\ island E *cen* Philippines

Ce·dar Rapids \ˈsē-dər\ city E Iowa

Cel·tic Sea \ˈkel-tik, ˈsel-\ inlet of the Atlantic in British Isles SE of Ireland, SW of Wales, & W of SW England

Central African Republic country N *cen* Africa; ✻, Bangui

Central America narrow portion of North America from S border of Mexico to South America — **Central American** *adj or n*

Central Valley valley of Sacramento & San Joaquin rivers in California between Sierra Nevada & Coast Ranges

Cey·lon \si-ˈlän, sā-\ **1** island in Indian Ocean off S India **2** — see SRI LANKA — **Cey·lon·ese** \ˌsā-lə-ˈnēz, ˌsē-, ˌse-, -ˈnēs\ *adj or n*

Chad \ˈchad\ country N *cen* Africa; ✻, N'Djamena — **Chad·ian** \ˈcha-dē-ən\ *adj or n*

Chad, Lake shallow lake N *cen* Africa at junction of boundaries of Chad, Niger, & Nigeria

Cha·gos Archipelago \ˈchä-gəs\ island group *cen* Indian Ocean; forms British Indian Ocean Territory — see DIEGO GARCIA

Chal·dea \kal-ˈdē-ə\ ancient region SW Asia on Euphrates River & Persian Gulf — **Chal·de·an** \-ˈdē-ən\ *adj or n* — **Chal·dee** \ˈkal-ˌdē\ *n*

Cham·pagne \sham-ˈpān\ region NE France

Cham·plain, Lake \sham-ˈplān\ lake between New York & Vermont extending N into Quebec

Chan·di·garh \ˈchən-dē-gər\ city N India N of Delhi

Chan·dler \ˈchan(d)-lər\ city SW *cen* Arizona

Chang \ˈchäŋ\ *or traditionally* **Yang·tze** \ˈyaŋ-ˈsē, ˈyaŋ(k)t-ˈsē; ˈyäŋ-ˈtsə\ river 3434 mi. (5525 km.) long *cen* China flowing into East China Sea

Chang·chun \ˈchäŋ-ˈchu̇n\ city NE China

Chang·sha \ˈchäŋ-ˈshä\ city SE *cen* China

Channel islands in English Channel including Jersey, Guernsey, & Alderney & belonging to United Kingdom

Charles \ˈchär(-ə)lz\ river 47 mi. (76 km.) long E Massachusetts flowing into Boston harbor

Charles, Cape cape E Virginia N of entrance to Chesapeake Bay

Charles·ton \ˈchär(-ə)l-stən\ **1** seaport SE South Carolina **2** city, ✻ of West Virginia

Char·lotte \ˈshär-lət\ city S North Carolina

Charlotte Ama·lie \ə-ˈmäl-yə, ˈa-mə-lē\ city, ✻ of Virgin Islands of the U.S.; on island of Saint Thomas

Char·lottes·ville \ˈshär-ləts-ˌvil, -vəl\ city *cen* Virginia

Char·lotte·town \ˈshär-lət-ˌtau̇n\ city, ✻ of Prince Edward Island, Canada

Chat·ta·noo·ga \ˌcha-tə-ˈnü-gə\ city SE Tennessee

Chech·nya \chech-ˈnyä, ˈchech-nyə\ republic of SE Russia in Europe; ✻, Grozny

Chelms·ford \ˈchemz-fərd\ town SE England

Che·lya·binsk \chel-ˈyä-bən(t)sk\ city W Russia

Cheng–chou — see ZHENGZHOU

Cheng·du *or* **Ch'eng–tu** \ˈchəŋ-ˈdü\ city SW *cen* China

Chennai — see MADRAS

Cher·no·byl \chər-ˈnō-bəl, (ˌ)cher-\ site N Ukraine of town abandoned after 1986 nuclear accident

Ches·a·peake \ˈche-sə-ˌpēk, ˈches-ˌpēk\ city SE Virginia

Chesapeake Bay inlet of the Atlantic in Virginia & Maryland

Chesh·ire \ˈche-shər, -ˌshir\ *or* **Ches·ter** \ˈches-tər\ former county W England bordering on Wales

Chester \ˈches-tər\ city NW England

Chev·i·ot \ˈchē-vē-ət, ˈche-\ hills along English–Scottish border

Chey·enne \shī-ˈan, -ˈen\ city, ✻ of Wyoming

Chi•ba \ˈchē-bä\ city E Japan on Honshu on Tokyo Bay E of Tokyo
Chi•ca•go \shə-ˈkä-(ˌ)gō, -ˈkò-, -gə\ city & port NE Illinois on Lake Michigan — **Chi•ca•go•an** \-ˈkä-gō-ən, -ˈkò-\ *n*
Chi•chén It•zá \chē-ˌchen-ēt-ˈsä, -ˈēt-sə\ ruined Mayan city SE Mexico in Yucatán Peninsula
Chich•es•ter \ˈchi-chəs-tər\ city S England
Ch'i–ch'i–ha–erh — see QIQIHAR
Chihli, Gulf of — see BO HAI
Chi•le \ˈchi-lē, ˈchē-(ˌ)lā\ country SW South America; ✱, Santiago — **Chil•ean** \ˈchi-lē-ən, chə-ˈlā-ən\ *adj or n*
Chim•bo•ra•zo \ˌchēm-bō-ˈrä-(ˌ)zō\ mountain 20,561 ft. (6267 m.) W *cen* Ecuador
Chi•na \ˈchī-nə\ **1** country E Asia; ✱, Beijing **2** sea section of the W Pacific; divided into East China & South China seas
Chin–chou *or* **Chinchow** — see JINZHOU
Chi•şi•nău \ˌkē-shē-ˈnaů\ *or* **Ki•shi•nev** \ˌki-shi-ˈnyòf; ˈki-shə-ˌnef, -ˌnev\ city *cen* Moldova; its ✱
Chit•ta•gong \ˈchi-tə-ˌgäŋ, -ˌgòŋ\ city SE Bangladesh on Bay of Bengal
Chong•qing *or* **Ch'ung–ch'ing** \ˈchůŋ-ˈchiŋ\ *or* **Chung•king** \ˈchůŋ-ˈkiŋ\ city SW *cen* China
Christ•church \ˈkrīs(t)-ˌchərch\ city New Zealand on E coast of South Island
Christ•mas \ˈkris-məs\ island E Indian Ocean SW of Java; governed by Australia
Chu•la Vis•ta \ˌchü-lə-ˈvis-tə\ city SW California S of San Diego
Chuuk \ˈchůk\ *or* **Truk** \ˈtrək, ˈtrůk\ islands *cen* Carolines, part of Federated States of Micronesia
Cin•cin•na•ti \ˌsin(t)-sə-ˈna-tē, -ˈna-tə\ city SW Ohio
Ci•u•dad Juá•rez \syü-ˈthäth-ˈhwär-es, ˈwär-; ˌsē-ü-ˈdad-\ city Mexico on Texas border
Ciudad Trujillo — see SANTO DOMINGO
Clarks•ville \ˈklärks-ˌvil, -vəl\ city N Tennessee NW of Nashville
Clear•wa•ter \ˈklir-ˌwò-tər, -ˌwä-\ city W Florida NW of St. Petersburg
Cleve•land \ˈklēv-lənd\ city & port NE Ohio on Lake Erie
Clyde \ˈklīd\ river 106 mi. (171 km.) long SW Scotland flowing into **Firth of Clyde** (estuary)
Coast Mountains mountain range W British Columbia, Canada; the N continuation of Cascade Range
Coast Ranges chain of mountain ranges W North America extending along Pacific coast W of Sierra Nevada & Cascade Range & through Vancouver Island into S Alaska to Kenai Peninsula & Kodiak Island
Cod, Cape \-ˈkäd\ peninsula SE Massachusetts
Coim•ba•tore \ˌkòim-bə-ˈtòr\ city S India
Cole•raine \kōl-ˈrān, ˈkōl-ˌ\ **1** district N Northern Ireland **2** port in Coleraine district
Co•logne \kə-ˈlōn\ city W Germany on the Rhine
Co•lom•bia \kə-ˈləm-bē-ə\ country NW South America; ✱, Bogotá — **Co•lom•bi•an** \-bē-ən\ *adj or n*
Co•lom•bo \kə-ˈləm-(ˌ)bō\ city, ✱ of Sri Lanka
Col•o•ra•do \ˌkä-lə-ˈra-(ˌ)dō\ **1** river 1450 mi. (2334 km.) long SW U.S. & NW Mexico flowing from N Colorado into Gulf of California **2** desert SE California **3** plateau region SW U.S. W of Rocky Mountains **4** state W U.S.; ✱, Denver — **Col•o•rad•an** \-ˈra-dᵊn, -ˈrä-\ *or* **Co•lo•ra•do•an** \-ˈra-dō-ən, -ˈrä-\ *adj or n*
Colorado Springs city *cen* Colorado E of Pikes Peak
Co•lum•bia \kə-ˈləm-bē-ə\ **1** river 1214 mi. (1953 km.) long SW Canada & NW U.S. flowing S & W from SE British Columbia into the Pacific **2** plateau in Columbia River basin in E Washington, E Oregon, & SW Idaho **3** city, ✱ of South Carolina
Co•lum•bus \kə-ˈləm-bəs\ **1** city W Georgia **2** city, ✱ of Ohio
Com•mon•wealth, the \ˈkäm-ən-ˌwel(t)th\ *or* **Commonwealth of Nations** *formerly* **British Commonwealth** the United Kingdom & most of the countries formerly dependent on it
Com•o•ros \ˈkä-mə-ˌrōz\ islands off SE Africa NW of Madagascar; country (except for Mayotte Island); ✱, Moroni
Con•a•kry \ˈkä-nə-krē\ city, ✱ of Guinea
Con•cord \ˈkän-ˌkòrd, ˈkäŋ-\ **1** city W California **2** town E Massachusetts NW of Boston **3** city, ✱ of New Hampshire
Con•go \ˈkäŋ-(ˌ)gō\ **1** *or* **Zaire** \zä-ˈir\ river over 2700 mi. (4344 km.) long W Africa flowing into the Atlantic **2** *officially* **Democratic Republic of the Congo** *formerly 1971–97* **Zaire** country *cen* Africa consisting of most of Congo River basin E of lower Congo River; ✱, Kinshasa **3** *or officially* **Republic of the Congo** country W *cen* Africa W of lower Congo River; ✱, Brazzaville — **Con•go•lese** \ˌkäŋ-gə-ˈlēz, -ˈlēs\ *adj or n*
Con•nacht \ˈkä-ˌnòt\ province W Ireland
Con•nect•i•cut \kə-ˈne-ti-kət\ **1** river 407 mi. (655 km.) long NE U.S. flowing S from N New Hampshire into Long Island Sound **2** state NE U.S.; ✱, Hartford
Constantinople — see ISTANBUL
Continental Divide line of highest points of land separating the waters flowing W from those flowing N or E and extending SSE from NW Canada across W U.S. through Mexico & Central America to South America where it joins the Andes Mountains
Cook \ˈkůk\ **1** inlet of the Pacific S Alas-

ka W of Kenai Peninsula **2** islands South Pacific SW of Society Islands belonging to New Zealand **3** strait New Zealand between North Island & South Island

Cook, Mount *or* **Ao·ra·ki** \au̇-ˈrä-kē\ mountain 12,349 ft. (3764 m.) New Zealand in W *cen* South Island in Southern Alps; highest in New Zealand

Cooks·town \ˈku̇ks-ˌtau̇n\ district *cen* Northern Ireland

Co·pen·ha·gen \ˌkō-pən-ˈhā-gən, -ˈhä-\ city, ✻ of Denmark

Cor·al Sea \ˈkȯr-əl, ˈkär-\ arm of the W Pacific NE of Australia

Coral Springs city SE Florida

Cór·do·ba \ˈkȯr-də-bə, ˈkȯr-thō-ˌvä\ city N *cen* Argentina

Cor·inth \ˈkȯr-ən(t)th, ˈkär-\ **1** region of ancient Greece **2** ancient city; site SW of present city of Corinth — **Co·rin·thi·an** \kə-ˈrin(t)-thē-ən\ *adj or n*

Corinth, Gulf of inlet of Ionian Sea *cen* Greece N of the Peloponnese

Cork \ˈkȯrk\ city S Ireland

Corn·wall \ˈkȯrn-ˌwȯl, -wəl\ *or 1974-2009* **Cornwall and Isles of Scilly** \ˈsi-lē\ former county SW England

Co·ro·na \kə-ˈrō-nə\ city SW California E of Los Angeles

Cor·pus Chris·ti \ˌkȯr-pəs-ˈkris-tē\ city & port S Texas

Cor·reg·i·dor \kə-ˈre-gə-ˌdȯr\ island Philippines at entrance to Manila Bay

Cor·si·ca \ˈkȯr-si-kə\ island France in the Mediterranean N of Sardinia — **Cor·si·can** \ˈkȯr-si-kən\ *adj or n*

Cos·ta Me·sa \ˈkōs-tə-ˈmā-sə\ city SW California

Costa Ri·ca \ˈrē-kə\ country Central America between Nicaragua & Panama; ✻, San José — **Cos·ta Ri·can** \-kən\ *adj or n*

Côte d'Ivoire \ˌkōt-dē-ˈvwär\ *or English* **Ivory Coast** country W Africa on Gulf of Guinea; official ✻, Yamoussoukro; seat of government, Abidjan

Cots·wold \ˈkät-ˌswōld, -swəld\ hills SW *cen* England

Cov·en·try \ˈkə-vən-trē\ city *cen* England

Craig·av·on \krā-ˈga-vən\ district *cen* Northern Ireland

Cra·ter \ˈkrā-tər\ lake 1932 ft. (589 m.) deep SW Oregon in Cascade Range

Crete \ˈkrēt\ island Greece in E Mediterranean — **Cre·tan** \ˈkrē-tᵊn\ *adj or n*

Cri·mea \krī-ˈmē-ə, krə-\ peninsula SE Europe extending into Black Sea — **Cri·me·an** \krī-ˈmē-ən, krə-\ *adj*

Cro·atia \krō-ˈā-sh(ē-)ə\ country SE Europe; ✻, Zagreb — **Croat** \ˈkrō-ˌat\ *n*

Croy·don \ˈkrȯi-dᵊn\ borough of S Greater London, England

Cu·ba \ˈkyü-bə, ˈkü-vä\ island in the West Indies; country; ✻, Havana — **Cu·ban** \ˈkyü-bən\ *adj or n*

Cum·ber·land \ˈkəm-bər-lənd\ river 687 mi. (1106 km.) long S Kentucky & N Tennessee

Cumberland Gap pass through Cumberland Plateau NE Tennessee

Cumberland Plateau mountain region E U.S.; part of S Appalachian Mountains extending from S West Virginia to NE Alabama

Cum·bria \ˈkəm-brē-ə\ county NW England

Cum·bri·an \ˈkəm-brē-ən\ mountains NW England chiefly in Cumbria county

Cu·par \ˈkü-pər\ town E Scotland

Cu·ri·ti·ba \ˌku̇r-ə-ˈtē-bə\ city S Brazil SW of São Paulo

Cush \ˈkəsh, ˈku̇sh\ ancient country NE Africa in upper Nile valley S of Egypt — **Cush·ite** \ˈkə-ˌshīt, ˈku̇-\ *n* — **Cush·it·ic** \ˌkə-ˈshi-tik, ku̇-\ *adj*

Cuz·co \ˈküs-(ˌ)kō\ city S *cen* Peru

Cymru — see WALES

Cy·prus \ˈsī-prəs\ island E Mediterranean S of Turkey; country; ✻, Nicosia — **Cyp·ri·ot** \ˈsi-prē-ət, -ˌät\ *or* **Cyp·ri·ote** \-ˌōt, -ət\ *adj or n*

Cy·re·na·ica \ˌsir-ə-ˈnā-ə-kə, ˌsī-rə-\ ancient region N Africa on coast W of Egypt — **Cy·re·na·i·can** \-ˈnā-ə-kən\ *adj or n*

Czecho·slo·va·kia \ˌche-kə-slō-ˈvä-kē-ə, -slə-, -ˈva-\ former country *cen* Europe divided into the independent states of the Czech Republic & Slovakia — **Czecho·slo·vak** \-ˈslō-ˌväk, -ˌvak\ *adj or n* — **Czecho·slo·va·ki·an** \-slō-ˈvä-kē-ən, -slə-, -ˈva-\ *adj or n*

Czech Republic country *cen* Europe; ✻, Prague

Dae·gu \ˈdā-gü\ *or* **Tae·gu** \ˈtā-gü, ˈdā-\ city SE South Korea

Daejeon — see TAEJON

Dahomey — see BENIN

Dairen — see DALIAN

Da·kar \ˈda-ˌkär, dä-ˈkär\ city, ✻ of Senegal

Da·ko·ta **1** *or* **James** river 710 mi. (1143 km.) long North Dakota & South Dakota flowing S into the Missouri **2** territory 1861–89 NW U.S. divided 1889 into states of North Dakota & South Dakota (the **Dakotas** \-təz\ )

Da·lian *or* **Ta–lien** \ˈdä-ˈlyen\ *or* **Lü·da** *or* **Lü–ta** \ˈlü-ˈdä\ *or* **Dai·ren** \ˈdī-ˈren\ city NE China

Dal·las \ˈda-ləs, -lis\ city NE Texas

Dal·ma·tia \dal-ˈmā-sh(ē-)ə\ region W Balkan Peninsula on the Adriatic — **Dal·ma·tian** \-shən\ *adj or n*

Da·ly City \ˈdā-lē\ city W California S of San Francisco

Da·mas·cus \də-ˈmas-kəs\ city, ✻ of Syria

Dan·ube \ˈdan-(ˌ)yüb\ river 1771 mi. (2850 km.) long S Europe flowing from

SW Germany into Black Sea — **Da·nu·bi·an** \də-ˈnü-bē-ən, da-, -ˈnyü-\ *adj*

Dar·da·nelles \ˌdär-də-ˈnelz\ *or* **Hel·les·pont** \ˈhe-lə-ˌspänt\ strait NW Turkey connecting Sea of Marmara & the Aegean

Dar es Sa·laam \ˌdär-ˌe(s)-sə-ˈläm\ city, historic ✻ of Tanzania

Dar·ling \ˈdär-liŋ\ river about 1700 mi. (2735 km.) long SE Australia in Queensland & New South Wales flowing SW into the Murray

Dar·win \ˈdär-wən\ city Australia, ✻ of Northern Territory

Da·vao \ˈdä-ˌvau̇, dä-ˈvau̇\ city S Philippines in E Mindanao on Davao Gulf

Dav·en·port \ˈda-vən-ˌpȯrt\ city E Iowa

Da·vis \ˈdā-vəs\ strait between SW Greenland & E Baffin Island connecting Baffin Bay & the Atlantic

Day·ton \ˈdā-tᵊn\ city SW Ohio

Dead Sea salt lake between Israel & Jordan; 1312 ft. (400 m.) below sea level

Death Valley dry valley E California & S Nevada containing lowest point in U.S. (282 ft. *or* 86 m. below sea level)

Dec·can \ˈde-kən, -ˌkan\ plateau region S India

Del·a·ware \ˈde-lə-ˌwer, -wər\ **1** river 296 mi. (476 km.) long E U.S. flowing S from S New York into Delaware Bay **2** state E U.S.; ✻, Dover — **Del·a·war·ean** *or* **Del·a·war·ian** \ˌde-lə-ˈwer-ē-ən\ *adj or n*

Delaware Bay inlet of the Atlantic between SW New Jersey & E Delaware

Del·hi \ˈde-lē\ city N India — see NEW DELHI

De·los \ˈdē-ˌläs\ island Greece — **De·lian** \ˈdē-lē-ən, ˈdēl-yən\ *adj or n*

Del·phi \ˈdel-ˌfī\ ancient town *cen* Greece on S slope of Mt. Parnassus

Democratic Republic of the Congo — see CONGO 2

De·na·li \də-ˈnä-lē\ *or unofficially* **Mount Mc·Kin·ley** \mə-ˈkin-lē\ mountain 20,320 *ft* (6149 *m*) *cen* Alaska Range; highest in U.S. and N. America; in **Denali National Park**

Den·mark \ˈden-ˌmärk\ country N Europe occupying most of Jutland & neighboring islands; ✻, Copenhagen

Den·ver \ˈden-vər\ city, ✻ of Colorado

Der·by \ˈdär-bē\ city N *cen* England

Der·by·shire \ˈdär-bē-ˌshir, -shər\ *or* **Derby** county N *cen* England

Der·ry \ˈder-ē\ *or* **Lon·don·der·ry** \ˌlən-dən-ˈder-ē\ city & port NW Northern Ireland

Des Moines \di-ˈmȯin\ city, ✻ of Iowa

De·troit \di-ˈtrȯit\ **1** river 31 mi. (50 km.) long between SE Michigan & Ontario connecting Lake Saint Clair & Lake Erie **2** city SE Michigan

Dev·on \ˈde-vən\ *or* **De·von·shire** \ˈde-vən-ˌshir, -shər\ county SW England

Dha·ka \ˈdä-kə\ city, ✻ of Bangladesh

Die·go Gar·cia \dē-ˌā-gō-ˌgär-ˈsē-ə\ island in Indian Ocean; chief island of Chagos Archipelago

Di·li \ˈdi-lē\ city & port N Timor, ✻ of East Timor

Di·nar·ic Alps \də-ˈna-rik\ range of the E Alps in W Slovenia, W Croatia, Bosnia and Herzegovina, & Montenegro

District of Co·lum·bia \kə-ˈləm-bē-ə\ federal district E U.S. coextensive with city of Washington

Djakarta — see JAKARTA

Dji·bou·ti \jə-ˈbü-tē\ **1** country E Africa on Gulf of Aden **2** city, its ✻

Dni·pro·pe·trovs'k *or* **Dne·pro·pe·trovsk** \də-ˌnye-prə-pə-ˈtrȯfsk\ city E *cen* Ukraine

Dodge City \ˈdäj\ city S Kansas on Arkansas River

Do·do·ma \dō-ˈdō-(ˌ)mä\ city, legislative ✻ of Tanzania

Do·ha \ˈdō-(ˌ)hä\ city & port, ✻ of Qatar on Persian Gulf

Dom·i·ni·ca \ˌdä-mə-ˈnē-kə\ island West Indies in the Leeward Islands; country; ✻, Roseau

Do·min·i·can Republic \də-ˈmi-ni-kən\ country West Indies in E Hispaniola; ✻, Santo Domingo — **Dominican** *adj or n*

Don \ˈdän\ river 1224 mi. (1969 km.) long SW Russia

Do·nets'k \də-ˈnyetsk\ city E Ukraine

Dor·ches·ter \ˈdȯr-chəs-tər, -ˌches-\ town S England

Dor·set \ˈdȯr-sət\ *or* **Dor·set·shire** \-ˌshir, -shər\ county S England on English Channel

Dort·mund \ˈdȯrt-ˌmu̇nt, -mənd\ city W Germany in the Ruhr

Dou·a·la \dü-ˈä-lä\ seaport W Cameroon

Dou·ro \ˈdȯr-(ˌ)ü\ *or Spanish* **Due·ro** \ˈdwe(ə)r-ō\ river 556 mi. (895 km.) long N Spain & N Portugal flowing into the Atlantic

Do·ver \ˈdō-vər\ city, ✻ of Delaware

Dover, Strait of channel between SE England & N France; the most easterly section of English Channel

Down \ˈdau̇n\ district SE Northern Ireland

Dow·ney \ˈdau̇-nē\ city SW California SE of Los Angeles

Down·pat·rick \dau̇n-ˈpa-trik\ town E Northern Ireland

Dra·kens·berg \ˈdrä-kənz-ˌbərg\ mountain range E Republic of South Africa & Lesotho; highest peak Thabana Ntlenyana 11,425 ft. (3482 m.)

Dres·den \ˈdrez-dən\ city E Germany

Du·bayy *or* **Du·bai** \(ˌ)dü-ˈbī\ **1** sheikhdom, member of United Arab Emirates **2** city, its ✻

Dub·lin \ˈdə-blən\ city, ✻ of Ireland

Dud·ley \ˈdəd-lē\ town W *cen* England

Duis·burg \ˈdü-əs-ˌbərg, ˈdüz-ˌ, ˈdyüz-ˌ\ city W Germany at junction of Rhine & Ruhr rivers
Du·luth \də-ˈlüth\ city & port NE Minnesota at W end of Lake Superior
Dum·fries \ˌdəm-ˈfrēs, -ˈfrēz\ burgh S Scotland
Dumfries and Gal·lo·way \ˈga-lə-ˌwā\ administrative subdivision of S Scotland
Dun·dee \ˌdən-ˈdē\ city E Scotland
Dun·gan·non \ˌdən-ˈga-nən\ district W Northern Ireland
Dur·ban \ˈdər-bən\ city and seaport E Republic of South Africa
Dur·ham \ˈdər-əm, ˈdə-rəm, ˈdu̇r-əm\ city N *cen* North Carolina
Du·shan·be \dü-ˈsham-bə, dyü-, -ˈshäm-, ˈdyü-ˌ; ˌdyü-shäm-ˈbā\ city, ✻ of Tajikistan
Düs·sel·dorf \ˈdü-səl-ˌdȯrf, ˈdyü-, ˈdœ-\ city W Germany on the Rhine
Ea·ling \ˈē-liŋ\ borough of W Greater London, England
East An·glia \ˈaŋ-glē-ə\ region E England
East China Sea — see CHINA
Eas·ter \ˈē-stər\ island Chile SE Pacific about 2000 mi. (3200 km.) W of Chilean coast
Eastern Cape province SE Republic of South Africa
Eastern Desert desert E Egypt between the Nile & the Red Sea
Eastern Ghats \ˈgäts, ˈgȯts, ˈgəts\ chain of low mountains SE India along coast
Eastern Hemisphere the half of the earth E of the Atlantic Ocean including Europe, Asia, Australia, and Africa
Eastern Roman Empire the Byzantine Empire from 395 to 474
Eastern Samoa — see AMERICAN SAMOA
East Germany — see GERMANY
East Indies the Malay Archipelago — **East Indian** *adj or n*
East London city S Republic of South Africa
East Pakistan the former E division of Pakistan consisting of E portion of Bengal; now Bangladesh
East River strait SE New York connecting upper New York Bay & Long Island Sound and separating Manhattan & Long Island
East Sea — see JAPAN, SEA OF
East Sus·sex \ˈsə-siks\ county SE England
East Timor *or* **Ti·mor–Les·te** \ˈtē-mōr-ˈlesh-ˌtā\ country SE Asia on E Timor; ✻, Dili
Ebro \ˈā-(ˌ)brō\ river 565 mi. (909 km.) long NE Spain flowing into the Mediterranean
Ec·ua·dor \ˈe-kwə-ˌdȯr, ˌe-kwä-ˈt͟hȯr\ country W South America; ✻, Quito — **Ec·ua·dor·an** \ˌe-kwə-ˈdȯr-ən\ *or* **Ec·ua·dor·ean** *or* **Ec·ua·dor·ian** \-ē-ən\ *adj or n*
Ed·in·burgh \ˈe-dᵊn-ˌbər-ə\ city, ✻ of Scotland
Ed·mon·ton \ˈed-mən-tən\ city, ✻ of Alberta, Canada
Edom \ˈē-dəm\ ancient country SW Asia S of Judaea & Dead Sea — **Edom·ite** \ˈēd-ə-ˌmīt\ *n*
Egypt \ˈē-jipt\ country NE Africa & Sinai Peninsula of SW Asia bordering on Mediterranean & Red seas; ✻, Cairo
Eire — see IRELAND
Elam \ˈē-ləm\ ancient country SW Asia at head of Persian Gulf E of Babylonia — **Elam·ite** \ˈē-lə-ˌmīt\ *n*
Elbe \ˈel-bə, ˈelb\ river 720 mi. (1159 km.) long N Czech Republic & NE Germany flowing NW into North Sea
El·bert, Mount \ˈel-bərt\ mountain 14,433 ft. (4399 m.) W *cen* Colorado; highest in Colorado & the Rocky Mountains
El·brus, Mount \el-ˈbrüz, -ˈbrüs\ mountain 18,510 ft. (5642 m.) Russia; highest in the Caucasus & in Europe
El·burz \el-ˈbu̇rz\ mountains N Iran
Eliz·a·beth \i-ˈli-zə-bəth\ city NE New Jersey
Elles·mere \ˈelz-ˌmir\ island N Canada in Nunavut
Ellice — see TUVALU
El·lis Island \ˈe-ləs\ island SE New York S of Manhattan; served as immigration station 1892–1954
El Mon·te \el-ˈmän-tē\ city SW California E of Los Angeles
El Paso \el-ˈpa-(ˌ)sō\ city W Texas on Rio Grande
El Sal·va·dor \el-ˈsal-və-ˌdȯr, -ˌsal-və-ˈ; ˌel-ˌsäl-vä-ˈt͟hȯr\ country Central America bordering on the Pacific; ✻, San Salvador
Ely, Isle of \ˈē-lē\ area of high ground amid marshes in East Anglia, England
En·field \ˈen-ˌfēld\ borough of N Greater London, England
En·gland \ˈiŋ-glənd, ˈiŋ-lənd\ country S Great Britain; a division of United Kingdom; ✻, London
English Channel arm of the Atlantic between S England & N France
En·nis·kil·len \ˌe-nə-ˈski-lən\ town SW Northern Ireland in Fermanagh district
Ephra·im \ˈē-frē-əm\ **1** hilly region N Jordan E of Jordan River **2** — see ISRAEL — **Ephra·im·ite** \ˈē-frē-ə-ˌmīt\ *n*
Equatorial Guinea *formerly* **Spanish Guinea** country W Africa including Mbini & Bioko; ✻, Malabo
Erie \ˈir-ē\ **1** city & port NW Pennsylvania **2** canal New York between Hudson River at Albany & Lake Erie at Buffalo; now superseded by New York State Barge Canal

Erie, Lake lake E *cen* North America in U.S. & Canada; one of the Great Lakes

Er·in \ˈer-ən\ poetic name of Ireland

Er·i·trea \ˌer-ə-ˈtrē-ə, -ˈtrā-\ country NE Africa; ✻, Asmara — **Er·i·tre·an** \-ən\ *adj or n*

Es·con·di·do \ˌes-kən-ˈdē-(ˌ)dō\ city SW California N of San Diego

Es·fa·han \ˌes-fə-ˈhän, -ˈhan\ *or* **Is·fa·han** \ˌis-\ city W *cen* Iran

Española — see HISPANIOLA

Es·sen \ˈe-sᵊn\ city W Germany in the Ruhr

Es·sex \ˈe-siks\ county SE England on North Sea

Es·to·nia \e-ˈstō-nē-ə, -nyə\ country E Europe on Baltic Sea; ✻, Tallinn — **Es·to·nian** \e-ˈstō-nē-ən, -nyən\ *adj or n*

Eswa·ti·ni \ˌe-swä-ˈtē-nē\ *or* **Kingdom of Eswatini** *or* **Swa·zi·land** \ˈswä-zē-ˌland\ country SE Africa between Republic of South Africa & Mozambique; administrative ✻, Mbabane; legislative ✻, Lobamba — **Swa·zi** \ˈswä-zē\ *adj or n*

Ethi·o·pia \ˌē-thē-ˈō-pē-ə\ *historically* **Abys·sin·ia** \ˌa-bə-ˈsi-nē-ə, -nyə\ country E Africa; ✻, Addis Ababa — **Ethi·o·pi·an** \-pē-ən\ *adj or n*

Et·na, Mount \ˈet-nə\ volcano 10,902 ft. (3323 m.) Italy in NE Sicily

Eto·bi·coke \e-ˈtō-bi-ˌkō\ former city Canada in SE Ontario; now part of Toronto

Etru·ria \i-ˈtrůr-ē-ə\ ancient country *cen* peninsula of Italy

Eu·gene \yü-ˈjēn\ city W Oregon

Eu·phra·tes \yů-ˈfrā-(ˌ)tēz\ river 1700 mi. (2736 km.) long SW Asia flowing from E Turkey & uniting with the Tigris to form the Shatt al Arab

Eur·asia \yů-ˈrā-zhə, -shə\ landmass consisting of Europe & Asia — **Eur·asian** \-zhən, -shən\ *adj or n*

Eu·rope \ˈyůr-əp\ continent of the Eastern Hemisphere between Asia & the Atlantic

European Union economic, scientific, & political organization consisting of Belgium, France, Italy, Luxembourg, Netherlands, Germany, Denmark, Greece, Ireland, Spain, Portugal, Austria, Finland, Sweden, Cyprus, Czech Republic, Estonia, Hungary, Latvia, Lithuania, Malta, Poland, Slovakia, Slovenia, Bulgaria, Romania, & Croatia

Ev·ans·ville \ˈe-vənz-ˌvil\ city SW Indiana

Ev·er·est, Mount \ˈev-rəst, ˈe-və-\ mountain 29,035 ft. (8850 m.) S Asia in the Himalayas on border between Nepal & Tibet; highest in the world

Ev·er·glades \ˈe-vər-ˌglādz\ swamp region S Florida now partly drained

Ex·e·ter \ˈek-sə-tər\ city SW England

Faer·oe *or* **Far·oe** \ˈfer-(ˌ)ō\ islands NE Atlantic NW of the Shetlands belonging to Denmark — **Faero·ese** \ˌfar-ə-ˈwēz, ˌfer-, -ˈwēs\ *adj or n*

Fair·banks \ˈfer-ˌbaŋks\ city E *cen* Alaska

Fai·sa·la·bad \ˌfī-ˌsä-lə-ˈbäd, -ˌsa-lə-ˈbad\ *formerly* **Ly·all·pur** \lē-ˌäl-ˈpůr\ city NE Pakistan W of Lahore

Falk·land Islands \ˈfȯ-klənd, ˈfȯl-\ *or Spanish* **Is·las Mal·vi·nas** \ˌēs-läs-mäl-ˈvē-näs\ island group SW Atlantic E of S end of Argentina; a British colony; ✻, Stanley

Far East the countries of E Asia & the Malay Archipelago — usually thought to consist of the Asian countries bordering on the Pacific but sometimes including also India, Sri Lanka, Bangladesh, Tibet, & Myanmar — **Far Eastern** *adj*

Far·go \ˈfär-(ˌ)gō\ city E North Dakota; largest in state

Faroe — see FAEROE

Fay·ette·ville \ˈfā-ət-ˌvil, -vəl\ city SE *cen* North Carolina

Fear, Cape \ˈfir\ cape SE North Carolina

Fer·man·agh \fər-ˈma-nə\ district SW Northern Ireland

Fernando Póo — see BIOKO

Fes \ˈfes\ city N *cen* Morocco

Fife \ˈfīf\ administrative subdivision of E Scotland

Fi·ji \ˈfē-(ˌ)jē\ islands SW Pacific; country; ✻, Suva — **Fi·ji·an** \ˈfē-(ˌ)jē-ən, fi-ˈ\ *adj or n*

Fin·land \ˈfin-lənd\ country NE Europe; ✻, Helsinki — **Fin·land·er** *n*

Flan·ders \ˈflan-dərz\ **1** region W Belgium & N France on North Sea **2** semiautonomous region W Belgium

Flat·tery, Cape \ˈfla-tə-rē\ cape NW Washington at entrance to Strait of Juan de Fuca

Flint \ˈflint\ city SE Michigan

Flor·ence \ˈflȯr-ən(t)s, ˈflär-\ *or Italian* **Fi·ren·ze** \fē-ˈrent-sā\ city *cen* Italy — **Flor·en·tine** \ˈflȯr-ən-ˌtēn, ˈflär-, -ˌtīn\ *adj or n*

Flor·i·da \ˈflȯr-ə-də, ˈflär-\ state SE U.S.; ✻, Tallahassee — **Flo·rid·i·an** \flə-ˈri-dē-ən\ *or* **Flor·i·dan** \ˈflȯr-ə-dən, ˈflär-\ *adj or n*

Florida, Straits of channel between Florida Keys on NW & Cuba & Bahamas on S & E connecting Gulf of Mexico & the Atlantic

Florida Keys chain of islands off S tip of Florida

Foochow — see FUZHOU

For·a·ker, Mount \ˈfȯr-i-kər, ˈfär-\ mountain 17,400 ft. (5304 m.) S *cen* Alaska in Alaska Range

For·mo·sa \fȯr-ˈmō-sə, fər-, -zə\ — see TAIWAN — **For·mo·san** \fȯr-ˈmō-sᵊn, fər-, -zᵊn\ *adj or n*

For·ta·le·za \ˌfȯr-tə-ˈlā-zə\ city & port NE Brazil on the Atlantic

Fort Col·lins \ˈkä-lənz\ city N Colorado
Fort–de–France \ˌfȯr-də-ˈfräⁿs\ city West Indies, ✻ of Martinique on W coast
Forth \ˈfȯrth\ river 116 mi. (187 km.) long S *cen* Scotland flowing E into North Sea through **Firth of Forth**
Fort Knox \ˈnäks\ military reservation N *cen* Kentucky SSW of Louisville; location of U.S. Gold Bullion Depository
Fort Lau·der·dale \ˈlȯ-dər-ˌdāl\ city SE Florida
Fort Wayne \ˈwān\ city NE Indiana
Fort Worth \ˈwərth\ city NE Texas
Fox \ˈfäks\ islands SW Alaska in the E Aleutians
Foxe Basin \ˈfäks\ inlet of the Atlantic N Canada in E Nunavut W of Baffin Island
France \ˈfran(t)s, ˈfräⁿs\ country W Europe between the English Channel & the Mediterranean; ✻, Paris
Frank·fort \ˈfraŋk-fərt\ city, ✻ of Kentucky
Frank·furt \ˈfraŋk-fərt, ˈfräŋk-ˌfu̇rt\ *or in full* **Frankfurt am Main** \(ˌ)äm-ˈmīn\ city W Germany on Main River
Frank·lin \ˈfraŋ-klən\ former district N Canada in Northwest Territories including Arctic Archipelago & Boothia & Melville peninsulas
Fra·ser \ˈfrā-zər, -zhər\ river 850 mi. (1368 km.) long Canada in S *cen* British Columbia flowing into the Pacific
Fred·er·ic·ton \ˈfre-drik-tən, ˈfre-də-rik-\ city, ✻ of New Brunswick, Canada
Free State *formerly* **Or·ange Free State** \ˈȯr-inj, ˈär-, -ənj\ province E *cen* Republic of South Africa
Free·town \ˈfrē-ˌtau̇n\ city, ✻ of Sierra Leone
Fre·mont \ˈfrē-ˌmänt\ city W California
French Guiana country N South America on the Atlantic; an overseas division of France; ✻, Cayenne
French Indochina — see INDOCHINA
Fres·no \ˈfrez-(ˌ)nō\ city S *cen* California SE of San Francisco
Frunze — see BISHKEK
Fu·ji, Mount \ˈfü-jē\ *or* **Fu·ji·ya·ma** \ˌfü-jē-ˈyä-mä\ mountain 12,388 ft. (3776 m.) Japan in S *cen* Honshu; highest in Japan
Fu·ku·o·ka \ˌfü-kü-ˈō-kä\ city Japan in N Kyushu
Ful·ler·ton \ˈfu̇-lər-tən\ city SW California
Fu·na·fu·ti \ˌfü-nä-ˈfü-tē\ city, ✻ of Tuvalu
Fun·dy, Bay of \ˈfən-dē\ inlet of the Atlantic SE Canada between New Brunswick & Nova Scotia
Fu·shun \ˈfü-ˈshu̇n\ city NE China E of Shenyang
Fu·zhou \ˈfü-ˈjō\ *or* **Foo·chow** \ˈfü-ˈjō, -ˈchau̇\ city & port SE China
Ga·bon \gä-ˈbōⁿ\ country W Africa on the Equator; ✻, Libreville — **Gab·o·nese** \ˌga-bə-ˈnēz, -ˈnēs\ *adj or n*
Ga·bo·rone \ˌgä-bō-ˈrō-(ˌ)nā, ˌkä-\ city, ✻ of Botswana
Gads·den Purchase \ˈgadz-dən\ area of land S of Gila River in present Arizona & New Mexico purchased 1853 by the U.S. from Mexico
Ga·la·pa·gos Islands \gə-ˈlä-pə-gəs, -ˈla-, -ˌgōs\ island group Ecuador in the Pacific 600 mi. (965 km.) W of South America
Ga·la·tia \gə-ˈlā-sh(ē-)ə\ ancient country *cen* Asia Minor in region around modern Ankara, Turkey — **Ga·la·tian** \-shən\ *adj or n*
Ga·li·cia \gə-ˈli-sh(ē-)ə\ **1** region E *cen* Europe now divided between Poland & Ukraine **2** region NW Spain on the Atlantic — **Ga·li·cian** \-ˈli-shən\ *adj or n*
Gal·i·lee \ˈga-lə-ˌlē\ hilly region N Israel — **Gal·i·le·an** \ˌga-lə-ˈlē-ən\ *adj or n*
Galilee, Sea of *or modern* **Lake Ti·be·ri·as** \tī-ˈbir-ē-əs\ lake N Israel on Syrian border; crossed by Jordan River
Gal·lo·way \ˈga-lə-ˌwā\ former administrative district of SW Scotland — see DUMFRIES AND GALLOWAY
Gam·bia \ˈgam-bē-ə, ˈgäm-\ *or* **the Gambia** *or* **Republic of the Gambia** country W Africa; ✻, Banjul — **Gam·bi·an** \-bē-ən\ *adj or n*
Gan·ges \ˈgan-ˌjēz\ river 1550 mi. (2494 km.) long N India flowing from the Himalayas SE & E to unite with the Brahmaputra and empty into Bay of Bengal through a vast delta — **Gan·get·ic** \gan-ˈje-tik\ *adj*
Gao·xiong \ˈgau̇-ˈshyu̇ŋ\ *or* **Kao–hsiung** \ˈkau̇-ˈshyu̇ŋ, ˈgau̇-\ city & port SW Taiwan
Garden Grove city SW California
Gar·land \ˈgär-lənd\ city NE Texas NNE of Dallas
Ga·ronne \gə-ˈrän, gä-ˈrȯn\ river 355 mi. (571 km.) long SE France flowing NW
Gary \ˈger-ē\ city NW Indiana on Lake Michigan
Gas·co·ny \ˈgas-kə-nē\ region SW France — **Gas·con** \ˈgas-kən\ *adj or n*
Gas·pé \ga-ˈspā, ˈga-ˌ\ peninsula SE Quebec E of mouth of the Saint Lawrence — **Gas·pe·sian** \ga-ˈspē-zhən\ *adj or n*
Gaul \ˈgȯl\ *or Latin* **Gal·lia** \ˈga-lē-ə\ ancient country W Europe chiefly consisting of region occupied by modern France & Belgium
Gau·teng \ˈgau̇-ˌteŋ\ province *cen* NE Republic of South Africa
Ga·za Strip \ˈgä-zə, ˈga-\ district NE Sinai Peninsula on the Mediterranean
Ge·ne·va \jə-ˈnē-və\ city SW Switzerland on Lake Geneva — **Ge·ne·van** \-vən\ *adj or n* — **Gen·e·vese** \ˌje-nə-ˈvēz, -ˈvēs\ *adj or n*

Geneva, Lake lake on border between SW Switzerland & E France

Gen·oa \ˈje-nō-ə\ *or Italian* **Ge·no·va** \ˈje-nō-(ˌ)vä\ city & port NW Italy — **Gen·o·ese** \ˌje-nō-ˈēz, -ˈēs\ *or* **Gen·o·vese** \-nə-ˈvēz, -ˈvēs\ *adj or n*

George·town \ˈjȯrj-ˌtau̇n\ **1** a W section of Washington, District of Columbia **2** city & port, ✻ of Guyana

Geor·gia \ˈjȯr-jə\ **1** state SE U.S.; ✻, Atlanta **2** *or* **Republic of Georgia** country SW Asia on Black Sea S of Caucasus Mountains; ✻, Tbilisi — **Geor·gian** \ˈjȯr-jən\ *adj or n*

Georgia, Strait of channel Canada & U.S. between Vancouver Island & main part of British Columbia NW of Puget Sound

Georgian Bay inlet of Lake Huron in S Ontario

Ger·man·town \ˈjər-mən-ˌtau̇n\ a NW section of Philadelphia, Pennsylvania

Ger·ma·ny \ˈjər-mə-nē\ country *cen* Europe bordering on North & Baltic seas; ✻, Berlin; divided 1946–90 into two independent states: the **Federal Republic of Germany** (West Germany; ✻, Bonn) & the **German Democratic Republic** (East Germany; ✻, East Berlin)

Get·tys·burg \ˈge-tēz-ˌbərg\ town S Pennsylvania

Gha·na \ˈgä-nə, ˈga-\ *formerly* **Gold Coast** country W Africa on Gulf of Guinea; ✻, Accra — **Gha·na·ian** \gä-ˈnā-ən, ga-, -ˈnī-ən\ *or* **Gha·ni·an** \ˈgä-nē-ən, ˈga-, -nyən\ *adj or n*

Ghats \ˈgȯts\ two mountain chains S India consisting of **Eastern Ghats** & **Western Ghats**

Ghent \ˈgent\ city NW *cen* Belgium

Gi·bral·tar \jə-ˈbrȯl-tər\ British colony on S coast of Spain including Rock of Gibraltar

Gibraltar, Rock of cape on S coast of Spain in Gibraltar at E end of Strait of Gibraltar; highest point 1396 ft. (426 m.)

Gibraltar, Strait of passage between Europe & Africa connecting the Atlantic & the Mediterranean

Gi·la \ˈhē-lə\ river 630 mi. (1014 km.) long SW New Mexico and S Arizona flowing W into the Colorado

Gil·bert \ˈgil-bərt\ town SW *cen* Arizona

Gilbert and El·lice Islands \ˈe-lis\ island group W Pacific; divided into Kiribati and Tuvalu

Gil·e·ad \ˈgi-lē-əd\ mountain region of NE ancient Palestine E of Jordan River; now in NW Jordan — **Gil·e·ad·ite** \-lē-ə-ˌdīt\ *n*

Gi·te·ga \gē-ˈtā-gä\ *or formerly* **Ki·te·ga** \kē-\ city, ✻ of Burundi E of former ✻ Bujumbura

Gi·za \ˈgē-zə\ city N Egypt on the Nile SW of Cairo

Gla·cier Bay \ˈglā-shər\ inlet SE Alaska at S end of Saint Elias Range

Glas·gow \ˈglas-(ˌ)kō, ˈglas-(ˌ)gō, ˈglaz-(ˌ)gō\ city S *cen* Scotland on the Clyde — **Glas·we·gian** \gla-ˈswē-jən, glaz-\ *adj or n*

Glen·dale \ˈglen-ˌdāl\ **1** city *cen* Arizona NW of Phoenix **2** city S California NE of Los Angeles

Glouces·ter \ˈgläs-tər, ˈglȯs-\ town SW *cen* England

Glouces·ter·shire \ˈgläs-tər-ˌshir, -shər, ˈglȯs-\ *or* **Gloucester** county SW *cen* England

Goa \ˈgō-ə\ state W India on Malabar coast

Goat Island island W New York in Niagara River — see NIAGARA FALLS

Go·bi \ˈgō-(ˌ)bē\ desert E *cen* Asia in Mongolia & N China

Godthab — see NUUK

Godwin Austen — see K2

Go·lan Heights \ˈgō-ˌlän, -lən\ hilly region NE of Sea of Galilee

Gol·con·da \gäl-ˈkän-də\ ruined city *cen* India W of Hyderabad

Gold Coast **1** — see GHANA **2** coast region W Africa on N shore of Gulf of Guinea E of Côte d'Ivoire

Golden Gate strait W California connecting San Francisco Bay with Pacific Ocean

Good Hope, Cape of \ˌgu̇d-ˈhōp\ cape S Republic of South Africa on SW coast of Western Cape province

Gorki — see NIZHNIY NOVGOROD

Gö·te·borg \ˌyœ-tə-ˈbȯr-ē\ city & port SW Sweden

Gram·pi·an \ˈgram-pē-ən\ hills N *cen* Scotland

Grand Banks shallow area in the W North Atlantic SE of Newfoundland

Grand Canyon gorge of Colorado River NW Arizona

Grand Canyon of the Snake — see HELLS CANYON

Grande, Rio — see RIO GRANDE

Grand Prairie city NE *cen* Texas W of Dallas

Grand Rapids city SW Michigan

Graz \ˈgräts\ city S Austria

Great Australian Bight wide bay on S coast of Australia

Great Barrier Reef coral reef Australia off NE coast of Queensland

Great Basin region W U.S. between Sierra Nevada & Wasatch Range including most of Nevada & parts of California, Idaho, Utah, Wyoming, & Oregon; has no drainage to ocean

Great Bear lake Canada in Northwest Territories draining through Great Bear River into Mackenzie River

Great Brit·ain \ˈbri-tᵊn\ **1** island W Europe NW of France consisting of England, Scotland, & Wales **2** UNITED KINGDOM

Great Dividing Range mountain system E Australia extending S from Cape York Peninsula into Tasmania — see KOSCIUSKO, MOUNT

Greater Antilles group of islands of the West Indies including Cuba, Hispaniola, Jamaica, & Puerto Rico — see LESSER ANTILLES

Greater London metropolitan county SE England consisting of City of London & 32 surrounding boroughs

Greater Manchester metropolitan county NW England including city of Manchester

Greater Sudbury — see SUDBURY, GREATER

Great Lakes chain of five lakes (Superior, Michigan, Huron, Erie, & Ontario) *cen* North America in U.S. & Canada

Great Plains elevated plains region W *cen* U.S. & W Canada E of the Rockies; extending from W Texas to NE British Columbia & NW Alberta

Great Rift Valley basin SW Asia & E Africa extending with several breaks from valley of the Jordan S to *cen* Mozambique

Great Salt Lake lake N Utah having salty waters & no outlet

Great Slave Lake lake NW Canada in S Northwest Territories drained by Mackenzie River

Great Smoky mountains between W North Carolina & E Tennessee

Greece \ˈgrēs\ country S Europe at S end of Balkan Peninsula; ✻, Athens

Green \ˈgrēn\ **1** mountains E North America in the Appalachians extending from S Quebec S through Vermont into W Massachusetts **2** river 730 mi. (1175 km.) long W U.S. flowing from W Wyoming S into the Colorado in SE Utah

Green Bay **1** inlet of NW Lake Michigan 120 mi. (193 km.) long in NW Michigan & NE Wisconsin **2** city NE Wisconsin on Green Bay

Green·land \ˈgrēn-lənd, -ˌland\ island in the North Atlantic off NE North America belonging to Denmark; ✻, Nuuk

Greens·boro \ˈgrēnz-ˌbər-ō\ city N *cen* North Carolina

Green·wich \ˈgre-nich, ˈgrēn-ˌwich, ˈgrin-ˌwich\ borough of SE Greater London, England

Green·wich Village \ˈgre-nich\ section of New York City in W Manhattan

Gre·na·da \grə-ˈnā-də\ island West Indies in S Windward Islands; independent country; ✻, Saint George's

Gren·a·dines, the \ˌgre-nə-ˈdēnz, ˈgre-nə-ˌ\ islands West Indies in *cen* Windward Islands; N islands part of Saint Vincent and the Grenadines; S islands dependency of Grenada

Groz·ny \ˈgrȯz-nē, ˈgräz-\ city S Russia in Europe; ✻ of Chechnya

Gua·da·la·ja·ra \ˌgwä-də-lə-ˈhär-ə, ˌgwä-thä-lä-ˈhä-rä\ city W *cen* Mexico

Gua·dal·ca·nal \ˌgwä-dᵊl-kə-ˈnal, ˌgwä-də-kə-\ island W Pacific in the SE Solomons

Gua·dal·qui·vir \ˌgwä-dᵊl-ki-ˈvir, -ˈkwi-vər\ river 408 mi. (656 km.) long S Spain flowing into the Atlantic

Gua·de·loupe \ˈgwä-də-ˌlüp\ two islands separated by a narrow channel in West Indies in *cen* Leeward Islands; an overseas division of France

Gua·lla·ti·ri \ˌgwä-yə-ˈtir-ē, ˌgwī-ə-\ volcano 19,882 ft. (6060 m.) high N Chile

Guam \ˈgwäm\ island W Pacific in S Marianas belonging to U.S.; ✻, Hagåtña — **Gua·ma·ni·an** \gwä-ˈmā-nē-ən\ *adj or n*

Gua·na·ba·ra Bay \ˌgwä-nä-ˈbär-ə\ inlet of the Atlantic SE Brazil on which city of Rio de Janeiro is located

Guang·dong \ˈgwäŋ-ˈdu̇ŋ\ *or* **Kwang·tung** \ˈgwäŋ-ˈdu̇ŋ, ˈkwäŋ-, -ˈtu̇ŋ\ province SE China bordering on South China Sea & Gulf of Tonkin; ✻, Guangzhou

Guang·zhou \ˈgwäŋ-ˈjō\ *or* **Can·ton** \ˈkan-ˌtän, kan-ˈ\ city & port SE China

Guan·tá·na·mo Bay \gwän-ˈtä-nä-ˌmō\ inlet of the Caribbean in SE Cuba; site of U.S. naval station

Gua·te·ma·la \ˌgwä-tə-ˈmä-lə, -tā-ˈmä-lä\ **1** country Central America **2** *or* **Guatemala City** city, its ✻ — **Gua·te·ma·lan** \-ˈmä-lən\ *adj or n*

Gua·ya·quil \ˌgwī-ə-ˈkēl, -ˈkil\ city & port W Ecuador

Guay·na·bo \gwī-ˈnä-(ˌ)bō, -(ˌ)vō\ city NE *cen* Puerto Rico

Guern·sey \ˈgərn-zē\ — see CHANNEL

Gui·a·na \gē-ˈa-nə, -ˈä-nə; gī-ˈa-nə\ region N South America on the Atlantic; includes Guyana, French Guiana, Suriname, & nearby parts of Brazil & Venezuela — **Gui·a·nan** \-nən\ *adj or n*

Guin·ea \ˈgi-nē\ **1** region W Africa on the Atlantic extending along coast from Gambia to Angola **2** country W Africa N of Sierra Leone & Liberia; ✻, Conakry — **Guin·ean** \ˈgi-nē-ən\ *adj or n*

Guinea, Gulf of arm of the Atlantic W *cen* Africa

Guin·ea–Bis·sau \ˌgi-nē-bi-ˈsau̇\ country W Africa; ✻, Bissau

Gui·yang \ˈgwā-ˈyäŋ\ *or* **Kuei–yang** \ˈgwā-ˈyäŋ\ city S China

Gulf States states of U.S. bordering on Gulf of Mexico: Florida, Alabama, Mississippi, Louisiana, and Texas

Gulf Stream warm current of the Atlantic Ocean flowing from Gulf of Mexico NE along coast of U.S. to Nantucket Island and from there eastward

Guy·ana \gī-ˈan-ə\ *formerly* **British Guiana** country N South America on the Atlantic; ✻, Georgetown — **Guy·a·nese** \ˌgī-ə-ˈnēz, -ˈnēs\ *adj or n*

Gwangju — see KWANGJU

Gwent \ˈgwent\ former county SE Wales

Gwyn·edd \ˈgwi-neth\ administrative area NW Wales

Hack·ney \ˈhak-nē\ borough of N Greater London, England
Ha·gåt·ña \hə-ˈgät-nyə\ *formerly* **Aga·na** \ä-ˈgä-nyä\ town, ✻ of Guam
Hague, The \thə-ˈhāg\ city, seat of government of Netherlands
Hai·kou \ˈhī-ˈkō\ city & port SE China
Hai·phong \ˈhī-ˈfȯŋ, -ˈfäŋ\ city & port N Vietnam
Hai·ti \ˈhā-tē\ country West Indies in W Hispaniola; ✻, Port-au-Prince — **Hai·tian** \ˈhā-shən\ *adj or n*
Ha·le·a·ka·la Crater \ˌhä-lā-ˌä-kä-ˈlä\ crater over 2500 ft. (762 m.) deep Hawaii in E Maui
Hal·i·fax \ˈha-lə-ˌfaks\ municipality & port, ✻ of Nova Scotia, Canada
Ham·burg \ˈham-ˌbərg; ˈhäm-ˌbu̇rg, -ˌbu̇rk\ city N Germany on the Elbe — **Ham·burg·er** \-ˌbər-gər, -ˌbu̇r-\ *n*
Ham·hung *or* **Ham·heung** \ˈhäm-ˌhu̇ŋ\ city E *cen* North Korea
Ham·il·ton \ˈha-məl-tən\ **1** town, ✻ of Bermuda **2** city & port, S Ontario, Canada on Lake Ontario
Ham·mer·smith and Ful·ham \ˈha-mər-ˌsmith-ənd-ˈfu̇-ləm\ borough of SW Greater London, England
Hamp·shire \ˈhamp-ˌshir, -shər\ county S England on English Channel
Hamp·ton \ˈhamp-tən\ city SE Virginia
Hampton Roads channel SE Virginia through which James River flows into Chesapeake Bay
Hang·zhou \ˈhäŋ-ˈjō\ *or* **Hang·chow** \ˈhaŋ-ˈchau̇, ˈhäŋ-ˈjō\ *or* **Hang–chou** \-ˈjō\ city E China
Han·ni·bal \ˈha-nə-bəl\ city NE Missouri on the Mississippi River
Han·no·ver *or* **Han·o·ver** \ˈha-ˌnō-vər, -nə-vər, *G* hä-ˈnō-fər\ city N *cen* Germany
Ha·noi \ha-ˈnȯi, hə-, hä-\ city, ✻ of Vietnam
Hao·ra \ˈhau̇-rə\ city E India on Hugli River opposite Calcutta
Ha·ra·re \hə-ˈrä-(ˌ)rā\ *formerly* **Salis·bury** \ˈsȯlz-ˌber-ē, -b(ə-)rē\ city, ✻ of Zimbabwe
Har·bin \ˈhär-bən, här-ˈbin\ *or* **Ha–erh–pin** \ˈhä-ˈər-ˈbin\ city NE China
Har·in·gey \ˈha-riŋ-ˌgā\ borough of N Greater London, England
Har·lem \ˈhär-ləm\ section of New York City in N Manhattan
Har·ris·burg \ˈha-rəs-ˌbərg\ city, ✻ of Pennsylvania
Har·row \ˈha-(ˌ)rō\ borough of NW Greater London, England
Hart·ford \ˈhärt-fərd\ city, ✻ of Connecticut
Hat·ter·as, Cape \ˈha-tə-rəs\ cape North Carolina on **Hatteras Island**
Ha·vana \hə-ˈva-nə\ city, ✻ of Cuba
Hav·ant \ˈha-vənt\ town S England
Ha·ver·ing \ˈhāv-riŋ, ˈhā-və-riŋ\ borough of NE Greater London, England
Ha·waii \hə-ˈwä-yē, -ˈwä-ˌē\ **1** *or* **Ha·wai·ian Islands** *formerly* **Sand·wich Islands** \ˌsan-(d)wich-\ group of islands *cen* Pacific belonging to U.S. **2** island, largest of the group **3** state of U.S., ✻, Honolulu
Hay·ward \ˈhā-wərd\ city W California SE of Oakland
Heb·ri·des \ˈhe-brə-ˌdēz\ islands W Scotland in the North Atlantic consisting of **Outer Hebrides** (to W) and **Inner Hebrides** (to E) — **Heb·ri·de·an** \ˌhe-brə-ˈdē-ən\ *adj or n*
Hel·e·na \ˈhe-lə-nə\ city, ✻ of Montana
Hellespont — see DARDANELLES
Hells Canyon \ˈhelz\ canyon of Snake River on Idaho–Oregon boundary
Hel·sin·ki \ˈhel-ˌsiŋ-kē, hel-ˈ\ city, ✻ of Finland
Hen·der·son \ˈhen-dər-sən\ city S Nevada
Hen·ry, Cape \ˈhen-rē\ cape E Virginia S of entrance to Chesapeake Bay
Her·e·ford and Wor·ces·ter \ˈher-ə-fərd-ᵊn-ˈwu̇s-tər\ former county W England
Hert·ford·shire \ˈhär-fərd-ˌshir, ˈhärt-, -shər\ *or* **Hertford** county SE England
Her·ze·go·vi·na \ˌhert-sə-gō-ˈvē-nə, ˌhərt-, -ˈgō-və-nə\ *or Serbian* **Her·ce·go·vi·na** \ˈk̲ert-sə-gō-vē-nə\ region S Europe; with Bosnia to the N forms Bosnia and Herzegovina — **Her·ze·go·vi·nian** \ˌhert-sə-gō-ˈvē-nē-ən, ˌhərt-, -nyən\ *n*
Hi·a·le·ah \ˌhī-ə-ˈlē-ə\ city SE Florida
Hi·ber·nia \hī-ˈbər-nē-ə\ — see IRELAND — **Hi·ber·ni·an** \-ən\ *adj or n*
Hi·ga·shi·ōsa·ka \hē-ˌgä-shē-ˈō-sä-kä\ city Japan in S Honshu E of Osaka
High·land \ˈhī-lənd\ administrative subdivision of NW Scotland
High·lands \ˈhī-ləndz\ the mountainous N part of Scotland lying N & W of the Lowlands
High Plains the Great Plains esp. from Nebraska southward
Hil·ling·don \ˈhi-liŋ-dən\ borough of W Greater London, England
Hi·ma·la·yas, the \ˌhi-mə-ˈlā-əz\ *or* **the Himalaya** mountain system S Asia on border between India & Tibet and in Kashmir, Nepal, & Bhutan — see EVEREST, MOUNT — **Hi·ma·la·yan** \ˌhim-ə-ˈlā-ən, hə-ˈmäl-(ə-)yən\ *adj*
Hin·du Kush \ˈhin-(ˌ)dü-ˈku̇sh, -ˈkəsh\ mountain range *cen* Asia SW of the Pamirs on border of Kashmir and in Afghanistan
Hin·du·stan \ˌhin-(ˌ)dü-ˈstan, -də-, -ˈstän\ **1** a name for N India **2** the subcontinent of India **3** the country of India
Hi·ro·shi·ma \ˌhir-ə-ˈshē-mə, hə-ˈrō-shə-mə\ city Japan in SW Honshu on Inland Sea
His·pan·io·la \ˌhis-pə-ˈnyō-lə\ *or Spanish* **Es·pa·ño·la** \ˌes-ˌpä-ˈnyō-lä\ island West Indies in Greater Antilles; divided between Haiti on W & Dominican Republic on E

Ho·bart \'hō-bərt\ city Australia, ✻ of Tasmania
Ho Chi Minh City \'hō-ˌchē-'min\ *formerly* **Sai·gon** \sī-'gän, 'sī-ˌ\ city S Vietnam
Hoh·hot \'hō-'hōt\ *or* **Hu·he·hot** \'hü-(ˌ)hā-'hōt\ city N China, ✻ of Inner Mongolia
Hok·kai·do \hȯ-'kī-(ˌ)dō\ island N Japan N of Honshu
Hol·land \'hä-lənd\ **1** county of Holy Roman Empire bordering on North Sea & consisting of area now forming part of W Netherlands **2** — see NETHERLANDS — **Hol·land·er** \-lən-dər\ *n*
Hol·ly·wood \'hä-lē-ˌwu̇d\ **1** section of Los Angeles, California, NW of downtown district **2** city SE Florida
Holy Roman Empire empire consisting mainly of German & Italian territories & existing from 9th or 10th century to 1806
Hon·du·ras \hän-'du̇r-əs, -'dyu̇r-; ȯn-'dü-räs\ country Central America; ✻, Tegucigalpa — **Hon·du·ran** \-ən\ *adj or n*
Hong Kong \'häŋ-ˌkäŋ, -'käŋ\ *or Chinese* **Xiang·gang** \'shyäŋ-ˌgäŋ\ special administrative region China on SE coast including Hong Kong Island & Jiulong Peninsula; chief city Victoria
Ho·ni·a·ra \ˌhō-nē-'är-ə\ town, ✻ of Solomon Islands
Ho·no·lu·lu \ˌhä-nə-'lü-(ˌ)lü, ˌhō-nə-\ city, ✻ of Hawaii on Oahu
Hon·shu \'hän-(ˌ)shü, 'hȯn-\ island Japan; largest of the four chief islands
Hood, Mount \'hu̇d\ mountain 11,235 ft. (3424 m.) NW Oregon in Cascade Range
Hoo·ver Dam \'hü-vər\ *or* **Boul·der Dam** \'bōl-dər\ dam 726 ft. (221 m.) high in Colorado River between Arizona & Nevada — see MEAD, LAKE
Hor·muz, Strait of \'(h)ȯr-ˌməz, (h)ȯr-'müz\ strait connecting Persian Gulf & Gulf of Oman
Horn, Cape \'hȯrn\ cape S Chile on an island in Tierra del Fuego; the most southerly point of South America at 56° S latitude
Horn of Africa the easternmost projection of Africa; variously used to refer to Somalia, SE or all of Ethiopia, often Djibouti, & sometimes Eritrea, Sudan, & Kenya
Horseshoe Falls — see NIAGARA FALLS
Houns·low \'hau̇nz-(ˌ)lō\ borough of SW Greater London, England
Hous·ton \'hyüs-tən, 'yüs-\ city SE Texas
Hsi–an — see XI'AN
Huang *or* **Hwang** \'hwäŋ\ *or* **Yellow** river about 3396 mi. (5464 km.) long N China flowing into Bo Hai
Hud·ders·field \'hə-dərz-ˌfēld\ town N England NE of Manchester
Hud·son \'həd-sən\ **1** river 306 mi. (492 km.) long E New York flowing S **2** bay, inlet of the Atlantic in N Canada **3** strait NE Canada connecting Hudson Bay & the Atlantic
Hu·gli *or* **Hoo·ghly** \'hü-glē\ river 120 mi. (193 km.) long E India flowing S into Bay of Bengal
Huhehot — see HOHHOT
Hull \'həl\ *or* **Kings·ton upon Hull** \'kiŋ-stən\ city & port N England
Hun·ga·ry \'həŋ-gə-rē\ country *cen* Europe; ✻, Budapest
Hunt·ing·ton Beach \'hən-tiŋ-tən\ city SW California
Hunts·ville \'hənts-ˌvil, -vəl\ city N Alabama
Hu·ron, Lake \'hyu̇r-ˌän, 'yu̇r-\ lake E *cen* North America in U.S. & Canada; one of the Great Lakes
Hy·der·abad \'hī-d(ə-)rə-ˌbad, -ˌbäd\ **1** city S *cen* India **2** city SE Pakistan on the Indus
Iba·dan \i-'bä-dᵊn, -'ba-\ city SW Nigeria
Ibe·ri·an \ī-'bir-ē-ən\ peninsula SW Europe occupied by Spain & Portugal
Ice·land \'īs-lənd, 'īs-ˌland\ island SE of Greenland between Arctic & Atlantic oceans; country; ✻, Reykjavik — **Ice·land·er** \'īs-ˌlan-dər, 'īs-lən-\ *n*
Ida·ho \'ī-də-ˌhō\ state NW U.S.; ✻, Boise — **Ida·ho·an** \ˌī-də-'hō-ən\ *adj or n*
Igua·çú *or* **Igua·zú** \ˌē-gwə-'sü\ river 745 mi. (1199 km.) long S Brazil flowing W
IJs·sel *or* **Ijs·sel** \'ī-səl, 'ā-\ river 70 mi. (113 km.) long E Netherlands flowing out of Rhine N into IJsselmeer
IJs·sel·meer \'ī-səl-ˌmer, 'ā-\ *or* **Lake Ijs·sel** freshwater lake N Netherlands separated from North Sea by a dike; part of former Zuider Zee (inlet of North Sea)
Ilium — see TROY
Il·li·nois \ˌi-lə-'nȯi\ state N *cen* U.S.; ✻, Springfield — **Il·li·nois·an** \ˌi-lə-'nȯi-ən\ *adj or n*
Il·lyr·ia \i-'lir-ē-ə\ ancient country S Europe and Balkan Peninsula on the Adriatic — **Il·lyr·i·an** \-ē-ən\ *adj or n*
Im·pe·ri·al Valley \im-'pir-ē-əl\ valley SE corner of California & partly in NE Baja California, Mexico
In·chon *or* **In·cheon** \'in-ˌchən\ city South Korea on Yellow Sea
In·de·pen·dence \ˌin-də-'pen-dən(t)s\ city W Missouri E of Kansas City
In·dia \'in-dē-ə\ **1** subcontinent S Asia S of the Himalayas between Bay of Bengal & Arabian Sea **2** country consisting of major portion of the subcontinent; ✻, New Delhi **3** *or* **Indian Empire** before 1947 those parts of the subcontinent of India under British rule or protection
In·di·an \'in-dē-ən\ ocean E of Africa, S of Asia, W of Australia, & N of Antarctica
In·di·ana \ˌin-dē-'a-nə\ state E *cen* U.S.; ✻, Indianapolis — **In·di·an·an** \-'a-nən\ *or* **In·di·an·i·an** \-'a-nē-ən\ *adj or n*
In·di·a·nap·o·lis \ˌin-dē-ə-'na-pə-lis\ city, ✻ of Indiana

Indian River lagoon 165 mi. (266 km.) long E Florida between main part of the state & coastal islands
Indian Territory former territory S U.S. in present state of Oklahoma
In·dies \ˈin-(ˌ)dēz\ **1** EAST INDIES **2** WEST INDIES
In·do·chi·na \ˌin-(ˌ)dō-ˈchī-nə\ **1** peninsula SE Asia including Myanmar, Malay Peninsula, Thailand, Cambodia, Laos, & Vietnam **2** *or* **French Indochina** former country SE Asia consisting of area now forming Cambodia, Laos, & Vietnam — **In·do–Chi·nese** \-chī-ˈnēz, -ˈnēs\ *adj or n*
In·do·ne·sia \ˌin-də-ˈnē-zhə, -shə\ country SE Asia in Malay Archipelago consisting of Sumatra, Java, S & E Borneo, Sulawesi, W New Guinea, & many smaller islands; ✻, Jakarta — **In·do·ne·sian** \-zhən, -shən\ *adj or n*
In·dore \in-ˈdȯr\ city W *cen* India
In·dus \ˈin-dəs\ river 1800 mi. (2897 km.) long S Asia flowing from Tibet NW & SSW through Pakistan into Arabian Sea
In·gle·wood \ˈiŋ-gəl-ˌwu̇d\ city SW California
In·land Sea \ˈin-ˌland, -lənd\ inlet of the Pacific in SW Japan between Honshu on N and Shikoku and Kyushu on S
Inner Hebrides — see HEBRIDES
Inner Mon·go·lia \män-ˈgōl-yə, mäŋ-, -ˈgō-lē-ə\ *or* **Nei Mong·gol** \ˈnā-ˈmän-ˌgōl, -ˈmäŋ-\ region N China
Inside Passage protected shipping route between Puget Sound, Washington, & the lower part of Alaska
In·ver·ness \ˌin-vər-ˈnes\ town NW Scotland
Io·ni·an \ī-ˈō-nē-ən\ sea, arm of the Mediterranean between SE Italy & W Greece
Io To — see IWO JIMA
Io·wa \ˈī-ə-wə\ state N *cen* U.S.; ✻, Des Moines — **Io·wan** \-wən\ *adj or n*
Ips·wich \ˈip-(ˌ)swich\ town SE England
Iqa·lu·it \ē-ˈka-lü-ət\ town Canada, ✻ of Nunavut on Baffin Island
Iran \i-ˈrän, -ˈran\ *formerly by outsiders* **Per·sia** \ˈpər-zhə\ country SW Asia; ✻, Tehran — **Irani** \-ˈrä-nē, -ˈra-\ *adj or n* — **Ira·nian** \i-ˈrā-nē-ən, -ˈran-ē-, -ˈrän-ē-\ *adj or n*
Iraq \i-ˈräk, -ˈrak\ country SW Asia in Mesopotamia; ✻, Baghdad — **Iraqi** \-ˈräk-ē, -ˈrak-\ *adj or n*
Ire·land \ˈī(-ə)r-lənd\ **1** *or Latin* **Hi·ber·nia** \hī-ˈbər-nē-ə\ island W Europe in the North Atlantic; one of the British Isles **2** *or* **Eire** \ˈer-ə\ country occupying major portion of Ireland (island); ✻, Dublin
Irish Sea arm of the North Atlantic between Great Britain & Ireland
Ir·kutsk \ir-ˈkütsk, ˌər-\ city S Russia near Lake Baikal
Ir·ra·wad·dy \ˌir-ə-ˈwä-dē\ river 1300 mi. (2092 km.) long Myanmar flowing S into Bay of Bengal
Ir·tysh \ir-ˈtish, ˌər-\ river over 2600 mi. (4180 km.) long *cen* Asia flowing NW & N from Altay Mountains in China, through Kazakhstan, & into W *cen* Russia
Ir·vine \ˈər-ˌvīn\ city SW California
Ir·ving \ˈər-viŋ\ city NE Texas NW of Dallas
Isfahan — see ESFAHAN
Is·lam·abad \is-ˈlä-mə-ˌbäd, iz-, -ˈla-mə-ˌbad\ city, ✻ of Pakistan
Islas Malvinas — see FALKLAND ISLANDS
Isle of Man — see MAN, ISLE OF
Isle of Wight \ˈwīt\ island England in English Channel
Isle Roy·ale \ˈī(-ə)l-ˈrȯi(-ə)l\ island Michigan in Lake Superior
Isles of Scilly **1** — see CORNWALL AND ISLES OF SCILLY **2** — see SCILLY
Is·ling·ton \ˈiz-liŋ-tən\ borough of N Greater London, England
Ispahan — see ESFAHAN
Is·ra·el \ˈiz-rē(-ə)l, -(ˌ)rā(-ə)l\ **1** kingdom in ancient Palestine consisting of lands occupied by the Hebrew people **2** *or* **Ephra·im** \ˈē-frē-əm\ the N part of the Hebrew kingdom after about 933 B.C. **3** country SW Asia; ✻, Jerusalem — **Is·rae·li** \iz-ˈrā-lē\ *adj or n*
Is·tan·bul \ˌis-tən-ˈbül, -ˌtan-, -ˌtän-, -ˈbu̇l, ˈis-tən-ˌ, *or with* m *for* n\ *formerly* **Con·stan·ti·no·ple** \ˌkän-ˌstan-tə-ˈnō-pəl\ city NW Turkey on the Bosporus & Sea of Marmara
Is·tria \ˈis-trē-ə\ peninsula in Croatia & Slovenia extending into the N Adriatic — **Is·tri·an** \-trē-ən\ *adj or n*
It·a·ly \ˈi-tə-lē\ country S Europe including a boot-shaped peninsula & the islands of Sicily & Sardinia; ✻, Rome
Itas·ca, Lake \ī-ˈtas-kə\ lake NW *cen* Minnesota; source of the Mississippi
Ivory Coast — see CÔTE D'IVOIRE — **Ivor·i·an** \(ˌ)ī-ˈvȯr-ē-ən\ *adj or n* — **Ivory Coast·er** \ˈkō-stər\ *n*
Iwo Ji·ma \ˌē-(ˌ)wō-ˈjē-mə\ *or* **Io To** \ˌē-(ˌ)ō-ˈtō\ island Japan in W Pacific SSE of Tokyo
Izhevsk \ˈē-ˌzhefsk\ *or 1985–87* **Usti·nov** \ˈüs-ti-ˌnȯf, -ˌnȯv\ city W Russia
Iz·mir \iz-ˈmir\ *formerly* **Smyr·na** \ˈsmər-nə\ city W Turkey
Jack·son \ˈjak-sən\ city, ✻ of Mississippi
Jack·son·ville \ˈjak-sən-ˌvil\ city NE Florida
Jai·pur \ˈjī-ˌpu̇r\ city NW India
Ja·kar·ta *also* **Dja·kar·ta** \jə-ˈkär-tə\ city, ✻ of Indonesia in NW Java
Ja·mai·ca \jə-ˈmā-kə\ island West Indies in Greater Antilles; country; ✻, Kingston — **Ja·mai·can** \-kən\ *adj or n*
James \ˈjāmz\ **1** — see DAKOTA **2** river

340 mi. (547 km.) long Virginia flowing E into Chesapeake Bay

James Bay the S extension of Hudson Bay between NE Ontario & W Quebec

James•town \ˈjāmz-ˌtau̇n\ ruined village E Virginia on James River; first permanent English settlement in America (1607)

Jam•shed•pur \ˈjäm-ˌshed-ˌpu̇r\ city E India

Ja•pan \jə-ˈpan, ja-\ country E Asia consisting of Honshu, Hokkaido, Kyushu, Shikoku, & other islands in the W Pacific; ✻, Tokyo

Japan, Sea of *also* **East Sea** arm of the Pacific between Japan & Korea

Ja•va \ˈjä-və, ˈja-\ island Indonesia SW of Borneo; chief city, Jakarta — **Ja•va•nese** \ˌja-və-ˈnēz, ˌjä-, -ˈnēs\ *n*

Jef•fer•son City \ˈje-fər-sən\ city, ✻ of Missouri

Jer•sey \ˈjər-zē\ — see CHANNEL

Jersey City city NE New Jersey on Hudson River

Je•ru•sa•lem \jə-ˈrü-s(ə-)ləm, -ˈrü-z(ə-)ləm\ city NW of Dead Sea, ✻ of Israel

Jid•da *or* **Jid•dah** \ˈji-də\ *or* **Jed•da** *or* **Jed•dah** \ˈje-də\ city W Saudi Arabia on Red Sea

Ji•lin \ˈjē-ˈlin\ *or* **Ki•rin** \ˈkē-ˈrin\ city NE China

Ji•nan *or* **Tsi•nan** \ˈjē-ˈnän\ city E China

Jin•zhou *or* **Chin–chou** *or* **Chin•chow** \ˈjin-ˈjō\ city NE China

Jiu•long \ˈjü-ˈlȯŋ\ *or* **Kow•loon** \ˈkau̇-ˈlün\ **1** peninsula SE China in Hong Kong opposite Hong Kong Island **2** city on Jiulong Peninsula

Jo•han•nes•burg \jō-ˈhä-nəs-ˌbərg, -ˈha-\ city NE Republic of South Africa

Jo•li•et \ˌjō-lē-ˈet\ city NE Illinois

Jor•dan \ˈjȯr-dᵊn\ **1** river 200 mi. (322 km.) long Israel & Jordan flowing S from Syria into Dead Sea **2** country SW Asia in NW Arabia; ✻, Amman — **Jor•da•ni•an** \jȯr-ˈdā-nē-ən\ *adj or n*

Juan de Fu•ca, Strait of \ˌwän-də-ˈfyü-kə, ˌhwän-\ strait 100 mi. (161 km.) long between Vancouver Island, British Columbia, & Olympic Peninsula, Washington

Ju•ba \ˈjü-bə, -ˌbä\ town, ✻ of South Sudan

Ju•daea *or* **Ju•dea** \ju̇-ˈdē-ə, -ˈdā-\ region of ancient Palestine forming its S division under Persian, Greek, & Roman rule — **Ju•dae•an** *or* **Ju•dean** \-ən\ *adj or n*

Ju•neau \ˈjü-(ˌ)nō, ju̇-ˈ\ city, ✻ of Alaska

Ju•ra \ˈju̇r-ə\ mountain range extending along boundary between France & Switzerland N of Lake of Geneva

Jut•land \ˈjət-lənd\ **1** peninsula N Europe extending into North Sea and consisting of main part of Denmark & N portion of Germany **2** the main part of Denmark

Ka•bul \ˈkä-bəl, -ˌbül; kə-ˈbül\ city, ✻ of Afghanistan

Ka Lae \kä-ˈlä-ā\ *or* **South Cape** *or* **South Point** most southerly point of Hawaii & of U.S.

Kal•a•ha•ri \ˌka-lə-ˈhär-ē, ˌkä-\ desert region S Africa N of Orange River in S Botswana & NW Republic of South Africa

Kalgan — see ZHANGJIAKOU

Ka•li•man•tan \ˌka-lə-ˈman-ˌtan, ˌkä-lē-ˈmän-ˌtän\ **1** BORNEO — its Indonesian name **2** the S & E portion of Borneo belonging to Indonesia

Ka•li•nin•grad \kə-ˈlē-nən-ˌgrad, -nyən-, -ˌgrät\ *formerly* **Kö•nigs•berg** \ˈkā-nigz-ˌbərg\ city & port W Russia

Kam•chat•ka \kam-ˈchat-kə, -ˈchät-\ peninsula 750 mi. (1207 km.) long E Russia

Kam•pa•la \käm-ˈpä-lä, kam-\ city, ✻ of Uganda

Kampuchea — see CAMBODIA

Kan•da•har \ˈkən-də-ˌhär\ city SE Afghanistan

Ka•no \ˈkä-(ˌ)nō\ city N *cen* Nigeria

Kan•pur \ˈkän-ˌpu̇r\ city N India on the Ganges

Kan•sas \ˈkan-zəs\ state W *cen* U.S.; ✻, Topeka — **Kan•san** \ˈkan-zən\ *adj or n*

Kansas City **1** city NE Kansas bordering on Kansas City, Missouri **2** city W Missouri

Kao–hsiung — see GAOXIONG

Ka•ra•chi \kə-ˈrä-chē\ city S Pakistan on Arabian Sea

Ka•ra•gan•da \ˌkär-ə-ˈgän-də\ *or* **Qa•ra•ghan•dy** \-dē\ city *cen* Kazakhstan

Kar•a•ko•ram Pass \ˌkär-ə-ˈkȯr-əm\ mountain pass NE Kashmir in **Karakoram Range** (system connecting the Himalayas with the Pamirs)

Ka•re•lia \kə-ˈrē-lē-ə, -ˈrēl-yə\ region NE Europe in Finland & Russia — **Ka•re•lian** \kə-ˈrē-lē-ən, -ˈrēl-yən\ *adj or n*

Ka•roo *or* **Kar•roo** \kə-ˈrü\ plateau region W Republic of South Africa W of Drakensberg Mountains

Kash•mir \ˈkash-ˌmir, ˈkazh-, kash-ˈ, kazh-ˈ\ disputed territory N subcontinent of India; claimed by India & Pakistan — **Kash•miri** \kash-ˈmi(ə)r-ē, kazh-\ *adj or n*

Ka•thi•a•war \ˌkä-tē-ə-ˈwär\ peninsula W India N of Gulf of Khambhat

Kath•man•du *or* **Kat•man•du** \ˌkat-ˌman-ˈdü, ˌkät-ˌmän-\ city, ✻ of Nepal

Kat•mai, Mount \ˈkat-ˌmī\ volcano 6715 ft. (2047 m.) S Alaska on Alaska Peninsula

Kat•te•gat \ˈka-ti-ˌgat\ arm of North Sea between Sweden & E coast of Jutland Peninsula of Denmark

Kau•ai \kä-ˈwä-ē\ island Hawaii NW of Oahu

Kau•nas \ˈkau̇-nəs, -ˌnäs\ city *cen* Lithuania

Ka·wa·sa·ki \ˌkä-wä-ˈsä-kē\ city Japan in E Honshu S of Tokyo

Ka·zakh·stan *also* **Ka·zak·stan** \ˌka-(ˌ)zak-ˈstan\ country NW *cen* Asia; ✻, Nur-Sultan — **Ka·zakh** *also* **Ka·zak** \kə-ˈzak, -ˈzäk\ *n*

Ka·zan \kə-ˈzan\ city W Russia

Kee·wa·tin \kē-ˈwā-tᵊn, -ˈwä-\ former district N Canada in E Northwest Territories NW of Hudson Bay; area now part of Nunavut

Ke·me·ro·vo \ˈkye-mə-rə-və\ city S *cen* Russia

Ke·nai \ˈkē-ˌnī\ peninsula S Alaska E of Cook Inlet

Kennedy, Cape — see CANAVERAL, CAPE

Ken·sing·ton and Chel·sea \ˈken-ziŋ-tən-ənd-ˈchel-sē, ˈken(t)-siŋ-\ borough of W Greater London, England

Kent \ˈkent\ county SE England — **Kent·ish** \ˈken-tish\ *adj*

Ken·tucky \kən-ˈtə-kē\ state E *cen* U.S.; ✻, Frankfort — **Ken·tuck·i·an** \-kē-ən\ *adj or n*

Ken·ya \ˈke-nyə, ˈkē-\ **1** mountain 17,058 ft. (5199 m.) *cen* Kenya **2** country E Africa S of Ethiopia; ✻, Nairobi — **Ken·yan** \-nyən\ *adj or n*

Key West \ˈwest\ city SW Florida on Key West (island)

Kha·ba·rovsk \kə-ˈbär-əfsk, k̲ə-\ city SE Russia

Kham·bhat, Gulf of \ˈkəm-bət\ *or* **Gulf of Cam·bay** \kam-ˈbā\ inlet of Arabian Sea in India N of Mumbai

Khar·kiv \ˈkär-kəf, ˈk̲är-\ *or* **Khar·kov** \ˈkär-ˌkóf, ˈk̲är-, -ˌkóv, -kəf\ city NE Ukraine

Khar·toum \kär-ˈtüm\ city, ✻ of Sudan

Khy·ber \ˈkī-bər\ pass 33 mi. (53 km.) long on border between Afghanistan & Pakistan

Ki·bo \ˈkē-(ˌ)bō\ mountain peak 19,340 ft. (5895 m.) NE Tanzania; highest peak of Kilimanjaro & highest point in Africa

Kiel \ˈkēl\ — see NORD-OSTSEE

Kiev — see KYIV

Ki·ga·li \kē-ˈgä-lē\ city, ✻ of Rwanda

Ki·lau·ea \ˌkē-ˌlä-ˈwā-ä\ volcanic crater Hawaii on Hawaii Island on E slope of Mauna Loa

Kil·i·man·ja·ro \ˌki-lə-mən-ˈjär-(ˌ)ō, -ˈja-(ˌ)rō\ mountain NE Tanzania; highest in Africa — see KIBO

Kil·lar·ney, Lakes of \ki-ˈlär-nē\ three lakes SW Ireland

Kings·ton \ˈkiŋ-stən\ city & port, ✻ of Jamaica

Kingston upon Hull — see HULL

Kingston upon Thames borough of SW Greater London, England

Kings·town \ˈkiŋz-ˌtau̇n\ seaport, ✻ of Saint Vincent and the Grenadines

Kin·sha·sa \kin-ˈshä-sə\ city, ✻ of Democratic Republic of the Congo

Ki·ri·bati \ˈkir-ə-ˌbas\ island group W Pacific; country; ✻, Tarawa

Kirin — see JILIN

Kirk·wall \ˈkər-ˌkwól\ town and port N Scotland, ✻ of Orkney Islands

Kishinev — see CHIŞINĂU

Ki·ta·kyu·shu \kē-ˌtä-ˈkyü-(ˌ)shü\ city Japan in N Kyushu

Kitch·e·ner \ˈkich-nər, ˈki-chə-\ city SE Ontario, Canada

Kitega — see GITEGA

Kit·ty Hawk \ˈkit-ē-ˌhók\ town E North Carolina

Klon·dike \ˈklän-ˌdīk\ region NW Canada in *cen* Yukon in valley of Klondike River

Knox·ville \ˈnäks-ˌvil, -vəl\ city E Tennessee

Ko·be \ˈkō-bē, -ˌbā\ city Japan in S Honshu

Ko·di·ak \ˈkō-dē-ˌak\ island S Alaska E of Alaska Peninsula

Ko·la \ˈkō-lə\ peninsula NW Russia bordering on Finland

Ko·rea \kə-ˈrē-ə\ peninsula E Asia between Yellow Sea & East Sea (Sea of Japan); divided 1948 into independent countries of North Korea & South Korea — **Ko·re·an** \kə-ˈrē-ən\ *adj or n*

Ko·ror \ˈkór-ˌór\ town, former ✻ of Palau

Kos·ci·us·ko, Mount \ˌkä-zē-ˈəs-(ˌ)kō, ˌkä-sē-\ mountain 7310 ft. (2228 m.) SE Australia in SE New South Wales; highest in Great Dividing Range & in Australia

Ko·so·vo \ˈkó-só-ˌvō, ˈkä-\ country S Europe in the Balkans

Kowloon — see JIULONG

Krak·a·tau \ˌkra-kə-ˈtau̇\ *or* **Krak·a·toa** \-ˈtō-ə\ island & volcano Indonesia between Sumatra & Java

Kra·kow \ˈkrä-ˌkau̇, ˈkra-, ˈkrā-, -(ˌ)kō, *Pol* ˈkrä-ˌküf\ city S Poland

Kras·no·dar \ˌkräs-nə-ˈdär\ city SW Russia

Kras·no·yarsk \ˌkräs-nə-ˈyärsk\ city S *cen* Russia

Kry·vyy Rih \kri-ˈvē-ˈrik̲\ *or* **Kri·voy Rog** \ˌkri-ˌvói-ˈrōg, -ˈrók\ city SE *cen* Ukraine

K2 \ˌkā-ˈtü\ *or* **God·win Aus·ten** \ˌgä-dwən-ˈós-tən, ˌgó-, -ˈäs-\ mountain 28,250 ft. (8611 m.) N Kashmir in Karakoram Range; second highest in the world

Kua·la Lum·pur \ˌkwä-lə-ˈlu̇m-ˌpu̇r, -ˈləm-, -ˌlu̇m-ˈ\ city, ✻ of Malaysia

Kuei–yang — see GUIYANG

Kun·lun \ˈkün-ˈlün\ mountain system W China extending E from the Pamirs; highest peak Muztag 25,340 ft. (7724 m.)

Kun·ming \ˈku̇n-ˈmiŋ\ city S China

Kur·di·stan \ˌku̇r-də-ˈstan, ˌkər-, -ˈstän; ˈkər-də-ˌ\ region SW Asia chiefly in E Turkey, NW Iran, & N Iraq — **Kurd** \ˈku̇rd, ˈkərd\ *n* — **Kurd·ish** \ˈku̇r-dish, ˈkər-\ *adj*

Ku·ril *or* **Ku·rile** \ˈkyu̇r-ˌēl, ˈku̇r-; kyu̇-ˈrēl,

kủ-\ islands Russia in W Pacific between Kamchatka Peninsula & Hokkaido Island

Ku•wait \kủ-ˈwāt\ **1** country SW Asia in Arabia at head of Persian Gulf **2** *or* **Kuwait City** city, its ✻ — **Ku•waiti** \-ˈwā-tē\ *adj or n*

Kuybyshev — see SAMARA

Kuz•netsk Basin \kủz-ˈnetsk\ *or* **Kuzbas** *or* **Kuz•bass** \ˈkủz-ˌbas\ basin S *cen* Russia

Kwa•ja•lein \ˈkwä-jə-lən, -ˌlān\ island W Pacific in Marshall Islands

Kwang•ju *or* **Gwang•ju** \ˈgwäŋ-(ˌ)jü\ city SW South Korea

Kwa•Zu•lu–Na•tal \kwä-ˈzü-(ˌ)lü-nə-ˈtäl\ province E Republic of South Africa

Ky•iv \ˈki-yē-ü, ˈkēv\ *or* **Ki•ev** \ˈkē-ˌef, -ˌev, -if\ city, ✻ of Ukraine

Kyo•to \kē-ˈōt-ō\ city Japan in W *cen* Honshu

Kyr•gyz•stan \ˌkir-gi-ˈstan, -ˈstän\ country W *cen* Asia; ✻, Bishkek

Kyu•shu \ˈkyü-(ˌ)shü\ island Japan S of W end of Honshu

Lab•ra•dor \ˈla-brə-ˌdȯr\ **1** peninsula E Canada between Hudson Bay & the Atlantic divided between the provinces of Quebec & Newfoundland and Labrador **2** the part of the peninsula belonging to the province of Newfoundland and Labrador — **Lab•ra•dor•ean** *or* **Lab•ra•dor•ian** \ˌla-brə-ˈdȯr-ē-ən\ *adj or n*

Lac•ca•dive \ˈla-kə-ˌdēv, -ˌdīv, -div\ islands India in Arabian Sea N of Maldive Islands

La•co•nia \lə-ˈkō-nē-ə, -nyə\ ancient country S Greece in SE Peloponnese; ✻, Sparta — **La•co•nian** \-nē-ən, -nyən\ *adj or n*

La•fay•ette \ˌla-fē-ˈet, ˌlä-\ city S Louisiana

La•gos \ˈlā-ˌgäs, -ˌgōs\ city, former ✻ (1960–91) of Nigeria

La•hore \lə-ˈhȯr\ city E Pakistan

Lake District region NW England containing many lakes & mountains

Lake•hurst \ˈlāk-(ˌ)hərst\ borough E New Jersey

Lake•wood \ˈlāk-ˌwủd\ city *cen* Colorado

Lam•beth \ˈlam-bəth, -ˌbeth\ borough of S Greater London, England

La•nai \lə-ˈnī, lä-\ island Hawaii W of Maui

Lan•ca•shire \ˈlaŋ-kə-ˌshir, -shər\ *or* **Lan•cas•ter** \ˈlaŋ-kəs-tər\ county NW England — **Lan•cas•tri•an** \laŋ-ˈkas-trē-ən, lan-\ *adj or n*

Lan•cas•ter \ˈlaŋ-kəs-tər, ˈlan-ˌkas-tər\ city NW England

Land's End \ˈlandz-ˈend\ cape SW England; most westerly point of England

Lan•sing \ˈlan-siŋ\ city, ✻ of Michigan

Lan•zhou *or* **Lan–chou** \ˈlän-ˈjō\ city W China

Laos \ˈlaủs, ˈlä-(ˌ)ōs, ˈlā-ˌäs\ country SE Asia in Indochina NE of Thailand; ✻, Vientiane — **Lao•tian** \lā-ˈō-shən, ˈlaủ-shən\ *adj or n*

La Paz \lä-ˈpäz, -ˈpäs\ city, administrative ✻ of Bolivia

Lap•land \ˈlap-ˌland, -lənd\ region N Europe above the Arctic Circle in N Norway, N Sweden, N Finland, & Kola Peninsula of Russia — **Lap•land•er** \-ˌlan-dər, -lən-\ *n*

La•re•do \lə-ˈrā-(ˌ)dō\ city S Texas on the Rio Grande

Larne \ˈlärn\ district NE Northern Ireland

Las•sen Peak \ˈla-sᵊn\ volcano 10,457 ft. (3187 m.) N California at S end of Cascade Range

Las Ve•gas \läs-ˈvā-gəs\ city SE Nevada

Latin America **1** Spanish America and Brazil **2** all of the Americas S of the U.S. — **Latin–American** *adj* — **Latin American** *n*

Latin Quarter section of Paris, France S of the Seine

Lat•via \ˈlat-vē-ə\ country E Europe on Baltic Sea; ✻, Riga

Lau•ren•tian Mountains \lȯ-ˈren(t)-shən\ hills E Canada in S Quebec N of the Saint Lawrence on S edge of Canadian Shield

Laurentian Plateau — see CANADIAN SHIELD

La•val \lə-ˈval\ city S Quebec NW of Montreal

Law•rence \ˈlȯr-ən(t)s, ˈlär-\ **1** city NE Kansas **2** city NE corner of Massachusetts

League of Nations political organization established at the end of World War I; replaced by United Nations 1946

Leb•a•non \ˈle-bə-nən\ **1** mountains Lebanon (country) running parallel to coast **2** country SW Asia on the Mediterranean; ✻, Beirut — **Leb•a•nese** \ˌle-bə-ˈnēz, -ˈnēs\ *adj or n*

Leeds \ˈlēdz\ city N England

Lee•ward Islands \ˈlē-wərd, ˈlü-ərd\ **1** islands Hawaii extending WNW from main islands of the group **2** islands South Pacific in W Society Islands **3** islands West Indies in N Lesser Antilles extending from Virgin Islands (on N) to Dominica (on S)

Le Ha•vre \lə-ˈhävrᵊ, -ˈhäv\ city N France on English Channel

Leh•man Caves \ˈlē-mən\ limestone caverns E Nevada

Leices•ter \ˈles-tər\ city *cen* England ENE of Birmingham

Leices•ter•shire \ˈles-tər-ˌshir, -shər\ *or* **Leicester** county *cen* England

Lein•ster \ˈlen(t)-stər\ province E Ireland

Leip•zig \ˈlīp-sig, -sik\ city E Germany

Le•na \ˈlē-nə, ˈlā-\ river about 2700 mi. (4345 km.) long E Russia, flowing NE &

N from mountains W of Lake Baikal into Arctic Ocean
Leningrad — see SAINT PETERSBURG
Le·ón \lā-ˈōn\ city *cen* Mexico
Ler·wick \ˈlər-(ˌ)wik, ˈler-\ town and port N Scotland in the Shetlands
Le·so·tho \lə-ˈsō-(ˌ)tō, -ˈsü-(ˌ)tü\ *formerly* **Ba·su·to·land** \bə-ˈsü-tō-ˌland\ country S Africa surrounded by Republic of South Africa; ✻, Maseru
Lesser Antilles islands in the West Indies including Virgin Islands, Leeward Islands, Windward Islands, Barbados, Trinidad, Tobago, & islands in the S Caribbean N of Venezuela — see GREATER ANTILLES
Le·vant \lə-ˈvant\ the countries bordering on the E Mediterranean — **Lev·an·tine** \ˈlev-ən-ˌtīn, -ˌtēn, lə-ˈvan-\ *adj or n*
Lew·es \ˈlü-əs\ town S England
Lew·i·sham \ˈlü-ə-shəm\ borough of SE Greater London, England
Lew·is with Har·ris \ˈlü-əs-with-ˈha-rəs, -with-\ island NW Scotland in Outer Hebrides
Lex·ing·ton \ˈlek-siŋ-tən\ **1** city NE *cen* Kentucky **2** town NE Massachusetts
Ley·te \ˈlā-tē\ island Philippines S of Samar
Lha·sa \ˈlä-sə, ˈla-\ city SW China, ✻ of Tibet
Li·be·ria \lī-ˈbir-ē-ə\ country W Africa on the North Atlantic; ✻, Monrovia — **Li·be·ri·an** \-ē-ən\ *adj or n*
Lib·er·ty \ˈli-bər-tē\ *formerly* **Bed·loe's** \ˈbed-ˌlōz\ island SE New York; site of the Statue of Liberty
Li·bre·ville \ˈlē-brə-ˌvil, -ˌvēl\ city, ✻ of Gabon
Lib·ya \ˈli-bē-ə\ country N Africa on the Mediterranean W of Egypt; ✻, Tripoli — **Lib·y·an** \ˈli-bē-ən\ *adj or n*
Libyan desert N Africa W of the Nile in Libya, Egypt, & Sudan
Liech·ten·stein \ˈlik-tən-ˌstīn, ˈlik-tən-ˌshtīn\ country W Europe between Austria & Switzerland; ✻, Vaduz — **Liech·ten·stein·er** \-ˌstī-nər, -ˌshtī-\ *n*
Lif·fey \ˈli-fē\ river 50 mi. (80 km.) long E Ireland
Li·gu·ria \lə-ˈgyu̇r-ē-ə\ region NW Italy on Ligurian Sea — **Li·gu·ri·an** \-ē-ən\ *adj or n*
Ligurian Sea arm of the Mediterranean N of Corsica
Li·long·we \li-ˈlȯŋ-(ˌ)gwā\ city, ✻ of Malawi
Li·ma \ˈlē-mə\ city, ✻ of Peru
Lim·a·vady \ˌli-mə-ˈva-dē\ district NW Northern Ireland
Lim·po·po \lim-ˈpō-(ˌ)pō\ river 1000 mi. (1609 km.) long Africa flowing from Republic of South Africa into Indian Ocean in Mozambique
Lin·coln \ˈliŋ-kən\ **1** city, ✻ of Nebraska **2** city E England
Lin·coln·shire \ˈliŋ-kən-ˌshir, -shər\ *or* **Lincoln** county E England
Line \ˈlīn\ islands Kiribati S of Hawaii
Lis·bon \ˈliz-bən\ *or Portuguese* **Lis·boa** \lēzh-ˈvō-ə\ city, ✻ of Portugal
Lis·burn \ˈliz-(ˌ)bərn\ district E Northern Ireland
Lith·u·a·nia \ˌli-thə-ˈwā-nē-ə, ˌli-thyə-, -nyə\ country E Europe; ✻, Vilnius
Lit·tle Rock \ˈli-tᵊl-ˌräk\ city, ✻ of Arkansas
Liv·er·pool \ˈli-vər-ˌpül\ city NW England
Li·vo·nia \lə-ˈvō-nē-ə, -nyə\ city SE Michigan
Lju·blja·na \lē-ˌü-blē-ˈä-nə\ city, ✻ of Slovenia
Lla·no Es·ta·ca·do \ˈla-(ˌ)nō-ˌes-tə-ˈkä-(ˌ)dō, ˈlä-, ˈyä-\ *or* **Staked Plain** \ˈstāk(t)-\ plateau region SE New Mexico & NW Texas
Lo·bam·ba \lō-ˈbäm-bə\ town, legislative ✻ of Eswatini
Lodz \ˈlüj, ˈlädz\ city *cen* Poland WSW of Warsaw
Lo·fo·ten \ˈlō-ˌfō-tᵊn\ islands NW Norway
Lo·gan, Mount \ˈlō-gən\ mountain 19,551 ft. (5959 m.) NW Canada in Saint Elias Range; highest in Canada & second highest in North America
Loire \lə-ˈwär, ˈlwär\ river 634 mi. (1020 km.) long *cen* France flowing NW & W into Bay of Biscay
Lo·mé \lō-ˈmā\ city, ✻ of Togo
Lo·mond, Loch \ˈlō-mənd\ lake S *cen* Scotland
Lon·don \ˈlən-dən\ **1** city SE Ontario, Canada **2** city, ✻ of England & of United Kingdom on the Thames; consists of **City of London** & Greater London metropolitan county — **Lon·don·er** \-də-nər\ *n*
Londonderry — see DERRY
Long Beach city SW California S of Los Angeles
Long Island island 118 mi. (190 km.) long SE New York S of Connecticut
Long Island Sound inlet of the Atlantic between Connecticut & Long Island, New York
Lon·gueuil \lȯŋ-ˈgāl\ city Canada in S Quebec E of Montreal
Lor·raine \lə-ˈrān, lȯ-\ region NE France
Los An·ge·les \lȯs-ˈan-jə-ləs\ city SW California
Lou·ise, Lake \lu̇-ˈēz\ lake SW Alberta, Canada
Lou·i·si·ana \lu̇-ˌē-zē-ˈa-nə, ˌlü-ə-zē-, ˌlü-zē-\ state S U.S.; ✻, Baton Rouge — **Lou·i·si·an·ian** \-ˈa-nē-ən, -ˈa-nyən\ *or* **Lou·i·si·an·an** \-ˈa-nən\ *adj or n*
Louisiana Purchase area W *cen* U.S. between Rocky Mountains & the Mississippi purchased 1803 from France
Lou·is·ville \ˈlü-i-ˌvil, -vəl\ city N Kentucky on the Ohio River
Low Countries region W Europe consisting of modern Belgium, Luxembourg, & the Netherlands

Low·ell \ˈlō-əl\ city NE Massachusetts NW of Boston
Lower 48 the continental states of the U.S. excluding Alaska
Low·lands \ˈlō-ləndz, -ˌlandz\ the *cen* & E part of Scotland
Lu·an·da \lu̇-ˈän-də\ city, ✻ of Angola
Lub·bock \ˈlə-bək\ city NW Texas
Lu·bum·ba·shi \ˌlü-büm-ˈbä-shē\ city SE Democratic Republic of the Congo
Luck·now \ˈlək-ˌnau̇\ city N India ESE of Delhi
Lüda *or* **Lü–ta** — see DALIAN
Lu·ray Caverns \ˈlü-ˌrā, lü-ˈ\ series of caves N Virginia
Lu·sa·ka \lü-ˈsä-kä\ city, ✻ of Zambia
Lü·shun \ˈlü-ˈshu̇n, ˈlue-\ *or* **Port Ar·thur** \-ˈär-thər\ seaport NE China; part of greater Dalian
Lu·ton \ˈlü-tᵊn\ town SE *cen* England
Lux·em·bourg *or* **Lux·em·burg** \ˈlək-səm-ˌbərg, ˈlu̇k-səm-ˌbu̇rk\ **1** country W Europe bordered by Belgium, France, & Germany **2** city, its ✻ — **Lux·em·bourg·er** \-ˌbər-gər, -ˌbu̇r-\ *n* — **Lux·em·bourg·ian** \ˌlək-səm-ˈbər-gē-ən, ˌlu̇k-səm-ˈbu̇r-\ *adj*
Lu·zon \lü-ˈzän\ island N Philippines
L'viv \lə-ˈvē-ü, -ˈvēf\ *or* **L'vov** \lə-ˈvȯf, -ˈvȯv\ *or Polish* **Lwów** \lə-ˈvüf, -ˈvüv\ city W Ukraine
Lyallpur — see FAISALABAD
Lyd·ia \ˈli-dē-ə\ ancient country W Asia Minor on the Aegean — **Lyd·i·an** \-ē-ən\ *adj or n*
Lyon \ˈlyōⁿ\ *or* **Lyons** \lē-ˈōⁿ, ˈlī-ənz\ city SE *cen* France
Ma·cao *or Portuguese* **Ma·cau** \mə-ˈkau̇\ *or Chinese* **Ao·men** \ˈau̇-ˈmən\ **1** special administrative region on coast of SE China W of Hong Kong **2** city, its ✻ — **Mac·a·nese** \ˌmä-kə-ˈnēz, -ˈnēs\ *n*
Mac·e·do·nia \ˌma-sə-ˈdō-nē-ə, -nyə\ **1** region S Europe in Balkan Peninsula in NE Greece, the former Yugoslav section & now independent country of North Macedonia, & SW Bulgaria including territory of ancient kingdom of Macedonia (**Mac·e·don** \ˈmas-ə-dən, -ə-ˌdän\ ) **2** *or now officially* **North Macedonia** country S *cen* Balkan Peninsula; ✻, Skopje; a former republic of Yugoslavia — **Mac·e·do·nian** \ˌmas-ə-ˈdō-nyən, -nē-ən\ *adj or n*
Mac·gil·li·cud·dy's Reeks \mə-ˈgi-lə-ˌkə-dēz-ˈrēks\ mountains SW Ireland; highest Carrantuohill 3414 ft. (1041 m.)
Ma·chu Pic·chu \ˌmä-(ˌ)chü-ˈpē-(ˌ)chü, -ˈpēk-\ site SE Peru of ancient Inca city
Mac·ken·zie \mə-ˈken-zē\ river 1120 mi. (1802 km.) long NW Canada flowing from Great Slave Lake NW into Beaufort Sea
Mack·i·nac, Straits of \ˈma-kə-ˌnȯ, -ˌnak\ channel N Michigan connecting Lake Huron & Lake Michigan
Ma·con \ˈmā-kən\ city *cen* Georgia
Mad·a·gas·car \ˌma-də-ˈgas-kər, -kär\ *formerly* **Mal·a·gasy Re·public** \ˌma-lə-ˈga-sē\ island country W Indian Ocean off SE Africa; ✻, Antananarivo — **Mad·a·gas·can** \ˌma-də-ˈgas-kən\ *adj or n*
Ma·dei·ra \mə-ˈdir-ə, -ˈder-ə\ **1** river 2013 mi. (3239 km.) long W Brazil flowing NE into the Amazon **2** islands Portugal in the North Atlantic N of the Canary Islands **3** island; chief of the Madeira group — **Ma·dei·ran** \-ˈdir-ən, -ˈder-\ *adj or n*
Ma·di·nat ash Sha'b \mə-ˈdē-ˌnə-tash-ˈshab\ city S Yemen
Mad·i·son \ˈma-də-sən\ city, ✻ of Wisconsin
Ma·dras \mə-ˈdras, -ˈdräs\ *or now officially* **Chen·nai** \ˈche-ˌnī\ city SE India
Ma·drid \mə-ˈdrid\ city, ✻ of Spain
Ma·du·rai \ˌmä-də-ˈrī\ city S India
Mag·da·len Islands \ˈmag-də-lən\ *or F* **îles de la Ma·de·leine** \ˌēl-də-lä-mäd-ˈlen, -mä-də-ˈlen\ islands Canada in Gulf of Saint Lawrence between Newfoundland & Prince Edward Island
Ma·gel·lan, Strait of \mə-ˈje-lən, *chiefly Brit* -ˈge-\ strait at S end of South America between mainland & Tierra del Fuego
Magh·er·a·felt \ˈmär-ə-ˌfelt, ˈma-k̲ə-rə-ˌfelt\ district *cen* Northern Ireland
Maid·stone \ˈmād-stən, -ˌstōn\ town SE England
Main \ˈmīn, ˈmān\ river 325 mi. (523 km.) long S *cen* Germany flowing W into the Rhine
Maine \ˈmān\ state NE U.S.; ✻, Augusta — **Main·er** \ˈmā-nər\ *n*
Ma·jor·ca \mä-ˈjȯr-kə, mə-, -ˈyȯr-\ *or Spanish* **Ma·llor·ca** \mä-ˈyȯr-kä\ island Spain in W Mediterranean — **Ma·jor·can** \-ˈjȯr-kən, -ˈyȯr\ *adj or n*
Ma·ju·ro \mə-ˈju̇r-(ˌ)ō\ atoll that contains ✻ of Marshall Islands
Mal·a·bar Coast \ˈma-lə-ˌbär\ region SW India on Arabian Sea
Ma·la·bo \mä-ˈlä-(ˌ)bō\ city, ✻ of Equatorial Guinea
Ma·lac·ca, Strait of \mə-ˈla-kə, -ˈlä-\ channel between S Malay Peninsula & island of Sumatra
Ma·la·wi \mə-ˈlä-wē\ *formerly* **Ny·asa·land** \nī-ˈa-sə-ˌland, nē-\ country SE Africa on Lake Nyasa; ✻, Lilongwe — **Ma·la·wi·an** \-ən\ *adj or n*
Ma·lay \mə-ˈlā, ˈmā-(ˌ)lā\ **1** archipelago SE Asia including Sumatra, Java, Borneo, Sulawesi, Moluccas, & Timor; usu. thought to include the Philippines & sometimes New Guinea **2** peninsula SE Asia divided between Thailand & Malaysia (country)
Ma·laya \mə-ˈlā-ə, mā-\ **1** the Malay Peninsula **2** former country SE Asia on Malay Peninsula; now part of Malaysia
Ma·lay·sia \mə-ˈlā-zh(ē-)ə, -sh(ē-)ə\ **1** the Malay Archipelago **2** the Malay Penin-

sula & Malay Archipelago **3** country SE Asia; ✻, Kuala Lumpur — **Ma·lay·sian** \mə-ˈlā-zhən, -shən\ *adj or n*

Mal·dives \ˈmȯl-ˌdēvz, -ˌdīvz\ islands in Indian Ocean SW of Sri Lanka; country; ✻, Male Atoll — **Mal·div·i·an** \mȯl-ˈdi-vē-ən, mal-\ *adj or n*

Ma·le \ˈmä-lē\ atoll containing national ✻ of Maldives

Ma·li \ˈmä-lē, ˈma-\ country W Africa; ✻, Bamako — **Ma·li·an** \-lē-ən\ *adj or n*

Mal·ta \ˈmȯl-tə\ islands in the Mediterranean S of Sicily; country since 1964; ✻, Valletta — **Mal·tese** \mȯl-ˈtēz, -ˈtēs\ *adj or n*

Malvinas, Islas — see FALKLAND ISLANDS

Mam·moth Cave \ˈma-məth\ limestone caverns SW *cen* Kentucky

Man, Isle of \ˈman\ island British Isles in Irish Sea; has own legislature & laws

Ma·na·gua \mä-ˈnä-gwä\ city, ✻ of Nicaragua

Ma·na·ma \mə-ˈna-mə\ city, ✻ of Bahrain

Man·ches·ter \ˈman-ˌches-tər, -chəs-tər\ **1** city S *cen* New Hampshire **2** city NW England

Man·chu·ria \man-ˈchu̇r-ē-ə\ region NE China S of the Amur — **Man·chu·ri·an** \-ē-ən\ *adj or n*

Man·hat·tan \man-ˈha-tᵊn, mən-\ **1** island SE New York in New York City **2** borough of New York City consisting chiefly of Manhattan Island

Ma·nila \mə-ˈni-lə\ city, ✻ of Philippines in W Luzon

Man·i·to·ba \ˌma-nə-ˈtō-bə\ province *cen* Canada; ✻, Winnipeg — **Man·i·to·ban** \-bən\ *adj or n*

Man·i·tou·lin \ˌma-nə-ˈtü-lən\ island 80 mi. (129 km.) long S Ontario in Lake Huron

Ma·pu·to \mä-ˈpü-(ˌ)tō, -(ˌ)tü\ city, ✻ of Mozambique

Mar·a·cai·bo \ˌma-rə-ˈkī-(ˌ)bō, ˌmär-ä-\ city NW Venezuela

Maracaibo, Lake extension of a gulf of the Caribbean NW Venezuela

Mar·a·thon \ˈma-rə-ˌthän\ plain E Greece NE of Athens

Mar·i·ana \ˌmer-ē-ˈa-nə\ islands W Pacific N of Caroline Islands; comprise Commonwealth of Northern Mariana Islands & Guam

Mariana Trench ocean trench W Pacific extending from SE of Guam to NW of Mariana Islands; deepest in world

Ma·rin·du·que \ˌma-rən-ˈdü-(ˌ)kā, ˌmär-ēn-\ island *cen* Philippines

Maritime Provinces the Canadian provinces of New Brunswick, Nova Scotia, & Prince Edward Island & formerly thought by some to include Newfoundland and Labrador

Ma·ri·u·pol \ˌma-rē-ˈü-ˌpȯl, -pəl\ *or 1949–89* **Zhda·nov** \zhə-ˈdä-nəf\ city E Ukraine

Mar·ma·ra, Sea of \ˈmär-mə-rə\ sea NW Turkey connected with Black Sea by the Bosporus & with Aegean Sea by the Dardanelles

Marne \ˈmärn\ river 325 mi. (523 km.) long NE France flowing W into the Seine

Mar·que·sas \mär-ˈkā-zəz, -zəs, -səz, -səs\ islands South Pacific; belonging to France — **Mar·que·san** \-zən, -sən\ *adj or n*

Mar·ra·kech \ˌma-rə-ˈkesh, ˈma-rə-ˌ, mə-ˈrä-kish\ city *cen* Morocco

Mar·seille \mär-ˈsā\ *or* **Mar·seilles** \mär-ˈsā, -ˈsālz\ city SE France

Mar·shall Islands \ˈmär-shəl\ islands W Pacific E of the Carolines; republic, in association with U.S.; ✻, Majuro

Mar·tha's Vineyard \ˈmär-thəz\ island SE Massachusetts off SW coast of Cape Cod WNW of Nantucket

Mar·ti·nique \ˌmär-tə-ˈnēk\ island West Indies in the Windward Islands; an overseas division of France; ✻, Fort-de-France

Mary·land \ˈmer-ə-lənd\ state E U.S.; ✻, Annapolis — **Mary·land·er** \-lən-dər, -ˌlan-\ *n*

Mas·ba·te \mäz-ˈbä-tē, mäs-\ island *cen* Philippines

Mas·e·ru \ˈma-sə-ˌrü, -zə-\ city, ✻ of Lesotho

Mash·had \mə-ˈshad\ city NE Iran

Ma·son–Dix·on Line \ˈmā-sᵊn-ˈdik-sən\ boundary between Maryland & Pennsylvania; often considered the boundary between N & S states

Masqat — see MUSCAT

Mas·sa·chu·setts \ˌma-sə-ˈchü-səts, -zəts\ state NE U.S.; ✻, Boston

Mat·a·be·le·land \ˌma-tə-ˈbē-lē-ˌland, ˌmä-tä-ˈbā-lā-\ region SW Zimbabwe

Mat·lock \ˈmat-ˌläk\ town N England

Mat·ter·horn \ˈma-tər-ˌhȯrn, ˈmä-\ mountain 14,691 ft. (4478 m.) on border between Switzerland & Italy

Maui \ˈmau̇-ē\ island Hawaii NW of Hawaii Island

Mau·na Kea \ˌmau̇-nä-ˈkā-ä, ˌmȯ-\ extinct volcano 13,796 ft. (4205 m.) Hawaii in N *cen* Hawaii Island

Mau·na Loa \-ˈlō-ə\ volcano 13,680 ft. (4170 m.) Hawaii in S *cen* Hawaii Island

Mau·re·ta·nia *or* **Mau·ri·ta·nia** \ˌmȯr-ə-ˈtā-nē-ə, ˌmär-, -nyə\ ancient country NW Africa in modern Morocco & W Algeria — **Mau·re·ta·ni·an** *or* **Mau·ri·ta·ni·an** \-nē-ən, -nyən\ *adj or n*

Mauritania country NW Africa on the Atlantic N of Senegal River; ✻, Nouakchott — **Mauritanian** *adj or n*

Mau·ri·tius \mȯ-ˈri-sh(ē-)əs\ island in Indian Ocean E of Madagascar; country; ✻, Port Louis — **Mau·ri·tian** \-ˈri-shən\ *adj or n*

May, Cape \ˈmā\ cape S New Jersey at entrance to Delaware Bay

Ma•yon, Mount \mä-ˈyōn\ volcano 8077 ft. (2462 m.) Philippines in SE Luzon

Ma•yotte \mä-ˈyät, -ˈyȯt\ island Comoros group; French dependency — see COMOROS

Ma•za•ma, Mount \mə-ˈzäm-ə\ prehistoric mountain SW Oregon the collapse of whose top formed Crater Lake

Mba•bane \ˌəm-bä-ˈbä-nā\ town, administrative ✻ of Eswatini

Mbi•ni \em-ˈbē-nē\ *formerly* **Río Mu•ni** \ˌrē-ō-ˈmü-nē\ mainland portion of Equatorial Guinea

Mc•Al•len \mə-ˈka-lən\ city S Texas

McKinley, Mount — see DENALI

Mead, Lake \ˈmēd\ reservoir NW Arizona & SE Nevada formed by Hoover Dam in Colorado River

Mec•ca \ˈme-kə\ city W Saudi Arabia; contains Islam's Great Mosque

Me•dan \mā-ˈdän\ city Indonesia, in N Sumatra

Me•de•llín \ˌme-də-ˈlēn, ˌmā-thā-ˈyēn\ city NW Colombia

Me•di•na \mə-ˈdī-nə\ city W Saudi Arabia

Med•i•ter•ra•nean \ˌme-də-tə-ˈrā-nē-ən, -nyən\ sea 2300 mi. (3700 km.) long between Europe & Africa connecting with the Atlantic through Strait of Gibraltar

Me•kong \ˈmā-ˈkȯŋ, -ˈkäŋ; ˈmā-ˌ\ river 2600 mi. (4184 km.) long SE Asia flowing from E Tibet S & SE into South China Sea in S Vietnam

Mel•a•ne•sia \ˌme-lə-ˈnē-zhə, -shə\ islands of the Pacific NE of Australia & S of Micronesia including Bismarck, the Solomons, Vanuatu, New Caledonia, & the Fijis

Mel•bourne \ˈmel-bərn\ city SE Australia, ✻ of Victoria

Mel•e•ke•ok \ˈme-lə-ˌkā-ˌȯk\ town, ✻ of Palau

Melos — see MÍLOS

Mel•ville \ˈmel-ˌvil\ **1** island N Canada, split between Northwest Territories & Nunavut **2** peninsula Canada in Nunavut

Mem•phis \ˈmem(p)-fəs\ **1** city SW Tennessee **2** ancient city N Egypt S of modern Cairo

Mem•phre•ma•gog, Lake \ˌmem(p)-fri-ˈmā-ˌgäg\ lake on border between Canada (Quebec) & United States (Vermont)

Men•do•ci•no, Cape \ˌmen-də-ˈsē-(ˌ)nō\ cape NW California

Mer•cia \ˈmər-sh(ē-)ə\ ancient Anglo-Saxon kingdom *cen* England — **Mer•cian** \ˈmər-shən\ *adj or n*

Mer•sey \ˈmər-zē\ river 70 mi. (113 km.) long NW England flowing NW & W into Irish Sea

Mer•sey•side \ˈmər-zē-ˌsīd\ metropolitan county NW England; includes Liverpool

Mer•ton \ˈmər-tᵊn\ borough of SW Greater London, England

Me•sa \ˈmā-sə\ city S *cen* Arizona

Me•sa•bi Range \mə-ˈsä-bē\ region NE Minnesota that contains iron ore

Mes•o•po•ta•mia \ˌme-s(ə-)pə-ˈtā-mē-ə, -myə\ **1** region SW Asia between Euphrates & Tigris rivers **2** the entire Tigris–Euphrates valley — **Mes•o•po•ta•mian** \-mē-ən, -myən\ *adj or n*

Mes•quite \mə-ˈskēt, me-\ city NE Texas E of Dallas

Meuse \ˈmyüz, ˈmə(r)z, ˈmœz\ river 580 mi. (933 km.) long W Europe flowing from NE France into North Sea in the Netherlands

Mex•i•co \ˈmek-si-ˌkō\ **1** country S North America **2** *or* **Mexico City** city, its ✻ — **Mex•i•can** \ˈmek-si-kən\ *adj or n*

Mexico, Gulf of inlet of the Atlantic SE North America

Mi•ami \mī-ˈa-mē\ city & port SE Florida

Miami Beach city SE Florida

Mich•i•gan \ˈmi-shi-gən\ state N *cen* U.S.; ✻, Lansing — **Mich•i•gan•der** \ˌmi-shi-ˈgan-dər\ *n* — **Mich•i•ga•ni•an** \ˌmi-shə-ˈgā-nē-ən, -ˈga-\ *n* — **Mich•i•gan•ite** \ˈmi-shi-gə-ˌnīt\ *n*

Michigan, Lake lake N *cen* U.S.; one of the Great Lakes

Mi•cro•ne•sia \ˌmī-krə-ˈnē-zhə, -shə\ islands of the W Pacific E of the Philippines & N of Melanesia including Caroline, Kiribati, Mariana, & Marshall groups — **Mi•cro•ne•sian** \-zhən, -shən\ *adj or n*

Micronesia, Federated States of islands W Pacific in the Carolines; country in association with U.S.; ✻, Palikir

Middle East the countries of SW Asia & N Africa — usually thought to include the countries extending from Libya on the W to Afghanistan on the E — **Middle Eastern** *adj*

Mid•dles•brough \ˈmi-dᵊlz-brə\ town N England

Middle West — see MIDWEST

Mid Gla•mor•gan \ˈmid-glə-ˈmȯr-gən\ former county SE Wales

Mid•i•an \ˈmi-dē-ən\ ancient region NW Arabia E of Gulf of Aqaba — **Mid•i•an•ite** \-ē-ə-ˌnīt\ *n*

Mid•lands \ˈmid-ləndz\ the *cen* counties of England

Mid•way \ˈmid-ˌwā\ islands *cen* Pacific 1300 mi. (2092 km.) WNW of Honolulu belonging to U.S.

Mid•west \ˌmid-ˈwest\ *or* **Middle West** region N *cen* U.S. including area around Great Lakes & in upper Mississippi valley from Ohio on the E to North Dakota, South Dakota, Nebraska, & Kansas on the W — **Mid•west•ern** \ˌmid-ˈwes-tərn\ *or* **Middle Western** *adj* — **Mid•west•ern•er** \ˌmid-ˈwes-tə(r)-nər\ *or* **Middle Westerner** *n*

Mi•lan \mə-ˈlan, -ˈlän\ *or Italian* **Mi•la•no**

\mē-ˈlä-(ˌ)nō\ city NW Italy — **Mil·a·nese** \ˌmi-lə-ˈnēz, -ˈnēs\ *adj or n*

Mí·los *or* **Me·los** \ˈmē-ˌlȯs\ island Greece

Mil·wau·kee \mil-ˈwȯ-kē\ city SE Wisconsin on Lake Michigan

Mi·nas Basin \ˈmī-nəs\ bay *cen* Nova Scotia; NE extension of Bay of Fundy

Min·da·nao \ˌmin-də-ˈnä-ˌō, -ˈnau̇\ island S Philippines

Min·do·ro \min-ˈdȯr-(ˌ)ō\ island *cen* Philippines

Min·ne·ap·o·lis \ˌmi-nē-ˈa-pə-lis\ city SE Minnesota

Min·ne·so·ta \ˌmi-nə-ˈsō-tə\ state N *cen* U.S.; ✻, Saint Paul — **Min·ne·so·tan** \-ˈsō-tᵊn\ *adj or n*

Mi·nor·ca \mə-ˈnȯr-kə\ island Spain in W Mediterranean — **Mi·nor·can** \mə-ˈnȯr-kən\ *adj or n*

Minsk \ˈmin(t)sk\ city, ✻ of Belarus

Mis·sis·sau·ga \ˌmi-sə-ˈsȯ-gə\ city Canada in S Ontario

Mis·sis·sip·pi \ˌmi-sə-ˈsi-pē\ **1** river 2340 mi. (3765 km.) long *cen* U.S. flowing into Gulf of Mexico — see ITASCA, LAKE **2** state S U.S.; ✻, Jackson

Mis·sou·ri \mə-ˈzu̇r-ē\ **1** river 2466 mi. (3968 km.) long W U.S. flowing from SW Montana to the Mississippi in E Missouri (state) **2** state *cen* U.S.; ✻, Jefferson City — **Mis·sou·ri·an** \-ˈzu̇r-ē-ən\ *adj or n*

Mitch·ell, Mount \ˈmi-chəl\ mountain 6684 ft. (2037 m.) W North Carolina in the Appalachians; highest in U.S. E of the Mississippi

Mo·bile \mō-ˈbēl, ˈmō-ˌbēl\ city SW Alabama on **Mobile Bay** (inlet of Gulf of Mexico)

Mo·des·to \mə-ˈdes-(ˌ)tō\ city *cen* California

Mog·a·di·shu \ˌmä-gə-ˈdi-(ˌ)shü, ˌmō-, -ˈdē-\ *or* **Mog·a·di·scio** \-(ˌ)shō\ city, ✻ of Somalia

Mo·hawk \ˈmō-ˌhȯk\ river E *cen* New York flowing into the Hudson

Mo·hen·jo Da·ro \mō-ˈhen-(ˌ)jō-ˈdär-(ˌ)ō\ prehistoric city in valley of the Indus NE of modern Karachi, Pakistan

Mo·ja·ve *or* **Mo·ha·ve** \mə-ˈhä-vē, mō-\ desert S California SE of S end of Sierra Nevada

Mol·da·via \mäl-ˈdā-vē-ə, -vyə\ region E Europe in NE Romania & Moldova — **Mol·da·vian** \-vē-ən, -vyən\ *adj or n*

Mol·do·va \mäl-ˈdō-və, mȯl-\ country E Europe in E Moldavia region; ✻, Chişinău — **Mol·do·van** \-vən\ *adj or n*

Mol·o·kai \ˌmä-lə-ˈkī, ˌmō-lō-ˈkä-ē\ island Hawaii ESE of Oahu

Mo·luc·cas \mə-ˈlə-kəz\ islands Indonesia E of Sulawesi — **Mo·luc·ca** \mə-ˈlə-kə\ *adj* — **Mo·luc·can** \-kən\ *adj or n*

Mom·ba·sa city & port S Kenya

Mo·na·co \ˈmä-nə-ˌkō\ country W Europe on Mediterranean coast of France; ✻, Monaco — **Mo·na·can** \ˈmä-nə-kən, mə-ˈnä-kən\ *adj or n* — **Mon·e·gasque** \ˌmä-ni-ˈgask\ *n*

Mon·go·lia \män-ˈgōl-yə, mäŋ-, -ˈgō-lē-ə\ **1** region E Asia E of Altay Mountains; includes Gobi Desert **2** country E Asia consisting of major portion of Mongolia region; ✻, Ulaanbaatar

Mo·non·ga·he·la \mə-ˌnän-gə-ˈhē-lə, -ˌnäŋ-gə-, -ˈhā-lə\ river N West Virginia & SW Pennsylvania

Mon·ro·via \(ˌ)mən-ˈrō-vē-ə\ city, ✻ of Liberia

Mon·tana \män-ˈta-nə\ state NW U.S.; ✻, Helena — **Mon·tan·an** \-nən\ *adj or n*

Mont Blanc \ˌmōⁿ-ˈbläⁿ\ mountain 15,771 ft. (4807 m.) SE France on Italian border; highest in the Alps

Mon·te·go Bay \män-ˈtē-(ˌ)gō\ city & port NW Jamaica on **Montego Bay** (inlet of the Caribbean)

Mon·te·ne·gro \ˌmän-tə-ˈnē-(ˌ)grō, -ˈnā-, -ˈne-\ country S Europe on the Adriatic Sea; ✻, Podgorica

Mon·ter·rey \ˌmän-tə-ˈrā\ city NE Mexico

Mon·te·vi·deo \ˌmän-tə-və-ˈdā-(ˌ)ō, -ˈvi-dē-ˌō; ˌmȯn-tā-vē-ˈthā-ō\ city, ✻ of Uruguay

Mont·gom·ery \(ˌ)mən(t)-ˈgə-mə-rē, män(t)-, -ˈgä-; -ˈgəm-rē, -ˈgäm-\ city, ✻ of Alabama

Mont·pe·lier \mänt-ˈpēl-yər, -ˈpil-\ city, ✻ of Vermont

Mon·tre·al \ˌmän-trē-ˈȯl, ˌmən-\ city S Quebec, Canada on **Montreal Island** in the Saint Lawrence

Mont·ser·rat \ˌmän(t)-sə-ˈrat\ island British West Indies in the Leeward Islands

Mo·ra·via \mə-ˈrā-vē-ə\ region E Czech Republic — **Mo·ra·vi·an** \mə-ˈrā-vē-ən\ *adj or n*

Mo·re·no Valley \mə-ˈrē-(ˌ)nō\ city S California

Mo·roc·co \mə-ˈrä-(ˌ)kō\ country NW Africa; ✻, Rabat — **Mo·roc·can** \-kən\ *adj or n*

Mo·ro·ni \mȯ-ˈrō-nē\ city, ✻ of Comoros

Mos·cow \ˈmäs-(ˌ)kō, -ˌkau̇\ *or Russian* **Mos·kva** \mäsk-ˈvä\ city, ✻ of Russia

Mo·selle \mō-ˈzel\ river about 340 mi. (545 km.) long E France & W Germany

Moyle \ˈmȯi(-ə)l\ district N Northern Ireland

Mo·zam·bique \ˌmō-zəm-ˈbēk\ **1** channel SE Africa between Mozambique (country) & Madagascar **2** country SE Africa; ✻, Maputo — **Mo·zam·bi·can** \ˌmō-zəm-ˈbē-kən\ *adj or n*

Mpu·ma·lan·ga \əm-ˌpü-mä-ˈläŋ-gä\ province NE Republic of South Africa

Mukden — see SHENYANG

Mul·tan \mu̇l-ˈtän\ city NE Pakistan SW of Lahore

Mumbai — see BOMBAY

Mu·nich \ˈmyü-nik\ *or German* **Mün·chen** \ˈmu̇en-kən\ city S Germany in Bavaria

Mun·ster \ˈmən(t)-stər\ province S Ireland

Mur·cia \ˈmər-sh(ē-)ə\ region & ancient kingdom SE Spain

Mur·ray \ˈmər-ē, ˈmə-rē\ river over 1560 mi. (2510 km.) long SE Australia flowing W from E Victoria into Indian Ocean in South Australia

Mur·rum·bidg·ee \ˌmər-əm-ˈbi-jē, ˌmə-rəm-\ river almost 1000 mi. (1609 km.) long SE Australia in New South Wales flowing W into the Murray

Mus·cat \ˈməs-ˌkät, -ˌkat, -kət\ *or* **Mas·qat** \ˈməs-ˌkät\ town E Arabia; ✻ of Oman

Muz·tag \müs-ˈtäg, məz-\ mountain 25,340 ft. (7724 m.) W China; highest in Kunlun Mountains

Myan·mar \ˈmyän-ˌmär\ *or unofficially* **Bur·ma** \ˈbər-mə\ country SE Asia; ✻, Nay Pyi Taw

My·ce·nae \mī-ˈsē-(ˌ)nē\ ancient city S Greece in NE Peloponnese

Myr·tle Beach \ˈmər-tᵊl\ city E South Carolina on the Atlantic

My·sore \mī-ˈsȯr\ city S India

Nab·a·taea *or* **Nab·a·tea** \ˌna-bə-ˈtē-ə\ ancient Arab kingdom SE of Palestine — **Nab·a·tae·an** *or* **Nab·a·te·an** \-ˈtē-ən\ *adj or n*

Na·goya \nə-ˈgȯi-ə, ˈnä-gȯ-(ˌ)yä\ city Japan in S *cen* Honshu

Nag·pur \ˈnäg-ˌpu̇r\ city E *cen* India

Nai·ro·bi \nī-ˈrō-bē\ city, ✻ of Kenya

Na·mib·ia \nə-ˈmi-bē-ə\ *formerly* **South–West Africa** country SW Africa on the Atlantic; ✻, Windhoek — **Na·mib·ian** \-bē-ən, -byən\ *adj or n*

Nan·chang \ˈnän-ˈchäŋ\ city SE China

Nan·jing \ˈnän-ˈjiŋ\ *or* **Nan·king** \ˈnan-ˈkiŋ, ˈnän-\ city E China

Nan·tuck·et \nan-ˈtə-kət\ island SE Massachusetts S of Cape Cod

Na·per·ville \ˈnā-pər-ˌvil\ city NE Illinois W of Chicago

Na·ples \ˈnā-pəlz\ *or Italian* **Na·po·li** \ˈnä-pō-lē\ *ancient* **Ne·ap·o·lis** \nē-ˈa-pə-ləs\ city S Italy on Bay of Naples — **Ne·a·pol·i·tan** \ˌnē-ə-ˈpäl-ə-tən\ *adj or n*

Nar·ra·gan·sett Bay \ˌna-rə-ˈgan(t)-sət\ inlet of the Atlantic SE Rhode Island

Nash·ville \ˈnash-ˌvil, -vəl\ city, ✻ of Tennessee

Nas·sau \ˈna-ˌsȯ\ city, ✻ of Bahamas on New Providence Island

Na·tal \nə-ˈtal, -ˈtäl\ former province E Republic of South Africa

Na·u·ru \nä-ˈü-(ˌ)rü\ island W South Pacific; country; ✻, Yaren — **Na·u·ru·an** \-ˈü-rə-wən\ *adj or n*

Nay Pyi Taw *or* **Nay·pyi·daw** \ˈnē-pyē-ˌdȯ\ site of ✻ of Myanmar

Naz·a·reth \ˈna-zə-rəth\ town of ancient Palestine in *cen* Galilee; now a city of N Israel

N'Dja·me·na \ən-jä-ˈmā-nä, -ˈmē-\ city, ✻ of Chad

Neagh, Lough \ˌläk-ˈnā\ lake Northern Ireland; largest in British Isles

Near East the countries of NE Africa & SW Asia — **Near Eastern** *adj*

Ne·bras·ka \nə-ˈbras-kə\ state *cen* U.S.; ✻, Lincoln — **Ne·bras·kan** \-kən\ *adj or n*

Neg·ev \ˈne-ˌgev\ desert region S Israel

Ne·gro \ˈnā-(ˌ)grō, ˈne-\ river 1400 mi. (2253 km.) long in E Colombia & N Brazil flowing into the Amazon

Ne·gros \ˈnā-(ˌ)grōs, ˈne-\ island *cen* Philippines

Nei Monggol — see INNER MONGOLIA

Ne·pal \nə-ˈpȯl, nā-\ country Asia on NE border of India in the Himalayas; ✻, Kathmandu — **Nep·a·lese** \ˌne-pə-ˈlēz, -ˈlēs\ *adj or n* — **Ne·pali** \nə-ˈpȯl-ē, -ˈpäl-, -ˈpal-\ *adj or n*

Ness, Loch \ˈnes\ lake NW Scotland

Neth·er·lands \ˈne-t͟hər-ləndz\ **1** *or Dutch* **Ne·der·land** \ˈnād-ər-ˌlänt\ *also* **Holland** country NW Europe on North Sea; ✻, Amsterdam; seat of the government, The Hague **2** LOW COUNTRIES — an historical usage — **Neth·er·land** \ˈne-t͟hər-lənd\ *adj* — **Neth·er·land·er** \-ˌlan-dər, -lən-\ *n* — **Neth·er·land·ish** \-ˌlan-dish, -lən-\ *adj*

Netherlands Antilles islands of the West Indies, formerly an overseas territory of the Netherlands; ✻, Willemstad

Ne·va \ˈnē-və, ˈnā-, nye-ˈvä\ river 40 mi. (64 km.) long W Russia; flows through Saint Petersburg

Ne·vada \nə-ˈva-də\ state W U.S.; ✻, Carson City — **Ne·vad·an** \-ˈva-dᵊn, -ˈvä-\ *or* **Ne·vad·i·an** \-ˈva-dē-ən, -ˈvä-\ *adj or n*

Ne·vis \ˈnē-vəs\ island West Indies in the Leeward Islands — see SAINT KITTS

New Amsterdam town founded 1625 on island of Manhattan by the Dutch; renamed New York 1664 by the British

New·ark \ˈnü-ərk, ˈnyü-\ city NE New Jersey

New Britain island W Pacific in Bismarck group

New Bruns·wick \-ˈbrənz-(ˌ)wik\ province SE Canada; ✻, Fredericton

New Caledonia island SW Pacific SW of Vanuatu; an overseas department of France; ✻, Nouméa

New·cas·tle \ˈnü-ˌka-səl, ˈnyü-\ city SE Australia in E New South Wales

Newcastle *or* **Newcastle upon Tyne** \ˈtīn\ city N England

New Delhi city, ✻ of India S of Delhi

New England section of NE U.S. consisting of states of Maine, New Hampshire, Vermont, Massachusetts, Rhode Island, & Connecticut — **New En·gland·er** \ˈiŋ-glən-dər\ *n*

New·found·land \ˈnü-fən(d)-lənd, ˈnyü-, -ˌland; ˌnü-fən(d)-ˈland, ˌnyü-\ island

Canada in the Atlantic — **New·found·land·er** \-lən-dər, -ˌlan-\ *n*

Newfoundland and Labrador province E Canada consisting of Newfoundland Island and Labrador; ✻, Saint John's

New France the possessions of France in North America before 1763

New Guinea **1** island W Pacific N of E Australia; divided between West Papua, Indonesia & independent Papua New Guinea **2** the NE portion of the island of New Guinea together with some nearby islands; now part of Papua New Guinea — **New Guinean** *adj or n*

New·ham \ˈnü-əm, ˈnyü-\ borough of E Greater London, England

New Hamp·shire \ˈhamp-shər, -ˌshir\ state NE U.S.; ✻, Concord — **New Hamp·shire·man** \-mən\ *n* — **New Hamp·shir·ite** \-ˌīt\ *n*

New Ha·ven \ˈhā-vən\ city S Connecticut

New Hebrides — see VANUATU

New Jersey state E U.S.; ✻, Trenton — **New Jer·sey·an** \-ən\ *n* — **New Jer·sey·ite** \-ˌīt\ *n*

New Mex·i·co \ˈmek-si-ˌkō\ state SW U.S.; ✻, Santa Fe — **New Mex·i·can** \-si-kən\ *adj or n*

New Neth·er·land \ˈne-t͟hər-lənd\ former Dutch colony (1613–64) North America along Hudson & lower Delaware rivers

New Or·leans \ˈȯr-lē-ənz, ˈȯr-lənz, ˈȯrl-yənz, (ˌ)ȯr-ˈlēnz\ city SE Louisiana

New·port \ˈnü-ˌpōrt, ˈnyü-, -ˌpȯrt\ **1** town S England in Isle of Wight **2** city SE Wales

Newport News \ˈnü-ˌpȯrt-ˈnüz, ˈnyü-ˌpȯrt-ˈnyüz, -pərt-\ city SE Virginia

New Providence island NW *cen* Bahamas; chief town, Nassau

New·ry and Mourne \ˈn(y)ü-rē-ən(d)-ˈmȯrn\ district S Northern Ireland

New South Wales state SE Australia; ✻, Sydney

New Spain former Spanish possessions in North America, Central America, West Indies, & the Philippines

New Sweden former Swedish colony (1638–55) North America on W bank of Delaware River

New·town·ab·bey \ˌnü-tᵊn-ˈa-bē, ˌnyü-\ district E Northern Ireland

Newtown Saint Bos·wells \ˈnü-ˌtau̇n-sənt-ˈbäz-wəlz, ˈnyü-, -sānt-\ village S Scotland

New World the Western Hemisphere including North America and South America

New York **1** state NE U.S.; ✻, Albany **2** *or* **New York City** city SE New York (state) — **New York·er** \ˈyȯr-kər\ *n*

New York State Barge Canal — see ERIE

New Zea·land \ˈzē-lənd\ country SW Pacific ESE of Australia; ✻, Wellington — **New Zea·land·er** \-lən-dər\ *n*

Ni·ag·a·ra Falls \(ˌ)nī-ˈa-g(ə-)rə\ falls New York & Ontario in **Niagara River** (flowing N from Lake Erie into Lake Ontario); divided by Goat Island into Horseshoe Falls, or Canadian Falls (158 ft. or 48 m. high) & American Falls (167 ft. or 51 m. high)

Nia·mey \nē-ˈä-(ˌ)mā, nyä-ˈmā\ city, ✻ of Niger

Ni·caea \nī-ˈsē-ə\ *or* **Nice** \ˈnīs\ ancient city W Bithynia; site at modern village in NW Turkey — **Ni·cae·an** \nī-ˈsē-ən\ *adj or n* — **Ni·cene** \ˈnī-ˌsēn, nī-ˈsēn\ *adj*

Ni·ca·ra·gua \ˌni-kə-ˈrä-gwə, ˌnē-kä-ˈrä-gwä\ **1** lake about 100 mi. (160 km.) long S Nicaragua **2** country Central America; ✻, Managua — **Ni·ca·ra·guan** \-ˈrä-gwən\ *adj or n*

Nice \ˈnēs\ city & port SE France on the Mediterranean

Nic·o·bar \ˈni-kə-ˌbär\ islands India in Bay of Bengal S of the Andamans

Nic·o·sia \ˌni-kə-ˈsē-ə\ city, ✻ of Cyprus

Ni·ger \ˈnī-jər, nē-ˈzher\ **1** river 2600 mi. (4184 km.) long W Africa flowing into Gulf of Guinea **2** country W Africa N of Nigeria; ✻, Niamey — **Ni·ger·ien** \ˌnī-ˌjir-ē-ˈen, nē-ˈzher-ē-ən\ *adj or n* — **Ni·ger·ois** \ˌnē-zhər-ˈwä, -zher-\ *n*

Ni·ge·ria \nī-ˈjir-ē-ə\ country W Africa on Gulf of Guinea; ✻, Abuja — **Ni·ge·ri·an** \-ē-ən\ *adj or n*

Nii·hau \ˈnē-ˌhau̇\ island Hawaii WSW of Kauai

Nile \ˈnī(-ə)l\ river 4160 mi. (6693 km.) long E Africa flowing from Lake Victoria in Uganda N into the Mediterranean in Egypt

Nil·gi·ri \ˈnil-gə-rē\ hills S India

Nin·e·veh \ˈni-nə-və\ ancient city, ✻ of Assyria; ruins in Iraq on the Tigris

Nip·i·gon, Lake \ˈni-pə-ˌgän\ lake Canada in W Ontario N of Lake Superior

Nizh·niy Nov·go·rod \ˈnizh-nē-ˈnäv-gə-ˌräd, -ˈnȯv-gə-rət\ *formerly 1932–89* **Gor·ki** \ˈgȯr-kē\ city W Russia

Nord–Ost·see \ˈnȯrt-ˈȯst-ˈzā\ *or* **Kiel** \ˈkēl\ canal 61 mi. (98 km.) long N Germany across base of Jutland Peninsula connecting Baltic Sea & North Sea

Nor·folk \ˈnȯr-fək\ city & port SE Virginia

Nor·man·dy \ˈnȯr-mən-dē\ region NW France NE of Brittany

North **1** river estuary of the Hudson between NE New Jersey & SE New York **2** sea, arm of the Atlantic E of Great Britain **3** island N New Zealand

North·al·ler·ton \nȯr-ˈtha-lər-tən\ town N England

North America continent of Western Hemisphere NW of South America & N of the Equator — **North American** *adj or n*

North·amp·ton \nȯr-ˈtham(p)-tən, nȯrth-ˈham(p)-\ town *cen* England

North·amp·ton·shire \-ˌshir, -shər\ *or* **Northampton** county *cen* England

North Cape cape New Zealand at N end of North Island

North Car·o·li·na \ˌker(-ə)-ˈlī-nə, ˌka-rə-\ state E U.S.; ✻, Raleigh — **North Car·o·lin·ian** \-ˈli-nē-ən, -ˈli-nyən\ *adj or n*

North Da·ko·ta \də-ˈkō-tə\ state N U.S.; ✻, Bismarck — **North Da·ko·tan** \-ˈkō-tᵊn\ *adj or n*

North Down district E Northern Ireland

Northern Cape province W Republic of South Africa

Northern Cook islands S *cen* Pacific N of Cook Islands

Northern Hemisphere the half of the earth that lies N of the Equator

Northern Ireland region N Ireland comprising 26 districts of Ulster; a division of United Kingdom; ✻, Belfast

Northern Mar·i·ana Islands \ˌmer-ē-ˈa-nə\ islands W Pacific; commonwealth in association with U.S.; seat of the government on Saipan

Northern Rhodesia — see ZAMBIA

Northern Territory territory N & *cen* Australia; ✻, Darwin

North Korea *or* **Democratic People's Republic of Korea** country N half of Korean Peninsula in E Asia; ✻, Pyongyang

North Las Vegas city SE Nevada

North Macedonia — see MACEDONIA 2

North Slope region N Alaska between Brooks Range & Arctic Ocean

North·um·ber·land \nȯr-ˈthəm-bər-lənd\ county N England

North·um·bria \nȯr-ˈthəm-brē-ə\ ancient country Great Britain in what is now N England and S Scotland — **North·um·bri·an** \-brē-ən\ *adj or n*

North Vietnam — see VIETNAM

North West province N Republic of South Africa

Northwest Passage sea passage between the Atlantic and the Pacific along the N coast of North America

Northwest Territories territory NW Canada consisting of the area of the mainland north of 60° between Yukon (territory) & Nunavut; ✻, Yellowknife

North York former city Canada in SE Ontario; now part of Toronto

North Yorkshire county N England

Nor·walk \ˈnȯr-ˌwȯk\ city SW California SE of Los Angeles

Nor·way \ˈnȯr-ˌwā\ country N Europe in Scandinavia; ✻, Oslo

Nor·wich \ˈnȯr-(ˌ)wich\ city E England

Not·ting·ham \ˈnä-tiŋ-əm\ city N *cen* England

Not·ting·ham·shire \ˈnä-tiŋ-əm-ˌshir, -shər\ *or* **Nottingham** county N *cen* England

Nouak·chott \nu̇-ˈäk-ˌshät\ city, ✻ of Mauritania

Nou·méa \nü-ˈmā-ə\ city, ✻ of New Caledonia

No·va Sco·tia \ˌnō-və-ˈskō-shə\ province SE Canada; ✻, Halifax — **No·va Sco·tian** \-shən\ *adj or n*

No·vo·kuz·netsk \ˌnō-(ˌ)vō-ku̇z-ˈnetsk, ˌnȯ-və-küz-ˈnyetsk\ city S Russia in Asia

No·vo·si·birsk \ˌnō-(ˌ)vō-sə-ˈbirsk, ˌnō-və-\ city S Russia in Asia

Nu·bia \ˈnü-bē-ə, ˈnyü-\ region NE Africa in Nile valley in S Egypt & N Sudan — **Nu·bi·an** \ˈnü-bē-ən, ˈnyü-\ *adj or n*

Nu·ku·a·lo·fa \ˌnü-kü-ä-ˈlō-fä\ seaport, ✻ of Tonga

Nu·mid·ia \nu̇-ˈmi-dē-ə, nyu̇-\ ancient country N Africa E of Mauretania in modern Algeria — **Nu·mid·i·an** \-dē-ən\ *adj or n*

Nu·na·vut \ˈnü-nə-ˌvüt\ semiautonomous territory NE Canada; ✻, Iqaluit

Nu·rem·berg \ˈnu̇r-əm-ˌbərg, ˈnyu̇r-\ *or German* **Nürn·berg** \ˈnœrn-ˌberk\ city S Germany

Nur–Sul·tan \ˌnu̇r-su̇l-ˈtän\ *or* **As·ta·na** \ä-stä-ˈnä\ city, ✻ of Kazakhstan

Nuuk \ˈnük\ *or Danish* **Godt·håb** \ˈgȯt-ˌhȯp\ town, ✻ of Greenland on SW coast

Ny·asa, Lake \nī-ˈas-ə, nē-\ lake SE Africa in Malawi, Mozambique, & Tanzania

Nyasaland — see MALAWI

Oa·hu \ō-ˈä-(ˌ)hü\ island Hawaii; site of Honolulu

Oak·land \ˈō-klənd\ city W California on San Francisco Bay E of San Francisco

Ob' \ˈäb, ˈȯb\ river over 2250 mi. (3620 km.) long W Russia in Asia flowing NW & N into Arctic Ocean

Oce·a·nia \ˌō-shē-ˈa-nē-ə, -ˈā-\ lands of the *cen* & S Pacific: Micronesia, Melanesia, Polynesia including New Zealand, & by some thought to include Australia & Malay Archipelago

Ocean·side \ˈō-shən-ˌsīd\ city SW California NNW of San Diego

Oder \ˈō-dər\ *or* **Odra** \ˈȯ-drə\ river about 565 mi. (909 km.) long *cen* Europe flowing from Silesia NW into Baltic Sea; forms part of boundary between Poland & Germany

Odes·sa \ō-ˈde-sə\ city & port S Ukraine on Black Sea

Ohio \ō-ˈhī-(ˌ)ō, ə-, -ə\ **1** river about 981 mi. (1578 km.) long E U.S. flowing from W Pennsylvania into the Mississippi **2** state E *cen* U.S.; ✻, Columbus — **Ohio·an** \-ˈhī-ō-ən\ *adj or n*

Oka·ya·ma \ˌō-kä-ˈyä-mä\ city Japan in W Honshu on Inland Sea

Okee·cho·bee, Lake \ˌō-kə-ˈchō-bē\ lake S *cen* Florida

Oke·fe·no·kee \ˌō-kə-fə-ˈnō-kē, ˌō-kē-\ swamp SE Georgia & NE Florida

Okhotsk, Sea of \ō-ˈkätsk, ə-ˈk̲ȯtsk\ inlet of the North Pacific E Russia in Asia
Oki·na·wa \ˌō-kə-ˈnä-wə, -ˈnau̇-ə\ **1** islands Japan in *cen* Ryukyus **2** island, chief of group — **Oki·na·wan** \-ˈnä-wən, -ˈnau̇-ən\ *adj or n*
Okla·ho·ma \ˌō-klə-ˈhō-mə\ state S *cen* U.S.; ✱, Oklahoma City — **Okla·ho·man** \-mən\ *adj or n*
Oklahoma City city, ✱ of Oklahoma
Old·ham \ˈōl-dəm\ city NW England
Old Point Comfort cape SE Virginia N of entrance to Hampton Roads
Ol·du·vai Gorge \ˈōl-də-ˌvī\ canyon N Tanzania SE of Serengeti Plain; site of fossil beds
Old World the half of the earth to the E of the Atlantic Ocean including Europe, Asia, and Africa & esp. the continent of Europe
Olym·pia \ə-ˈlim-pē-ə, ō-\ **1** city, ✱ of Washington **2** plain S Greece in NW Peloponnese
Olym·pic \-pik\ mountains NW Washington on Olympic Peninsula; highest Mt. Olympus 7965 ft. (2428 m.)
Olym·pus \ə-ˈlim-pəs, ō-\ mountains NE Greece
Omagh \ˈō-mə, -(ˌ)mä\ **1** district W Northern Ireland **2** town in Omagh district
Oma·ha \ˈō-mə-ˌhȯ, -ˌhä\ **1** beach NW France in Normandy **2** city E Nebraska on Missouri River
Oman \ō-ˈmän, -ˈman\ country SW Asia in SE Arabia; ✱, Muscat — **Omani** \ō-ˈmä-nē, -ˈma-\ *adj or n*
Oman, Gulf of arm of Arabian Sea between Oman & SE Iran
Omsk \ˈȯm(p)sk, ˈäm(p)sk\ city SW Russia in Asia
On·tar·io \än-ˈter-ē-ˌō\ **1** city SW California **2** province E Canada; ✱, Toronto — **On·tar·i·an** \-ē-ən\ *adj or n*
Ontario, Lake lake E *cen* North America in U.S. & Canada; one of the Great Lakes
Oran \ȯ-ˈrän\ city & port NW Algeria
Or·ange \ˈär-inj, ˈär(-ə)nj, ˈȯr-inj, ˈȯr(-ə)nj\ **1** city SW California **2** river 1300 mi. (2092 km.) long S Africa flowing W from Drakensberg Mountains into the Atlantic
Orange Free State — see FREE STATE
Or·e·gon \ˈȯr-i-gən, ˈär-\ state NW U.S.; ✱, Salem — **Or·e·go·nian** \ˌȯr-i-ˈgō-nē-ən, ˌär-, -nyən\ *adj or n*
Oregon Trail pioneer route to the NW U.S. about 2000 mi. (3220 km.) long from Missouri to Washington
Ori·no·co \ˌȯr-ē-ˈnō-(ˌ)kō\ river 1336 mi. (2150 km.) long Venezuela flowing into the Atlantic
Ork·ney \ˈȯrk-nē\ islands N Scotland
Or·lan·do \ȯr-ˈlan-(ˌ)dō\ city *cen* Florida
Osa·ka \ō-ˈsä-kä, ˈō-sä-ˌkä\ city Japan in S Honshu
Osh·a·wa \ˈä-shə-wə, -ˌwä, -ˌwȯ\ city SE Ontario, Canada on Lake Ontario ENE of Toronto
Os·lo \ˈäz-(ˌ)lō, ˈäs-\ city, ✱ of Norway
Oś·wię·cim \ˌȯsh-ˈfyen-chēm\ *or German* **Ausch·witz** \ˈau̇sh-ˌvits\ town S Poland W of Krakow
Ot·ta·wa \ˈä-tə-wə, -ˌwä, -ˌwȯ\ **1** river 696 mi. (1120 km.) E Canada in SE Ontario & S Quebec flowing E into the Saint Lawrence **2** city, ✱ of Canada in SE Ontario on Ottawa River
Ot·to·man Empire \ˈä-tə-mən\ former Turkish sultanate in SE Europe, W Asia, & N Africa
Oua·ga·dou·gou \ˌwä-gä-ˈdü-(ˌ)gü\ city, ✱ of Burkina Faso
Outer Hebrides — see HEBRIDES
Over·land Park \ˈō-vər-lənd\ city NE Kansas
Ox·ford \ˈäks-fərd\ city *cen* England
Ox·ford·shire \ˈäks-fərd-ˌshir, -shər\ *or* **Oxford** county *cen* England
Ox·nard \ˈäks-ˌnärd\ city SW California
Ozark Plateau \ˈō-ˌzärk\ *or* **Ozark Mountains** eroded plateau N Arkansas, S Missouri, & NE Oklahoma with E extension into S Illinois
Pa·cif·ic \pə-ˈsi-fik\ ocean extending from Arctic Circle to the Equator (**North Pacific**) and from the Equator to the Antarctic regions (**South Pacific**) & from W North America & W South America to E Asia & Australia — **Pacific** *adj*
Pacific Islands, Trust Territory of the grouping of islands in W Pacific formerly under U.S. administration: the Carolines & the Marshalls
Pacific Rim the countries bordering on or located in the Pacific Ocean — used esp. of Asian countries on the Pacific
Pa·dang \ˈpä-ˌdäŋ\ city Indonesia in W Sumatra
Pa·dre \ˈpä-drē, -drā\ island 113 mi. (182 km.) long S Texas in Gulf of Mexico
Pa·go Pa·go \ˌpä-(ˌ)gō-ˈpä-(ˌ)gō, ˌpäŋ-(ˌ)ō-ˈpäŋ-(ˌ)ō\ town, ✱ of American Samoa on Tutuila Island
Painted Desert region N *cen* Arizona
Pak·i·stan \ˈpa-ki-ˌstan, ˌpä-ki-ˈstän\ country S Asia NW of India; ✱, Islamabad — see EAST PAKISTAN — **Pak·i·stani** \ˌpa-ki-ˈsta-nē, ˌpä-ki-ˈstä-\ *adj or n*
Pa·lau \pə-ˈlau̇\ *or* **Be·lau** \bə-\ island group W Pacific in the W Carolines; country in association with U.S.; ✱, Melekeok — **Pa·lau·an** \pə-ˈlau̇-ən\ *n*
Pa·la·wan \pə-ˈlä-wən, -ˌwän\ island W Philippines between South China & Sulu seas
Pa·lem·bang \ˌpä-ləm-ˈbäŋ\ city Indonesia in SE Sumatra
Pa·ler·mo \pə-ˈlər-(ˌ)mō, pä-ˈler-\ city Italy, ✱ of Sicily
Pal·es·tine \ˈpa-lə-ˌstīn\ region SW Asia dating back to ancient times with unoffi-

cial, disputed, & fluctuating boundaries, but extending from E coast of Mediterranean Sea up to or beyond Jordan River — **Pal·es·tin·ian** \ˌpa-lə-ˈsti-nē-ən, -nyən\ *adj or n*

Pa·li·kir \ˌpä-lē-ˈkir\ town, ✻ of Federated States of Micronesia on Pohnpei Island

Pal·i·sades \ˌpa-lə-ˈsādz\ line of high cliffs 15 mi. (24 km.) long on W bank of the Hudson in SE New York & NE New Jersey

Palm·dale \ˈpäm-ˌdāl, ˈpälm-\ city SW California NE of Los Angeles

Pa·mirs \pə-ˈmirz\ elevated mountainous region *cen* Asia in E Tajikistan & on borders of China, India, Pakistan, & Afghanistan; many peaks over 20,000 ft. (6096 m.)

Pam·li·co Sound \ˈpam-li-ˌkō\ inlet of the North Atlantic E North Carolina between main part of the state & offshore islands

Pam·pa \ˈpam-pə\ city NW Texas

Pan·a·ma \ˈpan-ə-ˌmä, -ˌmȯ; ˌpan-ə-ˈmä, -ˈmȯ\ **1** country S Central America **2** *or* **Panama City** city, its ✻ on the Pacific **3** canal 40 mi. (64 km.) long Panama connecting Atlantic & Pacific oceans — **Pan·a·ma·ni·an** \ˌpan-ə-ˈmā-nē-ən\ *adj or n*

Panama, Isthmus of *formerly* **Isthmus of Dar·i·en** \ˌder-ē-ˈen\ strip of land *cen* Panama connecting North America & South America

Panama Canal Zone — see CANAL ZONE

Pa·nay \pə-ˈnī\ island *cen* Philippines in the Visayans

Pan·gaea \pan-ˈjē-ə\ land area believed to have once connected the landmasses of the Southern Hemisphere with those of the Northern Hemisphere

Pan·mun·jom *or* **Pan·mun·jeom** \ˌpän-ˌmu̇n-ˈjəm\ village on North Korea–South Korea border

Pao–t'ou — see BAOTOU

Pap·ua, Territory of \ˈpa-pyu̇-wə, ˈpä-pu̇-wə\ former British territory consisting of SE New Guinea & offshore islands; now part of Papua New Guinea

Papua New Guinea country SW Pacific; ✻, Port Moresby

Par·a·guay \ˈpa-rə-ˌgwī, -ˌgwā\ **1** river 1584 mi. (2549 km.) long *cen* South America flowing from Brazil S into the Paraná in Paraguay **2** country *cen* South America; ✻, Asunción — **Par·a·guay·an** \ˌpa-rə-ˈgwī-ən, -ˈgwā-\ *adj or n*

Par·a·mar·i·bo \ˌpa-rə-ˈma-rə-ˌbō\ city, ✻ of Suriname

Pa·ra·ná \ˌpär-ə-ˈnä\ river about 2500 mi. (4022 km.) long *cen* South America flowing S from Brazil into Argentina

Pa·ri·cu·tin \pä-ˌrē-kü-ˈtēn\ volcano Mexico on site of a former village

Par·is \ˈpa-rəs\ city, ✻ of France — **Pa·ri·sian** \pə-ˈri-zhən, -ˈrē-\ *adj or n*

Par·nas·sus \pär-ˈna-səs\ mountain *cen* Greece

Par·os \ˈpär-ˌȯs\ island Greece — **Par·i·an** \ˈpar-ē-ən, ˈper-\ *adj*

Par·ra·mat·ta \ˌpa-rə-ˈma-tə\ city SE Australia in New South Wales

Par·thia \ˈpär-thē-ə\ ancient country SW Asia in NE modern Iran — **Par·thi·an** \-thē-ən\ *adj or n*

Pas·a·de·na \ˌpa-sə-ˈdē-nə\ **1** city SW California E of Glendale **2** city SE Texas

Pat·a·go·nia \ˌpa-tə-ˈgō-nyə, -nē-ə\ region South America S of about 40° S latitude in S Argentina & S tip of Chile; sometimes thought to include Tierra del Fuego — **Pat·a·go·nian** \-nyən, -nē-ən\ *adj or n*

Pat·er·son \ˈpa-tər-sən\ city NE New Jersey

Pat·mos \ˈpat-məs\ island Greece SSW of Samos

Pat·na \ˈpət-nə\ city NE India on the Ganges

Pearl Harbor inlet Hawaii on S coast of Oahu W of Honolulu

Peking — see BEIJING

Pe·li·on \ˈpē-lē-ən\ mountain 5089 ft. (1551 m.) NE Greece

Pel·o·pon·nese \ˈpe-lə-pə-ˌnēz, -ˌnēs\ *or* **Pel·o·pon·ni·sos** \ˌpe-lə-pə-ˈnē-səs\ peninsula forming S part of mainland of Greece

Pem·broke Pines \ˈpem-ˌbrōk\ city SE Florida

Pen·nine Chain \ˈpe-ˌnīn\ mountains N England; highest Cross Fell 2930 ft. (893 m.)

Penn·syl·va·nia \ˌpen(t)-səl-ˈvā-nyə, -nē-ə\ state E U.S.; ✻, Harrisburg

Pe·o·ria \pē-ˈȯr-ē-ə\ **1** town SW *cen* Arizona **2** city N *cen* Illinois

Per·ga·mum \ˈpər-gə-məm\ *or* **Per·ga·mus** \-məs\ ancient Greek kingdom including most of Asia Minor

Perm \ˈpərm, ˈperm\ city E Russia in Europe

Pernambuco — see RECIFE

Persia — see IRAN

Per·sian Gulf \ˈpər-zhən\ arm of Arabian Sea between Iran & Arabia

Perth \ˈpərth\ city, ✻ of Western Australia

Pe·ru \pə-ˈrü, pā-\ country W South America; ✻, Lima — **Pe·ru·vi·an** \-ˈrü-vē-ən\ *adj or n*

Pe·tra \ˈpē-trə, ˈpe-\ ancient city NW Arabia; site in SW Jordan

Petrograd — see SAINT PETERSBURG

Phil·a·del·phia \ˌfi-lə-ˈdel-fyə, -fē-ə\ city SE Pennsylvania — **Phil·a·del·phian** \-fyən, -fē-ən\ *adj or n*

Phil·ip·pines \ˌfi-lə-ˈpēnz, ˈfi-lə-ˌpēnz\ island group approximately 500 mi. (805 km.) off SE coast of Asia; country; ✻, Manila — **Phil·ip·pine** \ˌfi-lə-ˈpēn, ˈfi-lə-ˌ\ *adj*

Phnom Penh \(pə-)ˈnäm-ˈpen, (pə-)ˈnȯm-\ city, * of Cambodia
Phoe·ni·cia \fi-ˈni-sh(ē-)ə, -ˈnē-\ ancient country SW Asia on the Mediterranean in modern Syria & Lebanon
Phoe·nix \ˈfē-niks\ city, * of Arizona
Phry·gia \ˈfri-j(ē-)ə\ ancient country W *cen* Asia Minor
Pic·ar·dy \ˈpi-kər-dē\ *or F* **Pi·car·die** \pē-kär-ˈdē\ region & former province N France bordering on English Channel N of Normandy — **Pi·card** \ˈpi-ˌkärd, -kərd\ *adj or n*
Pied·mont \ˈpēd-ˌmänt\ plateau region E U.S. E of the Appalachians between SE New York & NE Alabama
Pierre \ˈpir\ city, * of South Dakota
Pie·ter·mar·itz·burg \ˌpē-tər-ˈma-rəts-ˌbərg\ city E Republic of South Africa
Pigs, Bay of \ˈpigz\ *or* **Ba·hía de Co·chi·nos** \bä-ˈē-ä-t͟hā-kō-ˈchē-nōs\ bay W Cuba on S coast
Pikes Peak \ˈpīks\ mountain 14,110 ft. (4301 m.) E *cen* Colorado in a range of the Rockies
Pin·dus \ˈpin-dəs\ mountains W Greece; highest point 8136 ft. (2480 m.)
Pi·sa \ˈpē-zə, *It* -sä\ city W *cen* Italy W of Florence
Pit·cairn \ˈpit-ˌkern\ island South Pacific; a British colony
Pitts·burgh \ˈpits-ˌbərg\ city SW Pennsylvania
Plac·id, Lake \ˈpla-səd\ lake NE New York
Pla·no \ˈplā-(ˌ)nō\ city NE Texas N of Dallas
Plov·div \ˈplȯv-ˌdif, -ˌdiv\ city S Bulgaria
Plym·outh \ˈpli-məth\ **1** town SE Massachusetts **2** city & port SW England
Po \ˈpō\ river 405 mi. (652 km.) N Italy flowing into the Adriatic
Pod·go·ri·ca \ˈpȯd-ˌgȯr-ēt-sä\ city * of Montenegro
Po Hai — see BO HAI
Pohn·pei \ˈpōn-ˌpā\ island W Pacific in the E Carolines; part of Federated States of Micronesia
Po·land \ˈpō-lənd\ country *cen* Europe on Baltic Sea; *, Warsaw — **Pole** *n*
Pol·y·ne·sia \ˌpä-lə-ˈnē-zhə, -shə\ islands of the *cen* & S Pacific including Hawaii, the Line, Tonga, Cook, & Samoa islands, & often New Zealand among others
Pom·er·a·nia \ˌpä-mə-ˈrā-nē-ə, -nyə\ region N Europe on Baltic Sea; formerly in Germany, now mostly in Poland
Po·mo·na \pə-ˈmō-nə\ city SW California E of Los Angeles
Pom·peii \päm-ˈpā, -ˈpā-ˌē\ ancient city S Italy SE of Naples destroyed 79 A.D. by eruption of Vesuvius — **Pom·pe·ian** \-ˈpā-ən\ *adj or n*
Pon·ce \ˈpȯn(t)-(ˌ)sā\ city S Puerto Rico
Pon·do·land \ˈpän-(ˌ)dō-ˌland\ region S Republic of South Africa
Pon·ta Del·ga·da \ˌpȯn-tə-del-ˈgä-də\ city & port Portugal, largest in the Azores
Pont·char·train, Lake \ˈpänt-shər-ˌtrān, ˌpänt-shər-ˈ\ lake SE Louisiana E of the Mississippi & N of New Orleans
Pon·tus \ˈpän-təs\ ancient country NE Asia Minor — **Pon·tic** \ˈpänt-ik\ *adj or n*
Poole \ˈpül\ town S England on English Channel
Po·po·ca·te·petl \ˌpō-pə-ˈka-tə-ˌpe-tᵊl, -ˌka-tə-ˈ\ volcano 17,887 ft. (5452 m.) SE *cen* Mexico
Port Arthur — see LÜSHUN
Port–au–Prince \ˌpȯrt-ō-ˈprin(t)s, ˌpȯr-(t)ō-ˈpraⁿs\ city, * of Haiti
Port Jack·son \ˈjak-sən\ inlet of South Pacific SE Australia in New South Wales; harbor of Sydney
Port·land \ˈpȯrt-lənd\ **1** city SW Maine; largest in state **2** city NW Oregon
Port Lou·is \ˈlü-əs, ˈlü-ē\ city, * of Mauritius
Port Mores·by \ˈmȯrz-bē\ city, * of Papua New Guinea
Por·to \ˈpȯr-(ˌ)tü\ city & port NW Portugal
Por·to Ale·gre \ˈpȯr-(ˌ)tü-ä-ˈlā-grē\ city & port S Brazil
Port of Spain city NW Trinidad, * of Trinidad and Tobago
Por·to–No·vo \ˌpȯr-tō-ˈnō-(ˌ)vō\ city, * of Benin
Port Phil·lip Bay \ˈfi-ləp\ inlet of South Pacific SE Australia in Victoria; harbor of Melbourne
Port Said \sä-ˈēd, ˈsīd\ city & port NE Egypt on the Mediterranean at N end of the Suez Canal
Ports·mouth \ˈpȯrts-məth\ **1** city SE Virginia **2** city S England
Por·tu·gal \ˈpȯr-chi-gəl, ˌpür-tü-ˈgäl\ country SW Europe; *, Lisbon
Portuguese India former Portuguese possession on W coast of India; became part of India 1962
Port–Vi·la \pȯrt-ˈvē-lə\ *or* **Vila** city, * of Vanuatu
Po·to·mac \pə-ˈtō-mək, -mik\ river 287 mi. (462 km.) long flowing from West Virginia into Chesapeake Bay and forming boundary between Maryland & Virginia
Pough·keep·sie \pə-ˈkip-sē, pō-\ city & river port SE New York on the Hudson
Po·wys \ˈpō-əs\ administrative subdivision E *cen* Wales
Prague \ˈpräg\ *or Czech* **Pra·ha** \ˈprä-(ˌ)hä\ city, * of Czech Republic
Praia \ˈprī-ə\ town, * of Cape Verde
Prairie Provinces the Canadian provinces of Alberta, Manitoba, & Saskatchewan
Pres·ton \ˈpres-tən\ town NW England
Pre·to·ria \pri-ˈtȯr-ē-ə\ city Republic of

South Africa in the municipality of Tshwane, administrative * of the country
Prib·i·lof \ˈpri-bə-ˌlȯf\ islands Alaska in Bering Sea
Prince Ed·ward Island \ˈed-wərd\ island SE Canada in Gulf of Saint Lawrence; a province; *, Charlottetown
Prince Ru·pert's Land \ˈrü-pərts\ historical region N & W Canada consisting of drainage basin of Hudson Bay
Prince·ton \ˈprin(t)-stən\ borough W *cen* New Jersey
Prín·ci·pe \ˈprin(t)-si-pē\ island W Africa in Gulf of Guinea — see SÃO TOMÉ AND PRÍNCIPE
Pro·vence \prə-ˈvän(t)s, prō-ˈvä^{n}s\ region SE France on the Mediterranean
Prov·i·dence \ˈprä-və-dən(t)s, -ˌden(t)s\ city, * of Rhode Island
Pro·vo \ˈprō-(ˌ)vō\ city N *cen* Utah
Prud·hoe Bay \ˈprü-(ˌ)dō, ˈprə-\ inlet of Beaufort Sea N Alaska
Prus·sia \ˈprə-shə\ former kingdom, & later, state Germany — **Prus·sian** \ˈprə-shən\ *adj or n*
Pueb·lo \ˈpwe-ˌblō\ city SE *cen* Colorado SSE of Colorado Springs
Puer·to Ri·co \ˌpȯr-tə-ˈrē-(ˌ)kō, ˌpwer-tō-\ island West Indies E of Hispaniola; a self-governing commonwealth associated with U.S.; *, San Juan — **Puer·to Ri·can** \ˈrē-kən\ *adj or n*
Pu·get Sound \ˈpyü-jət\ arm of the North Pacific W Washington
Pu·ne \ˈpü-nə\ city W India, ESE of Mumbai
Pun·jab \ˌpən-ˈjäb, -ˈjab, ˈpən-ˌ\ region in Pakistan & NW India in valley of the Indus
Pusan — see BUSAN
Pyong·yang *or* **Pyeong·yang** \ˈpyȯŋ-ˈyaŋ, ˈpyəŋ-, -ˈyäŋ\ city, * of North Korea
Pyr·e·nees \ˈpir-ə-ˌnēz\ mountains on French–Spanish border extending from Bay of Biscay to the Mediterranean
Qaraghandy — see KARAGANDA
Qa·tar \ˈkä-tər, ˈgä-, ˈgə-; kə-ˈtär\ country E Arabia on peninsula extending into Persian Gulf; *, Doha — **Qa·tari** \kə-ˈtär-ē, gə-\ *adj or n*
Qing·dao \ˈchiŋ-ˈdau̇\ *or* **Tsing·tao** \ˈchiŋ-ˈdau̇, ˈ(t)siŋ-ˈdau̇\ city & port E China
Qi·qi·har \ˈchē-ˈchē-ˈhär\ *or* **Ch'i-ch'i-ha-erh** \ˈchē-ˈchē-ˈhä-ˈər\ city NE China
Que·bec \kwi-ˈbek, ki-\ *or French* **Qué·bec** \kā-ˈbek\ **1** province E Canada **2** city, its *, on the Saint Lawrence
Queens \ˈkwēnz\ borough of New York City on Long Island E of Brooklyn
Queens·land \ˈkwēnz-ˌland, -lənd\ state NE Australia; *, Brisbane — **Queens·land·er** \-ˌlan-dər, -ˌlən-\ *n*
Que·zon City \ˈkā-ˌsȯn\ city Philippines in Luzon; formerly * of the country
Qui·to \ˈkē-(ˌ)tō\ city, * of Ecuador
Ra·bat \rə-ˈbät\ city, * of Morocco
Rai·nier, Mount \rə-ˈnir, rā-\ mountain 14,410 ft. (4392 m.) W *cen* Washington; highest in Cascade Range
Raj·pu·ta·na \ˌräj-pə-ˈtä-nə\ *or* **Ra·ja·sthan** \ˈräj-ə-ˌstän\ region NW India S of Punjab
Ra·leigh \ˈrȯ-lē, ˈrä-lē\ city, * of North Carolina
Ran·cho Cu·ca·mon·ga \ˈran-(ˌ)chō-ˌkü-kə-ˈməŋ-gə, ˈrän-, -ˈmäŋ-\ city SW California
Rand·wick \ˈran-(ˌ)dwik\ municipality SE Australia in E New South Wales
Rangoon — see YANGON
Ra·wal·pin·di \ˌrä-wəl-ˈpin-dē, rau̇l-ˈ, rȯl-ˈ\ city NE Pakistan NNW of Lahore
Read·ing \ˈre-diŋ\ town S England
Re·ci·fe \ri-ˈsē-fē\ *formerly* **Per·nam·bu·co** \ˌpər-nəm-ˈbü-(ˌ)kō, -ˈbyü-\ city NE Brazil
Red \ˈred\ **1** river 1018 mi. (1638 km.) long flowing E on Oklahoma–Texas boundary and into the Atchafalaya & the Mississippi in Louisiana **2** sea between Arabia & NE Africa
Red·bridge \ˈred-(ˌ)brij\ borough of NE Greater London, England
Re·gi·na \ri-ˈjī-nə\ city, * of Saskatchewan, Canada
Re·no \ˈrē-(ˌ)nō\ city NW Nevada
Republic of the Congo — see CONGO 3
Ré·union \rē-ˈyü-nyən, ˌrā-üe-ˈnyō^{n}\ island W Indian Ocean; an overseas division of France; *, Saint-Denis
Reyk·ja·vik \ˈrā-kyə-ˌvik, -ˌvēk\ city, * of Iceland
Rhine \ˈrīn\ river 820 mi. (1320 km.) long W Europe flowing from SE Switzerland to North Sea in the Netherlands — **Rhen·ish** \ˈre-nish, ˈrē-\ *adj*
Rhine·land \ˈrīn-ˌland, -lənd\ *or German* **Rhein·land** \ˈrīn-ˌlänt\ the part of Germany W of the Rhine — **Rhine·land·er** \ˈrīn-ˌlan-dər, -lən-\ *n*
Rhode Is·land \rōd-ˈī-lənd\ **1** *or officially* **Rhode Island and Providence Plantations** state NE U.S.; *, Providence **2** — see AQUIDNECK — **Rhode Is·land·er** \-lən-dər\ *n*
Rhodes \ˈrōdz\ island Greece in the SE Aegean
Rho·de·sia \rō-ˈdē-zh(ē-)ə\ — see ZIMBABWE — **Rho·de·sian** \-zh(ē-)ən\ *adj or n*
Rhone *or French* **Rhône** \ˈrōn\ river 505 mi. (813 km.) long Switzerland & SE France
Rich·mond \ˈrich-mənd\ **1** — see STATEN ISLAND **2** city, * of Virginia
Richmond upon Thames borough of SW Greater London, England
Ri·ga \ˈrē-gə\ city, * of Latvia
Rio de Ja·nei·ro \ˈrē-(ˌ)ō-dā-zhə-ˈner-(ˌ)ō, -dē-\ city SE Brazil on Guanabara Bay
Rio Grande \ˌrē-(ˌ)ō-ˈgrand, -ˈgran-dē\ *or*

Mexican **Rio Bra•vo** \ˌrē-(ˌ)ō-ˈbrä-(ˌ)vō\ river 1885 mi. (3034 km.) long SW U.S., forming part of U.S.–Mexico boundary, and flowing into Gulf of Mexico

Río Muni — see MBINI

Riv•er•side \ˈri-vər-ˌsīd\ city S California

Riv•i•era \ˌri-vē-ˈer-ə\ coast region SE France & NW Italy

Ri•yadh \rē-ˈyäd\ city, ✻ of Saudi Arabia

Ro•a•noke \ˈrō-(ə-)ˌnōk\ city W Virginia

Roanoke Island island North Carolina S of entrance to Albemarle Sound

Rob•son, Mount \ˈräb-sən\ mountain 12,972 ft. (3954 m.) W Canada in E British Columbia; highest in the Canadian Rockies

Roch•es•ter \ˈrä-chəs-tər, -ˌches-tər\ city W New York

Rock•ford \ˈräk-fərd\ city N Illinois

Rocky Mountains *or* **Rock•ies** \ˈrä-kēz\ mountains W North America extending SE from N Alaska to *cen* New Mexico

Roman Empire the empire of ancient Rome

Ro•ma•nia \rü-ˈmā-nē-ə, rō-, -nyə\ *or* **Ru•ma•nia** \rü-\ country SE Europe on Black Sea; ✻, Bucharest

Rom•blon \räm-ˈblōn\ island group *cen* Philippines

Rome \ˈrōm\ *or Italian* **Ro•ma** \ˈrō-mä\ city, ✻ of Italy

Ro•sa•rio \rō-ˈzär-ē-ˌō, -ˈsär-\ city E *cen* Argentina on the Paraná

Ro•seau \rō-ˈzō\ seaport, ✻ of Dominica

Ros•tov–on–Don \rə-ˈstȯf-ˌän-ˈdän, -ˈstȯv, -ˌȯn-\ city S Russia in Europe

Ros•well \ˈräz-ˌwel, -wəl\ city SE New Mexico

Ro•ta \ˈrō-tə\ island W Pacific in the Marianas

Rot•ter•dam \ˈrä-tər-ˌdam, -ˌdäm\ city & port SW Netherlands

Ru•an•da–Urun•di \rü-ˈän-dä-ü-ˈrün-dē\ former trust territory E *cen* Africa bordering on Lake Tanganyika; now divided into Burundi & Rwanda

Rudolf, Lake — see TURKANA, LAKE

Ruhr \ˈru̇r\ **1** river 146 mi. (235 km.) long W Germany flowing NW & W to the Rhine **2** industrial district W Germany E of the Rhine in valley of Ruhr River

Rumania — see ROMANIA

Rupert's Land PRINCE RUPERT'S LAND

Rush•more, Mount \ˈrəsh-ˌmȯr\ mountain 5600 ft. (1707 m.) W South Dakota in Black Hills

Rus•sia \ˈrə-shə\ **1** former empire largely having the same boundaries as U.S.S.R. **2** SOVIET UNION **3** country E Europe & N Asia; ✻, Moscow

Ru•the•nia \rü-ˈthē-nyə, -nē-ə\ region W Ukraine W of the N Carpathians — **Ru•the•nian** \-ˈthē-nyən, -nē-ən\ *adj or n*

Ru•wen•zo•ri \ˌrü-ən-ˈzȯr-ē\ mountain group E *cen* Africa between Uganda & Democratic Republic of the Congo; highest Mount Margherita 16,763 ft. (5109 m.)

Rwan•da *formerly* **Ru•an•da** \rü-ˈän-dä\ country E *cen* Africa; ✻, Kigali — **Rwan•dan** \-dən\ *adj or n*

Ryu•kyu \rē-ˈyü-(ˌ)kyü, -(ˌ)kü\ islands Japan extending in an arc from S Japan, to N tip of Taiwan — **Ryu•kyu•an** \-ˌkyü-ən, -ˌkü-\ *adj or n*

Saar \ˈsär, ˈzär\ **1** river about 150 mi. (241 km.) long Europe flowing from E France to W Germany **2** *or* **Saar•land** \ˈsär-ˌland, ˈzär-\ region W Europe in valley of Saar River between France & Germany

Sac•ra•men•to \ˌsa-krə-ˈmen-(ˌ)tō\ **1** river 382 mi. (615 km.) long N California flowing S into Suisun Bay **2** city, ✻ of California

Sag•ue•nay \ˈsa-gə-ˌnā, ˌsa-gə-ˈ\ **1** river 105 mi. (169 km.) long Canada in S Quebec flowing E into the Saint Lawrence **2** city Canada in S Quebec

Sa•ha•ra \sə-ˈher-ə, -ˈhär-\ desert region N Africa extending from Atlantic coast to Red Sea — **Sa•ha•ran** \-ən\ *adj*

Sa•hel \ˈsa-hil, sə-ˈhil\ the S fringe of the Sahara

Saigon — see HO CHI MINH CITY

Saint Al•bans \ˈȯl-bənz\ city SE England

Saint Cath•a•rines \ˈka-th(ə-)rənz\ city Canada in SE Ontario

Saint Christopher — see SAINT KITTS

Saint Clair, Lake \ˈkler\ lake SE Michigan & SE Ontario connected by **Saint Clair River** (40 mi. or 64 km. long) with Lake Huron & draining by Detroit River into Lake Erie

Saint Croix \sānt-ˈkrȯi, sənt-\ **1** river 129 mi. (208 km.) long Canada & U.S. on border between New Brunswick & Maine **2** island West Indies; largest of Virgin Islands of the U.S.

Saint Eli•as, Mount \i-ˈlī-əs\ mountain 18,008 ft. (5489 m.) on Alaska–Canada boundary in **Saint Elias Range**

Saint George's \ˈjȯr-jəz\ town, ✻ of Grenada

Saint George's Channel channel British Isles between SW Wales & Ireland

Saint Gott•hard \sānt-ˈgä-tərd, sənt-, ˈgät-hərd\ pass S *cen* Switzerland in Saint Gotthard Range of the Alps

Saint He•le•na \ˌsānt-ə-ˈlē-nə, ˌsānt-hə-ˈlē-\ island South Atlantic; a British colony

Saint Hel•ens, Mount \sānt-ˈhe-lənz, sənt-\ volcano S Washington

Saint John \sānt-ˈjän, sənt-\ city & port Canada in New Brunswick

Saint John's \sānt-ˈjänz, sənt-\ **1** city, ✻ of Antigua and Barbuda **2** city, ✻ of Newfoundland and Labrador, Canada

Saint Kitts \ˈkits\ *or* **Saint Chris•to•pher** \ˈkris-tə-fər\ island West Indies in the Leeward Islands; with Nevis forms independent **Saint Kitts and Nevis**; ✻, Basseterre (on Saint Kitts)

Saint Law·rence \sānt-ˈlȯr-ən(t)s, sənt-, -ˈlär-\ **1** river 760 mi. (1223 km.) long E Canada in Ontario & Quebec bordering on U.S. in New York and flowing from Lake Ontario NE into the **Gulf of Saint Lawrence** (inlet of the Atlantic) **2** seaway Canada & U.S. in and along the Saint Lawrence between Lake Ontario & Montreal
Saint Lou·is \sānt-ˈlü-əs, sənt-\ city E Missouri on the Mississippi
Saint Lu·cia \sānt-ˈlü-shə, sənt-\ island West Indies in the Windwards S of Martinique; country; ✱, Castries
Saint Mo·ritz \ˌsānt-mə-ˈrits, ˌsaⁿ-mə-\ *or G* **Sankt Mo·ritz** \ˌzäŋkt-mə-ˈrits\ town E Switzerland
Saint Paul \ˈpȯl\ city, ✱ of Minnesota
Saint Pe·ters·burg \ˈpē-tərz-ˌbərg\ **1** city W Florida **2** *or 1914–24* **Pet·ro·grad** \ˈpe-trə-ˌgrad, -ˌgrät\ *or 1924–91* **Le·nin·grad** \ˈle-nən-ˌgrad, -ˌgrät\ city W Russia in Europe
Saint Thom·as \ˈtä-məs\ island West Indies, one of Virgin Islands of the U.S.; chief town, Charlotte Amalie
Saint Vin·cent \sānt-ˈvin(t)-sənt, sənt-\ island West Indies in the *cen* Windward Islands; with N Grenadines forms independent **Saint Vincent and the Grenadines**; ✱, Kingstown (on Saint Vincent)
Sai·pan \sī-ˈpan, -ˈpän, ˈsī-ˌ\ island W Pacific in S *cen* Marianas
Sa·kai \(ˌ)sä-ˈkī\ city Japan in S Honshu
Sa·kha·lin \ˈsa-kə-ˌlēn, -lən; ˌsä-kä-ˈlēn\ island SE Russia in W Pacific N of Hokkaido, Japan
Sal·a·mis \ˈsa-lə-məs\ ancient city Cyprus on E coast
Sa·lem \ˈsā-ləm\ city, ✱ of Oregon
Sa·li·nas \sə-ˈlē-nəs\ city W California
Salisbury — see HARARE
Salisbury Plain plateau S England; site of Stonehenge
Salop — see SHROPSHIRE
Salt Lake City city, ✱ of Utah
Sal·ton Sea \ˈsȯl-tᵊn\ saline lake about 235 ft. (72 m.) below sea level SE California; formed by diversion of water from Colorado River
Sal·va·dor \ˈsal-və-ˌdȯr, ˌsal-və-ˈ\ *or* **Ba·hia** \bä-ˈē-ə\ city NE Brazil on the Atlantic — **Sal·va·dor·an** \ˌsal-və-ˈdȯr-ən\ *or* **Sal·va·dor·ean** *or* **Sal·va·dor·ian** \-ē-ən\ *adj or n*
Sal·ween \ˈsal-ˌwēn\ river about 1500 mi. (2415 km.) long SE Asia flowing from Tibet S into Bay of Bengal in Myanmar
Sa·mar \ˈsä-ˌmär\ island *cen* Philippines
Sa·ma·ra \sə-ˈmär-ə\ *or 1935–91* **Kuy·by·shev** \ˈkwē-bə-ˌshef, ˈkü-ē-bə-, -ˌshev\ city W Russia, on the Volga
Sa·mar·ia \sə-ˈmer-ē-ə\ district of ancient Palestine W of the Jordan between Galilee & Judaea
Sam·ar·qand *or* **Sam·ar·kand** \ˈsa-mər-ˌkand\ city E Uzbekistan
Sam·ni·um \ˈsam-nē-əm\ ancient country S *cen* Italy — **Sam·nite** \ˈsam-ˌnīt\ *adj or n*
Sa·moa \sə-ˈmō-ə\ **1** islands SW *cen* Pacific N of Tonga; divided at longitude 171° W into American Samoa (or Eastern Samoa) & independent Samoa **2** *formerly* **Western Samoa** islands Samoa W of 171° W; country; ✱ Apia — **Sa·mo·an** \sə-ˈmō-ən\ *adj or n*
Sa·mos \ˈsā-ˌmäs, ˈsä-ˌmȯs\ island Greece in the Aegean off coast of Turkey
San·aa *or* **Sana** \sa-ˈnä, ˈsa-ˌnä\ city SW Arabia, ✱ of Yemen
San An·dre·as Fault \ˌsan-an-ˈdrā-əs\ zone of faults in California extending from N coast toward head of Gulf of California
San An·to·nio \ˌsan-ən-ˈtō-nē-ˌō\ city S Texas
San Ber·nar·di·no \ˌsan-ˌbər-nə(r)-ˈdē-(ˌ)nō\ city S California
San Di·ego \ˌsan-dē-ˈā-(ˌ)gō\ coastal city SW California
San·i·bel Island \ˈsa-nə-bəl, -ˌbel\ island SW Florida
Sand·wich \ˈsan(d)-(ˌ)wich\ town SE England
Sandwich Islands — see HAWAII
San Fran·cis·co \ˌsan-frən-ˈsis-(ˌ)kō\ city W California on San Francisco Bay & Pacific Ocean
San Joa·quin \ˌsan-wä-ˈkēn, -wȯ-\ river 350 mi. (563 km.) long *cen* California flowing NW into the Sacramento
San Jo·se \ˌsan-(h)ō-ˈzā\ city W California SE of San Francisco
San Jo·sé \ˌsäŋ-hō-ˈsā, ˌsan-(h)ō-ˈzā\ city, ✱ of Costa Rica
San Juan \san-ˈwän, ˌsän-ˈhwän\ city, ✱ of Puerto Rico
San Ma·ri·no \ˌsan-mə-ˈrē-(ˌ)nō\ **1** small country S Europe surrounded by Italy ENE of Florence near Adriatic Sea **2** town, its ✱ — **Sam·mar·i·nese** \ˌsa(m)-ˌma-rə-ˈnēz, -ˈnēs\ *n* — **San Mar·i·nese** \ˌsan-ˌma-\ *adj or n*
San Pe·dro Su·la \sän-ˈpā-(ˌ)thrō-ˈsü-lä\ city NW Honduras
San Sal·va·dor \san-ˈsal-və-ˌdȯr, ˌsän-ˈsäl-vä-ˌthȯr\ **1** island *cen* Bahamas **2** city, ✱ of El Salvador
San·ta Ana \ˌsan-tə-ˈa-nə, ˌsän-tä-ˈä-nä\ city SW California ESE of Long Beach
San·ta Bar·ba·ra \ˈbär-b(ə-)rə\ *or* **Channel** islands California off SW coast in the North Pacific
Santa Clara \ˈkler-ə\ city W California NW of San Jose
Santa Cla·ri·ta \klə-ˈrē-tə\ city S California N of Los Angeles
San·ta Fe \ˌsan-tə-ˈfā\ city, ✱ of New Mexico
Santa Fe Trail pioneer route to the SW

U.S. about 1200 mi. (1930 km.) long used esp. 1821–80 from vicinity of Kansas City, Missouri, to Santa Fe, New Mexico

San·ta Ro·sa \ˌsan-tə-ˈrō-zə\ city W California N of San Francisco

San·ti·a·go \ˌsan-tē-ˈä-(ˌ)gō, ˌsän-\ city, ✻ of Chile

San·to Do·min·go \ˌsan-tə-də-ˈmiŋ-(ˌ)gō\ *formerly* **Tru·ji·llo** \trü-ˈhē-(ˌ)yō\ city, ✻ of Dominican Republic

São Pau·lo \sau̇ⁿ-ˈpau̇-(ˌ)lü, -(ˌ)lō\ city SE Brazil

São To·mé \ˌsau̇ⁿ-tə-ˈmā\ town, ✻ of São Tomé and Príncipe

São Tomé and Príncipe country W Africa; ✻ São Tomé

Sap·po·ro \ˈsä-pō-ˌrō; sä-ˈpȯr-(ˌ)ō\ city Japan on W Hokkaido

Sa·ra·je·vo \ˌsa-rə-ˈyā-(ˌ)vō, ˌsär-ə-\ city SE *cen* Bosnia and Herzegovina, its ✻

Sa·ra·tov \sə-ˈrä-təf\ city W Russia, on the Volga

Sar·din·ia \sär-ˈdi-nē-ə, -ˈdi-nyə\ island Italy in the Mediterranean S of Corsica — **Sar·din·ian** \sär-ˈdi-nē-ən, -ˈdin-yən\ *adj or n*

Sar·gas·so Sea \sär-ˈga-(ˌ)sō\ area of nearly still water in the North Atlantic lying chiefly between 20° & 35° N latitude & 30° & 70° W longitude

Sas·katch·e·wan \sə-ˈska-chə-wən, sa-, -ˌwän\ province W Canada; ✻, Regina

Sas·ka·toon \ˌsas-kə-ˈtün\ city *cen* Saskatchewan, Canada

Sau·di Ara·bia \ˈsau̇-dē, ˈsȯ-dē, sä-ˈü-dē\ country SW Asia occupying largest part of Arabian Peninsula; ✻, Riyadh — **Saudi** *adj or n* — **Saudi Arabian** *adj or n*

Sault Sainte Ma·rie Canals \ˈsü-(ˌ)sānt-mə-ˈrē\ *or* **Soo Canals** \ˌsü\ three ship canals, two in U.S. (Michigan) & one in Canada (Ontario), at rapids in river connecting Lake Superior & Lake Huron

Sa·vaii \sə-ˈvī-ˌē\ island, largest in independent Samoa

Sa·van·nah \sə-ˈva-nə\ city & port E Georgia

Sa·voy \sə-ˈvȯi\ *or French* **Sa·voie** \sä-ˈvwä\ region SE France SW of Switzerland bordering on Italy — **Sa·voy·ard** \sə-ˈvȯi-ˌärd, ˌsa-ˌvȯi-ˈärd, ˌsa-ˌvwä-ˈyär(d)\ *adj or n*

Sca·fell Pike \ˌskȯ-ˈfel\ mountain 3210 ft. (978 m.) NW England; highest in Cumbrian Mountains & in England

Scan·di·na·via \ˌskan-də-ˈnā-vē-ə, -vyə\ **1** peninsula N Europe occupied by Norway & Sweden **2** Denmark, Norway, Sweden, & as used by some also Iceland & Finland — **Scan·di·na·vian** \ˌskan-də-ˈnā-vē-ən, -vyən\ *adj or n*

Scar·bor·ough \ˈskär-ˌbər-ō\ former city Canada in SE Ontario; now part of Toronto

Schel·de \ˈskel-də\ *or* **Scheldt** \ˈskelt\ river 270 mi. (434 km.) long W Europe flowing from N France through Belgium into North Sea in Netherlands

Schuyl·kill \ˈskü-kəl, ˈskül-ˌkil\ river 131 mi. (211 km.) long SE Pennsylvania flowing SE into the Delaware River at Philadelphia

Scil·ly, Isles of \ˈsi-lē\ island group SW England off Land's End

Sco·tia \ˈskō-shə\ SCOTLAND — the Medieval Latin name

Scot·land \ˈskät-lənd\ *or Latin* **Cal·e·do·nia** \ˌka-lə-ˈdō-nyə, -nē-ə\ country N Great Britain; a division of United Kingdom; ✻, Edinburgh

Scotts·dale \ˈskäts-ˌdāl\ city SW *cen* Arizona E of Phoenix

Scyth·ia \ˈsi-thē-ə, -t͟hē-\ ancient area of Europe & Asia N & NE of Black Sea & E of Aral Sea — **Scyth·i·an** \ˈsi-thē-ən, -t͟hē-\ *adj or n*

Se·at·tle \sē-ˈa-təl\ city & port W Washington

Seine \ˈsān, ˈsen\ river 480 mi. (772 km.) long N France flowing NW into English Channel

Sel·kirk \ˈsel-ˌkərk\ range of the Rocky Mountains SE British Columbia, Canada; highest peak, 11,555 ft. (3522 m.)

Se·ma·rang \sə-ˈmär-ˌäŋ\ city Indonesia in *cen* Java

Sen·dai \(ˌ)sen-ˈdī\ city Japan in NE Honshu

Sen·e·ca Falls \ˈse-ni-kə\ village W *cen* New York

Sen·e·gal \ˌse-ni-ˈgȯl, -ˈgäl, ˈse-ni-ˌ\ **1** river 1015 mi. (1633 km.) long W Africa flowing W into the North Atlantic **2** country W Africa; ✻, Dakar — **Sen·e·ga·lese** \ˌse-ni-gə-ˈlēz, -ˈlēs\ *adj or n*

Seoul \ˈsōl\ city, ✻ of South Korea

Ser·bia \ˈsər-bē-ə\ country S Europe in the Balkans; ✻ Belgrade

Serbia and Montenegro *or 1992–2003* **Yugoslavia** former country S Europe on Balkan Peninsula

Ser·en·ge·ti Plain \ˌser-ən-ˈge-tē\ area N Tanzania

Seven Hills the seven hills upon and about which was built the city of Rome, Italy

Sev·ern \ˈse-vərn\ river 210 mi. (338 km.) long Wales & England flowing from E *cen* Wales into Bristol Channel

Se·ville \sə-ˈvil\ *or Spanish* **Se·vi·lla** \sā-ˈvē-(ˌ)yä\ city SW Spain

Sew·ard Peninsula \ˈsü-ərd\ peninsula 180 mi. (290 km.) long W Alaska projecting into Bering Sea

Sey·chelles \sā-ˈshel(z)\ islands W Indian Ocean NE of Madagascar; country; ✻, Victoria — **Sey·chel·lois** \ˌsā-shəl-ˈwä, -ˌshel-\ *n*

Shang·hai \shaŋ-ˈhī\ city & port E China

Shan·non \ˈsha-nən\ river 230 mi. (370 km.) long W Ireland flowing S & W into the North Atlantic

Shar·on, Plain of \ˈsher-ən\ region Israel on the coast
Shas·ta, Mount \ˈshas-tə\ mountain 14,162 ft. (4316 m.) N California in Cascade Range
Shatt al Ar·ab \ˌshat-al-ˈa-rəb\ river 120 mi. (193 km.) long SE Iraq formed by flowing together of Euphrates & Tigris rivers and flowing SE into Persian Gulf
Shef·field \ˈshe-ˌfēld\ city N England
Shen·an·do·ah \ˌshe-nən-ˈdō-ə, ˌsha-nə-ˈdō-ə\ valley Virginia between the Allegheny & Blue Ridge mountains
Shen·yang \ˈshən-ˈyäŋ\ *or traditionally* **Muk·den** \ˈmu̇k-dən, ˈmək-; mu̇k-ˈden\ city NE China; chief city of Manchuria
Sher·brooke \ˈshər-ˌbru̇k\ city Quebec, Canada E of Montreal
Sher·wood Forest \ˈshər-ˌwu̇d\ ancient royal forest *cen* England
Shet·land \ˈshet-lənd\ islands N Scotland NE of the Orkneys
Shi·jia·zhuang *or* **Shih–chia–chuang** \ˈshir-ˈjyä-ˈjwäŋ, ˈshē-\ city NE China
Shi·ko·ku \shē-ˈkō-(ˌ)kü\ island S Japan E of Kyushu
Shi·raz \shi-ˈräz, -ˈraz\ city SW *cen* Iran
Shreve·port \ˈshrēv-ˌpȯrt\ city NW Louisiana on Red River
Shrews·bury \ˈsh(r)üz-ˌber-ē, -b(ə-)rē\ town W England
Shrop·shire \ˈshräp-shər, -ˌshir\ *or 1974–80* **Sal·op** \ˈsal-əp\ county W England bordering on Wales
Shu·ma·gin \ˈshü-mə-gən\ islands SW Alaska S of Alaska Peninsula
Siam — see THAILAND
Siam, Gulf of — see THAILAND, GULF OF
Si·be·ria \sī-ˈbir-ē-ə\ region N Asia in Russia between the Urals & the North Pacific — **Si·be·ri·an** \-ən\ *adj or n*
Sic·i·ly \ˈsi-s(ə-)lē\ *or Italian* **Si·ci·lia** \sē-ˈchēl-yä\ island S Italy SW of toe of peninsula of Italy; ✻, Palermo — **Si·cil·ian** \sə-ˈsil-yən\ *adj or n*
Si·er·ra Le·one \sē-ˌer-ə-lē-ˈōn, ˌsir-ə-, -lē-ˈō-nē\ country W Africa on the North Atlantic; ✻, Freetown — **Si·er·ra Le·on·ean** \-ˈō-nē-ən\ *adj or n*
Si·er·ra Ma·dre \sē-ˌer-ə-ˈmä-drā, ˈsyer-ä-ˈmä-thrā\ mountain system Mexico including **Sierra Madre Oc·ci·den·tal** \ˌäk-sə-ˌden-ˈtäl, ˌȯk-sē-ˌthen-ˈtäl\ range W of the *cen* plateau, **Sierra Madre Ori·en·tal** \ˌȯr-ē-ˌen-ˈtäl\ range E of the plateau, & **Sierra Madre del Sur** \ˈsu̇r, ˈsür\ range to the S
Sierra Ne·va·da \nə-ˈva-də, -ˈvä-\ **1** mountain range E California & W Nevada — see WHITNEY, MOUNT **2** mountain range S Spain
Sik·kim \ˈsi-kəm, -ˌkim\ former country SE Asia on S slope of the Himalayas between Nepal & Bhutan; state of India since 1975
Si·le·sia \sī-ˈlē-zh(ē-)ə, sə-, -sh(ē-)ə\ region E *cen* Europe in valley of the upper Oder; formerly chiefly in Germany now chiefly in E Czech Republic & SW Poland — **Si·le·sian** \-zh(ē-)ən, -sh(ē-)ən\ *adj or n*
Silk Road *or* **Silk Route** ancient trade route that extended from China to the Mediterranean
Sim·coe, Lake \ˈsim-(ˌ)kō\ lake Canada in SE Ontario
Si·mi Valley \sē-ˈmē\ city SW California W of Los Angeles
Sim·plon Pass \ˈsim-ˌplän\ mountain pass 6590 ft. (2009 m.) between Switzerland & Italy
Si·nai \ˈsī-ˌnī\ **1** mountain on Sinai Peninsula where according to the Bible the Law was given to Moses **2** peninsula extension of continent of Asia NE Egypt between Red Sea & the Mediterranean
Sin·ga·pore \ˈsiŋ-ə-ˌpȯr\ **1** island off S end of Malay Peninsula; country **2** city, its ✻ — **Sin·ga·por·ean** \ˌsiŋ-ə-ˈpȯr-ē-ən\ *adj or n*
Sinkiang Uighur — see XINJIANG UYGUR
Sioux Falls \ˈsü\ city SE South Dakota; largest in state
Skag·ge·rak \ˈska-gə-ˌrak\ arm of North Sea between S Norway & N Denmark
Skop·je \ˈskȯ-pye, -pyə\ city, ✻ of North Macedonia
Sla·vo·nia \slə-ˈvō-nē-ə, -nyə\ region E Croatia — **Sla·vo·ni·an** \-nē-ən, -nyən\ *adj or n*
Slo·va·kia \slō-ˈvä-kē-ə, -ˈva-\ country *cen* Europe; ✻, Bratislava
Slo·ve·nia \slō-ˈvē-nē-ə, -nyə\ country S Europe; ✻, Ljubljana
Smyrna — see IZMIR
Snake \ˈsnāk\ river NW U.S. flowing from NW Wyoming into the Columbia in SE Washington
Snow·don \ˈsnō-dᵊn\ massif 3560 ft. (1085 m.) in **Snow·do·nia** \snō-ˈdō-nē-ə, -nyə\ (mountainous district) NW Wales; highest point in Wales
So·ci·e·ty \sə-ˈsī-ə-tē\ islands South Pacific; belonging to France; chief island, Tahiti
So·fia \ˈsō-fē-ə, ˈsȯ-, sō-ˈ\ city, ✻ of Bulgaria
So·ho \ˈsō-ˌhō\ district of *cen* London, England
So·li·hull \ˌsō-li-ˈhəl\ city *cen* England
Sol·o·mon \ˈsä-lə-mən\ **1** islands W Pacific E of New Guinea divided between Papua New Guinea & independent Solomon Islands **2** sea, arm of Coral Sea W of the Solomons
Solomon Islands country, SW Pacific E of New Guinea; ✻, Honiara (on Guadalcanal)
So·ma·lia \sō-ˈmä-lē-ə, sə-, -ˈmäl-yə\ country E Africa on Gulf of Aden & In-

dian Ocean; ✻, Mogadishu — **So·ma·li·an** \-ˈmä-lē-ən, -ˈmäl-yən\ *adj or n*
So·ma·li·land \sō-ˈmä-lē-ˌland, sə-\ historical region E Africa consisting of Somalia, Djibouti, & part of E Ethiopia — **So·ma·li** \sō-ˈmä-lē, sə-\ *n*
Som·er·set \ˈsə-mər-ˌset, -sət\ *or* **Som·er·set·shire** \-ˌshir, -shər\ county SW England
So·nor·an \sə-ˈnȯr-ən\ *or* **So·no·ra** \sə-ˈnȯr-ə\ desert SW U.S. & NW Mexico
Soo Canals — see SAULT SAINTE MARIE CANALS
South Africa, Republic of *formerly* **Union of South Africa** country S Africa; administrative ✻, Pretoria; legislative ✻, Cape Town; judicial ✻, Bloemfontein — **South African** *adj or n*
South America continent of Western Hemisphere SE of North America and chiefly S of the Equator — **South American** *adj or n*
South·amp·ton \saů-ˈtham(p)-tən, saůth-ˈham(p)-\ city S England
South Australia state S Australia; ✻, Adelaide — **South Australian** *adj or n*
South Bend \ˈbend\ city N Indiana
South Cape *or* **South Point** — see KA LAE
South Car·o·li·na \ˌker(-ə)-ˈlī-nə, ˌka-rə-\ state SE U.S.; ✻, Columbia — **South Car·o·lin·i·an** \-ˈli-nē-ən, -ˈli-nyən\ *adj or n*
South China Sea — see CHINA
South Da·ko·ta \də-ˈkō-tə\ state NW *cen* U.S.; ✻, Pierre — **South Da·ko·tan** \-ˈkō-tᵊn\ *adj or n*
South·end–on–Sea \ˌsaů-ˌthend-ˌȯn-ˈsē, -ˌän-\ seaside resort SE England E of London
Southern Alps mountain range New Zealand in W South Island extending almost the length of the island
Southern Hemisphere the half of the earth that lies S of the Equator
South Georgia island S Atlantic E of Tierra del Fuego; administered by United Kingdom
South Island island S New Zealand
South Korea *or* **Republic of Korea** country S half of Korean Peninsula in E Asia; ✻, Seoul
South Seas the areas of the Atlantic, Indian, & Pacific oceans in the Southern Hemisphere
South Shields \ˈshēldz\ seaport N England
South Sudan country E Africa formed 2011 from the S part of Sudan; ✻, Juba
South Vietnam — see VIETNAM
South·wark \ˈsə-thərk, ˈsaůth-wərk\ borough of S Greater London, England
South–West Africa — see NAMIBIA
South Yorkshire metropolitan county N England
Soviet Central Asia portion of *cen* & SW Asia formerly belonging to U.S.S.R. and including the former soviet socialist republics of present-day Kyrgyzstan, Tajikistan, Turkmenistan, Uzbekistan & by some thought also to include Kazakhstan
Soviet Union *or* **U.S.S.R.** *or officially* **Union of Soviet Socialist Republics** country 1922–91 E Europe & N Asia; former union of 15 republics comprising present-day countries of Armenia, Azerbaijan, Belarus, Estonia, Georgia, Kazakhstan, Kyrgyzstan, Latvia, Lithuania, Moldova, Russia, Tajikistan, Turkmenistan, Ukraine, & Uzbekistan
So·we·to \sō-ˈwā-tō, -ˈwe-, -tü\ residential area NE Republic of South Africa adjoining SW Johannesburg
Spain \ˈspān\ country SW Europe on Iberian Peninsula; ✻, Madrid
Spanish America **1** the Spanish-speaking countries of America **2** the parts of America settled and formerly governed by the Spanish
Spanish Guinea — see EQUATORIAL GUINEA
Spanish Sahara — see WESTERN SAHARA
Spar·ta \ˈspär-tə\ ancient city S Greece in Peloponnese; ✻ of Laconia
Spo·kane \spō-ˈkan\ city E Washington
Spring·field \ˈspriŋ-ˌfēld\ **1** city, ✻ of Illinois **2** city SW Massachusetts **3** city SW Missouri
Sri Lan·ka \(ˌ)srē-ˈläŋ-kə, (ˌ)shrē-, -ˈlaŋ-\ *formerly* **Cey·lon** \si-ˈlän, sā-\ country having the same boundaries as island of Ceylon; ✻, Colombo — **Sri Lan·kan** \-ˈläŋ-kən, -ˈlaŋ-\ *adj or n*
Sri·na·gar \srē-ˈnə-gər\ city N India
Staf·ford \ˈsta-fərd\ town W *cen* England
Staf·ford·shire \ˈsta-fərd-ˌshir, -shər\ *or* **Stafford** county W *cen* England
Staked Plain — see LLANO ESTACADO
Stam·ford \ˈstam-fərd\ city SW Connecticut
Stan·ley \ˈstan-lē\ town, ✻ of Falkland Islands
Stat·en Island \ˈsta-tᵊn\ **1** island SE New York SW of mouth of the Hudson **2** *formerly* **Rich·mond** \ˈrich-mənd\ borough of New York City including Staten Island
Ster·ling Heights \ˈstər-liŋ\ city SE Michigan
Stir·ling \ˈstər-liŋ\ town *cen* Scotland
Stock·holm \ˈstäk-ˌhō(l)m\ city, ✻ of Sweden
Stock·port \ˈstäk-ˌpȯrt\ town NW England
Stock·ton \ˈstäk-tən\ city *cen* California
Stoke–on–Trent \ˈstōk-ˌän-ˈtrent, -ˌȯn-\ city *cen* England
Stone·henge \ˈstōn-ˌhenj, (ˌ)stōn-ˈ\ prehistoric assemblage of megaliths S England in Wiltshire on Salisbury Plain
Stone Mountain mountain 1686 ft. (514 m.) NW Georgia E of Atlanta
Stor·no·way \ˈstȯr-nə-ˌwā\ seaport NW Scotland; chief town of Lewis with Harris Island

Stra·bane \strə-ˈban\ district W Northern Ireland

Strath·clyde \strath-ˈklīd\ former region SW Scotland; included Glasgow

Strom·bo·li \ˈsträm-bō-(ˌ)lē\ volcano 2500 ft. (758 m.) Italy on **Stromboli Island** in Tyrrhenian Sea

Stutt·gart \ˈshtu̇t-ˌgärt, ˈstu̇t-, ˈstət-\ city SW Germany

Styx \ˈstiks\ chief river of the underworld in Greek mythology

Süchow — see XUZHOU

Su·cre \ˈsü-(ˌ)krā\ city, constitutional ✻ of Bolivia

Su·dan \sü-ˈdan, -ˈdän\ **1** region N Africa S of the Sahara between the Atlantic & the upper Nile **2** country NE Africa S of Egypt; ✻, Khartoum — **Su·da·nese** \ˌsü-də-ˈnēz, -ˈnēs\ *adj or n*

Sud·bury, Greater \ˈsəd-ˌber-ē, -b(ə-)rē\ city SE Ontario, Canada

Su·ez, Gulf of \sü-ˈez, ˈsü-ˌez\ arm of Red Sea

Suez, Isthmus of isthmus NE Egypt between Mediterranean & Red seas connecting Africa & Asia

Suez Canal canal 100 mi. (161 km.) long NE Egypt across the Isthmus of Suez

Suf·folk \ˈsə-fək\ county E England on North Sea

Sui·sun Bay \sə-ˈsün\ inlet of San Francisco Bay, W *cen* California

Su·la·we·si \ˌsü-lä-ˈwā-sē\ island Indonesia E of Borneo

Su·lu \ˈsü-(ˌ)lü\ **1** archipelago SW Philippines SW of Mindanao **2** sea W Philippines

Su·ma·tra \su̇-ˈmä-trə\ island W Indonesia S of Malay Peninsula — **Su·ma·tran** \-trən\ *adj or n*

Su·mer \ˈsü-mər\ the S division of ancient Babylonia — **Su·me·ri·an** \sü-ˈmer-ē-ən, -ˈmir-\ *adj or n*

Sun·belt \ˈsən-ˌbelt\ region S & SW U.S.

Sun·da \ˈsün-də, ˈsən-\ strait between Java & Sumatra

Sun·der·land \ˈsən-dər-lənd\ seaport N England

Sun·ny·vale \ˈsə-nē-ˌvāl\ city W California

Sun Valley resort center *cen* Idaho

Su·pe·ri·or, Lake \su̇-ˈpir-ē-ər\ lake E *cen* North America in U.S. & Canada; largest of the Great Lakes

Su·ra·ba·ya \ˌsu̇r-ə-ˈbī-ə\ city Indonesia in NE Java

Su·ri·na·me \ˌsu̇r-ə-ˈnä-mə\ country N South America between Guyana & French Guiana; ✻, Paramaribo — **Su·ri·nam·er** \ˈsu̇r-ə-ˌnä-mər, ˌsu̇r-ə-ˈnä-\ *n* — **Su·ri·nam·ese** \ˌsu̇r-ə-nə-ˈmēz, -ˈmēs\ *adj or n*

Sur·rey \ˈsər-ē, ˈsə-rē\ city Canada in SW British Columbia

Sut·ton \ˈsə-tᵊn\ borough of S Greater London, England

Su·va \ˈsü-və\ city & port, ✻ of Fiji on Viti Levu Island

Su·wan·nee \sə-ˈwä-nē, ˈswä-\ river 250 mi. (400 km.) long SE U.S. flowing SW into Gulf of Mexico

Sverdlovsk — see YEKATERINBURG

Swan·sea \ˈswän-zē\ city & port SE Wales

Swa·zi·land \ˈswä-zē-ˌland\ — see ESWATINI — **Swa·zi** \ˈswä-zē\ *adj or n*

Swe·den \ˈswē-dᵊn\ country N Europe on Scandinavia (peninsula) bordering on Baltic Sea; ✻, Stockholm

Swit·zer·land \ˈswit-sər-lənd\ country W Europe in the Alps; ✻, Bern

Syd·ney \ˈsid-nē\ city SE Australia, ✻ of New South Wales

Syr·a·cuse \ˈsir-ə-ˌkyüs, -ˌkyüz\ city *cen* New York

Syr·ia \ˈsir-ē-ə\ **1** ancient region SW Asia bordering on the Mediterranean **2** country S of Turkey; ✻, Damascus — **Syr·i·an** \ˈsir-ē-ən\ *adj or n*

Syrian Desert desert region between Mediterranean coast & the Euphrates in N Saudi Arabia, SE Syria, W Iraq, & NE Jordan

Table Bay harbor of Cape Town, Republic of South Africa

Ta·briz \tə-ˈbrēz\ city NW Iran

Ta·co·ma \tə-ˈkō-mə\ city & port W Washington S of Seattle

Taegu — see DAEGU

Tae·jon \ˈtā-ˈjən, ˈdā-\ *or* **Dae·jeon** \ˈdā-\ city *cen* South Korea NW of Taegu

Ta·gus \ˈtā-gəs\ *or Spanish* **Ta·jo** \ˈtä-(ˌ)hō\ *or Portuguese* **Te·jo** \ˈtā-(ˌ)zhü\ river 626 mi. (1007 km.) long Spain & Portugal flowing W into the North Atlantic

Ta·hi·ti \tə-ˈhē-tē\ island South Pacific in Society Islands

Tai·bei \ˈtī-ˈbā\ *or* **Tai·pei** \ˈtī-ˈpā, -ˈbā\ city, ✻ of Taiwan

T'ai–nan \ˈtī-ˈnän\ city SW Taiwan

Tai·wan \ˈtī-ˈwän\ *formerly* **For·mo·sa** \fȯr-ˈmō-sə, fər-, -zə\ **1** island off SE coast of mainland China; ✻, Taibei **2** strait between Taiwan & mainland of China connecting East China & South China seas — **Tai·wan·ese** \ˌtī-wə-ˈnēz, -ˈnēs\ *adj or n*

Tai·yuan \ˈtī-ˈywen, -ˈywän\ city N China

Tai·zhong \ˈtī-ˈjüŋ\ *or* **Tai·chung** \ˈtī-ˈchu̇ŋ\ city W Taiwan

Ta·jik·i·stan \tä-ˌji-ki-ˈstan, tə-, -ˌjē-, -ˈstän\ country W *cen* Asia bordering on China & Afghanistan; ✻, Dushanbe

Ta·kli·ma·kan *or* **Ta·kla Ma·kan** \ˌtä-klə-mə-ˈkän\ desert W China

Ta–lien — see DALIAN

Tal·la·has·see \ˌta-lə-ˈha-sē\ city, ✻ of Florida

Tal·linn \ˈta-lən, ˈtä-\ city, ✻ of Estonia

Tam·pa \ˈtam-pə\ city W Florida on **Tampa Bay** (inlet of Gulf of Mexico)

Tan·gan·yi·ka \ˌtan-gə-ˈnyē-kə, ˌtaŋ-gə-, -ˈnē-\ former country E Africa S of Kenya; now part of Tanzania

Tanganyika, Lake lake E Africa between Tanzania & Democratic Republic of the Congo

Tang·shan \ˈdäŋ-ˈshän, ˈtäŋ-\ city NE China

Tan·za·nia \ˌtan-zə-ˈnē-ə, ˌtän-\ country E Africa on Indian Ocean, including Zanzibar; legislative ✻, Dodoma; historic ✻, Dar es Salaam — **Tan·za·ni·an** \-ˈnē-ən\ *adj or n*

Ta·ra·wa \tə-ˈrä-wə, ˈta-rə-ˌwä\ island *cen* Pacific, contains ✻ of Kiribati

Tar·ry·town \ˈta-rē-ˌtaun\ village SE New York

Tar·sus \ˈtär-səs\ ancient city of S Asia Minor; now a city in S Turkey

Tash·kent \tash-ˈkent, täsh-\ city, ✻ of Uzbekistan

Tas·ma·nia \taz-ˈmā-nē-ə, -nyə\ *or earlier* **Van Die·men's Land** \van-ˈdē-mənz\ island SE Australia S of Victoria; a state; ✻, Hobart — **Tas·ma·nian** \taz-ˈmā-nē-ən, -nyən\ *adj or n*

Tas·man Sea \ˈtaz-mən\ the part of the South Pacific between SE Australia & New Zealand

Ta·try \ˈtä-trē\ *or* **Ta·tra** \ˈtä-trə\ mountains N Slovakia & S Poland in *cen* Carpathian Mountains

Taun·ton \ˈtȯn-tᵊn, ˈtän-\ town SW England

Tbi·li·si \tə-ˈbē-lə-sē, tə-bə-ˈlē-sē\ *or* **Tif·lis** \ˈti-fləs, tə-ˈflēs\ city, ✻ of Republic of Georgia

Te·gu·ci·gal·pa \tə-ˌgü-sə-ˈgal-pə, tā-ˌgü-sē-ˈgäl-pä\ city, ✻ of Honduras

Teh·ran \ˌtā-(ə-)ˈran, te-ˈran, -ˈrän\ city, ✻ of Iran; at foot of S slope of Elburz Mountains

Tel Aviv \ˌtel-ə-ˈvēv\ *or officially* **Tel Aviv–Ya·fo** \-ˈyä-fō\ city W Israel on the Mediterranean

Tem·pe \tem-ˈpē\ city S *cen* Arizona

Ten·nes·see \ˌte-nə-ˈsē, ˈte-nə-ˌ\ **1** river 652 mi. (1049 km.) long in Tennessee, N Alabama, & W Kentucky **2** state E *cen* U.S.; ✻, Nashville — **Ten·nes·se·an** *or* **Ten·nes·see·an** \ˌte-nə-ˈsē-ən\ *adj or n*

Te·noch·ti·tlan \tā-ˌnȯch-tēt-ˈlän\ ancient name of Mexico City

Tex·as \ˈtek-səs, -siz\ state S U.S.; ✻, Austin — **Tex·an** \-sən\ *adj or n*

Texas Panhandle the NW projection of land in Texas

Thai·land \ˈtī-ˌland, -lənd\ *formerly* **Si·am** \sī-ˈam\ country SE Asia on Gulf of Thailand; ✻, Bangkok — **Thai·land·er** \-ˌlan-dər, -lən-\ *n*

Thailand, Gulf of *formerly* **Gulf of Siam** arm of South China Sea between Indochina & Malay Peninsula

Thames \ˈtemz\ river over 200 mi. (322 km.) long S England flowing E from the Cotswolds into the North Sea

Thar \ˈtär\ desert E Pakistan & NW India (country) E of Indus River

Thebes \ˈthēbz\ **1** *or* **The·bae** \ˈthē-(ˌ)bē\ ancient city S Egypt on the Nile **2** ancient city E Greece NNW of Athens — **The·ban** \ˈthē-bən\ *adj or n*

Thes·sa·lo·ní·ki \ˌthe-sä-lō-ˈnē-kē\ city N Greece

Thim·phu \tim-ˈpü\ city, ✻ of Bhutan

Thi·ru·van·an·tha·pur·am \ˌtir-ü-və-ˌnən-tə-ˈpu̇r-əm\ city S India

Thousand Islands island group Canada & U.S. in the Saint Lawrence River in Ontario & New York

Thousand Oaks city SW California W of Los Angeles

Thrace \ˈthrās\ *or ancient* **Thra·cia** \ˈthrā-sh(ē-)ə\ region SE Europe in Balkan Peninsula N of the Aegean now divided between Greece & Turkey; in ancient times extended N to the Danube — **Thra·cian** \ˈthrā-shən\ *adj or n*

Thunder Bay city SW Ontario, Canada on Lake Superior

Tian·jin \ˈtyän-ˈjin\ *or* **Tien·tsin** \ˈtyen-ˈtsin, ˈtin-\ city NE China SE of Beijing

Tian Shan *or* **Tien Shan** \ˈtyen-ˈshän, -ˈshan\ mountain system *cen* Asia extending NE from Pamirs

Ti·ber \ˈtī-bər\ *or Italian* **Te·ve·re** \ˈtā-vā-rā\ river 252 mi. (405 km.) long *cen* Italy flowing through Rome into Tyrrhenian Sea

Tiberias, Lake — see GALILEE, SEA OF

Ti·bes·ti \tə-ˈbes-tē\ mountains N *cen* Africa in *cen* Sahara in NW Chad; highest 11,204 ft. (3415 m.)

Ti·bet \tə-ˈbet\ *or* **Xi·zang** \ˈshēd-ˈzäŋ\ region SW China on high plateau at average altitude 16,000 ft. (4877 m.) N of the Himalayas; ✻, Lhasa

Tier·ra del Fue·go \tē-ˈer-ə-(ˌ)del-fü-ˈā-(ˌ)gō, ˈtyer-ä-(ˌ)t͟hel-ˈfwā-gō\ **1** island group off S South America **2** chief island of the group; divided between Argentina & Chile

Tiflis — see TBILISI

Ti·gris \ˈtī-grəs\ river 1180 mi. (1899 km.) long Turkey & Iraq flowing SSE and uniting with the Euphrates to form the Shatt al Arab

Ti·jua·na \ˌtē-ə-ˈwä-nə, tē-ˈhwä-nä\ city NW Mexico on the U.S. border

Timbuktu — see TOMBOUCTOU

Ti·mor \ˈtē-ˌmȯr, tē-ˈ\ island S Malay Archipelago SE of Sulawesi; W half part of Indonesia, E half independent East Timor

Timor–Leste — see EAST TIMOR

Ti·ra·ne *or* **Ti·ra·na** \ti-ˈrä-nə, tē-\ city, ✻ of Albania

Ti·rol *or* **Ty·rol** \tə-ˈrōl\ *or Italian* **Ti·ro·lo** \tē-ˈrȯ-(ˌ)lō\ region in E Alps in W Austria

& NE Italy — **Ti·ro·le·an** \tə-ˈrō-lē-ən, tī-\ *or* **Tir·o·lese** \ˌtir-ə-ˈlēz, ˌtī-rə-, -ˈlēs\ *adj or n*

Ti·ti·ca·ca, Lake \ˌti-ti-ˈkä-kä, ˌtē-tē-\ lake on Bolivia–Peru boundary at altitude of 12,500 ft. (3810 m.)

To·ba·go \tə-ˈbā-(ˌ)gō\ island West Indies NE of Trinidad; part of independent Trinidad and Tobago — **To·ba·go·ni·an** \ˌtō-bə-ˈgō-nē-ən, -nyən\ *n*

To·go \ˈtō-(ˌ)gō\ country W Africa on Gulf of Guinea; ✻, Lomé — **To·go·lese** \ˌtō-gə-ˈlēz, -ˈlēs\ *adj or n*

To·kyo \ˈtō-kē-ˌō, -ˌkyō\ city, ✻ of Japan in SE Honshu on Tokyo Bay — **To·kyo·ite** \ˈtō-kē-(ˌ)ō-ˌīt\ *n*

To·le·do \tə-ˈlē-(ˌ)dō, -ˈlē-də\ city NW Ohio

Tol'·yat·ti \tȯl-ˈyä-tē\ city W Russia; NW of Samara

Tom·bouc·tou \tōⁿ-bük-ˈtü\ *or* **Tim·buk·tu** \ˌtim-ˌbək-ˈtü, tim-ˈbək-(ˌ)tü\ town W Africa in Mali near Niger River

Ton·ga \ˈtäŋ-gə, ˈtäŋ-ə, ˈtȯŋ-ä\ islands SW Pacific E of Fiji Islands; country; ✻, Nukualofa — **Ton·gan** \-(g)ən\ *adj or n*

Ton·kin, Gulf of \ˈtäŋ-kən\ arm of South China Sea E of N Vietnam

To·pe·ka \tə-ˈpē-kə\ city, ✻ of Kansas

Tor·bay \(ˌ)tȯr-ˈbā\ district SW England

To·ron·to \tə-ˈrän-(ˌ)tō, -ˈrän-tə\ city, ✻ of Ontario, Canada

Tor·rance \ˈtȯr-ən(t)s, ˈtär-\ city SW California

Tor·res \ˈtȯr-əs\ strait between New Guinea & Cape York Peninsula, Australia

Tou·louse \tü-ˈlüz\ city SW France

Tower Hamlets borough of E Greater London, England

Trans·vaal \tran(t)s-ˈväl, tranz-\ former province NE Republic of South Africa

Tran·syl·va·nia \ˌtran(t)-səl-ˈvā-nyə, -nē-ə\ region W Romania — **Tran·syl·va·nian** \-nyən, -nē-ən\ *adj or n*

Transylvanian Alps a S extension of Carpathian Mountains in *cen* Romania

Tren·ton \ˈtren-tᵊn\ city, ✻ of New Jersey

Trin·i·dad \ˈtri-nə-ˌdad\ island West Indies off NE coast of Venezuela; with Tobago forms the independent country of **Trinidad and Tobago**; ✻, Port of Spain — **Trin·i·da·di·an** \ˌtri-nə-ˈdā-dē-ən, -ˈda-\ *adj or n*

Trip·o·li \ˈtri-pə-lē\ **1** city & port NW Lebanon **2** city & port, ✻ of Libya

Tris·tan da Cu·nha \ˌtris-tən-də-ˈkü-nə, -nyə\ island South Atlantic, chief of the Tristan da Cunha Islands (part of British colony of Saint Helena)

Tro·bri·and \ˈtrō-brē-ˌänd, -ˌand\ islands SW Pacific in Solomon Sea belonging to Papua New Guinea

Trond·heim \ˈträn-ˌhām\ city & port *cen* Norway

Trow·bridge \ˈtrō-(ˌ)brij\ town S England

Troy \ˈtrȯi\ *or* **Il·i·um** \ˈi-lē-əm\ *or* **Tro·ja** \ˈtrō-jə, -yə\ ancient city NW Asia Minor SW of the Dardanelles

Truk — see CHUUK

Tru·ro \ˈtrůr-(ˌ)ō\ city SW England

Tshwa·ne \ˈchwä-nā\ municipality Republic of South Africa which includes city of Pretoria

Tsinan — see JINAN

Tsingtao — see QINGDAO

Tuc·son \ˈtü-ˌsän\ city SE Arizona

Tu·la \ˈtü-lä\ city W Russia S of Moscow

Tul·sa \ˈtəl-sə\ city NE Oklahoma

Tu·nis \ˈtü-nəs, ˈtyü-\ city, ✻ of Tunisia

Tu·ni·sia \tü-ˈnē-zh(ē-)ə, tyü-, -ˈni-\ country N Africa on the Mediterranean E of Algeria; ✻, Tunis — **Tu·ni·sian** \-zh(ē-)ən\ *adj or n*

Tu·rin \ˈtůr-ən, ˈtyůr-\ city NW Italy on the Po

Tur·kana, Lake \tər-ˈka-nə\ *or* **Lake Ru·dolf** \ˈrü-ˌdȯlf, -ˌdälf\ lake N Kenya in Great Rift Valley

Tur·key \ˈtər-kē\ country W Asia & SE Europe between Mediterranean & Black seas; ✻, Ankara — **Turk** \ˈtərk\ *n*

Turk·men·i·stan \(ˌ)tərk-ˌme-nə-ˈstan, -ˈstän\ country *cen* Asia; ✻, Ashkhabad — **Turk·me·ni·an** \ˌtərk-ˈmē-nē-ən\ *adj*

Turks and Cai·cos \ˈtərks-ənd-ˈkā-kəs, -ˌkōs\ two groups of islands West Indies at SE end of the Bahamas; a British colony

Tu·tu·ila \ˌtü-tü-ˈwē-lä\ island South Pacific, chief of American Samoa group

Tu·va·lu \tü-ˈvä-(ˌ)lü, -ˈvär-(ˌ)ü\ *formerly* **El·lice** \ˈe-lis\ islands W Pacific N of Fiji; country; ✻, Funafuti — see GILBERT AND ELLICE ISLANDS

Tyne and Wear \ˈtīn-ənd-ˈwir\ metropolitan county N England

Tyre \ˈtī(-ə)r\ ancient city, ✻ of Phoenicia; now a town of S Lebanon — **Tyr·i·an** \ˈtir-ē-ən\ *adj or n*

Tyrol — see TIROL — **Ty·ro·le·an** \tə-ˈrō-lē-ən, tī-\ *adj or n* — **Ty·ro·lese** \ˌtir-ə-ˈlēz, ˌtī-rə-, -ˈlēs\ *adj or n*

Tyr·rhe·ni·an Sea \tə-ˈrē-nē-ən\ the part of the Mediterranean SW of Italy, N of Sicily, & E of Sardinia & Corsica

Ufa \ü-ˈfä\ city W Russia NE of Samara

Ugan·da \ü-ˈgän-də, yü-, -ˈgan-\ country E Africa N of Lake Victoria; ✻, Kampala — **Ugan·dan** \-dən\ *adj or n*

Ukraine \yü-ˈkrān, ˈyü-ˌ\ country E Europe on N coast of Black Sea; ✻, Kyiv — **Ukrai·ni·an** \yü-ˈkrā-nē-ən\ *adj or n*

Ulaan·baa·tar *or* **Ulan Ba·tor** \ˌü-ˌlän-ˈbä-ˌtȯr\ city, ✻ of Mongolia

Ul·san \ˈül-ˈsän\ city SE South Korea

Ul·ster \ˈəl-stər\ **1** region N Ireland (island) consisting of Northern Ireland & N Ireland (country) **2** province N Ireland (country) **3** NORTHERN IRELAND

Ulu·ru \ü-ˈlü-rü\ *or* **Ayers Rock** \ˈerz\ outcrop *cen* Australia in SW Northern Territory

Um·bria \'əm-brē-ə\ region *cen* Italy in the Apennines

Un·ga·va \ˌən-'ga-və\ **1** bay, inlet of Hudson Strait NE Canada **2** peninsula region NE Canada in N Quebec

Union of South Africa — see SOUTH AFRICA, REPUBLIC OF

Union of Soviet Socialist Republics — see SOVIET UNION

United Arab Emir·ates \'e-mə-rəts, -ˌrāts\ country E Arabia on Persian Gulf; composed of seven emirates; ✱, Abu Dhabi

United Kingdom *or in full* **United Kingdom of Great Britain and Northern Ireland** country W Europe in British Isles consisting of England, Scotland, Wales, Northern Ireland, Channel Islands, & Isle of Man; ✱, London

United Nations political organization established in 1945 with headquarters in international territory in New York City

United States of America *or* **United States** country North America bordering on Atlantic, Pacific, & Arctic oceans & including Hawaii; ✱, Washington

Upper Volta — see BURKINA FASO — **Upper Vol·tan** \'väl-tᵊn, 'vōl-, 'vȯl-\ *adj or n*

Ural \'yu̇r-əl\ **1** mountains Russia & Kazakhstan extending about 1640 mi. (2640 km.); usually thought of as dividing line between Europe & Asia; highest about 6214 ft. (1894 m.) **2** river over 1500 mi. (2414 km.) long Russia & Kazakhstan flowing from S end of Ural Mountains into Caspian Sea

Uru·guay \'u̇r-ə-ˌgwī, 'yu̇r-\ **1** river about 1000 mi. (1609 km.) long SE South America **2** country SE South America; ✱, Montevideo — **Uru·guay·an** \ˌu̇r-ə-'gwī-ən, ˌyu̇r-\ *adj or n*

Ürüm·qi \'ᵫ-'rᵫm-'chē\ *or* **Urum·chi** \u̇-'rüm-chē, ˌu̇r-əm-'\ city NW China

Us·pa·lla·ta \ˌüs-pä-'yä-tä, -'zhä-\ mountain pass S South America in the Andes between Argentina & Chile

U.S.S.R. — see SOVIET UNION

Ustinov — see IZHEVSK

Utah \'yü-ˌtȯ, -ˌtä\ state W U.S.; ✱, Salt Lake City — **Utah·an** \-ˌtȯ(-ə)n, -ˌtä(-ə)n\ *adj or n* — **Utahn** \-ˌtȯ(-ə)n, -ˌtä(-ə)n\ *n*

Uz·bek·i·stan \(ˌ)u̇z-ˌbe-ki-'stan, ˌəz-, -'stän\ country W *cen* Asia between Aral Sea & Afghanistan; ✱, Tashkent

Va·duz \vä-'düts\ town, ✱ of Liechtenstein

Val·dez \val-'dēz\ city & port S Alaska

Va·len·cia \və-'len(t)-sh(ē-)ə, -sē-ə\ **1** region & ancient kingdom E Spain **2** city, its ✱, on the Mediterranean

Val·le·jo \və-'lā-(ˌ)ō\ city W California

Valley Forge locality SE Pennsylvania

Val·let·ta \və-'le-tə\ city, ✱ of Malta

Van·cou·ver \van-'kü-vər\ **1** city SW Washington on Columbia River opposite Portland, Oregon **2** island W Canada in SW British Columbia **3** city & port SW British Columbia, Canada

Van Diemen's Land — see TASMANIA

Van·u·atu \ˌvan-ˌwä-'tü, ˌvän-\ *formerly* **New Heb·ri·des** \'he-brə-ˌdēz\ islands SW Pacific W of Fiji; country; ✱, Port-Vila

Va·ra·na·si \və-'rä-nə-sē\ city N India

Vat·i·can City \'va-ti-kən\ independent state within Rome, Italy

Ven·e·zu·e·la \ˌve-nə-'zwā-lə, -zə-'wā-; ˌbā-nā-'swā-lä\ country N South America; ✱, Caracas — **Ven·e·zu·e·lan** \-lən\ *adj or n*

Ven·ice \'ve-nəs\ *or Italian* **Ve·ne·zia** \ve-'net-sē-ä\ city N Italy on islands in Lagoon of Venice — **Ve·ne·tian** \və-'nē-shən\ *adj or n*

Ven·tu·ra \ven-'tu̇r-ə, -'tyu̇r-\ city & port SW California

Ve·ra·cruz \ˌver-ə-'krüz, -'krüs\ city E Mexico

Ver·mont \vər-'mänt\ state NE U.S.; ✱, Montpelier — **Ver·mont·er** \-'män-tər\ *n*

Ve·ro·na \ve-'rō-nä\ city N Italy W of Venice

Ver·sailles \(ˌ)vər-'sī, ver-\ city N France, WSW suburb of Paris

Ve·su·vi·us \və-'sü-vē-əs\ volcano about 4190 ft. (1277 m.) S Italy near Bay of Naples

Vicks·burg \'viks-ˌbərg\ city W Mississippi

Vic·to·ria \vik-'tȯr-ē-ə\ **1** city, ✱ of British Columbia, Canada on Vancouver Island **2** island N Canada in Arctic Archipelago **3** state SE Australia; ✱, Melbourne **4** city & port, Hong Kong **5** seaport, ✱ of Seychelles — **Vic·to·ri·an** \vik-'tȯr-ē-ən\ *adj or n*

Victoria, Lake lake E Africa in Tanzania, Kenya, & Uganda

Victoria Falls waterfall 355 ft. (108 m.) S Africa in the Zambezi on border between Zambia & Zimbabwe

Vi·en·na \vē-'e-nə\ *or German* **Wien** \'vēn\ city, ✱ of Austria on the Danube — **Vi·en·nese** \ˌvē-ə-'nēz, -'nēs\ *adj or n*

Vien·tiane \(ˌ)vyen-'tyän\ city, ✱ of Laos

Vie·ques \vē-'ā-kās\ island Puerto Rico off E end of main island

Viet·nam \vē-'et-'näm, vyet-, ˌvē-ət-, vēt-, -'nam\ country SE Asia in Indochina; ✱, Hanoi; divided 1954–75 into the independent states of **North Vietnam** (✱, Hanoi) & **South Vietnam** (✱, Saigon) — **Viet·nam·ese** \vē-ˌet-nə-'mēz, ˌvyet-, ˌvē-ət-, ˌvēt-, -na-, -nä-, -'mēs\ *adj or n*

Vila — see PORT-VILA

Vi·la No·va de Ga·ia \'vē-lə-'nȯ-və-dē-'gī-ə\ city NW Portugal

Vil·ni·us \'vil-nē-əs\ city, ✱ of Lithuania

Vin·land \'vīn-lənd\ a portion of the coast of North America visited & so called by Norse voyagers about 1000 A.D.; thought to be located along the North Atlantic in what is now E or NE Canada

Vir·gin·ia \vər-'ji-nyə, -'ji-nē-ə\ state E U.S.; ✱, Richmond — **Vir·gin·ian** \-nyən, -nē-ən\ *adj or n*

Virginia Beach city SE Virginia
Virginia City locality W Nevada
Virgin Islands island group West Indies E of Puerto Rico — see BRITISH VIRGIN ISLANDS, VIRGIN ISLANDS OF THE UNITED STATES
Virgin Islands of the United States the W islands of the Virgin Islands; U.S. territory; ✻, Charlotte Amalie (on Saint Thomas)
Vi·sa·yan \və-ˈsī-ən\ islands *cen* Philippines
Vish·a·kha·pat·nam \vi-ˌshä-kə-ˈpət-nəm\ *or* **Vis·a·kha·pat·nam** \vi-ˌsä-\ city E India
Vis·tu·la \ˈvis-chə-lə, ˈvish-chə-, ˈvis-tə-\ river over 660 mi. (1062 km.) long Poland flowing N from the Carpathians
Vi·ti Le·vu \ˌvē-tē-ˈle-(ˌ)vü\ island SW Pacific; largest of the Fiji group
Vlad·i·vos·tok \ˌvla-də-və-ˈstäk, -ˈväs-ˌtäk\ city & port SE Russia on an inlet of Sea of Japan
Vol·ga \ˈväl-gə, ˈvȯl-, ˈvōl-\ river about 2300 mi. (3700 km.) long W Russia; longest river in Europe
Vol·go·grad \ˈväl-gə-ˌgrad, ˈvȯl-, ˈvōl-, -ˌgrät\ city S Russia in Europe, on the Volga
Vol·ta \ˈväl-tə, ˈvōl-, ˈvȯl-\ river about 300 mi. (485 km.) long Ghana flowing from **Lake Volta** (reservoir) into Gulf of Guinea
Vo·ro·nezh \və-ˈrȯ-nish\ city S *cen* Russia in Europe
Vosges \ˈvōzh\ mountains NE France on W side of Rhine valley
Wa·co \ˈwā-(ˌ)kō\ city *cen* Texas
Wad·den·zee \ˌvä-dᵊn-ˈzā\ inlet of the North Sea N Netherlands
Wake \ˈwāk\ island North Pacific N of Marshall Islands; U.S. territory
Wake·field \ˈwāk-ˌfēld\ city N England
Wa·la·chia *or* **Wal·la·chia** \wä-ˈlā-kē-ə\ region S Romania between Transylvanian Alps & the Danube
Wales \ˈwālz\ *or Welsh* **Cym·ru** \ˈkəm-ˌrē\ principality SW Great Britain; a division of United Kingdom; ✻, Cardiff
Wal·lo·nia \wä-ˈlō-nē-ə\ semiautonomous region S Belgium
Wal·sall \ˈwȯl-ˌsȯl, -səl\ town W *cen* England
Wal·tham Forest \ˈwȯl-thəm\ borough of NE Greater London, England
Wal·vis Bay \ˈwȯl-vəs\ town & port W Namibia on Walvis Bay (inlet of the Atlantic); formerly administered by Republic of South Africa
Wands·worth \ˈwän(d)z-(ˌ)wərth\ borough of SW Greater London, England
War·ren \ˈwȯr-ən, ˈwär-\ city SE Michigan
War·saw \ˈwȯr-ˌsȯ\ *or Polish* **War·sza·wa** \vär-ˈshä-vä\ city, ✻ of Poland
War·wick \ˈwär-ik\ town *cen* England
War·wick·shire \ˈwär-ik-ˌshir, -shər\ *or* **Warwick** county *cen* England
Wa·satch \ˈwȯ-ˌsach\ range of the Rockies SE Idaho & N *cen* Utah; highest Mount Timpanogos 12,008 ft. (3660 m.), in Utah
Wash·ing·ton \ˈwȯ-shiŋ-tən, ˈwä-\ **1** state NW U.S.; ✻, Olympia **2** city, ✻ of U.S.; having the same boundaries as District of Columbia — **Wash·ing·to·nian** \ˌwȯ-shiŋ-ˈtō-nē-ən, ˌwä-, -nyən\ *adj or n*
Washington, Mount mountain 6288 ft. (1916 m.) N New Hampshire; highest in White Mountains
Wa·ter·bury \ˈwȯ-tə(r)-ˌber-ē, ˈwä-\ city W *cen* Connecticut
Wei·mar Republic \ˈvī-ˌmär, ˈwī-\ the German republic 1919–33
Wel·land \ˈwe-lənd\ canal 27 mi. (44 km.) long SE Ontario connecting Lake Erie & Lake Ontario
Wel·ling·ton \ˈwe-liŋ-tən\ city, ✻ of New Zealand
Wes·sex \ˈwe-siks\ ancient kingdom S England
West Bank area Middle East W of Jordan River; occupied by Israel since 1967 with parts having been transferred to Palestinian administration since 1993
West Brom·wich \ˈbrä-mich\ town W *cen* England
West Co·vi·na \kō-ˈvē-nə\ city SW California
Western Australia state W Australia; ✻, Perth — **Western Australian** *adj or n*
Western Cape province SW Republic of South Africa
Western Ghats — see GHATS
Western Hemisphere the half of the earth lying W of the Atlantic Ocean & comprising North America, South America, & surrounding waters
Western Isles former administrative area of W Scotland consisting of the Outer Hebrides
Western Sahara *formerly* **Spanish Sahara** territory NW Africa; occupied by Morocco
Western Samoa — see SAMOA
West Germany — see GERMANY
West Indies islands lying between SE North America & N South America & consisting of the Greater Antilles, Lesser Antilles, & Bahamas — **West Indian** *adj or n*
West Midlands metropolitan county W *cen* England; includes Birmingham
West·min·ster \ˈwes(t)-ˌmin(t)-stər\ city N *cen* Colorado NW of Denver
West Pakistan the former W division of Pakistan now having the same boundaries as Pakistan
West·pha·lia \west-ˈfāl-yə, -ˈfā-lē-ə\ region W Germany E of the Rhine — **West·pha·lian** \west-ˈfāl-yən, -ˈfā-lē-ən\ *adj or n*
West Point site SE New York of United States Military Academy on W bank of Hudson River N of New York City
West Quod·dy Head \ˈkwä-dē\ cape;

most easterly point of Maine & of the Lower 48

West Sus·sex \ˈsə-siks\ county SE England

West Valley City city N Utah S of Salt Lake City

West Virginia state E U.S.; ✻, Charleston — **West Virginian** *adj or n*

West York·shire metropolitan county NW England; includes Wakefield

White sea NW Russia in Europe

White·horse \ˈhwīt-ˌhȯrs, ˈwīt-\ city, ✻ of Yukon, Canada

White Mountains mountains N New Hampshire in the Appalachians — see WASHINGTON, MOUNT

Whit·ney, Mount \ˈhwit-nē, ˈwit-\ mountain 14,495 ft. (4418 m.) SE *cen* California in Sierra Nevada; highest in U.S. outside of Alaska

Wich·i·ta \ˈwi-chə-ˌtȯ\ city S Kansas

Wichita Falls city N Texas

Wien — see VIENNA

Wight, Isle of — see ISLE OF WIGHT

Wil·lem·stad \ˈvi-ləm-ˌstät\ city, formerly ✻ of Netherlands Antilles

Wil·liams·burg \ˈwil-yəmz-ˌbərg\ city SE Virginia

Wil·ming·ton \ˈwil-miŋ-tən\ city N Delaware; largest in state

Wilt·shire \ˈwilt-ˌshir, -shər\ county S England

Win·ches·ter \ˈwin-ˌches-tər, -chəs-tər\ city S England

Win·der·mere \ˈwin-də(r)-ˌmir\ lake NW England in Lake District

Wind·hoek \ˈvint-ˌhu̇k\ city, ✻ of Namibia

Wind·sor \ˈwin-zər\ city S Ontario, Canada on Detroit River

Wind·ward Islands \ˈwind-wərd\ islands West Indies in the S Lesser Antilles extending S from Martinique but not including Barbados, Tobago, or Trinidad

Win·ni·peg \ˈwi-nə-ˌpeg\ city, ✻ of Manitoba, Canada

Winnipeg, Lake lake S *cen* Manitoba, Canada

Win·ni·pe·sau·kee, Lake \ˌwi-nə-pə-ˈsȯ-kē\ lake *cen* New Hampshire

Win·ston–Sa·lem \ˌwin(t)-stən-ˈsā-ləm\ city N *cen* North Carolina

Wis·con·sin \wi-ˈskän(t)-sən\ state N *cen* U.S.; ✻, Madison — **Wis·con·sin·ite** \-sə-ˌnīt\ *n*

Wit·wa·ters·rand \ˈwit-ˌwȯ-tərz-ˌrand, -ˌwä-, -ˌränd, -ˌränt\ ridge of gold-bearing rock NE Republic of South Africa

Wol·lon·gong \ˈwu̇-lən-ˌgäŋ, -ˌgȯŋ\ city SE Australia in E New South Wales S of Sydney

Wol·ver·hamp·ton \ˌwu̇l-vər-ˈham(p)-tən\ town W *cen* England NW of Birmingham

Worces·ter \ˈwu̇s-tər\ city E *cen* Massachusetts

Wran·gell, Mount \ˈraŋ-gəl\ volcano 14,163 ft. (4317 m.) S Alaska in **Wrangell Mountains**

Wro·claw \ˈvrȯt-ˌswäf, -ˌsläv\ city SW Poland in Silesia

Wu·han \ˈwü-ˈhän\ city E *cen* China

Wu·xi *or* **Wu–hsi** \ˈwü-ˈshē\ city E China

Wy·o·ming \wī-ˈō-miŋ\ state NW U.S.; ✻, Cheyenne — **Wy·o·ming·ite** \-miŋ-ˌīt\ *n*

Xi'·an *or* **Hsi–an** \ˈshē-ˈän\ city E *cen* China

Xianggang — see HONG KONG

Xin·jiang Uy·gur *or* **Sin·kiang Ui·ghur** \ˈshin-ˈjyäŋ-ˈwē-gər\ region W China between the Kunlun & Altai mountains

Xizang — see TIBET

Xu·zhou \ˈshü-ˈjō\ *or* **Sü·chow** \ˈshü-ˈjō, ˈsü-\ city E China

Yak·i·ma \ˈya-kə-ˌmȯ\ city S *cen* Washington

Ya·lu \ˈyä-(ˌ)lü\ river 500 mi. (804 km.) long SE Manchuria & North Korea

Ya·mous·sou·kro \ˌyä-mə-ˈsü-krō\ town, official ✻ of Côte d'Ivoire

Yan·gon \ˌyän-ˈgōn\ *formerly* **Ran·goon** \ran-ˈgün, raŋ-\ city, former ✻ of Myanmar

Yangtze — see CHANG

Yaoun·dé \yau̇n-ˈdā\ city, ✻ of Cameroon

Yap \ˈyap, ˈyäp\ island W Pacific in the W Carolines

Ya·ren \ˈyä-ˌrən\ district containing ✻ of Nauru

Ya·ro·slavl \ˌyär-ə-ˈslä-vᵊl\ city *cen* Russia in Europe, NE of Moscow

Yaz·oo \ya-ˈzü, ˈya-(ˌ)zü\ river W *cen* Mississippi

Ye·ka·te·rin·burg \yi-ˈka-tə-rən-ˌbərg, yi-ˌkä-ti-rēm-ˈbu̇rk\ *formerly* **Sverd·lovsk** \sverd-ˈlȯfsk\ city W Russia, in *cen* Ural Mountains

Yellow 1 — see HUANG **2** sea, section of East China Sea between N China, North Korea, & South Korea

Yel·low·knife \ˈye-lō-ˌnīf\ town, ✻ of Northwest Territories, Canada

Ye·men \ˈye-mən\ country S Arabia bordering on Red Sea & Gulf of Aden; ✻, Sanaa — **Ye·me·ni** \ˈye-mə-nē\ *adj or n* — **Ye·men·ite** \-mə-ˌnīt\ *adj or n*

Ye·ni·sey *or* **Ye·ni·sei** \ˌyi-ni-ˈsā\ river over 2500 mi. (4022 km.) long *cen* Russia, flowing N into Arctic Ocean

Ye·re·van \ˌyer-ə-ˈvän\ city, ✻ of Armenia

Yo·ko·ha·ma \ˌyō-kō-ˈhä-mä\ city Japan in SE Honshu on Tokyo Bay S of Tokyo

Yon·kers \ˈyäŋ-kərz\ city SE New York N of New York City

York \ˈyȯrk\ city N England

York, Cape cape NE Australia in Queensland at N tip of Cape York Peninsula

York·shire \-ˌshir, -shər\ former county N England

Yo·sem·i·te Falls \yō-ˈse-mə-tē\ waterfall E California in Yosemite Valley; includes two falls, the upper 1430 ft. (436 m.) & the lower 320 ft. (98 m.)

Youngs·town \ˈyəŋz-ˌtau̇n\ city NE Ohio

Yu·ca·tán \ˌyü-kə-ˈtan, -kä-ˈtän\ peninsula SE Mexico & N Central America including Belize & N Guatemala

Yu·go·sla·via \ˌyü-gō-ˈslä-vē-ə, ˌyü-gə-\ **1** former country S Europe including Serbia, Montenegro, Slovenia, Croatia, Bosnia and Herzegovina, & Macedonia; ✻, Belgrade **2** — see SERBIA AND MONTENEGRO — **Yu·go·slav** \ˌyü-gō-ˈsläv, -ˈslav; ˈyü-gō-ˌ\ *or* **Yu·go·sla·vi·an** \ˌyü-gō-ˈslä-vē-ən, -gə-\ *adj or n*

Yu·kon \ˈyü-ˌkän\ **1** river 1979 mi. (3185 km.) long NW Canada & Alaska flowing into Bering Sea **2** *or formerly* **Yukon Territory** territory NW Canada; ✻, Whitehorse

Yu·ma \ˈyü-mə\ city SW corner of Arizona on the Colorado

Za·greb \ˈzä-ˌgreb\ city, ✻ of Croatia

Zaire \zä-ˈir\ **1** river in Africa — see CONGO 1 **2** country in Africa — see CONGO 2 — **Zair·ean** *or* **Zair·ian** \zä-ˈir-ē-ən\ *adj or n*

Zam·be·zi *or* **Zam·be·si** \zam-ˈbē-zē, zäm-ˈbā-zē\ river about 1700 mi. (2735 km.) long SE Africa flowing from NW Zambia into Mozambique Channel

Zam·bia \ˈzam-bē-ə\ *formerly* **Northern Rhodesia** country S Africa N of the Zambezi; ✻, Lusaka — **Zam·bi·an** \ˈzam-bē-ən\ *adj or n*

Zan·zi·bar \ˈzan-zə-ˌbär\ island Tanzania off NE Tanganyika coast; united 1964 with Tanganyika forming Tanzania

Za·po·rizh·zhya *or* **Za·po·ro·zh'ye** \ˌzä-pə-ˈrēzh-zhyə\ city SE Ukraine

Zhang·jia·kou \ˈjäŋ-ˈjyä-ˈkō\ *or* **Kal·gan** \ˈkal-ˈgan\ city NE China NW of Beijing

Zhdanov — see MARIUPOL

Zheng·zhou *or* **Cheng–chou** \ˈjəŋ-ˈjō\ city NE *cen* China

Zim·ba·bwe \zim-ˈbä-bwē, -(ˌ)bwā\ *formerly* **Rhodesia** country S Africa S of Zambezi River; ✻, Harare — **Zim·ba·bwe·an** \-ən\ *adj or n*

Zui·der Zee \ˌzī-dər-ˈzā, -ˈzē\ — see IJSSELMEER

Zu·lu·land \ˈzü-(ˌ)lü-ˌland\ territory E Republic of South Africa on Indian Ocean

Zu·rich \ˈzu̇r-ik\ city N Switzerland